THE ENCYCLOPEDIA
AMERICANA
INTERNATIONAL EDITION

COMPLETE IN THIRTY VOLUMES
FIRST PUBLISHED IN 1829

GROLIER INCORPORATED

International Headquarters: Danbury, Connecticut 06816

Library of Congress Cataloging in Publication Data
Main entry under title:

THE ENCYCLOPEDIA AMERICANA.

Includes bibliographies and index.
1. Encyclopedias and dictionaries.
AE5.E333   1983   031   82-24191
ISBN 0-7172-0114-7   AACR2

RUSSIA

RUSSIA, a country that originated in eastern Europe and over the centuries grew into an empire extending to the Pacific Ocean. This article focuses on the history of Russia to the Revolution of 1917. For events following the overthrow of the Romanov dynasty, see RUSSIAN REVOLUTION and the UNION OF SOVIET SOCIALIST REPUBLICS—*History.*

Soviet historians include in the history of their country such phenomena as the growth of the Urartu kingdom in the Caucasus (founded in the middle of the 9th century B.C.) and of the vast Central Asian empire of the Achaemenids, founded by Cyrus the Persian in 549 B.C. However, Eastern Slavs (the ancestors of modern Russians) appeared first in the steppe north of the Black Sea and had no connection with such states.

The Eastern Slavs had been preceded in the steppe country by several peoples known to history. One of these were the Cimmerians, an Indo-European people mentioned by Homer in the *Odyssey.* Little is known about who they were or where they came from. They were scattered and replaced about 700 B.C. by the Scythians, whose realm ultimately extended from south of the Danube through the Caucasus and beyond. Goldwork in the Scythian "animal style" dazzles visitors to the Hermitage in Leningrad.

By about 200 B.C. the Scythians had been replaced in the steppe by the Sarmatians, a kindred people from the east. But Scythian fishing and trading colonies endured on the Crimean peninsula and the adjoining coastal areas. The coastal Scythians continued to buy grain from the Sarmatian-ruled steppe and to ship it to Greece after the Romans had become masters of the Mediterranean.

Beginning with the Goths, who settled in the Pontic or Black Sea steppe about 200 A.D., peoples unrelated to the Scythians and Cimmerians ruled the area. About 370 A.D. the Germanic-speaking Goths, who had originated in Scandinavia, were driven to the west by the largely Turkic-speaking Huns from the east. The Huns, who penetrated as far west as Gaul, scattered after their defeat at the Battle of Châlons in 451 by the Roman general Aëtius.

Another Turkic people, the Bulgars, made their appearance in the Pontic steppe in the 5th century, but in 558 they succumbed to the Avars, also an Altaic people. (Turkic is a subgroup of the Altaic linguistic group.) By the 640's the Bulgars had regained enough power to control a sizable area north of the Sea of Azov. But within a short time they had split in two—one horde occupying present-day Bulgaria and the other migrating to the vicinity of the junction of the Volga and Kama rivers, where by the late 10th century they had established a substantial state.

In the middle of the 7th century, a successor state to the western Turkic kaganate of Central Asia established itself in the region north of the Caucasus. This was the Khazar state. The Khazars held back invading Muslim Arabs and traded with the Byzantine Empire. Their rulers finally converted to Judaism.

The Slavs. The original Slavic homeland may have centered in what is today Poland and ranged from the Vistula River to the Dnieper River. Archaeologists trace proto-Slavic settlements there to about 1000 B.C. But not until the 1st century A.D. are Slavs mentioned in the historical writings of Pliny the Elder and, later, by Tacitus, who call them Venedi. The 6th century writers Procopius and Jordanes refer to the Slavs, who had appeared on the borders of the Byzantine Empire, as Antae and Sclaveni.

Probably some Slavs lived north and east of the Carpathians as early as the Scythian occupation of the steppe zone and outlasted all the non-Slavic states or hordes that followed.

KIEVAN RUS

By the 9th century the Eastern Slavs, who later became differentiated into Great Russians (or simply Russians), Belorussians, and Ukrainians, were divided into several tribes. They engaged in agriculture as well as hunting, fishing, the keeping of cattle and bees, and crafts, and traded with their neighbors in such products as furs, wax, and honey.

The Varangians. Such trade may have attracted Scandinavian or "Varangian" merchant-adventurers to eastern Slavic regions. Among these were the chieftains Askold and Dir, who occupied the town of Kiev on their way to attack Constantinople in 860. Soon after, Askold and Dir were dislodged from Kiev by Oleg, a Varangian leader of Novgorod. It seems probable that the state that came into being in the late 9th century, with Kiev as its center, was ruled by a Varangian dynasty founded by Oleg or perhaps by the earlier and even more shadowy Varangian Rurik, Oleg's predecessor in Novgorod. By the late 10th century the bulk of the state's population, which was Eastern Slavic, had absorbed its Varangian conquerors.

Kievan Rus (the origin of the word "Rus" is uncertain) was a state that came to consist of a group of principalities, of which Kiev itself was senior. The state's rulers, or grand princes, were able to threaten the Byzantine Empire and Constantinople itself. According to the 12th century *Kievan Primary Chronicle,* the empire was attacked by Oleg in 907 and by his successor, Igor, a clearly historical figure, in 941. Treaties between Rus and Byzantium signed in 911 and 944 as the result of such expeditions regulated their trade in precise fashion. The furs, wax, honey, and slaves that the Rus sent to Constantinople had to be levied from the Slavic tribes in annual winter expeditions. On one such expedition Igor was killed in 945. His widow, Olga, acted as

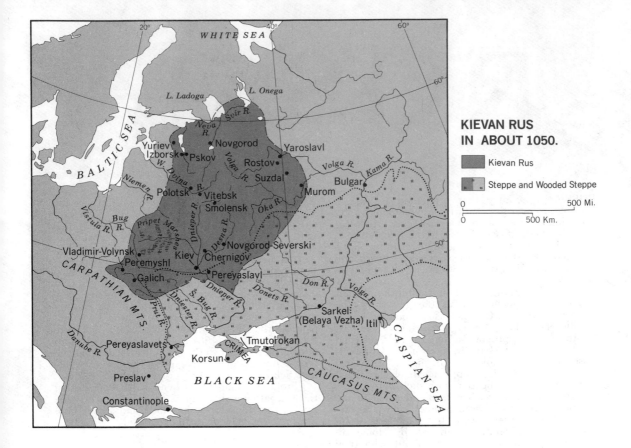

KIEVAN RUS
IN ABOUT 1050.

█ Kievan Rus

▓ Steppe and Wooded Steppe

regent for their son Svyatoslav I in his minority. She became a convert to Orthodox Christianity.

When Svyatoslav reached maturity, he won brilliant military victories over the Bulgars on the Volga and on the Danube. He considered making Pereyaslavets (Preslavets), near the mouth of the Danube, his capital. He also destroyed the Khazar state, eliminating a valuable buffer against Asian tribes moving westward across the steppe. In fact, the new Pecheneg horde that promptly appeared in southern Russia killed him in 972 and reportedly made his skull into a drinking cup.

Of his three sons, Vladimir emerged the victor in a struggle over the succession. Though at first a zealous worshiper of pagan gods, he converted to Orthodox Christianity about 988, and the people of Kievan Rus followed his lead. As a result the culture of Byzantium, the source of Orthodoxy, had far-reaching influence on the Kievan state's art, literature, law, and customs. But the Rus did not fall heir to the broader Byzantine Hellenic heritage, which was based on the Greek language. They had no need to learn Greek since Church Slavonic, not Greek, was the language of their liturgy. Church Slavonic was based on the Macedonian tongue and had been reduced to writing in the "Cyrillic" alphabet, invented for the purpose probably by a pupil of missionary Saint Cyril.

Christianized Rus in the Kievan period developed partly as a trading and partly as an agrarian society with a substantial class of slaves. Politically, it remained a federation of states rather than a single princedom. The princes might be limited in their power by local town assemblies (singular, *veche*) or a council of notables (*druzhina*, from which the boyar *duma* developed), in a manner varying from state to state.

The death of Vladimir I in 1015 was followed by internecine strife from which Yaroslav I ("the Wise") emerged as grand prince of Kiev in 1019. Kiev reached its highest point of development during his reign. Trade and intermarriage linked Kiev with states to the west. Russian princesses became queens of Poland, Hungary, Norway, and France.

Although Yaroslav won a decisive victory over the Pechenegs, a new group of Turkic invaders, the Polovtsy (or Cumans), began to threaten Rus soon after Yaroslav's death in 1054. A series of conflicts among Yaroslav's descendants prevented the Rus from organizing an effective defense against them. Vladimir II Monomakh (reigned 1113–1125) finally proved to be a match for the Polovtsy, and his domestic stature as a Christian prince commanded respect. He combated the abuses of usury and strove to inculcate concern for the welfare of all Rus. He was unable, however, to reverse the processes of decline.

His son Mstislav and nephew Yaropolk II kept peace in the realm until 1139. By then the princely families had multiplied, and with them contestants for the throne. In such regions as Novgorod the *veche* gained the upper hand over the prince, who might be invited and dismissed at will. The various principalities fought different enemies. In the west they confronted Finns, Lithuanians, Poles, and Hungarians. In the east they fought the Volga Bulgars and Polovtsy. Sometimes a principality allied itself with a foreign power against other princes of Rus.

Kiev gradually lost its authority as the unifying princedom. From 1139 to 1169 there were 17 princes in Kiev. In 1169, Andrew Bogolyubsky, prince of Suzdal, captured Kiev and sacked the city. He chose not to move his capital there but to Vladimir, a relatively new city south of Suzdal that had no strong notables or town assemblies to check his power.

Trade routes began to shift both northward and southward with the rise of the Italian and German cities and the capture of Constantinople by the Crusaders in 1204. Novgorod benefited from the shift, owing to its Baltic trade. The principalities of Galicia (or Lodomeria), with its capital city of Galich (Polish, Halicz; Ukrainian, Halych), and Volhynia, with its capital city of Vladimir-Volynsk, were united in 1199 and developed strength in the southwest. But Kiev lost its preeminence forever. Vladimir-Suzdal became the most important principality under Andrew Bogolyubsky's brother Vsevolod III "Big Nest" (reigned 1176–1212), but no new unity was reimposed on Rus. Therefore, when the Mongols invaded in force in 1237, resistance was feeble. However, the fact that no power in either Europe or Asia was able to check their advance suggests that even a healthy Kiev would probably have failed as well.

THE MONGOL PERIOD AND THE RISE OF MOSCOW

A raiding force from the Mongol armies of Genghis (Chinggis) Khan suddenly burst across the Caucasus and in 1223 met an army of Rus and Polovtsy at the Kalka River. The Mongols defeated the enemy and then immediately withdrew. In 1236 an army of perhaps 200,000 under Genghis' grandson Batu advanced on Europe and attacked the Volga Bulgars on the way. In the winter of 1237–1238 the Mongol cavalry overran most of Rus. They were halted before Novgorod only by the spring thaw. They leveled Kiev and continued west, in 1241 crushing the Poles and others at Liegnitz and defeating the Hungarians near Mohi.

The Golden Horde. In 1242, Batu's Mongols withdrew to the Russian steppe and established the so-called Golden Horde at Sarai on the lower Volga. From there they ruled Rus, officially from 1240 to 1480, though in fact their effective rule ended about 1450. The original Mongol conquest had devastated many towns and villages. But their rule was not harsh. After a short period in which some of their officials were stationed in the chief cities, the Mongols (or Tatars, as the Russians came to call these people, among whom Turkic elements soon predominated) generally left the principalities of Rus alone as long as tribute was paid to them. The Rus princes also had to be invested by the Mongol ruler, for a time in Karakorum and later in Sarai, and were required to furnish contingents to Mongol armies.

The effect of the Mongols on Russian development has long been a matter of scholarly debate. Some historians see Mongol influences in the shaping of Muscovite and, later, imperial Russian autocracy. Others point to Byzantine influences, and still others to indigenous ones.

The Struggle for Supremacy Among the Principalities. In the period following the Mongol conquest, there were three centers of power in Rus: Galicia-Volhynia, Novgorod, and Vladimir. In Galicia-Volhynia, an attempt was made to organize resistance to the Mongols. When it failed, the principality had to submit to Mongol rule once more. The boyars, or landowning notables, of Galicia and Volhynia were stronger than those in areas to the east, and they prevented the princes from consolidating their power. In the 14th century, Volhynia was annexed by Lithuania and Galicia by Poland.

Novgorod (officially, Lord Novgorod the Great) by the 12th century had gained both effective ecclesiastical autonomy and the power of limiting the prince's authority. Alexander Nevsky, chosen prince of Novgorod in 1236, defeated the Swedes by the Neva River (hence his appellation) in 1240. In 1242 he routed the Teutonic Knights in the "battle on the ice" of Lake Chud (Peipus).

The Novgorodians had to fight invaders from the west many times before and after Nevsky. Nevsky, however, chose to submit to the Mongols, believing that any other course was impossible. He began a policy of cooperation with the Horde, which was adopted by other princes of Rus who hoped thereby to keep the Mongol soldiers and officials at a distance. Novgorod governed itself through its *veche* and Council of Notables and expanded its commercial connections. It penetrated the northern forests all the way to the Urals and beyond, and traded actively with Gotland and the Germanic ports on the Baltic Sea before and after the rise of the Hanseatic League.

The beginnings of the Great Russian state, however, are to be found in the northeast in Vladimir. The son of Vsevolod III, Grand Prince Yuri, was killed in battle against the Mongols in 1238. In 1252 the Tatars removed one of his successors and installed Alexander Nevsky as grand prince. Nevsky's loyalty to the Tatars forestalled more than one punitive expedition that the khan had planned against Vladimir. His loyalty also led to greater Mongol toleration of Orthodox Christianity, though the pagan Mongols officially adopted Islam during the reign of Uzbek (1312–1342). In 1299–1300 the chief cleric, the metropolitan "of Kiev and all Rus," abandoned Kiev for Vladimir.

Upon Alexander Nevsky's death in 1263, his youngest son Daniel (died 1303) received the principality of Moscow. The town is first mentioned in the Chronicles under the year 1147. As its first resident prince, Daniel tried to make the state a solid base for his line. He and his successors annexed neighboring territories bit by bit. Yuri (reigned 1303–1325) competed with the grand princes of Tver, a state to the northwest, for the favor of the khans. Ivan I Kalita (reigned 1328–about 1341) succeeded in moving the seat of the metropolitan from Vladimir to Moscow in about 1326–1328, and also was awarded the title of senior grand prince. He was known for his financial sagacity as well as for his loyalty to the Tatars. During the reigns of Simeon the Proud (about 1341–1353) and Ivan II (1353–1359) and during the minority of Dmitri Donskoy (reigned 1359–1389), Metropolitan Aleksei gave his support to the Moscow principality (often referred to as Muscovy).

During this period large areas that once formed part of Kievan Rus came under Lithuanian control. At the same time that the people who came to be called Great Russians (or simply Russians) were mostly subject to the Tatars, those who were emerging as Belorussians and Ukrainians were gradually conquered by Lithuania. Grand Duke Gediminas (Polish, Gedymin; reigned 1316–1341) had unified and consolidated the pagan state of Lithuania in the Vilnius (Vilna) region and began its expansion to the southeast. Under Algirdas (Polish, Olgierd), Lithuania occupied Kiev in 1361 and went on to reach the Black Sea. In 1368 and 1372, Algirdas attacked Moscow, but the newly built stone walls of the Kremlin held against both assaults.

Ivan I, a 14th century grand prince of Moscow and Vladimir, is shown in the midst of his boyars in this miniature from a 16th century manuscript. Known as "Moneybags" (*Kalita*), he won protection from the Tatar khan by paying him tribute, which he raised from his subjects through heavy taxation. The tax collectors are shown extorting taxes by whipping Ivan's subjects.

Dmitri, grand prince of Moscow and Vladimir, leads his troops out of Moscow to confront the Tatars. He was later known as Dmitri Donskoy ("of the Don") because of his great victory in 1380 over the Tatar khan on the plain of Kulikovo beside the Don River. It was the first major Russian victory over the Tatars, to whom Russian princes had paid tribute since the 13th century.

Dmitri Donskoy made peace with Lithuania and defeated its ally, Tver. Most noteworthy, however, was his defeat of the Tatars, first in 1378 and then in the great Battle of Kulikovo in 1380, in which the Lithuanian and Ryazan armies failed to arrive in time to help the Tatar khan Mamai. Though Tokhtamysh, who replaced Mamai as khan, burned Moscow two years after Kulikovo, the khan reaffirmed Dmitri as grand prince.

Dmitri's son Vasili I (reigned 1389–1425) acquired new principalities, holding at bay both the Tatars and the Lithuanians. Nevertheless Lithuania, which had joined in a dynastic union with Poland in 1385, remained a serious threat to Muscovite lands. The Lithuanian ruler Jagiello (Lithuanian, Jogaila) had accepted Christianity in the Roman rite for himself and his followers, and thereafter the country was brought within the Polish cultural orbit, though 90% of its population remained Orthodox Slavs.

During the reign of Vasili II, son of Vasili I, the disintegrating Golden Horde lost control of the Crimea in 1430, of Kazan in 1436, and, after the death of Vasili II in 1462, of Astrakhan in 1466. Vasili was strong enough to establish a Tatar principality subject to himself in 1452, an event that marks Moscow's effective independence of the Horde.

Moscow, the Third Rome. Constantinople fell to the Ottoman Turks in 1453. Seeking Western aid against the Ottomans, Byzantium had agreed to a union of the churches under Rome at the Council of Florence in 1439. A council of Russian bishops repudiated the union (which soon collapsed) and in 1448 elected Iona as the metropolitan, terminating ecclesiastical dependence on the patriarch of Constantinople. By the time of Vasili II's death, Muscovy had become a realm of about 15,000 square miles (40,000 sq km).

Ivan III the Great succeeded his father, Vasili II, in 1462. He conquered Novgorod in the 1470's and Moscow's old rival Tver in 1485, thus becoming ruler of a Muscovy that had incorporated most of the Russian principalities. The few that remained were annexed by his son Vasili III, chiefly Pskov in 1510 and Ryazan in 1517. Vasili also wrested Smolensk from Lithuania.

Moscow's relations with its Tatar neighbors became less of a preoccupation when Ivan III formally renounced the tributary relationship in 1480. The army sent by the khan to punish him withdrew from the Ugra River without fighting. The remnants of the Golden Horde itself were destroyed by the Crimeans in 1502.

Ivan aspired to make Muscovy the new Byzantium. He took as his second wife Sophia (Zoë) Palaeologa, niece of the last Byzantium emperor, Constantine XI, and he adopted Byzantine symbols and ritual. The notion of Moscow as the "third Rome" was developed during the reign (1505–1533) of Vasili III, the son of Ivan III and Sophia. Vasili received the ambassador of the Holy Roman Empire, established diplomatic relations with the Ottoman sultan and the Mughul emperor, and permitted the establishment of a "German suburb," or Western colony, in Moscow.

During the period when Moscow was establishing its supremacy among the principalities, sometimes called appanages, some institutions comparable to those of Western feudalism developed, such as vassalage and immunities for subordinate princes and boyars. But the social system that developed in Russia did not parallel that of Western feudalism in all its particulars. For example, estates were inherited rather than granted for service.

Except in Novgorod, commerce and crafts did not flourish during the period. Most Russians were peasants but were not yet fully enserfed.

There were numerous slaves (singular, *kholop*), as in the Kievan period. The church did not suffer under the Muslim Tatars, and monastic lands became extensive and rich. Monks were important in the pioneering of settlements to the northeast, following the lead of Russia's most notable medieval saint, Sergius of Radonezh (died 1392).

IVAN IV THE TERRIBLE

In the period between the reign of Ivan III and the foundation of the Russian Empire by Peter I in 1721, fundamental changes occurred in the social-political structure of Muscovy. The development of Muscovy's trade and the growth of its cities were accompanied by the decline of the peasantry into serfdom. The freedom of the peasant to leave his landlord was reduced, and provisions were made for the landlord's recovery of peasants who had fled his estate.

During this period the minor princes and boyars, who made up the hereditary landlord class, were fast losing their political power, their lands, and even, in some cases, their lives, especially during the reign of Ivan IV (1533–1584). On the other hand the service landlords (*dvoryane*), with the support of Ivan III and his successors, increased in numbers and landholdings. Unlike the hereditary landowners, the *dvoryane* held title to their estates conditionally on either civil or military service to the state. The Muscovite grand princes, or czars, favored them over the boyars. It can be said that they created the *dvoryane* as the chief support of Muscovite absolutism.

Though the *dvoryane* formed a service class of gentry, service was also due from the minor princes, the boyars, and "free servants." Each of these was exempt from taxation. The taxed classes were mainly the merchants, artisans, and peasants.

Many of the minor princes and boyars were descended from rulers of Lithuania, Tatar states, or principalities of Rus that had been absorbed by Muscovy. Having lost their former power as they became mixed in a common pool of servitors to the Muscovite prince, they became preoccupied with matters of rank within their own class. The czars encouraged their rivalries for position by sanctioning *mestnichestvo* (literally, "system of placement"). In compliance with this system, the civil or military post assigned to a given minor prince or boyar had to reflect the rank of his family and himself in respect to all other members of his class.

The proud princes and boyars seem to have had several opportunities to consolidate as an aristocracy and limit the grand princes' power. However, for whatever reason, they never succeeded in doing so.

Early Years of Ivan IV's Reign. The three-year-old Ivan IV became grand prince on the death of his father, Vasili III, in 1533. At first his mother, Yelena Glinsky, acted as regent, treating the boyars with scant ceremony. She died suddenly in 1538. A period of intrigue and violence ensued in which the Shuiskys (the premier princely family, former rulers of Suzdal) and Belskys (headed by Vasili III's cousin) struggled for ascendancy, each attempting to mobilize both clerical and lay support.

Ivan IV seems to have been an intelligent and curious boy who suffered from the atmosphere of fear and brutality in which he grew up. Gradually ridding himself of the feuding princes,

Moscow's Kremlin, with its newly built walls, as it existed at the time of Ivan III the Great. It was Ivan's ambition to make Muscovy heir to the Byzantine Empire after Constantinople had fallen to the Ottomans in 1453.

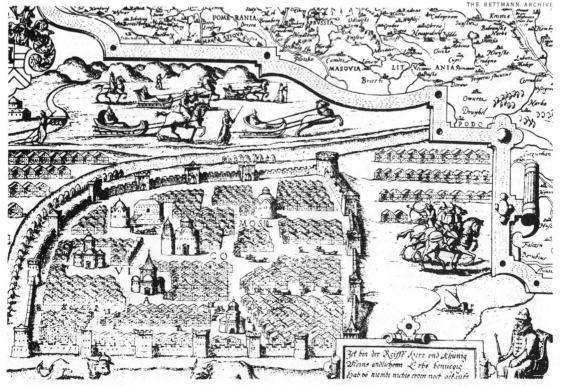

GROWTH OF RUSSIA FROM 1300 TO 1598.

- Muscovy about 1300
- Expansion to death of Vasili II, 1462
- Expansion to death of Ivan III, 1505
- Expansion to death of Fyodor I, 1598

Ivan in 1547 had himself crowned czar of all Russia by Metropolitan Makary (Macarius) and married Anastasia, a member of the boyar family of Romanov. A few months later a great fire destroyed much of Moscow, and mob violence threatened the czar himself. But a fairly tranquil period ensued, during which Makary and other advisers led him to summon the first assembly of the land, or *zemski sobor*, in 1549. To some extent it was comparable to the assemblies of estates of medieval western Europe.

In 1556 the military obligations of the land-owning class were specified. Each landowner had to begin military service at the age of 15 and serve for the rest of his life, if physically able. Compulsory service was now exacted of all land-holders, whether their estates were hereditary (singular, *votchina*) or based on service tenure (singular, *pomestie*). A standing force of *streltsy*, or musketeers, was also created.

Ivan's Wars. Though the Golden Horde had ceased to exist, the successor Tatar khanates of Kazan, Astrakhan, and the Crimea continued to raid Muscovite territory. On the west the Livonian Knights blocked Muscovy's access to the Baltic, and the dynastically united Poland-Lithuania overshadowed Ivan's realm.

Ivan first mounted a campaign against Kazan and succeeded in defeating it in 1552. The entire khanate was annexed in the next few years. In 1554–1556 his armies took Astrakhan and annexed that khanate also, thus acquiring for Muscovy the Volga Valley all the way to the Caspian Sea.

Since the Crimean Tatars had harassed Muscovy during the campaigns against Kazan and Astrakhan, Ivan's close advisers wished him to strike at the Crimea. But the czar's chief interest lay in trade with the West through the Baltic. This led him to undertake war against Livonia,

an adventure that was to last 24 years. Though much of Livonia fell to Ivan's armies, part of present-day Estonia was taken by Sweden, and the defeated Livonian Order secularized itself, its master accepting vassalage to the Polish king as duke of Courland.

When Russia succeeded in taking Polotsk, Lithuania offered peace in 1566. But Ivan, with the support of a *zemski sobor*, unwisely decided to continue the war. An increasingly Polonized Lithuania, which had been joined to Poland by dynastic ties since 1385, was politically united with Poland by the Union of Lublin in 1569. By this union the two countries gained a single sovereign and diet, although the two administrations and armies remained separate. Ivan now faced a more formidable enemy in a united Poland-Lithuania, and his resources were nearing exhaustion. A truce was arranged with Poland-Lithuania in 1582, and an armistice with Sweden was signed the following year. Muscovy was stripped of all its conquests along the Baltic and the Gulf of Finland.

Campaign Against the Boyars. In 1553, Ivan had fallen seriously ill. Thinking he was close to death, he demanded that the boyars swear allegiance to his son Dmitri. Their reluctance to do so made him increasingly suspicious of them. His distrust increased with the flight to Lithuania in 1564 of the boyar Andrei Kurbsky, one of his close companions. In December of that year, Ivan abruptly left Moscow for the nearby town of Aleksandrov, sending Moscow an ultimatum. To deal with the betrayal of princes and boyars, Ivan declared, he must be entrusted with the power to set up a state within a state, to be called the Oprichnina ("something set apart"). His ultimatum was accepted, and he returned a few weeks later to organize a new personal guard.

The new guards, known as Oprichniki, eventually numbered several thousand. They killed many boyars and other alleged enemies of the czar, and confiscated property wholesale. The rest of the realm was termed the Zemshchina, which the boyar duma and other previously existing administrative agencies continued to govern. But the Oprichniki were ordered to wipe out "treason" in both the Oprichnina and Zemshchina.

Closing Years of the Reign. Great social and economic damage was wrought by both the Livonian War and the domestic upheavals provoked by the czar's campaign against the boyars. The Oprichnina was abolished in 1572, perhaps because of Oprichnik inability to check the previous year's raid by Crimean Tatars, who reached and burned much of Moscow. Many Russians were in flight, joining Cossack settlements in the Ukraine and on the Don River.

The close of Ivan's reign was one of gloom, relieved in 1582 by the conquest of the khanate of Sibir (from which the name "Siberia" derives) by Yermak and his band of Cossacks, sent by the merchant-adventurer family of Stroganov. This event marked the beginning of Russian penetration to the Pacific Ocean, reached some 50 years later. Ivan died in 1584.

BORIS GODUNOV AND THE TIME OF TROUBLES

Two years before his death, Ivan IV had struck and killed his son and heir, Ivan, in a heated argument. Ivan was succeeded, therefore, by his next surviving son, Fyodor I. Fyodor was sickly and content to let his wife's brother, Boris Godunov, conduct much of the business of state. During Fyodor's reign, the patriarch of Constantinople agreed to elevate the metropolitan of Moscow to patriarch of Moscow, an act that other Eastern patriarchs later confirmed. The new see was to become the most important of the whole Eastern Orthodox Church.

A war with Sweden ended in 1595 with the reestablishment of Russia's western boundaries as

NATIONALMUSEET, COPENHAGEN

Ivan IV the Terrible, portrayed in an ikon dating from his reign, was the first Muscovite prince to be crowned czar and grand prince of all Russia. His struggles against the princes and boyars and his protracted wars left Russia in a state of economic and social collapse.

they had been before the Livonian War. Fyodor died in 1598, the last of the branch of Rurik that had ruled Moscow since Daniel. Ivan IV's youngest son, Dmitri, having been exiled to Uglich, had died there under mysterious circumstances in 1591. (Another son of Ivan's, also called Dmitri, to whom the boyars had been reluctant to give allegiance when Ivan became ill in 1553, had died soon after Ivan had recovered.)

Tobolsk was a well-established, fortified city when this 18th century engraving was made of it. It had been founded in 1587 at the confluence of the Irtysh and Tobol rivers in western Siberia. From there the Cossacks advanced eastward to the Pacific in the early 17th century, opening up the whole of Siberia to Russian settlement.

RADIO TIMES HULTON PICTURE LIBRARY

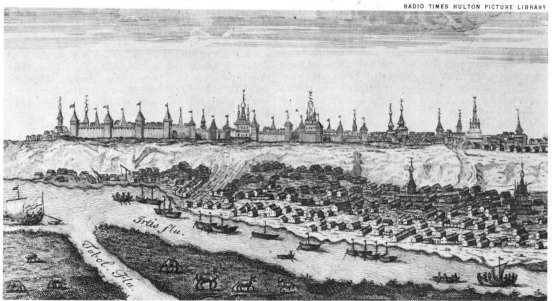

NOVOSTI, FROM SOVFOTO

Boris Godunov was crowned czar in 1598 after the death of the last of the Rurik dynasty of Muscovy. His reign began the 15-year period of civil disturbances and foreign invasions of Russia known as the Time of Troubles.

A series of theatrical yet fateful events took place in the period, known as the Time of Troubles, between Fyodor's death and 1613.

Boris Godunov. Boris Godunov was offered the throne, which he finally accepted, and ruled as czar from 1598 to 1603. He proved to be a skillful diplomat and able administrator. But famine and disease struck in 1601–1603. The princes and boyars opposed him, and though he exiled several of the Romanov family, forcing Fyodor Romanov to take monastic vows under the name Filaret, the opposition was not stifled. In 1603 a pretender to the throne appeared in Poland, who may have been a renegade church deacon named Grigori Otrepiev but who also may have believed he was truly Ivan's youngest son, Dmitri. Pushkin's play *Boris Godunov* and Mussorgsky's opera of the same name have popularized the suspicion current at the time that Boris was responsible for the real Dmitri's death. Modern scholars have found little evidence to confirm this.

The False Dmitris. The pretender, known as the First False Dmitri, had become a Roman Catholic in Poland and had fallen in love with a Polish noblewoman, Marina Mniszek. Raising an army with Polish and other Roman Catholic support, he entered Moscow in June 1605, a few weeks after Boris had died and his young son, proclaimed Fyodor II, had been murdered. The pretender was crowned czar and ruled for nearly a year. He married Marina Mniszek, who became czarina though she remained a Roman Catholic.

The support of the Roman Catholics for the new czar weakened when he put off fulfilling promises he had made to them. He was also distrusted by the boyars, who had welcomed (or used) him as a way of getting rid of Boris. In May 1606 the leader of the boyar faction, Prince

Vasili Shuisky, dethroned the pretender in a coup, burned his body, and fired the ashes from a cannon toward the west from which he had come.

Proclaimed czar as Vasili IV, Shuisky promised to make certain decisions in harmony with the boyar duma. At his instigation the real Dmitri was canonized, and his remains were brought from Uglich to Moscow, as part of a propaganda campaign to legitimize Shuisky's succession.

Outside Moscow, disorder was widespread. Many popular uprisings took place. The most dangerous was one led by a former slave, Ivan Bolotnikov, whose forces combined serfs and other lower-class elements with some landlords of the gentry class. Despite their challenge to authority and even property, they did not oppose the czarist system and for a time contended that Fyodor I's son Pyotr was with them. There never was a real Pyotr, and the false one was caught and killed, as was Bolotnikov after his defeat at Tula in 1607.

A new pretender, known as the Second False Dmitri, now appeared, claiming to be both the First False Dmitri and the real Dmitri. Marina Mniszek declared him to be her husband and joined him at his camp at Tushino near Moscow. Filaret served unofficially as his patriarch.

In 1609, Vasili Shuisky turned to the Swedes for help. The "Rogue of Tushino" fled to Kaluga. A delegation of Tushino gentry, abandoning the Second False Dmitri, visited the Roman Catholic king of Poland, Sigismund III, and invited the king's son Władysław to become czar. A document signed in February 1610 provided that he would rule with the *zemski sobor*.

In the spring of 1610 separate armies of Poles and the Second False Dmitri and Swedish units in the service of Vasili Shuisky were all near Moscow. In July an assemblage of Muscovites of different classes deposed Shuisky and forced him to become a monk. The Swedes had retreated northward. A Polish force entered Moscow, and the Muscovites accepted Władysław as czar. However, Sigismund III now strove to take the throne for himself, while the Swedes declared war on the Russians. In December 1610 the Second False Dmitri was slain by one of his own men, leaving the way clear for a national effort at resolving the crisis that would not be complicated by the "Rogue's" candidacy.

Resolution of the Succession Crisis. The effort was led by the church. The patriarch Hermogen announced that Russians were released from their allegiance to Władysław, and called on them to drive out the Polish Roman Catholic forces. The Poles promptly imprisoned him. Armies of gentry and Cossacks sprang up in various Russian cities, but they squabbled and hesitated. Several high clerics renewed their appeals for a national solution. The response of the city of Nizhni Novgorod was decisive. A butcher, Kuzma Minin, and Prince Dmitri Pozharsky organized an army there that reached Moscow in September 1612. The Poles, besieged in the Kremlin, surrendered in November. In early 1613 a *zemski sobor* convened, including representatives from the clergy, boyars, townsmen, and even some peasants. It elected 16-year-old Mikhail Romanov, kin to the old dynasty through Ivan IV's wife Anastasia. He was crowned in July as Michael I.

During the Time of Troubles, the boyars' bid for power and the lower classes' aspirations for a better life failed. It was the autocracy and its instrument, the service nobility, that emerged with their forces intact.

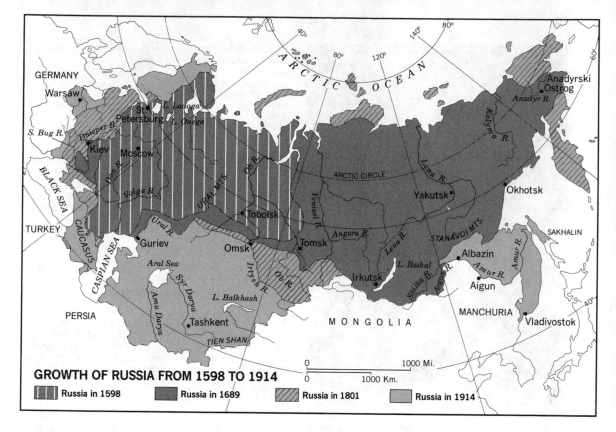

GROWTH OF RUSSIA FROM 1598 TO 1914

‖‖ Russia in 1598	■ Russia in 1689	⁄⁄ Russia in 1801	▨ Russia in 1914

THE EARLY ROMANOVS

The country's first need was for peace and
order. Peace with Sweden was concluded at
Stolbovo in 1617, with Sweden retaining the
shores of the Gulf of Finland, which it had regained during the Time of Troubles. In 1618,
Władysław of Poland attacked Moscow, reaching
its outskirts but failing to take the city. He then
accepted the Truce of Deulino, by which Poland
retained the provinces of Smolensk and Seversk
and returned its Russian prisoners, including the
czar's father, Filaret. Filaret officially became
patriarch in 1619 and in effect acted as regent
for his son. After the truce expired in 1632,
Władysław, now King Vladislav IV of Poland, defeated the Russians near Smolensk. By the Peace
of Polyanovka in 1634, Poland retained most of
the territory secured by the Truce of Deulino, but
Vladislav yielded his claim to the throne of Muscovy. Though the Cossacks of the Don region
captured the Turkish fortress of Azov in 1637
and offered it to Muscovy, a *zemski sobor* declined the offer out of prudence.

Filaret died in 1633 and Michael in 1645, to
be succeeded by his son Alexis. Known as "the
most gentle" czar despite his fits of temper,
Alexis was a devoted son of the church. (His
reign was idealized by some 19th century writers.)
He relied on the boyar Boris Morozov to run the
government, until an uprising in Moscow in 1648,
provoked by financial exactions and corruption,
led to Morozov's dismissal.

A new legal code was issued in response to
the unrest. Adopted in 1649, this *ulozheniye* is
often considered to mark the full arrival of serfdom for the landlords' peasants (as distinguished
from "state peasants" living on lands belonging
to the state). No limit was placed on the landlord's right to recapture fugitives from his estates.

The *ulozheniye* also terminated what remained of
the previously recognized right of peasants to
change their masters on St. George's Day. Thereafter, the gentry (*dvoryanstvo*) increasingly came
to treat the serfs as property. One result was to
accelerate the flight of peasants to the free
Cossacks of the Don and Dnieper valleys.

The Cossacks. Some of the Dnieper Cossacks
had established their forts, known collectively as
the Zaporozhian Sich ("stronghold beyond the
cataracts"), on islands in the lower course of the
Dnieper River in the Ukraine. They were known
as the Zaporozhian Cossacks. Poland, which had
gained control of the Ukraine when Lithuania
and Poland were united in 1569, allowed the
Dnieper Cossacks to govern themselves and elect
their own leaders.

As Poland attempted to impose Roman Catholicism on the Orthodox Ukrainians and as
Polish leaders pressed into the steppe, establishing large estates there, Cossack revolts broke out
and continued from 1624 to the 1650's. Several
times the Cossack *hetman* (headman) Bohdan
Chmielnicki (Ukrainian, Khmelnytzkyi; Russian,
Khmelnitsky) appealed to Alexis for protection
against the Polish Catholics. The czar and the
zemski sobor finally agreed to extend their protection, and in 1654 union was proclaimed, with
autonomy for the Ukrainians. Their autonomy
soon was abridged by Moscow.

War with Poland was the immediate result of
the union. It was concluded only in 1667 by the
Treaty of Andrusovo. By the terms of the treaty
Muscovy was awarded Smolensk and Chernigov.
The boundary of Muscovy was also extended to
the Dnieper River and across it to include the
city of Kiev.

Other Cossacks moving across Siberia reached
that part of the Pacific Ocean known as the
Sea of Okhotsk by 1640. In 1648 the Cossack

Nikon, shown in his patriarchal robes, introduced extensive reforms in the church that ultimately led to schism. He lost the support of Czar Alexis when he attempted to establish ecclesiastical autonomy within the state.

navigator Semyon Dezhnev sailed from the Arctic Ocean around the northeastern tip of Siberia, discovering the Bering Strait (as it would later be known). Furs were the main attraction of this vast eastern region, inasmuch as they figured prominently in state finance and were much in demand abroad. Although Russian administration followed the Cossack pioneers across Siberia, serfdom never did. As a result, the atmosphere was freer there than west of the Urals, though this was to change when exiles were sent to Siberia at a later date.

Farther south the Cossacks encountered the Chinese, and a series of clashes and disputes with them was concluded only in 1689 by the Treaty of Nerchinsk, which fixed the frontier in such a manner as to concede the Amur region to China. This frontier remained unchanged until 1858–1860.

In 1670–1671, Stepan ("Stenka") Razin, a *hetman* of the Don Cossacks, led a revolt against the Russian landlords. It spread up the Volga Valley. Certain Finnish and Turkic peoples of the region also rebelled. Razin was defeated, captured, and executed in 1671.

Church Reform and Schism. During Alexis' reign, a theological and moral revival took place. In 1652 an able but uncompromising cleric named Nikon was named patriarch. He undertook the correction of several errors in church books and rites. Nikon rode roughshod over the opposition, led by the archpriest Avvakum, and simultaneously made claims for ecclesiastical autonomy or even primacy in the state, which alarmed and then angered the czar. At the council of 1666–1667,

held in Moscow, Nikon was deposed as patriarch. But his reforms were upheld.

Those who opposed Nikon's reforms became known as Old Believers (*starovery*), Old Ritualists (*staroobryadtsy*), or simply Schismatics (*raskolniki*). They clung steadfastly to the old forms. A few died as martyrs, executed by the state, including Avvakum, who was burned in 1682. Many engaged in self-immolation, and in two decades more than 20,000 died in this manner. The only major split in the history of the Russian Church became permanent. Some managed to retain the services of the priesthood, while others were forced to do without. Merchants and prosperous peasants were prominent in the ranks of the Old Believers.

Alexis was succeeded by Fyodor III (reigned 1676–1682), his son by his first wife, Maria Miloslavskaya. During Fyodor's reign the *mestnichestvo* system was finally abolished (1682), thus reducing the power of the hereditary nobility.

PETER THE GREAT

Fyodor was survived by a sickly, slow-witted brother, Ivan. In the choice of a successor, Ivan was passed over in favor of Peter, the 10-year-old son of Alexis by his second wife, Natalia Naryshkina. Natalia was made regent. Within weeks, however, Ivan's 25-year-old sister Sophia led a coup that resulted in the proclamation of Ivan as the senior co-czar and Sophia as regent. The coup was carried out by the *streltsy*, among whom the Old Believers were strong.

The two boy czars had no say during Sophia's regency (1682–1689), and Ivan was to remain a nonentity. The regency was dominated by Sophia's chief adviser and lover, Prince Vasili Golitsyn, who devoted much of his attention to foreign affairs. In 1686 a treaty of "perpetual peace" was signed with Poland, generally confirming the borders of 1667.

In the west bank Ukraine (the Ukraine west of the Dnieper River) the decades after 1667 had been turbulent owing to continuing Cossack struggles with the Poles on the one hand and with the Crimean Tatars and Turks on the other. (The Crimea had been a vassal state of the Ottomans since 1475.) The treaty of 1686 provoked war with the Crimeans. Twice, in 1687 and 1689, Golitsyn led an army against them, suffering defeat. The second campaign was disastrous.

Peter spent much of his time roistering with his Western friends in the "German suburb," a place outside Moscow where foreigners could live. He also learned from them. In August 1689 a plot to place Sophia on the throne was foiled by troops loyal to Peter, and Sophia was confined to a convent. For several years more, Peter's mother and her lay and clerical advisers conducted the affairs of state. Only after she had died in 1694 did Peter become the effective ruler. Ivan V died in 1696.

Dynamic and tireless, Peter was to introduce a series of dramatic changes in Russian life, many of them designed to imitate West European states or to bring Russia into credible competition with them. He himself mastered the skills of soldier and sailor and several different crafts, and his curiosity extended to all branches of political, economic, and cultural affairs. His own youthful military games led to the creation of the first two Guards regiments, named Preobrazhenski and Semenovski after the villages in which the games took place. These regiments were to be powerful forces in war and peace for many decades thereafter.

Peter also indulged in time-consuming debauchery. His mother's attempt to domesticate him through marriage to Yevdokia (Eudoxia) Lopukhina in 1689 was unsuccessful. His entourage included such foreigners as Andrew Ostermann, son of a German pastor, the Scottish general Patrick Gordon, and the Swiss Francis Lefort. His friends ranged from such low-born Russians as Aleksandr Menshikov, who rose from selling pies on Moscow streets to become a prince, and a former swineherd, Pavel Yaguzhinsky, to scions of the most ancient noble families of Muscovy.

Peter's personal rule opened with a renewal of the war against the Turks and Tatars. Building a sizable fleet (Russia's first), he sailed it down the Don River and in 1696 captured Azov. He did not pursue the war, however, believing that he would need allies to defeat the Ottomans. To this end he formed the Great Embassy of 1697, a group of 250 with which he traveled incognito (not very successfully, however, since he was nearly seven feet tall and could be recognized easily). In a year and a half he visited Swedish, Prussian, Dutch, English, and Austrian (Habsburg) territories, observing and learning everything he could, from navigation to statecraft, though he gained no allies against the Turks.

The *streltsy*, many of whom had supported Sophia, raised a revolt to restore her to power. This brought him hurrying back to Moscow. Crushing the rebellion, Peter executed a thousand or more of them and compelled Sophia to take monastic vows. He forced his wife, whom he suspected of supporting the uprising, to do the same.

Acting on what he saw in the West, he ordered the upper classes, though not the peasants or clergy, to shave off their beards and adopt European dress. Also, he decreed the use of the Julian calendar. Although the Gregorian calendar, with its superior astronomical merits, had been introduced into Roman Catholic countries in 1582, several Protestant countries still followed the Julian calendar. Peter copied them in this and consistently chose to emulate Protestant rather than Catholic Europe.

(The Julian calendar, or "Old Style," is used in dating the events that follow, except when reference is made to events that are related to the West. In the latter case the Gregorian calendar is used, and the date is followed by the words "New Style.")

The Great Northern War. Abandoning the notion of a grand European alliance against the Turks, Peter hurriedly concluded peace with the Ottomans in 1700 and promptly joined in an adventure against Sweden, then at the height of its power. Augustus II, king of Poland (and, as Frederick Augustus I, elector of Saxony), had already enlisted Denmark as an ally against Sweden, and Peter joined them in the Great Northern War. In November 1700 he was besieging the Swedish fortress of Narva when the army of Charles XII, the brilliant young Swedish general and king, crushed and scattered the much more numerous Russian army. Unwisely considering Peter beaten, Charles became embroiled in inconclusive fighting with Augustus.

Raising another army, Peter sent it back to the northern Baltic area in 1701. Having driven the Swedes from the Neva River delta on the Gulf of Finland, Peter in 1703 began to build a new capital there, to be called St. Petersburg. A

THE MANSELL COLLECTION

Peter the Great is shown in a caricature as a barber cutting off a boyar's beard. On returning from western Europe in 1698, he tried to Westernize the Russians by having men of the upper classes shave off their beards.

fort built on an island in the Neva soon shielded the city, but Russia's ability to hold the Swedes at bay remained uncertain. In 1706, Poland was compelled to conclude peace with Sweden, and in early 1708 the Swedish army was ready to start for Moscow.

An uprising in 1707 of the Don Cossacks, led by Konrad Bulavin, resembled Razin's earlier rebellion. It soon spread widely. The Bashkirs on the Volga also revolted. These and other uprisings were responses to Peter's reforms and levies, designed to make possible the continuation of the war.

Charles XII diverted his attack south to the Ukraine, where the Dnieper Cossack *hetman* Ivan Mazepa stood ready to help him. Having crushed Bulavin's rebellion (though the Bashkir rising continued), Peter cut off Charles' supplies and won a decisive victory over the Swedes at Poltava in 1709, sending Charles XII and Mazepa fleeing from the scene to Ottoman sanctuary.

The Turks resumed war with Russia in 1710, and Peter and an inferior force found themselves encircled near the Prut River in the summer of 1711. Peter was fortunate to escape with a peace agreement, whereby he yielded Azov and, in effect, his aspirations for a footing on the Black Sea. Having built a northern navy (the southern one had been lost by the Turkish treaty), Peter at this time resumed the Great Northern War, with Saxony, Poland, Denmark, Hannover, and Prussia as his allies. He occupied most of Finland and the Baltic coast down to Riga, defeated the Swedish navy at sea, and later raided Sweden itself.

Peter the Great, proclaimed emperor in 1721 after his decisive victories over Sweden, is portrayed by Aert de Gelder, one of Rembrandt's most gifted students.

Peter and Frederick I, Sweden's new monarch, signed the Treaty of Nystad in 1721. Russia retained Livonia, Estonia, and the territory around the Gulf of Finland. In celebration of the treaty, Russia was proclaimed an empire, and Peter I was given the titles of emperor and "the Great." Russia had become a European power and thenceforth could not be threatened by either Sweden or Poland. The Ottoman Empire remained a formidable threat, however.

Russia was also firmly established beyond the Ural and the Caucasus mountains. The western and southern coasts of the Caspian Sea were annexed from Persia after a campaign in 1722–1723 but were retroceded in 1732. Commercial and diplomatic interests were pursued with the Turkic peoples of Central Asia as well as with India and China.

Domestic Reforms. Many of Peter's domestic reforms, undertaken during the wars of his reign, were influenced by military needs of the moment. But their general direction was shaped by his determination to imitate western Europe, especially its commercial and seafaring Protestant north. Peter created a new standing army equipped with artillery, whose nucleus was the Guards regiments but which also included separate Cossack detachments as well as ordinary Russian units of the line. He was the founder of the Russian navy, supplied by a new shipbuilding industry.

In 1711 he established the Senate, which was charged with the supervision of all governmental bodies. It was linked with the monarch by a procurator general. The first to be appointed was Pavel Yaguzhinsky. In place of the previous 50-odd *prikazy* (governmental departments), Peter formed "colleges" modeled on Swedish practice, which were supposed to make their decisions by majority vote. Originally colleges were set up for war, navy, foreign affairs, state income, state expenses, justice, financial oversight, commerce, and manufacturing.

Peter levied every indirect tax he could think of on the hapless population. In 1718 he instituted a tax on individuals in place of the previous tax on households. When taxes had been assessed by household, the tendency had been for more peasants to crowd into fewer households. As a result of the change from household to individual assessment, the village communes began to redistribute land on a regular basis so that the size of households would be related to the amount of land tilled. This redistribution enabled the individuals making up these households to pay their taxes from the produce of the land tilled.

Probably the result of this new tax was to strengthen the redistributory commune, characteristic of Great Russian areas. The village commune had had social and administrative functions for centuries. But the practice by which the commune also periodically redistributed land probably evolved in the 17th century on the lands of private landlords or gentry. Redistribution was introduced among peasants on state lands only later, in the reign of Catherine II. In the Ukraine the commune tended to be based on hereditary and not redistributory tenure.

The first modern census in Russia was taken in 1722. Its purpose was to assure that everyone paid the poll, or head, tax.

Indirect and direct taxation seem to have yielded in 1724 more than five times the revenue of 1680. A mercantilist-inspired tariff was also enacted in 1724 to protect metallurgical and textile industries either created or expanded by the czar.

In 1722, Peter issued a Table of Ranks (14 in number), which fixed the ranks through which members of the gentry (and others) were supposed to advance by merit in the civil and military service. Nongentry could become gentry for life by reaching the fifth rank. They could become hereditary gentry if they reached the ninth rank, and some did. Peter also promulgated a single-succession law in 1714, intended to terminate the division of land among all sons in a family. The Table of Ranks was in effect until 1917. The single-succession law was repealed in 1731.

Peter did the greatest violence to the sensibilities of his subjects with his ecclesiastical and cultural changes. When the patriarch died in 1700, Peter did not replace him. The patriarch's administrative functions were performed by Stefan Yavorsky, one of a series of 17th century clerics influenced by Polish Catholic methods. Yavorsky and other churchmen offended by Peter's Protestant leanings placed their hopes in the heir, Aleksei, son of Eudoxia. But Peter and his son became increasingly estranged. After several ultimatums, Peter tricked him into returning home from Austria. Aleksei died in Russia, probably under torture, in 1718.

By this time Stefan Yavorsky had lost influence, and Peter relied on Feofan Prokopovich, a bishop, to introduce in 1720 the Ecclesiastical Regulation for a new "college." Soon to be called the Most Holy Governing Synod, it administered the Orthodox Church. The whole settlement of church affairs, patterned on Lutheran models, was to determine church-state relations in Russia until 1917.

A series of "ciphering" schools were founded by Peter to educate the gentry, but they were not to last. Russia's educational system in the 18th century was to be based on the ecclesiastical seminaries created according to the Ecclesiastical Regulation, of which there were 46 in 1727. Instruction was mostly conducted in Latin, the language of Protestant as well as Roman Catholic scholasticism. Peter also wished to found a new Academy of Sciences. It was officially inaugurated under Catherine I, his successor, who was virtually illiterate.

SUCCESSION CRISES AND EUROPEAN ALLIANCES (1725–1762)

Catherine I was the daughter of a Lithuanian peasant. She had been Aleksandr Menshikov's mistress when Peter met her in 1705. The czar made her his mistress in that year and married her in 1712. Menshikov governed Russia during her reign. When she died in 1727, having designated Aleksei's son Pyotr (Peter's grandson) as her successor, Menshikov hoped to retain his power. However, Pyotr, on succeeding as Peter II in 1727, preferred the Dolgoruky family. He had intended to marry a Dolgoruky princess but died of smallpox at the age of 15.

Peter had not named a successor. The Supreme Privy Council, created during the reign of Catherine I, chose Anna Ivanovna, daughter of the co-czar Ivan V and widow of the duke of Courland. The council stipulated a series of "conditions" under which she could rule only by its consent. Anna accepted the conditions, but after becoming empress she used regiments of the Guards (which had already determined Catherine's succession in 1725) to repudiate the "conditions" and abolish the council.

Anna favored Germans during her reign—for example, Ostermann in foreign affairs and Ernst Johann Biron (Bühren), her lover and chief adviser. Biron is believed to have been responsible for the execution and exile of many thousands of her subjects. Anna designated as her successor the infant Ivan Antonovich, her grandnephew and the great-grandson of Ivan V. Anna died in October 1740 and was succeeded by the infant Ivan VI. His reign lasted only until November 1741 when Yelizaveta Petrovna, daughter of Peter the Great and Catherine I, supported by the Guards, seized the throne and was proclaimed Empress Elizabeth.

Elizabeth strove to link her own image with that of her father. Her abolition of capital punishment symbolized her break with Anna's repressive reign. However, she was not active as either a reformer or ruler, and the country's financial conditions deteriorated during her reign. As her successor she chose her sister's son, Karl Peter Ulrich, duke of Holstein-Gottorp, who had been raised as heir to the Swedish throne. Peter was brought to St. Petersburg at the age of 14. He disliked Russia and admired Prussia, especially its ruler Frederick the Great.

On Elizabeth's death in December 1761, Peter succeeded as Peter III. But after a reign of only six months, he was overthrown by another Guardist coup guided by his wife, Catherine, who had been born a princess of Anhalt-Zerbst. She came to terms with Russia more successfully than her husband and in time became known as Catherine the Great.

Domestic and Foreign Affairs. Between the reigns of Peter I and Catherine II significant changes had occurred. The gentry's situation had greatly improved. Their rights were codified, and their compulsory military service was reduced to 25 years in 1736 and finally abolished in 1762.

Since land tenure thereafter was no longer conditional on service, the concept of private property was introduced for the gentry, who were relieved of onerous obligations to the state. But the gentry's gain was the serfs' loss, because more than ever they were treated as the gentry's personal property, almost as slaves.

During this period Russia's foreign affairs centered on Europe, though the commercial treaty of Kyakhta was signed with China in 1727 and an Orthodox mission was established in Peking. From 1726 to 1761, Russia's chief ally was Austria, though Russia traded more with Britain than with Austria. In 1733–1735, Russia and Austria fought the War of the Polish Succession against France, long a supporter of Russia's old antagonists the Ottoman Empire, Poland, and Sweden. In that war the French candidate for the throne of Poland lost. In 1736–1739, Russia fought the Ottomans with Austrian support, but its gains were minor. In 1741–1743 a Russo-Austrian war against Sweden led to a small adjustment of the frontier in Finland in Russia's favor. In the War of the Austrian Succession (1740–1748), Russia played an insignificant role, but it confirmed the fears of Count Aleksei Bestuzhev-Ryumin, who managed foreign affairs under Elizabeth, that Prussia would become a threat to Russia.

In the "diplomatic revolution" of 1756, the old enemies Austria and France joined hands, while Prussia allied itself with Britain. In the ensuing Seven Years' War (1756–1763), Russia continued to fight alongside Austria but refused to declare war on Britain. In 1760, Russian forces reached Berlin. Prussia was saved from disaster at the last moment when Elizabeth died, and Peter III promptly made not only peace but an alliance with his hero Frederick the Great. The alliance was as short-lived as his reign.

In the course of these wars Russia became a full participant in Europe's dynastic struggles and produced such distinguished generals as Aleksandr Suvorov. But the cost of Russia's gains far exceeded their value.

CATHERINE THE GREAT AND PAUL I

Catherine II was acclaimed empress in 1762. She had no title to the throne under the law of 1722 and was not related by blood to previous sovereigns. Her claim rested solely on force. Her son (whose father may or may not have been Peter III) was an obvious alternative if discontented elements should try to replace her. One previous emperor, Ivan VI, was alive in prison at the start of her reign, but was killed according to prior instructions when an attempt was made to free him in 1764. Her task was to win acceptance, which she accomplished with patience and shrewdness. Her intelligence, education, and courage were impressive, and though her appetite for lovers was voracious, she was able until the last years to avoid letting her private passions interfere with matters of high policy.

Part of her strategy was to earn acclaim in the West and at home for her supposed devotion to the principles of the Enlightenment. Her sincerity in this regard has been both affirmed and denied, each side finding some apparent basis in evidence. In 1766 she summoned a legislative commission, for which she herself prepared a Nakaz (Instruction), drawing heavily on the writings of Montesquieu and Cesare Beccaria. After meeting for over a year (1767–1768), the commission was discharged without codifying the laws. But Catherine was praised for such measures by the *philosophes* of France. She exchanged letters with Voltaire and arranged for Diderot to come to St. Petersburg to instruct her. Both her own and Russia's reputation abroad were heightened by these gestures, whether this was justifiable or not.

The interruption of the commission was occasioned by the outbreak of war with the Ottoman Empire in 1768. The Russian army and navy acquitted themselves well, and in 1774 the Treaty of Kuchuk Kainarji yielded Russia a stretch of Black Sea coast and the ill-defined right to protect Balkan Christians. The Crimea had been occupied by Russia but was declared independent by the treaty. It was annexed, however, by Catherine in 1783.

In the fall of 1773, Yemelyan Pugachev, a Don Cossack, raised a rebellion which, due to the army's commitment to the war with the Turks, spread over a vast part of the Volga Valley and adjoining areas. Pugachev announced that he was Peter III and proclaimed the end of serfdom. It took the best efforts of Suvorov and the army to crush the revolt by late 1774.

The uprising led the empress to reform local government in 1775. She created new provinces (singular, *gubernia*), of which there were 50 by 1796. Each had an appointed governor, and the gentry participated in the administration. She confirmed gentry landownership and codified their privileges by the Charter of the Gentry (1785), giving members of the gentry in each province corporate legal status.

Prince Grigori Potemkin, one of Catherine's lovers and her ablest counselor, was associated with the colonization of the Black Sea coast. In 1787 the Turks declared war again and were again beaten. By the Treaty of Jassy in 1791 (1792, New Style), the Russian frontier was pushed to the Dniester River. The Turks never again were able to mount a serious threat to Russia.

In 1772, Russia, Prussia, and Austria agreed to the first partition of Poland, whose government had become increasingly weak. The partition brought the Russian border to the Dvina-Dnieper line. Poland's belated but broadly based effort at reform after the partition led to the constitution of 1791, which made the monarchy hereditary and provided for representative government to a degree unusual in Europe at the time. Russia and Prussia responded early in 1793 by partitioning Poland for the second time. Russia gained a great part of Belorussia and the Ukraine west of the Dnieper. Austria rejoined the other two powers in a third partition in 1795, which erased Poland from the map and gained Courland and a border along the Niemen and Western Bug rivers for Russia. The map was to be redrawn in the Napoleonic Wars. But Russian ascendancy in their land was to cause the Poles anguish for much of their later history. Under Catherine, Russia also joined the Armed Neutrality (1780) against Britain during the American Revolution and fought a brief war with Sweden, which left frontiers unchanged.

Russia's population, area, industry, and agricultural output grew rapidly in the 18th century. In Catherine's reign alone, foreign trade through both Baltic and Black Sea ports increased more than threefold.

The church suffered from the secularization of lands carried out in 1764 and from the growth of anticlerical feeling and religious indifference among the increasingly Westernized upper classes.

Catherine the Great professed admiration for the ideals of the Enlightenment while acting as autocratically and with as little concern for the improvement of the condition of the peasantry as any of her predecessors.

The cultural gulf widened between the often French-speaking gentry and the wretched and oppressed peasantry.

Catherine died in 1796, and her son Paul, having felt cheated of the throne for over 30 years, became emperor as Paul I. He was unpredictable and arbitrary in his personal behavior. He began his reign by undoing almost everything that his mother had done. Some of his decrees lasted, such as his law of succession to the throne (1797), which enacted primogeniture in the male line. Some did not, such as his 1797 law that limited serf labor on gentry estates.

In 1798, Russia joined the Second Coalition against France, and in the subsequent campaigns Suvorov performed perhaps the most brilliant feats of any Russian commander in history. However, Paul suddenly withdrew from the coalition and, siding with Bonaparte, prepared to attack the British in India and elsewhere. A palace revolution may already have been maturing, but this move seemed to trigger it. Paul was deposed and killed in March 1801.

ALEXANDER I

During the reign of Alexander I, Russia moved to the very center of the European stage, at least briefly. As a child Alexander had been taken away from his father, Paul, by his grandmother, Catherine II, and given an education in the style of the West and even of the Enlightenment, leaving him more familiar with French and English than with Russian. In the judgment of one historian, Alexander was partly "the pupil of La Harpe" (his tutor, a Swiss revolutionary) and partly "the drill-master of Gatchina" (his father's palace before 1796, where Alexander learned to admire Prussian military methods). Alexander developed enthusiasm also for secular constitutionalism and religious pietism. His ardor for pursuing one or another of these sets of ideas successively or simultaneously made him unpredictable and puzzling to his contemporaries.

He was undoubtedly privy to the plans of the conspirators who seized and murdered his father in March 1801, though he may not have sanctioned the murder. Alexander promptly abrogated several of Paul's repressive measures, recalled the expedition that had been sent to conquer India, and basked in widespread public approval.

He assembled an "unofficial committee" to reorganize the government, consisting of a circle of his young aristocratic friends, including Nikolai Novosiltsev, Pavel Stroganov, Viktor Kochubey, and Adam Czartoryski. It appears that Alexander even thought of ending absolutism and serfdom.

But the changes he introduced were much more modest. In 1802 he abolished Peter I's "colleges" and replaced them with ministries, each headed by a single man. At first there were eight: war, navy, foreign affairs, justice, interior, finance, commerce, and education. At the same time Alexander sought to make the Senate the country's highest administrative and judicial institution, an objective only partially achieved. In 1803 the "law on free agriculturists" enabled owners of serfs to emancipate them voluntarily into a status resembling that of the state peasants. Some 100,000 serfs, a tiny fraction of the total, eventually benefited from this law. Legislation enacted in 1804 ostensibly granted personal emancipation of the serfs of Livonia and Estonia but kept them bound to their lands. The results satisfied no one, and the laws were modified a few years later.

A new school system was enacted by a law of 1803. The country was divided into six educational regions, each to be endowed with schools and a university. A school for teacher training was revived in the capital (in 1819 becoming the University of St. Petersburg), and two new universities were founded in Kazan and Kharkov. Previously there were only three in the empire: a Russian university in Moscow, a Polish one in Vilna, and a German one in Dorpat.

The Napoleonic Wars and Their Aftermath. In 1805 the emperor was distracted from his domestic projects by the establishment of the Third Coalition against France. He had begun his reign by rapprochement with Britain while seeking to avoid trouble with Bonaparte. But the British reopened war with France in 1803, and Russia and Austria entered as allies of Britain in 1805, after Alexander had enunciated a set of war aims that included equitable frontiers and free political institutions for all European peoples. Gen. Mikhail Kutuzov led a Russian army against the French, but Napoleon, now emperor of the French, smashed a combined Austro-Russian force at Austerlitz in December 1805 (New Style). Austria abruptly made peace, but Russia did not. In October 1806, Prussia entered the war and was promptly defeated by Napoleon at Jena.

Just at that moment Alexander had to face a new enemy, the Ottoman Empire, though he was already involved in a war with Persia. The Russian annexation of part of Georgia in 1801 and of the rest in subsequent years was a cause of the wars with both Turkey and Persia. Russo-Turkish rivalry in the Balkans gave the French another way of encouraging Ottoman hostilities against Alexander.

Russian armies were battered at Eylau in East Prussia in February 1807 (New Style) and were defeated at Friedland in East Prussia in June. Alexander was ready to stop fighting. He signed the Peace of Tilsit, providing not only for peace but an alliance between France and Russia against Britain. In the following year, at Erfurt, the new alignment was reaffirmed. Russian reactions to it, however, were mixed. If Napoleon's Continental System, to which Russia now adhered, kept the products of the British from competing in Russian markets with those of local manufacturers, it also cut off Russia's exports of foodstuffs to Britain. The gentry were the sufferers.

Mutual distrust mounted despite Napoleon's encouragement of Russia's war with Sweden (1808–1809), which led to Russia's annexation of Finland. (Finland retained much of its autonomy under the Russian czars, their "grand dukes.") Alexander failed to provide other than nominal help to Napoleon in the 1809 war against Austria and was alarmed at the subsequent enlargement, at Austria's expense, of the grand duchy of Warsaw, Napoleon's own creation. Kutuzov was given command on the Turkish front, and his success was capped by the Treaty of Bucharest in May 1812, by which Russia obtained Bessarabia and peace.

During the period of the French alliance, Alexander had found a capable new adviser, Mikhail Speransky. In 1809, at Alexander's request, Speransky proposed a plan for a constitution. Only one part was put into effect: in 1810 a state council was created to assist the monarch in preparing sound legislation. Speransky also helped to reorganize the ministries and introduce a kind of merit system into the ponderous Russian bureaucracy. However, in the atmosphere of crisis prevailing in March 1812, Speransky was dismissed and exiled.

On June 24, 1812, Napoleon's Grande Armée invaded Russia. Over half a million men, a third of whom were French, forced the less than 200,000 Russian defenders to retreat. General Kutuzov was appointed commander and felt compelled to make a stand, which he did at the village of Borodino, in an exceptionally bloody battle, on September 7 (New Style).

He then retreated to the east and the Grande Armée entered Moscow. Almost at once the city began to burn. Alexander refused to make peace, and after only a month Napoleon withdrew. The supply system broke down, and both "General Winter" and Kutuzov's forces harassed the retreating French. Only a small fraction of the Grande Armée managed to cross the frontier.

Napoleon's nominal allies Prussia and Austria joined Alexander, and in the "Battle of the Nations" at Leipzig in October 1813 the French emperor suffered a crucial defeat. In March 1814, Alexander led the allied armies into Paris. Napoleon became "emperor of Elba" but managed to return, raise a new French army, and for a "Hundred Days" from March to June 1815, frightened the allies until his final defeat at Waterloo in July, a battle in which Russians did not participate.

The peace was made largely by the four chief powers who had defeated Napoleon and had formed a Quadruple Alliance: Russia, Prussia, Austria, and Britain. But other states also took part in the Congress of Vienna, which met from September 1814 to June 1815. The issue in which Russia was most concerned involved Poland. Alexander finally became ruler of a new kingdom

A large part of Moscow was destroyed by fire shortly after Napoleon's army had occupied the city in 1812. Abandoning the city, the army began the retreat to the west that ended in death for most of its soldiers.

of Poland centered on Warsaw, though Prussia and Austria regained substantial Polish territories. However, this settlement was reached only after Britain, Austria, and France secretly made an alliance against Russia and Prussia.

In September 1815, having undergone a pietist conversion in 1812, Alexander secured the reluctant adherence of several fellow monarchs to the Holy Alliance, which involved a vague commitment to Christian brotherhood. But it was the Quadruple Alliance that undertook to preserve the peace in a series of congresses: Aix-la-Chapelle (1818), Troppau and Laibach (1820–1821), and Verona (1822).

At Aix, France was admitted to what became the Quintuple Alliance. The congresses ceased to meet in 1822, but the three Central and East European monarchies continued to cooperate for some time, and no general war was to disturb Europe until 1914. In the success of the peacemaking (compared with other international settlements), Alexander deserves a substantial share of credit.

Alexander helped to impose a constitution on the returning Bourbon kings of France and defended constitutionalism elsewhere. He granted his own constitution to Poland and broadened the existing constitutional system of Finland. Hopes were raised that Russia itself might be given a constitution. In 1818, Alexander praised the new Polish constitutional institutions and expressed determination to extend them to Russia. Novosiltsev thereupon was directed to prepare a new constitutional draft, but it was never acted upon.

The czar's new chief adviser, Gen. Aleksei Arakcheyev, came to be regarded as a symbol of reaction, though this view is not quite just. He established a series of "military colonies," where soldiers could till the soil and live with their families. The idea had some merit, but it was spoiled by the pettiness and harshness of the regulations surrounding it. Laws of 1816–1819 changed the status of the peasants of Estonia, Livonia, and Courland, converting them into tenant farmers on the estates of their German landlords. But this was scarcely a solution to the problem of Baltic serfdom.

Alexander's earlier conversion to pietism had a curious effect in 1817, when Prince Aleksandr Golitsyn was appointed minister of a new, combined ministry of spiritual affairs and education. The Society of Jesus was banned and the Jesuits were expelled from Russia in late 1815, after surviving in that country alone because Catherine II had refused to publish the papal order of dissolution in 1773. Golitsyn was president of the Russian Bible Society and sought to make pietist Christianity the foundation of all worship and schooling. The archimandrite Photius was instrumental in leading the czar to dissolve the "combined ministry" and to dismiss Golitsyn in 1824.

The Decembrists. From 1816 on, a number of young officers, veterans of the Napoleonic Wars, had organized a series of secret societies akin to those in the contemporary West but also drawing on the traditions of Freemasonry, popular in Russia since the mid-18th century. In 1822 they were reorganized as the Northern Society and the Southern Society, the former led by Nikita Muraviev, the latter by Col. Pavel Pestel. The Northern Society was moderately liberal, whereas the Southern Society, especially Pestel, was inspired by French Jacobinism. Alexander knew something about these secret groups, but he took only halfhearted action against them.

The emperor's sudden death, in November 1825, while on holiday in Taganrog, gave the societies their chance. It was generally assumed that Alexander's oldest brother, Konstantin (Constantine), was the heir. But in 1820 he had renounced the throne to make a morganatic marriage, and the czar had designated his younger brother Nikolai as his successor. These arrangements remained secret.

On Dec. 14, 1825, the conspirator officers (later known as Decembrists) of the imperial guards led some 3,000 troops into the Senate Square in St. Petersburg. They clamored for the succession of Konstantin, although Nikolai had just been confirmed as Emperor Nicholas I. After some hesitation the square was cleared with gunfire, leaving many dead and wounded behind. A few months later, five leaders were hanged and many others exiled. A minor uprising in the south failed.

NICHOLAS I

Nicholas I's personality was less complex than that of Alexander. He had a forceful character and presence and was reputed to be the handsomest man in Europe. He shared his father's fondness for the order to be found in the barracks and on the drill field, and his readiness to keep order not only at home but abroad led to his sobriquet "the gendarme of Europe."

Nicholas' strong sense of duty and his determination to handle a wide range of matters himself made him waste time on detail. He preferred to rely on a series of institutions under his personal control, many linked to His Majesty's Own Chancery. He expanded these in 1826 to include the Second and Third Sections, dealing respectively with codification of law and the new gendarmerie (secret police). In 1836 the Fifth Section, dealing with state peasants, was added. In late 1837 this was converted into the Ministry of State Domains.

The first real codification of Russian law was carried out successfully by Speransky, who had been recalled to service in the capital. It took effect in 1835. Pavel Kiselev, as minister of state domains, sought, with mixed results, to improve the lot of the state peasants by reducing inequality in their allotments of land, expanding schooling for their children, and creating a system of limited self-government in their villages. Aleksandr Benkendorf was entrusted with the Third Section, which spread a wide net of informers and police throughout the country. Nicholas was determined to prevent any repetition of the Decembrist revolt.

From the moment of his accession, Nicholas had to contend with real and potential revolutionary movements abroad. He began by reluctantly supporting, up to a point, the Greek rebellion against the Ottomans that had begun in 1821. Ignoring an agreement with the British on what to do with the Ottoman Empire ("the sick man of Europe"), Nicholas imposed an ultimatum on Constantinople in the autumn of 1826. Complex negotiations ensued, in the midst of which, in October 1827, a combined Anglo-Franco-Russian squadron destroyed an Ottoman fleet in the Bay of Navarino.

But the British left the Russians to face the Turks alone in a war of 1828–1829. Before declaring war on Turkey, the czar concluded peace with Persia in the Treaty of Turkmanchai, ending a war that had begun in 1826 over territory in the Caucasus and giving Russia the part of Armenia around Yerevan (Erivan). In the Turkish war, fighting was fierce in both the Balkans and the Caucasus. The sultan accepted defeat by the Treaty of Adrianople (1829). Russia gained a little territory at the mouth of the Danube and in the Caucasus, a protectorate over the two "Danubian principalities," Moldavia and Wallachia (they nominally remained part of the Ottoman Empire), and other rights. Greek independence was secured, but Russian influence in Greece was thwarted when the new kingdom called a Bavarian prince to rule.

Revolutions in France and Belgium in 1830 were soon followed by revolution in Poland. Two and a half years earlier, Nicholas had sworn to uphold the Polish constitution when he was crowned king of Poland. Revolt in Warsaw was triggered by the czar's plans to use Polish troops along with Russian forces to suppress the French and Belgian uprisings. Grand Duke Konstantin, officially commander in chief of the Polish army and in fact the chief Russian official in Poland, was conciliatory toward the rebels. But in February 1831 a Russian army entered Polish territory, and Nicholas undercut popular support of the rebel leaders by taking measures to improve the lot of Polish serfs. Gen. Ivan Paskevich took Warsaw after heavy fighting in the autumn of 1831, and the revolt was crushed.

The Polish constitution of 1815 was replaced by the Organic Statute of 1832. Its provisions guaranteeing civil liberties were not put into effect. Paskevich became viceroy and virtual military dictator until he died in 1856. Schools were closed or russified, censorship was strictly enforced, and pressure was brought to bear on religious groups. In 1839 the Uniate Church (the church of Eastern rite under Roman obedience) of the kingdom was reunited with the Russian Church.

In 1833 the Russian minister of education, Sergei Uvarov, declared that education was to be based on the principles of Orthodoxy, autocracy, and nationality. His precise meaning was by no means self-evident, since the Westernized Uvarov knew and cared little for Russian traditions. But the motto served as justification for sharply curbing all opposition to the existing system.

Although public finance remained in a lamentable state, foreign trade doubled during Nicholas' reign as the export of grain through the Black Sea increased. The first significant Russian railway was opened in 1851 between St. Petersburg and Moscow. As industry grew, an increasing number of landlords accepted money rents (the *obrok* system) in place of labor services (the *barshchina* system). The serfs were permitted to earn the money due the landlord by engaging in some kind of industrial employment.

Russo-Turkish Relations. The Near East claimed the czar's attention again as Muhammad (Mehemet) Ali, the Ottoman viceroy in Egypt, rebelled against the sultan. Nicholas' support of the sultan promised to yield Russia greater influence over the Ottoman Empire. Russian troops landed at the Straits, and a few months later, in July 1833, Turkey and Russia signed the Treaty of Unkiar Skelessi, which provided for mutual support in case of attack by a third power. A secret article required the Turks to close the Straits to war vessels, thereby ensuring that Russia could not be attacked from the Black Sea. There was an erroneous suspicion, especially in Britain, that the secret article also permitted Russian warships free passage out of the Black Sea. Britain's growing fear of Russian designs in the Near and Middle East became an important element in international relations for the remainder of the century.

A second Egyptian-Ottoman conflict erupted in 1839, and Turkey was soon in grave danger. Complex diplomatic maneuvers led Britain and France to join the Austrian, Russian, and Ottoman empires in the Straits Convention of 1841, which barred all foreign warships from the Bosporus and Dardanelles in peacetime. Turkey was placed under continuing international supervision, in which Russia's role was no greater than that of any other power.

The revolutions of 1848, starting in France and spreading through Austria as far as the Danubian principalities, confirmed and heightened the czar's old fears of popular movements. His plans to send a Russian army westward were frustrated by revolutionary successes in Austria and Prussia. However, he did send an army into Moldavia and Wallachia, preserving Ottoman suzerainty there. He also dispatched Paskevich to Hungary with 170,000 men, who overthrew Lajos Kossuth's new regime in Budapest in August 1849 and restored Hungary to the Habsburgs. Nicholas also successfully supported Austria against Prussian efforts to unify Germany. Like Alexander in 1815, he appeared to be the arbiter of Europe. The appearance was soon to fade.

In 1850 a dispute about the Holy Places in Palestine began between France and Russia. But the ostensibly religious quarrel over Orthodox and Catholic privileges there was soon overshadowed by diplomatic maneuvers. International tensions grew with Russia's occupation of Moldavia and Wallachia in July 1853. Even then it seemed that diplomacy might preserve peace. But when Anglo-French naval squadrons entered the Straits, war broke out in October 1853 between the Russians and the Turks. Russia promptly destroyed a Turkish fleet at Sinop (Sinope). A few months later Britain and France entered the so-called Crimean War, to be joined later by Sardinia. Austria "astounded the whole world with its ingratitude" by compelling Russia to withdraw from the Danubian principalities, occupying them with its own troops. Prussia remained neutral, and Russia fought alone. Since Austrian troops now separated Russia from Turkey, the allies had to find another way to strike at the enemy.

Though there were minor engagements in the Caucasus and at sea from the Baltic to the Pacific, the focus became the allied landing in the Crimean peninsula and the siege of the great naval base at Sevastopol. Though it held fast for almost a year, the fortress fell in September 1855, seven months after the death of Nicholas I. The war exposed the inability of the Russian giant to hold even its own best fortifications against attack from the sea.

Westerners, Slavophiles, and Socialists. The reign of Nicholas I saw the emergence among the intelligentsia of two opposing views of Russia's past and future. One group was known as "Westerners" and the other as "Slavophiles." In the 1830's, Moscow students were shaken by Pyotr Chaadayev's *Lettre philosophique*, which argued that Russia had no cultural tradition worthy of the name. The Westerners, who saw this lack of a result of Russia's isolation from the West, included the mercurial though gifted critic Vissarion Belinsky, the future anarchist leader Mikhail Bakunin, and the radical Aleksandr Herzen (Gertsen).

The Slavophiles included Aleksei Khomyakov, who became a prominent lay theologian. An interest in the German philosophers Schelling and Hegel united the two groups, as did a determination to reform Russia. The Westerners favored institutional change, while the Slavophiles called for inner, moral transformation of the individual and society.

In the last years of Nicholas I's reign the first avowed socialists appeared in Russia in the Petrashevtsy group. Their teachings were not revolutionary. But in the panic created by the revolutions abroad, more than three dozen members were seized. Of these, 15 were sentenced to death and then reprieved at the very place of execution. The writer Fyodor Dostoyevsky shared this searing experience.

ALEXANDER II

The ruler who earned the sobriquet "czar liberator" and may have improved the lot of the ordinary Russian more than any other before or since was driven to reform by events rather than upbringing. Alexander II, the son of Nicholas I, had had as his tutor the dreamy humanitarian poet Vasili Zhukovsky, and as heir had demonstrated no particularly marked talents or interests, certainly not in reform. But in 1855 he became ruler as Russia faced defeat in the Crimean War. His first task was to make peace. By the Treaty of Paris, concluded on March 30, 1856 (New Style), all territories occupied by Russia were restored except a strip of Bessarabia on the Danube, which Russia was forced to cede to Moldavia. Both Russia and Turkey were forbidden to keep navies in or on the coast of the Black Sea.

The Great Reforms. In announcing the end of the war, the new emperor indicated that reforms would follow. A few days later he told the Moscow gentry that it was better to begin to abolish serfdom from above than to wait until it began to abolish itself from below. The startled gentry were not eager to embrace the cause of emancipation, but Alexander ordered officials to start work. On Feb. 19, 1861, a brief manifesto proclaimed serfdom abolished.

Long and complex laws prescribed the actual changes. The few household serfs were freed without land. The gentry's peasants received their freedom and roughly half of the gentry land they had been tilling for themselves except for a small but sometimes strategic area called "cut-offs" (*otrezki*). But they had to pay for the land they received. Determination of the exact size of peasant allotments and their price was left to each locality. If an ex-serf chose not to pay, he received only a quarter of his parcel. Only a small fraction took this option.

The ex-serfs of the gentry, who numbered over 20 million, were obliged to make "redemption payments" over the next 49 years to the state, which reimbursed the gentry in government bonds. Land was not transferred to the family or individual but to the existing village communes (singular, *obshchina* or *mir*), which had collective responsibility for apportioning taxes, selecting army recruits, and collecting the redemption payments.

Additional laws of 1863 and 1866 allotted land to the "appanage" (imperial family) peasants and the 19 million state peasants. The former received half again as much land per capita as the ex-serfs of the gentry, and the state peasants almost twice as much. In 1864 the serfs of the Polish nobility in the northwestern provinces and in Poland were granted land on terms substantially better than were given to the Russian serfs.

The 1861 legislation was both criticized and praised. The ex-serf was saddled with heavy burdens, and the commune was strengthened just when it was becoming a great obstacle to agricultural improvement. Nevertheless, human bondage was swept from Russian life.

Other so-called Great Reforms followed. In January 1864 institutions of elective local self-government called zemstvos were established at the level of the county (*uyezd*) and province (*gubernia*). Delegates to the county zemstvos were elected by town dwellers, peasant commune members, and individual landowners. The number of delegates that each of these three groups could elect was apportioned by how much land or other assets each group had. The delegates to the county zemstvos elected the delegates to the provincial zemstvos. The zemstvos managed schools, medical aid, roads, and many other local services and assisted peasant farmers with technical help. In time they employed many trained professionals. In 1870 the zemstvo system, at least in part, was extended to the government of towns.

In late 1864 an independent judiciary was established, and trials for major crimes were conducted before juries. Justices of the peace were created for minor civil and criminal cases. Most Russians were declared to be equal before the law. The legal reform was probably the most successful of the Great Reforms.

In 1874 all Russian males were made equally subject to military service. The term of service, which had been 25 years before 1859 and then 15 years, was reduced to six years. Soldiers were to be treated more humanely, and elementary education was introduced for all recruits.

The Great Reforms did much to hasten industrialization, expansion of the new professional, middle, and working classes, and the decline of the gentry as the key group in Russian society.

Much of Poland's autonomy was restored in 1862. Nevertheless an increasing number of Poles agitated for further change. An attempt to draft the radicals into the Russian army triggered an uprising in January 1863. But Poland had no army, as it had in 1830, and the peasants remained passive. The ill-equipped insurgents were crushed by Russian troops. The Russians rewarded the peasants by passing favorable legislation. But Poland was punished. The Organic Statute of 1832 became a dead letter, Poland was subjected to direct Russian administration, and russification affected education and the Uniate Church.

Reform in Finland followed a different course. The Finnish diet was reconvened in 1863 and met regularly thereafter. The "fundamental laws" could be changed only with the diet's consent, and until the end of the century constitutionalism was a reality in Finland.

The Polish revolt did not halt the reforms in Russia, but other factors slowed their pace. In 1866 an unstable student, Dmitri Karakozov, fired at the czar and missed. The immediate response was to appoint a new and reactionary minister of education, Dmitri Tolstoy. Already procurator of the Holy Synod at the time of his appointment, he handled both schools and church with repressive harshness, and his heavy-handed imposition of required classical studies was termed "Greco-Roman bondage." However, Tolstoy's restrictive regime did not prevent the emergence in the universities of many distinguished scholars, notably the chemist Dmitri Mendeleyev, the inventor of the periodic table of elements; the biologist Ilya Mechnikov, though after loss of his professorship in Russia he had to go to Paris to find adequate working conditions; Ivan Pavlov, the physiologist and student of the "conditioned reflex"; and Vasili Klyuchevsky, the foremost prerevolutionary historian.

In spite of the general slowing of reform in education, educational opportunities were generally widened. In 1865, girls from all social classes were admitted as day students to boarding schools that had previously been the exclusive preserve of girls of the privileged class. Although women were still barred from the universities, privately supported university-level courses were made available to them in 1869. With the help of the

THE BRITISH MUSEUM

Alexander II, known as the "czar liberator" for having abolished serfdom in 1861, introduced widespread reforms in Russia. They were insufficient to satisfy the extremist revolutionaries, one of whom assassinated him.

zemstvos, elementary education expanded in both town and country after 1864.

Diplomacy and War. During the reign of Alexander II, foreign affairs were managed more by the foreign minister, Aleksandr Gorchakov, than by the czar. Russia obtained France's support for the new principality of Rumania, formed between 1858 and 1866 by the union of Moldavia and Wallachia. When Napoleon III led an army into northern Italy in 1859 to expel the Austrians from the Italian peninsula, the czar gave Napoleon his support by a show of force on Austria's frontier. In the Polish insurrection, both France and Britain encouraged the Poles without actually helping them. But Alexander gained the support of Prussia, which feared that a Polish victory in Russian Poland might affect Prussian Poland. A revolution in Greece led to the dethronement of the Bavarian dynasty, which had ruled Greece since 1832. Russia joined Britain and France, in spite of their involvement in the Polish revolt, in arranging the accession of a Danish prince to the Greek throne.

In the tangle of diplomacy and brief wars by which the Prussian leader Otto von Bismarck achieved the unification of Germany, Russia maintained a neutrality benevolent toward Prussia in the Austro-Prussian War against Denmark over Schleswig-Holstein (1864), the Prussian war with Austria (1866), and the Franco-Prussian War (1870–1871). When the defeat of France became clear, Gorchakov denounced the Black Sea clauses of the Treaty of Paris in October 1870. Having come to regard the clauses as unwise in any case, the other powers acquiesced in March 1871. In 1873 a somewhat chastened Austria joined Russia and Prussia in the Three Emperors' League. Its significance remained vague.

In the meantime Russia had been active in Asia. Under the guidance of Nikolai Muraviev, governor general of Eastern Siberia, Russians penetrated the Amur Valley. In 1858 the Chinese and Russians signed the Treaty of Aigun, which gave to Russia the area north and west of the Amur River, from its junction with the Argun River to the Pacific. Though the Chinese did not ratify the treaty, they were obliged to sign an even more humiliating one with the Russians in 1860 after the Anglo-French occupation of Peking. In the Sino-Russian Treaty of Peking, the 1858 transfer of territory to Russia was confirmed, and Russia also gained the area between the Amur and Ussuri rivers and the Pacific. The present boundary accords with this treaty.

Although Russia extended its Pacific coast, it liquidated its possessions on the American continent in 1867 by the sale of Alaska to the United States for the sum of $7.2 million.

Russian control had been advancing in Central Asia, which belonged to no large recognized states, since the 1820's. In 1864, Gen. Mikhail Chernyayev was faced with the necessity of fighting the khanates of Bukhara and Khiva, which became Russian protectorates (1868 and 1873). The khanate of Kokand was simply abolished and annexed in 1876. Gen. Mikhail Skobelev completed the conquest of Central Asia by seizing the Trans-Caspian region. By 1884 the post-World War II Central Asian frontier was, with one minor exception, fixed.

In 1864, Foreign Minister Gorchakov declared that Russia, like the United States, France in Africa, and Britain in India, faced the difficulty of knowing where to stop in its annexation of territory. The British, not satisfied with such explanations, watched with alarm the Russian advances. But a war between Britain and Russia over Afghanistan and India that many expected was in fact avoided.

In Europe the Three Emperors' League soon foundered on conflicts of interest in the Balkans. In 1875 a revolt against the Turks broke out in Hercegovina and Bosnia, and soon Serbia and Montenegro declared war on the Ottomans. From the late 1860's, Pan-Slavist sentiment had been spreading in Russia. Though it never had the influence some outsiders attributed to it and only one significant official (Gen. Nikolai Ignatiev) ever subscribed to its unclear doctrines, Pan-Slavs helped to inflame public opinion after fighting broke out. The czar and Gorchakov, though neither was a revolutionary or a Pan-Slav, were reluctantly nudged in April 1877 into a war with Turkey. It was a war that international diplomacy had tried in vain to avert.

The military reforms of 1874 had still to take full effect. After some successes at the outset, Russian armies were thrown back. Nevertheless, the fortress of Plevna was taken by the Russians in late 1877, just after Kars in the Caucasus had fallen to them. With imperial armies approaching Constantinople in January 1878, the sultan accepted an armistice.

Peace was thought to have been made with the Treaty of San Stefano (March 1878), which would have created a large Bulgaria. But Austria and Britain forced the suspension of the agreement, and it was replaced by the Treaty of Berlin in July 1878. Russia gained some new territory in Bessarabia and the Caucasus. Serbia, Montenegro, and Rumania became fully independent of the Ottoman Empire. The proposed Bulgarian state was split into a small autonomous Bulgaria, an "Eastern Rumelia" with less autonomy, and a substantial Macedonian area that remained under Turkish rule. Other minor changes were made in the San Stefano map. A major item was the right of Austria to occupy Bosnia-Hercegovina, where the crisis had begun.

Much frustration and anger were expressed in Russia. A constitution for Bulgaria, where Russian troops remained for a short time, was authorized by Alexander II. Though the prince chosen by the Bulgarians was a nephew of the Russian empress, he proved far from an obedient instrument of St. Petersburg. Bismarck, conscious of Russian resentment against himself as the "honest broker" of the Congress of Berlin, signed a secret treaty of alliance with Austria in 1879. When Russia proposed an alliance with Germany, Bismarck countered by suggesting that the Three Emperors' League be revived. Negotiations to that end were completed in June 1881, a few months after Alexander II had been assassinated by a bomb thrown by a member of an extremist group, People's Will.

Revolutionary Ferment. In the 1860's new ideological enthusiasms—especially nihilism and socialism—swept the educated youth. The apostle of nihilism was the critic Dmitri Pisarev, who declared, "What can be broken must be broken." He placed his faith for human betterment in the new science of the day. Some of the Russian socialists of the period, such as Herzen, Bakunin, Sergei Nechayev, and Pyotr Tkachev, worked chiefly outside of Russia.

Inside Russia the first underground revolutionary manifestos appeared in 1861, and the mentor of the young radicals, Nikolai Chernyshevsky, was arrested the following year. In 1873–1874 more than 2,000 youths heeded Herzen's urging to go "to the people" by descending on peasant villages with their revolutionary message. The peasants often turned the puzzling intruders over to the police. A new society was formed in 1876. It took the name of Land and Freedom (Zemlya i Volya) and tried slightly altered tactics in a new but equally unsuccessful move "to the people" in 1877–1878.

The revolutionary Populists (narodniki), as they are sometimes called, abandoned the attempt to lead the masses to revolt, and turned instead to terrorism. The flogging of a prisoner by order of the military governor of St. Petersburg, Gen. Fyodor Trepov, led a young woman named Vera Zasulich to shoot and wound Trepov. A jury found her "not guilty." Thereafter, regular judicial rules were suspended in political trials. Terrorism became widespread. Several officials were assassinated. In 1879 the Land and Freedom society split on the issue of terrorism, the terrorists forming a group called the People's Will (Narodnaya Volya).

The People's Will made seven known attempts on the czar's life. One that blew up part of the Winter Palace in early 1880 led the czar to create a Supreme Executive Commission headed by Mikhail Loris-Melikov. A few months later he became minister of the interior, and the commission was dissolved. His policy combined both reform and the repression of revolutionaries. Dmitri Tolstoy was dismissed, censorship relaxed, and a plan drawn up for summoning zemstvo and municipal representatives to advise on laws before they were submitted to the State Council. Though the so-called Loris-Melikov constitution did not deserve that name, it recalled pleas by liberals after the zemstvo reform of 1864 that the czar "crown the edifice" of local self-government by creating a national representative assembly. He might have moved in such a direction. The Loris-Melikov plan was approved on the morning of March 1, 1881, by Alexander II, who was killed by a member of the People's Will a few hours later.

ALEXANDER III

Alexander III had become heir only after the death of his elder brother in 1865. His education had been neglected, but his private life was exemplary to an almost unprecedented extent among Russian monarchs. He had never been an ardent reformer, and the assassination of his father set him on a course of reaction that affected his successor as well.

He was considerably influenced by Konstantin Pobedonostsev, an intelligent, conservative thinker, able jurist, and procurator of the Holy Synod from 1880 to 1905. Pobedonostsev was instrumental in the shelving of the Loris-Melikov project for legislative consultation. Loris-Melikov was replaced as minister of interior by Nikolai Ignatiev, the Pan-Slav, who drew on earlier Slavophile ideas in planning the revival of the *zemski sobor*.

Pobedonostsev disapproved of Ignatiev's plan, and Ignatiev was replaced by Dmitri Tolstoy in 1882, assisted by A. D. Pazukhin. Together they charted a course of counter-reforms. In 1889 justices of the peace were abolished in most places, and appointed officials called land captains (*zemskiye nachalniki*) assumed their judicial functions and were assigned new administrative ones. In 1890 the zemstvo elections were made less democratic. In 1892 similar changes were made in municipal elections. The intent of these and other laws was to strengthen the declining gentry.

Certain measures did aid the peasantry: in 1881 redemption payments were reduced; in 1882 the State Peasant Bank was created to assist peasant purchase of land; a law, which went into effect in 1887, abolished the poll tax; and a law of 1889 regularized migration to Siberia. But the original aim of the emancipation laws, which was to make the ex-serfs landowners, was obscured by two decrees of 1893. One strengthened the village commune, making it more difficult for peasants to leave it. The other encouraged the repartition of land.

Alexander's reign witnessed a substantial acceleration in the growth of industry. The state built many railways, especially the Trans-Siberian (started in 1891). Tariffs were gradually raised, reaching a peak in 1891.

Foreign Policy. The newly revived Three Emperors' League was shaken by the Bulgarian crisis of 1885, when the unification of Bulgaria and Eastern Rumelia was proclaimed. Russian blunders resulted in the election of a pro-Austrian prince for Bulgaria, Ferdinand of Saxe-Coburg. Russia was left with a single ally, tiny Montenegro. Russo-Austrian rivalry over the Balkans prevented a second renewal of the Three Emperors' League in 1887. But Bismarck arranged a secret Reinsurance Treaty with Russia, despite Germany's continued alliance with Vienna. When Bismarck fell from power in 1890, however, Germany failed to renew the secret agreement.

At this point, two diplomatically isolated powers—France and Russia—startled Europe by their rapprochement. Their alliance was forged in several steps (1891–1894), ending in a military convention. French state loans helped to bring about the diplomatic marriage of St. Petersburg's reactionary monarchism with Paris' Third Republic.

Repression and the Eclipse of the Revolutionaries. Educational policy discouraged the secondary and higher education of the lower classes, and the ministry of education was given wide powers over the universities. New censorship regulations were issued in 1882. Russification was stepped up in Poland and the Baltic provinces, and attempts were even made to russify Central Asia. Though a conservative-minded committee recommended equal treatment for Jews, it was ignored, and new anti-Semitic legislation was enacted, leading to emigration of many Russian Jews and eventually to the formation of the Zionist movement (1897).

The 1880's were frustrating years for the revolutionaries. Most of the members of the People's Will were imprisoned. A single terrorist plot to murder Alexander III was foiled by arrests. Among the five executed was Lenin's brother Aleksandr Ulyanov. The failure of the movement "to the people" was followed by the failure of terrorism, and for the moment revolutionaries were at an impasse. As socialists abroad adopted Marxian orthodoxy, however, a new Liberation of Labor group was founded by Georgi Plekhanov in 1883 in Geneva, and small Marxist circles began to form inside Russia.

NICHOLAS II

Alexander's son, Nicholas II, resembled him in being a modest family man and a defender of autocracy. But Nicholas lacked his father's strength of character. He was married just after his accession in 1894 to Princess Alix of Hesse-Darmstadt. (She took the Russian name Alexandra.) They waited 11 years for the birth of a male heir, and when Aleksei was born in 1904 he was found to suffer from hemophilia. A year later the frantic parents were introduced to Grigori Rasputin, an unkempt *starets* ("holy man," in no sense a clergyman), who seemed to have the power to stop the czarevich's bleeding. Rasputin eventually gained considerable political influence, though it was much less than he was suspected of having.

Within a few months of his accession, the new emperor warned zemstvo leaders against the "senseless dreams" of any movement toward constitutionalism. He proposed no political changes and not only continued russification but unwisely extended it to Finland. A series of measures abridged the Finnish constitution and made Finns anti-Russian almost overnight. Ultranationalist groups multiplied in Russia. One consequence was the looting of Jewish property and the killing of over 100 Jews in the Kishinev pogrom in the spring of 1903. It was the first of any significance since 1881.

In the first decade of the reign, rapid economic growth continued under the direction of the minister of finance, Sergei Witte, who encouraged heavy industry and railway building. As industrial workers increased in number, so did strikes, leading the government to enact a law (1897) limiting the workday to 11½ hours.

Revolutionary activity revived. In the 1890's a series of public debates between Marxian socialists and socialists adhering to looser "populist" trends converted many university students to

Czar Nicholas II, the last Romanov ruler of Russia, his wife, and their five children. Nicholas holds his only boy and heir, Aleksei, who suffered from hemophilia.

socialism, and Marxism became fashionable. In 1898 the First Congress of the Russian Social Democratic Workers' party was held at Minsk, and the more peasant-oriented Socialist Revolutionary party took form soon afterward.

Russia and the Far East. An ill-conceived Far Eastern adventure absorbed most of the government's foreign interests in the early part of Nicholas' reign. Russia joined Germany and France in persuading the Japanese to give the Liaotung peninsula back to China after Japan's surprise victory over China in 1895. A grateful China allowed Russia to build the Chinese Eastern Railroad, substantially shortening the Chita-Vladivostok route. Russia also gained a sphere of influence in northern Manchuria and penetrated Korea, now formally independent. Another crisis, provoked by Germany's seizure of Kiaochow, enabled Russia to secure a 25-year lease of the Liaotung peninsula and the right to build a railroad connecting Port Arthur with the Chinese Eastern Railroad at Harbin. The Boxer Rebellion in China (1900) ended in Russian occupation of all Manchuria.

Alarmed by Russian expansion into Manchuria, the Japanese launched a surprise attack on the Russian fleet at Port Arthur in February 1904 (New Style) and captured the port in January 1905 (New Style). In several major battles between August 1904 and March 1905 (New Style) Russian armies were defeated near Mukden. In August the Japanese destroyed the Port Arthur fleet. In October 1905 a Russian fleet was sent from the Baltic to replace it. On arrival it was promptly sunk in Tsushima Strait by the Japanese (May 1905).

The 1905 Revolution and Its Aftermath. Russian autocracy faced its first major threat since the Decembrist uprising in the same year that the country met defeat in the Far East. After months of student disorders, scattered peasant uprisings, and mounting strikes, a priest named Georgi Gapon led unarmed workers to the Winter Palace in St. Petersburg on Jan. 9, 1905. They came to present their grievances to Nicholas. Troops fired on the crowd, killing over 100 people. The Revolution of 1905 is dated from this "Bloody Sunday." Protest and violence continued. Muti-

nies broke out in the army and navy, most notably on the battleship *Potemkin*.

The emperor agreed to convoke an advisory national assembly. In August he called for the creation of a national Duma, with advisory powers. But disorders continued, reaching a climax in a general strike in October, during which the first workers' soviets (councils) were created. The emperor made further concessions in his renowned October Manifesto, in which he promised to create a legislative assembly and to guarantee civil liberties. Witte, having just returned from concluding the Treaty of Portsmouth with Japan (Sept. 5, 1905, New Style), became Russia's first premier. By the terms of the treaty, Russia ceded to Japan the southern half of the island of Sakhalin, part of the South Manchurian Railway, and Russia's lease of the Liaotung peninsula.

The October Manifesto inaugurated a period of constitutional government. Two revolutionary parties, the Social Democrats and the Socialist Revolutionaries, were joined by some liberal Constitutional Democrats (Kadets) in demanding the formation of a constituent assembly, elected by universal, equal, secret, and direct suffrage, which would decide the political future of the country. But many moderates were satisfied with the emperor's proposed assembly, and they formed the Union of October 17 (later called the Octobrist party) to make the new system work.

The First Duma was elected on a broad franchise, though it fell short of the franchise demanded by the parties of the Left. The old State Council became a partly elective upper house. Nicholas promised that no bill could become law without the Duma's approval. But the Duma's budgetary powers were limited, and though Duma deputies could question ministers, the latter were responsible only to the czar. These and other matters were covered by the new Fundamental Laws of April 23, 1906.

The First Duma, which was dominated by the Kadets, met only from April to July. Their bill for expropriation, with compensation, of the lands of the gentry and others led the government to dissolve the Duma. In the Second Duma (February–June 1907), both the revolutionary Left and the Right gained at the expense of the moderates. The new premier, Pyotr Stolypin, dissolved it, at the same time changing the electoral law to produce a more conservative body. The change was contrary to the Fundamental Laws of 1906.

In November 1906, Stolypin had sponsored the first of several measures that were to make up the "Stolypin land reform." The reforms encouraged the peasant to leave the village commune and to consolidate his share of the land in a single plot. He was free to till his land from his old home in the village (*otrub*) or from a house on the farm itself (*khutor*). As a result, by 1916 about half of the peasant households in Russia had left or were in the process of leaving the communes. The consolidation of strips, an incredibly complex operation, moved more slowly.

The Third Duma lasted its allotted span of five years (1907–1912). Over 300 of the new total of 442 deputies supported Stolypin's government. Of these 300, about half were members of the Octobrist party, led by Aleksandr Guchkov.

Several revolutionary leaders despaired of further revolutionary activity in the immediate future and bided their time abroad. In 1903 the Social Democrats had split into Bolsheviks and Mensheviks. The former, led by Vladimir Ilich Lenin, insisted on a small, disciplined leadership; the latter preferred mass organization and action. The Socialist Revolutionaries had continued the terrorist traditions of the People's Will, assassinating two interior ministers in 1902 and 1904 and in 1906–1907 killing 4,100 officials down to the level of village police.

Stolypin halted the terrorism by creating special field courts-martial, which ordered over 1,000 revolutionaries to be hanged. The hangman's noose came to be known as the "Stolypin necktie." Stolypin was criticized for his impatience with legality, even by some who otherwise supported him. He also troubled moderates by his Russian nationalistic policies in Poland and Finland and by favoring Russians over Poles in the zemstvos that were being established in the western provinces. Stolypin was assassinated in 1911 by a double agent who was working for both the secret police and the terrorists.

The Third Duma extended zemstvos to three southeastern provinces, restored the justices of the peace and deprived land captains of judicial powers, introduced a system of workmen's insurance, and provided elementary education for more of the country's children. The Fourth Duma (1912–1917) was more conservative in its composition than the Third, and Stolypin's successors provided less effective leadership.

The Triple Entente and World War I. After 1905, Russia and Japan harmonized their differences with surprising success, and Russian attention was focused on Europe. Relations with Germany remained cool. An Anglo-Russian entente was signed in August 1907, compromising disputes over Persia, Afghanistan, and Tibet. Since Britain and France had reached an understanding in 1904, the result was a Triple Entente, which confronted the Triple Alliance of Germany, Austria-Hungary, and Italy.

The new foreign minister, Aleksandr Izvolsky, renewed Russian interest in the Balkans. In 1908 he agreed to Austrian annexation of Bosnia-Hercegovina in the forlorn hope that the Straits would be opened to Russian warships. In 1912 the Balkan states united to fight Turkey and defeated it. The division of the spoils led to a war in which Bulgaria was the sufferer at the hands of Serbia, Greece, and Montenegro. As in 1908, the Russian government was criticized in the press for failing to defend fellow Slavs. On June 28, 1914 (New Style), the archduke Franz Ferdinand, heir to the Austrian throne, was assassinated by Serbian terrorists in Sarajevo. Russia decided to support Serbia against any Austrian reprisals, believing a third Balkan humiliation would be unacceptable. By August the Triple Entente faced the Triple Alliance in World War I.

Government troops scatter unarmed demonstrators in St. Petersburg on Jan. 9, 1905. Several hundred civilians were killed or wounded on this "Bloody Sunday," which marked the beginning of the Revolution of 1905.

Rasputin, a mystic and debauchee, sits among his "court," which sometimes consisted of women of the aristocracy. Fearing that his influence over the empress would destroy the monarchy, conservatives murdered him in 1916.

Russian forces were hurled into East Prussia with insufficient preparation and were defeated at Tannenberg, though they may have saved France in the process by drawing German troops away from the Western front. In 1915 the Germans and Austrians pushed deep into the Russian Empire, to the edge of Riga and beyond Vilna. The Russian high command kept the army intact during the great retreat, but it produced great damage by pursuing a misconceived "scorched earth" policy all along the front. Millions of civilians were thrust into the interior.

In the summer of 1915 the czar himself assumed supreme command, an action only indirectly benefiting the war effort. In August 1916, Russia enjoyed its single substantial military success of the war when it took the offensive against Austria-Hungary in Galicia. Rumania was thereupon encouraged to enter the war against the Triple Alliance. It was promptly defeated, forcing the Russians to extend their front about 250 miles (400 km) and to refrain from pressing their advantage. There were successes on the Caucasian front against Turkey in the spring of 1916, and the supply and munitions situation was improving. All armies were war weary by 1917, but on balance the Russian war effort was no worse off than that of other combatants.

The Fall of the Romanovs. The political scene, however, was darkening. In 1915 many public organizations had sprung up to assist the war effort, including the Red Cross; the Union of Zemstvos and Towns, led by Georgi Lvov; and the War Industry Committee, headed by the Octobrist Guchkov. The emperor cooperated with such bodies for a time. But he refused to respond to the initiative of the moderate Progressive bloc, led by the Kadet leader Pavel Milyukov and supported by most of the Duma and the majority of the State Council.

While Nicholas II was at the front, the empress and Rasputin made many decisions and alienated virtually all segments of opinion. Several extreme conservatives organized the killing of Rasputin in December 1916 in order to save the monarchy. It was too late, and within two months unforeseen and spontaneous disorders in St. Petersburg toppled the Romanovs. The revolutionary leaders who were to bring the Soviet Union into existence were mostly abroad when the February Revolution of 1917 brought about the fall of the monarchy.

For a continuation of the country's history, see RUSSIAN REVOLUTION and the UNION OF SOVIET SOCIALIST REPUBLICS—*History*.

DONALD W. TREADGOLD
University of Washington

Bibliography
Auty, Robert, and Obolensky, Dimitri, eds., *Companion to Russian Studies 1: An Introduction to Russian History* (Cambridge 1976).
Billington, James H., *The Icon and the Axe: An Interpretive History of Russian Culture* (Knopf 1966).
Florinsky, Michael T., *Russia: A History and an Interpretation*, 2 vols. (Macmillan, N. Y., 1953).
Miliukov, Paul, *Russia and Its Crisis* (Collier Bks., 1962).
Pipes, Richard E., *Russia Under the Old Regime* (Scribner 1975).
Pushkarev, Sergei G., *The Emergence of Modern Russia, 1801–1917*, tr. by Robert H. McNeal and Tova Yedlin (Holt 1963).
Riasanovsky, Nicholas V., *A History of Russia*, 3d ed. (Oxford 1977).
Seton-Watson, Hugh, *The Russian Empire, 1801–1917* (Oxford 1967).
Treadgold, Donald W., *The West in Russia and China: Religious and Secular Thought in Modern Times*, 2 vols.; vol. 1, *Russia, 1472–1917* (Cambridge 1973).

For Specialized Study
Blum, Jerome, *Lord and Peasant in Russia from the Ninth to the Nineteenth Century* (Princeton Univ. Press 1961).
Jelavich, Barbara, *A Century of Russian Foreign Policy, 1814–1914* (Lippincott 1964).
Lyashchenko, Peter I., *History of the National Economy of Russia*, tr. by L. M. Herman (Macmillan, N. Y., 1949).
Venturi, Franco, *Roots of Revolution: A History of the Populist and Socialist Movements in Nineteenth-Century Russia*, tr. by Francis Haskell (Knopf 1960).
Vucinich, Wayne S., ed., *The Peasant in Nineteenth-Century Russia* (Stanford Univ. Press 1968).
Walkin, Jacob, *The Rise of Democracy in Pre-Revolutionary Russia* (Praeger 1962).
Weidlé, Wladimir, *Russia: Absent and Present*, tr. by A. Gordon Smith (Day 1952).
Yaney, George L., *The Systematization of Russian Government: Social Evolution in the Domestic Administration of Imperial Russia, 1711–1905* (Univ. of Ill. Press 1973).

RUSSIAN ART AND ARCHITECTURE are essentially the creation of the Slavic peoples of European Russia, beginning at the time of their conversion to Christianity in the 10th century. Russian art has roots, however, in the pagan art of earlier periods and has drawn successively on Byzantine and western European traditions. It has influenced adjacent areas, such as Armenia, Georgia, and Siberia, which were later to become part of the Russian Empire and then of the Soviet Union.

The history of Russian art and architecture falls into four major periods, reflecting the divisions of Russian political history: the medieval period of principalities influenced by Byzantine tradition, the Muscovite period dominated by Moscow, the Westernized period initiated by Peter the Great, and the Soviet era. Throughout its development, relatively constant elements in Russian art have been a humanizing tendency, a decorative sense, and patronage by the state.

MIDDLE AGES

The medieval period in Russia had two phases. The earlier, dominated by Kiev, lasted until the Mongol (Tatar) conquest in 1240. The later, which saw the rise of other states, ended with Moscow's gradual assumption of the role of a Third Rome, after the fall of Byzantium (Constantinople), the Second Rome, to the Turks in 1453.

In the 10th century, the Russians were loosely organized in a federation of largely self-governing principalities under the authority in military and foreign affairs of Kiev, in the Ukraine. At the command of Vladimir, grand duke of Kiev, they abandoned paganism in about 990 in favor of the Orthodox form of Christianity centered in Byzantium. So efficiently did they execute his instructions to destroy all objects connected with paganism that few vestiges of Russia's pre-Christian culture have survived. The exceptions are chiefly jewelry; amulets shaped like female deities, bears, or sun symbols; and stone idols. Certain pagan motifs, however, persisted in folk art, notably the tree of life, the Great Goddess, and animal designs derived from Persia or from the Scythians and Sarmatians, who inhabited southern Russia in early times.

Kiev's political preeminence was matched by its artistic achievements. Art also flourished in regional capitals, such as Vladimir, Suzdal, and especially Novgorod, which challenged Kiev's supremacy. All these Russian centers looked to Byzantium, source of their new faith, for their arts. Since the maintenance of Orthodoxy was their chief concern, they gave most of their attention to building churches. Russian princes also, however, quickly assimilated the Byzantine concept of kingship and built palaces to express it. But because most medieval secular work has long since perished, the period is represented almost entirely by religious works.

Architecture. Russia had a scarcity of building stone, but vast quantities of excellent wood were available to anyone for the cutting. Consequently, from pagan times on, wood was used for most building purposes, and Russians were noted for their woodworking skill. They used wood to build churches; modest, square or rectangular dwellings; and, in each city, a kremlin, or citadel, which included a castle or palace and at least one church within its walls. Oak was used to strengthen the walls surrounding the

NOVOSTI, FROM SOVFOTO

Icon of the brothers Florus and Laurus, two early Christian martyrs, school of Novgorod (14th century).

kremlin or the settlement around it and to pave the streets, as in 12th century Novgorod.

As a building material, however, wood has the disadvantages of being perishable and flammable. Therefore, few wooden medieval structures remain. Russian princes, to celebrate their new faith and authority, built their finest churches, monasteries, and palaces of stone. They had to hire Byzantine craftsmen to teach the Russians the new techniques of masonry.

Kiev. The four earliest cathedrals of Kiev were built in Byzantine style. They had the plan of a Greek cross within a square, rounded apses, barrel-vaulted roofs, and a low central dome flanked by several others. Domes, raised on low drums supported by squinches (arches) poised on piers or columns, were one of the most important Byzantine innovations to reach Russia. Interiors glowed with mosaics of glass, marble, stone, or brick tesserae and with frescoes.

Three of these Kievan cathedrals were destroyed or greatly damaged—Vladimir's Church of the Dime (Tithe; begun 989), by the Mongols; the Church of the Dormition (Assumption; begun 1073) in Pecherskaya Lavra (Monastery of the Caves), in World War II; and the sumptuous Church of St. Michael (begun 1108) in the Mikhail-Zlatoverkh (Dmitrov) Monastery, in the Stalinist era.

The fourth, Grand Duke Yaroslav's Cathedral of Hagia Sophia ("Divine Wisdom," commonly

St. Sophia; begun 1036), counterpart of Hagia Sophia in Byzantium, had its exterior altered in the baroque period but retains much of its original interior splendor. Unlike the small 11th century Byzantine churches, generally with three aisles and five domes, Yaroslav's church had five aisles and a large central dome, symbolizing Christ, surrounded by 12 smaller ones representing the apostles. Also, it was edged on three sides by a peristyle and had towers at the west corners containing stairs to the ruler's pew in the west gallery. The latter innovation was retained in the 12th century palace situated at Bogolyubovo.

Vladimir-Suzdal. In the late 12th century, regional capitals, such as Chernigov and Smolensk, built fine cathedrals on modified Byzantine lines. In the principality of Vladimir-Suzdal there evolved a distinctive style, which survives in a series of small churches of great elegance. They are cruciform in plan, their three aisles terminate in apses of full height, and their single domes rest on drums slenderer than those of Kiev. Each of the outer walls is divided into three vertical sections by some flat feature, such as a pilaster, and each is adorned with sculptured motifs of a figural, vegetal, or geometric character unique in Russian art. These churches are also interesting for their Romanesque elements stemming from the Western world. Representative of the fully developed style is the ornate Cathedral of St. Dmitri (begun 1193) in Vladimir.

Novgorod and Pskov. The architecture of Novgorod was launched by Vladimir of Kiev, who

Cathedral of St. Dmitri, Vladimir, with high apses, slender drum, and decorative reliefs (12th century).

SOVFOTO

commissioned a cathedral dedicated, like that in Kiev, to Hagia Sophia. Built of oak and roofed with "13 tops" (probably meaning "turrets"), it burned in 1045. A new stone replacement (completed 1052) is less ornate than Kiev's Hagia Sophia, having 3 aisles instead of 5, and 5 domes instead of 13. However, its plain, whitewashed, monolithic exterior, ornamented only by pilasters and a scalloped motif on the drums, already reflects Novgorod's fondness for simplicity and verticality. The stress on verticality is even stronger in the Cathedral of St. George (begun 1119) in the Yuriev Monastery built by Master Peter. Here the facades have the threefold division of Vladimir-Suzdal, and the domes are slightly pointed and reduced in number to three.

Novgorod, which had ceased to be dependent upon Kiev in the 11th century, escaped conquest by the Mongols. After a lull of a century, the arts regained their original impetus, and trade with the West expanded. New churches were built in a modification of the Novgorodian style. The threefold facade was retained, with restrained low-relief decoration. But the overall shape became cubelike, as the side apses, which had already been reduced in height and circumference in the exquisite Church of the Savior in nearby Nereditsa (1198; destroyed in World War II), gradually disappeared. Examples are the churches of St. Theodore Stratelates (about 1360) and Our Savior of the Transfiguration (1372), whose blind arcading on the remaining apse may reflect Western influence.

Roofs also changed, becoming completely vaulted, forming a scalloped or triangular-shaped gable on each side. Domes, usually single, stood on tall drums and gained a helmlike silhouette, which was later replaced by an onion shape, originating in Moscow. Free-standing, multistory towers were built for bells, new to Russia.

Like Novgorod, its satellite Pskov escaped the Mongols and also built new churches. They were small, with large porches and short, squat, waisted columns flanking the entrance to the nave. These churches were the earliest in which pendentives (spherical triangles) rather than squinches support the drum. Bell towers were similar to those in Novgorod.

The most advanced example of post-Mongol secular building was the stone palace built by Archbishop Vasili in Novgorod (1433). Its simple exterior contrasts sharply with the decorative brickwork of the princely palace in Uglich (1481), built in the Muscovite style. The Pogankiny mansion in Pskov, a rare example of a 17th century merchant's residence, suggests the domestic style of earlier centuries.

Painting. Medieval Russian painting includes frescoes, icons, and illumination, mostly done by monks. Like architecture, it was strongly influenced by Byzantine tradition in its formal, unrealistic, frontal style and religious subject matter and symbolism, but over the centuries it developed national and regional modifications.

Frescoes. The Byzantine artists who went to Kiev to adorn its churches were assisted by Russians, who made their influence felt even before they were able to replace their masters. As a result, although mosaic murals were never combined with painted ones in Byzantium, both mosaics and frescoes adorn the walls of Kiev's Hagia Sophia. Although they conform to Byzantine tradition, the humanistic element characteristic of Russian art is already apparent, as, for exam-

Cathedral of Hagia Sophia, Novgorod, showing the northern taste for simplicity and verticality (11th century).

ple, in the fresco portraits of Yaroslav's family (about 1045) in the nave, in contrast to the formality of contemporary Byzantine court portraiture. The early 12th century frescoes in Hagia Sophia's two towers are equally unique in Russian and Byzantine art for their secular content. One depicts the Byzantine emperor watching the hippodrome races. Others illustrate hunting, court, or theatrical scenes.

The early artists of Vladimir-Suzdal and Rostov drew on Kiev for inspiration and, at first, also worked under Byzantine masters. In the great fresco of the Last Judgment (begun 1194) in the Cathedral of St. Dmitri in Vladimir, a Byzantine master must have painted the 12 Apostles and the angels to their right, while the remaining angels appear to have been done by Russians.

Elsewhere Russians were producing works of great distinction. For example, the frescoes in the Church of the Savior in the Mirozhsky Monastery (1156), near Pskov, possess the intimacy and deep emotional content typical of the Pskovan school. Those adorning Pskov's Snetorgorsky Monastery (1313) display a spontaneity that was also characteristic of the region.

The finest work was done on Novgorodian territory. The frescoes in the Church of St. George in Staraya Ladoga (about 1167) display the clear lines and sense of movement that distinguish painting of the Novgorodian school. The *Last Judgment* in the Church of the Savior in Nereditsa was especially fine.

Byzantine influence revived in Novgorod with the arrival there about 1370 of the great Byzantine master Theophanes the Greek (Feofan Grek). Fragments of his murals in the Church of Our Savior of the Transfiguration show his elongated figures, subtle color, complex composition, and nervous, strongly highlighted style.

His influence was reflected in the Russian-painted murals in the Dormition Cathedral in Volotovo (1380; destroyed in World War II). The latter contrasted with the contemporary, Macedonian-influenced frescoes in the Church of the Savior in Kovalevo (destroyed in World War II).

By 1395, Theophanes was in Moscow, where he worked with Russian artists. He adorned the Church of the Birth of the Virgin, with the help of Semyon the Black and pupils; the Cathedral of the Archangel; and, with Prokhor of Gorodetz and the monk Andrei Rublev, the Annunciation Cathedral. During these years he also decorated the ducal palace with topographical and historical frescoes.

Rublev, an artist of great sensitivity and lyricism, the Fra Angelico of Russia, created the Muscovite school of painting. Examples of his frescoes are those painted with Daniil Chernyi in 1408 in the Dormition Cathedral in Vladimir.

Icons. Icons, religious panel paintings representing holy beings, were created for homes and for churches, especially for the high carved iconostasis (screen) introduced in the 14th century. Few survive from before the Mongol conquest, none definitely ascribed to Kiev. Although they adhere to Byzantine tradition, including the use of gold or silver for background and regalia, Russian elements are so much in evidence that few, even of the earliest icons, can be taken for Byzantine. Icons from Vladimir-Suzdal and Yaroslavl possess a patrician quality, which disappeared with the Mongol invasion. Novgorodian icons, which form the great majority, reflect the sturdier, more forthright outlook of a merchant people.

Of icons after the Mongol conquest, those of the Novgorodian school in the 14th and 15th centuries maintained such a high standard that they

METALWORK: (*Left*) Silver gilt censer with repoussé (17th century); (*Right above*) Gold cross with cloisonné, Byzantine style; (*Right below*) Gold cross with pearls (17th century).

represent the classical period in Russian icon painting. Their rhythmic, linear qualities, superb, brilliant colors, deep spirituality, and elimination of all unnecessary details stamp even the most Byzantine-influenced icons with the Novgorodian hallmark.

About the same time, the Moscow school of icon painting was developing, especially under Rublev. His rhythmical style, seen at its purest in the Old Testament *Trinity* (Tretyakov Gallery, Moscow), is distinguished by soft and delicate, yet precise and firm outlines; by the preponderance of curved lines unobtrusively contrasted with angular lines; by the sloping shoulders of his figures; and by clear, luminous, pastel colors. Other Muscovite painters acquired Rublev's elegance, combining it with brown flesh tints, multiple highlights, and elaborate architectural backgrounds. After Moscow's annexation of Novgorod in 1478, these elements, but without the elegance, began to influence and undermine the Novgorodian style.

Illumination. In book illumination, mostly religious, the Russo-Byzantine style was inspired by Byzantine tradition, yet, especially in Novgorod, it often incorporated non-Byzantine elements. These included elaborately interlaced initials, possibly influenced by Norse design; whole or truncated animals recalling Celtic, Romanesque, Russian, or even Scythian forms; and floral and geometric Russian motifs. Examples are the Svyatoslav Codex of 1073 and the exceptionally fine Khitrovo Gospels, perhaps by Rublev.

Decorative Arts—Metalwork. The tradition of metalwork in Russia is at least as old as the metal ornaments in a spirited animal style created by the Scythians. The pagan Slavs were too poor to work costly metals, but Kiev's Christian artisans produced for the church and the nobility exquisite vessels, jewelry, and other articles of filigree and cloisonné enamel on copper or gold. Cloisonné plaques for personal adornment were generally round or boat shaped, with Russian-inspired floral, geometric, or bird motifs. Religious plaques resembled their Byzantine prototypes.

The Vladimir-Suzdalian metalworkers produced superb damascene work, seen at its best in the 13th century panels of the doors of the Nativity Cathedral in Suzdal. The greater part of their output was chalices, censers, crosses, and book and icon covers for the church. Novgorod fashioned some vessels of distinctive scallop shape, with decorations sometimes showing Western influences.

Embroidery. Fine embroidery was made in convents from early medieval times. Most of the best work was for the church and followed Byzantine styles, but with regional modification. Commemorative portrait hangings, such as that of Saint Sergius of Radonezh, were embroidered in palace workshops from the 15th century.

MEDIEVAL PAINTING: (*Left*) Fresco by Theophanes the Greek (detail), from Church of Our Savior of the Transfiguration, Novgorod (14th century); (*Right*) Icon, the *Trinity* by Rublev, Moscow school (15th century).

MUSCOVITE PERIOD

In the 14th century, Moscow gradually began to emerge as the unifying force among the Russian principalities, most of which were still subject to Mongol rule. Dmitri Donskoy's victory over the Mongols at Kulikovo in 1380 quickened Moscow's creative spirit. Its prestige was enhanced by its assumption of leadership of the Orthodox community after the fall of Byzantium and by the marriage in 1472 of Ivan III to the niece of the last Byzantine emperor. Muscovite art reflected this rise in Moscow's fortunes.

Architecture—Wood. Muscovite stone architecture was greatly influenced by the long tradition of Russian architecture in wood. Although no medieval wooden buildings survive, churches of the 17th and 18th centuries faithfully reproduced the forms of the much older churches they replaced. They fall into four major types.

The first and most common was the cellular type. The church was raised on a substructure of storerooms and was surrounded by covered verandas reached by roofed staircases. The steeply pitched roof had at its center a small drum and dome or steeple, as in St. John's Church, near Rostov.

The second, or tent type, had a steeple shaped like a pyramid or tent. The steeple rose from amidst *kokoshnik* gables, so-called because their ace-of-spades shape resembled a *kokoshnik*, or medieval woman's headdress. These gables made a transition from the rectangular body of the church to the octagonal drum under the steeple, as in St. Clement's Church, at Una.

The third type had a tiered roof. On each facade, three or more tiers projected in rows of inverted-V-shaped gables, and an onion-shaped dome on a drum rose from the top, as in the Church of St. John the Forerunner in the Penovsky district.

The fourth and most spectacular type was multidomed. Each dome, piled in a central mass, rose from a shoal of *kokoshnik* gables, as in the Church of the Transfiguration in Kizhi.

Church of the Transfiguration, with *kokoshnik* gables and multiple onion domes, Kizhi (1714).

26c

These churches, regardless of their external differences, were divided internally into three sections—the trapeza, nave, and chancel. The trapeza was a low anteroom where worshipers could assemble for warmth, food, and talk. It was separated from the much higher nave by a thick wall designed to deaden the noise in the anteroom, but with slits cut in it to enable the overflow on feast days to follow the service. The nave was separated from the chancel by the iconostasis, whose central, or "Royal," doors revealed the altar.

An example of medieval and Muscovite domestic architecture is the palace at Kolomenskoe, near Moscow, built by Ivan I in the 14th century, subsequently rebuilt, and later destroyed. Known through early sketches and an 18th century model, it consisted of a series of square and rectangular sections under *kokoshnik* gables and tent-shaped turrets or steeply pitched roofs. The whole complex was as picturesque as an English half-timbered Elizabethan mansion, though less well ordered. Nobles' and merchants' houses followed a similar plan, including, for example, the mansion of the Stroganovs in Solvychegodsk, near Perm. Storerooms were on the ground floor and quarters for women and children on the top.

Stone. Muscovite stone architecture developed in the late 15th century, when Ivan III imported four Italian architects—Aristotele Fioravanti, Alevisio Novi, Marco Ruffo, and Pietro Solari—to strengthen the Kremlin with modern gunfire-resistant walls. He also employed them within the Kremlin but insisted that there they follow traditional Russian architecture.

The Kremlin's churches are a microcosm of the religious stone architecture of late 15th and early 16th century Muscovy. The Vladimir-Suzdalian style prevailed in the Dormition Cathe-

dral (begun 1475), built by Fioravanti after Ivan had sent him to study the churches of Vladimir, and in the Annunciation Cathedral (begun 1482), built by masons from Pskov and one of the first churches to copy wooden *kokoshnik* gables in stone. Pskovians also built the Cathedral of the Ordination (begun 1485), but in their native style.

In the Cathedral of the Archangel Michael (begun 1505), Novi combined such Russian basic elements as the cruciform interior ground plan and onion-shaped domes with such Renaissance decorative features as classical capitals, a cornice, and a row of flat, semicircular, fluted niches. The elegance of Moscow's developed ornamental styles is seen in the Church of the Savior Behind the Golden Lattice (1678). The original Terem Palace, also in the Kremlin, and the Old Printing House, in Moscow, are examples of secular Muscovite architecture.

A very different note is struck by two other important Kremlin buildings. The banqueting hall by Ruffo and Solari, called the Palace of Facets (begun 1487) after its faceted stone facade, is unique for its Italianate design. The novel bell tower of Ivan Veliky (begun 1532), built by the Italian Marco Bono, consists of Western-inspired, recessed, corniced tiers, whose outline was nonetheless attuned to that of the wooden tent-church.

The resemblance may have been intentional. For in 1532, Vasili III celebrated the birth of the future Ivan IV by building in Kolomenskoye the Church of the Ascension, which copied in masonry the features of wooden churches. Resting on a substructure, it is surrounded by verandas reached by covered staircases and is roofed with a tent-steeple rising from a cluster of superimposed *kokoshnik* gables.

Moscow Kremlin, with (*from right*) Ivan Veliky bell tower, Dormition Cathedral, and Archangel Michael Cathedral.

H. CARTIER-BRESSON, FROM MAGNUM

The Church of the Ascension launched a style of tent-roofed churches on a rectangular or octagonal plan, which quickly became so popular that in the mid-17th century Patriarch Nikon, zealously determined to maintain Byzantine traditions, forbade it in favor of domed churches. Fortunately two churches, which combined tent-roofs and domes and elaborated them in the baroque spirit, escaped his ban. They are the Church of the Beheading of St. John the Baptist in Dyakovo (begun 1553) and the brightly painted Cathedral of St. Basil the Blessed (begun 1555) in Moscow's Red Square.

Nikon's ban did not apply to churches built in the baroque style introduced through Poland and the Ukraine. Of two kinds, the more conservative were ornate yet basically traditional, as, for example, St. Nicholas Church in Khamovniki, Moscow (late 16th century), where the profuse decoration, chiefly around windows and doors, was a new departure. The Westernized baroque churches, such as those of the Intercession of the Virgin in Fili (1693), in a Moscow suburb, and of the Virgin of the Sign in Dubrovitzy (begun 1690), modified traditional forms. The cruciform interior plan is repeated on the exterior, with its four projecting arms rounded and an octagonal tower at its center. The Fili church is tiered, and its recessed superstructures are enlivened with domes. The Dubrovitzy church is one-storied, but its roof is ornamented with statues, never before so used. Neither of these baroque tendencies, however, continued.

Painting—15th and 16th Century Frescoes and Icons. The school of Moscow was at its height in the late 15th century under Dionysius, the third of the great masters of Russian painting, after Theophanes and Rublev. Working with his two sons and a team of artists, he frescoed the interiors of the Dormition Cathedral in Moscow and the Therapont Monastery and others and produced many icons. His fresco colors are light and gay, those in icons more subdued. In both forms his work, as a professional painter rather than a monk, is to some extent individualized in style. It is dramatic, and it reflects a new interest in aesthetics, perhaps influenced by the Italian architects in Moscow, and in depicting movement. Dionysius' profusely highlighted figures have small features, slender, elongated bodies, and swirling drapery. His backgrounds contain complex architectural compositions.

During the 16th century, new, often didactic themes appeared gradually in Muscovite icons, and several sequential scenes were presented on one panel. Although the reform-minded Council of the Hundred Chapters (1550–1551) advocated a return to Novgorodian tradition, and some artists complied, Muscovite tendencies generally continued. Panels became smaller, duller in color, and more crowded with additional figures and detail.

17th Century Icons and Murals. Toward the end of the 16th century, connoisseurs of icons sponsored a new style in the icons of the Stroganov school, by such men as Procopius Chirin and Istoma and Nazari Savvin. Trained in the workshops established by the Stroganov family in Solvychegodsk, they had developed a distinctive style while painting for the czar and the nobility in the Moscow Kremlin. Their jewel-like icons were in a richly colored, highly detailed, miniaturist style, with highlights in gold. Fine icons continued to be made after 1640 in the Palace of

TASS, FROM SOVFOTO

Cathedral of St. Basil, Moscow, painted and decoratively shingled in the Moscow baroque style (16th century).

Church of the Ascension, Kolomenskoye, stone copy of the wooden tent-roofed style (16th century).

SOVFOTO

TASS, FROM SOVFOTO

SOVFOTO

DECORATIVE ARTS: Ornamental wood carving from a building at Kolomenskoye (17th century); embroidered towel (detail), with tree-of-life motif.

Arms (Armory), which had become the artistic center of the country.

By the beginning of the 17th century, naturalism, as a result of Western influence, was already attracting Russian painters. Despite church opposition, they began to experiment with portraiture, realistic perspective, genre, and the naturalististic style, as seen in the icons of Simon Ushakov, Moscow's foremost artist. From about 1630, certain icons memorializing individuals—icons called *parsnuyas* from the Latin *persona*, or person—were a blend of traditional iconic and new Western trends.

Illumination and Illustration. Religious works in the 15th and 16th centuries continued to be illuminated in the Russo-Byzantine style. Secular works, such as the *Tale of Mamaev*, were illuminated in the Russo-Byzantine style in the 15th century. From the 16th century their painted illustrations reflect the influence of Western-inspired woodcuts by incorporating details of contemporary life.

Decorative Arts—Metalwork. Muscovite metalwork surpassed all previous Russian achievements, as skilled craftsmen in the Palace of Arms worked for the czar, the nobility, and the church, and the metalworkers' guild catered to the growing merchant class. In addition to religious articles, they produced a wide range of domestic wares, most characteristically loving-cups, wine tasters, and goblets. Such objects were made of plain or gilded copper, iron, silver, or gold and were often decorated with niello, repoussé, and vividly colored enamels.

Carving. Wood carving, at which the Russians have always excelled, flourished both as a professional and as a folk art. The forms and motifs of the Muscovite period recall earlier ones and continued into the early 20th century. Most professional carving was done for the church, as, for example, the Ludogoshchinsky Cross (1366). Figures in the round are rare, as a result of the Byzantine prohibition against statuary, but almost

life-size figures in very high relief are remarkable for their religious intensity. Many iconostases were exquisitely carved and painted, sometimes gilded, and fine work was lavished on church gates, the shingles of domes, and burial crosses.

Folk carving was chiefly on secular objects—carts, boats, furniture, looms, shuttles, tableware, stamps for decorating textiles and gingerbread, toys, and the frames of doors and windows. Motifs included vegetal and geometric forms and real and mythical animals.

Ceramics. Much excellent pottery had been made in Kiev, but after the Mongol invasion nothing of quality was produced anywhere in Russia until the late 16th century. From that time, Yaroslavl and Moscow made fine glazed tiles with pictorial designs to decorate churches and houses and the stoves used for heating.

Embroidery. In the Muscovite period many rich robes for clergy and nobility were embroidered in gold and silver thread to resemble imported brocades and velvets. Peasant women did cross-stitching or drawnwork on clothes and household linen, often using animal forms and the ancient tree-of-life and Great Goddess motifs.

WESTERNIZED PERIOD

As the early rulers of Kiev had been determined to transform Russia from a pagan to a Christian country, so Peter the Great set himself to propel Russia from the Middle Ages to the 18th century. As the Kievans turned to Byzantium for art and artists, so Peter looked to the West, importing artists and sending Russians to study abroad. His Westernizing policy ended the domination of religious art, just as his transfer of the capital to St. Petersburg (Leningrad) ended Moscow's political supremacy.

Architecture. Although Peter's Westernization had little effect on wooden peasant architecture, it greatly changed the style of churches, palaces, and country houses.

Early 18th Century. Aided by his first, and foremost, imported architect, the Swiss-Italian Domenico Trezzini, Peter began to build his new capital in 1703 on the Gulf of Finland, confronting the Western world. He was in such haste that he forbade building in stone and brick in the rest of Russia, and he often obliged both his foreign and Russian architects to complete work begun by a colleague. The city, planned by Trezzini and successively altered by the Frenchman A. J. B. Le Blond and the Russian P. M. Yeropkin, had a regular plan in the contemporary Western manner in contrast to the haphazard Russian cities. The architecture was Petrine baroque, a restrained blending of Peter's taste with Trezzini's interpretation of Dutch baroque, familiar to Peter from his travels abroad.

The first structure was Trezzini's citadel, the Fortress of St. Peter and St. Paul, with its great gate and cathedral surmounted by a bell tower and spire. The buildings on which Peter set most store were the wharves and the spire-crowned admiralty by I. K. Korobov, administrative buildings such as Trezzini's Twelve Colleges, and the three standardized types of houses that Peter had devised for the three social classes of the town's citizens. Other structures included the Kunstkamera (Cabinet of Curios) for Peter's collections, by the German G. J. Mattarnovi, and buildings by M. G. Zemtsov, Yeropkin, and other Russians.

St. Petersburg was more famous, however, for its palaces. That of Prince Menshikov at Oranienbaum, probably designed by the German Andreas Schlüter, was begun by J. G. Schädel and rebuilt in the late 18th century by Antonio Rinaldi. Schlüter may have designed Peter's intimate Summer Palace, built by Trezzini, Schlüter, and Schädel, with Peter himself doing much of the paneling. The great palace at Peterhof (Petrodvorets), with its formal gardens and fountains, was begun by Le Blond, architect of Louis XIV, on the pattern of Versailles and completed by J. F. Braunstein. On its grounds were the small palaces Mon Plaisir, possibly designed by Schlüter, and Marly, both built by Braunstein.

Late 18th and 19th Centuries. Although St. Petersburg remained essentially Peter's creation, it was further adorned in the mid-18th century by his daughter Elizabeth and her Italian architect, B. F. Rastrelli. He built palaces in an exuberant, strongly individual style that mixed baroque, rococo, and Russian elements. They generally had long facades broken by pillars and other details and covered with brightly colored stucco set off by white. Examples include the Winter Palace (originally begun for Peter), the Stroganov Palace, the Smolny Monastery complex, and, on the outskirts of the city, the enlarged palace at Peterhof and the Catherine Palace (named for Peter's wife) at Tsarskoye Selo (Pushkin).

In the late 18th century, Catherine the Great, who loved Roman architecture, imposed a more severe, neoclassical style. Using Russian and foreign architects, she commissioned such structures as the Hermitage Theater and the completion of the Catherine Palace, by Giacomo Quarenghi; the gate over the New Holland canal, by J. B. Vallin de la Mothe; the Tauride Palace, by I. E. Starov; and the palace in Pavlovsk, by Charles Cameron.

Where Catherine's buildings held an uneasy balance between the sedate work of Peter's architects and the ebullience of Elizabeth's, it took the genius of the Russian-born Italian Carlo Rossi to achieve complete cohesion. He worked at the beginning of the 19th century for Alexander I, who was even more of a classical purist than Catherine, deriving his style from Greece rather than Rome. Rossi coordinated the main buildings of the capital by designing splendid General Staff buildings to form the Palace Circus in front of the Winter Palace and by creating the brilliant Senate Square to the west.

In the same period, Thomas de Thomon built the stock exchange on the lines of a Greek tem-

TASS, FROM SOVFOTO

Palace at Peterhof, built for Peter the Great on the baroque pattern of Versailles (18th century).

Palace in Pavlovsk, built for Catherine the Great by Charles Cameron in neoclassical style (18th century).

NOVOSTI, FROM SOVFOTO

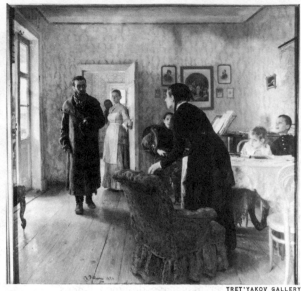

PETERSBURGIAN PAINTING: Levitsky's *Princess Dashkov* (1784); Repin's *Return of the Exile* (1884)

ple. A. D. Zakharov designed the more original Admiralty building, between the Winter Palace and Senate Square, which cleverly retained the spire from Peter's Admiralty. Good neoclassical work was still produced in the reign of Nicholas I, but the growth of the Slavophile movement led to the revival of the 17th century Muscovite style.

Painting and Graphics. Although icon painting continued as a local tradition, the major development in the capital was Westernized art. The Russians were especially outstanding in portraiture and graphics.

Portraiture. The striving for veracity and emotional intensity, already evident in icons, con-

Malevich's *Airplane Flying* (1914), a geometrical abstraction in the suprematist style he invented.

tinued in portraiture. True portraiture, produced in Moscow at the end of the 17th century but lacking in modeling, acquired polish and distinction only in St. Petersburg, under Peter's insistence, in the hands of I. M. Nikitin and A. M. Matveev. Only with D. G. Levitsky, a generation later, did it attain full artistry.

Russian forthrightness and the resulting intimacy are evident in the work of all these men, but especially in V. L. Borovikovsky's portrait of Catherine II walking her greyhound Tom. This work is in sharp contrast to the formal royal portraits of the West. The same spirit permeates the works of Russia's only truly great native sculptor, F. I. Shubin. Early 19th century portraitists, such as O. A. Kiprensky, were influenced by Byron and the Romantic movement.

Realism and the Avant-Garde. The growth of a social conscience, stimulated by such political events as the Napoleonic Wars and the Decembrist rising of 1825, led to a semi-satirical, semi-realistic movement in art, as, for example, in the paintings of P. A. Fedotov and V. G. Perov. After the Crimean War and the reforms of Alexander II, reform-minded artists led by I. N. Kramskoy founded the Society of Wanderers (Peredvizhniki) in 1870. Their purpose was to hold traveling exhibitions of realistic paintings revealing existing social evils. However, I. Y. Repin, the foremost realist painter, was never a member.

At the end of the 19th century, artists opposed to realism and interested in their European heritage, including A. N. Benois, L. S. Bakst, M. V. Dubozhinsky, M. F. Larionov, N. J. Goncharova, and the art patron Diaghilev, formed the World of Art (*Mir Iskusstva*) society. Taking the slogan "art for art's sake," they were the first Russians to concern themselves wholly with aesthetics rather than with spiritual meaning or with subject matter. Their stylized, exotic, brilliantly colored sets for Diaghilev's *Ballets Russes* transformed the European stage.

The Revolution of 1905 encouraged some artists to desire as much of a transformation in art as the terrorists did in politics. In their efforts to express the essence of their subject matter rather than its form, they discarded realism in favor of French-inspired cubism and other avant-garde movements. Larionov and Goncharova explored futurism and developed rayonism, which explored light radiating from objects. K. S. Malevich invented suprematism, an art movement dealing with basic geometric forms that led eventually to late 20th century minimal (primary-structure) art. Naum Gabo, Anton Pevsner, V. Y. Tatlin, and El Lissitzky developed constructivism, sculpture by assemblage that tried to incorporate movement. Wassily Kandinsky's emotionally inspired, nonobjective paintings contributed immeasurably to abstract expressionism.

Graphic Arts. As a part of the Westernizing process, Peter the Great encouraged the printing of books for both the quality and the mass market, many of them illustrated by naturalistic engravings. Many of the finer books were adorned with marvelously decorative chapter headings and tailpieces. In the 20th century, book illustration reached new heights of aesthetic achievement in the work of such World of Art members as Goncharova.

In the 18th century the popularity of the cheapest books was eclipsed by that of the *lubok,* or broadsheet. Decorated at first by woodcuts, later by engravings or lithographs, and often colored, they conveyed religious, political, and satirical subjects or simply songs and stories.

Decorative Arts. Russian metalwork of the 18th century included exquisite snuffboxes with painted enamel portraits and scenes. Craftsmanship perhaps reached its peak in the enameled and jeweled objects by the 19th century court jeweler K. G. (or Carl) Fabergé.

After much effort by Peter and Elizabeth, D. I. Vinogradov finally discovered the secret of porcelain. The Imperial Porcelain Manufactory was founded in St. Petersburg in 1750 and expanded by Catherine. It produced figurines, which became famous, and tablewares with armorial designs and, later, views and military subjects. Other porcelain factories were soon established.

SOVIET PERIOD

In the early Soviet period, some experimentation in art and architecture continued along with work in traditional styles. After a state decree in 1932, both artists and architects were required to belong to their respective unions, controlled by the government and serving the people.

Architecture. Soviet architecture has been chiefly concerned with constructing government buildings; industrial projects, such as dams and factories; and workers' housing. Notable early works, such as the Pravda building in Moscow by P. A. Gologov and the Dzerzhinsky Square complex in Kharkov by S. S. Serafimov and others, reflected the stark functionalism of the

Avtovo underground station, Leningrad, resplendent with marble floors, decorated columns, and chandeliers.

Comecon building, Kalinin Prospekt, Moscow, with curved walls of windows in austerely functional post-Stalinist style.

International style. During the Stalinist era in the 1930's and 1940's, most public buildings were in an ornate, grandiose, traditional style, labeled by one architect "proletarian classic." Examples are the University of Moscow and the Moscow and Leningrad subways, with decorations by the best artists. From the 1960's there was more emphasis on functional architecture, using prefabrication and other new techniques, as in the Central Lenin Stadium in Moscow.

Painting, Sculpture, and Graphics. Although the experimental work of pre-Revolutionary artists was invigorating Russian art and influencing art abroad, Lenin, as early as 1905, objected to it for possessing an existence of its own independent of everyday life. In 1919 he declared war on independent art and individualism, requiring that, in accordance with the views of Marx and Engels, artists glorify the worker as revolutionary hero and builder and defender of his homeland. Lenin instructed artists to revive the ideals of the Wanderers and emulate Repin. In 1921, assuming that easel painting, except for portraiture, had outlived its use, he demanded "monumental propaganda" works. Massive statues, often of perishable materials, were characterized by verticality and by modeling only for broad outlines. Immense paintings were executed in sweeping lines for street display.

Lenin's assertion that "pure art is dishonest" caused many distinguished artists to emigrate. Others stayed on, including former World of Art members K. S. Petrov-Vodkin and K. F. Yuon and some experimental artists, such as Malevich, Tatlin, and the constructivists Alexander Rodchenko, and, briefly, Lissitzky. Some helped to forge the social realist style demanded by the authorities, and some turned to industrial design. By the 1930's, easel painting had revived, and after World War II the importance of aesthetics came to be recognized. Nevertheless, easel painting has marked time.

In contrast, in graphic art, signal advances were made from the start. Lissitzky was outstanding in typography. The pictorial poster, introduced in 1918, reached a high standard, as designed by V. V. Mayakovsky and, later, A. A. Deineka. There was greatly expanded production of illustrated books, especially for children, a field in which V. A. Favorsky excelled.

TAMARA TALBOT RICE
Author of "A Concise History of Russian Art"

Bibliography

Buxton, David Roden, *Russian Mediaeval Architecture* (Cambridge 1934).

Gray, Camilla, *Great Experiment: Russian Art 1863–1922* (Thames 1962).

Hamilton, George H., *Art and Architecture of Russia*, 2d ed. (Viking 1976).

Lazarev, Viktor Nikitich, *Old Russian Murals and Mosaics* (Phaidon 1966).

Rice, Tamara Talbot, *A Concise History of Russian Art* (Thames 1963).

Vedier, Philippe, *Russian Art, Icons, and Decorative Arts* . . . (Walters Art Gallery 1959).

Voyce, Arthur, *Moscow Kremlin* (Univ. of Calif. Press 1954).

Worker and Collective Farm Woman by V. Mukhina, monumental stainless steel sculpture in social realist style (1937).

RUSSIAN CHURCH. This article outlines the development and growth of the Russian Orthodox Church from the time of the earliest conversions to Christianity in the 9th century up to the present day.

Origins. The first conversion of the Rus to Christianity dates from the days of the great Patriarch Photius (about 820–891) of Constantinople. A special bishopric seems to have been established for that period at Tmutarakan, near which the modern city of Krasnodar is located. An organized Christian community, with a cathedral church of the prophet Elias (Elijah) existed as early as 945 at Kiev. There were a considerable number of Christians in the retinue of Grand Prince Igor, who had to take an oath in the church at the signing of a treaty with Byzantium in 945. Igor's wife, Olga, was a Christian herself. Information about this early period is scanty and controversial. Apparently there were links with both Byzantium and the West, and a western bishop was about to go to Kiev. Of decisive importance was the conversion of Grand Prince Vladimir, the ruling duke of Kiev, probably in 989. He made Christianity the official religion in the Russian lands.

Early Organization. The expansion of the new religion was rather fast but not without resistance, and probably in many cases conversion was quite superficial. In any case, in the 11th century the church was firmly established in Russia, and a regular organization was inaugurated. The church was organized under the jurisdiction of Constantinople, as a special province of the Ecumenical Patriarchate, under the headship of a metropolitan, with residence at Kiev, who at an early date assumed the title "of the whole Russia." Several dioceses, including that of Novgorod in the north, were established under his primacy. Metropolitans were to be appointed and consecrated by the patriarch of Constantinople, and most of them were Greeks.

In the inner administration, however, the Russian Church enjoyed full independence. The Slavonic language was used in worship and in preaching. Links with the southern Slavs were strong at that time, and it was from Bulgaria that many Byzantine religious and other writings were circulated in Russia. Some new translations from Greek were made in Kiev and elsewhere.

The church had a national character from the very start, but the basis was Byzantine, if in a Slavic dress. The great cathedrals in Kiev and Novgorod were already erected by the 11th century and, like the famous church in Constantinople, dedicated to Hagia Sophia. The great underground monastery at Kiev, the Caves Lavra, dates from about the same time. How deeply Christianity penetrated the masses at that period it is difficult to say. But on the top level, Christian culture was already flowering, as can be seen by the numerous literary documents of that time, including the remarkable Russian *Chronicle*.

Later Organization. The Mongolian (Tatar) invasion and conquest in the 13th century accelerated the shift of political and national centers to the north, where Moscow soon became a new focus of national unification. The see of the metropolitan was translated to Moscow in 1328, although for a time the title was still "of Kiev and the whole Russia." Some Russian lands in the south and the west were incorporated in the newly formed Lithuanian dukedom, which ultimately was merged with the kingdom of Poland.

The onion-shaped domes of the Ostankino Church in Moscow are typical of Russian Orthodox churches.

For centuries there was a strong political tension between these two powers, Moscow and Poland-Lithuania, which affected the ecclesiastical situation. Finally the church was divided, and an independent metropole was established at Kiev.

After the Council of Florence (1439) had agreed on a plan for union of the Byzantine Church and Rome, a formal reason was found at Moscow to sever the link with Constantinople and to proclaim the autonomy of the Russian Church. A new metropolitan, Jonas, was consecrated by the Russian bishops in 1448. This is the date of the factual independence of the Russian Church. It was not, however, formally recognized by any church in the East until the end of the 16th century. The Byzantine union with Rome was very short-lived, but a new change radically affected the whole situation. When Constantinople (now Istanbul) was captured by the Turks in 1453, the Byzantine Empire collapsed. On the other hand, the political importance of Moscow was steadily growing, and the grand duke, or czar, of Russia was assuming the role of a protector of all subjugated Christians in the Turkish Empire. In 1589 the independence of the Moscow Patriarchate was officially recognized.

The situation was quite different in the west and the south. Toward the end of the 16th century Poland became one of the strongholds of Roman Catholicism. For various reasons bishops of the Orthodox Church in this realm decided to join Rome, under the condition that the Eastern rite and the existing church organization were to be retained. This move of the bishops was strongly opposed by the majority of clergy and laity, but union was enforced by the secular law (the Union of Brest, 1596), and the Orthodox Church ceased legally to exist in the realm. It continued, nevertheless, and in 1620 new bishops were consecrated, although they were not recognized by the government. The final settlement occurred only in 1632 with the election of the new metropolitan of Kiev, Peter Mogila. The Orthodox Church had to live in those parts in constant tension and conflict with the "Uniate" Church, as they derisively called the church of Eastern rite but of Roman obedience. The "Uniate" Church was strongly supported by the Polish government.

With the annexation of Kiev and other provinces in the south in the middle of the 17th century, the church of Kiev was incorporated into the Moscow Patriarchate, but not without resistance. The final unification of the church in Russia was achieved only in the 18th century, but the difference between the north and the south, caused by the difference in the historic past, has never been fully overcome. In the late 17th and 18th centuries, the influence of Kiev was overwhelming, despite the political domination of the north.

The chief and most tragic event of church life in Moscow in the 17th century was the great schism, the schism of the so-called Old Believers, who seceded from the main church in protest against the ecclesiastical reforms of the Patriarch Nikon (1605–1681), who wanted to adjust the forms and habits of the Russian Church to the contemporary Greek use. Millions seceded from the official church, were strongly persecuted by the state, and moved to the more remote areas of the realm and even abroad. The new movement was soon split into a number of competing branches, violently opposing each other on various issues. The schism has survived until the present, though reduced in size and without its original zeal and impetus. The fear of Western influence contributed to the obstinacy of the opposition. And, in fact, by the end of the 17th century, the cultural life of Moscow was strongly colored by the increasing influence of the West, coming chiefly through Poland. It was a preparation for that thorough Westernization of Russia that was undertaken by Peter I the Great (reigned 1682–1725).

Missions. The church in Russia has been from the very beginning a missionary body. In the early centuries Russians were concentrated chiefly in the western part of European Russia. Later they began steadily moving eastward and by the late 16th century penetrated into Siberia. The church followed the course of this colonization and in many instances even led the migration, especially in the north. The most impressive example of this early mission was the preaching of St. Stephen of Perm to the Zyrenians, a Finnish tribe, in the 14th century. Not only the native language was used for worship and instruction, but St. Stephen invented a new alphabet. He wanted to stimulate a native literary development but did not have much success. In the course of the 17th century new bishoprics were created in Siberia, and an Orthodox community was established even in Peking, China.

Culture. Links with the West were never fully missing. Novgorod was for a long period an active member of the Hanseatic League, and Western influence was felt there even in the field of religious art and literature. The most striking case of this influence dates from the late 15th century. Archbishop Gennadius of Novgorod decided to produce a complete code of the Bible in Slavonic. Ancient texts were used. But strangely enough, a Dominican monk, Benjamin, probably a Dalmatian, was invited to supervise the edition, and on the whole the final text seems to have been checked not by the Greek original, but by the Latin Vulgate. This Gennadius Bible (1499) was used for the first printed edition of the Slavonic Bible (Ostrog 1581), and at this point once more was edited and revised on the basis of the Greek tradition. Western influence was also quite obvious in the architecture of Moscow. Several of the Kremlin cathedrals were built by the Italian masters.

On the whole, however, the Muscovite culture retained the initial Byzantine inspiration. The cultural effort was concentrated in the field of religious art, and the great art of icon painting reached its climax in the 14th century. The unique perfection of the Russian icon is now commonly recognized. It is usual to put the greatest of Russian masters of that time, Andrei Rublev (about 1370–1430), on a par with the Italians Fra Angelico (1387–1455) and Paolo Uccello (1397–1475) and the Flemish brothers, Hubert (1366?–1426) and Jan (1370?–?1440) van Eyck. And even in this company Rublev is impressive for the balanced perfection of his art and its absorbing religious depth. This rise of the art reflected a deep spiritual movement in the church, a new monastic revival, started by St. Sergius (1314?–?1392) of Radonezh, founder of the famous Trinity Lavra (now the city of Zagorsk), near Moscow. It is true that this creative level was not retained, and one may witness a certain decline of icon painting, especially in the 17th century, but even at that time such great masters can be mentioned as Simon Ushakov and Procopius Chyrin. What was important was that Russian icon painting was not just an art but a sort of philosophy in colors. It was an artistic confession of the searching soul. By no means was there a stagnation in the field of culture, if the search found its expression only in the guise of art.

In the field of education, Moscow was in the rear. The first ecclesiastical school was organized in Kiev by Peter Mogila; in 1635 it was given the status of a college. Later this school became the Theological Academy of Kiev, surviving until the Russian Revolution. In the beginning the teaching was in Latin. From early in the 16th century until 1686, Kiev was in Poland, where the official language of education was Latin. But both the curriculum and the textbooks were simply borrowed from the Jesuit schools. The famous *Orthodox Confession* of Peter Mogila was made on a Roman pattern, and Roman Catholic influence was strongly felt in his liturgical enterprises. The process was similar to that in the Greek Church of that time. This new Kiev style was partially transferred to the north, to Moscow, where it provoked and promoted confusion and division.

Church and State. The Byzantine conception of the relation between church and state, as formulated early in the 6th century by Justinian I the Great and, later in the 9th century, in the *Epanagoge* of Basil I (reigned 867 to 883), was known in Russia from an early date. The theory professed a double authority (and accordingly a double allegiance): *sacerdotium* and *imperium,* or church and state. The assumption was that the two should abide and operate in perfect concord and agreement, respecting and recognizing each other's rights. The technical term for this settlement was *symphonia.* In practice, of course, the theory was never fully realized. It could not protect the church from the occasional or deliberate tyranny of the state, and yet it strongly emphasized an independent nature or character of the church.

In Russia this theory had no direct application until the consolidation of the national state. Local princes could not compete with the metropolitan of the whole Russia, backed in addition by the full authority of the ecumenical patriarch. The church was one in Russia, while the principalities were many. The tension grew steadily with the strengthening of the unified state. The Moscow state of the 16th century often intruded upon the church prerogatives, but the principle of duality and symphony was still faithfully kept.

The 17th Century. In the 17th century an unusual coincidence increased the factual authority of the church. Under Czar Michael (reigned 1613–1645), the first of the Romanov dynasty, the patriarchal throne was occupied by his father, Philaret, from 1619 to 1633. In addition, the czar was a weak man, but the patriarch was a great statesman of strong character. The crisis came in the middle of the century, under Czar Alexis I (reigned 1645–1676) and Patriarch Nikon. It may be true that Nikon used to overstep his rights, but he was acting still within the traditional Byzantine scheme. Nikon's deposition and condemnation in 1666, on the contrary, amounted to a departure from this scheme on the part of the state, not without some influence of the new Western conception of the supremacy of the state. Yet, in theory the old Byzantine conception was maintained.

The radical change was effected by Peter the Great. In some sense, the ground for his so-called ecclesiastical reform had been prepared by the previous development of relations between the state and church in Russia. But Peter formally espoused a new theory. He was strongly influenced by the Lutheran conception of an inclusive sovereignty of the local prince in all fields of national life, both temporal and spiritual. He claimed that the prince was the source of ecclesiastical jurisdiction, so that all authority in the church derived solely from him. By this theory the church had no independent status or standing at all, but was considered just an organ of the local or national state. It was a complete reversal of the Byzantine scheme.

Peter finally abolished the office of patriarch, in order not to have any chief bishop, and substituted instead an ecclesiastical college, or board, which had to be regarded as a state institution, deriving its power and authority from the monarch. This college was composed of a number of bishops, clergymen, and even laymen, appointed by the czar and acting on his behalf. A special officer, the high procurator, had to supervise the activities of the college, but he was not a member; he had the right of veto, but he had no vote. This reform met with strong resistance in the church and had to be enforced by pressure and violence. The new body was called the Holy Synod, but the title could not conceal the nature of the change. Peter could not rely upon the cooperation of the northern bishops and had to

select his own people for all offices in the church, chiefly from those who were educated in the south at Kiev or abroad. His chief adviser and assistant was Feofan Prokopovich (1681–1736), a learned but unscrupulous man and an ex-Uniate who was fully dependent upon Protestant sources, both in his theology and in his conception of the state and church relation. The new ideology was formulated in the *Ecclesiastical Reglement* (1721), a document of joint authorship by Prokopovich and Peter himself. It was not only a constitutional act but also an ideological pamphlet. Signatures of bishops and prelates to the document were extracted by an obvious pressure. Nor could so-called recognition of the reform by the Eastern patriarchs, who were led by political considerations, alter the antitraditional character of the venture.

The 18th Century. The new settlement was imposed by the power of the state, but it was never formally received by the church. The tension was so sharp in the early years of the new regime that it was necessary to make a rule that only persons from Ukraine should be promoted bishops and prelates. This rule was canceled only in the reign of Catherine II the Great (reigned 1762–1796). By a careful selection of bishops the crown was able to control the administration of the church, but it could not change its inner structure. The church was in effect in captivity, but inner freedom was never lost. An open attempt to change doctrines and rites made under Peter III (reigned 1762) led to the deposition of this monarch. Of course, it was not the main cause of his deposition, but this motive was strongly stressed in the acts of accession to the throne of his wife, Catherine II, and it was precisely this motive that gave to a palace plot the significance of a national event. Catherine II continued the ecclesiastical policy of Peter the Great, and it was in her reign that all church estates were secularized, and the church was deprived of its financial basis and independence (1764).

The 19th Century. The new system was finally consolidated only in the 19th century, under Alexander I (reigned 1801–1825) and especially Nicholas I (reigned 1825–1855). The high curator, who was originally a kind of state representative or commissar at the Holy Synod, had gradually become an independent head of a large administrative machine, parallel to the synodal administration and embracing various fields of ecclesiastical life. His representatives in the dioceses, without having any definite status in the church itself, in fact could control the whole administration. Bishops exercised their administrative authority through a diocesan consistory, composed of members of the clergy appointed by the Holy Synod, but the secretary to this body was an appointee of the high procurator. He played the same role on the local level that the high procurator played in Moscow.

However, no system is ever fully realized in practice, and one should not overlook the passive resistance that was quite strong even in the worst periods of captivity. An open protest was voiced in Alexander II's reign (1855–1881), and radical changes in the relationship between the church and the empire were openly discussed. No major step toward a reestablishment of a more normal situation from the church's point of view was taken, and in the days of Konstantin Petrovich Pobedonostzev, the high procurator from 1880

Troitse-Sergiyevo Monastery near Moscow was named for the popular Russian Saint Sergius, who was once its abbot. It was a place of pilgrimage for all social classes.

until 1905, pressure and control of the state was even increased.

The 20th Century. It is highly symptomatic that in 1904 an overwhelming majority of bishops, all of whom were appointees of the crown, formally insisted on abnormality of the regime. It was decided to convene a council of the church, and an impressive plan of reorganization was prepared and discussed. Again no action was taken.

The system inaugurated by Peter the Great upon a Western pattern collapsed in 1917. The council met in August of that year, the church administration was changed, and the office of patriarch was restored. The patriarch elected was Archbishop Tikhon (Vasili Ivanovich Belyavin, 1865?–1925), who had been the ruling archbishop of the Orthodox Church in North America for several years. The council had to work in a strained atmosphere of national catastrophe, revolution, and civil war, which could not fail to color the proceedings. But despite this unfavorable situation, it succeeded in passing an unusual amount of constitutional legislation that established the life of the church on the ground of strict ecclesiastical law. Unfortunately, most of these regulations could never be put in action under the Soviet regime.

Under the Soviets. The Russian Revolution in 1917 and especially the establishment of the Soviet rule completely changed the position of the church in Russia. It not only was separated from the state, which had occurred under a provisional government in 1917, but it was also persecuted. The reasons for persecution were manifold. The purpose was obvious: the church had to be deprived of all means of influencing the national

life, which was to be rebuilt on an antireligious pattern. For that reason the church was prohibited any educational activity, and missionary expansion in any sense became impossible. Destruction of churches, heavy taxation, deportation and execution of clergymen and active laymen—all these measures were but details in the general scheme of a complete transformation of the whole community into an irreligious body. The administration of the church was disrupted, and for a time no central administration existed.

The attempt to construct another organization to compete with the historical church, made by a group of clergy and sponsored by the government, failed to attract any considerable number of believers. Several groups were organized under such names as the Living Church, or the Renovated Church, in the early 1920's. They did not survive for long and ceased to exist long before World War II. In the meantime, order was restored and one of the old bishops, Sergius of Gorki (formerly Nizhni Novgorod) was permitted to assume the functions of an acting head. But his actions were controlled by the government.

During World War II the church participated in national defense and for that reason had to be reckoned with. Metropolitan Sergei (1867–1944) was proclaimed patriarch in 1943, but died soon afterward. Metropolitan Alexei (1877–1970) of Leningrad and Novgorod was elected his successor by the council of bishops in 1944. Diocesan administration was to a large extent restored, and some of the previously confiscated churches and monasteries were again put at the disposal of the church. Several training colleges for the ministry were established. However, "religious propaganda," understood in a wide sense, is still illegal.

In the late 20th century, Metropolitan Pimen of Kruititsky and Kolomna was elected Patriarch of Moscow on July 7, 1971, to succeed Patriarch Alexei. The church authorities were strongly controlled by a government council on ecclesiastical affairs. And, in fact, the church had to comply with the general policy of the state, which was inspired, as before, by antireligious principles. Available information on the actual situation of the church in Russia was incomplete and biased, the topic was controversial, and no impartial interpretation could be offered. The main problem was: to what extent can a Christian church cooperate with an avowedly antireligious state, without being involved in an inextricable compromise?

Inner Life. The inner life of the church was affected by the new policy of Peter the Great in a rather indirect manner—namely, through the school. In the course of the 18th century a network of seminaries was created in the country. A seminary was a kind of general high school, but it was administered by the church. There was special emphasis on religious subjects. The purpose was the training of the sons of the clergy, although not exclusively for the ministry. Up to the early 19th century these schools constituted the only school system in the empire. All these schools were built on the Kiev pattern—as Latin schools. There was no division of educational levels: the same schools included both elementary and graduate classes.

This type of school was changed only in the early years of the 19th century, when three groups of schools were established: elementary, in small towns; seminaries, in diocesan centers;

and theological academies, which were real graduate schools of theology. There were four of the last: at St. Petersburg, Moscow, Kiev, and Kazan. The Russian language had been used occasionally in the 18th century, but not much before the 1840's was it officially approved for the teaching of theology and philosophy. The school had a Western character. In fact it was a local version of a general type of ecclesiastical school in Europe of the 17th and 18th centuries.

Such an educational policy estranged the clergy from the people, both from the simple folks who had nothing to do with this imported scholarship and from the higher strata of the nation, which followed another line of development. Nevertheless, the contribution of these schools—including practically all the humanities in their curriculums—to the general culture of Russia cannot be exaggerated. Russian scholarship and learning had their roots in the traditions and experience of the ecclesiastical school, as was true of Western learning in the late Middle Ages.

Still, there was a tragic rift. The school knew little of the piety of the people. The emphatic tension between learning and piety in the Russian Church could not but distort and impoverish both of them. Thus, Russian theology of the 17th and 18th centuries employed an alien means of expression, which had been created and used for decidedly different purposes. It was impossible to express adequately the Eastern tradition in terms either of Reformation theology or of that of the Counter Reformation. But this was precisely what was persistently done, not only in Russia, but also in the Greek Church, until the mid-19th century and perhaps even later.

The whole situation was considerably changed in the course of the 19th century. The reasons for and factors in the change were manifold. First, there was a revival of contemplative monasticism, starting near the end of the 18th century, on the basis of the strict Byzantine tradition, and examples of its influence in wider fields than the religious can be traced even in Russian literature, as in the writings of Fyodor Dostoyevsky and Nikolai Gogol. Much later a rediscovery of the old religious art—of Byzantine and Russian iconography—contributed to the recovery of the ancient tradition.

The second influence was the biblical revival early in the 19th century, which led to a new translation of the Bible in the vernacular, ultimately published with the approval of the Holy Synod. At the same time systematic translation of the writings of the Church Fathers was undertaken. The work was conducted by the four theological academies and contributed much to the enlargement of theological perspective.

Next was the revival in the wider circles of the Russian intelligentsia, which began in the 1840's among the Slavophiles, of which Aleksei Khomyakov especially should be mentioned. It reached its climax in the early decades of the 20th century. It was an awakening of a creative approach to religion, and in spite of various aberrations and excesses it revitalized the church. This religious awakening was strongly felt also in various branches of culture: in literature, art, and philosophy. The movement's leaders were not exponents of a genuine Eastern tradition, and their thought was variously affected by many extraneous influences. But they did much to bring the religious theme to the attention of a wide group of Russian intellectuals. It is now recognized that Russian religious thought has a valuable contribution to make to the search for truth.

GEORGES FLOROVSKY, *Author of*
"Ways of Russian Theology"

Bibliography

Arseniev, Nicholas, *Russian Piety* (Am. Orthodox Press 1964).
Florovsky, Georges, *Ways of Russian Theology*, reissue (Nordland Pub. Co. 1977).
Kucharek, Casimir, *The Byzantine Slav Liturgy of St. John Chrysostom* (Alleluia Press 1971).
Marshall, Richard H., Jr., and others, eds., *Aspects of Religion in the Soviet Union* (Univ. of Chicago Press 1971).
Milynkov, Pavel N., *Religion and the Church* (Univ. of Pa. Press 1942).

RUSSIAN HISTORY. See RUSSIA for the history of Russia to 1917. See RUSSIAN REVOLUTION for the history of the Russian Revolution of 1917 and the subsequent Civil War. See the UNION OF SOVIET SOCIALIST REPUBLICS—*History* for the history of the Soviet Union.

The Russian Orthodox Church uses the liturgy of Saint John Chrysostom in Old Church Slavonic, except on special feasts such as Christmas (January 6) when the liturgy of Saint Basil is used. The Christmas liturgy of Saint Basil is here conducted by Pimen, Patriarch of Moscow and All Russia (*center*).

CYRILLIC ALPHABET—RUSSIAN FORM

MODERN RUSSIAN	SIMPLIFIED TRANSLITERATION	MODERN RUSSIAN	SIMPLIFIED TRANSLITERATION
А а	a	П п	p
Б б	b	Р р	r
В в	v	С с	s
Г г	g or gh	Т т	t
Д д	d	У у	u
Е е	e or ye	Ф ф	f
Ё ё	e or yo	Х х	kh
Ж ж	zh	Ц ц	ts
З з	z	Ч ч	ch
И и	i or y	Ш ш	sh
Й й	i or y	Щ щ	shch
К к	k	Ъ ъ	(*)
Л л	l	Ы ы	y
М м	m	Ь ь	(*)
Н н	n	Э э	e
О о	o	Ю ю	yu
		Я я	ya or ia

*Not usually transliterated

RUSSIAN LANGUAGE, the most important branch of the Slavonic family of languages in the Indo-European group. As the principal language of the Soviet Union and one of the five official languages of the United Nations, Russian has great international importance. Despite its rather formidable grammar and unfamiliar alphabet, the Russian language is simple and direct and admirably suited to every purpose that a modern language serves. Its literature, both prose and poetry, is among the greatest in the world, boasting such names as Tolstoy, Chekhov, Pushkin, and Dostoyevsky.

Russian is one of the eastern group of Slavonic languages. It is spoken by the largest of the Slavic races, the Great Russians. Great Russian should be carefully distinguished from the other members of its group, Little Russian, or Ukrainian, and White Russian, or Belorussian.

Russian is an excellent key for understanding such languages of the southern Slavonic group as Bulgarian, Serbo-Croatian, and Slovenian. Polish and Czech are in the western Slavonic group, but these have been influenced more by Latin than any other Slavonic language and hence have deviated further from the original Slavonic.

HISTORY

The morphological and syntactic development of Russian is made somewhat difficult to trace historically by the fact that Old Bulgarian, spoken by tribes along the Volga, became the ecclesiastical and literary language and remained so until the 17th century. Very early, however, the local spoken Russian of Kiev influenced Church Slavonic (Old Bulgarian) in both pronunciation and vocabulary, and in turn Church Slavonic affected the vernacular. Church Slavonic elements may still be observed in the Russian language, especially in phonetic and morphological peculiarities in words connected with intellectual and religious life. Church Slavonic, in a considerably modified form, of course, has remained the language of the Russian Orthodox Church: the Scriptures were written in it, and it was the language of church services up to the latest times. Thus, the history of Church Slavonic resembles in many of its aspects the history of Latin in the Roman Catholic Church.

The earliest written literature, chronicles and judicial documents, employed a language that was an admixture of the vernacular and Church Slavonic. In the 14th century Moscow displaced Kiev as a cultural center, and the local speech of Moscow, a combination of southern and northern dialects, influenced the written language. However, Church Slavonic still continued to influence the written language, though on a diminishing scale, until the 18th century. At that time, the great scientist, philologist, and poet Mikhail V. Lomonosov pointed out in his *Russian Grammar* the dependence of the literary language on Church Slavonic, a fact that had not been scientifically studied before. The literary language now began to fall more in line with the spoken language. Toward the end of the 18th century and the beginning of the 19th, especially through the efforts of Nikolai M. Karamzin and Aleksandr Pushkin, a literary norm for the Russian language was established.

CHARACTERISTICS

Russian is an extremely rich language, and by virtue of its structure capable of expressing the subtlest nuances of thought. Only a great people, said Ivan S. Turgenev, could possess such a language. As a member of the Indo-European family, Russian has developed in much the same way as other members of this family. As an inflected language, it resembles Latin and Greek in morphology.

Alphabet and Language Reform. The Russian, or Cyrillic, alphabet can be mastered in one lesson. Both Russian and Church Slavonic use the same alphabet, except that Peter the Great simplified the letters of Russian in 1708 by bringing them into closer conformity with the easier Latin letters of the West. Thus there is a current form known as the "civil alphabet" and the Church Slavonic alphabet, which is called *Kirilitsa*.

The civil alphabet was simplified still further after the 1917 Revolution. Before then there had been 36 letters, not counting the *ë*, which is not a separate letter and rarely occurs in this form except in grammars and texts intended for foreigners. In 1918 the Soviet government issued a "Decree on the Introduction of the New Orthography," which rejected as redundant four letters of the old alphabet. Hence the present alphabet has 32 letters. The decree effected further simplification: the hard sign was abolished at the end of words; a clarifying differentiation was introduced for spelling certain prefixes before unvoiced consonants; useless variations in the genitive endings of adjectives, pronouns, and participles were abolished; uniformity was given to the two nominative and accusative plural endings of all three genders; the masculine and neuter form of the third person plural pronouns was substituted for the old feminine form; the masculine and neuter form of the word "one" replaced the old feminine form; the genitive singular of the feminine personal pronoun became the same as the accusative. All these changes unquestionably made for simplification, and, as a result of such modifications, Russian became one of the most nearly phonetic languages in Europe.

Phonology. The pronunciation of Russian is not difficult. The chief obstacle for a person speaking a western European language is his tendency to make soft combinations hard. Before *e* and *i*, and before vowels beginning with *y*, such as *ya, ye,* and *yo,* all consonants, especially the dentals, are palatalized. This means they are sounded not with the top of the tongue pressing against the back of the teeth, but by touching the palate with the tongue higher up. Another difficulty is the hard *l* before *a, o,* and *u.* This is not pronounced as in English with the tip of the tongue at the root of the teeth, but rather with the tip of the tongue just touching the teeth. The uvula then vibrates, producing a kind of guttural *l* similar to a guttural *r.* Other sounds offer no particular difficulties.

However, a real obstacle for non-Russians learning the language is the variation in stress in Russian words. No definite rule for placing the stress is possible as in other Slavonic languages such as Polish and Czech. The stress is not always placed in the same position in the inflected forms of a single word. A few helpful generalizations regarding stress may be stated: (1) The stress in long (attributive) forms of an adjective is that of the nominative singular. (2) Pronouns are usually stressed on the case endings. (3) The majority of nouns are stressed throughout as in the nominative singular. Incorrect stress may sometimes lead to misunderstanding, especially in pairs of words that are spelled alike but stressed differently. Accurate handling of stress in Russian words can come only after an individual has had long experience in speaking the language.

Russian has comparatively few sounds that do not occur in English, and the variations in sound represented by each letter are usually regular. One peculiarity of the sound system is that there are two sets of vowels: hard vowels and soft, or "jotated," vowels. Pronunciation of a hard vowel varies according to whether it is stressed or unstressed and, if unstressed, according to its position in regard to the stressed vowel in the word. A soft vowel, whether it appears initially or follows another vowel, has the same range of sounds as the corresponding hard vowel but is preceded in each case by the sound "jot." There is a system of vowel mutation governed by definite rules, and also a regular system of consonant mutation, which likewise has its own rules.

Morphology. The Russian noun has three genders, two numbers, and six cases (a seventh,

the vocative, exists only in a few survivals). The genders are declined differently, but their plurals are virtually identical except for the genitive case. The neuter singular differs little from the masculine, but the feminine declensional forms are entirely different. A peculiarity in inflection is that words with soft endings are declined soft throughout. And there are many variations in the genitive and prepositional cases, owing chiefly to a confusion of the historic *o* and *u* declensions. During historic times Russian lost many of its grammatical forms, which can still be studied in Church Slavonic. One of these is the dual, which still exists in a sense after the numerals "two," "three," and "four," when the noun stands in the genitive singular, because that form frequently corresponded to the nominative dual.

In Russian, the attributive is transformed into the corresponding adjective or participle. Hence Russian is richer in adjectival forms than the languages of the West. Numerals are fully declined and are quite difficult. Although the nominal declension is complex, its syntactical application is rather simple, since an abundance of cases, each with a distinct function, obviates certain difficulties that are present in a language without grammatical endings.

Verbs. The verb system is an interesting combination of simplification and complexity. Little has survived of the intricate structure of the verb system in Church Slavonic, with its aorist and multiplicity of past tenses. Only one unconjugated past is left. The ordinary future is a compound of *I shall* and the infinitive, but in a large class of verbs, the present does duty for the future.

There are two conjugations, a wealth of participial forms, and gerunds from the old masculine nominative singular. As though to compensate for this relative simplicity in the conjugational system in a highly inflected language, a curious mechanism exists by which these few verbal forms are able to express by means of aspects most of the shades of meaning expressed in English through the tense structure.

The five tenses of the Russian verb are divided into two groups called the imperfective and perfective aspects. The imperfective aspect has three tenses: past, present, and future. The perfective aspect has only a past and a future. Each verb has two infinitives, from one of which the imperfective aspect is derived, from the other the perfective. The two infinitives are closely related. One may be formed from the other by (1) the addition of a prefix, (2) the expansion of one infinitive through insertion of a syllable, or (3) the alteration of a vowel preceding the infinitive ending. For a few verbs the two infinitives come from different stems. The imperfective tenses indicate iterative and durative actions. The perfective tenses indicate instantaneous actions or single and complete actions. The perfective aspect sometimes indicates also the performance of the action for a short time, or the beginning of the action, which is itself an instantaneous action. With such an instrument for nice distinction in meaning, it may be readily seen that Russian is capable of distinguishing shades of thought beyond the capacities of most other languages. Long training, of course, is necessary in order to make full use of the fine distinctions that are available from the various aspects of the verbs.

Russian does not ordinarily use the passive voice, and it has a very simple way of expressing the subjunctive with an unconjugated past tense and the addition of a particle. A reflexive is also used, which does not differ from the rest of the verbs, except for the addition of the unchanged reflexive ending.

Borrowings. The influence of Church Slavonic (Old Bulgarian) on spoken and written Russian has already been pointed out. Other foreign influences may be noted. Tatar has contributed names for many Oriental objects, such as weapons, garments, jewels, and some terms concerned with government. A few words have come from Finnish, and a good many words dealing with manners came from the more refined literary Polish.

Many Dutch and German words were imported after Peter the Great "opened his window on Europe." By the 18th century, which saw a full cultural rapprochement with the West, numerous words had been introduced. Most of them were French, but some were English or German. From that time also loanwords from international scientific terminology entered the Russian language. Since 1917, with the overthrow of the czarist regime, the Soviets have evinced a partiality for American words, not a few of them slang.

ERNEST J. SIMMONS, *Author of*
"Russian Fiction and Soviet Ideology" and
"Introduction to Russian Realism"

Bibliography

Dictionaries

Jaszczum, W., and Krynski, S., *A Dictionary of Russian Idioms and Colloquialisms* (Univ. of Pittsburgh Press 1967).
Müller, V. K., *English-Russian Dictionary*, 7th ed. (Dutton 1965).
Segal, Louis, ed., *Russian-English Standard Dictionary* (Praeger 1959).
Smirnitsky, A. I., *Russian-English Dictionary*, 7th ed. (Dutton 1966).
Waddington, Patrick, *A Basic Russian-English Vocabulary* (Crowell 1963).
Wedel, E., and Romanov, A., *Romanov's Russian-English, English-Russian Dictionary* (Barnes & Noble 1964).

Grammars

Birkett, George A., *Modern Russian Course*, 3d rev. ed. (Oxford 1947).
Buxton, Cyril R., and Jackson, H. Sheldon, *Russian for Scientists* (Wiley 1960).
Cornyn, William S., *Beginning Russian*, rev. ed. (Yale 1961).
Dewey, Horace W., and Mersereau, John, *Reading and Translating Contemporary Russian* (Pitman 1963).
Fayer, Mischa, *Basic Russian*, 2 vols. (Pitman 1959–1961).
Federov, Mikhail, and Kryukova, I. P., *Handbook of Russian Verbs*, adapted and ed. by C. V. James (Pergamon 1963).
Forbes, Nevill, *Russian Grammar*, 3d rev. ed. by J. C. Dumbreck (Oxford 1964).
Lemieux, Claude P., *Russian Conversation and Grammar*, 3d ed., 2 vols. (U. S. Naval Inst. 1960).
Maltzoff, Nicholas, *Russian Reference Grammar* (Pitman 1964).
Matthews, William K., *Russian Historical Grammar* (Oxford 1960).
Semeonoff, Anna, *A New Russian Grammar*, 12th rev. ed. (Dutton 1962).
Unbegaun, Boris O., *Russian Grammar* (Oxford 1957).
Ward, Dennis, *Russian for Scientists* (International Publications 1970).

Pronunciation

Boianus, Semen K., *Russian Pronunciation and Russian Phonetic Reader* (Harvard Univ. Press 1955).
Cheshko, L. A., *Russian Pronunciation*, ed. by C. V. James (Pergamon 1962).
Ward, Dennis, and Him, G., *Russian Pronunciation Illustrated* (Cambridge 1966).

RUSSIAN LITERATURE.

The literary tradition of Russia is both rich and varied. Its store of folklore is full of lyricism and charm, and its written literature, while developing later than those of some other countries, ranks among the finest in the world. Russian literature resounds with the names of such men of genius as Aleksandr Pushkin, Leo Tolstoy, Fyodor Dostoyevsky, and Anton Chekhov. In modern times, Soviet Russia has also produced a variety of brilliant literary figures, including Boris Pasternak, Aleksandr Solzhenitsyn, Yevgeni Yevtushenko, and Andrei Voznesensky.

Folk literature greatly influenced the work of several great Russian poets, Pushkin particularly, and its themes and imagery have been woven into ballet and opera as well. Soviet scholars have manifested a renewed interest in the country's rich folklore, and many collections and learned investigations of this material have been made.

One very important genre of Russian folk literature is the *bylina,* a long narrative poem in stressed verses. The themes are either historical events, usually related to the siege of Kazan (1552), or the legendary feats of heroes, such as Ilya of Murom. These poems were intoned by traveling professionals. The oldest extant texts were recorded from oral recitations by the Englishman Richard James in 1620. Later collections, published in the 19th century, include those by Kirsha Danilov and M. A. Rybnikov. Spiritual verses, *dukhovnye stikhi,* somewhat related to the *byliny* in style, were recited by wandering religious mendicants.

Russian folklore also contains many splendid songs about wedding ceremonials, harvest, death, feast days, and various superstitions. A popular type of short song was the *chastushka,* a four-line rhymed lyric. Perhaps the richest branch of Russian folklore, however, is its folktales, or *narodny skazki.* These tales resemble western European fairy tales, except that in Russian prose folktales the fairy remains invisible. As narratives these stories are highly original, artistic, and charming, with all manner of supernatural figures and events.

There are many published collections of Russian folktales, but among the earliest and best are those by Aleksandr N. Afanasiev (1855–1863) and by Nikolai Y. Onchukov (1903).

CONTENTS

LITERARY BEGINNINGS TO THE 18TH CENTURY

Medieval literature appeared somewhat late in Russia. The first documents date from the 11th century, about 50 years after the introduction of Christianity. They were in Church Slavonic, which Saint Cyril and Saint-Methodius created as a written language in the 9th century. Church Slavonic resembles Old Bulgarian. Slavonic remained the language of the Russian Orthodox Church and was used for all literary purposes until the 18th century, when it was displaced by the vernacular. Printing also was long delayed.

The vast panorama of the Russian Revolution was recorded by Nobel Prizewinner Boris Pasternak in his novel *Doctor Zhivago*. In this scene from the film version, czarist troops, with sabers drawn, attack protesters in Moscow.

The first book was published in 1564, but printing did not come into general use until the 18th century.

Kievan Period. The earliest literary remains are connected with the flourishing cultural development of Kiev, which lasted until about 1200. Religious writings, mostly sermons, were inspired by Byzantine Greek models. But some highly original examples of pulpit oratory have come down to us, among them the excellent 11th century *Eulogy on St. Vladimir* by Ilarion, metropolitan of Kiev, and the ornate and eloquent sermons of Cyril, bishop of Turov, who lived in the 12th century. The account of a pilgrimage to the Holy Land by Abbot Daniel the Palmer, also of the 12th century, is highly informative, and its whimsically realistic revelations of ecclesiastical trickery recall Chaucer's charming narratives.

Most remnants of early secular literature are chronicles (*letopisi*). These exist only in later compilations, although contemporary entries go back to about 1040. The chronicles contain valuable material for reconstructing the ancient history of Russia, and some have considerable literary merit. One of the best is *The Russian Primary Chronicle* imputed to Nestor, a 12th century monk and author. This *Chronicle* includes some delightful tales of mingled history and popular lore. It includes a notable secular piece, the *Instructions to His Children* of Vladimir Monomakh, grand prince of Kiev (reigned 1113–1125), which is a document of wise and pious counsel.

A considerable body of purely imaginative literature was probably written during the Kiev period, but the only substantial piece to survive is *The Song of Igor's Campaign* (12th century), discovered in 1795 and first published in 1800. This prose poem tells of the disastrous expedition of Prince Igor against the nomadic Polovtsy of the south. The work occupies a unique place in ancient Russian literature, and its unknown author was clearly a writer of great talent. The rich imagery, diction, and beautiful lyric interludes compare favorably with the best western European medieval verse. Later fragmentary remains in a similar vein have been preserved, some of them describing the Battle of Kulikovo (1380), but they are pale imitations of *The Song of Igor's Campaign*.

Post-Kievan Period. After the downfall of Kiev (1240), there was a period of strife between the several city-states, and not until the rise of Moscow were conditions again favorable for literary creation. The results, even then, were poor, since the new literature was ecclesiastical—Byzantine in spirit and monotonously formalized in style. Many sermons and lives of saints were written, and churchmen kept up the official chronicles. There were a few interesting exceptions. The *Domostroi*, generally ascribed to Sylvester, adviser to Ivan IV, the Terrible (reigned 1547–1584), was probably written earlier. Essentially a description of household management, this work reveals in stark detail the family pattern of the age: the father is a swaggering lord of creation, to whom mother, children, and servants owe absolute obedience. The most famous among polemical and historical writings is an exchange of letters between Ivan the Terrible and his former general, Prince Andrei Kurbsky. These show the czar's talents as a controversialist and master of biting invective. The most significant Muscovite literary performance came from the pen of the 17th century Archpriest Avvakum, the leader of the Old Believers in the church schism of the time. In several epistles Avvakum encouraged his followers to oppose religious and cultural innovations, but his chief work was his *Life* (1673), written in the vernacular and revealing a courageous personality and a masterful and original style.

The earliest Russian drama was imported from the West. Latin school dramas on religious themes were introduced into west Russian schools before 1600 and reached Moscow shortly thereafter. Most of these school dramas were influenced by the medieval miracle and mystery plays. The only originality in the Russian adaptations is in the comic interludes, where such Ukrainian types as the Cossack, the clerk, and the braggart Pole were introduced. School dramas, however, never became widely popular. They soon met the rivalry of a second importation from the West—secular plays of German origin, which had a great influence on the history of Russian drama.

A German Lutheran pastor, Johann Gottfried Gregori, living in a German suburb of Moscow, gave the first impetus to this new dramatic development during the reign (1645–1676) of Czar Alexis. In 1672, Gregori organized a troupe of actors to perform before the czar. For repertoire he drew upon printed collections of the plays of German strolling companies that he had known in his youth. These plays had been largely borrowed from the repertoires of companies of English actors performing in Germany. Among the plays selected by Gregori for translation and performance were *The Comedy of Queen Esther and the Haughty Aman* (acted in 1672), which was probably based on an English interlude, and *Temir Aksakovo* (acted in 1674), which unquestionably had as its ultimate source Christopher Marlowe's *Tamburlaine the Great*.

In the last years of the 17th century there were some successful school dramas such as the *Comedy of the Parable of the Prodigal Son*, written by Simeon of Polotsk in rhymed syllabic verse. However, under Peter the Great secular prose plays translated from the German again came into vogue, supplemented by translations of a few of Molière's dramas. Public theaters were opened, and the old school plays were now played only in seminaries and academies.

There is little literary worth in any of the early prose dramas, but some literary merit and originality can be claimed for verse drama. The verse plays of Saint Dimitri Tuptalo of Rostov and Feofan Prokopovich of Novgorod were real contributions to Russian drama. For example, in the *Nativity Play* of Saint Dimitri the dialogue of the shepherds before the apparition of the angels is most attractive for its quality of quaint humor in dealing with things solemn and holy. *Saint Vladimir* (1705) by Prokopovich, a tragicomedy on the theme of the introduction of Christianity into Russia, is almost classical in conception, and its verse represents the highest poetic level achieved at the time.

18TH CENTURY

Peter the Great to Catherine the Great. Peter the Great (reigned 1682–1725) opened a window to western Europe, and the whole country felt new energizing influences. Peter abolished the Old Church Slavonic script and simplified the alphabet. Some of the changes were suggested by Latin script. The vernacular came into use as the written language, although it continued for some time to be heavily influenced by Old Church Slavisms and foreign loanwords and expressions.

Ukrainian and White Russian scholars and clerics now began to introduce a Latinized scholasticism into Muscovite Russia. The forerunner of this development was Simeon of Polotsk, who had made many translations from Latin and published books of rhymed didactic verse. Two prelates of Ukrainian extraction and education, however, were more original as men of letters.

They were Saint Dimitri Tuptalo of Rostov and Feofan Prokopovich of Novgorod, both of whom also wrote plays. Prokopovich, in addition, was the greatest orator of his day. His *Spiritual Reglement* (1718) advocated the liberal reforms of Peter the Great.

Peter, whose feverish activity was directed toward practical improvement in Russia, cared little for culture as such, and imaginative literature did not flourish during his reign. A historian of the time, V. N. Tatishchev, forecast with some truth that it would take Russia seven generations to catch up with civilization in the West. A book typical of the literature in Peter's reign is *On Indigence and Wealth* by Ivan Pososhkov—a work erroneously thought to have anticipated the economic ideas of Adam Smith.

The reign of Anna Ivanovna, from 1730 to 1740, and of Elizabeth Petrovna, from 1741 to 1761, did little to promote literature. For the first time, French neoclassicism began to exercise a marked influence on Russian letters, as seen in the Horatian satires of Prince Antiokh Kantemir and in the dull odes of Vasili Trediakovsky, whose real contribution to literature was an able treatise on prosody. Mikhail Lomonosov was of infinitely greater stature. He is generally regarded as both the founder of modern Russian literature and the father of Russian science. In intellectual and artistic versatility, he was a kind of Russian Goethe. The language of his majestic odes sounds strikingly modern, and his pioneer studies in literary criticism and prosody were very important for his day.

The continuous history of both the Russian theater and drama really begins, during the reign of Elizabeth, with Aleksandr P. Sumarokov, who was not only a playwright but also an able literary writer and excellent songwriter. Sumarokov's tragedy *Khorev*, though influenced by outside sources, was the first Russian play. It was acted before the empress in 1747. To encourage this dramatic development, Elizabeth established in 1756 the first permanent Russian theater at St. Petersburg, with Sumarokov as director.

Sumarokov wrote several comedies and tragedies, but these are for the most part slavish imitations or mere adaptations of French neoclassical pieces. But as was so often to be the good fortune of later Russian dramatists, excellent acting rendered Sumarokov's plays acceptable as theater. Critics referred to Sumarokov as the "Russian Racine," which was a sobriquet that perhaps bears less of compliment than implication of plagiarism. Yet Sumarokov's efforts won him the title of "father of Russian drama." He did much to popularize the best plays of Corneille, Racine, Molière, and Voltaire in Russia.

Catherine the Great—Poetry and Prose. It has been said that Peter the Great created new bodies for the Russians, but Catherine the Great (reigned 1762–1796) put souls into them. Certainly her reign surpassed Peter's in encouraging cultural development. Influenced by French neoclassicism, Mikhail Kheraskov won the title of the Russian Homer with his vast epic poems *Rossiyada* (1779), on the taking of Kazan by Ivan the Terrible, and *Vladimir* (1785), about the introduction of Christianity into Russia.

However, better poets than Kheraskov wrote during Catherine's reign. The greatest was Gavrila Derzhavin. His *Ode to God* surpassed even Lomonosov's poetry, particularly in the splendor of its imagery. Of a lower order, but still highly competent, were the clever fables of Ivan Khemnitser and a very popular adaptation of La Fontaine's *Psyche* by Ippolit Bogdanovich.

Although the French neoclassical influence was dominant during Catherine's lifetime, English and German influences were also important. Several satirical journals appeared. Catherine herself seems to have started the first one in 1769. It was called *All Sorts and Sundries* and was inspired by the English journals *Tatler* and *Spectator* of Joseph Addison and Sir Richard Steele. The Freemason and pietist Nikolai Novikov edited a number of satirical journals, in which he boldly criticized social conditions. In 1773 the Empress suppressed all the journals, for Catherine affected liberalism only up to the point where it grew critical of her regime. She also suppressed the *Journey from St. Petersburg to Moscow* (1790) and imprisoned its author, Aleksandr Radishchev. This book attacked both serfdom and autocracy, and Soviet scholars now regard it as the starting point of revolutionary thought in Russia.

A foremost literary figure of Catherine's time was Nikolai Karamzin, whose most significant service was in the reform of the literary language. This reform lay in the direction of eliminating Church Slavisms and in following French syntactic and stylistic models. A group of literary conservatives unsuccessfully opposed these reforms. Their leader, Admiral Aleksandr Shishkov, argued for the preservation of archaic forms. However, Karamzin prevailed, and under his influence modern Russian literary prose took shape. His 12-volume *History of the Russian State* (1818–1826) is a masterful work. Influenced by Jean Jacques Rousseau and the 18th century English writers Samuel Richardson and Laurence Sterne, Karamzin also introduced the sentimental movement into Russian literature. His charming *Letters of a Russian Traveler* (1791) and his tremendously popular sentimental tale *Poor Liza* (1792) are both in this vein.

Drama. The interest in drama and theater was furthered by Catherine, who dabbled in playwriting herself. She wrote several satirical comedies, something that passes for a translation of *The Merry Wives of Windsor,* two historical plays that are classified as "imitations of Shakespeare," and still another play that was inspired by *Timon of Athens.*

Little good tragedy was written during Catherine's reign, except for Yakov Knyazhnin's *Vadim of Novgorod* (1789), which breathes a revolutionary political spirit. Comedy predominated, but it was largely influenced by the French neoclassical manner, though now with a firmer grasp on the realities of Russian life. Knyazhnin, an imitator of Voltaire, was a prolific writer of comedies, which on the whole are superior to his tragedies. They usually make excellent theater, but are not first-rate in characterization or dialogue. Perhaps his best comedies are *The Queer Fellows,* a satire on Russian Gallomania, and *An Accident with a Carriage,* a bold satire on serfdom. Even better as dramatic satire is the famous comedy *Chicane* (1798) by Vasili Y. Kapnist. This play is a vicious attack on officers of the law, who are painted as thieves and extortioners. Worthy of mention also is *The Miller, Wizard, Quack and Matchmaker* (1779), a comic work by Aleksander O. Ablesimov.

The greatest dramatist of the 18th century was Denis Fonvizin. His reputation rests on two comedies, *The Brigadier* (1769) and *The Minor* (1782). Both are prose works and reflect the influence of neoclassical French comedy, although Fonvizin's immediate model was the Danish dramatist Ludwig Holberg, whom he had read in German. *The Brigadier* is a social satire directed against the fashionable French semieducation so prevalent in Russia at the time. It is a well-constructed and amusing play. Fonvizin's masterpiece, *The Minor,* also a social satire, is more serious. Its main flaw is a conventional and uninteresting subplot. Attention is centered on the main plot and the vicious members of the Prostakov family: the domineering bully of a mother, her sheepish husband Prostakov (Mr. Simpleton), her furious brother Skotinin (Mr. Brute), and her son Mitrofan, who typifies brutal selfishness. The satire of the comedy is directed against the crude, barbaric natures of uneducated country gentry. Both characterization and dialogue are superior and strike a realistic note that was to be heard again in the best comedy of the 19th century.

EARLY 19TH CENTURY

Poetry. The bulk of literature written during Catherine's reign slavishly followed French, German, or English models. There was little originality, for Russian writers were still serving an apprenticeship to the authors of western Europe. In the first 40 years of the 19th century, however, Russian literature came of age in a wonderful flowering of poetry that was original in form and used native themes.

The towering genius of the period was Russia's greatest poet, Aleksandr Pushkin. Influenced at first by neoclassical 18th century French poets, he soon fell under the romantic spell of Lord Byron. Finally he developed his own original style, which was essentially realistic but cast in a lucid and classical form. His earliest long poem was *Ruslan and Lyudmila* (1818–1820), a semi-ironic and light romance. A series of verse tales followed—*The Prisoner of the Caucasus* (1820–1821), *The Robber Brothers* (1821), *The Fountain of Bakhchisarai* (1822), and *The Gypsies* (1824)—all inspired more or less by Byron's Oriental tales. In 1823, Pushkin began writing his masterpiece *Eugene Onegin,* a novel in verse, which he did not complete until 1830. He also wrote other long poems, including the inimitable *Bronze Horseman* (1833, published 1841), a wonderful series of folktales in verse and the finest collection of lyrics in Russian literature, as well as several plays and a substantial body of prose. His early death in a tragic duel shocked the country and left unfulfilled, despite his great achievements, the career of a poet who belongs among the foremost writers of the world.

The Pushkin Pleiad was a group of fine poets who were contemporary with Pushkin. The most talented of them was Yevgeni Baratynsky, a profoundly intellectual and serious poet who aspired, in his work, to a full union with nature. In striking contrast was the bright, clear, convivial poetry of Nikolai Yazykov. Others in the group were Denis Davydov, author of many fine poems on war and love; Prince Pyotr Vyazemsky, a witty poet and acute critic; Baron Anton Delvig, Pushkin's close friend and the author of a few chiseled lyrics; Kondrati Ryleyev, who was executed as a leader in the revolt of the Decembrists and who left a sheaf of noble and eloquent civic poems; Dmitri Venevitinov, whose few philosophical poems promised a lofty poetic future if he had

The Moscow Art Theatre specializes in great Russian drama, such as Chekhov's The Cherry Orchard.

lived; and Fyodor Glinka, whose verse combined deeply religious devotion with marked simplicity. Ivan Krylov, an older poet who did not belong to the Pushkin Pleiad, was the greatest Russian fabulist. His first book of *Fables* appeared in 1809, and he continued to write for years. The enormous popularity of his verse arose from his common sense and perfect mastery of language.

One of the geniuses of the age was Mikhail Lermontov. At his best, in a few perfect lyrics, in certain parts of his verse tales, and in his unsurpassed narrative romantic poem, *The Demon* (8th version, posthumously published 1842), he rivals Pushkin. He, more than Pushkin, deserves the title of the Russian Byron, though he was beginning to reject romanticism when he died.

This golden age of Russian poetry closed with Fyodor Tyutchev and Aleksei Koltsov. Koltsov's lyrics on the realities of peasant life, the first poetry of this kind in Russian, are excellent. Tyutchev's poetry is essentially metaphysical and is based on a pantheistic conception of the universe. Its prevailing pessimism derives from a constant dualism—a struggle between chaos and cosmos. His diction is faultless, and the love lyrics of his later years are cast in perfect 18th century classical style. Many years passed before Russia produced a body of verse in any way comparable to that of the first 40 years of the 19th century.

Fiction. Little prose fiction of distinction was written in Russia during the early 19th century. Some authors adhered to realism, others to romanticism, and still others produced a combination of the two styles. The realistic English and French picaresque tradition was represented in *A Russian Gil Blas* (1814) by Vasili Narezhny and in *Ivan Vyzhigin* (1829) by Faddei V. Bulgarin.

The popularity of Sir Walter Scott in Russia inspired historical romances of some merit. Mikhail N. Zagoskin wrote *Yuri Miloslavsky, or the Russians in 1612* (1829); Ivan I. Lazhechnikov

wrote *The Last Novik* (1831), *The Ice House* (1835), and *The Heretic* (1838); and Pushkin wrote *The Captain's Daughter* (1836). The Byronic prose tales of adventure of Aleksandr Bestuzhev-Marlinsky won wide popularity. The fiction of Prince Vladimir Odoyevsky and of Aleksandr Veltmann was less obviously romantic. And the romantic Byronic hero of Lermontov's prose masterpiece, *A Hero of Our Time* (1840), did not keep it from being a realistic and acute psychological study of human nature.

The greatest fiction writer of this period was Nikolai V. Gogol, who brilliantly combined the romantic and the realistic in his own special way. Much in his early collections of short stories, *Evenings on a Farm Near Dikanka* (1831–1832) and *Mirgorod* (1835), is sheer romanticism, but in some later tales he combines the romantic with an unusual power for realistic portraiture. After finishing his well-known play *The Inspector General* (1836), he began work on his masterpiece, the novel *Dead Souls* (1842, 1855). Here, with realism and sharp satirical intent, he created a series of unforgettable characters and revealed the vulgarity and ugliness of much of provincial life. The last years of Gogol's relatively short life were darkened by a religious mania that undermined his creative powers.

Nonfiction. Partly under the philosophical influence of Schelling and Hegel, a kind of intellectual revolution took place in Russia between 1825 and 1840. This revolution resulted in the formation of a class known as the intelligentsia, which later played so important a part in Russian political and social thought. By 1840 this movement had divided into two sharply opposing groups—the Slavophiles and the Westerners. The Slavophiles, who were strongly nationalistic, advocated a return to the virtues and traditions of old Russia. They upheld the Orthodox faith and the autocracy of the czar. Among the important Slavophile leaders were the brilliant religious thinker and poet Aleksei Khomyakov and the brothers Konstantin and Ivan Aksakov. However, few figures of notable literary ability were in the camp of the Slavophiles. The critic Apollon Grigoriev was an exception, for his best work is deeply imaginative and keenly perceptive. Nikolai Strakhov was an able though less profound critic, and the critical and philosophical writing of Konstantin N. Leontiev showed excellent literary talent.

The leader of the Westerners was the great literary critic Vissarion Belinsky, who felt that Russia's salvation lay in assimilating the progressive ideas of western Europe. The romantic idealism of Belinsky's early critical writing changed later to a demand for a literature of social significance and reform. His famous contemporary, Aleksandr Herzen, was also a Westerner. Herzen, obliged to leave Russia early in life, waged a political war against the Russian government from abroad through his journalistic writings. Herzen had artistic talent, and although most of his writing was political and social, his brilliant autobiography *My Past and Thoughts* (1855–1856) and his didactic novel *Whose Fault?* (1847) have high literary merit.

Belinsky established a tradition in literary criticism that was ably followed by Nikolai G. Chernyshevsky, Nikolai A. Dobrolyubov, and Dmitri Pisarev. They carried Belinsky's emphasis on social significance in literature still further, making the principal criterion of value in art its utilitarian value. Dobrolyubov's famous article *What Is Oblomovism?* (1859) amounts to a criticism of Russian life at the time. The radical trend begun by the Westerners became more emphatic about 1870 with the rise of the populists (*narodniki*). The populists stressed service to the people as the only possible atonement for the sins committed against the serfs by the educated class. Their principal leader was the critic Nikolai K. Mikhailovsky.

Drama. At the beginning of the 19th century there was little evidence of development in the drama. French neoclassicism gave way to a taste for sentimental plays, but no original work of value was written in this vein. Krylov wrote two rather successful satiric comedies, but the two most popular plays on the Russian stage were translations from the German melodramatist A. F. F. von Kotzebue.

During the first half of the 19th century four famous authors wrote plays. Two of these, authors, Pushkin and Lermontov, were primarily poets; the third, Gogol, was essentially a novelist, and only the fourth, Aleksander S. Griboyedov, was solely a dramatist.

Pushkin's first and longest play, *Boris Godunov* (1825), was an experiment—an attempt to write a Russian Shakespearean tragedy as a departure from the prevalent French neoclassical form. It is a historical play on the theme of Czar Boris Godunov, written in blank verse. Despite scenes of real dramatic beauty and occasional passages of stirring poetry, the play was not one of Pushkin's most mature works, and it has never won a secure place on the Russian stage. Pushkin's so-called "little tragedies," including *Mozart and Salieri* (1830), *The Feast During the Plague* (1830), *The Covetous Knight* (1836), and *The Stone Guest* (1836), are more interesting and more perfectly realized. They were not intended for acting, but are rather essays in the understanding of character and of dramatic situations. As such, they leave little to be desired, either as poetry or drama.

Lermontov had less merit than Pushkin as a dramatist. As a very young man he wrote three prose plays that deal with high-strung passions and melodramatic situations. His verse play, *The Masquerade* (1835), has more worth, but it is too melodramatic and the characters barely come alive. The play was revived with some success in Soviet Russia.

There are critics who insist that Gogol's *The Inspector General* (1836) is the greatest play in the Russian language. Certainly it is one of the greatest. The general theme, supplied to Gogol by Pushkin, of the hero who is mistaken by the people of a town for a government inspector, is magnificently developed from beginning to end. Gogol's originality, against the background of contemporary drama, is shown by the complete absence of the traditional love element and of any sympathetic characters. The play is a moral satire directed against corrupt and despotic officials. The characters are superbly drawn, and the dialogue, with its comic intensity, is among the most effective in Russian drama. The lasting popularity of this play rests in part on an underlying symbolism, which makes the speech and actions of its characters timeless despite their local application. Less known but almost as great is Gogol's exuberant comedy *Marriage* (1842).

The reputation of Griboyedov as one of the greatest Russian dramatists rests on one play, *Woe from Wit* (1822–1824). Full of brilliant wit, epigrams, and repartee, it has provided more clever quotable lines than any other single work in Russian literature.

MID-19TH CENTURY

Realistic Fiction. The classical Russian school of realism in fiction stems from Pushkin, not only from his prose tales, but also from his novel in verse, *Eugene Onegin*. Pushkin's style, his realistic descriptions of life on provincial estates, and such character creations as Eugene and Tatiana left a deep imprint on later fiction. In some ways Gogol followed Pushkin's path, though he also had great originality, especially in style and characterization. His humorous types are delightful, and the oppressed character of his famous tale *The Overcoat* (1842), illustrates a new "philanthropic trend" in Russian fiction. One of the earliest writers to reflect the influence of Gogol was Vladimir Sollogub, notably in his *Tarantas* (1844), a satirical account of a journey from Moscow to Kazan.

Soon the literary scene was populated with Pushkin's and Gogol's great followers, all of whom became known beyond Russia. One of the earliest was Ivan A. Goncharov. Belinsky hailed his first novel, *A Common Story* (1847), as a vital contribution to the new realistic school, but his masterpiece, *Oblomov* (1859), became a Russian classic. The hero Oblomov, a symbol of sloth and ineffectiveness, is a clear descendant of Pushkin's Eugene.

The realistic novel reached its peak with the three giants Ivan Turgenev, Fyodor Dostoyevsky, and Leo Tolstoy. Modern criticism considers Turgenev, who was strongly influenced by Pushkin, the least able of the three. His first substantial work, *A Sportsman's Sketches* (1847–1852), was poetic in style and showed sympathetic understanding of the oppressed serfs. In the novels *Rudin* (1856) and *A Nest of Gentlefolk* (1859), Turgenev used his favorite "weak hero" and "strong heroine" types—obviously inspired by Pushkin's Eugene and Tatiana. In *Rudin,* particularly, Turgenev, who was a Westerner, also showed his concern with social problems. In *On the Eve* (1860), Turgenev tried to rid himself of the "superfluous man" character type and to create an active hero. The critics were quick to point out that the new hero, Insarov, was a Bulgarian and not a Russian. The author's final answer to the demands of the critics for an active hero was Bazarov, in his masterpiece *Fathers and Sons* (1862). Radical critics, however, condemned Bazarov as a caricature of a revolutionist. Deeply offended, Turgenev spent most of his later life abroad, and although he continued to write, his later work fell off in power. Turgenev's novels are rich in human experience and social significance. His gallery of heroines, as well as his style, are among the best in Russian fiction.

Dostoyevsky, on the other hand, was quite outside the traditional development of Russian realism. His chief debt was to Gogol, who had pioneered in philanthropic fiction. Dostoyevsky followed Gogol's lead in his preoccupation with the downtrodden and oppressed. Thus the hero of his first tale, *Poor Folk* (1845), is a miserable copying clerk, like the hero in Gogol's *The Overcoat*. But unlike Gogol, who developed characters through external details, Dostoyevsky analyzed his characters from within. He was primarily interested in their souls. Dostoyevsky published a series of short stories from 1844 to 1849. In 1849 he was exiled to Omsk for his association with a radical group. He did not return to St. Petersburg or begin writing again until ten years later. With *Crime and Punishment*, published in 1866, he won widespread fame. The great novels that followed—*The Idiot* (1869), *The Possessed*, also called *The Devils* (1871–1872), and *The Brothers Karamazov* (1880)—made him one of the most celebrated authors in Russia. His novels have been discussed endlessly in Russia and abroad. Critics have found everything in them from grotesque, sensational misrepresentation of real life to the revelation of a new Christianity. His titanic characters, such as Raskolnikov, Prince Myshkin, Stavroghin, the Karamazov brothers, and the holy Zosima, undoubtedly reflect his own spiritual tragedy in the search for God. His attempted solutions for his characters do not always match the profundity and terrible realism of their tremendous conflicts and tragedies. Yet in his novels the fusion of the philosophical and imaginative fabric is complete, and his intense inner psychological analysis of characters is unique in world fiction.

Leo Tolstoy reverted to the Pushkin tradition of realism in both manner and subject matter. However, unlike Turgenev, he was not primarily concerned with contemporary problems of social significance in the works written before his spiritual change in 1880. Yet the original stamp of this colossal genius was placed on everything he wrote. His early works, such as *Childhood* (1852), *Boyhood* (1854), and *Youth* (1857), are, essentially, charming reminiscences. However, these works also reveal a realistic grasp on the experiences of life and a potential power of character analysis far beyond the talents of the older writer. These qualities reach their height in *War and Peace* (1865–1869) and *Anna Karenina* (1875–1877). Modern realism has never equaled the achievement of *War and Peace*. Each of the more than 500 characters has a distinct personality and speaks a distinct language. A Russian critic remarked that even the dogs in the book are individualized. Truth and simplicity, the two canons of Tolstoy's artistic faith, are scrupulously observed. And these same attributes, as well as the author's ecstatic love of life, appear throughout *Anna Karenina*.

After his spiritual struggle and conversion about 1880, Tolstoy professed to turn his back on art. Nevertheless, apart from the voluminous critical, moral, and religious works that he wrote after 1880, he produced a considerable body of imaginative literature of great merit, such as *The Death of Ivan Ilich* (1886), *The Kreutzer Sonata* (1889), *Hadji Murad* (written 1904; posthumously published 1911–1912), and *Resurrection* (1899). He also wrote several plays. Toward the end of his life he abandoned the psychological and analytical manner of his great period for a simple narrative style that would appeal to the masses. However, everything that he wrote, before and after his conversion, bore the indelible trace of his genius.

There were other fine 19th century realistic novelists who, though not in the same class with the giants, have a high place in Russian literature. The best novels of Aleksei F. Pisemsky are *The Petersburgher* (1853) and *A Thousand Souls* (1858). The first novel depicts uneducated people with rugged virtues and moral strength, and the second is a satire on genteel life. Pisemsky's heroes and heroines are vigorously drawn, both in his novels and in his plays. One of the great satirists in Russian literature was N. Shchedrin, the pen name of Mikhail Y. Saltykov. His *Golovlev Family* (1875–1880) is a satirical masterpiece, a social novel that portrays the sordid and crass lives of the ruble-hunting lower provincial gentry. Among the many radical journalists and novelists of the 1860's, the only outstanding one was Gleb Uspensky. His best work, *The Power of the Soil* (1882), portrays peasant life with humor and great sympathy.

Nikolai S. Leskov was the author of several minor classics. His novel *Cathedral Folk* (1872) is an amusing chronicle of provincial life. In his other novels and many short stories he produced a brightly colored canvas of Russian life in a humorous vein and in a style rich with folk idioms.

Poetry. The poets of the period were torn between the necessity of writing verse that reflected the civic problems of the day and of indulging in the poet's eternal search for truth and beauty. In trying to fulfill this double mission, Apollon N. Maikov and Yakov P. Polonsky were only partially successful. Count Aleksei K. Tolstoy, one of the greatest Russian writers of nonsense verse, also wrote exquisite lyric poetry and excellent dramas. The most celebrated realistic poet of the time was the radical Nikolai A. Nekrasov. His narrative poems *The Pedlars* (1863) and *Who Can Be Happy in Russia?* (1873–1876) are filled with keen, good-humored, shrewd satire and remarkable verbal power, always with undertones of poignant protest. Afanasi A. Fet was as conservative as Nekrasov was radical. His short, condensed lyrics are very beautiful.

Drama. The remarkable realistic development in fiction during the second half of the 19th century was accompanied by a similar realistic movement in acting and in playwriting. The famous actor Mikhail Shchepkin had established the great tradition of Russian realistic acting in the first half of the 19th century. This tradition was eventually developed into a theory of theatrical art by the celebrated actor and producer Konstantin Stanislavsky in his great Moscow Art Theater, founded in 1898. In its later development Russian scenic realism concentrated on social realism, on truth to the particular, that is on the least universal and most individual aspects of a given social milieu. All this found its first complete expression in original drama in the plays of Aleksandr N. Ostrovsky, one of the great Russian dramatists.

Between 1847 and 1886, Ostrovsky wrote about 40 plays in prose and eight in blank verse. With few exceptions, his plays are neither tragedies nor comedies, but tragicomedies. The subject matter of his early and most characteristic plays is life in Moscow, through which he chiefly satirizes bureaucrats and bourgeois merchants. Ostrovsky's first play, *The Bankrupt* (1849), later called *It's All in the Family*, was a sensational success, and it revealed at once his peculiar and rather original technique. He presented only unsympathetic characters, and he boldly discarded the ancient tradition of comedy—the poetic justice that punishes vice. His realism, which avoids both caricature and farce, is based on solid first-hand knowledge of the life described. All these traits were strengthened in the successful

Anna Karenina, by Leo Tolstoy, Russia's greatest novelist, was made into a classic motion picture in 1935, with Greta Garbo (*left*) as the doomed heroine and Fredric March (*in uniform*) as her lover Count Vronsky.

plays that followed: *Poverty Is No Disgrace* (1854) and *The Profitable Post* (1857). The play generally considered his masterpiece is *The Storm* (1860). It is his most poetic piece, a great poem of love and death, of freedom and thralldom. Notable later plays include *The Forest* (1871) and *Wolves and Sheep* (1875).

The only two contemporary dramatists who approached Ostrovsky's art were Aleksandr V. Sukhovo-Kobylin and Pisemsky. The best of the former's three plays is *Krechinsky's Wedding* (1855), a pure comedy of picaresque intrigue, in which the rogue triumphs over the stupidity of the virtuous character. The two other comedies, *The Affair* (1869) and *The Death of Tarelkin* (1869), are brutally cynical satires.

Pisemsky, essentially a novelist, began his dramatic career with comedies. But his most memorable work, *A Hard Lot* (1860), is one of the great tragedies in Russian dramatic literature. It is about the seduction by a squire of the wife of one of his serfs. The husband murders his wife and gives himself up to the law. The human conflict between the squire, who is legal master of the husband, and the husband, who is legal master of his wife, is worked out powerfully with a tragic inevitability that is classical in quality.

Turgenev, the great realistic novelist, thought early in his career that he might devote himself entirely to drama. His plays belong to the years between 1843 and 1852. They are largely experimental gropings after an adequate form of expression. The most actable is *The Provincial Lady* (1851), a light comedy with delicate characterizations. *A Month in the Country* (1850), a more interesting play, is a psychological study on the old theme of rivalry in love between a mature woman and a young girl. In its undramatic nature it is a forerunner of the plays of Anton Chekhov.

Drama was merely incidental in the extensive literary production of Tolstoy. Yet, one or two of his plays have an enduring place in the great dramatic literature of Russia. He succeeded though he possessed few of the essential qualities that make a dramatist. On the lighter side

are *The Contaminated Family* (1863), a delightful satire on the young generation, and *The Fruits of Enlightenment* (1889), an amusing social comedy which satirizes the vogue of spiritualism. However, Tolstoy's greatest and best-known play is *The Power of Darkness* (1887), a realistic tragedy of peasant life. The play embodies a favorite conviction of Tolstoy, the evil-begetting power of every evil action. Two more of his plays are worthy of comment: *The Light Shineth in Darkness* (unfinished; posthumously published 1911–1912) and *The Living Corpse* (written 1900; posthumously published 1911–1912). The first draws on Tolstoy's life, for it concerns a Tolstoyan moralist surrounded by an unsympathetic family. *The Living Corpse*, in point of view, is unique for Tolstoy. It reflects the mellow attitude of a kindly old man, free from Tolstoy's customary dogmatic moralizing, and full of sympathy for the abandoned drunkard in the play and even for the proud society mother.

Later in the 19th century there was a revival of historical verse plays, largely under the belated influence of Pushkin's *Boris Godunov*. In general all these plays are characterized by mediocre blank verse and by their failure to catch the flavor of old Russia, from which most of the themes were drawn. The movement was begun by the poet Lev A. Mey in his *Maid of Pskov* (1860), a conventionally pretty drama of the time of Ivan the Terrible. The best of the historical dramatists was Aleksei K. Tolstoy, whose famous trilogy, *The Death of Ivan the Terrible* (1866), *Czar Fyodor Ivanovich* (1868), and *Czar Boris* (1870), deserves its high reputation. The historical material is skillfully handled, the character drawing is adequate and sometimes brilliant, and the blank verse is superior to that in other contemporary historical plays.

LATE 19TH CENTURY TO THE REVOLUTION

Fiction and Poetry from 1880 to 1900. The towering shadow of Leo Tolstoy dominated fiction from 1880 to 1900. An early member of the new generation influenced by Tolstoy was Vsevo-

30g

lod M. Garshin, whose fame rests on his collected short stories. The most notable of these stories, particularly *The Scarlet Blossom* (1883), reveal a moral sensitivity and an infinite sympathy for the victims of man's inhumanity.

A. I. Ertel wrote *The Gardenins* (1898), a long novel about family life on a huge estate. Vladimir G. Korolenko was exiled to Siberia for radical activities, and he drew upon his experiences there in his tales. In stories like *Makar's Dream* (1885) he combines a delightful humor with a kind of radical idealism.

Korolenko's great rival was Anton Chekhov, whose first collected tales met with immediate success when they were published in 1885. His mature period, however, began in 1889, with the publication of *A Boring Story*. Here is found that mutual lack of understanding among characters and the psychological development of a mood that combine to form the "Chekhovian state of mind" so characteristic of his best-known tales, such as *The Duel* and *Ward 6*. These same qualities, along with deeper symbolic overtones, reappear in his famous plays.

Little excellent poetry was written during this period. The most popular of the social-minded poets was Semyon Nadson. His brief creative life was dedicated to themes of reform, but he lacked imaginative power and originality of expression. His rival for popular favor was A. N. Apukhtin, whose poetry is filled with a hedonist's regret for the lost pleasures of youth. The verse of Vladimir S. Soloviev rose above this undistinguished level. A brilliant philosophical thinker and a clever writer of nonsense verse, he was yet capable of embodying profound mystical experiences in beautiful lyrics.

Fiction after Chekhov. Because the radical movement of the 1880's and 1890's was driven underground by the czar's secret police, it could find no legal expression in literature. Yet a new force, Russian Marxism, had entered the struggle against autocracy, aided by a growing proletarian class. After the disastrous 1905 revolution, the Duma was established, but the high hopes of the revolutionists were blasted. A deep disillusionment with the whole radical movement followed, reflected in literature, in antipolitical individualism, and in the growth of aestheticism.

For a time the two most popular representatives of the new manner in fiction were Leonid Andreyev and Mikhail P. Artsybashev. Andreyev had two styles—the shrill, rhetorical style of *The Red Laugh* (1904) and the restrained, logical style of such celebrated short stories as *The Seven That Were Hanged* (1908). In general, the underlying theme of his fiction and plays was physical death and the annihilation of society, morals, and culture. Artsybashev echoed the same theme, but added that of sexual emancipation in his enormously successful and somewhat pornographic novel, *Sanin* (1907).

In striking contrast was the fiction of Maksim Gorky (the pseudonym of A. M. Peshkov). Gorky raised his voice on behalf of the lost men and women of Russia's lower depths and at the same time liberated Russian realism from its rather conservative tradition. Although Gorky began to publish long before the 1917 revolution, he lived to become the titular head of Soviet literature, which he profoundly influenced both by example and criticism. Gorky's early stories, published in three volumes in 1898–1899, reveal the cruelty and ugliness in the lives of the lowly creatures he met on his travels through southern Russia. The novels of his second period, including *Foma Gordeyev* (1899) and *Mother* (1906), depict the depraved life of provincial Russia and the unhappy lot of oppressed workers. In his last period he devoted himself largely to superb volumes of recollections. From 1925 until his death he worked on his epic novel, never completed, *The Life of Klim Samghin*, which presents the history of Russian life between 1880 and 1917. He draws a dark, cruel, and ugly picture but, rising above the gloom, there is always a ray of hope for a better and happier country.

Writers who reveled in outspoken realism and went as far toward revolutionary protest as the government would permit gathered around Gorky and his publishing firm, Znaniye. Two of them, Vikenti Veresayev (the pseudonym of Vikenti V. Smidovich), and A. S. Serafimovich (pseudonym of A. S. Popov), became popular in Soviet Russia for novels sympathetic to the ideals of the revolution. Serafimovich's *Iron Torrent* (1924) became especially popular. Some influence of Gorky appeared in the fiction of Aleksandr I. Kuprin, whose novel *The Duel* (1905) made him famous overnight. *The Shulamite* (1908) and *Yama* (1912), were also popular, but they were less powerful. A finer artist was I. A. Bunin, who first became known through his verse but achieved greater fame as a novelist. His most powerful novel was *Dry Valley* (1911–1912), the story of the disintegration of a landowning family.

The Symbolist Movement. There was one important reaction in the 1890's and early 1900's to writers such as Andreyev and Gorky and to the dominance of social significance and nihilistic thought in literature. It took form in a definite turning away from civic morality to aestheticism, from duty to beauty. Most participants in the new movement were intellectuals like Dmitri S. Merezhkovsky and his talented wife Zinaida Hippius, N. Minsky (the pseudonym of Nikolai M. Vilenkin), and V. V. Rozanov. Merezhkovsky is best known for his trilogy of historical novels—*Julian the Apostate* (1896), *Leonardo da Vinci* (1902), and *Peter and Alexis* (1905). However, he also played the philosopher and prophet, developing a curious antithetical approach to religion and morality. Rozanov was a critic and thinker of considerable power. His best works are *Solitary Thoughts* (1912) and *Fallen Leaves* (1913).

This emphasis on aesthetics and mysticism provided an easy transition to the remarkable symbolist movement, partly an offshoot of French symbolism. Valeri Bryusov established the movement with a collection of poems published in *The Russian Symbolists* (1894). He was a weaver of gorgeous imagery, but his verse often seems chill and premeditated. The early symbolist Konstantin D. Balmont was a more natural poet, yet there is more sound than sense in his *Under Northern Skies* (1894) and *Let Us Be Like the Sun* (1903). *The Cypress Chest* (1910) by Innokenti F. Annensky and *Cor Ardens* (1911) by Vyacheslav I. Ivanov were regarded in their day as fine collections of symbolist verse. The former was compressed, subtle, and precise; the latter, ornate and metaphysical.

One of the most remarkable authors of the symbolist movement was Fyodor Sologub, the pseudonym of the poet and novelist Fyodor Kuzmich Teternikov. He is best known for his famous novel *The Little Demon* (1907), whose hero, Peredonov, has become a symbol of concentrated nastiness. Perhaps the most original and most difficult of the symbolists was Andrei Bely, whose real name was Boris N. Bugayev. He was a brilliant critic and poet, but he too is best known for his novels, particularly *Petersburg* (1913–1916) and *Kotik Letayev* (1918). His style in the latter work suggests the writings of James Joyce. An author often associated with Bely, both as symbolist and prose stylist, was Aleksei M. Remizov. His tales of the ugliness of provincial life, *The Story of Stratilatov* (1909) and *The Fifth Pestilence* (1912), are written in ornamental, highly mannered prose.

In general, symbolist literature pointed in two clear directions: an aesthetic direction, emphasizing refinement of form, and a religious-mystical direction that usually involved the creation of dream worlds, often realistically described. Both tendencies fused in the work of the greatest of the symbolist poets, Aleksandr A. Blok. His early poems, such as those in *Verses about the Beautiful Lady* (1904), tell the history of his mystical "love affair" with a beautiful lady, who continued to haunt his later poems as he went through a long period of black despair. After 1917, he considered the revolution as a cleansing fire that would purify the soul of Russia. This attitude found expression in his greatest poem, *The Twelve* (1918), which is a miracle of revolutionary mysticism and metrical harmony. His radical enthusiasm later gave way to disillusion and chronic despair. He was perhaps the greatest Russian poet since Lermontov.

Drama. The founding of the Moscow Art Theater in 1898 by Stanislavsky and Vladimir Nemirovich-Danchenko ushered in a new development in Russian theater and drama. One of the first productions of the new theater in 1898 was Chekhov's *The Seagull*. Chekhov had written his first play, *Ivanov*, in 1887 and had followed up its success with several one-act comedies. In 1895 he wrote *The Seagull*, which was acted the next year in St. Petersburg. The performance was an utter failure, for neither director nor actors understood the play, and Chekhov vowed to abandon drama. However, Stanislavsky's production of *The Seagull*, in 1898, was a great success, and Chekhov turned with new energy to writing plays. There soon followed *Uncle Vanya* (1897), *The Three Sisters* (1901), and *The Cherry Orchard* (1903–1904), all of them triumphs.

These four plays constitute Chekhov's theater and represent quite a new direction in drama. There is no subject matter in Chekhov's plays, no plot, no action. In certain essentials the plays resemble his short stories. In a sense there is no hero or heroine; all the characters are equal. And the dialogue Chekhov employed is admirably suited to the expression of one of the favorite ideas of his tales—the mutual unintelligibility and strangeness of human beings who make no effort to understand each other. Further, his plays are steeped in emotional symbolism, and the dominant note is one of gloom, depression, and hopelessness. Stanislavsky's style perfectly suited the peculiar nature of Chekhov's plays and undoubtedly accounted for a good deal of their initial success on the stage. The Moscow Art Theater specialized in naturalistic realism, dispensed with all theatricality, abandoned the "star" system in theater, and concentrated on bringing out the inner life of each character.

Chekhov's highly original drama quickly inspired imitators, most of whom were bad. One of the first was Andreyev, who wrote about a dozen plays, several of which are still played. His Chekhovian realistic plays of Russian life, such as *Towards the Stars* (1906), *Days of Our Life* (1908), *Anfisa* (1910), and *Gaudeamus* (1911), are very poor imitations of Chekhov. Andreyev showed more originality, however, in another group of plays, symbolical dramas in conventional settings, such as *The Life of Man* (1907), *King Hunger* (1907), *Black Masks* (1909), *Anathema* (1910), and *He Who Gets Slapped* (1914). *The Life of Man* and *He Who Gets Slapped* won considerable success in productions both in Russia and abroad.

There is a curious avoidance of real life in Andreyev's plays, and the rhetorical prose and gaudy colors weary both the ear and eye. But their melodramatic effects often make for good theater, and for a time their philosophy of vanity, death, and the falseness of everything human had vogue. Some of the atmospheric details characteristic of Chekhov's work appear in the plays of Artsybashev, although he was additionally influenced by Strindberg. Artsybashev's psychological problem dramas, including *Jealousy* and *War*, are rather crude but they act well.

Gorky, whose dramatic efforts continued well into the period after the 1917 revolution, began as a patent follower of Chekhov. He wrote 15 plays, but only two or three won outstanding success on the stage. His first play, *The Petty Bourgeois* (1901), is a bitter picture of a middle-class family and a revolutionary locomotive engineer. It was eclipsed by *The Lower Depths* (1902), which was a sensational success. The play is a penetrating study of different types of human derelicts in an underground night's lodging. Gorky's dramatic system resembles that of Chekhov. The four acts, undivided into scenes, the absence of action, and the exaggerated development of conversations on the meaning of life all suggest Chekhov. The conversations particularly, but also the extraordinary realism of the settings and the unique characters, won unbounded applause for *The Lower Depths* both in Russia and abroad. Succeeding plays, among them *Summer People* (1905), *Children of the Sun* (1905), *The Barbarians* (1906), *Enemies* (1907), and *Vassa Zheleznova* (1910), were not very successful. However, *Yegor Bulychov and Others* (1932) was extremely well received in Soviet Russia. Its theme is the death of a capitalist on the eve of the Russian Revolution.

SOVIET LITERATURE THROUGH WORLD WAR II

Blok's *The Twelve* was in a sense the swan song of symbolism. The opposition was centered in two new groups. These were the acmeists, led by the poets Osip Mandelshtam, N. S. Gumilyov, and Anna Akhmatova, and the futurists, led by Igor Severyanin, Velemir Khlebnikov, and Vladimir Mayakovsky. The acmeists stressed clarity, precision, and a return to the established forms. The futurists demanded the destruction of all literary traditions in the name of a new flesh-and-blood art that would banish the pale aestheticism of the symbolists and the dry academism of classical writers. Soviet literature began in the shadow of this blatant revolt, and it was the immensely talented futurist poet Mayakovsky who first set his impress on the new movement. After 1917, Mayakovsky devoted all his ability and energy to the Revolution. His inspiration was the "social command" that he thought every Soviet poet must obey. He wrote many short pieces and plays, but his chief fame rests on several long narrative poems—*150,000,000* (1920), *Vladimir Ilich Lenin* (1924), and *Well and Good* (1927). He employed very remarkable sound effects and achieved visual effects with the short broken line for which he used various typographical tricks. No Soviet poet has been more honored than Mayakovsky. His only rival in popularity during those early days was Sergei Esenin or Yesenin, who regarded himself as the "last poet of the village." He had a fine lyric gift but was unable to adapt himself to the new order.

Certain definite tendencies began to emerge out of the confusion and conflicting literary demands that existed in the early years of Revolution and civil war. In 1917 the Proletcult was formed to direct the fight for a proletarian culture on an international scale. Two schools of thought promptly arose. One was the moderate group, supported by prominent government officials and certain writers known as "fellow-travelers," who argued that it was impossible to create a proletarian literature by official decree and that much of value could still be learned from bourgeois art and culture. The other consisted of the extremists, soon known as the "On Guard" group, who supported the idea of a government literary dictatorship and called for an uncompromising class-literature. A resolution of the central committee of the Communist party in 1925 declared in favor of the moderate school, and for a time the fellow-travelers were left free to write much as they desired.

Beginnings of Soviet Fiction. No Soviet fiction of any consequence was written until about the time of the New Economic Policy (1922–1928). The predominant themes of this early fiction were the stirring events of the Revolution and civil war, in which many of the young authors had participated. One of the first successful novels to depict revolutionary violence was *The Naked Year* (1922) by Boris Pilnyak (the pseudonym of Boris A. Vogau). *Armored Train 14–69* (1922) and *Colored Winds* (1922) by Vsevolod V. Ivanov treat guerrilla warfare in Siberia. Ivanov's characters are vivid, though astoundingly primitive in their emotions and actions. The extremely popular book *Chapayev* (1923), by Dmitri Furmanov, is an almost documentary narrative of the famous peasant partisan Chapayev, who commanded a division that saved Uralsk from the White forces. *Red Cavalry* (1926), by Isaak Babel, is more romantic in its treatment of violence. It is a collection of stories based on the author's experiences with Marshal Semyon M. Budenny's Cossacks.

On the whole, this early fiction eschewed the psychological analysis of the great 19th century Russian novelists and concentrated on straightforward realistic narrative. Before long, however, some Soviet novelists appeared who wrote on themes of revolution and civil strife, much in the manner of Leo Tolstoy, Dostoyevsky, and Chekhov.

One of the first was Konstantin A. Fedin. His novel *Cities and Years* (1922–1924), about a self-centered intellectual who eventually betrays the Revolution, aroused considerable interest. The flavor of Fedin's novel suggests Chekhov, and the spiritual doubt of his hero echoes Dostoyevsky. Dostoyevsky is even more in evidence in the fiction of Leonid M. Leonov, especially in the psychological development of character, as expressed in *The Badgers* (1924) and *The Thief* (1927).

Critics praised Leonov's fiction as a bridge between Soviet realists and classical writers of the past. In a sense the two periods are linked even more strongly in the work of Aleksei N. Tolstoy, a leading literary figure of Soviet Russia. Perhaps his most distinguished novel is *The Road to Calvary* (finished 1941), which pictures Russia before, during, and following the Revolution. *The Rout* (1926), the first novel of Aleksandr A. Fadeyev, shows the obvious influence of Leo Tolstoy in psychological insight and unrestrained realism. Fadeyev reveals an intimate knowledge of Siberia in *The Rout* (1927) and again more extensively in his best novel, *The Last of the Udegs* (1930–1940).

Fiction During the First Five-Year Plan. Under the First Five-Year Plan (1928–1932) a new attempt was made to regiment literature. The Russian Association of Proletarian Writers (RAPP) fell under the control of the critic Leopold Averbakh and a few close supporters, who dictated that the only themes suitable for Soviet writers were industrial reconstruction and agricultural collectivization under the Five-Year Plan, treated against a background of the class struggle. The results of this "planned literature" were for the most part unsatisfactory. Discontent became so great that in 1932 a government decree dissolved RAPP, and this extreme form of literary dictatorship came to an end. A general association of Soviet writers was set up to which all, Communists and non-Communists, were freely admitted.

Although most of the literature produced during the First Five-Year Plan hardly rose above the level of official propaganda or of skillful reporting, a few novels had superior merit. Fyodor V. Gladkov had, in 1925, anticipated the kind of fiction encouraged under the Five-Year Plan with his enormously popular *Cement*. Some years later he published *Energy* (1932–1938), a story of the men and women who built a power station on the Dnieper River. In *The Soviet River* (1930), Leonov depicted the establishment of a paper industry, and in *Skutarevsky* (1932) he described a large-scale electrification project. Although in both books he bores the reader with countless scientific technicalities, he shows, nevertheless, a typical Dostoyevskian concern for the "inner man" and his spiritual doubts. The subject of industrial reconstruction provided the theme for Pilnyak's fine novel *The Volga Flows into the Caspian Sea* (1930). *Time, Forward!* (1932) by Valentin Katayev is still more lively and artistic. Its theme is the competition of shock brigades in pouring cement, and the story is told with verve and excitement.

One of the greatest Soviet novelists, Mikhail A. Sholokhov, reached artistic maturity during this period. He began his long epic of Cossack life, *The Quiet Don*, in 1926. However, he interrupted it to write *Virgin Soil Upturned* (1932), the best novel written on the theme of agricultural collectivization during the First Five-Year Plan. A second part was published in 1960. Sholokhov finished *The Quiet Don* in 1940. The book covers eight years of its hero's experiences and development during World War I, the Revolution, and the civil war. It is an intensely moving story of a man's weakness and strength, reflecting the influence of Leo Tolstoy.

Meanwhile, up to this point, there was no lack in fiction of criticism of Soviet life. Satire aimed against the vices, foibles, and absurdities of Soviet officials was freely tolerated, provided it did not attack the accepted principles of the new order. Among the best-known satirists in fiction of the time were Y. I. Zamyatin, Ilya Ehrenburg, and Mikhail A. Bulgakov. Katayev's *The Embezzlers* (1928) is a delightful satire on two naïvely peculating Soviet officials. A number of humorous, popular satires were written in collaboration by Ilya Ilf (the pseudonym of Ilya A. Fainzilberg) and Yevgeni Petrov (the pseudonym of Yevgeni P. Katayev). The most widely read Soviet humorist, however, was Mikhail Zoshchenko, who published about ten volumes of short stories and novels. Beneath his humor there is always a deft criticism of the abuses of Soviet life.

Nor were ethical problems, such as the conflict of the new Communist conscience and ideals with traditional views of sex, love, marriage, and the family, neglected in the fiction produced during the First Five-Year Plan and even earlier. Two older writers who wrote on such problems were S. N. Sergeyev-Tsensky and Panteleimon Romanov. Yuri Libedinsky, in his later works, concerned himself with ethical and social problems, especially in his finest novel, *The Birth of a Hero* (1930), as did Yuri Olesha in his novel *Envy* (1927).

Fiction After the First Five-Year Plan. After 1932 there was less emphasis on themes dictated by "social commands" and greater emphasis on permanent values and universal constants of human behavior. Although the Communist conscience was still omnipresent, in such fine novels as Nikolai Ostrovsky's *How the Steel Was Tempered* (1934) and the unfinished *Born of the Storm* (1936), many other works of fiction expressed more universal emotions and human values.

Enthusiasm increased for the kind of historical fiction in which a Marxian approach was employed to reinterpret the past to conform with the present. Historical documentation was usually very careful and scholarly, and some of the novels were very interesting. In the brilliant historical novel *Peter the Great* (1929–1945), Aleksei N. Tolstoy treats the period of the famous czar as one of transition, symbolically parallel to the period of tremendous upheaval in Soviet Russia. Other noteworthy examples of this genre are *Razin Stepan* (1926–1927) by Aleksei Chapygin, *Tsusima* (1932–1935) by Aleksei Novikov-Priboi, and *Brusilov's Breakthrough* (1943–1944) by Sergei Sergeyev-Tsensky.

On the other hand, the historical novels of Yuri Tynyanov attempt to re-create literary figures of the past and the age in which they lived. Chief among them are *Kyukhla* (1925) and *Pushkin* (1936, 1943). In most historical novels the patriotic motive is strong, with emphasis on the heroism of the past as an example for the Soviet present. During World War II this trend developed into the most violent patriotism. Two themes predominate in the numerous war stories, poems, and plays that appeared after June 1941: love for the native soil and bitter hatred for the enemy.

After the war, the central committee of the Communist party severely condemned several prominent Soviet writers for alleged bourgeois tendencies and ordered literary efforts to be more communistic.

Poetry. Later Soviet poetry was deeply influenced by Mayakovsky's insistence, after 1917, on the socialist function of verse. However, the poets, like the novelists, were soon split into factions by the conflicting demands made by their Communist conscience and by "social commands." Demyan Bedny, an older writer regarded as a kind of poet laureate in the early days of the Revolution, was untroubled by these conflicts. Much of his ephemeral verse contained satirical and humorous commentaries on Soviet daily life.

However, many of the young proletarian poets, who were under Mayakovsky's influence, often lost themselves in the factional strife. They professed contempt for Russian bourgeois literature of the past and proclaimed their devotion to the Communist party and its aims. One of these poets was A. I. Bezymensky. In one of his best-known volumes of verse, *That Is How Life Smells* (1924), he asserted that his only real concern was for proletarian realities. After the dissolution of RAPP in 1932, Bezymensky and his strident leftism lost favor. Others among this group of young proletarian poets were Aleksandr Zharov, Nikolai Ushakov, Mikhail Golodny (the pseudonym of Mikhail S. Epstein), Mikhail Svetlov, and Vassili Kazin. Mayakovsky's chief follower was Nikolai Aseyev. His long poem, *Mayakovsky Begins* (1940), in honor of Mayakovsky's memory, strengthened Aseyev's position as one of the foremost poets of Soviet Russia.

Constructivism, a somewhat vague movement that developed out of futurism, had Ilya Selvinsky as its principal poetic adherent. Also somewhat influenced by this movement was Eduard Bagritsky, a highly talented poet with a fine lyric gift. The "poet's poet" of Soviet Russia, and certainly one of the most distinguished figures in literature, was Boris L. Pasternak, who began his career under the influence of the futurists. His long narrative poems, such as *Spektorsky* (1926) *and The Year 1905* (1927), seem uncongenial to his special lyric genius, which is more in evidence in his shorter pieces. He was very much an individualist, and although his language is often obscure and unorthodox in its syntactical structure, it is brilliantly successful in rhythmical effects. Another poet, at one time thought of as Pasternak's chief rival, was Nikolai Tikhonov, who developed his art in an independent fashion, largely as a medium for treating romantic subjects realistically.

In general, Soviet poets seemed unable to adapt themselves as easily as fiction writers to the new demands made on literature by the state. The discipline of verse was more severe, and it took a longer time for forms to crystallize and for faith to take root in the poetic consciousness. World War II brought the earlier promise of poetry to fuller realization. Something of a renaissance took place in Soviet war poetry. The older poets were being paced by such newcomers as Konstantin Simonov and Aleksandr Tvardovsky, and there was a definite transition from the often difficult, futuristic language of prewar poetry to a simple, uninvolved style, especially in many of the lyrics and ballads on war themes.

Literary Criticism. After the 1917 revolution, the old schools of historical-comparative and religious-philosophical literary criticism gave way to sociological and Marxist criticism, which examined literature from the point of view of social and economic evolution. Even earlier, a less purely Marxian approach had been formulated by such critics as Georgi V. Plekhanov, V. M. Frietsche, P. S. Kogan, V. L. Lvov-Rogachevsky, and Aleksandr Aleksandrovich Bogdanov (the pseudonym of A. Malinovsky). Bogdanov, the author of *Art and the Working Classes* (1918), became the principal theorist of the Proletcult.

This early Marxian literary criticism split into a right wing (Leon Trotsky, Vyacheslav P. Polonsky, Aleksandr Voronsky, Abram Lezhnev, and Anatoli V. Lunacharsky) and a left wing (G. Lelevich, G. Gorbachev, and Averbakh). Both factions accepted the doctrine of historical materialism and the critical method of both groups was to interpret literary works through an analysis of the economic and social structure of society. Their differences lay largely in the relative importance of these factors.

The most serious opponents of the Marxists in literary criticism were the formalists, who confined themselves largely to investigations of poetic speech and problems of style. Most of them were brilliant scholars. Their general thesis was that a work of art is the sum of the devices in it and that "form creates its content."

After 1932 the universal touchstone of Soviet literary criticism became "socialist realism." The term has various interpretations and applications. In its primary sense, socialist realism means a realism that is socialistic, reflecting socialist realities and a socialist mentality. Some Soviet critics, however, insisted that socialist realism must rest on socialist humanism. This concept was intended to broaden and ennoble the aims of art. The Soviet literature inspired by socialist realism was essentially optimistic in its definition of existence as activity, in its attempt to integrate literature and life, and in its effort to direct the changing present toward a more creative future.

Drama. Recognizing the educational and cultural value of the theater, the Soviet government gave every encouragement to the theater arts, and millions of people who had never seen a play became avid theatergoers. There was a great expansion and development of theatrical schools, of theories of acting and staging, and of other phases of the theater. The Moscow Art Theater continued to flourish after 1917, and other now famous theaters, among them the Meyerhold Theater, the Vakhtangov Theater, the Kamerny Theater, and the Realistic Theater, developed individual theories of dramatic art.

The Soviet plays written after 1917 were not markedly inferior in quantity or quality to those written in western Europe or the United States during the same period. Soviet drama, like fiction and poetry, mirrored the swift political, social, and economic changes in the USSR. Most of the dramatists first on the scene, such as Aleksei N. Tolstoy, Konstantin A. Trenev, Lunacharsky, Boris S. Romashov, and Sergei M. Tretyakov, belonged to the intelligentsia, and some had written plays before the Revolution. Several novelists who also wrote plays belong to this group, and some gained a permanent place in the Soviet theater. The plays of this group of dramatists reflected various styles, including romantic, realistic, and futuristic.

A second group of dramatists, some of proletarian origin, wrote plays mainly on civil war themes. Many of these works were poorly executed propaganda pieces. Among them are *The Echo* (1924) and *The Storm* (1925) by Vladimir N. Bill-Belotserkovsky and *The Band* (1924) by Gladkov.

Playwrights with post-Revolutionary training made up a third group. A few, among them Aleksandr N. Afinogenov, Vladimir M. Kirshon, Nikolai F. Pogodin, and V. V. Vishnevsky, wrote plays of enduring worth. Some of their outstanding plays are Afinogenov's *Fear* (1930) and *The Town of Dalekoye* (1935), Kirshon's *Bread* (1931), Pogodin's *Tempo* (1929) and *Aristocrats* (1934), and Vishnevsky's *First Cavalry Army* (1929). However, many plays of this period suffered from the monotonous and didactic propaganda patterns enforced by the dictatorial heads of RAPP, who required all writers to contribute their skill to the tremendous drive for industrial reconstruction and agricultural collectivization.

Generally, Soviet drama tended toward realism, and attempts were made to treat the problems and conflicts that grew out of the changing Soviet life. Straight propaganda plays, such as Mayakovsky's *Mystery-Bouffe* (1918) and *The Bedbug* (1929) and Tretyakov's *Roar China!* (1926)—the last a crude drama of foreign imperialism—soon wearied audiences. A few of the civil war plays, especially the *Armored Train 14-69*(1927), adapted by Vsevolod V. Ivanov from his book of the same name, and *Days of the Turbins* by Mikhail A. Bulgakov were well constructed and well acted.

The realistic trend in Soviet drama continued into the rest of the 1930's and the early 1940's. Effective anti-Nazi plays appeared both before and after the Nazis rose to power. Many Soviet plays of the time showed a deeper understanding of the individual's problems in a collectivist society. The didactic element was not eliminated, but dramatists were growing more concerned with the causes and effects of universal human behavior.

Contemporary dramatic concern with the past of the Russian people was reflected in historical plays, often dramatizations of famous novels, such as Leo Tolstoy's *War and Peace* and Aleksei N. Tolstoy's *Peter the Great*. This trend continued during World War II, after the German invasion of the Soviet Union in 1941. Other plays treated immediate war themes with stark realism. Among these were *The Russian People* (1942) by Simonov, *Invasion* (1942) by Leonov, and *Guerrillas of the Ukrainian Steppes* (1941) and *The Front* (1942) by Aleksandr Korneichuk.

SOVIET LITERATURE AFTER WORLD WAR II

Fiction. After World War II, many new writers emerged, among them Daniil Granin, Aleksandr Yashin, Andrei Bitov, Yuri Trifonov, and Anatoli Pristavkin. Themes from the war dominated their work. Several older writers, however, wrote memoirs of prewar life and the terror of the 1930's, and some focused on the aloneness of the individual. A few described the tempo of modern urban life.

The more relaxed atmosphere that prevailed following Stalin's death in 1953 led to the publication of anthologies, such as the two-volume *Literary Moscow* (1956), which attempted to introduce new writers and their work.

Konstantin Paustovsky, admired for his sensitive descriptions of the Russian landscape, often fictionalized his travel experiences and personal encounters. In the novella *Kara Bugas* (1932), he depicted the Caspian Sea, and one of his early novels was called *The Black Sea* (1936). His postwar *The Tale of Life* (1947–1961) consists of unhurried accounts of travels, friendships, work, and personal ideals. He edited an excellent postwar anthology of new writing, *The Tarusa Pages* (1961).

Vera Panova's war novel, *Companions* (1946), is characteristic of her style. The work, which has neither a central plot nor a hero, is loosely held together by the chain of events and incidents occurring on a hospital train. *The Factory* (1947) and *Bright Shores* (1949) bring out Panova's interest in ordinary people and in character traits, as well as her attention to detail. In *The Seasons* (1953) she concentrated on the problems of a schoolteacher. *A Sentimental Novel* (1958) is a partly fictionalized autobiography, which, like her other works, is marked by her even narrative style.

Yuri Nagibin wrote many stories about the war. However, he is better known for his tales about children, such as *The Winter Oak* (1953), and his stories about life in nature, including *The Chase* (1962). In this he is akin to the older author Mikhail Prishvin, who wrote essays, sketches, and stories lyrical in feeling, suggestive of folklore, and filled with details of ordinary life. Yuri Kazakov, who belonged to the younger set of postwar writers, dedicated his well-known story *Arcturus, a Hunting Dog* (1957) to Prishvin. It is a colorful and warm story about a blind dog's life in the woods. Kazakov's *The Loner* (1959) about the lonely yet good life of a buoy keeper on the banks of a river, vividly and sensitively describes the keeper's love of the place and his rich, fantasy life. Vasili Aksenov, on the other hand, describes an entirely different world in such works as *The Colleagues* (1960), *Ticket to the Stars* (1961), and *Oranges from Morocco* (1962), novels about modern, urban young men and women. His language is terse and exact. The forthright dialogue, often crude or slangy, reflects the young people's skepticism and their efforts to be sophisticated.

Viktor Nekrasov wrote in a direct and open style. His *Trenches of Stalingrad* (1946), about wartime heroism, *In the Native City* (1954), about the postwar disillusionment of returning soldiers, and *Kira Georgiyevna* (1961), about the sufferings of a former political exile, all rely on a narrative thread and easy, colloquial language. Vladimir Dudintsev, in his much-discussed *Not by Bread Alone* (1956), boldly asserted the right of the creative person to be different and imaginative in contemporary bureaucratic society. Nikolai Chukovsky wrote several historical novels, among them *The Baltic Sky* (1954), which describes the suffering and the sacrifices that went on during the Leningrad blockade in World War II.

Andrei Sinyavsky, author of *The Trial Begins* (1960), *Fantastic Stories* (1961), and *For Freedom of Imagination* (1971), as well as Yuli Daniel, author of *This Is Moscow Speaking* (1962), experimented with a new prose style called "phantasmagoric realism." Both came under severe government censure for alleged slander of their country in their works. Other writers who engaged in some prose experimentation included Yuri Dombrovsky in his *The Keeper of Antiquities* (1964) and Valentin Katayev in his *The Well* (1967).

Despite continued political repression, the best Russian writers emphasized the need for telling both historical and moral truths. Boris Pasternak's novel *Doctor Zhivago* (first published abroad in translation in 1957), movingly and brilliantly describes the life of a doctor-poet, from 1903 until his death in 1929. An epilogue brings the work up to 1943. Widely acclaimed in the West, the book was virtually ignored in the Soviet Union, and Pasternak was officially discouraged from accepting the Nobel Prize in literature offered to him in 1958. Lidia Chukovskaya's compassionate *The Deserted House* (1965) gives a finely differentiated account of an educated but politically unaware widow, who, though she loses her only son in the purges of the 1930's and suffers years of deprivation, fails to understand what was happening. The style is unobtrusive and economical; the scenes brief but full. The impact of the work lies in the contrast between ultimate values and actual fate. Nadezhda Mandelshtam's *Memoirs* (1970) is a detailed and generous account of the persecution of her husband, the poet Osip Mandelshtam. It lucidly expresses the humanistic tradition of Russian literature that goes back to the 19th century. In his novel *House in the Clouds* (1967), Vladimir Maksimov imaginatively and deftly dramatizes the difficulties of loneliness against a background of lyrical tenderness and stoic calm. Fyodor Abramov's *Two Winters and Three Summers* (1969) describes the sparse life of the inhabitants of the Archangel region after World War II, the desperation of some people, and the cynicism and opportunism of others. *The Wheel* (1971), by Andrei Bitov, is fresh and inventive both in concept and technique.

Aleksandr Solzhenitsyn became famous with his novel *One Day in the Life of Ivan Denisovich* (1962), the shattering account of a typical grueling day in a prison camp during the Stalin regime as expressed by a prisoner, a simple peasant. Solzhenitsyn's next work, *Matryona's House* (1963), describes a peasant woman's existence in her village. Both outstanding pieces, they reveal Solzhenitsyn's skill in realizing the idiosyncrasies of his characters. In both, an average person's average day, taken in the context of the particular surroundings and circumstances, unfolds step by step to be understood finally as an affirmation of genuine human values. Solzhenitsyn's larger novels, *The Cancer Ward* and *The First Circle* (both first published in English in 1968), are impressive dramatizations of painful personal experiences. Solzhenitsyn was awarded the Nobel Prize in literature in 1970 but was prevented from accepting it, as Pasternak had been, until after the Soviet government exiled him in 1974 and he moved to Switzerland.

Poetry. Poetry also flourished after World War II. From older, safe poets, like Leonid Martynov, to younger, bold ones, like Novella Matreyeva and Yuri Stepanov, the range of expression was broad. Poetry Day, established in the 1950's, was celebrated each December in Moscow and Leningrad with public readings and a published anthology of the works of many poets.

One of the best-known younger poets, Yevgeni Yevtushenko, wrote verse on topical subjects in an angular style, colloquial and aggressive in the manner of Mayakovsky. In such poems as *Zima Station* (1956) and *Babi Yar* (1961) and such collections as *Third Snow* (1955), *Promise* (1959), *Apple* (1960), *Tenderness* (1962), and *The Power Station of Bratsk* (1965), Yevtushenko exposed anti-Semitism in the USSR, urged modernity on Russia, and wrote of man's corruption by the easy life. By comparison, Andrei

Voznesensky's verse is more concise and more experimental. His poems, such as those in *Parabola* (1960), *The Triangular Pear* (1962), *Antiworlds* (1964), and *Achilles' Heart* (1966), are full of interesting assonances and are marked by vivid imagery and very strong rhythms. Some poems with broken rhythms, irregular lines, and slang or underworld cant protest the inhumanity of city life.

Joseph Brodsky wrote philosophical poems on broad, ethical themes. His *Poems* (1965) and *A Halt in the Wilderness* (1970) have an underlying tone of sadness and despair. They speak of man's solitude and, through skillfully linked metaphoric analogies, build a powerful poetic vision. The poetry of Bulat Okudzhava, on the other hand, is often carefree, lighthearted, and comic, filled with the easy rhythm of colloquial song. Many of his poems are intended to be accompanied by the guitar. *Johnny Morozov* (1959) and *The Paper Soldier* (1960) were very popular. The folk-song-like *From a Traveller's Diary* (1969) mingles old traditions with contemporary problems. Bella Akhmadulina wrote a private, mellifluous poetry. From *The Music Chord* (1962) to *Music Lessons* (1969) her emotional lyrics express a quiet strength and exquisite control of sound and sense in harmony.

Among the best of the older poets was Nikolaĭ A. Zabolotsky, whose first fine work, *Columns,* appeared in the 1920's. He received renewed recognition in *The Tarusa Pages,* following his release from prison, where he had been sent by the Stalin regime in the 1930's. His later poems, including *Old Tale* (1952), *Flight into Egypt* (1955), and *Poem of Spring* (1956), are beautifully measured and warmly lyrical. Boris Slutsky, however, also a former prisoner, returned to write somber satires, such as *When They Killed Beloyannis* (1956) and *A Quarter to Nine* (1956), and bitter political poems such as *Physicists and Lyricists* (1959) and *In the State There Is the Law* (1965). Slutsky's angry poems stand in great contrast to the elegiac beauty of Akhmatova's political *Requiem* (1961), dedicated to the political victims of the 1930's. Yevgeni Vinokurov, from *Word* (1962) to *Gesture* (1969), wrote with an accomplished lyricism.

Drama. After the war, more than 500 permanent Soviet theaters reintroduced foreign and classical plays. Among Russian plays, light satire and vaudevilles increased in popularity. The most celebrated comedian of his day, Raikin, always played to packed houses. In the Ukraine in the 1950's, more than half the repertory was light comedy. In Moscow and Leningrad, situation family comedies continued to be popular in succeeding decades.

The "well-made" socialist-realist dramas gradually yielded to plays depicting actual problems and conflicts of everyday life. Many plays of the 1950's and 1960's expressed disillusionment with life and concentrated on the probing of private lives. Nikolai-Fyodorovich Pogodin's *A Petrarchan Sonnet* (1957) sympathetically dramatizes a middle-aged industrialist's platonic love for a young librarian. Of Vera Panova's plays, the best remembered are *Farewell to White Nights* (1961), about the love life of Soviet youth, and *It's Been Ages* (1966), about a group of people caught in a snow storm at an airport. Leonid Zorin, a dramatist who won a gold medal at the Venice Festival for his film *Peace to the Newcomer* in 1961, wrote many plays. His *Warsaw Melody*

(1967), a two-part drama of love, fame, and disaffection, was staged by Ruben Simonov in the famous Vakhtangov Theater, with brilliant performances by Borisova and Ulyanov. Viktor Rozov's *Alive Forever* (1956), about young love and deep losses during World War II, was the basis of the highly successful Russian film *The Cranes Are Flying.* His *The Reunion* (1967) is about the lives of former members of a high school class. A more daring theme was treated by Aleksandr Volodin in his *My Elder Sister* (1961), which warns that collective narrowmindedness and philistinism can block individual liberty. Aleksei Arbuzov, in his *Irkutsk Story* (1959), produced by Okhlopkov, used a chorus as commentator.

The satirist and film scenarist Yevgeni Shvarts wrote biting social satire in the 1930's. Briefly staged before World War II, they were posthumously published in 1960. Among the best are *The Naked King* and *The Shadow,* both imaginative recastings of fairy tales into witty mockeries of bureaucracy and officialdom. Shvarts' achievement in these works was to link fable to facts with overwhelming histrionic force.

ERNEST J. SIMMONS[*]
Author of "Russian Fiction and Soviet Ideology"

Bibliography
General Literary History

Brown, Edward J., *The Proletarian Episode in Russian Literature, 1928–1932* (Columbia Univ. Press 1953).
Chadwick, Nora K., *Russian Heroic Poetry* (Macmillan 1932).
Freeborn, R. H., and others, *Russian Literary Attitudes from Pushkin to Solzhenitsyn* (Harper 1976).
Hayward, Max, and Crowley, Edward L., eds., *Soviet Literature in the Sixties* (Praeger 1964).
Lavrin, Janko, *Introduction to the Russian Novel* (McGraw 1947).
Lindström, Thaïs S., *A Concise History of Russian Literature,* vol. 1 (N. Y. Univ. Press 1966).
Mathewson, Rufus W., Jr., *The Positive Hero in Russian Literature* (Columbia Univ. Press 1958).
Reavey, George, *Soviet Literature Today* (Yale Univ. Press 1947).
Simmons, Ernest J., *Russian Fiction and Soviet Ideology: Introduction to Fedin, Leonov, and Sholokhov* (Columbia Univ. Press 1958).
Slonim, Marc, *Modern Russian Literature* (Oxford 1953).
Slonim, Marc, *Outline of Russian Literature* (Oxford 1958).
Slonim, Marc, *Soviet Russian Literature* (Oxford 1964).
Struve, Gleb, *Soviet Russian Literature, 1917–1950* (Univ. of Okla. Press 1951).
Swayze, Harold, *Political Control of Literature in the USSR, 1946–1959* (Harvard Univ. Press 1962).
Vickery, Walter N., *The Cult of Optimism: Political and Ideological Problems of Recent Soviet Literature* (Ind. Univ. Press 1963).
Zavalishin, Viacheslav, *Early Soviet Writers* (Praeger 1958).

Dramatic History and Criticism

Bruford, Walter H., *Chekhov and His Russia* (Oxford 1948).
Coleman, Arthur P., *Humor in Russian Comedy from Catherine to Gogol* (Columbia Univ. Press 1925).
Dana, Henry W. L., *A Handbook on Soviet Drama* (Am. Russian Inst. 1938).
Edwards, Christine, *The Stanislavsky Heritage* (N. Y. Univ. Press 1965).
Gorchakov, Nikolai, A., *The Theater in Soviet Russia,* tr. by Edgar Lehrman (Columbia Univ. Press 1957).
Houghton, Norris, *Moscow Rehearsals* (Harcourt 1936).
Macleod, Joseph, *The New Soviet Theatre* (Allen, G. 1943).
Markov, Pavel A., *The Soviet Theatre* (Gollancz 1934).
Roberts, Spencer E., *Soviet Historical Drama* (Nijhoff 1965).
Simmons, Ernest J., *Chekhov: A Biography* (Little 1962).
Van Gyseghem, André, *The Theatre in Soviet Russia* (Faber 1943).
Varneke, Boris V., *History of the Russian Theatre,* tr. by Boris Brasol (Macmillan 1951).
Welsh, David J., *Russian Comedy, 1765–1823* (Mouton 1966).

Tchaikovsky's *Swan Lake*, performed here by the Bolshoi Ballet, typifies the Romantic tradition in Russian music.

RUSSIAN MUSIC.

Viewed in historical perspective, the flowering of Russian music came very late. However, it compensated for this late beginning by a remarkable rapidity of development. In less than a century Russian music reached an equal rank with that of Western nations. Soon the world at large began to feel the impact of the musical language of such geniuses as Mussorgsky in the 19th century and Stravinsky in the 20th century. Tchaikovsky elevated symphonic writing to romantic greatness, and Rimsky-Korsakov brought orchestral writing to dazzling brilliance. Intense cultivation of music in all genres continued in Soviet Russia. Among Soviet composers the names of Prokofiev and Shostakovich became universally known.

From Glinka, "the Father of Russian Music," to the present day, the substance of Russian composition never departed radically from the basic structure of Russian folk music, characterized by a broad diatonic melody arranged in asymmetrical rhythms. There is something in this spaciousness of Russian folk melodies that suggests a correspondence to the immensity of the Russian land itself, with its great plains, rivers, and lakes, so that Russian folk music becomes a natural expression of this vastness. The role of Russian composers was to clothe the songs and rhythms of the Russian people in the cultural forms common to all civilizations, and in this coalescence lies the great achievement of Russian music.

TRADITIONAL MUSIC AND INSTRUMENTS

Folk Music. The first folk melodies of European Russia date from the 10th century. Asiatic Russia did not come into the national cultural complex until centuries later. Most ancient Russian folk songs are entirely *sui generis*. The first great alien influence—that from Byzantium—affected Russian religious music only. Russian folk song collectors gathered and published so much authentic material during the 19th and 20th centuries that the record of traditional folk songs is now remarkably complete.

In *Russian Folk Music in its Melodic and Rhythmic Structure* (1888), Peter Sokalsky made an interesting observation, that the older a song is, the narrower is its range. In the most ancient songs the melody usually consists of four notes of the diatonic scale in descending motion. The cadence of a falling fourth, characteristic of old Russian songs, is also typical of many themes in Russian symphonies and operas. At a later period, the basic range expanded to a fifth. With added flourishes a folk melody may attain a full octave, with the intervalic structure usually corresponding to a minor mode, which lends a melancholy lilt to the melody.

The rhythm of Russian folk songs is determined by characteristic groupings of two short notes followed by a long note—a familiar example is the *Song of the Volga Boatmen*. But Russian folk songs have a large incidence of uneven metrical units, such as 5, 7, or 11, to a phrase. Great Russian composers have used such typical time signatures as 5/4 (Glinka), 7/4 (Borodin), and 11/4 (Rimsky-Korsakov).

The first anthology of Russian folk songs, *Collection of Simple Russian Songs With Notes*, was published in 1782 by Vasili Trutovsky. The Russianized Czech Ivan Prach made a more important collection of 150 songs, which were noted down for him by Nikolai Lvov, an amateur musician. The publication of this work in 1790 found an immediate response, and a second edition appeared in 1806. The famous Italian composer Giovanni Paisiello expressed amazement at the beauty of these simple peasant songs, and Beethoven incorporated themes from them in the String Quartet, Opus 59, which he dedicated to Count Andreas Rasoumovsky, the Russian ambassador to Vienna. More songs were collected and classified during the 19th century. The most significant collection (1888) was by Nikolai Palchikov, who published 125 melodies with texts, all of which were gathered in the village of Nikolayevka, in Ufa province. Palchikov gave as many as eight versions of each song, enough to permit scholars to make general deductions regarding the chief characteristics of Russian folk music. Harmonizations of Russian folk songs, published by Tchaikovsky in 1868, Rimsky-Korsakov in 1877, Balakirev in 1886, and Liadov in 1894, further increased interest in the subject.

The beginning of scientific musical ethnography was made by Evgenia Lineva, who was the first to make phonograph recordings of Russian folk songs. In 1905 and 1912 she published two volumes of transcriptions of Russian folk songs under the general title *Peasant Songs of Great Russia in Folk Harmonizations Transcribed from Phonograms.* Each song begins with a solo, and is followed by a chorus in which the basic melody is freely embellished. The choruses usually have two or three individual parts, but Lineva found some four-part singing. She believed that Russian folk music is essentially polyphonic, but there is no proof that the ancient songs were anything more than single musical phrases, without secondary parts. The later polyphony of peasant choruses may have resulted from the influence of part singing in the church choirs.

Musical ethnography continued to advance after the 1917 revolution. Numerous collections of regional songs were published under the auspices of the Academy of Sciences, in the folklore series of the Institute of Anthropology, Ethnography, and Archaeology. Revolutionary songs of czarist times are included in the collection *Russian Folk Song* (1936).

Instruments. Folk music is deeply rooted in Russian folklore. In *The Chronicle of the Campaign of Igor* (about 1200), the legendary figure Bayan is a musician. According to the tale, "Bayan, as he recited the strife of bygone times, sent out ten falcons after a flight of swans, and the one that was first overtaken began her song. But in truth, brethren, not ten falcons did Bayan loose on the swans, but his wise fingers did he lay on living strings, and they by themselves sang the glory of the princes." The stringed instrument that Bayan played was the ancient *gusli,* a sort of zither or horizontal harp, with ten or more strings and a wooden sound chest. The *gusli* is no longer in practical use. Rimsky-Korsakov introduced a part for *gusli* in his opera *Sadko* to evoke the atmosphere of old Russia, but the part is usually performed on the harp. Other ancient stringed instruments are the *domra* (similar to the guitar, and played with a plectrum), and the *gudok* (a three-stringed instrument with a pear-shaped body, and played with a string bow). The *domras* were revived in Soviet Russia, and are often included in modern orchestral compositions.

In the Ukraine, the domra is called *kobza* or *bandura* (from the Polish *pandura*). The popular balalaika is in all probability a development of the *domra.* In the 18th century the balalaika assumed its familiar triangular shape. It usually has three strings and is plucked without a plectrum. An ensemble of balalaikas, organized by Vasili Andreyev early in the 20th century, gave many successful concerts in Russia and abroad.

Among old Russian wind instruments were the *rog* (diminutive, rozhok), a hunting horn; the *dudka,* a vertical flute; the *zhaleika,* a double reed with a single mouthpiece (the two pipes are connected at an angle); and the *svirel,* a panpipe composed of several reeds of different lengths, bound together. The nomenclature of these instruments varies according to locality and period. The Russian bagpipe, or *volynka,* prob-ably so named because of its supposed origin in the district of Volynia, consists of a goatskin bag and two pipes.

An interesting ensemble of Russian primitive instruments, an orchestra of hunting horns (*rog*), was initiated by Simeon Naryshkin in 1751. It consisted of 49 hunting horns of different sizes, ranging from three inches (7.6 cm) to 24 feet (7.3 meters) in length. The largest horn produced the note of low A under the bass clef staff. Each member of the ensemble could play only one note, and patient rehearsing was required to perform even a simple polyphonic composition. A witness to one of these events was a German resident of St. Petersburg, Jacob von Stählin, who described a successful performance in his memoir *News of Music in Russia* (1770).

Ancient Russian percussion instruments included drums, metal bars, and bells. The most interesting instrument was the *buben,* or tambourine. A huge *buben,* called a *nabat,* was so large that it took four horses to carry it and eight men to operate it.

Skomorokhi. The first musical entertainers mentioned in Russian history were the *skomorokhi,* or minstrels, who are spoken of as early as 1068 by Nestor, an 11th century Russian monk and chronicler, who complained in his chronicle that entertainments by the *skomorokhi* drew the people away from God, that churches stood empty while the populace amused themselves by playing on the *gusli* and blowing trumpets. According to 13th century sources, the *skomorokhi* played panpipes (*svirel*), string instruments (*gudok*), and tambourines (*buben*). In the 15th century they introduced a new type of entertainment, the puppet theater, which ultimately became the popular carnival play *Petrushka.*

The *skomorokhi* were so popular in medieval Russia that numerous villages in central Russia were named Skomorokhovo. As this popularity spread, the opposition of church and lay authorities grew stronger. In a decree in 1649, Czar Aleksei ordered ruthless persecution of the "godless *skomorokhi* with their *domras* and *gusli,*" and instructed police to destroy all musical instruments found among their possessions.

Very little is left of the musical compositions sung by the *skomorokhi.* However, a few songs and verses preserved in oral tradition are cited by Nikolai Findeisen, in his valuable two-volume work *Sketches of Music History in Russia from the Most Ancient Times to the End of the Eighteenth Century* (1928).

CHURCH MUSIC

Early Church Music. At the same time that Russian folk music was developing, the church established the foundations of formal musical learning. The pioneers were Greek and Bulgarian clerics who introduced Byzantine chant into Kiev after the Christianization of Russia. As early as the 11th century, texts with musical notation, derived from the Byzantine system of neumes, were in use in the Kiev churches and monasteries. By the 13th century in Russia, a native system of notation had emerged from the Greek system. The Russian system of notation was known as *znamenny* (from *znamya,* sign) or *kryuki* ("hooks," from the angular shape of the notes). In 1551, Ivan the Terrible established schools for teaching musical notation for use by church choirs. He had some knowledge of music and wrote several religious chants himself. Later still, the eight modes of the Russian *znamenny* chant were organized according to typical melodic figures, called *popyevki* (singing patterns). About 1700, the five-line notation, current in Europe, was universally adopted in Russian churches.

Later Church Music. The beginnings of polyphonic choral music date from the early 18th century. In 1713, Peter the Great formed a choir of 60 singers, and Russian noblemen organized private choruses. These *capellas* (from the Italian *cappella*, meaning chapel or choir) developed into the Russian choirs that became famous for their virtuosity. The *capella* founded by Peter the Great is still flourishing in Leningrad.

The father of Russian religious music in the polyphonic style was the late 18th, early 19th century composer Dmitri Bortnyansky, who studied in Italy, where he acquired the technique of part writing. His contemporary, Maksim Berezovsky, wrote many sacred works of high quality. The 19th century composer Aleksei Lvov, author of the czarist national anthem, also composed sacred music and wrote a treatise on the structure of Russian religious songs. Later both Tchaikovsky and Aleksandr Grechaninov contributed to the body of Russian religious music, writing in a free contrapuntal style.

CLASSICAL MUSIC

Beginnings. The initial impetus to secular music was given by the Italian musicians who were invited to Russia by the empresses Anna Ivanovna, Elizabeth Petrovna, and Catherine the Great in the 18th century. They included several world renowned names: Francesco Araja, Vincenzo Manfredini, Giuseppe Sarti, Tommaso Traetta, Giovanni Paisiello, and Domenico Cimarosa. These Italians were largely responsible for the flourishing state of opera and ballet in St. Petersburg during the second half of the 18th century. They acted as choir masters, teachers, concert players, and composers. The first opera with a Russian text, *Cephalus and Procris*, was composed by Araja to a libretto by Aleksandr Sumarokov and produced in St. Petersburg in 1755. Araja had poor knowledge of the Russian language, and the work's most serious defect is inaccurate conformity with the prosody of the libretto.

Influenced by Italian music, several Russian composers wrote operas during the reign of Catherine the Great. Among them were Evstigney Fomin, who wrote *Amerikantsy* (1788) to a romantic story set in Mexico, and Vasili Pashkevich, who composed *Fevey* (1786) to a libretto by Catherine the Great. The *Kalmuck Chorus* from *Fevey* is the earliest example of Orientalism in Russian music.

The National School. By the start of the 19th century, a national style of composition had begun to develop in Russian music. The Russian art song, often in the style of folk music and sometimes using folk themes, was cultivated by Aleksandr Alyabyev, Nikolai Titov, and Aleksandr Varlamov. Aleksei Verstovsky wrote an opera on a Russian subject, *Askold's Tomb* (1835), which, in spite of its Italianate idiom, has some Russian traits.

The acknowledged founder of the Russian national school of composition was Mikhail Glinka, who is to Russian music what Aleksandr Pushkin is to Russian literature. Glinka integrated the elements of Russian musical folklore into a musical language that can be called genuinely national. His first opera was produced in 1836,

SOVFOTO

Folk music is a popular Russian idiom. Members of this ensemble play the bandura, a Ukrainian instrument.

under the title *A Life for the Czar.* The subject was taken from Russian history, and he developed it in a purely national manner, especially in the songs and choral passages. His second opera, *Ruslan and Lyudmila* (1842), from Pushkin's poem, is remarkable for its brilliant color. Glinka's symphonic dance, *Kamarinskaya,* is the earliest example of orchestral treatment of Russian dance rhythms. In Glinka's songs and ballads, the vocal line of Russian verse received its perfect expression.

The music of Aleksandr Dargomyzhsky differs greatly from Glinka's. Less brilliant in color, it is rich in musical characterization. Dargomyzhsky's opera *Russalka* (1855) retains the traditional division into arias but is written in a distinctly Russian folk style. In his posthumously produced opera *The Stone Guest* (1868), Dargomyzhsky abandoned Italian modes in favor of operatic realism and replaced conventional recitative with vocal declamation.

The Mighty Five. Both Glinka and Dargomyzhsky remained little known outside Russia, but with the great symphonic and operatic works of Tchaikovsky, Rimsky-Korsakov, and Mussorgsky, Russia became a powerful factor in the general course of music history. The spirit of nationalism in Russian music was accentuated when five Russian composers known as the *Moguchaya Kuchka* (literally, "a mighty heap") formulated a set of musical aims. These composers were Mili Balakirev, Aleksandr Borodin, César Cui, Modest Mussorgsky, and Nikolai Rimsky-Korsakov. The epithet was bestowed on them by the Russian critic Vladimir Stasov. The individual talents and the contributions to Russian national music by these five composers were far from equal. Cui, a military engineer who wrote several operas in a conventional romantic style, had limited gifts. Balakirev played the role of spiritual head of the group and did much to inspire his companions with the ideals of Russian national art. But he wrote little, and only his Oriental fantasia *Islamey* (1869) survives the test of time. It is more appropriate, therefore,

History and folklore dominate Russian opera, as in Moussorgsky's *Boris Godunov* (above), about an early czar.

to speak of the "Mighty Three" of Russian music: Borodin, Rimsky-Korsakov, and Mussorgsky. Not one of them was a professional in the narrow sense of the word. Borodin was a professor of chemistry; Rimsky-Korsakov, a naval officer; and Mussorgsky, a government employee.

Of the three, Rimsky-Korsakov was the most prolific. In his many operas, he recreated the spirit of Russian folklore and history. He used Russian legends and folk tales in *The Snow Maiden* (1882) and *Sadko* (1894) and Russian history in *The Czar's Bride* (1893). In addition, he wrote operas to two fairy tales by Pushkin—*The Tale of Czar Saltan* (1900) and *Le Coq d'or* (1906). Rimsky-Korsakov's religious opera *The Tale of the Invisible City of Kitezh* (1907) shows the influence of Wagner's *Parsifal*. In the field of orchestral music, his symphonic suite *Scheherazade* (1881) was epoch-making in its colorful treatment of musical material in an allusive Oriental manner.

Borodin utilized elements of Russian Orientalism in his symphonic sketch *In the Steppes of Central Asia* (1880) and in the famous *Polovtzian Dances* from the opera *Prince Igor*, completed after his death by Rimsky-Korsakov and Glazunov. In a purely Russian style, Borodin created an epic work in his Second Symphony (1870), which without an explicit program paints a panorama of Russian *byliny* (epic chronicles).

Mussorgsky was regarded by his contemporaries as an erratic genius with inadequate technical equipment for the tasks he undertook. In historical perspective, however, he seems the greatest of the "Mighty Five" in boldness of musical invention and in profound understanding of the essence of Russian national folklore. Many of his harmonic procedures anticipated later developments in modern music. His greatest work is the opera *Boris Godunov* (1869). It is usually performed in the version prepared by Rimsky-Korsakov, in which certain crudities of orchestration and unconventional harmonic progressions are smoothed out. Dmitri Shostakovich also undertook reorchestration of *Boris Godunov* in 1941. Later, Mussorgsky's original score was restored, and the opera has been performed as composed, in Russia and abroad. Mussorgsky's opera

Khovanshchina, on a historical subject, was begun in 1873 and completed by Rimsky-Korsakov. In his short opera *Marriage* (1868), after Gogol's play, Mussorgsky applied the modern treatment of operatic dialogue. His piano suite *Pictures at an Exhibition* (1874) is remarkable for the variety of its characterization, from light humor to grandiose tonal painting. The suite became especially popular in the orchestral version by Maurice Ravel.

The cause of nationalism in Russian opera was ably served by Aleksandr Serov. His opera *Enemy Power* was posthumously produced in 1871 and is still in the Russian repertory. However, Serov's music lacks the revolutionary originality of Mussorgsky's work and the effectiveness of Rimsky-Korsakov's operatic panoramas. Similarly lacking in force are the numerous operas of Anton Rubinstein, who was the first great Russian pianist and the founder of the St. Petersburg Conservatory (1862). His opera *The Demon* (1875), after the dramatic poem by Mikhail Lermontov, and his piano pieces enjoy great popularity. Anton's brother, Nikolai Rubinstein, also a celebrated pianist, founded the Moscow Conservatory in 1866.

Tchaikovsky. The unique and solitary figure of Peter Ilich Tchaikovsky dominates Russian symphonic music in the second half of the 19th century. He stood aloof from his musical contemporaries and developed a style intensely individual, subjective, and often morbidly introspective. Although his music is unmistakably Russian, Tchaikovsky rarely resorted to literal quotations of Russian folk songs. His nationalism lies in his extraordinary power to create a Russian mood by expressing his own feelings.

Often described as a "melancholy genius," Tchaikovsky was capable of writing music filled with joyful energy. But the mood of his symphonic works was somber. The Fourth and Fifth symphonies express the inexorability of fate and the futility of struggle. The spirit of the Sixth Symphony, the *Pathétique* (1893), which Tchaikovsky conducted in St. Petersburg a few days before his death from cholera, is one of dejection. The musical quotation from the service for the dead, in the first movement of the *Pathétique* is characteristic. Tchaikovsky's symphonic poems, such as *Romeo and Juliet* (1869) and *Francesca da Rimini* (1876), are romantically somber, but the music itself has great vitality. His operas *Eugene Onegin* (1878) and *The Queen of Spades* (1890), both based on stories by Pushkin, are extremely popular in Russia. His splendid ballets —*Swan Lake* (1876), *The Sleeping Beauty* (1889), and *The Nutcracker* (1892)—are staples in the repertoires of dance companies all over the world.

St. Petersburg and Moscow Schools. Tchaikovsky and the "Mighty Five" greatly influenced the development of Russian music during the late 19th and early 20th centuries. The stronghold of the Romantic school was Moscow, where Tchaikovsky had taught at the conservatory, while the center for musical nationalists of the modern school was St. Petersburg, where the "Mighty Five" had flourished.

The heir of the nationalist School of St. Petersburg was Aleksandr Glazunov. He wrote symphonies, violin and piano concertos, chamber music and ballets, but no operas. As director of the St. Petersburg Conservatory (1906–1927), he played an important role in the education of the new generation of Russian composers. Anatol Liadov distinguished himself principally by short symphonic poems, such as *Baba-Yaga* (1904) and *Kikimora* (1909), in the folklore manner. Nikolai Tcherepnin is known chiefly for songs.

Tchaikovsky's followers cultivated the romantic type of symphonic, operatic, and vocal music. The greatest representative of the Moscow school was Sergei Rachmaninoff. His most enduring compositions are his piano works, which greatly elevated Russian pianistic style. His Piano Concerto in C Minor, No. 2 (1901) is a classic. His songs, poetic and lyrical, are in the Tchaikovsky tradition. Rachmaninoff spent his last 25 years chiefly in the United States, and his work of this period is less significant than his earlier music. Anton Arensky wrote effective piano and chamber music in a style resembling that of Rachmaninoff. Vasili Kalinnikov is remembered for his romantic First Symphony (1897).

Sergei Taneyev, Nikolai Medtner, Aleksandr Grechaninov, Mikhail Ippolitov-Ivanov, Reinhold Glière, and Sergei Vassilenko generally followed the Moscow school, with some stylistic departures toward the nationalists. Taneyev, who was a master of counterpoint, wrote a monumental treatise on contrapuntal technique. In his music, Taneyev adhered to a neoclassical type of composition without specific Russian traits. Medtner wrote almost exclusively for piano, in a style influenced by Chopin and Brahms. He left Russia in 1921 and settled in London in 1936. Grechaninov composed several operas, which follow the nationalist school in using subject matter from Russian epic legends. His songs and choral works reflect Russian romanticism. Grechaninov left Russia in 1925 and settled in the United States in 1939, where he continued to compose. In his compositions, Glière combined features of the nationalist school with romantic elements. Vassilenko adhered stylistically to the Moscow school but revealed some kinship with the nationalists in his operas.

Vladimir Rebikov merits a niche in the history of Russian music. At first a follower of Tchaikovsky, he was later attracted to modernism. He was the first Russian composer to use the whole-tone scale, not as an incidental device, but as a basic thematic structure.

MODERN MUSIC

Scriabin. The first true modernist of Russian music was Aleksandr Scriabin. His early piano works were strongly influenced by Chopin, and his orchestral music owed much to Wagner. However, Scriabin outgrew these influences to develop his own highly individual technique of composition. He moved from the harmonies of Liszt and Wagner to a style of composition in which tonality almost ceases to exist, and dissonances supplant concords. As a new harmonic basis, Scriabin made use of a six-note chord, which he called the "mystic chord." Religion and philosophy were important in his aesthetics, and his major works bear such indicative titles as *The Divine Poem* (1903), *The Poem of Ecstasy* (1907–1908), and *The Poem of Fire* (1909–1910). In *Poem of Fire,* also known as *Prometheus,* Scriabin included a part for a *clavier à lumières,* an instrument designed to produce sequences of colored lights. However, this color keyboard proved impractical. Shortly before his death, Scriabin made sketches for a pantheistic work called *Mysterium,* in which he intended to unite all the arts. Scriabin's music stands outside Russian national culture as a purely musical development of modern times, yet his technical innovations and his explorations in the field of new sonorities deeply influenced the new generation of Russian composers.

Stravinsky. The modern period of Russian national music is associated with Igor Stravinsky. His early works continued the tradition of Rimsky-Korsakov, with whom he had studied. The use of color in instrumental treatment and the programmatic depiction of Russian fairy tales, characteristic of Rimsky-Korsakov's last period, were the mainstays also of Stravinsky's early compositions. His *Firebird* (1910) is a symphonic panorama of Russian folklore, and *Petrushka* (1911) portrays the scenes of the Russian carnival. Both scores were written for Sergei Diaghilev's Ballets Russes in Paris. After their production, Stravinsky lived outside Russia, and in 1939 he went to the United States. Paradoxically, Stravinsky became the acknowledged leader of Western modernism through intensely Russian works. Perhaps his most revolutionary score was *Le Sacre du printemps* (1913), a modernistic representation of the rituals of pagan Russia. Here he broke with tradition and introduced polytonal and polyrhythmic innovations of unprecedented boldness; its Paris production by Diaghilev saw violent audience protests.

In 1924, Stravinsky's style changed toward neoclassicism. Among the works that reveal this influence are the ballet *Apollo Musagètes* (1927); the opera-oratorio *Oedipus Rex,* to a Latin text (1928); and *Symphony of Psalms* (1930). At this time, he also composed pastiches of music by other composers, such as *Le Baiser de la fée* (1928), a ballet based on themes by Tchaikovsky. Other works of Stravinsky's neoclassical period are *Capriccio* for piano and orchestra (1929); *Persephone* for tenor, choruses, and orchestra (1933–1934); *Concerto for Two Pianos* (1931–1934); *Jeu de cartes,* a "ballet in three deals" (1936); *Symphony in C* (1939); *Symphony in Three Movements* (1942–1945); the ballet *Orpheus* (1947); and the opera *The Rake's Progress* (1948–1951).

Throughout most of his career, Stravinsky resolutely opposed any specific systems of composition. In his last period, however, he adopted the serial technique as practiced by Arnold Schoenberg and Anton von Webern, putting it to use in his own distinctive manner. His first work that reflected such methods was the ballet *Agon*, completed in 1957. More explicitly serial was *Threni* for voices and orchestra (1958); *The Flood*, a musical play (1962); *Abraham and Isaac*, a sacred ballad (1963); and *Requiem Canticles* for voices and orchestra (1966).

Prokofiev and Miaskovsky. Sergei Prokofiev first became known as the composer of modernistic piano pieces that he himself performed brilliantly. In 1915 he wrote his first important orchestral work, *Scythian Suite*, evocative of ancient Russia and abounding in bold dissonances. In his early *Classical Symphony* (1917), destined to become his most popular symphonic work, Prokofiev demonstrated his mastery of the traditional style. He left Russia shortly after the Revolution and lived mostly in Paris, making frequent American tours. For Diaghilev's Ballets Russes in Paris he wrote the ballets *Buffoon* (1920) and *The Age of Steel* (1924). His opera *The Love for Three Oranges* (1921) was first performed in Chicago. In 1933 he returned to Russia and continued to compose prolifically. To his Soviet period belong the operas *Simeon Kotko* (1939) and *War and Peace*, after Tolstoy (1942–1952); the ballets *Romeo and Juliet* (1936) and *Cinderella* (1944); *Peter and the Wolf* (1936), a symphonic fairy tale for narrator and orchestra; and the cantata *Alexander Nevsky* (1940). Of his seven symphonies, the most distinctive besides the *Classical Symphony* is the Fifth Symphony (1944). His other important works include five piano concertos, two violin concertos, two cello concertos, nine piano sonatas, two violin sonatas, and numerous vocal works.

During World War II, Prokofiev composed an overture entitled *1941* (written 1941) and a cantata, *Ballad of an Unknown Boy* (written 1943), about a young Soviet partisan fighter who died for his country. At the end of the war he wrote a victory piece for large orchestra, *Ode to the End of the War* (1945). In 1948, along with other major Soviet composers, Prokofiev became the target of denunciation on the part of bureaucratic Communist party members. He sought to redeem himself with the opera *A Tale About a Real Man* (1948), glorifying a Soviet pilot, but it met with censure for its vestigial modernism.

In the annals of Soviet music, Nikolai Miaskovsky is often associated with his contemporary Prokofiev. Unlike Prokofiev, however, Miaskovsky never wrote for the musical theater but dedicated himself exclusively to instrumental music. He composed 27 symphonies, all of which were performed and published, 13 string quartets, a violin concerto, a cello concerto, and nine piano sonatas, as well as some songs. Despite his predilection for pessimistic moods expressed in characteristic minor tonalities, Miaskovsky adapted himself successfully to the compromising demands of Soviet music.

SOVIET MUSIC

The period after 1917 provides the music historian with many contrasts. The political revolution did not signal the advent of extreme radicalism in music. Ultramodernists attempted to discard the musical heritage of the past and to inaugurate a new revolutionary type of music, but such attempts failed because they were displeasing to the people. Adherents of proletarian music were equally unsuccessful in attempting to emphasize mass appeal and revolutionary subject matter. A compromise was effected in the formula of socialist realism, which postulates an art "socialist in content and national in form." Changing trends in Soviet musical aesthetics ran parallel with changes in the political and social structure of the Soviet Union.

The development of Soviet music may be divided into four phases: (1) the initial period, from 1917 to 1921, marked by the spirit of progressive innovation; (2) the period of conflicting trends, from 1921 to 1932, signalized by the rise and fall of proletarian music; (3) the period of socialist realism, from 1932 through World War II; and (4) the Soviet avant-garde.

Early Years. The famine and civil war during the early years of the Soviet regime did not encourage creative composition. Yet concert life continued, and the new audiences of soldiers and workers eagerly flocked to the opera houses and concert halls. Revolutionary ideology had little effect on the repertory, although there were attempts to inject a social note into familiar operas. Puccini's *Tosca* was rewritten as a story of the Paris Commune, and Meyerbeer's *The Huguenots* was changed to *The Decembrists*. Soon, however, the old librettos were restored.

The earliest opera on a Soviet subject was Arseni Gladkovsky's *For Red Petrograd* (1926), dealing with the Petrograd campaign of 1919. This was followed by Vladimir Deshevov's *Ice and Steel* (1930), based on the Kronstadt rebellion of 1921, and Lev Knipper's *The North Wind* (1930), on the subject of the Russian civil war. Ivan Dzerzhinsky's operas *And Quiet Flows the Don* (1934), a highly successful work based on the famous novel of Mikhail Sholokhov, and *Soil Upturned* (1937), also after Sholokhov, deal with Revolutionary events in Russia. In *Battleship Potemkin* (1937), Oles Tchishko depicted a sea mutiny under the czarist regime. The Ukrainian composer Boris Lyatoshinsky composed *Shchors* (1938), based on the life of a Ukrainian civil war hero of that name.

Although the early years of the Revolution saw few radical departures in the style of composition, there were many daring innovations in musical science and in performance. In Moscow, a conductorless orchestra, called *Persimfans* (for *Pervi Simfonicheski Ansamble*, or First Symphonic Ensemble), was organized in 1922 as a protest against the autocracy of orchestral leaders. For five years it presented numerous classical and modern works. In Moscow, in 1922, the Soviet engineer Léon Thérémin demonstrated the thereminovox, or theremin, the first electronic instrument, capable of unlimited variation of pitch and tone-color. A later development in electronic instruments was the emiriton, or electric piano, built in 1943 by a grandson of Rimsky-Korsakov.

When communications with western Europe were reestablished, Russian musicians became acquainted with the new music of Germany and France. The Association of Contemporary Music, formed in Leningrad in 1927, was active in presenting works by European modernists for several seasons. Machine music, as exemplified by Arthur Honegger's symphonic poem *Pacific 231*, had its adepts in Russia. Deshevov wrote *The Rails*, which imitated the noise of a railroad train in motion. Aleksandr Mosolov composed the industrial ballet *Factory*, which included a metal sheet in the orchestration for realistic effect.

Proletarian Music. In opposition to the modernists, a powerful movement arose in favor of a special type of proletarian music. The Russian Association of Proletarian Musicians (RAPM) issued a manifesto in 1924 proclaiming the principles of proletarian music. It opposed all "progressive" trends in modern music and all types of Western urban art, including jazz, in favor of revolutionary themes, in the tradition of Beethoven's *Eroica Symphony*. After several years of propaganda and controversy, which threatened to end creative activity in Russian music, the RAPM was dissolved by a government decree on April 23, 1932. This date was a landmark in the evolution of Soviet ideology in music.

Socialist Realism. After 1932, proletarian music was discredited and Stalin's formula of socialist realism was applied to music, within the framework of national art. A new crisis arose in January 1936, when the Moscow newspaper *Pravda* severely criticized the composer Dmitri Shostakovich—first, for "leftist deviation" and "naturalism" in his opera *Lady Macbeth of the District of Mtsensk* (1930–1932), and, second, for "oversimplification" in the treatment of a Soviet theme in the ballet *The Limpid Stream* (1934). The articles posed the problem of defining socialist realism and of drawing a clear line of demarcation so as to prevent the fallacies of "naturalism" and "oversimplification." The Shostakovich case became a cause célèbre in the annals of Soviet music because of the stature of the composer and his place in Soviet art.

Shostakovich. Dmitri Shostakovich grew up almost entirely under Soviet rule, and his talent developed with the evolution of Soviet ideology in general aesthetics. Shostakovich's works were satirical in character. His opera *The Nose* (1927–1928), based on a tale by Gogol, featured such effects as drunken hiccoughs, imitated by harp and violins, and the sound of a razor on the face. The part of the principal character, the Nose, was to be sung by a performer with his nostrils stuffed with cotton wads. There was an octet of janitors singing eight different advertisements. The opera was produced as an experimental spectacle in Leningrad in 1930.

The ballets of Shostakovich have the same satirical vein. His *The Golden Age* (1929–1930) contains a discordant polka that satirizes the Geneva disarmament conference. There are similar satiric strains in his symphonies. His First Symphony, written when he was 19, has become a standard of the orchestral repertoire in Russia and abroad. His second, called the *October Symphony*, and his third, *May First*, were less popular. After the rebuke administered by *Pravda*, Shostakovich abandoned programmatic music and returned to pure symphonic composition. His Fourth Symphony was judged unsuitable at its private performance in 1936, and the score was not published until 1962. Shostakovich returned to favor with his Fifth Symphony (1937), which was hailed in the Soviet press as a work in the best tradition of Russian music. The Sixth Symphony (1939) had little success, but the Seventh (1941), written during the siege of Leningrad, became world famous. This work depicts the struggle of the Soviets against the Nazi invasion, and its triumphant finale foretells the inevitable victory. There followed the Eighth Symphony (1943), the Ninth (1945), the Tenth (1953),

the Eleventh (1957), and the Twelfth (1960). The Thirteenth Symphony for orchestra, chorus, and solo bass (1962) aroused controversy on account of the text by the Soviet poet Yevgeni Yevtushenko, which dealt with the delicate problem of latent anti-Semitism in Russia; the score remained in manuscript. The Fourteenth Symphony (1969), is scored for soprano, bass, and small orchestra. Shostakovich wrote his Fifteenth Symphony for orchestra without chorus in 1971. His other works include two cello concertos (1959, 1966), two violin concertos (1955, 1967), two piano concertos (1933, 1957), 13 string quartets, two piano trios, a piano quintet, violin sonata, cello sonata, and piano pieces.

Stylistically, Shostakovich never deviated from his original conception of modern Russian music, lyrical and dramatic and freely dissonant, while keeping within the broad confines of tonality. His Eighth String Quartet and Tenth Symphony are thematically built on his Russian monogram in German as D, S (Es = E flat), C, H (= B natural phonetically transcribed). In his later works he occasionally applied 12-tone constructions. Shostakovich was the recipient of numerous Soviet prizes. On his 60th birthday in 1966 he was awarded the Order of Hero of Socialist Labor.

Khachaturian and Other Soviet Composers. Aram Khachaturian, an Armenian composer born in Georgia, achieved great popularity in Russia and abroad with his symphonies, concertos, and ballets, written in a coloristic, quasi-Oriental manner. The *Saber Dance* from his ballet *Gayane* (1942) has become universally popular. Another ballet, *Spartacus* (1954), gained wide acceptance in Russia. Khachaturian wrote three symphonies (1932, 1943, 1947); a brilliant piano concerto (1935); a violin concerto (1938); a cello concerto (1946); rhapsody concertos for violin (1961), for cello (1963), and for piano (1965); incidental music to Lermontov's play *Masquerade*; and chamber music. His wife, Nina Makarova, was also a composer. Khachaturian's nephew Karen Khachaturian wrote symphonies and chamber music.

A Soviet composer of prime importance was Dmitri Kabalevsky, who wrote in a melodious Russian manner, invigorated by a rhythmic élan. The overture to his opera *Colas Breugnon* (1938), after Romain Rolland, attained great popularity. He wrote several operas on Soviet subjects, including *At Moscow* (1943), *The Family of Taras* (1950), and *Nikita Vershinin* (1955); a *Requiem* in memory of the victims of World War II (1963); several symphonies; three piano concertos; a violin concerto; two cello concertos; and chamber music.

Ivan Dzerzhinsky successfully applied the formula of socialist realism to Soviet opera. In addition to *And Quiet Flows the Don* and *Soil Upturned,* he composed *The Tempest* (1940), *The Blood of the People* (1941), *The Blizzard* (1946), *Far From Moscow* (1948), *A Man's Destiny* (1961), and *Hostile Winds* (1969).

Tikhon Khrennikov pursued the ideals of socialist realism very energetically, and often acted as a spokesman for it. Accordingly, his music has a peculiar directness of purpose. He wrote the operas *In the Storm* (1939) and *Mother* (1957); a "musical chronicle," *White Nights* (1967); two symphonies; two piano concertos; a violin concerto; and chamber music.

Among conservative Russian composers, Boris

Asafyev wrote ballet music that achieved popularity in Russia. He also distinguished himself as a music critic under the name Igor Glebov. Yuri Shaporin adhered to the classical Russian school of composition and selected national subjects for his music. His works include *On the Kulikov Field* (1939), a patriotic cantata commemorating the Russian victory over the Tatars in the 14th century; *Chronicle of a Battle for Russian Land* (1944), an oratorio on the war with the Nazis; and *The Decembrists* (1953), a historical opera.

Most Russian composers of the older generation adapted themselves to the new revolutionary themes. During the Soviet period, Glière, composer of the monumental *Ilya Murometz Symphony* (1911), wrote a revolutionary ballet, *The Red Poppy* (1927). The Russian *Sailor's Dance* from this ballet became universally popular. Vassilenko wrote the patriotic opera *Suvorov* (1941). Maximillian Steinberg, a disciple and son-in-law of Rimsky-Korsakov, wrote a symphony (1933) celebrating the construction of a Siberian railroad. Several Jewish Soviet composers, among them Mikhail Gnessin, the brothers Aleksandr and Gregory Krein, and Aleksandr Veprik, cultivated Jewish themes. Julian Krein, Gregory's son, spent some years in Paris and then returned to Russia. He wrote mostly instrumental music. To these names should be added those of Lev Knipper, who composed symphonies as well as operas; Vissarion Shebalin, who wrote five symphonies and effective chamber music; and Vano Muradeli, a Caucasian composer of operas and symphonies in a colorful vein. Georgi Sviridov, composer of choral music in a grand Russian style, was greatly respected. His *Pathetic Oratorio* (1959) became a Soviet classic.

Several Russian composers emigrated after the Revolution. A number of them became United States citizens: Rachmaninoff in 1943, Grechaninov in 1946, and Stravinsky in 1945. Aleksandr Tcherepnin, the son of Nikolai Tcherepnin, lived mostly in Europe before settling in the United States in 1949. A highly prolific composer, he distinguished himself in opera, symphony, ballet, and chamber music and often appeared as a pianist for his own concertos and in recitals. Other Russian composers who settled in America included Nicolai Berezowsky, a gifted symphonist; Nikolai Lopatnikoff, who excelled in instrumental music in a neoclassical style; Vladimir Dukelsky, who after a notable beginning as a symphonic composer made a career as the writer of popular American songs under the name Vernon Duke; and Nicolas Nabokov, who wrote operas, oratorios, and symphonic works. Many celebrated Russian conductors, instrumentalists, and singers also left Russia after the Revolution. Among them were the famous basso Feodor Chaliapin, the conductor Serge Koussevitzky, the pianist Vladimir Horowitz, the violinists Jascha Heifetz and Nathan Milstein, and the cellist Gregor Piatigorsky.

Soviet Russia produced its own generation of virtuosos. They included the pianists Sviatoslav Richter, Vladimir Ashkenazy, Lazar Berman, and Emil Gilels; the violinists David Oistrakh, his son Igor, and Leonid Kogan; and the cellist Mstislav Rostropovich.

The Soviet Avant-Garde. The close cooperation between the USSR and the Western world during the crucial years of World War II opened the Soviet gates to many Western musical ideas, including modern techniques of composition. A temporary setback was inflicted on Soviet modernistic trends when the central committee of the Communist party, in its resolution of Feb. 10, 1948, administered a sharp rebuke to Soviet composers for their formalistic tendencies, expressly criticizing Prokofiev, Miaskovsky, and Shostakovich. Soviet composers had to make an adjustment to these authoritarian demands, but in 1958 the resolution was withdrawn. As a result, musicians who came to maturity after Stalin's death in 1953 felt free to proceed with bold experimentation. Shostakovich himself set an example in using an explicit 12-tone subject in his Twelfth String Quartet (1968). Tone-clusters, quarter-tones, and even aleatory devices began to appear in Soviet scores. Electronic music was practiced widely.

The most prominent Soviet composers of the avant-garde included Edison Denisov, Rodion Shchedrin, Sergei Slonimsky, Andrei Volkonsky, Alfred Schnitke, Leonid Grabovsky, Valentin Silvestrov, and Boris Tishchenko. Denisov, named after Thomas Edison by his father, an engineer, explored constructive sonorities. Shchedrin wrote effective ballets; his orchestral *Chimes* (1967) exploits impressionistic colors. Sergei Slonimsky was an uncompromising innovator. His *Concerto Buffo* for orchestra (1966) makes use of exotic percussion, quarter-tones, and other modernistic effects. In *Antiphones* for string quartet (1969) he applied nontempered scales. For the stage, Slonimsky wrote in a strong Russian style, and his opera *Virineya* (1967) enjoyed much success. Volkonsky, a pioneer of the avant-garde, was strongly criticized for his unorthodox type of composition but eventually regained his position in modern Soviet music. Schnitke composed music of grandiose dimensions, as exemplified by his symphonic *Poem of Cosmos* (1961). Grabovsky experimented in modern rhythms and dissonant counterpoint. Silvestrov wrote instrumental music in an abstract expressionistic manner. Tishchenko was adept at modernistic writing for piano. With the advent of the avant-garde, modern techniques finally acquired their rightful place in Soviet music.

Nicolas Slonimsky
Author of "Music Since 1900"

Bibliography

Abraham, Gerald, *Eight Soviet Composers* (Oxford 1943).
Asaf'ev, Boris, *Russian Music from the Beginning of the Nineteenth Century*, tr. by Alfred Swan (Am. Council of Learned Socs. 1953).
Bakst, James, *History of Russian-Soviet Music* (Dodd 1966).
Boelza, Igor, *Handbook of Soviet Musicians*, ed. by Alan Bush (1943; reprint, Greenwood Press, Inc. 1971).
Bush, Alan, *Music in the Soviet Union* (Workers Music Assn, Ltd. 1944).
Calvocoressi, Michel, and Abraham, Gerald, *Masters of Russian Music* (Knopf 1936).
Krebs, Stanley, *Soviet Composers and the Development of Soviet Music* (Norton 1970).
Leonard, Richard, *A History of Russian Music* (Funk 1968).
Montagu-Nathan, Montagu, *A History of Russian Music*, 2d rev. ed. (Biblo & Tannen 1969).
Sabaneev, Leonid, *Modern Russian Composers*, tr. by Judah Joffe (1927; reprint, Books for Libs., Inc. 1967).
Schwarz, Boris, *Music and Musical Life in Soviet Russia: 1917–1970* (Norton 1971).
Seaman, Gerald, *History of Russian Music*, vol. 1, *From its Origins to Dargomyzhsky* (Praeger 1967).
Stasov, Vladimir, *Selected Essays on Music*, tr. by Florence Jonas (Praeger 1969).

RUSSIAN ORTHODOX CHURCH. See Russian Church.

Street demonstrations by soldiers, workers, and peasants increased during the late spring of 1917 as the Provisional Government delayed in making the reforms that had been called for by the revolutionaries in February.

RUSSIAN REVOLUTION, a fundamental political and social upheaval that erupted in the Russian Empire in 1917. It began with the collapse of the centuries-old czarist regime in February and led to the overthrow of the Western-style Provisional Government and the establishment of the first national Communist political system in October. (Dates of events that precede Russia's adoption of the Gregorian calendar on Feb. 14, 1918, are given in Old Style or in both Old Style and New Style.) The Russian Revolution was followed by a bitter, devastating civil war (1918–1921), during which the Bolsheviks (renamed Communists in March 1918) defeated a variety of hostile military and political forces and consolidated their authority throughout much of the former Russian Empire.

ORIGINS OF THE REVOLUTION

The roots of the Russian Revolution are to be sought in the arbitrary, autocratic, and repressive czarist political and social system that evolved in the 16th–18th centuries, in the course of Russia's massive territorial expansion and rise into the ranks of the great European powers. Russia's geographical and often self-imposed cultural isolation from the West helped to shield Russia from the liberalizing influences of the French Revolution. Consequently, absolutism and the existing organization of Russian society survived virtually intact during the political convulsions of the late 18th and 19th centuries that shattered the traditional order throughout much of the European continent.

After Russia's defeat in the Crimean War in 1856, Czar Alexander II fostered significant reforms, among the most important of which were the abolition of serfdom and the creation of elected zemstvo institutions for limited self-government. However, the terms of the emancipation severely restricted opportunities for modernizing agriculture. At the same time the economic plight and ultimately the discontent of most peasants, who constituted the bulk of the Russian population, deepened.

A further weakness of the so-called Great Reforms was that no provision was made for any sort of representative body at the national level. In the last quarter of the 19th century, provision of a constitution and of a popularly elected parliament to complete the Great Reforms became the rallying cry of liberally inclined nobles, members of the intelligentsia, and articulate representatives of the numerically still very small urban business and professional classes.

Other factors contributed to political and social tensions in Russia around 1900. In addition to Great Russians, a host of religious and ethnic minorities lived within Russia's boundaries. The czarist government's policies of discrimination and persecution of non-Orthodox religious groups and its efforts to repress and to russify ethnic minorities stimulated discontent among the former and greatly intensified aspirations for independence among the latter.

At the same time Russia was in the throes of the industrial revolution that Britain had experienced a century earlier. An important side effect of Russia's rapid economic expansion was the creation of an indigenous working class and the development of new industrial centers. The Russian industrial revolution brought into being the same appalling living and working conditions that had existed during the early phases of the industrial revolution in Britain. Owing to these conditions, the rebelliousness of the Russian peasantry, hungry for more land, was quickly matched by the alienation and restlessness of the workers, a group whose ranks were constantly growing.

Alarmed by signs of popular discontent, the czarist government resorted to a variety of extraordinary measures aimed at molding an obedient citizenry and at preventing revolutionary activity. Nonetheless, by the first years of the 20th century, the more important opposition movements destined to play major roles in the revolution had been formed. These included the Marxist Social Democratic labor movement, the peasant-oriented Socialist Revolutionary (SR) movement, and the largely middle-class liberal movement. These three groups had significantly different aspirations for the future of Russia. Even within each movement there was little unanimity as to how the revolution would come about and what it would achieve. Thus, by 1905, Russian Social Democrats were split into the more moderate and orthodox Mensheviks and the ideologically flexible, more radically inclined Bolsheviks, led by Vladimir Ilich Lenin. Nevertheless, one common element united these diverse groups and subgroups: antipathy to the preservation of the autocracy.

In the wake of a disastrous war with Japan that began in 1904, opposition groups joined forces for the first time with peasants and factory workers in a concerted attack on the government. However, the resulting Revolution of 1905 did not end in a clear victory for either the government or the Russian public. Although the revised Fundamental Laws granted by Nicholas II in April 1906 transformed the Russian political system into a limited constitutional monarchy with a popularly elected legislature (the Duma), the arbitrary power of the czar remained vast. In the first two Dumas, elected on a broad but unequal and indirect franchise, the Constitutional Democratic (Kadet) party, the leading liberal political organization, sought to establish genuine parliamentary government on the Western model. However, the Kadets' efforts ended in failure. In June 1907 the Russian premier, Pyotr Stolypin, dissolved the Second Duma and enacted illegal electoral restrictions that severely narrowed the franchise and produced a Third Duma more attuned to the conservative attitudes of the monarchy and the upper classes.

In the light of these factors, there is no easy answer to the central, often-debated question: Would post-1905 Russia have been able to modernize without the violent political and social upheaval that erupted in 1917 if it had not suffered the additional strain of military defeats in World War I? In the past, most Western historians of Russia tended toward an optimistic view of late czarist Russia's prospects for survival and relatively peaceful modernization. They pointed to such measures as the granting of broad civil liberties; the legalization and generally free functioning of political parties and trade unions; the liberalization of regulations affecting higher education and the press; and the Duma's passage of important education and agrarian reforms (the Stolypin reforms) as signs that meaningful, enduring change was taking place and, more generally, that before the outbreak of the war, Russian politics and society were becoming more, not less, stable.

But a new generation of professional scholars, scrutinizing all aspects of Russian politics and society at that time, concluded, among other things, that the Stolypin reforms were not a viable, long-term solution to Russia's agrarian problems and, more basically, that on the eve of World War I the government again faced a steadily mounting political and social crisis. The findings of these historians strongly suggest that in 1914 the czarist order was close to bankruptcy and that the war crisis, far from being the primary cause of the revolution, postponed a political confrontation and a popular explosion that otherwise might have occurred sooner.

Initially, the Russian mobilization effort proceeded more quickly than the Central Powers expected or the government dared hope. But within two months of Russia's entry into the war in July 1914, the czarist army was dealt devastating defeats in the battles of Tannenberg and the Masurian Lakes. In the following spring the Austro-German armies launched a massive offensive that ended in the autumn with the Russian front pushed back hundreds of miles. By 1916 the willingness of Russia's front-line soldiers to fight was largely spent, and the disintegration of Russia's armed forces everywhere was well advanced.

Acute demoralization, however, was by no means peculiar to Russia's armed forces during World War I. But in Russia's case, the sinking morale among troops was accompanied by a growing political paralysis and government mismanagement of the war effort at home. Tending to view all expressions of public initiative as subversive, the wartime government endeavored to stifle such worthwhile civilian defense efforts as those by the zemstvos to mobilize industry and reorganize medical services. As the staggering reverses at the front in 1915 and the disintegration in the rear became widely recognized, the government of Nicholas II was subjected to open criticism not only by the old political opposition but also by conservative deputies in the Duma as well.

In an effort to bolster the military situation, Nicholas II took personal command of front-line troops in August 1915, leaving administrative matters at home in the hands of archreactionaries, headed by Empress Alexandra and her closest adviser, the notorious faith-healer Rasputin. The resulting scandalous political situation was coupled with rapidly deteriorating economic conditions, which grew particularly acute in the last months of 1916. By then, the urgent need for immediate political change was broadly acknowledged—in the court, the Duma, and the command of the army. Indeed, the regime of Nicholas II was so thoroughly discredited that the essential question was not whether it would survive but whether it would be overthrown by a palace coup or a revolution from below. For a more detailed account of the history of Russia before the Revolution, see RUSSIA.

THE FEBRUARY REVOLUTION

A popular revolt in Petrograd (formerly St. Petersburg), the Russian capital, forced Nicholas II from the throne. Preceded by a rising wave of antigovernment strikes, food riots, and street demonstrations, the overturn itself was neither planned nor directed by an organized political group. On February 22 (March 7, New Style), a lockout of indefinite duration was announced at the giant Putilov metalworking plant. On the following day, disturbances broke out among housewives who were waiting in long lines for bread; the wait was often in vain. These developed into spontaneous street demonstrations calling for the overthrow of the monarchy and an end to the war. By February 25 the popular explosion in Petrograd had become general. Cossacks sent to quell the disturbances demonstrated sympathy for rebelling workers, and units of the Petrograd garrison joined what had become a full-blown revolution.

By February 28, Petrograd was in the hands of insurgents, and the pattern was roughly similar throughout the empire. The czarist regime had become so thoroughly bankrupt that meaningful resistance to the overthrow of the old order failed to emerge. On March 2 (March 15, New Style), Nicholas II abdicated the imperial throne in favor of his brother, Grand Duke Mikhail. Mikhail, in turn, rejected the crown, at least until the convocation of a constituent assembly, and the more than 300-year reign of the Romanovs came to an abrupt end.

THE STRUGGLE FOR POWER

Two potential national governments emerged in the first days after the February revolution. These were the Provisional Government, created by a committee of Duma deputies and immediately acknowledged as the legal national authority, and the Petrograd Soviet of Workers' and Soldiers' Deputies, a revolutionary council formed spontaneously by socialist leaders and representatives of Petrograd factories and military units.

The Provisional Government at first was headed by Georgi Lvov (March 2–July 7) and subsequently by a brilliant trial lawyer and outspoken leftist Duma deputy, Aleksandr Kerensky (July 7–October 25). The political figures who initially accepted cabinet posts in the Provisional Government were, by and large, westernized liberals, to be joined belatedly by centrist or right moderate socialists. Members of the new cabinet were mainly intellectuals who admired Western political and economic institutions and, in the case of the liberals, possessed great concern for legality and the preservation of private property. Many of these men were also patriotic and nationalistic. Consequently, they strove to delay fundamental political decisions, such as land reform and independence for minority nationalities, until the convocation of a properly elected constituent assembly, long a basic demand of all Russian revolutionary groups. In the meantime, the Provisional Government concentrated its efforts on reestablishing order and bolstering the defense effort.

The Petrograd Soviet and the other local soviets that quickly sprang up in urban and rural areas around the country were made up of socialist leaders and rank-and-file representatives elected by workers, peasants, and military personnel. In May and June national conventions of workers', soldiers', and peasants' soviets formed permanent All-Russian Executive Committees. Taken together, these were not only numerically more representative but, by virtue of the loyalty they commanded among their constituents, they were potentially more powerful than the Provisional Government.

Until October 1917, when the executive bodies of the All-Russian Soviets became dominated by Bolsheviks, these institutions were effectively controlled by moderate socialists. Under their leadership the soviets recognized the authority of the Provisional Government and restricted their role to acting as guardians of the interests of the lower classes. Indeed, in early May, when the Provisional Government ap-

Aleksandr Kerensky (*right*), as minister of war, reviews Russian troops shortly before replacing Lvov as premier.

peared on the verge of collapse, several key moderate socialist leaders from the Petrograd Soviet accepted ministerial posts.

The moderate socialists' support of the Provisional Government was, at least in part, the result of doctrinal considerations. The Mensheviks remained committed to the orthodox Marxist assumption that a "bourgeois revolution," which the overthrow of the autocracy appeared to represent, had to be followed by an indefinite period of bourgeois-democratic rule. It followed that an underdeveloped Russia was not yet ripe for a socialist revolution. The Socialist Revolutionaries in the executive committees of the soviets, while not prevented by ideology from taking power into their own hands, shared with many Mensheviks the conviction that collaboration with military commanders and commercial and industrial groups was essential for Russia's survival in the war and as a bulwark against possible counterrevolution.

The postponement of fundamental political and social reforms until careful decisions could be made in peacetime doubtless seemed the only just course to the prominent liberals most responsible for shaping the Provisional Government's policies. But to hundreds of thousands of common soldiers, workers, and peasants who had little commitment to the war effort, and who resented the fact that the February revolution had brought them only meager social and economic gains, the prospect of postponing further reforms until peacetime made no sense at all.

By the late spring, growing segments of the lower classes viewed the Provisional Government as an instrument of the propertied classes, opposed to fundamental political and social change, and unconcerned about the needs of common citizens. Among the working classes the moderate socialists were increasingly criticized for their support of the government and the war effort, whereas the soviets were viewed as genuinely democratic institutions of popular self-rule.

Of the major Russian political groups competing for power and influence in 1917, only the Bolshevik party remained unfettered by association with the government and was therefore free to encourage its supporters to oppose it. On the eve of World War I, the Bolsheviks had achieved considerable success in attracting factory workers away from the more moderate Mensheviks. Much of this gain in support may have been lost during the war, when large numbers of these workers were shipped to the front and when local Bolshevik organizations were frequently decimated by arrests. But the party made a rapid recovery following the February revolution.

In April, Lenin returned to Russia from exile abroad and pointed the Bolshevik party toward an early socialist revolution. Subsequently, "Peace, Land, and Bread!" and "All Power to the Soviets!" became the party's key slogans. By tacit consent, Lenin's prerevolutionary conception of a small, united, centralized party was discarded. Decision making became more democratic and decentralized, the relatively free exchange of opinion was tolerated, if not encouraged, and tens of thousands of new members were welcomed into the party.

The fundamental weakness of the Provisional Government and the increasing strength of the Bolsheviks and other groups of the extreme left became strikingly apparent during the July days (July 3–5; July 16–18, New Style), when the government was at the mercy of crowds of armed

Lenin addresses a crowd while Trotsky stands beside the platform on the right. Less gifted as an orator than Trotsky, Lenin was the more skillful politician.
THE MANSELL COLLECTION

workers, soldiers, and Baltic fleet sailors demanding the creation of an exclusively socialist, Soviet government. But the moderately inclined Menshevik–Socialist Revolutionary soviet leadership steadfastly refused to assume power. Bolshevik leaders hung back from the decisive step of trying to overthrow the government. After the minister of justice released documents purporting to prove that Lenin was an agent of enemy Germany and it was announced that loyalist troops were on their way to Petrograd from the front, the rebellion fizzled out.

Non-Soviet historians have tended to view the July uprising as an abortive Leninist attempt to seize power. While it is true that the movement was in part an outgrowth of months of Bolshevik propaganda, what appears to have happened is that local Bolshevik organizations in the capital, responsive to their ultramilitant constituencies, encouraged the insurrection against the wishes of Lenin and a majority of the Central Committee. These leaders considered such action premature because it would be opposed by peasants in the provinces and soldiers at the front. The July uprising ended in an apparently decisive defeat for the Bolshevik party. The Bolsheviks were momentarily discredited even with the Left, both because of the party's apparent role in organizing the uprising and because of the German-agent charges against Lenin, who now went into hiding.

By the end of the July days, an initially successful Russian offensive had been turned by the Germans into another terrible rout of the Russian army. Kerensky became premier, heading a coalition government of liberals and moderate socialists who were most immediately concerned with restoring political authority and order at home and somehow shoring up the collapsing front. It appeared that a lull had been reached in the workers' movement and public opinion seemed to have shifted decisively to the right. Yet, despite a constant barrage of rhetoric by Kerensky, echoed by a host of resurgent civil and military rightist groups, none of the repressive measures proclaimed by the government at this time were fully implemented, nor did they achieve their objectives. More than this, the apparently increasing danger of counterrevolution heightened popular suspicions that the Kerensky government itself was part of the movement to stifle the revolution and helped dispel much of the bitterness and hostility toward the Bolsheviks that had developed among workers in the wake of the July uprising. By early August the party, with its apparatus intact, was embarked on a new period of growth.

For liberals and conservatives who had prematurely celebrated the demise of Bolshevism in July, the party's quick recovery and the numerous signs of deepening political and social crisis were shattering. Each day brought fresh reports of expanding anarchy among impatient, land-hungry peasants in the countryside; disorder in the cities; increasing militancy of factory workers; the government's inability to resist movements toward complete autonomy by the Finns and Ukrainians; the continuing radicalization of soldiers at the front and rear; catastrophic breakdowns in the production and distribution of essential supplies; and skyrocketing prices.

Under the weight of this news, many industrial and business figures, representatives of the landed class, military officers—in short, a broad spectrum of liberal as well as conservative

Troops of Gen. Lavr Kornilov turn in their arms in the late summer of 1917. Their march against Petrograd had been halted by Kerensky's government, which Kornilov had attempted to replace with his personal rule.

TASS, FROM SOVFOTO

opinion—even Allied representatives in Russia lost faith in Kerensky's capacity to stem the revolutionary tide. For some, the sole hope of restoring order at the front and arresting chaos at home seemed to lie in the establishment of a strong military dictatorship. At the end of August, they supported a rightist coup by Gen. Lavr Kornilov, commander in chief of the Russian Army. For a brief time, it appeared that Kornilov's troops would occupy the capital and that the Provisional Government would be overthrown. However, all political organizations to the left of the Kadets—the Mensheviks, Socialist Revolutionaries, anarchists, Bolsheviks, every labor organization of importance, and soldier and sailor committees at all levels—immediately banded together in defense of the revolution. Kornilov was forced to surrender without a shot fired.

The failure of Kornilov's coup demoralized the Kadets. The Mensheviks and Socialist Revolutionaries were weakened by interparty disputes over the nature and makeup of a future government. The big winners in the Kornilov affair were the Bolsheviks, whose increasing political strength was reflected in their newly won majorities in the Petrograd and Moscow soviets. In late September, Leon Trotsky, a Bolshevik, secured the key post of president of the Petrograd Soviet.

Kornilov's defeat testified anew to the great potential power of the Left. The flood of political resolutions adopted after the Kornilov affair demonstrated that there was a similarity between the professed Bolshevik program and the aspirations of the Russian lower classes. To be sure, the popular mood did not specifically reflect a desire for a Bolshevik government. Bolshevism was perceived at this time to stand for soviet power, for a strong but democratic government, genuinely representative of all socialist groups and ruling in the interests of ordinary citizens. Whether the Bolsheviks would ultimately translate this popular aspiration into a successful bid for exclusive power was still very much an open question.

THE OVERTHROW OF THE PROVISIONAL GOVERNMENT

Two weeks after Kornilov's defeat, Lenin, then still hiding in Finland, concluded that the moment was favorable for overthrowing the Provisional Government. He sent a series of frantic appeals to the Bolshevik Central Committee in Petrograd for the immediate organization of a popular armed uprising.

Lenin's impatience at this time was based on optimistic assessments of current political developments in Russia and of the prospects for revolutionary explosions abroad. He also seems to have feared that if the existing situation were not immediately exploited, another opportunity might not come again soon. Nonetheless, his insistent urgings were ignored by his party. This rejection was due partly to the stubborn efforts of such influential right-wing Bolsheviks as Lev Kamenev and Grigori Zinoviev, who objected to Lenin's appeals on basic, ideological grounds. But of even greater significance was the opposition of many militantly inclined Bolshevik leaders, like Trotsky, who shared in full Lenin's assumptions regarding the necessity and feasibility of an early socialist revolution in Russia. These leaders doubted that popular support for the "immediate bayonet charge" advocated by Lenin could be successfully mobilized. Because of their continuing interaction with workers and soldiers, they had a more realistic appreciation than Lenin did of the limits of the party's political authority among the masses and of the acceptance by the masses of the soviets as legitimate democratic institutions.

A second national Congress of Soviets of Workers' and Soldiers' Deputies was due to convene in Petrograd in October. Party leaders who were on the spot were ultimately forced to recognize that if the Bolsheviks usurped the prerogatives of the congress to act on the government issue, the party risked losing much of its hard-won popular support and, in all probability, would suffer as devastating a defeat as they had

The arrest of the Provisional Government by revolutionary forces in the October Revolution is dramatically portrayed in this Soviet painting. Aleksandr Kerensky, the premier, avoided arrest because he had already fled.

in July. At the same time, there was every hope that if the Bolsheviks continued to expand the party's political and military strength at the government's expense, and if it waited for the government to attack before actually launching an open insurrection, the prospects for success would be greatly enhanced.

The danger of such a course was that it might lead to the creation of a socialist coalition government, including moderates, rather than a government of the extreme Left. It appears that Lenin was one of the very few Bolshevik leaders to whom the enormous risk of a premature, independent, ultraradical course was outweighed by the desire to create an exclusively leftist regime at once.

Although with considerable wavering, caused largely by pressure for bolder action from Lenin, who by then had secretly returned to Petrograd, the Bolsheviks pursued precisely the course advocated by Trotsky and others. In mid-October, taking advantage of a counterrevolutionary scare generated by the government's announced intention of transferring the bulk of the radicalized Petrograd garrison to the front, the party superintended the creation of an ostensibly nonparty "defense" institution, the Military Revolutionary Committee of the Petrograd Soviet. Under the guise of defending the revolution and the coming Congress of Soviets, which was scheduled to open on October 25, the Military Revolutionary Committee secured the allegiance of virtually the entire Petrograd garrison, thus effectively disarming the government.

At dawn on October 24 (November 6, New Style), Kerensky responded to the Military Revolutionary Committee's usurpation of his command authority by initiating steps to suppress the Left, thereby assuring the success of the armed action against the government that Lenin had been demanding for more than a month. In the prevailing circumstances, only very meager and constantly dwindling numbers of Cossacks, military school cadets, and women soldiers were willing to side with the government.

Beginning on the afternoon of October 24, Bolshevik-led soldiers, sailors, and Red Guard detachments easily took control of key Petrograd bridges, transport and communications facilities, main public buildings, and munitions stores. On the following night, October 25 (November 7, New Style), revolutionary forces invaded the Winter Palace and arrested most of the cabinet. An exception was Kerensky, who earlier that day had fled to the front in a largely futile search for loyal troops. Later that same night, deputies to the Congress of Soviets approved a historic public manifesto, drafted by Lenin, announcing the Provisional Government's demise and proclaiming the congress' intention of immediately forming a revolutionary soviet, socialist government. Subsequently, the new administration was named the Council (Soviet) of People's Commissars. The congress approved Lenin's decrees on peace and land, promising Russia's prompt withdrawal from World War I (a peace treaty with the Central Powers was signed at Brest-Litovsk in March 1918) and transferring private and church lands to the soviets for distribution among the peasants.

THE CIVIL WAR

The Bolsheviks presented their overthrow of the Provisional Government as a defensive act on behalf of the soviets, thus legitimizing the insurrection in the eyes of supporters of the extreme Left. But, understandably, the new government did not accord with the deeply felt democratic principles of the moderate socialists. Most Mensheviks and Socialist Revolutionaries viewed the more broadly representative Constituent Assembly, soon to convene, as the legitimate forum for the creation of the future Russian political system. By refusing to participate in a Soviet coalition cabinet that included Lenin and Trotsky, the moderate socialists played into the hands of hard-line Bolsheviks like Lenin, who were hostile to any form of collaboration with more moderate groups. The ultimate result was an exclusively Bolshevik regime.

In the last days of October, Soviet forces rebuffed an attempt by Cossack troops loyal to Kerensky to retake the capital, and in succeeding weeks Soviet rule was established in Moscow and in other cities and towns throughout central Russia and beyond. Elections to the Constituent Assembly took place as scheduled in early November, and the assembly gathered in Petrograd on Jan. 5, 1918 (Jan. 18, New Style). When it became apparent that the delegates, an absolute majority of whom were Socialist Revolutionaries, were unwilling to accede to Lenin's demand that the Constituent Assembly recognize the authority of the Soviet regime, the delegates were forcibly dispersed.

In the months that followed, military officers and members of the former upper and middle classes (among them conservatives, liberals, and Socialist Revolutionaries) organized to combat the Bolsheviks. Also prominent on the White, anti-Bolshevik, side in the civil war that erupted in the spring of 1918 were sizable Cossack forces. In its uphill struggle for survival at this juncture, the Soviet regime had to contend with the rebellion of the Czech Legion, an army of 40,000 Czech and Slovak prisoners of war, whose original intent had been merely to leave Russia by way of Vladivostok, in order to fight on the side of the Entente on the Western front. The Bolsheviks' precarious political and military situation was further complicated by strong nationalist movements for independence in minority areas; by widespread local uprisings of anarchic "green" guerrilla forces, made up mostly of peasants; by the intervention and support of the Whites by foreign troops from Britain, France, Japan, the United States, and several other countries; by a war with newly independent Poland in 1920; and by a myriad of lesser military, political, economic, and social problems. In addition, the support of the revolutionary European proletariat that Lenin and Trotsky had confidently expected did not materialize.

There were many moments during the civil war when the tide of battle appeared to have swung decisively in favor of the Whites and when the Soviet regime seemed doomed. In May 1918 rebelling elements of the Czech Legion seized vast stretches of the Trans-Siberian Railroad and occupied cities and towns in eastern Russia and Siberia. Under their protection, a rival anti-Bolshevik government, dominated by Socialist Revolutionaries and headed by their leader, Viktor Chernov, was established in Samara (now Kuibyshev) on the Volga. Another major, more conservative, counterrevolutionary authority with national pretensions was established at Omsk, under Adm. Aleksandr Kolchak. Other rival movements and governments sprang up in the south and the far north.

In the summer of 1918, Gen. Anton Denikin's southern-based Volunteer Army, with the help of Don Cossack forces led by Gen. Pyotr Krasnov, cleared the Bolsheviks from the Don and Kuban regions. In July, however, attempts by Krasnov to take the strategically crucial city of Tsaritsyn (renamed Stalingrad in 1928 and Volgograd in 1961) ended in failure. This was a significant victory for the Reds. The Bolsheviks won another important victory in September 1918, capturing

Kazan and turning back a major, initially successful, offensive by the so-called People's Army, formed by the anti-Bolsheviks in Samara, and elements of the Czech Legion.

For the Bolsheviks, probably the most perilous time in the civil war was the late summer and fall of 1919. After having thwarted a strong spring offensive across the Urals by Kolchak's army, the Reds were confronted with a powerful drive by Denikin aimed at Moscow (which had become the capital of the Soviet state in March 1918) and a rapid strike on Petrograd launched from the Baltic by Gen. Nikolai Yudenich. For a brief time, it seemed that Petrograd and Moscow might both be occupied by the Whites. But in October, Yudenich's forces were stopped on the outskirts of Petrograd, and at about the same time a powerful Red Army counterattack halted Denikin just short of Tula, the gateway to Moscow.

The last White military threat of consequence was directed by Denikin's successor, Baron Pyotr Wrangel, in the summer of 1920. Upon the conclusion of an armistice between Soviet Russia and Poland the following October, the now more experienced and confident troops of the Red Army were free to deal harshly with this last echo of the civil war. Wrangel's army was driven into the Crimea, where the British helped evacuate some 130,000 White soldiers and civilians by sea to Constantinople (Istanbul).

Among often-cited reasons for the Bolshevik victory in the civil war, the following stand out. (1) The Bolsheviks' superior leadership.

Leon Trotsky in military uniform. As commissar of war, he welded the Red Army into an effective force that ultimately crushed White opposition in the civil war.

British sailors near Murmansk guard locomotives damaged by the Bolsheviks. The Bolsheviks considered the presence of even token Allied forces in Russia's Arctic ports a threat to their position in the civil war.

In this respect, Lenin's role in providing overall inspiration and political direction and Trotsky's contributions in building a formidable military arm, the Red Army, were of particular importance. (2) The broad appeal of the party's professed goals. As in 1917, the radical Bolshevik political and social program attracted support among workers and soldiers. Because White leaders either hedged on political issues or identified themselves with a return to the traditional order in the countryside, most peasants, who might otherwise have been expected to side with the Socialist Revolutionaries, remained aloof from the conflict. (3) Disunity among White leaders. The political and social goals of the widely scattered White movements varied dramatically. Cooperation and military coordination between them were virtually nonexistent. By contrast, the Bolsheviks were united in purpose and fiercely committed to victory. Also, the Bolsheviks controlled the populous central Russian heartland, including Petrograd and Moscow, thereby facilitating administration, resource procurement and allocation, and communications. More fundamentally, the political weakness of Russian conservatives, liberals, and moderate socialists during the pivotal revolutionary and civil war years was in large part a consequence of czarist Russia's peculiar political, social, and economic development.

Despite the success of Bolshevik forces, the civil war exacted a monstrous toll from the Bolsheviks and Russia. The bitter conflict and the resulting physical and human devastation left in their wake an economic and social crisis far worse than that of 1917. But of equal importance were the consequences for the Soviet regime's longterm development. The Bolsheviks had won the struggle for power in 1917 at least in part because they combined organizational cohesiveness with a degree of openness, democracy, and decentralization in the process of decision making that made their programs and policies responsive to popular aspirations and well tuned to rapidly changing political realities. In the course of the Bolsheviks' struggle for survival in the civil war, the democratic and decentralized character of the party was lost; the independence of the soviets was destroyed; an oppressive, centralized bureaucracy was reimposed throughout the entire country; and Russian political and economic life became subject to the will and dictates of the Bolshevik leadership.

ALEXANDER RABINOWITCH
Indiana University

Bibliography

Chamberlin, William Henry, *The Russian Revolution, 1917–1921*, 2 vols. (Macmillan, N. Y., 1935; Grosset 1965).

Charques, Richard, *The Twilight of Imperial Russia* (Phoenix House 1958; Oxford 1965).

Florinsky, Michael T., *The End of the Russian Empire* (Yale Univ. Press 1931; Collier 1961).

Katkov, George, *The Russian Revolution* (Harper 1967).

Keep, John L. H., *The Russian Revolution: A Study in Mass Mobilization* (Norton 1977).

Melgunov, S. P., *The Bolshevik Seizure of Power* (Clio 1972).

Rabinowitch, Alexander, *The Bolsheviks Come to Power: The Revolution of 1917 in Petrograd* (Norton 1976).

Radkey, Oliver H., *The Agrarian Foes of Bolshevism* (Columbia Univ. Press 1958).

Reed, John, *Ten Days That Shook the World* (International Pubs. 1919; Vintage 1960).

Rosenberg, William G., *Liberals in the Russian Revolution: The Constitutional Democratic Party, 1917–1921* (Princeton Univ. Press 1974).

Sukhanov, Nikolai N., *The Russian Revolution, 1917*, 2 vols. (Harper 1962).

Suny, Ronald G., *The Baku Commune, 1917–1918* (Princeton Univ. Press 1972).

Trotsky, Leon, *The History of the Russian Revolution* (Univ. of Mich. Press 1957).

RUSSIAN SOVIET FEDERATED SOCIALIST REPUBLIC (RSFSR) is the largest of the 15 union republics that make up the USSR. At its extremes it extends 5,000 miles (8,050 km) from east to west and 2,500 miles (4,025 km) from north to south. It has an area of approximately 6.6 million square miles (17 million sq km). This is more than 75% of the area of the USSR and encompasses 80% of European USSR and all of Siberia.

The republic is bounded on the north by the seas of the Arctic Ocean and on the east by seas of the Pacific Ocean. On the south there are North Korea, China, Mongolia, the Kazakh republic, the Caspian Sea, and the Azerbaidzhan and Georgian republics. To the southwest there are the Black Sea and the Sea of Azov, while on the west are the Ukrainian, Belorussian, Latvian, and Estonian republics, the Baltic Sea, Finland, and Norway. Included within the RSFSR is the detached oblast of Kaliningrad, which is on the Baltic Sea between Lithuania and Poland. Four of the largest rivers in the world—the Volga, Ob, Yenisei, and Lena—flow within the republic.

Most of the RSFSR consists of a series of great plains. Among the relatively few highlands are the Khibiny Mountains of the Kola Peninsula in the extreme northwest, the low Ural Mountains dividing European USSR from Siberia, and the Kuznetsk Basin in south central Siberia. In addition, there are the Baikal, Stanovoi, Sikhote Alin, Verkhoyansk, and Anadyr ranges in eastern Siberia. Between the Arctic Ocean and the Arctic Circle, the republic is composed mainly of tundra. From the tundra south to Leningrad in Europe, and nearly to the Trans-Siberian Railroad in Asia, the land is covered by a dense northern forest. Below this forest lies a partially wooded steppe, and in the southernmost areas there is a treeless black-soil steppe. The greater part of the population, industry, and agriculture is found in these two steppe zones. Though varying from region to region, the climate is generally dry and continental, with long subzero winters and short temperate summers.

Population and Political Divisions. In 1970 the republic had a population of 130,090,000, about 54% of the USSR total. About 80% of the inhabitants are Great Russians, the remainder comprising many different peoples, of which the most numerous are the Tatars, Ukrainians, Chuvash, Bashkirs, and Mordvinians.

For administrative purposes the republic is divided into 49 oblasts, 6 territories (*krais*), 16 autonomous republics, and 10 national districts (*okrugs*).

The largest cities with their 1970 populations, are Moscow (7,061,000, with suburbs), the capital; Leningrad (3,950,000, with suburbs), on the Baltic Sea; Gorky (1,170,000), and Kuibyshev (1,047,000), in the Volga Valley, Novosibirsk (1,161,000), in central Siberia; and Sverdlovsk (1,026,000) in the Urals.

Agriculture, Furs, and Fisheries. The RSFSR is a great agricultural land, producing most of the flax, potatoes, and rye of the USSR. In wheat growing it ranks third among the union republics, following the Ukraine and Kazakh republic. Hemp, sugar beets, vegetables, and sunflowers are also important crops. The area planted to crops is about 60% of the USSR total. Farms in the republic breed roughly half of the USSR's livestock. In addition, the world's largest herds of reindeer are raised in the RSFSR Arctic. Almost all the agriculture is socialized. The number of collective farms has steadily decreased as the smaller farms have been incorporated into larger units. During the 1960's the emphasis in agriculture shifted from collective farms to the larger state farms. The number of collective farms decreased by more than 65%, and the number of state farms doubled. There are no private farms, except for the kitchen gardens of rural residents.

Almost all the USSR's furs come from the republic's tundra and northern forest regions, and the latter also produce the largest part of the country's lumber. The RSFSR leads the other Soviet republics in fishing. The principal fisheries are located in the Pacific Ocean, Caspian Sea, Arctic Ocean, and Baltic Sea.

Mineral Production. The mineral resources of the republic are very large. About 90% of the USSR's coal deposits and over 50% of its iron and petroleum reserves are located in the republic. The Kuznetsk Basin encloses the world's second-largest coalfield, yielding in size only to the Appalachian reserves of the United States. Other coalfields are in the European Arctic, in areas south of Moscow, in the Urals, and along the Trans-Siberian Railroad throughout eastern Siberia. The largest iron deposits occur south of Moscow and in the Urals. The main oil fields are in the Ural-Volga region and the northern Caucasus, but huge deposits have also been discovered in western Siberia.

The Urals contain almost every known mineral, including sizable reserves of asbestos, bauxite, chromium, copper, nickel, phosphates, potash, sulfur, and zinc. The Kola Peninsula is the largest Soviet producer of phosphate fertilizer, and eastern Siberia mines most of the USSR's gold. The world's largest peat fields lie between Leningrad and Moscow and are mined extensively for fuel. Uranium deposits exist north of Leningrad, in the Urals, and in eastern Siberia.

Manufactures. Approximately two thirds of Soviet industry is in the RSFSR. From west to east the republic contains five main industrial concentrations: Leningrad, Moscow, the Volga Valley, the Urals, and the Kuznetsk Basin. Leningrad is the largest seaport and shipbuilding center of the RSFSR and is second only to Moscow as an urban industrial center. The Moscow industrial region, which includes the capital and surrounding districts, is the greatest industrial area of the republic. Most Soviet precision machines and textiles are manufactured there, and Moscow itself is a major center of the aircraft industry. Comparatively new industrially is the Volga Valley, which is a large producer of oil, gas, automobiles, tractors, airplanes, and riverboats. The Urals are the most important center for ferrous and nonferrous metallurgy. Nitrates, heavy machinery, railway rolling stock, tractors, and tanks are other important Ural products. Least developed is the Kuznetsk Basin, which, however, is the largest coal producer.

The republic produces about half the pig iron and chemical fertilizer and more than half the steel, machine tools, cement, and electric power in the USSR. It accounts for over 80% of the country's petroleum products and cotton textiles. Other leading products include motor vehicles, tractors, farm machinery, locomotives, railroad cars, cranes, computers, synthetic rubber, plastics, shoes, and medicines. Its industrial output is exceeded only by the United States.

The republic ships to other republics of the USSR machinery of all types, motor vehicles, railway rolling stock, airplanes, chemical fertilizer, synthetic dyes, rubber products, textiles, lumber, wood products, paper, and books. Its major imports from the rest of the USSR are coal, iron, oil and petroleum products, nonferrous metals, grain, cotton, silk, wool, hides, meat, butter, and fruit.

Transportation. Transportation is poorly developed in the RSFSR. There are few long-distance paved highways, and of the many large rivers only the Volga and its tributaries are used intensively for inland shipping. The huge Soviet-built canals—White Sea-Baltic, Moscow (formerly Moscow-Volga), and Volga-Don—usually operate below capacity. Coastal shipping is hampered by the freezing of most Arctic and Pacific ports each winter.

The backbone of the republic's transportation is the railroad network, which in European Russia is fairly dense and large. Most of Siberia, however, has only two major railroads—the largely electrified Trans-Siberian and the South Siberian, which extends from north Central Asia to the Lena River. Aviation is well developed, with airlines serving very remote regions, but sleds, sledges, carts, and pack animals are still used in the tundra and the northern forests.

Cultural Development. The RSFSR is a land of extremes. In contrast with the backwardness of the north, the republic as a whole has the highest cultural development of the USSR. About 70% of the country's scientists, engineers, and technicians are employed in the republic, and the Moscow and Leningrad oblasts alone contain 40% of the Soviet scientific research institutes and 70% of the industrial researchers. The Moscow and Leningrad ballets and the Moscow Opera are world famous. The two cities are also the leading educational centers of the country. The other Soviet republics copy the Russian republic's school system and law code, and most Soviet books are printed in the republic, particularly in Moscow and Leningrad.

Natives of other Soviet republics often resent cultural and economic domination by the RSFSR as unjust, compulsory Russification. In his last years, Joseph Stalin encouraged this Russification, which his successors have modified slightly. The vast size and industrial importance of the republic, however, naturally give it power.

Government. Like other Soviet republics, the RSFSR has a formal government consisting of a Supreme Soviet (legislature), elected on the basis of proportional representation; a presidium (standing legislative committee); and a council of ministers (cabinet). It has, however, fewer cabinet ministries than other Soviet republics, since USSR ministries govern the RSFSR directly in certain fields, such as police, the armed forces, and foreign affairs. Another distinctive feature is the existence of a special bureau for RSFSR affairs within the central committee of the USSR Communist party. Though ostensibly a democracy, the republic is in practice ruled by the Communist leaders of the USSR.

History. When the Bolsheviks seized power in Russia in November 1917, they at first permitted the larger minority peoples to secede. The remaining Russian territory was organized as the Russian Soviet Federated Socialist Republic. On July 10, 1918, the republic received its first constitution, which was federal in form and provided for autonomous republics, autonomous oblasts, and national districts for the small minority peoples remaining within the Russian federation.

During 1918–1920 much of the Russian republic itself rebelled against the rule of the Communists, restricting the domain of the new republic to part of European Russia. By 1920, however, the republic had reconquered most of the seceding areas, whose subsequent treatment was not uniform. The Ukraine, Belorussia, and the Caucasus were forced to become Soviet republics tightly allied with the RSFSR. Central Asia, although it was ethnically non-Russian, was reannexed by the RSFSR.

In 1922, as a result of RSFSR pressure, the Ukrainian, Belorussian, and Transcaucasian Soviet republics joined the RSFSR to form a new nation: the Union of Soviet Socialist Republics (USSR). A USSR constitution drafted by Stalin was formally adopted on July 6, 1923. In 1924, Uzbekistan and Turkmenia were detached from the republic, and in 1925 they became the fifth and sixth constituent republics of the USSR. Then, in 1929, the Tadzhik republic was created from RSFSR territory. The new USSR constitution of 1936 formed the Kazakh and Kirghiz republics from RSFSR regions. These five administrative changes removed all of Soviet Central Asia from the republic, which henceforth was confined to the predominantly Russian-inhabited Siberia and parts of the European Soviet Union.

In 1940 the Karelo-Finnish republic was formed, partly from newly annexed Finnish territory and partly from the Karelian autonomous republic of the northwestern RSFSR. In 1956, however, the RSFSR reannexed Karelia, which was reduced to the status of an autonomous republic. The official explanation for reincorporation was that Russians far outnumbered Karelians and Finns in the republic.

As a result of the USSR's victory in World War II, the RSFSR also annexed the East Prussian region of Königsberg, which was renamed Kalingrad oblast, as well as additional Finnish territory, Tuva, the Kuril Islands, and Southern Sakhalin.

During the 1970's the Soviet government attempted to slow industrial expansion in the European sector of the Russian republic and to accelerate exploitation of the huge new Siberian gas and oil fields.

ELLSWORTH RAYMOND
New York University

RUSSIAN THISTLE, a bushy weed with prickly leaves that is particularly troublesome in grainfields. Also known as tumbleweed, the Russian thistle (*Salsola kali tenuifolia*) is a member of the goosefoot family, Chenopodiaceae. It is native to Europe and Asia but now also grows wild in North America, particularly in prairie and plains regions. It reaches a height of about 2 feet (60 cm) and has a branched stem and inconspicuous flowers. In autumn the dead and dried branches form a mass that breaks away from the stem as tumbleweed. The tumbleweed is widely dispersed by the wind, scattering seeds.

RUSSIAN WOLFHOUND. See BORZOI.

RUSSO-FINNISH WAR. See FINLAND—*History;* WORLD WAR II—*Early Campaigns.*

RUSSO-JAPANESE WAR, a conflict fought in 1904–1905 that resulted in a victory for Japan. As a result, Japan gained territorial rights in Asia and won recognition as a major power.

In the late 1890's the Japanese were concerned over spreading Russian influence in Manchuria and Korea, on the mainland of Asia nearest to the Japanese islands. When the Russians acquired a lease on Port Arthur (Lushun) on the Liaotung Peninsula in China and established a naval base there, Japan decided to act.

On Feb. 8, 1904, without a declaration of war, Japanese torpedo boats struck suddenly at the Russian fleet in Port Arthur harbor. Japanese warships bombarded the shore batteries and began a close blockade of the port. Japan formally declared war on Feb. 10.

In the struggle that followed, Russia suffered from grave disadvantages. Its military establishment in the Far East was not large, and reinforcements and supplies had to pass over the single-track Trans-Siberian railroad, which stretched 5,500 miles (8,800 km) to Moscow. Japan, on the other hand, possessing plenty of shipping, had only a short sea passage from its home bases to the fighting zones.

In May 1904, the Russian army was driven out of Korea into Manchuria, where the principal land actions of the war were fought. The Japanese pushed northward, and in the Battle of Mukden (Feb. 21–March 10, 1905) broke the Russian power of resistance. Port Arthur had surrendered on Jan. 2, 1905, after a seven-month siege.

The main Russian naval strength was the Baltic Sea fleet, commanded by Adm. Zinovi P. Rozhestvensky, which left its home ports on Oct. 15, 1904, for a 10,000-mile (16,000-km) voyage to the Far East. In the North Sea a few days later, alarmed by a rumor of Japanese torpedo boats in the vicinity, the fleet fired on British fishing trawlers, damaging several of them and killing some fishermen. The incident nearly brought war between Britain and Russia.

Rounding the Cape of Good Hope, the Russian fleet headed for the base at Vladivostok, Siberia. On May 27, 1905, in Tsushima Strait, between Japan and Korea, it was intercepted by the Japanese fleet, commanded by Adm. Togo Heihachiro.

The ensuing battle was the first fleet action between ironclad warships. Japanese leadership, discipline, and gunnery were far superior. When the action ended the next day, only 6 of about 30 Russian ships escaped. The rest had been sunk or captured.

Peace talks, arranged by President Theodore Roosevelt, led to a treaty signed at Portsmouth, N. H., on Sept. 6, 1905. Russia yielded Port Arthur and the southern half of the island of Sakhalin and evacuated Manchuria. Japan's influence in Korea was recognized.

RUSSO-TURKISH WARS, a series of wars between Russia and Turkey that began in the 17th century and ended in the 20th century. The Turkish conquest of the Balkans, Bessarabia, the Crimea, the southern Ukraine, and the western Caucasus during the 15th and 16th centuries blocked Muscovite Russia from the Black Sea. As czarist Russia slowly expanded southward from Moscow, wars with Turkey were inevitable. The first conflicts were guerrilla raids by Don Cossacks against Turkish cities and ships. In 1637 these Cossacks captured the Turkish fortress of Azov near the mouth of the Don River. In 1642, however, Czar Michael Romanov refused to accept the fortress from the Cossacks because it was too remote from Moscow and too difficult for Russia to defend. Azov was soon recaptured by the Turks.

The first formal war between Russia and Turkey was fought during 1677–1681, when Sultan Mohammed IV invaded the eastern Ukraine, which Russia had recently annexed. The invasion was repelled, and Czar Fyodor III ended the war by concluding a 20-year truce. Five years later, in 1686, Russia and Poland jointly attacked Turkey in order to seize Turkish territory bordering on that of the two Christian allies. Russian invasions of the Crimea in 1687 and 1689 were unsuccessful. But Peter I the Great captured Azov (1696), and it was left in Russian hands by a 30-year truce concluded in 1700.

In 1710, Charles XII of Sweden, whom Peter had defeated at Poltava in 1709, induced Turkey to declare war on Russia. Peter's attempt to liberate the Balkans ended with his defeat near the Prut River, and to secure peace Russia returned Azov to Turkey. In 1736–1739, Russia, Austria, and Persia jointly attacked Turkey. Russian attempts to annex Bessarabia and the Crimea failed, however, and the Peace of Belgrade gave Moscow only a small Ukrainian area.

Two wars during the reign of Catherine II the Great finally gave Russia outlets on the Black Sea. Catherine began the first war (1768–1774) to punish Turkey for interfering in the internal politics of Russian-dominated Poland. Russian troops won great victories, capturing Azov, the Crimea, and Bessarabia. After a voyage from the Baltic Sea, a Russian fleet destroyed the Turkish Navy at Çeşme off the Turkish coast in 1770. By the Treaty of Kuchuk Kainarji, which terminated the war, Russia received the northern Caucasus, Azov, the eastern Ukrainian coast, and a protectorate over the Christians of Bessarabia. In addition, Turkey promised not to persecute its other Christian subjects. Russia later claimed that the treaty gave it a protectorate over all Christians under Turkish rule. Turkey also freed the Crimea, which Russia annexed in 1783.

Four years later, Turkey attacked Russia in order to regain the Crimea. Catherine's army invaded Bessarabia, and her fleet badly defeated the Turkish Navy in the Black Sea. By the Treaty of Jassy (1792), Turkey surrendered the western Ukrainian coast to Russia. The next war began in 1806, in the reign of Czar Alexander I. After a grave military defeat on the banks of the Danube, Turkey signed the Peace of Bucharest (1812), surrendering Bessarabia to Russia.

Wars After 1815. Having obtained the entire north coast of the Black Sea, Russia wished to control the Straits connecting this sea with the Mediterranean. To extend Russian influence toward the Straits, Czar Nicholas I fought two wars aiding Balkan revolts against Turkish rule. The first began in 1827 with a joint Russo-British-French defeat of a Turko-Egyptian fleet at Navarino. Then, declaring war in 1828, Russia invaded Bulgaria and forced Turkey to sign the Treaty of Adrianople (1829), which recognized Greek autonomy, made Russia the protector of Serbia and Rumania, and gave Russia most of the Caucasian coast on the Black Sea.

The next conflict was the Crimean War of 1853–1856, which Nicholas began after Turkey had refused to ally itself with Moscow or to permit Russian protection of all Christians in the Ottoman Empire. In 1854, Britain and France entered the war to aid Turkey. Badly defeated, Russia removed its warships from the Black Sea, lost part of Bessarabia, and relinquished its claim to exclusive protection over Ottoman Christians, by the terms of the Treaty of Paris in 1856.

During 1877–1878, Russia and its Balkan allies attacked Turkey to aid Bosnian, Hercegovinian, and Bulgarian revolts against Turkish rule. Russian troops swept through Bulgaria and reached the Sea of Marmara. By the Treaty of San Stefano (March 3, 1878), Rumania, Serbia, and Montenegro were freed from Turkish rule, Bosnia and Hercegovina became autonomous, Russia gained portions of Turkish Armenia, and a Russian protectorate was established over a huge autonomous Bulgaria extending to the Aegean Sea. Alarmed by the Russian success, the great powers forced Russia to accept the Treaty of Berlin (July 13, 1878), which transferred Bosnia and Hercegovina to Austria, withdrew Bulgaria from the Aegean, and abolished the Russian protectorate over Bulgaria.

When World War I began in 1914, Turkey quickly joined Austria and Germany against Russia. This Russo-Turkish war was ended by the Treaty of Brest-Litovsk (March 3, 1918), which gave Turkey the chief Armenian cities previously annexed by Russia. After the Russian civil war, Soviet Russia made peace with Turkey on March 16, 1921. Batumi and part of Armenia were placed under Soviet rule, and Kars, which had been annexed by czarist Russia, was restored to Turkey. Thereafter, Soviet-Turkish relations varied from friendship in the 1920's to verbal hostility from the 1930's onward, resulting from the USSR's expressed determination to secure control of the Straits. By the late 1960's, however, a thaw developed in Russo-Turkish relations, and the USSR began rendering sizable technical aid for the construction of Turkish industrial enterprises. See also EASTERN QUESTION.

ELLSWORTH RAYMOND
New York University

RUST, in botany, any of a large group of fungi that are parasites on other plants. Rusts attack all parts of a plant, causing a plant disease, also called rust. When attacked by the rust, the affected parts of the host plant develops reddish brown or orange pustular or blisterlike spots and streaks. The disease stunts the plant's growth and leads to the destruction of the plant.

Rust fungi have tiny threadlike filaments called *hyphae.* The hyphae enter a host plant through a stomate, or small opening, in a leaf or stem and obtain nourishment from the plant. The rust reproduces through spores, generally borne in an external club-shaped structure called a *basidium.* Autoecious rusts spend their entire life cycle on a single host plant, while heteroecious rusts require different hosts at various stages of their life cycle.

Most autoecious rusts are not serious economic pests. Two of them, the asparagus rust (*Puccinia asparagi*) and the flax rust (*Melampsora lini*), have been largely controlled by the development of species of asparagus and flax that are resistant to rust attack. Many heteroecious rusts, however, cause serious economic losses. One of the most important of these is the so-called stem rust of wheat, or the barberry-wheat rust (*P. graminis*). This species parasitizes on the barberry plant for part of its life cycle, causing little or no damage to the barberry, but during another stage of its life cycle, it attacks wheat and some other grains, causing severe damage. Efforts to control this rust have included the eradication of the barberry host and the development through hybridization and selection of strains of wheat resistant to the fungus.

Rusts make up the order Uredinales of the class Basidiomycetes of the division Fungi.

RUST, in metallurgy, is a reddish coating that forms on iron when it is corroded by the action of moist air. See also CORROSION.

RUSTICATION. See ARCHITECTURE—*Glossary of Architectural Terms.*

RUSTIN, rus'tən, **Bayard** (1910–   ), American civil rights strategist. He was born in West Chester, Pa., on March 17, 1910. He attended Wilberforce University, Cheyney State Teachers College, and the City College of New York. From 1941 to 1953 he was a staff member of the Fellowship of Reconciliation, and he was an early promoter of the Congress of Racial Equality. He was imprisoned as a conscientious objector during World War II.

Rustin helped to organize the civil rights march on Washington in 1963. His resistance to war and injustice took him to Africa, Europe, and Asia, where he provided leadership for indigenous protest. In 1964 he became executive director of the A. Philip Randolph Institute in New York City, a clearinghouse for civil rights groups.

C. ERIC LINCOLN
Union Theological Seminary, New York

RUSTON is a town in northern Louisiana, the seat of Lincoln parish, situated 31 miles (49 km) west of Monroe. The area has natural gas wells and farms that raise cotton, corn, vegetables, fruit, and cattle. Ruston's industries process lumber, milk products, and cottonseed oil, and manufacture industrial rollers and soft-drink bottles. Louisiana Polytechnic Institute is situated here. The town was settled in 1884 and has a mayor-council government. Population: 20,585.

RUTABAGA, rōōt'ə-bā-gə, an edible plant closely related to the turnip and grown for its smooth, thick, yellow or white tuber, or underground stem, which is fed to livestock and also eaten by man, particularly in Europe. It is also sometimes known as swede, Swedish turnip, and Russian turnip.

A biennial, the rutabaga (*Brassica napobrassica*) is a member of the mustard family, Cruciferae. It grows to a height of about 3 feet (90 cm) and has long, thick, shiny bluish green leaves and yellowish flowers. It grows best in northern areas with a cool climate. The flesh of the tuber is solid, stores well, and has a characteristic sweet flavor.

RUTEBEUF, rüt-bûf', French poet and satirist, who was a major figure in 13th century French literature. His works include exquisite lyric verse, as well as satires, *fabliaux,* and a play, *Le Miracle de Théophile.* See also FRANCE—*Literature* (The Middle Ages).

RUTGERS UNIVERSITY is a state-supported, co-educational institution of higher learning, with campuses in New Brunswick, Newark, and Camden, N. J. The school was founded as Queen's College by royal charter in 1766, the eighth college established in the American colonies. It acquired its New Brunswick site in 1808. In 1825 it was named Rutgers College in honor of its benefactor, the New York philanthropist Henry Rutgers. It became Rutgers College and The State University of New Jersey in 1917 and took its present name, Rutgers—The State University, in 1956.

The university consists of nine undergraduate colleges—two of arts and sciences, in New Brunswick (1766; also Rutgers College, for men) and in Newark; Douglass (1918; formerly New Jersey College for Women, for women); South Jersey; agriculture and environmental science; Livingston (for study of contemporary problems); engineering; nursing; and pharmacy. There are also two schools of law; a medical school; a graduate school; graduate schools of business administration, education, library service, and social work; and University College, an extension service in Camden, Jersey City, New Brunswick, Newark, and Paterson. The university offers bachelor's, master's, doctor's, and professional law degrees.

Enrollment in the early 1970's was about 32,000. The faculty numbered about 1,600.

RUTH, Babe (1895–1948), American baseball player. A powerful man, he hit 714 home runs during 22 seasons in the major leagues, a spectacular feat that revolutionized the game. Ruth was born in Baltimore, Md., on Feb. 6, 1895. He learned to play baseball at St. Mary's Industrial School in Baltimore, where he was sent when he was seven years old. He began his professional career with the Baltimore team in the International League in 1914, but before the close of the season he was sold to the Boston Red Sox of the American League. He became a notable lefthanded pitcher, but because of his prowess as a hitter he frequently was played at first base or in the outfield to insure his presence in the lineup. In 1919 he hit 29 home runs, regarded then as a remarkable feat. On Jan. 3, 1920, he was sold to the New York Yankees of the American League for $125,000.

In his 15 years with the Yankees, where he usually played right field, he dominated professional baseball. His left-handed slugging, always aiming at a home run, became the universal fashion, displacing the strategy of finesse. Although many followed his style, no one during his era approached his record of 714 home runs. He also hit 15 home runs in the 10 World Series in which he participated. He hit more than 50 in four different years; his peak was 60 in 1927. His lifetime batting average was .342. During his career he set or tied 76 batting or pitching records.

He was the greatest crowd attraction in baseball, and the highest paid player of his time. His top salary was $80,000 a year in 1930 and 1931. He left the Yankees after the 1934 season and shifted to the National League, playing briefly with the Boston Braves in 1935 and ending his activity as a coach with the Brooklyn Dodgers in 1938.

Statistics cannot describe Ruth's impact on baseball. His thunderous hitting captured the

Babe Ruth, baseball's great home-run hitter

public's imagination and restored its faith in the professional game, which had been severely shaken by the "Black Sox" World Series scandal of 1919. In 1936 he was one of the first players chosen for the baseball hall of fame.

Ruth was a tall man with a massive chest and shoulders and remarkably slender legs. His best weight was 215 pounds. His engaging simplicity and his theatrical gestures endeared him to millions. He was a born actor and struck out with as lusty and magnificent an air as he hit a home run. He was idolized particularly by children and returned their feeling warmly, often visiting hospitals with cheering words and gifts of autographed baseballs. A few years before his death in New York City on Aug. 16, 1948, he established the Babe Ruth Foundation for underprivileged children, and bequeathed to it a large part of his estate.

RUTH, BOOK OF, an Old Testament book that relates the story of the Jewess Naomi, an emigrant to Moab, where both her husband and two sons, who had married local women, died. She returned to Bethlehem with her daughter-in-law Ruth, who refused to desert her. A kinsman of Naomi's dead husband, Boaz, noticed Ruth as she gleaned barley. At Naomi's urging Ruth managed to remind Boaz of his duty to marry her under the levirate law. Boaz recognized his obligation and, after another relative officially renounced a prior claim, he married Ruth. According to the genealogy in 4:17b-22, which was a later interpolation, a son born to them is attached to the family of David.

The story of Ruth is fictional. It uses symbolic names: Naomi loses sons named Mahlon ("Weakness") and Chilion ("Consumption"), and she is deserted by a daughter-in-law named Or-Pah ("Disappointment"). Its careful construction and rapid narrative pace are typical of the ancient short story that is sometimes called a novella in technical writings. So is its didactic purpose. The story teaches the value of fidelity to family and to custom and emphasizes the benevolent omnipotence of God's providence, which extends even to the foreigner Ruth (2:12).

Concern for fidelity to traditional ties characterized the postexilic restoration, and the position of foreigners was a problem in Judea in the 5th century B. C. The Book of Ruth exalting a Moabitess seems to be a quiet polemic against the harsh treatment of foreign women witnessed under Ezra and Nehemiah (Ezra 10; Nehemiah 13:1–3). Further, the short story was a popular literary form in postexilic literature, as, for example, the books of Jonah and Esther. Finally, the Book of Ruth looks back to old times (4:7) and uses legal language characteristic of developed Judaism. Form and content, then, point to a late date of composition, probably the end of the 5th century B. C.

Palestinian Jews placed Ruth in the Writings, the third and latest part of the canon, but Hellenic Jews received it into the historical books. This divergence indicates acceptance into the canon after the development of the Diaspora, probably in the 2d century B. C.

DENNIS J. McCARTHY, S. J.
Pontifical Biblical Institute, Rome

RUTHENES, rōō-thēnz′, is the medieval Latin term for the inhabitants of ancient Kievan Russia. In modern times it has been used as a synonym for those Ukrainians who are also known as Little Russians, for the Ukrainian-speaking population of the regions of Galicia and Bukovina, and for those inhabitants of the northeastern districts of Hungary who speak a local Ukrainian dialect.

The term "Little Russians" began to fall into disuse before 1914, although the Czarist Russian government employed it officially until 1917. But neighboring countries with Ukrainian-speaking minorities continued to call these minorities Ruthenians. In addition, Ukrainian-speaking people who claimed a nationality distinct from Ukrainian or Russian retained the name.

The appellation "Ruthene" was most commonly used for the Ukrainian elements that were for a long time subjects of Poland and Hungary. They speak a Ukrainian dialect, and though they were formerly Eastern Orthodox, most later acknowledged the supremacy of the pope but preserved their own rites. After the partitions of Poland at the end of the 18th century, its Ruthenian subjects were divided between Russia and Austria. In 1806, Austria created the Uniate metropolitan archbishopric of Lwów (now Lvov) and in the same year restored the Lwów University. The Ruthenes in Hungary inhabited the territory southwest of the central Carpathian Mountains, along the present borders of Czechoslovakia, Hungary, and Rumania. Most of the people are engaged in agriculture, and the region, heavily forested and mountainous, was largely undeveloped until after World War II.

After World War I. At the end of World War I many Ruthenes, invoking the right to self-determination, aspired to become part of an independent or autonomous Ukrainian state, and a short-lived independent Ukrainian republic was proclaimed. The new state was overwhelmed by Bolshevik forces, and became part of the Soviet Union as the Ukrainian Soviet Socialist Republic. The Austrian Ruthenes were divided between Poland, which received Galicia, and Rumania, which received Bukovina. The Ruthenes of Bessarabia, a Russian province before 1918, went to Rumania.

On May 8, 1919, the Central National Council of the Ruthenes in Hungary declared union with Czechoslovakia, within which an autonomous province of Subcarpathian Ruthenia (Czech Podkarpatská Rus) was founded. The area of the province, whose capital was Uzhgorod, was 4,900 square miles (12,690 sq km). Its population was 725,000, of which 450,000, or about 62%, were Ruthenes.

Subcarpathian Ruthenia was the only region inhabited by Ruthenians to receive special political status between the two world wars. They enjoyed much more national and cultural freedom than their co-nationals in Poland, Rumania, and the USSR. But many of the Ruthenes in Czechoslovakia were dissatisfied in their new country, largely because they were never given the autonomy that had been promised them. The political situation was aggravated by the Great Depression and the general political instability of Europe. The Ruthenes desired either a full autonomy inside Czechoslovakia, or unification with the Ukrainian SSR, or full independence. Despite progress in all phases of life under Czechoslovak administration, Subcarpathian Ruthenia remained the most backward part of the state and had the highest rate of illiteracy.

Later History. On Oct. 11, 1938, after the historic Munich agreement, an autonomous Ruthenian government was formed within Czechoslovakia. But as a result of the so-called Vienna Award of Nov. 2, 1938, Germany and Italy gave Hungary the southern part of Ruthenia, including Uzhgorod (Hungarian Ungvár). What was left of autonomous Ruthenia was administered from Khust, the new capital. On March 15, 1939, after the second partition of Czechoslovakia, an independent Carpatho-Ukrainian state was proclaimed. This was followed by immediate occupation by the Hungarians.

During World War II the former Czechoslovak Ruthenia was a part of Hungary. In the meantime, the Soviet Union acquired the Ukrainians of Poland as a result of the Molotov-Ribbentrop pact of 1939 and retained most of them after World War II. The Soviet Union has controlled Bessarabia and the northern part of Bukovina since 1944.

Czechoslovak Ruthenia, which had been freed from the Hungarians by Soviet troops in 1944, was briefly returned to Czechoslovakia. By the treaty of June 29, 1945, however, it was transferred to the Soviet Union and became the Transcarpathian oblast of the Ukrainian republic on Jan. 22, 1946. In that year, the Soviet government suppressed the Ruthenian Church and imprisoned some of its clerics. In 1965 the Pope designated Josif Slipyj, the head of the Ruthenian church, as cardinal.

The area of the oblast is approximately 4,980 square miles (12,900 sq km), and its population (1970) is 1,057,000, of which about 70% are Ukrainians. About 28% of the population is urban. The capital is Uzhgorod, which has a population (1970) of 65,000. See also TRANSCARPATHIAN OBLAST.

WAYNE S. VUCINICH
Stanford University

RUTHENIUM, rōō-thē′nē-əm, is a hard white metal in the platinum group of chemical elements. Its discovery in 1844 is generally credited to an Estonian chemist, Karl Kraus, although the oxide of the metal was first isolated in 1827 by Emile Osann, a German physician. The name ruthenium derives from a medieval Latin name for Russia, since the metal was first found in the Ural Mountains in association with other ores of the platinum group. Such ores, which also occur in North and South America, are the source of ruthenium, which is extracted from them by a complex chemical process.

Uses. Ruthenium is alloyed with metals such as iridium, osmium, palladium, platinum, and rhodium to increase their hardness. It is also alloyed with titanium to improve the corrosion resistance of that metal. Ruthenium is electrodeposited to make very durable electrical contacts, and it is a useful catalyst in some chemical reactions.

Properties. Ruthenium is located in Group VIII of the periodic table of the elements. It can exist in oxidation states of 1 through +8, but the most common valence is +3. Its atomic number is 44, and its atomic weight is 101.07. The metal has a specific gravity of 12.4, and its hardness is comparable to that of iridium. It melts at about 2250° C (4080° F). There are 16 isotopes of the element. Seven are stable, of which the most abundant is ruthenium-102.

Ruthenium is very resistant to corrosion, but it oxidizes to the tetravalent and octavalent forms (RuO_2 and RuO_4) when heated to about 800° C (1470° F). The octavalent form explodes at that temperature. The metal is not attacked by hot or cold acids except in the presence of potassium chlorate, when it again oxidizes explosively. It combines with halogens and sodium peroxide or other caustic oxidizing mixtures. The most common compound of the metal is ruthenium trichloride ($RuCl_3$). Numerous complex salts are also known.

Further Reading: Avtokratova, Tatiana, *Analytical Chemistry of Ruthenium* (Davey 1964).

RUTHERFORD, ruth′ər-fərd, **Ernest** (1871–1937), British physicist who won the 1908 Nobel Prize in chemistry for working out the theory of radioactive disintegration of elements. Rutherford was born in Spring Grove (now Brightwater), near Nelson, New Zealand, on Aug. 30, 1871. He attended Canterbury College, Christchurch, New Zealand, receiving his undergraduate degree in 1894 and winning a scholarship to Trinity College, Cambridge University. There he worked under the tutelage of the physicist Joseph John Thomson. Rutherford first devoted himself to a subject dear to Thomson's heart—the conduction of electricity through gases—but this work familiarized him with the delicate experimental technique needed in his forthcoming studies in the field of radioactivity. It was only a short while after Rutherford arrived in England that the German physicist Wilhelm Konrad Roentgen, in 1895, announced the discovery of X rays and in effect began the revolution in modern physics that was to include the quantum theory, radioactivity, and relativity.

In 1898, Rutherford became professor of physics at McGill University in Montreal. There, with the English chemist Frederick Soddy, he applied himself for almost 10 years, to untangling the processes of radioactive disintegration. Al-

NATIONAL PORTRAIT GALLERY
Ernest Rutherford pioneered in studies of the atom.

pha and beta radiation—which Rutherford named—were carefully distinguished and then used to follow radioactive transformations of uranium and thorium through chemical manipulations. Rutherford showed that radioactivity involved a natural transmutation of the radioactive elements. He returned to England in 1907 as professor of physics at Victoria University of Manchester.

Perhaps Rutherford's most important investigation was that of the scattering of alpha particles by thin gold sheets. Together with his assistants Hans Geiger and Ernest Marsden, he used alpha particles to probe the structure of the atom. In the course of this work he proved that the alpha particle was really the nucleus of the helium atom. He further concluded that the atom must consist of a small positively charged nucleus around which electrons circle. It was this model that Niels Bohr used in 1913 as the basis for his famous model of the atom. In 1917, Rutherford became the first man to change one element to another when he bombarded nitrogen atoms with alpha particles and converted them to oxygen atoms.

Rutherford was honored in England by being appointed director of the Cavendish laboratory at Cambridge in 1919 and was raised to the peerage in 1931 as 1st Baron Rutherford of Nelson. He died in Cambridge on Oct. 19, 1937.

L. Pearce Williams°, *Cornell University*

Further Reading: Andrade, Edward N., *Rutherford and the Nature of the Atom* (Doubleday 1964).

RUTHERFORD, ruth′ər-fərd, **Margaret** (1892–1972), British actress, noted for the eccentrics that she portrayed in a career that spanned 47 years and included roles in more than 100 plays and 30 films. She was born in London on May 11, 1892. At first a teacher of elocution and piano, she began her theatrical career when she joined the Old Vic as a drama student in 1925. Her performance in *Short Story* (1935) brought

Margaret Rutherford in *Murder, She Said* (1962)

her recognition as a comedienne, and many other successes followed. She recreated some of her stage roles in films, among them *Blithe Spirit* (1945), *The Importance of Being Earnest* (1947), and *The Happiest Days of Your Life* (1950). Her film work probably became best known when she played the eccentric sleuth Jane Marple in the Agatha Christie mysteries *Murder, She Said* (1962), *Murder Ahoy!* (1964), and others.

She was married in 1945 to producer-actor Stringer Davis, with whom she often appeared. For her services to the theater she was named a Dame of the British Empire in 1967. She died in Buckinghamshire, England, on May 22, 1972.

HOWARD SUBER
University of California, Los Angeles

RUTHERFORD, Mark. See WHITE, WILLIAM HALE.

RUTHERFORD, ruth′ər-fərd, a borough in northeastern New Jersey, is in Bergen county, 9 miles (14 km) west of midtown New York City. Fairleigh Dickinson University was founded here in 1942 and one of its three coequal campuses is here. The poet William Carlos Williams was a resident of Rutherford.

The community was laid out in 1862 on the Kingsland and Berry land grants, and was originally known as Boiling Springs. In 1875 the name was changed in honor of John Rutherford, a U. S. senator from New Jersey (1791–1798), who was a friend of John Jay, first chief justice of the United States, whose farm was nearby on the Passaic River. The borough was incorporated in 1881. Population: 19,068.

RUTHVEN RAID, rōōth′vən, the arrest and detention of King James VI of Scotland by a group of nobles resentful of the influence on him of several favorites, notably Esme Stuart, the 1st duke of Lennox.

On Aug. 23, 1582, the king, then 16 years old, was forced or persuaded to go to the home of William Ruthven, the 4th Baron Ruthven, who had recently been created 1st earl of Gowrie, at Perth. There James was detained by the conspirators, who wished him to accede to certain demands. Under pressure, the young king denounced Lennox and another close associate, the earl of Arran. James escaped in June 1583 and made Arran his chancellor, Lennox having died in France. Earl Gowrie was accused of treason, but pardoned.

RUTILE, rōō′tēl, or titanium dioxide, is the most common titanium mineral. It is used to coat welding rods and to color porcelains and in the production of paint and ink pigments, paper, glass, plastics, creams, and powders. Brookite and octahedrite are less common minerals with the same composition but different crystal structures. See also TITANIUM.

Crystals of rutile, ordinarily somewhat translucent, have a diamondlike luster and are reddish brown to black—the name "rutile" comes from Latin *rutilus*, or "red." Transparent crystals show fire and brilliance, but their low hardness reduces their suitability for gems.

Synthetic rutile is made by the flame-fusion process and is sold as a gem under the names titania and miridis, among others.

Rutile occurs in detrital black sands and in granite, pegmatite, schist, and other rocks, and in quartz veins in these rocks. One form of quartz containing needlelike rutile crystals is called *sagenite*. The largest rutile producer is Australia. Commercial quantities are found in Florida and Virginia in the United States.

Composition, TiO_2; hardness, 6–6.5; specific gravity, 4.2; crystal system, tetragonal.

RUTLAND, rut′lənd, a county in east central England, is in the East Midlands about 30 miles (50 km) southwest of The Wash, an inlet of the North Sea. Rutland, sometimes called Rutlandshire, is the smallest county (152 square miles, 390 sq km) in England. It consists principally of undulating agricultural land not more than several hundred feet above sea level. Near the center of the county is the Vale of Catmose. The Welland River forms Rutland's southern border, separating it from Northampton.

There are no large industries in Rutland. Barley, wheat, potatoes, and oats are grown in the county. Cheese-making is important. Ironstone, limestone, and sandstone from Rutland's quarries were used in building Buckingham Palace and other notable structures. The county has many fine stone houses and churches.

Oakham is the principal town and administrative center of Rutland. There are a few small industries in and around Oakham. At Uppingham there is a boys' school that was founded in the 16th century.

In the 10th century, Rutland was given to Queen Elfthryth by her husband, Edgar, king of the English. In the next century it passed to Edith, wife of Edward the Confessor. During the Middle Ages the Forest of Rutland was a favorite hunting area. Keepers of the forest are recorded as early as the 12th century. The hunting tradition was preserved by a notable pack of foxhounds at Cottesmore. Population: (1961) 23,504.

GORDON STOKES
Author of "English Place-Names"

RUTLAND, rut'lənd, a city in western Vermont, the seat of Rutland county, is situated in the valley of Otter Creek, about 50 miles (80 km) southwest of Montpelier. The range of the Green Mountains, dominated by Killington Peak (4,241 feet or 1,290 meters), the second highest in Vermont, is a few miles east of the city. The mountains offer year-round recreational opportunities.

Rutland is known as the Marble City because of the nearby marble quarries. The city has stone-finishing plants and makes stone-working machinery. Other manufactured products include scales, fire clay, jet turbine components, medical supplies, dresses, and printed business forms.

Rutland was chartered in 1761 and settled in 1769. It was named for Rutland, Mass., the town from which the first land grantee came. It became a village in 1847 and a city in 1892, with a mayor-council government. Population: 18,436.

RUTLEDGE, rut'lij, **Ann** (1814?–1835), American historical figure. She was the daughter of James Rutledge, a tavern owner at New Salem, Ill., where in 1831 she became acquainted with Abraham Lincoln. She was betrothed to John McNamar, a storekeeper using the name McNeil, who was on a prolonged visit to the East when she died in Sand Ridge, Ill., on Aug. 25, 1835. There is evidence that Lincoln was deeply moved by her death. In 1866, Lincoln's former law partner, William Herndon, spun the romantic story of their deep love, which has become a legend. Most historians regard it as unsubstantial, supported only by vague recollections and suppositions long after the event.

RUTLEDGE, rut'lij, **Edward** (1749–1800), American lawyer and legislator, who was the youngest signer of the Declaration of Independence. Born in Charles Town, S. C., on Nov. 23, 1749, the youngest of seven children, Edward followed the conservative path and views of his brother, John. After studying law in London, he returned to South Carolina in 1773, was admitted to the bar, and married the daughter of the wealthiest planter in the colony.

In 1774, through the influence of John Rutledge, Edward was elected to the South Carolina legislature, which later that year sent both brothers as delegates to the Continental Congress. With John absent in South Carolina, Edward vacillated on the independence issue, but finally voted favorably for the Declaration of Independence and signed it with the other delegates.

Returning to South Carolina in 1777, Rutledge became an artillery captain, was captured, imprisoned, and later freed in a prisoner exchange. From 1782 to 1798 he served in the state legislature, where he was staunchly conservative in his views, and developed a prosperous law partnership with Thomas Pinckney. Rutledge was a Federalist presidential elector in 1788, 1792, and 1796. Elected governor of South Carolina in 1798, he served until his death, on Jan. 23, 1800, in Charleston, S. C.

RUTLEDGE, rut'lij, **John** (1739–1800), American public official and judge, who was governor of South Carolina during the American Revolution. A delegate to the Convention of 1787, he was a signer of the U. S. Constitution.

Born in Charles Town (now Charleston), S. C., he studied law in London and returned to South Carolina in 1760. A member of the provincial legislature from 1761, he was a delegate to the Continental Congress (1774–1775), where he favored self-government within the British empire. He served on the committee that framed the constitution of South Carolina in 1776 and became president of the General Assembly. Distrustful of democracy, he resigned as president in protest against a move to liberalize the constitution.

As governor of South Carolina (1779–1782), Rutledge directed the war effort from North Carolina after Charleston fell. He was a delegate to the Congress of the Confederation (1782–1783) and was judge of the court of chancery of South Carolina (1784–1791). At the federal Convention of 1787, he reflected the views of wealthy planters and urged congressional election of the president. Appointed to the U. S. Supreme Court in 1789, he resigned to become chief justice of South Carolina in 1791. His appointment in 1795 as U. S. chief justice was not confirmed by the Senate after he publicly criticized Jay's Treaty. He died in Charleston, on July 18, 1800.

RUTLEDGE, rut'lij, **Wiley Blount, Jr.** (1894–1949), American judge, who was a liberal member of the Supreme Court, especially vigorous in his defense of civil liberties. He was born in Cloverport, Ky., on July 20, 1894. He was educated at the University of Wisconsin and taught in high schools in Indiana, New Mexico, and Colorado. After receiving a law degree at the University of Colorado, he was admitted to the bar and practiced law at Boulder, Colo. Subsequently he was associate professor of law at the University of Colorado, then professor and dean of the school of law at Washington University, St. Louis, and at the College of Law, State University of Iowa. In 1939, President Franklin D. Roosevelt named him an associate justice of the U. S. Court of Appeals in the District of Columbia, and four years later appointed him an associate justice of the Supreme Court of the United States. Here he served until his death on Sept. 10, 1949, at York, Me. He joined with Justices Hugo L. Black, Frank Murphy, and William O. Douglas as a consistent champion of civil liberties during the "rebirth" of the court after the conservative "Nine Old Men" period.

RUWENZORI RANGE, rōō-ən-zōr'ē, mountains in east central Africa, rising along the boundary between Uganda and Zaïre (formerly Congo), just north of the equator. The range is about 75 miles (120 km) long from north to south and about 40 miles (65 km) wide.

In contrast to the other elevated areas of East Africa, the Ruwenzori Range is not volcanic but is a remnant of the old Archean floor of Africa, which has proved resistant to erosion. A huge faulted block, it stands in lofty isolation in the western Great Rift Valley, bounded by lines of fracture. Lake Albert lies to the north and Lake Edward to the south.

Description. The higher sections of the Ruwenzori Range, consisting of snow-capped peaks and glaciers, are divided into six groups, all rising above 14,000 feet (4,200 meters). They are separated by deep gorges. The highest massif is Mt. Stanley (Ngaliema), which reaches an elevation of 16,763 feet (5,109 meters) at Margherita Peak.

Mountains of the Ruwenzori Range in the distance separate Uganda from Zaire.

Above 9,000 feet (2,700 meters) the Ruwenzori Range is almost continuously covered by heavy cloud. Humidity is always high, and the mean annual rainfall exceeds 200 inches (5,000 mm). The numerous swift torrents have cut deep gorgelike valleys on both flanks of the range. Those flowing west drain to the Semliki River, which links lakes Edward and Albert. The eastward-flowing streams are less rapid, and many enter Lake George, from which water reaches the Semliki by way of the Kazinga Channel and Lake Edward.

Vegetation. The range's lower slopes, formerly forested, are now mostly grass-covered up to 7,500 feet (2,300 meters). Some agriculture is practiced on these slopes. Above the grass, to about 11,000 feet (3,300 meters) are dense forests and bamboos. Higher still the vegetation consists of tree heaths, lobelias, and grass until the snow line is reached at about 14,000 feet (4,200 meters). There is evidence to suggest that in the past the snow line was as low as 4,000 feet (1,200 meters) above sea level.

Exploration. The Ruwenzori Range is commonly, though not universally, identified with the Mountains of the Moon, described by the ancient geographer Ptolemy as a source of the Nile River. The first European to see the range was the explorer Henry Morton Stanley, who called the mountains Ruwenzori ("rainmaker"). Margherita Peak was first scaled by an expedition led by the Duke of the Abruzzi in 1906.

Copper and cobalt are mined in the Ruwenzori's eastern foothills at Kilembe, Uganda.

ROBERT W. STEEL
University of Liverpool

RUY BLAS, roo′ē blàs, is a verse drama by Victor Hugo, written in 1838. Its plot, alternating gaiety with bloody tragedy, makes the play Hugo's most popular contribution to romanticism.

RUYSBROECK, rois′brōōk, **Jan van** (1293–1381), Flemish mystic writer. Ruysbroeck (or Ruisbroeck) was born in Rysbroeck, south of Brussels, Duchy of Brabant (now Belgium). He is not only the greatest mystic writer the Netherlands produced but also one of the glories of Dutch literature. He was ordained a priest in 1317, and was vicar at St. Gudule Church in Brussels. Seeking more solitude he retired, together with two companions to the Soniën Forest, where he founded the abbey of Groenendael, whose first prior he became.

His entire life was devoted to his writings. His mysticism is related not so much to the teachings of St. Thomas Aquinas as to the Platonic-Plotinic concepts. Part of his work is a reaction against the pantheistic tendencies of Bloemaerdinne and her followers and against the mysticism of Meister Eckhart.

His masterwork, *Die chierheit der gheestelicker brulocht* (The Adornment of the Spiritual Marriage), is a purely mystical and symbolic treatise, while some of his other works deal with the way of life in monasteries and convents. His language is brilliant, although some passages are verbose and full of elaborate symbolism. His influence outside the Netherlands was considerable. The mystics Johannes Tauler and Heinrich Suso knew his writings. During his lifetime some of them were translated into Latin. A complete Latin translation appeared in 1532. His ideas penetrated France, Germany, and Spain and contributed greatly to the evolution of Roman Catholic mysticism in Europe. Ruysbroeck died at Groenendael on Dec. 2, 1381.

RUYSBROECK, William of. See RUBRUQUIS, GUILLAUME.

RUYSDAEL, Jacob van. See RUISDAEL, JACOB VAN.

River Landscape, by the 17th century Dutch painter Salomon van Ruysdael.

RUYSDAEL, rois'dàl, **Salomon van** (c. 1600–1670), Dutch painter of landscapes, especially of river scenes. Ruysdael was born in Naarden, the son of the burgher J. J. de Goyer. The name Ruysdael was probably taken from a castle where the family once lived. The spelling with a "y" distinguishes Salomon from his more famous nephew, the painter Jacob van Ruisdael.

Ruysdael may have trained under the Haarlem landscape painters Esaias van de Velde and Pieter de Molijn, both of whom influenced his style. He joined the Haarlem painters' guild in 1623. Most of his works were landscapes of the flat Dutch countryside, with a cart track or river, a clump of trees, and a wide clouded sky. Earlier works, like the paintings of his contemporary Jan van Goyen, tend to be tightly drawn and soberly colored, with the river or track forming a diagonal across the canvas. Examples are *River Landscape* (about 1630; Rijksmuseum, Amsterdam) and *River Bank* (1632; Kunsthalle, Hamburg). Later works were more freely drawn, vividly colored, and open in composition, as in *Ferry* (1647; Musées Royaux des Beaux Arts de Belgique, Brussels). Ruysdael also did a few still lifes. He was buried in Haarlem on Nov. 3, 1670.

RUYTER, roi'tər, **Michiel Adriaanszoon de** (1607–1676), Dutch admiral, who fought the English and French fleets in 17th century wars. He was born at Flushing, the Netherlands, on March 24, 1607. He went to sea before he was 12, and passed his life in the Dutch merchant service and the navy. He became a vice admiral in 1653.

De Ruyter's seamanship and his development of an effective order of combat and tight fleet discipline enabled him to win most of his battles in the Northern War (1658–1659), the Anglo-Dutch wars of 1665–1667 and 1672–1674, and the war with France (1672–1678).

Among his achievements were his victory over the English in the Four Days' Battle (June 1–4, 1666), off the North Foreland; his raid (June 1667) on shipping in the Medway River, only 20 miles (32 km) from London); his repulse of an English raid on Schoonveldt Channel, the Netherlands, on May 28, 1673, and his triumph over the French at the Battle of Texel on Aug. 11, 1673.

In 1676, de Ruyter was sent to the Mediterranean to fight the French. He was wounded in the naval Battle of Messina on April 22, and died on his ship off Sicily, on April 29.

RUŽIČKA, rōō'zhĕch-kä, **Leopold** (1887–1976), Croatian-Swiss chemist, who shared the 1939 Nobel Prize in chemistry with the German chemist Adolf Butenandt for synthesizing higher terpenes, including sex hormones. Ružička was born in Vuková, Croatia (now Yugoslavia) on Sept. 13, 1887. He was educated at the Technical High School in Karlsruhe, Germany, and the University of Basel and became a Swiss citizen in 1917. He taught at the University of Utrecht (1926–1929) and at the Technology Institute in Zürich until 1957. He died in Zürich on Sept. 26, 1976.

Beginning in 1916, Ružička undertook the study of naturally occurring odoriferous compounds, most importantly the musk constituents civetone and muskone. He showed that each had a ring structure with 17 and 15 members, respectively, whereas until that time it was thought that rings with more than 8 members could not exist in nature or be prepared as stable compounds. He and his assistants also undertook the study of terpenes and developed the "isoprene rule" that higher terpenes can be considered to be composed, basically, of isoprene (C_5H_8) units —the simplest being the monoterpenes ($C_5H_8)_2$, or $C_{10}H_{16}$. Through the work of Ružička and others, the structure of cholesterol and the bile acids was determined in the 1920's. In the 1930's he and Butenandt became the first men to synthesize the sex hormones androsterone and testosterone, starting from cholesterol.

Lake Kivu, on Rwanda's western border, is the largest of the country's many lakes. It separates Rwanda from Zaire (Congo).

CHARLOTTE KAHLER, PHOTO TRENDS

RWANDA, rōō-on′də, is a republic in east central Africa. Before independence it was linked with neighboring Burundi in the Belgian-administered UN trust territory of Ruanda-Urundi. It became independent on July 1, 1962.

Located at the crossroads of Africa, slightly south of the equator, the tiny mountain republic of Rwanda lies in the very heart of the central African rift valley. Its physical landscape, suggesting a tropical Switzerland, evokes bucolic charm as well as grandiose beauty. Its recent history, by contrast, is a tale of civil strife and social upheaval.

Rwanda's transition to independence was accompanied by a serious tribal conflict between the Tutsi ruling caste and the Hutu masses. A Hutu revolt, which resulted in untold casualties, ended the country's traditional monarchy. Rwanda emerged from the struggle imbued with a sense of republican austerity and committed to socialism and democracy. But its paucity of economic resources and the growing pressure of overpopulation on the land remain critical problems.

The Land. Rwanda covers an area of 10,169 square miles (26,338 sq km). It is a country of mountains and plateaus, interspersed with deep valleys. Much of the landscape consists of hills and valleys scattered with eucalyptus trees and banana groves, alternating with patches of luxuriant pastures. Elevations range from 4,800 feet (1,500 meters) on the shores of Lake Kivu in the west to nearly 15,000 feet (4,600 meters) in the volcanic Virunga mountain range in the northwest. The mountains separate the Nile Basin from the Congo Basin. Lake Kivu, which is the largest of the country's many lakes, forms part of Rwanda's border with Zaire (formerly Congo).

Although Rwanda lies near the equator, its high elevation makes its climate temperate. The average annual temperature in most of the country is about 68° F (18° C), with only small seasonal variations. The region around Lake Kivu is generally hotter and more humid. Rwanda's average annual rainfall varies between 40 and 50 inches (1,000–1,300 mm). The amount varies

markedly according to the season, with the major rainy season from February to May.

The whole western region of Rwanda is ideal for herding and the cultivation of food crops. But it quickly shades off in the east into the savanna zone, which may range from arid and treeless grassland to acacia scrublands and bamboo forests. A major strain on land resources stems from the high density of the cattle population—approximately 3 million head. The large number of cattle has tended to accelerate the process of erosion on deforested hill sides, with disastrous effects on soil productivity.

The People. Rwanda had a population of about 3.7 million in 1971. With about 364 persons per square mile (140 per sq km), it is one of the most densely populated countries in Africa. It is estimated that the population is increasing at the high rate of 2.9% annually.

Traditional Rwandan society was organized into hierarchical strata roughly coinciding with the three major ethnic groups—Tutsi, Hutu, and Twa. The Tutsi, also known as Batutsi or Watutsi, represent approximately 4% of the total population. Formerly the dominant caste, these tall, cattle-raising people exercised the political control over the other groups. The Hutu, or Bahutu,

---

INFORMATION HIGHLIGHTS

Official Name: Republic of Rwanda.
Head of State: President.
Head of Government: President.
Area: 10,169 square miles (26,338 sq km).
Boundaries: *North,* Uganda; *east,* Tanzania; *south,* Burundi; *west,* Zaire (Congo).
Population: 3,700,000 (1971).
Capital: Kigali (1970 population, 17,000).
Major Languages: Kinyarwanda and French (both official).
Major Religions: Christianity; tribal.
Monetary Unit: Rwanda franc.
Weights and Measures: Metric system.
Flag: Red, yellow, and green vertical stripes. A large black letter "R" is in the center of the yellow stripe. See also FLAG.
National Anthem: *Rwanda Rwacu.*

who account for 85% of the population, are primarily farmers and previously worked the land for its Tutsi owners. The pygmoid Twa, or Batwa, 1% of the population, are hunters and potters.

Using their cattle as a lever of economic and social power to subdue the indigenous Hutu and Twa populations, the Tutsi eventually developed a highly centralized system of government. The Rwanda monarchy was essentially a Tutsi monarchy. Through an elaborate system of rituals and traditions the Tutsi managed to give a sanction of legitimacy to the premise of inequality on which the country's social and political system was established.

With the spread of Western education and Christianity, Rwandan peasants became increasingly dissatisfied with their inferior position. The resulting conflict of interest between the ruling aristocracy and the subordinate castes culminated in widespread ethnic violence in 1959, followed by a massive exodus of Tutsi people. The reversal of traditional statuses following the revolution led to the emergence of a political system in which power lies exclusively in the hands of the Hutu elites.

The Hutu and Tutsi share the same Bantu language, Kinyarwanda, as well as similar cultural traditions. About half the people practice their traditional religion; the remainder are Christians, chiefly Roman Catholics. Primary school facilities have been expanded, but few students attend secondary schools. The National University of Rwanda, founded in 1963, had an enrollment of about 400 in the early 1970's.

There are almost no real villages in Rwanda. Today, as in the past, the hill is the primary focus of social and economic activity. Urban growth has remained limited to the perimeter of the capital city, Kigali, which had a population of about 17,000 in 1970. Thus traditional life styles are still very much in evidence, as shown by the continuing influence of the clientage system and the persistence of kinship and regional loyalties. Despite the impression of stability, regional and communal tensions within the country continue to hamper the political modernization of Rwanda.

Economy. With a per capita income of about $40 a year, Rwanda is one of the poorest coun-

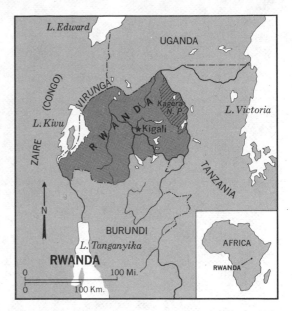

tries in Africa. Its economy has not progressed very far beyond the subsistence level because of the lack of significant mineral resources and the absence in the past of incentives for development.

The economy is based almost completely on agriculture and livestock raising. Subsistence crops include sorghum, maize, manioc, beans, and bananas. The principal export crop is coffee. The production of coffee underwent a substantial increase in the late 1960's, rising from 8,600 tons in 1966 to 15,500 tons in 1970. But these gains were largely nullified by the decline in world prices for coffee.

To offset Rwanda's overwhelming dependence on coffee exports, steps have been taken to expand tea and pyrethrum plantations, in particular through the establishment of farming communities known as *paysannats*. With aid from the European Development Fund a total of about 30,000 families had been installed in *paysannats* by the beginning of 1969.

CHARLOTTE KAHLER, PHOTO TRENDS

Banana plantation near Kigali is a producer of one of Rwanda's main food crops. Bananas are eaten raw, cooked as a vegetable, and used for making a type of beer.

Contour cultivation of hilly land helps prevent soil erosion, which is a serious problem in Rwanda.

As in most other pastoral societies of East Africa, the herding of cattle has had more than economic significance in Rwanda. Although their role in contemporary society is no longer associated with social and ethnic distinctions, cattle remain a very familiar sight. The most fertile areas of the country have been heavily overstocked and overplanted. Efforts are being made to reduce the density of the cattle population and to increase the value of the cows through the promotion of commercial cattle ranching. But the importance attached in the past to the ownership of cattle is one reason why the adjustment of agricultural production to the requirements of a fast-growing population has proved such a difficult task.

Mineral exports represent a small percentage of Rwanda's foreign exchange earnings. Small quantities of cassiterite, wolframite, and colombo-tantalite are mined in the northern and eastern regions. Manufacturing is primarily for local consumption and includes food processing and the production of textiles and chemicals. Tourism is being promoted, mainly in the scenic Lake Kivu area and to Kagera National Park, which shelters many species of wildlife.

In the absence of railroads and an adequate road network, Rwanda's rugged terrain hampers economic and social development. An international airport at Kigali was expanded to accommodate large jets in 1968.

History and Government. The first known inhabitants of what is now Rwanda were the Twa. The region was later occupied by the Hutu, and then by the Tutsi. The kingdom of Rwanda developed its present territorial base partly through conquest and partly through peaceful assimilation.

Under the leadership of a royal clan, successive waves of Tutsi pastoralists spread their domination over the indigenous Bantu societies, whose customs and traditions they gradually assimilated into their own. The critical step in this process of conquest and assimilation took place in the region near Kigali during the reign of the Tutsi king Ruganzu Bwimba, probably in the 15th century. The most spectacular conquests, however, took place in the reign of Mwami (King) Kigeri Rwabugiri, in the latter half of the 19th century. At the inception of colonial rule, most of the Hutu people were already incorporated in the fold of the Tutsi monarchy.

Rwanda was made part of German East Africa in the late 19th century. After World War I, Rwanda and Burundi were administered by Belgium as the League of Nations mandate of Ruanda-Urundi, which became a UN trust territory following World War II. The Belgians, like the Germans, governed Rwanda through its traditional authorities, retaining the established structure based on Tutsi supremacy.

The system of indirect rule aimed at maintaining the legitimacy of the monarchy. But it did not prevent the penetration of Westernizing influences, which had a shattering impact on Rwanda's indigenous societies.

With the development of revolutionary aspirations among the peasantry in the years following World War II, tensions increased between the Tutsi aristocracy and the Hutu elite. In the 1956 Bahutu Manifesto the Hutu for the first time formally demanded equal rights, and violent clashes erupted in several parts of Rwanda in 1959. Large numbers of Tutsi fled to neighboring countries, the number of refugees reaching an estimated 200,000 in the 1960's.

Neither willing nor able to stem the tide of Hutu unrest, Belgium lent the full support of its administrative apparatus to the Hutu. In 1960 a provisional government was set up, composed primarily of members of the all-Hutu Parti de l'Emancipation des Masses Hutu (Parmehutu). Grégoire Kayibanda, leader of Parmehutu, became premier. In January 1961 the government declared Rwanda a republic and deposed Mwami Kigeri V. The following September the Parmehutu scored a landslide victory in legislative elections, and, in a UN-sponsored referendum conducted at the same time, the monarchy was formally abolished. Kayibanda was elected president in October. Rwanda became formally independent on July 1, 1962. But sporadic ethnic violence continued long after independence.

The 1962 constitution declared Rwanda to be a "democratic, social, and sovereign republic" with a president and 47-member National Assembly. President Kayibanda was reelected in 1965 and 1969, but in July 1973, Maj. Gen. Juvénal Habyarimana led a coup and established a military government. In August 1973 a cabinet was formed with Habyarimana as president. A national congress was elected and took its place in January 1976. Late in 1978 a new constitution was approved in a national referendum. Habyarimana was reelected president and promised an early return to civilian government.

Rwanda's closest diplomatic ties are with Belgium and France. It is a member of the United Nations, the Organization of African Unity, and the Organisation Commune Africaine, Malgache et Mauricienne (OCAM).

RENÉ LEMARCHAND*
University of Florida

Bibliography
Lacger, Louis de, *Le Ruanda* (1961).
Lemarchand, René, *Rwanda and Burundi* (Praeger 1970).
Linden, Ian and Jane, *Church and Revolution in Rwanda* (Manchester Univ. Press 1977).
Louis, William Roger, *Rwanda-Urundi, 1884–1919* (Oxford 1963).
Maquet, Jacques J., *The Premise of Inequality in Ruanda* (Oxford 1961).
Vansina, Jan, *L'Évolution du Royaume du Rwanda des origines à 1900* (1962).

Tall Rwandan dancer is a Tutsi (Watusi). The Tutsi people are noted for their great height.

VICTOR ENGELBERT, PHOTO RESEARCHERS

RYAN, Thomas Fortune (1851–1928), American financier and promoter. He was born on a small farm in Lovington, Nelson county, Va., on Oct. 17, 1851. Orphaned at 14, he worked as a messenger in Baltimore and for a brokerage firm in New York City. He became a partner in his own brokerage firm, and at 23 he bought a seat on the New York Stock Exchange.

Beginning in 1883, Ryan was involved in a bitter and complex struggle for control of New York City's street railway lines, which was marked by the use of political influence, by lawsuits, and charges of overcapitalization and stock watering. In 1906, after he tried to merge his surface transit interests with the new subway system, Ryan retired from the transportation fields. Most of his companies went bankrupt. He later invested in tobacco, banking, and life insurance enterprises. At the invitation of Leopold II, king of the Belgians, he exploited the mineral resources of the Belgian Congo.

William C. Whitney, an associate of Ryan, called him "the most adroit, suave, and noiseless man" in American financial history. Ryan died in New York City on Nov. 23, 1928.

RYAZAN, rē-ə-zan', was a medieval Russian principality. Its first center, now called Old (Staraya) Ryazan, lay on the Oka River. Ryazan emerged as a principality in the early 1100's, united at first with the Murom principality to the north. It was often in conflict with the principality of Vladimir, later absorbed by Moscow.

In 1237, Ryazan suffered a devastating invasion, including the razing of the capital, by Batu Khan's Golden Horde. A new capital, Pereyaslavl-Ryazanski, was founded about 30 miles (48 km) upstream on the Oka. The Golden Horde at times supported Ryazan, but as the Horde's strength ebbed, Moscow expanded. In 1456 the eight-year-old prince of Ryazan was placed under Moscow's protection, and for practical purposes, Ryazan's independence ended. Moscow made Ryazan a province about 1517.

RYAZAN, rē-ə-zan', is a city in the USSR in the Russian republic and is the capital of Ryazan Oblast. Also transliterated Riazan, it is about 115 miles (185 km) southeast of Moscow on the west bank of the Trubezh River, one mile (1.6 km) above its confluence with the Oka River. Its historic buildings include the Uspenski (Assumption) and Arkhangelski cathedrals in the area enclosed by the ancient kremlin. It is principally a manufacturing center, producing agricultural and other machinery, electronic equipment, clothing, and foodstuffs. Ryazan Oblast is an agricultural region with an area of about 15,290 square miles (39,600 sq km).

In 1237, after the destruction of the principality of Ryazan's capital, Old (Staraya) Ryazan, by the Mongols, the princes of Ryazan moved upstream 30 miles (48 km) to Pereyaslavl-Ryazanski, renamed Ryazan in 1778. After its absorption by Moscow in the early 16th century, Ryazan was one of a chain of strong points established across Moscow's southern border from the Dnieper River to the Volga. Inhabited by Cossacks, these outposts were closely associated with the expansion southward of Muscovite Russia. Population: (1971) of the city, 365,000; of the oblast, 1,409,000.

W. A. DOUGLAS JACKSON
University of Washington

Albert Ryder's *Siegfried and the Rhine Maidens* (painted between 1880 and 1900) is an imaginative interpretation of moonlight on foliage and water.

RYBINSK, ri-byinsk′ is a city in the USSR in the Russian republic. It is on the Volga River, about 150 miles (241 km) northeast of Moscow and 50 miles (80 km) northwest of Yaroslavl. It is a river port and manufacturing center and the site of a dam built on the Volga near the mouth of the Sheksna River to create the Rybinsk Reservoir, which at that time formed the largest artificial lake in the USSR, with an area of 1,800 square miles (4,660 sq km). The dam, completed in 1941, and improvements in the nation's canal system enhanced the city's commercial importance. A large hydroelectric plant is associated with the dam. The city produces river craft, printing and power machinery, cables, matches, and lumber. There is a museum of regional history.

The first mention of a Slavic settlement at the site, then within the jurisdiction of the powerful prince of Novgorod, was in 1137. From the 15th to the 18th century, the principal economic activity of the town, then known as Rybnaya Sloboda, was fishing. Both its old and its present name, which dates from 1777, derive from the Russian word *ryba*, meaning "fish." The town's commercial importance began with the opening of the Mariinsk Canal in 1810, linking the Volga with St. Petersburg (now Leningrad), the capital, via the Sheksna and Mologa rivers and Lake Onega. By 1910, Rybinsk was the busiest port on the upper Volga. From 1946 to 1957 it was known as Shcherbakov, after a Bolshevik leader who was born in the city. Population: (1970) 222,000.

W. A. DOUGLAS JACKSON
University of Washington

RYDBERG, rid′bûrg, **Viktor** (1828–1895), Swedish man of letters, who was the last and perhaps the greatest of the idealists in the typically Swedish romantic manner. Abraham Viktor Rydberg was born in Jönköping, Sweden, on Dec. 18, 1828. After studying at the University of Lund, he was a contributor, from 1855 to 1876, to the Göteborg journal *Handels-och sjöfartstidning*, which published many of his writings. The novels

Fribytaren på Östersjön (1857; *The Pirate of the Baltic*) and *Den siste athenaren* (1859) established his reputation. The latter was translated into English as *The Last Athenian* (1869) and was also translated into German and Danish. With his very successful *Bibelns lära om Kristus* (1862; *The Teachings of the Bible about Christ*), Rydberg turned to theology. This interest is also reflected in *Medeltidens magi* (1865; *The Magic of the Middle Ages*) and in *Romerska sägner om apostlarna Petrus och Paulus* (1874; *Roman Legends of the Apostles Peter and Paul*). Rydberg's *Romerska dagar* (1877; *Roman Days*) is a collection of essays on various aspects of the archaeology of Italy.

Rydberg was an active champion of liberalism. His later interests ranged over wide areas of study—aesthetics, philosophy, psychology, religion, and also history, which he taught for some years in Stockholm. He also wrote poetry and made a translation of Goethe's *Faust*. Rydberg was not honored by election to the Swedish Academy until 1877, though he had long been one of his country's foremost writers. He died in Stockholm on Sept. 21, 1895.

EDWIN H. ZEYDEL
Author of "Ludwig Tieck and England"

RYDER, rī′dər, **Albert Pinkham** (1847–1917), American painter, who sought to express on canvas his gropings toward the mystery of nature and the ineffable. Ryder was born in New Bedford, Mass., on March 19, 1847. A childhood by the water led to his lifelong interest in painting the sea. An eye ailment, contracted during childhood, cut short his education after he graduated from grammar school, and the affliction plagued him throughout his life.

Moving with his family to New York City about 1868, Ryder briefly attended the National Academy of Design. But his development was primarily a matter of realizing his own highly personal vision, a process that he analogized to an inchworm's clinging to the end of a twig and revolving in the air at it reaches for something beyond. Even art seen on his trips to Europe in 1877,

1882, 1887, and 1896 had little effect on his work.

A simple, unworldly man, Ryder had a considerable circle of friends but lived as a recluse out of devotion to his work, especially toward the end of his life. He spent hours studying the effects of moonlight and foliage, and he worked and reworked canvases for years, loading them with rich impasto layers of pigment, improperly applied and heavily varnished, causing them to deteriorate even in his lifetime.

Gradually Ryder's style departed from his early representation of nature's outward appearance to a concern with subjective visionary themes, often inspired by the Bible or Shakespeare, in which nature reflected the emotions of man. His most fruitful period was 1880 to 1900, after which his eyesight rapidly failed. Famous seascapes of these years are *Toilers of the Sea* (Metropolitan Museum of Art, New York), *Jonah*, and *Flying Dutchman* (both National Gallery, Washington). The *Forest of Arden* (private collection) and *Siegfried and the Rhine Maidens* (National Gallery) are forest scenes bathed in a mysterious light. In such works, Ryder's subordination of detail to the plastic relationships of masses endeared him more to later viewers familiar with abstract movements than to his contemporaries.

Ryder gained slight recognition in his own time, although he became a member of the National Academy in 1906. Eventually, however, he won a place with Winslow Homer and Thomas Eakins among the foremost American painters of the late 19th century. As an indication of his fame, the number of forgeries of his work is several times greater than the 160 or so authenticated paintings. Ryder died in Elmhurst, N. Y., on March 28, 1917.

Further Reading: Goodrich, Lloyd, *Albert Pinkham Ryder* (Braziller 1959); Rogers, Meyric R., *Four American Painters* (Museum of Modern Art Publications, Reprint Series, 1970); Sherman, F. F., *Albert Pinkham Ryder* (1920).

RYE, a municipal borough in southeast England, is about 55 miles (90 km) southeast of London near where the Rother and Tillingham rivers merge and flow into the English Channel. About 1350, Rye had the honor of being added to the original Cinque Ports (Five Ports) that were designated to defend England against invaders.

For the next three centuries, Rye flourished as a seaport. Gradually its harbor silted over, and Rye now stands on an isolated hill. There are a number of antiquities that interest visitors at this seaside resort. At its highest point is Ypres (pronounced locally, "Wipers") Tower, a defensive strong point erected in the 12th century.

The parish church dates from the Norman period and has a 16th century clock. Edward III directed that walls be built around the town, and one of the gates, the Land Gate dating from the 14th century, remains. Population: (1961) 4,438.

RYE, a city in southern New York, in Westchester county, is on the north shore of Long Island Sound, 24 miles (39 km) northeast of New York City. It is a community of homes, many of whose residents commute to New York. Rye has a number of private yachting and golf clubs. Playland, an amusement park developed by the county, is at Rye Beach.

Municipal offices are situated in the Square House, one of the oldest buildings in the city, where George Washington and the Marquis de Lafayette stayed. Kirby's Tide Mill, built in 1770, is the only one of its kind remaining in the state.

John Jay, first chief justice of the United States, is buried in the Jay cemetery on the Boston Post Road.

Settled in 1660, Rye is the second-oldest community in Westchester county. It was incorporated as a village in 1904 and became a city, the smallest in the county, in 1942. The city adopted the council-manager form of government in 1959. Population: 15,083.

RYE is a cultivated plant (*Secale cereale*) of the grass family, Gramineae. The wild ancestor of rye and the place of its first domestication are unknown, but it probably originated in the eastern Mediterranean region or in western Asia, where wild species of *Secale* are still found. The problem is further complicated by the frequent escape of rye itself from cultivation and its persistence for a time as a wild plant. The terms "wild rye" and "ryegrass," which are often applied to species of *Elymus* or *Lolium*, are misnomers, since these genera are only distantly related to rye.

Uses. Historically rye is the latest addition to the list of cereals, and economically it is one of the less important. It was not known to the ancient Greeks or Egyptians or the Semitic races and never has been grown extensively in India or southeastern Asia. In Roman literature it was mentioned first by Pliny near the beginning of the Christian era. The Saxons took it to Britain about 500 A.D.

In Europe rye has long been used for making black bread. In the United States the grain is also used to make bread, but its main uses are as food for livestock and in the manufacture of alcohol and alcoholic beverages, especially whiskey. The plant is used often as a winter cover crop to prevent soil erosion and as a pasture in early spring. When plowed under before flowering time, it provides good green manure. The tough straw has little value as stock food, but it is used for bedding and as a packing material. It has been used also in the manufacture of coarse paper.

In primitive agriculture, rye and wheat were often grown together in the same field. This practice may have been due to the difficulty in separating the two kinds of grain when they had become mixed. It may also have worked as a good agricultural gamble, since wheat gives better yields than rye under good conditions, and rye the better yield under poor conditions. The quality of the bread made from the grain mixture depended on the amount of wheat present. Rye is deficient in the glutinous proteins that give wheat dough the elasticity necessary for good leavening, so that pure rye bread is heavy and compact compared to wheat bread.

Description and Culture. Botanically, rye resembles wheat in many ways, and the two are so closely related that rye will hybridize with some varieties of wheat. The individual plant consists of a cluster of tall, stiff, unbranched stems produced by a profuse basal branching of the seedling. The flowers are borne in a terminal spike 4 to 6 inches (10–15 cm) long, along the axis of which the two- or three-flowered

Rye grain resembles wheat grain but is more slender.

spikelets are arranged alternately. The small leaf, or bract, standing below each flower has a long, bristlelike appendage, or awn. The plant bears an abundance of pollen and depends almost completely on cross-pollination to reproduce. The grain of rye is longer and more slender than that of wheat, and it separates from the chaff when threshed. At any time during its development, rye can be distinguished from wheat by the bluish green tint of its stem and leaves.

Rye has few stable agricultural varieties. This may be due to its limited variability and to the fact that necessary cross-pollination makes it difficult to produce pedigreed lines. The diploid chromosome number is 14. Polyploids have been produced artificially, and some of these have shown promise, but they have not been fully utilized.

Rye is usually sown in late summer or early fall, about a month earlier than wheat, and develops as a winter annual, maturing in June or July. Some varieties may be sown in the spring. It often produces a fair crop on soils too poor or too dry for wheat and is less damaged by extreme cold, but it also responds well to better conditions.

Rye is grown extensively in the USSR, which produces nearly half the world's total rye crop, and in eastern Europe. Not more than 2% or 3% of the world crop is produced in the United States, where Kansas, Nebraska, North Dakota, and South Dakota are leading states.

Diseases. Rye is susceptible to the usual array of fungus and insect enemies of the cereals, but the damage done is less than in the case of wheat. The ergot fungus is, however, of peculiar significance. (See ERGOT.) It causes the developing rye grain to become a large, purplish or black, hardened mass that contains several highly toxic substances. Certain mysterious epidemics that have attacked local populations in Europe since medieval times have been traced to the use of rye flour contaminated with these poisons.

See also CEREALS; GRASS.

PAUL WEATHERWAX
Formerly, Indiana University

Further Reading: U. S. Department of Agriculture, *Growing Rye* (USGPO 1959); Wilson, Harold K., *Grain Crops*, 2d ed. (McGraw 1955).

RYE HOUSE PLOT, a conspiracy to assassinate King Charles II of England and his brother, the duke of York (afterward James II), which was devised by a group of extreme but obscure Whigs. The attempt was to be made in April 1683 as the king and the duke, traveling from Newmarket to London, passed Rye House, near Hoddesdon, Hertfordshire, which belonged to Richard Rumbold, one of the plotters. The plan miscarried and was revealed to the authorities by informers who implicated some of the Whig leaders, alleging that they were planning an armed insurrection.

Three of these leaders—William Russell, Arthur Capel, 1st earl of Essex, and Algernon Sidney—were charged with treason in connection with the Rye House plot, of which they probably had no knowledge. The earl of Essex died in the Tower of London, apparently a suicide, and the others were beheaded.

RYE WHISKEY is a distilled liquor that is made in the United States. By federal regulation, it must be distilled from a mash containing at least 51% rye, or must be a combination of such whiskeys. It is aged in new charred oak barrels, but its age when it is sold is not stipulated by regulation. Rye usually tastes younger than bourbon whiskey of the same age.

Rye whiskey was first distilled in western Pennsylvania in the 18th century by Scots and Irish settlers, who found it easier to transport and sell the whiskey than the grain from which it was produced.

See also DISTILLED SPIRITS; WHISKEY.

RYEGRASS, any of several species of grasses of the genus *Lolium,* some of which are important forage grasses. *Lolium* grasses generally have long, narrow, flat leaves and slender flowering spikes. Although not closely related to rye, they are classified with rye, wheat, and barley in the grass tribe Hordeae. Two species, the perennial, or English, ryegrass, *L. perenne,* and Italian ryegrass, *L. multiflorum,* are important forage grasses of northern Europe and the British Isles and they also have been naturalized in North America.

A number of superior varieties of these have been produced by selection and hybridization. *L. perenne,* a short-lived perennial, is often used in lawn mixtures to produce quickly a ground cover that will die out as the better but more slowly growing species take its place. Because of their deep root systems, this and other species of *Lolium* are also used to prevent erosion and improve soils by bringing up nutrients from the subsoil.

L. temulentum, commonly known as darnel, is supposed to be the biblical tare. Its harmful effects are due to a poisonous fungus that grows in the developing grain. It is difficult to separate the grains of this weed from those of wheat or barley at threshing time, and the fungus is not visible externally.

RYKOV, rī'kôf, **Aleksei Ivanovich** (1881–1938), Russian political leader. Of peasant stock, he was born in Saratov on Feb. 25 (Feb. 13, Old Style), 1881. As a young man he began revolutionary activities in Saratov, and at the University of Kazan he joined the Russian Social Democratic Workers' party. He met Vladimir Ilich Lenin in Geneva and became a close collaborator of the Bolshevik leader. Rykov was elected to the party's central committee at the Third Congress, and in the revolution of 1905 he was active in Moscow. Between 1907 and 1914, he was arrested frequently for revolutionary activity and exiled, but he escaped each time.

After the revolution in March 1917, he returned from exile in Narym, where Stalin had also been banished, and played a prominent part in the Bolshevik Revolution. He was appointed commissar of the interior in the first Soviet government. Soon afterward, he resigned from the government and the central committee of the party in protest against Lenin's hard policy toward other socialist parties, but he was appointed chairman of the Supreme Council of the National Economy in March 1918.

Rykov attained the peak of his influence and prominence during the years of the New Economic Policy (NEP). In 1922 he was elected to the Politburo and was reelected until 1930. On Lenin's death in 1924, Rykov succeeded him as chairman of the Council of People's Commissars (premier). Favoring the concessions granted the peasants under the NEP, he came out strongly against Leon Trotsky in 1926–1927. After Joseph Stalin's sharp turn to the left, Rykov continued to oppose a rapid tempo of industrialization at the expense of the peasantry and fought Stalin's policy of liquidating the kulaks. In 1929 he recanted and became a staunch advocate of the first five-year plan. Nevertheless, he was denounced in 1930 as a "right deviationist" and was ousted as premier and Politburo member.

With others, Rykov was condemned at the Moscow treason trial of 1938 as an agent of foreign intelligence services plotting to overthrow the Soviet regime. After publicly confessing guilt on March 13, he was condemned to death and was shot in Moscow on March 14.

After 1957, official criticism of him became less severe. Authoritative Soviet works referred to Rykov and certain of his codefendants as "capitulators" and "agents of the kulaks in the party," but not as foreign agents.

ALBERT RESIS, *Northern Illinois University*

RYLE, rīl, **Gilbert** (1900–1976), English philosopher of the linguistic analysis school. Ryle was born in Brighton on Aug. 19, 1900. He was a scholar of Queen's College, Oxford, where he gained three first classes in honors examinations and was an oarsman of prowess. He became a tutor at Christ Church in 1925. In World War II he was a major in the Welsh Guards. He was Waynflete professor of metaphysical philosophy at Oxford from 1945 until his retirement in 1968. He died in Yorkshire on Oct. 6, 1976.

Ryle's philosophy is notable chiefly for two things. The first is his conception of the task of philosophy. He holds that philosophical problems arise from "category mistakes," the use of concepts in fields where they do not apply. We may say, for example, that the rain began at 4 o'clock, and also that time itself began 6,000 or 6 million years ago. To suppose that time— or the universe—can begin in the sense in which an event in time can begin is to commit a category mistake. Philosophic problems vanish when once the terms employed are distinguished and defined. Nothing is more useful for this purpose than the study of ordinary usage, and Ryle is a leader of the school of linguistic analysis.

Ryle's second contribution was made in his *Concept of Mind* (1949). In this influential book he disputes the traditional view that mind is totally distinct from body, a "ghost in the machine." What we really mean by mind, he insists, is a certain kind of behavior. To say that a person is intelligent is to say that when confronted by difficulties he acts in a certain way. There is nothing in mind that cannot be publicly observed and studied. The book aroused much controversy, many critics contending that it was a return to behaviorism and a denial that consciousness had any distinct existence.

BRAND BLANSHARD
Author of "Reason and Analysis"

RYMER, rī'mər, **Thomas** (1641–1713), English critic and antiquarian, who introduced the critical theories of the French neoclassicists and formalists to England. Rymer was born at Yafforth, Yorkshire, England, and attended Cambridge University. He studied law at Gray's Inn and was admitted to the bar in 1673. In 1678 he published a play in rhymed verse, *Edgar, or the English Monarch,* which was never performed.

Rymer then turned his attention to the criticism of drama, and in *The Tragedies of the Last Age* (1678), he severely criticized the works of Beaumont and Fletcher because they did not adhere to classical notions of tragedy. In *A Short View of Tragedy* (1692) he condemned Shakespeare's *Othello* as "a bloody farce without salt or savour." In 1692 he was appointed historiographer to the king and was commissioned to prepare a collection of English treaties and conventions, entitled *Foedera, conventiones, literae et cujuscunque generis acta publica*... (Vol. 1, 1704). By 1735, 20 volumes were published, covering the period from 1101 to 1654. The last five were edited after Rymer's death, in London, on Dec. 14, 1713, by Robert Sanderson, his assistant.

RYSWICK, Peace of, riz'wik, the peace treaty that ended the War of the League of Augsburg (1689–1697), which in Britain was called the War of the Grand Alliance and which in North America was named King William's War. It was arranged through Sweden's mediation between France and the League of Augsburg allies. Plenipotentiaries of the warring nations met in the village of Ryswick (Rijswijk), near The Hague, where on Sept. 20, 1697, conventions were signed by France with the United Provinces, Britain, and Spain. Representatives of the Holy Roman Empire signed on October 30, and Europe was again at peace.

France, although it had won a series of victories, was exhausted and made important concessions. The Dutch received a favorable commercial treaty. Britain gained recognition of King William III, architect of the League of Augsburg, from France, and France's promise not to help James II. French rule was confirmed over Nova Scotia, and Strasbourg and Alsace, sought by the empire, remained in the possession of France. See also AUGSBURG, LEAGUE OF.

RYUKYU ISLANDS, rē-ōō′kū, a Japanese archipelago extending in an arc of 650 miles (1,050 km) between Kyushu, the southernmost of Japan's four main islands, and the Chinese island of Taiwan.

The Ryukyus separate the East China Sea from the Pacific Ocean. Their total area is 1,338 square miles (3,465 sq km). In Japanese they are called Ryukyu-retto or Nansei-shoto; in Chinese, the Liu-ch'iu Islands.

Land and People. The Ryukyus consist of three major island groups (*gunto* in Japanese), with a total population (1965 census) of 1,120,369. The northern group is the Amami Islands (population, 186,193), including the Tokara Islands. The central group is the Okinawa Islands (812,-339), including Okinawa, Iheya, the Kerama Islands, Ie, and Kume. The southern group is the Sakishima Islands (121,837), consisting of the Yaeyama and Miyako groups and scattered islands, one cluster of which, the Senkaku (Tiaoyutai) group, is claimed by China.

Okinawa is the largest and most populous island in the Ryukyus. Naha, the archipelago's major seaport and largest city, is located there. It is the administrative center of Okinawa prefecture, which consists of the Okinawa and Sakishima island groups. The Amami Islands are part of Kagoshima prefecture, the seat of which is in Kyushu.

The climate of the Ryukyus is subtropical, with high humidity, but monsoonal winds reduce the discomfort. The average annual temperature is 70°F (21°C) and the average annual rainfall measures 84 inches (2,100 mm). In summer destructive typhoons may sweep over the islands. Indigenous wildlife includes poisonous snakes, wild boar, and black rabbits.

Agriculture has long been the principal occupation of the islanders, the chief products being sugarcane, sweet potatoes, bananas, pineapples, rice, and soybeans. Fishing is a leading industry. Manufactured goods include foodstuffs, clothing, ceramics, and tobacco products. The maintenance of U. S. military bases and the servicing of their personnel are important to the economy of Okinawa.

The inhabitants of the Ryukyu Islands resemble other Japanese in physical appearance. The Ryukyuan language differs in many respects from Japanese. The educational system follows the Japanese pattern. The University of the Ryukyus, on Okinawa, was established in 1950 with U. S. help.

History. Ruled by independent kings in early times, the Ryukyu Islands came under Chinese domination in the 14th century. After a Japanese invasion in the 17th century the inhabitants were obliged to pay tribute to both masters. Commodore Matthew Perry of the U. S. Navy visited Okinawa in 1853 but failed to persuade his government to build a naval base there. China relinquished its claims in the Ryukyus in 1874, and five years later Japan incorporated the islands into its empire.

Okinawa became an important objective of U. S. forces in World War II, and the campaign to take the island from the Japanese was the last major battle of the conflict. More than 100,000 Japanese and 12,000 U. S. personnel were killed during the bitter fighting. Civilian casualties were extremely heavy.

After the war the Ryukyus remained under U. S. administration, and Okinawa was developed as a strategic U. S. airbase. By the peace treaty with Japan, effective in 1952, Japan retained "residual sovereignty" over the Ryukyu Islands. The Tokara group was returned to Japanese jurisdiction in 1951 and the rest of the Amami Islands in 1953.

Okinawa became a major base for U. S. operations in Vietnam in the mid-1960's. The American military effort increased the island's prosperity but provoked strong opposition in the Ryukyus and Japan.

On May 15, 1972, Okinawa and the other Ryukyu islands still under administration of the United States were restored to full Japanese control. The United States continued to maintain large military facilities on Okinawa under provisions of the U. S.-Japanese mutual security treaty, requiring the United States to consult with Japan before moving any U. S. forces on Japanese soil into combat.

RYUN, rī′ən, **Jim** (1947–   ), American track athlete. James Ronald Ryun was born in Wichita, Kans., on April 29, 1947. A lanky youth, he began to train seriously for middle-distance running at the age of 15. Finishing last in 1964 in a race against seven collegians, Ryun nevertheless became the first high school student to run a mile in less than four minutes. He reached the semifinals of the Olympic 1,500-meters in 1964.

In 1965, Ryun entered the University of Kansas, where his first high school track coach, Bob Timmons, was then coaching. In 1966 and 1967, Ryun set world records in the half mile (1:44.9), the mile (3:53.3 and then 3:53.1), and the 1,-500 meters (3:33.1). He received the Sullivan Trophy of the Amateur Athletic Union as the outstanding U. S. amateur athlete of 1966.

Perhaps affected by the high altitude of Mexico City, Ryun finished second in the Olympic 1,500-meter run in 1968. He lost again in that event in 1972, falling down during a heat.

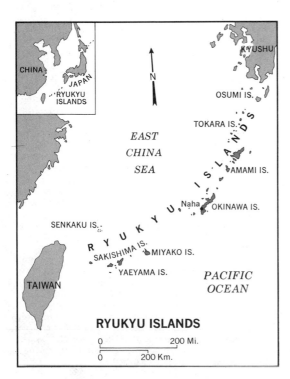

EAST CHINA SEA

PACIFIC OCEAN

CHINA

JAPAN

RYUKYU ISLANDS

TAIWAN

KYUSHU

OSUMI IS.

TOKARA IS.

AMAMI IS.

Naha OKINAWA IS.

SENKAKU IS.

SAKISHIMA IS. MIYAKO IS.

YAEYAMA IS.

RYUKYU ISLANDS

N

RYUKYU ISLANDS

0   200 Mi.

0   200 Km.

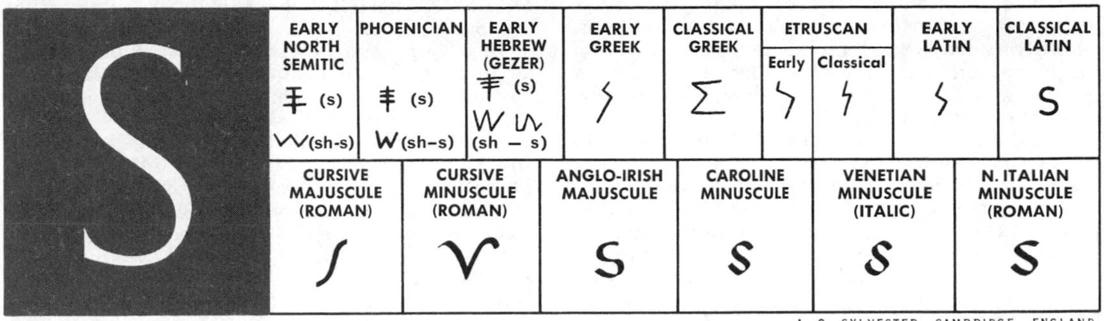

	EARLY NORTH SEMITIC	PHOENICIAN	EARLY HEBREW (GEZER)	EARLY GREEK	CLASSICAL GREEK	ETRUSCAN		EARLY LATIN	CLASSICAL LATIN
						Early	Classical		
S	⊥ (s) ᾱᾱ(sh-s)	ᚇ (s) W (sh-s)	⊥ (s) W ᾱ (sh — s)	ζ	Σ	ξ	ξ	ζ	S
	CURSIVE MAJUSCULE (ROMAN)	CURSIVE MINUSCULE (ROMAN)	ANGLO-IRISH MAJUSCULE	CAROLINE MINUSCULE	VENETIAN MINUSCULE (ITALIC)	N. ITALIAN MINUSCULE (ROMAN)			
	ʃ	⋎	S	S	S	S			

DEVELOPMENT OF THE LETTER S is illustrated in the above chart, beginning with the early North Semitic letter. The evolution of the majuscule (capital) S is shown at top; that of the minuscule (lower-case) at bottom.

S, es, is the 19th letter and the 15th consonant of the English alphabet and of all the alphabets derived from the Latin. The ancient North Semitic alphabet, the ancestor of all the existing alphabets, had four sibilants, or hissing sounds, which still exist in modern Hebrew: *zayin, sam'ekh, tsade,* and *shin. Shin* became the Greek letter *sigma* (*s*), and through the Etruscan alphabet it passed into the Latin and hence into all west European languages. The development of the shape of the letter *s* throughout its history is shown in the chart above, as well as in the alphabet chart in the article ALPHABET.

Pronunciation. S is the principal sibilant in the English alphabet. Actually, it is a fricative, representing two chief sounds: one voiceless, or hard and sharp, as in "saint" or "salt"; the other voiced, or soft and flat, as in "rose" or "reason." In the second case the sound would be more accurately denoted by *z*. At the beginning of words, *s* is generally voiceless; in other positions it is somewhat irregular. In the initial position the *s* sound is produced by emission of breath while the end of the tongue is brought close to the front palate just behind the gums.

Often *s* has the sound of *sh*, especially in the termination *-sion* when the *s* is preceded by a consonant, as in "declension," "mansion." But when preceded by a vowel, the *s* in this termination sounds like *zh* or French *j*, as in "intrusion," "collision." (In modern Hebrew the sounds *s* and *sh* are denoted by the same letter, *shin,* the sounds being distinguished by the dot added above this letter—to the right for the *s* sound and to the left for the *sh* sound.) There are exceptions to the foregoing more or less general rules for the sounds of *s*. For instance, in such words as "sugar," "sure," "surely," the *s* is pronounced *sh,* although it is initial.

In many words, such as "island" or "viscount," the *s* is mute, and its omission lengthens the preceding vowel. In some instances the High German *s* became *t* in English (*Wasser,* "water"; *das,* "that"). In some words of Latin or French origin the *sh* sound acquired the spellings *ch* ("machine"), *ci* ("social"), *ti* ("martial"), and *sci* ("conscience").

Other Uses of S. Both the capital and the lowercase forms of *s* are used as symbols or abbreviations for a number of words (see ABBREVIATIONS). In academic use, S is a grade, rating a student's work as satisfactory.

DAVID DIRINGER
Author of "The Alphabet"
Further Reading: See the bibliography for ALPHABET.

SA, Nazi paramilitary group. See GERMANY—*History;* STORM TROOPERS.

SÁ DE MIRANDA, sà thə mē-raɴ'də **Francisco de** (1481–1558), Portuguese poet, who introduced Italian Renaissance verse forms and poetic ideas into Portugal. Sá de Miranda was the illegitimate child of Inês de Melo and Gonçalo Mendes de Sá, a canon of Coimbra. He was legitimized in 1490.

After studying law, Sá de Miranda settled in Lisbon, where he attended the court of King Manuel I. In 1521 he went to Italy, traveling to Milan, Florence, Rome, and Sicily. During his five-year stay in Italy, he absorbed the techniques and ideas of such great contemporary figures as Giovanni Ruccellai, Jacopo Sannazzaro, Ariosto, and Francesco Guicciardini, as well as of such earlier literary giants as Dante, Boccaccio, and Petrarch. After returning to Portugal, he remained in Lisbon for a few years before settling at his estate, where he devoted himself to literary pursuits. He died at Tapada in 1558.

Sá de Miranda's important works include his eclogues *Alexo* and *Basto* and his many sonnets, which reflect his brilliant utilization of Italian verse forms. He also wrote fine elegies, epigrams, and satires, as well as two prose comedies, *Os Estrangeiros* and *Os Vilhalpandos.*

SAADI, sä-dē' (1184?–1291), was a Persian Sufi poet, whose works combined a warmth of feeling and entertainment with religious mystical thought. An alternate form of his name is Sadi. His original name was Muslih ud-Din, but he later adopted the name Saadi, which was derived from the name of the rulers of Shiraz, his native city.

After studying in Baghdad and spending many years traveling, Saadi settled in Shiraz, where he enjoyed the favor of several Persian rulers. The Persians had high regard for his golden maxims, which they considered a treasure of true wisdom, and for his pure, simple, and elegant style.

Saadi's most famous works are the *Bustan* (1257; *Fruit Garden*) and the *Gulistan* (1258; *Rose Garden*). There is also a collection (*Diwan*) of lyric poems, in Arabic and Persian. The *Bustan,* entirely in verse, is a collection of histories, fables, and moral instructions. The *Gulistan,* written in both verse and prose, contains personal recollections, aphorisms, and advice. His collected works appear in Persian and have been translated into English.

SAADIAH BEN JOSEPH, sä′dē-ə ben jō′zəf (882–942), Babylonian Jewish scholar and philosopher, whose originality and broad interests made him the most significant Jewish author of his day. A prolific writer, Saadiah wrote about 100 Hebrew and 200 Arabic works.

Saadiah ben Joseph, who is often referred to as Saadia Gaon, was born in Dilaz, Faiyum, Egypt. From 915 on he traveled through Palestine and other countries, finally settling in Babylonia where in 928 he was appointed gaon, or head, of the Academy of Sura. Following a quarrel with the exilarch David ben Zakkai, who was one of a line of Jewish civil and judicial rulers of the exiles in Babylon, Saadiah was deposed, but was reinstated in 937. Saadia's known works include a polemic (915) against the heretical Karaite sect and other powerfully argued writings against heretics. In his main philosophical work, the *Kitab al-Amanat wal-I'tiqadat* (*Book of Beliefs and Opinions*), written in Arabic in 933, Saadiah follows both Aristotle and the Muslim *kalam*, a liberal theological and philosophical system. He denies any conflict between faith and reason and attributes eternal existence, omnipotence, and omniscience to God.

Most of Saadiah's *halakhic* (religio-legal) writings are in Arabic, although some of his *responsa* (decisions on questions of ritual) are in Hebrew. His *Sepher Ha-Galuy*, written in Hebrew, contains an account of his difficulties and was intended as a model for composition. His prayer book, which was published in Jerusalem as the *Siddur of Saadiah Gaon* in 1941, was intended to standardize Jewish prayers. The *Siddur* contains rubrics, in Arabic, and *piyyutim* (religious poems), written in an artificial and difficult Hebrew. Saadiah's translation of the Bible into Arabic is called the *Tafsir* and is accompanied by commentaries in Arabic on most of the biblical books.

Saadiah was also a renowned Hebrew lexicographer. His great lexicon, the *Agron*, with explanations in Arabic, was one of his earliest works and is extant only in fragments. He compiled a list of words occurring only once in the Bible, the *Hapax Legomena*. His Hebrew grammar, *Kutub al-lugha* (*Books of Language*), was written in Arabic and consists of 12 parts.

En route to Babylonia in 921, Saadiah became involved in a controversy with the Palestinian rabbi Aaron ben Meir, who was determined on drastic changes that would have greatly complicated the Jewish calendar. In his *Sepher Zikkaron* he vigorously refuted the Palestinian claim to final authority in such matters, thereby establishing the Jewish calendar now in use. Saadiah died in Sura, Babylonia (modern Iraq).

RAPHAEL PATAI
Fairleigh Dickinson University

Further Reading: Malter, Henry, *Saadia Gaon: His Life and Work* (1921).

SAALE, zä′lə, is the name of two German rivers. The Saxoman Saale rises in the Fichtelgebirge in northeast Bavaria and flows north across Thuringia for 265 miles (426 km) into the Elbe in East Germany. It has dams with large reservoirs and is navigable for the last 100 miles (160 km) from Naumburg.

The Franconian Saale rises in northwest Bavaria near the Bavarian-Thuringian border. It flows southwest for 84 miles (135 km) to join the Main River at Gemünden in West Germany.

SAALFELD, zäl′felt, a town in East Germany on the Saale River, is on the northwestern slopes of the Thuringian Forest, in a region long noted for mining. There are iron and steel works nearby, and the town produces electrical machinery and paper goods.

The town, established about 1200, has several fine buildings dating from the Middle Ages. These include a 13th century Franciscan monastery, now used as a museum; a late 13th century castle; a 14th century church; and the 16th century town hall. From 1680 to 1735 the town was the capital of the duchy of Saxe-Saalfeld. Population: (1970 est.) 33,405.

SAAR. See SAARLAND.

SAAR RIVER, zär, rises in the northern Vosges Mountains of France, where it is called the Sarre, and flows northward through Moselle and Bas-Rhin departments. It enters West Germany at Saareguemines and continues north to join the Moselle River 5 miles (8 km) southwest of Trier. The Saar is approximately 150 miles (240 km) long.

SAARBRÜCKEN, zär-brük′ən, a city in West Germany, is on the Saar River near the French border and 100 miles (160 km) southwest of Frankfurt-am-Main. Although essentially a modern city, there are some interesting historic buildings. The 18th century Ludwigskirche is built on the plan of a Greek cross and has an octagonal tower. St. Arnual's Church is 13th–14th century Gothic, with a Baroque tower. There is an 18th century castle that belonged to the counts of Nassau-Saarbrücken.

The city is the capital of the Saarland and the center of the state's industrial and cultural life. It serves as a rail center for a large industrial and coal-mining region and manufactures steel products, machinery, cement, chemicals, and clothing.

Saarbrücken became the capital of the Saar Territory in 1919, after having frequently changed hands between France and Germany. In 1957, when the territory became the Saarland, a state of West Germany, Saarbrücken continued as the capital. Population: (1969 est.) 131,461.

SAAREMAA, sä′re-mä, an island in the Baltic Sea, is included within the territory of the Estonian republic of the USSR. Alternate forms of the name are Sarema and Saare. The Swedish form is Ösel and the Russian is Ezel. It is at the mouth of the Gulf of Riga, 13 miles (20 km) from the mainland. It is separated from Hiiumaa Island to the north by Soela Sound, and is connected with Muhu Island to the northeast by a causeway. The southwestern end of the island elongates into a 20-mile (32-km) peninsula. The island covers an area of 1,046 square miles (2,709 sq km), and its irregular coast forms a few harbors near which the towns are located. The principal town and port is Kuressaare (Kingisepp) on the southern coast. The chief occupations of the inhabitants are fishing and agriculture.

Dominated by the Knights of the Sword, or Livonian Knights, from the 13th to the 16th centuries, Saarema was conquered by Denmark about 1560, passed to Sweden in 1645, and to Russia in the early 18th century. At the close of World War I it became a part of Estonia, which passed under Russian rule in 1940.

EERO SAARINEN'S Hockey Rink (1958) at Yale University is designed with an upswept roof suspended from steel cables.

SAARINEN, sä'ri-nen, **Eero** (1910–1961), American architect. He was an outstanding figure in the generation that followed the great pioneers of modern architecture—Frank Lloyd Wright, Mies van der Rohe, and Le Corbusier. Unlike them, Saarinen never formulated an easily identifiable style. His airport terminals, embassies, university buildings, and monuments are alike only in the boldness of their design. He believed that the roots of architecture lay "in life itself—the way the building is used and a love for the people who use it."

Early Years. Saarinen was born in Kirkkonummi, Finland, on Aug. 20, 1910, the son of the Finnish architect Eliel Saarinen. The family emigrated to the United States in 1923. After graduating from the Yale School of Architecture in 1934, Saarinen worked with his father. Their joint designs included the General Motors Technical Center, Warren, Mich. (completed 1957), in the clean, rectilinear International style.

In 1940, the year he became a United States citizen, Saarinen collaborated with Charles Eames on a molded plywood chair that won an award in the Museum of Modern Art's organic furniture design contest. His other furniture designs included the so-called womb chair in 1948 and pedestal furniture that were made of molded plastic in the 1950's.

Maturity. Saarinen emerged as a leading architect in 1948, when he won the competition for the Jefferson National Expansion Memorial in St. Louis with a design for a catenary arch of stainless steel, 630 feet (195 meters) high (built 1962–1964). For the Massachusetts Institute of Technology he designed the Kresge Auditorium (1955), with a triangular, thin-shell dome, which is poised above three isolated points of support and is completely glazed between them. The adjacent chapel is an unbroken cylinder of brick. The roof of the Ingalls Hockey Rink (1959), Yale University, hangs from a parabolic arch 228 feet (71 meters) long. Movement dominates the design as though to express the activity within.

Saarinen designed the United States embassies in Oslo (1959) and London (1960) and the immense Bell Laboratories (1962) at Holmdel, N. J. The laboratories' curtain walls of silvered reflecting glass can exclude as much as 75% of the sun's heat.

Saarinen's most sensational work is the TWA terminal (1962) at the Kennedy International Airport, New York, with concrete roofs that seem to leap into the air. The curving forms of the terminal, completely plastic in approach, evince Saarinen's youthful interest in sculpture. Less dramatic but no less open, and even more functional, is the Dulles International Airport (1962) in Chantilly, Va., which includes a mobile waiting room.

Saarinen also designed the partially underground Vivian Beaumont Repertory Theater for the Lincoln Center for Performing Arts and the new CBS building, both in New York City. The CBS building, Saarinen's only skyscraper, was New York's first reinforced concrete tower. His John Deere administrative center in Moline, Ill., is made of unpainted Cor 10 steel, which will develop a protective coating of rust. Saarinen died in Ann Arbor, Mich., on Sept. 1, 1961.

EVERARD M. UPJOHN, *Coauthor of* "*History of World Art*"

Further Reading: Saarinen, Aline B., ed., *Eero Saarinen on His Work* (Yale Univ. Press 1962); Temko, Allan, *Eero Saarinen* Braziller 1962).

SAARINEN, sä'ri-nen, **Eliel** (1873–1950), Finnish-American architect, who was one of the pioneers in modern design. His progressive rejection of eclecticism and his corresponding emphasis on functionalism paralleled the work of other progressive and influential European architects—Ragnar Ostberg, Peter Behrens, Otto Wagner, and H. P. Berlage.

Career in Europe. Gottlieb Eliel Saarinen was born in Rantasalmi, Finland, on Aug. 20, 1873. He was trained at the Polytechnic Institute in Helsingfors (now Helsinki) from 1893 to 1897. His Finnish Pavilion for the Paris Exposition of 1900 won distinction for its simple, forthright design. His picturesque studio-home at Hvitträsk (1902), in its straightforward handling of pine and granite, reveals his respect for Finnish tradition and his lifelong sensitivity to the special qualities of materials.

Saarinen's most important building prior to World War I was the Helsinki Central Station (1910–1914), a monumental handling of internal space and external masses. It showed only the faintest trace of tradition in its design and was restrained in its independent decoration. In his design for the Chicago Tribune building (1922), Saarinen accepted the setback principle, causing the masses of his towering skyscraper to seem to grow spontaneously from bottom to top. Although his design won only second prize, it

ELIEL SAARINEN'S Central Station (1910–1914), Helsinki has bold, clearly marked masses suitable to its function.

MONKMEYER

had more influence on subsequent skyscrapers than the first-prize design.

Career in the United States. Saarinen emigrated to the United States in 1923 and taught architecture at the University of Michigan. From the late 1920's he was associated with various educational enterprises of the Cranbrook Foundation at Bloomfield Hills, Mich. In the 1920's and 1930's he designed the Cranbrook School for Boys, the Kingswood School for Girls, the Institute of Science, and the several buildings of the Cranbrook Academy of Art. The earlier buildings show traces of eclecticism, while the later have a simplified classic style complemented by the decorative sculpture of Carl Milles. As head of the academy from 1934 to 1948 and then of the graduate school of architecture, Saarinen and his wife Loja, a distinguished designer and weaver, shaped the educational program in architecture and arts and crafts.

Saarinen later worked in partnership with his son Eero. Their Kleinhans Music Hall, Buffalo, N. Y. (1938), is a functional building whose external massing expresses its interior form. The acoustics are almost perfect. The Tabernacle Church of Christ, Columbus, Ind. (1940), exhibits two of Saarinen's favorite motifs—a slender tower, opposing its verticals to surrounding horizontal masses, and a sunken pool mirroring the building. The one-story Crow Island School, Winnetka, Ill. (1939), is light, airy, and spacious, with furniture scaled to the child. The music pavilion (1940) at the Berkshire Music Center at Tanglewood, near Lenox, Mass., has a quadrant-shaped plan. The striking pavilion opens on spacious lawns.

Saarinen became a U. S. citizen in 1945. He received many awards. His books include *The City: Its Growth, Its Decay, Its Future* (1943) and *Search for Form* (1948). He died in Bloomfield Hills on July 1, 1950.

EVERARD M. UPJOHN, *Coauthor of "History of World Art"*

Further Reading: Christ-Janer, Albert William, *Eliel Saarinen* (Univ. of Chicago Press 1948).

SAARLAND, zär'länt, a state in West Germany since 1957, is a major industrial district, bordered on the south and southwest by French Lorraine and on the west by Luxembourg. It was formerly called the Saar Territory or Saar. It comprises the undulating hill country south of the Hunsrück Mountains and has an area of 991 square miles (2,567 sq km). The Saarland's main river is the Saar. Of the state's population of 1,127,400 (1969), nearly 75% is Roman Catholic and the remainder mostly Protestants. The capital is Saarbrücken, an industrial city of over 130,000 people.

The Saarland is one of the most important industrial districts in Europe. Its chief product is coal, mined, in the region between Neunkirchen and the Saar River. There are also large iron and steel industries, which are centered in Neunkirchen, Saarbrücken, Völklingen, Homburg, and St. Ingbert. For iron ore, Saarland industries must rely on the supplies of French region of Lorraine.

About one third of the working force of the Saarland is employed in mining or in iron and steel production. In addition, there are machine manufacturing plants, chiefly in Saarbrücken, and large glass and ceramic industries, mainly in St. Ingbert and Mettlach.

History. In the Middle Ages the area was broken into a number of territories, of which the largest was the countship of Saarbrücken. From 1381 it belonged to the dynasty of Nassau and was known as Nassau-Saarbrücken. In 1681 the French acquired a small bridgehead over the Saar River. Louis XIV had the Marquis de Vauban build the strong fortress of Saarlouis. During the Napoleonic era (1801–1814), the Saarland, together with the whole west bank of the Rhine, was under French domination. By the second Peace of Paris (1815), France was forced to cede Saarlouis and the surrounding area, and almost all of the Saarland became a district of the Prussian Rhine province.

The great Saar industries were built principally in the early 20th century. In 1919, under the terms of the Versailles Treaty, the area

SAARLAND

0   20 Mi.
0   20 Km.

now called Saarland was separated from Germany and set up as Saar Territory, under the supervision of the League of Nations. The separation took place ostensibly in order to give France the Saar's coal as reparation for destroyed French mines. France, however, hoped to incorporate the Saar within its own territory.

The Versailles Treaty had stipulated that a plebiscite, held after 15 years, would decide whether the Saar was to be French or German. By 1935 it was obvious that the vote would not favor France. On the other hand, due to the rise of Adolf Hitler in Germany, there was speculation that the people of the Saar might prefer the continuation of the existing regime. A proposition to this effect was included as a third option in a plebiscite on Jan. 13, 1935. The result, however, was an overwhelming vote in favor of union with Germany. The League of Nations then returned the Saarland to Germany, but only after Germany had paid for the coal mines that, under the Versailles Treaty, had become the property of France.

After World War II the French organized the former Saar Territory as a special region within their zone of occupation. A referendum in October 1947 favored economic union with France, and in 1948 an autonomous Saar entered into a customs union with France. When West Germany was freed of Allied controls in 1949, and as it gained in prosperity, the desire of the Saarlanders for reunion with West Germany grew. In 1954 a Franco-West German agreement proposed to make Saarland a European territory, but this was rejected in a 1955 plebiscite. In 1956 a new Franco-West German agreement, providing for full political integration of the Saarland with West Germany, was signed. This settlement became effective on Jan. 1, 1957, and played an important part in hastening the reconciliation of France and Germany.

HAJO HOLBORN
Author of "A History of Modern Germany"

SAAVEDRA LAMAS, sä-ä-vä-thrä lä'mäs, **Carlos** (1878–1959), Argentine lawyer, who received the Nobel Peace Prize in 1936. He was born in Buenos Aires on Nov. 1, 1878. In 1903 he graduated summa cum laude from the University of Buenos Aires, where he afterward taught political economy and constitutional law.

From 1932 to 1938, Saavedra Lamas served as Argentina's foreign minister. In 1933 he drafted an antiwar pact that was signed by 13 Latin American nations, the United States, and Italy. While presiding over the Chaco Peace Conference in 1935, he helped to end the war between Bolivia and Paraguay. In 1936 he presided over the assembly of the League of Nations. He was president of the University of Buenos Aires (1941–1943) and a professor there (1943–1946). He wrote books on law and on ways to preserve peace. He died in Buenos Aires on May 5, 1959.

SABAEANS, sə-bē'ənz, one of the three major peoples in the history of ancient South Arabia, the other two being the Minaeans and the Himyarites. The Sabaeans (Arabic, *Saba'*) were the first South Arabian people to step within the threshold of civilization. They are the Sheba of the Old Testament (Gen. 10:7; 25:3) and the Sabai of the 8th century B. C. cuneiform inscriptions of Mesopotamia. The earliest Western reference to them occurs in Greek writings of the second half of the 3d century B. C. Their habitat was the southwestern corner of the Arabian peninsula, now called Yemen. The fertility of this rain-favored land, its proximity to the sea, and its strategic location on the route to India gave it decided advantages over Hejaz in the north, and made it the seat of a flourishing culture long before the rise of Islam.

Until the last quarter of the 19th century, firsthand knowledge of this South Arabian civilization was fragmentary and meager. Islam did not encourage the study of any pre-Islamic civilizations, and explorations were forbidden. A Danish scholar and traveler, Carsten Niebuhr, was the first to announce (1772) the existence of South Arabic inscriptions. A French Jew, Joseph Halévy, was the first European to penetrate inner Yemen (1869–1870). Disguised as a rabbi from Jerusalem seeking alms for the Jews, he brought back 685 inscriptions from 37 localities. He was followed by Eduard Glaser, whose explorations between 1882 and 1894 yielded some 2,000 inscriptions extending as far back as the 7th century B. C. The inscriptions are written in alphabetic characters, somewhat related to Phoenician, and reveal what the Sabaeans and other South Arabians had to say about themselves.

Inscriptions, classical writings, and excavations, show that the South Arabians achieved a high degree of civilization and prosperity based upon agriculture and trade. Their religion was in essence a planetary astral system in which the cult of the moon god, known to the Sabaeans as Almaqah (health giving), prevailed. During at least the last millennium before Christ and two centuries after Christ, they almost monopolized the international trade of the Red Sea and the Indian Ocean, as well as the land trade that took frankincense, myrrh, spices, condiments, and other tropical products through Arabia into the Mediterranean. Some of these products came from India or East Africa. Incense was highly prized for ritual use and for Egyptian mummification. In their heyday the Sabaeans had colonies or trading posts all the way through North Arabia. The Queen of Sheba—if historical—must have come from one of these. She is named Bilqīs in Muslim tradition.

By the mid-8th century B. C., the Sabaeans had established a kingdom of their own with Marib as its capital. The kingdom lasted until about 115 B. C. In the first period, ending about 450 B. C., a priest-king, bearing the title Mukarrib Saba, stood at the head of the state. In the second period the ruler appears shorn of his priestly character and bearing the title Malik (king of) Saba.

Marib lies about 60 miles (100 km) east of Sana, the present capital of the Yemen Arab Republic, at an elevation of 3,900 feet (1,200 meters). It has been visited by few Westerners. Its historical fame rests on its dam (*sadd*), a remarkable engineering feat intended to create an artificial reservoir between hills for irrigation. The older portions of the dam were constructed in the mid-7th century B. C. by Sumhualay Yanuf and his son Yathaamar Bayyin.

Arab historians ascribe the decay of South Arabian civilization to the "bursting of the great dam" shortly before the rise of Islam. In fact, the decay was due to a variety of economic and political causes, one of which was a shift in the trade routes.

PHILIP K. HITTI
Author of "History of the Arabs"

Further Reading: Faris, Nabih A., *The Antiquities of South Arabia* (Princeton Univ. Press 1938); Fakhry, Ahmed, *An Archaeological Journey to Yemen* (Service des Antiquités de l'Égypte 1951–1952); Hitti, Philip K., *History of the Arabs*, 10th ed. (St. Martins 1970); Schoff, W. H., tr., *The Periplus of the Erythraean Sea* (Longmans 1912).

SABAH, sä′bä, is a state of Malaysia. It was formerly British North Borneo. See also BORNEO; MALAYSIA.

SABATIER, sà-bà-tya′, **Paul** (1854–1941), French chemist, who shared the 1912 Nobel Prize in chemistry with Victor Grignard for his research on the role of catalysts in organic syntheses. He was born in Carcassonne on Nov. 5, 1854, obtained his doctorate in 1880 from the University of Toulouse, and joined the faculty there.

Sabatier's key discovery in catalytic chemistry —made in 1897 with Jean Baptiste Senderens— was that hydrogen combines with unsaturated hydrocarbons in the presence of finely divided nickel. This became the basis for industrial processes such as the production of gasoline and fuel oil from coal and of margarine from cottonseed oil. He died in Toulouse on Aug. 14, 1941.

SABATINI, sab-ə-tē′nē, **Rafael** (1875–1950), Anglo-Italian author of historical novels. Sabatini was born in Jesi, Italy, on April 29, 1875, the son of an Italian tenor and an English soprano, and was educated in Switzerland and Portugal. At 17 he could read and write six languages, an accomplishment that encouraged him to begin a business career in Liverpool, England. After 10 years of writing commercial correspondence to foreign firms, he began to write short stories. In 1904 he wrote his first novel, *The Tavern Knight.*

Often called "the modern Dumas," Sabatini was the author of over 40 historical novels, biographies, and plays. His best-known novels are *Scaramouche* (1921), *Captain Blood* (1922), and *The Sea Hawk* (1915), all of which were made into movies. Other novels chronicled the further adventures of Scaramouche and of Captain Blood. Sabatini died in Adelboden, Switzerland, on Feb. 13, 1950.

SABBAT, sab′ət, a periodic gathering of witches. The term is possibly derived from the Hebrew Sabbath or from the French *s'ebettre,* meaning "to frolic." Belief in the sabbat is traceable back to the 14th century. Details of the occurrences were derived primarily from those tortured by the Inquisition as suspected witches. The sabbat could take place on almost any day of the week. It began shortly before midnight and ended at dawn. The sabbat reportedly included homage to the devil, a banquet on the flesh of young children, and dancing, and it always culminated in a sexual orgy.

SABBATAI ZEBI, sab-ə-tī′ tsə-vē′ (1626–1676), was a Jewish pseudo-messiah. Sabbatai Zebi was born in Smyrna, Turkey. Influenced by cabalistic (mystical) studies and subject to manic-depressive psychosis that probably were augmented by the horrors of the 1648–1649 massacres of Jews by the Ukrainian leader Bohdan Chmielnicki, he developed the delusion that he was the long-awaited Messiah of the Jews. After traveling through Rhodes and Tripoli, he went to Egypt where he married an eccentric young girl, named Sarah, who, for her part, was convinced that it was her destiny to be the Messiah's bride. On reaching Palestine in 1665, he was hailed as Messiah by the "prophet" Nathan of Gaza. Though the rabbis of Jerusalem excommunicated Sabbatai, his following continued to increase, and soon Jews all over the world became his fervent adherents.

In 1666 he went to Constantinople to depose the sultan, but was arrested, confined to the fortress of Gallipoli, and finally given a choice between death and the acceptance of Islam. He chose the latter. Many of his followers, however, were not shaken in their faith in him even by this act of apostasy, and accepted his explanation that his conversion and sufferings were willed by God as a trial for the Messiah and an atonement for the sins of Israel. Growing impatient with his activities the Turks finally banished him to the remote citadel of Dulcigno in Albania, where he died in 1676. The Sabbataian movement led to the rise of the Dönmeh and finally, in the 18th century, of the Frankist sect.

RAPHAEL PATAI
Fairleigh Dickinson University

SABBATH, the weekly day of rest and religious observance. The term is derived from its use as the Hebrew *Shabbath,* denoting the seventh day of the week, or Saturday. Most Christians observe the Sabbath on Sunday, although some sects such as the Seventh Day Adventists keep it on Saturday. The Muslim Sabbath is Friday. This article deals with the Jewish observance. For Christian customs, see SUNDAY; for Muslim practice, see ISLAM—*Islamic Worship.*

Origins. The Jewish Sabbath is kept from sunset on Friday until sunset on Saturday. It is observed in Hebrew ritual as a holy day in which man is required to withdraw from mundane affairs in order to experience a foretaste of paradise on earth. The biblical law of the Sabbath observance constitutes the fourth of the Ten Commandments: "Six days shalt thou labor, and do all thy work; but the seventh day is a sabbath unto the Lord thy God; in it thou shalt not do any manner of work, thou, nor thy son, nor thy daughter, nor thy man-servant, nor thy maid-servant, nor thy cattle, nor thy stranger that is within thy gates" (Exodus 20:9–10 and Deuteronomy 5:13–14, *The Holy Scriptures According to the Masoretic Text*).

The reason given for resting on the Sabbath is twofold. First, the day has to be kept holy because God made heaven and earth in six days, "and rested on the seventh day, wherefore the Lord blessed the Sabbath day and hallowed it" (Exodus 20:11). Second, the day serves as a reminder that "thou wast a servant in the land of Egypt, and the Lord thy God brought thee out thence" (Deuteronomy 5:15). As strictly interpreted, the penalty for desecrating the Sabbath was death: "whosoever doeth any work in the Sabbath day, he shall surely be put to death" (Exodus 31:15).

Postbiblical Jewish law devoted much attention to determining in precise detail the various kinds of work forbidden on the Sabbath, although any of them was considered permissible if it had to be performed in order to save a human life. These rules are contained especially in the tractate "Sabbath" of the Mishna and the Babylonian Talmud, upon which are based all the subsequent codification of Sabbath observances.

Scholarly research has sought to establish a relationship between the Hebrew Sabbath and the Babylonian Sabattu, a periodic unlucky day on which people abstained from any activity or undertaking. Whatever the original connection, the Hebrew Sabbath developed a completely different character.

Traditional Observances. Ever since the 1st century A. D., the Sabbath has been a day of spiritual and intellectual enjoyment, expressed most characteristically in prayer and study. Traditionally, men begin the holy day by attending synagogue services about an hour prior to the commencement of the Sabbath on Friday evening, while the women remain at home and light the Sabbath candles. Upon the men's return from the synagogue, the *Kiddush* ("Sanctification"), a benediction over a cup of wine, is recited, and then the Sabbath meal, consisting of specially delightful food, is served. Whenever the wife is in a ritually pure state, marital intercourse on the Sabbath night is recommended by the rabbis.

The Sabbath morning is again spent in the synagogue, where, in addition to the regular morning (*Shaharit*) service, the *Mussaf* (or "Supplement") prayers are said, and the weekly portion is read from the Pentateuch. The afternoon is spent in leisure, or in studying the sacred books. In the late afternoon a repast kept hot since the day before is set out at the "third banquet" amidst singing and learned discussion. This is followed, after sunset, by the Havdalah ("separation"), the valedictory benedictions over a candle, spices, and wine which signify the end of the Sabbath.

RAPHAEL PATAI
Fairleigh Dickinson University

SABELLI, sə-bel′ī, was the name given by the Romans to the peoples of ancient Italy who spoke Oscan. This designation included a number of groups with little political unity. These people spread over much of central Italy during the 5th century B. C., occupying Campania and Lucania. The Sabelli usually imposed their own language and merged with the local population. Among the Sabelli peoples are the Frentani, Lucani, Mamertini, Sabines, and Samnites.

SABER. See FENCING.

SABER-TOOTHED TIGER, any of several large extinct cats that had very long curved daggerlike teeth in their upper jaw. They ranged over Europe, Asia, Africa, North America, and South America. They first appear in the fossil record in the early Oligocene Period, some 40 million years ago, and probably became extinct only about 20,000 to 30,000 years ago. The extinction of the saber-toothed tiger is often given as an

COURTESY OF THE AMERICAN MUSEUM OF NATURAL HISTORY
Restoration of a saber-toothed tiger (genus *Smilodon*)

example of an inadaptive trend in evolution, supposedly evidenced by the development of such long canine teeth that the animal's bite became ineffective. This is incorrect. The Saber-toothed tiger most likely became extinct because its prey animals died out, and it was not agile enough to compete with faster predators for the available food.

SABIANS, sā′bē-ənz, are members of a Gnostic sect with Judaeo-Christian overtones. The name was also applied to a pagan sect in Syria. The Gnostic Sabians (Mandaeans), a sect of uncertain origin, perhaps dating from the 4th or 5th century A. D., practiced baptism and cleansing of sin by immersion. Their name derives from the Arabic *al-Sabiah*, which comes from a Semitic stem meaning "to immerse."

The Sabians (Mandaeans) are mentioned three times in the Koran, which accorded them the toleration guaranteed to the "people of the Book," notably Christians and Jews. The Sabians, who flourished on the marshy plains near the southern Euphrates River, also became known as the Christians of St. John the Baptist.

Muslim writers confused the Sabians with a pagan community in Harran (ancient Carrhae in northern Syria), which presumably adopted the baptism rite to secure the Koran's tolerated status. These pseudo-Sabians, who were actually moon worshipers, were overrun by the Mongols in the 13th century. However, a small community of real Sabians has survived, chiefly in Iraq. Under the name of al-Subba, the sect is especially noted for delicate metalwork in Baghdad.

PHILIP K. HITTI
Author of "History of the Arabs"

SABIN, sā′bən, **Albert Bruce** (1906–   ), American virologist, who developed an oral vaccine against poliomyelitis. Sabin was born in Bialystok, Russia (now in Poland) on Aug. 26, 1906. His family moved to the United States in 1921. He attended New York University, obtaining his medical degree in 1931, and served his internship at Bellevue Hospital before joining the staff of the Rockefeller Institute in 1924. In 1939 he joined the staff of the medical school at the University of Cincinnati and the Children's Hospital Research Foundation.

Sabin devoted his career to the development of protective vaccines against viruses that cause death and crippling illness in children. In particular he worked many years to produce an oral, live-virus vaccine against the three identified strains of poliomyelitis, in contrast to the inactivated-virus approach of Jonas Salk. The work of both men was based on the researches of Nobel Prize-winners John F. Enders, Frederick C. Robbins, and Thomas H. Weller.

After breeding millions of polio viruses, Sabin eventually developed strains that did not cause paralysis of the central nervous system, even when injected into the brains of monkeys. Sabin tried out the vaccine on numerous volunteers, including himself, before offering it to the scientific community in 1957 for massive field tests. The tests proved successful, as did those of oral polio vaccines independently developed by two other U. S. scientists, Hilary Koprowski and Herald Cox. See also POLIOMYELITIS.

SABIN, sā′bən, **Florence Rena** (1871–1953), American anatomist. Sabin was born in Central City, Colo., on Nov. 9, 1871. She received her medical degree in 1900 from Johns Hopkins University, joined the staff there, and later became the first woman to be made a full professor at Johns Hopkins. Her researches there were devoted to the determination of the origins of the lymphatic system and of blood vessels and cells in the developing embryo. In 1925 she became the first woman member of the National Academy of Sciences. That same year she went to the Rockefeller Institute for Medical Research to investigate cellular mechanisms of bodily defense against infections, especially tuberculosis. She retired to Denver, Colo., in 1938 but became active in the reformation of Colorado's public health laws. She died in Denver on Oct. 3, 1953.

SABIN, sā′bən, the unit of sound absorption of a surface. A sound absorption of one sabin is equivalent to the sound absorption of a perfectly absorbing material that has a surface area of 1 square foot (0.093 sq meter). The sabin is named after the American physicist Wallace C. Sabine.

SABIN VACCINE, sā′bən, an oral vaccine against poliomyelitis developed by the American virologist Albert Bruce Sabin. See SABIN, ALBERT BRUCE; POLIOMYELITIS.

SABINE, sā′bĭn, **Wallace Clement** (1868–1919), American physicist. He was born in Richwood, Ohio, on June 13, 1868, and graduated from Ohio University in 1886. Sabine attended Harvard, became a professor of physics and mathematics there, and died in Cambridge, Mass., on Jan. 10, 1919.

In 1895, Sabine was asked to improve the acoustics of a new lecture hall. From this beginning he worked out the principles of architectural acoustics. He laid down three general acoustical rules: the sounds must be loud enough, their quality must be unchanged, and successive sounds must not overlap. He defined a standard reverberation time as the time a sound takes to fall to one millionth of its original intensity, and established a standard of sound absorption in terms of the area of an open window—a perfect absorber, since all sounds falling on the window pass through it. (See SABIN.) He found that a room's reverberation time is defined by its volume divided by its total absorptivity, and he determined an optimum time of reverberation.

SABINES, sā′bīnz, a people of ancient Italy. They were one of the Sabelli groups and were concentrated in the hilly country northeast of Rome. They were a people of deep religious feeling. Their habits were simple and their lives virtuous.

From earliest times the Sabines were represented among the population of Rome, and the legend of the rape of the Sabine women by the wifeless followers of Romulus was probably fabricated to explain this admixture. They were conquered in 449 B. C., and again in 290 B. C. They were admitted to full Roman citizenship in 268, after which they disappeared as a separate people.

SABINIAN, sə-bin′ē′-ən (died 606), was pope from 604 to 606. Sabinian was a deacon of Rome when he was elected pope in March 604. He was consecrated on September 13. During Sabinian's tenure as Pope Gregory I's ambassador to the Byzantine court, Patriarch John the Faster of Constantinople assumed the title of ecumenical patriarch, a move Gregory saw as a threat to Roman authority. He chided Sabinian for not opposing the step more vigorously. Sabinian's reign was occupied chiefly with fending off the attacks of the Lombards in Italy.

SABLÉ, sä′blə, **Marquise de** (c. 1599–1678), French patroness of letters, whose salon in Paris attracted many famous literary figures. She was born Madeleine de Souvré in Touraine and was married to the Marquis de Sablé in 1514. A woman of intelligence and beauty, she frequented the famous salon of the Marquise de Rambouillet at the Hôtel de Rambouillet.

In 1646, together with her friend the Countess de Maure, the Marquise de Sablé began to hold salons at her Paris home. Antoine Arnauld, La Rochefoucauld, and Mmes. de Sévigné and de La Fayette were frequent visitors. The discussions that took place at her salons helped La Rochefoucauld formulate his famous *Maximes* (1665), precise and highly literate analyses of human behavior. Her own *Maximes*, published in 1678, are not entirely of her authorship. In her later years the Marquise de Sablé retired to the celebrated convent of Port Royal, where she died in 1678.

SABLE, one of the most valuable of furbearing animals. Although the name sable is often used interchangeably with marten, it should be applied only to the true, or Russian, sable, *Martes zibellina*. The soft, durable fur of this animal is used to make coats, stoles, and trimmings.

The Russian sable is a small weasellike animal found in parts of northern Europe and

Sable, *Martes zibellina*, at Soviet fur farm. It is a solitary animal that feeds on mammals and birds.

TASS, FROM SOVFOTO

Asia. It grows to a length of about 18 inches (45 cm), not including its bushy foxlike tail. Its coat varies from yellowish to dark brown above with gray markings on the face and tawny on the throat and underparts. It spends most of its time alone in trees, traveling from branch to branch. A vicious animal, it feeds on birds, squirrels, and other small animals. The mating season is in the summer, and after a gestation period of about nine months, the female produces a litter of usually four blind hairless kittens.

SABLE, Cape, the southern tip of Florida and the southernmost point of the mainland of the United States. The Florida Keys are south of the cape. Cape Sable is in the Everglades National Park and is noted for its beaches.

SABLE ANTELOPE, a large, handsome forest-dwelling antelope, *Hippotragus niger,* found in southern and eastern Africa. It has annulated, or ringed, horns that curve backward and sometimes reach a length of 3.5 feet (1 meter), long pointed ears, a mane at the nape, and a tufted tail. A bull stands about 4.5 feet (1.5 meters) at the shoulders and weighs about 500 pounds (225 kg). Females and young often associate in herds led by a single adult bull. They roam freely, grazing on grass. The young, born after a gestation period of about 270 days, are reddish until their third year. At least one variety, the giant sable antelope, *H. n. variani,* is considered endangered and is now known only in Angola.

SABLE ISLAND, Canada, is in the North Atlantic Ocean, about 180 miles (288 km) east of Halifax, Nova Scotia. About 25 miles (40 km) long and 1 mile wide, it is the exposed portion of a submerged sandbank about 75 miles (120 km) long. The name "sable" is the French for "sand." The island is being gradually worn away by the sea; formerly it was twice as long as it is now. It has been the scene of hundreds of shipwrecks, and for this reason it has often been called "the graveyard of the Atlantic."

Sable Island's only year-round inhabitants are the crews of a weather station and a radar installation. There are no trees on the island, and

the only vegetation is beach grass and small bushes. About 200 wild horses, descendants of animals cast ashore from a wreck some centuries ago, roam the island's eastern portion.

In the early 1970's, a test strike on the island found what engineers believed might be important oil deposits. Jurisdiction over Sable Island has long been an issue between the governments of Canada and of Nova Scotia province. The residents' votes have been counted with those of Halifax county, and any legal matters have been ruled upon by the Halifax courts.

SABOTAGE, sab'a-täzh, is the obstruction of an industrial or other process, with the intention of slowing it or bringing it to a halt. The term is most often applied to the destruction of equipment, although it may be extended to cover any act of obstruction, such as refusal to work or interference with the work of others.

Sabotage has a long history in industrial labor strife. During the early years of the Industrial Revolution, the weavers of England, seeing their livelihood threatened by the rapid spread of the factory system, often sabotaged the newly introduced power-operated machinery.

Sabotage has also been widely used as a clandestine political weapon in wartime, particularly in factories engaged in the production of goods essential to the conduct of war. During both world wars the intelligence service of the belligerent powers tried to place agents in the work forces of enemy manufacturing plants for the express purpose of industrial sabotage, thus creating a major problem for the agencies of counter intelligence.

The word "sabotage" derives from the French *saboter,* an expression meaning "to clatter one's wooden shoes" (*sabots*), or to work clumsily. Centuries after the term was coined, France gave the world one of its most spectacular examples of sabotage on a national scale. During the German occupation of that country in World War II, the French underground, or *Maquis,* accomplished prodigies of destruction and disruption. They hampered the movement of German troops by dynamiting trains, bridges, and roads, slowed operations in factories by various acts, kidnapped or murdered key personnel, and generally reduced the usefulness of France to the Germans as a military base and as a supplier of goods.

Sable antelope, *Hippotragus niger*

MARK BOULTON, FROM NATIONAL AUDUBON SOCIETY

SACAGAWEA, a Shoshone, was the only woman to travel with the Lewis and Clark expedition. She was a guide and helped avoid conflict between whites and Indians. The painting is by N. C. Wyeth.

SABRATHA, sab'rə-thə, was a Punic and Roman city in northwestern Libya, on the Mediterranean Sea about 40 miles (65 km) west of Tripoli. It was one of the three *emporia*, or commercial cities, of ancient Tripolis.

The first permanent settlement of Sabratha was made by the Carthaginians in the 4th century B. C. The city reached its peak of prosperity under the Romans in the 2d century A. D. Sacked by the Austurians in the 4th century, Sabratha flourished again under Byzantine rule from the 6th century until it fell to the Arabs in 643.

Sabratha's extensive ruins include the Roman and Byzantine walls that enclosed the city. There are also remains of the Roman forum, baths, theater, and temples, and Christian churches.

SABRE-TOOTHED TIGER. See SABER-TOOTHED TIGER.

SACAGAWEA, sak-ə-gə-wē'ə (1784?–1884), American Indian guide of the Shoshone tribe, the only woman to accompany the Lewis and Clark Expedition. Her Minnetarre name, *Tsa-ka-ka-wias*, means Bird Woman, and her Shoshone name, *Bo-i-naiv*, means Grass Maiden. Her name is also spelled *Sacajawea* and *Sahcargarweah*.

She was betrothed in infancy, but was captured by the Minnetarres when a child and later gambled away to a Frenchman named Toussaint Charbonneau, whose wife she became and with whom she was living in the Dakotas when Lewis and Clark reached there. Charbonneau and Sacagawea were engaged as guides and spent the winter at Fort Mandan, where Sacagawea's son, Baptiste, was born on Feb. 11, 1805. Sacagawea displayed remarkable ability as a guide, leading the way to her own country which she had not seen since a child. On one occasion she rescued from an overturned canoe the records of the expedition. She led the party to her own people on Aug. 17, 1805, where she was immediately recognized. Her shrewd sense and good counsels prevailed over her brother's determination to destroy the whites for their goods. Finding all her people dead except her brother and the child of a dead sister she immediately adopted the sister's child, and according to the custom of her people never admitted the sister's child to be other than her own. Sacagawea accompanied the party to the ocean, which was reached on Nov. 7, 1805, and returned with Captain Clark by way of the

Yellowstone, which region she also knew well.

Upon their return to the Minnetarre country Charbonneau refused to accompany the explorers to civilization, and Sacagawea remained with him. She then disappeared until she was found, an old woman, in the Shoshone Agency. She told a clear and intelligible story. She died in the Shoshone Agency in Wyoming on April 9, 1884.

SACCHARIN, sak'ə-rən, is a sweetening agent that is about 300 to 500 times sweeter than ordinary sugar and is widely used as a sugar substitute. Its main use has been as a sweetener in diet sodas and other low-calorie beverages and foods. Many diabetics turn to saccharin-sweetened foods and beverages because their bodies cannot properly metabolize sugar. However, since in some cases of diabetes there is evidence that saccharin may contribute to hypoglycemia and insulin shock, diabetics should consume saccharin-sweetened substances only under medical supervision.

In June 1978 the U. S. Food and Drug Administration required that all stores selling foods and beverages containing saccharin must post notices that the additive may be a health hazard. The FDA's decision was reached on the basis of several studies indicating that saccharin causes bladder cancer in rats. In the most nearly definitive study, carried out in Canada, rats fed saccharin amounting to 5% of their diet showed a marked increase in the incidence of bladder cancer. The significance of the Canadian study has been contested on several grounds, including the fact that the saccharin used was not pure and that rats are more susceptible to bladder cancer than other mammals.

SACCHETTI, säk-kāt'tē, **Franco** (c. 1330–1400), Italian writer and poet, best known for his novellas (tales) in the style of those in Boccaccio's *Decameron*. Sacchetti probably was born in Ragusa of a noble family. He settled in Florence, where he was a merchant and government official. He was noted for his common sense, good humor, and liberal-minded piety.

Sacchetti's novellas, begun in 1390, numbered about 300, but only 200 have survived. They have no framing situation, as does the Decameron, but in general relate the reactions of various characters to the odd things that happen to them. Sacchetti's poetry includes sonnets, *canzoni*, *ballate*, madrigals, and *cacce* (hunting songs).

SACCO-VANZETTI CASE, sak'ō-van-zet'e, the trial and conviction of Nicola Sacco, shoemaker, and Bartolomeo Vanzetti, fish peddler, who were executed in Massachusetts on Aug. 23, 1927, for holdup murders that were committed in South Braintree on April 15, 1920. The paymaster and the guard of the Slater and Morrill Shoe Factory had been shot dead and robbed of $15,776. Intense interest in the case, in the United States and in other countries, stemmed from a belief that Sacco and Vanzetti had been accused by sheer accident and convicted not on the evidence but largely because of unpopular political, social, and religious views.

The early 1920's was a time of widespread anti-alien and anti-radical hysteria. Sacco and Vanzetti, both Italian-born members of the Galleani anarchist group, feared raids in the Boston area and were shocked by the discovery of the body of a radical friend, Salsedo, outside a building where the authorities had detained him. Trying to dispose safely of radical literature from the home of other friends, Sacco and Vanzetti arranged to borrow the car of an associate, Mike Boda, that had been left for repair at Johnson's garage in West Bridgewater.

The police, who had been searching for a Buick car in which the Braintree murderers had escaped, found a stolen Buick in a nearby woods. This was identified as the car also used, presumably by Italians, in an attempted holdup in Bridgewater on Dec. 24, 1919. When the police learned that Boda's car was in the Johnson garage, they instructed Johnson to let them know if it was called for.

Sacco, Vanzetti, Boda, and an acquaintance named Orciani arrived at the garage on the evening of May 5, 1920, and Johnson's wife telephoned the police. Because Johnson, meanwhile, had told Boda the car could not be driven without new license plates, the men left. Within the hour, Sacco and Vanzetti were arrested on a trolley car bound for nearby Brockton.

The police found a Colt revolver on Sacco and a Harrington & Richardson on Vanzetti. After the police called witnesses to the two crimes at South Braintree, both men were charged with the murders. However, Vanzetti alone was charged with the attempted holdup in Bridgewater, because on that particular day Sacco had been at his job.

Tried first before Judge Webster Thayer for the Bridgewater holdup, Vanzetti was convicted. The case against him rested entirely on identification by eyewitnesses. However, many of their statements made to Pinkerton detectives right after the holdup (but available to the defense only many years after the trial) were greatly at variance with the witnesses' own trial testimony.

The trial of both men for the Braintree murders, also before Judge Thayer, began in Dedham, Mass., on May 31, 1921. The state's evidence consisted primarily of identification by witnesses, expert ballistic testimony interpreted as concluding that one of the mortal bullets had been fired from Sacco's pistol, and "consciousness of guilt."

The claim of the prosecution was that the defendants, when arrested, acted as though they meant to use the guns they were carrying, and that both told falsehoods. At the trial the defendants sought to ascribe these falsehoods to fears arising from their radical connections. Thus the issue of radicalism was injected into the trial by the defense. Many students of the case believe the cross-examination of Sacco, especially, was highly improper.

The defense produced "alibi" witnesses, ballistics experts, and many witnesses to the crime, who denied Sacco's or Vanzetti's participation. Sacco's alibi was strong. He testified that he had gone to Boston on the day of the murders to inquire about a passport at the Italian consulate, and this was corroborated.

After the conviction of both defendants on July 14, 1921, the defense filed a number of motions for a new trial. All motions were heard by Judge Thayer and all denied in 1924. In 1926, appeals were argued before the Supreme Judicial Court of Massachusetts. This court affirmed, only on the ground that it could find no legal error. Later, another motion was made before Judge Thayer based on a statement by Madeiros, a fellow prisoner of Sacco, that he, not the defendants, had been a party to the murder. The defense contended that the Braintree crime had been committed by a gang of Providence, R. I., criminals led by the Morelli brothers. This motion was also denied and the denial upheld in 1927.

On April 9, 1927, Judge Thayer imposed sentence of death. Each defendant declared his innocence. Vanzetti, in an impassioned declaration of his socialist beliefs, wrote: "Never in our full life could we hope to do such work for tolerance, for justice, for man's understanding of man as now we do by accident. Our words—our lives—lives of a good shoemaker and a poor fish peddler—all! That last moment belongs to us—that agony is our triumph."

Petitions for clemency followed. Gov. Alvan T. Fuller appointed, as an advisory committee, President A. Lawrence Lowell of Harvard, President Samuel W. Stratton of Massachusetts Institute of Technology, and former Probate Judge Robert Grant. Both governor and committee heard defense counsel and interviewed witnesses. On Aug. 3, 1927, the governor denied clemency.

The committee's report was severely criticized by much of the press, especially the report's handling of the charge of prejudice against Judge Thayer. The Lowell Committee had characterized the hostility of the judge's private statements about the defendants as "a grave breach of decorum," but concluded that his remarks had not affected his conduct of the case or influenced the jury. A motion for revocation of sentence, filed by the defense because of Judge Thayer's prejudice, was denied by him. Attempts to obtain redress in the federal courts failed.

Immediately before the executions were carried out, demonstrations, sometimes with violence, took place in many parts of the world. Upton Sinclair's novel, *Boston,* is perhaps the most authentic work the case inspired, and Maxwell Anderson's play, *Winterset,* the most imaginative. Some writers have claimed that Vanzetti was innocent but Sacco guilty. This opinion rests mainly on ballistic tests made many years after the trial, which are not conclusive. It is generally agreed, however, that there should indeed have been a new trial, at which all significant information brought to light in the interim could have been considered by a jury.

OSMOND K. FRAENKEL
A General Counsel, American Civil Liberties Union
Further Reading: Fraenkel, Osmond K., *The Sacco-Vanzetti Case* (reprint, Russell, 1969); Frankfurter, Felix, *The Case of Sacco and Vanzetti* (reprint, Grosset 1962); Russell, Francis, *Tragedy in Dedham: The Story of the Sacco-Vanzetti Case* (McGraw 1971).

SACHER-MASOCH, zä′кнər-mä′zôкн, **Leopold von** (1836–1895), German novelist, from whose name the word "masochism" is derived. He was born in Lemberg, Germany, on Jan. 1, 1836. His novels were realistic in style and dealt with peasant life and Jewish themes. In some of them he described the aberration of deriving sexual pleasure from suffering pain and humiliation, which led to the coinage of the word "masochism."

His most famous works are *Das Vermächtnis Kains* (4 vols., 1870–1877; *The Legacy of Cain*) *Falscher Hemelion* (1873; *False Ermine*), and *Die Messalinen Wiens* (1874; *The Messalinas of Vienna*). Sacher-Masoch died in Lindheim, Hesse, on March 3, 1895.

SACHEVERELL, sə-shev′ər-əl, **William** (1638–1691), English parliamentarian. He entered Parliament for Derbyshire in 1670 as a Whig and bitterly opposed court policy, especially the secret treaty with France. A leader in investigating the "Popish Plot" and impeachment of Lord Arundel and the five popish lords (1678), he first suggested the Exclusion Bill to deny James the succession.

Richard Onslow, speaker of the House of Commons, called him the "ablest parliament man of Charles II's reign." Sacheverell died in Barton, Nottinghamshire, England, on Oct. 9, 1691.

SACHS, zäks, **Curt** (1881–1959), German musicologist. He was born in Berlin on June 29, 1881. Sachs studied music history and art history at the University of Berlin, earning a Ph. D. in 1904. Later he studied musicology with Hermann Kretzschmar and Johannes Wolf. In 1919, Sachs became curator of the Berlin State Museum of Musical Instruments and in 1920, professor at the National Academy of Music. He also taught at the University of Berlin.

After the Nazis came to power in 1933, Sachs left Germany, going first to Paris and then to New York, where he settled in 1937. He taught at New York University and at Columbia. Sachs was a consultant to the New York Public Library (1937–1952) and headed the American Musicological Society (1948–1950). His major works include *The History of Musical Instruments* (1940), *Our Musical Heritage* (1948), and *Rhythm and Tempo* (1953). He died in New York City on Feb. 5, 1959.

SACHS, zäks, **Hans** (1494–1576), German poet, who is the most famous of the 16th century *Meistersinger* (Mastersingers), master craftsmen who wrote poems and songs as an avocation.

Life. Sachs was born in Nuremberg on Nov. 5, 1494, the only son of Jorg Sachs, a tailor, and his wife, Christina. Hans attended the local Latin school from 1501 to 1509, when he was apprenticed to a shoemaker. At this time also he received instruction from Leonhard Nunnenpeck, a weaver, in the art of the mastersong. Sachs spent his years as a journeyman in southern Germany, Austria, and the Rhineland. After returning to Nuremberg in 1516, he became a master shoemaker and subsequently a mastersinger. In 1519 he married Kunigunde Creutzerin, by whom he had seven children. He became famous four years later with his poem *The Wittenberg Nightingale,* in which he praised and supported Martin Luther and the Reformation. Sachs remained in Nuremberg throughout his long life, working as a cobbler and composing mastersongs, plays, and poems. For many years he was one of the official examiners at Nuremberg's singing school of new aspirants to the title of mastersinger. He died in Nuremberg on Jan. 19, 1576.

Works. Sachs began to collect his poems in 1517. His first efforts at drama date from 1518. Evidence of his wide reading is reflected in such titles as *Gismundo and Guisgardo, Lucius Papirius Cursor, Lady Poverty and Lady Luck, Lucretia,* and *Virginia.* His learning is also apparent in his translations of the classics and of Italian and French literature.

Sachs' purpose, whatever he was writing, was to point a moral, usually a practical one about coexisting with one's fellowmen. The story is told in plain language with little attempt at subtle characterization, motivation, or descriptive setting. The moral is clearly stated at the end. Sachs' greatest talent lay in his presentation of the scenes he knew best—the life of the petty bourgeoisie of his time. This talent is particularly evident in his Shrove Tuesday plays, with their emphasis on crudely realistic comedy. Their spirit is often indicated in their titles, such as *The Baker's Boy in the Convent, The Cobbler and the Liver Sausage,* and *The Parson and the Adulterous Peasants.* His play *The Wet Man* is typical. In it, a man works all day in the rain. When he comes home, his wife tells him to go to the well for water since he is already wet. He fetches the water and pours it over her, remarking that, since she, too, is now wet, she can go to the well. The moral of the story is: don't let your wife make a fool of you.

Sachs was a prolific author, producing an enormous number of lyrics, fables, tragedies, comedies, and narrative poems. A list of his own, compiled in 1567, shows 4,275 mastersongs, many with original melodies, 1,700 narrative poems, and 208 dramas. Thus, although he did not write for a living, it is clear that literature was his principal occupation.

The image of Sachs as the industrious shoemaker who spontaneously produced poetry after his day's work is an idealized oversimplification. This picture of Sachs was evoked by Richard Wagner in his great comic opera *Die Meistersinger von Nürnberg,* first performed in 1868. Wagner's work and, earlier, the praise of Goethe inflated Sachs's literary reputation in the 19th century. In fact, however, Sachs' poetic gifts were very limited, and he is much more interesting as a social observer and commentator.

W. T. H. JACKSON, *Author of "Medieval Literature: A History and a Guide"*

Further Reading: Könnecker, Barbara, *Hans Sachs,* with bibliography (1971); Taylor, Archer, *The Literary History of Meistergesang* (Oxford 1937).

SACHS, zäks, **Julius von** (1832–1897), German botanist, who is considered the founder of experimental plant physiology. Sachs was born in Breslau, Silesia (now Wrocław, Poland), on Oct. 2, 1832. He studied at Prague and received his doctorate in 1856. After holding other academic positions, he was appointed professor of botany at Würzburg in 1869, a position he held until his death, in Würzburg, on May 29, 1897.

Sachs devoted the major portion of his studies to plant metabolism and the determination of the relative importance of various minerals in plant nutrition. He clarified the process of respiration in plants and showed that chlorophyll is located in plant cells in special bodies that were later named chloroplasts. He found that sunlight plays the essential role in the absorption of carbon dioxide by these bodies and that starch appears in the chloroplasts immediately following the absorption. In addition, he carried out research on phototropism and geotropism and studied the mechanism of water transport in plants. A respected teacher, Sachs wrote several important works, of which the best known is *Lehrbuch der Botanik* (1868).

SACHS, zäks, **Nelly** (1891–1970), German-Swedish poet, whose deeply moving verse, full of dramatic symbolism and poignant imagery, powerfully delineates the age-old theme of the suffering of the Jewish people. She shared the Nobel Prize in literature in 1966 with the Israeli author Shmuel Agnon.

Nellie Sachs was born in Berlin on Dec. 10, 1891. She began writing poems and playlets as a young girl, but her youthful efforts attracted little critical notice. After reading the novel *Gösta Berling* by Selma Lagerlöf, she began to correspond with the Swedish author, who helped Miss Sachs and her mother escape from Nazi Germany to Sweden in 1940. Miss Sachs learned Swedish and earned a living by translating Swedish literary works into German. Gradually she developed her unrhymed, strongly rhythmic style and a preoccupation with the theme of Jewish martyrdom. A selection of her work was translated into English and published as *O the Chimneys* (1967). She died in Stockholm, May 12, 1970.

SACKVILLE, Thomas (1536–1608), English statesman and poet. He was born in Withyham parish, Sussex; became a student of the Inner Temple; and was later called to the bar. At the Temple he wrote the last two acts of the *Tragedie of Gorboduc*, first performed in London in 1561 and printed in 1565. As a poet, he is best known for his contributions to *A Mirror for Magistrates* (1st ed., 1559), a collection of early Elizabethan narrative poetry, which was started by William Baldwin, George Ferrers, and others. Sackville's contributions, which first appeared in the 1563 edition of the *Mirror*, were a poetical preface—the *Induction*, which has been called the greatest English poem between Chaucer's *Canterbury Tales* and Spenser's *Faerie Queen*—and *Complaint of Henry Duke of Buckingham*.

From 1557 to 1563, Sackville sat in the Parliaments of Queen Mary and Queen Elizabeth. He was knighted and created Baron Buckhurst in 1567. Between that time and 1598, he carried out a number of delicate missions at home and in foreign countries, and in 1599 he was rewarded by the office of lord high treasurer, confirmed as a lifetime post by James I. In 1604 he was created earl of Dorset. Sackville died in London on April 19, 1608. See also GORBODUC; MIRROR FOR MAGISTRATES.

Further Reading: Swart, J., *Thomas Sackville: A Study in Sixteenth Century Poetry* (Wolters 1949).

SACKVILLE-WEST, Victoria Mary (1892–1962), English novelist and poet, who is best known for her novel *The Edwardians*. She was the daughter of the 3d Baron Sackville and was born at Knole, Sevenoaks, Kent, on March 9, 1892. In 1913 she married Harold Nicolson, journalist and diplomat. *The Edwardians* (1930), a witty commentary on the social scene of the post-Victorian era, was followed by *All Passions Spent* (1931), in which the heroine, in her desire to be an artist, fights against conventions.

She also wrote several nonfiction works, including *Knole and the Sackvilles* (1922), an account of her home and family. *Pepita* (1937) was a fictionalized biography of her maternal grandmother, who was a Spanish dancer. Miss Sackville-West died at Sissinghurst Castle, Kent, on June 2, 1962.

SACO, sô'kō, is a city in southern Maine, in York county, across the Saco River from Biddeford, about 15 miles (24 km) south of Portland. Its industries make textile products, shoes, rawhide products, and clothing. The York Institute Museum has a fine-arts collection. Thornton Academy (coeducational) was founded in 1811.

Saco and Biddeford were both settled in 1630. The communities were called Saco until 1718 and Biddeford until 1762. Saco was renamed Pepperellboro, but resumed its original name in 1805. It was chartered in 1867 and has a mayor and board of aldermen. Population: 12,921.

SACRAMENT, generally understood as a formal rite of the Christian church and a symbol of a spiritual reality. The word "sacrament" is derived from the Latin *sacramentum*, which in its original use was employed for the oath taken following enrollment in the Roman armies. A legal use of the same word referred to a deposit made by those engaged in court action, with the understanding that the loser forfeited his *sacramentum* to the state treasury, which, as some suppose, employed the money for sacred purposes. The fact that the word, in its root and significance, suggests something set apart as holy, indicates that both the military and the legal *sacramentum* were regarded as having some religious character.

Ecclesiastical Usage. The term is more generally employed in contemporary usage to describe a sacred religious practice, although it can also have the connotation of a holy mystery. Hence, it is related to *mysterion*, the Greek term employed to describe some hidden truth or reality that is made known to men through the revelation of God. It is with its ecclesiastical usage, however, that this article is concerned, since that is the sense of the word in ordinary speech.

Ecclesiastical Definition. In this connection the term "sacrament" can be used in a general or in a narrower meaning. In the former, it is defined by St. Augustine as *signum sacrum* or *signum rei sacrae* (sacred sign or sign of a sacred reality), a definition that has been generally accepted by Christian theologians. The Anglican Book of Common Prayer gives a fuller statement, "an outward and visible sign of an inward and spiritual grace." The sacramental idea suggests that there is a general principle running through the created world, in which corporeal or material things are the expressive media for unseen, but genuine, realities of a spiritual kind. Values, ideals, and purposes are operative in, and their reality is expressed through, such material and corporeal realities. Goodness is known and seen through good acts; beauty, through beautiful objects; love, through loving persons. More significantly, it is said that God is known in this fashion. Saint Thomas Aquinas wrote: "Through signs that can be perceived by the senses, the mind is stimulated in its aim towards God." Catholic Christianity (the ancient, undivided

Christian Church and those churches—such as the Anglican, Roman, and Eastern Orthodox—that claim continuity with it) has maintained that the normal means for reaching the divine Reality is through such sacramental impressions of God.

Physical contacts, material realities, things done in the realm of the visible, tangible, corporeal, or sensible, are for Catholic Christianity the most effective way in which states of mind, attitudes, beliefs, and certainties of many sorts may be stimulated and even inaugurated, as well as deepened and enriched. Central in this pattern of material expression of spiritual reality is the Incarnation of God in Christ, in which it is believed that God employed, sacramentally, a human life as his means of self-expression in the created order.

Definition According to Rite. When this general sense of the word "sacrament" is restricted to the ecclesiastical rites of worship, the definition of Hugh of St. Victor is adequate: "a corporeal or material element offered to the senses, which from likeness represents, from institution signifies, and from consecration contains, some invisible and spiritual grace." This definition includes four points that have generally been maintained as essential to a sacrament:

(1) The sacrament must have a sign that is a visible reality. This may be the pouring of water, as in Baptism; the bread and wine of the Lord's Supper, Holy Communion, or Mass; the laying-on of hands, as in ordination and confirmation.

(2) Further, the sacrament must have some spiritual grace or gift, which is conveyed to the faithful recipient. In Baptism this is forgiveness of sin and incorporation into the Church of Christ; in the Lord's Supper, the body and blood of Christ; in Ordination, the grace of ministry; in Confirmation, the strengthening for responsible Christian life.

(3) The sacrament must in some sense have been divinely instituted. It cannot be a mere human invention, but in one way or another must have attached to it the promise of the divine purpose, whether by explicit institution, as in the Last Supper of Jesus with his disciples, the Holy Communion, or by some more general direction which has led to such a rite, as in the Unction of the sick.

(4) Finally the sacrament must be efficacious in that it conveys or contains that which it professes to do. The view is held in Catholic Christianity that sacramental rites are not merely edificatory or teaching signs but actually effect some result through their performance.

This definition has been further refined by theologians, such as Aquinas, in order to include the following ideas: *matter* of the sacrament, or some external and visible thing such as the eucharistic elements of bread and wine; *form of* the sacrament, or words that explicitly state the intention for which the rite is being performed; *minister* of the sacrament, or a person properly authorized to conduct the rite; *benefit,* or the good result which follows. A *valid* sacrament is one in which all these conditions are met. In the Eucharist, or Holy Communion, another term is introduced, the *res* of the sacrament, the underlying reality that it contains and conveys. In the Eucharist this is the body and blood of Christ.

Sacraments as Symbol and Instrument. From the definition quoted above from Hugh of St. Victor, the phrases "from likeness represents and from institution signifies" introduce another set of ideas that have, especially in recent years, been much emphasized by theologians, particularly Anglicans, such as Oliver Chase Quick: a sacrament is both a *symbol* and an *instrument.* By symbol is meant that there is in a sacramental rite some likeness that, in Hugh's phrase, "represents" what is being commemorated or conveyed.

Hence the bread and the wine in the Eucharist from likeness represent the body and blood of Christ, in this instance by divine institution; or in Baptism, the pouring of water represents, from likeness, the washing away of sin (dirt), which soils the personality of the recipient. On the other hand, the sacrament is not merely symbolic, since it is a sign that effects what it symbolizes. It is thus instrumental.

To some degree this notion of the sacrament rests back upon the Aristotelian conception of "efficient cause," and is suggested by Aquinas in his general discussion of the subject in the *Summa Theologica* where he uses the illustration of a woodman's ax effectual in felling a tree. The Reformed theologians of the 16th century were divided on this matter, some resting content with a merely significatory understanding of the sacrament, and others, as in England, insisting that a sacrament is an "effectual sign."

Number of Sacraments. Throughout Christian history the problem of the number of ecclesiastical sacraments has been a matter of theological discussion. All Christians, except the Society of Friends, have accepted Baptism and the Eucharist as sacraments "generally necessary to salvation," in the sense that their use is the normal way of admission to, and participation in, the benefits of Christ, although there have been widely differing interpretations of the sense in which this is true. On the other hand, Catholic Christianity, in both eastern and western forms, has said that there are five other rites, of a sacramental nature, that may properly be called sacraments. These are: Confirmation; Marriage; Absolution, or Penance; Holy Orders, or the rite of setting-apart for the ministry; and Unction, or the Anointing of the sick or dying. It was not until the Middle Ages that the number was set at seven, and even this does not provide for the variety of less formal rites and actions or objects which in western Catholicism are called sacramentals.

Meaning of the Sacraments. In the full scheme of seven sacraments, certain of the group are believed to be effective in conveying character or status in the relation of the recipient to God and Christ. In Baptism, the person receiving the sacrament is made a member of the Body of Christ, the Church; in Confirmation, he is given the special status of a communicant; and in Ordination, he receives the position of an ordained person with particular rights that attach to this office. In this meaning of character the three sacraments are said to be "indelible"; that is, they can never be repeated because the status that has been granted is a permanent status. Protestant theologians have tended to deny this view, especially as regards Ordination, but in the Anglican Church, the Roman Catholic, and Eastern Orthodox churches it has usually been held.

Finally, the more traditional Christian view is that the sacraments are effectual apart from the moral character of the minister. This is the basic meaning of the concept of their operation *ex opere operato*. The Anglican Articles of Religion state this in the phrase: "That the unworthiness of the minister hindereth not the sacraments." In this way, it is said, the recipient is not dependent upon the intangible factor of ministerial holiness or intention. However, it is always considered necessary that a minister shall have at least this much by way of "intention"; he shall purpose to do what the church itself intends, even if his understanding of this is not complete. The sufficient guarantee that he so intends is his use of the normal matter and form that the church has prescribed and the fact that he is himself a properly authorized person to perform the rite.

Various Interpretations. The interpretation of sacraments differs in the various Christian denominations and churches. The outline already given is in general that of Catholic Christianity, including the Anglican Communion. The Reformed churches of the continent of Europe, with their offspring in other parts of the world, have variations on this view. Calvinism and Lutheranism, as well as the followers of Zwingli (the Reformed Church, properly speaking), have tended to take a less systematic view, holding that the efficacy of the sacraments is due to the blessing of Christ and that the formalized scheme is not necessary for an understanding of their operation. In some of these groups, great emphasis is placed on the faith of the recipient. However, all Christians have maintained that, in one way or another, "faith is the means whereby we receive the sacrament."

It is important to observe, however, that in recent years there has been a much stronger emphasis, throughout Christianity, on the importance of the sacramental idea in general and the significance of sacramental rites within the Christian Church. This has been associated with the liturgical movement of the Roman Catholic Church and with similar movements found in other denominations. See also BAPTISM; CONFIRMATION; EUCHARIST; LORD'S SUPPER.

W. NORMAN PITTENGER
Cambridge University

Further Reading: Rahner, Karl, *The Church and the Sacraments*, tr. by W. J. O'Hara (Herder & Herder 1963); Schillebeeckx, Edward, *Christ: The Sacrament of the Encounter With God*, tr. by Paul Barrett (Sheed 1963); Shepherd, Massey H., *The Worship of the Church* (Seabury 1952).

SACRAMENTALS are objects, prayers, and rites that are a source of spiritual blessing when used by the faithful in a proper way. According to Roman Catholic theology sacramentals are like sacraments in that they are signs of a spiritual reality, but they differ from them in that sacramentals are instituted by the church rather than by Christ. They derive their efficacy from the prayer and blessing of the church. Religious objects blessed by a priest, such as rosaries, crucifixes, holy water, and images of Christ, the Blessed Virgin, or the saints, are sacramentals, as are various actions, such as the sign of the cross. Other sacramentals include rites and prayers that are part of the administration of the sacraments, as, for example, the blessing of the water and the anointing with oil in Baptism. Anglicans and Eastern Orthodox also recognize the use of sacramentals but do not in all instances share the same theology on the subject.

SACRAMENTO, the capital of California and the seat of Sacramento county, is in the north-central part of the state, 85 miles (137 km) east of San Francisco. Its setting at the confluence of the Sacramento and American rivers in the fertile Central Valley is picturesque, with the coastal mountains rising to the west and the rugged Sierra Nevada to the east.

The city is built around the state capitol building, which is situated on a sloping terrace in a park containing trees and plants from all over the world. The building, constructed of California granite and white painted brick and topped by a huge gold dome, resembles the U. S. Capitol. Most of the streets are broad and straight, and many are lined with trees. Flowers abound throughout the year. There are so many camellias that the city has become known as the "Camellia Capital of the World."

Economy. Sacramento's economy is widely based, relying on industry, agriculture, military installations, and government. The city is a missile and rocket center engaged in the nation's space programs. The power pack that lifted the first U. S. satellite into orbit was built here. Among the many products manufactured in Sacramento are aircraft parts, military weapons, defense systems, radiators, bricks, chemicals, liquid gas, soap, caskets, paint, scales, furniture, paper plates, bags, and pencils. Foods such as soups, cake mixes, potato chips, and sausages are also made here, and many of the major U. S. meat packing and food processing companies are located in the city, where they prepare and package meats and vegetables, fruits, and other crops from the Central Valley for marketing throughout the nation. The valley's chief crops include barley, rice, nuts, corn, sugar beets, tomatoes, wheat, and alfalfa.

There are three major military installations in or near Sacramento. These are Mather Air Force Base, McClellan Air Force Base, and the Sacramento Army Depot. The state government offices and agencies also exert a great economic influence.

Sacramento is an important transportation center. It is the junction of two mainline transcontinental rail carriers, the Southern Pacific and the Western Pacific, and has one of the nation's largest switching yards. It offers movement of goods to all parts of the United States on carload, piggyback, and container freight cars.

Although situated so far inland, Sacramento is a port that can handle oceangoing vessels. In 1963, the Sacramento-Yolo Port District deepwater ship channel was completed, connecting the city's facilities with San Francisco Bay.

Education, Culture, and Recreation. The city maintains three junior colleges, and the California State University at Sacramento is situated here, as is the McGeorge School of Law, a branch of the University of the Pacific.

The Crocker Art Gallery contains a fine collection of drawings and paintings, including works by Leonardo da Vinci, Michelangelo, Rembrandt, and Albrecht Dürer. The State Indian Museum contains exhibits illustrating the artifacts and ways of life of the California Indians. The Sutter's Fort State Historical Monument is a restoration of the fortified trading post, ranch house, and workshop of Sacramento's first settler. The Old Sacramento historical area includes many buildings of the 1850–1870 period. In the 1970's, a 9-acre (3.6-hectare) historic park was developed here by the state.

The California capitol building in Sacramento stands at the eastern end of Capitol Mall.

The Sacramento Symphony presents a full season of concerts and gives free concerts for young people. There is also a Sacramento Civic Ballet.

The Sacramento Capitols play Continental League professional football, and the Camellia Bowl Festival of Sports, held every December, features numerous sports activities. There is a Camellia Festival every spring, and the California State Fair is held here at the end of every summer.

History. In 1839, John Augustus Sutter, a German-born Swiss citizen, received permission from the Mexican government to establish a colony in the interior of northern California. He settled with his party on the south bank of the American River near its confluence with the Sacramento, and began raising crops and livestock and building his fort. Soon after the occupation of California by American forces in 1846, Sutter found such a good market for his produce along the northern California coast that he had several hundred men working for him.

In January 1848, Sutter's chief carpenter, James W. Marshall, discovered gold in the trail-race of Sutter's mill at Coloma, on the south fork of the American River northeast of the present site of Sacramento. Within a few months, the gold rush was on.

Although prices soared to unbelievable heights, Sutter's merchandising enterprises did not prosper, because his workers left him to look for gold, his stock was stolen, and squatters settled on his land. To save some part of his holdings, he deeded a parcel along the Sacramento River to his son, who had a townsite plotted. The town that sprang up was called Sacramento, after the river which ran beside it, and it quickly became a supply and recreational center for miners.

The town was ravaged by flood in 1849, but the following year it had a population of 6,820, and was incorporated. In the next few years, fire, floods, and cholera swept the community, but the town aspired to being the state capitol, and in 1854 it was so designated.

In 1857, the Sacramento Library Association was founded. Among its sponsors were four young men who made railroad history in the next few years—Collis P. Huntington, Leland Stanford, Charles Crocker, and Mark Hopkins.

In 1860, when the Pony Express was inaugurated, Sacramento became its western terminus. Three years later it was incorporated as a city. In 1863, the Central Pacific Railroad began laying tracks east from Sacramento to meet the Union Pacific, giving the nation its first transcontinental rail route in 1869.

By the time the great gold rush had ended, the main supports of the city's present-day economy had been laid, and the search for quick riches gave way to the development of agriculture in the area. Steadily the modern city took shape. Dams were built on the American and Sacramento rivers to produce electricity for the area and to control the floods that had tormented the city.

After World War II, more diverse industry came to the city. A ten-year plan (1951–1961) drawn up by the Citizens Redevelopment Advisory Committee launched a rebuilding program to replace run-down areas with low-income housing, parks, and boulevards. The rebuilding in downtown Sacramento continued into the 1980's.

Government and Population. Sacramento has a nine-member city council, including a mayor, that hires a city manager. Population (metropolitan area) 1,014,002; (city) 275,741.

SACRAMENTO RIVER, in central California, rises in the northern part of the state, near Mount Shasta, and flows southward about 320 miles (512 km) to join the San Joaquin River flowing from the south. Their waters empty into Suisun Bay, an arm of San Francisco Bay. The Sacramento and San Joaquin are the principal rivers of California, draining the great Central Valley between the Sierra Nevada and the Coast Ranges. This valley is one of the foremost agricultural regions of the United States. Among the important tributaries of the Sacramento are the Pit and the Feather rivers.

The Sacramento is a key factor in the Central Valley Project, which was begun in the 1930's to provide flood control, store water for irrigation of farmlands and to supply California's cities, and to furnish hydroelectric power. Shasta Dam, on the Sacramento below the mouth of the Pit, and Keswick Dam, farther downstream, are major units in this development.

SACRÉ-COEUR BASILICA, sà'krā-kûr', a French pilgrimage church in Paris at the summit of the Butte Montmartre. It is a popular tourist attraction.

Initiated privately by Catholics, it was decreed by law in 1873 as a national votive offering after the Franco-Prussian War, to be dedicated to the Sacred Heart of Jesus. The enormous cost was met entirely by private donation.

Work was begun on the church in 1876, according to a design by Paul Abadie, and after his death in 1884 was continued by a number of architects. The church was completed in 1914 and consecrated in 1919.

The building, of white stone and concrete, is in the 12th century Byzantine-Romanesque style, on cruciform plan with numerous domes and cupolas. The campanile by Lucien Magne contains one of the largest bells in the world. The main dome is visible from all over Paris and was a favorite subject for painters, such as Maurice Utrillo.

SACRED COLLEGE OF CARDINALS, the body of churchmen in the Roman Catholic Church who elect the pope and administer the offices of the Roman Curia. They are named by the pope and must be bishops. See CATHOLIC CHURCH, ROMAN—*Organization.*

SACRED HEART OF JESUS, in recent centuries, one of the most widespread devotional practices in the Roman Catholic Church. It is based on the church's teaching with regard to its founder, Jesus Christ, who is both God and man. He is but one single person having both the nature of God and the nature of man. Since Jesus Christ is a divine person, the second person of the Blessed Trinity who has become man, his heart is truly "the divine Heart which wrought our salvation," to which is owed "honor and glory forever." Hence devotion is directed to the person of Jesus Christ, to his living, sentient heart, and to that heart as a symbol of the love that he has for his heavenly Father and for men.

This devotion has a manifold purpose: to honor Christ, the Saviour of mankind; to seek that men's hearts be inflamed with love for him whose love for them is recalled by thought of his sacred heart; and to make reparation for injuries committed against him. Scriptural foundation for the devotion is found in the many references to the heart as the seat of thought, will, and affection, to Christ's own words, "Learn of me, because I am meek, and humble of heart" (Matthew 11:29), and other texts.

Development of Devotion. Although there are patristic and medieval references to the heart of Christ, as in the writings of such saints as Cyril, Cyprian, Basil, Ambrose, Francis of Assisi, Bonaventura, Bernard of Clairvaux, Gertrude, and Mechtilde, it was in the 17th century, partly in reaction against Jansenism, that the devotion began to spread most rapidly and widely among Roman Catholics. Chief among those who promoted it were Saint Jean Eudes, Blessed Claude de la Colombière, and especially Sainte Marguerite Marie Alacoque, a nun of Paray-le-Monial, France, whose letters contain records of private revelations that have become known as the "promises of the Sacred Heart." The 12th of these, "the great promise," reads: "The all-powerful love of My Heart will grant to those who shall communicate on the first Friday of

FRENCH GOVERNMENT TOURIST OFFICE

SACRÉ-COEUR BASILICA, built on a hill in Montmartre, overlooks the city of Paris.

nine consecutive months the grace of final perseverance." Closely connected with this devotion is that to Jesus Christ in the Holy Eucharist, with the attendant practice of frequent reception of Holy Communion. The devotion has inspired many beautiful prayers, including notably the *Litany of the Sacred Heart,* the *Morning Offering,* and acts of consecration to the Sacred Heart.

The Society of Jesus has long taken a leading part in promoting the devotion. The League of the Sacred Heart, commonly known as the Apostleship of Prayer, founded in France in 1844 by Father Francis X. Gautrelet, has a membership of over 30 million. Various religious communities, both of men and of women, have been dedicated to the Sacred Heart. Celebrated on the Friday after the octave of Corpus Christi, and usually falling in June, the month dedicated to the devotion, the feast of the Sacred Heart was established in 1765 by Pope Clement XIII and extended to the universal church by Pope Pius IX. Pope Leo XIII consecrated the human race to the Sacred Heart, and Pope Pius XI decreed that this consecration be renewed each year on the feast of Christ the King.

JOHN K. RYAN
The Catholic University of America

Further Reading: Bainvel, J., *Devotion to the Sacred Heart,* ed. by G. O'Neill, tr. by E. Leahey (1924); Dachauer, Alban J., *The Sacred Heart* (Bruce 1959); Dalgairns, John B., *The Devotion to the Sacred Heart of Jesus,* 3d ed. (1910); Stierli, Josef, ed., *Heart of the Saviour,* tr. by P. Andrews (Herder 1957).

SACRIFICE. The word "sacrifice" has two radically different connotations, and failure to recognize this opposition has often caused confusion in theological thinking.

Secular Definition. The modern secular use of the word describes voluntary deprivation, and its definition may be epitomized in "giving up." What is given up—possessions, happiness, reputation—is always of some value to the sacrificer. It is frequently destroyed, or it may pass into the possession of someone else, who is not, however, regarded as the recipient of a sacrifice. The deprivation is always effected so that the sacrificer may achieve a purpose that to him or to some other person or cause, is of greater value than that of the object sacrificed. Illustrations of this are seen in the expression "He sacrificed his position for his principles" and "The soldier made the supreme sacrifice." The Oxford Dictionary gives the date 1706 when "sacrifice" was first used as a verb in this sense. As a noun it had been so used much earlier.

The word came into use through the Christian Church, which had taken it from the religions that formed the milieu of its early life, the Greek, Jewish, and Roman, in which it was invariably used with reference to cult, having no secular significance whatever. To understand the meaning of the word we must turn to these three religions.

RELIGIOUS BACKGROUND

"Sacrifice" comes from the Latin noun *sacrificium* and the verb *sacrificare*, which are blanket terms for any religious act in which a thing is made sacred, that is, given to a deity and made his property. If what was made sacred was an animal or a cereal for the purpose of preservation of the life power of the deity, thus keeping him favorable, it was burned in order that the food, sublimated into smoke, might rise to the upper air where the deities lived. A handful of food thrown into the hearth fire by the father of the family at a meal was a *sacrificium*. Instruments used in the process of public sacrifices, temples where the process was carried on, and articles of adornment of the temples were likewise made sacred. Rites of lustration or purification with the purpose of warding off demons or evil influences were also called sacrifices.

The rules and ceremonies for these rites were meticulously preserved from early days in the *jus divinum*, which was the body of regulations for keeping people in the good graces of the gods, as the *jus civile* prescribed the regulations for keeping them in the good graces of the city or state.

Greek Rites. The Greek language had no such blanket term to describe religious rites. Rites in honor of the deities of the upper air (Olympus) were called *thusiai*. Those offered to chthonic powers were called *sphagia*.

Thusiai were always offered by daylight, preferably in the morning. Certain parts of the animal victims, the steaks, were burned on a *bomos*, a large stone or a pile of stones raised higher than the worshipers. The remainder was eaten by the worshipers as part of the rite. The act of burning the flesh for the deities was *thuein* or *hiereuein*. The rites were concluded by music and dancing. Their purpose was to honor the friendly deities.

Sphagia were offered by night. The rite was described by the verbs *sphagiazein*, meaning to

slaughter, *enagizein*, meaning to make taboo, and *holokautein*, meaning to burn wholly. The victims were burned on an *eschara*, a rude stone laid as close as possible to the ground or in a trench dug for the purpose. None of the animal was eaten, and the whole eerie rite was performed in silence. The purpose was placation or aversion of unloved powers.

Our translations of all these Greek words have come through the Latin and have lost the sharp distinction between the rites. *Thusiai* and *sphagia* have both become "sacrifices." All the words describing the rite have become "to sacrifice." *Bomos* and *eschara* have both become "altars." The result is that we hear of two kinds of Greek sacrifice, thus confusing rites that should be sharply distinguished.

Jewish Rites. Jewish rites were likewise described by different vocabularies, with no blanket term to group them together. The best known was the *zevach*, which was, in most ways, a counterpart of the Greek *thusia*, by which it is translated in the Septuagint. In Judaism, after the return from the captivity, the *holah* gained increasing significance. In this rite an animal was wholly burned on an altar, and none of it was eaten by priest or people. This was not a rite of aversion or placation. As the smoke of the *zevach* carried the choice parts of the victims to the sky, where Yahweh (a Hebrew name for God) lived, and was thus an offering of the best part of the food to the deity, the *holah* was considered as offering the whole animal to the deity, thus becoming the greatest possible gift that could be offered. Long after Yahweh was considered to have no physical form, both these rites were continued with increasingly analogical interpretation.

When the Hebrew Bible was translated into Greek, *zevach* was easily rendered by *thusia*. Translation of *holah* gave difficulty. All Greek rites in which an animal was wholly burned were rites of placation and aversion but *holah* was honorific and could not be rendered by *holocauton*. The translators ingeniously coined other words from the same Greek roots, but differently spelled and with slightly different endings. When the Greek Bible passed into Latin the distinction was lost. Roman religion had no rites equivalent to Greek *holocauton*, and the Greek was Latinized into *holocauston* (wholly burned). This came into the Douay version as "holocaust." The King James version tried to remedy this by coining the compound word "whole-burnt offering."

The oldest sacrificial rite continuing to the present day is the Jewish annual Pesach (translated "phase" and "pasch" in the Douay version and as "passover" in the King James version). It preserves the primitive communal meal, with no burning of any part on an altar by priests. The blood of the animal was smeared upon the doorposts of the house where the rite was performed, as a prophylactic against dangerous misfortune.

In addition to these sacrifices, Judaism had many rites of purification, which probably arose from taboo rites. One could not worship if he were taboo, and the taboo had to be solemnly removed before one could participate in worship. Judaism early extended its taboos to include moral disqualifications. Underlying all those rites was the fundamental principle that sacrificial worship was an act of the group and not of an individual. Therefore every individual in the group, as well as the group as a whole, must be free from physical and moral taboo, whether conscious of it or not. The place of worship, the altar, must likewise be free from deliberate or accidental contact that it might have had with a taboo person.

The common method of purification was smearing or sprinkling with blood, the principle of life. This might be performed as a special act, but it was always a necessary preparation for offering a sacrifice. The natural source of the blood was the animal to be sacrificed.

The name, Day of Atonement, uses a 16th century word to translate Greek and Hebrew words that described purification but had no suggestion of reconciliation. On that day alone the sins of priest and people were solemnly transferred to the scapegoat, which was then not sacrificed but driven "into the wilderness" by acolytes, who had to be purified from their contacts with the sin-laden beast.

Here was the only instance in which the "laying on of hands" was specifically interpreted. This was probably because the meaning was different from the customary use of the term. In every Jewish sacrifice the worshiper had first to lay his hand upon the beast before he killed it. This is never explained as transfer of sins. It was probably a means of some sort of identification of the worshiper with the victim, which was to be offered, at least in part, to Yahweh.

Sacrifice as Worship. These rites would be better understood if the word "sacrifice" were confined to the rites of worship as the solemn acts for which purification was a necessary preparation and in which some solemn act was performed with an animal that had been killed for the purpose.

The death of the animal was an incidental, necessary fact in order that the sacrifice might be performed. It was not a factor of the sacrifice. The death of all individual animals or cereals that we eat is still a necessary fact or event occurring either before or during the process of eating the food. It cannot be regarded as a factor of the meal. Thus the death of the animal was never on the altar. For obvious physical reasons the beast was slain as near the altar as was in keeping with whatever reverence accompanied the sacrifice. After the victim was killed there were three possibilities for disposal of the carcass: (1) The worshipers might eat all of it. (2) They might eat part and sublimate part into smoke for the gods. (3) They might burn all of it.

The first method was that of the Jewish Pesach, the Greek *bouphonia,* the strange rite or the 'Aisāwa, a Muslim fraternity in Algeria, and in many other primitive rites, all of which had their origin in days before men had any concept of deities. The common meal of the early family or clan or tribe was the method by which the life power and the qualities of the animal were appropriated by those who participated in the feast. Totemistic concepts of "eating the god" may well have contributed to the development of the rite.

With the growing conviction that the mysterious life powers, which men wanted to appropriate, were sentient beings, it was simple to picture the smoke of their roasts ascending to those beings. It was but a step to the conviction that a portion of the meat should be sent up to the gods. Thus may well have arisen the regular, official sacrifices we see most highly developed

among the Greeks and Hebrews, the *thusia* and the *zevach.* In both these sacrifices the idea of thanksgiving was highly developed, expressed in Greek by the word *eucharistia,* which passed into Christianity.

We are able to reconstruct the ritual acts of both Greek and Hebrew sacrifices, which were remarkably similar. In both were three distinct parts, the preparation, the sacrifice proper, and, except in the *holah,* the meal, accompanied and followed by music.

In both religions the preparation consisted of purification from normal and accidental uncleanness from daily living and from acts and crimes that constituted barriers to worship. In Greek rites this was accomplished by lustration. In Jewish rites it was accomplished by manipulation of the blood of the victim and included the altar as well as the worshipers. At the end of these rites the animal was killed and dissected. In Jewish rites this killing was prescribed to be done by the worshiper.

The priests then performed the sacrifice itself by burning on the altar the choice parts of the flesh of the victim. Homer gives elaborate descriptions of this in two places in the *Iliad* and two in the *Odyssey,* with almost identical words in all four passages. The sacrifice, except the *holah,* was followed by the meal, for which meticulous rules are prescribed in Greek inscriptions. For large, official sacrifices the music was as elaborate as possible. The aim was always to make the sacrifice as large as possible, burning as many victims as could be provided.

From biblical Judaism comes the sacrifice in which none of the victim was eaten. The animal was flayed because his hide was the perquisite of the priests in both Greek and Jewish sacrifices. The burning of all the remainder upon the altar lent itself easily to lofty spiritual interpretation.

Decline of Sacrifices. There was no possible connection between this whole-burnt offering and the Greek aversion and placation rites to which reference has been made. With the destruction of the Temple in 586 B. C., Hebrew sacrifices came to an abrupt conclusion. The priests and the better part of the people were banished to Babylonia. They were convinced that no Jewish sacrifices could be offered outside the Temple in Jerusalem. Judaism became a sacrificeless religion until the return from the captivity and the building of a second Temple more than a century later. During this time the tradition of the sacrifices and their ritual were reduced to writing in the Pentateuch (Torah), which forms the sole early source for study.

All Jewish sacrifices had to be accompanied by an offering of cakes of fine flour called the *minchah,* translated in the Douay version as "oblation of sacrifice," in the King James version as "meat offering," and in the Jewish version as "meal offering." In certain instances, this could even be substituted for an animal sacrifice.

With the establishment of synagogues in Palestine after the return from the captivity and the dispersion of the people into distant lands, it became increasingly difficult for a Jew to go to Jerusalem, where alone sacrifices could be offered. Pious folk who could afford them might make occasional pilgrimages, but for the greater part of Judaism sacrifices were impossible. They learned to content themselves with prayer, fasting, almsgiving, and reading of the Torah as adequate surrogates for sacrifice. Thus by the time of Jesus, Judaism had been largely weaned from this worship. With the destruction of the Temple in 70 A. D., Jewish sacrifices were brought to an end. Greek sacrifices took another two centuries to peter out.

Sacrifice for Omens. In Babylonia the study of the configurations of the liver seems to have been the principal reason for religious slaughtering of animals. The will of the gods could be ascertained by careful study of the contour and markings of a sheep's liver. Babylonian tablets abound in meticulous directions for this study. For removal of the liver the animal had to be killed. Once more the death of the victim was a fact but not a factor of the rite. After examination of the liver, some disposition of the carcass had to be made, and this disposition developed into elaborate rites. All of this is reflected in Latin rites.

In Greek sacrifices the killing of the animal afforded a good opportunity to examine the organs for omens. This examination was usually an incidental accompaniment of the rite and not the primary purpose of it. The Jewish law positively forbade liver omens of any kind.

Roman Sacrifices. Roman sacrifices were of an entirely different kind. The personalities of Roman deities were not so clearly developed as those of the Greek gods and the Hebrew Yahweh. The Roman rites were also strongly influenced by the Etruscans, who may originally have come from Babylonia. The Babylonian influence can be seen particularly on the emphases in Roman rites upon the study of omens. Indeed among the Romans the primary purpose of the rite was the study of omens shown by the *exta,* the name given to the organs below the diaphragm. The animal, adorned with fillets and ribbons to mark it as holy, was led to the altar, where it had to go willingly. It was further sanctified by sprinkling pieces of cake and pouring wine upon it. After the animal was killed, the *exta* were dissected, carefully examined, cooked, and laid upon the altar fire with selected pieces of flesh. The remainder of the flesh lost its sanctity and became the property of the priests. The whole sacrifice was performed in silence, save for weirdly playing pipes to drown other noises.

The burning of the *exta* was a necessary sequel to the examination for omens. These organs had been used for a solemn purpose and could therefore be used for no other. With the rise of the concept of deities, the examination for omens could well be interpreted as learning the will of the god. The burning of the *exta* would be sending them up to the god. The addition of pieces of flesh marked a definite offering of some kind.

The normal Roman sacrifice had no common meal. A very few minor rites are found in which such a meal was eaten, but these rites were not encouraged by the *jus divinum* and were in no way official. The gladness, joy, and thanksgiving that marked Greek and Hebrew sacrifices were no part of Latin rites. When Latin became the chief language of the Mediterranean world the same *sacrificia* was employed to describe all other rites, even though they were totally different in purpose and technique.

ORIGIN AND DEVELOPMENT OF SACRIFICES

Much that has been said of the origin of sacrifice has been marked by the confusion of thinking that came from Roman use. It is impossible to group together honorific rites with glad thanksgiving, aversion rites with weirdness and horror, omen rites and purification rites, and try to find a single origin for the whole conglomeration.

Causations. Fear of misfortune, taboo, and demons may well explain most of the aversion rites and may have given rise to many of the purification rites, while omen rites, desire to learn the will of the gods, may have descended from methods of gratifying the natural desire to probe the future. Omens were derived from those phenomena unexplainable by known causes. The deities as the life powers were naturally regarded as the ultimate cause of these phenomena and might well reveal their plans by the markings of the liver, which, as its name in English indicates, was supposed to be the seat of the life-soul because it is the bloodiest organ of the body.

The "gift-theory," suggested by Edward B. Tylor in *Primitive Culture* . . . (1871; 5th ed., 1929), may well explain the continuance of sacrifices and their development. It does not explain their origin, which antedates any concept of deities. Men were led by worship to know their deities. They did not invent worship because they believed in deities.

Totemism, studied in detail by James George Frazer in *Totemism and Exogamy* (1910), and *The Golden Bough, a Study in Magic and Religion* (1911–1926), may well have marked the first clear step toward the idea of a worshiper's appropriating the power of the deity within himself, as seen in the rites in which the victim was wholly eaten. However, we have not solved the problem of how totemism arose. We realize also that totemism makes no contribution to the origin of the better-known and more regularly observed sacrifices.

The only common origin of sacrifice, omen rites, and rites of purification and aversion seems to have been primitive man's conviction that, in addition to the physical objects that formed his environment, there were invisible and unpredictable powers that made themselves known through those physical environments. Some of these seemed friendly and some inimical. One kind of rite tried to establish union with the former. A totally different kind tried to banish the latter.

Christian Concepts of Sacrifice. The Greek word *thusia* was used by early Christians to describe the work of Jesus, the ideal of Christian living, and the Eucharist, which was always the great act of worship of Christians until the 16th century and has continued so in the Roman, Orthodox, and Anglican communions. When this word was translated into Latin as *sacrificium,* the confusion of thinking that has marked many Christian writers began. The confusion was complicated by the assumption that the death of the victim was a factor, as well as a fact, in the sacrifice. This was climaxed by identifying the sacrifice solely with the death of Jesus. This was possibly the unlucky first step toward the modern concept of sacrifice as the very reverse of what it was in days when its significance was solely cultic.

ROYDEN KEITH YERKES
Author of "Sacrifice in Greek and Roman Religion and Early Judaism"

Further Reading: Gray, George B., *Sacrifice in the Old Testament* (Oxford Univ. Press 1925); Hubert, Henri and Mauss, Marcel, *Sacrifice: Its Nature & Function,* tr. by W. D. Halls (Univ. of Chicago Press 1964); Yerkes, Royden K., *Sacrifice in Greek and Roman Religion and Early Judaism* (Scribner 1952).

SACRILEGE, sak′rə-lij, the profanation of a holy place or thing, and by extension of meaning, any act that blasphemously misuses or desecrates divine things, names, persons, or places.

The origin of sacrilege as a quasi-legal term is in the Code of Justinian, which made robbery from churches a crime punishable by death. The concept, however, has earlier sources in regulations, such as those for Greek temples and for the Temple in Jerusalem, where trespass was sacrilegious and punishable in some cases by death.

Only since the 19th century has the legal action for profanation of church buildings and associated crimes been similar to that for like secular offenses.

SACROILIAC, sak-rō-il′ē-ak, in man, a joint, or articulation, in the lower back between the sacrum, a triangular bone formed by the fusion of the five sacral vertebrae, and the ilium part of each hip bone. Shaped like a narrow slit, the sacroiliac joint is surrounded by very strong ligaments, including the ventral sacroiliac ligament, the dorsal sacroiliac ligament, and the interosseus ligament. The joint is capable of very little movement. Although injuries to the sacroiliac joint were once thought to be responsible for many cases of lower back pain, it is now known that the sacroiliac joint is very stable and that most pain attributed to the sacroiliac is due to disturbances in intervertebral disks.

SACRUM, sak′rəm, a large, triangular bone that is part of the vertebral column in man. Formed by the fusion of five sacral vertebrae, the sacrum is located at the dorsal part of the pelvis, inserted wedgelike between the hip bones. Its base articulates with the last of the lumbar vertebrae and its apex with the coccyx. The pelvic surface is concave, increasing pelvic capacity, while the dorsal surface is convex and narrower.

SADAT, sä-dät′, **Anwar el-** (1918–1981), Egyptian army officer and political leader, who succeeded Gamal Abdel Nasser as president of Egypt in 1970. He was born in the village of Talah Minufiya on Dec. 25, 1918. After attending the Abbasiyah Military Academy in Cairo, he became closely associated with Nasser and other officers strongly opposed to British control of Egypt.

Sadat spent several years in prison in the 1940's for his anti-government activities. Reinstated in the army in 1950, he was a leading participant in the military coup that overthrew King Faruk in 1952.

Sadat served on the new regime's Revolutionary Command Council and held the posts of minister of state, chairman of the National Assembly, editor of the newspaper *al-Jumhuriya,* and vice president of Egypt. Following Nasser's death on Sept. 28, 1970, he became president. In 1971 he survived a coup attempt by Vice President Ali Sabry and other highly placed politicians. Afterward he enjoyed enormous popularity and, most important, prestige within the army.

In 1972, Sadat expelled Soviet military advisers from Egypt because the Soviet Union apparently was unwilling to support renewed hostilities with Israel. The president's chief problem with Israel had been the recovery of the Sinai Peninsula, Egyptian territory lost in the 1967 war. Sadat's saber rattling in 1972 and 1973 was taken seriously by few world leaders, and because of this the Egyptian strike across

EDDIE ADAMS/CONTACT

Egyptian President Anwar el-Sadat sacrificed prestige in the Arab world by signing a peace treaty with Israel.

the Suez Canal into Sinai in October 1973 was a tactical success. Despite subsequent Egyptian reverses, the war forced Israel to begin negotiating on more flexible terms than in the past. Essential to the war and its promising aftermath for Egypt was Sadat's enlistment of oil-producing Arab states to apply an oil embargo against the United States and other nations.

After the war, Sadat staked his reputation on a rapprochement with the United States. He received President Nixon in Egypt in 1974, met with President Ford in Austria in 1975, and maintained a close personal relationship with U. S. Secretary of State Henry Kissinger. Under agreements between Egypt and Israel, negotiated in 1974 and 1975 with Secretary Kissinger's help, Sadat regained control of strategic Sinai territory and oil, enhancing his stature in the Arab community and in the world.

In November 1977, Sadat made the dramatic announcement that he would go to Israel if that would further the chances for peace in the Middle East. In his subsequent speech before the Israeli parliament, he called for Israeli withdrawal from all Arab lands occupied in the 1967 war. After meetings with U. S. President Carter at Camp David, Md., Sadat and Israeli Prime Minister Menahem Begin signed a preliminary peace agreement in September 1978 and a formal peace treaty in March 1979. Sadat and Begin shared the Nobel Peace Prize for 1978.

Sadat gained for Egypt phased withdrawal of Israeli forces from the rest of Sinai and billions of dollars of U. S. aid, including arms. But generally the Arab world reacted bitterly, suspending Egypt from the Arab League and imposing political and economic sanctions. Until his assassination in Cairo on Oct. 6, 1981, he continued to press Israel for Arab autonomy in the West Bank of the Jordan and the Gaza Strip.

SADDLE. See HORSEMANSHIP AND RIDING.

SADDUCEES, saj'ə-sēz, a sect or party of the
Jews during the last three centuries preceding the
fall of Jerusalem and the end of the old Jewish
state (70 A. D.). The history of the party and
the facts as to its constituency, beliefs, and
practices are only imperfectly known.

Sources. The statements in Josephus and the
New Testament, our most important evidence, are
not altogether satisfactory. The New Testament
writers may have been indirectly influenced by
Pharisaic prejudice, while Josephus, writing to
please and interest Greek and Roman readers,
limits himself to a few somewhat general and not
altogether consistent observations. In the New
Testament the Sadducees are linked with the
Pharisees as opponents of Jesus (Matthew 16:1,
6, 12). They are said to have denied the resurrection of the body (Matthew 22:23) and also
the existence of angels or spirits (Acts 23:8). As
influential priests and members of the Sanhedrin
the Sadducees officially opposed the early preaching of the Apostles (Acts 4:1; 5:17). They sat
side by side with Pharisees in the Sanhedrin, or
supreme council of Judaism (Acts 23:6), although the two parties were hostile to each other.

Josephus, the Jewish historian, tells us that
the Sadducees did not believe in fate, that is,
Providence, or in the immortality of the soul
(Antiquities 13:5, 17:2, 4; 20:9). They emphasized human free will and responsibility and
were more austere and inclined to severity in
judgment than were the Pharisees. They rejected
tradition and held the written law alone to be
authoritative. They belonged mainly to the more
wealthy and aristocratic circles and were not influential with the mass of the people. Josephus
doubtless knew more about the Sadducees than
he set down in his writings. It must be remembered that the evidence of both Josephus and the
New Testament holds good mainly for only the
very last period of Jewish history, when these
Sadducees were only a shattered remnant of a
once great and powerful party.

Origins and Role. There is no trace of any
distinct parties in postexilic Judaism until about
180 B. C., when the close contact with Hellenism
consequent on the Seleucid supremacy over
Palestine led to an ardent Hellenizing propaganda
and consequently to a cleavage of the Jewish
community into two factions, the conservative
and the radical or Hellenistic. But it is a mistake
to identify the Sadducees with the latter, who
were willing to sacrifice even the law itself in
favor of conformity to Greek ideas and practices.
The conservatives stood for steadfast loyalty to
the law and Jewish customs and prejudices. But
within the conservative ranks, to which the
majority of the people belonged, two tendencies
were operative. Some, with loyal acceptance of
the law and reverence for it as the supreme
religious authority, were content with the Law
as written. They opposed an accumulation of
traditional interpretation as authoritative. Dogmas not explicitly taught in the Law might be
refused assent.

On the other hand, there were those who
sought to make the law ever more comprehensive
and universally applicable through exegesis or
interpretation. Such interpretations became an
ever-enlarging body of tradition as binding as the
Law itself. This was the party of the scribes,
ardent students of the Law, while the other
tendency was mainly represented by the priests
and aristocracy. The scribal position was essen-

tially that Israel was fundamentally a church, a
religious organization. The opposite position allowed full room for the conception of Israel as a
political entity, a nation among the nations of the
world. In the reorganization of the Jewish state
under the Asmonean priest-princes (142–63 B. C.),
the party of the scribes became definitely organized as the Pharisees. The group or party
opposed to the Pharisees was known as the
Sadducees. The name is probably derived from
Zadok, chief priest during Solomon's reign, and
originally applied to the priestly aristocracy of
Jerusalem. Since the priests were the dominant
influence in the group it was applied to all of
them. Because they were dominated by the
priestly class, it is perhaps best to understand
their position on the Law as an attempt to preserve the prerogatives of the priests as its interpreters. There is no evidence, however, that
these were so strictly organized as was the case
with the Pharisees. In general, the Asmonean
rulers were inclined to favor the Sadducees. The
Pharisees thus became the party of opposition.

The nonpriestly aristocracy also generally sided
with the government, that is, were counted as
Sadducees. The numbers of this generally patriotic, conservative party were sadly diminished in
the civil strife preceding the Roman occupation
(63 B. C.) and in the wars between Herod and
Antigonus, the last Asmonean prince. Its representation in the Sanhedrin was reduced and its
hold on the people greatly diminished. In
Herod's later years the party seems to have
bettered its condition, but it never again recovered its earlier power and influence. As a
party it ceased to exist with the fall of Jerusalem
in 70 A. D. and the complete disorganization of
Judaism that ensued. The view advocated above
is somewhat different from the traditional one,
which takes the Sadducees to have been, as a
party, somewhat irreligious, inclined to Hellenism, worldly, and with little reverence for the
Law and sacred things in general. That some
Sadducees were such is probably true, but it
certainly is not correct so to characterize the
party as a whole.

Literature. The Sadduciac type of thought is
represented in Jewish literature by such works
as Ecclesiastes in the Old Testament, by Ecclesiasticus and 1 Maccabees in the Apocrypha,
and possibly by the Testaments of the Twelve
Patriarchs and the Book of Jubilees in the
Pseudepigrapha, extrabiblical religious literature.
A most interesting Sadduciac work was discovered in the Cairo genizah and published in
1910 under the title *Fragments of a Zadokite
Work*. It gives evidence of the existence of a
reform party or sect within the Zadokite circle
that originated about 200 B. C. and was still in
existence as late as near the beginning of the
Christian era, the date of the fragment.

EDWARD E. NOURSE
Formerly, Hartford Theological Seminary

Bibliography

Bokser, Ben Z., *Pharisaic Judaism in Translation* (Block
1935).
Charles, R. H., *Fragments of a Zadokite Work* (Oxford
1912).
Hartford, R. T., *The Pharisees* (1924).
Leszynsky, R., *Die Sadducäer* (1912).
Schärer, E., *Geschichte des jüdischen Volkes im Zeitalter
Jesu Christi,* 4th ed. (1907).
Wellhausen, Julius, *Die Pharisäer und die Sadducäer*
(1874).
Zeitlin, Solomon, *Religious and Secular Leadership*
(Dropsie College 1943).

SADE, sàd, **Marquis de** (1740–1814), French author and libertine, from whose name the word "sadism" is derived. His best-known work is *Justine, or The Misfortune of Virtue,* a novel about a girl who undergoes sexual maltreatment.

Donatien Alphonse François, Count de Sade, popularly known as the Marquis de Sade, was born in Paris on June 2, 1740. He saw military service from 1754 to 1763 and then served in several posts, including that of governor-general of Bresse and Bugey. After an incident in Marseille involving young girls, de Sade was tried in absentia for poisoning and sodomy. He was sentenced to death but was reprieved by the king. He continued his licentious ways for the next 30 years and was often arrested. He was finally committed in 1803 to the lunatic asylum at Charenton, where he died on Dec. 2, 1814.

De Sade's works have been both dismissed as trite pornography and praised for brilliance of style, profundity of thought, and psychological insights that anticipated Freud. Apart from *Justine* (1791), his major works are *The One Hundred Days of Sodom* (1785), *Juliette, or the Luxuries of Vice* (1792), *Philosophy in the Boudoir* (1795), and *The Crimes of Love* (1800). He also wrote plays for the Comédie Française.

Further Reading: Lely, Gilbert, *Marquis De Sade,* tr. by Alec Brown (Grove 1970).

SADI, Persian poet. See SAADI.

SADISM, sā′dizm, is the infliction of pain for the purpose of pleasure. Cruelty, aggressively enjoyed, comprises the sadist's sexual urge. Rather than being a fusion of sexual and aggressive urges, aggression is the means by which a sadist obtains sexual gratification. The German neurologist Baron Richard von Krafft-Ebing coined the term sadism from the name of the Marquis de Sade, a French novelist during the Revolution, who wrote about his own sadistic acts and thought that a lust for destruction was natural.

Uncomplicated sadism is unusual. More often sadism occurs as a part of a complementary pair with masochism, in which sexual excitement and gratification are achieved by enduring pain inflicted on the self as an object. Sadomasochism, furthermore, is not infrequently accompanied by other perversions. The variety and degree of sadistic behavior makes it difficult to establish statistical incidence.

In his study of childhood sexuality, Sigmund Freud recognized that sadistic impulses, like other parts of the sexual drive, are natural but normally undergo profound changes in the course of every individual's maturation, except among those whose sadism is constitutionally of very high intensity and is reinforced at each stage of development. Under stress, such persons are prone to immature self-defense, with the repetition of sadistic acts experienced in childhood.

According to some psychiatrists, sexual deviates troubled with sadism usually come for treatment because of anxiety and depression. Initiation of treatment on their own improves prognosis. However, the more primitive the sadistic act and the closer to primal anxiety, the more difficult is the treatment.

HENRY I. SCHNEER, M. D.
State University of New York

Further Reading: Freedman, Alfred M., and Kaplan, Harold I., eds., *Comprehensive Textbook of Psychiatry:* "Sexual Deviations," by Irving Bieber, Sandor Lorand, and Henry I. Schneer (Williams & Wilkins 1967).

SADO, sä-do, is an island in Japan. Administered as part of Niigata prefecture, it lies off the west coast of Honshu Island, 32 miles (51 km) from the city of Niigata. Its area is 331 square miles (857 sq km).

Sado has a diversified surface culminating in Mt. Kimpoku, which reaches 3,872 feet (1,180 meters) above sea level. South of the mountain is the town of Aikawa, with a noted ancient gold mine, now exhausted. Ryotsu, the chief port, is 18 miles (29 km) northeast of Aikawa. Sado's industries include rice cultivation and fishing. Population: (1965) 102,925.

SADOWA, zä-dō′və, **Battle of,** the decisive engagement in the Austro-Prussian War (or Seven Weeks' War) of 1866, in which the Austrians were overwhelmed. It was fought near the Bohemian towns of Sadowa and Königgrätz, and is sometimes called the Battle of Königgrätz.

On July 3, following the plan of Count von Moltke, Prussian chief of staff, three Prussian armies converged on the inferior Austrian troops under General von Benedek. Austria's defeat at Sadowa outweighed its success in Italy, and it was soon forced to sue for peace.

SÁENZ PEÑA, sä′äns pä′nyä, **Roque** (1851–1914), Argentine president. His administration was notable for the electoral reforms that brought democracy to Argentina.

A member of the conservative oligarchy and son of a president (Luis Sáenz Peña, 1823–1907), he was born in Buenos Aires on March 19, 1851. Educated in Argentina, he traveled in Europe and entered Argentine politics in the 1870's. Among his government posts were those of minister of foreign affairs and ambassador to Spain and to Italy. As Argentina's delegate to the first Pan-American Conference (1889–1890), he opposed the U. S.-sponsored all-American customs union because of Argentina's economic ties to Europe.

With the opposition Radical party abstaining, Sáenz Peña was elected president in 1910. He regarded himself as nonpartisan and pushed through the conservative Congress many of the reforms demanded by the Radicals, including universal male suffrage, the secret ballot, and voter registration. He died in office on Aug. 9, 1914.

SAFAD, sə-fäd′, is a town in Israel, northwest of the Sea of Galilee. Alternate forms of the name are Zefat (Hebrew) and Safed. Because of its elevation (2,720 feet, or 829 meters), it is a popular summer and health resort. Several industries have been established by the state.

The town had a Jewish community in the 11th century, but it was probably destroyed by the Crusaders, who built a fortress there. Jews returned, and in the 16th century, following the expulsion of Jews from Portugal and Spain, Safad became a center of Jewish learning and mysticism and one of the four Jewish holy cities in Palestine. In 1948, when Israel achieved independence, it was the scene of fierce Arab-Israeli fighting. Population: (1969) 13,100.

SAFAVIDS, sə-fä′wēdz, a dynasty that ruled Iran from 1501 to 1736. An alternate spelling of the name is Safawids. The Safavid order, founded in 1301, became a revolutionary Muslim Shiite movement in the 15th century. See also IRAN—*History;* PERSIAN ART.

Moshe Safdie's *Habitat,* a prefabricated, multiple-unit housing structure, was built for Expo 67 in Montreal.

SAFDIE, saf'dē, **Moshe** (1938–   ), Canadian architect, who designed prefabricated, multiple-unit housing structures. He was born in Haifa, Israel, on July 14, 1936, went with his family to Canada in 1954, received an architecture degree from McGill University, and then studied with the American architect Louis I. Kahn.

Safdie won wide acclaim at Montreal's Expo 67 with Habitat—a mass-produced, prefabricated apartment complex of stepped reinforced concrete blocks. Despite imposed modifications of his original design, the project established that the repetitive identical unit could encourage imaginative grouping and produce high-quality, low-cost industrialized housing.

After his success with Habitat, Safdie pushed its concept further. He designed a 300-unit hillside cluster in San Juan, Puerto Rico, and a similar project with 4,500 units in Israel. A belief that architecture ought to respond flexibly to changing human patterns underlies his design for the student union at San Francisco State College, where individual hexagonal units can be rearranged even after original assembly. His book *Beyond Habitat* (1970) calls for a visionary "housing machine" that would allow every man to structure his dwelling to suit his own needs.

KATHERINE G. KLINE
Albright-Knox Art Gallery, Buffalo, N. Y.

SAFE, a strongly built container for valuable objects. The two main kinds of safes are the *money safe* and the *record safe.* A money safe is designed primarily to provide protection against the theft of valuables. A record safe is designed primarily to ensure that valuables will not be destroyed by fire.

Money Safes. Cash, jewelry, negotiable securities, and similar valuables are stored in a money safe to thwart burglars. The basic money safe has a heavy round door and steel walls that are at least 1 inch (2.5 cm) thick. It can be in-

stalled in a wall or welded into place at a desired location. Sometimes the basic money safe is enclosed in a reinforced-concrete block that has a steel cladding, which discourages removal of the safe by burglars and greatly increases the safe's resistance to drills, sledges, explosives, and metal-cutting torches.

A money safe also can be built with special features. For instance, special alloys are used to cover the front and door of a money safe to provide protection against attack with a carbide drill. Similar protection is provided by using Relsom bars, which cause the drill to bind and shatter. Also, layers of copper are used in the front of a safe and around its door to provide protection against attack with an acetylene torch. The copper rapidly carries heat away from the area to which the torch is applied and thus hinders the melting of the plate. Another protective measure is the use of a relocking mechanism that automatically throws two or three emergency bolts into action when the lock of a safe is jarred by cutting tools or explosives.

MONEY SAFE for cash, jewels, and securities. Such safes resist attack by torch or tool.

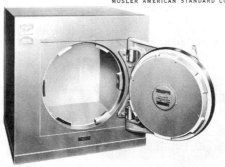

Record Safes. Personal records, business records, and similar documents are stored in a record safe to protect them from fire. A record safe has rectangular doors and steel walls built thinner than those of a money safe. The walls of a record safe are lined or filled with a thermal insulating material such as an asbestos compound. The insulation markedly decreases the rate of heat transfer to the inside of a safe.

Record safes are classified on the basis of their ability to keep papers intact while subjected to a high temperature in a test furnace, to withstand rupture when placed in the test furnace, and to withstand a 30-foot (10-meter) test fall while still hot. Record safes that pass such tests are given certifications by the Underwriters' Laboratories and the Safe Manufacturers National Association.

The contents of record safes are relatively vulnerable to burglary, and the contents of money safes are relatively vulnerable to fire. Consequently, safes should be used for the purpose for which they are designed.

Historical Background. Various methods for safely keeping treasure, jewels, and other valuables have been in use since the beginning of recorded history. The ancient Egyptians, Greeks, and Romans used wooden boxes to store valuables. Wooden boxes, some bound with iron bands and some equipped with locks, were in use in Europe during the Middle Ages and the Renaissance. Perhaps the first all-metal strongbox was built in France in 1820. It had double walls, the space between which was filled with an insulating material. Daniel Fitzgerald of New York City built a similar safe in 1843. Since then, safes have been improved by using stronger metals, more fire-resistant insulating materials, and more complex locks. In addition, modern safes can be protected by sophisticated alarm systems.

A RECORD SAFE'S fire-resistant walls protect personal records, business records, and other papers

MOSLER AMERICAN STANDARD CO.

SAFETY is the condition of being free from the danger of harm. As a legal concept, it implies a state of relative security from accidental injury or death due to measures designed to guard against accidents. Laws that encourage the maintenance of safety standards are often called safety laws.

See ACCIDENTS; AIR SAFETY; AUTOMOBILE SAFETY; COAL—*Coal Mining and Production;* COAST GUARD, UNITED STATES; HOMEMAKING— *Safety in the Home;* LIFESAVING; MINING—*Safety;* NUCLEAR ENERGY—*Nuclear Fission Reactors* (Operating Problems).

SAFETY GLASS is a laminated or heat-treated glass that reduces injuries stemming from broken glass. The first safety glass, introduced about 1910, consisted of two sheets of glass with a thin sheet of cellulose nitrate between them. In the 1920's cellulose acetate replaced cellulose nitrate, and about 1936 this design was superseded by laminated glass with polyvinyl butyral sheeting. This safety glass is used mainly for automobile windshields. When struck, the glass may break but the fragments adhere to the plastic sheeting. The sheeting also serves to cushion the blow.

SAFETY LAMP, a portable shielded-flame lamp used in mines to detect the absence of adequate oxygen or the presence of firedamp, a violently explosive mixture of air and methane. The safety lamp signals the presence of firedamp by an elongation of its flame. When insufficient oxygen is present, the flame becomes dim or goes out.

The miner's safety lamp was invented by Sir Humphry Davy in 1815. The key feature of the lamp is a wire mesh cylinder enclosing the flame. The mesh cylinder shields the flame and prevents ignition of firedamp by cooling the hot combustion products of the flame below the temperature at which firedamp ignites. The development of satisfactory safety lamps greatly reduced the frequency of deaths from firedamp explosions and asphyxiation.

SAFETY MATCH, a match that lights only when struck across a chemically prepared friction surface. Wooden safety matches are struck on the side of the box in which they are contained. Book safety matches are struck along a strip on the cover. See also MATCH INDUSTRY.

SAFETY RAZOR, a razor with a guard for the blade to prevent deep cuts in the skin. The safety razor was invented by the American manufacturer King C. Gillette in 1895, and it was first marketed by his company in 1903. See also RAZOR.

SAFETY VALVE, a valve set to open at a pressure safely below the bursting pressure of a boiler, hot-water heater, compressed air tank, or other container. The valve's resistance to opening typically is provided by a spring with an adjustable tension or by a lever with an adjustable weight. When this set resistance is overcome by excessive pressure in the container, the valve opens. The valve is built so that it stays open until the pressure in the container is reduced by a specified amount. Any adjustments in the settings at which a safety valve opens and closes must be made by licensed personnel. See also VALVE.

SAFFARIDS, sə-fär′idz, a Muslim dynasty that reigned in Persia from the early 860's until after 900. It took its name from its founder, Yaaqub Ibn al-Layth al-Saffar. This minor dynasty is significant because it represented a national revival within Persia, it inspired the first real Muslim military challenge to the temporal authority of the caliphate at Baghdad, and it encouraged Shiism, the Muslim sect that was destined to win all Iran in a later century.

Yaaqub and his three brothers raised a small body of troops in their native province of Seistan, which today lies in eastern Iran and southwestern Afghanistan. Eventually Yaaqub was able to force the governor of the Tahirid dynasty to leave Seistan. In 861, Yaaqub took over much of the area of modern Afghanistan. He then moved west toward the heart of Iran to seize the provinces of Kerman and Fars.

Alarmed by Yaaqub's rising power, the caliph tried to pacify him by naming him amir, or governor, of the area of his conquests. Still unsatiated, Yaaqub marched toward Baghdad, but he was defeated in 876. After his death in 879, his army proclaimed his brother Amr as successor.

The caliph granted Amr authority over the vast area of Transoxiana in 898. In attempting to occupy the area, however, Amr was defeated and taken prisoner. He was sent to Baghdad, where the caliph had him executed in 902. Amr's descendants struggled to maintain their authority for the next decade, and some years later two members of the family exerted limited power until the mid-10th century.

SAFFLOWER, saf′lou-ər, an important plant native to India but now widely distributed in warm regions throughout the world. The flowers of safflower yield a dye and the seeds an oil, and the leaves are eaten as a salad vegetable.

The safflower plant, *Carthamus tinctorius*, is a member of the composite family, Compositae. It grows from 1 to 3 feet (30–90 cm) tall and has spiny-toothed oval, oblong, or lance-shaped leaves. Its orange-yellow flower heads, about 1 inch (2.5 cm) in diameter, are surrounded by prickly bracts.

The flower heads of safflower yield both a red and a yellow dye. The red dye has been used since ancient times for cloths, especially silk, and in rouge. Safflower is raised commercially for dyestuffs in Bengal and southern France.

Safflower oil is extracted from the seeds by pressing or by treatment with a solvent. The oil has long been used in paints, varnishes, and soaps. It is popular as a salad and cooking oil for people on low-cholesterol diets because it is rich in unsaturated fatty acids. Safflower is an important oil crop in Egypt, India and the Far East. It is also processed in the United States.

SAFFRON, saf′rən, a crocus whose flowers yield a deep yellowish orange substance also known as saffron and used as a flavoring and coloring agent. The saffron, *Crocus sativa*, is a member of the iris family, Iridaceae. It grows about 18 inches (46 cm) tall and has long narrow leaves that arise directly from an underground stem, or corm. The long fragrant flowers are purple or sometimes white. The flower's style, or female reproductive part, is bright red and when dried yields an aromatic agent that is used to color and flavor foods and medicines and was once valued as an antispasmodic drug. Saffron has been cultivated in Mediterranean regions since ancient times.

SAFI, saf′ē, is a major port of Morocco. Located on the western coast of the country, it is about 85 miles (137 km) northwest of Marrakech. It is the chief outlet for Marrakech and the phosphate center of Youssoufia (formerly Louis-Gentil). Safi also exports sardines and has an important canning industry. A citadel built by the Portuguese when they occupied the city in the 16th century still stands. Population: (1969) 125,000.

SAFID RUD, sə-fēd′ rōōd′, a river in northeast Iran, is formed by the junction of the Qizil Uzun and Shah Rud at Manjil. An alternate form of its name is Sefid Rud. It breaks through the Elburz Mountains in a long gorge and runs onto the Gilan plain. The river forms a delta before reaching the Caspian Sea east of Resht. A dam below Manjil is used for power generation, flood prevention, and irrigation. Its length from Manjil is about 60 miles (97 km).

SAGA, sä-gä, is a city in Japan, on Kyushu Island, 25 miles (40 km) southwest of Fukuoka. It is the capital of Saga prefecture. The city is a seaport at the head of the Ariakeno-umi (gulf) and a distribution point for the agricultural products of the prefecture. It has cotton textile and ceramicware industries. It was formerly a castle town of the Nabeshina clan.

The prefecture occupies part of the Hizen Peninsula of Kyushu, between the Korea Strait on the north and the Ariakeno-umi on the south. Its area is 929 square miles (2,406 sq km). The Tsukushi Plain, its rich agricultural region, produces rice, sweet potatoes, and silk. The town of Arita is noted for its porcelains—the Arita, Imari, and Nabeshima wares, fine specimens of which are highly prized by collectors. The industry dates back to the early 17th century.

Saga prefecture was one of the areas where Chinese and later Western cultural influences first entered Japan. In Tokugawa times (1603–1867) it was part of the powerful feudal barony of Hizen. Population (1970): of the city, 143,-454; of the prefecture, 838,468.

Flower head of the safflower, *Carthamus tinctorius*

GRANT HEILMAN

SAGA, säg′ə, a word cognate with German *sage* ("a short tale")—with which, however, it must not be confounded in meaning—and with English *saw* ("saying"). In its limited and original meaning and without qualification, a saga is a story or group of stories in prose, of a historical character, relating in a series of episodes the whole life history of a Scandinavian hero and written down in Norway or mainly in Iceland during the Middle Ages. The historical events that the sagas narrate took place mostly in the period extending from the time of Iceland's settlement, in the late 9th century, to the middle of the 11th century. That was the heroic age of the Icelandic people. At first, the sagas were nothing but oral transmissions from one tale-teller to another. Their composition began about the middle of the 12th century and lasted for about 100 years.

Other Meanings of Saga. In a wider sense the word "saga" is applied to any narration of events of the past, mythical as well as historical in character, but possessing the traits of the genuine saga. In these tales some legendary champion, from whom the saga takes its name and in whom the important events are centered, is the hero. Heroic achievement and marvelous adventure, fact and fancy, are mingled freely. In the course of generations the saga undergoes important changes, acquires accretions, and takes on a more or less poetic and artificial character.

Finally, the saga is consigned to writing and handed down as a kind of rudimentary epic. Works of that kind, in which the historic element is found in greater or less degree, are frequently identified by the terms saga, myth, legend, märchen, epopee, and epos. But when these terms are so applied, they are used without clear distinction of meaning.

In the last stage of its development, the word "saga" has come to mean any free creation of the popular fantasy, sometimes incredible or even burlesque in character. Here the historical element is entirely lacking. In its widest sense, saga is sometimes used to include the entire body of the history and mythology of a people or their literature or some division of it. Hence we read of the Norse, German, Irish, or Greek sagas and of saga poetry, saga cycles, heroic sagas, beast sagas, the Cú Chulain saga, the Karl saga, the Njáls saga. In Norse mythology, Saga is also the name of a goddess.

Classification. The Icelandic sagas are so numerous and diverse that they defy strict classification. Under one system, three principal classes may be identified—historical, mythical, and romantic. Sagas may also be grouped geographically, according to the part of the country in which they arose or in which their scenes are located, or as major and minor sagas, the latter being more distinctly local in character and simpler in plot and interest than the former.

Historical Sagas. At least three works belong to the historical class. The well-known *Landnámabók* (*Book of Settlements*) contains a list of all the notable men who settled in the island up to 930 and includes much that is valuable on the religion, laws, and customs of the people. It is preserved only in a version dating from the 13th–14th centuries. *The Islendingasögur* (*Sagas of Icelanders*) embodies the lives and achievements of celebrated Icelanders and the fortunes of great Icelandic houses from 950 to 1130. The *Biskupasögur* (*Sagas of Bishops*) contains biog-raphies of Icelandic bishops who flourished in the 11th and 12th centuries. These biographies constitute an ecclesiastical history of Iceland, and although they are of less literary interest than the secular materials, they are of the utmost historical value.

It would be difficult to say how much is to be regarded as authentic history in *Nóregs Konungasögur* (*History of the Norwegian Kings*)—also called *Heimskringla* (*Ring of the World*), from the words with which it opens. This was the work of the greatest of all Icelanders, Snorri Sturluson, who was born about 1178 in West Iceland and became distinguished as a statesman, scholar, poet, and sagaman. It was written about 1230 and gives the history of the kings, chiefly of Norway. The Icelanders never lost the feeling of connection with the motherland, with which their country had a close relationship, especially in the time of Harold I (Harald Haarfager, or "Harold Fairhair"), when Iceland was settled, and of Olaf Tryggvason, when it was converted to Christianity. The *Heimskringla* possesses all the most excellent features of the best saga art.

Of historical importance also is the *Sturlungasaga* (*History of Sturla*), which is a collection of later *Islendingasögur*, telling of events that happened as late as the year 1250. The tales belonging to this saga arose in West Iceland about the beginning of the 14th century and contain some of the finest narrative passages in the whole body of Icelandic literature.

Mythical Sagas. Sagas treating of the old heroic legends belong to the mythical class. Some of these—like the *Volsünga Saga,* which is a prose rendition of the Nibelung story as given in the Eddic lays—are the common property of all the Germanic peoples. Others, like the *Frithjofs Saga,* are particularly Scandinavian.

Romantic Sagas. The romantic sagas—the *Riddarasögur,* for example—are mostly translations or adaptations of foreign (chiefly French) courtly epics and romances of chivalry, such as the tales of Troy, Alexander the Great, Charlemagne, King Arthur and the knights of the Round Table, and Barlaam and Josaphat. They were written down in the 13th century and became favorites two centuries later. They are purely literary and have no historic value. The *Fornaldarsögur* (*Tales of the Past*) deals with the early history of Iceland and is partly of a fairy and romantic character, telling of Viking voyages, love adventures, and battles involving *berserkers* (invulnerable warriors) and monsters.

Others. The simplest form of the saga is the *tháttr,* or short tale, treating of a single episode in the life of a distinguished Icelander. There are also sagas dealing with the Faeroes (islands in the North Atlantic Ocean), the Orkney Islands, Norway, Denmark, Greenland, and Vinland. Among the many minor sagas may be mentioned the *Gíslasaga,* the story of an outlaw poet, Gísli Sursson, set in northwestern Iceland; the *Bandamannasaga* (*The Confederates*), which, quite exceptionally, is humorous and is sometimes called the first comedy in western Europe; the *Víga-Glúmssaga,* the story of a grasping peasant, set in northeastern Iceland; the *Fóstbrœdhrasaga* (*The Foster Brothers Saga*), most of which takes place in the Icelandic colony in Greenland in the 11th century; the *Eríkssaga Raudha* (*The Saga of Eric the Red*), which tells of Eric's discovery of Greenland in the early

980's; and the *Grœnlendingasaga* (*Saga of the Greenlanders*), set in Greenland and containing tales of voyages to the coast of North America.

Four Masterpieces. The following are the greatest of the Icelandic sagas: (1) The *Eyrbyggjasaga* (*Saga of Eyrbyggja*), which covers a period of about 140 years (890–1030), was written probably by a cleric about 1225. It is remarkable for the great variety and richness of its adventure and for the light it throws on the manners and customs of the period. Its style is serious, measured, and realistic. (2) The *Egilssaga*, which takes its name from that of the skald (poet) Egill Skallagrímsson, portrays the life of the 9th and 10th centuries. As his sources, its author made use of oral traditions, other saga material, and Egill's own poems and put the whole into writing about the year 1200. (3) The *Laxdœlasaga* is, for the modern reader, the most romantic and one of the most attractive sagas. The incidents took place between 910 and 1026, and the scene is laid among the people of Laxátals in West Iceland. Here, too, the author, who was also probably a cleric, made masterly use of his sources, some of which may have been Irish, both oral and written. (4) The saga universally recognized as the ripest and most brilliant product of the saga art is the *Njálssaga*. It is composed of two originally independent sagas, those of Gunnar and Njál, and belongs to the south of Iceland. It is designed on the most liberal scale and is remarkable for the masterly way in which its plot—full of intrigue, love, and hate—has been handled and for its character-drawing and simple and effective style.

The Sagaman's Art. In Iceland and Ireland, more than anywhere else in western Europe, storytelling was a necessary part of every assembly. The professional sagaman wandered from place to place, told his stock-in-trade, received entertainment and rewards in return, and gathered material for new stories. Because they were of oral transmission, these tales, whether historical or legendary in character, always used the oral saga as a background, even when later they were thought fit to be consigned to writing. Almost all the events narrated in them took place between the years 950 and 1030. That was the Saga Age of Iceland, when life, in a material sense, was almost barbarous and factional fights were frequent. The sagaman made the most of the abundant stuff at hand for heroic narrative. His heroes are represented as being almost more than human. They belong, for the most part, to the ruling class. The author gives a short account of the hero's family; youth and manhood; loves, friendships, and enmities; great deeds; and death, which was usually of a tragic character. They were based almost entirely on actual happenings and were in close relation to the lives of those for whom they were recited or written. Thus the sagas convey a wonderfully faithful picture of life not only in the Scandinavian world during those centuries but also among the other Germanic peoples who once lived in similar circumstances but have left no such record of their own past.

The very language in which the sagas are couched is conducive to the appearance of reality. It is in prose and very often in the form of dialogue. As the sagaman's main object was to move his hearers, he told his tales in unaffected language—the everyday language of the people. Like a dispassionate observer, showing no sympathy with either the events or their heroes, he was content to assemble the incidents and to relate them with brevity and restraint. The result, however, is much more than a mere impersonal folktale. Surprisingly, the essential rules of all good storytelling seem to have been clearly fixed at that early date, and they were observed to perfection. Dramatic irony and suspense; the orderly, steady progression of the scenes; the recurrence of personages familiar from other sagas, the chief figure in one becoming a subordinate character in another; the incidental mention of unheroic details—all these techniques add to the interest of the saga. One thing the Icelandic sagaman—like the contemporary Irish *sgéulaidhe*—could do supremely well, and that was to tell a story. The Icelandic sagas stand apart both as a notable phenomenon in literary history and as an absolutely independent creation of the northern mind. See also EDDAS and the Index entry *Saga*.

JOSEPH DUNN
Formerly, The Catholic University of America

Bibliography

Andersson, Theodore M., *The Icelandic Family Saga: An Analytic Reading* (Harvard Univ. Press 1967).
Andersson, Theodore M., *Problems of Icelandic Saga Origins* (Yale Univ. Press 1964).
Bekker-Nielsen, Hans, *Old Norse-Icelandic Studies: A Select Bibliography* (Univ. of Toronto Press 1967).
Craigie, William A., *Icelandic Sagas* (1913; reprint, Kraus Reprint 1968).
Einarsson, Stefán, *A History of Icelandic Literature* (Johns Hopkins Press 1957).
Hallberg, Peter, *Icelandic Saga*, tr. by Paul Schach (Univ. of Neb. Press 1962).
Hannesson, Jóhann S., *Sagas of Icelanders: A Supplement to Islandica*, vols. 1 and 24 (Cornell Univ. Press 1958).
Hermannsson, Halldór, *Bibliography of the Icelandic Sagas and Minor Tales* (1908; reprint, Kraus Reprint).
Hermannsson, Halldór, *Old Icelandic Literature: A Bibliographical Essay* (1933; reprint, Kraus Reprint).
Hermannsson, Halldór, *Sagas of the Kings and the Mythical-Heroic Sagas* (1937; reprint, Kraus Reprint).
Hermannsson, Halldór, and others, eds., *Islandica*, 39 vols. (Cornell Univ. Press 1908–1958).
Jones, Gwyn, ed., *Erik the Red and Other Icelandic Sagas* (Oxford 1961).
Ker, William P., *Epic and Romance*, 2d ed. (Dover 1908).
Sveinsson, Einar O., *Njáls Saga: A Literary Masterpiece*, ed. by Paul Schach (Univ. of Neb. Press 1971).
Turville-Pétre, Gabriel, *Origins of Icelandic Literature* (Oxford 1953).

SAGAN, sȧ'gäN, **Françoise,** the pen name of Françoise Quoirez (1935–   ), French author, who is best remembered for her highly successful novel *Bonjour Tristesse*. She was born in Cajarc, France, on June 21, 1935. After attending various private schools, she studied at the Sorbonne in Paris but left without taking a degree.

In 1953, when she was 18, Miss Sagan began to write *Bonjour Tristesse*, a skillfully told story of an unhappy, cynical teenage girl set on preventing the remarriage of her widowed father. The novel was an instantaneous success at its publication in 1954 and was awarded the Prix des Critiques in the same year. It also quickly became an international best seller and was translated into some 20 languages. It appeared in the United States in 1955.

Miss Sagan's other works include the novels *A Certain Smile* (1956), *Those Without Shadows* (1957), *Aimez-Vous Brahms?* (1959), and *The Wonderful Clouds* (1962). She also wrote several plays and collaborated with the composer Michel Magne on a ballet, *Le Rendez–vous manqué* (1958).

SAGASTA, sä-gäs'tä, **Práxedes Mateo** (1827–1903), Spanish prime minister and political leader. He was born in Torrecilla en Cameros on July 21, 1827, and became an engineer. He was exiled in 1856 and 1866 for opposing Isabella II's government. He returned to Spain in 1868 and helped lead the revolution that led to her dethronement. Sagasta then served in several ministerial posts and briefly (1871–1872) as prime minister under King Amadeus. He retired after the accession of Alfonso XII in 1874.

In 1880, Sagasta returned to active politics with the founding of the Liberal party under his leadership. During the next two decades he served five times as prime minister. He was severely criticized for Spain's defeat in the Spanish-American War (1898) and for signing the peace treaty with the United States. He died on Jan. 5, 1903.

SAGE, Russell (1816–1906), American financier, whose fortune endowed a number of philanthropies. He was born in Verona Township, Oneida county, N. Y., on Aug. 4, 1816. He was a successful wholesale grocer in Troy, N. Y., from 1839 until 1857. He was an alderman of Troy and served as a Whig member of Congress from 1853 to 1857. In 1863, Sage moved to New York City and began large-scale investing in Western railroads and other enterprises. Jay Gould was his partner in many operations. In the 1880's, Sage became a banker.

In 1891, a visitor to his office, who was refused a loan of $1,200,000, exploded a bomb. The bomber and a clerk were killed, but Sage recovered from severe injuries. He died at Lawrence Beach, N. Y., on July 22, 1906.

His second wife was Margaret Olivia Slocum Sage (1828–1918), whom he married in 1869. She played an important role in the management of his fortune and after his death applied huge sums to philanthropy. Among these were the Emma Willard School for girls and Russell Sage College, both in Troy. With an initial gift of $10 million, she established in 1907 the Russell Sage Foundation for the improvement of social and living conditions in the United States. The foundation conducts research in collaboration with other institutions to promote the use of knowledge of the social sciences.

SAGE is an herb (*Salvia officinalis*) widely used as a seasoning for foods, especially sausages and dressings for poultry and pork. The term "sage" is also applied to a wide variety of other plants, including sagebrush, that resemble *Salvia officinalis* in odor or color.

Sage is a small shrubby plant, usually not more than 18 inches (46 cm) high. Its usually whitish green leaves are highly aromatic. The flowers, borne in early summer, are usually blue but sometimes are pink or white. For use as a seasoning, the leaves should be gathered when young, before flower stems develop. They are most aromatic when fresh, but can be preserved by being dried slowly in moderately warm, preferably moving, air.

SAGE GROUSE, a large grouse, *Centrocercus urophasianus*, native to the dry sagebrush areas of western North America. It usually has mottled gray, black, or buff plumage. The male reaches a weight of 6 to 8 pounds (2.7–3.6 kg) and a length of some 30 inches (75 cm), much of

ALAN PITCAIRN, FROM GRANT HEILMAN

Sagebrush *(Artemisia tridentata)*

which is accounted for by a long slender tail. In complex courtship displays, the male erects his tail like an extended fan, bows deeply, vibrates partly open stiffened wings, displays orangelike inflated gular, or throat, sacs, and utters resonant booming and groaning noises in competition with other males. The female alone builds the nest, incubates the clutch of seven eggs, and cares for the young.

SAGEBRUSH, any of several species of undershrubs found abundantly in arid, alkaline regions of western North America. Sagebrushes are classified in the genus *Artemisia* of the composite family, Compositae. The best-known species is the common shrub *A. tridentata*, known as bitter sage or blue sage. It varies from dwarfed shrub size to almost treelike proportions. It has stalkless wedge-shaped leaves that are generally silvery gray and small yellowish or whitish flower heads. Sagebrush is eaten by many animals. The pungent odor of sagebrush, which resembles that of the cooking herb also known as sage (*Salvia officinalis*), permeates large areas of the Far West.

SAGINAW, sag'ə-nô, is a city in eastern Michigan, the seat of Saginaw county, situated on the Saginaw River about 15 miles (24 km) south of Saginaw Bay of Lake Huron and about 80 miles (128 km) northwest of Detroit. The surrounding area raises sugar beets and has coal, oil, and salt deposits. The city's industries make automobile parts, metal products, fabricated metals, machinery, and food products.

The Saginaw Art Museum has displays of Indian artifacts, paintings, and sculpture.

A trading post was built in 1816 by Louis Campau near the city's present site. A council house was erected, and here on Sept. 24, 1819, a treaty was concluded between Lewis Cass, governor of Michigan Territory, and the Chippewa Indians that ceded large tracts of land to the United States.

The fur traders developed a small community, but as the settlement grew the lumber industry superseded the fur trade. In the latter half of the 19th century, Saginaw was one of the lumbering centers of the nation. The industry declined as indiscriminate cutting diminished the forests. Exploitation of the salt and coal deposits dominated the economy for a time, until manufacturing enterprises began to grow.

Saginaw was incorporated as a city in 1857. East Saginaw was chartered two years later, and the two municipalities were consolidated in 1889 into Saginaw city. With the adoption of a new charter in 1936, a city manager-council government was formed. Population: 77,508.

SAGITTA, sə-jit′ə, a constellation of the Northern Hemisphere. See CONSTELLATION.

SAGITTARIA, saj-ə-târ′ē-ə, any of a genus, *Sagittaria,* of wholly or partly aquatic plants, some of which are popular aquarium plants. Members of the water plantain family, Alismaceae, Sagittaria are widely distributed in tropical and temperate regions of the world. Handsome plants, they have erect or floating lancelike, elliptical, or arrowshaped leaves and whorllike flowers with white petals carried well above the waterline. The common arrowhead, *S. latifolia,* grows in the mud along rivers and ditches. Very ornamental, it has whorls of flowers arising from the center of a cluster of large, erect, sagittate leaves. Its thick fibrous rootstock produces starch-rich tubers that were a food staple for some Indian tribes.

SAGITTARIUS, saj-ə-târ′ē-əs, is a summer constellation of the Northern Hemisphere. One of the 12 signs of the zodiac, it lies across the ecliptic between the other signs Capricornus and Scorpius. In Greek mythology the constellation represented the learned centaur Chiron, depicted as an archer aiming his arrow toward Scorpius. Part of Sagittarius has a dipperlike shape and has come to be known as the "Milk Dipper" because it lies next to the Milky Way.

Sagittarius is fairly conspicuous even though its two brightest stars, Kaus Australis and Nunki, have magnitudes of only 1.95 and 2.14, respectively. The western region of the constellation is of particular interest because the Milky Way in that area represents the central regions of our galaxy. Numerous globular and open clusters of stars that surround the galactic center can be observed there, including M17, M18, and M23. To the east, M55 is a globular cluster that is bright enough to be observed with the naked eye. The constellation also includes several famous nebulosities, such as M8, the Lagoon Nebula; M17, the Omega, or Horseshoe, Nebula; and M20, the Trifid Nebula. Also located in Sagittarius is the point at which the sun's path reaches its greatest yearly angular distance south of the equator—that is, the Northern Hemisphere's winter solstice, about December 22.

SAGO, sā′gō, is a starchy product that is extracted from the trunks of certain palms and cycads. It is a basic food for people in the southwestern Pacific Ocean region, from which it is also an important export. Rich in carbohydrates, sago is easily digested and is often used in special diets. Sago flour is used in bakery products and puddings and as a thickener for soups and sauces.

Palms of the genus *Metroxylon,* which grow primarily in Indonesia, Malaysia, Fiji, and the Moluccas, are the principal source of sago. The palm tree has a stout trunk that may be smooth or spiny in different varieties and that rises to about 40 feet (12 meters). It is surmounted by large, pinnate leaves and bears spherical, scaly fruit. The tree thrives in freshwater swamps, with little need for cultivation. It flowers only once, usually between the ages of 12 and 15 years, after which it dies. The fruit seldom contains fertile seeds, and propagation is primarily by means of shoots, or suckers, that grow at the base of older stems.

The maximum amount of sago is obtained from palm trees that are felled just before they begin to flower, and the yield from a single palm cut at this time frequently amounts to about 200 pounds (90 kg) of commercial sago. The tree trunk is cut into sections, and the hard, thick rind is split to expose the pith, which is scooped out. The material is then processed into the meal with water, a paste is formed that may be rubbed through sieves to produce the hard, shiny grains that are known commercially as pearl sago.

SAGUARO, sə-gwä′rō, the largest cactus in the world. It is also spelled *sahuaro.* The saguaro, *Carnegiea gigantea,* is found in desert regions in the southwestern United States and in adjacent areas of Mexico. The saguaro has a columnar trunk and sometimes grows to a height of 60 feet (18 meters). It is sparsely branched and has stout strong spines. A succulent, the saguaro accumulates reserves of water in its leaves and stem. White flowers, generally about 4 inches (10 cm) long and 2 inches (5 cm) wide, occur at the tips of the stem and branches. The red, egg-shaped fruit is edible. The saguaro has been grown in greenhouses but generally does not do well under cultivation.

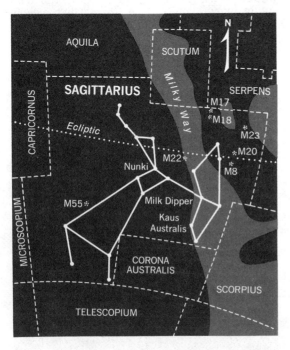

FRED MANG, JR., NATIONAL PARK SERVICE

Saguaro cacti stand in huge weird forests in the Saguaro National Monument near Tucson, Arizona.

SAGUARO NATIONAL MONUMENT, sə-gwǎ′rō, is in southern Arizona, east and west of Tucson. The Rincon Mountain section is about 7 miles (11 km) east of the city; the Tucson Mountain section is about the same distance west of the city.

The monument displays thousands of saguaro cacti, which mark the flora in parts of the southwestern United States and northwestern Mexico. The plant has the shape of a candelabrum; the main stem may grow as high as 50 feet (15 meters). The Rincon Mountain section has many giant specimens that are decaying with age. In the Tucson Mountain area, the plants tend to be smaller, younger, and more vigorous.

The monument presents striking contrasts of climate, flora, and fauna at different altitudes. At 3,100 feet (940 meters), the plant life is typical of dry desert conditions. At the top of Mica Mountain (8,666 feet or 2,632 meters), the plants are those of lower elevations in southern Canada.

In the Rincon Mountain section, a 9-mile (15 km) drive through the Cactus Forest offers a scenic route. There are hiking trails and picnic areas in both sections of the monument, but no facilities for camping or lodging.

The monument's area exceeds 78,000 acres (31,500 hectares), of which 63,000 acres (25,- 500 hectares) are in the Rincon Mountain area.

SAGUENAY RIVER, sag′ə-nā, in southeastern Quebec, Canada. It rises in Lac St-Jean and flows southeast for about 125 miles (200 km) to the St. Lawrence River at Tadoussac. It issues from the lake in two channels, the Grande Décharge and the Petite Décharge, which unite beyond the Île d'Alma to form the main stream.

In its entire course, the river drops more than 300 feet (90 meters).

Below the city of Chicoutimi, 60 miles (96 km) from the St. Lawrence, the river broadens to become a fjord. Hills on both sides create a great gorge; Capes Eternity and Trinity, 30 miles up the river, are about 1,500 feet (450 meters) high. Thousands of tourists, drawn by the spectacular scenery, take steamboat excursions up the river each year.

A number of hydroelectric stations are powered by the river's rapids, and there are pulp and paper mills along its banks. At Arvida is a large aluminum plant. Chicoutimi, at the head of navigation, has varied industries.

The Saguenay was first visited by Jacques Cartier in 1535. Samuel de Champlain explored its lower reaches in 1603. For many years it was an important route for explorers, missionaries, and fur traders.

SAGUIA EL HAMRA. See SPANISH SAHARA.

SAGUNTO, sä-gōōn′tō, a town on the east coast of Spain, is in Valencia province, about 15 miles (24 km) north of Valencia. South of the town, on the site of the ancient Saguntum, are the well-preserved remains of a Roman theater and of medieval fortifications. North of Sagunto are the ruins of a Roman circus. The town processes agricultural products, has brandy and wine distilleries, and manufactures iron and steel.

The town was an Iberian settlement before the Greeks established a colony in the 3d century B. C. About 225, Rome, wary of growing Carthaginian power, concluded a treaty with Hasdrubal guaranteeing the independence of Saguntum. In 219, Hannibal and the Carthaginians attacked the town, which withstood an eight-month siege before falling. The capture of Saguntum was an immediate cause of the Second Punic War.

The Moors seized the town in the 8th century A. D. and it remained under their control until King James I of Aragón captured it in the late 13th century. The Moors called the town Murviedro, a name it retained until 1877. Population: (1960) 15,210.

SAHA, sä′hä, **Meghnad** (1893–1956), Indian physicist. He was born in Seoratali, Dacca (now in Bangladesh), on Oct. 6, 1893, and received a master's degree in applied mathematics in 1915. He became interested in quantum theory and astrophysics and by 1919 had developed the equation on high-temperature ionization that bears his name. His paper on stellar spectra appeared in 1921. The work extended classical gas thermodynamics and kinetics to plasmas and was very important in the interpretation of stellar spectral lines. Saha later became active in the development of scientific institutes in India and in national economic planning involving technology. He died in New Delhi on Feb. 16, 1956.

SAHAPTIN INDIANS, sä-hap′tin, a linguistic stock of North American Indians, who inhabited a section of the northwestern plateau along the Columbia River and its tributaries in northeastern Oregon, southeastern Washington, and southwestern Idaho. An alternate spelling is Shahaptian. Well defined linguistically, the family was fairly homogeneous in its customs. A principal tribe, the Nez Percé, is sometimes called the Sahaptin. See INDIAN, AMERICAN.

Sand dunes of the Sahara, the world's largest desert.

SAHARA, sə-har'ə, the great desert of northern Africa and the largest in the world. It extends from the Atlantic Ocean on the west to the Red Sea on the east, and from the Atlas Mountains and Mediterranean Sea on the north to the savannas of the Sudan region on the south. With an area of more than 3 million square miles (8 million sq km), the Sahara is divided among the countries of Morocco, Algeria, Tunisia, Mauritania, Mali, Niger, Chad, Senegal, Libya, Egypt, and Sudan, and the territory of Spanish Sahara. Parts of the desert are known by separate names, such as the Eastern or Arabian Desert between the Nile River and the Red Sea, and the Libyan Desert along the border between Egypt and Libya.

The Sahara has an estimated population of 2 million, excluding the densely settled Nile Valley, which is usually considered apart from the surrounding desert. The principal language of the people of the Sahara is Arabic and their religion is Islam.

Land and People. The northern Sahara, from southern Morocco to Egypt, is composed of rocky plateaus (*hamadas*), gravel-covered plains (*regs*), and areas of shifting sand dunes (*ergs*). Oases occur wherever water is available, as along the intermittent streams that flow into the Sahara

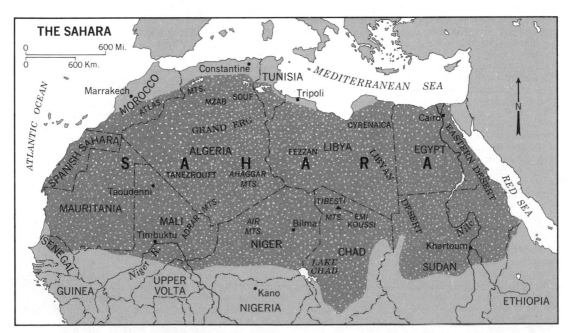

THE SAHARA

from the Atlas Mountains and at artesian springs and wells. Nomadic tribes graze sheep and goats in the desert during the period of winter rains, but during the dry summer most of the nomads move north to the Atlas Mountains or high plateaus.

Contrasts in landforms, peoples, and oases have led to the recognition of distinctive areas. For example, the Mzab region in Algeria is inhabited by people of Berber origin, who comprise a sect of Islam and live in cities located on rocky hills or mesas. Nearby is the Souf, where date palms are planted in basins scooped out of loose sand and the people are mostly of Arab origin. The Fezzan, in southern Libya, is a large basin of gravel (reg) surface, and its people, the Fezzanis, maintain a separate tradition. Cyrenaica, in northeastern Libya, is a rocky plateau with coastal settlements and interior pasturages, and is the home of the Sanusi people.

The central part of the Sahara, in southern Algeria and along Libya's borders with Niger and Chad, consists of high plateaus and mountains. The major uplands of this region are the Ahaggar, Aïr, and Tibesti mountains. The latter region has the highest peaks of the Sahara, including the extinct volcano Emi Koussi, which rises to a height of 11,204 feet (3,415 meters). The Ahaggar and Aïr regions are inhabited mainly by Tuaregs, while the Tibesti mountains are occupied by a Negroid people, the Tebu.

The southern Sahara, from Mauritania across the Lake Chad region to the northern part of the Republic of Sudan, consists of low plateaus and broad plains. Date palms are found only in rare spots. One of the few resources is salt, which is mined at Taoudeni and Bilma. Nomads graze goats and cattle on the southern margins of the desert during the season of summer rains, migrating south during the dry winter. The peoples are mostly of mixed Hamitic and Negro origin, but certain Saharan areas in West Africa have predominately Tuareg or Arab populations.

Climate and Vegetation. Arid climate and sparse vegetation are characteristic features of the Sahara. In central parts precipitation averages less than 1 inch (25 mm) a year, but it increases to more than 5 inches (125 mm) along the outer margins. It is one of the world's hottest areas, with mean annual temperatures reaching over 100° F (38° C) in some places.

In the interior, rainfall is so light and rare that forage for camels or goats is available only at intervals, and the nomadic population is very sparse and mobile. In the extremely dry Tanezrouft region of southern Algeria, vegetation is entirely absent and there are neither oases nor nomads. In more favored spots, wells and springs provide water for the date palms, barley fields, and vegetable gardens of the oases. The margins of the Sahara, with seasons of light rain, support a nomadic population.

Economy. From the 10th century to the close of the 19th century, trans-Saharan camel caravans crossed the desert to trade. They carried cloth and other manufactured goods from the cities of Barbary—such as Marrakech, Constantine, and Tripoli—to Sudanese centers—such as Timbuktu and Kano—and returned with cargoes of gold, leather, and slaves. Camels are still widely used for local trade and travel, but trans-Saharan transportation is now provided mostly by trucks and airplanes.

The Sahara has been found to be rich in minerals. It is a major source of oil, especially in parts of Libya and Algeria. Iron ore is mined in Mauritania. The Saharan region is also a principal source of natural gas.

BENJAMIN E. THOMAS
University of California at Los Angeles

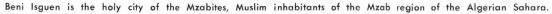

Beni Isguen is the holy city of the Mzabites, Muslim inhabitants of the Mzab region of the Algerian Sahara.

RODNEY W. ANGOVE, FROM BLACK STAR

SAHARANPUR, sə-här′ən-pŏŏr, is a city in India, in Uttar Pradesh state, 90 miles (145 km) northeast of Delhi. It is a railroad junction and a marketplace for the agricultural products of the district, as well as a manufacturing center for the local cotton, tobacco, and sugar. Saharanpur contains railroad shops and a paper mill and is known for its wood carvings. Also in the city are government botanical gardens, a fruit research institute, and an aviation training center. Population: (1970) 228,000.

SAICHO, sī-chō (762–822), was a Japanese Buddhist monk who established the Tendai sect in Japan. He is also known as Dengyo Daishi. See JAPAN–*Religion and Philosophy* (Buddhism).

SAID, sä-ēd′, **Sayyid** (1791–1856), Arab ruler of Muscat and Oman and of Zanzibar, who created a commercial empire in East Africa. He was born Said Ibn Sultan near Muscat and was the son of the ruler of Muscat and Oman. He became sayyid, or ruler, in 1806.

About 1840, Said moved his permanent residence to the island of Zanzibar, from where he eventually dominated the east coast of Africa from Kilwa in the south to Mogadishu in the north. During his long rule Zanzibar became the economic center of East Africa, and he greatly strengthened the island's economy by encouraging the cultivation of cloves. He also played a leading role in organizing the commercial penetration of the interior of East Africa.

Said maintained close relations with Britain, with which he signed two anti-slave trade treaties. He also signed commercial treaties with France and the United States. He died in October 1856.

SAID IBN SULTAN. See SAID, SAYYID.

SAID PASHA, sä-ēd′ pả′shä (1822–1863), was viceroy of Egypt from 1854 to 1863. He was born in Cairo on March 17, 1822, the fourth son of Muhammad Ali. Educated in Paris, Said succeeded his uncle Abbas I as viceroy in July 1854.

One of Said's first actions after coming to power was to grant a concession for the construction of the Suez Canal to Ferdinand de Lesseps, a French diplomat. The canal, begun in 1859, was not completed until 1869, after Said's death. The Viceroy allowed many of his father's social and economic reforms to wither, and because of his heavy spending Egypt fell deeply in debt to European creditors. Said died in Alexandria on Jan. 18, 1863.

SAIDA. See SIDON.

SAIGA, sī′gə, a sheeplike antelope, *Saiga tatarica*, that has an unusually inflated nasal region. A gregarious species, the saiga roams in herds in desert and steppe regions of Siberia and eastern Russia, feeding on shrubs and grasses. Its dense, furry, yellowish brown summer coat turns white and woolly in winter. The male stands about 30 inches (75 cm) at the shoulders and has amber-colored, slightly curved horns.

SAIGO TAKAMORI, sī-gō tä-kä-mō-rē (1827?–1877), was a Japanese patriot. He was born in Kagoshima, Kyushu Island. Saigo was a samurai and an enthusiastic partisan of the emperor, whom he supported in opposition to the dominant Tokugawa shogunate. He took an important part in the restoration of power to the emperor in 1868 and was appointed commander in chief of the army. In 1873, after his desire to attack Korea was overruled, he resigned. Four years later he was one of the samurai who, displeased with the Western ideas of the throne, launched the Satsuma rebellion. When his forces were defeated he committed ritual suicide. Saigo was not stigmatized as a rebel, and he became the hero of the imperial restoration.

SAIGON, sī-gon′, the former capital of South Vietnam, is on the Saigon River, about 50 miles (80 km) from the South China Sea. It is adjacent to the city of Cholon, and the two are governed as a single metropolis.

PETER WERLE, FROM PHOTO RESEARCHERS

SAIGON, because of its Western architecture, tree-lined streets, and handsome parks, has a European look. The city was built largely in the 19th and 20th centuries when Vietnam was under French administration.

Saigon, which resembles a Western city, is the commercial center for the southern part of Vietnam. Cholon is Chinese in character and is more industrial. Among the principal products of the metropolis are foodstuffs, soap, bicycles, cotton fabrics, rubber goods, and varnish. Food-processing establishments include fruit-packing plants, breweries, distilleries, and rice mills. The nearby delta of the Mekong River is one of the great rice-growing areas of Asia, and rice was Saigon's chief export until production was drastically reduced by the Vietnam War. Foreign trade was handled by a large number of export-import firms, owned and operated mostly by resident Chinese.

Metropolitan Saigon is connected with Da Nang and Hué in the north by a railroad along the coast and is joined by rail with My Tho and Loc Ninh to the south. Saigon is connected with most cities in the country by a network of highways. Tan Son Nhut airport in suburban Saigon is a busy international terminal and a major military air base. Linked by canals to the Mekong River and served by an extensive inland waterway system, the city is the largest port of southern Vietnam. Its extensive port facilities include shipyards and a naval base.

The former University of Saigon, founded in 1917 as the Université Indochinoise, is Vietnam's oldest university. It is now named the University of Ho Chi Minh City.

History. Saigon originated as a Khmer settlement. During the 17th century it became part of the kingdom of Vietnam. The city was within the territory that became the French colony of Cochin China in the 1860's.

During World War II, Saigon was occupied by the Japanese, who used it is a base for operations in other parts of Southeast Asia. When Vietnam was divided into two states in 1954, Saigon was made the capital of South Vietnam.

The city, which has wide, tree-lined boulevards and many public parks, underwent many physical and socioeconomic changes as a result of the Vietnam War. It was occupied peacefully by Communist forces on April 30, 1975, and was renamed Ho Chi Minh City. Much of the population, which had been swollen by a vast influx of refugees, was resettled in the countryside. Population: (1976) 3,460,500.

SAIGYO, sī-gyō (1118–1190), was a Japanese wandering priest-poet, the first of a series of such poets, who are much admired in Japan. He was a master of the *tanka*, a poem consisting of 31 syllables in five lines. Saigyo was born to a samurai family. At the age of 23 he left his family and abandoned his military career to become a Buddhist priest. Afterward he spent most of his life traveling in Japan. He died at the Kosenji temple in Osaka.

Saigyo lived during a time of instability and civil strife. The power of the aristocracy at Heian (Kyoto), the imperial capital, was in decline, and with it the brilliant Heian court life. A new class of provincial military leaders was coming into prominence. Saigyo's poetry expresses a new spirit contrasting with the courtly love poetry of the preceding centuries. It is characterized by a love of nature and deep religious feeling. Saigyo was well represented in the *Shinkokinshu* (*New Collection from Ancient and Modern Times*), the eighth of the imperial anthologies of Japanese poetry (1206).

SAIKAKU. See IHARA SAIKAKU.

SAILCLOTH is a strong fabric suitable for making sails. The earliest sails probably were made of materials such as animal skins or reeds. Greek and Roman ships had cloth sails but were mainly propelled by oars. By about 1600 ships of the major European countries used sailcloth woven from flax fibers. After about 1850 cotton canvas was widely used for sails. Since about 1950 the synthetic fiber Dacron has been popular for sailboats. Dacron sails are lighter and stronger than cotton sails and they dry more quickly than cotton. See also Dacron.

SAILENDRA, shī-len′drǝ, a Buddhist dynasty of Java and the Sumatra-based maritime empire of Śrivijaya. The Śailendras (Shailendras) apparently disappeared from Java and appeared in Sumatra in the mid-9th century, though possibly they ruled Śrivijaya before then. A king of Mataram in Java was married to a Śailendra princess. It has been suggested that he defeated the last Javanese Śailendra ruler, and that the latter made his way to Sumatra and became king of Śrivijaya.

In Java the Śailendras built the Borobudur and other great monuments. As lords of Śrivijaya they controlled sea trade between China and India, reaching the height of their power by 1025. Palembang, Śrivijaya's capital, was a noted center of Buddhist learning.

SAILFISH, any of a group of large marine sport fishes with very long rays and dark spots on the large sail-shaped dorsal fin. Sailfish also have spearlike snouts, or bills, and ridges on the sides of the caudal peduncles just in front of their tails. They are found in warm coastal waters throughout most of the world. The Pacific sailfish (*Istiophorus orientalis*) is the largest species, reaching a length of more than 11 feet (3.3

AMERICAN MUSEUM OF NATURAL HISTORY

The sailfish gets its name from its large dorsal fin.

meters) and a weight of more than 200 pounds (90 kg). The Atlantic sailfish (*I. albicans*), one of the most popular game fishes along the East Coast of the United States, is somewhat smaller. Folding their "sails" against their bodies, sailfish swim very rapidly, sometimes striking at smaller prey fishes with their bills. Sailfish, together with spearfish and marlin, are classified in the family Istiophoridae of the order Perciformes.

SAILING. See NAVIGATION; SHIP—*Sailing Vessels*; YACHTS AND YACHTING.

SAINT, SAINTE. All geographic names beginning "Saint" or "Sainte" are entered under those headings, even though practice elsewhere may be to use the abbreviated forms "St." and "Ste." Names beginning "Saint" are alphabetized before names beginning "Sainte." "São" is used for Portuguese place-names and "San" and "Santa" for Spanish and Italian place-names.

Entries on persons whose last names begin with the abbreviated form "St." are under "St." but alphabetized as though "St." were spelled out. Entries on saints of the church are under their given names or surnames.

SAINT, a person who is regarded as an exemplar of virtue by reason of his deeds and life. In the Roman Catholic Church a person is declared a saint through the process of canonization. (See CANONIZATION.) In this case the title affirms the belief of the church that the person is in heaven and hence is worthy of honor. In Christian theology, saints, besides serving as exemplars, may also intercede with God on behalf of the faithful. Saints are also found in other religions, such as Islam and Buddhism. In Islam the function of the saint is similar to that in Christianity. In Buddhism, particularly the Mahayana form, the saint (*bodhisattva*) is one who is qualified for entrance into the state of Nirvana but who delays his entry in order to assist all sentient beings. (See BUDDHA AND BUDDHISM.) This article will treat the development of the concept of saints in Christianity.

Biblical Usage. English translations of the Old Testament, particularly the King James Version, frequently translate the Hebrew word for "holy" as "saint." The Hebrew people were holy because of their special covenant relation to God. They were the holy people of God, set aside for his service, and hence saints (Leviticus 19:2). The term "saint" was also used in a more general sense to indicate a pious and observant Jew (Psalm 31:23).

In the New Testament and in the writings of Saint Paul, the term "saint" was frequently used of the faithful Christian (Acts 9:13). Saint Paul frequently used it in the opening greeting of his epistles, as in the Epistle to the Colossians which reads "To the saints and faithful brethren of Christ at Colossae" (1:2). In the Gospel of Matthew, Christ tells the Apostles that they will have a special role in heaven (19:28). One is a saint by virtue of his special relationship with Christ, who alone is holy (Philippians 1:1). On the last day, when Christ will come to judge the world, his saints will participate, and at that time their holiness will be manifested to all (I Thessalonians 3:13).

The Cult of Martyrs in the Early Church. In the early church the term "saint" was applied to all who willingly suffered martyrdom for their faith. The place of death and burial became a place of cult, where the liturgy of the Eucharist was celebrated. The practice of placing relics of the martyrs in the altar also became common at this time. However, only the cult of those martyrs who received the approbation of the local bishop was permitted. By the 4th century the Fathers of the Church, in particular St. John Chrysostom and St. Cyril of Jerusalem, were encouraging the faithful to ask the saints to intercede for them with God.

By the end of the 4th and the beginning of the 5th century the custom of including confessors (those who had witnessed to their faith in Christ by their lives) among the saints became common.

A distinction between the type of worship offered to God and that offered to the saints was made about this time. Worship given to God was designated by the Greek word *latria*, which is translated by the modern English word "worship" or, traditionally, "adoration"; that given to the saints was called in Greek *dulia*, which in English would be "veneration." By the 6th century the names of the saints began to be included in the prayers of the Mass as celebrated in Rome.

Lives of the saints prepared for the edification of the faithful were common by the 8th century and flourished throughout the Middle Ages. Popular devotion during this period fostered a tendency to create highly fanciful tales, with no historical value, about the saints. Superstitious practices also developed. Some of the faithful prayed to the saints not as though they were intercessors with God, but as though they were the direct source of favors.

The Reformation to the Modern Era. During the Renaissance and Reformation many of the lives of the saints were subjected to critical analysis and were rejected as fanciful and dangerous. Among the Reformers, particularly the Calvinists and the Zwinglians, the practice of veneration of the saints was done away with because it was felt that it detracted from the unique mediatorship of Christ, was unscriptural, and was hopelessly interwoven with superstition. The Thirty-nine Articles of the Church of England (which was later subscribed to by the other churches of the Anglican Communion) expressly condemn the "Romish doctrine" of the "Invocation of Saints" (Article 22). In later years, however, the interpretation of this article has been disputed, many theologians considering that it was opposed only to the excesses of the time.

In 1563 the Roman Catholic Council of Trent, while it encouraged devotion to the saints, stressed that the saints are venerated and not worshiped, and that Christ is the sole mediator of man. The faithful should pray to the saints to ask their intercession with Christ for whatever assistance they might need.

Since the Oxford Movement in the 19th century, the veneration of saints in the churches of the Anglican Communion has become more common. Church buildings have long been dedicated to saints, and their feasts form part of the Anglican liturgical calendar.

Most Protestant churches do not have any veneration of the saints, but church buildings are frequently dedicated to them.

The Roman Catholic Church has subjected the universal liturgical calendar of saints' feasts to critical evaluation. In 1969 the feasts of some saints whose historical reality was questionable or whose universal appeal was doubtful were removed. If a local cult of the saint was still active, however, his feast might still be observed locally. In general, the day of the saint's death was to be the day of his feast since that day is regarded as the time of his birth into the glory of heaven. The regulations had to do with the liturgical observance of these saints' feasts. The church did not raise the question of whether these figures are saints.

See also articles on individual saints; BEATIFICATION; HAGIOGRAPHY.

PATRON SAINTS

Among Christians, particularly Roman Catholics, various saints have been traditionally associated with a disease or disability, an occupation, profession, or other activity. Their intercession with God has been sought through prayer for cures or for the protection and fostering of one or another activity. Their designation as patron saints usually arose through popular devotion. In some few instances the Roman Catholic Church has officially named patron saints. In the list below these are indicated by an asterisk.

Occupations

Accountants: St. Matthew
Actors: St. Genesius
Advertisers: St. Bernadino of Siena*
Anesthetists: St. René Goupil
Architects: St. Thomas the Apostle; St. Barbara
Artists: St. Luke
Astronomers: St. Dominic
Athletes: St. Sebastian
Authors: St. Francis de Sales
Aviators: Our Lady of Loreto; Ste. Thérèse of Lisieux; St. Joseph of Cupertino

Bakers: St. Elizabeth of Hungary; St. Nicholas
Bankers: St. Matthew
Barbers: Sts. Cosmas and Damian; St. Louis
Bookkeepers: St. Matthew
Booksellers: St. John of God
Builders: St. Vincent Ferrer
Butchers: St. Anthony of Egypt; St. Hadrian; St. Luke

Carpenters: St. Joseph
Comedians: St. Vitus
Cooks: St. Lawrence; St. Martha

Dentists: St. Apollonia

Editors: St. John Bosco
Engineers: St. Ferdinand III

Farmers: St. George; St. Isidore
Firemen: St. Florian
Fishermen: St. Andrew
Florists: St. Dorothy; Ste. Thérèse of Lisieux

Gardeners: St. Dorothy; St. Adelard; St. Tryphon; St. Fiacre; St. Phocas
Grocers: St. Michael

Hospital Administrators: St. Basil the Great; St. Frances Cabrini
Hunters: St. Hubert; St. Eustachius

Infantrymen: St. Maurice

Jewelers: St. Eligius
Journalists: St. Francis de Sales*
Jurists: St. Catherine of Alexandria; St. John of Capistrano

Laborers: St. Isidore; St. James; St. John Bosco
Lawyers: St. Ivo; St. Genesius; St. Thomas More
Librarians: St. Jerome

Mariners: St. Michael; St. Nicholas of Tolentino
Medical Social Workers: St. John Regis
Medical Technicians: St. Albert the Great
Merchants: St. Francis of Assisi; St. Nicholas of Myra
Metalworkers: St. Eligius
Miners: St. Barbara
Musicians: St. Gregory the Great; St. Cecilia; St. Dunstan

Nurses: St. Camillus de Lellis and St. John of God*; St. Agatha; St. Alexius; St. Raphael

Painters: St. Luke
Pharmacists: Sts. Cosmas and Damian; St. James the Greater
Philosophers: St. Justin; St. Catherine of Alexandria
Physicians: St. Pantaleon; Sts. Cosmas and Damian; St. Luke; St. Raphael
Poets: St. David; St. Cecilia
Policemen: St. Michael
Postal Workers: St. Gabriel
Priests: St. Jean-Baptiste Vianney*
Printers: St. John of God; St. Augustine of Hippo; St. Genesius
Public Relations Specialists: St. Bernadino of Siena*
Radiologists: St. Michael*

Occupations

Sailors: St. Cuthbert; St. Brendan; St. Eulalia; St. Christopher; St. Peter Gonzales; St. Erasmus
Scholars: St. Brigid
Scientists: St. Albert*
Sculptors: St. Claude
Seamen: St. Francis of Paolo
Secretaries: St. Genesius
Singers: St. Gregory; St. Cecilia
Skiers: St. Bernard
Social Workers: Ste. Louise de Marillac*
Soldiers: St. Hadrian; St. George; St. Ignatius; St. Sebastian; St. Martin of Tours; St. Joan of Arc
Stenographers: St. Genesius; St. Cassian
Students: St. Thomas Aquinas; St. Catherine of Alexandria
Surgeons: Sts. Cosmas and Damian

Tailors: St. Homobonus
Tax Collectors: St. Matthew
Taxi Drivers: St. Fiacre
Teachers: St. Gregory the Great; St. Catherine of Alexandria; St. Jean Baptiste de la Salle*
Theologians: St. Augustine; St. Alphonsus Liguori
Workingmen: St. Joseph
Writers: St. Francis de Sales*

Family Members

Brides: St. Nicholas of Myra
Children: St. Nicholas of Myra
Housewives: St. Anne
Mothers: St. Monica

The Ill and the Handicapped

Barren Women: St. Anthony of Padua; St. Felicitas
Blind: St. Odilia; St. Raphael
Bodily Ills: Our Lady of Lourdes
Cancer Patients: St. Peregrine
Deaf: St. Francis de Sales
Dying: St. Joseph; St. Barbara
Eye Sufferers: St. Lucy
Headache Sufferers: St. Teresa of Ávila
Heart Patients: St. John of God
Invalids: St. Roch
Mentally Ill: St. Dympna
Rheumatism: St. James the Greater
Sick: St. Michael; St. John of God and St. Camillus de Lellis*
Throat Sufferers: St. Blaise

Miscellaneous

Acolytes: St. John Berchmans
Boy Scouts: St. George
Emigrants: St. Frances Cabrini*
Falsely Accused: St. Raymond Nonnatus
Foreign Missions: St. Francis Xavier*; Ste. Thérèse of Lisieux*
Foundlings: Holy Innocents
Hospitals: St. Camillus de Lellis and St. John of God*; St. Jude Thaddeus
Pilgrims: St. Alexius; St. James
Poor Souls: St. Nicholas of Tolentino
Prisoners: St. Dismas; St. Barbara; St. Joseph Cafasso
Searchers for Lost Articles: St. Anthony of Padua
Travelers: St. Anthony of Padua; St. Nicholas of Myra; St. Christopher; St. Raphael
Universities: Blessed Contardo Ferrini
Youth: St. Aloysius Gonzaga; St. John Berchmans*; St. Gabriel Possenti

SAINT ALBANS, ôl'bənz, is a municipal borough, cathedral city, and market town in southeastern England, in Hertfordshire, about 20 miles (30 km) northwest of London. It is a dormitory suburb for London and has some industry.

Printing is important in St. Albans. The third printing press in England was set up here in the late 15th century. Other industries include the manufacture of electrical goods and textiles, and herb and seed growing.

The city is named after the first English martyr, St. Alban, a Roman soldier converted to Christianity about 300 A.D. An abbey was built in 793 on the hill where he is said to have been beheaded by the Romans. Only a gateway remains of the original building. The present structure, one of the most remarkable Christian buildings in England, has been extended and altered and represents many styles of architecture.

The abbey is in the form of a Latin cross, with a length of 547 feet (270 meters) and breadth of 206 feet (60 meters). The nave, nearly 300 feet (90 meters) long, is the longest medieval nave still standing. The Norman parts of the abbey were built of flint and bricks from the Roman town of Verulamium across the River Ver. Verulamium was once the capital of Roman Britain. Population: (1961) 50,276.

SAINT ALBANS, ôl'bənz, a city in northwestern Vermont, the seat of Franklin county, is about 30 miles (48 km) north of Burlington and 15 miles south of the border of Canada. It is the trading and shipping point of an area that has dairy farms and produces hay and timber. The city has railroad shops and grain mills and manufactures pulp and paper and flashlights.

St. Albans was the scene of a violent incident in the American Civil War. On Oct. 19, 1864, Confederate Lieut. Bennett H. Young and about 30 armed mounted men, most of them escaped war prisoners, entered the town from Canada. In a flurry of fighting, several citizens were killed or wounded. The raiders, remaining in town less than an hour, seized $200,000 from the banks, but failed in an attempt to burn the town. They fled back to Canada, where Young and twelve of his men were captured. They were later released by Canadian authorities, who decided that Canada had no jurisdiction in the case.

St. Albans was settled in 1763. It became a town in 1788 and a city in 1897. Government is by mayor and council. Population: 7,308.

SAINT ALBANS, ôl'bənz, a city in western West Virginia, in Kanawha county, is situated 12 miles (19 km) west of Charleston, at the confluence of the Coal and Kanawha rivers. It is the center of a region that has coal mines and natural gas fields, and dairy, poultry, and vegetable farms.

The site of St. Albans was explored in 1774 and was settled about 1790. Government is by mayor and council. Population: 12,402.

SAINT ALBERT, a town in central Alberta, Canada, is on the Sturgeon River, 11 miles (17 km) northwest of Edmonton. It is the center of a diversified agricultural area. The community grew around a mission station established in 1861. A bridge here was said to have been one of the first built in Canada west of the Great Lakes. Population: 31,996.

SAINT ANDREWS is a city in east central Scotland, in Fifeshire, noted for its golf courses, university, and ancient buildings. It is 30 miles (48 km) northeast of Edinburgh. Situated just south of the River Eden estuary, on the North Sea, St. Andrews was formerly an important Scottish seaport. Its name is said to derive from relics of St. Andrew, brought here in the 4th or 8th century.

Saint Andrews has four famous golf courses. The course starting from the Royal and Ancient Golf Club House is regarded as the course from which the game developed to worldwide popularity. Championship matches are played here.

The cathedral was founded in 1160 and was eventually consecrated in the presence of King Robert the Bruce in 1318. It was more than 350 feet (105 meters) long. The town was the chief bishopric of Scotland before 908. In 1472, St. Andrews was named by the pope to be the archiepiscopal and metropolitan see of the Roman Catholic Church in Scotland. Only the west and east ends of the cathedral, and parts of its south wall, are still standing.

The former episcopal palace, now known as the castle, is in ruins. There are remains of an Augustinian priory built in 1144. St. Rule's Chapel, dating probably from the same year, consists now simply of a square slender tower. During the Reformation, St. Andrews declined in importance. After a sermon by John Knox, the Scottish Protestant reformer, in 1559, the cathedral was partially sacked and the episcopal palace demolished. Population: (1961) 9,888.

SAINT ANDREWS, University of, a coeducational institution of higher learning in St. Andrews, Scotland. Founded by a group of scholars, who obtained a charter from Bishop Henry Wardlaw in 1412, it is the oldest Scottish university. Women were admitted in 1892.

St. Andrews consists of the faculties of arts, science, and divinity. There are two constituent colleges—St. Mary's and the United College of St. Salvator and St. Leonard. The university maintains two medieval churches and a 17th century library, which contains collections of rare books and manuscripts. Enrollment, about 400 in the 19th century, increased to about 2,600 in the early 1970's, when the faculty numbered about 270.

SAINT-ARNAUD, saN-tàr-nō, **Armand Jacques Leroy de** (1798–1854), marshal of France, who commanded the French army in the Crimean War. He was born in Paris on Aug. 20, 1798, and joined the army in 1817. After 1837, he served three tours of duty in Algeria, where he was successful in fighting against the Kabyle tribes. By 1851, he was a general of division.

In October 1851, he was appointed minister of war. He played an important part in December of that year in the coup d'etat that enabled Louis Napoleon to seize the government and become the emperor Napoleon III. Saint-Arnaud was made a marshal of France.

In 1854, Saint-Arnaud resigned as war minister to lead the French forces to the Crimea. His troops fought with the British under Lord Raglan to win the Battle of the Alma River on September 20, but within a few days his health impelled him to relinquish his command. He died at sea on September 29 while on a ship bound for France.

The City Gate in the wall of the Castillo de San Marcos is one of many tourist attractions in St. Augustine.

SAINT AUGUSTINE, ô'gəs-tēn, a city in northeastern Florida, the seat of St. Johns county, is on the Atlantic Ocean, about 40 miles (64 km) south of Jacksonville. It is situated on a peninsula formed by the San Sebastian River on the west, the Matanzas River and Bay on the east, and the Intercoastal Waterway on the south. Anastasia Island, which is connected to the city by bridges, partially shelters it from the Atlantic Ocean.

St. Augustine, which was founded in 1565, is the oldest city in the United States. Because of its historical interest and its mild climate, it is one of the most frequented resorts in the nation.

The city is in an agricultural region that produces livestock, cabbage, and potatoes, and dairy and poultry products. These are all processed in St. Augustine. Processing of seafood caught in the nearby waters is also important. St. Augustine is a world leader in the building of shrimpboats. Other industrial activity includes airplane modification and engine repair and bookbinding.

Places of Interest. One of the most interesting relics of the city's past is the Castillo de San Marcos (1672), which is the last of nine reconstructions of the wooden fort built in 1565. It is a symmetrical structure built of coquina, a native shell rock, with four bastions and a moat and walls that range in thickness from 9 to 13 feet (2.7–3.9 meters). It has been established as a national monument to preserve the oldest masonry fort in the nation. A portion of the Cubo Line, a palisaded wall that ran from the fort to the San Sebastian River to protect the city from attacks by land, has been restored, and

the City Gate, an 1808 reconstruction of the one built into the wall in 1704, is still standing. Nearby is the zero milestone of the old Spanish Trail, which ended in San Diego, Calif., making it the first highway to cross the entire continent.

The St. Augustine National Cemetery, the oldest documented national cemetery in the United States, contains the bodies of 105 men who were killed in an Indian massacre in 1842. The Oldest House is maintained as a museum, with exhibits depicting life in colonial times.

A large area on and around St. George Street has been reconstructed. There are numerous old houses and shops here, including a wooden school house, the Old Spanish Treasury, and the Rodriquez-Avero Sanchez House, which contains a Museum of Yesterday's Toys. Also of interest are the Cathedral of St. Augustine, Government House (1690), and the St. Francis Barracks.

Fort Matanzas National Monument is 14 miles (20 km) south of the city. Fort Matanzas was built in 1742 to supplement the Castillo de San Marcos.

Museums include the Lightner Municipal Exposition, and the Museum of Pirate and Lost Treasure of the Spanish Main. The Fountain of Youth Memorial Park contains a planetarium and an Indian burial ground.

A pageant reenacting the city's founding is given each summer at the St. Augustine Amphitheater on Anastasia Island across the Bridge of Lions. St. Augustine Beach, 5 miles (8 km) southeast of the city, offers swimming and fishing recreation.

History. In 1565, Don Pedro Menéndez de Avilés, captain of the Spanish fleet, arrived here on August 28, the feast of St. Augustine. Eleven days later he officially founded the settlement, naming it after the saint, and planned its development as a military post.

St. Augustine was sacked and burned by Sir Francis Drake in 1586, and by the English buccaneer John Davis in 1668. In 1702 the town was taken and burned by a band of Carolinians. Gen. James Oglethorpe, the British governor of Georgia, led a joint expedition of Georgians and Carolinians against St. Augustine in 1740, but failed to take the city. Fort Matanzas was built in 1742. In 1743, Oglethorpe was defeated in another attack.

In 1763, Florida fell by treaty to the British, and St. Augustine thrived as an export center. The Spanish regained control in 1783 and kept it until Florida was ceded to the United States in 1821.

In 1835, during the Seminole War, Maj. Gen. Francis L. Dade, with a command of 139 men, was surprised by the Indians, and he and all but four of his men were killed. During the Civil War, St. Augustine was under Confederate rule from January 1861 to March 1862, when Union troops assumed control. During the 1880's the capitalist Henry Flagler developed St. Augustine into a thriving resort, and it continues as such today.

Government and Population. St. Augustine has a commission form of government. Population: 11,985.

SAINT BASIL'S CATHEDRAL, an ornate example of Russian architecture, stands in Red Square, Moscow.

OLGA DIAMOND, PHOTO RESEARCHERS

SAINT AUGUSTINE GRASS, a widely used lawn grass. See GRASS—*Lawn Grasses;* LAWN.

SAINT BARTHÉLEMY, săn-bȧr-tāl-mē', an island of the French West Indies and part of the overseas Department of Guadeloupe, is geographically one of the northern Leeward Islands. It is in the Caribbean Sea, 12 miles (19 km) southeast of St. Martin and 125 miles (201 km) northwest of Guadeloupe. St. Barthélemy is an irregularly shaped island with a rocky surface, about 11 miles (18 km) long and 2.5 miles (4 km) wide. It is protected from erosion by the sea by a chain of reefs. There is a well-protected port at Gustavia, in the Bay of Carenage on the western side of the island.

Although the island is dry and nearly treeless, the soil is fertile. Vegetables are cultivated in some of the valleys, and bananas, cassia, tamarinds, and sassafras are exported. The tourist industry is important to the economy and there is fishing in the surrounding waters.

St. Barthélemy was occupied by the French in 1648. It was ceded to Sweden in 1784, but in 1877 the French bought it back. Slavery was abolished on the island in 1848. Population: (1970 est.) 2,200.

SAINT BARTHOLOMEW'S DAY MASSACRE, bär-thol'ə-mū, was the name given to the murder of French Huguenots in Paris on Aug. 24, 1572, Saint Bartholomew's Day. The slaughter of French Protestants quickly spread to the provinces, and about 20,000 Huguenots were ultimately killed by Roman Catholic mobs. The prime responsibility for the massacre was borne by Catherine de Médicis, who opposed the influence of the Protestant leader Adm. Gaspard de Coligny over her weak son, King Charles IX.

After an attempted assassination of Coligny failed on August 22, Catherine convinced Charles that the Protestants were planning to murder him, and Charles authorized the massacre of August 24. Catholic leaders, among whom the Guise family was prominent, were able to take advantage of the concentration in Paris of notable Protestants who had attended the marriage of Henry of Navarre (the future Henry IV), the Huguenot leader, to Marguerite de Valois, Charles IX's sister, earlier in August. In addition to damaging France's relations with Protestant countries, the killings strengthened Protestant opposition to the house of Valois.

SAINT BASIL'S CATHEDRAL, baz'əlz, a 16th century Russian church on Red Square in Moscow, now a museum. Commissioned by Ivan IV to commemorate his victories over the Mongol khanates of Kazan and Astrakhan, it was dedicated to the Virgin but is called the Cathedral of St. Basil the Blessed. The church, built between 1555 and 1560 by Postnik and Barma, combines the stone, Byzantine domed style and the wooden, Russian tent-shaped style. The stone structure is dominated by a high, octagonal tower over a central chapel. This tower is surrounded by eight smaller towers over four large octagonal chapels on the main axes and four small polygonal ones between. They are enclosed by a gallery built later. The towers and their onion-shaped domes are heavily carved and, though originally whitewashed, have been polychromed since the 17th century, creating an exotic splendor.

SAINT-BENOÎT-SUR-LOIRE, saN-be-nwä′sür-lwàr′, is a village in France, renowned for its Romanesque church. It is in Loiret department, about 20 miles (32 km) southeast of Orléans.

The area was a center of druidic worship before a Benedictine abbey named Fleury was established in the 7th century. When barbarians destroyed Monte Cassino, the monastery in Italy where Saint Benedict (French, Saint Benoît) was buried, Fleury sent representatives who recovered the remains of Benedict and his sister, Saint Scolastica. The relics were returned to Fleury, which renamed itself after Saint Benedict. The imposing church raised over his crypt was built between 1067 and 1218 and is an outstanding example of Romanesque architecture, especially the belfry and choir. The monastic buildings were destroyed in the French Revolution. Restoration of the church was begun in the 19th century. Population: (1962) 553.

SAINT BERNARD DOG, bər-närd′, a large, powerfully built, heavily coated dog that is famous for helping to rescue people lost in snowstorms in the Alps. The dog stands 25 to 30 inches (64–76 cm) tall at the shoulder and weighs about 165 pounds (75 kg). It has a massive skull with a rather squarish muzzle and high set ears that droop sharply to the side of the head. It also has broad sloping shoulders, a very broad back, strong legs, broad feet, and a rather long and bushy tail.

The St. Bernard generally has a very dense, coarse, short-haired coat, but some long-haired varieties have been developed. The coat is usually red and white with white markings on the chest, feet, noseband, ruff, and tip of the tail.

The St. Bernard was most likely developed in Switzerland from a large Asian dog carried to Europe by the Romans. The breed gets its name from the Hospice of Saint Bernard, where it has long been kept by the monks to help them in rescuing lost travelers. The dogs were probably first brought to the monastery in the late 17th century.

Saint Bernards have an excellent sense of smell that helps them locate people lost in snowstorms or buried in avalanches. They are also excellent pathfinders, never losing their way. By the 1970's they were credited with saving more than 2,500 lives.

The Saint Bernard, a large mastiff

EVELYN M. SHAFER

LOUIS H. FROHMAN, FROM RAPHO-GUILLUMETTE

Basilica of Saint-Benoît-sur-Loire is one of the finest examples of Romanesque architecture in France.

SAINT BERNARD PASSES, saN-ber-nàr′, are two passes, Great and Little St. Bernard, that cut through the Alps. Great St. Bernard runs from Switzerland to Italy, while Little St. Bernard connects France and Italy. The roads from the passes meet in Aosta, Italy.

Great St. Bernard, one of the highest passes in the Alps, crests at 8,111 feet (2,472 meters). It is 15 miles (24 km) east of Mont Blanc and leads from Martigny in Valais Canton to Aosta. The Romans, who called it Alpis Poenina, built a road through the pass in the 1st century A. D. In the late 10th century Saint Bernard of Menthon established at the summit the hospice famous for rescuing stranded travelers. St. Bernard dogs were bred for this rescue work. Because of its height, the pass was closed during the winter months until 1964, when an all-weather tunnel was built under the highest point of the pass.

Little St. Bernard is about 10 miles (16 km) south of Mont Blanc and links the French valley of the Isère, on the west, with Dora Baltea Valley in Italy. Its highest point is 7,177 feet (2,188 meters).

The pass is one of the easiest in the Alps and may be the route Hannibal used to enter Italy in 218 B. C. It was known as Alpis Graia by the Romans, who used it as a main road to Gaul. The hospice on this pass was also founded by Saint Bernard.

SAINT BONIFACE, bon'ə-fãs, a city in southeastern Manitoba, Canada, is on the east bank of the Red River, opposite Winnipeg, the capital of the province. It is a railroad and industrial center, with large stockyards and meat-packing plants, grain elevators, flour mills, dairies, breweries, oil refineries, and factories producing sheet metal, paint, and soap.

St. Boniface is the seat of a Roman Catholic archdiocese. The cathedral, when it was built in 1908, was one of the largest church edifices in Canada. A majority of the city's inhabitants are of French descent.

The community originated in a mission and settlement in 1818. It was incorporated as a city in 1908 but became part of Winnipeg in 1972.

SAINT-BRIEUC, saɴ-brē-û', a city in Brittany, is in northwestern France, 55 miles (88 km) northwest of Rennes and near the English Channel. The capital of Côtes-du-Nord department, it is the department's administrative, commercial, industrial, and tourist center. It is on a plateau between the Gouët River and its tributary, the Gouëdic, near the outlet of the Gouët into the Gulf of St.-Malo. Manufactures include iron, steel, and agricultural implements.

The city dates from the 5th century, when a Welsh missionary, Saint Brieuc, established a monastery there. St.-Brieuc has had a turbulent history, especially during the Reign of Terror of the French Revolution. The Cathedral of St.-Étienne, built in the 13th and 14th centuries, served as a fortress during Breton wars in the 14th century. The cathedral, which has been restored several times, has two large towers at the front. The ruined tower of Cesson stands in the Gouët estuary, where St.-Brieuc's port, Le Légué, is located. Population: (1968) 50,281.

SAINT CATHARINES, a city in southern Ontario, Canada, is situated on the Welland Canal, about 35 miles (56 km) east of Hamilton and just south of Lake Ontario. It is the center of the Niagara fruit-growing region. Large vessels traversing the canal can be accommodated in its docks. The city's industries include shipbuilding and ship repair, food packing and canning, and the manufacture of automotive and airplane parts, electrical apparatus, paper products, slide fasteners, and oil burners.

Ridley College, an Anglican Church school for boys, is in St. Catharines. The community was incorporated as a city in 1876. Population: 124,018.

SAINT CHARLES, a city in northeastern Illinois, in Kane and Du Page counties, is situated on the Fox River about 35 miles (56 km) west of the center of Chicago. The surrounding area is chiefly farmland. The city makes metal and plastic products. St. Charles was founded in 1834 and was incorporated in 1839. Government is by a mayor and council. Population: 17,492.

SAINT CHARLES, a city in eastern Missouri, the seat of Saint Charles county, is on the Missouri River, about 20 miles (32 km) northwest of the center of St. Louis. It is the shipping center of an agricultural area, and has industries that make dresses, beer, dairy products, aluminum products, and electronic devices.

Lindenwood College, a coeducational institution affiliated with the Presbyterian Church, is in St. Charles. The Sacred Heart Academy was founded in 1818.

St. Charles was settled in 1769 by French pioneers. For a short time the territory was under Spanish rule, and then was receded to the French. It became part of the United States in the Louisiana Purchase (1803).

The community was incorporated in 1795. It was the state's first capital from 1821 to 1825. St. Charles received its city charter in 1849. Government is by mayor and council. Population: 37,379.

SAINT CHRISTOPHER was the original name of an island in the Caribbean Sea now better known as St. Kitts. See SAINT KITTS.

ST. CLAIR, Arthur (1736–1818), American general, whose career was marked by military and political failures. He was born in Thurso, Scotland, on March 23, 1736. As an ensign in the British Army, he served in Canada during the French and Indian War. With inherited money he bought tracts of land in Pennsylvania, becoming the colony's largest resident landowner west of the Alleghenies.

Joining the Continental Army at the start of the American Revolution, he was a colonel in the unsuccessful invasion of Canada in 1775, and a brigadier general under Washington's command in the battles of Trenton and Princeton in the winter of 1776–1777. As a major general, he was named commandant of the important post of Fort Ticonderoga in 1777, but in a short time he surrendered the fort when confronted by a British force. He was court-martialed but exonerated.

In 1785, he became a delegate to the Continental Congress, and in 1787 he was its president. Later that year he was named governor of the Northwest Territory.

In 1791, the federal government chose him to lead a small army against the Miami Indians. Poorly trained and equipped, his troops were surprised and routed at their camp near the site of Fort Recovery, on the Wabash River in western Ohio. St. Clair was officially freed of blame for the defeat, but resigned his command. He continued as territorial governor. Some of his attitudes, especially his opposition to the entrance of Ohio to the Union, made him widely unpopular, and he was removed from office by President Thomas Jefferson in 1802. St. Clair retired to Westmoreland county, Pa., where he lived in poverty until his death on Aug. 31, 1818.

SAINT CLAIR, Lake, in central North America, the smallest lake in the Great Lakes system. It is connected with Lake Huron, to the north, by the St. Clair River, and with Lake Erie, to the south, by the Detroit River. Lake St. Clair is bisected by the border between the United States and Canada. Michigan is the western shore, and Ontario is the eastern shore. Part of Detroit is situated at the lake's southwestern corner.

Roughly circular in shape, the lake is about 33 miles (52 km) in diameter. Its area is about 466 square miles (1,300 sq km), and its maximum depth about 26 feet (7 meters).

Although dredging is needed to keep the channel open, the lake is an integral part of the Great Lakes shipping route for vessels carrying bulk cargoes of iron ore, coal, wheat, and limestone. Oceangoing ships that use the St. Lawrence Seaway also traverse the lake.

SAINT CLAIR RIVER, in central North America. It flows southward from Lake Huron for 40 miles (64 km) into Lake St. Clair. Although it is called a river, it is actually one of several connecting channels in the Great Lakes system. It forms part of the boundary between the United States and Canada, with Michigan on the western shore and Ontario on the eastern.

The gradient in the channel is slight, and minimal dredging makes it possible for large vessels to use the passage. The only large communities along its course are Port Huron, Mich., and Sarnia, Ont., which are opposite each other at the northern end.

SAINT CLAIR SHORES is a city in southeastern Michigan, in Macomb county. It is on Lake St. Clair, about 12 miles (19 km) northeast of the center of Detroit. It is a residential community whose population has increased more than 400% since 1950. Beaches and marinas and private docks for pleasure boats line the lake shore. St. Clair Shores was incorporated as a village in 1925 and as a city in 1950. Government is by a council and city manager. Population: 76,210.

SAINT-CLOUD, saN-klōo′, is a town in France in the department of Hauts-de-Seine. It is on a slope overlooking the Seine River, about six miles (10 km) west of the center of Paris. Its name is derived from Clodoald, or Cloud, a grandson of Clovis, who founded a monastery on the site of the town.

The magnificent château, destroyed during the Franco-Prussian War, was the residence of several French rulers. In 1799, Napoleon staged the coup d'etat of 18 Brumaire at St.-Cloud, and in 1810 he married Marie Louise in the château. Charles X issued the July Ordinances from the château in 1830. Napoleon III, who had been proclaimed emperor in 1852 while he was at the château, declared war on Prussia from it in 1870. The fine park of the château, with its beautiful fountains, remains, and there is a horse-racing track. These, together with an excellent view of Paris, makes St.-Cloud a favorite resort. Population: (1968) 28,162.

SAINT CLOUD, a city in central Minnesota, is on the Mississippi River, 60 miles (96 km) northwest of Minneapolis. It is the seat of Stearns county, and parts of the city are in Benton and Sherburne counties.

Quarries that produce colored granite, which were established here in 1870, are a major industry. The city has large railroad shops, and manufactures refrigerating equipment, paper and paper products, iron and brass products, and optical goods. It also is a center for processing dairy products.

St. Cloud State College is situated here. St. John's University for men and the College of St. Benedict for women are a few miles west of St. Cloud, at Collegeville and St. Joseph, respectively. The Stearns County Historical Museum is in St. Cloud.

The community was settled in 1853 and platted in 1854. Before the first railroad reached here in 1866, it was a terminus of the Hudson's Bay Company, which brought furs down from the Red River valley in wooden oxcarts.

St. Cloud was incorporated as a village in 1856 and as a city in 1868. Government is by mayor and council. Population: 42,566.

HANS HANNAU, FROM RAPHO-GUILLUMETTE

Christiansted is the capital and principal port of the island of St. Croix, in the U. S. Virgin Islands.

SAINT CROIX, kroi, the largest of the Virgin Islands of the United States, is in the Caribbean Sea, about 40 miles (64 km) south of St. Thomas and about 90 miles (145 km) southeast of San Juan, Puerto Rico. It is 23 miles (37 km) long and 6 miles (10 km) across at its widest point. The terrain of the island ranges from arid and rocky in the east, through rolling upland pastures, to lush tropics, in the west. Mountains rise abruptly from the northeastern shore of St. Croix. The principal towns and ports are Fredericksted, on the west coast, and Christiansted, on a bay on the northern side of the island. St. Croix is the agricultural center of the island group. Sugarcane has been phased out as a major crop, but vegetables are cultivated and livestock is raised. The principal industries include rum distilling, alumina reduction, and oil refining.

St. Croix was discovered by Christopher Columbus in 1493. During the next two centuries it was settled for brief periods by the Dutch, French, Spanish, and English. It was purchased by Denmark in 1733 and by the United States in 1917. Population: 49,013. See also VIRGIN ISLANDS OF THE UNITED STATES.

SAINT CROIX ISLAND NATIONAL MONUMENT, kroi, in eastern Maine, Washington county, is an island in the St. Croix River—which is the border between Maine and New Brunswick, Canada—near its mouth at the Atlantic Ocean. The monument was established in 1949 to commemorate the colony established briefly on the island in 1604 by the French explorers Samuel de Champlain and sieur de Monts (Pierre du Quast).

SAINT-CYR, saN-sēr', **Laurent de Gouvion** (1764–1830), a marshal of France. He was born in Toul on April 13, 1764. He went to Paris to study art, but in 1792 joined the army to fight in the revolutionary wars. He served in the Rhine campaign and quickly rose in rank. In 1801 he was named ambassador to Madrid.

St.-Cyr fought in the Polish campaign in 1807–1808 and in 1812 led an army that defeated the Russians at the Battle of Polotsk. In recognition of the victory, he was created marshal. He was Louis XVIII's minister of war for three months in 1815 and again in 1817–1819. St.-Cyr was created marquis in 1817. He died in Hyères on March 17, 1830.

SAINT-CYR-L'ÉCOLE, saN-sēr'lā-kôl', is a town in France in Yvelines department, three miles (5 km) west of Versailles. Madame de Maintenon founded a school for the daughters of impoverished noblemen in the town in 1686. Racine wrote two plays, *Esther* and *Athalie*, for performances at the school. Madame de Maintenon retired to the school after the death of Louis XIV in 1715 and was buried in its chapel. During the French Revolution, the school was abolished.

In 1808, Napoleon transferred to its building the famous military academy that he had founded at Fontainebleau, south of Paris. The academy was destroyed during World War II and was subsequently moved to Coëtquidan, in Brittany. Population: (1968) 16,001.

SAINT DAVID'S, a village in southwestern Wales, in West Pembrokeshire, is near St. David's Head—a promontory on the Atlantic Ocean, which is the westernmost point in Wales. The town, which is the metropolitan see of Wales, is noted for its beautiful cathedral and was long a place of pilgrimage. It is a market for an agricultural area.

The cathedral is dedicated to St. David, the patron of Wales, who is said to have built a church and monastery here about 550. No traces of either remain. The present cathedral, the largest in Wales, was built mostly in the late 12th century, and is primarily in the transitional Norman style. Also of interest in the town are the ruins of the Bishop's Palace, built mainly between 1280 and 1350, and the partly ruined Tower Gate. Population: (1961) 1,690.

ST. DENIS, den'is, **Ruth** (1877–1968), American dancer, choreographer, and teacher, who was one of the pioneers of modern dance. Ruth Dennis was born in Newark, N. J., on Jan. 20, 1877. She was dancing in plays and musicals, as Ruth St. Denis, when a cigarette poster of the Egyptian goddess Isis inspired her to be a concert artist specializing in Oriental dance. She performed *Radha* at her first concert, in New York City in 1906, and then toured Europe and the United States. Her repertoire, including *Green Nautch*, *Egypta*, *O-Mika*, and *White Madonna*, was danced barefoot, usually in Oriental costume, and emphasized rippling arm movements and striking poses with scarves and veils.

In 1914, Ruth St. Denis and Ted Shawn became partners and were married that year. Together they founded the Denishawn company and school in 1915. Like her husband, St. Denis was interested in the religious roots of dance and believed that dancers should be trained in all traditions. The school, in Los Angeles and

BROWN BROTHERS

Ruth St. Denis with Ted Shawn in a joint recital.

other cities, provided such training for the great dancers Martha Graham, Doris Humphrey, and Charles Weidman. The company, with St. Denis as soloist, introduced American audiences to serious ethnic dance.

St. Denis and Shawn separated in 1932 to work independently. St. Denis continued to dance, sometimes at Shawn's school in Jacob's Pillow, Mass. She was involved in the Society of Spiritual Arts (founded 1931) and the Church of the Divine Dance (founded 1947). She also taught—for example, at the School of Natya (founded with La Meri in New York in 1940) and at Adelphi College—and lectured and filmed her dances. She died in Los Angeles on July 21, 1968.

SAINT-DENIS, saNd-nē', is a city in France noted for its Gothic church. It is an industrial suburb of Paris, 6 miles (10 km) north of the center of the capital in Seine-St.-Denis department.

The abbey and basilica of St. Denis, the latter containing the tombs of a number of French monarchs, are the primary points of interest. The abbey, founded in 626 by King Dagobert I, is located on the traditional site of the grave of St. Denis, patron saint of France. Rebuilt in the 18th century, it now houses a school for the daughters of members of the Legion of Honor. The present basilica, built in 1136–1147 and enlarged in the 13th century, was the first large structure in the Gothic style and served as a model for later buildings. Among the royalty buried there were Louis XII and Anne of Brittany, Henry II and Catherine de' Médicis and Louis XVI and Marie Antoinette. Though most of the royal ashes were scattered during the French Revolution, the tombs and sarcophagi, many with extremely fine sculptures, remain. Population: (1968) 99,268.

SAINT-DENIS, saND-nĕ', is the capital of the French overseas department of Réunion in the Indian Ocean. Situated on the northern coast of the island, St.-Denis is built on a long, narrow beach shut off on the land side by a range of high volcanic mountains.

The city is Réunion's administrative and commercial center. It is connected with the island's other towns by a railroad running along the northern and western coasts. Its port is at Pointe-des-Galets, about 10 miles (16 km) to the west. Population: (1967) 67,550.

SAINT ELIAS, ē-lī'as, **Mount,** on the border between Alaska and Yukon Territory, Canada, rising to a height of 18,008 feet (5,475 meters). It is the second highest peak in the St. Elias Mountains. Mount Logan (19,850 feet or 6,000 meters) is the highest.

Mount St. Elias is about 300 miles (480 km) east of Anchorage, Alaska, and only about 25 miles (40 km) from the Gulf of Alaska. The Malaspina Glacier rises on its slopes. The mountain was sighted from the sea by Vitus Bering on July 16, 1741. It was first climbed by the Duke of the Abruzzi in 1897.

SAINT ELMO'S FIRE is the bluish glow that sometimes is seen at the tips of trees, spires, masts, or other tall objects in a thunderstorm. The phenomenon, an ionization process known as *point discharge,* represents an accumulation of positive charge at elevated points because of the attraction of negative charge on storm clouds, when the electrical field is very intense.

The name of the phenomenon derived from that of a 4th century saint, Erasmus, whom sailors took as their patron. The glow was believed to be a manifestation of his protection. Peter Gonzales, a 13th century friar, later became the "Saint Elmo" of Iberian sailors.

SAINT-ÉTIENNE, saN-tā-tyen', is an important industrial city in France. The capital of Loire department, it is on the Furens River, 32 miles (51 km) southwest of Lyon. Situated in a high-quality coal field, it produces steel and armaments, bicycles, machinery, chemicals, and textiles, particularly silks, which have been manufactured there since the 16th century.

Saint-Étienne developed an important coal trade in the 14th century and began the manufacture of firearms for the state in the 16th century under Francis I. There is an arms museum with items from all parts of the world. Population: (1968) 213,468.

SAINT EUSTATIUS, ū-stā'shəs, is an island of the Netherlands Antilles, situated about 175 miles (282 km) east of Puerto Rico. Geographically it is one of the Leeward Islands, but politically it belongs to what the Dutch call the Windward Islands of the Netherlands Antilles. St. Eustatius (in Dutch, *Sint Eustatius*) is a volcanic island with an area of 11.8 square miles (30.6 sq km). Its capital is Oranjestad.

The island, commonly called *Statia,* opened its first hotel in 1971. It has a growing tourist trade. The official language is Dutch, but English is more widely spoken. The island was sited by Christopher Columbus in 1493 and colonized by the Dutch in 1636. It was a prosperous trading center in the 17th and 18th centuries. Population: (1971 est.) 1,600.

SAINT-ÉVREMOND, saN-tā-vrə-môN', **Seigneur de** (1614–1703), French wit and litterateur, whose writings anticipated the spirit of the French Enlightenment. Charles de Marguetel de Saint-Denis, the Seigneur de Saint-Évremond, was born at St.-Denis-le-Gast in January 1614. He was educated for the judiciary but chose a military career and served as an officer in the Thirty Years' War. His opposition to Cardinal Mazarin's policies brought him into royal disfavor, and in 1661 he fled to England where he remained, except for the period between 1665 and 1670, which he spent in Holland. He received a pension from King Charles II of England and was a brilliant member of the London salon of Hortense Mancini, duchess of Mazarin. He died in London on Sept. 29, 1703.

Saint-Évremond's *Comédie des académistes,* written in 1643 and published in 1650, is a satire on the early French Academy. His famous *Conversation du maréchal d'Hocquincourt avec le père Canaye* (1658) is a satire of excessive trust in religious belief. He also was a literary critic and had considerable influence in England.

SAINT-EXUPÉRY, saN-tāg-zü-pā-rē', **Antoine de** (1900–1944), French aviator and writer, whose works lyrically portray the pioneer days of aviation. He was born in Lyon on June 29, 1900. After serving as a military flier, he became a commercial pilot in 1926 and flew early airmail routes in France, North Africa, and South America. After rejoining the French Air Force at the outbreak of World War II, he escaped occupied France and went to the United States by way of North Africa in 1940. In 1942, Saint-Exupéry joined the Allied forces in North Africa and undertook a number of reconnaissance missions. He failed to return from a flight over the Mediterranean on July 31, 1944.

Antoine de Saint-Exupéry, French aviator and writer

UPI

Saint-Exupéry described his early flying experiences and the thoughts they inspired in *Courrier-Sud* (1928; Eng. tr., *Southern Mail,* 1933), *Vol de Nuit* (1931; Eng. tr., *Night Flight,* 1932); and *Terre des Hommes* (1939; Eng. tr., *Wind, Sand and Stars,* 1939). These books present graphic descriptions of a pilot's existence, combined with poetic musings on the meaning of life and civilization.

Saint-Exupéry recounted his experiences in the war in *Pilote de Guerre,* which was published first in an English version as *Flight to Arras* (1942). He also wrote and prepared the illustrations for a fantasy for children, *Le Petit Prince* (1943; Eng. tr., *The Little Prince*), which became a classic.

SAINT FRANCIS, a city in southeastern Wisconsin, in Milwaukee county, is on Lake Michigan immediately south of Milwaukee. It is a residential suburb, incorporated in 1951, and is governed by a mayor and council. Population: 10,042.

SAINT GALL. See SANKT GALLEN.

SAINT-GAUDENS, gô'dənz, **Augustus** (1848–1907), American neoclassical sculptor, who adopted the best standards of French taste and technique without being bound by tradition. Saint-Gaudens was born in Dublin, Ireland, on March 1, 1848, and was taken to the United States in childhood. He was apprenticed to a cameo cutter and then studied for three years at the École des Beaux Arts, Paris. There followed three more years of study in Rome before he returned to the United States in 1892. As a sculptor in New York, he was part of a circle that included the architects H. H. Richardson, Stanford White,

Augustus Saint-Gaudens' statue the *Puritan* (Deacon Samuel Chapin) in Springfield, Mass.

MUSEUM OF FINE ARTS, SPRINGFIELD, MASS.

and Charles McKim and the artist John La Farge. He worked in Cornish, N. H., from 1885 until his death on Aug. 3, 1907.

Saint-Gaudens' sculpture, in a majestic style that was at once polished and free, consists chiefly of monumental bronze statues of heroes. They include *Admiral Farragut* (1881; Madison Square, New York); *General Sherman,* on horseback, led by Victory (1903; entrance to Central Park, New York); *President Lincoln* (1887; Lincoln Park, Chicago); and the striking *Puritan,* with Bible and cudgel (1887; Springfield, Mass), the embodiment of the unswerving Puritan ideal. Especially moving is the meditating draped figure on the *Adams Memorial* (1891; Rock Creek Cemetery, Washington, D. C.).

Saint-Gaudens also designed bronze medals authorized by Congress and a number of bronze and marble plaques in bas-relief. With La Farge, he decorated Trinity Church, Boston, and carved two caryatids for the Cornelius Vanderbilt mansion in New York City (Metropolitan Museum of Art).

Further Reading: Hollingsworth, B., *Augustus Saint-Gaudens* (1948).

SAINT GEORGE'S, a town in the southeastern West Indies, is the capital, chief port, and commercial center of Grenada and the administrative center of the Windward Islands. It is considered to be one of the most beautiful ports in the Caribbean. The town overlooks St. George's Bay in the Caribbean Sea on the southwestern coast of Grenada.

St. George's derives much of its income from a large tourist trade, and it is an important insurance center. Industry includes brewing, tobacco, and the manufacture of paper and paper products. Population: (1970) 6,634.

SAINT-GERMAIN, Treaty of, saN-zher-maN', the peace agreement between the Allies and defeated Austria after World War I. It was signed at St.-Germain-en-Laye on Sept. 10, 1919. It was the complement of the Treaty of Versailles and settled the territorial and political status of Austria. It was ratified by the Austrian legislature on October 17.

The treaty recognized Austria as a republic, thereby ending the rule of the Habsburg monarchy, and fixed new boundaries for the state. The Austro-Hungarian Empire disappeared, with several states receiving parts of its territory. Hungary, Czechoslovakia, and the Kingdom of the Serbs, Croats, and Slovenes (later Yugoslavia) were established as independent states; Italy received the South Tirol and some smaller parcels; Bukovina was assigned to Rumania; and newly independent Poland regained areas it had lost to the Habsburgs in the 18th century.

Austria also pledged to recognize the independence of all territories formerly part of the Russian Empire and to honor all agreements made since 1917 by the Soviet government. Austria further agreed to respect the political, racial, and religious rights of all peoples within its boundaries. The Austrian Army was limited to 30,000 men; all Austrian warships had to be surrendered to the Allied powers; and no naval or air forces were allowed to be retained. Another clause provided for the apportionment of its war debt among the successor states of the empire. Important conditions were drawn up affecting Austria's ports, waterways, and railways.

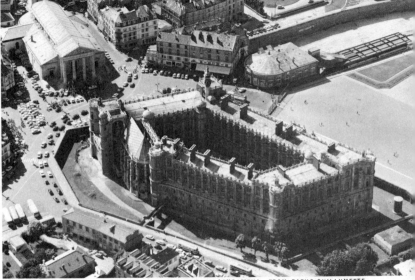

Château of Saint-Germain-en-Laye, the home of French kings before Versailles was built, houses the National Museum of Antiquities.

SAINT-GERMAIN-EN-LAYE, saN-zher-maN'näN-lā', a town in France that was once a royal residence, is in Yvelines department, 13 miles (21 km) west of Paris. Its location on a height above the Seine River and bordering a forest have made it a favorite summer resort of Parisians. The terrace of St.-Germain is one of the finest promenades in Europe and commands an extensive view of the valley of the Seine.

The château, or castle, built by Louis VI in the 12th century was rebuilt by Charles V about 1370. Francis I, Louis XIV, and other kings made many additions to the original château, and Henry II started a New Château, which was largely demolished in the late 18th century. The pavilion of Henry IV remains from the New Château. Henry II, Charles IX, and Louis XIV were born in these royal residences. The original château houses a national museum of antiquities.

Because of its association with the crown, the town is linked with numerous royal acts. By the Edict of St.-Germain-en-Laye (1570), Catherine de Médicis ended the third War of Religion. Treaties signed in 1679 ended hostilities between Louis XIV and Brandenburg at the end of the Third Dutch War. The treaty between the Allies and Austria was signed in the town in 1919. Population: (1975) 37,509. See also SAINT GERMAIN, TREATY OF.

SAINT-GOTHARD, got'ərd, is a pass through the Alps in Switzerland. The name is also given to a mountain group through which the pass cuts. Part of the Lepontine Alps, these mountains form a nucleus in the great watershed of Europe. Each of its slopes give rise to an important river —the north to the Reuss, the south to the Ticino, the west to the Rhône, and the east to the Rhine. All these rivers rise within a circuit of 10 miles (16 km) from the center of the range.

For several centuries the pass had a hospice at the summit (6,808 feet; 2,075 meters). Today there is a hotel. Only a bridle path existed through the pass until 1830, when an excellent carriage road was completed. The modern highway follows the same route. A railway tunnel runs underneath the pass between Göschenen on the north and Airolo, Italy, on the south, thus directly connecting the railway system of northern Italy with those of Switzerland and western and central Germany. The tunnel built in 1872–1882, is about 9¼ miles (15 km) long.

SAINT HELENA, hə-lē'nə, is an island in the South Atlantic Ocean, 1,200 miles (1,930 km) west of Africa and 700 miles (1,130 km) southeast of Ascension Island, the nearest land. It is best known as the place where Napoleon Bonaparte was exiled. Together with the smaller Ascension Island and the Tristan da Cunha island group, it forms a British colony.

St. Helena, of volcanic origin, is rugged and mountainous, rising to 2,685 feet (818 meters) at Mount Actaeon. The island is 10.5 miles (17 km) long and 6.5 miles (10.5 km) wide, with about 8,600 acres (3,480 hectares) of tillable land. The chief crops are potatoes, sweet potatoes, and vegetables. There is no industry, and the island does no exporting. There is only one good harbor, St. James's Bay, which serves Jamestown, the capital of the colony and only town on the island.

St. Helena was discovered in 1502 by the Portuguese navigator João da Nova Castella on a return trip from India. It was uninhabited. The Dutch claimed it in 1633 but did not take possession. The British held it from 1659 except for a brief Dutch occupation in 1673. It was an important port of call for vessels sailing between Europe and the Indian Ocean until the Suez Canal opened in 1869, shifting trade to the Mediterranean. Napoleon was exiled here from 1815 until his death in 1821, and Longwood House, where he lived, is a Napoleonic museum maintained by the French government. St. Helena became a crown colony in 1834. Ascension Island was annexed to the colony in 1922 and the island of Tristan da Cunha in 1938. Population: (1977) 5,216.

SAINT HELENS, Mount, a volcanic peak of the Cascade Range in southwestern Washington, about 45 miles (72 km) northeast of Portland, Oreg. It is one of a long series of Cascade peaks extending about 700 miles (1,127 km) from Lassen Peak, California, to Mt. Garibaldi, British Columbia, and forming a section of the volcanic "Ring of Fire" around the Pacific from South America to Alaska, Japan, and Indonesia.

Mount Saint Helens was named by Capt. George Vancouver in 1792 for Lord St. Helens, Britain's ambassador to Spain. The Klickitat Indians had named it *Tah-one-lat-clah* ("Fire Mountain"). A symmetrical, snow-capped cone rising to 9,677 feet (2,950 meters), the "Mt.

Fuji of America" had been built up during the past thousand years over the remains of an ancient volcano. Prior to 1980, it had erupted every 100 to 150 years, most recently in 1857.

After a series of earthquakes beginning in March, Mt. Saint Helens erupted violently on May 18, 1980, sending tons of ash and debris 12 miles (19 km) into the sky; leveling thousands of acres of Douglas fir forest; filling valleys, lakes, and rivers with mud and debris; killing vast numbers of animals, birds, and fish; and leaving more than 50 persons dead or missing. Some 1,300 feet (396 meters) of the mountaintop were blown away, leaving a crater nearly a mile (1.6 km) wide and 2,500 feet (762 meters) deep. Two lesser eruptions in March 1982 resulted in no loss of life or major damage.

SAINT HELIER, hel′yər, the capital of Jersey in the Channel Islands, is situated on the east shore of St. Aubin's Bay in the English Channel, on the south side of the island. It is a port and trading center and a popular summer resort. The town is dominated by the 19th-century Fort Regent, which stands at the summit of a steep cliff. The 16th century Elizabeth Castle is on an islet in the bay. On another islet is what is said to be the hermitage of St. Helier, a 6th-century martyr. In the town itself is a church dating back to the 14th century. When the French attempted to seize control of Jersey Island in 1784, they were defeated in a battle fought in St. Helier's Royal Square. Population: (1971) 28,135.

SAINT HYACINTHE is a city in southern Quebec, Canada, on the Yamaska River, 34 miles (54 km) east of Montreal. It is an industrial city, the center of a network of railroads and highways. Its manufactures include textiles, machinery, paper and wood products, and shoes. The Casavant organ factory is located here.

The Seminaire de Saint Hyacinthe, founded in 1811, and the Collège de Saint Maurice, which is affiliated with the University of Montreal, are here. Saint Hyacinthe was founded in 1760. It was incorporated as a town in 1849 and as a city in 1857. Population: 38,246.

SAINT IVES is a municipal borough in the southwesternmost part of England, in Cornwall. It is on St. Ives Bay, a part of the Atlantic Ocean, about 15 miles (24 km) northeast of Land's End. It is a seaside resort and artists' colony noted for its beaches and beautiful landscapes. Saint Ives was named for the 5th century Irish martyr Saint Ia. A 15th century church dedicated to him still stands. Population: (1971) 9,710.

SAINT JAMES, a city in southeastern Manitoba, Canada, forming a western suburb of Winnipeg. Founded in 1853 on the Assiniboine River as a parish settlement of the Church of England, it was incorporated as a municipality in 1921 and as a city in 1956. Chiefly residential, the city contains Winnipeg International Airport, a Royal Canadian Air Force base, and the Manitoba Institute of Technology. Population: 41,731.

SAINT JAMES'S PALACE, a royal residence in London, England, is at the western end of Pall Mall opposite St. James's Park. It was built in 1532 for Henry VIII, who demolished a leper hospital on the site. The original building was largely destroyed by fire in 1809. It was rebuilt

in a different style. The chief survivals of Henry VIII's palace are the gatehouse and the Chapel Royal, whose ceiling may have been designed by the court painter Hans Holbein.

Adjoining the palace are York House, where the Duke of Windsor stayed when he was Prince of Wales, and Clarence House, which was added in 1825 and restored in 1949 as a residence for Princess Elizabeth (later Queen Elizabeth II) and her family.

Following Henry VIII, St. James's Palace was also the official residence of Edward VI, Mary, and Elizabeth I. Charles I stayed here on the night before his execution in 1649. The palace was the birthplace of Charles II, James II, Mary II, Anne, and George IV. Queen Victoria moved the royal residence to nearby Buckingham Palace, but the English court is still known as the Court of St. James's.

SAINT JAMES'S PARK, a 93-acre (38-hectare) park in London, England, is south of St. James's Palace and east of Buckingham Palace. It is beautifully landscaped, contains a lake, and affords views of the two palaces. The park was created by Henry VIII and finally rearranged by George IV.

SAINT-JEAN, saɴ-zhän′, is a city in southern Quebec, Canada, on the Richelieu River, 20 miles (32 km) southeast of Montreal. The name is often anglicized as St. Johns. The city manufactures silk products, hosiery, paper, and food products. It is the site of Dawson College, a branch of McGill University, and of the Collège de Saint Jean de Richelieu, which is affiliated with the University of Montreal.

Fort St.-Jean, built on the site of the community in 1749, was besieged for a month in 1775 before being taken by Continental forces led by Gen. Richard Montgomery. It was later retaken.

The community of St.-Jean was the terminus of Canada's first railroad, constructed in 1836 from la Prairie on the St. Lawrence River, 16 miles (25 km) to the northwest. Population: 35,640.

SAINT-JEAN-D'ACRE. See ACRE.

SAINT-JEAN-DE-LUZ, saɴ-zhäɴd-lüz′, is a port and fashionable resort town in the Basque country of southwestern France. It is in Pyrénées-Atlantiques department, about 12 miles (20 km) southwest of Bayonne at the mouth of the Nivelle River on the Bay of Biscay. The composer Maurice Ravel was born across the river in the neighboring town of Ciboure.

The most striking feature of the town is the 13th century Basque-style church, in which Louis XIV married Marie-Thérèse of Spain in 1660. Plain on the exterior, the church has a richly decorated interior with painted wooden panels and with wooden galleries, reserved for men. Population: (1968) 10,206.

SAINT JÉRÔME, saɴ zhā-rōm′, a city in southern Quebec, Canada, is situated on the Rivière du Nord, about 33 miles (52 km) northwest of Montreal. It manufactures quality paper, woolens, rubber and leather footwear, and wood products. It was settled in 1834 and was incorporated as a village in 1856. It became a town in 1881 and achieved the status of a city in 1950. Population: 25,123.

SAINT JOAN is a play by George Bernard Shaw, written and produced in 1923. It is one of Shaw's best and most popular plays.

Saint Joan is based on the life of Joan of Arc. Joan is inspired by heavenly voices to lead the French to victory against the English. Successful at first, she triumphantly crowns the dauphin, Charles, king of France. But she is captured later by the English and is tried and burned.

In Shaw's view, Joan was burned because she was a threat to the religious and secular establishments. She communed directly with God, ignoring the intermediary role of the church. She addressed herself to the people without consulting the feudal nobility.

In an epilogue, learning of her canonization, Joan offers to revisit earth. Rejected again, she cries, "O God that madest this beautiful earth, when will it be ready to receive Thy saints? How long, O Lord, how long?"

The play had its first production in New York, with Winifred Lenihan as Joan. London saw it in 1924, Sybil Thorndike playing the title role. Katharine Cornell starred in it in 1936.

ST. JOHN, Henry. See BOLINGBROKE, 1ST VISCOUNT.

ST. JOHN, J. Hector. See CRÈVECOEUR, MICHEL-GUILLAUME JEAN DE.

ST. JOHN, sin'jən, **Oliver** (1598?–1673), English parliamentarian and judge. He began the practice of the law in London in 1619. He was imprisoned, but soon pardoned, for circulating a seditious document in 1629. He established a reputation as an astute counsel by defending Lord Saye and John Hampden in their 1637 trial for refusing to pay the ship money levy.

St. John's sympathies with parliamentary government and his marriage to a cousin of Cromwell led him to support the Puritan Revolution. A leading figure in the Long Parliament of 1640, he was the probable author of its Root and Branch Bill and Militia Bill. He served as solicitor general (1641–1643), acted as attorney general (1644), supported Cromwell against Parliament (1647), and became chief justice of the Court of Common Pleas (1648). In 1652 he was a member of the commission that secured a treaty with Scotland.

After Cromwell dissolved the Rump Parliament in 1653, St. John was inactive in government. He refused to participate in the trial of Charles I and cooperated with Gen. George Monk (Monck) in restoring the monarchy (1660). Defending himself in the *Case of Oliver St. John,* he denied any complicity in the expulsion of royalists from Commons, the establishment of the Commonwealth, or the execution of Charles. He received only light punishment for his association with Cromwell and the Commonwealth, being disallowed to hold public office. After 1662 he lived abroad; he died on Dec. 31, 1673.

SAINT JOHN, a city in southern New Brunswick, Canada, the seat of St. John county, is situated at the mouth of the St. John River on the north shore of the Bay of Fundy, 585 miles (940 km) east of Montreal, Quebec. About 1 mile (1.6 km) from the center of the city are the Reversing Falls on the St. John River. At high tide in the bay, the flow of the river is reversed.

St. John was the first city in Canada to be incorporated. It retains much of the charm of its past. The city has extensive piers and drydocks, and its chief industries are shipping and shipbuilding and repair. It also has sugar and oil refineries and paper mills.

A branch of the University of New Brunswick is in the city. The New Brunswick Museum contains exhibits of all types of arts and sciences and history. There are also many old buildings and historical landmarks in the city, the most interesting of which are the Old Loyalist Burial Ground, with graves dating from 1784; Barbour's General Store, a restoration of an old general store; and the Loyalist House, which stands virtually as it was built in 1810.

The site of St. John was first visited on the feast of St. John the Baptist (June 24) in 1604, by Samuel de Champlain. Fort La Tour was built at St. John in 1631 but was destroyed soon after by the Sieur d'Aulnay Charnisay, who established a fort on the opposite side of the harbor. Fort Charnisay was occupied by garrisons from time to time until about 1700 when it was left to fall into ruin. In 1758 it was rebuilt by the English and renamed Fort Frederick. English traders settled here in 1762.

The modern city developed in 1783 with the arrival of the United Empire Loyalists. This wave of colonization made New Brunswick a province, and by royal charter St. John was incorporated as a city in 1785, the first in British America. It was also the first in Canada to adopt a commission form of government. In 1877 a disastrous fire destroyed more than half the city, and many of the old wooden buildings were replaced by brick ones. Population: 80,521.

SAINT JOHN, the third-largest of the Virgin Islands of the United States, is in the Caribbean Sea, 3 miles (5 km) east of St. Thomas and about 80 miles (129 km) east of San Juan, Puerto Rico. The island is about 9 miles (14 km) long and 5 miles (8 km) wide. St. John's terrain is rugged, with mountains of volcanic origin and an irregular coast. A bay forest on St. John supplies leaves for the rum industry in Charlotte Amalie on St. Thomas. The Virgin Island National Park, dedicated in 1956, is on St. John.

The island was discovered by Christopher Columbus in 1493. It was taken by Denmark in 1684, but not settled until 1716, when the Danes built a number of sugar plantations here. The island was shaken by a slave revolt in 1733, when the blacks held the island for six months, but the plantation owners again gained control. The island was also a hideout for buccaneers. It was sold to the United States in 1917. Population: 2,360. See also VIRGIN ISLANDS OF THE UNITED STATES.

SAINT JOHN OF JERUSALEM, Knights of, a religious and military order, also known as the Knights Hospitalers, that was founded in the Middle Ages. Originally called the Order of St. John of Jerusalem, then Knights of Rhodes, and ultimately Knights of Malta, it is the oldest religious-military institution and therefore takes precedence over the other orders that followed its example, such as the Knights Templar and the Teutonic Knights.

The Hospital of St. John of Jerusalem was founded in the mid-11th century in Jerusalem by merchants from Amalfi, Italy, to aid the increasing number of pilgrims who were visiting the

GREEK NATIONAL TOURIST OFFICE

The Grand Master's Palace and the Street of the Knights bear witness to the splendor of Rhodes when it was ruled by the Knights of St. John of Jerusalem.

LOUIS H. FROHMAN

Holy Land. A monk named Gerard, rector of the hospital during the siege of Jerusalem by Godfrey of Bouillon during the First Crusade, was the first master of the order. During his mastership (1100–1120) the order extended its influence in the Middle East and Europe, building hospitals on routes to the Holy Land. Pope Paschal II, by the bull of Feb. 15, 1113, recognized the order and put it under the protection of the papacy, a practice continued by later popes.

Under Raymond du Puy, who succeeded Gerard, the Knights' mission became more militaristically oriented, as it helped wage war against the Muslims. At the same time, the order was becoming immensely rich through donations and bequests, and subsidiary chapters were established throughout Europe. It became a military force that for centuries formed the advance guard of Christian Europe.

As it assumed knightly-military functions in addition to religious ones, the order divided itself into soldier-brothers, or knights of justice; servant brothers; and clerks, or chaplains. When the Latin Empire of Constantinople was founded in 1204, the order, from such fortresses as the famed Krak des Chevaliers in Syria, acted as a militia, while continuing its hospital work. Their last stronghold in the Holy Land was at Acre. After the collapse of the Latin Empire in 1261 and the fall of Acre in 1291, the Knights settled on Cyprus until they took the island of Rhodes from the Seljuk Turks in 1309. Their fortification of Rhodes made it Christendom's strongest outpost against the Muslims.

On Rhodes the order was divided into the *langues*, or tongues, of Provence, Auvergne, France, Italy, Aragón, Castile and Portugal, England, and Germany. The members of each *langue* lived together and had their own leader. The order's main offices were distributed among the *langues*. The symbol of the order came to be a white cross on a black robe.

Muslim leaders frequently attacked the Knights on Rhodes, and in 1522, after heroically resisting a siege by Suleiman the Magnificent, the Knights capitulated and left the island. Holy Roman Emperor Charles V's cession of Malta to the Hospitalers (1530) confirmed the sovereignty of the order at a time when it was defeated and homeless. Suleiman used his fleet to attack Malta in 1565, but after a siege that lasted five months the Knights defeated Suleiman's powerful Muslim force.

Later History. With Napoleon's expedition to Egypt, in 1798, Malta came into the possession of the French and later passed to the British, who by the Treaty of Amiens (1802) undertook to restore it to the order. In 1814, however, the Treaty of Paris legalized British possession. From Malta the order went successively to Messina, Catania, and Ferrara, coming finally to Rome in 1831.

In 1879, after a long period of lieutenancy, Pope Leo XIII restored the title of grand master, with the usual powers. The modern organization that subsequently emerged has stressed charitable activities, particularly care of the sick, and has expanded beyond Europe.

Further Reading: Peyrefitte, Roger, *Knights of Malta*, tr. by Edward Hyams (Criterion 1959); Riley-Smith, Jonathan, *Knights of St. John in Jerusalem and Cyprus* (St. Martins 1967).

SAINT JOHN'S, capital of Newfoundland. An important seaport with a fine harbor, the city is a center for Newfoundland's commercial fishing fleet.

SAINT-JOHN PERSE. See PERSE, SAINT-JOHN.

SAINT JOHN RIVER, in eastern Canada, is the principal river in the province of New Brunswick. It is about 400 miles (644 km) long. It rises in Somerset county, Maine, and for 75 miles (120 km) forms the boundary between the United States and Canada before entering New Brunswick. The river empties into the Bay of Fundy at St. John, New Brunswick. At the mouth are the Reversing Falls, rapids that fall 17 feet (5 meters) in which the flow of the river is reversed at high tide in the bay.

Large steamers navigate the river as far as Fredericton, a distance of 85 miles (137 km), while smaller craft ascend to Woodstock, 150 miles (241 km) from the mouth.

SAINT JOHN'S, the capital of Antigua—one of the Leeward Islands in the West Indies—is a city on the northwestern side of the island, on a small bay of the Caribbean Sea. It is the commercial center of Antigua and its chief port. The island has no natural deep-water harbors, but in 1968, St. John's opened a new dredged-out harbor with extensive facilities for bunkering and storing. The principal commodities handled by the port are sugar, cotton, foodstuffs, machinery, and lumber.

The city is also a popular resort. Places of interest include the cathedral, the custom house, and the old residence of the English governors. The area was settled by the British in 1632. Population: (1970) 21,814.

ST. JOHN'S, the capital of Newfoundland province, is the easternmost city in Canada. It is on the Atlantic Ocean in the northern part of the Avalon peninsula in southeastern Newfoundland, 565 miles (909 km) east of Port-aux-Basques, which connects by ferry with Sydney, Nova Scotia. St. John's harbor is almost landlocked, admitting ships through the Narrows, which are flanked by cliffs that are 500 feet (152 meters) high. The city is built on slopes overlooking the harbor.

St. John's, one of the oldest settlements in North America, has always been an important shipping center. It is situated on the chief Atlantic shipping lanes, 1,213 miles (1,952 km) northeast of New York City and 1,829 miles (2,942 km) west of Liverpool, England. The city is also one of the leading centers of the codfish industry in Canada, and fish packing, fish processing, and the manufacture of fish products are important. Other industry includes shipbuilding, lumber, and textiles.

The Memorial University of Newfoundland, dedicated to the men of Newfoundland and Labrador who were killed in World War I, was founded as a college in 1925 and incorporated as a university in 1949. St. John's is also the center of extensive oceanographic studies. The university maintains its own art gallery. Other museums include the Newfoundland Naval and History Museum; the Newfoundland Museum, with historical exhibits; and the Arts and Culture Centre. Signal Hill National Park is the site of the last battle between the French and English for control of the Atlantic coast. At Cabot Tower atop the hill, Guglielmo Marconi in 1901 received the first wireless message sent across the Atlantic Ocean.

The city has two cathedrals, the Basilica of St. John the Baptist (Roman Catholic), a modified Romanesque structure, and the Cathedral of St. John the Baptist (Anglican), a Gothic building. The Old Garrison Church, a wooden structure, was built in 1836 for the use of the military. The Confederation Building houses the provincial government headquarters.

It is generally believed that the site of St. John's was discovered by John Cabot on the feast of St. John the Baptist (June 24) in 1497. Its first settlers were probably members of the crews of fishing fleets who were left behind during the winter to prepare for the next season's fishing. In 1540 there were 20 houses in St. John's. From here, in 1583, Sir Humphrey Gilbert took possession of the island in the name of Queen Elizabeth I of England. A large barter trade was carried on here among the French, Portuguese, Basque, and English fishermen, and as early as 1641 the American colonies began trading with St. John's.

A bitter struggle between France and England over Newfoundland ended in 1762, when Col. William Amherst, with the Highlanders and the Royal American Regiment, recaptured the city from the French, who had briefly occupied it. During the 19th century, St. John's suffered enormous losses from three fires. In the 20th century the wooden buildings were mostly replaced by stone structures.

St. John's is governed by a mayor and a council. Population: (1981) 83,770.

SAINT JOHN'S BREAD. See CAROB.

SAINT JOHNS RIVER, in northeastern Florida, one of the major rivers in the state. Its source is in the swamps around Lakes Helen Blazes and Saw Grass in Brevard county, about 15 miles (24 km) west of Melbourne. It flows generally northward, broadening occasionally into lakes, of which Lake George is the largest. At Jacksonville, it turns eastward and empties into the Atlantic Ocean.

The river is about 285 miles (456 km) long. In its lower reaches, it is several miles wide, and even 150 miles (240 km) upstream, its width is about a mile. As far as Jacksonville, about 15 miles from the sea, it is navigable by large ocean-going ships, and smaller vessels can go to Sanford, 200 miles (320 km). From Palatka to its mouth (86 miles or 137 km) the river is part of the Intracoastal Waterway.

Through much of its course, the river's banks are lined with luxuriant subtropical vegetation. The water hyacinth (*Eichhornia crassipes*) has choked the channel and must be cleared constantly.

The French built Fort Caroline near the river mouth in 1562. The St. Johns River was a route for early travelers into Florida's interior.

SAINT-JOHN'S-WORT, wûrt, is a common plant of central Europe which has become a serious weed in parts of the United States, particularly on the Pacific Coast and in the intermountain area. Though used to designate many plants of the genus *Hypericum*, the term "Saint-John's-wort" is most commonly applied to *H. perforatum*. Flowers are perfect and numerous, borne in a cymose panicle, yellow in color, and showy when they occur in large masses. The dried pods and foliage turn a milk-chocolate brown in the fall and are readily detected among other plants by this coloring.

H. perforatum is a shallow-rooted perennial with opposite leaves bearing pellucid glands that show as clear spots on the leaves (perforate). A clean smooth herb two to three feet in height and growing in dense patches, it has a sticky resinous juice containing hypericin, a poison with unique properties. When the herb is eaten in large quantities by white or spotted animals, the white areas on the animals are photosensitized and in the sunlight become sore, resulting in loss of condition and even death in severe cases.

ALDEN S. CRAFTS
University of California at Davis

SAINT JOHNSBURY is a town in northeastern Vermont and the seat of Caledonia county. It is at the junction of the Passumpsic and Moose rivers, about 37 miles (59 km) northeast of Montpelier. The manufacture of maple sugar has made the community famous.

St. Johnsbury also makes platform scales, which have been a major product since 1831, when Thaddeus Fairbanks obtained the first patent. It also produces paper, gloves, and cattle feed.

The Fairbanks Museum of Natural Science and the St. Johnsbury Athenaeum, a library and art gallery, are points of interest. The St. Johnsbury Academy was founded in 1842.

Settled in 1786 by Jonathan Arnold of Rhode Island, St. Johnsbury was named for Jean de Crèvecoeur, who wrote *Letters from an American Farmer*. It became the county seat in 1856. Government is by town manager. Population: 7,938.

SAINT JOSEPH, a city in southeastern Michigan, the seat of Berrien county, is on Lake Michigan at the mouth of the St. Joseph River, about 25 miles (40 km) north of the Indiana state line. The city of Benton Harbor is directly across the river.

St. Joseph is in a resort area where fruit farming and commercial fishing are important. The city makes machinery, castings, rubber goods, hosiery, paper boxes, and dairy products.

The area around the mouth of the St. Joseph River was visited by early explorers and missionaries. The Sieur de La Salle built Fort Miami here in 1679. The first permanent settlement, about 1830, was made on high ground, the site of the present city. The community was incorporated as a village in 1836 and as a city in 1891. Government is by commission and manager. Population: 9,622.

SAINT JOSEPH, a city in northwestern Missouri, the seat of Buchanan county, is on the Missouri River, about 50 miles (80 km) north of Kansas City. It is a railroad and highway center and a major trading point for 15 counties in Missouri, Iowa, Nebraska, and Kansas.

The city lies in a rich agricultural region. Meat-packing and the processing of dairy products are among its leading industries. Its manufactures include concrete, structural steel, wire rope, auto cables, fire fighting equipment, boats, chemicals, and paper products.

Points of interest include the Albrecht Gallery Museum of Art; the St. Joseph Museum, which has historical and natural history collections; the Pony Express Stables Museum; and the Jesse James House, the last home of the outlaw Jesse James. Eugene Field, the journalist and poet, lived in St. Joseph, which he memorialized in his verses, *Lovers' Lane, Saint Jo.*

Founded by Joseph Robidoux of St. Louis, who established a trading post on the site in 1826, the town of St. Joseph was laid out in 1843. It was incorporated two years later and became the county seat in 1846.

In the mid-19th century, St. Joseph was the departure point for thousands of settlers and adventurers who developed the Far West. Parties bound for the Oregon Territory and the gold-fields of California pushed their wagons through the town, which became a huge supply depot. The Missouri River offered an easy route to and from the East, and the first railroad did not reach St. Joseph until 1859. The famous Pony Express service was established between St. Joseph and California in 1860.

St. Joseph was incorporated as a city in 1851. Government is by mayor and council. Population: 76,691.

SAINT-JUST, saN-zhüst', **Louis Antoine Léon** (1767–1794), French revolutionary. He was born in Decize, France, on Aug. 25, 1767. The son of an army officer, he was well educated at Soissons and Reims. The writings of Jean Jacques Rousseau influenced him to join the French revolutionary movement and to support Maximilien Robespierre, whose friend and close associate he later became. Elected to the National Convention in 1792, he demanded in his first speech that the deposed King Louis XVI be judged not as a citizen, but as an enemy.

Like Robespierre, Saint-Just was an inexorable adherent of Rousseau's political theories, believing

Basseterre is the capital and principal port of the island of Saint Kitts, in the Caribbean area. It exports the agricultural products raised in the hilly land of the island's interior.

that through stern virtue a perfect state could be created to bring happiness to the world. Because of his own incorruptibility and his youthful good looks, he was known as the "archangel of the revolution." During the Reign of Terror (1793–1794), he, Robespierre, and Georges Couthon formed a ruthless triumvirate in the Committee of Public Safety. He collaborated in the destruction of the Girondists (a moderate faction) and in the downfall of Jacques René Hébert, Georges Jacques Danton, and their followers.

France had been attacked by a coalition of European monarchies, and Saint-Just was at times sent into the field to supervise defensive operations. On returning from a successful campaign in 1793 to drive the enemy forces back across the Rhine, he became president of the Convention. He was recalled from another military mission in 1794 to assist Robespierre in quelling political opposition. On July 27 he attempted to defend Robespierre in the Convention, but he failed and was arrested. He was guillotined in Paris the following day with Robespierre, Robespierre's brother Augustin, and Couthon. Their deaths and the execution of other Robespierrists in the days that followed ended the Reign of Terror. See also FRANCE—*History;* FRENCH REVOLUTION.

Further Reading: Bruun, Geoffrey, *Saint-Just, Apostle of the Terror* (Shoestring Press 1966, reprint of 1932 edition).

SAINT KILDA, the westernmost island of the Outer Hebrides, is in the Atlantic Ocean, about 140 miles (225 km) west of the mainland of northern Scotland. It is about 3 miles (5 km) long and 2 miles (3 km) wide, and has a rugged terrain. Its name comes from the Norse *Kilde,* or "Well," after the ancient well found there. Its older name is Hirta ("death or gloom"). In 1930 the island was evacuated—there were fewer than 40 people living there—and made into a bird sanctuary. The name St. Kilda is also applied to some nearby smaller islands.

SAINT KITTS is a Caribbean island in the Leeward group, about 200 miles (320 km) east-southeast of Puerto Rico. It is also called St. Christopher. Together with the islands of Nevis and Anguilla, it is a self-governing state associated with Britain. See also SAINT KITTS-NEVIS-ANGUILLA.

St. Kitts is an oval-shaped, mountainous volcanic island covering an area of 68 square miles (176 sq km). It has a pleasant tropical climate with a mean temperature of about 79° F (26° C). The chief products are sugar, molasses, cotton, coconuts, tropical fruits, and salt. These are exported through Basseterre, the capital and principal city, which is also a distributing point for merchandise bound for nearby islands. The population is largely of African descent, but much of the farmland is in sugar and cotton plantations owned by the European minority.

Called Liamuiga (fertile island) by the Carib Indians who once inhabited it, St. Kitts is said to have been discovered by Christopher Columbus in 1493. The first island in the area to be settled by British colonizers (1623), it was often referred to as the "mother colony of the West Indies."

France also founded a settlement in the 1620's, and the island was a bone of contention between the two powers until awarded to Britain by the Treaty of Versailles in 1783. Population: (1966) 37,150.

SAINT KITTS-NEVIS-ANGUILLA, sănt-kits', nē'vəs-ang-gwil'ə, a Caribbean state associated with Great Britain, was created in 1967 and granted internal autonomy, with Britain retaining responsibility for its defense and foreign affairs. The constituent islands—St. Kitts (or St. Christopher), Nevis, and Anguilla—had previously been associated as a unit in Britain's Leeward Islands colony (1871–1956) and as a member of an autonomous West Indies federation (1958–1962). Nevertheless, Anguilla, the smallest of the three, rebelled against the new state and, in 1969, was briefly occupied by British troops. In 1971, colonial status was restored, but in 1976 Anguilla was granted special self-governing status within the state. Population: (1974 est.) 65,000.

SAINT LAMBERT, saɴ län-bâr', a city in southern Quebec, Canada, is on the eastern shore of the St. Lawrence River opposite Montreal, with which it is connected by the Victoria Bridge. Primarily a residential city, St. Lambert has industries that manufacture fountain pens, electrical machinery, metal products, and wooden sashes and doors. The city was incorporated in 1921. Population: 20,557.

ST. LAURENT, saN lô-rän′, **Louis Stephen** (1882–1973), Canadian political leader, who was prime minister from 1948 to 1957, the second French Canadian to hold that office.

He was born in Compton, Quebec, on Feb. 1, 1882. He graduated from Laval University in 1902 and took a law degree there in 1905. Admitted to the bar in 1905 and to the law faculty of Laval in 1914, he achieved prominence as a lawyer, especially in constitutional cases. He served as president of the Canadian Bar Association from 1930 to 1932 and was later made honorary life president.

Inexperienced in politics, St. Laurent was brought into the cabinet in 1941 by Prime Minister W. L. Mackenzie King to serve as minister of justice and attorney general. He was elected to Parliament from Quebec East in 1942. In 1946, still in the King cabinet, he became secretary of state for external affairs. Despite considerable anti-French sentiment, he succeeded King as party leader and as prime minister in 1948. He retired from active politics in 1958, and he died, in Quebec City, on July 25, 1973.

While still minister of justice, St. Laurent began to play a significant role in Canada's international relations. He was among its delegates to the San Francisco Conference (1945), headed the delegations to the first sessions of the United Nations General Assembly (1946, 1947), and made Canada's successful bid for a seat on the UN Security Council. He claimed for Canada a major role in negotiating the World War II peace treaties, and it was he who first voiced the concept of the North Atlantic Treaty Organization. Under his guidance Canada often played the role of mediator in international disputes. Domestically, he was instrumental in making Newfoundland a province of Canada (1949) and in developing the Canadian supreme court as a court of final appeal. His greatest contribution as prime minister was in leading Canada to maturity within the Commonwealth of Nations and as an international power.

Louis St. Laurent, prime minister of Canada (1948–1957)

NATIONAL FILM BOARD OF CANADA

SAINT LAURENT, saN lô-rän′, a city in southern Quebec, Canada, is on Montreal Island, immediately northwest of Montreal. It is a residential city with steel and light manufacturing enterprises. The College de St. Laurent is situated here.

A mission was established on the site of the community in 1720. The town was founded in 1845 and became a city in 1955. Population: 65,900.

SAINT LAWRENCE RIVER AND GULF, a river and a gulf in eastern Canada. The river, one of the major streams in North America, is the outlet of the Great Lakes. It issues from Lake Ontario and flows northeast, widening beyond the city of Quebec to form a broad estuary that eventually merges with the Gulf of St. Lawrence north of the Gaspé Peninsula. The gulf opens into the Atlantic Ocean through Cabot Strait, between Cape Breton Island and Newfoundland, and the Strait of Belle Isle, which separates Newfoundland from Labrador.

The river and gulf are part of a continuous waterway (the Great Lakes–St. Lawrence system) from Duluth, Minn., at the western extremity of Lake Superior, to the Atlantic. Since 1842, through treaty arrangements, the river has been open to ships of the United States on a basis of equality with those of Canada, but only since 1958, when a series of great locks and dams was completed between Montreal and Ogdensburg, N. Y., has the stream been navigable by deep-draft oceangoing vessels. See also ST. LAWRENCE SEAWAY.

The River. From Lake Ontario to the head of its estuary near Quebec, the St. Lawrence River is roughly 300 miles (500 km) long. It forms the boundary between New York state and the province of Ontario along the first third of this stretch and subsequently flows through Quebec province. The estuary itself is almost as long as the river proper.

The St. Lawrence begins its run at the northeastern end of Lake Ontario as a broad, sluggish stream whose arms wind among the so-called Thousand Islands—some 1,500 picturesque islands and islets that have long attracted vacationers. Between Ogdensburg and Montreal, which is the largest city along its banks, the stream moves more swiftly. Here occur the many shoals and rapids that were the most formidable obstacles to waterborne transportation. Even along this stretch, however, there are several "pools," or basins, where the river spreads to a width of 2 miles (3 km) or more.

A few miles upstream from Montreal, the St. Lawrence receives its first major tributary, the Ottawa River. Below the city the river slows, widens, and receives the Richelieu, which flows north from Lake Champlain. Far downstream, the Saguenay, flowing from the east, swells the volume of water in the estuary, which eventually reaches a width of about 90 miles (145 km).

The Gulf. The Gulf of St. Lawrence is a broad, nearly landlocked body of water between Nova Scotia, New Brunswick, eastern Quebec, and the island of Newfoundland, which blocks what would otherwise be its spacious eastern entrance. From December to April, drifting ice menaces shipping both in the gulf and in the two straits which give access to the ocean. Important islands in the gulf include Anticosti, Prince Edward Island, and the Magdalen Islands.

The St. Lawrence River forms the eastern end of the St. Lawrence Seaway.

Economic Importance. The St. Lawrence Valley is one of Canada's major farming and industrial areas, noted for its paper mills, timber, dairy products, grains, and fruit. Commercial development was spurred by the increase in river traffic that followed completion of the seaway and by the expansion of hydroelectric power facilities that was a part of the seaway project. In the gulf area fishing is an important industry.

Geology. The St. Lawrence system is comparatively young by geological standards, being a relic of the last ice age. It took form when the continental ice fields retreated toward the Arctic, leaving a maze of lakes and swamps, worn-down uplands, terminal moraines, and deeply etched valleys. Larger glacial lakes were eventually reduced to the present linked Great Lakes, through which a continual current flows eastward, making these lakes, in a sense, the western extension of the St. Lawrence River.

History. The first European of record to sail up the St. Lawrence was the Frenchman Jacques Cartier in 1535. He called it the River of Canada, but the name St. Lawrence, which he had bestowed on the outer gulf in 1534, came to be preferred for the whole system.

The river long served the French as their principal highway into the interior. The St. Lawrence Valley was a major battleground of the French and Indian War (1754–1763), and the defeat of the French at Quebec by the British in 1759 was one of the decisive events in Canadian history, precipitating the collapse of the French empire in North America.

WILLIAM R. WILLOUGHBY*
St. Lawrence University, New York

SAINT LAWRENCE SEAWAY, a navigable waterway of North America, connecting the Great Lakes with the Atlantic Ocean. Improved through the efforts of Canadian and United States engineers in the late 1950's, it was officially opened as a deep waterway on June 26, 1959. A related hydroelectric project was completed the previous summer. The seaway's opening marked the consummation of an undertaking that had been vigorously advocated, and equally vigorously opposed, for half a century.

St. Lawrence System. The St. Lawrence–Great Lakes system, some 2,350 miles (3,800 km) in length, has its source in the St. Louis River, which enters Lake Superior at Duluth, Minn. From this point, the waterway follows the Great Lakes to the northeastern end of Lake Ontario, where the St. Lawrence River itself begins. The river flows northeast until it enters the Gulf of St. Lawrence and, eventually, the Atlantic Ocean. See also ST. LAWRENCE RIVER AND GULF.

Prior to 1959 most of the seaway was deep enough for large-scale navigation. From the open ocean to Montreal, the river had a depth of about 35 feet (over 10 meters) and could accommodate all but the largest oceangoing vessels. From Ogdensburg, N. Y., to the head of the lakes, the waterway had a minimum depth of 25 feet (7.6 meters), easily navigable by specially built lake steamers carrying up to 25,000 tons.

But in between these two long stretches of open navigation, from Montreal to Ogdensburg, a distance of less than 120 miles (195 km), river navigation was impeded by dangerous shoals and rapids. Through this section all traffic was obliged to pass through a series of 14-foot-deep (4 meters) canals, containing a total of 22 locks, built by Canada before 1903. Only small canallers of less than 3,000 tons were able to squeeze through these restricted channels. It was the removal of this "bottleneck" that was the major objective of the construction program carried out by Canada and the United States in 1954–1959.

Power Project. Works designed principally to provide hydroelectric power, but which contributed incidentally to the navigation project, were built by New York state and the province of Ontario in the International Rapids section, between Ogdensburg, N. Y., and Cornwall, Ontario. These works included a power dam (later named the Saunders-Moses Dam) across the north channel at Barnhart Island, connecting the lower end of this island with the Canadian mainland; a spillway dam (Long Sault Dam) across the south channel, connecting the upper end of Barnhart Island with the American mainland near Massena, N. Y., and, upstream, a control dam (Iroquois Dam) across the river in the vicinity of Iroquois Point, below Ogdensburg.

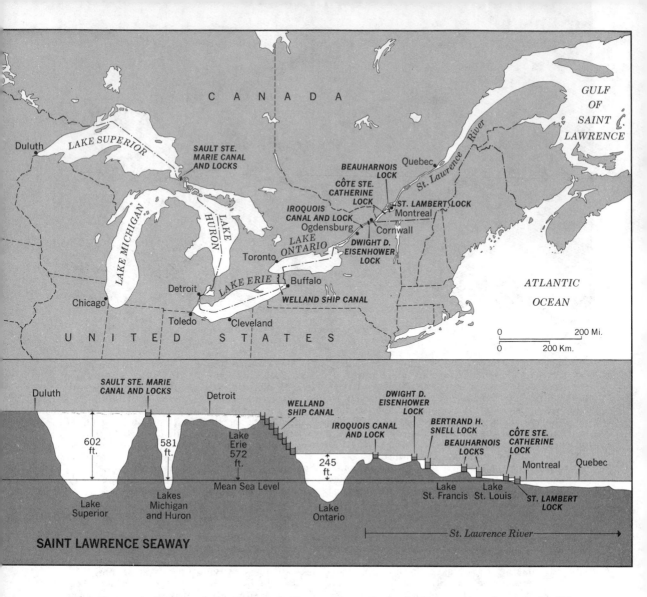

The map shows the Great Lakes–St. Lawrence region with labels including Duluth, LAKE SUPERIOR, LAKE MICHIGAN, LAKE HURON, SAULT STE. MARIE CANAL AND LOCKS, Chicago, Detroit, Toledo, Cleveland, LAKE ERIE, Buffalo, WELLAND SHIP CANAL, Toronto, LAKE ONTARIO, Ogdensburg, IROQUOIS CANAL AND LOCK, CÔTE STE. CATHERINE LOCK, BEAUHARNOIS LOCK, Quebec, ST. LAMBERT LOCK, Montreal, Cornwall, DWIGHT D. EISENHOWER LOCK, St. Lawrence River, GULF OF SAINT LAWRENCE, ATLANTIC OCEAN, CANADA, UNITED STATES.

Scale: 0 – 200 Mi. / 0 – 200 Km.

Profile diagram labeled SAINT LAWRENCE SEAWAY: Duluth; SAULT STE. MARIE CANAL AND LOCKS; Detroit; WELLAND SHIP CANAL; DWIGHT D. EISENHOWER LOCK; IROQUOIS CANAL AND LOCK; BERTRAND H. SNELL LOCK; BEAUHARNOIS LOCKS; CÔTE STE. CATHERINE LOCK; Montreal; Quebec; Lake Superior 602 ft.; Lakes Michigan and Huron 581 ft.; Lake Erie 572 ft.; Mean Sea Level; Lake Ontario 245 ft.; Lake St. Francis; Lake St. Louis; ST. LAMBERT LOCK; St. Lawrence River.

The Power Authority of the State of New York directed the state's share of the construction, while the Ontario Hydro-Electric Power Commission supervised the province's share. The job was completed in less than five years, costing the state and province each approximately $300 million and providing each with over 800,000 kilowatts of additional electricity.

Navigation Project. The two federal governments accepted the responsibility for constructing the works intended exclusively for navigation. The United States' share included the digging of the Wiley-Dondero ship channel to bypass the power-project spillway dam at Barnhart Island. This canal, which is 10 miles (16 km) long and 27 feet (8 meters) deep, has two locks, the Dwight D. Eisenhower Lock at the upstream end and the Bertrand H. Snell Lock at the downstream end. Each is 860 feet (260 meters) long and 80 feet (24 meters) wide. The United States also dredged the Thousand Islands section, between Ogdensburg and Lake Ontario, to 27 feet. In addition, by the mid-1960's the United States had completed the deepening of the connecting channels of the Great Lakes.

Canada constructed a short canal and a lock (Iroquois Lock) to bypass the Iroquois Control Dam. It also built a canal and two locks (Upper and Lower Beauharnois) between lakes St. Francis and St. Louis, and, farther downstream, another canal and two more locks (Côte Ste. Catherine and St. Lambert) to bypass the Lachine Rapids near Montreal. All the locks were comparable in size to those built by the United States. The Canadians also deepened the Welland Ship Canal, between lakes Erie and Ontario, to 27 feet and dredged portions of the 70-mile (110 km) Cornwall-Montreal section.

The United States share of the navigation project was directed by the U. S. Army Corps of Engineers, with the St. Lawrence Seaway Development Corporation exercising general supervisory control. The Canadian share was supervised by the St. Lawrence Seaway Authority of Canada. The cost of the project to Canada was about $340 million. The United States was estimated to have spent nearly $150 million on work in the International Falls section alone.

Seaway Operations. The principal responsibility for the operation of the St. Lawrence Seaway—defined as including both the Montreal–Lake Ontario section and the Welland Canal section—was vested in Canada's St. Lawrence Seaway Authority. Through agreement between

Ships passing through the locks of the St. Lawrence Seaway near Cornwall, Ontario.

the cooperating governments, a system of tolls was instituted, with both nations sharing in the proceeds. The system involved double charges. One charge was based on the gross registered tonnage of the vessel making the transit. The other was based on the character of the cargo, with the rate-per-ton on general cargo (packed and packaged goods, including all manufactured goods) being fixed at a level more than twice as high as that on bulk cargo (ore, grain). Tolls for partial transits of the seaway were prorated.

Peak months for traffic on the St. Lawrence Seaway are May to October, with normal winter conditions making the waterway virtually useless from mid-December to early April. As anticipated, seaway traffic increased steadily after the deep waterway was opened. Cargo tonnage through the Montreal–Lake Ontario section rose from an annual average of slightly more than 10 million tons in the mid-1950's to more than 50 million tons in the early 1970's. During the same period, Welland Canal cargo tonnage increased from less than 20 million tons to more than 60 million tons per year.

The traffic rise was soon causing congestion, especially in the older, Welland Canal section of the seaway. In 1967 a six-year project was launched to build a new 8-mile (13-km) channel bypassing the city of Welland, Ontario, where drawbridges had impeded rapid movement. Other improvements included the introduction of a modern traffic control system that reduced the average time of transit through the Welland Canal and its eight locks from 24 hours in 1964 to 14 hours in 1970. A similar computerized control system was also introduced in the Montreal–Lake Ontario section.

Benefits. The navigation and power projects sparked an industrial and agricultural boom in the entire Great Lakes–St. Lawrence region. Increasing quantities of grain, newsprint, wood pulp, machinery, and automobiles were shipped through the waterway to eastern and European markets, while ever-growing shipments of Labrador iron ore traveled up the St. Lawrence to the steel mills of the Midwest. Many cities on the Great Lakes developed their harbors to handle the increased volume of shipping.

To take advantage of the cheap, abundant St. Lawrence power, both the Reynolds Aluminum Company and General Motors established factories in or near Massena, N. Y., at the lower end of the International Rapids section, and the Aluminum Company of America greatly expanded its Massena production program. Many other industries also settled near the new power sites. On the Canadian side, much of the output of the new generating stations was fed into a large power grid that served nearly 2 million customers throughout eastern Ontario. In this area, as in much of northeastern New York and southwestern Quebec, benefits in the form of additional jobs, expansion of service industries, increases in land values, and money generated for school building and other public improvements have been impossible to calculate.

HISTORY

The ambitious project of 1954–1959 was only one of many undertaken to improve navigation along this system since the discovery of the St. Lawrence River by Jacques Cartier in the 16th century.

Early Canalization. From the early 18th century, the Canadians conducted a program of channel dredging and canal construction that by 1903 provided a 14-foot (4.25-meter) waterway from the Atlantic to Lake Erie. Beginning in 1823, the United States carried out improvements in the connecting channels of the Great Lakes which, by 1914, provided 21-foot (6.4-meter) navigation for upbound and 25-foot (7.6-meter) for downbound traffic, from the eastern end of Lake Erie to the western end of Lake Superior.

By the 1930's the Canadian-built, 28-mile-long (45-km) Welland Ship Canal, bypassing Niagara Falls, made it possible for vessels of 25-foot draft to navigate between Lake Ontario and Lake Erie. Nearly 20 years in the building (1913–1932), the Welland Canal overcame the 326-foot (99-meter) difference in the water levels of the two lakes by means of eight huge locks with minimum depths of 30 feet (9 meters) over the sills. It required only the deepening of some of its connecting channels to meet seaway specifications.

But passage along the St. Lawrence proper above Montreal remained limited to vessels of shallow draft. And because of the rapid growth of commerce and the steady increase in the size of ships, even the most improved channels were soon outmoded. Rail rates were high, and the railroads proved incapable of moving all of the wheat and manufactured goods pouring out of the Great Lakes region. Both in the United States and in Canada an insistent agitation arose for an improved St. Lawrence waterway.

Studies and Agreements. In response to this pressure, the two federal governments requested the International Joint Commission, which was created in 1911 to deal with boundary water problems, to conduct studies and make recommendations with respect to the improvements of St. Lawrence navigation between Montreal and Lake Ontario. After extensive hearings and investigations, the commission, composed of three members from each country, concluded that the waterway should be cooperatively improved and suggested that this could be accomplished most economically in the International Rapids section through a combined navigation-power project.

Although the conclusions of the commission were greeted with satisfaction by most Americans and by some Canadians, Prime Minister Mackenzie King's Liberal government of the 1920's was reluctant to enter into treaty negotiations with the authorities at Washington. Canada at that time had ample supplies of electricity and adequate transportation facilities. The utility and shipping interests of Montreal were strongly opposed to the combined project. The country was deeply in debt, and many Canadians rejected any partnership arrangement with the powerful, somewhat unpredictable United States. But following the coming to power of the Conservatives under Richard Bennett in July 1930, negotiations were started, culminating in the St. Lawrence Deep Waterways Treaty of July 19, 1932.

The treaty provided for the cooperative construction of a 27-foot waterway from Lake Superior to the Atlantic. It also provided for the development of the potential electrical power of the International Rapids section, the power and the costs to be shared equally by the two countries. President Franklin D. Roosevelt, as well as spokesmen for the Midwest and many advocates of public power, urged prompt Senate approval of the treaty. Opposition was expressed by railroad and shipping interests, Eastern port and Gulf of Mexico representatives, the private utility companies, and the coal-mining industry. The U. S. Senate, voting on March 14, 1934, failed to give the treaty the two-thirds majority approval necessary for ratification.

In March 1941, after World War II had created a great demand for electrical and shipbuilding facilities, a new U. S.-Canadian understanding was signed. It differed from that of 1932 in two important ways: (1) it included plans for the redevelopment of Niagara Falls, as well as the previous proposals for navigation and power development; and (2) it was designated an "agreement," making it subject to approval by a simple majority of each of the houses of the U. S. Congress. Japan's attack on Pearl Harbor caused Congress to defer action, and for several years thereafter the project's history was a succession of hearings and reports, setbacks and defeats.

Power Priority Plan. As one way of ending the impasse, New York and Ontario officials, early in 1948, proposed the separation of the power phase from the navigational, arguing that the state and province could then proceed at once with power development, leaving the two federal governments to carry out later the proposed navigation improvements. In December 1950, however, the U. S. Federal Power Commission (FPC) rejected New York's application for a power license and recommended that the federal governments proceed at once with the combined navigation-power projects. Again, the U. S. Congress took no action to approve the 1941 agreement.

In June 1952 the two federal governments submitted joint applications to the International Joint Commission (IJC) asking for the construction of the power works in the International Rapids section by Ontario Hydro and a United States entity. Three months later the FPC agreed to reconsider New York's application. The IJC speedily granted the requested permission, but 21 months elapsed before FPC and court hearings on New York's application were completed and Washington finally designated the New York Power Authority as the cooperating entity.

The long delay placed a serious strain on U. S.-Canadian relations but also gave Congress a final opportunity to obtain for the United States a share in the seaway. It seized this opportunity by passing the Wiley-Dondero Act, signed by President Dwight D. Eisenhower on May 13, 1954, creating the St. Lawrence Development Corporation and calling for Canadian-American cooperation in developing a 27-foot channel from Lake Erie to the Atlantic Ocean. After U. S. officials had given certain assurances regarding the construction and operation of the waterway, the Canadian government agreed to readmit the United States into a partnership arrangement. This ended the purely political phase of the project and at last cleared the way for the beginning of construction in late 1954.

WILLIAM R. WILLOUGHBY*
St. Lawrence University

SAINT-LÔ, saN-lō′, a town in Normandy and the capital of Manche department, is in northern France. It is on a rocky hill dominating the Vire River, about 48 miles (77 km) southeast of Cherbourg. Of Gallic origin, it was renamed in the 6th century for Laudus, or Lô, Bishop of Coutances. In the Middle Ages it was a weaving center, and it still manufactures textiles.

The 14th–16th century Church of Notre Dame was ruined in World War II, when the town, a German strong point, was almost totally destroyed by Allied forces in 1944. The medieval walls, uncovered by bombing, have been excavated. The architecture of the rebuilt town is quite original, combining traditional Norman and modern styles. The Memorial Hospital, built through Franco-American efforts, has a mosaic by Ferdinand Léger. Population: (1968) 18,615.

The St. Louis, Mo., riverfront is dominated by the stainless steel Gateway Arch designed by Eero Saarinen.

SAINT LOUIS, lо̄о'əs, a city in eastern Missouri, is the most populous municipality in the state and in the Mississippi River valley. Surrounded by, but independent of, St. Louis county, the city is situated on the west bank of the Mississippi River, just south of its confluence with the Missouri. It is a major manufacturing, transportation, commercial, educational, and cultural center.

St. Louis' eastern border, dotted with low bluffs, follows a crescent bend in the Mississippi for 19 miles (31 km). Tall office buildings, as well as an occasional high-rise apartment dwelling, mark the skylines of both the downtown area along the river and Clayton, a suburb immediately west of the city limits. St. Louis has developed a diversity of economic activity, which has provided stability in periods of economic decline. But the city's economic position has lagged behind newer metropolitan areas since World War II.

Metropolitan Area and Population. St. Louis is the core city of a standard metropolitan statistical area that covers over 4,000 square miles (10,000 sq km). This area, as defined for census purposes, comprises the city of St. Louis; the four Missouri counties of St. Charles, Jefferson, Franklin, and St. Louis; and the two Illinois counties of Madison and St. Clair. The Illinois and Missouri sections are linked by eight bridges spanning the Mississippi River. The oldest is Eads Bridge, which was opened in 1874, and the others are MacArthur, Chain of Rocks, McKinley, Jefferson Barracks, Clark, Veterans Memorial, and Poplar Street bridges, all of which are of steel construction.

The population of the city of St. Louis declined 27.2% between 1970 and 1980, reflecting the flight to the suburbs that was a feature common to metropolitan areas throughout the country during this period. While it was taking place, the population of the St. Louis urbanized area and that of the entire metropolitan area decreased by about 2% each.

Since the 1960's political boundaries have increasingly divided the area on the bases of race and social and economic status. Residents of St. Louis county have a higher average income and educational level than do residents of the city. Most of the blighted and slum areas are found near the central and older part of the city, while a substantial portion of new housing has been constructed in the suburban areas. The rapid increase in school enrollments in the county in comparison with the city indicates where a larger proportion of younger families are establishing homes.

University City, a suburb adjoining the western boundaries of the city of St. Louis, represents a notably integrated community. But most of the black population is concentrated within the city limits of St. Louis, especially in the northern and central sections. According to the 1980 census, blacks constitute about 45% (206,386) of the city's population.

The City Plan Commission has estimated that

INFORMATION HIGHLIGHTS

Population: *City,* 453,085; *metropolitan area,* 2,356,460.
Area: 61 square miles (158 sq km).
Elevation: Mean altitude of 465 feet (142 meters), with elevations varying from 400 to 500 feet (120–150 meters) above sea level.
Climate: Humid continental, with four distinct seasons—spring and autumn are moderate, winter is relatively cold, summer is hot; average annual temperature is 54°F (12°C); annual precipitation averages 37 inches (940 mm).
Government: Mayor and 28-member board of aldermen, all elected for 4-year terms.

29% of the city's housing stock is in poor condition, 40% in fair condition despite some code violations, and 31% in good condition. The "better" housing tends to be concentrated in south St. Louis, with an enclave of very spacious homes on broad, tree-lined private streets in the west end.

Economy. Manufacturing, which is well diversified, occupies the largest sector of the local economy. The major industry is the production of transportation equipment, including several assembly plants of major automobile manufacturers and the manufacture of jet aircraft and space capsules. Other important industries include food processing and the manufacturing of primary metals, fabricated metal products, non-electrical machinery, and chemicals. The St. Louis industrial area is the only one in the United States producing six basic metals—iron, lead, zinc, copper, aluminum, and magnesium. A number of major firms have their national headquarters in the city.

St. Louis has long been a leading wholesale trade center, and, although it has suffered in recent years from competition with Dallas and Fort Worth, the wholesale industry is still one of the largest employers of labor in the metropolitan area. Wholesale activities employing the greatest numbers of persons are machinery; groceries and related products; motor vehicles and automotive equipment; electrical goods; and dry goods and apparel. St. Louis is also the leading hog market in the United States, a major processor of raw furs, and one of the nation's principal grain markets.

The city has long served as a retail shopping center for eastern Missouri and southern Illinois. Before World War II, retail sales were concentrated in the core area of St. Louis, where three large department stores were located. Increased demand for passenger car parking space and the growth of the suburban population have led all the large retailers to establish branch stores in outlying shopping centers. The four types of retailing in order of employment are general merchandise stores, eating and drinking places, food stores, and apparel and accessory stores.

An important financial center, St. Louis is the home of the Federal Reserve Bank for the Eighth District.

To support industrial needs, St. Louis has an unlimited supply of high quality water from the Mississippi, Missouri, and Meramec rivers and from wells throughout the area. Water for the city is supplied by a city-owned system, while country areas are supplied by a privately owned utility company. Fuel from Texas, Louisiana, and Oklahoma is supplied by natural gas and pipeline companies. Extensive refining facilities are located on the east side of the Mississippi at Wood River and East St. Louis. The coalfields of southern Illinois supply an abundance of coal for heavy industries in the St. Louis area. Electric power is supplied by a privately owned company.

Transportation. As an interior transportation center, St. Louis ranks second only to Chicago. The area is served by numerous railroad trunk lines, several short lines, and switching railroads. All principal railroads use Union Station and the switching tracks owned and operated by the St. Louis Terminal Railroad Association.

Major U. S. highways carry passenger traffic and motor freight in and out of the St. Louis area. Overnight freight deliveries are made within a wide radius of St. Louis. Regular service to and from St. Louis is provided by motor-freight companies and bus lines.

St. Louis is the country's busiest inland port. Located on the Mississippi River Waterway, which comprises over 13,000 navigable miles (21,000 km), St. Louis industries can take advantage of low barge rates for moving heavy nonperishable products. Service to New Orleans is available the year round, and service to Minneapolis and St. Paul is available eight months of the year. The Chain of Rocks Canal, constructed and operated by the Missouri-Illinois Bi-State Authority, has improved river traffic by bypassing a long curving stretch of the Mississippi.

The city of St. Louis owns and operates a large commercial airport (Lambert-St. Louis International Airport) with a modern terminal building, considered one of the showplaces of the area. The airport accommodates the largest of modern jetliners. In addition, a number of small fields are available for private planes. Proposals for a regional airport have generated controversy over its location, with political leaders in the city usually preferring a nearby site in Illinois and county political leaders generally preferring a Missouri site.

Education and Cultural Life. St. Louis has long been recognized as a leading educational and cultural center of the Midwest. Its public schools are given high ratings by the state department of education and by private accrediting agencies. Many parochial schools and privately supported schools are available in both the city and the county. The St. Louis city-St. Louis county junior college district is a leader in the nation's junior college movement.

Higher Education. Among the institutions of higher education are Washington University, St. Louis University, Webster College, and Harris Teachers College. The University of Missouri maintains a growing campus in the city. Southern Illinois University has a campus at nearby Edwardsville.

Concordia Theological Seminary and Eden Theological Seminary (at Webster Groves) are major institutions training young persons for the clergy. There are several Roman Catholic colleges for women, including Fontbonne College, Maryville College of the Sacred Heart, and Notre Dame College, which are affiliated with St. Louis University. There are also schools of nursing and a distinguished school of pharmacy.

Communications Media. Two outstanding daily newspapers are published in St. Louis. The *Globe-Democrat* has been published under its present name since 1875. The *Post-Dispatch*, which exercises national influence, has been operated by members of the Pulitzer family since 1878. The area is served by 19 radio stations and 5 television stations.

Libraries and Museums. Both the city and county of St. Louis maintain public, tax-supported libraries, with central library facilities as well as branches and mobile units. The St. Louis Mercantile Library Association, which administers a subscription library of some 200,000 volumes, was founded in 1846 and is one of the oldest of its kind west of the Mississippi River. The St. Louis University Library has a collection of documents on microfilm from the Vatican Library in Rome.

Specialized libraries in the area include a law library maintained by the Law Library Asso-

The Climatron, a geodesic dome in the Missouri Botanical Garden, has plant life of seven different climates.

ciation and libraries maintained by the Missouri Botanical Garden, Missouri Historical Society, and the Jefferson Memorial in Forest Park.

The Jefferson Memorial Museum preserves numerous Jefferson manuscripts and houses a museum of Missouriana. It also has a collection of trophies received by Charles A. Lindbergh after his flight to Paris in the *Spirit of St. Louis* in 1927, a flight sponsored by St. Louis businessmen.

The City Art Museum, situated at the crown of Art Hill in Forest Park, has a large collection of masterpieces of painting, drawing, sculpture, and the applied arts, and outstanding collections brought to St. Louis for special exhibits. One of the most widely used symbols of the city is the equestrian statue of Louis IX (St. Louis) of France in front of the museum.

Old locomotives, streetcars, buses, trucks, and horsedrawn equipment are displayed in the Museum of Transport. Exhibits of science and nature and a dinosaur display may be viewed in the Museum of Science and Natural History.

Recreation and Entertainment. The city of St. Louis maintains many public parks, swimming pools, playgrounds, softball and baseball fields, tennis courts, golf courses, a skating rink, and lakes stocked for fishing. St. Louis county and its municipalities also operate extensive park and playground facilities. Forest Park, a 1,400-acre (567-hectare) park maintained by the city, is one of the major attractions of the metropolitan area. It includes the art museum, the Jefferson Memorial, the municipal theater, the Jewel Box (used for seasonal flower displays), the zoological gardens, the planetarium, and the Steinberg Skating Rink.

The Missouri Botanical (Shaw's) Garden, an outstanding showplace, was founded by Henry Shaw, a St. Louis philanthropist, in 1858 and opened to the public in 1860. It comprises a city garden of 75 acres (30 hectares), a 1,600-acre

(650-hectare) arboretum at nearby Gray Summit, and a tropical extension in Balboa, Panama. The garden's more than 11,000 species constitute the largest collection of plant life in the Western Hemisphere. A major attraction of Shaw's Garden is the Climatron, a geodesic dome covered with a plastic skin, which displays plant life common to seven different climates.

Music and Theater. Musical organizations include the fine St. Louis Symphony Orchestra. It performs in Powell Symphony Hall, a magnificent renovated motion-picture theater in midtown St. Louis. The city also has an opera company, a little symphony, and numerous chamber music societies.

During the summer months, the St. Louis Municipal Theatre (Muny Opera) presents light opera and musical comedies in Forest Park, in the largest outdoor theater (12,000 seats) in the United States. Also during the summer, the Mississippi River Festival, under the auspices of the St. Louis Symphony and Southern Illinois University at Edwardsville, provides concerts of classical and popular music in Edwardsville.

A commercially operated theater presents plays that have had successful runs on Broadway in New York City. Repertory theater is available at the Loretto-Hilton Center of Webster College.

A showboat, tied up at the levee near Eads Bridge, presents old-fashioned melodrama, and the *Admiral*, a vessel equipped with dining and dancing facilities, makes regular excursions on the Mississippi River.

Sports. St. Louis is the home of the Cardinals of the National Baseball League, the Cardinals of the National Football League, and the Blues of the National Hockey League. The architecturally impressive Busch Memorial Stadium, situated near the riverfront, has a seating capacity of 50,000 and is the site of professional baseball and football games. It also houses the St. Louis Sports Hall of Fame.

The St. Louis Planetarium, in Forest Park, was designed by the St. Louis architect Gyo Obata.

The city's universities sponsor basketball teams, and amateur baseball and soccer leagues play regular schedules in local parks. Elaborate bowling establishments are available, and some of the leading national professional bowlers make their headquarters in St. Louis. Professional prizefights and wrestling shows are available.

Social Season. The social season in St. Louis is ushered in by the Veiled Prophet Ball and Parade. In an elaborate ceremony the Veiled Prophet, a mysterious monarch who presides over his mystical kingdom of Khorassan, crowns a "queen of love and beauty" to preside over the social season. The Veiled Prophet (whose identity has not been revealed since his first visit to the city in 1878) and his queen and maids of honor lead a parade of highly decorated floats designed by a leading St. Louis artist.

Buildings and Other Places of Interest. Many public buildings, such as City Hall, the Public Library, Kiel Municipal Auditorium, the U.S. Customs and Courthouse, the Civil Courts Building, the Municipal Courts Building, and Soldiers Memorial are grouped around Memorial Plaza, which is situated just west of the downtown business district. The Old Courthouse, located near the riverfront, was the site of the first trial of the Dred Scott case in 1846.

The widely admired Spanish pavilion, built for the New York World's Fair of 1964–1965, was reerected on a site in the vicinity of the sports stadium in downtown St. Louis and formally dedicated in 1969. But efforts to maintain it as a focus of tourist interest (with restaurants, a theater, and exhibition hall) have not proved financially successful. A replica of Columbus' flagship the *Santa Maria,* moored at the St. Louis riverfront, is open to the public.

The 10-story Wainwright Building, designed by Louis Sullivan and completed in 1891, had a vital influence on all skyscraper architecture. The terminal building at Lambert-St. Louis International Airport, the Climatron in Shaw's Garden, and the Planetarium in Forest Park have all won national architectural awards.

Among the historic churches of St. Louis are the Episcopal Christ Church Cathedral, built between 1859 and 1867, and the Roman Catholic Church of St. Louis of France, erected in 1831–1834 and until 1914 the cathedral of the St. Louis archdiocese. The Cathedral of St. Louis, begun in 1907 and dedicated in 1914, is an imposing, ornately decorated structure of Byzantine design.

Two residences, rich in historical associations, are maintained as museums: the Eugene Field House, where the journalist and poet was born in 1850, and the Robert Campbell House, the antebellum home of one of the city's pioneer families. Aloe Plaza, opposite Union Station, includes a pool and fountain noted for their 14 cast bronze figures sculpted by Carl Milles. The sculpture, called *The Meeting of the Waters,* symbolizes the meeting of the Mississippi and Missouri rivers.

In 1941, a 37-block area on the riverfront was cleared for the establishment of a memorial to Thomas Jefferson and the Louisiana Purchase, but its construction was delayed for 20 years. Known as the Jefferson National Expansion Memorial, the site is under the jurisdiction of the National Park Service. The distinguishing feature of the memorial is Gateway Arch, a huge, 630-foot-high stainless steel arch. Designed by Eero Saarinen to symbolize the gateway to the West, it dominates the downtown riverfront. Visitors are carried to its observation deck in passenger gondolas attached to each leg of the arch.

Government. Besides the government of the city of St. Louis, some 150 governmental units exercise political authority in the St. Louis city-county area. These are over 90 municipalities, plus numerous school districts and fire protection districts, and a public water district. The metropolitan sewer district serves an area including all of the city and most of the county, and the Bi-State Authority includes areas in both Missouri and Illinois.

Health Facilities. The metropolitan area has a large number of public and private hospitals.

The Washington University Medical School is part of one of the outstanding medical centers in the United States. Efforts of the Alliance for Regional Community Health, Inc. (ARCH) to reduce the rate of hospital bed expansion in the county—since such expansion is construed as placing a disproportionate burden for servicing low-income patients on city-based hospitals—have provoked controversy and resistance.

City Government. St. Louis was first incorporated as a town on Nov. 9, 1809. It was given the status of a city under a special legislative charter in 1823. The city was part of St. Louis county until 1876, when it was separated from the county under provisions of the 1875 state constitution. The separation was accomplished by a local election, when both a plan of separation and a home-rule charter for the city were approved. The city's boundaries were extended to increase its size from 18 to 61 square miles (47–158 sq km), and the city assumed the responsibilities of both a municipality and a county within its boundaries. The manner in which this separation occurred has made it legally impossible for the city to extend its boundaries as its population spilled over its 1876 territorial limits.

The governmental structure of St. Louis is provided by its home-rule charter, approved in 1914. The city government is a mayor-council form. The mayor and the board of aldermen are elected for four-year terms. One alderman is elected from each of the city's 28 wards, and a president of the board is elected at large. Except for the city comptroller, who is popularly elected, major administrative officers are appointed by the mayor.

The service functions of the city are administered by directors of streets, public welfare, parks, recreation and forestry, health and hospitals, public safety, and public utilities. These directors, in addition to a president, constitute the board of public service. A comprehensive merit system, administered by a three-man civil service commission and a director, covers all regular administrative officers of the city.

Since the city is required to perform county functions within its borders, a complete set of county officers is elected and supported by city taxes. These officers, including the recorder of deeds, sheriff, coroner, treasurer, public administrator, license collector, and collector of revenue, operate under state statutes and cannot be integrated into the regular city governmental machinery. Since they operate outside the merit system, they furnish substantial job patronage to the party in power. The police department is administered by a board of police commissioners composed of four members appointed by the governor, with the mayor serving as an ex-officio member. Twice in 10 years (1950 and 1957) proposed new city charters were drafted by boards of freeholders but were defeated at the polls.

County Government. Prior to 1950, St. Louis county was governed, like all rural counties of Missouri, by a county court composed of 3 elected judges and 12 popularly elected administrative officers. In 1950, the county voted to take advantage of the county home-rule privileges granted in the 1945 state constitution. The new home-rule charter provided for a seven-member council to exercise legislative power and a popularly elected county supervisor to be the chief executive. Although the supervisor has extensive executive power, including preparation of the annual budget, his authority is restricted by the fact that the highway engineer, recorder of deeds, sheriff, coroner, and prosecuting attorney are directly elected and therefore not responsible to him.

Merger Efforts. Numerous efforts have been made to integrate the government of St. Louis city and county and to reduce the number of local governments in the area, but each attempt has suffered defeat at the polls. A plan to merge the county and its local governments with the city was presented to the voters in 1926, and although it was given a favorable vote in the city, it failed to pass in the county. In 1930, an attempt to coordinate the government of the city and county in a federated plan by means of a state constitutional amendment was defeated.

In 1956–1957, the Metropolitan St. Louis Survey, directed by members of the faculties of Washington and St. Louis universities, conducted a comprehensive survey of governmental relations in St. Louis city and county. Following the issuance of its report, a board of freeholders was selected to prepare a plan of governmental cooperation for submission to the voters. At an election held in 1959, the plan was defeated in both the city and the county.

History. French and Spanish Period. St. Louis was founded in 1764 by Pierre Laclède, a merchant from New Orleans, whose trading company had been granted exclusive rights to the Indian trade of the region by the French director general of Louisiana. Accompanied by his 14-year-

The Rest House in Forest Park, St. Louis. The 1,400-acre (566-hectare) park is one of many in the city.

AMERICAN AIRLINES

old stepson, Auguste Chouteau, Laclède outfitted and led an expedition up the Mississippi River to find a site for a trading post for his company.

He explored northward along the Mississippi and chose for settlement a site on the west bank of the river, below its confluence with the Missouri. A party of 30 men and boys landed there on Feb. 14, 1764, and on the following day they began to erect buildings for a permanent settlement. It was named in honor of King Louis XV of France and his patron saint, Louis IX. The nickname "Mound City" perpetuates the memory of the Indian mounds found in the vicinity of the settlement.

Fort Chartres, a French outpost on the Illinois side of the river, passed to British control in 1765 in pursuance of treaty agreements concluded in 1763 transferring French territory east of the Mississippi to Britain. Many French and French Canadians in the Illinois country then moved across the river to Laclède's village. By 1772, St. Louis had a population of 399 whites and 198 slaves.

In 1770 a Spanish lieutenant governor arrived at St. Louis to carry out the secret terms of the Treaty of Fontainebleau (1762–1763), by which France ceded all of Louisiana west of the Mississippi to Spain. Under Spanish rule St. Louis became the seat of government for Upper Louisiana. In 1780, during the American Revolution, residents of St. Louis successfully repelled a British-inspired attack by Indians and French Canadians on their garrison.

Early American Period. Although France regained legal possession of the Louisiana Territory by the Treaty of San Ildefonso of 1800, the United States, prior to the actual resumption of French control, acquired the region as part of the Louisiana Purchase in 1803. The formal transfer of Upper Louisiana to the United States took place on March 9, 1804. Thereafter, St. Louis was the seat of government for the district of Louisiana, and, from 1812 to 1821, was the capital of the territory of Missouri. While the population of St. Louis (1,039 in 1800) was chiefly French prior to its incorporation within the territory of the United States, American migrants from Virginia, Kentucky, and Tennessee subsequently moved into the area. By 1821, the population had reached 5,600.

During the first four decades of the 19th century, St. Louis served as the center of the trans-Mississippi fur trade. Large firms, such as the Missouri Fur Company, originated by Manuel Lisa in 1808, and the American Fur Company, founded by John Jacob Astor in 1827, were established to organize, finance, and outfit the expeditions. After 1840, however, the fur trade rapidly lost its dominance in the city's economy.

The development of the steamboat and the railroad locomotive played important roles in the commercial growth of St. Louis. The *Zebulon M. Pike,* the first paddle-wheeler to reach St. Louis, docked at its port in 1817. From 1830 to 1860 the steamboat was the main carrier of freight and passengers on both the Mississippi and Missouri rivers. During this period, St. Louis suffered a temporary setback when a fire, which began at the waterfront on May 4, 1849, devastated a large part of the city and was followed by a catastrophic cholera epidemic.

Steamboat activity reached its crest at St. Louis in the 1850's, the arrivals numbering over 5,000 in 1859. But railroads soon displaced the steamboats in the city's economic life. On July 4, 1851, the Pacific Railroad Company began to build west from St. Louis, and the expansion of railroad mileage in the east connected St. Louis with the Atlantic Coast by 1863. In 1872, the city received almost 3 million tons of freight by rail, compared with under 900,000 tons by river.

Large numbers of German and Irish immigrants arrived in St. Louis between 1830 and 1870. A wave of German immigrants entered the city after the failure of the revolutions of 1848 in Europe, and by 1850 one third of the population was German-born. By 1870, the population included over 65,000 German-born residents and 34,000 natives of Ireland.

During this period, the impress of German culture on St. Louis became strong and durable. Four daily newspapers including the *Westliche Post,* founded in 1857 by Carl Daenzer and later edited by Carl Schurz, were supported by the Germans. One of the first public kindergartens in the United States, reflecting German pedagogy, was established in St. Louis in 1873. Gymnastic societies (*turnvereins*) and singing societies (*gesangvereins*) also flourished.

Civil War and Later 19th Century. The abolitionist sentiment of the Germans in St. Louis was responsible, at least partially, for the city's support of the Union cause in the Civil War. Although interests were divided during the war (there were about 1,500 slaves in St. Louis in 1860, but they did not constitute an important factor in the local economy), no military engagements were fought within the city itself. The St. Louis Arsenal was under the command of Union officers, and on May 10, 1861, federal troops forced the surrender of Camp Jackson, a pro-Southern military training camp on the western outskirts of the city. Besides functioning as a military supply base, St. Louis served as a hospital center and as the headquarters of the Western Sanitary Commission, founded by Dr. William Greenleaf Eliot to care for the sick and wounded.

After the Civil War, industrial expansion was accompanied by the emergence of a notable cultural movement. The manufacture and processing of iron and steel, leather, food, clothing, and building materials developed into leading industries. Concurrently, St. Louis became the center of a philosophical movement inspired by Hegel. Initiated by Henry Conrad Brokmeyer, a Prussian immigrant, the movement was institutionalized in 1866 as the St. Louis Philosophical Society. The following year the society launched the *Journal of Speculative Philosophy,* which was edited until 1893 by the educator and philosopher William Torrey Harris.

Early 20th Century. The beginning of the 20th century brought both fame and notoriety to St. Louis. The Louisiana Purchase Exposition, held in the city in 1904, received worldwide acclaim. In 1910 the first international aviation meet in the United States was held at Kinloch Park, near the present site of the international airport.

But the decade was marred by widespread municipal corruption. Between 1900 and 1904, Joseph W. Folk, a young circuit attorney, proved that a street railway franchise had been obtained through bribery, exposed corruption in connection with garbage disposal and utility operations, and ultimately secured the conviction of nine members of the municipal assembly for bribery or perjury.

While St. Louis shared in the general prosperity following World War I, the Prohibition Amendment administered a severe blow to the city's brewing industries. In desperate efforts to remain in business, brewers turned to the production of malt, syrup, yeast, corn products, and vitamins.

During the Great Depression almost $70 million was expended in the city for direct relief between 1932 and 1937. The 1930's also saw the growth of industrial labor unions, an effective smoke-abatement ordinance (1939), and, with the repeal of Prohibition in 1933, the revival of the brewing industry.

Later 20th Century. Although the city's first public housing projects were completed in 1943, an aggressive campaign against urban blight was not launched until the 1950's. In 1955, voters approved two important bond issues: a $110 million bond issue, the largest in the city's history, for general improvements, including provisions for hospitals, expressways, parks, slum clearance, and a planetarium; and an accompanying $16 million bond issue authorizing public school improvements. Additional bond issues were approved in 1962 to continue the city's plan for improving physical facilities.

The Third Street Interregional Highway, a 2-mile (3-km) expressway, was opened to traffic in 1955, and in 1961 the Mark Twain Highway (Interstate 70) was opened from downtown St. Louis to St. Charles, 8 miles (13 km) west of the city limits. One of the principal bottlenecks at the city's approaches was eliminated in 1958 with the opening of a 4-lane expressway bridge, with a span of 4,028 feet (1,244 meters) across the Missouri River at St. Charles.

Seven public housing projects were completed by 1956. Further implementing the bold plans designed to replace the slums of the downtown and central district, the city's Land Clearance and Redevelopment Authority approved a project in 1957 for the industrial and residential redevelopment of the Mill Creek Valley, a 465-acre (188-hectare) depressed area.

In 1961 the city enacted a law barring religious or racial discrimination in places of public accommodation, and for the first time a black was appointed to a municipal cabinet post. The first black congressman from St. Louis was elected in 1968.

In the 1970's a spirit of misgiving and concern seemed to be the prevailing mood. Contributing to this feeling were population loss and the decline of the central city. St. Louis shared with other "inner cities" the severe problems of urban decay, poverty, and taxpayer resistance to the passage of proposals for bond issues and school taxes. Indeed, one study declared St. Louis to be "the most abandoned city" in the United States. However, by the 1980's there appeared to be a renaissance, notably in the rehabilitation of housing through grants to private developers and in capital improvements.

MERLE KLING
Washington University, St. Louis

Bibliography

Bollens, John C., ed., *Exploring the Metropolitan Community* (Univ. of Calif. Press 1961).
Coyle, Elinor M., *Saint Louis: Portrait of a River City* (Folkestone 1970).
Kirschten, Ernest, *Catfish and Crystal* (Doubleday 1965).
McDermott, John F., ed., *The Early Histories of St. Louis* (St. Louis Hist. Doc. Foundation 1952).
Witman, Arthur, *St. Louis* (Doubleday 1969).

SAINT-LOUIS, saN-lwĕ′, is a port city in Senegal. It is situated in the northwestern part of the country, largely on the small St.-Louis Island in the Senegal River, about 15 miles (25 km) from the Atlantic Ocean. The city is linked to the mainland by several bridges, and it is connected by rail with Dakar, about 160 miles (260 km) to the southeast.

In the past, St.-Louis' strategic location on one of Africa's great arterial waterways made it a major river port and seaport. But it has been handicapped in the 20th century by the competition of Dakar and by a sandbar that obstructs the river's mouth and prevents deeper-draft ships from reaching the port. Nevertheless, the city has remained a major trade center for the developing Senegal River valley. Its chief exports are peanuts and hides and skins.

History. St.-Louis, which was founded as a fort by French traders in 1659 and named for King Louis XIV, was the first permanent French settlement in West Africa. It was occupied by the British from 1757 to 1779 and again from 1809 to 1817. In the 19th century it became the principal French base for the conquest of the interior of West Africa. St.-Louis acquired full communal status in 1873.

The city served as the capital of French West Africa federation from 1895 until it was superseded by Dakar in 1902. From then until 1958, St.-Louis was the administrative center for the federation's territories of Senegal and Mauritania. Nouakchott then became the capital of Mauritania and Dakar of Senegal. Population: (1976) 88,000.

SAINT LOUIS PARK, lōō′əs, a city in eastern Minnesota, in Hennepin county, immediately west of Minneapolis. It is a residential suburb of the Twin Cities, Minneapolis and St. Paul, but it is also a commercial and industrial center, with warehouses and commercial office buildings. Industry includes printing and graphic arts, and the manufacture of plastic and rubber parts, precision machined parts, paint, cast aluminum cookware, peanut butter, window and door frame units, and canvas products.

St. Louis Park was settled in the 1850's, and by the 1860's schools had been opened and a local government was beginning to take form. It was incorporated as a village in 1886 and as a city in 1954. It has a council-manager form of government. Population: 42,931.

SAINT LOUIS UNIVERSITY, lōō′əs, a private, Roman Catholic, coeducational institution in St. Louis, Mo., owned and operated by the Society of Jesus. It was founded as St. Louis Academy in 1818 by Louis W. Du Bourg, bishop of Louisiana. The school was renamed St. Louis College in 1820 and came under Jesuit control in 1827. It granted its first baccalaureate in 1830 and adopted its present name in 1832. It offers bachelor's through doctor's degrees.

The university comprises the College of Arts and Sciences, the School of Business Administration, the School of Nursing and Allied Health Professions, the College of Philosophy and Letters, the School of Social Service, the School of Divinity, the School of Law, the School of Medicine, and the Graduate School. The Pius XII Memorial Library has a unique microfilm collection of documents from the Vatican Library. The total enrollment is about 10,000 students.

SAINT LUCIA, lū'shə, a Caribbean island, second largest of the Windward Islands of the Lesser Antilles. St. Lucia is an independent state, formerly associated with Britain. Situated about 200 miles (320 km) north of Trinidad, it is separated from St. Vincent to the southeast by the St. Vincent Passage, and from Martinique to the south by the St. Louis Channel.

The island is about 28 miles (45 km) long, with a maximum width of about 14 miles (22.5 km). Its area is about 238 square miles (616 sq km). It is mountainous and scenic. The highest peak, at 3,145 feet (959 meters), is Morne Gimie, but the most spectacular are Gros Piton and Petit Piton, two ancient forest-covered volcanic cones that rise abruptly from the sea near Soufrière on the west coast. Nearby are the hot sulfurous springs for which the town was named. Many short rivers intersect the mountains, and some flow into broad, fertile valleys.

The climate is tropical, tempered by northeast trade winds. The dry season occurs from January to April and the rainy season from May to August. Annual rainfall varies from 55 inches (1,400 mm) on the south coast to 140 inches (3,550 mm) in the interior. Temperatures average from about 70° F to 80° F (21°–27° C.).

The people of St. Lucia are mainly of African or mixed African and European descent. The official language is English, although there is also a local patois that owes much to early French domination of the island. The capital, chief population center, and best harbor is Castries, with some 45,000 inhabitants in the city and suburbs.

The economy is chiefly agricultural. Bananas replaced sugar as the main export crop in the late 1950's. Cocoa beans, coconut oil, and copra also are exported. Industries include rum making, fishing, and brick manufacturing. In the late 1970's a large oil-transshipment terminal was being built on St. Lucia. There are an adequate road system and two airfields.

In 1958, St. Lucia became a unit in the 10-member West Indies Federation, a virtually autonomous British dependency within the Commonwealth of Nations. In 1962 it joined an eight-member group in forming a new federation with similar ties. On March 1, 1967, the island became independently associated with Britain, acquiring full internal self-government, while Britain retained responsibility for foreign affairs and defense. The associated status ended on Feb. 22, 1979, when St. Lucia attained full independence. The British monarch continues to be head of state and to be represented by a governor general, who appoints the prime minister. Parliament consists of a Senate and House of Assembly, and there is a supreme court.

History. Neither the date of St. Lucia's discovery nor the identity of its discoverer has been established. England tried unsuccessfully to settle the island in 1605. A second English attempt, begun in 1638, also failed, due to fierce attacks by the native Carib Indians. French claims to the island were confirmed by treaty with the Caribs in 1660. St. Lucia subsequently changed hands several times before being captured by the British in 1803 and ceded to them by the Treaty of Paris in 1814. From 1838, it was part of Britain's Windward Islands administrative group. Population: (1970 est.) 115,000.

RICHARD E. WEBB°
Former Director, Reference and Library Division,
British Information Services, New York

SAINT-MALO, saɴ-mȧ-lō', a port in Brittany, is in northwestern France in Ille-et-Vilaine department, 47 miles (76 km) north of Rennes. It is at the mouth of the Rance River, with the old city perched on a small island connected to the mainland by a causeway called Le Sillon. Almost totally destroyed in World War II, the town was reconstructed and is one of Brittany's great tourist attractions and resort areas.

The town takes its name from Saint Malo, a Welsh monk, who arrived in the 6th century. It came under the bishops of Aleth, who helped build it into a great port by the 12th century. The magnificent ramparts that surround the town were begun in the 12th century, and the castle was added in the 14th and 15th centuries. The castle's great keep is used as a history museum. During the 16th century it was independent for four years, and in the next two centuries prospered as a commercial port and as a haven for privateers. Marine industries continue to be important to the economy. Among the famous natives of the town are the explorer Jacques Cartier and the writer François-René de Chateaubriand. Population: (1975) 45,030.

SAINT MARC, saɴ mark, a town on the west coast of Haiti, in L'Artibonite department, is on St. Marc's Bay in the Gulf of Gônave, 44 miles (71 km) northwest of Port-au-Prince. It is a shipping center for the fertile valley that encloses it. The chief exports are coffee and logwood. Near the town is Crête à Pierrot, a headland which was strongly fortified by English engineers and occupied by Haitian soldiers during the war of independence. Population: (1971 est.) 15,988.

SAINT MARK'S BASILICA. See BYZANTINE ART AND ARCHITECTURE; SAN MARCO; VENICE.

SAINT MARTIN is one of the Leeward Islands in the Caribbean Sea. It lies 155 miles (250 km) east of Puerto Rico. The northern 20 square miles (52 sq km) is French and is called Saint-Martin. Its capital is Marigot and it is administered as part of the Overseas Department of Guadeloupe. The remaining 15 square miles (40 sq km), called Sint Maarten, is Dutch. Its capital, Philipsburg, is the seat of the territorial government of an administrative district that is part of the Netherlands Antilles.

The island is hilly and is populated mainly by English-speaking blacks. It was settled by the French and the Dutch in the 1640's. The early cane sugar and sea salt industries died out by the early 20th century, when many of the inhabitants abandoned St. Martin to work on more prosperous islands. An economic revival, based on tourism, rum distilling, and commercial fishing began in the 1950's. Population: French part (1974) 6,191; Dutch part (1974) 10,310.

SAINT MARYS was the first settlement in the state of Maryland. In 1634, Gov. Leonard Calvert sailed up the Potomac River to Saint Marys River, bought land from the Indians, and established a settlement near the mouth of the river. A Jesuit mission was established, but liberty of worship prevailed. Though Saint Marys was the capital of Maryland and for a number of years the only town in the province, it remained no more than a small settlement. In 1694, the capital was moved to Annapolis.

SAINT MARYS RIVER, in North America, is part of the boundary between Michigan, in the United States, and Ontario, in Canada. The river issues from Lake Superior and flows into Lake Huron. It is about 63 miles (100 km) long. At the Lake Huron end, it is divided by two large islands into two channels.

The river falls about 20 feet (6 meters) between Lake Superior and Lake Huron. As a part of the waterway of the Great Lakes, it carries an immense volume of shipping, principally iron ore and wheat vessels. Canals near Sault Ste. Marie, Mich., and Sault Ste. Marie, Ont., known as the Soo Canals, carry the traffic around the rapids. (See SAULT SAINTE MARIE CANALS.) Navigation of the river is closed by ice during the winter months.

SAINT MATTHEWS, a city in northern Kentucky, in Jefferson county, is just east of Louisville. It is principally a residential city, whose citizens work in Louisville, but there is some light industry. Lumber and paper are the chief products manufactured. St. Matthews was incorporated in 1950. It is governed by a mayor and council. Population: 13,354.

SAINT MICHAEL'S MOUNT is a small island off the southwest coast of England, in Mount's Bay, 3 miles (5 km) east of Penzance, Cornwall. The island is about 1 mile (1.6 km) in circumference and rises, pyramid-shaped, to about 270 feet (82 meters). It can be reached by causeway at low tide only. The town of Marazion is half a mile (0.8 km) to the north.

Edward the Confessor founded a monastery on the mount in the early 11th century and put it under the direction of the Benedictine abbey of Mont-Saint-Michel in Normandy. Under Henry VIII, the island passed to secular control. Crowning the mount is an ancient castle of the St. Aubyn family, which incorporates parts of the former monastery. The castle has a tower topped by a stone cupola, or lantern, known as "St. Michael's Chair"—an ancient lighthouse.

During the Middle Ages the mount was a popular place of pilgrimage and a fortress. It is now the property of the National Trust.

SAINT-MIHIEL, saN-mē-yel', is a town in northeastern France in Meuse department, on the Meuse River. The town, founded by the Gauls, was called Châtillon until the 8th century, when it adopted its present name from its Benedictine abbey. In the 16th century a brilliant artistic school developed under the sculptor Ligier Richier, earning St.-Mihiel the name of "the Florence of Lorraine." The many monuments in the town date mostly from the 17th and 18th centuries.

Its capture by the Germans in 1914 isolated the key fortress of Verdun and endangered the Paris Basin. Attacks on the St.-Mihiel Salient failed until September 1918. In the first major U. S. offensive in the war, troops under Gen. John J. Pershing drove the Germans from their bridgehead on the Meuse, removing a German threat and enhancing the reputation of the U. S. Army. Population: (1968) 5,262.

SAINT-MORITZ, sänt mô-rits', is a fashionable and popular ski and health resort in eastern Switzerland in Graubünden canton. The German form of its name is Sankt Moritz, and the Romansch form is San Murezzan.

The town is in the Upper Engadine Valley and consists of St. Moritz-Dorf (village) and St. Moritz-Bad (baths). The Dorf is at 6,080 feet (1,853 meters), and the springs, which were known to the Romans, are somewhat lower. There is a 12th century leaning tower and the remains of a druid stone system. The town's economy revolves around tourists, who are attracted by the many ski slopes, fine hotels, and the beautiful setting. Population: (1970) 5,699.

SAINT-NAZAIRE, saN-nȧ-zȧr', is a port city in France in Loire-Atlantique department. It is at the mouth of the Loire River, about 37 miles (60 km) northwest of Nantes. The well-equipped docks extend about three miles (5 km) and can accommodate the largest vessels. St.-Nazaire is also a major manufacturing and metallurgical center.

The town has an ancient granite dolmen and menhir. It is thought to have been the site of an old Gallo-Roman seaport named Corbilo. It developed commercially in the late 19th century. During World War II it was an important German military and submarine base, which was ultimately destroyed by Allied bombing. Population: (1968) 63,289.

SAINT-OMER, saN-tô-mâr', is a town in France in Pas-de-Calais department, 22 miles (35 km) southeast of Calais, on the Aa River. It is situated in an area of reclaimed marshlands where polders are intensively cultivated in market gardens. It is a shipping center for fruits and vegetables, and its products include cement, bricks, sugar, and hosiery.

St.-Omer had its origin in a village that grew up around the monastery of St. Berlin, founded by Saint Omer in the 7th century. The old cathedral, the basilica of Notre Dame, built in the 13th–15th centuries, has a fine south portal. The 17th century courthouse was designed by François Mansart. Located in the borderlands between Flanders (modern Belgium) and France, St.-Omer became permanently a part of France in 1677, when Louis XIV captured it. During part of World War I it was headquarters for the British Army. Population: (1968) 18,205.

SAINT PATRICK'S CATHEDRAL is a Roman Catholic cathedral in New York City. It is on the east side of Fifth Avenue, opposite Rockefeller Center. It is a Gothic Revival structure designed by James Renwick. The building is shaped like a Latin cross, with the vestibule and nave constituting the long arm. Where the nave and transepts cross each other, the clergy choir, the sanctuary, and the high altar begin. Beyond the altar is a polygonal apse and the Lady Chapel.

St. Patrick's Cathedral was built mainly of granite, but wood and plaster were used in the vault to obviate the need for flying buttresses. The exterior length of the building is 332 feet (101 meters), and the exterior breadth is 174 feet (53 meters). The height to the top of the spire is 330 feet (100 meters). The seating capacity is about 3,000. At the time of its consecration in 1910, it was the eleventh-largest church in the world. Today it is surrounded by skyscrapers, which tend to dwarf it.

In 1850, Archbishop John Hughes proposed building the cathedral as a replacement for the older St. Patrick's Cathedral (still standing) on Mott Street, in downtown Manhattan. The cornerstone was laid in 1858, and the new cathedral was dedicated in 1879. The spires were added in 1887, and the Lady Chapel was constructed by Charles T. Matthews in 1901–1906.

SAINT PAUL, the capital of Minnesota and the seat of Ramsey county, is on the Mississippi River, at the mouth of the Minnesota River, just below the head of navigation on the Mississippi. The city is built on bluffs along the north bank of a large northeastward bend in the Mississippi and on the opposite bank where the river curves southward again.

St. Paul adjoins Minneapolis to the west and northwest. The two municipalities are together known as the Twin Cities. The Twin Cities are the center of a metropolitan area that covers five entire counties—Anoka, Dakota, Hennepin, Ramsey, and Washington.

St. Paul was once a city with narrow winding streets that made it look more like an older city in the northeastern states than one that had developed from a midwestern pioneer town. Now it is a modern city with streets in a gridiron system—except where natural hills and the bends in the Mississippi prevent it—and streamlined office buildings. The city has a 200-acre (81-hectare) area of office buildings surrounding the state capitol and a large shopping district, both

St. Patrick's Cathedral, on New York City's Fifth Avenue, was designed in the Gothic Revival style.

LOUIS GOLDMAN, FROM RAPHO-GUILLUMETTE

of which were built up during the 1960's and 1970's.

Economy. St. Paul became a steamboat terminus on the Mississippi in the 1820's, and is still an important shipping center. St. Paul and its metropolitan area serve a regional market that includes eight states and two Canadian provinces. Besides air and rail facilities for shipping, St. Paul is the terminus of many barge lines and is one of the largest motor freight centers in the United States.

St. Paul is a major industrial center. Among the great number of products manufactured are computers, guidance systems, textiles and apparel, household appliances, and paper. The city is also a center for automobile assembly, merchandising firms, graphic arts, and printing and publishing. There are stockyards, food processing plants, and breweries, and the lumber and plastics industries are important.

Education, Culture, and Recreation. There are a number of institutions of higher learning in St. Paul. These include the College of St. Catherine and the College of St. Thomas (Roman Catholic), Concordia College (Lutheran), Hamline University (Methodist), Macalester College (Presbyterian), and Bethel College and Seminary (Baptist). The St. Paul (Roman Catholic) Seminary and the College of Agriculture of the University of Minnesota are also in the city.

Museums in the city include the St. Paul Arts and Science Center, which in addition to exhibits houses a repertory theater; the Minnesota Museum of Art; the Science Museum, which contains a natural history museum and exhibits in other scientific fields; the Musical Instrument Museum, including exhibits and a library for the use of music students; and the Arts and Science Center in the state capitol complex. The Minnesota Historical Society and the Ramsey County Historical Society also maintain museums, as does the Catholic Historical Society of St. Paul. Macalester College and Hamline University maintain their own art galleries.

The Gibbs Farm Museum has agricultural implements in use between 1850 and 1930. Its displays recreate farm life in Minnesota.

St. Paul has a chamber orchestra and two opera companies—the St. Paul Opera Association, which presents an ambitious repertory of both standard and unusual works, including world premieres, and the St. Paul Civic Opera, which offers light operas and operettas. The Minnesota Theatre Company performs regularly at its home in the Livingstone Theatre. During the summer the University of Minnesota Players offer old plays aboard a showboat on the Mississippi.

Recreation. Each January, St. Paul holds a 10-day Winter Carnival, which features a wide variety of winter sports events, including ski jumping, dogsled and skimobile racing, ice yachting, tobogganing, and speed skating. The Minnesota State Fair is held in St. Paul. The annual event runs for 10 days, ending with Labor Day, and attracts participants and spectators from all parts of the state and beyond.

The Twin Cities area has a number of professional sports teams that play in nearby Bloomington. These include the Minnesota Twins baseball team, the Minnesota North Stars of the National Hockey League, and the Minnesota Vikings of the National Football League. The University of Minnesota's football team also plays there. St. Paul itself provides facilities for

The Minnesota state capitol building in St. Paul was designed by Cass Gilbert and overlooks the city.

skiing. Its highest ski slide is in Battle Creek Park.

Places of Interest. The state capitol was constructed of more than 20 varieties of marble, limestone, sandstone, and granite. It is surmounted by a dome of white Georgia marble. Buildings housing government agencies surround the capitol, making up the capitol complex.

The City Hall and Courthouse is an unusual contemporary building. Its entrance concourse is of marble, and each of its 18 stories is finished in a different variety of wood from a different country. In the council chamber are paintings of St. Paul's pioneer days and of its later life. On the concourse is a 36-foot (11-meter) onyx statue, *The Indian God of Peace.* The god is represented standing with a group of Indians smoking peace pipes crouched at his feet. The statue, which was designed by the Swedish sculptor Carl Milles, is mounted on a base which slowly oscillates to reveal details.

The Cathedral of St. Paul, which was designed by E. L. Masqueray and built in 1906–1915, is generally modeled on St. Peter's Basilica in Rome. It has a monumental arch at the entrance, a central rose window, and a huge dome. The nave is flanked by two large chapels, and there are six smaller chapels beyond the sanctuary.

The city has a large number of parks, the most interesting of which are Indian Mounds Park and Como Park. The former, on a bluff overlooking the Mississippi, is believed to be the burial place of Sioux Indian chieftains. Como Park is the site of a large zoo and of a conservatory that has extensive floral displays and tropical plants.

History. In the winter of 1766–1767 a New Englander named Jonathan Carver ascended the Mississippi and Minnesota rivers in search of a northwest passage to the Pacific Ocean, and stopped at the site of St. Paul to investigate an Indian burial ground. In 1803 the Louisiana Purchase brought the lands west of the Mississippi within the domain of the United States. The U. S. government soon sent out expeditions to explore the new lands and bring them under U. S. authority. Lt. Zebulon M. Pike set out from St. Louis in 1805 and bought acreage from the Indians around the confluence of the Minnesota and Mississippi rivers. The land was intended as a site for a military base, but squatters soon settled on the land. In 1819, Col. Henry Leavenworth established an army post on the Minnesota River on the site of Mendota (now a suburb just south of St. Paul), but the following year, the post was moved across the river, where Col. Josiah Snelling built Fort St. Anthony, later renamed Fort Snelling.

Under the protection of the fort, an Indian agency and a fur trading post were established at Mendota, and Roman Catholic and Protestant missionaries came to minister to both the Indians and the community of white settlers that had grown up around the fort. In 1840, these settlers and all the others who were living on federal lands in the area were expelled. A French Canadian trader, Pierre "Pig's Eye" Parrant, led a group of the evicted squatters to a Mississippi river landing near Fort Snelling, where they built up a settlement called Pig's Eye. The following year, Father Lucian Galtier built a log chapel and dedicated it to St. Paul. The settlers later adopted the name of the patron saint for their community.

In 1846 a post office was opened in St. Paul. In 1847 the town was platted and a school was opened. Steamboats began regular service, bring-

131

LOUIS H. FROHMAN

A. F. KERSTING

St. Paul's Cathedral, Christopher Wren's masterpiece, is dominated by a great neoclassical dome. The imposing interior, inspired by the baroque, has an arched nave leading to the altar.

ing up the river settlers and goods for trade, and St. Paul became the headquarters for the American Fur Company, which had had a trading post at Mendota since 1821.

The Minnesota Territory was created in 1849, and St. Paul became its capital. In September of the same year, the first Territorial Legislature assembled here, and in November the settlement was incorporated as a town. St. Paul was chartered as a city in 1854. When Minnesota became a state in 1858, the city retained its status as capital. The legal limits of St. Paul were extended to the Minneapolis line in 1884.

Until about 1890, St. Paul's economy depended largely upon trade and transportation, but at the turn of the century, industry began to develop. In the 20th century the city took on importance as an educational and cultural center.

Government and Population. St. Paul has a commission form of government. Population: of the Minneapolis-St. Paul statistical metropolitan area, 2,114,256; of the city, 270,230.

SAINT PAUL ISLAND is situated near the middle of the southern Indian Ocean, about 2,800 miles (4,500 km) east of South Africa and 2,000 miles (3,200 km) north of Antarctica. Except for Amsterdam Island, 60 miles (97 km) to the north, the nearest island is 900 miles (1,450 km) away. St. Paul is a volcanic crater about 3 square miles (8 sq km) in area. It was discovered by Portuguese sailors in the 16th century and was briefly settled in the 18th century by fishermen from Réunion. It has been a part of the French Southern and Antarctic Territories since they were formed in 1955.

SAINT PAUL ISLAND is one of the Pribilof Islands in the Bering Sea. It is a U. S. possession. See PRIBILOF ISLANDS.

SAINT PAUL'S CATHEDRAL is a 17th century English church in London. Built by Sir Christopher Wren in a baroque-influenced style, the great domed structure on Ludgate Hill is one of the chief architectural glories of the city. St. Paul's, which replaces two earlier churches, is the first cathedral to be constructed for Anglican worship. It contains many tombs and monuments.

History. According to tradition, the site of St. Paul's was once occupied by a Roman temple. A Christian church was built there in the early 7th century by Bishop Mellitus and dedicated to St. Paul by the newly converted King Æthelbert of Kent. Destroyed by fire, it was replaced by a Norman cathedral built from the late 11th to the 13th century and given an Early English Gothic choir. The Norman church, later known as Old St. Paul's, was damaged by fire in the 16th century and given a classical facade by Inigo Jones in the early 17th century.

The Great Fire that swept London in 1666 destroyed much of Old St. Paul's. Wren was asked to design a new cathedral. Construction began in 1675 and was completed in 1710, an unusually short period, since cathedrals usually took centuries. Wren oversaw the entire process. The cathedral was repaired in 1915 and after World War II. In 1958 a chapel was dedicated to the memory of Americans based in Britain who died in the war.

Style. The design of St. Paul's was a compromise between austere Calvinist architecture and rich Catholic baroque, just as Anglicanism tried to avoid the extremes of the two denominations. It was also a compromise between Wren's preference for a centralized church on the plan of a Greek cross and the Anglican clergy's demand for a traditional, long Gothic church on the plan of a Latin cross. Thus St. Paul's has a

St. Peter's Basilica (*right*), the largest church in the world, is surmounted by a giant dome that was designed by Michelangelo. The nave (*above*) as seen from a point above the high altar.

long nave and choir but domed rather than ribbed vaulting and a huge dome in the center rather than at the east end. The west facade consists of two tiers of paired Corinthian columns, flanked by a pair of baroque towers.

Wren's special interest was in creating a dome that would dominate the London skyline, as the spire of Old St. Paul's had done, yet be pleasingly shallow when seen from within. He solved the problem by building three shells, one inside the other. The shallow inner dome of stone has a central eye lit by the windows of a lantern on top of the outer dome. The lantern is supported by a brick and stone cone hidden between the inner and outer domes. The outer dome of lead over timber rests on a high drum surrounded by a balustrade. Just below the interior dome is a whispering gallery. Although views of the church have been partly obstructed by 20th century high-rise buildings, the structure is still an architectural masterpiece.

SAINT PETER, a city in southern Minnesota, the seat of Nicollet county, is on the Minnesota River, 67 miles (108 km) southwest of Saint Paul. It is the center of a grain, livestock, and poultry farming area.

Gustavus Adolphus College, a coeducational Lutheran institution, is in the city. The Old State Capitol Building was erected in 1857 after it was proposed to move Minnesota's capital from Saint Paul when the territory entered the union the next year. The move failed.

Saint Peter was founded in 1853 and incorporated in 1865. It is governed by a mayor and council. Population: 9,056.

SAINT PETER PORT is the capital of Guernsey, the second-largest of the Channel Islands at the western end of the English Channel. It is on the east side of the island and has a deepwater port which is protected by a rocky islet on which stands the 12th-century Castle Cornet. The town of St. Peter Port is spread out on slopes overlooking the harbor, with steps connecting the different levels in places. Near the harbor is the 15th century Town Church. The house in which the French author Victor Hugo lived in 1855–1870 is a museum. Population: (1961) 15,804.

SAINT PETER'S BASILICA is the central church of Roman Catholicism. An Italian church in Vatican City, Rome, it is on a site that is believed to be the grave of St. Peter. Built in the 16th and 17th centuries to replace an earlier church, St. Peter's is a masterpiece of Renaissance and baroque style. It is also the largest church in the world. It is not a cathedral; the seat of the pope as bishop of Rome is St. John Lateran. However, St. Peter's has been used for most papal ceremonies since 1870.

Early History. The site of St. Peter's was once a Roman cemetery. An early pope built a chapel there to mark what is believed to be the grave of the Apostle Peter, martyred by Nero. About 320, Emperor Constantine began to construct a church, later known as Old St. Peter's, on the site. A T-shaped basilica, it was focused on the tomb of St. Peter, which lay at the crossing of the transepts, and was entered by an atrium at the eastern end of the five-aisled nave.

By the time of the return of the popes from Avignon in the 15th century, Old St. Peter's was in decay. Nicholas V began to rebuild the choir.

16th Century. Julius II decided that a whole new church was needed and put Bramante in charge. Bramante seems to have designed a church on the plan of a Greek cross, in a square, with a great central concrete dome, like that of

133

Bayfront Auditorium in St. Petersburg, Fla., faces Tampa Bay. It accommodates theatrical and sports activities.

the Pantheon, over St. Peter's tomb. The cornerstone of one of the piers supporting the dome was laid in 1506. After Bramante's death in 1514, Raphael took on the project. To suit those who wanted a long nave, which would cover the area of Old St. Peter's and provide for processions, he modified Bramante's design to make a Latin-cross plan. Meanwhile the nave of Old St. Peter's continued to be used. After the delay caused by the sack of Rome in 1527, Antonio da Sangallo the Younger made a huge wooden model of a Latin-cross church.

Michelangelo, who replaced Sangallo in 1547, returned to Bramante's Greek-cross plan and designed a new ribbed stone dome and a facade with huge paired pilasters. Much construction was completed by his death in 1564. Giacomo della Porta built the dome (1585–1590) in a more pointed version of Michelangelo's design. It is 435 feet (133 meters) high.

17th Century. When Paul V finally decided on a Latin-cross plan, Carlo Maderno added a long nave with side chapels, replacing the old nave in 1612 and giving the church a total length of 636 feet (194 meters). He also built the facade, a modification of Michelangelo's design, with colossal engaged columns and pilasters and a loggia (balcony) above the center door where the pope makes public appearances. The facade balances the transepts but blocks a view of the dome. The church was dedicated in 1626.

The vast baroque interior of St. Peter's holds 50,000 people. Bernini made the bronze baldacchino (1630) with twisted supports, which shelters the main altar, above the tomb of St. Peter. On the wall of the apse is his Chair of St. Peter (1656), a sculpture centered on a bronze throne containing the ancient ivory-covered wooden chair believed to have belonged to Peter. Bernini also executed the equestrian statue of Constantine and the tombs of Urban VIII and Alexander VII. Among other important sculptures are the medieval bronze statue of St. Peter, its right foot worn down by the kisses of the faithful, and Michelangelo's marble *Pietà*. The altars are adorned with mosaic copies of baroque paintings. Bernini also created the oval piazza (1656–1667) surrounded by colonnades, which forms a magnificent setting for St. Peter's.

SAINT PETERSBURG, a city on the west coast of central Florida, in Pinellas county, is situated at the south end of Pinellas Peninsula, which separates Tampa Bay from the Gulf of Mexico. The city is connected to Tampa and its environs by bridges across the bay, and to Bradenton and Sarasota by the twin-span 15-mile (25-km) Sunshine Skyway Bridge across lower Tampa Bay and a part of the Gulf of Mexico. St. Petersburg, which has a subtropical climate, is principally a resort and residential city. It has been called the "Sunshine City."

The city's industry includes electronics and engineering design and research, but the economy is chiefly based upon tourism. There are many beaches along St. Petersburg's 33 miles (53 km) of waterfront, and parks and recreational areas are found throughout the city. Major facilities include the Bayfront Auditorium, which can accommodate three events—theater, sports, or a meeting—at the same time, and the municipal pier building. The latter building is a 5-tiered inverted pyramid structure that was built in 1972 to replace the old Million Dollar Pier, which from 1926 to 1967 had been a landmark of the city. It is built at the end of a long pier which has fishing and swimming facilities, and contains restaurants and meeting halls.

The Festival of States, established in 1896, is held each March. This 10-day celebration features dances, banquets, concerts, art exhibits, sports events, and marching band competitions. It is climaxed by a parade.

St. Petersburg is the home of Florida Presbyterian College and St. Petersburg Junior College. The College of Law of Stetson University and a branch of the University of Southern Florida are also here. The principal museums are the Museum of Fine Arts, the Science Center of Pinellas County, the St. Petersburg Historical Museum, and the Art Club of St. Petersburg.

The area of St. Petersburg was settled in 1846. The city itself was founded by John C. Williams of Detroit, who purchased the land in 1876 and secured the building of its first railroad in 1888. It was incorporated in 1892, and has a council-manager form of government. Population of the Tampa–St. Petersburg metropolitan area, 1,569,134; of the city, 238,647.

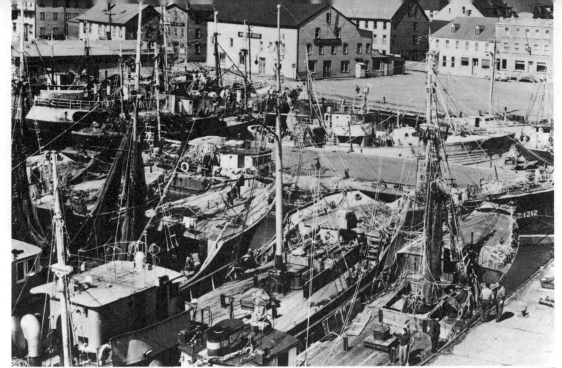

St. Pierre, capital of St. Pierre and Miquelon, and the fishing fleet that is the islands' economic mainstay.

SAINT PETERSBURG, Russian city renamed Leningrad in 1924. See LENINGRAD.

SAINT-PIERRE, Bernardin de. See BERNARDIN DE SAINT-PIERRE, JACQUES HENRI.

SAINT-PIERRE, saN-pyar′, a small port town on the island of Martinique in the French West Indies. It is on the northwest side of the island, on the Bay of St. Pierre in the Caribbean Sea, about 11 miles (18 km) northwest of Fort-de-France, the capital. Mont Pelée, a volcano more than 5,100 feet (1,555 meters) high is about 4 miles (6 km) north of the town.

St.-Pierre was founded in 1635, and grew into the leading port and commercial center in the French West Indies. Then, in February 1902, Mont Pelée, thought to have been extinct, began to give signs of activity. On May 8, it erupted, spewing a fiery cloud of gas and ash over the city, completely destroying it and killing all but two of the residents, who numbered about 30,-000. Although the site was resettled, St.-Pierre never regained its former importance. It is now visited by tourists, who come to see the ruins and the Musée Volcanologique. Population: (1962) 5,434.

SAINT PIERRE AND MIQUELON, saN pyâr′, mē-klôn′, an island group in southeastern Canada, just south of Newfoundland, that is about 10 miles (16 km) southwest of Newfoundland's Burin Peninsula. Miquelon is about 3 miles (5 km) northwest of St. Pierre and 15 miles (25 km) west of the peninsula.

Miquelon is actually two islands joined by a slender, 10-mile (16-km) long sandbar isthmus. Grande Miquelon is to the north, Langlade, or Petite Miquelon, is south of the isthmus. There are several islets off the northern and eastern coasts of St. Pierre and just northeast of Miquelon. The islands are rocky, with little vegetation, and have a cold, foggy climate.

Most of the territory's population lives on St. Pierre's 10 square miles (26 sq km), although Miquelon's 83 square miles (215 sq km) are also inhabited. The capital and commercial center of the territory is the town of St. Pierre on the east coast of St. Pierre.

The chief industries are fishing and the processing of fish—salting, drying, canning, and freezing codfish. The islands' entire economy depends on the nearby Grand Banks fisheries. St. Pierre's harbor is kept virtually ice-free by the passing Gulf Stream. There are some minor enterprises, such as mink and silver-fox farming, whose animals are raised on fish. Nearly all consumer goods must be imported.

The population of the islands is of French origin and speaks French. The territory has compulsory primary education, provided mainly by Roman Catholic schools, and a small secondary and vocational educational system. Most of the population is literate.

History. The Territory of St. Pierre and Miquelon Islands is all that remains of the old French colonial empire in northern North America. Breton, Basque, and Norman fishermen were fishing off the islands early in the 16th century, and in 1535 Jacques Cartier claimed the islands for France. The present population is descended largely from French Canadians who were expelled by the British from Newfoundland and Acadia in the 18th century.

The islands were several times occupied by the British, but have been in continuous French possession since 1816. They had the status of a colony until Jan. 1, 1947, when they became a partially autonomous overseas territory of France with representation in the French Parliament and French Union.

The islands voted in 1958 to retain their status as a territory of France, but the French government decided to make them a department of France, and this change was given final approval by the French Senate on July 9, 1976. The islands send a deputy and a senator to the French Parliament. Population: (1974) 5,840.

SAINT-QUENTIN, saN-kän-taN′, is a city in France in Aisne department, about 80 miles (129 km) northeast of Paris, at the junction of the Somme River and St.-Quentin Canal. It has a collegiate church built between the 12th and 15th centuries, and a 15th-century town hall in Flamboyant Gothic style. The principal manufactures are textiles, machinery and sugar.

The city, which is of Roman origin, was a place of pilgrimage during the Middle Ages because of the tomb of St. Quentin, who was believed to have been martyred here during the reign (284–305) of Emperor Diocletian. Because of its strategic location, it figured conspicuously in a number of wars, notably in 1557, when it was besieged by the Spanish; in 1871, when it was the scene of a crucial battle in the Franco-Prussian War; and in 1918, during World War I. Population: (1968) 63,932.

SAINT-RÉMY DE PROVENCE, saN-rā-mē′ də prô-väNs′, is a town in France in Bouches-du-Rhône department, 12 miles (19 km) northeast of Arles. Its chief industry is growing flower, vegetable, and grain seeds.

Slightly south of the modern town are the ruins of the ancient town of Glanum, founded by the Greeks and later taken by the Romans. Little remains from the Greek era, but from Roman times there is a splendid mausoleum and a triumphal arch, the oldest in the region. Both date from the 1st century A. D. Attached to the 12th century priory of St.-Paul-Mausolée is a church in the Romanesque style characteristic of Provence. Population: (1962) 4,420.

SAINT-SAËNS, saN-säNs′, **Camille** (1835–1921), French composer, organist, and pianist, who is famous for such works as his opera *Samson et Dalila* and his instrumental suite *Le Carnaval des animaux.*

Life. Charles Camille Saint-Saëns was born in Paris on Oct. 9, 1835. He began to compose at the age of 6 and appeared publicly as a pianist at 10. After private study, he attended the Paris Conservatory, winning a first prize as an organist in 1851, but failing to win a Prix de Rome. His First Symphony was heard in Paris in 1853, eliciting a letter from Charles Gounod saying that the 18-year-old composer had "the obligation to become a great master." Saint-Saëns was organist at the churches of St.-Merry (1853–1857) and the Madeleine (1858–1877) in Paris and then retired to compose, conduct, and play his own works.

A notable pianist and teacher, Saint-Saëns was a leader in French musical life for almost 70 years. He was showered with public honors, including membership in the Institut de France (1881), a Grand Cross of the Legion of Honor (1913), and numerous honorary degrees. As a representative of the French government at the Panama-Pacific Exposition in San Francisco, Calif., in 1915, the composer conducted his own choral work with orchestra, *Hail California.* After appearing as pianist-composer in Dieppe in August 1921, Saint-Saëns went on a vacation to Algiers where he died on Dec. 16, 1921.

Works. Saint-Saëns, a composer of exquisitely made but seldom profound music, was dazzlingly prolific and not stringently self-critical. The enormous body of his works shows compositions of great distinction among many mere potboilers. He was especially known late in life for his biting

CULVER PICTURES

Camille Saint-Saëns, French composer.

opposition to most modern tendencies in art. His finest achievements include the opera *Samson et Dalila* (first performed 1877); his Third Symphony (with organ, 1886); the symphonic poems *Le Rouet d'Omphale* (1872), *Phaéton* (1873), *Danse macabre* (1875), and *La Jeunesse d'Hercule* (1877); *Le Carnaval des animaux,* for two pianos and orchestra, including the famous cello piece *The Swan* (1922; composed 1886); the Second (1868), Fourth (1875), and Fifth (1896) piano concertos; the Third Violin Concerto (1881); the First Cello Concerto (1873); the *Introduction et rondo capriccioso* for violin and orchestra (1913; composed 1863); and many pieces for chamber ensembles, piano, and both solo voices and chorus. Saint-Saëns, a noted wit, also wrote several books, in both prose and verse, of continuing interest and value.

HERBERT WEINSTOCK
Coauthor of "Men of Music"

Further Reading: Brook, Donald, *Five Great French Composers* (Rockliff 1946); Harding, James, *Saint-Saëns and His Circle* (Chapman 1965).

SAINT-SIMON, saN-sē-môn′, **Count de** (1760–1825), French social scientist and philosopher. Claude-Henri de Rouvroy was born in Paris on Oct. 17, 1760. Intermarriage within the Saint-Simon family made him a relative, though distant, of his illustrious earlier namesake, Louis de Rouvroy, Duke de Saint-Simon, political historian. At 19, Claude-Henri was an officer in the French expeditionary force sent to support the American colonists in their War of Independence, an experience that awakened his interest in social questions. That interest grew immeasurably toward the end of the 18th century, with the outbreak of the French Revolution. He concluded that society was sick and determined to be its savior. Except for the interlude of the Terror, during which he barely escaped the guillotine, Saint-Simon dabbled in land speculation, convinced that substantial means were essential to the fulfillment of his mission. He amassed a fortune but squandered it on an ambitious program of travel and study. When he began to write, he was already impoverished. By 1810 he was virtually penniless.

Out of the maze of Saint-Simon's works, one principle emerges: that the science of man must be developed along "positive" lines and made to govern the planned economy of progress. World leadership should be entrusted to the scientific elite, who alone are capable of substituting international cooperation for international strife and of teaching man how to tame nature for the sake of his own welfare and happiness.

With this end established, the means remained to be worked out. Faithful at first to 18th century doctrine, Saint-Simon clung to mathematics and Newtonian physics as the fountainhead of all science, including the social sciences. Thus he wrote *Lettres d'un habitant de Genève* (1803), *Introduction aux travaux scientifiques du XIXe siècle* (1808), *Esquisse d'une nouvelle Encyclopédie* (1810), and *Travail sur la gravitation universelle* (1813).

However, Saint-Simon's *Mémoire sur la science de l'homme*, also written in 1813, testifies to a change of heart. He now placed his reliance in the budding life sciences: physiology, psychology, history, and economics. From this ensued his prophetic vision of a technocratic state or superstate, guided by experts, organized for productive labor by *industriels*, or businessmen, and bent on suppressing the political rivalries or economic inequities that breed war. This theory he set forth in *De la réorganisation de la société européenne* (1814), *L'industrie*, in collaboration with Auguste Comte (1816–1818), *Le politique* (1819), *L'organisateur* (1820), *Catéchisme des industriels* (1823–1824).

Finally in the twilight of his life, he restored the doctrine of religious feeling as a positive factor and indeed as the prime mover of mankind in *Le nouveau Christianisme* (1825).

Saint-Simon died in Paris on May 19, 1825. Posthumous fame succeeded his lifelong obscurity. His doctrine was extolled and not infrequently modified by a number of disciples, and Saint-Simonism proved to be a seminal force of the first magnitude. All subsequent social planners—romanticists, positivists, Marxists, advocates of modern capitalism and of the corporate state—in some way or other have been indebted to it. See also SOCIOLOGY.

JEAN-ALBERT BÉDÉ
Columbia University

Further Reading: Charléty, Sébastien, *Histoire du Saint-Simonisme*, rev. ed. (1931); D'Allemagne, Henri René, *Les Saint Simoniens 1827–1837* (1930); Leroy, Maxime, *La vie véritable du comte Henri de Saint-Simon* (1925); Manuel, Frank E., *The New World of Henri Saint-Simon* (reprint; Univ. of Notre Dame Press 1963).

SAINT-SIMON, saN-sē-môN′, **Duke de** (1675–1755), French memorialist and historian. Louis de Rouvroy, Duke de Saint-Simon, was born in Paris on Jan. 16, 1675. He entered the army in 1691 but ruined his prospects by opposing Louis XIV on matters of precedence. In 1702 he left the army because he had not received an anticipated promotion and went to the court in spite of Louis' coolness toward him.

Outside of minor diplomatic missions, he spent most of his time at Versailles, in relative isolation. His political hopes, shattered at the death in 1712 of Louis, Duke of Burgundy, Louis XIV's grandson and heir to the throne, were revived when another friend, Philip II, Duke d'Orléans, became regent for Louis XV in 1715. Saint-Simon's caste prejudices and lack of flexibility, however, sharply limited his influence, and he withdrew from public life, in bitterness and disappointment, after the death of Orléans in 1723. Retiring to his country estate, he worked on his *Mémoires*, which were still unpublished when he died in Paris on March 2, 1755.

Writings. Even though they embody notes and impressions recorded as far back as 1694, the *Mémoires* were specifically written as an expansion and refutation of the Marquis de Dangeau's *Mémoires*, an insipid work of monarchical adulation by a fellow courtier. Saint-Simon disapproves strongly of Louis XIV, whom he compares unfavorably to his father, Louis XIII. Louis XIV is viewed as the chief artisan of a social upheaval in which the old aristocracy was supplanted by a coalition of bourgeois ministers and various upstarts from the judicial and other low-ranking nobility. The privileges granted by the King to his illegitimate children are another cause of indignation.

Inordinately proud of his title of "duke and peer," Saint-Simon devotes much attention to matters of etiquette. His tendency to reduce most political problems to questions of court precedence often verges on the ludicrous in the modern reader's eyes, but it betrays an acute consciousness of the nobility's loss of power and should be viewed as a futile attempt to remedy a hopeless situation. Later historians, favorable to either the bourgeoisie or the King, often underestimate his historical insights. He discerns with great penetration what in modern times would be called the totalitarian aspects of the new absolute monarchy. He paints an impressive fresco of court life and an immense gallery of historical portraits in a language that, thanks to an aristocratic contempt for literary pretensions and a complete disregard of classical rules, has lost none of its archaic picturesqueness, vivacity, and descriptive force.

RENÉ GIRARD
The Johns Hopkins University

Further Reading: Saint-Simon, Duc de, *Memoirs*, ed. by W. H. Lewis, rev. ed. (Macmillan 1964); Saint-Simon, Duc de, *Mémoires*, ed. by Jose Lupin, 2 vols. (1951).

SAINT SIMONS ISLAND, in southeastern Georgia, in Glynn county, is on the Atlantic coast about 7 miles (11 km) east of Brunswick, with which it is connected by a causeway. It is one of the Sea Islands, that once were famous for the quality of their cotton. The unincorporated area of St. Simons is occupied by residences and summer homes. James Edward Oglethorpe, governor of Georgia colony, built Fort Frederica here in 1736, and in the Battle of Bloody Marsh (1742) his victory over the Spaniards established British control of the southeastern part of what is now the United States. Fort Frederica was created a national monument in 1945.

SAINT SOPHIA, or Sancta Sophia, in Istanbul, Turkey, is one of the world's most important Byzantine structures. See HAGIA SOPHIA.

SAINT THOMAS, a city in southern Ontario, Canada, the seat of Elgin county, is on Kettle Creek, just above the north shore of Lake Erie. It is midway between the U. S. cities of Detroit, Mich., and Buffalo, N. Y., and 18 miles (29 km) south of London, Ontario. The city is an important railway center, with repair shops and factories that manufacture rolling stock and equipment. Other industry includes automobile assembly and the manufacture of steel and paper products. St. Thomas also serves the surrounding rich agricultural region.

Alma College, a junior women's college affiliated with the University of Western Ontario, is here, as is the Elgin County Pioneer Museum. The area was settled about 1810. It became a village in 1852 and a county town in 1861, and was incorporated as a city in 1881. Population: (1976) 28,165.

SAINT THOMAS, the second-largest of the Virgin Islands of the United States, is in the Caribbean Sea, about 40 miles (64 km) east of Puerto Rico. It is about 14 miles (23 km) long and 2 miles (3 km) wide.

The island is of volcanic origin, and has a rugged terrain and a deeply indented coast. The largest settlement is Charlotte Amalie, which is the capital of the Virgin Islands of the United States and has one of the finest natural harbors in the Caribbean. St. Thomas' principal industry is tourism. Bay rum, produced from leaves of the West Indian bayberry, is the chief export. The main campus of the College of the Virgin Islands is in Charlotte Amalie.

St. Thomas was discovered by Christopher Columbus in 1493, but not colonized until 1657, when a short-lived Dutch community settled here. There was a Danish colony briefly in 1666, and in 1672 the Danes founded a permanent settlement at St. Thomas Harbor. It was sold to the United States in 1917. Population: of the island, 44,218; of Charlotte Amalie, 11,756.

See also VIRGIN ISLANDS OF THE UNITED STATES.

SAINT-TROPEZ, saN-trō-pā′, is a popular Riviera resort town in France on the Gulf of St.-Tropez, a striking Mediterranean bay. The town is in Var department, about 37 miles (60 km) northeast of Toulon. Favored by painters and writers, it has also been popularized as a fashionable resort, particularly by film stars.

The town is named after Tropez, a Christian who, according to legend, was beheaded and cast adrift, coming to shore at the town's site. The citadel dates from the 16th century, when the town was an independent republic. Population: (1968) 6,151.

SAINT VALENTINE'S DAY. See VALENTINE'S DAY.

SAINT VALENTINE'S DAY MASSACRE, a multiple killing of rival gangsters by henchmen of Al Capone on Feb. 14, 1929, in Chicago. "Scarface Al," head of a huge crime syndicate, stayed immune from prosecution after his gunners, disguised as policemen, lined up seven members of the notorious George ("Bugs") Moran gang against a garage wall and shot them all. See also CAPONE, AL.

SAINT VINCENT, Earl of. See JERVIS, JOHN.

SAINT VINCENT AND THE GRENADINES, a Caribbean country in the Windward Islands of the Lesser Antilles. It comprises St. Vincent, the principal island, and the Grenadines, a group of some 600 small islands strung out in a line between St. Vincent and Grenada to the south. The total area is approximately 150 square miles (390 sq km). St. Vincent island is about 18 miles (29 km) long and 11 miles (18 km) wide. The larger Grenadine islands include Bequia, Canouan, Mayreau, Mustique, Union, and Carriacou. The population is largely of African descent, with some Carib Indian admixture. Portuguese and East Indian laborers were imported after the abolition of slavery in the 19th century. The capital and chief town is Kingstown, on St. Vincent.

Of volcanic origin, St. Vincent is traversed from north to south by a rugged mountain chain that reaches its maximum elevation of 4,048 feet (1,234 meters) in the volcano of Soufrière, which has had damaging eruptions in 1821, 1902, and 1979. The climate is tropical, tempered by the trade winds, so that the mean temperature is about 80° F (27° C). The annual rainfall varies from about 150 inches (3,810 mm) in the mountains to about 60 inches (1,520 mm) on the southeastern coast. There is a dry season from December to April.

There is a modest tourist industry, but the country's economy is largely agricultural. Principal exports are bananas, arrowroot, coconuts, cotton, sugar, cassava, and peanuts. The island of Carriacou in the southern Grenadines produces Sea Island cotton. There is an airport at Arnos Vale, and there are regular ship connections with Jamaica and Trinidad.

St. Vincent is said to have been discovered by Christopher Columbus in 1498, when it was populated by Carib Indians. In 1627 the British king granted it to the earl of Carlisle, but the island was left undisturbed to the Caribs until 1763, when it was ceded to the British crown in perpetuity. The French took the island in 1779 and held it until it was returned to Britain by the Treaty of Versailles in 1783. In 1795 the Caribs, aided by French allies from Martinique, launched a revolt and overran St. Vincent, burning the sugarcane fields and killing the British settlers.

ST. VINCENT AND THE GRENADINES

Order was restored the following year by British troops under Sir Ralph Abercromby. More than 5,000 Caribs were deported to the island of Roatán off the coast of Honduras.

From 1958 to 1962, St. Vincent was an independent member of the Federation of the West Indies. In 1968 the island became a member of the Caribbean Free Trade Association, and the following year it became an associated state of the United Kingdom. The northern Grenadines, from Bequia to Petit St. Vincent, were administered by St. Vincent, while Carriacou and islets south of it were administered by Grenada.

Moves for independence were initiated by a resolution of the St. Vincent House of Assembly in 1976, seeking termination of the associated statehood. On Oct. 27, 1979, Saint Vincent and the Grenadines became an independent monarchy within the Commonwealth of Nations. The British monarch is represented by a governor general. Population: (1975) 100,427; (1979 est.) 110,000.

See also GRENADINES.

SAINT VINCENT, Cape, a promontory in Portugal and the most southwesterly point of continental Europe. It juts into the Atlantic Ocean, about 60 miles (97 km) west of Faro.

The cape has a lighthouse on top of a 175-foot (53-meter) cliff, inside a 16th century monastery. Nearby are the ruins of the town established in the 15th century by Prince Henry the Navigator, who founded there a school for navigators and an observatory. Several important naval battles were fought off the cape. In a key engagement in 1797, a British fleet under Sir John Jervis defeated superior Spanish forces.

SAINT VITUS DANCE, the name sometimes applied to Sydenham's chorea, a disease characterized by involuntary jerking of parts of the body. See CHOREA—*Sydenham's Chorea.*

SAINTE ANNE DE BEAUPRÉ, saN-taN' də bō-prā', a town in Montmorency county, Quebec, Canada, that contains the shrine of Sainte Anne, mother of the Virgin Mary. It is located on the north shore of the St. Lawrence River, 22 miles (35.4 km) northeast of Quebec city. The shrine was built on land given for a church by Étienne de Lessard in 1658. The first major miracle recorded took place in 1662, when three shipwrecked sailors were tossed up on the shore near the Church of Ste. Anne. The church, which was popularly known as the sailor's chapel, rapidly became a place of pilgrimage.

In 1878 the shrine was entrusted to the Redemptorist Fathers. A large basilica, which was still unfinished in the early 1970's, is on the site of an 1876 structure destroyed by fire in 1922. One of the major attractions is a cyclorama of Jerusalem on the day of Christ's crucifixion. Population: 3,292.

SAINTE-BEUVE, saNt-büv', **Charles Augustin** (1804–1869), French literary critic, whose works, interpreting literature as a product of social and historical forces, were widely influential in both England and America.

Life and Early Works. He was born in Boulogne-sur-Mer, France, on Dec. 23, 1804. After studying science in Paris, he entered medical school in 1823 but devoted only four years to medicine, combined with literary journalism, before turning entirely to literature.

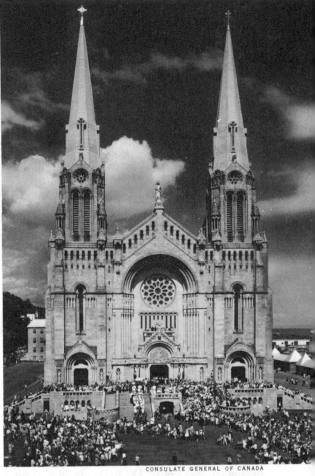

CONSULATE GENERAL OF CANADA

Basilica of Sainte Anne de Beaupré, site of many reported miracles, attracts thousands of pilgrims annually.

Having become a contributor to the *Globe,* a liberal and philosophical journal, Sainte-Beuve collected his articles and published them as his first book under the title *Tableau historique et critique de la poésie française au XVIe siècle.* (1828). The book contained a review of Victor Hugo's *Odes et ballades,* and this piece of friendly criticism initiated a fruitful but short friendship between the two men. Sainte-Beuve later became the lover of Mme. Hugo, and the discovery of the affair led to a complete break in 1834. In this period of his life Sainte-Beuve was also very much attracted by Saint-Simonism and by Lamennais, but later he renounced romanticism in all forms and turned to scientific literary criticism. In his "romantic period" he published three volumes of verse—*Vie, poésies et pensées de Joseph Delorme* (1829), *Consolations* (1831), and *Pensées d'août* (1837)—and his only novel, *Volupté* (1834).

Sainte-Beuve was appointed keeper of the Mazarin Library in 1840 but lost the position as a consequence of the Revolution of 1848. In 1854 he became professor of Latin poetry at the Collège de France but was unable to lecture because the strongly anti-Bonapartist students, resenting his support of the emperor, interrupted him whenever he appeared in the classroom. He was transferred to the École Normale Supérieure and taught there until 1865, when he was appointed to the Senate. By that time he had become critical of the Second Empire and had regained his popularity by his defense of freedom of speech and thought. He died in Paris on Oct. 13, 1869.

Major Works. The most famous of Sainte-Beuve's literary essays were the critical articles published in newspapers and journals—first in the *Constitutionnel* and later in the *Moniteur* and the *Temps.* The entire series was republished in 28 volumes, of which the best are entitled *Causeries du lundi* (15 vols., 1851–1862). The remainder were collected in *Nouveaux lundis* (13 vols., 1863–1870). He also published *Portraits littéraires* (1832–1839), *Portraits de femmes* (1844), *Portraits contemporains* (1846), and *Chateaubriand et son groupe littéraire* (1861).

Works of Sainte-Beuve published posthumously include *P. J. Proudhon, sa vie et sa correspondance* (1872); *Lettres à la princesse* (1873), which are letters to Mathilde, cousin of Napoleon III; *Correspondance* (1877–1878); and *Nouvelle correspondance* (1880). Sainte-Beuve also wrote a history of the Jansenists, *Histoire de Port-Royal* (5 vols., 1840–1860).

Bibliography

Barlow, Norman H., *Sainte-Beuve to Baudelaire: A Poetic Legacy* (Duke Univ. Press 1964).
Giese, William F., *Sainte-Beuve: A Literary Portrait* (1931; reprint, Greenwood Press, 1974).
Harper, George M., *Charles-Augustin Sainte-Beuve* (1909; reprint, Books for Libs. 1970).
Lehmann, Andrew G., *Sainte-Beuve: A Portrait of the Critic. 1804–1842* (Oxford 1962).
Marks, Emerson R., ed., *The Literary Criticism of Sainte-Beuve* (Univ. of Neb. Press 1971).
Nicolson, Sir Harold George, *Sainte-Beuve* (1957; reprint, Greenwood Press, 1977).

SAINTE CHAPELLE, saNt shà-pel', a 13th century French chapel in Paris, is a masterpiece of Gothic architecture. Ste. Chapelle was commissioned by Louis IX to house the reputed crown of thorns and other relics brought back from the Crusades. Replacing an old chapel in the courtyard of the royal palace, now the Palace of Justice, it was built in the 1240's, probably by Pierre de Montreuil, and was restored in the 19th century.

Ste. Chapelle is one of the early examples of the *rayonnant* Gothic style, which stressed height and expanse of glass. The structure consists of a lower chapel for the palace servants and an upper chapel for the court. The latter is flooded with light from the 15 vivid stained glass windows that virtually form its walls. The jewel-like effect is heightened by the painted and gilded columns and vaulting. Other saintes chapelles include those at Riom and Vincennes.

SAINTE-CLAIRE DEVILLE, saNt-klâr' də-vēl', **Henri Étienne** (1818–1881), French chemist. He was born on the island of St. Thomas, then a Danish possession, on March 11, 1818. The son of a French consul, he was educated in France and in 1843 obtained doctorates in medicine and science. In 1859 he became a chemistry professor at the Sorbonne, where he remained until his death, in Boulogne-sur-Seine, on July 1, 1881.

Sainte-Claire Deville studied aluminum metallurgy in the 1850's. The method he developed for the commercial production of the metal reduced its cost greatly, although it remained expensive until new production methods were developed later in the century. (See ALUMINUM—

History.) He also studied the metallurgy of platinum and the platinum group of elements, investigated the dissociation of gas molecules at high temperatures, and was the first chemist to prepare nitrogen pentoxide.

SAINTE-FOY, saNt-fwä', a city in southeastern Quebec, Canada, in Quebec county, is situated on the northern slope of the escarpment that constitutes the north bank of the St. Lawrence River, just south of Quebec City. It is mainly residential, but there is some scattered light industry.

Within the city limits is the Cité Universitaire, the main campus of Laval University. Laval, the oldest French-language university in North America, moved to Ste.-Foy from Quebec City between 1949 and 1966. St. Lawrence College—affiliated with Laval since 1959—is also here.

A parish was established at Ste.-Foy in 1636, changing the village's name to Notre Dame de Foy, but the older name persisted. In 1760 the Duke de Levis, in a battle here, defeated the English in their attempt to retake Quebec. Ste.-Foy was incorporated as a city in 1955. Population: 68,883.

SAINTES, saNt, is a town in France in Charente-Maritime department, on the Charente River, 47 miles (76 km) southeast of La Rochelle. It is a regional transportation and commercial center and has foundries and machinery and distilling industries.

The town was the chief settlement of the Santones and in Roman times was called *Mediolanum.* There is a Roman amphitheater and a triumphal arch of Germanicus Caesar, both from the 1st century A. D. Until the 19th century the arch was on a bridge across the Charente.

During the Middle Ages, Saintes became the center of the county, and later the province, of Saintonge. Medieval buildings include the Church of Ste.-Marie-des-Dames, which is primarily Romanesque, and the Romanesque Church of St. Eutrope, named after Eutrope (Eutropius), first bishop of Saintes. Population: (1968) 28,138.

SAINTES-MARIES-DE-LA-MER, Les, saNt-mä-rē-də-lä-mâr', a village and beach resort in France, in the Camargue region of Provence. It is on the Mediterranean Sea in Bouches-du-Rhône department, 18 miles (29 km) southwest of Arles.

Its name derives from the ancient Provençal tradition that Mary Magdalene, Mary (sister of the Virgin), Mary (mother of John and James), and Sara, their black servant landed at the town's site after being driven from the Holy Land. The relics of the last three are preserved in the 12th century Romanesque, fortified church, which has long been the object of pilgrimages. They are held in May and October, with Gypsies, who venerate Sara, flocking to the May ceremonies. Population: 904.

SAIONJI KIMMOCHI, sī-ōn-jē kĕm-mō-chē, **Prince** (1849–1940), the last of the *genrō,* or "elder statesmen" of Japan. These were men who, having participated in the Meiji Restoration and held high government office, had retired to serve as a body of influential advisers to the emperor.

Born in Kyoto, the son of Tokudaiji Kinzumi, he was adopted into the Saionji family. He played a small part in the restoration of imperial power in 1868 and subsequently founded the

Meiji Law School and a newspaper that helped popularize Western liberal ideas. Prime minister in 1906–1908 and 1911–1912, he received the title of prince in 1920. He died in Okitsu on Nov. 24, 1940.

SAIPAN, sī-pän', is the second-largest island (after Guam) of the Marianas group in the western Pacific Ocean. Of volcanic origin, it is hilly and has an area of 47 square miles (122 sq km).

Saipan was controlled by Spain from 1565 until it was purchased by Germany in 1899. Japan received the island, along with the other Marianas except Guam, as a League of Nations mandate in 1920. Saipan was taken by U. S. forces in 1944 and became the site of a large U. S. airbase. In 1962 it became the headquarters of the U. S. Trust Territory of the Pacific. Population: (1971 est.) 10,458.

SAIS, sā'əs, was a city of ancient Egypt. Located in the Nile delta, the site is now occupied by the village of Sa el-Hagar. Little remains of the ancient city.

Sais was the chief shrine of the goddess Neith and was also a shrine of the god Osiris. The city became politically important when two of its princes ruled Lower Egypt as the 24th dynasty (725–710 B. C.). The 26th, or Saite, dynasty ruled all of Egypt from 664 B. C. until it was defeated by the Persians in 525 B. C.

SAITAMA, sī-tä-mä, is a prefecture in Japan just north of Tokyo. Except in the west the terrain is level. Saitama is a main producer of vegetables for the Tokyo market. Other agricultural products are green tea and silk. Manufactures include textiles and machinery.

The prefecture of Saitama has an area of 1,467 square miles (3,800 sq km). Its capital is Urawa. Population: (1970) 3,866,472.

SAIVISM, shī'vizm, or *Shaivism,* is the devotional movement centered around the Hindu god Shiva (Śiva). See also SHIVA.

SAKAI, sä-kī, is a seaport and industrial city in Japan, in Osaka prefecture. It is situated on Osaka Bay and is separated from the city of Osaka on the north by the Yamato River.

An ancient trading port, Sakai began to decline in importance when foreign trade was severely restricted in the first half of the 17th century. Its ruin was completed by the silting of the harbor entrance in the early 18th century. With the dredging of the harbor in modern times, Sakai resumed its place in international trade and became a producer and exporter of iron, steel, and petrochemicals. It also manufactures and ships machinery, textile goods, bicycles, and cutlery. Population: (1970) 594,367.

SAKE, sä'kē, a fermented rice beer, is the national beverage of Japan. It is often called a wine because it is not effervescent like beer and it has a high alcoholic content—12% to 16%. It is said to be named after Osaka, Japan. Sake is colorless and is usually served warm.

SAKHALIN, sə-кнu-lyēn', is an island of the USSR in the northern Pacific Ocean. It is separated from the Soviet mainland to the west by the Tatar Strait and from the Japanese island of Hokkaido on the south by La Pérouse Strait.

About 590 miles (950 km) from north to south, this mountainous island has an area of about 29,700 square miles (76,925 sq km). Two mountain ranges run north and south, with a central valley between them. The principal rivers are the Tym and the Poronai, navigable for a short distance and teeming with fish. The climate is very severe. Yuzhno-Sakhalinsk is the main city and the administrative center.

Fishing is the most important occupation, though many people engage in forest industries. Pulp and paper are produced in the south. Coal is mined in the west, and there are oil wells in the north. A pipeline carries petroleum across the Tatar Strait to the Soviet mainland.

Japanese colonists settled in the southern part of the island in the late 18th century, and Russians arrived in the north in the 19th century. The two powers ruled jointly until 1875, when Russia obtained the southern part by ceding the Kuril Islands to Japan. By the Treaty of Portsmouth (1905), which followed Russia's defeat in the Russo-Japanese War, Japan regained the southern portion, which they called Karafuto. After World War II, the USSR was ceded the southern part, as well as the Kurils. Since 1947, Sakhalin and the Kurils have formed Sakhalin oblast. Population: (1970 est.) 600,000.

SAKHAROV, sə-кнä'rôf, **Andrei Dmitriyevich** (1921–   ), Soviet physicist, who contributed to the development of the Soviet thermonuclear (hydrogen) bomb. He graduated from Moscow University in 1942 and published a study, *The Excitation Temperature in Gas Discharge* in 1948. In 1950, Sakharov and the theoretical physicist Igor Y. Tamm proposed the use of an electrical discharge in a plasma confined in a magnetic field to obtain a controlled thermonuclear reaction. In 1968, Sakharov circulated an essay titled *Progress, Coexistence, and Intellectual Freedom,* advocating atomic disarmament, U. S.–Soviet cooperation in solving world problems, and intellectual freedom in the USSR. He was subsequently vilified in the Soviet press, and on Jan. 22, 1980, he was arrested, stripped of his awards, including Hero of Socialist Labor, and isolated with his wife in Gorky.

Sakharov was born in Moscow on May 21, 1921. He became a member of the Lebedev Institute of Physics in Moscow and was elected to the Soviet Academy of Sciences. He won the 1975 Nobel Peace Prize, and his wife accepted the award for him when he was not permitted to go to Oslo. *My Country and the World* (Eng. ed., 1975) urged Soviet political amnesty.

SAKI, sä'kē, the pseudonym of Hector Hugh Munro (1870–1916), British satirist, who is best known for his fictional pieces distinguished by gaiety of dialogue and narrative.

He was born in Akyab, Burma, on Dec. 18, 1870. After being educated in grammar schools in Exmouth and Bedford, England, he returned to Burma in 1893 and was commissioned in the Burma police. The following year he reappeared in England, where he delighted readers of the *Westminster Gazette* with political sketches in the Lewis Carroll manner. These sketches, issued under the name of Saki (cupbearer in the *Rubáiyát of Omar Khayyám*), were later published in 1902 as *The Westminster Alice.* From 1902 to 1908 he traveled in Europe as foreign correspondent for the *Morning Post.*

After Saki had been sidetracked into his only serious study, *The Rise of the Russian Empire* (1900), he turned to writing the short stories, published as *Reginald* (1904) and *Reginald in Russia* (1910), on which his reputation rests. He was killed in action during World War I, on Nov. 13, 1916, at Beaumont-Hamel, France.

Reginald and *Reginald in Russia,* as well as *Chronicles of Clovis* (1911) and *Beasts and Superbeasts* (1914), reveal Saki's whimsical humor and biting wit at their best. Although he is not neglecting his penchant for political satire in these stories, he frequently portrays blithely irrepressible young men and strange and exotic animals in fantastic settings. With his fondness for flaying the pretentiously self-righteous and the negatively dull, Saki reveals a flippant annoyance with adults and a contrasting sympathy and understanding for their victims, children. Stylistically, his lack of conventional plot structure is usually more than compensated for by the fertility of his imagination and by his mastery of the unexpected phrase. In addition to his short stories Saki also wrote several plays and a fine novel, *The Unbearable Bassington* (1912).

Further Reading: Spears, George J., *The Satire of Saki: A Study of the Satiric Art of Hector H. Munro* (Exposition 1963).

ROBERT HERMES, FROM NATIONAL AUDUBON SOCIETY
Pale-faced saki (*Pithecia pithecia*)

SAKI, sak'ē, any of several South American medium-sized monkeys that have a long bushy nonprehensile tail and long hair that usually forms a beard on the chin and a ruff around the face. The monkeys have a somewhat humanlike face with a sad expression and humanlike legs and hands. They usually may be found in forests along the banks of rivers, feeding on fruits, other plant matter, and small animals.

Sakis are scientifically classified into two genera, *Pithecia* and *Chiropotes,* within the family Cebidae.

SAKKARA. See Saqqara.

SAKTI. See Shakti.

SALADIN, sal'ə-din (1138–1193), sultan of Egypt and Syria and founder of the Ayyubid dynasty. The Arabic form of his name is Salah al-Din Yusuf Ibn Ayyub. Of Kurdish parentage, Saladin was born in Tikrit, Mesopotamia, in 1138 and, when still an infant, was taken by his family to Baalbek, where his father served as commander of the garrison. Later his family moved to Damascus.

In 1164 young Saladin, whose name means "the bounty of religion," reluctantly interrupted his theological career to join his uncle Shirkuh on a military campaign against Egypt, home of an unorthodox caliphate and occasional ally of the Latin Kingdom of Jerusalem. Saladin played an important role in his uncle's campaigns, and after Shirkuh's death in 1169 he was made commander of the Syrian troops in Egypt. In 1171, when al-Adid, the Fatimid caliph, died in Cairo, Saladin took over the reins of government, while recognizing the overlordship of the Abbasid caliphate in Baghdad. With the government of Egypt went Cyrenaica and Hejaz.

When Nur ad-Din, Sultan of Damascus, died in 1174, Saladin managed to annex Muslim Syria, with which went northern Mesopotamia as far as Mosul. The Baghdad caliph did not hesitate to confirm him in his new position as sultan of Egypt and Syria. Secure in his newly consolidated kingdom, Saladin proceeded to realize the greatest ambition of his life, to rid the remaining part of Syria—namely, Palestine—of the Crusaders.

On July 4, 1187, his army met the forces of the King of Jerusalem and his allies at Hattin, above Tiberias, and dealt them a crushing defeat. Of the prisoners, King Guy- of Lusignan was treated in a manner worthy of his high office, but Renaud de Chatillon, lord of the stronghold of the Krak des Chevaliers, who had violated treaty obligations, was cut down with the victor's own scimitar. Jerusalem was entered on October 2, and the humane treatment of his Frankish inhabitants stood in sharp contrast with that accorded the Muslims in 1099 when the city was captured by the Crusaders.

Almost all the coast towns, Tyre excepted, fell into Saladin's hands. But those between Acre and Jaffa were ceded to the Crusaders after Saladin's failure to relieve Acre, which fell in 1191, of the siege by Richard the Lion-Hearted and his allies. The Franks enjoyed the advantage of possessing a fleet, which Saladin lacked. An armistice concluded with Richard in 1192, however, underlined the extent of Saladin's achievements, for the Christians were left with only a ribbon of land along the coast. The Muslims retained the interior, including the holy city of Jerusalem, which greatly reduced the power of the Crusader states.

Saladin lived less than six years after his dramatic capture of Jerusalem. On March 4, 1193, he died in Damascus, where his tomb, beside the Ummayyad mosque, is still visited and revered. He brought unity to a divided Muslim area, instilled in its people the spirit of *jihad* (holy war), and dealt the Crusader states blows from which they never recovered. In history and legend, Eastern and Western, his name has survived as that of a champion of chivalry. See also Ayyubid; Crusades.

PHILIP K. HITTI
Author of "History of the Arabs"

Further Reading: Slaughter, Gertrude, *Saladin* (Exposition 1955).

In Salamanca, a 16th century cathedral with a stone-encased tower rises above the banks of the Tormes River.

SALAL, sə-lal′, a spreading evergreen shrub with glossy foliage that is sometimes used for Christmas decorations. The salal, *Gaultheria shallon*, also called shallon, is a member of the heath family, Ericaceae. It is found along the Pacific coast of North America north to British Columbia. It grows from 1 to 2 feet (30–60 cm) tall and has ovate or roundish leaves, 1.75 to 4 inches (4.5–10 cm) long, shiny above and paler below. White or pinkish urn-shaped flowers, about 0.5 inch (1.2 cm) long, occur in axillary or terminal racemes. The many-seeded, purplish black fruit has a spicy aromatic odor and is eaten by many birds and animals.

SALAMANCA, sä-lä-mäng′kä, is a city in Spain and the capital of Salamanca province. It lies 107 miles (171 km) northwest of Madrid, occupying three hills on the north bank of the Tormes River. The city, which manufactures chemicals and food products, is the commercial center for the province.

Architecturally, it is one of Spain's most interesting cities, and it has numerous and magnificent ecclesiastical and educational institutions. The Plaza Mayor, built in 1729–1733 and one of the finest squares in Europe, is surrounded by an arcade supported by Corinthian columns. The New Cathedral, begun in 1513, adjoins the 12th century Romanesque Old Cathedral. The New Cathedral is a fine example of Flamboyant Gothic, with an elaborate portal, lofty dome, and graceful interior columns. The main building of the university is opposite the New Cathedral. The College of the Archbishop, also known as the Irish College, is a colossal and sumptuous 15th century edifice with a fine facade. There are many other medieval buildings, including handsome residences and palaces.

In ancient times the city was called Salmantica and Helmantica and was an important city of the Vettones. In 222 B.C. it was taken by Hannibal and, after being ruled by the Romans, became important under the Visigoths. It was ravaged by the Moors before it was retaken by Christian forces late in the 11th century. In 1543, Philip II married Maria of Portugal in the city. During the Peninsular War, in 1812, the future Duke of Wellington led British forces to a notable victory there over the French.

The Province. The province has an area of 4,829 square miles (12,313 sq km), the greater part of which is covered by oak and chestnut forests. The principal rivers are the Tormes, Douro, Yeltes, Agueda, and Alagón. Cereals, hemp, olive oil, and wine are the main products. There are some mineral deposits, but mines have not been intensively developed. Population: (1969 est.) of the city, 116,500; of the province, 401,100.

SALAMANCA, University of, sä-lä-mäng′kä, a secular coeducational institution of higher learning in Salamanca, Spain. Founded by royal decree of Alfonso IX of León in 1219, it was chartered by Ferdinand III of Castile in 1243 and then reorganized in 1254 by Alfonso X. Pope Alexander IV extended various privileges to Salamanca in 1255, and Pope Martin V drew up new constitutions for it in 1422. The university ranked with the other famous medieval universities. It became a center for theological study, reached the high point of its development in the latter part of the 16th century, when its enrollment exceeded 6,000.

Salamanca came under secular control in 1838, and its theological faculty was dismissed in 1868. In the latter part of the 19th century it had only a few hundred students. The modern institution has faculties of philosophy and letters, science, law, and medicine. In the early 1970's its students numbered over 4,000; faculty, about 180. In 1940 the Pontifical University of Salamanca under the control of the Spanish hierarchy was founded to replace the dismissed theological faculty.

SALAMANDERS, like frogs and other amphibians, live in moist environments. Salamander larvae, like the marbled salamander (*top right*), live in the water, where they are conspicuous by their bushy external gills. Adult salamanders, like the green salamander (*top left*), the dusky salamander (*top center*), and the tiger salamander (*left*), seek out moist shady environments on land.

SALAMANDER, sal′ə-man-dər, any of a large group of amphibians with tails. They resemble lizards superficially but lack scales and have a smooth moist skin. The group includes hellbenders, newts, mud puppies, and giant salamanders. Salamanders frequent moist, wooded, and shaded areas. They are absent from Australia and from Africa south of the Atlas Mountains. Nineteen species are recorded from Europe, and fewer than 100 are known to occur in the United States and Canada. In Asia and Latin America, the salamander fauna is imperfectly known, but it is probable that the total number of living species in the world is close to 500.

Salamanders range in size from less than 2 inches (5 cm) to the giant salamander, which may be more than 5 feet (1.5 meters) long. Salamanders have four limbs, terminating in clawless feet. Some are brightly colored, others are dull and dark, and still others have almost transparent skin. In adult salamanders the body is divided into distinct head, trunk, and tail regions. Teeth are present in both jaws, even in the larval stages, and in most species the number of teeth increases during the process of growth.

Some salamanders live on land and some in water. They are generally active at night or on rainy days, searching for food, such as insects, snails, worms, and other small animal matter. Many salamanders breed in moist situations on land. Usually the male deposits sperm that the female picks up, and the eggs, which are covered with jelly, are then fertilized internally before they are laid. Some species of salamanders breed in water, however, and in some of these the eggs are fertilized after they are laid. The larvae breathe through external gills that later disappear in those species whose adult forms live on land. Salamanders, like most amphibians, can regenerate a lost tail or limb.

Salamanders and newts make up the order Caudata of the class Amphibia. Anatomical evidence points to their descent from the more primitive Lepospondyli perhaps 200 million years ago during Triassic times. They retain many characteristics of their primitive ancestors but generally have fewer bones in the head and shoulder girdle. One widely accepted classification of salamanders divides them into the following five natural groups or suborders.

Cryptobranchoidea. Members of this group have a more generalized skeleton than do other salamanders. They retain many primitive habits, including external fertilization of the eggs. Only two families are included in the suborder: the Hynobiidae, with five genera confined to Europe and Asia; and the Cryptobranchidae, with two genera, *Andrias* in eastern Asia and *Cryptobranchus* in eastern North America. The cryptobranchids are incompletely metamorphosed salamanders derived from the hynobiids, some of which are terrestrial and others of which are lungless, brook-dwelling forms.

Ambystomidea. This group contains the single family Ambystomidae. Its members are North American derivatives of hynobiid ancestry. Many of the species are terrestrial, and fertilization is internal, although the eggs are usually laid in the water. *Rhyacotriton,* a mountain stream form of western North America, has its lungs reduced to mere vestiges.

Salamandroidea. This group contains three families. The most primitive members of the group are those in the family Salamandridae, with species widely distributed in the Northern Hemisphere. The terrestrial salamanders of Europe (principally *Salamandra* and related genera) are grouped together with the newts, all species in the family being characterized as metamorphosing forms having teeth on the roof of the palate behind the internal nares. The only live-bearing salamanders belong to the genus *Salamandra*.

The family Amphiumidae contains only one species, *Amphiuma means*, an inhabitant of the southeastern United States. This eel-like salamander has an incomplete metamorphosis, the limbs are greatly reduced, and there are only two or three toes. It is a derivative of the same stock that led to the salamandrids.

The third, most important, and most widely distributed family derived from the same stock is the Plethodontidae. The family includes brook dwellers as well as terrestrial species, many of which inhabit mountainous areas. The center of distribution is North America, but representatives are present in Europe and South America. They are all lungless and possess a groove extending from the nostril to the edge of the snout. The groove seems to be concerned with olfaction.

Proteida. The single family in this group, the Proteidae, forms a natural group of uncertain ancestry. Included are the mud puppies (*Necturus*) of eastern North America and the European blind salamander or olm (*Proteus*). None of the proteids metamorphose into adult forms. They spend their lives as permanent larvae with external gills. Lungs also are present.

Meantes. This group, containing two genera in the single family Sirenidae, is confined to the southeastern United States. The genus *Siren* has two species, the great siren (*S. lacertina*) and the lesser siren (*S. intermedia*). The genus *Pseudobranchus* has only one species, the dwarf siren (*P. striatus*). All three species, like the proteids, are permanent larvae that differ from all others in having lost the hind limbs.

CHARLES M. BOGERT
The American Museum of Natural History

Further Reading: Bishop, Sherman C., *Handbook of Salamanders* (Comstock Publishing Associates 1967).

SALAMIS, sal'ə-mis, was the main city of ancient Cyprus. Its ruins, which include a Roman forum and aqueduct, are in eastern Cyprus, about 6 miles (10 km) north of Famagusta.

Probably dating from Mycenaean times, it traditionally was founded by Teucer, a native of the Greek island of Salamis, after the Trojan War. The city fell to all the major powers, including the Persians, Ptolemies, and Romans. About 200 B. C. its harbor began to silt up, and it declined in importance. In 115–117 A. D., the Jewish population revolted, killing thousands of Cypriotes.

SALAMIS, sal'ə-mis, is an island off the coast of Greece, in the Saronic Gulf of the Aegean Sea, about 10 miles (16 km) west of Athens. It covers an area of about 39 square miles (101 sq km) and has an irregular shape and rocky surface. It is separated on the east and west from the mainland by narrow, winding channels that give access on the north to the beautiful Bay of Eleusis, which has the appearance of a lake. Olives are grown, and vineyards flourish. The modern town of Salamis, with a population of 18,317 (1971), is on the island's west coast.

A decisive naval battle between the Athenian and Persian fleets was fought off the island in 480 B. C., during the Persian Wars. The Persians, hoping to trap the Greeks, blocked the western channel and advanced up the eastern channel. The Greeks retreated to form a battle line and then sailed into the Persians. Rammed and prevented from maneuvering by their own reserves, the Persians were routed. They never again challenged the Athenians at sea. The island later fell to the Macedonians but was restored to Athens in the 3d century B. C.

SALARY GRAB, the popular name for the precipitous increase in federal salaries in the United States in 1873. The Constitution provides for the compensation of the president, senators, representatives, justices, and federal officers from the federal treasury. The act of March 3, 1873, provided that the president's salary be increased from $25,000 to $50,000, that of the chief justice from $8,500 to $10,500, those of the vice president, cabinet officers, associate justices, and speaker of the House from $8,000 to $10,000, and of senators and representatives from $5,000 to $7,500.

Another act, March 4, 1873, made the salary increases of members of Congress retroactive for the previous two years. This, the essence of the "salary grab," aroused so much indignation that the laws were repealed by Congress on Jan. 20, 1874, except those affecting the salaries of the president and justices.

SALAZAR, säl-ə-zär', **António de Oliveira** (1889–1970), prime minister of Portugal. He was born on April 28, 1889, in Vimieiro, near Santa Comba Dão in the province of Beira Alta. His parents were António de Oliveira and Maria do Resgate Salazar, small landowners. In his youth Salazar attended the village school. In 1900 his strong religious inclinations led him to enter the seminary at Viseu, but after eight years he left to teach school in Viseu. In 1910 he entered the University of Coimbra, where he was an outstanding student in economics. He graduated in 1914 and joined the teaching staff of the university. In 1918 he obtained a chair as professor of economic sciences, and soon became well known for his writings on finance and economic matters.

In January 1921, Salazar was one of three Catholic Center deputies elected to Parliament. He attended only one session and returned in disgust to his teaching duties at Coimbra, where he continued to study and write. In May 1926, when the parliamentary regime was replaced by a military dictatorship, Salazar was offered the post of finance minister. He accepted but resigned five days later because of the confusion he found in the government. On April 27, 1928, Gen. António Carmona became provisional president, and Salazar was again asked to serve as finance minister. He accepted, but only on the condition that he receive broad powers. The result was that he was in virtual control of the government. On July 5, 1932, he became prime minister, retaining the post of finance minister as well until 1940.

In 1933 a constitution was written that reflected Salazar's ideas of government, combining authoritarianism with the ethical principles embodied in the 19th century papal encyclical *Rerum novarum*. The constitution declared Portugal to be a unitary and corporative state. The new order came to be known as the Estado Novo (New State).

António Salazar, prime minister of Portugal (1932–1968)

Salazar was friendly with Gen. Francisco Franco, the leader of the Nationalists in the Spanish Civil War, and recognized his regime in 1938. In 1942, Spain and Portugal signed an alliance, called the Iberian Pact. During World War II, Salazar kept Portugal neutral, although in 1943 he made concessions to Britain and the United States in the Azores. In 1949 he brought Portugal into the North Atlantic Treaty Organization (NATO).

Salazar's austere regime was not unopposed. In 1935 there was a revolt in the armed forces, and in 1937 an attempt was made against his life. He was later faced with new internal opposition, as well as an armed revolt in the Portuguese African colony of Angola, the loss of the enclave of Goa to India, and Chinese hostility to Portuguese possession of Macao. Salazar was always self-effacing and austere, remote from the people.

In September 1968, after being incapacitated by a brain hemorrhage, he was succeeded as prime minister by Marcelo Caetano. Salazar died in Lisbon on July 27, 1970.

GREGORY RABASSA, *Queens College*

Bibliography

Derrick, Michael, *The Portugal of Salazar* (Books for Libs. 1972).

Egerton, F. Clement, *Salazar* (Transatlantic 1944).

Ferro, Antonio, *Salazar: Portugal and Her Leader* (Ryerson Press 1939).

Garnier, Christine, *Salazar: An Intimate Portrait* (Farrar, Straus 1954).

Kay, Hugh, *Salazar and Modern Portugal* (Hawthorn Bks. 1970).

SALÉ, sà-lä′, is a city on the Atlantic coast of Morocco, just north of Rabat, of which it is a suburb. It produces carpets and pottery.

Salé was founded in the 11th century and soon became a flourishing commercial port. In the 17th century, as a semi-independent republic, it was a haven for pirates who became known as Salle rovers. Population: (1971) 155,557.

SALE, in law. See SALES.

SALEM, in Massachusetts, is one of the oldest New England seaports. It lies on Salem Bay, 15 miles (24 km) northeast of Boston, and is the seat of Essex county. Salem is an industrial city that produces electrical goods, leather goods, and chemicals. It also attracts tourists interested in witchcraft, maritime history, architecture, and Nathaniel Hawthorne.

Points of Interest. Salem has taken care to preserve its historical associations. Many houses remain from the 17th century, including the Witch House, home of Judge Jonathan Corwin, where accused witches were examined; the Pickering House; the Retire Beckett House; the Hathaway House; and the House of Seven Gables, the supposed setting of Hawthorne's novel. Handsome neoclassical houses built for merchants and sea captains of the 18th and early 19th centuries may be seen along Chestnut Street and elsewhere. Among them are the Ropes Mansion, the Crowninshield-Bentley House, and two by Samuel McIntire—the Peirce-Nichols House and the Pingree House.

Some of these houses are maintained by the Essex Institute, which also has a historical museum and a fine library. The Peabody Museum has outstanding maritime exhibits. At the Salem Maritime National Historic Site, Derby Wharf, Derby House, and the Custom House, where Hawthorne worked, recall Salem's great seafaring days. Pioneer Village re-creates the rough 1630 settlement, and the Salem Witch Museum presents narrated scenes of the witch trials.

History. Salem, called Naumkeag by the Indians, was settled in 1626 by Roger Conant and others from Plymouth and Cape Ann. After John Endecott and other colonists arrived from England in 1628, the settlement became the first outpost of the Massachusetts Bay Company, later centered in Boston. The town was incorporated in 1630 as Salem. The first Puritan Congregational Church, led for a time by Roger Williams, was established in Salem in 1629.

In 18th century Salem, shipbuilding and trade with the West Indies and Europe flourished, encouraged especially by privateering during the American Revolution, when Salem was the only major port not captured by the British. After the war, Salem ships voyaged to China and the East Indies, making fortunes for such families as the Derbys, Crowninshields, and Nicholses. Maritime activity dwindled in the 1830's, as Salem harbor could no longer accommodate the new larger ships, and was gradually replaced by manufacturing. Salem was incorporated as a city in 1836. It is governed by a mayor and council. Population: 38,220.

Witchcraft Trials. In 1692, Salem was swept by a hysterical fear of witchcraft. That spring some young girls seemed to go into convulsions and accused the Rev. Samuel Parris' West Indian slave Tituba and other persons of bewitching them. They were probably inspired by Tituba's voodoo tales and possibly influenced by Cotton Mather's account of four bewitched girls in Boston in 1688. A judicious application of discipline, discretion, and distraction might have ended the matter. Instead, the girls attracted great attention and in self-protection extended their accusations. Salem citizens, like most other Europeans and Americans, believed in witches, and they were also uneasy about French and Indian attacks on New England. They readily accepted the girls' fantasies and the findings of a

WITCH HOUSE in Salem, Mass., built in 1642, was the home of Jonathan Corwin, the judge at the witchcraft trials in 1692. Restored by private owners, it is now a museum.

MASSACHUSETTS DEPARTMENT OF COMMERCE

special court, which ignored wise clerical advice and English judiciary rules. No one dared protest lest he too be accused. Consequently, several hundred persons were arrested, many were imprisoned, and 19 were hanged. Giles Corey was pressed to death for refusing to plead.

The madness abated in September, when Gov. Sir William Phips, petitioned by Boston clerics to exclude "spectral evidence" from consideration, dissolved the court. Eventually, most of the members confessed their error. Twenty years later the Massachusetts legislature annulled the convictions and made reparation to the victims' heirs.

SALEM, a town in southeastern New Hampshire, in Rockingham county, is on the Massachusetts border, 30 miles (48 km) north of Boston. It is a residential community with only a little light industry. Rockingham Park is well known for its horse races. The Salem Historical Museum maintains exhibits and there is a recreation park on Canobie Lake.

Salem was incorporated in 1750 and grew slowly until the 1960's when the population more than doubled in 10 years. The community is governed by a town manager and selectmen. Population: 24,124.

SALEM, a city in southwestern New Jersey, the seat of Salem County, is situated on Salem Creek near its confluence with the Delaware River. It is 39 miles (63 km) southwest of Camden. Its manufactures include canned food products, glass, and floor coverings.

Salem was founded as a Quaker colony by John Fenwick in 1675. The Friends Burial Grounds date back to 1676. The Friends Meeting House was built in 1772 and was still in use 200 years later. The Salem County Historical Society has a museum. Salem was incorporated as a village in 1695, and as a city in 1858. It is governed by a mayor and council. Population: 6,959.

SALEM, a city in western Ohio, in Columbiana County, is 69 miles (111 km) southeast of Cleveland. Machinery and machine parts and fabricated metal products are manufactured.

Salem was founded by Quakers from Salem, N. J., in 1806. It was incorporated as a village in 1830, and as a city in 1887. It is governed by a mayor and council. Population: 12,869.

SALEM, a city in northwestern Oregon, the capital of the state, in Marion and Polk counties, is on the Willamette River about 50 miles (80 km) south of Portland and some 60 miles (97 km) east of the Pacific coast. Salem is the seat of Marion county. It is situated in a diversified agricultural area that produces livestock, dairy cattle, and poultry; grain, hay, and seed crops; fruits, nuts, and vegetables.

The city's principal industries are food processing; lumber and wood products; machinery; electrical products and batteries; sand, gravel, and concrete products; and textiles.

Salem is the home of Willamette University, the oldest university (1842) in the Pacific Northwest, and of Western Baptist Bible College. The Salem Art Association–Bush House and Bush Bar Art Center, in the Bush House (1877–1878), contains art galleries and a library of art. Also of interest are the Pioneer Museum and the Yaguina Bay State Lighthouse.

The state capitol (1938) is a striking building of white Vermont marble, designed by Francis Keally. The dome is surmounted by *The Pioneer*, a sculptured figure of heroic size by Ulric Ellerhusen. Near the entrance to the capitol is a bronze statue, *The Circuit Rider*, by Alexander Phimister Proctor, a memorial to Robert Booth, one of the itinerant preachers who served Oregon's pioneer settlements. Within the capitol, the history of the state is depicted in murals by Barry Faulkner and Frank H. Schwartz.

Jason Lee, a Methodist Episcopal missionary to the Indians, established a mission station here in 1840 and the next year founded a manual

OREGON STATE CAPITOL, in Salem. Completed in 1938, it stands at the head of a wide, sweeping mall.

training school for Indians. A town was laid out in 1848 and lots were bartered for wheat. In 1851, the legislature voted to make Salem the capital of the Oregon Territory. It was retained as tentative capital of Oregon when statehood was granted in 1859, and was officially voted the permanent Oregon state capital in 1864. The decison was ratified by a vote of the electorate in that year.

Salem was incorporated as a city in 1860. It is governed by a council and city manager. Population: 89,233.

SALEM, an independent city in southwestern Virginia, is situated on the Roanoke River in the Blue Ridge mountains, 7 miles (11 km) west of Roanoke. Although it is independent of any county, Salem is the seat of Roanoke County. It is a summer resort and manufactures machinery, medicines, brick, clothing, and furniture. It is the home of Roanoke College, a coeducational Lutheran institution.

Salem was founded by James Simpson in 1802 on land from a grant made to Gen. Andrew Lewis in 1761. It was incorporated as a town in 1806, and became an independent city in 1968. Population: 23,958.

SALERNO, sä-ler′nō, is a city in Italy and capital of Salerno province. It is 30 miles (48 km) southeast of Naples.

The old city, with its cramped, irregular streets, slopes down from the crest of a hill dominated by the ruins of Castello di Arechi, a Lombard fortress built originally by the Romans and refortified by the Normans. The modern sector of the city—rebuilt after World War II devastation—extends downward in a fanlike pattern of streets from the old city to the sea. Salerno's chief architectural monument is the 11th century Norman Cathedral of San Matteo (Saint Matthew), rebuilt in the 18th century and later partially restored. It contains the tomb of Pope Gregory VII. According to legend, the body of Saint Matthew was brought here in the 10th century and buried in the crypt.

Leading industries include food processing, the manufacture of textiles and ceramics, and iron, stone, and cement works. Much of the city's trade passes through its own port, built in 1260 and enlarged in modern times.

The Province. The province, in the southern part of Campania, is generally mountainous and hilly and is traversed by Apennine ranges. The chief level stretches are along the coastal plain, where agriculture is the principal occupation. The province has an area of 1,900 square miles (4,921 sq km).

History. A Roman outpost was established near the site of the present city to pacify the local inhabitants in the late 3d century B. C. In 194 B. C. a Roman colony, Salernum, was founded on the site of a Greco-Italic settlement. It was sacked by Samnites during the Social War of 90–88 B. C.

In 646 A. D. the city became part of the Lombard duchy of Benevento. The duchy was divided in 839, and Salerno became the capital of the principality of Salerno. With help from the Frankish Emperor Louis II, it survived the Muslim siege of 871–872 and rose gradually to a peak of political importance early in the 11th century. The principality fell to Robert Guiscard, a Norman leader, in 1076, but the city, with its celebrated medical school and grand court, continued to flourish until sacked in 1194 by Emperor Henry VI.

Though rebuilt, it was eclipsed by the aggrandizement of Naples under Frederick II of Sicily. The city's later history followed that of the kingdoms of Sicily and Naples.

During World War II, Salerno and the beaches extending southward to the mouth of the Sele River and Paestum were the scene of a fierce battle in September 1943 between the entrenched German troops and Allied forces landing from the sea. Population: (1969 est.) of the city, 150,700; of the province, 975,100.

SALES, an important branch of modern commercial law. The term "sale" has usually been defined as an agreement whereby one person, called the *seller,* transfers the general property interest in some specific chattel to another person, called the *buyer,* for a consideration, called the *price.* Although this definition makes it appear that the law of sales might consist of a few simple rules only, this body of law is among the most complex in the collection of commercial laws in the United States. Indeed, Article 2 of the Uniform Commercial Code (1952) is the longest and perhaps the most radical, or innovative, article of the code.

Origin of the Law of Sales. Like other branches of commercial law, the modern law of sales originated in the Law Merchant, a body of rules and customs employed by the merchants of the Middle Ages to resolve their commercial disputes. These rules, though largely unwritten, were known and relied on by most men of commerce. See also Law MERCHANT.

In the 18th century two distinguished English judges, Lord Holt and Lord Mansfield, incorporated the Law Merchant into the common law and made it the operating doctrine for commercial disputes in all English courts. Thus, the English common law, at one sweep, was enriched by a well-developed body of commercial law, including the law of sales. In the 18th and early 19th centuries, sales law continued to develop in England and in the United States along common law lines with new rules and principles being developed on the basis of experience.

First Codifications. By the end of the 19th century, many judges and lawyers thought the law of sales had matured to such a degree that its codification could be undertaken. They felt that certainty of result would be promoted by stating all the rules of sales law in a single statute. Accordingly, in 1888, Mackenzie D. Chalmers, a scholar of great distinction, was commissioned to codify the law of sales in Britain. He was instructed to "reproduce as exactly as possible the existing law." In spite of this instruction, Chalmers relied heavily on sales concepts and rules that had developed in the late 17th and early 18th centuries. As a consequence, his efforts, which culminated in the British Sale of Goods Act in 1893, represented a codification of norms that appears to have lagged behind the then-current commercial doctrine and practice.

In the United States, codification of the sales law was assigned in 1902 to Samuel Williston of the Harvard Law School, who, impressed with Chalmers' work in England, followed it closely. Consequently, his Uniform Sales Act (1906), with a few important exceptions, was almost identical with the British Sale of Goods Act.

The Uniform Sales Act and the British Sale of Goods Act thus represented "old" law at the times they were promulgated. Strong sentiment developed in the United States to repeal the Uniform Sales Act even before most states enacted it into law.

The Uniform Commercial Code. In 1936 the Merchants Association of New York, calling the Uniform Sales Act obsolete, asked Congress to enact a new federal sales law. Their bill was withdrawn when the National Conference of Commissioners on Uniform State Law agreed to undertake a revision of the sales law. This group found that a complete reconsideration of all commercial law was imperative. This conviction ultimately led to the preparation of the Uniform Commercial Code (1952), a statute now enacted into law in every state of the United States except Louisiana.

Article 2 of the Uniform Commercial Code is the basic sales law of the United States and a model for the world community of commerce.

Any body of sales law must provide rules that answer four basic questions: (1) How is a sales contract formed? (2) What are the terms of a sales contract? (3) How is the contract performed? (4) What remedies are available if performance is not rendered?

Article 2 of the Uniform Commercial Code is organized along the lines of these questions and gives elaborate answers to them. The first part of Article 2 sets out definitions and general principles that are applicable, thus permitting the substantive parts of the article (those determining rights and legal powers) to be stated efficiently, without undue qualification or repetition.

The second part of Article 2 answers the question, How is a sales contract formed? Basically it provides that the simple contract rules apply to the formation of sales agreements, but these rules are modified by 10 sections that provide rules for special situations. The most interesting and innovative of these rules are those that (a) validate the firm offer (section 2–205); (b) permit a modified agreement to be effective though not supported by consideration (section 2-209); (c) resolve the "battle of conflicting forms"—that is, settle the dispute that occurs where the seller uses a different form from that used by the buyer (section 2–207); and (d) provide a statute of frauds that is applicable to the sale of goods at a price of $500 or more (section 2–201).

The third part of Article 2 answers the question, What are the terms of a sales contract? Here the code announces a principle of freedom of contract and states that the express terms of an agreement are to be given effect. This principle, however, is limited by a doctrine of unconscionability (section 2–302), which permits a court to strike from the sales contract any harsh or oppressive term. Often the parties to a sales agreement do not specify all of the terms of the transaction. In that case, part three provides a methodology for filling in the missing terms.

The fourth, fifth, and sixth parts of Article 2 describe how sales contracts are to be performed. In essence these parts state that the seller must get the right goods to the right place at the right time, and that the buyer must be there, ready, willing, and able to accept the goods and pay for them. Relief from strict rules of performance is provided for in unusual and harsh situations.

The seventh and last part of Article 2 answers the final question, What remedies are available if performance is not rendered? The remedies, though fraught with technicalities, thrust in the direction of putting the aggrieved party in the same financial position he would have occupied had the sales contract not been breached. See also COMMERCIAL LAW.

WILLIAM D. HAWKLAND
School of Law
State University of New York at Buffalo

Further Reading: Hawkland, William D., *A Transactional Guide to the Uniform Commercial Code* (Joint Committee on Continuing Legal Education of the American Law Institute and the American Bar Association, 1964).

SALES TAX, a levy on the sale, or on receipts from the sale, of a broad range of commodities. The amount of the tax is calculated as a flat percentage of the selling price. The term "sales tax" usually designates the "general" sales tax as opposed to the excise tax, which is a selective tax on the sale of a specific commodity or group of commodities, such as cigarettes, or all tobacco products.

In the United States the general sales tax has been a major fiscal instrument of state governments, many of which have derived more than half of their revenues through this levy since World War II. The tax has also been imposed by local governing bodies. The federal government has preferred the excise tax to the sales tax.

Other countries have made liberal use of the sales tax at the national level. France raises considerable revenue through a multiple-stage, or turnover, tax, collecting a percentage of the amount of the sale each time a commodity changes hands along the route from the raw materials supplier to the user of the finished product. Other nations have relied on the value added tax, which is closely related to the turnover tax in that it is applied at each stage of the production-distribution cycle, although it is based not on the total selling price at each stage but on the value added to the commodity while it was in the possession of the seller. In the United States, the sales tax is usually a single-stage tax applied at the retail level.

The sales tax, whose origins are almost as ancient as the concept of taxation itself, is often attacked as a "regressive" tax, that falls most heavily on the poor, who must spend a greater proportion of their income on basic necessities. The tax becomes more "proportional," or equitable, when food is specifically exempted from the list of commodities upon which the tax is levied. See also TAX.

SALESIAN SOCIETY. See BOSCO, SAINT JOHN.

SALIC LAW, sā′lik, was the law of the Salian Franks. Before the barbarian tribes settled within the Roman Empire, their law was unwritten custom transmitted by oral tradition. The Salian Franks, like each of the other tribes, lived by their own law. Indeed, men continued to live by the principle of *personality of law,* that is, laws affecting persons, into the 13th century. The Salic law reflects this practice and also the later impact of Roman civilization on tribal culture. The law was probably written down for the first time, in Latin, about 500 A. D., before the Franks converted to Christianity. As one of the earliest of surviving barbarian codes, it is a valuable source for the conditions of primitive Germanic life. Later additions show the growing influence of Christianity.

Although, from the late 14th century, royal lawyers made the rule against inheritance by females of *terra salica* part of fundamental public law, the original Salic code was concerned with private and with procedural law, especially penal law. Most of the articles constitute a tariff, that is, fines to be paid on *compositions* or transactions such as bodily injury, cattle theft, and the like. Other provisions indicate Frankish views on marriage, the family, or property. Salic principles greatly influenced the laws of other tribes—the Lombards and Bavarians, for example. Also, until *territoriality of law,* that is, laws of a particular

country, replaced *personality of law,* relating to persons, Salic law was the tribal law most often invoked.

An enormous number of manuscript problems complicates study of the Salic law and frustrates the editing of a definitive text. A critical discussion of these problems and the existing texts may be found in Simon Stein, "Lex Salica, I" and "Lex Salica, II," *Speculum,* vol. 22, pp. 113–134, 395–418, 1947.

PETER RIESENBERG
Washington University, St. Louis, Mo.

SALICYLIC ACID, sal-ə-sil′ik, or orthohydroxybenzoic acid, $C_6H_4(OH)(COOH)$, is a white, crystalline substance used in making aspirin (acetylsalicylic acid), dyes, and perfumes, and sometimes as a fungicide.

SALIENTIA, sā-lē-en′shē-ə, an order of amphibians that includes the frogs, toads, and their close relatives. It is also known as order Anura. All adult members are tailless and most have strong hind limbs for leaping and swimming. See also AMPHIBIA; FROG; TOAD.

SALIERI, sä-lyä′rē, **Antonio** (1750–1825), Italian composer and conductor. He was born in Legnago on Aug. 18, 1750. After the death of his parents he went first to Venice and, in 1766, to Vienna, under the guardianship of the Viennese court composer Florian Gassmann. Gassmann saw to his protégé's education and presented him to Emperor Joseph II. Salieri's first success, the comic opera *Le donne letterate* (1770), led to his appointment as court composer after Gassmann's death in 1774.

Although Vienna was Salieri's permanent home, he spent considerable time in Italy and France. In Paris he studied with Gluck, who recommended him to the Académie de Musique to compose the music for a new opera. The work, *Les Danaïdes* (1784), was a triumph. Salieri's greatest opera, *Tarare,* was successfully produced in Paris in 1787 and created a sensation in Vienna in 1788, under the title *Axur, re d'Ormus,* with a revised libretto in Italian by Lorenzo da Ponte. Da Ponte was also the librettist for Mozart, whom Salieri is known to have intrigued against and whom Salieri was unjustly accused of fatally poisoning.

A remarkably prolific composer, Salieri wrote some 39 operas as well as a sizable body of sacred music. He was active in the musical life of Vienna, serving, apart from court composer, as court conductor and as a director of the opera for many years. In addition, he was the teacher of such composers as Beethoven, Schubert, and Liszt. He died in Vienna on May 7, 1825.

SALINA, sə-lī′nə, a city in central Kansas, the seat of Saline county, is on the Smoky Hill River, 91 miles (155 km) north of Wichita and 112 miles (180 km) west of Topeka. Situated in a winter wheat and livestock area, it has grain storage facilities, flour mills, and meat and poultry packing plants. Its principal industry not related to agriculture is aircraft manufacture. The city is also the home of Marymount College, a Roman Catholic institution, and of Kansas Wesleyan University.

Salina was platted in 1858 and was incorporated as a city in 1870. It is governed by a city manager and council. Population: 41,843.

SALINAS, sä-lē′näs, **Pedro** (1891–1951), Spanish poet, scholar, and critic. He was born in Madrid on Nov. 27, 1891. After attending the University of Madrid, he studied at the Sorbonne in Paris. In 1918 he became professor of Spanish literature at the University of Seville and later held a similar post at the University of Madrid. After the beginning of the Spanish Civil War in 1936, Salinas settled in the United States, where he taught at Wellesley College and then at Johns Hopkins University. He died in Boston, Mass., on Dec. 4, 1951.

Salinas' early works include a volume of poetry, *Presagios* (1923) and a modern version of the great Spanish epic *Poema de mio Cid* (1925). In 1933 he published *La voz a ti debida*, an exquisite love poem that ranks among the finest in Spanish literature. The poems he wrote after going to the United States reflect a preoccupation with the intense loneliness often experienced by modern man. Among his later collections are *El Contemplado* (1946) and *Todo más claro y otros poemas* (1949). His major critical works include studies of Jorge Manrique (1947) and of Rubén Darío (1948).

SALINAS, sə-lē′nəs, a city in west central California, the seat of Monterey county, is at the northern end of the Salinas Valley, about 100 miles (160 km) south of San Francisco. The name "Salinas" comes from the Spanish word for salt, and refers to the salt marshes that once covered much of the area. The Salinas Valley is now an irrigated agricultural region famous for its vegetables and dairy products. Lettuce is the principal crop of the valley. Processing plants in Salinas prepare the harvest for shipment, and can fruits and vegetables.

The California Rodeo is held in Salinas every summer. The Salinas Valley Museum and the Youth Science Center of Monterey County are in the city. The author John Steinbeck was born here, and the area figures prominently in his fiction.

Salinas was founded as a stage depot in 1850 by Elias Howe. It was incorporated in 1874 and is governed by a council and manager. Population: 80,479.

SALINGER, sal′ən-jər, **J. D.** (1919–   ), American writer, whose novel *Catcher in the Rye* claimed wide readership among the post-World War II generation. Jerome David Salinger was born in New York City on Jan. 1, 1919, the son of a prosperous importer. He entered New York University in 1936 but quit to learn the importing business in Germany and Poland. In 1938 he entered Ursinus College in Pennsylvania but left there after a few months to study writing under Whit Burnett at Columbia University. Salinger served in the U. S. Army from 1942 to 1945, landing in France on D-Day.

Salinger's first published work, *The Young Folks,* appeared in Burnett's *Story* magazine in 1940. Other short stories followed in *Collier's, Esquire,* and the *Saturday Evening Post.* A short version of *The Catcher in the Rye* was accepted for publication in 1946 but was withdrawn by the author. A long work, *The Inverted Forest,* appeared in 1947, but Salinger did not attract wide attention until *A Perfect Day for Bananafish* was published in *The New Yorker* magazine in 1948. Thereafter he wrote almost exclusively for *The New Yorker.*

The Catcher in the Rye appeared at last in 1951, followed by *Nine Stories* in 1953, the year that Salinger moved to Cornish, N. H. After his marriage in 1955 to Claire Alison Douglas (divorced, 1967), he wrote sparingly and only about the fictional Glass family. These stories were collected in *Franny and Zooey* (1961) and *Raise High the Roof Beam, Carpenters, and Seymour: An Introduction* (1963).

Salinger's work was received more enthusiastically by post-World War II American youth than that of any other writer, but the opinion of critics varied. *The Catcher in the Rye* is an unparalleled portrait of a hypersensitive urban adolescent. With *Nine Stories*, it presents Salinger's view of the "phoniness" of modern life. His later writings, however, became increasingly affected. See also CATCHER IN THE RYE.

WARREN G. FRENCH
Author of "J. D. Salinger"

Further Reading: French, Warren, *J. D. Salinger* (Twayne 1963); Grunwald, Henry A., ed., *Salinger: A Critical and Personal Portrait* (Harper 1962).

SALISBURY, solz′ber-ē, **1st Earl of** (1563–1612), English political leader. He served Queen Elizabeth I as secretary of state and from 1603, the year of the accession of James I, he was James' leading minister.

The second son of William Cecil, Lord Burghley, Elizabeth's chief minister, Robert Cecil was born on June 1, 1563. Groomed for statesmanship, Robert was educated privately because of a back deformity and marked physical frailty, and later he attended Cambridge University. At the age of 21 he entered the House of Commons. He first joined Elizabeth's government as his father's associate, but his subsequent advancement was due to ability. Elizabeth made him her representative in Commons from the outset of his membership there, and he acted as her secretary of state from 1590 until he was named officially to the office in 1596.

Cecil opposed the attempt of the Earl of Essex to seize power from Elizabeth in 1599–1600, and he negotiated successfully for a successor to Elizabeth. He maintained a secret correspondence with James VI of Scotland to prepare for James' accession to the English throne, and he became chief minister when the King acceded as James I of England in 1603. In 1606, James rewarded Cecil with the earldom of Salisbury. As events were to prove, this reward ultimately permitted Commons to "win the initiative" from the crown, for James was deprived of Cecil's leadership in Commons.

Throughout the period of his service to James, Salisbury used his influence to keep the political actions of the King within the general pattern of Elizabeth's policies, thereby easing the transition from the Tudor period to the Stuart period. Salisbury died in Marlborough on May 24, 1612.

FREDERICK G. MARCHAM
Cornell University

SALISBURY, solz′ber-ē, **3d Marquess of** (1830–1903), British prime minister. His long tenure in office in the late 19th century and spanning the turn-of-the-century period was the heyday of Britain's "splendid isolation."

Born in Hatfield, Hertfordshire, England, on Feb. 3, 1830, Robert Arthur Talbot Gascoyne Cecil was a direct descendant of Robert Cecil, 1st Earl of Salisbury. He inherited his abilities from a family noted for political brilliance. He sat as a Conservative in the House of Commons from 1853 to 1868, when he succeeded to his father's title and entered the House of Lords. In 1866 he had become secretary for India, but his opposition to the extension of the franchise led him to resign the post the next year to lead an unsuccessful revolt against his own party's Reform Act.

When the Conservatives were returned to power in 1874, Salisbury was again secretary for India, and from 1878 to 1880 he was foreign minister. As such, he demanded that the treaty of San Stefano, which Russia had imposed on Turkey and which partitioned the Balkans, should be submitted to European scrutiny. At the subsequent Berlin congress, where he and Prime Minister Benjamin Disraeli represented Britain, Russia's encroachments were limited and Turkey was propped up as a barrier between Russia and British interests in the Mediterranean.

Salisbury was prime minister in 1885–1886, 1886–1892, and 1895–1902, a total of 13 years and 10 months. His governments passed important social legislation, especially with regard to land reform, but opposed any concession to Irish nationalism. Except for a few months in 1886 and from 1900 to 1902, when his health began to fail, he was personally responsible for foreign affairs. He resigned in July 1902 and died in Hatfield on Aug. 22, 1903.

Salisbury's policies were marked by flexibility, moderation, and an ability to distinguish between the essential and secondary interests of Britain. Always willing to compromise in colonial dispute that did not threaten the security of Britain's existing empire, he was uncompromising on problems threatening the security. In 1898 he risked war with France to assert British predominance in the Nile Valley. In relations with the great powers, Salisbury strictly avoided entangling alliances. He argued consistently that Britain, as a parliamentary state, could not commit itself to act in future circumstances in a predetermined way. Its actions, he thought, must depend on public feeling at the time they are taken. By the turn of the century a sense of insecurity had led his countrymen to the view that his isolationism was dangerous, and his principles were abandoned by his successors.

JOHN BROWN
University of Edinburgh

SALISBURY, sôlz'ber-ē, **5th Marquess of** (1893–1972), British political leader. A strongly principled Conservative, he held numerous cabinet posts, mainly in foreign and colonial affairs.

Robert Arthur James Gascoyne-Cecil was born in Hatfield, Hertfordshire, England, on Aug. 27, 1893, a scion of one of the most distinguished titled families in England, prominent in government for some 400 years. He was educated at Eton and Oxford and fought in France in World War I. First elected to the House of Commons in 1929, he remained a member until he was called to the House of Lords as Baron Cecil in 1941. He was leader of the Lords from 1942 to 1945, and, after succeeding to the marquessate in 1947, was leader again from 1951 to 1957.

Lord Salisbury served in the cabinet as undersecretary for foreign affairs (1935–1938), paymaster-general (1940), dominions secretary (1940–1942 and 1943–1945), colonial secretary (1942), lord privy seal (1942–1943), and lord

president of the council (1952–1957). In 1938 he resigned office in opposition to Neville Chamberlain's foreign policy, and in 1957 he resigned again in opposition to the release of Archbishop Makarios, the rebellious Greek primate of Cyprus. That year he was decisive in promoting the appointment of Harold Macmillan as prime minister. After 1945, Salisbury led the Lords away from obstruction of the Labour government's social reforms. From 1965 he opposed sanctions against Rhodesia. He died in Hatfield on Feb. 23, 1972.

A. J. BEATTIE
London School of Economics

SALISBURY, sôlz'ber-ē, a town in the northwestern corner of Connecticut, in Litchfield county, is about 45 miles (72 km) northwest of Hartford. It is a residential and year-round resort community. A point on the southern slope of Mount Frissell, in the northern part of the town, is the highest elevation in the state (2380 feet or 725 meters).

The Hotchkiss School for boys is in the Lakeville section of Salisbury and Salisbury School for boys is also in the town. The Scoville Library, organized in 1803, is the oldest tax-supported library in the United States.

Salisbury was settled in 1719 and incorporated in 1741. Iron mines in the mountains were worked in the 18th and early 19th centuries and Salisbury produced munitions for the Continental armies in the Revolution. Population: 3,896.

SALISBURY, sôlz'ber-ē, a municipal borough, in south central England, on the Avon River in Wiltshire, 22 miles (35 km) northwest of Southampton. It was founded in 1220, when townspeople from Old Sarum, a town 1½ miles (2 km) to the northwest, began a cathedral at Salisbury. The town became known as New Sarum, which is its official title today.

The cathedral was dedicated in 1260 and is said to be a unique example of perfect Early English architecture, except for its tower and spire that were added about 1330. The graceful spire, 404 feet (123 meters) high, is the tallest in England. The cathedral library contains one of four original copies of Magna Carta.

In medieval times, Salisbury was a center of the woolen industry, but it is now a market town with some minor industries. It is also a tourist center, particularly since Stonehenge, a Stone Age monument on Salisbury Plain, is only 9½ miles (15 km) north of the city. Population: (1961) 35,492.

SALISBURY, sôlz'ber-ē, a city in southeastern Maryland, the seat of Wicomico county, is at the head of navigation of the Wicomico River, 106 miles (170 km) southeast of Baltimore. It is the chief trading, manufacturing, and distributing center on the Delmarva Peninsula, which lies between the Atlantic Ocean and Chesapeake Bay and is often referred to as the Eastern Shore. The region is a major poultry-raising area, and also grows fruits and vegetables. Salisbury's industries include lumber, cabinetmaking, food processing, textiles, and machinery. Salisbury State College is in the city.

Salisbury was founded in 1732 and incorporated in 1854. It was occupied by Union troops during the Civil War. Government is by mayor and council. Population: 16,429.

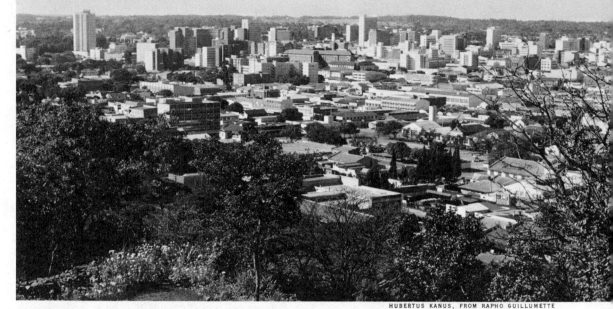

Salisbury, the capital and largest city of Rhodesia, is situated on a plateau nearly a mile above sea level.

SALISBURY, sôlz′ber-ē, a city in west central North Carolina, the seat of Rowan county, is 32 miles (51 km) southwest of Winston-Salem. It is the center of an industrial area that manufactures machinery, textiles, furniture, chemicals, paper products, rubber products, and glass. Catawba and Livingstone Colleges are here. Places of interest include the Rowan Museum, the Old Stone House (1766), and the Civil War prison grounds and cemetery.

Salisbury was founded in 1753 and was incorporated as a city in 1770. During the Revolutionary War, British Gen. Charles Cornwallis pursued American Gen. Nathanael Greene through Salisbury. During the Civil War, a Salisbury prison held some 10,000 Union prisoners, more than half of whom died. The city has a council-manager form of government. Population: 22,677.

SALISBURY, sôlz′ber-ē, is the capital of Zimbabwe and its main commercial, industrial, and transportation center. It is situated in the northeastern part of the country, at an elevation of more than 4,800 feet (1,500 meters).

The surrounding area has gold mines, farms, and cattle ranches. Tobacco is the chief commercial crop, and Salisbury is one of the world's largest tobacco markets. The city's industries include food and tobacco processing and the production of fertilizers, clothing, and construction materials. Railroads connect Salisbury with the neighboring countries of Zambia, Mozambique, and South Africa. An international airport is located near the city. Zimbabwe's National Gallery, the Queen Victoria Memorial Library, and the University of Zimbabwe are all located in Salisbury.

Salisbury was settled in 1890 by the Pioneer Column, the first large group of European settlers and prospectors to arrive from South Africa. The settlement, originally called Fort Salisbury, was named for Lord Salisbury, the British prime minister. It became a municipality in 1897 and a city in 1935. When Southern Rhodesia became a separate British colony in 1923, Salisbury was made its capital. From 1953 to 1963 it was also the capital of the Federation of Rhodesia and Nyasaland. It remained the capital of Southern Rhodesia, which declared its independence from Britain as Rhodesia in 1965, and then of Zimbabwe. Population: (1969) 385,530.

SALISH INDIANS, sā′lish, a linguistic stock of North American Indians, who inhabited the Pacific Northwest from the ocean to eastern British Columbia and Washington and into Idaho and Montana. The dialects of the Salishan linguistic family have been grouped into 16 subdivisions. Cultural differences among the Salish tribes in part reflected differences between coastal and inland environments. The tribe designated as Salish is more popularly known as the Flatheads. See FLATHEAD INDIANS.

SALIVARY GLANDS, sal′ə-ver-ē, the glands that secrete saliva in the mouth. In man and other carnivores the salivary glands have three main functions. They secrete ptyalin, the initial enzyme in digestion. They lubricate ingested food and clean the mouth. And they excrete bodily wastes, notably urea in persons with nephritis, sugar in severe diabetics, or certain drugs such as mercury, lead, and potassium iodide. Controlled by the pituitary gland, the salivary glands also plan an important role in the excretion of sodium and potassium.

Description. In man the salivary glands are divided into three principal pairs, located in the walls of the oral cavity and opening directly into it. The *parotid,* the largest of the salivary glands, is below and in front of the external ear in subcutaneous tissue. It overlies the masseter, or chewing, muscle and communicates with the mouth through Stensen's duct, which is generally found opposite the second molar tooth. The *submaxillary* salivary gland, the next largest, is under the jaw and empties into the mouth from paired ducts, called Wharton's ducts, that lie on either side of the frenulum of the tongue. The smallest salivary glands, the *sublinguals,* are in the floor

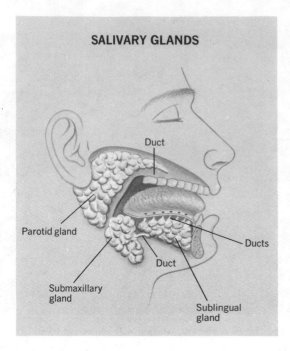

SALIVARY GLANDS

Duct

Parotid gland

Submaxillary gland

Duct

Ducts

Sublingual gland

of the mouth and open into the several folds of the undersurface of the tongue, close to Wharton's duct. Mucous alveoli, or sacs, predominate in this gland. All the salivary glands are richly supplied with blood vessels and lymphatics and are innervated by both sympathetic and parasympathetic nerve fibers.

Functions. The body carefully controls the amount of saliva secreted. Approximately 1 quart (0.9 liter) of saliva is produced daily, about 98% of which is water. A dry mouth sometimes signifies a low blood plasma level and may indicate a patient that is a poor surgical risk with a tendency to go into shock.

The main digestive enzyme produced by the salivary glands is ptyalin. This enzyme acts directly on ingested starch to convert it into the disaccharide maltose. This reaction requires an alkaline, neutral, or faintly acid medium. Little actual digestion of starch occurs in the mouth, but food covered with saliva when it reaches the fundus of the stomach is protected from the acids of gastric juice for a considerable time, thus allowing starch digestion to continue. The remainder of starch digestion is performed by the enzymes of the pancreas and of the small intestines.

The cleansing action of saliva is of great importance in the removal of culture media for the growth of bacteria. Food particles, shed epithelial cells, and foreign debris are swept away by saliva to be deactivated by hydrochloric acid in the stomach. In conditions where salivary secretion is suppressed, as in high fevers or the rapid loss of an essential body fluid, the mouth is deprived of its supply of saliva and becomes foul, and bacteria multiply.

Diseases. The human salivary glands, particularly the parotid, are subject to certain diseases. Parotid swelling, for example, is the first clinical sign of the virus infection mumps. Certain types of tumors, rich in mucin, also occur in the parotid. These tumors are usually benign and respond well to complete surgical excision. The salivary

glands may also become infected through the ducts connecting them with the oral cavity.

In Other Animals. In all animals the salivary glands are adapted to meet the needs of the particular animal. The woodpecker, for example, has unusually large submaxillary salivary glands that assist the bird in trapping insect prey on its sticky tongue. Similarly, the swift uses its own saliva, which is rich in a glutinous substance, to construct its nest.

REAUMUR S. DONNALLY, M. D.
Washington Hospital Center
Washington, D. C.

SALK, sôk, **Jonas Edward** (1914–　　), American medical research scientist, who developed the first vaccine against poliomyelitis. Salk was born in New York, N. Y., on Oct. 28, 1914. He obtained his medical degree from New York University College of Medicine in 1939 and later went to the University of Michigan's School of Public Health. In 1947 he became head of the University of Pittsburgh's Virus Research Laboratory and taught preventive medicine.

From 1942 to 1947 Salk also worked for the Army on the development of a vaccine against influenza. The experience that he gained prepared him to undertake the work that was to bring him world fame. In 1949 the U. S. microbiologist John Enders and his group at Harvard University developed a way to culture polio virus for study in quantity, enabling Salk and his own group to begin their own efforts to prepare an inactivated polio virus that could serve as an immunizing agent against the disease. By 1952 they prepared and successfully tested such a vaccine, and in 1954 massive field tests were successfully undertaken. In the rush of activity caused by the public excitement that soon followed, some poorly prepared vaccine samples led to a number of fatalities, but Salk's vaccine was used thereafter with great success. In 1963, Salk became director of the Salk Institute for Biological Studies at San Diego, Calif. See also POLIOMYELITIS.

Jonas Edward Salk, developer of Salk polio vaccine.

THE NATIONAL FOUNDATION—MARCH OF DIMES

SALK VACCINE, sôk, a vaccine against poliomyelitis developed by Jonas Salk. See POLIOMYELITIS; SALK, JONAS.

SALLUST, sal'əst (86–?34 B.C.), Roman historian and politician. Gaius Sallustius Crispus, known as Sallust, was born in Amiternum, became a quaestor, and in 52 was a tribune. After being expelled briefly from the Senate on charges of immorality in 50, he was reappointed quaestor in 49 by Julius Caesar, whom he later served as praetor in Africa and then proconsular governor of Numidia. Having acquired great wealth, he returned to retirement in Rome, where he built a large estate whose gardens are known as the Horti Sallustiani.

Of Sallust's historical works, two monographs have survived intact: *Bellum Catilinae*, which was probably published in 43, and *Bellum Iugurthinum*, which appeared about 41. The first, an account of the conspiracy of Catiline, was not prepared from original documents, and its chronology and facts are distorted. It aims at the explanation of motive and general development and is of value for its literary rather than its historical qualities. Sallust concurs in Cicero's estimate of Catiline. The second work, an account of the Jugurthine War of 111–105 B.C., shows evidence of the use of original sources as well as of the author's own experience in Africa. But it, too, is of more interest for its portraiture than its history.

His greatest work, the five books of the *Historiae*, a history of the republic from 78 to 67, has survived only in fragments. Sallust was influenced by the Greek historian Thucydides. His style, consciously archaic, is graphic and effective. The best Latin text with an English translation is John C. Rolfe's *Sallust*.

SALMASIUS, sal-mā'shəs, **Claudius** (1588–1653), French classicist, best known for his controversy with John Milton over the divine right of kings. Claude de Saumaise, commonly known by the Latin form of his name, Claudius Salmasius, was born in Semur-en-Auxois, Burgundy, on April 15, 1588. He studied at Paris, where he became a Protestant, and at Heidelberg, where in 1609 he discovered an important 10th century manuscript of Greek poetry, which later became known as the *Palatine Anthology*. Trained as a lawyer, he preferred a scholarly career, but his Protestantism also prevented him from succeeding his father as magistrate.

Salmasius was named a professor at the University of Leiden in 1631 and remained there except for a year (1650–1651) at the court of Queen Christina of Sweden. Salmasius died in Spa in the Spanish Netherlands on Sept. 3, 1653.

Besides Latin and Greek, Salmasius was acquainted with Hebrew, Arabic, Persian, Coptic, Syriac, and other ancient languages. He published more than 80 works, the most important among them being a commentary on Gaius Solinus' *Polyhistor*, called *Plinianae exercitationes in C. Julii Solini polyhistora* (1629). *Salmasius' Defensio regia pro Carolo I* (1649) supported the theory of the divine right of kings and attacked the regicide parliamentary government of England. More importantly, it evoked the celebrated reply from the pen of John Milton, *Pro populo Anglicano defensio contra Claudii anonymi, alias Salmasii defensionem regiam* (1651). Salmasius probably undertook the work at the behest of Charles II.

SALMON, sam'ən, any of a large group of streamlined fishes that are among the most important sport and commercial food fishes. All· salmon have a characteristic small adipose fin positioned on the dorsal surface of the body opposite the anal fin.

ATLANTIC SALMON

The Atlantic salmon (*Salmo salar*) is native to the rivers of both sides of the North Atlantic Ocean. Its body is moderately long and only slightly compressed, the greatest depth being about one fourth the total length without the caudal fin. The scales, which are comparatively large, number about 120 in the lateral line. The dorsal fin has 11 rays and the anal fin 9 rays. The color, like the form, varies with sex, age, food, and condition. The adult is brownish above and silvery on the sides, with numerous small black spots, often X- or XX-shaped, on the head, body, and fins and with red patches along the sides of the male. Young salmon have about 11 dusky crossbars, besides black and red spots. The average adult weighs 10 to 30 pounds (4.5–9 kg), but specimens of over 80 pounds (36 kg) have been recorded.

North American Range. The original natural range of the Atlantic salmon in North America stretched from Greenland to Long Island Sound. In fact, the vast abundance of salmon was one of New England's chief attractions for settlers in colonial times. The Merrimack River is reported to have been so filled with them during the

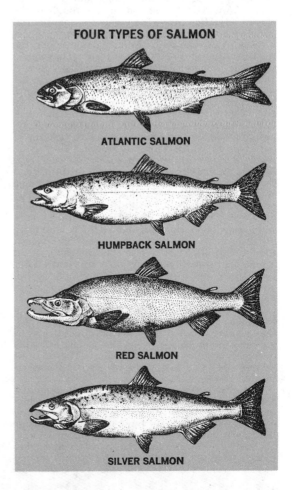

FOUR TYPES OF SALMON

ATLANTIC SALMON

HUMPBACK SALMON

RED SALMON

SILVER SALMON

An Atlantic salmon on its way to its spawning waters leaps the rapids of the Matamek River in Quebec.

spring migration that they sometimes crowded the fish near the banks out onto land. There was a gradual decline in the numbers of Atlantic salmon due to overfishing in the rivers and the damming of the upper streams for milling and other purposes. Now Atlantic salmon range throughout the North Atlantic from Massachusetts to Iceland and from northern Spain to Scandinavia.

Habits and Feeding. Adult salmon enter the rivers and work their way upstream. They spend two years or more in the sea, but little is known about their habits during this time. While in the sea, salmon feed on crustaceans, small shrimps, and young crabs. Young salmon that stay only two years in the sea remain small; size increases with the length of time passed in the sea. Salmon probably do not go very far from the mouth of the river in which they were born. They enter rivers in the spring as soon as the water has reached a moderate degree of warmth, and they therefore appear in southern rivers much earlier than in northern ones. They are in magnificent condition and make their way upstream with extraordinary persistence and force, overcoming swift rapids, climbing cataracts, and leaping unbroken falls as high as 12 feet (36 meters), though only the strongest can accomplish so great a feat, and sometimes only after repeated efforts. When in rivers, salmon eat little or nothing but are sometimes hungry enough to grasp at an angler's bait.

Having reached, as near as time and circumstances permit, the sources of the stream, the females deposit their eggs in vast quantities. The males simultaneously void their milt so that fertilization takes place at once. The Atlantic salmon does not die after spawning and may return to the sea.

Growth and Development. In North America, river salmon spawn late in the fall. The development of the embryo is soon checked by the winter cold, so that it does not burst the shell of the egg until early spring. At this time, the embryo salmon has a slender, half-transparent trunk, less than 1 inch (2.5 cm) long, and carries an immense ovoid sac—the yolk sac—suspended be-

neath. During the next six weeks it takes no food but is supported and nourished by the yolk sac, whose substance is gradually absorbed into the rest of the body. Not until the sac has nearly disappeared does the salmon really look like a fish and begin to seize and swallow food. It now puts on a mottled coat with several heavy, dark bars across its sides and with bright red spots, larger and fewer than those of a trout. It therefore looks very unlike the adult salmon but much like a young trout. In this stage it is termed, in Scotland and England, a *parr,* and was formerly thought to be a wholly different species from the salmon.

The parr stage lasts a year or two in British rivers, and the few observations that have been made in the United States and Canada indicate that its duration is more likely to be two years than one in North American rivers. The parr, which at first is little over 1 inch (2.5 cm) long, has good teeth and a good appetite. Beginning to feed at a season of the year when the water is filled with small insects and other more minute creatures, it grows rapidly, probably increasing its weight 30 or 40 times during its first summer. In two years it reaches a length of 6 to 8 inches (15–20 cm), and its bright red spots and dark bars are replaced by a silvery coat like that of the adult salmon. It is now termed a *smolt* and is ready to go to sea, where it finds a rich feeding ground and rapidly increases in size.

In American rivers north of New Brunswick, Canada, as in those of northern Europe, the salmon returns from the sea when it has attained a weight of 2 to 6 pounds (0.9–2.7 kg). It is then termed a *grilse.* In Canadian rivers in general, grilse occur in great numbers, coming in from the sea at a later date than the adults but, like them, ascending to the upper waters and mingling freely with them. Grilse are seldom seen in the rivers of the United States, yet it by no means follows that the salmon in these streams do not pass through the same phases of growth as those of Canada and northern Europe, or that the growth is more rapid. It is merely that in the grilse stage the salmon of the United States generally lack the instinct, or perhaps have not undergone some glandular change, that impels their more northern relatives to seek fresh water.

Grilse exhibit to a great degree the characteristics of the adult salmon. The main external differences are a shorter head, a slenderer form, and a difference in color and markings. They are remarkably active and agile, leaping to great heights. The male is sexually well developed and mates with the adult salmon, but the female is immature. Like the adult, grilse abstain from food, and consequently lose weight, during their stay in fresh water.

PACIFIC SALMON

There are five species of salmon on the Pacific coast of North America, all belonging to the genus *Oncorhynchus:* the quinnat, Chinook, or king salmon (*O. tschawytscha*); the red, sockeye, or blueback (*O. nerka*); the humpback or pink (*O. gorbuscha*); the silver or coho (*O. kisutch*); and the dog or chum (*O. keta*). The features that distinguish the Pacific from the Atlantic salmon are not marked and consist chiefly in a larger number of rays in the anal fin and of branchiostegals, gill rakers, and pyloric caeca.

The steelhead (*Salmo gairdneri*), technically a trout but popularly regarded as a salmon, also inhabits the waters of the Pacific coast and adds to the importance of the salmon tribe.

Quinnat, Chinook, or King Salmon. The quinnat is also known as the Chinook, king, Columbia River, Sacramento, or tyee salmon. It is the finest of the Pacific salmons. Not only is it superior in food qualities, but it attains a much larger size and has a wider geographical range and a greater value per pound.

The quinnat has a robust body, conical head with small eyes, and deeply forked caudal fin. The color above is dusky, sometimes with a bluish or greenish tinge; the sides and belly are silvery; and the head is dark with a metallic luster. The back and the dorsal and caudal fins have numerous round black spots.

When fresh from the ocean, it is a very handsome, well-formed fish, greatly resembling the Atlantic salmon, though less symmetrical and graceful. It is of a uniform rich red color, which becomes paler or streaked at the approach of the spawning season. Its value for canning is enhanced by the persistence of the red color of the meat after cooking. No other salmon compares with it in size. In the Yukon River in Alaska it reaches a weight of over 100 pounds (45 kg). Farther south it runs smaller, although in the Sacramento River specimens weighing 50 or 60 pounds (23–27 kg) are not rare; 22 pounds (10 kg) is a fair average weight in the Columbia River and 16 pounds (2.7 kg) in the Sacramento. Its known range is practically from Monterey Bay in central California to the Yukon, but it probably ranges farther north.

The quinnat has been introduced into Japan, Australia, New Zealand, and Europe, but efforts to acclimatize it on the Atlantic coast of the United States have been unsuccessful.

While in the sea, quinnat salmon probably do not wander very far from the mouths of the rivers they have left, and for this reason usually return to spawn in the rivers in which they were hatched. They prefer the larger rivers, like the Sacramento, the Columbia, the Nushagak, and the Yukon. They are very persistent in ascending the rivers to spawn, and have been seen crowding up the rivulets that form the headwaters of the Sacramento until nearly half of their bodies were exposed to the air. No matter how far the headwaters of a river are from the ocean, some of the salmon will press forward until they are stopped by impassable obstructions or by water too shallow for them to swim in. On reaching the headwaters, they remain for a week or two before proceeding to the spawning grounds. Their rate of progress varies with the season and probably depends to a great extent on the rainfall and the state of the river. Rain, roily water, or high water always hastens their progress.

When the quinnat first come from the ocean, the sexes are almost identical in appearance, but as the time for spawning approaches, they start to differentiate, and during the spawning season the differences become more marked. The fully developed ova of the female give her a round, plump appearance. The male grows very thin. His head flattens, the upper jaw curves like a hook over the lower, and the eyes become sunken. Large, powerful, white doglike teeth appear on both jaws, and the fish acquires a gaunt and savage appearance. As soon as quinnat reach fresh water, their appetites decrease, their throats begin to narrow, and their stomachs shrink. At first this process does not entirely prevent them from feeding, but it changes them enough to enable them to overcome the temptation to return to their well-stocked feeding grounds in the ocean. Moreover, the longer they remain in fresh water, the greater the changes, and the desire to turn back for food is correspondingly lessened. This alteration comes about gradually, increasing day by day from the time they leave tidewater, until at the near approach of the spawning season their throats and stomachs become entirely incapable of receiving food, and the desire to feed leaves them entirely. The great reserve of flesh and

Netted salmon are hauled aboard a small fishing boat. Most commercially caught salmon are canned.

CANNED SALMON INSTITUTE

SALMON FISHING is both a sport and an industry. Scottish smoked salmon is world famous.

TOM HOLLYMAN, FROM PHOTO RESEARCHERS

blood that they bring with them from the ocean enables them to keep the vital organs active until their mission up the freshwater streams is accomplished.

The spawning season of the quinnat varies in different rivers and, considering the entire Pacific coast, lasts at least six months. A few days before they are ready to spawn, the quinnat salmon uses its head and tail to hollow out elongated cavities in the gravel beds of the river where there is some current. Here in due time the eggs and milt are deposited. The eggs drift into the crevices in the pile of stones thrown up below the hollow, sink to the bottom, and remain in that protected position during incubation. The young also remain in the cavity until the umbilical sac is absorbed. The eggs and young are liable to destruction by freshets but are comparatively safe from other injurious influences. The quinnat is not so prolific as the Atlantic salmon. It produces an average of 300 to 400 eggs to each pound of the parent weight. Like all Pacific salmon, they do not return to the sea but die on or near their spawning grounds.

As the salmon ascend the rivers, they are caught by gill nets, fyke nets, pounds, weirs, seines, wheels, and other devices. In the Sacramento and Columbia the greater number are caught as they head upstream by means of gill nets drifting with the current or tide. In the rivers they are comparatively safe from natural enemies except otters, ospreys, and fishers, but immense numbers are destroyed at the mouths of the streams by seals and sea lions.

Red, Sockeye, or Blueback Salmon. If we consider the entire West Coast, the red salmon is probably more numerous than all the others combined. It is known in different regions as the blueback, redfish, Fraser River salmon, and sockeye or sauqui. Since 1914, when the route to its spawning grounds was temporarily blocked, it has not returned in abundance to the Fraser River.

For canning purposes the red salmon is only slightly inferior to the quinnat, for the color of its flesh is a rich red that persists after canning. Large quantities are canned in Alaska, particularly on Kodiak Island, and its commercial importance to the territory is indicated by the fact that about half the value of Alaskan canned salmon consists of fish of this species. Comparatively few red salmon are sold fresh in the United States.

The red salmon is next to the smallest of the salmons. The body is rather slender; the caudal fin, much forked; the anal and the dorsal fins, low. The color above is bright blue, the sides are silvery, and there are no spots. The maximum weight is about 15 pounds (6.8 kg), but the fish rarely weighs over 8 pounds (4 kg), and the average weight is scarcely 5 pounds (2.2 kg). In various lakes where it weighs only 0.5 pound (0.22 kg) when mature, it is called the little redfish. The red salmon ranges from Humboldt Bay, Calif., to the Far North, but in general it ascends only those rivers that rise in cold, snow-fed lakes. Except in the breeding season, its color is a clear, bright blue above and silvery on the sides and belly. At the spawning period the back and sides become red, and the male develops an extravagantly hooked upper jaw. This fish is also found landlocked. In lakes it is called silver trout; in streams, redfish.

Humpback or Pink Salmon. The humpback is the smallest Pacific salmon. Its weight averages only 5 pounds (2.2 kg) and rarely reaches 10 pounds (4.5 kg). The color is bluish above and silvery on the sides. The hind part of the back, the adipose fin, and the tail have numerous black spots. The largest spots, which are oblong in shape, are on the tail. Its range is from Alaska, where it is abundant, to California, and it also runs off Japan. In food qualities the fresh-run humpback is scarcely inferior to any other salmon. While the flesh has a very fine flavor, it is paler than that of other red salmon, and the species was formerly neglected by canners. By the 1960's, however, humpback salmon exceeded red salmon in quantity landed and in economic value among the varieties of salmon along the U.S. Pacific coast.

The humpback salmon generally seeks the smaller streams for the purpose of spawning and deposits its eggs a short distance from the sea, sometimes within only a few rods of the ocean. At Kodiak Island, Alaska, where it is often very abundant, it arrives in the latter part of July, the run continuing for only a few weeks. Spawning takes place in August.

Silver or Coho Salmon. The silver salmon is also known as the silversides, skowitz, kisutch, hoopid salmon, and coho salmon. It is a beautiful fish, with a graceful form and a bright silvery skin. The body is long; the head, short and conic; the snout, blunt; the eye, small; the fins, small, the caudal fin being deeply forked. The color above is bluish green, and the sides are silvery and finely punctulated. Spots are few and obscure on the head, back dorsal fin, adipose dorsal fin, and the upper rays of the caudal fin. Its flesh, which is fairly good, usually has a bright red color, but this fades on cooking. Canned in large quantities, it is also well adapted for quick freezing for the market. Its average weight in the Columbia River and Puget Sound is 8 pounds (3.6 kg), but in Alaska it is nearly 15 pounds (6.8 kg). Its range is from San Francisco to northern Alaska and as far south on the Asian coast as Japan. It runs up the rivers to spawn in the autumn or early winter, when the waters are high, but usually does not ascend great distances from the ocean.

Dog or Chum Salmon. The dog salmon has the form of the quinnat, but its head is longer and more depressed. The color is dusky above and on the head and paler on the sides. There are sometimes very fine spots on the back and sides. The tail is either a plain dusky color or finely spotted, with a black edge, and the other fins are blackish.

The dog salmon is dried in large quantities by the Alaskan natives. Its average weight is 12 pounds (5.5 kg) and the maximum about 20 pounds (9 kg). It is found from San Francisco to Kamchatka, being especially abundant in Alaska, and also occurs off Japan. The enlargement and distortion of the jaws give the species a very repulsive look, and its large teeth give it its common name. When it has just arrived from the ocean, its flesh has a beautiful red color and is not unpalatable, but it deteriorates rapidly in fresh water. The dog salmon spawns in shallow rivers and creeks.

Steelhead. In form, size, and general appearance, the steelhead resembles the salmon of the Atlantic coast, and it is distinguished from other Pacific coast salmon by its square tail, small head, round snout, comparatively slender form, light-colored flesh, and habit of spawning in the spring. It is slenderer than the quinnat and consequently not so heavy for its length. Its average weight in the Columbia is about 8 pounds (3.6 kg), although it sometimes reaches 30 pounds (13.6 kg).

This fish, popularly regarded as a salmon, is now generally accepted as the silvery, sea-run form of the rainbow trout (*Salmo gairdneri*). It is found from San Diego north to Alaska and, in its rainbow phase, in eastern and central North America. Its color varies considerably with the locality.

The steelhead begins to enter the Columbia in the fall and is then in prime condition. Like the quinnat, it ascends rivers for long distances and has been found almost as far up the tributaries of the Columbia as the ascent of fish is possible. Since the greatest quantities of steelheads are caught in the spring, when the fish are spawning and are in a deteriorated condition, they are not generally esteemed as food, but when they come fresh from the sea and are in good condition, their flesh is excellent. As the demand for salmon has increased, steelheads have been used for canning, and they form a noteworthy part of the canned salmon from the Columbia River. In Washington, where they are regarded by law as a sport fish, their capture or processing for sale is prohibited, but they may be taken for commercial purposes in Oregon.

C. W. COATES[*]
Formerly, New York Zoological Society

Bibliography

Haig, Brown, Roderick, *Return to the River: A Story of Chinook Run* (1941; reprint, Morrow 1965).
Harris, Walter, *Salmon Fishing in Alaska* (Barnes, A. S. 1967).
Hasler, Arthur D., *Underwater Guideposts, Homing of Salmon* (Univ. of Wis. Press 1966).
Jones, John W., *The Salmon* (Collins 1959).
Koo, Ted S., ed., *Studies of Alaska Red Salmon* (Univ. of Wis. Press 1962).
Netboy, Anthony, *Atlantic Salmon: A Vanishing Species* (Faber 1968).
Netboy, Anthony, *Salmon of the Pacific Northwest* (Binfords 1958).
Schwiebert, E., *Salmon of the World* (Winchester 1970).

SALMONBERRY, sam′ən-ber-ē, a raspberry, *Rubus spectabilis*, native to the Pacific coast of North America from Alaska south to California and east to Idaho. It is cultivated for its showy reddish flowers and edible, salmon-colored berries. Salmonberry is also the name of a white-flowered raspberry, *R. parviflorus*, of western North America, whose fruit is not edible.

SALMONELLA, sal-mə-nel′ə, is a genus of bacteria that frequently cause infections in man and other animals. There are over 300 types of Salmonella classified in the family Enterobacteriaceae. These bacteria are aerobic, or oxygen-dependent, rod-shaped, gram-negative bacteria. They are generally motile and usually do not produce spores.

Salmonella infections, commonly called *salmonellosis*, most often affect the gastrointestinal tract but may be generalized. The infection may range in severity from very mild, almost imperceptible, to very serious, sometimes even fatal, as in such a disease as typhoid. Salmonella are transmitted through the feces and urine of infected persons or occasionally animals, with feces-contaminated hands a common vector.

SALMONELLOSIS, sal-mə-ne-lō′səs, is an illness caused by an infection with a bacterium of the genus *Salmonella*. A common type of salmonellosis, is a form of food poisoning caused by eating food contaminated with *Salmonella* and characterized by nausea, vomiting, diarrhea, and abdominal pain. Another form of salmonellosis is paratyphoid fever. See also FOOD POISONING; TYPHOID FEVER.

SALOME, sə-lō′mē (died before 62 A. D.), was the granddaughter of Herod the Great and the daughter of Herodias and Philip the Tetrarch. She was instigated by her mother to ask Herod Antipas for the head of John the Baptist as a reward for her dancing. She is unnamed in the gospel accounts (Matthew 14:6; Mark 6:22), but named by Josephus, the Jewish historian. John the Baptist had condemned Herod Antipas' marriage to his brother Philip's wife and was imprisoned by him. Salome danced for Herod on his birthday and was promised anything she asked. According to Josephus, who calls her the daughter of Herod Antipas and Herodias, she was first married to her uncle Philip and then to Aristobulus, king of Lesser Armenia.

SALOME, sal′ə-mā, is an opera in one act by Richard Strauss, first performed at Dresden in 1905. Its text, a German translation of Oscar Wilde's play, elicited protests at first because of its decadence, but it was ultimately recognized as an undoubted masterpiece.

Salome, in Wilde's retelling of the biblical story, lusts after the imprisoned prophet Jokanaan, who denounces her family. King Herod desires his stepdaughter, Salome, and promises to give her anything if she will dance for him. She performs the erotic dance of the Seven Veils and asks for the head of Jokanaan on a silver platter. After trying to dissuade her, Herod grants her wish. In the famous final scene of the opera, Salome sings passionately to the severed head and kisses its dead lips. Horrified, Herod has her killed. Strauss' revolutionary score matches the story, seething and pulsating, screaming and thundering at appropriate moments.

Roman ruins blend with modern apartment buildings in Salonika, Greece. The pillars of the triumphal Arch of Galerius (303) depict his victory over the Persians.

SALOMON, sal′ə-mən, **Haym** (1740–1785), American patriot and financier of the American Revolution. Salomon was born in Lissa, Poland, of Jewish-Portuguese ancestry. Persecuted as a Polish revolutionary, he fled to America in the early 1770's and gravitated to the patriot cause. He was arrested by the British in 1776, but worked to undermine the loyalty of Hessian troops in his assignment as interpreter. After his release, he became a merchant in New York, but was again arrested in 1778, implicated in a plot to destroy British ships and warehouses.

Escaping to Philadelphia, Salomon acquired wealth as a banker. He freely loaned Robert Morris, the Continental superintendent of finance, more than $350,000. He negotiated the war subsidies from France and Holland, and when Continental money was withdrawn, he distributed $2,000 in specie to relieve distress among the poor of Philadelphia. The government's indebtedness to Salomon, estimated at $660,000, was never repaid to him or his heirs. He died penniless in Philadelphia, on Jan. 6, 1785.

SALON, sà-lôn′, is a French term referring to a fashionable assemblage, generally of literary, artistic, and political figures, held regularly in a private home. Although the French salon extended into the 20th century, the most famous such gatherings occurred in the 17th and 18th centuries. They were usually presided over by a hostess, often celebrated in her own right. These meetings were marked by brilliant conversation and discussions on aesthetic, philosophic, and political subjects. Some salons were politically influential, while others limited themselves to intellectual activity. Among the most important salons were those of Mlle. de Scudéry, Mme. Scarron, Mme. d'Épinay, and Mme. de Staël.

Salon, in art, refers to a gallery for art exhibitions in France, such as the salons of the Louvre. The term also refers to regular exhibitions of works by living artists in France. The first such salon dates from the 17th century.

SALONIKA, sə-lon′ə-kə, a seaport on the Gulf of Salonika in the Aegean Sea, is the second-largest city in Greece. Situated in northeastern Greece, it is the capital of the region of Macedonia and of the province (nomos) of Salonika. Its name is transliterated from Greek as Thessalonike or Thessaloniki. Its Latin form is Thessalonica. In ancient times the town was called Therma.

Lying at the head of a bay, the city rises from the port area, where the 15th century White Tower is a famous landmark, to the acropolis, topped by a Venetian citadel, also built in the 15th century. The lower city, ravaged by fire in 1917 and rebuilt on a modern plan, is traversed from east to west by a Roman road, the Via Egnatia. It runs from the Vardar Gate on the west to the Kalamaria Gate on the east. The arch of Galerius, built in the early 4th century, spans the road on the east. The walls of the upper city were begun in the late 4th century and subsequently rebuilt and altered many times. The white, crenellated walls with guard towers are a distinctive feature of the city.

Much of the city's architecture reflects the centuries of Byzantine and Ottoman Turk rule that preceded Salonika's reversion to Greece in 1912. The early Christian churches were converted into mosques, and when they were reconverted to Christian structures, their minarets were destroyed.

St. Sophia, built on a Greek cross plan in the 8th century, is similar to the celebrated architectural masterpiece of the same name in Istanbul, Turkey, and has mosaics from the 10th century. St. George's, a church converted to a mosque in the late 16th century and reestablished as a Christian church in the 20th century, contains early Christian mosaics dating from the 5th century. The 5th century basilica of St. Demetrius was reconstructed after having been destroyed in the 1917 fire. The Archaeological Museum has artifacts from several periods of the city's history. The Aristotelian University of Salonika was founded in 1925. Attached to it is the university's center for Byzantine research.

The city's economy revolves around the port, which is the center of commerce for Macedonia and much of the Balkans. It exports a wide variety of agricultural and industrial products. Major railroad lines converge on the city, which has one of Greece's main petroleum refineries. Textiles, carpets, food products, and machinery are manufactured.

History. Therma is mentioned in connection with Xerxes' march through Greece in the early 5th century B.C. In 315 B.C. it was refounded by Cassander, who named it after his wife, a sister of Alexander the Great. During the Roman-Macedonian wars of the 2d century B.C., it was the chief station of the Macedonian fleet. After the Roman occupation it became the first city of Greece. It was an early seat of the Christian church, and Saint Paul addressed two epistles to the Thessalonians, the members of the Christian community in the area.

During the barbarian invasions, it was the most important stronghold of the Byzantine Empire and a thriving commercial center. In medieval times it was taken by the Saracens (904), the Normans of Sicily (1185), and, after several attempts, by the Ottoman Turks (1430). The Turks murdered many of the Christian inhabitants, converted churches to mosques, and incorporated the city into the Ottoman Empire.

In 1912, during the first Balkan War, Greeks retook the city, which was ceded to Greece by the Treaty of London in 1913. King George I, visiting the city in March 1913, was assassinated. The city served as a major Allied base in World War I. In World War II it was a key objective of the Germans, who exterminated the large Jewish population before they withdrew in 1944. Population: (1971) of the city, 339,496; of the province, 550,563.

SALPINGITIS, sal-pən-jīt'əs, is an inflammation of the Fallopian, or uterine, tube. The major symptom is usually pain in the lower quadrant of the abdomen, usually more severe on one side. A vaginal discharge and previous episodes of pain may also be reported by the woman. A pelvic examination usually reveals tubal enlargement and cervical tenderness. Diagnosis, however, may be difficult, and the condition must be differentiated from acute appendicitis and ectopic pregnancy as well as from other abdominal disorders. Salpingitis may sometimes be caused by the tubercle bacillus, gonorrhea bacillus, or other infecting agents. In some cases—for example, pyosalpingitis—pus may occlude the tube, causing sterility.

SALSETTE ISLAND, sal-set', north of Bombay, India. See BOMBAY.

SALSIFY, sal'sə-fē, is a hardy plant, *Tragopon porrifolius,* that is sometimes cultivated for its edible root. The plant, which has an oysterlike flavor, is also sometimes known as *oyster plant* or *vegetable oyster.*

Salsify grows wild in southern Europe. It attains a height of about 4 feet (1.2 meters) and has narrow grasslike leaves and solitary showy purple heads of ligulate, or straplike, flowers. The flowers open in the morning and close before noon. The long, tapering, carrot-shaped taproot, also called salsify, is white and fleshy. The salsify fruits are plumed and float through the air like those of a dandelion. The salsify and related species are sometimes called goat's beard because of the long silky beard, or pappus, of the seeds. A hardy plant, salsify may be cultivated in northern gardens but needs a long growing season. Closely related black salsify (*Scorzonera hispanica*) of Spain has yellow flowers and a blackish-skinned root similar to that of true salsify.

SALT, a category of chemical compounds, comparable to the categories "acid" and "base." In common usage the term is applied to one particular salt, sodium chloride, known as common salt. (See SALT, in mineralogy.) In chemistry the term includes a large number of compounds that share certain physical and chemical characteristics. These compounds occur in vast quantities in the earth's crust, particularly as rock-forming minerals, and they constitute the greater portion of the solid materials dissolved in the ocean. Certain salts are essential to the metabolism of living organisms and to the productivity of soils.

A salt always consists of a positively charged ion other than the hydrogen ion of acids, and a negatively charged ion other than the hydroxyl (OH⁻) group of bases. Thus salts, like acids and bases, are electrolytes—that is, substances that in solution conduct electricity by a transfer of ions. Almost all salts are also ionic in the solid state, with the ions arranged in a crystal lattice structure. Salts generally have high melting and boiling points. Their solubility in water depends upon the combination of ions in a given salt, and in solution they generally exhibit the characteristic color and other physical properties of these ions.

Formation. A salt may be formed by replacing the hydrogen ions of an acid with metallic ions such as sodium (Na^+) or with other positively charged radicals such as ammonium (NH_4^+). A salt may also be formed by replacing the negatively charged hydroxyl groups of a base with nonmetallic ions such as chlorine (Cl^-) or with other negatively charged radicals such as the sulfate group (SO_4^-). In fact, salts were originally defined as one of the products of the reaction of acids with bases, the other product being water. This kind of reaction is known as neutralization. For example:

$$HCl + NaOH \rightarrow NaCl + H_2O$$
hydrochloric   sodium   sodium   water
acid   hydroxide   chloride

$$H_2SO_4 + 2NH_4OH \rightarrow (NH_4)_2SO_4 + H_2O$$
sulfuric   ammonium   ammonium   water
acid   hydroxide   sulfate

Other kinds of reactions may also be used. For example, common salt is also prepared by reacting metallic sodium directly with hydrochloric acid, yielding NaCl and hydrogen gas.

$$2HCl + 2Na \rightarrow 2NaCl + H_2$$

Some salts may also be formed by the direct combination of the constituents of the salt, as in the reaction of the elements mercury (Hg) and sulfur (S) to form the salt mercury sulfide (HgS). New salts are sometimes produced through an exchange of ions between different salts combined in solution. For example, adding a solution of barium chloride to one of sodium sulfate yields the salts barium sulfate and sodium chloride.

$$BaCl_2 + Na_2SO_4 \rightarrow BaSO_4 + NaCl$$

Kinds and Names of Salts. Salts are classified as normal, acid, or basic, depending on their composition. They may also be grouped in other ways, such as inorganic or organic salts, depending on the nature of the acids from which they are derived.

Normal Salts. Normal salts, such as NaCl or any of the other salts mentioned thus far, do not contain hydrogen or hydroxyl ions that can provide acid or base reactions in solution. Such salts have two-part names, the first part indicating the positive ion and the second indicating the negative ion. An -ide suffix is given to the negative ion if it does not contain any oxygen: thus, sodium chloride. If it does contain oxygen, as in SO_4^-, an ending such as -ate or -ite is used, depending on the original acid. Thus the salts of sulfuric acid, H_2SO_4, are sulfates, whereas those of sulfurous acid, H_2SO_3, are sulfites. Further variations in the oxidation state of the anion may be indicated by using the prefixes per- or hypo- with the name of the anion, as in sodium persulfate for the compound $Na_2S_2O_8$, and sodium hypophosphite for NaH_2PO_2.

Acid Salts. A salt that contains at least one hydrogen ion as well as the other positive ion is called an acid salt, because the hydrogen is available to act as an acid in reactions of the salt with other chemicals. An acid salt represents the incomplete neutralization of an acid that contains more than one hydrogen ion. For example, phosphoric acid (H_3PO_4) contains three hydrogens. The normal sodium salt of the acid is Na_3PO_4. However, two acid salts are also possible: NaH_2PO_4, in which two hydrogens are still available, and Na_2HPO_4, in which one hydrogen is available.

Methods of naming acid salts vary. In the above examples, the composition can be indicated by giving the positive ion an appropriate prefix: thus, disodium phosphate and monosodium phosphate, respectively. The two acid salts might also more simply and less precisely be called sodium acid phosphates, or the number of hydrogens could be indicated, as in sodium dihydrogen phosphate, and so forth.

Basic Salts. A salt that contains at least one hydroxyl ion is called a basic salt, because the hydroxyl is available in solution to act as a base. For example, the normal salt produced by the reaction of HCl with aluminum hydroxide ($Al(OH)_3$) is $AlCl_3$. However, two basic salts can also be formed: $Al(OH)_2Cl$ and $Al(OH)Cl_2$. Basic salts are named simply by placing the word "basic" or "dibasic" before the name of the normal salt.

Double Salts and Complex Salts. The salts described thus far have been simple salts, but many double salts and complex salts also exist. A double salt consists of two simple salts in combination, such as $MgCl_2 \cdot KCl$, where the ions are sufficiently close to the same size to fit into the same crystal lattice. When placed in solution, all of the components of such double salts are available as ions. A complex salt contains two different kinds of metal ions or equivalent positive ions: for example, $Cu(NH_3)_4Cl_2$ and $K_2Cr_2O_7$. Solutions of complex salts also usually yield all of the metal ions, with exceptions such as the second example above, potassium dichromate, in which the metal ions are bound in complex ions.

Other Definitions of Salts. Modern theories of acids, as developed by the Danish chemist Johannes Brønsted and the American Gilbert Lewis, have also enlarged the chemical definition of salts. Thus a salt may be described as any aggregate of ions, atoms, or molecules joined by a coordinate covalent bond, according to the Lewis theory of acids. However, the ordinary concept of a salt is still that of an electrovalent compound. See also ACID; BASE.

Further Reading: Greenstone, Arthur, and others, *Concepts in Chemistry* (Harcourt 1966).

SALT, in mineralogy, is the mineral halite, or sodium chloride (NaCl). It is an essential part of the diet of mammals, including man, and an important commercial chemical. Salt is widely distributed and has been a leading item of trade throughout man's history. One indication of its high value in ancient times is the word "salary," which derives from *salarium,* the Latin word for money allotted to Roman soldiers for the purchase of salt. The salt produced in those times was often very impure. Thus the biblical phrase about salt that had "lost its savor" probably was an allusion to crude salt that had been exposed to water, with subsequent removal of the true salt content from a residue of clay or marl. Today large amounts of high-quality salt are produced by many different countries around the world.

The physiological role of sodium chloride in the human body is not discussed in this article, but it can be pointed out that human blood is a saline solution and that gastric juices contain about 0.6% hydrochloric acid, the chlorine of which derives from salt. The sodium of the salt serves in the regulation of osmotic pressures in the body and protects against excessive loss of water. When salt is lost in great amounts through perspiration, the loss can be made up with salt tablets. On the other hand, modern diets usually contain considerably more salt than the body actually needs, in which case the excess is excreted. In certain pathological conditions, common salt or any other ionizable sodium compound must practically be excluded from the diet. See DIET.

Uses. The most familiar use of salt is in the seasoning of food in the kitchen and at the table. Table salt is finer in grain than the ordinary commercial product. In damp weather, salt tends to cake by taking up moisture from the atmosphere. The tendency to cake is reduced by adding very small amounts of substances such as magnesium or sodium carbonate, calcium phosphate, or corn sugar. In regions where amounts of iodine in water and soil are low, a small amount of potassium iodide is added to table salt to provide iodine needed by the body.

Commercial salt has many uses, among which the preservation of food is probably the most familiar. At one time salt was mixed with crushed ice in all kinds of refrigeration operations, to produce temperatures well below that of melting ice alone. Modern refrigerating methods have cut down on this use, but salt is still employed in the preservation of butter, cheese, fish, and meat, and in the freezing and packing of ice cream. Commercial salt is also an important material in the leather industry, in the preservation of hides. Pressed salt blocks are a common sight in pastures and stock-feeding pens. Finally, salt is used on icy sidewalks and streets to melt the ice and prevent more ice from forming, although this use can be damaging to road surfaces, soils, and vehicles.

The chemical industries are major users of sodium chloride. When a solution of salt is electrolyzed, the products are chlorine, caustic soda (sodium hydroxide), and hydrogen. Caustic soda is also made in smaller quantities by the action of calcium oxide on a solution of sodium carbonate, but the latter compound is itself derived for the most part from salt. In fact, besides being the source of metallic sodium and of chlorine, sodium chloride is the source of practically all the leading compounds of these two elements. Included are the sodium compounds used in the textile, glass, soap, enamel, lumber, and tanning industries. The valuable industrial chemical hydrochloric acid is for the most part produced by the action of concentrated sulfuric acid on dry salt, while sodium cyanide is derived from the reaction of salt and calcium cyanamide.

Properties. In chemistry, common salt is only one of a large number of electrolytic compounds classified as salts. (See SALT.) In mineralogy, sodium chloride is known as halite. The compound occurs as a mineral in the form of crystals or in granular or compact deposits. The isometric crystals generally are cubic in form and are transparent to translucent. While the pure compound is colorless to white, impurities may give the mineral a reddish, yellowish, or bluish tinge. Halite has a hardness of 2.5 and a specific gravity of 2.16.

Sodium chloride is a stable compound even at high temperatures. It melts without decomposing at 800°C (1472°F) and becomes a vapor at 1440°C (2624°F). Its solubility in water does not change greatly with temperature. Thus at the freezing point of water, 100 parts by weight of water can hold 35.6 parts by weight of salt in solution, whereas at the boiling point the salt capacity of the same amount of water is increased only to 39.1 parts by weight of salt. This property is of use in the recovery and crystallization of salt.

Larger salt crystals that are grown from small ones are usually cloudy. However, if they are allowed to grow very slowly, large and perfectly transparent crystals can be obtained for use in optical instruments. Since the crystals have a tendency to take up water from the atmosphere, the instruments must be kept in rooms at controlled humidities.

Within a cubic crystal of salt, the ions of sodium and chlorine are arranged alternately, one ion at each corner of the cubic cells of which the crystal is composed. When an electric current is passed through a concentrated solution of the compound, chlorine and hydrogen gas are given off, while sodium and hydroxyl (OH) ions are left behind.

Occurrence. The oceans of the world contain the larger percentage of the sodium chloride in the earth's crust. Of the total content of 3.7% by weight of dissolved solids in ocean water, common salt represents about 2.8% by weight, or about two thirds of the dissolved materials. Some lakes and inland seas contain much higher percentages of salt. These bodies of water represent an extensive concentration of such solids through the building up of the materials from inflowing rivers and streams and the subsequent evaporation of water in the lakes. The Great Salt Lake in the United States has a salt content of about 15% by weight, of which about four fifths is common salt, or sodium chloride. The Dead Sea lying between Israel and Jordan has a salt content nearly twice that of the Great Salt Lake, but sodium chloride constitutes only about two fifths of the total weight of solids of that body of water. The remaining solids consist of a variety of other salts.

There are deposits of solid salt throughout the world, some of them several thousand feet in thickness. Such deposits represent the solids left behind by the evaporation of ancient lakes and seas. In some cases they lie far underground, while at other sites they may be exposed on the earth's surface through geological processes such as erosion. One particular kind of salt formation is the salt dome, formed by the nearly vertical intrusion of salt upward through overlying rock deposits. These domes are often used as sources of commercial salt, and they may also be associated with other valuable minerals such as sulfur and petroleum. (See SALT DOME.) Salt may also be obtained in the form of highly concentrated brines from wells that tap underground streams flowing through salt deposits.

Rock salt and salt from salt domes are produced in quantity in Austria, Czechoslovakia, East and West Germany, Britain, Poland, the Soviet Union, Spain, and the United States. Among the leading states in the United States are Kansas, Michigan, New Mexico, New York, and Ohio. Louisiana and Texas, in particular, derive large amounts of salt from domes. Many maritime countries, including France, India, Italy, Portugal, the Soviet Union, and Spain, produce salt by the evaporation of sea water. In the United States, California and Texas are major users of this method, while the Great Salt Lake in Utah is another source of the compound. Other salt-producing countries are Australia, Brazil, Canada, Chile, China, France, Japan, Mexico, the Netherlands, and Rumania.

Production. Salt is produced in quantities that exceed those of most if not all other commercial chemicals, and of most metals except iron. Originally the primary method of production was that of evaporation from sea water. This method is still of great importance in dry maritime regions with long summer seasons, but the greater proportion of salt produced in the world today is derived from rock salt and salt domes. Most of the salt sold or used by producers is in the form of concentrated brine.

Salt Deposits. Salt may be obtained from domes by ordinary mining techniques or by "solution mining," in which fresh water is pumped down into the dome and the dissolved salt solution pumped back up to the surface for recovery. Rock salt is quarried by the usual excavation methods used in such operations. The average purity of rock salt is of the order of 98%, the most common impurities being calcium and magnesium sulfates or the chlorides of those metals. If the salt is sufficiently pure, it is simply crushed and ground and then separated by screens into different size grades and packaged. In some countries, impurities such as gypsum or anhydrite may be picked out by hand. Another technique makes use of the "transparency" of sodium chloride crystals to thermal radiation. When the quarried material is exposed to such radiation, the impurities pick up heat, whereas the salt does not. The material is passed along a belt coated with a thermoplastic material to which the impurities cling as the salt is thrown free, since the warmer impurities in turn warm the plastic and cause it to stick to them.

Salt quarried from deposits containing greater amounts of impurities may be treated in a number of ways. The salt can be melted and recrystallized to separate the impurities. This is done either alone or in the presence of a mixture of sodium carbonate and silicon dioxide, or of calcium carbonate and sodium nitrate. Air may be passed through the mixture to burn away carbonaceous materials in the salt, which is then crystallized and separated from the slag for grinding and screening. The impure salt may also be leached with a mixture of pure salt solution and dilute hydrochloric acid, dissolving the impurities in the material. Afterwards the salt is filtered, washed with more pure salt solution, dried, ground, and graded.

Evaporation Methods. When salt is obtained by the solar evaporation of sea or lake water, the water may first be run into shallow ponds where sparingly soluble substances such as calcium carbonate and calcium sulfate are precipitated and removed. The partially purified and somewhat concentrated solution is then run to another set of ponds. There a fairly pure sodium chloride precipitate is deposited through further evaporation. The remaining solution contains the more soluble salts such as the chlorides of potassium, magnesium, and calcium. This solution, called a bittern, is discarded.

The most common method of producing sodium chloride from brines is in multiple vacuum evaporators. Heat is supplied to the first of the series of evaporators by steam in pipe coils, or in steam chests through which the brine is circulated in pipes. A vacuum pump and condenser are connected to the last evaporator in the series. Steam coming from the brine in the first evaporator is passed into the steam chest of the next evaporator in line, where it condenses and produces a vacuum over the liquid from which it came. Its latent heat of condensation causes the brine around the steam chest it has entered to boil. The vapor from this process passes on to the next evaporator, and so on down the series. In the last evaporator, the vapor is condensed by cool water, and the vacuum is instead produced by a pump. Such evaporators are usually equipped with conical bottoms connected to receivers called salt boxes, in which the salt collects. The brine usually is given a preliminary

treatment with calcium oxide to remove most of the impurities.

A somewhat inefficient system of evaporation occurs in a "grainer" pan or trough with steam coils raised slightly above the bottom of the pan. The tiny cubes of salt that form at the surface float temporarily because of surface tension and while floating are surrounded by a rectangular rim. The crystal ultimately takes the form of an inverted hollow pyramid, called a "hopper" crystal. The salt crystals then sink to the bottom of the grainer and are drawn out on a board to the discharge end by reciprocating rakes.

Insoluble products such as calcium sulfate may be removed from salt brines by passing the hot, concentrated brine through cylinders that are packed with pebbles. The undesired material is deposited on the pebbles. At intervals the cylinder is drained and rotated and the deposits ground off and discarded. In this process, the final crystallization is done in grainers.

WILLIAM T. READ
Former Chemical Adviser, United States Army

Further Reading: Bersticker, A. C., and others, eds., *Symposium on Salt* (North Ohio Geological Society 1963); Borchert, Hermann, and Muir, Richard O., *Salt Deposits* (Van Nostrand-Reinhold 1964); Kaufmann, Dale W., ed., *Sodium Chloride* (reprint, Hafner Pub. Co. 1968); United States Bureau of Mines, *Minerals Year Book* (USGPO, annually).

SALT AGREEMENTS. See ATOMIC WEAPONS CONTROL; DISARMAMENT.

SALT DOME, in geology, a plug of salt that has penetrated upward through overlying rock strata to within a few hundred feet of the surface of the earth. The structure is usually roughly cylindrical and may have a vertical dimension of as much as 6 miles (10 km). Such domes

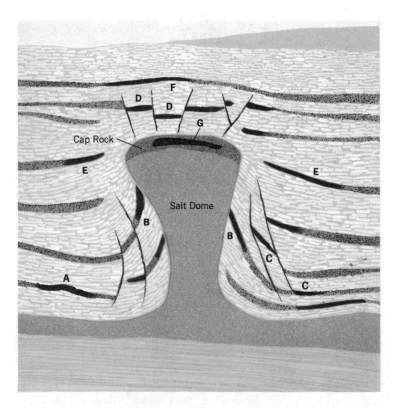

A SALT DOME deforms overlying strata when it wells upward. If the strata are permeable and bear oil and gas, their deformation produces different kinds of traps for the minerals. The subsidence of surrounding strata forms trap A, while the impermeable salt dome itself provides traps at points B. Rock fractures around and above the dome at points C and D are further places where oil and gas, respectively, can collect. Tapering beds provide traps E, while beds that arch upward above the dome form traps such as F. Insoluble constituents from the salt mass may accumulate above the salt dome, forming a cap rock that can also trap minerals, as at point G.

are found throughout the world. At a few locations, such as Iran, the tops of some domes are exposed by the erosion of overlying rocks.

Salt domes represent upwellings from layers of salt left behind by the evaporation of ancient seas and then covered by subsequent deposits of sediments. As the weight of the sediments increased, the salt became plastic and eventually forced its way upward at weaker points in the overlying material. The deformed strata surrounding such upwelling domes often provided traps for oil, gas, and other minerals. The cap rocks that formed above salt domes along the coast of the Gulf of Mexico have proved to be particularly rich in mineral deposits.

SALT GLAND, a gland in birds that excretes salt. Salt glands are larger in marine birds than in land species and have been studied in herring gulls, pelicans, cormorants, eider ducks, and petrels. An outgrowth of the nasal cavity, the salt gland is made up of branched tubular glands arranged about a central cavity.

The salt gland supplements the excretory function of the kidneys, and in some species it plays an even more important role than the kidneys in excreting excess sodium chloride. A similar function is effected by the rectal gland of some fishes, notably the spiny dogfish, *Squalus acanthias.*

SALT GRASS, any of various grasses that grow in coastal salt marshes or interior alkaline regions. There are four known species, two of which are the seashore salt grass, *Distichlis spicata,* and the desert salt grass, *D. stricta.* Seashore salt grass has stems 4 to 16 inches (10–40 cm) tall and numerous leaves. It forms dense colonies along the coast from Nova Scotia to Florida, the Gulf Coast, and the coast from British Columbia to California. Desert salt grass is found in alkaline soils in Saskatchewan, the western United States, and Mexico. Near the Great Salt Lake, Utah, it has been used for grazing.

SALT HAY is hay made from salt grass or grass growing in tidal marshes. It is popular as a winter mulch, or protective covering. Light yet dense, it is used by commercial pansy growers and others to reduce evaporation, prevent soil erosion, and enrich the soil. See also MULCH.

SALT LAKE. All lakes contain some salts and other solids in solution, but those in which the percentage of salt equals or exceeds that of the ocean are generally called salt lakes or seas. The Dead Sea, for example, is about seven times as salty as the ocean. Other famous salt lakes include the Aral and Caspian Seas and Great Salt Lake in Utah. Such lakes often have little or no outflow, and some are natural evaporating pans where deposits accumulate to the extent that they are commercially important.

The materials dissolved in a salt lake consist primarily of common salt, or sodium chloride, but other salts such as magnesium or calcium sulfate may also be present in quantity, depending on the nature of the rocks and soil in the drainage area feeding the lake. Thus some lakes in volcanic regions, such as Natron and Nagadi lakes in eastern Africa, are rich in calcium carbonate and other minerals derived from volcanic rocks. The salt content also varies with the ratio of the rate of inflow to the rate of evaporation.

THE CHURCH OF JESUS CHRIST OF LATTER-DAY SAINTS

"This Is the Place" Monument commemorates the arrival of the Mormon pioneers in the Salt Lake valley.

SALT LAKE CITY, the capital of Utah and the seat of Salt Lake county, is in the northern part of the state. It is the largest city in Utah and is a hub of a vast portion of the mountainous regions of the West. Salt Lake City was founded by members of The Church of Jesus Christ of Latter-day Saints (Mormons). The church still has great influence here, making the city rich with the historical and cultural qualities of this religious denomination. It is sometimes called the "Mormon Capital."

The physical setting is magnificent. The city is bordered on the east and southwest by the striking peaks of the Wasatch Range, and on the northwest by the Great Salt Lake. The main part of the city is built on terraces and benches, geological remains of old Lake Bonneville, the prehistoric source of the Great Salt Lake.

The original streets were laid in a grid pattern, intersecting squarely in compass directions and numbered and named according to their relation to Temple Square, the center block of the city. Each square block is 10 acres (4 hectares) in area. The old streets were built wide enough to permit a horse and wagon to make a full circle. The generous width of the streets allows for the efficient flow of modern traffic, making it appear as though the city planners had great foresight. The beauty of the streets is enhanced by an abundance of trees and well-kept lawns.

THE CHURCH OF JESUS CHRIST OF LATTER-DAY SAINTS

TEMPLE SQUARE is dominated by the six-spired Mormon Temple. The oval building is the Tabernacle.

Economy. Salt Lake City began as a farming community but has grown into an economically thriving city with industry, commerce, mining, and finance. The mountains around the city furnish nonferrous metals, notably copper, lead, zinc, silver, and gold. The Bingham Copper Mine is located a few miles to the west. From this single mine, more than $7 billion in minerals has been removed, making it a leader in world production. Oil refineries receive crude oil from neighboring states and distribute it by pipeline throughout the Rocky Mountain region.

The irrigated Salt Lake valley is a profitable agricultural region that produces meat and dairy products and supplies beets to the regional sugar refineries. The city is also a shipping and wholesale center for many goods and services between Denver and the Pacific Coast.

Federal defense expenditures are allocated to Salt Lake City for the production of missiles, rocket engines, and electrical apparatus. A branch of the Federal Reserve Bank of San Francisco has made Salt Lake City a center for banking throughout the region. The economy is also stimulated by a thriving tourist trade.

Education, Culture, and Recreation. The University of Utah, in Salt Lake City, is the oldest university west of the Mississippi River. It was founded in 1850 as the University of Deseret. It now offers undergraduate work in some 90 fields and gives graduate degrees in more than 70 areas, accomplished through 11 professional schools. There are more than 100 permanent buildings on the campus, more than half of which were built after 1960 on land returned to the University by Fort Douglas, a U. S. military reservation.

Westminster College is supported by the local Protestant denominations. Other institutions of higher learning include the L. D. S. Business College, Stevens-Henager Junior College and the state-operated Utah Technical College.

In the 19th century, Mormon missionaries traveling throughout the world encouraged converts to their religion to come to Salt Lake City. As a result, the city today has an international atmosphere. Life in the city is enriched by the Utah Symphony Orchestra, the Salt Lake Opera Association, Ballet West, and the world-famous Mormon Tabernacle Choir, which performs in the tabernacle on Temple Square, accompanied by the great 11,000-pipe organ.

Collections of art and pioneer relics are exhibited in the State Capitol and in the Daughters of Utah Pioneers Memorial Building, among other places. In the summer a musical play entitled *Promised Valley* is presented nightly.

The gigantic Salt Palace, located in the center of the city, is the home of Utah's professional basketball and hockey teams and provides a place for visiting entertainers to perform. There is also a 15,000-seat arena-type Special Events Center at the University of Utah.

Liberty Park occupies 100 acres (40.5 hectares) and provides boating and picnicking facilities, a bandstand, and an aviary. Another park, Memorial Grove, is dedicated to the men who died in World War I. City attractions are a wax museum, a planetarium, and a zoo.

The nearby mountains are rich with recreational activities. Their canyons provide hiking, hunting, fishing, winter sports, and spectacular sightseeing. For other diversions, one can float without effort in the Great Salt Lake or witness record-breaking land speeds in the auto races on the nearby Bonneville Salt Flats.

Places of Interest. The copper-domed State Capitol, spectacular in itself, commands a majestic view from its location on Capitol Hill. The city and many surrounding communities can be viewed from here in a sweeping panorama.

At the mouth of Emigration Canyon, which is just east of the city, is a monument commemorating the entrance of Mormon pioneers into the valley. The monument is named after the exclamation said to have been made by their leader, Brigham Young, upon first seeing the site of the present city: "This is the Place."

Most of the notable places of interest are inseparable from the dominant culture of the Mormon Church. Temple Square with its carefully kept grounds is notable among these. The 6-spired granite temple was under construction for 40 years (1853–1893). Blocks of granite for walls 16 feet (5 meters) thick were hauled by oxteam from quarries 20 miles (32 km) away. Atop the temple is a golden statue representing the Angel Moroni of the Book of Mormon—one of the Mormon scriptural works. Only members in good standing are allowed into the temple.

Open to all, however, and on the same grounds, is the tabernacle, shaped much like a turtle's back. It has no interior supports, which for the time it was built (1867) makes it an architectural wonder.

Also on Temple Square is the Assembly Hall, which was built from leftover stone used on the temple. In addition, there is a museum and a visitors' center. The square also contains a monument to the state bird, the seagull, which appeared in flocks to devour hordes of crickets that threatened to destroy the first harvest in the valley.

Salt Lake City boasts one of the first department stores in the United States. ZCMI (Zion's Co-operative Mercantile Institution) was founded in 1868. The Beehive House and Lion House, former residences of Brigham Young, are also of public interest.

History. Because of prejudice against their religion and unique life style, early Mormons were forced more than once to abandon prosperous communities they had established. When this began to happen again in Nauvoo, Ill., Brigham Young and others planned an exodus to a "land that nobody wanted." Although they had planned a spring migration, difficulties with neighbors forced them to leave in midwinter, causing hardship, death, and immense sacrifice.

On July 22, 1847, the first of the Mormon pioneers, Orson Pratt and Erastus Snow, reached the Salt Lake valley. The main party of 147—including their leader, Brigham Young—entered two days later, on July 24, 1847. This date is still celebrated yearly as Pioneer Day in Utah.

Development. Crops were planted on the day of arrival. The hard ground of the dry valley broke plows, so mountain streams were diverted to soften and water the land. The year after the arrival of the pioneers, the valley became territory of the United States as a result of a treaty with Mexico. In 1849 an immigration service was begun to aid converts to the Mormon faith from Europe and elsewhere. Funds were advanced for travel to Salt Lake City and were paid back after arrival.

In March 1849 the Mormon leaders here drafted a constitution for a vast territory encompassing some 200,000 square miles (18,580 sq km) of territory between the Rockies and the Sierra Nevada, which they called the State of Deseret—the name coming from a word in the Book of Mormon meaning "honeybee." Salt Lake was its capital. In 1850 the U. S. Congress reduced the "state" to a much smaller Utah Territory, and in 1851, Salt Lake was incorporated as the City of the Great Salt Lake. At the same time the capital was moved to Fillmore, but it was moved back five years later.

The gold rush of 1849 brought with it the first taste of prosperity. Prospectors and speculators raced to the West Coast through Salt Lake City, bringing goods and scarce money with them. Trading became the order of the day as Mormons supplied the needs of the gold rushers in return for their treasures from the East Coast.

Later 19th Century. The practice of plural marriage, theocracy, and exclusivist economic arrangements made the Mormons suspect to outsiders. Conflict developed between the Mormons and the U. S. government, and in 1858 the Mormons received word that a force of the U. S. Army was on its way to put down their "rebellion." Stunned by the news, the Mormons deserted Salt Lake City, leaving behind only enough men to burn the city if "outsiders" attempted to assume control of Mormon homes. There was no open confrontation, and the inhabitants returned to their homes. The troops did not remain in the city, but stayed at nearby Camp Floyd until the outbreak of the Civil War. In 1862, Fort Douglas was established on a bench overlooking Salt Lake City, and federal troops continued to "keep an eye on the Mormons."

The completion of the transcontinental railroad in 1869 stimulated mining and industry here and the establishment of non-Mormon interests. The following year the locally built Utah Central Railroad connected Salt Lake City with the transcontinental junction at Ogden. Eventually the Gentile miners, farmers and bankers coalesced with the Mormons to form the foundation of the city's present-day economy. In 1896, Utah was admitted to the Union, with Salt Lake City as its capital. The city has grown and prospered since without much unusual incident.

Government and Population. Salt Lake City has a commission type of government. Population: of the metropolitan area, 936,255; of the city, 163,697.

LEONARD J. ARRINGTON
Utah State University

Bibliography

Arrington, Leonard J., *Great Basin Kingdom: an Economic History of the Latter-day Saints, 1830–1900* (Harvard Univ. Press 1958).
Morgan, Dale Lowell, *The Great Salt Lake* (McClelland 1947).
Rose, Josephine, and Dougan, Terrell, *This is the Place* (Published by the authors 1971).
Stegner, Wallace, *Mormon Country* (Duell 1942).
Utah State Historical Society, *The Valley of the Great Salt Lake* (1967).

SALT MARSH, a shore area covered with plants that is periodically flooded by the action of tides. See TIDAL MARSH.

SALT RIVER, in south central Arizona, flows westward from sources in Apache county about 200 miles (320 km) into the Gila River near Phoenix. Four dams form lakes that supply irrigation for farming. See ARIZONA—*The Land.*

SALTA, säl′tä, a city in northern Argentina, the capital of Salta province, is on the Río Arias in the Lerma Valley of the Andes Mountains, about 140 miles (225 km) north of Tucumán and 1,000 miles (1,609 km) northwest of Buenos Aires. It is the commercial center for the surrounding agricultural region, which produces sugarcane, wine grapes, and tobacco. The city's industry includes meatpacking, oil refining, leather, flour, and cement. Tourists are attracted to Salta because of its nearby thermal springs and its festivals, including a fiesta celebrating the city's deliverance from a severe earthquake in 1692.

The city has many old buildings and many new ones are in the colonial style. The old cathedral contains images of the Cristo del Milagro and the Virgin Mary that were sent from Spain in 1592. It is believed that the earthquake of 1692 miraculously came to an end because these images were carried through the streets. Also of interest in Salta are the Cabildo, now a museum, and the Convent of San Bernardo. The city was founded in 1582 by Hernando de Lerma, then governor of Tucumán. Population: (1960) 117,400.

SALTBUSH, any of several herbs and shrubs found along oceans and in salt desert areas. See ATRIPLEX.

SALTEN, zäl′tən, **Felix** (1869–1945), Austrian author, who wrote *Bambi* (1923), one of the best-loved classics of children's literature. This charming and poignant tale of a family of deer and their animal friends was first translated into English in 1928. A motion-picture cartoon of *Bambi* was made in 1942 by Walt Disney. In addition to *Bambi* and other children's books, Salten wrote novels, essays, and plays.

Salten was born in Budapest on Sept. 6, 1869, but lived mostly in Berlin and Vienna. After 1938 he lived in Hollywood and in Zürich, Switzerland, where he died on Oct. 8, 1945.

SALTILLO, säl-tē′yō, a city in northern Mexico, the capital of the state of Coahuila, is in the Sierra Madre Oriental at an altitude of 5,145 feet (1,068 meters). It is 53 miles (85 km) southwest of Monterey and about 550 miles (885 km) by road north of Mexico City.

Saltillo is an industrial city and the center of a rich agricultural and mining region. Fruits, cotton, and grain are grown in the vicinity and coal, silver, gold, lead, and other metals are mined in the surrounding mountains. The city itself has woolen, silk, and cotton mills. Handicrafts are manufactured here, and the serapes are particularly sought after. Saltillo is also a summer resort, popular for its cool, dry mountain air. Institutions of higher learning include the University of Coahuila; the Technological Institute, an agricultural college; and the Interamerican University, which offers summer programs for U. S. students.

The city is a mixture of modern and Spanish colonial architecture. Particularly notable are the 18th-century cathedral, the governor's palace, and the Alameda (park).

Saltillo was founded about 1555. From 1824 to 1836 it was the capital of a territory which included what is now the state of Texas. In 1847, during the War of Independence, the Mexicans were defeated by U. S. forces at nearby Buena Vista. Population: (1966 est.) 121,996.

SALTO, säl′to, a city in northwestern Uruguay, the capital of Salto department, is situated on the Uruguay River, at the head of navigation for large vessels, about 250 miles (400 km) northwest of Montevideo, the capital of the country. Concordia, Argentina, is directly across the river. Salto is the shipping and trading center of the department, which has many large cattle ranches and diversified farms. Famous orange and tangerine groves are near the city. Population (1967 estimate): 53,000.

SALTON SEA, sol′tan, in extreme southern California, in Imperial and Riverside counties about 80 miles (128 km) northeast of San Diego, is a brackish body of water about 30 miles (48 km) long and about 10 miles (16 km) wide, situated about 240 feet (72 meters) below sea level. It is the largest lake in the state.

The Salton Sea lies in the Salton Trough, which extends to the southeast as the Imperial Valley, a rich farming region, and to the northwest as the Coachella Valley. The area was once covered by the upper waters of the Gulf of California. After it was cut off by the broadening of the delta of the Colorado River delta, it sank below sea level, and became a salt-covered depression, known as the Salton Sink.

Floods in the Colorado River to the eastward in 1905–1907 broke the levees built for irrigation projects and inundated the depression creating a body of salt water covering about 450 square miles (1,260 sq km). The lake that was formed had no outlet, but evaporation has reduced its area. A waterfowl sanctuary is situated at the lake's southern end.

SALTPETER is a common name for potassium nitrate, or niter. A similar substance known as Chile saltpeter is sodium nitrate.

The name saltpeter means "rock salt," since the compound has a cooling, saline taste and is sometimes found as a crust on rock and earth surfaces. It is also a constituent of some soils. The white crystals are translucent and have a glassy luster. Saltpeter was once used in gunpowder and is still used in black powders as well as in fluxes and in the manufacture of matches, glass, and nitrogen compounds. The liquid salt is a powerful oxidizing agent.

Composition, KNO_3; hardness, 2; specific gravity, 2.1; crystal system, orthorhombic.

SALTYKOV, sul-ti-kôf′, **Mikhail Evgrafovich** (1826–1889), Russian novelist and satirist, who often wrote under the pseudonym Nikolai Shchedrin. Saltykov was born in Spas-Ugol, in Tver province, on Jan. 27 (Jan. 15, Old Style), 1826. After studying at the Noblemen's Institute in Moscow, he went to the Imperial Lyceum at Tsarskoe Selo, near St. Petersburg, in 1838. Following his graduation in 1844 he entered the civil service in St. Petersburg and soon became involved with the radical intellectuals in the city. One of his early stories, *An Intricate Affair* (1848), which condemned social inequities, resulted in his transfer to a lesser post in Vyatka. During his eight years there he wrote his successful satirical character studies of bureaucrats, *Provincial Sketches* (1856), using the pseudonym N. Shchedrin to protect himself from official censure.

Saltykov returned to St. Petersburg in 1856 and held various civil-service posts until his retirement in 1868. He then became coeditor, with the poet Nikolai Nekrasov, of the periodical *Fatherland Notes* and devoted himself exclusively to literature. His novel *The Golovlev Family* (1875–1880), a satire about a landed provincial family, is considered his masterpiece. He died in St. Petersburg on May 10 (April 28, Old Style), 1889.

SALUKI, sə-loo′kē, a hound considered to be the oldest known breed of domesticated dog. A graceful dog, the saluki generally resembles a greyhound in overall form. The male saluki stands 23 to 28 inches (58–71 cm) tall at the shoulder and weighs 40 to 60 pounds (18–27 kg). Females are often considerably smaller. The saluki has a long narrow head with deep-set eyes and long ears that hang close to the head. The neck, shoulders, and thighs are well muscled. The tail is long, set low, and well weathered on the underside with long, silky hair. The coat is smooth, soft, and silky. It may be a solid color of white, cream, tan, fawn, golden, or black, or a combination of colors.

The saluki, also called a gazelle hound, is a sight hound, relying more on its keen eyesight than on its sense of smell when hunting. It is very fast and has been used to hunt gazelles, hares, and other fast-moving animals. Very sturdy and sure-footed, the saluki can run over all kinds of rough terrain.

Carvings depicting dogs that appear to be salukis have been found in excavations dating from 2100 B.C. and possibly even centuries earlier. The saluki was the royal dog of the ancient Egyptians and was prized throughout the Middle East. It is known to have been brought to England in 1840.

BERNARD P. WOLFF, FROM PHOTO RESEARCHERS

In Salvador, Brazil, the town on the hill is linked by elevators (*left*) with the port below.

EVELYN M. SHAFER

The saluki may be the oldest breed of domestic dog.

SALUS, sā′ləs, in Roman mythology, was the goddess of safety and health. She was often identified with the Greek Hygieia and was represented on coins in the same manner. In Rome the temple to Salus on the Quirinal was reputedly built in 302 B.C. The *augurium salutis,* in which the gods were asked whether it was permissible to pray for the *salus* (welfare) of the people, was held annually on a day when there were no wars.

SALVADOR, säl-va-thôr′, a port city on the east coast of central Brazil, the capital of the state of Bahia, is on All Saints Bay of the Atlantic Ocean, about 750 miles (1,207 km) north of Rio de Janeiro. It is divided into the Upper City, which is built on a long cliff overlooking the bay, and the Lower City, which extends from the foot of the Upper City and is connected to it by elevators and switchback roads.

Salvador is one of Brazil's chief ports. Tobacco, sugar, lumber, diamonds, and petroleum are exported from here and manufactured goods are imported. The city's industry includes shipbuilding and repair, tobacco processing, sugar refining, woodworking, and textiles.

A large number of baroque colonial churches are scattered throughout Salvador. The cathedral and the chapel of the convent of São Francisco are especially noteworthy. Other relics of Salvador's past include several old forts in and around the city, many old houses, and several lighthouses and marketplaces.

Salvador was the first formally established settlement in Brazil. It was founded under the name Bahia in 1549 by order of King John III of Portugal, to keep the Spanish, French, and Dutch out of the Brazilian colony. The city became a thriving slave market and the leading port of the colony, and until 1763 was the capital of Brazil. Salvador declined somewhat during the 19th century, but grew rapidly in the 20th century. Population: (1970) 1,000,600.

SALVADOR, El. See EL SALVADOR.

A salvage vessel equipped with cranes begins the work of raising a sunken vessel in the Suez Canal.

SALVAGE, Marine. The word "salvage" has many meanings, but it may be defined broadly as the recovery of articles or materials that would otherwise be abandoned to complete destruction. This applies on land or sea. The following account deals only with marine salvage.

Salvaging Ships. The physical acts of refloating sunken or stranded vessels together with any cargoes on board are defined as salvage operations. The towing of disabled vessels to safe ports is not properly considered to be salvage but service rendered. However, towage service when performed by salvors after a vessel is refloated may be considered as a part of a salvage operation.

Every case is classified primarily as (1) sinking, or (2) stranding. Each presents its individual problems demanding the use of certain methods or combinations of methods. These are determined by the salvage engineer, whose highly specialized knowledge can be acquired only by experience over many years plus common sense application of physics. Local knowledge of existing and potential weather conditions as far as they affect the method and timing of the operation is of great importance.

The cause of the casualty—whether a sinking or a stranding, resulting from collision with other ships, or damage occasioned by explosion, fire, striking submerged rocks, reefs, or objects—and the depth of water in which the ship lies determine the physical and economic feasibility of the undertaking.

In stranding cases, the essential factors in refloating are the nature of the shoreline where the vessel lies, the degree of exposure to effects of wind and sea, the season of the year, the range of tidal differences between high and low, and the weights of cargo, fuel, and water that can be removed to lighten the dead weight of the vessel as it lies on the sea bottom to increase the buoyancy. Equally important for the economic consideration is the known existing damage to vessel and cargo, the probable increase in damage to the vessel by pounding on the sea bottom before or during refloating or due to the jettisoning of cargo to increase buoyancy.

The methods of refloating a sunken ship are determined by the damage that caused the ship to sink, the depth of water in which it lies, tidal or other currents, probable weather conditions expected during salvage operations, and availability of necessary equipment and skilled personnel such as divers. Paramount in any operation is the salved value of ship and cargo balanced against the estimated cost of the refloating and restoration of the vessel to comply with classification and government requirements.

Salvage operations are usually undertaken by professional salvage companies, which maintain salvage vessels fully equipped with the anchors, cables, wires, ropes, portable pumps, air compressors, large and small machine tools, drilling and blasting tools, diving gear for numbers of divers, and a variety of bolts, nuts, pipe, steel plates, timber planks and caulking materials, air and water hose, and an infinite number of other items. Salvage vessels are specially designed and built for the intended service. They must be fast and powerful, capable of traveling long distances, of towing the salvaged ships to safe ports of repair, and must be seaworthy to combat the severest gales with their attendant wave conditions. Modern salvage ships represent the investment of many hundreds of thousands of dollars.

The crews who man such ships are trained specialists. They must have great endurance and willingness to undertake the inherent hazards of the employment.

The chief salvage officer must have many qualifications, including seamanship, engineering and mechanical ability, knowledge of naval architecture and physics, and a working acquaintance with chemical reactions that generate dangerous gases. He must have vision, courage, and ability to command.

The salvage ships' crews are usually divided into two groups: (1) deck and engineer officers and deck and engine room unlicensed personnel, who navigate and maneuver the ship and maintain the entire crew; (2) the salvage crew, which is composed of assistant salvage officers and divers; divers' tenders; machinists; carpenters; pump engineers; electricians; and signalmen, who include radio operators, riggers, launch engineers, and seamen. The numbers employed vary with the magnitude of the operation. For operations on very large ships several salvage ships with full crews are frequently required.

Refloating a Stranded Vessel. A stranded vessel must first be lightened by removal of portable weights of cargo, ballast, fuel, and water to restore necessary buoyancy.

If the bottom is damaged and leaking, the inflow of water must be controlled by pumping, patching, or the application of compressed air to force the water out.

If patching is practicable and conditions permit, divers may fit patches on the outside of the hull. If outside patching cannot be done because of lack of space between the ship and sea bottom or because of rough sea conditions, inside patches may be used. These are usually made by sealing the ruptures with quick-setting concrete reinforced to withstand the pressure of the water outside.

Where no patching is practicable, the damaged compartments may be sealed off at the decks and bulkheads above water in such a manner as to render them airtight. Sufficient pressure of compressed air from the portable compressors is then forced into the sealed compartments to overcome and eject water from the outside.

The lack of buoyancy necessary to float is measured in tons. The draft of the vessel at the forward and after ends immediately before stranding, minus the draft at both ends at high tide as the vessel rests on the bottom, when computed by the tons per inch of immersion, as shown by the dead weight carrying scale, gives the amount of weight necessary to be removed.

Heavy anchors are placed at predetermined positions offshore in deeper water. Attached to the anchors are chains, wires, or heavy rope cables, the other ends of which are on the deck of the stranded ship. Tackles secured to the shipboard end of the cables are so engaged to the ship's winches, capstans, or windlass that the pulling power is multiplied. When the necessary excess weights of cargo, fuel, and water have been removed, heavy strains are imposed on the cables and tackles, dragging the vessel out into deep water. Frequently the way to deep water is obstructed by rocks that must be drilled, blasted, and removed by divers before the ship can be moved out.

The removal of weights of cargo is accomplished by transfer to barges or to the land by trolley lines. If such removal is not practical, the cargo may be discharged into the sea, that is, jettisoned. This is a sacrifice for the benefit of all concerned. The costs of this voluntary act are apportioned among those who benefit.

Refloating a Sunken Vessel. The prime consideration in undertaking salvage of a sunken vessel is the depth of water, whether the ship is partly submerged or entirely submerged. How deeply is the vessel submerged? Is the vessel upright, on one side, or bottom up? Loaded, partly loaded, or empty? Is it a passenger vessel, a dry cargo vessel, or a tanker?

The inevitable calculations must be made regarding cost of salvage, cost of restoration, and resultant net value if successful.

If the vessel is only partly submerged in comparatively shallow and protected waters, such as the U.S. Navy warships that were bombed at Pearl Harbor, patching and pumping would be the selected method.

UPI

Two salvage ships support a freighter raised from the bottom of the Kiel Canal, Germany.

If the vessel is completely submerged in an upright position and the depth of water permits, cofferdams of steel or wood may be erected to extend either the ship's sides or, in some cases, the coamings of the hatches up above the water line. If this is done and the damaged portions of the lower hull are sealed by patching, the vessel may be pumped out. Great care must be exercised to prevent the vessel from capsizing during the raising. At Pearl Harbor the battleship *California* was patched and all openings into the hull closed and cofferdams erected to extend 16 feet (5 meters) higher than the submerged quarterdeck. The *Oklahoma* capsized bottom up in sinking, so that the hull had to be rolled right side up before the patching could proceed and the cofferdams built.

Submerged and stranded tankers usually may be floated by the introduction of compressed air into the cargo tanks to expel the water.

Salvage of Cargo. Cargo in wrecked and sunken ships is frequently salvaged by divers even if the vessel is not recovered. Over $5 million was recovered from the British steamer *Egypt* salvaged at more than 400 feet (120 meters) depth off the coast of France in 1922.

LEBBEUS CURTIS
Rear Admiral, USNR (Ret.)
Former Salvage Officer, Pacific Fleet

SALVARSAN, sal'vər-san, is a trade name for arsphenamine, the compound that Nobel laureate Paul Ehrlich discovered as a treatment for syphilis, ushering in the era of chemotherapy. Chemotherapy is the administration of drugs that injure or kill disease-producing organisms without damaging the host. The compound was also known as "606" because it was the 606th arsenic compound that Ehrlich and his co-workers tested in searching for an effective drug. It was replaced in the 1940's by the antibiotics.

SALVATION is a theological term signifying a state of healing and fulfillment. See BUDDHISM—*Doctrines and Principles;* CHRISTIANITY—*Doctrine and Practices;* HINDUISM—*Beliefs and Practices.*

THE SALVATION ARMY

THE SALVATION ARMY was founded by William Booth, who preached to the poor and outcasts of society in London's East End in the 19th century (*left*). Booth began many programs to meet the urgent needs of those to whom he preached the Gospel. The Salvation Army carries on his work throughout the world, adapting itself to new needs and different societies. At the Bronx Citadel Day Center in New York City (*below*) Salvation Army personnel provide additional educational opportunities for the children of working mothers.

THE SALVATION ARMY

SALVATION ARMY, The,

an international Christian, religious, and charitable movement, organized and operated along military lines. Its original and still paramount purpose is to lead men and women into a right relationship with God. However, it is best known for its social welfare services that are offered to all without distinction of nationality, social class, color, or creed.

Origin and Development. The movement was founded by William Booth, who was born in Nottingham, England, in 1829. He married Catherine Mumford in 1855 and was ordained a minister of the Methodist New Connexion in 1858. He decided to become an evangelistic preacher in 1861 and devote himself to work among the unchurched poor. In 1865 he began to preach in the East End of London, a wretchedly poor slum. At first, Booth expected to send his converts to regular established churches. However, because his converts were so poor and many were former thieves, prostitutes, drunkards, and gamblers, they were not at home in the churches and often were not welcome there. His work was organized under the name of the Christian Mission, and soon the converts were needed to help handle the large crowds who came to hear him preach.

By the end of the first year, Booth had 300 workers. Four years later there were 3,000. They hailed their leader as "General," a shortened form of his title of General Superintendent. In 1878, Booth changed the name from Christian Mission to the Salvation Army. He organized it along military lines for the sake of efficiency, with himself as General.

Early in his work, Booth recognized that little could be done for the salvation of a man's soul if his body was cold and hungry, and he began to provide for the physical needs of his converts at his mission stations. In 1890 he published *In Darkest England and the Way Out*, which detailed the horrors of poverty in Victorian England and offered a comprehensive plan for rescuing the "submerged tenth" of the population. His ideas included the formation of self-help communities where the poor could be trained and employed and ultimately resettled overseas where opportunities were greater. It provided for rescue homes" for inebriates, discharged prisoners, and "fallen women," and for a "poor man's bank" and a "poor man's lawyer." While Salvation Army welfare services expanded rapidly, Booth never marshalled the resources needed for the success of his ambitious program.

All of the eight children of William and Catherine Booth served the Salvation Army in various capacities. The eldest son, Bramwell, succeeded his father as general upon Booth's death in 1912. Ballington Booth resigned from the Army in 1896 and founded the Volunteers of America. Under the 30-year leadership (1904–1934) of Evangeline Booth, Army work in the United States expanded greatly and received substantial financial support from the public. Catherine Mumford Booth, wife of the founder, was known as the "Mother of the Army." She published a pamphlet called *Female Ministry* in 1859, and in 1860 began to preach in public, an almost unheard-of thing for a woman.

By the early 1970's the Salvation Army was at work in 77 countries and had over 25,000 officers in charge of 16,000 Corps (combination church and neighborhood welfare centers) and approximately 3,000 social welfare agencies including hospitals, schools, rehabilitation centers, and other institutions.

Work in the United States. Salvation Army work officially commenced in the United States in 1880, when Commissioner George Scott Railton and a party of seven women officers landed in New York. In its early years the Salvation Army was derided by many who found its marching, singing, street meetings, and uniforms vulgar and irreverent. Its meetings were often attacked and stoned by rowdies. Army members served jail terms for disturbing the peace, and several lost their lives. Over the years its mode of operation became accepted, and its many contributions made it beloved. It is now established in the 50 states and Puerto Rico. In the early 1970's in the United States there were 5,000 officers, 1,100 Corps, and an enrollment of 327,000 soldiers or members who give voluntary service in the Corps.

Organization. The administrative head of the Salvation Army is the General, who is chosen by the High Council made up of Commissioners and other leading officers from all parts of the world. International headquarters are located in London. The United States is divided into four administrative regions with headquarters in New York, Chicago, Atlanta, and San Francisco. National headquarters are in New York. The national commander is the chief officer. The Salvation Army is incorporated as a nonprofit religious and charitable organization. All property and revenues are in the custody of a board of trustees.

Officer Training. Officers in the United States are trained in four Schools for Officer Training. Upon completion of a two-year course of formal study and practical field experience, the cadet is commissioned a lieutenant. He, or she, is also an ordained minister who performs marriages and other ministerial duties. The officer may advance to captain, major, brigadier, lieutenant colonel, colonel, lieutenant commissioner, and commissioner. Officers serve where they are assigned and receive a modest living allowance based on rank and number of children.

Worship and Doctrine. Salvation Army services tend to be informal and lively. There are ceremonies for the enrollment of soldiers and dedication of children comparable to acceptance into church membership and baptism of children. The Lord's Supper, or Communion service, is not observed. The commanding officer fulfills the function of a minister or priest. Open-air services and music are used to attract newcomers.

The beliefs of the Salvation Army are summed up in its Foundation Deed of 1878. Besides a recognition of the Bible as the only rule of Christian faith and practice, the doctrines affirm belief in God as the Creator and Father of all mankind; a Trinity of Father, Son, and Holy Ghost; Jesus Christ as the Son of God and Son of Man; sin as the great destroyer of man's soul and society; salvation as God's remedy for man's sin and man's ultimate and eternal hope made available through Christ; sanctification as the individual's present and maturing experience of life set apart for the holy purposes of the Kingdom of God; and an eternal destiny of triumph over sin and death.

COL. C. EMIL NELSON
The Salvation Army

Further Reading: Collier, Richard, *General Next to God: Story of William Booth and the Salvation Army* (Dutton 1965; Sandall, Robert, *The History of the Salvation Army* (Nelson 1968).

SALVIA, sal've-ə, any of a large genus of herbs and shrubs found in temperate and tropical regions of the world. The *Salvia,* or sage, genus is classified in the mint family, Labiatae. Some species are cultivated for their leaves, which are used as a seasoning, and some species are grown for their attractive showy flowers. Among some of the ornamental species are thistle sage (*Salvia carduacea*) of California, grown for its white wooly foliage and bluish flowers, and scarlet sage (*S. splendens*), a species native to Brazil, that is widely used in gardens as summer bedding because of its attractive whorls of scarlet flowers. Common, or garden, sage (*S. officinalis*), native to the Mediterranean region, is widely cultivated for its leaves, which are used as a seasoning. See also SAGE.

SALVINI, säl-vē'nē, **Tommaso** (1829–1916), Italian actor. He was born in Milan on Jan. 1, 1829. As a boy he showed a talent for acting, so his father, an actor, had him trained for the theater. At 16 he began his stage career but left in 1849 to take part in the war of Italian independence. He was made a corporal and served throughout the siege of Rome. He returned to the stage the following year and soon began to study for the roles he later played with such success—Orosmane in Voltaire's *Zaïre,* the title roles in Alfieri's *Saul* and *Oreste,* and various parts in Shakespeare, including roles in *Hamlet, Othello,* and *King Lear.*

Having achieved great success in Italy, Salvini toured Europe. In 1873 he made his debut in the United States, playing in *Othello* in New York City. On a later visit (1886) he appeared as Othello, with Edwin Booth as Iago. Salvini died in Milan on Jan. 1, 1916.

SALWEEN RIVER, säl-wēn', in southern Asia. The Salween rises in eastern Tibet and flows southeast and south through the Chinese province of Yünnan and eastern Burma. At Moulmein, Burma, it empties into the Gulf of Martaban of the Bay of Bengal. In Tibet and Yünnan it has cut deep gorges, in part parallel and close to those of the Mekong and Yangtze rivers. Although the Salween has a length of about 1,750 miles (2,800 km) it has little commercial importance because it is mostly unnavigable.

SALZA, zäl'tsä, **Hermann von** (1170?–1239), German grand master of the Teutonic Knights. Appointed grand master about 1210, he became councillor to Frederick II, Holy Roman emperor, whom he accompanied in the attack upon the Saracens at Damietta, Egypt, in 1221. He was also with the emperor on the Fifth Crusade, in 1229. Under Salza the Knights helped extend German influence in eastern Europe, heading Christianizing expeditions into Hungary and Transylvania. As a result of Salza's friendship with the Emperor, the Knights in 1226 were made overlords of Prussia, the future center of their power.

In 1230, Salza was instrumental in effecting a reconciliation between Frederick and Pope Gregory IX, and in 1235 he helped resolve the conflict between Frederick and Henry, his elder son, who had headed a rebellion of the German princes. Powerfully supported by Pope and Emperor alike, Salza was able to raise his order to the height of its power, with all privileges enjoyed by older orders. He died in Barletta, Italy, on March 19, 1239.

The Hohensalzburg fortress (*upper right*), dating from the 11th century, dominates the city of Salzburg.

SALZBURG, zälts′bŏŏrкн, is a city in west central Austria and the capital of Salzburg province. It is near the West German border, 75 miles (121 km) southeast of Munich. The city lies in a beautiful valley, on both sides of the Salzach River, above which tower the wooded slopes of the Salzburg Alps. On the east bank is the Kapuzinerberg (Capuchins' Hill) and on the west is the Mönchsberg (Monks' Hill), on which, dominating the city, looms the 11th century fortress of Hohensalzburg, the largest completely preserved fortress in central Europe.

Besides its Alpine setting, the city is noted for its fine buildings and its world-famous summer music festival, which has been augmented by spring and autumn concert series. Most of its best buildings, including the 17th century cathedral and the Residenz, the former archiepiscopal palace, are from the baroque period and show a strong Italian influence. Mozart was born in the city, and, although little honored during his life, he now has a statue in the Mozartplatz, his birthplace is a museum, and his music dominates the festival.

Originally a Roman settlement known as Juvavum, the city grew up around an 8th century monastery. It took its modern name, meaning "castle of salt," from the area's rich salt mines. A famed religious stronghold, it was for over 1,000 years the seat of the archbishops of Salzburg, who ranked among the most powerful princes of the Holy Roman Empire. The stern ecclesiastical bond was broken in 1802 when the see was secularized. Since then the city has been alternately in Austrian and German hands.

The Province. The province is mountainous, with the Hohe Tauern and Salzburg Alps containing some of the world's most beautiful mountain panoramas. Its numerous Alpine resorts and spas draw a large tourist trade, the province's leading industry. There is limited agriculture and some mining of salt and metals. The province has an area of 2,762 square miles (7,154 sq km). Population: (1971) of the city, 127,455; of the province, 399,681.

SALZGITTER, zälts′gi-tər, an industrial city in West Germany, is near the border with East Germany, in the foothills of the Harz Mountains. It is in the state of Lower Saxony, about 15 miles (24 km) southwest of Brunswick. A market center during the Middle Ages, it did not begin to develop industrially until the 1930's.

The original town of Salzgitter took the name of Salzgitter-Bad, for its saline springs. In 1937 the government began building smelters and steel plants in Salzgitter to exploit the area's iron-ore deposits, the largest in Germany. The town of Salzgitter and numerous surrounding villages were combined into a municipal district that was known as Watenstedt-Salzgitter from 1942 to 1951. In addition to various types of steel, made from local ore, the city manufactures coke, chemicals, textiles, machinery, food products, and radio and television sets. Population: (1969 est.) 118,000.

SALZKAMMERGUT, zälts′käm-ər-gŏŏt, is an Alpine district in Austria, some 230 square miles (596 sq km) in area. It lies in the provinces of Styria, Upper Austria, and Salzburg. The district derives its name from its extensive deposits of salt, and its name means "property of the salt administration."

It has been called the "Austrian Switzerland" because of its magnificent lakes and mountainous scenery, and it is a popular resort area. The lakes include Atter, Traun, Hallstätt, and St. Wolfgang. Dachstein, 9,830 feet (2,996 meters) in height, is the highest peak. The principal resort town of the Salzkammergut is Bad Ischl, in Upper Austria.

SAMAL, sä'mäl, is a small island in the southern Philippines. It is located in Davao Gulf, which indents the southern coast of Mindanao Island. The island shelters Davao harbor to the west.

About 17 miles (27 km) long and 13 miles (21 km) wide, Samal has an area of 96 square miles (249 sq km). The island has a general elevation of 820 feet (250 meters). The soil is fertile, and cacao is the chief cash crop. High-quality timber is also produced. The island is administered as part of Davao del Norte province. Population: (1960) 33,103.

SAMANIDS, sə-mä'nidz, a native Persian dynasty that ruled in eastern Persia (Iran) and Transoxiana, in Central Asia, in the 9th and 10th centuries. The dynasty was named for Saman, a Persian noble who converted to Islam. His grandsons served the Baghdad caliphate, and Nasir I, a great-grandson, became governor of Transoxiana in 875. His successor expanded his rule to include Khurasan and established his capital at Bukhara.

Persian literature and art flourished under the Samanid rulers. In the late 10th century, under pressure from the Turks on the north and the Ghaznavids on the east, the dynasty weakened. Its last ruler, Abdul-Malik II, was overthrown in 999.

SAMAR, sä'mär, is an island in the eastern Philippines. One of the Visayan group, it is separated from Luzon on the north by San Bernardino Strait and from Leyte on the southwest by the narrow San Jaunico Strait. It is bounded on the east by the Pacific Ocean, on the south by Leyte Gulf, and on the west by the Samar Sea.

With an area of 5,050 square miles (13,080 sq km), Samar is the third-largest island of the Philippines, after Luzon and Mindanao. With several offshore islands it constituted a province until it was divided in the 1960's into three new provinces—Eastern Samar, Northern Samar, and Western Samar.

The Land. Samar is primarily rugged, with level plains confined to the coastal areas. A central mountain chain traverses the island from northwest to southeast and is divided near the center by the Ulut River valley. The highest point is Mt. Capotoan, which rises to 2,789 feet (850 meters) in the north central area. Another group of mountains in the extreme northwest reaches elevations between 1,700 and 1,800 feet (520–550 meters).

Samar has a number of short, navigable rivers, including the Oras, Ulut, Suribao, and Gatubig. There are also four lakes. Dense tropical forests are found in the interior. Rainfall averages about 100 to 170 inches (2,540–4,320 mm) a year throughout the island.

The People. The population of Samar and its offshore islands was 1,024,336 in 1970. Most of the people are members of the Samar-Leyte (Waray-Waray) group, the sixth-largest cultural-linguistic group in the Philippines. They are primarily Roman Catholics, although there are also a number of Protestant communities. The Samaran language is a member of the Malay-Polynesian linguistic family. The population is primarily rural, living in small villages. The largest city and major port is Catbalogan, on the west coast.

Economy. Agriculture is the principal economic activity. Rice is the chief subsistence crop, followed by sweet potatoes and cassava. Coconuts, hemp, and bananas are grown for export. Iron ore and copper are mined. Fishing and lumbering are also important.

History. Samar was known to early Spanish explorers as Ibabao. An unsuccessful rebellion against Spanish rule erupted on the island in 1649. From 1735 to 1768, Samar was combined into a single province with Leyte.

Samar came under Japanese control during World War II in 1942 and was retaken by American forces in October 1944. The waters around the island were the scene of a series of engagements known as the Battle for Leyte Gulf (October 23–26), in which Allied sea and air forces defeated an attempt by the Japanese Navy to halt the invasion of the Philippines.

SAMARA, su-mä'rə, the former name of Kuibyshev, a city in the USSR. See KUIBYSHEV.

SAMARIA, sə-mâr'ē-ə, was the capital of the ancient kingdom of northern Israel. It was also the region of northern Palestine that was named for the capital city. The site of the city of Samaria is located 42 miles (67 km) north of Jerusalem, near the modern village of Sebastiyeh, Israel. According to I Kings 16:24, the hill on which the city was built was purchased by Omri, king of Israel (reigned about 876–869 B.C.). Omri built a fortified city on the site and made it the capital of the northern kingdom of Israel. His successor, Ahab, continued the construction. Archaeological investigations have revealed a large and well-planned city with an extensive royal quarter. The city's greatest period of prosperity occurred during the reign of Jeroboam II (about 786–746 B.C.) when the kingdom expanded to include parts of Syria and Transjordan.

After the death of Jeroboam the city entered a period of decline with the ascendancy of the Assyrian Empire. The city fell to the Assyrian armies of Sargon II in 721 B.C. Sargon deported most of the inhabitants and settled other conquered peoples in it. Samaria became an administrative center for the Assyrian Empire. With the breakup of the empire, Samaria came under Babylonian control in 612 B.C. and passed to Persian control in 539 B.C. It was successively part of the Macedonian, Ptolemaic, and Seleucid empires. In 107 B.C. it again became part of a Jewish kingdom when it fell to the forces of John Hyrcanus, Hasmonean ruler of Palestine. Samaria became the seat of a Roman province in 63 B.C. It regained some of its prominence under Herod the Great, who rebuilt it and renamed it Sebaste in 30 B.C. Herod also constructed a temple of Emperor Augustus in the city. During the Jewish revolt of 66 A.D. the city was burned by rebels, but it was soon rebuilt. Under the empire of Constantine (about 280–337 A.D.) Sebaste became the seat of an episcopal see. It was occupied by Muslim Arabs in 634 A.D.

The region of northern Palestine became known as Samaria after the split of Solomon's kingdom into northern Israel and Judah in the 9th century B.C. The boundaries of Samaria changed with the successive ruling powers, and its extent can only be roughly given. It was bounded on the north by the valley of Jezreel and extended south as far as Jericho and the valley of Aijalon. In the east it was bounded by the Jordan River and in the west by the coastal plain of the Mediterranean.

SAMARITANS, sə-mar'ə-tənz, a Jewish sect whose center of worship is Mount Gerizim in northern Israel. The name is familiar to many through the parable of the Good Samaritan recorded in Luke 10:25–37. The origins of the Samaritans are difficult to trace. They claim descent from the Israelite tribes of Ephraim and Manasseh. A large portion of the Samaritan population was deported after the Assyrian conquest of the region in 721 B.C., and other conquered peoples from Cutha, Babylon, and Hamath were resettled in the area. Traditional Judaism looked upon the Samaritans, whom they usually called Cuthites, as a mixed race and not really Jews. The Samaritans maintained that not all the Jews were deported from Samaria and that many returned from exile. The Jews also claimed that the Samaritans obstructed the efforts of Ezra and Nehemiah to rebuild the temple in Jerusalem after the return from the Babylonian exile. They refer to themselves as *Shamerin,* meaning "observants," rather than *Shomeronim,* which means "inhabitants of Samaria." The traditional antipathy between the two has made the historical accounts on both sides unreliable.

The Samaritans built a temple of their own on Mount Gerizim in opposition to the Jerusalem temple. Josephus, the Jewish historian, gives the date of its building as sometime during the reign of the last Persian king, Darius Codommanus (335–330 B.C.). Josephus also related a story about Manasseh, a priest of Jerusalem who was exiled because he married the daughter of Sanballat, the Persian governor of Samaria. He indicates that it was Manasseh who originally requested permission for a temple, a request that was granted by Alexander the Great in 332 B.C. after he had conquered the area. When Samaria was under the control of the Hellenizing ruler Antiochus IV Epiphanes (reigned 175–163 B.C.) the Samaritans had their temple dedicated to Zeus Hellenios. It was destroyed by the Hasmonean ruler John Hyrcanus in 109 B.C.

The Samaritans joined with the Jews in their revolt against Roman authority in 66 A.D. and shared in the retribution exacted, losing about 12,000 persons. They also shared in the Jewish dispersion throughout the Roman Empire. Samaritan enclaves are recorded in Egypt and Rome. They were constantly harassed by Christian rulers but enjoyed a minor revival in the 4th century when a number of new synagogues were constructed by Baba Rabba, a Samaritan leader. All their privileges and rights were revoked by Emperor Justinian in 529 A.D. They came under Muslim rule in 636. Little was known of the Samaritans until European scholars became interested in them in the 16th century. In 1616, Pietro della Valle secured a copy of the Samaritan Pentateuch and other writings. By the mid-20th century fewer than 200 Samaritans remained, mainly in Nablus, near Mount Gerizim.

Beliefs. The Samaritans believe that God is incorporeal, without associate, and indescribable. Moses is a unique being, the "light of the world," and the prophet par excellence who intercedes with God for his followers. The Torah was written by God and is immutable. Mount Gerizim is the place chosen by God for worship of Him, and is the center of the world. Streams of living water will flow from it at the end of the world. There will be a day of vengeance and reward in which the evil will be condemned to eternal fire and the good will enter Eden.

The Samaritans conceive of their history as consisting of two periods: one of God's favor during which the temple on Mount Gerizim endured; and the second, one of God's displeasure, which has lasted since the temple's destruction. They look to the restoration of the temple with the coming of the *Taheb,* or "restorer," who will usher in a new eschatalogical age in which the temple and the sacrificial cult will be restored.

Samaritan theology shows some Muslim influences. For example, reference to God as being without associate has a direct parallel in Muslim descriptions of God. Similarly, the way in which Moses is described is very much like Muslim descriptions of the prophet Mohammed.

Language and Literature. The Samaritan language is a dialect of western Aramaic. However, since the Samaritans have been under Muslim domination, Arabic has been used except for liturgical and scholarly purposes. The principal piece of Samaritan literature is the Samaritan Pentateuch, which is written in Hebrew but in an archaic script. There are estimated to be about 6,000 variants in the Samaritan text, as compared with the Masoretic Hebrew version. Some of the variants reflect Samaritan religious views—for example, after Exodus 20:17 a command to build a temple on Mount Gerizim is introduced. During the period of Hellenistic domination some works were written in Greek. Excerpts from these works have been preserved in Eusebius of Caesarea's *Ecclesiastical History.*

Other early works include the *Discourse of Marqeh,* which is a sermon on Moses by a 4th century A.D. theologian, and a series of hymns called the *Duriān,* which was written by Amran Darah. Later works include a translation of the Pentateuch into Arabic prepared by Abul Hasan (Judah ha-Leir) in the 12th century and revised in the 14th century by Abul Barakat. Two 10th century works are also of interest: the *Kafi,* which is a compendium of ritual by Joseph of Askar, and the *Tabah,* or "potpourri," which is a collection of ritual and doctrinal discussions.

Further Reading: Gaster, Moses, *The Samaritans* (Search 1925); id., *Samaritan Eschatology* (Search 1932); Montgomery, J. A., *The Samaritans* (1907).

SAMARIUM, sə-mar'ē-əm, symbol Sm, a hard, brittle, silvery metal, is one of the rare-earth, or lanthanide, series of elements. It was discovered spectroscopically by the French chemist Paul Émile Lecoq de Boisbaudran, who isolated its trivalent oxide from the mineral samarskite, for which the element is named. Samarium is used to dope calcium fluoride crystals for lasers, as a catalyst in certain organic reactions, and in the ceramics industry. Along with other rare earths, it is used for carbon-arc lighting. The isotope Sm–149 is a good neutron absorber for nuclear reactors. Samarium salts are used as sensitizers for infrared-sensitive phosphors.

The atomic number of samarium is 62, and its atomic weight is 150.35. It has 18 known isotopes, of which 7 occur naturally. The specific gravity of the metal is about 7.5. Its melting point is 1072° C (1961.6° F), and its boiling point is 1900° C (3452° F). The metal ignites in air at about 150° C (302° F). Its more common valence state is $+3$, but it also forms divalent ($+2$) compounds. Samarium is obtained commercially by extraction from monazite. It is also found in gadolinite and other minerals in association with other rare earths.

SAMARKAND, sam'ər-kand, is a city in the USSR in the Uzbek republic. It is about 170 miles (275 km) southwest of Tashkent, at an altitude of 2,358 feet (719 meters), in the fertile valley of the Zeravshan River. It is the administrative center of Samarkand oblast. The chief industries are the manufacture of wool, cotton, silk, leather, and food products, and machinery. One of the oldest cities in Central Asia, rich in history and architecture, Samarkand is made up of a native section with squat yellow buildings crowded along narrow winding streets and a Russian section with wide streets lined with poplars and other trees.

History and Monuments. The city was first mentioned by the Greeks in the 4th century B.C. as Maracanda, the capital of Sogdiana. The origin of the name is probably Persian, but its exact meaning is unknown. When captured by Alexander the Great in 329 B.C., it was a large and flourishing city, located on the Silk Road between China and the West.

Overrun by the Arabs early in the 8th century, Samarkand was later governed by the Samanids (874–999), who were vassals of the Baghdad caliphs. The city became a center for the manufacture of rag paper, introduced by the Chinese, which replaced parchment and papyrus. Arab hegemony was brought to a close at the end of the 10th century by Muslim Turks, who established the Kara Khanid state. Conquered in 1130 by Seljuk Turks, named after Seljuk, their leader, Samarkand was shortly taken by the Kara Khitai Mongolian nomads from the east. A local uprising against the Kara Khitai was successful, but Samarkand fell to the forces of Genghis Khan in 1220, suffering much destruction.

With the disruption of the Mongol Empire in the second half of the 14th century, Samarkand in 1370 became the center of a new Mongol Empire, the empire of Timur. Timur, or Timur the Lame (Tamerlane), was a Turkicized Mongol from Kesh (now Shakhrisyabz) on the Kashka

Samarkand has a large population of Uzbeks, central Asians different culturally and racially from Russians.

FRANCES MORTIMER, FROM RAPHO-GUILLUMETTE

TASS, FROM SOVFOTO

In Samarkand the Bibi Khanum, completed in 1504, represents the finest in 15th century Muslim architecture.

Darya to the south. When Timur's empire reached its zenith, Samarkand ruled over the lands from the Aral Sea on the north to the Persian Gulf on the south and from Anatolia on the west to India on the east.

Timur made his capital a prosperous and beautiful city. Magnificent buildings, representing the finest in 15th century Muslim architecture, were erected. Among these are the Bibi Khanum, dating from 1399–1404, a group of buildings including a madrasa, or college, built by Timur's favorite Chinese wife. The most famous of all is the Gur Emir Mausoleum, Timur's tomb, built in 1405. Made of native baked clay, it suffered in succeeding centuries from the ravages of time and earthquakes. Restored in 1958, it still reveals an impressive sky-blue, ribbed cupola and walls ornamented with blue mosaic.

Timur's grandson, Ulugh Beg, a learned astronomer and mathematician, turned Samarkand into a renowned center of learning. In 1437 he built an observatory, the ruins of which were uncovered in 1908. Equally famous was the Ulugh Beg Madrasa (1421) facing the Registan, a square in the center of the old city. Two other madrasas, modeled on the Ulugh Beg, were subsequently erected on the square, the Shir Dor in 1619 and the Tillia Kari in 1647. Other mosques and mausoleums built outside the city, such as the Shah-i-Zindah, are neither so large nor so impressive as the Bibi Khanum or the Registan groups. The Shah-i-Zindah Mosque, built by Timur to honor a nephew of Mohammed who reputedly died in the City, contains the tombs of Timur's relatives.

Samarkand was seldom visited by Europeans between the 15th century and the 19th. But the most splendid account of its medieval glory is given by Ruy González de Clavijo, an emissary of Henry III of Castile to Timur's court in 1403–1406. During subsequent centuries Samarkand fell under Chinese jurisdiction and the emir of Bukhara. In 1868 it was captured by the Russians and formally ceded to Russia by Bukhara. Samarkand and other lands taken from the emirate were formed into the Zeravshan district and, in 1887, the region of Samarkand. In 1888 the Trans-Caspian Railroad reached Samarkand from the west, and it later extended eastward to Tashkent. By 1908, Samarkand was a city of more than 80,000, with a significant Russian minority.

Samarkand was the birthplace (1904) of a Muslim reform movement known as Dzhadidism and was an important center of Turkestani nationalism. On Nov. 28, 1917, the revolutionary Soviet government established itself in the city. From 1924 to 1930, when Tashkent was made the capital, Samarkand was the capital of the Uzbek republic. In 1933 the Uzbek State University was established in the city on the base of a pedagogical academy.

The Oblast. The oblast is one of the main areas of the Uzbek republic. Formed in 1938, it has an area of 12,300 square miles (31,857 sq km). The three main cities are Dzhizak, Katta-Kurgan, and Samarkand, the oblast center. The Trans-Caspian Railroad crosses the oblast on the route from Krasnovodsk to Tashkent. Uzbeks make up a majority of the population.

Dominated by uplands in the north and southeast, the oblast is drained by the Zeravshan River, which occupies a broad central valley. Beyond the mountain in the northeast, the oblast includes part of the very dry Golodnaya Step (Hungry Steppe). Precipitation is low, varying from about 7 inches (180 mm) in the lowlands to over 15 inches (380 mm) in the mountains. Though winter temperatures may fall below freezing, the frost-free period lasts for over 200 days.

Essentially agricultural, the oblast depends on the waters of the Zeravshan for irrigation. About two thirds of the irrigated area is in cotton, but grains are also grown, along with vegetables, potatoes, melons, and grapes. Silkworms and karakul sheep are raised. Industries include cotton ginning, wine production, and food processing. Tungsten and molybdenum are mined at Lyangar in the mountain range of the Nura Tau in the north. Population: (1971) of the city, 272,000; of the oblast, 1,511,000.

W. A. Douglas Jackson
University of Washington

SAMARRA, sa-mur′rä, is a city in Iraq, on the east bank of the Tigris River, 70 miles (97 km) north of Baghdad. It was founded in 836 during the reign of the Abbasid Caliph al-Mutasim by his Turkish general Ashnas to serve as a new residence for the caliph and his Turkish mercenary army.

The site had already been inhabited in prehistoric times. The name, going back to pre-Muslim times, has been interpreted on the coins of the caliphs of Samarra as *Surra man raa*—"delighted is he who sees [it]." Between 836 and 892 eight Abbasid caliphs ruled from Samarra. Now a vast field of ruins, the ancient city has yielded a large amount of material, which forms the main basis for knowledge of the art of the period. It was unearthed during excavations (1911–1913) under the German archaeologists Friedrich Sarre and Ernst Herzfeld.

One of the largest cities ever built by the Muslims, Samarra had an enormous number of palaces. Caliph al-Mutawwakil alone is said to have built 24 palaces in the mid-9th century. There were also many large houses, enclosures, bath halls, mosques, military depots, shops, workshops, stables, prisons, and resthouses. The most important buildings were the main palace of the caliphs, the Jausaq al-Khaqani on the Tigris, built by al-Mutasim; the Palace of Balkuwara and the Great Mosque, built by al-Mutawwakil; and the Mosque of Abu Dulaf, built by the same caliph in his new town north of Samarra, Jafariya.

Of the Jausaq al-Khaqani only the Bab al-Amma, a triple *iwan* (*ivan*) arched gateway leading to the caliph's apartments, is still standing on the high bank of the Tigris. A flight of steps leads up from a vast water basin. The general layout of this immense palace structure has been recorded in the excavations by Herzfeld and a model has been built in the Baghdad Museum. It is one of the most monumental architectural endeavors ever undertaken. Built on an axial system there are series of enormous courts surrounded by *iwan* halls and barrel-vaulted apartments, a cross-shaped domed throne room, and a vast variety of smaller, secondary adjacent buildings or building complexes.

The Great Mosque of al-Mutawwakil, built between 846 and 852, is an immense rectangle, about 784 by 512 feet (239 by 156 meters), of which only the thick walls of baked brick are still standing. The interior structure—the roofs of the prayer hall, nine naves deep on the qibla side, and the arcades, four naves deep on the east and the west sides and three naves deep on the north side, all resting on marble columns—has completely disappeared.

Still standing intact is the minaret (al-Malwiya), standing beyond the north wall of the mosque. It is a 175-foot (53-meter) high massive tower with a spiral staircase running around on the outside to the top.

The Mosque of Abu Dulaf, built between 859 and 861, follows the same principle, but brick piers have replaced the marble columns, and the scale, 699 by 443 feet (213 by 135 meters), inside is somewhat smaller. The minaret follows the al-Malwiya model.

Styles of Decoration. The palaces and many of the houses were decorated with carved and molded plaster panels. Three distinctly different styles can be distinguished. Style A (Herzfeld, Style III), closely follows the pre-Abbasid, late classical tradition. Vine leaves and grapes, and freely growing scrolls set into rectangular or polygonal panels, are cut into the plaster on the wall. Style B (Herzfeld, Style II) is a combination of the more naturalistic Style A and somewhat stylized floral forms in abstract and semiabstract designs. In addition, the patterns are no longer cut but are molded on the wall. Style C (Herzfeld, Style I) is entirely abstract, composed of infinite patterns of curvilinear forms only vaguely reminiscent of the plant and floral forms from which they originated. The patterns of this style are again molded, probably in large panels on the ground, which were put on the walls when dry.

The first style (A) has a strong light-and-shadow-contrast effect because of deep undercutting and elaborate surface tooling. The second style (B) has a rather flat effect, eliminating most of the contrasts. Style C, being entirely molded without any surface tooling and no strong modulation of the relief, has completely eliminated any contrast effect.

A great deal of pottery has been unearthed in Samarra, decorated with various patterns in many different techniques. There are molded relief wares with interlace patterns with small rosettes and floral forms and white glazed wares with small inscriptions in cobalt blue and green running-glaze patterns, decorating the rims in straight imitation of Chinese T'ang wares.

In addition, there are white glazed wares with beautifully simple patterns of leaves, rosettes, and trees, in cobalt blue and luster-painted wares with a light ground painted in various shades of brown and yellow, or with a bright, tomato-red ground painted in yellow and purple. This last technique is also used on tile work, of which small fragments have been preserved.

The most important contributions of the Samarra artists are undoubtedly their wall paintings, which decorated large surfaces in the palaces and houses. Only small fragments have been preserved, but it has been possible to reconstruct larger compositions. These include dancers, scenes of struggles between beasts and men, animals, and a monumental acanthus scroll composed of calices set one within the other, with human figures and animals (from the *harim* in the Jausaq Palace).

ERNST GRUBE, *Metropolitan Museum of Art*
Author of "World of Islam"

Further Reading: Creswell, Keppel A. C., *Early Muslim Architecture*, part 2 (Oxford 1941); Lloyd, Seton, *Ruined Cities of Iraq* (Oxford 1944).

SAMARSKITE, sə-mär′skĭt, is a rare mineral composed of a very complex mixture of columbium and tantalum oxides with oxides of rare-earth elements and other metals such as calcium, iron, lead, tin, titanium, and uranium. Because samarskite is rare, it is not an important source of the rare earths, as are other complex minerals such as monazite. Samarskite is named after a 19th century Russian mine official, V. Y. Samarsky, who discovered the mineral in the Ural Mountains.

Crystals of the mineral are velvety black and have a glassy to resinous luster. However, samarskite usually occurs in a massive form. It is always found in pegmatites. The most notable site of the mineral is in Brazil. In the United States, samarskite has been found in Colorado, Connecticut, Maine, and North Carolina.

Composition, complex mixture of metal oxides; hardness, 5–6; specific gravity, 4.1–6.2; crystal system, orthorhombic.

SAMBA, säm′bə, a dance of Brazilian origin with African influences. The samba, or *batuque*, has a syncopated rhythm in $2/4$ time. As a Brazilian folk dance, especially popular at Carnival, it is fast and violent, danced by a soloist in the middle of a circle of dancers. The ballroom version, which spread to many countries, is a more restrained dance, in which partners do a quick two-step, tilting backward on the forward steps and forward on the backward steps.

SĀMKHYA, sang′kyə, one of the six orthodox systems of philosophy in Hinduism. The Sāmkhya, which means "reason" or "enumeration," is an analysis of nature. The basic text is attributed to Kapila. See also HINDUISM—*Formal Philosophies*.

SAMMARTINI, säm-mär-tē′nē, **Giovanni Battista** (1701–1775), Italian organist and composer, whose work led to the development of the modern symphonic form. He was born in Milan, where he received his musical training and served as an organist in several churches. He was *maestro di cappella* of the Milanese Convent of Santa Maria Maddalena from 1730 to 1770. The composition of his first symphony in 1734 led to his development of the form along lines later, followed by Joseph Hayden. Sammartini also participated in the evolution of 18th century chamber music procedures. Christoph Willibald Gluck was his pupil. Sammartini died in Milan on Jan. 15, 1775.

A prolific composer, Sammartini is said to have written more than 2,000 works, including symphonies, chamber pieces, operas, an oratorio, and much liturgical music. Most of it remains unpublished, but there are some scholarly modern editions.

Giuseppe Sammartini (c.1693–c.1750), Giovanni's brother, was also a musician and composer.

HERBERT WEINSTOCK
Coauthor of "Men of Music"

SAMNITES, sam′nīts, an ancient people inhabiting the mountainous region of Samnium in south-central Italy. Samnium was bordered by Latium to the west, Apulia to the east, Lucania and Campania to the south and southwest, and by districts occupied by Marsians, Paelignians, and Frentanians to the north.

An Oscan-speaking people, probably of Sabine origin, the Samnites maintained a confederation of four states—Caraceni in the north, Pentri in the center, Caudini in the southwest, and Hirpini in the south. The confederacy, which probably did not have a general council, functioned best in war, when the executive officers of the union's communities chose a war leader to command its army. The Samnites were mostly farmers, who dwelt in usually unfortified villages, but were formidable fighters.

Their efforts to conquer more fertile fields from neighboring Campanians, Lucanians, and Apulians, with whom Rome was allied, induced Roman intervention and resulted in the traditional three Samnite Wars, the first of which, in 343–341 B. C., is perhaps purely legendary. In the second (326?–304), during which a surrounded Roman army surrendered at the Caudine Forks in 321, the Samnites failed to expand into Apulia, Lucania, and southern Campania. After their defeat in the third war (298–290), the Samnites were compelled to become Roman allies. But this alliance failed to prevent some of the Samnites from supporting Pyrrhus, king of Epirus, who conducted military campaigns in Italy during 280–275, or from aiding Hannibal, who occupied central Italy from 216 to 209, during the Second Punic War (218–201).

Samnite resistance to Roman supremacy ended in the Social War of 90–88, when their armies were slaughtered. Thereafter the survivors gradually were Romanized, and as a nation the Samnites ceased to exist in the late 1st century B. C. Among the principal Samnite communities were Aufidena, Bovianum Vetus, Caudium, and Beneventum, now called Benevento, which was the most important.

P. R. COLEMAN-NORTON
Formerly, Princeton University

View of the sea from the Samoan home of author Robert Louis Stevenson.

SAMOA, sə-mõ′ə, is a group of islands in the South Pacific Ocean about 2,300 miles (3,500 km) southwest of Hawaii. It is divided politically into two parts. West of longitude 171° W is Western Samoa, an independent nation. To the east is American Samoa, an unincorporated territory of the United States.

The islands of Western Samoa include Savaii, Upolu, Apolima, Manono, and five uninhabited islets off the east coast of Upolu. American Samoa consists of the islands of Tutuila, Aunuu, the Manua group (Tau, Olosega, and Ofu), Rose Island, and Swains Island, a coral atoll 210 miles (340 km) to the northwest.

Europeans discovered Samoa in 1722, but missionaries and traders did not arrive until the middle of the 19th century. An agreement between Britain, Germany, and the United States in 1899 awarded Western Samoa to Germany and the eastern islands to the United States. New Zealand administered Western Samoa as a League of Nations mandate after World War I and as a UN trusteeship from the end of World War II until the territory became independent in 1962.

The Land. The principal islands of the Samoan archipelago are coral-fringed summits of a submarine volcanic range. The larger islands are mountainous and rugged, rising to 6,094 feet (1,857 meters) on Savaii. The largest islands of Western Samoa are Savaii, with an area of 703 square miles (1,821 sq km), and Upolu, with 430 square miles (1,114 sq km). Tutuila, the largest island of American Samoa, has an area of 52 square miles (135 sq km).

Lying within 15° of the equator, the Samoan islands have a rainy tropical climate. Coastal temperatures average nearly 80° F (27° C) and vary little during the year. From May to November southeast trade winds moderate the heat slightly. Annual rainfall generally exceeds 100 inches (2,500 mm) and is greatest on the southeastern slopes, totaling 200 inches (5,000 mm) on Tutuila. The wetter part of the year is the season of light and variable winds—December to April—when tropical cyclones occur most frequently.

The warm, moist climate favors a dense rain forest, but grasses and scrubs predominate on the more recent laval flows of Savaii. Coastal forests have been replaced by settlements and cultivated land. Thickets of mangrove remain in a few areas of brackish water near river mouths. Native animal life consists mainly of a few species of birds and reptiles.

The People. About five sixths of the roughly 200,000 Samoans live in Western Samoa. The islands' largest urban settlement is Apia, a group of villages along the harbor on Upolu. It is the capital and principal port of Western Samoa. Pago Pago, another chain of villages, stretches along the shore of Pago Pago harbor on Tutuila. It is the capital and chief port of American Samoa. Other settlements in the islands are villages located mainly on the coasts.

The Samoans are a brown-skinned, large-bodied Polynesian people. Their language, considered to be the oldest Polynesian tongue in use today, was unwritten until missionaries set it down in the Latin alphabet in the 19th century. Although the Samoans have been converted to Christianity, they retain many of the beliefs and rites of their former animistic religion. Leading denominations are the Congregational Christian Church of Western Samoa, Roman Catholic, Methodist, Mormon, and Seventh-day Adventist.

Samoan society is organized around extended families, each headed by a chief, or *matai*, who is responsible for the family's welfare. The Samoan dwelling, or *fale*, has an oval roof, thatched with sugarcane leaves and supported on wooden poles. Western technology has gradually replaced stone cutting tools and a large variety of fishhooks, scrapers, and knives made from shell. Early Samoans were master boat builders and navigators. They fashioned textiles from coconut and pandanus fibers and a cloth, called *tapa*, from the bark of the paper mulberry plant.

Until the second half of the 20th century Samoans were largely indifferent to Western material culture and the rewards of persistent labor, but trade, communications, and education have been growing forces for change. New Zealand established schools, an agricultural college, and a teachers college in Western Samoa, where there are also several church schools. In American Samoa the United States maintains an extensive program of education for both children and adults, incorporating an educational television network. Pago Pago has a community college.

History to 1899. Samoa was probably settled by voyagers from Melanesian islands to the west during the 1st millennium B.C. Archaeological and linguistic evidence suggests that their earlier cultural origins were in Southeast Asia. The first European to reach Samoa was Jacob Roggeveen, a Dutch navigator, who sailed through the Manua group in 1722 without landing. The French explorer Louis Antoine de Bougainville found the archipelago in 1768 and named it the "Navigators' Islands." Visits by other Europeans did not result in any significant settlement until 1830, when John Williams landed on Savaii in 1830 to establish a mission for the London Missionary Society.

American interest in the islands began in 1839 with a survey by the U. S. Exploring Expedition under Lt. Charles Wilkes. In 1872, Comdr. Richard W. Meade of the USS *Narragansett* negotiated with High Chief Mauga for the use of Pago Pago as a coaling station.

International rivalry in the islands culminated in an agreement between Britain, Germany, and the United States in 1889, providing for a neutral state of Samoa. But the Samoans were unable to maintain an effective government, and, under the Convention of 1899, Britain withdrew, leaving the western islands to Germany and the remainder to the United States.

WESTERN SAMOA

The Economy. The basic economy of Western Samoa is subsistence agriculture. Principal crops are taro, yams, bananas, breadfruit, and papayas. Coconut palms provide food, oil, fiber, utensils, and building materials. Pigs and poultry supplement the diet, especially on ceremonial occasions. Fishing has declined from its former importance. A copra trade developed from early commercial contacts with Europeans, and cacao and bananas later were established as export crops. Coconut plantations are grazed by beef cattle in some areas to control undergrowth.

Manufacturing activities are concerned primarily with food processing and the making of furniture and handicrafts. A sawmill at Asau on Savaii operates in conjunction with logging by a U. S. company under a long-term timber lease. After a change in government policy in 1965, hotel and airport development increased, and tourism became important.

Government. The constitution of Western Samoa provides for a "head of state," who is the chief executive. The office was first held jointly by representatives of two royal lines—Tupua Tamasese Mea'ole, who died in 1963, and Malietoa Tanumafili II. After the death of Tanumafili, the head of state will be chosen by the legislature for a five-year term.

The head of state appoints a prime minister and cabinet from the Legislative Assembly to serve with him on the Executive Council. The assembly consists of 45 Samoan members, elected by the *matais*, and 2 European members, elected by universal adult suffrage. The chief justice of the Supreme Court, appointed by the head of

Map of Samoa, with the three largest islands shown separately at right. Western Samoa, formerly administered by New Zealand, became independent in 1962. The eastern islands have been under U. S. administration since 1899.

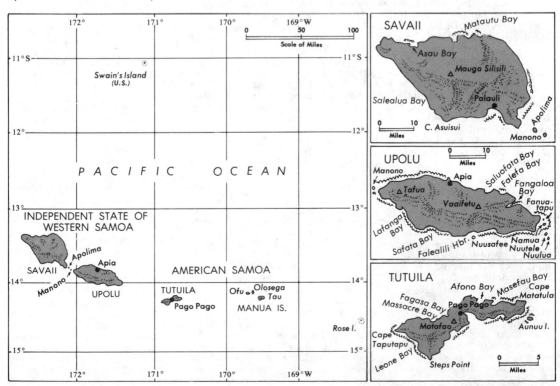

state, presides over the judicial system, and the department of police and prisons is responsible for law and order. The *matai* system prevails in matters of local government.

In international affairs New Zealand frequently represents Western Samoa. But Western Samoa is a member of the South Pacific Commission and has been active in conferences dealing with problems of the Pacific Islands. The state is a member of the Commonwealth of Nations and was admitted to the United Nations on Dec. 15, 1976.

History. Although there had been earlier contacts with explorers and missionaries, the modern history of Western Samoa began with the arrival of German traders in 1856. August Unshelm and his successor, Theodor Weber, maintained a trading base at Apia and extended their activities to other South Pacific islands, developing plans for German colonization. But these plans came into growing conflict with the interests of Britain and the United States, and sporadic wars among Samoan chiefs disrupted the political scene during the latter half of the 19th century.

Under the Berlin Treaty of 1889 the three Western powers agreed to the creation of an independent kingdom in Samoa, but native wars broke out again. The three Western states revoked the Berlin Treaty by the Convention of 1889, in which Britain renounced all claims to Western Samoa in favor of Germany.

Shortly after the outbreak of World War I, a New Zealand force occupied Western Samoa, and, in 1920, New Zealand was awarded a League of Nations mandate over the islands. During the first 16 years of the mandate there was increasing agitation against New Zealand officials by a native organization, the Mau a Pule, until a change in administrative policy was made. Following World War II the League of Nations mandate was converted to a UN trusteeship, and on Jan. 1, 1962, Western Samoa became an independent nation.

AMERICAN SAMOA

American Samoa has a total area 76.1 square miles (197 sq km). Its 1980 census population is 32,395.

The Economy. The policies of the U. S. territorial administration and the scarcity of suitable land have not favored the development of plantation agriculture in American Samoa. Tropical fruits, starchy root crops, and vegetables are grown locally, but additional food has to be imported. Commercial fishing fleets supply tuna canneries at Pago Pago, which provide the leading export. A nearby factory makes cans for the tuna industry, and another manufacturing plant exports coconut products. Mats, basketware, and other handicrafts are minor exports.

After the completion of a hotel in 1965 an increasing number of tourists visited Pago Pago, and additional facilities were developed near Tafuna Airport. Air services connect the territory with Hawaii, Tahiti, Fiji, and Western Samoa. Pago Pago is also a port of call for cruise ships.

Government. The U. S. Department of the Interior administers American Samoa as an unincorporated territory whose people are U. S. nationals but have no vote in federal elections. The president of the United States appoints the territory's governor, who is chief executive, and a secretary, who assists the governor and acts as lieutenant governor. The governor appoints heads of executive departments to deal with local affairs. The legislature consists of the Senate and House of Representatives. Senators are elected for four years from among the *matais*, according to Samoan custom. Representatives are chosen by popular vote and serve for two years. An elected delegate represents Swains Island in the lower house but does not have voting privileges.

Judicial authority is vested in a high court and five district courts. Fundamental rights are protected by the constitutions of both the United States and the territory. Local government is organized in a system of political districts, counties, and villages. In each village a council of chiefs elects one of its members as mayor.

History. Separate political status for American Samoa was established by the Convention of 1899, under the terms of which Britain and Germany gave up their claims to the islands of eastern Samoa. Following ratification of the treaty in 1900, the United States negotiated with leading chiefs the cession of Tutuila and Aunuu, and the chiefs of the Manua islands agreed to a similar transfer of authority in 1904. But it was not until Feb. 20, 1929, that the deeds of cession were accepted by the U. S. Congress. Swains Island, relinquished by Britain, was annexed by the United States in 1925.

The U. S. Navy administered American Samoa from 1900 to 1951 and maintained an active naval station at Pago Pago. By executive order President Harry Truman transferred administration of the islands to the secretary of the interior, effective July 1, 1951. The first territorial constitution was approved by the Samoans in 1960. A revised constitution was adopted in 1967.

HOWARD J. CRITCHFIELD
Western Washington State College

Bibliography

Cumberland, Kenneth B., *Southwest Pacific*, rev. ed. (Praeger 1969).
Davidson, James W., *Samoa mo Samoa, the Emergence of the Independent State of Western Samoa* (Oxford 1967).
Gilson, R. P., *Samoa 1830 to 1900* (Oxford 1970).
Guiart, Jean, *Arts of the South Pacific* (Braziller 1963).
Mead, Margaret, *Coming of Age in Samoa* (Morrow 1928).
Pitt, David, *Tradition and Economic Progress in Samoa* (Oxford 1970).

SAMOGITIA, sam-ō-jish'ē-ə, is a historical region of western Lithuania, with its center in the Samogitian Highlands north of the lower Neman (Niemen) River. Its Lithuanian name is Žemaitija. The region's chief cities are Raseiniai in the south and Telšiai in the north. In the Middle Ages the area was inhabited by the Samogitians, or Zhmud, a Lithuanian people, and was conquered by the Teutonic Knights. It was recovered for united Poland-Lithuania in 1410.

SAMORI TOURÉ. See Touré, Samori.

SAMOS, sä'môs, is a Greek island in the Aegean Sea, one of the Sporades, or Greek Archipelago. It is about 1 mile (1.6 km) off the Turkish coast and 45 miles (72 km) south of İzmir. It is about 27 miles (43 km) long, has a maximum width of 12 miles (19 km), and is 194 square miles (502 sq km) in area. Limen Vatheos, on the northern side of the island, is the chief port and has been the capital since the 1800's. The former capital, Khora, on the south side, stands on the site of the ancient Temple of Hera. Samos, with Icaria and the Phournoi island group, forms the province (*nomos*) of Samos. The island has a population of over 40,000.

The island has several good harbors and is traversed by two rocky, barren mountain ranges, the highest peak of which is Mount Kerketeus (4,725 feet; 1,440 meters). The land is very fertile. Olive groves are plentiful on the lower mountain slopes, and grapes, figs, cotton, and tobacco are grown. Wine making and cigarette manufacture are the chief industries. There are also small deposits of marble, silver, iron, lead, and emery. Barges and sailing vessels are built from native timber at Tigani.

Samos was colonized by the Ionians about 1000 B.C. By the 7th century B.C., it was a leading Greek commercial center. The island passed to the Persians in the 6th century, but regained its freedom after the victory of Mycale in 479. Samos was captured by the Romans in 84 B.C.

The island assumed a leading role during the Greek war of independence (1821–1830), but it came under Ottoman suzerainty in 1832. It was taken by the kingdom of Greece during the Balkan Wars in 1912–1913, and Greek sovereignty was confirmed under the Treaty of Lausanne on July 24, 1923.

SAMOSET, sam'ə-set (died c. 1653), American Indian sachem of the Pemaquid (sometimes called Monhegan) tribe. His name is an English corruption of Osamoset, which translates literally as "he walks over much."

It was Samoset who startled the Pilgrims of Plymouth Colony by greeting them, in their own tongue, "Welcome, Englishmen!" in March 1621, when he introduced them to Massasoit, the Wampanoag chieftain. Pleased by the gifts he received, Samoset was instrumental in helping the colonists establish themselves in the first few years after their arrival. With Unongoit, he signed the first deed conveying land between Indians and the English, when in 1625 some 12,000 acres (4,900 hectares) of Pemaquid territory were "sold" to John Brown of New Harbor, Me.

There has always been some uncertainty as to how Samoset learned English—this despite Gov. William Bradford's clear statement, in his history of Plymouth, that the sachem had never been in England but had learned the language through contact with English fishermen who frequented the Maine coast. The argument that Samoset was actually an Englishman named Capt. John Somerset was effectively disposed of by Albert Matthew in *The Indian Sagamore Samoset* (1901).

Little is known of Samoset's life. No portrait exists, and he is described only as tall and straight, with long hair.

FREDERICK DOCKSTADER
Museum of the American Indian

SAMOTHRACE, sam'ə-thrās, is an island of Greece in the northeastern part of the Aegean Sea, east of Thasos. Almost oval in shape and about 71 square miles (184 sq km) in area, Samothrace (Samothraki) is rugged. It has no good harbor. Mount Phengari (5,249 feet; 1,600 meters) is the highest point in the Aegean Islands. Samos' chief products are grain, olive oil, honey, hides, and sponges. It has a population of about 4,000.

Samothrace was settled before the 6th century B.C. from Samos. Usually allied with Athens, it was subsequently ruled by Macedon—with short interludes of Ptolemaic and Seleucid control—until Rome took it in the 2d century B.C. and made it a free community under Roman control. It passed to the Eastern Roman Empire in 395 and was seized in 1456 by the Turks, who lost it to the Greeks in 1912.

The most notable archaeological find on the island is the *Winged Victory of Samothrace*, found in 1863 and now in the Louvre Museum in Paris. Twentieth-century excavations have revealed more of the ruins of the Sanctuary of the Great Gods, a theater, a stoa, a cemetery, and much pottery.

SAMOYED, sam-ə-yed', a northern breed of dog originally developed as an all-round guard, hunting, and sled dog among the Samoyed peoples in the region of northern Siberia between the Urals and the Lena River. The Samoyed first achieved fame outside Russia as a result of its wide use as a sled dog by Fridtjof Nansen, Luigi Amadeo, Roald Amundsen, and other polar explorers. Nearly all modern Samoyeds outside the Soviet Union are descended from polar expedition dogs.

The Samoyed stands about 19 to 23 inches (48–58 cm) at the withers and weighs about 40 to 60 pounds (18–27 kg). It has a white coat made up of an outercoat of long harsh guard hairs and a soft woolly undercoat that insulates it from summer heat as well as winter cold. The Samoyed is intelligent, alert, very lively, loyal, and friendly. It makes an excellent but not vicious watchdog and a gentle companion. In the United States it is still widely trained as a sled dog.

Further Reading: Ward, Robert H., and Dolly, *The Complete Samoyed* (Howell Book House 1971).

Samoyeds are playful pets as well as strong sled dogs.

EVELYN M. SHAFER

SAMOYED, sam-ə-yed′, a group of languages spoken in western Siberia and northeasternmost Europe, which, together with the Finno-Ugrian group, form the Uralic family. On the basis of their affinity and probable history, the Samoyed languages are usually divided into North and South Samoyed. North Samoyed consists of Yurak Samoyed, with 25,000 speakers, who are called Nentsy by the Russians and occupy the Nenets National District of the Russian SFSR; Yenisei Samoyed, with 300 speakers; and Tagvi, or Avam, Samoyed, with 700 speakers. South Samoyed, whose only living member is Ostyak Samoyed, also called Selkup, has 4,000 speakers.

About seven groups are known to have spoken South Samoyed in the 18th and 19th centuries, but most of them have since been Russified, Turkified, or Mongolized. The northern Samoyed are mainly reindeer breeders and fishermen; their southern kinsmen practice agriculture.

Samoyed folklore and ethnology have been collected by Soviet and Finnish scholars. Samoyed alphabets, created in the 1930's by Soviet experts, have contributed to a steady growth of native literature.

ROBERT AUSTERLITZ, *Columbia University*

SAMPAN, sam′pan, a light, flat-bottomed boat used in Far Eastern rivers, canals, and harbors for fishing, ferrying, carrying small cargoes, or as a home. The Chinese sampan is a wedge-shaped vessel without a keel, averaging 12 to 14 feet (3.5–4 meters) in length and 4 feet (4.3 meters) in width. It usually has an awning of matting that forms a cabin and is propelled by oars of twisted rattan. Some have sails.

A Japanese sampan is a boat with a broad, flat keel. It is usually propelled by one or more sculls, but may have sails or a motor instead.

The Hawaiian sampan is a fishing boat built along the lines of an Oriental sampan, but propelled by a diesel motor.

SAMPHIRE, sam′fir, a fleshy perennial herb, *Crithmum maritimum,* found along the seacoasts of the British Isles, western continental Europe, and the Mediterranean. It is sometimes grown as a salad plant or for ornament and may be planted in locations removed from the coast. It thrives in a sunny exposure on sandy or gravelly soils. A member of the parsley family, Umbelliferae, the samphire grows 1 to 2 feet (30–60 cm) tall and has three-parted leaves divided into short linear segments. Its white or yellowish flowers are very small and are borne in compound umbels. The fruit is ovoid and about 0.25 inch (0.6 cm) long. The name samphire is also used in the United States for glassworts (genus *Salicornia*). See GLASSWORT.

FRANK G. LIER, *Columbia University*

SAMPLER, a piece of linen, canvas, or other fabric recording specimen stitches and patterns. During the Renaissance, an experienced embroiderer stitched sample patterns on a piece of fabric for reference. From about the 16th to the mid-19th century, girls of upper-class families in Europe and European colonies made samplers of stitches and designs both for reference and as indications of their skill. With the development of machine stitching in the 19th century, samplers ceased to be a part of a girl's education. In the 20th century they became collector's items.

The age of a sampler, especially of an English or American product, can often be determined by the shape of the fabric and the character of the designs. The earliest samplers were long and narrow and displayed a variety of designs scat-

SAMPLERS. (*Left*) Sampler by Mary Varick of New York (1789) offers seven maxims and a portrait of Washington, reflecting America's new independence. (*Above*) Bordered sampler by Harriet Holt (1803) is rare in its use of human hair and isinglass window panes.

tered at random. Some designs were embroidered in colored silks. Others might be samples of cutwork, drawn work, or needlepoint lace, done in white thread. Gradually the designs came to be placed in orderly rows, which, combined with rows of alphabets and numerals, made a harmonious whole. The name of the maker and the date were often added. By the late 17th century, pious inscriptions, mottoes, verses, and biblical quotations had appeared.

Samplers of the 18th century were shorter and wider and had fewer types of designs and stitches. The tent stitch, satin stitch, and cross stitch were popular. The designs tended to be organized less like a pattern sheet and more like a picture. They usually were enclosed in a border, at first geometric, then floral. In addition to alphabets, numerals, name, date, and verse, the designs often included figures of people, birds, animals, or other objects.

Samplers of the 19th century were often without borders, and the scenes showed perspective and background. Some gave examples of darning stitches arranged around a basket or vase of flowers. Many after 1820 were worked in wool.

Further Reading: Bolton, Ethel S., and Coe, Eva J., *American Samplers* (Mass. Society of the Colonial Dames of America 1921); Christie, Grace, *Samplers and Stitches* (Batsford 1948).

SAMPLING. See MARKETING; PUBLIC OPINION; STATISTICS.

SAMPSON, sam′sən, **William Thomas** (1840–1902), American admiral. He was born at Palmyra, N. Y., on Feb. 9, 1840, and graduated first in his class at the U. S. Naval Academy in 1860. In various posts he contributed to the renaissance of the U. S. Navy.

He headed the court of inquiry that gave the opinion that the sinking of the battleship *Maine*, in the harbor of Havana, Cuba, on Feb. 15, 1898, was caused by external means. The sinking was one cause of the Spanish-American War that year. Sampson commanded a fleet that blockaded six Spanish warships in the harbor of Santiago de Cuba. On July 3, while Sampson in his flagship was en route to a conference at Siboney, east of Santiago, the Spanish ships tried to escape. Sampson turned and headed west, but when he arrived, the Spaniards had surrendered after a fight to a squadron headed by Commodore Winfield Scott Schley. Sampson cabled that the victory had been won by the fleet under his command, and a controversy arose between him and Schley. A court of inquiry censured Schley for some of his battle actions, but Congress failed to give Sampson any recognition. Sampson died at Washington, D. C., on May 6, 1902.

SAMSON, sam′sən, a hero of the tribe of Dan, about whom a cycle of popular tales is preserved in the Book of Judges (chapters 13–16). He did great damage to the Philistines, early archenemies of Israel. His name is found among other West Semitic names in texts from Nippur in Babylonia. The name Samson is related to the Hebrew word *shemesh* meaning sun. The stories are of a secular nature, except for allusions to his being driven by the spirit of the Lord and the story of his birth, which is a fascinating tale linked with a rock altar that still exists near Zorah (modern Sar′ah, Israel).

Biblical Story. Samson's birth was foretold by an angel to the wife of Manoah who had been barren for many years. He was to be a Nazarite from birth and drink no wine or cut his hair, both part of the Nazarite vows. Only the vow concerning the cutting of his hair was observed by Samson, for the Bible story relates he drank freely.

Samson wedded a Philistine maiden. At the festivities he propounded a riddle, based on his experience with a lion, and offered a wager for its solution by some of the Philistines. The girl begged Samson to tell her the answer secretly, but when he finally complied she betrayed the answer to the Philistines. To pay the lost wager, Samson went down to Ashkelon and slew 30 Philistines, taking their spoil. Upon his return, he found his bride given to another, so in revenge he set fire to the standing grain of the Philistines. He then took refuge in the rock of Etam, but the Philistines sent a force to demand his extradition. He gave himself up to the Judeans, but on being brought to the Philistines he broke his bonds and, seizing the jawbone of an ass as weapon, he smote the Philistines. The story provides a popular etymology of the name Ramath-lehi, which means "height of the jawbone" and of a spring found there.

Next Samson went to a harlot at Gaza, an event related without any moral stricture. The Philistines planned to seize him when he left the city in the morning, but he carried off the gates of Gaza, using them as a shield for protection, and took them to Hebron some 38 miles (60 km) away. Thereupon he became enamored of another Philistine maiden, Delilah. Instigated by the Philistines to find out the secret of Samson's strength, Delilah learned that it lay in his long hair. Samson was shorn of his locks while asleep and was overpowered by the enemy. His eyes were put out, and he was taken to Gaza, where he had to turn the mill in prison. However, as his hair grew again, his strength returned. During the festival for the Philistine god Dagon, Samson was brought to a temple where he was mocked. But grasping the middle pillars of the temple, he caused the whole structure to collapse, thus killing all those within the building, including himself, and those on the roof. His relatives obtained his remains and buried them in the family tomb.

The Samson theme was interpreted by John Milton in his poetic drama *Samson Agonistes* (1671) and by Camille Saint-Saëns in his opera *Samson et Dalila* (1877).

EMIL G. KRAELING
Author of "Rand McNally Bible Atlas"

SAMSON AGONISTES, sam′sən ag-ə-nis′tēz, is a poetic drama by John Milton. Probably, but not certainly, his last work, it was published with *Paradise Regained* in 1671. In form a classical tragedy in blank verse with choral odes in irregular meters, it is based on the biblical account of Samson in Judges 13–16. The action occurs on the last day of Samson's life, at the time he is a prisoner of the Philistines, "eyeless in Gaza," in a state of despondency because of his realization that his yielding to temptation has caused the triumph of the Philistine god Dagon over the true God Jehovah.

The five scenes or acts serve as "provocative incidents" that arouse Samson from lethargy and despair. As a result of visits from his old friends, his father, his wife, and a giant who boasts that he, rather than Samson, is the strongest man in the world, Samson feels his strength returning, obeys the command of his enemies that he appear before them in the temple in which they are riotously celebrating their victory, performs incredible feats of strength, and finally deliberately pulls down the pillars of the temple, destroying all the Philistine aristocracy and himself and causing Jehovah to triumph over Dagon.

The drama is a remarkable fusion of the Hellenic and the Hebraic spirits. In form it is an adaptation of Greek tragedy, particularly that of Sophocles and Euripides, but parallels in structure and mood to the Book of Job are equally impressive. The final impression of Milton's Samson is very different from that of the simple strong man of Judges, since Milton interprets his Samson psychologically, with the result that he becomes much more human and complex than the original. Milton was peculiarly able to understand Samson because of the close analogies with his own life. Like Samson, Milton had believed himself "called" to perform some great work for the glory of God, but after having been diverted from writing poetry for nearly 20 years, several of which he spent in the service of the Commonwealth government, he found himself blind and a prisoner of the Royalist party, which had triumphed over the Puritans at the time of the Restoration.

Samson Agonistes is the greatest example of classical drama in English. It is also the most moving of Milton's major works because of his sympathetic understanding of the main character, the growing tension of the "provocative incidents," and the mood of the ending, in which Milton has given the finest English example of the Greek catharsis, by means of which pity and terror are finally resolved and the audience is left "calm of mind, all passion spent."

MARJORIE H. NICOLSON, *Author of "John Milton: A Reader's Guide to His Poetry"*

Bibliography

Crump, Galbraith M., ed., *Twentieth Century Interpretations of Samson Agonistes* (Prentice-Hall 1968).

Krouse, F. Michael, *Milton's Samson and the Christian Tradition* (Princeton Univ. Press 1949).

Nicolson, Marjorie H., *John Milton: A Reader's Guide to His Poetry* (Farrar, Straus 1963).

Parker, William, *Milton's Debt to Greek Tragedy in Samson Agonistes* (1937; reprint, Barnes & Noble 1969).

Stein, Arnold, *Heroic Knowledge: An Interpretation of Paradise Regained and Samson Agonistes* (1957; reprint, Shoe String 1965).

SAMSON ET DALILA, sän-sôn′ ä dä-lē-lä′, is an opera in three acts by Camille Saint-Saëns, first produced in German at Weimar in 1877. The libretto is by Ferdinand Lemaire, after the biblical story. Among the most renowned numbers in the opera are Dalila's *Amour, viens aider ma faiblesse;* Samson and Dalila's duet, *Mon coeur s'ouvre à ta voix;* Samson's *Vois ma misère, hélas!;* and the orchestral *Bacchanale.*

The work is set in Gaza. Samson rouses his fellow Israelites to rebel against the Philistines and himself slays Abimelech, satrap of Gaza. The victorious Israelites are rejoicing when Philistine maidens, including Dalila, whom Samson has loved earlier, try to seduce the Israelite leaders. Dalila tries to use her charms to extract from Samson the secret of his great strength. He fends her off at first but at last falls victim to her wiles. Learning that his strength lies in his long hair, she cuts it off. He is then subdued by the Philistines, who blind him.

The blinded Samson languishes in a prison for a while before Philistine soldiers drag him off to grace a victory orgy in the temple of the god Dagon. At the orgy the Philistines, led by Dalila, pour scorn on Samson. He invokes his God, praying for a brief return of his strength. As Samson stands between the two largest pillars supporting the temple, his prayer is answered. He grasps the pillars, pulling them down, and the temple thunders down upon the drunken Philistines, Dalila, and Samson himself.

HERBERT WEINSTOCK
Coauthor of "Men of Music"

SAMSUN, säm-sōōn′, is a city in Turkey on the Black Sea and capital of Samsun province. It is about 200 miles (322 km) northwest of Ankara. Samsun is an important commercial center and is Turkey's second most important tobacco port. It also exports grain, wool, and hides and manufactures cigarettes.

Athenian Greeks from Miletus founded a colony in 562 B. C., calling it Amisus. Romans conquered it in the 1st century B. C., and it later passed to the Byzantine Empire. In the late 11th century Amisus was besieged by the Turks who, failing to take it, built the stronghold of Samsun 1.5 miles (2.5 km) to the southeast. Christian Amisus and Muslim Samsun stood side by side until 1425, when the Ottomans marched on Amisus. Genoese traders in Amisus set the city on fire and fled by ship. It was never rebuilt. Samsun kept its importance until the Russian annexation of the Crimea in 1783 cut off its most important source of trade.

The city was rebuilt after a disastrous fire in 1869, and its commerce revived with the development of steam navigation. In 1919, Kemal Atatürk landed at Samsun on his way to the interior to organize resistance to the Greek invasion. An equestrian statue commemorates his landing.

The province, with an area of 3,626 square miles (9,391 sq km), has a fertile coastal strip, which widens at the river mouths, backed by the rugged, wooded Canik Mountains. The province produces the highest quality tobacco in Turkey. Population: (1970) of the city, 134,272; of the province, 822,318.

SAMUDRAGUPTA, sə-mōō-drə-gōōp′tə, was an Indian emperor who reigned from about 330 to 375/380 A. D. The son and successor of Chandragupta I, founder of the Imperial Gupta dynasty, he made the Gupta Empire the paramount power of India.

Samudragupta has been called the Napoleon of India because of his extensive conquests. His father had established a powerful state consisting of parts of Bihar, Bengal, and Uttar Pradesh in northern India. Samudragupta extended his patrimony westward to the Chambal and Yamuna (Jumna) rivers, northward to the Himalaya foothills, eastward to the Brahmaputra, and southward to the Narbada River. Beyond these limits other rulers became his vassals.

Although Samudragupta was a Hindu, he followed a policy of religious tolerance in his domains. He was a patron of religion, the arts, and scholarship. He was a learned man in his own right and a talented musician and poet. See also GUPTA.

Further Reading: Gokhale, Balkrishna G., *Samudra Gupta* (Asia Pub. 1962).

SAMUEL, sam'ū-əl, was an Israelite religious leader of the 11th century B. C., who annointed Saul and then David as kings of Israel. What is known about him is reported in I Samuel in the Old Testament.

Biblical Portrayals. Various ideas concerning him were held by later tradition. The story of his birth shows that he was a Nazarite, was connected with the temple at Shiloh, and became the successor of Eli. That the temple was destroyed at this time (Jeremiah 7:12 ff.) is not related. In I Samuel 9–10 he is a seer, living in an unmentioned town in the district of Zuph. He is a man to whom one could turn for clairvoyant information, but who was respected and served as God's agent in selecting and anointing a king for Israel. Another report regards him as a prophet who lived at Shiloh and received divine revelations there (3:20). Again he is a leader of a band of ecstatic prophets at Ramah (19:18 ff.). He is also portrayed as a judge who traveled about and held court at Bethel, Mizpah, and Ramah (7:15), and whose sons exercised the same function at Beersheba (8:1–2). A late story has him play a prophetic role while judging at Mizpah (7:3–14). He promises divine help if Israel will put away foreign gods. By prayer and sacrifice he brings about God's intervention and the defeat of the enemy, and raises a memorial stone named "stone of help" (Ebenezer). The defeat of the Philistines is definitive. The writer of this particular story saw no necessity of further Philistine wars.

Kingship. But the main interest in the figure of Samuel centers about his relation to kingship and the first kings. The old story of I Samuel 9 and following thinks of the monarchy as a great blessing and of Samuel as taking the lead in establishing it. Not so the story that has been put before it in chapter 8. Here he is grieved by the public desire for a king and draws a discouraging picture of that institution. He subsequently, at Mizpah, arranges the election of a king by lot (10:17 27), and in a farewell discourse in chapter 12 takes the same dim view of the monarchy.

Samuel's falling out with Saul is vividly reported in chapter 15, although it is anticipated in the incident related in 13:8–15. While the narrative contains a fine prophetic saying (15:22), its characterization of Samuel as an exponent of extermination makes the modern reader sympathize with Saul. A narrative giving Samuel credit for selecting and anointing David in secret as the next king is put immediately after the story of Saul's rejection (16:1–13). Therewith Samuel's active role ends. David takes refuge with him at Ramah on fleeing from Saul, according to 19:18–24, which is in part a variant of 10:10–2). But the incident is colorless. The death of Samuel is reported twice (25:1, 28:3). In the second instance it is because it is part of a separate story, and the information was required to explain Saul's request of the witch of Endor to bring up the spirit of Samuel. This story gives the Samuel-Saul cycle a powerful conclusion.

Samuel loomed as an important figure in later biblical literature. Jeremiah mentions him in the same breath with Moses (Jeremiah 15:1). In the Apocrypha the encomium of Sirach likewise exalts him (Ecclesiasticus 46:13–20).

EMIL G. KRAELING
Author of "Rand McNally Bible Atlas"

SAMUEL, Books of, two historical books of the Old Testament. They were treated as one book in Hebrew manuscripts until the 15th century. In the Septuagint, the Greek translation of the Old Testament, they were divided and called I and II Kings, while what is now called I and II Kings was entitled III and IV kings. The Books of Samuel really are part of a continuous work, which probably began with Deuteronomy and concluded with II Kings, and was compiled in the 6th century B. C.

Composition and Dating. The Books of Samuel represent the interweaving of various sources, which help to explain the repeated stories and conflicting accounts found throughout the books. Many biblical scholars believe that at least two strands of tradition are represented, which they label J and E. Most would not go so far as to identify these strands with the J and E traditions found in the Pentateuch, although they have many similar characteristics, but would prefer to see them as paralleling the Pentateuchal sources and arising out of much the same circumstances. The J source is traceable back to the late 10th century B. C., while E is considerably later and can probably be dated in the 7th century B. C. In general the J tradition is believed to be closer to the events related and more historically reliable. For the most part, J is also more favorably disposed toward the monarchy. It is believed that the work was compiled just before the Babylonian Exile in the 6th century B. C.

Divisions. The portion of this historical work found in I and II Samuel may be divided into five main sections. The first tells of Samuel's birth and youth and of his activities as a man (I Samuel 1–7). The second treats of Samuel and Saul (I Samuel 8–15). The third deals with Saul and David (I Samuel 16 to II Samuel 1). The fourth describes the reign of David (II Samuel 2–8). The fifth is concerned with events in David's family (II Samuel 9–20). There follows an appendix of diverse materials (II Samuel 21–24).

Content. In the first section of the Books of Samuel there are two easily recognizable independent units: the story about the birth and youth of Samuel (I Samuel 1–3) and the one about the Ark of the Covenant (4:1 to 7:1; continued in II Samuel 6).

In the second section there are three different versions of the founding of the monarchy: (1) I Samuel 8; 10:17–25. (2) Chapters 9:1 to 10:16. (3) Chapter 11, in which the editor injected 11:12–14. While the second story is ancient, the third is probably the one closest to historical fact, except for the exaggerated size of Saul's force in 11:8, for which some late copyist may be responsible. In this story Saul's rise is due to his own initiative and the act of the people. There is no thought of priestly or prophetic mentors. An independent unit is the account of the uprising against the Philistines, in which Jonathan is the hero (chapters 13–14). Valuable information about Saul's wars and about his family is given in 14:47–52. A story with a prophetic slant and portraying Samuel in an awesome light is the one that recounts his break with Saul (chapter 15).

The third section is devoted to David and his relation to Saul. A preliminary story implants the idea that Samuel had elected and anointed David in secret in advance of any further happenings (I Samuel 16). There are a number of versions

concerning how David became a servant of Saul:
(1) A musician is recommended to dispel Saul's
melancholy, and David is chosen for the post
(16:14–23). (2) As visitor to the army in the
field, David offers to fight Goliath and is interviewed by Saul (17:1–54). (3) Saul meets
David after his successful combat and keeps him
in his entourage (17:55 to 18:5). A new theme
is introduced in 18:6 and following: Saul's jealousy and his desire to kill David. There are
several versions of David's peril and escape. (1)
Saul's attempt to kill David with a spear. Michal,
David's wife, helps David to escape (19:9–18).
(2) Jonathan finds out for David what his father's
intentions are and gives him warning, whereupon
David departs (20:1–42). (3) David, having
made a hasty escape, obtains food and a weapon
from the priest Ahimelech of the sanctuary at
Nob (21:2–10).

David becomes a brigand leader in southern
Judea. Here Abiathar, son of the priest of Nob,
comes to him and tells of Saul's vengeance on
that whole city. David makes him his priest
(chapter 22). David saves a city threatened by
the Philistines, but leaves it when Saul is about
to besiege it and goes to the wilderness of Ziph
(23:1–14). There are several accounts of how
David spared Saul when the latter was in pursuit
of him; one is localized at Engedi (chapter 24),
the other in the wilderness of Ziph (chapter 26).
One pursuit of David had to be called off because of a Philistine raid (23:24–29). The completely independent story of Nabal (chapter 25)
reveals how David made his living and gained a
wife. There are two versions of his taking refuge
with King Achish of Gath (21:11–16 and chapter 26). The second is well supported by what
follows, and reveals David's skill in playing a
double role. Achish plans to take him along on
the campaign against Israel.

An independent story of Saul's visit to the
witch of Endor is introduced (28:3–25), which
is one of the most impressive Old Testament narratives. The mobilizing Philistines send David
home, and the story of his return and his pursuit of the Amalekites is then presented. He
cleverly sends some of the spoil to Judean towns
(chapters 29–30). The first book ends with the
Battle of Gilboa and the sad fate of Saul and
his sons. But the Saul-David theme actually carries through II Samuel 1. Here David receives
the news of Saul's death but slays the bringer of
the tidings.

The fourth section progresses more simply.
David becomes king at Hebron, while Abner sets
up a son of Saul, Ishbosheth in Transjordan. The
Israelites are defeated by the Judeans. Abner
is slain by Joab while on a diplomatic mission
to Hebron. Ishbosheth is murdered, whereupon
the Israel tribes offer David their crown. He captures Jerusalem and makes it his capital, bringing
in the Ark of the Covenant. A prophecy of the
court prophet Nathan assures him of the perpetuity of his house. A summary account of his
military achievements and a list of his officials
are given.

The fifth section consists in the main (II
Samuel 9–20) of a single historical narrative, the
climax and conclusion of which have been cut off
and put in I Kings 1–2. It is the story of the
Davidic succession, written by a man close to
the events. The leading candidates for the succession are eliminated, leaving the way free for
Solomon to obtain the throne.

SAMUELSON, Paul Anthony (1915–   ),
American economist, who received the Alfred
Nobel Memorial Prize in Economic Science in
1970. Samuelson is celebrated for the breadth
and versatility of his contributions to economic
theory and for his ability to alternate between
abstract analysis and the day-to-day matters of
national economic policy. He is responsible for
fundamental advances in the theory of consumer
behavior, capital and interest, international trade,
public finance, welfare economics (the pure
theory of economic policy), and fiscal and monetary policy. His *Economics*, published first in
1948 and in its eighth edition in 1971, is the
standard elementary college textbook in economics in many countries.

Contributions. Samuelson's early work was
summed up in his *Foundations of Economic Analysis* (1947). It laid down a unified treatment
of the basic decision units in the economy: the
consuming household and the producing firm.
The book also showed how the theories of demand and supply could be deduced in parallel
from the postulate that consumers maximize their
satisfaction and firms maximize their profits, both
taking as given the market prices of goods and
productive inputs. The power of this conception
manifested itself in the observation that many
properties of a competitive economic system
could be deduced by treating the system as if it
were itself engaged in maximizing some appropriate defined quantity.

Another important unifying idea to emerge
from this early work is that the dynamic stability
of an economic system (its behavior over time
if it is disturbed from equilibrium) contains information on its comparative-statical properties
(the way its position of rest or equilibrium depends on underlying data).

In a series of papers that began in 1954,
Samuelson revived, clarified, and extended the
analysis of a fundamental problem in public finance: the production and allocation of public
goods. These are commodities that—like national
defense and an attractive environment and unlike
food and clothing—can be enjoyed by many people without diminishing the amount left over for
enjoyment by others. Such goods, he contended,
are natural objects of government spending.

In another series of articles, he analyzed the
conditions under which free trade in movable
goods could substitute for the mobility of labor
and other productive services, and thus lead
toward equalization of wages and other rewards
among trading countries.

He was one of those who refined and applied
the insights of the English economist John Maynard Keynes to the study of business cycles and
economic stabilization.

Life. Samuelson was born in Gary, Ind., on
May 15, 1915, and studied economics at the University of Chicago, graduating in 1935, and at
Harvard (Ph. D. 1941). From 1940 he taught
economics at the Massachusetts Institute of Technology. He was the first winner of the John
Bates Clark Medal of the American Economic
Association (1947). He was president of the
American Econometric Society in 1951 and a
member of the editorial board of *Econometrics*.
He wrote voluminously on current economic
problems and advised many government agencies
and public figures.

ROBERT M. SOLOW
Massachusetts Institute of Technology

Samurai armor of the 16th century. Such armor was worn by the daimyos, who were feudal barons.

SAMURAI, sam'ə-rī, warriors of feudal Japan. The word *samurai* is derived from the verb *samurau*, which means "to serve," and was used in the early Middle Ages in Japan to denote the soldiers on guard duty at the emperor's palace. Subsequently, it was taken to include all members of the warrior class who owed loyalty and service to a feudal superior. The number of samurai was excluded from the official census figures issued in the 18th century, but it has been estimated that they comprised about 6% of the population.

The samurai formed the leading class in Japanese society. From the beginning of the 17th century it was followed in order of precedence by those of the farmer, the artisan, and the trader. There were many gradations of rank within the warrior class, from the simple soldier to the well-to-do vassal living on his estate and ready to serve his overlord at call. The samurai code of behavior is known as Bushido.

History. Before the rigid division of classes was introduced about 1615, the well-to-do samurai constituted a rural gentry of considerable strength, since many of them owned much land and controlled a numerous peasantry. They took part in the endemic warfare that lasted throughout the Middle Ages until after the beginning of the Tokugawa shogunate early in the 17th century. As new methods of warfare developed, particularly after the introduction of firearms in 1542, the mounted samurai, with sword, spear, and bow, had to give way on many occasions to men armed with muskets and to a lower class of foot soldier, the *ashigaru,* so that their military importance tended to diminish. They did, however, constitute the solid, dependable warrior group. When under the Tokugawa regime after 1615 the country was divided into some 270 fiefs governed by chieftains (daimyos), a great number of samurai took service with their former commanders and lived on land granted to them.

The long era of peace after 1615 raised difficult problems for the samurai. Some of them held important official posts in the fiefs or in the central government offices, but many had to find work in the towns, and others sank in the social scale. But in general they preserved the ethos of their class, some reaching the highest pinnacle in political life, others devoting themselves to literature and the arts or to political philosophy. It was principally men of samurai birth who organized the revolution of 1868, by which the feudal hierarchy was overthrown and a constitutional monarchy developed.

Social legislation in 1871 led to the absorption of the samurai into the mass of the people, and soon after their stipends were commuted on unfavorable terms. Thus, many samurai fell into misery, but as a class they rose to the occasion, and before long they were dominant in both central and provincial government. See also BUSHIDO.

SIR GEORGE B. SANSOM, *Author of "Japan, a Short Cultural History"*

SAN ANDREAS FAULT, an-drā'əs, a large fault that extends northwestward from the Gulf of California through the state of California for several hundred miles. See diagram "San Andreas Fault" in the article EARTHQUAKE.

SAN ANGELO, an'jə-lō, a city in western Texas, the seat of Tom Green county, is situated at the junction of the North and Middle Concho rivers, about 180 miles (288 km) northwest of Austin. It is the trading center for the Edwards Plateau region, noted for raising cattle, sheep, and goats, and for producing oil.

The city is a livestock center and one of the nation's foremost markets for wool and mohair. Among the leading industries are food processing, and making stone, clay, and glass products. Goodfellow Air Force Base is nearby.

Angelo State College is in the city. The Fort Concho Restoration and Museum, an outpost that resisted Indian raids, is an attraction. Lakes Nosworthy and North Concho on the city's outskirts provide fishing and water sports.

Settlement began in 1867 with the founding of Fort Concho. A trading center grew up near the fort and in 1882 became the county seat. The city was incorporated in 1888, and is governed by council and manager. Population: 73,240.

SAN ANSELMO, an-sel'mō, a city in western California, in Marin county, is at the north end of Ross Valley, about 16 miles (26 km) north of downtown San Francisco. It is a residential community. San Anselmo is the site of the San Francisco Theological Seminary of the United Presbyterian Church in the United States of America. Nearby Mount Tamalpais is a popular recreational area, with wooded slopes, lakes, streams, and hiking trails.

The city was part of the old Mexican grant of Punta de Quintin. The portion known as Cañada de Anselmo later became known as San Anselmo. "Anselmo" was the name of a baptized Indian; the "San" was added to conform with the neighboring towns of San Rafael and San Quentin. Incorporated in 1907, it is governed by a mayor and council. Population: 11,927.

The Alamo in San Antonio, defended against the Mexicans in 1836, is the "Cradle of Texas Liberty."

SAN ANTONIO, an-tō′nē-ō, the third-largest city in Texas, the seat of Bexar county, is situated on the nonnavigable San Antonio River, about 190 miles (304 km) west of Houston. It is a major manufacturing city and the banking, transportation, and retail trade center of south-central Texas.

San Antonio was a focal point of the early history of Texas. The Alamo, a shrine of Texas independence, is in San Antonio. Today, the city displays a variety of the old and new, a modern and progressive city with the charm of the Spanish-American influences that helped to shape its character.

The skyline of downtown San Antonio is dominated by the Tower of the Americas (750 feet, or 225 meters), but one level below the narrow streets of the business district is the peaceful San Antonio River. Lined with boutiques, shops, and restaurants, the beautified banks, called the Paseo del Rio, are the delight of tourists. By riverboat, visitors can approach the Convention Center, which adjoins the HemisFair Plaza complex, built in 1968 as an international exposition. This blending of the picturesque and the practical is everywhere evident in the downtown district and immediate environs.

As the city spreads out into many suburban sections served by enclosed shopping malls, it is a typical sprawling metropolis. The generally flat terrain slopes into rolling hills only in the northwest quadrant. An expressway system connects the suburbs and the city's downtown central section.

In the 1980 census, San Antonio's population was 786,023. More than half were of Hispanic descent, and about 7% were blacks. The population of the metropolitan area was 1,071,954.

Within the city limits lie five incorporated cities: Alamo Heights, Balcones Heights, Castle Hills, Olmos Park, and Terrell Hills. The combined population of these cities was about 20,000, and many of their residents were employed in San Antonio proper. San Antonio's area is about 184 square miles (476 sq km).

San Antonio adopted council-manager government in 1952. The mayor and the 11 members of the City Council are the only elected officials of the city government.

The Economy. Originally established in 1718 as a Spanish military post, San Antonio has always been militarily important. American troops have been stationed in San Antonio since Texas became a state. Fort Sam Houston is the headquarters of the U. S. 5th Army and the location of the Brooke Army Medical Center. The San Antonio Air Material Area, known for its logistics and maintenance operations, is at the Kelly Air Force Base, as is the U. S. Air Force Security Service. "Gateway to the Air Force" is the name applied to Lackland Air Force Base, an Air Force Training Command Base. Randolph Air Force Base is the headquarters for the Air Training Command. The Aerospace Medical Division and the School of Aerospace Medicine are located at Brooks Air Force Base.

San Antonio is one of the leading livestock centers and one of the largest produce exchange markets in the United States. Although there are no major oil developments in the area, it is the commercial headquarters for the south Texas petroleum producing district. Twenty-five percent of the wool and 85% of the mohair produced in the United States are grown west of San Antonio.

There is a wide diversification in manufacturing, from the fabrication of executive airplanes to church furniture, from storage batteries to stained-glass windows. The production of clothing and the processing of food products are important. Products of the metal industry include structural steel; steel forms; and equipment for food handling, commercial refrigeration, and electronic data processing. The retail, wholesale, and service trades, the military payroll, and tourist and convention income also contribute to the economy.

Education and Cultural Life. Nine independent school districts provide public education in the San Antonio area. Private schools include many in the Catholic parochial system and others that are nondenominational or Protestant supported. One of the most famous is the Texas Military Institute, where Gen. Douglas MacArthur was once a student. The two junior colleges are St. Philip's College and San Antonio College. The five institutions of higher learning are Trinity University (founded 1869), St. Mary's University (1852), Incarnate Word College (1881), and Our Lady of the Lake College (1896).

Good libraries are housed in the colleges and universities and on military bases. The modernized San Antonio public library system has strong regional branches and mobile libraries that serve all Bexar county. The Hertzberg Circus Museum, a nationally known collection of circus memorabilia and documents, is housed in the Main Library Annex.

The Institute of Texan Cultures, located in the HemisFair Plaza, through exhibits and films shows the contributions of the 26 ethnic groups who settled in Texas. The Lone Star Hall of

Wildlife and Ecology is one of the outstanding exhibits at the Witte Memorial Museum. The McNay Art Institute is dedidcated to modern art. The San Antonio Art Museum, occupying a renovated brewery, opened in 1981. The city's symphony orchestra is recognized nationally.

The Southwest Research Institute does applied research for industry, government agencies, and individuals in such areas as mineral technology, physics, chemistry, engines, electronics, and ocean engineering. Biomedical research is done by the Southwest Foundation for Research and Education, which is endowed by national organizations and supported by grants. A citizen-supported Research and Planning Council conducts research into governmental problems.

The Media. Communications in San Antonio reflect the bilingualism of its population. Three of the 15 radio stations broadcast in Spanish, as does one of the five television stations. There are also five FM stations. The three daily newspapers are the San Antonio *Express* (established 1865), the San Antonio *News* (1918), and the San Antonio *Light* (1889). Of the 11 weekly newspapers, one is in Spanish.

Places of Interest. The Alamo, "Shrine of Texas Liberty," situated in the center of the downtown area, is the outstanding tourist attraction in San Antonio. Within the enclosure are the chapel in which the Americans made their desperate stand against the Mexican Army in the Texas Revolution of 1836, two museums of Texas relics, and a Library of Texana.

Within walking distance of the Alamo is the Arneson River Theatre, where the San Antonio River separates the stage from the grass-covered seats terraced on the bank of the river. Above it is the block-long La Villita, or Little Town, a restored residential section where the houses reflect the two nationality groups that have greatly influenced San Antonio—Spanish and German. It is also an arts and crafts center.

The four missions established about the same time as the Alamo (1718) are interesting: Mission Concepcion, San Francisco de la Espada Mission, San Juan Capistrano Mission, and Mission San José, a state and national historic site, which contains a famous rose window.

Other sights in the San Antonio area are the Spanish Governor's Palace, used by the Spanish governors as home and office; Buckhorn Hall of Horns, a collection of horns from almost every kind of horned animal; and the San Antonio Zoo in Brackenridge Park. This city park is also well known for the four early Texas homes rebuilt on its grounds. More than 75 other parks and playgrounds and several golf courses and swimming pools are also part of the city's extensive park and recreation program.

Annual Events. San Antonio is known as the Fiesta City, with its entertainment year climaxed in the week of April 21 by the Fiesta de San Jacinto, commemorating Texas independence from Mexico. A magnificent Battle of Flowers Parade; an illuminated night parade, Fiesta Flambeau; and a river pageant, a parade of illuminated decorated barges floating on the San Antonio River, highlight a week of varied entertainment. During Fiesta Week the visitor realizes anew the elements that have blended to make San Antonio fascinating—the Mexican-Spanish culture, the old West, and the modern city with its important military installations.

The San Antonio Livestock Exposition is held annually in February. Rodeo shows, livestock exhibits, and commercial displays promote the ranching and farming industry.

History. When members of a Spanish expedition discovered the San Antonio River on June 13, 1691, they came upon a Coahuiltecan Indian village, Yanaguana, along the upper headwaters of the stream. They named the site San Antonio de Padua in honor of the saint whose feast day it was.

No permanent settlement was made until 1718, when Father Antonio de San Buenaventura y Olivares, a Franciscan, and Martin de Alarcón, the Spanish governor of Coahuila and Texas, established a town, Villa de Bejar (later called Bexar); a fort, Presidio de Bejar; and the Mission San Antonio de Valero (later known as the Alamo). The Franciscan brothers at Mission San Antonio de Valero and the four other missions in the area taught the Indians Christianity and Spanish methods of farming.

The missions were secularized in 1793 after an epidemic had wiped out most of the Indian population. After the secularization of the Mission San Antonio de Valero, Mexican troops were quartered in the plaza area.

Spain sent 56 colonists from the Canary Islands in 1731. Their settlement, San Fernando de Bejar, was located a little west of Presidio de Bejar. Marauding Indians and economic hardships made their life difficult. By 1791 the three settlements, San Fernando de Bejar, Villa de Bejar, and Mission San Antonio de Valero, had come to be considered as one, San Antonio de Bejar. Their population totaled 1,333.

Except for a brief period, San Antonio remained under Spanish rule until 1821, when Mexico won its independence from Spain. Colonists from the United States, who had been allowed to settle in Texas, soon rebelled against the tyranny of Mexican rule. The Mexican dictator, Gen. Antonio López de Santa Anna, sent Gen. Martin Perfecto de Cos to San Antonio to put out

The San Antonio River, bordered by gardens, shops, and restaurants, threads the downtown section of the city.

TEXAS HIGHWAY DEPARTMENT

STEVES HOMESTEAD in San Antonio, built in 1876, is a museum of furniture of the Victorian period.

this spark of rebellion. The Mexicans were defeated, and the articles of surrender were signed in the Cos House restored now in La Villita.

Two months later, in February 1836, Santa Anna himself marched toward San Antonio. Lt. Col. William Barrett Travis, the gallant commander of the small band of Americans quartered in San Antonio, made the decision to stay and fight so that the ill-organized Texan army would have time to mobilize. The valiant band of 183 soldiers withdrew from the town into the Alamo enclosure, which was only an improvised fort, offering little protection against a Mexican army estimated at over 6,000. On March 6, 1836, the Mexicans scaled the walls, and all the Alamo's defenders were killed. See also ALAMO.

The cry "Remember the Alamo" inspired the Texan army one month later when Gen. Sam Houston successfully led it against Santa Anna at San Jacinto. See SAN JACINTO, BATTLE OF.

Texas became a republic in 1836, and San Antonio was incorporated on June 5, 1837. For a few years it was almost a deserted town, due to lack of protection against the harassment of Indians and Mexican troops. These conditions were changed when Texas was admitted to the Union (1845), and San Antonio soon showed some population growth.

After the Civil War in the 1860's and 1870's, San Antonio was known as a wild West town, but that boisterous era faded as it began to develop commercially and culturally. HemisFair '68, a world's fair marking the city's 250th anniversary, drew millions of visitors. Today, the city combines the easy tempo of life in a mild and warm climate with the accelerated pace of progress, and retains the charm of its Spanish-American origins side by side with its importance as a commercial and military center of the Southwest.

IRWIN SEXTON
Director, San Antonio Public Library

Bibliography

Curtis, Albert, *Fabulous San Antonio* (Naylor 1955).
Green, Rena Maverick, ed., *Samuel Maverick, Texan, 1803–1870* (Privately printed © 1952).
Lord, Walter, *A Time to Stand* (Harper 1961).
Ramsdell, Charles, *San Antonio: a Historical and Pictorial Guide* (U. of Texas Press 1959).

SAN BENITO, bə-nē′tō, a city in extreme southeastern Texas, in Cameron county, is in the lower Rio Grande valley about 18 miles (28 km) northwest of Brownsville. It is part of the Brownsville-Harlingen-San Benito metropolitan area. Situated in an irrigated agricultural region, San Benito is a center for processing citrus fruits and vegetables. Tourism is also important to the economy.

Mexican ranchers from José de Escandón's colony, holding royal land grants from Spain, settled the area in 1771. San Benito was founded in 1904 and was incorporated in 1910. Government is by council and city manager. Population: 17,988.

SAN BERNARDINO, bûr-nər-dē′nō, a city in southwestern California, the seat of San Bernardino county, is about 60 miles (96 km) east of the center of Los Angeles. It is a trade center for the San Bernardino Valley, whose agricultural products include citrus fruits, grapes, truck crops, milk, and poultry.

Industries in and near the city include the manufacture of steel, cement, water softeners, building materials, clothing, and lumber. San Bernardino is also a rail transportation center. Aerospace Corporation and the Norton Air Force Base, which is situated within the city limits, deal with missiles.

Local cultural groups provide music and drama for the city. The annual National Orange Show, first held in 1915, has permanent exposition buildings in the city, including an auditorium with a capacity for 12,000 spectators. The San Bernardino Valley College here is a 2-year junior college. Within a short distance of the city are mountain resorts in the San Bernardino National Forest, which attract skiers in the winter and campers in the summer.

The original settlement was named San Bernardino when the Spanish missionary Father Francisco Dumetz arrived in the valley in 1810 on the feast of St. Bernardino of Siena. In 1851 a Mormon colony settled in San Bernardino, which was incorporated as a town in 1854. The Mormons were recalled to Utah by Brigham Young in 1857. In 1863, San Bernardino was disincorporated, and in 1886 it was reincorporated as a city of the fifth class. It is governed by a mayor and council. Population: 118,794.

SAN BERNARDINO MOUNTAINS, bûr-nər-dē′nō, in southern California, are in San Bernardino and Riverside counties, about 100 miles (160 km) east of Los Angeles. The range extends approximately north and south for about 55 miles (88 km) from Cajon Pass at the eastern end of the San Gabriel Mountains to San Gorgonio Pass at the northern end of the San Jacinto Mountains. Although some geographers regard them as part of the Coast Ranges, they may be considered a continuation of the Sierra Nevada.

The average height of the range is about 6,000 feet (1,820 meters). San Gorgonio Mountain, the highest peak in southern California, rises to 11,485 feet (3,490 meters), and San Bernardino Mountain to 10,630 feet (3,230 meters).

Much of the range is encompassed in the San Bernardino national forest, and there are many recreational sites. Arrowhead and Big Bear are popular summer and winter resorts. The Rim of the World Drive loops 45 miles (72 km) over a high scenic route.

SAN BERNARDINO STRAIT, bûr-nər-dē'nō, a waterway in the Philippines, between the southeastern point of Luzon and the northwestern tip of Samar. It forms the main channel for shipping from the Pacific Ocean to Manila and the South China Sea by way of either the Sibuyan Sea or the Visayan Sea.

During World War II the strait was one of the scenes of the Battle for Leyte Gulf, a decisive U. S. victory over the Japanese fleet. See also LEYTE GULF, BATTLE FOR.

SAN BRUNO, broo'nō, a city in western California, in San Mateo county, is about 12 miles (19 km) south of the center of San Francisco, just west of San Francisco international airport. Its industries that include lithography, wire products, sheet metal fabricating, airline repair bases, and flower growing. A national archives and records center is situated here. The famous Tanforan race track was destroyed by fire in 1964, and a regional shopping center now stands on the site of the track.

The first airplane flight on the Pacific took place at Tanforan in 1910, and in 1911 Eugene Ely took off from Tanforan and made the first plane landing on a naval vessel.

A creek and a mountain near the site of the community were named for Saint Bruno in 1775 by Capt. Bruno de Heceta, exploring for the Spanish navy. The community, which began to develop about 1862, was named for these. The city was incorporated in 1914. Government is by council and manager. Population: 35,417.

SAN CARLOS, kär'ləs, a city in California, is situated 2 miles (3 km) west of the south end of San Francisco Bay, about 25 miles (40 km) south of the center of San Francisco. It is a flower growing and shipping center. San Carlos was incorporated in 1925 and is governed by council and manager. Population: 24,710.

SAN CLEMENTE, klə-men'tē, a city in southwestern California, in Orange county, is on the Pacific Ocean about 60 miles (96 km) southeast of the center of Los Angeles. The surrounding area is largely agricultural, and the city produces cut flowers and deals in eggs, strawberries, and Valencia oranges.

Tourism is important to the economy. The former home of President Richard M. Nixon is a place of interest, as is San Clemente Beach state park nearby.

San Clemente, a community of homes with red tile roofs, was founded in 1925, during the housing boom that followed World War I. It was incorporated in 1928 and is governed by a council and manager. Population: 27,325.

SAN CRISTÓBAL ISLAND, kris-tō'bəl, one of the Galápagos Islands, in the Pacific Ocean, about 600 miles (950 km) west of Ecuador. It is also known as Chatham Island. All the islands belong to Ecuador and are a national park.

San Cristóbal, the easternmost of the group, is about 26 miles (41 km) long. Of volcanic origin, its highest elevation is about 4,500 feet (1,308 meters). It is the site of the town of San Cristóbal, the islands' administrative center. San Cristóbal is the most fertile of the Galápagos. The inhabitants grow sugarcane, coffee, and yucca. They also raise cattle and engage in fishing. Population: (1962) 1,404.

AMERICAN AIRLINES

THE CONVENTION CENTER in San Diego, Calif., is part of a large complex of municipal buildings.

SAN DIEGO, dē-ā'gō, is a city in southern California, near the border of Mexico about 100 miles (160 km) southeast of Los Angeles. It is a port of entry and the seat of San Diego county. The site of the first European settlement in California, it was named for San Diego (St. James) de Alcalá.

A rapidly growing city, San Diego has been known in the past for its naval bases, its prominent role in early aviation development, and its proximity to Mexico. Since World War II, however, it has prospered upon a variegated commercial foundation that has included industry, agriculture, research, trade, tourism, and the city's great appeal as a place to live.

The style of life in San Diego features outdoor activity, encouraged by a diversified landscape, two spacious bays, and a kindly climate with persistent sunshine. The creative arts are generously supported and promoted, as by art sales in public parks. Performances of music and live drama, some of these also in the open air, are frequent and well attended.

Setting and Physical Features. San Diego stands on land that rises gradually from the Pacific shore onto mesas or foothills of The Laguna mountain range. These are separated by numerous canyons that separate the 25 to 30 communities that make up the city. The climate is mild and semiarid, with an average temperature of 63° F (17° C) and annual rainfall of about 10.4 inches (265 mm).

San Diego covers about 392 square miles (1,015 sq km), including inland water. The limits touch Escondido to the north and National City in the south. The shoreline at the west runs from south to north along San Diego Bay, with its naval and commercial shore installations, and around the natural deepwater harbor to Point Loma. Northward from the point are Ocean Beach, the narrow Mission Beach peninsula (which encloses Mission Bay Aquatic Park), Pacific Beach, LaJolla, Torrey Pines Park, and Del Mar Heights, all part of greater San Diego. Also part of the city is South San Diego, at the Mexican border, an agricultural community connected to the city proper by a legal corridor running through San Diego Bay.

193

The city of San Diego, Calif., is on the east shore of San Diego Bay, a 12-mile (19-km) long natural harbor.

Places of Interest. The Community Concourse in the downtown area contains the City Administration Building, the Civic Theater, and an exhibit hall and convention center. Also downtown, and less than a mile from San Diego Bay, is the 1,400-acre (567-hectare) Balboa Park, which is the home of the world-famous San Diego Zoo. The park also includes the Museum of Man; the Fine Arts Gallery, with many originals by old masters; the Natural History Museum; Spanish Village and the Institute of Art, both of which feature local artists; the Aerospace Museum, with historical aircraft and aviation mementos; the Hall of Champions, commemorating local sports personalities; and the new Hall of Science and Planetarium. The park also retains many landmarks from the Panama-California Exposition of 1915–1916 and the California-Pacific International Exposition of 1935–1936, including the House of Pacific Relations, the Spreckels Organ Pavilion, the recreated Casa del Prado, and a reproduction of Shakespeare's Globe Theater.

To the north and inland, in Presidio Park, is the original site of San Diego de Alcalá, Junípero Serra's first mission in Upper California, founded in 1769. Here, too, is the Spanish presidio (military garrison) and Fort Stockton. Archaeological discoveries on the presidio site and historical materials relating to San Diego are on display. Nearby is the terminus of El Camino Real, the "king's highway" running north to Monterey, pioneered by Don Gaspar de Portolá.

Old Town, just west of the presidio, was the city's first civilian settlement and still contains restored early Spanish, Mexican, and American period homes. Part of Old Town is now a state park. The present Mission San Diego is 6 miles (10 km) to the east, in Mission Valley.

Point Loma was the site of LaPlaya, the beach where, during the early 19th century, traders cured cattle hides for export to New England. Toward the southern end of this peninsula are Fort Rosecrans and a military cemetery, and at the southern tip, on a bluff, is Cabrillo National Monument, with an 1855 lighthouse.

The *Star of India,* an iron-hulled sailing ship built in 1863 and fully restored, is a maritime museum at the harbor waterfront. The Wild Animal Park is at the northeast city limits, and Sea World, a large aquarium in Mission Bay Aquatic Park, features performing sea animals.

Tide pools with small marine life abound along the shore, especially at LaJolla Cove, where there are also caves formed by wave action. North of LaJolla is Torrey Pines State Park, preserving groves of these rare trees. Glider enthusiasts soar along the nearby ocean cliffs, within sight of a city-owned tournament-quality golf course. Offshore here is an underwater park.

Recreation. Aquatic sports and ocean fishing are enjoyed most of the year, as is land recreation, with a multitude of parks, tennis courts, and golf courses in the vicinity. Mountains and deserts to the east attract campers, hikers, cyclists, and, in winter, skiers. The Stadium in Mission Valley is the home of major league football and baseball teams and the California State University, San Diego, football team.

Education and Cultural Life. Public elementary and private schools are numerous. Publicly supported adult education centers and junior colleges also serve the city, and there are several private business and technical schools. Colleges and universities include San Diego State University, the United States International University, the University of San Diego, Point Loma College, the California School of Professional Psychology, the Scripps Institution of Oceanography, and a campus of the University of California. Palomar Observatory, with the 200-inch (508-cm) Hale telescope, is situated on a peak about 65 miles (105 km) northeast of the city. The

Salk Institute for Biological Studies, a research center, is at LaJolla.

The San Diego Public Library operates a central downtown building and a growing system of branches and bookmobiles. Among the notable special collections in the main building are those on local history and the history of printing. The San Diego County Library is also headquartered in the city, and there are several specialized business and scientific libraries.

San Diegans support numerous year-round little theater groups, including the pioneer Old Globe in Balboa Park with its summer Shakespeare festival. The city's symphony orchestra and its opera company have extensive seasons, and the Civic Light Opera Company sponsors open-air productions. Musical events as well as art exhibitions are held in the LaJolla Museum of Contemporary Art and in adjacent Sherwood Hall.

Media. There are more than 30 radio stations and several local television channels, plus some cable TV services. The San Diego *Union* (morning) and *Tribune* (evening), two newspapers under single ownership, furnish the city with daily and Sunday news coverage. There are several weekly neighborhood newspapers.

Population. There were 17,700 people in San Diego in 1900, 147,995 in 1930, 573,224 in 1960, and 696,769 in 1970. By the mid-1970's, it displaced San Francisco as California's second-largest city. At the 1980 census, the population totaled 875,538, while that of the metropolitan area was 1,861,846.

Ethnically, the population is fairly typical of most U. S. cities, although there may be more than the average number of persons with Spanish surnames, mainly people of Mexican or Philippine descent. Portuguese tuna fishermen and their families populate parts of Point Loma. Despite its popularity with retired people, San Diego is predominantly a city of young families attracted to the area by pleasant living conditions.

Economic Life. San Diego derives its economic sustenance from many sources: electronics, aerospace suppliers, nuclear and oceanographic research, fishing, marine products, retail and wholesale distribution, imported goods, and clothing manufacture. The city is headquarters for some large banks and savings and loan companies, a motel group, a large scheduled airline, and an extensive chain discount house. Tourism is also a major income producer in a city favored by an excellent climate and generous hotel, motel, and convention accommodations. San Diego has long been a military center, with much of its income derived from the armed forces.

The harbor, including the shore facilities of other cities adjoining San Diego Bay, is managed by the San Diego Unified Port District. Several hundred merchant ships flying about two dozen national flags enter port yearly. There are docking and loading facilities, waterfront parks, boat marinas, and water sports areas.

Truck gardening, dairy farms, and small cattle ranches operate within the San Diego city limits, while lemon, orange, and avocado groves flourish in outlying areas. The production of dairy products and eggs is important in the city's economy. Sand and rock are mined within the city limits, and salt is recovered from seawater in a modern plant.

Naval Installations. San Diego is a hub of naval activities. It includes the 11th Naval District headquarters, a supply depot, naval ship and air stations, training centers for Navy and Marine recruits, a naval hospital, and an electronics laboratory. A large fleet, ranging from aircraft carriers to atomic submarines, is stationed in San Diego. The Coast Guard maintains bases with rescue aircraft and patrol ships.

Transportation and Communications. The heaviest passenger traffic into the city is by automobile on Interstate 5 from the north and Interstate 8 from the east. Several scheduled commercial airlines use San Diego International Airport (called Lindbergh Field), operated by the Port District. Private aircraft fly from Lindbergh Field and from city-operated Montgomery and Brown fields. San Diego is served by bus, truck, and railroad companies. A trolley line, opened in 1981, links downtown San Diego with the Mexican border. A bridge has replaced the ferries that once were the most direct link between downtown San Diego and Coronado, on the long peninsula that shelters San Diego Bay.

Government. San Diego is a charter city under California law. It is one of the largest U. S. cities with a council-manager form of government, which was established in 1931. The mayor and eight councilmen are elected for four-year terms, and they appoint a city manager. The elections are nonpartisan.

History. A Portuguese navigator in Spanish service, Juan Rodríguez Cabrillo, discovered San Diego Bay on Sept. 28, 1542, naming it San Miguel. Don Sebastián Vizcaíno, who entered it on Nov. 10, 1602, renamed the bay San Diego.

Father Junípero Serra, a Franciscan, led a Spanish expedition that established a mission to the Indians and a presidio near the bay in 1769. Because of conflicts between soldiers and Indians, Father Serra moved the mission to its present site in 1774.

The British explorer George Vancouver entered the harbor in the *Discovery* on Nov. 27, 1793. Occasional American ships followed in later years. Trade in cattle hides between American shippers and local herd owners became lucrative after the establishment of Mexican rule in 1822.

The Mexican War in 1846 brought the U. S. sloop *Cyane*, under Capt. Samuel duPont, into the

MISSION SAN DIEGO, in Presidio Park, was the first Spanish mission in Upper California.

JOSEF MUENCH

bay on July 29, 1846. Troops under John C. Frémont disembarked and raised the U. S. flag over the Old Town plaza. U. S. soldiers led by Gen. Stephen W. Kearny had come westward from Kansas and on December 6 fought a costly battle against loyal Californians under Gen. Andrés Pico at San Pasqual, northeast of San Diego.

The town's first newspaper, the *Herald*, was founded in 1851 but failed in 1860, leaving San Diego without a newspaper until 1868, when the present *Union* began to publish. A year earlier, Alonzo E. Horton in effect founded modern San Diego by purchasing an unsuccessful 1,000-acre (405-hectare) development in the present downtown area. Horton built a wharf, laid out streets, gave land to churches, and, in 1870, opened a hotel opposite the new town's plaza.

An 1870 gold strike at Julian, in the mountains to the northeast, and several land booms increased the population rapidly. The Santa Fe Railway arrived in 1885, and the financier John D. Spreckels and others brought added improvements. From a high of 40,000 in the 1880's, however, San Diego dropped in population to 17,000 near the turn of the century, as real-estate enterprises failed. The city's later growth came as a result of U. S. Navy investments, the industrial progress nurtured by several wars, and the city's encouragement of civilian industries.

San Diego's sunny climate was largely responsible for making it a favorite production and testing site of the pioneers of aviation. In 1883, John J. Montgomery flew the first successful glider flights at Otay Mesa, and on Jan. 26, 1911, Glenn H. Curtiss piloted the first successful seaplane flight, taking off from San Diego Bay. Charles Lindbergh had his airplane, *Spirit of St. Louis*, built here in 1927. After World War II, the Atlas missile, a vital cog in the U. S. space program, was assembled in San Diego.

Marco G. Thorne
City Librarian, San Diego Public Library

Further Reading: Federal Writers Project, *San Diego: A California City* (AMS Press 1975, repr. of 1937 ed.); Morgan, Neil, and Blair, Tom, *Yesterday's San Diego* (Seemann 1976); Pourade, Richard F., *The History of San Diego*, 6 vols. (Union-Tribune Pub. Co. 1961–1967).

SAN DIMAS, dē'məs, a city in southwestern California, in Los Angeles county, is about 25 miles (40 km) east of the center of Los Angeles. Plastic objects are made. The Voorhis campus of California State Polytechnic College is in the community. The Frank G. Bonelli regional county park is of interest.

San Dimas was founded in 1862 and the community was incorporated as a city in 1960. Government is by council and city manager. Population: 24,014.

SAN FERNANDO, fər-nan'dō, a city in southwestern California, in Los Angeles county, is situated at the northern end of the San Fernando Valley, about 20 miles (32 km) northwest of the center of Los Angeles. It manufactures and assembles electronic parts and makes garments. The church and monastery of the Mission San Fernando Rey de España, founded on Sept. 8, 1797, have been restored.

White men entered the valley in the 1760's and gold was found here in 1842. The community was laid out in 1874 and was incorporated as a city in 1911. Government is by mayor and council. Population: 17,731.

SAN FRANCISCO, a city in California, is noted for the beauty of its setting and the buoyant spirit of its people. It occupies the tip of a narrow and hilly peninsula, a site with a dramatic quality that visitors rarely fail to recognize. Thanks to its favorable location on a spacious, land-locked harbor, and with easy access by water to a large area rich in natural resources, the city has long been the financial, commercial, and cultural center of northern California.

CONTENTS

A visitor's first impression of San Francisco's dramatic setting is enhanced on closer acquaintance by the sweeping views of sky, land, and water from many elevated spots; by clusters of picturesque buildings clinging precariously to nearly perpendicular hillsides; and, perhaps most striking of all, by the gridlike pattern of the city streets. The streets, with few exceptions, were laid out without regard to the contours of the land, and in consequence many ascend the hills at angles too steep to permit vehicular traffic of any kind.

But not all the qualities that set San Francisco apart from other cities result from its physical setting. Much of its present individuality springs from the circumstances of its early history. The city of today dates from the gold rush. The discovery of gold in January 1848 marked the city's true beginning, although the spot had then been occupied for more than half a century, and a frontier village of some 200 inhabitants had grown up there. The shiploads of adventurers from every corner of the world gave the early settlement a cosmopolitan flavor that has persisted to the present.

Upon landing, those who spoke the same language and shared the same background tended to band together, and so established a group of smaller communities within the larger settlement. A number of these remain today, adding a further picturesque note to the modern city. Among the more colorful of such "foreign quarters" are Chinatown, the Italian quarter, and the Japanese cultural center, fronting on Geary Boulevard a few blocks beyond Van Ness Avenue.

Many important changes took place in the city during the 1960's and the 1970's, including the completion of several large-scale urban renewal projects, the building of many tall hotels and apartment and office buildings in the central

---

INFORMATION HIGHLIGHTS

Location: Northern California, on the northern tip of a peninsula with the Pacific Ocean on the west, the Golden Gate on the north, and San Francisco Bay on the east.

Population: *City,* 678,974 (14th in U. S.); *metropolitan area* (San Francisco-Oakland), 3,250,630.

Area: 45 square miles (117 sq km)

Elevation: Sea level to 925 feet (280 meters) atop Mt. Davidson.

Climate: Temperature averages 60° F (15° C) in summer, 51° F (10° C) in winter; rainfall averages 20.8 inches (533 mm).

Government: Mayor and 11-member board of supervisors.

area, and the construction of the Bay Area Rapid Transit System. But notwithstanding these and other major modernization projects, many of the features that lent distinction to the earlier city remain. These include the quaint but still serviceable cable cars, the many green open spaces (in particular the Presidio and the magnificent Golden Gate Park), and Fisherman's Wharf, Twin Peaks, and Ocean Beach. Perhaps the most pleasing of all are the alternate periods of swirling fog and brilliant sunshine that envelop the city, and everywhere unexpected views of row on row of terraced houses slanting down steep hillsides toward the water's edge.

1. Physical Features

San Francisco, standing midway on the long northern California coastline, is surrounded on three sides by water—the Pacific Ocean, the Golden Gate, and San Francisco Bay—and is accessible by land only from the south. The city is dominated by a series of steep-sided hills, the highest of which, Mt. Davidson, has an altitude of 925 feet (280 meters). Other elevated spots include Telegraph, Nob, and Russian hills, close to the downtown district; Twin Peaks, near the geographical center of the city; and Bernal Heights, in the Mission district to the south. Overlooking the ocean, the Golden Gate, and the bay are Sutro Heights, Land's End, and Pacific Heights.

San Francisco Bay, one of the world's best harbors, is some 50 miles (80 km) long and 3 to 12 miles (5–19 km) wide. It is connected to the north with San Pablo and Suisun bays, into which empty the Sacramento and San Joaquin rivers. A number of islands dot the bay, the largest of which are Angel Island, Yerba Buena, Alcatraz (once the site of a federal prison), and the man-made Treasure Island, the site of the 1939–1940 Golden Gate International Exposition.

San Francisco's climate is without extremes of heat or cold. The prevailing westerly winds off the ocean tend to make it "an air-conditioned city," with cool summers and mild winters. Flowers bloom throughout the year, and warm clothing for evening wear is the rule at all seasons. Morning fogs are frequent from May to August, but are usually dissipated by midday.

2. Description

Almost from the beginning San Francisco has been divided into several clearly defined neighborhoods. The original village was built on the shore of Yerba Buena Cove. During the gold-rush period, hotels, shops, and places of entertainment were grouped about the old Spanish plaza. The lower slopes of Telegraph, Nob, and Rincon hills served as residential districts. Although the passage of time has brought many changes, traces of this original pattern may still be seen.

Business Districts. The present financial district, centering on Montgomery and California streets, occupies part of the site of the original cove. Nob and Telegraph hills have remained favorite residential areas, but Rincon Hill was taken over by factories and warehouses and today serves as an anchorage for cables supporting the San Francisco-Oakland Bay Bridge. Beginning about 1880, the hotel, theater, and retail shopping center moved toward the southwest, and today is grouped about Union Square. As the city's growth continued, new housing spread

JOSEF MUENCH

The Golden Gate Bridge, at the entrance to San Francisco Bay, links San Francisco and its northern suburbs.

outward, covering the hills and intervening valleys and stopping only when it reached the water's edge to the north, east, and west.

Other well-known districts include the Embarcadero, a 200-foot (60-meter) wide thoroughfare that follows the curving bay shore · from China Basin to Fisherman's Wharf. It is flanked on the water side by a long series of piers, where the ships of many nations take on and discharge passengers and freight. The factories and warehouses of the industrial district lie south of Market Street.

Residential Areas. Homes on Telegraph, Nob, and Russian hills have long been favored because they have excellent views and are conveniently close to the downtown area. Since the 1960's, however, an increasing number of private residences have been replaced by tall apartment buildings. The area known as the Mission, a section of picturesque wooden buildings facing on slanting streets, grew up about the venerable Mission Dolores. Other attractive residential neighborhoods include Pacific Heights and Sea Cliff, both overlooking the Golden Gate, and several newer subdivisions on the wooded hillsides south of Twin Peaks.

The largest and the most distinctly San Franciscan residential areas are the Richmond district, fronting on the ocean to the north of Golden Gate Park, and the Sunset district, on the ocean to the south of the park. They both

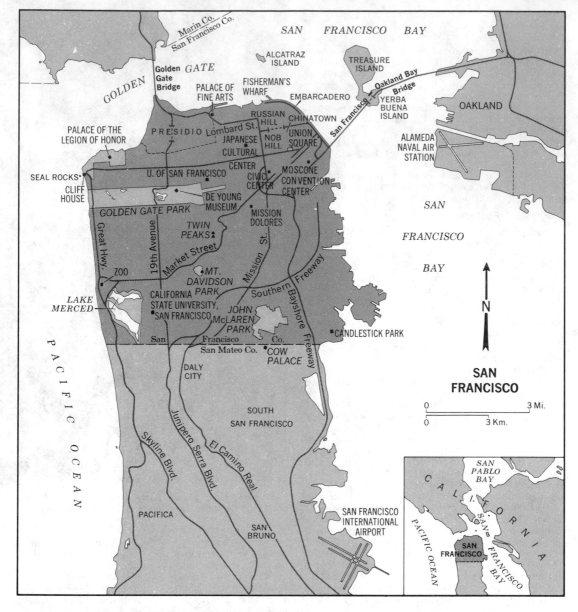

occupy several hundred acres of former sand hills that have been solidly built with row on row of one-story cottages, each occupying the full width of its narrow lot and each with a small garden and bay window facing the street.

3. Places of Interest

San Francisco is one of the most exciting and cosmopolitan cities in the United States. Visitors cannot help but fall under the spell of the city's magnificent setting, with its white buildings sitting on the many hills that overlook the surrounding waters. With its historic buildings, beautiful parks, and wide range of cultural, recreational, and nighttime activities, San Francisco is one of the tourist's favorite cities.

Historical San Francisco. The two oldest of San Francisco's historic buildings are the Mission Dolores at 16th and Dolores streets and the former Commandant's House (now the Officers' Club) in the Presidio. Dating from 1776, they were the first houses built within the borders of the present city. Both were unpretentious structures, their thick walls made of adobe bricks and their tile roofs supported by hand-hewn timbers lashed together by thongs of cowhide and fastened with wooden pegs. They were permitted to fall into partial ruin during the Mexican regime but were subsequently restored.

Adjoining the mission to the south is San Francisco's first cemetery, where many pioneers of the Mexican and early American period are buried. In front of the Officers' Club at the Presidio are three ancient cannons, part of the original defenses of the harbor. Two were cast in Madrid in the early 1500's, and the third bears the date 1679. Another historic building in the Presidio is Ft. Point, which long guarded the southern portal of the Golden Gate. Standing on the site of the original adobe fort put up by the Spanish in 1794, the present massive brick structure, which once mounted more than 100 cannons, was completed in 1857.

The old Spanish plaza, now called Portsmouth Square, was the center of the early city and is rich in historical associations. About it were grouped the trading posts and living quarters of the original settlers, and the hotels, theaters, and gambling casinos of gold rush days. In the northwest corner stood the small customhouse above which the American flag was first raised on July 9, 1846. At one corner of the square—beneath which a city-owned parking facility has been built—is a handsome monument to the author Robert Louis Stevenson, who frequented the spot during his stay in San Francisco in 1879.

Popular Attractions. Adjoining Portsmouth Square on the west is San Francisco's colorful Chinatown, a veritable city within a city and the largest Chinese quarter outside the Orient. Grant Avenue from Bush Street to Columbus Avenue is the heart of Chinatown. Fronting on it and on neighboring streets and alleys are the bazaars, restaurants, markets, and temples that make the district a major attraction.

Another picturesque spot is Fisherman's Wharf, at the foot of Taylor Street. There the boats of the fishing fleet tie up before a group of restaurants serving the many varieties of seafood found in Pacific Coast waters. A few blocks west of Fisherman's Wharf is the Maritime Museum, which displays interesting material relating to the city's history as a world seaport. Also near the wharf are the Cannery and Ghirardelli Square, each a picturesque complex of galleries, shops, and restaurants occupying respectively an old fruit-packing plant and a former chocolate factory.

Other points of interest are the Cliff House and Fleishhacker Zoo, both on the ocean front; the Japanese Cultural and Trade Center; and Coit Tower, rising 210 feet (64 meters) atop Telegraph Hill. The Latin Quarter, where many artists reside, is near the base of Telegraph Hill. The old Barbary Coast in North Beach is much changed from the days when its dance halls and gambling resorts were known to sailors from all over the world.

Parks and Squares. The most celebrated of San Francisco's many open spaces is Golden Gate Park, which contains more than 1,000 acres (400 hectares) and extends inland from the beach for more than 4 miles (6 km). When the city acquired the property in 1870, it was a waste area of barren sand hills interspersed with clumps of stunted oaks. Over the years this unprepossessing spot was transformed into an attractively wooded area of lakes, gardens, and scenic driveways, together with tennis courts,

bowling greens, and numerous other recreational facilities. Also within the park are an art museum, aquarium, planetarium, music concourse, and a charming and popular Japanese tea garden.

The Presidio, occupying more than 1,500 acres (600 hectares) at the northernmost tip of the peninsula, has been a military reservation since 1776 and now serves as headquarters of the U. S. Sixth Army. Today much of its surface is covered with thick stands of cypress and eucalyptus trees, with scenic drives along the ocean side. Overlooking the bay are numerous military installations, including parade grounds, an airstrip, a hospital, workshops, warehouses, and living quarters for officers and men.

Other open spaces include Union Square, center of the retail shopping district; Sigmund Stern Memorial Grove, scene of open-air summer concerts; Twin Peaks Park; and, in a district now given over to factories and warehouses, quaint, oval-shaped South Park, where in the 1850's and 1860's the city's elite made their homes.

Notable Buildings. A number of impressive public buildings are grouped about the Civic Center Plaza, including the two-blocks-square City Hall with its 309-foot (94-meter) dome, the Civic Auditorium, Public Library, and State Building. Across Van Ness Avenue from City Hall are the Municipal Opera House and the Veterans' Memorial Building. All are faced with California granite and form a harmonious unit architecturally. Nearby is the 20-story Federal Office and Courts Building, completed in 1963. The Louise M. Davies Symphony Hall, part of the Performing Arts Center, was completed in 1980. The George Moscone Convention Center, a major unit of the South of Market urban-renewal project, was opened on Dec. 2, 1981.

During the 1960's and the 1970's a group of lofty new buildings sprang up in the downtown district. Among the tallest are the 52-story headquarters of the Bank of America, the 42-story Security Pacific National Bank Building in the Embarcadero Center development, and the headquarters building of the Transamerica Corporation, a pyramid-shaped structure of 48 stories topped by a 212-foot (65-meter) spire. Construction in the Union Square area has included several hotels of 30 stories or more and lofty additions to two existing hotels: the St. Francis and the San Francisco Hilton.

These graceful row houses on Hyde Street in San Francisco are remnants of the city's 19th century domestic architecture.

The San Francisco skyline, looking northward across Richardson Bay to the mountains of Marin county.

Sports and Festivals. Always a pleasure-loving city, San Francisco lends support to numerous festivals, ranging from Chinese New Year and the annual Columbus Day celebrations to horse shows, rodeos, regattas, and the East-West football game. In the field of professional sports the city has been represented in baseball since 1959 by the San Francisco Giants and in football since 1946 by the Forty-Niners. Since 1971 the home games of both teams have been played at Candlestick Park in the southeast corner of the city, with a capacity of 52,000 for baseball and 62,000 for football.

4. Education and Cultural Life

The cultural climate of San Francisco is reflected not only in its support of art, music, and the drama but also in its appreciation of good food and wines and other adjuncts to gracious living.

Education in the city is a more than usually complex operation because of the diverse racial backgrounds of its residents. The city maintains a comprehensive public school program ranging from kindergarten to college level. It also provides a variety of courses for non-English-speaking groups, both children and adults.

Colleges and Universities. The largest school of higher education in the city is California State University, San Francisco, which dates from 1899.

Other institutions of higher education include the city-supported City College of San Francisco and the long-established University of San Francisco (founded in 1855). The city is the site of the San Francisco Art Institute, and a number of departments of the University of California, among them the Hastings College of Law and the schools of medicine, dentistry, pharmacy, and nursing. Elsewhere in the bay area are the Berkeley campus of the University of California, Stanford University, Mills College, and the Catholic schools of St. Mary's and Santa Clara.

Cultural Diversity. The varied cultural and racial heritage of San Francisco residents is reflected in the number and variety both of its newspapers and its churches. There are two major dailies—the *Chronicle* and the *Examiner*. The city also has more than a dozen daily or weekly papers published in Chinese, Japanese, Italian, German, Spanish, Russian, and the Scandinavian languages.

Most groups also have their own places of worship. In addition to the many churches and synagogues there are several Chinese temples and Buddhist shrines.

Museums and Libraries. More than two million persons annually visit the three leading art galleries—the M. H. De Young Memorial Museum in Golden Gate Park, the San Francisco Art Museum in the Civic Center, and the Palace of the Legion of Honor in Lincoln Park. Other collections of artistic, historical, and scientific material are on display at the California Historical Society, the Society of California Pioneers, and the California Academy of Sciences.

The public library system consists of the main library in the Civic Center and more than 20 branches throughout the city. There are also a number of important private libraries, including that of the Mechanics' Institute, which has been in existence since 1855.

Performing Arts. In the forefront of musical activities are the city-financed symphony orchestra and opera company, both nationally recognized for the quality of their productions. The city also maintains a municipal chorus and, through its Art Commission, sponsors an annual outdoor art show in the Civic Center.

5. The People

Perhaps to a greater extent than any other American city, San Francisco's population is made up of people of many racial strains. This is due in part to its geographical position and to its long-standing trade with countries bordering on the Pacific. Even in days before the gold rush, the residents, then predominantly of Spanish ancestry, included a sprinkling of Americans, Europeans, Kanakas from the Hawaiian Islands, natives of Chile and other South or Central American countries, and an occasional Chinese. It was, however, the discovery of gold that gave the city the markedly cosmopolitan quality it has retained to this day.

Boatloads of adventurers from both hemispheres joined the rush that followed, some to leave after a few months in the diggings, others to remain permanently. Thus San Francisco has long had its French, German, Italian, Chinese, Japanese, and other ethnic colonies, each retaining the customs of its homeland and having its own churches and newspapers. In the 20th century large numbers of blacks arrived in the city, settling largely in the Fillmore and Hunters Point districts.

In 1980, San Francisco had a population of 678,974, a loss of 5.1% from the 1970 figure of 715,674. The decline in population in the 1970's was due mainly to the city's confined area, which has not been changed in more than 100 years, and to the fact that here, as in many other cities, there has been a movement to the suburbs, where greater living space is available. The number who daily enter and leave the city is close to 250,000, of whom approximately 40% pass over the San Francisco-Oakland Bay Bridge, 40% by highway or rail from down the peninsula, and 20% over the Golden Gate Bridge.

During the 20th century a number of significant changes have taken place both in the number and composition of the city's residents. Between 1900 and 1950 population more than doubled. Since 1950, however, it has fallen off by nearly 100,000, a decline of 12.4%. In 1900 the nonwhite residents—most of whom were Chinese—numbered only 5.1% of the total population. By 1950 that percentage had risen to 10.5%, and by 1970 to 28.6%. During the 1970–1980 decade the trend continued, reaching 42% by 1980, when the city had 147,426 Asians and 86,414 blacks. Filipinos, American Indians, Koreans, Hawaiians, and Polynesians also showed substantial gains in population. Thus, San Francisco maintains its reputation as a melting pot of the races.

6. The Economy

San Francisco has long been one of the nation's leading centers of transportation, industry, and finance. Favored by nature with a magnificent land-locked harbor, it faces in three directions an extensive area rich in agricultural lands, minerals, lumber, oil, and other natural resources. From the beginning, its maritime commerce has been a prime factor in the city's economy, and over the years docking facilities have kept pace with the port's mounting foreign and domestic trade. In 1962 the city took over control of the waterfront from the state, and an extensive program of modernization began.

The greatest tonnage of shipping passing through the Golden Gate is in crude oil and

SAN FRANCISCO CONVENTION & VISITORS BUREAU

Ocean Beach is on San Francisco's Pacific shore. This view looks south from Cliff House.

A cable car, the unofficial symbol of San Francisco, climbs one of the city's steep hills.

AMERICAN AIRLINES

At Fisherman's Wharf, small fishing boats jostle each other near some of San Francisco's most popular eating places.

petroleum products, with agricultural products a close second. San Francisco's chief import is green coffee, which is processed at a number of plants on the city's waterfront.

Fully as important as its ocean-borne commerce is the city's trade with the interior. The rivers that drain California's central valleys enter the bay through a cleft in the Coast Ranges, which forms a natural gateway for the flow of a varied two-way traffic. Thus for more than a century San Francisco has enjoyed a major share of the trade with inland points. This trade originated with the Sierra Nevada gold camps in the 1850's and was expanded to the Nevada silver mines in the 1860's and 1870's. Since then San Francisco has received the products of the farms, ranches, and cattle ranges of the Sacramento and San Joaquin valleys; the forests to the north and east; and the orchards and vineyards of the coastal region.

The city's industrial growth has kept pace with other phases of its economy. Leading industries include food processing and the manufacturing of fabricated metals, machinery, and clothing. San Francisco is also a major printing and publishing center. In the field of finance, the largest groups are banking and insurance, both of which rank among the most important in the western United States.

7. Transportation

For well over a century San Francisco was the point through which passed a major share of the traffic flowing between California and the rest of the world. During the earlier period the movement of men and goods was almost entirely by water. Ships docking at San Francisco's harbor engaged in the transpacific trade. Regularly scheduled steamers ran to Panama or Nicaragua and others operated in coastal waters and in the bay and the rivers that empty into it.

Later, transportation by water was supplemented, and in some cases supplanted, by other means. The building of wagon roads and later of local railroads made once remote inland points readily accessible. The completion of the first transcontinental railroad in 1869 provided a direct link with the rest of the nation.

Road, Rail, and Air Transportation. San Francisco is connected with countless other points, both near and distant, by a network of high-ways, railroads, and airlines. Major rail lines provide nationwide transportation of freight, as do numerous highway trucking companies. With the decline of passenger traffic by rail after World War II there has been a corresponding increase in other facilities. Motor buses operating over the West Coast's excellent highway system provide frequent passenger service throughout the area.

The rise of commercial aviation led to the founding of a city-owned air terminal. Since it opened in 1927, the San Francisco International Airport has undergone a continuous expansion of facilities that has made it one of the largest and busiest in the nation.

Ferries and Cable Cars. Two colorful features of local transportation have been the ferryboats plying the waters of the bay and the picturesque cable cars, which over the years have become a sort of unofficial symbol of the city. With the building of the San Francisco-Oakland and the Golden Gate bridges in the mid-1930's, the ferryboats have disappeared. The historic cable cars, their routes gradually reduced from 58 miles (93 km) to less than 10 miles (16 km), were temporarily retired in 1982 to undergo a $58.2 million renovation.

Automobile Congestion. The Municipal Railroad, which, besides the cable lines, operates streetcars and buses serving all parts of the city, has for years been fighting a losing battle with private automobiles for a major share of the traffic. The consequence is that in San Francisco, as in most American cities, congestion on the downtown streets has become an ever more serious problem.

With the aim of solving that difficulty and of relieving congestion on the trans-bay bridge, in 1962 the voters of San Francisco, Alameda, and Contra Costa counties approved a bond issue of $793 million for the building of the Bay Area Rapid Transit System (BART). The first such facility to be built in the United States in many years, BART consists of 75 miles (120 km) of high-speed electric railway, serving the east bay communities and linking them with San Francisco by means of a 3.6-mile (5.8-km) tunnel beneath the bay. Included in the plan is a two-level subway beneath Market and Mission streets to be used both by the interurban trains and the city streetcars.

Ghirardelli, on the north shore of San Francisco, was once a chocolate, spice, and textile plant, but now it houses shops, theaters, and both indoor and outdoor restaurants and bistros.

8. Government

San Francisco has a consolidated city and county government. Legislative powers are vested in an 11-member board of supervisors, 5 or 6 members of which are elected every 2 years for 4-year terms. Other elected officers include the mayor, district attorney, sheriff, public defender, and judges of the superior and municipal courts, all serving 4-year terms.

The mayor has veto power over legislation passed by the board of supervisors. He appoints a chief administrative officer, a controller, and members of various boards, commissions, and agencies. Members of the board of education are nominated by the mayor and confirmed by the voters.

Prior to the American conquest of California, the pueblo of Yerba Buena (now San Francisco) was governed by an *alcalde* (mayor) and an *ayuntamiento* (town council). The first *alcalde* was Francisco de Haro, who was elected in 1834, and Mexican *alcaldes* continued to serve until Aug. 6, 1846, when Washington A. Bartlett, a lieutenant in the U. S. Navy, was appointed to the post.

On April 15, 1850, San Francisco was granted its first charter by the newly organized California legislature. Six years later the legislature authorized the consolidation of the city and county governments and the formation of a board of supervisors. In 1861 a new charter was adopted, which remained in force until May 26, 1898. One of the provisions of the 1898 charter was that it authorized the municipal ownership and operation of public utilities. Over the years this has resulted in the city's acquiring its own airport and street transportation system, and in the development of the large Hetch Hetchy project in Yosemite National Park, which supplies water and electrical power to San Francisco and nearby communities. The 1898 charter remained in force until Jan. 8, 1932, when it was superseded by a charter that has served ever since.

9. History

Although pioneer explorers had cruised along the California coast as early as the mid-16th century, all failed to see the narrow cleft in the hills that marked the entrance to San Francisco Bay. Consequently, more than 200 years passed before the bay itself was known to the world.

Spanish and Mexican Control. Spain had laid claim to Alta California as part of its New World empire. But it was not until the 1760's that Spanish officials in Mexico City, alarmed at rumors that other nations were plotting to take over the California territory, dispatched an expedition northward to establish permanent settlements there.

The expedition, led by Gaspar de Portolá, governor of Baja California, reached San Diego in the summer of 1769 and continued up the coast. They were looking for Monterey Bay, which had been discovered and described in glowing terms by Sebastián Vizcaíno in 1602. The group passed Monterey Bay without recognizing it and in late October made camp on the lower San Francisco peninsula while Portolá dispatched a scouting party under José Francisco Ortega to explore the country ahead. On Nov. 2, 1769, Ortega's party reached the crest of a ridge of hills and saw spread out before them the great body of water now known as San Francisco Bay.

During the next few years several other parties visited the spot. An expedition headed by Capt. Pedro Fages explored the east side of the bay in March 1772. In August 1775 the supply ship *San Carlos*, piloted by Juan Manuel de Ayala, sailed through the Golden Gate, and is believed to be the first vessel to enter the harbor.

Eight months later Juan Bautista de Anza reached the site of the future city, having led a party of soldiers and settlers from northern Mexico for the purpose of founding permanent settlements on the bay. On March 28, 1776, he chose the spots where a mission and presidio (garrison) were to be built. Both establishments were founded later that year, and the first phase of the city's evolution began. During the next half century and more, members of the remote settlements lived quiet, pastoral lives. The few soldiers at the presidio had little to occupy their time. The mission padres tried—with indifferent success—to convert the Indians to Christianity and to teach them the white man's skills.

By the 1830's the region's long period of isolation was drawing to a close. Hunters and trappers were entering the California province from the east and north, and the visits of whalers and Boston trading ships were growing more frequent. The latter were attracted by a brisk trade in hides and tallow with the cattle ranches

SAN FRANCISCO CONVENTION & VISITORS BUREAU

The Peace Pagoda in the Japanese Cultural and Trade Center was a gift from the people of Japan.

in the back country. In 1835 the growing activity of the port led to the building of the first house on Yerba Buena Cove, which was so-named because of a sweet-smelling shrub that grew on the nearby hillsides. Other houses, most of them combination residences and trading posts, followed, and in 1839 a Swiss surveyor, Jean Jacques Vioget, laid out the first streets of the village of Yerba Buena. When the United States took over the province of California in 1846, Yerba Buena was a frontier town of approximately 200 inhabitants. Early in 1847 its name was changed to San Francisco.

The Gold Rush. The discovery of gold in the Sierra foothills on Jan. 24, 1848, led to a concerted rush on the city. The argonauts appeared in such numbers that supplies and services of every sort were quickly exhausted. Many of the newcomers were obliged to live in tents or improvised shelters of earth or brush and to cook their meals over campfires. Shiploads of merchandise were brought ashore and dumped on the beach for lack of storage space. Buildings about the plaza were converted into gambling resorts and returned huge profits to their operators. Because everything was in short supply, prices rose to fantastic heights. Abandoned ships were drawn up on the mud of the cove, connected by piers with the land, and made to serve as hotels, shops, and warehouses. Hundreds of buildings of canvas or wood were hastily erected to house stores, banks, and offices, and when these were swept away in the frequent fires, they were promptly rebuilt.

By 1850, San Francisco's population had grown to nearly 35,000 from 800 in 1848. It was a time of violence and lawlessness, for among those who had joined the rush were the reckless and unruly from half the world. Their depreda-

tions became so flagrant that in 1851 and 1856 concerned citizens organized viligante committees. The vigilantes rounded up the ringleaders and, having hanged some and banished others from the city, forcibly restored order.

From the mid-1850's the yield of the goldfields declined steadily. However, this was offset by an increase of farming and industry, and the city's growth continued. On the downtown streets substantial structures of brick or stone replaced the earlier wooden buildings. Factories and warehouses rose in the new industrial district, and acres of residences spread over the sides and crests of the nearby hills. The discovery of rich silver deposits in Nevada in 1859 and the opening of the transcontinental railroad a decade later ushered in another period of sustained prosperity. By 1900, San Francisco had a population of more than a third of a million and had become the ninth-largest city in the nation.

Earthquake and Rebuilding. The earthquake and fire of April 18, 1906, took 500 lives and destroyed 3,000 acres (1,200 hectares) in the heart of the city. Tens of thousands were made homeless. Undeterred by that calamity, the residents set about rebuilding their city on a more impressive scale. By 1915, when San Francisco celebrated the opening of the Panama Canal by the Panama-Pacific International Exposition, all traces of the disaster had disappeared.

The Modern City. In the 20th century San Francisco has maintained and consolidated its position as the financial, commercial, and cultural center of the large and rich area it serves. Among noteworthy events have been the building of the two bay bridges, the development of city-owned public utilities, and the carrying forward of several large-scale urban development projects. In World War II it was a major shipping point of men and supplies to the Pacific fronts, and in 1945 delegates gathered there to write the United Nations Charter.

With the completion in 1974 of the Bay Area Rapid Transit System, San Francisco entered a new phase of its evolution. This means of fast transportation spurred new construction, and by 1980, Market Street was solidly lined with highrise structures from the Ferry Building to Fourth Street. The George R. Moscone Convention Center, the first unit of a large South of Market urban-renewal project, was opened on Dec. 2, 1981.

After the assassination in November 1978 of Mayor George Moscone and City Supervisor Harvey Milk, Dianne Feinstein, who served out the balance of Moscone's term, was elected in 1979 to a four-year term as the city's first woman mayor.

OSCAR LEWIS, *Author of*
"San Francisco: Mission to Metropolis"

Bibliography

Beebe, Lucius, and Clegg, Charles, *San Francisco's Golden Era: A Picture Story of San Franciso Before the Fire* (Howell-North 1960).
Bronson, William, *The Earth Shook, the Sky Burned* (Doubleday 1959).
Dillon, Richard, *Embarcadero* (Coward-McCann 1959).
Galvin, John, ed., *First Spanish Entry into San Francisco Bay, 1775* (Howell Bk 1971).
Gilliam, Harold, *San Franciso Bay* (Doubleday 1957).
Lewis, Oscar, *San Francisco: Mission to Metropolis,* 2d ed. (Howell-North 1980).
McGloin, John B., *San Francisco: The Story of a City* (Presidio Press 1979).
Olmsted, Roger, and Watkins, Tom H., *Here Today: San Francisco's Architectural Heritage* (Chronicle Bks 1968).
Thomas, Gordon, and Witts, Max M., *San Francisco Earthquake* (Stein & Day 1971).

SAN FRANCISCO, University of, a Roman Catholic coeducational institution of higher learning, situated on a 27-acre (11-hectare) campus near the center of San Francisco, Calif. It was founded in 1855 and was chartered in 1859 as St. Ignatius College. The present name was adopted in 1930.

The university comprises colleges of liberal arts, science, and business administration; schools of law and nursing; a graduate division; and an evening college. Bachelor's and master's degrees and four education credentials are offered. The interdisciplinary Institute of Chemical Biology incorporates a master's program with research.

SAN FRANCISCO CONFERENCE. See UNITED NATIONS—*Origins.*

SAN FRANCISCO OPERA, a program of regular opera organized as a part of the San Francisco War Memorial in 1922. The new War Memorial Opera House opened on Oct. 15, 1932, with Claudia Muzio and Dino Borgioli in Puccini's *Tosca.* Before that date, performances had been held in the Auditorium on Grove Street. At first the season was two weeks long, but by 1929 it had been expanded to more than six, with a preliminary season in Portland, Oreg., and postseason performances in southern California. Later the season was extended from September through November, with performances also in March. Gaetano Merola was chief conductor and general director from 1923 until his death in 1953. Kurt Adler became general director in 1953.

Opera stars for the regular company have been recruited largely from New York's Metropolitan and the Chicago opera, as well as from abroad. The opera's orchestra is drawn from the San Francisco Symphony. Representative novelties and revivals performed at the San Francisco Opera after World War II included Sir William Walton's *Troilus and Cressida* (American premiere, 1955), Francis Poulenc's *Les Dialogues des Carmélites* (American premiere, 1957), Alban Berg's *Wozzeck* (1960), Giuseppe Verdi's *Ernani* (1968), and Richard Wagner's *Siegfried* (1970).

SAN FRANCISCO SYMPHONY ORCHESTRA, an important American orchestra formed in 1911 by the Musical Association of San Francisco. Its early years, under Henry Hadley (1911–1915), were difficult. The organization was plagued by insufficient financial backing, inadequate concert and library facilities, and inability to engage musicians on a permanent contract basis. Some of these problems were partly solved under Alfred Hertz (1915–1930), but the orchestra still failed to prosper. A series of guest conductors did not improve matters, and in 1934 concerts were suspended.

In 1935, however, public support for the orchestra was voted, a more vigorous administrative board was set up, and the renowned conductor Pierre Monteux was engaged. Under Monteux's leadership, the San Francisco Symphony rapidly gained in stature and became one of the foremost orchestras in the United States. After Monteux's resignation in 1953, it was led by Enrique Jorda (1955–1963). Josef Krips became conductor in 1964 and was succeeded by Seiji Ozawa in 1970. Dutch conductor Edo de Waart, guest conductor from 1975 to 1977, succeeded Ozawa in 1977.

THEODORE C. KARP
University of California, Davis

SAN GABRIEL, gä′brē-əl, a city in southwestern California, in Los Angeles county, is a residential suburb, about 9 miles (14 km) east of the center of the city of Los Angeles. It has some light industry, notably plastics and automobile supplies. The Mission San Gabriel Arcángel, now a parish church, contains some of California's first mission art.

San Gabriel was settled by Franciscan missionaries, who founded the mission in 1771. For more than a century, the settlement was the closest point of civilization on the western side of the Mojave Desert, making it a gateway to the Pacific coast. In 1781, the Spanish governor Felipe de Neve set out from San Gabriel to found the pueblo that grew into the city of Los Angeles. San Gabriel received its city charter in 1913. It has a council-manager form of government. Population: 30,072.

SAN GENNARO, sän jen-nä′rô, is the Italian name of Saint Januarius, the patron saint of Naples. On his feast day, September 19, there are joyous festivals in Naples and among Neapolitans abroad, especially in the Italian section of New York City. See JANUARIUS, SAINT.

SAN GERMÁN, säng her-män′, a town in Puerto Rico, is on the Guanajibo River, about 110 miles (177 km) southwest of San Juan. It is the second-oldest settlement in Puerto Rico, and has many old buildings. The Porto Coeli Church is notable. The Inter American University is in the town. Chief industries are electronics and textiles. San Germán was settled at the mouth of the Guanajibo in 1511, but was moved upstream in 1573. Population: 32,941.

SAN GIMIGNANO, sän jē-mē-nyä′nō, is a town in central Italy in Siena province, 18 miles (30 km) northwest of Siena. The town's medieval appearance has made it a popular tourist center, and visitors are the main source of income. There are distilling and ironworking industries.

The most striking reminders of the Middle Ages are the town's towers, of which 13 remain. In the mid-14th century there were as many as 76. For many years the Palazzo del Podestà, begun in 1288 and over 160 feet (59 meters) high, set a standard for later towers. In the Palazzo Communale is the town museum, which has paintings by many Florentine and Sienese artists, including Benozzo Gozzoli, Filippino Lippi, and Pinturicchio. There are frescoes by Gozzoli in the 12th century collegiate church and in the 13th century Church of St. Augustine.

An independent republic in the early Middle Ages, San Gimignano was torn between the Guelph and Ghibelline factions in the town. In 1352 the town placed itself under Florence. Population: (1971) 7,652.

SAN ILDEFONSO, sän ēl-dä-fôn′sō, a village in Spain, is the site of the former royal palace of La Granja. In the Sierra de Guadarrama, 7 miles (11 km) southeast of Segovia, it is at an altitude of over 3,900 feet (1,190 meters) and is a summer resort. The village grew up around a grange (granja), or farm, cultivated by monks.

Philip IV wanted to emulate France's Versailles, and had the palace begun in 1721. It is a rectangular building with an imposing facade, and it has extensive gardens with fountains. Philip, who abdicated at San Ildefonso in 1724,

MISSION SANTA CLARA, a replica of the building that was constructed in 1797, stands on the University of Santa Clara campus, just west of San Jose.

THE UNIVERSITY OF SANTA CLARA

and his wife, Elizabeth Farnese, are buried in the palace chapel. By the Treaty of San Ildefonso (1796), Spain was tied to the French republic. It was at the palace that Ferdinand VII in 1832 confirmed the revocation of the Salic Law and then restored it, thus giving women the right of succession.

SAN JACINTO, Battle of, jə-sin′tō, the engagement that decided the independence of Texas from Mexico. Fought on April 21, 1836, on the banks of the San Jacinto River, near the present Houston, Tex., it was a complete victory for the Texans, who were led by Gen. Sam Houston, over the Mexican forces of Gen. Antonio López de Santa Anna.

Colonists from the United States and Europe had become increasingly restive under Mexican rule, and on March 2, 1836, declared their independence as a republic and set up a provisional government. Santa Anna, the Mexican military dictator of the region, recaptured the town of San Antonio and killed all the outnumbered defenders of the citadel of The Alamo on March 6, 1836. See ALAMO.

On March 11, Houston mustered 374 men at Gonzales, 60 miles (96 km) east of San Antonio. This was the only armed group resistance remaining in the new republic. Retreating eastward before Santa Anna's advance, Houston attracted recruits to his ranks. By April 20, when the opposing forces were in touch at a ferry over the San Jacinto, Houston had 800 men against Santa Anna's 910. Houston knew that Santa Anna was expecting a reinforcement of about 500 men, but he coolly waited until they arrived. He said later that he "did not want to take two bites at a cherry."

On the morning of April 21, Houston attacked. His surprise was complete. Within 20 minutes, resistance was overcome. Almost the entire Mexican force was killed, wounded, or captured. Santa Anna was made a prisoner.

The Texans suffered losses of only 16 killed and 24 wounded. Houston was among the wounded. Santa Anna signed armistice terms that provided that all the divisions of his army should evacuate Texas. The massacre of The Alamo was avenged, and the independence of Texas was established. Houston was president of a permanent government that was inaugurated in October. The San Jacinto battleground, along the Houston Ship Channel east of Houston, is now a state park.

SAN JOAQUIN RIVER, wo-kēn′, in central California, rises in a small glacier southeast of Yosemite National Park on the slopes of the Sierra Nevada in Mono county. It flows southwest into Fresno county and then turns northwest to join the Sacramento River in a delta at Suisun Bay, an arm of San Francisco Bay. The San Joaquin is about 350 miles (560 km) long. It is navigable by small craft as far as Stockton, 50 miles (80 km) from its mouth.

The San Joaquin Valley is part of the Central Valley of California, one of the richest agricultural regions in the United States. A series of dams have diverted the river's water to provide irrigation. In its upper reaches, the San Joaquin receives tributaries flowing from the Sierra Nevada, and in Fresno county it is joined by the Kings River, which carries the waters of the Tulare system of lakes.

SAN JOSE, hō-zā′, a city in western California, the seat of Santa Clara county, is 7 miles (11 km) below the southern tip of San Francisco Bay and 50 miles (80 km) southeast of downtown San Francisco. The city lies in the Santa Clara Valley, with the Santa Cruz Mountains to the west and the Mount Hamilton arm of the Diablo

Range to the east. It is traversed by the Coyote and Guadalupe rivers, which carry water only in the spring. The city is the center of a large and rapidly growing metropolitan area of industry, shopping malls, and homes.

San Jose is the processing and shipping center for the surrounding agricultural region, which raises wine grapes, plums, and apricots. The city also produces electronic components, computers, electric motors, food machinery, bakery products, beer, carpets, clothing, paper board, fabricated rubber products, cans, and motor vehicles. The Ames Research Facility of the National Aeronautics and Space Administration (NASA) and the Naval Air Station, both at nearby Moffett Field, are major influences on the economy of San Jose.

The city is the home of San Jose State College. Founded in 1862, this is the oldest public educational institution in California. The San Jose City College is also here. Cultural events include symphony concerts, operas, and plays.

There are a number of museums in the city, including the Rosicrucian Egyptian Museum and Art Gallery, the Rosicrucian Science Museum and Planetarium, the San Jose Historical Museum, the State House Museum, the Triton Museum of Art, and the Youth Science Institute. San Jose State College has its own art gallery. Also of interest is the New Almaden Quicksilver Mines Exhibit.

On the campus of the University of Santa Clara, just west of San Jose, is a replica of the Mission of Santa Clara built in 1797. Alum Rock Park, a 687-acre (278 hectare) municipal playground 6 miles (10 km) east of San Jose, contains mineral springs and scenic formations that attract thousands of visitors annually. Water sports facilities are provided by the many water conservation reservoirs around the city. The Municipal Rose Garden has one of the finest rose collections in the United States.

San Jose is the oldest civic settlement in California. It was founded by Spanish colonizers on Nov. 29, 1777, and named the Pueblo de San José de Guadalupe in honor of St. Joseph and after the Guadalupe River, on which the town was situated. After the territory came under the U. S. flag, San Jose became, in 1849, the first capital of the state of California, although statehood was not achieved officially until 1850. The first state legislature convened here from December 1849 to May 1851, when the seat of government was transferred to Vallejo.

The first city in California to be chartered (1850), San Jose developed economically as a supply base for gold prospectors and, after the completion of a rail line to San Francisco in 1864, as a distribution point for the burgeoning agricultural wealth of the Santa Clara valley. The growth of manufacturing industries to supply all of the region's farm equipment needs added to the city's importance.

San Jose has the council-manager form of government. The population of the city and its metropolitan area has grown rapidly since World War II. The city had 68,457 residents in 1940, and 95,280 in 1950. In the next decade, mostly as a result of annexations, the city's population more than doubled to a total of 204,196 in 1960. The 1970 census showed that it had more than doubled in the decade of the 1960's. In this period, the metropolitan area gained more than 50%. Population (city): 629,546, (metropolitan area): 1,295,071.

SAN JOSÉ, sän hō-zä′, the capital of Costa Rica, is situated in a broad valley at an altitude of about 3,850 feet (1,173 meters), near the geographical center of the republic, about 70 miles (113 km) east of Puntarenas—a city on the Pacific Ocean—and 80 miles (129 km) west of Limón—a city on the Caribbean Sea. It is also

The National University of Costa Rica, in San José, is housed in a fine group of modern buildings.

the capital of San José province, which stretches westward from the city, down the mountain slopes leading to the Pacific and stopping at the border of the narrow Pacific province of Punta-renas. San José province is an important coffee-growing region. Stock is also raised, and sugar-cane, cacao, vegetables, and fruit are grown. The city is the trade center for the province, and is also an important industrial center. Wine and beer, chocolate, canned foods, leather goods, and furniture are manufactured here. San José is also the home of the University of Costa Rica, which was inaugurated in 1941.

San José, by far the largest city in Costa Rica, is laid out in a gridiron pattern. Its architec-ture is a mixture of Spanish colonial and modern styles. The National Palace, which houses the offices of the national congress, contains a fine collection of portraits of Costa Rican statesman. The National Museum has Mayan gold orna-ments and other precolonial relics and a large collection of Central American pottery. One of the city's most imposing buildings is the Na-tional Theater, a lavish Renaissance building with marble, beaten gold, and velvet furnish-ings. Other places of interest include the Mu-nicipal Palace, which houses the city government offices; the National Library; and the Cathedral.

Because earthquakes are common in the city, most of the older buildings in San José are no more than four stories high. But with the de-velopment of more sophisticated building meth-ods in the mid-20th century, higher buildings became safer, and skyscrapers began to appear in the city, notably the towering social security building. Just west of the city is La Sabana, a beautiful plain that contains one of San José's most elegant residential suburbs. The National Stadium is situated on this plain.

The city was founded in 1736 by settlers from nearby Cartago who called it Villa Nueva. After Costa Rica attained independence in 1821, San José fought for a short time with Cartago. In 1823, the capital of the republic was moved from Cartago to San José. By then the sur-rounding coffee plantations had begun to pros-per and San José became the center of the coffee trade. The city continued to grow rapidly in the 20th century. Population: city (1978), 242,704; metropolitan area (1977), 395,401.

SAN JUAN, säng hwän', a city in northwestern Argentina, the capital of San Juan province, is situated in a valley of the Andes Mountains, on the Río San Juan, about 100 miles (161 km) north of Mendoza and 600 miles (965 km) north-west of Buenos Aires. It is the commercial cen-ter for the province's agriculture and mining and has local trade with Chile. The province produces grapes, olives, and grain, and is im-portant for stock raising. Gold, silver, iron, copper, and coal are mined in the province. There is a national college in the city. The birthplace of the Argentine statesman and edu-cator Domingo Faustino Sarmiento is a museum.

The city was founded in 1562 and called San Juan de la Frontera because of its situation on the Indian frontier. In 1592 it was moved 4 miles (6 km) south because of continual flood-ing in the original location. It became a Roman Catholic diocese in 1834 and an archdiocese in 1934. In 1944 an earthquake destroyed most of San Juan. The city was slowly rebuilt. Popula-tion: (1970) 112,582; (1980 est.) 400,000.

SAN JUAN, säng hwän', is the capital and largest city of Puerto Rico. It is on the northern coast of the island, on the Atlantic Ocean, about 1,000 miles (1,600 km) southeast of Miami, Fla., and 1,690 miles (2,720 km) southeast of New York City. San Juan is the chief commercial, indus-trial, shipping, and governmental center of the Commonwealth of Puerto Rico and a popular vacation resort.

The city is made up of Old San Juan (San Juan Antigua), on a rocky island in the Atlantic, and several districts on the mainland. The old city contains many of the governmental and business offices. It is connected by bridges to Santurce, directly south of the island, which is the largest of the mainland districts. Other dis-tricts are Hato Rey, Guaynabo, and Río Piedras. The San Juan metropolitan area also includes the adjacent municipalities of Carolina, Trujillo Alto, Guaynabo, Cataño, and Bayamón.

Economy. San Juan is a highly industrialized city, and a large portion of Puerto Rico's manu-facturing is centered in the metropolitan area. The wide range of products made here includes rum and other beverages, drugs, chemicals, cloth-ing, cement, and jewelry. A large portion of the goods manufactured in Puerto Rico is shipped to the United States from San Juan's port. A great deal of the city's manufacturing is the re-sult of a government program to bring new in-dustries to the island. The program had its begin-nings in Operation Bootstrap, which was initiated in 1948 to bolster Puerto Rico's then lagging economy.

The government headquarters of the com-monwealth are in San Juan, as are the main offi-ces of all of the island's public corporations. There are also some U. S. government offices here and a number of U. S. military installa-tions. Luxury resort hotels are strung along the city's beaches on the Atlantic, just southeast of Old San Juan. The tourist industry contributes significantly to the city's economy.

RESTORED SPANISH HOUSES in San Juan, Puerto Rico, help recreate an Old World atmosphere.

COMMONWEALTH OF PUERTO RICO

Education and Culture. The main campus of the University of Puerto Rico and the Puerto Rico Junior College are located in the Río Piedras district of San Juan. The College of the Sacred Heart is in Santurce.

The Institute of Puerto Rican Culture, a government organization that promotes the island's indigenous culture, has an art gallery in Old San Juan, and its orchestra gives concerts here and elsewhere in the commonwealth. The government also sponsors the Puerto Rican Conservatory and the Symphony Orchestra of Puerto Rico, which were formed under the renowned cellist Pablo Casals. The Festival Casals, held each spring, is widely acclaimed.

Puerto Rican culture is emphasized in San Juan's museums. The arts are exhibited in the Museum of Colonial Architecture; the Museum of Puerto Rican Art; the Santos Museum, which exhibits antique *santos* (small religious figures carved from wood); and La Casa del Libro, where exhibits are devoted to the art of the book. The Museum of the Puerto Rican Family and the Pharmacy Museum show other aspects of Puerto Rican culture. The University of Puerto Rico maintains its own museum of art, history, and archaeology.

In the 17th century Fort San Jerónimo there is a museum of military history. The Museum of Conquest and Colonization houses artifacts unearthed in the vicinity of a house that was built in 1508 by Juan Ponce de León, Puerto Rico's first governor.

Places of Interest. The northwest tip of Old San Juan is dominated by the massive fort of El Morro, part of which dates back to 1539. Portions of the old wall that surrounded the city in the 17th century are still standing, including the San Juan Gate, the main entrance to the city through the old wall, first opened in 1635. Fort San Cristóbal was built between 1766 and 1772 to defend the land side of the city and aid El Morro in defending the coast.

A number of other early buildings also remain standing, and many of them have been restored by the government. The Cathedral of San Juan de Bautista, started in 1540 to replace an older cathedral that was destroyed in a hurricane, contains the tomb of Ponce de León. San José Church dates back to 1532. Also of interest is La Fortaleza, built in 1540 as the town's first fort but converted into the governor's mansion in 1640 and remodeled in 1896.

History. Juan Ponce de León and about 50 Spanish colonists settled at nearby Caparra in 1508. In 1521 the community was moved to the present site of San Juan. Subjected to frequent attacks from European privateers, the city gradually built up fortifications to protect itself.

San Juan, which had been the island's capital from the beginning, retained its status when Puerto Rico came under U.S. administration in 1898. During the 20th century the city spread out to the mainland and grew rapidly.

Government and Population. San Juan is governed by a city manager and an administrative board. Population: (1980) of the city, 422,701; of the metropolitan area, 1,083,664.

SAN JUAN BOUNDARY DISPUTE, a controversy between the United States and Britain over possession of the San Juan Islands in Puget Sound. The British-American treaty of 1846 fixed the boundary between western United States and

COMMONWEALTH OF PUERTO RICO

Luxury hotels face the beach in San Juan. Old Fort Jerónimo, in the foreground, has been restored.

Canada at 49° north latitude to the middle of the channel separating Vancouver Island from the mainland. But the treaty was vague as to the precise channel. The United States claimed it was Haro Strait, whereas Britain claimed it was Rosario Strait. Consequently, both claimed the San Juan Islands, which lie between.

The so-called "Pig War" ensued. Local authorities of both nationalities attempted to collect taxes in the disputed territory. The height of hostilities—and absurdity—was reached in 1859, when a pig belonging to Charles J. Griffin, an Englishman, raided the vegetable garden of Lyman A. Cutler, an American, and was shot. Troops of both countries rushed in. The U.S. 9th Infantry was led by Capt. George Pickett.

With war threatening, both nations agreed to arbitration. During the cooling off period, British and American soldiers stationed on opposite ends of San Juan Island vied in the exchange of parties. In 1872, Emperor William I of Germany awarded the islands to the United States. The islands now belong to the state of Washington.

SAN JUAN CAPISTRANO, hwän kap-ə-strä'nō, a city in southwestern California, is in Orange county, near the Pacific Ocean, 60 miles (96 km) south of Los Angeles.

It is the site of the Mission San Juan Capistrano, which was founded on Nov. 1, 1776 and was dedicated by Father Junípero Serra. It was named for St. John of Capistrano, the Crusader. Construction was completed in 1806. Built in the form of a cross, 180 by 90 feet (54 by 27 meters), the stone church was regarded as a remarkable example of mission architecture. It had seven domes and a tall campanario or belfry. In 1812, an earthquake destroyed much of the church, and 29 persons were killed.

A statue of Father Junípero Serra graces the garden of Mission San Juan Capistrano, which he dedicated in 1776.

The mission is remarkable for having a second church, called Padre Serra's church, which is built of adobe. This has been restored.

It is said that flocks of swallows have nested in the ruined church for many years, arriving from their winter homes in the south on St. Joseph's Day, March 19, and departing on October 23, St. John's Day—the death day, not the feast day. Visitors come to the mission each year to witness these flights. According to legend, the birds have been late only once, delayed by a storm at sea.

The community of San Juan Capistrano, which was incorporated as a city in the 1960's, grew around the mission. Population: 18,959.

SAN JUAN DEL NORTE, säng hwän del nôr′tä, is a town in the southeastern corner of Nicaragua and the capital of Río San Juan department. It is on the northern channel of the delta of the Río San Juan.

The British occupied the town, then called Greytown, from 1848 to 1850 to keep the United States from digging a canal across Nicaragua. The British gave up the town after the signing of the Clayton-Bulwer Treaty, agreeing that neither the United States nor Britain would have dominion over the area. During the gold rush of 1849, San Juan del Norte was an important transfer point and trading station on the sea route to California.

In the 20th century the town's harbor silted up, preventing its further use by ships. Population: (1971 est.) 720.

SAN JUAN HILL, Battle of. See SPANISH-AMERICAN WAR.

SAN LEANDRO, lē-an′drō, a city in western California, in Alameda county, is a southern suburb of Oakland, east of San Francisco Bay. Machinery, lumber, paper and metal products, glass, and chemicals are its chief industries. It is also an important horticultural center, and a cherry and flower festival is held annually. San Leandro was settled in 1836 and incorporated in 1872. It has a council-manager form of government. Population: 63,952.

SAN LORENZO, lə-ren′zō, an unincorporated area in western California in Alameda county, is situated on the eastern shore of San Francisco Bay between San Leandro and Heyward, about 10 miles (16 km) south of the center of Oakland. It is a residential village, and is a part of the Greater San Francisco-Oakland Metropolitan area. Population: 20,545.

SAN LUIS OBISPO, lōō′əs ō-bis′kō, is a city in western California, the seat of San Luis Obispo county, on San Luis Obispo Bay of the Pacific Ocean, about 160 miles (256 km) northwest of Los Angeles. It is in an agricultural area. The city manufactures metal furniture and electronic products. State, county, and city offices employ a large part of the labor force.

California State Polytechnic College and Cuesta College are in the city. The San Luis Obispo County Historical Museum has archaeological and historical displays. The Mission of San Luis Obispo de Tolosa, established on Sept. 1, 1772, by Fray Junípero Serra, has been restored and serves as a parish church.

The community grew around the mission. It became a pueblo in 1844 and was incorporated as a city in 1856. Government is by council and manager. Population: 34,252.

SAN LUIS POTOSÍ, san lwēs pō-tō-sē′, is a state in north-central Mexico. Most of its land area lies on Mexico's Northern Plateau at an average elevation of about 6,000 feet (1,800 meters). The climate here is moderate and the soil fertile, but agriculture is generally confined to irrigated areas due to the insufficient rainfall. There is a smaller section in the southeast, separated from the plateau by the Sierra Madre Oriental and lying in a semitropical area with elevations averaging less than 1,000 feet (300 meters). Here sugar, coffee, tobacco, fiber plants, and tropical fruit are cultivated. In this region is the state's only important river, the Pánuco, which flows eastward out of the mountains to empty into the Gulf of Mexico at Tampico. The easternmost point on the state's boundary is some 30 miles (48 km) from the gulf.

Livestock provides hides and wool for export, and some rubber is exported. But the leading economic activity is mining, concentrated in the southwest, where mines have been worked since the 1770's. The capital city of San Luis Potosí, situated in this area, has large processing plants. Silver, lead, gold, copper, mercury, and cinnabar are the principal ores mined. The total area of the state is 24,417 square miles (63,670 sq km). Population: (1970) 1,281,996.

SAN LUIS POTOSÍ, sän lwēs pō-tō-sē, is a city in the east central part of Mexico. It is the capital of the state of San Luis Potosí and an important mining center. It is situated 225 miles (360 km) northwest of Mexico City in an arid region at an elevation of some 6,100 feet (1,850 meters), which gives it a moderate climate. Many of the buildings, including the governor's palace and the Church of El Carmen, an example of extreme baroque, are constructed of a distinctive rose-colored stone, and the city's many domes and towers are covered in colored, glazed tile. The region was one which the Aztecs had not conquered before the arrival of the conquistadores. The Spaniards at first overlooked the riches of the area and merely erected a series of strongholds to protect their lines of communication with Zacatecas, where they had established mines.

San Luis Potosí was founded about 1550, being named for King Louis IX of France (St. Louis). The "Potosí" was added later in allusion to the great Bolivian mining district whose name had become a synonym for fabulous wealth. The discovery of gold precipitated a rush in 1590, but operations were badly conducted, and for some 30 years after 1620 the town was almost completely abandoned in the belief that the mineral wealth of the surrounding region was exhausted. Further discoveries, particularly of silver, subsequently restored its prosperity.

During the internal struggle against the Emperor Maximilian in the 1860's, the city was for a time the provisional capital of the government of Benito Juarez. Later, the so-called "Plan of San Luis," a call for reform that helped to kindle the revolution of 1910, was drawn up in this city.

Mining and the processing of ores are the greatest local industries, but there are also cotton and woolen manufactures, breweries, and flour mills. The city is connected by highway and rail with the Gulf port of Tampico, some 200 miles (320 km) to the east. Population: (1970) 230,-039.

SAN MARCO, sän mär′kō, the main piazza (square) of Venice. The piazza is the center of a beautiful complex of buildings in Byzantine, Gothic, and Renaissance styles, reflecting Venice's history as a rich center of trade. It was the scene of state ceremonies and is still the focus of civic life. The piazza is dominated by St. Mark's Basilica (a cathedral since 1807). This 11th century church in the Byzantine style of a Greek cross with five domes was later embellished with marble panels, mosaics, Gothic pinnacles, and four gilded bronze horses (4th–3d century B. C.), giving an exotic, fantastic effect.

Near St. Mark's are the campanile (1912 replica of 10th century original), with the adjoining Logetta di San Marco (16th century) by Sansovino and the clock tower (late 15th century). The remainder of the piazza is surrounded by the arcaded buildings of the Procuratie (16th–19th century), before which are outdoor cafés. On the southeast corner the piazza opens into the smaller Piazzetta, bordered by the Palazzo Ducale (14th century) on the east, the Canale di San Marco on the south, and the Old Library (16th century) by Sansovino on the west.

The Piazza San Marco is the focal point of Venice. It is dominated by the imposing campanile (bell tower), behind which are St. Mark's Basilica (*left*) and the ducal palace (*right*). Arcaded buildings line the other sides.

San Marino's walled fortresses crown the three peaks of Mt. Titano. The castles, which afford outstanding views of the countryside, are linked by a path.

SAN MARCOS, mär′kəs, a city in south central Texas, the seat of Hays county, is on the San Marcos River, 30 miles (48 km) south of Austin. It is an agricultural, business, and recreational center. Its principal industries are meatpacking, feed processing, fish hatcheries, and tourism.

The river has a flow of clear, cold water, and there are parks and caves along its banks. The city's Aquarena Springs has an underwater theater and glass-bottom boats that take passengers over underwater gardens. Southwest Texas State College and the San Marcos Baptist Academy are in the city.

San Marcos was settled in 1845, and when Hays county was organized three years later, the town became its seat. It has a council-manager form of government. Population: 23,420.

SAN MARCOS, University of, mär′kōs, a coeducational institution of higher learning in Lima, Peru. Founded by a decree of Charles V of Spain in 1551, it vies with the University of Mexico, also founded in 1551, for the honor of being the oldest university in the New World. It was controlled by the Dominicans until 1571, when it was placed under secular control.

In 1961 three levels of study were established: general liberal arts and professional and doctoral programs. Among available fields of study are mathematics and physics; chemistry and chemical engineering; geology and geography; biology; pharmacy and biochemistry; veterinary science; dentistry; medicine; psychology and social science; law and political science; philosophy, psychology, and art; linguistics, literature, and philology; education; and economics. In the early 1970's the enrollment in the university was over 20,000 students.

SAN MARINO, mə-rē′nō, a city in southwestern California, in Los Angeles county, is a residential suburb. It lies at the edge of the Sierra Madre, 11 miles (18 km) east of the center of the city of Los Angeles and just southeast of Pasadena. It is the seat of the internationally known Henry E. Huntington Library and Art Gallery, which houses unique books and paintings. (See Huntington Library.)

San Marino was settled about 1852 and incorporated in 1913. It has a council manager form of government. Population: 13,307.

SAN MARINO, sän mä-rē′nō, is an independent republic, perhaps the oldest in Europe, in the central Apennines. Surrounded by Italian territory, it lies southwest of Rimini and near the coast of the Adriatic Sea. It takes its name from Marinus, an early Christian acclaimed as a saint (Italian, San Marino).

The republic has an area of about 24 square miles (61 sq km) and a population (1970) of about 19,000. Approximately 4,000 people live in the capital, also named San Marino. The people, proud of their independent heritage, are of Italian stock. The language is Italian, and the religion is Roman Catholic.

Much of the republic is coextensive with steep Mt. Titano (2,421 feet; 738 meters). The mountain's three main peaks, each commanded by a castle, are represented on San Marino's coat of arms. The capital city, perched on the side of the mountain, has several old castles, a 10th century church rebuilt in the 14th century, and the basilica San Marino. The 19th century neo-classic basilica was raised over the ruins of an earlier structure and contains the crypt of Saint Marinus. The only other major town is Serravalle, given to the republic in 1463 by Pope Pius II in return for San Marino's help in opposing Sigismondo Malatesta.

The main sources of revenue are tourism and the republic's distinctive postage stamps. San Marino has a customs union with Italy and receives payments from Italy in exchange for permitting Italian state monopolies on tobacco and

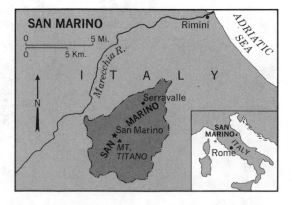

other items. Many of the people are farmers, growing corn, grapes, and other fruit and raising livestock. Wine, building stone, ceramics, and textiles are exported.

History and Government. Traditionally, the history of the republic begins in the 4th century A. D., when Marinus, a Christian stone-cutter fleeing the persecutions of the Emperor Diocletian, settled on Mt. Titano. Although its early history is obscure, San Marino had emerged as a democratic republic by about 1,000. During the Middle Ages it was generally successful in avoiding the partisan entanglements of the era. After the mid-13th century it was protected by the Montefeltro family. It briefly came under the control of Cesare Borgia in 1503. In 1631 the papacy, through Pope Urban VIII, recognized its independence. Cardinal Alberoni tried to subjugate it in 1739, but independence was restored in 1740. In 1849, Giuseppe Garibaldi's followers found refuge in San Marino.

The republic became more closely associated with Italy after 1862, when it placed itself under the protection of the new kingdom of Italy. During World War II, San Marino was officially neutral, but it was occupied by German troops and, as a result, was bombed by the Allies. From 1945 until 1957 it was ruled by a Communist-Socialist coalition, which made it the only European state outside the Iron Curtain that was under Communist rule.

San Marino is governed by a Grand and General Council of 60 members, elected every 5 years by popular vote. Women may vote but may not hold office. Executive powers are exercised by a Congress of State, which has 10 departments, and 2 captains regent. The captains regent serve six-month terms, with new officers invested with medieval ceremony each April 1 and October 1. The captains regent and the members of the Congress of State are chosen by the council from among the council members.

José de San Martín, a liberator of South America.

Government Palace, rebuilt in the late 19th century, retains the original Tuscan-Gothic style.

SAN MARTÍN, sän mär-tēn', **José de** (1778–1850), Argentine general and liberator. Known as the "Liberator of the South," he shares with Simon Bolívar the glory of having expelled the Spanish power from continental South America.

Early Career. The son of a prominent Spanish official, he was born in Yapeyú, in northern Argentina, on Feb. 25, 1778. At the age of nine he was sent to Madrid to obtain a military education. Commissioned second lieutenant in 1793, he rose through the ranks to lieutenant colonel in 1808. He participated with distinction in campaigns on the Portuguese frontier, in Africa, and in the Peninsular War. In 1812 he resigned his commission and embarked for Argentina, where he tendered his services to the revolutionary government and independence movement.

General and Liberator. Evaluating his role as military rather than political, San Martín determined to liberate Argentina by striking at the citadel of Spanish power in Peru. On Feb. 3, 1813, he defeated the Spanish forces at San Lorenzo on the Paraná. Promoted to general in 1814, he succeeded Gen. Manuel Belgrano in command of the Army of Upper Peru, which had suffered shattering defeats on the Bolivian plateau. Late that year, San Martín had himself appointed military governor of the region of Cuyo, comprising four future Argentine provinces. Here he matured his plan to conquer Peru by invading Chile and advancing northward by sea.

In January 1817, Gen. San Martín set out from Mendoza at the head of a seasoned army of 4,000 men on the 17-day march across the Andes through the Uspallata Pass. At Chacabuco, on February 12, he routed the hastily assembled Spanish forces. Then dividing his army, he sent a part to destroy the Spanish nuclei in southern Chile while leading the main body in the invasion of the central and northern areas. On March 17,

1818, he occupied Santiago, but two days later was badly defeated at Cancha Rayada. However, his decisive victory at the Maipo River on April 5 retrieved his fortunes and proved the death blow to the Spanish power in Chile.

Having declined the presidency of liberated Chile in favor of Bernardo O'Higgins, one of his chief lieutenants, San Martín now prepared for the second phase of his plan by constructing a fleet capable of dominating the Pacific and of convoying his army to Peru. On Aug. 23, 1820, he set sail from Valparaiso with an army of 4,500. Debarking at Parascas on September 8, he occupied the coast as far as Pisco, some 150 miles (240 km) south of Lima, the capital. Minor victories culminated in the battle of Pisco (December 6) in which the Spanish general and most of his artillery were captured. At the Conference of Puchanca (June 2, 1821), he rejected terms that did not concede absolute independence. Resuming his advance, he occupied Lima on July 9.

Proclaiming Peru's independence on July 28, 1821, San Martín assumed the title of "protector." In this role he expelled the majority of Spanish citizens, reformed the inhuman system of Indian labor exploitation, abolished slavery, and initiated a system of annual redemptions of quotas of living slaves.

Meeting with Bolívar. To rout the remaining Spaniards from the Peruvian highlands and to plan for the political future of Latin America, the natural step was collaboration with Bolívar, the liberator of the north. The celebrated secret meeting between San Martín and Bolívar at Guyaquil on July 26, 1822, has remained a subject of speculation. San Martín emerged deflated, for he resigned his protectorship and military command to the new Peruvian congress in September and returned to Argentina, a simple citizen.

Retirement. With his daughter, San Martín sailed for Europe in 1824. He remained in voluntary exile until his death in Boulogne, France, on Aug. 17, 1850. His remains were reinterred in the cathedral in Buenos Aires in 1880.

Argentina regards José de San Martín as its greatest revolutionary hero. Actually the liberator's plans were continental more than national, for he favored a centralized constitutional monarchy for Latin America. Apolitical and self-effacing, he removed himself from the political chaos of liberated Argentina and deferred to the stronger personality of Bolívar.

Further Reading: Metford, John C., *San Martín, the Liberator* (McLeod 1950); Rojas, Ricardo, *San Martín, Knight of the Andes* (Doubleday 1945).

SAN MATEO, mə-tā'ō, a city in western California, in San Mateo county, is on San Francisco Bay, about 15 miles (24 km) southeast of the center of San Francisco. It is a residential community with commercial and shopping centers that serve a large area. The College of San Mateo is in the city. Coyote Point on the bay front is of interest. San Mateo was founded in 1863. It has a council-manager form of government. Population: 77,640.

SAN MIGUEL, sän mē-gel', a city in eastern El Salvador, the capital of the department of San Miguel, is on the Río Grande de San Miguel, about 75 miles (120 km) southeast of San Salvador, the nation's capital. It is the center of an agricultural area, and there is some silver and gold mining nearby. The city has a little industry, notably vegetable oil processing.

San Miguel was founded in 1530 and retains much of its old world charm. The 18th-century cathedral, old Spanish residences, and the gardens of the church of Chinameca are especially noteworthy. Population: (1970) 59,304.

SAN PABLO, pab'lō, a city in western California, in Contra Costa county, is about 15 miles (24 km) in an air line northeast of San Francisco. Bathroom fixtures are the chief manufactured product. Contra Costa College is in the city. San Pablo is governed by a mayor and council. Population: 19,750.

SAN PEDRO is a port in southwestern Ivory Coast. Opened in 1971, it was developed by the government to serve as a major outlet for forest products from the interior. The town is intended to serve the growing western region of the country, which has an important agricultural and mineralogical potential. Population: (1972) 14,000.

SAN PEDRO DE MACORÍS, sän pä'thrō thā mäkō-rēs', a port city in the southeastern Dominican Republic, the capital of San Pedro de Macorís province, is situated at the mouth of the Río Higuamo on the Caribbean Sea, about 40 miles (64 km) east of Santo Domingo. Sugar and molasses are manufactured here.

San Pedro de Macorís attained great prosperity in the early 20th century as a center for the export of sugar and molasses. The city's elegance and thriving cultural life earned it the name of the "Little Paris of the Caribbean." In the 1930's most of the exporting was shifted to Santo Domingo, and San Pedro de Macorís declined in importance. Population: (1970) 42,500.

SAN RAFAEL, rə-fel', a city in western California, the seat of Marin county, is about 15 miles (24 km) north of downtown San Francisco, to which the Golden Gate Bridge provides access. It is a residential community, with some light industry, including electronics; printing and publishing; and the processing of foods, lumber and wood products, and chemicals.

Of interest are the Civic Center designed by Frank Lloyd Wright and a replica of the old mission. Museums include the Louise Boyd Natural Science Museum, the Pony Express History and Art Gallery, and the museum of the Marin County Historical Society. The Dominican College of San Rafael offers degrees in liberal arts.

The San Rafael Arcángel Mission was founded on Dec. 14, 1817, as a health retreat for priests and colonists. A community grew up around it, and San Rafael was incorporated in 1874 and became a city in 1913. It has a mayor-council form of government. Population: 44,700.

SAN REMO, san rä'mō, is a Mediterranean seaport and popular resort in Italy, on the Riviera, 10 miles (16 km) east of Ventimiglia. The town is terraced, with the old upper town's narrow, crooked streets lined with lofty buildings, often connected by arches. The old town contrasts sharply with the modern structures and promenades of the lower town. Among San Remo's attractions are the Cathedral of San Siro, begun in the 12th century. Its major export is cut flowers. Population: (1969 est.) 50,300.

SAN REMO CONFERENCE, san rä'mō, a meeting held on April 19–26, 1920, in San Remo, Italy, to discuss the results of World War I. The leading participants were Britain, France, and Italy, represented by David Lloyd George, Alexandre Millerand, and Francesco Nitti, their respective heads of government. They were joined by representatives of Japan, Greece, and Belgium.

The most important result of the conference was agreement on the basic peace treaty with Turkey. (See SÈVRES, TREATY OF.) The conferees also agreed on independence for Middle East territories, assigning them as mandates for an interim period. Britain received Iraq and Palestine, while France was given Syria (including Lebanon).

SAN SALVADOR, san sal'və-dôr, a city in El Salvador, became the capital of this Central American republic in 1840. The city is in a valley near the volcano San Salvador, at an elevation of 2,100 feet (640 meters). It is 120 miles (195 km) southeast of Guatemala City and some 20 miles (32 km) from the Pacific port of La Libertad, with which it is connected by rail.

A well-planned city, San Salvador is built on a modified gridiron pattern, with wide streets and several parks. Due to the threat of earthquakes, its houses tend to be low and surrounded by open areas. Noteworthy structures include the National Palace, where the legislature meets; the Casa Blanca, residence of the president; the cathedral; and several buildings of the National University, including its observatory. An important industrial center, the city has factories producing soap, silk and cotton textiles, cigars, sugar, and beer. It is also a thriving commercial hub.

San Salvador was founded in 1528 by Jorge de Alvarado, brother of the Spanish conquistador Pedro de Alvarado. From 1831 to 1839 it was the capital of a federation of Central American states. The city was all but destroyed by earthquakes in 1854, 1873, and 1917 and has also been devastated by floods. Population: (1969) 349,725.

SAN SEBASTIÁN, san sə-bas'chən, is a city in northern Spain on the Bay of Biscay, at the mouth of the Urumea River. A major port and the capital of Guipúzcoa province, it is a natural and fortified stronghold, 10 miles (16 km) from the French border. Fishing is one of the main occupations, and there are numerous port-related industries. Other industries include the manufacture of chemicals, electrical equipment, metal products, and phonograph records.

San Sebastián, with its striking combination of mountain and seashore scenery, is Spain's most fashionable resort city and was a summer residence of the royal family. The old town lies on a peninsula, at the tip of which is Monte Urgull, a hill topped by the Castillo de la Mota. The principal buildings of interest are the churches of Santa María and San Vicente, built in the 18th and 16th centuries, respectively. The modern city extends around the Bay of La Concha, on which the former royal palace is located, and along both banks of the Urumea.

The city has sustained several sieges, the most memorable of which was in 1813, when English and Portuguese forces under the future Duke of Wellington took it by storm and burned it. The San Sebastián Pact, a republican manifesto, was signed in the city in 1930 and led to the fall of the monarchy. Population: (1969 est.) 156,300.

SAN STEFANO, san stef'ə-nō, **Treaty of,** a peace treaty of the Russo-Turkish War, concluded March 3, 1878, at San Stefano, a port on the Sea of Marmara.

By its terms an autonomous Bulgaria, extending from the Danube to the Aegean, was established under Russian protection. Rumania, Serbia, and Montenegro were recognized as independent. Bosnia and Hercegovina were granted autonomy. Russia was to receive a huge war indemnity and parts of Turkish Armenia. The Berlin Congress, held in June and July, greatly altered the provisions of San Stefano, which were considered too favorable to Russia. See also BERLIN CONGRESS; RUSSO-TURKISH WARS.

PLAZA LIBERTAD is in the center of San Salvador, the capital of the Central American republic of El Salvador.

San Xavier del Bac, a Spanish mission near Tucson, Ariz., was founded before 1700.

SAN XAVIER DEL BAC, san zā′vē-ər del bak, is a Spanish mission in the Santa Cruz Valley nine miles south of Tucson, Ariz. One of the most beautiful of the Spanish missions in the New World, it has been called the "White Dove of the Desert." The original church was founded several miles north of the present site before 1700 by Father Eusebio Francisco Kino, a Jesuit missionary to the Indians. In 1751 the Indians plundered the crude adobe structure and drove the Jesuits from the area. A second structure was built, but this was destroyed by a party of raiding Apaches.

The present church was constructed between 1782 and 1797 by the Franciscan Order. It is a cruciform edifice, built of adobe with a stone foundation and a covering of fine cement. It faces south. The façade, highly ornamented with scroll work adorned with the arms of the Franciscan Order, is well preserved. Two towers, one unfinished, surmount the front. Over the main chapel is a massive dome of splendid proportions and lightness. Several fine frescoes depicting the life of Christ remain.

The missionaries left San Xavier in 1828, after which the Papago Indians preserved it. The missionaries returned in 1911 and have established the mission as a church and school for the Papagos.

SANA, son-a′, is the capital city of Yemen Arab Republic. It is in the center of the country, about 90 miles (145 km) northeast of the Red Sea port of Hodeida, to which it is linked by a modern road built with Communist Chinese aid. It lies in a valley about 7,750 feet (2,362 meters) high.

The city is surrounded by a wall, which is pierced by eight gates. The old quarter has most of Sana's elaborately decorated mosques, including the Great Mosque. It was erected on the site of a 6th century Christian church and has a Kaaba similar to the one at Mecca. The former royal palace was severely damaged in Yemen's 1962 revolution. Sana is an important trade center, dealing chiefly in coffee and dried fruit, especially raisins. Sword blades and gold and silver jewelry are manufactured.

Of great antiquity, the city was the center of an early Himyarite kingdom and in the Middle Ages was ruled by Ethiopians. In the 16th century, and again from 1872 to 1918, it was under Turkish control. Its importance grew after Yemen became independent following World War I. Population: (1964 est.) 100,000.

SANBORN, Franklin Benjamin (1831–1917), American author, journalist, and humanitarian, who financially aided John Brown in his raid on Harpers Ferry. Sanborn was born in Hampton Falls, N. H., on Dec. 15, 1831, and was educated at Harvard. After graduating in 1855 he took an active part in the abolitionist movement, becoming secretary of the Massachusetts Free Soil Association. He met John Brown in 1857 and lent support to his efforts. Acquainted with Brown's plans for a raid, he attempted to dissuade him but eventually arranged for money to be given to him. In the investigation that followed the Harpers Ferry incident Sanborn narrowly escaped prosecution.

Sanborn, an active journalist most of his life, contributed to the Springfield *Republican* (1856–1914) and edited the Boston *Commonwealth* (1863–1867) and the *Republican* (1868–1872). He was a founder of the American Social Science Association in 1865 and edited its journal for 30 years. In 1863 he became secretary of the Massachusetts State Board of Charities, the first board of its kind in the United States, and instituted a system of inspection and reports of charitable institutions.

Among the many books written by Sanborn are *The Life and Letters of John Brown* (1885) and biographies of his friends Henry D. Thoreau (1882), A. Bronson Alcott (1893), and Ralph Waldo Emerson (1901). Sanborn died in Plainfield, N. J., on Feb. 24, 1917.

SANCHI, sän′chē, is a village in India famous for its ancient Buddhist stupas, or reliquary structures. It is situated in Madhya Pradesh state, about 23 miles (37 km) northeast of the city of Bhopal.

Sanchi's stupas date back to the reign of Emperor Asoka (Ashoka) in the 3d century B. C. The best known is the Great Stupa, a huge hemispherical mound of masonry that stands 54 feet (16 meters) high and is 120 feet (36 meters) in diameter. It is enclosed by a stone railing with four high *torana* (gateways). See also TEMPLE—*India* (Buddhist).

SANCHO III, saɴ′shōō (990?–1035), king of Pamplona (Navarre), called "the Great." The son of García III of Pamplona, Sancho succeeded his father about 1000. He began to expand his realm by seizing the counties of Sobrarbe and Ribagorza to the east and then laid claim to lands stretching through the county of Barcelona as far as the Mediterranean.

Sancho married a daughter of the count of Castile and in 1028 claimed Castile as part of his wife's inheritance. He successfully pursued Castilian claims to lands on the Leonese border, then entered León and declared himself its emperor in 1034. At this point Sancho was at least titular head of most of the Christian states in Spain. He died the next year and his empire was fragmented among his four sons.

SANCHO PANZA, sän′chō pän′zə, is the squire of the deluded hero of Cervantes' novel *Don Quixote* (1605 and 1615). Sancho, a naïve rustic, is recruited by the Don, who fancies himself a knight errant, with promises that the poor peasant will rule an island. He accompanies the Don on all his adventures and is near him when he dies. Cervantes beautifully contrasts the self-deluding, sophisticated knight with the direct, realistic squire. See also DON QUIXOTE.

SANCTI SPÍRITUS, sangk′tē spē′rē-tōōs, a city in central Cuba, in Las Villas province, is on the Río Yayabo, about 45 miles (72 km) southeast of Santa Clara and 20 miles (32 km) north of Tunas de Zaza, a port on the Caribbean Sea. It is the commercial center for the surrounding agricultural area, and sugar and cigars are manufactured here. Sancti Spíritus was founded in 1514 by Diego Velásquez de Cuellar. The city still has many of its old buildings, which are of Spanish colonial design with a Moorish flavor. Population: (1970) 57,700.

SANCTIONS, International, penalties applied against a state in order to make it comply with international law. Sanctions are applied by, on behalf of, at the request of an international organization representing the international community. They are directed against a state or group of states that has violated or threatens to violate an international obligation, especially the obligation to refrain from military aggression.

Until the recent past, individual states or groups of states have used various measures "short of war" to bring other states to terms—for example, suspension of diplomatic relations, trade embargoes, so called pacific blockade, naval demonstrations, military intervention, and even the shelling of cities. The two first-mentioned measures, and possibly the third, are still permissible under international law. But one of the principal aims of the League of Nations was to do away with the unilateral use, or threat, of force. Instead, the Covenant of the League of Nations, for the first time in history, intended to create a system under which the international community as a whole would, if the need arose, impose international sanctions.

The League of Nations. The idea of international sanctions was embodied primarily in Article 16 of the Covenant of the League of Nations, which stated that if any League member resorted to war in disregard of its Covenant obligations, this was to be deemed an act of war against all members. The members, therefore, were "immediately" to apply the following sanctions against an offending state: (1) the severance of all trade or financial relations with it; (2) the prevention of "all intercourse" between their own nationals and those of the Covenant-breaking state; and (3) the prevention of all financial, commercial, and personal intercourse between the nationals of the offender and the nationals of any other state. The article further provided for the possibility of military sanctions.

The League of Nations never applied military sanctions. But when Italy, under the Fascist regime of Benito Mussolini, flagrantly attacked Ethiopia in 1935, the League decided on an embargo against Italy, especially on petroleum and its derivatives. The plan did not succeed, however, because Mussolini was able to obtain the necessary gasoline and oil despite the embargo.

The United Nations. The Charter of the United Nations gives the Security Council a very wide scope. Under Article 39 of the Charter, once the Security Council has determined that there exists "any threat to the peace, breach of the peace, or act of aggression," it "shall make recommendations, or decide what measures shall be taken . . . to maintain or restore international peace and security." In accordance with Articles 41 and 42, such measures may "include complete or partial interruption of economic relations of rail, sea, air, postal, telegraphic, radio, and other means of communications, and the severance of diplomatic relations"; or of "such action by air, sea, or land forces as may be necessary to maintain or restore international peace and security [including] demonstrations, blockade, and other operations by air, sea, or land forces of Members of the United Nations."

Such actions are not necessarily conceived as "sanctions," so that they do not necessarily put the stigma of lawbreaker on the state or states against which they are directed. Furthermore, since the Security Council may take any action of this kind if it finds that a "threat to the peace" exists, such intervention may be decided upon by the council if no actual acts of war have occurred. The Security Council invoked compulsory economic sanctions against Rhodesia in 1966 after Rhodesia's white-minority government unilaterally declared its independence from Britain.

JOHN H. E. FRIED
City University of New York

Further Reading: Doxey, Margaret P., *Economic Sanctions and International Enforcement* (Oxford 1971); McDougal, Myres S., and Feliciano, Florentino P., *Law and Minimum World Public Order* (Yale Univ. Press 1961).

SANCTIS, Francesco de. See DE SANCTIS, FRANCESCO.

SANCTUARY, a sacred or consecrated place such as a temple, church, or mosque. Sanctuaries were formerly recognized as places of refuge for fugitives and criminals. Such refuges were known among the ancient Greeks and Romans and among the Jews (Numbers 35). From the early 4th century, Christian churches were considered places of sanctuary, and the practice was recognized and regulated in 392 by a decree of Emperor Theodosius I. The right of sanctuary continued to be acknowledged all through the Middle Ages. It was based in part on the sanctity of the consecrated church but also on the duty of a Christian priest to show mercy to an offender, to intercede for him, and to persuade him to repentance instead of handing him over for immediate execution. The system provided a useful check on acts of summary private vengeance in time of disorder, but, with the growth of more effective judicial systems, came to be regarded as an abuse.

In 13th century England, the practice was that a felon who sought sanctuary was required to "abjure the realm" within 40 days. He would be granted a safe conduct to the coast; but he was *ipso facto* held guilty, his goods were confiscated, and he was forbidden to re-enter the kingdom without royal permission. If he failed to abjure within the 40 days he could be forced out of sanctuary by starvation. Besides this general right of sanctuary for felons, claimed by all churches, certain ecclesiastical and secular places acquired, by royal grant, the privilege of giving sanctuary for longer periods and for criminals other than felons.

In the 15th century there were several parliamentary petitions seeking to restrict the right of sanctuary. In 1529, Henry VIII required those abjuring the realm to be branded on the thumb. In 1530 he substituted permanent imprisonment for exile and in 1540 he reduced the number of recognized sanctuaries by about half. The right of sanctuary throughout England was abolished by a statute of 1624. A few districts continued to assert a customary right of immunity from arrest within their borders—notably the part of London called Alsatia, which became a notorious resort of criminals. These remaining privileges were abolished in 1697. Events on the Continent followed a similar course: the right of sanctuary was restricted in the later Middle Ages, and abolished between 1750 and 1850.

BRIAN TIERNEY, *Cornell University*

SANCTUARY, a novel by the American author William Faulkner, published in 1931. It deals with the thwarted efforts of an honest lawyer to bring justice and order to a small town in Mississippi. It may be read as an allegory of the corruption of the society of the Old South. The bootlegger Popeye represents progressive modernism and materialistic exploitation, and the lawyer Horace Benbow, idealistic, but impotent, historic tradition.

Temple Drake, a 17-year-old college girl from an upper-class family, provokes the disreputable Popeye into raping her. Popeye also kills Tommy, a moonshiner, and takes Temple, who witnessed the crime, to a brothel in Memphis. Benbow tries to convict Popeye of Tommy's murder, but Temple falsely testifies against an innocent man, who is lynched for the crime. Ironically, Popeye is accused and executed for a murder he did not commit.

SAND, sänd, **George,** the assumed name of the French novelist Amandine Aurore Lucie Dupin, Baroness Dudevant (1804–1876). She was born in Paris on July 1, 1804. In *Histoire de ma vie* (4 vols., 1854–1855), a major masterpiece, she dwelt at length on her strange pedigree.

Aurore's father, Maurice Dupin, had married Sophie Delaborde, a humble Parisian modiste. But he could claim a real, though tarnished, kinship to royalty. His mother, Mme. Dupin-Francueil, was a natural daughter of that 18th century hero of love and war Count Hermann Maurice de Saxe, himself the illegitimate son of Augustus II, king of Poland. Aurore's grandmother, a cultured woman and an accomplished musician, embodied the spirit of the old aristocracy, although she, who had known and befriended Jean Jacques Rousseau, shared Rousseau's passion for country life, and had become, on her estate at Nohant, near Châteauroux, a member of the landowning gentry. All these strands were to appear in the texture of George Sand's career.

As Wife and Mother. The "rustic-aristocratic" side of Aurore's life seemed to prevail at first. She was four years old when her father died, and she spent most of her youth at Nohant, under the wing of Mme. Dupin-Francueil. Even her marriage, at the age of 18, to Casimir, Baron Dudevant, followed the accepted pattern. She was a dutiful wife at first, bore him two children, Maurice and Solange, and let her growing resentment of him and his prosaic ways smolder for eight years before she left him, in early 1831.

Liaisons with Sandeau and Musset. The next four or five years were those of her "romantic rebellion." She led a bohemian life in Paris, associating with young artists and writers, flouting every convention, and herself often smoking cigars or wearing masculine costume. A liaison with the writer Jules Sandeau heralded her literary debut. They published a few stories in collaboration, signing them "Jules Sand." As a consequence, she adopted, for her first independent novel, the name that made her famous. That novel, *Indiana* (1832; Eng. tr., 1881), and others in rapid succession—*Valentine* (1832), *Lélia* (1833), *Jacques* (1834), and so on—testified to the prodigious facility of her pen. All of these novels averred her hostility to current social norms and advanced flamboyantly the claims of romantic feminism, which met with much public opposition.

Meanwhile, George Sand compounded her *succès de scandale* by embarking on what may have been the wildest love affair of the century. She and the poet and playwright Alfred de Musset, six years her junior, traveled together to Venice, came back separately, and went through innumerable quarrels and reconciliations until the final break in 1835. This tempestuous episode became the source of much literary material: Musset's *Nuit de Mai* (1835–1837) and *Confession d'un enfant du siècle* (1836) and George Sand's *Elle et lui* (1859), as well as her exquisite *Lettres d'un voyageur* (1834, 1836).

Chopin and a Social Cause. The fires of rebellion and passion abated thereafter, and George Sand's next celebrated liaison—that with the composer and pianist Frédéric Chopin, though not tranquil by any means—actually suggests on her part a feeling of possession induced by pity. The composer, already stricken with tuberculosis, aroused the mother complex, always very strong in her (her children have been called the great-

BETTMANN ARCHIVE

George Sand, French writer, dressed as a man

est love of her life). She nursed him—as is evident from *Un hiver à Majorque* (1841), describing her stay on the island of Majorca with him—and hovered over him until he grew impatient of her solicitude.

Meanwhile, the "plebeian" chord was awakening in her heart, and she transferred to the people the powers of love that she had been squandering on men. Spurred on by such noted advocates of social betterment as Félicité Robert de Lamennais, Michel de Bourges, and Pierre Leroux, she began writing humanitarian, broadly "socialistic" novels. *Mauprat* (1837), a work of transition—on the theme of a brute, Bernard de Mauprat, transformed by love—is also a most interesting effort. There followed *Spiridion* (1838–1839), *Les sept cordes de la lyre* (1840), *Le compagnon du tour de France* (1840), *Consuelo* (1842; Eng. tr., 1846), *Le Meunier d'Angibault* (1845), and *Le péché de Monsieur Antoine* (1847)—each a persistent call, under the guise of fiction, for the reconstruction of society and the mating of classes through the practice of evangelical love.

"Good Lady of Nohant." The revolution of 1848 occurred at time when George Sand was conceiving serious doubts about the possibility or wisdom of immediate reform. She had initiated the series of pastoral idylls, cast in the beloved countryside around Nohant, that remain today her most enduring title to fame—*La mare au diable* (1846; Eng. tr., *The Haunted Pool*, 1890); *François le champi* (1850; Eng. tr., *Francis the Waif*, 1889). Idylls they are, but they preach, too, a return to the soil as the true haven of peace, virtue, and happiness.

To be sure, the outbreak of the revolution rekindled George Sand's ardor. She offered her services to the provisional government, wrote articles for the *Bulletin de la République*, composed her *Lettres au peuple*, and so on. When the June days came, however, with the repression that ensued, she returned to Nohant, there to exploit further the rustic vein of her inspiration—*La petite Fadette* (1848; Eng. tr., *Fanchon the Cricket*, 1864) and *Les maîtres sonneurs* (1853). As time went on and she grew old most gracefully, the novels that still issued from her fertile brain took on a quasi-patriarchal hue. Her sentimental indulgence henceforth included the gentry itself in her rose-colored view of country life. *Les beaux messieurs de Bois-Doré* (1858), *Jean de la Roche* (1860), *Le Marquis de Villemer* (1861), and *Mademoiselle de la Quintinie* (1863) are faded pastels by now. But in the "good lady of Nohant" who painted them—ever close to the people, ever kindhearted and hospitable to all—there emerges, fully recognizable, a replica of Mme. Dupin-Francueil, *née* Aurore de Saxe, with her undefinable aura of aristocratic prestige, taste, and beauty. She died at Nohant on June 8, 1876. See also the Index entry, *Sand, George*.

JEAN-ALBERT BÉDÉ
Columbia University

Bibliography

Caro, Elme M., *George Sand* (1888; reprint, Kennikat 1970).
Doumic, René, *George Sand: Some Aspects of Her Life and Writings*, tr. by Alys Hallard (1910; reprint, Kennikat 1971).
Maurois, André, *Lélia: The Life of George Sand*, tr. from the French by Gerard Hopkins (Harper 1953).
Schermerhorn, Elizabeth W., *The Seven Strings of the Lyre: The Romantic Life of George Sand* (Houghton 1932).
Seyd, Felizia, *Romantic Rebel: The Life and Times of George Sand* (Viking 1940).
Spoelberch de Lovenjoul, Vicomte Charles de, *George Sand: Étude bibliographique sur ses ouvres* (1929 ed.; reprint, Burt Franklin 1967).
Winwar, Frances, *The Life of the Heart: George Sand and Her Times* (Harper 1945).

SAND, in common usage, is the silica sand that constitutes many beaches and desert dunes. In geology, however, sand is any loose material consisting of small mineral or rock particles ranging from angular to almost spherical in shape, and it is defined and graded by the size of these particles. For very coarse sands the range is 1 to 2 millimeters (0.04–0.08 inch); for coarse sands, 0.5 to 1 mm; for medium sands, 0.25 to 0.5 mm; for fine sands, 0.12 to 0.25 mm; and for very fine sands, 0.06 to 0.12 mm. When such particles are consolidated, they form sandstones.

The most common constituents of sands are quartz and feldspar. Also often present are complex mixtures of clays and many other minerals, some of which may be economically important in themselves. For example, black sands are rich in the titanium mineral rutile, while greensand contains glauconite. Silica, or quartz, sands are usually up to 95% silica and have many applications. They are used in glass manufacture and water filtration, as abrasives, and for making foundry molds. Ordinary grades of sand are also widely used in the building industry for making mortar, plaster, and concrete. Other grades of sand are employed in the manufacture of pottery, scouring soaps, and explosives.

Geologically, sands are detrital deposits formed by the erosive action of running water, ocean waves, glaciers, or wind. They may be formed in place, or they may be transported and concentrated by these agencies. Silica sands are usually derived from the disintegration of igneous or other rocks, whereas calcium-rich sands result

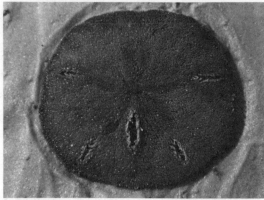

Living five-holed sand dollar (*top*). The five holes are clearly visible in the sand dollar skeleton (*bottom*).

mostly from the grinding up of shells, corals, or limestone beds by wave action. Granite forms a quartz-feldspar sand known as feldspathic, or arkose, sand, while basic rocks form ferromagnesian, or graywacke, sand. Deposits of these different sands accumulate as beaches, offshore bars, dunes, moraines, and river deltas. See also BEACH; DELTA; DUNE; EROSION; MORAINE; SANDSTONE.

SAND CREEK MASSACRE, an attack on Nov. 29, 1864, by Col. John M. Chivington and perhaps 750 cavalrymen on an encampment of Indians in Kiowa county, Colo. After three years of killing and pillaging by Indian bands in the new Colorado Territory, Black Kettle and other Cheyenne and Arapaho chiefs surrendered to military authorities at Fort Lyon in the fall of 1864. Ordered to leave the vicinity of the post, the 200 Indian warriors and some 500 women and children settled on Sand Creek, 40 miles distant. There, at dawn on November 29, they were surprised by Chivington's troops, who inflicted appalling losses on the helpless Indians. Estimates of the number of Indians slain, including women and children, range from 150 to 500. Chivington claimed the higher figure, and also reported 9 of his soldiers killed.

The soldiers were hailed as heroes at first, but investigations by Congress, a military commission, and the Commissioner of Indian Affairs elicited enough testimony to discredit Chivington.

SAND DOLLAR, any of a group of flattened circular invertebrate animals that are found in shallow coastal waters, usually just beneath the surface of the sand. They are also sometimes known as sea cakes.

Sand dollars are classified in several genera of the class Echinoidea of the phylum Echinodermata. They are closely related to sea urchins and to starfish.

Sand dollars may be as small as 0.5 inch (1.2 cm) in diameter, but most are usually from 2 to 4 inches (5–10 cm) across. The body is enclosed in a limy shell, known as a test, through which protrude ambulacral, or tube, feet and many very fine spines. On the aboral, or upper, surface of the sand dollar, these spines keep the sand out, while on the oral, or under, surface, they function together with the tube feet to allow the sand dollar to crawl slowly on the sand.

Food, such as seaweed and very small marine animal matter, is swept into the centrally located mouth by hairlike cilia on the spines. Many sand dollars also have elongated slitlike holes, or lunules, perforating the shell in a symmetrical arrangement. The function of these openings is not known.

SAND DUNE. See DUNE.

SAND FLEA. See CHIGOE.

SAND GROUSE are any of a family of highly gregarious terrestrial birds that inhabit the plains and sandy deserts of the tropical regions and central parts of Eurasia and Africa. They are related on one hand to pigeons (family Columbidae) and on the other hand to grouse (family Gallinae).

Sand grouse are usually from 9 to 16 inches (23–40 cm) long and they generally resemble doves. They have short bills, short necks, long pointed wings, and short legs with feathered tarsi. Their plumage is dense. It may be sandy, buff, reddish brown or gray above, and it is often spotted or marked. Their faces and breasts are frequently boldly marked, and their tails are often barred.

Pin-tailed sand grouse (*Pterocles alchata*)

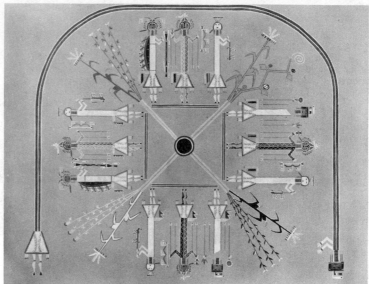

This Navaho sand painting depicts a lake, in the center, from which grow corn and other plants. Surrounding the lake are rainbow bars. The gods invited to the ceremony stand on the bars.

Generally grouped in large flocks, sand grouse fly at regular hours, usually dawn and dusk, to special watering holes. They immerse their bills to sip and suck water. They feed during the day on seeds, berries, buds, and small insects.

Sand grouse nest in depressions, or scrapes, on the ground. The two or three eggs are white, buff, or greenish and often marked. Both parents incubate the eggs and care for the downy young, which leave the nest shortly after hatching.

The 16 known species of sand grouse are classified in two genera: *Syrrhaptes* and *Pterocles*, making up the family Pteroclidae of the order Columbiiformes.

SAND PAINTING is the making of a design on the earth or a floor with colored sand or other pulverized mineral or organic matter such as charcoal, meal, or rice. It is also the design itself. Sand painting, also called dry or earth painting, is traditional among such widely distributed peoples as Pueblo, Navaho, and Plains Indians, Hindus, and Australian aborigines as part of religious ritual. The abstract designs are handed down by demonstration.

SAND PIPE, a kind of long, cylindrical tube that is found primarily in limestone deposits, such as the chalk cliffs of England and France. The tubes are called sand pipes because they are commonly filled with sand or gravel that has fallen or washed down from overlying deposits. Over geological time the sand may consolidate to form sandstone.

Sand pipes range up to 60 feet (nearly 20 meters) in depth and from 6 to 12 feet (2–4 meters) in diameter. They are probably formed by the dissolving action of groundwater on limestone, especially when the water is charged with carbon dioxide after seeping down from soils rich in decaying organic matter.

SAND SHARK, any of a family, Carchariidae, of fierce-looking sharks found in shallow water in temperate and tropical seas, generally swimming constantly. Along the American coast, the sand tiger, or sand shark, *Carcharias taurus*, is found from Maine to Florida, and a separate population is found around Brazil. It and some closely related species are also known to occur around South Africa, in the eastern Atlantic and Mediterranean, and around the coasts of Argentina, Australia, Japan, China, and India. The sand shark is not known to attack humans along the American coast, but around South Africa it is considered very dangerous and is known to attack without provocation.

The largest sand shark taken was 10 feet 5 inches (3.2 meters) long and weighed about 300 pounds (136 kg). It is unusual among sharks in that it can swallow air and retain it in its stomach, thus allowing the stomach to function as a hydrostatic organ, much like the air bladder of other fishes. Females begin to bear young when they are about 7 feet (2.1 meters) long. Two embryos develop, one in each horn of the uterus.

SAND SPRINGS, a city in northeastern Oklahoma, in Tulsa county, is on the Arkansas River, about 7 miles (11 km) west of Tulsa. It makes corrugated boxes, oil-field pipe and equipment, fiber glass, plastics, steel products, and porcelain and cement products. Sand Springs was incorporated in 1916 and is governed by council and manager. Population: 13,246.

SANDAGE, san'dij, **Allan Rex** (1926–   ), American astronomer. Sandage was born in Iowa City, Iowa, on June 18, 1926. He obtained his doctorate in astrophysics from the California Institute of Technology in 1953. Joining the staff at Mt. Wilson and Palomar observatories, he undertook a study of the stellar populations of globular clusters, which he determined to be the oldest objects in our galaxies. In the early 1960's he participated in the identification of the objects now known as quasars, and in 1963 he observed that the nucleus of radio galaxy M82 is undergoing an explosion. His work on red shifts in galactic spectra supported the theory that the universe expands and contracts.

SANDALWOOD is a fragrant hardwood obtained from trees that grow in southern India, Malaya, and other countries in the Orient. The main source of sandalwood is *Santalum album*, a small evergreen tree native to India. The heartwood of *S. album* is yellow-brown, very hard, and close grained. It is made odorous by the presence of an oil, which is even more abundant in the roots. The oil is distilled from the roots and heartwood chips and is mainly used as a perfume, especially in India. Sandalwood is widely used in India and China for fans, boxes, carvings, and other articles of inlaid work. Buddhists in those countries use sandalwood for cremations and incense. The Brahmans use powdered sandalwood in pigments for making caste marks.

Red sandalwood is obtained from *Pterocarpus santalinus,* a small leguminous tree found in southern India, Ceylon, and the Philippines. This wood is used in making a dye that gives wool a red-brown color.

SANDALWOOD ISLAND. See Sumba.

SANDBLASTING is the use of a blast of air or steam laden with sand. Sandblasting is used to clean, grind, cut, or decorate hard surfaces such as those of glass, stone, or metal. For instance, sandblasting is used to clean the exteriors of stone buildings, to remove scale from metal surfaces, to blast through metal stencils to cut lettering or designs on stone monuments or buildings, and to etch designs on glass vases.

SANDBUR, any of several annual or perennial plants whose seeds are enclosed by prickly burs. The field sandbur, *Cenchrus pauciflorus,* has stems 8 to 36 inches (20–90 cm) long and usually two spikelets in each bur. It is found in sandy open ground in most states of the United States, Baja California, and southern South America. The coast sandbur, *C. incertus,* has stems 10 to 40 inches (25–100 cm) tall and one to three spikelets in each bur. It grows in open sandy soil in southeastern and southern coastal states. The dune sandbur, *C. tribuloides,* has conspicuously hairy burs. It inhabits loose sands in the West Indies, along the Gulf Coast from Florida to Louisiana, and along the Atlantic Coast from New York to Florida.

SANDBURG, Carl (1878–1967), American poet and biographer of Abraham Lincoln. He was born of Swedish peasant stock in Galesburg, Ill., on Jan. 6, 1878. He grew up in Galesburg, a town of 15,000 residents in his boyhood, which nevertheless boasted three colleges. Here, in a building of Knox College, Abraham Lincoln and Stephen A. Douglas had had one of their historic debates in 1858, and the town abounded in stories of its hero, Lincoln, which were among young Sandburg's first impressions. He went to the Galesburg public school for four years, and to the Swedish Lutheran summer school. At 13 he finished the eighth grade and had to go to work. His first job was driving a milk wagon, and as he drove along, he recited his favorite pieces of prose and verse. He was especially fond of the Bible and Thomas Gray's *Elegy.* Later he worked as a bootblack and porter in a local barber shop, where he listened to the customers' talk about local history and arguments about politics, and became engrossed in the affairs of his state.

Early Years. When the Spanish-American War broke out in 1898, Sandburg enlisted, saw active service in Puerto Rico, and was war correspondent for the Galesburg *Evening Mail.* In September 1898 he entered Lombard College, a local institution, receiving free tuition for his war service. But in 1902, at the time of examinations and diplomas, he wandered off and was never graduated. Nevertheless, Philip Green Wright, professor of English at Lombard, published

BROWN BROTHERS

Carl Sandburg, 20th century American poet and biographer of Lincoln, collected and sang American folk songs.

Sandburg's first little book, *In Reckless Ecstacy* (1904). For two years after college, Sandburg was a genuine hobo, taking temporary jobs on newspapers and peddling stereoscopic views. Roaming about the country, north, south, east, and west, he got to know America in the songs of her farmhands, cowboys, rivermen, and Negro stevedores, strumming on his guitar as he went.

In Chicago, where he became associate editor of the *Lyceumite,* Sandburg met Winfield R. Gaylord, organizer of the Social-Democratic party in Wisconsin, and Gaylord offered him the position of party organizer. Sandburg liked the city of Milwaukee because of its strong civic consciousness, and made it his base. There he married Lillian Steichen in 1908 and, to support his growing family, went into advertising, wrote features for the Milwaukee *Journal and Daily News,* and worked spasmodically at his free verse poetry, influenced by Walt Whitman. In 1912 he returned to Chicago, and in 1916 his *Chicago Poems* came out, followed by *Cornhuskers* in 1918, which won its author half of the Poetry Society Prize. In 1914 he won the Levinson Prize offered by *Poetry Magazine.* When the United States entered World War I in 1917, Sandburg was sent abroad by the Newspaper Enterprise Association as special correspondent in Sweden and Norway.

Later Years and Major Works. Upon his return from Europe, Sandburg worked 13 years for the Chicago *Daily News.* In 1920 he published *Smoke and Steel,* for which he shared the Poetry Society Prize with Stephen Vincent Benét. *Slabs of the Sunburnt West* appeared in 1922 and also his *Rootabaga Stories* for children. Meanwhile, he was painstakingly collecting Lincoln material for his great biography, leaving Chicago for the seclusion of a farm with his wife and three daughters. In 1926 his *Abraham Lincoln: The Prairie Years* came out in two volumes, bringing financial relief. Sandburg labored 16 years more to bring out *Abraham Lincoln: The War Years* (4 vols., 1939), which won the Pulitzer Prize for history in 1940, and another Civil War volume, *Storm Over the Land* (1942). Meanwhile, *The American Songbag*, a collection of folk songs, appeared in 1927, one year before *Good Morning America*, the Harvard Phi Beta Kappa poem for 1928. *The People, Yes* followed in 1936, perhaps his greatest poetic work.

Sandburg is regarded as the representative poet of the prairie West. An inherently simple man, he rose from the humblest beginnings and did not fear hard work. He created for himself a new technique in poetry, celebrating industrial and agricultural America. Sometimes his verse becomes propaganda. *Always the Young Strangers*, published in 1953, is autobiographical, telling of his life in Galesburg and the role of the Swedes in settling the Middle West. Sandburg died in Flat Rock, N. C., on July 22, 1967.

Laura Benét
Author of "Famous American Poets"

Further Reading: Callahan, North, *Carl Sandburg: A Biography* (N. Y. Univ. Press 1970); Crowder, Richard, *Carl Sandburg* (Twayne 1964); Durnell, Hazel B., *The America of Carl Sandburg* (Univ. Press of Washington, D. C., 1966).

SANDE, san'dē, **Earl** (1898–1968), American jockey. He was born in Groton, S. Dak., on Nov. 13, 1898. Sande won his first race at 15 and was paid $1 of the $10 purse. He eventually won 967 races, and his horses collected purses of nearly $3 million. Man o' War was one of his mounts.

Sande reached the peak of his career in the early 1920's as a rider for the Rancocas Stable of Harry F. Sinclair. He won the Kentucky Derby on Zev in 1923 and then rode Zev to victory over Papyrus, winner of the Epsom Derby, in a match race for a purse of $80,000. Seriously injured in 1924, Sande recovered to win the 1925 Kentucky Derby, on Flying Ebony, and after a brief retirement he won the derby again on Gallant Fox in 1930. Damon Runyon wrote of "a handy guy like Sande,/Bootin' them babies in." After uneven success as a trainer, Sande made a brief comeback attempt as a jockey in 1953. Having lost all his money, he died in Jacksonville, Oreg., on Aug. 20, 1968.

SANDERLING, a small sandpiper, *Crocethia alba*, common along seacoasts throughout the world. A member of the sandpiper family, Scolopacidae, it is well known for its long migrations, often breeding in Arctic regions and migrating to southern Argentina for the nonbreeding season.

The sanderling grows to a length of about 8 inches (20 cm) and has gray and white plumage. In summer the adults have a distinctive reddish breast. Like some other running birds, the sanderling lacks a hind toe and has a streamlined three-toed foot. It feeds on crustaceans and insects and has been known to follow closely behind turnstones and to dart in and steal some food when the turnstone turns over a stone or other object looking for food. Sanderlings usually lay four eggs in a depression on the ground. Both parents incubate the eggs and sometimes perform distraction rituals to guard their nest.

SANDERS, Liman von. See Liman von Sanders.

SANDHURST, Royal Military Academy at, sand'-hûrst, a training school for potential officers of the British Army, situated near Camberley, Surrey, about 30 miles (56 km) southwest of the center of London. It is often called simply "Sandhurst."

A royal military academy was established in 1802 at Great Marlow. The institution was moved to Sandhurst in 1812. Until after World War I, officers for the artillery, engineers, and signals were trained at the Royal Military Academy at Woolwich. A decision to concentrate all training at Sandhurst was made in 1940, but World War II postponed its implementation until 1947.

Most cadets enter the academy at the age of 19 and after an intensive course of about a year and a half receive commissions in various branches of the services.

SANDINO, sän-dē'nō, **Augusto César** (1893–1934), Nicaraguan guerrilla leader. He was born in 1893, the son of a coffee planter, and was educated in the state schools. In 1926 he joined the Liberal insurrection with a force of some 800 men, during the fighting with the Conservatives. In May 1927 the United States decided to intervene and to impose peace and disarmament on both sides, but the agreement negotiated at Tipitapa on May 3, 1927, was not recognized by Sandino, who refused to lay down his arms. He retired to the mountains of northern Nicaragua, and there successfully defied all efforts by the U. S. Marines to capture him.

When, on Jan. 3, 1933, the last marines were withdrawn from Nicaragua, Sandino and some 500 followers were still in defiant liberty, and had aroused the support of much of Latin America. On Feb. 2, 1933, Sandino made a peace agreement with President Juan Sacasa, and with 100 followers embarked on a cooperative farming project on the Coco River. Subsequently, however, conflicts arose between his followers and the national guard, and on Feb. 21, 1934, he went to the capital city of Managua to discuss with President Sacasa various means of terminating this friction. Sandino's assassi-

A sanderling, *Crocethia alba*, running before the surf

nation followed a dinner with the president; he, his brother Socrates, and two aides were seized by national guardsmen, taken to the airport, and shot. "Maladministration in the national guard" was first blamed, but within a week a movement was under way to justify Sandino's execution. An offer of amnesty by the government in the interests of peace was accepted by most of Sandino's followers. Whether Sandino is regarded as a "bandit," the official U. S. view, or as a patriot, his stand against intervention aroused anti-U. S. feeling in Latin America, which was mitigated only by the Good Neighbor Policy of President Franklin D. Roosevelt.

SANDOMIERZ, sän-dô′myesh, is a town in southeastern Poland in Kielce province, about 50 miles (80 km) southeast of Kielce on the Vistula River. It manufactures glass, rubber products, and textiles.

It became the capital of the principality of Sandomierz in the 12th century. Many buildings, including a 14th century castle, remain from the Middle Ages, when it was one of Poland's most prosperous towns. It was later under Austrian and Russian rule before being returned to Poland in 1919. Population: (1964 est.) 14,200.

SANDOZ, san′dōz, **Mari** (1901–1966), American novelist and historian of the western frontier. Mari Susette Sandoz was born in Sheridan county, Nebr., the daughter of Swiss immigrants. She studied intermittently at the University of Nebraska and taught school. In 1935 she published *Old Jules,* a biography of her father, which won the Atlantic Monthly Prize. In 1947 she began teaching writing at the University of Wisconsin. She died in New York City on March 10, 1966.

Miss Sandoz wrote more than 20 books on the history and folklore of the Nebraska plains and the cattle country of the Old West. She is noted for her colorful writing style and her meticulous research. Her best nonfiction includes *Crazy Horse* (1942), *The Cattlemen* (1958), and *These Were the Sioux* (1961). Her outstanding novels are *Slogum House* (1930), set in late 19th century Nebraska, and *Capital City* (1939), about the descendants of the Midwestern pioneers.

SANDPAPER is a sand-coated paper or fabric used chiefly for smoothing wood surfaces. Sandpaper is made by applying adhesive to one side of the paper or fabric and then depositing sand through a sieve, which controls the grain size. Sandpaper is less abrasive than glass paper in finishing wood. It is intermediate between glass paper and emery in smoothing a metal surface. See also ABRASIVES.

SANDPIPER, any of a large family of small to medium-sized shorebirds. There are approximately 75 species comprising the family Scolopacidae. The group is related to other families of shorebirds, such as the plovers and the oyster catchers, and, less closely, to the gulls, terns, and auks. The term "sandpiper" refers to the habits of these birds of running along sandy beaches uttering thin, piping notes. Sandpipers are good table birds, but their sociable habits and fearlessness permitted gunners to shoot unreasonable numbers. A number of species became very rare, and laws were passed protecting sandpipers throughout the year in Canada and the United States. In addition to the more typical sandpipers, the family Scolopacidae also contains some specialized or unusual types, such as the woodcock, snipe, and curlew.

The vast majority of the members of the sandpiper family nest in the Northern Hemisphere. They are especially abundant in the far north where the numerous pools and abundant insect life of the arctic tundra during the brief northern summer provide them with ideal nesting conditions. The nest is usually a mere depression in the sand or grass. Four rather large and pointed eggs are laid. When arranged with the pointed ends together at the center of the nest the eggs form a circle that the parent bird is just barely able to cover. Young sandpipers are long-legged, attractive little creatures, covered with buffy and yellowish down. They follow their parents as soon as they leave the shell and pick up their own food.

The plumage of sandpipers is attractive but not brilliant. In general, the feathers are mottled with gray and brown to match the background of sand and marsh. During the nesting season a brighter plumage is usually acquired, and the breast then is often reddish or chestnut. Unlike most birds the female sandpiper is in many species somewhat more brightly colored and larger than her mate. When this is the case, the female is often the more aggressive partner during courtship, while the male is left to perform most of the duties of incubation. There are others, however, such as the pectoral sandpiper (*Erolia melanotos*) and the ruff (*Philomachus pugnax*), in which the male is larger and more colorful.

Because the Arctic regions are completely unsuitable for sandpipers during the long winter months, the northern nesters are birds of powerful flight. Many of them nest right around the Arctic region with little variation from continent to continent and in the autumn fly thousands of miles to the south to winter in southern Africa, Argentina, and even in the Hawaiian Islands, New Zealand, and Australia. Others are more hardy and winter on the seacoasts north to the latitude of Long Island or New Jersey.

Sandpipers live mostly on small insects and other aquatic creatures. Their long legs and bills enable them to wade through shallow water and mud in search of their food. As a rule, they do not swim, though a few have the toes partially webbed or "semipalmated." Most sandpipers are highly gregarious and move about in large flocks. These flocks may contain but a single species or several species of about the same size. When in flight the members of a flock wheel and turn in perfect unison, as though guided by a single instinct.

The commonest and best-known sandpiper in North America is the spotted sandpiper (*Actitis macularia*). This bird is by no means restricted to the coast but is also found along almost every creek or pond on the continent. It is known to the farm boy as the "tip-up" because of its habit of teetering nervously up and down on its slender legs. This habit, shared by many species of birds that live along bodies of water, is thought to aid such species in judging distance. The spotted sandpiper is smaller than a robin, grayish above and white below, with black spots on the breast. These spots are lost during the winter and are absent at all seasons in the closely related common sandpiper (*A. hypoleucos*) of the Old World.

HUGH HALLIDAY, FROM NATIONAL AUDUBON SOCIETY

Least sandpipers (*Erolia minutilla*), the smallest of all sandpipers

Among those species that nest in the far north and migrate or winter along our ocean beaches, there are a number of species of small size, such as the least sandpiper (*Erolia minutilla*), the red-backed sandpiper (*E. alpina*), and the semipalmated sandpiper (*Ereunetes pusillus*). Some of these are no larger than sparrows and are most amusing and attractive as they run rapidly up and down the beaches following each receding wave in search of food. They are often known collectively as "peeps," and the hunter of a past generation would shoot large numbers of them to make "peep pie." Two related species, the purple sandpiper (*Erolia maritima*) of the North Atlantic and the rock sandpiper (*E. ptilocnemis*) of the North Pacific, are hardy enough to pass the winter along northern seacoasts and are only slightly migratory.

Another large and well-known group of sandpipers is that comprising the genus *Tringa*. It includes among American species the solitary sandpiper, and the two species of yellowlegs, and in the Old World the redshanks, the greenshanks, and the green and wood sandpipers. These are birds of larger size. The greater yellowlegs (*T. melanoleucus*), for example, stands about 1 foot (30 cm) high. When feeding it dashes about very actively in shallow water in pursuit of minnows and aquatic insects. The species of this genus are often called "tattlers" because of their loud, piercing cries, which seem to warn geese and other waterfowl of the presence of a hunter. The solitary sandpiper (*T. solitaria*) migrates along inland streams and ponds. As it alights it has the habit, shared by some other shorebirds, of gracefully elevating its wings above the back and then quickly folding them. Unlike its relatives, the solitary sandpiper does not nest on the ground but prefers to lay its eggs in an old nest of a robin or some such tree-nesting bird. One of the finest species of American sandpipers is the Bartramian sandpiper (*Bartramia longicauda*), or "upland plover" as it is called, though it is not a true plover. It is a bird of grassy plains and fields, seldom seen along beaches. About 12 inches (30 cm) in length, it is handsomely marked with brown and gray. All the notes of this bird are musical. The call note is a bubbling warble,

often heard as this bird migrates over at night. On the nesting grounds the upland plover mounts high in the air and, sailing on motionless wings, utters a long-drawn, haunting whistle. Such aerial songs or display flights are characteristic of a number of shorebirds. In winter the upland plover migrates all the way to the pampas of the Argentine. This species is a very close relative of the curlews.

DEAN AMADON
American Museum of Natural History

SANDRINGHAM, san'dring-əm, a royal estate in eastern England, in Norfolk County, is 7.5 miles (12 km) northeast of King's Lynn. It includes Sandringham House, a 200-acre (80-hectare) park, York cottage, and the Church of Mary Magdalene. The royal family are frequent visitors. Since the end of World War II, farming has been done on the estate to contribute to the royal economy.

In 1861 land consisting of 7,000 acres (2,833 hectares) was purchased and an Elizabethan-style house was built on it as a country residence for the Prince of Wales, who later became King Edward VII. George VI was born in York cottage and died in Sandringham House.

SANDS, Robert Charles (1799–1832), American editor, poet, and author, best known for his life of John Paul Jones. Sands was born in Flatbush, N. Y. (now part of Brooklyn), on May 11, 1799. He graduated from Columbia in 1815 and was admitted to the bar in 1820, but he devoted himself mainly to literature. In 1824 he established and edited the *Atlantic Magazine,* which later became the New York *Review,* and William Cullen Bryant joined him as editor from 1825 to 1827.

From 1827 until his death in Hoboken, N. J., on Dec. 17, 1832, Sands was on the editorial staff of the *Commercial Advertiser.* He wrote with Bryant and Congressman G. C. Verplanck a series of essays published in the form of an annual, *The Talisman* (1828–1830), in which appears one of his longest poems, *The Dream of the Princess Papantzin*. His *Life and Correspondence of John Paul Jones* was published in 1831.

SANDSTONE is a sedimentary rock formed by the consolidation of ancient beds of sand. Sometimes the sand grains were compacted solely by the weight of later, overlying deposits. More commonly they are held together by some kind of cementing material that partially or completely fills the spaces between the grains.

Physical Characteristics. When a sandstone is broken apart, it is usually the cementing material that fractures. The individual grains remain unbroken, giving to the fresh surface the granular appearance and feel that is characteristic of the rock. Sandstones that contain little cementing material are easily disintegrated into their original fragments of sand. The color of the stone depends upon its mineral composition. Most sandstones are light, ranging from white to buff, gray, and yellow, but they may also be red, brown, green, or other colors.

Sandstones usually were formed by the deposition of sand in marine waters and along beaches and the later compaction of these deposits. Some lake- and stream-deposited formations are also observed. All sandstones deposited in shallow waters may show ripple and wave marks as well as the impressions or traces of various animals. Generally they are more finely grained than the sandstones compacted from beach deposits, as are the occasional sandstones formed from wind-deposited dunes. The latter may show wind ripples.

Composition and Classification. The grains of a sandstone are primarily quartz and feldspar. Some sandstones also contain mica grains as well as fragments of many other kinds of rock. The cementing material, or matrix, can vary widely in composition. Among the most common constituents are clay minerals, calcite, hematite, limonite, and silica. A rock consisting almost entirely of cemented calcite fragments could also, in theory, be classified as a sandstone, but in fact it is called a limestone.

Sandstones are commonly separated into four major classes according to their mineral composition: quartzite, arkose, graywacke, and subgraywacke. Quartzite is the richest in silica, both in the matrix and in the grains themselves. Arkose sandstone is richer in feldspar than is quartzite. Graywacke represents a mixture of rounded to angular quartz, feldspar, and mica grains in a wide range of cementing materials. The name, which means "gray grit," refers to the coarse texture of the stone. Subgraywacke sandstone contains less feldspar than graywacke does, and its quartz grains are more rounded.

Sandstones may also be classified according to the size range of their sand grains, in the same way that sands are graded. See SAND.

Importance to Man. Throughout history, sandstone has been widely quarried and used as a building material, since sandstone in general is more easily cut and shaped than are hard rocks such as granite. The sandstone dimension-stone industry is decreasing in importance, but the rock is still significant as a construction material in the form of the crushed stone used in making concrete. Crushed sandstone is also employed in making pottery, porcelain, glass, abrasives, and foundry molds.

Sandstone beds themselves are of great importance to man, since they are commonly aquifers, or water-bearing layers of rock. They also often contain great deposits of oil and gas.

Further Reading: Spock, Leslie E., *Guide to the Study of Rocks* (Harper 1953).

SANDUSKY, san-dus′kē, a city in north-central Ohio, the seat of Erie county, is on Sandusky Bay of Lake Erie, 60 miles (96 km) west of Cleveland. It is a port of entry and an important shipping point for coal, and has extensive lake fishery operations. The city is also a manufacturing center, its products including boats, machinery, metal goods, plastics, paper, crayons and chalk, rubber goods, fertilizers, glues and pastes, lighting fixtures, and chemicals.

The surrounding region is farmland that grows fruits, which are processed in the city. The area's vineyards supply Sandusky's noted wineries. There are also deposits of sand, gravel, and clay nearby, which contribute to the city's industries.

The area was explored early by the French, and by 1749, English traders were frequenting the region. In 1763 a fort was built, but it was burned down the same year by Indians in the Pontiac Conspiracy. In 1813, Commodore Oliver Hazard Perry defeated a British squadron in the Battle of Lake Erie, fought at Put-in-Bay, north of Sandusky.

In 1816, settlers from New England called the place Portland, but when its plat was enlarged in 1818, the name was changed to Sandusky City, based on the corruption of an Indian word meaning "at the cold water"—referring to the cool springs nearby.

Sandusky City was made the seat of Erie county in 1838. The word "City" was dropped from its name and it was incorporated in 1845. Sandusky has a commission form of government. Population: 31,360.

SANDWICH, 4th Earl of (1718–1792), English political leader. John Montagu was born on Nov. 3, 1718. He was educated at Cambridge, traveled extensively, and in 1739 returned to England where he took his seat in the House of Lords and joined the Whig partisans led by the Duke of Bedford.

He served as first lord of admiralty in 1748, 1763, and from 1771 to 1782. He was appointed ambassador to Madrid in 1763, but before he could depart on his mission he was made one of the principal secretaries of state. While in this office, he took part in the prosecution of a former friend, John Wilkes. In 1768 he became postmaster general.

As first lord of the admiralty, he made his own gain and party interest of paramount importance, and his insufficient equipment of the navy was said to have caused much of the disaster that it encountered in those years. His administration was on the whole disastrous. Perhaps no man in the 18th century was held in more bitter contempt in England, partly because of his excessively immoral personal life, and he lived in virtual retirement after 1782. The Earl was the reputed inventor of the sandwich, for eating as a timesaver at the gaming table. He died in London on April 30, 1792.

SANDWICH, a market town on the southeastern coast of England, in the county of Kent, is on the Stour River at its mouth on the English Channel, about 60 miles (96 km) east of London. The tower of St. Clement's Church is a good example of Norman architecture, and there are Roman ruins. From the 11th century, Sandwich was one of the Cinque Ports. (See CINQUE PORTS.) In the 16th century, its harbor silted up. Population: (1961) 4,234.

SANDWICH, a town in southeastern Massachusetts, is situated on Cape Cod, about 60 miles (97 km) southeast of Boston. It is a typical old Cape Cod community and attracts many tourists. Places of interest include the Sandwich Glass Museum, with exhibits of the glassware for which the town was famous in the 19th century; the Hexie House and Dexter's Grist Mill; the Dexter Estate; the Heritage Plantation of Sandwich, which houses a general museum of transportation, American craftsmanship and military exhibits; and Yesteryear's Museum, an extensive collection of Caucasian and Oriental dolls, which is housed in the town's first parish meeting house, built in 1638.

Sandwich was settled in 1637 and incorporated in 1639. Population: 8,727.

SANDWICH ISLANDS. See HAWAII—*History.*

SANDWORM, any of various sand-dwelling marine worms that are often used as bait by fishermen. Sandworms are frequently found near the low-tide line along the seacoast of North America, often living in burrows lined with mucus from the worms' bodies. Some sandworms (genus *Nereis*) are known as clam worms. (See also CLAM WORM.)

Most sandworms are about 5 or 6 inches (12.5–15 cm) long and have segmented bodies. The sexes are separate, and the worms undergo a rather complex life cycle.

Sandworms are members of the class Polychaeta of the phylum Annelida.

SANDY HOOK, in eastern New Jersey, in Monmouth county, is a low, sandy peninsula that extends northward into the Atlantic Ocean from Atlantic Highlands. Its northern tip, or hook, which is 16 miles (24 km) south of New York City, is at the southern side of the entrance to Lower New York Bay.

The peninsula is about 5 miles (8 km) long and less than 1 mile (1.6 km) wide. Fort Hancock, a U. S. Army installation, is near the northern end, and a lighthouse, built in the late 1760's, stands at the northern tip.

In 1962, the federal government leased a large part of Sandy Hook to New Jersey for use as a state park. The park contains facilities for fishing and ocean bathing, and preserved natural areas, notably a holly forest. In the 1970's a proposal was made to include all of Sandy Hook in a Gateway National Recreation Area, which would include a total of 26,000 acres (10,522 hectares).

SANDYS, sandz, **Sir Edwin** (1561–1629), English parliamentarian, who was a major promoter of colonization in Virginia. The second son of Edwin Sandys, archbishop of York, and older brother of George Sandys, the poet and colonist, he was born in Worcestershire, England, on Dec. 9, 1561. He graduated from Corpus Christi College, Oxford, in 1579, studied law, traveled abroad, and entered Parliament. At first a strong supporter of James I, upon whose coronation in 1603 he was knighted, Sir Edwin became a behind-the-scenes leader of the parliamentary opposition, though he retained the favor of the king.

Sandys joined the Virginia Company of London (London Company) in 1607 and served as its treasurer from 1619 until 1624, when the company was dissolved and its interests vested in the crown. He was also a director of the East India Company and of The Somers Islands Company. Though he never visited Virginia, he maintained an interest in the affairs of its settlers until his death in October 1629, meanwhile sitting as an elder statesman of the parliamentary opposition.

SANDYS, sandz, **George** (1578–1644), English poet, traveler, and Virginia colonist, whose use of the heroic couplet paved the way for its use by Dryden and Pope. Sandys was born in Bishopsthorpe, Yorkshire, on March 2, 1578. He studied at Oxford and later traveled in France, Italy, Turkey, Egypt, and Palestine, publishing an account (1615) of his journeys that was of considerable ethnological and geographical value. He was appointed treasurer of the Virginia Company in 1621, succeeding his brother, Sir Edwin, and sailed for Virginia soon afterward. He was treasurer until 1625 and was appointed a member of the council in 1624 and again in 1626 and 1628. In 1631, after some controversy concerning his alleged infringements of the rights of other settlers, he returned to England.

While in Virginia, Sandys completed his translation of the first ten books of Ovid's *Metamorphoses* (1626), upon which his reputation as a poet largely rests. His use of a very syntactically balanced form of the heroic couplet anticipated the efforts of Dryden and Pope, who made it the major vehicle of English neoclassical poetry in the 18th century. He also was the author of *A Paraphrase upon the Psalms of David and upon the Hymnes Dispersed throughout the Old and New Testaments* (1636) and translated Hugo Grotius' *Christ Passion* from the Latin (1640). Sandys died in Boxley, near Maidstone, Kent, on March 4, 1644.

SANFORD, Edward Terry (1865–1930), American judge. He was born in Knoxville, Tenn., on July 23, 1865. He was educated at the University of Tennessee and at Harvard University (LL. B. 1889), and was admitted to the Tennessee bar in 1888. He was U. S. assistant attorney general in 1907–1908 and U. S. district judge for eastern and middle district of Tennessee in 1908–1923. He served as an associate justice of the U. S. Supreme Court from 1923 until his death in Washington, D. C., on March 8, 1930.

Sanford wrote opinions in some important cases, including *Gitlow* v. *New York* (1925), from which Holmes and Brandeis dissented, which upheld a conviction for publishing a communist manifesto. But he took a more liberal view in a later opinion on a similar subject.

SANFORD, a city in central Florida, the seat of Seminole county, is situated on Lake Monroe and the St. Johns River, about 20 miles (32 km) northeast of Orlando. Among the industries in the city and the surrounding area are citrus fruit packing and shipping, the manufacture of boats, mobile homes, women's knit dresses and suits, men's and boys' shirts and pajamas, commercial telephone equipment, and capacitors. Research and development of electronic systems are carried on.

The community grew up around Mellonville, a trading post established in 1837 near a fort. In 1870, Henry Shelton Sanford bought land here, including the townsite, and the city was named in his honor. Government is by council and manager. Population: 23,176.

SANFORD, a town in southwestern Maine, in York county, is on the Mousam River about 35 miles (56 km) southwest of Portland. It is an industrial center that manufactures aircraft and aircraft components, acrylic plastic sheets, shoes, plastic heels and dowel lifts, woolen yarns, carpeting, electronic components, and woven labels.

The land for the site of the town was purchased from the Indians in 1661, but no permanent settlement was made until about 1740. The community was first called Phillipstown in honor of one of the original grantees. It was incorporated in 1768 and named for Peleg Sanford, stepson of the grantee. Industrial development began in 1867, when a factory began making carriage robes and blankets.

The town of Sanford includes the unincorporated areas of Sanford Center and Springvale. Government is by a town meeting and a board of selectmen. Population: 18,020.

SANFORD, a city in central North Carolina, the seat of Lee county, is a shipping and industrial center, about 40 miles (64 km) southwest of Raleigh. The city is important for its tobacco market. Its industries include textiles, wearing apparel, electronics, construction, furniture, brick and tile, and machinery.

Sanford was incorporated in 1874. It has a mayor-council form of government. Population: 14,773.

SANGALLO, säng-gäl'lō, a family of 15th and 16th century Florentine architects and military engineers, who worked in various Italian cities in the Renaissance style. Members of the Giamberti and Cordiani families, they were called Sangallo from their home near the Porto San Gallo. The most important were the brothers Giuliano and Antonio and their nephew Antonio.

GIULIANO DA SANGALLO (C. Giamberti; c. 1445–1516) did his most important work in and around Florence. The Villa di Poggio a Canaiano for Lorenzo dé Medici was built in the style of a Roman temple, on a raised terrace, with a columned and pedimented facade. The Church of the Madonna delle Carceri in Prato was one of the first churches in Italy to be built on a Greek-cross plan. Giuliano also built the monastery of Santa Maria Maddalena dei Pazzi, the sacristy of the Church of Santo Spirito, the Palazzo Strozzi, and fortifications. He began the Basilica of Loreto and worked on St. Peter's in Rome.

ANTONIO DA SANGALLO THE ELDER (A. Giamberti; c. 1455–1535) at first built fortifications, such as those at Civita Castellana for Cesare Borgia. Late in life he built at Montepulciano the Church of San Biagio on a Greek-cross plan and several classical palaces.

ANTONIO DA SANGALLO THE YOUNGER (A. Cordiani; 1483–1546) worked chiefly in and near Rome. He built several churches, including Santa Maria di Loreto and the Pauline Chapel in the Vatican, and was assigned to St. Peter's. He also built the Mint, the Palazzo Farnese (a model for later Roman palaces), other palaces and villas, and the defenses for Civitavecchia and other cities.

SANGAMON INTERGLACIAL STAGE, sang'gə-mən, the most recent of the three North American interglacial stages that are generally recognized by geologists in the chronology of the ice ages of the Pleistocene Epoch. The Sangamon interglacial lies between the Wisconsin and the preceding Illinoisan periods of extended glaciation. The corresponding time and rock divisions in European geology are the Riss-Würm interglacial and the Würm and Riss glaciations, respectively. Such divisions and their dating are very imprecise, but the Sangamon interglacial may be considered to have begun somewhat more than 100,000 years ago and to have ended approximately 70,000 years ago.

SANGER, sang'ər, **Frederick** (1918–   ), British biochemist, who was a pioneer in establishing the chemical structure of proteins. He received the 1958 Nobel Prize in chemistry for his work on the structure of proteins, particularly that of insulin.

Life. Sanger was born in Rendcombe on Aug. 13, 1918. The son of a physician, he was educated at Bryanston School and at St. John's College, Cambridge University, where he received his doctor's degree in biochemistry in 1943. From 1940 he did research in biochemistry at Cambridge, holding the Beit Memorial Fellowship for Medical Research from 1944 to 1951. In the latter year he joined the staff of the British Medical Research Council, where he became head of the division on protein chemistry. In 1954 he was elected a fellow of the Royal Society, London. His publications consisted chiefly of papers in biochemical periodicals.

Contributions to Science. Sanger's early work involved the study of the free amino groups of proteins. Proteins consist largely of amino-acid residues, arranged sequentially in polypeptide chains. In order to determine their chemical structure, these chains can be fragmented by hydrolysis to shorter chains (oligopeptides) and then to free amino acids.

Sanger sought to identify the free amino groups of proteins by substituting for them DNP (dinitrophenyl) radicals. For this purpose he used FDNB (1-fluoro-2, 4-dinitrobenzene), a chemical that is now commonly known as Sanger's reagent. After substitution, the proteins were hydrolyzed, and the resulting yellow N-DNP derivatives of amino acids were separated by partition chromatography. (See CHROMATOGRAPHY–*Partition.*) These procedures found additional application in assessing chemical damage to–and thus impoverishment of–the nutritive value of proteins, and in analyzing amino acids.

Beginning in 1945, Sanger spent more than 10 years applying these and other techniques to investigating the structure of insulin, the antidiabetic hormone. Evidence obtained through crystallography and other physicochemical means had already indicated that the insulin protein has low molecular weight and high homogeneity. Even so, Sanger's contemporaries thought him overambitious in attempting to analyze the structure of insulin.

Sanger's technique in carrying out his analysis was to make a partial breakdown of the insulin protein into oligopeptides small enough to be separated and identified by the methods then available. By piecing together the information he had obtained, he established by 1955 the arrangement of the 51 amino-acid residues composing the molecule of ox insulin. He discovered that the insulin molecule was made up of two chains, with 20 amino-acid residues in the A-chain and 31 in the B-chain.

Sanger also showed that insulin preparations from different mammals had similar molecular structures, except for the amino-acid sequence comprising positions 8, 9, and 10 in the A-chain of the molecule. Several groups of chemists in following years confirmed Sanger's structure of the insulin molecule by using it as the basis for the chemical synthesis of insulin in the laboratory.

Because Sanger's work demonstrated that insulin is a chemical entity in the organic chemist's sense, scientists were encouraged to study the structures of other proteins. Other important consequences of his work were, firstly, the establishment of a chemical basis for the phenomenon of species specificity in proteins, which shed new light on their evolution; and, secondly, the discovery that protein-splitting enzymes attack the same linkages in proteins as in oligopeptides. Sanger later developed precise ultramicro methods for studying protein structures in connection with genetic problems.

R. L. M. SYNGE
Nobel Prize Winner in Chemistry, 1952

SANGER, Margaret (1883–1966), American birth-control advocate who was a founder and leader of the birth-control movement in the United States. She promoted the idea of birth control as a basic human right that should be available to all.

Margaret Sanger was born in Corning, N. Y., on Sept. 14, 1883, sixth of the 11 children of Michael and Anne Purcell Higgins. She attended Claverack College, then studied nursing at White Plains (N. Y.) Hospital and at Manhattan Eye and Ear Hospital. In 1900 she married William Sanger, an architect. To supplement the family income after the birth of her second son, Mrs. Sanger worked as an obstetrical nurse in the lower East Side of Manhattan. She was divorced from Sanger, but retained his name professionally, and in 1922 married the industrialist Noah H. Slee.

Margaret Sanger, pioneer advocate of birth control.

The turning point of Mrs. Sanger's life had come in 1912, when a young tenement mother died in her arms of a self-induced abortion. Mrs. Sanger determined to emancipate women from what she viewed as the servitude of unwanted pregnancy. In 1913 she went to Europe, where contraceptive knowledge was more advanced. While studying there she coined the term "birth control."

After returning to the United States in 1914, she founded the magazine *Woman Rebel* to advance her views. In defiance of New York law, she opened in 1916 the first birth-control clinic in the United-States in the Brownsville section of Brooklyn. The clinic was soon raided, and Mrs. Sanger was arrested and jailed. Despite numerous other arrests and formidable opposition, she pursued her cause. Through speaking tours in the United States and in Europe, and by means of published articles, she gradually interested some influential people. In 1917, with the help of suffragette leaders, she founded the National Birth Control League, which became the Planned Parenthood Federation of America.

Mrs. Sanger was instrumental in organizing the first International Birth Control Congress, which met in Geneva, Switzerland, in 1927. The culmination of her work came in 1952, in Bombay, India, when the International Planned Parenthood Federation was established, with Margaret Sanger as its first president. She died on Sept. 6, 1966, in Tucson, Ariz.

SANGER is a city in central California, in Fresno county, about 15 miles (24 km) east of Fresno. Electric wiring, automobile heaters, and blue jeans are manufactured. Grapes, oranges, plums, and peaches are packed and shipped, and frozen foods are processed. Sanger was incorporated in 1911 and is governed by a council and city manager. Population: 12,558.

SANGIHE ISLANDS, säng'ē, in Indonesia, midway between the northeastern tip of Sulawesi (Celebes) and the southermost point of Mindanao in the Philippines. The Sangihe group, which is volcanic and subject to earthquakes, includes Sangihe, Siau, Tahulandang, and several smaller islands. The largest, Sangihe, is about 30 miles (50 km) long and 8 to 17 miles (13–27 km) wide. It contains the chief port, Tahuna. The islands' total area is 314 square miles.

The group has a wet tropical climate and fertile volcanic soil. The chief products are nutmeg, coconuts, manila hemp, and timber. The people of the islands were converted to Christianity during the period of Dutch rule, which lasted from 1677 to 1949. Population: (1961) about 125,000.

SANGSTER, Charles (1822–1893), Canadian poet, one of the first to use Canadian themes in verse. Sangster was born in Kingston, Upper Canada (now Ontario), on July 16, 1822. He became editor of the Amherstburg *Courier* in 1849, but shortly afterward he returned to Kingston and became a journalist. He also worked in the post office department at Ottawa from 1868 to 1886. Sangster died in Kingston on Dec. 9, 1893.

The highly patriotic character of Sangster's verse is credited with greatly advancing the cause of confederation in Canada. He was the author of *Saint Lawrence and the Saguenay* (1856) and *Hesperus and Other Poems* (1860).

SANHEDRIN, san-hed'rin, the highest Jewish court and chief legislative council, which functioned from postexilic times until after the destruction of the Temple in Jerusalem in 70 A. D. The Great Sanhedrin consisted of 71 members, with the high priest as its president. The Sanhedrin was also the name given to lower courts of 23 members that existed in the larger Jewish communities. The word *sanhedrin* is derived from the Greek word meaning "assembly." According to rabbinical tradition the institution of the Sanhedrin can be traced to the time of Moses and the council of elders mentioned in Numbers 11: 10–24, but most scholars reject this view.

Origins and Early History. It is most likely that the Sanhedrin developed from the council of elders, alluded to in Ezra 5:5 and Nehemiah 2:16, that helped organize the exiles who had returned from Babylon. Some scholars believe that there were actually two Great Sanhedrins, one that dealt purely with religious questions of the interpretation of the Mosaic Law and another whose province was civil matters. It would seem more likely that one Sanhedrin existed, the extent of whose authority changed as Palestine came under the domination of one or another power.

The Sanhedrin was an aristocratic body whose president was the chief priest, a hereditary office. Its members were drawn from the priestly families, the scribes, and teachers of the law. It had representatives of both the Sadducaic and the Pharisaic parties among its members.

Roman Period. When the Romans under Pompey took control of Palestine in 63 B. C., the monarchy was destroyed. John Hyrcanus II was appointed high priest and ethnarch of the Jews. Gabinius, proconsul of Syria from 57 to 55 B. C., deprived Hyrcanus of civil authority and divided Jewish territory into five districts, each with its own sanhedrin. Julius Caesar restored Hyrcanus as high priest and ethnarch in 47 B. C., and it seems that the power of the Jerusalem Sanhedrin was also restored.

Herod the Great (reigned 37–4 B. C.) effectively controlled the Sanhedrin by making the office of high priest no longer hereditary and by successively appointing seven high priests. In 6 A. D., Palestine was segmented and placed under Roman procurators. Under direct Roman control most of the internal rule of the Jewish populace was in the hands of the Sanhedrin. However, the Roman authority could by-pass it any time it saw fit. It is disputed whether the Sanhedrin had the power to inflict the death penalty. In the case of Christ, their decision was referred to Pilate, the Roman procurator (John 18:31).

The high priest convened the sessions of the Sanhedrin. After the death of Herod the Great the high priest was appointed by the Roman authorities, who took care to choose from the priestly families. Agrippa II, who was allowed by the Romans to assume the title of king, was also given the authority to name the high priest in 49 A. D. The rebellion of 66 A. D., which ended in the destruction of the Temple in Jerusalem in 70 A. D., also brought about the effective destruction of the Sanhedrin's political authority. Thereafter, it dealt only with religious questions. The Sanhedrin that was established by the council of Jamnia in 90 A. D. had only moral force and was primarily an assembly of teachers and scholars.

Further Reading: Hoenig, Sidney B., *The Great Sanhedrin* (Bloch 1953).

SANIDINE, san'i-dēn, or glassy feldspar, is a variety of orthoclase. The mineral is commonly found as relatively large, often transparent crystals embedded in geologically recent igneous rocks. See FELDSPAR–*Potash Feldspars.*

SANITARY ENGINEERING is the branch of engineering that deals with the promotion and conservation of the public health, comfort, and convenience. See AIR POLLUTION; INSECT CONTROL; SEPTIC TANK; WASTE DISPOSAL; WASTEWATER; WATER POLLUTION; WATER SUPPLY.

SANITATION is the application of measures to make environmental conditions favorable to health. See PUBLIC HEALTH; WASTEWATER; WATER POLLUTION; WATER SUPPLY.

SANKEY, sang'kē, **Ira David** (1840–1908), American evangelist known for his hymn singing. Sankey was born in Edinburg, Pa., on Aug. 28, 1840. He worked as a clerk in a bank in Newcastle, Pa., of which his father became president in 1857, and, after serving with the Union Army in the Civil War, he again took a position with his father, who had become a collector of internal revenue. Meanwhile, Sankey had sung in the choir of the Methodist Church at Newcastle and had been chosen its choir leader and superintendent of its Sunday school.

Sankey was also active in the Young Men's Christian Association and was made a delegate to its convention in Indianapolis in 1870. It was here that he met Dwight L. Moody, the evangelist with whom he was intimately associated until Moody's death in 1899. In 1873 they went to Britain to conduct evangelistic services. Sankey's contribution was his singing. Although his voice was not a great one, the simplicity and expressiveness of his singing profoundly moved audiences. When the evangelists returned to the United States in 1875, they carried on an extensive evangelistic crusade. Royalties from their very popular hymn collections, *Sacred Songs and Solos* (1873) and *Gospel Hymns* (1875–1891), were given largely to support the Northfield School in Massachusetts, which Sankey had established. Sankey died in Brooklyn, N. Y., on Aug. 13, 1908.

SANKHYA, säng'kyə, or *samkhya,* one of the six orthodox philosophies of Hinduism. See also HINDUISM–*Formal Philosophies.*

SANKT GALLEN, zängkt gäl'ən, is a city in Switzerland and capital of Sankt Gallen canton, which is in the northeastern section of the country. The French form of its name is Saint-Gall. The city is in the northeastern part of the canton, on the Steinach River, about 50 miles (80 km) east of Zürich. It is an industrial center manufacturing textiles, chemicals, and food products.

Saint Gall, a Celtic missionary, settled along the Steinach in 612 and was later joined by disciples. The city grew up around a Benedictine abbey, established in the 8th century, that became a noted center of learning during the Middle Ages. The most imposing structures in the city, the cathedral and the adjacent abbey buildings, attest to the prominent role of religion in the city's history. The cathedral, built in 1755–1768, is a baroque structure with two richly decorated towers at the front. The interior decoration is also lavish, particularly the chancel. There are frescoes on the central dome and numerous murals. The abbey library, the Stiftsbibliothek, designed and built during the cathedral's construction, contains thousands of rare manuscripts and books. The splendor of the rococo interior, with dazzling parquet floors, painted ceilings, and intricate woodwork, overshadows the valuable collections.

The Canton. The canton is in the German-speaking section of Switzerland, and the majority of the people are Roman Catholics. Sankt Gallen surrounds the half-cantons of Appenzell Inner Rhoden and Appenzell Ausser Rhoden and is bounded on the north by Lake Constance and Thurgau canton and on the west and south by Zürich, Schwyz, Glarus, and Graubünden cantons. On the east is the Rhine River, which separates the canton from Liechtenstein and forms most of its Austrian border.

It has an area of 777 square miles (2,012 sq km) and varies in altitude from 1,309 feet (399 meters) at Lake Constance to more than 10,000 feet (3,050 meters) in the Alps in the south. The canton is a center of the Swiss textile industry, producing muslin, laces, and embroideries. It was admitted to the Swiss Confederation in 1803. Population: (1970) of the city, 80,852; of the canton, 384,475.

SANLÚCAR DE BARRAMEDA, sän-lōō′kär thä vär-rä-mä′thä, is a city in southwestern Spain in Cádiz province, in the region of Andalusia. It is a seaport at the mouth of the Quadalquivir River, 17 miles (27 km) north of Cádiz, and is a summer resort. Among the buildings of interest are several convents and the palace of the dukes of Medina Sidonia, which contains valuable art treasures. The St. George Hospital (1517) was founded by King Henry VIII of England.

The chief occupations of the inhabitants are fishing and growing wine grapes. Andalusia's characteristic wine, manzanilla, is matured in cellars in the city. Its location on the Quadalquivir below Seville made Sanlúcar an important port at the height of the Spanish Empire. Columbus embarked from Sanlúcar in 1498 on his third voyage to the New World, and Magellan sailed from the town in 1519 to begin his global voyage. Population: (1960) 32,580.

SANNAZARO, sän-nä-dzä′rō, **Jacopo** (1458–1530), Italian poet and epigrammatist, who is most famous for his *Arcadia* (1504), a lyric pastoral poem that influenced the English poet Philip Sidney. Sannazaro was born in Naples on July 28, 1458. After study under A. Pontano (Pontanus), he was admitted to the Arcadian Academy as *Actius Sincerus*, the name he selected to be known by, according to the prevailing custom. He spent several years in foreign travel and on his return to Naples soon became famous as a poet and courtier. His verse attracted the attention of King Ferdinand I of Naples and his sons Alfonso and Frederick. When Frederick ascended the throne in 1496, he gave Sannazaro the villa of Mergellina and a pension of 600 ducats. In 1501, when Frederick was forced into exile by Louis XII, Sannazaro accompanied him to France and remained with him until his death in 1504.

During this period Sannazaro completed *Arcadia*. Written in Italian, it is an allegorical and semiautobiographical account of the unrequited love of Sincero, who retires to Arcadia

SWISS NATIONAL TOURIST OFFICE

The cathedral in Sankt Gallen, built between 1755 and 1768, is noted for its baroque and rococo interior.

and the life of a shepherd. Sannazaro's subsequent works include *De partu Virginis* (1526), a Latin poem that earned him the title of the "Christian Virgil," and his collected *Sonetti e canzoni* (1530). His elegance of expression, no less than the poetical beauty of his thoughts, give him a distinguished place among poets of the Renaissance. Sannazaro died in Naples on April 27, 1530. See also ARCADIA.

SANS-CULOTTES, sän-kü-lôt′, a term applied from 1789, during the French Revolution, to France's lower classes—the shopkeepers, artisans, and workers. The term means "without knee-breeches" and was used by aristocrats, who wore knee-breeches, to refer contemptuously to those who wore long trousers. The name was associated with the republicans of Paris who worked with the Jacobins. As applied by the sans-culottes to themselves, it was a complimentary name like "patriot." The last five days (six in leap years) of the Revolutionary Calendar were festivals called the sans-culottides.

SANSEVIERIA, san-sə-vēr′ē-ə, a genus of tropical plants with stiff upright leaves. Commonly known as snake plants, sansevieria are popular, hardy houseplants. See SNAKE PLANT.

SANSKRIT, san'skrit, is the oldest stage of the Indo-Aryan subfamily of Indo-European languages.

History. Bands of Indo-European speakers seem to have emerged from the country north of the Caspian Sea into the Middle East in the first half of the 2d millennium B. C. Some of them, after various vicissitudes, settled in Iran, where their language developed into the Iranian languages called Old Persian, Avestan, Middle Persian, and later Pahlavi, Persian, and others. The other branch seems to have experienced various wanderings. From proper names and other material in their records some are known to have formed an element in the Mitannian and Kassite kingdoms of northern Syria and Mesopotamia (about 16th–14th centuries B. C.). Their much better known linguistic brethren went east toward India and invaded the Indus Valley, probably in the first half of the 2d millennium B. C.; the chronology is very uncertain. Here these horse and cattle nomads seem to have met a people with a highly developed urban civilization (the Harappa culture). Apparently they destroyed what they found and enslaved the people.

The invaders were Indo-Aryan speakers, and the native people were possibly Dravidian speakers. The Indo-Aryans finally settled for a time in the Punjab (upper Indus Valley) and there produced at least the earlier parts of the Vedic ritual literature. They spoke a number of dialects, one of which is the nucleus of the old Vedic language. There are, however, traces of other dialects in this literature. For example, it is usually held that both *l* and *r* of Indo-European became *r* in the basic Vedic language, but that in another dialect of the time both *l* and *r* became *l*, and that some words with *l* were borrowed from this dialect into the basic Vedic language.

As time went on within the Vedic period, which probably is to be considered as ending about the middle of the 1st millennium B. C., there was expansion of the Indo-Aryan speakers eastward down the Ganges Valley. In time and in space new dialects evolved among all classes of the people. The language spoken in everyday life diverged more and more from the old language of the ritual, and even before the end of the Vedic period many speakers of Indo-Aryan were using dialects that had features later found in Middle Indic (Prakrit). Some forms of this type were even used when new ritual literature was composed, and some of the latest ritual compositions were included even in the first of the compilations known as the Vedas—the Rig Veda (*Ṛgveda*). There was also borrowing into the Vedic language of words from the Dravidian languages of the original population, both the people of the Harappa culture and the inhabitants of the Ganges Valley whom the invaders met in their eastward expansion.

A concern for verbal accuracy in ritual utterances seems to have troubled the Vedic peoples very early. At some time in the Vedic period this concern led to the growth of a technique for preserving accuracy—namely grammar—in the sense of describing accurately the sounds and forms of the desirable utterances and in the further sense of prescribing what was desirable and teaching what was to be avoided. A long series of Vedic grammarians, whose works are the *Prātiśākhyas*, culminated, through stages whose details are far from certain, in Panini (about the 5th century B. C.). He, however, described in his grammar—the *Aṣṭādhyāyī*, or "eight-chaptered work"—his own spoken language, which was not quite the same as the old Vedic and was also not the Middle Indic that some communities were already speaking. He was interested in some Vedic forms but gave them only as divergences from the dialect that he spoke and was primarily interested in describing. His language was as much a true Old Indic as Vedic was, but a somewhat different dialect. He was born in Salatura in what is now the North-West Frontier province of Pakistan, but this fact throws little light on the nature of the local dialects of his time.

From Panini's time on, spoken dialects diverged more and more from the norm he had described, but with minor exceptions all who wrote with an eye to acceptance by the learned followed his description. They wrote, and even learned in their schools to speak, in a literary language that was less and less the language of everyday life. To this literary language they gave the name Sanskrit (*saṃskṛta*), the "polished" or "cultivated" or "refined" or "perfected" language, as opposed to the everyday languages, which they called Prakrit (*prākṛta*), the "natural" languages. The literary Sanskrit, as the heir of the Vedic religious tradition, became the vehicle of Hindu culture and has remained down to the most recent times the language in which traditional Hinduism of India has found its expression through its learned custodians, the Brahmans. The situation is very like that of Latin, which was the vehicle of the classical and medieval culture of Europe and still lives today in the liturgical and other writings of the Roman Catholic Church.

Description. The two dialects of Old Indic—Vedic and Sanskrit—are in structure very like Latin and classical Greek. They have complex inflectional systems for nouns, adjectives, pronouns, and verbs. Nouns, adjectives, and pronouns have the categories of number (singular, dual, plural), gender (masculine, feminine, neuter), and case (nominative, accusative, instrumental, dative, ablative, genitive, locative, vocative). The Vedic verb has categories of voice (active and middle), mood (indicative, subjunctive, optative, imperative), tense (present, imperfect, perfect, aorist, future), number, and person. The present stems of verbs show a large number of different types, formed by various suffixes and infixes and by reduplication. In addition to the simple verb, there are secondary verb types—passive, causative, desiderative, intensive—and some combinations of these (for example, a passive of the causative), which show forms in most of the categories of the simple verb. Like the Indo-European languages in general, this language has many combinations of verb forms with adverbial prefixes, with the meanings of the combinations very often not obtainable by a simple addition (compare English *understand*). The Sanskrit verb system differs from the Vedic in that it shows fewer of the categories (for example, the subjunctive is almost totally disused and the aorists are moribund), but since Panini taught much of the Vedic verb system there was a tendency for learned literary men to use many of the strictly Vedic forms in order to show their erudition. As in Latin and Greek, stems, suffixes, and prefixes often have several different phonetic forms depending on their phonetic surroundings. This feature applies also to words within sentences: for example, *nalo vadati* (Nala is speaking), *nalaḥ pacati* (Nala is cooking), *nalas tiṣṭhati* (Nala is standing), with three forms of the nominative singular meaning "Nala." Again, as in Latin and Greek, sometimes a number of different categories are carried by one unanalyzable form: for example, in such a form as *asmi* ("I am") the unanalyzable suffix *-mi* is first person, singular number, present tense, indicative mode, active voice. And the same category is often represented by very different forms in different word classes.

This highly complex morphology was described by Panini in a degree of detail and systematic lucidity that was not achieved for Latin and Greek or for the modern languages of Europe until recent times. When Sanskrit became known to Europeans toward the end of the 18th century, it was learned in the traditional way, through the medium of Panini's grammar. With this systematic guide, the English scholar Sir William Jones announced—in 1786 in a famous address that he delivered in Calcutta—that Sanskrit, Greek, and Latin "have sprung from some common source which, perhaps, no longer exists." He suspected that the Germanic and the Celtic languages probably had the same origin. This was the seed from which sprang Indo-European comparative grammar, the branch of linguistics that sets forth in all detail the relationship posited by Jones. His "perhaps" has turned out to be "certainly." At times his clear vision was neglected and it was suggested that Sanskrit was really the common source of the other languages. After this was firmly proved to be incorrect, it was for a long time held that Sanskrit was at least more archaic in its sounds than the other languages of the group. Even this has turned out to be only partly correct. The vowel system of Sanskrit is less archaic than that of classical Greek (for example, *a*, *e*, and *o* of Indo-European have all become *a* in Sanskrit but have remained separate in Greek), and its consonant system shows a good deal of change through palatalization and other modifications. On the other hand, the Vedic language preserved more traces of the old Indo-European system of semivowels than has any other of the languages. In spite of all the Sanskrit changes, the sys-

tematic relationships of the Indo-European vowels were partially preserved in Sanskrit (the ablaut system), and the Hindu grammarians' systematic description of the relationships put scholars on the right path toward a lucid understanding of the much richer system seen in Greek. Sanskrit is only one of the Indo-European languages and not the one with the oldest records (Hittite holds that position with at least one document datable in the 17th century B. C.). The material, however, that Sanskrit yields for Indo-European studies and its historical role in those studies still make it one of the primary languages in that branch of linguistic discipline.

MURRAY B. EMENEAU
University of California, Berkeley

Further Reading: Burrow, Thomas, *The Sanskrit Language*, 2d ed. (Barnes & Noble 1965); Lamman, Charles R., *Sanskrit Reader* (Harvard Univ. Press 1883); Macdonell, Arthur A., *A Practical Sanskrit Dictionary* (Oxford 1924); Macdonell, Arthur A., *Sanskrit Grammar for Students*, 3d ed. (Oxford 1927); Monier-Williams, M., *Dictionary of English and Sanskrit* (Verry 1970); Perry, Edward D., *Sanskrit Primer* (Columbia Univ. Press 1959).

SANSKRIT LITERATURE. See INDIA—*Literature* (Classical Literature).

SANSOVINO, sän-sō-vē′nō, **Andrea** (c. 1460–1529), Florentine sculptor of the High Renaissance. Andrea Contucci, known as Sansovino, from his birthplace, was born in Monte San Savino, Tuscany. He was trained in Florence under Antonio Pollaiuolo and worked with Bertoldo di Giovanni and Giuliano da Sangallo. In 1491, Lorenzo de' Medici sent him to Portugal to work for John II. Sansovino remained there until 1501, except for the years 1493–1496, which he spent sculpting reliefs for the Baptistery in Florence.

From 1501 to 1513, Sansovino worked chiefly in Florence and Rome. In Florence he executed such sculptures as the *Christ and St. John* over the door of the Baptistery (1502) and the altar for the Corbinelli in the Church of Santo Spirito. In Rome he carved the elaborate tombs of the cardinals Ascanio Sforza and G. B. della Rovere in the Church of Santa Maria del Populo and the *Virgin, Child, and St. Anne* for the Church of San Agostino (1512). He also carved a *Madonna* and

Andrea Sansovino's *Baptism of Christ* stands over the east portal of the Baptistery in Florence.

The Palazzo Corner della Cà Grande (1532), Venice, was designed by Jacopo Sansovino.

a *St. John the Baptist* for the Cathedral of Genoa. In 1513 he was entrusted by Leo X with the sculpture for the Holy House of the Virgin in the Church of the Holy House in Loreto. He completed three reliefs there—the *Annunciation,* the *Nativity,* and *Jeremiah.*

Sansovino's work, influenced by Raphael and classical sculpture, blends classical severity of style and subordination of detail with the freshness of the Renaissance spirit grounded in a thorough study of nature. The expression and action of his figures are full of feeling, yet they never overstep the bounds of dignity and moderation. Sansovino died in Monte San Savino.

SANSOVINO, sän-sō-vē′nō, **Il** (1486–1570), Italian architect and sculptor, who brought to Venice the High Renaissance style. Jacopo Tatti (Il Sansovino) was born in Caprese, near Florence, on July 2, 1486. He was trained and adopted by the Florentine sculptor Andrea Sansovino, whose name he took. Sansovino worked in Florence (1511–1517) and in Rome (1518–1527), where he was part of Bramante's circle. Works of this period, influenced by Andrea Sansovino and by classical sculpture, include, in Florence, *Bacchus* (Bargello) and *St. James* (Duomo) and in Rome, the tombs of Cardinal G. Michiel and Bishop Orso (San Marcello), and the *Madonna del Parto* (San Agostino).

After the sack of Rome in 1527, Sansovino settled in Venice, where as state superintendent of building, he built many palaces, churches, and civic structures, ornamenting them with sculpture. The Palazzo Corner (Ca' Grande, designed 1532), with its two column-fronted stories above a rusticated ground floor, so successfully combined classical architecture with the Venetian style that it became the model for later palaces.

His masterpiece, the Old Library (begun 1536; completed by V. Scamozzi, 1588) consists of two long low stories with arcades and balus-

trades, a design borrowed by Palladio. The facade is enriched by sculptured figures, festoons, and other motifs. The Logetta (1537, rebuilt 1902), at the base of the Campanile, is adorned with four classical bronzes, stone reliefs, and, inside the portico, the charming terra-cotta *Madonna with Child and St. John the Baptist.*

Sansovino's Venetian sculptures, powerful and fluid yet restrained, include the *Madonna and Child* (1534; Arsenal) and the huge *Mars* and *Neptune* on the stairs in the courtyard of the Palazzo Ducale (1554). He died in Venice on Nov. 27, 1570.

SANTA ANA, an′ə, a city in southwestern California, is the seat of Orange county. It is on the Santa Ana River, just west of the Santa Ana Mountains, and is situated 15 miles (24 km) east of Long Beach and 35 miles (56 km) southeast of Los Angeles. It is the center of the agricultural Santa Ana Valley. The city's industry includes the manufacture of aircraft, electronic parts, rubber goods, fiber glass, engines, and radios.

Places of interest include the Charles W. Bowers Memorial Museum, which contains exhibits of early California history and Indian artifacts; the Orange County Historical Society museum; and Movieland of the Air, which contains a large collection of antique aircraft. Santa Ana College is a junior college.

Santa Ana was founded in 1869, and was incorporated in 1886. It has a council manager form of government. Population: 204,023.

SANTA ANA, sän′tä ä′nä, is a city in western El Salvador and the capital of Santa Ana department. It is situated at an altitude of about 2,100 feet (640 meters) in a mountain-encircled valley, about 35 miles (56 km) north of San Salvador and 20 miles (32 km) east of the Guatemala border. It is the commercial center for the valley, which produces coffee and sugarcane, and the business center of western El Salvador. Santa Ana has one of the largest coffee mills in the world. Sugar refining is also important and there is some light industry.

The city has an impressive Gothic cathedral and a number of other fine old buildings, including the Renaissance Theater and the colonial-style Church of El Calvario. Lake Coatepeque, a popular resort, is 12 miles (19 km) west of Santa Ana. Population: (1969 est.) 102,300.

SANTA ANNA, sän'tä ä'nä, **Antonio López de** (1795?–1876), Mexican general and revolutionary. He was born at Jalapa on Feb. 21, 1795(?). He entered the army at 15, and attained public prominence as a supporter of the self-proclaimed emperor Augustín de Iturbide in 1822. After having expelled the royalists from Vera Cruz, Santa Anna took command in that city, where he led a revolt that sped Iturbide's retirement.

New Revolts. After the defeat of the federal party in 1822, Santa Anna retired to his estate; but he emerged again in 1828 in support of Vicente Guerrero's claims to the presidency, in which the latter supplanted Anastasio Pedraza. In 1829 the Spanish invasion furnished Santa Anna a favorable opportunity, and as minister of war and commander in chief at the head of the federal forces he compelled Barradas to capitulate at Tampico, September 11. He soon joined with Anastasio Bustamante in overthrowing Guerrero, and setting up the former in his place, but also, in 1832, led in the overthrow of Bustamante himself, and the restoration of Pedraza. In 1833 Santa Anna was chosen president, and soon after renounced the party of the Federalists, and put himself at the head of the Centralists, who desired the centralization of power in the executive government. His popularity with the army was not shared by the nation at large. On May 11, 1835, he defeated an insurgent army on the plains of Guadalupe, and as the blow was fatal to the Republicans he was shortly afterward named dictator. The federal constitution was abolished and the governors of the several states became dependent on the central power.

The Alamo. Texas, however, having long felt rebellious, now broke out into a revolution to try to attain independence. Santa Anna attacked San Antonio in February 1836, stormed the Alamo, killed its defenders, and pursued the Texans under Sam Houston. But on April 21, at the Battle of San Jacinto, his forces were routed and he himself was taken prisoner. Santa Anna secured his release by a treaty recognizing the independence of Texas. This was repudiated by Mexico, which suspended his dictatorship.

He was permitted to go to the United States, and after his return to Mexico in 1837 lived in retirement for a year. He offered his services to his country against the French in 1838, and taking command of the troops, repelled the assault on Veracruz on December 5, and forced the enemy to retire. In this engagement he lost a leg, a casualty that helped restore him to popular favor. He again became a leader of the Centralists, and from October 1841 to June 1844 was virtual dictator under the title of president.

Clashes with the United States. The new constitution of June 12, 1843, under which he was formally elected president, increased his dictatorial powers, the exercise of which led to a fresh revolution, in which he was overthrown. He was

CULVER PICTURES

Antonio López de Santa Anna, victor at the Alamo.

taken prisoner in January 1845 and banished. But at the prospect of war with the United States, he was recalled in July 1846, and was first appointed generalissimo and then, in December, provisional president.

At the opening of 1847, Santa Anna led an army of 20,000 against the American troops under General Taylor, and fought the Battle of Buena Vista, February 22–23, in which he was defeated. On April 18 he was attacked and defeated at Cerro Gordo by General Scott. Immediately after the Battle of Chapultepec the city of Mexico fell and was entered by the Americans (September 14). Santa Anna, escaping from the city, briefly continued a desultory warfare; but on April 5, 1848, having resigned the presidency, he received permission to retire from the country, and sailed for Jamaica, whence he continued on to Venezuela.

In 1853, Santa Anna was recalled and elected president for one year. But after setting up an odious despotism, he proclaimed himself in December 1853 president for life, with the title of Serene Highness and the right to nominate his successor. Revolution followed in 1854, and when he saw in 1855 that his cause was lost, Santa Anna fled from the capital to find refuge in Cuba, Venezuela, and Saint Thomas. In this absence he was tried and condemned for treason, and his estates were confiscated. He returned to Mexico during the 1864 French occupation, but was not permitted to remain. In 1867 he again returned, but was once more exiled and went to live in the United States. Finally, after the death of Juárez and the amnesty of 1874, he was permitted to reside in his own country. He died in Mexico City on June 20, 1876.

Further Reading: Callcott, Wilfred H., *Santa Anna: The Story of an Enigma Who Once Was Mexico* (reprint, Shoe String 1964).

SANTA BARBARA, a city in southwestern California, the seat of Santa Barbara county, is on the Santa Barbara Channel of the Pacific Ocean, 95 miles (153 km) northwest of the center of Los Angeles. It is protected to the south by the Santa Barbara Islands and to the north by the Santa Ynez mountains, upon whose slopes the city is built. Its mild climate, the beauty of the city, and its historical attractions draw millions of tourists every year.

The principal tourist attraction is the Santa Barbara Mission, sometimes called the "Queen of the Missions." The mission was founded in 1786, but the present building, which blends Spanish and Moorish architecture, was constructed in 1815 to replace one destroyed by an earthquake three years earlier. The church is a rectangular building of native sandstone with massive square front towers of solid masonry topped by arcaded, domed belfries. A mission house, a patio for the monks and a cemetery make up the remainder of the mission, which is one of the best-preserved in California. Damage caused by an earthquake in 1925 was repaired.

Santa Barbara has tried to retain the atmosphere of its past. Old buildings still stand—notably the mission and the county courthouse. Many of the city's later houses and buildings are in the Spanish colonial style, with white walls and red tile roofs. Even newer buildings are designed in this tradition. The city is carefully landscaped, and flowers are in bloom the year round.

In addition to tourism, the city's economy is based on electronics and aerospace research and on light industry, particularly the assembling of electronic component parts. Fishing is also important. Although oil drilling is prohibited on shore in the Santa Barbara area, petroleum and natural gas are produced from wells about 5 miles (8 km) off shore. Ruptures in the oil wells have created pollution problems.

The University of California at Santa Barbara is west of the city on a 600-acre (243-hectare) seaside campus; the Santa Barbara City College, a public junior college is here; and Westmount College, an interdenominational liberal arts school, is in suburban Montecito. The Santa Barbara area is also the home of the Brooks Institute of Photography and of the Music Academy of the West.

Among the city's museums are the Museum of Art, the Museum of Natural History, the Santa Barbara Historical Society, and the Faulkner Memorial Art Gallery in the public library. The Santa Barbara Botanic Garden is located on the site of the Old Mission Dam and Aqueduct, built in 1806.

Santa Barbara has its own symphony orchestra. Little theaters provide live drama in the city. The International Cymbidium Orchid Show is held here. There are many spectator sports events, including polo and horse shows. Swimming, fishing, and boating are favorite recreations in Santa Barbara. The yacht harbor is one of the city's most distinctive features. Every August, the four-day Old Spanish Days in Santa Barbara is held, recreating an early California fiesta.

The area of Santa Barbara was first sighted in 1542 by Juan Rodríguez Cabrillo, who claimed it for Spain. Sebastián Vizcaíno anchored offshore on Dec. 4, 1602, and the ship's priest named the channel and shoreline in honor of St. Barbara, whose feast it was. In 1782, the Viceroy of Mexico sent a group here to found a presidio, or fortified settlement. The mission was founded on the day of the feast of St. Barbara in 1786.

In 1846, Commodore Robert Field Stockton claimed the land and flew the American flag over it. The garrison he left was driven out by Mexican forces, but Col. John C. Frémont retook the post. In 1848, Mexico ceded California to the United States by treaty.

The city was incorporated in 1850. It is governed by a mayor and council. Population (metropolitan area): 298,660; (city): 74,542.

SANTA BARBARA ISLANDS, a group off the coast of southern California, from 20 to 60 miles (32 to 96 km) from the mainland, south and southeast of Santa Barbara. There are eight islands of various sizes, arranged in an irregular line from north to south: San Miguel, Santa Rosa, Santa Cruz, Anacapa, San Nicolas, Santa Barbara, Santa Catalina, and San Clemente.

JOSEF MUENCH

Mission in Santa Barbara, built in 1786, is one of the most beautiful churches in California. It is often called the "Queen of the Missions."

JOSEF MUENCH

Avalon, on Santa Catalina Island in the Pacific Ocean, is 27 miles (43 km) southwest of Los Angeles, Calif.

SANTA CATALINA ISLAND, kat-ə-lē'nə, part of southern California, in the Pacific Ocean about 25 miles (40 km) south of Long Beach. One of the Santa Barbara Islands, it is separated from the mainland by San Pedro Channel.

The island is about 22 miles (35 km) long with an average width of 4 miles (6 km). It is hilly and wooded, with many deep gorges. In 1919, William Wrigley bought the island and developed it as a resort. The surrounding waters abound in fish. The small city of Avalon (population 1,520) is the only community situated on the island.

The island was discovered in 1542 by Juan Rodríguez Cabrillo, a Portuguese navigator in Spanish service, who named it San Salvador. Sixty years later, Sebastián Vizcaíno, a Basque navigator, renamed it in honor of St. Catherine of Siena.

SANTA CATARINA, saɴn tə kȧ-tə-rē'nə, is a state in southern Brazil. It is bounded on the north and south, respectively, by the states of Paraná and Rio Grande do Sul, and on the west by Argentina. The eastern boundary is a long, well-indented shoreline on the South Atlantic. The capital, Florianópolis, is situated on an offshore island, the Ilha de Santa Catarina, which was once fortified by the Portuguese. The area of the state is more than 37,000 square miles (96,000 sq km).

A narrow coastal area is separated from the highland plateau of the interior by a pair of mountain ranges that parallel the coast. These mountains are bisected by several river valleys. A hot, humid, rainy climate prevails along the coast, while the interior upland has a more temperate climate, with distinct seasons and occasional frosts. The population pattern is similarly varied, with Brazilians of Portuguese descent concentrated along the coast, and the inland areas settled largely by the descendants of late 19th-century German immigrants.

The state is well wooded, producing excellent timber. Other economic mainstays of Santa Catarina are coal, which is exported to other parts of Brazil, and agriculture, the principal occupation in the upland. Major farm products include corn, wheat, potatoes, tobacco, and fruit. There are some food processing industries. A railroad crosses the state, but transportation facilities have remained generally underdeveloped. Population: (1970) 2,911,479.

SANTA CLARA, a city in western California, in Santa Clara county, is just west of San Jose and about 45 miles (72 km) south of San Francisco. It is noted for its dried fruits, particularly prunes. Other industry includes construction, electronics, canning, and the manufacture of paper and fiber glass. Points of interest are the old Mission—a replica of the third mission building on this site—and the de Saisset Art Gallery and Museum, both on the campus of the University of Santa Clara, and the Triton Museum of Art, which has an extensive collection of American art.

The Mission Santa Clara de Asis was founded by Franciscan missionaries in 1777, and the surrounding community was incorporated as Santa Clara in 1852. The University of Santa Clara, founded as a missionary school in 1851, was incorporated in 1875. The city has adopted a council-manager form of government. Population: 87,700.

SANTA CLARA, sän'tä klä'rä, a city in Cuba, the capital of Las Villas province, is situated near the geographical center of the island, about 160 miles (257 km) southeast of Havana. It is the commercial center of an agricultural region that raises cattle, coffee, sugarcane, and tobacco. The city's industries include rum distilling, tanning, and sugar refining. Furniture, cigars, and soft drinks are manufactured here. Santa Clara is also the seat of a public university.

The city was founded in 1689 by a group of settlers from the coastal town of Remedios, who were trying to escape from constant attacks by pirates. Santa Clara was built on the site of the ancient Indian town of Cubanacan, which, it is said, Christopher Columbus mistook for the seat of Kubla Khan. Locally, Santa Clara is sometimes called Villa Clara. Population: (1970) 131,500.

NORCROSS

CULVER PICTURES

The modern concept of the jolly, bearded Santa Claus (*left*) is based on the cartoons of Thomas Nast, like the one above that appeared in *Harper's Weekly* in 1881.

SANTA CLAUS, san'tə klôz', is a legendary American figure who traditionally brings gifts to children at Christmas. The popular image harks back to a historical person, Saint Nicholas, who was a 4th century bishop of Myra in what is now Turkey. Little is known of Saint Nicholas' life, but many traditions have grown up about him. He is supposed to have been elected bishop while still a very young man and to have been imprisoned during Diocletian's persecutions. One story about him is that he secretly provided three bags of gold as the dowry for three sisters, the daughters of an impoverished merchant. One of the bags of gold, which he tossed through a window at night, happened to fall into a stocking hung by the chimney to dry. The custom of hanging Christmas stockings is said by some to have originated in this way.

He was a very popular saint among Eastern Christians, and his cult was introduced into Germany by the Byzantine princess Theophano, who became the wife of Emperor Otto II (reigned 973–983). It spread to England, where some 400 churches were dedicated to him. In the west, Saint Nicholas became known as the patron saint of children, apparently through some fanciful elaborations of his kindness to the three sisters. One of these tales was that he restored to life three children who were killed by a wicked innkeeper, who had cut up their bodies and pickled them in brine. During the Middle Ages, particularly in Germany and England, a popular festival of the "boy bishop" was celebrated on December 6, Saint Nicholas' feast day. A young boy was elected bishop for a day and, robed in full episcopal regalia of miter, cope, and crozier, led a parade through the town.

American Development. The Dutch, although largely Protestant, retained their attachment to Saint Nicholas whom they called Sinter-Klaas. It was they who were responsible for his introduction to the American scene. Dutch settlers in New Amsterdam (now New York) kept the festival on December 6 and the practice of giving gifts to children. The English settlers took over the idea. Sinter-Klaas became Santa Claus, and was gradually associated with Christmas.

Washington Irving in his *Knickerbocker's History of New York* (1809), doubtlessly influenced by the Dutch origins, described him as a rotund, jolly figure, wearing a wide-brimmed hat and smoking a long-stemmed pipe. The current popular image of Santa Claus owes much to Clement C. Moore's poem *A Visit from St. Nicholas* (1823). It was he who added the reindeer and sleigh, the twinkling eye, and "laying his finger aside of his nose." The fur suit seems to have been a contribution from Germany, where Saint Nicholas was pictured often as a furry imp called "Pelz Nichol." Thomas Nast, a political cartoonist, developed the popular picture of Santa Claus, first in a cartoon in *Harper's Illustrated Weekly* in 1863 and again in an 1866 issue in which his *Santa Claus and His Works* appeared. Interestingly, the broad-brimmed hat became in Nast's imagination a soft furry cap.

The idea of Santa Claus has parallels in other countries. The Reformation influence downgraded the role of saints, so in Germany the image was replaced by the Christ Child, who in popular legend became Kris Kringle. Father Christmas was the English variant, although the American Santa Claus has spread to England as well as to Canada and Australia.

SANTA CRUZ, sän'tä krōōth', **Marquis de** (1526–1588), Spanish admiral, who formed the Spanish Armada. Álvaro de Bazán, 1st Marquis de Santa Cruz, was born in Granada on Dec. 12, 1526. Under Don John of Austria he played a brilliant role in the defeat of the Turks in the key sea Battle of Lepanto in 1571 and in the capture of Tunis in 1573. His victory off Terceira (1583) secured the Azores for Spain and completed the Spanish conquest of Portugal.

Created captain general of the ocean the same year, he began proposing the conquest of England to King Philip II. His plan was accepted, and he was commissioned to organize and command the requisite fleet. He was unjustly reproached by the King for long delays in its preparation. Santa Cruz died in Lisbon on Feb. 9, 1588, a few months before the "Invincible Armada" at length sailed under the command of the incompetent Duke de Medina-Sidonia.

SANTA CRUZ, sän'ta krōōs, **Andrés de** (1792–1865), Bolivian soldier and political leader. He was born in La Paz in 1792, a mestizo who claimed descent on his mother's side from the royal Incas. He entered the Spanish Army and rose to the rank of colonel. Captured by the patriots in 1820, he was persuaded to adopt their cause, became a general in the army, and led an invasion of Upper Peru in 1823.

In 1826–1827 he was acting President of Peru under Bolívar. In 1829 he was elected President of Bolivia for a term of 10 years and also received the title of grand marshal. His measures were progressive and the country enjoyed great prosperity under his administration. From the first he adhered to his purpose of uniting the Pacific coast republics, and his successful invasion of Peru in 1836 was followed by his proclamation of the Peruvian-Bolivian confederation. In 1839 a Chilean army under Gen. Manuel Bulnes invaded Bolivia and defeated Santa Cruz at Yungay. He resigned, and spent the rest of his life in exile in Europe. He died in 1865 in St. Nazaire, France.

SANTA CRUZ, sän'tä krōōs, the southernmost province of Argentina, is bounded on the north by Chubut province, on the west and south by Chile, and on the east by the Atlantic Ocean. Its southeastern tip is on the Strait of Magellan. The capital is Río Gallegos. Sheep farming is the basis of the economy. Santa Cruz became a province in 1957. Population: (1970) 84,457.

SANTA CRUZ, sän'tä krōōs, a city in the isolated eastern part of Bolivia, the capital of Santa Cruz department, is on the Río Piray, about 300 miles (483 km) by air east of La Paz. It is the commercial center of an agricultural area that produces sugarcane, citrus fruits, and cattle. The city's industry includes lumber and oil refining. During the 1970's Santa Cruz was developing as a communications link between Bolivia and its neighboring countries. There is a public university here. The cathedral has a collection of colonial hand-wrought silver.

The city was settled in 1561 by Spanish colonists who came from Paraguay. It remained a small city out of touch with the rest of the nation until 1954, when a highway was built, connecting Santa Cruz with the populous western part of Bolivia. In the next two decades it grew rapidly. Population: (1969 est.) 108,700.

SANTA CRUZ, san'ta krōōz, a city on the west coast of California, the seat of Santa Cruz county, is on the north shore of Monterey Bay, about 75 miles (120 km) south of San Francisco. It is a vacation resort and has some light industry, including the processing of food and lumber and the manufacture of furniture and electronics equipment. Fishing is also important, and the surrounding agricultural region produces vegetables. There is a branch of the University of California here. Places of interest include a reconstruction of the old mission, the museum of the Santa Cruz Art League, and the Santa Cruz Museum.

The Mission Santa Cruz was founded in 1791 and secularized in 1834. Whaling ships frequently stopped here to buy green food, and by 1840 the redwood lumber business was prospering. The city was chartered in 1866. It has a council-manager form of government. Population: 41,483.

SANTA CRUZ DE TENERIFE, sän'tä krōōth thä tä-nä-rĕ'fä, is the capital of the Spanish province of Santa Cruz de Tenerife, one of two provinces comprising the Canary Islands. The city is situated on the northeastern coast of the island of Tenerife. It has an excellent harbor and is a major port. The beauty of its natural setting, its mild climate, and its fine beaches have made the city an important tourist resort. Population: (1969) 170,000.

SANTA CRUZ ISLANDS, san'tə krōōz, an archipelago in the South Pacific Ocean, administered as part of the British Solomon Islands Protectorate. The island group lies south of the Solomon Islands and north of the New Hebrides.

The Santa Cruz Islands have a combined area of 380 square miles (980 sq km). The group consists of the main islands of Ndeni (Santa Cruz), Vanikoro, and Utupua, and many small islands. The larger islands are volcanic and mountainous, and most of them are surrounded by coral formations. One of the islands, Tinakula, is an active volcano.

The climate is hot and humid, but the soil is very fertile and the vegetation is luxuriant. Small amounts of copra and timber are exported.

The people of the Santa Cruz Islands are primarily Polynesians. The first European to discover the archipelago was the Spanish navigator Álvaro de Mendaña de Neyra in 1595. In World War II, U. S. and Japanese naval-air forces clashed near the islands on Oct. 26, 1942. Population: (1970) 3,828.

SANTA FE, sän'tä fä, a city in northwestern Argentina, the capital of Santa Fe province, is on the Río Salado del Norte near its confluence with the Río Paraná, about 300 miles (483 km) northwest of Buenos Aires. It has a large port with modern facilities, and is the center of an agricultural region. The city's industries include flour milling, zinc and copper smelting, and the export of grain. The Universidad del Litoral is here.

Places of interest include Government House; the churches of La Merced and San Francisco; and the Cabildo, where the Argentine constitution of 1853 was adopted. Santa Fe was founded in 1573 and became a center for Jesuit missionaries. It later fought in vain to stem the growing economic influence of Buenos Aires over the nation. Population: (1960) 208,900.

The Palace of the Governors in Santa Fe, built about 1610, is now part of the Museum of New Mexico.

SANTA FE, san'tə fā', is the capital of New Mexico and the seat of Santa Fe county. The city is in the north central part of the state, on the Santa Fe River, which flows into the Rio Grande 22 miles (35 km) west of the city. It is situated at an altitude of nearly 7,000 feet (2,135 meters) in the Sangre de Cristo Mountains. Southeast of Santa Fe are the Ortiz Mountains, to the south are the Sandia, and to the west the Jemez Mountains. The city is 62 miles (100 km) northeast of Albuquerque, the state's largest city.

Santa Fe is one of the oldest settlements in the United States. Although it has been a state capital only since 1912, it has been the seat of a government since 1610. The city, which is built around a central plaza, has retained much of its Indian-Spanish heritage. Old adobe houses, with tiled roofs and shady patios, and Indian and Spanish shops still line the narrow, winding streets, lending an air of Old World charm. Many of the newer buildings are also of Spanish colonial and territorial architecture, and the new state capitol, a high pillbox building, is a modern adaptation of the Spanish colonial tradition.

A large number of the city's residents are of Spanish descent, and both Spanish and English are spoken in the city. A number of Indian villages cluster on the edge of the city. Sante Fe's mingling of American, Spanish, and Indian cultures, bilingual tradition, and unique atmosphere have earned it the nickname of "the city different," making it attractive to tourists.

Economy. The city derives much of its income from tourism and from the sale of Indian arts and crafts. The state government operations also contribute greatly to the economy. Santa Fe has a little light industry that makes electronic instruments, textiles, aluminum ware, gypsum, and pumice products.

Culture and Education. Santa Fe is a thriving center of the arts. The city's chief cultural attraction is its summer opera season. The Santa Fe Opera offers some of the most ambitious works in any repertory. Although standard works are also given, each year the company produces one or more works in their world or American premieres. The season, which runs through June and July, is attended by audiences that come from all parts of the world.

The operas are performed in a modern, partly roofed, open-air theater built into a mountainside 5 miles (8 km) north of the city. It was constructed in 1968 to replace one that had burned down a year earlier.

The arts and crafts colony was begun in 1923. Most of the city's artists gather here to work and display their creations. Weavers, potters, and other handicraftsmen work in the colony.

Pueblos and Museums. Near the city are many Indian pueblos of interest to anthropologists. Santa Fe itself was an Indian village before it was settled by Europeans in 1609 or 1610, and artifacts are still being uncovered here. One of the most interesting of the ancient sites is Bandelier National Monument, 41 miles (66 km) west of the city.

A number of museums display Indian arts and crafts and the Indian way of life. These include the Museum of Navajo Ceremonial Art, the Museum of New Mexico, the "Old Cienega Village" Museum, the Institute of American Indian Arts, and the School of American Research. Other museums are the International Institute of Iberian Colonial Arts and the New Mexico Military Museum.

Higher Education. Higher education is supplied by two Roman Catholic institutions, The College of Santa Fe and St. John's College. Both offer four-year degree programs.

Places of Interest. The city is full of reminders of its rich history. The Mission of San Miguel of Santa Fe, although it has a remodeled facade, is believed to be the oldest church in the United States. Construction was begun on it in 1621. The Cristo Rey church is said to be the largest adobe structure in the United States. The Cathedral of Saint Francis of Assisi, the first church between Durango, Mexico, and St. Louis, Mo., to achieve the status of cathedral, was built between 1869 and 1886 by Archbishop John Baptist Lamy, who was the model for the principal character in Willa Cather's novel *Death Comes for the Archbishop.*

The Palace of the Governors, on the plaza, is a long, low building with massive walls that was built about 1610 as the Spanish capitol of the Southwest. For 300 years it served as a seat of government for Spanish, Mexican, Confederate, and American administrations. Lew Wallace stayed here while he was governor of New Mexico Territory (1878–1881) and writing part of his novel *Ben Hur*. It is reputedly the oldest public building still standing in the nation.

Other places of interest include the Scottish Rite Temple, a replica in part of the Alhambra in Granada, Spain; Our Lady of the Light Chapel; and the old Santa Fe National Cemetery.

Recreation and Special Events. The mountains around Santa Fe offer many opportunities for recreation. Aside from hunting and fishing, there are facilities for skiing at the Santa Fe Ski Basin, 16 miles (25 km) from the city through the Santa Fe National Forest.

Thoroughbred and quarterhorse races are held at Santa Fe Downs from mid-May to Labor Day. The Rodeo de Santa Fe takes place in July.

On Labor Day weekend, a three-day festival is held to commemorate the reconquest of New Mexico from the Indians in 1692. During the fiesta, which has been celebrated since 1712, the events of the historic event are reenacted.

History. In the winter of 1609–1610, Pedro de Peralta, the third Spanish governor of the Province of New Mexico, founded Santa Fe on the ruins of an old Indian pueblo. He named it *La Villa Real de la Santa Fe de San Francisco de Asis* (The Royal City of the Holy Faith of St. Francis of Assisi), later shortened to Santa Fe. He built a palace fortress, laid out a public square, and walled the square with adobe.

The Mission Supply, a pack train service, was started between Mexico City and Santa Fe to provide settlers and missionaries with materials unavailable on the frontier, but colonization was slow. Trouble with the Indians developed, and in 1680, after a battle with the Indians, the settlers abandoned the city. The Indians held Santa Fe until 1692, when the Spanish retook it with little opposition.

Beginning in 1739, French colonial traders began to find their way to the city, and in 1792 the first round trip was made over a route that later became the famous Santa Fe Trail from Missouri. Soon after, Mexico obtained its independence from Spain in 1821, and the city came under the new republic's government. American traders came in, and regular trade was established.

In the Mexican War, American troops took the city in a bloodless victory in 1846. In 1862, during the American Civil War, the city was held by the Confederates for two weeks. It was retaken by Union forces and remained under their control. When New Mexico was admitted into the union in 1912, Santa Fe became the state's capital, as it had been the capital of all of its previous governments.

Government and Population. Santa Fe has a council-manager government. Population: 48,953.

SANTA FE SPRINGS, san'tə fã, is a city in southern California, in Los Angeles county, about 10 miles (16 km) southeast of the center of Los Angeles. It is a major center of oil production and makes oil well equipment, clay pipe, and chemicals. It was incorporated as a city in 1957. Population: 14,559.

SANTA FE TRAIL, san'tə fã, a famous 19th century overland trade route in the United States by which caravans traveled from western Missouri up the valley of the Arkansas, then southwest through Raton Pass in Colorado to Santa Fe, N. Mex. Trapping parties had ventured to Santa Fe but had run into Spanish restrictions and penalties.

In 1821, William Becknell, a trader from the hamlet of Franklin, Mo., organized an expedition of 20 or 30 plainsmen for the purpose of "trading for Horses and Mules, and catching Wild Animals...." Struggling upward over the difficult Raton Pass, he blundered into an encampment of Mexican soldiers. Startled to be told by the troops that Mexico had won independence, he realized his luck. With Spanish rule removed, American traders would be cordially welcome in Santa Fe. Laden with Mexican silver dollars, he returned to Franklin, to be known henceforth as "father of the Santa Fe trade."

Although the pioneering work had been done in opening up the trail, it was still essential to map good roads and improve methods of travel. Becknell continued to help solve these problems, leading another expedition in 1822 by way of the Cimmaron desert, a trip of great hardship that also had a profitable ending. As steamboats expanded their routes, Franklin, Mo., was gradually succeeded by Independence and Westport as the chief outfitting stations for traders. The Atchison, Topeka, and Santa Fe railroad displaced the old trail in 1880.

The Santa Fe Opera's new open-air theater is built into the side of a mountain north of the city.

ALAN STOKER, SANTA FE CHAMBER OF COMMERCE

SANTA ISABEL, sän'tä ē-sä-vel', now called Malabo, is the capital and chief port of Equatorial Guinea. It is situated on the northern tip of the island of Fernando Po (Macias Nguema Biyogo) in the Gulf of Guinea.

The city was founded by the British as Clarencetown, or Port Clarence, in the 1820's, and was renamed Malabo by the constitution of 1973. Its chief export is cacao. Other exports include coffee, tropical woods, bananas, and palm oil. Population: (1970 est.) 20,000.

SANTA MARÍA, sän'tä mä-rē'ä, **Domingo** (1825–1889), president of Chile. He was born in Santiago, and was educated in the National Institute and at the University of Chile. He held a number of cabinet posts and other offices, including minister of finance, supreme court justice, minister of the court of appeals, and minister of war during the War of the Pacific against Bolivia and Peru.

Santa María was president of Chile from 1881 to 1886. He concluded the war successfully and suppressed the last uprising of the Araucanian Indians. Laws were passed requiring civil registration of births, deaths, and marriages; public cemeteries were removed from the control of the church; and freedom of worship was granted. The Roman Catholic Church did not support his government. In another reform, property qualifications for voting were dropped. Santa María died in Santiago in July 1889.

SANTA MARIA, saɴn'tə mə-rē'ə, an island in the Atlantic Ocean, is the easternmost island in the Azores, which belong to Portugal. It has an area of 37 square miles (96 sq km) and rises to 1,936 feet (590 meters) at Pico Alto. Its only port is Vila do Pôrto, a town of over 5,000. The island's airport is a major stopover on transatlantic flights. See also AZORES.

SANTA MARIA, san'ta mə-rē'ə, a city in southwestern California, in Santa Barbara county, is on the Santa Maria River, 8 miles (13 km) east of the Pacific Ocean and about 75 miles (120 km) northwest of Santa Barbara. It is the center of a farming area that produces flower seeds, vegetables, and grains. There are many oil wells in the area. The city's industries include food processing, sugar refining, and the manufacture of sound recordings, tire molds, cable, and marine hardware. Vandenberg Air Force Base, an aerospace center, is about 20 miles (32 km) to the southwest.

In 1871 the first building was constructed on the site of Santa Maria. Settlement remained sparse until oil was discovered here in 1902. The community then grew rapidly and was incorporated in 1905. It has a council-manager form of government. Population: 39,685.

SANTA MARTA, sän'tä mär'tä, a city on the northern coast of Colombia, the capital of Magdalena department, is built on cliffs overlooking a deep bay on the Caribbean Sea, about 450 miles (724 km) north of Bogotá. It is at the base of the Sierra Nevada de Santa Marta, which rise to a height of nearly 19,000 feet (5,790 meters) less than 30 miles (48 km) to the east. Santa Marta is an important banana shipping port. It was founded in 1525, and it is the oldest city in Colombia. Population: (1972 est.) 141,-300.

SANTA MONICA, a city in southwestern California, in Los Angeles county, is on Santa Monica Bay of the Pacific Ocean. It is situated about 15 miles (24 km) west-southwest of the center of Los Angeles.

It is an industrial city and the retail center of a large area. It has many fine homes, and its ocean beaches attract tourists and residents of the area.

The principal economic activities include aircraft and aerospace industries and the manufacture of electronic components for aerospace systems, ball-point and nylon-tipped pens, plastic components, and laser devices and systems. Extensive research in electronic development is carried on.

The Santa Monica Art Association and the Santa Monica symphony orchestra are among the cultural attractions.

The name Santa Monica is believed to have been given to the site by members of the party of Gaspar de Portolá, the Spanish explorer, on St. Monica's Day, May 4, 1770. According to legend, a soldier who watched a small waterfall dropping into a shadow compared the waters to the tears shed by St. Monica for her wayward son Augustine.

The city was founded in 1875 and was incorporated in 1886. It is governed by a council and manager. Population: 88,314.

SANTA PAULA, pô'lə, a city in southwestern California, in Ventura county, is about 60 miles (96 km) northwest of the center of Los Angeles. Fruit is grown in the area and there are many oil wells. The city makes paper containers, drinking cups, and light plastics. The California Oil Museum has exhibits depicting the history of the oil industry in the state.

Santa Paula was incorporated in 1902 and is governed by a council and administrator. Population: 20,552.

SANTA ROSA, rō'zə, a city in northwestern California, the seat of Sonoma county, is about 15 miles (25 km) east of the Pacific Ocean and 50 miles (80 km) north of San Francisco. It is the center of a fruit-growing and dairy- and poultry-farming region. Some of California's finest wines are produced in the area. The city's principal industries are fish packing, fruit processing, lumber, optical coating, and the manufacture of machinery, clothing, and shoes.

Luther Burbank, the horticulturist who developed more than 800 new varieties of plants, lived in Santa Rosa from 1875 until his death in 1926. The Luther Burbank Memorial Gardens, where Burbank is buried, is open to the public. The Codding Museum contains history and natural history exhibits. The Jesse Peter Memorial Museum in Santa Rosa Junior College houses exhibits of natural history, and Indian artifacts.

Just north of Santa Rosa is the Petrified Forest, containing silicified and opalized redwood trees. About 20 miles (32 km) northwest of the city is the Armstrong Redwoods State Park, which contains a natural theater amidst the giant trees. Fort Ross State Historic Park, which is about 30 miles (48 km) northwest of Santa Rosa, is a restoration of a trading post that was established by Russian fur traders in 1812.

Santa Rosa was founded in 1833 and incorporated in 1868. It has a council-manager form of government. Population: 83,205.

SANTA SOPHIA, or Sancta Sophia. See Hagia Sophia.

SANTANA, sän-tä′nä, **Pedro** (1801–1864), Dominican soldier and political leader. He was born in Santo Domingo on June 29, 1801. A lawyer and wealthy landowner, he led the revolt by which Santo Domingo separated from Haiti. He was elected president of the "independent State of Spanish Haiti" in November 1844 for a four-year term. After his term ended, he was recalled in 1849 to repel Haitian aggression. Reelected to the presidency in 1853, he served until 1857, repelling two more Haitian attacks in the interim.

Santana seized the government in 1858, but despairing of maintaining order, agreed to the country's annexation by Spain in 1861. He died in Santo Domingo on June 14, 1864.

SANTANDER, sän-tän-der′, **Francisco de Paula** (1792–1840), Colombian patriot and political leader, who is regarded as the founder of New Granada (Colombia). He was born in Rosario de Cúcuta, New Granada, in April 1792. For his services in the war of liberation he was promoted to general of division in 1817 and especially distinguished himself in 1819 during the victory of Simon Bolívar at the Battle of Boyacá.

When Colombia's constitution was adopted in 1821 he was inaugurated vice president, with Bolívar as president. However, actual administration of the government was exercised by Santander, and he and Bolívar came into conflict over the latter's goal of a centralized autocratic state. Following Santander's reelection in 1827, Bolívar deposed and exiled the vice president. After Bolívar's death in 1830, Santander returned to New Granada, was elected president, and served from 1832 to 1837. He died on May 5, 1840, in Bogotá.

SANTANDER, sän-tän-der′, is a city in northern Spain and the capital of Santander province. One of Spain's chief ports, it is on the Bay of Santander, an inlet of the Bay of Biscay. The city has shipping industries and is a popular resort because of its splendid beaches. The cathedral, originally Gothic but with later additions, has a fine crypt containing a Moorish font. Near the city are the famous caves of Altamira, with prehistoric wall paintings and engravings as much as 20,000 years old.

The province covers an area of 2,044 square miles (5,294 sq km). It is enclosed on all sides but the north by mountains and possesses extensive forests and important iron and lead mines. It also produces large quantities of grain. Along the coast, fishing is the main occupation, while livestock raising is prevalent in the uplands. Population: (1969 est.) of the city, 144,800; of the province, 475,300.

SANTARÉM, saNN-tə-räNm′, is a city in Portugal on the lower Tagus River, about 45 miles (72 km) northeast of Lisbon. The capital of Santarém district, it is the commercial center for one of Portugal's most productive agricultural regions. It is also a tourist center known for its bullfights.

Its strategic position above Lisbon has made the city important since Roman times, when it was first called Scalabis and later Praesidium Julium. It was a Moorish stronghold from 715 until the mid-1100's. Population: (1960) 16,449.

SANTAYANA, san-tē-an′ə, **George** (1863–1952), American philosopher, poet, and literary critic. Although Spanish was his native tongue, all of Santayana's very considerable literary work was composed in English, a language he learned to write with great descriptive accuracy and evocative force. His best essays, though not his poetry, are a lasting part of the literary heritage of the English language. His contributions to philosophy, for which he is best known, represent his view that philosophy is the art of articulating a vision of the "large facts" of human life. For Santayana, truth is absolute, but our knowledge of it is marred by the bias of our perspectives. The most we can expect, therefore, is an adequate account of things from the human point of view.

Life. Santayana was born in Madrid, Spain, on Dec. 16, 1863. His father was a minor official in the Spanish civil service, and his mother was the Spanish widow of an American businessman. When he was nine, his mother took him to Boston, where he attended Boston Latin School. He received his B. A. from Harvard in 1886 and his Ph. D. a few years later, after writing his dissertation on the German philosopher Hermann Lotze. In 1889, Santayana joined Harvard's outstanding philosophy department. Success in the classroom and a measure of acceptance by Cambridge society did not satisfy him. In 1912, when savings and a small inheritance made him financially independent, he resigned his post and left for Europe never to return.

During his years at Harvard, Santayana published several works, including a collection of poetry, *Sonnets and Other Verses* (1894); an influential study of aesthetics, *The Sense of Beauty* (1896); and the five-volume *The Life of Reason* (1905–1906), on which generations of American naturalist philosophers were raised.

After leaving the United States, Santayana devoted the rest of his life to what he liked best —philosophical reflection and literary work, including his mature philosophic works, his only novel, *The Last Puritan* (1935), and his autobiography. A modest, sedentary man, he viewed the world as his host and not as his home. To many, his personality seemed distant and aloof. Even his three-volume autobiography, *Persons and Places* (1944), *The Middle Span* (1945), and *My Host the World* (1953), indicates little private emotional involvement. However, this is the result of deliberate choice and literary strategy. The very people who thought of Santayana as a "cold fish" found themselves, when in need, the beneficiaries of his anonymous generosity.

At the outbreak of World War II, Santayana was in Italy, isolated from friends and funds. He moved into the nursing home of the Blue Sisters in Rome, where he continued intellectually active almost until his death on Sept. 26, 1952.

Thought. For Santayana, philosophy is a symbolic expression of the values and of the perceptions that structure a way of life. The notion of the translation of human interests into the shared language of symbols plays a central role in his early work. *The Life of Reason* is an account of the way in which human creativity embodies itself in common sense, society, religion, art, and science. Starting from the premise that all ideals have a natural ground, he traces the patterns of human activity and the development of values and institutions. For him, all the arts of men are responses of a variable human nature to the assaults of the changing environment. Reason, itself a physical force within individuals, works to harmonize our impulses and to forge a world in which their satisfaction would be secure.

Santayana was raised in the Roman Catholic faith, which as an adult he neither practiced nor renounced. Although widely regarded as an atheist, he had, in fact, an extraordinary sensitivity to the highest flights of religious imagination. From the early *Interpretations of Poetry and Religion* (1900) to the sympathetic and perceptive treatment of Christ in *The Idea of Christ in the Gospels* (1946), he worked for a better understanding of the function of religion. The role of religious statements is to express our predicaments and moral resolves. Taken literally they are false; as symbols, however, they reveal deep truths about the condition and aspirations of man.

Scepticism and Animal Faith (1923) heralded the development of Santayana's mature philosophy. The system was fully worked out in *The Realms of Being* (4 vols., 1927–1940). Here the focus shifts to ontology—the nature and types of reality. His search for an honest and relevant philosophy leads him to reject the subjectivist tradition of modern thought. The rationalistic criterion of absolute certainty dooms the quest for knowledge to futility. Yet we act with perfect confidence in a treacherous world. It is evident, therefore, that we know much more than a thorough skepticism can allow. Philosophy must proceed by explicating and systematizing the commitments implicit in our confident action. This confidence Santayana calls "animal faith," which, if trusted, reveals to us the real spatio-temporal matrix of our actions.

Following Aristotle, Santayana analyzes this world of space and time into matter and form (essence), but he denies purposiveness in nature, lodging all causation in the material component of substance. Matter, indefinite in its potentiality, and essence, infinite in the number of its specific forms, constitute two of the "realms" or types of being. The history of matter taking form is the history of the world: the eternal record of this is the realm of truth. All knowledge presupposes intelligent but powerless spirit (consciousness), the fourth irreducibly different sort of being.

Santayana views good and bad as relative to the actual nature or "psyche" of individuals. The animal psyche, soon to be extinguished without trace, cannot gain ultimate satisfaction. But it is possible for some or perhaps all of us to transcend (though not abandon) the endless instrumentalities of life and engage in the timeless contemplation or enjoyment of whatever essence may be presented. This liberation through absorption in immediacy is "the spiritual life."

The theory of the spiritual life is perhaps the central part of Santayana's philosophy. We have the evidence of his disciplined, austere existence to prove that this is the ideal he tried to actualize in his own life. His calm life, balanced vision, and high ideals are an appropriate legacy for our distracted age.

JOHN LACHS, *Vanderbilt University*

Further Reading: Arnett, Willard E., *George Santayana* (reprint; Washington Sq. Press 1968); Cory, Daniel, *Santayana: The Later Years* (Braziller 1963); Lachs, John, ed., *Animal Faith and Spiritual Life* (Appleton 1967); Munitz, Milton K., *The Moral Philosophy of Santayana* (Columbia Univ. Press 1939); Schilpp, Paul A., ed., *The Philosophy of George Santayana* (Northwestern Univ. Press 1940).

SANTIAGO, sän-tyä'gō, a city in Chile, is the capital of the republic and of Santiago province. It is one of the four largest cities of South America. It is situated on the Mapocho River, about 60 miles (95 km) east southeast of the Pacific port of Valparaíso.

Santiago stands on a wide plain at an elevation of about 1,700 feet (520 meters), backed by the massive, snow-clad peaks of the Andes to the east. It has a moderate climate, with temperatures averaging 45° F (7° C) in winter (June-September) and 70° F (21° C) in summer (December-March), and annual rainfall seldom exceeding 15 inches (370 mm).

The city is the focus of the commercial, industrial, and cultural life of Chile and is the seat of virtually all the nation's major governmental agencies. Located at the northern end of the long Central Valley (called the "breadbasket of Chile"), it is a major food-processing and distributing point. It is also one of Latin America's greatest textile centers. Other manufactures include chemicals, glassware, paper, machinery, metal products, and furniture. Roads and railroad lines link Santiago with northern and southern Chile, several Pacific ports and Argentina. The city has an international airport.

Description. Though built on hilly ground, Santiago is notable even among Latin American cities for its spacious avenues and many parks. The widest of its boulevards, the Avenida Bernardo O'Higgins, or Alameda, occupies a dry riverbed.

The city's dominant physical features are two small mountains. Santa Lucía Hill, the lesser of the two, rises on the south bank of the Mapocho near the downtown business district. Once the fortified heart of the city, this hill has been converted into a landscaped open area that has been called one of the most attractive urban parks in the world. Across the river and a few blocks to the north, the Hill of San Cristóbal rises some 1,200 feet (365 meters) above street level. At its summit is a large statue of the Virgin Mary, a gift from the people of France. On San Cristóbal's lower slopes is one of Latin America's largest zoological parks.

Santiago has many tall office and apartment buildings, but retains much that is old. Parts of its cathedral, much rebuilt because of periodic earthquake damage, date back to the mid-16th century. The cathedral faces the Plaza de Armas, Santiago's central square.

Other outstanding buildings include the early 19th century Presidential Palace (Palacio de la Moneda), the Congressional Palace, and the National Library and Historical Museum. The city has three universities, including the state-run University of Chile, which succeeded the University of San Felipe, founded by royal decree in 1738. The hub of the city's cultural life is the Municipal Center, which stages orchestral, dance, and operatic performances.

The Province. Santiago province covers about 6,560 square miles (16,000 sq km) in the northern part of the fertile Central Valley, which extends from the Argentine border to the Pacific coast. The principal river is the Maipó. Copper is mined in the mountains to the east. The main seaport, San Antonio, is connected by rail with the capital city and supplements Valparaíso as a shipping point for the products of the province. Much of the land area is in farms, producing corn, wheat, barley, oats, and a variety of vegetables and

Santiago, capital of Chile, seen from Santa Lucia Hill, is a city of broad avenues and massive buildings.

fruit. The province is famous for its wines and has many small vineyards.

Due principally to manufacturing activity in and around the city of Santiago, the province is responsible for more than one third of the total value of Chilean industrial production. Besides the capital and San Antonio, important cities include San Bernardo and Melipilla.

History. The Spaniard Pedro de Valdivia, who marched south from Peru to conquer Chile, founded the city of Santiago in 1541. It figured prominently in the wars of liberation in the early 1800's. José de San Martín occupied the city in 1817, after crossing the Andes from Argentina, and in the following year Santiago became the capital of an independent Chile.

The city has been buffeted by earthquakes in every century of its existence. One of the worst, in 1617, virtually destroyed the town. The once serious threat of inundation by the rampaging Mapocho River has been reduced by flood control projects.

Population: (1970) of the city of Santiago, 510,246; of the metropolitan area, 2,900,000; of the province, 3,218,155.

SANTIAGO DE COMPOSTELA, sän-tyä′gō thä kôm-pōs-tä′lä, is a city in Spain in the region of Galicia. It is in La Coruña province, 34 miles (55 km) south of the city of La Coruña. Since the Middle Ages, when the relics of Saint James the Greater were discovered, the city has been a center for pilgrims from throughout Europe. Santiago is the Spanish form of Saint James.

The tradition of Saint James' removal to Spain appears to date from the 7th century. By the tradition, the body of Saint James, who was martyred about 44, was cast adrift in a boat, finally washing up on the coast of Galicia, where he was buried. His tomb was miraculously discovered in the 9th century and became a rallying point for Spanish Christians fighting the

Moors. The city grew around the tomb. The festival of Saint James begins each year on July 25, with processions and fireworks.

Into Santiago's small urban area are crowded over 40 churches as well as convents and monasteries, hospitals, and a university, founded in 1532. Physically and psychologically the city is dominated by its superb Romanesque Cathedral of St. James, begun about 1075 and completed in 1211. According to tradition, it contains the tomb of the apostle, whose silver sepulcher lies in a crypt under the main altar. The principal entranceway is from the Plaza Mayor, through the Obradoiro. Just inside is the Pórtico de la Gloria, showing scenes from the Last Judgment, which is the most magnificent of the masterpieces carved from Galician granite by the medieval builder and sculptor Maestro Mateo. Santiago's shrine became the goal of thousands of pilgrims from throughout the medieval Christian states, and their contributions resulted in the still impressive splendor of the city.

Surrounded by low mountains, the city is inland from the Atlantic shores of Galicia's famous estuaries (*rías*). Fairs and cattle markets for the surrounding livestock region are held in the city. Such handicrafts as wood carving are important, and there are small factories manufacturing drugs, furniture, tires, and leather goods. Population: (1969 est.) 46,000.

SANTIAGO DE CUBA, sän-tyä′gō thä kōō′vä, a city in Cuba. The capital of Oriente province, Santiago is the principal seaport in eastern Cuba. It is situated on a virtually landlocked bay on the southern coast, less than 50 miles (80 km) west of Guantanamo and about 475 air miles (765 km) east-southeast of Havana. The bay is connected with the Caribbean by a long, winding channel. The city is in the center of an agricultural region and not far distant from mines that yield copper, iron, and manganese.

245

Santiago de Cuba was founded in 1514 by the island's Spanish conqueror, Diego Velásquez, who was buried in the cathedral. It was the capital of Cuba from 1522 to 1589. It was captured and plundered by French invaders in 1553 and by the British in 1662. During the Spanish-American War, U. S. forces achieved victory by storming San Juan Hill and other heights overlooking Santiago (July 1, 1898) and destroying a Spanish fleet outside of the harbor (July 3). Population: (1966 est.) 250,000.

SANTIAGO DE LOS CABALLEROS, sän-tyä'gō thä lōs kä-vä-yä'rōs, a city in the north central Dominican Republic, the capital of Santiago province, is on the Río Yaque del Norte, about 35 miles (56 km) south of Puerto Plata, the republic's chief Atlantic port. It is the marketing, processing, and distribution center of an agricultural area, where tobacco, rice, cacao, and coffee are grown.

Santiago de los Caballeros was settled in 1504 by 30 Spanish gentlemen. It survived earthquakes, fires and insurrections to become in the 20th century the second-largest city in the republic. Population: (1970) 155,200.

SANTIAGO DEL ESTERO, sän-tyä'gō thel äs-tā'rō, a city in north central Argentina, the capital of Santiago del Estero province, is on the Río Dulce, about 575 miles (925 km) northwest of Buenos Aires. It is the commercial center for the province's agricultural and lumber industries, and a resort city.

Santiago del Estero, founded in 1553 by Spanish colonists from Peru, is the oldest continuous settlement in Argentina. It has a Gothic church and Franciscan convent dating from about 1570. Population: (1960) 80,395.

SANTILLANA, sän-tē-lyä'nä, **Marqués de** (1398–1458), Spanish poet, and the leading literary figure of his time in Spain. Iñigo Lopéz de Mendoza, Marqués de Santillana, was born in Carrión de los Condes, Palencia, Spain, on Aug. 19, 1398. He was a learned and courtly warrior serving John II of Castile. Beginning as an imitator of the troubadors, he composed numerous *serranillas* (pastoral or mountain songs) notable for their simplicity, natural tone, and beauty of form and expression. His didactic and allegorical poetry won him less popularity. Nevertheless such doctrinal poems as the *Diálogo de Bías contra fortuna* and *El centiloquio* are particularly beautiful and vigorous. A learned man familiar with the Trecento Italian writers and such French masterworks as the *Roman de la rose*, he introduced the Italianate sonnet to Spain and produced able imitations of Petrarch. His dramatic and allegorical poem *La comedieta de Ponça*, in *arte mayor* verse form, is also imitative of the Italian masters.

Santillana established a personal library unusual for his time. In his well-known *Prohemio* (1449), an introduction to his poems, he was one of the first Spaniards to write learned commentaries on the epochal works of literature, starting with Homer and the Bible. Santillana died in Guadalajara on March 25, 1458.

ROBERT J. CLEMENTS
New York University

SANTO DOMINGO, an island in the Caribbean Sea. See HISPANIOLA.

SANTO DOMINGO, sän'tō thō-mēng'gō, is the capital city of the Dominican Republic. Santo Domingo was also the early name of the Caribbean island of Hispaniola, on which the city is located, and the former name of the Dominican Republic, which shares the island with the Republic of Haiti. From 1936 to 1961 the city was called Ciudad Trujillo, for President Rafael Leonidas Trujillo Molina, the Dominican Republic's dictatorial ruler.

Situated on the island's southern coast, about 150 miles (240 km) east of the Haitian capital of Port-au-Prince, Santo Domingo is Hispaniola's largest city and one of the largest in the Caribbean area. It functions as the center of Dominican commercial, industrial, civic, and cultural life. It is also the republic's principal port, exporting sugar, coffee, tobacco, timber, cacao, and some manufactured products. Its location in one of the country's two most intensively cultivated valleys makes it also a local marketing center for agricultural produce. There are food processing plants, sugar and textile mills, woodworking plants, and other light industries. The climate is warm, with high humidity the rule.

The harbor, which has few natural advantages, was artificially transformed into one of the Caribbean's best during the 1930's, with the addition of breakwaters, a long concrete wharf, and other improvements. The port handles at least half of the nation's foreign trade. There is also a large international airport.

The city grew up on the right bank of the Ozama River, spreading westward along the Caribbean shore from the river's mouth. A broad, tree-lined boulevard, the Avenida George Washington, runs along the waterfront. There are many parks, both in the area occupied by the "old city" near the river and in the more modern sections that lie to the west of it.

Contemporary architecture predominates, due to the ambitious building program undertaken under Trujillo after much of the city had been leveled by the hurricane of Sept. 3, 1930, the most destructive of many that have battered the town. Outstanding older structures that survived the storm and have been restored include the Cathedral of Santa María, with its elaborate tomb containing the remains of Christopher Columbus; the Government Palace; and the Alcázar de Colón, part mansion and part medieval fortress, which was once occupied by Diego Columbus, the discoverer's son. Notable modern buildings include those of University City, housing the faculties of the University of Santo Domingo.

History. Santo Domingo can fairly claim to be the oldest continuously settled community founded by Europeans in the Western Hemisphere. It was established by Bartholomew Columbus, the brother of Christopher, in 1496, on the left bank of the Ozama, a few miles east of San Cristóbal, where the Spaniards had discovered gold deposits. Six years later, the settlement, briefly known as Santiago de Guzmán, was destroyed by a hurricane, but the survivors began immediately to build across the river, near the present site of the cathedral.

For several decades, Diego Columbus and others ruled in considerable splendor in Santo Domingo. By 1550, the gold mines were exhausted and the Indians, who furnished slave labor, had been virtually exterminated by European diseases and warfare. The city's subsequent decline might have resulted in its abandonment had

The Alcázar de Colón in Santo Domingo was once occupied by Diego Columbus, son of Christopher Columbus.

it not become established as an important seat of Spanish administration in the New World. In 1586 the English privateer Sir Francis Drake raided and sacked the town.

A sugar economy gradually became established in the Santo Domingo area, supporting the city while Spanish power in the Caribbean declined during the 17th and 18th centuries. The Haitians held the city from 1822 until 1844, when it became the capital of an independent Dominican Republic. Anarchy led to Santo Domingo's occupation by U. S. marines from 1916 to 1924. Population: (1970) 671,400.

SANTO TOMÁS, University of, sän'tō tō-mäs', in Manila, Philippines. It is also called the Catholic University of the Philippines, a title bestowed by Pope Pius XII in 1947. Santo Tomás was founded by Spanish Dominicans in 1611. Classes in the arts, philosophy, and theology were first conducted in 1619, and schools of civil and canon law were added in 1734. The institution was granted the title "royal" by Charles III of Spain in 1785 and the title "pontifical" by Pope Leo XIII in 1902.

Until the 1920's the school was in the old, walled part of Manila. It began to transfer to a larger campus in 1927. This was used by the Japanese as a concentration camp for American and Allied civilians during World War II, at one point holding as many as 7,000 internees. The university expanded rapidly after the war, reaching an enrollment of over 30,000 by the 1970's.

The institution has schools of civil law, canon law, sacred theology, philosophy, engineering, arts and letters, medicine and surgery, and pharmacy; colleges of science, architecture and fine arts, education, commerce and business administration, and nursing; and a graduate school.

SANTORIN, san-tō-rēn', is an island in the Aegean Sea, perhaps the site of Atlantis. See THERA.

SANTOS, saɴn'tōōs, is a large city in southeastern Brazil. The chief port of São Paulo State, it is situated on São Vicente Island just off the Atlantic coast, some 200 miles (320 km) by air southwest of Rio de Janeiro and less than 30 miles (48 km) southeast of the state's capital, São Paulo, which is the largest city in South America.

The climate at Santos is generally warm and humid, with a mean temperature of 72° F (22° C) and an average annual precipitation of over 80 inches (2,000 mm). The heavy rainfall is caused by moist ocean air impinging against the almost wall-like coastal escarpment of the Serra do Mar, which rises abruptly to a height of nearly 3,000 feet (900 meters). São Paulo city, behind the crest of the escarpment, is connected with Santos by a twisting but broad superhighway and an efficient cable railway.

Santos grew slowly from the time of its settlement by Portuguese (1507) until the middle 1800's, when it became the dominant coffee-shipping port for Brazil. Its growth later accelerated with that of the state. Shipping both the agricultural products of the interior and the industrial goods of metropolitan São Paulo, Santos exports and imports more than 40% of the total value of Brazil's foreign trade goods, and is a major terminal of domestic coastal shipping as well. The economically active part of the population engages mainly in transport and storage activities and other business related to the port, which has the largest dock area in Latin America. The city processes wheat flour, sugar, salt, and fish products. Steel is made and petroleum refined in the suburbs.

Due to extensive building since World War II, Santos has a modern aspect, with many new office and apartment buildings in evidence, but there remain several buildings, monuments, and ruins that date back to the colonial 16th and 17th centuries. Santos is also a seaside resort, with impressive beaches at São Vicente and Guarujá. Population: (1970) 345,459.

SANTOS-DUMONT, saɴɴ'tōōz-dü-môɴ', **Alberto** (1873–1932), Brazilian aviation pioneer, who in 1906 made the first official airplane flight in Europe. He was born João Gomes on July 20, 1873, near São Paulo, later changing his name to Palmyra and then to Santos-Dumont. As a youth he showed an aptitude for mechanics and had conducted many experiments in gliding and ballooning before he went to Paris at the age of 18 to further his studies in aeronautics.

After several years of inventing, Santos-Dumont built his first airship. It was a cigar-shaped bag 80 feet (24 meters) long that was filled with hydrogen and powered by a small gasoline engine.

Between 1897 and 1901, Santos-Dumont built six other small airships. On Oct. 19, 1901, after several attempts, he won the Deutsch Prize of 100,000 francs for his flight in his sixth airship from St. Cloud around the Eiffel Tower and back again, a distance of about 7 miles (11 km). The flight took just under half an hour and was the first of its kind.

Santos-Dumont then turned his attention to heavier-than-air craft. On Oct. 23, 1906, he made the first officially observed successful flight in a powered biplane in Europe and won the Archdeacon Prize. His first successful monoplane, called the *Demoiselle* because of its small size, was a canvas-covered bamboo frame

São Francisco River, in Brazil, drops 275 feet (82 meters) in rapids at Paulo Afonso Falls.

CARL FRANK, PHOTO RESEARCHERS

mounted on bicycle wheels. Even with its engine it weighed only 259 pounds (116.5 kg).

By 1908, French designers had come to the fore, and Santos-Dumont lost his leading position in the world of aviation. As he retired into obscurity the horrors of war haunted him, and each fatal aviation disaster in World War I intensified his belief that the airplane had become a curse. In addition, on his return to Brazil in 1928, an airplane accident occurred in which 14 fliers who had flown out to escort his ship were killed. In 1932 a revolt in São Paulo against the government further depressed him, and he committed suicide on July 24.

Elizabeth B. Brown
Former Historical Librarian,
Institute of Aerospace Sciences

SANUSI, sə-nōō'sē, a Muslim order in Arabia and North Africa, founded in the 19th century, that eventually became a political movement. It was established by Muhammad Ibn Ali al-Sanusi (1787–1859), who was born in Algeria and settled in the Hejaz, Arabia, early in the 19th century. He was greatly influenced by the Syrian theologian Ahmad Ibn Taymiyah (1263–1328), whose writings were his spiritual guide.

Al-Sanusi aimed at a revival of the simplicity of the early days of Islam and the purification of Muslims. The Sanusi (Senusi) order made rapid progress among the Bedouin of the Hejaz, but al-Sanusi was forced to leave. He moved his activities to Cyrenaica, where in 1843 he founded his first African *zawiyah* (monastery), which became the mother house. Under his leadership and that of his son Muhammad al-Mahdi, the order spread rapidly, mainly in Cyrenaica, Tripolitania, and central Africa, until it had a large membership and about 130 monasteries.

Al-Mahdi was succeeded in 1902 by his nephew Ahmad al-Sharif, who was occupied primarily with foreign threats. He led the Sanusi resistance to the French in the Sahara and to the Italians after their invasion of Libya in 1911. During World War I the Sanusi sided with the Central Powers and made an unsuccessful attack on British-occupied Egypt. After the war the Allies forced al-Sharif to relinquish his command, and he was succeeded by his cousin Muhammad Idris.

After acknowledging Italian sovereignty over the coastal parts of Libya, Idris established himself as emir (prince) of the interior of Cyrenaica. Hostilities with Italy were renewed with the advent of Fascism, and Libya was reduced to an Italian colony in 1931. The Sanusi helped defeat the Axis forces in Libya during World War II, and, in 1951, Idris became the first king of independent Libya. In 1969 he was deposed by a military coup that abolished the monarchy.

Nicola A. Ziadeh
American University of Beirut

SÃO FRANCISCO, souɴ fran-sêsh'kōō, a river in northeastern Brazil, which with its tributaries, constitutes the largest river system within the Brazilian Highlands. It is about 1,800 miles (2,880 km) long.

The river rises in the Serra de Canastra in southwest Minas Gerais state at an elevation of just over 4,200 feet (1,276 meters). It flows northward, descending in a series of small falls and rapids, separated by gentle gradients, to about 1,548 feet (470 meters) at the city of Pirapora. Much of the river's length is aligned,

THE VIA ANCHIETA, a super-highway in São Paulo state, links the city of São Paulo with resort towns like Santos and Guaruja.

by a rift valley, parallel to the east coast of Brazil. In its last 150 miles (240 km), it cuts eastward toward the coast and enters the Atlantic Ocean 60 miles (96 km) northeast of Aracaju.

The river's drainage basin, whose area is 239,000 square miles (619,000 sq km), is commonly divided into three parts. The Upper Basin, above the rapids at Pirapora, is an unnavigable section of the river. The Middle Basin, where most of the river is navigable from Pirapora to within 80 miles (128 km) of its mouth, contains 75% of the basin's area and slightly over half its population. In the Lower Basin, a short navigable section of the river flows through the moist *zona da mata* of northeastern Brazil.

An important break in the river's course is the famous Paulo Afonso Falls, 150 miles (240 km) from its mouth, where the river drops 275 feet (82 meters) in a spectacular series of cascades. A large hydroelectric project has been built at the falls.

The Upper Basin and Lower Basin have generally adequate rainfall and moderately high population densities. The vast Middle Basin suffers from low and unpredictable rainfall and is sparsely populated. Some subsistence crops are grown along the banks, but the area's principal economic activity is raising low-quality livestock.

KEMPTON E. WEBB, *Columbia University*

SÃO LUÍS, soun lwēs, a city on the northern coast of Brazil, the capital of Maranhão state, is situated between the bays of São Marcos and São José on São Luís Island, which is actually a peninsula that is cut off from the mainland only by a narrow channel. It is about 250 miles (402 km) southeast of Belém. São Luís has a good harbor on São Marcos Bay at the mouths of the navigable Mearim and Itapecuru rivers, and ships the tropical agricultural products of the region, as well as lumber and hides. São Luís' industries include cotton milling, sugar refining, and food processing.

The city was founded by the French in 1612 and named for King Louis XIII. It was taken by the Portuguese in 1615. A number of Brazil's leading writers were born here, earning the city the name of the "Athens of Brazil." Population: (1970) 210,000.

SÃO MIGUEL, soun mē-gâl′, an island in the Atlantic Ocean, is the largest island in the Azores, which belong to Portugal. It has an area of 288 square miles (746 sq km). It is made up of two mountainous volcanic sections separated by a central hilly region. Fruits and vegetables are raised on the fertile soil, and wine is produced. With Santa Maria, São Miguel forms Ponta Delgado district, named after the island's chief port, a town of over 22,000. See also AZORES.

SÃO PAULO, soun pou′lōō, a state of southern Brazil, is Brazil's most economically productive region, accounting for nearly two thirds of the nation's industrial production, a third of its gross national product, and more than 40% of its tax revenues. The capital is São Paulo, South America's largest city. The chief seaport is Santos.

São Paulo is bounded on the southeast by the Atlantic Ocean. Its coastline is about 300 miles (500 km) long. The state is bounded by Rio de Janeiro state on the northeast, Minas Gerais on the north, Mato Grosso on the west, and Paraná on the south.

The land surface of the state rises abruptly from the narrow Atlantic coastal plain to the 2,900-foot (880-meter) high crest of the Serra do Mar escarpment, within a few dozen miles of the coast. The land beyond the crest slopes downward toward the northeast, away from the sea. As a result, the southeastern third of the state has elevations generally exceeding 2,000 feet (610 meters), while the northwestern boundary at the Paraná River lies at about 500 feet (150 meters) elevation.

The state's coolest temperatures and greatest rainfall occur in the areas of high elevation not far from the coast, with as much as 150 inches (3,800 mm) of rain falling in some districts. Nearly all of the streams in the state rise in the uplands near the coast and eventually flow into the Paraná.

Although the rain forest and precipitous slopes of the coastal zone have discouraged agricultural exploitation, the semideciduous forests of the interior have attracted pioneer planters for over 100 years. The fertile, weathered-lava soils of this region proved ideal for coffee growing, to which the state owed its initial prosperity.

JERRY FRANK

São Paulo is the capital of São Paulo state and one of Brazil's fastest-growing industrial cities.

History. Throughout colonial times, the area that is now the state was crossed by numerous groups of gold and diamond seekers. Except for a few small mining communities, the region remained unsettled and economically stagnant.

After the 1850's, however, the rising world demand for coffee resulted in the establishment of coffee plantations in the São Paulo city area and their subsequent spread westward along the river valleys into the interior. Railroads provided the all-important surface links between the agricultural interior, the trade center of São Paulo city, and the shipping port of Santos. The special character of the population of the state is due mainly to the immigration of settlers from Europe (particularly Italy) since the mid-1880's.

Fortunes from coffee were invested in the new manufacturing enterprises that sprang up in or near the capital city after 1920. Since the mid-1930's, further industrialization, highway building, and the mechanization and diversification of agriculture (cereal grains, cotton, tobacco, truck farming) more than compensated for the decline in coffee production and raised São Paulo to economic preeminence among the Brazilian states. Population: (1979 est.) 22,291,400.

KEMPTON E. WEBB
Columbia University

SÃO PAULO, souɴ pou'lōō, is a city in southern Brazil. It is South America's largest city and the greatest industrial center in Latin America. Though its population in 1883 was only 35,000, São Paulo had grown into a city of more than 1,250,000 by 1940. In the next 40 years it swelled into a metropolis of more than 8 million people. Its rapid and sustained growth from the 1940's to the 1980's led some demographers to predict that it could have a population of 26 million by the year 2000.

Setting. São Paulo is situated 200 miles (320 km) west of Rio de Janeiro, in the eastern part of the state of São Paulo, of which it is the capital. (See SÃO PAULO, state.) It stands just behind the crest of the Serro do Mar escarpment at an elevation of about 2,500 feet (760 meters). It is 33 miles (53 km) northwest of Santos, its port on the Atlantic coast.

Although it is located on the Tropic of Capricorn, it enjoys a temperate, healthful climate due to its high elevation and frequent cloud cover. The average annual temperature is 67° F (19° C), with few extreme readings recorded either in summer (December to March) or winter (June to September).

Unlike a typical Latin American city with broad, tree-lined avenues radiating from a spacious old plaza, São Paulo resembles a large city in North America. Its streets, laid out in the late 19th and early 20th centuries with little planning or thought to the future, tend to be narrow and congested, especially in the downtown area. The effect of crowding is only slightly mitigated by several small parks and one larger one, the Parque Dom Pedro II.

The central business district is the so-called Triangulo, a triangular piece of flat-topped terrace along the southern side of the shallow valley of the Tiete River, a small stream that flows through the city from east to west. As recently as 1949, only three buildings in this area exceeded 12 stories. Twenty years later, a traveler approaching the city by air saw the Triangulo as a virtually unbroken mass of reinforced concrete and glass buildings ranging in height from 20 to 35 stories. Brazil's shortage of structural steel has inhibited the construction of taller buildings.

Economy. The "urban agglomeration" that is São Paulo contains most of the industrial facilities of São Paulo state. The metropolitan area accounts for at least half the total value of industrial production in Brazil.

Manufacturing has been the motive force behind the city's growth since the mid-1930's. From a solid base that included the production of consumer goods, textiles, and food and tobacco products as well as myriad activities connected with the marketing of the agricultural goods of the inland farms, São Paulo launched into heavy industry. Such industry has come to include car manufacturing (with giant Ford, General Motors, and Volkswagen plants in operation), metallurgy, chemicals and pharmaceuticals, transport equipment, furniture, paper, synthetic rubber, electrical goods, and other production. Predictably, the city also became a headquarters of Brazilian and foreign banking operations.

Urban Problems. São Paulo's rapid expansion has brought gigantic problems. Although the city is fairly well connected with outlying districts by highway and railroad, including a cable railway that climbs the escarpment from Santos, the downtown area is glutted with automobiles and buses and seriously polluted by their fumes. Furthermore, despite a higher concentration of cars than occurs in any major world city except Los Angeles, Calif., a 1972 survey revealed that 60% of the roads within the spreading metropolitan city limits remained unpaved in that year. Serious lags also developed in the provision of such services as water supply, sewage disposal, telephones, and public lighting.

In the 1970's more than 350,000 people a year flooded into the city—many more than were being absorbed by São Paulo's new industries. Tens of thousands of the new arrivals were forced to find shelter in the *favelas*—shanty towns with shacks fashioned out of empty crates and hammered tin cans, constructed in whatever outlying area had not yet been developed by realtors. At least a third of the city's residents were living in accommodations that lacked running water.

Hope for the future rested with a basic urban plan, introduced in the late 1960's and designed to impose some control on the city's growth until 1990. São Paulo's taxing capacity as a municipality gave it at least the potential to finance the improvements needed in public services and housing, provided that the vast influx of indigent families from rural Brazil could be slowed. A key element of the urban plan was the building of a 270-mile (430-km) subway and the construction of a complex of peripheral highways that are designed to reduce traffic congestion in the central city.

City Life and Institutions. Paulistas, as the residents of the city are called, live in an atmosphere of hubbub and bustle unusual in Latin American cities, and display a tendency toward independence and entrepreneurial initiative. The typical Paulista is a relatively recent arrival who came to the city to make his fortune, and his interests and activities often reflect this preoccupation.

Despite the city's business orientation and its many social problems, it has many of the cultural advantages and amenities of a more settled metropolis. It has four universities, including the University of São Paulo, one of Brazil's leading educational institutions.

São Paulo is a major center of medical research, with over 200 hospital organizations, several of which are teaching hospitals. There are more than 100 libraries, many concert halls and motion-picture theaters, more than a dozen radio broadcasting stations, and several television stations. The principal newspaper, *O Estado de São Paulo*, has one of the largest circulations in Brazil.

History. São Paulo was founded by Jesuits in 1554, on the feast day of Saint Paul (January 25). It was little more than a jumping-off place for diamond and gold prospectors until the early 19th century, when it became prominent briefly as a center of agitation for Brazilian independence from Portugal.

In 1822, Dom Pedro of the Portuguese royal house (later Emperor Pedro I of Brazil) chose the city as the site for the proclamation of national independence. The city's growth began with the spread of coffee cultivation over the interior of the state in the last half of the 19th century. By 1890, São Paulo was serving the coffee boom as a center of marketing and finance and as a collection point from which the product was sent by railroad to the port of Santos for shipment overseas.

Coffee financiers were largely responsible for the establishment and support of the processing facilities that began to turn the city into a light industrial center in the early 1900's. Contributing to São Paulo's subsequent growth were such natural advantages as its altitude and relatively cool climate, which protected it from the serious epidemics that afflicted lower-lying, more tropical cities such as Rio de Janeiro. Population: (1978 est.) 8,300,000.

KEMPTON E. WEBB
Columbia University

SKYSCRAPERS like these are typical of the architecture of São Paulo, a thoroughly modern city.

MANCHETE, FROM PICTORIAL

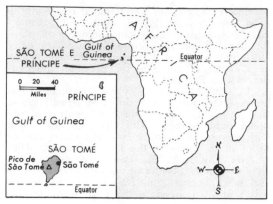

Location map of São Tomé e Príncipe.

SÃO TOMÉ E PRÍNCIPE, soun tōō-mâ′ ē prĕn′sĕ-pē, formerly a Portuguese overseas province in the Gulf of Guinea off the west coast of Africa, became an independent republic on July 12, 1975. It consists of two islands: São Tomé, about 150 miles (240 km) northwest of Cape Lopez, Gabon; and Príncipe, about 90 miles (145 km) northeast of São Tomé.

The Land. The islands, which have a combined area of 372 square miles (964 sq km), form part of a volcanic arc stretching from the Cameroon Mountains to the island of Annobón to the southwest. São Tomé is about 30 miles (50 km) long and 20 miles (30 km) wide. It is mountainous, with peaks over 3,500 feet (1,000 meters) in height. The highest is Pico de São Tomé, which rises to 6,640 feet (2,024 meters). Príncipe, about 10 miles (16 km) long and 5 miles (8 km) wide, is less rugged.

Located close to the equator, the islands have a typically tropical climate, with high temperatures and heavy rainfall. The rainy season lasts from September through May. Both islands were originally covered by tropical rain forest, but today virgin forest remains only in the mountainous centers.

The People. The country had a population of about 70,000 at independence in 1975. Most of the inhabitants live on São Tomé. The capital, on São Tomé island, is also called São Tomé.

The indigenous inhabitants are descendants of the original Portuguese colonists and Africans from the coast of Guinea. The official language is Portuguese, and the principal religion is Roman Catholicism.

The Economy. The soil is exceptionally fertile. Sugar cultivation produced considerable prosperity in the 16th century, but competition from Brazil caused a commercial decline that lasted for two centuries. The introduction of coffee and cacao in the early 19th century initiated an economic revival, and the islands were one of the world's major producers of cacao prior to World War I.

The main export product of the islands is cacao, supplemented by coffee, palm oil, copra (from coconuts), and bananas. The trees are cultivated on large European-owned plantations by African contract laborers from Angola, Mozambique, and the Cape Verde Islands. São Tomé e Príncipe exports most of its production and imports most of its food and manufactured goods. There is generally a favorable balance of trade. Portugal buys most of the islands' exports, except cacao, and supplies most of the imports.

History. The Portuguese navigators Pedro Escobar and João de Santarém discovered São Tomé late in 1470 and Príncipe early in 1471. The islands were settled by Portuguese and by mainland Africans brought as slaves. They were declared a Portuguese overseas province in 1522, but were occupied briefly by the Dutch in the mid-17th century.

Early in 1974 the new revolutionary government in Portugal promised independence to Portugal's possessions in Africa. A Gabon-based group, the Movement for the Liberation of São Tomé and Príncipe, headed by Manuel Pinto da Costa, was ready to take control. On July 12, 1975, the islands became the independent Democratic Republic of São Tomé and Príncipe, and Costa was proclaimed its first president.

RICHARD J. HOUK*, *De Paul University*

SAÔNE-ET-LOIRE, sôn-ā-lwär′, is a department in east central France, in Burgundy. It stretches from the Loire River on the southwest to beyond the Saône on the northeast and has an area of 3,331 square miles (8,627 sq km). The capital is Mâcon. Mâcon and Beaujolais wines are produced. Le Creusot is an important industrial center. Population: (1969) 550,362.

SAÔNE RIVER, sôn, a river in central France. It rises in the Faucilles hills of the Vosges, about 15 miles (24 km) southwest of Épinal. It flows southwest to enter Saône-et-Loire department, where it receives the Doubs River. The Saône turns south at Chalon and flows along the borders of Saône-et-Loire, Ain, and Rhône departments toward Lyon, where it joins the Rhône. Its total length is about 300 miles (483 km), most of which is canalized.

SAP, a fluid found in plants, consists mainly of water in which many substances have dissolved. The water enters the plant through the roots from the soil. Two kinds of sap may be distinguished: *crude* sap and *elaborated* sap. Crude sap ascends from the roots through the xylem to the leaves. It carries water and minerals that are needed as raw materials for growth and for food manufacture that takes place in the leaves. Elaborated sap descends from the leaves, distributing the foods manufactured there to various parts of the plant where they are needed.

Cohesive forces originating in the leaves appear to be chiefly responsible for the ascent of crude sap. The sap is thought to be "pulled up" the stem by the resultant tension, sometimes as high as nearly 400 feet (120 meters) in the tallest trees. Most of the water taken into the plant from the soil passes out of the plant eventually in the form of vapor from the leaves. However, some of it, as crude sap, may leave the plant in liquid form, a phenomenon known as *guttation*. Guttation is especially noticeable on lawn grasses in the early morning when the sap appears as large drops at the tips of the leaves and is commonly mistaken for dew. The flow of elaborated sap may result in part from pressures developed in the leaves. Girdling, or the removal of a ring of bark from the trunk of a tree, results in a tree's eventual death because the elaborated sap, which travels through the inner bark, can no longer reach the roots and provide them with the foods needed.

Some sap is of direct economic importance. The sap of the sugar maple is, for example, the source of maple sugar and syrup, and the sap of certain century plants (*Agave*) is used to make the beverages pulque and mescal in Mexico.

JOHN W. THIERET
University of Southwestern Louisiana

SAPAJOU, a medium-sized monkey. See also CAPUCHIN.

SAPIR, sə-pēr′, **Edward** (1884–1939), American anthropologist and linguist. He was born in Lauenburg, Germany (now Lebork, Poland), on Jan. 26, 1884. The son of a Jewish cantor, he migrated with his family to the United States in 1889. He was raised from early childhood in New York City, attended Horace Mann School and Columbia University (A. B., 1904) on scholarships, and received his doctorate from Columbia in 1909. His original fields of study were the Germanic and Semitic languages, but he was drawn into anthropology and American Indian language study by the influence of Franz Boas. Beginning in 1907 he held posts successively at the universities of California and Pennsylvania, as chief of the division of anthropology in the Geological Survey of Canada (1910–1925), and at the University of Chicago. From 1931 to 1939 he was Sterling professor of anthropology and linguistics at Yale University, where he chaired the newly founded department of anthropology. There, as at Chicago, he attracted students from a broad spectrum of related fields: anthropology, linguistics, sociology, psychology, and psychiatry. Sapir died in New Haven on Feb. 4, 1939.

Though his field research was primarily among the Indians of the western United States and Canada, his range of linguistic interests covered most of the world. Through the study of language as a communicative medium and of semantics as concerned with its accuracy, he became interested in personality and its relations to the environing culture. His book *Language, An Introduction to the Study of Speech* (1921), is as much concerned with symbolic and communicative aspects as with technical linguistics. As chairman (1934–1935) of the division of anthropology and psychology of the National Research Council, he was able to advance the convergence of interest, which he pioneered, between anthropology and psychiatry. His basic views are to be found in "The Emergence of the Concept of Personality in a Study of Cultures" (*Journal of Social Psychology,* 1934). He also made major contributions to cultural anthropological theory and method, as in *Time Perspective in Aboriginal American Culture: A Study in Method* (1916), and to folklore.

Sapir's impact, both direct and indirect, remains strong in linguistics and anthropology. In a comparatively brief teaching career, he trained or influenced many of the present leading figures in these fields. His writings, some reprinted many times, are a part of their contemporary literature. In addition to his scholarly gifts, he was a poet, musician, and champion of human rights. His poetry appeared in *Poetry, The New Republic, The Dial, The Canadian Forum, The Nation,* and other magazines. His talents as a writer added much to the readability of his scholarly productions.

ROBERT F. G. SPIER, *University of Missouri*

The sapodilla tree is a broadleaved tropical evergreen.

SAPODILLA, sap-ə-dil′ə, a handsome, evergreen, white-flowered tree, *Achras zapota,* of the sapodilla (Sapotaceae) family. It is native to southern Mexico and to adjacent Central America but it is now grown throughout the tropical regions of the world, including southern Florida. The sapodilla tree is the chief source of chicle, a key ingredient in chewing gum. See also CHICLE.

The fruit of the sapodilla tree is 3 to 4 inches (8 to 10 cm) in diameter. The skin is brown, thick, and rough. The soft yellow-brown or red-brown flesh, which is often granular, has a sweet agreeable flavor. It contains several hard glossy brown or black seeds. The fruit may be eaten out of hand or in salads, or it may be pulped and used in sherbets or ice cream. Also, jam or marmalade may be made from it.

JOHN W. THIERET°
University of Southwestern Louisiana

SAPONIFICATION, sə-pon-ə-fə-kā′shən, is a form of hydrolysis in which an ester reacts with an alkali to form an alcohol and a salt of the ester. The reaction is best known for its use in making soap. See also HYDROLYSIS; SOAP.

SAPONIN, sap′ə-nən, any of a certain group of chemicals occurring in soapberry, soapwort, and a number of other plants. These plants have long been used as soap substitutes in various countries, because the saponins produce quantities of lather when the plants are shaken with water. A commercial product also called saponin is derived from such plants and used as a foaming and emulsifying agent and detergent.

Saponins are glycosides, or chemicals that yield sugars when hydrolyzed. However, one kind also yields steroids, while another kind yields certain terpene derivatives. Saponins are poisonous in the bloodstream because they dissolve red blood cells.

See also GLYCOSIDE.

SAPONITE, sap′ə-nīt, is a clay mineral that has a high magnesium content. See CLAY—*Montmorillonite Group.*

SAPPHIRE, saf'ir, is a name given to all gem varieties of corundum except those of reddish color, which are called ruby. The word sapphire used alone always refers to the blue gemstone. Those of other colors are called, for example, yellow sapphire or pink sapphire, and when colorless are called white sapphire. Stones that show a starlike optical effect when cut in a convex shape are called star sapphires. The effect is produced by reflections from tiny needle-shaped inclusions of the mineral rutile in the sapphire's crystal structure.

Sapphires other than those of blue color are often sold under the names of other gems with the word oriental as a prefix. Thus, oriental emerald is a name that has been given to green sapphire, and oriental topaz is called yellow sapphire. In the literature of antiquity and the Middle Ages, colorless sapphire was often referred to as a form of diamond, and other gemstones, now given specific names of their own, were often called sapphires.

Uses. Sapphire is best known as a gem, but because of its hardness—9 on the Mohs scale—it is also used industrially as thread guides, orifices in oil furnaces, and small spheres in ball-point pens. Because of its unusual dielectric properties it is used in electrical instruments, and because of its transparency and resistance to heat it is used as windows in high-temperature furnaces. Its transparency to ultraviolet and infrared radiation also makes the stone of use in optical instruments.

Sources. The finest sapphires come from Kashmir, and their color is described as Kashmir blue. Occasional fine stones of the same quality from other sources are also called Kashmir sapphires. Most mines produce a variety of colors. Other important producing districts are near Bangkok in Thailand, near Mogok in Upper Burma, Ceylon, Afghanistan, and central Queensland, Australia. The best star sapphires come from Ceylon. Some fine sapphires have also been mined in the United States in an area south of the Missouri River in central Montana.

Although a few sapphires have been mined from crystalline rocks, the great majority have come from placer deposits in stream beds. Prior to World War I they were extensively mined for use as jewel bearings in watches and in electrical measuring instruments such as household meters. The finer stones were sold as gems, but most of the income from the mining operations came from the sale of industrial-quality stones. Then, in the mid-1920's, synthetics supplanted natural stones as jewel bearings. However, a few natural stones are still produced today from irregularly operated mines in East Asia and in Australia. Natural sapphire as a gemstone has not been completely replaced, however, because the fine blue Kashmir sapphires have never been duplicated artificially.

Artificial Sapphires. In 1902, Auguste Verneuil, a French scientist, developed the process for making synthetic gem sapphires. The basic material is powdered corundum (Al_2O_3), which gives carrot-shaped crystals called *boules* when fused. A small amount of iron and titanium imparts a blue color, a cobalt a green color, nickel and magnesium a yellow color, and more than 5% of chromic oxide (Cr_2O_3) a deep red color. The process has been called the flame-fusion method because an oxyhydrogen flame is used, the oxygen carrying the powder into the center of the flame. Crystallographic orientation may be controlled by using small seed crystals onto which the fused droplets fall. Star sapphires were first manufactured in 1947 by adding about 1% of titanium dioxide (TiO_2).

See also CORUNDUM; GEMS.

C. B. SLAWSON
Coauthor of "Gems and Gem Materials"

SAPPHO, saf'ō, Greek poet of the late 7th and 8th centuries B. C., who was one of the greatest of the ancient classical lyricists. She was born on the island of Lesbos, Greece, probably in the late 7th century B. C. Little is known for certain of her life, but she was married and had a daughter. Stories of her love for Phaon and of her suicide are doubtless fictions. The date of her death is unknown.

Sappho was the most famous of Greek woman poets. Her collected works were apparently arranged according to type into nine books in ancient times. There were many poems. The famous "few, but roses all" may mean "short (poems) but roses." No continuous manuscript of Sappho is extant; two poems of greater length, possibly complete, have survived through quotation by later critics, Dionysius and the Pseudo-Longinus, and some epigrams, of doubtful authenticity, are preserved in *The Palatine Anthology*. There are also fairly extensive papyrus fragments, some representing almost complete poems.

Sappho showed little interest in politics, though civil wars are said to have disturbed her life. Mostly, she wrote short lyrics to and about girls she favored, with informal hymns, apparently not for choral presentation, addressed to divinities, such as Hera and Aphrodite. There was also a group of wedding poems. Elsewhere, Sappho is bitter, and sometimes sententious. Most characteristic are simple love lyrics that described the state of her own feelings with regard to her favorite girls.

Sappho's poetic language is apparently not a literary dialect but the Aeolic vernacular of Lesbos. It is frank, simple, and exquisitely arranged in meters that, though intricate, are easily read, lacking the bewildering scale and length of choral strophes. She may well have invented several types of line and stanza, including the one named after her. The Sapphic stanza is a four-line stanza, the first three lines of which have 11 syllables each, and the fourth line, five syllables. Sappho's strength is in the effortless adaptation of feeling to form. She was well known in Rome. Catullus translated one poem, borrowed lines elsewhere, and used some of her meters. Horace used the Sapphic stanza frequently.

RICHMOND LATTIMORE
Author of "Greek Lyrics"

Further Reading: Bowra, Sir Cecil Maurice, *Greek Lyric Poetry: From Alcman to Simonides*, 2d ed. (Oxford 1961); Lattimore, Richmond, *Greek Lyrics*, 2d ed., (Univ. of Chicago Press 1960); Lobel, Edgar, and Page, Denys L., eds., *Poetarum Lesbiorum Fragmenta* (Oxford 1955); Page, Denys L., *Sappho and Alcaeus: An Introduction to the Study of Ancient Lesbian Poetry* (Oxford 1955).

SAPPINGTON, an unincorporated area in eastern Missouri, in St. Louis county, is situated just west of the city of St. Louis. Sappington lies within the townships of Concord, Gravois, and Bonhomme. It was undeveloped until the 1960's, when it was built up as a residential suburb of St. Louis. Population: 10,603.

SAPPORO, säp-pô-rō, the largest city in northern Japan, is situated in southwestern Hokkaido Island, about 500 miles (800 km) north of Tokyo. It lies on the Toyohira River.

The city is the capital of Hokkaido prefecture. It also serves as the processing and distribution center for the agricultural plain of Ishikari, on which it lies. Sapporo's chief manufacturing industries are food processing, lumber milling, and printing.

The city was laid out in 1871 on a rectilinear plan and has wide, tree-lined streets. It is the home of Hokkaido University. There are botanical gardens with alpine flora in the city and hot springs nearby. The climate is cold, and Sapporo is a winter sports center, with skiing grounds in the suburbs and ski jumps nearby. The city was host to the 1972 Winter Olympic games. Population: (1970) 1,010,123.

SAPROLITE, sap'rə-līt, is a disintegrated rock that still retains some of its former texture and structural appearance. The soft, reddish or brownish material is produced in humid tropical and subtropical regions by the chemical decay of rock strata and consists primarily of clays and silts. Formations of saprolite may extend to depths of 300 feet (100 meters). The material is easily excavated, but because of its weak and plastic nature it is unable to support heavy engineering structures.

SAPROPHYTE, sap'rə-fīt, a nongreen plant that lives on dead or decaying plant or animal matter. Mushrooms, molds, and some other fungi and certain species of bacteria are saprophytes. A few flowering plants, including Indian pipe and some members of the orchid family, are saprophytes. Saprophytes lack chlorophyll and therefore cannot manufacture their own food through the process of photosynthesis, but they possess certain enzymes that enable them to break down decaying organic matter and absorb the nutrient particles. Saprophytes that cannot live any other way are termed *obligate* saprophytes, while plants that are usually parasitic but that under certain conditions become saprophytes are termed *facultative* saprophytes.

SAPSUCKER, either of two species of North American woodpeckers making up the genus *Sphyrapicus*. The sapsuckers differ from other woodpeckers chiefly in their feeding habits. They eat more vegetable matter, especially the sap or soft inner bark of trees. They secure this inner bark, called cambium, by chiseling neat rows of circular pits or squarish holes through the outer bark. They then eat the cambium and with the tips of their tongues lap the drops of sap that accumulate. They also eat the insects that are attracted by the flowing sap. The sapsucker's tongue and the muscles that control it are quite different from those of other woodpeckers. The tongue is not extensible and ends in a soft brush rather than as a dart, as in other woodpeckers. Sapsuckers occasionally do quite a good deal of damage to trees, especially in orchards, but they also perform a useful function of destroying some harmful insects.

The sapsuckers are about 9 inches (23 cm) long. Their plumage is handsomely variegated, either black and white or red and yellow. The best known and most abundant is the common, or yellow-bellied, sapsucker (S. *varius*), which is

Yellow-bellied sapsucker (*Sphyrapicus varius*)

widely distributed in the wooded regions of Canada and the United States. Williamson's sapsucker (S. *thyroideus*) is rarer and is restricted to the pine forests of the western mountains. It has a white patch on each wing and a red throat patch.

CHARLES VAURIE[*]
The American Museum of Natural History

SAPULPA, sə-pul'pə, a city in central Oklahoma, the seat of Creek county, is in an agricultural region, 15 miles (24 km) southwest of Tulsa and 100 miles (160 km) northeast of Oklahoma City. It is an industrial city and the center of an area that is rich in oil and natural gas. Its chief industries are meat packing and the manufacture of glass, pottery, bricks, furnaces, tanks, and tools.

William Sapulpa, a Creek Indian, established a trading post on this site in the early 1880's. A settlement was founded in 1888, and in 1898 it was incorporated as the city of Sapulpa. It has a council-manager form of government. Population: 15,853.

SAQQARA, sə-kär'rə, was the necropolis of the ancient Egyptian city of Memphis. Its remains still stand 3 miles (5 km) west of the Nile, on the border of the Libyan Desert and 15 miles (24 km) southwest of Cairo. It is one of the main archaeological sites of Egypt.

The oldest remains at Saqqara (Sakkara) are mud brick mastabas dating from the beginning of Egyptian history. Tombs were built by the kings of the 1st and 2d dynasties at both Saqqara and Abydos, and it is uncertain which necropolis has the real graves and which has cenotaphs.

Saqqara is the site of the world's first large structure in stone, the stepped pyramid of King Djoser of the 3d dynasty. Designed by the royal architect Imhotep, the tomb rises in six steps and originally reached a height of 200 feet (60 meters). The pyramid dominates the scene of a mortuary complex including a temple, courtyards, and an enclosure wall.

The first king of the 5th dynasty, Userkaf, built his pyramid at Saqqara, but his successors were buried at Abusir, to the north. The last rulers of the dynasty returned to Saqqara, and

The Step Pyramid of King Djoser dominates the skyline at Saqqara, near Cairo.

the pyramid of King Unis was the first to have the funerary literature known as Pyramid Texts inscribed on its interior walls. The 6th dynasty kings were also buried at Saqqara.

Around the pyramids stand the mastaba tombs of the nobility. The Serapeum, the burial place of the sacred Apis bulls, dates from the Late Kingdom.

SARABAND, sar'ə-band, an old dance developed in Spain. The saraband, probably imported from Central America to Andalusia, was a wild street dance and song, criticized by 16th century Spanish writers for its lascivity and suppressed by Philip II. It was gradually purified in European court ballets and ballrooms of the 17th century. The dance was in triple time, with allowance for variations of steps. Some versions, closer to the original, were fast and performed with bells on the legs and with castanets. Others were slow, stately processional dances done with gliding steps accented on the second beat. This type became the slow movement in the musical suite. Quick sarabands continued into the 18th century, especially in the theater.

SARACENS, sar'ə-sənz, was the general term applied by Christians during the Middle Ages to Islamic peoples, both Arab and Turkish. The term is still in limited use. The Saracens mentioned by classical writers were a tribe living in northern Arabia. In succeeding centuries its application was extended to cover all Arabs and then to describe all Muslims. The Saracens invaded France in the early 8th century but were stopped by Charles Martel. Their cultural influence, particularly in architecture, was especially noticeable in Sicily, which they held from the 9th century to the 11th.

SARACOĞLU, sä-räj-ō-gloo', **Sükrü** (1887–1953), Turkish prime minister. He was born in Ödemis, received a superior education, and became a lawyer. After World War I he joined the nationalist movement of Mustafa Kemal (Kemal Atatürk) and was elected to the Grand National Assembly in 1923. He held a number of cabinet posts, including minister of justice, in which he fostered Atatürk's Westernization program. He was appointed foreign minister by President İnönü in 1938.

As foreign minister he followed a policy of strict neutrality in World War II. After he became prime minister in 1942, Saracoğlu continued Turkey's neutrality, although with some anti-Axis bias, until Turkey declared war on Germany and Japan in 1945. He left office in 1946 but retained his seat in the Grand National Assembly until 1950. He died in Istanbul on Dec. 27, 1953.

SARAGAT, sä-rä-gät', **Giuseppe** (1898–   ), president of Italy. He was born in Turin on Sept. 19, 1898. He attended the University of Turin and became a banker. He joined the Socialist party in 1922. When Mussolini banned opposition parties in 1926, Saragat went into exile and opposed the Fascists until he could return to Italy after Mussolini's overthrow in 1943.

In 1946 he was elected president of the Constituent Assembly that drew up Italy's new constitution. Opposing the Socialists' plans to work with the Communists, Saragat left the party in 1947 to form the more moderate Social Democratic party but continued to serve in the cabinets of numerous governments. In an attempt to stabilize Italian politics, Saragat developed the "opening to the left" that brought a center-left coalition to power in 1963. Saragat served as foreign minister in the new government until late 1964, when he succeeded Antonio Segni as president. Saragat left office in 1971.

SARAGOSSA, sä-rä-gō'sä, the traditional capital of Aragón, is a city in northern Spain, 160 miles (258 km) west of Barcelona and situated on the south bank of the Ebro River. It is the capital of Saragossa province. The name is also spelled Zaragoza. The city is the major industrial, commercial, and communications center for the region. Its manufactures include agricultural machinery, textiles, chemicals, and glass.

The old city lies between the river, which is spanned by a 15th century arched bridge, and the curving Calle del Coso, which follows the line of the medieval walls. The Cathedral of La Seo was begun in 1119 on the site of a mosque. The Cathedral del Pilar, begun in 1681 and containing some paintings by Goya, commemorates the appearance of the Virgin before Saint James in 40 A. D. Among the Moorish structures is the Castillo de la Aljafería. The University of Saragossa, founded in 1474, is noted for its medical school.

Originally an Iberian settlement, it was taken by the Romans in the 1st century B. C. Under Augustus it was called Caesaraugusta, from which its modern name is derived. It became an early center of Christianity before falling to the Suevi and the Visigoths in the 5th century. The Moors captured the city about 712.

In 1118, Alfonso I of Aragón liberated Saragossa from the Moors, and it began three centuries of prosperity as the capital of the kingdom of Aragón. Its importance declined somewhat when the royal court shifted to Castile in the late 15th century. In 1808–1809, during the Peninsular War, the city heroically withstood a French siege, in which half the city's population died, before capitulating. One of the most staunch defenders was the Maid of Saragossa.

The Province. The province, which reaches the lower Pyrenees on the north, has an area of 6,615 square miles (17,133 sq km). It is divided northwest-southeast by the Ebro. Irrigation canals parallel part of the river on either bank, providing water for farms that raise sugar beets, grain, and other crops. The province receives little rainfall, and most of the rural population lives in the few fertile valleys. Industry and commerce are concentrated around the capital city. Population: (1969 est.) of the city, 434,900; of the province, 741,800.

SARAH, sâr'ə, was the wife of the biblical patriarch Abraham and the mother of Isaac. She was childless when God promised Abram that he would be the sire of a great people, changing Abram's name to Abraham and that of Sarai, as she was called, to Sarah (Genesis 17:15). See also ABRAHAM.

SARAI, sä-rī', was the name of two capitals of the Mongols' Golden Horde. The first, established in the 13th century by Batu-Khan, was northwest of modern Astrakhan. In the 14th century the capital was moved to a new site, also called Sarai, or Sarai-Berke, east of modern Volgograd. See also GOLDEN HORDE.

SARAJEVO, sar-ə-yā'vō, the site of the assassination of Archduke Francis Ferdinand, which precipitated World War I, is a city in central Yugoslavia. Its name is also spelled *Serajevo* and *Sarayevo*. The capital of the Bosnia and Hercegovina republic, the city is on the Miljacka River, 125 miles (200 km) southwest of Belgrade. It is the economic and communications center of Bosnia and has steel, jewelry, carpet, weaving, and tobacco industries. The city is the seat of a Roman Catholic archbishop, an Orthodox metropolitan, and the most important Muslim religious official in Yugoslavia.

Sarajevo was long under Turkish control, and the old Turkish quarter occupies the hilly eastern section. Among the city's many mosques are the Begova, or Chusrev Beg, the country's principal mosque, which was completed in 1531 and is one of Yugoslavia's most beautiful Ottoman buildings. Between the Begova and the river is the Turkish bazaar, a jumble of narrow alleys and small shops, which continues to be a lively center of

SPANISH GOVERNMENT TOURIST OFFICE

The Cathedral del Pilar in Saragossa, Spain, along the banks of the Ebro River. It is built on the site where, by tradition, the Virgin, descending from heaven on a marble pillar, appeared before Saint James.

Minaret of Begova mosque pierces Sarajevo's skyline in the old Turkish quarter. Begova, one of the most striking Ottoman structures in Yugoslavia, is the country's principal mosque.

EASTFOTO

trade. Across the river is the Careva mosque, also built in the 16th century. Beyond the Careva is the city's carpet factory. The national museum, the university, and the 19th century town hall are also of interest.

The first recorded mention of Sarajevo is in the early 15th century, when there was a fortress called Vrh-Bosna. In 1429 the Turks captured this fortress and founded the town of Bosna-Sarai, the forerunner of Sarajevo, below it. Austrian forces under Prince Eugene burned the town in 1697.

The Turks made it the capital of Bosnia-Hercegovina in 1851, and it continued as the capital when the region passed to Austria-Hungary in 1878. It soon became a center of Serbian nationalism, and on June 28, 1914, Austria's Archduke Francis Ferdinand was assassinated in the city. Austria-Hungary used his death as an excuse to attack Serbia, precipitating World War I. After the war, the city was incorporated into Yugoslavia. Population: (1971) 210,000.

SARANAC LAKE, sar′ə-nak, a village in the Adirondack Mountains of northern New York, in Franklin and Essex counties, is on the Saranac River, near Lower Lake Saranac, about 50 miles (80 km) southwest of Plattsburgh. It is a vacation resort and a medical research center. Tourism, dressmaking, and the manufacture of wood products are its chief industries.

Saranac Lake was settled in 1819 and incorporated in 1892. In 1884 Edward Livingstone Trudeau established a tuberculosis sanatorium near the village. The English author Robert Louis Stevenson stayed here in 1887–1888, and his cabin is still a tourist attraction. In 1894, Trudeau opened a laboratory for the study of tuberculosis and in 1930 the Will Rogers Memorial Sanitorium opened. Saranac Lake is governed by a city manager. Population: 5,578.

SARASOTA, sar-ə-sō′tə, a city in western Florida, the seat of Sarasota county, is on Sarasota Bay, an inlet of the Gulf of Mexico, 55 miles (88 km) south of Tampa. It is the winter quarters of the Ringling Brothers Barnum and Bailey

Circus. The surrounding area produces citrus fruits and celery. Industry in the city includes electronics, aviation, boat building, and the manufacture of mobile homes.

Places of interest include the Circus Hall of Fame; the Ringling Museums, including an art museum of 16th, 17th, and 18th century masterpieces, the Ringling Museum of the Circus, and a large reference library on Baroque art; the Bellm Cars and Music of Yesterday museum; and the Sarasota Jungle Gardens. Sarasota was founded in 1896 and incorporated in 1902. It has a council-manager form of government. Population: 48,868.

SARASWATI, Dayanand. See DAYANAND SARASWATI.

SARATOGA, sar-ə-tō′ga, a city in western California, in Santa Clara county, is about 40 miles (64 km) southeast of the center of San Francisco. A winery is among the principal industries. The Saratoga campus of West Valley junior college is here. Saratoga was incorporated as a city in 1956. Government is by mayor and council. Population: 29,261.

SARATOGA, Battles of, two battles of the American Revolution, which are commonly known by other names. See AMERICAN REVOLUTION—*Important Battles*.

SARATOGA SPRINGS, sar-ə-tō′ga, is a city in eastern New York, in Saratoga county, about 25 miles (40 km) north of Albany. It is often called "Saratoga." It has been for many years a health and pleasure resort, and has textile, electronic, and packaging industries.

The beneficial qualities of the mineral springs, which were known to the Indians, have attracted visitors since soon after the Revolution. During the mid-19th century, many hotels, notably the United States—once said to be the largest in the world—made the community one of the most famous resorts of the time. Since 1935, many of the springs have been in a state reservation.

Horse racing began at the Saratoga race track about 1850, and for many years the August race

Saratoga Springs, a famous summer resort, was a haven for fashionable society during the 19th century.

meeting was one of the most important in the United States. The National Museum of Racing in the city has exhibits relating to the thoroughbred horse and horse racing.

Other places of interest include the Saratoga Historical Museum and Walworth Museum, and the Hathorn Gallery, affiliated with Skidmore College for women, which is in the city. The Saratoga battlefield, scene of Revolutionary War battles, the second of which was an American victory that was the turning point of the war, is east of the city.

The site of the city was ceded by the Indians to the Dutch in 1684. The community was incorporated as a village in 1829 and as a city in 1915. Population: 23,906.

SARATOV, sä-rä′tôf, is a city in the USSR, in the Russian republic. It is the capital of Saratov oblast and is on the Volga River, about 450 miles (650 km) southeast of Moscow. It is an important industrial and cultural center of the lower Volga Valley.

Saratov's principal industries are steel fabrication, petrochemicals, and glass. Machinery plants manufacture electric steel furnaces, diesel engines, bearings, and refrigerators. The chemical industry is based on an oil refinery and yields synthetic alcohol, acetylene, and synthetic fibers. Some of the raw material is obtained from small oil and gas fields nearby. The Saratov hydroelectric station, completed in 1970, is upstream near Balakovo.

Saratov arose in 1590 as a fortress guarding Russian trade on the Volga River against the hostile nomads of the steppe to the east. In the 19th century it developed as a center for the grain trade of the surrounding region. The city has a university founded in 1909, an opera, and a conservatory. Nikolai G. Chernyshevsky, a 19th century Russian revolutionist, was born in the city.

The Oblast. Saratov oblast covers an area of 39,000 square miles (101,000 sq km) on both banks of the Volga. It is a major wheat-growing region of European Russia, and beef cattle and sheep are raised. Industrial centers, in addition to the capital, include Engels, across the Volga from Saratov, and the new chemical center of

Balakovo. Population: (1970) of the city, 757,-000; of the oblast, 2,454,000.

THEODORE SHABAD
Editor of "Soviet Geography"

SARAWAK, sə-rä′wäk, a state of Malaysia. See BORNEO; MALAYSIA.

SARAZEN, sar′ə-zən, **Gene** (1902–   ), American golfer. He was born in Harrison, N. Y., on Feb. 27, 1902. Beginning his golf career as a caddy in Rye, N. Y., Sarazen quickly rose to prominence as a player. He first qualified for the U. S. Open when he was 18 years old, and he won the Open championship in 1922 when only 20. He then defeated Walter Hagen in a 72-hole match for the unofficial world's championship. Though a contemporary of such great players as Hagen, Bobby Jones, and others, Sarazen did well in major tournaments. He repeated his U. S. Open triumph in 1932, also won the British Open in 1932, and won the Professional Golf Association championship in 1922, 1923 (defeating Hagen on the 38th hole), and 1933.

Sarazen's most spectacular victory came in the 1935 Masters tournament, when his double eagle deuce on the 15th hole of the final round gained him a playoff against Craig Wood, which Sarazen won. Sarazen, who was short and stocky, was the first golfer to win all four of the major tournaments cited above. He narrowly missed a third U. S. Open title in 1940, losing a play-off to Lawson Little. He also represented the United States in four Ryder Cup matches against Britain. During a long career, Sarazen was also a golf instructor and a club professional. He was a strong player into the late 1940's.

SARCODINA, sär-kə-dī′nə, is the class of protozoa, or unicellular animals, that includes the amoebas. All members of this class characteristically have cytoplasmic extensions, or pseudopodia, that function as organs of locomotion and for trapping food particles. Sarcodinians are found in both fresh and marine water, and some live on moist surface soils. Most are solitary or free-living, but some are parasitic and colonial. See AMOEBA.

SARCOIDOSIS, sär-koi-dō′sis, is a systemic inflammatory disease characterized by the appearance of nodules and scar tissue in the lungs, lymph nodes, bones, and various other organs of the body. The disease occurs throughout the world, most commonly affecting people between the ages of 20 and 40. In the United States it is much more common among Negroes than among Caucasians. The cause of sarcoidosis is not known.

Diagnosis of sarcoidosis is frequently difficult because the symptoms are often minimal and vague. There may be some generalized signs of mild fever, weight loss, and lack of energy, but other symptoms, which depend on the particular organs involved, often do not appear until there is extensive tissue involvement.

There is no specific treatment. Cortisone and other adrenocortical steroids are sometimes administered to suppress the inflammatory process. In many cases, there is a spontaneous remission.

SARCOMA, sär-kō′mə, a type of cancer consisting of a malignant tumor that arises in bone, muscle, or connective tissue. Sarcomas can be further classified according to the specific tissue in which they develop and according to the degree of malignancy present. Sarcomas are differentiated from other types of cancer—for example, from carcinomas that arise in the skin or epithelial or glandular tissue, from leukemia that develops in bone marrow, and from lymphoma that arises in lymph nodes. See CANCER—*Classification;* TUMOR.

SARCOPHAGUS, sär-kof′ə-gəs, a stone or terracotta coffin. The term, which was used by the Greeks and Romans, comes from Greek words meaning "flesh" and "eat." The Romans believed that the Greeks once made sarcophagi of a stone that disintegrated bodies quickly. This explanation is doubtful.

The earliest sarcophagi were made by the Egyptians to represent a palace. Later Egyptian coffins, however, were usually wooden and shaped like a mummy. In the Hellenized Middle East and in Greece, boxlike marble sarcophagi were made with reliefs on the four sides and with gabled lids. The Etruscans produced stone or terracotta sarcophagi of the same shape but often with a recumbent figure of the deceased on the lid. In

the Roman Empire, both pagan and Christian sarcophagi were carved on three or four sides and had gabled lids or lids of the Etruscan type.

SARD, särd, is a brownish variety of chalcedony. See CARNELIAN; CHALCEDONY.

SARDANAPALUS, sär-dən-ə-pā′ləs, was the legendary last king of Assyria, who according to the ancient account was the 30th and most dissolute in a line of effete sovereigns. Supposedly when Arbaces, a satrap of Media, beseiged the Assyrian capital, Sardanapalus burned himself, his queen and concubines, and the treasures of his palace in an enormous conflagration.

The story is told by Diodorus Siculus (1st century B.C.), whose source was Ctesias, a Greek physician at the Persian court 400 years earlier. For many centuries Sardanapalus was mistakenly identified with the historical Ashurbanipal, Assyria's last great ruler. His brother Shamash-shum-ukin, king of Babylonia, died under similar circumstances. The legend is the subject of Byron's tragedy *Sardanapalus* and of Delacroix's painting *The Death of Sardanapalus.*

SARDINE, sär-dēn′, any of a variety of small fishes of the herring family, Clupeidae, widely used as a canned food. Sardines are free-swimming, fast-moving fishes that inhabit the open and upper waters of the seas. They are generally iridescent, with silvery bellies and green or blue backs sometimes spotted with black.

Along with the herring, sardines are among the most primitive marine fishes. Anatomically they are distinguished, for example, by a two-lobed nonfunctional lung. They are true bony fishes (teleosts) with one short dorsal fin near the middle of the back, no lateral line, and no scales on the head.

Sardines, together with herring and menhaden, feed on plankton. In the North Sea about 2 million tons (net weight) of herring consume from 50 to 60 million tons annually of zooplankton—minute crustaceans, larval forms, and fish eggs.

The species of sardines canned depends on the part of the world in which they are caught and processed. *Clupea pilchardus* is found in the Mediterranean and off the Atlantic coasts of

An Etruscan sarcophagus of the 4th century B.C., found at Tarquinia, Italy. The reclining figure of the deceased is characteristic of Etruscan sculpture.

Sardines trapped in a large seine are hoisted aboard a Norwegian fishing vessel by means of a bucket net.

Spain, Portugal, France, and north to the British Isles. *Clupea harengus* is found in the North Atlantic and the Baltic, including the waters off Canada and the United States, principally Maine. Off Norway is found *Clupea spratus.* California catches and cans *Sardinops caerulea.* South Africa has *Sardinops ocellata;* the west coast of South America, *Sardinops sagax;* Japan, *Sardinops melanosticta;* Australia, *Sardinops neopilchardus;* the west coast of North Africa, *Clupea sagax* and *Clupea eba.*

Fishing. To catch sardines, fishermen use seines, drift nets, or ring nets that float in the upper waters where the sardines swim. Sardines are usually fished at night when they rise to feed on the surface animal plankton, which also rises at night.

In Maine, fishermen use traps or weirs to catch sardines. The weirs are large circular or heart-shaped stationary enclosures formed by upright stakes and netting into which the fish are diverted by barriers across their course. The fishing vessels pull alongside the trap, and the sardines are removed by means of a power-operated dip net or a suction hose. After the fish are caught and placed in the hold of the vessel, from 200 to 300 pounds (90.7–136 kg) of salt are sprinkled over each 1,200 to 1,500 pounds (544–680 kg) of fish. California sardines are caught mostly by purse seiners.

Important sardine fisheries are also found in the United Kingdom, Norway, Denmark, Sweden, Finland, Portugal, France, Spain, South Africa, and Iceland. The fish are handled differently and the seasons are different in each country.

Canning. Sardine canning methods vary considerably depending on the locality and custom but consist essentially of washing, salting, cooking, drying, packing, and sterilizing.

In France, Spain, and Portugal, the fish are dried, fried in oil, and packed. In Scandinavian countries a smoking process is commonly used to cook and dry the fish before packing.

In the United States high labor costs have accelerated the development of mechanical devices for packing canned sardines. Although a frying process similar to the French method is used in Maine, most of the sardines packed in that state and many of the larger sardines packed in California are cooked by live steam.

JOSEPH PILEGGI.[*]
National Marine Fishery Service

SARDINIA, sär-din′ē-ə, the second-largest island in the Mediterranean Sea, constitutes, with some small neighboring islands, a special region of Italy, with limited autonomy. The Italian form of its name is *Sardegna.* The island, whose capital is Cagliari, is about 120 miles (193 km) southwest of central Italy. It is separated from the Italian mainland by the Tyrrhenian Sea and from Corsica, 7.5 miles (12 km) to the north, by the Strait of Bonifacio. Sardinia is hot and dry during the summer. In the winter it is warm and has light rainfall. The population of the region, which is divided into three provinces, was 1,495,-300 in 1969.

The Sardinians are a hardy, honest, haughty, and clannish people. They are also hospitable, generous, and devoted to the Catholic Church. Because of Sardinia's isolation and the strong attachment of its people to the past, especially in the mountainous districts, the Sardinians have preserved many of their customs. Their language has a closer affinity to Latin than modern Italian has, although different dialects prevail in different sections of the island.

The Land. The island, which has an area of 9,196 square miles (23,818 sq km), is about 165 miles (265 km) long and 90 miles (145 km) wide. The coastline is varied, with a large gulf on each side of its four sides and many small harbors and bays. The Gulf of Cagliari, on the south, is the most important. Off the northeast coast there are a number of small islands, including Caprera, which was the refuge of the patriot Giuseppe Garibaldi, and La Maddalena, which has a naval base.

Approximately 90% of Sardinia is mountainous or hilly. A chain of mountains cuts across the northern part from southwest to northeast. The Monti del Gennargentu rise to 6,016 feet (1,834 meters) in the east of the central part of Sardinia. In the northwest there is the Plain of Sassari, while in the south the Campidano Plain, the most fertile section of the island, runs from the Gulf of Oristano on the west to the Gulf of Cagliari on the south. The area near Iglesias in the southwest is rich in minerals.

The largest river is the Tirso, which rises in the high plateau of Budduso, forms the artificial Lake Omodeo, and empties into the Gulf of Oristano on the west. The Flumendosa rises in the Monti del Gennargentu and flows to the east coast. The Coghinas, whose source is in the Marghine Mountains, discharges into the Gulf of Asinara.

The island's main city is Cagliari, the historic and regional capital. Situated at the head of the Gulf of Cagliari, it is Sardinia's only large industrial center and the focus of commerce. Its population is 219,852 (1968). Other important cities are the provincial capitals of Sassari—the only other city with a population of more than 100,-000—and Nuoro and the mining center of Iglesias.

Economy. Numerous development plans have been promoted in an effort to advance Sardinia's economy in both the agricultural and industrial sectors. One plan initiated landholding reforms, while the Cassa per il Mezzogiorno (Fund for the South), begun in 1950, helps finance public works, especially hydroelectric and irrigation projects. Other plans have committed the national government to investments designed to invigorate the economy and lift the standard of living.

Sardinia's industries are chiefly agricultural.

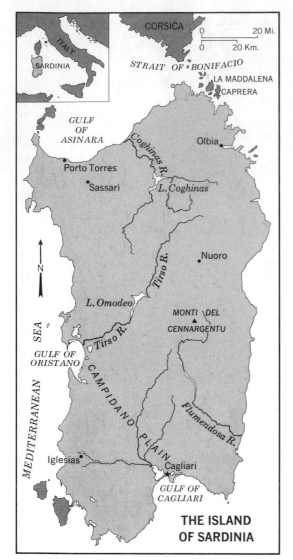

THE ISLAND OF SARDINIA

Agricultural production has been increased through the introduction of modern equipment and cultivation methods. The main products are wheat, barley, beans, and wine. Sardinia provides 75% of Italy's cork production. Olives, tobacco, and, along the coasts, fruits are also grown. The mountainous areas are devoted to pasture, with sheep, goats, and cattle the principal livestock.

Nonagricultural industries include mining, fishing, tourism, and some manufacturing. Mining, particularly near Iglesias, produces lead, zinc, copper, iron, manganese, coal, and smaller amounts of several other minerals. Salt pans are concentrated near Cagliari and Carloforte. Fishing is limited and is pursued primarily by mainland immigrants. Tourism has shown steady increases but has been hampered by the island's lack of modern facilities.

Although there are several main roads running east-west and north-south, Sardinia's road network is not dense. The principal towns are connected by railroad. The primary ports are Cagliari, Olbia, and Porto Torres. Cagliari is the chief commercial port, and Olbia, in the northeast, is the main passenger port.

Government. In 1948, Sardinia was made a special region of Italy, with limited autonomy. The regional government has the authority to enact local legislation and to levy local taxes. Its legislative and administrative powers extend over a wide field of local affairs, including local police, public health, public works, and some areas in industry and agriculture. Legislative functions are in the hands of a regional council, and there is an executive branch with a president.

History. Little is known about the earliest inhabitants of Sardinia, though many interesting monuments of its prehistoric civilization have been preserved. These include the so-called *domus de gianas* ("houses of the spirits"); the *tombe dei giganti* ("tombs of the giants"), long underground chambers; and the *nuraghi,* conical towers built of large blocks of unmortared stone. Thousands of the *nuraghi,* some perfectly preserved, may still be found, especially near Abbasanta, Barumini, and Silanus. They were used in defense, in guarding forts and passes, and as homes and bronze foundries. Who these early Sardinians were is not certain, but it is probable that the southern part of the island was inhabited by Ibero-Balearic settlers from Spain and later by Phoenicians from Africa.

In the 6th century B. C. the island was occupied by the Carthaginians, supposedly under Sardus, the son of Maceris or Hercules. The island was presumably named for this Sardus, who was later worshiped as Sardopater. About this same period, the Greeks founded a colony at Olbia, about which little is known. Under the Carthaginians, Sardinia was developed as a grain-growing center and, after passing to Rome in 238 B. C., became one of the chief Roman granaries.

Middle Ages. About the middle of the 5th century A. D., Vandals invaded the island and remained in control until 534, when they were expelled by the Byzantines. The Goths overran Sardinia in 550, but the Byzantines retook the island three years later. Sardinia was a province of Byzantium until the early 8th century, when the island suffered a series of invasions by the Saracens.

About 1000, a Saracen chief succeeded in establishing himself at Cagliari, but he was driven out by the Pisans, with the help of the Genoese, in 1015–1016. A bitter dispute between the Pisans and the Genoese over the ownership of Sardinia followed, with the papacy and the Holy Roman Empire deciding in favor of Pisa. The dominion of the Doria and the Visconti families was established in the northern section, the marquisate of Massa and Malaspina at Bosa, and the marquisate of Gherardesca at Iglesias. Meanwhile the island was divided into four *giudicati,* or regions: Cagliari, Arborea, Logudoro, and Gallura. For the next seven centuries the *giudicati* were nearly always at war with each other, depending in turn on the help of Pisa, Genoa, and the papacy. Only the relatively prosperous *giudicato* of Arborea tried several times to free the island from outside domination.

In 1164, Emperor Frederick I Barbarossa bestowed the title of king on Barisone, *giudice* of Arborea, but his authority was never effective. In 1239, Emperor Frederick II arranged a marriage between his illegitimate son Enzio, on whom he conferred the title of king of Sardinia, and Adelasia, the heiress of Gallura and Logu-

The port of Alghero, located on the western coast of Sardinia, is a center for coral and lobster fishing.

doro. In 1249, at the Battle of Fossalta, Enzio fell into the hands of the Bolognese, who kept him prisoner in Bologna for the rest of his life. After their defeat at the naval Battle of Meloria in 1284, the Pisans were obliged to surrender Sassari and Logudoro to Genoa.

Spanish Influence. In 1297, Pope Boniface VIII invested King James II of Aragón with Sardinia. However, it was not until 1326 that Alfonso of Aragón (later Alfonso IV) succeeded in driving the Pisans out of Cagliari. After their occupation of Arborea in 1403, the Aragonese abolished the title of *giudice*, replacing it with a feudal marquisate. By 1421 the Spanish occupation of Sardinia was complete, the island being governed by viceroys who convoked the Cortes (assembly) every 10 years.

Sardinia remained a Spanish province until the War of the Spanish Succession, when, in 1708, Cagliari capitulated to a British fleet. The Treaty of Utrecht in 1713 assigned Sardinia to Archduke Charles of Austria. In 1717, however, Giulio Cardinal Alberoni occupied Cagliari for Spain, but Spanish possession was brief. By the Treaty of London of 1718, Sardinia was given to Victor Amadeus II, duke of Savoy, to compensate him for the loss of Sicily. He took possession of the island in 1720 and assumed the title of king of Sardinia.

Rule of Savoy. Although a despot, Victor Amadeus reigned with prudence and zeal. In 1730 he abdicated in favor of his son, Charles Emmanuel III, during whose reign of 43 years the prosperity of the island was substantially increased. However, all remnants of free institutions in Sardinia were abolished.

In 1799 the young ruler of Savoy and Sardinia, Charles Emmanuel IV, was compelled to retire to Sardinia, while the French plundered his possessions on the mainland. In 1802 he abdicated in favor of his brother Victor Emmanuel I, who remained in Cagliari until 1814.

The arrangements made by the Allies in accordance with the Treaty of Paris in 1814 and the final act of the Congress of Vienna in 1815 imposed on Italy boundaries roughly corresponding to those of the pre-Napoleonic era. To the kingdom of Sardinia, now reconstituted under Victor Emmanuel I, France ceded its old provinces of Savoy and Nice. The Allies also insisted on the cession to Sardinia of the territories of the former republic of Genoa, in order to strengthen Sardinia as a buffer state between France and the smaller states of central Italy. For the island's later history, see SARDINIA, KINGDOM OF.

Further Reading: Guido, Margaret, *Sardinia* (Praeger 1964); Houston, James M., *The Western Mediterranean World* (Praeger 1967); Warne, Osmond H., *Your Guide to Sardinia* (Int'l. Pubs. Serv. 1965).

Sardinian woman dries wool on bushes after having washed it in river. Sheep are raised in the mountains.

SARDINIA, sär-din'ē-ə, **Kingdom of,** a realm established in 1720, when the island of Sardinia, added to the territories of the house of Savoy by the Treaty of London in 1718, gave its name to the kingdom that later spearheaded the movement for a unified Italy. (For the history of Sardinia to 1815, see SARDINIA.)

Besides the island, the kingdom included Savoy, Nice, Piedmont, and some minor accessions made after 1720. Its capital was Turin, in Piedmont. The mainland parts of the kingdom were overrun by the armies of the French during the Napoleonic Wars, but in 1815, by agreements made at the Congress of Vienna, the kingdom was reconstituted to include Sardinia, Piedmont, Savoy, Nice, and Liguria.

After the fall of Napoleon, the political climate of the Sardinian kingdom changed radically. The spirit of the French Revolution had created a popular demand for a constitution—a demand opposed by the nobility and rich bourgeoisie. The liberals organized themselves into secret societies, and under the most important of these, the Carbonari, they attempted on March 10, 1821, to enforce their demands by an appeal to arms. Victor Emmanuel I preferred to abdicate rather than grant the constitution. Charles Felix, his successor and brother, who reigned until 1831, put down the insurrection with an iron hand. After Charles Felix died without issue, Charles Albert, the head of the cadet branch of the family, ascended the throne on April 27, 1831.

First Italian Constitution. Aroused to action by Young Italy (*Giovane Italia*), a secret political society established by the revolutionary patriot Giuseppe Mazzini in 1831, the Italian peninsula was plagued with numerous revolts and uprisings. Charles Albert conceived the idea of expelling the Austrians from Italy and establishing a unified kingdom. In this idea he was seconded by several political reformers: Cesare Balbo, Giacomo Durando, Massimo d'Azeglio, and Vincenzo Gioberti. After granting a liberal constitution to his subjects on March 4, 1848, Charles Albert declared war on Austria and placed himself at the head of the movement. The Lombards welcomed him as their savior. Meanwhile, Parma, Modena, and Lombardy declared themselves parts of the Sardinian kingdom. Brilliant victories were won by the Sardinian troops at Goito, Valeggio, and Monzambano.

Soon, however, the King of the Two Sicilies and other rulers, who had at first supported Charles Albert under the pressure of their people, deserted the cause. The feeble army of Charles Albert, fighting alone against Austria, suffered a crushing defeat at Custoza on July 24, 1848. On August 9, at Salasco, Charles Albert sued for an armistice, which, however, he abrogated on March 12, 1849, to resume hostilities. Defeat and retreat followed in rapid succession, ending in the bloody rout at Novara on March 23. That evening Charles Albert abdicated in favor of his son, Victor Emmanuel II, who on March 29 took his oath under the constitution that his father had granted. Charles Albert died in exile in Portugal on July 28.

Victor Emmanuel II and Cavour. The reign of Victor Emmanuel II was inaugurated by a treaty of peace with Austria by which Sardinia was bound to pay a heavy indemnity toward the expenses of the war. The independence and the territory of the Sardinian kingdom were preserved intact. Under Victor Emmanuel II, the economic, political, and social institutions of the kingdom were greatly developed and improved. A fierce contest with the Roman Catholic Church and the religious corporations of the country terminated wholly to the advantage of the state. In October 1850, Camillo Benso di Cavour entered the Sardinian cabinet as minister of agriculture and commerce. Cavour became the prime minister in November 1852, and under his able leadership the peninsula was eventually united under the house of Savoy.

In January 1855, Cavour entered into an alliance with France and Britain, calling for Sardinia's participation in the Crimean War. At the peace conference in Paris in 1856, as the delegate of Sardinia, Cavour outlined Italy's case for unification before the assembled powers. The conference took no action on his demands for the emancipation of Lombardy from Austrian rule, the secularization of the Roman government, the withdrawal of French troops from Rome, and the reform of the government of Naples. But Cavour nevertheless scored important gains. The question of Italian unification had been brought to the attention of all Europe, and the kingdom of Sardinia had taken upon itself the office of protector of Italy.

Pursuing this policy further, Cavour had a secret meeting with Emperor Napoleon III of France in July 1858 at Plombières, where a Franco-Sardinian alliance was formed against Austria for the liberation of northern Italy. War began on April 29, 1859, and a series of brilliantly fought victories by the combined French and Italian forces fostered the hope of the ultimate success of the Italian cause. Napoleon, however, without consulting anyone, arranged an armistice with Emperor Francis Joseph I of Austria on July 11. The terms of peace provided for the liberation of Lombardy, the creation of an Italian confederacy with the pope as its honorary president, and the retention of the region of Venetia by Austria.

Meanwhile, the war had had its repercussions in other states of the peninsula. The duchies of Modena, Parma, and Tuscany, as well as Romagna, declared their intention of uniting with the kingdom of Sardinia. To secure Napoleon's consent to this union, Victor Emmanuel, in March 1860, ceded Savoy and Nice to France, after which he formally proclaimed the annexation of Romagna and the Italian duchies. For this act he was excommunicated by the pope.

Unification of Italy. Serious disturbances had also been occurring in Sicily. On May 5, 1860, Giuseppe Garibaldi with his army of 1,200 volunteers left Quarto, near Genoa, determined to free the Kingdom of the Two Sicilies from Bourbon rule. Following a swift and heroic campaign, the entire island of Sicily was freed by July 20. Within a month Garibaldi crossed the Strait of Messina and landed in Calabria, on the mainland.

While he moved northward against the Bourbon army, the troops of Victor Emmanuel crossed the frontier of the Papal States and on September 18 defeated Gen. Léon Juchault de Lamoricière at Castelfidardo. A few days later, on October 1–2, Garibaldi won a brilliant victory on the banks of the Volturno River. The Sardinian army, moving southward, entered the Two Sicilies on October 15. On November 8, in Naples, Garibaldi presented Victor Emmanuel with the results of the plebiscite in the Two Sicilies, which favored its annexation to Sardinia.

The first Italian parliament, including deputies from all the newly annexed regions, met in Turin on Feb. 18, 1861. The deputies soon approved a bill proclaiming the kingdom of Italy, which was sanctioned by the King on March 17, 1861. The formal date for the transformation of the kingdom of Sardinia into the kingdom of Italy is March 17. See also ITALY—*History*.

Further Reading: Mack Smith, Denis, *Cavour and Garibaldi, 1860* (Cambridge 1954); Whyte, Arthur J. B., *The Evolution of Modern Italy, 1715–1920* (Blackwell 1944).

SARDIS, sär′dis, was the capital of ancient Lydia, in Anatolia, on the site of the present village of Sart, Turkey, 35 miles (55 km) northeast of İzmir (Smyrna). Sardis, or Sardes, stood in the valley of the Hermus (now the Gediz) River, below Mt. Tmolus (now Boz Dağ). It was a wealthy trading center on the routes between the Aegean Sea and the interior. Its strong citadel was destroyed by the Cimmerians in the 7th century B. C., but the town recovered and flourished, becoming the luxurious capital of the proverbially rich Croesus (reigned 560–546 B. C.). In 546 B. C. it was captured by the Persian king Cyrus the Great, who incorporated Lydia into his realm. The Greeks burned Sardis' acropolis in 499.

Under the Romans, the city prospered in spite of great destruction by an earthquake in 17 A. D., but after the rebuilding of Byzantium as Constantinople (dedicated 330 A. D.), Sardis gradually lost its commercial importance. In 1306 it was ceded to the Seljuk Turks, and in 1402 was taken by Timur (Tamerlane), who presumably destroyed it, since it disappears from history. Organized excavations, begun by the American Society for the Excavation of Sardis in 1910, have yielded important archaeological remains, the chief sites being a Lydian necropolis, the acropolis, the Hellenistic temple of Artemis, and a synagogue. See also LYDIA.

SARDONYX, sär′don-iks, is a cryptocrystalline variety of quartz that is sometimes used as a gem. The stone is made up of reddish brown layers of sard that alternate with white layers of chalcedony. See also QUARTZ.

SARDOU, sàr-dōō′, **Victorien** (1831–1908), French playwright who enjoyed a worldwide reputation during his lifetime. He was born in Paris on Sept. 7, 1831. Having given up the study of medicine to pursue a career as a dramatist, he supported himself in various employments until the failure of his first play, *La taverne des étudiants* (1854), and other disappointments led to a breakdown in health. He slowly recovered under the ministrations of Mlle. de Brécourt, an actress whom he married in 1858. Through his wife, he met the famous actress Virginie Déjazet, who became the star of his first successful play, *Les Premières Armes de Figaro* (1859).

Comedies and historical dramas followed in rapid succession, invariably winning large audiences but not escaping disparagement from the critics. Like his predecessor Eugène Scribe, on whom his technique was modeled, Sardou had great facility for creating dramatic situations, but his characterizations were often sketchy and rarely penetrated below the surface. He was elected to the French Academy in 1877.

Among Sardou's comedies of manners are *Les Pattes de mouche* (1860), *Nos Intimes* (1861), and *La Famille Benoîton* (1865). The historical comedy *Madame Sans-Gêne* (1893) was written with Émile Moreau for the actress Réjane. Sarah Bernhardt appeared in the title role of *Fédora* (1882), a play with a Russian setting. Sardou's other works include *Rabagas* (1872), a political comedy, and *Divorçons* (1880), a satire on divorce. Sardou died in Paris on Nov. 8, 1908.

SAREMA. See SAAREMAA.

SARGASSO SEA, sär-gas′ō, a region of the North Atlantic Ocean, between the West Indies and the Azores. On the west and south the boundaries of the Sargasso Sea are clearly defined by the Gulf Stream, but on the east and south they are less distinct. The name of the region is derived from the floating masses of brown gulfweed (*Sargassum*) that accumulate there. The seaweed is the home of many forms of small animals, and the area is the breeding ground of the European and North American eel.

The Sargasso Sea is a region of converging ocean currents and prevailingly calm winds, and its deep blue waters are characteristically warm and clear. These features, in combination with the prevalence of seaweed, gave rise to the erroneous legend that the Sargasso was an "island of lost ships," where galleons lay becalmed in the entangling snares of the weed. See GULF STREAM for a map of the area.

SARGENT, sär-jənt, **John Singer** (1856–1925), American painter, who worked chiefly in Europe. First acclaimed for his elegant, yet realistic portraits, Sargent was later recognized for his impressionistic watercolors.

Early Years. Sargent was born in Florence, Italy, on Jan. 12, 1856, the son of a prominent Philadelphia physician and his artistically inclined wife, who induced her husband to live abroad. Encouraged by his mother, Sargent studied art in Florence. In 1874 he entered the Paris studio of the fashionable portraitist Carolus-Duran, who gave his pupil a thorough training influenced by Velázquez and the impressionists. There Sargent acquired the realistic approach, interest in light, and virtuoso technique that characterize his work.

Sargent showed at the Paris Salon of 1877, at the age of 21. The next year he won honorable mention with the picturesque genre scene *Oyster Gatherers of Cancale* (1878; Corcoran Gallery, Washington). In 1879 and 1880 he traveled to Spain to study Velázquez, to Morocco, and to Haarlem to study Franz Hals. The result was copies of Velázquez' works and the dramatic *El Jaleo* (1882; Gardner Museum, Boston), a genre scene of a Spanish dancer and musicians. He also did portraits. These early works were usually in dark, rich tones and were often unusual in their use of empty space and diagonals. Outstanding examples are the *Daughters of Edward D. Boit* (1882; Museum of Fine Arts, Boston), *Robert Louis Stevenson* (1885; J. H. Whitney collection), and the famous portrait of Mme. Gautreau in a black décolleté gown, *Madame X* (1884; Metropolitan Museum, New York), which was attacked for its too realistic and provocative presentation of a vain and handsome woman.

Middle Years. Lacking commissions in Paris, Sargent moved to London in 1885. Unmarried,

John Singer Sargent's *Madame X* (1884)

he devoted himself to painting. He remained in London except for summer excursions on the Continent and frequent trips to the United States. He had visited the United States for the first time in 1876 and had become a citizen. His painting trips, starting in 1887, centered in Boston.

Sargent's portraits gradually won great popularity. Such works as *Carnation, Lily, Lily, Rose* (1885–1886; Tate Gallery, London) reveal his particularly warm sentiment toward children. His portraits of the rich and aristocratic, in pale tones, have an aloof elegance that recalls the great tradition of English portraiture. Among his English sitters were Graham Robertson, Lord Ribblesdale, Ellen Terry, and the Wertheimer family (all in the Tate) and the Wyndham Sisters (Metropolitan). His American sitters included Henry James, Theodore Roosevelt, John D. Rockefeller, and Isabella Stewart Gardner.

Sargent has been criticized for superficiality, facile technique, lack of creative insight, and lack of interest in the modernist movements of his time. His compensating virtues were his spontaneity, his unusual composition, his use of light to hide or reveal shapes, and his powers of observation. He had the realist's feeling for the idiosyncrasies of the sitter and always claimed that in his portraits he did not judge but merely chronicled. For all his dash and sparkle, his works are faithful documents of the Victorian and Edwardian upper class.

Sargent was elected to the Royal Academy in 1897. He refused a knighthood in 1907 on the grounds that he was a U. S. citizen.

Later Years. After having completed several hundred portraits, Sargent virtually abandoned that lucrative field to concentrate on murals and watercolors. Beginning in 1890 he worked for 26 years on murals for the Boston Public Library. To verify his conception of their subject, the history of religion, he journeyed to Greece, Egypt, and the Middle East. He also did murals for Widener Library at Harvard University and for the Boston Museum of Fine Arts.

Sargent's watercolors are of scenes in the Alps, Italy, the Mediterranean islands, and the Rocky Mountains, as, for example, the *Piazzetta* (Brooklyn Museum) and *Lake O'Hara* (Fogg Art Museum, Harvard). In their dazzling light and free brushwork they admirably capture the atmosphere of the locale. His oil landscapes are similar.

At the request of the British government, Sargent went to the front in 1918 to paint scenes of World War I. Although he was stricken with influenza, he did produce *Gassed* (1918). He died in London on April 15, 1925.

Further Reading: Downes, William H., *John S. Sargent, His Life and Work* (Little 1925); Mount, Charles M., *John Singer Sargent* (Norton 1955); *Private World of John Singer Sargent* (Corcoran Gallery 1964).

SARGENT, sar'jənt, **Winthrop** (1753–1820), American soldier and territorial governor. Born in Gloucester, Mass., on May 1, 1753, he graduated from Harvard College in 1771. During the American Revolution he attained the rank of major. He became secretary of the newly organized Ohio territory in 1787 and the same year was appointed by Congress to the administrative post of secretary of the Northwest Territory. Sargent served as acting governor during the frequent absences of the governor, Gen. Arthur St. Clair, and for a period after St. Clair's defeat by the Indians in 1791. From 1798 to 1801, Sargent served as the first governor of the Mississippi Territory.

A Federalist in politics, Sargent pursued many scientific and historical interests, publishing papers on American antiquities and on the natural sciences. He died near New Orleans, La., on Jan. 3, 1820.

Winthrop Sargent (1825–1870), his grandson, was a prominent historian. His books include *The History of an Expedition Against Fort Duquesne, in 1755 . . .* (1855) and *The Loyal Verses of Joseph Stansbury and Doctor Jonathan Odell, Relating to the American Revolution* (1860).

SARGON, sär'gon, or Sargon of Akkad (Agade), was the founder of the first Semitic dynasty of ancient Mesopotamia. His Akkadian name was Sharrum-kin. He wrested power in Sumer (southern Iraq) from Lugalzaggesi, the ruler of Umma, about 2350 or 2300 B. C. Sargon's empire may have reached as far as Lebanon and into Anatolia (Turkey). The northern part of Sumer became known as Akkad, the name of the capital he built. The site of this city has not been identified with certainty.

Sargon's rise to power was the culmination of a long process of infiltration by Semitic peoples into southern Mesopotamia. His dynasty lasted over 100 years. During his reign Akkad was one of the most splendid cities of the ancient world, with a seaborne trade extending to India and East Africa.

SARGON II, sär'gon, king of Assyria (reigned 721–705 B. C.). He completed the conquest of Samaria (Israel) begun by his predecessor, Shalmaneser V, and afterward subjugated the major unconquered states of Syria. In his greatest campaign he broke the power of Urartu (Armenia).

Sargon built a new capital, Dur Sharrukin (modern Khorsabad, Iraq). It contained a magnificent palace adorned with remarkable stone reliefs, some of which are in the Louvre, Paris. See also ASSYRIA—*Late Assyrian Empire* (Second Phase); and ARCHITECTURE—*Mesopotamian and Persian.*

SARK is one of the Channel Islands, in the English Channel, about 25 miles (40 km) west of the Cherbourg Peninsula of France. The island is 3.5 miles (4.6 km) long and 1.5 miles (2.4 km) wide and consists of the Great Sark and the Little Sark, which are connected by an isthmus called the Coupée. There are three small harbors—La Maseline, Creux, and Havre Gosselin. The privately-owned islet of Brechou is nearby. Sark has impressive coastal cliffs, and the Gouliot Caves and the Venus and Jupiter Pools—natural depressions in the rock—are noteworthy. Fishing, agriculture, and tourism are the supports of the economy.

Like the other Channel Islands, Sark is a British possession, but it is not a part of the United Kingdom. The island is governed by a hereditary seigneur, or dame, who appoints a seneschal (chief magistrate) and also by the Court of Pleas, a parliamentary body composed of hereditary tenants and elected deputies. Population: (1971) 493.

SARMATIANS, sär-mä'shənz, an ancient nomadic pastoral people, closely related to the Scythians. They spoke an Indo-European language and were known as excellent horsemen and fierce warriors. They lived east of the Don River until the 3d century B. C., when they began moving west, displacing the Scythians.

One branch of the Sarmatians, the Roxolani, eventually settled along the Black Sea near the mouth of the Danube, while another, the Iazyges, crossed the Carpathians to the Danube plain. These branches and the Alani often came into conflict with the Romans, but they were kept out of the Roman Empire until pressure from German tribes drove them west in the 2d century A. D. They subsequently dispersed. The term "Sarmatia" is vague and is used to refer to their original homeland around the lower Don and to their territory in the Danube region.

SARMIENTO, sär-myän'tō, **Domingo** (1811–1888), Argentine political leader and educator. He was born in San Juan on Feb. 15, 1811. In 1829 he fought in the insurrection against the Gaucho dictator Juan Manuel Ortiz de Rosas and was exiled in 1835 to Chile. There he established a brilliant career as a literary figure, educator, and political thinker. His most famous book, *Facundo* (1845), ostensibly a biography of a political enemy, presents Sarmiento's enlightened and progressive political philosophy.

In 1852, after the defeat of de Rosas, Sarmiento returned to Argentina and a political career. He was minister to the United States from 1864 to 1868. As president of Argentina from 1868 to 1874, he gave the country one of its most successful and progressive administrations. From 1875 to 1888 he reorganized Argentina's school system. Sarmiento's extensive writings, largely devoted to educational theory, appeared in a collected edition of 52 vols. (1885–1903). He died in Asunción, Paraguay, on Sept. 11, 1888.

Further Reading: Bunkley, Allison W., *The Life of Sarmiento* (Greenwood 1952).

SARMIENTO DE GAMBOA, sär-myän'tō thä gämbō'ä, **Pedro** (c. 1530–c. 1592), Spanish navigator. He was born in Galicia. He spent some time exploring the coast of Peru, then in 1579 he was ordered to take possession of the Strait of Magellan and intercept the English admiral Sir Francis Drake, who was plundering Spanish ships off the coast of South America. Drake, however, evaded him.

In 1581, Sarmiento was sent again to fortify the strait, this time in joint command with Diego Flores Valdés, who deserted him, taking all but four ships. In 1583, Sarmiento founded San Felipe, a colony on the shores of the strait, and garrisoned it with 300 men. In 1584 he set sail for Europe, but was captured and imprisoned by the English. All but two of the men in San Felipe died of starvation, earning the colony the name of Port Famine.

SARNATH, sär-nät', was an ancient religious center in India, 5 miles (8 km) north of present Varanasi (Benares). The site contains the Deer Park where Gautama Buddha delivered his first sermon after his enlightenment. Sarnath was one of the most important places of Buddhist pilgrimage. It was destroyed by Afghan invaders at the end of the 12th century.

At the site is a modern temple as well as ruins of ancient monasteries and stupas and the broken pillar of Asoka. The pillar's lion capital, depicted on the state emblem of India, is in the Sarnath Museum. Under the Imperial Guptas, Sarnath was the center of a great school of sculpture. The museum houses notable works of Buddhist art.

SARNIA, sär'nē-ə, a city in southwestern Ontario, Canada, on Lake Huron and the St. Clair River, is directly across the river from Port Huron, Mich., with which it is connected by bridges and a railroad tunnel.

Situated on the waterway of the Great Lakes, Sarnia is a large port and one of Canada's major industrial centers. Along the river south of the city is the nation's greatest concentration of petrochemical industries. Sarnia is the terminus of oil pipelines from Texas and Alberta, and possesses huge oil refineries. Fiber glass, synthetic rubber, glycol, and carbon black are among the chemical products that are made. Automotive parts are among other important manufactures.

Sarnia ranks as one of the busiest lake ports in Canada, and there are many docks and grain elevators. Flour mills are near the waterfront.

The first settler arrived on the site in 1807, but the community was not founded until 1833. Originally known as The Rapids, its name was changed in 1836 to Port Sarnia, at the suggestion of a lieutenant governor of Upper Canada, who formerly had been lieutenant governor of Guernsey, in the Channel Islands, which the Romans had called Sarnia. The word "Port" was later dropped from the name. Population: 50,892.

SARNOFF, sär′nôf, **David** (1891–1971), American industrialist who pioneered in bringing radio and television into millions of homes in the United States. By his hard work and relentless drive, he rose from a job as office boy to the chairmanship of the giant RCA Corporation, formerly the Radio Corporation of America (RCA). While serving in various executive positions with RCA, he led the company's entry into radio broadcasting and reception in the 1920's and black-and-white and color TV broadcasting and reception in the 1940's and 1950's.

Sarnoff was born on Feb. 27, 1891, in Uzlian in the Russian province of Minsk. David, four younger children, and his mother, Leah, left Russia and joined his father, Abraham, in New York City in 1901. After his father died, David quit school and went to work as an office boy for the Commercial Cable Company in 1906. His first fame came in April 1912, when he was a wireless (radiotelegraphy) operator with the American Marconi Company. Sarnoff picked up the message that the S.S. *Titanic* had run into an iceberg and was sinking, and for three days he constantly sat at his radio equipment, taking messages giving the names of survivors. In 1915 he wrote a memo to the management of American Marconi proposing a plan to bring "music into the home by wireless," but his idea was ignored.

The American Marconi Company was absorbed by the newly created RCA in 1919, and Sarnoff became general manager of RCA in 1921. Seizing the opportunity to impress RCA's directors with the potential of radio, he helped give a blow-by-blow broadcast of the Dempsey-Carpentier boxing match in 1921. This broadcast was a great popular success. Sarnoff became vice president of RCA in 1922, and within three years the company's radio receiver sales totaled $83 million. Another of Sarnoff's visions was realized in 1926 with the formation of the National Broadcasting Company (NBC), the first radio chain in the United States. In the late 1920's, Sarnoff successfully drove for the acquisition of the Victor Talking Machine Company, putting down objections by saying, "We'll combine radio and the phonograph in the same set."

Sarnoff foresaw a future for television as early as 1923, the same year Vladimir Zworykin invented the iconoscope. When Zworykin joined RCA in 1930, Sarnoff said he wanted an all-electronic TV system rather than one that used a mechanical scanner. Nine years later, after at least $20 million had been spent on all-electronic television, Sarnoff appeared before a TV camera at the New York World's Fair and said, "Now we add radio sight to sound."

During World War II, Sarnoff served as a communications consultant and became a brigadier general in 1944. Thereafter, he was addressed as "General." After the war he pumped millions of dollars into the development and successful acceptance of color TV sets that could receive black and white as well as color. Sarnoff died in New York City on Dec. 12, 1971.

SAROYAN, sə-roi′ən, **William** (1908–1981), American short-story writer, novelist, and playwright. He was born in Fresno, Calif., on Aug. 31, 1908, the son of Armenian immigrants somewhat like those he often pictured affectionately in his work. He first gained recognition in 1934 for the short story *The Daring Young Man on the Flying Trapeze,* a mixture of fantasy and realism, which

CENTRAL PRESS, FROM PICTORIAL PARADE

William Saroyan, American author and playwright

became the title story of a collection published that year. This work was marked by the exuberant, impressionistic style and the sympathetic portrayal of character for which Saroyan became known. Some of his best stories appeared in the autobiographical collection *My Name Is Aram* (1940). His longer fiction includes the novel *The Human Comedy* (1942), the partly autobiographical story of a boy who delivers telegrams; *Boys and Girls Together* (1963), a novella about a young writer and his wife; the novel *One Day in the Afternoon of the World* (1964), about an aging author; and the autobiographical *Not Dying* (1963).

The play *My Heart's in the Highlands* (1939) was a Broadway success, and *The Time of Your Life* (1939), was widely acclaimed. The latter, about a collection of eccentrics in a waterfront bar, won a Pulitzer Prize, which Saroyan declined because of his belief that commerce should not patronize art. His other plays include *Love's Old Sweet Song* (1941) and *The Beautiful People* (1941), which was included in the collection *Three Plays* (1941). Saroyan died in Fresno, Calif., on May 18, 1981.

Further Reading: Floan, Howard R., *William Saroyan* (Twayne 1966).

SARPI, sär′pē, **Paolo** (1552–1623), Venetian statesman and historian who attacked the papacy in his history of the Council of Trent. Sarpi, who is also known as Fra Paolo and Paulus Servitus, was born in Venice on Aug. 14, 1552. A Servite monk, Sarpi devoted himself until middle age to a wide range of studies. He was a friend of Galileo, and his thought reflects the empiricism of the scientific movement. As tension increased early in the 17th century between the aggressively centralizing Counter-Reformation papacy and Venice, with its long tradition of political and religious independence, Sarpi was appointed consultant in theology and canon law to the republic. During the interdict of 1606–1607 of Venice by the papacy, he took a leading part in fashioning the theoretical weapons that enabled Venice to resist papal pressure, thereby winning for himself the permanent enmity of Rome. He then continued his attack on the papacy by writing his monumental *History of the Council of Trent*, which was smuggled out of Venice and first published in London in 1619.

Sarpi conceived of the church universal as a loose federation of local churches, and his history of the Council of Trent aims to show how the papacy had imposed a tyranny over the whole by skillful manipulation. Widely translated, it fixed for centuries the unfavorable Protestant image of modern Roman Catholicism, but it is also important as an early effort to apply the insights of the political historiography of the Italian Renaissance to church history. Sarpi has often been regarded as a kind of secret Protestant, but there is little evidence to support this view. The essential motive of his career was devotion to Venice. Sarpi died there on Jan. 15, 1623.

WILLIAM J. BOUWSMA
University of California, Berkeley

SARPSBORG, särps′bôr, is a town in southeastern Norway on the Glomma River, 45 miles (72 km) southeast of Oslo. Hydroelectric works on Sarpsfoss falls, on the Glomma, supply power for paper mills—chiefly in Borregård, a southeastern suburb —textile and electrical equipment factories, and chemical works. Sandesund, a southwestern suburb, is the city's port, with lumber an important export.

Founded by Olaf II (St. Olaf) in 1016, Sarpsborg was the meeting place of the Borgarthing, an ancient legal body. The town was destroyed by the Swedes in 1567 and was not rebuilt until 1838. Population: (1971 est.) 13,338.

SARRAUTE, sä-rōt′, **Nathalie** (1900–   ), French novelist, a leader of the "New Wave" in French literature and creator of the "anti-novel." Nathalie Tcherniak was born in Ivanovo, Russia, on July 18, 1900, and moved with her family to France when she was three. She studied law at the Sorbonne and at Oxford and practiced law until 1942, when she began to devote full time to writing. In 1925 she married Raymond Sarraute.

Miss Sarraute's first book, *Tropismes*, a collection of short pieces, was published in 1939 (Eng. tr., *Tropisms*, 1964). Her *Portrait d'un inconnu* (1947; Eng. tr., *Portrait of a Man Unknown*, 1958) has a preface by Jean-Paul Sartre, in which he calls it an "anti-novel." It avoids standard plot, characterization, and chronology for a more direct communication of feelings and experiences. Her later novels include *Martereau* (1953; Eng. tr., 1959) and *Les Fruits d'or* (1963; Eng. tr., *The Golden Fruits,* 1964).

SARSAPARILLA, sas-pə-ril′ə, any of several plants of the genus *Smilax*, characteristically tough twining shrubs with square or round prickly stems, small flowers, and shining leaves. They are indigenous to Central America, southern Mexico, northern South America, and such West Indian islands as Jamaica. The name "sarsaparilla" is derived from the Spanish *zarza* ("shrub") and *parrilla* ("little vine").

The dried roots of a sarsaparilla plant are used in the form of an extract or syrup to provide flavoring or a scent. The roots chiefly are used as a flavoring additive in root beer and other soft drinks. Sarsaparilla was once considered an alterative—that is, a drug that would alter the body's metabolism in a generally beneficial way. This theory is no longer accepted.

ISAAC ASIMOV
Boston University

SARTHE, sàrt, is a department in northwestern France. The capital is Le Mans, an industrial city of 140,520 (1968). Chiefly agricultural, the department produces grains, fodder, vegetables, apples (for cider), and other fruits. Percheron horses are bred, and cattle and other livestock are raised. It is drained by the Sarthe River and its tributaries, the Huisne and Loir. Population: (1971) 471,000.

SARTI, sär′tē, **Giuseppe** (1729–1802), Italian composer, celebrated in his time for his melodious operas. He was born in Faenza and was baptized there on Dec. 1, 1729. He was a student of the eminent teacher-composer Giambattista Martini and went on to become the teacher of another noted composer, Luigi Cherubini. Sarti became the most celebrated composer of Italian operas of his day and enjoyed international acclaim. He held a succession of important posts in Italy and at foreign courts, notably those of director of Italian opera at the court of King Frederick V of Denmark; *maestro di cappella* of the Milan Cathedral; and, for the last 18 years of his life, court composer to Catherine the Great of Russia and her successors. He died in Berlin, Germany, on July 28, 1802.

Sarti composed cantatas, oratorios, sonatas, and other music, but he was primarily an opera composer, writing some 75 works in that genre. They are all well-wrought, highly singable operas in the best 18th century Italian style, but as enjoyable as they would undoubtedly be today, they remain in oblivion. Only a snippet of his great operatic output is heard today—a tune from his opera *Fra due litiganti il terzo gode* (1782) that Mozart quoted in *Don Giovanni* (1787). Sarti's other operas include *Vologeso* (1754), *Siroe* (1779), and *Il trionfo della pace* (1783).

EDMOND STRAINCHAMPS, *Rutgers University*

SARTO, Andrea del. See ANDREA DEL SARTO.

SARTOR RESARTUS, sär′tər rə-sär′təs, is the spiritual autobiography of the Scottish essayist and historian Thomas Carlyle. It was first published serially in *Fraser's Magazine* (1833–1834) and then in book form in the United States (1836) and England (1838). *Sartor Resartus* ("The Tailor Retailored") reveals the main themes of Carlyle's transcendental thought and the stylistic qualities of his prose. In order to bring his extravagant, often grotesque, humor into play, Carlyle writes as an editor organizing the papers of an eccentric German professor, Diogenes Teufelsdröckh ("God-born devil's-dung"), professor of Things in General at Weissnichtwo ("Know-not-where"). In Book I, an explanation of his "clothes philosophy," Carlyle insists that just as clothes hide the real body so do the material objects of the earth merely suggest the spiritual reality behind them. Book 2, more personal, deals primarily with Carlyle's own spiritual struggles. In Book 3 he applies the clothes philosophy to the social institutions of his day.

The prose of *Sartor Resartus* is distinctly Carlylean—poetic, colorful, highly connotative, and allusive. It is marked by the author's imaginative command of language and his passionate concern to convey concretely and graphically the truth as revealed to him. Most moving are the chapters entitled "The Everlasting No," "Centre of Indifference," and "The Everlasting Yea," which brilliantly portray Carlyle's rebirth after a period of desolation.

MICHAEL TIMKO, *Queens College*

SARTRE, sàr′trǝ, **Jean-Paul** (1905–1980), French writer, who won fame as the intellectual and literary leader of existentialism, the philosophy that swept Europe after World War II. In novels, plays, essays, and philosophical works, he expounded his theory that life has no meaning or purpose beyond the goals that each man sets for himself. Sartre refused the Nobel Prize for literature in 1964. He said that it was not fair to the reader to add the weight of such extraneous influences to the power of a writer's words.

Sartre was born in Paris on June 21, 1905, and graduated from the École Normale Supérieure in 1929. He taught philosophy, mostly in provincial high schools, until he was drafted into the army at the start of the World War II. He was captured by the Germans but escaped and became a leader in the resistance movement. After the war, he devoted full time to writing and political activity. In 1946 he founded a monthly literary and political review, *Les Temps modernes*. He died in Paris on April 15, 1980.

Works. Sartre's first novel, *La Nausée* (1938; Eng. tr., *Nausea*, 1949) expressed the idea that human life has no purpose. The long philosophical essay *L'Être et le néant* (1943; Eng. tr., *Being and Nothingness*, 1956) linked this idea closely with the concept of man as terrifyingly free and responsible in anguish for the choices he makes. A more optimistic view of existentialism, a philosophy Sartre did much to make famous in the immediate postwar period, appeared in the play *Les Mouches* (1943; Eng. tr., *The Flies*, 1946) and in the lecture *L'Existentialisme est un humanisme* (1946; Eng. tr., *Existentialism and Humanism*, 1948). However, Sartre afterward declared that the lecture was "a mistake," and his later plays and novels continued to insist upon his early vision of man as a "useless passion." His failure to complete the intended series of four novels with the overall title *Les Chemins de la liberté* (*Paths of Freedom*)— *L' Age de raison* (1945; Eng. tr., *The Age of Reason*, 1947), *Le Sursis* (1945; Eng. tr., *The Reprieve*, 1947), and *La Mort dans l'âme* (1949; Eng. tr., *Iron in the Soul*, 1950)—confirmed this impression, and his growing interest in Marxism failed to give him an optimistic view of human history. His philosophical work *La Critique de la raison dialectique* (1960) is an attempt to reconcile Marxism with existentialism, but its main theme is the inevitability of conflict between men.

Aesthetically, Sartre's most successful works are his first novel, his short stories in the volume *Le Mur* (*The Wall*, 1939; Eng. tr., *Intimacy*, 1949), and his drama. Two plays stand out: *Les Mains sales* (1948; Eng. tr., *Dirty Hands*, 1949) and *Les Séquestrés d'Altona* (1959; Eng. tr., *The Condemned of Altona*, 1960). Both deal with the problem of liberty and responsibility, both end with the suicide of the main character, and both combine exciting drama with the intelligent presentation of moral and political ideas. His one-act play *Huis clos* (1944; Eng. tr., *No Exit*, 1947) has become a popular theater piece. Sartre's literary criticism includes essays on William Faulkner (1938), Charles Baudelaire (1946), and Jean Genet (1952; Eng. tr., *Saint Genet*, 1963). His theory that literature must take sides in political issues was expressed in *Qu'est-ce que la littérature?* (1948; Eng. tr., *What Is Literature?*, 1949). In 1964 he published the first volume of a projected two-volume autobiography, *The Words*. The second volume was abandoned. In 1971 and 1972 he published three volumes of a work on Flaubert. The projected fourth volume never appeared. See also EXISTENTIALISM.

PHILIP THODY, *Author of "Jean-Paul Sartre"*

Jean-Paul Sartre, French existentialist writer

Bibliography

Aron, Raymond, *Marxism and the Existentialists* (Simon & Schuster 1970).

Bauer, George, *Sartre and the Artist* (Univ. of Chicago Press 1969).

Greene, Norman, *Jean-Paul Sartre: The Existentialist Ethic* (Univ. of Mich. Press 1960).

Peyre, Henri, *Jean-Paul Sartre* (Columbia Univ. Press 1968).

Savage, Catharine, *Malraux, Sartre, and Aragon as Political Novelists* (Univ. of Fla. Press 1965).

Sheridan, James F., *Sartre: The Radical Conversion* (Ohio Univ. Press 1969).

Thody, Philip, *Jean-Paul Sartre: A Literary and Political Study* (Hamilton, H. 1960).

SASEBO, sä-se-bō, a seaport city in Japan, is in Nagasaki prefecture on the western side of Kyushu Island, near the mouth of Omura Bay. The city has shipbuilding, machinery, and food processing industries.

Sasebo was an obscure village until 1886, when its development as one of Japan's chief naval bases began. Heavily bombed during World War II, the port was subsequently rebuilt for expanded commercial use and for U. S.-Japanese security needs. Population: (1976 est.) 251,607.

ANNAN PHOTO

On the spacious prairies of Saskatchewan, grain elevators rise above vast fields of wheat.

Coat of arms

SASKATCHEWAN

CONTENTS

SASKATCHEWAN, sas-kach′ə-wän, is the central of the three Canadian provinces, Alberta, Saskatchewan, and Manitoba, known as the Prairie Provinces. It is part of a northern extension of the Great Plains area that includes the Midwestern states of the United States. The province takes its name from the Cree Indian word for its largest river.

Saskatchewan is a land of broad expanses and blue skies, in which the play of light and shadow on the clouds is an impressive part of the landscape. Like its sister province, Alberta, Saskatchewan has no saltwater coastline, but unlike Alberta it has no Rocky Mountains. Its settled parts are popularly called "prairie," although only a small fraction of the province is true prairie. It is mostly rolling grassland in its southern third, and lake and forest country in the north. The northern half of the province is nearly uninhabited wilderness.

1. The Land

Saskatchewan's boundaries are wholly manmade and very regular. The province extends about 335 miles (539 km) from east to west and 760 miles (1,220 km) from north to south. Its total area is 251,700 square miles (651,942 sq km), of which 13% is water. Almost a third of the province (mainly in the settled parts) lies between 1,800 and 2,400 feet (550–730 meters)

ANNAN PHOTO

Fast-river fishing in Lac la Ronge Provincial Park in the western part of the province.

above sea level, sloping generally north and east to 900 feet (270 meters) or less. The highest point is in the Cypress Hills in the southwest corner, rising to 4,546 feet (1,386 meters).

Barely two fifths of Saskatchewan is privately owned. Provincial forests account for over 100,000 square miles (250,000 sq km) of territory, and the rest consists of provincial and national parks, Indian reserves, and other federal and provincial crown lands.

Geologically, Saskatchewan has only two small unglaciated areas, both in the south. The rest is predominantly sedimentary rock formations, with a vast northern expanse of the Precambrian shield, which cuts across several provinces.

Although high hills are rare, the Saskatchewan landscape is marked by numerous dramatic valleys, through which rivers flow roughly west to east. The most important rivers are the North and South Saskatchewan, which drain much of the Canadian prairies and join near Prince Albert before emptying into Lake Winnipeg in Manitoba. The South Saskatchewan was dammed in the 1960's to provide electrical energy, creating Lake Diefenbaker, one of the province's largest lakes, over 80 miles (130 km) in length. Other rivers include the Qu'Appelle, Souris, and Assiniboine in the south and the Churchill in the north.

The province has hundreds of natural lakes, especially in the north, where many are still unnamed. The largest is Lake Athabasca, which Saskatchewan shares with Alberta.

Climate. Saskatchewan has a typically continental climate, with wide seasonal and daily variations in temperature. The average January temperature ranges from 0° F (−18° C) in the southwest to −20° F (−29° C) in the northeast. July temperatures range from 67° F (19° C) in the south to 57° F (14° C) in the north. Temperatures of −65° F (−54° C) and above 110° F (43° C) have been recorded.

The year is generally dry, with cycles of moister periods. Winter blizzards and summer thunderstorms are common. Annual precipitation is between 12 and 16 inches (305–407 mm), over half of which falls in the growing season, May to September.

Vegetation. Saskatchewan's vegetation varies from grassland in the south to forest in the north. About 40% of the total area of the province is occupied agricultural land, and two thirds of that is in crops or summer fallow. About 20% of the total area of the province is productive forest land, while the remaining 40% is still classified as nonproductive.

The forests of Saskatchewan are largely aspen, spruce, poplar, and pine. The huge trees common to the Pacific coast and the Great Lakes basin are not found in the province, although relatively large trees will grow when cultivated, as will many hardy fruit trees.

The southern grasslands, which in the past supported many major types of wild grasses, have been converted wherever possible to the grains and seed-oil plants that make Saskatchewan a chief supplier of wheat, rye, barley, oats, and rapeseed.

Animal Life. The conversion of the land to agricultural use has pushed many formerly common wild mammals to the point of extinction. Bison are now found only in parks or on an occasional farm, and grizzly bears are rarely seen. The black bear and the mountain lion have been virtually eliminated from the settled areas. How-

A herd of buffalo in Moose Jaw Wild Animal Park. Many kinds of wildlife abound in the sparsely populated areas of Saskatchewan.

ever, the smaller predators—lynx, bobcat, coyote, and wolf—all thrive, feeding on the rodents and rabbits with which the plains are generously endowed, or on the province's broad supply of moose, elk, caribou, deer, and antelope.

The province's fresh waters supply large quantities of game fish, with northern pike, lake trout, rainbow trout, walleyed pike, and brook trout especially numerous. The commercial fishery harvests more than 10 million pounds a year. This catch includes brine shrimp harvested in several saline lakes in the south.

Saskatchewan is a flyway for an almost bewildering variety of waterfowl, with the great blue heron and many species of crane prominently represented. Among the game birds are the ptarmigan (in the far north), and several varieties of duck (mallard, canvasback, pintail, teal), grouse (sharptailed, ruffed), and partridge (Hungarian, chukar). The grasslands provide nesting material and food for a wide range of songbirds.

Conservation. A resident of the province would have to be unusually imperceptive to be unaware of the teeming wildlife or of the difficulties of conserving it. Saskatchewan has been spared many major problems of industrialization and urbanization. But the use of synthetic fertilizers and pesticides, which inevitably find their way into its river systems, has created both problems and controversy.

Since all major rivers rise to the west of Saskatchewan, pollutants can also reach the province from sources beyond its jurisdiction. In the early 1970's the public was warned that fish from several bodies of water should not be eaten because of their mercury content. But no one has demonstrated how the province's agricultural economy could maintain the quality or quantity of its production without chemical aids.

2. The People

The population of Saskatchewan has never exceeded 1 million and in absolute numbers has remained remarkably stable for over 40 years. According to the 1981 census the province had a population of 968,313, concentrated in the southern half. This represented an increase of about 4% since 1971.

Under the supervision of a conservation officer, commercial fishermen haul in a catch of tullibees (whitefish), netted through the ice of Last Mountain Lake.

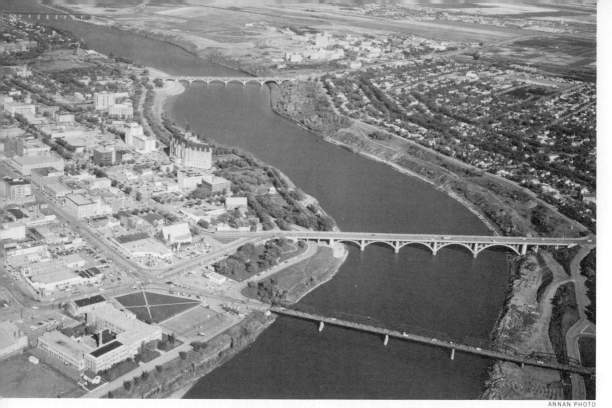

Saskatoon, one of Saskatchewan's two major cities, is situated on both sides of the South Saskatchewan River.

The urban-rural distribution, however, has changed greatly, the farming population declining from 61% in 1931 to 20.9% in 1976. The split between urban and rural (including farm and nonfarm rural) was 55.5% urban; 44.5% rural.

Major Cities. Saskatchewan's urban areas have been among the fastest growing in Canada. About one third of the province's population live in the cities of Regina, the capital, and Saskatoon. Regina is located in the southern portion of the settled area, while Saskatoon is in the northern part of the settled region.

Since the two cities are approximately equal in size but 160 miles (258 km) apart, they in effect give the province two economic capitals, each of which dominates a large empire for the distribution of goods and services. Rivalry between the two is intense in everything from rates of growth to securing new industry.

Components of the Population. The area was known only to Indians, fur traders, and a few explorers until the late 19th century. It began to fill up with settlers in the 1870's and 1880's. The population was near 100,000 at the beginning of the 20th century, then sextupled to 648,000 by 1916, and passed 900,000 by 1931.

The immigrants who poured into the province in its earlier years came from eastern Canada, the United States, and Europe. They were attracted by generous homesteading grants of land, and, for many of the Europeans, by freedom from compulsory military service. Probably few parts of the world are peopled by a higher proportion of descendants of "draft-dodgers."

The immigrants settled in homogeneous communities. For example, in Cannington Manor upper-class Britishers tried to transplant their whole way of life, even fox hunting. Cannington Manor failed, but other settlements did not. To this day both small towns and farming areas are recognizably Ukrainian, German, French-Canadian, and so on, with the old languages still spoken and the songs and dances and artistic traditions maintained. Sometimes one can observe "Canadianization" in a single family. The grandparents speak only their mother tongue, and a few are still illiterate; the parents are literate and bilingual in the mother tongue and English; the children speak and write only English.

Of Saskatchewan's population, about 40% is of British origin, 19% German, 9% Ukrainian, 6% Scandinavian, and about 6% French. Sizable groups are of Polish, Dutch, Austrian, and Hungarian descent. The proportion of persons of Asian origin is small (probably less than 5,000),

POPULATION—GROWTH AND DISTRIBUTION

Year	Population	Change (percent)	Percent Urban	Percent Rural
1901..	91,279	...	6.1	93.9
1911..	492,432	539.5	16.1	83.9
1921..	757,510	53.8	16.8	83.2
1931..	921,785	21.7	20.3	79.7
1941..	895,992	−2.8	21.3	78.7
1951..	831,728	−7.2	30.4	69.6
1961..	925,181	5.1	43.0	57.0
1971..	926,242	0.1	53.0	47.0
1981..	968,313	4.5	...*	...*

*Not available.

LARGEST CENTERS OF POPULATION

City	1981	1971	1961
Regina	162,613	139,469	112,141
Saskatoon	154,210	126,449	95,526
Moose Jaw	33,941	31,854	33,206
Prince Albert	31,380	28,464	24,168
Yorkton	15,339	13,430	9,995
Swift Current	14,747	15,415	12,186
North Battleford	14,030	12,698	11,230
Weyburn	9,523	8,815	9,101
Estevan	9,174	9,150	7,728
Lloydminster*	6,034	8,691	5,667
Melfort	6,010	4,725	4,039

*Partly in Alberta.

SASKATCHEWAN

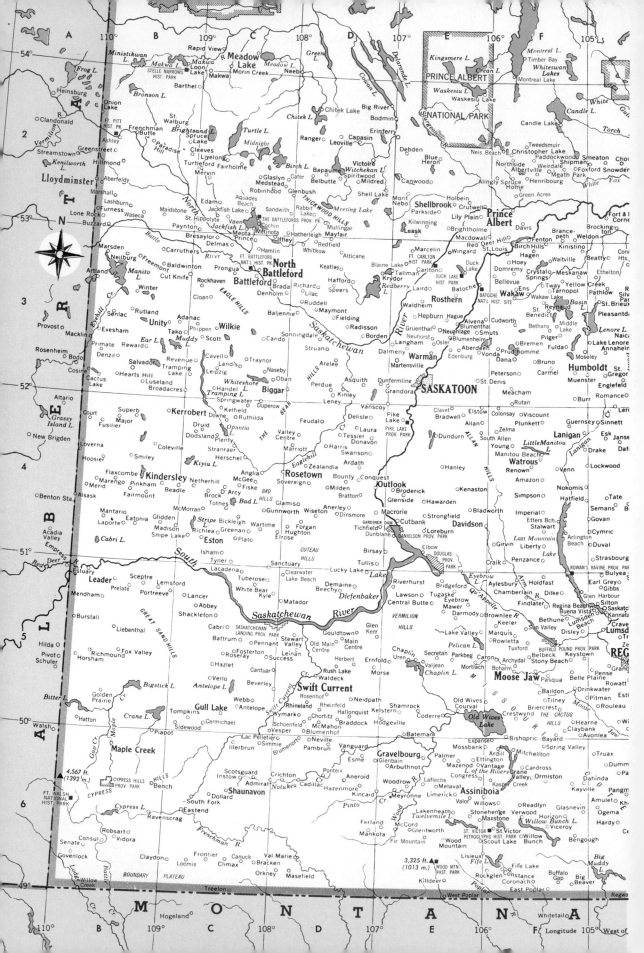

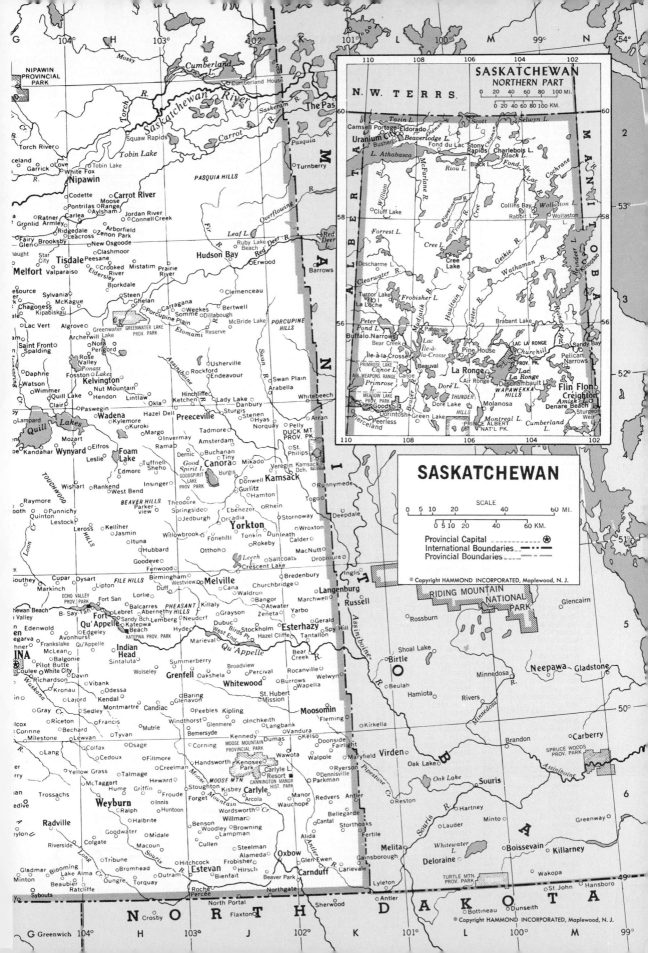

SASKATCHEWAN

‡Population of metropolitan area.

Regina is the capital and largest city of Saskatchewan.

but this group is highly urbanized and is concentrated in particular occupations, and thus it is a noticeable fraction of the population. Indians, who are overwhelmingly rural, number about 45,000. In addition there are a few hundred blacks.

Religion. The religious affiliations of Saskatchewan's population present a similar mosaic. The largest religious body is the United Church of Canada, with 32% of the church members. The second largest is the Roman Catholic Church, with 26%, followed by the Anglican (10%), Greek Catholic (4%), and Greek Orthodox (4%), and there are significant groups of Presbyterians, Baptists, Pentecostals, and Jehovah's Witnesses. Religion has often been an important factor in Saskatchewan politics.

3. The Economy

Agriculture has remained the major economic activity in Saskatchewan and wheat the most important crop. But by the 1960's about 60% of the net value of the province's production was earned by nonagricultural activities, especially mining. The present status of Saskatchewan's economy represents a remarkable comeback from the depths of poverty it reached during the drought years of the 1930's.

Saskatchewan ranks fifth or sixth among the ten provinces in wealth, depending on the current state of grain crops and world sales. Apart from a few small local industries, all of its major products—grain, meat, potash, and oil—are consumed outside its borders. The provincial economy is therefore vulnerable to the fluctuations of both consumption and prices over which it has no control.

Agriculture. In the decades since World War II the number of farms has decreased, while the size of the average farm has increased. Saskatchewan is one of the world's most important wheat-producing regions, and some 60% of its cropland is in wheat. In a good year the wheat harvest yields at least 500 million bushels. Other crops include barley, oats, rye, and rapeseed.

Saskatchewan's first large crop was buffalo bones, which were gathered in central locations for shipment east to be ground up for fertilizer. But that crop could be reaped only once, and was succeeded by the rapid development of the grasslands.

Livestock raising has become an increasingly important part of the economy. Beef cattle predominate, followed by hogs.

Mining. Virtually all mineral development has taken place since World War II. Discoveries of oil, natural gas, uranium, and potash have made mining the second most important segment of the economy. In the late 1970's, Saskatchewan produced 58 million barrels of oil and 43 million cubic feet of natural gas annually. It possesses the world's largest and highest-grade potash deposits. Most of this development has been in the settled portions of the south, but uranium is mined in the north, especially near Lake Athabasca.

Manufacturing and Power. Manufacturing has made great progress since World War II, but by the 1970's the province's labor force in manufacturing remained less than 1% of the Canadian total. The province's resource base does not provide for the production of either consumer goods or machinery. Manufacturing activities include chiefly oil refining and food processing. The labor

Giant combines harvest wheat on the plains near Regina.

union movement is small, and its largest locals are in essential areas such as marketing.

Saskatchewan's vast reserves of natural gas have been developed as a prime source of energy. Gas supplies most of the province's homes with heat. Another major resource, fresh water, has also been exploited. Millions of gallons of fresh water are required daily by the potash mines, and several rivers have been harnessed to provide hydroelectric power.

Transportation. Marketing is of particular relevance in Saskatchewan, for the movement of raw materials and farm machinery places heavy de-

Hummingbird No. 1, near Gladmar. Millions of barrels of oil are produced each year in Saskatchewan.

mands on a transportation system that must serve a large and often thinly settled region. Transportation is also vulnerable to outside forces, and prairie farmers are regularly irritated by dock or railway strikes hundreds of miles away and by shortages of ships or boxcars. The storage of goods held for export is another essential part of the system, and the prairie elevator is a familiar sight.

The transportation system has been under pressure for years because, as elsewhere, the trains needed to develop the region in the first place, moving hundreds of thousands of people in and harvests of wheat out, have been rendered largely obsolete by trucks and planes. Saskatchewan is crossed by two east-west railways, with the Canadian Pacific passing through Regina, in the south, and the Canadian National serving Saskatoon, to the north. But the loss of passenger and local freight revenue annually increases the railways' desire to eliminate trains and close stations.

Local transportation has been transferred to roads, and Saskatchewan reputedly has the largest per capita road mileage in existence. The settled part is crisscrossed with a grid of road allowances 1 or 2 miles (1.6–3.2 km) apart, most of them trails, which in dry weather are as passable as pavement, but which may be closed by snow or rain. These lead to a system of all-weather graded roads and a network of highways linking

SASKATCHEWAN'S CHANGING ECONOMIC BASE: NET VALUE OF COMMODITY PRODUCTION
(In millions of dollars)

	1960	1965	1970
Agriculture	525	710	425
Manufacturing	116	139	201
Construction	191	241	226
Mining	165	292	328
Electric power	32	49	66
Other natural resources	8	4	13

Source: Treasury Department, Saskatchewan

the major cities and towns. The Trans-Canada Highway crosses the province through Regina. The road system, though sometimes apparently primitive, is crucial to Saskatchewan rural life and to many of the recreational activities of the townspeople.

The roads are supplemented by local air service, and flying farmers are sufficiently numerous to have an association. The province has no major international airport, but access to Canada's fourth busiest airfield, at Winnipeg, Manitoba, is not difficult.

Saskatchewan's waterways are now used primarily for recreational purposes, though ferries cross the rivers at several places. Although there are a few larger vessels on northern lakes, the only boats seen in the settled part are those used for fishing and water skiing.

Tourism. In the competition to attract visitors, Saskatchewan's lakes and rivers must be rated as its principal resources, providing opportunities for everything from ice fishing in January to the hunting of waterfowl in late autumn. The province is gradually becoming more accessible to camper trailers and is acquiring a modest population of small pleasure boats, snowmobiles, and other playthings for vacationers. By comparison with other provinces, however, its tourist trade is growing at a slow rate. Saskatchewan's remote location and its harsh winter climate would seem to mitigate against its becoming an affluent resort area within the very near future.

Research and Development. Fundamental research to promote industry has been dominated by the University of Saskatchewan, the Saskatchewan Research Council, and National Research Council laboratories, which are on the university campus. Experimental farms and stations are operated by the federal and provincial governments. A growing number of government departments and branches, such as those interested in geology, archaeology, and zoology, have been undertaking research.

4. Government

The structure of the government of Saskatchewan is superficially like that of the other provinces, although local traditions, as elsewhere, have shaped its use. The titular head of the government is the lieutenant governor, who is appointed by the federal cabinet. Although he has vast powers on paper, any genuine use of them usually precipitates a crisis. His real duties are ceremonial, the provincial equivalent of those of a constitutional monarch.

Actual authority is vested in the premier and his cabinet. The premier is the leader of the majority party of the Legislative Assembly, and he and the cabinet ministers must (by custom) be members of the assembly.

Members of the Legislative Assembly are elected by simple plurality vote from 61 single-member constituencies. The assembly has a maximum term of five years, but is often dissolved on the advice of the premier before that limit is reached. It meets regularly early in the new year for a 10- or 12-week session. But sessions have been growing longer, and extra summer or fall sessions have become increasingly common.

Judiciary. All judges above the rank of magistrate are appointed by the federal government. The judiciary is a pyramid with local magistrates' courts at the bottom, above which are district courts, the court of queen's bench, and the ap-

Potash storage building near Esterhazy. Saskatchewan has the world's largest deposits of potash.

Chief cities, industries, products, and resources.

The Saskatchewan Legislative Building, in Regina.

peals court. All levels may hear cases under federal, provincial, or municipal law. Appeals may be made to the federal court or the Supreme Court of Canada.

Local Government. Local government is divided among the various cities, towns, villages, and rural municipalities. All perform the usual housekeeping functions in regard to utilities and roads. These units are not important bases of political power, although collectively their associations are among the most influential pressure groups, essentially conservative where the reorganization of local government is concerned.

Municipal governments in Saskatchewan are based on a congressional model, with provisions for direct and separate election of mayors and councils.

PREMIERS OF SASKATCHEWAN

Name	Party	Dates of Office
Walter Scott	Liberal	1905–1916
William Melville Martin	Liberal	1916–1922
Charles Avery Dunning	Liberal	1922–1926
James Garfield Gardiner	Liberal	1926–1929
James Thomas Milton Anderson	Conservative	1929–1934
James Garfield Gardiner	Liberal	1934–1935
William John Patterson	Liberal	1935–1944
Thomas Clement Douglas	CCF[1]	1944–1961
Woodrow Stanley Lloyd	CCF	1961–1964
W. Ross Thatcher	Liberal	1964–1971
Allen E. Blakeney	NDP[2]	1971–1982
Grant Devine	PC[3]	1982–

[1]CCF—Cooperative Commonwealth Federation
[2]NDP—New Democratic party, successor to CCF
[3]PC—Progressive Conservative party

Public Finance. Approximately one third of Saskatchewan's annual budget is devoted to education and another third to highways. Both were relatively inexpensive items when they were originally assigned to provincial jurisdiction, and the provinces were permitted to levy only direct taxes. The disparity between Saskatchewan's constitutional responsibilities and its fixed sources of income underlies much of its public finance. Although the province is more affluent than in the past, it still relies on federal grants.

Social Services. Saskatchewan has been a pioneer in many fields of welfare and administration. It created a publicly financed hospitalization system in the late 1940's and a similar medical care system in the 1960's. It also led the way in introducing collective bargaining in the public service, in making automobile insurance compulsory, in accomplishing numerous advances in welfare legislation and subsidized geriatric centers, and in establishing a public transportation system with a fleet of buses and a flying ambulance service.

Many of these governmental innovations were the work of the Cooperative Commonwealth Federation (CCF), a party that formed the first socialist administration in North America in 1944. But the CCF built largely on older traditions. The immediate ancestors of thousands of prairie residents came to virtually free land on railways built on governmental initiative, and they have always regarded government as just one more instrument for accomplishing collective ends. Saskatchewan therefore has always had a mixed public-private enterprise economy.

Political Parties. The Saskatchewan voter rarely feels an obligation to vote for the same party in provincial and federal elections, largely because they are held on different issues. The major provincial parties are the Liberal party, which dom-

GOVERNMENT HIGHLIGHTS

Representation in the Parliament of Canada: 6 senators, appointed by governor general, retiring at 75; 12 members of House of Commons, elected by people of province.

Provincial Government: Lieutenant governor (formal head, appointed by federal government as representative of the crown); Legislative Assembly, 61 members, elected for maximum of five years; premier and executive council (cabinet) supported by, and members of, Legislative Assembly.

Voting Age: 18 years, provincial elections; 18 years, federal elections.

inated the government until 1944; the New Democratic party (NDP), formed by a merger of the CCF and the Canadian Labour Congress, and which was in power from 1971 to 1982; and the Progressive Conservative party (PC), which won a landslide victory in the 1982 election.

Federal and provincial parties with the same name often have very different leanings. Thus having the same party in power in Saskatchewan as in the national parliament is no guarantee of federal-provincial cooperation. The provincial Liberal government of 1964–1971 was more conservative than the federal Liberal government.

Party lines have not entered local politics. Although local politicians are often chosen as candidates in provincial and federal elections, municipal politics are nonpartisan or bipartisan.

5. Education and Cultural Life

Saskatchewan's school system, apart from a few private institutions operated in the main by church groups, is public and decentralized. The department of education has broad responsibilities for curriculum standards and levels of local expenditure. But the local boards, within provincial guidelines, are highly autonomous.

Elementary and Secondary Education. In the late 1960's, Saskatchewan initiated a nongraded school system. The traditional 12 elementary-secondary grades were replaced by 4 divisions, each consisting of a 3-year program. About 230,000 students are enrolled in the province's schools.

In the past, education in the province, reflecting the ethnic backgrounds of the population, was racked by struggles over the language to be used for instruction. Since particular ethnic groups were predominantly Catholic, the issue of religion invariably became involved. Powerful pressure groups were generally successful in suppressing all languages other than English, as well as barring the use of public schools for religious instruction. In the larger urban areas separate schools were established that were financed and controlled by Catholic taxpayers.

The larger centers thus have two school systems, public and separate, under different elected school boards. Since the 1960's, with the ancient battles over language apparently ended, there has been a trend towards the liberalizing of restrictions on French and other languages in the schools, partly in response to federal policies encouraging bilingualism.

Higher Education. The publicly supported University of Saskatchewan has a large campus at Saskatoon. Its Regina campus was considerably smaller; this campus became the separate University of Regina in 1974.

The university from the start developed with a strong consciousness of the community it serves.

It has operated a farm as part of its facilities at Saskatoon, and faculty members have done outstanding work in developing hardy strains of wheat and in improving farming techniques and machinery. Extension programs have been established for general as well as academic education. The Saskatoon campus has also acquired a strong northern interest, with an Institute for Northern Studies. It also has an Institute for Space and Atmospheric Studies, which has pioneered in study of the aurora borealis.

The university has several strong scientific departments, and nonscientific work has included noteworthy studies in history, economics and economic history, law, and political science, as well as creative work in art, music, and drama.

A plains study program was instituted at the University of Regina. Two religious colleges are affiliated with the university: Campion College, operated by the Roman Catholic Church, and Luther College, supported by the Lutheran Church.

Libraries. The province has a widely used public library system, which includes municipal institutions in the urban areas and regional libraries that serve rural areas. For specialized purposes these can be supplemented by the legislative library in Regina, the university libraries, and the provincial archives. Books in languages familiar to various ethnic groups are kept in the regional libraries.

Museums. Saskatchewan has some unusual collections of particular relevance to its past. The museum at the Royal Canadian Mounted Police

Tourists visit the chapel in a tour of the barracks of the Royal Canadian Mounted Police, Regina.

ANNAN PHOTO

The Museum of Natural History, Regina, exhibits Canadian plants and animals in their natural habitats.

barracks in Regina is as famous as its crime laboratories. The Western Development Museum (Saskatoon, North Battleford, and Yorkton) houses comprehensive samples of machinery from the province's pioneering days. The Museum of Natural History in Regina has a highly professional exhibition of flora and fauna mounted in reconstructed natural habitats.

Scattered throughout the province are historical museums related directly to local events. These include the museum at Batoche, the site of the major battle in the Riel Rebellion of 1885, and several forts that were key points in fur-trading times.

The leading art collections are the Norman Mackenzie Gallery in Regina and the Mendel Art Gallery in Saskatoon. Both galleries have permanent and traveling exhibitions and are heavily patronized.

Other Cultural Activities. Both Regina and Saskatoon have symphony orchestras. The music faculty of the university's Regina campus offers regular productions, including operas, and the Saskatoon campus presents an annual series of professional concerts arranged by the music department. Both cities support semiprofessional theatrical companies, which are sometimes augmented by outside stars, and the university's drama faculty presents plays. Several amateur companies perform in their localities.

Lively art colonies exist in Regina and Saskatoon, primarily at the university and near the art galleries, but artists are at work throughout the province. Indian art, except for the commercial varieties aimed at the tourist trade, is not deeply rooted in most parts of Saskatchewan, but rock paintings have been discovered in the north. Indian patterns and artifacts derived from Indian sources have enjoyed a renaissance that began in the 1960's.

Saskatchewan churches, particularly rural structures built by immigrants, contain some striking religious art that reveals its European sources, both in the architecture and the interiors.

Media. The province's broadcasting stations and newspapers serve their communities well with conventional coverage of local affairs and sports. But the broadcasting outlets are merely links in national chains in which Saskatchewan's market is relatively small. Almost all of the programming originates outside the province. The two largest dailies—the Regina *Leader-Post* and the Saskatoon *Star-Phoenix*—are owned by absentee interests and rely almost exclusively on wire services and syndicates for material from outside the province.

One benefit of the media's status is that residents are not isolated from the rest of Canada but are thoroughly integrated into a North American system. It also means that authentic Saskatchewan media are found only in the weeklies, of which there are several dozen, and a few small radio stations. The largest weekly is *The Western Producer*, published by the Saskatchewan Wheat Pool, the province's biggest marketing cooperative. The same press publishes books with prairie themes.

The local services of the media are outstanding. They not only cover news events but disseminate invaluable reports on weather threats to crops and police messages about dangerous road conditions and prison escapees. In a province where the population averages fewer than 5 per square mile (about 2 per sq km), the value of such assistance is often beyond price.

6. Recreation

Almost all of Saskatchewan is suitable for one or more of man's chief methods of relaxing. Roughly half the province is untouched by roads, and fishermen and hunters must fly in. Even in the major cities, the wilderness is often as close as the golf courses, and stray deer still wander into town. The natural hazards of the golf course in Prince Albert National Park include bear and foxes.

National and Provincial Parks. Prince Albert National Park lies just north of the city of Prince Albert. The park, one of the most popular in Canada, covers roughly 1,500 square miles (3,600 sq km) of forest and lake country.

The province maintains 14 parks, covering considerably more area, in all regions typical of the Saskatchewan landscape except for the north-

FAMOUS RESIDENTS OF SASKATCHEWAN

Adaskin, Murray (1906–   ), composer.
Coldwell, Major James William (1888–   ), legislator, leader of federal CCF, 1940–1958.
Davin, Nicholas Flood (1843–1901), newspaperman and legislator.
Diefenbaker, John George (1895–1979), prime minister of Canada, 1957–1963; leader of the opposition 1956–1957 and 1963–1967.
Dumont, Gabriel (1838–1906), Riel's chief lieutenant during 1885 rebellion.
Haultain, Frederick William George (1857–1942), political leader and judge.
Howe, Gordie (1928–   ), hockey star.
Hurley, Robert (1894–   ), painter.
McCourt, Edward A. (1907–1972), scholar and author.
McNaughton, Andrew George Latta (1887–1966), Canadian commander overseas, World War II, and administrator.
McPhail, Alexander James (1883–1931), farm leader.
Partridge, Edward Alexander (1862–1931), farm leader.
Piapot (1816–1908), Indian chief.
Poundmaker (1826–1886), Indian chief.
Sapp, Allan (1929–   ), painter.
Vickers, Jon (1926–   ), operatic tenor.

ern tundra. They provide a wide variety of camping and boating facilities. Cypress Hills Provincial Park is unique—a geological aberration in which are found flora and fauna not indigenous elsewhere in the province. Other provincial parks include Moose Jaw Wild Animal Park in the south central area and Moose Mountain Provincial Park in the southeast.

There are also several dozen regional parks, designated areas in which golf courses and other recreational facilities are established primarily to serve a district's local residents. Additional campsites and picnic facilities are located along the main highways.

Regular Events. Sightseeing attractions are available throughout the year. They range from a Trappers' Festival with dogsled races in Prince Albert to an active program of football, baseball, and hockey. There is an annual indoor track meet that features international athletes. The only fully professional team is the Saskatchewan Roughriders, a football squad based in Regina. Saskatchewan is a major supplier of hockey players, and many of the National Hockey League's stars played first on the plains.

Several cities and towns have regular summer and winter events, including music festivals and week-long exhibitions, or fairs, often identified with revivals of pioneer practices. The largest are Regina's Buffalo Days and Saskatoon's Saskachimo.

7. History

Saskatchewan's history is impressive first for the peaceful nature of the white man's occupation and second for the importance of the cooperative movement. The Saskatchewan region was originally inhabited by Indians, particularly the Cree, who followed the buffalo herds until their virtual disappearance in the 1870's. The first white man to see the area was Henry Kelsey, who arrived in 1690 as an agent of the Hudson's Bay Company.

Early Settlers. Explorers and fur traders soon arrived in increasing numbers, and Ft. Lacorne, the first trading post, was built in 1753. The first permanent European settlement in the area was Cumberland House, built in 1774 by the Hudson's Bay Company. After the Dominion of Canada was formed from the British North American colonies in 1867, the British government acquired the Northwest Territories, including present-day Saskatchewan, from the Hudson's Bay Company in 1870.

By the mid-19th century the fur trade had declined, and permanent agricultural settlements began to be established. Settlers were encouraged by the government's offer of free homesteads, and the completion of the transcontinental Canadian Pacific Railway in 1885 was a great stimulus to settlement.

Riel Rebellion. Whether the Indians were too few in number to defend their land or were deceived by the white man's promises, the Riel Rebellion in 1885 was the first and last violent confrontation. The rebellion was an uprising of some of the Indians and *métis*, persons of mixed French and Indian blood. It was quickly suppressed, and the *métis* leader Louis Riel was hanged for treason.

Formation of the Province. When the Northwest Territories received parliamentary representation in 1887, one of the electoral districts was called Saskatchewan. The population continued to grow and in 1905 became large enough to justify the formation of two provinces—Saskatchewan and Alberta.

Between 1905 and World War I, Saskatchewan's population increased rapidly, with an influx of immigrants from eastern Canada, the United States, Britain, and continental Europe. The pioneers created a highly productive agricultural economy. But the Depression and serious drought of the 1930's created much hardship and political unrest.

World Wars I and II. A summary of Saskatchewan's history would be incomplete without reference to the province's contributions in two world wars. Thousands of its citizens served in both, but conscription created more difficulties

Qu'Appelle Hall is one of the residence halls for men at the University of Saskatchewan, Saskatoon.

GIBSON PHOTOS LTD

ANNAN PHOTO

Ukrainian church near Insinger. A large segment of the Saskatchewan population is of Ukrainian origin.

former nationals of states with which Canada was at war. For the wartime election of 1917 the federal government took no chances, and in a special franchise act it simply eliminated from the voters' lists all former nationals of certain countries who had become Canadians after 1902. In 1942, during World War II, when the federal government asked in a plebiscite if the electorate would relieve it of its promise not to enact conscription, the largest "no" votes outside Quebec were in rural Saskatchewan.

Political History. The Liberal party governed Saskatchewan from 1905 to 1929 and again from 1934 to 1944, when demands for more radical solutions to the province's problems brought to power the Cooperative Commonwealth Federation (CCF). In the 1960's the CCF merged with the Canadian Labour Congress to form the New Democratic party (NDP). The Liberals won again in 1964 but lost to the NDP in 1971. In 1982 the NDP lost to the Progressive Conservatives.

Cooperative Movement. Every major aspect of Saskatchewan's social and political life has been affected by the cooperative movement. Although the movement was not itself political, the Liberal party in its early years, and subsequently the CCF and later the NDP, were concerned with translating into political action the same talents and skills that went into organizing stores and other marketing agencies. The Saskatchewan government is the only one with a full minister of cooperatives and cooperative development.

A similar manifestation was seen in the 1920's, when several Protestant churches in Canada were uniting into the United Church of Canada. The amalgamation was marked by much bitterness elsewhere, but in Saskatchewan it was found that church union had already been quietly accomplished in community after community.

The cooperative movement has manifested itself in a wide range of activities connected with the manufacture and distribution of goods and services. The Saskatchewan Wheat Pool is the largest grain elevator company. Federated Cooperatives Limited is the wholesaler for several hundred retail outlets. One of the largest oil refineries is a co-op. Paralleling this structure is the credit union movement.

Willing Partner. Saskatchewan has been a willing partner in the federation of Canada. Through both its prosperous growth under federal auspices down to 1930 and its subsequent extreme destitution under the combined burdens of depression and drought, it has been, in character, a cooperative province, and its comparative affluence after World War II has not altered its view of its role in the nation. The province's citizens reserve the right to rail endlessly about the iniquities of federal and eastern interests whose policies are dominant, but separatism has not flourished in Saskatchewan.

NORMAN WARD
University of Saskatchewan

on the plains than anywhere else in Canada, except Quebec. During World War I, farmers generally were concerned over the loss of desperately needed manpower to the army, and Saskatchewan, with the most heavily agricultural economy in the country, was hard hit.

The province's difficulties were compounded by the fact that a high proportion of its population was of European extraction, some of whom had escaped from conscription abroad and opposed it in Canada, and some of whom were

HISTORICAL HIGHLIGHTS

1690	Henry Kelsey, Hudson's Bay Company agent, became first white man to see area of present-day Saskatchewan.
1753	Fort Lacorne, the area's first trading post, was built.
1774	First permanent settlement, Cumberland House, was established.
1870	Northwest Territories, including present-day Saskatchewan, acquired by Canada from the Hudson's Bay Company.
1873	North West Mounted Police organized.
1876	Chief Sitting Bull and Sioux Indians fled into the Northwest Territories from the United States after defeating Gen. George Custer at a battle on the Little Bighorn River.
1882	Canadian Pacific Railway, first rail link with east, reached area.
1885	Riel Rebellion quickly suppressed.
1887	Northwest Territories received parliamentary representation.
1905	Saskatchewan created as a province.
1909	Sir Wilfrid Laurier, prime minister of Canada, laid cornerstone for University of Saskatchewan.
1924	Saskatchewan Wheat Pool organized by farmers.
1929	First non-Liberal government formed.
1935	Riot of unemployed workers in Regina.
1944	First socialist government in North America elected.
1957	John Diefenbaker, Saskatchewan member of Parliament, became prime minister of Canada.
1965	South Saskatchewan Dam completed.

Bibliography

Bennett, John William, *Northern Plainsmen* (Aldine Pub. 1969).
Fowke, Vernon Clifford, *National Policy and the Wheat Economy* (Univ. of Toronto Press 1957).
Gray, James Henry, *The Winter Years: The Depression on the Prairies* (Macmillan 1966).
Lipset, Seymour Martin, *Agrarian Socialism: The Cooperative Commonwealth Federation* (Doubleday 1968).
McCourt, Edward A., *Saskatchewan: The Traveller's Canada* (St. Martins 1967).
Ward, Norman, and Spafford, Duf, eds., *Politics in Saskatchewan* (Longmans 1968).

SASKATCHEWAN, University of, sas-kach'ə-wän, a coeducational, nondenominational university in Saskatoon, Saskatchewan, Canada. A campus of the university in Regina became the University of Regina in 1974. The institution was established by legislative act in 1907. The Regina branch was established as Regina College in 1911 by the Methodist Church. The university assumed responsibility for its operation in 1934 and decided to create a second campus there in 1959.

In Saskatoon, the university overlooks the South Saskatchewan River. Included among the components of the site are a university farm and experimental plots. The campus is a center of scientific, industrial, and agricultural research.

Faculties at Saskatoon are those of arts and science; agriculture; commerce; education; engineering; home economics; law; medicine, which also directs the program in nursing; dentistry; pharmacy; and veterinary medicine. Courses in theology are available through affiliated colleges of various denominations.

Institutions associated with the Saskatoon campus include St. Thomas More College (Roman Catholic), College of Emmanuel and St. Chad (Anglican), Lutheran Theological Seminary, and St. Andrew's College (United Church of Canada), all at Saskatoon. St. Joseph's College (Ukrainian Orthodox) at Yorktown and St. Peter's College (Roman Catholic) at Muenster are also affiliated with the university.

The university has been noted for its work in the creative arts, economics, and science. It operates a farm on which hardy strains of wheat have been developed.

The university grants bachelor's, master's, and, in some areas, doctor's degrees. Enrollment at the Saskatoon campus numbers about 10,000, while that at the formerly affiliated campus at Regina numbered about 4,000.

SASKATCHEWAN REBELLION. See RIEL, LOUIS; SASKATCHEWAN—*History.*

SASKATCHEWAN RIVER, sas-kach'ə-wän, a river in south central Canada. It has two main branches, the North Saskatchewan, with the Brazeau, Clearwater, Vermilion, and Battle rivers as tributaries; and the South Saskatchewan, with the Oldman, Bow, and Red Deer rivers as tributaries. The two branches have their source in the watershed of the eastern ranges of the Rockies. They flow generally eastward through Alberta and Saskatchewan to unite about 25 miles (40 km) east of Prince Albert, Saskatchewan. The combined stream sweeps northeast and southeast, receives the Carrot River from the south after entering Manitoba, and empties into Lake Winnipeg. It is the fourth-longest river in Canada, measuring some 1,200 miles (1,930 km).

The Saskatchewan River was discovered by the Sieur de La Vérendrye in 1741 and first came into prominence as a water route for rival companies seeking to tap the fur riches of the Canadian Northwest. The drainage area is one of Canada's great agricultural regions. Irrigation began in 1901 in Alberta. In the 1960's a gigantic hydroelectric earth dam was built on the South Saskatchewan in the vicinity of Elbow, Saskatchewan. Industrial and municipal uses of the river's flow have sharply increased water-utilization and pollution-control problems.

Prominent landmarks at the University of Saskatchewan at Saskatoon are the Arts Building *(left)* and Library.
SASKATCHEWAN INFORMATION SERVICE

SASKATOON, sas-kə-toon', a city in south-central Saskatchewan, Canada, is on the South Saskatchewan River, about 150 miles (240 km) northwest of Regina. It is the commercial and distributing center of a huge grain-producing region and the terminus of highways, railroads, and airlines.

One of the grain elevators in the city, which holds 5.5 million bushels (192,500,000 liters), was built and is operated by the Canadian government. The city has flour and cereal mills, meat-packing plants, dairy-product processing establishments, and a potash plant. The railroads employ a large proportion of the labor force.

Saskatoon is a handsome city, noted for its wide streets, parks, and fine homes. Six bridges, including three railroad spans, cross the river.

The city is the home of the University of Saskatchewan. A number of museums are in the city, including that of the Saskatoon Gallery and Conservatory Corporation, which exhibits paintings, sculpture, and the graphic arts; the Museum of Ukrainian Culture; the Western Development Museum; and the Nutana Collegiate Institute. Several museums and the W. P. Fraser Memorial Herbarium are associated with the university.

Saskatoon was founded as the administrative center of a temperance colony set up in the Canadian Northwest under the auspices of the Temperance Colonization Society of Ontario. By arrangement with the Canadian government, the society acquired a tract of land on both sides of the South Saskatchewan River. In 1882 a party headed by John N. Lake came west and chose the site for the colony's future capital. The name "Saskatoon" derives from a Cree Indian word *Mis-sask-a-too-mina,* referring to an edible berry found in the vicinity.

The original settlement was on the east bank of the river, but when the first railroad was built in 1890, its station was on the west bank, and a new community arose there, called West Saskatoon. The older settlement was called Nutana, meaning "firstborn." Both communities were incorporated as the city of Saskatoon in 1906. Population: 154,210.

SASSAFRAS, sas'ə-fras, is the colloquial and generic name of three species of trees in the laurel family, Lauraceae. Two are native to eastern Asia, and one is native to eastern North America. *Sassafras albidum* extends from Maine, southern Ontario, and Michigan to Texas and Florida. It may approach 100 feet (30 meters) in height and 6 feet (2 meters) in diameter, but it is usually smaller, sometimes even shrubby. The bark is dark red-brown and deeply furrowed; young twigs are green. The leaves are four to six inches (10 to 15 cm) long. They generally are oval on older branches but often mitten-shaped or three-lobed on younger shoots and twigs. In autumn the leaves turn various shades of yellow, orange, pink, and deep red. The flowers, which appear as the leaves emerge, are yellowish green, not showy, and are staminate or pistillate, usually on different trees. The staminate flowers have six perianth parts, nine stamens, each opening by four valves, and three pairs of glands. In the pistillate flowers, there are six staminodia and one pistil. The pistil ripens into a blue drupe that is eagerly devoured by birds, which thus disperse the seed of the tree. The heartwood of sassafras is dark or orange-brown and resistant to decay. It is sometimes used for fence posts and rails.

In contrast to its present distribution, sassafras is found in both Europe and North America in fossil form as far back as the Lower Cretaceous. It was widespread in Europe, Greenland, and North America in the Upper Cretaceous, and survived in Europe until near the end of the last glacial period.

All parts of the sassafras tree are strongly aromatic. Early explorers and settlers in the New World were told by the Indians that it would cure diverse ills, and it was eagerly sought and shipped to Europe. However, like other panaceas, it was not effective. Oil of sassafras, derived especially from the roots and wood, is used to some extent in scenting perfumes and soaps. Leaves and pith, dried and powdered, were used as a thickener for soups. Roots of sassafras were dried and steeped to make sassafras tea, but the tea was banned by the U.S. Food and Drug Administration for use or sale in interstate commerce because of its carcinogenic qualities.

It has long been known that oil of sassafras in high dosages is highly toxic. Laboratory tests revealed that safrole, its main constituent, can induce malignant tumors in livers of rats. It may no longer be used in flavoring beverages, such as root beer. However, safrole-free extracts of sassafras may be safely used under certain conditions listed in federal regulations.

EDWIN B. MATZKE, *Columbia University*

SASSANIAN ART. See PERSIAN ART.

A large sassafras tree (*Sassafras albidum*). The leaves of the sassafras (inset) have a distinctive shape.

JOHN H. GERARD, FROM NATIONAL AUDUBON SOCIETY

N. E. BECK, JR.
FROM NATIONAL AUDUBON SOCIETY

SASSANIAN DYNASTY, sə-sän'ē-ən, Persian rulers of Iran from the 3d to 7th century A. D. The Sassanians, or Sassanids, had their capital at Ctesiphon in Iraq. Their official religion was orthodox Zoroastrianism.

The dynasty was named for Sassan, who was probably a grandfather of Ardashir I. Ardashir established Sassanian power in Iran by defeating and killing his Parthian overlord, Artabanus, about 224. Ardashir's son Shapur I (reigned 240–272?) defeated and captured the Roman emperor Valerian in 258 or 259. The Sassanian empire reached its height of prestige and power under Chosroes I (Khosrau; reigned 531–579). The last ruler, Yazdigird III, died in 652 after Iran had been overrun by the Arabs under the banner of Islam. Sassanian institutions greatly influenced the Abbasid Arab empire.

SASSARI, säs'sä-rē, is an Italian city in northeastern Sardinia and the capital of Sassari province. Most of the city is modern, but there is a medieval quarter with narrow, winding streets. The city is an agricultural trading center and produces various foodstuffs.

The province, which covers an area of 2,903 square miles (7,519 sq km), is generally mountainous. Farming, livestock raising, and mining are the mainstays of the economy. Population: (1969 est.) of the city, 91,200; of the province, 402,200.

SASSETTA, säs-set'tä (c. 1400–1450), was a Sienese painter whose imaginative work was a transition from the charming, pious Sienese Gothic style to the more realistic approach of the Florentine Renaissance. Stefano di Giovanni, called Sassetta since the 18th century, was trained in Siena and entered the painters' guild before 1428. He produced chiefly altarpieces for Sienese and other churches. Although much has been attributed to him, relatively few undisputed works survive. Among them are panels of an altarpiece for the Arte della Lana, or wool merchants' guild

(1423–1426; Pinacoteca, Siena, and other places); the *Madonna of the Snow* (1430–1432; Florence, Coll. Contini Bonacossi); and the masterly polyptych for the Church of San Francesco in Sansepolcro (1444; some panels National Gallery, London). Nearly as important is the *Adoration of the Magi* (Siena, Coll. Chigi-Saracini) and its upper part, *Journey of the Magi* (Metropolitan, New York).

These works show the influence of Sienese painting and the International Gothic style in their brilliant color, gold background, elegant line, and religious devotion. They also have, however, a more sophisticated handling of spatial relationships, more lifelike figures, and architectural elements, which suggest Sassetta's knowledge of Masaccio, Masolino, Ghiberti, and other masters of the early Florentine Renaissance.

SASSOFERRATO, säs-sō-fä-rä'tō, is the pseudonym of the Italian painter Giovanni Battista Salvi (1609–1685). He was born in Sassoferrato, Ancona, on Aug. 25, 1609. He studied under his father and under Il Domenichino in Naples. In Rome he was greatly inspired by the paintings of Raphael, whom he copied. He died in Rome or Florence on Aug. 8, 1685.

Il Sassoferrato was a skilled copyist, and as such he is chiefly remembered. His work, which reflects an earlier style, consists mainly of Madonnas portrayed in a sentimental manner. His paintings are displayed in several European museums, and there is a Madonna in New York City's Metropolitan Museum of Art.

SASSOON, sə-sōon', **Siegfried** (1886–1967), English author, whose writings reveal his passionate pacifism. He was born in Brenchley, Kent, on Sept. 8, 1886. As an army officer in World War I, he became imbued with the hatred of war that he expresses in his poetry. Though wounded, decorated, and promoted to captain, he renounced his part in the conflict and became a crusading pacifist. Politicians, profiteers, and "patrioteers"

SASSETTA'S *Journey of the Magi* (15th century) is the upper part of an altarpiece panel.

all were targets of his bitter, passionate satire in *The Old Huntsman* (1917), *Counterattack* (1918), and *Satirical Poems* (1926). His subsequent volumes of poetry—*The Heart's Journey* (1928) and *Vigils* (1935)—though quieter and more reflective, still reveal the spiritual laceration the war had inflicted on him. His *Collected Poems 1908–1956* appeared in 1961.

Sassoon's prose works are largely autobiographical and hence carry forward the same theme, but in a tempered mood. The first volume of a fictionalized autobiography, *Memoirs of a Fox-Hunting Man* (1928), was awarded the Hawthornden Prize in 1929. This was followed by two other volumes, and the whole was published as a trilogy entitled *The Complete Memoirs of George Sherston* (1937). The work contrasts Sassoon's life as a sporting gentleman with his martial experiences. His later prose includes *The Weald of Youth* (1942) and *Siegfried's Journey, 1916–1920* (1945). Sassoon died in Warminster, Wiltshire, on Sept. 1, 1967.

SATAN. See DEVIL, THE.

SATARA, sä-tä′rə, is a city in India, in western Maharashtra state. It is located about 115 miles (185 km) southeast of Bombay, at an elevation of 2,200 feet (670 meters), just beneath a rugged eastward spur of the Western Ghats. A trading center, it is also an educational center.

The city is dominated by its famous fort, built in 1192 on a commanding mesa characteristic of the western edge of the Deccan Plateau. Satara was the capital of the independent Maratha kingdom established by Shivaji (Śivājī) in the late 17th century. Under the British from 1848 to 1947, the city was the headquarters of Satara district. Population: (1961) 44,353.

MAUREEN L. P. PATTERSON
The University of Chicago

SATAVAHANA, sä-tə-vä-hə-nə, a dynasty of ancient India. The period of its establishment, the duration of its rule, the number of its kings, and the reasons for its disappearance are all uncertain. Probably the dynasty was founded in the 2d century B. C. and lasted some 450 years.

The founder was Simuka, a member of the Satavahana family of Andhra, the territory between the Godavari and Krishna (Kistna) rivers in the Deccan. The Satavahanas rose to power under his son or nephew Shatakarni (Śatakarni) I. Gautamiputra Shatakarni, probably in the early 2d century A. D., made himself master of the Deccan and claimed to have defeated the Shakas, or Śakas (Scythians), Yavanas (Indo-Greeks), and Pahlavas (Indo-Parthians), thus acting as a defender of southern India from foreign invaders. One of his successors, Vasishthiputra Shatakarni, was defeated by the Shaka satrap Rudradaman I, but Satavahana power was restored by the dynasty's last great ruler, Shri Yajna Shatakarni.

The Satavahanas were orthodox Hindus and were tolerant of other faiths. They patronized art and literature and promoted a flourishing trade and agriculture in their realm.

SATELLITE, in astronomy, a secondary body, or moon, that revolves around one of the primary bodies, or planets, of the solar system. See SOLAR SYSTEM—Table 2, and individual entries on the planets that have satellites.

SATELLITE, Artificial. The first known suggestion that men might launch and make use of an artificial satellite of the earth appeared in a story in 1869, *The Brick Moon*, written by the U. S. clergyman and author Edward Everett Hale. The brick moon of the tale was placed in orbit in order to serve as a navigational aid to ships at sea. Whatever other merits the story may have had, the use of an artificial satellite was a far-reaching concept that was not realized until nearly a century had passed.

In the 1920's and 1930's the concept received some attention by pioneers in rocketry and astronautics such as Konstantin Tsiolkovsky of the Soviet Union and Hermann Oberth of Germany. They pointed out some of the advantages that would be obtained by placing rocket-launched satellite payloads into orbit, particularly if men were aboard. It was the development of successful large rockets in World War II that started the real growth of artificial satellite studies in the late 1940's, primarily in the United States and the Soviet Union. The space age may be said to have begun with the orbiting of Sputnik 1 by the USSR in October 1957.

The launch of Sputnik 1 took the world by surprise—not least for the fact that it was the USSR, not the United States, that had taken this first step into space. The Soviet Union received an additional boost in prestige one month later when it orbited Sputnik 2 with a dog aboard. In the United States many political, social, and scientific institutions came under criticism as the nation pondered how it had managed to fall so far behind in astronautics. In particular, the quality of science and engineering curricula was questioned. Committees dealing with astronautics were established by the National Advisory Committee for Aeronautics and by Congress, and the Defense Department set up an agency to deal to a great extent with space matters.

Among other steps taken by the United States, the Army finally was given permission to orbit an earth satellite. At the same time, new life was injected into the Navy's faltering Vanguard program, begun in 1955. By the end of January 1958, a small Explorer I was sent into orbit about the earth by the Army, soon to be followed by other Explorers and several Vanguards. The National Aeronautics and Space Administration (NASA) was also established. The USSR maintained a lead in space science and technology for some time, but by the end of the first decade of the space age both nations were launching satellites at so regular a rate that the world press paid scant notice. Astronautics was becoming almost commonplace.

Many hundreds of satellites—large and small, long-lived and short-lived, simple and complex, successful and unsuccessful—have since been sent into space. The United States has conducted a variety of satellite programs in astronomy, and satellites have been used to study energetic particles coming from outer space as well as ionospheric and other geophysical phenomena. Some satellites have been used to determine the response of biological specimens to weightlessness, radiation, and other space conditions.

The USSR, Britain, France, and Canada have developed satellites for a number of purposes. The USSR has tended to group most of its unmanned satellite launches under the Cosmos program. Britain has concentrated on the Ariel series of ionospheric research satellites, while the Canadian have cooperated on the International Satellite for Ionospheric Studies project by developing the Alouette satellites for measuring electron-density distribution and variation in the ionosphere, and cosmic radiation flux. Mainland China, West Germany, Italy, Japan, Australia, and India have launched satellites with their own or another country's rockets.

This article is concerned primarily with technological aspects of artificial satellites, but some consideration is given to possible future manned orbital programs. For a discussion of manned and unmanned space probes and the history of space exploration, see SPACE EXPLORATION.

USES OF SATELLITES

Through the centuries, astronomers were severely handicapped by having to make observations from the bottom of a thick and often turbulent atmosphere that blocks out many space phenomena completely and attenuates or distorts many others. The development of aerial vehicles and, later, of sounding rockets provided a means for lifting instruments above at least part of the atmosphere. However, it was only with the launching of artificial satellites that scientists were able to escape the effects of the atmosphere in making astronomical observations.

The development of satellites was of special importance to geophysicists, in that they were able to make long-duration measurements over many different latitudes and longitudes. Because satellites remain in flight for extended periods, they can monitor phenomena of changing intensities and can detect phenomena that may occur only briefly or at widely scattered locations. For these and other reasons, satellites are used routinely by the major spacefaring nations and also by smaller industrial powers.

Unmanned satellites perform six primary functions. (1) They are used to investigate the characteristics of the upper atmosphere, including the exosphere. (2) They study the nature of the earth's space environment, including energetic particles, interplanetary matter, electromagnetic radiation, gravitational and magnetic fields, and the interaction of these phenomena and the atmosphere. (3) They are used to study celestial objects from a vantage point beyond the atmosphere. (4) They carry out biological experiments. (5) They perform essentially nonscientific tasks in applied technology, such as communications, education by television relay, weather observation, aid to navigation, geodetic surveying and mapping, and military reconnaissance and surveillance. (6) Some satellites are used in support of manned orbital operations such as the U.S. Apollo program.

ORBITING OF SATELLITES

Satellites usually are launched from a relatively few fixed sites. Among those in the United States are NASA's installation at Cape Kennedy, Fla., and the adjacent Eastern Test Range of the Air Force, which also operates the Western Test Range at Vandenberg Air Force Base. A smaller site is NASA's Wallops Island Station in Virginia. One major USSR installation called Baikonur is at Tyuratam in Kazakhstan and another at Plesetsk near Archangel. In Australia the principal site is at a desert testing range named Woomera. Such bases provide full logistical support for the assembly, checkout, and launching of space vehicles. They are preferred to mobile

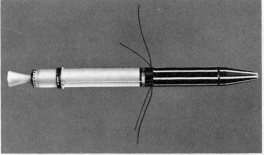

EXPLORER 1 (top), the first U. S. satellite, was orbited on Jan. 31, 1958. It found the Van Allen radiation belts. Vanguard 1 (bottom) followed it into space on March 17, 1958, to provide scientists with geodetic data.

and shipboard launchings because the sites are tied in with a network of geodetic control stations, and hence their geographical locations are very accurately known. This is an important factor in determining correct orbits. Large sites also possess their own radar and optical tracking stations and telemetry installations and the many other facilities needed to support and monitor satellite programs. Finally, multiple or simultaneous launchings can be made at such sites, a desirable capability for certain missions.

Checkout and Testing. Extensive checkout and testing must be done prior to launching a satellite, even though this has been carried out by its manufacturer. There are several reasons for this, such as possible exposure and damage in transport, different environmental conditions at the launch site, and possible incompatibility of the satellite with the launch vehicle. The complicated checkout and preflight testing of the launch vehicle usually are conducted at the same time. Included are a systems test, a test for vehicle compatibility with the satellite, a range and vehicle prelaunch checkout, and final checkout and countdown ending in lift-off. All these steps take place while vehicle and satellite are together on the launch pad except for the first phase of the systems test, which is an assembly check.

Even with these checks, several constraints still must be considered. First of all, safety factors have to be taken into account. The carrier vehicle must be fired into a predetermined flight path, or *launch corridor*, through the atmosphere, and must stay within range of the tracking station. If the vehicle deviates from its corridor at any time in flight, it is signaled to

ESSA 3, launched in 1966—one of a series of American satellites for photographing the earth's cloud cover.

destroy itself by the range safety officer. Wind velocities and other meteorological conditions must be known, because they can affect a flight path. In addition, it is desirable to launch rockets in an eastward direction in order to take advantage of the added final orbital speed provided by the earth's rotation. Attention also must be paid to the so-called *launch window*—the time during which a given mission can most economically commence, in terms of the propulsive capabilities of the carrier vehicle. Thus, if a satellite is to be placed in a specific orbital plane, calculations are made to determine the precise time when the plane passes through the point where the satellite is injected into orbit. Every second of delay in launch increases the velocity that must be achieved by the launch vehicle. If the vehicle's capabilities are exceeded, the mission is *scrubbed* until a later date.

Attaining Orbit. In order for a satellite to be orbited, it must be propelled at a velocity that imparts enough energy to keep it in that orbit without application of additional force. If the orbit is low, the resistance of the outer atmosphere will cause the satellite to *decay*—that is, to lose orbital speed and reenter the atmosphere. The higher above the earth the orbit is, the longer the lifetime of the satellite, but perturbing forces still must be taken into account. Thus the flattening of the earth at its poles can disturb a satellite that is in fairly low orbit, whereas the effects of the attraction of the sun and the moon must be considered for a very high orbit. These and other perturbing forces can be cancelled out by fitting a satellite with an on-board propulsion system that compensates for the forces. The term *station keeping* is used to describe the act of correcting for perturbing forces.

SATELLITE SUBSYSTEMS

Artificial satellites can be described in terms of a number of major subsystems, which are discussed separately below. Some simple satellites

have few such subsystems, including the balloon satellites used for air density measurements. Others, like the Orbiting Astronomical Observatories, are very complex and have most if not all of the different kinds of subsystems.

Structure. The basic structure of a satellite is developed only after thorough study is made of its intended uses, the kind of orbit it will have, its predicted useful lifetime, its instrumentation and power supplies, its internal environmental control needs, the capabilities of its carrier vehicle, and so forth. The structure should be of the lowest weight that will still provide adequate strength. Simplicity of design is sought, both to reduce manufacturing costs and to ease the installation of instruments and other subsystems. Special problems are created by the use of equipment such as explosive bolts for separating experimental packages, extended booms for the mounting of experiments, and nuclear power elements. Other design problems are the need for freedom from internally induced magnetic fields, for sufficient mechanical insulation to reduce vibration and noise, and for protection from radiative and micrometeoric impingements.

Satellite shapes have evolved from the simple cylinders and globes of the earliest craft to forms that are often quite bizarre. Basically cylindrical shapes are to some extent still popular, however, because they readily permit spin stabilization along the axis of symmetry. The addition of experimental packages and the desire for independent units, or *modules*, have greatly changed satellite design. Thus one shape often used is the polygon cylinder, consisting of a series of instrument bays. Hatbox shapes have been employed in some communications and weather satellites, such as Tiros, while orbiting observatories often are elongated and have many booms. Extended "paddle" shapes on which solar cell units are placed are very common. They are used where the main structure cannot, or should not, accommodate all the units required to meet the satellite's power needs.

Additional design constraints are imposed by capsules that have to reenter the atmosphere and be recovered. The U. S. Biosatellite 2, for example, which returned from a 45-hour mission on Sept. 9, 1967, with numerous biological specimens aboard, consisted of three main components: an adapter section that remained in orbit, a reentry vehicle, and the biocapsule that incorporated the experiments and supporting equipment, recovery parachutes, and a radio beacon. The reentry vehicle was a blunt cone about 40 inches (100 cm) in diameter. The forward part of the vehicle was made of fiberglass and had to be covered completely with a phenolic nylon heat shield in order to absorb the heat generated by reentry into the atmosphere.

Power Supply. The task of a satellite's power supply subsystem is to accept the original power in whatever form it comes, condition it properly, and then relay it to the necessary on-board equipment. The amount of electrical power required may range from a few watts to hundreds of watts, depending on the instrumentation and communications load and on the desired lifetime of the satellite. Power can be supplied by short-lived fuel cells or batteries, or by long-lived solar cells or the radioisotope devices that have been used but are still in the development stage.

Solar cells are by far the most common choice. They take advantage of the abundant solar energy available in space by converting it directly into electrical energy (the photovoltaic process). The cells are used in association with chemical batteries, which provide power during the portions of orbit when the satellite is in the shadow of the earth. Thus the cells can supply power directly to the equipment, or they can be used to recharge the chemical batteries. Solar cells are reliable and have often been used on scientific and applications satellites. For example, 33,000 solar cells were used on the U. S. OGO 4 (Orbiting Geophysical Observatory) orbited in 1967, supplying approximately 560 watts of electrical power. The cells, however, are relatively heavy and expensive, take up considerable volume, and can be damaged by micrometeorites and corpuscular radiation.

In fuel cells a fuel is oxidized to produce power. The ratio of weight to energy provided makes fuel cells less attractive than other power sources, but they are acceptable for short missions.

Among other possibilities are turbogenerators that produce power from the heat of the sun or of nuclear reactions, and thermionic generators that produce power from sunlight. For example, SNAP devices (Systems for Nuclear Auxiliary Power) have been used on some U. S. satellites. In these devices, radioisotopes or small reactors produce heat that is then converted into electricity. Thermionic systems powered by radioisotopes are relatively lightweight.

Communications. The technique of making physical measurements from a distance is called *telemetry.* The inputs of a satellite's telemetric system are received by any one of many sensors, while its outputs are the encoded information that it transmits to ground receivers for storage and later analysis. This communication of data is essential to the function of almost all satellites. The ability to receive signals is also necessary in order to trigger the return of data or, if possible, to correct some malfunction.

Special antennas, receivers, transmitters, and power supplies are used in spaceborne communications subsystems. They must be of high reliability and low weight. To facilitate ground tracking, most satellites also are fitted with beacons or transponders. In addition they normally contain such devices as encoders, commutators, analog-to-digital converters, and voltage frequency regulators. The latter permit signal conditioning in order to transfer the output in a useful format down to earth. This is called *encoding.* Data usually are stored temporarily in tape recorders or magnetic core memory units rather than transmitted continuously.

Internal elements of a satellite's communications subsystem are subjected to radio-frequency interference, or "crosstalk," that must be reduced to a minimum. Depending on the instruments aboard, there often is magnetic interference as well. This may be reduced by rewiring or by using substitute materials. Design engineers often are forced to make compromises in developing antennas for a given craft, since the antennas should interfere as little as possible with the coverage or "look angle" of the instruments. Antennas may be affected adversely by changing heating conditions, by rapid spinning of the satellite, and by weak signals. A further complication is that they often must be steerable.

CENTRE NATIONAL D'ÉTUDES SPATIALES

DIADÈME SATELLITE was one of a series of French spacecraft designed to observe the shape of the earth.

Scientific Instrumentation. Electronic and other instruments are installed on a satellite for the purpose of detecting, measuring, recording, telemetering, processing, and analyzing quantities encountered in space. Without instruments, satellites could undertake only a small number of useful missions, such as the air density measurements made by observing the changing orbits of large balloon satellites from the ground. The

ARIEL 3, a British satellite, was launched on May 5, 1967, to study ionization in the earth's atmosphere.

BRITISH AIRCRAFT CORPORATION

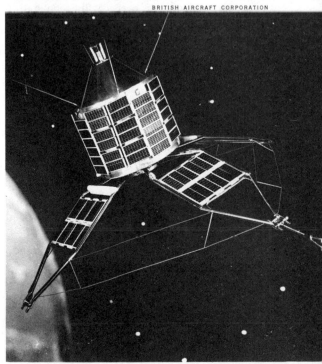

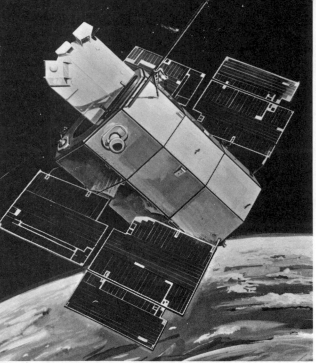

OAO 2 (Orbiting Astronomical Observatory) was sent into orbit on Dec. 7, 1968, to make telescopic studies from above the obscuring effect of earth's atmosphere.

principal element of these instruments is the *sensor*, the component that converts an input signal into a quantity that is measurable by another part of the instrument. Normally the input stimuli are converted into electrical signals. An instrument may have a single sensor, or it may have multiple sensors and other equipment.

Satellite instruments should be light, small, and highly reliable. They should be relatively insensitive to vibration, shock, and magnetic disturbances, and operate over a wide temperature range. The instruments must be compatible with adjacent instruments and be able to put out conditioned signals. Also, they must be easily stored, checked out, and calibrated, and have an adequate capacity for data storage. Finally, they must be able to operate either in a vacuum or in a sealed bay on the satellite.

Large satellites often house many instruments that perform compatible experiments—that is, experiments that do not interfere with one another. Smaller satellites tend to study specific phenomena only. For example, the U.S. Explorers and similar small craft in general carry only a few specialized instruments.

Most satellite instruments developed thus far have been used to detect and measure geophysical phenomena, but a number have been developed for studying astrophysical phenomena and problems in the biosciences. There are instruments for measuring trapped radiation high above the earth, for performing aeronomy studies, and for undertaking research in ionospheric physics and solar physics. Among these numerous instruments are the neutral mass spectrometer, the Langmuir probe, and the electrostatic analyzer for studying plasmas; the radiometer; the ionization chamber; the micrometeorite detector; the scintillation counter; the helium magnetometer; the coronagraph; and the Geiger-counter telescope.

Engineering Instrumentation and Environmental Control. The engineering instrumentation subsystem is used to determine, at any given time, the operational condition of a satellite. Various points on board are monitored, and the data are transmitted to earth. Temperatures, switching positions, outputs of the power supply, pressures, intensity of sunlight, and other quantities may be measured. These measurements often permit ground controllers to diagnose difficulties aboard the satellite and, perhaps, to take corrective steps.

The function of the environmental control subsystem, in turn, is to protect the satellite from its space environment and from the internal environment created by the equipment aboard. One of the principal engineering problems, in this respect, is the maintenance of internal temperatures within acceptable limits. Excess heating is the greatest concern, but low temperatures also can be a problem for certain instruments. A satellite can be made to rotate so that no one side is excessively heated. Special paints or surface finishes can be applied to reflect more or less heat, as desired, in sensitive areas. Louvers and vanes have been developed for the same purposes. Occasionally, thermoelectric cooling techniques are used and conduction paths established.

Adequate protection also must be provided against external radiation fluxes and magnetic forces, as well as against internal radiation fluxes, if nuclear power sources are used in the satellite. Structural members and instruments must be insulated from mechanical stresses that are present in the launch operation. Instruments are protected against electric power surges and radiofrequency interference by the use of circuit breakers and regulators and by efficient circuit design and component arrangement.

Guidance and Attitude Control. In guiding and controlling a satellite, there must be some means of sensing the path it is following and its position at any given instant. Attitude information can come through ground studies of signal enhancement from the satellite transmitter. Sun sensors, horizon scanners, star trackers, and magnetic field measurements aboard the craft also can provide the necessary attitude data.

A satellite often must be oriented in space in a particular way in order to perform its assigned functions or to operate efficiently. If weather satellites such as Tiros and Nimbus were not fixed in attitude so as always to be pointed toward the earth, for example, they could not provide information on terrestrial cloud cover. Reaction devices of several kinds can be used to maintain a certain orientation or to shift a satellite into a new attitude. Thus, a device somewhat like a yo-yo can be released radially outward in order to stop a satellite from spinning, or the horizon sensors that provide attitude information can be used to lock the satellite onto the horizon. Some craft incorporate inertia wheels operated by electric motors. Others exchange angular momentum through magnetic couplers, gravity gradient devices, aerodynamic surfaces, or solar pressure vanes. Springs and viscous fluids occasionally are used on satellites to damp out undesired internal motions.

Large satellites like the U.S. orbiting observatories have a variety of attitude-control mechanisms and devices. In the OGO 4, for example, the elements include infrared horizon scanners, servomechanisms, cold gas jets, and electrically driven flywheels. The scanners ascertain that the bottom of the satellite is always pointed toward the earth, and they provide error signals to the flywheels and jets that turn the OGO 4 on its roll and pitch axes. Sun sensors furnish error signals for control of yaw motion and the rotation of the extended solar panels, while other elements maintain the attitude of experiment packages with respect to the satellite's orbital plane.

Propulsion. More and more applications satellites are equipped with on-board rocket engines that provide limited maneuverability. Such satellites may have to change orbits, to undertake maneuvers in order to maintain a predetermined orbit, to commence reentry maneuvers, or to brake during descent and just before landing. On the other hand, on-board propulsion has been used on scientific satellites only to a limited extent.

A station-keeping capability is most important for communications satellites in particular, especially those with a 24-hour period that keeps them above a fixed point on the earth's surface. Thus the Intelsats—the craft owned by the International Telecommunications Satellite Consortium—incorporate a twin hydrogen-peroxide rocket-propulsion system. This provides boost thrust for final injection into synchronous orbit and for station keeping thereafter. The satellites are designed to maintain desired positions for up to five years.

Computers. Computers are used increasingly in artificial satellites. They can store data on the performance of the craft, provide for internal checking routines, store scientific information measured during the mission, time various events, and initiate predetermined sequential actions.

SPACE STATIONS

Salyut. On April 19, 1971, the Soviet Union placed the 18-ton Salyut 1 space station in orbit. It had a forward compartment for docking manned Soyuz spacecraft, a biological laboratory, a compartment for scientific instruments, and a compartment for propulsion equipment.

Soyuz 10, manned by cosmonauts Vladimir Shatalov, Alexei Yeliseyev, and Nikolai Rukavishnikov, docked with Salyut 1 on April 23, 1971, but the crew did not transfer to the space station. Soyuz 11, carrying Viktor Patsayev, Vladislav Volkov, and Georgi Dobrovolsky, was launched on June 6, 1971, and docked with Salyut 1 soon after attaining orbit. Patsayev and Volkov entered Salyut 1 and made medical and biological tests, while Dobrovolsky remained on Soyuz 11. On June 29, 1971, the three cosmonauts rode Soyuz 11 back to earth, but they all died during the landing phase as a result of loss of compression in the crew cabin. The Salyut 1 space station fell from orbit in October 1971.

Salyut 2, weighing 27.5 tons, was rocketed into orbit at an altitude of about 150 miles (240 km) on April 3, 1973. Other Salyuts were launched soon afterward, and a number of dockings with Soyuz spacecraft were completed in the ensuing years as new space records were set and broken.

In 1975, cosmonauts Pyotr Klimuk and Vitali Sevastianov remained aboard the Salyut 4 space station for 63 days. In 1977–1978, cosmonauts Yuri Romanenko and Georgi Grechko spent 96 days in Salyut 6. In 1978, cosmonauts Vladimir Kovalenok and Aleksandr Ivanchenkov orbited in Salyut 6 for 139 days. In 1979, cosmonauts Valeri Ryumin and Vladimir Lyakhov spent 175 days in Salyut 6, and in 1980, Ryumin and Leonid Popov were launched in Soyuz 35 for an extended space voyage in Salyut 6. They were joined briefly by other cosmonauts launched in Soyuz 36 and an improved spacecraft, Soyuz T2, later in 1980.

Skylab. The 118-foot (36-meter) long, 85-ton Skylab, the first American space station, was rocketed into orbit on May 14, 1973. Skylab orbited the earth at an altitude of about 270 miles (435 km) and made one revolution every 93 minutes. The National Aeronautics and Space Administration's initial plans called for three 3-man crews to travel to the space station, live there for about one or two months, and then return to earth. The broad objectives of this project were to study the physiology of man in space, the physics of the sun, and the resources of the earth.

The space station included an orbital workshop, an airlock module, a multiple docking adapter, and a telescope mount. The workshop was a cylindrical two-story cabin 48 feet (14.6 meters) long and 22 feet (6.7 meters) in diameter. It had crew quarters, storage areas for food and water, and a large window. The crew quarters included individual sleeping compartments, sit-down and stand-up toilet facilities, a collapsible shower stall, exercise equipment, and a work area for experiments.

The airlock module, 16 feet (4.9 meters) long and having a maximum diameter of 22 feet (6.7 meters), was located between the workshop and the multiple docking adapter. It contained communications, environmental, and electrical equipment and a passage to enable astronauts to go outside Skylab for repairs or other tasks.

The multiple docking adapter, which was 17 feet (5.2 meters) long and 10 feet (3 meters) in diameter, provided the docking port for the ferry spacecraft that brought astronauts to the Skylab and returned them to earth when their space mission was completed.

The telescope mount contained eight telescopes, primarily for observing ultraviolet and X-ray emissions from the sun that cannot be studied on earth.

Skylab gradually lost altitude and came down on July 11, 1979, scattering debris over the Indian Ocean and southwestern Australia as it made its fiery descent into the atmosphere.

Mission of Skylab 1 Crew. On May 25, 1973, Capt. Charles Conrad, Jr., Comdr. Joseph P. Kerwin, and Comdr. Paul J. Weitz rode a 15-ton Apollo spacecraft to rendezvous with Skylab. After nine tries, the Skylab 1 crew latched the Apollo's nose into the Skylab's multiple docking adapter. The next day, they set up a parasol over a part of the Skylab's skin where micrometeorite and heat shielding had been ripped away during launch. As a result, the temperature in Skylab was dropped from about 120° F (50° C) to near a normal 70° F (21° C).

On May 30, the astronauts began to take pictures of the earth to increase man's knowledge of mineral resources, crops and forests, pollution, and weather. On June 7, Conrad and Kerwin went outside the space station and cut a strap that was keeping the single remaining solar-cell wing from being extended. The wing was deployed successfully, thereby restoring much of the space station's electric power supply. The crew returned to earth on June 22 after living in Skylab in a weightless environment for a record 28 days.

Mission of Skylab 2 Crew. On July 28, an Apollo spacecraft with Capt. Alan L. Bean, Maj. Jack R. Lousma, and Owen K. Garriott, a civilian scientist, was launched on a voyage to link up with Skylab. The Skylab 2 crew docked their Apollo ferry craft at the space station that same day.

On August 6, Lousma and Garriott went outside Skylab and erected a 12-foot (3.6-meter) by 24-foot (7.3-meter) sunshade and loaded new film in the solar telescope cameras. In doing so, they set a record for the longest space walk—6 hours and 31 minutes of activity outside a space vehicle.

During their record 59.5 days in space, the astronauts also made photographic surveys over broad areas of the earth to locate mineral resources and survey crops and forests. The crew took many thousands of photographs of the earth and sun, and used 18 miles (29 km) of magnetic tape to record data from observations of the earth. They returned to earth on Sept. 25, 1973.

Skylab 3 Crew. Astronauts Gerald Carr, Edward Gibson, and William Pogue were launched in an Apollo spacecraft on Nov. 16, 1973, entered the Skylab space station, and set a new record of 84 days in a weightless environment before returning to earth on Feb. 8, 1974. They performed new medical tests, photographed comet Kohoutek, repaired an air-cooling system, and took thousands of photographs of the sun and earth and made miles of magnetic tapes recording data about the earth's surface. On their return to earth, doctors found them wobbly-legged but apparently in better condition than the Skylab 1 and 2 crews, whose missions also had broken endurance records.

SATELLITES IN THE FUTURE

Unmanned satellites undoubtedly will be orbited at an increasing rate in years to come. In addition, a number of projected manned programs are of importance in this discussion of the future of artificial earth satellites. Previous manned orbital flights are described in more detail in the article SPACE EXPLORATION.

Unmanned Programs. Besides the meteorological, communications, and navigational satellites that are standard by now, one kind of applications satellite certain to provide great benefits is the Earth Resources Technology Satellite (ERTS). This satellite of the 1970's is designed to provide additional means of gathering information in broad areas such as agriculture, forestry, physical and cultural geography, geology, mineral resources, cartography, hydrology, and oceanography.

For example, the mining and petroleum industries spend millions of dollars each year searching for metallic ores, oil, and other deposits. An ERTS can make photographic, infrared, radar, radiometer, and other surveys of the earth in support of ground search efforts. The ability of its instrumentation to identify gross terrain features and major fault lines that generally are associated with oil or mineral wealth will be of special importance, particularly for the inaccessible regions of the globe.

In the area of water resources, these satellites can be used to help predict water reserves, irrigation requirements, and impending floods. Pictures taken from space can help to determine the extent and depth of snow cover, which in turn could lead to predictions of runoff for irrigation and power production, and of flooding. Similarly, space monitoring of the state of plant growth and vigor in an area can assist in detecting incipient drought conditions and other potential ecological disasters. Broad area examinations of the amounts of water in lakes and ponds can help in predicting potential water reserves for nearby large cities.

Manned Programs. In the Soviet Union, after completion of the Vostok and Voskhod flights in 1965, there was a lull of more than two years in manned space efforts. Then, in 1967, the Soyuz series of flights began. As the United States moved toward the achievement of manned lunar landings, the Russians chose instead to center efforts on the near-earth space environment—perhaps in part because of technological difficulties in developing sufficiently powerful boosters. The first step in Soviet plans for a long-lasting orbiting space station was the Salyut orbiting laboratory, flown and manned for the first time in 1971.

In the United States, following the completion of the earth-orbital Mercury and Gemini series in 1966, there was a marked decrease for a while in attention directed toward strictly manned orbital operations. This was understandable, since the moon was the objective for manned flights that continued until the end of

SALYUT SPACE STATION in the foreground of this drawing was launched and manned by the Soviet Union for the first time in 1971. The Soyuz spacecraft in the background is shown making the approach for docking so that its cosmonauts can transfer to the orbiting laboratory.

1972. Plans have been made, however, for orbital laboratories with a relatively few astronaut-scientists aboard; and other plans include large, permanent space stations with large crews.

Joint U.S.-Soviet Mission. With completion of Skylab, the U.S. manned space program originally was to have ended until planned space-shuttle tests could be made in the late 1970's. However, in 1972 the United States and Soviet Union agreed on the joint Apollo-Soyuz mission that was completed in July 1975. On July 15, astronauts Thomas Stafford, Vance Brand, and Donald Slayton were launched from Cape Canaveral, Fla., in an Apollo spacecraft, and cosmonauts Aleksei Leonov and Valery Kubasov were launched from Kazakhstan, USSR, in a Soyuz spacecraft. The two spacecraft met over the Atlantic Ocean on July 17 and remained docked for two days while the crews moved back and forth between them. The Soyuz crew returned to earth on July 21, and the Apollo crew returned on July 24.

Large Space Stations of the Future. Beyond the limited plans of the immediate future, space scientists of both the United States and the Soviet Union look forward to a time when there will be more sophisticated space stations capable of sustaining dozens and perhaps eventually hundreds of men in orbit for periods ranging from weeks to years. A variety of sizes and shapes has been proposed, but the most popular and logical appears to be the wheel or centrifuge shape. That is, a broad-diameter, spinning, wheel-shaped station would provide a sensation of artificial gravity at the rim, due to the action of centrifugal force. At the core, or center, of the station, zero and near-zero gravity conditions would exist, forming a useful site for the docking of ferry vehicles from the earth. See also SPACE EXPLORATION.

FREDERICK I. ORDWAY, III*
Coauthor of "History of Rocketry and Space Travel"

Further Reading: Ordway, Frederick I., *Pictorial Guide to the Planet Earth* (Crowell 1975); Porter, Richard W., *The Versatile Satellite* (Oxford 1977).

SATEM, an Indo-European language group. See CENTUM AND SATEM LANGUAGE GROUPS.

SATIE, sȧ-tē', **Erik** (1866–1925), French composer, whose eccentric but witty and original compositions won him a significant place in modern French music.

Erik Alfred Leslie Satie was born in Honfleur on May 17, 1866. He was taken to Paris as a youngster and briefly studied at the conservatory there. Publishing his first piano pieces in 1887, Satie began his career of humorous mystification by calling them his Opus 62. After several years of pursuing a bohemian existence, he resumed serious musical study, attending classes given by Vincent d'Indy and Albert Roussel at the Schola Cantorum. Satie's wit, intense originality, and seemingly revolutionary theories won him influential admirers among younger musicians. In his honor, the conductor Roger Desormière and the composers Darius Milhaud and Henri Sauguet founded the "Ecole d'Arcueil," named for the Paris suburb in which Satie lived after 1898. Although the general public often regarded him as a mountebank and poseur, his music gradually won nonprofessional admirers. Satie died in Paris on July 1, 1925.

Many of Satie's compositions are written in an extremely simple, bare style and have deliberately meaningless titles. His most notable works include the "symphonic drama" *Socrate*, from a text after Plato, for four sopranos and chamber orchestra; the ballets *Parade* (1917), *Mercure* (1924), and *Relâche* (1924); and incidental music to such plays as Joséphin Péladans *Le Fils des étoiles* (1891), with the prelude orchestrated by Maurice Ravel, and *Le Prince de Byzance* (1891), H. Mazel's *Le Nazaréen* (1892), J. Bois' *La Porte heroïque au ciel* (1893), and Maurice de Geraudy's *Pousse l'amour* (1905). Satie also write songs and a large number of piano pieces, the most familiar of which are *Gymnopédies* (1888), with two of the three pieces later orchestrated by Claude Debussy, *Gnessiennes* (1890), *Trois Moraeaux en forms de poire* (1903), and *Trois Préludes flasques* (1912).

HERBERT WEINSTOCK
Coauthor of "Men of Music"

SATIN is a silk, rayon, nylon, or cotton fabric with a satin weave. In a satin weave using a filling effect, the warp (vertical yarn) does not cross the filling (horizontal yarn) as often as in a plain weave. For example, in an eight-shaft satin weave using the filling effect, the vertical yarn shows on the face of the fabric once in every eight interlacings, and the horizontal yarn shows on the face in seven out of eight interlacings. As a result the fabric has an even, close, and smooth face, which gives satin its luster. In contrast, in a plain weave the vertical yarn shows on the face of a fabric once in every two interlacings.

There are various kinds of satin. A satin-damask fabric has a pile (raised surface) or a decorative pattern. Slipper satin has a silk warp and a cotton filling. Light fabrics called Indian or Chinese satins are plain, damasked, striped, open-worked, or embroidered satins.

The luster of satin-weave fabrics and the ease with which they drape make them popular for garments such as evening dresses, bridal gowns, and capes. Their smoothness makes them excellent for lingerie, ribbons, and linings.

Satin was first made of silk yarns in ancient China. See also DAMASK; TEXTILE.

SATIN SPAR, the common name for fibrous minerals that are sometimes cut and polished to make beads or gemstones. Satin spar most commonly is a variety either of gypsum or of the somewhat harder calcite. See CALCITE; GYPSUM.

SATINFLOWER. See STAR-OF-BETHLEHEM.

SATINWOOD is any wood yielded by various species of trees of the rue family (Rutaceae). West Indian satinwood is a product of *Zanthoxylum flavum*, a small tree that grows in the West Indies and Florida. This wood is hard, heavy, and finely textured. It has a satiny luster and an oily feel, and it is creamy to golden yellow. When freshly cut, the wood has an odor like that of coconut. It has long been used for the manufacture of fine furniture. Antique satinwood furniture is usually made from this kind of satinwood. Another New World species of satinwood tree, *Z. elephantiasis* of the West Indies, Mexico, and Central America, yields concha satinwood, which is yellowish with a green cast, turning dull brown.

East Indian satinwood is the product of *Chloroxylon swietenia,* a tree native to India and Ceylon. The wood is pale to golden yellow and is frequently mottled. The various satinwoods, which take a high finish, are used mainly for furniture, cabinetwork, and brush backs.

SATIRE is both a specific literary genre and a literary manner. As a genre, it has reference to a poetic form originated in the 2d century B.C. by the Roman satirist Lucilius; practiced with distinction by his successors, Horace, Persius, and Juvenal; and best described by Quintilian in his *Institutio oratoria* (about 95 A.D.). This formal verse satire, written in Latin hexameters, was dramatic, with the Satirist, through a dialogue with an Adversary, exposing vice and folly by means of critical analysis. Alexander Pope's *Epistle to Dr. Arbuthnot* is an 18th century English example.

In its more frequent sense, satire is a literary manner in which the follies and foibles or vices and crimes of a person, mankind, or an institution are held up to ridicule or scorn, with the intention of correcting them. This manner may be present in many art forms and may employ many methods. Satire is also applied to magic songs and ritualistic invective in Greek, Old Irish, and Arabic literatures, where the ritual curse was believed to have powerful effects.

The word *satire* is derived from the Latin *(lanx) satura* ("full plate"; "plate filled with various fruits"—hence, a medley). But its origin often has been confused with the satyr play of Greek drama—the fourth play in the dramatic bill, with a chorus of "goat men" and a coarse comic manner. This latter etymology is false, but it has influenced—and confused—English ideas about satire.

The Nature of Satire. Although satire is often comic, its object is to evoke not mere laughter but laughter for a corrective purpose. It always has a target—such as pretense, falsity, deception, arrogance—which is held up to ridicule by the satirist's unmasking of it. Because the satirist usually cannot speak openly or does not wish to do so, he chooses means that allow him to utter the unspeakable with impunity. His viewpoint is ultimately that of the cold-eyed realist, who penetrates sham and pretense for a didactic purpose. The portrayals generally are at variance with outward appearances, but they contain recognizable truth, and it is this truth that gives the satirist his license to attack.

The simplest direct form of satire is invective—forthright and abusive language directed against a person or cause and making a sudden, harsh revelation of a damaging truth. Another form of direct satire is exaggeration, in which the good characteristics are passed over and the evil or ridiculous ones are emphasized. Caricature is an example. Indirect satire usually employs a plot through which the characters render themselves ridiculous by their actions and speech. Irony, burlesque, travesty, and parody are modes and forms of indirect satire. Typical methods are contrasts between statement and action, allegorical treatment (men as animals, for example), and understatement.

Two modes of satire are given the names of their great Roman practitioners, Horace and Juvenal. Horatian satire is urbane; the satirist is a man of the world who smiles at the foibles of his fellowmen without indignation. Juvenalian satire is harsh; the satirist is an enraged moralist who denounces the vices and corruptions of his fellowmen. Alexander Pope is a Horatian satirist; Jonathan Swift, a Juvenalian one.

Early Periods. There have been few ages when man has not employed satire to comment on his fellowman. In antiquity, it was present in the invectives of the Greek lyric poet and lampoonist Archilochus, the animal fables of Aesop, the comedies of Aristophanes, and the character sketches of Theophrastus, as well as in the verse of the Romans previously mentioned—Lucilius, Horace, Persius, and Juvenal—and in the dialogues of Lucian. In the Middle Ages, the beast fables and beast epics, such as those about Reynard the Fox, were numerous. The 14th century English poet Geoffrey Chaucer was on occasion a master satirist, as was the 16th century French author François Rabelais, in *Gargantua and Pantagruel.* The early 17th century brought great satiric work—Cervantes' *Don Quixote* in Spain and Ben Jonson's comedies in England. Somewhat later came Molière's comedies in France.

The Great Period. The great modern age of satire was the neoclassic period, when the satiric spirit was everywhere present and a return was made to formal verse satire. Notable among English verse satires of the later 17th century were Samuel Butler's attack on the Puritans in the mock-epic *Hudibras* and John Dryden's poems, such as *Absalom and Achitophel,* on the Titus Oates conspiracy, and *Mac Flecknoe,* on Thomas Shadwell. The 18th century brought such major English verse satires as Pope's *The Dunciad,* on contemporary writers, and his *Imitations* of Horace; John Gay's parody *The Beggar's Opera;* and Samuel Johnson's Juvenalian poems *London* and *The Vanity of Human Wishes.*

Satiric prose also flourished in the British Isles, especially in the early 18th century. It included Jonathan Swift's harsh attacks on corruption in religion in *A Tale of a Tub* and on mankind in *Gulliver's Travels,* as well as his devastating shorter pieces, such as *A Modest Proposal* and other tracts on the plight of the Irish. Gentle satire found a civilized voice in the essay periodicals, particularly Addison and Steele's *The Tatler* and *The Spectator.*

Satire also flourished in France in the neoclassic age. Examples include La Fontaine's great poetic work *Fables;* Voltaire's philosophical tale *Candide;* La Rochefoucauld's pithy *Maxims;* and Montesquieu's critique of French and Persian beliefs, fashions, and institutions in *Lettres persanes (Persian Letters).*

Later Times. The 19th century was not particularly friendly to satire. But, in England, Lord Byron produced a substantial amount of satiric verse, including his great unfinished *Don Juan.* William Makepeace Thackeray produced much satiric prose, and the satiric spirit was vigorously present in W.S. Gilbert's comic librettos and Oscar Wilde's essays and plays. Twentieth century England has produced satiric drama by George Bernard Shaw, essays and fiction by Max Beerbohm and Aldous Huxley, and verse by T.S. Eliot. In France, masterful satire appeared in the fiction of Anatole France.

Satire in America. The chief period of satire in America paralleled that in England. The essays and verse of such writers as Benjamin Franklin, the Hartford Wits (Timothy Dwight, Joel Barlow, and others), and Philip Freneau were harmonious in spirit with the satire of the neoclassic age.

Later satirists included Mark Twain, Finley Peter Dunne, Ambrose Bierce, Sinclair Lewis, and E. E. Cummings. Contemporary examples are found in the work of the so-called black humorists, such as Joseph Heller's novel *Catch 22*. But the United States has not had a truly great age of satire. See also the Index entry *Satire*.

C. HUGH HOLMAN
Author of "A Handbook to Literature"

Further Reading: Bloom, Edward A. and Lillian D., *Satire's Persuasive Voice* (Cornell Univ. Press 1979); Knox, E.V., *The Mechanism of Satire* (Folcroft 1973); Pollard, Arthur, *Satire* (Methuen 1970); Sanders, Charles, *The Scope of Satire* (Scott 1971).

SATO EISAKU, sä-tō ä-sä-kōō (1901–1975), Japanese political leader, who was prime minister from 1964 to 1972. He was born in Yamaguchi prefecture, Honshu, on March 27, 1901. He was the adopted son of Sato Matsusuke and the younger brother of Prime Minister Kishi Nobusuke.

After graduation from the Tokyo University law school in 1924, Sato entered the ministry of railways, which sent him to study in Europe and the United States in 1934–1937. He rose in the ministry to become chief of the bureau of control and vice minister for transportation. After World War II he held posts in several cabinets. He was also in charge of preparations for the 1964 Summer Olympics in Tokyo.

Sato succeeded Ikeda as prime minister and as president of the Liberal-Democratic party later in 1964. Under Sato's leadership, Japan continued its rapid economic growth. Sato continued Japan's reliance on a collective security system under the U.S.–Japan security treaty. Reflecting Japan's "nuclear allergy," he advocated nonproliferation of nuclear weapons.

Sato visited the United States in November 1967 seeking the return of Japanese territories under U.S. administration. As a result, the Bonin Islands were restored in 1968. Again in Washington the next year, he obtained an agreement under which the United States returned the southern Ryukyu Islands, including Okinawa, in May 1972. Sato retired in July of that year.

Sato was co-winner of the 1975 Nobel Peace Prize. He died in Tokyo on June 2, 1975.

JOYCE C. LEBRA, *University of Colorado*

SATRAP, sä'trap, the governor of a satrapy, or province, of the Achaemenid Persian Empire. The satrap (*khshathrapavan*, "protector of the kingdom") was appointed by the king. His responsibilities included collecting taxes, supervising the local administration, and ensuring internal security. Darius I reorganized the provincial system to check the power of the satraps and made certain local officials responsible only to the king. But afterward, as the empire declined, many satraps became virtually independent.

After the Macedonian conquest, the satrap system was retained by Alexander the Great and his Seleucid successors. The Shaka (Saka) rulers of states in northern and western India—princes of Iranian origin and their Indianized descendants—were also known as satraps (*kshatrapas*).

SATURDAY is the seventh day of the week. It was the original day of the Sabbath prescribed in the Bible and is still observed as such by Jews and some Christians. The first component of the word comes from Latin *Saturnus* ("Saturn") and the second from Old English *dæg* ("day").

SATURN, sat'ərn, the second-largest planet in the solar system and the sixth in order of increasing distance from the sun. It is 9 1/2 times farther from the sun than the earth is. Situated between Jupiter and Uranus, Saturn is almost 100 times as massive as the earth and yet consists mostly of the light gases hydrogen and helium.

Surrounding Saturn is a miniature solar system consisting of the planet's satellites (moons) and beautiful rings. Almost all of the moons are made of comparable amounts of ice and rock, in contrast to the planets of the inner solar system, which consist almost entirely of rock. The largest satellite, Titan, is bigger than the planet Mercury and has an atmosphere within which organic molecules—relatives of the ones that make up life—are continually being produced. Located closer to the planet than almost all the satellites, the rings consist of countless numbers of icy snowballs in orbit about Saturn. The space between the satellites and above and below the rings is not empty, but is filled with a very low density gas and with energetic, electrically charged particles that form belts similar to the earth's Van Allen radiation belts.

One of five planets bright enough to be seen with the unaided eye, Saturn was known to the astronomer-priests of ancient civilizations, who carefully charted its changing position with respect to the stars. It was first observed through a telescope in 1610 by Galileo Galilei, who discovered the rings of Saturn but did not understand their geometry. Later observations over the next several centuries resulted in the solution of this mystery, the discovery of nine of Saturn's moons, the definition of the large-scale architecture of the rings, and the finding of weather patterns in the atmosphere of Saturn.

NASA's unmanned spacecraft Pioneer 11 visited the Saturn system in September 1979. Subsequent flybys were made in November 1980 and August 1981 by two Voyager spacecraft, which carried more sophisticated collections of instruments. Observations conducted from these spacecraft resulted in many major findings, including the discovery of several new rings and satellites, the detection of the planet's magnetic field and its associated radiation belts, and the detailed definition of the weather patterns and winds in Saturn's atmosphere.

Density and Composition. A rocky object occupying the same volume as Saturn would weigh about ten times more than Saturn. In fact, even such a volume of water would weigh twice as much as Saturn. Detailed mathematical models that match Saturn's observed mass and volume imply that Saturn consists of two major components: a very deep fluid envelope that is made up almost entirely of hydrogen and helium, as is the sun; and a central denser core made of rocks and perhaps liquid water, methane, and ammonia. The core of Saturn has a mass of 15 to 20 times that of the earth and extends out to about 7,500 miles (12,000 km) from the center of the planet, while the envelope has a mass of 75 to 80 times the mass of the earth and ranges from 7,500 to 37,000 miles (12,000 to 60,000 km) from the center.

Atmosphere. The uppermost fraction of the fluid envelope represents the observable portion of Saturn's atmosphere. Molecular hydrogen accounts for about 90% of all the atmospheric gases. Helium atoms make up almost all the rest, with water vapor, methane, and ammonia

Saturn and its rings, as seen by Voyager I from 11 million miles (18 million km).

present at about a 0.1% level in the warmer regions of the atmosphere. Much smaller amounts of other hydrogen-containing molecules and even carbon monoxide are also present in the gas mixture.

Because Saturn is much more distant from the sun than is the earth, temperatures in its observable atmosphere are generally much colder than those in the earth's atmosphere. The coldest temperature, about −306°F (−188°C), occurs at a pressure about 0.1 that at the surface of the earth (or, equivalently, 0.1 bars). At higher altitudes, in Saturn's stratosphere, the temperature rises as a result of the absorption of sunlight by gaseous methane and small smog particles. (The smog particles may be generated chiefly by ultraviolet sunlight converting gaseous methane into a combination of complex polymers made of carbon and hydrogen atoms.)

At lower altitudes, in the troposphere, the temperature rises steadily with depth. It is so cold in the upper troposphere that some types of gases are expected to condense and form cloud layers. The most prominent of these clouds are those made of water at about the 81°F (27°C) and 20-bar level and of ammonia ice at the −189°F (−123°C), 1.5-bar level.

The visual appearance of Saturn is determined chiefly by a combination of the stratospheric smog particles, the ammonia cloud, and coloring agents that are present within and outside this cloud. As with Jupiter, the most basic feature of Saturn is an alternating set of bright, whitish zones and dark-colored belts. Both types of bands are oriented along latitudinal lines. In the zones the ammonia clouds may be somewhat denser, caused perhaps by rising air motions within them. The bands of Saturn are much more muted in appearance than those of Jupiter, due to a thicker layer of smog particles on Saturn that partially masks the underlying features.

Near Saturn's equator the winds at the altitude of the ammonia clouds blow chiefly from west to east at astonishing speeds of up to 1,100 miles per hour (480 meters per second), or about two thirds the speed of sound in that locality on Saturn. This jet stream has a peak speed of about four times that of the equatorial jet of Jupiter and extends about twice as far, ranging from about 40°S to 40°N. At higher latitudes the wind speeds are much less and tend to alternate between blowing to the west and to the east, as they do at midlatitudes in Jupiter's atmosphere.

Magnetic Field. Saturn's magnetic field is about two thirds as strong as the earth's field at their respective surfaces. However, because Saturn is much bigger than the earth and field strengths decrease sharply with distance from their sources, a source strength of 600 times that for the earth is required to produce Saturn's magnetic field. This source strength for Saturn is still 30 times smaller than that for Jupiter. It is thought that for all three planets, magnetic fields are generated in highly conducting regions of their interiors by the "dynamo" process, whereby fluid motions are partly converted into magnetic energy. In the case of Jupiter and Saturn, this highly conducting region occurs in the deep reaches of their fluid envelope, where the pressures are so high that molecular hydrogen is both dissociated into atoms and stripped of its electron, thus becoming a metal.

Excess Heat. On planets of the inner solar system, such as the earth, there is almost an exact balance between the amount of sunlight absorbed by them and the amount of heat they radiate to space. However Saturn, like Jupiter, radiates to space about twice the amount of sunlight it absorbs. On Jupiter the current excess heat appears to be due to the slow loss of heat from the interior that was built up during an early rapid contraction. However, this same factor can account for only about one third of the excess heat from Saturn. The additional heat could be due to the fact that helium does not mix well with metallic hydrogen at the cooler temperatures inside Saturn. Just as oil and water form separate layers when mixed together, some of the heavier helium sinks toward the planet's center, releasing gravitational energy, which is subsequently radiated as heat.

Satellites. A total of 21–23 moons are known to be in orbit around Saturn. The number of known moons was 17 until the Voyager-spacecraft photographs revealed four or six more. They range in distance from 2.3 R_s (the moon designated as 1980 S28) to as far as 216 R_s (Phoebe) from the planet's center, where R_s is Saturn's equatorial radius (37,000 miles or 60,000 km). By far the largest satellite is Titan, which has a diameter of 3,180 miles, (5120 km). It is slightly larger than Mercury and slightly smaller than Mars. All the remaining satellites are comparable in size to large asteroids, with diameters varying from 950 miles (1530 km) for Rhea down to 20 miles (30 km) for 1980 S28.

The mean density—mass per unit volume—of the larger satellites lies between 1 and 2 grams per cubic centimeter, with the moons lying closer to Saturn tending to have values closer to the low end of this range. Such values imply that Saturn's satellites are made of a mixture of rock and ice. The proportion of ice varies from about 75% for Mimas and Tethys to about 50% for Titan. In contrast, water constitutes only about 0.01% of the earth's mass. Water is probably the dominant type of ice in the satellites, but some ices may contain ammonia and methane.

Craters represent a widely occurring feature across the surfaces of the satellites of Saturn, as they do virtually everywhere in the solar system, including the earth's moon. These bowl-shaped excavations are formed when a small stray body, such as a comet or asteroid, collides with a satellite or planet. The smaller satellites, such as Mimas, have high crater densities, which imply that its surface dates from almost the time of the formation of Saturn—4.6 billion years ago.

Parts of the surfaces of the larger satellites Dione and Rhea have much lower crater densi-

ties than other portions. It is likely that these variations reflect early volcanic epochs, when molten ice and rock, derived from their interiors, poured across parts of their surfaces, erasing craters that had already formed there.

Large cratering events can profoundly affect the smaller satellites. Mimas has a "giant" crater that measures 80 miles (130 km) across, which equals about one third the size of the satellite. This crater is 6 miles (10 km) deep and has surrounding walls that are 3 miles (5 km) high and a central mound of material that stretches 4 miles (6 km) above the crater floor. If the impacting body had been any larger, it might have destroyed the satellite. In fact, such a cataclysmic collision may have produced 1980 S1 and 1980 S3 by fragmenting a larger parent body. They have nearly identical distances from Saturn.

Iapetus, one of the largest satellites, shows a remarkable variation in brightness across its surface. The hemisphere facing the direction of its orbital motion is five times darker than the opposite hemisphere. This extreme variation in brightness may be due either to internal causes, such as volcanic flooding of parts of its surface, or to external causes such as the coating of parts of its surface with outside dust, perhaps derived by crater excavation of the tiny outermost moon, Phoebe.

The largest moon of Saturn, Titan, is the only satellite in the solar system known to have a substantial atmosphere. At its surface the atmospheric pressure reaches a value of 1.6 bars, thus exceeding the corresponding value of 1 bar for the earth's atmosphere. As in the earth's atmosphere, molecular nitrogen is the most abundant gas in Titan's atmosphere. However, in contrast to the earth's atmosphere, the remaining gases contain hydrogen atoms, with the atmosphere

Schematic diagram of the rings visible through earth-based telescopes. (From the earth they can never be seen face-on, as here). The earth, the moon, and the distance between them are shown on same scale as Saturn.

The extraordinarily beautiful and complex rings, photographed by Voyager I from about 5 million miles (8 million km). Within Cassini's division *(dark gap),* previously thought empty, many thin rings can be seen.

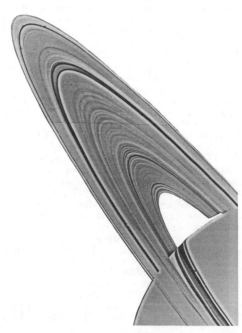

KEY FACTS ABOUT SATURN

Mass	6.28×10^{23} tons (5.69×10^{26}kg) (about 95 times that of the earth)
Mean diameter	72,000 miles (116,000 km) (9.1 times that of the earth)
Mean density	43 pounds/cubic foot (0.69 grams/cm^3) (12.5% of the earth's)
Surface gravity[1] at equator	29.7 feet (9.0 meters) per second per second (93% of the earth's)
Escape velocity[2] at equator	22.1 miles (35.6 km) per second (3.2 times that of the earth)
Magnetic field	0.2 gauss at equator, 0.5 at poles (about 65% of the earth's)
Mean distance from sun	887 million miles (1,427 million km)
Mean orbital velocity	5.99 miles (9.64 km) per second
Revolution period (sidereal year)[3]	29.46 earth years
Rotation period (sidereal day)[4]	10.68 earth hours
Number of satellites	21–23

[1]Rate at which a freely falling body is accelerated by gravity.
[2]Speed needed by a departing object in order never to be pulled back down by the planet's gravity.
[3]Time required for the planet to complete one revolution around the sun with respect to the fixed stars.
[4]Time required for the planet to complete one rotation about its axis with respect to the fixed stars.

consisting of a few percent methane, a few tenths of a percent molecular hydrogen, and much smaller amounts of ethane, acetylene, and hydrogen cyanide. Gases other than nitrogen and methane are produced within the atmosphere when ultraviolet sunlight and high-energy particles fragment methane and nitrogen.

Hydrogen cyanide—a molecule consisting of single atoms of hydrogen, carbon, and nitrogen—represents a unique molecule that has not been found anywhere else in the solar system. It is particularly interesting in that it is a key intermediate material in the chemical sequence that may have led to the origin of life on the earth. However, the temperatures on Titan are too cold to permit any significant amounts of water vapor to exist in its atmosphere or liquid water on its surface, and so not all the ingredients needed to make life-forming molecules are present.

As on Saturn, atmospheric chemistry results not only in the production of complex gases but also tiny smog particles. Because the smog particles extend throughout the bottom 200 miles (300 km) of the atmosphere (on the earth they are largely confined to the bottom mile, or 1–2 km), they totally obscure our view of the surface. The smog particles play an important role in the heat balance of the atmosphere. Because they are good absorbers of sunlight and poor emitters of heat radiation, the middle portion of Titan's atmosphere (above 60 miles, or 100 km) is heated to temperatures of about $-171°F$ ($-113°C$), whereas the temperature reaches a value as low as $-333°F$ ($-203°C$) at an altitude of 30 miles (50 km), where little sunlight penetrates. At still lower altitudes, the temperature gradually rises, reaching a value of $-292°F$ ($-180°C$) at the surface.

Besides the smog particles, which are probably a complex organic polymer made of carbon, nitrogen, and hydrogen atoms, condensation clouds of methane may exist in the lower 30 miles of the atmosphere. Liquid pools of methane and solid glaciers of methane ice may cover parts of Titan's surface, in which case the amount of methane in the atmosphere is controlled by the temperature of the surface.

Rings. The rings of Saturn are one of the most beautiful sights in the sky, surrounding the planet with a pale golden halo. They are a very flat and broad disk of material and lie in the planet's equatorial plane. They are subdivided into a number of separate rings, each of which, in turn, consists of a number of ringlets. The two brightest rings, the ones easily seen with a telescope, are the somewhat fainter outer A ring and the brighter inner B ring. The inner edge of the B ring is located only 20,000 miles (32,000 km) above Saturn's cloud tops, while the outer edge of the A ring is situated at an altitude of 47,000 miles (76,000 km). The A and B rings are separated by a 2,200-mile (3,500-km), dark but not totally empty zone, known as Cassini's division after its discoverer. Lying inside the B ring are the faint C ring and still fainter D ring, while the narrow, faint F and G rings and the broad and very faint E ring are located at progressively increasing distances beyond the A ring. The entire ring system spans a radial distance of about 140,000 miles (230,000 km), yet its brightest portions have a vertical extent of less than a few kilometers.

The rings consist of a very large number of tiny bodies traveling in independent orbits about Saturn. Energy-dissipating collisions between adjacent ring particles have led to the almost complete elimination of random up-and-down motions, but have not affected their common circular motion in the direction of the planet's rotation. This is why the rings are so flat. The particles in the rings are made almost entirely of water ice and range in sizes between about 0.5 inch (1 cm) about 30 feet (10 meters). However, much smaller, microscopic particles are also present in some parts of the rings, such as the B ring, the outer part of the A ring, and the F ring. Also, moonlets having sizes between about 0.5 mile and 30 miles (1–50 km) are suspected to be present in many parts of the rings and to be responsible for much of the fine structure seen in the Voyager pictures. Bodies of such sizes tend to create empty regions around themselves through their gravitational interaction with much smaller bodies. In a similar way, somewhat larger moons that lie just outside some rings help to determine the location of their edges. For example, moons 1980 S26 and 1980 S27 (125 miles, or 200 km in diameter) are situated on either side of the F ring.

Magnetosphere. As with Mercury, the earth, and Jupiter, the strong magnetic field of Saturn deflects the flow of the solar wind and creates a protected region called the magnetosphere. The outer boundary of the magnetosphere lies close to the orbit of Titan on the upstream side of the solar-wind flow and at greater distance on the downstream side. High-energy, electrically charged ions and electrons are present throughout most of this region, although they are almost totally absent close to the planet because there the ring particles efficiently absorb them. Neutral and electrically charged gases of low energy also are present within the magnetosphere. Much of the high- and low-energy gases in the magnetosphere may derive from atoms that escape from the top of Titan's atmosphere and from fragmented water molecules from the surfaces of ring particles.

JAMES B. POLLACK
Space Science Division
NASA Ames Research Center

Further Reading: Beatty, J. Kelly, and others, eds., *The New Solar System* (Sky Publishing, 1981).

SATURN, sat'ərn, a Roman god of agriculture, was the husband of Ops and father of Picus, another agricultural god. Saturn was the god of sowing and harvest and is represented as bearing a sickle. The origins of his worship are unclear, but he was later identified with the Greek god Cronus, who, driven from his supreme throne by Zeus, went to Latium, set up his kingdom there, and taught the people the practice of agriculture.

His reign in Rome was regarded as the Golden Age. His throne was shared with Ops, afterward identified with Rhea, and in the 6th century B.C., during the reign of the last king of Rome, Lucius Tarquinius Superbus, a temple to Saturn was built at the foot of the Capitol. This was later used as Rome's treasury (*Saturni Aerarium*). The Tables of Law and Senate decrees were also kept there. The foundations of this temple and eight pillars still remain at the western end of the Forum. The statue of Saturn was swathed in woolen bandages except during the Saturnalia, his festival in December, when it was uncovered.

SATURN ROCKET. See ROCKETS; SPACE EXPLORATION—*Principles of Space Flight.*

SATURNALIA, sat-ər-nāl'yə, was a Roman festival commemorating the happy period under Saturn, when freedom and equality reigned and violence and oppression were unknown. It probably began as a harvest celebration, but this connection was later lost.

Originally it was marked on December 17, but its length was later extended. During the Saturnalia, public business ceased, masters and slaves changed places, and some moral codes were relaxed. Feasting prevailed, and gifts were exchanged, usually candles and small clay dolls. It was similar to the Christian festival of Christmas. The statue of Saturn, bandaged the rest of the year, was unwrapped.

SATURNINUS, sat-ər-nī'nəs, **Lucius Appuleius** (died 100 B.C.), Roman revolutionary democrat and popular orator, who opposed the power of the Senate. He served as quaestor in Ostia in 104 B.C. and was elected tribune of the plebeians in 103 and again in 100.

While a tribune he worked closely with Gaius Marius, a plebeian general who was consul. Saturninus granted lands to Marius' veteran troops and passed a controversial grain law. These measures were popular with the lower classes but aroused opposition among the aristocrats, whom Saturninus attempted to curb by establishing a permanent court of treason. During his second tribunate he allied himself with Marius and Gaius Glaucia, a praetor. Marius became alienated, however, when an opponent of Saturninus and Glaucia was murdered, and Marius had the two men outlawed. With Glaucia, Saturninus was stoned to death.

SATYAGRAHA, sə-tyä'grə-hə, Gandhi's technique of nonviolent action. See GANDHI, MOHANDAS.

SATYR, sāt'ər, in Greek mythology, was a spirit of the woods and hills, animal-like in desires and behavior. The Roman counterparts of the satyrs were the fauns. The satyrs are represented as grotesque creatures, of human form for the most part but with the tail of a horse or with the little horns, pointed ears, and often the legs of a goat. There is no clear distinction between satyrs and sileni, although classical authors often represent sileni as old satyrs.

The poet Hesiod made them brothers of the nymphs and called them worthless and mischievous. They are lustful creatures, fond of dancing and revelry. The sculptor Praxiteles showed a satyr pouring wine. Satyrs were generally cowards except when aroused by desire or wine. They are associated with Dionysus, the Greek god of fertility, as his attendants. In Greek literature they are first clearly recognizable in satyr-plays such as Euripides' *Cyclops.*

SATYR PLAY, sāt'ər, in ancient Greek literature, a short, comic play performed after a trilogy of classical tragedies. The satyr play, which included a chorus of satyrs, was often based on the same myth as the tragedies.

SAUCONITE. See CLAY—*Montmorillonite Group.*

SAUD, sä-ōōd' (1902–1969), king of Saudi Arabia. His full name was Saud Ibn Abd al-Aziz Ibn Abd al-Rahman al-Faisal Al Saud. The son of Ibn Saud, he was born in Kuwait in January 1902. He participated in many of his father's military campaigns, despite eye problems that troubled him throughout his life. He was named crown prince in 1933 and succeeded his father in 1953.

Saud promoted Arab dignity and rigidly opposed Israel, while trying to maintain good relations with Western nations. Although Saudi Arabia had vast oil revenues, Saud was unable to deal with economic problems, and there was a financial crisis in 1958. His brother Faisal was given administrative powers, and rivalry with Faisal continued after the King resumed his powers in 1960. Saud was deprived of his executive powers in early 1964 and was deposed in favor of Faisal in November. Saud lived in exile in Europe until his death in Athens on Feb. 23, 1969.

Saud, king of Saudi Arabia from 1953 to 1964.

PICTORIAL PARADE

J. ALLAN CASH, FROM RAPHO GUILLUMETTE

The mountains of Saudi Arabia, in the Hejaz, are traversed by road from the Red Sea to Mecca and Medina.

CONTENTS

SAUDI ARABIA, sȧ-o͞o′dē ə-rä′bē-ə, the largest nation in the Middle East east of the Suez Canal, is a kingdom occupying nearly nine tenths of the Arabian Peninsula. The country, whose population is overwhelmingly Muslim, is the birthplace and heartland of Islam. Although the Saudi dynasty seized power in 1902, the present kingdom was established in 1932 after Ibn Saud, its founder, brought together under his rule the majority of the peninsula's diverse tribes.

Saudi Arabia's desert terrain, its arid climate, scarce resources (except oil), and relatively small population have influenced its history through the ages. Although the birthplace of the Prophet Mohammed and the starting point for the great Arab empires that determined the history and culture of the Middle East and North Africa for centuries, the peninsula faded into the background of world history shortly after the Prophet's death, as the centers of Arab civilization moved to richer and more fertile regions.

At the beginning of the 19th century there was a flurry of religious revival in Arabia when the Wahhabis, Islamic fundamentalists, gathered sufficient strength to break out of their homeland, invade Iraq, capture Mecca, the holiest site in Islam, and threaten Damascus. But the Wahhabi movement was crushed by a joint Turkish-Egyptian expeditionary force and was quiescent for the rest of the century.

Under the leadership of Ibn Saud, a direct descendant of the earlier Wahhabi leaders, fundamentalist Islam and Saudi political ambitions converged to become a powerful force at the beginning of the 20th century. Winning one victory after another, Ibn Saud established a new and powerful bedouin monarchy. Although militarily and politically dominant in the peninsula, the new Saudi kingdom was poor in natural resources, backward in its economic and social development, and relatively primitive in its governmental administration. Not until oil was discovered in 1936 and later exploited in large quantities did Saudi Arabia attract world attention. At first, the oil interests were British, but by the end of World War II, U. S. companies dominated the petroleum concessions. With the emergence of strong nationalist sentiment in the decades that followed, the Saudis placed ever greater pressure on foreign oil companies to turn over both profits and control to their government.

INFORMATION HIGHLIGHTS

Official Name: The Kingdom of Saudi Arabia (al-Mamlaka al-Arabiya as-Saudiya).
Head of State: King.
Head of Government: President of the Council of Ministers (Prime Minister).
Area: approximately 850,000 square miles (2,200,000 sq km).
Elevation: Highest point approximately 9,000 feet (2,750 meters).
Population: estimated (1971) between 5,000,000 and 8,000,000.
Capital: (royal) Riyadh; (administrative) Jidda.
Major Language: Arabic.
Major Religious Group: Sunnite Muslim.
Monetary Unit: Saudi rial.
Weights and Measures: Metric system.
Flag: Green, with an Arabic inscription in white, "There is no god but Allah, Muhammad is the prophet of Allah," and a white sword.

1. The Land

Saudi Arabia's major geographical regions correspond roughly to its four major political subdivisions. They are the Nejd ("highland") in central Arabia; the Hejaz ("barrier") along the upper Red Sea coast; Asir ("difficult region") along the Red Sea between the Hejaz and Yemen; and the Eastern Province, or Hasa ("sandy ground with water"), along the Persian Gulf.

The Four Regions. The largest region, the Nejd, is Saudi Arabia's heartland, containing the cities of Riyadh, Anaiza, and Buraida. It is a gently sloping steppe rising from 2,000 feet (600 meters) in the east to 5,000 feet (1,525 meters) in the west. Some four inches (100 mm) of rain fall annually, producing scrub vegetation just barely capable of supporting the flocks of nomadic herdsmen. Its two great deserts are the Nafud in the north and the narrow Dahna in the south. In the stony and sandy deserts, especially in the north and east, there are several oases with settled agricultural populations. During the day the temperature varies from 130° F (54° C) to nearly freezing in the winter. However, night temperatures, even during summer, are comfortable.

The Hejaz, 150,000 square miles (388,500 sq km) in area, stretches along the Red Sea from the Gulf of Aqaba south to Asir. Its coastal plain is separated from the interior highlands by the western mountain slopes. Wadis (valleys that are normally dry, but carry runoff water during the winter rainy season) provide water, making settlement of the highlands possible. Roads connect the ports of Jidda and Yanbu (Yenbo) on the Red Sea coast with the holy city of Medina, 2,500 feet (762 meters) above sea level in the interior highlands. Mecca, the holiest city of Islam, is on the western side of the escarpment dividing the coastal plain from the mountainous interior.

Asir, south of the Hejaz, has a fertile western coastland, which receives up to 12 inches (300 mm) of rainfall a year, more than any other part of the kingdom, and is consequently among the most heavily populated areas. The mountains rising from the coastal plain are terraced for agriculture. In the interior, mountains continue to rise, with several peaks southeast of Mecca reaching heights of over 8,000 feet (2,500 meters).

The Eastern Province (Hasa) extends south along the Persian Gulf from Kuwait. It contains the oil that is the principal source of Saudi Arabia's national income. The area is formed of sedimentary rock, gravel, and sand, common oil-producing land formations typical of the Middle East. Annual precipitation is sparse, sometimes less than 4 inches (100 mm). During the day, temperatures often reach 120° F (50° C). The oil port at Ras Tanura is the terminal for the pipeline from the Dhahran oil fields. Dammam, also on the coast, is the terminus of a railroad to Riyadh in the Nejd. The oasis of Hasa, probably Saudi Arabia's largest, supporting an estimated 200,000 people, is in the Eastern Province. It has 60 or more springs and is famous for its dates. Hofuf and some 40 other towns and villages are in the oasis.

In the southern part of Saudi Arabia, extending eastward some 750 miles (1,200 km) from the borders of Asir to the Persian Gulf, is the immense desert called the Rub al-Khali (The Empty Quarter). It is the largest continuous body of sand in the world and covers about 200,000 square miles (518,000 sq km). Parts of it are uninhabited except after infrequent rains, when bedouins move in to take advantage of the sparse pasturage.

Plant and Animal Life. Because rainfall is scanty and capricious and since there are no large streams, vegetation is light except in Asir and the southern Hejaz coastal regions. Camel pasturage springs up after the winter rains. There are no large forests, although large trees such as the tamarisk grow in some regions.

The government has taken measures to protect the increasingly rare species of gazelles, which were once more numerous. In the highlands there are mountain goats, wildcats, troops of baboons, wolves, hyenas, foxes, and smaller animals. Birds such as wild eagles, hawks, and falcons are found. The oases abound in small birds such as the cuckoo, thrush, and swallow.

There are many varieties of tropical fish in coastal waters, and the possibilities of commercial fishing on a large scale have now been appreciated. Whales and dolphins can be found in the Persian Gulf.

Locusts breed in the desert and are the scourge of Saudi Arabia. Swarms have been known to fly 1,500 miles (2,500 km) nonstop and have been seen 1,200 miles (2,000 km) at sea. The bedouins consider them a delicacy, roasting, boiling, or drying them in the sun.

2. The People and Their Way of Life

The vast majority of the inhabitants of Saudi Arabia are Arabs, descended from indigenous tribes, with past infusions of African and Asian blood from neighboring countries. Because of the small amount of immigration, there has been little change for centuries in the ethnic composition of Saudi Arabia. There are, however, small ethnic minorities, principally those settled in the coastal towns and those who have come either on pilgrimages or to work in the expanding oil industry.

Different Arabic dialects are spoken, although that of the bedouins is considered the purest since it most resembles the language of the prophet Mohammed and has not been greatly influenced by foreign tongues.

Perhaps over 90% of the Saudis are Sunnite Muslims of the puritanical Wahhabi sect of the Hanbalite school. There are also small groups of Shiite Muslims in eastern Arabia.

Social life is organized along family and tribal lines, with the patriarch playing a dominant role. Loyalties are still primarily given to the family, the clan, and the tribe rather than to any political entity.

The rigid Islamic religious pattern imposes a conservative stamp upon society, and all aspects of life are still guided by literal interpretations of the Koran. Islamic practice governs relationships between man and woman, parents and children, family and tribe. Even food and dress are determined by age-old Islamic tradition.

Although over 90% of the people of Saudi Arabia are still illiterate, a formal system of education was initiated during the early 1930's. An indication of growing pressure for social change is the increased demand for the education of women, who have finally been admitted to state schools. Several private schools for girls have been established at Mecca and Medina in response to the demands for changing the traditional lowly status of women.

Average life expectancy is estimated at be-

ARAMCO

Oil, which dominates the economy of Saudi Arabia, is obtained in the deserts of the Eastern Province (Hasa).

tween 30 and 40 years. Most of the population is under 20 years of age. While records are not kept, the nomadic birthrate is believed to be one of the highest in the world. It is balanced by very high infant, child, and maternal mortality rates.

About two thirds of the total population of Saudi Arabia is believed to be nomadic or semi-nomadic. About 12% are settled cultivators, and some 22% are urban dwellers. The nomadic bedouins herd camels and also graze flocks of sheep and goats. Large numbers of seminomads also own communal lands, which some cultivate. Herding has declined in relative importance due to the decreasing dependence on the camel as a means of transport and to the expansion of agriculture.

Pastoral life keeps the bedouins on the move over the deserts. Because of the need for portable shelter, they live in tents woven from goat hair. These "people of the camel" are completely dependent on the animal for transportation, food, and shelter. They live on camel's milk for months at a time when in the desert. At other times they support themselves by their flocks of sheep and goats, the surplus products of which they supply to the settled population.

The average family settled in a town or village lives in a one- or two-storied two-room mud hut. One room may be shared with the family livestock. Village architecture varies regionally. In some parts of Asir, African influence is apparent in the use of reeds to construct beehive huts. In desert regions most houses are built of brick made by mixing mud and straw. Palm or other wood may be used for beams and doors.

Most villagers are subsistence farmers who live from their scanty grain crops, chiefly wheat. The farmers walk to work from their village homes. In many of the villages there are also smiths, tinkers, shopkeepers, and masons.

In larger and older villages there is usually a suq (marketplace) where biweekly or monthly markets are held. The suq also serves as a gathering place for special occasions. In more sparsely settled regions, one suq may serve a number of small, neighboring hamlets. Close to the village suq may be a mosque, generally a simple rectangular mud brick or stone building of one or two stories. Since Saudis are strict observers of simplicity in their practice of Islam, they frown upon the use of the minaret or dome in tombs and mosques. The kuttub (kuttab), or Muslim religious school, is held in one of the mosque rooms.

There is little difference between the characteristic clothing of the nomad and that of the settled population. However, only among the bedouins will one see men with plaited hair, and only city dwellers wear Western-style shoes rather than sandals. Men usually wear ankle-length, long-sleeved white shirts, and on their heads cotton kerchiefs held in place by black ropelike cords. Women wear black robes and veils, although in the cities some wear Western dresses under their black garments.

Slavery was legal in Saudi Arabia until it was abolished in 1963. It was then estimated that there were as many as half a million slaves, although there was no accurate count. Slave trading and the importation of slaves were prohibited by a 1927 treaty with Britain, although smuggling from Africa continued in spite of British naval patrols. Slaves enjoyed a relatively high social status and were accepted as part of the families they served. Many ascended to the highest government posts; one even became King Ibn Saud's prime minister.

3. The Economy

Although the discovery of oil in 1936 transformed Saudi Arabia's economy, raising crops and herding have remained the traditional occupation of most Saudis.

Agriculture. From the 1930's on, agriculture became increasingly important as the government settled more nomads on the land, expanded cultivated areas, and experimented with new farming techniques. Yet even today it is estimated that only 1% of the total land area is cultivated, though 15% is estimated to be cultivable. Surveys indicated that the land under cultivation could be increased substantially if the numerous potential water supplies were developed. At the present time, 80% of the land under cultivation is irrigated, but by rudimentary methods: some 70% of the water used has to be lifted from wells or pits by animal power or centrifugal pumps. Furthermore, primitive farming methods are still widespread in spite of the successful experimental projects the government has established with the aid of foreign specialists.

Agricultural produce is still so limited that the country must import much of its food supply. The townspeople especially are dependent on food imports. The policy of nomad settlement has also increased dependence on food imports, since many of the new settlers require long periods of time before they can become productive and self-sustaining.

Dates are the principal cash crop throughout the country, except in Tihama, where grain sorghums predominate. Most of the cultivated areas in the oases are devoted to the date palm, and the fruit is the only food export other than coffee.

Dates are a staple food throughout Arabia. The date stones and the spathes of the date palm are used for animal fodder, the ribs and leaves of the palm for firewood, the trunk for construction, and the fiber for cordage and matting.

Other major agricultural products, none of which is sufficient to meet the country's needs, are wheat, rice, corn, alfalfa, barley, and grapes. Cotton, melons, and fruits are grown on a smaller scale. Coffee is cultivated in the Asir highlands near the Yemen border. Annual crop production fluctuates widely according to the water supply.

Camels, sheep, and goats, once abundant, have decreased considerably in number because of drought and the decline in stock raising. The single-humped camel is still the most important animal, providing a principal source of meat, milk, hide, and transport across the desert. Cattle do not thrive because of the heat and aridity. Horses, although a prestige animal among the bedouins, have never been of great economic importance. In the past they were used by raiding parties, but with improved security conditions their value has declined. Donkeys are still beasts of burden in mountainous regions, but they cannot be used for long distances across the desert, where camels serve best.

The Oil Industry. The modern petroleum industry came to Saudi Arabia in 1932 when a subsidiary of the Standard Oil Company of California struck oil in neighboring Bahrain. Prior to 1932, drilling rights in Saudi territory had not been greatly valued. But the Bahrain discovery led California Arabian Standard Oil Company (Casoc) to sign a concession with Saudi Arabia in 1933, to run for 60 years. With the discovery of oil in 1936, Saudi Arabia no longer had to depend on date exports and income from the pilgrims to Mecca and Medina for revenues.

Today the petroleum industry dominates the economy of Saudi Arabia. By the early 1970's, oil was the source of more than 90% of the national income, providing over 97% of the country's total exports and about 95% of the exports to its major trading partners, including the United States and Britain. Saudi Arabia has also become a major supplier of oil for western Europe and Japan. Production increased from 594.6 million barrels in 1963 to 3,096 million in 1974. Oil income yielded more than $25 billion in cash payments in the mid-1970's. The country's oil reserves are the world's largest, slightly less than one fourth of the world's total. With new fields discovered in 1975, oil reserves rose to more than 170 billion barrels.

Aramco. In 1944 the name of the American concession holder was changed to Arabian American Oil Company (Aramco). Aramco included the California Standard Oil Company and the Texas Oil Company (Texaco), which had joined the enterprise in 1936. In 1946, arrangements were made for the Standard Oil Company (New Jersey) and the Socony-Vacuum Oil Company (later the Socony Mobil Oil Company) to become Aramco partners. As part of its program to nationalize the petroleum industry, Saudi Arabia by 1976 had reached agreement with Aramco to assume complete control of the concession.

Other concessions in the former Saudi-Kuwait Neutral Zone are held by the Getty Oil Co. and the Japanese-owned Arabian Oil Co.

After 1938, the American concessions exported enough crude oil to supply the needs of several European industrial nations. Most of this oil

ARAMCO

While his camels drink their fill, a young bedouin nomad fills his goatskin water bag at a desert watering place.

came from about 200 wells in the Eastern Province and its offshore area. Aramco also constructed a major refinery and accompanying installations on the Persian Gulf at Ras Tanura.

A major installation is Tapline, the Trans-Arabian Pipeline that connects the Abqaiq oil field and Ras Tanura with the Lebanese oil port of Sidon on the Mediterranean coast slightly over 1,000 miles (1,600 km) away. Completed in 1950, Tapline, built by Aramco and the Tapline Company, an Aramco affiliate, traverses the desert of northern Saudi Arabia, Jordan, southern Syria (occupied by Israel in 1967), and Lebanon. Shipment of oil from the Eastern Province to the Mediterranean by Tapline avoids the 3,600-mile (5,790-km), nine-day tanker voyage by way of the Suez Canal. Tapline is linked with the various oil fields in eastern Saudi Arabia through a network of internal pipelines and is today the principal means of shipping Saudi oil to Western markets.

Industry and Labor. Building construction is second only to oil production in industrial importance. It is an offshoot of the oil industry, which both creates the market and supplies the funds for construction. Most materials for building, such as cement and steel, are imported but local contractors have been employed in constructing Aramco buildings. Aside from the oil and building industries, Saudi Arabia is limited in its industrial development. However, steps are being taken to overcome this limitation. Under a $140 billion 5-year economic plan announced in May 1975, a projected $13 billion would be invested in heavy industry by 1980, and large investments would be made in housing, highways, power lines, water supplies, and ports.

Few of the people possess technical, administrative, or managerial skills, although a growing number of younger men educated in the West have begun to acquire them. Until after World

303

The goal of pilgrims to Mecca is the Kaaba, which is covered with a black cloth. The Black Stone, which is an object of veneration, is set into the side of the Kaaba.

ARAMCO

War II, only foreign entrepreneurs had the technical knowledge or capital available to undertake significant business enterprises.

Mineral resources other than oil are meager. They include gold, silver, lead, and copper. There has also been some production of salt, gypsum, and limestone. However, the means for estimating the production of these commodities are lacking.

Handicrafts have developed on a small local scale and include weaving and fine embroidery work. Some 2% to 3% of the people are engaged in pearling, fishing, and shipbuilding, ancient Persian Gulf occupations practiced for centuries by Arabs of the port towns. In spite of the vast resources of the seas surrounding Arabia, fishing is still a marginal occupation.

Although there are no available statistics on the distribution of Saudi Arabia's labor force, it is clear that modern industrial opportunities exist only in the oil industry and its ancillary enterprises. Those parts of the population not involved in these industries are engaged in traditional employment or are self-employed. Next to agriculture, the nonindustrial field employing the greatest number of people is government service, now rapidly expanding in public administration, and in medical, military, educational, religious, and similar activities. Craftsmen and traders are a small but rapidly growing group.

Although there is no direct government legislation on labor unions, they are in effect prohibited. Nevertheless, labor in the oil and ancillary fields has become increasingly aware of its potential bargaining power, particularly in view of the growing strength of labor unions in nearby Arab countries. In the years after the 1967 Arab-Israeli war, labor unrest among Palestinians working in Saudi Arabia increased and there have been occasional unauthorized strikes.

Finance and Trade. Because modern finance is relatively new in Saudi Arabia, and banks still play a very small part in the domestic economy, few Saudis use domestic banks for savings, although there are large Saudi deposits in banks abroad. Until the Saudi Arabian Monetary Agency was established in 1952, there was no central bank. Most private commercial banks have been foreign owned.

Oil provides more than 97% by value of

the country's total exports. Exports in 1971 went chiefly to western Europe (52%), Asia (27%), South America (6%), and Africa and North America (about 5% each).

The United States is by far the country's most important source of imports, followed by Lebanon, Japan, Britain, and West Germany. The principal imports have been motor vehicles and parts, building materials, foodstuffs, textiles, machinery, electrical equipment, and pharmaceuticals. There is little internal trade except of petroleum products produced by Aramco and food and livestock produced by local bedouins.

Transportation and Communication. Saudi Arabia's only operating railroad is the 357-mile (575-km) government-owned line connecting Dammam with Riyadh. It was opened in 1951. The old Turkish-built Hejaz railway, which formerly connected Medina with Syria, was abandoned in 1924. A paved highway, to link all the main centers, is constantly being expanded. Hard-surfaced roads link the main towns of Hejaz and the Eastern Province with Riyadh.

Jidda, on the Red Sea, and Dammam, on the Persian Gulf, are the two principal ports. Ras Tanura, on the east coast, is used for loading oil tankers. In Riyadh, Jidda, and Dhahran there are modern airports. Within the kingdom the Saudi Arabian Airlines has a monopoly.

There are government-owned telephone and telegraph services and radio stations at Mecca, Medina, and Jidda, and an American-operated station at Dhahran.

4. History and Government

Although Islam was born in Mecca and Medina, two principal cities of present-day Saudi Arabia, the main centers of Islamic development moved northward after the death of the Prophet Mohammed in 632. After the 7th and 8th centuries, the Arabian Peninsula was isolated for nearly 1,000 years. For the history of the Arabian Peninsula from the beginning to the 18th century, see ARABIA—*History.*

In the 18th century, Mohammed Ibn Abd al-Wahhab became the religious guide of Mohammed Ibn Saud, chief of the small north Arabian principality of Dariya. The followers of Mohammed Ibn Abd al-Wahhab, the Wahhabis, were Muslim fundamentalists who opposed various innovations introduced into the religion and sought to return to the practice of Islam as preached by the Prophet Mohammed.

The fusion of Wahhabi religious fervor and the political acumen of the Sauds won the new movement a large and zealous bedouin following and enabled Mohammed Ibn Saud's son, Abd al-Aziz, to expand his father's principality to the Red Sea. After the Wahhabis captured Mecca in 1803, the Ottoman sultan sent Egyptian forces to destroy the movement. Finally, after three expeditions, the first Wahhabi-Saud empire was crushed in 1818.

For the next 30 years the Wahhabi-Saud movement was quiescent. Then the Sauds opened a new offensive against the Rashids, an Ottoman-backed clan of northern Arabia. Fighting continued periodically for the rest of the 19th century, with fortune passing from one side to the other. In 1902, Abd al-Aziz Ibn Saud, a descendant of the first Wahhabi-Saud leader, led a group of a few dozen tribesmen to capture the seat of Rashid power in Riyadh, which he later made the capital of the renewed Saudi Arabian kingdom. After defeating the Rashids, Ibn Saud successively conquered most of the other tribes in central Arabia until, by the beginning of World War I, he had become the most powerful leader and ruler of the largest area in the peninsula. His success was due not only to military prowess, but also to his attaining leadership of the Wahhabi movement. As spiritual leader, he inspired in his bedouin followers a religious loyalty higher than their devotion to their tribes and towns. Wahhabi missionaries encouraged the growth of Ikhwan ("brotherhood") communities in a religio-political system much like that established by the Prophet Mohammed. Within a few years the movement united central Arabia in a unity symbolized by Ibn Saud.

After the Turco-Italian War of 1911–1912 and the Balkan Wars, Turkey, which had controlled parts of the peninsula since the 16th century, withdrew many of its troops from Arabia. During 1913, Ibn Saud used the opportunity to stage a surprise attack on the remaining Ottoman garrisons along the Persian Gulf and to seize the area that is now the Eastern Province (Hasa). The Turks barely had time to respond to these attacks on their empire before World War I broke out.

During World War I, the British established contact with Ibn Saud and his principal rival in the Arabian Peninsula, the Hashemite sharif of the Hejaz, Hussein Ibn Ali. Hussein proclaimed himself king of the Arab countries, but the British recognized him only as king of the Hejaz. However, they extended to him more assistance during the war than they did to Ibn Saud. The British foreign office favored Hussein, while Britain's India office subsidized Ibn Saud. The two rivals were kept apart only through energetic British warnings that their respective subsidies would be terminated if they fought each other and that British military support would go to whichever side was attacked.

Unification and Independence. At the end of the war, when the British subsidies were no longer paid, Ibn Saud was free to attack Hussein and other rivals in the peninsula. He extended his authority throughout the peninsula by destroying the last remnants of the Rashid amirate and seizing its capital at Hail. By 1925 he had also defeated Hussein's forces, conquering the

Hashemite kingdom of the Hejaz, including the holy cities of Mecca and Medina. A few months later Asir, between the Hejaz and Yemen, was incorporated in the Saudi kingdom when its tribal leader decided to join it to Ibn Saud's territories.

In 1934, Ibn Saud defeated neighboring Yemen but generously refrained from seizing any of its territories. Relations between the two kingdoms remained friendly until the 1962 revolution, which overthrew the Yemeni monarchy.

Until the early 1930's, local tribal chiefs exercised extensive power in the more remote regions of Saudi Arabia. However, after rounding out his territorial acquisitions, Ibn Saud sought to consolidate his political authority. An initial measure was the formation of the kingdom of Saudi Arabia in 1932 from the various provinces taken over in the previous three decades.

When it was established, the kingdom of Saudi Arabia had indefinite borders, a situation that complicated its relations with Jordan, Iraq, Kuwait, Yemen, Iran, and the Persian Gulf principalities. Most of the border disputes with these neighboring countries have been settled, although there are still conflicting claims to border areas in the south and along the Gulf where oil is believed to exist.

Evolution of the Government and the Military. With the establishment of the kingdom, government continued to be based on the tribal system and Islamic law. No written constitution was adopted. However, although the king was theoretically an absolute monarch with powers limited only by the Koran, he ruled within the limitations set for a paramount chief, since he was subject to the traditions and customs prevailing among the country's bedouin tribes and city clans.

Ibn Saud obtained acceptance of new forms of government by establishing them within the framework of the customary and traditional forms

Irrigation makes possible a limited amount of farming in Saudi Arabia. This is a field of Egyptian clover.

Jidda, on the Red Sea. The city is a busy port and the headquarters for the diplomatic corps.

of Islamic tribal society. A quasiconstitutional system evolved from the great number of decrees issued by Ibn Saud on such matters as taxation, border control, and the other affairs of concern to a modern nation. Nevertheless, the government still asserts that all public law derives from the Koran, which is the basic law of the country. Justice is administered by religious courts on the basis of the Koran. There are no legislative bodies or political parties.

In consolidating his power, Ibn Saud made extensive use of his newly created regular army, which was equipped with modern weapons and airplanes. As the regular army increased in strength, its younger officers were considered politically unreliable, even dangerous, because of their "Western" ideas. To balance their influence, prestige, and power, the White Army, or National Guard, was organized from tribal levies. Many of its members were associated with the Ikhwan and noted for their extraordinary mobility and the respect they commanded even among various unruly elements of the population. While the regular army was under the jurisdiction of the defense ministry, the White Army reported directly to the king through his ministers. Proposals to integrate the armed forces were resisted by the government because of the unpredictable political consequences.

After the 1930's the petroleum industry brought to Saudi Arabia not only Western workers and administrators but Western machines, techniques, and concepts. Life became far more complex. The traditional tribal form of government was now inadequate to cope with the increasing complexities in the practical affairs of government. A direct consequence of the growing modernization was the creation of the first Council of Ministers in 1953, the year in which Ibn Saud died and was succeeded by his eldest son, King Saud. After that, the absolute monarchy evolved toward monarchical-ministerial rule in which the prime minister and cabinet played an increasingly authoritative role.

During the reign of King Saud (1953–1964), his brother, Crown Prince Faisal, was prime minister for several long periods, during which the brothers engaged in a power conflict. Prince Faisal attempted to end many of the worst abuses of government in 1958 when he tightened financial controls and enacted a decree centralizing responsibility and specifying the jurisdiction of each minister. The decree empowered the Council of Ministers to draw up policies on all foreign and domestic affairs and charged it with implementing them. The impact of the 1958 reorganization was substantial. The king was no longer an absolute monarch but one whose powers were subject to considerable limitation.

Political power shifted back to the royal family when King Saud relinquished control over the government to Crown Prince Faisal in 1964. In November 1964, Saud was deposed by a Saudi family council, and Faisal became king as well as president of the Council of Ministers, with extensive powers to appoint and dismiss government officials.

Despite Faisal's reassertion of royal prerogatives, pressure from younger members of the Saud family and from the growing middle classes forced him to modify many of the restrictive Islamic practices that circumscribe life in the country. Education was expanded and university enrollment increased. Larger numbers of Saudis were sent to Western colleges and technical schools. Restrictions were lifted on the kinds of music to which people could listen, and women were permitted to appear on government radio and television stations. Cameras were no longer confiscated from visitors on the ground that it is sacrilegious to reproduce the human image. Legislation was enacted to encourage foreign banks and other businesses. However, despite promises of political reform and a constitution, the trend was toward increasing the strength of the monarch. Even the traditional consultative council of notables and members of the royal family atrophied from disuse.

Foreign Affairs. Saudi Arabia's strong attachment to the Arab cause is evidenced by its becoming one of the original members of the Arab League and by its participation in the boycott and blockade of Israel. However, the conservative character of the country has led to frequent diplomatic crises with Egypt and Arab radical nationalists, who regard the kingdom as a reactionary vestige of an outmoded era.

In 1962, after the revolution in Yemen, the Saudi government sent military assistance to the ousted monarch of Yemen. Since Egypt at the same time supported the new republican government, a head-on clash loomed between the two countries. Direct conflict was averted when the United States and the United Nations elicited promises from both countries to desist from giving aid to Yemen.

Although Saudi Arabia did not participate in the 1967 war against Israel, the consequences of Arab defeat affected the country. As a result of Egypt's defeat, Saudi Arabia withdrew all troops from Yemen, making possible a peaceful settlement of the dispute. Saudi Arabia then established relations with the new Yemen republic. In July 1974 a long-held dispute with Abu Dhabi was settled.

King Faisal took the lead in rallying the Islamic world against Israeli occupation of Jerusalem and other Arab lands. Since the 1973 Arab-Israeli war, Saudi Arabia has given strong diplomatic and financial support to Egypt, Jordan, Syria, and the Palestinians. President Nixon visited Faisal in June 1974 and was told that there could be no Middle Eastern peace until Israel had withdrawn from Arab territories taken in the 1967 war, and the Palestinians had been granted sovereignty.

Saudi Arabia played a prominent role in efforts of the Organization of Petroleum Exporting Countries (OPEC) to obtain a larger share of income from oil produced by Western companies. By 1973 it became clear that oil would be used as a weapon against countries whose policies were disliked. Within a year, OPEC had quadrupled the price of oil per barrel, and a temporary embargo had been placed on shipments to the United States and the Netherlands. Meanwhile, by late 1976, Saudi Arabia had reached agreement with Aramco to assume complete control of the oil concession.

In the midst of this shift in power from the Western oil companies to the nations of the Middle East, Faisal was assassinated by a nephew during a reception at the royal palace on March 25, 1975. He was succeeded by his brother, Crown Prince Khalid.

DON PERETZ[*]
*Director, Program in Southwest Asian
and North African Studies
State University of New York, Binghamton*

Bibliography

De Gaury, Gerald, *Faisal, King of Saudi Arabia* (Praeger 1967).
Dickson, Harold R., *The Arab of the Desert*, 3d ed. (Barnes & Noble 1959).
Howarth, David, *The Desert King: Ibn Saud and His Arabia* (McGraw 1964).
Lipsky, George A., *Saudi Arabia: Its People, Its Society, Its Culture* (Human Relations 1959).
Philby, Harry St. John, *Saudi Arabia* (Praeger 1955).
Sanger, Richard H., *The Arabian Peninsula* (Cornell Univ. Press 1954).
Twitchell, Karl S., *Saudi Arabia*, 3d ed. (Princeton Univ. Press 1958).
Winder, R. Bayly, *Saudi Arabia in the Nineteenth Century* (St. Martins 1966).

SAUGUS, sô′gəs, a town in eastern Massachusetts, in Essex county, is a residential community, about 10 miles (16 km) north of Boston. The Saugus Iron Works National Historic Site attracts many tourists. It includes the Iron Master's House, a reconstruction of the first successful integrated ironworks in America. The historic building, built of English oak brought from England by the builder, contains a blast furnace, a forge, and a rolling and slitting mill. The old "Scotch" Boardman House is also of interest.

The town, originally called Hammersmith, was settled around 1630. The ironworks was established in 1643. Saugus was one of the first American communities to manufacture shoes and woolens. The town was incorporated in 1815. It has a council-manager form of government. Population: 24,746.

SAUK INDIANS, sôk, a North American tribe of Algonkian stock originally situated in eastern Michigan, where the Saginaw Bay is named for them. Woodland dwellers, they lived in bark lodges and cultivated vegetables but were generally more nomadic and more warlike than their neighbors.

The Sauk were first encountered by 17th century French Jesuit missionaries in the Green Bay area of Wisconsin, where they had fled before the advancing Iroquois. They became closely associated with the Fox after jointly taking up arms against the French in 1733. The united tribes moved to Missouri, where they were friendly with the Spaniards in the late 1770's; then to Illinois, where they came increasingly into conflict with the white settlers. In 1832 the Sauk fought the Black Hawk War over lands ceded to the U. S. government. Simultaneously they had to fight the Sioux, Omaha, and Menominee. Defeated by the U. S. Army, they succeeded in driving their Indian foes from Iowa and took refuge with the Fox there. See BLACK HAWK WAR; FOX INDIANS.

After further land cessions the Sauk moved to Kansas and finally to Indian Territory (Oklahoma) in 1867.

SAUL, sôl, was the first king of Israel. He reigned from about 1020 to about 1000 B. C. Much of the tradition about him is legendary, appropriate to the heroic age in which he lived. The short summary of his reign in the Bible (I Samuel 14:47–52) reads like an epitaph and is probably contemporary or at least based upon contemporary sources.

Saul was the son of Kish, a leading member of the tribe of Benjamin, and was born at the family home at Gibeah, near Jerusalem. His reign marked the transition from the old local rule of the judges to that of the kingship over the united nation. Although Saul's own territory was relatively small, he was a "king" whose rights were recognized by tribes other than his own. A powerful and successful warrior, he gained control of surrounding peoples in Moab, Ammon, Edom, Zobah, and the Philistine coast.

There are various accounts in the Bible of Saul's choice to be king, and of the beginning of kingship in Israel. Some viewed it as apostasy from the divine theocracy. This critical attitude of the kingship was probably a later view. According to others, God directed the prophet Samuel to anoint Saul as king at Gilgal. A third view is that popular demand raised Saul to kingly leadership, especially after his victories over the Ammonites (I Samuel 11). No doubt, as with the early kings of Greece, Rome, Scotland, England, and other lands, the initiative of the chieftain himself had much to do with his becoming king. Saul's reign was one of increasing peace and prosperity for the small land of Israel, and thus prepared for the greater reign of his favorite and successor, David. Precisely how long he reigned is not known, for the Hebrew text of I Samuel 13:1 is defective: "Saul was . . . years old when he began to reign; and he reigned . . . and two years over Israel. It is estimated that he reigned for 20 years.

The whole story of Saul, like the stories of the judges, is based on legend and oral tradition handed down for several generations. Its real significance, for the biblical writer or compiler, is the religious meaning it conveys. From the later or Deuteronomic point of view, which was strongly theocratic, the very idea of kingship was a mistake. Hence, in one of the stories, Samuel is described as warning the nation against choosing a king. The accounts of Saul's mental malady, his jealousy of David, his vengeance on the priests of Nob, his repulse of the Philistine invasion, the battle in the forest, his death by suicide, the hanging of his body and those of his sons on the walls of Beth Shean and their rescue by the loyal men of Jabesh—these are found in the later chapters of I Samuel and lead up to the beautiful elegy attributed to David in II Samuel 1:19–27. The whole story is straight from Israel's heroic age, and the interspersed lyrics belong to its "border ballads."

FREDERICK C. GRANT
Formerly, Union Theological Seminary

Further Reading: Albright, William F., *From Stone Age to Christianity* (Johns Hopkins 1940); Bright, John, *A History of Israel* (Westminster 1959).

SAULT SAINTE MARIE, sōō sänt mə-rē′, a city on the northeastern tip of Michigan's Upper Peninsula, the seat of Chippewa county. It is situated on the south bank of St. Mary's River, which forms the boundary between the United States and Canada, and on the Sault Ste. Marie Canals, which carry ship traffic between Lake Superior and Lake Huron. It is connected by bridge with Sault Ste. Marie, Ontario, which is directly across St. Mary's River.

The Michigan city is in an agricultural area that specializes in dairy farming and stock raising. Hydroelectric power is produced along the "Sault" (rapids) in the river. The maintenance of the canal locks, which handle a large part of the nation's freight ships, is important. The manufacture of lumber and veneer are the principal industries.

Lake Superior State College is in the city. Places of interest include the home of Henry Rowe Schoolcraft, the American ethnologist who had headquarters where he studied Indian life in the 1820's; the Chippewa County Historical Society, and the John Johnson Home (1796), which is one of the oldest houses in the state.

Étienne Brulé landed at the site of Sault Ste. Marie in 1618 when he was searching for a northwest passage. Other explorers followed, and in 1668 the Jesuits established a mission here under Father Jacques Marquette, making Sault Ste. Marie the oldest permanent settlement in Michigan. In 1787 the region became a U. S. territory by treaty with the French, and in 1820 Gen. Lewis Cass negotiated treaties with the

local Indians and built Fort Brady. The city was incorporated in 1887. It has a council-manager form of government. Population: 14,448.

SAULT SAINTE MARIE, sōō sänt mə-rē′, a city in central Ontario, Canada, the seat of Algoma county, is situated on the north bank of St. Mary's River, which serves as a boundary between Canada and the United States. On the opposite bank is the U. S. city of Sault Ste. Marie, Michigan. The city is in a forested region, where hunting and fishing are rewarding.

It is one of Canada's chief ports. Ships pass through its canal locks which circumvent the "Sault" (rapids) in St. Mary's River, thereby allowing traffic between lakes Superior and Huron. The most important industries are steel, paper, chemicals, and lumber.

Places of interest include Wosguhaegun, a replica of an early Hudson's Bay Company trading post, where pioneer life is reproduced. The museum on St. Joseph Island consists of a pioneer church, school, and barn.

The Sault Ste. Marie area was long popular among the Indians for its proximity to three of the Great Lakes—Superior, Huron, and Michigan. It was visited by French explorers, fur traders, and missionaries throughout the 17th century. A post was established by the North-West Fur Company in 1783. It was incorporated as a town in 1887 and as a city in 1912. Population: 82,697.

SAULT SAINTE MARIE CANALS, sōō sänt mə-rē′, are on the United States-Canada border, on the St. Marys River between the twin cities of Sault Ste. Marie, Mich., and Sault Ste. Marie, Ont. They are a vital link in the Great Lakes waterway, which carries a huge volume of ship and barge traffic, principally of iron ore and grain. They are often called the Soo Canals.

The river, which connects Lake Superior with Lake Huron, drops about 20 feet (6 meters). The canals, which are two parallel routes, one on the U. S. side and one on the Canadian, bypass the rapids of the river. Each was built and is operated by the nation in whose territory it is situated.

The canal on the Michigan side, which is 1.6 miles (2 km) long, has two channels. Each channel has two locks. Two of these locks are 1,350 feet (405 meters) long and 80 feet (24 meters) wide. They are among the largest locks in the world. The Canadian canal is 1.4 miles (2 km) long and has one lock.

The need for a canal to avoid the river's rapids and so complete a water route through the Great Lakes was recognized in the 18th century. A canal was built on the Canadian side in 1799, but was destroyed by American troops in the War of 1812. Beginning in 1855, construction was carried on by the U. S. and Michigan state government, with locks being replaced from time to time. The Canadian canal was built in 1895.

SAUMUR, sō-mür′, is a town in the Loire Valley of France, in Maine-et-Loire department, 28 miles (45 km) southeast of Angers. The main part of the town is on the south bank of the Loire River, but it also occupies an island and has spread to the north bank. Its chief products are dry and sparkling wines, religious articles, and mushrooms.

The town grew up under the protection of the château of the counts, later dukes, of Anjou. Several strongholds occupied its promontory. The present château was built in the late 14th century, altered in the 16th. The Church of Notre Dame de Nantilly has Romanesque and Gothic features and a splendid collection of tapestries. A Protestant bastion in the 16th century, Saumur declined after the Revocation of the Edict of Nantes (1685), when about half the inhabitants emigrated. It revived somewhat when France's noted cavalry school was established in the town in 1763. Much of the town was damaged in 1940. Population: (1971 est.) 21,551.

SAURASHTRA, sou-räsh′trə, is a peninsula in western India. It is also called Kathiawad (Kathiawar). See KATHIAWAR PENINSULA.

SAURISCHIAN, sô-ris′kē-ən, any of the "reptile hip" dinosaurs, one of the two major kinds of dinosaurs. Among the better-known saurischian dinosaurs was *Tyrannosaurus* and *Diplodocus*. See also DINOSAUR.

SAUROPODA, sô-rop′ə-də, any of a group of large plant-eating saurischian, or "reptile-hip," dinosaurs. See DINOSAUR.

SAUSAGE is chopped and seasoned meat usually stuffed into a long round casing, or skin. Sausage meat commonly is pork or a mixture of pork and beef, although other meats such as poultry and veal sometimes are used. Sausage casings are made from cleaned and soaked intestines of animals, reconstituted collagen, or cellulose materials.

Virtually all processed meats—frankfurters, bolognas, fresh and smoked sausage, luncheon meats and cold cuts, and specialties such as braunschweiger and slender-sliced varieties—are categorized as sausages.

The case of preparation and the wide selection of sizes, flavors, and ingredients have increased the popular demand for sausages of all types. As the age of casual living and convenience continues, the demand for sausage is expected to continue to grow.

Sausage products are excellent sources of protein, B vitamins, and minerals. Also, they are considered economical because there are no bones or waste.

More than 200 different kinds of sausages are marketed. They may be classified into five main groups: fresh sausage, uncooked smoked sausage, cooked sausage, cooked smoked sausage, and dry sausage.

Fresh sausage is made from selected cuts of fresh meat not previously cured. Pork usually is the main ingredient, although beef sometimes is used. This style of sausage includes fresh pork sausage in bulk, patty, chub, or link form and fresh country-style pork sausage. Fresh sausage must be kept under refrigeration, and it should be cooked thoroughly before being served. Frying, baking, broiling, and outdoor grilling are favorite methods of cooking pork sausage. Low cooking temperatures are advised.

Uncooked smoked sausage includes smoked country-style pork sausage and smoked country-style sausage, mettwurst (a fermented type), kielbasa, and Polish and Italian pork sausage. They should be kept under refrigeration and must be cooked before being served. Some varieties of

kielbasa and Polish and Italian sausage are precooked by the manufacturers. Also, some persons consider Italian sausage as fresh sausage.

Cooked sausage usually is prepared from fresh uncured meats, although occasionally some cured meats are used. Cooked sausages, which are thoroughly precooked and ready to serve, include cooked salami, kosher salami, cooked fresh and smoked thüringer, liver sausage, blood sausage, and tongue.

Cooked smoked sausage includes the frankfurter, bologna and berliner, wieners and Vienna-style sausage, garlic knoblauch or knackwurst sausage, and German-type mortadella. All of these have been smoked before, during, or after cooking. They may be served cold or heated.

Dry sausage is made in dozens of varieties. The two main kinds of dry sausages are salamis and cervelats; both are made in hard and soft styles. Salamis usually are more highly seasoned than cervelats. The amount and kind of spice used in their manufacture and the temperature of processing determine their flavor. Dry sausage products include farmer, holsteiner, thüringer, goettinger, goteborg, and landjaeger cervelats; alessandri, alpino, arles, German, kosher, Hungarian, and Italian salamis; frizzes, gothaer, cappicola, mortadella, lyons, pepperoni, and some chorizos. They keep indefinitely in a cool place and are ready to serve without cooking.

Historical Background. Sausages have been made at least since Greek and Roman times. Some sausage formulas were originated by the Spartans. The Romans made a sausage consisting of fresh pork and bacon finely minced with nuts and flavored with pepper, cumin seed, bay leaves, and potherbs. By the end of the 19th century, several European cities, including Milan, Bologna, Lyon, Frankfurt am Main, and Vienna (Wien), were noted for their sausages.

CHOLM G. HOUGHTON
American Meat Institute

SAUSAGE TREE, an African tree, *Kigelia pinnata,* that is widely grown in tropical climates because of its attractive flowers and unusual fruit. The tree grows to a height of 20 to 50 feet (6–15 meters) and has compound leaves and purplish red, bell-like flowers. The sausage-shaped fruits, which hang from cordlike stems, are 1 to 2 feet (0.3–0.6 meter) long and weigh from 5 to 12 pounds (2–5 kg).

SAUSSURE, sō-sür′, **Ferdinand de** (1857–1913), Swiss linguist, who had an important influence on the development of structural linguistics. Saussure was born in Geneva on Nov. 26, 1857, and was educated at the universities of Geneva, Leipzig (where he received a doctorate in 1880), and Berlin. He taught at the École des Hautes Études in Paris (1881–1891) and at the University of Geneva, where he was a professor of Indo-European linguistics and Sanskrit (1901–1913) and after 1907 also professor of general linguistics. His most important work was *Cours de linguistique générale* (1916; Eng. tr., *Course in General Linguistics*, 1959), a collection of his lectures published posthumously. Saussure and his followers held that since languages differ in all aspects of structure, they cannot be fitted into a general framework but must be studied separately. His work provided a basis for subsequent studies in structuralism. Saussure died in Geneva on Feb. 22, 1913.

SAUSSURE, sô-sür′, **Horace Bénédict de** (1740–1799), Swiss geologist and meteorologist and the first scientific explorer of the Alps. Saussure was born in Conches, near Geneva, on Feb. 17, 1740, the son of a Swiss agricultural expert, and became a professor of physics and philosophy at Geneva when he was 22 years old. In 1787, in the course of geological journeys, he became the first traveler (rather than guide) to reach the summit of Mont Blanc, where he measured the mountain's height barometrically. He described his Alpine travels in the four-volume *Voyages dans les Alpes* (1778–1796). Saussure's work on glaciers and the effects of erosion was important in the growth of geological interest in the study of mountains.

Saussure also discovered several minerals and developed the hair hygrometer approximately to its present form. He died in Geneva on Jan. 22, 1799.

Nicolas Théodore de Saussure (1767–1845), his son, was a pioneer in experimental physiology.

SAUTERNE, sô-tûrn′, is a sweet white wine that is produced from grapes grown around Sauternes, a village in Gironde department near Bordeaux, France. Similar types of wines are produced in other countries under this name.

SAUVEUR, sō-vûr′, **Joseph** (1653–1716), French physicist and mathematician who pioneered in establishing the field of musical acoustics. He was born in La Flèche, France, on March 24, 1653, and was named a professor of mathematics at the Collège de France in 1686. Sauveur died in Paris on July 10, 1716.

In 1700, Sauveur gave an explanation of stationary waves, using the concepts of node and antinode. That same year he discovered the beats produced by the interference of two waves of slightly different frequencies, and he established a fixed standard of pitch. Sauveur also studied vibrating strings and organ pipes and observed the existence of harmonics. In addition, he made experiments to determine the hearing limits of the human ear.

In mathematics, Sauveur successfully applied the calculus of probabilities in analyzing the results of games of chance.

SAVA RIVER, sä′vä, the longest river within Yugoslavia, with a length of 583 miles (938 km). The Sava Dolinka and Sava Bohinjka, its headstreams, rise in the extreme northwest in the Julian Alps and join near Radovljica. The Sava flows southeasterly through Slovenia, Croatia, where it is part of the Croatia-Bosnia border, and Serbia to join the Danube at Belgrade.

SAVAGE, Michael Joseph (1872–1940), New Zealand political leader, who was prime minister from 1935 to 1940. He was born in Benalla, Victoria, Australia, on March 7, 1872. After emigrating to New Zealand in 1907, he became active in that country's labor movement and was one of the principal founders of the Labour party in 1916.

Savage was elected to Parliament in 1919. He became deputy leader of the Labour party in 1923 and leader in 1933. He headed the election campaign that led to a Labour victory in 1935 and became prime minister, forming New Zealand's first Labour government. A wide range of social legislation was passed during his administration, including the establishment of a 40-hour work week, a public housing and works program, and farm price stabilization. Savage died in Wellington on March 26, 1940.

SAVAGE, Richard (1698?–1743), English poet and playwright, best known as the subject of one of the finest biographies in Samuel Johnson's *Lives of the English Poets*. He became Johnson's friend when Johnson first arrived in London.

Savage claimed to be the illegitimate son of Anne, Countess of Macclesfield, by Richard Savage, Earl Rivers, but that child probably died in infancy. More likely, Savage was the son of the illegitimate child's nurse, and was born in London, on Jan. 10, 1698.

After a scant education, Savage was apprenticed to a shoemaker, but he soon turned to literature. He published *The Convocation*, a poem about a religious controversy, in 1717. His comedy *Love in a Veil* was performed in 1718, followed in 1723 by his tragedy *Sir Thomas Overbury*, in which he played the title role. His best poems, *The Bastard* and *The Wanderer*, appeared in 1728 and 1729, respectively.

Savage killed a man in a tavern brawl in 1727 and escaped hanging only through the influence of Lady Hertford. He was granted a pension by Queen Caroline in 1732, but when she died in 1737, he was left without an income. Savage led a stormy life, getting into trouble repeatedly because of his satires and his way of life. Pope and other literary friends tried to help Savage, but he finally died in a debtors' prison in Bristol on Aug. 1, 1743.

SAVAII, sä-vī′ē, is one of the chief islands of Western Samoa. See SAMOA.

SAVANG VATTHANA, sä-väng vä-tä-nä (1907–), king of Laos, succeeded his father, King Sisavang Vong, in 1959. He was born on Nov. 13, 1907, and was educated in Paris. A conservative, Savang Vatthana accepted the restoration of French control over Laos in 1946 after World War II. In return for support of the Indochinese Federation, the French confirmed the sovereignty that his father, the king of Luang Prabang, had assumed over a unified Laos in 1945. As crown prince, Savang Vatthana often represented the throne in foreign affairs.

In 1975 the coalition government of neutralists, rightists, and the communist Pathet Lao, under Souvanna Phouma, collapsed, and Savang Vatthana abdicated. From 1975 to 1977 he acted as adviser to the People's Democratic Republic of Laos but was subsequently arrested.

CONSTANCE M. WILSON
Northern Illinois University

SAVANNA, sə-van′ə, a tropical or subtropical grassland that usually contains scattered trees and shrubs. It is also spelled savannah. It usually develops in areas where there is fairly heavy rainfall—40 to 60 inches (1.0–1.5 meters) a year—interrupted by distinct dry seasons. In the dry seasons, savannas are subject to extensive burning, and in some cases they are maintained through periodical burning or heavy grazing that restore nutrients to the soil.

The main areas of savannah in the world are in Africa, South America, Australia, and southern Asia. See also ECOLOGY—*Major Biomes of the World;* GRASSLAND—*Types of Grasslands.*

Shade trees draped with Spanish moss frame Wormsloe House (1733), a plantation house near Savannah, Ga.

SAVANNAH, sǝ-van'ǝ, in eastern Georgia, the seat of Chatham county, is built on a bluff overlooking the Savannah River 18 miles (29 km) west of its mouth on the Atlantic Ocean. It is 273 miles (440 km) by road southeast of Atlanta and 154 miles (248 km) north of Jacksonville, Fla. The city is the birthplace of the colony of Georgia, and it is among the most interesting historically.

Savannah's homes recall Georgian England. Its gardens and grilled gateways and fences are constant reminders of its past. The city is spotted with majestic, moss-veiled oaks, and is checkerboarded with parks and squares. The wealth of flowers and tropical plants gives it an atmosphere rare among American cities. Savannah's beauty is complemented with a mild climate. The nearby ocean moderates winter weather and tempers the summer heat.

The Savannah metropolitan area is highly industrialized. The principal products manufactured here are paper, refined sugar, wall board, superphosphates, synthetic nitrogen, asphalt roofing and other petroleum products, edible oils, paint pigments, metal containers, processed seafoods, wood products, trailer-truck bodies, and aircraft. The city is also an important center of shipbuilding and ship repair, and is a major land-water transshipping center.

Principal exports are lumber, naval stores, paper products, fertilizers, and machinery. Principal imports are petroleum products, titanium dioxide ore, gypsum rock, Chilean nitrates, and raw sugar. At one time, Savannah was the second-largest cotton port in the United States, but the growth of manufacturing has diminished the importance of cotton in the city.

Armstrong State College and Savannah State College provide 4-year degree programs. The Coastal Empire Arts Festival, a week-long event promoting the arts, is held every spring. Museums in Savannah include the Telfair Academy of Arts and Sciences, the Ships of the Sea Museum, the Savannah Science Museum, and the Factors' Walk Museum, with Civil War exhibits.

Savannah's history is commemorated by many monuments and old buildings. Efforts to preserve or restore many fine examples of early 19th century architecture have met with some success. In the early 1970's, the Historic Savannah Foundation purchased a number of old houses and restored certain areas to the distinction that they formerly possessed.

Points of interest in Savannah include the birthplace of Juliette Gordon Low, the founder of the Girl Scouts; the Georgia Historical Society; and Christ Episcopal Church, where John Wesley preached in 1736. The present building dates from 1840.

In Chippewa Square stands a bronze figure, executed by Daniel Chester French, honoring Gen. James Oglethorpe, the founder of Savannah. Fort Pulaski, near the city, is a national monument.

Gen. Oglethorpe founded Savannah in 1733. It became the seat of government when Georgia was made a royal province in 1754. In 1777, Savannah became the capital of the colony of Georgia, one of the original 13 colonies, but it was captured by the British the following year. Combined French and American troops failed to retake the city in a battle later that year, and Savannah remained in British possession until the close of the Revolutionary War.

The city was chartered in 1789, and rapidly grew as a cotton center. During the Civil War, it was a major Confederate supply depot. It was taken by Gen. William T. Sherman on Dec. 21, 1864, at the end of his March to the Sea. After the war it was slowly rebuilt as a cotton port. During the 20th century the city has turned toward manufacturing.

Savannah is governed by a mayor and council. Population: metropolitan area (including all of Chatham county): 230,728; the city, 141,390.

311

SAVARY, sȧ-vȧ-rē', **Anne Jean Marie René** (1774–1833), French general. He was born in Marcq, Ardennes, on April 26, 1774, and joined an infantry regiment in 1790. In 1798 he served as aide-de-camp to General Desaix on the French expedition to Egypt. After the Battle of Marengo in 1800, he was appointed adjutant to Bonaparte and soon rose high in his confidence, playing a key role in the execution of the Duke d'Enghien in 1804. He became a division commander in 1805.

In 1808, Bonaparte sent Savary to Madrid, where he conducted the negotiations that led to the kidnapping of Spain's Ferdinand VII in Bayonne, France. Created duke de Rovigo, Savary succeeded Joseph Fouché as minister of police in 1810. On Bonaparte's return from Elba in 1815, Savary reaffirmed his allegiance to the Emperor and was appointed inspector general of gendarmes. He was imprisoned in 1815 on Malta, where he began his *Memoirs*, but escaped after seven months. He returned to France in 1819 and was acquitted on charges of contributing to Napoleon's flight from exile. In 1831–1833 he returned to active duty as military commander of Algiers. He died in Paris on June 2, 1833.

SAVATE, sȧ-vat', was a French form of boxing in which the contestants used their feet rather than their fists. Its name is taken from the French word *savate* ("old shoe"). The sport was popular in France, particularly among the lower classes in the cities, before the introduction of the English form of boxing. Savate was most in vogue during the 18th century. Thai boxing, a favorite sport in Thailand, is similar to savate.

In an attempt to retain, in the face of the growing popularity of English boxing, some aspects of the historic French sport, Charles Lecour and his son Hubert developed *la boxe française* ("French boxing") in the 19th century. This new sport combined kicking with punching with the fists. Although there was some initial enthusiasm for the sport, French boxing never gained wide acceptance and in the 20th century was confined to infrequent exhibitions.

SAVERY, sā'vər-ē, **Thomas** (c. 1650–1715), English inventor. Savery was born in Shilstone, near Plymouth, about 1650. He became a military engineer and also experimented with mechanical devices. His most significant invention, a machine for raising water, was the first practical mechanical application of steam power. The pumping device was not used in mines, as had been intended, but it was used in water supply systems for country houses and for mill wheels. The patent, granted in 1698, was later extended to 1733. Thus Thomas Newcomen had to enter partnership with Savery in order to exploit his own invention, the first truly successful steam engine. Savery died in London in May 1715.

SAVIGNY, säv'in-yē, **Friedrich Karl von** (1779–1861), German jurist. He was born in Frankfurt am Main, on Feb. 21, 1779, and was educated at the universities of Marburg, Jena, Leipzig, and Halle. He taught law at the universities of Marburg, Landshut, and Berlin, and from 1842 to 1848 he was minister for the revision of legislation in Prussia.

In the field of legal philosophy, Savigny is considered by many the founder or at least the leading exponent of the "historical school" of jurisprudence. Early in 1814, Anton Friedrich Justus Thibaut, a professor of law at Heidelberg, had advocated the codification of German law, both as a means of rationalizing the law and of bringing the German states closer together. Other writers suggested adopting already existing codes, such as those of France, Austria, or even Prussia. Savigny attacked all these proposals. He denounced the current theories of rationalism, which assumed the possibility of deducing legal theories from general and universal principles, irrespective of past history and national peculiarities. Savigny contended that law is an expression of the common consciousness of the people, or *Volksgeist*, in just the same way as their language and constitution are. Law, he argued, can grow only organically and almost unconsciously, and not by means of formal rational legislation. His attack on codification was so successful that Germany did not get a civil code until 1900.

As part of his thesis, Savigny emphasized the importance of knowing and understanding the history of law. His works included a standard history of Roman law in the Middle Ages, *Geschichte des römischen Rechts im Mittelalter* (6 vols., 1815–1831). This was of immense importance as the first "modern" history of the subject using the now standard critical techniques, based on a vast amount of research into primary sources. It can largely be credited with creating a group of scholars interested in legal history.

Possibly Savigny's other most important work was his *System of Modern Roman Law* (8 vols., 1840–1849), a detailed and scholarly analysis of Roman law as developed in Europe. Most modern scholarship in the field is indebted to it.

In Germany, Savigny's influence on law teaching was immense. He had a hand in founding one university, Berlin, and advising on the improvement of others, such as Heidelberg. The fact that a man of his aristocratic background had entered the teaching profession and fought for its advance had an important impact in a country as conscious of aristocracy as Germany was at the time. He died in Berlin on Oct. 25, 1861.

B. J. HALÉVY, *Osgoode Hall Law School of York University, Toronto*

SAVILE, sav'əl, **George** (1633–1695), English political leader and essayist. He was born in Thornhill, Yorkshire, on Nov. 11, 1633. He was educated in Shrewsbury, and in France and Italy.

On the death of Cromwell, Savile distinguished himself by his exertions on behalf of Charles II. In 1669 he was appointed a commissioner of trade, in 1672 became a member of the privy council, and in 1682 was created 1st Marquis of Halifax and lord privy seal. Under James II, Lord Halifax was made president of the council, but he was dismissed from office because he opposed the repeal of the test and habeas corpus acts. From this time Halifax continued in opposition and contributed to the elevation of William III to the throne. He died on April 5, 1695, in London.

Halifax was the author of a variety of political tracts, which were admired for their combination of irony and vigorous statement. His principal pamphlets included *Maxims of State, The Character of a Trimmer, Character of King Charles II, Anatomy of an Equivalent,* and *Letter to a Dissenter.* An edition of his complete works was published in 1912.

SAVINGS, in economic theory and analysis, are the portion of current income that is not spent on currently consumed goods and services. Individuals or business firms *save* when they spend less than their full income on current consumption. They *dissave* when their expenditures on current consumption exceed their income.

The process of saving obviously increases the net assets of the saver. This is true not only for individuals and businesses but also for national economies. In fact, savings and the growth of assets play a critical role in a nation's economic growth.

The ability of a society to add to its stock of productive equipment and other capital assets is limited by the volume of savings that is available. If a high proportion of national income is devoted to the purchase of goods and services for current consumption, the rate of savings will be low. Then the bulk of a nation's productive capacity will be used for the output of goods and services that, while satisfying current wants and needs, do not add to the nation's productive facilities. This situation is characteristic of most underdeveloped countries, where a low level of income makes it difficult to sustain personal and business savings. In wealthier industrialized nations, on the other hand, the level of personal and business income readily accommodates a relatively high savings rate. The resultant savings permit increased investment in machines, education, resource development, and other sources of expanded output. The savings add to the productiveness of human labor and make a valuable contribution to the rising standards of living.

Importance of Savings Units. Savers may be classified into three broad categories: (1) individuals, (2) business corporations, and (3) government. The extent to which each of these sectors contributes to total national savings varies widely from one country to another. Personal and business savings tend to be proportionately larger in the more advanced countries, particularly in those with free-enterprise economies. In contrast, government savings assume greater importance in underdeveloped nations and in nations with a high measure of state control over industry and commerce.

In the United States, household savings represent by far the most important source of total national savings. Long-run trends indicate that U. S. households—including farms and unincorporated business enterprises—save about 12% of income after taxes. This includes savings through the purchase of consumer durable goods. Fluctuations around this long-term average include substantial advances in the savings rate during periods of prosperity and full employment, followed by declines in periods of economic recession and increasing unemployment. Most households are net savers over the years, as is evidenced by the small proportion of households having no net worth. In total, the factor of household savings generally accounts for roughly three fourths of total annual savings in the United States.

Corporate savings in the United States tend to average about 35% of corporate income after taxes and dividend payments, although this rate is subject to wide fluctuations as business conditions change. Since World War II, local and state governments have established an annual savings rate of about 5%, and the federal government has saved annually between 5 and 10% of its current revenues.

The Utilization of Savings. To some extent in the United States, and to an even greater extent in most other countries, a substantial portion of total savings funds is employed directly by the savers themselves. A substantial part of individual savings, for example, is employed in the purchase of homes and durable goods. Similarly, the savings of many business corporations are used directly for the acquisition of plant, equipment, and other capital assets. In the case of government, savings most often represent the outlay of current revenues for such projects as streets, schools, hospitals, and other forms of public investment.

Many savings units accumulate savings far in excess of their need for real investment in tangible assets. In advanced countries, a variety of institutions channel these savings funds into productive uses. The most important of these institutions are commercial banks, savings banks, savings and loan associations, and insurance companies. Each of these types of institution receives a more or less steady inflow of savings funds, which through the lending process are placed at the disposal of savings users. Through a somewhat different process, investment banking houses engaged in marketing corporate and municipal securities also serve to channel savings funds into productive channels.

An individual's savings may be reflected in several ways. If he utilizes the savings funds directly, the process of saving probably will be reflected in increased ownership of real property. On the other hand, the savings may result in increased ownership of financial assets, such as bank balances, shares in savings and loan associations, stocks and bonds, or some other form of liquid assets. In the latter case, the proceeds of the individual's savings have been placed at the disposal of other economic units.

Motives for Saving. The considerations that may stimulate individuals to save are not subject to precise enumeration, but at least the following motives appear to be of major importance: (1) the desire to provide for future contingencies, both expected and unexpected; (2) the desire to acquire durable tangible assets (particularly household assets) that add to the convenience or pleasure of living; and (3) financial reward.

The manner in which individuals manage their savings funds bears a close relationship to the particular purpose for which savings are accumulated. Savings in the form of contributions to retirement funds, life insurance premium payments, and participation in Christmas savings clubs, for example, are manifestations of the desire to provide for future contingencies.

GROWTH OF SAVINGS DEPOSIT OF $100

(At selected rates of interest, compounded monthly)

Years	5%	5½%	6%	7%	8%
1	105.12	105.64	106.17	107.23	108.30
2	110.49	111.60	112.72	114.98	117.29
3	116.15	117.89	119.67	123.29	127.02
4	122.09	124.55	127.05	132.21	137.57
5	128.34	131.57	134.89	141.76	148.98
10	164.70	173.11	181.94	200.97	221.96

Interest as an Incentive. The capacity of savings funds to earn a rate of return, in the form of interest, provides an incentive to save. This is true even in those instances where savings funds are not being set aside for the purchase of specific durable assets. The ability of savers to obtain financial reward from direct investment in capital assets, or from lending their funds to direct investors, has long been considered a major stimulant to savings.

Even in the Soviet Union, for example, the state bank follows the practice of paying interest on savings funds deposited with it by individuals. This practice represents not only a departure from Communist ideology but also a recognition of the importance of savings to the achieving of economic growth.

Besides encouraging savings, interest rates also serve the function of allocating savings funds to those sectors of the economy in which savings can be used most profitably. With allowances for the degree of risk involved, savings will tend to flow into the hands of those users who can put the funds to most profitable use, because those users will be able to pay higher rates of interest for the use of savings funds.

LESLIE C. PEACOCK
Crocker-Citizens National Bank, San Francisco

Further Reading: Goldsmith, Raymond W., *A Study of Saving in the United States,* 3 vols. (Princeton Univ. Press 1955–1956); Heller, Walter W., and others, eds., *Savings in the Modern Economy: A Symposium* (Univ. of Minn. Press 1953).

SAVINGS AND LOAN ASSOCIATIONS are financial institutions whose main function is to promote thrift and home ownership. For savers, they provide a way to set aside funds, and they offer the safety of insurance, a reasonable rate of return, and ready access to those funds. For borrowers, they provide financing for home ownership with a mortgage tailored to needs. These associations are often referred to as "specialty shops of finance" because of their emphasis on home financing.

Savings associations are the leading source of home financing in the United States and hold over 40% of the total home mortgage debt outstanding. They rank second only to commercial banks as thrift institutions that accept the liquid assets of individuals. The associations have been the fastest growing type of financial institution in the years since World War II.

Savings associations conduct operations in all 50 states and in the District of Columbia, Puerto Rico, and Guam. Pennsylvania has the greatest number of associations, but California ranks first in the dollar amount held by institutions.

Organization. For the most part, savings associations operate as local institutions. Most of their savers live near the association, most of the loans held by the association are granted on properties situated within a short distance of the office, and the association's board of directors is made up mainly of local persons, who are familiar with the community.

Every savings and loan association operates under a charter, which is a contract between a government agency and the association. The charter enables the association to operate as a corporation and specifies the conditions under which it can operate. An association may obtain a charter from the federal government through the Federal Home Loan Bank Board, or from its own state through the state's supervisory authority.

Most savings associations operate as mutual organizations. In those cases, they do not issue capital stock—the savers and borrowers are the owners of the institution. Federal regulations require that all federally chartered associations be mutual institutions. Most states permit only mutual institutions, but some states authorize both mutual and permanent stock companies. Permanent stock companies are different from mutual institutions in that they issue capital stock, and the stockholders are owners of the corporation.

Practically every phase of operation of a savings and loan association, whether under federal or state charter, is covered by legislation and regulation. The institutions are closely supervised and subject to periodic examination to determine the extent to which their operations are in accord with laws and regulations, to evaluate their financial condition, to establish the integrity and accuracy of their records, and, finally, to ensure the safety and efficiency of their procedures in conducting day-to-day business operations.

Savings Facilities. Savings associations offer a wide range of accounts from which to choose. The regular savings account may be opened with any amount, and additions may be made in any amount at any time. Investment certificates are available to those who wish to make a lump-sum investment. These certificates are usually issued in fixed amounts, and withdrawals are made for the full amount of the certificate. Most associations also offer special types of accounts for the systematic saver who wishes to put aside a definite amount of money each week or each month.

The savings contract is also flexible as to the ownership of the account. Available variations include individual accounts, multiple-owner accounts, trust accounts, and corporation and organization accounts.

Savings associations pay out dividends to savers for use of their funds. Dividends may be credited directly to the saver's account and are compounded if left in the account. Dividends also may be paid out to the saver by check. Savings associations commonly return a somewhat higher yield to their savers than other similar types of investments.

Investment Powers. Savings associations invest the bulk of their funds in loans secured by a mortgage on real estate. The association has a legal claim against certain parcels of real property should the borrower default on his obligation to repay the loan. Thus, the association's loans are backed up by a claim against real property through which the association may seek to recover its investment.

Most loans held by savings associations are secured by an amortized mortgage on single-family, owner-occupied residences. These loans are made to construct a new home or to purchase an existing home. Other loans may be made on apartments, shopping centers, industrial parks, churches, motels, hotels, or other real properties. Some savings associations may make loans to finance the education of college students.

The loans held by associations differ in the interest rate, the down payment, and the term or maturity. The differences depend on the degree of risk involved and conditions in the market. The level of risk is determined through analysis of the ability of the borrower to repay the debt, along with the ability of the property to stand as security for the debt over a prolonged period of time.

Many associations also make some use of programs sponsored by the Federal Housing Administration and the Veterans Administration. The major portion of the loans held by associations, however, are conventional loans based on the association's own mortgage plan, without government guarantee or insurance.

Most loans granted by savings associations are direct-reduction loans. The borrower agrees to repay the debt in equal monthly installments over a fixed period. The monthly payment is used first to cover the interest charge, and second to reduce the amount of principal outstanding. Interest is charged each month on the balance outstanding. As a result, the proportion of the monthly payment used to cover interest declines gradually as the principal is repaid, and the proportion applied to reduce the principal increases gradually.

Savings associations offer many other flexible features in a mortgage loan contract. For example, many associations permit the borrower to pay off his loan ahead of the contract schedule without incurring a penalty for prepayment. Another flexible provision that is often used enables the borrower to obtain additional funds under specified conditions without having to rewrite the existing mortgage.

Federal Home Loan Bank (FHLB) System. Congress established the Federal Home Loan Bank System in 1932 to serve as a central credit organization for the savings and loan business. The system is composed of (1) the Federal Home Loan Bank Board, (2) 12 regional Federal Home Loan banks, and (3) the member institutions. All federal savings and loan associations must be members. State-chartered associations may become members upon application and approval of the FHLB.

An important function of the system is to provide associations with a source of funds that would enable them to meet unusual withdrawal demands from savers. In addition, the Federal Home Loan banks were set up to help member institutions meet the demand for mortgage funds when the immediate inflow of savings dollars is not sufficient to do the job. Another important responsibility of the system is to supervise the nationwide system of federal savings and loan associations.

Federal Savings and Loan Insurance Corporation (FSLIC). Similar in purpose and structure to the Federal Deposit Insurance Corporation, the FSLIC was created in 1934 to stimulate confidence in thrift and home-financing institutions. The majority of savings and loan associations are members of the FSLIC, and state-chartered associations that qualify are eligible to become members. The FSLIC guarantees that every saver with an account in a member association will get back every dollar he has invested, up to $20,000 per account. If an insured institution defaults, the government agency undertakes to reimburse each qualified, insured account for the full amount covered by the insurance provisions as soon as possible. Reimbursement may be by cash payment or by making available another account, equal to the insured account, in a newly formed institution in the same community or in another insured institution.

History. Savings associations in the United States are direct descendants of the British building societies organized in the 1770's. The Oxford Provident Building Association, organized in 1831 in Frankford, Pa. (now a part of Philadelphia), was the first such organization in the United States.

The first associations were all voluntary and incorporated. There was no public supervision of their activities. Members subscribed to a certain number of shares in the organization, toward which they made monthly payments. When sufficient funds were available for a loan, members submitted bids for the use of the funds to purchase a home or to finance the building of one. When the last member paid his loan and the shares matured, the organization was declared to be terminated.

During the 1850's a more permanent form of organization became popular. In contrast to the earlier terminating association that issued a single series of stock and dissolved after each member had received a loan, the serial plan involved issuing successive series of stocks so that the association continued in existence despite termination of individual series.

The next stage of development resulted from a growing preference of members for the permanent share plan. Under this plan, which began its rise to prominence in the 1870's, shares were issued at any time. The associations began to establish separate accounts for each savings customer.

Savings associations grew steadily during the late 1800's and early 1900's. The rise of the savings and loan business to leadership in thrift and home financing took place in the decade following World War II. Challenged by a great postwar housing shortage, savings and loan managements developed a broader outlook on their mission and placed great emphasis on attractive quarters, choice locations, and business-promotion activities.

Effective trade organizations existed at the national and state levels. Key statutory changes took place in the 1950's at the federal and state levels, enabling associations to provide more flexible mortgage contracts and more flexible savings plans. But the underlying source of the postwar growth was the sound basic purpose of savings and loan associations: to promote thrift and home ownership.

ARTHUR M. WEIMER
Indiana University

SAVINGS BANK. See BANKS AND BANKING— *Mutual Savings Banks.*

SAVINGS BONDS are debt obligations issued by governmental bodies to tap the savings of individuals. To make these securities as attractive as possible to the general public, governments usually sell them in small denominations and at many locations. Savings bonds often offer especially attractive terms not made available to purchasers of other securities offered by the same government. For this reason, savings bonds often are not eligible for purchase by commercial banks or other types of financial institutions.

Why Bonds Are Issued. When a government is eager to induce individuals to purchase savings bonds, it is almost always attempting to avoid inflationary pressures on the economy. A government borrows money because its level of spending has exceeded the amount of revenue obtained through tax collections. If the government can attract the savings of the populace into purchase of government securities, then savings already in the hands of the public will be turned over to the government and will finance the deficit—the gap between the level of government spending and the amount of tax collections.

If the savings of the public cannot be tapped, the deficit nevertheless must be financed, because the government must pay for all the goods and services it has purchased. In such a case, the government must either print new money or borrow from financial institutions. Often the only way the government can borrow from financial institutions is by allowing the commercial banking system to create new deposit money and pay for the government bonds with this newly created money.

Whether the government prints new money or borrows newly created money from the commercial banks or from the central bank, the final result is the same, because more money has been created. If the nation is not able to increase its output of goods and services, this increased money supply will lead to price and wage increases and inflationary pressure. Thus governments try to finance their deficits by borrowing from the public as much as they possibly can in periods when the economy is near capacity operation and cannot expand its output—a condition that occurs, for instance, in wartime.

Advantages and Disadvantages. To the public, the advantage of savings bonds is usually their high degree of safety. Because they are guaranteed by the government, they are as riskless as the nation's currency itself. Generally they are offered with terms for repayment fixed in advance so that the buyer is sure of the redemption value if he needs to get his investment money back before the bonds mature.

In some cases, however, because the amount of repayment has been determined in advance and because the amount of interest income paid has been fixed, savings bonds have failed to attract the public. Rising prices and pressures of inflation make fixed-income securities unattractive to savers, because the amount returned on maturity—even with interest added—often buys fewer goods and services than the money originally invested could have purchased at the time the securities were bought. Therefore some nations have issued savings bonds whose redemption value and interest are not fixed in advance, but are tied to some other item that reflects changes in the value of the currency over time, such as a cost-of-living index, the price of gold coins, or the cost of electric power. Britain has had savings bonds on which no interest is paid. Instead, all the interest that would accrue to holders of the bond issue is pooled and then distributed to the winners of a lottery in which only these savings-bond holders participate.

Because tapping the savings of the public is often so important to a nation's economic stability, the promotional efforts devoted to selling savings bonds often exceed those connected with the sale of all other government securities.

PAUL S. NADLER, *New York University*

SAVINKOV, sȧ′vyin-kôf, **Boris Viktorovich** (1879–1925), Russian revolutionary, who opposed both the czarist and Bolshevik regimes. While a student in St. Petersburg (now Leningrad) in the late 1890's, he joined the Socialist Revolutionary party. He became a leading member of its most militant wing and helped arrange the assassinations of V. K. Plehve, the interior minister and

police chief, in 1904 and Grand Prince Sergei in 1905. Arrested and sentenced to death, he escaped to Switzerland in 1906.

He served in the French Army during World War I and returned to Russia after the revolution in early 1917. In August he was appointed vice minister of war in Aleksandr Kerensky's government. Savinkov opposed the Bolshevik takeover and promoted revolts in Russia before fleeing in late 1918. He subsequently tried to organize resistance from Poland until the Polish-Soviet treaty in 1921. Apprehended while secretly attempting to reenter Russia in 1924, he was condemned to death, but the sentence was commuted to 10 years' imprisonment. He reportedly committed suicide in prison in Moscow.

SAVOIE, sȧ-vwȧ′, is a department in southeastern France in the Savoy Alps, on the Italian border. It was formed in 1860 from the southern half of Savoy, a region ceded to France by the kingdom of Sardinia. The Rhône River forms its northern boundary, separating it from Haute-Savoie. The capital is Chambéry. Tourism is a mainstay of the economy, and there are numerous ski resorts. There are hydroelectric stations in the mountains, and agriculture is carried on in the valleys. The area is 2,389 square miles (6,187 sq km). Population: (1971) 298,500.

SAVONA, sä-vō′nä, is a Mediterranean seaport in northwestern Italy, in the region of Liguria. It is the capital of Savona province, a hilly area in which vegetables, wine grapes, flowers, olives, and other fruits are raised. The city is situated amid vine-covered hills and orange groves on the Riviera, 25 miles (40 km) southwest of Genoa. The late Renaissance cathedral, completed in 1602, is near the Sistine Chapel, built by Pope Sixtus IV. Also of interest are the 16th century Church of St. John the Baptist, the castle (1542), and the museum and art gallery.

The city is a center of the iron industry and also manufactures machinery, glass, leather, and sulfur. Its port handles imports of coal, petroleum, iron, and grain and exports of foodstuffs and manufactured products.

As Savo the city was a thriving commercial center under the Romans. It was also prosperous during the Middle Ages until its capture by the Genoese in 1528. After World War II its economy was helped by new superhighways linking it with Genoa and Turin. Population: (1969 est.) of the city, 78,700; of the province, 289,100.

SAVONAROLA, sä-vō-nä-rô′lä, **Girolamo** (1452–1498), Italian friar and religious reformer, who exerted great influence in Florence during the 1490's. His uncompromising character eventually alienated many people and helped to bring about his fall and martyrdom.

Early Life. He was born in Ferrara on Sept. 21, 1452, into a family of cultured merchants attached to the court of the Este family, which ruled Ferrara. He received strict moral training and an early education of a medieval and scholastic nature from his grandfather, a physician and scientist. After studying Latin, drawing, and music, Savonarola undertook humanistic studies at Ferrara, winning a mastership in liberal arts. He then began to study medicine.

But he was more attracted to the study of theology and still more to religious meditation and asceticism. In 1475 he abandoned his studies and his family to enter the monastery of San Domenico at Bologna, considered the leading as well as the most severe of the Dominican order in Italy. Very little need be noted of his novitiate years there. Probably upon the insistence of his superiors, he was trained to deliver sermons and to teach. Having completed theological studies, he was sent to Florence in 1482 to serve as a reader at the monastery of San Marco.

First Years in Florence. At that time Florence was the intellectual and cultural center of the peninsula, the cradle of humanism and of the Renaissance. For centuries the guide and model in the political evolution of the Italian communes, it was under the ambitious and enlightened rule of the powerful Medici family, represented in these years by Lorenzo the Magnificent. In such a setting, Savonarola's visions of a moral reformation, a religious renewal, and a political restoration based upon democratic principles acquired new worth, greater urgency, and universal meaning.

Savonarola began speaking in minor churches and monasteries and also (1484) in San Lorenzo, the parish church of the Medici, with little or no success. To the Florentines, who were accustomed to elegant humanistic rhetoric, Savonarola spoke in an unadorned style. His crude pronunciation was obscured by peculiarities of dialect, and he used biblical references instead of the poetic and classical allusions then in fashion. Sermonizing at San Gimignano in 1485–1486, he began to speak in a prophetic vein, inspired by increasing asceticism and by revelations. In these years he composed his famous poem *Oratio pro ecclesia*.

He left Florence in 1487 to become a master in the studium (school of theology) of the Dominican monastery at Bologna. In the following years he preached at Ferrara, Mantua, Brescia, Pavia, and Genoa. In 1490, at the request of his friend and admirer Giovanni Pico della Mirandola, he was called back to Florence by Lorenzo. Soon after his return in 1491 he was elected prior of San Marco. He did not thank Lorenzo for this appointment, as was customary, nor did he acknowledge Lorenzo's rich gifts to the monastery.

Broadening his activities as a reader, he took up sermonizing again, first in San Marco, then (1491) in the cathedral, and (1492) again in San Lorenzo, winning greater success with the people, who were stirred by his inspired and fiery words. At this time he was called to the deathbed of Lorenzo to give his blessing. That he refused to give Lorenzo his benediction is a legend invented by his followers, the *Piagnoni* (weepers).

In 1493 he spoke at Bologna in a still more prophetic vein, calling for repentance in view of the imminent invasion of Charles VIII of France and the election of the dissipated and ambitious Cardinal Rodrigo Borgia to the pontificate as Alexander VI. At this time Savonarola succeeded in having the monastery of San Marco separated from the Lombard congregation, thus attaining an autonomy that facilitated his reform of the Dominican order. This reform he hoped to extend to the city of Florence and from there to all Christianity.

Charles VIII's arrival in Tuscany drove Lorenzo's son, Piero de' Medici, from Florence in 1494. The friar's pacificatory counsels prevented excessive violence in this political overturn. Sev-

ALINARI—ART REFERENCE BUREAU

SAVONAROLA was martyred when he attempted to reform Florentine government and the Catholic Church.

eral times Savonarola acted as an ambassador to the French King, and his actions increased the conqueror's respect for the city, which his troops soon evacuated on Nov. 28, 1494. Florence, for its part, pursued a policy of friendship toward France, in spite of threats from the Pope, Holy Roman Emperor Maximilian I, Venice, Milan, and Spain, who were joined together in the "Holy League."

Height of Influence. Florence again became a republic, almost isolated among the other Italian states, but inspired by the words and example of the friar who was regarded as a prophet and worker of miracles. The time had come to set up a democratic government that would make it possible to achieve Savonarola's ideals for reform. The constitution of 1494 was intended to transform Florence into a perfect Christian and civil republic, on a theocratic base but without clerical domination. It resembled that of Venice, where interference by the church was avoided.

This political arrangement remained unchanged until 1530, except for periods of Medici rule, and soon resulted in a complete reform of public life and morality. The Florentines again experienced spiritual fervor, industry, austerity, and sobriety. *Monti di pietà* (pawnshops under religious jurisdiction) were established, and the system of taxation was revised. During the carnivals of 1497 and 1498 the *bruciamenti della vanità* (burning of the vanities) took place, in which immoral books and frivolous objects were burned on the Piazza della Signoria. It is highly improbable that valuable works of art were destroyed in these bonfires. Savonarola showed the highest consideration for art, and artists like Sandro Botticelli, Michelangelo, Simone Pollaiuolo, and Fra Bartolommeo drew inspiration from him.

Nevertheless, many were dissatisfied, either because of personal interests or because they favored the return of the Medici. His opponents were known as *Compagnacci* (bad company), *Palleschi* (ballers, from the gold balls on the Medici arms), and *Arrabbiati* (angry ones). Although Piero de' Medici attempted unsuccessfully in 1497 to return to Florence, he usually preferred using indirect methods, pleading for the Pope's intervention. Alexander VI had invited Savonarola to Rome in 1495, but the friar, citing poor health, declined the invitation. In the months that followed he was ordered by the Pope to abstain from sermonizing. When this ban seemed to be lifted in 1496, he began his famous sermons on the prophet Amos, castigating Roman corruption. In the same year he gave his sermons on the prophecies of Micah, and, during Advent, the terrible ones on Ezekiel, continuing them in 1497. The Pope offered him a cardinal's hat, but Savonarola refused it, clearly indicating his determination to become a martyr rather than a compromiser.

Fall and Martyrdom. Famine, war, and plague afflicted Florence, increasing Savonarola's difficulties, which were made more acute by governments favorable to the Medici. In May 1497, incited by the friar's enemies, Alexander VI issued a papal letter of excommunication, the validity of which was dubious and which the Pope himself seemed to regret. In February 1498, outraged by the proposal that he receive absolution in return for Florence's entering the anti-French league, Savonarola returned to the cathedral pulpit to preach on Exodus. The city was threatened with an interdict if he was not surrendered to Rome, and the chief magistrates ordered him to stop his sermons. In San Marco, Savonarola contemplated the possibility of summoning a council for the reform of the church, but he took no action.

When Savonarola was challenged to a "test by fire" by a Franciscan friar, Francesco di Puglia, his disciple Fra Domenico da Pescia volunteered to undergo the test. The trial did not take place because of the evasions of the challengers, but the sympathy of the populace was alienated from Savonarola when the spectacle failed to materialize. The following day, Palm Sunday, a turbulent crowd besieged San Marco, demanding Savonarola's surrender. When the chief magistrates issued an order for his appearance, he presented himself at the Palazzo Vecchio. He was imprisoned, and outbreaks of violence against the friar and his followers ensued.

Tried for heresy, Savonarola underwent grueling cross-examination and cruel torture. Confessions extorted from him were read to the populace in his absence. After a third and last trial, the Apostolic commissioners pronounced him and his brother friars Domenico da Pescia and Silvestro Maruffi "heretics and schismatics." Delivered to the secular arm, they were hanged and their bodies were burned on the Piazza della Signoria on May 23, 1498, in the presence of the entire populace. Their ashes were scattered in the Arno, but various relics were collected by devout citizens. The sentiments of the *Arrabbiati* prevailed throughout the city for a while, but the *Piagnoni* soon regained their strength, and the republic lasted until 1512.

Evaluation. Incorruptible, although excessively severe, Savonarola was personally above suspicion, filled with sincere zeal, and always

obedient in spite of his rebellious attitude. The spiritual reform he envisioned was based on his own inner perfection, and he wished to carry it into effect "within" the church, acting according to the dictates of Christian conscience. Living at a time of crisis—a spiritual and religious crisis, a crisis of humanistic culture and of national politics—he sought to channel the ferment of the age into a vast reform based on his own ideals.

Although Savonarola was well aware of the church's decadence and the unworthiness of some of the popes, he always remained loyal and obedient to the church itself, accepting his unjust condemnation as a necessary sacrifice. For this reason, in spite of apparent resemblances, he differs profoundly from the later religious reformers. His rehabilitation began immediately after his death, and his doctrine, when examined by synods and councils, was always adjudged perfectly orthodox.

Bibliography

De La Bedoyère, Michael, *The Meddlesome Friar and the Wayward Pope* (Doubleday 1958).

Ridolfi, Roberto, *Life of Girolamo Savonarola*, tr. by Cecil Grayson (Knopf 1959).

Roeder, Ralph, *Savonarola: A Study in Conscience* (Brentano 1930).

Symonds, John Addington, *The Age of the Despots*, new ed. (Putnam 1960).

Van Paassen, Pierre, *A Crown of Fire* (Scribner 1960).

T. H. EVERETT

Winter savory (*Satureia montana*)

SAVORY, săv′ə-rē, any of several aromatic mints of the genus *Satureia*, especially summer savory, *S. hortensis*, and winter savory, *S. montana*, which are used in cookery. Summer savory is an erect annual that grows up to 12 inches (30 cm) tall. It has pink flowers and oval leaves, the latter being used for flavoring meats, soups, salads, or other dishes. Winter savory is an erect perennial that grows up to 16 inches (40 cm) tall. It has tough lance-shaped leaves, which are used in cookery to give a flavor similar to that of thyme.

Savories are native to lands bordering the Mediterranean Sea, but they now are widely grown in home gardens.

SAVOY, sə-voi′, is an area of southeastern France that was ceded to France by the kingdom of Sardinia in 1860. Today it is divided into two departments, Haute-Savoie and Savoie. See Haute-Savoie; Savoie.

SAVOY, sə-voi′, **House of,** one of the oldest dynasties in western Europe. The French form of the name is *Savoie,* and the Italian form is *Savoia.* The history of the house may be conveniently divided into the periods of the countship, the dukedom, and the monarchy. The counts ruled from about 1024 to 1416, when the realm was raised to a dukedom, which lasted until 1713. In 1713 the head of the house became a king. The monarchs ruled, successively, as kings of Savoy, Sardinia, and Italy until 1946.

Background. The territory of Savoy formed part of ancient Gaul and from 122 B. C. until 407 A. D. was in the possession of the Romans, who divided it into two provinces, the Graian and Pennine Alps. In 407 it was seized by the Burgundians, but with Burgundy it became subject to the Franks in 534. Savoy was later included in the Carolingian Empire, and on its dissolution in 887, Savoy was granted by the Diet of Tribur to Rudolph, King of Transjurane Burgundy and, with that kingdom, was united to Arles.

On the accession of the last king of Arles to the throne of the Holy Roman Empire as Conrad II in 1027, the more powerful nobles of northwestern Italy became direct vassals of the Holy Roman Emperor. These included Humbert I the Whitehanded (Umberto Biancamano), Count of Savoy and Maurienne.

The Countship. Under Humbert I, the first of his family to take a prominent place among the northern Italian princes, the house of Savoy asserted its rule over the Alpine region controlling the two St. Bernard passes and the Mont Cenis Pass between France and Italy. Through marriage, warfare, and diplomacy, successive counts sought to enlarge their domain and to strengthen their position. In the late 11th century Humbert's nephew, Amadeus II, through the claims of his mother, Adelaide, heiress to the marquisate of Susa, added nearly the whole of Piedmont to the original possession of the house. In the early 12th century Amadeus III arranged key marriages in France.

Amadeus' grandson Thomas I, who ruled from 1188 to 1233 and who supported Emperor Frederick II in his contest with the papacy, obtained important accessions in Chambéry, Turin, Vaud, and other lordships. Like his father Thomas, Amadeus IV was a firm supporter of the Emperor. Amadeus obtained the submission of the city of Turin and ceded Piedmont to a brother, Thomas, Count of Maurienne.

Peter II, who ruled from 1263 to 1268, and his brother Boniface acquired influence and wealth in England through their niece, Eleanor of Provence, who married Henry III in 1236 and was the mother of Edward I. Peter became earl of Richmond, and Boniface was made archbishop of Canterbury. Peter, who reorganized the government, had no real claim to Savoy because he was a younger son.

Peter's nephew Amadeus V the Great reached the throne in 1285, and during his long reign (1285–1323) he regularized succession by male primogeniture to avoid further interfamily struggles. Amadeus VI the Green Count supported France at the beginning of the Hundred Years' War. In 1364 he answered an appeal for a crusade, and in 1382 he accompanied Louis of Anjou to Naples. Amadeus VII the Red Count acquired Nice near the end of the century, thus providing Savoy with a Mediterranean outlet.

The Dukedom. In 1416, Holy Roman Emperor Sigismund elevated Amadeus VIII to duke and freed Savoy from its imperial feudal obligations. Abandoning public life in 1439, Amadeus VIII was elected antipope by the Council of Basel, in opposition to Eugene IV, and was crowned as Felix V in 1440. The papal schism ended when Felix resigned as pope in 1449.

A series of weak rulers followed Amadeus until the senior male line became extinct in 1496. The title passed to the nearest collateral heirs, Philibert II and his brother, Charles III, who ruled from 1504 to 1553. Charles aided Emperor Charles V against Francis I of France, and, after losing some lands to the Swiss Confederation, he was deprived of all his territories by France. At the Peace of Câteau–Cambrésis (1559), Emmanuel Philibert the Iron Head regained most of Savoy. His son, Charles Emmanuel I, made numerous unsuccessful attempts to improve his position during his 50-year reign (1580–1630). Subsequent dukes followed a cautious policy of subservience to either France or Spain. Opportune shifts of allegiance by the last duke, Victor Amadeus II, during the War of the Spanish Succession (1702–1713) led to the elevation of Savoy to a kingdom by the Peace of Utrecht.

The Kingdom. The Peace of Utrecht increased Savoy's territory on the Italian mainland and also granted it the island of Sicily. However, Spain forced Victor Amadeus II to exchange Sicily for Sardinia in 1720. Charles Emmanuel III gained additional slight territorial concessions in Italy after the wars of the Polish Succession (1733–1735) and Austrian Succession (1740–1748). The mainland provinces fell under French control from 1792 to 1815. Restored to power by the Congress of Vienna (1815), Victor Emmanuel I tried to eradicate French reforms and changes. After the 1820 revolts he abdicated in favor of his younger brother, Charles Felix. The latter's death, following the upheavals of 1831, ended the senior branch of the house of Savoy.

The cadet branch of Savoy-Carignano, descended from the youngest son of Charles Emmanuel I, came to the throne with Charles Albert in 1831. He supported Italian nationalists against Austria, as did his son, Victor Emmanuel II, who reigned from 1849 to 1878 and who became the first king of a united Italy in 1861. Social, political, and economic problems beset his son, Humbert, who was assassinated by an anarchist on July 29, 1900. The first 15 years in the reign of Victor Emmanuel III, the last king, saw Italy rallying anew around the monarchy. But World War I upset the balance, and postwar unrest threatened the country.

In 1922, Victor Emmanuel brought the Fascists to power, subsequently accepting their domestic dictatorship and foreign aggression, which made him emperor of Ethiopia (1936) and king of Albania (1939). After Italy's defeat (1943) in World War II, many demanded Victor Emmanuel's abdication. The King at first refused but finally withdrew in favor of his son, Humbert II, on May 9, 1946. The Italian people rejected the monarchy in a referendum, and Humbert left Italy for exile in Portugal on June 14, 1946. His departure ended over 900 years of dynastic history for the house of Savoy. See also ITALY— *History;* SARDINIA, KINGDOM OF.

SAVOY OPERAS. See GILBERT AND SULLIVAN OPERAS.

WESTINGHOUSE

A diamond-tipped saw cuts through a prestressed concrete floor plank 1 foot (30 cm) thick and 8 feet (2.4 meters) wide. This floor is used in office buildings.

A chain saw powered by a small gasoline engine makes it possible for one man to cut far more timber than two men using a manual crosscut saw.

MCCULLOCH CORP.

SAW, a tool whose cutting edge is a row of sharp teeth. Saws are manufactured for use in cutting wood, metal, plastics, fabrics, meat, concrete, or any material that is softer than the saw blade. They usually are categorized as hand saws, stationary and portable power saws, and industrial power saws. Hand saws and power saws are used by craftsmen and laymen. Industrial saws are normally used in the logging, manufacturing, and construction industries.

Major Types of Saws. Hand saws used for cutting wood include rip, crosscut, back, dovetail, compass, keyhole, coping, turning, pruning, veneer, flooring, miter-box, and docking saws. Hand saws used for cutting metal include the metal-cutting hand saw and the hacksaw. Meat and frozen foods are cut with a butcher's saw or a kitchen saw.

Stationary power saws include the table saw, the overarm (radial) saw, the band saw, and the jigsaw. Portable power saws include hand electric power saws, which have a circular blade, saber and bayonet saws, which have a narrow reciprocating blade; and chain saws, which have teeth anchored to a chain belt.

In power saws, only the blade needs to be changed to obtain the required variety of cutting. There are various kinds of blades, including crosscut, rip, combination, plywood, planer, concave, metal-cutting, and masonry blades.

Selection of Saws. The selection of a hand saw depends on the type of work to be done. A 26-inch (64-cm) crosscut usually has 8 tooth points per inch and is used for rough-sawing boards to length. A 20- to 24-inch (51-61 cm) crosscut usually has 10 to 12 points per inch and is used for fine cuts. Backsaws, dovetail saws, and miterbox saws, which are primarily used for making joints, have 12 to 15 points per inch. Keyhole, compass, and coping saws are used for cutting irregular shapes. The less common ripsaw cuts parallel to the wood fiber. It is 26 inches long and most commonly has 5.5 points per inch.

Metal-cutting hand saws are available in the conventional hand-saw shape with 15 tooth points per inch or as a hacksaw, which has a 14- or 32-point blade held rigidly in a metal frame. Butcher saws are similar to hack saws but have longer blades. They contain about 11 tooth points per inch.

Power table saws usually have ¾ to 3 h.p. motors and have circular blades 6 to 14 inches (15-36 cm) in diameter. The shaft speed should be 3,450 rpm. These saws are capable of cutting material to width and length, as well as cutting rabbet, dado, plow, miter, and tenon joints.

Band-saw blades have teeth shaped on narrow bands of metal tensioned between two pulley wheels, with the cutting action toward the table. Blades are specialized for cutting wood, metal, plastic, fabric, or foodstuffs in straight or irregular shapes.

Power jigsaw blades, which reciprocate vertically by means of a pulsating lower shaft and a spring-loaded upper shaft, are used for cutting irregular shapes.

Radial-arm saw blades are attached directly to the shaft of the motor, which is suspended over a table via a yoke and overarm to a rear column. Blade sizes range in diameter from 8 to 20 inches (20-50 cm), and industrial saw blades are as large as 44 inches (118 cm) in diameter. They are mainly used as cutoff saws but can be used for cuts similar to those of a table saw.

Power hand saws are patterned from the stationary machines, with sizes being designated by blade diameter or length.

Care of Saws. Hand saws and power-saw blades must be kept clean for efficient use. Wet or dry abrasive paper along with varsol or kerosene as a lubricant will polish the metal sufficiently. Any rubbing should be done parallel to the manufacturer's machining.

Usually, the teeth of saws are set alternately to allow cutting clearance. Hand saws can be set with a hand-operated saw set. Circular saw blades can be set with a punch and anvil or by a machine. Blades can be sharpened by hand filing or by special grinding wheels, but such tasks should be done by an experienced person.

History. The saw is one of the oldest tools known to man. Probably, the first saws were naturally jagged-edged rocks. The origins of manufactured saws go back to the flint saws used by the Magdalenian culture in southern France as early as 8000 B.C. The Egyptians used saws made of copper or bronze by 3000 B.C.

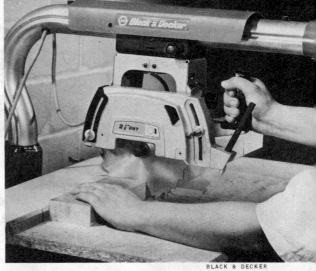

BLACK & DECKER

GLOSSARY OF SAW TERMS

Angle of Cut.—The angle between the blade and the material being cut; it is 45° for crosscut saws and 60° for ripsaws.
Binding.—Pinching of the blade due to inadequate set.
Crown.—The curved cutting edge of a hand saw.
Cutting Angle.—The angle contained within a tooth.
Heel.—The rear end of a hand saw.
Jointing.—Trimming the cutting edge of a blade to ensure uniform tooth length.
Kerf.—The width of a cut made by saw teeth.
Kink.—A sharp bend in a blade, making it useless.
Lip Clearance.—The angle at the back edge of a tooth to allow entry clearance into the material.
Points per Inch.—The number of tooth points per inch of blade.
Rake.—The face angle of a tooth as it enters material.
Set.—The alternate bending of teeth to allow cutting clearance.
Skew Back.—The curved back edge of a handsaw to achieve lightness.
Toe.—The front end of a hand saw.

BLACK & DECKER   THE STANLEY WORKS

A radial arm saw makes a crosscut through a 2-by-4 board with ease (*top*). It will also bevel crosscut, miter, bevel miter, rip, bevel rip, dado, and plow. The three-speed jigsaw (*left*) cuts along curved or irregular lines. It can also make patterns in openwork. The circular saw (*right*), the most common power saw, has teeth around the periphery of the disk. Large circular saws are used by sawmills to cut logs into lumber.

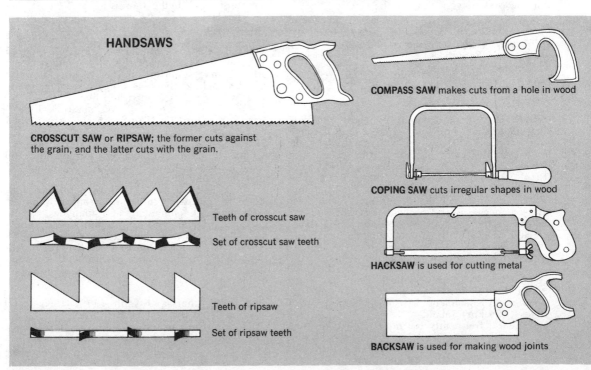

HANDSAWS

CROSSCUT SAW or **RIPSAW**; the former cuts against the grain, and the latter cuts with the grain.

Teeth of crosscut saw

Set of crosscut saw teeth

Teeth of ripsaw

Set of ripsaw teeth

COMPASS SAW makes cuts from a hole in wood

COPING SAW cuts irregular shapes in wood

HACKSAW is used for cutting metal

BACKSAW is used for making wood joints

Common sawfish (*Pristis pectinatus*)

Ancient bronze saws have been found in Germany, Switzerland, France, Spain, Hungary, and Italy, and a stone mold for casting saws was found in Sweden. Other finds include ancient Egyptian bronze saw blades with inserted jeweled teeth, Tahiti shark's-teeth saws, and copper wire with inbedded diamonds, used by the Incas.

Efficient saws were not made until iron was discovered. Even greater advances were made after the invention of steel by the Chalybes about 1400 B.C. Efficiency was achieved with carefully shaped and set teeth, with blades tapered from cutting edge to back edge of the saw.

Circular saws can be traced back to about 400 B.C., since Hippocrates is said to have used a drum saw to cut disks out of skulls. Samuel Miller of England is credited with the invention of the first circular wood saw in 1777. William Newberry of England patented the band saw in 1808. Others who developed the blade efficiency include Miss Crepin, a Frenchwoman, and M. Perin, a French inventor who was responsible for the present versatility of the saw.

W. MALCOLM SHARP
Southern Alberta Institute of Technology

Further Reading: DeCristoforo, Romeo J., *Modern Power Tool Woodworking* (Magna 1967); Hammond, James J., and others, *Woodworking Technology* (McKnight 1966); Harris, Edward, *Cabinetmaking and Building Construction* (McGraw 1967); Olson, Delmar W., *Woods and Woodworking for Industrial Arts* (Prentice-Hall 1964).

SAWFISH, any of a family of highly modified sharklike fishes characterized by a long flattened rostrum that is equipped with toothlike scales and resembles a saw. In addition to several fossil forms dating back to the Cretaceous Period, more than 70 million years ago, there are six living species, making up the genus *Pristis*, family Pristidae, of the order Raiiformes. The best-known species is the common sawfish, *P. pectinatus*, of the Gulf of Mexico and the Atlantic Ocean. It is usually considered large at 18 feet (5.5 meters), but specimens over 30 feet (9 meters) long and weighing more than 5,000 pounds (2,250 kg) have been reported. Other species live in warm seas throughout the world. All of them appear to ascend rivers for some distance, and specimens have been reported 200 miles (124 km) inland.

Sawfish frequently use their sawlike rostrums to slash through schools of small fishes, killing or stunning them, or to stir bottom-dwelling prey animals from their hiding places. They also use their saws in defense. Sawfish are ovoviviparous, producing up to 27 living young at a time.

Sawfish are of little importance, either commercially or as sport fish. Their skin, like that of some sharks, produces shagreen, and the liver has a high yield of oil. The "saws" of sawfish are also sometimes sold as curios.

JOHN D. BLACK
Northeast Missouri State Teachers College

SAWFLY, any of a large family (Tenthredinidae) of insects in the same order (Hymenoptera) as ants, bees, and wasps. The name "sawfly" refers to the sawlike sheath of the female fly's ovipositor. With the serrated edge of the sheath, the female makes incisions in leaves and stems in which she lays her eggs. Like wasps, bees, and other hymenopterous insects, sawflies have biting mouth parts and two pairs of transparent wings. They are easily distinguished from these related insects by their abdomens, which are not constricted at the thorax.

The larvae of sawflies resemble caterpillars but have at least six pairs of prolegs. Perhaps because they all feed on living vegetable and many are slimy, sawfly larvae are often referred to as slugs. The currant slug (*Pteronides ribesi*) often damages currant bushes. Other harmful sawflies include the pear slug, rose slug, grape slug, willow sawfly, and turnip fly.

WILLIAM D. FIELD°
Formerly, The Smithsonian Institution

SAWU, sä'vōō, is an island in Indonesia, between Timor and Sumba. It covers an area of 160 square miles (400 sq km) and is 23 miles (37 km) long and 10 miles (16 km) wide.

Sawu has a fertile soil, yielding tobacco, millet, corn, beans, cotton, and tropical products such as betel, cinnamon, and mangoes. There are also buffalo, wild boars, and deer. Horses and tobacco are the chief exports.

The island once consisted of five principalities, subject to the Dutch government of Timor. It became part of Indonesia in 1949. Population, including nearby islands: (1961) 78,785.

SAX, sáks, **Charles Joseph** (1791–1865), and **Antoine Joseph,** known as Adolphe (1814–1894), Belgian makers of musical instruments. They were father and son, and both were born in Dinant. In 1815, Charles Joseph Sax set up a factory in Brussels, where he produced musical instruments of many kinds. Adolphe worked as an apprentice under his father and then went to Paris, where he was very successful, showing a special aptitude for altering and improving instruments. His father joined him there, and the Saxes' most renowned and controversial innovations were popularized in Paris after 1842.

The most famous of these were the saxophones, a family of metal instruments—keyed, with a conical bore (as in oboes), and played by a single beating reed (as in clarinets). The saxophones, which are hybrid woodwind brasses, blend well with both standard wind groups. The saxophone was popular in military bands, and some serious composers scored pieces for it. But it underwent a period of eclipse until it became prominent in jazz bands, after 1915. Other instruments developed by the Saxes include the family of saxhorns; the mixed bugle-trumpet, called the saxtromba, or saxotromba; and the altered tubas (really bass saxhorns), known as saxtubas.

HERBERT WEINSTOCK, *Author, "Men of Music"*

SAXE, sȧks, **Maurice de** (1696–1750), marshal of France, who was one of the most successful commanders in French military history. Hermann Maurice was born in Goslar, Germany, on Oct. 28, 1696, the natural son of Frederick Augustus I of Saxony (later King Augustus II of Poland). He began his military career while still a boy, serving under Prince Eugene of Savoy in 1709–1710. His father made him count of Saxony (comte de Saxe, French form) in 1711.

He entered the service of France in 1719 and attracted attention through his innovative training methods. In 1726 he was elected duke of Courland and, except for Polish and Russian opposition, might have married its duchess, the future Empress Anna Ivanovna of Russia. He returned to France, where he wrote *Mes rêveries*,

an original treatment of war and military life. In 1734, during the War of the Polish Succession, he won promotion to lieutenant general.

His most notable victories were in the War of the Austrian Succession (1740–1748). In 1741 he captured Prague in a brilliant surprise night attack and in 1744 was made marshal of France. Saxe scored a major success in 1745 when his victory at Fontenoy helped France gain control of the Austrian Netherlands. He followed this with victories at Raucoux (Rocour, 1746) and Maastricht (1748) and was made marshal general of France by Louis XV. After the war he retired to the château of Chambord, which had been granted to him for life and where he died on Nov. 30, 1750. Through one of his many mistresses he was an ancestor of George Sand.

SAXE, sȧks, the French form of Saxony, is often used in English as an identifying prefix for various Saxon realms. For Saxe-Laurenburg and Saxe-Wittenberg, see SAXONY. For other realms using this prefix, see SAXON DUCHIES.

SAXHORN, a family of valved brass musical instruments, closely akin to the tuba. The saxhorn is shaped somewhat like a large trumpet, with a deep cup mouthpiece extending from it at a right angle. It is of a semiconical bore, with a marked expansion in the last section leading to the bell, which has only a moderate flare. The saxhorn may have either three or four valves and may be made in a variety of ranges. It was devised by Antoine Joseph (Adolphe) Sax and was patented by him in Paris in 1845. It is widely used in military bands.

SAXIFRAGE, sak'sȧ-frij, any of various plants of the genus *Saxifraga* (rock breaker). Some grow wild in the crevices of rocks, while others are cultivated for their white, yellow, pink, or purple flowers. Saxifrages generally are low-growing plants found in temperate, subarctic, and arctic regions, mainly in mountainous or rocky terrain. Saxifrages in the eastern United States include *S. virginiensis*, which has small white flowers, and *S. pennsylvanica*, which has greenish white or purple flowers. The London pride, *S. umbrosa*, cultivated in European gardens, has small pink and white flowers clustered on a stem about 1 foot (30 cm) high. The aizoon saxifrage, *S. aizoon*, native to arctic regions, is widely grown for its whitish purple-spotted flowers.

SAXO GRAMMATICUS, sak'sō grȧ-mat'i-kȧs (1150?–?1220), Danish historian. A native of Denmark, he appears to have been the secretary of Archbishop Absalon of Lund, under whose auspices he wrote a history of the Danish kingdom and its dependencies from earliest times to 1186. This work, *Historia Danica* or *Gesta Danorum*, is written in brilliant Latin, which Erasmus praised. Saxo chose as his models ·the later Roman historians, especially Valerius Maximus, yet in some of his expressions and in his mode of representation he is quite medieval.

The work is divided into 16 books, the earlier of which give a highly colored and imaginative account of ancient Danish history as learned from tales and traditions and is full of living pictures of old heroic wars and adventures. The first nine books are not reliable history, but when the writer approaches his own time his history is of the greatest value.

Maurice de Saxe, Marshal of France.

LAUROS-GIRAUDON

SAXON DUCHIES, the general term applied to the former German duchies of Thuringia—Saxe-Altenburg, Saxe-Coburg, Saxe-Meiningen, and Saxe-Weimar. From the 13th century these territories had belonged to the margraves of Meissen, who through Frederick I the Warlike, a member of the Wettin family, became electors of Saxony as well. In 1485 the Wettin family divided its possessions between Ernest and Albert, the grandsons of Frederick the Warlike. The elder brother Ernest received the Wittenberg lands, on which the electoral dignity rested, and most of Thuringia. Albert was given the margravate of Meissen with Dresden and Leipzig and the title of duke of Saxony. See SAXONY, German electorate and kingdom.

The protection of Martin Luther and the cause of the Reformation brought the Ernestine line into conflict with Holy Roman Emperor Charles V, the defender of Roman Catholic interests. Charles V, supported by Duke Maurice of Saxony, Albert's nephew, defeated and captured Elector John Frederick in 1547, during the Schmalkaldic War. The Wittenberg lands and the electoral dignity were given to Maurice and remained thereafter with the Albertine line.

John Frederick, assuming the title of a duke of Saxony, was confined to the rule of Thuringian territories. Since no laws of primogeniture were established until late in the 18th century, these territories experienced a series of partitions, reunions, and redivisions, which reached an end only on May 1, 1920, when most of the Saxe territories and the principalities of Reuss and Schwarzburg formed the state of Thuringia within the Weimar Republic. In 1945 this state became part of the Soviet occupation zone, but it ceased to exist as such in 1952 when all states in East Germany were dissolved and were replaced by smaller administrative units.

Ernestine Partitions. The division of the Thuringian lands began after the death in 1554 of Duke John Frederick, who had taken his seat in Weimar and had founded the University of Jena as a center of orthodox Lutheranism. In 1554 his four sons partitioned the duchy into the four duchies of Weimar, Gotha, Coburg, and Altenburg. With the expiration of the lines of Coburg, Gotha, and Eisenach by 1640, their lands came to the sons of Duke John of Weimar.

One of John's sons, Ernest I the Pious of Gotha-Coburg, also inherited Altenburg in 1672, but his possessions were splintered when they were divided among his seven sons after his death in 1675. William, an elder brother of Ernest the Pious, ruled Weimar and Eisenach, which his heirs split into Saxe-Weimar, Saxe-Jena, and Saxe-Eisenach. But in 1741 a reunion took place under Duke Ernest Augustus I of Weimar, who finally bound his succession by a law of primogeniture. The duchy, which became a grand duchy in 1815, of Saxe-Weimar-Eisenach retained its territorial identity thereafter. It received some small additional territories at the Congress of Vienna in 1815.

Saxe-Coburg passed after the death of Ernest the Pious to his son Albert and in 1699 to Albert's younger brother, Duke John Ernest of Saxe-Saalfeld. His descendants retained Coburg until 1918 and Saalfeld until 1826, when there was a redivision of territories. Frederick I, eldest son of Ernest the Pious, had received, in 1679, Gotha and Altenburg, which remained under the rule of his descendants to the expiration of the line in 1825. In 1826, Ernest III of Saxe-Coburg-Saalfeld gave Saalfeld to Saxe-Meiningen and received Gotha, thereupon calling himself Duke Ernest I of Saxe-Coburg-Gotha. His brother Leopold became king of the Belgians in 1831 and his younger son Albert became consort of Queen Victoria of England. After the death of his son Ernest II in 1893, Alfred, Duke of Edinburgh, a son of Queen Victoria, assumed the government. He was followed in 1900 by his nephew, Charles Edward, who abdicated in November 1918. Gotha then joined the new state of Thuringia, and Coburg went to Bavaria.

In 1826 the ruler of Saxe-Hildburghausen, a duchy that had also existed since 1679, ceded his territory to Saxe-Meiningen and became duke of Saxe-Altenburg, the easternmost of the Saxon duchies, located in the hills and valleys of the Saale and Pleisse rivers, while Saxe-Meiningen was farthest to the west along the Werra River. Of the four Saxon duchies existing after 1826—Saxe-Weimar-Eisenach, Saxe-Coburg-Gotha, Saxe-Altenburg, Saxe-Meiningen—all but the last sided with Prussia in the struggle for German unification. Saxe-Meiningen joined Austria in the war of 1866 and was occupied by Prussian troops. Its Duke Bernhard was forced to abdicate in favor of his son, George II, who, with all the other Saxon dukes, joined the North German Confederation and subsequently the German Empire.

The largest and most important of all the duchies was Saxe-Weimar-Eisenach. From 1741 it consisted chiefly of two major sections: the region around Eisenach at the northwestern tip of the Thuringian Mountains, and the Weimar-Jena territory covering the north-central slope of these mountains. The duchy became world famous in the second half of the century when its ruler, Duke Charles Augustus, brought to its capital city, Weimar, and to the University of Jena the leading spirits of the great German civilization of the age. Wieland, Herder, Schiller, and Goethe spent their best years in Weimar, while the University of Jena attracted, apart from Schiller, philosophers of the rank of Schelling, Hegel, Fichte, and Fries. In 1816, Grand Duke Charles Augustus was one of the first German princes to give his country a constitution and grant complete freedom from censorship.

It was from Saxe-Weimar-Eisenach that the national movement of German students, the Burschenschaft, took its origins. Weimar remained a center of German arts under the successors of Charles Augustus. It was often referred to as the capital of German culture, in contrast to Potsdam as the capital of Prussian-German power politics. Such considerations contributed to the choice of Weimar as the meeting place of the German Constituent Assembly in 1919, which drafted the constitution of the first German republic.

HAJO HOLBORN
Author of "A History of Modern Germany"

SAXONS, a Teutonic tribe first mentioned in history by the geographer Ptolemy in the 2d century A. D. The German form of their name is Sachsen. They were settled in the southern part of the Cimbric Peninsula, supposedly present-day Schleswig. From here they advanced during the 3d and 4th centuries beyond the Elbe and Weser rivers. Some of the Saxons, together with the Angles, migrated in the 5th and 6th centuries to England. See also ANGLO-SAXONS.

The remaining Old Saxons, as those on the Continent were called, expanded in the meantime throughout a considerable part of northwestern Germany. The Elbe and Saale rivers were the boundaries of their eastward extension, and in the south, they bordered on the Hessians and Franks. In the west the Rhine north of the Lippe River formed the border. Along the coast of the North Sea the Frisians maintained themselves as a separate tribe.

The Saxons were composed of four major groups: Westphalians, Angrarians (Engerns), Eastphalians, and (in Holstein) Nordalbingians. They conducted continuous warfare with the Franks. After a long series of bloody wars (772–804), Charlemagne subjugated them. The Saxons were forced to accept Christianity, and several bishoprics were established in their territory. The Saxons continued to live under their own laws, which Charlemagne had collected and which formed a collection called the *Lex Saxonum.*

HAJO HOLBORN
Author of "A History of Modern Germany"

SAXONY was an early duchy in northwestern Germany, inhabited in the 3d century A. D. by the Germanic Saxons. The German form of the name is Sachsen. With the dissolution of Charlemagne's empire in the 9th century, there emerged the tribal duchy of Saxony, which combined the low-German territories between the Rhine and the Elbe rivers.

Saxony was one of five German tribal or "stem" duchies into which the East Frankish Empire tended to dissolve. Otto, son of a Saxon noble named Liudolf, was named the first duke of Saxony in 880, and in 908 he acquired Thuringia also. His son Henry the Fowler was elected German king as Henry I in 919. His son, Otto I, succeeded him as king and became Holy Roman emperor in 962, beginning the Saxon line of emperors that ruled until 1024.

In 960, Otto I gave the duchy to a relative, Hermann Billung, who extended it eastward, though his authority was largely restricted to the northern parts. After the expiration of the Billung dynasty in 1106, Count Lothair of Supplingburg became duke of Saxony. Soon after becoming emperor as Lothair II in 1125, he gave the duchy to his son-in-law, Henry the Proud, Duke of Bavaria, a member of the Guelph family. But in 1138, Emperor Conrad III took the duchy from Henry and bestowed it on the Ascanian margrave of Brandenburg, Albert the Bear. Henry the Lion, son of Henry the Proud, refused to acknowledge the Ascanian claim and in 1142 was again granted the duchy. He extended the Saxon power as far as the Oder River and the Baltic Sea. But simultaneously he became the most powerful opponent of the universal aspirations of the Hohenstaufen, or Ghibelline, emperors. His struggle with Emperor Frederick I resulted, in 1180, in the loss of all his fiefs. See also GUELPHS AND GHIBELLINES.

Saxony was then divided. Cologne received the duchy of Westphalia, and other territories went to the archbishops of Bremen and Magdeburg and the bishops of Osnabrück, Paderborn, Minden, Hildesheim and Halberstadt. The counts of Oldenburg, Lippe, and Holstein were made imperial princes. The Guelph dynasty retained only the lands of Brunswick and Lüneburg, in the center of the old tribal duchy of Saxony, popularly called Lower Saxony. In subsequent centuries, Brunswick-Lüneburg emerged as the most important state, its rulers becoming electors of Hannover in 1692. Only in 1946 were the major parts of the old Saxon duchy united again in the state of Lower Saxony, one of the nine states forming West Germany.

In the 12th century the Ascanians received Lauenburg and the country around Wittenberg on the Elbe, which were the only parts of the former duchy that retained the name Saxony and the ducal title. The Golden Bull of 1356 raised Saxony-Wittenberg to an electorate of the empire. Upon the expiration of the Ascanian line of Saxony-Wittenberg, Emperor Sigismund gave the electorate in 1423 to Frederick I the Warlike, a member of the Wettin family. As margrave of Meissen and landgrave of Thuringia, Frederick ruled the lands to the south. See also SAXONY (electorate and kingdom).

HAJO HOLBORN
Author of "A History of Modern Germany"

SAXONY was a German electorate and kingdom. The main part of the state of the Wettin dynasty was the march or mark Meissen (Misnia), the land north of Bohemia, west of Silesia, east of Thuringia, and south of the old Saxony and Brandenburg. In the 13th century the margraves of Meissen became landgraves of Thuringia as well. Frederick I the Warlike, who founded the University of Leipzig in 1409, acquired in 1423 the duchy of Saxony-Wittenberg, which gave him the rank of elector. Soon the name Saxony was applied also to the region called Meissen.

His grandsons, Ernest and Albert, divided the territories between them in the Leipzig partition of 1485. Ernest received most of Thuringia, Saxony-Wittenberg, and the electoral title, while Albert as duke of Saxony ruled Meissen and northern Thuringia. In 1502, Elector Frederick III the Wise founded the University of Wittenberg, from which Luther's Reformation started in 1517. Frederick and his early 16th century successors, John the Constant and John Frederick, protected Luther's precepts against the decrees of the Roman Catholic Church and of Holy Roman Emperor Charles V.

The Emperor defeated and captured John Frederick in the Schmalkaldic War of 1546–1547. As a result of John Frederick's defeat, the Ernestine line of the house of Wettin lost Wittenberg and the electoral title. Both went to Duke Maurice of the Albertine line, who was an ally of Charles V, though in 1552 he led the rebellion of German princes that blocked the plans of religious and imperial restoration forever. The Ernestines remained confined to Thuringia. In the absence of strict laws of primogeniture, which were not established until the late 18th century, they divided their territories into a number of duchies of which Saxe-Weimar, Saxe-Altenburg, Saxe-Coburg, and Saxe-Meiningen were historically significant. See also SAXON DUCHIES.

Albertine Electorate. The historical role of Saxony in the 16th century was to a large extent made possible by the advanced economic development of the region. It was then one of the chief mining regions of the world, producing silver, copper, precious stones, tin and salt, and was a center of textile industries. Under Elector Augustus, Saxony received an excellent administration from which Leipzig especially profited in its rise as the great emporium of central Germany.

During the Thirty Years' War (1618–1648), Saxony fought first with Gustavus Adolphus (Gustav II) of Sweden against the German Emperor Ferdinand II, who supported Catholic interests. In 1635, however, Saxony concluded the Peace of Prague with the Emperor and as a consequence suffered much devastation by Protestant armies in the years thereafter.

After 1648 the rise of absolutism proved irresistible. At the same time the court developed great luxury, which reached its height under Frederick Augustus I, known as Augustus the Strong, who during his reign from 1694 to 1733 made Dresden one of the most beautiful baroque cities on the Continent. Frederick Augustus, after joining the Roman Catholic Church, also became king of Poland in 1697 as Augustus II. Saxony lost thereby its leadership of the Protestant princes of northern Germany, which fell to the rising Brandenburg-Prussia. The Polish ambitions forced Saxony to side with Austria, and Saxony suffered severely in the mid- and late 18th century in the wars of Frederick II of Prussia, whose highest though unfulfilled, ambition was the conquest of Saxony.

Kingdom of Saxony. In the Napoleonic Wars, Elector Frederick Augustus III joined France after the defeat of Prussia in 1806–1807. Enriched by Prussian territory and raised to king of Saxony as Frederick Augustus I, he became a member of the Confederation of the Rhine. Napoleon also gave the crown of the grand duchy of Warsaw to the new Saxon king in 1807. In the Battle of Leipzig in 1813, Frederick Augustus was captured, but at the Congress of Vienna in 1815, Austria's foreign minister, Prince von Metternich, saved the existence of the kingdom of Saxony, which Prussia wanted to annex. Saxony was compelled, however, to cede to Prussia over 50% of its territories, among them the region of Wittenberg, which in the 15th century had given it the name Saxony. See also SAXONY, province of Prussia.

Saxony became a member of the German Confederation in 1815 and joined the Prussian Customs Union (Zollverein) in 1833. In 1831 the country received a constitution. During the German revolution of 1848–1849 the liberal and democratic movements showed great strength but were defeated. The expansionist policies of Prussian Chancellor von Bismarck were opposed by the Saxon government of Count Friedrich von Beust, but Saxony was beaten by Prussia in the Austro-Prussian War of 1866. Bismarck accepted Saxony as a member of the North German Confederation in 1867 and of the German Empire in 1871.

Modern Saxony. The collapse of the empire and the revolution of November 1918 forced the abdication of the last king, Frederick Augustus II, and Saxony became a state within the Weimar Republic. When Hitler abolished all state rights in Germany in 1933, Saxony came under the control of a Nazi governor, Martin Mutschmann. After 1945, Saxony became one of the five states of the Soviet occupation zone and in 1949 of East Germany. In 1952 all the states were abolished and were replaced by smaller administrative units.

Saxony from 1815 to 1952 covered an area of 9,366 square miles (24,259 sq km). It was the fifth largest state in area in the German empire, and had the third largest population. Its southern frontier toward Bohemia ran along the ridges of the Erzgebirge, the Elbsandsteingebirge, and Lusatian Mountains. Most of Saxony is mountainous and hilly. Only the northern sections around Leipzig and Meissen are part of the north German plain. Since the late Middle Ages it has been one of the most densely populated areas in Germany.

Saxony's modern industrialization in the late 19th century made it the most industrialized state of Germany. There is some hard coal in the Zwickau region, as well as small iron mining. More important is brown coal (lignite) mining, chiefly around Leipzig. Uranium is mined in the Erzgebirge region. The overwhelming group of Saxon industries include textile, machine, metalware, electrical equipment, optical and glass, clock, paper, and furniture manufactures. To these may be added some specialized branches of industry such as the renowned porcelain works of Meissen and the printing trade of Leipzig, the greatest center of German book production in the 18th and 19th centuries. Leipzig was not only the largest industrial city of Saxony but also one of the greatest commercial centers on the Continent. Other important cities are Dresden, Freiberg, Karl-Marx-Stadt, Plauen, Zittau, and Zwickau.

HAJO HOLBORN
Author of "A History of Modern Germany"

SAXONY, was a former province of Prussia. Since World War II it has been part of East Germany. Under the terms of the Congress of Vienna peace settlement of 1815, King Frederick Augustus I of Saxony ceded over 50% of his lands to Prussia (see SAXONY, German electorate and kingdom). Most of these territories, including Wittenberg, the region along the middle Elbe River, and northern Thuringia, were brought together with former Prussian territories between the Elbe River and the Harz Mountains and formed after 1816 the Prussian province of Saxony. Magdeburg became the capital of the new province, which consisted of three governmental districts (Magdeburg, Merseburg, and Erfurt), covering altogether an area of 15,955 square miles (41,323 sq km). The population of the province passed 2 million by 1871 and reached 3,400,592 in 1933.

The province contained in the north some of the most fertile agricultural areas of Germany on which was also based an important sugar industry. Around the Harz, remnants of the medieval mining of copper, lead, silver, and sulfur survived. The most important resources were the large lignite (brown coal) deposits and salt mines around Halle and Bitterfeld. They favored the development of large chemical industries. By 1933 one fifth of Germany's basic chemical production was located in Saxony. During World War II the Nazis built many factories for manufacturing synthetic materials in the province. The great lignite deposits served as the chief source of electric power.

In 1945 the province of Saxony became part of the Soviet occupation zone. By adding the small state of Anhalt, the Russians formed the state of Saxony-Anhalt in 1945. In July 1952 this state was eliminated when all states in East Germany were abolished and replaced by smaller administrative units.

HAJO HOLBORN
Author of, "A History of Modern Germany"

Coleman Hawkins playing tenor saxophone.

BROWN BROTHERS

SAXOPHONE, sak'sə-fōn, is the name of a group of wind musical instruments. Saxophones consist of a conical brass tube sounded by a mouthpiece that is fitted with a single reed similar to that of the clarinet. The sound is also similar to that of the clarinet, but it is deeper and more mellow. The soprano saxophone is usually straight, but the other saxophones, which are held vertically, curve up at the bottom. The crook, or upper section, is detachable. When in place, it curves in the opposite direction of the bell, toward the player's mouth. At intervals along the tube there are openings controlled by key mechanisms.

The saxophone was developed by Antoine Joseph (Adolphe) Sax, who patented it in Paris in 1846. It soon became popular in military bands, where it supplied a good tonal link between the clarinets and the tenor brasses. Later, it was accepted in symphony orchestras, and it became prominent in jazz bands.

SAY, sā, **Jean Baptiste** (1767–1832), French economist, who enunciated the doctrine that became known as Say's Law of Markets, an economic thesis for many years. He was born in Lyon, on Jan. 5, 1767, but as a young man was engaged in business in England. Returning to France at the outbreak of the French Revolution, he became a journalist noted for his skill in expounding the economic principles of Adam Smith with force and clarity. From 1816 he was a professor of political economy at various institutions.

Say's Law of Markets held that a supply of goods generates a demand for the goods. Satisfying this demand, he believed, would ensure full employment and avoid economic depressions.

Say added the entrepreneur to the classical list of land, labor, and capital as a factor in production. He regarded the entrepreneur as a combining and creative force among the other three factors.

Say's most important book was *Traité d'économie politique,* published in 1803. A sixth edition appeared in 1846. Say died in Paris on Nov. 16, 1832.

SAYAN MOUNTAINS, sä-yän', a mountain system in the USSR, in southern Siberia. The Eastern Sayan, which forms part of the USSR-Mongolian border, is over 600 miles (965 km) long and extends northwest-southeast to about 100 miles (160 km) from the southern end of Lake Baikal.

The highest peak is Munku Sardyk (11,453 feet, or 3,491 meters). The Western Sayan stretches northeast 400 miles (645 km) from the Altai Mountains to the Eastern Sayan. Both Sayan ranges are cut by the Yenisei River and its numerous tributaries.

SAYERS, sā'ərz, **Dorothy Leigh** (1893–1957), English writer, best known for detective stories featuring the elegant and sophisticated sleuth Lord Peter Wimsey. She was born in Oxford on June 13, 1893. After graduation from Somerville College, Oxford, in 1915, she taught briefly and then joined a London advertising agency as copywriter. Her first detective novel, *Whose Body?* (1923), introduced Wimsey, who subsequently appeared in such stories as *Unnatural Death* (1927), *Strong Poison* (1930), *The Nine Tailors* (1934), and *Gaudy Night* (1935). In 1933, after she had left the agency, she published the mystery *Murder Must Advertise,* which is set in an advertising firm.

Miss Sayers' other works include theological essays, among them, *The Mind of the Maker* (1941), and a partial translation of Dante's *Divine Comedy* (1949, 1955). She died in Witham, Essex, on Dec. 17, 1957.

SAYRE, sâr, **Francis Bowes** (1885–1972), American public official and diplomat. Born in South Bethlehem, Pa., on April 30, 1885, he graduated from Williams College in 1909 and Harvard Law School in 1912. In 1912–1913 he was deputy assistant district attorney of New York county. Assistant to the president of Williams College (1914–1917), he joined the Harvard faculty in 1917 and was a professor there from 1924 to 1934. On a leave of absence in 1923–1925 he acted as consultant to the government of Siam (later Thailand) in negotiating treaties with nine European governments.

Appointed assistant U. S. secretary of state in 1933, Sayre followed an antiprotectionist philosophy in negotiating reciprocal trade agreements. He was high commissioner to the Philippine Islands from 1939 to 1942 and escaped from Corregidor by submarine. His later posts included U. S. deputy director of Foreign Relief and Rehabilitations Operations (1943) and U. S. ambassador to the UN Trusteeship Council (1947–1952).

Sayre married Jessie Woodrow Wilson, daughter of the President, in the White House in 1913. She died in 1933, and in 1937 he married Mrs. Elizabeth Evans Graves, who survived him at his death in Washington, D. C., on March 29, 1972. His son, Francis B. Sayre, Jr., became dean of Washington Cathedral in 1951.

SAYREVILLE, sâr'vil, a borough in eastern New Jersey, in Middlesex county, is on the Raritan River, about 18 miles (28 km) southwest of Newark. Its industries produce chemicals, film, plastic containers, tile and brick, and cookies and crackers. The borough was incorporated in 1919 and is governed by a mayor and council. Population: 29,969.

SAYVILLE, an unincorporated community in southeastern New York, is in Suffolk county on Long Island. It is on Great South Bay of the Atlantic Ocean, about 50 miles (80 km) east of New York City. A part of the town of Islip, it is a residential and resort community where boating and fishing are popular. The harvest of oysters, clams, and scallops has been an aid to the economy. The Edwards House, built in the late 18th century and owned by the Sayville Historical Society, is a museum. Sayville was organized in 1838 as Sevell. In the application for a post office, the name was spelled as Sayville, and so it remained. Government is by the town of Islip. Population: 11,680.

SAYYID AHMAD KHAN, sī'id ä'mäd кнän (1817–1898), Indian educator, who was the leader of the Islamic community in India during the latter 19th century. He was born in Delhi on Oct. 17, 1817. He entered the civil service of the British Indian government in 1837, and during the Indian Mutiny (1857–1858) he was instrumental in saving many European lives.

Sayyid sought to harmonize Islamic culture in India with Western learning rather than bring about a cultural synthesis with the Hindu community. In 1869, he founded a college at Ghazipur that used Western teaching methods. After its success he established the Anglo-Oriental College at Aligarh in 1875. In 1920 it became the Aligarh Muslim University.

Sayyid retired from the government service in 1876, but later served on India's legislative council. He died in Aligarh on March 2, 1898.

SAZONOV, su-zô'nôf, **Sergei Dmitriyevich** (1861–1927), Russian foreign minister. He was born in Ryazan province on Aug. 10 (July 29, Old Style), 1861, and entered the diplomatic service in 1883. He became assistant foreign minister in 1909 and foreign minister in 1910.

Sazonov tried to maintain good relations with Britain and France while advancing Russian interests in the Balkans and the Middle East. His support of Serbia against Austria-Hungary brought Russia into World War I in 1914. His advocacy of an autonomous Poland led to his dismissal in 1916. After 1917 he served in Paris as the anti-Bolshevik foreign minister. He died in Nice, France, on Dec. 23, 1927.

SCAB, any of several plant diseases characterized by localized areas of scaly, crusty, corky tissue on fruits and twigs, or by olive-colored velvety spots on leaves. Diseased fruit is often dwarfed or misshapen. Common on apple, cucumber, peach, pear, and pecan trees, scab diseases cause severe losses. In the United States, for example, the average scab-caused loss of apples amounts to over ten million bushels annually.

Except for the common potato scab, which is caused by a soil-inhabiting actinomycete, most scab diseases are caused by various fungi. Apple scab, for example, is caused by the fungus *Ven-*

turia inaequalis, which has two distinct phases in its life cycle. One phase, the imperfect, or *Fusicladium,* stage, lives on the fruit and leaves, while the other, the perfect, or *Venturia,* stage, is found on the dead leaves. With favorable moisture and temperature conditions during blossom time, the ascospores of the *Venturia* stage invade young leaves and fruit and soon develop into olive-colored patches of *Fusicladium* conidia. The conidia are disseminated by rain or mist to other susceptible tissue.

Precisely timed fungicidal sprays such as captan or dodine are widely used for scab control in order to produce marketable fruit. There is evidence, however, that the apple scab fungus may be resistant to some fungicides.

JERRY T. WALKER, *University of Georgia*

SCAB, a crust that forms on the surface of a cut, abrasion, or ulcer. The scab covers the injured area while healing takes place and usually falls off when healing is complete.

SCABBARD FISH, or cutlass fish, any of a family (Trichiuridae) of more than 20 species of long, narrow, laterally compressed fishes that somewhat resemble a scabbard or cutlass in shape. The name scabbard fish is applied especially to fishes of the genus *Lepidopus.* The game fish *L. caudatus,* which ocurs in the eastern Atlantic, Indian, and South Pacific, reaches a length of 5 to 6 feet (1.5–1.8 meters) with a weight of only about 6 pounds (2.7 kg).

One of the most widely distributed members of the family is the cutlass fish *Trichiurus lepturus,* a food fish found in the Atlantic, India, and western Pacific oceans.

SCABIES, skā'bēz, is the infestation of man by mites. It is also known as the "seven-year itch." In other animals the condition is called *mange.* The mite, *Sarcoptes scabei,* is hardly larger than the point of a pin. It painlessly burrows into the uppermost layer of the skin and lays its eggs. Although an ordinary infestation comprises only about 10 to 20 burrows, an infested individual usually has dozens of intensely itchy papules and tiny blisters that are caused by an allergic reaction provoked by the infestation. There are very effective scabicides, such as lindane (Kwell) and benzyl benzoate (Topocite), that destroy the mites when applied carefully to the skin according to a particular regimen. Since scabies is transmitted from person to person, all close personal contacts of an infected person must be treated.

STEPHEN E. SILVER, M. D., *Lawrence and Memorial Hospital, New London, Conn.*

SCABIOUS, skā'bē-əs, any plant of the genus *Scabiosa,* which is characterized by plant flowers that bloom in showy heads at the top of a long stalk. The field scabious, *S. arvensis,* is a perennial with purple flowers. It is native to Europe but has been naturalized in the United States. Sweet scabious, *S. atropurpurea,* is an annual with purple, lavender, maroon, scarlet, pink, or white flowers that grow on stalks up to about 3 feet (1 meter) tall. It is native to southern Europe but has been naturalized in California. Field and sweet scabious are easily grown in garden soil in a sunny place. The seeds can be planted in midspring. The grown plants produce blooms that are excellent as cut flowers.

La Scala, in Milan, Italy, is one of the world's foremost opera houses.

SCAD, any of several species of fishes of the family Carangidae. The big-eyed scad, *Trachurops crumenophthalmus,* is widely distributed in tropical seas and is an important food fish in some regions. The mackerel scads (genus *Decapterus*) include several small species, such as the silvery-colored *D. Macarellus* and the round scad, or cigarfish, *D. punctatus,* both of which are found in the western Atlantic.

SCAEVOLA, sē'vō-lə, **Gaius Mucius,** legendary Roman hero. When Lars Porsena, an Etruscan chieftain, besieged Rome, perhaps in the 6th century B. C., Gaius Mucius offered to kill him. Captured and threatened with death, Gaius Mucius held his right hand in an altar fire to show his indifference to pain. Impressed, Porsena freed Gaius Mucius and made peace with Rome. Gaius Mucius then took the name Scaevola, meaning "left-handed." Scaevola was also the name of an amulet worn by Roman children.

SCAEVOLA, sē'vō-lə, **Quintus Mucius** (died 82 B. C.), Roman jurist and political leader. The son of Publius Scaevola, a famous jurist, Quintus compiled the first systematic examination of Roman civil law, a study that was the basis for many later commentaries.

As consul in 95 B. C. with Lucius Licinius Crassus, Scaevola instituted a law that removed illegally registered people from the citizenship rolls, which helped to provoke the Social War of 90–88. Scaevola was later sent as proconsul to the province of Asia and reorganized its government. Appointed *pontifex maximus* in 89, he gave, by custom, free legal advice. He was murdered in 82 by political opponents.

SCALA, skä'lä, **Can Grande della** (1291–1329), Italian nobleman, who was lord of Verona. He was the most distinguished member of the family that ruled the city from 1277 to 1387. Another form of his name is Can Francesco, and of the family name, Scaliger.

During a time of constant political and military struggles in Italy, the family supported the Ghibellines, who sided with the Holy Roman Empire, and opposed the Guelphs, who sided with the papacy. Can Grande was made imperial vicar by Emperor Henry VII and during the wars against the Guelphs extended his territory to make Verona one of the most powerful northern Italian states. He was also noted as a patron of the arts.

SCALA, La, skä'lä, one of the great opera houses of the world, in Milan, Italy. La Scala—more correctly called the Teatro alla Scala—is the leading theater for the presentation of Italian opera in Europe, although operas of all nationalities are performed there.

La Scala was built by the architect Piermarini, on the order of Empress Maria Theresa, to replace the Royal Ducal Theatre, which had burned down. It opened on Aug. 3, 1778, with a performance of Antonio Salieri's *Europa riconosciuta.* Many of the greatest 19th and 20th century Italian operas received their premieres at La Scala, including masterpieces by Donizetti, Bellini, Rossini, Verdi, and Puccini. The theater was extensively remodeled in 1867. During the 1920's, it enjoyed one of its most brilliant periods, under the directorship of Arturo Toscanini. It was damaged by a World War II air raid, in 1943, but was carefully restored and reopened in 1946.

SCALAR, skā'lər, a quantity that has only a numerical magnitude. Physical quantities such as length, mass, time, volume, and speed are scalar quantities. Each of them can be specified by a number and the proper units—for instance, a speed of 10 miles (16 km) per hour. In contrast, a vector quantity has both a numerical magnitude and a specified direction in space. Physical quantities such as force, velocity, and acceleration are vector quantities. Each of them must be specified by a direction as well as a number and units—for instance, north at a velocity of 10 miles per hour.

SCALARE, skə-lar'ē, a popular aquarium fish that is strikingly barred with black and silver and has long pointed fins. A member of the family Cichlidae, the scalare, *Pterophyllum scalare,* is also known as a freshwater angelfish. It is native to tropical rivers of South America. Several melanistic varieties, called black angels, have been developed by breeders.

SCALE, in music, a succession of pitches, arranged in an ascending or in a descending order, that provide the tonal material of music. The word derives from the Italian *scala*, meaning "ladder."

Basic Scales. Until the end of the 16th century, Western music used the medieval modes, or scales, that were named after the ancient Greek modes but otherwise did not correspond to them. The medieval modes ("church modes" or "ecclesiastical modes") were gradually superseded by the seven-tone major and minor scales (diatonic scales) that became the basis for most Western music. The major scale corresponds to the medieval Ionian mode; the minor scale is an adaptation of the Aeolian and Dorian modes. See MODES.

All major scales are structurally alike, consisting of whole tones ("t" in diagrams), except between the third and fourth and the seventh and the eighth degrees, which consist of semitones ("s" in diagrams). The major scale in the key of C is:

The three forms of the minor scale (A minor) are, in order shown, harmonic, melodic ascending, and melodic descending.

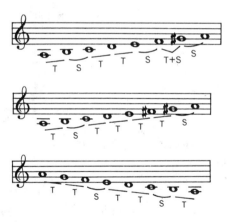

In the tuning system of equal temperament, adopted in the 1700's, a scale may begin on any of the 12 notes of the piano keyboard, using sharps or flats (usually shown by a key signature) to form the proper order of whole tones and half tones. As a result, there are 12 major and 12 minor diatonic scales. All the tones in these scales may be combined in one scale—the chromatic scale—which consists of 12 successive semitones. This all-inclusive scale is an enrichment of the diatonic scales and supplies the tonal resources of modern music, unrestricted by the limits of the diatonic system. See CHROMATICISM.

If the chromatic scale ascends, it is convenient to write it with sharps, thus:

If it descends, it is convenient to write it with flats, thus:

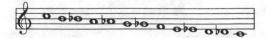

Other Scales. The diatonic scales formed the basis of practically all European music through the 19th century, albeit with a constantly increasing use of chromatic notes. About 1900, progressive composers started using other scales. The medieval modes were "rediscovered" and were introduced into symphonic music by Ralph Vaughan Williams and Gustav Holst, who based their works on modal English folk tunes. Claude Debussy wrote in the whole-tone scale (six whole tones to the octave); its tonal ambiguity was particularly appropriate for his impressionistic style. Paul Hindemith developed a scale based on the harmonic series of overtones. Other exotic scales were adopted to add color and variety to the diatonic system: the primitive pentatonic scale of Chinese and Japanese music; the so-called Gypsy scale of Hungarian music, with its two augmented seconds; and the quarter-tone scale, with 24 semitones to the octave, for which a quarter-tone piano was devised.

The 12-tone system of Arnold Schoenberg is not based on a true scale. Instead it uses the 12 tones of the chromatic scale in a different order for each piece, the possible combinations being infinite. See ATONAL MUSIC.

With the invention of electronic means of producing notes, there was no restriction whatsoever on the number of pitches that could be used, and most electronic composers have abandoned the familiar seven-tone major and minor scales.

CHARLES N. HENDERSON, *Director of Music St. George's Church, New York*

SCALE. See BALANCE; WEIGHING MACHINES.

SCALE INSECTS comprise more than 2,000 species of insects in which the bodies of adult females are so modified that they bear little resemblance to ordinary insects. Scale insects are usually tiny and inconspicuous, generally occurring on fruit, stems, and leaves, although some occur on the roots of plants. Although scales are individually tiny, they sometimes infest plants in such enormous numbers that they appear to encrust plant parts. They include many of the most destructive crop pests.

Adult females of most species are permanently attached to the plant, unable or uninclined to move. They are wingless and typically degenerate in body form, with missing or reduced eyes, legs, and wings. Their mouthparts are adapted for piercing plant tissues and sucking the juices. Adult males are two-winged flies as adults. They have no mouthparts and do not feed in this stage.

There are two types of scale insects, the soft scales and the armored scales. The bodies of the soft scales are soft in the nymphal stages, but adult females have thick, tough, often very convex integuments on their backs. Adult females do not lose their antennae or legs, and they can move to some extent, although they usually appear to remain sessile. Soft scales, like mealybugs, excrete honeydew.

Armored scales are economically the most important scale insects. They are usually smaller

GRANT HEILMAN

A twig infested with terrapin scale, a soft scale

than soft scales, and the bodies of adult females are more highly modified for a sessile life. Shortly after they are established on a host plant, the females lose their legs, and their antennae are reduced. Their bodies are hidden by a protective scale made up of secreted wax and the skins cast off in molting.

With their close relatives the mealybugs, the scale insects make up the family Coccidae.

SCALIGER, skal'ə-jər, **Joseph Justus** (1540–1609), French scholar and author, whose works on ancient chronology greatly influenced modern historical scholarship. He was born in Agen, France, on Aug. 4, 1540, the son of Julius Caesar Scaliger. He learned Latin from his father and began the study of Greek at the University of Paris but was largely self-taught in Greek language and literature. He also acquired a reading knowledge of Hebrew and Arabic.

In 1563, Scaliger became the tutor of a young French nobleman, Louis d'Abian, who was to be his patron for the next 30 years. He traveled throughout Europe with his patron. During this period he became a Protestant, a fact that probably hindered his advancement in France. To escape the religious upheavals there, he went to Geneva in 1572 and taught in the academy of Geneva for two years. He then returned to France, where he resided with his patron's family and produced much of the work that made him famous. In 1593 he became a professor of history at the University of Leiden, a position that he held until his death in Leiden on Jan. 21, 1609.

In *De emendatione temporum* (1583), Scaliger reconstructed the ancient system of chronology, subjecting classical views to the judgment of sound historical scholarship. His *Thesaurus temporum* (1606) was an enlargement of his earlier work, and on the basis of both he has been called the founder of the science of chronology. He also was noted for his textual criticism of Latin authors, especially his editions (1579, 1600) of Manilius' poem *Astronomicon*. Scaliger's claim of descent from the Della Scala family of Verona

was attacked in 1607 by Caspar Scioppius, a Jesuit spokesman. Scaliger replied in *Confutatio fabulae Burdonum* (1608), but this work failed to establish his claim to noble lineage.

SCALIGER, skal'ə-jər, **Julius Caesar** (1484–1558), French classical scholar of Italian birth, who gained a wide reputation for learning through his works on grammar, literary criticism, and natural science. Scaliger was born in Riva, on Lake Garda, on April 23, 1484. He claimed descent from the Della Scala family that ruled Verona in the 13th and 14th centuries, but the claim is suspect. Little is known of his early life. He left Italy in 1525 and was appointed physician to the bishop of Agen (ancient Aginnum), France. He married a French woman and became a French citizen. The scholar Joseph Justus Scaliger was the 10th of his 15 children. Scaliger died in Agen on Oct. 21, 1558.

He became known as a scholar in literary matters through his attacks in 1531 and 1536 on Erasmus' *Ciceronianus*, a satire ridiculing the stylistic excesses of Ciceronians. In *De causis linguae Latinae* (1540), Scaliger made one of the earliest attempts to analyze the principles of Latin grammar. In *Poetices libri VII*, published posthumously in 1561, he used Greek and Latin poetics and rhetoric as a basis for literary criticism. In the natural sciences, his contributions took the form of commentaries on the works of standard authors. These included the dialogue *De plantis* (1556), on a book of plants wrongly attributed to Aristotle; and two incomplete commentaries, one on Aristotle's *Historia animalium* and another on Theophrastus' *Peri phyton historia,* both published posthumously.

SCALLION, skal'yən, a type of onion that has a thick basal portion. It is also known as a green onion. The term scallion is also applied to leeks and shallots. See also ONION.

SCALLOP, skal'əp, any of a group of marine bivalve mollusks in which the soft body is enclosed by circular hinged shells that are characteristically ridged radially and have wavy edges. Scallops are found throughout the world and are highly esteemed for their edible adductor muscles, also often called scallops.

Scallops with their shells open, revealing the tentacles and beadlike eyes that fringe the shell

ROBERT C. HERMES, FROM NATIONAL AUDUBON SOCIETY

Scallops are from 2 to 6 inches (5–15 cm) across. Directly beneath the shell is a fleshy layer of tissue, known as the *mantle*. The edges of this mantle are equipped with many well-developed *ocelli*, or eyes, that the scallop uses to locate nearby moving objects. Scallops generally do not attach themselves to the ocean bottom but swim rapidly. They propel themselves by alternately opening the valves of their shells, letting the water in, and then closing the shells, forcibly ejecting water. Unlike other mollusks, the scallop has only a single large muscle, the adductor, controlling the opening and shutting of the shell valves.

There are many species of scallops, classified in several genera, making up the family Pectinidae, of the class Pelecypoda, phylum Mollusca. One of the most common species is the Atlantic bay scallop, *Aequipecten irradians*, found along the eastern coast of the United States. Other important scallops are the giant Pacific scallop, *Pecten caurinus*, of the Alaska coast and the giant deep-sea scallop, *P. magellanicus*.

SCALP, the covering of the top of the head. A fibrous tissue layer connects the scalp to the underlying skull. The scalp itself is composed of several layers, including skin, subcutaneous tissue, and muscle.

SCALPING, the removal of all or part of an enemy's scalp, with hair attached, usually for use as a trophy or occasionally for religious or medicinal purposes. A common practice was to cut a small area slightly larger than a silver dollar from the crown of the head and remove it by a firm yank. Sometimes the entire skin of the head, face, and ears was taken, though this was rare. A favorite target was the "scalp lock": a braid or length of hair that had religious importance and was worn as a challenge. Once removed, the scalp might be offered as a sacrifice or "food" to a divinity. More often it was stretched on a hoop, dried and painted on the underside in red or black for use in war ceremonies, attached to the village scalp pole, or used as a decoration. Although the act was not always fatal (depending upon the size of the wound), the enemy usually was killed before being scalped. Sometimes he was scalped alive, then released and sent home as a warning or a challenge.

The origin of the custom has long been a cause for controversy, with some apologists denying it as aboriginal in the Western Hemisphere. The archaeological and linguistic evidence, however, removes any doubt as to its existence in pre-Columbian America. Indeed, it seems obviously related to the head-trophy cult common throughout the Americas, as does the *tsantsa* or "shrunken head" trophy of the Jivaro Indians of Ecuador. Though practiced in the Old World, notably in central and northeastern Europe, it is uncertain why scalping seems to have been more prevalent in the New World, particularly in North America. It was most common in the East and Southeast, secondarily in the Plains and Southwest. The scalp bounties offered by white colonists and governments greatly influenced the spread, and during inter-European warfare in North America, Englishman scalped Englishman and even offered rewards for the scalps of other whites as well as Indians.

FREDERICK J. DOCKSTADER, *Former Director, Museum of the American Indian*

SCAMANDER. See XANTHUS.

SCAMMONY, skam'ə-nē, is a twining perennial plant native to dry regions of Asia Minor. It has arrowhead-shaped leaves, white or purplish flowers similar to wild morning glories, and a fleshy root. Sap from the root formerly was used as a purgative. The drug was obtained from the plant by first making incisions in the large taproot and catching the sap as it exuded. Then the sap was mixed with scrapings from the root and dried for use.

Scammony, *Convolvulus scammonia*, is classified in the family Convolvulaceae, the morning-glory family.

SCAMOZZI, skä-môt'sē, **Vincenzo** (1552–1616), Italian architect, who was a follower of Andrea Palladio. He was born in Vicenza and was trained by his father, a carpenter-architect. As a result of his travels in Italy, Austria, Germany, and France, Scamozzi wrote a guidebook to the antiquities of Rome, a travel diary, and the treatise *L'Idea dell'architettura universale* (1615), a long academic work but the first of its kind to mention medieval buildings.

Scamozzi's first major building was the Villa Pisani at Lonigo—a hilltop house modeled on Palladio's Villa Rotonda at Vicenza. His domestic architecture had some influence on Palladio's English follower, Inigo Jones.

Scamozzi completed several of Palladio's works, notably the church of San Giorgio Maggiore in Venice and the Teatro Olimpico at Vicenza, to which he added the permanent stage set. He designed a similar theater at Sabbioneta. In Venice, he designed the Procuratic Nuove on the Piazza San Marco to blend with Jacopo Sansovino's library. Scamozzi's design for a new cathedral in Salzburg, although not executed, influenced subsequent architecture there. He died in Venice on Aug. 7, 1616.

SCANDERBEG. See SKANDERBEG.

SCANDINAVIA is a term for the three northern European kingdoms of Denmark, Norway, and Sweden. Culturally and historically, the Scandinavian nations are usually considered to include Iceland, under Danish rule between the 14th and the 20th centuries, the Faeroes, and Finland, under Swedish domination from the 13th century to the 19th.

Geographically, the Scandinavian peninsula includes only Norway and Sweden and a portion of northern Finland. The mountains extend to the Atlantic on the western, or Norwegian side, of the peninsula, but end in slopes that lead to the Baltic on the Swedish side. The Danish peninsula and islands belong to the northern European plain. The languages and ethnographic, political, and cultural development of the people, however, are so closely related as to be historically inseparable.

See also articles on individual countries in Scandinavia.

SCANDINAVIAN LANGUAGES. See DANISH LANGUAGE; NORWEGIAN LANGUAGE; SWEDEN—*Language*.

SCANDINAVIAN LITERATURE. See DENMARK—*Literature*; NORWEGIAN LITERATURE; SWEDEN—*The Culture*.

SCANDINAVIAN MYTHOLOGY.

The pagan beliefs of Scandinavia have been transmitted by Christian writers and are therefore only fragmentarily known. Thanks, however, to the diligence of medieval Icelandic scholars, they are more fully preserved than those of any other Germanic tribe.

The chief sources of information are the two Eddas (See also EDDAS). The *Elder,* or *Poetic, Edda* is a collection of some 30 mythological and heroic poems discovered in 1643 and probably composed between the 9th century and the 13th. The *Younger,* or *Prose, Edda* was written by Snorri Sturluson in the early 13th century as a handbook of poetics. Supplementing these two major sources are the poems of the *skalds,* or court poets, who even after the coming of Christianity used mythological allusions to adorn their verses. There are also a few runic inscriptions, occasional comments by classical writers (especially Tacitus in his *Germania*), and the writings of the 11th century German historian Adam of Bremen and of the 12th–13th century Danish historian Saxo Grammaticus. Other sources include the sagas of Norway and Iceland, Finnish folklore, and the evidence of pagan worship offered by Scandinavian place-names.

Modern scholarship has revealed that the system of mythology presented in Snorri's *Edda,* on which most accounts of Scandinavian paganism are based, represents only the very last stages of this religion as practiced in Norway and Iceland of the Viking age, from about 800 to 1050. In the Viking age it was already strongly influenced by Christianity and pervaded with literary and poetic fantasy. The truth seems to be that Scandinavian mythology was never a unified body of doctrine but an aggregate of local practices of worship that varied from age to age and from country to country.

Snorri's Mythology. The system of the *Prose Edda* is a complete cosmogony, covering the entire existence of the world. Creation is described as the spontaneous result of a union between heat and cold in a chasm called Ginnungagap. The giant Ymir and the cow Audhumla thus came into being, and through some further links generated Odin and his brothers. They created the visible world from the body of Ymir and made the first human couple, Ask and Embla, from two trees.

Conflicts quickly arose between men and giants (*jotnar*), so that the gods had to protect men by creating in the midst of the universe a fortress called Midgard (the earth). In the center of it they had set their own dwelling, Asgard, and outside the wall lay the home of the giants—Jotunheim, a name adopted in modern Norway to designate the wildest mountain region of the country. In Asgard there were 12 chief gods, each with his own palace, but all under the leadership of Odin, father of the gods and ruler of the world. His name appears as Wuotan (Old High German), Wodan (Old Saxon), and Woden (Anglo-Saxon) and is the basis of the English word "Wednesday." The greatest shrine of the gods was the ash tree Yggdrasill, which spread its branches over the entire world and whose roots extended into Asgard, Jotunheim, and Niflheim, the deepest cavern of darkness. This ash tree, with its constant process of growth and destruction, is a symbol of the universe and its changing fate.

Odin was married to Frigg—from whom "Friday" is derived—and one of his sons was Thor (as in "Thursday"), the god of thunder and the protector of man against the giants, who are clearly associated with the hostile forces of nature. Balder, the god of innocence, was another son of Odin and the husband of Nanna. He was slain with a dart of mistletoe by the blind god Hoth (Hodr) at the instigation of Loki, and his death was the great tragic climax in the life of the gods. Tyr (as in "Tuesday"), the one-handed, was the god of war, while Njord and his son Frey were gods of fertility who belonged to an originally hostile and older group of gods called the *Vanir.* Another member of this group was Frey's sister, Freya, the goddess of love and beauty.

To make life more interesting, the gods had in their midst the evil and mischievous Loki, descended from the giants and himself the parent of certain fearful monsters like the Fenris wolf, the Midgard serpent, and Hel, the female keeper of the dead. Loki was the central figure of innumerable adventures in which he alternately tricked and helped the gods. In the end he suffered for his crimes by being chained in a way reminiscent of the fate of the Greek god Prometheus. Thor was also involved in a number of adventures, some of them bordering on the burlesque, while Odin's adventures displayed a more subtle cunning. In addition to Frigg and Freya, there were several other goddesses who were known collectively as the Asynjur.

Odin was the particular protector of warriors, and he sent his Valkyries ("the choosers of the slain") to bring him heroes who had died on the battlefield. In his Valhalla ("the hall of the slain") they fight and feast until the day of the final world battle when they go forth as Odin's host. This was the famous Ragnarok, "doom of the gods," not "twilight" as Richard Wagner understood it, which will be introduced by three years of world war and three years of icy winter. After a veritable Armageddon between the gods and the giants, all will be destroyed by fire. A new world will rise out of the sea, and a new age will begin when Balder returns from Hel, and "the mighty one [Odin] who rules all" descends to create a new, just, and happy race of men.

Origins of the Myths. Snorri interpreted the gods as being heroic men who had immigrated from Asia and were elevated to divinity. Early German mythographers thought that an original monotheism had degenerated into a disgraceful polytheism. Scholars like Max Müller and Viktor Rydberg made much of the idea that the gods were allegories of nature. All these views have been abandoned in the light of a renewed examination of the evidence.

The foundation of a scientific study was laid by the German mythologist Jacob Grimm in his *Deutsche Mythologie* (1835), although he made the error of assuming that the mythology of the Eddas was of general Germanic origin. Later in the 19th century, folklorists like Wilhelm Schwartz and Wilhelm Mannhardt distinguished between the "lower" mythology, or universal belief in nature spirits, and the "higher" mythology, which had been developed out of the former by a priestly class. The Dane Henry Peterson showed that Odin had not always been the chief god, and that in many places, especially in Norway and Iceland, Thor had been the most popular deity. In 1881, the Norwegian philologist

Elseus Sophus Bugge, tried to prove that much of Snorri's cosmogony exhibited Christian-classical influences, and later scholars, such as Axel Olrik, Kaarle Krohn, and C. W. von Sydow, have confirmed certain details of this theory. Norwegian scholars like Magnus Olsen and Oluf Rygh have extracted from place-names further valuable information concerning actual worship.

It has been shown that the content of the Eddas is myth, which often differs sharply from faith and rite, and is far more easily influenced by cultural contacts. The Germanic peoples were in constant touch with nations to the south and learned from them in varying ways and degrees. Like other elements in their culture, the conceptions of their gods underwent constant growth and development.

Among the earliest historical knowledge of the Germanic peoples is the fact that primitive fertility practices were associated with a goddess called Nerthus, who Tacitus claimed was the favorite German deity in the 1st century A. D. But the name is identical with the male Scandinavian Njord, an older god who plays a fairly modest role in the Eddas. Fertility is further suggested by the name Frigg, which is cognate with the Greek Priapus, as well as by Frey and Freya. Another old god is Tyr, who was probably at one time an important sky god, for he bears the same Indo-European name as the Sanskrit Dyaus, the Greek Zeus, and the Latin Jupiter. Tyr, however, is definitely a minor god in the Eddas.

These early gods seem to have been partly displaced by Thor, who was very popular in Scandinavia before the birth of Christ. But in the following centuries the worship of Odin, whose name is cognate with the Latin *vates*, or "inspired prophet," and the German *wehen*, "to blow", who was known as a wind god and the leader of the souls of the dead, spread north from the Rhine Valley of Germany. His association with magic, cunning, and poetry appealed to the Viking chieftains of Scandinavia, while the common people continued to worship the robust, earthy Thor. Last of all came such a figure as Balder, who can hardly be anyone but Christ. There is not a single place-name to indicate that a temple to him had ever been raised, and his own name means simply "lord."

According to Jan de Vries, such elements as the world tree may go back to common Indo-European beliefs or, as Adolf Schröder maintains, they may have been borrowed from the Middle East, as parallels can be found in Persian, Iranian, and Greek myths. Similar influences can be traced in the concept of Ragnarok, with its obvious parallels in the Apocalypse and in Iranian religion.

Although it seems impossible to disentangle all the details of its development, it is clear that Scandinavian mythology is neither a wholly native nor a wholly borrowed product. Once definite personalities for the gods had developed, it was a short step to filing out their biographies with the most miscellaneous folklore material, and from this aggregate the poets and mythographers created the fascinating structure known as the mythology of the Eddas. Originally a faith, this mythology developed into literature and became a source of poetic metaphor for the skalds of the Viking age. It was this sophisticated form of Scandinavian religion that Snorri Sturluson recorded. The actual rites of worship he either did not know or as a Christian did not care to record.

EINAR HAUGEN, *Harvard University*

Bibliography

Branston, Brian, *Gods of the North* (Vanguard 1955).
Brøndsted, Johannes, *The Vikings*, tr. by Estrid Bannister-Good (Penguin 1960).
Colum, Padraic, *The Children of Odin* (1920; reprint, Macmillan 1962).
De Vries, Jan, *Altgermanische Religionsgeschichte*, 2 vols., 2d ed. (1956–1957).
Ellis, Hilda R., *The Road to Hel* (1943; reprint, Greenwood 1968).
Munch, Peter A., *Norse Mythology*, tr. by Sigurd B. Hustvedt (1926; reprint, AMS Press 1970).
Polome, Edgar C., ed., *Old Norse Literature and Mythology* (Univ. of Tex. Press 1969).
Sturluson, Snorri, *Prose Edda of Snorri Sturluson*, tr. by Jean I. Young (Univ. of Calif. Press 1964).

SCANDIUM, skan′dē-əm, symbol Sc, is a silvery white metallic element found widely scattered in the earth's crust. Its only specific ore is the rare mineral thortveitite, a mixed scandium-yttrium silicate found in commercially available quantities only in Iceland, Norway, and the Malagasy Republic, but it also occurs in minerals such as davidite. It makes up approximately 0.0006% by weight of the earth's crust, and is usually found in very small amounts associated with such elements as iron, magnesium, tin, and zirconium. It is also present in the atmosphere of many stars. The man-made isotope, scandium-47, is used as a tracer element, and metallic scandium improves the performance of a nickel alkaline storage battery when present in the anode.

In 1871 the Russian chemist Dmitri Mendeleyev predicted the existence and many of the properties of a then undiscovered element, which he named eka-boron. In 1879, Lars Nilson of Sweden succeeded in extracting from a mixture of rare earths a new element that had almost identical properties with those predicted by Mendeleyev. Nilson named the new element scandium in honor of his native Scandinavia.

Scandium has an atomic weight of 44.96 and an atomic number of 21 and is located in Group IIIB of the periodic table. Its normal valence state is 3. There is only one natural isotope. The element has a melting point of 1539° C (2802° F) and a boiling point of 2727° C (4941° F). Its density is 2.992. Most of its salts are white in the solid state and colorless in water solution. The oxide and other scandium compounds are used as catalysts.

THOMAS D. O'BRIEN, *University of Nevada*

SCANNING ELECTRON MICROSCOPE. See ELECTRON MICROSCOPE—*Scanning Electron Microscopes.*

SCAPA FLOW, skap′ə flō, is a bay in the southern part of the Orkney Islands, north of Scotland, that covers about 50 square miles (130 sq km). Nearly surrounded by islands and accessible from the sea only by a few defensible small channels, it was the principal anchorage and base of the Royal Navy in both World Wars.

Scapa Flow is bounded by the islands of Mainland, or Pomona, on the north, Burray and South Ronaldsay on the east and southeast, and Hoy on the southwest and west. Its three principal exits are westward by Hoy Sound into the Atlantic Ocean, eastward by Holm Sound into the North Sea, and southward by Hoxa Sound into Pentland Firth.

In World War I, the passages into Scapa Flow were defended by mines, submarine nets, and other obstacles. At the start of World War II, some of these were not in place, and on Oct. 14, 1939, a German U-boat penetrated the anchorage and sank the battleship *Royal Oak*.

After the armistice that ended World War I (Nov. 11, 1918), the ships of the German High Seas Fleet surrendered and were interned in Scapa Flow. On June 21, 1919, the ships were suddenly scuttled and abandoned by their crews. Germany was compelled to surrender other tonnage to the Allies in compensation.

SCAPEGOAT, in anthropology, an animal, object, or person to which are transferred the sins, ritual impurities, sickness, or other misfortunes of a community or individual. The term originated in a mistranslation of Hebrew words meaning "goat for Azazel," which occur in Leviticus 16. Azazel was possibly a name designating an evil spirit of the wilderness.

Leviticus 16 describes the annual Day of Atonement ritual, in which the people of Israel presented two goats as sin offerings before God. One goat, chosen by lot, was sacrificed and its blood sprinkled on the mercy seat in the tabernacle. The second animal was the goat for Azazel—wrongly "scapegoat" (escaping goat) in the King James Version and "emissary goat" in the Douay Version. The high priest placed both his hands on this goat while confessing the sins of all the people. It was then released into the wilderness, symbolically carrying with it the sins of the nation.

The scapegoat concept—the idea of getting rid of one's troubles by transferring them to a symbolic figure—is widespread. The ancient Greeks had an annual festival at which two human scapegoats—a deformed or criminal man and woman—were scourged out of the city. The Babylonians beheaded a ram, rubbed its body against the walls of the temple to absorb any impurity that might be present, and then cast its head and body into the river. In Iran, broken pots were tossed over the walls of the village on New Year's Eve to rid the village of all the misfortunes of the preceding year. In Japan sins or misfortunes were transferred to rags, rice stalks, or paper figures which were then thrown into the river.

These acts are essentially magical, based on the belief that the effects of sin and misfortune can be gotten rid of by transferring them ritually to a symbol which is then cast away. In modern society the transference is more often psychological than physical.

ELIZABETH E. BACON
Michigan State University

SCAPEGOAT, in psychology, is a term used broadly to denote the phenomenon of blaming another person or group of persons for one's own shortcomings and frustrations. Thus, the practice is a form of projection. The person or group who are recipients of the blame may be chosen for traditional reasons or because they are relatively defenseless.

The choice of the scapegoat is an irrational process. The batter who strikes out at a crucial point in a baseball game may accuse the umpire of unfairness rather than admit his own lack of skill. The person who fails to achieve an ambition may project his self-esteem by blaming a race or an ethnic group rather than confess his own incompetence. The scapegoat is, therefore, a convenient alibi for want of success. Young children soon learn from their elders that some racial or ethnic groups are traditionally regarded as acceptable victims of aggressions and hates arising from frustrations. Such traditions may be exploited in times of stress by political groups. An example of such a phenomenon was the anti-Semitic policy of the Nazis in Germany in the 1930's and 1940's.

A special type of scapegoating is to blame others for moral lapses, real or fancied, which the "scapegoater" would actually like to commit. His own sense of guilt or unconscious envy of the supposed offender, who may be quite innocent, causes the "scapegoater" to demand harsh retaliative action. Vituperation or even physical acts of hostility may be directed against the scapegoat in the vain hope of regaining or finding peace of mind.

PHILIP L. HARRIMAN
Editor of "Encyclopedia of Psychology"

Further Reading: Hilgard, Ernest, *Introduction to Psychology*, 3rd ed. (Harcourt 1962); Krech, David, and Crutchfield, Richard S., *Elements of Psychology* (Knopf 1965).

SCAPOLITE, skap'ə-līt, a series of silicate minerals resembling feldspars in composition and feldspathoids in structure. Their transparent to translucent crystals are prismatic and have a coarse to faintly fibrous appearance and glassy luster. They range from white to gray, pale green, or reddish.

Scapolites occur in crystalline schists, gneisses, and amphibolites, and are also found in metamorphosed limestones that are in contact with igneous rocks.

The end members of the scapolite series are *marialite*, or $Na_4Al_3(Al,Si)_3Si_6O_{24}(Cl,CO_3,SO_4)$, and *meionite*, in which the sodium (Na) in the formula is completely replaced by calcium (Ca). The elements and radicals grouped in parentheses replace one another in the series. Intermediate series members are also known as *wernerite*, *dipyre*, and *mizzonite*.

Composition, given above; hardness, 5–6; specific gravity, 2.6–2.8; and crystal system, tetragonal.

SCAPULA, skap'yə-lə, a large, flat, triangular-shaped bone that forms the shoulder blade. See also SHOULDER.

SCAR, a mark that remains after the healing of a wound. It is tough fibrous connective tissue that grows in, replacing tissue that has been destroyed or injured. Scars may form in any tissue of the body, including heart and other muscle tissue, liver, and skin.

SCARAB, skar'əb, any of a large family of beetles found throughout the world. There are more than 30,000 known species, making up the family Scarabaeidae of the order Coleoptera. Adult scarab beetles are robust and distinctly oval to almost circular in outline, often with stout spiny legs used for digging. They characteristically have a club on the end of each short and usually elbowed antenna. The club is composed of several flattened plates that can be closed compactly like pages in a book. The forewings are hard and often highly polished and beautifully

The sacred scarab (*top*) pushes a small ball of dung with its hind legs, bracing itself with its forelegs against the ground. In ancient Egypt the scarab, often carved in stone (*below*), was a symbol of the sun.

colored. Scarab larvae, or "grubs," are white or yellowish white, fat, wrinkled, and almost always bent in a semicircle.

Many species of scarab beetles feed on manure. They also roll together balls of dung in which to lay their eggs, thus providing food for their grubs. Many scarabs feed on the roots of plants as grubs and on leaves as adults. Others eat fungi, and a few feed on carrion.

Many scarabs are serious pests. May beetles, often called June bugs, are common leaf chafers and seriously damage lawns and pastures. Adult rose beetles destroy roses, grapes, and other garden plants. In the United States the most destructive of the scarab beetles is the Japanese beetle (*Popillia japonica*).

In Egypt the species *Scarabaeus sacer*, whose circular shape and bright golden tints suggest the shape and luster of the sun, was believed to be one of the forms under which the sun-god appeared and was thus held to be sacred. Accordingly, seals, amulets, and beads were made in the stylized shape of the beetles, and these artifacts are also known as scarabs.

The sacred scarab was important in art and religion for thousands of years. It was the symbol of immortality because it was observed to enter the soil and later reappear as though resurrected. Tremendous numbers of scarabs were often found on the surface of the mudbanks along the Nile River, and this supported the belief in spontaneous generation.

WILLIAM D. FIELD
Smithsonian Institution

SCARAMOUCH, skar'ə-mōōsh, is a stock character originating in Italian *commedia dell'arte.* It is spelled Scaramuccia in Italian and Scaramouche in French. At first classed as a servant, the character came to be a type of poltroon and braggart, recognizable by his black costume. The 17th century Italian comic actor Tiberio Fiorillo was associated with the role for some 50 years and may have created it. He played the part in Italy before performing it in Paris, where, after 1640, he spent most of his time. Fiorillo used body expression more than dialogue to portray the character. Molière, who admired Fiorillo, borrowed from his great characterization for some of his own characters. The Englishman Joseph Grimaldi, the foremost clown of the 19th century, was another celebrated Scaramouch.

SCARBOROUGH, skär'bə-rə, a municipal borough in northern England, is on the east coast in the North Riding of Yorkshire, 40 miles (64 km) north of Hull. Scarborough is the most popular of the Yorkshire holiday resorts. Its seaward frontage is divided into two wide bays by a headland 290 feet (88 meters) high and crowned with the ruins of a Norman castle.

On the south side of the headland is the harbor, used by small coastal ships and fishing vessels. From the harbor extends the South Bay, sheltered by low cliffs laid out with gardens. Here are splendid beaches and the spa, a modern establishment on the site of the 17th-century development that was built around the mineral springs discovered here in 1620. For 200 years the old spa had been a center of fashion, but after the original buildings burned down in 1876, Scarborough became known less for its springs than for its invigorating climate.

The North Bay is less sandy than the South Bay, except at its northern end, but there are a number of gardens here, and an open-air theater with its stage on an island.

The seaward part of the castle headland is guarded by a deep ditch and rampart, the only approach being by a narrow causeway. The principal ruin is the castle keep, where George Fox, founder of the Religious Society of Friends (Quakers) was imprisoned in 1665–1666. In addition to the castle ruins, there are on the headland remains of an early Iron Age settlement and of a Roman signal station from about 370 A. D. Population: (1971) 44,370.

H. GORDON STOKES
Author of "English Place-Names"

SCARLATINA. See SCARLET FEVER.

SCARLATTI, skär-lät'tē, **Alessandro** (1660–1725), Italian composer, who was the founder of the Neapolitan school of opera. He was born in Palermo, Sicily, on May 2, 1660. As a boy he was sent to Rome to study music with Giacomo Carissimi, a renowned composer of oratorios. In Rome, while still very young, Scarlatti became *maestro di cappella* to former Queen Christina of Sweden. He similarly served the viceregal court at Naples in the 1690's. In 1703 he became assistant to Antonio Foggia at the Roman Church of Santa Maria Maggiore, succeeding Foggia as *maestro* in 1707. After 1709 he returned to Naples to head the royal chapel. Scarlatti also taught briefly at the Conservatorio di Santa Maria di Loreto, in Naples, but he chiefly took in private pupils, the most renowned of whom were

Alessandro Scarlatti, early Italian opera composer

his son Domenico Scarlatti and the North German opera composer Johann Adolf Hasse. Scarlatti died in Naples on Oct. 24, 1725.

Although Scarlatti wrote in most of the musical forms current during his lifetime, his reputation was made mainly as an opera composer. He wrote some 115 operas, of which about 50 survive. Not all of these, however, are in full score. He conducted the earliest known of them, *Gli equivoci nel sembiante* (also known as *L'errore innocente*), in Rome before his 20th birthday. His later operas became stylistically noteworthy for his increasing use of the *aria da capo*, an essentially musical rather than dramatic device, and for his employment of recitatives accompanied by orchestra rather than the usual harpsichord. His first operas are generally believed to have been: *Olimpia vendicata* (first performed in Naples, 1685); *La Rosmene* (Naples, 1688); *La Statira* (Rome, 1690); *Pirro e Demetrio* (Naples, 1694); *La caduta de' Decemviri* (Naples, 1697); *Il prigioniero fortunato* (Naples, 1698); *L'Eraclea* (Naples, 1700), with the earliest known operatic septet; *Il Tigrane* (Naples, 1715), regarded as his masterpiece; *Il trionfo dell'onore* (Naples, 1718), the oldest surviving Neapolitan-style opera; and *La Griselda* (Rome, 1721), his 114th and the last of his surviving operas.

Scarlatti's operas strongly influenced Handel and other composers of *opera seria*. In the later eras of "reform," however, they were decried as antidramatic because of their concentration on the music and neglect of stage action. His other compositions, many of which are of the highest caliber, include about 14 oratorios, perhaps 200 Masses, much other sacred music, madrigals, some 700 cantatas, serenatas, duets, sinfonie for small orchestra, chamber music, and numerous harpsichord solos.

HERBERT WEINSTOCK
Author of "Music as an Art"

Further Reading: Dent, Edward Joseph, *Alessandro Scarlatti: His Life and Works* (Longmans 1905).

SCARLATTI, skär-lät′tē, **Domenico** (1685–1757), Italian composer and keyboard virtuoso. Giuseppe Domenico Scarlatti was born in Naples on Oct. 26, 1685. He was the son of the composer Alessandro Scarlatti, with whom he studied. At the age of 16, he was an organist-composer at the Neapolitan royal chapel. The first two of his several operas were produced when he was 18. After further study at Venice, he held court positions in Rome and from 1714 to 1719 acted as *maestro di cappella* at the Vatican. In 1719 or 1720 he went to Lisbon, becoming court musician to Princess Maria Barbara, daughter of King John V of Portugal. When she married the future Ferdinand VI of Spain in 1729, Scarlatti went to Madrid, receiving appointment as her *maestro de cámara* when she became queen of Spain in 1746. Except for brief visits to Italy, he remained in Madrid for the rest of his life. He died in Madrid on July 23, 1757.

Although Scarlatti was renowned in his lifetime both as an extraordinary harpsichordist and as a composer in many forms, his modern reputation rests preponderantly on his more than 600 sonatas and other pieces for the harpsichord. Brief, ceaselessly inventive, largely cast in homophonic texture, these crisp, expressive pieces (they are not sonatas in the modern sense) influenced most later composing for harpsichord and piano. They are notable for their free style and for their intimate relation to the instrument. They make frequent use of swift runs in thirds and sixths, rapid repetitions of notes that require great digital dexterity, broken chords in oblique or contrary motion, wide skips, the crossing of the hands on the keyboard, and shaping ornamentation. The basic repertoire of the modern harpsichord joins Scarlatti's pieces to those of Couperin, Rameau, Bach, and Handel.

Many of Scarlatti's harpsichord pieces were published during his lifetime. Subsequent partial editions have been numerous. From 1906 on the standard edition was that of Alessandro Longo, whose numbering of the pieces still is widely used, but the scholarly investigation of the harpsichordist Ralph Kirkpatrick has resulted in the gradual substitution of his numbering of Scarlatti's works for Longo's.

HERBERT WEINSTOCK, *Author, "Music as an Art"*

Further Reading: Kirkpatrick, Ralph, *Domenico Scarlatti*, rev. ed. (Princeton Univ. Press 1955); Sitwell, Sacheverell, *Background for Domenico Scarlatti, 1685–1757* (Greenwood 1935).

SCARLET FEVER is an acute, contagious respiratory infection characterized by sore throat, a diffuse skin rash, and later by desquamation, or scaling off, of the skin. It is sometimes known as *scarlatina.* Scarlet fever is caused by infection with any serological type of group A streptococcus that produces erythrogenic toxin—that is, a toxin that produces a rash.

The disease, which occurs primarily in the first decade of life, was an important cause of death in children prior to the 20th century. Since then the incidence has declined markedly, and death is now rarely observed. Important advances in the study of scarlet fever were made by the American husband-and-wife team of George Frederick Dick and Gladys Henry Dick, who developed the so-called Dick test for determining susceptibility to scarlet fever.

The group A streptococcus responsible for scarlet fever characteristically causes an infection of the throat and tonsils, which is associated with sore throat, headache, fever, and tender, enlarged lymph nodes at the angle of the jaw. The onset is sudden, with an incubation period of two to three days. Vomiting may be an early symptom in the young child. When a skin rash does not appear, the disease is termed streptococcal sore throat, still one of the common respiratory infections. The development of a skin rash is dependent on two factors. First, the streptococcus must produce erythrogenic toxin. Second, the patient must be susceptible to this toxin. Many individuals are not susceptible, presumably because they have been infected previously with strains of streptococci that produce small amounts of toxin. The toxin stimulates the production of immune bodies, which subsequently neutralize toxin when it is produced by a new group A streptococcal infection.

Those patients who contract scarlet fever develop the rash within 48 hours of the first symptoms. The eruption appears first on the sides and front of the neck, spreads down the chest and abdomen, and finally involves the extremities. The palms and soles are usually not involved. The rash begins as a diffuse erythema with super-imposed small red spots. It fades on pressure, and it is intensified in the folds of the skin. It persists for only a few hours in a mild attack but for as long as five days in a severe case. During convalescence a branny desquamation occurs, especially over the ears, palms, and soles. In scarlet fever the tongue is usually covered by a white coat through which red spots are observed—the "strawberry tongue." Later, the coat is lost, and the tongue is more like a raspberry.

The complications of scarlet fever and streptococcal sore throat are identical, although suppurative, or pus-producing, foci are more common in scarlet fever. These include otitis media, mastoiditis, peritonsillar abscess, pneumonia, empyema, and arthritis. Rheumatic fever, with involvement of the heart, occurs in about 3% of patients. Nephritis sometimes follows scarlet fever and is caused by certain types of group A streptococci.

Scarlet fever is spread by intimate contact with a patient or carrier. It is not spread by airborne particles or contaminated fomites. Treatment of the disease is now relatively simple. Penicillin is the drug of choice, but other antibiotics are also effective. Early and adequate therapy eliminates most of the serious complications, including rheumatic fever and acute nephritis. Furthermore, penicillin kills the streptococci so that the patient is rendered noninfectious a few hours after treatment is started. Thus rigid quarantine is no longer a necessary public health procedure.

CHARLES H. RAMMELKAMP, M. D.
Case Western Reserve University

SCARLET LARKSPUR, a perennial herb, *Delphinium cardinale*, with bright scarlet flowers, which in the United States is native to southern California.

The larkspurs make up a genus of about 200 species of annual or perennial herbs of the buttercup family, including some of the hardiest and most attractive of garden flowers. The scarlet larkspur is an erect or arching perennial, two to three feet (0.6–0.9 meter) high, with flowers in long clusters (racemes).

SCARLET LETTER, a novel by the American author Nathaniel Hawthorne, published in 1850. *The Scarlet Letter* is Hawthorne's masterpiece and is generally considered one of the greatest American works of the 19th century.

The Plot. The scene is Boston in the 1640's. Hester Prynne, who has borne a child out of wedlock, has been sentenced to stand for three hours before the pillory and thenceforth to wear the scarlet letter "A" that proclaims her an adulteress. Despite the pleas of two clergymen—the saintly John Wilson and his young colleague, Arthur Dimmesdale—she steadfastly refuses to name her lover. But Dimmesdale is the man, and the triangle is completed by the arrival, under the name of Roger Chillingworth, of the elderly physician with whom Hester had contracted a loveless marriage several years before. Chillingworth wishes to find Hester's lover and revenge himself. Suspecting Dimmesdale, he takes up lodgings with the young minister.

Hester had sinned and been punished, and she has become an outcast. But as an outcast she has also been set free. "Standing alone . . . she cast away the fragments of a broken chain. The world's law was no law for the mind." Hers is the only emancipated intellect in New England. She lives simply, supporting herself and her daughter Pearl by her needlework, and the austerity of her outward life is such that the community tacitly accepts her, the scarlet letter becoming no more than a piece of background.

Meanwhile, Dimmesdale is suffering the torments of unconfessed sin, a torment fiendishly augmented by Chillingworth, who had early guessed the secret. At his first interview with Hester, Chillingworth had made her swear never to reveal his identity, and not until seven years have passed does she muster the courage to tell Dimmesdale the truth. In a famous scene the lovers maintain that what they did had "a consecration of its own" and that Chillingworth's sin is worse than theirs, for he had "violated, in cold blood, the sanctity of a human heart." Hester and Dimmesdale dream briefly of flight; Chillingworth knows it. The one place where he cannot follow is the scaffold. There, before the pillory, Dimmesdale at last makes a public confession, and there, broken by guilt, he dies in Hester's arms.

Commentary. Hawthorne began his novel where a conventional work would end. His concern is not with the moment of passion but with the psychology of the participants and with moral problems deeper than the worldly code. Repeatedly, in the short stories that preceded *The Scarlet Letter* and in the romances that followed it, he brooded over the interrelations of good and evil and their disconcerting tendency to merge or to reverse themselves.

A reversal of conventional values in the novel is evident. The adulterers are treated sympathetically, and the cuckolded husband becomes the villain, whose deepest offense lies in his probing of Dimmesdale's heart. To Hawthorne, the unpardonable sin is invasion of privacy, treating people as specimens, not as individuals.

DELANCEY FERGUSON
Formerly, Brooklyn College

SCARLET MACAW, mə-kô', *Ara macao*, the largest and most striking and colorful of the Mexican parrots. The scarlet macaw grows to a length of 3 feet (1 meter). In plumage it is predominantly scarlet, with a band of yellow across the wings and considerable blue on the wings and back. Like other macaws, the scarlet macaw has a long pointed tail and a face partially bare of feathers. Macaws are monogamous and lay two or three white eggs.

SCARLET MITE, any of the many red carnivorous mites found in grass and among weeds. The young of some scarlet mites are parasites of spiders and other insects.

SCARLET PIMPERNEL, pim'pər-nel, a novel of adventure by the Hungarian-born English author Baroness Orczy. Published in 1905, *The Scarlet Pimpernel* was a huge success and was dramatized later that year by the author and her husband, Montague Barstow. It was made into a film in 1935. Baroness Orczy wrote a number of less successful sequels.

The action of *The Scarlet Pimpernel* revolves around a stalwart young English nobleman who, during the French Revolution, assumes the airs of a fop to fend off suspicion while he intrigues to get aristocrats out of France and away from the Reign of Terror. He can be identified in his secret rescue missions by a signet ring, which bears the image of a scarlet pimpernel blossom.

SCARLET RUNNER, a climbing bean plant that has bright red flowers and long pods containing edible red-and-black seeds. It is a perennial in warm climates but is grown as an annual elsewhere. The plant, which is native to tropical America, was cultivated in Mexico as early as about 6000 B.C. Some varieties of the scarlet runner now are grown in Mexico, Britain, and continental Europe for their edible beans. In the United States, the plant primarily is grown for its ornamental flowers. The scarlet runner, *Phaseolus coccineus*, belongs to the genus *Phaseolus*, as do the kidney bean and the lima bean.

SCARLET TANAGER. See TANAGER.

SCARRON, skà-rôn', **Paul** (1610–1660), French poet, playwright, and novelist, whose vigorous wit is most vividly displayed in the novel *Le Roman comique*. Scarron was born in Paris on July 4, 1610. A member of a good family of Piedmontese origin, he led a fairly carefree life for almost 30 years. At 19 he became an *abbé*, entered the service of a bishop, went to Rome, and eventually attained a dominant position in fashionable literary circles. An attack of fever, followed by rheumatism, left him a hopeless cripple. His spirit was unbroken, however, and his house in Paris became the rendezvous of a somewhat libertine group amused by Scarron's bitter mockery of himself and the world. His talents were admired, and he might have been prosperous if he had not sacrificed his pensions, one by one, to the demands of his circle.

In 1652, Scarron married the beautiful, well-born, but poverty-stricken Françoise d'Aubigné, later to become the famous Mme. de Maintenon and finally the wife of Louis XIV. Mme. Scarron turned his turbulent gatherings into a well-regulated salon. Scarron died of his infirmities, in Paris, on Oct. 7, 1660.

Scarron was a wickedly clever versifier. Unfortunately, he never finished his *Virgile travesti*, a parody of the *Aeneid*, which showed him to be a master of burlesque. He was happier in his comedies, notably *Jodelet, ou le maître valet* (1643), which created a stock type, the sort of person whose absurdities cause helpless laughter. The valet Crispin in *L'Écolier de Salamanque* (1654) was also a long-lived type.

Scarron's finest achievement, however, is *Le Roman comique,* an unfinished novel that protested against the preciosity of current French fiction. Here, as elsewhere, Scarron borrowed boldly but artistically from Spanish novels. The unfinished state of some of his most important works, however, makes it difficult to assess him.

SCARSDALE, a village in southern New York, in Westchester county, about 20 miles (32 km) north of the center of New York City. It is a suburban residential community, whose character is maintained by zoning laws that protect against encroachments by industry or "look-alike" housing. The village and the township of Scarsdale are coterminous.

The Manor of Scarsdale was established in 1701 by a deed of grant from King William III of England to Caleb Heathcote, who named the manor after his native district in Derbyshire. During the Revolutionary War, the British general Sir William Howe set up his headquarters at Griffin House here in October 1776, just before the Battle of White Plains. Griffin House is one of several 18th century houses still standing.

Scarsdale was incorporated as a village in 1915. It is governed by a village manager, who is responsible to an elective board of trustees. Population: 17,650.

SCAT, any of a small family of tropical Indo-Pacific fishes that are very popular in aquariums, largely because of the beautiful coloring of the young. About six species are classified in several genera that make up the family Scatophagidae of the order Perciformes. They are primarily marine fishes, but some enter shallow brackish water.

Scats are less than 12 inches (30 cm) long and have four anal spines. In the common scat, *Scatophagus argus,* the young has black spots and orange-red bands extending down the dorsal surface of the body, but the adult loses the bright coloring and has only the spots. Scats of the genus *Selenotoca* are silvery.

The common scat (*Scatophagus argus*)

The Tyndall effect can be observed in nature when the rays of a setting sun break through gaps in a cloud bank. As the light is scattered by dust particles in the atmosphere, sunbeams become visible as ribbons of light in the sky.

SCATTERING OF LIGHT, a process whereby a ray of light is altered in direction after colliding with a particle but is not altered in wavelength. The extent to which a beam of light is scattered by particles increases as the size of the particles increases.

A narrow beam of light traveling through distilled water or through a solution of small crystalloid molecules is not noticeably scattered by the particles it meets. If the water or solution is viewed from a direction at right angles to the beam, no light is visible. Such a liquid is said to be optically clear. However, if the beam of light passes through a colloidal solution containing particles with a diameter of approximately 100 nanometers (100×10^{-9} meter), scattering becomes noticeable. If the solution is viewed at right angles to the beam, a cone of light is distinctly visible. This difference in the optical properties of colloidal and crystalloidal solutions which was first pointed out by the British physicist John Tyndall in 1868, is called the Tyndall effect. Light can also be scattered by large enough particles suspended in air. For instance, we see evidence of a Tyndall effect whenever a sunbeam, entering an otherwise dark room, is clearly marked out by the floating dust motes about us.

The Tyndall effect is made use of in the ultramicroscope, which can be used to detect particles not large enough to be seen directly through ordinary microscopes. This is done by viewing the particles at right angles to a beam of light and discerning them by the light they scatter.

The efficiency with which light is scattered varies directly as the fourth power of the frequency of the light. This means that violet light, which roughly has a frequency twice the frequency of red light, is scattered roughly 16 times more than the red light is. Sunlight passing through our inevitably dusty atmosphere gives evidence of this. The light at the blue end of the spectrum is scattered to a far greater extent than the light at the red end. For this reason our daylight sky is so beautifully blue in color (or cigarette smoke sometimes has a bluish cast). We are seeing it by the light of the scattered portion of the spectrum.

Tyndall was the first to explain the blue sky in terms of the scattering of light, but the mathematical analysis of the effect of the frequency of light, the particle size, and the refractive index was carried through in detail by Lord Rayleigh in 1871. As a result, the phenomenon is often called *Rayleigh scattering.*

When the sun is near the horizon, its light travels through a greater thickness of air before reaching the eye, so that scattering is more extensive. Enough light is removed from the blue end of the spectrum to make the sky seem greenish, and the sun itself, visible by the still unscattered light at the red end of the spectrum, seems orange or even red. Sunset is more marked than sunrise in this respect, for by the end of the day man and other life forms have done much to increase the dustiness of the air. When this dustiness is further increased by the massive effects of a volcanic eruption, sunsets are particularly impressive. In fact, after the eruption of Krakatau, in Indonesia, in 1883 sunsets of unearthly beauty were seen the world over for more than a year.

See also AEROSOL; LIGHT—*Behavior of Light.*
ISAAC ASIMOV, *Boston University*

Further Reading: Chandrasekhar, S., and Elbert, Donna D., *Illumination and Polarization of the Sunlit Sky on Rayleigh Scattering* (Am. Phil. 1954); Kerker, Milton, *Scattering of Light and Other Electromagnetic Radiation* (Academic Press 1969); Newton, Roger G., *Scattering Theory of Waves and Particles* (McGraw 1966).

SCAUP, skôp, are compact diving ducks that usually have a black head and white back. They are abundant and are found on all continents except South America. See Duck.

SCEPTER, sep'tər, a staff symbolizing sovereign power. From early times a staff, originally a weapon, has indicated secular or religious authority. Examples are the scepters held by monarchs, the rods of Moses and Aaron, and the croziers of bishops. Others included the batons of Greek messengers and judges, Roman centurions, and modern field marshals and the maces used by certain officers of the British Parliament and of the U. S. House of Representatives.

SCÈVE, sâv, **Maurice** (1500/1510–c. 1560), French poet, who was the principal member of the Lyonese circle of poets. They followed their own literary directions and inclinations, independent of the court poets and theorists of the Pléiade. Living on the busy route leading to and from Italy, the Lyonese group, which included Louise Labé and Pernette du Guillet, was more susceptible to minor literary currents in Italy than were its rivals in the Loire Valley.

Scève was born in Lyon, the son of a city official. His alleged discovery in Avignon in 1533, where he was studying, of the tomb of Laure de Noves, Petrarch's fatal love, first brought him into prominence. King Francis I, himself a poet, was delighted.

Very likely it was the Petrarchan sequence of sonnets and *canzoni* to Laura that inspired Scève's major work, *Délie, objet de plus haulte vertu* (1544), a sequence of *dizains* (ten-line stanzas built on four rhymes) addressed to an ideal woman. *Délie* is obviously an anagram of *l'Idée*, a Platonic ideal, although some scholars have identified her with the Lyonese bluestocking Pernette du Guillet. These love poems fascinated, baffled, and irritated Scève's contemporaries and rivals by their obscurity. The highly refined and carefully worked out poems are still difficult to understand, although scholars have traced their conceits and symbolism to sources in iconology, mythography, cabala, alchemy, lapidaries, bestiaries, Scripture, natural science of antiquity, and the vocabulary of late Petrarchism and neo-Platonism.

Scève was not as prolific as his rivals in the Pléiade group. Among his minor works are a pastoral, *La saulsaye* (*Willow Grove*), and *Microcosme*, a philosophical history in verse of man the microcosm, as the humanists called him. Because of Scève's intriguing symbols and imagery, he has experienced a great revival of interest from the period of Symbolism in late 19th century French poetry to the present.

ROBERT J. CLEMENTS
New York University

Further Reading: Saulnier, Verdun L., *Maurice Scève*, 2 vols. (1948–1949); Scève, Maurice, *Sixty Poems*, tr. by Wallace Fowlie (A. Swallow 1949); id., *Oeuvres Complètes*, ed. by B. Guégan (1927).

SCHACHT, shäкнт, **Hjalmar Horace Greeley** (1877–1970), German financier. He was born in Tingleff, Germany (now Tinglev, Denmark) on Jan. 22, 1877. His mother was an American of Danish descent, and he spent most of his boyhood, to the age of 12, in the United States.

Active in banking in Germany from 1903, he became director (1916) of the Nationalbank für Deutschland, which by fusion expanded in 1922 into the Darmstädter and Nationalbank. In 1923, next to Hans Luther, he contributed most toward ending German inflation and creating a stable new currency. Schacht was made Reich currency commissar and in December 1923 president of the Reichsbank. In 1929 he was Germany's chief delegate at the Paris conference that drafted a new plan of German reparations, and he accepted the resulting Young Plan. In April 1930, however, he renounced the plan, which had been approved by The Hague conference of governments, because of the provisions for its execution on which the conference had agreed. Schacht also resigned as Reichsbank president.

In 1931 he assisted in effecting an alliance of the German Nationalist and the Nazi parties in the so-called Harzburg front. In March 1933, Adolf Hitler made him Reichsbank president. He remained until 1939, serving in addition as Reich minister of economics in 1934–1937. In four years Schacht managed to bring the German economy, which in 1932 had reached the bottom of the depression, to a state of high productivity and full employment. The end and means of his policies were German rearmament.

When he became convinced that Hitler intended to use the new armed forces for aggression, however, Schacht became an opponent of the regime. He was arrested and held in the Dachau concentration camp in 1944. Brought to trial as a war criminal before the International Military Tribunal at Nuremberg, he was acquitted in 1946. He was held by German denazification courts until 1948 and afterward was active as a banker. His memoirs, *76 Jahre meines Lebens*, appeared in 1953. He died in Munich on June 4, 1970.

HAJO HOLBORN
Author of "A History of Modern Germany"

SCHAFF, shaf, **Philip** (1819–1893), American church historian and theologian who was a co-originator of the "Mercersburg theology." Schaff was born in Chur, Switzerland, Jan. 1, 1819. He studied at the universities of Tübingen and Halle and received his theological degree at Berlin in 1841. He lectured at Berlin, where he was much influenced by the scholar Johann A. W. Neander.

Schaff went to the United States in 1844 to teach church history and literature in the Theological Seminary of the German Reformed Church at Mercersburg, Pa. His inaugural address, published as *The Principle of Protestantism* (1845), displayed his great interest in church union. He viewed the history of the Christian Church as a divinely appointed development that would lead eventually to the blending of the values of Catholicism and Protestantism in an evangelical Catholicism. Charges of heresy were leveled against him before the Reformed Synod, but he was exonerated. Schaff was very critical of the revivalism of American Protestantism and joined with his colleague John W. Nevin in the development of the "Mercersburg theology," which sought a return to the theological heritage of the Reformation, urged liturgical renewal, and stressed ecumenism.

In 1864 Schaff became secretary of the New York Sabbath Committee and in 1870 joined the faculty of the Union Theological Seminary in New York City. Among the 80 publications that brought him recognition as a theological scholar

Schaffhausen is on the Rhine River. The Munot fortress on the hill was built between 1564 and 1585.

1208. It was ruled first by its abbots, then by the Habsburgs, and after 1415 by its trade guilds. The city joined the Swiss Confederation in 1501.

The Canton. The northernmost of the Swiss cantons, Schaffhausen lies almost entirely north of the Rhine, with two of its three separate sections almost surrounded by West Germany. Its area is 115 square miles (298 sq km). A large majority of the population is Protestant and German-speaking.

The canton includes the southern fringes of the Black Forest and slopes down in the south to the Rhine Valley, where the population is concentrated. Over half the people live in the capital and its industrial suburb, Neuhausen. The famous Rheinfall ("Falls of the Rhine") are at Neuhausen. Cultivated lands produce cereals, vegetables, and fruits, and manufactures include watches, jewelry, and aluminum. Hydroelectric plants on the Rhine supply power. Population: (1970) of the city, 37,035; of the canton, 72,854.

SCHARNHORST, shärn'hôrst, **Gerhard Johann David von** (1755–1813), Prussian general, who was the chief creator of the modern Prussian military system, which was the foundation of the German armies of the 20th century. He was also the father of the Prussian general staff. He educated the first generation of officers, among them Karl von Clausewitz, who was the theoretician of the later army.

Scharnhorst was born at Bordenau, Hannover, Germany, on Nov. 12, 1755, the son of a farmer. He became an artillery officer in the Hannover army in 1778. He transferred to the Prussian service in 1801, and three years later he was knighted.

He was chief of staff of one of the two Prussian armies that were decisively beaten by Napoleon Bonaparte's troops in the double battle of Jena and Auerstadt on Oct. 14, 1806. He was captured by the French but was soon exchanged. In the Battle of Eylau (Feb. 7–8, 1807), in which Russian and Prussian troops for the first time fought Napoleon to a temporary stalemate, he proved his superior strategic judgment.

After the Peace of Tilsit (July 9, 1807), which left a badly mutilated Prussia, Scharnhorst was appointed director of the war ministry and chief of staff of the Prussian Army. In close association with Baron Karl vom und zum Stein and Prince Karl August von Hardenburg, he reformed the Prussian military system. Learning from the examples of the American and French revolutions, he abolished the mercenary character of the army, which he transformed into a national force based on universal conscription. The Peace of Tilsit had limited the Prussian Army to 42,000 men, and Scharnhorst could therefore only prepare plans for a national guard, but by rapid training and change of conscripts he created at least a reserve. Corporal punishment was abolished, and military discipline was generally adjusted to that of a citizens' army.

After Napoleon's defeat in Russia in 1812, Scharnhorst directed the mobilization of Prussian forces for the war of liberation, but he was severely wounded in its first battle at Grossgörschen (Lutzen) on May 2, 1813, and died in Prague, Bohemia, on June 28, 1813.

HAJO HOLBORN
Author of "A History of Modern Germany"

were his *Creeds of Christendom* (3 vols., 1877) and *History of the Christian Church* (5th ed., revised and enlarged; 7 vols., 1882–1892). He was editor of the English translation of Johann Peter Lange's *Commentary on the Holy Scriptures* (25 vols., 1865–1880) and of a translation and adaptation of Johann J. Herzog's *Realenzyklopädie,* called *The Schaff-Herzog Encyclopedia of Religious Knowledge* (3 vols., 1882–1884).

Schaff participated in the preparation of the Revised Version of the Bible and founded the American Society of Church History in 1888. He died in New York City on Oct. 29, 1893.

ROBERT T. HANDY
Union Theological Seminary

SCHAFFHAUSEN, shäf-hou'zən, is a city in Switzerland and the capital of Schaffhausen canton. The city is on the north bank of the Rhine River, 23 miles (37 km) north of Zürich. It is an important rail and manufacturing center, producing metal goods, textiles, and watches.

A river port in the Middle Ages, it derived its name from the skiff houses along the riverbank where cargoes were handled. The town grew around the All Saints Abbey, founded about 1050, of which the Romanesque minster remains. The inscription on its bell is said to have inspired Schiller's *Song of the Bell.* Monastery buildings now contain an important national museum. Other historic buildings include the 16th century circular fortress, the Munot. Schaffhausen became a free imperial city about

SCHAUMBURG, shoum'bûrg, is a village in northeastern Illinois, in Cook and Du Page counties. It is about 30 miles (48 km) northwest of Chicago, of which it is a suburb. It is principally a residential community, but there is some light industry. Schaumburg was built up during the 1960's. Before then it was only sparsely settled. Population: 18,730.

SCHAUMBURG-LIPPE, shoum'bŏŏrκн-lip'ə, was formerly an independent German state, with its capital at Bückeberg. Since 1946 it has been a district in the West German state of Lower Saxony. It is in the northwest, east of the Weser River, and has an area of 131 square miles (339 sq km). It has rolling hills and is primarily agricultural.

Schaumburg-Lippe was formed in 1643 from a part of the once extensive medieval countship of Schaumburg (or Schauenburg) and a section of the countship of Lippe. It was ruled by a branch of the Lippe family and became a principality in 1807, the year in which it joined the Confederation of the Rhine. It was also a member of the German Confederation, created in 1815 as a replacement for the Holy Roman Empire. After the Austro-Prussian War of 1866, Schaumburg-Lippe joined Prussia and other German states north of the Main River in the North German Confederation. It entered the German Empire in 1871. After 1866, Schaumburg-Lippe was surrounded by Prussian territory. The last prince, Adolf, abdicated on Nov. 16, 1918. Statehood was retained under the Weimar Republic and the people twice (1926, 1930) declined to unite with Prussia. The Nazis placed it under a governor in 1933, and it was included in Lower Saxony after World War II.

SCHECHTER, shek'tər, **Solomon** (1847–1915), Rumanian-born Jewish scholar and theologian who formulated the philosophy of Conservative Judaism. Schechter was born in Focsani, Rumania, on Dec. 7, 1847. He studied at Vienna and Berlin before going to England in 1882, where he lectured at Jews' College in London. In 1890 was appointed reader in rabbinical literature at University College, Cambridge. After 1899 he also taught Hebrew at the University of London. In 1896 he identified one of the Genizah fragments and in 1897 took from Cairo to Cambridge an invaluable store of these Hebrew and Arabic manuscripts.

A leader of the Conservative wing of Judaism, Schechter opposed the Reform movement and as a Zionist believed that that movement should be religious in nature and not merely nationalistic. He went to the United States in 1902 to become president of the Jewish Theological Seminary in New York City. He became chief spokesman for Conservative Judaism.

He was an editor of the first edition of *The Jewish Encyclopedia* and of the English translation of the Hebrew Bible published in 1917. Among his many published works are *Studies in Judaism* (1896). Schechter died in New York City on Nov. 19, 1915.

SCHECHTER CASE, shek'tər, a landmark decision of the U.S. Supreme Court, which held in *Schechter Poultry Corp.* v. *United States* (1935) that the National Industrial Recovery Act providing for self-regulation of industry is unconstitutional.

SCHEELE, shā'lə, **Carl Wilhelm** (1742–1786), Swedish chemist who was the uncredited discoverer of oxygen. Scheele was born in Stralsund, Sweden (now Germany), on Dec. 9, 1742. Seventh in a family of eleven children, he was apprenticed to an apothecary in Göteborg, Sweden, at the age of 14 and remained a pharmacist for the rest of his life—in Malmo, Stockholm, Uppsala, and, after 1775, in Koping. In those days pharmacists prepared their own drugs, and minerals, not infrequently becoming deeply engaged in chemical research.

As a discoverer of new substances, Scheele was unparalleled in the history of chemistry. Among organic compounds he isolated tartaric acid early in his career and gallic acid, malic acid, citric acid, and oxalic acid in the last years of his short life. Among inorganic compounds he was the first to isolate the toxic gases hydrogen sulfide, hydrogen fluoride, and hydrogen cyanide. He also discovered the colored compound copper arsenite—now called Scheele's green—and was the first to demonstrate the presence of calcium phosphate in bone.

It is in connection with the chemical elements, however, that he achieved his greatest fame. He either discovered or greatly contributed to the discovery of manganese, nitrogen, oxygen, tungsten, barium, molybdenum, and chlorine. Yet it was Scheele's misfortune that in each case the credit for the discovery went elsewhere. Thus, he actually isolated and described chlorine in 1774 but did not recognize it as an element. The credit went to Sir Humphry Davy in 1810 for demonstrating its elementary nature. Worse yet, Scheele discovered oxygen as early as 1771, but the description of his experiments was delayed through the negligence of his publisher, so that Joseph Priestley, whose discovery was three years later than Scheele's, published first and received the credit.

There remains to Scheele, however, the fact that the mineral from which he first obtained tungstic acid in 1781 is still called scheelite in his honor.

Scheele suffered from severe rheumatic attacks in the last years of his life. He died in Koping on May 21, 1786, at the age of 43. He never married until three days before his death, and then only in order that the widow of the former owner of the pharmacy that Scheele had purchased in 1776 might inherit and once again own it.

ISAAC ASIMOV
Boston University

SCHEELITE, shā'līt, or calcium tungstate, is an important ore of tungsten in the United States. Elsewhere, wolframite is the more important ore of the metal. Scheelite is named after the Swedish chemist Carl Scheele.

Crystals of the mineral are translucent to transparent and have a glassy to diamondlike luster. They may be white, yellow, brown, or green. The mineral commonly occurs in crystalline or granular masses and is found in granite pegmatites and metamorphic deposits. The most important occurrences of scheelite in the United States are in Nevada and California. The mineral is also found in Australia, Czechoslovakia, England, and Germany.

Composition, $CaWO_4$ (molybdenum also usually present); hardness, 4.5–5; specific gravity, 5.9–6.1; crystal system, tetragonal.

SCHEFFEL, shef'əl, **Viktor von** (1826–1886), German poet and writer of popular historical novels. Joseph Viktor von Scheffel was born in Karlsruhe on Feb. 16, 1826, and studied law at the universities of Munich, Heidelberg, and Berlin. He held a government post in Frankfurt am Main and had a law practice in Säckingen. His first success as a writer was his charmingly humorous epic poem, *Der Trompeter von Säckingen* (1854). He then resigned his post and moved to Heidelberg, where he hoped to become a professor, but an eye ailment forced him to put aside his ambition. He died in Karlsruhe on April 9, 1886.

In 1857, Scheffel published *Ekkehard, eine Geschichte aus dem zehnten Jahrshundert,* which, because of its romantic appeal, became one of the most popular novels of the day. Set in the 10th century at the monastery of St. Gall, it is based on sound historical study and relates the history of a young monk who writes the famous Latin poem *Waltharius,* the tale of Walter of Aquitaine and his betrothed, Hildegund of Burgundy. Scheffel's collection of student songs, *Gaudeamus, Leiden aus dem Engeren und Weiteren* (1868), was also very successful. Among his other works are the historical novels *Heigeido* (1857) and *Juniperus, Geschichte eines Kreuzfahrens* (1867).

SCHEFFLERA, shef'lər-ə, any of several shrubby tropical plants of the genus *Schefflera* of the family Araliaceae. The plants are excellent for decorative landscaping in warm regions, and their showy smooth foliage makes them desirable as houseplants. The umbrella tree, *S. actinophylla,* is well suited for growing as a houseplant in a pot or tub.

This native of Australia has leaves consisting of five stemmed leaflets arranged like fingers at the end of a main stalk. Scheffleras are best raised from seeds. They prefer a well-drained, porous soil enriched with fertilizer. The genus is named for the German botanist G. C. Scheffler.

Schefflera, a tropical plant popular as a houseplant.

ROCHE (1509)

SCHEHERAZADE, shə-her-ə-zäd', is the heroine of the frame story of the *Arabian Nights.* Scheherazade, a daughter of the Grand Vizier of the Indies, marries the antifeminist Sultan Shahriar, who ·has vowed to marry a new wife every day and kill each bride the following morning. Scheherazade saves herself by beginning to tell a new tale to her husband every night and refusing to finish it until the next. After she has told 1,001 tales, the sultan is convinced of her worthiness and makes her his consort.

Rimsky-Korsakov composed a symphonic suite, *Scheherazade* (1888), which was based on the *Arabian Nights.* In 1910 the suite was adapted for a ballet, which centers on the action of the work's prologue.

SCHEIDEMANN, shī'də-män, **Philipp** (1865–1939), German political leader. He was born in Kassel on July 26, 1865, and was a member of the Social Democratic party from his youth. He edited the party's newspaper, served as a deputy in the Reichstag, and in 1911 became secretary of the party.

Although in the early years of World War I he rallied his party in support of the government, toward the end he joined with Matthias Erzberger of the Center party in advocating a "peace without annexations or indemnities." In 1918 he was briefly secretary of state without portfolio in the cabinet of Prince Max of Baden, but after the internal revolution and the abdication of Emperor William II, Scheidemann gave up his post and, on November 9, proclaimed the new German republic. In February 1919 he was elected president of the republic's first ministry, but he resigned in June in protest over the Treaty of Versailles, which he refused to sign. He sat in the Reichstag again as Social Democratic deputy after 1920 but left Germany after Hitler took power in 1933. Scheidemann died in Copenhagen on Nov. 29, 1939.

SCHEIDT, shīt, **Samuel** (1587–1654), German composer. He was born in Halle and studied music in Amsterdam. He became the organist of the Halle Moritzkirche in 1608 or 1609 and by 1620 was *Kappelmeister* to the Margrave of Brandenburg. He died in Halle on March 30, 1654.

Reacting against the superficial, "coloristic" compositions of his time, Scheidt composed sacred organ music of sober, powerful expressiveness. He made extensive use of fugue and prepared the way for the extended works of the northern baroque, or Gothic, style. He was important in the evolution of Protestant church music, being among the first to write true organ chorales. His numerous compositions include a Mass, Magnificats, figured chorales, fantasias, toccatas, hymns, sacred concertos, dances, and *70 Symphonien . . .* with figured bass.

HERBERT WEINSTOCK
Coauthor of "Men of Music"

SCHELDT RIVER, skelt, a northern European river that rises in northeastern France, crosses western Belgium, and enters the North Sea through the Netherlands' Zeeland province. The French name for the river is Escaut, and the Flemish and Dutch name is Schelde. Its source is near Le Catelet. It flows past Ghent and up to Antwerp, Belgium's principal port.

The Scheldt is 270 miles (435 km) long, and almost all of it, due to an extensive system of locks, is navigable. Its principal tributaries are the Lys (which joins it at Ghent), the Dender, and the Rupel.

Navigation rights on the Scheldt River were long a source of irritation between Belgium and the Netherlands. Since 1925 a joint commission has exercised jurisdiction over the river.

SCHELER, shā′lər, **Max** (1874–1928), German philosopher who was an early advocate of the phenomenological approach in philosophy. Scheler was born in Munich on Aug. 22, 1874. He studied at the University of Jena, where he came into contact with the spiritualism of Rudolf Christoph Eucken and the neo-Kantianism of Otto Liebmann. After meeting Edmund Husserl in 1901, Scheler found that he too had been moving toward a more complete philosophy of experience without the artificial limitations of traditional empiricism and rationalism. His subsequent reference to himself as a cofounder of phenomenology was not accepted by Husserl, although Scheler became a coeditor of the latter's *Jahrbuch für Philosophie und phänomenologische Forschung* and contributed a two-part work, *Der Formalismus in der Ethik und die materiale Wertethik* (Formalism in Ethics and Material Ethics), to its first two volumes (1913, 1916). In 1919 he became a professor of philosophy at the University of Cologne.

After a period of formal adherence to Roman Catholicism (about 1920 to 1924), Scheler saw a threat to the individual in the dogmas of the church and renounced natural theology as conceived on the basis of Thomism. For its proper instatement he looked to an antischolastic version of Augustinianism, freed from the accretions of history and founded by a phenomenological philosophy that viewed existence with fresh eyes. In this manner the immediate contact of the soul with God was to be revealed and demonstrated.

Scheler reacted in his way to many of the leading intellectual movements of his time. The central idea of historical materialism was appropriated by means of a "sociology of knowledge," with the economic factor subordinated to a pluralistic view and to a "philosophical anthropology" that provided for spiritual values. An opponent of the evolutionary theory, he defended the interests of supernaturalism. He wrote feelingly in defense of Germany in World War I, and he has been charged with anticipating some aspects of Nazi ideology. Scheler died in Frankfurt am Main on May 19, 1928.

MARVIN FARBER
State University of New York

Further Reading: Farber, Marvin, *Naturalism and Subjectivism* (Thomas 1959); Scheler, Max, *The Nature of Sympathy,* tr. by Peter Heath (Yale Univ. Press 1954); id., *On the Eternal Mind,* tr. by Bernard Noble (Harper 1961).

SCHELLING, shel′ing, **Friedrich Wilhelm Joseph von** (1775–1854), German idealist philosopher who laid the foundation for the development of Hegelian idealism. Schelling was born in Leonberg, Württemberg on Jan. 27, 1775. He studied theology at Tübingen and in 1798 became a professor at the University of Jena, where he soon found fame and admiration. For a while he was a friend and colleague of Fichte. After serving as a professor at Würzburg from 1803 to 1806, he was called to the Munich Academy. From 1820 to 1826 he taught at the University of Erlangen. He accepted a call to Berlin in 1841, but gave up his teaching career in 1846. Schelling died in Ragaz, Switzerland, on Aug. 20, 1854.

With Fichte and Hegel, Schelling was one of the greatest German idealists. His intellectual influence is seen both in his impact on transcendental philosophy and in his work on the philosophy of nature, history, and art. While he is frequently viewed as a link between Fichte and Hegel, he is less often recognized as the first notable critic of post-Kantian idealism. This facet of his thought is recognizable in his shift, in the interpretation of nature and history, from a rational dialectic, which regards the order and development of being as the same as the order and development of thought, to an existential dialectic, which seeks to ground the conditions of thought in the datum of experience.

The Newtonian mechanical vision of the world was effectively demolished by the critical philosophical work of Hume and Kant. Schelling, like Fichte, at first attempted to describe the way in which man's intellect must be supposed to operate in the process of knowing. He tried to state the means whereby man knows the universe and the process whereby the intellect grasps reality. Fichte saw the world as the scene of man's duty and the basis of his moral freedom, but Schelling adopted a more objective account of reality and prepared the way for Hegelian absolute idealism. In his view, reality was identical with the necessary movement of thought, evolving dialectically. Although he differed in many ways from Hegel, he laid the foundation for much of the latter's philosophy. For Schelling, as for Hegel, the real is the rational process of the world developing toward its realization in the final, unified expression of ultimate truth. It is possible to know the world completely by tracing reflectively the logical process whereby the movement of nature and history necessarily comes to pass. The goal of the process is a completed state of self consciousness. Schelling called the universal mind, whose developments constitute this process, absolute identity. Hegel called it the ideal.

In his later philosophy, Schelling went beyond Hegel as he grew increasingly discontented with the logical pantheism of his earlier system. He turned to a voluntarism that in some ways anticipated Schopenhauer and Nietzsche, and launched an attack on all forms of rationalism. The universe, he taught, cannot be assumed at the outset to be a rational system. Rather, form and order are derived from the attempt to impose a logical structure on an originally chaotic impulse or force. From 1809 on he endeavored to develop a "metaphysical empiricism" by means of which he could show that rational order is a hypothetical construct requiring confirmation by the concrete events of nature and history. In addition, he sought to show that the categories of religion are ultimately more meaningful expressions of the content of the real. Schelling has thus been identified as one of the formative figures in the development of the philosophy of existence.

PAUL C. HAYNER
California State College at Fullerton

Further Reading: Schelling, Friedrich W. J. von, *The Ages of the World,* tr. by Frederick Bolman (Oxford 1942); id., *On Human Freedom,* tr. by James Guttmann (Open Air 1936).

SCHENCK, shengk, **Robert Cumming** (1809–1890), American congressman and diplomat. He was born in Franklin, Ohio, on Oct. 4, 1809. Graduated from Miami University in 1827, he was admitted to the bar in 1831 and began to practice law in Dayton, Ohio. He entered politics with a term in the Ohio legislature (1841–1843), then served as a Whig leader in the U. S. House of Representatives from 1843 to 1851. From 1851 to 1853 he was U. S. minister to Brazil.

On the outbreak of the Civil War, Schenck was commissioned brigadier general of volunteers. He fought in both battles of Bull Run, sustaining serious wounds in the second. Commissioned a major general in August 1862, he was in command at Baltimore until his resignation in 1863 to return to Congress, where he served as a Republican until 1871.

Appointed U. S. minister to Britain, he held that post from 1871 to 1876, when he resigned in the aftermath of an unfortunate involvement in a mine promotion scheme. The Utah silver mine of which he was a director had been using his name in attempting to sell stock in Britain. Though Schenck's own integrity was not questioned, it was considered out of keeping for a diplomat to have been connected with such a venture. Schenck retired from public service and practiced law in Washington, D. C., where he died on March 23, 1890.

SCHENCK v. UNITED STATES, shengk, a landmark decision of the U. S. Supreme Court in 1919 in which the court held that speech cannot be punished unless there is a "clear and present danger" that it will lead to evils Congress has a right to prevent. See also CIVIL RIGHTS AND LIBERTIES.

SCHENECTADY, skǝ-nek'tǝ-dē, is a city in eastern New York state, the seat of Schenectady county, on the south bank of the Mohawk River and the State Barge Canal, 13 miles (20 km) northwest of Albany. It is part of the Albany-Schenectady-Troy metropolitan area, whose population is 720,786.

Schenectady is a major industrial city. Its principal manufactured products are electrical, atomic, and jet machinery and materials, including large turbines and generators and large and small motors; diesel locomotives; insulating materials; and chemicals and plastics. Extensive industrial research and development is carried on, especially in the field of environmental measurement devices.

The city is the seat of Union College and University. The college, founded in 1795, was the birthplace of Greek-letter social fraternities in the United States. Its campus was designed on the first comprehensive plan for a college campus, drawn in 1812 by the French architect Joseph Jacques Ramée. The university, an association of independent institutions, formed in 1873, includes a medical college, a law school, and a college of pharmacy, all situated in Albany.

The Schenectady Museum on Nott Terrace Heights maintains museums of art, natural history, science and technology, and a planetarium. It conducts an active program throughout the year. The Schenectady County Historical Society organizes exhibits of Indian artifacts and local history.

History. The Mohawk Indian name for the site of Schenectady was *Schonowe* (big flats).

The name *Schenectady* means "at the end of the pine plains," referring to the old portage between the Hudson River near Albany and the Mohawk River, which led across a flat country covered with scrub pine trees.

The first settlement was Dutch. Arent Van Curler purchased land from the Indians in 1661, and the next year fur traders and farmers around Albany built homes there. The community was burned and many of its inhabitants were massacred in an Indian raid on Feb. 8, 1690, but it was soon rebuilt.

Schenectady was chartered as a city in 1798. Its economy had long benefited from the stream of pioneers moving westward up the Mohawk valley. With the opening of the Erie Canal in 1825, the city's period of industrial growth began. Shipyards built craft for canal and river traffic. A locomotive works was established in 1848, the beginning of an industry that is still identified with Schenectady. The creation of the General Electric Company's great plant in 1892 founded Schenectady's other famous industry. A slogan was coined: "The city that lights and hauls the world."

Schenectady is governed by a city council and a city manager. Population: 67,972.

SCHERZO, sker'tzō, is a term that is applied to a movement in a musical composition. The term is the Italian word for "joke." In modern music it refers to a playful, humorous, or capricious movement of a symphony, sonata, or concerto. It evolved from the minuet and trio movement, as developed by Haydn, and is generally written in this form. The term, however, was used long before Haydn's time to indicate either outright musical jokes or simply playful music. The most notable early example is Monteverdi's *Scherzi musicali* (1628).

Beethoven found the scherzo a congenial channel of expression for his boisterous sense of humor, and in his hands it attained a recognized importance. Later composers also wrote scherzos, although their character is often light and graceful rather than humorous. The term is also sometimes given to independent compositions, such as Chopin's scherzos for the piano.

SCHIAPARELLI, skyä-pä-rel'lē, **Elsa** (1890–1973), Italian-French couturiere, known for her international influence on women's fashions. She was born in Rome, reportedly on Sept. 10, 1890, the daughter of a University of Rome professor, and died in Paris on Nov. 13, 1973. For a time she wrote scripts in New York City, and in the 1920's went to France, of which she later became a citizen. In Paris she began to design and manufacture pullover sweaters and in 1927 set up her first workshop on the Boulevard St. Germain. She soon established herself in haute couture with her designs for sportswear, town suits, evening dresses, and other costumes, moving to larger quarters first on the Rue de la Paix (1929) and then on the Place Vendôme (1935), where she also set up a perfume business.

Mme. Schiaparelli's flair was for understanding the spirit of the age. She was always startled by some "eccentricity," which rapidly became the mode. Her "shocking pink," for instance, introduced a new note into the color spectrum of fashion, and it was she who brought the long reign of the cloche to an end by sticking a sock sideways on her head and calling it a hat.

After lecturing in the United States during World War II, she reopened the Place Vendôme establishment in 1945, and in 1949 she opened a branch in New York City to mass-produce her creations. She told the story of her career in her book, *Shocking Life,* published in 1954.

JAMES C. LAVER
Author of "Taste and Fashion"

SCHIAPARELLI, skyä-pä-rel'lē, **Giovanni Virginio** (1835–1910), Italian astronomer who first reported observing straight-line markings on Mars. He was born in Savigliano on March 14, 1835. After graduating from the University of Turin, he studied in Berlin and under Friedrich von Struve in Pulkovo, Russia. He then joined the staff at the Brera Observatory in Milan and later became its director. He died in Milan on July 4, 1910.

Schiaparelli devoted his studies primarily to the solar system. He investigated comets, discovered the minor planet Hesperia in 1861, and observed vague markings on the planet Mercury. In 1887 he published the first accounts of his observations of markings on the surface of Mars. He described them as a linked system of straight lines and called them *canali,* meaning "channels." The word was mistranslated as "canals," which only reinforced the speculations of a few prominent astronomers such as Percival Lowell that the markings were suspiciously artificial and could indicate the presence of intelligent life on Mars. The markings, in fact, were an optical illusion. See also MARS.

SCHICK, shik, **Béla** (1877–1967), Hungarian-American pediatrician who developed the Schick test for determining susceptibility to diphtheria. Schick was born in Boglár, Hungary, on July 16, 1877. He received his doctorate from Karl Franz University in Graz, Austria, and took up practice in Vienna. He was also associated with the University of Vienna from 1902 to 1923. He then went to the United States, where he became a citizen in 1929. He served as a consulting pediatrician at Mount Sinai Hospital in New York City and at several other institutions, and from 1936 to his retirement he was clinical professor of children's diseases at Columbia University. He died in New York on Dec. 6, 1967.

Schick developed his diphtheria test while at the University of Vienna. He first revealed the process in 1908 and then perfected the technique in 1913. The test showed that the number of infants susceptible to the disease increases up to one year of age but decreases thereafter. (See also DIPHTHERIA.) Schick also wrote extensively on scarlet fever, tuberculosis, the nutrition of children, and allergies.

SCHICK TEST, shik, a skin test given to determine immunity to diphtheria. It was developed by the Hungarian pediatrician Béla Schick. The test involves the injection of a small amount of diphtheria toxin under the skin. The appearance of a red spot near the injection site within 48 hours indicates susceptibility to diphtheria and the need for vaccination.

SCHIEDAM, sКНē-däm', is a city in the Netherlands, in South Holland province, near the confluence of the Schie and Nieuwe Maas rivers, 3.5 miles (6 km) west of Rotterdam. Its principal industry is the distilling of gin, which is exported throughout the world. It also has important shipyards and plants producing glass, chemicals, and machinery. The town is intersected by numerous canals.

Notable buildings include a 17th century town hall and the 15th century Church of St. John. Schiedam was chartered in 1273 and flourished as a fishing port and trade center in the Middle Ages. It was later superseded by Rotterdam. Population: (1971 est.) 83,313.

THE MINNEAPOLIS INSTITUTE OF ARTS
Egon Schiele's portrait of Paris Von Gütersloh (1918).

SCHIELE, shē'lē, **Egon** (1890–1918), Austrian painter and draftsman of the expressionist school. He was born in Tulln on June 12, 1890. Trained at the Vienna Academy of Fine Arts, he was influenced by Gustave Klimt, who, as founder of the Vienna Secession, worked in the decorative, linear *Jugendstil* (art nouveau).

Schiele's nudes and landscapes, in oil and pencil, had a sharp linear quality with strong color accents, as, for example, *Girl in Black Stockings* (1911; private collection). These works and his portraits have a personal intensity that links him to the expressionists. The portraits, painted with harsh brushstrokes and dissonant colors, emphasize hands, as, for example, *The Painter Paris Von Gütersloh* (1918; Minneapolis Institute of Art). Although drafted into the army in 1915, Schiele continued to paint and took part in the Secessionist exhibition of 1918. He died of influenza, in Vienna, on Oct. 31, 1918.

SCHIFF, shif, **Jacob Henry** (1847–1920), German-born American financier. He was born in Frankfurt-am-Main, Germany, on Jan. 10, 1847. He went to the United States in 1865. Five years later, he joined the brokerage firm of Kuhn, Loeb & Co., and became its president in 1885.

Schiff was involved in the financing of many important railroads, especially the Pennsylvania and the Baltimore and Ohio. He backed Edward H. Harriman of the Union Pacific in his struggle with James J. Hill of the Great Northern for control of the Northern Pacific. Schiff also engaged in industrial financing. Among his clients were the American Smelting and Refining Company, the Westinghouse Electric Company, and the Western Union Telegraph Company. He was interested in enterprises in Mexico and other countries. In 1904, during the Russo-Japanese War, he obtained a $200 million loan for Japan.

Schiff's intellectual and philanthropic activities were widespread. He established the Semitic Museum at Harvard University, created departments of Semitic literature in the New York Public Library and the Library of Congress, and aided the Jewish Theological Seminary. He was a founder of the American Jewish Committee and gave liberally to help Jews in want during World War I. Schiff died in New York City on Sept. 25, 1920.

SCHIKANEDER, shē-kä-nä′dər, **Emanuel Johann** (1751–1812), German actor, singer, impresario, and author, best known as the librettist of Mozart's opera *The Magic Flute.* He was born in Straubing, Germany, on Sept. 1, 1751. In 1773 he set out as a wandering theatrical musician and soon functioned as actor, singer, director, and playwright. When his troupe visited Salzburg, Austria, in 1780, he met the Mozart family. He pursued his multiple professions at Graz, Pressburg, and Budapest, then settled in Vienna in 1784. In 1789 he became manager of the Theater auf der Wieden.

Among the numerous librettos that Schikaneder wrote was *The Magic Flute,* composed as a Singspiel (an opera including spoken dialogue) by Mozart in 1790–1791. Schikaneder sang the role of Papageno when the opera was first produced, in Vienna, in 1791. He later founded the Theater an der Wien and managed it from 1801 to 1806. He then suffered severe financial losses and died, insane, in Vienna on Sept. 21, 1812.

HERBERT WEINSTOCK
Coauthor of "Men of Music"

SCHILLER, shil-ər, **Ferdinand Canning Scott** (1864–1937), English philosopher, who was a leading English pragmatist. Schiller was born in Ottensen, near Hamburg, Germany on Aug. 16, 1864. Educated in England at Rugby and Oxford University's Balliol College, he was instructor in philosophy at Cornell University from 1893 to 1897. He returned to Oxford, where from 1897 to 1926 he was tutor in philosophy and fellow of Corpus Christi College. From 1929 to 1936 he taught at the University of Southern California. Schiller died in Los Angeles, Calif., on Aug. 6, 1937.

Schiller was much influenced by the American philosopher William James, whom he met at Cornell. He became England's leading exponent of pragmatism, in a version he variously called humanism, voluntarism, and personalism. Rejecting both absolutism and naturalism, he insisted that man, as the starting point and the goal of all experience, must be the only measure of any system of ideas. An enthusiastic and stimulating man, he wrote a number of books, notably *Riddles of the Sphinx* (1891), *Studies in Humanism* (1907), *Logic for Use* (1929), and *Our Human Truths,* a collection of his last writings published posthumously (1939).

CULVER PICTURES
Friedrich von Schiller, German poet and dramatist

SCHILLER, shil′ər, **Friedrich von** (1759–1805), German dramatist, poet, historian, philosopher, and aesthetic theorist, who was one of the giants of German literature. Schiller and his contemporary Goethe are the chief representatives of German classicism.

The Rebellious Youth. Johann Christoph Friedrich von Schiller was born in Marbach, Württemberg, on Nov. 10, 1759. His father was an officer and surgeon in the army of Duke Karl Eugen of Württemberg. Young Schiller received his early education (1766–1773) in the "Latin School" in Ludwigsburg. However, his plan to prepare himself for the study of theology at Tübingen was thwarted by the Duke, who ordered him to attend the Karlsschule, a military academy newly founded by the Duke himself. Schiller attended the academy (located in Stuttgart after 1775) from 1773 to 1780. The strict military discipline and spirit of the school were repugnant to the young pupil and did much to shape his early writings.

In 1780 the young rebel was dismissed from the academy after writing the essay *Versuch über den Zusammenhang der tierischen Natur des Menschen mit seiner geistigen (On the Relation Between Man's Animal and Spiritual Nature).* Without a degree, Schiller was given the socially inferior position of assistant regimental medical officer at Stuttgart.

Schiller's early readings, surreptitiously obtained, included the works of Friedrich Gottlieb Klopstock; Lessing's play *Emilia Galotti;* and the *Sturm und Drang* ("Storm and Stress") playwrights. His first drama, *Die Räuber (The Robbers),* was begun in 1777 and finished in 1780. It was published in 1781 and first performed in Mannheim in January 1782. The work was a tremendous success and established its author as a born dramatist who instinctively found the pathos of the stage language and who knew how to achieve genuine theatrical effects. Schiller, who had left his medical post at Stuttgart without the Duke's permission, was present at the performance.

When the Duke further curtailed Schiller's liberty by threatening him with dismissal if he did not cease "the writing of comedies and of all nonmedical works," he fled from Württemberg in September 1782, with his friend, the musician Andreas Streicher. Schiller's second play, *Die Verschwörung des Fiesko zu Genua* (*Fiesco; or, the Genoese Conspiracy*), did not find favor with the Mannheim theater director, Baron Heribert von Dalberg. The play was not performed until October 1783, at Frankfurt am Main. Fearing persecution by the Duke, Schiller then took refuge, in December 1782, in the home of Frau Henriette von Wolzogen in Bauerbach. Here he wrote his third drama, the middle-class tragedy he called first *Luise Millerin* and then *Kabale und Liebe* (*Cabal and Love*, or *Intrigue and Love*), which was given its first performances in Frankfurt am Main and Mannheim on, respectively, April 13 and April 15, 1784. In the first three dramas Schiller's unbridled genius gave full vent, in massive attacks, to his hatred of vice, of the arbitrariness of tyrants, and of the corruption at the courts of his day.

The Theater-Poet. On Sept. 1, 1783, Schiller was given the post of theater-poet at the Mannheim theater, with the stipulation that he provide three plays a year. However, his contract was not renewed in the following year. During his stay at Mannheim he fell passionately in love with Charlotte von Kalb, the wife of a French captain. He found surcease from the conflict between his passion and duty in two poems, *Freigeisterei der Leidenschaft* (*Freethinking of Passion*, later called *The Struggle*) and *Resignation*.

Schiller left Mannheim for Leipzig in April 1785 and then went on to Dresden. At this time he began his lifelong friendship with Christian Gottfried Körner, at whose homes in Leipzig and Dresden he stayed for two years. In Dresden he wrote the hymn *An die Freude* (*To Joy*), later set to music by Beethoven in the fourth movement of the Ninth Symphony; worked on his fourth drama, *Don Carlos*; studied history; and occupied himself with various social and philosophical questions.

In 1787, Schiller left Dresden because he had been offered a position as theater-poet at Hamburg, but he stopped at Weimar. Through Charlotte von Kalb he had met Duke Karl August of Saxe-Weimar in Darmstadt in 1785. The Duke appointed him a counselor in the services of the little duchy after Schiller had read to him the first act of *Don Carlos*. However, the Duke did not, as it turned out, provide the expected financial help. *Don Carlos* was first performed in Hamburg on Aug. 29, 1787, after Schiller had revised it for the stage.

Compared with the three previous dramas, *Don Carlos* might be called a purification. Through repeated revisions, this historical drama gradually lost its Storm and Stress style and became an idealistic play of ideas. The family tragedy of the royal house of Spain in the 16th century was changed to a drama promulgating enlightened humanitarian ideas that could not yet be realized in the Spain of the Inquisition. As Schiller became more and more concerned with

the presentation of political concepts—freedom, especially freedom of thinking and world citizenship—he tried to make the Marquis of Posa and the man in whom he placed his hopes, Carlos, the precursors of a better time.

The Historian. In 1789, Schiller became professor of history at Jena. During the years between 1787 and 1792, in Weimar and at Jena, he devoted himself almost exclusively to the study of history and to writing on historical subjects. The two major works of this period are his *Geschichte des Abfalls der vereinigten Niederlande* (1788; *The Defection of the Netherlands*) and *Geschichte des dreissigjährigen Krieges* (1791–1793; *The History of the Thirty Years' War*).

On Feb. 22, 1790, Schiller married Charlotte von Lengefeld. In the following year, a lengthy illness forced him to give up his professional duties. His affliction left him a semi-invalid. Fortunately, he received financial aid for the next three years from Prince Friedrich Christian von Schleswig-Holstein-Songerburg-Augustenburg and the finance minister Count Ernst von Schimmelmann.

The Philosopher. The years from 1792 to 1796 were given over almost entirely to the study of philosophy and aesthetics. Among the essays Schiller wrote during this time were *Über Anmut und Würde* (*On Grace and Dignity*); *Über das Erhabene* (*On the Sublime*); *Briefe über die ästhetische Erziehung des Menschen* (*Letters On the Aesthetic Education of Man*); and *Über naïve und sentimentalische Dichtung* (*On Naïve and Sentimental Poetry*).

The study of Kant brought about a decisive turn in Schiller's development. He had studied the writings of Leibniz and Anthony Ashley Cooper, Lord Shaftesbury. Shaftesbury had already overcome the mechanistic concept of nature of the Enlightenment. He understood nature as a teleologically interwoven entity imbued with the divine spirit. Schiller took from Leibniz and Shaftesbury the concept of harmony that plays an important role in the views of the world and of art during the classical period. Kant had presented morality and reason as opposites. Schiller set up the ideal of their conciliation in aesthetic harmony. Beauty and grace must join the moral act. In the "beautiful soul" the physical and the moral state of man enter into free interplay. The "beautiful soul" is by nature harmonious. However, if duty and desire do not agree, man shows dignity and sublimity in overcoming desire. The conflict between the harmonious development of all powers in man and the sublimeness in self-control and in action is resolved by an evolutionary consideration: Harmony was a reality in nature at one time. Civilization has broken it only to lead it to new harmony in a civilization that is, in turn, nature again. Aesthetic training has as its goal the realization of his cultural ideal.

In 1795, 1796, and 1797, Schiller wrote a number of poems of deep philosophical content: *Das Mädchen aus der Fremde* (*The Girl from Abroad*), *Die Teilung der Erde* (*The Division of the Earth*), *Pegasus in der Dienstbarkeit* or *Pegasus in Joche* (*Pegasus Under the Yoke*), *Die Ideale* (*The Ideals*), *Das Ideal und das Leben* (*The Ideal and Life*), *Der Spaziergang* (*The Walk*), and *Die Worte des Glaubens* (*Words of Faith*).

The Friend of Goethe. The friendship and alliance between Schiller and Goethe began in

July 1794, after a chance meeting in Jena. Goethe's artistic powers were reactivated through Schiller's influence, and soon the two worked together on Schiller's journal *Die Horen* (1795–1797). In 1797, in Schiller's *Musenalmanach* (*Almanac of the Muses*), they published the *Xenien,* a collection of mostly satirical epigrams dealing with or attacking contemporaries for their lack of appreciation for *Die Horen* and the *Musenalmanach.* The 1798 *Musenalmanach* included such popular ballads of Schiller's as *Der Taucher* (*The Diver*); *Der Ring des Polykrates* (*Polycrates' Ring*), *Die Kraniche des Ibykus* (*The Cranes of Ibycus*), *Der Kampf mit dem Drachen* (*The Fight with the Dragon*), *Die Bürgschaft* (*The Pledge*), and *Das Eleusische Fest* (*The Eleusian Festival*). The well-known *Das Lied von der Glocke* (*The Song of the Bell*) was published in 1799.

In December 1799, Schiller moved to Weimar, where he assisted Goethe in the direction of the court theater by adapting many plays for that stage, including Goethe's *Egmont.* Schiller's historical dramatic poem in three parts, *Wallenstein,* was first performed there in late 1798 and early 1799.

The Historical Dramatist. In his next historical play, *Maria Stuart,* first performed on the Weimar stage on June 14, 1800, Schiller applied the analytical technique of Euripides. The drama begins after Mary, Queen of Scots, has been sentenced to death. She is the passive heroine, her suffering the substance of a tragedy whose plot concerns whether or not the sentence will be carried out. Schiller believes that Mary is responsible for Darnley's death, a postulate that is historically uncertain. However, the dramatist does not believe that Mary was involved in a plot against Elizabeth's life. Mary learns to consider the injustice done her by Elizabeth as moral justice, as atonement for her early crime. The realistic sensualist turns into an idealist: "God considers me worthy of atoning for my early severe blood guilt through this undeserved death." For Schiller, it is not Elizabeth but Mary who is the true queen in spiritual bearing and outer beauty. Elizabeth's vanity is hurt. Her dramatic development leads downward from the height of power to gradual humiliation and isolation. The meeting of the two queens, in which Mary shows herself as spiritually superior to Elizabeth, is a dramatic device and not based on historical fact.

The "romantic tragedy" *Die Jungfrau von Orleans* (*The Maid of Orleans*), Schiller's next drama, was first staged in Leipzig in 1801 and in Weimar on April 23, 1803. Voltaire's cynical treatment of Joan of Arc in *La Pucelle d'Orléans* had challenged Schiller to write his idealizing "drama as legend" (in Benno von Wiese's phrase), a work that is neither classical nor historical, but romantic and poetic. Neither the trial nor the burning at the stake is used. The miracle world of the legend is taken seriously. The miraculous is a poetic allegory for the presentation of the supernatural. Joan's tragic conflict is between her mission and her person as a human being. Since she fights for God's cause, her mission must be free from all human concerns. She must be pure. She represents Schiller's concept of the sublime. When she falls in love with her enemy, Lionel, it is shown that the saintly has fallen victim to the world. Her power declines. "She must be purified in strict service" until she sacrifices herself to her superhuman mission and attains transfiguration as a result of her heroic death on the battlefield.

In *Die Braut von Messina* (*The Bride of Messina*), first performed with great success at Weimar on March 19, 1803, Schiller approached the dramatic form of the ancients by employing choruses. The theme of the hostile brothers, so popular with the Storm and Stress writers (and also the theme of Schiller's *Die Räuber*), is taken up again. The analytical technique and inescapable fulfillment of the prophecy that the brothers will find death through their sister are reminiscent of the fate drama of the ancients.

Wilhelm Tell is Schiller's last completed play and stands at the zenith of the German classical drama. First given in Weimar on March 17, 1804, it has become popular at folk festivals in both Germany and Switzerland. The Swiss peoples' struggle for their liberty has become the symbol for the struggle for freedom and true democracy of all peoples that are oppressed. While working on another drama, *Demetrius,* Schiller succumbed to tuberculosis. He died in Weimar on May 9, 1805.

Achievement. Schiller's dramatic work shows an impressive development, improvement, and enhancement from the Storm and Stress plays of his youth to the mature, classically perfect verse drama of his last years at Weimar. He is one of the greatest dramatists Germany has produced. With his sure instinct for what is effective on the stage and his keen awareness of the "great concerns of humanity," his work belongs to the most original and important in world literature. His ability to address directly and inspire people of all walks of life, and to make them share the high buoyancy of his ethical ideals, was and has remained unique despite the attempts of many imitators. "The stage is to be considered a moral institution," he said. To the stage was to be assigned the high mission of supporting religion and the law. "The jurisdiction of the stage begins where the field of worldly law ends." The leitmotiv of almost all of Schiller's dramas is the idea of liberty, which rings again and again and is often made the main theme. But liberty for Schiller is not arbitrariness of the individual, but rather the ethical postulate of human dignity as set forth in Kant's philosophy.

FREDERIC E. COENEN, *Former Editor*
"Studies in the Germanic
Languages and Literatures"

Bibliography

Ellis, John M., *Schiller's Kalliasbriefe and the Study of the Aesthetic Theory* (Mouton 1969).
Ewen, Frederic, *Prestige of Schiller in England, 1788–1859* (Columbia Univ. Press 1932).
Frey, John R., ed., *Schiller 1759–1959: Commemorative American Studies* (Univ. of Ill. Press 1959).
Garland, Henry B., *Schiller, the Dramatic Writer: A Study of Style in the Plays* (Oxford 1969).
Kerry, Stanley S., *Schiller's Writings on Aesthetics* (Manchester Univ. Press 1961).
Kostka, Edmund K., *Schiller in Russian Literature* (Univ. of Pa. Press 1965).
Longyear, R. M., *Schiller and Music* (Univ. of N. C. Press 1966).
Mann, Thomas, *Last Essays,* tr. by Richard and Clara Winston and others (Knopf 1959).
Miller, Ronald D., *Schiller and the Ideal of Freedom: A Study of Schiller's Philosophical Works with Chapters on Kant* (Clarendon Press 1970).
Schiller, Johann Christoph Friedrich von, *A Schiller Symposium in Observance of the Bicentenary of Schiller's Birth* (Univ. of Tex. Press 1960).
Stahl, Ernest L., *Friedrich Schiller's Drama: Theory and Practice* (Oxford 1954).
Witte, William, *Schiller and Burns and Other Essays* (Macmillan, N. Y., 1959).

SCHILLER PARK, shil′ər, is a village in northeastern Illinois, in Cook county, about 15 miles (24 km) northwest of the center of Chicago. Foods are processed and packaged, and tools, clamping devices, and electrical appliances are made. O'Hare International Airport is northwest of the village. Population: 11,458.

SCHINKEL, shing′kəl, **Karl Friedrich** (1781–1841), German architect and artist in the neoclassical style. He was born in Neuruppin, Brandenburg, on March 13, 1781, and studied architecture in Berlin under Friedrich Gilly and in Rome. Although he began his architectural practice in 1798, until 1816 he was principally a painter of romantic landscapes noted for their classical and Gothic architecture. He designed his first major public building, the Neu Wache ("new gatehouse") in Berlin in 1816. This was followed by a series of public buildings and palaces, designed or remodeled, in Berlin or Potsdam. Schinkel also designed stage sets, among which was one for Mozart's *The Magic Flute* (1815), interiors, furniture, jewelry, silver, gardens, and medals, including the famed Iron Cross.

Schinkel's best-known works include, in Berlin, the Royal Theater (1818–1821), the Altes (Old) Museum (1823–1830), and the War Memorial on the Kreuzberg (1818), and, in Potsdam, the Charlottenhof (1826), which he remodeled, and the Nikolaikirche (1830–1837). He also designed a projected palace (1834) on the Acropolis in Athens for King Otto of Greece.

Most of the buildings Schinkel designed are in a correct, precise, classical style that, though cold in its perfection, helped to reform German architecture. His designs in the Gothic revival style, notably the ill-proportioned Werderesche Kirche (1821–1831) in Berlin, are less acceptable to modern taste. Schinkel used a style of his own in the Bauakademie (Academy of Architecture) and in the project for a library in Berlin in the 1830's, which strikingly anticipated the work of the American Louis Sullivan, the Netherlander Hendrik P. Berlage, and other forerunners of modern architecture. Form, suitably decorated, followed function, but since Schinkel's patrons preferred Greek or Gothic revival, he was never able to develop a personal style. He died in Berlin on Oct. 9, 1841.

HERBERT D. HALE
Formerly, "Art News" Magazine

SCHIPA, skē′pä, **Tito,** pseudonym of the Italian tenor Raffaelo Attilio Amedeo (1889–1965). He was an intensely musical man, gifted with a voice of unique lyric timbre. He was born in Lecce on Jan. 2, 1889, and studied to be a composer but went into singing instead. Schipa made his operatic debut at Vercelli in 1911 and went on to sing at major Italian and South American opera houses. He created the role of Ruggiero in the premiere of Puccini's *La Rondine* at Monte Carlo in 1917.

Schipa went to the United States in 1919. There he sang with the Chicago Civic Opera (1919–1932) and the Metropolitan Opera, New York (1932–1934; 1940–1941). He sang the leading tenor roles in *La Sonnambula, The Barber of Seville, Lakmé, La Traviata, Lucia di Lammermoor, Tosca,* and other operas. Schipa continued to perform to critical acclaim long past the age at which most tenors retire. He died in New York City on Dec. 16, 1965.

EVELYN M. SHAFER

The schipperke is an excellent small watchdog.

SCHIPPERKE, skip′ər-kē, a small black dog that has a closely docked tail and a foxlike head with erect small ears. The breed's origin is uncertain. It may have been developed from the Leuvenaar, a breed of small dogs now extinct, or it may have derived from larger dogs of the northern spitz group or from a Belgian sheepdog, also now extinct. By the latter part of the 19th century, when the breed received official recognition in Belgium, it was the most popular house dog there and was also used as a watchdog on barges and canal boats. The modern schipperke is an excellent watchdog, suspicious of strangers, and it is good with children. It can be used as a hunter of small game and makes a particularly good rabbit dog.

The schipperke has a thick, somewhat harsh outercoat of straight hairs and an undercoat of warm, fine hair. The undercoat is thin on the midbody but dense about the neck region, where it forms a ruff, and about the hindquarters, where it forms a culotte. The dog's height is about 11 inches (28 cm) at the shoulder, and its standard weight is not over 18 pounds (8 kg).

SCHIPPERS, ship′ərs. **Thomas** (1930–1977), American conductor. He was born in Kalamazoo, Mich., on March 9, 1930, and was a prodigy as a pianist and organist. While studying at the Curtis Institute in Philadelphia, he won an award in a Philadelphia Orchestra contest for young conductors. Schippers made his debut with the Lemonade Opera, in New York City, in 1948. From 1951 to 1954 he was conductor of the New York City Opera.

Schippers appeared as a guest conductor of the New York Philharmonic in 1955 and in the same year made debuts at the Metropolitan Opera, New York, and La Scala, Milan. He conducted a number of world premieres of operas by Gian-Carlo Menotti and appeared frequently at the annual Festival of Two Worlds, in Spoleto, Italy. He also conducted the premiere of Samuel Barber's *Antony and Cleopatra*, which opened the new Metropolitan Opera House at Lincoln Center, New York City, in 1966. Schippers became conductor of the Cincinnati Symphony in 1970. He died in New York City on Dec. 16, 1977.

SCHIRMER, shûr'mər, a music-publishing firm in New York City. G. Schirmer, Inc., has a huge catalog of publications, whose titles include not only editions of music from the standard repertory but also many works by young American composers. The firm also publishes *The Musical Quarterly* (founded in 1915); *Baker's Biographical Dictionary of Musicians* (first published in 1900), which has become a standard reference; and other books on music and related subjects.

Schirmer's dates from the 19th century. In 1854, Gustav Schirmer, whose grandfather made musical instruments in Germany, became manager of the New York publishing firm of Kerksieg & Breusing. In 1861 he and Bernard Beer took control of the company, renaming it Beer & Schirmer, and in 1866 it became G. Schirmer. An allied engraving and printing plant was established in 1866. After Schirmer's death in 1893, the firm passed to his sons and has continued to remain within the family.

SCHIRRA, Walter Marty, Jr. See ASTRONAUTS; SPACE EXPLORATION—*Early Apollo Flights.*

SCHISM, siz'əm, a formal separation from the discipline and authority of a church or a religious body. A break in the organizational unity of a church does not necessarily imply a difference in doctrine. See GREAT EASTERN SCHISM.

SCHIST, shist, is a class of medium to coarse-grained metamorphic rock that possesses a variety of cleavage called schistosity, or foliation, whereby the rock breaks along parallel surfaces. Schistosity is caused by the parallel arrangement of platy minerals such as the micas as the rock undergoes metamorphism. Schists are classified according to their mineral composition. The different kinds result from the regional, or large-scale, metamorphism of sedimentary and igneous rocks of different composition. The term *metamorphic grade*, as applied to schists, refers to the degree of change there has been from the mineralogy and texture of the original rock. See also SCHISTOSITY.

Mica schists are schists derived from the metamorphism of sedimentary shales and shaly sandstones. There is a sequence of mica schists of increasing metamorphic grade, each of which contains characteristic minerals. Chlorite schists contain muscovite, chloritoid mica, and chlorite. With increased metamorphism, biotite mica also appears. Garnet-mica schists contain garnet as well, which replaces the chlorite and chloritoid. Staurolite-kyanite schists are highly metamorphosed mica schists in which muscovite and chlorine have mostly disappeared, leaving mainly biotite mica, staurolite, and kyanite. With still higher metamorphism, mica schists grade into gneisses.

If mica schists are derived from shaly sandstones, they contain more quartz and plagioclase feldspar and fewer mica-rich minerals. Calcareous schists result from the metamorphism of calcareous shales and contain, in addition to mica, the metamorphic minerals talc, tremolite amphibole, and diopside pyroxene. Greenschists result from the regional metamorphism of basic and semibasic igneous rocks. Their green color is due to chlorite, epidote, and actinolite amphibole, and they also contain white plagioclase feldspar. Magnesian schists derive from ultrabasic igneous rocks and are made up predominantly of antigorite serpentine, chlorite, and talc.

SCHISTOSITY, shis-tos'ə-tē, is a form of foliation in some coarser-grained metamorphic rocks, in which prismatic minerals are concentrated in closely spaced planes along which the rocks split readily. See FOLIATION; SCHIST.

SCHISTOSOMIASIS, shis-tə-sō-mī'ə-səs, is a chronic infectious disease of man caused by certain blood flukes of the genus *Schistosoma*. Also known as bilharziasis, it is one of the most serious parasitic infections of man, affecting millions of people in tropical and subtropical regions of Africa, Asia, and the West Indies. The fluke, called a shistosome, requires a snail host for part of its life cycle. The disease is transmitted through snails and water contaminated with the infective larvae, or *cercarias*, of the flukes. The larvae enter the circulatory system and concentrate in the blood vessels of the pelvic and intestinal regions. The symptoms and course of the disease depend on the particular infecting fluke and the degree of infestation.

One form of the disease, called intestinal schistosomiasis, is caused by S. *mansoni*. Its initial signs may include itching, hives, anorexia, headache, and diarrhea and other abdominal symptoms, followed several weeks later by high fever, chills, and more severe gastrointestinal symptoms, including bloody diarrhea. This phase of the disease may subside gradually over a period of several months or in severe cases may lead to anemia accompanied by swelling of the spleen and liver. A closely related form of the disease, eastern schistosomiasis, or katayama, is caused by S. *japonicum*. It resembles the intestinal form but is generally more severe, affecting the liver earlier and causing death within a few years. Another form, often called vesical schistosomiasis, is caused by S. *haematobia* and commonly affects the genitourinary system.

All forms of schistosomiasis are treated with antimony-containing compounds that kill the flukes, but these drugs often produce serious side effects. Therefore, new pharmaceutical agents continue to be tested.

SCHIZOMYCETES, class that includes all bacteria. See BACTERIA AND BACTERIOLOGY.

Schist with laminar layers deformed into wavy pattern.

T. N. DALE, U. S. GEOLOGICAL SURVEY

SCHIZOPHRENIA, skit-sə-frē′nē-ə, is a mental disorder characterized by many symptoms that in different combinations involve feelings, thoughts, actions, and relations with the surrounding world. As a consequence of these symptoms, the schizophrenic adopts a way of living that differs from that prevailing in the society of which he is a part. He seems to confuse fantasy with reality and to live in a private world, at least where certain areas of living are concerned. The schizophrenic often entertains false beliefs, or delusions. He may, for example, think that he is the victim of persecutors. He may also have perceptual experiences without appropriate external stimulations. For instance, he has hallucinations of hearing voices although nobody is talking to him, or he perceives apparitions without a corresponding external object. Although etymologically the term "schizophrenia" means a division or splitting between the different parts of the psyche, the term as used by psychiatrists does not mean split personality.

Unlike other mental diseases that were well recognized as clinical entities in ancient times, schizophrenia was differentiated and considered as a separate entity only toward the end of the 19th century, predominantly by the German psychiatrist Emil Kraepelin, who named the disorder *dementia praecox*. The Swiss psychiatrist Eugen Bleuler coined the term "schizophrenia," after convincing himself that a dementia state is by no means the ineluctable outcome of the disorder, as Kraepelin had believed.

Occurrence. Schizophrenia is the most common of those serious mental illnesses called psychoses. The disorder affects a little less than 1% of the general population. In the United States more hospital beds are occupied by schizophrenics than by patients affected by any other disease. Every year schizophrenics constitute from 20% to 25% of first admission to public psychiatric hospitals. Because of the relative youth of most patients at admission and their long stay, schizophrenics make up 55% of the resident population of these hospitals.

Schizophrenia may occur at any time from puberty to the age of 40. After the age of 45 the risk of developing the illness is sharply decreased. Childhood schizophrenia has been described by many psychiatrists, but not all psychiatrists agree that such cases belong in the same clinical category as adult schizophrenia.

Types of Schizophrenia. There are four major types of schizophrenia: simple, paranoid, hebephrenic, and catatonic. The *simple type* is characterized by an impoverishment of the personality. The onset is insidious and often unnoticed. The patient isolates himself and seems to lose interest in his surroundings. His thinking processes are superficial and refer only to concrete things or situations. His emotions lack depth, and his judgment is inadequate.

The *paranoid type* is characterized by delusions, often of persecution but occasionally grandiose in content. For instance, the patient may consider himself a great inventor or believe that he is a great historical figure of the present or of the past. Hallucinatory experiences and special ways of thinking tend to support these false beliefs, or delusions.

The *hebephrenic type* has many characteristics similar to those of the paranoid type, but the disintegration of the personality is more pronounced. The patient's behavior is obviously inappropriate, silly, and bizarre, and his affective reactions to situations and people appear either shallow or incongruous.

The *catatonic type* is characterized by unusual motor behavior. The patient may be in a state of immobility and assume statuesque positions. He often presents the symptom known as waxy flexibility. He maintains positions of the body in which he is put, even if these positions are uncomfortable, and remains in these positions for long periods of time. He may be mute and comply with others' wishes to an extreme degree, or he may become negativistic and resist any attempt to direct him. Occasionally, states of immobility are interrupted by unpredictable periods of excitement.

Some psychiatrists distinguish three other types of schizophrenia: the *schizo affective type,* characterized by additional symptoms and by moods of elation or depression; the *undifferentiated type,* characterized by severe but not sufficiently specific behavior and thinking disorder; and the *pseudoneurotic type,* presenting predominantly neurotic symptoms with psychotic episodes of brief duration.

Symptoms. Some symptoms occur in all types of schizophrenia. The patient seems to have changed his relation to the world. He often hallucinates or has special referential attitudes. He thinks that facts or events in the world around him have a special meaning or a purpose connected with his own life. One symptom—either overt or hidden—that seems to be present in all types of schizophrenia is a thinking disorder. Abstract concepts are represented in a concrete frame of reference. This type of cognition is similar to the one found in the dreams of normal people. Freud attributed this type of thinking to what he called the primary process—the system that rules the unconscious more than the other parts of the psyche.

Causes. Many theories have been advocated to explain the cause of schizophrenia. Some psychiatrists believe that the disorder is caused by environmental psychological factors, while others think that it is due to organic causes, and still others find the cause in a combination of psychological and organic factors.

The American psychiatrist Adolph Meyer considered schizophrenia the result of what he called a longitudinal progressive maladaptation that resulted from faulty habits and disorganizations of habits. Although the Austrian physician and neurologist Sigmund Freud did not attempt to enunciate a total theory of schizophrenia, he added new partial understandings of the disorder. As a result of Freud's psychoanalytic studies, schizophrenic symptoms came to be interpreted as having a symbolic meaning. Actually, it was the Swiss psychologist Carl Jung who applied Freud's theory and interpretation of dreams to schizophrenia. According to Jung, a schizophrenic thinks and acts as a normal person does in his dreams. Jung believed that the disorder is caused by an unusual strength of what he called the collective unconscious, so that an abnormal number of atavistic tendencies hinder adjustment to present life.

Still another theory of schizophrenia was presented by the American psychiatrist Harry Stack Sullivan, who stressed the importance of a person's early interpersonal relations, especially to poor parent-child relationships. The individual in such a situation grows up with great anxiety and lack of self-esteem. If at adolescence or later, repeated traumas occur to his sense of self-regard, the patient may go through a sequence characterized by distortions, lack of consensual validation, and finally by a state of schizophrenic panic.

The present author believes that psychological environmental factors have a great, but not exclusive, importance in the causation of schizophrenia. If an individual responds to an unhealthy family environment in ways that distort and magnify the environmental abnormality, he may begin to deal with reality in an inappropriate manner.

Several authorities have stressed the importance of heredity as a cause of schizophrenia. Some have ascertained statistically that schizophrenia occurs more frequently in some families than in others, though not frequently enough to permit the recognition of a transmission that is in accord with the known laws of heredity. It seems probable that only a potentiality for schizophrenia is transmitted genetically and that certain environmental pressures tend to change this potentiality into a clinical problem in some individuals.

Still other investigators have tried to find a biochemical error that may be responsible for schizophrenia. One reported that he had isolated in the blood serum of patients a substance—taraxein—that might cause schizophrenic symptoms. Other researchers have attributed the condition to a deficiency of serotonin, a chemical present in the blood and brain. Still other investigators have carried out extensive histological investigations of brain tissue, but they have failed to find any anatomical abnormality in schizophrenics.

Treatment. Most schizophrenic patients are treated by physical methods, a minority by psychotherapy. Drug therapy is the most common physical method. It consists of the administration of large doses of tranquilizers, the most common of which is chlorpromazine (Thorazine). Other methods of treatment include electric-shock therapy and insulin treatment. Psychosurgery involving the separation of certain areas of the brain, especially in the frontal lobes, is now rarely used. Increasing numbers of patients are treated by a form of psychotherapy that represents a modification of traditional psychoanalysis.

The pessimism that used to prevail concerning the effects of treatment seems to be disappearing. Although statistics about the final results of treatment are unreliable, it appears that a large number of patients treated by physical therapy have a complete remission of symptoms, particularly if treatment is initiated at the onset of the illness. Other patients improve but have some residual defects. Only a hard core never recover. Psychotherapy, when successful, brings about not only a removal of symptoms of schizophrenia but also an integration of personality that is generally superior to that preceding the onset of the disorder.

SILVANO ARIETI, M. D.
Author of "Interpretation of Schizophrenia"

Further Reading: Arieti, Silvano, *Interpretation of Schizophrenia* (Brunner 1955); Arieti, Silvano, ed., *American Handbook of Psychiatry* (Basic Bks. 1966); Bellak, Leopold, and Loeb, Laurence, eds., *The Schizophrenic Syndrome* (Grune & Stratton 1969); Rosenthal, David, and Kety, S. S., *The Transmission of Schizophrenia* (Pergamon 1968).

SCHLEGEL, shlä'gəl, **August Wilhelm von** (1767–1845), German critic, literary historian, and translator. His translations of plays by Shakespeare helped to make them as popular in Germany as in England.

Life. Schlegel was born in Hannover, Germany, on Sept. 8, 1767. He studied at Göttingen and then wrote for Schiller's journal *Die Horen*. Schlegel's most important involvement in the German romantic movement extended from 1796 to 1800 in Jena, where he collaborated with his brother Friedrich on the *Athenaeum*, a journal of romantic literature.

In 1803, Schlegel accepted a post as tutor to the children of Mme. de Staël, the famous French woman of letters, who, having been banished from France by Napoleon for political activity, moved to her estate at Coppet on Lake Geneva. From Schlegel she derived some of her ideas about the glorious age of Goethe in German literature, which she incorporated in her book on her views of Germany, *De l'Allemagne*. Schlegel traveled with Mme. de Staël to Italy, Switzerland, France, and Sweden, and remained with her until her death in 1817. He then accepted a post as professor at the University of Bonn, which he held until his death, in Bonn, on May 12, 1845.

Schlegel lacked the originality of his younger brother, but he was an able interpreter of the latter's ideas to the creative romantic writers and to the general public. In his *Vorlesungen über schöne Literatur und Kunst,* lectures delivered in Berlin from 1801 to 1804, as well as in his more celebrated and expanded series of lectures *Über dramatische Kunst und Literatur,* held in Vienna in 1807–1808, he contrasted the earth-bound solidity of the literature of the ancients with the longing for the infinite inherent in romanticism. The latter signified for him a synthesis of northern and medieval Roman Catholic elements.

Translations. Schlegel's greatest claim to fame rests on his very skillful and gifted translations, to which he brought an instinctive feeling for the form and content of other literatures. He translated 17 of Shakespeare's plays, which were published in 10 volumes (1797–1810). Between 1825 and 1833 a revision of these plays and the translation of the remaining ones were accomplished in an inferior manner under Ludwig Tieck's supervision by Tieck's daughter Dorothea and by Wolf Heinrich von Baudissin. This so-called Schlegel-Tieck rendering of Shakespeare became the standard one in Germany and made the playwright almost more popular there than in England. Schlegel also made masterly translations from the Romance languages in his *Blumensträusse italienischer, spanischer und portugiesischer Poesie* (1804), which included selections from Dante, Petrarch, Boccaccio, Tasso, Cervantes, and Camões. In addition, he achieved an excellent translation of five plays of Calderón de la Barca in his *Spanisches Theater* (2 vols., 1803–1809), which initiated the Spanish dramatist's influence on German poetry. Similarly, Schlegel's Hindu studies—the publication of the journal *Indische Bibliothek* (1823–1830) and editions of the *Bhagavad Gītā* (1823), *Rāmāyaṇa* (1829), and *Hitopadeśa* (1829)—marked the beginning of Sanskrit scholarship in Germany.

Schlegel justly called himself a "cosmopolitan of art and poetry." As a creative writer, he was rather weak, but he excelled in the sonnet.

PERCY MATENKO
Brooklyn College

Bibliography

Schlegel, August W. von, *A Course of Lectures on Dramatic Art and Literature*, tr. by John Black (1846).
Schlegel, August W. von, *Sämmtliche Werke*, 12 vols., ed. by Eduard Böcking (1846–1847).
Schlegel, August W. von, *Verlesungen uber schöne Litteratur und Kunst*, 3 vols., ed. by Jakob Minor (1884).
Tymms, Ralph, *German Romantic Literature* (Methuen 1955).
Zeydel, Edwin H., *Ludwig Tieck, the German Romanticist* (Princeton Univ. Press 1935).

SCHLEGEL, schlä'gəl, **Friedrich von** (1772–1829), German critic, aesthetician, and writer, who was the leading critic of the German romantic school. Through the brilliant aphorisms that he called "fragments" and other writings, he became the fountainhead of the philosophical ideas that were later adopted and implemented by the creative romantic writers.

Life. Karl Wilhelm Friedrich von Schlegel was born in Hannover, Germany, on March 10, 1772. He started to prepare for a legal career but switched to the study of art, classics, and philosophy at the universities of Göttingen and Leipzig.

In 1796, Friedrich joined his elder brother August Wilhelm, also a critic, in Jena and began to develop his aesthetic ideas of romanticism, which became strongly influenced by Fichte's philosophy. During a sojourn in Berlin (1797–1799) he met Moses Mendelssohn's daughter, Dorothea Veit, whom he married in 1804. From 1798 to 1800 he and his brother edited the *Athenaeum*, a periodical that became the official organ of the Jena romantic group. He and his wife were converted to Roman Catholicism in 1808, and in the following year he joined the Austrian foreign office. From 1815 to 1818 he served as secretary of the Austrian legation at the German Confederation in Frankfurt. Schlegel died in Dresden, Saxony, on Jan. 12, 1829.

Critical Theories. One of Friedrich's chief contributions to German aesthetic theory was his definition of romantic poetry as "progressive universal poetry," in which romantic "becoming" was contrasted with the limited perfection of antiquity. He also demanded a blending of different literary forms and developed the idea of romantic irony. This theory, a result of his misunderstanding of Fichte's doctrine of the absolute ego, expressed partly the writer's desire to assert his independence from his work by a deliberate attempt to destroy its illusion. Essentially, however, it represented his realization of the discrepancy between the created work and the unattainable ideal of the work that the author had in mind.

Friedrich's most comprehensive statement on romantic theory was his *Gespräch über die Poesie* (1800). In it he set up Dante, Cervantes, and Shakespeare as the legitimate rulers of modern poetry. He urged a new mythology comprising a synthesis of Spinoza's pantheism and physics and stressed the importance of the "fantastic" and "sentimental" (the subjective and spiritual) element in the romantic novel. Schlegel was one of the first to assign to Goethe his proper place in literature by treating him in his total development, in every branch of writing, as the representative of an entire age.

Through his *Über die Sprache und Weisheit der Indier* (1808), Friedrich became the founder of Oriental studies in Germany and was even one of the sources of inspiration for Goethe's *Westöstlicher Divan*. Finally, he made a contribution to the art of modern living in his unfinished and unsuccessful but provocative novel *Lucinde* (1799). In this work love was regarded as a noble synthesis of physical and spiritual elements, and the ideal of the modern, emancipated woman was thus anticipated.

PERCY MATENKO
Brooklyn College

Bibliography

Gundolf, Friedrich, *Romantiker* (1930).
Preitz, Max, *Friedrich Schlegel und Novalis: Biographie einer Romantikerfreundschaft in ihren Briefen* (1957).
Reiff, Paul, *Die Ästhetik der deutschen Fruhromantik*, ed. by Theodor Geissendoerfer (Univ. of Illinois Press 1946).
Schlegel, Friedrich von, *Literary Notebooks, 1797–1801*, ed. by Hans Eichner (Univ. of Toronto Press 1957).
Tymms, Ralph, *German Romantic Literature* (Methuen 1955).
Walzel, Oskar F., ed., *Friedrich Schlegels Briefe an seinen Bruder August Wilhelm* (1890).

SCHLEICHER, shli'кнər, **Kurt von** (1822–1934), German military and political leader. He was born in Brandenburg on April 7, 1882. He entered the army in 1900 and became a friend of General von Hindenburg's son Oskar. After joining the general staff in 1913, Schleicher made a number of other advantageous contacts, particularly with Gen. Wilhelm Groener and Gen. Hans von Seeckt.

After Hindenburg became president in 1925, Schleicher's importance increased, and by 1928 he was a major general in the army ministry. In his attempt to make the army the guiding force in Germany, Schleicher engaged in numerous intrigues, which led to his appointment as war minister in 1932 in the cabinet of Chancellor Franz von Papen, whom he succeeded on Dec. 2, 1932. Schleicher was unable to create a coalition government with Hitler, and he was forced by Hindenburg to resign on Jan. 28, 1933. Schleicher and his wife were murdered in Berlin on June 30, 1934, during the "night of the long knives," in which many of Hitler's opponents were eliminated.

SCHLEIDEN, shlī'dən, **Matthias Jakob** (1804–1881), German botanist, who, with Theodor Schwann, is credited with formulating the cell theory. Schleiden was born in Hamburg on April 5, 1804. Educated for the law, he was not a success in that profession and gave it up to follow his interest in botanical science. In 1839 he became professor of botany at Jena, where he remained until 1862. He then worked as a private teacher until his death in Frankfurt on June 23, 1881.

Schleiden quickly grasped the significance of Robert Brown's discovery of the cell nucleus, announced in 1833. From it, he developed his concept of the cell and its origin. He considered the cell to be the basic individual of the plant kingdom, and the multicellular plant to be a colony of cellular individuals. The growth of the plant consisted of the production of new cells and their development. His proposed origin of new cells from the cytoblastema—that is, the nucleus—within the old cell was completely wrong, but it took over 30 years of development of the techniques of microscopy to discover how new cells are produced and the true role of the nucleus in the process of mitosis.

Schleiden's concept of the development of the plant embryo, published in 1837, was original with him. His predecessors had considered the pollen grain to be comparable to the sperm of animals in the fertilization of the ovum, whereas Schleiden believed the pollen to be comparable to the ovum itself. He thought that the pollen tube inserted a mass into the embryo sac, which he likened to the uterus, and that it was nourished there and developed into the embryo. This view was controversial until the truth of the development of the embryo from the fertilized ovum was established by Wilhelm Hofmeister in 1849.

Schleiden's third important theory, that the parts of the flower are essentially modified leaves and develop from buds that are leaf buds, is useful in understanding the great variety of flowers and the abnormalities that occasionally appear. However, from the modern viewpoint, it is typical of the morphological thinking of his predecessors.

Working in an era when the life sciences were emerging from the stage of description and classification into a modern science, Schleiden scorned dogma, discarded teleological explanation, and preached the inductive method. His two-volume textbook *Grundzüge der wissenschaftlichen Botanik* (1842–1843; Eng. tr., *Principles of Scientific Botany*), was the first of its kind and long a model for its successors. His writings are filled with violent polemic and ruthless criticism of other scientists—a feature that made them attractive to the younger generation of botanists. Erroneous as most of his ideas were, they were those of a pioneer and so clearly stated that the errors were readily corrected.

J. WALTER WILSON
Brown University

Further Reading: Singer, Charles, *A History of Biology*, rev. ed. (Schuman 1950); Taylor, Gordon Rattray, *The Science of Life* (McGraw 1963).

SCHLEIERMACHER, shlī′ər-mä-ᴋʜər, **Friedrich Ernst Daniel** (1768–1834), German theologian and philosopher, who is generally acknowledged as the most influential Protestant theologian between the Reformation and the 20th century. He was a major source of developments in the philosophy and psychology of religion, as well as in theological interpretation.

Life. Schleiermacher was born in Breslau, Germany, on Nov. 21, 1768. He studied at the Moravian Brethren's schools at Niesky and Barby (1783–1787) and at the University of Halle (1787–1789). He was professor of theology and philosophy at Halle (1804–1806) and of theology at Berlin (1810–1834). He also preached regularly throughout his career, notably as chaplain to the Charité Hospital in Berlin (1796–1802) and at Trinity Church, Berlin (1808–1834).

In keeping with his own ideal of the "prince of the church," who unites theological discipline with leadership in the practical life of church and culture, his career embraced many-sided activities in church, state, education, and society. From 1796 to 1802 he was a participant in the Berlin circle of romanticists and an intimate associate of Friedrich Schlegel. He published translations of Plato (1804–1805). After the Napoleonic invasions, Schleiermacher was one of the creative spirits in the rebuilding of German life and in the establishment of the University of Berlin in 1810. He was also a member of the Academy of Sciences from 1811. As church leader, he urged union of the Reformed and Lutheran groups, advocated freedom of the church from state control, and developed an influential pattern for theological studies (*Kurze Darstellung des the-*

ologischen Studiums, 1811; Eng. tr., *Brief Outline of the Study of Theology*, 1850). A political and social liberal, he argued for economic equality, social insurance, and shorter working hours for labor.

Major Works. In the work that made him famous, *Uber die Religion; Reden an die Gebildeten unter ihren Verächtern* (1st ed., 1799; Eng. tr. from 2d ed., *On Religion; Speeches to its Cultured Despisers*, 1893), Schleiermacher rejects the common assumption that religion is essentially beliefs or moral principles. Reflecting the influence of the Moravian pietism and of the romantics, he argues that religion is rather an irreducible feeling or intuition of the infinite in the finite, a "sense and taste for the infinite," which belongs to the deepest level of human awareness and expresses in manifold forms an original and universal disposition of mankind. He thus defends both the integrity and independence of religion, which need not and cannot be justified by anything other than itself, and its essential place in culture. In his more philosophical works, religion took its place as one of the domains in a universal science of mind. In his greatest work, *Der christliche Glaube* (1st ed., 1821–1822; Eng. tr., from 2d ed., *The Christian Faith*, 1928), he describes the essence of religion more specifically as the consciousness of absolute dependence. In Christianity, this relationship to God takes the form of the experience of redemption from sin which he interpreted as lack of God consciousness through Jesus Christ. Church doctrines are to be viewed as descriptions of the religious affections, and the task of systematic theology is the explication of the contemporary consciousness of the religious community, as a guide for the practical work of the church.

Schleiermacher died in Berlin, on Feb. 12, 1834. His collected works, consisting largely of lecture notes, were published in three series: theological writings, sermons, and philosophical and miscellaneous (30 vols., 1835–1864), plus 4 volumes of letters (1858–1863).

CLAUDE WELCH
University of Pennsylvania

Bibliography
Barth, Karl, *Protestant Thought: From Rousseau to Ritschl*, tr. by Brian Cozens (Harper & Row 1959).
Brandt, Richard B., *The Philosophy of Schleiermacher* (Greenwood 1941).
Dillenberger, John, and Welch, Claude, *Protestant Christianity Interpreted Through Its Development* (Muhlenberg 1954).
Dilthey, Wilhelm, *Leben Schleiermachers* (1870).
Pfleiderer, Otto, *The Development of Theology in Germany since Kant*, tr. by J. F. Smith (1890).

SCHLEMMER, shlem′ər, **Oskar** (1888–1943), German painter and sculptor of abstract human figures in space. Schlemmer was born in Stuttgart on Sept. 4, 1888. He was trained at the Stuttgart Academy and, later, while in Berlin, was influenced by the work of Cézanne, Seurat, the cubists, and other avant-garde painters.

From 1920 to 1929, Schlemmer taught first sculpture and then stage design at the Bauhaus, where he was exposed to the advanced architectural theories of Gropius. He then taught at the Breslau Academy (1929–1932) and the Berlin Academy (1932–1933).

After some early Cézannesque landscapes, Schlemmer, by 1912, had entered his personal realm of stiff, expressionless, machinelike figures carefully interrelated in imaginary architectural space. He pursued this theme in such paintings as *Figures Resting in Space* (1925; Marlborough Gallery, London), *Fourteen Figures in an Imaginary Architecture* (1930; Wallraf-Richartz Museum, Cologne), and *Bauhaus Staircase* (1932; Museum of Modern Art, New York). Schlemmer further explored this theme in his colored cement reliefs for the Bauhaus in Weimar (1919–1923; destroyed by the Nazis) and in his ballet *Treader Ballet* (first performed in Stuttgart in 1922).

Forbidden by the Nazis to teach, Schlemmer moved to Eichberg in southern Germany. His later work, such as the *Window* series (1942; private collection), was in watercolor, with looser brushstrokes and softer shapes. He died in Baden-Baden on April 13, 1943.

SCHLESINGER, shlā′zing-ər, **Arthur Meier** (1888–1965), American historian. He was born in Xenia, Ohio, on Feb. 27, 1888. He studied at Ohio State University (B. A., 1910) and Columbia University (Ph. D., 1917). His doctoral dissertation, *The Colonial Merchants and the American Revolution,* was awarded the Justin Winsor prize of the American Historical Association. After teaching in the history departments of Ohio State University and the State University of Iowa, Schlesinger joined the Harvard University faculty in 1924, becoming Francis Lee Higginson professor of American history in 1939 (emeritus after 1954). He also held many visiting professorships in the United States and other countries and served on many civic and professional committees. Schlesinger died in Boston, Mass., on Oct. 30, 1965.

Schlesinger's books include *New Viewpoints in American History* (1922); *Learning How to Behave* (1946); *Paths to the Present* (1949); and *Prelude to Independence* (1958). Perhaps his greatest contribution to American historiography, however, was as an editor of the 13-volume series, "A History of American Life" (1929–1948). The central problem of the series, only partially resolved, was integration of a mass of facts regarding social, economic, and intellectual development —virtually all phases of American history not encompassed by political history. Because of Schlesinger's concern with "the uncommon importance of common folk and common things," the series is of great importance in the history of American history. His own volume in the series, *The Rise of the City, 1878–1898* (1933), is one of the best integrated and a classic statement of urbanization as a theme in American history. At the same time, Schlesinger's conception of the "urban interpretation of history" should be read in the light of William Diamond's perceptive critique of this approach.

EDWARD N. SAVETH
New York State University at Fredonia

SCHLESINGER, shlā′zing-ər, **Arthur Meier, Jr.** (1917–   ), American historian. He was born in Columbus, Ohio, on Oct. 15, 1917. Graduated from Harvard in 1938, he was a member of the university's Society of Fellows (1939–1942) and then served with the Office of War Information and the Office of Strategic Services. He was a member of the Harvard history faculty from 1946 to 1961.

A prolific scholar and journalist, Schlesinger has contributed to many scholarly and popular periodicals. His first book was the biography *Orestes A. Brownson: A Pilgrim's Progress* (1939). Then came *The Age of Jackson* (1945), which

MUSEUM OF MODERN ART, NEW YORK, GIFT OF PHILIP JOHNSON
Bauhaus Stairway (1932) by Oskar Schlemmer

won the Pulitzer Prize in history. The book was, however, criticized by some historians, who felt that he ascribed to labor an inordinate influence on the rise of Jacksonian democracy and underestimated the role of the American middle class and its laissez-faire aspirations. *The Vital Center* was published in 1949.

Schlesinger's major undertaking is a multivolume and highly dramatic history, *The Age of Roosevelt,* of which the first three volumes are *The Crisis of the Old Order* (1957), *The Coming of the New Deal* (1959), and *The Politics of Upheaval* (1960). These attracted a wide readership and mark great advances in technique, synthesis, and presentation.

Schlesinger, an active Democrat, was a cofounder of Americans for Democratic Action, and served on the staff of Adlai Stevenson during the latter's two unsuccessful candidacies for president. Schlesinger worked for the election of John Kennedy in 1960 and was appointed in 1961 a special assistant to President Kennedy for Latin American affairs. He resigned in 1964, after the president's assassination. In 1967 he was named Albert Schweitzer professor of humanities of the City University of New York.

His book about the Kennedy administration, *A Thousand Days* (1965), won the Pulitzer Prize in biography and a National Book Award. Schlesinger's many honors also include a Bancroft prize and a Parkman prize.

EDWARD N. SAVETH
New York State University at Fredonia

Friedrichstadt, like many other small towns in Schleswig-Holstein, retains its old-fashioned grace and beauty.

SCHLESINGER, shles'in-jer, **James Rodney** (1929–   ), American public official. He was born in New York City on Feb. 15, 1929. After receiving B. A., M. A., and Ph. D. degrees from Harvard, he taught economics at the University of Virginia. His lectures at the Naval War College, published under the title *The Political Economy of National Security,* led to his employment by the Rand Corporation, where he specialized in strategic analysis, with emphasis on nuclear weapons.

Schlesinger's public career, which began in 1969, was notable for his serious, intellectual approach to issues, his capacity for hard work, and an outspoken and direct manner not typically found in the federal bureaucracy. As assistant director of the Bureau of the Budget, he formulated an energy policy for the Nixon administration. As chairman of the Atomic Energy Commission (1971–1973), Schlesinger sought to shift the commission from the role of protector of the nuclear industry to guardian of the public interest. Though he often sided with environmentalists, he approved an allegedly hazardous nuclear test in the Aleutian Islands, even bringing members of his family to view the explosion.

In 1973, during the period of the Watergate scandals, President Nixon named Schlesinger director of the Central Intelligence Agency (CIA). Seeking to restore the CIA's damaged reputation, he dismissed many CIA employees engaged in clandestine operations and put more emphasis on the gathering and analysis of intelligence. Later in 1973, Schlesinger became secretary of defense and sought to reverse the downward trend in the defense budget. He endeavored to achieve balances in conventional forces in Europe, in stra-

tegic nuclear weapons, and in naval power. His criticism of the policy of détente with the Soviet Union led to his dismissal by President Ford in 1975. He served President Carter as an adviser on energy policy in 1977 and as the first secretary of energy from 1977 to 1979. He then joined the Center for Strategic and International Studies at Georgetown University.

SCHLESWIG-HOLSTEIN, shlās'vĭкн hôl'shtĭn, is one of the states of West Germany. The modern state, which has an area of approximately 6,045 square miles (16,655 sq km), is somewhat smaller than the historical realm of Schleswig-Holstein, because North Schleswig is part of Denmark. The state lies between Denmark on the north, the Baltic Sea and the North Sea on the east and west respectively, and the Elbe River, with Hamburg, on the south. On its southeastern frontier it borders on the Mecklenburg section of East Germany. The state also includes the German North Frisian Islands and the islands of Helgoland in the North Sea and Fehmarn in the Baltic.

The mainland terrain is part of the great North German plain. The eastern part is slightly hilly and contains the most productive land. The central part is largely barren, and the west coast consists of fertile marshland. The principal rivers are the Eider, which separates Schleswig in the north from Holstein in the south, and the Trave, which flows into the Baltic at the port of Lübeck.

The state has a population of 2,591,000 (1978 est.). Prior to World War II the inhabitants were solidly Low Saxon and Frisian, but in 1945 and the years thereafter the state absorbed more than 600,000 Germans expelled from parts of eastern Germany placed under Polish and Russian administration.

The capital and largest city of Schleswig-Holstein is Kiel, a Baltic seaport and former naval base of over 275,000 inhabitants. The two next most populous cities are Lübeck, with almost 250,000 people, and Flensburg. Both are also Baltic ports.

Economy. The basis of Schleswig-Holstein's economic life is agriculture, which employs 76% of the land. About 8% is woodland. The most productive agricultural activities are cattle breeding and dairy farming. The state's milk products are marketed throughout Germany, and the Holstein cow is known worldwide. There is also an extensive fishing and shipping trade, with its chief port in Kiel. Kiel is adjacent to the Baltic gate of the 60-mile (97-km)-long Kiel Canal, connecting the Baltic and North seas. The city's Howaldt shipyards, owned by the government, are among the most active in Europe.

Schleswig-Holstein also has a modest oil industry, which is based on production from Holstein wells. Brunsbuttelkoog, where the Kiel Canal enters the estuary of the Elbe River, has terminals for imported oil to be refined.

History. Holstein appeared in history around 800 A. D. as the northernmost part of the tribal duchy of Saxony that was subjugated and Christianized by Charlemagne. From the early 12th century the counts of Schauenburg (Schaumburg) were the rulers. They conducted successful wars against the Danish kings, as a result of which they received the duchy of Schleswig as a Danish fief in 1386. Schleswig originally had been organized by Holy Roman Emperor Otto II in 975 as the northern mark of the empire, but was ceded by Emperor Conrad II to King Canute the Great of Denmark in 1027. When the line of Schauenburg counts expired, the estates of Schleswig and Holstein elected the Danish king Christian I as their ruler in 1460. He promised that Schleswig and Holstein should remain "forever undivided."

The Congress of Vienna in 1815 made Holstein, but not Schleswig, a member of the German Confederation, a settlement that was to prove untenable in the age of growing nationalism. So far the differences between Danes and Germans, who lived side by side in Schleswig, had been inconsequential. The rapid growth of national sentiment, however, turned Danes and Germans against each other. The Danish national liberals became known as the Eider Danes because their foremost demand was the full incorporation of Schleswig, separated from Holstein by the Eider, into the Danish state. The expected expiration of the ruling line of the Danish dynasty led the Danish government in 1846 to announce the right of succession of the Glücksburg line in all its territories, whereas under Germanic law another line of the royal house, the dukes of Augustenburg, could claim Schleswig and Holstein.

When the Eider Danes gained power in Copenhagen in the revolutionary year of 1848, the people of Schleswig-Holstein formed a government of their own. In their role as representatives of the German Confederation, Prussian troops drove the Danes from Schleswig-Holstein, but Russia, Britain, and Sweden threatened to assist Denmark, and the passing of the revolutionary tide in Germany made the German gov-

ernments desist from supporting Schleswig-Holstein. The German Confederation returned the two duchies to Denmark in 1851–1852. In the London Protocol of May 8, 1852, the great powers recognized the right of succession of the Glücksburg line in the duchies, which, however, were to remain separate from Denmark.

In November 1863 the new Danish king Christian IX, under the influence of the Eider Danes, gave Denmark and Schleswig a common constitution, whereupon Frederick, Duke of Augustenburg, who was backed by public opinion in Germany, claimed the throne of Schleswig-Holstein. The Prussian chancellor, Otto von Bismarck, won Austrian cooperation against Denmark, which, having violated the London Protocol, was not actively supported by Britain and Russia. In the German-Danish War of 1864 the Danes were driven from Schleswig-Holstein, which they ceded to Austria and Prussia in the Peace of Vienna of Oct. 30, 1864.

The Austro-Prussian conflict over the disposal of the duchies led to the Austro-Prussian War of 1866. In the Peace of Prague, Austria ceded its rights in Schleswig-Holstein to Prussia, but Article 5 of the peace treaty contained the provision that a plebiscite should be held in northern Schleswig to enable the Danes living there to opt for Denmark. Bismarck frustrated the execution of Article 5 and persuaded the Austrian government to annul it.

From 1867 to 1945, Schleswig-Holstein was a province of Prussia, into which the free city of Lübeck was incorporated in 1937. Meanwhile, after World War I, the Allied powers had decided to hold a plebiscite to determine the future of North Schleswig. Two plebiscite areas, northern and southern, were formed in North Schleswig. The northern area voted (1920) 70% for union with Denmark, with which it was then joined, while the southern area, voting 80% for Germany, remained German. Small Danish and German minorities have continued living on both sides.

HAJO HOLBORN
Author of "A History of Modern Germany"

SCHLEY, slī, **Winfield Scott** (1839–1911), American naval officer. He was born in Frederick county, Md., on Oct. 9, 1839, and graduated from the U. S. Naval Academy in 1860. He led the expedition that in 1884 rescued the survivors of the Greely Arctic exploring party.

In the Spanish-American War (1898), Schley, a commodore, commanded a cruiser squadron in Cuban waters under Rear Adm. William T. Sampson, who had been promoted over Schley. On July 3, 1898, Schley's cruisers defeated the Spanish fleet when it tried to escape from the harbor of Santiago de Cuba, where it had been blockaded. Sampson's flagship was a short distance away and did not take part in the battle. A controversy arose over who had been in command, and a court of inquiry censured some aspects of Schley's conduct, although a minority supported him. Schley died in New York City on Oct. 2, 1911.

SCHLICK, shlik, **Moritz** (1882–1936), German philosopher, who was the founder of the Vienna Circle of logical positivist philosophers. The work of this group has had perhaps the most lasting influence of any school of thought in the 20th century. Schlick was born in Berlin on April 14, 1882. He took his doctorate in physics under Max Planck at the University of Berlin (1904) and throughout his life maintained a strongly scientific orientation in his philosophical work and writings. He taught at the universities of Rostock and Kiel and after 1922 was professor of the philosophy of inductive sciences at the University of Vienna. Schlick was assassinated in Vienna, Austria, on June 22, 1936, by a mentally deranged student. With his death the Vienna Circle ceased to meet.

Schlick's contributions to philosophy were, in the order of their importance, in the theory of knowledge, the logic of science, ethics, and philosophy of life and culture. To him, philosophy was the logical clarification of the basic concepts, assumptions, and methods of human knowledge and conduct. He expounded a refined analysis of the concept of truth, essentially as the one-to-one correspondence of statements to facts. Purely logical and mathematical truths were viewed as "analytic," that is, as valid on the basis of definitions and meaning postulates. Schlick was a staunch empiricist in that he emphasized experience—ultimately direct observation—as the basis of validating all factual claims to knowledge. He repudiated the "a priori," or knowledge of matters of fact on the basis of pure reason alone. In this connection he criticized incisively the views of Kant and the Neo-Kantians, as well as the conventionalistic doctrine of Jules Henri Poincaré. Schlick was among the very first to appreciate the philosophical significance of Einstein's theory of relativity. He also contributed illuminating analyses in the philosophy of physics and biology.

In his epoch-making work *Allgemeine Erkenntnislehre* (1918; 2d ed., 1925; *General Theory of Knowledge*), Schlick held a realistic view of empirical knowledge, brilliantly arguing for the existence of physical objects as independent of the acts of observation. Later, mainly under the influence of Rudolf Carnap and Ludwig Wittgenstein, he tempered this view in the direction of a nonmetaphysical positivism or empirical realism. Schlick's ethics was a psychologically refined utilitarianism. His philosophy of life and culture was a highly liberal and optimistic view of human goals and values.

His other major books were *Fragen der Ethik* (1930; Eng. tr., *Problems of Ethics*, 1939); *Gesammelte Aufsätze* (1938; *Collected Papers*); and *Grundzüge der Naturphilosophie* (1948; Eng. tr., *Philosophy of Nature*, 1949). See also LINGUISTIC ANALYSIS.

HERBERT FEIGL
University of Minnesota

SCHLIEFFEN, shlē′fən, **Alfred von** (1833–1913), German general, who as chief of the army general staff from 1891 to 1906 devised "the Schlieffen Plan of 1905," by which Germany theoretically could wage a victorious war on two fronts.

When World War I began in 1914, the German armies followed some basic tenets of this plan. But Schlieffen's successor as chief of the general staff, Gen. Helmuth von Moltke, made radical modifications that weakened its execution and caused its failure.

A staff officer through most of his career, Schlieffen was a thinker and planner on a grand scale. His plan was drawn for a simultaneous war against France on the west and Russia on the east. He envisaged a sweep by huge German forces through the Netherlands and Belgium—disregarding any neutrality of those countries—and along the French coast in an arc whose hinge was at Metz. When this advance, wheeling counterclockwise, extended below Paris, the armies would continue east to strike the French armies massed in Alsace and Lorraine and destroy them. After the expected quick victory in France, adequate forces would go to the Russian front.

Between 1905, when Schlieffen completed his plan, and the outbreak of war in 1914, events impinged on the plan. Russia recovered rapidly from defeat in the Japanese War of 1904–1905 and expanded and improved its army. France introduced compulsory military training and developed an aggressive military spirit. The Saar coal mines and the Rhineland industrial area that lay in front of the eastern French armies had become increasingly important to the German armament industry and had to be defended.

Von Moltke adhered to the general concept of the plan but made radical changes in detail. The German armies stalled before Paris and were driven back in the First Battle of the Marne. The French held in the east, and there began the long and bitter struggle of mass armies that led to Germany's defeat.

VINCENT J. ESPOSITO
Formerly, United States Military Academy

Further Reading: Ritter, Gerhard, *The Schlieffen Plan*, tr. by Andrew and Eva Wilson (Praeger 1958).

SCHLIEMANN, shlē′män, **Heinrich** (1822–1890), German archaeologist, who discovered the site of the ancient city of Troy. He was born in Neubukow, Mecklenburg, Germany, on Jan. 6, 1822. The son of a poor Protestant minister, he became a grocer's apprentice at the age of 14. Soon after, he was shipwrecked on his way to South America and landed in the Netherlands, where he found work in business. In an amazingly short time, he acquired a knowledge of all the major European languages, adding ancient and modern Greek in the 1850's.

In 1846, as the agent of a number of Dutch firms, Schliemann went to St. Petersburg, Russia, where he soon opened an import business of his own and amassed a considerable fortune. He was in California in 1850, when that state entered the Union, and he thus acquired U. S. citizenship. After traveling in 1858–1859, he decided to wind up his St. Petersburg business to devote himself to archaeological work. In 1868 he went to Greece.

Archaeological Work. Schliemann's study and love of Homer's writings had led him to believe that there was a substantial body of historical facts behind the legendary elements of the Homeric poems. He became convinced that the site of Troy was Hissarlik, Turkey, and he undertook an excavation there at his own expense in 1870–1872. He continued the excavation at intervals until 1890, working with Wilhelm Dörpfeld from 1882. Schliemann's estimate that Homeric Troy had stood on this site proved correct. But by 1890 it was shown that even older settlements had existed at Hissarlik.

In 1876–1878, Schliemann successfully excavated ancient Mycenae, the city that Homer said was ruled by Agamemnon, the king who led the Greeks against Troy. He uncovered the tombs of the Mycenaean kings, with their great riches. Schliemann also excavated at Orchomenos, Marathon, and Tiryns. He died in Naples, Italy, on Dec. 25, 1890.

Schliemann's excavations were the first to allow a view of the Mycenaean civilization. At the time of his death, the self-taught archaeologist had revolutionized the understanding of Greek history. Schliemann's books included *Ithaka, der Peloponnes und Troja* (1869); *Mykenä* (1878); *Ilion* (1881); *Orchomenos* (1881); and his autobiography (1892).

HAJO HOLBORN
Formerly, Yale University

Further Reading: Payne, Robert, *Gold of Troy* (Funk 1958); Thompson, George S., *Heinrich Schliemann, Discoverer of Buried Treasure* (Macmillan 1964).

SCHLÜTER, shlü′tər, **Andreas** (1664–1714), German sculptor and architect whose work offers some of the best examples of the late baroque style in Germany. Schlüter was born in Hamburg, Germany. He was a pupil of his father, the sculptor Gerhard Schlüter, and traveled considerably in Italy as a young man. In 1691 he entered the service of John III Sobieski, king of Poland, and in 1694 he was called to Berlin as court sculptor to the Prussian king, Frederick I. From 1695 to 1706 he carved 76 keystones for the Zeughaus ("arsenal") in Berlin. These consisted of ornamental helmets and a Medusa on the exterior and, remarkably, more than 20 heads of dying warriors in the courtyard. From 1698 to 1703 he worked on an equestrian statue of Frederick William, the "Great Elector," with four slaves at the base of the pedestal. This monument, now in the forecourt of the Schloss Charlottenburg in Potsdam, is one of his best-known works and one of the best examples of German baroque statuary.

Meanwhile, as court architect, Schlüter also worked on plans and decorations for the Berlin Palace, which had to be pulled down after World War II. The Münzturm ("Mint Tower") in the royal palace compound was built on a sandy foundation and had to be destroyed by the architect in 1706. This and other reverses cast Schlüter into disgrace. In 1713 he left Prussia to become chief architect of the Russian court at St. Petersburg (now Leningrad), where he died in 1714.

Schlüter's work on the Berlin Palace and some of his other lost works are known from drawings and photographs. His magnificent baroque tombs of Frederick I and his queen in the Cathedral of Berlin and an elaborate pulpit in the Marienkirche there remain untouched.

HERBERT D. HALE
Formerly, "Art News" Magazine

SCHMALKALDIC LEAGUE, shmäl′käl-dik, the league that was formed in 1531 for the military defense of Martin Luther and his associates against the efforts of Holy Roman Emperor Charles V to crush the new religious movement of the Reformation or to render it helpless economically. The league was organized in the German town of Schmalkalden and included the Protestant princes and delegates from several free cities. Among its leaders were Philip of Hesse and John the Constant and his son John Frederick, electors of Saxony.

The defense of the Protestant movement offered at Augsburg in 1530—that the "evangelical" doctrine differed in no way from essential Roman Catholic doctrine and had to do merely with "a few so-called abuses"—was not acceptable to the Catholic Church and could not be conscientiously maintained in the face of imperial investigation. (See also AUGSBURG CONFESSIONS.) The Protestant forces then organized the Schmalkaldic League. The idea of a military league was offensive to many, to whom it meant disloyalty and revolution, but this was answered by the theory that the local territorial princes were responsible directly to God, the emperor being only their elected head.

The league was of short duration. Originally founded for 6 years, it was then extended for 10 more. In view of the Turkish danger, the Emperor was forced to compromise and to grant temporary toleration to the Protestants (1532). Thus Württemberg, Pomerania, Saxony, and Brandenburg were won for the Protestant cause. But in the Schmalkaldic War (1546–1547), the Emperor, with the help of Maurice, Duke of Saxony, succeeded in crushing the league. See also CHARLES V.

FREDERICK C. GRANT
Union Theological Seminary

SCHMIDT, shmit, **Helmut** (1918–   ), chancellor of West Germany. He was born in Hamburg on Dec. 23, 1918. In World War II he served on the Russian and Western fronts, and was captured by the British toward the end of the war. In 1946 he joined the Social Democratic party and in the following year became the first national chairman of the Socialist Students League. He managed the transportation administration of Hamburg state from 1949 to 1953.

Schmidt became a deputy in the Bundestag in 1953. From 1962 to 1965 he directed the department of domestic affairs of Hamburg state. He returned to the Bundestag in 1965 and served as the Social Democratic floor leader from 1967 to 1969. He was defense minister from 1969 to 1972 and subsequently finance minister (1972–1974). On May 6, 1974, Chancellor Willy Brandt resigned after an East German spy was discovered on his staff. His party chose Schmidt to succeed Brandt. On May 16 the Bundestag elected him the fifth chancellor of West Germany. He and his coalition of Social Democrats and Free Democrats were returned with a larger majority in the 1980 election. In October 1982, Schmidt received a no-confidence vote in the Bundestag and was replaced as chancellor.

SCHMIDT, Kaspar. See STIRNER, MAX.

SCHMIDT, shmit, **Maarten** (1929–   ), Dutch-American astronomer. He was born in Groningen, the Netherlands, on Dec. 28, 1929, and obtained his doctorate from the University of Leiden in 1956. In 1959 he went to the United States to join the staff of the California Institute of Technology, where he became a professor of astronomy in 1964.

Schmidt studied the structure, dynamics, and evolution of galaxies and stars. In the early 1960's his interest was drawn to a number of radio sources that another astronomer, Allan Sandage, had identified with light sources that appeared to be stars. However, their spectra were not starlike. Schmidt suggested that the spectral lines of these quasi-stellar sources, or "quasars," represented a large shift toward the red end of the spectrum and hence that the objects lay enormous distances away. This was largely adopted by astronomers as a working hypothesis. See also QUASAR.

SCHMIDT, shmit, **Wilhelm** (1868–1954), German linguist and ethnologist. He was born in Hörde, Westphalia, on Feb. 16, 1868. After joining the Roman Catholic missionary Society of the Divine Word, he was ordained in 1892.

Father Schmidt taught languages and ethnology at the society's St. Gabriel Mission Seminary in Mödling, near Vienna, and from 1918 also taught ethnology and the science of religion at the University of Vienna. The German invasion of Austria in 1938 forced him to leave the country for Switzerland, where he lectured at the University of Fribourg until 1951. He died in Fribourg on Feb. 10, 1954.

Schmidt was largely self-taught in linguistics and ethnology. A series of papers that he wrote on the languages of southern Asia, Oceania, and Australia soon made him famous.

In ethnology he was mainly concerned with problems of religion and social organization. Following up ideas first expressed by the British folklorist Andrew Lang, Schmidt opposed the importance accorded by scholars to animism and tried to show that the original religion of the most primitive tribes was a relatively pure monotheism. He adopted and made broader application of the German ethnologist Fritz Graebner's *Kulturkreise* theory of cultural diffusion, becoming its most outstanding advocate. [Proponents of this theory held that clusters of culture traits had been diffused over wide areas from each cluster's center of origin.] The theory never won wide acceptance, however, and was finally abandoned even by Schmidt's former students.

Schmidt wrote more than 600 books and papers. The periodical *Anthropos*, which he founded in 1906, became the most prominent international review of ethnology and linguistics. His books include the 12-volume *Der Ursprung der Gottesidee* (1912–1955), parts of which appeared in English as *The Origin and Growth of Religion;* and *Handbuch der Methode der kulturhistorischen Ethnologie* (1937), translated as *The Culture Historical Method of Ethnology.*

Although Schmidt did not do fieldwork, he encouraged missionaries to study the cultures and languages of the peoples among whom they were working, and he published their reports. Expeditions that he organized—such as those to study the Indians of Tierra del Fuego, the Negritos of Asia, and the Pygmies of Africa—resulted in a vast enrichment of anthropological and linguistic knowledge. Various of his views may not stand the test of time, but he ranks among the great figures of modern anthropology.

ROBERT HEINE-GELDERN
Formerly, Institut fur Volkerkunde
University of Vienna

SCHMIDT-ROTTLUFF, shmit-rŏt'lŏof, **Karl** (1884–1976), German painter and woodcut artist of the expressionist school. Karl Schmidt, who called himself Schmidt-Rottluff from his birthplace, Rottluff, Saxony, was born on Dec. 1, 1884. Like E. L. Kirchner, Erich Heckel, and Fritz Bleyl, he studied architecture in Dresden and in 1905 founded with them *Die Brücke* ("The Bridge"), the beginning of modern art in Germany. In 1911 he moved with the group, augmented by other members, to Berlin, where he remained.

Die Brücke, until it disbanded in 1913, produced paintings, lithographs, and woodcuts in an expressionistic style. Their vivid colors and flat, simplified forms reflected the influence of

Karl Schmidt-Rottluff's woodcut *Road to Emmaus* (1918)

Fauvism, cubism, African sculpture, and the work of Van Gogh and Munch. Schmidt-Rottluff's painting was perhaps the boldest and most dissonant in color and the most abstract. Examples are *Resting in the Studio* (1910; Kunsthalle, Hamburg) and *Rising Moon* (1912; private collection). His style moved from brutal, flailing brushwork toward more settled definition of objects in planes that increasingly showed perspective. His woodcuts, of exceptional quality, were stiffly drawn in strong patterns of black and white. Many done during World War I were of religious themes, such as *Road to Emmaus* (1918).

Between 1923 and 1930, Schmidt-Rottluff visited Italy and France. He taught at the Prussian Academy of Art (1931–1933) but was forbidden by the Nazis to paint. In 1947 he was appointed to the Berlin Academy of Art. His later work lost none of its earlier power. He died in West Berlin on Aug. 10, 1976.

SCHMITT, shmit, **Bernadotte Everly** (1886–1969), American historian. He was born in Strasburg, Va., on May 19, 1886, and graduated from the University of Tennessee in 1904. Three years at Oxford University as a Rhodes scholar kindled Schmitt's interest in Anglo-German relations, and diplomatic history thereafter became his specialty. He received an M. A. degree at Oxford in 1913, having also earned a doctorate in history at the University of Wisconsin in 1910.

Teaching first at Western Reserve University and from 1925 to 1946 at the University of Chicago, Schmitt became perhaps the leading American scholar concerned with the causes of the outbreak of World War I. In 1915 he completed his *England and Germany, 1740–1914* (1916) a pioneering book on the tension between the great powers. Another work, published in two volumes, dealt with much the same theme and was entitled *The Coming of the War, 1914* (1930). For this book Schmitt won the 1931 Pulitzer Prize for history. In these studies Schmitt generally refuted the "revisionist" notion that Germany was free of blame as a major cause of World War I. A more limited work, *The Annexation of Bosnia, 1908–1909* (1937), also concerned itself with the implications of Germany's behavior prior to the war.

Schmitt's other books include two volumes he edited, *Some Historians of Modern Europe* (1942) and *Poland* (1945), and *The Origins of the First World War* (1958). From 1929 to 1946, Schmitt edited the *Journal of Modern History,* and from 1949 to 1952 he was the U. S. editor in chief of the captured "Documents on German Foreign Policy, 1918–1945."

In 1960, Schmitt became president of the American Historical Association, and a selection of his papers and addresses was brought out as *The Fashion and Future of History* (1960). He died in Alexandria, Va., on March 22, 1969.

ANDREW F. ROLLE
Occidental College

SCHMITT, shmēt, **Florent** (1870–1958), French composer. He was born in Blâmont, France, on Sept. 28, 1870. He studied music in Nancy and Paris, including composition with Jules Massenet and Gabriel Fauré. After winning a Prix de Rome in 1900, he worked in Rome from 1900 to 1904 and then traveled widely in central and eastern Europe before settling permanently in Paris in 1906.

Schmitt was a prolific composer from his youth, and he added copiously to his long list of compositions until he was well into his ninth decade. He also wrote extensively about music and from 1919 to 1939 was music critic for the Parisian newspaper *Le Temps.* He died in Neuilly-sur-Seine, a suburb of Paris, on Aug. 17, 1958.

Schmitt wrote in most musical forms. His style was predominantly impressionistic and programmatic but was marked by contrapuntal and rhythmic experimentation and by vigorous employment of percussion. Except for the orchestral suite that he arranged from his score for the ballet *La Tragédie de Salomé* (1907), his music is no longer frequently performed.

HERBERT WEINSTOCK
Coauthor of "Music as an Art"

SCHMOLLER, shmōl'ər, **Gustav Friedrich** (1838–1917), German economist. He was born in Heilbronn, Württemberg-Baden, on June 24, 1838. For many years he taught political science at the universities of Halle, Strasbourg, and Berlin and exercised great influence in the spheres of education and government. Through his governmental associations he was able to place his disciples in many important academic posts. He was known as "the professor-maker." He was a member of the Prussian Staatsrat (1884) and the Herrenhaus (1899).

Schmoller emphasized above all the accumulation of factual historical material. He attacked the classical economists' static, deductive analysis of an unreal "economic man" and insisted that economics should be studied dynamically and inductively, in the context of history and sociology.

A follower of such German economists of the historicist school as Wilhelm Rescher, Karl Knies, and Bruno Hildebrand, he was also identified with the Verein für Sozialpolitik (Society for Social Science). Methodologically he had much in common with a tradition that led from the Marquis de Condorcet to Karl Marx, but he differed from Marx in his emphasis on induction. Schmoller's impact and that of his followers have been felt principally in economic history.

Schmoller died in Bad Harzburg, Lower Saxony, on June 27, 1917.

SCHMUCKER, shmuk'ər, **Samuel Simon** (1799–1873), American Lutheran theologian, who was a leader of the Lutheran General Synod. He was born in Hagerstown, Md., on Feb. 28, 1799. A graduate of Princeton Theological Seminary, he helped found and was first professor (1826–1864) of the Gettysburg Theological Seminary. He also founded and was first president (1832–1834) of Pennsylvania (now Gettysburg) College. He published more than 40 works in behalf of low-church Lutheranism and of interdenominational unity. Schmucker died in Gettysburg, Pa., on July 26, 1873.

SCHNABEL, shnä'bəl, **Artur** (1882–1951), Austrian pianist. He was born in Lipnik, Austria (now in Czechoslovakia), on April 17, 1882. A prodigy, he studied piano with Theodor Leschetizky in Vienna from 1891 to 1897. In Berlin he became a noted chamber music performer, taught at the Hochschule für Musik, and gradually emerged as a foremost interpreter of Beethoven's piano music.

The rise of the Hitler regime forced Schnabel to settle outside Germany. In 1939 he went to New York, where he had made his American debut in 1921, and remained there for a time. His Carnegie Hall series of all the Beethoven piano sonatas became famous, and he won high critical acclaim for his playing of Brahms and Schubert.

Schnabel was, in addition, a notably successful teacher. He also composed, in surprisingly advanced dissonant and even atonal manners. He published two books—*Betrachtungen über Musik* (1933; Eng. tr., *Reflections on Music,* 1934) and *Music and the Line of the Most Resistance* (1942). He died in Axenstein, Switzerland, on Aug. 15, 1951.

KARL ULRICH SCHNABEL (1909–   ), his son, also became a pianist and composer. He made his New York debut in 1937 and later became a U. S. citizen.

HERBERT WEINSTOCK
Coauthor of "Men of Music"

SCHNAUZER, shnou'zər, a breed of dog that generally has a long head with arched bristly eyebrows, a moustache, and whiskers, and a compact body covered with a stiff wiry coat. It occurs in three sizes. See GIANT SCHNAUZER; MINIATURE SCHNAUZER; STANDARD SCHNAUZER.

SCHNEIDER, shnī'dər, **Alexander** (1908–   ), Lithuanian-American violinist. He was born in Vilnyus (then part of Russia), on Dec. 21, 1908. After studies at the conservatory in Frankfurt am Main, Germany, he served as concertmaster for the symphony orchestra there from 1925 to 1933, when he joined the Budapest String Quartet as second violinist. From 1933 he lived mainly in the United States.

Schneider collaborated with the noted Spanish cellist Pablo Casals in the establishment of annual music festivals at Prades, France, beginning in 1950, and at San Juan, Puerto Rico, beginning in 1957. Thereafter he became increasingly active as a performer and as a conductor of baroque music. He also taught with notable success and made many phonograph recordings, both as performer and conductor.

HERBERT WEINSTOCK
Coauthor of "Men of Music"

SCHNITZER, Eduard. See EMIN PASHA.

Arthur Schnitzler, Austrian playwright

SCHNITZLER, shnits′lər, **Arthur** (1862–1931), Austrian dramatist and novelist, whose works delved into the psychological problems of the society in which he lived. He often dealt with the themes of sexuality and marriage.

Life. Arthur Schnitzler was born in Vienna on May 15, 1862. His father was a well-known throat surgeon, whose patients included many of Vienna's leading actors and opera stars. The son also became a physician, receiving his M. D. from the University of Vienna in 1885, but his associations with his father's theatrical patients stimulated him to write playlets even while he was studying medicine and during his early years as a practicing physician.

As editor of the medical journal *Internationale klinische Rundschau* from 1887 to 1894, Schnitzler wrote reviews and articles dealing mainly with psychotherapy. He hailed the approach to psychic phenomena of young Sigmund Freud, who later stated that Schnitzler's poetic intuition led to some of the same conclusions as his own researches. For nonscholarly publications Schnitzler used the pseudonym Anatol, a name he also selected for the hero of his first playlets, written between 1889 and 1892. After 1894, Schnitzler devoted himself exclusively to literature, writing a large number of plays, novels, and short stories. He died in Vienna on Oct. 21, 1931.

Early Works. In the seven one-act episodes that make up *Anatol* (published in 1893; Eng. tr., 1911), the dramatist depicted with wit and delicate humor the graceful philandering of a frivolous and melancholy dandy. In frivolity, Anatol sought escape from the sad contemplation of oncoming age and the inevitability of death. Schnitzler's first full-length play, *Das Märchen* (*A Fairy Tale*, 1891) attacked the double standard of morality on the ground of logic and defended it on the basis of male psychology. In *Liebelei* (1895; Eng. tr., *Light-o'-Love*, 1912), he presented the game of love as viewed by the woman and showed that what might be merely a gay flirtation for the man could be laden with deepest tragedy for the girl. *Reigen* was written in 1897 but, because of censorship, was not published until 1903 (Eng. tr., *Hands Around*, 1920). In this work he sardonically depicted in ten dialogues the roundelay of sexuality and the hypocrisy of a social order in which healthy instincts were reduced to selfish lusts, and tragic passions degenerated into petty vices. A French film version of his work, *La Ronde* (1950), became a classic in its own right.

Mature Works. As Schnitzler grew older, the frivolous bachelor and the unmarried "sweet" girl ceased to occupy the center of his attention. His finest narrative and dramatic works then dealt with the problems of married life. In *Zwischenspiel* (1906; Eng. tr., *Intermezzo*, 1915), he explored the possibility of absolute truthfulness in marriage. He presented an ultramodern couple who were finally forced to realize that no lasting marriage could be built on such unstable pillars as frankness and individual liberty. In other plays and in stories, he illustrated that an excess of personal freedom must lead to a disintegration of personality, and he showed that understanding, if carried too far, can operate as a paralyzing force.

In *Der einsame Weg* (1903; Eng. tr., *The Lonely Way*, 1915), Schnitzler wrestled with the tragedy of loneliness, the inevitable fate of all who eschew responsibilities. Later, in *Das Weite Land* (1911; Eng. tr., *The Vast Domain*, 1923), he offered the complexity of existence as the ultimate explanation for the paradoxical behavior of his dramatic characters. He regards the soul as a vast panorama in which there is room for both love and treachery, faith and faithlessness, or adoration of one person and longing for another.

In the autobiographical novel *Der Weg ins Freie* (1908; Eng. tr., *The Road to the Open*, 1913) and in the play *Professor Bernhardi* (1912; Eng. tr., 1913), Schnitzler grappled with the problem of anti-Semitism and laid bare a moral and social condition that even then caused suffering and bewilderment to many in Europe.

Evaluation. Schnitzler is a dramatist of ideas who explores the psychic streams that course between human beings. Apparent contradictions in his works result from his anxiety to view each problem from different angles. As the many possibilities encased in every situation are unlocked, the sharp distinctions between truth and fiction, reality and illusion, waking life and dream life, and necessity and freedom disappear, to be replaced by an awareness of the relativity of all knowledge and experience, a deep distrust of all dogmas, and a solemn awe before the insoluble mystery of all creation. The world becomes surcharged with magic, a fragrant mist overhangs all objects, and daily scenes take on a semblance of fairyland. Schnitzler in his plays thus blends realism and romanticism, oversophistication and charm, autumnal moods and sentimental glamour, brooding melancholy and a skeptical affirmation of life.

SOL LIPTZIN
Author of "Arthur Schnitzler"

Further Reading: Allen, Richard H., *Annotated Arthur Schnitzler Bibliography* (Univ. of N. C. Press 1966); Reichart, H. W., and Salinger, H., eds., *Studies in Arthur Schnitzler* (AMS Press 1963); Swales, M. W., *Arthur Schnitzler: Professor Bernhardi* (Pergamon 1972).

SCHNORR VON CAROLSFELD, shnôr fôn kä′rōls-felt, **Julius** (1794–1872), German religious and historical painter, who was part of the German Pre-Raphaelite School called the Nazarenes. He was born in Leipzig on March 26, 1794, and studied art under his father, Hans Veit Schnorr. In 1818 he went to Rome, where he painted frescoes based on Ariosto's epic poem, *Orlando Furioso,* on the walls of the Villa Massimi. This villa was also decorated by Peter von Cornelius, Johann Friedrich Overbeck, and Philipp Veit, who, with Schnorr, were members of a group of artists called the Nazarenes. The Nazarenes were moved by the same ideals as the Pre-Raphaelites in England: a return to the piety and purity of the art of the Middle Ages. From 1825 to 1846, Schnorr worked in Munich on decorations for the Royal Palace. He taught at the Munich Academy from 1827 to 1846 and at Dresden from 1846 until his death there, on May 24, 1872.

In his lifetime, Schnorr was best known for his frescoes in the Munich Residenz, his illustrations for the *Bibel in Bildern,* religious paintings, and the stained-glass designs in the Glasgow Cathedral and St. Paul's in London. Later, his precise and observant portrait drawings were more appreciated.

HERBERT D. HALE
Formerly, "Art News" Magazine

SCHOENBERG, shŭn′bĕrĸн, **Arnold** (1874–1951), Austrian-American composer, who exerted a revolutionary influence on 20th century music by his abandonment of the traditional tone system for a 12-tone, or 12-note system, known in Europe as dodecaphony. His compositions, often discordant, raucus, and bewildering to the uninitiated, sometimes provoked audiences to storms of protest. At his death, however, few critics, whether sympathetic or hostile, would deny the significance of his contributions as composer, theorist, and teacher.

Life. Schoenberg (originally Schönberg) was born in Vienna on Sept. 13, 1874. At the age of eight he began studying the violin. Later, he taught himself the cello and composed chamber music for amateur groups with whom he played. He soon came to the attention of the composer and teacher Alexander von Zemlinsky, who taught him counterpoint and engaged him to play the cello in the Polyhymnia Orchestra. In 1899 he composed his first important work, the tone poem *Verklärte Nacht,* a sextet for strings.

In 1901, through the influence of Richard Strauss, Schoenberg obtained a teaching position at the Stern Conservatory in Berlin. He returned to Vienna in 1903, when he met Gustav Mahler, who arranged to have several of his works performed. Schoenberg's works were met with hostility in Vienna, and the young composer returned to Berlin in 1911 and taught at the Academy of Art and again at the Stern Conservatory. He conducted his own works in Amsterdam (1911), St. Petersburg (1912), and London (1914), gaining international recognition as well as evoking opposition. After serving in the Austrian Army from 1915 to 1917, he taught in Mödling (near Vienna) and in Amsterdam. He was a professor at the Prussian Academy of Arts in Berlin from 1925 to 1933, when he was dismissed by the Nazi government because he was a Jew.

Schoenberg left Germany and went to the United States in 1933. He taught at the Malkin Conservatory in Boston and at the University of

RICHARD FISH, FROM COLUMBIA RECORDS
Arnold Schoenberg, leading 20th century composer.

California in Los Angeles. He became an American citizen in 1940. Schoenberg died in Los Angeles on July 13, 1951.

Works. Schoenberg's early compositions were romantic in character and traditional in form. The most notable of these is the *Gurre-Lieder* (1911), a song cycle for a gigantic orchestra, chorus, and soloists, which, though Wagnerian in concept, marked a departure by introducing new orchestral effects and using solo instruments in contrast with the full orchestra.

The works that followed approached atonality, and in *Pierre Lunaire* (1912), a melodrama for recitation and chamber orchestra, Schoenberg developed the technique known as *Sprechstimme*—half singing, half speaking—which was later to be used by many important opera composers. Schoenberg's early operas *Erwartung* (1909), a monodrama, and *Die glückliche Hand* (1913) are in an expressionistic mode.

Between 1914 and 1924, Schoenberg developed his revolutionary 12-tone system. In this system, a particular ordering of the 12 tones of the chromatic scale is adopted for a given work. This ordering—called a 12-tone set, or row—is then designated as prime, and by means of certain transformations, the entire work is derived from it. The first large-scale 12-tone work was the Quintet for Winds (1924).

Schoenberg worked almost exclusively in the 12-tone idiom thereafter. His most important later works include the String Quartet No. 3 (1926), Six Pieces for Men's Chorus (1930), Pianoforte Pieces (1929 and 1932), String Quartet No. 4 (1936), Violin Concerto (1936), Prelude to a "Genesis" Suite (1944), *Ode to Napoleon* (1943), Fantasia for Pianoforte and Violin (1949), and the operas *Von Heute auf Morgen* (1929) and *Moses und Aron* (1951). His books include *Harmonielehre* (1911; *Theory of Harmony*) and *Style and Idea* (1951).

The influence of Schoenberg's music and theory was wide even during his own lifetime. While his most important disciples were Alban Berg and Anton von Webern, few composers of the mid-20th century were unaffected by his work.

SCHOENHEIMER, shŭn′hī-mər, **Rudolf** (1898–1941), German-American biochemist who first used radioactive isotopes in biochemical research. He was born in Berlin on May 10, 1898, and obtained his doctorate from the University of Berlin in 1923. With the advent of Hitler he went to the United States, where he joined the staff of the College of Physicians and Surgeons at Columbia University. Depressed by the outbreak of war in Europe, he committed suicide in New York City on Sept. 11, 1941.

Schoenheimer began to use isotopic tracers for research purposes in 1935, when deuterium—a heavy isotope of hydrogen—first became available in sufficient quantity. By "tagging" fat molecules with deuterium and feeding them to laboratory animals, he found that ingested fat is stored in animal tissues and the stored fat then used at a rapid rate of turnover. He also employed a heavy isotope of nitrogen in order to study the movement of amino acids in organisms. See also BIOCHEMISTRY—*Research Methods.*

SCHOFIELD, skō′fēld, **John McAllister** (1831–1906), American general in the Union Army during the Civil War. He was born in Gerry, N. Y., on Sept. 29, 1831, and graduated from the U. S. Military Academy in 1853.

At the start of the Civil War, he was chief of staff to Gen. Nathaniel Lyon in the 1861 operations in Missouri and later commanded the department of Missouri. In February 1864, as a major general, he took command of the 23d Corps and of the Army of the Ohio.

Schofield commanded one of the three armies of Gen. William T. Sherman in the campaign against Atlanta in the spring and summer of 1864. In November, Schofield's corps was sent to join Union forces concentrating at Nashville, Tenn., under Gen. George H. Thomas. Part of this assignment was to block the Confederates led by Gen. John B. Hood, who were advancing northward into Tennessee. On Nov. 30, Hood was repulsed by Schofield at Franklin, Tenn., in one of the war's fiercest battles. Schofield's corps shared in the final operations in North Carolina in the spring of 1865.

After the war, Schofield held various commands, and from 1888 until 1895, when he retired as a lieutenant general he was commanding general of the army. He died in St. Augustine, Fla., on March 4, 1906.

SCHOFIELD BARRACKS, skō′fēld, a U. S. Army installation in Hawaii, is on the central plateau of the island of Oahu, about 20 miles (32 km) northwest of the center of Honolulu. It was established in 1909 and named for Gen. John McAllister Schofield, a Union leader in the Civil War, who had reported in 1872 on the military value of the site. Schofield Barracks became an important training camp during World War I. It was strafed on Dec. 7, 1941, by the Japanese aircraft that bombed nearby Pearl Harbor. Life at the installation during the period just before World War II is described in James Jones' novel *From Here To Eternity* (1951).

SCHOLA CANTORUM, skō′lə kan-tôr′əm, a trained choir that sings the parts of the liturgy not sung by the priest or the laity in Roman Catholic and Anglican churches. It literally means "school of singers." Pope Gregory I established the first *schola* in the 6th century.

SCHOLARSHIPS. A scholarship is a type of financial award given to college students in recognition of past or potential academic achievement. The terms "scholarship" and "fellowship" are sometimes used interchangeably. Generally, however, a scholarship is awarded to undergraduates, while a fellowship is given for graduate study. See FELLOWSHIP.

Scholarships are offered by colleges and universities themselves; by federal, state, and local governments; and by corporations, foundations, labor unions, fraternal and service clubs, religious groups, and other nonacademic organizations. They may be in the form of the remission of certain fees, of a credit toward the payment of college charges, or of an outright grant of funds to be used for college expenses. In addition, at many colleges and universities groups of alumni offer athletic scholarships to outstanding high school athletes so they may participate in intercollegiate sports.

Scholarship awards have been a significant factor in the increase in college and university enrollment. It is estimated that student financial assistance of various types totals some $450 million annually.

Currently, most scholarship programs are related to financial need, although need is not necessarily a prerequisite. The College Scholarship Service, an organization sponsored by the College Entrance Examination Board, has devised a financial aid form that is now used by over 1,600 colleges and universities in a cooperative effort to achieve some uniformity in assessing need. A detailed report on such factors as annual income, investments, debts, and dependents is submitted to the College Scholarship Service, which duplicates copies and sends them to the colleges as requested, along with a confidential analysis of need and a recommended award.

Government Programs. The federal government, through a program of grants, loans, and student employment, has sought to make a college education possible for all qualified students. Many states also have extensive scholarship aid programs.

The National Defense Student Loan Program has aided more than 1.5 million students. Undergraduates may borrow up to $1,000 annually, to a $5,000 maximum, while graduate or professional students may borrow as much as $2,500 a year, to a total of $10,000. Repayment can be spread over a 10-year period, and there are forgiveness provisions for borrowers who become public school teachers.

Other types of federally aided programs include college work-study, a program of employment for students from middle- or upper-income families, when the need criterion may not justify a National Defense Student Loan, and educational opportunity grants, a program of direct grants in which the student receives a nonobligating award of funds, based on exceptional need and evidence of academic or creative promise. The higher education legislation enacted by Congress on June 8, 1972, authorizes "basic" grants up to a maximum of $1,400 per year, less what the family can contribute, to students needing financial assistance to attend college.

Private Programs. The National Merit Scholarship Corporation, established in 1955 and maintained largely by the financial support of the Ford Foundation, administers the largest independently supported undergraduate scholarship program in the United States. Approximately 95% of U. S. high schools participate in the Merit Program, with 1,000 National Merit scholarships offered for one year.

Additionally, more than 175 corporations and other organizations sponsor some 2,000 scholarships, ranging in value from $100 to $1,500 a year for four college years. While scholars are selected without regard to need, the amount of the reward is adjusted to the actual need of the recipient.

Publications. Information on scholarships may be obtained through the *Student Information Bulletin*, published by the National Merit Scholarship Corporation, and *Federal Aids for College Students*, published by the U. S. Office of Education. The College Scholarship Service of Princeton, N. J., also provides announcements of available scholarships.

EDWARD ALVEY, JR.
*Mary Washington College of the
University of Virginia*

SCHOLASTIC APTITUDE TEST. See COLLEGES AND UNIVERSITIES—*Admissions Requirements and Procedures;* TESTING—*Special Testing Programs.*

SCHOLASTICISM is the philosophy that developed in the Middle Ages in the schools of the Carolingian Empire and in the medieval universities and that traditionally has been highly regarded by the Roman Catholic Church. Scholastic philosophy may be characterized by three things: (1) a basic "realism" that connotes a belief that all knowledge is derived through the senses; (2) an emphasis on methodology by which philosophical truth is arrived at from sense data by a process of induction governed by strict rules of logic; and (3) a close association with theology, because Scholasticism developed in a Christian context and was frequently utilized to elucidate theological points.

Origins and Growth. Charlemagne (about 742–814) invited leading scholars of the church to his court and established a Palatine school and a series of cloister and diocesan schools throughout his empire. Out of these medieval centers of learning arose Scholastic philosophy. The term "Scholastic," or the Latin "doctor Scholasticus," was applied not only to teachers of the seven liberal arts in these Carolingian institutions and the seats of learning established later, but also to teachers of theology and philosophy. The term gradually came to be applied only to the latter group.

The development of Scholasticism may be divided into three major periods: (1) early—850–1200, that is, from the time of Johannes Scotus Erigena to John of Salisbury and the Arab scholastics; (2) high point—1200–1500, that is, from Alexander of Hales to the rise of Renaissance humanism, when the medieval universities were the great centers of Scholasticism; and (3) modern—1500–mid-20th century, that is, from a period in which Scholasticism declined into an overly formalistic methodological system to the revival of Scholasticism as exemplified by the work of Étienne Gilson and Jacques Maritain.

The first period is characterized by the controversy regarding the primacy of universals. The second period is marked by the fusion of Aristotelianism with dogmatic theology, the delimitation of the spheres of faith and reason, and the controversy regarding the primacy of the will over the intellect. The early part of the third period was a time of the decline of Scholasticism, when its rigorous methodology became an end in itself instead of a means of reaching philosophical truth. Beginning in the late 19th century Scholasticism again achieved its traditional balance between insight and method and began to be accepted again as a viable philosophical system.

In the first period the chief figures were Johannes Scotus Erigena, who was the earliest notable Scholastic and who fused Neoplatonism with Christian theology; Gerbert, who became Pope Sylvester II and was renowned for his investigations in mathematics and the natural sciences; Roscellinus, who was the reputed originator of Nominalism; Peter Lombard, who was the author of the famous *Sentences* upon which many later Scholastics wrote commentaries; William of Champeaux, who championed realism against Peter Abelard's modified Nominalistic position; Anselm of Canterbury, who constructed an ontological argument for the existence of God; Peter Abelard, who was the originator of conceptualism; and John of Salisbury, who was a part of a reaction to a one-sided Scholastic culture.

The major figures of the second period include Alexander of Hales, who was one of the originators of the "summa," a sort of encyclopedia of theology and natural science that attained vogue in this period; Bonaventure, who held that philosophy was subservient to theology; Albertus Magnus, who was the most learned man of his age in the natural sciences; Thomas Aquinas, who fused Aristotelianism with Christian theology; Duns Scotus, who was an advocate of the primacy of the will against the determinism of the Thomists; and William of Occam, who was an important Nominalist and an opponent of the temporal power of the papacy.

The early schoolmen possessed among other works a meager part of the logical treatises of Aristotle, Plato's *Timaeus*, the writings of Boethius, Cicero, Seneca, Augustine, Martianus Capella, and Dionysius the Pseudo-Areopagite. The schoolmen of the dominant period of Scholasticism possessed the whole body of Aristotelian writings and the works of Arab and Jewish commentators on them.

One of the fundamental characteristics of the first two periods of Scholasticism was the confusion between the roles of philosophy and theology. Philosophy was understood in a broad sense as the search for truth and wisdom and thus included the natural sciences and other branches of knowledge. In the Christian context of the times, revelation and the reasoned reflection upon it, theology, were considered valid sources of truth and proper data for philosophical speculation. Theology most frequently received the preeminent role because its truth, based on revelation, was accepted as more certain than truth obtained by reason alone. Philosophy was regarded as the "handmaid of theology," and its role was to help organize and elucidate doctrine. Scholastic philosophy was peculiarly well suited to this role because of the rigorous logical force of its methodology. Gradually the spheres of theology and philosophy became more clearly delineated, and philosophy itself became limited to the search for truth based upon reason alone. The Nominalist controversy did much to clarify the roles of the two sciences. Yet it is safe to say that throughout there was an intimate connection between the two. Not until the rise of humanism in the 15th century did philosophy and theology become completely separate and often violent opponents.

Early Period. The most important question for early Scholasticism was the ontological significance of logical genera, or universals. In this controversy the Scholastics split into two great parties, the realists and Nominalists. Realism is the doctrine that genera and species have existential reality, that is, they are entities, and extreme realists regarded such universals as existing apart from and independent of particulars. The formula for the extreme realists was that universals exist *ante rem* ("before the particular"). The moderate realists held that they exist *in re* ("in the particular). The extreme opposition was formed by the Nominalists, who maintained that universals, or genera, are only class names and have no existence apart from the name. A middle party was formed by the conceptualists or sermonists, who maintained that universals are concepts and have ideal existence as notions in the mind, or, as Abelard more specifically held, the word becomes universal by means of predication. The formula for Nominalism and conceptualism is that universals exist *post rem* ("after the particular").

These discussions of the Middle Ages were mainly exercises in abstract dialectic, although they were carried on with great subtlety and genius in logical analysis. However, the question acquired an important bearing by involving the doctrine of the Trinity and the existence of God. According to the realists the greater the universality, the greater the reality; the wider the concept the more extensive its being. God, as the most universal notion, has the most complete reality; as *ens generalissimum* he is *ens realissimum*. Further, the Nominalists regarded as real only the individual, concrete thing. The realists urged against this that according to Nominalism, only the three persons (as individuals) of the Trinity have reality; therefore, there is no Godhead and we have tritheism. Anselm maintained that the universals existed before particular things in the mind of God. The most memorable of the controversies on the subject took place in Paris between William of Champeaux and Abelard, in which the latter gained a dialectic victory.

Highpoint. Scholasticism reached its complete formulation in Thomas Aquinas, who developed a system of philosophy by the fusion of Aristotelianism with Christian theology and who sought to correlate more precisely than his predecessors had the spheres of faith and reason. Reality and truth are one continuous realm, although certain truths transcend reason and are apprehended only by faith. Faith and revelation do not contradict reason; they transcend it.

An absorbing question for the Scholastics of this period was the psychological question of whether primacy belongs to the will or to the intellect. Does the will determine our ideas, or do our ideas determine the will? Thomas Aquinas was a determinist, while John Duns Scotus represented the voluntarists. Is it the will or the intellect that is decisive in determining character? On the side of the primacy of the intellect were arranged Thomas Aquinas, the medieval Aristotelians, the German mystics, and the Dominicans; while on the side of the will were Duns Scotus, the Augustinians, William of Occam, and the Franciscans. On the question of universals, Aquinas and Duns Scotus took similar ground,

namely, that of moderate realism. Both maintained that the universals exist in the mind of God (*ante rem*) as ideas before creation, substantially and immanently in things (*in re*), and as notions and names employed by the individual mind (*post rem*).

The philosophy of the Arabs during the Scholastic era is essentially Aristotelianism combined with elements of Neoplatonism, particularly the emanation theory. Their interest was mainly in medicine, natural science, and mathematics. The chief Arabic philosophers were al-Farabi, Avicenna, al-Ghazzali, and Averroës. They were important as the carriers of Aristotelianism and the seeds of natural science into Europe through Spain. The Jewish philosophy of the Scholastic period is partly the cabala and Aristotelianism. The most important figure, however, was Maimonides, who combined the philosophy of Aristotle with Hebrew theology.

Modern Period. Scholasticism went into a period of decline in the 15th century. Humanistic critics with their emphasis on rationalism poked fun at the semantic squabblings of the Scholastics, and Reformers, such as Martin Luther, criticized it for obscuring and perverting the teachings of Christ as found in the Gospels. Thus by the 16th century the term "Scholastic" had become pejorative, signifying obscure and irrelevant mental exercises of little practical use.

Various schools of Scholastic thought were formed as Scholasticism lost its vitality, and these schools were followed by various religious orders, whose almost exclusive property Scholasticism gradually became. The Dominicans adhered strictly to the teachings of St. Thomas Aquinas. The Franciscans generally followed the teachings of Duns Scotus. The Jesuits followed Aquinas, but soon one of their own members, Francisco Suarez, was making positive contributions. However, it would be unfair to characterize the entire early period as one of decline, for there were a number of prominent thinkers, including Suarez, Tommaso de Vio Cajetan, John of St. Thomas, and Francisco de Vitoria. As Scholasticism began to come to grips with a new era of a divided Christendom, rising nationalism, and a developing science, new subjects began to dominate its discussions. There was a considerable controversy over the relation between grace and free will as well as discussions on the origins of civil power, the morality of war, and the basis of moral law. However, in the 17th and 18th centuries Scholasticism was utilized in the teaching of philosophy and theology in seminaries and religious houses of the Catholic Church but had little influence outside that world.

A revival of interest in Scholasticism, particularly in Thomism, was spurred by Pope Leo XIII in his encyclical *Aeterni Patris* (1879), in which he urged a return to Thomistic philosophy. This was in part caused by the difficulties of accommodating Catholic doctrine to the dominant philosophies of the day, Kantianism and Hegelianism. In 1879, to further the renewal, Pope Leo created the Roman Academy of St. Thomas to prepare critical texts of the works of St. Thomas. He also ordered the creation of an institute at Louvain University in Belgium for the study of Thomism. By 1917, Thomism had become the required system of philosophy in all Roman Catholic seminaries and church-sponsored universities. Scholasticism in its Thomistic form came to be called the "perennial philosophy," by which was meant that it could be adapted to meet the needs of each age.

However, it was not until the 20th century that Scholasticism again began to win acceptance in the world at large as a viable philosophical system. Such Scholastic philosophers as Étienne Gilson and Jacques Maritain became known as competent philosophers in a world that had become greatly different from the one that gave rise to Scholasticism.

Bibliography

Chenu, Marie Dominique, *Towards Understanding St. Thomas,* tr. by A. M. Landry and D. Hughes (Regency 1964).

Copleston, Frederick, *History of Philosophy:* Vol. 2, *Medieval Philosophy* (Newman 1950); Vol. 3, *Late Medieval and Renaissance* (Newman 1953).

Delhaye, Philippe, *Medieval Christian Philosophy,* tr. by S. J. Tester (Hawthorn 1960).

Knowles, David, *The Evolution of Medieval Thought* (Random House 1962).

Pieper, Josef, *Scholasticism: Personalities and Problems of Medieval Philosophy* (McGraw-Hill 1960).

SCHOLLANDER, shol'ən-dər, Donald Arthur

(1946–   ), American swimmer. He was born on April 30, 1946, in Charlotte, N. C., and grew up near Portland, Oreg. He left home at the age of 15 to join the Santa Clara, Calif., Swim Club. Within a year Schollander had set a U. S. record for the 440-yard freestyle. In 1962 he tied the world record for the 200-meter freestyle and in 1963 became the first swimmer to break 2 minutes in that event. Nicknamed "The Machine," he had great technical ability and a powerful kick.

In 1964, at age 18, Schollander became the first swimmer to win four Olympic medals in one year. He set an Olympic record of 0:53.4 in the 100-meter freestyle and a new world and Olympic record of 4:12.2 in the 400-meter freestyle. He swam on the winning 400- and 800-meter freestyle teams. He was named the outstanding U. S. amateur athlete of 1964 and excelled in swimming at Yale University. In 1968 he lowered his 200-meter freestyle mark to 1:54.3. In the 1968 Olympics he swam on the winning U. S. 800-meter freestyle team and placed second in the 200-meter freestyle.

SCHOMBERG,

shōm'berkн, **Duke of** (1615–1690), European soldier, who died at the Battle of the Boyne. Friedrich Hermann, the future duke of Schomberg, was born in Heidelberg, Germany, on Dec. 6, 1615, the son of an official at the court of the Elector Palatine. His mother was the daughter of an English lord.

He was educated in Sedan, Paris, and Leiden. He served under Prince Frederick Henry of Orange (1633) in the Thirty Years' War, and he subsequently fought with the Swedish Army in Germany (1634), the Dutch Army (1639–1650), the French Army (after 1650), and the Portuguese Army (1660–1668). He was naturalized in France in 1668 and became a French marshal in 1675. A Protestant, he was forced to leave France after the revocation of the Edict of Nantes in 1685 and attached himself to the court of Frederick William, Elector of Brandenburg.

He commanded a Prussian force sent to aid William of Orange in 1688 and went to England with William during the Glorious Revolution that overthrew James II. Made duke of Schomberg and an English citizen in 1689, he was sent to Ireland in August of that year to command the troops fighting the deposed James. William crossed to Ireland in 1690, and he and Schomberg moved against the Catholics. In the fateful Battle of the Boyne on July 12, 1690, in which the Catholics were routed, Schomberg was killed by Irish cavalry.

SCHÖNBERG, Arnold.

See Schoenberg, Arnold.

SCHÖNBRUNN PALACE,

shûn-broon', an 18th century Austrian palace in the baroque style, in Hietzing, a suburb of Vienna. The palace and park, inspired by Versailles, were built as a royal summer residence in the reigns of Charles IV and Maria Theresa. The original design, by J. B. Fischer von Erlach, was much altered. The building, begun in 1695, has richly decorated apartments in the rococo style. Major features of the vast park, planned by Ferdinand von Hohenberg and begun in 1765, are a botanical garden, a menagerie, and a gloriette (columned arcade).

Schönbrunn Palace, near Vienna, was built in the 18th century as a royal summer residence.

MARTIN SCHONGAUER'S engraving *Christ Carrying the Cross,* one of a series portraying the Passion of Christ. Schongauer was Germany's most important engraver before Dürer.

SCHONGAUER, shōn'gou-ər, **Martin** (c. 1450–1491), German painter and engraver, who was the most important engraver before Albrecht Dürer and one of the greatest German painters. Schongauer was born in Colmar, Alsace, probably between 1445 and 1450, the son of Caspar Schongauer, an Augsburg goldsmith who had moved to Colmar about 1440. Little is known of Schongauer's early life, but it is assumed that he learned technique in his father's workshop.

Schongauer was influenced by the Flemish painter Roger van der Weyden. The quality of Schongauer's painting was such that he was known as "Martin Schön" ("Martin the Beautiful"), "Hübsch ["the Handsome—Charming, Fine"] Martin," and in Italy, "Bel Martino." His engravings were circulated throughout Europe in his lifetime and were used as models in many workshops. Dürer especially was influenced by Schongauer's engravings, and he journeyed in 1492 to Colmar to meet the master, unaware that Schongauer had died in 1491 in Breisach, where he had been called in 1489 to paint frescoes in the cathedral.

Religious subjects predominate in Schongauer's existing work, which consists of some 50 original drawings, more than 100 copper engravings, and only a few paintings. Of the paintings that can be attributed to him with certainty, the most important are the large panel *Virgin in the Rose Bower* (1473; Church of St. Martin, Colmar) and the monumental *Last Judgment* frescoes in Briesach.

SCHOOL is commonly applied to any of various kinds of educational institutions, such as elementary and secondary schools and colleges and universities. For articles relating to schools and their curriculums and activities, see the Index entries beginning *Education.*

SCHOOL ADMINISTRATION. See EDUCATION—*Educational Administration.*

SCHOOL BOARD. See EDUCATION—*Educational Administration.*

SCHOOL DISTRICT. See EDUCATION—*Educational Administration.*

SCHOOL FOR SCANDAL, a comedy by the Irish dramatist Richard Brinsley Sheridan, produced in 1777 at Drury Lane Theatre, London. It ran 20 nights the first season, 65 nights the second season, and has been a favorite ever since. *The School for Scandal* is a crowded fabric of situations derived from a broad reading of earlier English comedy and from an intimate acquaintance with the stage. Action is more important than speech, and events follow each other in rapid succession. Although scandal is spoken in the play, none is actually seen in the action. There is little repartee. Dialogue serves not as a fencing of wits—which is usually the case in 18th century comedies—but as the rapid patter of character, manipulated through a foreordained intrigue. To keep the conversation moving rapidly is the first requirement. Therefore a spirit of raillery is maintained.

The story of *The School for Scandal* revolves around efforts to keep apart the young lovers Charles Surface and Maria, and around the problems of the young Lady Teazle and her elderly husband, Sir Peter. Charles' brother, Joseph, a full-blooded hypocrite, manages to keep things in a state of upset between both couples. He does this by spreading scandal—in which he is aided by Lady Sneerwell, who is herself in love with Charles—and by trying to corrupt the country-bred Lady Teazle and woo Maria for himself. After much confusion, including a famous scene in which characters make discoveries about each other by hiding behind screens and in closets, everything is put to rights by Sir Oliver Surface, the uncle and benefactor of Charles and Joseph, who has discovered the entire truth while in disguise.

SCHOOL LUNCH PROGRAM, a federally sponsored program, administered by the U. S. Department of Agriculture (USDA), that provides free or reduced-price lunches to students in American public or private nonprofit elementary and secondary schools. The program is authorized by the National School Lunch Act of 1946, as amended. One fifth of the cost is borne by the federal government, one fifth by state and local authorities, and three fifths by the students. Schools are eligible to participate if they pro-

A schooner of the type widely used in the late eighteenth century for fishing and cargo in coastal waters.

vide nutritious meals as determined by USDA standards and if their food service is nonprofit. The USDA also purchases some of the food used in the program. Students may receive lunches at less than the standard charge or without charge if school authorities determine a need and provided that the student is not identified in any special way (by race, for example) or discriminated against. Other federal programs have made funds available for setting up and maintaining food service facilities in schools.

SCHOOLCRAFT, Henry Rowe (1793–1864), American explorer and ethnologist. He was born in Watervliet, N. Y., on March 28, 1793, and was educated at Union and Middlebury colleges. In 1820 he was a geologist with an exploring expedition, under Gen. Lewis Cass, to the Lake Superior copper region and the upper Mississippi. He became Indian agent for the tribes of Lake Superior in 1822, with headquarters first in Sault Sainte Marie and later in Michilimackinac (or Mackinac). He commanded the 1832 expedition that discovered the sources of the Mississippi. In 1836 he concluded an important treaty with the Chippewa Indians, whereby the northern third of the lower peninsula and the eastern half of the upper peninsula of Michigan Territory were ceded to the United States. Soon afterward he was appointed acting superintendent of Indian affairs and disbursing agent for the northern department.

In 1847 he began the preparation, under government appointment, of his elaborate *Historical and Statistical Information Respecting the History, Condition and Prospects of the Indian Tribes of the United States* (1851–1857). For the first five volumes an appropriation of nearly $30,000 per volume was made by Congress. The sixth and last was published at the expense of the War Department. The beautifully printed work was copiously illustrated with steel engravings by Seth Eastman. It was the first means of introducing Indian legend and tradition to the general reader and gained a considerable reputation as a work of scholarship. Schoolcraft died on Dec. 10, 1864, in Washington, D. C.

SCHOONER, skōō′nər, a sailing vessel with two or more masts, having only fore-and-aft-rigged sails. This type of rigging enables the vessel to sail closer to the wind than a square-rigged ship can. Schooners are also easily maneuverable and can be handled by smaller crews. They were first built by American colonists in the early 18th century and were used extensively as merchant and fishing vessels until the second decade of the 20th century, when they were replaced by steamships. Today schooners are generally used as yachts.

The typical schooner of the 18th and early 19th centuries—which engaged in the American coasting trade and, to a lesser extent, in transoceanic trade—was a two-masted vessel with foresail, mainsail, topsails, staysail, and one or more jibs. A schooner that is rigged with a square fore-topsail and topgallant sail, is called a topsail schooner.

About 1840, larger vessels of three or more masts came into use, and for the rest of the century, American shipbuilders constructed ever larger schooners. Schooners built in the 1880's and 1890's were often quite large, ranging from 2,000 to 3,000 tons and having four, five, or even six masts. These schooners were generally constructed for the foreign trade. The only seven-masted schooner was the 5,200-ton *Thomas Lawson*, built at Fore River, Mass., in 1902. Its sails were raised by a donkey engine, making it possible to sail it with a relatively small crew.

Although the schooner was always a favorite and distinctive American rig, it was used in the 19th century by French and English shipbuilders. Today's schooner yachts usually have only two masts with triangular sails on the after side.

SCHOPENHAUER, shō′pən-hou-ər, **Arthur** (1788–1860), German philosopher, best known for his pessimism and his interpretation of reality in terms of a nonrational "will." Most contemporary philosophers find his metaphysical system unacceptable. But his vision of man as both the product and victim of blindly operating forces that he can neither understand nor control, as resident in a godless world that is far from congenial to him, and as ceaselessly striving and suffering, to no purpose, is one that cannot be lightly dismissed. These views make Schopenhauer seem much more modern than most thinkers of his time.

Life and Works. Schopenhauer was born in Danzig on Feb. 22, 1788. His father was a successful businessman, who left him a substantial inheritance that made him financially independent. He studied philosophy at Göttingen and Berlin and received his doctorate from the University of Jena in 1814. His dissertation, *On the Fourfold Root of the Principle of Sufficient Reason,* which was published the same year, reflects Kant's great influence on him. His next book, *On Vision and Colors,* appeared in 1816. His most important work, *The World as Will and Idea* (1818) received little attention at the time, but it did enable him to become a lecturer at Berlin. His academic career was short. Hegel was also at Berlin, and Schopenhauer's quixotic attempt to challenge Hegel's influence was a complete failure. Schopenhauer retired to private life in 1831, but continued to write, publishing *On the Will in Nature* (1836) and *The Basis of Morality* (1841). He also published a greatly expanded edition of *The World as Will and Idea* (1844) and a two-volume collection of essays entitled *Parerga and Paralipomena* (1851). He died in Hamburg on Sept. 21, 1860.

It was only with the appearance of his last book that he began to receive widespread attention. Throughout his life he lived in isolation,

Arthur Schopenhauer, German philosopher.

resentful of the world's neglect, hostile toward other thinkers, and generally unable to form satisfying relationships with others. His abrasive personality contributed greatly to his isolation. He was arrogant and contemptuous, moody and rather paranoid, deeply cynical and pessimistic. While he was an astute critic of other philosophers, he could not tolerate criticism. Yet had he been differently disposed, he might have been incapable of developing as important a philosophical position as he did.

Metaphysics. Schopenhauer was convinced by Kant of the necessity of distinguishing between the phenomenal world or things as they are perceived by us, and "things in themselves." Like Kant, he believed that it was illegitimate either to speculate *a priori* about the latter or to apply to them categories appropriate to the phenomenal world. But whereas Kant had concluded that "things in themselves" and their relation to the phenomenal world were thus unknowable, Schopenhauer did not. The aim of his metaphysics is "to present to rational knowledge the whole manifold of the world generally . . . comprehended in a few abstract concepts." The most fundamental of these concepts are "will" (*Wille*) and "idea" (*Vorstellung*).

He begins with the Kantian proposition that "all that exists for knowledge . . . is only object in relation to subject, perception of a perceiver, in a word, idea." Further, he considers it illegitimate to attribute reality to anything if we do not and cannot experience it or something like it. The only objects we can ever experience, however, are objects we might perceive, and all perceptible objects exist only as perceptions or "ideas" of perceiving subjects. The form as well as the content of these perceptions is dependent upon the experiencing subject. The whole world is experienced only as a network of "ideas" and so must be conceived accordingly. In short, "the world is idea."

That the world is more than simply "idea," however, is suggested by the fact that we, the experiencing subjects, are more than this and are also more than "pure knowing subjects." We act as well as perceive, in accordance with a dynamic principle that Schopenhauer terms "will." Indeed, it is this nonrational principle, and not reason, that determines most of what we do in the course of our lives. It is in terms of "will" that our essential nature is to be conceived. Reason is but one faculty among others that has emerged in the course of our development as active beings. And if we are essentially "will," this suggests that the rest of the world might be similarly constituted, when considered as it is "in itself." Indeed, since "will" is the only principle in addition to "idea" of which we have any experience, it is only in terms of "will" that anything may be added to the conception of the world as "idea." "Thus if we hold that the material world is something more than merely our idea, we must say that . . . it is that which we find immediately in ourselves as *will.*"

The obvious and important differences between inanimate objects, plants, animals, and men are attributed to differences in the degree of complexity of "will" involved in each case. Each kind of thing is associated with a distinct and rather Platonic "Idea" or eternal essence, but all are manifestations of the same underlying dynamic principle. "In all . . . forms of . . . nature, it is one and the same will that reveals itself."

However, while they all are thus essentially one, existing things are in constant conflict by their very nature as manifestations of "will." Those that are more complex emerge and sustain themselves only through a "subduing assimilation" of simpler ones, which in turn resist the attempt. Things of the same type compete for the means of their existence. These conflicts inevitably result in suffering, with the consequence that wherever there is "will," there is suffering. ("Suffering" here encompasses the whole range of kinds of distress to which a species is susceptible.)

This suffering, however, is to no real purpose. The most that is achieved through the struggle by which it is caused is the opportunity to continue the struggle. The attainment of pleasure does not counterbalance suffering, for pleasure is merely the relief experienced upon the removal of a particular occasion of suffering. No goal is reached, no end accomplished, no good realized. This, together with his abhorrence of pointless suffering, leads Schopenhauer (revealing the influence of Buddhism on his thought), to conclude that the struggle for existence is worse than senseless and that oblivion is preferable to life.

Ethics. The central feature of Schopenhauer's morality is the alleviation of suffering. He contends that suffering is abhorrent wherever it occurs and that therefore one ought to do all one can to diminish suffering everywhere. We tend to attach greater importance to our own suffering than to that of others. However, reason "places other individuals completely on the level with myself and my own fate." Thus to concern oneself solely with one's own suffering is to act selfishly, while to concern oneself equally with that of others is to act morally.

However, since suffering is inseparable from life at the level of "will," Schopenhauer goes on to advance a personal ethic of withdrawal from active engagement in the world of "will." In it he assigns an important role to aesthetic and philosophical contemplation. In both sorts of contemplation, which for him are ultimately one and the same, one temporarily ceases to relate oneself to objects in an active way and shifts one's attention to the "Ideas" or eternal forms of which concrete objects are merely manifestations. In so doing, one "forgets his individuality, his will, and only continues to exist as pure subject." As such, one rises above the world of "will." Art no less than philosophy is thus viewed as an essentially cognitive enterprise, in which, however, the natures of things are represented directly, rather than conveyed through the medium of concepts.

The temporary attainment of a contemplative stance, however, does not transform one permanently into a will-less subject. The "will" in the individual inevitably reasserts itself, driving him back into the world of striving and suffering. Thus the only true deliverance attainable, short of death, is that which may be achieved through the direct suppression of the "will," by means of a systematic program of asceticism. Schopenhauer rejects suicide only because he regards it as a last desperate expression of the "will" rather than a successful suppression of it.

Through denying and ultimately eradicating every impulse that impels one toward involvement in the world of existence, the true ascetic achieves a kind of death in life in which he effectively no longer exists as "will." Schopenhauer suggests that one "who has attained to the denial of the will to live . . . is filled with inward joy and the true peace of heaven." But his ultimate ideal, like that of Buddhism, is not a society of true ascetics. Rather, it is the utter annihilation of the "will" and all of its manifestations: "No will: no idea: no world."

Significance. Schopenhauer may be viewed as a transitional figure between Kant and such later thinkers as Nietzsche, Bergson, and Freud. He also played an important role in the rebellion against Hegelian Idealism, and in the post-Idealist revival of interest in Kant. He was one of the first modern philosophers to break radically with the Judeo-Christian world view and to incorporate certain elements of Eastern thought into his philosophy. These characterizations, however, do not do him justice. He is even more significant considered in his own right; for his conception of reality and man's nature and his position concerning the meaningfulness of human life are as unsettling as they are original and important in the history of philosophy.

RICHARD SCHACHT
University of Illinois

Further Reading: Copleston, Frederick C., *Schopenhauer, Philosopher of Pessimism* (Burns 1946); Gardiner, Patrick, *Schopenhauer* (Penguin 1963); Wallace, William, *Life of Schopenhauer* (1890); Zimmern, Helen, *Arthur Schopenhauer: His Life and His Philosophy*, rev. ed. (Scribner 1932).

SCHOTTKY, shot′kē, **Walter** (1886–), German physicist, who developed the tetrode, a four-element vacuum tube. He was born in Zurich, Switzerland, on July 23, 1886, and received doctorates in engineering, technology, and natural research at the University of Berlin. In 1914 he found that electron emission from a heated metal is enhanced by applying a strong electric field at the surface of the metal. This effect is now called the Schottky effect. About 1919 he devised the tetrode, the first multigrid vacuum tube. In 1935 he noted that a lattice vacancy was created in a crystal by displacing an ion from its site within a crystal to the surface of the crystal. Such a lattice vacancy is now called the Schottky defect. In 1940 he proposed a theory of the rectifying action at the contact between a metal and a semiconductor, where such action depends on a barrier layer at the surface of contact. Later, metal semiconductor diodes, which are called Schottky barrier diodes, were built.

SCHREINER, shrī′nər, **Olive** (1855–1920), South African writer, who was widely known for her militant feminism and attacks on bigotry. She was born on March 24, 1855, in Wittebergen Reserve, Cape Colony, where her father was a Lutheran missionary. Largely self-educated, she was employed for a time as a governess before going to Britain in 1881. She returned to South Africa in 1889 and died in Cape Town on Dec. 11, 1920.

Miss Schreiner had taken with her to Britain her manuscript of *The Story of an African Farm*, which was published in 1883 under the pseudonym Ralph Iron. This outspoken novel, critical of Christianity and enthusiastic in its support of militant feminism, brought her immediate fame. Her other books included *An English South African's View of the Situation* (1899) and *Women and Labour* (1911), neither of which achieved the popularity of her first work.

SCHRÖDINGER, shrü′ding-ər, **Erwin** (1887–1961), Austrian theoretical physicist, who shared the 1933 Nobel Prize with Paul Dirac for his wave-mechanical interpretation of atomic phenomena. Schrödinger was born in Vienna, on Aug. 12, 1887. He was educated at the University of Vienna, where his prime interests were mathematics and physics. He held various professorships and in 1927 succeeded Max Planck at the University of Berlin. There he joined Albert Einstein, Max von Laue, and Planck to form the strongest center of theoretical physics in Germany. Upon Hitler's rise to power, Schrödinger moved first, in 1933, to Oxford, England, and eventually, in 1940, to the newly created Dublin Institute for Advanced Study. He spent his last few years in Austria, where he died, in Vienna, on Jan. 4, 1961.

Schrödinger's early research dealt with statistical mechanics, X-ray diffraction, and relativity. His familiarity with Einstein's work made him receptive to the suggestion by Louis de Broglie in 1924 that just as electromagnetic radiation has particle characteristics, so should matter have wave characteristics. In 1926 he elaborated this idea into his theory of wave mechanics. The matrix mechanics, or quantum mechanics, advanced by Werner Heisenberg the year before was soon seen to be a mathematically different way of expressing the same analysis of the structure of the atom that Schrödinger had made. Decades earlier, Planck had introduced discrete or quantum conditions into the heretofore accepted continuum of nature. Niels Bohr had then imposed quantization of the orbital electrons in atoms, explaining the observed spectral lines as energy emitted or absorbed when an electron jumped from one fixed orbit to another. Schrödinger saw how the frequencies of these lines could be explained as the differences between frequencies of standing waves belonging to orbital electrons, and was able logically to predict various atomic properties understood earlier only on an empirical basis. See also QUANTUM THEORY.

LAWRENCE BADASH
University of California, Santa Barbara

SCHUBERT, shōō′bərt, **Franz Peter** (1797–1828), Austrian composer, who developed and brought to its highest form the German *lied*, or art song. Using verses by such authors as Goethe, Schiller, Heine, and Shakespeare, he achieved an exquisite fusion of poetry and music, in which the music brilliantly expresses and underscores the emotion and meaning of the words. In addition to art songs, Schubert also wrote masterful symphonies, chamber music, piano music, and church music.

LIFE

Early Years. Schubert was born in Vienna on Jan. 31, 1797. His father, of Moravian peasant stock, was a schoolteacher in the Viennese suburb of Lichtenthal. His mother, a native of Silesia, had been a cook. Franz was the 13th of 14 children, nine of whom died in infancy.

Schubert's first musical impressions were of the chamber music sessions of his father and older brothers, one of whom, Ferdinand, later became fairly well known as a composer of church music. Schubert received his first music instruction at home, starting piano lessons when he was six and violin lessons when he was eight. He was then turned over to the parish choirmaster, Michael Holzer, who taught him singing and music

theory. When Franz was 11, he sang and played the violin in the parish church. He also made his first timid attempts to write music.

In October 1808, Schubert was sent to the Stadtkonvikt, a boarding school attached to the imperial court in Vienna. There, students were taught music as well as other subjects in return for their services as choristers. During his student days at the Stadtkonvikt, Schubert composed several works, among them a fantasia for piano duet (1810) and his first song *Hagars Klage* (1811). During his last months at the school and for some time after he left, he studied with the Italian composer Antonio Salieri.

Schubert's mother died of typhus in 1812, and he left the Stadtkonvikt in 1813. He attended a teacher training school for about a year and in 1814 took a job as a teacher in the school in which his father also taught. Now he began to compose feverishly in every spare moment, between classes and at night. In the next two years he experimented with a great variety of musical forms, producing several chamber works, symphonies, Masses, operas, and songs. Among his most famous songs of this period are *Gretchen am Spinnrade* (1814) and *Erlkönig* (1815).

Middle Years. In 1816, Schubert was granted a leave of absence from his teaching job. A friend, Franz von Schober, arranged for lodgings for Schubert, who supported himself erratically by giving music lessons. Schober was one of several artist friends of Schubert who gave him financial assistance from time to time. However, Schubert's financial difficulties did not prevent him from enjoying the lively bohemian literary, musical, and artistic life of Vienna. His friends often gathered to play his music. After Schober introduced the baritone Johann Michael Vogl to Schubert, the singer became a regular interpreter of Schubert's songs at many of these gatherings, which became known as Schubertiads. Soon the songs were being sung throughout Vienna. One of the most beautiful songs written during this period is *An die Musik* (1817), to a text by Schober. Schubert went back to teaching in 1817 but resigned the next year.

In the summer of 1818, and again in 1824, Schubert was employed as music teacher to the family of Count Johann Esterházy at their country estate in Hungary. Schubert's enthusiasm for Hungarian folk music and gypsy airs dated from this time. Out of the experience came such works as the *Divertissement à l'Hongroise* (1824), a piano composition for four hands. In the fall of 1818, Schubert was commissioned to write an operetta, *Die Zwillingsbrüder* (first performed in 1820 with Vogl in the lead). During the summer of 1819 he wrote the famous *Trout Quintet in A Major*.

The year 1821 saw the first publication of any of Schubert's compositions. *Erlkönig* appeared in April 1821, and thereafter his works were published regularly. In the following year he wrote one of his best-known orchestral works, the beautiful and haunting *Unfinished Symphony*. Through most of 1823, Schubert was ill, stricken with a venereal disease. Yet, though he was bedridden part of the time, he continued to compose, producing the great song cycle *Die schöne Müllerin*, set to words by Wilhelm Müller; the incidental music to *Rosamunde;* and two operas, *Die Verschworenen* and *Fierrabras*.

Last Years. After spending the summer of 1824 with the Esterházy family in Hungary, Schubert returned to Vienna refreshed. Among his compositions of 1824 and 1825 were the String Quartet in D Minor (*Der Tod und das Mädchen*), *The Lady of the Lake* songs, and the Piano Sonata in A Minor. In 1826, Schubert petitioned for the post of vice kapellmeister to the imperial court, but was not accepted. He suffered a great blow early in 1827 with the death of his lifelong idol, Beethoven. The two men met for the first and only time in March 1827, one week before Beethoven's death. Schubert was a torchbearer at the funeral. In the summer of 1827 he was elected as a representative to the Vienna Philharmonic Society, an honor that gave him much pleasure. Among his most important works of 1827 are the magnificent song cycle *Die Winterreise*, set to words by Müller, and the Trio in E-Flat Major for piano, violin, and cello.

Schubert's health had been declining since 1823, and as his condition worsened he suffered from attacks of anxiety and despondency. Fortunately, his creative powers seemed little affected by his bad health and impoverished circumstances. He wrote many of his most ambitious works in the last year of his life—the Symphony in C Major, known as the *Great*, the String Quintet in C Major, the cantata *Miriams Siegesgesang*, the Mass in E-Flat Major, and the beautiful song cycle *Schwanengesang*, containing such songs as *Der Atlas* and *Der Doppelgänger*, both to texts by Heinrich Heine. In March 1828 he arranged the only public concert of his works in his lifetime and enjoyed a great success.

In October 1828, Schubert contracted typhoid fever. He died in Vienna on Nov. 19, 1828. In accordance with his wishes, he was buried near Beethoven in the Währing Cemetery. About 60 years later, the bodies of both composers were disinterred and reburied in the Central Cemetery of Vienna.

WORKS

Schubert's music combines elements of both classicism and romanticism. His works were largely cast in classical forms, and he is therefore often regarded as the last composer of the classical school that included Haydn, Mozart, and the young Beethoven. However, the highly emotional and subjective quality of his music, its rich melodies and exquisite lyricism, also mark him as one of the first great romantic composers.

Art Songs. Schubert derived inspiration from the poetry he set to music to a far greater extent than any earlier composers of songs. He achieved the perfect union of the two arts. Furthermore, he increased the importance of the piano accompaniment, to balance with the vocal part and help establish mood and atmosphere.

Schubert wrote over 600 *lieder*, from brief strophic pieces to such long ballads as *Adelwold und Emma* (1815). In some of his earlier songs he inclined toward exalted topics, but as he matured his songs became more purely lyrical and personal. Among his most famous songs are *Gretchen am Spinnrade, Erlkönig, Heidenröslein* (1815), *Rastlose Liebe* (1815), *Der Wanderer* (1819), *Du bist die Ruh'* (1823), and *Who is Silvia?* (1826). *Die Forelle* (1817; *The Trout*), gave its name and theme to the *Trout Quintet in A Major*. *Der Tod und das Mädchen* (1817) served as a theme for the variations that constitute the slow movement of the string quartet of that name.

Schubert's predilection for delicate nuances and sudden reversals of mood found an ideal out-

BROWN BROTHERS

Franz Schubert, Austrian Romantic composer

let in his song cycles—compositions for groups of topically connected poems. In general, it was his custom in these cycles to write music for a number of poems by the same author, finding an appropriate and distinctive expression for each literary work. He wrote two cycles to words by the German poet Wilhelm Müller: *Die schöne Müllerin* (20 songs) and *Die Winterreise* (24 songs). Some of his most famous *lieder* are in these two groups. Other cycles are *Schwanengesang* (1828), a group of 14 songs, six of them to poems by Heinrich Heine. The celebrated *Ständchen* is from this cycle. *The Lady of the Lake* (1825) contains songs set to parts of the long poem of that name by Sir Walter Scott.

Symphonies. Schubert's first three symphonies, written between 1813 and 1815, might strike the listener as exercises in form and orchestration. The Fourth Symphony in C Minor (1816), the *Tragic*, and the Fifth Symphony in B-Flat Major (1816), were modeled on symphonies of Mozart and Haydn. The Sixth Symphony in C Major (1818), the *Little*, shows marked signs of Beethoven's influence. The Seventh Symphony in B Minor (1821) exists only as a sketch. Schubert never orchestrated it.

About 1822, Schubert's style took on a new and more personal quality, becoming increasingly lyrical and delicate. This quality was apparent in the symphony written at about that time, the Eighth Symphony in B Minor, the *Unfinished*. The exact date of its composition is unknown. Schubert's reasons for not completing it remain a mystery. It is assumed that he intended to complete the work, for the first nine bars of a scherzo movement were fully written and the rest of the movement sketched out. Whatever the explanation, the Eighth Symphony is a masterpiece.

One of Schubert's last works, written in the year of his death, was the Symphony in C Major, the *Great*. Acclaimed in later years for its melodic beauty and exciting rhythmic drive, it lay in obscurity until Robert Schumann, on a visit to Vienna in 1838–1839, discovered it in a pile of manuscripts in the possession of Ferdinand Schubert. Schumann sent it to Felix Mendelssohn, who conducted it at Leipzig in 1839 but failed to get it established as part of the symphonic repertoire. The symphony was abandoned and forgotten until it was rediscovered in the late 19th century.

Chamber Music. Schubert composed a sizable body of chamber works. These include some 20 string quartets, of which three were lost and a few left unfinished; the String Quintet in C Major; the *Trout Quintet* for piano, viola, cello, violin, and double bass; the Octet in F Major (1824); and the Trio in B-Flat Major and the Trio in E-Flat Major (both 1827).

Many of the string quartets were written during Schubert's musical apprenticeship, when he was between 15 and 19. The popular Quartet in C Minor (1820) is happy and cheerful, if somewhat superficial. The *Der Tod und das Mädchen* quartet is more profound, resembling the *Great C-Major Symphony* in rhythmic intensity and harmonic richness.

Piano Music. Schubert wrote some 14 or 15 completed sonatas. Four of these, the A Minor (1823), A Minor (1825), D Major (1825), and G Major (1826), are similar in structure and tend to weaken in the last movement. None has the graceful, purely pianistic figurations that characterize the best sonatas of Mozart and Beethoven. However, in Schubert's last three sonatas, written in 1828, he shows his mastery of the form. Of the three sonatas, C Minor, A Major, and B-Flat Major, the last is probably the most frequently played.

Among Schubert's shorter compositions for the piano are the six *Moments musicaux* (1823–1827) and the eight *Impromptus* (1827). The *Impromptus* are historically important as the first major departure from the dominant sonata form in 19th century piano music. They also have intrinsic merit as charming little mood pieces.

Operatic Music. Schubert's operas failed for various reasons, perhaps the most important being that he never found an adequate libretto. *Die Zwillingsbrüder* and *Die Zauberharfe*, both produced in 1820, held the stage only briefly. He wrote incidental music to Helmina von Chézy's play *Rosamunde*, which had two performances in Vienna in 1823 and was then forgotten. The music was rediscovered by Sir George Grove and Sir Arthur Sullivan during a visit to Vienna in 1867. The charming score survives as ballet music.

Church and Choral Music. Schubert's Masses and choral works are generally not on a par with his other vocal music. Many music historians, however, consider them the point of departure for the great church music of the later 19th century Austrian composer Anton Bruckner. Schubert's approximately 100 cantatas, psalms, hymns, and other choral pieces have moments of great beauty.

ANN M. LINGG[*]
Author of "Mozart, Genius of Harmony";
"Mephisto Waltz, the Story of Franz Liszt"

Bibliography

Deutsch, Otto Erich, *Schubert: A Documentary Biography*, tr. by Eric Blom (Dent 1947).
Hutchings, Arthur, *Schubert* (Pellegrini & Cudahy 1949).
Einstein, Alfred, *Schubert: A Musical Portrait* (Oxford 1951).
Porter, Ernest G., *Schubert's Song Technique* (Dobson 1961).
Abraham, Gerald, ed., *Music of Schubert* (Norton 1947).

SCHULBERG, shōōl'bûrg, **Budd** (1914–   ), American writer of tough, realistic fiction. He was born in New York City on March 27, 1914, and was raised in Hollywood, where he observed at first hand the movie world he later described so vividly. Between 1937 and 1939, after graduating from Dartmouth College in 1936, he published several short stories about Hollywood.

Among these stories was one that later became the novel *What Makes Sammy Run?* (1941), which chronicles the rise of Sammy Glick from office boy to movie tycoon. Schulberg's second novel, *The Harder They Fall* (1947), exposed racketeering in professional prizefighting. *The Disenchanted* (1950), concerning the final days of an alcoholic has-been genius who goes to Hollywood to do a screenplay, is probably based on F. Scott Fitzgerald. Another novel, *Sanctuary Five* (1970), deals with the socialist takeover of a Caribbean island, probably Cuba, and its figurehead president, who takes refuge in a neutral embassy.

In 1954, Schulberg won an Academy Award for the screenplay *On the Waterfront*. He also collaborated on stage versions of *The Disenchanted* (1958) and *What Makes Sammy Run?* (1964).

SCHULLER, shōōl'ər, **Gunther** (1925–   ), American composer and horn player, known also as an active proponent of modern music and jazz. He was born in New York City on Nov. 22, 1925, the son of a violinist in the New York Philharmonic. He attended the Manhattan School of Music, began the study of the French horn at the age of 14, and while still in his teens played the horn in the Ballet Theatre Orchestra, New York City, and the Cincinnati Symphony. Later he appeared as horn soloist with the Metropolitan Opera Orchestra, devoted much of his time to composition and work with groups interested in modern music and jazz, and in 1967 became president of the New England Conservatory of Music.

As a composer, Schuller was influenced by such atonal, or 12-tone, composers as Webern and Schoenberg. But he also admired Stravinsky and other nonatonalists, and his 12-tone works reflect both influences, even as his jazz compositions fuse jazz with music in the classical tradition. Among his many compositions are Concerto for Horn and Orchestra (1944), *Atonal Jazz Study* (1948), *Fantasy,* for unaccompanied cello (1951), and *Fanfare* (1968). His books include *Horn Technique* (1962) and *Early Jazz: Its Roots and Musical Development* (1968).

SCHULZ, shōōlts, **Charles Monroe** (1922–   ), American cartoonist, creator of the widely popular comic strip *Peanuts.* Schulz was born in Minneapolis, Minn., on Nov. 26, 1922. After graduation from high school in St. Paul, Minn., he studied art through a correspondence course, served in World War II, and then began to draw a comic strip for a St. Paul newspaper. In 1948 he sold his first cartoons to the *Saturday Evening Post.* His rise to fame began in 1950, when the United Feature Syndicate bought his idea for a comic strip, naming it *Peanuts.*

Featuring child characters with mature attitudes, Charlie Brown and Lucy, and a philosophical dog, Snoopy, *Peanuts* became one of the most widely syndicated features of all time. It inspired television series and the musical comedy *You're a Good Man, Charlie Brown* and provided the basis for numerous *Peanuts* books, as well as a line of greeting cards. See also COMICS.

SCHUMAN, shoo'mən, **Frederick Lewis** (1904–1981), American political scientist and writer. He was born in Chicago, Ill., on Feb. 22, 1904. Educated at the University of Chicago, where he received his Ph. D. in 1927, he served on its faculty from 1927 to 1936, when he became professor of political science at Williams College. From 1938 to 1968 he was Woodrow Wilson professor of government at Williams and then joined the faculty of Portland State University. He died in Portland, Oreg., on May 19,1981.

A lecturer and contributor to magazines, he was probably best known for his books. These include: *International Politics* (1933, 7th ed. 1969); *Night Over Europe* (1941); *Russia Since 1917* (1957); *Government in the Soviet Union* (1961); and *The Cold War: Retrospect and Prospect* (1962).

SCHUMAN, shoo'män, **Robert** (1886–1963), French political leader who promoted European economic unity through the Schuman Plan. He was born in Luxembourg (city) on June 29, 1886. He was brought up in Lorraine, then a province of Germany, attended German universities, and began the practice of law in Metz. Because he refused to serve in the German Army in World War I, he spent the war years in a German prison.

In 1919, when Lorraine was returned to France, he was elected to the French Chamber of Deputies as a representative of Moselle. He was a member of the PDP (Parti Démocratique Populaire) and concentrated on finance. After World War II, during which he had been imprisoned by the Germans and later fought with the French Resistance, he returned to the Chamber of Deputies. He was a founder of the MRP (Mouvement Républicaine Populaire), a reform-oriented party of liberal Catholics who worked for European unity. He became finance minister in 1946 and again in 1947, and in November of that year was chosen premier. Strikes were settled in a few weeks, but he lost power in July 1948 over his military budget. In August he again became premier briefly.

From 1948 to 1952 he was foreign minister in all cabinets, but he refused to serve in the cabinet of Pierre Mendès-France because of the chamber's refusal to ratify the European Defense Community, which Schuman ardently supported. In 1950, while foreign minister, he advanced the Schuman Plan, which proposed to put national coal and steel resources under a supranational authority. It went into force in 1952 as the European Coal and Steel Community (ECSC) and became a forerunner of the Common Market.

In February 1955 he became minister of justice in the cabinet of Edgar Faure. In 1958 he was elected to the Fifth Republic's first National Assembly, and from 1958 to 1960 he was president of the European Parliament Assembly. He died near Metz on Sept. 4, 1963.

SCHUMAN, shoo'mən, **William Howard** (1910–   ), American composer and teacher, whose works form an important body of mid-20th century American music. .He was born in New York City on Aug. 4, 1910. He studied privately under Max Persin, Charles Haubiel, and Roy Harris and received degrees from Columbia University. Thereafter he taught (1935–1944) at Sarah Lawrence College and was president (1945–1962) of the Juilliard School of Music and president (1962–1969) of Lincoln Center in New York City.

Schuman's music, which is characterized by energetic rhythm patterns and long, flowing lines, includes symphonies, choral and chamber works, and ballets. The Boston Symphony Orchestra gave the first performances of his symphonies *American Festival Overture* (1939), Symphony No. 3 (1941), and *Symphony for Strings*, No. 5 (1943). His *Secular Cantata No. 2* (1943) won a Pulitzer Prize. Works on American themes include the popular *New England Triptych* (1956) and Symphony No. 10, *American Muse* (1976).

Further Reading: Schreiber, Flora R., and Persichetti, Vincent, *William Schuman* (Schirmer 1954).

SCHUMAN PLAN. See SCHUMAN, ROBERT.

SCHUMANN, shoo'män, **Clara** (1819–1896), German pianist. Clara Wieck was born in Leipzig on Sept. 13, 1819. A child prodigy, she studied piano with her father, Friedrich Wieck, and made her debut when she was nine. In 1831–1832, accompanied by her father, she made a concert tour through the musical centers of Germany and France and soon received international recognition as an established virtuoso. One of her father's pupils was the composer Robert Schumann. Clara and he fell in love and, in spite of strong opposition on Wieck's part, were married in 1840.

For 16 years, until Schumann's death in 1856, she shared his work and successes. Thereafter she pursued her public career alone, devoting herself to furthering recognition of her husband's genius as well as that of their friend Johannes Brahms. For many years she was principal piano teacher in the conservatory at Frankfurt am Main. She died there on May 20, 1896.

SCHUMANN, shoo'män, **Elizabeth** (1885–1952), German-American soprano, who was one of the leading lieder singers of her day and who specialized in operas by Mozart and Richard Strauss. She was born in Merseburg, Germany, on June 13, 1885, and made her opera debut with the Hamburg Opera in 1910. In 1919 she was engaged by the Vienna State Opera, where she sang for 23 years. Meanwhile, she had sung in most of the leading opera houses, making her New York debut at the Metropolitan in 1914 as Sophie in Strauss' *Der Rosenkavalier*. She also sang regularly at the Salzburg festivals from 1922 to 1935.

In 1938, after the Nazi takeover of Austria, Miss Schumann moved to the United States. She made a number of concert tours in which she performed Strauss songs with the composer accompanying her. She taught at the Curtis Institute of Music, Philadelphia, from 1938 until her death, in New York City, on April 23, 1952.

SCHUMANN, shoo'män, **Robert Alexander** (1810–1856), German composer, who was one of the most ardent of the German romantic composers. He was the master of all the musical forms of his time except opera. Nevertheless, his single completed opera, *Genoveva*, has much fine music, especially the overture. Schumann's genius was particularly suited to piano music and to German art songs, or *lieder*. His compositions for the piano rank with the best ever written, and his *lieder* rival those of Schubert and Brahms. Although Schumann wrote music for orchestra, it is usually overly orchestrated. However, he was an outstanding composer of chamber music, especially for combinations in which the piano is used.

Schumann possessed a multipersonality, which he recognized and wrote about in his music journal *Neue Zeitschrift für Musik*. He perceived in himself three main traits, which are reflected in his music. He called the brash hero Florestan; the romantic dreamer Eusebius; and the introspective philosopher Raro. Schumann even created the *Davidsbündler*, or Society of David, a group to oppose the Philistines—people who either do not like or understand art, or who prefer pseudo-art, such as a popular kind of conventional music that changes but little through the years. He was also a gifted author, and his writings are amusing and interesting as well as informative. They represent some of the finest musical criticism ever written.

Early Years. Schumann was born in Zwickau, Saxony, on June 8, 1810. His father was an author and bookshop owner, who started a publishing house in Zwickau. Thus Robert was exposed early to literature, which was an important influence on his music and on his prose writings. Schumann started piano lessons when he was about six. However, his all-consuming interest in music did not begin until 1819, when he heard a concert by the great pianist Ignaz Moscheles, an experience that left an indelible impression. He then made rapid progress as a pianist and began to compose.

In 1828, Schumann passed his Lyceum examinations with distinction. His diary of this time mentions the writer Jean Paul, who exerted a profound influence on him. Schumann reluctantly enrolled as a law student at Leipzig University, but he did not attend classes faithfully. He spent hours in discussions with friends on art and life and considerable time writing poetry in the style of Jean Paul, as well as composing. At this time, also, Schumann began to hear the songs of Schubert and became a lifelong champion of Schubert's music.

For a brief period in 1828–1829, Schumann studied piano with the celebrated teacher Friedrich Wieck and met Wieck's daughter, Clara, then nine years old, who later married Schumann. Clara was to become a great pianist in her own right and did much to advance the cause of her husband's music after his death.

Another important development during this eventful time in Schumann's life was his tormenting fear of insanity. Unfortunately, this fear had a real basis, for he was confined to an asylum during the last years of his life.

Schumann's brief encounter with law studies left him convinced that music should be his life's work. He had already discovered that he could express himself better emotionally through improvising at the piano than through literary endeavors. However, to placate his mother, Schumann, in 1829, went to Heidelberg, taking up law at the university there. Through a Heidelberg law professor, Justus Thibaut, who had published a book on musical aesthetics, Schumann received a training in "music appreciation," hitherto unknown to him, since Thibaut's home was the scene of a great variety of *Hausmusik*, or home concerts.

In 1830, Schumann heard Paganini, the great violin virtuoso, and the effect on him was profound. One result of this experience was that in 1832 and 1833, Schumann adopted Paganini's brilliant *Caprices* for piano. During the same period, he composed his Opus 1, the *Abegg Variations*. The title is significant for two reasons.

THE BETTMANN ARCHIVE

Robert Schumann, the great German Romantic composer, and his wife, Clara, a leading pianist of the day.

Abegg was the family name of one of his female acquaintances, and the letters of the name are all musical notes. Schumann used them as a theme, employing a technique called *soggetto cavato*, literally, "carved out melody." He used this device again in the *Carnaval* piano suite (1834–1835) with the musical letters in his own name employed with great imagination. In German the theme is: s (e flat), c, h (b natural), and a. Another example of *soggetto cavato* are his fugues on the name BACH (Opus 60, 1845). In German the theme is: b flat, a, c, and h.

Schumann returned to Leipzig in 1830 to resume his studies with Wieck. His mother had reluctantly consented to his continuing music study, apparently convinced by a letter from Wieck, and Schumann moved in with the Wieck family. Although Wieck admired Schumann's gifts, he was more interested in the career of his daughter, a child prodigy, who was in demand for concert performances. Robert and Clara were virtually inseparable when she was not away playing concerts; however, Clara was still a child, and the first love between them was only familial. The absence of Wieck, on tour with Clara, forced Schumann to find another teacher, and he settled on the conductor Heinrich Dorn, who began by teaching him thorough-bass.

Schumann had many other passionate interests at this time. He discovered Chopin, also a struggling young man in 1830, and was completely captivated by him. (Both men were the same age.) He began a novel, *Die Davidsbündler*, in which Florestan and Eusebius, two of the personifications of his personality traits, probably first appeared. His diary of the period contains frequent mention of them. Schumann also published his first music, the *Abegg Variations*, as well as an article on Chopin, printed in the *Allegemeine musikalische Zeitung* in 1831.

Middle Years. In 1831, Schumann continued to compose piano music and to study such works as Bach's *Art of Fugue.* Opus 2, the delightful *Papillons,* was composed and published in 1832. The format of *Papillons* is an extended cycle of short "character pieces" that are based on romantic ideas and ideals. The first 23 opuses, for piano, represented new concepts in piano writing, both in the techniques required to play them and in the subtle harmonic colorations that were being developed simultaneously, though along different lines, by Chopin and Liszt. This outburst of piano music occupied Schumann for almost a decade. Opus 23 is dated 1839. Among his other important piano works of the 1830's are *Toccata,* three piano sonatas, *Symphonic Variations, Scenes from Childhood,* and *Kreisleriana.*

During this decade of intensive composition for piano, several important events occurred. In 1832, Schumann attempted to strengthen his fingers by wearing a mechanical device that permanently damaged the fourth finger of his right hand. This spelled the end of any hopes he had for a concert career.

In the same year Dorn, whose relationship with Schumann was far from harmonious, decided to end the lessons. Left on his own, Schumann studied some excellent works, among them Friedrich Wilhelm Marpurg's treatise on the fugue and Bach's *Well-Tempered Clavier.* In 1834, Schumann and some friends formed the *Neue Zeitschrift für Musik,* which Schumann edited until 1844. The *Neue Zeitschrift für Musik* was unusual in that it favored new music, in addition to praising true greatness in old music. Almost all of the other contemporary music periodicals were very conservative.

In 1834, Schumann became engaged to a young student of Wieck's, Ernestine von Fricken. It is thought that one of the reasons he subsequently broke off with her was that he discovered that she was not the blood daughter of the wealthy Baron von Fricken but an illegitimate girl, who had been taken into the von Fricken family. Another reason may have been his growing passion for Clara.

The love affair of Robert and Clara reads like a 19th century novel. They fell in love gradually. As he watched a delightful, talented child blossom into a beautiful young woman, he forgot Ernestine. Wieck, however, would not give his blessing and tried everything in his power to keep them apart. The marriage finally took place in 1840, after Schumann went to court to obtain legal consent.

Later Years. After the lovers were married, Schumann literally burst into song. The year 1840 has been called the "song year," and one masterpiece followed another. As with his piano pieces, Schumann liked to group songs together in cycles. Among the greatest song cycles of 1840 are *Myrthen, Liederkreis, Frauenliebe und Leben,* and *Dichterliebe.* However, he continued to write songs throughout his life. In 1841, known as the "symphony year," Schumann wrote his Symphony No. 1 in B flat major, called the *Spring,* and the Symphony No. 2, later revised (1851) as the Symphony No. 4 in D minor. His other important symphonic works include the Symphony No. 2 in C major (1845–1846) and the Symphony No. 3 in E flat major, called the *Rhenish* (1850). In 1842, the "chamber music" year, he completed such masterworks as the Quintet for piano and strings.

The Schumanns had numerous friends in the world of music. One was Felix Mendelssohn, who had been named conductor of the Leipzig Gewandhaus Orchestra in 1835. Mendelssohn became "Felix Meritas" in Schumann's writings. Perhaps their dearest friend was Brahms, whose genius was recognized by Schumann after hearing the younger composer's earliest piano works.

By the late 1840's, Schumann suffered increasingly from bouts with mental illness. He had made suicide attempts earlier in his life, and long periods of great depression now began to affect his work. Many lofty conceptions for works were never fulfilled, and the finished works were not always up to Schumann's previous standards. Some masterpieces were written, however, among them the Piano Concerto in A minor (1845); incidental music to Byron's drama *Manfred* (1848–1849); many fine piano pieces; *Scenes from Goethe's Faust* (1844–1853); and the Cello Concerto in A minor (1850). Most of the other compositions are the work of a sick mind. The Schumanns' move to Dresden in 1844 and to Düsseldorf in 1850 only made matters worse. At Düsseldorf, Schumann was engaged as municipal music director, but was unsuccessful. Beginning in 1852 the symptoms of severe illness became more frequent, and in 1854 he was committed to an asylum at Endenich, near Bonn. He died there on July 29, 1856.

Evaluation. A great part of Schumann's music is in the permanent concert repertoire by virtue of its lovely melodies, unusual harmonic effects, and strong rhythmic patterns. Unlike several romantic composers, Schumann has not been in and out of favor through the years. His work has enjoyed a continuous and steadfast popularity.

KENNETH BLANCHARD KLAUS
Author of "The Romantic Period in Music"

Bibliography

Abraham, Gerald, ed., *Schumann: A Symposium* (Oxford 1952).
Brion, Marcel, *Schumann and the Romantic Age,* tr. by Geoffrey Sainsbury (Macmillan, N. Y. 1956).
Brown, Thomas Alan, *The Aesthetics of Robert Schumann* (Philosophical Lib. 1968).
Klaus, Kenneth Blanchard, *The Romantic Period in Music* (Allyn 1970).
Plantinga, Leon B., *Schumann as Critic* (Yale Univ. Press 1967).

SCHUMANN-HEINK, shōō'män-hīnk, **Ernestine** (1861–1936), Austrian-American contralto, regarded as one of the greatest opera singers of her time. Her voice was rich and full, her style eloquent, and her technique impeccable. She was born Ernestine Rössler in Lieben, near Prague, on June 15, 1861. She studied voice at Graz and made her opera debut at Dresden in 1878 as Azucena in Verdi's *Il Trovatore.* She sang in Wagner's *Ring* cycle at Covent Garden, London, under the baton of Gustav Mahler in 1892 and sang in all performances of the *Ring* given at Bayreuth in 1896–1906, with the exception of 1904.

Mme. Schumann-Heink made her American debut in Chicago as Ortrud in Wagner's *Lohengrin.* The following year she appeared at the Metropolitan, New York, in the same role. Her success was so great that she remained in the United States and became a U. S. citizen in 1908. At Dresden, in 1909, she created the role of Klytemnestra in Richard Strauss' *Elektra.* Her later years were devoted to concert work, and in 1932, at the age of 71, she gave a farewell performance at the Metropolitan, as Erda in the *Ring.* She died in Los Angeles, Calif., on Nov. 17, 1936.

SCHUMPETER, shōōm′pā-tər, **Joseph Alois** (1883–1950), American economist. He was born in Triesch, Moravia (now Czechoslovakia) on Feb. 8, 1883. In 1909, he became professor of economics at the University of Chernovtsy, Austria (now in the USSR) and for the rest of his life he taught economics, except for service as Austria's minister of finance in 1919 and 1920. His other teaching posts were at the University of Graz, the University of Bonn, and, from 1932, Harvard University.

Although trained in the Austrian school of economics, Schumpeter, with his complex economic thought, did not fit into a "school." He was, however, deeply interested in the Lausanne school, which is strongly inclined toward the use of mathematics, and he took part in the founding of the Econometric Society in 1930.

Schumpeter's writings established him as an authority on both economic theory and the history of economic thought. In *The Theory of Economic Development* (1912) he was the first economist to analyze aggressive capitalism from the premise that it stems from large and innovative corporations. His *Business Cycles* (1939) filled out Schumpeter's theories by presenting much mathematically oriented research on the theory, history, and statistics of the capitalist process. His other works that became standard references included *Capitalism, Socialism, and Democracy* (1942) and the large *History of Economic Analysis* (1954), which was published after his death. Schumpeter died at Taconic, Conn., on Jan. 8, 1950.

SCHURZ, shōōrts, **Carl** (1829–1906), German-American political leader, editor, and writer. He was born in Liblar, near Cologne, Prussia, on March 2, 1829. He studied at the University of Bonn, in 1848, was co-publisher of a revolutionary journal, and in 1849 escaped to the Palatinate upon the failure of an insurrection which he promoted at Bonn. He took part in the defense of Rastatt and upon its surrender fled to Switzerland. In 1850 he returned to Germany, going then to Scotland and to Paris, where he was a correspondent for the German press, and, after a year in London, went to the United States. He lived in Philadelphia until 1855, then moved to Madison, Wis. Schurz identified himself with the Republican party, and by his speeches made himself an important factor in influencing the German ethnic sector of the state against slavery. He entered legal practice at Milwaukee, was a member of the National Republican Convention of 1860, and assisted largely in the framing of its platform. He greatly helped the election of Lincoln by brilliantly attacking Stephen A. Douglas at Cooper Union in New York.

President Lincoln appointed him minister to Spain, but in December 1861 he resigned to enter the army, receiving a commission as brigadier-general of volunteers. He distinguished himself at the second Bull Run, or Manassas, and was promoted major-general. In 1863 he commanded a division at Chancellorsville, held temporary command of the 11th corps at Gettysburg, and took part at Chattanooga.

After the war he returned to professional practice, in 1865–1866 was Washington correspondent of the New York *Tribune*, and was appointed by President Johnson a special commissioner to report on the workings of the Freedmen's Bureau. In 1868 he was temporary

chairman of the convention that nominated Grant, whom he actively supported. In 1869–1875 he was senator from Missouri. He vigorously opposed many of the leading measures of the Grant administration, and in 1872 helped to organize the Liberal Republican party, which nominated Horace Greeley for president. In 1876 he supported Rutherford B. Hayes for president; Hayes made him secretary of the interior. Schurz introduced competitive examinations for posts in the civil service, and ably advocated forest protection on public domains. From the close of the Hayes administration to 1884, he was editor of the New York *Evening Post*, and his speeches and articles were numerous and noteworthy. He died on May 14, 1906, in New York City.

SCHUSCHNIGG, shōōsh′nik, **Kurt von** (1897–1977), Austrian chancellor. He was born in Riva, on Lake Garda, on Dec. 14, 1897. He became a lawyer, entered parliament in 1927, and founded the Ostmärkische Sturmscharen, an organization to uphold Austrian independence.

As minister of justice in 1932–1934 and educational minister in 1933–1934, Schuschnigg helped Chancellor Dollfuss repress the Social Democrats. When Dollfuss was assassinated in 1934, Schuschnigg succeeded him as head of the semifascist state. He tried to maintain Austrian independence while pursuing a friendly policy toward Germany. When Nazi demands became insistent in 1938, Schuschnigg announced a plebiscite on independence. Before it could be held, he was forced to resign, and German troops occupied Austria. He was imprisoned during World War II. He then emigrated to the United States, where he taught for 20 years before returning to Austria. He died near Innsbruck on Nov. 18, 1977.

SCHUSTER, shōō′stər, **Alfredo Ildefonso** (1880–1954), Italian cardinal and archbishop of Milan. He was born in Rome on Jan. 18, 1880, entered the Benedictine monastery of St. Paul-outside-the-Walls, and was ordained on March 19, 1904. He served as master of novices (1904–1916) and as prior (1916–1918). In 1918 he was made abbot nullius of St. Paul-outside-the-Walls.

Schuster was a noted liturgical scholar and historian. His monumental liturgical commentary, *Liber Sacramentorum* (9 vols., 1919–1929), and his book on St. Benedict, *Storia di San Benedetto e dei suoi tempi* (1943), are his most important works. Pope Pius XI named him archbishop of Milan and made him a cardinal, personally consecrating him a bishop on July 21, 1929. Schuster's generally tolerant attitude toward the Fascist regime caused some comment, but his personal sanctity was never questioned. He died in Venegono, Italy, on Aug. 30, 1954.

SCHUSTER, shōōs′tər, **Sir Arthur** (1851–1934), German-British physicist. He was born in Frankfurt am Main on Sept. 12, 1851, obtained a doctorate from Heidelberg, and in 1869 became a British subject. He collaborated with Rayleigh at the Cavendish Laboratory in determining the value of the absolute ohm. From 1881 to 1907 he worked at Owens College in spectroscopy, terrestrial magnetism, optics, and the mathematical theory of periodicity. He made the first photograph of the spectrum of the sun's corona, and he showed that current is conducted through a gas by ions. Schuster was knighted in 1920 and died, in Twyford, on Oct. 14, 1934.

SCHÜTZ, shüts, **Heinrich** (1585–1672), German composer, who was one of the great geniuses of 17th century German music and the most important precursor of Johann Sebastian Bach. Although famous primarily as a composer of religious music, he is also remembered for his *Daphne* (1627; now lost), the first German opera, and for some fine madrigals.

Schütz' contributions to German music were enormous. He brilliantly translated and incorporated elements of the *nuove musiche*, or new music, of Italy into his own compositions, producing a superb synthesis of Italian and German styles without sacrificing the spirit of the German tradition. Influenced by Giovanni Gabrieli, his teacher, and by Claudio Monteverdi, Schütz created splendid choral works in which the text was given heightened dramatic importance. Among his greatest compositions are *Musikalische Exequien* (1636), a requiem for soloists and choir; *Christmas Oratorio* (1664); and four magnificent Passions, written in his old age.

Schütz was born in Köstritz, Saxony, on Oct. 8, 1585. He was admitted to the chapel of Kassel as a choirboy in 1599. The Landgrave Moritz of Hesse-Kassel saw to his education, and in 1608, Schütz went to the University of Marburg to study law. However, he was more interested in music, and in 1609, sponsored by the Landgrave, he traveled to Venice, where he studied under Giovanni Gabrieli until 1612.

Schütz returned to Germany in 1613 and after serving as court organist in Kassel, went to Dresden. There, in 1617, he became conductor of the electoral chapel, a post he held, with sporadic interruptions, thereafter. Schütz revisited Venice in 1628. From 1633 to 1635 he served as court conductor in Copenhagen, returning in the same capacity in 1637–1638 and 1642–1645. Although Schütz repeatedly asked to be relieved of his post in Dresden, his resignation was never accepted. He died in Dresden on Nov. 6, 1672.

SCHUTZSTAFFEL (SS), shōōts'stä-fəl, an elite German Nazi organization, also known as the Blackshirts. It was formed in 1925 under the Storm Troopers (SA) to provide protection for Hitler. It began its real growth in 1929, when Heinrich Himmler became its leader, and its influence expanded after Hitler took power in 1933. In a purge of June 30, 1934, the SS triumphed over the SA, whose leaders were eliminated.

The SS quickly built up vast power within the Nazi state, becoming the main exponent of the party's "racial" policies and taking over the Gestapo, the secret police. During World War II, starting from a small base, the Waffen SS, the organization's military arm, grew to about 500,000 men and rivaled the regular army in influence. The SS was also responsible for the extermination policies in eastern Europe, and it directed the concentration camps.

SCHUYLER, skī'lər, **Philip John** (1733–1804), American soldier and political leader. A prominent New York landowner and businessman, he was also a Revolutionary War general, and he served in the Continental Congress and in the first U. S. Senate.

Schuyler was born to a landed family in Albany, N. Y., on Nov. 20, 1733. He served in the French and Indian War, rising to the rank of major, then went to England in 1761 to settle colonial war claims. Returning in 1763, he developed lumbering and milling on his Saratoga property. In 1764 he acted as commissioner to determine the boundary between New York and Massachusetts, and he later helped settle the New Hampshire boundary. As a representative in the New York Assembly in 1768, he earnestly defended the side of the colonists.

A delegate to the Continental Congress in 1775, Schuyler served on the committee to frame rules for the Continental Army. On June 19, 1775, he was appointed one of the four American major generals and was placed in command of the department of northern New York. Planning to invade Canada, he reached Lake Champlain, where he left a subordinate in command of Fort Ticonderoga. Early in 1776 he led an expedition to Johnstown, N. Y., and captured British military stores. On July 4, 1777, Ticonderoga was evacuated by Gen. Arthur St. Clair, but the Americans effected a masterful retreat engineered by Schuyler. Superseded by Gen. Horatio Gates on August 4, Schuyler, at his own insistence, was court-martialed for alleged neglect of duty in permitting the capture of Fort Ticonderoga. He was acquitted and vindicated in 1778. The following year he resigned from the army.

In 1779–1780, Schuyler was again a delegate to the Continental Congress, and in 1780 he also was chairman of a committee concerned with reorganizing army staff departments. He entered the New York State Senate in September 1780 and actively supported the Federalist campaign to secure New York's ratification of the U. S. Constitution. With Rufus King, he represented New York in the first U. S. Senate (1789–1791). Reelected in 1797, after another term in the New York senate, he served until his retirement in 1798. He died in Albany on Nov. 18, 1804. Schuyler's daughter, Elizabeth, was the wife of Alexander Hamilton.

SCHUYLERVILLE, skī'lər-vil, is a village in eastern New York, in Saratoga county, on the Hudson River, about 32 miles (51 km) north of Albany. It has many historic associations. The first settlement, made in 1649, was burned in an Indian raid in 1745. This had been called Saratoga, from an Indian word meaning "the place of swift waters."

The community, which was situated on the strategic line of communications between New York City and Canada, was rebuilt. The decisive Battles of Saratoga in the American Revolution were fought in the nearby countryside and are commemorated in the Saratoga national historic park, 8 miles (12 km) south of Schuylerville.

The village was incorporated in 1831 under its present name, in memory of Gen. Philip Schuyler, a leader of the Revolution. Population: 1,256.

SCHUYLKILL RIVER, skōōl'kil, in southeastern Pennsylvania, rises in Schuylkill county, flows generally southeast, and enters the Delaware River at Philadelphia. It is about 150 miles (240 km) long. Among the larger communities along its banks are the cities of Pottsville, Reading, Pottstown, and Norristown. Some of Philadelphia's port facilities are along the river. Philadelphia has obtained part of its water supply from the Schuylkill.

The river's name is derived from a Dutch word, *schuilkil*, which means "hidden channel."

SCHWAB, shwob, **Charles Michael** (1862–1939), American industrialist, who was a leading entrepreneur in the expansion of the steel industry. He was born in Williamsburg, Pa., on Feb. 18, 1862. His formal education was slight before he went to work in the Edgar Thomson Steel Works, owned by the Carnegie brothers. In 1887, he was made superintendent of the Homestead Steel Works, another Carnegie property, but returned to Thomson two years later.

In 1892, after a disastrous strike at the Homestead works had been crushed with bloodshed, Andrew Carnegie sent Schwab to restore harmony and put the plant in efficient operation. He achieved this, and in 1897 he became president of the Carnegie Steel Company, Ltd.

In 1901, he arranged the gigantic sale of the Carnegie steel interests to J. Pierpont Morgan, and the subsequent organization of the United States Steel Corporation, of which he became president at Morgan's insistence.

Two years later he resigned to head the Bethlehem Steel Corporation, of which he had bought control. He built this company into one of the major steel enterprises in the world. Its success in filling arms contracts for the Allies in World War I made it a rival of United States Steel. From April to December 1918, Schwab was chairman of the Emergency Fleet Corporation, created by President Woodrow Wilson to spur shipbuilding for the war.

After the war, Schwab invested heavily in various directions. Some of the ventures failed, and the Great Depression further injured his interests. His vast fortune, with which he had endowed many philanthropies, dwindled, and he was virtually insolvent when he died in New York City on Sept. 18, 1939.

SCHWANN, shvän, **Theodor** (1810–1882), German physician and scientist, who articulated the theory that all living things are made up of cells. Schwann was born in Neuss, Prussia, on Dec. 7, 1810, and was educated in Neuss, Cologne, and Bonn. He began his medical studies in Würzburg and from 1833 continued them at Berlin, then the foremost German university. There he came under the commanding influence of the physiologist Johannes Müller. Even when Schwann later departed from his professor's philosophy of biology, Müller's ideas formed the backdrop and the counterweight to the newer, more materialistic biological concepts of many of Schwann's generation. In 1834, Schwann received his M. D. and license.

Though trained in medicine, Schwann followed a common 19th century pattern by making his mark in the laboratory. He completed his most important research very early in his career while still under Müller. In 1839 he assumed a chair of instruction in Louvain, Belgium, and henceforth ceased to be an innovative force in the life sciences. From 1848 to 1879 he taught at the University of Liège. He died, honored but isolated, in Cologne on Jan. 11, 1882.

Work. Schwann's scientific work employed a variety of mechanical, chemical, and microscopical techniques. After early inquiries into the mechanics of muscle contraction in 1836, he turned to the chemical investigation of digestion. Experimenting with the artificial digestion of egg white by acids, also in 1836, he was able to isolate a factor in the stomach that produced this effect without itself being consumed. Calling the substance pepsin, he thus uncovered the first of the proteolytic enzymes.

In 1837, Schwann anticipated Pasteur by experimentally refuting the spontaneous generation of ferments. Growing first out of this work were his microscopical researches, which demonstrated that fermentation was due to yeast organisms. His most celebrated contribution was also microscopical: the cell theory of the *Microscopical Investigations . . .* (1839). Uniting all the functions of plants and animals under one physiological concept, that of the living cell, he provided a critical leading idea for the biological sciences. His analogy between the formation of cells and crystals—an error soon to be corrected by Robert Remak and Rudolf Virchow—reflected the complexity of the philosophical posture of biology at the time.

RUSSELL C. MAULITZ
Duke University School of Medicine

Further Reading: Coleman, William, *Biology in the Nineteenth Century* (Wiley 1971); Maulitz, Russell, "Schwann's Way: Cells and Crystals," *Journal of History of Medicine and Allied Sciences*, vol. 26, October 1971.

SCHWARZ-BART, shvärts-bärt', **André** (1928–), French novelist. He was born in Metz on May 23, 1928. He studied at the Sorbonne, and during World War II he was active in the French resistance. After the war he worked in a factory in Les Halles, a Paris district.

Schwarz-Bart's best-known novel is *Les Derniers des justes* (1959; Eng. tr., *The Last of the Just,* 1960). It is a semihistorical account of the persecution of the Jews, traced through 36 generations of a single family. It begins with a pogrom in England in 1185 and culminates in the death of Ernie Levy at Auschwitz, a Nazi concentration camp, during World War II. The 36 "just men" of the novel represent "the hearts of the world multiplied," into which we "pour all our griefs." Schwarz-Bart was awarded the Prix Goncourt in 1959. In 1967 he was the winner of the Prix de Jerusalem.

SCHWARZENBERG, shvär'tsən-berkH, **Prince Felix zu** (1800–1852), Austrian prime minister. He was born in Krummau, Bohemia, on Oct. 2, 1800, the nephew of Prince Karl Philipp. He entered the army in 1818 and transferred to the diplomatic corps in 1824. He served in several European capitals and became closely linked with Prince Metternich, the foreign minister.

When the European revolutionary disorders of 1848 broke out, Schwarzenberg first fought with the Austrian armies in Italy and then returned to Vienna. Metternich had been forced from office early in the year, and in November, Schwarzenberg was chosen to fill the vacant post. In December he forced the abdication of the feebleminded Emperor Ferdinand in favor of the young Francis Joseph.

As prime minister he sought to restore Austria's prestige and power through centralization. Early in 1849 the Reichstag drafted a constitution for a federal, decentralized Austria. He dissolved the Reichstag and issued the Stadion Constitution, establishing a centralized state. On Dec. 31, 1851, he had this constitution abolished, which made Francis Joseph an absolute ruler. During this period Schwarzenberg tried to increase Austria's influence in Germany while attempting to contain Prussia. He died in Vienna on April 5, 1852.

SCHWARZENBERG, shvär'tsən-berĸн, **Prince Karl Philipp zu** (1771–1820), Austrian field marshal. He was born in Vienna on April 15, 1771, and entered the army in 1787. During the Napoleonic Wars against France, Schwarzenberg advanced rapidly, becoming a general in 1796. He served with distinction in the battles of Hohenlinden (1800), Ulm (1805), and Wagram (1809).

After Austria made peace with France in 1810, he conducted the negotiations that led to the marriage of Napoleon and Marie Louise, daughter of Emperor Francis I. Schwarzenberg then commanded the Austrian contingent that accompanied Napoleon to Russia. On his return he urged Austria to renew hostilities with France. He was made a field marshal in 1813 and led the allied forces to a victory over the French at Leipzig. Schwarzenberg suffered a stroke in 1817 and died in Leipzig on Oct. 15, 1820.

SCHWARZKOPF, shvärts'kôpf, **Elisabeth** (1915–　　), German soprano. With her exquisite voice, impeccable style, and warm personality, Elisabeth Schwarzkopf excelled in both opera and lieder. She was born in Jarotschin, Poland, on Dec. 9, 1915. She studied voice in Berlin and made her opera debut in 1938 at the Berlin City Opera as one of the Flower Maidens in *Parsifal*. She went on to sing Zerbinetta in

NORMAN GRYSPEERDT
Elisabeth Schwarzkopf in Strauss' *Der Rosenkavalier*

Richard Strauss' *Ariadne auf Naxos* in 1943, after which she joined the Vienna State Opera.

Following World War II, Elisabeth Schwarzkopf gained international fame. She sang Eva in the performance of *Die Meistersinger* that inaugurated the postwar Wagner festivals at Bayreuth, and she made her American debut in San Francisco in 1953. Noted for her roles in operas by Mozart and Strauss, she was particularly acclaimed as the Marschalin in Strauss' *Der Rosenkavalier*. She retired from opera in 1971 but continued to sing lieder.

SCHWARZWALD. See BLACK FOREST.

SCHWEITZER, shvī'tsər, **Albert** (1875–1965), Alsatian-German scholar and humanitarian, and founder of the Schweitzer Hospital in Lambaréné, Gabon, Africa. Dr. Schweitzer won fame in four well-defined fields—music, theology, philosophy, and medicine—as well as in the more general but nonetheless supremely important area of spiritual example and charismatic personal witness.

Schweitzer's remarkable accomplishments in all these fields are readily documented. He was one of the great church and concert organists of his time, and he himself designed and built some of the world's great organs on which he played. His performances commanded such a following that for many years he helped to support his humanitarian endeavors in Africa by giving organ concerts throughout Europe. He was also an authority on Bach, and his biography of the composer, *J. S. Bach* (1905), is a standard work.

As a social philosopher and religious thinker, Schweitzer belonged in the first rank. His humanistically oriented study *The Quest of the Historical Jesus* (1906) is one of several theological works that would have assured him fame even if he had never left Europe to go to Africa.

Schweitzer's central precept, "Reverence for Life," became something of a catch phrase. However, anyone who soberly thinks through the meaning and implications of this expression will have come a long way toward understanding Schweitzer's thought and teachings. He stood against the increasing prevalence of violence in his time, and his respect for the fragility and wonder of life is in marked contrast to the lack of concern for human existence that has plagued and disfigured so much of the 20th century.

Schweitzer began the medical-missionary phase of his life at the age of 30, when he abandoned a successful career as a musicologist and religious educator to study medicine. After acquiring a medical degree, he went to Africa, where he founded a medical settlement that performed prodigies of service to the sick.

Schweitzer's greatness, however, ultimately rests less on his tangible achievements than on his importance as a symbol. More important than what he did for others was what others accomplished because of his example. Wherever Schweitzer's story was known, people were affected and their lives changed. For instance, Larimer Mellon, a member of one of the wealthiest American families, was so deeply moved by Schweitzer's selfless dedication that he returned to college in his late thirties, took a medical degree, and, with his wife, founded the Albert Schweitzer Hospital in Haiti.

Early Years. Albert Schweitzer was born in Kaysersberg, Alsace, on Jan. 14, 1875. His father was an Evangelical Lutheran pastor, who soon moved the family to the village of Gunsbach, where young Schweitzer lived until he was nine. In 1885 he was sent to live with his scholarly great-uncle in Mulhouse, so that he could study at the gymnasium there. Until his graduation in 1893, Schweitzer lived by the stern, unfrivolous (though not unkind) standards of his great-uncle's generation—an experience that intensified his precocious interest in politics, theology, and other serious concerns. During these years, Schweitzer also took lessons from the master organist Eugène Münch.

University Days. In the fall of 1893, Schweitzer enrolled in the University of Strasbourg, where he remained until 1914, except for a year's man-

ASSOCIATED NEWSPAPERS

ALBERT SCHWEITZER, scholar and musician, who spent his life as a medical missionary in Africa.

Bibliography

Cousins, Norman, *Dr. Schweitzer of Lambaréné* (1960; reprint, Greenwood Press 1973).
Franck, Frederick, *Days with Albert Schweitzer: A Lambaréné Landscape* (1959; reprint, Greenwood Press 1974).
Hagerdorn, Hermann, *Albert Schweitzer: Prophet in the Wilderness*, rev. ed. (Collier Books 1962).
Schweitzer, Albert, *Out of My Life and Thought* (Holt, 1933).
Schweitzer, Albert, *The Theology of Albert Schweitzer for Christian Inquirers*, ed. by E. N. Mozley (Gordon Press 1977).

SCHWENKFELDERS, shvengk'felt-ərz, followers of the Reformation theologian Kaspar Schwenkfeld. Schwenkfeld, a native of Silesia, was greatly influenced by Martin Luther. He visited Luther several times at Wittenberg but disagreed with him on a number of important points. Schwenkfeld wanted a complete separation of church and state. He also did not accept the Lutheran interpretation of the Eucharist, believing that the bread and wine were only symbols. He rejected the cardinal principle of Lutheranism—justification by faith—because he felt that justification was a positive regeneration imparted by Christ.

Schwenkfeld evolved a theory that Christ's humanity became gradually divinized and published this view in *Konfession und Erklärung* (1540). This position made him particularly unwelcome among orthodox Protestants as well as Catholics. He was forced to leave Silesia and went to Strasbourg and other southern German cities. Schwenkfeld died in Ulm, Dec. 10, 1561.

Schwenkfeld attracted a small group of followers. They were persecuted particularly in Silesia in the early 18th century. Many fled to Saxony and Holland. A group of about 200 went to Philadelphia, Pa., in 1734. It is this branch that has survived. Their church was incorporated in 1909 as the Schwenkfelder Church and has a congregational polity. The Schwenkfelders number a little more than 2,000.

SCHWERIN, shvä-rēn', is a city in East Germany and the capital of Schwerin district (bezirk), an agricultural region with an area of 3,348 square miles (8,671 sq km). The city is on Lake Schwerin (German, Schweriner See) and is 60 miles (97 km) east of Hamburg and 20 miles (32 km) south of the Baltic Sea. A number of small lakes surround the city. It is a rail and road junction and manufactures machinery, food products, and cigarettes. Peat is cut from the large bogs near the city.

Originally a Wendish settlement, Schwerin was first mentioned in 1018 and received its charter in 1161. From 1167 to 1648 it was the seat of a bishopric. It passed to the duchy of Mecklenburg in the 14th century, when its Gothic cathedral was begun. Schwerin was the capital of Mecklenburg-Schwerin from 1621 to 1934, when it became the capital of Mecklenburg. The former palace of its dukes was built in 1845–1857 on an island between Lake Schwerin and another lake. Population: (1979 est.) of the city, 117,406; of the district, 589,000.

SCHWINGER, shwing'gər, **Julian Seymour** (1918–), American physicist who shared the 1965 Nobel Prize in physics with the Japanese physicist Shinichiro Tomonaga and the American physicist Richard Feynman. Schwinger was born in New York, N. Y., Feb. 12, 1918. He won his doctorate from Columbia University in 1939 and worked

datory military service and brief stays in Paris. During the first 12 years of this period he studied theology and philosophy, laying the foundation for his later writings on the life of Jesus, the Synoptic Gospels, and the meaning and direction of civilization. He earned his doctorate in philosophy in 1899, with a thesis on Kant, and later held a series of administrative and teaching posts at the university.

In 1905, when Schweitzer was 30, he decided to make good on an earlier resolve that after his thirtieth birthday he would devote all his energies to helping mankind. Accordingly, to the dismay of his friends and colleagues, he undertook intensive studies at the university's medical school with the purpose of fitting himself for service as a medical missionary to the Congo. His medical studies were paid for largely by organ concerts, teaching, and royalties from his book on Bach. In 1912 he married Helene Bresslau, who had studied nursing in preparation for the Congo venture. They had a daughter, Rhena, born in 1919.

Lambaréné. In 1913, Schweitzer took his medical degree, and he and his wife went to Lambaréné, in what was then French Equatorial Africa. There they founded the Schweitzer Hospital, on the Ogooué River "at the edge of the primeval forest," where, during subsequent decades, many thousands of Africans received treatment.

Meanwhile, despite his personal modesty, Schweitzer became a figure of larger-than-life proportions, and, in recognition of his accomplishments as a humanitarian and as a force for peace, he was awarded the 1952 Nobel Peace Prize. Schweitzer died at Lambaréné on Sept. 4, 1965, after which his daughter and colleagues carried on his work there.

NORMAN COUSINS
Author of "Dr. Schweitzer of Lambaréné"

under J. Robert Oppenheimer at the University of California before joining the Harvard faculty in 1945. Two years later he was made a full professor while still under 30 years old.

Schwinger's work in theoretical physics led to the formulation of quantum electrodynamics, with important consequences for the physics of elementary particles. Tomonaga and Feynman carried out similar investigations independently.

SCHWITTERS, shvit'ərs, **Kurt** (1887–1948), German artist, who made collages and junk sculpture. Schwitters was born in Hannover on June 20, 1887. Trained at the Dresden Academy, he painted academic portraits for a living, but his real interest lay in expressionism, dadaism, constructivism, and the de Stijl movement. In 1919 he began to make collages of street trash—old tram tickets, bits of newspapers, scraps of cloth, and string—which he called *Merzbilden*. He gave this dadaist rubbish aesthetic meaning by subtle organization reflecting cubism and de Stijl. He also built the first *Merzbau*, a towering construction of junk, in his Hannover home (destroyed). From 1923 to 1932 he edited *Merz* magazine, supporting dadaism and constructivism.

To escape the Nazis, Schwitters fled to Norway, where he built another *Merzbau*, and then to England. He began a third *Merzbau* before he died in Ambleside, Westmoreland, on Jan. 8, 1948.

SCHWYZ, shvēts, is a town in central Switzerland and the capital of Schwyz canton. The canton, which has an area of 351 square miles (909 sq km), was one of the original Forest Cantons that formed the nucleus of the modern Swiss state. Switzerland's name is derived from Schwyz. Most of the population is German-speaking and Roman Catholic. The town is at the foot of the Great and Little Mythen peaks and is 3 miles (5 km) from Brunnen, its port on Lake Lucerne. There is a 17th century town hall, decorated with scenes from Swiss history, and a number of 16th and 17th century homes.

In the mid-13th century, Schwyz was a small community of freemen subject to the Holy Roman emperor. When its independent status was challenged, Schwyz banded with the cantons of Uri and Unterwalden in 1291 to renounce rule by the Habsburgs. An attempt by the Habsburgs to reassert authority was turned back at the Battle of Morgarten in 1315. Despite its small size, Schwyz was a leading force in the later growth of the Swiss Confederation. Population: (1970) of the town, 12,194; of the canton, 92,072.

SCIATICA, sī-at'i-kə, is pain along the course of the sciatic nerve. The pain may be caused by pressure, inflammation, or disease of the nerve or by compression or trauma to the roots of the nerve in the sacral portion of the spinal cord. Such compression may be due to arthritis of the spine, to so-called slipped disk, or to an injury. The pain of sciatica generally follows the course of the nerve, traveling from the lower back into the buttocks, through the pelvic region, and down the back of the thigh. It then follows the branches of the sciatic nerve, which extends down the lower leg into the foot. Tingling and unusual feelings sometimes occur with the pain, and there may be associated muscle weakness. The treatment of sciatica depends on its cause. Symptomatic relief includes rest, the administration of analgesics, and the application of heat.

SCIENCE, History of. The origins and development of several major divisions of science are discussed in separate articles of *The Encyclopedia Americana.* These include ASTRONOMY, BIOLOGY, BOTANY, CHEMISTRY, GEOLOGY, MATHEMATICS, MEDICINE, PHYSICS, and ZOOLOGY. In addition, many entries on specialized scientific fields include historical discussions, and there are individual biographies of all the important scientists. Further entries dealing with the history of science can be found by consulting the Index entry *Science, History of.* The present article is concerned with the nature of the history of science, the special problems that it presents to the historian, and the study and teaching of that discipline.

Introductory Definition. If science is defined as systematized positive knowledge, or what has been taken as positive knowledge at different ages and in different places, then the history of science is the description and explanation of the development of that knowledge. For example, considering all that is known today in astronomy, how did man obtain that knowledge? It is a very long story that goes back to prehistoric times when men began to observe the sun, moon, stars and planets, and to wonder about them. Today's knowledge has been reached only through a painstaking process of inquiry and discovery, and many, many errors. If the acquisition and systematization of any such knowledge is, as many think, the only human activity that is truly cumulative and progressive, the importance of the study of the history of science is apparent, and in this broad sense becomes the keystone of all historical investigations.

SURVEY OF SCIENTIFIC DEVELOPMENT

The definition of the history of science given above can be better understood if it is illustrated with an outline of the way that the scientific experience of mankind was gradually developed until it reached its present depth and complexity. It must be emphasized that this outline is not intended as a history of science but simply as a general view of it, enough to give the reader some awareness of the many kinds of investigations involved.

Any history of science must begin with an account of the dawn of science, as revealed through the studies of anthropology and archaeology. Many questions face the investigator. How did early men invent and fashion their tools? How did they domesticate animals and learn the tricks of husbandry? How did they obtain the rudiments of arithmetic, geometry and astronomy? How did they find the best foods for health and the best drugs for sickness? How did they learn to navigate the waters, to hunt and fish, to lift and transport heavy stones, to dig for ores and smelt them, to make bronze implements and later iron ones? How did they discover the ways of social life in families and tribes, the methods of economy and government? How did they develop a language and means of recording it? Did they achieve a kind of social or historical consciousness, and if so, how did they gratify it? How were artistic and religious needs awakened in them, and what did they do to obey them? These are but a few of the innumerable questions that must be answered in order to understand the level of knowledge that man had attained before the curtain of recorded history rose.

The earliest cultures represented by written documents occurred in Egypt, Mesopotamia, India, and China. An account of these cultures cannot be given by historians of science without the collaboration of Orientalists able to decipher and to interpret those documents. The historians must extract from these studies all the data pertinent to their own quest and then seek to explain them with respect both to the field of science and to the cultures being studied.

Greek and Roman Times. The first culture to undertake true scientific inquiry was that of the ancient Greeks. After the violent upheavals caused by the discovery of iron and use of iron weapons, the Greeks began to explain the universe and themselves in a deeper way. The earliest of those Greeks were settled along the western coast of Asia Minor, in Sicily, and south Italy. From them came the basic elements of mathematics, astronomy, mechanics, physics, geography, and medicine. Few of their writings have been preserved, and what is known of their achievements in scientific inquiry is derived from fragments and secondary sources.

The golden age of the Greeks in science coincided with their golden age in literature and art, which took place primarily in the Athens of the 5th and 4th centuries B.C. The 5th century witnessed great philosophers such as Democritus and Leucippus, who developed a form of atomic theory; mathematicians such as Hippocrates of Chios; astronomers such as Philolaus; and physicians such as Hippocrates of Cos, "the father of medicine." That golden century was brought to a close by the political murder of Socrates in 399 B.C.

The 4th century was even richer in scientific achievements and was dominated by two of the greatest personalities in history. The first half of the century was dominated by Plato, founder of the Academy of Athens, and the second half by Aristotle, founder of the Lyceum in the same city. So far-reaching was the influence of these men that to this day every thinking man, every scientist, may be said to be in some sense either a Platonist or an Aristotelian.

The political ruin of Hellenic Greece caused such deep changes all around that scholars are agreed in using a new name to designate the new culture, which developed chiefly from the 3d century B.C. on. The center was no longer in Athens but in Alexandria and other Greek cities established outside of Europe. The new Hellenistic culture was immortalized by the deeds of 3d century anatomists such as Herophilus and Erasistratus, and of mathematicians and astronomers such as Euclid, Aristarchus, Archimedes, Eratosthenes, and Apollonius. The last three of these men flourished in the second half of the 3d century, while the astronomer Hipparchus became an important scientific figure in the late 2d century B.C.

The end of the Hellenistic age merged with the Roman age, because Rome had become the political master of the Greek world just before the Christian era began. Roman science was but a reflection of the Greek. A few scientific books of some interest were written in Latin, however—by Lucretius and Cicero, in the 1st century B.C., and in the succeeding 1st century A.D. by Celsus, Pliny, and Frontinus. Yet, until the 7th century, all the outstanding names in science were still Greek, the two greatest of all being the 2d century astronomer and geographer Ptolemy and the physician Galen. These two giants dominated the golden age of the Roman Empire. Later appeared more mathematicians and astronomers,

such as Diophantus and Pappus in the 3d century, Theon of Alexandria in the 4th, and in the 5th his daughter Hypatia—famous as the only noted woman scholar of ancient times—and Proclus; philosophers such as Philoponus and Simplicius in the 6th century; and physicians such as Oribasius in the 4th century, Aetios and Alexander of Tralles in the 6th, and Paulus Aegineta in the 7th century.

Middle Ages. Thereafter followed the time of the Muslim conquest of a great part of the Mediterranean world, and the era known as the Middle Ages. It is impossible to describe here even in briefest manner all the complexities of medieval history. From the 9th century to the 11th, all of Greek knowledge was translated into Arabic and the best new scientific books were written in Arabic. After the 11th century, the whole was gradually retranslated into Latin, and to a lesser extent into Hebrew. The greatest physician of the early Middle Ages was the 11th century ibn-Sina (Avicenna) and the most original scientist was his contemporary al-Biruni. The leading mathematicians and astronomers of that period of the 9th to 11th century were all writing in Arabic—al-Khwarizmi, al-Farghani, and al-Battani in the 9th century, Abul-Wefa in the 10th, Omar Khayyam and al-Zarqali in the 11th—as were the leading philosophers, the 9th century al-Kindi, the 10th century al-Farabi, and ibn-Sina and al-Ghazzali, both of the 11th century. Arabic culture was international, extending from the far west of Spain and Morocco to as far east as India. It was interracial and it was also interreligious, for it included not only Muslims but also Jews and Christians. Later medieval thought was dominated by three giants, the Muslim ibn-Rushd (Averroës), the Jew Maimonides (both 12th century), and the 13th century Christian Saint Thomas Aquinas.

The Renaissance. Two major developments in the 15th century radically changed the course of the Western world. These were the invention of typography, about the middle of the century, and the geographical discoveries initiated by Henry the Navigator and reaching a climax at the end of the century with the voyages of Columbus and others. These geographical discoveries continued during the 16th century and immeasurably increased human experience in many directions. As for the discovery of printing, it did not mean simply a far greater diffusion of ideas than had been possible before, but also the production of *standard* texts and, a little later, *standard* illustrations. For the first time the progress of knowledge could be registered as soon as it was made, standardized, and transmitted to every corner of the civilized world. Until this period East and West had worked together, but now the Muslim East, increasingly inhibited by religious obscurantism, rejected printing and ceased to cooperate with the Western world.

The discovery of printing was so pregnant that it is well to consider it the beginning of a new period, the so-called Renaissance, which was almost exclusively Western as far as science is concerned. If the Renaissance is defined as the period 1450 to 1600, one of its main characteristics was the recovery of the texts of the Greek classics, most of which had been known only through Latin translations of Arabic translations. In other respects, however, the Renaissance was essentially the continuation of the Middle Ages. There were a few giants such as Leonardo da

Vinci, Nicolaus Copernicus, Andreas Vesalius, Vannoccio Biringuccio, Rodolphus Agricola, Ambroise Paré, Pierre Belon, Konrad von Gesner, Tycho Brahe, William Gilbert, and Simon Stevin, and a few rebels such as Philippus Aureolus Paracelsus and Bernard Palissy, but modern science cannot be said to begin in earnest until the 17th century with such men as Francis Bacon, Galileo Galilei, Johannes Kepler, and René Descartes.

The Growth of Academies. During the Renaissance, printing shops had become numerous, and the number of printed books increased immeasurably thereafter. The steady accumulation of knowledge was guaranteed. Another powerful means of controlling and recording the progress of science was the establishment of academies. The first academies of science date from the 17th century: the Accademia dei Lincei in Rome (1603–1630), the Accademia del Cimento in Florence (1657–1667), the Royal Society in London (1662), and the Academie des Sciences in Paris (1666). The books and journals sponsored by those academies, and a few other journals such as the *Journal des savants* of Paris (1665) and the *Acta eruditorum* of Leipzig (1682), guided the activities of men of science wherever they were working. Almost all the leading scientists were fellows of at least one of these academies, and it would be possible to describe the development of science in innumerable directions on the basis of the academic publications alone.

The Birth and Development of Modern Science. The main monuments of modern science, however, are the great treatises such as the *Principia mathematica* of Sir Isaac Newton (1687), the *Traité de la lumière* of Christiaan Huygens (1690), and a great many others, too many to be listed here. Indeed, in the 17th and 18th centuries, the number of distinguished men of science is so great that an enumeration of them would be impossible even in a longer general review. It is more interesting to point out that these scientists were distributed all over Europe. It became clearer than ever that scientific activities are international. The history of science as observed in any one country, however great, is very incomplete, because some of the essential work was done in other countries. Even such a small country as Switzerland produced its full share of scientific heroes: Paracelsus, Gesner, the Bernoullis, Albrecht von Haller, Leonhard Euler, Lambert, Steiner, and others. Young America started making her own gifts with Benjamin Franklin, John Winthrop, and Benjamin Thompson (later Count Rumford).

In the 19th century, science developed so fast and in so many directions, with almost incredible luxuriance and yet with so much steadiness, that even the best observers were deceived and became a little too optimistic. They believed that science was approaching a stage of perfection. For a while it seemed that further progress would consist simply in obtaining an infinity of new data to complete the schemes of the naturalists, or in making physical measurements with greater precision and expressing results with a greater degree of finality.

This peaceful and optimistic climate was upset toward the end of the 1800's, when there began a series of inventions and purely scientific developments that radically changed the material conditions of life and caused the 20th century to seem so different from preceding centuries that to many modern eyes the whole past tends to be a separate world. Many of these life-changing inventions were not fully developed until the end of the 19th century, but thereafter their growth was so rapid and their diffusion so intense that they became essential parts of the 20th century environment. Dynamos, electric motors, telegraphs, telephones, internal-combustion engines, phonographs, aviation, cinema, wireless, radio, television, methods of refrigeration, plastics—each of these words could easily be amplified into many volumes.

The purely scientific discoveries of that era were equally revolutionary. They upset many sciences as deeply as inventions upset ways of life, and their potential effects on the fate of mankind are profound. It will suffice here to refer to the discovery of X rays by Wilhelm Konrad Roentgen in 1895, of radioactivity by Antoine Henri Becquerel in 1896, and of psychoanalysis by Sigmund Freud in 1900 and after; to the rediscovery of Mendelism in 1900; to the discovery of the theory of quanta by Max Planck in 1901, of the theory of mutations by Hugo De Vries in 1901–1903, of radium by Pierre and Marie Curie in 1903, of the special and general theories of relativity by Albert Einstein in 1905 and 1916, and of the disintegration of the atom by Baron Rutherford in 1919.

THE STUDY OF THE HISTORY OF SCIENCE

Men of science and technicians want to know the latest results. They may consider previous results as obsolete and disregard them. The historian of science, however, is interested not only in the newest results but also in the whole evolution of thought and discovery that led to them and made them possible. The historian of science appreciates the fruits of present knowledge, but he wants to know the tree of knowledge with all its roots and branches.

Development of the History of Science. Since the 18th century, at least—that is, since the time of Giovanni Battista Vico, Montesquieu, and Voltaire—the concept of history has become more and more comprehensive. At first historians were concerned mainly with political and military history, but gradually they learned to attach more attention to arts and letters, religion, and economics. Thus the old political history was transformed into something much broader that might be called the history of culture. The historical field was also extended in a geographical way. Early historians were concerned only with the history of their own people. Under Greek and Roman influence the geographical field was increased, but a great many centuries were to elapse before historians obtained a better knowledge of all the nations and included this knowledge in the scope of their own studies and their conception of mankind.

It was only in relatively recent times that the importance and centrality of the history of science was realized, and even today many historians do not realize it fully. There were a few pioneers in this field by at least the end of the 17th century. Among them were such men as the Swiss Daniel LeClerc and Albrecht von Haller; the Germans J. C. Barkhausen, J. C. Heilbronner, Johann Beckmann, A. F. Hecker, Abraham Gotthelf Kastner, and Johann Friedrich Gmelin; the Englishmen John Freind, Joseph Priestley, and Adam Smith; the Swede Olaf Celsius; and the French Jean Étienne Montucla and Jean Sylvain Bailly.

However, the first man to introduce this theme in a broader context and to increase its circulation was the 19th century French philosopher Auguste Comte, who developed it in his *Cours de philosophie positive*. His views were discussed by another French philosopher, Antoine Augustin Cournot, in 1861, but the real inheritor of Comte's thought and the first great teacher of the history of science was Paul Tannery. In the 20th century his example was followed by many scholars in various countries. The history of science became a full-fledged discipline.

It is to be expected that philosophers would become especially interested in the history of science, because the philosophical implications of scientific work are not clear until science is considered in terms of the manner of its growth. That is, in order to understand a function, it does not suffice to consider only the last points in the curve that represent it. The whole curve must be taken into account. And the historian of science cannot accomplish his task satisfactorily unless he understands the philosophical implications of science. Many men of science were primarily inventors and technicians, avoiding philosophy, yet none grew up in a philosophical vacuum. Every scientist is influenced by the religious and philosophical conceptions of his time, whether he is aware of them or not.

Methods of the Historian of Science. The methods that the historian of science uses are necessarily the same as those used by other historians, but as they must be applied to scientific facts and theories, the historians of science must receive a scientific preparation as well as a purely historical one. It is impossible to understand and to appreciate scientific documents without adequate scientific knowledge. All the difficulties of the history of science stem from the necessity of a double education. Much bad work has been done by historians who did not know science and also by men of science who had no idea of historical methods and did not even realize that such methods existed.

The main point is that knowledge of any kind is worthless unless it is as accurate as conditions permit. It is here that the conflict of methods appears. A physicist fully aware of all the difficulties of physical measurements may be trusted to do his best to overcome these difficulties. The same man is likely not aware of historical difficulties and of the need of historical precision. On the other hand, while the historian must also try to be as accurate as possible, he must remember that the same degree of precision is not required in every case. For example, when the length of an object is mentioned, the unit varies with the needs. It may be expressed in microns, millimeters, yards, or miles. In the same way, it may be necessary to give the time and date of an event very exactly, say 9 A. M., March 21, 1591 (Gregorian), whereas in other cases, it may suffice to say March 1591, or 1591, or "toward the end of the 16th century." All those expressions are accurate, though their degrees of accuracy vary considerably. To use a higher degree of precision than the circumstances warrant is a form of pedantry, notwithstanding the obvious fact that when the historian is investigating any subject he should note the dates and other facts with as much precision as possible.

Historical methods are on the whole less tangible and more delicate than physical methods, and therefore more difficult to set forth. This is due to the fact that the subject matter of history is human and therefore capricious, even when that matter is the development of science. The reactions of a man of science are infinitely more complex than are those of the objects that he is studying.

The methods required to investigate ancient or medieval science are, of course, more complex than those needed to explain modern events. In the case of contemporary events described in familiar language, it is hardly necessary to study the background, which is known well enough, or to consider linguistic difficulties. On the other hand, when the historian tries to appreciate the trigonometrical facts included in Arabic books written in Baghdad in the 9th century, he must be able to evoke the culture of that place and period, understand the Arabic language and Islamic religion, and so forth. That kind of work is not simply historical but philological as well. The basis of the work is always what the philologists call the establishment of the text. That is, in the case just mentioned, the historian must determine as exactly as possible what was written by al-Khwarizmi, by Habash al-Hasib, and by al-Battani; he must establish the text of their very words, either as written by themselves or quoted by others; and it is only after that has been done that the trigonometry ideas of these men can safely be investigated. Merely to assume, instead, that al-Battani may have written this or that, is worthless and perverse.

Thus, within the historical field, the establishment of a text implies a very special and complex training. Philological and historical methods can be learned only through personal experience in their use, and that process of learning is never fully completed.

TEACHING OF THE HISTORY OF SCIENCE

Because the history of science is a new discipline, the teaching of it is very recent. The first professorship was established at the Collège de France in 1892, but the appointment of unqualified professors defeated the grand aim. Even today, some university administrators have yet to appreciate (1) the importance of such studies; (2) the need of entrusting them to competent scholars equipped with the necessary scientific, historical, and philosophical training; and (3) that such work, being difficult and still in the experimental stage, must be a full-time occupation. Too often such teaching has been entrusted as a kind of side job to men who, however eminent in other science fields, were not qualified to teach the history of science. However, the teaching of the history of science is organized fairly well, though in different ways, in various European and Asian universities such as London, Paris, Frankfurt am Main, Moscow, and Ankara, and in various U. S. universities such as Harvard, Wisconsin, Cornell, Yale, Johns Hopkins, and Brown, among others. It is possible in those universities to continue these studies up to the degree of Ph. D. in the history of science.

History of Science as Opposed to the History of Particular Sciences. It should be noted that the history of science is essentially different from the history of particular sciences or of particular techniques.

To consider technology first, the explanation of its development implies a large amount of economic or sociologic research. Inventions are made to answer definite needs, and each new invention of any importance creates new needs and causes an endless chain of other inventions. For example, the discovery of the first steam engine opened up an enormous branch of technology. Not only were those engines and their accessories gradually improved, but their availability also suggested new technical departures such as railways and steamships, and a great many other machines. Therefore, the historian of any branch of technology must be familiar with patent literature, and with all kinds of industrial and commercial ramifications, and even with legal problems, with all of which the historian of science would hardly concern himself.

On the other hand, the historian of science must try to take into account every branch of science and investigate their interrelationships, which are frequent and complex. Indeed, his main purpose is to explain the development of the whole tree of science, a tree that never ceases to grow. He must explain how the progress of one science affected the progress of other branches. For example, the development of microscopes and telescopes implied the possible solution to certain physical and chemical problems and other technical difficulties, since better microscopes influenced the progress of natural sciences, and better telescopes accelerated astronomical progress and enabled man to conceive a universe or universes immeasurably larger than the universe of his ancestors. Furthermore, because the historian of science is writing for scientists and learned men in many different fields, he can never assume that the scientific knowledge of his readers is sufficient to understand the intricacies of any specific problem. For example, the historian of chemistry expects his readers to know chemical technicalities, but the historian of science cannot entertain the same expectations. A general treatise on the history of science is thus less technical than one on chemical history, but what it loses on that side it gains in broadness of outlook. The historian of chemistry is more of a technician in his writings, whereas the historian of science is more of a humanist.

Diversity of Points of View. Because the history of science is a field of endless complexity and incredible size, it would be foolish to say that there is one way to study it or to teach it, and no other. In fact there are many ways and many points of view, each of which is acceptable and useful and none of which is exclusive of the others. There is the point of view of the historian, who wishes to understand as fully as possible the culture of a nation or of a period; the point of view of the professional man of science, who would explore the origin and development of his own field of knowledge; the point of view of the man of letters, who would include science in his survey either because great men of science are—or should be—distinguished authors, or because no writer can help having some kind of scientific background; and the point of view of the philosopher, whose main concern is to show the complex relationship between science and philosophy and how much either influenced the other. In addition there are at least three other points of view—the logical, psychological, and sociological —that deserve to be examined more carefully at this point.

Logical Point of View. Logicians and teachers of the positive contents of science try to unravel the logical concatenation of scientific facts and to give a logical interpretation of discoveries. Students of the history of science may be surprised by the results of such inquiries, for the chronological order of discoveries is often very different from the logical one, and what some people call the logic of science is largely casual and retrospective. Nevertheless it is worthwhile and helpful to explain discoveries in their logical order, even though they were not always made in that order. That is, teachers of a vast subject such as inorganic chemistry or theoretical mechanics must put fundamental notions first in spite of the fact that these notions may have been the very last to be discovered. Their main concern is not historical order but the teaching of science as simply and clearly as possible.

Psychological Point of View. Another set of historians is interested in the individual aspects of scientific work. They ask themselves questions such as the following: How did it happen that a given scientist made such or such a discovery? Is it to be explained in rational or emotional terms? How does he compare with other scientists and with people of his time and environment in general? How was his temper affected by work or play, by success or failure? How was he influenced by his social environment, and how did he influence it in turn? How did he express and reveal himself, or fail to reveal himself? What was the quality of his spirit? Was he concerned with social, moral, or religious issues, or was he indifferent to the world around him, blind to everything except the narrow field of his research? Not only the psychologist but also the humanist tries to answer such questions, for the answers may tend to shake some popular myths about the unemotional nature of the scientific process and to help further in assessing the role that the scientist is able to or should play in the world at large.

Social Point of View. Instead of considering men of science individually and trying to find the individual roots of their activities, an investigator may choose to consider them as members of a social group and study the social pressures to which they may have been submitted. According to the Marxist philosophic system of dialectical materialism, for example, science is explained primarily, if not exclusively, in social and economic terms. There is a core of truth in such explanations, since science does not develop in a social vacuum. Men of science are citizens, whom the state or their employers can use and abuse in many ways. If the scientist is a physicist or astronomer, his opportunities will depend upon the laboratory or observatory to which he has been admitted, and his freedom will be limited by the good or bad will of administrators or fellow workers.

Yet there is another viewpoint. This is that nobody can completely control the human spirit —that a scientist may be helped or inhibited by social factors but that his scientific ideas are not totally determined by them. At any rate, honest men of science have often continued activities detrimental to their material interests. Historians of science should describe such conflicts as carefully as possible, thereby helping the rest of mankind to understand various forms of society and the psychology of exceptional men such as great scientists.

A vast literature devoted to the problems of the impact of society on science and of science on society may be classified under the general heading "Science and Society." Sociologists are tempted to restrict their interest in the history of science to these problems and their endless implications.

The Uses of the History of Science. There are obviously many theoretical motives for studying the history of science. A man of science would study that history in order to throw light upon his own task and to increase his enjoyment of it; a philosopher, to relate science to philosophy and to account for some variations of the latter; a psychologist, to explore the peculiarities and possibilities of the human mind; a sociologist, to understand more clearly the many relationships between scientists and the social groups to which they belong; and other such reasons might be found.

However, the people who study a subject for theoretical reasons are probably exceptional. Most students submit themselves to definite training for practical reasons, such as qualifying themselves for a trade or profession. Looking at it from their angle, then, the study of the history of science will complete the training of scientific teachers, since to teach well requires a kind of perspective that can be obtained only by historical inquiries. Furthermore, the study of the history of science will improve the qualifications of students for many parascientific positions having to deal directly or indirectly with scientific pursuits, such as those of librarians, editors, curators of museums, and school or government administrators.

GEORGE SARTON
Author of "Horus: A Guide to the History of Science"

Bibliography

Bernal, John D., *The Emergence of Science*, vol. 1 (reprint, MIT Press 1971).
Butterfield, Herbert, *The Origins of Modern Science*, rev. ed. (Free Press 1965).
Butterfield, Herbert, and others, *A Short History of Science: A Symposium* (Doubleday 1959).
Clagett, Marshall, ed., *Critical Problems in the History of Science* (Univ. of Wis. Press 1969).
Crombie, Alistair C., *Medieval and Early Modern Science*, 2 vols. (Harvard Univ. Press 1961).
Dampier, William C., *A History of Science and its Relations with Philosophy and Religion*, 4th ed. (Cambridge 1966).
Fowler, William S., *The Development of Scientific Method* (Pergamon 1962).
Gillispie, Charles C., *The Edge of Objectivity: An Essay in the History of Scientific Ideas* (Princeton Univ. Press 1960).
Hall, Alfred R., *The Scientific Revolution, Fifteen Hundred to Eighteen Hundred: The Formation of the Modern Scientific Attitude*, rev. ed. (Beacon Press 1966).
Joravsky, David, *Soviet Marxism and the Nature of Science, 1917–1932* (Columbia Univ. Press 1961).
Keenan, Boyd R., ed., *Science and the University* (Columbia Univ. Press 1966).
Lark-Horovitz, Karl, and Carmichael, Eleanor, *Chronology of Scientific Development, 1848–1948* (American Association for the Advancement of Science 1948).
Sarton, George, *Ancient Science and Modern Civilization* (Univ. of Neb. Press 1964).
Sarton, George, *History of Science: Ancient Science Through the Golden Age of Greece* (reprint, Norton 1970).
Sarton, George, *History of Science: Hellenistic Science and Culture in the Last Three Centuries B. C.* (reprint, Norton 1970).
Sarton, George, *Horus: A Guide to the History of Science* (Chronica Botanica 1952).
Singer, Charles, *From Magic to Science* (Smith, P. 1960).
Singer, Charles, *A Short History of Scientific Ideas to 1900* (Oxford 1959).
Thorndike, Lynn, *A History of Magic and Experimental Science*, 8 vols. (Columbia Univ. Press 1923–1959).
Wolf, Abraham, *A History of Science, Technology, and Philosophy in the 16th and 17th Centuries*, 2 vols. (Smith, P. 1951).
Wolf, Abraham, *A History of Science, Technology, and Philosophy in the Eighteenth Century*, 2 vols. (Smith, P. 1952).

SCIENCE FICTION, currently known by the initials SF, is commonly defined as fiction in which some aspect of science forms an element of the plot or background. But 20th century SF authors, editors, and critics maintain that an exact definition is difficult—if not impossible—to come by, even as they question that "science fiction" is a suitable name for the genre. The reasons have to do with disagreement about what specific works or what body of literature it includes, as well as with the origin and connotations of the term.

History. The term "science fiction" and its variant "scientification" were coined by an American electrical engineer, Hugo Gernsback, to identify the tales used to enliven the content of popular-science magazines—among them, *Modern Electrics*—that he published in the first decades of the 20th century. The popularity of these tales, together with a burgeoning interest in new inventions and technology, led to the appearance in the 1920's of specialized pulp magazines devoted exclusively to "science fiction," the first of these being Gernsback's *Amazing Stories*. By the 1930's the term, especially in the United States, had become closely associated in the public mind with pulp fiction, or trash.

At the same time, the new term "science fiction" had been appropriated as a label for a large body of speculative and prophetic works, not merely dating to such 19th and early 20th century masterpieces as Jules Verne's *From the Earth to the Moon* and *Twenty Thousand Leagues Under the Sea* and H. G. Wells' *The Invisible Man* and *The Time Machine*, but going back to classical and even biblical times. Literary historians, if not the general public, recognized that the prophet Ezekiel was writing "science fiction" when he described the flaming wheels in the sky (Ezekiel 1)—surely a fair approximation of a contemporary UFO (Unidentified Flying Object) report. The Greek satirist Lucian wrote science fiction in such dialogues as his *Icaromenippus*. Savinein Cyrano de Bergerac wrote it in his 17th century comic "histories" of voyages to the moon and the sun. Rabelais had written science fiction in the preceding century, and Voltaire continued the tradition in 18th century France.

Later examples, in Britain and the United States, of "mainstream" writers who have also written science fiction include Rudyard Kipling, Mark Twain, E. M. Forster, Aldous Huxley, C. S. Lewis, Graham Greene, John Cheever, Anthony Burgess, and Kingsley Amis. Orwell's *Nineteen Eighty-four* has some of the qualities of science fiction, and so does Golding's *Lord of the Flies*. The list is endless.

The contemporary SF author, editor, and critic Damon Knight has said of the genre: "SF means what you are pointing at when you talk about it." Frederick Pohl calls it "the literature of consequences"—a fine tool for investigating the results of human acts and inventions. Isaac Asimov states that there are three kinds of SF: "What if...," "If only...," and "If this goes on...." Many SF stories contain more than one of these motifs, and it is often suggested that speculative fiction might be a far more accurate term, serving at least to help separate SF from its more encompassing parent, fantasy.

Science and SF. To many observers, "science fiction" is a misnomer. The word "science," both as defined in dictionaries and as understood by the public at large, has no fixed meaning—or at

Arthur C. Clarke's story *The Sentinel* was spectacularly translated to the screen as *2001: A Space Odyssey.*

least none that is helpful in defining and delimiting a literary genre. Yet the root of the word "science"—*scientia,* meaning "knowledge"—is apt. To regard SF as "knowledge fiction" is to come closest to its special nature. Its basic ingredient is knowledge—knowledge extrapolated or new knowledge—cast in a narrative that delineates its effects on society or the individual. If this "knowledge" aspect can be extracted from a story, leaving a cohesive narrative, then the original is ersatz SF—for example, the cowboy story set on Mars, instead of in Texas.

Use of the word "science" to designate a kind of fiction has had some interesting side effects. In a science-worshipping culture, it becomes fashionable or amusing to derogate science, even as in Boccaccio's day it was fashionable or "brave" to scandalize monks and nuns. Such acts represent an obverted acknowledgment of authority, if not a diverted form of worship. Today's science, daily passing miracles while at the same time threatening human existence, has become an unpredictable and totipotent deity, to which obeisance must be made. And a form of popular literature with "science" as part of its name makes an opportune target of derogation.

It is probably for this reason that many readers—and virtually all serious critics—have refused to recognize that SF contains as much true excellence, as well as trash, as any other

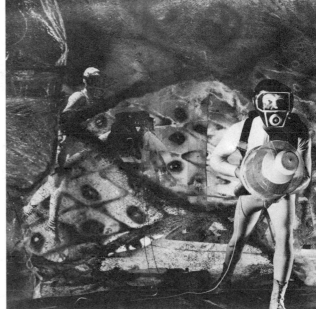

In the film *Fantastic Voyage* (1966) miniaturized men and instruments travel through the human bloodstream.

Novels by Jules Verne, early SF writer, have been made into successful motion pictures. In Walt Disney's interpretation of *20,000 Leagues Under the Sea* (1954), Captain Nemo's *Nautilus* plies treacherous waters.

form of writing. Yet the same public and the same critics have no difficulty in seeing a spectrum of excellence in other fields, such as mystery-detective or Western stories. The fact is that the best writing in contemporary SF is quite as good as the best anywhere. Ray Bradbury, Arthur C. Clarke, D. G. Compton, Samuel R. Delaney, Robert A. Heinlein, R. A. Lafferty, Ursula K. LeGuin, and Kurt Vonnegut, Jr., among many others, produce writing that is of the highest quality.

Current Status. Since about 1930, SF has carried with it an ardent and highly articulate following of "fans," who produce their own amateur periodicals and critiques and meet all over the world in clubs, conferences, conventions, and symposiums. The World Science Fiction Convention (World Con), which is held annually, is the scene of the "Hugo" trophy award, named after pioneer Hugo Gernsback, for the year's best novel, novelette, dramatic presentation, or other SF form. The Science Fiction Writers of America (SFWA) provides the "Nebula" trophy, produces anthologies, and functions in matters of collective concern to SF authors.

A new development is the astonishing growth in the number of courses in SF as literature offered at the college and university level. Virtually nonexistent in the mid-1960's, these courses numbered more than 100 half a decade later. Teachers and scholars in the field have organized a Science Fiction Research Association, with an official journal, *Extrapolation*.

SF magazines continue to publish despite rather severe competition from paperback anthologies of new fiction and the appearance of SF in general magazines. There are several volumes of annual "best" SF and numerous anthologies of reprinted stories. The number of hardcover SF books that are so called—and of books that are indeed SF but not so called—continues to rise, as does the number of SF books by "mainstream" authors. Of the last-named group, Michael Crichton's *Andromeda Strain* (1969) and Vladimir Nabokov's *Ada* (1970) became best sellers.

SF is immensely popular in Japan, France, and Britain, and in each it has its "fan" followers. It is a recognized force in Soviet literature. The Swedish writer and critic Sam J. Lundwall reports an upsurge of SF in Rumania, Poland, East and West Germany, Italy, and the Scandinavian countries.

The SF film and cinema came into being with *The Laboratory of Mephistopheles* (1897) by pioneer genius Georges Méliès and reached a new peak with Stanley Kubrik's *2001: A Space Odyssey* (1968), based on Arthur C. Clarke's story *The Sentinel*. In between, there have been hundreds of SF films of all degrees of quality. The Japanese are particularly notable for ingenious and charming special effects and model work. In television there have been many single productions and a number of series, most notably *Star Trek*, proving repeatedly that SF and the visual media are admirably suited to each other.

THEODORE STURGEON
SF Writer, Author of "More Than Human"

Further Reading: Ellison, Harlan, ed., *Again, Dangerous Visions* (Doubleday 1971); Franklin, H. Bruce, ed., *Future Perfect* (Oxford 1968); Knight, Damon, *In Search of Wonder*, 2d ed. (Advent Pubs. 1967); Lundwall, Sam J., *Science Fiction* (Ace Bks. 1971); *Science Fiction Hall of Fame*, vol. 1, ed. by Robert Silverberg (Doubleday 1970), and vol. 2, ed. by Ben Bova (Doubleday 1973); Wilson, Robin Scott, ed., *Clarion* (Signet Bks. 1971).

SCIENTOLOGY is a quasi-scientific and religious discipline that claims to be both "the study of knowledge in its fullest sense" and "an applied religious philosophy." The Church of Scientology depends on the second claim, but in the early days of the movement its theory was described as "an exact science."

Origins and Development. The founder of Scientology was an American, L. (Lafayette) Ron Hubbard. In 1950 he published *Dianetics: the Modern Science of Mental Health*, a best seller describing a therapy for "all inorganic mental ills and all organic psycho-somatic ills." By 1952 an international organization had been incorporated, now known under the name of Scientology. In 1955 the movement took on a religious direction with the creation of the Founding Church of Scientology in Washington, D. C., and New York. Hubbard carries on intensive communication with followers in the English-speaking countries and in Denmark, France, and Sweden.

Teachings and Practices. As a psychological technique, *Dianetics* depends on analysis of mental functioning into activities of the *analytical* and the *reactive* minds, which correspond roughly to the *conscious* and *unconscious* of psychoanalysis. Survival, said to be the primary goal of human mental organization, is served differently by the two activities. The analytical mind is the organ of experience and stores recoverable memories. The reactive mind stores what are called *engrams*, the sensory traces of painful events, of moments when one was unconscious, or even of prenatal injuries.

Dianetic therapy consists of reducing the power of engrams or converting them into memories by reviewing one's past with a person called an *auditor*. It stresses good communication techniques. In Scientology a device called an *E-meter*, which is similar to a skin galvanometer, helps by indicating emotionally charged words. A novice or *preclear* becomes a *clear* by long discipline in discharging such engrams, and then is able to become an auditor of others or a minister of the church.

Criticism and Conflict. Authorities in psychoanalysis deny that the unconscious can be so neutralized and they are therefore opposed to Scientology. The Federal Food and Drug Administration, reacting to the early quasi-medical claims of Scientology, raided the Washington church in 1963. The church won an appeal in 1971 on the basis of freedom of religion. The literature of Scientology and E-meters now carries disclaimers of intent to cure diseases. How practically motivated the newer religious emphasis of Scientology was is a moot question. Formal religious services seem to play no major part in the activities of the church. Scientology does, however, bear comparison with Christian Science.

The central idea in subsequent Scientology doctrine is that man is a *thetan*, a preexistent spiritual being which in life possesses a body and a mind. This idea shows the influence of Eastern religions on Hubbard and also suggests some Gnostic traditions.

JOHN B. SNOOK
Barnard College

Further Reading: Hubbard, L. Ron, *Dianetics: The Modern Science of Mental Health* (Paperback Library 1968); id., *Scientology: A New Slant on Life* (American Saint Hill Organization Church of Scientology 1965); Rowley, Peter, *New Gods in America: An Informal Investigation* (McKay 1971).

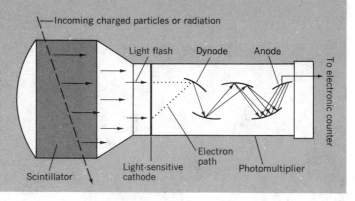

SCINTILLATION COUNTER

When fast-moving charged particles pass through the scintillator, it emits flashes of light. The light flashes strike the cathode of the photomultiplier tube, causing an ejection of electrons. The electrons are multiplied in the tube and then passed to an electronic counter, which counts electrical pulses.

Incoming charged particles or radiation

Light flash · Dynode · Anode

To electronic counter

Scintillator · Light-sensitive cathode · Electron path · Photomultiplier

SCILLY ISLANDS, sil′ē, an archipelago in the Atlantic Ocean, about 30 miles (48 km) west of Land's End in Cornwall, England. The group, sometimes called the Isles of Scilly or the Scilly Isles, constitutes the southwesternmost part of England. Within an area of 6.3 square miles (16.3 sq km) are some 140 islets and rocks, totaling 4,041 acres (1,635 hectares). St. Mary's is the largest. The islands are composed of coarse granite, with a few metalliferous veins. Seaside cliffs are dotted with caves that have been hollowed out by the Atlantic, and there are reefs and shoals around the islands that make navigation perilous in rough weather.

St. Mary's Tresco, St. Martin's, St. Agnes, and Bryher are inhabited. The weather is mild, giving rise to an early flower- and vegetable-growing industry for the London market. There is commercial fishing around the islands, and tourist trade on St. Mary's at Hugh Town, the largest community in the island group. Star Castle, built at Hugh Town in 1593, is now a hotel.

The ruins of a 10th century abbey are found on Tresco. Also here are fortifications known as Oliver Cromwell's Tower and King Charles' Tower. The tropical gardens at the residence of Augustus John Smith, proprietor of the islands from 1834 to 1872, are particularly noteworthy. Bronze Age burial mounds and prehistoric remains are found on a number of the islands. Bishop Rock lighthouse, built in 1858 and rebuilt 30 years later, is situated on an outlying rock to the southwest. There are other lighthouses on Round Island and at Peninnis Head on St. Mary's.

Athelstan conquered the Scilly Islands in 938, and sent monks to build an abbey on Tresco. Henry I handed the islands over to the abbot of Tavistock, but Henry VIII took them back when the monasteries were dissolved in 1539. Queen Elizabeth leased them to Sir Francis Godolphin in 1568 and he later built Star Castle as a home for his family. Prince Charles was sheltered by the Godolphin family at Star Castle before he fled to Jersey in 1645. In 1834 the islands were leased to Augustus John Smith. They were handed over to the crown again in 1933. The Scilly Islands are governed by a county council and are part of the St. Ives parliamentary division. Population: (1961) 2,288.

SCINTILLATION COUNTER, sint-əl-ā′shən, an instrument for detecting fast-moving charged particles or various kinds of radiation. Basically, it consists of a scintillator and a photomultiplier tube. When it is used to count particles, an electronic counter is connected to the photomultiplier tube.

The scintillator is a solid or liquid substance that emits flashes of light when it absorbs energy from particles or radiation entering the instrument. These light flashes fall on the light-sensitive cathode of the photomultiplier tube, causing an ejection of electrons from its cathode. In this way the photomultiplier tube converts the light flashes to electrical pulses, which can readily be measured or counted.

The scintillator can be produced in a wide variety of sizes, shapes, and compositions to make the instrument especially suitable for some particular application. Inorganic crystals, organic crystals, liquids, powders, plastics, or glasses are used in making a scintillator. Inorganic crystals, such as sodium iodide crystals activated with thallium, are particularly useful for detecting gamma rays. Organic crystals, such as transtilbene or terphenyl crystals, are especially useful for counting particles at very high rates. Liquids, such as terphenyl dissolved in toluene, are used in large, relatively low-cost instruments.

Scintillating instruments are used in laboratories for basic research. They also are used in detecting radiation hazards and in exploring for radioactive minerals.

See also ELECTRONICS—*Electron Tubes* (Phototubes); PHOSPHOR.

SCIOTO COMPANY, sī-ō′tō, a land speculation corporation formed in 1787 for the purpose of acquiring a large tract in the Ohio country along the Ohio and Scioto rivers bordering land held by the Ohio Company. The principal speculators were Col. William Duer, secretary of the national treasury board, which handled land sales, and the Rev. Menasseh Cutler, who had negotiated land sales for the Ohio Company. Duer and his associates, who included government officials, were not able to purchase Western lands directly because of their positions. They arranged to acquire the land indirectly through Cutler, whom they took into the Scioto Company. Under pressure from Duer, Congress authorized the land sale, and the treasury board sold Cutler some 1.8 million acres (730,000 hectares) at about 8 cents an acre for the Ohio Company and an option for an additional 5 million acres (2 million hectares) at 66⅔ cents an acre. The option was turned over to the Scioto Company.

The investors proposed to finance their purchase by selling shares in the company at high prices in Europe, keeping the greater part to resell later at a profit. Joel Barlow, a former Ohio Company agent, represented them in Paris. Barlow overextended himself, selling tracts not actually owned and inducing emigration, which the speculators had not provided for. The French settlers lured to the "city" of Gallipolis suffered from lack of supplies, and most were unable to get title to their lands.

ALINARI-ART REFERENCE BUREAU

Scipio Africanus Major, Roman victor over Hannibal.

SCIPIO AFRICANUS MAJOR,

SCIPIO AFRICANUS MAJOR, sip'ē-ō af-rə-kā'nəs (236 B. C.?–183 B. C.), Roman general, who defeated Hannibal and led Rome to victory in the Second Punic War (218–201). His given name was Publius Cornelius Scipio. He was a member of a powerful Roman family and the son of Publius Scipio, a noted Roman general who played a key role in the early stages of the war.

Destined to be the most renowned Roman of his generation, the youthful Scipio saved his father's life in the Battle of the Ticinus River (218), which inaugurated the Second Punic War in Italy. As military tribune, he rallied the Roman remnant after the disastrous defeat at Cannae (216). After acting as aedile (212), Scipio went as proconsul (210) to Spain, where he soon captured Cartagena, the chief Carthaginian base. Then by spirited leadership, by revising Roman military tactics, by attracting Spanish allies to his side, and by brilliant campaigning, he so completely conquered the Carthaginians during 208–206 that Punic control of the peninsula collapsed and the Romans acquired almost all the Iberian Peninsula.

Returning to Rome, Scipio became consul in 205 and received Sicily as his province. There he organized the Roman invasion of Africa, which he began in 204. Scipio was so successful that the Carthaginians sued for peace, summoning Hannibal, their greatest general, from Italy in 203. Hannibal's return inspired renewal of hostilities, which ended in the Battle of Zama (202). At Zama, Scipio, the first Roman to employ cavalry effectively, decisively defeated Hannibal's Carthaginians. Scipio dictated harsh terms of peace in 201 and returned to Rome, where he celebrated a triumph and received the surname Africanus, to which later Romans added Major to distinguish him from his grandson, whose capture of Carthage in the Third Punic War won him the surname Minor.

Later Career. After the war, Scipio held a number of public offices—censor (199), chief of the Senate (199, 190), and consul (194)—but was less successful in making policy than in waging war. His military experience was utilized in 190, when he served as legate to his brother Lucius, who conducted the war against King Antiochus III the Great of Syria. The crushing defeat of Antiochus at Magnesia in Asia Minor was due to Scipio's plans, though illness prevented his participation in battle.

Scipio's return from Asia was robbed of acclaim by an accusation that he and his brother had accepted bribes from Antiochus. Though the truth has been clouded by conflicting testimony, it is evident that the prosecution was engineered by Scipio's political enemies. After a dramatic acquittal, Scipio retired to his Campanian villa at Liternum, where he passed his last years in privacy.

P. R. COLEMAN-NORTON[*]
Formerly, Princeton University

Further Reading: Liddell Hart, Basil H., *A Greater Than Napoleon, Scipio Africanus* (1926; reprint, Biblo & Tannen 1971); Scullard, H. H., *Scipio Africanus: Soldier and Politician* (Cornell Univ. Press 1970).

SCIPIO AFRICANUS MINOR,

SCIPIO AFRICANUS MINOR, sip'ē-ō af-rə-kā'nəs (185 B. C.–129 B. C.), Roman general, who commanded Roman forces that defeated Carthage in the Third Punic War (149–146 B. C.). The son of Lucius Aemilius Paulus, he was adopted by Publius Cornelius Scipio, his uncle and the elder son of Scipio Africanus Major. In his early years he bore the name Publius Cornelius Aemilianus, to which were later added the agnomens Africanus and Numantinus.

Scipio participated in the Battle of Pydna (168), in which his natural father concluded the Third Macedonian War (171–167), and then served as military tribune in Spain (151), where he won distinction. The outbreak of the Third Punic War saw Scipio still a subaltern, but his gallant conduct in Africa and his general's commendation gained for him the consulate in 147 and command of the Roman forces besieging Carthage. In 146 he captured Carthage, which he razed, selling the inhabitants into slavery and sowing the area with salt. He organized the Punic domains into the Roman province of Africa and returned to Rome, where he celebrated a triumph. To his inherited agnomen Africanus he added the additional agnomen Minor (the Younger) to distinguish him from his grandfather.

Scipio became censor in 142 and headed a legation to the eastern Mediterranean countries in 140–139. Rome's constant military failures in Spain led to his election as consul in 134. He successfully concluded the war there by capturing Numantia (133) after a long siege, receiving another triumph in Rome in 132 and another agnomen, Numantinus.

Perhaps more important than Scipio's military exploits was his patronage of the intellectuals who constituted the influential Scipionic Circle. His acquaintance with Greek literature and philosophy was above that of his Roman contemporaries, and he was a great orator. In politics he championed the conservative party against the democratic party, led by his brothers-in-law and first cousins, Tiberius Sempronius and Gaius Sempronius Gracchus. Scipio's sudden death in Rome, after political disorders, has been ascribed to assassination, but no evidence for this claim exists.

P. R. COLEMAN-NORTON[*]
Formerly, Princeton University

Further Reading: Astin, A. E., *Scipio Aemilianus* (Cornell Univ. Press 1967).

SOME TYPES OF SCISSORS AND SHEARS

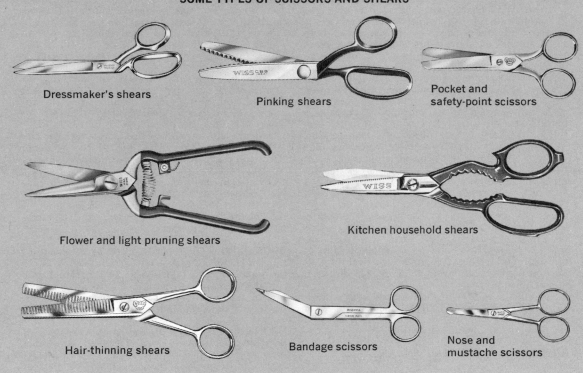

Dressmaker's shears

Pinking shears

Pocket and safety-point scissors

Flower and light pruning shears

Kitchen household shears

Hair-thinning shears

Bandage scissors

Nose and mustache scissors

SCISSORS AND SHEARS are cutting instruments that operate by the action of the opposed edges of two blades. The blades, usually made of steel, are joined by a pivot pin or screw. There are handles at the ends of the blades. Scissors differ from shears only in size. Any instrument less than 6 inches (15 cm) long is called a scissors, whereas larger tools are called shears.

Most scissors have identical round or slightly oval handles, providing openings for the thumb and first finger. Scissors are commonly named for their uses—for example, buttonhole scissors, embroidery scissors, and manicure scissors. Many shears have unlike handles, one with a small opening for the thumb, the other with a long oval opening for the four fingers. Tailor's shears are usually of this type, as are sheep shears. Pinking shears, used in sewing, have a special blade that cuts a serrated edge. Tin shears are ruggedly constructed, as are pruning shears.

Spring shears of tempered bronze or iron were made in ancient Rome. The effectiveness of scissors was greatly improved when Benjamin Huntsman produced shear steel at Sheffield, England, in the 1740's. The durability of scissors and shears was improved after the introduction of stainless steel by Harry Brearley in England in 1912.

SCISSORTAIL, a beautiful flycatcher, *Muscivora forficta,* found in the southeastern United States and in Mexico. It has a deeply forked tail and two very long outer tail feathers that it crosses and recrosses like a pair of scissors while in flight. Scissortails are about 14 inches (35 cm) long. They are usually gray above and white below with salmon coloring on the sides and scarlet at the base of the crown feathers. Like other New World tyrant flycatchers of the family Tyrannidae, the scissortail feeds on insects it catches in flight and on small fruit. See also FLYCATCHER.

SCITUATE, sit'ū-āt, a town in eastern Massachusetts, in Plymouth county, is situated on Massachusetts Bay in the Atlantic Ocean, 20 miles (32 km) southeast of Boston. It is a residential community and a seaside resort. Some lobster fishing is done in the nearby waters. Places of interest in the town include the lighthouse, the Old Stockbridge Grist Mill, and the Scituate Historical Society's museum.

Scituate was settled in 1628 and incorporated in 1636. Its name is from an Algonquian word for "cold stream." Scituate early became an important shipbuilding center. Among the persons of note who have lived here are the poet and playwright Samuel Woodworth, who was inspired by a local well to write his popular poem *The Old Oaken Bucket* (1817), and the abolitionist and women's rights advocate Samuel May and his niece Louisa May Alcott, author of *Little Women* (1868–1869). Government is by town meeting and selectmen. Population: 17,317.

SCLERA, sklir'ə, the outermost coat of the eye. The sclera is a tough, opaque, white coat commonly known as the "white of the eye." It covers approximately the posterior five sixths of the surface of the eyeball and is continuous with the outer sheath of the optic nerve. A thin vascular tissue called the *choroid* separates the inner part of the sclera from the photosensitive part of the eye, the *retina.* See EYE—*Structure of the Human Eye.*

395

SCLERODERMA, sklir-ō-dûr′mə, is a relatively uncommon chronic disease of connective tissue in human beings. Also known as *progressive systemic sclerosis*, it is characterized by diffuse sclerosis, or hardening, of the connective tissues of the skin and internal organs. The disease affects both sexes and all ages but most commonly occurs in middle-aged women. Its cause is unknown.

The early symptoms of scleroderma are variable and may include cutaneous manifestations such as hyperpigmentation and edema followed by a hardening of the skin and the development of a shiny, waxy appearance and eventually a masklike expression. Other symptoms depend on the particular internal organs involved. If, for example, lung tissue is affected, dyspnea may develop. If the esophagus or other organs of the digestive system are involved, various gastrointestinal signs may develop. Involvement of the kidneys may lead to renal insufficiency, and changes in the musculoskeletal system may produce muscular weakness. The disease is generally slowly progressive, but often is marked by periods of remission, and in some cases there is spontaneous recovery. There is no specific treatment for scleroderma, but the adrenal cortical steroids are frequently employed to alleviate early inflammatory phases.

A mild, localized form of scleroderma, known as *morphea*, characterized by local patches or streaks of scleroderma, is a benign disorder with no systemic involvements.

SCLEROSIS, MULTIPLE. See MULTIPLE SCLEROSIS.

SCOFIELD, skō′fēld, **Paul** (1922–   ), British actor. David Paul Scofield was born in Hurstpierpoint, Sussex, on Jan. 21, 1922. He studied at the Croydon Repertory Theatre School and the Mask Theatre School in London. He first attracted wide attention when he played (1946–1947) at the Shakespeare Memorial Theatre, Stratford-upon-Avon. Thereafter he appeared in a wide variety of plays, including *The Seagull* (1949), *Ring Round the Moon* (1950), *The River Line* (1952), *Venice Preserved* (1953), and *The Power and the Glory* (1956).

Scofield won international acclaim for his interpretation of Hamlet at the Moscow Art Theatre and then in London in 1955. He appeared as Sir Thomas More in *A Man for All Seasons* (London, 1960; New York, 1960–1961) and in the film version of that play (1966). The latter brought him both the U.S. Academy Award and the British Film Academy Award.

SCOLECITE, skol′ə-sīt, is hydrous calcium aluminum silicate, or $Ca(Al_2Si_3O_{10}) \cdot 3H_2O$. Its glassy crystals are transparent to white. A member of the zeolite mineral family, scolecite resembles natrolite. See NATROLITE.

SCOLIOSIS, skō-lē-ō′səs, is a lateral curvature of the spine, or backbone. It affects about 2% of the population. Scoliosis may be functional, due to bad posture, or structural, due to a malformation of the spine or injury to associated muscles. See also CURVATURE OF THE SPINE.

SCONE, skōōn, **Stone of,** the coronation stone of Scottish kings from Kenneth I (called McAlpin), until it was carried off to England by Edward I in 1296. Kenneth I (died about 858 A. D.) was said to have brought the Stone of Destiny from Dunstaffnage to Scone, in East Perthshire, Scotland. John de Baliol, after his coronation in Scone in 1292, did homage to Edward I as lord paramount. But Edward conquered Baliol and sent the stone to England. Used in the coronation of every monarch from William I, with two exceptions, the stone was stolen from Westminster Abbey on Christmas Day, 1950, by Scottish nationalists but returned on April 11, 1951.

SCOPAS, skō′pəs, Greek sculptor of the 14th century B. C., who, with Praxiteles and Lysippus, was one of the foremost sculptors of his time. Scopas was born in Paros, possibly the son of a sculptor. He is considered of the Athenian school, although he worked in many parts of the Greek world. According to Pliny and Pausanias, he collaborated on the Mausoleum of Halicarnassus, designed and did some sculpture for the Temple of Athena Alea in Tegea, and worked on the Temple of Artemis at Ephesus. Fragments from the pediments of Athena's temple (National Museum, Athens), which may be his, include heads showing strong emotion, conveyed by open mouth and deep-set eyes, in an expressive manner suggesting later Hellenistic developments. Reliefs from the Mausoleum (British Museum, London), possibly his, give a similar effect.

Ancient writers mention numerous statues made by Scopas for various Greek cities, some of which have been identified in Roman copies or on coins. Among them are a *Nereid* (Museo Ostiense, Ostia) and a *Triton* (Vatican) from a marine group, the *Lansdowne Heracles* (J. P. Getty Museum, Malibu, Calif.), *Pothos* (Museo Capitolino, Rome), a much-praised *Maenad* (Staatliche Kunstsammlungen, Dresden), and a *Meleager* (Vatican).

Paul Scofield, in the 1966 film *A Man for All Seasons*

CULVER PICTURES

BROWN BROTHERS

Clarence Darrow (*left*) conducted the defense and William Jennings Bryan assisted the prosecution in the Scopes case, which generated a spate of books opposing the teaching of the theory of evolution.

WIDE WORLD

SCOPES TRIAL, skōps, a celebrated case that was brought in 1925 against a high school biology teacher, John T. Scopes, by the state of Tennessee. Responding to pressure by militant Protestant fundamentalists in the Southern states, the legislature of Tennessee passed a penal statute in March 1925 that made it unlawful to teach in any public school "any theory which denies the story of the Divine creation of man as taught in the Bible, and to teach instead that man is descended from a lower order of animals."

The governor of Tennessee approved the law on March 13, and the American Civil Liberties Union (ACLU) immediately offered to defend any teacher willing to test the law. An interested businessman in Dayton, Tenn., enlisted a youthful biology teacher, John Thomas Scopes, to make a test. Scopes was indicted, and trial in Dayton was set for July. William Jennings Bryan, the orator and political leader, volunteered his services to the prosecution. A similar offer was made to the defense by Clarence Darrow, the foremost criminal lawyer of his day. Darrow was aided by Arthur Garfield Hays of New York, counsel to the ACLU, and by Dudley Field Malone, a liberal Roman Catholic.

The trial ran 11 days, taking place before a single judge, from July 10 to July 21, and attracted worldwide attention from the press and public. H. L. Mencken was one of the prominent reporters who covered the trial.

The rulings of the court barred any testimony on constitutional questions of civil liberties. Also, the court refused to consider any testimony that related to the validity of the Darwin theory of evolution. The judge said that the sole question at issue was whether Scopes had, or had not, actually taught the theory of evolution. The climax was a devastating cross-examination by Darrow of Bryan which revealed Bryan as less than an expert witness on the Bible, and profoundly uninformed on biological science. Bryan's difficulties on the witness stand may well have contributed to his sudden illness and death five days after the trial ended.

Scopes was convicted and fined $100. He appealed to the Tennessee supreme court, which some months later unanimously reversed the conviction on the ground that only a jury could impose a fine in excess of $50. It did not pass on the constitutionality of the statute and thus prevented a contemplated appeal to the United States Supreme Court. The widely publicized "monkey trial," however, so harmed the fundamentalists' drive for similar laws in other states that they succeeded in only two, Mississippi and Arkansas. There, the laws were entered on the statute books in 1926 but not enforced until nearly 40 years later, when an Arkansas teacher brought suit resulting in the state supreme court upholding the law. On appeal to the U. S. Supreme Court, in a unanimous decision, *Epperson v. Arkansas* (1968), held that it violated the constitutional ban against establishment of religion. Tennessee did not repeal its law until 1967.

ROGER N. BALDWIN
Former Director
American Civil Liberties Union

Bibliography

Bryan, William Jennings and M. E., *Memoirs of William Jennings Bryan* (reprint, Haskell House 1970).
Darrow, Clarence S., *The Story of My Life* (reprint, Scribner 1960).
Hays, Arthur Garfield, *Let Freedom Ring*, rev. ed. (reprint, Plenum Press 1971).
Scopes, John T., and Presley, James, *Center of the Storm* (Holt 1967).

SCOPOLAMINE, skō-pol'ə-mēn, is a drug obtained from the henbane shrub (*Hyoscyamus niger*) and related shrubs of the nightshade family, Solanaceae. Also known as hyoscine, it is closely related to atropine and is one of the oldest drugs known in medicine.

Scopolamine is used medically to dilate the pupils of the eye, often an aid to ophthalmologic diagnosis. It also affects automatic nerve fibers and acts to inhibit the secretion of several glands, including the salivary and sweat glands, and as an antispasmodic to relax the smooth musculature of the stomach and intestine. Its chief use perhaps is in preanesthesia to produce sedation before the administration of an anesthetic for surgery. The side effects of scopolamine include dryness of the mouth and blurred vision.

The first page of the score, in manuscript, of Johannes Brahms' *Tragic Overture* (1880).

SCOPUS, Mount, skō'pəs, peak in Israel, just northeast of Jerusalem that has always been important to the city's defense. Another form of its name is Scopas. Its height is 2,736 feet (834 meters). In the Israeli-Arab war of 1948–1949 it was held by the Israelis, but it was surrounded by Arab territory. After the six-day war of 1967, the Israelis incorporated it into Jerusalem. It is the site of the Hebrew University and the Hadassah Medical Center.

SCORE, in music, the manuscript or transcript of a composition showing the various instrumental or vocal parts on separate staffs, one above the other. It is so-called from the bars drawn (or scored) through the staffs so that notes to be played or sung together are in vertical alignment. Although the earliest known form of score dates from the 11th century, the modern instrumental score came into being with the rise of orchestral music, beginning in the late 16th century.

In an instrumental score, the parts are arranged according to the classes of instruments, usually with the woodwinds (flutes, piccolo, and others) on the upper staffs, followed in descending order by the brasses (horns, trumpets, trombones, and tuba), the percussion instruments (timpani, drums, and others), and the strings. In a choral score, the soprano parts are on the upper staffs, followed in descending order by the contraltos, tenors, and basses.

SCORESBY, skôrz'bē, **William** (1789–1857), English Arctic mariner and scientist. He was born at Cropton, near Whitby, on Oct. 5, 1789. He accompanied his father on trips to the Greenland whale fishery and attended Cambridge University between voyages. During his trips he began to chart Arctic regions.

Scoresby invented a diving device that led to his discovery that Arctic waters were warmer at the bottom than on the surface. In 1820 he published *An Account of the Arctic Regions and Northern Whale Fishery* (2 vols.), a pioneer work on Arctic science.

In 1822, Scoresby surveyed and charted some 400 miles (644 km) of Greenland's east coast. Scoresby Sound was named for him. He then returned to England and studied for the ministry. He was ordained in 1825 and held several clerical posts before retiring in 1847. He continued with his scientific studies of magnetism and made two trips to the United States and one to Australia. Scoresby died in Torquay, Devonshire, on March 21, 1857.

SCORIA, skôr'ē-ə, in geology, is a bubbly, dark, and cinderlike volcanic rock. It forms by cooling suddenly after ejection from a volcanic vent, under pressure, as a foamy liquid.

SCORODITE, skôr'ə-dīt, is a mineral arsenate of ferrous iron. Its translucent crystals are pale green to brownish and have a glassy to diamondlike luster. The mineral also occurs in an earthy form. It is usually found in metallic veins in association with other arsenic-bearing minerals, or as a deposit of hot springs.

Composition, $FeAsO_4 \cdot 2H_2O$; hardness, 3.4-4; specific gravity, 3.1-3.3; crystal system, orthorhombic.

SCORPIO, skôr'pē-ō, is a form of the name of the constellation Scorpius. See SCORPIUS.

GORDON SMITH, FROM NATIONAL AUDUBON SOCIETY

SCORPION young (*top*) pass through the early stages of their development on their mother's back. (*Right*) A tropical scorpion (*Centruroides gracilis*) with its prey, killed by the scorpion's venomous tail stinger.

LUNT, FROM ANNAN

SCORPION, skôr′pē-ən, a predaceous arthropod of the order Scorpiones (or Scorpionida). Scorpions are the most primitive land arachnids and the oldest, being known from Silurian fossils, and they may have been the first land animals. These flattened, distinctively segmented animals are characterized by the presence of a poisonous sting on the end of the abdomen, the five terminal segments of which are sharply narrowed to form a long, ringed, movable tail. The tail is curled over the back so that the curved, spine-like sting is in position to strike insects, spiders, and other small living animals that the scorpion preys on. The upper side of the cephalothorax (a combined head and thorax) is a flat carapace bearing a pair of large median eyes and a group of two to five small eyes on each side margin. The cephalothorax is broadly joined to the abdomen, as in solpugids and pseudoscorpions, not narrowed to a slender waist, as in such distant relatives as whip scorpions and spiders. The four pairs of walking legs are similar and relatively slender. Held out in front to test the terrain is a pair of long, robust pedipalpi provided with stout pincers similar to those of lobsters, which are used to hold the prey. A small but strong pair of jawlike chelicerae in front of the mouth aid in crushing the body of the victim.

The scorpion digests the soft parts of its prey by discharging a digestive fluid over them. The predigested food is then sucked through the mouth by the pharynx, which serves as both a pump and a strainer. As in all arachnids, the genital products are voided through a pore that opens on the ventral face of the second abdominal segment. Immediately behind are a pair of comb-like pectines found only in scorpions and thought to have a sensory function.

Scorpions are solitary, nocturnal creatures that attack each other as readily as any other suitable prey. During mating the male extrudes to the ground a complicated spermatophore. He then grasps the forelegs of the female and dances her into a position to accept the sperm mass. Whereas most arachnids lay eggs, the scorpions are viviparous, bringing forth living young. The newly born scorpions mount the back of the mother and stay there until after their first molt, usually for about a week. During this period they consume the food stored in their bodies. The belief that these weak, tiny babies feed upon the body of the mother has no basis in fact. No less a fable is the classic story that scorpions commit suicide by stinging themselves when they are helplessly cornered or surrounded by a ring of fire. During frantic efforts to escape, the victim stings at random, sometimes striking its own body before succumbing.

The venom of most scorpions causes mild to severe local reactions at the site of the sting. A few species of relatively small size, belonging mostly to the family Buthidae, are known to cause pronounced neurotoxic reactions in man and warm-blooded animals. These species occur in several parts of the world. Probably the most notorious are several species of *Centruroides* from western and southern Mexico. These were formerly responsible for the mortality of as many as 1,500 persons a year, mostly young children. The paving of streets, improved sanitation, and the wearing of shoes have sharply reduced the danger of these species, which abound in these areas and often enter houses. Two allied species occur in Arizona where they have gained a most unsavory reputation, with several recorded fatalities. Serums that are very effective in alleviating the severe symptoms are available.

Scorpions abound in humid tropical areas and in hot deserts, where they are represented by many species. The giants are great black creatures from tropical Africa, frequently 7 inches (180 mm) long, and the average size for the whole order is about half that length. Thirty or more species are found in the United States, chiefly in the South and Southwest, but some penetrate north to Virginia in the East and even farther north in the West, where they range into the Canadian provinces of British Columbia, Alberta, and Saskatchewan.

Other arachnids frequently associated with the true scorpions because of their common names but which for the most part are not closely allied are the following: The pseudoscorpions (order Chelonethi) are tiny forms rarely exceeding one-fourth inch (6 mm) in length that resemble scorpions but have the abdomen rounded behind and without trace of whip or tail. The wind scorpions or solpugids (order Solifuges) are active, tailless creatures notable for the tremendous size of their chelicerae. The whip scorpions (order Pedipalpi), narrow-waisted types lacking a caudal sting, are a somewhat heterogeneous group, some having a slender, jointed, whiplike tail, others being tailless and having the first legs tremendously elongated into lashlike whips.

WILLIS J. GERTSCH*
Emeritus Curator of Arachnida
Department of Entomology
The American Museum of Natural History

Further Reading: Comstock, John H., *The Spider Book*, rev. by W. J. Gertsch (Comstock Publishing Associates 1948); Savory, T. H., *Arachnida* (Academic Press 1964); Snow, Keith R., *Arachnids* (Columbia Univ. Press 1970); Stahnke, Herbert L., "Scorpions of the United States," *Turtox News*, vol. 22 (1944).

SCORPION FISH, skôr′pē-ən, any of a family of poisonous fishes that live on or near the ocean bottom, often in rocky areas. Also known as rockfish, scorpion fish are found in temperate or tropical marine waters. Included in the Scorpaenidae family are the tropical turkeyfish or lionfish, the deadly stonefish, the rosefish, and many other species.

Scorpion fish are usually less than 1 foot (30 cm) long, but some reach a length of 3 feet (90 cm). Some are rather somberly colored, while others are brightly colored and spectacular. The dorsal, anal, and ventral fins have sharp spines that can inflict a painful wound. In many species venom glands are associated with these fin spines. Scorpion fish feed on other smaller fish, and most bear live young.

Many scorpion fish are good food fishes. One species in particular, the rosefish (*Sebastes marinus*), marketed as ocean perch, is increasingly popular.

California scorpion fish (*Scorpaena guttata*)

JEANNE WHITE, FROM NATIONAL AUDUBON SOCIETY

SCORPION FLY, skôr′pē-ən, any of an order of small to medium-sized insects that generally have two pairs of long narrow membranous wings and an elongated head forming a turned-down beak with chewing mouthparts. Male scorpion flies also have pincerlike organs that resemble scorpions' stingers on the ends of their abdomens. A few species are wingless.

There are about 300 species of scorpion flies making up the order Mecoptera. They are widely distributed throughout the world but are not of any significant economic importance. Adults are frequently found in moist places where there is rank vegetation. Females lay eggs in masses on the ground, and the larvae, which resemble caterpillars but have more abdominal legs, live in burrows. Both adults and larvae are scavengers, feeding on dead insects and other animal matter. Some species also eat vegetable matter. Some species of scorpion flies habitually hang by their long legs from some supporting object and are known as hanging flies.

SCORPIUS, skôr′pē-əs, also called Scorpio, is a summer constellation of the Northern Hemisphere. One of the 12 signs of the zodiac, it lies across the ecliptic between Sagittarius, Centaurus, and Libra. (See also ZODIAC.) In one of the tales from Greek mythology, Scorpius was the scorpion ordered by the gods to kill the hunter Orion by stinging him in the foot. The stars that were considered to form the scorpion's claws were later separated from the rest of the constellation by the Romans and made into the constellation Libra.

Scorpius is a bright, easily observed constellation. It occupies a dense region of the Milky Way in which star clusters and nebulae abound. Its brightest star, the red supergiant Antares, or "rival of Mars," is one of the sky's 20 brightest stars. Antares was venerated in ancient times. Antares has a small companion that is visible only through powerful telescopes. Other bright stars in the constellation include ε, θ, κ, and λ Scorpii. The star μ Scorpii is a naked-eye double, while β Scorpii is easily separated into a double star by small telescopes. Only a few of the many star clusters in the constellation can be mentioned. The large M4 and the condensed but bright M80 are both globular clusters, while M6, M7, and oc 6124 are all striking open clusters.

SCORZALITE. See LAZULITE.

LYNWOOD M. CHACE, FROM NATIONAL AUDUBON SOCIETY

Scotch pine (*Pinus sylvestris*)

SCOTCH PINE is a widely distributed pine tree used for lumber, windbreaks, and ornamental plantings. A native of Europe, it is found over most of that continent and much of northern Asia. There are dense growths of Scotch pines in northern Germany and the USSR. In eastern North America, the tree has been widely planted for forestry purposes.

Scotch pine, *Pinus sylvestris*, attains a height of 60 to 150 feet (18–46 meters) and has a straight trunk up to 5 feet (1.5 meters) in diameter. It has twisted boughs, 1.5- to 3.5-inch-long (4- to 9-cm) blue-green needles borne in sheathed clusters of two, and short-stalked cones that usually are less than 2 inches (5 cm) long. The heartwood, which is reddish brown, lasts as well as oak and is well adapted to indoor or outdoor construction work. The wood gives good results with paints, varnishes, and stains, and it is easily glued.

SCOTCH PLAINS is a township in north central New Jersey, in Union county, in a valley east of Watchung Mountain, about 22 miles (35 km) southwest of the center of New York City. It is mainly a suburban residential area.

The township contains the Stage House Inn, formerly Ye Old Historic Inn, which dates back to 1737. Also of interest is the Frazee House.

This was occupied during the American Revolution by Mrs. Elizabeth ("Aunt Betty") Frazee, who when offering bread to the British commander Lord Cornwallis avowed that she did so "in fear and not in love."

The site was settled in 1684 by Scottish Presbyterian and Quaker immigrants, who named it Scots Plains, in memory of their leader, George Scot, who had died en route. The name later became Scotch Plains. Scotch Plains was a part of the borough of Elizabeth until 1794. It was a part of Westfield (1794–1877) and of Fanwood township from 1877 until 1917, when it became an independent township. It has a council-manager form of government. Population: 20,774.

SCOTCH TERRIER. See SCOTTISH TERRIER.

SCOTCH WHISKY is a liquor distilled from a fermented mash of barley that has been dried over a peat fire, and aged in casks (often used sherry casks). Most modern commercial Scotch whisky is blended with grain whiskies to produce a lighter liquor.

Malt whisky was being made in Scotland as early as the 12th century, but was little known outside of that country until the late 1700's. As wider distribution became possible, the pure Scotch malt whisky began to be blended with others. Today Scotch may contain a blend of up to 50 different whiskies. It is also made outside of Scotland, but with less success. See also DISTILLED SPIRITS—*Whiskey*.

SCOTER, skō'tər, any of a genus, *Melanitta*, of diving ducks. The white-winged scoter (*M. fusca*) and the black, or common, scoter (*M. nigra*) inhabit northern Europe, Asia, and North America. The surf scoter (*M. perspicillata*) is restricted to North America.

Scoters are usually from 19 to 21 inches (48–53 cm) long. Males are generally velvety black and females brown. The bill is broad and long and in the male is brightly colored and has a knob at its base. The surf scoter has two white patches on its head, and the white-winged scoter a white patch on the wing. Scoters nest around fresh water but move to sea after the breeding season. There, they congregate in large flocks not far from the shore. They fly heavily, close to the water, but are very good divers. Their food consists chiefly of shellfish, especially mussels. See also DUCK.

CHARLES VAURIE
The American Museum of Natural History

SCOTISTS. See DUNS SCOTUS, JOHN; SCHOLASTICISM.

Common Scoter (*Melanitta nigra*), a diving duck.

ERIC HOSKING F. R. P. S., FROM NATIONAL AUDUBON SOCIETY

Scotland

CONTENTS

INFORMATION HIGHLIGHTS

Political Status: A political division of the United Kingdom of Great Britain and Northern Ireland; formerly a separate kingdom.

Area: 30,412 square miles, or 78,767 sq km (32% of the total area of the United Kingdom).

Popuation: (1971 census): 5.2 million (9.5% of the population of the United Kingdom).

SCOTLAND forms the northern part of the island of Great Britain. It is bounded on three sides by the sea—the Atlantic Ocean on the north and west and the North Sea on the east—and it borders England on the south. Politically, it is part of the United Kingdom of Great Britain and Northern Ireland. Administratively, it is divided into 33 counties and the four major cities, which rank as "counties of cities." The largest city, Glasgow, an industrial center with a population of more than one million, is the third-largest city in the United Kingdom. The others are Edinburgh, the capital and cultural center, Aberdeen, and Dundee.

United with England since 1707, Scotland still maintains a separate identity. The land gives an impression of ruggedness quite unlike the low-lying English countryside and the soft greenness of Ireland, though this distinction does not hold throughout. The Scots themselves are usually distinguishable from the English in speech and mannerisms. Their sense of separatism was derived from a long history of independence before union and fostered by geographical remoteness and economic backwardness. Resistant to conformity, the Scots doggedly adhere to traditional ways while participating fully in the mainstream of modern life. Scottish nationalism, born of economic discontent, also has a positive aspect— that of preserving what is uniquely Scottish, preventing total absorption by Britain or Europe.

The following article deals mainly with the unique features of the Scottish countryside, with the Scottish people and their way of life, with the economy, government, law, and history of Scotland, and with Scottish contributions to the arts. For general information relating to Scotland as a part of Britain and especially for modern history, see GREAT BRITAIN AND NORTHERN IRELAND, UNITED KINGDOM OF.

1. The Land

A country of striking natural beauty, Scotland is characterized by rugged hills and by deep glacial lakes known as *lochs*. It is almost entirely surrounded by the sea, which encroaches in deeply penetrating inlets and forms estuaries known as *firths*, at the mouths of rivers. The total area of 30,412 square miles includes inland waters and 186 inhabited coastal islands.

Scotland's greatest length, from Dunnet Head in the northeast to the Mull of Galloway in the southwest, is usually stated at 287 miles (462 km), but if the northern Orkney and Shetland islands are taken into account, the country stretches for nearly 450 miles (724 km). The breadth of the mainland attains 150 miles (240 km) at its widest point between Applecross in the west and Buchan Ness in the east, but it is generally much less and drops to 24 miles (39 km) between Loch Broom in the west and the Dornoch Firth in the east. The border isthmus separating Scotland from England comprises the Solway Firth, the Cheviot Hills, and the lower reaches of the Tweed River. Here the breadth is about 60 miles (97 km), although the irregu-

The rugged Scottish landscape at Loch Alsh is the setting for Eilean Donan castle, once shelled by the English and a surviving reminder of the land's stormy history.

lar and largely artificial border line measures full 100 miles (161 km).

Land Regions. Traditionally, Scotland is divided geographically into the Highlands, the Central Lowlands, and the Southern Uplands, each with boundaries largely defined by geological features. Some authorities would add as a separate region the eastern corner around Aberdeen. Although this area falls into the Highlands as usually defined, it is essentially Lowland in character. In any case, much the larger part of Scotland consists of the Highlands—that is to say, mountain plateaus broken up by broad valleys, or *straths*, and narrower valleys, or *glens*. Apart from narrow strips of comparatively fertile coastline, which are much broader and more extensive on the east coast than on the west coast, the population is concentrated in the valleys.

The Highland zone itself is split into two sections by the Great Glen of Scotland, which runs from Inverness on the east coast to near Fort William on the west. This natural depression with its chain of lochs was used for the construction of the Caledonian Canal. Southwest of the Great Glen lie the Grampian Mountains, traversing the country from northeast to southwest and presenting, on their precipitous northern slopes, some of Scotland's wildest scenery. Ben Nevis (4,406 feet, or 1,343 meters), in the southwestern Grampians, is the highest mountain in the British Isles. Four summits of the Cairngorm Mountains, a northernly group of the Grampians, exceed 4,000 feet (1,200 meters),

and 543 other hills in the Highland zone are over 3,000 feet (900 meters). It is a common ambition of climbers to ascend all these hills, often called Munroes, after the compiler of the first list of them, Sir Hugh T. Munro.

South of the Highlands and occupying the "waist" of Scotland are the Central Lowlands. Their northern boundary may be taken to run from a few miles north of Glasgow northeastward almost to Aberdeen; their southern boundary, from south of the town of Ayr northeastward to Dunbar. Although described as Lowlands, this area contains an almost continuous line of hills between Renfrewshire in the southwest and the Sidlaw Hills, northwest of Dundee, but with natural gaps used by roads and railways. The highest hill in this region is Ben Cleuch (2,363 feet or 720 meters), in the detached range of the Ochil Hills in Fife. Between the Sidlaw Hills and the Highlands lie Strathmore, a fertile lowland area, and around Edinburgh the Lothian plain. Between these and other truly Lowland areas are often large tracts of moorland.

The Southern Uplands, the southernmost division of Scotland, are not very clearly marked off from the Central Lowlands. They consist of country not unlike the Highlands, but on a smaller scale and less elevated. The hills are usually rounded and grass-grown and the valleys wider and less rugged. The highest peak in this area is Mount Merrick (2,764 feet, or 842 meters), in the Galloway district. Many other hills in the Uplands exceed 2,000 feet (600 meters).

The greater part of Scotland, as at Loch Carron, consists of Highlands cut through by broad and narrow valleys.

Barley and oats are the principal cereals grown in the Central Lowlands. Below, a harvest near Stirling.

Coasts and Islands. The west coast of Scotland is generally a wild, deeply indented mountain wall. Sea lochs or firths run deeply into the land and are themselves studded with islands. The Firth of Clyde, for example, encloses the islands of Arran, Bute, and The Cumbraes. The east coast also includes long sections of steep cliffs broken up by extensive stretches of low, sandy coast. The chief inlets on the east—the firths of Forth and Tay on the southeast, and the Moray, Cromarty, and Dornoch firths on the northeast—run far back into the coastal plain. The north coast is deeply indented by several narrow sea lochs, which have more in common with the western than with the eastern inlets.

There are nearly 800 islands in all, most of them uninhabited. Only a handful of these, including several used for lighthouses, lie off the east coast. Close to the north of the Scottish mainland lie the Orkney Islands and far to the northeast of them, the Shetlands, outposts of the early Norsemen. However, the great bulk of the Scottish islands are found on the west coast. They are mostly divided into two groups: (1) the Inner Hebrides, reached by short ferries and stretching from Skye in the north to Islay in the south; and (2) the Outer Hebrides, sometimes called the "Long Island," 30 miles (48 km) or more out to sea, stretching from Lewis with Harris, which together make up one island, in the north, to Berneray in the south. Still farther to the west is the small group of islands collectively called St. Kilda.

Rivers and Lakes. Scotland is famous for its rivers and lakes. Many of the largest rivers enter the sea as firths named for the rivers, as, for example, the firths of Forth and Clyde. Except for the Clyde, kept open by continual dredging, Scotland has hardly any navigable rivers. The

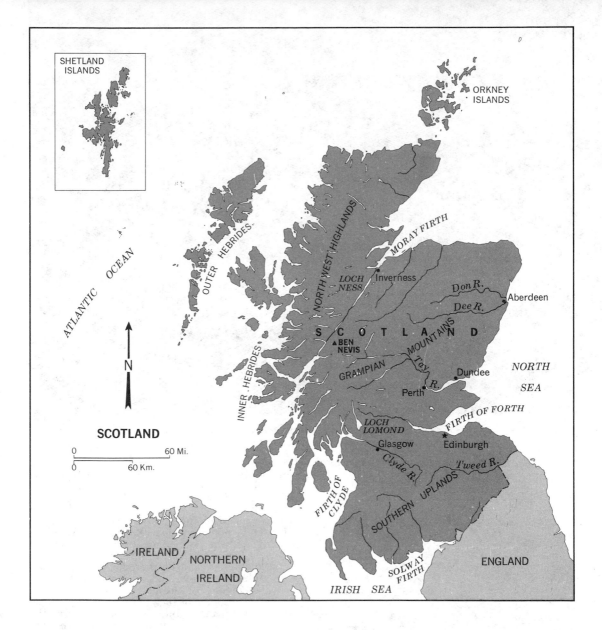

Tay, Tweed, and many other rivers are well known for their salmon fishing.

There are few lakes in the Southern Uplands or Central Lowlands, the best known being St. Mary's Loch, in the Border country, and Loch Leven, known for its angling matches, near Kinross. The Highland zone contains a great many lakes, including Loch Lomond (28 square miles, or 72 sq km), the largest lake in all of Britain. Loch Katrine, in the heart of the Trossachs, is the source of Glasgow's water supply, and Loch Earn, near Perth, is a headquarters for water sports. Loch Maree, in Ross county, and lochs Lochy, Ness, Nevis, and Oich, in Inverness, are among those noted for their magnificent settings. Loch Ness has been a subject of a centuries-old controversy over an alleged monster in its depths.

Geology. Scotland provides fascinating study for the geologist. The older Precambrian rocks are prominent in the Highlands and Outer Hebrides, although subsequent changes have complicated their geology. The Central Lowlands are composed mainly of Paleozoic rocks. Their extensive carboniferous strata make this area one of the important mineral fields of Britain. The Southern Uplands are largely Silurian and Ordovician.

There is much evidence of volcanic activity and also of the successive ice ages, when frost broke up the mountain cliffs, and glaciers gouged out valleys. Raised beaches, many of them well above present sea level, show the effect of the pressure and subsequent melting of the ice cap. The breaking up of the elevated plateau, of which Scotland once consisted, by erosion and denudation by water and ice gave the country its present contours. The mountains consist often of harder rocks that resisted change, while the softer rocks were trenched and furrowed in all directions by the action of the elements.

It is notable in northern Scotland that the rivers running to the west coast have short, relatively steep courses, while the rivers flowing east are longer and less rapid. Also notable in this region is the "crag and tail" formation of many of the hills—that is, a steep west face backed by a ridge that drops gradually to the east.

Skye, the largest island of the Inner Hebrides, is celebrated for its scenic mountainous moorland.

Peat is gathered on Barra, in the Outer Hebrides. In remote areas peat is still used for fuel.

Natural Resources. Scotland's natural resources are limited. They are confined largely to the Central Lowlands, where the soil is fertile and where there are extensive deposits of coal, iron, slate, granite, and other minerals. Only fragments remain of the natural pine forests of the Highlands, notably in the Mar district, Aberdeen county, and the Rothiemurchus Forest, Inverness. In good seasons, heather honey is produced in large quantities, and heather shoots supply food and shelter for grouse and other game birds.

The dream of exploiting Scotland's peat mosses as a source of fuel and power has scarcely been implemented. But rivers and lochs of the Highlands have been utilized to produce relatively cheap electric power for the area and surplus power for other districts, and electricity is being produced from nuclear plants. The fresh waters themselves are important to the Scotch whisky industry. A large-scale government afforestation program has made forestry important in the Southern Uplands, but the Border country is best known for its sheep raising.

The surrounding seas no longer afford much good fishing, though rivers and lakes offer trout and salmon.

Climate. For a country lying so far to the north, the climate of Scotland is reasonably mild in winter owing to the prevalence of southwest Atlantic winds and the direction taken by warm water currents along its western coasts. No month has an average temperature below freezing. In winter the west is slightly warmer than the east, but in summer, differences in temperature are erratic and unimportant.

The west coast and especially the western hills have a much heavier rainfall than the east coast and even the Central Highlands. The mountains near Fort William receive more than

NOEL HABGOOD, FROM PHOTO RESEARCHERS

Oban is a resort facing a picturesque bay. McCaigs Folly, an uncompleted circular structure, overlooks the town.

150 inches (3,800 mm) of rain in an average year, while parts of the coastal strips in the east have less than 25 inches (635 mm). July and August often tend to be wet, especially in the Highlands.

DAVID B. HORN, *Author of "Great Britain and Europe in the Eighteenth Century"*

Further Reading: Dunnett, Alastair I., *Scotland in Color* (Viking 1970); Linklater, Eric, and Smith, Edwin, *Scotland* (Viking 1968); O'Dell, Andrew C., and Walton, Kenneth, *The Highlands and Islands of Scotland* (Nelson 1962).

2. The People

Although the traditional division of all Scots into Highlanders and Lowlanders still has meaning, it has been an oversimplification. The Shetlanders with their Norse blood and traditions and the mixed Gaelic-Norse population of the Hebrides never fitted into either category. Intermarriage has helped to blur a real dividing line and to make the Scots one people. The modern population moves freely among the three main geographical regions and the Orkney and Shetland islands.

The most important distinction regarding the Scots is that to be made between the bulk of the population that lives in or within easy traveling distance of the big towns and the minority that lives in the Highlands glens or border valleys or on the islands.

Since the end of the 18th century, there has been a steady drift from country to town. Attempts to reverse this process have been unsuccessful. Derelict cottages and ruined farmsteads are noticeable throughout the Highlands, the western islands, and the Border country. The hard life and the paucity of opportunity in these isolated areas are unacceptable to the younger and more ambitious people. Many small com-

The Scottish Highland breed of cattle resists the cold weather and survives on scant feed.

BRITISH TOURIST AUTHORITY

munities, particularly in the western Highlands and islands, consist almost entirely of elderly people. Increasingly tourism is the major industry in these beautiful, but remote, pockets.

Population. In 1755, the first attempt to calculate the population of Scotland, partly by enumeration and partly by estimate, yielded a figure of 1,265,000. By the time of the first official census in 1801, this figure had risen to 1,608,420. In the next 120 years the population trebled before entering a slight decline in the 1920's.

Emigration has been a continual drain on Scotland's population. Although the 19th and 20th centuries brought some immigration, especially from Ireland, there was a net loss. The high birthrate of the 19th century made emigration necessary, and periods of economic distress intensified the problem. It has been calculated that about 900,000 persons left Scotland in the first 30 years of the 20th century. Since most of these were young people, Scotland was left with an unduly high proportion of older persons. This has been a factor in the economic difficulties the country has since encountered.

The 1971 census of Britain showed a population of about 5,227,700 in Scotland. This was the highest figure recorded in any census. However, the increase over 1961, estimated at 48,000, was only half that of the increase in the previous decade. A rise in the birthrate has been offset by continued losses through emigration. Over two fifths of the population lives in less than one twentieth of the country's area.

The most populous counties are Lanark (containing Glasgow), Midlothian (with Edinburgh), Ayr, Renfrew, Fife, and Aberdeen. All counties of cities, except Glasgow, and all large burghs, except Greenock, showed population gains in the 1950's and 1960's.

Language. In their search for a common identity the Scots are not aided by language. There are at least two tongues, with their variations, spoken in Scotland, though some linguists would not consider either a distinct language. These are Scottish Gaelic, spoken mainly by a tiny fraction of the population residing in the western Highlands and western islands, and Lowland Scots, the Scots vernacular form of English descended from the northern dialect of Middle English. English is, in fact, the language of Scotland, though it normally is not the English of London. Even in the Lowlands dozens of dialects of the vernacular can be distinguished, ranging from accented standard English to speech incomprehensible to the English and to many Scots.

Gaelic was the Scots vernacular until about the 16th century, when it yielded to Lowland Scots, retreating to the remote western areas. The surviving Scots vernacular has been so influenced by English and, in some areas, by Scandinavian languages that it is barely discernible as a distinct tongue. Some common features different from English pronunciation include the *a* or *ai* sound substituted for ō, as in "stane" for "stone," and the *u* or *ui* for *oo* or *u,* as in "buik" for "book," as well as the trilled *r*. Spelling of the Scots vernacular is far from uniform, and English has long been the standard written language. See also CELTIC LANGUAGES.

Clan System. A remnant of tribalism and feudalism, the clan, or genealogical kin unit, has vanished as a political or economic entity, though it survives, in corrupted form, out of sentiment and commercialism. It is a normal feature of primitive communities to base society on the family and kin. What gave longevity to Celtic tribalism in Scotland was the physical framework of the country, which led to the formation of many small, detached settlements having little contact with each other.

After the long Wars of Independence, culminating in the Battle of Bannockburn in 1314, the central government was not strong enough to impose a common pattern on the whole country. Each region formed a unit with some characteristics of a family and of a kingdom. The clan chief ruled over his clan, most of whom believed that they were bound to him by ties of blood as well as of obligation. In the disturbed state of the country it was to the chief's interest not to wring the maximum profit from the clan territory, but to gain control of a reliable body of able-bodied fighting men. When the clan chief was also the feudal lord of the district, and son succeeded father both in hereditary land tenure and feudal office, his local authority became unchallengeable. Strictly speaking, the clan system was restricted to the Highlands, but a similar kinship structure evolved in the Border regions.

The association of tartans with clans was a creation of the 18th century. The wearing of the tartan, a plaid fabric characteristic of a clan, had been forbidden after the last Jacobite rising (1745–1746), and, when it again became lawful in 1782, clan tartans developed rapidly. The commercialization of the Highlands, which actually destroyed the clan system, popularized the tartan pleated skirt, or kilt. See also CLAN.

Housing. The prehistoric colonizers of Scotland were often cave dwellers. But by Roman times the inhabitants seem to have lived mostly in hill forts, sometimes connected with underground shelters or stores. About the same period are usually dated the brochs, or open circular towers of dry-stone masonry, which are most numerous in the Orkney and Shetland islands, the Hebrides, and the northern Highlands. The Celtic monasteries consisted of wooden or wattled huts, but these were replaced by beehive stone buildings, just as the early wooden castles of the Norman barons were transformed into the massive stone fortresses of the later Middle Ages.

In the towns, timber continued in regular use, although many burgh houses also were built solely of stone. Many of these houses still exist and some of them, skillfully modernized, make comfortable living quarters. In the country districts regional influences played an important part, but dry-stone walls of great solidity, tiny or no windows, and thatched roofs with no adequate outlet for smoke from a central fire were common features. In the 19th century, lime was often used to bind the dressed stones together, and corrugated iron took the place of thatch. The animals, which had shared accommodations with the human occupants in the original windowless "black houses," were now separately provided for in byres and stables. The black houses lingered longest in the western islands and Highlands.

The worst modern slums are in the center of the big towns. The local councils are gradually demolishing them and removing their inhabitants to new houses, usually on the outskirts. Glasgow has been largely redeveloped, and its "overspill" has created several new towns. In the redevelop-

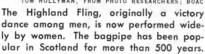

The Highland Fling, originally a victory dance among men, is now performed widely by women. The bagpipe has been popular in Scotland for more than 500 years.

ment of central urban areas, the scarcity of building sites has resulted increasingly in construction of multistory apartment buildings. Since 1960, government assistance has been given to four categories of housing; slum clearance and redevelopment, accommodation for overspill population, houses to meet the needs of incoming industry, and houses for the aged. The housing shortage remains severe because low rents stimulate demand, and high taxes preclude new private construction.

Food and Drink. Many traditional Scottish foods are giving way to packaged and frozen products, but some specialties remain popular. Fish, available in great variety, is prepared in appetizing ways. Apart from the characteristic salmon and sea trout, there are haddocks and other whitefish in profusion, such as the "finnan haddie" (really Findon haddock, after the village of Findon, Kincardine), and the Arbroath "smokie." Finnans usually are split open before smoking, and smokies are smoked whole. Various ports specialize in herring, which can be split open and kippered slowly above oak and birch chips, or pickled in brine, or heavily smoked and cured. The Aberdeen-Angus breed of cattle and the Blackface mutton are world renowned. Game—venison and grouse—is available. Heather honey has an unmistakable bouquet and flavor. The slow ripening of a Scots summer yields soft fruit of excellent quality.

Soup is a Scottish specialty, of which there are endless variations, the best known being broth, a thick soup made with mutton or beef, vegetables, and barley, and cock-a-leekie made with a fowl and lots of leeks. White and black puddings made from oatmeal, suet, and onions lead on to haggis, the traditional pudding containing organ meats of a sheep or calf boiled within the stomach of the animal along with other ingredients. Milk is often prepared in the form of curds and whey or as crowdie, a kind of farm cheese. Scottish breakfasts, based on porridge, are hearty and healthy. Edinburgh restaurants are famous for their teas, accompanied by tea bread, cakes, scones, shortbread, and jams in profusion. Scotch whisky, produced in large quantities for export, also is consumed at home. Scottish brewers make excellent beer, which also is exported.

Religion. The national church, the Church of Scotland, is Presbyterian in government. Each parish has its kirk session, which elects an elder to represent it at the presbytery governing a group of parishes. The presbyteries are grouped in synods, and once a year representatives of the presbyteries meet in a General Assembly at Edinburgh and elect a moderator or chairman. The history of the Church of Scotland since the early 18th century has been largely a record of secessions by dissatisfied minorities. Much the most notable of these was the Disruption of 1843, which took place over the claim of congregations to appoint ministers. In 1929, however, there was a reunion that brought the great majority of Presbyterians back into an enlarged, established church, although there are a number of small, dissenting groups, especially the Free Presbyterians of the northwestern Highlands and islands.

The Roman Catholics are the second-largest religious community in Scotland. Partly owing to Irish immigration, they have gained in numbers and importance. The Episcopal Church of Scotland, the affiliate of the Church of England, is small in numbers but, being supported by many nobles and gentry, has a disproportionately strong influence.

Other Christian denominations represented in Scotland include Congregationalists, Baptists, Methodists, and Unitarians. There are also Jewish synagogues and Mormon missions.

Education. Although Scottish education had a long history before the Reformation, the Reformers' *First Book of Discipline* gave it impetus. Beginning in the 16th century, the church tried to establish schools in every parish.

409

Scottish pubs, such as this one near a Glasgow shipyard, are centers of social life for workingmen.

In the 19th century, education came to be recognized as a function of the state, and the Education (Scotland) Act of 1872 transferred responsibility for primary schools to elected school boards and made school attendance compulsory. Successive acts have in effect created a comprehensive national system of education under the ultimate control of the Scottish Education Department, but with wide powers given to local education committees. These last consist largely of members elected by the ratepayers (local taxpayers) as town and county councilors, but also of members with special knowledge and experience of education. Primary and secondary education in schools provided by these authorities is usually free. It is financed chiefly by central government grants and local taxation. The Education (Scotland) Act of 1945 made the local education authorities responsible for the physical well-being of all children and young persons. In addition to the publicly financed schools, there are numerous independent secondary schools in the towns and a few private boarding schools on the English public school model.

Scotland has four universities that were founded in the 15th and 16th centuries: St. Andrews (1411), Glasgow (1451), Aberdeen (1494), and Edinburgh (1583). The University of Dundee dates from 1881. Institutions founded in the 18th and 19th centuries that were given university charters during the period of expansion in higher education of the 1960's include Heriot-

Watt University in Edinburgh and the University of Strathclyde in Glasgow. Stirling University was founded in 1964. In addition there are teacher training colleges and technical institutes.

DAVID B. HORN, *Author of*
"Great Britain and Europe in the Eighteenth
Century" and "A Short History of the
University of Edinburgh, 1556–1889"

Bibliography

Burleigh, John H. S., *Church History of Scotland* (Oxford 1960).
Daiches, David, *Paradox of Scottish Culture* (Oxford 1964).
Donaldson, Gordon, *Scots Overseas* (Fernhill 1966).
Finlay, Ian, *Scotland Past and Present* (McBride 1957).
Knox, Henry M., *Two Hundred and Fifty Years of Scottish Education* (Oliver 1953).
McCallum, Neil, *It's an Old Scottish Custom* (Vanguard 1952).
McIntosh, Angus, *Introduction to a Survey of Scottish Dialects* (Nelson 1953).

3. Economy

The economy of Scotland, though Scotland is an integral part of Britain and has a broadly similar pattern of economic activities, nonetheless presents several distinctive features. While goods, labor, and capital have enjoyed unrestricted movement between Scotland and England since the act of union in 1707, the Scottish economy has experienced relatively severe cyclical and structural unemployment together with heavy emigration of skilled labor from time to time. The economy has tended to remain unduly dependent on industries suffering periodic decline or those at a competitive disadvantage.

These factors, coupled with a lack of appropriate investment since 1945, help to explain why throughout the 1960's, Scotland's per capita gross domestic product averaged only 89% of the national figure, and unemployment persisted at twice the national level. Economic growth nevertheless has kept pace at least with the rest of Britain. Both the index of industrial production and the total domestic income rose substantially in the 1960's and early 1970's.

Population, Emigration, and Employment. Scotland's population (1971 census) of 5,227,700 is very unevenly distributed. It is densely concentrated in the Central Lowlands from the region west of Glasgow to the North Sea coastal area between Edinburgh and Aberdeen. Less than one fifth of the people live north and west of this central industrial belt, so that the Highlands and islands continue to be an economic region with special problems of development. These areas and the counties bordering England have become virtually depopulated after steadily shrinking since the mid-19th century.

More generally, Scotland has for generations experienced an outward movement of its people. Even in the period from 1951 to 1968 net emigration from Scotland removed 87% of its natural increase in population, though net losses by migration since have been diminishing.

Employment remained virtually constant at 2,100,000 from 1960 to 1970. Declines in male employment were offset by gains in female employment. The work force in the early 1970's was divided among service industries (50.5%), manufacturing (34.8%); construction (9.2%), mining (2.3%), and agriculture and others (3.2%).

Agriculture, Forestry, and Fishing. Employing approximately 68,000 workers, these primary activities are relatively more important to the Scottish economy than are their counterparts in the rest of Britain. Farms, which are noted for beef cattle (Aberdeen-Angus and Shorthorn), lamb, and livestock and dairy products, contribute about 11% to the total national farm output. Crops add only half as much as livestock to output, and the traditional oats has given way to barley as the major cereal grown. Root crops are important. Three fifths of Britain's turnips and rutabagas and one sixth of its potatoes are grown in Scotland. Pasture, permanent and rotational grazing, accounts for 65% of the land in agricultural use. Additionally, a vast amount of acreage in hilly or mountainous areas is rough grazing land suitable only for extensive sheep or cattle raising, a distinctive characteristic of Scottish farming.

Britain's entry into the European Economic Community (EEC) is likely to benefit most branches of Scottish agriculture because productivity per worker compares favorably with European practice. This is especially true of beef production, but the more subsidized hill sheep farms and dairy herds may encounter difficulties when Britain adopts the agricultural policy of the EEC.

Forests, mostly coniferous, whether publicly owned by the Forestry Commission or in private estates, have become a significant factor in land use. Their area rose from 1.4 million acres (570,000 hectares) in 1953 to 1.6 million acres (640,000 hectares) in 1970.

Fishing is mainly for haddock, herring, cod, and whiting in coastal and more distant waters of the North Sea. The industry employs almost 10,000 men and 2,750 vessels.

Traditional Industries. Coal mining, iron and steel manufacturing, papermaking, shipbuilding, textiles—particularly jute spinning and weaving—and whisky distilling have played a dominant role in Scotland's industrial fortunes since the mid-19th century. However, coal mining and shipbuilding have declined sharply since the late 1950's. Few coal mines remain in operation, and despite a remarkable increase in per capita productivity, coal mining remains unprofitable.

Shipbuilding, concentrated largely on the upper and lower reaches of the Clyde River, underwent drastic reorganization during the 1960's. Much of this change arose from a 1966 report of a government investigation, which promised financial aid for mergers in the industry. Tonnage launched fell by 40% and employment by 20,000 workers as firms were amalgamated or liquidated.

Iron founding and papermaking also suffered upheaval through falling demand, company mergers, and exposure to competitive imports of Scandinavian pulp and paper products when the European Free Trade Area removed tariffs in 1968. Textile output as a whole stagnated, though Scots knitted woolen garments maintained a reputation for quality. Of Scotland's traditional products, only whisky enjoyed a boom throughout most of the postwar period, though expanding production created few extra jobs.

Industrial Development. Even before the Committee of Inquiry into the Scottish Economy submitted its report in 1961, it had been widely recognized that Scotland had too small a share in Britain's growth industries. These rapidly expanding sectors were either science- and research-based activities—such as electronics and chemicals—or assembly-line production, typified by the motor vehicle and office equipment factories. Guided by administrative controls and stimulated

FENNO JACOBS, FROM BLACK STAR

Scotch whisky owes its popularity in part to a slow aging process and its distinctive spring water.

by fiscal incentives, a number of new industries gained ground in Scotland during the 1950's and 1960's. Two big motor assembly plants were established, one in Bathgate designed to produce commercial trucks and farm tractors, the other in Lynwood, near Glasgow, geared to assemble compact private cars. Firms already prominent in light engineering and electronics opened factories in central Scotland, producing computers, instruments, business machines, aircraft, and airplane engines.

While many British concerns were involved, North American enterprise also contributed substantially to the diversification and updating of Scotland's industrial economy. By 1969, 89 U. S. companies had established manufacturing plants in Scotland, employing 73,000, or 10% of all those engaged in manufactures and yielding 12% of total output in Scotland.

In the fuel and power industries, a start was made with nuclear-powered generation of electricity, and natural gas and oil discoveries offshore in the North Sea were being developed in the early 1970's. Technically advanced but expensive hydroelectric generating capacity had previously brought extensive social benefits in the northwestern half of the country.

Transport developments since the 1960's have included steady increases in air traffic, road construction, and the completion of major bridges over the rivers Forth, Tay, and Clyde. Branch railway lines have been greatly reduced.

Herring fishing is an important factor in the economy of the Shetland Islands. A crew unloads its catch at Scalloway harbor.

Government Assistance. The local employment acts of 1960 and 1963 provided for government assistance to so-called "development districts," areas with unemployment above 4.5%, which was applicable to almost all of Scotland. Previously somewhat neglected, Scotland has received above average per capita levels of public investment since 1963, especially for schools, housing, roads, and environmental services. New towns were developed in central Scotland at East Kilbride, Cumbernauld, Glenrothes, Livingston, and Irvine.

Under the industrial development act of 1966, firms setting up in Scotland obtained cash grants from the government, and between 1967 and 1974, manufacturers in the development districts were paid a labor subsidy known as the regional employment premium. Although these incentives for regional industrial development stimulated Scotland's economic expansion, they were extremely costly as a method of creating employment.

Banking and Finance. Since the mid-19th century, Scotland has been notable for the scale and influence of its commercial banks and investment trusts. The Bank of Scotland dates from 1695. In 1958 a committee studying the British monetary system described Scotland as one of the relatively "overbanked" countries of the world, so strong was its branch banking tradition. The number of branches has been steadily reduced as three major commercial banking groups have been formed by mergers. These new groupings continue to exercise their right, sanctioned by the bank charter act of 1844, to issue their own bank notes.

The investment trust is a Scottish invention of the 1870's. In the early 1970's investment trusts registered in Edinburgh, Dundee, Aberdeen, and Glasgow accounted for a third of all British investment trust assets. Unlike the commercial banks, which have tended to concentrate on Scottish business, the investment trusts have worldwide interests.

There are seven major life insurance companies in Scotland, but building societies are, on the contrary, much less in evidence in Scotland than in England. This may reflect the fact that, since the late 1940's, 80% of all houses built in Scotland have been government financed, compared with 50% of houses built in England. Scotland has had to overcome a legacy of bad housing conditions, requiring substantial public subsidy if rents were to continue at low levels and slum clearance to proceed apace.

Tourism. No account of Scotland's economy is complete without noting that the greater part of the country, being sparsely populated, hilly, and abounding in lochs, inlets, and islands, is well endowed as a tourist mecca. A steadily growing number of holiday accommodations and improved facilities for both winter and summer vacation pastimes—including skiing, mountaineering, angling, sailing, and golf—have produced an expanding tourist trade. It is believed that more than 4.25 million residents of Britain vacation in Scotland each year, and 700,000 visitors arrive from overseas.

IAN G. STEWART
University of Edinburgh

Further Reading: Campbell, Roy H., *Scotland Since 1707: The Rise of an Industrial Society* (Barnes & Noble 1965); McGrone, Gavin, *Scotland's Future* (Kelley 1969).

4. Government

The government of Scotland is the government of the United Kingdom of Great Britain and Northern Ireland. Scottish representatives sit in Parliament with their English, Welsh, and Irish counterparts, and since the late 19th century the Scots have held the office of prime minister with disproportionately high frequency. Yet, a feeling of Scots nationalism persists, and there has been a movement for a degree of separatism or some reconstruction of the central government.

Government administration in Scotland is subject to the control of the department of the secretary of state for Scotland (Scottish office), a ministry of the central government in London. The Scottish system of local government is complex and in some respects archaic. Reform movements have been directed toward bringing administrative districts and taxing authorities more in line with population distribution.

The Scottish Ministry. While the act of union in 1707 gave the British Parliament ultimate control of the government of Scotland, in practice the crown retained control, acting through a Scot-

Sheep raising for the wool industry represents a practical land use for the Highlands and islands. A herd moves through the narrow streets of Inverness en route to railway shipping yards.

tish nobleman appointed as a third British secretary of state responsible for Scottish administration. Later, the crown depended on an active party politician who, with some assistance from the Scottish lord advocate and other legal officers, virtually ruled Scotland as "manager." Sometimes it was the lord advocate who acted as an omnicompetent minister for Scotland.

The first step toward the present system was the institution of the office of Scottish secretary in 1885. A member of the British cabinet, he was the head of the Scottish office, manned by civil servants, and had special responsibility for public order and education. Functional boards of experts previously established, such as those supervising lunatic asylums and prisons, manufacturing, fisheries, health, housing, and poor relief, long retained independence of action, but were gradually regrouped, staffed by civil servants, and brought under the control of the Scottish secretary.

The powers of the secretary were steadily extended, and in 1926 he was granted the improved status of secretary of state. Acts of 1928 and 1939 reorganized the old boards as departments within the secretary of state's office.

Ancient crafts skillfully practiced in modern Scotland include textile work and metalwork. Tartan may be woven on hand-worked looms as well as in factories. Silversmithing dates from medieval times.

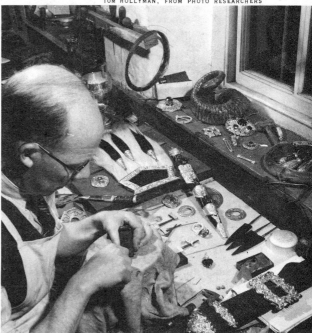

Hunting grouse remains a popular pastime and social event for Scotsmen and for tourists.

Since 1939, with minor changes for efficiency, the secretary of state for Scotland has directly controlled the whole executive government of Scotland. His office is divided into four administrative departments: agriculture and fisheries, education, home and health, and development, each headed by a secretary based in St. Andrew's House in Edinburgh. A permanent undersecretary of state, who is the principal adviser of the secretary of state, presides over the whole organization. While the secretary of state and his officials make many executive decisions, most of their work is supervisory and advisory.

The secretary of state for Scotland does not depend entirely on his civil servants for advice. Since 1952 he has had the assistance of three parliamentary undersecretaries, politicians like himself, as well as a minister of state senior to the undersecretaries. In addition, he can consult the Scottish law officers, the lord advocate, and the solicitor general. The vast extension of Scottish office functions justifies this division of labor. It should be noted, however, that the secretary of state does not have complete control of all government business in Scotland. A number of London-based departments, such as the ministry of labour and national service, operate in Scotland, and occasionally functions are transferred from the Scottish office to one of these United Kingdom departments. In addition, there is a growing number of semipublic or wholly public commissions responsible for economic development in a particular field.

Local Government. Prior to May 1975, Scotland was divided for administrative purposes into 480 local units (four counties of cities—Edinburgh, Glasgow, Aberdeen, and Dundee—and 21 large burghs, 176 small burghs, 33 counties, and 196 districts). A government white paper in 1963 proposed a drastic reorganization of local govern-

ment machinery in the interest of greater efficiency. By the Local Government (Scotland) Bill enacted Oct. 25, 1973, Scotland's local government was completely reorganized, effective May 16, 1975. Under the new plan for local government, the counties were abolished and were replaced by nine regions—Highland, Grampian, Tayside, Fife, Lothian, Central, Borders, Strathclyde, and Dumfries and Galloway. These regions in turn were divided into a total of 53 districts. In addition, the reorganization plan created the three island areas of Orkney, Shetland, and the Western Isles.

Each of the newly created units has a council with councilors elected for four-year terms, and a chairman elected each year by the councilors. The functions allocated between regions and districts are much the same as between counties and districts in England. The first councilors under the reorganization plan were elected in May 1974, pending the official coming into existence of the plan on May 16, 1975.

A Local Government Boundary Commission in Scotland, similar to corresponding commissions in England and Wales, was created to advise the secretary of state on electoral matters and the boundaries of local authorities. A commissioner for local administration has the authority to investigate any complaints of maladministration that may be brought by the public. This commissioner deals directly with the council concerned in settling the complaint.

DAVID B. HORN*, *Author of "Great Britain and Europe in the Eighteenth Century"*

Further Reading: MacCormick, Neil, ed., *Scottish Debate: Essays on Scottish Nationalism* (Oxford 1970); Milne, Sir David, *The Scottish Office and Other Scottish Government Departments* (Oxford 1958); Pryde, George S., *Central and Local Government in Scotland Since 1707* (1968); Wolfe, J. N., ed., *Government and Nationalism in Scotland* (Aldine 1969).

5. Law

In medieval times the law administered in Scotland derived from several independent sources. Canon and civil law, largely mediated through clerics, and the pithy legislation of the Scottish Parliament were the most rational elements. These were supplemented by feudal and burgh customs.

Until the establishment of a central professional judiciary in 1532, no consistent and controlled development of the national legal system was possible. In 1681, Sir James Dalrymple, 1st Viscount Stair, most eminent of Scottish judges, published the first edition of his *Institutions of the Laws of Scotland,* which laid the foundations of modern Scots law. Stair, in effect, restated the civil law of Scotland in accordance with the most enlightened European civilian thought of the natural-law school. Up to the Napoleonic Wars, those aspiring to practice in the Scottish courts usually prepared themselves by studying civil or Roman law at the great European law schools, mainly those of France or the Netherlands. Thus, the foundations of Scots law, apart from land law, are civilian or Romanistic. (See CIVIL LAW.) Though Scots law has not been codified, special authority is given to the institutional works of a few outstanding writers, such as Stair. Especially during the 19th and 20th centuries, however, indirect English influences on Scots law have had the effect of producing to some extent a mixed or hybrid system comparable to that of South Africa, Quebec, Ceylon, or Louisiana.

Civil Procedure. Scottish civil law, like Roman law, divides those under full age into pupils and minors. The age of puberty is 14 for males and 12 for females, though 16 is now by statute the minimum age for marriage. A minor in Scots law has considerable contractual capacity, especially if his father is dead and no curator has been appointed. He may also marry or make a will of movables without parental consent. Divorce has been recognized since the Reformation in the 16th century. Grounds include adultery, desertion, cruelty (including habitual drunkenness), incurable insanity, and presumed death. A testator's power to dispose as he chooses of his estate by will is restricted by the recognition given by Scots law to the legal rights of the widow, or widower, and children, which may extend to one half or two thirds of the movable estate.

In Scots civil litigation, a person can be bound by an informal gratuitous contract or indeed by a bare promise. Thus a person can sue to enforce a benefit that was promised to him under a contract to which he was not a party. The rules applicable in *contract* are generally Romanistic, but English influences affect certain branches of the law, especially commercial contracts. Thus, though in general under Scots law a real right cannot be transferred by contract without delivery, an exception to this rule is made in the case of sale. Scots law provides comprehensive remedies against unjust enrichment to recover money or property that have come into the possession of another contrary to the intention of the true owner, or where the purpose for the transfer cannot be achieved.

In the law of *delict*, the theory of Scots law is that there is a general right of redress for the willful or negligent infliction of unjustifiable harm. Besides this general right, there are also a number of delicts specified by name, with particular rules of their own. The English concept of *trespass* as an actionable tort is unknown to Scots law, but a delictual action can be brought in respect of damage caused to land or buildings by an intruder. Threatened intrusion and persistent intruders may be restrained by *interdict*, called "injunction" by the English. Scots law grants money damages by way of solace for wounded feelings, as, for example, grief resulting from bereavement or affront to the personality due to insult. Thus slander is actionable, even without publication to a third party.

The Scots law regarding acquisition and transfer of movables is in the main founded on civil-law principles. Apart from minor exceptions, it is impossible to constitute security over movables without transferring possession. Land law is still in theory feudal, and subinfeudation is familiar, the service having been commuted into a perpetual payment known as feu-duty.

Criminal Procedure. Scottish criminal law reached maturity later than private law and thus avoided the disadvantages of the premature rigidity that affected English law. Thus, Scots law, through judicial decision, developed liberal doctrines regarding insanity, diminished responsibility, and provocation, which only in relatively modern times have been partly adopted into English law.

In Scotland, unlike England, the more serious crimes are not covered by legislation. Apart from legislation, the sources of Scottish criminal law are to be found in the practice of the criminal courts influenced to some extent by the civil and canon law and mediated through the institutional writers and justiciary reports. Criminal prosecution in Scotland is essentially a public and not a private duty. The lord advocate, or his representatives, ultimately decide when to prosecute, the nature of the charge, and the appropriate procedure, whether that of the high court of justiciary or sheriff court.

CHARLES MAY, FROM BLACK STAR

Edinburgh's main thoroughfare, Princes Street, is bordered by public gardens. View is from the monument to Sir Walter Scott.

Pretrial procedure in Scotland is conducted in private and therefore cannot be reported in the press. Further, all publicity that might influence opinion for or against the accused before trial is absolutely forbidden. Both prosecution and defense must disclose their witnesses, and documents they will produce, to each other before trial, and, while the accused is entitled to ample notice of the charge alleged against him, he, for his part, is required to notify before trial any special defense, for example, alibi. Trial in solemn procedure—that is, for a serious crime—is before a judge and jury of 15. The verdict may be by simple majority and may be in one of three forms: guilty, not guilty, and not proven. The latter two are verdicts of absolute acquittal.

See also GREAT BRITAIN—*Government* (Judicial System; Scotland).

T. B. SMITH, *University of Edinburgh*

Further Reading: Gloag, William M., and Henderson, Robert C., *Introduction to the Law of Scotland*, 6th ed., ed. by Andrew D. Gibb and Norman M. L. Walker (Green 1957); Smith, Thomas Broun, *A Short Commentary on the Laws of Scotland* (Stevens 1962).

6. History

Scotland had a long history of fierce independence, resisting onslaughts by Romans, Anglo-Saxons, and the English, until the act of union in 1707 united England and Scotland under one king and parliament. A progression of events, including union of the crowns of England and Scotland in 1603, and questions of economic viability made union inevitable in 1707. Once effected, however, many Scots felt regretful and resentful, evaluating Scotland as the junior partner in the merger. The union has survived and prospered. The Scots and the English alike consider themselves British, but Scottish nationalism flickers periodically, usually in negative response to poor economics.

Before 1286. The earliest inhabitants of Scotland have left few traces of their presence during the Old Stone Age (before about 8000 B. C.). They may all have been visiting hunters and fishermen. In the New Stone Age (about 4000–2000 B. C.), however, two colonizing movements can be clearly traced. One of these started in the Mediterranean and reached the western and northern coasts of Scotland by way of the Bay of Biscay along an old trade route from the Mediterranean to the Baltic. The other came from the European continent across the North Sea to the east coast. Settlements were made about the same time by these colonists on the western and eastern coasts, and the river valleys were followed inland. These newcomers were agriculturists who reared cattle and owned domestic animals, and they gradually colonized Scotland. The western people, characterized anatomically as longheaded, are noted for their burial cairns, each containing a series of chambers attached to a kind of family vault, while the roundheaded eastern colonists buried their dead individually in short cists (graves lined with stone slabs).

In the centuries before the birth of Christ, new settlements were made by Celtic peoples, familiar with the working of iron, who lived in organized communities under chieftains in hill forts. It was for defense against them that the Romans, after failing to conquer Scotland, constructed the walls from the Tyne River, England, to the Solway Firth, and from the Clyde River to the Firth of Forth. Punitive expeditions were made beyond the walls from time to time, but northern Scotland remained little influenced by the Romans. Even the south, though militarily occupied at times, had virtually no contact with Roman civilization.

Picts, Scots, Britons, Angles, Norsemen. Before the withdrawal of the Roman legions from Britain, Scots from Ireland were establishing their power in what is now Argyll. Soon afterward the Angles began to occupy Lothian, and the Britons who had lived under Roman rule were driven westward. Thus, by about 600 A. D. four peoples were living on the Scottish mainland. The Picts occupied most of the Highlands, except for the Scots colony in Dalriada (Argyll), while the western Lowlands (Strathclyde) were held by partially Romanized Britons and the southeastern Lowlands (Lothian) by the Angles. For a time it seemed likely that the Angles would extend their sway to the north and west, but their progress was decisively checked by the Picts at the Battle of Nechtansmere (685).

The Norse raids and invasions added a fresh element to the population and it was largely owing to the needs of defense that Kenneth MacAlpin (Kenneth I) secured recognition as ruler of a united Pict-Scot kingdom, sometimes called Alban (about 843). Not until after the Battle of Carham (1016 or 1018) was Lothian finally added to Alban. In 1034, Strathclyde, after a long period as a satellite state, was also incorporated in a united kingdom of Scotland, which did not at first include the islands or the northernmost mainland counties. Caithness and Sutherland were recovered from the Norsemen by William the Lion (William I, reigned 1165–1214), though royal authority there was merely nominal until the reign of James IV. After the Battle of Carham (1016 or 1018) was Lothian Hebrides and the Isle of Man (1266). But here, too, until the reign of James IV, the lords of the Isles were more often in practice independent sovereigns than Scottish vassals. Orkney and Shetland were pledged to Scotland by Christian I of Denmark in 1468–1469 as part of his daughter's dowry on her marriage to James III and since then have been part of the Scottish kingdom. Geographic, but not political, unity was thus established.

Development of Christianity. Saint Ninian and Saint Kentigern were among the earliest Christian missionaries known to have worked in Scotland, but the Irish Scot, Saint Columba, probably did most to Christianize the Highlands from his base on Iona during the second half of the 6th century. The Celtic Church was a powerful missionary body, but it lacked the close-knit Roman organization. Defeated at the Synod of Whitby (664), the Celtic clergy retired to Scotland and within half a century both Picts and Scots had accepted the Roman supremacy and customs. Dunkeld, the ecclesiastical capital, was soon superseded by St. Andrews. Saint Margaret, an English princess who married Malcolm III, did much in the late 11th century to bring the Scottish Church into closer touch with the reforms effected in the Roman Catholic Church. Under her sons, who reigned in the first half of the 12th century, regular dioceses were developed, Continental orders of monks were introduced, and a parochial system started. The payment of tithes for the support of parish churches was made compulsory.

The youngest of Queen Margaret's sons, David I (reigned 1124–1153), had spent much time at

In Glasgow, municipal buildings face George Square. Known as the City Chambers, they were built in 1889.

CHARLES MAY, FROM BLACK STAR

the English court and had married an English heiress. He reorganized the whole fabric of the Scottish Church and state on Anglo-Norman lines. The old Celtic use of collateral succession to the crown was replaced by primogeniture. Land was granted to Anglo-Norman nobles, who held it from David I and acted as his lieutenants in the maintenance of law and order. Sheriffs were established in the royal castles to do justice, collect taxes and rents, and generally carry out the king's orders, while many burghs were created to serve as military strongholds and trading posts. Particularly in the north, the new system supplemented rather than replaced the old Celtic practices, but even there it proved a unifying factor.

Emergence of the Border with England. In spite of his English connections, David I pursued the policy of his predecessors of expansion southward, and due to English weakness in the reign of Stephen, he succeeded in mastering the northern counties of England. However, Henry II recovered control of these lands on his succession to the English throne. In an attempt to regain them for Scotland, William the Lion was captured at Alnwick in 1174 and forced to accept the Treaty of Falaise, by which he recognized that his whole kingdom was held as a fief from the English king. Suzerainty over the kingdom of Scotland was surrendered by Richard I of England in 1189 in exchange for funds needed to finance his crusade.

Thus, the frontier was fixed in practice during the 13th century by the Tweed River, the Cheviot Hills, and the Solway Firth, and for about 100 years there was a period of comparative peace between England and Scotland. Partly for this reason, the reigns of Alexander II (1214–1249), successor to William the Lion, and Alexander III (1249–1286), are sometimes regarded as Scotland's golden age. A system of centralized government was established, trade and agriculture prospered, and the Hebrides were recovered from the Norse kings.

From the Wars of Independence to the Union of the Crowns: 1286–1603. The deaths of Alexander III and, four years later, his infant granddaughter Margaret, the maid of Norway, on her way to become queen of Scots, enabled Edward I of England to secure recognition by the Scots of his claim to be feudal superior of all Scotland. John Balliol (reigned 1292–1296) was chosen king of Scotland, and after his coronation at Scone he paid homage to Edward I as lord paramount. Treated as a vassal, Balliol was goaded into defiance, trusting partly to the alliance he had made with England's enemy, France, in 1295. Thus began the Scottish Wars of Independence.

Edward's campaign in Scotland in 1296 was a complete success, and Balliol had to resign his crown. William Wallace then rose and routed an English army at Stirling Bridge (1297), only to be completely defeated the following year at Falkirk. Edward was preoccupied with French wars and internal opposition, but by 1305 he had captured Wallace and regained control of Scotland. The Scottish cause was unexpectedly taken up and carried to a successful conclusion by an Anglo-Norman noble, Robert the Bruce (Robert I, reigned 1306–1329), whose grandfather had been the chief rival to Balliol in the competition for the Scottish throne.

Although he had murdered his most dangerous rival, John (the Red) Comyn, in the Franciscan church in Dumfries in 1306, shortly before assuming the crown, Bruce was supported by most of the Scottish clergy and lesser gentry. While Edward II of England was wrangling with his barons, Bruce steadily extended his power in Scotland. Victorious at Bannockburn in 1314, he secured the freedom of his adopted country, al-

"ILLUSTRATED," FROM BLACK STAR

Robert the Bruce defeated the English at Bannockburn in 1314. Statue is at Stirling Castle.

though this was not formally recognized until 1328 by the Treaty of Northampton.

Bruce died the following year, and the new and ambitious king of England, Edward III, gave support against Bruce's son, David II (reigned 1329–1371), to Edward Balliol (son of King John Balliol) and reopened the Wars of Independence. Edward Balliol defeated David II's supporters near Perth in August 1332 and was crowned king at Scone the following month, acknowledging Edward III as his feudal superior. In 1334 he ceded to Edward III the southern counties of Scotland from Haddington to Dumfries, while David II went into exile in France. The Scots nationalists soon defeated Balliol, but David II, when attempting to invade England as France's ally in the Hundred Years' War, was taken prisoner at Neville's Cross (1346). To secure the return of their king in 1357, the Scots undertook to pay an enormous ransom. By making heavy taxation necessary, this helped foster regular representation of the burghs in Parliament. Until his death in 1371, David II's Anglophile tendencies threatened Scottish independence.

The Crown Versus the Barons. By this time the ultimate results of the Normanization of Scotland were evident. The Anglo-Norman nobles, originally intended to serve as agents of the central government, became more independent. The central government under Robert II (reigned 1371–1390), grandson of Robert Bruce and founder of the Stuart (Stewart) dynasty, and his son, Robert III (reigned 1390–1406), was unable to control them, while Gaelic tribalism in the Highlands and islands revived.

For the whole of the 15th century and the first half of the 16th, the main theme of Scottish history was the continuous struggle between the crown and the barons. The Stuart kings suffered from a fundamental weakness in that they were merely a noble house raised to the throne. At the beginning of this period the great nobles were already overmighty subjects, owning great tracts of land within which they ruled as petty kings, supported by hereditary grants of judicial and fiscal privilege made to their ancestors by the crown. The kings could only hope to destroy these too powerful subjects by invoking the help of some of their rivals. The result was that the destruction of one noble house was usually accompanied by the rise of another house equally threatening to the monarchy. The Scottish Parliament, which took shape in the 14th century, was mainly a feudal assembly and the Scottish Commons were incapable of giving to the crown even the modest measure of support sometimes offered by their English contemporaries to their king.

James I (reigned 1406–1437), son of Robert III, after his return from a long period of imprisonment in England, set the pattern for most of his successors. From 1424 his rule was inspired by a determination to put down the nobles and reestablish effective royal authority. His assassination by a malcontent clique brought his son, a child of six, to the throne as James II (reigned 1437–1460). The second James broke the power of the earls of Douglas (1455) and was killed besieging Roxburgh Castle, which had been held by the English since the Wars of Independence. His son, James III (reigned 1460–1488), was more interested in the arts and sciences than in government or war. His reign was marked by almost continuous baronial unrest and opposition, culminating in his defeat in battle near Stirling and in his murder afterward.

James IV (reigned 1488–1513) soon gained the upper hand of the nobles and reduced most of the country to obedience. He temporarily increased the royal revenue from crown lands by substituting for short leases permanent tenures in exchange for a fixed annual feu-duty, but continued inflation soon reduced the advantages of the new system. He also developed the practice of diverting to the crown a substantial share of the revenues of the church, which owned almost half the wealth of Scotland. He negotiated with European states and signed a treaty of perpetual peace with England in 1502. His marriage to Margaret Tudor, elder daughter of Henry VII of England, a year later, was destined to bring about the union of the crowns of England and Scotland in 1603. Reverting to the traditional alliance with France, James IV invaded England with a large army, only to be completely routed and killed at Flodden in 1513.

The Reformation; Mary, Queen of Scots. Another minority followed, with faction fights between the nobles until James V (reigned 1513–1542) became old enough to establish his personal government in 1528. The burning of Patrick Hamilton, a young reformist, as a heretic at St. Andrews in the same year made the Reformation a live issue for Scotland. It was closely linked with the main problem of the reign, relations with England. James V was a conservative on both questions. Declining Henry VIII's invitation to join with him against the pope, he adhered to the alliance with France. His half-hearted invasion of England led to another military disaster at Solway Moss (1542), followed shortly by his death a few days after he had received news of the birth of a daughter to his second wife, Mary of Guise.

This infant princess was to become Mary, Queen of Scots (reigned 1542–1567). Sent to France when only five years old, to preserve her from the English, she grew up a Frenchwoman and was married to the dauphin Francis, who became king of France, as Francis II, in 1559.

At this time, James V's widow, Mary of Guise, governed Scotland as regent, and French garrisons had been established in Scotland. National resentment at foreign rule reinforced the nascent Protestantism of some of the nobles and of many middle-class townspeople. Riots occurred and churches were destroyed. John Knox thundered against "the monstrous regiment [government] of women." The reformist lords known as the "Congregation" secured the backing of an English fleet and army and, after the death of Mary of Guise (1560), the French garrison surrendered at Leith. The Treaty of Edinburgh that year virtually ended the Franco-Scottish alliance and pointed the way to close association with the old enemy, England. Also in 1560 the Scottish Parliament denied papal supremacy and forbade the celebration of the Mass in Scotland.

The question of what was to be substituted for the old church was a basic issue in Scotland for over 100 years. Although the Reformation Parliament adopted a Confession of Faith, Queen Mary, who returned to Scotland in 1561 after her husband died, never accepted it. Most of the dignitaries and priests of the old church held office until they died or resigned, and the monasteries were not dissolved. The Reformers found great difficulty in obtaining control of sufficient resources to enable them to set up the new church on a national basis. There were no funds to carry out the far-reaching plans for hospitals, poor relief, and a national system of education, as set out in the *First Book of Discipline* (1561). At first superintendents had been appointed to exercise a measure of supervision over former church dioceses, but the rise of the Presbyterians, led by Andrew Melville, led to a frontal attack on the historic position of the bishops and to the demand for complete parity of ministers as set out in the *Second Book of Discipline* (1578). Presbyteries, synods, and a General Assembly composed of ministers and elders were established, and the new constitution of the church was approved by Parliament in 1592.

The effective reign of Mary, Queen of Scots, from 1561 was short and inglorious. John Knox and his associates were implacably hostile to a Roman Catholic queen, and she showed no flair for government. Her approach to politics was to try to play off one faction of the nobles against another. Her marriage to Lord Darnley (Henry Stuart), a possible successor to the English throne, made Elizabeth I of England suspicious of her intentions, and when Darnley was found murdered in 1567, Queen Mary was believed to have been an accomplice of the murderers. Mary then married James Hepburn, 4th Earl of Bothwell, a step that cost her both Roman Catholic and Protestant support. While a prisoner in Lochleven Castle, she was compelled to abdicate in favor of her infant son by Darnley, James VI (reigned 1567–1625), later James I of England (reigned 1603–1625). She escaped, only to be

John Knox House, Canongate Street, Edinburgh, where the Protestant reformer reportedly lived in the 1560's.

defeated by the regent, her half-brother, the Earl of Moray, at Langside (1568). Politically bankrupt, she crossed into England, but the civil war she had started did not end until 1573.

James VI; Union of the Crowns. During James VI's minority, Scotland was governed once again by regents, and factious strife followed on the end of the civil war. Esmé Stuart, created duke of Lennox in 1581 by James VI, tried to restore French influence and managed to bring about the execution of the Anglophile regent, James Douglas, 4th Earl of Morton, in 1581. Lennox' opponents, however, seized the young King, locked him up in Ruthven Castle, and governed the country in his name (1582–1583).

By this time James VI was old enough, at 17, to take over the government. Escaping from Ruthven Castle, he soon got rid of the Ruthven lords. His ambition was to become king of England as great-great-grandson of Henry VII and the legitimate successor to Elizabeth I. This meant that although he flirted from time to time with the continental Catholic powers, his policy had to be basically Protestant and Anglophile. Even the execution of Mary, his mother, at Fotheringhay Castle in 1587, did not seriously impair the good relations between England and Scotland. James reaped the reward of his complaisance. On Elizabeth's death in 1603, he was recognized as the rightful king of England. Thus the crowns of England and Scotland were united.

From the Union of the Crowns to the Union of the Kingdoms: 1603–1707. James VI had firm ideas about royal prerogative. Even before 1603, he had worked to strengthen the reputation and power of the monarchy. Knowing bishops to be useful in securing state control of the church, James succeeded in reestablishing the office of bishop, though shorn of much of its powers. The ancient constitution of the Scottish Parliament made the bishops especially useful to the king, owing to their role in electing the lords of the articles, the committee of the Parliament often entrusted with its lawmaking powers.

James' removal to London greatly strengthened the monarchy. No longer was he personally in danger from lawless nobles and Calvinist fanatics. Backed by the greater resources of England, he sat in London and governed all Scotland with his pen. Both Parliament and the General Assembly could be packed, and the Scots privy council could be relied on to carry out the King's wishes. Only on one occasion did James revisit his native country, but he continued to take an active interest in its government. The union of 1603 was a personal union, and James would have liked to bring the two countries closer together. His rather halfhearted efforts were resisted in both countries, and it was only in ecclesiastical affairs that James made much progress. The Five Articles of Perth (1618) strengthened the position of the Scottish bishops and enforced on the Scots a more ritualistic form of church service and sacraments.

Scotland and the English Civil War.
James VI knew when to stop, but his successor Charles I (reigned 1625–1649), unfamiliar with his Scots subjects, set out to complete what his father had begun. A book of canons, which altered doctrine, was published in 1635. Changes in ritual were enforced by the issue in 1637 of a service book, similar to the English Book of Common Prayer, which had not been sanctioned either by Parliament or General Assembly. The use of this new form of service at the High Kirk of Edinburgh (the present Church of St. Giles) led to disturbances in the church, followed by rioting in the streets. Since other steps taken by Charles I had alienated most of the Scots nobles, all classes joined to sign the national covenant of 1638, which professed loyalty to the King but bound its signatories to resist these innovations in religion. Twice Charles tried to reduce Scotland by force in the first and second Bishops' Wars (1639–1641), but the Scots army defeated him and advanced into northern England. This disaster brought to an end Charles' 11-year tyranny in England and made possible the work of the English Long Parliament.

When the civil war began in England, the Scots Presbyterians naturally sympathized with the opponents of the King. In exchange for a promise to establish the presbyterian system of church government in Scotland, England, and Ireland, the Scots, by the solemn league and covenant of 1643, agreed to give active support to the English Parliament with its Presbyterian majority. Scots regiments fought against the King, especially at Marston Moor (1644), but James Graham, 1st Marquess of Montrose, a former Covenanter, changed sides and raised a Highland army to fight for Charles I. The Presbyterian forces were strong enough to defeat Montrose at Philiphaugh (1645), but by this time it was clear that control of the English Parliament was passing from the Presbyterians to the Independents, who hated presbytery as much as episcopacy and would never carry out the bargain of 1643.

After his final defeat in England, Charles I offered to establish Presbyterianism in Scotland for three years. A Scots army then invaded England, only to be routed at Preston (1648). When the English Parliament executed Charles I in 1649, the Scots proclaimed his son king as Charles II. This new threat to Puritan ascendancy was destroyed by Oliver Cromwell's victories at Dunbar (1650) and Worcester (1651). Cromwell sought to conciliate the Scots by offering them an incorporating union with England with some representation in the London Parliament and freedom to trade with the English colonies. This did not survive long enough to prove its value, but it was a precedent for the future.

Revolution of 1688.
The Restoration of 1660 brought back the old system in Scotland much more completely than in England. Parliament was again controlled by the king through the lords of the articles and the privy council. The Episcopalian system was reimposed and maintained in spite of the armed protests of Presbyterian extremists at Rullion Green, in the Pentland Hills, in 1666 and at Drumclog in 1679. Captive Covenanters were often punished by transportation to the American colonies. In 1687, however, Charles II's successor, James VII of Scotland and James II of England (reigned 1685–1688) offered toleration. Many were prepared to accept this, but others refused to share a toleration granted equally to Catholics.

Scotland accepted the Revolution of 1688 as it had accepted the Restoration—without having done anything effectual to bring it about. Whereas in England the Revolution was conservative, in Scotland it really was revolutionary. The Scottish Parliament was freed from the lords of the articles and became a sovereign lawmaking assembly (1690). Even more revolutionary was the establishment of the Church of Scotland as a Presbyterian national organization. The General Assembly met in 1690 for the first time since 1653. This turn of events was due largely to the refusal of most of the Episcopalian clergy to take the oaths of allegiance to William III and Mary, which convinced William that he must depend on the Presbyterians.

Need for Union.
In some ways the most important result of the Revolution was the union of the English and Scottish parliaments (1707). As long as the king governed Scotland and kept control of the Scottish Parliament, no one in England felt any need for closer union. Once the Scottish Parliament had escaped from royal control, however, William III (reigned 1689–1702) found himself expected to serve two masters. By adopting the Darien Scheme of colonizing the Panama area in America against the will of Spain, the Parliament threatened to ruin his foreign policy, which required good relations with Spain.

When, under Queen Anne, England engaged in the War of the Spanish Succession while Scotland continued to sympathize with England's enemy, France, political and strategic arguments for complete union became overwhelming from the English point of view. The Scots would have preferred a federal style of union, which England would not accept. Forced to choose between England and France, they thought the interests of the Presbyterian Church were safer with Protestant, though Episcopalian, England than with Roman Catholic France. Also the bribe of free trade with England's colonies tempted Scots mer-

Holyrood Castle, Edinburgh, was the residence of Mary, Queen of Scots, from 1561 to 1567.

chants, though they realized that economic union with England would mean the ruin of some Scottish industries protected by tariffs. What Scotland felt most was the loss of its Parliament. The Scots did, however, retain their legal system and Presbyterian Church.

After Union. The union of the parliaments ended the political history of Scotland as an independent state, but facilitated the economic and cultural developments that made the 18th century the most prosperous and distinguished period of Scottish history. Glasgow flourished on the profits of trade with North America, above all in tobacco, and became the hub of Scottish industry. The trade with England in beef cattle prospered. New crops, especially turnips and potatoes, were introduced. Grasses were planted on arable land, and regular rotations of crops developed. Fallowing, draining, liming, and manuring became normal agricultural practice. Landlords granted long leases to their tenants and showed them how to increase yields. Large-scale forestry, shelter belts, and fields enclosed by dry-stone dikes became features of the Scottish landscape. Government funds helped to extend the linen industry and herring fisheries. Revenues from estates confiscated from the Jacobite supporters of the exiled Stuarts were devoted to founding spinning schools and encouraging home weaving. The metallurgical and chemical industries operated on a large scale.

Edinburgh produced or drew to itself leading historians and philosophers, scientists and architects, painters and literary men, doctors and surgeons. The fierce concentration on religious controversies moderated, though the embers still glowed and came to life in such episodes as the anti-Catholic riots of 1779.

End of Jacobitism. For half a century after the union the basic political issue in Scotland was between supporters of the House of Hanover and union with England, and supporters of the House of Stuart and an independent Scotland. On two occasions this led to civil wars—in 1715 and 1745–1746—but on neither occasion was there the slightest chance of a permanent Stuart victory. Only massive help from the court of France could have turned the tide, and this was not forthcoming. Even if it had been, the appearance of French fleets and armies on British coasts and battlefields would have provoked a national reaction fatal to the Stuart cause. By mid-18th century, Jacobitism, or support for the exiled Roman Catholic Stuart pretenders, was moribund.

The end of political Jacobitism left the field clear for new political issues, but these were slow to develop. The 45 members elected by Scottish constituencies to the British House of Commons under the act of union and the 16 Scottish peers elected by their fellow peers to sit in the British House of Lords normally supported the government and thus exerted more influence than they could have done if disunited. The act grouped Scottish burghs into single member constituencies, which, while as corrupt as the English borough constituencies of the day, were difficult to manage owing to local rivalries. The revival of genuine two-party politics is usually ascribed to the influence of the French Revolution. The friends of France and liberty organized themselves and held conventions in Edinburgh, but their leaders soon were arrested and transported. The movement was driven underground, where it became associated with the early activities of trade unions in the industrial areas.

Emigration from the Highlands. The end of the clan system in the Highlands and the changing use of land—not to support the largest possible number of able-bodied men but to provide the maximum return in cash—led to emigration of many Highlanders, mostly to other parts of Britain but also overseas and particularly to North America. Estates formerly capable of supporting the clansmen were often transformed into sheep runs or vast stretches of deer forest. Those who refused to leave their old homes often were forcibly evicted. The land clearances and lack of employment embittered the Highlanders and contributed to Scottish radicalism in the 19th century.

Political Reforms. In the Lowlands the revolutionary radicals of the 1790's gave way to sober Whigs, who in 1802 founded the *Edinburgh Review*, long the standard-bearer not only of Scottish but of British Whiggism. Facing an uphill struggle to secure reform, they were not helped by radical demands for annual parliaments and universal suffrage, which were accentuated by the spread of the Industrial Revolution and the misery of the surviving handloom weavers.

The first important Whig victory was the Scottish Parliamentary reform act of 1832, which gave votes to shopkeepers, artisans, and farmers and added eight seats to Scotland's representation in the British Parliament. Scotland now could be depended on to return a large Whig or Liberal majority. Municipal reform followed in 1833. The self-electing corporations were replaced by councils elected by the householders, who were further authorized to elect commissioners of police and to levy rates on the inhabitants of the burghs for purposes of local government. The second reform act (1867–1868) gave votes to many members of the working classes, and the third (1884–1885) granted manhood suffrage. Because seats were allocated on a strict population basis, Scotland received 72 seats out of 670. This was subsequently increased to 74, then reduced to 71 by the abolition of the university franchise in 1948. Dissatisfaction with government extended from the state to the church, where lay patronage led to the disruption of 1843, which split the national church for nearly a century.

Practical grievances and feelings of inferiority led to the development of Scottish nationalism, which is widely supported but divided against itself. The movement characteristically draws most of its strength from the industrial west. The excessive development of heavy industries in this area, with only partial success at diversification, still remains the main Scottish economic problem.

Economic difficulties continued to spur emigration in the 20th century despite a growing countertrend of immigration mainly from England and Ireland. Financially Scotland became sounder, but this had insufficient effect on the standard of living of the ordinary Scot. The creation and development of the cabinet office of the secretary of state for Scotland and the reorganization and extension of government social services for Scotland were aimed at improving conditions for all the Scots and bringing the highlanders and islanders into the mainstream of British life.

DAVID B. HORN, *Author of
"Great Britain and Europe in the
Eighteenth Century"*

Bibliography
Brown, Peter H., *History of Scotland*, 3 vols. (reprint, Octagon 1971).
Dickinson, William Croft, and Pryde, George S., *A New History of Scotland*, 2 vols. (Nelson 1961–1962).
Linklater, Eric, *Survival of Scotland* (Doubleday 1968).
Mitchison, Rosalind, *A History of Scotland* (Methuen 1970).
Rait, Sir Robert, and Pryde, George S., *Scotland*, 2d ed. (Praeger 1954).

7. The Arts

The Anglian form of Scottish literature emerged full grown with the Wars of Independence (1296–1328)—full grown as a self-conscious part of the developed European culture of the 14th century, with characteristics persisting into modern times. Chronicles preserve scraps of songs, by no means primitive. John Barbour enlivened his *The Brus,* a verse biography of Robert Bruce, with romantic decoration of factual report. Andrew of Wyntoun, in his rhymed *Oryginale Cronykil of Scotland,* moved from biblical and national legend to the files of the diocese of St. Andrews. Other writers worked in the common fields of romance and morality. Henry the Minstrel (known also as Blind Harry) in the late 15th century harked back to Barbour in *The Actis and Deidis . . . of Schir William Wallace,* with a heavier admixture of romance almost overwhelming his facts. While a captive of the English in about 1423, King James I wrote *The Kingis Quair (The King's Book),* a love-allegory on his own marriage to an English bride. He had learned to write English verse after the courtly Anglo-French style of Geoffrey Chaucer. Once restored to the throne, James had no leisure for elaborate works of art, but in more settled times new Scottish poets cultivated the same style.

The two most prominent poets in this style were Robert Henryson and William Dunbar, both working in the late 15th and early 16th centuries. Not mere "Scottish Chaucerians," they paid homage to Chaucer and John Lydgate. In *The Testament of Cresseid,* Henryson produced an appendix to Chaucer's *Troilus and Criseyde* worthy of its original. But the two poets also formed an elaborate poetic diction and rhetoric of their own. Henryson is the master of the quiet meditative strain in Scottish literature, and, especially in his fables, a keen observer of men and beasts. Dunbar has few equals in any language in versatility and technical ingenuity and in fantastic visualization. A court poet and a satirist uninhibited by courtly decorum, he is denied a place among the world's greatest literary figures by his lack of humane philosophy.

Gavin Douglas, who was a skillful allegorist in the same school, is remarkable for the first translation of Vergil's *Aeneid.* This work represented a deliberate departure from chivalric adaptation into scholarly humanism.

Darkness descends with the Battle of Flodden (1513). Of 21 Scottish poets named by Dunbar in his *Lament for the Makaris,* only a few are identifiable. Only one or two battered volumes survive to show that Walter Chepman and Andrew Myllar of Edinburgh printed works of the "makars" (Scottish poets) about 1508. Except for the manuscript collections of John Asloan, George Bannatyne, and Sir Richard Maitland (Lord Lethington), most of Henryson, Dunbar, and the rest would have disappeared during that time of violence and feuds. Douglas' *Aeneid* was printed in London, where he died in exile.

This article deals with the Anglian element of Scottish literature, composed chiefly in languages descended from the Northern dialect of Middle English and emerging as Lowland Scots, standard English, or a mixture of both. For a discussion of Scottish Gaelic literature, see CELTIC LITERATURES— *Scottish Gaelic Literature.*

High atop Castle Rock, Edinburgh Castle dominates Scotland's historic capital.

The chaotic state of the realm occupied Maitland and Sir David Lindsay, both state officials who knew the facts and spoke their minds. Lindsay, a strong humorist unrestrained by overrefinement, remained popular for generations as the fearless champion of the common people, critical alike of the church, the nobility, the administration, and the king himself. He stands out by his use of dramatic form in *Ane Satyre of the Thrie Estaitis*—a work that is long, formless, voluble, earnest for all-round reform, coarse, and impressive in its plain dignity. In the same way the *Gude and Godlie Ballatis* (ballads) of the three Wedderburn brothers James, John, and Robert mainly translations of the Psalms and of German hymns, varied from spiritual depth to ribald mockery.

Histories abound from the 14th century to the 16th. John of Fordun, writing in the late 14th century, covered the period to the mid-12th century in the *Scotichronicon*. Other major historical works in Latin were published by John Major and Hector Boece in Paris, John Leslie in Rome, and George Buchanan, a scholar and Latin poet of European renown, in Edinburgh. In translation by John Bellenden, Boece's *Historiae Scotorum* was copied in Raphael Holinshed's *Chronicles* for Shakespeare to read. In the vernacular, John Knox gave his version of events in his *History of the Reformation in Scotland* (1644), and Robert Lindsay of Pitscottie wrote, in purer Scots, a *Chronicle* colored with odd passages of emotion and comedy.

Besides Buchanan, Scots figured well as Latin poets. The *Deliciae Poetarum Scotorum*, an anthology edited by Arthur Johnston, himself one of the best of them, was published in Amsterdam in 1637. Scots kept contact with the Continent and knew the poetry of Italy and France as well as that of England. Alexander Hume, a religious poet, Alexander Scott, an amorous one, Alexander Montgomerie, William Fowler and others blended classical, Italian, and French styles with their inherited tradition. James VI was a patron and colleague. Scotland, however, failed to produce a poet masterful enough to create and impose a Scottish stylistic and linguistic medium as England did, in Edmund Spenser. There was no vernacular version of the Scriptures, and the English Bible became familiar to people at large.

Effect of the Union of the Crowns. After James VI inherited the English throne (as James I) in 1603, some of his poets went south with him. Of those who remained in Scotland, some like William Drummond of Hawthornden cultivated the international muses in pure English. Scottish writers had to face an alternative either to address all the king's subjects, most of whom knew only southern English, or to be content with a local audience, who might understand both dialects. James Graham, 1st Marquess of Montrose, ranks among the Cavalier poets. Others, like William Hamilton of Gilbertfield and Robert Sempill of Beltrees exploited the "popular" style, regional in speech and subject.

When the Revolution of 1688 brought relative stability to the land, this popular speech and style were assumed to be the only Scottish way of writing. Allan Ramsay, writing mainly in the first half of the 18th century, set the pace. At his best he was regional in painting the manners of the rougher parts of Edinburgh, provincial in his attitude to Londoners like Joseph Addison and Alexander Pope, and national in his reprinting of the old makar poems. Robert Fergusson was provincial in his English verses, regional and admirable as the poet of the Edinburgh streets and clubs. In the late 18th century, Robert Burns proved that regional poetry in Scots could be as central to mankind as the regional poetry of London or Paris. Though not a scholar of the old poetry, Burns seized upon the lyrical part of the popular tradition and made himself the master of it.

Many other men were collecting ballads and traditional songs. Eighteenth century Scotland was achieving a remarkable literary revival, and men were following the wider opportunities far

423

beyond its borders. James Thomson brought the memories of his Border childhood to fruition in *The Seasons*. Tobias G. Smollett, drawing on his early experiences as a naval surgeon in *Roderick Random* and looking fondly homeward in *The Expedition of Humphry Clinker*, became one of the early masters of the novel. Two philosophers, David Hume and Adam Smith, set Scotland in the main intellectual current of Europe. History absorbed the energies of many writers, such as Hume, Smollett, Sir David Dalrymple (Lord Hailes), and William Robertson. James Boswell immortalized Samuel Johnson in a masterpiece of biography by the same process of sympathetic imagination as Barbour and Lindsay had used in their times, though in different associations.

A striking accession to the country's literary strength in this period was the beginnings of assimilation of the Celtic culture of the Highlands. From Barbour onward the writers of "Inglis" had been consistently hostile to the Gaelic tradition. Now, however, *The Works of Ossian* by James MacPherson, alleged translations from a 3d century Gaelic bard, captivated Scotland and the European world.

These were the great days of Scottish authorship, and they lasted another generation, through the early 19th century. A group of young Scottish lawyers scored a striking success with a new periodical, the *Edinburgh Review* (founded in 1802), devoted to science, travel, history, economics, politics, and literary criticism.

In 1805, Walter Scott scored in a different fashion with *The Lay of the Last Minstrel*, followed it up with more poetry, and then, in 1814, began again in prose with *Waverley*. At this stage, two images of Scottish literature and the Scottish scene coexisted: the pragmatical-factual of the *Edinburgh Review* school and the romantic of Scott. The division has its truth, but it ignores the political excitement of the reviewers and the social and ethical value of Scott. Scott did not take his poetry or his novels too seriously, but his native force carried him into European popularity.

The 19th and 20th Centuries. Thereafter the shadows of Burns and Scott lay too heavily on the land for healthy growth. James Hogg had a natural gift for lyrical expression but little else. Thomas Campbell lacked confidence in his own powers. John Gibson Lockhart came close to Boswell as biographer of his father-in-law, Scott. His tragic novels were somewhat undernourished. John Galt, admirable in the documentary way, lacked staying power and critical control. The many lyricists fell back too easily on the local and popular fashion. The young lions of *Blackwood's Magazine*, founded in 1817, roared none too convincedly.

A repressive Calvinistic church and the materialism of an industrial age are blamed for the weakness of the 19th century. They did not help, but the new generation had lost sense of direction. Thomas Carlyle looked to Germany but found nothing positive to cure his innate dissatisfaction. He is best, and most Scottish, in his historical work. Lesser men lacked confidence. Authorship, whether in Scots or English, dwindled into an accomplishment. Robert Louis Stevenson suffered from extreme physical weakness. He fought it gallantly, and at least did not make it his theme. In John Davidson a sense of power was frustrated in negation and gloom. James M. Barrie translated the minor popular fashion into terms of the novel. Later he showed skill in handling the resources of the theater, but had little to say.

During World War I, Scotland lost its promising youth in battle. The survivors felt the need for a new start. One result was an interest in drama. The apparently capricious flights of the Scottish imagination, however, are not easily controlled in dramatic form. Scottish drama, as in the 18th century effort of John Home, had been amateurish. In the postwar revival, James Bridie (pseudonym of O. H. Mavor), a deeply humane artist, merely disconcerted the critics, and other promising playwrights never received the encouragement that might have matured the dramatic arts into real fruition.

The novel suffered from the same uncertainty. Lewis Grassic Gibbon (pseudonym of James Leslie Mitchell) had most power, but his theme is a lament over a lost and synthetically conceived peasantry. Few of those handling contemporary themes have his depth. An exception is Neil M. Gunn, a novelist of vision and sensitivity.

A renaissance period in Scottish poetry beginning after World War I initiated the so-called "Lallans revival." Feeling they could best express the soul of Scotland in the Scots language, poets modified the dialect of the Lowlands into a literary form known as Lallans. Hugh McDiarmid (pseudonym of Christopher M. Grieve) recovered the long meditative poem and gave to the lyric an intensity it had lost. He created an elaborate literary diction in Lallans, going beyond the mixture of dialects of Burns and Stevenson in search of a Scots language capable of true poetic expression. Other successful writers of the Lallans revival continuing into the middle and later 20th century include Sydney Goodsir Smith, Douglas Young, and Alexander Scott.

In the pens of lesser poets, the Lallans' technique is too much a cult speech. The basic problem is that the Scots language is too little standardized or developed as a written language—much less as a literary tool. Its inadequacy is suggested by McDiarmid's later drift into English for the wide themes he explores. Rejecting Lallans, William Soutar wrote unusual poetry in traditional Scots. Outstanding poets writing in English include Edwin Muir, Norman MacCaig, and George Bruce. They have managed to convey the sense of Scotland in English, while making the language Scottish in rhythm and tone.

W. L. RENWICK
Emeritus, University of Edinburgh

MUSIC

In considering Scottish music, one must distinguish between folk and art music. The former is profuse and varied, while the latter is sparse and has made little impact. The reasons for this are complex and obscure, involving economic, political, geographical, and religious factors, none of which favored the growth of a sophisticated art but did permit a lively folk tradition.

The early 16th century was the golden age of Scottish art music. Churches and *sang sculs* ("song schools") were producing scholarly and gifted priest-composers, the greatest being Robert Carver and Robert Johnson, and the king's court was also a center of considerable musical activity. The Reformation helps to account for the lack of extant manuscripts—an important survivor is the *St. Andrews Psalter* (1566)—and for the subsequent dearth of composers.

Abbotsford House, in Roxburghshire, was the home of Scottish poet and novelist Sir Walter Scott.

A few 17th century manuscripts have come to light, containing secular vocal and instrumental music, much of it English in origin.

When 18th century Edinburgh became an important cultural center, public concerts and musical societies were instituted. In the 19th century this institutional progress continued—in Glasgow as well as Edinburgh. John Reid, a soldier and amateur musician, left money to found the Edinburgh University chair of music (1839). The Glasgow Athenaeum School of Music, now the Royal Scottish Academy of Music, was founded in 1890. Three years later the Scottish National Orchestra was founded in Glasgow. And a chair of music was established at the University of Glasgow in 1930.

Led by Alexander Campbell Mackenzie, a nationalist school of composers arose in the late 19th century. Although they formed the most coherent revival since pre-Reformation times, their works are seldom heard today.

In the 20th century, the Edinburgh International Festival of Music and Drama, started in 1947, has gained worldwide recognition as an outstanding annual musical event. Prominent composers of the 20th century include Erik Chisholm, Robert Crawford, C. Thorpe Davie, Ian E. Hamilton, Thea Musgrave, and Robin Orr.

Modern living has dealt a death blow to folk music as a vital means of expression, and, since it depended on oral tradition, much has been lost. Until the mid-20th century, little attempt was made to preserve what remained. The School of Scottish Studies (founded in 1951 at Edinburgh University), has collected and collated hundreds of tunes. Scottish folk song can be classified roughly into three types: the Hebridean, which makes extensive use of the pentatonic scale; the Highland, which includes much instrumental music; and the Lowland, which was so popular in 18th century London that what many people regard today as Scottish folk song was in fact confected for the London music hall.

The bagpipe, now Scotland's national instrument, was introduced in the 15th century. The clarsach and the Jew's harp are much older. In the 18th and 19th centuries, Niel Gow, William Marshall, and others helped to establish the violin as a solo instrument and also for accompanying dancing. In Scotland, perhaps more than elsewhere, folk music has been debased by commercialism and ignorance of the true tradition.

WALTER R. CAIRNS
Edinburgh University Press

VISUAL ARTS

Scotland has contributed much less to the graphic arts than to literature and scholarship. Beginning with the symbolic carved stones of the Picts and the Celtic crosses on the island of Iona, the Scottish artistic tradition culminates in the medieval cathedrals and Renaissance castles, though these seem usually to have been designed by foreign craftsmen. In modern times the "Scottish baronial" style of architecture flourished in the hands of native architects in the 17th century and developed in the 18th century into the classical style associated with Robert Adam and others of his family.

To the 17th century can also be traced the beginning of a native school of painters specializing in portraits. One of the earliest of these was John Scougall, who painted Henry, Prince of Wales, before 1612. A contemporary, George Jamesone, may have been a pupil of Peter Paul Rubens. Several painters with the surname Scougall flourished later in the 17th century along with Jamesone's pupil, Michael Wright. Among the foreign painters who worked in Scotland during the 17th and early 18th centuries was John

425

Baptist Medina, whose son John and grandson John also painted many 18th century portraits. Medina's best pupil, William Aikman, was forced by comparative lack of demand to move to London. The younger Allan Ramsay, son of the poet of the same name, also migrated to London and became court painter to George III.

Indubitably the greatest Scottish portrait painter was Henry Raeburn. Working in the late 18th and early 19th centuries, he painted nearly all the outstanding men and many of the most attractive women of Edinburgh. During this period David Wilkie made his reputation by painting everyday episodes, such as *Blind Man's Buff* and *The Penny Wedding*. A contemporary of theirs, John Thomson of Duddingston, a minister of the kirk, was the first Scottish painter to specialize in landscape. The 18th century portrait medallions of James Tassie of Pollokshaws have never been excelled.

The founding of the Royal Scottish Academy in 1826 was a landmark in Scottish painting, though the contributions of the early Victorians are now disregarded. Attention focuses on the pioneer achievements of William McTaggart who, before 1870, anticipated the French impressionists in their preoccupation with light and their ability to transfer to canvas vivid perceptions of the outdoors. After McTaggart there emerged the Glasgow school of Scottish painters, whose works are exhibited in the art galleries of the world. This tradition continued into the mid-19th century and beyond in the work of Samuel J. Peploe, F. C. B. Cadell, Stanley Cursiter, William G. Gillies, and Anne Redpath.

Similarly, in architecture, the massive Gothic and classical buildings designed by some of the Victorian architects fell out of fashion, and "Balmorality" was coined as a term of abuse for the spurious Scottish baronial style affected by others.

The design of Charles Rennie Mackintosh for the Glasgow School of Art building (erected 1897–1907) is usually regarded as the opening of a new architectural era in Scotland, marked by functionalism and occasionally by exhibitionism.

DAVID B. HORN, *Author of*
"Great Britain and Europe in
the Eighteenth Century"

Bibliography
Craig, David, *Scottish Literature and the Scottish People, 1680–1830* (Hillary House 1961).
Farmer, Henry G., *History of Music in Scotland* (Hinrichsen 1947).
Finlay, Ian, *Art in Scotland* (Oxford 1948).
Finlay, Ian, *Scottish Crafts* (Chanticleer 1948).
McLaren, Moray, *The Wisdom of the Scots* (Joseph, M. 1961).
Wittig, Kurt, *The Scottish Tradition in Literature* (Oliver 1958).

SCOTLAND, Church of, the national, free, established church of Scotland. The Church of Scotland was not formally constituted until 1560, but there were early leaders with Reform leanings. Patrick Hamilton exemplified the Lutheran influence and was burned for heresy at St. Andrew's in 1528. George Wishart, who was burned for heresy in 1546, opened the door to the Reform tradition of the Swiss. However, it was John Knox who was the major vehicle for the introduction of the Reform ideas of Calvin and Zwingli. The Parliament of 1560 denied the authority of the pope in Scotland and adopted the "Scottish Confession" of Faith and the *First Book of Discipline* by which the new church was to be governed. The Scottish Reform leader Andrew Melville's *Book of Discipline* (1578) was much more presbyterian in tone.

Presbyterian-Episcopal Conflicts. For more than a century after its original creation the Church of Scotland vacillated between the episcopal and presbyterian forms of church government. Following the abdication of Mary, Queen of Scots, in 1567 the church was administered by the General Assembly. Bishops still existed, and according to the Concordat of Leith (1572) they were to be appointed by the king. Some presbyteries were established by the assembly, but the system was by no means complete. Under James VI, the General Assembly gave the bishops some real authority in 1610. From 1610 to 1638 and from 1661 to 1689 an episcopal polity was in force. In the other periods presbyterian forces predominated. The Westminster Assembly, which was appointed by the Long Parliament in 1643, resulted in the Westminster Confession (1647), which was accepted by the General Assembly of the Scottish Church. It was strongly Calvinistic in doctrine and outlined a presbyterian church government. In 1690, William of Orange, the new king of England, consented to the Westminster Confession and to a presbyterian form of government for the Scottish church. The Church of Scotland has been presbyterian ever since.

Secessions and Disruption. In 1712 the English Parliament passed a law reestablishing the right of patronage in Scotland. This act was at the root of much later turmoil in the church. In the 18th century, two major breaks occurred, centering on a conflict between a more liberal group influenced by Enlightenment concepts and a more traditional party. An evangelical and traditional group, led by Ebenezer Erskine, seceded from the church in 1733, and another evangelical group under Thomas Gillespie seceded to become the Relief Presbytery in 1761. Within the Church of Scotland itself the evangelical emphasis began to dominate by the early 19th century.

The patronage issue was the basic cause of the Disruption of 1843, in which a third of the ministers left to form the Free Church of Scotland. The immediate cause of the break was the blocking by the courts of the veto power of local congregations over the appointment of a minister found unacceptable to the majority.

Free Church and Reunion. The established church was gradually freed of government control. The administration of the care and education of the poor became a state responsibility in 1845, and the educational system came under state control in 1874. In 1874, Parliament abolished the patronage system, clearing the way to a reunion with the Free Church. This was finally accomplished in 1929, following the passage of various bills that entirely freed the church from state control. About half the population of Scotland are baptized in the Church of Scotland, but only about 7% are regular communicants.

SCOTLAND YARD is the popular name for the headquarters of the metropolitan police of London, England, and for the police themselves, especially the Criminal Investigation Department. The present headquarters, opened in 1967, is a 20-story glass and concrete building that stands in Victoria Street, near the Houses of Parliament. The former red-brick building on the Thames Embankment was opened in 1890 by Commissioner of Police James Monro, who named it New

Scotland Yard. For 61 years previously, the headquarters had been situated at 4 Whitehall Place, just off Whitehall. It derived its name, Scotland Yard, from a medieval palace, dating back to the 13th century, that once stood on the site and was used to house kings and queens of Scotland during state visits to England.

History. The metropolitan police force was first recruited in 1829, sponsored by the home secretary, Sir Robert Peel, whose name provided the new police, in top hats and belted coats, with the nicknames "peelers" and "bobbies." These men replaced the so-called Bow Street Runners, a small body of paid police organized in London in the mid-18th century by Henry Fielding, magistrate and novelist. The disciplined activities of the Bow Street Runners soon reduced the capital's crime statistics. However, in their early years they were far from popular and received little cooperation from the public.

In 1842, following a manhunt for an Irish coachman who had committed a brutal murder and who was caught, convicted, and hanged, the first plainclothes Yard men went on duty. At once there was an outcry against these "agents provocateurs" and "police spies." They were likened to agents who had brought several continental police forces into disrepute. But several sensational arrests resulted in trials that turned the tide of public opinion, and by 1868, when the first commissioner, Sir Richard Mayne, died, the detective department was firmly established. Nine years later a turf scandal involving three senior Yard detectives resulted in an outcry against police corruption. Chiefly as a result of the findings in the trial of the accused men, the Criminal Investigation Department (CID) was formed in 1878 under Howard Vincent.

The first specialists of the CID were the special branch members, formed to deal with Fenian terrorists. After World War I the flying squad was formed to combat automobile bandits and other criminals. The flying squad absorbed the ghost squad, formed after World War II. This was a group of men and women who roamed the crime world, passing information to headquarters but keeping themselves in the background so as to remain unknown. A similar specialist squad, the fraud squad, was set up after World War II.

Criminal Investigation. The Yard's CID employs all types of criminal investigative techniques. It includes the criminal records office, fingerprint and photography divisions, the fraud and drug squads, the flying squad, the criminal intelligence branch, the metropolitan police laboratory, and the training school for detectives. The fingerprint department maintains criminals' fingerprints for the whole of Britain. The Yard's fingerprint system was adopted in the early 1900's by the Federal Bureau of Investigation of the United States, and it is used by most other modern police forces.

The Yard has its own forensic laboratories, and a special office is manned night and day for handling internal communications and exchanges of information with the International Criminal Police Commission (Interpol), with headquarters in Paris. The information room handles the metropolitan 999 telephone emergency service for police. The Yard directs all activities of the metropolitan police force, including traffic control and regulation of cabs and buses and their drivers. In direct combating of crime, it is responsible only for the metropolitan district, except for the City of London, or financial area, which has its own police force. Local police forces frequently call on the Yard for help in solving difficult cases, almost invariably murder cases.

Changes. In 1972 the incoming metropolitan police commissioner, Robert Mark, announced sweeping organizational changes. The select 3,200-member detectives branch would henceforth be under the supervision of senior officers in the uniformed branch at headquarters, rather than simply reporting, as formerly, to senior plainclothes officials. The commissioner also announced that all police branches would now be interchangeable; detectives could switch to the uniformed force, and policemen on the beat could transfer to the detective branch.

Scotland Yard men have figured in many international exploits. As early as 1864, Detective Inspector Richard Tanner pursued a man wanted for murder to the United States. Chief Inspector Frank Froest once followed an absconding financier to South America and arrested him. In 1910 a chief inspector sailed for Canada to arrest an American, Dr. Hawley Harvey Crippen, for the murder of his wife, following the receipt of a message from a ship in mid-Atlantic—the first use of radio in apprehending a fugitive criminal.

Many writers, including Charles Dickens, Wilkie Collins, and Sir Arthur Conan Doyle have found inspiration for professional police characters in the reports of cases solved by Yard men.

LEONARD GRIBBLE
Author of "Triumphs of Scotland Yard"

SCOTLANDVILLE, an unincorporated area of East Baton Rouge parish (county) in southern Louisiana, is on the east bank of the Mississippi River, just north of the city of Baton Rouge. It is a residential community and the seat of Southern University and the state Agricultural and Mechanical College. Population: 22,557.

SCOTS LAW. See GREAT BRITAIN AND NORTHERN IRELAND, UNITED KINGDOM OF—*Government* (Judicial System—Scotland); SCOTLAND—*Law.*

SCOTT, Charles Prestwich (1846–1932), English journalist, who edited the Manchester *Guardian* for many years. Scott was born in Bath on Oct. 26, 1846, and was educated privately until he entered Corpus Christi College, Oxford (M.A., 1869). He immediately began work on *The Scotsman* of Edinburgh. In 1871 he joined the Manchester *Guardian*, owned by his cousin, John Edward Taylor, son of the paper's founder. In 1872, aged 26, Scott was made editor, and he continued in that post for 57 years, until his resignation in 1929. On Taylor's death in 1905 he became principal proprietor as well. He was a Liberal member of Parliament from 1895 to 1906. Scott died in Manchester on Jan. 1, 1932.

The *Guardian*, established as a weekly on May 5, 1821, had become a daily in 1855. Under Scott it supported the Liberal party and attained editorial influence, especially after 1885. It sometimes backed unpopular causes, but Scott saw the accomplishment of many reforms.

Scott organized a remarkable staff. A man of patriarchal appearance, he refused special honors and titles. His high concept of journalism earned him tributes and made the *Guardian* one of the world's most respected newspapers.

ROBERT W. DESMOND
Formerly, University of California, Berkeley

SCOTT, Dred. See DRED SCOTT CASE.

SCOTT, Duncan Campbell (1862–1947), Canadian poet, whose work shows his concern for the plight of Canadian Indians. He was born in Ottawa on Aug. 2, 1862, and educated at Stanstead College, Quebec. He entered the federal Department of Indian Affairs in 1880 and was its permanent head from 1913 to his retirement in 1932. He died in Ottawa on Dec. 19, 1947.

Scott had a profound sympathy for the Indians, which was reflected in much of his poetry. For example, his finest and most original verse, *The Forsaken* and *The Onondaga Madonna,* gives vivid expression to their fears for the future of their race. His unfamiliar Indian themes and his austere style prevented him from being a "popular" poet, but in time he came to be recognized as one of the leading spirits of Canadian poetry.

Scott's short stories—for example, *In the Village of Viger* (1896)—are noteworthy both for a flawless technique and for a keen understanding of the French-Canadian way of life. His publications include *The Magic House* (1893), *Labour and the Angel* (1898), *New World Lyrics and Ballads* (1905), *Via Borealis* (1906), and *The Circle of Affection* (1947).

SCOTT, George Campbell (1927–   ), American stage and film actor, known for his individuality and the intensity and strength of his characterizations. He was born in Wise, Va., on Oct. 18, 1927, but grew up in Pontiac, Mich., where his family established residence during his childhood. After serving in the U. S. Marine Corps (1944–1948), he entered the University of Missouri in 1950 to study journalism but soon turned to acting. He gained experience in stock companies and in 1957 made his New York City debut in a production of *Richard the Third.* Subsequently he appeared in other Shakespearean

George C. Scott in the title role of *Patton* (1970)

roles and in such plays as *The Wall* (1960) and *Desire under the Elms* (1963).

Scott's first film, *The Hanging Tree* (1959), was followed by successes that included *Anatomy of a Murder* (1959) and *The Hustler* (1961), both of which brought him Academy Award nominations, *Dr. Strangelove* (1964), and *Petulia* (1968). For *Patton* (1970), he received an Academy Award, which he declined because of his dislike for "that whole superstructure and the phony suspense and the crying actor clutching the statue to his bosom. . . ." He also appeared on television.

SCOTT, Sir George Gilbert (1811–1878), English architect, who became the leading practitioner of the Gothic Revival style. He was born in Gawcott, Buckinghamshire, on July 13, 1811. After a routine apprenticeship, he designed public buildings but was not able to indulge his taste for Gothic architecture until about 1840. In 1844 he won a competition for designing St. Nicholas' Church, Hamburg, the spire of which still remains, after the bombing of World War II. For this work he achieved immediate renown, and he became the builder or restorer of an unparalleled number of churches and other edifices. Harry S. Goodhart-Rendel, in *English Architecture Since the Regency* (1953), thus sums up Scott's activities: "That an architect who, during a working career of forty years, built or interfered with nearly five hundred churches, thirty-nine cathedrals and minsters, twenty-five universities and colleges, and many other buildings besides, was a remarkable man it would be foolish to deny."

As a restorer, Scott brashly did away with many fine non-Gothic objects, and for this reason, among others, his work was controversial in his own time. To most people he is best known for the Albert Memorial in Hyde Park, London, erected to the memory of Prince Albert, Queen Victoria's consort. Severe critics consider this elaborate work to be the reduction to absurdity of Scott's interpretation of the Gothic Revival. Scott was knighted in 1872. His writings include *Personal and Professional Recollections* (1879). He died in London on March 27, 1878.

SCOTT, Hugh Doggett, Jr. (1900–   ), American legislator. He was born in Fredericksburg, Va., on Nov. 11, 1900. He received a B. A. from Randolph-Macon College in 1919 and a law degree from the University of Virginia in 1922. He practiced law in Philadelphia and was assistant district attorney there from 1926 to 1941. He was a Navy intelligence officer in World War II.

A progressive Republican, Scott served in the U. S. House of Representatives (1941–1945 and 1947–1959) from Pennsylvania, and was national chairman of his party (1948–1949) during Gov. Thomas E. Dewey's second unsuccessful presidential campaign. First elected to the U. S. Senate in 1958, Scott became successively the assistant Republican leader and then, on the death of Sen. Everett Dirksen in 1969, the Republican leader. Noted for his acerbic wit in debate, Scott defended President Nixon's Vietnam policies against a number of antiwar senators. But he opposed Nixon on a U. S. Supreme Court nomination and on an administration attempt to dilute the Voting Rights Act. Scott vigorously defended Nixon's role in Watergate until the final flood of evidence. He announced his retirement in 1976.

SCOTT, Sir Richard William (1825–1913), Canadian political leader. He was born in Prescott, in what later became the province of Ontario, on Feb. 24, 1825. Of United Empire Loyalist stock and a Roman Catholic, he started his career as a Bytown (Ottawa) lawyer in 1848, turned to politics, and served in the legislatures of United Canada (1857–1863) and, after Confederation, Ontario (1867–1873). Called to the Senate in 1874, he served as secretary of state and registrar general (1874–1878) under Prime Minister Alexander Mackenzie, and again in those positions (1896–1908) under Sir Wilfrid Laurier, and he was also the Senate Liberal leader from 1902 to 1908.

Scott is remembered chiefly as father of the Separate School Act of 1863, under which the first adequate provision was made for Roman Catholic separate schools in Upper Canada. He also helped enact the Canadian temperance, or Scott, Act of 1878, and was a leader in the selection of Ottawa as the national capital. In 1909 he was knighted. He died in Ottawa on April 23, 1913.

R. G. PRODRICK
Assistant Chief Librarian
University of Toronto

SCOTT, Robert Falcon (1868–1912), English Antarctic explorer, whose last expedition was an epic of heroism and frustration. The Norwegian explorer Roald Amundsen beat Scott by a month and three days in a race to be the first man to reach the South Pole, and Scott and his four companions died on the return journey.

Scott was born in Stoke Damerel, near Devonport, on June 6, 1868. Although he was a delicate boy, he was accepted as a cadet in the Royal Navy, and to the navy, which shaped even his attitude to polar exploration, he remained dedicated all his life.

In 1886, Scott joined the West Indies squadron. This was a prophetic event because its commander, Albert Hastings Markham, was a famous Arctic explorer, and Markham's cousin, Sir Clements Robert Markham, became president of the Royal Geographical Society and chief patron of Scott's expeditions.

As a lieutenant, Scott qualified as a torpedo specialist, which was then the most modern branch of naval science. This, too, had its future effect, giving him an understanding of scientific matters that proved valuable to a leader of two Antarctic expeditions that contributed greatly to science.

First Expedition. A chance meeting with Sir Clements Markham, in London in 1899 proved to be the turning point in Scott's career. The Royal Society and the Royal Geographical Society were then organizing the National Antarctic Expedition, and Markham offered Scott the leadership. On this expedition (1901–1904), in the *Discovery*, Scott named King Edward VII Land and with Ernest Shackleton and others made the first deep penetration in land to latitude 82° 17′ S. The first advances were also made beyond the rim of the polar plateau.

Plans for the Future. In 1905, Scott, who was now a captain, returned to the navy. However, he continued to prepare for a return to Antarctica and experimented with the first motorized tracked snow vehicles. Meanwhile news of Shackleton's success in reaching to within 97 miles (156 km) of the South Pole accelerated these preparations.

In 1910, Scott sailed in the *Terra Nova*, carrying with him dog teams, ponies, and the new motor sledges. Despite Norwegian advice, he chose to transport by means of ponies and men on this last expedition. The motor sledges, because they were experimental, were used chiefly only around the base. Scott, a deeply sensitive man behind the stern mask of naval discipline, abhorred the Norwegian practice of using and then slaughtering and eating those dogs that became surplus as sledge loads lightened during the journey.

Scott's first setback came in Melbourne, Australia, with the news that Amundsen, who had planned to go to the Arctic, was proceeding to Antarctica instead. The next shock was learning that Amundsen was at a base on the Bay of Whales that was 60 miles (96 km) nearer the Pole than Scott's.

Last Expedition. Scott nevertheless persevered, first with depot-laying journeys and then with the main expedition. By Dec. 30, 1911, despite a blizzard, he had ascended the Beardmore Glacier to the plateau, surpassing Shackleton's record, although at telling cost to his men. One party then turned back, and two were left. One was the polar party under Scott, with Edward A. Wilson, Capt. Lawrence E. G. Oates, and Edgar Evans, a seaman. The other was the last supporting party under Scott's second-in-command, Lt. Edward R. G. R. Evans (knighted in 1935 and created 1st Baron Mountevans in 1945), with Lt. H. R. Bowers and two seamen.

With Bowers included at the last minute, Scott's party set out on Jan. 4, 1912, for the South Pole, 178 miles (284 km) away, hauling their sledges themselves. They reached the South Pole on January 17.

But it was too late. The Norwegian flag was flying at the site, and messages told of Amundsen's arrival there on Dec. 14.

Then came the forlorn return, through blizzards, with scurvy daily weakening the party. First Evans died, after a serious fall. A month later, Oates, badly frostbitten and aware that he was gravely hampering his comrades, walked out into a driving storm in a supreme act of self-sacrifice. Finally, toward the end of March, not far from a well-stocked depot, Bowers, then Wilson, then Scott died—with 165 miles (264 km) to go.

In his last diary entry on March 29, Scott wrote: "We shall stick it out to the end, but we are getting weaker, of course, and the end cannot be far. It seems a pity, but I do not think I can write any more."

On Oct. 30, 1912, their bodies were found in a snowed-up tent on the Ross Ice Shelf. With them were their notebooks and specimens that they had never discarded despite their weight, and Scott's diaries and last messages to the world. These reveal the qualities of Scott as a man and a leader, his intense patriotism, and his courage.

See also AMUNDSEN, ROALD; ANTARCTICA; POLAR EXPLORATION, SOUTH.

LAURENCE P. KIRWAN
Royal Geographical Society

Further Reading: Gwynn, Stephen L., *Captain Scott* (Harper 1930); Kirwan, Laurence P., *History of Polar Exploration* (Norton 1960); Lashly, William, *Under Scott's Command*, ed. by Alec Robert Ellis (Taplinger 1969); Mountevans, Edward R. G. R., 1st Baron, *Man of the White South: The Story of Captain Scott* (Nelson 1958).

SCOTT, Sir Walter (1771–1832), Scottish poet and novelist. He began his literary career as a collector of ballads and the author of popular narrative poems of romantic adventure, and went on to develop the genre of the historical novel. Most of Scott's novels, which blend realism and local color with romance and elements of the Gothic, are set in the immediate or distant past. They usually center on a fictional hero or heroine but incorporate real persons, places, and historical events. Scott carefully developed his characters, often using appropriate colloquial speech patterns, and he carefully set the scenes of his action after a thorough research of the period. He thus successfully evoked the epoch he was attempting to recreate. His novels, notably *Waverley, The Monastery, Ivanhoe,* and *The Heart of Midlothian,* had a significant influence on 19th century fiction in Britain and throughout Europe, and the genre he created is still popular.

THE BETTMANN ARCHIVE

SIR WALTER SCOTT, 19th century Scottish poet and author of the romantic Waverley Novels.

LIFE

He was the son of Walter Scott, a writer to the signet (solicitor), and Anne, daughter of John Rutherford, professor of medicine at Edinburgh University. Scott was descended on both sides from famous border families. His father belonged to a younger branch of the Buccleuch family, one of the oldest in Scotland. This heritage appealed to Scott's romantic side and fostered his love for Scottish history and antiquities, thus profoundly influencing his future both as a man and as a writer.

Early Life. Scott was born in Edinburgh on Aug. 15, 1771. An early illness, now believed to have been poliomyelitis, left him lame in the right leg, but the fresh country air at Sandyknowe, his grandfather's farm, and nearby Kelso, where he spent much of his boyhood and early manhood, saved his life. He grew up to be over six feet in height and of great strength and physical endurance. He attended Edinburgh High School (1779–1783) and studied art and law at Edinburgh University (1783–1786 and 1789–1792).

In 1786, Scott was apprenticed to his father and was called to the bar in 1792. He never liked pleading cases, and sought appointments that would give him financial security. He was made sheriff depute of Selkirk in 1799 and a principal clerk of session in 1806.

In 1797, after an unsuccessful courtship of Williamina Belsches of Fettercairn, Scott married Margaret Charlotte Carpenter, daughter of Jean and Marguerite Volaire Charpentier of Lyon. A rumor, long current, that Margaret Charlotte was the illegitimate daughter of her guardian, the Marquess of Downshire, was ultimately disproved. The Scotts had five children: a son born in 1798, who lived only one day; Charlotte Sophia, who married John Gibson Lockhart, Scott's ultimate biographer; Walter; Anne; and Charles. Almost every year after his marriage, Scott lived five months in Edinburgh, at 39 Castle Street, and seven months in the country. His country homes were at Lasswade (1798–1804) and at Ashiestiel (1804–1812) and Abbotsford (1812–1832), both on the River Tweed.

Years of Fulfillment. In the early 1800's, Scott began publishing poetry and quickly became popular, but he wished to rely on his legal profession, and not on literature, for his livelihood. His salaries as sheriff and principal clerk were adequate to enable him to live in the style he desired, but the latter office, to which he had been appointed in 1806, offered no salary until 1812, and he undoubtedly had to rely on literary earnings to supplement his income.

To what extent Scott hoped to increase his earnings through his connection with James Ballantyne, his printer at Kelso, is difficult to say. Scott, who had an eye for good printing, advised him to transfer his press to Edinburgh, assuring him of ample employment. Ballantyne complied, and Scott fulfilled his promise by having his friend print most of his works. Scott became a secret partner in 1805, and henceforth his life was inextricably bound up with that of his printer. At this time Scott was in his prime, both physically and mentally, and he planned many new publications to keep Ballantyne's presses occupied. Within ten years he edited over 50 volumes of miscellaneous works, the most important being an edition of John Dryden (18 vols., 1808) and an edition of Jonathan Swift (19 vols., 1814).

In politics Scott was not a strong party man, but for a few years after 1806 he adopted a more aggressive policy. He withdrew his support from the *Edinburgh Review*—a Whig periodical put out by his publisher Archibald Constable—and in 1809 took a leading part in the establishment of the *Quarterly Review,* a Tory journal published in London. He declined the editorship but contributed frequently to its pages. Not content with these indirect blows at Constable, he set up James Ballantyne's brother John as a publisher. John was quite unfitted for the task, and the publishing business was doomed to failure from the start. By 1813 the firm was in such difficulties that only Scott's strong will and cool head kept it from bankruptcy. The firm was rescued with the help of Constable, who thereby tightened his hold on Scott as his principal publisher, to Scott's ultimate ruin.

In 1814, Scott published anonymously his first novel, *Waverley*, which was a great success. With the publication of this book, the pattern of his life had changed. Sheltered behind the cloak of anonymity, he ceased to be outwardly a man of letters. By continuing his habit of writing before breakfast he appeared a man of leisure when not engaged in his legal duties.

From 1814, Scott's main preoccupations were the expansion of his Abbotsford estate a few miles down the Tweed from Ashiestiel; building his house; settling his family for life; steering the Ballantyne business through troubled waters; and entertaining an ever-widening circle of friends. When purchased and renamed by him in 1811, Abbotsford was a farm of 120 acres. The estate had increased tenfold by 1825, the result of 13 purchases. Overemphasis has always been put on Scott's "yerd-hunger" (*yerd* is a Scottish and Northern English form of the word "earth"), but it is usually not realized how much the building of his house—carried on in two stages, 1817–1819 and 1822–1825—taxed his time and energies. The importance Scott attached to his house is shown by his reluctance to leave Scotland when building operations were in full swing.

As soon as *Waverley* was out in 1814, Scott set out with the lighthouse commissioners on their voyage of inspection around the coasts of Scotland, visiting the Orkney and Shetland islands. In 1815 he visited France. Wherever he went, he gathered material for his books.

Scott was created a baronet by King George IV in 1820. In 1822, Scott organized, with unremitting labor and tact, the celebrations for the visit of the King to Edinburgh. In 1825, Scott's elder son, Walter, who was then a lieutenant in the 15th Hussars, married Jane Johnson, heiress of Lochore in Fife. Walter's regiment was stationed in Ireland, and in the summer of 1825, Scott, with his daughter Anne and John Gibson Lockhart, visited the couple at Dublin and toured the island, calling on the Irish novelist Maria Edgeworth at Edgeworthstown. This was the last unclouded year of Scott's life.

Final Years. In January 1826, Constable went bankrupt, dragging down Scott and Ballantyne, whose finances were closely linked with his. Scott refused to take refuge in bankruptcy and accepted responsibility for all of Ballantyne's debts, which amounted to about £120,000. He applied for a trust to administer Ballantyne's affairs and pledged himself to pay off every penny of his liabilities. In assessing blame, it should be understood that Scott's only fault was his trust in Constable's stability. It is contrary to the known facts to say that Scott was extravagant in buying land and building Abbotsford or that he gambled on future unwritten-novels. From his writing he is said to have earned over £100,000 (only a portion of which he spent on Abbotsford), and he ought, therefore, to have died a rich man. But Constable never paid Scott in cash, and Scott never knew the value of bills and counterbills exchanged between Ballantyne and Constable. Scott was content to believe that he was spending far less than he was earning, and to give guidance to Ballantyne in negotiating bills as and when the occasion arose, deferring the final settlement in the belief that Constable could easily meet all his obligations when called on to do so.

When the crash came, Scott faced the issue stoically. His *Journal*, which he began to keep in 1825, is a record of a cheerful, indomitable spirit that adversity could not break. Lady Scott died in May 1826. Scott's own health deteriorated rapidly, and his lame leg began to trouble him, curtailing his outdoor activities. In 1830 he suffered a paralytic stroke, which was followed by others, but he continued to write for as long as he possibly could.

By 1831 his doctors, insisting on complete rest, prescribed a visit to Italy, and he sailed from Portsmouth, arriving at Naples in December. For the next six months, through mistaken kindness, he was taken sightseeing and kept in a constant whirl of engagements so that he lost strength instead of gaining it. Arriving back at Abbotsford in July 1832, he lingered on, with only intervals of consciousness, until his death on September 21. He was buried beside his ancestors in Dryburgh Abbey on the banks of his beloved Tweed. From the profits of his writings all his debts were ultimately paid.

Scott was succeeded by his elder son Walter, who died childless in 1847, when the baronetcy became extinct. His younger brother had predeceased him, unmarried, in 1841, and Anne had died, unmarried, in 1833. The succession to Abbotsford, therefore, fell to the children of Sophia and Lockhart.

WORKS

The foundations of Scott's literary career were unconsciously laid, for as a young man he had no ambitions to be an author. He was, nevertheless, storing up the materials out of which he created future works. From childhood Scott was a voracious reader of history, romances, poetry, and drama—not only in English, but also in Latin, French, Spanish, Italian, and German. His memory was so tenacious that he forgot nothing that interested him. An acute observer, he acquired an intimate knowledge of every type of character, a knowledge he used later in portraying with fidelity characters in all walks of life, from kings to beggars. He numbered among his many friends men and women differing in politics and religion and from all social levels, for, though a Tory, he was a democrat in his daily life and writings.

An early love for old ballads led to his first major work, *Minstrelsy of the Scottish Border* (2 vols., 1802; 2d ed., 3 vols., 1803). While collecting these ballads, he was also attracted to German literature, and his first publication, *The Chase and William and Helen* (1796), consisted of translations from Gottfried A. Bürger. His next publication was a translation in 1799 of Goethe's play *Götz von Berlichingen*. The Gothic element, which appears in varying degree throughout his work, was due to this early interest in contemporary German literature.

The Narrative Poems. Scott's rise to fame as a poet was rapid. His name had already spread before the *Minstrelsy* brought him further into prominence. A ballad that he wrote himself for that collection proved to be too long and was published as *The Lay of the Last Minstrel* (1805). Its success was immediate, and Scott followed this with *Marmion* (1808), for which Constable had offered 1,000 guineas before it was written. With *The Lady of the Lake* (1810) he reached the highest point in his poetical career. *Rokeby* appeared in 1813, and in that year he was offered, but declined, the poet laureateship. His last major poem was *The Lord of the Isles* (1815). His others, all minor, were *The Vision of Don*

Roderick (1811), *The Bridal of Triermain* (1813), *The Field of Waterloo* (1815), and *Harold the Dauntless* (1817).

Scott himself said that the emphasis in *The Lay* had been on style and in *Rokeby* on character. It was the novelty and vivaciousness of his style that had made Scott the most popular poet of his day. It was the character drawing of *Rokeby* that made him a novelist. He had, unconsciously perhaps, been experimenting, and in *Rokeby* he found the outstanding gift that gives him his place in English literature today. For full expression Scott's genius required a medium that gave him complete freedom, and he found that medium in the novel. But he was an immediate success as a novelist only because he had served his apprenticeship in storytelling, plot construction, and character drawing in verse.

The Waverley Novels. Scott claimed that he gave up the writing of long poems because Lord Byron had beaten him at it, but the real reason for his decision was that Scott knew that he had exhausted his vein of narrative poetry. He was keenly alive to the wants of the public and confident of his own ability to satisfy them, and so he turned back to an early attempt of 1805 to write a prose romance. This was *Waverley*, which he completed rapidly, and it was published anonymously by Constable on July 7, 1814. Its success was never in doubt, and Scott found that from the rich stores of his mind he could produce one novel after another with no effort beyond the physical act of writing. Though suspicion fell on him, he maintained his anonymity until the financial crash compelled him to avow authorship publicly on Feb. 23, 1827.

Guy Mannering (1815) followed *Waverley* after seven months. The next, *The Antiquary* (1816), professed to be the last by the unknown author. These three formed a sort of trilogy of Scottish manners, covering the years 1745 to 1804. Then, under the pseudonym of Jedediah Cleishbotham he began writing four series of novels under the title *Tales of My Landlord*. The first series (1816) was *The Black Dwarf* and *Old Mortality;* the second (1818) consisted of *The Heart of Midlothian;* the third (1819) contained *The Bride of Lammermoor* and *A Legend of Montrose;* and the last series (1831) was made up of *Castle Dangerous* and *Count Robert of Paris*. Between the first and second series, *Rob Roy* (1817) had appeared by the "Author of 'Waverley,'" and this designation was the most commonly used after that. All the novels to 1819 dealt with Scotland, and so their author came to be known as the "author of the Scotch novels," a title that lasted until the end of his life, in spite of the fact that with *Ivanhoe* in 1819 he crossed the Border and produced a novel with a wholly English setting. Similarly, all of Scott's novels have become known as the Waverley Novels.

After the success of *Ivanhoe*, which was set in the 12th century, Scott allowed his imagination to wander in time and space for the settings of his novels. He went to 15th century France for *Quentin Durward* (1823), the Crusades in the Holy Land for *The Talisman* (1825), India for *The Surgeon's Daughter* (1827), and 15th century Switzerland for *Anne of Geierstein* (1829). England provided the settings for *Kenilworth* (1821), involving the Earl of Leicester and Queen Elizabeth I; *The Fortunes of Nigel* (1822), placed in the Jacobean era; *Peveril of the Peak* (1823), which centers on a "popish plot" to overthrow King Charles II; and *Woodstock* (1826), about the English Civil War. It is among these non-Scottish novels that we must look for Scott's best work after 1819. The Scottish ones of this period—*The Monastery* and *The Abbot* (both 1820), *The Pirate* (1821), *St. Ronan's Well* (1823), *Redgauntlet* (1824), *The Fair Maid of Perth* (1828), and *Castle Dangerous*—do not take first rank, although *St. Ronan's Well*, as the only novel of contemporary manners, and *Redgauntlet*, because of its autobiographical interest, are both important in a study of Scott.

Last Works. Scott's *Life of Napoleon* was published in 9 volumes in 1827. This had entailed a vast amount of reading and a visit to France in 1826, ostensibly to collect material. He continued to write novels, but, encouraged to concentrate on works that required neither research nor invention, he also wrote *Tales of a Grandfather* (1828–1831), dealing with Scottish and French history for young readers, *The History of Scotland* (1829–1830), *Letters on Demonology and Witchcraft* (1830), and introductions and notes to new editions of the poems and novels that are valuable for his own account of his development as a poet and for the genesis of the novels.

For a listing of separate articles on works by Scott, see the Index entry *Scott, Sir Walter*.

JAMES C. CORSON, *Author of "Bibliography of Sir Walter Scott, 1797–1940"*

Bibliography
The Standard Editions of Scott's Works are those published by Robert Cadell at Edinburgh, including *The Waverley Novels*, 48 vols. (1829–1833); *Poetical Works*, 28 vols. (1834–1836); and *Miscellaneous Prose Works*, 28 vols. (1834–1836).
Gordon, Robert C., *Under Which King: A Study of the Scottish Waverley Novels* (Barnes & Noble 1969).
Grierson, Sir Herbert J. C., ed., *Letters of Sir Walter Scott*, 12 vols. (1932–1937); reprint, AMS Press 1971).
Grierson, Sir Herbert J. C., *Sir Walter Scott, Bart., A New Life* (1938; reprint, Landsdown Press 1971).
Johnson, Edgar, *Sir Walter Scott: The Great Unknown*, 2 vols. (Macmillan 1970).
Lockhart, John Gibson, *Memoirs of the Life of Sir Walter Scott, Bart.*, 2 vols. (Houghton 1902).
Scott, Sir Walter, *Journal*, ed. by John G. Tait and W. M. Parker (Clarke, Irwin 1950).
Young, Charles A., *The Waverley Novels* (Folcroft 1907).

SCOTT, William (1745–1836), English judge known for his important decisions in Admiralty law. He was born on Oct. 17, 1745, near Newcastle-on-Tyne, son of a Newcastle tradesman. He won a scholarship to Oxford University and, after his graduation in 1764, was a tutor there until 1776 and lecturer in ancient history until 1785. In 1776 he inherited his father's shipping business, gaining practical experience that later proved of value. In 1777 he began to study law at the Middle Temple in London, and was called to the bar in 1780.

In 1782, Scott was named advocate general of the lord high admiral's office and in 1798 a judge of the high court of Admiralty, a position he held for the next 30 years. In this capacity he became in effect the father of British maritime law and therefore, indirectly, of the maritime law of the United States. Knighted in 1788, he was raised to the peerage as Baron Stowell of Stowell Park in 1821. For the previous 20 years he had represented Oxford University in the House of Commons. He died at Earley Court, Berkshire, on Jan. 28, 1836.

SCOTT, Winfield (1786–1866), American general, who from 1841 until his retirement in 1861 was general in chief of the U. S. Army. He was born near Petersburg, Va., on June 13, 1786. He left William and Mary College in 1805 because he disapproved of the irreligious feelings among the students. He was admitted to the Virginia bar in 1806 and continued to practice law until he joined the Army in 1808.

He was commissioned a captain, but his career began shakily when he was court-martialed and suspended for a year (1810) for calling his superior officer, Gen. James Wilkinson, as great a traitor as Aaron Burr.

Promoted to lieutenant colonel in the War of 1812, he served in the Battle of Queenston Heights in Canada, but was forced to surrender. Exchanged and promoted to colonel, he led the attack on Fort George (May 27, 1813), where he was wounded in a powder magazine explosion.

As a brigadier general, he was a gallant leader in the Battle of Chippewa on July 4–5, 1814. On July 25 he was the hero of the Battle of Lundy's Lane, where he was wounded twice. He declined an appointment as secretary of war but accepted a gold medal from Congress and the rank of brevet major general.

Scott was assigned to lead troops in the Black Hawk War against the Sac and Fox Indians in Illinois in 1832, but the war ended before Scott saw action. In the same year, Scott commanded federal troops in the harbor of Charleston, S. C., during the nullification crisis. (See SOUTH CAROLINA—*History.*) His tact and vigor were largely responsible for averting a civil war at that time.

He served in the Seminole and Creek Indian campaigns in Florida (1835–1836). His talent for diplomacy in critical situations was tested successfully in touchy incidents along the border with Canada in 1837 and 1839. (See CAROLINE AFFAIR; AROOSTOOK WAR.) In 1838 he superintended the removal of the Cherokee Indians from their lands in Georgia to a reservation west of the Mississippi River. Scott received 57 votes on the first ballot as a candidate for the presidential nomination in the Whig Convention of 1839. On June 25, 1841, he became general in chief of the Army. He was called "Old Fuss and Feathers" because of his stern sense of discipline and formality.

During the Mexican War, Scott proved a valiant and resourceful leader in the field in the 1847 campaign. His successes included the siege and capture of Veracruz (March 26), with a loss of fewer than 20 killed; his sunrise attack on the Mexican army at Cerro Gordo (April 18); the occupation of Jalapa (April 19) and Perote (April 22); the battles of Contreras and Churubusco (August); the storming of Chapultepec (September 13) and the entry into Mexico City on the next day. He received another gold medal from Congress.

Scott was nominated for president by the Whigs in 1852 but lost to Franklin Pierce, carrying only the electoral votes of Vermont, Massachusetts, Kentucky, and Tennessee. In 1855, as a brevet lieutenant general, he rendered distinguished service in 1859 on the Pacific coast in the San Juan Boundary dispute with Britain.

At the outbreak of the Civil War, Scott remained loyal to the Union despite his Southern birth. He foresaw a long and difficult struggle and approached it with deep strategic insight. He planned carefully for the defense of Wash-

CULVER PICTURES

Gen. Winfield Scott, a hero of two wars.

ington, D. C., the national capital. He opposed vigorously the pressures that led to the premature commitment of untrained troops in the First Battle of Bull Run (July 21, 1861), a disastrous Union defeat. Wait, he said, until an army is properly mustered and prepared.

But by now, Scott's age was beginning to tell. Younger men slighted him. He doubted the wisdom of the choice of Maj. Gen. George B. McClellan as commander of the Army of the Potomac, and the tension between them may have contributed to Scott's retirement, at his own request because of ill health, on Oct. 31, 1861. President Lincoln, visiting Scott's home with his entire cabinet, remarked, "I cannot but think we are still his debtors." Scott died at West Point, N. Y., on May 29, 1866.

EARL SCHENCK MIERS
Author of "The General Who Marched to Hell"

Further Reading: Elliott, Charles W., *Winfield Scott, the Soldier and the Man* (Macmillan 1937); Smith, Arthur Douglas Howden, *Old Fuss and Feathers: The Life and Exploits of Winfield Scott* (Greystone 1937).

SCOTT, a township in western Pennsylvania, in Allegheny county, is situated on Chartiers Creek, 4 miles (6 km) southwest of downtown Pittsburgh, of which it is a suburb. Scott township is mainly residential, but the steel and electrical industries are important here, and sausage casings are also made. At the edge of the township is Bower Hill, where in 1794, at the climax of the Whiskey Rebellion, a mob of insurrectionists burned the home of federal excise collector, Gen. John Neville.

Scott was created in 1861 from a part of the township of Upper St. Clair, and named for Gen. Winfield Scott. Coal mining began here in 1883 and for a while was the township's chief industry. In the mid-20th century, Scott grew rapidly as a residential suburb. It has a commission form of government. Population: 20,413.

SCOTTI, skôt′tē, **Antonio** (1866–1936), Italian singer. He was born in Naples on Jan. 25, 1866. After his debut as Amonasro in Verdi's *Aïda*, Scotti, a baritone, sang successfully throughout Europe. Both his London debut at Covent Garden, in 1899, and New York debut at the Metropolitan Opera, also in 1899, were in the title role of Mozart's *Don Giovanni*.

An able dramatic singing actor, Scotti remained on the Metropolitan roster until a farewell appearance there in 1933, in Franco Leoni's *L'Oracolo*, an opera that he had made popular by his characterization of Chim-Fen. His noted roles also included Scarpia in *La Tosca*, Rigoletto, and Falstaff. His recording with Enrico Caruso of the third-act tenor-baritone duet from Verdi's *La forza del destino* is a landmark in recording history. He died in Naples on Feb. 26, 1936.

HERBERT WEINSTOCK, *Coauthor, "Men of Music"*

SCOTTIE. See SCOTTISH TERRIER.

SCOTTISH CLANS. See CLAN–*Scottish Clans*.

SCOTTISH DEERHOUND, a large, rough-coated sight hound long used for hunting deer and other large game. Developed in Scotland by the 16th or 17th century, the breed was also known as the Scotch greyhound or the Highland greyhound. During much of its history the breed was owned largely by Highland chieftains, and for a time no one of rank lower than earl could own one. Although it is not legal to hunt antlered game with dogs in the United States, deerhounds have been used there for hunting wolves, coyotes, and rabbits.

The deerhound's body formation is similar to that of the smaller greyhound. Its harsh, wiry, heavy coat is adapted to the moist, cold climate of Scotland. The standard weight ranges from 85 to 110 pounds (38–50 kg) for dogs and 65 to 95 pounds (30–43 kg) for bitches. Its strength and speed were desirable for hunting the large deer of Scotland, often weighing 250 pounds (113 kg). As pets they are tractable, companionable, and known for their devotion to their masters.

Scottish deerhound, originally bred for hunting deer

EVELYN M. SHAFER

SCOTTISH LITERATURE. See SCOTLAND–*The Arts.*

SCOTTISH TERRIER, popularly known as the Scottie, a rough-coated terrier originally developed in the Scottish Highlands for hunting foxes, badgers, and other pest animals. Once called the Aberdeen terrier, it was officially recognized as a separate breed with the establishment of a breed club in Britain in 1882.

Scotties are double-coated dogs, having dense undercoats of short, soft hairs, and dense outer-

EVELYN M. SHAFER

The Scottish terrier, often known as the Scottie

coats of harsh, wiry hairs. Although the most common coat color is now black, Scotties can also be wheat colored, gray, or brindle of various colors. In the first standard for Scotties, the most desirable color was given as red brindle with black muzzle and ear tips.

The Scottie has a compact, strong, body with powerful hindquarters. Its standard height at the shoulder is 10–11 inches (25–28 cm) and its weight is 19–22 pounds (8.5–10 kg) for dogs and 18–21 pounds (8–9.5 kg) for bitches.

SCOTTO, skôt′tō, **Renata** (1933?–   ), Italian soprano, who was a singing actress of unusual ability. She was born in Savona, Italy, on Feb. 24, 1933 or 1934. She studied voice in Milan and made her operatic debut there as Violetta in *La Traviata* at the Teatro Nazionale in 1953. Later that year she made her La Scala, Milan, debut in a small role in Catalani's *La Wally*. She soon was in demand throughout Italy because of her well-schooled voice and attractive personality. She achieved international fame when she successfully substituted for Maria Callas in *La Sonnambula* at the 1957 Edinburgh Festival. She made her Metropolitan Opera debut in 1965, triumphing as Butterfly, and from the early 1970's centered her operatic activity in the United States.

Although she began as a light soprano, she gradually undertook heavier roles. An accomplished vocal technician, with great facility in pianissimo singing, Scotto also had interpretive gifts that deepened as the top of her range showed signs of wear from the demands made on it. She made a powerful effect in televised opera and recorded a long list of complete roles.

WILLIAM ASHBROOK
Author of "The Operas of Puccini"

SCOTTS BLUFF NATIONAL MONUMENT, in western Nebraska, is in the North Platte River valley near the city of Scottsbluff. It consists of a high bluff of flesh-colored Brule clay and sandstone that was a landmark for pioneers traveling the Oregon Trail in the early and middle 19th century. It was declared a national monument in 1919 to preserve something of the old trail which so many thousands of pioneers followed westward.

The monument covers an area of 3,084 acres (1,248 hectares), stretching from the North Platte River to Dome Rock, an isolated formation to the southwest. The bluff itself, which resembles a ruined castle on a hilltop, rises 750 feet (229 meters) above the river plain, and is divided in two by Mitchell Pass. A paved road leads to the top of the bluff, affording a spectacular view. There is a museum of pioneer life at the base.

SCOTTSBORO CASE, the prosecution of nine Negro boys who were indicted in Scottsboro, Ala., on March 31, 1931, on charges of having raped two white girls in a railroad freight car. Doctors who examined the girls after the alleged rape testified that no rape had occurred. However, eight of the boys were convicted and sentenced to death. The case became a *cause célèbre* when Northern liberals and radicals, believing the Negroes to be victims of racial bias, came to their support. The U.S. Supreme Court in *Powell* v. *Alabama* (1932) and *Norris* v. *Alabama* (1935), reversed convictions obtained in the case in Alabama courts, in the former instance because the defendants had not been permitted adequate counsel, in the latter because of improper selection of the jury. In further proceedings in Alabama, 1935–1937, four defendants were again convicted, one being sentenced to death, a penalty later commuted to life imprisonment, and the others to imprisonment ranging from 75 to 99 years. Indictments against the remaining five were dropped, and four were released; the fifth received a 20-year sentence for assaulting an officer during an earlier attempt to escape.

Over a period of years, four of the five still imprisoned were released by the Alabama board of pardons and paroles, the only one to remain in prison being Heywood Patterson, the alleged ringleader, who was serving a 75-year term. Patterson escaped in 1948 and fled to Michigan, which refused to return him to Alabama: in 1950 he was convicted in a Michigan court of manslaughter in the stabbing of another Negro, and two years later died in prison. The last-known survivor of the nine, Clarence Norris, paroled in 1946, fled to the North, and was granted a pardon in October 1976. The Scottsboro case was widely exploited by Communists for propaganda purposes. But the eventual freeing of most of the defendants was due chiefly to the efforts of the Scottsboro defense committee, a predominantly liberal, non-Communist body.

Further Reading: Carter, Dan T., *Scottsboro: A Tragedy of the American South* (La. State Univ. Press 1979).

SCOTTSDALE, a city in central Arizona, in Maricopa county, adjoining the city of Phoenix, which is to its west. Its warm, sunny winters have made it a popular winter resort. It is also known as an arts and crafts center. The city's largest industries are tourism and electronics. Aerial mapping and the manufacture of wearing apparel are also important.

The Taliesin West architectural school founded by Frank Lloyd Wright is located here, and a number of galleries show the work of Scottsdale artists. Also of interest in the city are the museums of the Railroad and Mechanical Society and the Red Brick Schoolhouse (1909).

Scottsdale was founded in 1896 by Winfield Scott, a homesteader and former army chaplain. It became a town in 1913 and a city in 1961. During the 1960's the city annexed much of the surrounding area, increasing its population during that decade by 576.5%. It has a council-manager form of government. Population: 88,364.

SCOTUS, John Duns. See DUNS SCOTUS, JOHN.

SCOURING RUSH. See HORSETAIL.

SCRABBLE, a trademarked and copyrighted word game in which letter tiles marked with various score values are used to form interlocking words, crossword fashion, on a playing board. Two to four players compete by counting score values of 1 to 10 marked on the letter tiles used, and by placing words to cover places, including premium places, on the board. Each player starts with seven tiles, and play continues until all tiles have been drawn and one of the players has used all his letters, or until all possible plays have been made. The values of letters not used when play ends are deducted from a player's score. If one player has used all his letters, his score is increased by the total of the unplayed letters of all the other players.

Scrabble, a game based on ideas developed by Alfred M. Butts, New York City architect, was introduced in 1948 by the Production & Marketing Company of Newtown, Conn., and is manufactured by the Selchow & Righter Company, New York City. It is related to anagrams, a traditional game employing letter tiles that is said to have been played since the Middle Ages. Scrabble became widely popular among English-speaking peoples, and was adapted to other languages including Dutch, French, German, Italian, Norwegian, Spanish, Russian, and Afrikaans. The distribution of letters and score values is varied in accordance with frequencies of letter use in each language.

SCRANTON, William Warren (1917–), American political leader. He was born in Madison, Conn., on July 19, 1917. After serving as a pilot during World War II, he received his law degree from Yale in 1946. He then practiced law in Scranton, Pa., a city named for his ancestors, among them the industrialist George Whitfield Scranton (1811–1861). He was an assistant to the secretary of state in 1959 and 1960.

Scranton was elected to the U.S. House of Representatives in 1960 as a Republican. As governor of Pennsylvania from 1963 to 1967, he inaugurated a state sales tax and a program to encourage industrial development. Scranton, a leader of the progressive wing of the Republican party, made an unsuccessful attempt to win the presidential nomination in 1964. As student protests grew during the Indochina war, Scranton was named chairman of the President's Commission on Campus Unrest. He was U.S. ambassador to the United Nations in 1976–1977.

SCRANTON, a city in northeastern Pennsylvania, the seat of Lackawanna county, is on the Lackawanna River, about 120 miles (193 km) north of Philadelphia and 135 miles (217 km) northwest of New York City. The Pocono Mountains are to the southeast of the city.

Scranton is an industrial and trading center. Among its products are electrical machinery, metal goods, textiles, wearing apparel, leather goods, color television tubes, processed foods, paper, and printing. The city's railroad repair yards are also important to its economy.

Facilities for higher education include the University of Scranton and Marywood College, both private Roman Catholic institutions; Lackawanna Junior College; and a branch of Pennsylvania State University. The International Correspondence Schools, believed to be the largest organization of its kind in the world, are here. The Everhart Museum of Natural History, Science, and Art and the Lackawanna Historical Society help advance both education and culture. Nay Aug Park contains a zoo, botanical gardens, and a model coal mine.

In 1786 the Abbott brothers, Philip and James, came from Connecticut, and founded a gristmill on Roaring Brook. About 1800 the Slocum brothers, Ebenezer and Benjamin, took over the Abbott holdings and named the area first Unionville, then Slocum Hollow. The Slocums began a charcoal furnace for iron manufacture. The Scranton brothers, George and Selden, built the iron industry into a major one by means of a new smelting process. In 1845, they named the community Harrison in honor of President William Henry Harrison, but a few years later the name was changed to Scrantonia, in their honor, and in 1851 it was shortened to Scranton. The community was incorporated as a borough in 1853 and as a city in 1866.

In the 1880's the Scranton Steel Company was founded. It later merged with the Lackawanna Iron and Coal Company to form the Lackawanna Iron and Steel Company. In 1902 the departure of this company to Buffalo, N.Y., dealt a heavy blow to Scranton's economy, but this was offset by the growing importance of the coal industry, which earned the city the name of "the Anthracite Capital of the World." By 1920, however, the coal industry had waned, and after World War II the city quickly grew into the industrial center it is today.

Scranton has a mayor-council form of government. Population: of the metropolitan statistical area (Lackawanna county), 227,908; of the city, 88,117.

SCRAPIE, skrăp'ē, is a slowly progressive, fatal disease of the nervous system of sheep. It is characterized by compulsive rubbing or scraping against fixed objects and by uncoordinated movements. It has been transmitted experimentally to sheep, goats, and various rodents by injecting tissue, especially brain tissue, from an infected animal. Passage from animal to animal can be continued indefinitely. The clinical disease may appear months or even years after injection of infected tissue. Since the 1960's two fatal degenerative diseases of the human nervous system, kuru of the primitive Fore people of New Guinea and the rare Jakob-Creutzfeldt syndrome, have been found to be similar to scrapie. Thus scrapie has a scientific importance greater than the relatively·small economic loss that it causes farmers.

There has been much speculation on the nature of the causal agent of scrapie. Progress in the identification of the agent has been slow, because it can only be detected indirectly by its ability to produce disease. Until the late 1960's it was thought that the transmissible agent of scrapie was a virus because the agent passes filters that retain all particles larger than a virus and because it apparently multiplies when passed through animals. But the scrapie agent has not been seen under the electron miscroscope; does not stimulate the production of antibodies, a characteristic of viruses; shows marked resistance to boiling and to various chemicals, including betapropiolactone, that destroy viruses; and is highly resistant to doses of ultraviolet light that are lethal to viruses. These findings indicate that the scrapie agent does not contain nucleic acid, the genetic material of viruses. The size of the scrapie agent—about one half that of the smallest known virus—plus its tendency to stick to larger particles have added to the difficulties of purifying and characterizing the agent.

    I. H. PATTISON, *Institute for Research on Animal Diseases, Compton, England*

SCREAMER, any of a family of aquatic birds found in tropical and subtropical parts of South America. The three species of screamers, making up the family Anhimidae, are thought to be distantly related to waterfowl, but they resemble turkeys in size and appearance. Their plumage is brown or gray with black and white areas, and in two species the head is crested. The legs are massive, long, and equipped with long, powerful toes. The front edge of each wing is armed with two long, sharp spurs with which they can deliver crippling blows. The horned screamer (*Anhima cornuta*) has a spinelike projection, about 5 inches (12.5 cm) long, that curves forward from the forehead. Screamers inhabit marshes and other parts of the tropical forests and pampas, wading and swimming and feeding on the vegetation. Their screamlike calls, uttered day or night, carry long distances.

    CHARLES VAURIE
    American Museum of Natural History

Black-necked screamer (*Chauna chavaria*)

Entertainments at the House of Pleasure, a painting on gilded paper by an anonymous 17th century artist, decorates this Japanese screen, one of a pair.

SCREECH OWL, or scops owl, any of about 36 species of small owls that make up the genus *Otus*. Screech owls have hornlike ear tufts and blackish streaks on their plumage. In the New World they range from southern Canada to Brazil, and in the Old World they are found in Europe, Asia, and Africa. In North America the term "screech owl" usually refers particularly to *O. asio*, of which there are about 15 subspecies. Many of the subspecies have two color phases, one sooty to grayish and one reddish. Sometimes both phases appear in a single brood. The screech owl feeds on a wide variety of insects, mice and other small mammals, and birds. Its characteristic call is a series of quavering plaintive whistles, usually on a descending scale.

Screech owls that have taken over a woodpecker's hole

SCREEN, an architectural structure that serves to partition or enclose, or a piece of furniture that protects from heat, light, or drafts. Screens may be ornamental as well as functional and are often works of art.

Architecture. A choir screen traditionally separates the clergy in the choir or side chapel from the laity in the body of the church. In Roman Catholic churches the choir screen is often pierced or cut out to reveal the altar. Many medieval cathedrals have elaborate carved stone choir screens with statues. Smaller churches have carved, often painted, wooden choir screens. A rood screen is a choir screen that supports a rood (crucifix) or a rood loft (gallery) bearing a rood. Ornate wrought-iron grilles form the choir screens in some French, Italian, German, and especially Spanish churches, where they are called *rejas*. In Orthodox churches the choir screen, or iconostasis, is a solid partition adorned with painted images and cut by three doors.

Other architectural screens are the altar screen (reredos), a carved or painted screen behind the altar; and the hall screen, a solid carved partition separating the great hall of a Tudor or Elizabethan house from the passage to the kitchen. In Islamic and modern architecture, a screen wall, outside a building and bearing no weight, conceals a view or gives shelter from sun or wind. Window screens may be wire mesh in frames, as in Western houses, or wooden or stone lattices or iron grilles, as in Islamic and Oriental buildings.

Furniture. A folding screen may shield a person from view or drafts or divide a room. Chinese screens, generally tall and many-paneled, are of painted silk, embroidered silk or tapestry, carved wood inlaid with jade or porcelain, or incised or painted lacquer. Lacquer screens exported from Coromandel in the 17th and 18th centuries were especially popular in the West. Japanese screens, usually low with up to six panels, in pairs, are of paper with painted scenes.

An 18th century fire screen, when placed near a chair, gave protection from the direct heat of an open hearth.

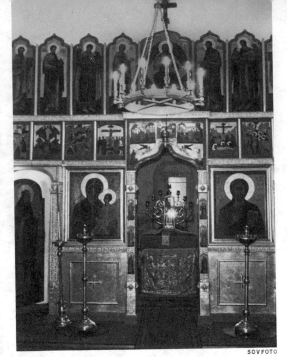

An Orthodox iconostasis, or choir screen, with doors, an altar, and painted religious images and scenes.

European screens are Oriental imports or of wood panels, painted leather or paper, embroidery, tapestry, or fabric to match other furniture. A fire screen, one panel of similar materials, on feet or sliding on a pole, gave protection from the direct heat of an open fireplace in European rooms. Fire screens of solid metal or, later, of wire mesh protected against flying sparks.

SCREW, a threaded metal or plastic device for fastening things together or transmitting motion. It is one of the six simple machines, in effect being an inclined plane wound spirally around a cylinder or cone.

Threads. The spiral ridge around the cylinder or cone is called a thread. It has a uniform section whose shape depends on the work the screw is designed to do. A thread on the outside of a cylinder or cone is called an *external,* or *male,* thread. A mating thread on the inside of a hollow cylinder or cone is called an *internal,* or *female,* thread. On a cylinder, the thread is a straight or parallel thread. On a cone or part of a cone, the thread is a taper thread. The thread is a right-hand thread if, when viewed from the head, the screw turns in a clockwise direction to recede. The thread is a left-hand thread if it turns counterclockwise to recede. The top of a thread is called the *crest.* The bottom of the groove is called the *root.* The distance from one crest to the next is called the *pitch.* The axial movement during one complete rotation is called the *lead.* A single thread is a single helix from one end to the other. Its lead is equal to its pitch. Single threads are used for fastening and for measuring, as on the screw of a micrometer. Threads used for imparting motion may be multiple. A double thread comprises two distinct threads with the angle of the helix increased to allow room for the second thread. The threads start 180° apart. Triple threads start 120° apart. Quadruple threads start 90° apart for rapid advance of the screw. The lead of a double thread is twice as long as its pitch, and the lead of a triple thread is three times as long as its pitch.

Three types of threads are used for fastening: a V thread at a 60° angle with a sharp crest and root; a V thread at a 60° angle with crest cut off and root filled in (American standard); and a Whitworth thread with a 55° angle and rounded crest and root (English standard). The United States, United Kingdom, and Canada agreed in 1948 on the American type as a standard thread. Three types of threads are used for transmitting motion: the square thread; the Acme thread, which has a 29° angle and squared-off crest and root; and the buttress thread, which has one face vertical and the other at a 45° angle.

Fasteners. Screws, bolts, and nuts depend on their threads for holding power. They make excellent fasteners, especially for parts that may be disassembled at some future time. Friction between the threads of a bolt and its nut tends to prevent unscrewing except when vibration is great. Bolts are generally distinguished from screws because they pass completely through the parts being joined and are fastened by a nut on the threaded end. A screw does not require a nut. Instead, it passes entirely through only one of the parts and seats directly in threads in the second part. A metal part in which a machine screw is seated can be drilled and tapped with mating threads. A wood screw (made of metal for use in wood) makes its own thread in the wood into which it is driven, as does a self-tapping machine screw used in sheet metal and relatively soft materials.

Screws and bolts are identified either by their application or the shapes of their heads. They include wood screws, machine screws, setscrews, cap screws, thumbscrews, lag screws or bolts, carriage bolts, stove bolts, eyebolts, and studs. They are made of iron, steel, copper, brass, bronze, aluminum alloy, or plastics such as nylon. Screwheads commonly are countersunk and flat so as not to protrude from the surface of the part through which they are inserted. They generally are slotted so that they can be driven in place with a screwdriver. Bolt heads usually are square or hexagonal to provide gripping surfaces for a wrench. Nuts are perforated square or hexagonal metal blocks threaded internally to mate with the thread of the bolt and avoid binding. When pulled up with a wrench, they draw and hold the parts together. The various kinds of nuts include full nuts, cap nuts, machine-screw nuts, wing nuts, castellated nuts, and knurled nuts. They may be used with a washer (ring of metal), leather, or other material around the bolt to form a seat to protect the surface against which it is drawn or to lock it in place against loosening by vibration. Lock washers are split or toothed, with sharp, canted ends or corners that bite into the joining faces and prevent counterrotation.

Screw machines turn out billions of screws and bolts annually. Essentially they are fully automatic turret lathes with one or more spindles. The multiple-tool holder is pivoted so that each tool in turn is brought into action for turning and threading bar stock, forming the head, and cutting off. Special screws and bolts can be made in a screw-cutting lathe with a single-edge cutting tool, or by using chasers or comb tools controlled by master screws.

Screw Machines. As part of a mechanical device, the screw is an efficient and extremely useful form of inclined plane. The mechanism consists of a frame, a screw, and a sliding member. One of the earliest is Archimedes' screw, which raises water from one level to another. Other screw machines include the screw conveyor for moving bulk materials through a trough; the household meat grinder, which forces meat through a cutter; and the carpenter's auger, which disposes of chips by conveying them up the thread.

The screw also is important in machine tools such as lathes and milling machines, where it produces a slow, feeding motion in the cutter or the work piece in clamps and vises. It closes the jaws to hold the work piece firmly. It also is useful in precise measurement and adjustment, as in micrometers, surveying instruments, and astronomers' telescopes; in propellers on airplanes and ships; and in jackscrews for raising and adjusting heavy loads. For instance, an automobile jack can lift and hold a ton or more by working a simple hand lever against a screw through a pawl and ratchet. See also INCLINED PLANE; SIMPLE MACHINE.

FRANK DORR, *Former Associate Editor*
"Popular Science Monthly"

SCREW PINE, any of various shrubs or trees of the genus *Pandanus* of the screw pine family, Pandanaceae. Screw pines are natives of the tropics, especially Malaysia and the islands of the Pacific and Indian oceans. About 150 species are known. They have stiff, long, narrow leaves in tufts at the ends of the branches or of the main stem. In some species the leaves are prickly on the margins and on the midrib beneath. Many species develop aerial roots from the trunk and branches that, after the base of the trunk decays, become the plant's only support. The unisexual flowers are without petals and occur in dense clusters that terminate the branches and are subtended by bracts. The woody, fibrous, or pulpy fruits are aggregated into compact round or cylindrical heads. Screw-pine leaves are woven into matting, hats, containers, and other articles. The fruits, seeds, and very young leaves of some species are edible. Several species are used as house or conservatory plants.

JOHN W. THIERET[*]
University of Southwestern Louisiana

SCREWWORM FLY, a parasitic species, *Callitroga americana*, or blowfly. See BLOWFLY.

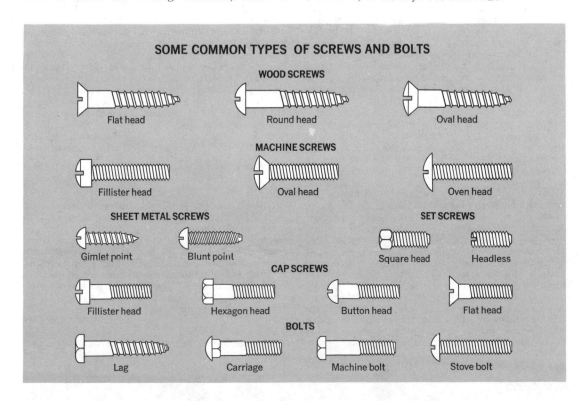

SOME COMMON TYPES OF SCREWS AND BOLTS

WOOD SCREWS
Flat head — Round head — Oval head

MACHINE SCREWS
Fillister head — Oval head — Oven head

SHEET METAL SCREWS
Gimlet point — Blunt point

SET SCREWS
Square head — Headless

CAP SCREWS
Fillister head — Hexagon head — Button head — Flat head

BOLTS
Lag — Carriage — Machine bolt — Stove bolt

BROWN BROTHERS

Aleksandr N. Scriabin, Russian composer

SCRIABIN, skryả'byin. **Aleksandr Nikolayevich** (1872–1915), Russian composer. He was born in Moscow on Jan. 6, 1872. After musical studies in Moscow, he went on a European tour in 1895–1896, playing mostly his own Chopinesque piano pieces. His fame as a composer grew gradually. From 1898 to 1903 he taught at the Moscow Conservatory. Then, given financial assistance by a wealthy patron, he settled in Switzerland, where he composed the orchestral work *The Divine Poem,* first played in Paris in 1905. He toured the United States as soloist, playing his own compositions, in 1906–1907. In 1908 his *Poem of Ecstasy* was given its premiere in New York City by the Russian Symphony Orchestra, under Modest Altschuler. In 1910, Serge Koussevitzky hired Scriabin as piano soloist for a musical tour by boat down the Volga River. It was for Koussevitzky that he wrote *Prometheus,* also known as *The Poem of Fire,* an astonishing work for orchestra, piano, and color organ. Scriabin played the piano part at its first performance (without the color organ), in Moscow, in 1911, under Koussevitzky. Altschuler gave it with color organ at Carnegie Hall, New York City, in 1915. Scriabin was heard in public for the last time, in Petrograd, on April 15, 1915. He died in Moscow on April 27, 1915.

Of Scriabin's many compositions, mostly for orchestra and for piano, only the *Poem of Ecstasy, Prometheus,* and a few short pieces are now played with any frequency. However, his practices and his theories had some influence on later composers. He experimented restlessly with new harmonies, especially of chromatic texture, and with a "mystic chord" (C, F♯, B♭, E, A, D) built up in fourths, which he based on a highly personal interpretation of theosophical doctrines. A strange, unhappy man, Scriabin intended his largest works as artistic syntheses with religious significance, but he lacked the constructive ability to evolve musical forms of enough solidity to achieve his ambitions.

HERBERT WEINSTOCK
Coauthor of "Men of Music"

SCRIBE, skrēb, **Eugène** (1791–1861), French dramatist. Augustin Eugène Scribe was born in Paris on Dec. 24, 1791. In a prolific dramatic career, he wrote more than 400 plays, frequently with collaborators, between the production in 1815 of his *Une Nuit de la garde nationale,* a one-act vaudeville, and his death 46 years later. A contemporary of the Romantic group, he did not align himself with their school or aesthetics but was intent on appealing to the less artistic and less idealistic bourgeoisie, whose purely materialist conception of life he shared. For them he created a new dramatic genre. After having resurrected the 18th century vaudeville, a short comedy interlaced with musical interludes based on a contemporary event, he decided, much in the manner of Molière, to give this genre greater breadth and timeliness. The increased emphasis he thus gave to mores resulted in the creation of the *comédie-vaudeville,* and by gradually abolishing the music and extending and strengthening the intrigue, he turned his plays into real comedies. Scribe was elected to the French Academy in 1836. He died in Paris on Feb. 20, 1861.

Although lacking in distinction, depth, and vigor, Scribe's style is nevertheless agreeable and correct. He contributed significantly to the development of the French theater through his technique of plot construction. Exponent of the "well-built play" (*pièce bien faite*), he is a master craftsman who weaves one scene into another so skillfully that his effect is spellbinding. Prime examples of his technique are *Bataille des dames* (1851), wherein suspense is created by a series of minor crises, and *Le Verre d'eau* (1840), a historical drama of intrigues at the court of Queen Anne of England, built on the theory that great events are produced from small, apparently insignificant causes. Among French dramatists influenced by his mastery of plot technique were Alexandre Dumas *fils,* Émile Augier, and Victorien Sardou.

Other plays by Scribe that deserve mention are *Bertrand et Raton* (1833), a historical comedy; *Une Chaîne* (1841), a comedy; and *Adrienne Lecouvreur* (1849), a tragedy. Scribe also wrote libretti for operas, including *La Dame blanche* (1825), *La Muette de Portici* (1828), *Fra diavolo* (1830), *Robert le diable* (1831), *La Juive* (1835), *Les Huguenots* (1836), and *Le Prophète* (1849). He amassed a fortune and was extremely generous to collaborators.

SIDNEY D. BRAUN
Author of "Dictionary of French Literature"

Further Reading: Arvin, Neil C., *Eugène Scribe and the French Theater, 1815–1860* (Harvard Univ. Press 1924).

SCRIBES, skrībz, in Jewish history and religion, men who served as writers or recorders and, in later times, as interpreters of the law and in related capacities. In the days of the Hebrew monarchy (up to 586 B.C.), the scribes were mostly court officials who specialized in penning letters and documents and functioned as recording secretaries. Some served prophets, writing down their extemporaneous speeches, as, for example, in Jeremiah 36. In some cases the scribal skill was passed on within certain families (I Chronicles 2:55).

In the 5th century B.C. the Jewish priest and scribe Ezra rose to a high position in the court of the Persian king Artaxerxes I and became the leader of the Jewish exiles who returned to Palestine (Ezra 7). Thereafter, the tasks of the scribes grew more varied: some specialized in the copying of the scrolls of the Mosaic Law (Torah), phylacteries (*tefillin*), and doorpost scrolls (*mezuzoth*); others in recording important communal events; and others in writing marriage contracts, letters of divorce, and other legal papers.

In the last two centuries B. C., the importance of the scribes' position increased, and they became interpreters of the law, teachers, preachers, and judges. From among their ranks were elected the members of the Great Assembly, the central legislative body of Jewish Palestine. The tradition-abiding Jewish majority held the scribes in great respect, and their legal decisions were accepted as mandatory. It was probably because of the great legal authority wielded by the scribes that the early Christians, who embraced doctrines contrary to the teachings of the scribes, were opposed to them and accused them of hypocrisy, as, for example, in Matthew 23, Luke 11, and Mark 7. ·

Following the 1st century A. D., the title "scribe" fell into disuse, and the scribes' legislative functions were continued by the Talmudic sages, the rabbis.

RAPHAEL PATAI
Theodor Herzl Institute

SCRIBNER, skrib′nər, an American family of publishers.

CHARLES SCRIBNER (1821–1871), the founder of the family publishing house, was born in New York City on Feb. 21, 1821. He graduated in 1840 from the College of New Jersey (later Princeton University) with a law degree, but ill health caused him to give up the law. In 1846 he entered publishing in partnership with Isaac D. Baker. Except for 1871–1878, the firm has continued in the Scribner name alone since Baker's death (1850). From 1878 it was known as Charles Scribners' Sons.

Scribner established a reputation for quality books ranging from philosophy to popular fiction. The firm's early periodicals were *Hours at Home* (1865–1870) and *Scribner's Monthly* (1870–1881). Scribner died in Lucerne, Switzerland, on Aug. 26, 1871.

CHARLES SCRIBNER (1854–1930), the son of the preceding, was born in New York City on Oct. 18, 1854. He graduated from Princeton in 1875 and became head of the firm after the death of his older brother John Blair Scribner in 1879. He continued to direct it for 51 years—until 1930, when he was succeeded as president by his younger brother Arthur Hawley Scribner. Charles sold the earlier periodicals and founded *Scribner's Magazine* (1887–1937). He attracted leading authors, including Robert Louis Stevenson, Henry van Dyke, Ring Lardner, and Ernest Hemingway. He donated equipment and quarters to establish the Princeton University Press. He served as a trustee of Princeton University, was influential in banking circles, helped secure the international copyright law (1891), and helped form the American Publishers' Association (1900). Scribner died in New York City on April 19, 1930.

CHARLES SCRIBNER (1890–1952), the son of the preceding, was born in New York City, on Jan. 26, 1890. He entered the publishing firm after graduating from Princeton in 1913. After service as a lieutenant in the Quartermaster Corps in World War I, he returned to Scribner's in 1918 and became president in 1932. He was also president of Princeton University Press and a director of Bantam Books, Inc., and Grossett & Dunlap, Inc. Scribner died in New York City on Feb. 11, 1952.

CHARLES SCRIBNER, JR. (1921–   ), a son of the preceding, was born in Quoque, N. Y., on July 13, 1921. After graduating from Princeton in 1943, he served in the United States Navy (1943–1946) during and after World War II and was discharged as a lieutenant. He then joined the family publishing firm as advertising manager and became president of Charles Scribners' Sons in 1952 and president of Princeton University Press in 1957.

SCRIMSHAW, skrim′shô, is a useful or ornamental article of whalebone, whale ivory, or walrus tusk carved by sailors or others. The term also means the process of carving such objects. Variations of the word include scrimshandy, scrimshander, and scrimshonter.

Scrimshaw was developed by sailors on 18th and 19th century whaling ships to pass the many hours of idleness on long voyages. They worked chiefly with saws, files, and, especially, jackknives to produce a great variety of objects. Such objects included the jagging wheel (for crimping piecrust), with a handle shaped like a fish, siren, bird, dragon, or fiddleback; busks (corset stays); boxes, baskets, and birdcages; cane handles; fans; and bracelets and rings. Decorative scenes, such as whaling incidents, were often incised in the ivory and rubbed with black or red pigment to emphasize the lines. Examples of scrimshaw may be seen in the museums of former whaling towns in New England.

Scrimshaw was introduced by whalers to Eskimos in the late 19th century. Eskimo craftsmen incised bow-drill handles, pipes, and other objects with scenes of Eskimo life.

Scrimshaw is the art of carving on whale or walrus bone.

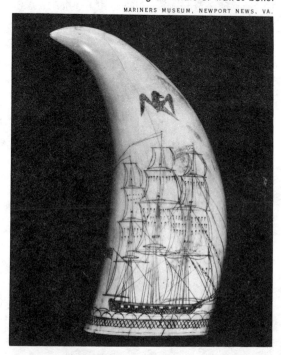

SCRIP is a certificate indicating that the bearer is entitled to some payment not yet received. Scrip may be exchanged for cash or for a permanent certificate under stated conditions. Scrip serves to conserve cash for the issuing body. Most commonly, scrip represents fractional rights to shares of stock when a stock dividend or stock split is declared by a corporation. Less frequently, it consists of temporary certificates awaiting permanent stock or bond certificates. Scrip has also been used to pay bond interest in lieu of cash.

Municipal governments and business corporations have issued scrip as wage payments to employees in times of severe cash shortage. Fractional paper money issued by the United States government in the Civil War period, which were called "shinplasters," was another form of scrip, as was the "invasion currency" carried by Allied troops in World War II.

WILLIAM N. KINNARD, JR.
University of Connecticut

SCRIPPS, an American family who created an extensive chain of American newspapers.

EDWARD WYLLIS SCRIPPS (1854–1926), who founded the chain, was born near Rushville, Ill., on June 18, 1854, and educated in the local schools. He entered journalism in Detroit in 1872 and worked on the *Evening News,* founded by his half-brother James Edmund Scripps in 1873. In 1878 he founded the Cleveland *Penny Press* (later known as the *Press*). With James providing most of the capital, he acquired the St. Louis *Evening Chronicle* in 1880 and the Cincinnati *Penny Post* (later the *Post*) in 1881. Scripps also sponsored the establishment of the *Kentucky Post* in 1885, dated Covington, Ky., but published in Cincinnati. A controversy with James in 1879 over the Cleveland paper's financial operation foreshadowed a quarrel in 1889 over control in Cincinnati and other differences that resulted in a split between the two.

After 1889, Scripps formed a partnership with Milton Alexander McRae, which was joined by George H. Scripps, another half-brother of Edward, in 1894, and resulted in the formation of the Scripps-McRae League of Newspapers. At least as early as 1887 the newspapers in Detroit, Cleveland, St. Louis, and Cincinnati, with the Kentucky edition added, constituted the first daily newspaper chain or group in the United States. Minus the Detroit paper after 1889, the group was to establish or purchase, and sometimes also to suspend, newspapers in many Midwestern and Southern cities. Scripps always held at least 51% of the stock in every paper, giving him control. In 1893 Scripps acquired an interest in the San Diego *Sun,* and between that year and 1909 he purchased or established other Western dailies to form the Scripps Coast League of newspapers, operated independently.

Altogether, in a career spanning half a century, Scripps controlled at various times more than 30 daily newspapers. His promotion of afternoon newspapers—inexpensive, nonpolitical, liberal, and made to appeal to women as well as men—contributed to a virtual revolution in journalistic practices. In 1907 he formed the United Press Associations (since 1958 the United Press International). He sponsored several newspaper syndicates, including the Newspaper Enterprise Association (1902) and Science Service (1920).

A millionaire by the mid-1890's, Scripps became active in philanthropy. With his half-sister Ellen Browning Scripps, he endowed the Scripps Institution of Biological Research at La Jolla, Calif., now the Scripps Institution of Oceanography, a division of the University of California. Scripps died aboard his yacht, in Monrovia Bay, Liberia, on March 12, 1926.

JAMES GEORGE SCRIPPS (1886–1921), Edward Wyllis Scripps' eldest son, assumed active direction of the Scripps enterprises following differences between his father and Milton Alexander McRae that ended the Scripps-McRae partnership in 1914. A quarrel between father and son in 1920 resulted in James' removal from general direction, although he retained control of five of the West Coast newspapers.

ROBERT PAINE SCRIPPS (1895–1938), another son of Edward Wyllis Scripps, directed the main group of former Scripps-McRae newspapers after 1920. These were reorganized as the Scripps-Howard Newspapers in 1922, with Robert associated in a new partnership with Roy W. Howard.

JAMES EDMUND SCRIPPS (1835–1906), half-brother of Edward Wyllis Scripps, became a journalist in Chicago and then in Detroit, where he was part owner of the *Tribune* and in 1873 founded the *Evening News* (now the *News*). Later associated with his half-brother and George H. Scripps, his brother, in newspaper enterprises, he broke with Edward Wyllis in 1889 and thereafter concentrated entirely on his Detroit interests.

ELLEN BROWNING SCRIPPS (1836–1932), sister of James Edmund Scripps and half-sister of Edward Wyllis Scripps, was associated with both of them professionally and financially in journalistic undertakings. Moving to La Jolla, Calif., about 1891, she was partly responsible for the town's development, made benefactions to the town of Rushville, Ill., and founded the Scripps College for women at Claremont, Calif., now part of the Claremont Colleges.

ROBERT W. DESMOND
Formerly, University of California, Berkeley

Further Reading: Cochran, Negley, *E. W. Scripps* (Harcourt 1933); McCabe, Charles R., ed., *Dammed Old Crank: A Self Portrait of E. W. Scripps Drawn from His Unpublished Writings* (Harper 1951); Stewart, Kenneth, and Tebbel, John, *Makers of Modern Journalism* (Prentice-Hall 1952).

SCROFULA, skrof′yə-lə, is a lumpy swelling along the sides of the neck and above the clavicle, caused by a tuberculous infection of lymph glands. Scrofula most commonly results from infection with *Mycobacterium tuberculosis,* where the primary infection is pulmonary, and the organisms reach the lymph nodes by direct drainage through the lymphatics or by spreading through the blood stream. It may also result from an atypical infection with a scotochromogen, with the primary infection in the throat or tonsils. Virtual eradication of tuberculosis from dairy herds and the pasteurization of milk have made scrofula due to *M. bovis* rare. Most scrofula infections are amenable to drug therapy, although scotochromogen infections are less responsive to such therapy and sometimes necessitate surgical removal of the lymph glands.

DONALD ARMSTRONG, M. D.
Memorial Sloan Kettering Cancer Center

SCROGGS, skrogz, **Sir William** (1623?–1683), English judge, who has been called in print "one of the worst judges that ever disgraced the English bench." He was born in Deddington, Oxfordshire, England. He was educated at Oxford

University, and was called to the bar, after studying law at Gray's Inn, in 1653. Appointed chief justice in 1678, he became notorious for his brutality and partiality in conducting the trials of Roman Catholics implicated in the Popish Plot fabricated by Titus Oates in that year. He was impeached by the House of Commons but was never brought to trial. However, in 1681 he was removed from office by Charles II, who granted him a pension. He died in London on Oct. 25, 1683.

SCROLLS, Dead Sea. See DEAD SEA SCROLLS.

SCROOGE, skrōōj, **Ebenezer,** the central character in Charles Dickens' *A Christmas Carol* (1843). He is the employer of Bob Cratchit, a poor clerk, whose son, Tiny Tim, is a cripple. Scrooge, "a squeezing, grasping, covetous old hunks," has visions of Christmas past, present, and yet to come. The dreams have a miraculous effect upon him, making him cheerful and loving. The character so captured the popular imagination that his name is synonymous with miserliness.

SCROPE, skrōōp, **George Julius Poulett** (1797–1876), English geologist and political economist. He was born in London on March 10, 1797, with the surname of Thomson, but when he married he assumed his wife's surname. Scrope made extensive geological field trips and witnessed the eruption of Mount Vesuvius in 1822. His works, such as *Geology of Central France* (1827), contributed to theories of the action and source of energy of volcanoes, and they marked the beginning of the modern science of volcanology. Together with the efforts of Sir Charles Lyell, these researches helped to replace Neptunian theories of the earth's history with the uniformitarian theory that earth-shaping processes have operated in a similar manner throughout geological time. Scrope died in Fairlawn, near Cobham, on Jan. 18, 1876.

SCROTUM, skrō'təm, in male human beings, a cutaneous pouch containing the testes and parts of the spermatic cord. It is divided into two lateral portions by a ridge, or raphe, the left portion usually hanging lower than the right. The light brownish, very thin outer skin is thrown into folds and covered with sebaceous follicles and hair. See TESTIS.

SCRUB TYPHUS is a rickettsial disease caused by *Rickettsia tsutsugamushi*, or *R. orientalis*, transmitted to man by the larval, or "chigger," stage of certain mites and occasionally by infected rodents. Also known as *tsutsugamushi fever*, it occurs in eastern and southeastern Asia and was a major problem for soldiers during World War II, especially in rural and jungle areas.

After an incubation period of 10 to 18 days, a small pink lesion usually develops in the skin of the groin, buttocks, or other hairy regions. It slowly develops into a small reddish lesion with a black center. Enlarged lymph glands develop in the adjacent area, and soon chills, fever, headache, and prostration develop. By the end of the first week of fever, a pinkish skin rash occurs on the chest and abdomen and gradually spreads over the entire body, except for the face and hands. In severe cases, abnormalities of the blood, heart, and lungs develop.

In its early stages the disease must be differentiated from typhus fever, malaria, dengue fever, and other somewhat similar diseases. Diagnosis is confirmed on the basis of specific blood serum tests. Untreated scrub typhus may be fatal, but in properly treated cases, the mortality rate is negligible. Within 24 to 36 hours after treatment with chloramphenicol or the tetracyclines is begun, toxic signs abate, fever disappears, and the rash and lesion regress.

HERBERT L. DuPONT, M. D.
University of Maryland School of Medicine

SCRUBBIRD, either of two species of Australian birds, making up the family Atrichornithidae. They resemble large wrens but are closely related to lyrebirds. The noisy scrubbird, *Atrichornis clamosa*, of western Australia is about 8.5 inches (22 cm) long and has dark brown plumage with a whitish throat and breast. It is known for its loud ringing whistles and cracking noises. The rufous scrubbird, *A. rufescens*, of eastern Australia is slightly smaller and also has dark brown plumage but has its throat and underparts tinged with orange-brown. Scrubbirds are nearly flightless. They search the jungle for insects and small snails and their eggs. The nest, generally dome-shaped, is made of grass and rootlets plastered with a pulpy substance.

SCUBA DIVING. See DIVING, PROFESSIONAL.

SCUDÉRY, skü-dā-rē', **Madeleine de** (1607–1701), French novelist and woman of letters. She was born in Le Havre on Nov. 15, 1607. In 1638 she joined her brother in Paris, where he was pursuing a literary career. She assisted him in his work and began writing her own works, with which he helped and which he published under his name. Mlle. Scudéry also became a frequenter of the famous salon at the Hôtel de Rambouillet, from which she drew much of the material she used in her romances.

Mlle. Scudéry's most famous novels are *Artamène, ou le Grand Cyrus*, 10 vols. (1649–1653) and *Clélie*, 10 vols. (1654–1660), in which she used characters and settings from Persian and Roman worlds to express contemporary French notions of romance. In *Le Grand Cyrus* the hero, Artamène, was really the Prince de Condé, and in volume 10 she introduced herself under the name "Sappho." Her own salon, the Société du Samedi, was opened in 1552 after the Hôtel de Rambouillet salon had ended. Mlle. Scudéry died in Paris on June 2, 1701.

SCULLING. See ROWING.

SCULPIN, skul'pən, any of a family of fishes that generally have the eyes on top of a large head and sharp spines in front of the gills. There are about 300 species, making up the family Cottidae, order Perciformes. Most are bottom-dwelling fish. Many are marine, found in cold waters, but some live in brackish water and some in fresh water. Sculpins range from a few inches to more than 2 feet (60 cm) in length. They are often scaleless or only partially scaled and usually have two dorsal fins and large fan-shaped pectoral fins. One of the most common species is the Pacific staghorn sculpin, *Leptocottus armatus*, which is equipped with hooks on its opercle, or gill cover. It is found abundantly in bays from Alaska to Lower California. Other members of the family include the cabezone and the sea raven. See also CABEZONE.

Sculpture styles range through Michelangelo's Renaissance *Moses*, in marble; the wood mask of the primitive Kwaki-utl of the Pacific Northwest; and N. Gabo's modern *Linear Construction, Variation,* of synthetic threads.

SCULPTURE

CONTENTS

SCULPTURE is the branch of the fine arts that is primarily concerned with the creation of expressive form in three dimensions. It includes a wide range of different kinds of art works, extending from free-standing, independent objects, through various forms of high, medium, and low relief, to extreme forms of low relief that are little more than raised drawings.

Techniques. Works of sculpture are produced by three main processes: (1) *carving*, a reductive process in which the desired form is reached by removing the surplus from a block or similar mass of material; (2) *modeling*, an additive process in which the form is built up in a plastic material; and (3) *constructing* or *assembling*, in which the sculpture is created by joining ready-made objects and units of material that already

have a shape of their own. Materials may also be shaped by *hammering*, as in metal forging and repoussé, or by *incising*, as in glyptic art (engraving of cameos, seals, and other gems). *Casting* is an important process in the production of many kinds of sculpture, although its main use is as a method of reproducing rather than shaping forms.

Materials. Almost any material capable of being shaped three-dimensionally may be used for sculpture. Hard, durable materials, such as stone, metal, wood, concrete, terra cotta, ivory, bone, and, more recently, plastics, have generally been preferred. But work has also been produced in more perishable materials, such as leather, feathers, soap, ice, and snow. Even edible materials, such as bread dough, cake icing, and butter, have been used. The shaping of these materials involves a great variety of technical skills and processes. Some sculptors are specialists in stone carving, bronze founding, or the like. Others work in a variety of materials, sometimes employing specialist craftsmen to carry out certain aspects of the work, as, for example, metal casting or the laborious initial stages of stone carving.

444

Formal Elements. The principal formal elements of sculpture are mass and space. Although these are inseparable in the sense that neither can exist without the other, it is the shaping of the masses—the solid material bulk of the sculpture—that has traditionally claimed most of the sculptor's attention. Only during the 20th century have sculptors become fully aware of the positive role that space may play as an element in the design of their work. Textural qualities, color, line, and the play of light and shade may also make an important contribution.

Size. Sculpture varies in size from the minute scale of coins, medals, cameos, and ivories to the colossal scale of the Statue of Liberty, the Christ of the Andes, and the relief frieze of the great Altar of Pergamon.

Setting. Some sculptures are completely self-contained and exist as independent, even portable, objects in their own right. The great majority, however, are integrated or linked in some way with the structure of a building, a piece of furniture, a vessel, an implement, a musical instrument, or the like, or are designed for a special environment, such as a garden, a town square, or the interior of a building.

Purpose. Sculptural images have served many important religious and civic purposes. Such works include temple sculpture, religious icons, ritual objects, tomb figures, and various kinds of commemorative sculpture such as grave steles, triumphal arches, columns, portraits, war memorials, and tomb effigies. Works of a lighter nature include garden sculpture, fountains, body ornaments, and a wide variety of decorative sculpture. In the 20th century a great deal of sculpture has been produced for purely aesthetic purposes, to be appreciated as an end in itself.

1. Techniques and Materials

Carving—Stone. Stone has been almost universally employed as the chief material for monumental sculpture for a number of reasons. It is readily available in large quantities in most parts of the world. It is durable, weather resistant, homogeneous in texture, and uniform in hardness. And it has been the principal material used for the important buildings with which most monumental sculpture is associated.

The techniques used for stone carving depend on both the hardness of the stone itself and the quality of the metal tools available at the time. Gothic sculpture, mostly carved in softer stones with metal chisels, was usually cut boldly and deeply with considerable undercutting, deep shadows, and strong detail. Before the development of modern tools, harder stones, such as granite, were usually pulverized with hammers and then rubbed down with emery and similar abrasive materials, producing, for example, the smooth continuous surfaces and shallow detail of much Egyptian sculpture. All stones, however, are heavy and lacking in tensile strength and therefore encourage a massive and compact treatment without vulnerable projections or thin, easily fractured, supporting shapes. The ankles of free-standing figures, for example, are almost always given extra support.

Some sculptors have preferred to overcome rather than submit to the natural limitations of stone. A great deal of Hellenistic, Roman, and post-Renaissance European stone sculpture is very freely and openly carved out of a number of jointed blocks of stone. It often emulates the freedom of design, as seen, for example, in the outspread limbs and flying draperies of metal sculpture.

In *direct stone carving,* the main masses are first roughed out of the block, and the final detail is approached gradually by progressing from larger containing shapes to smaller contained ones. This systematic process imposes a characteristic order on the design of direct stone carvings. This order and other features are lost in indirect carving.

In *indirect carving* the design is first modeled in clay. This original model is then cast in plaster and handed over to a professional carver, who uses a pointing machine—a kind of three-dimensional tracing machine—for reproducing the design in stone. Inevitably the result has the plastic quality of modeling rather than carving.

Small-scale carvings in hard stones, such as jade, rock crystal, and agate—some of which are harder than steel—require special techniques of grinding, drilling, and abrading.

Wood. Because wood is affected by the weather and is subject to attack by insects or fungi, it does not survive the passage of time as well as stone. Nevertheless, it has been extensively used, mainly for indoor sculpture. It is the principal material of tribal sculpture in Africa, Oceania, and North America, and it has been used by every advanced civilization.

Both hardwoods and softwoods are used for sculpture. They are carved with either gouges or adzes, which are kept extremely sharp in order to cut through the bundles of wood fibers without splitting them.

Wood is a relatively light material with considerable tensile strength along its grain. It may therefore be carved openly, with more projections and thinner shapes than stone. It is also easily jointed for building up large works or for creating extensions into space, such as the arms of a crucifix. Boxwood, pear, and other close-grained woods may be carved on a small scale with a wealth of delicate detail. Open-grained woods, such as elm or pine, are better used on a large scale. Gothic wood sculpture shows the kind of complex designs that may be carved in wood, while the large elm figures of the 20th century sculptor Henry Moore show the kind of openness that may be achieved.

Ivory. Ivory, obtained from elephant, mammoth, walrus, hippopotamus, and narwhal tusks, is available in only relatively small pieces. The tusks may be carved solid or sawed into panels and carved into reliefs. Because it is dense and hard, ivory may be carved with great delicacy into small, intricate designs. Tools include various saws, chisels, knives, rasps, and drills.

Modeling. The chief plastic materials used for modeling are clay, wax, and plaster, although other materials, such as concrete, plasticine, stucco, and synthetic resins, can be used. A modeled sculpture may be an end in itself and be made rigid and permanent either through the self-setting properties of the material used (plaster, concrete, stucco) or, if it is ceramic sculpture, by firing in a kiln. A great deal of modeling, however, is merely the first stage in the process of producing a permanent sculpture by casting in another material, such as bronze, aluminum, fiberglass, or concrete.

Clay is the most widely used of all modeling materials, mainly because it is universally available, easy to cast from, extremely plastic, and convertible by firing into one of the most imperishable of all substances. It may also be manipulated with great freedom and fluency, either directly with the hands or with a variety of modeling tools. The chief of these are spatulas for applying the clay and wire-loop tools for removing it.

In ceramic sculpture, the clay model itself is preserved as the finished product. Various kinds of clay may be used and fired to different temperatures to produce earthenware, stoneware, or porcelain. Small sculptures may be modeled in smooth refined clays. Larger works are made from tougher clays with ingredients such as sand and grog (crushed once-fired clay), which give them a coarse, open texture. The ceramic sculptor does not have to consider the problems of casting, unless his work is to be reproduced by slip casting or press molding, and he may therefore model complex, open forms and highly textured surfaces. To withstand the stresses of firing, however, all but the thinnest clay masses must be hollow and of a rather even thickness. Most ceramic sculpture is kept fairly compact in design to prevent breakage.

Modeling in clay and wax is an extremely immediate process preferred by many sculptors who want to leave the traces of their personal handling of the material as a kind of sculptural calligraphy on the finished form. A metal casting may then be thought of primarily as a means of rendering a modeled sculpture permanent. The metal serves merely to fix the plastic, modeled appearance of the original forms. This approach is typical of the work of Auguste Rodin and Jacob Epstein in the 19th and 20th centuries. Sometimes, however, the sculptor works with the qualities of the metal itself in mind and removes all superficial evidence of the plasticity of clay or wax, as in Benin and Indian bronzes.

Modeled sculpture intended for casting in metal may be designed with great freedom. There is no initial block of material to impose limits on its spatial extension, and the metal itself has so much tensile strength that attenuated and extended forms present no problems. A bronze or aluminum figure may easily be made to rest on one foot or to extend its arms freely into space. During the modeling stages, heavy clay models must be adequately supported inside by an armature of metal or wood.

Plaster and stucco are sometimes used for interior, decorative, relief sculpture, but their fragility limits their use for free-standing or exterior work. Today, the process of modeling directly in plaster for reproduction by metal casting has become widespread. This method cuts out the laborious process of converting a clay original into the plaster master cast required by a metal foundry.

Wax is used mainly as a preliminary material for small metal castings. Its main advantage is that it may be melted out of a mold, leaving a cavity to be filled with the molten metal. For larger metal cast sculptures, wax may be modeled as a finishing layer over a core of refractory material. This wax-coated model is then cast by the lost-wax process described below.

Casting. In casting sculpture there must be an original model, a mold taken from this model, and a cast taken from the mold. All three may be made in a number of materials and by a variety of processes.

There are three main types of molds employed in sculpture. (1) *Waste molds* are used for producing a single cast. After the mold has been filled with the casting material, it is broken away from the cast in pieces, hence the term "waste mold." (2) *Piece molds* are constructed in a number of sections over the original model in such a way that they can be easily removed without damaging the model. They are used when the original model must be preserved undamaged or when a number of casts are to be taken from the same mold. (3) *Flexible molds* of gelatine, rubber compounds, or flexible synthetic materials are used for reproducing rigid original models and for producing a number of casts. The flexibility of the mold enables it to be pulled away easily from undercut and complex surfaces without damage to the original model or cast.

Metal-cast sculpture is produced in two main ways: the lost-wax (*cire-perdue*) process and sand casting. The *lost-wax process* is used for the finest casts. Except for the smallest sculpture, it requires a model consisting of a layer or shell of wax over a core of refractory material. In the direct lost-wax process, the sculptor fashions the model directly in thick, malleable wax laid over a roughly shaped core. In the indirect lost-wax process, he first makes a clay model, casts it in plaster, and from the cast makes a flexible mold, which he coats with melted wax to form a hollow wax shell. He fills the shell with refractory material.

The procedure is then the same for both the direct and indirect processes. The wax-covered model is invested with (enclosed in) a mold made of a refractory material, in which channels allow the molten metal to flow and mold gases to escape. The invested model is heated and the wax melted out. Molten metal is poured in to replace the wax. After cooling, the mold is broken away from the metal cast and the core removed. The cast is then cleaned and worked on directly with metal-working tools.

Sand casting is mainly an industrial process used for producing fairly rough metal castings in relatively simple shapes without surface refinement or detail. A mold made of cohesive casting sand is built up in pieces around the original model, and a sand core is suspended inside the mold, leaving a gap to be filled with molten metal. Simple, solid, sand castings are often produced today by burying a model made of expanded polystyrene in casting sand and pouring molten metal straight onto it. The polystyrene disappears as gases, leaving a cavity to be filled by the metal. This technique is sometimes known as the *lost-pattern process*.

Concrete and various types of cast-stone sculpture are usually produced by casting in plaster waste molds made from clay originals. Lightweight, economical, and durable casts are now widely made by laying up synthetic resins reinforced with glass fiber in plaster molds.

Assembling and Constructing. Assembling as a complete method of producing sculpture is a recent development, but the principle is not entirely new. Wooden masks and figures made by many tribal peoples were often augmented by cloth, beads, mirrors, ropes, nails, feathers, shells, wickerwork, or other materials; and some Western religious sculptures, especially Madonnas and saints, are fully clothed, crowned, and set in niches or small stage sets, in which miscellaneous objects are assembled.

TECHNIQUES AND MATERIALS

Carved marble *Despair* (1885) by Rodin, showing the contained, fluently muscled figure emerging from the block of stone.

Cast bronze Chinese Buddhist altarpiece (6th century) from the Wei dynasty, having thin, pierced forms and delicate detail.

Welded iron and steel construction of found objects ("Untitled"; 1962) by Richard Stankiewicz.

Detail of carved-wood ceremonial pole (*right*) from southwestern New Guinea, with openwork form.

Modeled-clay vessel (*left*) from pre-Columbian Peru, with a stirrup spout and shaped like a puma.

No special techniques are required for assembled sculpture. Its components (ready-made, found objects, or junk) may be put together loosely in a variety of ways.

Constructed sculpture usually consists not of ready-made objects but of preformed units—for example, rods, sheets, tubes, planks, threads—in a variety of materials. These may be joined by any suitable method, such as gluing, welding, riveting, and screwing. A great deal of modern direct-metal sculpture and wood sculpture is constructed. As a method of producing sculpture, construction lends itself most readily to open, spatial rather than solid, massive designs. It displays a closer identity between structure and form than is possible with sculpture that is carved or modeled in a homogeneous mass.

Finishing. Surface finishes for sculpture are either applied or natural.

Applied. The most common applied finish is color. Almost all sculpture before the Renaissance was colored. The strong coloring of sculpture sealed in Egyptian tombs has often survived almost intact. Greek marble nudes, now colorless through exposure, were originally tinted with wax colors and had painted or inlaid eyes. Medieval sculpture was brilliantly painted and gilded and heavily patterned. Indian sculpture was usually finished off with a coat of gesso, in which fine detail was modeled, and then painted. Most of the tribal sculpture of Africa, Oceania, and North America was boldly colored. Many ceramics in all periods have been colored by combinations of slip, glazes, and enamels.

Frequently, color was applied not by the sculptors themselves but by painters. On Greek reliefs, painters were also expected to insert important details.

Sculpture from the Renaissance to the 20th century was usually uncolored, but in the 20th century the use of color revived. Metal and wood sculpture is often sprayed with cellulose paints, and fiberglass may be painted on the surface or colored all through.

Natural. The natural beauty of stone, wood, or metal may be brought out by smoothing and by applying polishes or lacquers, which may also act as preservatives. Some stones will take a high polish, achieved by rubbing down when wet with a series of coarse to fine abrasives. Wax is sometimes used for a final gloss. Wood is usually finished by either scraping or sandpapering and is then waxed or oiled to bring out its color and grain.

Metal sculpture may be rubbed down with emery and steel wool and polished with metal polish to bring out its natural luster. It may have its color changed by gilding, electroplating, or patinating. Patinating, applied chiefly to bronze, is the treatment of that metal by a chemical that changes its natural golden color to a variety of green, blue, brown, or black, which ancient bronzes acquired through the corrosive effects of exposure to sea water, earth, or weather. Metal sculpture may also be decorated by engraving, etching, enameling, or other techniques.

Other Materials. Sculptors today make use of any material, natural or man-made, or any technique that may serve their purpose. Some of the more commonly used materials are plastics, such as perspex, polythene, polystyrene foam, resin reinforced with glass fiber, and nylon; fabrics; foam rubber; glass; water; air, as in inflatable sculpture; and artificial light. The use of these new materials and the introduction of electrically powered movement in kinetic sculpture may require a considerable knowledge of specialized techniques and machinery.

L. R. ROGERS
Author of "Sculpture"

Bibliography

Clarke, Geoffrey, and Cornock, Stroud, *A Sculptor's Manual* (Reinhold 1968).
Lanteri, Edward, *Modelling and Sculpture: A Guide for Artists and Students* (Dover 1965).
Mills, John W., *The Technique of Casting for Sculpture* (Reinhold 1967).
Read, Herbert Edward, *The Art of Sculpture* (Pantheon Bks. 1956).
Rich, Jack C., *The Materials and Methods of Sculpture* (Oxford 1947).
Rogers, Leonard R., *Sculpture* (Oxford 1969).

2. History—Ancient

Sculpture, in the round and in relief, was first produced by Paleolithic man. Since then, there have been few societies in which sculpture has not played an important role.

The three-dimensionality and durability of sculpture have made it the generally preferred medium for the expression of man's most deeply felt ideas about himself and his place in the cosmos. It has served as a means of representing gods, mythical beings, kings, heroes, and other important personages and of recording major events in the spiritual life of a community.

Our view of the sculpture of the past is somewhat distorted by the accidents of survival. Virtually all ancient sculpture in perishable materials has disappeared, including most wood sculpture. Only works in stone, fired clay, ivory, bone, or metal remain. Even the limited amount of surviving metal sculpture is out of all proportion to what was produced, since vast quantities of sculpture in bronze or precious metals have been melted down.

Sculpture is usually closely related in both style and content to the other arts. It follows its own laws of development, but it interacts with the other arts, is affected by the same geographic, economic, and political circumstances, and expresses the same fundamental religious, social, and philosophical attitudes and beliefs.

The development of urban civilization, with its concentration of power and wealth and its need for palaces and temples, created the conditions for the growth of monumental figure sculpture in Sumer and Egypt between 4000 and 3000 B. C. The development of large-scale sculpture in the ancient world shows an increasing mastery over the movement of the figure. Sculptors gradually liberated their work from its architectural background and from the spatial straitjacket imposed on it by the shapes of the blocks from which it was carved.

Middle Eastern—Mesopotamian. The great ancient civilizations of Mesopotamia—Sumerian, Babylonian, and Assyrian—only occasionally produced sculpture of a quality comparable with the superb and sustained achievement of Egypt. Concentration on the development of a strong sculptural tradition was hampered by the unsettled political life of the region, by a rather pessimistic, joyless religious outlook, and by a lack of good, easily available stone.

The first Mesopotamian civilization, and probably the first of all civilizations, was that of Sumer, a region of city-states, such as Erech (Uruk), Ur, and Lagash. Sumerian sculpture consists in the main of stiff, isolated figures,

Gudea of Lagash, a compact, stone Sumerian figure (before 2000 B. C.).

Winged lion, an Assyrian gate guardian, in alabaster (9th century B. C.).

which are entirely frontal and are formed around a rigid vertical axis. The most impressive works are a number of statues of Gudea, a ruler of Lagash. They are compact, concentrated, and energetic. Their powerful, simple forms have been greatly admired by 20th century sculptors as examples of direct stone carving. Relief sculpture shows no evidence of a conception of spatial depth, but in at least one work—the victory stele of Naramsin—the composition is bold and original. One of the finest Sumerian sculptures, from Ur, is the well-known rampant goat and tree, constructed of wood, gold, and lapis lazuli.

Little sculpture of real merit has survived from the 1,000 or so years of the Babylonian Empire, which replaced the Sumerian city-states. The best-known work is the large stone stele of Hammurabi, which records that king's code of laws and is surmounted by a bold relief showing him facing the sun god.

The Assyrians maintained their empire by a rule of terror. Their major sculptural achievements were associated with the great palaces built by their autocratic emperors, such as the palaces of Sargon at Khorsabad, of Ashurbanipal at Nineveh, and of Ashurnasirpal at Nimrud. The finest works are the gigantic, powerful, human-headed winged bulls that guard the entrances of the palaces and the low relief friezes that occupy the interior walls.

The narrative friezes from the palaces of Ashurbanipal and Ashurnasirpal glorify the emperors, showing their cruelty and invincibility in war and their bravery as hunters. Assyrian reliefs have no spatial depth, everything being arranged in registers and flattened out to lie in the surface plane. They contain a wealth of detail about military life, but their main glory is their treatment of animals. Horses and lions,

in particular, are represented with great feeling for their grace and strength.

The winged bulls, the larger relief figures, and the free-standing figures are rigidly posed and harsh, with an overemphasis on surface details at the expense of plastic form. In this aggressive art there appears to be no concern for the gentler aspects of humanity or interest in the female figure, which is so beautifully represented in Egyptian sculpture.

Iranian. The Persian Empire absorbed Assyria and Babylonia and profited from their artistic traditions. The Achaemenid emperors built enormous palaces, the greatest of which are at Persepolis and Susa, and decorated their staircases and audience halls with splendid sculpture—stone columns topped by bulls arranged back to back, stone processional relief friezes, and brightly colored glazed brick reliefs. The conventions and general style of the reliefs owe much to Assyrian examples, but they are gentler and more decorative and graceful. This change of mood reflects the Persian rulers' more optimistic religion and humane conception of justice.

Steppe. The art of nomadic peoples, such as the Scythians, who roamed the steppe regions between China and Europe, is sometimes known as the "animal style." It is an art mainly of small portable metal objects—weapons, harness trappings, and ornaments—in which animal themes, treated with the utmost freedom, become a basis for complex, semiabstract designs. The influence of this art was widespread in China, Europe, and the Middle East. It is believed to be connected with the stylized art of prehistoric Iran and with the much later (first half of the 1st millennium B. C.) bronzes of Luristan.

Egyptian. An astonishingly consistent tradition of sculpture flourished in Egypt for about 30

Mycerinus and His Queen (Old Kingdom Egyptian), in slate, with a blocklike, severely frontal pose.

ures in wood and metal. The composition of the sculpture is governed by strict conventions, and in larger works the poses are severely limited. The figures stand bolt upright, kneel, squat, or sit either on seats or cross-legged. All are uncompromisingly frontal, with their main planes conforming to the faces of a cubic block. But despite its limited movement, Egyptian sculpture at its best, especially during the Old Kingdom, shows a profound grasp of the plastic essentials of both the male and female figure and is unsurpassed in its dignity and power. At its worst it is stiff and stereotyped.

The need to make sculptured doubles of the dead encouraged the development of portraiture, in which Egyptian sculptors excelled. The Old Kingdom, the 12th dynasty, and the Amarna period of the 18th dynasty are outstanding for portrait heads. The bodies rarely show individuality.

Relief sculpture is rich in representations of scenes of everyday life—farming, hunting, craft activities, feasting, and the like. Even though the planimetric conventions that govern the composition of reliefs and the construction of the figure are strict, the reliefs are astonishingly vivid and informative. A notable feature is their sympathetic observation of the character and behavior of animals and birds. Superb examples are found in reliefs from the tombs of Ti and Mereruka (5th and 6th dynasties) at Saqqara. The refinement and elegance that the crisp, linear Egyptian style of low relief could achieve is evident in the reliefs in the tomb of the Vizier Ramose at Thebes (18th dynasty).

One of the most remarkable periods of Egyptian sculpture occurred under the pharaoh Akhenaton (Amenhotep IV) during the 18th dynasty. It is known as the Amarna period, after this ruler's capital city. This amazing man instituted a new monotheistic religion and encouraged a relaxation of the traditional conventions of Egyptian art, making it more naturalistic and human. A famous work of this period is the colored bust of his queen, Nefertiti.

Aegean. During the 3d and 2d millennia B. C., three civilizations—Cycladic, Cretan (Minoan), and Mycenaean—preceded Greek civilization proper in the eastern Mediterranean. Of the early civilization of the islands known as the Cyclades, little survives except marble tomb figures. Most of these are slender, girlish figures with abstract, flattened forms totally different in spirit from the full-bodied, fleshy Old Stone Age "Venuses." The abstraction is sometimes carried to a point where the sculpture becomes a mere violin-shaped abbreviation for the female figure.

Cretan civilization centered on great palaces, such as those at Knossos and Phaestos, but produced no temples or monumental sculpture. Its smaller sculpture, however, is extremely sophisticated, differing from all previous work in its organic, flowing naturalism and exuberant movement. Notable works are snake goddesses in ivory and ceramic and reliefs on steatite vases.

Mycenae, on the Greek mainland, succeeded Knossos as the center of civilization in the Aegean. Its main sculptural achievements were in goldsmithing, but one striking monumental work has survived—the heraldic relief of two lions over the Lion Gate. The two famous gold cups found on the mainland at Vaphio may be Cretan. Their repoussé reliefs show a new understanding of space and a naturalism that foreshadows Greek work of 1,000 years later.

centuries, from about 3110 B. C. until its decline when it came into contact with Greek and Roman art. The site of Egyptian civilization—the Nile Valley, a fertile strip cut off from invaders by mountains and deserts—favored this kind of cultural continuity, as did the conservative Egyptian social system and religion. Sculptors worked in a wide variety of materials, including hard stones, such as diorite and granite; soft stones, such as alabaster and limestone; and wood, ivory, bronze, gold, and ceramics.

That sculpture was the main art form was due primarily to the Egyptians' view of life after death. Most of the sculpture is associated with tombs. These were regarded as the homes of the dead, which had to be equipped with everything the occupant would need for continuance of his life in the afterworld. Much of this equipment was provided in the form of sculptural representations in the round and in relief. The occupant's own continued existence was assured by mummification and by placing his sculptured "double" in the tomb. The quality of the tomb and its contents depended on the occupant's wealth and status. The tombs of the pharaohs, who were divine kings, were particularly splendid, as we know from Tutankhamen's tomb, which was discovered with all its contents intact.

Egyptian sculpture in the round ranges in scale from the colossal rock-cut figures of the Temple of Amon at Abu Simbel to minute fig-

Greek. In sculpture—as in drawing, philosophy, literature, science, and politics—the contribution of Greek civilization makes a radical break with the past. Influences from Mesopotamia, Egypt, and other sources are apparent in the early stages, but a distinctively Greek quality soon becomes dominant. The major periods were the Archaic (from the 7th to the early 5th century B. C.), the Classical (early 5th century to about 330 B.C.), and the Hellenistic (about 330 to 30 B. C.).

The main functions of Greek sculpture were defined early in the Archaic period as the decoration of architecture, the representation of gods, heroes, and mythical events, the commemoration of the dead, and the provision of offerings to the gods. The principal materials of monumental sculpture were marble, which was plentiful and excellent for sculpture, and bronze. Large-scale stone sculpture was first produced around 660 B.C. The making of life-size bronzes, however, did not begin until well over 100 years later, after technical advances in hollow-bronze casting opened up the possibility. During the Classical period, bronze was the main material for free-standing sculpture. Very few original works have survived, but numerous Roman stone copies give some idea of the range and quality of Greek bronzes. It is important to remember that great experimental sculptors such as Myron, Polyclitus, and Lysippus worked in the freer medium of metal sculpture.

The two main preoccupations of Greek sculptors were with (1) the plastic structure and principles of movement of the human body itself and (2) the interplay of the freer linear and sheet forms of drapery with the volumes and surfaces of the body. The knowledge they acquired led them toward an increasing naturalism and also served as a basis for their attempts to create perfect ideal types of human beauty. These aspects of Greek sculpture have had a profound effect on the development of Western sculpture and painting until the 20th century. They are so familiar that we tend not to see what tremendous achievements they were.

Archaic. The direction taken by Archaic sculpture is best exemplified in the development of standing male nude figures (*kouroi*). The earliest figures are stiffly posed in a manner derived directly from Egyptian sculpture—completely frontal and conceived from the outside in relation to the four faces of a stone block. In many instances they have considerable charm and a direct vigor that is lacking in later work, but they show only a rudimentary grasp of the internal structure of the figure, and their detail is highly schematic. By the end of the Archaic period and the beginning of the Classical period, they show a considerable knowledge of the anatomy and principles of movement of the figure. This is evident in two works from the early 5th century B. C. in the subtle movement and fully plastic surfaces of the famous sculpture of a boy attributed to Critius and in the splendidly mature and rather ponderously energetic figure of the more than life-size bronze of Zeus, or Poseidon, found near Artemisium (Artemision).

The development of drapery follows a similar course, from the shallow, stylized, decorative folds of the costumes of the early standing female figures (*korai*) to the richer, more fluent modeling of the long fluted tunic of the bronze charioteer of Delphi (about 470 B.C.).

PHOTO BULLOZ

Winged Victory of Samothrace (Hellenistic Greek), in marble, having a graceful and realistic form.

New developments also take place in relief, away from the largely pictorial aspects of pre-Greek reliefs toward a more three-dimensional sculptural approach in which figures are undercut and made to stand out from the background. In the magnificent frieze of the Siphnian Treasury of Delphi, the figures are made to overlap three or four deep and to occupy a narrow stage-like space in front of the background. Pedimental sculpture carries this process even further, until by the end of the Archaic period the figures are completely freed from their background, as in the sculptures at Aegina.

Classical. Understanding of the structure and mobility of the figure reached new heights during the Classical period. Beginning with such works as Critius' boy, it reached its peak in the sculpture designed by Phidias for the Parthenon, especially in such works as the majestic Dionysus; the three goddesses, with their rich, cascading draperies; and the processions and cavalcades of the frieze. Different in spirit from the grand conceptions of Phidias were the reticent bronzes of Polyclitus. This intellectual sculptor wrote a treatise on the proportions of the figure, now lost. His work exemplifies a tendency of Greek sculpture to achieve canons of ideal proportion and completely controlled and intelligible structure and movement. His main theme was the nude male athlete. In the work of these great 5th century sculptors, the

Capitoline Brutus, Etruscan or Roman bronze portrait bust (3d century B. C.), with finely detailed features.

Greek tendencies toward idealization and naturalism reached a state of perfect balance.

In later Classical sculpture of the 4th century, new types of sensibility were at work. Praxiteles introduced a new kind of softness and fluency to the surfaces of his figures and in the *Aphrodite of Cnidus* perfected the female nude. Lysippus developed a canon of slender proportions, differing from the canon of Polyclitus, and experimented with a greater rotational movement of the figure. Portraiture also took a new direction, away from the idealized portraits of the 5th century toward a new interest in the uniqueness of the individual person. Numerous excellent funerary reliefs suggest a calm melancholy in the face of death, as poignantly expressed in the quiet scene on the stele of Hegeso, in which the dead girl and her maidservant are calmly examining a necklace.

Hellenistic. After the conquests of Alexander the Great, new centers for the production of sculpture were established in the empire, especially in Asia Minor and Rhodes, and Greek sculpture became much more varied and complex. In general, there was a loss of religious feeling, along with a growing interest in the observation of the natural world—a concern with the real and unique rather than the ideal type. This resulted in the production of grotesque figures—in attempts to express violent emotions and fleeting moods—and in the creation of settings, including landscapes, for figures. The marvelous *Winged Victory of Samothrace,* with windblown garments whipping and swirling around the sensuous form; the tortuous, complex *Laocoön* group; and the great relief frieze from the Altar of Zeus and Athena, Pergamum, typify many of the new qualities achieved in Hellenistic sculpture.

Mention should be made of the rich Greek tradition of small-scale sculpture. Splendid small bronzes were produced throughout the whole period. Many of these are freer in movement than large-scale sculpture, and they cover a wider range of subjects. Terra cottas were also popular, the best known being the single figures and charming, intimate groups from Tanagra in eastern Greece.

Etruscan. Although greatly influenced by Greek sculpture, the Etruscan predecessors of Rome in ancient Italy (8th to 1st century B. C.) made a distinctive contribution to the history of sculpture. Their favorite materials were bronze, terra cotta, and soft stones. Among their notable achievements are small elongated bronze figures, which are greatly admired today, and sarcophagi with portrait figures reclining on their lids and relief panels on their sides.

Roman. The practical and realistic Romans fell completely under the spell of Greek sculpture. It was first filtered to them by way of the Etruscans, but little remains of this earlier sculpture of the Roman Republic. With the growth of the Roman Empire and the conquest of Greek territory, however, more direct influences were brought to bear as the Romans plundered, imported, and copied thousands of Greek statues and employed Greek sculptors to work for them.

The most distinctively Roman sculpture is portraiture and narrative relief. Roman stone, terra-cotta, and bronze busts are among the most realistic and revealing portrayals of character in the history of world art. They provide an incomparably frank record of the features of many great personalities of the time.

Roman relief owed much to Greek and Etruscan sources, which it developed in new directions. Perhaps the most extraordinary example of Roman relief is the continuous narrative relief band that winds up the Column of Trajan and depicts with vivid detail Trajan's victorious campaigns in the Dacian wars (101–107 A. D.). Important developments in relief also took place on the side panels of Roman sarcophagi. By representing depth vertically in what is known as bird's-eye perspective, Roman artists were able to depict scenes in depth without destroying the flatness of a surface and with considerable decorative effect. This aspect of Roman relief influenced Italian late Gothic and early Renaissance sculptors, such as Nicola and Giovanni Pisano. Another development that greatly influenced medieval sculpture was the arcaded relief panel in which a number of individual figures and groups were represented within a series of architecturally framed niches. With the decline of Rome and the growth of Christianity, Roman art lost interest in realistic representation and acquired a more other-worldly quality.

Byzantine. The Byzantine era began when the capital of the empire was transferred from Rome to Byzantium in 330 A. D. The decline of naturalism, apparent in the later stages of Roman art, became even more marked in Byzantine art. Monumental sculpture, disapproved of by the church, declined and virtually ceased. But sculptural talent, found an outlet in small-scale work, especially in a tradition of ivory carving that combined a splendid sense of decoration and a lively narrative skill with a profound spirituality.

L. R. ROGERS
Author of "Sculpture"

Bibliography

Bazin, Germain, *The History of World Sculpture,* tr. by Madeline Jay (Studio Vista 1970).
Carpenter, Rhys, *Greek Sculpture* (Univ. of Chicago Press 1960).
Frankfort, Henri, *The Art and Architecture of the Ancient Orient,* 4th rev. ed. (Penguin 1969).
Pope-Hennessy, John, ed., *A History of Western Sculpture:* vol. 1, *Classical Sculpture* by George M. Hanfmann (N. Y. Graphic 1967).
Smith, William S., *The Art and Architecture of Ancient Egypt* (Penguin 1958).

3. History—Western

Apart from the great stone Celtic crosses of Northumbria and Ireland and the intricately decorated wood-carved doorways of Scandinavian churches, almost no large-scale sculpture of merit was produced in Europe from the end of the Roman Empire, in the 5th century, until the late 11th century. This does not mean that the wonderful flowering of monumental Romanesque sculpture in the 12th century was without roots.

Early Medieval. The preceding art of the early Middle Ages—Byzantine, Carolingian, and Ottonian—was incomparably rich in miniature three-dimensional art in ivory and in gold and other metals. This was one of the main channels by which motifs and techniques were developed and transmitted from the ancient world to Romanesque sculptors. Moreover, a vital tradition of ornamental art, related to the early animal art of the steppes, existed among the barbarian tribes that overran Europe and were later converted to Christianity. This art of fantastic beasts and intricate decoration—again on a small scale in jewelry, harness equipment, weapons, and the like—was to make a major contribution to Romanesque, particularly in northern Europe. Nearer the Mediterranean, where Roman remains were abundant, Romanesque sculpture became more classical in spirit.

Romanesque. Sculpture known as Romanesque (11th and 12th centuries) is largely religious art. It owed its development to the increasing wealth of the church, to the practice of making pilgrimages, and to an enormous expansion of monasticism. The building of churches along the pilgrimage routes to Santiago de Compostela, Spain, and the building problems set by new liturgical needs in the monasteries provided the basis for the development of sculpture.

The greatest achievements of Romanesque are in architectural sculpture, especially in carved column capitals and portals. Figures and other motifs, almost always in relief, are made to fit into the architectural framework, often by radically distorting their natural shape. This integration of sculpture and architecture is perfectly exemplified in the royal portal of the Chartres cathedral (late Romanesque). Some excellent large free-standing sculpture was produced, but usually in materials other than stone. It includes crucifixes, Madonnas, lecterns, and candlesticks in wood or metal.

The principal function of Romanesque sculpture was to give expression to the truths of revealed religion. The art of the monks, like the monks themselves, was concerned more with the transcendental world than with the world of nature. On the whole, it is either remote and severe or visionary and expressionistic.

The patronage of the Cluniac monks in France provided the impetus for the most outstanding school of Romanesque sculpture. The great tympana (semicircular areas above doors) of the churches at Autun, Moissac, and Vézelay are among the most powerful religious sculptures of all time. Even today, without their original coloring, their visions of the Last Judgment, Pentecost, and Christ in Majesty are awe-inspiring. One of the greatest Romanesque sculptors is known to us by name, since he took the unusual step of putting his name, Gislebertus, on his tympanum at Autun, where he was active from 1125 to 1135. He was responsible for the excellent column capitals at Autun and for the one great nude of the period, the Eve of Autun.

Splendid sculpture is also found in many churches in Spain. The portals of the great pilgrimage center, Santiago de Compostela, and the beautiful reliefs in the cloister of the monastery of Santo Domingo de Silos near Burgos are outstanding. Among the most notable examples of Romanesque carving in Italy are the 12th century work of Wiligelmo at Modena and Benedetto Antelami at Parma.

German Romanesque sculptors excelled in metalwork. Ottonian bronze founders made the superb gates for St. Michael's at Hildesheim and produced others that were exported to such places as Novgorod in Russia and Gniezno (Gnesen) in Poland. Prominent examples of free-standing German sculpture are the candle-bearing figure in the cathedral at Erfurt and the vigorous, monumental lion erected in 1166 as a memorial in Brunswick to Henry the Lion. The latter was the first secular memorial sculpture produced in the West. A great school of ivory and metal sculptors flourished in the area of the Meuse Valley. A splendid example of this Mosan art is the bronze baptismal font (early 12th century) by Renier de Huy in the Church of St. Barthélemy at Liège.

Wood-carved sculpture of a high order was produced during Romanesque times. Two excellent examples are the lectern supported by the figures of the four Evangelists in the parish church at Freudenstadt, Germany, and the Catalan *Majestad de Battlo* in Barcelona. Both have kept much of their original polychrome.

Gothic. The change from Romanesque to Gothic was a gradual one, occurring at different times (about 1150–1250) in various parts of Europe. The new spirit in sculpture, as in architecture, was a natural development of the fundamental premises laid down in Romanesque. Some authorities see its beginnings in the royal portal of the Chartres cathedral and in the work of Benedetto Antelami in Italy. Others regard these as the final flowering of Romanesque.

These are the chief ways in which fully developed Gothic differs from Romanesque: (1) Whereas Romanesque figures are conceived in relief as an outcrop from the background and are completely dependent on it, Gothic figures are conceived organically around an axis of their own. They are not spread out over the background but move autonomously against it. (2) Gothic sculpture reveals a growing interest in the natural world—in plants and animals—and in the real behavior of drapery and the structure of the figure. (3) It is more humanistic than Romanesque. The hieratic quality of Romanesque gives way to the expression of ordinary human feeling such as the tender smile of the Vierge Dorée ("Golden Virgin") of Amiens.

Early Gothic. The first real flowering of Gothic was in the Île-de-France in the 2d quarter of the 12th century. A comparison of the architecturally disciplined severity and unnatural proportions of the jamb figures of the royal portal at Chartres with the more mobile, freer forms of those of the north and south transepts illustrates the direction in which early Gothic sculpture was developing. A major influence on the development of Gothic in this area was the classicism of the Mosan goldsmiths, especially the great Nicholas of Verdun. This classical aspect of Gothic monumental sculpture reached

Romanesque stone capital, with distorted shapes, sculpted by Gislebertus for Autun Cathedral (12th century).

Madonna and Child, finely carved in ivory, in the stiff, hieratic Byzantine style (11th century).

its zenith in such figures as the Visitation group in the Reims cathedral. By the mid-13th century the Gothic style had spread from the workshops of such places as Reims, Paris, Amiens, and Chartres to the rest of Europe, and an enormous amount of sculpture was being produced.

Late Gothic. The noble statues of the founders in the cathedral of Naumburg, Germany, reflect the high ideals of chivalry of the 13th century. But the influence of court tastes in the 14th century led to a loss of seriousness and high ideals in much of the sculpture—a substitution of charm and fashionable elegance for the deep religious feeling of early Gothic. By the 15th century, however, court influences waned, and the tastes of the new burgher class introduced a more solid, down-to-earth quality into sculpture. A great center for sculpture at this time was Burgundy, where the finest sculptor of the period, Claus Sluter, worked. The prophets on his *Well of Moses* and the figures on the portal of the Carthusian monastery of Champmol, near Dijon, have a massiveness and dignity that strike a new note in sculpture.

The late Gothic sculpture of the 15th and early 16th centuries is especially rich in works for the interiors of churches. This was the great period of medieval wood carving, the richest examples of which were made in Germany, Austria, and Flanders. The greatest works of the period are the wooden altarpieces of such sculptors as Veit Stoss, Tilman Riemenschneider, and Michael Pacher. Other major achievements in Gothic sculpture are the splendid tradition of recumbent tomb effigies, the free-standing groups representing the entombment of Christ, and the devotional statues, especially the Madonnas.

Italian Gothic. Gothic sculpture in Italy follows a rather different course from that of northern Europe, and in many respects it anticipates the Renaissance. The names of most of its greatest artists are known to us. They include Nicola Pisano and his son Giovanni, who carved a magnificent group of marble pulpits; Arnolfo di Cambio; Tino di Camaino; Lorenzo Maitani; and Andrea Pisano, who made the first of the great bronze sculptured doors for the Baptistery of the Florence cathedral.

Renaissance. No abrupt transition took place from Gothic to Renaissance sculpture. The new attitudes began to emerge within the context of Italian Gothic and only gradually gained the ascendancy. This happened first in Florence, which became the leading center for Renaissance sculpture during the 15th century, its greatest period being 1400–1450.

An account of Italian Renaissance sculpture cannot deal with the development of a general period style. It must be an account of the work of a number of artists, each with his own individual style. Artists, whose status was formerly that of craftsmen, became accepted in 14th century Florence as the intellectual equals of philosophers, writers, and musicians. They were open to influence from the wave of humanism, which was affecting the intellectual life of the city with its new rational, questioning attitudes, its concern with natural phenomena, its interest in the ideas of the classical world, and its confidence in the mental and physical capacities of man. The nature of patronage changed, too. The church lost its virtual monopoly as powerful commercial guilds and wealthy private patrons began to commission sculpture.

Gothic realism in (*left*) the stone *Visitation* (about 1220), Reims Cathedral, and (*center*) Riemenschneider's *St. James* (15th–16th century), in wood. Renaissance classicism in (*right*) Donatello's bronze *David* (about 1432).

Early Renaissance. One of the two greatest masters of the early 15th century was Ghiberti. In spirit he was primarily a Gothic artist, but in his masterworks, the two pairs of bronze doors with relief panels that he made for the Baptistery in Florence, there is much that is Renaissance in spirit. His use of perspective pictorial space in the later pair of doors is a particularly Renaissance feature.

The other great master, Donatello, is the supreme genius of the period and probably the most inventive and versatile of all sculptors. He affected the whole course of development of sculpture in his own time, and even in the 20th century he influenced such sculptors as Epstein and Manzu. His early marble *St. George,* for the Church of Orsanmichele, expresses in its alert, youthful confidence something of the spirit of the early Florentine Renaissance. His Gattamelata monument, a portrait statue of Erasmo da Narni in bronze is the first monumental equestrian statue of the modern world. His bronze *David* is the first large free-standing nude, and his relief panel *St. George Slaying the Dragon,* which was placed beneath the statue of Saint George, is the first example of the use of the new science of perspective in relief sculpture and of the low-relief technique known as *stiacciato*. In his old age Donatello reached new heights of expressiveness in his intensely personal bronze pulpits of San Lorenzo, Florence, and his tragic, emaciated *Magdalene.*

Among other great 15th century figures were Luca della Robbia, a marble carver and maker of glazed terra-cotta sculpture whose work is imbued with a serenity and sweetness quite foreign to the complex character of Donatello, and Jacopo della Quercia, whose powerful, dramatic marble reliefs on the portal of San Petronio in Bologna influenced Michelangelo. Bernardo Rossellino, in his marble tomb of Leonardo Bruni in Florence, set a pattern for sculptured wall tombs that was followed by his younger brother Antonio and by Desiderio da Settignano and many others. Agostino di Duccio developed a personal style of linear low relief, which is at its best in the Tempio Malatestiano in Rimini. The greatest sculptor of the late 15th century was Andrea del Verrocchio, whose best-known works are his *David* and his equestrian statue of Bartolommeo Colleoni in Venice, both in bronze.

High Renaissance and Mannerist. The High Renaissance period, beginning about 1500, is dominated by the towering personality of Michelangelo. Generally regarded as the most powerful genius in world sculpture, he introduced an entirely new kind of feeling into sculpture —a disturbing sense of frustrated power, with energetic, muscular bodies struggling against the restrictions of their own material being. His most important sculptures, in marble, are those associated with his long, unfinished projects for the tomb of Pope Julius II in Rome and the Medici tombs in Florence and the two unfinished Pietàs of his old age. His youthful *Pietà* and gigantic *David* are especially popular.

The tortured poses and complexity of Michelangelo's work contributed to the Mannerist phase of sculpture. The violent movement, affected poses, and unnatural proportions of Mannerism are found in the metalwork of Benvenuto Cellini and the bronzes and marbles of Giovanni da Bologna (Giambologna). An important aspect of Mannerist sculpture is its success, partic-

Bernini's *Ecstasy of St. Teresa* (1645–1652), in marble, exemplifies exuberance of Italian baroque.

ularly noticeable in Giambologna's marble *Rape of the Sabines*, in creating compositions that may be viewed all round without any one point of view predominating.

Some of the most notable sculptors outside Italy to be influenced by the Renaissance were Michel Colombe, Francesco Primaticcio, Jean Goujon, and Germain Pilon in France and Peter Vischer the Younger in Germany. Pilon's bronze statue of King Henry II for the royal tomb at St.-Denis is one of the outstanding original works of the century. Alonso Berruguete, a Spaniard who returned to Spain after training in Florence and Rome, produced a number of remarkable works, including a polychrome wooden altarpiece for San Benito el Real, Valladolid, and an alabaster *Transfiguration* for Toledo cathedral.

Baroque and Rococo. By the end of the 16th century Mannerism was in decline and new trends in sculpture were beginning to emerge. These culminated in the work of Giovanni Lorenzo Bernini, the greatest sculptor of the 17th century and virtually the creator of the baroque style. New kinds of seriousness in religion and religious art, which were demanded by the Counter-Reformation and the Council of Trent, fostered the development of the new style. The center of baroque was Rome, where the patronage of the popes, especially their commissions for St. Peter's, gave Bernini and other baroque sculptors opportunities to execute works on a grand scale.

Characteristic features of Bernini's new approach to sculpture include the following: (1) He helped break down the barriers between architecture, painting, and sculpture. In the Cornaro chapel, for example, his sculptural group, *Ecstasy of St. Teresa*, is the centerpiece of a complex conception involving other sculptured figures, the architectural setting itself, and paintings. (2) His work featured an openness and freedom of design, with fluttering draperies, outstretched limbs, and open contours. (3) He preferred types of action that are not resolved within the sculpture itself. His *David*, for example, peers intently out into the space occupied by the viewer toward an implied Goliath. (4) He used a variety of materials in one sculptural work. For the papal tombs of Urban VIII and Alexander VII, Bernini used white and colored marbles and bronze. (5) An increased realism in the use of textures appeared in his work. Stone lost its stoniness and took on the qualities of flesh, hair, cloth, and the like. This is apparent even in such early works as *Pluto and Proserpine* and *Apollo and Daphne.*

The sculpture of the period 1600–1750 moves between the full-blooded baroque style of Bernini and a more restrained classical version. The work of Bernini's two greatest contemporaries, Alessandro Algardi and François Duquesnoy, was more restrained, and their influence on 17th century sculpture was greater than his. Algardi's best-known work is the marble relief *The Meeting of Pope Leo I and Attila*, in St. Peter's. Other prominent Italian baroque sculptors are Melchiorre Caffà, Ercole Ferrata, Camillo Rusconi, and Giovanni Battista Foggini.

In France the baroque style flourished under Louis XIV in a toned-down classical manner that suited the tastes of the court. Most of this marble sculpture is conceived in allegorical terms with themes from classical mythology. François Girardon's delightful group *Apollo Attended by the Nymphs*, created for the grotto of Thetis at Versailles, is strongly classical (Hellenistic) in spirit. Pierre Puget, a more completely baroque sculptor, whose masterpiece is the *Milo of Crotona*, received little recognition in his lifetime.

In Spain and Latin America the emotionalism of the baroque style was combined with an intense realism, involving the use of actual cloth and hair and naturalistic color. The greatest works are extravagant gilt wood altarpieces, such as that of San Esteban, Salamanca, by José Churriguera.

Rococo art, which developed primarily in France, was a variation of baroque rather than a radical departure from it. It lacks the high seriousness of baroque and is lighthearted, playful, sentimental, and decorative. The idealized prettiness of Étienne Maurice Falconet's marble female figures and the erotic playfulness of the small terra-cotta groups by Clodion (Claude Michele), such as *Satyr Crowning a Bacchante*, are typically rococo.

The development of baroque and rococo in central European churches provided the climax of the integration of architecture, sculpture, and painting that Bernini initiated. Wood and stucco were the preferred materials for the extravagant sculptural decoration of these churches. Among the best-known examples are works by Ignaz Günther and Egid Quirin Asam in Bavaria and Domenikus Zimmermann and Joseph Anton Feuchtmayr in Swabia.

Fountain sculpture is an outstanding aspect of the baroque and rococo periods in Rome. The dynamism and other elements of the baroque style encouraged extravagant fantasy and playfulness in design, as in Bernini's Triton Fountain and Fountain of the Four Rivers. The later Trevi Fountain is especially popular.

Neoclassical. The strong vein of classicism that runs through the baroque period came to the fore around 1750. The study of antique sculpture and rejection of baroque at this time received much of its impetus from the work of the German scholar J. J. Winckelmann, who became the chief theorist of neoclassicism. Interest in classical culture was also stimulated by the excavations at Pompeii and Herculaneum.

A return to the idealization and purity of Greek art was already apparent in the work of Jean Antoine Houdon. But this became more uncompromising in the marbles of Antonio Canova, whose *Theseus and the Minotaur* is the first significant example of the neoclassical approach.

From its beginnings in Rome, neoclassicism became a widely international movement. England was an important center, with Thomas Banks, John Flaxman, and Richard Westmacott among its leaders. Other important sculptors were Bertel Thorvaldsen in Denmark, who, apart from his own work, restored classical sculpture, and Gottfried Schadow in Germany.

The imitation of classical sculpture, which soon became recognized as the mainstay of a sculptor's education in the academies, received vast official support during the late 18th and 19th centuries in Europe and the United States. This revivalist sculpture was based mainly on the study of plaster casts of Greek originals and Roman copies, and its cold white marble perfection seldom approaches anywhere near the spirit of genuine classical sculpture.

Romantic and Realistic. The 19th century was an extremely complex period in the history of sculpture. The growth of a wealthy bourgeoisie affected tastes and patronage. Private individuals and public bodies rather than the church and the court commissioned sculpture, and their preference was for the naïvely realistic and sentimental. Statues were erected in vast quantities to commemorate local dignitaries, musicians, writers, and the like, and public buildings and parks were not considered complete without sculptural decoration. Classical, allegorical, medieval, and exotic themes were among the most popular. Rival attitudes and schools argued the merits of different approaches to art, and the conservative artistic establishment was bitterly opposed by a struggling Romantic movement. In sculpture, as in painting, the opposition to academic sterility developed mainly in France.

One of the first and most original Romantic sculptors was A. A. Préault, who attempted to express a new range of feelings and ideas through the medium of relief. François Rude's *The Marseillaise* on the Arc de Triomphe in Paris is a vigorous mixture of elements from various styles, strongly Romantic in feeling. Jean Baptiste Carpeaux modeled with great freedom and exploited the possibilities of an "unfinished" surface, which showed something of his handling of the medium. Jules Dalou produced realistic studies of peasants and workmen in their everyday clothes.

The Romantic and realist tendencies in France culminated in the work of Auguste Rodin, unquestionably one of the world's greatest sculptors. He detested the formulas of academic classical sculpture, although he loved Greek sculpture itself, and he admired and studied Donatello and Michelangelo. Principally a modeler, he handled his material with incredible facility and used the human figure as a vehicle for the expression of complex and powerful feelings. He cultivated the romantic possibilities of the incomplete sculptural fragment and of fluently modeled "unfinished" surfaces. Through unremitting study of the anatomy and movement of the human body, he was able to express in the poses of his figures and the ripple of muscle and tendon on their surfaces all kinds of inner tensions and feelings that were utterly beyond the range of his contemporaries. Some of the most important works among his prolific output are *The Gates of Hell,* a long project based on Dante's *Divine Comedy;* a monumental statue of Balzac; and *The Burghers of Calais,* all in bronze.

Modern. Two major changes that have taken place in the art of sculpture during the 20th century have made it different from the sculpture of any previous period. First, there has been an almost complete abandonment of the naturalistic Greco-Roman tradition, which had dominated Western sculpture since the Renaissance. This has opened the way for a vast diversity of new approaches to sculptural representation and for a much fuller appreciation of nonnaturalistic styles of sculpture, such as African, Oceanic,

Serene spirit of neoclassicism is typified by Canova's *Pauline Bonaparte Borghese as Venus Victrix* (1808), in marble.

Reclining Nude with Guitar (1928), by J. Lipchitz, is a cubist abstraction, carved in basalt, that integrates mass and space.

pre-Columbian American, Archaic Greek, and Romanesque. Influences from these other styles have played an important part in the development of modern sculpture. The availability of museum collections and photographic reproductions has made modern sculptors the heirs of all the world's sculpture.

Second, the art of sculpture has expanded its scope to include nonfigurative (abstract or nonobjective), as well as figurative, sculpture. From Paleolithic times to the early 20th century, sculpture had been a representational art, with the human figure and animals as its main themes. Today many sculptors start from entirely new premises, treating sculpture as an art that is concerned with the whole realm of three-dimensional expressive form and that, like music, need not take its point of departure from anything in nature.

As a result of these two fundamental changes of attitude, sculptors now explore new realms of imagery and new possibilities in the relations of mass and space, and they experiment with a wide range of new techniques and processes.

Realist and Expressionist. Many 20th century sculptors have continued to take the human figure as their main theme and to work in traditional materials and techniques. The immediate followers of Rodin—Aristide Maillol, Émile An-

toine Bourdelle, and Charles Despiau—were inspired by his example as a free artist following his own personal direction, but they reacted against his highly individual romantic style. Maillol—in his *Mediterranean*, for example—eschewed Rodin's fluent surfaces and treated the figure as a composition of carefully proportioned and balanced convex volumes. His work achieves a new kind of monumental repose. Other later sculptors who have produced figure sculpture in realist or expressionist styles include Wilhelm Lehmbruck, Ernst Barlach, Jacob Epstein, Käthe Kollwitz, Gaston Lachaise, Carl Milles, Elie Nadelman, Marino Marini, and Giacomo Manzu.

Cubist. Although cubism was primarily a movement in painting, it made an interesting and extremely influential contribution to sculpture. The early cubist reliefs that Picasso made from wood, cardboard, paper, and other materials around 1914 were forerunners of much constructed and assembled sculpture. The cubist painters' technique of disintegrating natural forms into simplified planes and subsequently reconstituting those forms into semiabstract designs of convex and concave surfaces was taken up in the sculpture of Jacques Lipchitz, Henri Laurens, Ossip Zadkine, Alexander Archipenko, Raymond Duchamp-Villon, and Umberto Boccioni. Cubist sculptors always took their starting point from

(Left) Brancusi's marble *Seal* (1943) abstracts and refines nature into pure yet subtle form. (Below) Giacometti's bronze *Woman with Her Throat Cut* (1932) surrealistically suggests a mutilated skeleton.

Recumbent Figure (1938), in green Hornton stone, is typical of Henry Moore's abstract treatment of form—the incorporation of empty space in a smooth, simplified mass.

natural form, and their work usually retains some element of representation.

Constructivist. In all the sculpture of the past the primary element was mass, and the weight and solidity of sculptural materials were emphasized. This traditional approach was forcefully rejected by the constructivist movement, which started in Russia in the early 20th century. Some of its initiators, such as Vladimir Tatlin and Alexandr Rodchenko, faded from public view in Russia. But the brothers Naum Gabo and Antoine Pevsner continued to develop constructivism in the West, and it is now a major and highly fruitful aspect of world art.

Space is the primary element of the constructivist. Linear components such as rods, wires, and threads, together with sheets of transparent plastic and metal, are used in preference to solid volumes. They are made to define movement in space and to enclose space. In the open structures of constructivist sculpture, many new materials and techniques are employed and complete nonobjectivity is essential. This aspect of modern sculpture is closely connected with developments in modern architecture—for example, its new methods of construction, use of transparent surfaces, and rejection of massiveness.

Brancusi. The work of the great Constantin Brancusi is the opposite of constructivism. It stresses weight and volume—the tactile aspects of three-dimensional form. Brancusi used the traditional materials of sculpture—stone, wood, and metal—and refined and abstracted shapes taken from nature (heads, torsos, birds, animals) to produce apparently simple but in fact extremely subtle solid forms. His influence was considerable, and sculptors such as Jean Arp, Barbara Hepworth, and Henry Moore owed much to him.

Surrealist. The cubists and constructivists and Brancusi were concerned mainly with aspects of form. Many other 20th century sculptors, especially those inspired by surrealism, explored new kinds of imagery or content. The surrealists' investigations into the realm of fantasy and dream imagery, pursued mainly in paintings, had a profound effect on modern sculpture. The sculptures of René Magritte and Max Ernst are direct products of surrealism. Surrealist fantasy is important in the work of Alberto Giacometti—for example, his construction The Palace at 4 A. M. and bronze Woman with Her Throat Cut.

The metamorphosis of forms and the blending of forms from different realms of nature are common surrealist devices that many modern sculptors have adopted. The haunting insectlike and treelike figures of Germaine Richier and the monsters that Eduardo Paolozzi fabricated from technological junk are examples of this. But perhaps Henry Moore's works in wood and stone—blending the shapes of the reclining female figure with the forms of bones, caves, landscape, rocks—are the most profound of this kind. Much of the fascination of Claes Oldenburg's work also depends on the transmutation of objects from one realm of form to another. What is normally rigid and hard becomes disturbingly soft and deflated.

Found-Object. The piecing together of found objects in an assemblage opened up new possibilities for the content and imagery of sculpture, especially when the objects were chosen for their poetic evocations rather than their merely formal properties. This category of sculpture includes the boxes of Joseph Cornell, the wooden reliefs of Louise Nevelson, the "ready-mades" of Marcel Duchamp, the "junk" sculptures of Baldaccini César and John Chamberlain, and some of the work of Edward Kienholz. Among the best-known uses of found objects are Picasso's effective Bull's Head, made from the saddle and handlebars of a bicycle, and the baboon's head, in Baboon and Young, which is cast from a toy automobile.

Environmental Construction. The concept of sculpture as objects to be viewed from outside has been rejected by the creators of sculptured environments. Their aim is to create a total setting, often a kind of room, in which the spectator may move about. This almost theatrical art form may include sculptured or cast figures and actual objects, as in the work of George Segal and the tableaux of Edward Kienholz, or it may be an abstract environment using lighting effects and various types of constructed forms, as in the work of Lucas Samaras and Yayoi Kusama. The Merzbau constructions of Kurt Schwitters (begun in 1920) are probably the first work of this kind.

Direct-Metal. The decade of the 1950's has been called the "Iron Age" of modern sculpture because so many sculptors had turned to working directly in metal by welding and forging rather than casting. This method of producing sculpture was started by Picasso and Julio Gonzalez around 1930, and Gonzalez continued to be one of the best and most original sculptors using the medium. Reg Butler, Lynn Chadwick, Alexander Calder, Theodore Roszak, Seymour Lipton, and Eduardo Chillida all produced excellent direct-metal sculptures. But the greatest sculptor to use the medium was David Smith. His *Cubi* series, made shortly before his death in 1965, out of sheet stainless steel, gave the medium a monumental seriousness not previously achieved.

Primary-Structure. In the 1960's a group of sculptors began to produce extremely simple sculpture, usually on a large scale and fabricated with great precision, often by industrial craftsmen, to the sculptor's specifications. The impact of these primary structures (sometimes called minimal sculpture) is direct and powerful. They are completely abstract and nonsymbolic, and all trace of personal expression is removed from their surfaces in an effort to achieve anonymity. Notable work of this kind has been produced by Philip King, Donald Judd, William Tucker, Tony Smith, Ronald Bladen, and many others.

Other Forms. The immensely varied activities of modern sculptors have led to the production of many types of art work that can only be included under the term "sculpture" if its definition is stretched well beyond traditional limits. One of the most important developments is the inclusion of actual motion as an element in the work. Pioneers in this field were Naum Gabo, Marcel Duchamp, Laszlo Moholy-Nagy, and Alexander Calder. Movement may be caused by air currents, as in Calder's mobiles, or by water, magnetism, or electrically powered devices.

Light, too, is frequently used as a feature of sculpture. The electronically controlled "luminodynamic" constructions of Nicolas Schöffer, which project changing patterns of light into space, are notable achievements in this field.

Also difficult to classify are the various kinds of three-dimensional art that do not aim to produce possessable objects. This antiobject art takes many forms, including some that involve the performance of operations on landscape, such as painting the seashore and wrapping mountains, cliffs, and buildings in plastic.

L. R. ROGERS
Author of "Sculpture"

Bibliography

Bazin, Germain, *The History of World Sculpture*, tr. by Madeline Jay (Studio Vista 1970).
Hammacher, Abraham M., *The Evolution of Modern Sculpture: Tradition and Innovation* (Abrams 1969).
Kultermann, Udo, *The New Sculpture: Environments and Assemblages* (Praeger 1968).
Pope-Hennessy, John, ed., *A History of Western Sculpture:* vol. 2, *Medieval Sculpture* by Roberto Salvini (Joseph, M. 1970); vol. 3, *Sculpture: Renaissance to Rococo* by Herbert Keutner (N. Y. Graphic 1969); vol. 4, *Sculpture: Nineteenth and Twentieth Centuries* by Fred Licht (N. Y. Graphic 1967).

4. History—Oriental

The sculpture of the Orient, notably that of India, China, and Japan, is today recognized as one of the great sculptural traditions of world art. Profoundly religious in nature and usually created by anonymous craftsmen, it is an art that takes its place beside the medieval sculpture of Europe as one of the great spiritual expressions of mankind. The purpose of this art was to help the believer visualize the deity as an aid in worship. Sculpture as a fine art, made for purely aesthetic purposes, did not exist in the Orient until modern times, when, especially in Japan, a school of sculpture based on Western prototypes came into being.

Indian—Indus Valley Civilization. The most ancient of the Oriental sculptural traditions is that of India, where remarkable works were produced by the Indus Valley, or Harappan, civilization, which flourished from about 2500 B.C. It is sometimes also referred to as the Indo-Sumerian civilization because it has striking similarities to the somewhat older culture of ancient Sumer. Small statues in stone, clay, or copper have been excavated at numerous Indus Valley sites, notably at Harappa and Mohenjo-Daro in what is now Pakistan. Human figures or animals were represented both in three-dimensional images and in low relief on numerous engraved seals.

Buddhist. This early period of Indian art was followed by the Vedic age, when Aryan tribes invaded India from the northwest before 1200 B.C. According to some scholars, they probably destroyed the already weakened Indus Valley civilization. Consequently, little art of any kind was produced in India for the next 1,000 years. Not until the reign of the Buddhist King Ashoka (Asoka) during the 3d century B.C. did a new school of sculpture arise, under Buddhist inspiration. Elaborate carving often decorated early Buddhist monuments such as cave temples, stupa mounds erected in memory of the Buddha, and other structures. Especially famous are the stupas at Bharhut and Sanchi and the free-standing sanctuary at Bodh-Gaya. Images of pre-Buddhist tree nymphs (*yakṣī*) and reliefs representing scenes from Buddhist legend are particularly fine. However, Buddha as a person never appears.

David Smith's stainless steel *Cubi XVII* (1963), one of a series of direct-metal constructions.

With the reign of the Indo-Scythian (Kushana) King Kanishka (1st or 2d century A. D.), Buddhist art changed greatly. In the Gandhara region of northwestern India, there arose a new school of sculpture, which is usually referred to as the Greco-Buddhist because it employs Indian Buddhist iconography but artistic forms derived from Greek and Roman art. At the same time another school of art closer to the native Indian tradition flourished in Mathura in northern India. In both of these sculptural traditions the Buddha and his saints, or Bodhisattvas, were now represented in human form. It was at this time, during the first three centuries A. D., that the standard iconographical types, such as the Buddha seated in the Yogi position and the standing Buddha, were evolved.

The golden age of Indian Buddhist sculpture took place under the Gupta dynasty (4th–6th century A. D.). Following carefully prescribed iconographical and aesthetic canons, the sculptors of this age produced images that are among the great masterpieces of world art. They had a profound influence on the Buddhist art of Southeast Asia, China, and Japan. In these images the Buddha is usually shown dressed in a monk's garment and with his curly hair cut short, indicating that he had renounced the world. He has the third eye (*ūrnā*) and the protuberance on his head (*uṣnīṣa*), symbols of his supernatural powers. His expression is always serene; the smile hovering over his lips shows that he is the Enlightened One, who has overcome the world and has achieved inner peace and harmony. Great emphasis is also placed on his hand gestures (mudrā) which express the various qualities associated with sacred beings. The Bodhisattvas, on the other hand, are always dressed in the garments of Indian princes, with skirts, scarves, and jewels, for Shakyamuni Buddha himself had been a royal prince before his Enlightenment.

The center of the Gupta school was at Sarnath in northern India, but fine examples of this type of art may be found all over India, especially at the great cave temples of Ajanta. The preferred medium was stone, but bronze, clay, and ivory images also exist. The style of these statues represents a synthesis of the Gandhara and Mathura schools and represents the classical statement of Indian Buddhist art.

Hindu. By the 7th century, Hinduism, which incorporated the ancient Vedic religion, had replaced Buddhism as the chief religion of India. From that time most Indian sculpture was created under Hindu auspices. Hinduism taught the worship of the Hindu gods, especially Shiva and Vishnu with their female counterparts Parvati and Lakshmi, as well as a huge pantheon of other deities, demons, and sacred animals—all of which were represented in Hindu sculpture.

It is difficult to select among the many great artistic movements of Hindu India. The most famous of the early Hindu sculptures, dating from the 7th and 8th centuries, are the elaborate cave temples carved out of rock at Ellora, in central India; at Elephanta, an island near Bombay; and at Mamallapuram in southern India, near Madras. These temples consist of architectural elements adorned with figures and scenes, in which the dynamic spirit of Hinduism finds powerful expression, combining a deeply spiritual feeling with great emphasis on sensuous beauty.

The next phase of Hindu art is best exemplified by the free-standing temples at Khajuraho in northern India and at Bhuvanesvara and

B. ROWLAND, JR.

Stone head of Buddha (3d–4th century), with third eye and cranial protuberance, from Gandhara, India.

Konarak in Orissa, which are decorated with thousands of magnificent sculptural images dating from the 10th to the 13th century. Here the sensuous aspect of Hindu art is very evident in the loving (*maithuna*) couples, who symbolize the love of the soul for the deity in terms that, for the Western viewer at least, often border on pornography in their explicitness.

This art came to an end, at least in northern India, as Islam, brought to the subcontinent by invaders in the 11th and 12th centuries, gradually took hold. Only in the south did Hindu sculptural tradition continue to flourish. The finest creations of the southern school were the bronze images created under the Chola dynasty (10th–13th century). Representing Shiva as Nataraja, or Lord of Dance, and his beautiful wife, Parvati, these metal images are among the great achievements of Indian art. However, even in the south, Hindu art began to decline in the 15th century. On a folk level fine carvings, usually made of wood, were produced in later times.

Central and Southeast Asia. From India proper both Buddhist and Hindu sculpture spread throughout the Indian-influenced world. To the north, in Afghanistan and Central Asia, a late form of Greco-Buddhist sculpture flourished between the 4th and 6th century. Later, Tibet and Nepal, where a form of Buddhism known as Lamaism developed, produced a sculpture that included many Hindu and native Tibetan elements. It usually took the form of strange, esoteric bronze or clay images of divinities with bizarre shapes and demonic expressions. This Lamaist art has been a vital force into modern times.

To the southeast, Indian Buddhist art exerted a powerful influence in Ceylon, Java, Burma, Thailand, and Cambodia. Many critics regard the great stupa mound at Borobudur in central Java as the single greatest monument of Buddhist art in all Asia. The most persistent of these traditions of Buddhist sculpture is that of Thailand, where fine Buddhist sculptures have been made for over 1,000 years. The best of them, especially those of the early period, are among the master-pieces of Buddhist art.

The single greatest school of religious sculp-ture of Southeast Asia is that of Cambodia, which, under the Khmers (10th–13th century) produced some of the supreme masterpieces of Buddhist as well as Hindu art. Best known are the architectural carvings on the great temples at Angkor Vat and Angkor Thom, impressive both for their huge scale and their artistic excellence. However, numerous individual images, some of them colossal in scale, others small, often of metal, are equally fine. In fact, the Cambodian statues of this period are equal to the best sculp-tures produced in India at the time.

Chinese. In China, where painting and calligra-phy have always been regarded as the major art forms, sculpture has never played a very promi-nent role. Nevertheless the Chinese sculptural tradition is also a very old one and has produced some very fine works.

Early Dynastic. The beginning of the Chinese sculptural tradition can be traced back to the first historical dynasty, the Shang, which lasted from about 1500 to about 1000 B. C. The main works produced at this time were small-scale representations of animals in the form of bronze vessels as well as marble or jade carvings, which no doubt had some religious or magical signifi-cance. With the succeeding Chou dynasty (about 1000 B. C.–about 250 B. C.), sculpture began to play a more important role. Now the human figure was also represented, and splendid images of dragons, tigers, and horses were produced. The main media employed continued to be bronze and jade, but clay and wood were also used. There was no large-scale sculpture until the Han dynasty (200 B. C.–200 A. D.), when carvings of horses and stone reliefs were pro-duced. The most common Han images, however, were the clay grave figures that were placed in the tombs to accompany the dead into the spirit world.

Six Dynasties. A new chapter in the history of Chinese art started with the Six Dynasties period (220–589 A. D). This period saw the introduction of Buddhism, which completely transformed the religious and cultural life of the nation. From this time on most of the sculpture produced was devoted to the Buddhist religion and intended for Buddhist temples. The earliest of these images date from the late 4th and early 5th cen-turies but the finest of them come from the late 5th and early 6th centuries. Their basic concept and iconography are clearly derived from India but the artistic style of these statues, especially those produced under the Wei dynasty, reflects the more abstract and linear conventions of Chi-nese art. Most remarkable are the often huge stone carvings at such great cave temples of northern China as Yunkang at Shansi and Lung-men at Honan. However, the numerous small gilt bronze images representing Buddhas and Bodhisattvas are equally fine as works of art. Secular sculpture played a minor role and usually took the form of grave figures.

T'ang. The Six Dynasties period was followed first by the short-lived Sui period and then by the T'ang period (618–906), regarded by many critics as the greatest age in Chinese art. Bud-dhism continued to flourish during this era, and huge numbers of Buddhist images of all kinds were produced. Stone carvings from the T'ang period at Lungmen and at another famous cave temple, T'ien-Lung-Shan, are representative of the finest work of this time. In their increased naturalism and fuller forms, these stone carvings clearly reflect the renewed Indian influence. Other statues were made of gilded bronze, lacquer, wood, clay, or precious metals, all ex-

Hindu sculpture from the 11th century: (*left*) lov-ing couple, stone, from a temple at Khajuraho, north India, and (*below*) Shiva Nataraja, Lord of the Dance, bronze, Chola period of south India.

Chinese tomb sculpture: (*above*) a spirited horse with trappings, realistically modeled in terra cotta and polychromed, from the T'ang period, and (*below*) a white jade pendant of a winged dragon, symbol of fertility and rainmaking, with rhythmic form and incised decoration, from the late Chou period.

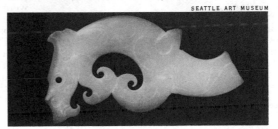

Miroku, a meditating Japanese Bodhisattva (Asuka period), in bronze, in the Chinese style.

ecuted with great skill and a highly developed aesthetic sense. The T'ang period, an age of material wealth and splendor, also produced a good deal of purely secular art. The finest examples of T'ang secular art include stone carvings of horses and clay grave figures.

Sung, Ming, and Ch'ing. After the severe persecutions of Buddhists in the mid-9th century, Chinese sculpture declined, and though some fine carvings were still produced during the Sung and Ming periods, the great period of Chinese sculpture was over. The best of the Sung sculptures were carved in wood and painted in bright colors and were marked by a gentler and more relaxed style than had prevailed earlier. Ming sculptures are outstanding for their realism in the representation of human beings and animals. However, they lack the expressive power and aesthetic refinement of many earlier works. The best of the late Chinese sculptures are the graceful porcelain and jade figurines made during the late Ming and Ch'ing periods (17th–early 20th century). Decorative in intent, they can be charming indeed at their best.

Japanese—Prehistoric. In Japan, sculptures may be found among the oldest archaeological remains of the Jomon period (3d–1st millennium). These earliest sculptures, made of clay, take the form of female fertility images with large insect eyes and stylized bodies in which the thighs and breasts are emphasized. During the Grave Mound period (about 200–600 A. D.), hollow clay figures known as *haniwa* were produced in large quantities. Unlike the Chinese grave figures, on which they were probably based, they

were not placed in the tombs but in a circle around the grave mounds and were thought of as substitutes for the human sacrifices performed in ancient times. Their forms are simple and highly abstract, with an emphasis on cylindrical shape that makes them very appealing to modern taste. Although most of the *haniwa* represent humans, others take the form of animals, houses, or boats, which gives them a historical as well as a purely aesthetic interest.

Asuka and Nara. The historical era of Japanese art begins with the Asuka period (552–650), when Buddhism and Buddhist art were introduced from the mainland. Based on Korean and Chinese models, the works of the Asuka period, especially those at Horyu-ji temple in Nara, are among the masterpieces of Japanese sculpture. The preferred artistic media were bronze, wood, and clay. Stone, which had played such a major role in India and China, was hardly used in Japan.

The images produced in the subsequent Nara period (650–794) were even more accomplished and were largely based on T'ang Chinese prototypes. The most famous of these images is the giant bronze Buddha at Todai-ji temple in Nara. Unfortunately this image was badly damaged in later times. Particularly fine examples of sculpture of this period are also the lacquer statues representing celebrated Buddhist teachers as well as the Buddhist deities and the dramatic clay figures of the various guardian deities.

Heian. With the Heian period (794–1185), sculpture developed a more indigenous, typically Japanese style, no longer following continental models. The preferred medium was wood, and

HOLLIS COLLECTION, NEW YORK

The god Fudo, a fierce Japanese Buddhist guardian deity, in wood, from the Kamakura period.

the forms, softer and warmer, were in keeping with the refinement and elegance of the times. Although the subjects treated were still largely Buddhist, Shinto deities were also represented. Prominent also among Heian sculptures were the masks used in the *bugaku* dance.

Kamakura. The last great period of Japanese sculpture was the Kamakura period (1185–1392). One of the most famous statues of this time is the enormous Buddha of Kamakura, which is some 42 feet (13 meters) high. Also well known are the great guardian figures, carved by the famous sculptor Unkei, which are at the entrance gate to the Todai-ji temple in Nara. Outstanding for their realism and their sense of drama, these statues are among the best ever made in Japan.

14th–19th Century. With the 14th century and the decline of traditional Buddhism, sculpture ceased to play a major role in Japanese art. The only original creations of the later centuries are the No masks, which originated during the 15th century in the Muromachi period and continue to be made to the present day, and the small *netsuke* carvings, representing all kinds of legendary and folk figures, which served as toggles of the medicine cases and tobacco pouches worn by the Japanese men of the Edo period (1603–1867) Although often charming and interesting for their subjects, these miniature carvings are hardly a major form of artistic expression. Only the folk carvings of this period preserve some of the expresive power of earlier sculptures.

HUGO MUNSTERBERG
Author of "Sculpture of the Orient"

Bibliography

Kidder, J. Edward, *Masterpieces of Japanese Sculpture* (Tuttle 1961).
Lee, Sherman E., *A History of Far Eastern Art* (Abrams 1964).
Munsterberg, Hugo, *Chinese Buddhist Bronzes* (Tuttle 1967).
Munsterberg, Hugo, *Sculpture of the Orient* (Dover 1972).
Rowland, Benjamin, *The Art and Architecturè of India*, 3d rev. ed. (Penguin 1967).
Sirén, Osvald, *Chinese Sculpture from the Fifth to the Fourteenth Century* (Scribner 1925).
Sivaramamurti, Calembus, *South Indian Bronzes* (Verry 1963).

5. History—African, Oceanian, Pre-Columbian

The traditional art of the various peoples of sub-Saharan Africa, Oceania, and pre-Columbian North and South America is often referred to as "primitive." The term here does not mean immature or inept but suggests that the cultures of these peoples, largely unknown to the West before the 15th century, were close to the basic demands of life. These peoples lacked one or more of such attributes of civilization as cities, consolidation of political power, written language, and scientific technology. Their art, however, rooted in their religious, economic, and social concerns, was enormously significant to them.

Primitive sculpture ranged from monumental figures of divinities or ancestors to masks, small fetish figures, vessels, and tools. Many objects were used in rituals or ceremonies to ensure bountiful harvests, cure illness, mark rites of passage, or divine the future. Some ritual objects were imbued with supernatural power to achieve a desired end. Other objects indicated rank or status.

The motifs of primitive sculpture were based not on the realistic representation of human or animal forms but on creative, sometimes abstract, interpretations of these forms. The styles in which these forms were rendered varied greatly from one culture area to another and within a culture area.

The primitive sculptor used stone, bone, or shell tools, or, in African tribes, metal. In most cultures, he underwent a lengthy apprenticeship to learn the use of his tools and materials and the style traditional to his tribe or village. He could, however, interpret traditional forms in his own way. His work, often technically proficient and sensitively creative, was largely for chiefs, priests, or other leaders.

African. The sculpture of Black Africa, developed by Negro tribes in West Africa and central Africa, has a vitality and expressiveness that make it highly esteemed. Most of it is carved in wood, although terra cotta, ivory, and metal were also used. Because the ancestor cult was important to most tribes, many figures and masks commemorated ancestors or served as ritual containers of their power as spirits. Other sculpture represented deities or mythological beings or denoted rank.

Baulé. The Baulé people of the Ivory Coast made commemorative ancestor figures and ritual deity and ancestor masks. Both types are naturalistic but not representational. By their rhythmic shaping and proportion, refined surface planes, and lyrical flow of outlines, they are, rather, the sculptor's creative interpretations of nature. Baulé human masks are often similar expressively to their carved human figures, but their animal masks are often nonnaturalistic.

Yoruba, Ife, and Benin. The tribes of Nigeria produced outstanding sculpture in a variety of media. The Yoruba made naturalistic wooden figures and masks for rites honoring their many nature gods. These carvings depend on life forms or genre subjects, expressed in an emphatic, sculptural style. Mass and volume are equally stressed. Shapes are clearly defined, ample in

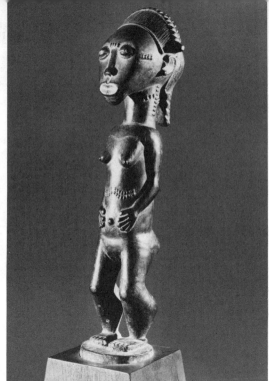

African sculpture: (*above*) a hollow bronze head (about 1550) from Benin, Nigeria. Originally a carved elephant tusk was fitted into the open top. (*Right*) a wooden figure of a woman, carved by the Baulé of the Ivory Coast for use in ancestral rites.

scale, and complexly related, proportioned to lead the eye to the enlarged head. Yoruba sculptures are far more often painted than those of other African tribes. Colors are arbitrary, accentuating the expressive parts.

From the Yoruba kingdom of Ife (11th–19th century) come superbly modeled, idealistic heads in terra cotta and in bronze. According to tradition, the sculptors of the kingdom of Benin (13th–18th century) acquired the art of casting bronze from Ife. Using the lost-wax process, the royal Benin workshops made small figures in the round, reliefs, and hollow heads. The heads, some from the 15th century, were placed on the altar of the oba, or king. They had carefully defined surfaces, and into the open tops of some were fitted elephant tusks carved in spiraling bands from the base to the tip with realistic representations of the oba and court life. The early bronzes of Ife and Benin are remarkably close in quality to those of ancient China or Renaissance Italy.

Ashanti. The Ashanti of Ghana also worked in metal. In contrast to the idealized forms of Ife, their small bronze figures for weighing gold dust are impressionistic. They depict genre subjects, fantastic birds and animals, proverbs, religious subjects, and geometric forms.

Bambara. The stylized sculpture of the Bambara tribes of Mali include large and small female figures and distinctive stylized antelope masks. The masks refer to the Bambara belief that in ancient times the Creator dispatched to earth a fabulous antelopelike animal to teach the people agriculture. Attached to basketry caps, the masks were worn by men in ritual dances at the sowing and harvesting seasons.

Cameroon and Congo. The sculpture of tribes in central Cameroon includes human and animal forms carved as masks, figures, or posts flanking doorways. Their forceful style relies on rough-textured, vigorous forms, which are large, often massive, and emphatically defined, rather than on fluid, decorative surfaces. Figures have dramatic forms and often contorted poses, which convey a sense of movement.

In the Congo, sculpture of the Bayaka and Basonge tribes somewhat resembles that of Cameroon. Forms are dynamic and stylized but without the vigor and scale of Cameroon sculpture.

Oceanian. The sculpture of Oceania is that of the racially varied peoples of Australia and four regions of Pacific islands—Indonesia, Melanesia, Micronesia, and Polynesia. These peoples developed a wealth of sculptural styles that makes generalization difficult. Aesthetically the most important and, often, spectacular sculpture is that of Melanesia and Polynesia.

Melanesian. The widely diverse sculpture of isolated Melanesian groups should be seen in the context of several allied elements in Melanesian culture. One element was the belief in power residing in ancestors and especially in supernatural beings. Another element was prolonged socioreligious ceremonies, often taking years to complete, which gave loosely organized peoples a strong sense of the continuity of time. A third element was large, men's houses, which were ceremonial centers and repositories of sacred figures, masks, and drums.

The profusion of sculpture from the Sepik River area of north central New Guinea has the most distinctive of the many Melanesian styles. Ancestors were often honored at death by a carved and painted figure or mask. Sometimes their skulls were covered with modeled clay or paste and painted to resemble the ancestors as they had appeared at ceremonial occasions during their lifetime. Supernatural beings were represented by carved figures, frequently having a hallucinatory, surrealistic appearance. Masks or other decorative sculptures were attached to the high front gables of men's houses. Sepik River masks and figures generally conveyed a sense of the spiritual power residing in them through vigorous forms combined in original, dramatic ways. Their bizarre character was usually intensified by bright paint and feathers, leaves, seeds, and shells.

In the Papuan Gulf area of southern New Guinea, masks, sometimes 10 feet (3 meters) high, representing supernatural beings, were made anew for each ceremonial. These masks had a lower part carved in wood to resemble an open-snouted crocodile and an upper part consisting of a tall framework of palmwood covered with bark cloth.

On New Ireland, ceremonial, clan-owned sculpture in the form of single figures, horizontal or vertical compositions, or masks was in an open-work style. Carved-out, or negative, spaces worked with solid forms to produce an extraordinarily vital and noble open design.

Polynesian. No art could more completely express the culture to which it belonged than the art of Polynesia. It involved concepts of rank, based on descent from deified ancestors; mana, a spiritual power inherent to a greater or lesser degree in all animate and inanimate things; and taboo, which stipulated protocol to protect people from contact with sources of greater or lesser mana than their own. Polynesian sculptors, who were specialists in particular areas of their art, worked in wood, stone, and shell. They made figures and such implements as clubs, combs, and paddles, and decorative carving on houses and canoes. Many of the forms were intended to evoke the power of their remote ancestors.

Polynesian three-dimensional sculpture has self-sufficient forms, to which polychromy is unimportant. Its expressive significance depends on the shapes and their relationship, as seen in the figurative carvings of Samoa, the Cook Islands, Tahiti, and nearby islands. Figures are stylized but basically naturalistic.

In the stylized sculpture of the Marquesas Islands the proportions are heavy and rather remote from reality. The surfaces are often carved with complex, basically rectilinear designs, which are comparable to the allover tattooing designs common to the islands. Similarly, the elaborate, curvilinear surface designs on the figurative art of the Maori of New Zealand are related to the rich Maori tattooing patterns. The figures are relatively static but convey a fierce aggressiveness.

Hawaiian sculpture has one of the most significant of Polynesian styles. It is dramatic in its three-dimensional forms and in its association of negative spaces with solid, volumetric forms. Almost grotesque figures with strongly defined shapes suggest movement through their inherent, dynamic, sculptural force.

On Easter Island are huge, roughhewn stone figures, half figures, and busts, some more than 30 feet (9 meters) high. Presumably they were set up on a sanctuary wall to commemorate clan ancestors. The figures are rendered purely sculpturally with sharp-cut brows, deep-set eyes, straight-lipped mouths, and heavy, projecting

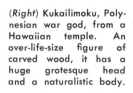

(*Left*) Polynesian wall panel from a Maori council house in New Zealand. It is of carved wood and has curvilinear surface decoration that resembles Maori tattoos.

DOMINION MUSEUM, WELLINGTON

(*Right*) Kukailimoku, Polynesian war god, from a Hawaiian temple. An over-life-size figure of carved wood, it has a huge grotesque head and a naturalistic body.

GRANGER COLLECTION

Giant Easter Island roughhewn stone heads of clan ancestors were probably set on low walls on open-air sanctuary platforms.

jaws and chins, all suggesting a contained, moody, or introverted quality.

In contrast are small, well-polished wooden figures under 2 feet (60 cm) high. These emaciated, skeletized forms may be ancestor figures. They and other small figures of lizards, birds, and grotesques are carefully carved with elaborate descriptive detail.

North American. The Indian and Eskimo groups of North America produced masks, figures, and implements reflecting the differences in their geography and culture.

Eastern, Southern, and Southwestern. The tribes of the eastern woodlands carved and painted wooden ceremonial masks, of which the Iroquois "false faces," with round eyes, large, distorted noses and mouths, and attached horsehair, were superb examples. Tribes from the southern woodlands and prairie carved stone pipes in human and animal forms. Pueblo Indians in the Southwest fashioned wooden, leather, and cloth masks and small wooden dolls representing kachinas, or benevolent spirits.

Northwestern Coast. Some of the finest examples of American Indian sculpture were produced by the Kwakiutl and Tlingit tribes of the northwest coast. The area, abounding in cedar forests and salmon streams, provided the wealth and leisure to hold innumerable religious and social ceremonials requiring many works of art. Most of it was carved in cedar and polychromed.

Kwakiutl masks, hung with cloaks of shredded cedar bark, were worn by dancers in secret-society rites and in potlatch ceremonies for the prestigious giving away of wealth. Designs were inherited or acquired by warfare or other means. The masks were derived from human, animal, or hybrid forms. Shapes were frequently aggressive and dynamic. Some masks had movable parts; others were very large.

The Kwakiutl also made monumental "totem poles" from huge red cedar trees. They were polychromed in light stains, especially red, black, yellow, and white. These memorials displayed lineage through a complex arrangement of hu-

man and animal forms. Their dramatic shapes and expressions can almost be called baroque.

Tlingit masks, largely ancestral designs or insignia of rank, were smaller than Kwakiutl masks and often more naturalistic. Tlingit memorial poles, made of the slender yellow cedar of the area, were slimmer than Kwakiutl poles. Figures and masks were arranged in separated horizontal bands around the poles. Small forms and delicate colors, including a unique blue-green, give Tlingit sculpture a rococo quality.

Eskimo. Early Eskimo hunters in the far north, working in walrus-tusk ivory, stone, and wood,

Carved jade deity figurine, with werejaguar head in Olmec style, is from a pre-Columbian tomb in Mexico.

Pre-Columbian sculpture: (*left*) Chacmool figure (11th–15th century), lying before a Toltec-Mayan temple with feathered-serpent columns, Chichén Itzá, Yucatán; (*above*) Mayan relief (709) of a penitent kneeling before a priest, Yaxchilan, Mexico.

carved small implements and figures of animals and humans with incised abstract or skeletal designs. Animals were of great importance, both as the main item of sustenance and as a source of spiritual power. Many types and styles of wooden ceremonial masks evolved, combining distorted human, animal, and imaginary forms. Some were asymmetrical. Others were composites with attachments, some movable, of wood, bone, feather, and shell. In the mid-20th century, Eskimos produced polished, naturalistic, small stone sculpture that showed great feeling for animal life.

Middle American and Andean. The peoples of Middle America (Mexico and Central America) and the Andes, who were richer and more highly organized than the tribal groups of North America, are considered civilized rather than primitive. Their art is discussed here, however, because it has common roots with tribal art and because these peoples lacked such elements of civilization as political consolidation, in Middle America, and writing, in the Andes.

Olmec. Underlying the later agricultural societies that developed in Middle America was the Olmec civilization (about 12th–5th century B. C.) at La Venta and other centers on the southeastern coast of Mexico. Olmec tombs, covered by the ubiquitous Middle American pyramid, have yielded human figurines and carved celts in clay, jade, and serpentine, together with pottery in figural shapes. Typically the bond tends to be chunky and the head to have a long cranium, long, narrow eyes, and a half-open, down-at-the corners mouth.

Colossal basaltic stone figures and heads, up to 8 feet (2.4 meters) high, apparently were set in relation to architectural forms. Believed to be memorial generic "portraits" of important persons, they have heavy facial features and headdresses like football helmets. Remarkably fantastic and powerful is the werejaguar head, the fundamental style for all Olmec deities, which appeared in all sizes and materials, but especially in much-prized jade.

Zapotec and Teotihuacán. Successors to the Olmec were the Zapotec in western Mexico (about 550 B. C.–900 A. D.) and Teotihuacán in the Valley of Mexico (about 2d century B. C.–6th century A. D.). The "danzantes" stone figures in low reliefs lining the entrance to a Zapotec pyramid tomb at Monte Alban show Olmec influence strongly. The Zapotec also carved jade figures and modeled fairly large clay urns representing figures with elaborate headdresses.

The sculpture of Teotihuacán tends to be rigid, formal, and highly symbolic. Each step of a famous five-step pyramid called the Temple of Quetzalcoatl (the feathered-serpent god) is richly carved with alternating heads of the rain god and the feathered-serpent god. Teotihuacán also produced distinctive stone masks of open-mouthed humans and many hand-molded small clay heads and figurines.

Maya. The elaborate Maya civilization was at its height first in southeastern Mexico and Guatemala (about 300 B. C.–900 A. D.) and then, remodeled by Toltec invaders, to the north in Yucatán (about 900–1200). In the early period in such ceremonial centers as Tikal and Yaxchilan, stone roof combs, high walls raising from temple roofs, were decorated with carved openwork or reliefs. Stone stelae were carved in high and low relief with stylized human, animal, and hybrid forms and square glyphs recording the date and other matters. Stone or stucco reliefs adorned the stairways, facades, and interiors of temples and palaces. Most of this work was painted. The Maya also modeled elegant clay figurines.

In the later Mayan period in Uxmal, Chichén Itzá, and other centers, the roof comb was replaced by the flying facade, an upward continuation of the front wall. Stelae were rare, but facades were carved with allover geometric patterns and projecting figures and heads.

Toltec. The militaristic Toltec civilization (10th–12th century), which centered at Tula in the Valley of Mexico and extended to Yucatán, created new styles. Pyramids and other structures were decorated with low-relief friezes in a linear style painted red, white, and black. They showed ceremonial scenes of combat or human sacrifice and jaguars and eagles symbolizing military societies. An important innnovation was great columns at temple entrances carved to represent the feathered-serpent god. They were made in three parts, the head forming the base, the body rising above it, and the tail and rattles extended to support the lintel. There were large and small multipartite columns in the form of caryatids and atlantes. Especially famous are the Chacmools, large recumbent human figures with hollowed abdomens to hold offerings.

Aztec. The Aztec civilization (15th–16th century), similar to the Toltec, produced reliefs incorporating figures and hieroglyphs and, most notably, free-standing stone sculpture. Many Aztec deity figures, such as the Mother of the Gods, 8 feet (2.4 meters) high, are colossal and grotesque. Some figures have skulls instead of heads, and some are rendered in simple, strong, naturalistic forms and stress volume and heavy masses. Many of these are roughly four-sided, suggesting the original stone block.

Mochica. The Mochica culture in Peru (3d century B. C.–1st century A. D.) was distinguished by its fine polished pottery, painted red, white, and black. Many vessels were modeled realistically in the form of human or animal figures or emotionally expressive portraits. Some were topped by a stirrup-spout consisting of a tubular loop and spout.

Tiahuanaco. Monumental stone sculpture is characteristic of the Tiahuanaco civilization, which flourished in Peru and Bolivia about 1000 A. D. The most famous is the Gateway of the Sun, a monolithic structure about 9 feet (2.7 meters) high. Across the top is a frieze in very low relief with incised detail, consisting of a conventionalized human figure, with a short blocklike body and large rectangular head flanked by rows of rectangular, condor-headed running figures. There are also huge, free-standing stone figures, including one almost 24 feet (7.3 meters) high. All are blocklike and proportioned to emphasize the large, rectangular head. The Tiahuanaco style influenced later Andean sculpture.

PAUL S. WINGERT
Author of "Primitive Art"

Bibliography

Dockstader, Frederick, *Indian Art in America* (Burns & MacEachen 1962).
Dockstader, Frederick, *Indian Art in Middle America* (N. Y. Graphic 1964).
Laude, Jean, *Arts of Black Africa* (Univ. of Calif. Press 1971).
Linton, Ralph, and Wingert, Paul S., *Arts of the South Seas* (Museum of Modern Art 1946).
Mason, J. Alden, *Ancient Civilizations of Peru* (Penguin 1969).
Wingert, Paul S., *Primitive Art* (Oxford 1962).

SCUP, either of two common marine fishes of the Atlantic coast of the United States. Both species are commonly known as porgies and belong to the porgy and sea-bream family, Sparidae. The northern scup, *Stenotomus chrysops*, a valuable food fish, is found from Maine to North Carolina and is most abundant in Middle Atlantic waters. After spawning it winters off Virginia and North Carolina at depths of 150 feet (46 meters, or 25 fathoms). The southern scup, or fair maid, *Stenotomus aculeatus*, ranges from Virginia to Texas.

The Scup is a deep-bodied fish, nearly oval in outline. It has large fins, a forked caudal tail, and caninelike teeth. It is only about 3 inches (7.5 cm) long at the end of its first year, but attains a length of 12 to 14 inches (30–35 cm) and a weight of 1 to 2 pounds (0.45–0.9 kg) at maturity. The adult is silver blue above and iridescent blue below. The young are marked with six dusky vertical bars, which gradually disappear as the fish matures. Scups are bottomliving fish, feeding on mollusks, small crustaceans, and worms.

JOHN D. BLACK[°]
Northeast Missouri State Teachers College

SCURVY is a deficiency disease caused by the lack of vitamin C (ascorbic acid) in the diet. This deficiency causes increased fragility of the capillaries and incomplete deposition of cement substances between the cells. As a result, the teeth become loose, and there is bleeding from the gums, under the skin, around the bones, and in the joints. Wounds heal defectively, and the bones become more brittle. In chronic conditions anemia may be present.

Causes and Prevention. Human beings are susceptible to scurvy because they lack the enzyme system responsible for a portion of the biological synthesis of ascorbic acid. Monkeys and guinea pigs also lack this enzyme system and are likewise susceptible. Because ascorbic acid reserves are rapidly lost, foods containing it should be eaten daily. The U. S. Food and Nutrition Board of the National Academy of Sciences recommends 35 to 60 milligrams of vitamin C as a normal adult requirement. However, many studies indicate that requirements for specific vitamins probably vary greatly among individuals and in the same individual at different times.

Ascorbic acid needs may be met by including fruits, particularly citrus fruits or juices, and fresh vegetables, especially the green leafy variety, in the diet. Potatoes, turnip greens, and strawberries are other good sources of ascorbic acid.

Better eating habits and improved distribution of foodstuffs in the developed regions of the world have virtually eliminated scurvy among adults. It may occur, however, in exceptional situations of greatly restricted food supply or in persons with unusual eating habits that exclude scurvy-preventing foods from the diet.

Scurvy in infants resembles the adult disease. The developing bones become fragile, and there is bleeding in the membranes surrounding the bones. The similarity between infantile scurvy and the adult form was established in 1883 by Sir Thomas Barlow, who first distinguished between scurvy and rickets. Infantile scurvy became widespread with the general introduction of bottle-feeding of infants on heated, sterilized cow's milk. Both the pasteurization and evaporation processes reduce the vitamin content of milk, thus making it necessary to provide supplementary sources of ascorbic acid in the infant diet. Scurvy is no longer prevalent among infants in the United States because of the inclusion of fruit juices and vegetables rich in vitamin C in their diet.

History. The earliest references to scurvy tell of its occurrence among soldiers, sailors, and prisoners, and during periods of famine. The ancient Greek physician Hippocrates describes soldiers who suffered from pains in the legs, gangrene of the gums, and loss of teeth—classic symptoms of scurvy. The disease plagued the Crusaders, explorers of the New World, mariners on long voyages around Africa, pioneers on the westward trek across North America, and soldiers in the American Civil War.

Epidemics of scurvy were once common among sailors on long sea voyages because of their diet of dried, salted, and preserved foods and the virtual absence of fresh fruits and vegetables. The South African city of Cape Town was settled to provide the crews of ships with a resting place to recover from the disease and to supply vessels with fresh vegetables before they sailed around the Cape of Good Hope.

Classic studies made in 1749 by James Lind, a Scottish naval surgeon, established that scurvy is caused by a dietary deficiency. He conducted well-designed therapeutic trials aboard a ship at sea to show that oranges and lemons cured scurvy. In 1753 he summarized this evidence, substantiated by other observations, in A Treatise on the Scurvy. He proposed a method for the preservation of citrus fruit juice that would prevent scurvy aboard ship. It was not until 1795, however, that Sir Gilbert Blane succeeded in gaining approval for a recommendation that lime juice be issued to all British naval vessels—a custom responsible for the use of the term "limey" to denote a British sailor. The Merchant Shipping Act of 1854 broadened the fight against scurvy by making a similar issue compulsory in the British merchant marine.

WILLIAM J. DARBY, M. D.*
Vanderbilt University School of Medicine

SCUTAGE, skū'tij, was a fee inaugurated in 11th century England, by which feudal vassals were released from their obligation to supply knights for royal wars. The term "scutage" ("shield money") dates from the 12th century, but the practice derived from the ancient Anglo-Saxon *fyrdwite,* a fine levied on disobedient warriors. William the Conqueror revived this as voluntary payment by which ecclesiastical vassals could commute their obligatory knightly service. A set sum was levied for each knight's fee or service owed, and the proceeds were used to hire mercenaries for the royal army. In the 12th century the option of paying scutage was extended to lay vassals. The reviving money economy made commutation advantageous to vassals who could not afford improved cavalry equipment, and the king welcomed increased independence from feudal loyalties as well as increased efficiency. Thus scutage marked both an important military innovation and a departure from the earlier agrarian society.

Henry II greatly expanded the collection of scutage in his preparation for the attack on Toulouse in 1159, but under Richard I (reigned 1189–1199) its convenience as a tax overshadowed its voluntary origins. King John's attempt to levy frequent and increased scutages for unsuccessful wars encouraged the baronial resistance that culminated in the Magna Carta in 1215. Thereafter scutage was illegal without the consent of the barons. It contributed later to the decline of the feudal nobility, whose military function was eclipsed by the new mercenary armies. By the 14th century, more remunerative parliamentary subsidies rendered scutage obsolete, but it was not abolished until the reign (1660–1685) of Charles II.

JOHN W. MCKENNA
*Author of "Henry VI of England
and the Dual Monarchy"*

SCUTARI, a city in Albania. See SHKODËR.

SCUTARI, a city in Turkey. See ÜSKÜDAR.

SCUTARI, Lake, skōō'tä-rē, largest lake in the Balkans, on the Yugoslavia-Albania border. The Albanian form of its name is Ligen i Shkodrës, and the Serbo-Croation form is Skadarsko Jezero. Fed partly by the Moraca River and drained by the Bojana, it was once an inlet of the Adriatic Sea. It is about 25 miles (40 km) long and from 4 to 7.5 miles (6.5–12 km) long. Shkodër, Albania, lies at its southeastern tip.

SCUTUM. See CONSTELLATION.

SCYLLA, sil'ə, in Greek mythology, was the daughter of King Nisus of Megara. She fell in love with King Minos of Crete when he came to attack Megara. To help Minos, Scylla cut from her father's head a lock of purple hair that had made Megara invulnerable to capture. After Minos captured Megara, and Nisus was slain, Scylla was transformed into a sea bird or, by some accounts, into a fish. Nisus himself was changed into an eagle that constantly pursued his transformed daughter to punish her for her crime.

SCYLLA AND CHARYBDIS, sil'ə, kə-rib'dəs, are two navigational hazards at the mouth of the Strait of Messina, between the Italian mainland and Sicily. They are represented in Greek mythology as two sea monsters. Scylla is a promontory on the mainland. Navigation around the promontory was considered dangerous by the ancients, although it is not regarded as especially difficult by modern sailors. Charybdis (modern Garofalo) is a whirlpool nearly opposite the entrance to the harbor of Messina in Sicily. It is regarded as dangerous to navigation even for modern ships, and must have been extremely hazardous in ancient times. The familiar expression "between Scylla and Charybdis" means to be confined to a choice between two equally dangerous situations.

In Homer's *Odyssey,* Scylla is described as a monster with 12 feet, 6 necks, and 6 mouths with triple rows of teeth, who lived on a rock on the Italian coast. She wore a girdle of dogs' heads around her loins. When Odysseus sailed near her she seized six of his men. According to one legend, she was changed from a beautiful woman into a monster through the jealousy of Circe or Amphitrite. Latin authors sometimes confused this Scylla with Scylla, daughter of King Nisus. (See SCYLLA.) Homer represents Charybdis as a figure sitting opposite Scylla on a low rock under a fig tree, sucking in and belching forth water three times a day. Odysseus barely escaped being drawn into the whirlpool.

SCYTHE, sīth, a farm tool, wielded with two hands, for cutting grass, grain, or other crops. It consists of a long curved metal blade attached to a long wooden handle. The scythe was developed from the sickle, which has a shorter blade and a shorter handle and is worked with one hand.

The scythe was in use in Europe at least by the time of the Roman Empire. It became equipped with its characteristic short bar handle projecting from the long handle about the 12th century. Scythes with a half circle of bent willow attached near the blade to gather the cut stems were in use in Flanders by the end of the 15th century. Scythes with curved instead of straight handles came into use by the end of the 1600's.

The scythe was increasingly used in reaping wheat, oats, barley, and other crops until the invention of mechanical reapers in the 1830's. Since then, it has largely been supplanted for harvesting crops.

Further Reading: Singer, Charles, and others, *A History of Technology*, vols. 2 and 3 (Oxford 1954–1958).

SCYTHIANS, sith'ē-ənz, a group of closely related tribes, called Scyths, that lived in a region of southeastern Europe in ancient times. Herodotus, in the 5th century B. C., wrote that they lived in the south Russian steppe between the Carpathians and the Don River. To some other Greeks, Scythia was a much vaguer term denoting the little-known area far to the north and northeast of the Black Sea.

Since the Scythians were one of many similar nomadic nations inhabiting a region where borders were variable and ill-defined, the confusion among the Greeks is understandable. It is clear, however, that Herodotus can safely be followed when he defines Scythia as the section of the plain bordered on the west by the lower Danube and the Carpathians, on the east by the Don River and the Kuban Valley, on the south by the Black Sea and the Caucasus, and on the north by the thick forest that stretches along the edge of the fertile grassland. The Scythians proper are those tribes that occupied this territory from about 700 B. C. and formed a single cohesive political entity until the 4th century B. C., when the nation was splintered into several groups.

Early History. Though there is considerable controversy about the exact origin and race of the Scythians, the weight of the evidence indicates that they were an Indo-European people who spoke an Iranian language akin to Old Persian. Undoubtedly they had mingled with such other peoples as the Turks, Mongols, and Huns, but the scant linguistic evidence and the physical type of most skeletal remains support the Indo-European designation. They probably settled in the north central section of the Eurasian steppes, perhaps in the Altai region, early in the 2d millennium B. C., but until the end of the 8th century B. C. nothing is known about their activities.

About 800 B. C., during the Chou dynasty of China, the Emperor Hsüan drove the warlike Hsiung-nu from his borders. This seems to have started a chain reaction of migrations, as each eastern tribe was driven to attack its western neighbor. At the end of the 8th century the Scyths were attacked by the Massagetae from the east, and the Scythians, in turn, crossed the Volga and fell upon the Cimmerians, driving them through the Caucasus and into Asia Minor.

WALTER CHANDOHA

A farmer cuts timothy with a scythe.

Most of the Scyths passed through the Caucasus and took over the region around Lake Van. They first appear in Assyrian records from the reign of Esarhaddon (680–699 B. C.). At first they seem to have fought against the Assyrians and later allied with them against the Mannai, Medes, Babylonians, and others at various times. In the last third of the 7th century they were at the height of their power. Herodotus says that they ruled all Upper Asia for 28 years, but the statement cannot be taken in a literal sense for there is no evidence that they actually attempted to create and rule an empire. They were sufficiently powerful, however, to roam and plunder in whatever direction they chose. They conducted raids as far south as Egypt, and in Palestine the city of Beth-shan (modern Beisan) was renamed Scythopolis, probably in testimony to a Scythian occupation.

Decline. When the Babylonians and Medes first marched upon Nineveh (615–614 B. C.), the Scyths helped the Assyrians to repel the attack. Two years later, however, the Scyths were persuaded to desert Assyria and to join the attack against it, and Nineveh fell to the invaders in 612. Shortly afterward, the Scythians took Carrhae (modern Haran, Turkey), the new capital and last stronghold of Assyria. It was not long before the Medes turned upon their Scythian allies, killing some and driving most of them back through the Caucasus into Scythia. Many Scyths, however, remained on the southern shores of the Black Sea and in parts of Armenia, forming permanent settlements.

Though their great moment of power had passed, the Scythians were still able, about 512, to beat off a great expedition led against them by

471

the Persian King Darius I before his attack upon Greece, and later still, about 325, they met and defeated the army of Zopyrion, one of Alexander the Great's generals, who had been sent to drive them from Thrace. But in the 4th and 3d centuries B. C. the Scyths were steadily driven from their lands by the Sarmatians, a kindred nation from the east. By the end of the 3d century the south Russian steppe was known as Sarmatia, and the Scythians no longer existed as a single nation, though tribes of them remained in the Balkans and in the Asian section of the steppes.

Way of Life. Like most nomads, the Scythians kept cattle and moved seasonally in search of grass. They were expert horsemen and seem to have been the first horse-riding people in southern Russia. They were able to use bows and arrows from horseback in the manner of the Parthians. Their clothing was suited to an equestrian life—tight trousers of felt or leather, high soft boots, and a short tunic covered by a jacket with a hood for the head. All their garments were elaborately tooled with stylized designs. About the women's dress there is less certainty, but they appear to have worn long robes and veiled headdresses. They rode with the children and perhaps lived in large covered wagons. Some authorities assert that they fought alongside the men.

Though the Scythians had no fixed places of worship, no altars, and apparently no ritual apparatus, they worshiped several gods. First of all there was the great goddess Tabiti, a goddess of fire and probably a mother goddess, since, like Artemis, she is depicted with wild animals. Other gods were Papoeus, whom Herodotus identifies with Zeus; gods of earth, sun, and moon; and one corresponding to Ares, the god of war. To the latter they sacrificed human captives.

In war the Scythians were savage. They scalped and beheaded their enemies, often making cups from their skulls. These cups were sometimes used to drink the blood of a slain adversary. For war the nation was divided into three divisions, each with its own commander. Though the king possessed great power, all tribesmen of the warrior class enjoyed various political rights.

Not all Scyths were warriors, however. Part of the nation consisted of tribes that cultivated the land and were subject to the warrior tribes of the Nomad and Royal Scyths. These latter lived between the Dnieper and the Don rivers and grew wealthy on the farming and exports of the agricultural Scyths: the Callipidae on the Bug, the Alazones and the Aroteres east of the Dniester, and the Georgi near the Dnieper. Scythian wheat exports as well as fish, timber, and slaves were extremely important to the Greek cities on the Black Sea and especially to Athens and its confederacy.

The Scyths were polygamous, and sons customarily inherited their fathers' wives. The favorite wife, however, would be buried with the husband. Burials were most elaborate, as can be seen from numerous well-preserved tombs along the Kuban and at Pazirik. Burial chambers consisting of four rooms were built for kings and perhaps for men of rank. These were filled with personal possessions, food, wine, the favorite wife, and the head servants. The abundance of gold and silver objects in the tombs attests to the wealth of the kings and to Scythian skill in metalwork. Outside the burial chamber the man's favorite horses would be slain, and the whole would be heaped over with a mound of earth.

Art. Scythian art was almost completely decorative, adorning objects of everyday use such as saddles, blankets, rugs, clothing, swords, and vases. For this reason it was omnipresent, and there were many skilled craftsmen. As might be expected from a nomadic people, animals form the principal artistic motif. Naturalistic, stylized, and imaginary creatures often appear together in a single design. In the best examples of this art there is a rhythm and vitality that is quite admirable.

The Scythian animal style was developed into the Sarmatian polychrome style, which in turn was adopted by the Goths and introduced into central Europe. In the Middle Ages the influence of Scythian animal designs also penetrated northern Europe through contact between the Scandinavian countries and Russia.

See also GOLDWORK AND SILVERWORK.

Further Reading: Herodotus, *History,* tr. by George Rawlinson, 4th ed. (1880); Minns, Ellis H., *Scythians and Greeks* (Biblo & Tannen 1913); Rice, Tamara Talbot, *The Scythians* (Praeger 1957); Rostovtzeff, Michael I., *Iranians and Greeks in South Russia* (Oxford 1922).

Scythian bowl of the 4th century B. C. The silver vessel is covered with goldwork that depicts the life of Scythian warriors.

A. W. AMBLER, FROM NATIONAL AUDUBON SOCIETY   WILLIAMS, FROM ANNAN

Two sea anemones—ringed anemone (*left*) and aggregated anemone (*right*)—common in coastal Pacific waters.

SDS. See STUDENTS FOR A DEMOCRATIC SOCIETY.

SEA. See OCEAN, THE.

SEA ANEMONE, a-nem′ə-nē, is the popular name for some 1,000 species of polyp or coelanterate of the order Actiniaria in the class Anthozoa. These brightly colored, flowerlike animals are found in all seas, but they are generally more numerous and larger in temperate and warm waters. Most of them live singly, but some form colonies.

Unlike the closely related stone corals, sea anemones never form an internal limy skeleton but may form a superficial one in the ectoderm. Generally they live attached to rock pilings or the like, but a few burrow in sand or mud. Some fix themselves as commensals to shells inhabited by hermit crabs. A few are truly parasitic in jellyfishes.

Physical Characteristics. Despite their popular name, only a few of these animals resemble anemone blossoms. The majority look like dahlias or chrysanthemums. . The typical sea anemone has a stout, more or less cylindrical, body that is topped by a broad, flat disk. The disk contains a slitlike mouth surrounded by whorls of simple hollow tentacles, which resemble flower petals. From the mouth a short, tubular gullet, or esophagus, reaches into the cavity of the body. It is connected to the body walls by radiating septa, or mesenteries, that divide the body cavity into a corresponding number of sacs. The esophagus communicates with the sacs through a central space into which the septa do not reach. A pair of ciliated grooves, or siphonoglyphs, extend along opposite sides of the esophagus and into the corresponding corners of the mouth. These always remain open and are the seat of

inflowing and outflowing currents of water. The grooves provide both a means of respiration and an outlet for the removal of waste matter from the body.

The body walls, as well as the tentacles, which are outgrowths from them, are very contractile and largely composed of muscles arranged in a circular and a longitudinal layer. The circular layer is for extension; the longitudinal layer, for retraction. These muscles have special relations to the mesenteries. The mesenteries are vertical radiating septa reaching from the mouth disk or peristome to the base, and from the body wall to the esophagus, but ending freely below the esophagus. They are not strictly radial in arrangement but are grouped in pairs, almost always, like the tentacles, in some multiple of six. The mesenteries corresponding to the siphonoglyphs differ in structure from all of the others and are termed directive; the others form different classes according to the order and degree of development. The intermesenteric sacs may further communicate by one or two pores in each mesentery.

Along the edges of the septa the testes and ovaries are developed from the cells lining the gastric cavity. Digestive cells are also found in the same region, as well as an area filled with stinging thread cells, or nematocysts.

Sea anemones may be distinguished by the arrangement of their septa and tentacles and, less importantly, by their color and form. Most species, particularly the tropical varieties, are beautifully colored. The average size of a sea anemone is 2½ to 3 inches (64–76 mm) in diameter and 4 inches (100 mm) in height.

Food and Reproduction. Sea anemones are carnivorous, but, having very limited powers of locomotion, they depend on the food that falls on their tentacles or peristome. The food is paralyzed by stinging cells or captured by the tentacles and passed through the mouth into the gastric cavity for digestion. The undigested portion of the food is ejected through the mouth. The sea anemone is capable of consuming a large amount of food and of growing rapidly. If it is starved, it will shrink almost to the point of disappearance, without losing its form.

Reproduction is achieved both asexually, by budding and fission, and sexually. In sexual reproduction the eggs and spermatozoa are usually produced by different individuals. The eggs are fertilized in the gastric cavity and escape from the mouth in most cases as minute, free-swimming larvae, or planulae. These soon attach themselves to a substrate and develop mouths, tentacles, and mesenteries, until the adult structure is attained.

SEA BASS, any of the family Serranidae of marine fishes, many of which are important food and game fishes. Among the common species are the striped bass, the black sea bass, the kelp bass, the sand bass, and the spotted sand bass. See Bass.

SEA BREAM, any of various species of the family Sparidae, some of which are important food and game fishes. Most are found in tropical and temperate marine waters, but a few are found in colder waters and in freshwater.

SEA COW, any of the three genera of aquatic mammals in the order Sirenia, which is made up of the families Dugongidae and Trichechidae. The Trichechidae family consists of three species of the single genus *Trichechus* that are commonly called manatees. The Dugongidae family consists of two species, the *Dugong dugon* and the extinct *Hydrododamalis gigas*, or *H. stelleri*, which is commonly known as Steller's sea cow. See Dugong; Manatee.

Steller's sea cow, which was confined to the waters around the Bering Strait, was a dugonglike animal with a small head, no teeth, and a laterally lobed tail. Sought for its meat and oil, it was hunted to extinction within a century after its discovery in 1741 by German naturalist Georg Wilhelm Steller.

SEA CUCUMBER, any of a group of marine animals with elongated tubular bodies. Sea cucumbers are found in all seas of the world at all depths, usually lying on the bottom on one flattened side. They are classified in the class Holothuroidea of the phylum Echinodermata.

Sea cucumbers range in length from 1 inch (2.5 cm) to almost 5 feet (1.5 meters). They are very often brownish but may range in color from black to bright yellow and red stripes. Its skeleton consists of microscopic ossicles embedded in a leathery and somewhat slimy skin. Its mouth is surrounded by a ring of five or more small tentacles which are used to extract microscopic organic matter from the sand. A coiled digestive system stretches from the mouth to the anus. Respiration occurs through a complex of tubules, called the respiratory tree, which is attached near the end of the intestine.

Sea cucumbers move somewhat caterpillarlike through waves of muscular contractions, sometimes aided by small tube feet. A few species reproduce asexually, but most species reproduce sexually. In some the eggs are fertilized externally, but in other species the eggs are fertilized and hatched internally with the young discharged through the anal rupture. If disturbed, a sea cucumber may eviscerate itself and later regenerate any parts lost in the process.

SEA DAYAK. See Dayak.

SEA ELEPHANT. See Elephant Seal.

SEA FAN, a horny coral that grows in a flat, fanlike form. Sea fans are found in most warmer coastal seas, where their yellow, orange, or reddish hue often adds much color to the coral reefs. Sea fans, which may grow to a height of 15 inches (37.5 cm) or more, represent the skeletons of many colonial polyps, each of which has eight tentacles. A common species along the coast of Florida and the West Indies is *Gorgonia flabellum*.

SEA FEATHER is the name applied to any of several marine coelenterates, particularly the sea pen (*Pennatula*), in which the colony of cells has a feathery form and the stem or shaft of the colony has a calcareous or horny axis that is

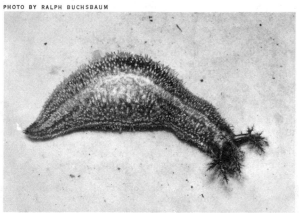

SEA CUCUMBERS. *Below:* A sea cucumber (*Pentacta pygmaca*) with numerous tube feet and with branched tentacles surrounding its mouth. *Left:* Closeup of the tentacles of another species, *Cucumaria miniata.*

JOHN TASHJIAN TACOMA AQUARIUM

Sea feather or sea pen *(Ptilosarcus quadrangularis)*

embedded in the mud of the sea bottom. Sea feathers may grow to a height and width of about 18 inches (45 cm) and are often reddish or yellowish.

SEA GOOSEBERRY, a small gelatinous invertebrate animal found in seas throughout the world. See COMB JELLY.

SEA GRAPE, any of various tropical shrubs or small trees of the genus *Coccolaba*, especially the plant *C. uvifera*, which inhabits sandy shores of Florida and tropical America. It has glossy heart-shaped leaves, small greenish flowers, and purplish berries. The berries, which resemble grapes, are edible and are sometimes used to make jelly. Sea grapes are classified in the buckwheat family, Polygonaceae.

SEA GULL. See GULL.

SEA GULL, a play by Anton Chekhov, first performed in St. Petersburg in 1896. Unacclaimed at its premiere, *The Sea Gull* enjoyed a sensational success two years later when it was staged by Konstantin Stanislavsky and Vladimir Nemirovich-Danchenko at their Moscow Art Theatre. *The Sea Gull* (or *Seagull*) became the symbol of this theater, permanently linking its name with that of Chekhov.

A favorite on the Russian stage, the play became widely popular in Europe and the United States in the first quarter of the 20th century. It has continued to be an organic part of the national repertory in the Soviet Union. In *The Sea Gull,* Chekhov replaced conventional stage tricks, external action, and dramatic climaxes with a new theatrical language based on understatement, psychological portraiture, hints, allusions, and descriptions of moods.

The Sea Gull has no central hero but depicts the destinies and relationships of its various characters. Treplev, a young writer, is frustrated in his search for new literary forms and in his hopeless love for Nina, a delightful girl who dreams of becoming an actress. Nina, however, is in love with Trigorin, a middle-aged author, who, despite his popularity, doubts his own talent. He seduces Nina out of vanity and boredom and then deserts her. When Treplev sees Nina again, she is no longer the fresh, free, and happy creature that he adored. Trigorin has ruined her life and her fate has been much like that of a sea gull that Treplev once senselessly shot and showed her. However, she is still determined to be an actress and her feelings toward Treplev have not changed. The other characters in the play are equally unsuccessful and form a melancholic background of sorrow and disappointment. Their sad life stories are projected with compassionate realism, typical of Chekhov's manner, and their deceptively trivial dialogues reveal their intimate feelings.

SEA HARE, a gastropod mollusk of the genus *Apysia,* sometimes called *Tethys.* It is found in most seas, generally in muddy or sandy tracts. The animal is sluglike in appearance and brightly colored, usually yellowish or greenish. When

The sea grape has small, purplish, edible berries.

ROBERT HERMES, FROM NATIONAL AUDUBON SOCIETY

The sea hare has front tentacles that resemble hare's ears.

DOUGLAS P. WILSON, F. RP.S.

disturbed it emits a purple protective fluid. The mantle is oblong, flexible, and transparent and has side lobes, used as fins, that extend over the sides and back to cover the rudimentary shell. Gills are located at the center and posterior portions of the dorsal surface. The sea hare has four tentacles, rhinophores believed to be organs of taste. The front tentacles resemble the ears of a hare, thus giving the animal its popular name. The eyes are at the base of the two rear tentacles. The length of the sea hare ranges from a few inches to more than 16 inches (40 cm).

Seaweed is the sea hare's chief food, but small crustaceans, mollusks, and annelids are also consumed. The animal's mouth is equipped with quick, muscular lips, and its stomach is compound, consisting of a crop, muscular gizzard, and accessory cavities. The sea hare is hermaphroditic. It deposits its eggs in long strips.

The sea hare is in the subclass Opisthobranchia of the order Tectibranchia. It was considered poisonous by the ancients, but it is actually harmless to man, except for an acrid substance that is produced by some species and that irritates the human skin.

SEA HORSE, a small marine fish of the genus *Hippocampus*, in the family Syngnathidae, closely related to the pipefish. It is widely distributed in the temperate and tropical waters of the world. The sea horse is so named because of its distinctively horselike head, general body shape, and upright position. It is covered with bony plates arranged in rings and has an elongated tubiform snout and a toothless mouth. The sea horse lacks a caudal fin but has small pectoral, dorsal, and anal fins. It also has a prehensile tail, which it uses to attach itself to seaweed or other available supports.

The sea horse is capable of a variety of color changes, enabling it to be relatively inconspicuous

The sea horse, despite its appearance, is a fish.

DOUGLAS FAULKNER

in its natural habitat. An Australian species has numerous dermal flaps covering its body and tail, giving it a remarkable resemblance to the seaweed in which it lives.

Most adult sea horses are about 6 inches (15 cm) long, but sizes may range from 2 inches (5 cm) to 12 inches (30 cm). The best known species is the common sea horse (*H. hudsonicus*), found off the Atlantic coast of the United States, southward from Cape Cod.

The male sea horse has a brood pouch on its abdomen into which the female places eggs for hatching. As many as 200 young escape from this pouch after an incubation period of 40 to 50 days. The diet of the sea horse consists of plankton animals, primarily small crustaceans.

The sea horse has long been a popular aquarium fish, but is difficult to maintain because it must be supplied with running sea water.

JOHN D. BLACK
Northeast Missouri State University

SEA ISLANDS, a chain of low-lying islands in the Atlantic Ocean, off the coasts of South Carolina, Georgia, and northern Florida. In South Carolina the most important of these islands include James, Johns, Edisto, Port Royal, St. Helena, Parris, and Hilton Head; in Georgia they include Tybee, Ossabaw, St. Catherines, Sapelo, St. Simons, Jekyll, and Cumberland islands; and in Florida, Amelia Island. A number of the islands are connected to the mainland by bridges and causeways.

Some of the Sea Islands are resorts and some have wildlife refuges and parks. Fort Frederica National Monument is on St. Simons.

Parris Island is the site of a U. S. Marine installation. The chief crops of the island are corn, peanuts, and potatoes. Shrimp, crabs, and oysters are caught in large quantities.

English and Spanish contended for control of the Sea Islands in the 18th century. Later, the islands were famous for the quality of their cotton. After the Civil War, freed slaves received land on the islands, and their descendants, called Gullah, still reside here. See also FORT FREDERICA NATIONAL MONUMENT; GULLAH.

SEA KALE is a perennial plant, *Crambe maritima*, of the mustard family. It is native to Europe, where it grows along the Atlantic and Baltic coasts.

Sea kale is cultivated for its young asparaguslike shoots, which are used as a vegetable after they are blanched. The shoots are blanched either by covering the crown to a depth of a foot or more with loose fine earth or by putting an opaque box over the plant. Sea kale is grown only rarely in the United States.

JOHN W. THIERET*
University of Southwestern Louisiana

SEA LAMPREY, lam'prē, a lamprey, *Petromyzon marinus*, of the Atlantic coasts of North America. See LAMPREY.

SEA LAVENDER is the common name for plants of the genus *Limonium* of the leadwort family, Plumbaginaceae. The genus contains about 150 species of perennial or rarely annual herbs occurring on seacoasts and in deserts, salt meadows, and salt marshes the world over, but is most numerous in the Old World. Some species are occasionally cultivated in gardens. The leaves

Sea lions, aquatic mammals with webbed feet, or flippers, are found in arctic, temperate, and tropical waters of the world.

A. W. AMBLER, FROM NATIONAL AUDUBON SOCIETY

of sea lavenders are confined to the base of the plant. The many small blue, lavender, yellow, or white flowers are borne in branched clusters and are usually arranged along one side of the stems. The flower clusters of some species retain their color well in dried bouquets.

Five species of sea lavenders are native to the United States, all in coastal marshes. One of these is found in California, the other four in the eastern states.

JOHN W. THIERET
University of Southwestern Louisiana

SEA LETTUCE is a pale green seaweed, *Ulva lactuca*, whose crinkly fronds are sometimes used in salads.

SEA LILY, any of a large group of crinoids, stalked echinoderms, that spend their entire lives attached to the sea bottom. Sea lilies are found in almost all seas, usually at moderate depths or in deep water. The sea lily has a more or less cup-shaped body, or corona, that has five or more feathery arms that give the animal a flower-like appearance. A long, usually joined, stalk extends from the bottom, or aboral surface of the body, and firmly anchors the sea lily to the sea bottom. See also CRINOID.

SEA LION, any of four genera of aquatic mammals related to the fur seal. It is found in arctic, temperate, and subtropical waters around the world, especially along the coasts of North and South America, southern Africa, Australia, New Zealand, and some oceanic islands. The sea lion has an elongated body with a short tail, a dog-like head, and four webbed feet, or flippers. Its hind flippers can be turned forward to help support the body, and the animal can walk on four feet. It is classified with the fur seal in the family Otariidae in the suborder Pinnepedia. The sea lion has only one layer of coarse hair, although fine underhairs are present, distinguishing it from the fur seal, which has a distinct underfur. The length of the sea lion ranges from 5 to 12 feet (150–350 cm), and its color from reddish brown to black.

The sea lion feeds on crustaceans, cephaloids, sea birds, and fish. They are gregarious and gather in rookeries during the summer, where the males have harems of 10 to 20 females. One pup is born to each female after about a year. One species, the California sea lion (*Zaophus californianus*), is used as a performing seal.

SEA MOUSE, any of about 26 species of marine worms making up the genus *Aphrodite*. Closely related to bloodworms, feather dusters, and sandworms, sea mice are found throughout the world, generally occurring in subintertidal depths to 600 meters or more on mud, rock, or coralline bottoms.

These rather broad worms are named sea mice because of their oval shape, convex above and flat below, and their creeping or wriggling movement. In the sea mouse, the dorsal or upper surface is iridescent, the sides have brilliant prismatic colors, and the ventral or lower surface is pale flesh-colored or roughened by many small papillae. The bright colors are due to diffraction of light through the mass of hairlike felt and setae that cover the body. The felt protects the underlying soft parts of the body and conceals the 15 pairs of scales, or elytra, that cover the back of the worm.

Sea mice range in size from a fraction of an inch to about 8 inches (20 cm). They have 35 to 40 body segments, indicated by serially arranged thick needle-shaped spines directed laterally. The head, a small lobe at the anterior end, is usually concealed except for a pair of long slender palpi, or feelers. The mouth leads through a spacious buccal cavity to a cylindrical, muscular proboscis with four jaws and then extends to an alimentary tract that has complex pinnately divided diverticula. The anus is posterior.

SEA OTTER, a fur-bearing marine animal of the genus *Enhydra*, found in the waters of the North Pacific Ocean. It is classified in the subfamily Lutrinae of the weasel family, Mustelidae, in the order Carnivora. The sea otter is a sturdy, thickset animal with a broad, flattened head,

STUART B. HERTZ

The sea otter lives in northern Pacific waters. The otter above is floating on his back while holding a rock on his belly. He smashes shellfish on the rock to open them and get at the meat.

PRO PIX, FROM MONKMEYER

small ears, and short limbs. Its hind feet are large, broadly webbed, and flipperlike. Its forefeet are disproportionately small but agile enough to use rocks as hammers to break open shellfish. An adult weighs about 80 pounds (36 kg), stands 10 to 12 inches (25–30 cm) at the shoulders, and has a head and body length of 35 to 40 inches (25–30 cm) and a tail length of 10 to 12 inches (25–30 cm).

The brownish black fur of the sea otter is soft, full, deep, and finely grizzled. The animal was so widely hunted during the 18th and 19th centuries that by 1910 it was almost extinct. Today it is internationally protected and is increasing in number.

Originally a friendly animal, the sea otter is now suspicious and distrustful of man and never comes ashore even to breed. It spends almost its entire life offshore in the floating kelp beds of the Pacific. It is believed that the animal pairs for life. The female gives birth to a single pup nine months after mating, not in a den or nest, but on the floating kelp. The pup is born fully furred and with its eyes open. The mother otter floats on her back and her pup rests, sleeps, and is nursed on her breast. The pup is not weaned for six months and may stay with its mother for a year or until the next pup is born. The animal reaches maturity in four years.

The sea otter feeds on crustaceans, shellfish, and other forms of life found on the ocean floor. It may go down 100 feet (30 meters) or more in search of food. Its original range extended from California to Alaska, and from the Kamchatka Peninsula to the Kuril Islands. The killer whale is one of its few natural enemies.

GEORGE G. GOODWIN
The American Museum of Natural History

SEA PINK, the common name for a genus, *Armeria,* of small perennials cultivated in rock gardens. See also THRIFT.

SEA ROBIN, any of numerous species of fish of the family Triglidae, found in shallow temperate and tropical waters in all parts of the world. The popular name derives from its reddish color and large, winglike pectoral fins. The sea robin has a large head encased in bony plates, a flattened snout, and an elongated, tapered body covered with small scales. The larger species reach a length of 2 to 3 feet (60–90 cm). The first three

rays of the long pectoral fins are separated from the fin web and also from one another. The rays have special sensory organs at the ends, which are used by the fish to propel itself along the bottom, to turn over rocks and other small objects, and to sense the small fishes and crustaceans it feeds upon.

Numerous species of the genus *Prionotus* inhabit the warmer North American seas. The best known are the short-winged sea robin (*P. carolinensis*), whose pectoral fins are red and less than half as long as the body, and the long-winged sea robin (*P. strigatus*), whose pectorals are brown and more than half as long as the body. Both are common as far north as Cape Cod. The short-winged fish is also found in Massachusetts Bay. Several related species are found on the Pacific coast and elsewhere. Some are called flying fish. Large numbers of sea robins are caught by fishermen, but even though their flesh is excellent, they are not considered food fish.

WOMETCO MIAMI SEAQUARIUM

Bighead sea robin is found in shallow Atlantic waters.

SEA SERPENT, a large, apparently mythical, marine animal, also called sea monster, whose supposed existence has been reported for many centuries. Early Norse legends contained descriptions of sea serpents in Scandinavian waters. The first printed account of such a monster—based on hearsay but with a picture—appeared in Konrad von Gesner's *Historium animalium* (1551–1558). The Norwegian missionary Hans Egede claimed to have sighted a sea serpent off the Greenland coast in 1734 and wrote a report of his observations. Since his time, many reports of such beasts have been made. These include reports by a British steamer and a German submarine during World War I and a report by the steamer *Santa Clara* in 1947.

The most-publicized sea serpent of recent times is the so-called Loch Ness monster, named after one of the larger freshwater lakes in Scotland. It is described as being 60 feet (18 meters) or more in length, with a small head, a long slender neck, and a trunk either slender or thickened at the middle. Witnesses allegedly saw loops of the body, or a fin on the back and two pairs of flippers, above the surface of the water. No animal or parts of one fitting this description have washed ashore or have been collected.

Several well-known examples of marine life might provide a basis for reports of sea serpents. These include long strands of seaweed moved by wave action, several porpoises leaping out of water in single file, or giant squids moving their long tentacles at the surface of the water. The creature probably most responsible for the reports is the oarfish, *Regalecus glesne*. It is 20 or more feet (6 meters) in length and has a slender head and narrowly compressed tapering body that is crested along the head and back. Although it is thought to live in the deeper regions of the sea, it has been observed swimming at the surface, and several have been cast ashore in Bermuda, California, and elsewhere. There is also a long slender shark, *Clodoselache*, which is found in the deep waters of the Pacific.

Sea monsters have been compared with the plesiosaurs, slender marine reptiles that inhabited the seas in Cretaceous times. Some were 40 to 50 feet (12–15 meters) long. They had a small head, a long neck (up to 22 feet, or 6.7 meters), and two pairs of slender paddle-shaped limbs.

Although there is a tendency to discount sightings of sea serpents, the sea still holds some surprises. The discovery in 1938 of several live specimens of the coelacanth—a member of a fossil group 100 million to 250 million years old—is one example. Some zoologists believe that the sea serpent may be a marine animal that is yet to be discovered.

TRACY I. STORER
Coauthor of "General Zoology"

Further Reading: Gould, Rupert T., *The Case for the Sea Serpent*, reprint (Singing Tree 1969); id, *The Loch Ness Monster and Others* (Bles 1934); Heuvelmans, Bernard, *In the Wake of the Sea Serpents* (Hill and Wang 1968); Ley, Willy, "The Great Unknown of the Seas," *Exotic Zoology* (1959).

SEA SLUG is the name given to any of the shellless marine snails of the order Nudibranchia in the subclass Opisthobranchia. Sea slugs are found in nearly all the seas, from shallow water to depths of several fathoms. A few, such as those of the genus *Glaucus*, are pelagic, living in the open ocean at or near the surface.

Sea slugs have an extraordinary range of coloration. They may be a solid color—red, blue, or even black—or they may be a mixture of colors forming stripes or a marbled effect. Sometimes the external gills, rhinophores, and pallium appendages are differently colored. Sea slugs range in length from about ⅛ inch (3 mm) to 6 inches (150 mm). The gill, when present, is external and located on the back in the rear portion of of the animal. See also SNAILS AND SLUGS.

Most, if not all, sea slugs are predaceous, feeding mainly on sessile animals, such as hy-

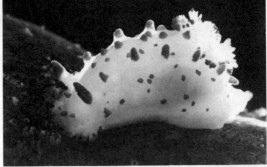

Sea slugs—*Triopha carpenteri* (above) and *Glossodoris macfarlandi* (below)—are found throughout the world.

droids and sponges. All are hermaphraditic, both sexes being contained in a single individual.

WILLIAM J. CLENCH[*]
Museum of Comparative Zoology
Harvard College

SEA SQUIRT, a cylindrical or spherical sea animal of the class Ascidacea in the subphylum Tunicata of the phylum Chordata. It is found along or near the shores of all the seas. The sea squirt is enclosed in a tunic lined with a membranous mantle containing muscle fibers and blood vessels. Most sea squirts attach themselves on one side to rocks, the sea floor, or some other substantial surface. The free side has two open ings, or siphons. Water enters the inhalant siphon and goes into the throat, where microscopic organisms are strained out and sent to the gullet and intestine. The exhalant siphon squirts the filtered water far away from the animal to avoid having it inhaled again. The larva of the hermaphraditic sea squirt has a notochord, which is lost during metamorphosis. This larval notochord has led scientists to believe that the sea squirt is distantly related to the vertebrates.

A common sea squirt, *Ciona intestinalis*, found along the Atlantic and California coasts, usually near shore.

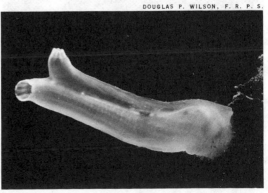

SEA TURTLE, any of several species of turtles that spend almost their entire lives in the sea, coming ashore only to lay eggs. The sea turtles are classified in two families—the leatherback in the family Dermochelidae and the green turtle, loggerhead, and a few other species in the family Chelonidae. See also GREEN TURTLE; LEATHERBACK; LOGGERHEAD.

SEA URCHIN, any of a large group of marine animals that have a globular shape and many projecting spines. They are classified in the class Echinoidea; the word "echinoid" comes from the Greek for "hedgehoglike," an apt description of these animals. Sea urchins are found in shallow and deep water from polar to tropical seas. All live on the bottom, where they prefer rocky habitats, but some may be found on sand.

The sea urchin has a rigid internal shell, or test, that is formed by joined skeletal plates. The regular echinoid test is radically symmetrical and marked by regularly arranged tubercules on which the spines are set. The test wall is formed by an alternation of five interambulacral plates, which are imperforate, and five ambulacral plates, which are pierced by pores that hold slender tube feet. A cycle of genital plates at the aboral end surrounds a membranous periproct, the area containing the anus. One of the genital plates contains the *madreporite*, a porous plate that allows fluids to pass in and out of the water-vascular system.

The spines of most sea urchins are sharp and pointed, but some are club-shaped. Those of a number of species have poison glands. The spines are used in locomotion, to cover the aboral surface with pebbles or other objects, and for protection. A few sea urchins use their spines and jaws to bore into rocks or even steel pilings. Several kinds of small, jawed appendages—the *pedicellariae*—are set among the spines. These are used to keep the surface clean, to repel small invaders, and—in some species—to aid in subduing prey.

The mouth of the sea urchin lies in the center of a membranous peristome and is equipped with a remarkably complex jaw apparatus called *Aristotle's lantern*. The ambulacral system centers in a water ring surrounding the mouth and a stone canal extending to the madreporite.

Purple sea urchin (*Strongylocentrotus purpuratus*). Sea urchins feel and move by means of slender tentacle-like tube feet interspersed among rigid spines.

GRANT HEILMAN

Radial canals run on the inner surface of the test to connect the ring canals and tube feet. In many sea urchins, muscles associated with Aristotle's lantern pump coelomic fluid in and out of a whorl of peristomal gills, facilitating respiratory exchange. Two nerve rings encircle the mouth, giving rise to radial nerves, which follow the radial water canals.

Sea urchins move about with their oral surface downward, using either spines or tube feet or both. Species using spines for locomotion are the fastest, some reaching speeds of 7 feet (2 meters) per minute. Sea urchins feed on algae, dead matter, and sessile or sedentary animals. Feeding is slow. Two or three weeks may be required to consume a clump of seaweed. To reproduce, sea urchins shed eggs and sperm into the sea. Zygotes give rise to unique pluteus larvae, which undergo a complex metamorphosis.

Sea urchins are in the subclass Regularia of the class Echinoida. Modern species may be placed in three orders: Lepidocentroida, largely extinct and now abyssal, with a somewhat flexible test; Cidaroidea, with a very large primary spine and several small spines on each interambulacral plate and with the interambulacral plates crossing the peristome to the mouth ring; and Diadematoida, with the interambulacral plates extending only to the peristomal border.

PAUL A. MEGLITSCH
Drake University

Further Reading: Boolootián, R. A., ed., *Physiology of Echinodermata* (Interscience 1966); Hyman, L. H., *The Invertebrates*, vol. IV, "Echinodermata" (McGraw 1955).

SEABEE, a member of the U. S. Navy Construction Battalions (CB's) that were organized in World War II to build naval bases and other installations in combat areas. Early in the war, civilian workers under contract were used for this work. But their doubtful status under the laws of war, which was demonstrated by the capture and execution by the Japanese of workers on Wake Island in December 1941, indicated that such personnel should be organized into military units. Seabee battalions of 1,000 men each were formed under the command of officers of the Navy's civil engineer corps. They received combat training and wore a special insignia—a flying bee wearing a sailor's cap and carrying a tommygun, a wrench, and a hammer.

The Seabees built airfields, harbor facilities, and temporary buildings for shops, barracks, and warehouses. Some units were organized as stevedores. They had much freedom of action in completing their assignments and made a notable record. Their peak strength of more than 258,000 men was reached in June 1945. After World War II, the Seabees were retained as part of the postwar naval organization.

JOHN D. HAYES
Rear Admiral, U. S. Navy (Retired)

SEABORG, sē'bôrg, **Glenn Theodore** (1912–), American nuclear chemist who shared the 1951 Nobel Prize in chemistry with Edwin M. McMillan "for their discoveries in the chemistry of the transuranium elements." A pioneer in the field of nuclear chemistry and physics, Seaborg was a codiscoverer of the transuranium elements with atomic numbers from 94 through 102.

Seaborg also helped to discover several radioactive isotopes; the actinide concept of the position of heavy elements in the periodic table;

the neptunium radioactive series; and a chemical separation method for the manufacture of plutonium. As an administrator, he served as chancellor of the Berkeley·campus of the University of California (1958–1961) and as chairman of the U. S. Atomic Energy Commission (1961–1971).

Seaborg was born in Ishpeming, Mich., on April 19, 1912. In 1937, after graduating from the University of California (B. A., 1934; Ph. D., 1937), Seaborg joined the university's faculty at Berkeley, where he became a full professor in 1945. In 1940 he began collaborating with McMillan in the latter's research on the elements beyond uranium and was part of the team that isolated plutonium (atomic number 94) in 1940. Seaborg took over direction of this research in 1941, and that same year he and his associates isolated the isotope U-233 from thorium and established thorium's nuclear-fuel potential. They identified americium (95) and curium (96) in 1944; berkelium (97) in 1949; californium (98) in 1950; einsteinium (99) in 1952; fermium (100) in 1953; mendelevium (101) in 1955; and nobelium (102) in 1958.

Seaborg and his group recognized that the newly discovered family of transuranium elements resembled the rare-earth family in that both sets of elements added electrons to inner atomic orbits to increase their atomic numbers. They identified these two sets as actinides and lanthanides.

See also TRANSURANIUM ELEMENTS.

ISAAC ASIMOV
Author of "Search of the Elements"

SEABURY, sē′ber-ē, **Samuel** (1729–1796), American clergyman who was the first bishop of the Protestant Episcopal Church in America. Seabury was born in North Groton, Conn., on Nov. 30, 1729. He graduated from Yale College in 1748 and three years later took a course in medicine at the University of Edinburgh. He did not, however, practice medicine, but began studying theology instead. Ordained in the Church of England in 1753, he returned to America in 1754 and became rector of Christ Church, New Brunswick, N. J. In 1757 he received the pastorate of Grace Church, Jamaica, L. I., and in 1766, of St. Peter's, Westchester, N. Y.

In 1775, because of his Loyalist sympathies, Seabury had to leave his parish and go to New York City, where he resided during most of the Revolutionary War. He wrote numerous articles in support of the Tory cause, of which he was one of the ablest advocates, and was imprisoned for a time for his loyalty to the king. However, when peace was declared, he became a loyal supporter of the United States.

In 1783, after the war, 10 out of the 14 Episcopal clergymen in Connecticut assembled at Woodbury to consider action concerning the organization of the church under the changed civic conditions. They elected Seabury as the first Episcopal bishop in America. He then sailed for England and waited in London more than a year for consecration by the English bishops. Owing to the connection between the Church of England and the state, various political reasons stood in the way, and he finally decided to apply to the Scottish bishops, who were not under the jurisdiction of the Church of England. On Nov. 14, 1784, Seabury was consecrated in Aberdeen by the bishop and coadjutor-bishop of that see and by the bishop of Moray and Ross.

Returning to the United States, he assumed his episcopal duties and became rector of St. James' Church, New London. Seabury's jurisdiction was recognized over Rhode Island, Connecticut, and later Massachusetts, but the validity of his consecration was denied by many, partly because of prejudice caused by his former political attitude. Two bishops were consecrated for the southern and middle Atlantic states in England in 1787. All three were eventually recognized by the General Convention in 1789 and a single Episcopal Church assured.

Seabury exercised a great deal of influence on the final shape of the constitution and liturgy of the Protestant Episcopal Church in the United States, although he was not entirely happy with its final form. A man of strong views, he was also a man of great simplicity, humility, and self-sacrifice, and his services were of inestimable value to the Episcopal Church in the United States. Seabury died in New London, Conn., on Feb. 25, 1796.

Further Reading: Steiner, Bruce E., *Samuel Seabury: A Study in the High Church Tradition* (Ohio Univ. Press 1972).

SEABURY, sē′ber-ē, **Samuel** (1873–1958), American judge, who was counsel and prime mover in an investigation of corruption in New York City. This earned him a national reputation as a foe of boss rule and champion of honest city administration.

He was born in New York City on Feb. 22, 1873, and was educated at home and in New York private day schools. He received the LL. B. degree from the New York Law School in 1893, and he was admitted to the bar in 1894. Elected justice of the city court of New York in 1901, he was in 1906 elected a justice of his state's supreme court for a 14-year term. He resigned in 1914 when elected associate justice of the New York state court of appeals. He resigned his justiceship in August 1916 and the next month was nominated by the Democratic party as its candidate for governor, but lost the election to Charles Whitman. In 1930 he was appointed referee of the appellate division, 1st judicial department, New York, to investigate conditions in the magistrate courts.

In the following year, Gov. Franklin D. Roosevelt appointed him to hear charges filed against the district attorney of New York county. Also in 1931 he was counsel of The New York State Joint Legislative Committee to investigate the affairs of New York City. His 1931–1932 investigations revealed widespread corruption in the city government, and as a result, Mayor James J. Walker and other officials resigned. These developments led to the election in 1933 of reform candidate Fiorella La Guardia, Seabury's choice as mayor. Seabury died on May 7, 1958, in East Hampton, N. Y.

SEAFORD, sē′fərd, an unincorporated area in southeastern New York, in Nassau county and Hempstead township, is situated on the south shore of Long Island, about 25 miles (40 km) east of the center of New York City. It is on South Oyster Bay adjacent to the unincorporated areas of Wantagh, to the west, and Massapequa, to the east. Seaford is almost entirely a residential community, and many residents commute to New York City. The Nassau County Museum of Natural History is here. Population: 17,379.

Fur seals breed in large colonies, or rookeries, like this one on Tyuleny Island in the Sea of Okhotsk.

SEAL AND SEAL FISHERIES.

SEAL AND SEAL FISHERIES. Seals are aquatic mammals with streamlined, torpedo-shaped bodies, doglike heads, and four webbed feet, or flippers. Most seals are marine dwelling and are found mainly on seacoasts and islands in the higher latitudes of both hemispheres. They swim with great ease and can remain under water for long periods but must return to land or ice to give birth.

Seals are classified in the order Pinnipedia, which has three families: (1) Otariidae, six genera and 12 species of eared seals, including the fur seals and sea lions; (2) Phocidae, 13 genera and 18 species of true, earless, or hair seals; (3) Odobenidae, including only the single species of walrus. Seals are all carnivorous and were formerly classified as a suborder of the Carnivora. This article deals with the eared seals, especially the fur seals, and the earless or true seals. For information on the walrus, see WALRUS.

The fur seals, which breed in the North Pacific, are commercially valuable for their pelts. The hair seals, abundant in cold regions, are hunted for their meat and skins and for the oil extracted from their blubber, which is used as a lubricant and in the leather industry and in soap manufacture. The commercial value of furs, leather, and oil products throughout history has brought some species of seals perilously close to extinction, but most species increased under government protection in the 20th century.

SEALS

Physical Characteristics. The average body size of seals is greater than that of the carnivores. The smallest seal is the ringed seal, which at maturity is about 55 inches (1.4 meters) long and weighs almost 200 pounds (90 kg). The largest is the male southern elephant seal, which reaches a length of 256 inches (6.5 meters) and a weight of 8,000 pounds (3,630 kg). Depending on the social organization of the species to which it belongs, the male seal may be slightly smaller than the female, as in the case of the monk seal, crabeater seal, leopard seal, and Weddell seal; it may be about the same size as the female, as are most of the Phocidae; or it may be much larger as are all Otariidae.

The blubber of the seal, a thick subcutaneous layer of fat, may make up more than 45% of the body weight. It provides thermal insulation and reserve energy during lactation and the fasts characteristics of most, if not all, seals, as well as buoyancy in the water.

The calls of seals range from the quiet notes of the Weddell seal and the high chirping bird-like call of the Ross seal to the booming staccato challenge of the northern elephant seal, which can be heard within a radius of more than 1 mile (1.6 km) away.

Behavior. Some seals, such as the harbor seal, remain on land much of the time. Others, such as the northern fur seal, may spend six to eight months of the year at sea. Many of the subpolar species living at the edge of the ice have developed migratory patterns in response to seasonal advantages in food and protection. Outside the water the usual habitat for fur seals is an island, offshore rock, sandbar, ice floe, or—less often—a broad mainland or extensive body of shore ice.

Seals are more sociable or gregarious than land animals. Several species, such as the fur seals, are solitary in winter, but they gather in the summer on rookeries (breeding grounds). The population of a rookery may vary from a few individuals to more than a million animals within a radius of 50 miles (80 km).

The food of seals is exclusively flesh, consisting of various types of fish, cephalopods, shellfish, macroplankton, seabirds, and—in some cases—other seals. While seaweed fragments are occasionally found in the stomach, these are probably ingested by accident. The diet varies greatly with the species of seal.

Life Cycle. The courtship display and mating routine differ with each seal species or family, but polygamy is highly developed in all the fur seals. Depending on the species, the average harem varies, some having about 15 females for one male, others as many as 40 females for a single male. Among the hair seals, polygamy is highly developed only in the elephant seal, which has an average harem of 20, and moderately developed in the gray seal, which has an average harem of 10.

The average life-span of a female northern fur seal is 8–12 years, but some live 20–30 years. The harp seal may live for more than 30 years and is sexually active in its 20's. Seals seldom live beyond the age of 40. Due to many and varied causes, natural mortality is quite high, especially among the young. Seals are also killed by various marine predators, including large sharks, killer whales, and polar bears.

Fur Seals. The fur seals are remotely descended from the bears, or bearlike ancestors, and were appropriately called "sea bears" by their discoverers. Each fur-seal population is usually an independent, self-perpetuating unit. The fur seals belong to two distinct groups or genera of the family Otariidae—*Callorhinus* and *Arctocephulus*.

Callorhinus. The northern fur seals (C. ursinus) breed in the summer and fall on the Pribilof and Komandor (Commander) islands in the Bering Sea, on Robben Island in the Sea of Okhotsk, the Kurile Islands off the coast of Japan, and on San Miguel Island off the California coast. In winter and early spring they are widely dispersed over the North Pacific Ocean, southern Bering Sea, Sea of Japan, and Sea of Okhotsk.

The hardy old bulls are the first to reach the rookeries, arriving in the spring, but the great majority of the seals arrive in July. Each bull selects a summer home along the shore where he may induce the greatest number of cows to join him. The younger, less experienced bulls are forced to take up less advantageous locations and consequently acquire fewer cows for their family groups (harems). The harem of an older bull may have as many as 100 cows, whereas that of a younger bull may be made up of only a few. Once a cow has joined the group there can be no amiable separation. The bull watches over his family, and no immature animals, except for those newly born (pups), are allowed to intrude where harems are established.

Each cow gives birth to one pup—conceived the summer before—usually a few hours after she arrives at the rookery. The pups are jet black and weigh about 12 pounds (5.4 kg) at birth. At maturity a northern fur seal bull weighs about 500 pounds (225 kg) and a cow about 90 pounds (40 kg). Adult males have a high mortality rate and rarely reach 20 years of age, but occasionally a female lives for more than 25 years.

The peak of the fur seals' southward departure from the Pribilof Islands is in early November. This migration extends to the latitude of southern California and Japan and is reached in December. The movement back north begins in the early part of the spring.

Arctocephalus. The South African fur seal (A. pusillus) is a coastal species with a rather limited range. Since no distant migrations are undertaken, the bulk of the population is confined to about 100 miles (160 km) from land. The range extends along the coasts of South West Africa and the Cape of Good Hope province of South Africa. Exploited commercially for more than 300 years, it is the most widely known of all Species of Arctocephalus.

The South American fur seal (A. *australis*) ranges from Brazil to the Strait of Magellan and northward to southern Peru, and to the Galápagos Islands and the Falkland Islands. They are divided into three subspecies.

Sea Lions. The five species of sea lions are closely related to fur seals, but their pelts consist chiefly of coarse outer hairs and lack the dense undercoat of fine hair that makes the pelts of fur seals commercially valuable. See also SEA LION.

Hair Seals. All hair seals belong to the family Phocidae. These seals are not considered in the same category as fur seals and are not as valuable commercially. Of the three Pinnipedia families, the hair seals are the most highly specialized for aquatic life. The neck is short and the head can be raised. There are no external ears. The posterior limbs are adapted for swimming to such an extent that they are not used by the animal on land. In contrast, the fur seal uses only its

Sea lions are also members of the seal family. This South American bull is protecting his harem and pups.

GEORGE HOLTON, FROM PHOTO RESEARCH

Gray seals (*Halichoerus grypus*) are hair seals that inhabit the temperate waters of the North Atlantic. These gray seals rest on the rocks of one of the Farne Islands, off the coast of Northumberland, England.

LONDON DAILY EXPRESS

anterior limbs for swimming and can move rapidly on land in an undulating lope.

Certain of the hair seals have pushed into high latitudes and to the edge of the permanent ice, others have persisted in subtropical waters, and a few are relict in lakes. Like all other pinnipeds, the phocids have failed to multiply in warm seas. The family is very large, with many of the species broken down into subspecies in order to include isolated forms.

Northern Hair Seals. The harp seal (*Pagophilus groenlandicus* or *Phoca groenlandicus*) is a deep-sea animal that breeds on drifting pack ice in the North Atlantic and the adjoining waters of the Arctic Ocean. They are nowhere resident the year around but make long and regular migrations. Populations are found from the coast of Labrador eastward to the Kara Sea, off the coast of Siberia.

The ringed seals (*Pusa hispida* or *Phoca hispida*) are divided into six subspecies. In general they inhabit the edge of the Arctic ice, in the Arctic Ocean, and they occasionally range to the North Pole. They are found on sea ice along northern Eurasia, Greenland, and North America and in landlocked lakes of extreme western Europe. Their range extends south to Hudson Bay and Labrador, the Sea of Okhotsk, northern Japan, and the northern Bering Sea. They are the most common and widely distributed of all seals in the Soviet Union—principally because the USSR has an extensive ice-bordered coastline—and they are the most important of all seals in the economy of the natives of the far north. Some biologists include the Caspian seal (*P. caspica*) and Baikal seal (*P. sibirica*) as subspecies of *P. hispida*. The Baikal and Caspian seals are confined to landlocked Lake Baikal, to a cluster of small lakes near the Baltic, and to the Caspian Sea.

The harbor seals (*Phoca vitulina*) are divided into five subspecies. They are distributed around the rim of the Arctic Ocean and along its arms extending southward along the shores of Eurasia and North America. The northern limit of their range is perhaps Ellesmere Island. The southern limits are Portugal and North Carolina in the Atlantic Ocean and northern Lower California and China in the Pacific. They are also found in the Baltic. The hooded seal (*Cystophora cristata*) is another species of hair seal found in the north.

Southern Hair Seals. The crabeater seal (*Lobodon carcinophagus*) is by far the most populous of the four truly Antarctic seals. A more appropriate name for them would be "krilleater." They are semigregarious in their habits and are found in the seas around Antarctica, following the edge of the pack ice.

The southern elephant seals (*Mirounga leonina*) are circumpolar in distribution. Some authorities give subspecific rank to those of the Falkland, Macquerie, and Heard island groups. The other southern hair seals are the Weddell seal (*Leptonychotes weddelli*) and the leopard seal (*Hydrurga leptonyx*).

See also ELEPHANT SEAL; GRAY SEAL; HAIR SEAL; HARBOR SEAL; HARP SEAL; LEOPARD SEAL.

SEAL FISHERIES

Seals were hunted with such enthusiasm during the 19th century that many species would have become extinct had they not finally come under the protection of international agreements and restrictive regulations. As it happened, the world seal population had been severely reduced by the beginning of the 20th century and several species of seals were thought to have vanished altogether.

Worldwide sealing declined sharply after World War II, and the population of many formerly harvested species began to increase. Some of the southern fur seals once considered extinct began to appear again and by the 1970's were once more seen throughout their former ranges.

Northern Fur Seal Fisheries. From time immemorial, the Indians of the northwest coast of North America followed the custom of spearing seals from canoes as the animals passed along their shores from February to May. The number of animals taken, primarily for food, was small and probably never exceeded a few thousand a year.

The slaughter of the fur seals in the North Pacific started shortly after the discovery of the Pribilof Islands in 1786. In the 50 years that followed, about 2 million seals were killed. In 1835 the Russian management, worried about the future of the seal population, imposed restrictions on shore killings on the Pribilofs. The herds responded to this conservation measure, and in 1867, when the United States acquired the islands along with Alaska, there were about 2 million seals.

New Zealand sea lions (*Neophoca hookeri*), closely related to fur seals, are the most playful of the pinnipeds and often come on land. Since their pelts are valuable for leather, slaughter by man has greatly reduced their numbers.

During the first 40 years of U. S. ownership of the Pribilofs, the sealing privilege was leased to private companies. More than 2.3 million skins of fur seals were taken, for which $9.5 million was paid into the U. S. treasury. Although sealing operations on shore were regulated, the unregulated killing of seals at sea, known as pelagic sealing, took a heavy toll.

Unlike sealing on land, where it is possible to select the animals to be killed according to sex and age, pelagic sealing was extremely wasteful. For many years there was no way to stop it, since it was carried on in waters beyond the control of countries possessing the rookeries. The sealing fleet expanded from one vessel in 1879 to 122 by 1891. It reached its peak in 1894, when the ocean catch from the Pribilof herds totaled 143,000 animals. After that the catch grew increasingly smaller and in 1902 was only about 15,000 seals, but the decline of the Pribilof seal herds continued.

In 1911, when the once great fur seal population had dwindled to about 200,000 animals, the United States, Britain, Japan, and Russia agreed to put a stop to pelagic sealing and conserve the seal under the terms of the North Pacific Fur Seal Convention, which remained in force until terminated by Japan in 1942. From 1942 to 1957 the Pribilof herds were protected by a provisional agreement between the United States and Canada, and in 1957, a new convention, similar to that of 1911, was concluded by the United States, the Soviet Union, Japan, and Canada. Principally it prohibited the killing of fur seals at sea except for certain numbers that might be taken for scientific research and those hunted by aborigines using primitive weapons. The convention included a provision whereby Canada and Japan each would receive 15% of the sealskins taken by the U. S. commercial operation on the Pribilofs and—subject to certain stipulations—a similar percentage of Russia's commercial take.

All land harvesting of seals is now done under the Soviet government on Robben Island and the Komandor Islands and under the control of the U. S. government on the Pribilof Islands, where Aleut residents work under the supervision of the Fish and Wildlife Service. On the Pribilofs, most of the skins are taken in July and after preliminary preparation are shipped to a factory, where they are dressed, dyed, machined, and finished under government contract and sold at public auction. The Pribilofs are capable of producing more than 60,000 skins a year. Thanks to conservation measures, the summer population of the northern fur seal has risen to about 1.3 million, most of which originate on the Pribilof Islands.

Southern Fur Seal Fisheries. Toward the end of the 18th century, fur-seal hunting in the Southern Hemisphere began, and it grew rapidly in importance. Early in the 19th century it assumed gigantic proportions. It first began at the Falkland Islands about 1784, and according to the old accounts, millions of animals were taken during the next 15 years. Fur seals were present in such numbers that as many as 800 or 900 a day were killed with clubs on a single small islet. As a result, fur seals on the Falklands became extinct about 1800. Sealing trips were made to the west coast of South Africa as early as 1790, later to the South Georgian rookeries (in the Falkland

Harbor seals are found in northern waters, usually in harbors or even in rivers. They do not form rookeries.

Fur seals are slaughtered under government supervision, as here on St. Paul Island in the Pribilofs.

Islands Dependencies), and then off the coasts of Chile, Patagonia, Australia, and the Antipodes Islands; off the Crozet, Prince Edward, South Shetland, and Kerguelen islands; and elsewhere.

There were about 60 vessels in the southern fur-seal fleet in 1801. The United States, Britain, Portugal, Germany, Russia, and France were represented. The yield of furs was taken mostly to the Canton (China) market, where they were exchanged for teas and silks. Since sealing was highly profitable, there was an indescriminate and exterminating slaughter of herds. As a result, the once abundant and valuable seal fisheries of the Southern Hemisphere were severely depleted. Some rookeries never recovered, but a few have improved enough under government supervision to be again commercially valuable.

By the 1970's, fur seals were again increasing in the Southern Hemisphere on most of the islands where they were once abundant. They are protected and managed on the coasts of South Africa and on Lobos Island, off Uruguay. South Africa produces about 20,000 pelts annually and Uruguay about 1,000.

Hair-Seal Fisheries. Although the hair seals are universal in their distribution, they occur in numbers sufficient to support fisheries only in a few areas, notably the waters along the west coast of Greenland and the coasts of Newfoundland, Labrador, and the Gulf of St. Lawrence; on Jan Mayen Island and in its surrounding waters; and in the White Sea. The Caspian Sea also supports a fishery. Small isolated groups of hair seals, of local importance only, are found along both coasts of the United States and Canada, around the British Isles and Norway, in the Baltic, on the islands of the south seas, along both coasts of South America, and in Alaskan and Siberian waters.

The once extensive hair-seal fishery of the South Atlantic, South Pacific, and Antarctic regions was primarily for the capture and use of the elephant seal. Carried on with whaling and fur sealing, it was exclusively for oil. Once abundant, the population was unrestrictedly exploited but was brought under protective management early in the 20th century and began increasing.

The Newfoundland hair-seal fishery, once the most important in the world, rapidly declined in the mid-20th century until it was placed under the protective management of Canada. The hair-seal fishery of Jan Mayen Island—which had been second only to that of Newfoundland and prosecuted by vessels from Norway, England, and Germany—showed early signs of depletion, and despite attempts at regulation it was seriously depleted by the end of the 19th century. Substantial catches are made annually at Novaya Zemlya (a Soviet archipelago in the Arctic Ocean) and in the White and Caspian seas. Many hair seals are taken annually along the Alaskan and Siberian coasts of the North Pacific and Arctic oceans by native peoples for food and clothing.

The number of hair seals caught through the years has followed a downward trend paralleling that of ships and men employed. Until about 1860 the average annual take was more than 500,000. From 1860 until the early part of the 20th century, the catch averaged well above 200,000 annually, but after World War I it dropped to an average of less than 125,000. Another colorful, highly speculative industry rich in adventure, romance, and tragedy seemed to be disappearing.

JOSEPH PILEGGI
National Marine Fishery Service

Bibliography

King, Judith E., *Seals of the World* (British Mus. Natural Hist. 1964).
Maxwell, Gavin, *Seals of the World* (Houghton 1967).
Riley, Frances, *Fur Seal Industry of the Pribilof Islands 1786–1960,* Fishery Leaflet 516, U. S. Bureau of Commercial Fisheries (USGPO 1961).
Scheffer, Victor B., *Seals, Sea Lions and Walruses: A Review of the Pinnipedia* (Stanford Univ. Press 1958).
Scheffer, Victor B., *Year of the Seal* (Scribner 1970).

SEAL BEACH, a city in southwestern California, in Orange county, is on the Pacific Ocean, about 7 miles (11 km) southeast of Long Beach. It is almost entirely residential, but there is a little light industry scattered through the city. A U. S. Naval Weapons Station is located here, and there are rich oil fields nearby. Seal Beach was incorporated in 1915. During the 1960's its population increased by 250%. The city has a council-manager form of government. Population: 25,975.

SEAL FISHERIES. See SEAL AND SEAL FISHERIES.

SEAL OF THE UNITED STATES. See GREAT SEAL OF THE UNITED STATES.

SEALAB, sē′lab, any of a series of human habitats used in the U. S. Navy's Deep Submergence Systems Project. The series began in 1964 when four men lived for ten days submerged in Sealab I off the coast of Bermuda. See also DEEP-SEA EXPLORATION—*Manned Descents.*

SEALING WAX is a plastic preparation applied to folded papers, envelopes, or documents to fasten them and receive impressions of identifying seals. In the Middle Ages it was made of beeswax, Venice turpentine, and vermilion or other pigment. Later lac or, in inferior grades, rosin, was substituted for wax. Sealing wax has generally been replaced by the gummed envelope.

SEALS are dies bearing symbols or inscriptions indicating ownership, and the impressions they make. The die, or stamp, usually of hard clay, stone, or metal, is incised, modeled, or cut in relief and is pressed into soft clay, wax, lead, paper, or other material. It may be a cylinder seal, consisting of a clay cylinder with modeled figures; a stamp seal, consisting of a cut surface on the end of a block or cone or other shape or with a handle on the back; or a seal ring. Fre quently the modeling or cutting is so fine as to make the seal a work of art.

Seals were used in ancient times before written signatures were common, and later along with signatures. They were affixed to the closings of documents and letters (clay or wax tablets or papyrus or parchment rolls or sheets), boxes, jars, doors, or other objects to show ownership or authority or to prevent tampering. Royalty and state officials, religious leaders, towns and universities, and private individuals in various civilizations all used seals. The Sumerians invented the cylinder seal. The Greeks, Romans, and medieval Europeans had stamp seals and also seal rings, often with exquisitely carved gemstones. Chinese stamp seals, used with ink, were an early form of printing. See also GREAT SEAL; GREAT SEAL OF THE CONFEDERACY; GREAT SEAL OF THE UNITED STATES.

SEALYHAM TERRIER, sē′lē-ham, a long-coated terrier originally developed as a hunter of badgers, foxes, and otters. Its name is derived from Sealyham, Haverfordwest, Wales, the estate of a Captain John Edwardes, who developed the breed in the latter half of the 19th century, largely by shooting instantly the many dogs that failed any of his strict requirements for aggressiveness, courage, and tenacity. The breed was officially recognized in 1911 by both the Kennel Club of Great Britain and the American Kennel Club.

EVELYN M. SHAFER

The Sealyham terrier was developed in the late 1800's.

The Sealyham has a long, hard, wiry coat. Its color is usually all white, but some have brown, badger-colored, or lemon markings on the head and ears. It has a broad, deep chest, a fairly long neck, and powerful hindquarters. The standard weight for dogs is not over 20 pounds (0.9 kg) and for bitches not over 18 pounds (0.8 kg). The standard height is not over 12 inches (30 cm) at the shoulder.

SEAMAN, a person below the rank of officer who is employed on any type of vessel navigating a sea, lake, channel, or river. Originally limited to those who could "hand, reef, or steer" a sailing vessel, the term was subsequently broadened to include everyone performing services in a subordinate capacity that are members of a ship's company.

Early Hardships. Nautical skill has never been the exclusive attribute of any one race or nation. The Phoenician and Greek seafarers of antiquity, the Polynesian and Scandinavian mariners up to 1000 A. D., and the European and American seamen of more recent times—all proved their mastery of the art of seamanship and contributed to the increase of geographical knowledge and the growth of international trade. Throughout the centuries, seamen shared the same hardships: hunger, thirst, exposure to the elements, inadequate wages, and the perils of the sea. Shipmasters, who frequently were merchants trading for their own account, did not scruple to increase the profits of the voyage by cheating seamen of their wages, providing inadequate food and accommodations, and imposing fines and forfeitures upon the slightest pretext. Flogging and even more barbaric corporal punishments were the accepted methods of enforcing a discipline so rigorous as sometimes to lead, almost inevitably, to murder, mutiny, and desertion. By the nature of their employment, seamen were cut off for long periods from contact with home, and those who survived the hazards of ill treatment, shipwreck, and disease afloat often returned as strangers in their own country, practiced in skills ill suited to earning a living ashore. It is scarcely surprising that the buccaneers of the 17th and 18th centuries were almost all renegade seamen, for that was an age in which seamen were trained to fight as well as to sail.

At the end of the 19th century, the status of merchant seamen represented a unique survival of a medieval system of employment long since obsolete in other occupations. A seaman was bound to his ship for a stated term and was liable to forcible recapture and return if he attempted to leave before its expiration. During that period he was subject to the commands of his employer, upon whom he was directly dependent for food, shelter, and other necessities of life.

The technological and scientific progress that accompanied the Industrial Revolution had brought about some improvements: steam propulsion reduced the length of voyages, steel hulls afforded somewhat better living accommodations, and modern medicine succeeded in eliminating many of the diseases previously endemic on shipboard. However, the remarkable improvement in the 20th century was largely due to enactment by many maritime nations of special laws designed to protect the seaman against his employer's cupidity and his own improvidence. The United States took the lead in legislation of this type.

Modern Statutory Protection. From the legal standpoint, seamen have long been regarded as "wards of the legislature." In 1897 the U. S. Supreme Court explained that seamen were treated "as deficient in that full and intelligent responsibility for their acts which is accredited to ordinary adults and as needing the protection of the law in the same sense as minors and wards." The result was a complicated series of statutes regulating virtually every aspect of the seaman's employment.

As early as 1790, however, Congress had provided that the so-called shipping articles, or agreement between the master and crew, must set forth in writing the scope of the voyage, the time of service, and the amount of wages. Subsequent legislation prescribed the form of this contract, which, in order to avoid any possibility of fraud or duress, must be executed in the presence of an official shipping commissioner and posted in a part of the vessel accessible to the crew. A shipping commissioner must likewise supervise the paying-off and discharge of seamen. Outside the United States this function is performed by the American consul, who, in addition to arranging for the support and repatriation of sick or destitute seamen, also investigates disputes arising on board American vessels in foreign ports.

To assure payment of his wages, a seaman is given a maritime lien of the highest priority against the ship. The vessel owner cannot limit his liability for such claims, even if the ship becomes a total loss. Any unjustified failure to pay wages promptly after completion of the voyage makes the vessel owner liable for double wages for every day's delay. So important is the seamen's right to wages that, under American law, any seaman, including those aboard foreign vessels in U. S. ports, is entitled to demand payment of one half of the wages then owing at every port where his ship loads or discharges cargo during the voyage. However, advance payment of wages is prohibited, and, with few exceptions, a seaman's wages cannot be allotted, assigned, or subjected to legal attachment. The master still retains the right to make forfeitures of wages for offenses such as desertion, absence without leave, and willful damage to the vessel, her stores or cargo. In cases of continued willful disobedience

of lawful commands at sea the offender may be placed in handcuffs and kept on a bread-and-water diet.

Laws have also been enacted to regulate the size, warmth, and cleanliness of crew quarters aboard ship, the adequacy of water and provisions, availability of medicines and proper clothing, and the number of hours worked. Under traditional maritime law a seaman injured or falling sick while in the service of the ship is entitled to support and medical care at the shipowner's expense. In U. S. ports the Public Health Service provides free hospitalization and medical care to crews of American vessels.

Seamen have been given broad rights to sue the shipowner for negligence or for the unseaworthiness of the vessel, regardless of their own fault. For this purpose the term "seaman" has been judicially expanded to include a vessel's master as well as other classes of shipboard employees, such as stewardesses, barbers, and musicians.

These statutory safeguards of the American seaman's rights have been accompanied by an unprecedented rise in real wages, a development that is attributable largely to the growing importance of seamen's unions. The first united union was formed in 1895, but the process of organization was slow and frequently bloody. Seamen were individualistic by nature, worked in small, relatively isolated units, and were necessarily subject at all times to strict discipline. Despite the dwindling of their membership in the depression years after World War I, the maritime unions were instrumental in obtaining passage of an act in 1936 requiring that not less than 75% of the unlicensed crew of every American vessel be U. S. citizens. After World War II, they attained a dominant role in the American shipping industry through collective bargaining agreements obligating shipowners to employ only those seamen furnished through the union hiring halls. American seamen's unions have since joined with similar organizations in other countries to protect their gains by attempting to raise the standards of shipboard employment on vessels of other flags.

The International Labor Organization, a specialized agency of the United Nations, has also played an important part in the preparation of multilateral conventions designed to improve the health and safety of seamen.

ELLIOTT B. NIXON, *Member, New York Bar*
Editor, "American Maritime Cases"

SEARCH, RIGHT OF. See BLOCKADE; CONTRABAND; INTERNATIONAL LAW; SEARCH AND SEIZURE.

SEARCH AND SEIZURE, the examination or inspection by an officer of the law of a suspect's premises or person, in order to discover stolen, contraband, or illicit property, or some evidence of guilt, to be used in the prosecution of a criminal action. In the United States, protection against the abuse of this practice is provided in the 4th Amendment to the Constitution, which forbids "unreasonable search and seizure," and is also provided in similar state constitutional provisions. The 4th Amendment, together with its state constitutional counterparts, condemns arrests or searches on mere suspicion, as, for example, simply on the basis of an anonymous phone call.

"Probable Cause." The amendment provides that the police may invade a man's privacy or curtail his liberty only upon "probable cause" or "reasonable grounds." This standard has been defined by the courts to mean those apparent facts or circumstances that would cause a reasonably discreet and prudent man to believe that a criminal offense has been, or is being committed, as charged.

So far as the police are armed with "probable cause," the arrest or search is valid, even though the person involved turns out to be innocent. But if the police act arbitrarily or indiscriminately, their conduct is illegal, even though it turns out that they happened to guess correctly on a particular occasion. As the courts have expressed it, a search or seizure is "good or bad when it starts and does not change character from its success." Were it otherwise, officers would "be encouraged to proceed in an irregular manner on the chance that all will end well."

Searches Contrasted with Arrests. In one important respect, the rules governing searches are more restrictive than those governing arrests: searches require a warrant, a written authorization by a magistrate to the police to arrest or search. Arrests without a warrant, even though there is ample opportunity to secure one, are valid if based on "probable cause." The person may then be searched, as may the area "within his immediate control," in order to protect the arresting officer against attack by hidden weapons or to prevent the destruction of incriminating evidence in the arrested person's possession. However, unless the search itself is incident to an initial lawful arrest and confined to the area within the arrested person's reach, a search of a home, however "reasonable" or "probable" the belief that contraband or articles offensive to the law will be found inside, is generally still invalid when not made pursuant to a warrant. Thus, without some compelling necessity such as the need to move swiftly to prevent the imminent destruction of incriminating evidence in the house, or the need to stop and search a moving vehicle, the police may not bypass the magistrates. Even when emergency conditions justify dispensing with the need for a search warrant, they do not permit dispensing with the need for "probable cause."

"Stop and Frisk." In 1968 the U. S. Supreme Court held that, under certain circumstances, a police officer who lacks adequate grounds to make a full search or technical arrest may nevertheless briefly detain and "frisk" a person on the street or other public place. The Court utilized a "balancing of interests" test, ruling that the "reasonableness" of each particular invasion of a citizen's privacy should be determined by balancing law enforcement interests against the magnitude of the intrusion involved. Thus, it concluded that when an officer has reason to believe that "criminal activity may be afoot and the person with whom he is dealing may be armed and presently dangerous," even though the officer lacks traditional "probable cause," he may constitutionally conduct a carefully limited search of the outer clothing of such person in order to discover weapons which might be used to assault him.

Supreme Court Interpretation. All state constitutions contain a clause similar to that of the 4th Amendment, often using its precise wording. Even if such a state guaranty were to be repealed, every person would still be protected against illegal arrests or searches by state or city police, for though the 4th Amendment is addressed to federal agents only, the U. S. Supreme Court has held that the security of one's privacy against arbitrary intrusion by the police is "implicit in the concept of ordered liberty" and thus enforceable against the states under the due process clause. The court has also ruled that the federal constitution bars the use of illegally seized evidence, and likewise of leads or clues obtained from such evidence, in state as well as federal criminal prosecutions. This is known as the "exclusionary rule." But in 1971, newly appointed Chief Justice Warren Burger expressed much disenchantment with the rule. He doubted that it significantly deterred police from acting illegally and maintained that, whatever the rule's benefits, it was not worth "the high price it extracts from society–the release of countless guilty criminals." His unhappiness with the rule, and criticism of it by judges and law enforcement officials, indicated that the rule was in considerable jeopardy.

See also WARRANT; WIRETAPPING.

YALE KAMISAR
University of Michigan Law School

SEARCH WARRANT. See WARRANT.

SEARCHLIGHT, an optical device for projecting a narrow, high-intensity light beam over distances up to many miles. The beam is projected by means of a concentrated light source of extremely high brightness placed at the focal point of a lens or mirror.

Uses. By World War I, powerful searchlights had been developed for military applications such as coast defense and aircraft detection, for long-range signaling, and for aids to navigation. Electronic techniques developed in World War II made the searchlight obsolete for aircraft detection and other detection applications. However, new applications have been found for them, and they are still widely used. Searchlights are used on aircraft in antisubmarine warfare, on tanks for tactical combat applications, and in advance combat areas for indirect illumination of battlefields by atmospheric scattering of light. They also are used as solar simulators in space research and as components of a variety of measuring and signaling devices. In everyday life, searchlights have a variety of uses, such as helping firemen fight fires or illuminating buildings to highlight them at night.

Design and Performance. Most searchlights use parabolic reflectors rather than lenses because reflectors with large light-collecting angles are free from spherical and chromatic aberrations, which severely limit the capability of lenses. A theoretical-point source of light at the focal point of a perfect parabolic reflector would produce a beam of exactly parallel rays. In fact, however, all light sources, however small, have extent and thus are not actually point sources.

Searchlight beams are fully formed at a relatively short distance from the light. From there on, they have characteristic angular distributions of light intensity, with divergences ranging from about 1° to 10°. If a fully formed beam is projected through a vacuum, the illumination at any point is inversely proportional to the square of the distance between the point and the light source. In such circumstances, the attenuation,

A searchlight display by U. S. Navy ships in Los Angeles harbor during a Harbor Day celebration.

or decrease in illumination, depends only on distance. However, if a light beam is projected through air, the beam is also attenuated by scattering and absorption caused by dust, moisture, and the air molecules themselves.

Attenuation due to the inverse square law and the atmosphere drastically limits the useful range of a searchlight. When the range of a searchlight under a given set of conditions is several miles, the increase in light-source intensity required to obtain a relatively small increase in range is very large. If the atmosphere is at all hazy, the required increase in intensity may be extremely high.

The most effective light sources for searchlights are those with very high brightness, notably the carbon arc. The high-intensity carbon arc, developed by the German inventor Heinrich Beck between 1906 and 1910 is the most intense light source for searchlights. Water-cooled carbon arcs have been operated with brightnesses of 2,-000 candles per square millimeter (c/mm^2). High-intensity carbon arcs generally operate in the range from 500 to 1,500 c/mm^2. For comparison, the brightness of the sun as seen from the earth's surface, is about 1,600 c/mm^2.

Mercury and mercury-xenon short-arc lamps are widely used as light sources in small searchlights. They do not attain the brightness of carbon arcs, but they do not require complex carbon-feed mechanisms and can operate for many hours without attention.

Where simplicity and reliability are of most importance and high intensity and small beam divergence of less importance, incandescent lamps may be used as light sources in searchlights, even though the maximum brightness of a tungsten-filament incandescent lamp is only about 20 c/mm^2. Incandescent light sources have been used in tank-mounted searchlights and in airborne searchlights for search and rescue.

Research and Development. The development of large powerful searchlights, with reflectors 10 feet (3 meters) in diameter and carbon arcs consuming as much as 600 kilowatts of power, reached a peak in World War II. The maximum beam intensity of many of the more powerful searchlights was several billion candles. Since then, researchers have concentrated on the development of new light sources, new reflector designs, and new fabrication techniques. For in-

stance, research in plasma physics may eventually result in the development of a practical light source with a brightness greater than that of the high-intensity carbon arc.

THEODORE H. PROJECTOR, *Consulting Engineer*

Further Reading: Illuminating Engineering Society of America, *Lighting Handbook*, 5th ed. (1972).

SEAS, Freedom of. See HIGH SEAS.

SEASICKNESS is a form of motion sickness that some persons experience on shipboard. It results from random and multidirectional movement of the ship.

Symptoms. Confusion, dizziness, loss of appetite, nausea, and vomiting are symptoms of seasickness. The onset of these symptoms is usually abrupt, and the symptoms increase in intensity with higher seas. They cease when the victim has become accustomed to the motion or when calm water or land is reached.

Cause. Seasickness is believed to result from a combination of kinesthetic, visual, and psychological factors. Kinesthetic disturbances affect the semicircular canals of the inner ear, which are the chief controls of body balance. When balance is lost on steady ground, nerve impulses from the limbs reach the inner ear and are transmitted to the brain. The brain integrates the impulses and transmits corrective impulses back to the limbs to right the body. However, during the accelerating and decelerating motions of the deck of a ship, haphazard impulses from the limbs become difficult to integrate and the sense of balance is disrupted.

Visual factors may increase the incidence and severity of seasickness symptoms. On land, the horizon is fixed at one level and serves as orientation in space. When the horizon is viewed from a moving vessel at sea, however, it may appear to rise, shift, or tilt too fast or too inconsistently for the visual sense to follow.

The psychological factor is believed to be a paramount cause of seasickness. Some or all of the symptoms may result from anxiety at the loss of secure, steady body support.

Prevention. Drugs such as antihistamines, parasympathetic depressants, and sedatives are often successful in preventing attacks of seasickness if taken beforehand. These drugs include dimenhydrinate, diphenhydramine, and phenobarbital. The drugs may be prescribed alone or in different combinations, and in doses to suit the individual.

A number of other measures besides drugs are helpful in minimizing seasickness. Taking a position near the center of the ship serves to reduce motion. A conscious attempt should be made to keep the eyes open and to adapt to a shifting horizon. Breathing should be easy; it should not be in short gasps, nor should the breath be held. Finally, one should let the body "hang loose" and adapt to the ship's motion instead of becoming tense.

Once a sensitive person's balance apparatus becomes adapted to the unsteadiness of a sea vessel in motion, subsequent voyages are usually tolerated with progressively fewer symptoms. In some cases, adaptation is never achieved, and sea travel must be avoided. Such persons usually are subject also to airsickness and car sickness—two other forms of motion sickness.

HERBERT S. BENJAMIN, M. D.
Cedars of Lebanon Hospital, Los Angeles

SEASIDE is a city on the west coast of California, in Monterey county. It is on the south shore of Monterey Bay, an inlet of the Pacific Ocean, about 80 miles (129 km) south of San Francisco. The city is principally a residential community. Ford Ord, a U. S. Army post, is nearby. Seaside was founded in 1900 and incorporated as a city in 1954. It has a council-manager form of government. Population: 36,567.

SEASON, one of the four divisions of the year, as determined by the changes in the relative lengths of day and night as the earth moves around the sun. These changes affect the amount of heat received from the sun at a given time of year, which in turn affects average temperatures. The differences between the seasons are most evident in the temperate regions of the earth and least evident near the equator. The polar regions always remain cold, but temperatures fluctuate on a seasonal basis.

The seasons exist because the earth's axis of rotation is inclined at an angle to the plane of the ecliptic—that is, the plane of the earth's orbital path around the sun. This means that as the earth moves around the sun in the course of a year, the orientation of its Northern and Southern Hemispheres slowly changes. From about March 21 to September 23, more of the Northern than the Southern Hemisphere faces toward and is warmed by the sun. The situation is reversed from September 23 to March 21.

Thus, beginning with March 21 in the Northern Hemisphere, the seasons run as follows: *spring,* March 21–June 22; *summer,* June 22–September 23; *autumn,* September 23–December 22; and *winter,* December 22–March 21. The seasons are reversed in the Southern Hemisphere, with spring beginning about September 23.

See also EQUINOX; SOLSTICE; and individual articles on the seasons.

SEASONING is an ingredient, such a a condiment, spice, or flavoring, that is added to food primarily for the savor it gives. See HERBS AND SPICES.

SEATO. See SOUTHEAST ASIA TREATY ORGANIZATION.

SEATTLE, sē-at′əl, is a city in western Washington, the seat of King county. An important seaport and port of entry, sometimes called the "Gateway to the Orient" or the "Gateway to Alaska," Seattle is the largest metropolis of the Pacific Northwest, with a half million citizens within its city limits and about a million and a half in its metropolitan area. It is situated between the east shore of Puget Sound and a freshwater lake (Lake Washington). It is about 680 air miles (1,100 km) north of San Francisco, Calif., and some 175 miles (280 km) south of Vancouver, British Columbia, Canada.

The city offers a beautiful prospect. It is built on a series of hills, some of which rise to heights of over 500 feet (150 meters) and all of which command views of the bays and lakes that surround the community. Snowcapped peaks of the Olympic range are to be seen to the west, while Mt. Rainier raises its symmetrical, ice-encrusted volcanic cone in the southeast. Other peaks of the Cascade Range are visible to the east and northeast.

Seattle's geographical location favored its growth as a trade and transportation hub and, eventually, as a manufacturing center. It possesses outstanding educational and cultural facilities, chief among which is the University of Washington, founded in 1861, only 10 years after the area was settled.

The city covers a land area of nearly 90 square miles (235 sq km). Lake Washington forms the eastern boundary, and two other lakes—Union, largely surrounded by industrial plants, and Green, bordered by parks—are within the city limits.

The eastward drift of weather from the Pacific Ocean gives Seattle a mild but moist climate. In winter, prevailing winds blow from the warmer latitudes to the southwest. In summer, cool air moves down from the Gulf of Alaska. The average maximum daily temperature in July is 75° F (24° C), and the normal January minimum is 36° F (2° C). The average annual precipitation has been about 32 inches (810 mm), less than that in many U. S. cities, although frequent overcast days give the city the reputation of being rainy. Of the total annual rainfall, 75% is recorded from October through March. Average snowfall is less than 9 inches (230 mm) per year.

Economic Life. Though dominated to a degree by a major aerospace industry, Seattle's economy is sustained by a diversity of other manufacturing activities and by the trade passing through its excellent port facilities. Its geographical situation makes it a center of road, rail, and air traffic.

Port of Seattle. The Great Circle route for shipping between Seattle and the Orient is 1,000 miles (1,600 km) shorter than the southerly route from California by way of Hawaii. Ships outbound from Seattle sail 125 miles (200 km) through Puget Sound and the Strait of Juan de Fuca to reach the open Pacific. Seattle is the principal port for shipments to Alaska, and carries on extensive trade with ports on the Gulf of Mexico and the Atlantic coast by way of the Panama Canal.

The city's largest natural harbor is curving Elliott Bay, which has a wide entrance and a shoreline nearly 10 miles (16 km) long. The harbor is very deep. One of the most important adjuncts of the port is a ship canal, 8 miles (13 km) long, dug by the U. S. Army Engineers in

Pacific Science Center and the Space Needle are on the site of Seattle's Century 21 Exposition of 1962.

1916, connecting Lake Washington with Puget Sound by way of Lake Union. Locks almost as large as those of the Panama Canal lower ships 26 feet (8 meters) from fresh to salt water. The canal made Lake Union an extension of the industrial waterfront and led to further expansion of Seattle's maritime industry.

Seattle receives imports from more than 40 nations, principally Canada, Mexico, and Japan, while exports go to over 70 countries, the leading markets being Japan, Korea, and India. The chief commercial imports are lumber and wood products, limestone and lime rock, gypsum rock, bananas, newsprint, oil and petroleum products, fish and canned salmon, electronic equipment, and automobiles, trucks, and parts. Leading commercial exports are wheat, barley, wheat flour, coal, lumber, rye, beans, oats, and apples.

Seattle's major harbor and airport facilities are administered by the Port of Seattle, a municipal corporation embracing a territory with boundaries coextensive with those of King county. The corporation is independent of any city, county, or state agencies. It is governed by a board of three port commissioners, elected for six-year terms. The Port Commission operates 14 of the largest piers and terminals on the Seattle waterfront. It also operates the Foreign Trade Zone, established by Congress in 1949 as a service to foreign traders. Here goods from foreign countries may be entered without payment of duty, stored indefinitely, manipulated in almost any way, and reshipped abroad with no duty on reexport.

Manufacturing. The Boeing Airplane Company has its main plant on the Duwamish River just beyond the city limits. The company was born during the era of wooden aircraft, using the plentiful supplies of lumber in the area. During World War II it experienced enormous expansion as it mass-produced the B-17 "Flying For-

tress," the country's most reliable bomber. Continuing to expand after the war, Boeing supplied bombers and jet stratotankers for the U.S. Strategic Air Command and later concentrated on jet planes for commercial service and the development of missiles.

Shipbuilding, a huge industry in Seattle during World Wars I and II, now is confined to fishing boats, barges, and pleasure craft. Other manufactured products include electronic, nautical, medical, and dental instruments; luggage; building materials; machinery and fabricated metal products; heating equipment; plastics; cosmetics and perfumes; toys; pharmaceuticals; chemicals; lighting fixtures; paints; canvas and rubber products; and clothing.

The industries based on natural resources, with which Seattle has been historically identified—forest products, agriculture, and fishing—remain important but no longer dominate the economy. The forest-products industry has developed from simple tree felling and lumber cutting to a diversified complex that produces plywood, furniture, office and school fixtures, pulp and paper, and chemicals.

The West Coast's largest fishing fleet still sails from Seattle, but out of the old agricultural and fishing economy has grown a more complicated food-processing industry that produces flour, prepared mixes, cereals, animal feeds, beer, wine, candy, and dried, canned, and frozen fruits, vegetables, and seafoods. Recreational opportunities in the area have spurred the manufacture of ski equipment, fishing gear, and other sporting goods.

Transportation and Communications. Seattle is served by many railroads, among them the Chicago, Milwaukee, St. Paul and Pacific, the Great Northern, the Northern Pacific, and the Union Pacific. The Seattle-Tacoma International Airport, south of Seattle proper, is used by Northwest Orient, Pan American, United, Western, and Japan airlines and several smaller lines.

Seattle is on U.S. Highway 99, the north-south Pacific Coast road, and U.S. Highway 10 enters the city from the east across the Lake Washington Floating Bridge, built in 1940. The bridge, which spans the lake on floating pontoons, is considered an outstanding engineering achievement. Washington State Ferries, the world's most extensive automobile ferry system, connects Seattle with the Olympic Peninsula, several islands in Puget Sound, and the city of Victoria, British Columbia.

Education. Enrollment in Seattle's public schools exceeds 100,000. Private schools in the city include the Cornish School of Music, Dance, Art, and Drama; the Helen Bush-Parkside School, for girls and younger boys; the Saint Nicholas School, Forest Ridge Convent, and Holy Names Academy, for girls; and Lakeside School and St. Joseph's, for boys.

The University of Washington, which opened in 1861 as the territorial university, occupies a 640-acre (2,592-hectare) campus overlooking Lake Washington and Lake Union, with fine views of the Cascade Range and Mt. Rainier. Among its modern structures are the Medical-Dental Center, an engineering building, and a student union. The sports stadium seats 55,000. A crew house, holding 24 shells, furnishes facilities for Washington crews, which have ranked among the nation's best.

Also in the city are Seattle University (Roman Catholic, coeducational), which opened in

The Floating Bridge takes motor traffic eastward from Seattle across Lake Washington to Mercer Island.

1900, and Seattle Pacific College (Free Methodist, coeducational), which began as a seminary in 1893.

Churches and Hospitals. Among Seattle's many churches and synagogues, St. James' Cathedral is the seat of the Roman Catholic archdiocese of Seattle, and the Cathedral Church of St. Mark's is the seat of the Protestant Episcopal diocese of Olympia. The city has more than 30 hospitals, a large children's hospital, a medical school at the University of Washington, and several schools of nursing.

Culture. The cultural life of Seattle received a boost with the creation after 1962 of the Seattle Center, a spacious and modern complex occupying the land upon which the Century 21 Exposition (see below) had stood. The center has a number of museums, theaters, and other attractions, including the Opera House, home of the city's symphony orchestra. The Seattle Symphony, among whose conductors have been Sir Thomas Beecham and Milton Kamins, presents a full season of concerts and also neighborhood programs. The Seattle Center Playhouse, supported by the University of Washington, is a renowned repertory theater company.

Libraries. The Seattle Public Library moved into a new $4.5 million building in the downtown area in 1960. It possesses more than a million volumes, with an annual circulation of nearly 4 million. The system includes a municipal reference library, many branch libraries, and a library for the blind with more than 20,000 talking books. Special services include film, technology, art, music, education, and business and economics departments. Nonstudents may use the University of Washington's main and specialized libraries.

Museums and Galleries. The Seattle Art Museum in Volunteer Park has one of the notable collections on the Pacific Coast. Other galleries are the privately endowed Frye Art Museum and the Henry Art Gallery on the university campus. The Washington State Museum, also on the campus, has an extensive collection of Northwest Indian, Eskimo, and Aleut artifacts. The Museum of History and Industry in the Arboretum has a collection ranging from the obstetrical instruments of Seattle's first physician to space helmets, and from a dugout canoe to *Slo-Mo-Shun IV*, the Seattle-built boat that revolutionized the design of hydroplanes.

Also of interest are the Seattle Art Museum Pavilion and the Pacific Science Center, both located at the Seattle Center.

Art and Literature. Seattle is the home of the Northwest school of painters, including Mark Tobey and Morris C. Graves. Tobey was influenced by Chinese art and, after a visit to China in 1934, developed "white writing," a technique reminiscent of Chinese calligraphy. In 1958 he became the first American since Whistler to win the grand prize at the Venice Biennale. Graves, who was also strongly influenced by Oriental techniques and philosophy, is noted for his mystical impressions of the flora and fauna of the mist-wrapped shores of Puget Sound.

No school of writers has arisen in Seattle to match its painters, but Vernon Louis Parrington won the Pulitzer Prize in history in 1928 for his *Main Currents in American Thought,* and Theodore Roethke won the Pulitzer Prize for poetry in 1954 for *The Waking.* Seattle's best-known popular writer was Betty MacDonald, author of *The Egg and I* (1945).

Media. Seattle has two major newspapers, the morning *Post-Intelligencer* and the evening *Times.* There are also many community, foreign-language, and special-interest papers. Some two dozen radio broadcasting stations operate in the vicinity, and there are several television channels, including an educational channel.

Places of Interest. Points of interest to visitors include Pioneer Place, with its totem pole; Boeing Field, with its fleet of jet planes; and the Pike Street public markets, where farmers sell their own produce in stalls overlooking the harbor. The Civic Auditorium provides seating and committee rooms for 7,500 persons and is used by international, national, and regional conventions. Restaurant experts rate Seattle among the 10 top cities in the United States for dining places. Many of these specialize in foreign foods. Boat trips in the harbor, through the Chittenden locks to Lake Union and Lake Washington and to British Columbia are popular. Mt. Rainier is an easy drive by automobile.

Recreation and Parks. Seattle's mild climate makes possible a wide variety of outdoor recreation all year. The Puget Sound country claims the largest per capita boat ownership in the world. Saltwater fishing, mostly for salmon, has no closed season and requires no license. Skiing

Seattle is the leading port of the Northwest. Its waterfront is backed by the business district skyscrapers.

is the major winter sport, with many ski areas situated within a few hours' drive of the city. A week-long Sea Fair in August features water sports climaxed by a hydroplane race.

Forty-five parks, totaling 3,500 acres (1,420 hectares), offer opportunities for golfing (3 municipal courses), swimming (outdoor pool, indoor pools, and at least 10 beaches), and other sports. Major park areas include Seward Park, Woodland Park (with a zoo), Lincoln Park, and Volunteer Park. Smaller parks with views are Kinnear, Kerry, Belvedere, Duwamish Head, and Magnolia. Connecting the scattered parks is a scenic boulevard system that skirts Lake Washington or overlooks Puget Sound.

In 1976 the Kingdome, the West Coast's first domed stadium, opened. It is the home of Seattle's four major league sports teams—the Mariners (baseball), Sounders (soccer), SuperSonics (basketball), and Seahawks (football). The Kingdome also is the scene of rock concerts, circuses, and boat shows.

Flour mills, whose product is shipped from the port, stand by a dock on Seattle's West Waterway.

Century 21 Exposition. The Century 21 Exposition was held in Seattle in 1962. It was the first major international exposition held in the United States since 1939 and one of the few profitable ones. Its theme was "Man in Space," and its purpose was to depict life in the 21st century. The U. S. State Department, acting on an earlier proclamation by President Dwight D. Eisenhower, invited all nations on the United States diplomatic list to participate.

The dominant structure of the exposition was a 600-foot (180-meter) tower, the Space Needle, topped by a revolving restaurant. Other features were monorail commuter service from downtown Seattle to the fairgrounds; a U. S. science pavilion with a simulated "ride through space"; and "Coliseum Century 21," depicting life in the next century. There were also exhibits of art, commerce, and industry. Several structures, including the Space Needle, were kept when the area became a civic center and convention site.

Government. Seattle has a nonpartisan mayor-council government. The mayor and nine councilmen are elected for four-year terms, as are the comptroller, treasurer, corporation counsel, and various board members. The city owns and operates the power, water, and transit systems. The water supply is chiefly the pure mountain water impounded on Cedar River in the Cascade Range.

History. The Seattle area's first settlers, a group of five pioneering families from Illinois, arrived in the fall of 1851, after Olympia and other communities to the south had been founded. The Illinoisans settled on a point at the south end of Elliott Bay, which they named New York. Other settlers derisively called it Alki, a local Indian word meaning "by-and-by."

The Early Decades. Within a month, the pioneers were cutting pilings for shipment to San Francisco, where the building boom stimulated by the gold rush had raised lumber prices to $200 per 1,000 board feet. Because the beach at Alki Point proved unsuitable for loading lumber, most of the settlers moved in March 1853 to the east side of Elliott Bay, where the city's business section now stands. In May a plan of the town was recorded with the territorial government. The community was named for Chief Seattle of the friendly Duwamish and Suquamish tribes. Incorporation as a city did not come until 1869.

For some years, timber was virtually the only cash crop. When Henry Yesler, a lumberman from Ohio, arrived with capital enough to build the first steam mill, two of the pioneers, David Maynard and Carson Boren, shifted the stakes on their waterfront claims to make room for him. Yesler's mill, at a point where the clay bluff dipped almost to sea level, gave the community an industrial base. The trail down which horses pulled logs to the mill, known locally as the "skid road," grew into a street lined with cafés and saloons catering to loggers and sailors, and it helped to fix the term "skid road" (often corrupted to "skid row") in American usage.

In January 1856 an Indian attack on the town was dispersed by fire from the U. S. S. *Decatur*. Only two white men were killed and two houses burned, but continuing Indian troubles in the hinterland slowed development of the Puget Sound region. Nevertheless, a university was established in Seattle in 1861.

One problem of the community was the shortage of marriageable women. Men outnumbered women 10 to 1 among Seattle's white population. In 1864, Asa Mercer, the young president of the university, journeyed east and escorted back 11 young women, who quickly found husbands. In 1866 he made a second trip and returned with about 30 more marriageable women, or "Mercer girls," as they came to be called.

The influx of Chinese laborers, imported to help build the railroads that were then pushing westward, worried white workmen, who feared that the newcomers would depress wages. On Feb. 7, 1886, extremists in Seattle rounded up a number of Chinese and tried to deport them on a steamer bound for San Francisco. A volunteer home guard rallied to protect the Chinese, and five rioters were wounded, one fatally, before order was restored. On June 6, 1889, a flaming glue pot in a print shop touched off a fire that destroyed most of the city's business district. Reconstruction of the area permitted the replacement of wooden buildings by masonry.

Seattle's citizens had hoped that their city would be the first in Washington Territory to become the terminus of a transcontinental railroad, but they were disappointed in 1873, when the Northern Pacific built its lines to Tacoma. In 1893, however, James J. Hill chose Seattle as the western terminus of the Great Northern Railway, and three years later he helped to persuade the Nippon Yusen Kaisha shipping line to use Seattle as its port of entry, giving the city an early lead in competition for trade with the Orient. Hill, who had obtained vast holdings of western lands for building the railroad, sold 900,000 acres (364,500 hectares) of timber to Frederick Weyerhaeuser, a Midwestern lumberman, and reduced long-haul rates for lumber by 60%, opening the Midwest market to Puget Sound lumber.

The 20th Century. With a new business district, a railroad, and shipping facilities, Seattle was able to capitalize on the discovery of gold in Yukon territory and Alaska. When the S. S. *Portland* docked on July 17, 1897, with what was described as "nearly a ton" of gold, Seattle interests exploited the publicity to depict the city as the gateway to the northern goldfields.

Money brought by the gold rush enabled Seattle to finance a major program of civic improvements. To level space for the expanding business district, millions of cubic yards of earth were sluiced from the steep downtown hills. Much of this was used for fill to create factory sites on the tidal flats. The Alaska-Yukon-Pacific Exposition in 1909–1910, held on grounds that became part of the university campus, drew an estimated 3.75 million visitors. Ten cities adjacent to Seattle chose to be annexed, and during

A parade of small craft moves from Lake Union through a canal to Lake Washington as the yachting season opens.

the decade 1901–1910, Seattle's population tripled, jumping from 80,000 to nearly 240,000.

The opening of the Panama Canal in 1914 increased maritime trade with Atlantic ports and Europe, and during World War I shipbuilding boomed. Growing employment and profits stirred labor union activity. The Industrial Workers of the World (IWW) were preaching violence in Puget Sound lumber camps and along Seattle's skid road. The American Federation of Labor's craft unions were more conservative but restless.

When, in 1919, the U. S. Shipping Board sought to eliminate the cost of living differential that western yards had enjoyed over eastern yards, the Metal Trades Council voted to strike, and 110 other unions went out in sympathy. On Feb. 6, 1919, Seattle experienced the first general strike in the history of the United States. All industry and most business houses and transportation lines closed down, but the strike petered out after six days.

The political power of labor, which had been considerable during the war, waned for a time after the general strike. A series of municipal scandals involving bootlegging, vice, and irregularities in the city's purchase of the privately owned street railway system led to the election in 1926 of a reform candidate, Bertha K. Landis, the first woman mayor of a large American city.

The depression years of the 1930's saw the rise of the left-wing Washington Commonwealth Federation and the business-oriented Cincinnatus movement, but both groups disappeared during World War II. The Western Conference of Teamsters, organized by Dave Beck in 1937 as a division of the International Brotherhood of Teamsters, exercised great political and economic power in the city for 20 years. Beck became international president of the union in 1952, but resigned in 1957, after a congressional committee revealed his improper use of union funds. Beck's influence in Seattle ended and that of the Teamsters was reduced.

During the 1960's, Seattle remained heavily dependent on the Boeing complex and its large payroll. The firm, which increasingly specialized in commercial jets, rockets, and space vehicles, employed one of every five Seattle workers. Consequently, by the early 1970's, the area was being seriously affected by reductions in federal spending for aerospace projects. Some of the slack was taken up as the city developed containerization facilities, computerized traffic scheduling techniques, and other improvements designed to exploit its advantages as a transportation hub, particularly in the growing trade between the American Midwest and Japan.

Politically, Seattle has become relatively independent. Voters have tended to elect Republicans to the U. S. House of Representatives, Democrats to the U. S. Senate and to state executive offices, and both to the state legislature. City offices are nonpartisan. Population: (1980) of the city, 493,846; of the metropolitan area, 1,607,469.

Bibliography

Binns, Archie, *Northwest Gateway* (Binford 1949).
Eichenbaum, J., and others, *Seattle* (Ballinger Pubs. 1976).
Morgan, Murry *Skid Road: An Informal Portrait of Seattle*, rev. ed. (Univ. of Wash. Press 1981).
Peterson, Bob, *Seattle Discovered* (Madrona Pubs. 1976).
Sale, Roger, *Seattle, Past to Present* (Univ. of Wash. Press 1976).
Satterfield, Archie, and others, *The Seattle Guidebook*, 5th ed. (Writing 1981).

SEAWEED is a mass or growth of marine plants, most often algae. Seaweed is widely distributed in the oceans, occurring from tide level to considerable depths, floating freely or anchored to the bottom. Some seaweeds are important economically for food, fertilizer, or other uses. See ALGAE.

SEBACEOUS GLAND, sǝ-bā'shǝs, a tiny, oil-producing gland found in the integument, or skin, of mammals. In man, sebaceous glands are found throughout the skin, except for the thick skin of the palms and soles. They are usually associated with hair follicles and are particularly abundant on the scalp, forehead, and chin. Large compound sebaceous glands are found in the nose and external ear, and specialized sebaceous glands occur on the upper eyelid.

Sebaceous glands develop from outpocketings of epithelium and open by means of short ducts into parts of the hair follicles. Their product, called *sebum*, consists of an oily secretion mixed with protein constituents of the cells of the gland, which disintegrate as they give off their secretions. Sebum on the surface of the skin helps keep the skin and hair soft and flexible and aids in preventing excess absorption or loss of water from the body surface.

Overactivity of the sebaceous glands plays a role in several skin conditions, including acne vulgaris and seborrheic dermatitis, or seborrhea. In some cases sebum may become clogged in the duct opening, and a blackhead may result. Occasionally the duct of a sebaceous gland may become obstructed, and the gland itself becomes distended and filled with sebaceous material, forming a sebaceous cyst, or wen.

SEBASTIAN, sǝ-bas'chǝn, **Saint,** 3d century Roman Christian martyr who was a frequent subject for Renaissance artists. Nothing certain is known about him except that he was martyred early in the reign (284–305) of Emperor Diocletian and was buried on the Appian Way, presumably near where the Basilica of St. Sebastian now stands. According to later legend, he was born in Narbonne in Gaul, of Milanese parentage, and became a captain in the Praetorian Guards. Sebastian is said to have effected many secret conversions and miraculous cures before Diocletian discovered that he was a Christian and sentenced him to be shot to death with arrows. Nursed by the Christian woman Irene, the saint survived. But he fearlessly confronted the Emperor again and was beaten to death with clubs. Renaissance painters most often depict him transfixed with arrows. He is variously shown as an old soldier, a young man, or a heroic figure. His feast day is January 20.

SEBASTIAN, sǝ-bas'chǝn (1554–1578), king of Portugal. He was born in Lisbon on Jan. 19, 1554, after the death of his father, Prince John. Sebastian succeeded his grandfather, John III, in 1557 and came of age officially in 1568. During his minority the regency was exercised first by his grandmother Catherine, sister of Emperor Charles V, and from 1562 by his great-uncle, Cardinal Henry, who succeeded Sebastian as king. A religious fanatic, obsessed with a desire to win military glory, Sebastian projected a great crusade against the Muslims of North Africa. An initial fiasco in Morocco in 1574 failed to blunt his enthusiasm.

Another opportunity came when a war of succession broke out in 1578 in the kingdom of Fez and Morocco. Sebastian, in the hope of winning glory for Christianity and Portugal, agreed to support one of the claimants. He collected a fleet and an army and sailed for Morocco in June 1578. The expedition was met at Alcazarquivir by the host of Mulei Malek, who held the throne. On Aug. 4, 1578, Sebastian's forces were routed, and he was killed.

Sebastian had no heirs, and succession to the throne was disputed. Philip II of Spain had strong claims that he reinforced with his army after Henry's death in 1580, and Portugal became a Spanish possession. Soon after the battle, rumors began to spread that Sebastian was still alive. Supporters of this movement, known as Sebastianism, believed that the King would return to save Portugal. Several pretenders claimed to be Sebastian in the years immediately following his death.

SEBASTIANO DEL PIOMBO, sä-bäs-tyä′nō däl pyōm′bō (1485?–1547), Italian painter, whose mastery of color influenced Raphael and other Renaissance painters. Sebastiano Luciani was born in Rome, probably in 1485. Early in his life he decided to devote himself to music. However, about 1500 he turned to painting and studied under Giovanni Bellini and Giorgione. He was particularly influenced by the latter, notably in regard to color.

After Giorgione's death in 1510, Sebastiano went to Rome, where he became acquainted with Michelangelo. He also was a friend of Raphael, who was influenced by his chromatic technique, but their friendship turned to animosity when he

Sebastiano del Piombo's portrait of Pope Clement VII

ALINARI-ART REFERENCE BUREAU

tried to vie with Raphael. Sebastiano's *Raising of Lazarus* (commissioned 1516; National Gallery, London) was undertaken in direct competition to Raphael. While Sebastiano was adept at such group paintings, his chief merit lay in single figures and portraits. Two of his most striking portraits are those of Andrea Doria (1526; Galleria Doria Pamphili, Rome) and Pope Clement VII (1526; Museo di Capodimonte, Naples).

Sebastiano returned to Venice after the sack of Rome in 1527. There he did one of several versions of *Christ Bearing the Cross*. Back in Rome in 1529, he became a favorite of Pope Clement, who, in 1531, created him Piombatore Papale (keeper of the papal seals)—hence his surname. Thereafter, his duties curtailed his artistic production. He died in Rome on June 21, 1547.

SEBASTOPOL. See SEVASTOPOL.

SEBORRHEA, seb-ə-rē′ə, is a condition in which the sebaceous glands of the skin become overactive, secreting an excess amount of sebum, which gives the skin an oily appearance and sometimes leads to the formation of oily scales. It is often associated with the development of blackheads and secondary infections of the skin. Seborrhea most often occurs on the face, particularly the forehead, nose, and chin. Seborrhea or seborrheic dermatitis of the scalp increases the production of dandruff. There is no specific treatment for seborrhea. Frequent cleansing of the skin to remove excess oil is essential and astringent lotions are sometimes applied to the skin. See also DANDRUFF.

SECANT. See CALCULUS—*The Geometrical Meaning of the Derivative*; CIRCLE; TRIGONOMETRY.

SECAUCUS, sē-kô′kəs, a town in northeastern New Jersey, in Hudson county, is on the Hackensack River, which forms part of its western border, about 3 miles (5 km) west of the center of New York City. It adjoins Jersey City, which is to its north. Secaucus is a residential town and a large warehouse center. It was incorporated as a borough in 1900 and as a town in 1917. Government is administered by a mayor and council. Population: 13,719.

SECESSION, si-sesh′ən, is the formal withdrawal from a political organization, such as a state, empire, or federation. The term originated in ancient Rome, where on three occasions between 494 and 287 B.C. the oppressed plebeians seceded from the republic by marching out of the city and refusing to return until their grievances were redressed. In modern terms such action would be considered more of a strike or rebellion, for secession implies an attempt by a community or province to break away permanently from a larger organization and assume self-government. Because political organizations normally do not recognize such a right, secession is usually a revolutionary act.

Secession: Ancient and Modern. In the ancient world the northern Israelite tribes successfully seceded from the Davidian kingdom after the death of Solomon in 933 B.C. and founded the separate kingdom of Israel. In 5th century Greece a number of cities attempted to secede from the League of Delos, dominated by Athens, but they were held in subjection. Rome showed statesmanship in preventing the secession of Italian cities in 91–88 B. C. by granting citizenship to their inhabitants.

Among the numerous instances of successful secession in the modern world were Belgium's separation from the kingdom of Netherlands by armed rebellion in 1830 and Norway's peaceful break with Sweden in 1905. In Latin America, secession, successful or attempted, has been frequent. Notable examples were the secession of Venezuela and Ecuador from Gran Colombia in 1830, and of Panama from Colombia in 1903.

Of worldwide significance has been the demand of colonial peoples for the right to secede from the empires of European powers. Before the 20th century such secession was accomplished only by force, as in the case of the American colonies held by Britain and Spain. The British conceded self-government to southern Ireland in 1922 only after failing to crush an Irish rebellion, but after 1945 they accepted the partial or complete secession of various Asian and African peoples. The Dutch yielded to the secession of Indonesia in 1949. After the French had unsuccessfully fought rebellion in Indochina, the government, in 1958, recognized a general right of secession for colonial dominions; yet France struggled to hold on to Algeria through more than seven years of warfare, until 1962. Portugal continued to resist independence movements in its overseas provinces. The Soviet Union, immediately after its 1917 revolution, accepted the secession of Poland, Finland, and the Baltic states. But it disallowed such rights in subsequent years and reincorporated the Baltic states in 1940.

Except for the continued process of the breakup of colonial empires, secession in the second half of the 20th century has largely meant the dissolution of states and federations relatively newly constituted in relation to the history of nations. Examples include the peaceful end of the West Indian Federation (Jamaica and Trinidad-Tobago) in 1962 and the withdrawal of Singapore from Malaysia in 1965; the bloody, unsuccessful secessionist movements in Katanga province, the Congo (later Zaïre) in 1960 and in Biafra, Nigeria, in 1969; and the equally disastrous, but successful, secession of Bangladesh from Pakistan in 1971.

In U. S. History. According to the states' rights interpretation of the U. S. Constitution, the individual states, in forming the Union, had merely delegated certain limited powers to the federal government, retaining full sovereignty. Any state, therefore, was legally entitled to withdraw from the partnership if it decided that its rights were being violated. This theory was opposed by early nationalists—such as Chief Justice John Marshall and Daniel Webster—who argued that the federal government was fully sovereign within the spheres assigned to it, and that it derived its powers directly from the people and was not merely a league of states. Hence, under no circumstances was there any right of secession. Before the Civil War such problems of constitutional interpretation evoked numerous debates, for any section of the Union that felt its interests injured by federal policies was likely to assert a states' rights theory. Opposition to federal power was sectional rather than statist, and there was no consistency in the attitudes of different sections.

New England, which had been strongly nationalist as long as the Federalist party controlled the federal government, changed to states' rightism after the Republican victory of 1800. Extremists continued to advocate secession down to 1814 but were defeated in the Hartford Convention of that year, which merely recommended certain amendments to the Constitution. Subsequent changes in federal policies ended discontent in New England but led to a steady growth of states' rights sentiment in the South. The South developed various grievances against federal economic policies, especially with reference to the tariff, and was increasingly alarmed by the growth of antislavery sentiment in the North. Its philosophical leader, John C. Calhoun, trying to find a moderate alternative to secession, asserted that any state could "nullify" a federal act that violated its rights. But when South Carolina attempted to nullify the tariff in 1832, the compromise ending the dispute did not recognize nullification.

During the following 28 years virtually all of the political spokesmen for the South came to accept the states' rights view, differing on the expediency of secession, while the North became generally nationalistic.

Following the election of Abraham Lincoln to the presidency in 1860, secessionists won control in the South. Between Dec. 20, 1860, and Feb. 1, 1861, conventions in seven states voted for dissolution of federal ties, and after the outbreak of the Civil War they were joined by four others. Their main justification was the alleged Northern interference with Southern rights with respect to slavery. Some Northern leaders at first were inclined to accept secession, but after Lincoln called for volunteers to defend the Union, the North rallied to his support.

Since the defeat of the South in 1865, there has been no instance of formal secession in the United States, though secession remains a theoretical possibility for extreme states' rightists. On another level, there has been a recurrent movement among some circles in New York City to secede from New York state and join the Union as the 51st state.

See also CIVIL WAR; CONFEDERATE STATES OF AMERICA; STATES' RIGHTS; UNITED STATES—*Sectional Conflict and Preservation of the Union, 1815–1877.*

HENRY B. PARKES*, *Author of "The American Experience"*

SECOND, the basic unit of time measurement. One second is $\frac{1}{60}$ of a minute and $\frac{1}{86,400}$ of a day. Its length was first defined in the metric system in terms of the mean solar day. (See DAY.) However, since the earth's rotation rate—the basis of the solar day—actually varies, the *ephemeris second* was accepted by international convention in 1956. Its length is defined as $\frac{1}{31,556,935.9747}$ of the tropical year that ended at midnight, Dec. 31, 1899. See YEAR.

The use of a specific year avoids the problem of a varying solar year but presents other problems in scientific work. In 1967 the length of the second was redefined in terms of atomic radiation in order to create a precise and readily available standard. One second is given as the duration of 9,192,631,770 cycles of the radiation emitted by a cesium-133 atom as it passes from one specified transition state to another. This duration was set to be as close as possible to that of the ephemeris second, but the two values will diverge with time.

The ruins of Hadrian's Villa, the largest imperial country estate in the Roman Empire, are near Tivoli, close to Rome. The estate, with palaces, theaters, baths, gardens, pools, and colonnades, was like a small city.

SECOND CENTURY. In the first years of the 2d century A. D. the two largest empires of the ancient world—those of Rome and the Han dynasty of China—were at their maximum extent. About 180 A. D. both began their decline. The Roman Empire, surviving the crisis of the next century, continued in the West until 476 and in the East until the Turks took Constantinople in 1453. The downfall of the Han Empire was more precipitous. After the Han dynasty's final collapse in 220, China remained divided for more than 350 years.

Between Rome and China in the 2d century stretched the territories of the Parthians in Iran and the Kushans in northern India and part of Central Asia. Thus most of the culturally advanced portion of the Eastern Hemisphere was divided among four states. Trade routes by land and sea connected all the civilized areas of the hemisphere and extended even beyond the limits of the "known" world—across the Danube and Black Sea into northern Europe and over the Sahara into West Africa. Trade routes also provided avenues of cultural interpenetration.

South of the Mediterranean region there were centers of civilization in northeastern Africa and southern Arabia. However, the African kingdom of Meroe in Sudan had passed its zenith by the end of the 1st century, and the kingdom of Aksum in northern Ethiopia did not reach the peak of its development until the 4th century. For South Arabia the 2d century was a turning point. The prosperity of this area depended on its monopoly of the Arabian Sea trade with India, and competition from Greek merchantmen in the ser-

vice of Rome began to make itself felt. By the 6th century the ruin of the South Arabian trading centers was complete.

To the east, Hindu civilization flourished in peninsular India during the 2d century under the Satavahana dynasty. The beginnings of Southeast Asian kingdoms appeared in the lower Mekong Valley, central Vietnam, and the northern Malay Peninsula. Japan was still in the prehistoric stage of its cultural development.

Unknown to the peoples of the Eastern Hemisphere were the centers of advanced culture in Mexico, Central America, and Peru. The Maya civilization was rapidly developing toward maturity in the 2d century, but the birth of the Aztec and Inca empires lay far in the future.

1. Roman Empire

Many scholars agree with Edward Gibbon in looking back to 2d century Rome as the acme of ancient civilization. Gibbon wrote in the *Decline and Fall of the Roman Empire,* "If a man were called to fix the period in the history of the world during which the condition of the human race was most happy and prosperous, he would, without hesitation, name that which elapsed from the death of Domitian to the accession of Commodus"—that is, from 96 to 180 A. D.

When the 2d century began, the Roman Empire embraced the whole civilized world of the West, around the shores of the Mediterranean Sea, an area between 1,500 and 2,000 miles (2,400–3,000 km) from north to south and about 3,000 miles (5,000 km) from west to east. It encompassed an area of nearly 2 million square

A cast of part of the relief on Trajan's Column in Rome shows the Romans at top defending a fortress under attack by the Dacians, inhabitants of what is now Rumania. The relief, 200 yards long, spirals around the tall column and illustrates other events of Trajan's Dacian campaigns.

miles (5 million sq km) of fertile and productive land, with a population that has been estimated at between 75 million and 100 million.

Politically, the empire was still a military monarchy, but during the period between Domitian and Commodus a series of able rulers, the ablest since Augustus, governed this vast region with justice and efficiency. Men were aware of the signal benefits of the new era, following the tyrannies of such rulers as Caligula, Nero, and Domitian. Early in the 2d century Trajan forbade Pliny the Younger, the governor of Bithynia, to pay attention to anonymous informers against the Christians because such a procedure was "unworthy of our enlightened age." In turn, the governor repeatedly stressed the "tranquility and public order" that characterized the new era.

THE EMPERORS OF THE 2D CENTURY

The period comprising the final years of the 1st century and most of the 2d century was the age of the five "good" emperors: Nerva (reigned 96–98), Trajan (reigned 98–117), Hadrian (reigned 117–138), Antoninus Pius (reigned 138–161), and Marcus Aurelius (reigned 161–180). Following them, a swift decline that began with Commodus (reigned 180–192) led to the vast disorder and mounting crises of the succeeding centuries.

Pertinax and Didius Julianus each reigned briefly in 193 but were quickly succeeded by Septimius Severus (reigned 193–211), who was the choice of the army. The legions had made and unmade rulers in the days of the triumvirs (1st century B. C.) and again in the year of the four emperors (69). From the reign of Commodus onward they were once more to play an increasing role in the making and unmaking of monarchs. Against the background both of what went before and what followed, the reigns of the five good emperors appeared to later historians and to contemporaries alike a kind of golden Indian summer, which lingered for almost a century before the frosts and storms of the long dark winter set in.

Nerva. Marcus Cocceius Nerva, a distinguished senator and jurist, was chosen by the Senate to succeed the despotic Domitian, who was assassinated in September 96. Since Nerva was 66 years old, it was obvious that his election was only a temporary solution. Yet even in his brief reign he did much to reestablish peace and confidence, especially in remote regions of the empire. His crowning achievement was the appointment of his successor, Trajan, the ablest administrator and general in the army.

Trajan. More than anyone else, Trajan (Marcus Ulpius Traianus) laid the foundations of prosperity and internal peace that endured through most of the 2d century. His conquest of Dacia (roughly modern Rumania) in 101–102 and 105–107 extended the European boundary of the empire beyond the Danube. During the Dacian wars he took large supplies of precious metals and 50,000 able-bodied prisoners. With the aid of this reserve of wealth and manpower he overcame an inherited public deficit and embarked upon a vast program of public works. Trust funds were set up for the care of the poor and for public education of freeborn children, partly no doubt in the interest of encouraging the free Italian population to raise large families in the face of rising foreign-born groups. The impetus to architecture continued through the reign of Hadrian, and the impressive ruins of forums, baths, theaters, basilicas, circuses, hippodromes, aqueducts, and harbors attest to the wealth and magnificence of the period.

Dacia remained Roman until the Gothic invasions of 250–270. The whole later history of Europe would undoubtedly have been very different had the Roman Empire enjoyed another century of peace and prosperity and been able to extend its border beyond the Rhine to the Elbe, the Oder, or the Vistula. If this had occurred, a much shorter line could have been completed via the Carpathians to the mouth of the Danube —one that might later have held the barbarians in check.

Trajan continued Rome's expansion in the east. The commercially strategic Nabataean kingdom in northwestern Arabia, conquered in 105, was made a Roman province. Afterward a road was built from Syria to the Gulf of Aqaba, and a Roman fleet was stationed in the Red Sea. In his war with Parthia (113–117), Trajan annexed Armenia and conquered Mesopotamia, including the Parthian capital, Ctesiphon. He died while

"Cavalcade" relief from the base of Antoninus Pius' Column illustrates an ancient funerary rite in which mounted soldiers rode three times around the grave or pyre. The center figures are participants in the second part of the ceremony, consisting of parades, races, and mock combats.

returning from an expedition against the Parthians, and his annexation of Armenia and Mesopotamia was promptly repudiated by Hadrian.

Hadrian. Hadrian (Publius Aelius Hadrianus) was a very different person from Trajan, his cousin. Hadrian reversed Trajan's aggressive policy, strengthening existing frontiers instead of expanding them. He was a patron of literature and art, and especially generous to the ancient Greek cities, where classical civilization had been born. The ruins of his villa at Tivoli still testify to his unbounded enthusiasm for the arts, mythology, and archaeology. Like most of the good emperors, he was tolerant and cosmopolitan, and he enthusiastically promoted the common welfare. More than half of the Emperor's time was spent in the provinces, Hellenizing, Romanizing, and organizing their social and political life. He encouraged the work of the great jurists in collecting, codifying, and expounding the whole body of Roman law. He attracted men of ability to the civil service, and he instituted the famous Roman postal system.

Hadrian precipitated a war with the Jews when he ordered the erection of a pagan city, Aelia Capitolina, on the ruins of Jerusalem. The whole Jewish world rose in revolt in 132, and the rebellion was suppressed in 135 only after bitter fighting. Hadrian's increasing megalomania and self-identification with deity led also to the opposition of the Christians, who refused to acclaim him *dominus et deus.*

Hadrian's Tomb, now the Castel Sant'Angelo, in Rome, originally consisted of a square base supporting a round structure planted with trees on top. Above the trees rose an altar bearing a sculpture of a chariot drawn by four horses and driven by Hadrian as the ruler of the earth.

501

A martial emperor who hated war, Marcus Aurelius is seen as a conqueror in the Piazza Campidoglio, Rome.

Hadrian's plaintive death song, the often quoted *Animula, vagula, blandula* ("Little soul, little wanderer, little darling, soon to go down to the cold, pale, naked underworld, never to smile again . . ."), is not the language of the great emperor in the heyday of his power and magnificence, and should not be viewed as characteristic of him. The man was sick, physically and mentally; indeed he was dying. But the verses do reflect the enfeeblement of spirit that was sapping the inner vitality of the empire, for all its external splendor and apparent prosperity.

Antoninus Pius. Much less is known about Antoninus Pius (Titus Aurelius Fulvus Boionius Arrius Antoninus), who had been adopted by Hadrian as heir to the throne. What Marcus Aurelius says of him is convincing evidence that Antoninus' 23-year reign must have been one of the happiest in all history. He was a true "father of his country." During his reign "all the provinces flourished," and by his economical administration the treasury accumulated a large surplus.

In this peaceful period the spread of Oriental cults took on new impetus. Along with them went a renewed emphasis on astrology as well as a greater propaganda for popular philosophy. During his reign, in 147, the 900th anniversary of the founding of Rome was celebrated. The Alexandrians hailed him as the World Redeemer Heracles, the benefactor of all mankind.

Marcus Aurelius. Perhaps the most interesting of the good emperors was the last, Marcus

Aurelius Antoninus, who reigned for 19 years. More about him as a man is known than about any other Roman emperor, since his *Meditations* contains his whole life philosophy. It is one of the noblest documents of ancient Stoic piety and speculation, and along with the works of Seneca and Epictetus it is the fullest exposition of the later Roman type of Stoicism.

But it was Marcus' ill fortune to be compelled to face the accumulated liabilities and the mounting misfortunes that had resulted from the long era of prosperity following Trajan. During these years the Parthians in the east and the German tribes north of the Danube had bided their time and were now ready to try to seize territory of what they assumed to be an enfeebled Rome.

Under the able generalship of Avidius Cassius, the Romans repulsed the Parthians, destroying Ctesiphon and Seleucia, its sister city across the Tigris, in 164. The victory was a costly one. The Roman troops brought home with them a plague, which spread everywhere and decimated the population of the west and north. It lasted for many years and may have contributed to that strange loss of vitality that characterized the decline of the empire in the following centuries.

The restive northern tribes, which invaded the Danube Valley and northeastern Italy in 167, were completely defeated by 180. But the effort required the absence of the emperor from Rome during much of this time.

This absence was most unfortunate for Marcus, both personally and publicly. These were the years when Commodus, his son and successor, was growing up. Lacking firm parental restraint, the young prince became spoiled and irresponsible. Marcus' choice of Commodus as his successor blots out much of the solid achievement of his difficult but nobly pursued career.

Commodus. The ill-starred reign of Lucius Aelius Aurelius Commodus lasted for 12 years. The poison of autocratic power seems to have unbalanced his mind. He persecuted the Senate, renamed Rome "Colonia Commodiana" after himself, and renamed the months after his own names and titles. He planned to appear publicly as the incarnation of Hercules on Jan. 1, 193, in the roles of both consul and gladiator. But he was assassinated on New Year's Eve, 192, by members of his palace staff.

Close of the Century. The 2d century ended in gloom and foreboding of worse things to come. The reigns of Commodus' successors Pertinax and Didius Julianus were short-lived. Then, in 193, began the dynasty of the Severi, who were oriented toward the East and had little regard for Roman traditions. The slow decline of the *Imperium Romanum* had begun.

PEACE AND PROSPERITY IN THE EMPIRE

While it lasted, the era of peace and prosperity under the good emperors brought to the world blessings that have never been wholly lost or forgotten. There was no serious threat or invasion from without or of revolution from within. For three generations and more, men lived in a civilized society and passed on to their barbarian neighbors the inheritance of learning, art, letters, philosophy, and the science of government—an inheritance accumulated since the Hellenistic age.

The Hellenizing process begun in the East by Alexander the Great was now being carried to its conclusion in the West. For example, Greek was still spoken and written in Italy, Gaul, and North Africa. Hermas in Rome and Saint Irenaeus in Gaul wrote in Greek, and the persecuted churches in Vienne, near Lyon, wrote their accounts of the martyrdoms in Greek. The Latin version of the Bible was begun about 150, but previously the Greek text had served in North Africa, Italy, and Gaul. Even the *Meditations* of Aurelius were written in Greek.

Government. The 2d century emperors were virtually absolute dictators, since the Senate had declined in influence for over 100 years. But the government was efficient, staffed largely by men of the equestrian order. Taxes were moderate and were collected now by officials rather than by tax farmers. The law was studied scientifically and was accurately codified. Vast building operations were undertaken not only in Rome but also in the provinces, especially under Hadrian. The city governments were well organized, public schools were established, and farm relief was provided through government loans, the interest being used to educate poor country children. Slavery was dying out, and it was easier for slaves to obtain freedom. World trade had expanded; even silk from China and cotton from India could be purchased in the West.

Intellectual and Religious Life. Some of the great writers of later antiquity lived during the 2d century: the historians Tacitus, Dio Cassius, Suetonius, and Arrian; the philosophers Epictetus and Marcus Aurelius; the essayist and biographer Plutarch; the satirists Lucian and Juvenal; the novelist Apuleius; the orator Dio Chrysostom; the traveler Pausanias; the physician Galen; the geographer and astronomer Ptolemy; and the writers of famous letters, Pliny the Younger and Marcus Cornelius Fronto. Among Christian writers, some of the later New Testament authors belong to the early 2d century, and following them were the Apologists and Tertullian and Saint Irenaeus. Yet with all the intellectual and religious activity of the age, there was little indication of fresh progress. Rhetoric—that is, oratory—was still the crown of education, not philosophy, science, or history.

The ancient religious cults were dying. For the majority of the population astrology and the Oriental mysteries had taken their place—such cults as those of Isis, Cybele, Attis, and, above all, Mithras. For the educated, a refined type of personal philosophy sufficed, usually Stoicism or a revived and purely spiritual type of Platonism.

The most vital religious movement of the period was Christianity. The persecutions thus far had been only local and sporadic, usually outbursts of mob violence, as in Bithynia in 112 and Vienne in 177. The widespead official efforts to stamp out the new religion came later, under emperors Decius and Diocletian.

Spread of Roman Culture. The civilizing mission of Rome was accomplished not by coercion or restraint or by force of arms or the transplanting of populations, but by the peaceful methods of example, public education, the just administration of law, a widespread commerce, and the establishment of cities, towns, and country villas in which the urbane Roman type of life was cultivated, exemplified, and enjoyed. Roman civilization was thus made attractive to multitudes of peoples along the far-flung frontiers of the empire and among the nations only recently incorporated within it.

Whatever it had been originally, Roman civilization was now a self-sustained culture, expanding by its own inner attractiveness to other peoples. The tragedy, for all later history, is that it ended too soon, before its task was done and before it had reached and transformed more of the barbarian peoples to the north and east, whose onslaughts on the Roman world in the 4th and 5th centuries almost extinguished European civilization. Where Roman culture had really taken root, it survived to some extent the Dark Ages that followed and in turn passed on its blessings to the new peoples.

This culture was not limited to the aristocracy, although naturally it was centered in the upper classes. Emperor Caracalla's grant of Roman citizenship in 212 to all freemen throughout the empire was only the climax of a long process of education and preparation for responsibility. This process was more marked in the provinces than in Rome itself, where a large part of the populace still lived on the dole and where it was possible for landless farmers and vintners from every part of Italy and for the drifting unemployed of a whole empire to gather and be fed.

Economic Conditions. It is estimated that the city of Rome in the 2d century had a population of over one million, of whom perhaps a fifth were idle, supported by the state, both fed and amused at public expense. The same luxury and extravagance were found in the provinces, though to a lesser degree. Unfortunately, this luxury and the general superficial prosperity that made it possible did not prevent the extinction of many of the upper-class and upper-middle-class families. The equestrian class grew, but only by adoption and recruitment from outside.

Economically, a kind of stagnation seems to have been increasing. The rich had most of the wealth and lacked all incentive to increase it. The poor were content with "bread and circuses."

A typical Roman shop sign, found near the port of Ostia, shows that the tradesman was a grinder.

ALINARI-ART REFERENCE BUREAU

HUBERTUS KANUS, FROM RAPHO GUILLUMETTE

Hewn from rock, the "Treasury" at Petra was probably a temple. Petra, now in Jordan, was the capital of the Nabataean kingdom, conquered by Rome in 105.

The middle class, in between, seemed satisfied with free public baths, public spectacles, free education, and the general security and opulence that surrounded them, and above all with the comparative freedom to pursue any religious cult or philosophy that attracted their attention or interest.

In the eastern provinces, manufacturing was thriving, and the finished wares of Syria and Asia Minor were as well known in Rome as Egyptian grain and cotton goods. The port of Ostia near Rome was a thriving headquarters of Mediterranean trade. It had completely outstripped Puteoli (Pozzuoli), which was too remote for the transshipment of the vast cargoes of food and other supplies destined for the metropolis. Trade and transport were well developed and thus had an immense effect upon the spread and establishment of a widespread common culture.

FREDERICK C. GRANT
Union Theological Seminary

2. Iran

The Parthians, a nomadic people of Central Asia, invaded the plateau of Iran about 250 B. C. At that time Iran was part of the Greek Seleucid empire. During the next century the Parthians took the place of the Seleucids as rulers of Iran and Mesopotamia. From the mid-1st century B. C. there was constant warfare between the Parthians and Romans, with fortune favoring alternately one side and the other. Armenia, lying between them, was a main source of contention.

Despite striking victories over the Parthians in the 2d century A. D., the Roman emperors came to realize that they could not permanently extend their power beyond the Euphrates River into Mesopotamia and the plateau of Iran. Nor were the Parthians ever able to establish themselves in the Roman East. Parthian military might proved to be strongest in a defensive role. The repeated Roman invasions of the 2d century did, however, greatly weaken the Parthian, or Arsacid, dynasty, which was replaced by the native Persian Sassanian dynasty early in the 3d century.

3. India

From the 2d century B. C. to the 1st century A. D. a series of foreign peoples from the northwest established themselves in India. Greeks, Shakas (Śakas), Pahlavas, and Kushans invaded in that order. The last three groups each broke the power of its predecessor in the northwestern part of the subcontinent and founded a power base of its own there. All four peoples played a part in the history of India during the 2d century A.D., but only the Kushans and Shakas had a major role.

At its height under Kanishka, the Kushan domain covered much of northern India and extended through Afghanistan into Central Asia. The Kushans came into conflict with the Parthians to the west and the Han dynasty rulers of China to the northeast. Kanishka, who ascended the throne sometime between 78 and 144, ruled for 23 years. He adorned his capitals—Purushapura (Peshawar) and Mathura—with celebrated monuments and invited eminent philosophers and poets to his court. One of his great achievements was his summoning of the fourth Buddhist council to discuss theology and doctrine. As a result, Buddhist missionaries were sent to Central Asia and China, where their faith took new root. After Kanishka's death Kushan power gradually declined, and in the 3d century the kingdom disintegrated.

South of the area under Kushan control, the Shakas, who had become dominant in part of western India, contended with the Satavahana, or Andhra, dynasty of the Deccan. Early in the 2d century the Satavahanas gained the advantage under Gautamiputra Shatakarni. This ruler claimed to have defeated the Shakas, Yavanas (Greeks), and Pahlavas. By the middle of the century their fortunes were briefly reversed by the Shaka prince Rudradaman, who deprived the Satavahanas of much of their territory. Subsequently the Satavahanas recouped their losses, but in the 3d century their kingdom began to break apart. The Satavahanas were upholders of Brahman orthodoxy, though tolerant of other faiths. Trade and agriculture flourished under their rule.

In the far south during the 2d century the Tamils were rapidly evolving political and economic structures comparable to those that had developed to the north. The Satavahanas sped this process by providing a cultural and commercial link between northern and southern India.

4. China

In China, the 2d century represented a major turning point, the transition from the power and prosperity of the ancient Han Empire to the refeudalization and impoverishment that marked the Six Dynasties period. At the beginning of the century the Later Han Dynasty of the Liu family had reached its peak, its armies having just established control of Central Asia to the Caspian Sea. To the south, Chinese power extended through the province of Tongking (Tonkin) in what is now northern Vietnam. By the end of the century, however, the glory of the Han was over and a kind of dark age set in.

Through the first half of the century, Chinese power was gradually eroded by social and economic changes. The continued growth of great landed estates forced increasing poverty on the peasants, many of whom became semi-serfs under the control of great landlords. Growing factionalism at the court centered around the great families, eunuchs, Confucian-inspired officials, and relatives of empresses. The emperors became pawns of these political groups. There were repeated protests and demonstrations by students at the imperial university, who may have numbered 30,000.

Factionalism brought widespread loss of faith in the Han system, and central power became meaningless as the great landlords and generals created new provincial power bases. By 180, warlords were struggling for power in the provinces.

Peasant impoverishment created the basis for a massive peasant rebellion, a prototype of those that recurred throughout the history of traditional China. Out of their desperation, peasants created a religious movement centered on certain faith-healers and aimed at establishing an agrarian utopia with land and equality for all. In 184, peasant armies arose throughout China in the Yellow Turban Revolt. Although crushed by warlord military forces, the rebels destroyed what remained of Han central power. Members of the Liu family continued to reign, however, until 220.

Warlords like the flamboyant adventurer-poet Ts'ao Ts'ao, the aristocratic Liu Pei, and the Sun brothers (all of whom became semi-mythical heroes) succeeded in establishing their control over the three major regions of China. They thus created conditions that soon led to the division

Clay model of a Chinese manor house dates from about 150 A.D. The house was made of timber and rammed earth. Birds on the roof may represent departed spirits.

Bodhisattva from Gandhara in northwest India. A bodhisattva is a merciful being who renounces Nirvana to help men attain release from the cycle of rebirth.

EVENTS OF THE SECOND CENTURY

102	Death of Chinese general Pan Ch'ao: beginning of decline of Han dynasty's power in Central Asia.
105	Roman conquest of the Arab Nabataean state (capital: Petra).
117	Death of Emperor Trajan; accession of Hadrian. Roman Empire at its greatest extent.
135	Revolt of the Jews (from 132) suppressed by Hadrian.
138	Death of Roman Emperor Hadrian; accession of Antoninus Pius.
144	Latest date for start of Kanishka's 23-year reign over Kushan empire (earliest date: 78).
161	Death of Roman Emperor Antoninus Pius; accession of Marcus Aurelius.
164	Romans destroyed Parthian cities of Ctesiphon and Seleucia. Returning soldiers spread plague (165–166) throughout Roman Empire.
180	Death of Marcus Aurelius, last of the five "good" Roman emperors; accession of Commodus.
180	Commodus made peace with the Germans, ending 13 years of war but renouncing final Roman victory.
184	Yellow Turban peasant revolt in China.
192	Founding of the state of Champa in Vietnam.
193	Septimius Severus was made Roman emperor by the Army.

of China into the Three Kingdoms. Ts'ao Ts'ao's power was partly based on his use of Hsiung-nu (Hun) forces, which set the pattern for foreign invasions that marked the next four centuries.

The 2d century also brought much creative activity. The world's first water-powered mills appeared, and Chinese developed a proto-porcelaineous ceramic ware. The earliest known examples of pure rag-content paper date from this time. The mathematician and poet Chang Heng built a seismograph that showed the direction of the centers of earthquakes.

Near the beginning of the century, China's greatest woman scholar, Pan Chao, completed a major historical work, the *Han Shu*, which had been started by her father and brother. This work was the first Chinese dynastic history, setting a model that was followed down to the 20th century. Intellectually, the century witnessed a revival of classical ideas, especially of Taoism and Legalism. A new religious fervor developed among Chinese, laying the basis for the great age of Buddhism that followed.

JAMES R. SHIRLEY
Northern Illinois University

Bibliography

Balazs, Étienne, *Chinese Civilization and Bureaucracy:* "Political Philosophy and Social Crisis at the End of the Han Dynasty" (Yale Univ. Press 1964).
Boak, Arthur E. B., and Sinnigen, William, *A History of Rome to 565 A. D.*, 5th ed. (Macmillan 1965).
Cambridge University Press Editors, *The Cambridge Ancient History*, vol. 11: *The Imperial Peace, A. D. 70–192* (1965).
Cary, Max, *History of Rome: Down to the Reign of Constantine*, 2d ed. (Macmillan 1964).
Fitzgerald, Charles P., *China: A Short Cultural History*, 3d ed. (Praeger 1961).
Frye, Richard N., *The Heritage of Persia* (World Pub. 1963).
Ghirshman, Roman, *Iran* (Penguin 1954).
Majumdar, Ramesh C., *The History and Culture of the Indian People*, vol. 2: *The Age of Imperial Unity* (Bharatiya Vidya Bhavan 1951).
Parker, Henry M. D., *A History of the Roman World, from A. D. 138 to 337*, 2d ed. (Macmillan 1958).
Reischauer, Edwin O., and Fairbank, John, *East Asia: The Great Tradition* (Houghton 1960).
Rostovtzeff, Mikhail I., *Social and Economic History of the Roman Empire*, 2d ed. rev. by Peter Fraser (Oxford 1957).
Salmon, Edward T., *A History of the Roman World, from 30 B. C. to A. D. 138*, 6th ed. (Barnes & Noble 1968).
Thapar, Romila, *A History of India*, vol. 1 (Penguin 1966).
Warmington, Eric H., *The Commerce Between the Roman Empire and India* (Cambridge 1928).
Wheeler, Mortimer, *Rome Beyond the Imperial Frontiers* (Philosophical Lib. 1954).

SECOND INTERNATIONAL. See INTERNATIONAL.

SECOND WORLD WAR. See WORLD WAR II.

SECONDARY EDUCATION. See EDUCATION– *Secondary Education.*

SECORD, sē'kôrd, **Laura Ingersoll** (1775–1868), Canadian Loyalist. Born in Great Barrington, Mass., on Sept. 13, 1775, she moved to Canada after the American Revolution. In 1813, during the War of 1812, she overheard plans by U. S. troops billeted in her house for an attack on Beaver Dam. Crossing the American lines, she rushed 20 miles (32 km) to warn the British. She died in Chippawa, Ontario, on Oct. 17, 1868.

SECRET BALLOT, or Australian ballot, an official list of candidates and proposals, issued only at a polling place, where it is marked in secret. See BALLOT; ELECTION.

SECRET SERVICE, U. S., a federal law-enforcement agency of the Department of the Treasury. It was established on July 5, 1865. The responsibilities and jurisdiction of the director of the Secret Service and his staff and agents include: (1) protection of the president of the United States and certain other officials; (2) detection and arrest of counterfeiters; (3) the carrying out of other specified duties, such as supervision of the Executive Protective Service, which protects the White House, and of the Treasury Security Force, which protects the Treasury buildings and vaults; and (4) the offering and payment of rewards for services and information contributing to the apprehension of criminals.

The duties of the Secret Service are defined in an act of Congress, Title 18, U. S. Code, section 3056, which amended earlier regulations.

Origin. In 1865, President Abraham Lincoln, at his last cabinet meeting, approved creation of the Secret Service in the Treasury Department to fight counterfeiters. Not only Lincoln but two more presidents, James A. Garfield and William McKinley, would be victims of assassins before the Secret Service, the only general law-enforcement agency of the federal government at that time, was in 1901 assigned the function of protecting presidents.

Tragedies and near-tragedies, from one administration to another, gradually expanded the agency's duties to include responsibility for the protection of the president-elect, then Woodrow Wilson (1913); the president's immediate family (1917); the vice president, then Alben W. Barkley (1951); the vice president-elect (1962); former presidents and their wives (1965); the widow of a former president until her death or remarriage, and the children of a former president until they reach the age of 16—an aftermath of the assassination in 1963 of President John F. Kennedy (1968); major presidential and vice presidential candidates (1968); visiting heads of foreign governments and, at the president's direction, other foreign dignitaries and U. S. officials abroad (1971).

Early History. For nearly half a century after it was established in 1865, the Secret Service investigated not only counterfeiting, its primary responsibility, but also various violations of federal law that were later assigned to other government agencies. Agents uncovered opium smuggling, extortion rackets by organized crime, and even an attempt to steal Lincoln's body from its tomb. In 1871 the Secret Service went after the Ku Klux Klan and within three years had jailed more than a thousand of that organization's hooded terrorists.

In the Spanish-American War, agents tracked down an elusive Spanish spy ring that was operating in Canada. They located the headquarters of the spy ring in Montreal, and exposed Lt. Ramón Carranza, naval attaché of the Spanish legation, as the mastermind of the operation. Carranza was banished from Canadian soil by the government of Canada, and with the arrest of other spies in the United States, the Secret Service effectively put an end to the Spanish espionage apparatus.

President Theodore Roosevelt in 1907 sent Secret Service agents west to investigate suspected frauds involving government-owned land. Thousands of acres were being offered free to homesteaders but wound up in cattle empires. When the Secret Service exposed huge land frauds, including some questionable practices by congressmen, Congress told the agency to mind its own business—counterfeiting. Some Secret Service agents were transferred to the Department of Justice, to launch the forerunner of the Federal Bureau of Investigation.

During World War I, President Woodrow Wilson persuaded Congress to lift its restrictions on the Secret Service long enough for agents to go after a German sabotage network. When an agent snatched a plotter's briefcase, the whole scheme was uncovered. At President Calvin Coolidge's order, agents secretly investigated the Teapot Dome oil scandals—a plot hatched to make millions out of the government's oil reserves. Secretary of the Interior Albert B. Fall was convicted as a result of the Secret Service investigations, and others were fined or fled the country. Then, once again, the Secret Service returned to concentrate mainly on catching counterfeiters and protecting presidents.

Counterfeiting. To protect the nation's money, the Secret Service is charged by law with detecting and suppressing the counterfeiting and forgery of obligations and securities of the United States, including currency, checks, and bonds. See COUNTERFEITING.

In carrying out this major responsibility, the Secret Service is sending more agents undercover to catch counterfeiters. Despite the sharp rise in the production of phony money, particularly through the use of high-speed presses, agents are still able to seize most of the counterfeit bills before they can be passed. Because the leaders of organized crime frequently deal in counterfeit money and forged government checks and bonds, Secret Service agents are assigned to the attorney general's strike forces against organized crime.

Protection of the President. The Secret Service was charged with protecting presidents in 1901, after William McKinley was assassinated. Congress, however, did not vote money for presidential protection until 1906, or make the assignment permanent until 1951. Because the Secret Service protects around the clock, agents followed President Wilson when he was courting Mrs. Edith Bolling Galt, kept vigil with President Coolidge at his dying son's bedside, and traveled through submarine-infested waters with President Franklin D. Roosevelt during World War II. Because the Secret Service guards against kidnapping, as well as assassination and bombing, agents go to school with the president's children, accompany them on their dates, and are never far away on their honeymoons. The agency had successfully protected presidents for six decades until President John F. Kennedy was assassinated in Dallas, Texas, on Nov. 22, 1963. The tragedy marked a turning point for the Secret Service.

An investigation commission headed by Chief Justice Earl Warren concluded that the Secret Service lacked men and facilities to keep up with the increased complexities of protecting presidents; that it provided no guidelines to other agencies to spot potential risks; and that it had no liaison for reporting these risks. Carrying out the Warren Commission's recommendations to modernize the Secret Service, the force was increased in less than a decade from 361 to 1,200 agents, while its budget rose from $7.6 million to $62.6 million. By the early 1970's, the agency had some 60 district offices. Guidelines detailing which "risks" to report, from subversives to mal-

contents, were issued to other agencies, and twenty times more information poured in, all to be fed to the Secret Service's massive new computers. In the new close liaison, intelligence-gathering agents pay daily calls on more than a dozen government offices.

Although the agency keeps many of its protective methods secret, it publicly discloses some procedures. At inaugurations the president is shielded by bullet-proof glass; heavy armor plate in the floor of his parade reviewing stand protects him against planted bombs; and helicopters hover above to make sure the sky is safe. In a motorcade the president rides in a limousine with armor-plated sides and bullet-resistant glass. Agents ride on the car's rear platform and more agents follow, their eyes on the crowd and their compact machine guns within reach. Air-to-ground communications with a helicopter alert the agents to possible roof-top snipers or to disturbances ahead.

Presidential protection is as good as highly trained men and modern equipment can make it. Stressing preventive intelligence, the agency screens some 20,000 potential threats a year, and keeps known revolutionaries and persons with mental or emotional disturbance under surveillance when the president comes to town. Security planning for trips is more detailed than ever, and the Secret Service trains local police in protective techniques. Protection is to be as thorough but as inconspicuous as possible, befitting the leader of a democracy.

Yet, as the Warren Commission recognized, the president's desire for frequent, easy access to the people can complicate the protective task. No agents rode on the corners of the Kennedy car in the Dallas motorcade because the President had asked them not to do so. President Lyndon B. Johnson often strode into milling throngs where agents could not protect him. Even former President Harry Truman chided him for the risks he took. Later, President Johnson admitted to Secret Service agents that he realized he had been inconsiderate.

Sen. Robert F. Kennedy's assassination, on June 5, 1968, the night he won the California Democratic presidential primary, precipitated another major role for the Secret Service. Within hours, President Johnson ordered the Secret Service to protect all presidential candidates. Congress soon passed legislation calling for similar protection. In all, 11 candidates were guarded before the 1968 election. Between elections, the 526 agents who are recruited in order to protect major candidates in election years join in the hunt for counterfeiters. During the 1972 presidential primary elections some editorial writers protested that Secret Service protection put a barrier between candidates and the people, and a congressman protested because he was asked for identification, but the candidates themselves did not protest. They knew how real the danger could be, as evidenced by the fact that on May 15, 1972, Gov. George Wallace of Alabama was shot and critically wounded by a would-be assassin on the eve of his primary victory in Maryland.

To combat "an escalating risk of assassination," the National Commission on the Causes and Prevention of Violence proposed in 1969 that Congress require television stations to grant free time to candidates near election day, in order to reduce exposure to possible snipers' bullets. Because Congress did not act, the Secret Service remains the principal shield when presidents and would-be presidents address the people.

Other Responsibilities. The climate of dissension, of bombings, and of spiraling crime all prompted vast expansion in the 1970's of Secret Service responsibilities and of the uniformed force it supervises.

After attacks on Washington's diplomatic colony had increased more than seven times in the 1960's, President Richard M. Nixon ordered the White House police, supervised by the Secret Service, to guard foreign missions in the nation's capital, as well as the White House and buildings where presidential offices are situated. Legislation in 1970 changed the name of this special force to the Executive Protective Service, officially expanded its duties to cover the 117 embassies, and increased its size from 250 to 850 men and women. Where this force patrols, crime has dropped. One patrol uncovered a bomb outside a Portuguese Embassy office. When they were still known as White House police, these presidential guardians battled Puerto Rican nationalists trying to invade Blair House, the temporary White House, in order to kill President Harry S Truman. In the shootout, one policeman was slain, and two were wounded.

The other uniformed force under Secret Service supervision is the Treasury Security Force, which safeguards the billions of dollars and securities stored in the main Treasury building's underground vaults. This force also guards the Treasury building and its cash room, where many government workers cash paychecks and the public exchanges paper money and coins.

Training. The Secret Service prides itself on being an elite force. Prospective agents must be college graduates, preferably with at least a "B" average and in the top quarter of their class, and they must have completed courses in police science and criminology. Candidates must also be over 21, pass a written Civil Service examination, and undergo a thorough character investigation.

Trainees begin on-the-job training in a designated field office, where they learn to handle weapons, observe court procedures, and meet fellow agents, police, and prosecutors. After a short time, the trainees go to Washington for the seven-week course that is given to all Treasury enforcement agents. Another three-month period of field training is followed by specialized courses at the Secret Service training school. There they learn how to spot forgeries and counterfeits, and how to ward off threats to the president's safety. They are taught fire fighting, defensive tactics, and shooting at night, and are advised on how to proceed when talking to the mentally ill. They practice driving the president's car under varying conditions, and also the technique of clinging to the steps of the "follow-up" car. Later, they may be sent to universities to broaden their background and increase their value to the service. The first women to become special agents were sworn in on Dec. 15, 1971. They are given the same training and the same assignments as the men.

MIRIAM OTTENBERG, *Investigative Reporter*
Washington (D. C.) "Evening Star"
Author of "The Federal Investigators"

Further Reading: Dorman, Michael, *The Secret Service Story* (Delacorte 1967); Neal, Harry E., *The Story of the Secret Service* (Grosset 1971); Reilly, Michael F., and Slocum, William J., *Reilly of the White House* (Simon & Schuster 1947).

SECRET SOCIETIES are associations whose existence, membership, purpose, or ritual is not revealed to nonmembers. The degree of secrecy varies widely, from organizations in which all except ritual is public, to clandestine groups whose very existence is only suspected. Although not universal, secret societies are found in many countries and among both primitive and civilized peoples.

In the ancient world, secret societies were chiefly religious, or at least professedly so, but in ancient times religious and temporal power were so closely associated that it was difficult, if not impossible, to draw a dividing line. There were the mystery cults of Osiris and Serapis in Egypt, of Orpheus and Dionysus in Greece, of Cybele of Phrygia, and of Mithras in Persia. All tended to surround the worship of the gods with elements of secrecy and awe, and helped to keep the ignorant masses in submission to the hierarchy and all that it represented.

In the Middle Ages, secret societies often resorted to repression in their exercise of power. The secret courts of Westphalia were virtually vigilante committees, bound to secrecy by the nature of their objectives. In more recent times, politics, religion, crime, and a desire for fraternal association have all inspired the creation of secret societies.

Secret Societies Among Primitive Peoples. All primitive societies use secret symbolic acts to test the novice psychologically or physically. The societies conduct initiation rites and rituals that stress the traditions of the organization. The ritual is designed to give the initiates a sense of passing from an inferior to a superior status, often with a feeling of psychological rebirth. Secrecy gives both prestige and social solidarity to members, but such secrecy must be enforced, either by oath or by threats of penalties for divulging the secret.

In addition to such rites of passage as the initiation into manhood, which all boys in a primitive society shared and which was involuntary, many preliterate tribes have had secret societies of the more restrictive type. These differ widely in purpose according to region. Among Indians of the northwest coast of North America, membership was limited to men of noble birth. Among the Pueblo Indians, on the other hand, every man belonged to some society. The dances were public, and the societies sought to promote the welfare of the whole community. In Melanesia a man often joined several societies. The emblems gave insurance against theft of property, and membership in some restricted societies raised a person's rank in the tribal councils. Here, as in many societies, members advanced through a series of grades, and only a few achieved the highest levels.

Secret Organizations in Civilized Society. Secret societies may be divided generally into (1) religious groups, (2) political and economic societies, (3) criminal societies, and (4) fraternal organizations.

Religious Groups. Most secret societies are partly religious in origin, but often acquire secular attributes. In western Africa, the high priests of the tribal men's and women's societies are more powerful than political chiefs and in effect control the government. In China in 1900, the Boxers and other secret societies led the Boxer Rebellion against Europeans. The White Lotus Society, founded in the 4th century by a

The Ku Klux Klan, one of the largest secret societies in the United States, marches in Washington, D. C., in 1925.

Buddhist with Manichaean leanings, worked for the downfall of the Sui, Yüan, and Ming dynasties, and was active in the T'ai-p'ing Rebellion in the mid-19th century.

In the Middle East, the Assassins, a secret order of the Ismailite sect of Muslims, attained political power in the late Middle Ages by terrorist killings of their enemies and emerged in the 19th century as the respectable Ismaili sect under Aga Khan I. The Knights Templar, formed as a religious and military order to fight the Saracens, became wealthy through business dealings with the enemy. Similarly, the Spanish Garduña, founded by Christian refugees to drive out the Moors, came to terrorize Christians as well as Moors and Jews for the sake of plunder.

Political and Economic Societies. The secret societies that arose in the 19th and 20th centuries have been chiefly political and benevolent. The struggle for freedom in Italy gave birth to powerful secret organizations that continued to exist after Italian unity had been gained, and they caused considerable anxiety to the authorities. Ireland has also had a large number of secret political societies, including the United Irishmen, the Fenians, and the Irish Republican Army. In Russia, members of a revolutionary society known as the People's Will assassinated Alexander II in 1881, and was an ever-present menace to autocratic government.

Secret societies formed specifically for political action tend to disappear when the crisis ends. In this category would fall the Jacobins of the French Revolution, the Omladina in the Balkans, the Mau Mau and the Red Hand in Africa, and the Land and Liberty in czarist Russia.

In the United States, the Ku Klux Klan, which first flourished in the South after the Civil War, had political objectives, principally to remove Negroes from public offices and to restore white rule. During a revival in the 1920's, the Klan placed greater emphasis on the religious aspect of its philosophy, opposing Catholics, Jews, and the foreign-born. Notorious for its acts of terrorism, the Klan kept its membership secret, and Klansmen appeared in public dressed in full-length white robes and face masks.

The only political party in the United States with a fetish for secrecy was the American party. Its members were popularly known as "Know-Nothings" because they professed ignorance when asked about the organization. The party, rooted in anti-Catholic sentiment, flourished in the 1850's.

Criminal Societies. Secret societies of specific criminal intent have included the Mafia and Camorra in Italy, the Thugs in India, and the Brotherhood of the Beggars in 16th and 17th century England. In the United States a transplanted Mafia and a secret mob known as Murder Incorporated appeared. In the 19th century, the Molly Maguires, a society of the Pennsylvania coal regions that engaged in acts of terrorism and murder, was suppressed by the state and its leaders were executed.

Fraternal Organizations. Certain societies function with a moderate amount of secrecy, usually limited to initiation, special rites, and signs of recognition. These are essentially fraternal organizations that emphasize good fellowship, mutual aid, or philanthropy. Among names well known internationally are the Masonic Order, with origins that traditionally date back at least to the time of King Solomon; the Independent Order of Odd Fellows; the Knights of Columbus; and the Ancient Order of Hibernians.

College fraternities and sororities, most of them designated by Greek letters, are also regarded as secret societies.

See also FRATERNAL SOCIETIES; FRATERNITIES AND SORORITIES; MYSTERY CULTS; and names of individual organizations.

Further · Reading: Butt-Thompson, Frederick W., *West African Secret Societies* (reprint, Argosy 1969); Daraul, Arkon, *A History of Secret Societies* (reprint, Bernhill 1966); MacKenzie, Norman, ed., *Secret Societies* (Holt 1968); Webster, Hutton, *Primitive Secret Societies*, 2d ed. rev. (reprint, Octagon 1968).

Secretary bird (*Sagittarius serpentarius*)

SECRETARY BIRD, a long-legged terrestrial bird of prey found in open grasslands in Africa south of the Sahara. Named for its elongated crest feathers that resemble a bunch of quill pens stuck behind the ears of a 19th century clerk, the secretary bird, *Sagittarius serpentarius*, is the only member of the family Sagittariidae of the order Falconiformes.

The imposing bird stands 4 feet (1.2 meters) tall and has a rather long neck, large wings, and a long narrow tail. Both sexes are pale gray with black wing tips, thighs, tail, and crest. Bare skin about the eyes is orange. The secretary bird feeds on reptiles, small mammals, birds, and insects, which it chases on the ground and kills with repeated blows of its feet. It is adroit at hunting snakes and wards off the strikes of venomous snakes with its wings.

The female alone incubates the two or three reddish white eggs on a bulky platform nest made of sticks and built in a low tree. Both parents feed the downy young.

GEORGE E. WATSON, *Smithsonian Institution*

SECRETIN, si-krēt'ən, is a hormone produced by cells lining the duodenal part of the small intestine when acid contents of the stomach enter the intestine. Secretin enters the bloodstream and is carried to the pancreas, where it stimulates the secretion of pancreatic juice. It also stimulates bile secretion by the liver. See DIGESTION—*The Pancreas*; HORMONE.

SECRETION is the process of active production and discharge of substances by living cells. The process occurs in both plants and animals, and the secreted substances may be gaseous, liquid, or solid. Plants, for example, secrete nectar and a rigid cellulose cell wall, and animals secrete hormones, enzymes, and skeletal parts, such as shells, among other substances.

Many secretions are produced in highly specialized cells grouped into complex structures called glands. Ductless glands that release their product—a hormone—directly into the bloodstream are called *endocrine* glands. *Exocrine* glands release their secretion into special ducts to an internal or external body surface. Among familiar exocrine glands are those that produce milk, tears, sweat, mucus, and various digestive juices.

Secretion is the result of work performed in intracellular metabolism and requires oxygen consumption and the release of carbon dioxide and heat. The nature, quantity, and rate of secretion of all cells is controlled by a complex interrelationship of many factors, including regulatory impulses of the autonomic nervous system and the level of hormones in the bloodstream.

See also ENZYME; GLAND; HORMONE.

SECTIONALISM is a term denoting differences between the North and South before the American Civil War. See UNITED STATES: *Sectional Conflict and Preservation of the Union*.

SECULAR GAMES, Roman games held to celebrate the end of one *saeculum*, or generation, and the beginning of another. The length of a *saeculum* was variously fixed at 100 or 110 years, but the games were actually held at irregular intervals. Under the republic they were known as the Tarentine games, from a place in the Campus Martius, called Tarentum, where they were celebrated. Nothing is known of their origin beyond the fact that they were celebrated in honor of Pluto and Proserpina for the purpose of averting from the state some great calamity.

Under Augustus Caesar they were revived in 17 B. C. with considerable pomp, occupying three days and nights, and were accompanied by sacrifices to Jupiter, Juno, and other superior deities. For this occasion Horace wrote his *Carmen Saeculare* in honor of Apollo and Diana. The secular games were celebrated on numerous subsequent occasions, including centennials of the building of Rome.

SECULARISM is an ethical system founded on the principles of natural morality and independent of revealed religion or supernaturalism. Secularism was first proposed as a formal philosophical system by George J. Holyoake about 1846, in England. Its first postulate is freedom of thought, that is, the right of every man to think for himself. Implied in this postulate as its necessary complement is the right to difference of opinion upon all subjects of thought. This right would be negated without the right to assert that difference. Finally, secularism asserts the right to discuss and debate all vital questions, such as opinions regarding the foundations of moral obligation, the existence of God, the immortality of the soul, and the authority of conscience.

Secularism does not maintain that there is no other good but the good of the present life, but it does maintain that the good of the present life is a real good, and to seek that is good. It aims to find that material condition in which it shall be impossible for man to be deprived or to be poor. In this life there are, it asserts, material agencies that cannot be neglected without folly or hurt, and that it is wisdom, mercy, and duty to attend to them. It does not combat the postulates of Christianity, nor does it say there is no light or guidance save in nature. Rather, it maintains that there is light and guidance in secular truth, whose conditions and sanctions exist independently, act independently, and act forever.

SECURITIES AND EXCHANGE COMMISSION (SEC),

a federal agency created by the U. S. Congress in 1934 to protect investors. It performs legislative and judicial as well as executive functions. The president names the SEC's five commissioners with the advice and consent of the Senate, and he selects one of the five to serve as chairman. No more than three commissioners may be members of the same political party, and the five-year term of one commissioner expires each year.

The creation of the SEC followed two decades of regulation at the state level. State laws were not displaced, but, standing alone, they were considered inadequate. The stock market crash of 1929, the Depression that followed, and the ensuing Senate investigation led to federal regulation of the securities aspects of the economy.

The SEC functions under the provisions of seven statutes, which have civil and criminal sanctions attached:

The Securities Act of 1933 is concerned essentially with the distribution of stocks, bonds, and other securities to the public. The issuing company must first file a registration statement with specified information, including independently certified financial statements. The statement, before it becomes effective, is examined by financial experts, lawyers, accountants, and engineers on the SEC staff. The SEC has no authority under this statute to approve any security or to pass on its merits. It may only assure that the registration statement is accurate and complete. A prospectus containing the basic information about the security must be given to each buyer.

The Securities Exchange Act of 1934 deals with trading in securities after their distribution. All stock exchanges, as well as all brokers or dealers in the so-called over-the-counter market, must register with the SEC. Broad provisions guard against fraud and manipulation. Buying on credit is regulated by the board of governors of the Federal Reserve System, whose margin rules are enforced by the SEC. The disclosure provisions of the 1933 act are supplemented by the 1934 act: certain publicly owned companies must register and file periodic reports; solicitations of proxies to vote their securities are subject to SEC rules; and there are controls with respect to trading by their officers, directors, and principal stockholders.

The Public Utility Holding Company Act of 1935 and the Investment Company Act of 1940 are specialized statutes. Because of evils that a Federal Trade Commission study revealed in the field of electric and gas holding companies, the 1935 act required corporate simplification and geographical integration of each holding company system. The Investment Company Act generally regulates so-called mutual funds and other investment companies. Congress passed the Investment Advisers Act of 1940 to register investment advisers.

The Trust Indenture Act of 1939 assures that bonds offered to the public will have independent corporate trustees to protect and enforce bondholders' rights. Chapter X of the Bankruptcy Act (1938) makes the SEC an impartial adviser to the federal courts in reorganizing publicly held corporations in financial difficulties.

LOUIS LOSS
Harvard University

SECURITIES MARKET, an organized exchange set up to facilitate the purchase and sale of stocks and bonds. Such markets, also known as stock exchanges, provide potential investors with a wide range of information regarding the securities in which they deal, and they enhance the liquidity of stocks and bonds by offering a ready market in corporate and government securities. They also enable the issuers of new securities, whether governments or private corporations, to gain quick access to investment capital. Membership in organized exchanges consists of various kinds of brokers, dealers, and traders, who function in a regulated auction market. See also STOCK EXCHANGE.

SECURITY COUNCIL, United Nations. See UNITED NATIONS—*Covenant and Charter.*

SECURITY-WIDEFIELD is an unincorporated area in central Colorado, in El Paso county. It is adjacent to the southern part of Colorado Springs, just east of the Rocky Mountains, at an altitude of more than 6,000 feet (190 meters). It is a residential community that is divided into two sections, Security and Widefield. Many of the residents work at Fort Carson, an adjacent U. S. Army post. The post was opened in 1942 as Camp Carson. It was made a permanent installation in 1954. Population of Security-Widefield: 15,297.

SEDAINE, sə-dân', **Michel Jean** (1719–1797), French dramatist and librettist. He was born in Paris on July 4, 1719, and worked as a stonemason and architect. Self-educated, he published in 1760 *Recueil de pièces fugitives,* a collection of fables, dialogues, and philosophical letters. His real success, however, was in the theater. His most famous play, *Le Philosophe sans le savoir* (1765), is a domestic drama that followed Diderot's concept of *drame bourgeois,* that is, a play that is neither a comedy nor a tragedy. His other plays include the comedy *La Gageure imprévue* (1768) and the tragedy *Maillard ou Paris sauvé* (1771).

Sedaine, who was elected to the French Academy, also wrote librettos for comic operas, including *Rose et Colas* (1764), *Les Sabots* (1768), and *Richard Coeur de Lion* (1748). He died in Paris on May 17, 1797.

SEDALIA, si-dāl'yə, a city in west central Missouri, the seat of Pettis county, lies in gently rolling farmlands, about 100 miles (160 km) southeast of Kansas City. It is an industrial and agricultural center. Dairy products, eggs, and poultry are processed. Among the products manufactured in the city are glass, textiles, shoes, prefabricated houses, truck bodies, housewares, disinfectants, dog food, and chemicals. Photo processing and steel fabrication are also important.

The Pettis County Museum contains exhibits on military affairs, farm life and agriculture, the sciences, nature, and history, as well as items of general interest, costumes, and Indian artifacts. The Missouri State Fair is held in Sedalia each August.

In 1857, Gen. George R. Smith bought 1,000 acres (405 hectares) of land in Pettis county in anticipation of the railroad's passage through the area. He filed a plat for a city here called Sedville, after his daughter Sarah, whom he called "Sed." In 1860, Smith filed a second plat, including Sedville, and called it Sedalia. The first passenger train arrived in 1861, but before Sedalia could establish a local government, the Civil War broke out and it became a Union military post. It was finally incorporated in 1864, when it was also named county seat in place of Georgetown. Sedalia was chartered as a city in 1889. It is governed by a mayor and a council. Population: 20,927.

SEDAN, sə-dän', is a town in France, in the department of Ardennes, on the east bank of the Meuse River, about 7 miles (11 km) from the Belgian frontier. Until the 15th century it was an ecclesiastical holding. It then passed to the house of La Marck, which began its huge 15th century castle, and the house of La Tour d'Auvergne. It was the birthplace of Henri de la Tour d'Auvergne, Viscount de Turenne. A center of Protestant resistance in the early 17th century, it was finally surrendered to the French crown in 1642. Jean Baptiste Colbert, finance minister under Louis XIV, established a lace factory in Sedan, and textiles are still a mainstay of the economy.

Sedan was the scene of the disastrous French defeat on Sept. 1, 1870, in the Franco-Prussian War. (See SEDAN, BATTLE OF.) In World War I, two U. S. divisions reached the outskirts on Nov. 6, 1918, but a French division was given the honor of liberating it. In World War II its capture in May 1940 inaugurated the German invasion of France. Population: (1968) 22,998.

SEDAN, sə-dan', **Battle of,** in the Franco-Prussian War, fought on Sept. 1, 1870, at Sedan in northeastern France. It was a disaster for the French. The Emperor Napoleon III and his large army surrendered as prisoners. The war ended four months later in a Prussian victory.

After France declared war on July 15, 1870, the French were repulsed in battles along the eastern frontier. One wing of their army, under Marshal Achille F. Bazaine, was driven into the fortress city of Metz. The other wing, led by Marshal Marie E. P. M. de MacMahon, moved to relieve the city.

Trapped in a bend of the Meuse River at Sedan, the French took severe punishment in an all-day battle on September 1. Finally the Emperor, who had been present to inspire the troops, surrendered with 83,000 men. See also FRANCO-PRUSSIAN WAR.

The defeat at Sedan festered in the French national consciousness for many years. In November 1918, near the end of World War I, American troops were halted in a drive on Sedan to permit the French to retake the city and avenge the old disaster.

SEDAN CHAIR, sə-dan', a one-passenger vehicle carried by two bearers that was a fashionable mode of transportation in European cities during the 18th century. It consists of an enclosed chair with side windows and a hinged front door, and is often luxuriously cushioned and decorated. Long horizontal poles extend along its sides and beyond the chair. The bearers stand between the poles—one in the front and one in the back—to carry it. The sedan chair was known in ancient Assyria and Persia and introduced to Europe in the 16th century. It was used mostly in the Orient after the early 19th century.

SEDATIVE, an agent that tends to calm, moderate, or tranquilize, allaying irritability, nervousness, or excitement. Sedatives are classed as central-nervous-system depressants—that is, they reduce the excitability of the central nervous system. Low doses of most sedatives produce relaxation and a lessening of anxiety, while higher doses produce drowsiness. In large or excessive doses, most sedatives produce sleep or even general anesthesia, but in normal doses they do not produce unconsciousness. Among the common sedatives are the barbiturates, including phenobarbital (Luminal), amobarbital (Amytal), and secobarbital (Seconal); and miscellaneous agents such as chloral hydrate, paraldehyde, and the bromides. Alcohol is also a sedative. Many of the barbiturates are known colloquially as "goof balls," "downs," or "yellow jackets." Since the 1960's barbiturate abuse has become an increasingly serious drug-abuse problem.

Sedatives are useful medically in the treatment of conditions in which a slight depression of the central nervous system is desirable. Examples of such conditions include hyperthyroidism, or overactivity of the thyroid gland; motion sickness; and certain heart conditions in which excessive excitement should be avoided. Sedatives are also often useful and are sometimes prescribed, generally for a limited period of time, to help patients affected by severe anxiety, tension, or worry.

Most sedatives are habit-forming and if taken in excessive doses, poisonous. The use of two or more different sedatives at the same time—for example, a barbiturate, or "sleeping pill," along with an alcoholic beverage—is particularly dangerous and can produce serious and possibly fatal consequences. See also BARBITURATE; CHLORAL HYDRATE; DRUG ADDICTION AND ABUSE.

SEDDON, sed'ən, **James Alexander** (1815–1880), American political leader, who was secretary of war for the Confederacy. He was born in Fredericksburg, Va., on July 13, 1815. After graduating from the University of Virginia law school in 1835, he began practice in Richmond. He served in the U. S. House of Representatives (1845–1847 and 1849–1851), where he was associated with John C. Calhoun. As a member of the Virginia delegation to the Washington Peace Conference of February 1861, Seddon upheld the right of peaceful secession. In July of that year he represented Virginia at the provisional Confederate Congress. Confederate President Jefferson Davis appointed him secretary of war in November 1862.

Frail and gaunt, Seddon was described by frontier novelist John Beauchamp Jones as resembling "an exhumed corpse after a month's interment." Nevertheless he proved to be an able secretary. Maintaining good relations with his president and congress, he had more influence on military strategy than any other civilian adviser to Davis. After the fall of Atlanta in 1864, he recommended the utilization of Negro slaves in the Confederate Army. He resigned in January 1865, when the waning military fortunes of the Confederacy prompted congressional demands for cabinet reorganization. Imprisoned by federal authorities at the end of the Civil War, he was soon released and devoted himself to farming at his home near Richmond. Seddon died in Goochland county, Va., on Aug. 19, 1880.

EDWIN A. MILES
University of Houston

SEDDON, sed'ən, **Richard John** (1845–1906), New Zealand political leader, who was prime minister from 1893 to 1906. He was born in Eccleston, Lancashire, England, on June 22, 1845. He went to Australia in 1863 and then to New Zealand in 1866, where he prospered as a storekeeper in the goldfields.

Seddon entered national politics with his election to Parliament in 1879. He became a cabinet member in the Liberal government of John Ballance in 1891 and succeeded him as prime minister two years later. During his administration, Seddon introduced a wide range of social legislation, including women's suffrage and old-age pensions. He encouraged the introduction of state fire insurance and state construction of housing for workers. He sent New Zealand troops to aid Britain during the South African War. Seddon died at sea on June 10, 1906.

SEDER. See PASSOVER.

SEDGE, any of various grasslike plants of the family *Cyperaceae* (sedge family), especially perennial plants of the genus *Carex*. The 700 or more species in the genus *Carex* are widely distributed in temperate and Arctic regions, with a few native to mountains in the tropics. Most frequently sedges inhabit wet marshes and the edges of streams and ponds, where they grow in coarse tufts.

The plants have a three-angled, solid stem and usually narrow, three-ranked leaves, which may have harsh cutting edges. Their flowers are unisexual. The floral axes vary from long slender spikes to short compact spikes, according to species. The fruit is a lens-shaped or three-angled achene surrounded by a papery sheath. A few species are grown as decorative plants, while others are grown as sand or soil binders.

HOWARD W. SWIFT*
New York Botanical Garden

A planting of sedge (Carex aurea stricta).

T. H. EVERETT

SEDGWICK, Adam (1785–1873), English geologist. He was born in Dent, Yorkshire, on March 22, 1785. Graduating from Cambridge in 1808, he became professor of geology there in 1818. He pioneered in developing a scientific basis for the study of geology. His most distinguished work was his investigation of Paleozoic and crystalline rocks in England, Scotland, and Wales. He established an orderly succession for the rocks in the mountains of northern Wales, and with the Scottish geologist Sir Roderick I. Murchison he made an intensive study of the rock formations of Devonshire. This work introduced the terms "Cambrian" and "Devonian" into the geological time scale. Sedgwick died in Cambridge on Jan. 27, 1873.

SEDGWICK, John (1813–1864), American general, who was one of the most reliable Union leaders in the Civil War. He was born at Cornwall, Conn., on Sept. 13, 1813, and graduated from the U. S. Military Academy in 1837. He fought in the Seminole War in Florida (1837–1838) and in the major engagements of the Mexican War (1846–1847), being promoted twice for bravery.

When the Civil War began, he was promoted quickly through the grades of lieutenant colonel and colonel to brigadier general of volunteers. In the Peninsular Campaign (June 1862) he commanded a division, and was wounded at the Battle of Glendale on June 30. He was made a major general on July 4, 1862.

He was wounded at the Battle of Antietam (Sept. 17, 1862). In the Battle of Chancellorsville (May 1–4, 1863), he commanded two corps. While Gen. Joseph Hooker moved to attack the Confederates from the west, Sedgwick was ordered first to hold and then to attack the Confederates' eastern wing at Fredericksburg, but his drive was halted, and he was forced to retreat. Commanding the VI corps, then the largest in the army, Sedgwick arrived on the second day of the Battle of Gettysburg and took part in its later stages.

When Gen. U. S. Grant opened his drive into Virginia in May 1864, Sedgwick led his corps into the Battle of the Wilderness (May 5–6) and repulsed a Confederate attack on the Union right flank. He was killed by a sniper at the Battle of Spotsylvania on May 9.

Sedgwick was a steady rather than a brilliant leader. He was greatly admired by his officers and men, who called him "Uncle John."

SEDGWICK, Robert (c.1613–1656), American colonist and soldier. Born in Woburn, England, he emigrated to Charlestown, Mass., in 1636. One of the first settlers there, he operated a brewery and later helped establish iron works. As a London-trained artilleryman, he assisted in organizing the Military Company of Massachusetts in 1638, and two years later became its captain. Several times a deputy in the General Court, he was elected major general of Massachusetts colony in 1652.

Under orders from Oliver Cromwell, protector of England, Sedgwick organized an expedition against the Dutch of New Netherlands in 1654, but peace interfered, and instead he captured several French ports in the Penobscot region of Maine. In 1655 he participated in a British expedition against Spain in the West Indies, and he was made major general and governor of Jamaica. He died there on May 24, 1656.

SEDIMENTARY ROCKS are rocks formed by the consolidation of ancient sediments over geological time. Most of the sediments derived from the fragmenting or chemical disintegration of older rock materials. The particles were then carried by water, glaciers, or winds and deposited elsewhere. Sedimentary deposits of organic and inorganic materials also accumulated on the floors of former oceans. See ROCKS–*Sedimentary Rocks*.

SEDITION is a common law offense that is less than treason but that may be preliminary to it. In American law, as provided in the Smith Act of 1940, penalties for sedition may be imposed on anyone who knowingly or willfully advocates the duty or propriety of overthrowing or destroying the government of the United States, or of any state or possession thereof, or political subdivision therein, by force or violence. Publication of writing, or participating in the organization of any group, advocating such policies are also offenses under the Smith Act. Treason, by distinction, implies not merely advocacy but an overt act aiming at overthrow of government. In *Pennsylvania* v. *Nelson* (1956) the U. S. Supreme Court decided that Congress in passing the Smith Act intended to occupy the field of sedition, and thus superseded state statutes. See SMITH ACT.

In the United Kingdom, the offense of sedition consists of acts done, words spoken and published, or writings capable of being a libel, with an intention either (1) to bring into hatred or contempt, or to excite disaffection against, the sovereign or the government and constitution of the United Kingdom or either House of Parliament, or the administration of justice; or (2) to excite subjects unlawfully to attempt the alteration of government institutions; or (3) to incite others to criminal disturbance of the peace; or (4) to raise discontent or disaffection or to promote ill-will and hostility between different classes of subjects. The law is set forth in the Criminal Libel Act of 1819 and in Stephen's Digest.

The combination of two or more persons to further a seditious intention constitutes seditious conspiracy. An intention is not seditious if it is to show that the sovereign has been misled or mistaken, or to point out defects in the government or constitution with a view to their reformation; or to advocate the lawful alteration of any matter. Corrupt or malicious motives must not be imputed. The rare prosecutions in the 20th century suggest that an attempt to incite violence against the institutions and laws of the state or a section of the community must be shown, as in *R.* v. *Caunt* (1947), although *R.* v. *Wallace Johnson* (1940) A. C. 231 (Privy Council, Gold Coast) is to the contrary. See also TREASON.

OLIVE M. STONE
Reader in Law, London School of Economics and Political Science

SEDLEY, Sir Charles (1639–1701), English lyric poet and dramatist. He was born in Aylesford, Kent, in March 1639. He attended Oxford but left before graduating to assume his baronetcy. Sedley was one of the most versatile lyric poets of his day, and his love poems remain excellent examples of the art.

Sedley's dramatic works were less successful. His first play, *The Mulberry Garden* (1668), a comedy adapted from Molière's *School for Husbands*, mixed romantic scenes in heroic couplets with realistic ones in prose. His second play was a tragedy, *Antony and Cleopatra* (1677), written in rhymed couplets. Sedley returned to comedy in *Bellamira, or the Mistress* (1687), a prose version of Terence's *Eunuchus. The Grumbler* was published posthumously.

In later life Sedley was a member of Parliament, where he consistently opposed the policies of James II. He died in London on Aug. 20, 1701.

SEDOV, sye-dôf', **Leonid Ivanovich** (1907–　　　), Soviet physicist, who contributed to the development of Sputnik, the first artificial satellite. He was born in Rostov-on-Don on Nov. 14, 1907, graduated from Moscow University in 1930, and received his Ph. D. in 1938. Sedov became a professor at Lomonosov State University in 1937, dean of the school of hydrodynamics in 1951, and head of the Mathematics Institute of the Academy of Sciences in 1953. His research included work on hydrofoil theory, gas dynamics, and the theory of flareups of novae and supernovae. He also made studies of interplanetary travel. He was head of the Soviet delegation at several international astronautical congresses and served as president of the International Astronautic Federation.

SEDUCTION is an act that may be either a crime or a civil injury (tort). Because the elements of each kind of seduction vary according to the jurisdiction, a general definition cannot be universally applicable. Seduction was not a crime at common law, but it is a statutory offense in most states of the United States.

The *crime* may be broadly described as the obtaining by a man of illicit sexual intercourse with a woman through a promise of marriage or by other means of persuasion. Consent is an essential element of seduction, and the law usually specifies that consent must have been obtained by an unconditional promise of marriage. Although such a promise need not be binding, if the victim believes in it and consents in reliance on it, the law applies insofar as legal action against the seducer is concerned. Thus a married man may be guilty of seduction—if not adultery—if his victim is unaware of his marital condition. The previous chaste character of the injured woman is generally a prerequisite, though this does not necessarily connote virginity, because a widow or divorcee can be the victim of seduction. In most states, marriage of the parties operates to bar criminal prosecution.

The *civil injury*, in common law, provided liability for the seduction of a daughter or servant. Because the basis of the injury was considered to be the immediate and possibly eventual loss of services, the cause of the action belonged to the father or master.

In many states the common-law action has been altered and enlarged so that the seduced female herself may recover damages. The essential factors to be proved in a civil action for seduction are enticement or persuasion resulting in sexual intercourse, and the chastity of the victim at the time of the offense. A woman who marries her seducer cannot, as a general rule, recover damages for the seduction.

Seduction can be committed only against an unmarried woman. Homosexual intercourse with a minor would be sodomy, pederasty, or some other statutory crime, rather than seduction.

RICHARD L. HIRSHBERG
Attorney at Law

SEDUM, sē′dəm, a genus of plants of the family Crassulaceae. There are about 350 species in the genus, with about 30 of them occurring wild in the United States and Canada. Most sedums are perennial plants that inhabit the temperate and colder regions of the Northern Hemisphere. Some sedums are cultivated for their great diversity of foliage or for their showy clusters of pink, white, yellow, or reddish purple flowers. They are preeminently useful for rock gardens and for cultivation in poor soil because they are remarkably hardy under adverse conditions. Some sedums are creeping plants that prefer barren rocks and spread luxuriantly over them, thus earning their common name of stonecrop, whereas others grow erect. The sedums are easily propagated by seeds or offshoots, and they have great vitality.

Sedum acre, called the wall pepper, is a common creeping plant covered with yellow starlike flowers; it is fond of sunny, rocky places. One of the handsomest species is the old-fashioned border plant, *S. spectabile,* which has upright stems and broad clusters of purple flowers. *S. telephiodes* and *S. roseum* grow in great masses on mountain ledges, and the latter is notable for its rose-scented roots. *S. telephium* is the orpine or live-forever, so called because a cut branch will grow outdoors and perhaps bloom. See also ORPINE.

SEE, Thomas Jefferson Jackson (1866–1962), American astronomer. See was born near Montgomery City, Mo., on Feb. 19, 1866. After graduating from the University of Missouri in 1889, he went to Germany to study at the University of Berlin, obtaining his doctorate in 1892. Returning to the United States, he participated in the organization of the astronomy department of the University of Chicago and the establishment of Yerkes Observatory at Williams Bay, Wis. After two years at the Lowell Observatory in Flagstaff, Ariz., he joined the staff of the U. S. Naval Observatory in 1899. In 1903 he was placed in charge of the Mare Island Chronometer and Time Station off the coast of California, where he remained until his retirement. See died in Oakland, Calif., on July 4, 1962.

Although he had an unremarkable career and made no important contributions to science, See is remembered for his numerous controversial papers on astronomical subjects and his unfailing knack for espousing the discredited side of scientific theories. Thus among his publications were *Discovery That Aether Waves Are the Cause of Universal Gravitation* (1927), *Nonsensical Theory of Expanding Universe Demolished* (1940), *All the Disturbances of the Moon's Motion Fully Explained* (1942), and *Invariability of Sidereal Day* (1949–1950). An early admirer, William Larkin Webb, wrote a biography in 1913 titled *Brief Biography and Popular Account of the Unparalleled Discoveries of T. J. J. See.*

SIMONE D. GOSSNER, *Editor, Time-Life Books*

SEE, an episcopal diocese. The term is derived from Latin *sedes,* meaning "chair." It refers most properly to the throne of the bishop, which came to symbolize his office, and by extension it means the territory over which he presides. "See city" is often used to refer to the center of a bishop's activity and the place in which the bishop's cathedral and throne are physically located. See also HOLY SEE.

SEEBECK, zā′bek, **Thomas Johann** (1770–1831), German physicist who in 1821 made the first discovery of a thermoelectric effect. Seebeck was born in Reval (now Tallin, Estonian SSR) on April 9, 1770. He studied at Berlin and Göttingen and became a friend of Goethe, with whom he worked on a theory of color and the effect of colored light. Also, Seebeck built a polariscope and studied the rotational effect of sugar solutions on plane-polarized light. He became a member of the Berlin Academy in 1818 and three years later discovered the thermoelectric effect that is now called the Seebeck effect in his honor. He also devised a thermocouple and used it to measure temperature. Seebeck died in Berlin on Dec. 10, 1831.

See also THERMOELECTRICITY.

SEEBECK EFFECT, zā′bek, a thermoelectric effect in a closed circuit that includes two conductors made of different metals and two junctions at different temperatures. It was discovered by Thomas J. Seebeck in 1821. See also THERMOELECTRICITY.

SEEBOHM, sē′bōm, **Frederic** (1833–1912), English lawyer and economic historian. Born in Bradford on Nov. 23, 1833, he was educated at the Bootham School in York. He read law in London, and was called to the bar in 1856. Although he was active in local government and business, his greatest contribution was in economic history. He produced important studies: *The English Village Community* (1883), which made English history less provincial and interpreted it in the light of general economic evolution; *The Tribal System in Wales* (1895), which gave as realistic a picture of tribal customs as the former work had done in surveying the open field system; and *Tribal Custom in Anglo Saxon Law* (1902), which provided a study of the tribal solidarity of kindred. He died in Hitchin, England, on Feb. 6, 1912.

SEECKT, zākt, **Hans von** (1866–1936), German general, who secretly revived the German army after World War I. He was born at Schleswig, Germany, on April 22, 1866, and joined the army in 1885. From 1899, he served on the general staff, the core of the German military machine. In World War I, he was chief of staff of armies in Poland and Serbia and of the Turkish army.

Some terms of the Treaty of Versailles were drawn to prevent the resurgence of a militarily powerful Germany that might start a war of revenge. The German general staff was abolished, and the army was limited to 100,000 men. Tanks, heavy artillery, and aircraft were prohibited.

Seeckt was named commander in chief of this shadow army. He secretly trained the small officer corps in the theories of duties beyond their ranks, ensuring that in another war they could re-create the general staff. He emphasized the principle of close coordination of all branches of the armed forces, including the air force, to create mobile power. He was certain that men and materiel would eventually be available.

Seeckt was dismissed in 1926 after a dispute with President Paul von Hindenburg, but he had formed the nucleus of an army that Adolf Hitler found ready to his hand when he came to power in 1933. Seeckt was a military adviser to Chiang Kai-shek in China in 1934 and 1935. He died in Berlin on Dec. 27, 1936.

SEED, the reproductive structure of seed plants. A typical seed consists of the *embryo*, or rudimentary plant; *endosperm*, or stored food; and the coats that form the protective layers on the surface. The embryo is the most essential part of the seed, consisting of the *plumule*, or *epicotyl*, that form the rudimentary stem; the *cotyledon* or *cotyledons* that are the seed leaves; the *hypocotyl*, or portion connecting the cotyledons; and the *radicle*, or rudimentary root. The embryo varies greatly in size and form in different seeds. In the mature bean seed, for example, the embryo fills the seed, while in the orchids or American holly the embryo is just a mass of undifferentiated cells at the time of seed maturity. At germination, or sprouting, the plumule develops into the shoot and the radicle into the root. The cotyledons may or may not appear above ground. In some cases, they function as real leaves, turning green and carrying on photosynthesis for a while. In the hypocotyl region of the embryo axis, the transition from stem to root tissues of the new plant takes place.

Seed formation usually follows fertilization of the egg nucleus of the ovule by a male nucleus from the germinating pollen grain. The fertilized ovule then develops into the embryo of the seed. The endosperm, or stored food for the young embryo, develops after the second male nucleus from the pollen tube conjugates with two other nuclei in the embryo sac. This double fertilization occurs in most angiosperms, but the resulting endosperm is not always present in the mature seed, since it may be used up by the developing embryo, as in the case of many legumes. In the gymnosperms, the endosperm tissue is entirely gametophytic, being produced by the ovule without any fertilization.

Although seed formation is usually dependent upon a fertilization process, seeds may be formed from certain parts of the ovary normally considered as purely vegetative. Such seeds, containing both embryo and endosperm, are formed by the dandelion, for example. The development of seeds without prior fertilization is known as *apomixis*.

Seeds, the ripened ovules of flowers, are usually contained in fruits that develop from ovaries. If the fruits are dry and indehiscent, they may be called seeds. Such fruits are the *caryopsis*, or grain, the *achene*, characteristic of Compositae; the *schizocarp*, illustrated by Umbelliferae; and the *nut*.

Food stored in seeds is a source of energy for the germination and early development of the seedling, but it is also of the utmost importance for the nutrition of man and other animals. Seeds are rich sources of carbohydrates, fats, and proteins as well as of mineral matter and other accessory foods. Many valuable ingredients of medicines are also found in some seeds.

Dispersal of Seeds. Seed dispersal is of prime importance for the survival and distribution of plants over the surface of the earth. Many seeds have become adapted to dispersal by various agents, including wind, water, birds, fur-bearing animals, and man.

The wind is one of the principal agents for the dispersal of seeds. A large number of plants rely entirely on the small size of the seed and its light weight for distribution. Among these are orchids, poppies, and gentians, which produce capsules opening in various ways to expose the minute seeds within them to the wind. Other seeds or fruits have developed special structures to facilitate dispersal by wind. Winged seeds are characteristic of lily, tulip, and pine, for example, and maple and elm are among those plants with winged fruits. Many grasses also have wings on specialized coverings of the seeds. The so-called parachute seedpod of *Aristolochia*, a native of the Philippines, represents an extreme adaptation for dispersal by wind. When its seeds are ripe, the pods split to form six parts suspended by a thread attached to the stem of the vine. The split pod hangs upside down on the vine, and the seeds are shaken out by the wind. Many members of the family Compositae, such as the dandelion, have seeds with a tuft of fine hairs that facilitate wind dispersal.

Water may play an important part in the transportation of seeds for long distances. The distribution of the coconut palm over the surface of the earth, for example, is thought to be due in part to the germination of ocean-borne nuts that drifted or were carried by the current from their original location. Mature seeds of aquatic plants such as water lilies are covered with a gelatinous substance that gives buoyancy for their flotation away from the parent plant.

Birds are especially important in the dispersal of seeds associated with juicy pulp, such as berries and cherry. Seeds carried by fur-bearing animals are principally those of grasses or of weeds equipped with spines, such as cocklebur, tick trefoils, and sandburs. Human beings also carry such seeds on their socks or other parts of their clothing. Ants have been observed to disseminate the seeds of *Trillium* and bloodroot.

Many plant families do not depend on any special agent but have developed mechanical devices for ejection of their seeds. Pressures and tensions develop in the mature fruits, throwing the seeds out. In the legume family, pods may twist into spirals, while touch-me-not pods simply collapse. In violets, the pods split into three valves that press on the enclosed seeds to release them. In the wood sorrels, the outer seed coats turn inside out with enough pressure to cast the enclosed seeds for some distance. In witch hazel, the inner, woody layer of the mature, drying seed capsule curves inward, producing pressure that is enough to shoot the seeds out of the capsule with some force.

Germination. Seedsmen, nurserymen, and home gardeners have all experienced difficulty at one time or another in the germination of seeds. If the seeds possess a dormant embryo, or impermeable seed coats, as is the case of many trees and shrubs, there are very definite and simple procedures that may be used to bring about germination. If, on the other hand, the embryos are not dormant, but the seeds still fail to germinate under ordinary conditions, some other treatment must be given. Some common seeds have special germination requirements.

Certain specific temperature conditions are necessary for the germination of many forms. For example, wild columbine seeds germinate very poorly at a constant temperature as high as 77° F (25° C) but give excellent germination if the daily temperature alternates between 59° and 77° F (15°–25° C). Annual delphinium or larkspur seeds show very poor seedling production at temperatures about 59° F (15° C) but can be induced to germinate at temperatures as high as 80° F (27° C) by pretreatment on a moist medium for one, two, or three weeks at temperatures of

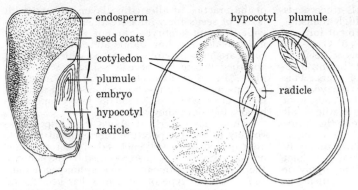

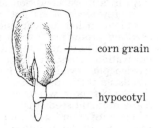

ANATOMY OF CORN AND BEAN SEED

endosperm
seed coats
cotyledon
plumule
embryo
hypocotyl
radicle

hypocotyl   plumule
radicle

STAGES IN GERMINATION OF A CORN SEED

corn grain

hypocotyl

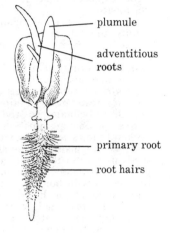

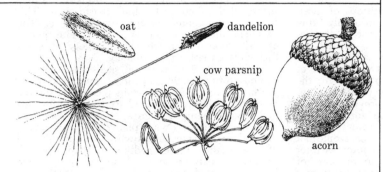

SOME DRY INDEHISCENT FRUITS MAY BE CALLED SEEDS

oat
dandelion
cow parsnip
acorn

plumule

adventitious roots

primary root

root hairs

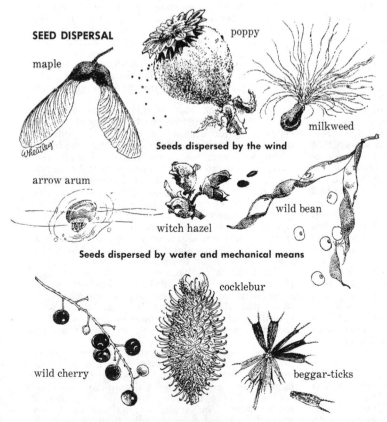

SEED DISPERSAL

maple

poppy

milkweed

Seeds dispersed by the wind

arrow arum

witch hazel

wild bean

Seeds dispersed by water and mechanical means

cocklebur

wild cherry

beggar-ticks

Seeds dispersed by birds and mammals

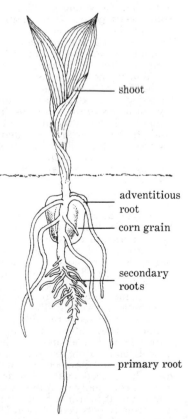

shoot

adventitious root

corn grain

secondary roots

primary root

about 50° or 60° F (10° or 15° C). Lettuce seeds can also be made to germinate at high temperatures normally inhibitive by pretreatment for four days in a moist condition at 40° F (5° C).

Many weed seeds not only show a delay in germination but are capable of distributing their seedling production over a period of years. This fact is demonstrated repeatedly by the years of cultivation necessary to get rid of weeds in a garden plot, even if care is taken to eradicate all weeds as they appear and to prevent the introduction of new weed seeds. The soil contains many dormant seeds that produce plants promptly when cultivation, excavation, or erosion give them the moisture, temperature, and oxygen supply or light exposure that is required for them to germinate.

Dormancy. Seed dormancy is a term used to signify the failure of viable seeds to germinate when they are placed under conditions of moisture and temperature that would ordinarily bring about sprouting. This is in contrast to the so-called dormancy of the dry, resting seed. The term *afterripening* signifies the preparation of the seed for resumption of growth. Dormancy is of definite advantage to the continuance of the species in that germination under conditions unfavorable for seedling survival is prevented. This is true for many temperate-zone forms whose seeds mature in the autumn. If germination took place immediately, the young seedlings would not be able to withstand the rigorous winter weather and would all be killed. Again, in the case of certain desert annuals, dormancy at maturity prevents germination at the close of a rainy growing season and the beginning of a dry season, conditions that the young seedlings could not survive. Some seeds possess impermeable seed coats that prevent their germination for years or even for centuries. This feature characterizes many of the legumes, as well as some other forms, and permits their distribution in time instead of space. In addition to the numerous seeds that are dormant in the dry state, there are many that have a prolonged primary dormancy or an induced secondary dormancy in the wet state. The most common example of the latter are weed seeds of various kinds that remain ungerminated and fully viable for years in the soil. Experiment has shown that some seeds fully imbibed with water live for as long as 60 years buried in the soil. This has also been demonstrated in many cases where unusual plants have appeared on excavated or bombed sites.

A type of low intensity dormancy is exhibited by many seeds at maturity but which disappears after a period of dry storage. This is characteristic of many grains and flower seeds and of some vegetable seeds, notably lettuce.

It has long been known that certain seeds, especially of the legume family, possess coats that prevent the absorption of the water necessary for germination. Among the known methods for making the coats permeable are shaking or mechanical scarification, soaking in concentrated sulphuric acid or alcohol, and hot water or other special temperature treatments.

Many plants, especially those of the temperate zone, have seeds with dormant embryos. The method commonly used to break this dormancy is pretreatment in a moist medium at low temperature, usually between 32° and 50° F (0°–10° C). This process has been used by nurserymen for a long time, and it is termed *stratification* because of the practice of alternating layers of sand with layers of seeds for winter treatment. Some seeds with dormant embryos do not afterripen in a moist medium at low temperatures because their coats are impermeable to water, which must be absorbed before the necessary changes can take place. In these cases, it is essential to make the coat permeable by mechanical or chemical treatment, after which a period at low temperature breaks the dormancy.

The seeds described above that respond favorably to low temperature pretreatment become afterripened while still enclosed in the seed coats, and once growth has been resumed by the embryo, the green plant appears above ground in a short time. Another type of dormancy has been found in which the seed germinates to form a root without any pretreatment, but once the root is formed, low temperature must be given to break the dormancy of the shoot or the bud that forms it. This has been designated as *epicotyl dormancy*. The two-year lilies, the tree peony, and several species of *Viburnum* belong in this category of seeds that undergo epicotyl dormancy.

When all the coats of seeds of some rosaceous forms, such as peach, apple, and hawthorn, are removed, a certain percentage of the embryos, which require cold stratification for normal development, will grow at greenhouse temperatures to form dwarf plants. In such physiological dwarfs, normal growth is readily initiated after exposure of the seedling to a cold period. Finally, an extreme type of dormancy is shown by seeds of such forms as *Convallaria*, *Smilacina*, and *Trillium*. These require pretreatment at low temperature to break the dormancy of the root, a period at high temperature to permit the root to grow, another period at low temperature to break epicotyl dormancy, and a second period at high temperature to permit the growth of the afterripened epicotyl to form a green shoot.

The causes of physiological dormancy are not known, though many of the chemical and physical changes that accompany the breaking of dormancy are known.

Storage. Seed storage methods are very important in the maintenance of viability of all seed types. The performance of any seed depends less upon its actual age than upon the conditions under which it has been stored. Experiments have demonstrated that temperature and moisture are of vital importance. It has been known for a long time that low temperature is more desirable than higher temperature, but temperatures above freezing, especially between 40° F (5° C) and freezing, have been considered adequate. The truth is, however, that a very moist atmosphere at 40° F often brings about more rapid deterioration than ordinary room temperature. This emphasizes the fact that a cool place is not always the best place to store seeds. Evidence has shown the superiority of below-freezing temperatures to those just above freezing for maintaining seed viability. This difference becomes significant as the storage period lengthens to more than ten years.

Seeds with high moisture content deteriorate more rapidly than those with low moisture, provided they will tolerate drying. Sealed containers are beneficial to maintain low moisture content. There is more rapid degeneration of seeds stored in sealed containers that are opened and sealed repeatedly than of seeds in sealed containers that are never opened from the time of storage to the time of testing. Under adverse temperature and humidity conditions, there may be a favorable effect of reduced oxygen supply.

Some seeds are short-lived by virtue of the fact that they do not tolerate drying. Among these are citrus seeds and those of many tropical plants. Even these may have the life-span extended by adjustment of moisture content and storage at a temperature of about 40° F (5° C).

Testing. Seed testing and analysis of agricultural and vegetable seeds to determine, as nearly as possible, the actual planting value of the seed lot and to be sure of the purity of the seeds have become general practice. Seed laws in many parts of the world specify certain standards that must be met before seeds can be offered for sale. This has resulted in the development of special sampling and testing equipment and prescribed, detailed methods for testing the germination and purity of all types of commercial seeds. Important parts of this testing deal with an examination of the seed sample for noxious-weed content and for other impurities, with the origin of the seeds, and with trueness of variety. Possible pathological conditions are also tested, and procedures are being developed to test the seeds as hosts and carriers of disease organisms. Progress has been made in the standardization of national and international rules for seed testing in the interest of uniformity and of world trade.

In order to get a true index of the planting quality of seeds, their germination capacity must be tested under special conditions required by that seed. In most cases the tests are very simple, since the seeds germinate easily. However, light is required for germination of many grasses and some vegetable seeds, and potassium nitrate may be substituted for light requirement in some cases. Prechilling moist seeds at low temperature, high temperature treatment, combinations of low and high temperatures in daily alternations, mechanical abrasion of the seed coat, soaking in water, and predrying are some of the special procedures used to test these seeds.

In addition to the microscopic examination of seeds for purity and identification, sometimes other methods have to be used to determine variety. For example, Italian ryegrass can be distinguished from perennial ryegrass by a fluorescence examination of the roots under ultraviolet light. Italian ryegrass roots fluoresce, while the others do not.

SEED INDUSTRY

The seed industry comprises the development, production, collection, cleaning, packaging, marketing, and shipping of seeds, which are a vital part of the economy of the world. The functioning of this very complex and highly important industry requires special services of geneticists and plant breeders, who work to develop superior seeds; physiologists, who investigate the nutrition and other growth characteristics of the plant; plant pathologists, who are constantly working on disease problems; growers, who must learn the highly specialized techniques of seed production; and equipment manufacturers, who must supply the apparatus and materials necessary for the different phases of the industry.

Hybrid corn is an example of one of the most important of all crop developments. Geneticists have greatly improved a plant that has been in use for thousands of years by the establishment of pure lines and the subsequent hybridization of these lines to produce seeds that possess hybrid vigor manifested in the plants grown from them. The parent plants are grown side by side in large, isolated fields and are pollinated by wind. Only pollen from the male parent must be allowed to fall on the silks of the female parent, and possible fertilization by any other male must be prevented, a costly expense. It should also be pointed out that a double cross is used in hybrid corn seed production. The first cross is between two inbred lines, and the second involves the crosses of these inbreds. This process must be repeated each year. The superiority of hybrid seed corn is best demonstrated by the rapid rise in its use from a small beginning in 1933. Now, the great majority, and in some areas 100% of the corn acreage in the United States is planted with hybrid seed. The production and sale of hybrid corn seed is an important industry in the United States and in other nations. Since the 1940's hybrid corn has been introduced into many countries. Researchers are still scouting regions of Central and South America for promising corn varieties, hoping to develop still better strains of corn.

In addition to the seeds grown for feed, for man, or for livestock, there is a large and thriving flower seed industry. The importance of tree seeds, also, should not be overlooked. They are required for reforestation of lands denuded by erosion, burning, or cutting and are essential in conservation and timber production and the maintenance of a food supply for wildlife.

LELA V. BARTON[*]
Boyce Thompson Institute for Plant Research

Further Reading: Barton, Lela V., *Bibliography of Seeds* (Columbia Univ. Press 1967).

SEED FERN, any of an order, Cycadofilicales, of extinct treelike or vinelike plants that resembled ferns but reproduced through seeds. Also known as *pteridosperms*, they became extinct about 100 million years ago.

SEED PLANTS are plants that bear seeds. There are two major types of living seed plants: gymnosperms, in which the seed is naked, and angiosperms, in which the seed is enclosed in an ovary. See GYMNOSPERM; PLANTS AND PLANT SCIENCE.

SEEGER, Alan (1888–1916), American poet. Seeger was born in New York City on June 22, 1888. After graduating from Harvard University in 1910, he did desultory writing, both in prose and poetry. Although he rebelled against many literary conventions, he employed traditional verse forms. In 1912 he went to live in Paris, where he continued his writing and attended classes in painting. At the outbreak of World War I in 1914, he enlisted in the French Foreign Legion as a private. Despite his intense individualism, he was an excellent soldier and won the Croix de Guerre and the Médaille Militaire. He was killed in action at Belloy-en-Santerre, France, on July 4, 1916.

Most of Seeger's better-known poems were inspired by the war. These include his prophetic *I Have a Rendezvous with Death*, which was first published after he had been killed in battle. His *Collected Poems*, with sonnets as well as poems on war themes, was published in 1916. His *Letters and Diary* appeared in 1917.

Pete Seeger, a leading American folksinger, also composed folk songs and collected old songs and ballads.

SEEGER, Pete (1919–   ), American folksinger, folklorist, and composer, who was one of the leaders of the folk-music revival in the United States in the 1940's and 1950's. He was born in New York City on May 3, 1919. He left Harvard after two years to learn folk music at its source by traveling through the South and Southwest and in Mexico.

Seeger was a founding member of the Almanac Singers in 1940, and in 1941–1942 he toured with the pioneering American folksinger Woody Guthrie. In 1948, Seeger joined the Weavers, a vocal group that made some of the first folk recordings to become widely popular. From 1957 he was a solo performer, and his reedy baritone voice and five-string banjo were heard on college campuses, at folk-music concerts and festivals, and on radio and television. With his relaxed, intimate style, he usually succeeded in getting all types of audiences to sing along with him.

Seeger wrote such successful songs as *Where Have All the Flowers Gone?* (with Lee Hays), *If I Had a Hammer*, and, in collaboration with the Weavers, *Kisses Sweeter Than Wine*. Among his albums of recordings are *Frontier Ballads*, children's songs, work songs, and African freedom songs. His book of ballads and autobiography, *The Incompleat Folksinger*, was published in 1972.

SEEING EYE, the trademark of Seeing Eye, Inc., of Morristown, N. J., for guide dogs trained to lead blind people. Besides Seeing Eye, Inc., several other organizations around the world train guide dogs for the blind. In the United States, the principal organizations include Guiding Eyes for the Blind, Yorktown Heights, N. Y.; Guide Dogs for the Blind, San Rafael, Calif.; and Leader Dogs for the Blind, Rochester, Mich.

The main qualities looked for in potential guide dogs are intelligence, docility, tractability, eagerness to please, and a calm, sweet disposition. At Guiding Eyes for the Blind, which maintains its own breeding program, the breeds most often found with these qualities are Labrador and golden retrievers. Other breeds used include German shepherds and, to a lesser extent, smooth-haired collies, bouviers des flandres, and boxers.

Puppies selected for training as guide dogs are socialized by raising them in foster homes rather than in kennels. When the dog is about a year old, it begins extensive training in a school for guide dogs. There it learns the basic obedience commands: "come," "sit," "down," and "stay." It then is trained in a harness to lead its owner rather than to walk in the "heel" position. The harness enables the dog's owner to sense its movements. The dog learns to stop at curbs and stairways, to avoid obstacles (including overhead obstacles), to cross busy streets, to move through crowded stores, and to travel on buses or other means of public transportation. In all these situations the dog is taught to avoid meandering and to take the initiative in avoiding possible hazards rather than merely to obey specific commands.

To learn how to use a guide dog, a blind person typically spends about a month at the guide-dog school learning both how to direct and how to follow the lead of the dog. Most of the training is "on location" on town and city streets and shopping centers and stores.

Dogs were occasionally used as guides for the blind at least as early as the 17th century. The use of a guide harness, which links man and dog much more closely than does a leash, was first proposed by an Austrian clergyman, Johann W. Klein, in *Textbook for Teaching the Blind* (1819).

Well-trained dogs can help blind people find their way safely through hazardous areas such as train stations.

SEERSUCKER is a cloth with puckered stripes produced by slack-tension weaving. Every other warp yarn is held under normal tension during the weaving, but the intervening yarns are slack. When the filling yarns are woven into place, the flat yarns pucker, while the yarns under normal tension remain straight. The resulting cloth has a pattern of alternating puckered and flat stripes, with the stripes in the warp direction.

SEFERIS, sə-fer'is, **George,** pen name of the Greek poet and diplomat Georgios Seferiades (1900–1971). His verse captures the classical character of modern Greece and the tragic experience of its people in the 20th century. Seferis was the first Greek man of letters to win the Nobel Prize for literature (1963). He also served his country in diplomatic posts, including those of ambassador to Lebanon, Syria, Iraq, Jordan, and Britain, and the United Nations.

Life. Georgios Seferiades was born of Greek parents in Smyrna (now İzmir), Turkey, on Feb. 29, 1900. His childhood in that largely Greek city on the Aegean Sea became a major source of inspiration in his later years, and it was there that he wrote his first poetry at the age of 14. He left Smyrna at the beginning of World War I to continue his education in Athens, graduating in 1917 from the First Classical Gymnasium.

Seferis studied law and literature at the University of Paris from 1918 to 1924. During this period he came to know French poetry intimately, began to compose some of the poems published in his first volume, and earned a degree in law. After a visit to London in 1924–1925 to perfect his English, Seferis returned to Athens to enter the Greek foreign service. He remained a career diplomat until his retirement in 1962, serving in London, Cairo, Johannesburg, Pretoria, Ankara, and Beirut, among other foreign posts. His final diplomatic appointments were ambassador to the United Nations (1956–1957) and ambassador to Britain (1957–1962). His work as a diplomat became especially significant during the Cyprus crisis of the 1950's, when he contributed tact and wisdom to the negotiations that resulted in the London Agreement (1959) making Cyprus independent of British rule.

Seferis married Maria Zannou in 1941. After his retirement, he and his wife lived in Athens, where he died on Sept. 20, 1971.

Writings. Seferis' first volume of poems, *Strophe* (1931), demonstrated that an original voice had come into Greek letters, a voice that was entirely contemporary, yet rich in echoes from the long Greek poetic tradition that began with Homer. In the six volumes that followed, *E Sterna* (1932), *Mythistorema* (1935), *Gymnopaidia* (1936), *Tetradio Gymnasmaton* (1940), *Emerologio Katastromatos I* (1940), and *Emerologio Katastromatos II* (1944), the poet perfected a sparse yet subtle style that remained both individual and influential. The younger generation of poets in Greece showed a great debt to Seferis' work.

Seferis also extended the range of his themes in these six volumes, creating out of personal materials a profound and moving portrait of his nation's mood before and during World War II. His two later volumes, *Kichle* (1947) and *Emerologio Katastromatos III* (1955), reveal a mature poet of genius surveying the destiny of his people, and of modern man generally, with unique compassion and understanding.

Seferis also earned a reputation as a distinguished critic and translator. He played a crucial role in introducing to his countrymen such major poets as Ezra Pound and T. S. Eliot, and he commented with insight on the principal writers in his own tradition.

EDMUND KEELEY
*Coeditor and Translator of
"George Seferis: Collected Poems"*

SEGESTA, sē-jes'tə, was an ancient city in northwest Sicily, near the modern town of Calatafimi. Its extensive remains include an unfinished temple dating from the 5th century B. C., walls, houses, a temple of Demeter, a 3d century theater, and baths.

Although not Greeks, the Segestans were Hellenized by the 5th century. Athens tried to aid the city in its quarrel with Selinus, the traditional enemy of Segesta, in 415 but was badly defeated. Segesta became allied with Carthage after the Carthaginians sacked Selinus in 409. Agathocles, tyrant of Syracuse, took the city in 307 and killed many of the inhabitants, but Segesta recovered and continued as an ally of Carthage. In 262 during the First Punic War, Segesta turned on Carthage and surrendered to Rome. After raids by the Saracens, the city was abandoned in the 10th century A. D.

SEGHERS, zā'gərs, **Hercules Pietersz** (1589/1590–?1638), Dutch landscape painter and etcher, who was the first to print intaglio plates in color. It is thought that he was born in Haarlem. He studied under the Flemish landscape painter Coninxloo in Amsterdam and by 1612 was a member of the Haarlem guild. Between 1614 and 1631 he lived in Amsterdam. From the subject matter of his work—predominantly mountains—it is thought that he may have traveled during this time through the Alps to Italy. Later records place him in Utrecht and then in The Hague, where he was last heard of in 1633. It is assumed that he died there in the late 1630's.

Seghers' known work includes a number of etchings and four or five signed paintings, none of which is dated. The latter are chiefly awe-inspiring mountain landscapes, combining dark colors with broad streaks of golden light, such as *Landscape* (Uffizi, Florence). As an etcher, Seghers not only printed intaglio plates in color but experimented with different colored papers, using light lines on a dark ground and sometimes tinting his prints by hand.

Further Reading: Collins, Leo C., *Hercules Seghers* (Univ. of Chicago Press 1953).

SEGNI, se'nyē, **Antonio** (1891–1972), prime minister and president of Italy. He was born in Sassari, Sardinia, on Feb. 2, 1891. He graduated from the University of Rome in 1913 and then served in World War I. He subsequently taught law at the universities of Perugia (1920–1925), Cagliari (1925–1929), Pavia (1929–1931), Sassari (1931–1954), and Rome (1954–1955).

Segni entered politics in 1919 as an antifascist member of the Italian Popular party, the predecessor of the Christian Democratic party. After World War II, Segni was elected to the Constituent Assembly that drafted the Italian constitution, and in 1948 he became a member of the Chamber of Deputies. While minister of agriculture (1946–1951), he played a prominent part in obtaining land-reform legislation.

After serving as minister of public information in 1954, Segni became prime minister in a coalition government that ruled (1955–1957) without the support of the left. Strongly pro-Western, Segni served for a second time as prime minister in 1959–1960 and was foreign minister in 1960–1962. He was president of Italy from 1962 to 1964, when he resigned after suffering a stroke. He died in Rome on Dec. 1, 1972.

SEGO LILY, sē′gō, is the common name for the perennial herb *Calochortus nuttallii*, a member of the lily family found most widely in the United States from the Dakotas and Nebraska to California and New Mexico. Like true lilies, the sego lily grows from an underground bulb. Its stiff, erect stem reaches a height of 12 to 24 inches (30–61 cm), with ashy green leaves. The petals, one to two inches (25–51 mm) long, are exquisitely beautiful in their wide range of colors: blue, pink, lilac, yellow, and white. The sego lily is the state flower of Utah.

SEGOVIA, sə-gō′vē-ə, **Andrés** (1893–), Spanish guitarist, who was a leading figure in the revival of interest in the classical guitar and its music. He was born in Linares on Feb. 17, 1893. He was mainly self-taught, though much influenced by an earlier master, Francisco Tárrega. His first public performance was at the age of 16, in Granada, in 1909. It was followed by a long series of successes in Europe and North and South America. His debut in New York City in 1928 was a triumph both for Segovia as a musician and for the guitar as an instrument in the concert hall. The critics were deeply impressed by his technical virtuosity and profound musical imagination. In the decades that followed, Segovia continued playing throughout the world, and his reputation grew.

Andrés Segovia, Spanish classical guitarist

Segovia's scholarly studies and transcriptions of music written for other instruments greatly extended the repertoire for the guitar. In addition, many modern composers, including Manuel de Falla, Joaquín Turina, and Mario Castelnuovo-Tedesco, wrote for him. Segovia also gained an outstanding reputation as an interpreter of Bach, Handel, Mozart, and other classical composers.

SEGOVIA, sə-gō′vyä, is a city in central Spain and the capital of Segovia province. The city is about 40 miles (65 km) northwest of Madrid and lies between the Eresma and Clamores rivers, just above their confluence. Segovia was a major textile center in the Middle Ages. Today it is of minor industrial importance.

The city is primarily interesting for its history and architecture. Established about 700 B. C., it became an important Roman settlement in the 1st century B. C. Its magnificent Roman aqueduct, built from unmortared granite, probably in the early 2d century A. D., is still in use and is Segovia's most imposing monument.

Segovia was taken by the Moors in the early 8th century and retaken by Alfonso VI in 1079. The Alcázar, a fortified castle used as a residence by the kings of Castile, was started by Alfonso and has many later additions. The cathedral, a late Gothic structure built in the 16th century, is the most striking ecclesiastical building, but there are also notable Romanesque and Gothic churches. Outside the old city walls is the former Convent of Santa Cruz, founded by King Ferdinand and Queen Isabella, and across the Eresma is the Gothic monastery of El Parral, founded in 1477.

The Province. The province, part of Old Castile, is a thinly populated tableland of 2,683 square miles (6,949 sq km). It is separated on the east from New Castile by the Sierra de Guadarrama. The province produces grain, hemp, and vegetables and raises livestock. Granite, marble, and limestone are quarried. Population: (1970) of the city, 41,880; of the province, 162,770.

SEGRÈ, sə-grā′, **Emilio Gino** (1905–), American high-energy nuclear physicist, who shared the 1959 Nobel Prize in physics with Owen Chamberlain for their discovery of the antiproton in 1955.

In their work, Segrè, Chamberlain, and two other scientists used the bevatron particle accelerator at the Lawrence Radiation Laboratory of the University of California. By means of the bevatron, the scientists accelerated a stream of protons to an energy of 6.2 billion electron volts (GeV) and directed them at a copper block. When the high-energy protons struck the copper target, they created many subatomic particles, a few of which were antiprotons. In other work, Segrè was a codiscoverer of slow neutrons and the elements technetium, astatine, and plutonium.

Segrè was born in Tivoli, Italy, on Feb. 1, 1905. He received his Ph. D. from the University of Rome in 1928 and taught physics there (1930–1936) and at the University of Palermo (1936–1938). In 1938 he became a research assistant at the University of California. From 1945 to 1946 he was a group leader at the Los Alamos Scientific Laboratory in New Mexico. After World War II, he returned to the University of California as a professor of physics. See also ANTIMATTER.

SEGREGATION is the physical separation or isolation of races by law or custom. In the United States, Negroes have been most directly affected by such segregation, and it is concerning their status that the great bulk of legislation, litigation, and controversy has centered.

Early Attitudes. Although the full legal segregation of Negroes was a relatively late phenomenon in American race relations, the system derived from attitudes that were part of the justification and defense of slavery. The basic assumption of the slave system was the alleged innate and permanent inferiority of the Negro race. Under slavery, the status of the great majority of Negroes was fixed, and there was no need for segregation to establish their inferior station. At the same time, the nature and requirements of slavery accustomed the upper levels of both races in the South to a degree of association and intimacy rarely equaled in other parts of the country.

After the emancipation of the slaves, many Southerners and some Northerners were disposed to regard the freedmen as an addition to the despised caste of pre-Civil War free Negroes and to treat them in the same way. The so-called black codes enacted in the South in 1865–1866 restricted freedmen's rights in various ways. At least two states barred them from first-class railway coaches, and Texas required railroads to provide separate coaches for them. These abortive "Jim Crow" laws were quickly repealed by Reconstruction legislatures, though discrimination often continued without legal sanction. As race relations worsened, Negroes in the South withdrew voluntarily from the white churches, and their children were placed in separate schools.

The conservative white governments that overthrew Reconstruction retained many pre-Civil War attitudes and discriminatory practices established since emancipation but, for more than a decade, showed no disposition to increase segregation. Freedmen were often denied their civil rights and discriminated against by railroads, hotels, and inns, but the era of genuine segregation, when the principle was deliberately applied to all possible areas of contact between the races, was yet to come. Extremists were held in check by conservative rulers who found the Negro a useful ally in politics, and who had no strong motive for aggression against him.

Growth of Segregation. The way to full segregation was opened by several events. Economic unrest and depression in the 1890's brought forward politicians free of conservative restraints. The conservative governments were attacked by a Populist movement that attracted Negro allies, and to strengthen their position, many conservatives now promoted white supremacy movements to unite their own race at the expense of the subordinate one. Moreover, many of the agrarian radicals of the Populist movement were themselves not immune from appeals to race. The Supreme Court of the United States approved the "separate but equal" principle in *Plessy* v. *Ferguson* in 1896 and legal disfranchisement in *Williams* v. *Mississippi* in 1898. Northern resistance was softened by imperialistic adventures beginning with the Spanish-American War of 1898, and Southern ideas of racial superiority were used to justify U. S. rule of colonial people.

The first segregation laws of importance were those requiring separation of the races aboard trains, and by 1892 seven Southern states had

such laws. Up to 1900 this was the only segregation law adopted by a majority of Southern states, but in the first two decades of the 20th century the movement rushed forward at great speed. The Jim Crow waiting room in railway stations was provided for by nearly all Southern states by 1910. Next to be required were segregated streetcars. Much of the system was contributed by city ordinances or local regulations enforced without the formality of statute law. By one means or another, however, the races were separated in theaters and amusement parks, in hospitals and auditoriums, in jails, stockades, and convict camps, and in institutions for the blind and deaf, for paupers and feebleminded, for the insane, the tubercular, and the juvenile delinquent. Often without the prompting of the law, separate drinking fountains, toilets, elevators, stairways, exits, and entrances were provided and designated by signs. The movement continued until walls of segregation separated the races in almost every conceivable circumstance.

Start of Reform. About 1940 the tide of public opinion began to turn, and in the years following World War II a movement of formidable strength was directed against the segregation system. It was fostered by civil rights organizations of both races in the North and South, by churches and labor unions, and by a new assertiveness among the Negroes themselves. It was aided indirectly by two wars and a cold war of propaganda, by urbanization and northward movement of Negro population, and by industrialization in the South. It received encouragement from both the major national political parties and great assistance from presidential directives that virtually eliminated segregation among federal employees and among personnel of the military services. The most effective pressures upon the South were decisions of the federal courts that weakened segregation on trains and common carriers, in housing and working conditions, and in publicly supported colleges and professional schools.

Many Southern states, in the attempt to maintain "separate but equal" conditions, made important strides in improving facilities for Negroes, especially in their school systems. However, the Supreme Court decision in *Brown* v. *Board of Education* (1954), held segregation in the public schools to be "inherently unequal" and therefore unconstitutional. School desegregation proceeded steadily but slowly after that ruling. A full decade passed, and many federal court orders were issued, before all of the Southern states had begun even token integration. Although about half of the biracial school districts in the Deep South were officially desegregated by the mid-1960's, less than 2% of the Negro pupils actually attended integrated schools. In the North, de facto school segregation continued, as a result of residential segregation. As this situation came under attack, many school districts took steps to correct "racial imbalance."

Progress in 1960's and 1970's. By the 1960's the tempo of desegregation had accelerated in many areas, often stimulated by economic boycotts and protest demonstrations by organized civil rights groups. Segregated hotels, restaurants, retail stores, and recreational facilities yielded to the pressures. Several states and cities passed antidiscrimination statutes affecting housing and employment. The sweeping federal civil rights act of 1964 flatly forbade segregation in all privately owned public facilities subject to any form of federal control under the interstate commerce clause of the U. S. Constitution. Other federal legislation, notably the civil rights acts of 1957 and 1960 and the voting rights law of 1965, were aimed primarily at guaranteeing Negro suffrage. These laws and the federal court decisions requiring strict proportional representation in Congress and in state legislatures broadened and strengthened the Negro's participation in government.

Other important Supreme Court decisions include *Jones* v. *Alfred H. Mayer Co.* (1968), ruling that under the power given Congress to enforce the 13th Amendment, the Civil Rights Act of 1866 had made it illegal for 100 years for anyone to refuse to sell or rent to anyone because of race or color; and *Swann* v. *Charlotte-Mecklenberg Board of Education* (1971), a unanimous decision that busing children as a means of dismantling dual school systems was constitutional.

Segregation is partly a private matter that cannot be eliminated by legislation alone. It persists in many areas of American life, in both North and South. Nevertheless, official opposition has placed segregationists on the defensive. Where segregation exists, it is frequently denied or excused, indicating that it is in retreat.

See also CIVIL RIGHTS AND LIBERTIES; CIVIL RIGHTS MOVEMENT.

C. VANN WOODWARD
Yale University

Further Reading: Knapp, Robert B., *Social Integration in Urban Communities* (Teachers' College 1960); McEntire, Davis, *Residence and Race* (Univ. of Calif. Press 1960); Muse, Benjamin, *Ten Years of Prelude: The Story of Integration Since the Supreme Court's 1954 Decision* (Viking 1964); Myrdal, Gunnar, and Others, *An American Dilemma: The Negro Problem and American Democracy*, rev. ed. (Harper 1962); Woodward, C. Vann, *The Strange Career of Jim Crow*, rev. ed. (Oxford 1966).

SÉGUIER, sā-gyā′, **Pierre** (1588–1672), chancellor of France. He was born in Paris on May 29, 1588, into a family of wealthy lawyers. After entering the royal administration, he became an intendant in 1621 and in 1624 was made one of the presidents of the Parlement of Paris.

Séguier was appointed chancellor in 1635 and strengthened his hold on this important office by supporting Cardinal Richelieu and his successor, Cardinal Mazarin. In 1639, Séguier suppressed a revolt in Normandy, and in 1642 he directed the prosecution of the Marquis de Cinq-Mars, an opponent of Richelieu. After Richelieu's death in 1642, Séguier succeeded him as "protector" of the Académie Française. During the Fronde rebellion (1648–1653), Séguier was attacked and had to give up his seals of office, which were restored in 1656. After Louis XIV assumed direct rule in 1661, Séguier directed the trial of Nicolas Fouquet, superintendant of finances, and helped revise the legal system. He died in St.-Germain-en-Laye on Jan. 28, 1672.

SEGUIN, sə-gēn′, a city in south central Texas, the seat of Guadalupe county, is on the Guadalupe River, about 33 miles (52 km) northeast of San Antonio. Seguin makes metal products, aircraft parts, textiles, and food products. Texas Lutheran College is in the city. Los Nogales Museum and Sebastopol, a house built in 1853, are points of interest. Settled in 1832, Seguin was incorporated in 1853. It is governed by a council and manager. Population: 17,854.

SEGURA RIVER, sā-gōō′rä, a river in southeastern Spain. It rises in Jaén province and flows some 200 miles (320 km) in a generally easterly direction to empty into the Mediterranean Sea southwest of Alicante. Its chief tributary is the Mundo River. The waters of the Segura feed irrigation systems around the cities of Cieza, Murcia, and Orihuela, and its falls generate power at several hydroelectric stations. The Segura was known as the Tader in Roman times.

SEHESTED, sē′es-tăth, **Hannibal** (1609–1666), Danish court official. He was born on the island of Ösel (now Saaremaa). Educated abroad, he returned to Denmark in 1632 and held posts at the court of Christian IV. Sent to Sweden to negotiate a treaty and propose a marriage between Denmark's Crown Prince Frederick and Gustavus Adolphus' heiress, Christina, he was unsuccessful. Some years later he married his sovereign's daughter Christine, and in 1642 he was appointed viceroy of Norway.

During Christian's second war with Sweden (1643–1645) he ably supported the Danish cause, invading Sweden four times. Thereafter, in order to strengthen the defense against Sweden he continued to improve Norway's finances and economy and build up its navy. His enemies in the Danish Rigsråd forced him into exile in 1651. Frederick III recalled him in 1660, the year in which the power of Sehested's opponents in the Rigsråd was broken. After his return, Sehested negotiated an advantageous peace with Sweden and was rewarded with high offices. He became a close adviser of Frederick and began centralizing the administration. He died in Paris on Sept. 23, 1666.

SEI SHONAGON, sā shō-nä-gôn (c. 1000 A. D.), was a Japanese author who wrote *The Pillow Book*. Little is known about her except that she was a court lady in the service of Empress Sadako and was a contemporary of Lady Murasaki, the author of *The Tale of Genji*.

Sei Shonagon's *Pillow Book* is a collection of writings that includes her observations of court life and her judgments of people and things categorized under such headings as "annoying," and "moving." She is sometimes tender and lyrical, but often she is witty and scathing in her commentaries on the people around her. Her vivid and sparkling prose style is much admired, and her discursive essays are the prototype of a literary form popular in Japan. *The Pillow Book* is also a valuable source of information about the aristocratic society of the Heian period.

Further Reading: Sei Shonagon, *The Pillow Book of Sei Shonagon*, tr. and ed. by Ivan Morris, 2 vols. (Columbia Univ. Press 1967).

SEICHE, sāsh, a standing oscillation of the water in a lake, harbor, or similar water basin. The term was first applied to the phenomenon as observed in Lake Geneva, Switzerland.

Standing oscillations in water basins are initiated by events such as a storm or even a sudden drop in atmospheric pressure. The oscillation period ranges from a few minutes to more than an hour, as determined by the size and shape of the basin. Long, narrow basins are particularly likely to develop seiches. In a bay or small sea connected with the open ocean, the seiche may be reinforced by lunar tides if their periods correspond closely. The best-known example is the large seiche in the Bay of Fundy.

SEIGNORIALISM, sañ-yôr′ē-əl-izm, was the system of dependent land tenure that existed throughout medieval Europe. The term, derived from the French word *seigneurie* (lordship), has the same meaning as the word *manorialism,* derived from the English word *manor* (landed estate). It may be defined as the system of land tenure adhering between the lord and his dependent tenants who worked the land, and also as the administrative and legal processes that preserved this system.

Seignorialism should be distinguished from feudalism. Feudalism was the political, military, and social system of the nobility of the Middle Ages, whereas seignorialism was the economic base upon which it rested. Though not wholly accurate, it is justifiable to apply seignorialism to economic systems such as existed at certain times in Russia, the Middle East, China, Japan, and French Canada, where the term feudalism is less appropriate. Throughout most of the Middle Ages, seignorialism and feudalism complemented each other. It must be emphasized, however, that seignorialism appeared first in response to the basic economic requirement of survival and that only later did feudalism develop and come to be superimposed upon seignorialism. Of the two, seignorialism was the more fundamental; without it, feudalism could never have functioned.

Origin of Seignorialism. Seignorialism developed in the late Roman Empire in the West when imperial authority was disappearing, German tribes were overrunning the provinces, and the economy was disintegrating to one of land and simple barter. During this turbulent age the powerful landlord consolidated his economic and political position over large areas of land. As the one individual capable of offering a degree of security and protection, he drew to him less fortunate persons. Men with small plots surrendered them to him in return for protection. They lost ownership of the land but received back its possession, which they and their heirs could enjoy so long as they performed various economic services. Men without land came to the lord from whom they sought protection and enough land to provide sustenance. Like the others, they became his economic dependents and had to perform economic services.

Roman law called these plots held by tenants *precaria* because customarily as the result of a prayer (*preces*) the lord received man and land under his protection, or granted out some of his land. Sometimes these lands were called benefices (*beneficia*) because they had been granted as a boon by the lord. Whether called *precaria* or *beneficia,* such land was said to be held by precarious tenure because possession depended on the performance of services. For many centuries the lord was the only instrument of law and order, providing for his tenants both the means of survival and local government. Seignorialism developed in the early Middle Ages to provide a subsistence level of life for most of the inhabitants of Europe.

To debate whether seignorialism was more Roman or Germanic in origin is fruitless. All that need be understood is that in the late Roman imperial period large estates called *latifundia* were controlled by great landlords and cultivated by economically dependent peasants (*coloni*) who had lost their legal freedom by the 4th century and had become tied to the soil. These individuals, the *adscripti glebae* of Roman law,

were the prototype of the medieval peasant. When the Germans appropriated the empire, they brought with them a similar agrarian system of dependent tenure. During the early Middle Ages the two systems fused to form the classic medieval seignorialism.

However efficient as an economic system between the 4th and 12th centuries, when normal economic activity and money had virtually disappeared, seignorialism did not provide the necessary political and military services required by the Germanic states that replaced the empire. This was strikingly evident to the Carolingians in the 8th century, when they were faced with the defense of western Europe against the Magyars from the east and Saracens from the south. To fight successfully against the cavalry of these warlike antagonists, the Carolingians mounted heavily armed warriors on big war chargers. In this fashion the knight was created, and he proceeded to dominate the battlefield for the next 600 years.

Lacking the money to outfit and maintain this expensive fighter, the Carolingians resorted to granting men landed estates (seigniories or manors) in return for providing knight service. The land, buildings, peasants, and appurtenances so granted, comprised the fief (*feodum*) of the man (vassal) and served as his recompense for supplying military services and performing political duties. The vassal in turn could obtain knight service by the same method, granting fiefs from his land to men who became his vassals. So it was that subinfeudation and the feudal hierarchy developed, resting upon the honorable relationship of free and noble men who formed the feudal aristocracy. Every possessor of a fief, whether king, great lord, or simple vassal, was a lord because the fief brought with it all the privileges and obligations of the seigniory.

Though at times composed of but one seigniory, a fief generally included a number of seigniories scattered about the countryside. Each was a landed unit of economic exploitation with its unfree peasants. Just as the lord of the seigniory had to perform services to hold his fief, his peasants had to perform menial economic tasks to hold their parcels of land. Here, then, was the fundamental difference between feudalism and seignorialism. The former included only free aristocratic men who performed honorable services for their fiefs. The latter included as well the unfree peasants who worked the seigniories composing the fief and whose relation to the lord rested upon the performance of ignoble economic tasks in return for a small piece of land and protection.

Functions of Seignorialism. The chief purpose of the seigniory was agricultural. Although no generalization about the land system is entirely accurate, it may be said that each seignory usually included a fortified dwelling (manor house) or castle for the lord and his family, with his farm buildings, gardens, and orchard. Near the manor house were the cottages of the peasants, clustered about the church, mill, and wine press. In addition, the lord held arable land, pasture for his cattle, meadow for his hay, forest for wood and hunting, and pond and stream for fishing. All these made up the lord's demesne and provided for the maintenance of his family.

The remaining land of the estate was distributed to the peasants in small equalized plots. Varying in area from 20 to 30 acres (8–12 hectares), these plots were seldom concentrated but were distributed in strips throughout three fields. This was the open-field system that generally divided the land into three large fields, each containing strips of arable land held by lord and peasants. Each year one field lay fallow while the others were cultivated. Such a system of land rotation provided the only defense against soil exhaustion.

All the work was cooperative. The peasants plowed, sowed, cultivated, and harvested the lord's and their own strips. They shared the meadow and pasture and had rights to wood and stream. The routine services, called labor services, or *corvée*, consisted not only of agrarian work but of repairing roads, bridges, and castles. The extra tasks demanded at plowing and harvesting time were called boon services. The peasants had to pay yearly rents of agrarian produce to the lord. They were also responsible for other special payments that included *formariage* (*merchet*), a payment permitting the peasant's daughter to marry outside the seigniory; *mainmorte* (*heriot*), a type of inheritance tax; *chevage*, a head tax; and *banalités*, fees collected from local market trade.

The real political master of the peasants was the lord. He taxed them when he saw fit, secured military service from them in emergencies, and rendered justice to them in the seignorial court. By virtue of their economic strength and military prestige, most lords were able to acquire political powers. The mass of men lived under this system of economic dependency with no chance of escape from their bondage to the land until the revival of economic activity in the 11th and 12th centuries. This revival introduced a money economy into western Europe, thereby enabling the peasant to commute his services for money and to attain his freedom. The long decline of seignorialism and feudalism had begun.

Decline of Seignorialism. By the 15th century, seignorialism had disappeared from most of western Europe. Vestiges remained in France until 1789, and in Germany it did not completely die until the revolution of 1848. In Russia it survived until abolished by Czar Alexander II in 1861. Throughout central Europe, it lasted with certain modifications into the 19th century. In large areas of the Middle East, forms of a seignorial system are still found. Even in the 20th century, vast expanses of Asia followed an agrarian system similar to seignorialism. It could be found in Central and South America up to the 19th century. The French introduced a seignorial system into Canada in the early 17th century. Though its most oppressive aspects of tenure were removed by legislation in the 19th century, not until 1941 did the Seignorial Rent Abolition Act of the Province of Quebec end all vestiges of seignorialism.

BRYCE D. LYON
Brown University

Bibliography

Bloch, Marc, *French Rural History*, tr. by Janet Sondheimer (Univ. of Calif. Press 1966).
Blum, Jerome, *Lord and Peasant in Russia from the 9th to the 19th Century* (Princeton Univ. Press 1961).
Cambridge Economic History of Europe, Vol. I—The Agrarian Life of the Middle Ages, rev. ed., ed. by M. M. Postan (Cambridge 1966).
Duby, Georges, *Rural Economy and Country Life in the Medieval West*, tr. by Cynthia Postan (Univ. of S. C. 1968).
Neilson, Nellie, *Medieval Agrarian Economy* (Holt 1936).

SEINE-ET-MARNE, sen-ā-màrn', is a department in north central France, east of Paris. It is near the center of the Paris Basin and is named for the Seine and Marne rivers, which cut through it. It is an agricultural area and produces Brie cheese. It includes the forest of Fontainebleau and the former royal palace. The capital in Melun. Population: (1971 est.) 639,500.

SEINE-MARITIME, sen-mä-rē-tēm', is a department in northeastern France, in the old province of Normandy and bordered on the north by the English Channel. It was formerly called Seine-Inférieure and includes the lower Seine River. Its main cities are Rouen, the capital, and Le Havre. It is a fertile agricultural area. Population: (1971 est.) 1,151,400.

SEINE RIVER, sen, a historically and economically important river in France. It rises at a height of 1,545 feet (471 meters) in the Plateau of Langres, about 18 miles (30 km) northwest of Dijon, It flows in a northwesterly direction to empty into the English Channel at Le Havre. Its winding course has a length of 482 miles (775 km). Curious phenomena of the lower river are the tidal bores, several feet high, which sweep in from the sea. The banks in this area are protected by dikes.

Several major rivers and many minor streams join the Seine, including the Yonne, the Marne (at Paris), and the Oise. Important cities along the river are the port of Le Havre, at the mouth; historic Rouen, with its fine cathedral; and Paris, the heart of the country. The first settlement at Paris was on an island in the Seine, Île de la Cité. Below Paris the river winds through a pleasant countryside in a series of broad loops and enters the sea by a long estuary.

The river carries an enormous volume of barge traffic, and certain parts of the river, such as between Nanterre and Paris, are crowded with port facilities. Canals, designed for barges, link the Seine with the Loire, Rhône, Meuse, Scheldt, Saône, and Somme rivers.

SEINE-SAINT-DENIS, sen-saNd-nē', is a department in France on the northern and eastern edge of Paris. It was created in 1964, with the reorganization of departments in the Paris area. It is a heavily industrialized section of greater Paris, and its capital is Bobigny. Its area is 91 square miles (235 sq km). Population: (1971 est.) 1,329,000.

SEIPEL, zī'pəl, **Ignaz** (1876–1932), Austrian chancellor. He was born in Vienna on July 19, 1876. An ordained Catholic priest, he held professorships at Salzburg (1909–1912) and Vienna (1917–1918). Through his book *State and Nation* (1916), Seipel became prominent. He was designated leader of the Christian Socialists in the assembly in 1919.

In 1922 he succeeded Johann Schober as chancellor. On June 1, 1924, he was shot and seriously wounded, and in November he resigned as chancellor. In October 1926 he again became chancellor, as well as foreign minister, and he tried with some success to revive Austria's economy. A critic of parliamentary democracy, Seipel supported the Heimwehr, a fascist organization. He resigned as chancellor in 1929 and was an unsuccessful presidential candidate in 1930. He died in Pernitzon on Aug. 2, 1932.

SEISMOGRAPH, sīz'mə-graf, an instrument for recording movements of the ground caused by earthquakes, explosions, or other phenomena that release mechanical energy into the earth. The record, called a seismogram, shows the oscillation sequences as the waves arrive at the seismograph site, delayed and modified by their travels through the earth.

An inertial seismograph senses ground movements by observing their effects relative to a mass supported in a pendulumlike structure in the instrument. The detected displacements may be very small, so in order to produce a seismogram directly, early seismographs used mechanical levers to magnify and enscribe the record on a moving strip of smoked paper. The sensitivity of such devices was limited by mechanical friction, a problem avoided in improved instruments that magnified readings optically and recorded them on photosensitive paper. In modern seismographs the detector, called a seismometer, first converts the movements to electrical signals by a transducer that most often takes the form of a coil moving with the mass in the field of a magnet. The signals can write a magnified photographic record when connected to a sensitive mirror-galvanometer. At most seismic stations a number of such instruments with different characteristics are used for routine data acquisition. More elaborate seismographs use electronic amplification and filtering before the signals are displayed for visual reading or recorded on magnetic tape for computer processing. Portable instrumentation of this kind is used extensively for geophysical exploration, and a number of seismographs may be combined in a network or in an array.

The usable magnification of a seismograph is limited by the microseismic noise continuously generated by storms at sea and by large-scale weather activity. In addition, occasional higher-frequency seismic noise may be caused by local weather or by man-made activities. Seismographs designed for large magnification have a reduced response to such noise background. Seismometers may be located underground at carefully selected sites where the lower noise level allows magnifications of more than 100,000 times for short-period seismographs operating in the frequency

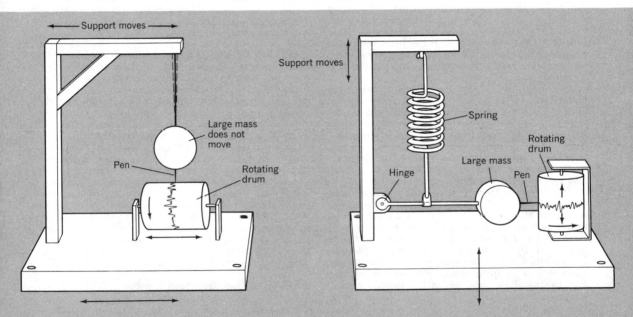

The basic operating principle of an inertial seismograph is the inertia of a large mass relative to motions of the framework in which it is suspended, such motions being caused by earthquakes or other earth disturbances. The pendulum-like system at left, above, would detect horizontal motions and the system at right vertical motions. In practice such systems are refined by magnetic and electronic devices. Otherwise the motions of the system would be too small to read, and the pendulum would tend to develop its own natural frequencies and obscure the readings.

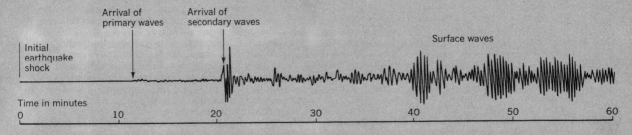

A typical record, or seismogram, made by a sensitive seismograph, in this instance of an earthquake more than 5,000 miles (8,000 km) from the recording station. First to arrive are the primary or longitudinal waves. These are followed by the secondary or transverse waves, and finally by the surface waves of the earthquake.

band of 1 to 5 hertz, or cycles per second, and magnifications of a few thousand times for seismographs operating in the range of 1 cycle per 15 to 100 seconds. On the other hand, a sensitive seismograph can be overloaded by local earthquakes. Lower-sensitivity accelerographs that operate only when triggered by larger motions are installed at many earthquake-prone locations as standby instruments. Seismoscopes, which record only peak displacements, are also widely used for engineering seismology.

Strain seismographs record deformations of the ground directly by measuring small changes in the distance between two points. The daily cycles of tidal strain are only about one part in one billion. However, much smaller deformations can be detected by instruments using electronic sensors or laser interferometers. Such seismographs, which are installed in many places, extend the range of seismic observations to very long periods of time and open new fields of research by recording the changes of strain in the earth associated with earthquakes.

See also EARTHQUAKE; SEISMOLOGY.

F. KOLLAR
*Department of Energy,
Mines and Resources, Canada*

SEISMOLOGY, sīz-mol′ə-jē, is the branch of earth science concerned with the study of natural earthquakes, man-made earthquakes, and related phenomena.

Seismologists study the elastic waves generated by an earthquake. There are two main kinds: body waves that radiate into the earth's interior, and surface waves that propagate along its surface. Because body waves experience relatively little distortion and attenuation as compared with other carriers of information about the earth's interior such as heat flow, they are the best carriers of such data. Surface waves are also useful, because they convey additional information about earth structures near the surface. The information on earth structures and focal mechanisms obtainable from such studies is complemented by the study of seismic disturbances generated by nuclear and chemical explosions. Explosions are useful because the source mechanism is less complex than for most earthquakes, and the location and detonation times generally are known precisely. The application of refraction and reflection techniques in conjunction with explosions has brought about man's most detailed knowledge of the structure of the earth's crust.

A major advance in the understanding of earthquake activity on a global scale has come about by integrating regional activity with the essential postulate of plate tectonics—that the earth's surface may be divided into a number of rigid plates, or caps, whose boundaries are the seismic belts of the world. It is the relative motion between the caps that generates earthquakes. In the oceans, earthquakes are confined to narrow strips, whereas in the continents they are generally spread over a wide belt. The origin and importance of this difference are not fully understood.

The source mechanism of earthquakes has also become the object of much study. Intensive measurements of ground motion and deformation, gravity variations, and, in some cases, magnetic fluctuations near the source of shallow-focus earthquakes have contributed greatly to man's understanding of the complex processes taking place in a source region. Evidence indicates that most of the relative motion between adjacent plates occurs in the form of *creep,* a slow process that does not generate detectable seismic waves. It is only in "locked" regions where creep cannot take place that there is a buildup of energy and earthquakes occur.

Seismological studies and techniques have contributed to the welfare of society. Oil exploration companies utilize seismic techniques to locate oil- and gas-bearing formations. Engineering seismologists study the effects of violent ground disturbances on buildings and other structures and advise on earthquake-resistant designs. Evidence that earthquakes can be triggered by injecting fluid into the earth or by exploding nuclear devices underground has enhanced man's understanding of earthquake mechanisms. It has also reinforced the judgment that the possibility of earthquake prediction in certain active tectonic regions is drawing nearer.

See also EARTHQUAKE; GEOLOGY—*Geological Processes.*

H. S. HASEGAWA
*Department of Energy,
Mines and Resources, Canada*

Further Reading: Richter, Charles F., *Elementary Seismology* (Freeman 1958).

SEISTAN, sās-tän′, is a region of eastern Iran and southwestern Afghanistan. It consists of a depression with an area of about 7,000 square miles (18,000 sq km), which attracts the drainage of several rivers. Only one of these, the Helmand, is a permanent stream. The rivers normally empty into several lagoons, or *hamun,* but in high flood they form a large marshy lake, the Hamun-i-Helmand. Although Seistan (Sistan) has a desert climate, irrigation makes possible the cultivation of wheat, barley, cotton, and maize, supporting a population of about 300,000.

Under the Achaemenid dynasty of ancient Iran (Persia), the region was known as Zranka (in Greek, Drangiana). After its conquest by the nomadic Shakas (Sakas) from the north, it became known as Shakastan, from which the name Seistan is derived. The present Iranian-Afghan border through the region was fixed in 1905.

SEIXAS, sā′shəs, **Gershom Mendes** (1745–1816), American patriot and rabbi. He was born in New York City on Jan. 14, 1745, the son of a refugee from Lisbon, Spain, who settled in New York about 1730.

In 1766, Seixas became rabbi of the Spanish and Portuguese Synagogue in New York. On the outbreak of the Revolution he espoused the American cause, choosing to close the synagogue rather than continue it under British rule. While the majority of his congregation went to Philadelphia, he settled in Stratford, Conn. In 1780 he was asked to organize a synagogue in Philadelphia, the Mikve Israel.

Largely through his efforts, a modification in the test clause in the Pennsylvania constitution was made on Dec. 23, 1783, whereby Jews were no longer disqualified from holding public office. After the British evacuation of New York in 1784, the old synagogue was reestablished, and Seixas resumed his former charge. From 1787 to 1815, he was a trustee of Columbia College. When Washington was inaugurated in 1789, Seixas was selected to take part in the ceremonies. Seixas died in New York City on July 2, 1816.

SEJANUS, si-jā'nəs, **Lucius Aelius** (died 31 A. D.), adviser of the Roman Emperor Tiberius. He was the son of a Roman knight and had influential political connections through his mother's family. After the accession of Tiberius in 14 A. D., Sejanus and his father were made co-commanders of the Praetorian Guard. Sejanus soon became the sole commander and he acquired the complete confidence of Tiberius. He increased the power of the guard by quartering the cohorts in one camp.

As his influence over Tiberius grew, Sejanus also developed power over the Senate, particularly after the death in 23 of Drusus Caesar, the son of Tiberius. Sejanus later was implicated in the murder of Drusus. To increase his personal power, Sejanus also plotted against several other members of the imperial family and he encouraged Tiberius' decision to retire to Capri in 26.

After the Emperor's withdrawal, Sejanus' authority was unchallenged. The suspicions of Tiberius were finally aroused in 31, shortly after Sejanus had become consul, and the Emperor was convinced that his favorite was plotting to overthrow him. Sejanus was then imprisoned, condemned to death, and executed on the same day in Rome.

SEKONDI-TAKORADI, sek'ən-dē tä-kō rä'dē, is the principal seaport and third-largest city of Ghana. It was formed by the amalgamation of the cities of Sekondi and Takoradi in 1946.

Sekondi became a major port and commercial center after the completion in 1903 of a railroad to the mineral and timber resources of the interior. It was superseded by the deep-water harbor at Takoradi in 1928.

The chief exports of Sekondi-Takoradi are cacao, timber, manganese, and bauxite. Industries include sawmilling and the processing of cacao beans, tobacco, and palm products. The city is linked by rail with Kumasi in the north and with Accra, the national capital, in the east. Population: (1970) 160,868.

SELAGINELLA, sə-laj-ə-nel'ə, is a genus of mostly tropical plants with small scalelike leaves and propagated by spores. The species are very numerous and widely distributed in warm regions.

Selaginella (*Selaginella canaliculata*)

T. H. EVERETT

They are generally quadrangular, with the two lower rows of small one-veined leaves larger than the upper two rows, thus giving a flattened look to the fronds.

Selaginellas are generally creeping plants, and they often form mosslike mats of foliage. However, in some species supported by other plants, they are erect, and in still other cases, climbing. Selaginellas, with their verdant foliage, sometimes iridescent, or changing in hue, are cultivated in greenhouses as pot plants, for edgings, and for hiding bare earth.

S. lepidophylla, a Mexican species, growing in flat rosettes, although not very beautiful, is one of the familiar resurrection plants, because it becomes desiccated in time of drought and revives when the moist conditions return. When dried out, it rolls its branches inward and forms a ball. See also LYCOPSIDA.

SELANGOR, sə-lang'ər, is one of the states of the federation of Malaysia. Located on the western coast of the Malay Peninsula, it is bounded on the north by Perak, on the east by Pahang, on the southeast by Negri Sembilan, and on the south and west by the Strait of Malacca.

Selangor has an area of 3,160 square miles (8,180 sq km). Its coastline is about 100 miles (160 km) long, and the state extends inland a distance of about 50 miles (80 km) to a north-south mountain range that forms its border with Pahang. There are several short rivers, including the Selangor, Klang, and Langat.

Almost half the people of Selangor are Chinese, and about a sixth are Indian. Malays accounts for most of the remaining third of the population. Shah Alam replaced Kuala Lumpur as the state capital in 1978, though Kuala Lumpur remained the capital of the federation. Other towns in Selangor are Port Swettenham, the chief port, and Klang, an important rubber center.

Selangor has a well-developed economy. Coal and tin are mined, and there are important rubber estates. Coconuts, rice, and pineapples are cultivated on a considerable scale. Fishing is also an important part of the economy. Kuala Lumpur is connected by rail with Klang and Port Swettenham, and with Singapore to the south and Penang to the north.

The Dutch drove the sultan of Selangor from the state in 1784, and he was eventually forced to acknowledge their suzerainty. Following the Dutch evacuation of Malaya, British influence became paramount. The sultan made a commercial treaty with the British governor of Penang in 1818. Selangor was placed under British protection in 1874, and it became one of the Federated Malay States in 1895.

Occupied by Japanese forces from 1942 to 1945 during World War II, Selangor became part of the Federation of Malaya in 1948 and of the Malaysian federation in 1963. Population: (1970) 1,630,366.

SELASSIE, Haile. See HAILE SELASSIE.

SELBORNE, sel'bôrn, **1st Earl of** (1812–1895), English judge, whose highly important achievement was the complete reform of the judicial system. Roundell Palmer was born on Nov. 27, 1812, in Mixbury, Oxfordshire. After graduating at Christ Church, Oxford University, in 1834, he studied law and was called to the bar in 1837; in 1849 he became a queen's counsel.

From 1847 until 1857 he was member of Parliament for Plymouth, and in 1861 he was elected to the House of Commons for Richmond, Yorkshire, thereupon becoming solicitor general in the cabinet of Lord Palmerston. As attorney general (1863–1866) he advised the government on matters arising from the American Civil War.

In 1872 he entered the cabinet of William Ewart Gladstone as lord chancellor, being made Baron Selborne; his most important work in this office was to help to draft and to ensure passage of the Judicature Act through Parliament the following year. This act removed vast numbers of outmoded legal technicalities, arranged a fusion of law and equity, and set up a logical court system. He lost the office of lord chancellor with the fall of the Gladstone government in 1874, but resumed it when the Liberals again returned to power in 1880. In 1882 he received an earldom, but in 1885 he severed his connection with the Liberals because of differences with Gladstone on home rule for Ireland. He died in Petersfield, Hampshire, on May 4, 1895.

SELDEN, George B. (1846–1922), American inventor and patent attorney who until 1911 held the patent under which most automobiles were manufactured in the United States. Selden was born in Clarkson, N. Y., on Sept. 14, 1846. He studied law and became a lawyer in 1871. In 1879 he applied for a patent on a vehicle that had a Brayton two-cycle engine, running gear, driving wheels, a propeller shaft and clutch, and a carriage body, but he delayed issuance of the patent until 1895. In 1903 the Association of Licensed Automobile Manufacturers was formed, and each member agreed to pay Selden a royalty of 1.25% of the retail price of all automobiles sold. The Ford Motor Company refused, however, and Selden brought a suit against it in 1903. A 1909 court decision upheld Selden, but a 1911 decision held that Ford was not guilty of infringement because it was using the Otto four-cycle engine. Selden then went into automobile manufacturing but failed. He died in Rochester, N. Y., on Jan. 17, 1922.

SELDEN, John (1584–1654), English jurist, antiquary, Orientalist, and political leader. He was born in Salvington, Sussex, on Dec. 15, 1584. After studying at Oxford University he moved in 1602 to London and studied law at Clifford's Inn, most important of the inns of chancery. Two years later he was admitted to the Inner Temple, and was called to the bar in 1612. His *Duello, or Single Combat* (1610) and some legal writings were followed by *Titles of Honour* (1614), a work of permanent value, and *Analecton Anglo-Britannicon* (1615), a history of civil government in Britain before the Norman Conquest. With publication of *De Diis Syriis* (1617), a study of polytheism, he attained a European reputation as an outstanding Orientalist, and this was enhanced by treatises on rabbinical law.

However, great controversy arose among the English clergy with appearance of his *History of Tythes* (1618), which admitted a legal right to the clergy, but denied their divine right. The work was suppressed and Selden was brought before the privy council and made to renounce his views. He was believed instrumental in getting Parliament to deny in 1621 that it owed its rights and privileges to the crown, and for this he was imprisoned in the Tower of London. First elected a member of the House of Commons in 1623, he labored for the advancement of civil and religious liberty. He supported the impeachment in 1626 of George Villiers, 1st Duke of Buckingham, and two years later he helped draft the Petition of Right and spoke in support of it in the House of Commons. In 1629 he was once more sent to the Tower, for his part in securing the resolution in the House against the levying of tonnage and poundage. Released in 1630, he ceased political activity for awhile and turned again to writing. Among his other well-known works were *Mare Clausum* (1635), a claim for English control of the narrow seas, and *Privileges of the Baronage of England* (1642).

In 1640 he was elected to the Long Parliament, and there, in 1641, he helped draft the articles of impeachment of Archbishop William Laud. He took part as a lay member in the Westminster Assembly of divines, endeavoring to moderate the fanaticism, and thereafter he was appointed keeper of the rolls and records of the Tower of London. He died in London on Nov. 30, 1654. He is best remembered, however, for his *Table Talk* (1689), reports of over 20 years, for he was an engaging conversationalist whose close friends included Ben Jonson and the Earl of Clarendon. Jonson had early described him as "living on his own, the lawbook of judges of England, the bravest man in all languages."

SELDEN, an unincorporated area in southeastern New York, in Suffolk county, is near the center of Long Island, about 6 miles (10 km) south of Port Jefferson. It is a residential community with some industry. Suffolk County Community College is here. Population: 11,613.

SELDES, sel'dəs, **Gilbert Vivian** (1893–1970), American author and critic of the communications media. He was born in Alliance, N. J., on Jan. 3, 1893. He graduated from Harvard in 1914 and became music critic of the Philadelphia *Evening Ledger*. After military service in World War I he worked for several New York newspapers and in 1930 began his own column in the New York *Journal*. He was a program director for the Columbia Broadcasting System (1937–1945) and dean of the Annenberg School of Communications, University of Pennsylvania (1959–1963). He died in New York City on Sept. 29, 1970.

In 1924, Seldes published *The Seven Lively Arts*, which examined the effects of comic strips, films, vaudeville, and popular songs on American society. He wrote two other major works on the media: *The Great Audience* (1950), which analyzed the organization and influence of films, radio, and television, and *The Public Arts* (1956), which dealt primarily with television.

George Seldes (1890–), his brother, was also an author. He is best known for his exposés of censorship of the press, including *You Can't Print That!* (1929).

SELECTIVE SERVICE. See CONSCRIPTION.

SELECTMAN, an executive officer in New England towns that have government by town meeting or representative town meeting. Usually three or more selectmen are elected for one- to four-year terms. The first selectman functions like the mayor in a mayor-council system.

SELENE, Roman goddess. See LUNA.

SELENITE. See GYPSUM.

SELENIUM, sə-lē′nē-əm, symbol Se, is the 70th most abundant element in the earth's crust. Discovered in 1817 by Swedish chemist Jöns Jakob Berzelius, it was named for the moon (Greek, *selene*) because its sister element tellurium was named for the earth (Latin, *tellus*).

Uses. Selenium is a semiconducting metalloid that conducts electricity in one direction only. It is used in the production of rectifiers. Because the electrical conductivity of gray selenium increases on exposure to light, the element is also used in photoelectric cells and in xerography. In the glass and ceramics industries, selenium serves in producing ruby glass and colored glazes. Other uses include the vulcanization of rubber and the preparation of lubricants, pharmaceuticals, and medicines. Selenium compounds are used in pigments. Sodium selenate (Na_2SeO_4) improves the corrosion resistance of chromium plate and of aluminum and its alloys.

Properties. Selenium is located in Group VIA of the periodic table, the oxygen family of elements. Its atomic number is 34, and its atomic weight is 78.96. There are six stable isotopes, of which selenium-80 and selenium-78 are the most abundant. The element exists in several allotropic forms. At room temperature it is most commonly a gray hexagonal solid, but it is also found as a red monoclinic solid and a black or red amorphous solid. The gray form has a specific gravity of 4.79, melts at 217° C (422.6° F), and boils at about 685° C (1265° F). Liquid selenium is black. When it is cooled rapidly, the amorphous solid forms.

Chemically, selenium is similar to sulfur. It has oxidation states of −2, 4, and 6. Active metals reduce selenium to its selenide, or negative valence form, while less active metals form covalent compounds with the element. Selenites (SeO_3^{-2}) and selenates (SeO_4^{-2}) are analogous to sulfites and sulfates and are good oxidizing agents, as are selenic acid (H_2SeO_4) and selenium dioxide (SeO_2). The latter is formed as selenium burns in oxygen, with a pale blue flame. Hydrogen selenide (H_2Se), a gas formed by the action of acids on metal selenides, is toxic and has a disagreeable odor.

All selenium compounds are toxic, except for copper and lead selenides. Their physiological effects resemble those of arsenic, causing lung and liver damage, vomiting, diarrhea, and abdominal pain or cramps. Small doses, however, can be tolerated in medicines. Contact with selenium or its salts may cause dermatitis. Some plants accumulate toxic concentrations of selenium from soils. No more than three parts per million of the element has been suggested as the safe concentration limit in foods.

Occurrence and Production. Selenium occurs in igneous rocks and as selenides of base metals, and is found in sulfide deposits of copper, zinc, nickel, and silver. It is produced by treating electrolytic copper refinery "slimes" that contain selenides. These are converted to water-soluble selenites by smelting, roasting, or direct oxidation, and then reduced to the metal. Treatment of flue dust formed in sulfuric acid manufacture also yields selenium.

HERBERT LIEBESKIND
The Cooper Union, New York

Further Reading: Bagnall, Kenneth, *The Chemistry of Selenium, Tellurium, and Polonium* (Elsevier 1966).

SELENIUM CELL, sə-lē′nē-əm, a photoelectric cell that has a layer of metal deposited on a layer of selenium. Light falling on the cell generates an electric current. Selenium cells are widely used in light meters. See also LIGHT METER; PHOTOELECTRIC CELL.

SELEUCIA, si-lōō′shə, is the name of several ancient cities in Asia founded by Seleucus I Nicator, one of the successors of Alexander the Great.

The most celebrated of these cities was Seleucia-on-the-Tigris, which was established about 312 B.C. about 20 miles (32 km) southeast of modern Baghdad. Seleucus made it his capital, to replace Babylon. The city was on the Tigris and was connected to the Euphrates River by a canal, which helped to make it one of the richest commercial cities in the ancient world. It also became the center of Hellenistic culture in the Middle East. The number of its inhabitants at the time of its greatest prosperity is estimated to have been about 600,000, chiefly Greeks and Macedonians.

During the decline of the Seleucid dynasty the city became independent. Its great wealth attracted the pillaging tribes of southern Armenia and Media, by whom it was partially plundered several times. Parthians took control of the area in the early 1st century A.D., but they allowed the city to retain its Greek character. The Roman Emperor Trajan burned the city in 116. It was rebuilt, but in 164, when it had a population of about 300,000, the Roman Avidius Cassius burned it again, and from that time it was deserted and became as desolate as Babylon itself.

Seleucia Pieria, another important city, was founded by Seleucus about 300 B.C. It was near the mouth of the Orontes River in Syria, close to the modern Syrian-Turkish frontier. Initially a capital of Seleucus, it soon became the port for Antioch. Its natural strength was improved by fortification. It occupied a very prominent place in the wars between the Seleucids and the Ptolemies. Antiochus IV made it a free city, a status that was upheld by Pompey in 64 B.C. The Romans made improvements in the harbor and used it as a naval base. Saint Paul sailed from the city on his first mission. In the 6th century A.D. it fell into complete decay.

Seleucia Tracheotis, a city of Cilicia on the Calycadnus (Göksü) River, was also built by Seleucus. It was once a rival of Tarsus, and on its site are many ancient ruins, including a castle. The modern Turkish town of Silifke occupies the site. There was also a city called Seleucia in Persia. Founded by Alexander the Great as Alexandria, it was rebuilt as Seleucia by Antiochus I of Syria. Among the other cities of the name were Seleucia in Mesopotamia on the Euphrates, on the Belus in Syria, in Pisidia, and in Pamphylia.

SELEUCIDS, si-lōō′sidz, dynasty founded in Syria by Seleucus I Nicator, one of the ablest generals of Alexander the Great and eventually a successor to a large part of Alexander's divided empire. The Seleucids ruled from 312 to 64 B.C. As his share of the empire, Seleucus I received in 321 the satrapy of Babylon, from which he conquered eastward as far as the Indus River by 302. In 301, in alliance with Lysimachus, a fellow-successor of Alexander, Seleucus defeated Antigonus I, King of Macedonia and another general and successor of Alexander, at Ipsus. In the division of the Macedonian empire that followed the death of Antigonus at Ipsus, Seleucus added Syria and the eastern part of Asia Minor to his domain.

In northern Syria he established Antioch, named after his father, which became the capital of the kingdom. He also founded several cities named Seleucia after himself, chief among which was Seleucia-on-the-Tigris, which served as the capital of the eastern satrapies. These cities were peopled by Macedonian and Greek colonists, enjoyed civic independence, and developed into important centers for the diffusion of Greek language and culture. Educated Syrians began to study Greek and write in it, but the countryside retained its old speech and way of life. Next to colonization, the establishment of a standard calendar for western Asia was perhaps the greatest achievement of the period. The year 312 B.C. is reckoned as marking the birth of the Syrian monarchy and the starting point of the Seleucid era.

Successors of Seleucus. The kingdom established by Seleucus, who died in 280, was hardly ever at rest. His immediate successors, Antiochus I Soter and Antiochus II Theos, fought indecisively against Ptolemy II, King of Egypt and son of another general and successor of Alexander, for the possession of Palestine. Antiochus III the Great, during his long reign from 223 to 187, reconquered the Iranian territory as far as India and carried Seleucid arms almost to the Egyptian border. But his attempt to conquer Greece brought him into conflict with the growing power of Rome, to which he was forced to cede all the territory beyond the Taurus Mountains and to pay a heavy war indemnity. In his wars he made effective use of the elephant. This animal became a Seleucid emblem and figured on the coins. Apamea-on-the-Orontes served as a depot where war elephants, mostly imported from India, were bred and trained.

Of the remaining sovereigns—there were about 26 in all—one of the best known was Antiochus IV Epiphanes, whose invasion of Egypt in 169 resulted in the occupation of its lower part. As an enthusiastic champion of Hellenism, he tried to impose its culture upon his subjects, particularly the Jews of Palestine, thus provoking the Wars of the Maccabees (167–160). The spoils of the Temple of Jerusalem helped to finance his lavish program of public buildings.

Among his 2d century successors, Antiochus V Eupator was a feeble and corrupt ruler, Alexander Balas was dissolute, and Demetrius II Nicator could not hold his own against the Parthians. Antiochus VII Sidetes restored the royal line and carried on war against the Jews, who were enjoying a period of independence under the Maccabees.

The Seleucid state had become so weak by the 1st century that Tigranes I, King of Armenia, ventured to invade Syria and penetrated as far south as Acre in 69. Five years later Pompey the Great, the Roman general, appeared on the scene, overthrew Antiochus XIII Asiaticus, and organized Syria into a Roman province. By that time the regions of Bactria, Parthia, Armenia, and Judaea had been lost.

Economy and Government. Syria was the backbone of the Seleucid kingdom. Syrian trade, both domestic and foreign, was of great consequence to the entire realm and to its population.

It was the Seleucid policy to promote commercial relations with the Greco-Roman world. The main inland highways were guarded by chains of strong colonies, which also provided adequate halts for the caravaners. Dura-Europos, founded around 300 by Seleucus I on the desert road between Syria and Mesopotamia, was such a colony and soon developed from a strong fortress into an important emporium.

The political institutions of the Seleucid realm were a strange mixture of Greek and Middle Eastern elements. The king not only enjoyed absolute power, but also was surrounded by a divine halo of Oriental origin. Some of the late kings, like Balas, assumed Semitic titles. The language of the court was, of course, Greek. Both army and navy were the king's. In its early stages the army consisted of Macedonians and Greeks recruited from the realm. Its nucleus was the phalanx. While the fleet at no time played a decisive part in any of the recorded battles, it performed a useful function in cooperating with the active army and in protecting military transport. The fleet was manned mostly by Phoenicians.

PHILIP K. HITTI
Author of "History of Syria"

Further Reading: Bevan, Edwyn R., *House of Seleucus*, 2 vols. (1902; reprint, Barnes & Noble 1966); Hitti, Philip K., *History of Syria, Including Lebanon and Palestine* (Macmillan 1951); Rostovtzeff, Michael I., *The Social and Economic History of the Hellenistic World*, 3 vols. (Oxford 1941).

SELF-DEFENSE, in law, is the almost universally respected right of the individual to take such measures as may be needed to protect his person or other legally recognized interests and, within certain limits, to protect the person and interests of third parties. Thus a person is not held legally responsible for the harm he may cause in the exercise of this right to respond to an attack, if the response is justifiable according to the specific requirements of the particular legal system.

The early common law, characterized by a theory of strict liability, recognized the right of self-defense, but required payment of compensation for any harm caused during exercise of the right. Subsequent law, although it endorsed the proper exercise of self-defense, maintained a curious distinction between *justifiable* and *excusable* homicide. Deadly force was regarded as justified only to repel a felony, and an obligation to retreat was imposed in the face of lesser crimes. However, modern Anglo-American law regards as justified the use of such force as may be necessary either in the defense of one's own person or property or the defense of another person or his property.

Practically, this "right to take the law into one's own hands" is founded on the urgent necessity to protect the individual and his or her lawful interests in those circumstances in which the legal machinery created for the purpose can be of no avail. One is not obliged passively to suffer the wrongful harming or destruction of one's person or interests, but the law also requires that the response be both necessary and proportionate to the apprehended harm. Excessive force results in full or partial responsibility for the harm done by the person who acts in self-defense.

H. H. A. COOPER, *Deputy Director*
Criminal Law Education and Research Center
New York University

SELF-INCRIMINATION. See FIFTH AMENDMENT; IMMUNITY.

SELFRIDGE, sel'frij, **Harry Gordon** (1864?–1947), American-born British merchant. He was born at Ripon, Wis., probably on Jan. 11, 1864. He worked in Chicago for the wholesale-retail firm of Field-Leiter, later Marshall Field & Co., becoming a partner in 1890. Leaving Marshall Field in 1904, he bought the firm of Schlesinger & Mayer and sold it in four months for a large profit.

On March 15, 1909, after an advertising campaign unprecedented in England, Selfridge opened the department store of Selfridge & Co., Ltd., in Oxford Street, London. Shrewd publicity, attractive displays, and imaginative merchandising helped make the store one of the largest in Europe. Selfridge later sold his share in the enterprise and took over William Whitely & Co., an old rival. He also combined other stores in London and Dublin, and formed a chain in several provincial cities. He became a British citizen in 1937. Selfridge died in London on May 8, 1947.

SELIGMAN, sel'ig-mən, **Edwin R. A.** (1861–1939), American economist, teacher, and editor, noted for theoretical contributions in the areas of public finance and taxation. Edwin Robert Anderson Seligman was born in New York City on April 25, 1861. His father, an international banker, had him tutored at home until the age of 11 by Horatio Alger, Jr., son of the famed author of rags-to-riches novels. At 14, Seligman entered Columbia University, where he mastered several languages. He later studied abroad and, in 1885, joined the Columbia faculty, becoming a professor of political science (1904–1931).

Seligman was a founder and president (1902–1904) of the American Economic Association. In such works as *The Shifting Incidence of Taxation* (1892) and *The Income Tax* (1911), he did much to clarify and popularize the concept of progressive taxation, or taxation based on the ability to pay. His *Economic Interpretation of History* (1902) had a considerable influence among historians.

In his later years, Seligman established the *Encyclopedia of the Social Sciences* and was its first editor in chief (1827–1835). He died in Lake Placid, N. Y., on July 18, 1939.

SELIM I, se-lēm' (1467–1520), Turkish sultan. He was a son of Bayezid II whom he dethroned in 1512 during a power struggle in which he overcame his brothers Corcud and Ahmed. The Persian Shah Ismail I, founder of the Safavid dynasty, had been Ahmed's ally. Before proceeding against Ismail, Selim, a Sunnite Muslim, is said to have slaughtered 40,000 of his Shiite subjects, who were the Persians' coreligionists and perhaps in sympathy with them. Ismail was completely defeated at Chaldiran in Armenia on Aug. 23, 1514, and Selim captured Tabriz.

The Mamluk sultan of Egypt, whom Selim accused of being allied with Ismail, was overwhelmed by Selim's Turks, well equipped with muskets and artillery, at Marj Dabiq, north of Aleppo, on Aug. 24, 1516. Syria then fell into Turkish hands, and in January 1517 Selim captured Cairo, adding Egypt to the Ottoman domain. His advance had been helped by the hatred the subject populations had for the Mam-luks. Selim transferred to Constantinople the puppet Abbasid caliph whom the Mamluks had maintained at Cairo, and the caliphal privileges and finally the title were absorbed by Selim's successors. Even more important, the holy cities of Arabia acknowledged the Ottoman sultan as their protector. Selim died near Çorlu on Sept. 20, 1520.

SELIM II, se-lēm' (1524?–1574), a Turkish sultan. He was the son of Suleiman I, whom he succeeded in 1566. Known as Selim the Drunkard, he was engrossed in the pleasures of his court. Selim relied principally on Mohammed Sökölli, grand vizier from 1560 to 1579, whose policy was pro-Venetian and anti-Spanish, and a Portuguese Jew, the financier Joseph Nasi.

During Selim's reign the Turks captured Tunis from Spain in 1569 and took Cyprus from the Venetians in 1570–1571. A Christian fleet inflicted a severe defeat on the Ottomans in the naval Battle of Lepanto in 1571. Selim, who died in Constantinople (Istanbul) on Dec. 12, 1574, was succeeded by his son Murad III.

SELIM III, se-lēm' (1761–1808), a Turkish sultan. He was born in Constantinople (Istanbul) on Dec. 24, 1761, the son of Mustafa III. Selim succeeded his uncle Abdul-Hamid I in 1789, during the war with Russia and Austria, who coveted the Ottoman lands in Europe.

After this conflict ended in the Treaty of Jassy (1792), Selim began a determined effort to reform the Ottoman state, particularly the finances and armed forces. He was an admirer of European civilization and recruited European advisers to help with his Westernization programs. Although he raised a small corps armed and trained in the European fashion, little was accomplished because of resistance by the Janissaries and religious leaders and the inertia of a ponderous administrative system.

Egypt, occupied by the French under Napoleon in 1798, was returned to Turkey in 1801. Continued Russian expansion led to an understanding between Selim and Napoleon and to war with Russia in 1806. In 1807, however, the sultan was overthrown and imprisoned by a rising of the Janissaries, who replaced him with Mustafa IV. Selim was strangled in Constantinople on July 28, 1808, as loyal forces approached the city. They captured it and made Mahmud II, Selim's nephew and pupil, the sultan. See also TURKEY–*History*.

SELINUS, si-lī'nəs, was an ancient Greek city on the southwestern coast of Sicily. It is on an isolated site about 8 miles (13 km) southeast of Castelvetrano. The modern Italian form of its name is Selinunte. It was founded in the 7th century B. C. and flourished during the 5th century.

Its traditional enemy, Segesta, after receiving ineffective aid from Athens in 415, called in the Carthaginians, who sacked Selinus in 409. It never recovered, though it became a Carthaginian tributary and was quickly repopulated. In 250 the Carthaginians razed the city and moved the inhabitants to Lilybaeum (modern Marsala). The remains include temples, walls, and an acropolis, none in a good state of preservation. Some of the fine sculptures on the temples were removed to the National Archaeological Museum in Palermo.

SELJUKS, sel-jōōks', originally Turkoman tribesmen, who in the 10th century fought their way into western Asia and established dynasties in Persia, Mesopotamia, Syria, and Asia Minor. Tradition derives the name from Seljuk, the chieftain of an Oghuz (Ghuzz) tribe that had settled in the Bukhara region and embraced Islam, of the Sunnite variety.

Great Seljuks. The history of the Seljuks assumes major importance in 1055 when Togrul (Tughrul, Togrul Beg), grandson of Seljuk, having pushed his conquest through Persia, entered the Abbasid capital, Baghdad, and was received by the Caliph al-Qaim as a deliverer from the domination of a Persian Shiite dynasty, the Buwayhids (Buyids). Al-Qaim bestowed on Togrul the title of "sultan."

Togrul was succeeded by his nephew, Alp Arslan, who in 1071 inflicted a crushing defeat on the Byzantine army at Manzikert (Malazkirt). This disaster, from which the Byzantine Empire never fully recovered, opened Asia Minor to an influx of Turkomans and Turks, in whose control it has remained.

Alp's son and successor, Malik Shah, who was ably served by his illustrious Persian vizier, Nizam al-Mulk, ruled a sultanate extending from Afghanistan to the Byzantine borders and is considered the greatest of his line. During his reign the frontiers were extended by various chieftains to Syria, Palestine, and western Asia Minor. New roads were opened, mosques built, canals dug, and large sums expended on caravansaries. After Malik Shah's death in 1092, civil wars among his young sons and their supporters and other disturbances led to the breakup of his house, although the main line, the Great Seljuks, maintained a nominal suzerainty in Persia until 1157.

Syrian Seljuks. The founder of Seljuk power in Syria was Tutush, son of Alp Arslan, who gained possession of Aleppo in 1094. His sons ruled at Aleppo and Damascus. Various Seljuk dynasts ruled in North Syria from 1078 to 1171.

Rum Seljuks. More important than the Seljuks of Syria were the Rum (meaning, Roman, or Western) Seljuks who ruled in Asia Minor from 1077 to about 1300, becoming independent with the decline of Great Seljuk power. This branch was founded by Suleiman ibn Qutulmish, a cousin of Alp Arslan, who was put in charge of the conquered territory and established himself at Nicaea (İznik), not far from Constantinople, in 1077. The Rum Seljuk capital was moved to Iconium (Konya) in 1084.

Hemmed in between the Byzantines on the northwest and the states the Crusaders established at Antioch (Antakya) and Edessa (Urfa) on the southeast, the Rum sultanate was limited to central Asia Minor. Nevertheless, trade flourished with the Italian merchant republics and the kingdom of Little Armenia in Cilicia, and sultans and princes vied in building mosques, madrasas (mosque schools), and other public buildings that still attract students and visitors. Gradually, however, Asia Minor became partitioned into rival petty principalities, which were overcome by the Mongol onslaught in the mid-13th century. One of these principalities was that of the Ottoman Turks, cousins of the Seljuks and, beginning with the 14th century, their heirs.

PHILIP K. HITTI
Author of "History of the Arabs"

SELKIRK, sel'kûrk, **5th Earl of** (1771–1820), Scottish humanitarian who founded the Red River Settlement in Canada. Thomas Douglas was born on June 20, 1771, on St. Mary's Isle in Kirkcudbrightshire, Scotland. He was educated at Edinburgh University, and succeeded to the earldom in 1799. Convinced that the poverty of the Scottish highland peasantry could only be ameliorated by emigration, Selkirk obtained grants of land in Upper Canada which later became Ontario, and on Prince Edward Island. In 1803 he sailed with the first emigrants, who settled near Orwell Bay, P. E. I. The other settlement, Baldoon, failed. In 1809 he acquired, through relatives, a substantial interest in Hudson's Bay Company, which in 1811 allotted him 116,000 acres near present-day Winnipeg. The first settlers for this colony sailed the same year, and founded the Red River Settlement by constructing Fort Douglas in 1812.

However, the ruthless hostility of the North West Company, an association of fur traders, brought on armed confrontation in 1816, during which a number of persons were killed, and the Scottish colonists were driven out of Fort Douglas. Selkirk, who was en route from Montreal with a force he had recruited there, retaliated by seizing the headquarters of the North West Company at Fort William, and dispatched a party that regained Fort Douglas in January 1817. Long litigation ensued, and Selkirk's opponents won heavy damages against him for the false arrest of two Nor'westers. Broken in both fortune and health, he died in Pau, France, on April 8, 1820. With the Red River colony, however, he laid the foundations of Winnipeg and Manitoba.

SELKIRK, sel'kûrk, **Alexander** (1676–1721), Scottish sailor, whose solitary sojourn on a Pacific island inspired Daniel Defoe's *Robinson Crusoe*. He was born in Largo, Fifeshire, Scotland, in 1676, the son of a shoemaker, and went to sea as a youth.

In May 1703 he joined William Dampier's privateering expedition to the South Seas, as sailing master on the galley *Cinque Ports*. After quarreling with his captain, Thomas Stradling, Selkirk was put ashore at his own request in October 1704 on the island of Más a Tierra, the largest of the Juan Fernández group, 400 miles (640 km) west of Chile.

He remained there until February 1709, when he was picked up by the vessel *Duke*, commanded by Woodes Rogers. He was appointed a mate and received command of a captured prize ship. He returned to England in 1711, but went back to sea and died on Dec. 12, 1721, when he was master's mate of the *Weymouth*.

The essayist Richard Steele, who met Selkirk, told his story in *The Englishman* (No. 26, Dec. 5, 1713). Rogers wrote of it in his *Voyage Round the World* (1712). Defoe evidently used some of this material in his yarn. There is no reason to believe that Selkirk left a journal.

SELKIRK, sel'kûrk, a town in southeastern Manitoba, Canada, is on the Red River, 23 miles (37 km) north of Winnipeg. It is an important steel-manufacturing center. A fort was built here in 1767, and an Indian mission was founded in the 1830's. It was planned in the 1870's to bridge the river for the Canadian Pacific Railroad, but quicksands made this impossible, and the railroad crossed at Winnipeg. Population: 10,037.

SELKIRK, sel'kûrk, a county in southeastern Scotland, is bounded on the north by Midlothian, on the east by Roxburgh, on the south by Dumfries, and on the west and northwest by Peebles. It is also known as Selkirkshire. It is roughly 24 miles (39 km) long and 12 miles (19 km) wide. The terrain is hilly, with the slopes becoming gentler and more rounded in the east. Selkirk's chief rivers are the Yarrow and the Ettrick, which flow into the Tweed, where it briefly cuts across the county in the north. Galashiels is the largest town, but the royal burgh of Selkirk is the county town.

The county is chiefly agricultural. Sheep and cattle are raised, and the chief crops are fodder, oats, turnips, and barley. The principal industry in the towns is wool. Yarn, tweeds, and hosiery are produced. There is a large tannery in Galashiels.

Selkirk is noted for the beauty of its scenery. William Wordsworth, Sir Walter Scott, and other poets have been inspired by the Valley of the Yarrow. St. Mary's Loch is the largest in southern Scotland. Man-made places of interest include the ruins of Newark Castle, which was the seat of a royal hunting ground in the days of King James I. Also noteworthy is the mansion of Ashiestel on the banks of the Tweed, where Sir Walter Scott lived from 1804 to 1812. The famous author was sheriff of Selkirk from 1799 to his death in 1832.

Selkirk was held by the Romans, who had a camp in the Ettrick Valley. It was a part of the British kingdom of Strathclyde and then a part of the Saxon kingdom of Northumbria. In the early part of the 11th century it was annexed to Scotland. Population: (1971), 20,868.

SELLERS, Peter (1925–1980), British character actor and comedian, known especially for his talent for vocal mimicry. He was born in Southsea, Hampshire, on Sept. 8, 1925, to a family active in show business. After attending St. Aloysius College in Highgate, he served in the

Peter Sellers, British film comic, portrayed a French detective in *The Pink Panther* (1964) and its sequels.

UNITED ARTISTS

Royal Air Force (1943–1946), and then spent several years doing comic impersonations in London vaudeville houses. He became well known in Britain through a zany radio series *The Goon Show* (1949–1959), which he helped originate.

Sellers made his stage debut in the farce *Brouhaha* in London in 1958. In the meantime he had appeared in motion pictures—among them, *Orders Are Orders* (1955), *The Ladykillers* (1956), and *The Naked Truth* (released in the United States as *Your Past Is Showing!* 1958). He made his first major impression on U. S. film audiences in *The Mouse That Roared* (1959), in which he played the parts of a prime minister, a duchess, and a constable. For his role as a self-important shop steward in *I'm All Right, Jack* (1959), he won a British Film Academy Award. His numerous other pictures include *Lolita* (1962); *Dr. Strangelove* (1964), in which he played four different roles; *The Pink Panther* (1964) and its sequels, in which he played the blundering Inspector Clouseau; and *Being There* (1979), for which he was nominated for an Academy Award. He died in London on July 24, 1980.

SELLING. See ADVERTISING; BROKER; MARKETING; SALES.

SELMA, sel'mə, a city in central Alabama, the seat of Dallas county, is on the Alabama River, about 50 miles (80 km) west of Montgomery. Situated in "the black soil belt," the city is a distributing point for the produce of the region, which includes cotton, livestock, and forage crops. Among the city's manufactures are farm machinery, lumber, lawnmowers, tables, bricks, and cigars.

Selma was settled in 1816, and in the early 19th century was the center of a prosperous cotton planting region. A number of fine homes dating from before the Civil War remain. During the war, Selma was a major Confederate supply depot, and there was a navy yard on the river. On April 2, 1865, a week before the war ended, Selma was wrecked by Union cavalry, which occupied the town after a brief engagement.

Selma was incorporated as a city in 1920. In 1965, it was a focus of civil rights demonstrations. On March 7, Dr. Martin Luther King, Jr., headed about 500 blacks who attempted to organize a protest march to the state capitol at Montgomery. Police broke up the demonstrators. A federal court ruled that the blacks had a constitutional right to march to petition the governor with regard to voting rights, and on March 21 a large number of marchers left Selma, protected by National Guardsmen. The march was peaceful, and reached Montgomery on March 25.

Selma is governed by a mayor and council. Population: 26,684.

SELSYN, sel'sin, a *self-synch*ronous electromechanical system for transmitting small torques over a distance without using a rigid mechanical connection. A selsyn is also called a synchro system. See also SYNCHRO.

SELWYN, sel'win, **George Augustus** (1809–1878), British prelate, who was the first Anglican bishop of New Zealand. He was born in Hampstead, England, on April 5, 1809. He was educated at Cambridge and was appointed bishop of New Zealand in 1841.

Having learned the Maroi language on the

voyage to New Zealand, Selwyn soon won the trust of the Maori people. He visited many of the South Sea islands and created a separate missionary diocese in Melanesia. During the first Maori War in the mid-1850's, Selwyn was unpopular with the Maoris because he was an Englishman and with the British settlers because he was a defender of Maori rights. But his promotion of a biracial New Zealand eventually won him the respect of both races.

Selwyn returned to Britain in 1867 and became bishop of Litchfield. He died in Litchfield on April 11, 1878. Selwyn College, Cambridge, incorporated in 1882, was built by public subscription in his memory.

SELYE, sel'yə, **Hans** (1907–   ), Canadian physician noted for his concept of biological stress. Selye was born in Vienna, Austria, on Jan. 26, 1907. He received both an M. D. degree (1929) and a Ph. D. (1931) at the German University, Prague. In 1932 he joined the faculty of McGill University in Montreal, Canada, and in 1945 he became head of the Institute of Experimental Medicine and Surgery in Montreal.

Selye's investigations into the effect of environmental stress on man and other animals tended to show that one of its chief effects is the release of adrenal-gland hormones, which normally lead to an appropriate adaptation to the stress-causing situation. Under certain conditions, however, particularly long-continued stress with continued release of hormones, it appeared that the adaptation mechanism malfunctions, leading to pathological effects such as ulceration and high blood pressure. Selye held that this malfunctioning causes a variety of diseases, including certain rheumatic and kidney disorders, which he called "diseases of adaptation."

SELZNICK, selz'nik, **David Oliver** (1902–1965), American motion picture producer. He was born in Pittsburgh, Pa., on May 10, 1902. He began his career in the film industry as an assistant story editor with Metro-Goldwyn-Mayer in 1926. The next year he went to Paramount as a producer and in 1931 became vice president in charge of production at RKO-Radio. He returned to Metro-Goldwyn-Mayer in 1933, becoming chief producer of Hollywood's largest studio. The first of the expensively cast films subsequently associated with his name was *Dinner at Eight* (1933), which was followed by several lavish filmings of literary works, such as *David Copperfield* and *Anna Karenina* (both 1935).

Because he found the administrative apparatus of a large studio unwieldy, he worked only in his own independent organizations from 1936. The culmination of his career—and perhaps of the entire Hollywood golden age—was attained in his production of *Gone with the Wind* (1939). His other films include *The Prisoner of Zenda* (1937), *Intermezzo* (1939), *Duel in the Sun* (1946), and *A Farewell to Arms* (1957). He died in Hollywood, Calif., on June 22, 1965.

SEMANTICS, si-man'tiks, is the study of meanings. The term is derived through Greek *sēmainein* ("to signify," or "mean"). It is concerned with the relation between words or other symbols and the objects or concepts to which they refer, as well as with the history of meanings and the changes they undergo. As an empirical study of word meanings in existing languages, semantics is a branch of linguistics. As an abstract study of the relation between symbols and what they mean, semantics is a branch of logic, in philosophy. (See LINGUISTIC ANALYSIS.) Semantics also became important to literary criticism, especially after the publication of such works as C. K. Ogden and I. A. Richards' *The Meaning of Meaning* (1923).

General semantics—as a doctrine and educational discipline developed by Alfred Korzybski, Wendell Johnson, S. I. Hayakawa, and others—is intended to promote understanding and cooperation among people through training in the critical use of words and other symbols. See also the Index entry *Semantics*.

SEMAPHORE, sem'ə-fôr, a visual signaling system, especially one that uses different positions of movable arms to represent letters, numbers, or other information. It is known that the early Greeks communicated over short distances by means of torches and flags, and that the Romans made use of towers. With the invention of the telescope about 1600, the range of visual signaling could have been greatly increased. A signaling system based on use of the telescope was described by Robert Hook late in the 17th century, but it remained for the French engineer Claude Chappe to put Hook's idea to use in 1794.

Chappe's semaphore had a line of towers spaced within sight of each other between Paris and Lille, a distance of 144 miles (230 km). A pivoted wooden beam with arms at the end was mounted on each tower. The positions of the beam and arms were read by means of a telescope and passed on from tower to tower. The system could convey a message over the 144-mile route in two minutes, thus providing a means of communication previously unmatched in speed. Other nations adopted Chappe's system, but it was largely superseded by the electric telegraph about 1850. However, a modified form of Chappe's system has survived because Hutton Gregory a telegraph engineer, introduced it for signaling on British railroads in the early 1840's.

Another semaphore system was developed from the post and arm. In this system, the message sender holds a flag in each hand and moves his arms to different positions. The U. S. Navy uses semaphore flags, each half red and half yellow, for short-range signaling. See also SIGNALS AND SIGNALING.

SEMARANG, sə-mä'räng, a city in Indonesia, is a seaport in northern Java and the capital of Central Java province. It is situated on the Java Sea at the mouth of the Semarang River, 260 miles (415 km) east of Djakarta.

Semarang is the primary commercial and industrial center of central Java. It is connected with Djakarta, Surabaja, and other Javanese centers by road, rail, and air routes. Its port is protected by a long jetty, but most ships anchor in a roadstead up to 3 miles (5 km) offshore, transferring cargo and passengers by lighter. During the December-March monsoon season, this anchorage often becomes unsafe.

The city's major industries include the manufacture of machinery and textiles and metalworking. Fishing is also an important commercial activity. The principal exports are rubber, coffee, sugar, cassava, and kapok.

Semarang is composed of two districts—an old town near the coast and a newer town farther inland. River silting and the development of coastal ponds for fish culture have left the harbor and its associated old town somewhat separated from the newer sections of the city and the hill suburb of Tjandi, which is 500 feet (150 meters) above sea level.

Semarang first came under Dutch control in 1678. It was occupied by the Japanese in 1942 during World War II and afterward became part of the Republic of Indonesia, proclaimed in 1945. Population: (1971) 633,000.

SEMELE, sem′ə-lē, in Greek mythology, was a princess of Thebes. The daughter of King Cadmus and Queen Harmonia, she was one of the lovely mortals who caught Zeus' roving eye. By Zeus she conceived a famous son, Dionysus.

Hera, Zeus' jealous wife, discovered her husband's affair with Semele and, to avenge herself, prompted the girl to ask her lover to appear in his Olympian splendor. Since he had sworn to deny her nothing, he had no alternative, and his radiance scorched her to death. Zeus, however, was able to save the unborn Dionysus, with whom she was pregnant, and to mature him in his thigh. Most accounts add that Semele's son later led her out of the underworld to heaven.

LIONEL CASSON, *New York University*

SEMEN, sē′mən, is a viscid, whitish fluid produced in the human male reproductive tract. It is also known as *seminal fluid*. It consists of large numbers of spermatozoa, the male reproductive cells, or gametes, produced in the testes and suspended in the secretions of several accessory glands, including the seminal vesicles, Cowper's gland, and the prostate gland. These secretions provide a favorable environment and nutrient material for the sperm. The fluid is usually neutral to slightly alkaline and serves as the vehicle in which sperm are maintained in the male reproductive tract and transferred to the female genital tract. It is usually released from the body by ejaculation. See HUMAN REPRODUCTION–*Accessory Sexual Structures;* SPERM.

SEMENOV, sə-myô′nôf, **Nikolai Nikolayevich** (1896–   ), Soviet physical chemist who shared the 1956 Nobel Prize in chemistry with Sir Cyril Hinshelwood "for their research on the mechanism of chemical reaction." Semenov was born in Saratov on April 16, 1896. He graduated from Leningrad University in 1917, worked at the Leningrad Physicotechnical Institute from 1920 to 1931, and became director of the Institute of Chemical Physics, Moscow, in 1931. In 1944, he became professor of physical chemistry at Moscow University.

Semenov did research on vapor condensation on solid surfaces, the ionization of salt vapors under the action of electronic impulses, the combustion and detonation of explosives, and chain reactions. In particular, he investigated the competition between ordinary reactions and chain reactions. In chemical chain reactions the reaction, once started, sustains itself by the interaction between the starting materials and transitory products (especially free radicals) continually formed and destroyed during the reaction. Semenov established some of the conditions that influence the formation of a chain reaction.

SEMICIRCULAR CANAL. See EAR–*Structure of the Human Ear.*

SEMICONDUCTOR, a material that conducts an electrical current less easily than does a metal such as copper or aluminum but much better than an insulator such as glass or ceramic. In both metals and semiconductors, electrical current is conducted by electrons that are free to move through the material under the influence of a voltage. However, there are far fewer free electrons in a semiconductor than in a metal. Furthermore, the number of free electrons in a semiconductor can be strongly dependent on temperature, whereas the number of free electrons in a metal is virtually unaffected by temperature.

Many different substances are semiconductors. For example, the elements silicon, germanium, and selenium are semiconductors, as are the chemical compounds indium antimonide, lead telluride, and cadmium sulfide. Most of the known semiconductors are crystalline solids, although some are noncrystalline materials. The scientific study of semiconductors is a branch of solid-state physics. See also SOLID-STATE PHYSICS.

Applications. Semiconductors are the active materials of most solid-state electronic devices, including transistors, diode rectifiers, light-emitting diodes, solar cells, light sensors, infrared detectors, and injection or p-n junction lasers. Semiconductor devices, especially the transistor, have revolutionized electronics, making possible such developments as small portable radios and large-scale electronic computers.

Probably the first semiconductor devices were selenium light sensors, which were used in the late 19th century. Several other types of devices were developed in the first half of the 20th century. However, widespread interest in semiconductors began in 1948 with the invention of the transistor. Continuing research on semiconductors is providing additional useful new materials and devices.

Properties. The most characteristic property of a semiconductor is a large increase in its electrical conductivity with temperature; this increase occurs over certain temperature ranges. Michael Faraday first observed this property in silver sulfide in 1833. It results from the fact that the number of electrons free to conduct current can increase sharply with temperature in a semiconductor. The conductivity also can be changed greatly by such influences as light, magnetic field, pressure, or tiny amounts of impurities in the material. This variety of properties not only makes semiconductors useful in various practical devices but also makes them interesting scientifically.

The properties of a semiconductor follow from the structure of the material. The atoms are joined mainly by sharing their valence (outershell) electrons in *covalent bonds;* that is, a valence electron from one atom cooperates with another from an adjacent atom to form each bond. Covalent bonding can be understood fully only by means of the quantum theory, but it is sufficient here to think of the bonds simply as rodlike electronic bridges connecting the atoms. The bonding is entirely covalent in an element such as silicon. In a compound such as indium antimonide the adjacent atoms are different elements, and the bonding force is partly ionic; that is, the atoms are partially ionized with opposite electric charges and therefore attract each other. See also BOND; VALENCE.

The structure of silicon, the most widely used semiconductor, provides an example for

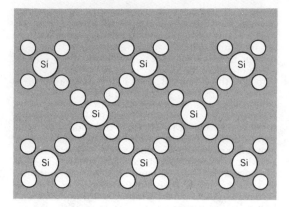

Fig. 1. In this two-dimensional model of a tiny volume of a silicon crystal, the silicon atoms (large circles) are bonded together by pairs of valence electrons (small circles). Since all valence electrons are locked up in bonds, silicon is a poor electrical conductor. Conductivity can be increased by the presence of impurity atoms, such as phosphorus or aluminum, which contain more or less than four valence electrons.

understanding the basic properties of semiconductors. Silicon has four valence electrons, so that each atom in its crystal is covalently bonded to four others, as shown in Fig. 1. In this model all the valence electrons are immobilized in bonds, so that there are no charges able to move through the crystal to conduct an electrical current when a voltage is applied to the crystal. At temperatures above absolute zero, thermal energy frees a tiny fraction of the bonding electrons, and these become conduction electrons. The fraction freed increases rapidly with temperature but remains small up to the melting point of the material. At room temperature pure silicon has only about one free electron per ten trillion bonding electrons. Other forms of energy, such as light, can also release bonding electrons. The minimum amount of energy required to excite an electron so that it is free from its bond is called the *energy gap* of the semiconductor.

When an electron is excited out of a bond, an empty electronic state, or "hole," remains. An electron from another bond can then move into this hole and leave a hole in its bond, and so on. One can think of a hole as a positively charged particle that changes place with a negatively charged electron. This is a second method of conduction. It is customarily described in terms of holes acting as positively charged carriers of electrical current. Conduction by the equal numbers of electrons and holes created by breaking interatomic bonds is called *intrinsic* because it results from the atoms and structure of the semiconductor itself.

The energy levels that the bonding electrons and the excited conduction electrons occupy actually are distributed over two almost continuous bands, called, respectively, the *valence band* and *conduction band*. They are separated by the energy gap of the semiconductor. The energy bands, which result from the wave properties of electrons, are beyond the scope of this article. However, the use of energy-band concepts is not essential to an adequate general understanding of the properties of semiconductors.

Now suppose that one silicon atom in Fig. 1

is replaced by an *impurity* atom such as phosphorus. It has five valence electrons instead of four, and it has one more proton in its nucleus than silicon. Four of these electrons bond covalently with the four surrounding silicon atoms. The fifth electron is not needed for bonding, but it is attracted weakly by the extra phosphorus proton. This electron can be freed for conduction by much less energy than that required to free a bonding electron. However, a conducting hole is not simultaneously created, as in an intrinsic semiconductor, because the electron is not freed from a bond. Impurity atoms with such extra valence electrons are said to make a semiconductor *n*-type because they provide conduction only by negative charges, the excess electrons.

Suppose next that one silicon atom in Fig. 1 is replaced by an impurity atom such as aluminum. It has only three valence electrons and one less nuclear proton than silicon. One of the bonds then lacks an electron and therefore contains a hole. This hole is attracted weakly by the aluminum atom. However, it can be freed by small energies to conduct current without simultaneous creation of a conducting electron. Impurity atoms with fewer valence electrons than the number needed for bonding are said to make a semiconductor *p*-type because they provide conduction only by holes, which act as *positive* charges.

The *n*-type and *p*-type semiconductors are analogous, differing only in the opposite signs of their charge carriers. Conduction determined by electron donors or acceptors in a semiconductor is called *extrinsic*. Extrinsic semiconductors are very useful because their properties can be adjusted by controlling their impurity concentrations and type.

P-N Junctions. A semiconductor crystal can be made *p*-type and *n*-type in adjacent regions to form *p-n* junction, as shown in Fig. 2. Many different semiconductor devices have single or multiple *p-n* junctions. To understand the properties of *p-n* junctions, recall that opposite charges

Fig. 2. P-N junction. A. When a positive voltage is applied to the *p* side of the junction and a negative voltage to the *n* side, electrons and holes are injected across the junction, carrying a substantial current. B. With applied voltages reversed, electrons and holes move away from the junction, and little current flows.

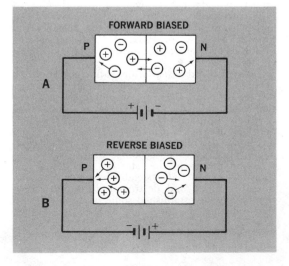

attract each other, whereas like charges repel. Thus, if one applies a so-called forward voltage across a *p-n* junction, as shown in Fig. 2a, holes are forced (*injected*) from the *p* region into the *n* region, and electrons are forced from the *n* region into the *p* region. As a result a substantial current flows. However, if the voltage is reversed, as shown in Fig. 2b, the holes and electrons in the *p* and *n* sides are drawn away from the junction, leaving a more nearly insulating layer. As a result, very little current flows. A *p-n* junction therefore acts as an electrical rectifier, which can convert alternating current into direct current.

The *p-n* junctions have other interesting and useful properties. Especially important are those involving light energy. When holes are injected into the *n* region by an applied forward voltage, an equal number of conduction electrons is drawn from the electrical contact into the *n* region to preserve the over-all electrical neutrality of the material.

An analogous result occurs in the *p* region, with holes being drawn into the *p* region to compensate for injected electrons. The injected hole and electron concentrations in both regions are higher than those without the applied voltage. The natural tendency of any physical system is to achieve its lowest possible energy state. This causes *recombination* of electrons and holes; that is, the free electrons drop into the holes, and the energy lost can be emitted as light. This effect is the basis of light-emitting diodes and injection or *p-n* junction lasers. Its inverse, the creation of a voltage across a *p-n* junction by electron-hole pairs excited by light, is used in solar cells and in *p-n* junction light sensors.

Preparation. Semiconductors are usually prepared as highly pure, nearly perfect single crystals that are grown by several different methods. Most common is slow solidification of molten material onto a single-crystal seed placed in contact with the melt, such as in the Czochralski and zone-melting techniques. Single crystals also can be grown by gradual condensation of atoms or molecules from a vapor onto a single-crystal substrate. See also CRYSTAL—*Crystal Growing*.

Semiconductors can be *doped* with selected impurities during crystal growth to achieve desired properties. Typical concentrations are only one impurity atom per every thousand to billion semiconductor atoms, and yet the impurities affect the semiconductor properties greatly. The *p-n* junctions generally are made either by diffusing *p-* or *n*-type impurities into a crystal of the opposite type at a high temperature, or by introducing impurities of each type consecutively during crystal growth.

See also ELECTRONICS—*Microelectronics*; TRANSISTOR.

DONALD LONG
Honeywell Corporate Research Center

Bibliography

Blakemore, John S., *Solid State Physics* (Saunders 1969).
Holden, Alan, *The Nature of Solids* (Columbia Univ. Press 1965).
Long, Donald, *Energy Bands in Semiconductors* (Wiley-Interscience 1968).
Wolf, Helmut F., *Semiconductors* (Wiley-Interscience 1971).
Wright, Donald A., *Semi-Conductors* (Methuen 1966).

SEMICONDUCTOR DIODE, dī'ōd, a two-terminal solid-state device characterized primarily by its ability to rectify electric current—that is, to pass current readily only in one direction. Because semiconductor diodes not only can rectify but also perform many other functions, they are used in almost every type of electronic equipment. Another main type of diode is the vacuum-tube diode. See also ELECTRONICS—*Electron Tubes*.

A semiconductor diode is a small, solid semiconductor crystal that is permeable to electrons. Current flow in only one direction is achieved by creating an electrical barrier within the semiconductor or at its surface. Passage of current is allowed when the barrier is reduced by applying a "forward" voltage, but current is blocked when the barrier is increased by applying a "reverse" voltage.

The rectifying barrier can be formed in two ways. In a *metal-semiconductor diode,* the barrier is formed near the surface of the crystal in the region where the metal contacts the semiconductor. The first semiconductor point-contact diodes had barriers of this type. In a *p-n junction diode* the barrier is formed within the semiconductor crystal between a *p* region that passes current with positive charges (called holes) and an *n* region that passes current with negative charges (electrons). The *p* and *n* regions are formed by adding selected impurities to the crystal.

Compound Semiconductor Diodes. Most semiconductor diodes are made from silicon or germanium, but some are made from compound materials such as gallium arsenide or gallium phosphide. Compound semiconductors are particularly useful in *p-n* junction diodes that function as energy conversion devices. These devices include laser diodes, which use an energy conversion process to generate a coherent beam of monochromatic radiation; electroluminescent diodes, which emit noncoherent light when current is passed through them; and diodes used as solar cells, which convert light into electrical energy.

SEMICONDUCTOR DIODES AND THEIR FUNCTIONS

Type	Function
Rectifier	
Silicon or germanium p-n junction diode	Conversion of ac power to dc power
Selenium plate rectifier	Conversion of ac power to dc power
Small-Signal Diode	
Varactor	Voltage-dependent capacitor
Varistor	Current-dependent resistor
Backwards diode	Low-resistance rectifier
Schottky diode	High-frequency, fast switching
Point-contact diode	High-frequency, fast switching
Voltage Regulator	
Zener diode	Constant-voltage source
Negative-Resistance Device	
Tunnel diode	High-frequency oscillator, switch
Read diode	High-frequency oscillator
Energy Converter	
Solar cell	Light (radiation) detector
Photodiode	Light (radiation) detector
Laser diode	Light-beam source
Electroluminescent diode	Light source

History. The first practical use for the diode was in the early 20th century when a lead sulfide, zincite, or silicon carbide semiconductor crystal was placed in contact with a thin flexible wire, called a *cat's whisker*, to form a signal detector in a radio receiver. By 1920 the vacuum tube almost completely replaced this early point-contact diode as the detector.

During World War II, silicon point-contact diodes were used at frequencies as high as 3,000 megahertz. This success prompted renewed interest in silicon and germanium, which led to development of the point-contact transistor in 1947 and the semiconductor p-n junction in 1949.

During the 1950's and the 1960's, the p-n junction diode replaced the vacuum-tube diode for most functions. Compared with a vacuum-tube diode, a p-n junction diode is much smaller, more rugged, more reliable, requires no warm-up time, operates with smaller voltages, generates less heat, and costs less.

FRED D. ROSI, *RCA Corp.*

SEMINARY. See THEOLOGICAL EDUCATION.

SEMINOLE INDIANS, sem'ə-nōl, a North American Indian tribe of the Southeastern United States. A Muskogean-speaking people, they evolved as a distinct tribe at about the time of the American Revolution, formed basically around a nucleus of Oconee Indians. The Oconee, a Hitchiti subdivision of the Creek people of Georgia, had migrated to Florida in the mid-1700's. Florida, then Spanish territory, was a refuge area for many remnant Indian groups, including the Yamasee, Apalachicola, Yuchi, and Okmulgee, and also for runaway Negro slaves. From these peoples emerged the entity known as the Seminole. The Creek term *simanóle*, meaning "runaways" or "those who separate," indicates their status. The surviving Florida Seminole call themselves *Ikaniúksalgi*, or Peninsula People.

In 1842–1843, after the second Seminole War, the main body of the Seminole, usually estimated at about 3,800 people, was removed as part of the Five Civilized Tribes to Indian Territory in Oklahoma. There, some 3,000 of their descendants remain. A small group split off in 1850 under the leadership of Wild Cat (Coacoochee) and settled in Mexico, near Eagle Pass, Texas. More than 1,000 Seminole live in central and southern Florida, descendants of the perhaps 300 survivors who remained in the wilds of the Everglades until the U. S. government gave up the struggle to relocate them. Divided into two major groups, Mikasuki and Cow Creek, they inhabit four reservations: Seminole, Dania, Brighton, and Big Cypress. Another group lives along the Tamiami Trail in southern Florida.

The Florida Seminole are tall and are darker than most Indians, due to frequent intermarriage with Negroes. The men live by fishing, small-game hunting, and manual skills, and the women are adept at crafts. Vegetables and tobacco are raised. The traditional platform homes, called *chickees*, are built of palmetto thatch mounted on posts above the boggy land, though most Seminole live in more modern dwellings.

The culture of the Oklahoma Seminole differs little from that of the other members of the relocated Five Civilized Tribes. All share living conditions similar to those of the poorer rural whites of the state. Once numbered among the most isolated of the U. S. Indian tribes, the Seminole have, since World War II, welcomed contacts, seeking education and modern facilities.

See also CREEK INDIANS; SEMINOLE WARS.

FREDERICK J. DOCKSTADER
Museum of the American Indian

Further Reading: Cotterill, Robert S., *The Southern Indians* (Univ. of Okla. Press 1954); McReynolds, Edwin C.. *Seminoles* (Univ. of Okla. Press 1957).

SEMINOLE WARS, sem'ə-nōl, the campaigns waged by the United States against the Seminole Indians. The first, a short struggle in 1817–1818, was in a sense a continuation of the Creek War (1813–1814). It was fought largely out of U. S. ambition—spurred especially by Gen. Andrew Jackson—for possession of Spanish Florida, which fell to the United States shortly afterward. The second, usually referred to as the Seminole War proper (1835–1842), was the fiercest war waged against the American Indians. It left more than 1,500 soldiers and uncounted civilians dead, at a cost of well over $20 million. The Seminole Wars created an indelible blot on Indian-white relations because of the evident duplicity of the U. S. government.

Both conflicts grew out of frictions engendered by the War of 1812, the presence of many Negro slaves who had fled to the Seminole Indians for protection, the failure of the government to control Georgia and Florida slave raiders, and the injustices of treaties negotiated with the Seminole under questionable circumstances.

The campaigns of the second war were an outstanding demonstration of guerrilla warfare by the Seminole. The war chiefs Jumper, Alligator, Micanopy, and Osceola, leading 3,000–5,000 poorly armed warriors, were pitted against four U. S. generals and more than 200,000 troops. As the hostilities dragged on, the frustrated U. S. forces turned more and more to desperate measures. Gen. Thomas S. Jesup seized Osceola under a flag of truce and imprisoned him, confident that this would end the resistance. Although Osceola died in prison in 1838, other Seminole leaders took up the battle, and the war continued. A nominal end to the hostilities came in 1842, but no peace treaty was ever signed. Most of the Seminole were removed west to Indian Territory, but a few hundred escaped into the Everglades, where their descendants still live.

FREDERICK J. DOCKSTADER
Museum of the American Indian

Further Reading: Foreman, Grant, *Indian Removal* (Univ. of Okla. Press 1953); Josephy, Alvin M., Jr., *The Patriot Chiefs* (Viking 1961); Tebbel, John W., and Jennison, Keith W., *The American Indian Wars* (Harper 1960).

SEMIPALATINSK, syi-myi-pu-lá'tinsk, is a city in the USSR, in the northeast Kazakh republic, on both banks of the Irtysh River. It is the third-largest Kazakh city and the capital of Semipalatinsk oblast. The city was founded in 1718 as a Russian frontier fortress, and during the 19th century it grew into a central Asian commercial city. The relocation of factories from west of the Ural Mountains during World War II spurred its growth. It has large food processing, building materials, and textile industries.

The oblast, bounded on the southeast by China, has an area of about 67,600 square miles (175,085 sq km). Most of it is flat, with mountain ranges only in the center and along the eastern frontier. The Irtysh is the largest river. Grain and cattle are raised in the north, while sheep-herding predominates in the southern desert. There are valuable mineral deposits. Population: (1970) of the city, 236,000.

SEMIPRECIOUS STONE, a gemstone, usually of a softer mineral, that is considered less valuable than a fine-quality diamond, emerald, ruby, or sapphire. However, the term is imprecise. See also GEM—*Value.*

SEMIRAMIS, si-mir'ə-mis, is a figure of ancient Southwest Asian history, legend, and mythology. The historical Semiramis, called Sammuramat by the Assyrians, was the wife of the Assyrian king Shamshi-Adad V (reigned 823–811 B. C.) and the mother of Adadnirari III (reigned 810–783). She was queen regent during the minority of her son from about 810 to 806.

Semiramis seems to have been a Syrian princess, since her name, which was originally Shemiramat ("the goddess Shemi is exalted"), is found in Hebrew as Shemiramoth and has good Syrian parallels. She occupied a more important place than any other known Assyrian queen, and her dates agree well with the tradition preserved by Herodotus. Thus the identification appears certain. Her husband's last known triumph was the conquest of Babylonia, and therefore Herodotus' statement that she built great irrigation works at Babylon is reasonable. Her armies are said to have fought in Armenia and Media.

The legendary Semiramis appears first in the works of the Greek historian Ctesias (about 400 B. C.). There she is said to be a daughter of the Aramaean goddess Atargatis (a form of Astarte and Ishtar) and the wife of Ninus, the legendary founder of the Assyrian Empire. She herself is supposed to have had a long reign, during which she enlarged the empire enormously. At her death, she left her throne to her son Ninyas and was turned into a dove.

The legendary Semiramis enjoyed tremendous popularity as the Syrian and Armenian Shamiram, and many monuments were attributed to her. She is the protagonist of Calderón's drama *The Daughter of the Air,* Voltaire's tragedy *Sémiramis,* and Rossini's opera *Semiramide.*

W. F. ALBRIGHT
Formerly, Johns Hopkins University

SEMIRARA ISLANDS, sä-mē-rä'rä, in the central Philippines, between Mindoro and Panay. The Semirara group consists of three main islands (Semirara, Caluya, Sibay) and several islets. It has an area of about 50 square miles (130 sq km). The chief economic activities are coal mining, coconut cultivation, and fishing. The islands, inhabited by Visayans, are part of Antique province. Population: (1960) 5,993.

SEMITE, sem'īt, a person whose native tongue belongs to the Semitic language family. The term "Semitic" is properly used only in reference to language. It should never be used in connection with race or religion. Ancient Semites included the Akkadians, Assyrians, Babylonians, Canaanites (including the Phoenicians), Carthaginians, and Hebrews. Modern Semites include the Arabs, many Ethiopians, and native Israelis.

The Semites originally inhabited a common area, probably in the neighborhood of Arabia, and spoke a common language called Proto-Semitic. Before 2500 B.C. many of them migrated in successive waves to Mesopotamia, regions along the Mediterranean coast, and the Nile Delta. Several distinct states eventually emerged, each with a Semitic language and its own culture and religion. Among these states were Babylonia and Assyria. The Hebrews, who migrated to Palestine, were the founders of the first major monotheistic religion, which gave rise to modern Judaism and made important contributions to Christianity and Islam. See also SEMITIC LANGUAGES.

SEMITIC LANGUAGES are the languages spoken by the nations of whom Shem was considered the common ancestor. The word Semitic comes from the Septuagint form of the name Shem. Shemitic, derived directly from the Hebrew, is much less frequent. The Semitic languages form a group somewhat like the Aryan group, although the relationship of the different languages is much closer. The members of the group do not entirely correspond to the list of the descendants of Shem given in Genesis 10:21–31. Elam, for example, which is included, in 10:22, was not a Semitic people, while the Canaanites, including the Sidonians, who were Semitic, are given in 10:15 among the descendants of Ham. Such facts indicate that the table of nations in Genesis 10 was not entirely ethnological, but at least partly geographical: the nations were grouped according to their geographical distribution in the time of the writer.

General Divisions. The Semitic languages are often divided into two main divisions, Northern and Southern. But the Northern Semitic languages can be divided into three groups, Eastern, Northern, and Middle, which are separated from one another by differences very nearly as great as those between the two divisions first mentioned. It seems better, therefore, to recognize the general division as having four members or branches —Eastern, Northern, Middle, and Southern Semitic languages.

The Eastern Branch. The Eastern branch includes the Babylonian and Assyrian languages. Assyrian is really a dialect of Babylonian, there being but very slight phonetic differences between the two, although the difference is somewhat greater in the form of the characters. Babylonian is found much earlier than Assyrian and also continues somewhat later. The Babylonian inscriptions thus far found begin probably about 4000 B.C, possibly somewhat earlier, and extend to the capture of Babylon in 538 B. C. Babylonian was also used later as a literary language under the Persian and Greek rulers of Babylonia. Assyrian inscriptions extend from about 1800 B. C. to shortly before the fall of Nineveh in 606 B. C.

The Northern Branch. The Northern Semitic, or Aramaic, branch includes many languages and dialects, to all of which the general term Aramaic is applied. The oldest Aramaic literature is found in northern Syria in the inscription of Zakkūr, 9th–8th century B. C., and in the inscriptions from Senjirli, of the 8th century B. C., some words on Assyrian and Babylonian tablets being only a little later. The language of these inscriptions differs very much from the later Aramaic languages and resembles the Canaanite language in many particulars. The Aramaic languages are divided into two principal branches, Western and Eastern, the geographical distribution of which was largely in harmony with these names. Western Aramaic may be called one language, with the following principal dialects: biblical Aramaic, being the language of portions of the Old Testament books of Daniel and Ezra and of a few words elsewhere in the Old Testament; Targumic Aramaic, usually so called, the language of the Palestinian Targums; the similar language of most of the Gemara of the Palestinian Talmud and of the Palestinian Midrashim, which is also found in small parts of the Mishna, and also of the Babylonian Gemara; Samaritan, the language of the Samaritan Targum to the Pentateuch; the language of some Jewish inscriptions and papyri from Egypt, dating somewhat before the time of Christ; the language of the few Aramaic words found in the New Testament; the language of the inscriptions found in Tadmor or Palmyra; and the language of the Nabataean inscriptions found in Idumea and vicinity. The only modern representative of Western Aramaic is the language spoken at the present time by a few people near Damascus, in and near the village of Malula. This language is written in the Syriac character, but it belongs to the Western Aramaic class.

Eastern Aramaic includes Syriac; Mandaic, the language of the Christian sect of Mandaeans who lived east of the Tigris; and the language of the most of the Babylonian Gemara. Syriac was the language of the Christian Aramaeans and was employed in an extensive literature, chiefly of an ecclesiastical nature, extending from the 2d to the 13th century A. D., including the translation of the Bible known as the Peshitta. The word Syriac means the same as Aramaic and was adopted by the Aramaeans from the Greeks, because the word Aramaic had come to be used as meaning heathen. After the separation of the two sects known as the Nestorians and Jacobites, each developed its own dialect, known as the Nestorian and the Jacobite, respectively. The actual dialectical differences are slight, chiefly in the pronunciation of the vowels. In writing, somewhat different forms of the characters were used and the vowels were represented by entirely distinct systems—in the Nestorian dialect by dots and in the Jacobite by characters borrowed from the Greek. The modern representative of the Nestorian branch is the language used by the Nestorian Christians, in parts of Persia, especially in the city of Urmia and vicinity, in some villages in Kurdistan, and in portions of Mesopotamia. This language shows many changes from ancient Syriac, those in the verb being especially striking, while the vocabulary has received a large number of foreign words, especially from Arabic, Persian, and Kurdish.

Further, this language has forms not found in Syriac but preserved in other Aramaic languages as well as in some of the other Semitic languages, so that it is evidently descended not from ancient Syriac itself but from a closely related dialect. There are four principal dialects of modern Syriac, that used in Urmia and vicinity, that of northern Persia and some adjacent regions in Turkey, that of Kurdistan, and that of Mosul and vicinity. While the language is the same in all, there are many dialectical variations. The modern representative of the Jacobite Syriac is the language of Tur Abdin, in the western part of Kurdistan. Although this language is similar to the modern Nestorian language, there are many differences.

The chief general feature that distinguishes the Eastern and Western Aramaic languages is the preformative of the imperfect. This is *y* in all the Western Aramaic dialects, although a few forms with *l* are found in biblical Aramaic, and *n* in all the Eastern, although Mandaic and the Babylonian Talmud have *l* along with *n*. In modern Syriac the verbal form is so much different that no preformative is used.

The Middle Branch. The middle Semitic branch is also called Canaanite, for all its languages are often included under the general term Canaanite.

The only one of these languages in which much literature has survived is the Hebrew. Nearly all of the Old Testament is in ancient Hebrew. Aside from this, the oldest Hebrew documents are probably about 75 inscribed potsherds found at Samaria in 1910, written in ink with a reed pen, containing brief business memoranda. These are usually ascribed to the time of Ahab, the first half of the 9th century B. C. A small limestone calendar tablet was found at Gezer in 1908 and is assigned to the 8th century. The Siloam inscription is usually dated about 700 but is possibly much later. Various inscribed Hebrew seals have been found, dating perhaps from the 8th century on. Coins with Hebrew characters are from the 2d century B. C. to the 2d century A. D. New Hebrew or Mishnaic Hebrew is found chiefly in the Mishna and also somewhat in the Gemara and in related works. To a certain extent, the Jews have continued to use Hebrew as a literary language to the present time, but the bulk of their later literature was produced in the Middle Ages. The language as thus used is ordinarily similar to Mishnaic Hebrew. Hebrew, modernized by the coinage of new words, is one of the two official languages of the State of Israel, the other being Arabic.

The Phoenician has much that is identical with the Hebrew, while the differences are slight, affecting the vowels more than the consonants, although the vocabulary shows some variations. It is found in inscriptions from Phoenicia and its colonies, prominent among the latter being Carthage, where the language was called Punic. Considerable portions are also found quoted in works of Latin and Greek authors, chiefly in the play *Poenulus* of the Roman dramatist Plautus. Most of the Phoenician inscriptions are from the 4th century B. C. and later. Some are as old as the 6th century, while the oldest inscription may belong to the 8th century or a little earlier. The inscription of Eshmunazar, from the time of Alexander the Great, is the most important. In this group are also included the Canaanite, Moabite, Ammonite, and Edomite languages. The last two are known only from the proper names found in the Old Testament and the inscriptions of other nations. The Moabite is known from that source and also from the Moabite stone, written by Mesha, king of Moab, and dating from about 850 B. C. The Canaanite, aside from information given in the Old Testament, is known from glosses found in the Tell el-Amarna tablets about 1400 B. C. All four are substantially identical with Hebrew, the Canaanite and Moabite (which are known more fully than the other two) showing slight dialectical variations. Moabite and Phoenician, like Hebrew, have *waw* consecutive with the imperfect. Some of the Philistine proper names given in the Old Testament are Semitic. It is generally agreed, however, that the nation was not Semitic, but perhaps learned and used the common Canaanite language after its arrival in Palestine.

The Southern Branch. The Southern Semitic branch is sometimes called the Arabic group because the Arabic language is its most important representative. Under Arabic may be included ancient, or classical, Arabic; its descendant, modern Arabic; and southern Arabic, often improperly called Himyaritic, including the closely related dialects of Sabaean and Minaean. The great work in ancient Arabic is the Koran, composed by Mohammed, although a few poems are older than this sacred work. Printed modern Arabic is substantially the same wherever it is found and does not differ greatly from the ancient language. The spoken language, however, is divided into many dialects, of which the most important are those of Syria, Egypt, Mesopotamia, Tunis, Malta and Oman, and Zanzibar. Under the general head of modern Arabic may be included the extensive Arabic literature from soon after the time of Mohammed to the present time. Sabaean and Minaean are found in inscriptions, chiefly in southern Arabia. These are of uncertain date, although it is now often claimed that the earliest Minaean inscriptions are earlier than 1000 B. C., while the oldest Sabaean are somewhat later.

Modern representatives of these dialects are found in the present dialects of the same region, of which little is known. Two of them are the Mahri and the Socotri. Included in the Southern Semitic branch is also Ethiopic, or more properly Geez. This was probably a descendant of Sabaean. The ancient Ethiopic was the language of Abyssinia. It closely resembles the Arabic dialects, sharing with them some of their most characteristic features, while in many other respects it differs greatly from them. It was the spoken language of Abyssinia until approximately the 13th century A. D.

The earliest known literature comes from about 500 A. D. Most of the literature consists of translations from other languages. The most important documents are the translation of a part of the Bible, made about 500 A. D., and the apocryphal book of Enoch, which is a translation from a lost original. Modern representatives of the language in the same region are the Tigré, the Tigrina, and, with extensive incorporation of foreign elements, the Amharic, together with dialects related to the Amharic, such as the Harari and Gurague.

Some scholars class the Egyptian language as Semitic. It seems evident, however, that it is not but that very early in prehistoric times it was subjected to strong Semitic influences. Doubtless these influences can be attributed to invaders from Asia.

The Written Characters. The written character of the Babylonian and Assyrian languages is the cuneiform. The writing is partly ideographic and partly syllabic—but not at all alphabetic. According to the common view, however, the cuneiform was not the invention of the Babylonians but was taken by them from the earlier inhabitants of the land, the non-Semitic Sumerians. It was originally a picture writing, like the hieroglyphics of the Egyptians, but has been so largely conventionalized that in most cases the resemblance to the original picture has been lost. The Assyrian forms, when they differ from the Babylonian, show modifications in the direction of greater conventionalizing and increased regularity. Aside from the cuneiform, all Semitic languages use an alphabet, consisting entirely of consonants, which goes back to the same original forms. Ethiopic is an apparent exception, in that the vowels are written with the consonants—that is, each consonant has six or more different forms according to the vowel following it. These forms have such a resemblance to those of the other Semitic languages, however, and in particular to the Sabaean that is written without vowels, that it is probable that the earliest form contained simply the consonants and that the modifications of form for the expression of the vowels show a later development.

What is commonly regarded as the earliest form of the Semitic alphabet is usually called the Phoenician, a name given to it by the Greeks because they obtained it from the Phoenicians. But the Phoenician alphabet at the time of our earliest knowledge, about the 8th century B. C., was practically identical with the forms found about the same time among the other Canaanites and the Aramaeans.

The origin of this alphabet is doubtful. The common view at present is that it was derived from certain Egyptian characters, although some regard it as taken from the Babylonian. After the Greeks obtained this alphabet, it passed from them to the Romans and then to the many modern alphabets derived from the Greek and Latin. The earliest inscriptions known in this alphabet are probably the ostraka from Samaria in Hebrew, of the 9th century; the Hebrew Gezer inscription, of the 8th century; the Moabite stone, about 850 B. C., in the Moabite language; a Phoenician inscription, of about the same date; the Siloam inscription, about 700 B. C., in Hebrew; and the Zakkūr inscription and the inscriptions from Senjirli, about the 8th century B. C., in Aramaic. All have substantially the same forms. Within the next few centuries two types gradually arose, the old Hebrew and the Aramaic, or square, characters.

The old Hebrew was used in the writing of Hebrew till the Jews adopted Aramaic as their vernacular, which was at any rate before the time of Christ, when they naturally came to use ordinarily the Aramaic form of character for the Hebrew as well. The Samaritans have always used the old Hebrew form of character, with many changes, especially in the direction of greater elaborateness. The only modern use of this form of character is in the Samaritan of the present day.

The earliest Syriac character, known as the Estrangela, was a cursive writing developed from the Aramaic form. From this came the later Syriac forms, both Nestorian and Jacobite, as well as the Arabic characters, including both the Kufic and the Neskhi.

The southern Arabic characters, found in Sabaean and Minaean, differ greatly from the characters already mentioned and are perhaps earlier than any other forms that have been found. They are to be traced, however, to the same common character in an early form. The Ethiopic character is a development of the southern Arabic form.

The Ethiopic language and the Assyrian and Babylonian are written from left to right. All the other Semitic languages are written from right to left.

General Characteristics of the Semitic Languages. The modern Semitic languages and dialects have been greatly changed by the influence of the other languages with which they have been brought in contact. Therefore, the modern languages should not receive a prominent place in the consideration of the general characteristics of the Semitic languages, although the modern languages may offer confirmatory testimony in some particulars.

Some general characteristics of the ancient Semitic languages may well be noted, keeping in mind a comparison with other languages, especially with the Aryan group. It is not claimed, of course, that the characteristics that will be named have no similarities elsewhere but rather that they may fairly be considered general characteristics of the Semitic group, as they could not be of any other group.

The Semitic languages divide the letters into two general classes, consonants and vowels, and the consonants are the more important. Roots are composed only of consonants, while the vowels are used, along with consonantal changes, to express modifications of the fundamental root idea. Although the vowels are thus important, it is in a domain entirely subordinate to the consonants. The result of this is that originally, in all the languages except the Assyro-Babylonian and Ethiopic, only the consonants were written and the vowels were added by means of small marks, for the most part above or below the consonants. In fact, it was only in comparatively late times that the vowels were written at all. The inscriptions—such as those of Phoenicia and of Senjirli, the Moabite stone, and the Siloam inscription—have no vowels. In the Assyro-Babylonian the vowels are expressed, but the characters are usually supposed to have been borrowed, as has already been noted. In the Ethiopic the vowels are expressed by slight changes in the form of the consonant, a feature, however, that is probably to be regarded as a late development, although it goes back to the earliest known literature. Originally, it is probable that only the consonants were written.

Originally the Semitic languages were characterized by the possesssion of a large number of gutturals, some of them very peculiar. In the course of time, however, part of these were lost by most of the languages, the Arabic preserving them the most fully.

The Semitic roots are almost entirely triliteral, that is, each consists of three consonants. An occasional root is found containing four or more consonants, but these are exceptional. On the other hand, the belief is growing that many of the triliteral roots, especially some of the so-called weak roots, were originally biliteral. But here the tendency of the languages toward triliterality is seen plainly from the fact that to a large extent these roots have assumed the appearance of triliterality.

The relation between nouns and verbs is very close. In fact most of the features of inflection are the same in both, the noun features being the earlier.

A prominent characteristic of verbal inflection, with many similarities in the nouns as well, is the development of many different stems or conjugations from the same root. These are formed partly by internal change in consonants and vowels and internal additions and partly by external additions. Thus one stem has an intensive meaning, another a causative, another a reflex, and so on. In the original Semitic there must have been many different stems. Some have been lost in each language. The Ethiopic has preserved the largest number of stems, the Arabic the next largest, and then the Assyrian. These stems afford a very concise way of expressing many different shades of meaning connected with a single root idea, each of which would in most languages require either the use of a compound verb or the addition of separate words for its expression.

The languages use pronominal suffixes attached to nouns, verbs, and prepositions. These are really shortened forms of the pronouns. With nouns they have the force of a genitive; with prepositions, of a dative; and with verbs, ordinarily of an objective accusative.

The languages are distinctly objective. The personal standpoint of the speaker or writer counts for little. In the verb, the third person is the simple uninflected form, the starting point of the inflection. (In the Aryan languages the first person is the starting point.) The present time, the time of the speaker or writer, is of little importance in comparison with the past and future. The use of the tenses is often based upon an assumed standpoint. So also many phases imply the assumption of a standpoint other than that of the writer or speaker.

Certain phenomena may be classed together under the general statement that they show a lack of development in the languages. This is not, however, due to lack of time or of favoring circumstances, because these features are ordinarily found to characterize in a similar way all the languages at all times and under all circumstances. These phenomena indicate rather psychological characteristics of the people, their natures are not complex, they show limitations in some directions. Certain developments that are common in Aryan languages, the Semites did not feel to be necessary. Among these characteristics are the following:

Most of the Semitic languages have only two tenses, usually called the perfect and the imperfect. There is difference of opinion as to whether these differed in their fundamental meaning from some of the tenses of the Aryan languages. The later forms of several of the languages developed a present tense from a participle, which is only suggested in the earlier usage. In general, the Semitic tense usage is thus much less fully developed than the Aryan. Moods also are relatively undeveloped. They are found only in connection with the imperfect tense—even the imperative being derived from it—and in most of the languages they are not widely used.

The nouns have only two genders, masculine and feminine.

There is an almost entire absence of compound words, either nouns or verbs, except in proper names.

The syntax is in many particulars of a simple and undeveloped kind. There is a strong tendency to leave much in the relation of clauses and sentences to inference. This leads to the very frequent use of parataxis. There is but a small number of particles of every kind. In most of the languages the original case endings have been lost, but there has been no great development of prepositions to take their place. There is also a scarcity of adjectives in most of the languages, so that nouns are frequently used in place of adjectives.

Relation to the Primitive Language. No existing language can be called the common mother of the other Semitic languages, or even the most primitive in every respect. Each of the languages is probably in some features more primitive than any other. But the Arabic preserves far more that is primitive both in grammatical forms and syntactical usage than any other of the languages. This is in spite of the fact that the known Arabic literature is very late. The Arabs in their desert home remote from other nations changed the language less than other peoples in a short space of time.

Thus the Arabic preserves the case endings, which have been largely lost in the other Semitic languages, except in the Assyro-Babylonian, where they are often used indiscriminately. The Arabic preserves the original endings —sometimes consonants but more often vowels— both in verbs and nouns, which are largely lost elsewhere. The Arabic retains in most cases the original vowels, which in the other languages undergo various changes, such as heightening, shortening (volatilization), and contraction, although the Ethiopic has also retained many of these. The formation of the plural nouns by internal changes—the broken plurals—which is so prominent a feature of the Arabic, is found elsewhere only in Ethiopic. This was probably a primitive feature.

See also ALPHABET; ARAB CIVILIZATION—*Language;* ASSYRIOLOGY; BABYLONIA; ETHIOPIC LANGUAGE AND LITERATURE; HEBREW LANGUAGE AND LITERATURE.

GEORGE RICKER BERRY
*Author of "The Old Testament
Among Semitic Religions"*

Bibliography

Brockelmann, Carl, *Grundriss der vergleichenden Grammatik der semitischen Sprachen,* 2 vols. (1908–1913).
Brockelmann, Carl, *Semitische Sprachwissenschaft* (1906).
Caspari, C. P., *A Grammar of the Arabic Language,* rev. ed., tr. and ed. by William Wright (Cambridge 1968).
Driver, Godfredy R., *Semitic Writing from Pictography to Alphabet* (Oxford 1954).
Gray, Louis H., *Introduction to Semitic Comparative Linguistics* (Columbia Univ. Press 1934).
Leslau, Wolf, *Annotated Bibliography of Semitic Languages of Ethiopia* (Mouton 1965).
Lidzbarski, Mark, *Handbuch der nordsemitischen Epigraphik* (1897).
Lindberg, O. E., *Vergleichende Grammatik der semitischen Sprachen* (1898).
Littmann, E., *Semitic Inscriptions* (1905).
Moscati, Sabatino, ed., *Introduction to the Comparative Grammar of Semitic Languages: Phonology and Morphology* (Harrassowitz 1964).
Nöldeke, Theodor, *Die semitischen Sprachen,* 2d ed. (1899).
O'Leary, De L. E., *Comparative Grammar of Semitic Languages* (1923).
Renan, Ernest, *Histoire générale et système comparé des langues semitiques,* 5th ed. (1878).
Wright, William, *Lectures on the Comparative Grammar of Semitic Languages* (Cambridge 1890).

SEMMELWEIS, zem'əl-vīs, **Ignaz Philipp** (1818–1865), Hungarian physician, who did pioneering work in the control of puerperal, or childbed, fever, an often fatal septicemia resulting from bacterial infection of the female genital tract after childbirth. Semmelweis was born in Buda, Hungary, on July 1, 1818. He received his degrees of doctor of medicine and master of midwifery in 1844 from the University of Vienna.

While working at Vienna's Allgemeines Krankenhaus, Semmelweis noticed that women who gave birth before entering the hospital and who had not therefore undergone internal examination during labor had a much lower rate of mortality from puerperal fever than did the women who had delivered in the hospital and had been examined. The idea that puerperal fever was a communicable disease had been suggested as early as 1795 by the Scottish doctor Alexander Gordon, but Semmelweis was unfamiliar with the meager literature on the subject.

While Semmelweis was investigating the problem, his friend and colleague Jakob Kolletschka died after a small scalpel wound incurred during an autopsy had become infected. Semmelweis noticed that the pathological changes that occurred were identical to those that occurred in women who died of puerperal fever. He reasoned that poisons were transmitted from putrid to healthy tissues, by the scalpel in the case of Kolletschka, and by the fingers of the obstetrician when he examined a woman during labor. The students who usually went from the autopsy room directly to the delivery rooms were the obvious link.

Semmelweis posted an order on May 15, 1847, requiring all such students to scrub their hands thoroughly in a solution of chlorinated lime before entering the maternity ward. Within six months the mortality rate from puerperal fever fell and continued to fall after that when Semmelweis ordered all students to scrub before every examination. Semmelweis was attacked by many of the outstanding scientists of his day and was not reappointed to Allgemeines Krankenhaus. He returned to Budapest to teach. His theories, with supporting evidence, were published in *Die Atiologie, der Begriff und die Prophylaxis des Kindbettfiebers* (1861; *The Cause, Nature, and Prevention of Puerperal Fever*), but his views did not gain general acceptance until after his death, in Vienna, on Aug. 13, 1865.

SEMMERING, zem'ə-ring, is a village in Austria in the Semmering Pass, southwest of Vienna. The pass is the lowest (3,215 feet, or 980 meters) and most easterly Alpine pass. Beneath the pass is the world's first mountain railroad tunnel, built in 1848–1854. It is about 1 mile (1.6 km) long. The railway begins at Gloggnitz, Lower Austria, and is carried along the face of precipices by means of 15 tunnels and 16 viaducts to Mürzzuschlag, Styria.

The climate and beautiful scenery have made the Semmering region a popular health resort and winter sports center.

SEMMES, semz, **Raphael** (1809–1877), American naval officer, who commanded Confederate raiders in the Civil War. He was born in Charles county, Md., on Sept. 27, 1809, and became a midshipman in the U. S. Navy in 1826. He was promoted to lieutenant in 1837 and saw action in the Mexican War. He resigned in February 1861 and volunteered for the Confederate Navy.

With the rank of commander, he was assigned to command the *Sumter,* then berthed at New Orleans. It was only a packet steamer, but Semmes directed its conversion into an armed raider and sailed on June 30. Operating in the West Indies and the Atlantic, Semmes burned or captured a number of Union merchant vessels until the *Sumter* was blockaded at Gibraltar, and he abandoned the ship.

Semmes was ordered to take command of the *Alabama,* which was then being built for the Confederacy in England. From Aug. 24, 1862, Semmes cruised the waters of the world for nearly two years, destroying more than 70 Union ships and virtually disrupting the Union maritime trade.

In June 1864, Semmes put in to Cherbourg, France, with the *Alabama* badly in need of repair. Here he was blocked by the Union warship *Kearsarge.* On June 19, Semmes sallied out to fight. After a brief engagement, the *Alabama* was in a sinking condition and was abandoned. Semmes and most of the crew were rescued.

Following the war, Semmes practiced law in Mobile, Ala., where he died on Aug. 30, 1877.

SEMPER, zem'pər, **Gottfried** (1803–1879), German architect. He was born in Hamburg on Nov. 29, 1803. He studied law at the University of Göttingen but changed to the study of architecture. He then took a journey through Italy, Sicily, and Greece. In Berlin he became the pupil of Karl Schinkel, who recognized his talent and educated him to fill the place of professor of architecture in the Dresden School of Building. Between 1837 and 1841, Semper built several important structures in Dresden, including the court theater. In 1849 he traveled to Paris and London. In London he undertook the arrangement of the statuary in Kensington Museum. He continued active up to the time of his death, in Rome, on May 15, 1879.

Semper's most important buildings were erected in Dresden and in Vienna, where his work is still a commanding feature of city architecture. He was an uncompromising adherent of the Renaissance style, as founded on the Roman structures of the later empire, especially those of the forums. Semper's buildings are distinguished by harmony of composition, purity, and moderation of detail.

SEN, Keshab Chandra. See KESHAB CHANDRA SEN.

SEN-NO-RIKYU, sen-nō-rē-kū (1521–1591), was a Japanese tea master, who perfected the tea ceremony (*cha-no-yu*). He was born in Sakai to a wealthy family. His real name was Sen-no-Soeki, but he adopted the pseudonym Rikyu, which expresses scorn of riches and honors.

Rikyu studied under the tea master Takeno Sho-o and was initiated into Zen Buddhism by the priest Kokei Sochin. Under the patronage of Toyotomi Hideyoshi, the most powerful man in Japan, Rikyu became an arbiter of taste whose rulings on the etiquette of the tea ceremony were accepted as standards. He applied the principles of Zen, which pervaded the ceremony, and in the spirit of *wabi* ("rustic simplicity") he adopted the type of tea house seen in mountain villages. His influence extended to the arts, because he encouraged styles of severe beauty for the bowls and utensils used in the tea service. He was also a master of flower arrangement. Rikyu eventually lost the favor of Hideyoshi, and in 1591 he committed ritual suicide.

SENA, sā'nə, an Indian dynasty that ruled in Bengal from about 1100 to about 1250. The Senas, Hindus of south Indian origin, came into prominence in Bengal under Samantasena. His grandson Vijayasena, the first independent ruler of the line, defeated the Buddhist Palas in Bengal. Vijayasena's successor, Ballalasena, wrote religious works and reputedly instituted a marriage system called Kulinism, in which a woman marries a man of higher caste than her own. Kulinism was widely practiced in Bengal until the 19th century.

Ballalasena's son Lakshmanasena brought the dynasty to its height of power by his conquests. A patron of the arts, he invited poets such as Jayadeva and Dhoyi to his capital, Vijayapura. About 1200, Lakshmanasena was defeated by the Muslim general Ikhtiyar-ud-din Muhammad Khalji and fled to the east, where he died soon afterward. His sons preserved the Senas' independence in eastern Bengal against the Muslims until the mid-13th century.

SÉNANCOUR, sā-näN-kōōr', **Étienne Pivert de** (1770–1846), French novelist and essayist. He was born in Paris on Nov. 16, 1770. Destined by his father for the priesthood, he went to Switzerland in 1789 to avoid entering a seminary. His marriage the following year to a young Frenchwoman in Fribourg was not happy. During the French Revolution he was included in the list of emigrants, and most of his fortune in France was lost. He returned to France in 1803 and died in St. Cloud on Jan. 10, 1846.

Sénancour was a great admirer of Jean Jacques Rousseau, who inspired much of his *Rêveries sur la nature primitive de l'homme*, published in Paris in 1799. Sénancour's best-known work, *Obermann* (1804; *The Superman*) is an autobiographical novel written in the form of letters, in part describing solitary wanderings in the forest of Fontainebleau and Switzerland. It attracted no notice until it was discovered by Sainte-Beuve in 1833. *Obermann*, originally written in an earlier version called *Aldomen* (1795), is filled with the melancholy of the *mal de siècle* but also has a real and delicate feeling for nature, with some philosophical passages that are highly original. It was translated into English by A. G. Waite in 1903.

Sénancour's other writings include *De L'Amour selon les lois primordiales* (1805) and *Isabelle* (1833), another epistolary novel. The influence of Goethe's *Werther* is recurrent in Sénancour's writings, some of which have a strong poetic fervor.

SENATE, an assembly or council with the highest deliberative and, usually, legislative functions. The word is derived from the Latin *senatus*, which means literally an assembly of old men. In ancient Rome the senate was the supreme council of state. The upper houses of the legislatures of several modern countries, including France, Italy, Canada, Argentina, and the United States are known as senates, as are the governing bodies of certain universities.

Bicameral (two-house) legislatures are the rule in most nations, though the upper house is not always known as the senate. As members of the upper house of a bicameral legislature, senators generally enjoy more prestige than do other legislators. Even though the lower house actually may exercise more power, a certain elitism exists in the senate. This is due, in large part, to its smaller size and to the manner of election or appointment of senators, which makes them less directly responsible to the voters. See also CONGRESS OF THE UNITED STATES; LEGISLATION; SENATE, UNITED STATES.

Roman Senate. Originally an advisory council of patricians during the monarchy in ancient Rome, the senate became the chief governing body in the state. Under the republic, the senate admitted plebeian members and exercised broad legislative and administrative powers. Virtually unhampered in its handling of foreign affairs and in controlling finance, it also was influential in selecting magistrates. The senate remained prestigious under the empire, for theoretically it provided the formal acceptance of the emperor's claim. It gradually lost its independence. Functions became subordinate to imperial decrees, then merely consultative. Senators frequently failed to attend sessions. Though existing in form, the senate had declined before the actual fall of Rome. See ROME (History).

SENATE, one of the two equal branches of the Congress of the United States. Like its counterpart, the House of Representatives, it was created by the Constitutional Convention in 1787 and began work in 1789, after the ratification of the Constitution. The Senate has two members for each state in the union and has grown in size as the nation has added states. Thus it began with 22 senators—two of the original 13 states had not yet ratified the Constitution—and presently has 100 members. As a result of the major compromise between states' rights and popular representation that was necessary in the 1787 convention, the Senate was conceived to be directly representative of the states. Presumably senators would also be more representative of the upper social classes than the more democratic House. Senators were elected by state legislatures from 1789 until 1913, when the Constitution was amended to provide that they be elected directly by the voters.

Qualifications, Perquisites, and Membership. The Constitution provides that a senator must be 30 years of age, have been a citizen of the United States for 9 years, and be a resident of the state from which he is elected.

Senators receive a basic salary of $60,662.50, plus supplementary tax benefits and honoraria from speeches—the same as for members of the House of Representatives.

Senators also receive $300,000 to $500,000 annually to pay a staff, the sum being determined by the population of each senator's state. The average senator has about 20 staff members in Washington and several in offices in his home state. Funds are also provided to senators for renting office space in the state, travel, office supplies, postage, and telephone and telegraph. In addition, senators can use the mails free for official business, participate in a generous retirement program, and enjoy immunity from some kinds of arrest and legal action.

The average senator is a white male lawyer and a war veteran. Most senators who are not lawyers are businessmen. Few women or blacks have been elected to the Senate (for example, in the 97th Congress that met in January 1981, there were only two women and no black members of the Senate).

The average senator, unlike the average member of the House of Representatives, can usually count on gaining statewide visibility and perhaps regional or national notice as well if he chooses to speak on important issues of the day. A number of presidential candidates—both those who declare themselves to be candidates and those who are nominated—have been senators.

Elections. Until 1913, state legislatures elected senators. Thus the party affiliation of the senator was dependent on which party controlled the state leigslature, which in turn was dependent on state elections. Since 1913, senators have had whole states as their constituencies. Every senator has a six-year term, with one third of the seats up for election every even-numbered year. The two seats for any given state are up for election in different years. Since World War II about three fourths of the senators whose term expired in a given year have sought reelection. About four fifths of the incumbents running win reelection. Thus any given Senate typically meets with about 85 to 90 incumbent senators and 10 to 15 "freshmen." This phenomenon helps create stability in the Senate.

Until about 1880 the average senator at any given time had been in the Senate about four years. By the 1890's the average senator had served more than seven years. With some variations this held true until the 1960's, when the average length of service climbed to more than ten years. At the same time the average age of senators remained almost constant.

Organization and Rules. The Senate, despite its relatively modest size, has a complex organizational structure and elaborate rules. It relies on standing committees and subcommittees to process most of the substantive legislation flowing through the body. Its substantive business amounts to between 7,000 and 20,000 bills introduced in both houses and up to 500 public laws and several hundred private laws enacted per year. In 1981 there were 15 standing committees and more than 100 subcommittees, select committees, and special committees. Given the multiple memberships of senators—most served on two or three committees and a large number of subcommittees—many decision-making meetings were necessarily attended by only a few senators and staff members. Virtually every senator is the chairman or ranking minority member of some subcommittee. In such a situation a senator who wishes to develop influence over the subject matter of one or two of his subcommittees can do so and can, in effect, become a spokesman for the Senate as a whole.

Given the limited number of senators and the large number of staff members, who work both for individual senators and for committees, the staff is important in the Senate in helping shape legislative products. Many staff members become professionals who remain in the Senate bureaucracy even if the senator for whom they work leaves the Senate.

Both parties in the Senate have also evolved organizational structures that help shape the conduct of business. The floor leaders of the two major parties in the Senate did not emerge as consistently important individuals until the 1880's. A single majority leader and minority leader were not routinely elected until the period between 1911 and 1913. Since that time they have been elected consistently and have, in fact, taken the leading roles as spokesmen for their party to the public, to the president, and within the Senate, although different individuals have performed the role very differently. Other leaders include the party whips, who are, in effect, assistant floor leaders who perform tasks at the discretion of the floor leaders; the chairmen of the party conferences, which are meetings open to all members of the party; and the chairmen of the party policy committees, which were created after World War II.

The formal presiding officer of the Senate is the vice president of the United States, although he spends little time in the Senate. His importance in the body is usually limited to those occasions on which he has an opportunity to cast the deciding vote on a controversial measure because the senators themselves are evenly divided. This may happen only a few times during his four-year term. The Senate also elects a president *pro tempore* who is supposed to preside in the absence of the vice president. In reality, most presiding is done by junior senators.

The Senate has 44 rules, some of which are quite elaborate. Much of the time, however, the Senate proceeds on the basis of "unanimous consènt" agreements worked out between the floor leaders of the two parties. This gives the Senate considerable flexibility as it conducts its legislative business.

The one rule for which the Senate is widely known is that pertaining to the cloture of debate. The Senate's traditions include "unlimited debate." A relatively small number of senators can, by manipulating the rules and procedures of the Senate, prevent legislative action for a number of days or weeks or even months. In 1917 the Senate created a procedure whereby two thirds of the senators could close debate. On March 7, 1975, the Senate amended the rule so that a vote by three fifths of the Senate's full membership (60 senators) would suffice to invoke cloture. In the years between 1917 and 1975, the two-thirds cloture rule had been invoked 24 times. See also CLOTURE; FILIBUSTER.

Senate Development and Impact on Public Policy. Before the Civil War the Senate enjoyed periods in which it appeared to dominate public policy. This was especially true in the 1830's, 1840's, and 1850's, when the country and the Senate were violently divided over the issue of slavery. Leading senators such as Daniel Webster, Henry Clay, and John C. Calhoun dwarfed lackluster presidents as spokesmen for contending views on slavery and on other issues as well. After the Civil War the Senate underwent a period in which power was centralized in the hands of leading party figures, senators began serving much longer periods, seniority became the criterion for advancement to committee chairmanships, and various party committees and organizations were established. This process was basically completed by 1895, and the "modern" Senate had come into being: a Senate with important, although not always dominant, party leaders constrained by the presence of large numbers of career senators advancing in large part by seniority.

The Senate has three exclusive Constitutional powers in addition to a number of powers it shares with the House of Representatives. First, the Senate sits as a court in cases in which impeachments against federal officials have been brought by the House. Conviction requires a two-thirds vote. In its entire history the Senate has received only 12 cases and has convicted only 4 individuals, all federal judges. The most famous impeachment case was the one in which the Senate acquitted President Andrew Johnson by one vote in 1868.

Second, the Senate must confirm presidential nominations by majority vote. In the 91st Congress (1969–1971) more than 134,000 nominations were received, most of them of military officers. The nominations that receive most attention are those for cabinet positions and for the Supreme Court. Other federal judges and ambassadors also require Senate confirmation and sometimes involve controversy. The Senate usually confirms appointments, sometimes after lengthy hearings. But the Senate has also shown its willingness to rebuff the president. This occurred in the cases of 8 individuals nominated for cabinet positions, the last of which was in 1959 when President Eisenhower's nominee for secretary of commerce was rejected, and of 11 individuals nominated for the Supreme Court, including 2 nominees put forward by President Nixon. The Senate has also refused to take action on other nominees, thus causing a president to withdraw the nomination to replace it with another one.

Third, the Senate must, by two-thirds vote, ratify treaties the president makes with foreign governments. On 11 occasions the Senate has refused to grant ratification, although in all cases the supporting votes outnumbered the opposing votes. The most important such occasion was in 1920, when the Senate rejected the Treaty of Versailles, which contained the Covenant of the League of Nations as well as the peace terms with Germany. By contrast, the Senate in 1960 rejected a relatively minor protocol involving compulsory settlement of disputes arising under sea law. The Senate has ratified all other treaties, but sometimes only after lengthy debate.

In addition to its special powers the Senate shares with the House general responsibility for processing a vast amount of legislation each year. On some measures senators and their staff members initiate legislative proposals. On other measures they work closely with representatives of the executive branch or with the private sector to generate legislative proposals. On some measures the Senate reacts to initiatives coming from the House. On many measures both the House and the Senate are basically reacting to initiatives coming from the executive branch. They can pass these measures as proposed, amend them before passing them, or reject them. Usually both the Senate and the House make some sort of input to any major piece of legislation before it returns to the president for his signature.

During the 1950's a group of liberal Senators generated a number of ideas that later became law, and during the 1960's the Senate supported liberal domestic legislation far more often than the House did. Beginning in the late 1960's the Senate sought to reassert itself as an independent influence in foreign affairs, largely as a negative reaction to the U. S. military involvement in the war in Indochina.

In general, senators are jealous of their prerogatives and wish to maintain their independence of the president and of the House of Representatives. Nevertheless, the modern Senate has cooperated closely with those entities during the several major bursts of lawmaking activity that have produced the basic domestic and foreign programs characteristic of the national government in the 1960's and 1970's. Much of the time political and institutional conditions prevent swift and dramatic action, but when the conditions permit such action the Senate has shown itself capable of participating fully and importantly in the shaping of major changes in public policy.

For more information on the committee system, on how a bill becomes a law, and on the relationship between the Senate and the executive branch, see CONGRESS OF THE UNITED STATES.

RANDALL B. RIPLEY
The Ohio State University

Bibliography

Haynes, George H., *The Senate of the United States: Its History and Practice*, 2 vols. (1938; reprint, Russell & Russell 1960).
Huitt, Ralph K., and Peabody, Robert L., *Congress: Two Decades of Analysis* (Harper 1969).
Matthews, Donald R., *U. S. Senators and Their World* (Univ. of N. C. Press 1960).
Pettit, Lawrence K., and Keynes, Edward, eds., *The Legislative Process in the U. S. Senate* (Rand McNally 1969).
Ripley, Randall B:, *Power in the Senate* (St. Martins 1969).

SENDAI, sen-dī, a city in Japan, is situated near the east coast of Honshu Island, 190 miles (305 km) northeast of Tokyo. It is the capital of Miyagi prefecture.

Sendai is known as the "metropolis of woods" because of its many groves of trees. It is the seat of Tohoku University with a noted metals research institute. The city manufactures foodstuffs, chemicals, machinery and other metal products, and timber and wood products.

The community developed as the castle town of the 17th century feudal lord Date Masamune. The castle stood on Aoba Hill, which has a commanding view of the city and surrounding area. Population: (1970) 545,065.

SENDAK, sen'dak, **Maurice Bernard** (1928–), American writer and illustrator of children's books. He was born in Brooklyn, N. Y., on June 10, 1928. While attending high school, he worked part time as a background illustrator for the *Mutt and Jeff* comic strip. After attending the Art Students League in New York City, he was chosen to illustrate Marcel Aymé's *The Wonderful Farm* (1951). The success of this book brought him commissions to illustrate for other leading authors of children's books, including Ruth Krauss, Meindert DeJong, and Janice Udry.

With *Kenny's Window* (1956), Sendak began doing both text and pictures. His popular books, marked by fantastic drawings, include *Very Far Away* (1957), *The Sign on Rosie's Door* (1960), the Caldecott Medal winner *Where the Wild Things Are* (1963), and *In the Night Kitchen* (1970). See also LITERATURE FOR CHILDREN.

SENDER, sān-der', **Ramón José** (1902–), Spanish author, critic, and educator. He was born in Alcolea de Cinca, Spain, on Feb. 3, 1902, and was educated at the University of Madrid. From 1925 to 1930 he was the editor of *El Sol*. For the next six years he worked as a free-lance writer and novelist until he fought for the Republicans in the Spanish Civil War (1936–1939). He then went to Mexico, where he continued to write novels until 1942, and to the United States, where he was professor of Spanish literature at Amherst College, the University of Denver, and the University of New Mexico.

Sender is one of the few contemporary Spanish novelists to have won a worldwide audience. His work, distinguished by its realism and compassion, includes *Pro Patria* (1934), *Counter-Attack in Spain* (1938), *A Man's Place* (1940), *The Affable Hangman* (1954), and *Requiem for A Spanish Peasant* (1960).

SENECA, sen'ə-kə (c.55 B. C.–c.37 A. D.), Roman educator, called Seneca the Elder, who was the father of the more famous Lucius Annaeus Seneca, philosopher and statesman. His first name is not certain, but it appears to have been either Marcus or Lucius.

Seneca was born about 55 B. C. in Corduba (now Córdoba), Spain. He went to Rome as a young boy and studied public speaking, which, befitting a man destined for politics or law, was the cornerstone of higher education in Rome. He died about 37 A. D.

Seneca was the author of two textbooks on rhetoric: a collection of *controversiae* (five books of the original ten are extant) and a collection of *suasoriae* (seven have survived). A *controversia* was a highly hypothetical law case to argue in mock court (for example, "a man who has lost his weapons in battle seizes some from a hero's tomb, fights bravely, puts them back—and is subsequently charged with sacrilegious violation of the tomb"). A *suasoria* was an imaginary deliberation on the appropriate action to take during a famous crisis ("the 300 Spartans at Thermopylae consider whether they ought to retreat") or an imaginary exhortation during a famous crisis (for example, an impassioned appeal to Hannibal to cross the Alps). The two collections, along with seven surviving prefaces to the individual books, are a key source of information about the nature of this all-important phase of Roman education and letters.

Further Reading: Duff, John Wight, *A Literary History of Rome in the Silver Age* (Scribner 1927).

SENECA, sen'ə-kə, **Lucius Annaeus** (c.4 B. C.–65 A. D.), Roman philosopher and statesman, who was the most brilliant thinker and writer of his time. He was the second son of the Roman educator and author, Seneca the Elder.

Life. Lucius was born in Corduba (now Córdoba), Spain, about 4 B. C. His family was wealthy and of equestrian rank, and he was taken to Rome as a boy to be educated for the law and an official career. He also attended with enthusiasm the lectures of several noted Pythagorean, Stoic, and Cynic philosophers. He gained great fame for eloquence and entered the Senate through the quaestorship. However, in 41 A. D., at the instance of Empress Messalina, who accused him of an intrigue with Julia Livilla, sister of the late emperor, Caligula, he was banished to Corsica. From there he sent to his mother, Helvia, the charming *Consolatio*, but exhibited little fortitude in his exile. Finally, in 49, Agrippina, who, after the execution of Messalina, had married Emperor Claudius, secured Seneca's recall that he might act as tutor to her son Domitius (later Emperor Nero). At Nero's accession in 54, Seneca wrote the curious political satire (still extant) on the death of Claudius, commonly known as *Apocolocyntosis*, meaning "pumpkinification," a word formed upon the analogy of apotheosis ("deification").

During the first years of the new reign, Seneca, in conjunction with Sextus Afranius Burrus, prefect of the Praetorian Guard, was on the whole successful in keeping Nero within the bounds of humanity. Agrippina, ambitious and cruel, was determined to rule the state through her son, and Seneca seems to have palliated the latter's excesses in order to destory his mother's influence over him. Finally, when Poppaea Sabina, with whom Nero had become infatuated, induced him to order the assassination of his mother, Seneca wrote for the Emperor a letter to the Senate, asserting that Agrippina had conspired against the Emperor's life and had committed suicide upon being discovered.

The death of Burrus in 62 made Seneca's position quite insecure. Nero fell into the hands of men like the infamous Ofonius Tigellinus, and money was needed to meet the Emperor's extravagant expenditures. Seneca, who had become enormously wealthy, foresaw his probable ruin, and offered to resign to Nero all that he had. Upon receiving a negative answer, couched in terms of specious affection, Seneca retired into the country, near Rome, and lived with utmost simplicity. In 65 A. D., he was implicated in the conspiracy of Gaius Calpurnius Piso and was ordered to commit suicide. His wife Paulina insisted on dying with him. As described in the affecting account in Tacitus' *Annals*, he opened the veins of his arms. Paulina's life was barely saved by her slaves, but Seneca, after suffering prolonged agony, during which he displayed the utmost serenity, was finally suffocated in a vapor bath.

Works. Seneca's moral essays embrace various so-called dialogues, including: *On Peace of Mind, On Anger, On the Shortness of Life;* three *On Clemency,* addressed to Nero; and seven *On Benefits,* as well as 20 books of *Letters to Lucilius.* With these may be grouped the seven books of *Naturales Quaestiones,* which handle physics as a basis for ethical reflections. He also left nine tragedies, composed rather to be read aloud than to be acted, and so rhetorical in substance that, though fine passages are not lacking, they are declamations rather than real poetry. They had, however, a great influence on the drama of the 16th century.

Assessment. Seneca was undoubtedly an earnest seeker after truth and right, and the Roman world was much his debtor for the wise and humane administration of the state during the "golden quinquennium" of Nero. But he lacked real strength of character, and in his connection with Nero too often acquiesced in permitting positive evil in order that a greater good might be accomplished.

But as a man of letters, Seneca was incomparably the most brilliant figure of his time. He was an extremely prolific writer, his subjects were exceedingly varied, and his ideas were usually nobly conceived and eloquently expressed. In striking contrast to the turgid style of Cicero, he loved short, epigrammatic sentences. He was an expert in the use of every variety of rhetorical ornamentation, which, in harmony with the prevailing taste, he carried to excess. Though by no means a profound thinker, Seneca was broadminded and sympathetic in his presentation of the ethical principles, mainly Stoic, by which he believed man's daily life should be guided. Indeed, he was considered by certain Fathers of the Church to have been a Christian, and there are 14 extant letters, undoubtedly spurious, of a correspondence with St. Paul.

NELSON G. McCREA
Formerly, Columbia University

Bibliography

Clemen, Wolfgang H., *English Tragedy Before Shakespeare* (Methuen 1961).
Mendell, Clarence W., *Our Seneca* (reprint, Shoe String 1968).
Reynolds, Leighton D., *Medieval Tradition of Seneca's Letters* (Oxford 1965).
Seneca, *Works,* ed. by E. Hermes and others (Teubner Series 1902–1914).
Tobin, Ronald W., *Racine and Seneca* (Univ. of N. C. Press 1971).

SENECA INDIANS, sen'ə-kə, a tribe of North American Indians belonging to the Iroquois family, and one of the Five (later Six) Nations League of the Iroquois, founded about the year 1570. Their own name, *Tsonondowanenaka* or *Tsonondowaka* ("people of the great hill or mountain") probably refers to the lofty eminence south of Canandaigua Lake. The term Seneca is a Mohawk rendering of the name, which has passed through Dutch to English hands. With the Mohawk and the Onondaga, the Seneca constituted the elder phratry, or subdivision, of tribes in the social and political organization of the confed-

eration, while the junior phratry was composed of the Oneida and the Cayuga.

The earliest-known council fire of the Seneca people was established south of Canandaigua Lake, while their territory comprised the region environing Seneca and Canandaigua lakes and extended westward to Genesee River. As a member of the league, the Seneca were called *Honĕñninhohoñte,* meaning "They are fixed to a door or door-flap." This signified that the Seneca people were the political doorkeepers of the league, not because, as was commonly asserted, they stood at the western frontier of the territory of the confederation, but because being at first averse to joining the league, they were finally persuaded to do so by being granted the honor of the office of doorkeeper and of official executioner. Their last two league chiefs or rulers were charged with the duty of ascertaining the good or evil designs of any alien who might seek to enter the jurisdiction of the confederation. It had been the policy of the Dutch of New Netherland to maintain an alliance with the league to guard against French encroachments. After 1664 the English pursued the same policy. During the American Revolution, the Seneca espoused the cause of Britain against the colonies.

Skaniadariio, or Handsome Lake, who was the founder of the reformed pagan Iroquoian religion that is in vogue today among the various northern Iroquoian peoples, was a Seneca. On the migration, or probably expulsion, of the Awenrehronon from the headwaters of Genesee River, N. Y., in 1639, and on the later defeat of the Neutral Nation (so-called by the French because of their neutrality during some of the Iroquois-Huron Wars) about 1649–1650, and of the Eries about 1654–1657, the Seneca moved some of their settlements and colonies westward toward Lake Erie and along the Allegheny River.

In 1657 there were 11 different alien tribes or peoples represented among the Seneca, thus indicating how well they exercised the right of adoption to replace their great losses in the almost interminable wars of the league, which had then lasted about 75 years. The earliest estimate of the number of the Seneca, in 1660 and 1677, gave them about 5,000. In 1825 those in New York were reported at 2,325. Twenty-five years later, they were estimated at 2,712, with over 200 more on the Grand River reservation in Canada. About the same estimation was given in 1909. In the 1960's their population was reported to be more than 4,100.

In the late 20th century, the Seneca are represented by several different bodies of people dwelling in diverse places, including New York state, Oklahoma, Pennsylvania, and Ontario. Of the several tribes formerly constituting the League of the Iroquois, the Seneca are the most progressive in the arts and knowledge of civilization. With incidental exceptions, the history of the Seneca previous to the American Revolution is virtually that of the league. See also IROQUOIS INDIANS.

SENECAN SERIES, sen'ə-kən, the series of rocks deposited in the Senecan Epoch of the Lower Upper Devonian Period, about 370 million years ago. The name is derived from Lake Seneca in New York, where the sedimentary rocks dating from that period of geological time were first observed. The Senecan rocks succeed the Erian Series and underlie the Chautauquan Series. See also DEVONIAN PERIOD—*Geology.*

GEORGE GERSTER, FROM RAPHO-GUILLUMETTE

Dakar, the westernmost city on the African continent, is the capital and chief seaport of Senegal.

SENEGAL, sen-ə-gôl′, is a republic in the westernmost part of Africa. It has been in longer continuous contact with Europe than any other part of Subsaharan Africa. Formerly administered by France, it became independent in 1960.

During the colonial period Senegal was the political and economic center of the Federation of French West Africa. After independence, the republic followed a policy of cooperation with other African states and maintained close relations with France and the Western bloc. But Senegal's stability and prosperity came under increasing economic pressures, partly because the country had lost the regional primacy it enjoyed under French administration.

The Land Senegal has an area of about 76,000 square miles (197,000 sq km). The independent republic of Gambia forms an enclave along the Gambia River, separating the major part of Senegal from its southern region, the Casamance. Most of the country consists of rolling plains at an elevation of less than 650 feet (200 meters). But in the southeast, plateaus forming the foothills of the Fouta Djallon mountains reach elevations of about 1,600 feet (490 meters).

The Senegambia region is drained by four major rivers, all flowing from east to west and emptying into the Atlantic Ocean. The Senegal River, which forms Senegal's northern border, is navigable throughout the year as far upstream as Podor. The Saloum River, in the central part of the country, has become an important mercantile link since the growth of the city of Kaolack as a major peanut-exporting port. The Casamance River in the extreme south can be used by vessels as far inland as Ziguinchor, the largest southern city. But the Gambia River, the most navigable stream and the natural highway of the Senegambia region, lies mostly in Gambia.

Senegal has three distinct vegetation zones, determined by the annual rainfall. From the Senegal River south to a line drawn from the town of Thiès to the lower Falémé River is the *Sahelian zone*. This is a transitional semidesert area

---

INFORMATION HIGHLIGHTS

Official Name: Republic of Senegal.
Head of State: President.
Head of Government: Premier.
Area: 76,000 square miles (197,000 sq km).
Boundaries: *North,* Mauritania; *east,* Mali; *south,* Guinea and Portuguese Guinea; *west,* Atlantic Ocean. The Republic of The Gambia penetrates over 200 miles (300 km) into Senegal.
Population: 4,000,000 (1971).
Capital: Dakar (1969 population, 400,000).
Major Languages: French (official), Wolof, Fulani, Mandingo.
Major Religions: Islam, animism, Christianity.
Monetary Unit: CFA franc.
Weights and Measures: Metric system.
Flag: Tricolor of green, yellow, and red vertical stripes. A green star is at the center of the yellow stripe. See also FLAG.
National Anthem: "Pluck your koras, strike the balafons."

551

MICHEL RENAUDEAU, FROM DE WYS

Sacks of peanuts, a major agricultural product of Senegal, are taken by truck to ports for shipment to France.

where the average yearly rainfall is approximately 14 inches (350 mm). The Sahelian zone is characterized by rough grasses interspersed with scattered thorny shrubs and small acacia bushes. South of the Sahelian lies the *Sudanic zone,* where the rainfall varies up to 35 inches (900 mm) a year. Vegetation becomes steadily thicker toward the southern limits of the Sudanic zone just north of the Gambia River. Grass is more abundant, there are many silk-cotton and baobab trees, and the acacia bushes become larger. Between the Gambia River and the Casamance River is the *Casamance zone,* which has an annual rainfall ranging from 35 to 60 inches (900–1,500 mm).

The southwest, with many small winding creeks, is a region of marshy swamps and localized tropical forests. In the nonforested areas the vegetation is heavy, reflecting the greater precipitation. North of Cape Verde, where the semidesert area reaches the sea, drifting sand and the action of wind and water have created long, sandy beaches. The hilly and rocky site of Cape Verde provides shelter for the excellent natural harbor of Dakar. The coastal region south of Cape Verde is basically mudflat and mangrove forest, intersected by many creeks. Almost all the creek and river estuaries are blocked by sandbars.

Most of the land in Senegal is only of marginal usefulness. Along the many creeks and rivers, mangrove forests block all but the most modest attempts at agriculture, and saline intrusion also limits productivity. On the coast north of Cape Verde the sandiness of the soil restricts farming, and in the Casamance the forested areas are not suitable for anything but subsistence agriculture. The soils are leached of their minerals in the Casamance and in central Senegal. The soils of the rest of the country are iron-heavy or too sandy to be very fertile. The best farming regions are the plains that extend southeastward from Cape Verde to the Gambia River and in the floodplain of the middle Senegal River.

Senegal's climate is marked by contrasts. The coastal regions, particularly north of Dakar, receive good sea breezes from early November through February, giving the area one of the most pleasant climates in Africa. The average January temperature of Dakar is a mild 73° F (23° C). The temperature rises sharply in the interior of northern Senegal because of its proximity to the Sahara. South to the Casamance the humidity increases, with less modifying effects from offshore winds.

There is a definite dry and wet season throughout Senegal. The wet season in the Sahelian zone is from June to October, in the Sudanic zone from May to October, and in the Casamance from May to December.

The People. Although most of Senegal's 4 million people live in rural areas, about 10% reside in Dakar, the capital. Dakar was the administrative center of French West Africa and after World War II the third-greatest French seaport. A hub of air travel between Africa, Europe, and the Americas, the city is noted for its sophistication and high cost of living. Other important cities are Kaolack (1971 population, 95,000), Thiès (90,000), Rufisque (58,200), and St.-Louis (57,900).

Ethnic Groups. Senegal's population has a complex ethnic pattern consisting of several major groups and numerous smaller ones. The Wolof comprise about 36% of the population; the Fulani, about 17%, the Serer about 16%; and the Tukulor, about 6%.

The Wolof were among the first Africans to come in contact with European traders. Even before the 19th century, some Wolof had accepted Western culture, and they have come to dominate the city and town life of Senegal. The Serer people are closely related culturally and linguistically to the Wolof. They live chiefly in the territories of their ancient kingdoms of Sine and Saloum, in western Senegal. These are the country's most productive peanut-growing areas.

The Fulani (Fula, Peul), who are scattered from Senegal to Cameroon, probably originated in the ancient kingdom of Tekrur along the middle Senegal River. Most of the Senegalese Fulani in the north are nomadic pastoralists. In the region of the Gambia River and in the Casamance they have intermarried to a large extent with other groups, and many have become settled farmers. The Tukulor, who speak Fulani, live south of the middle Senegal River.

The Mandingo, one of the most important peoples in Africa, are represented in Senegal by a small number of farmers in the central and eastern regions. Three different Mandingo dialects are discernible—the Malinke, Gambian, and Serahuli. Small groups of Lebu are found in the fishing villages adjacent to the Dakar area. The dominant people of the Casamance are the Diola. In the extreme north there is a small resident population of Berbers from Mauritania.

Tribal diversity in Senegal prevented any single group from controlling the entire region. Nevertheless, despite differences in language, culture, and economic pursuits, two unifying forces have emerged in the 20th century. One consists of the French language, culture, education, and political forms bequeathed to independent Senegal. The other is Islam.

Education. French is the official language of Senegal and the medium of instruction in the schools. The educational system is modeled on that of France, with modifications to accommodate local needs and traditions. Its development was enhanced by Senegal's position as the center of the French West African federation. The federation's most important secondary schools were located in Senegal, and the University of Dakar became one of Africa's greatest centers of learning.

In the early 1970's, about 50% of the children of primary school age attended classes. The University of Dakar had nearly 4,000 students, including over 2,000 from other countries.

Religion. About 86% of the population is Muslim. The Tijaniyya brotherhood of Islam is particularly strong, except around Diourbel where the Mouride sect exercises great influence. Much of Senegal was converted to Islam only in the late 19th century. The Serer and Diola have remained largely unconverted.

Economy. Senegal's predominantly agricultural economy has long been dependent on one crop. Peanuts, introduced in the late 19th century, provide about 80% of the total export earnings. Millet, sorghum, and rice are also cultivated, and commercial fishing is a growing industry. Some cattle are raised for export by the Fulani, but most of the country's livestock does not enter the market economy.

Although manufacturing is a relatively small sector of the economy, Senegal is the most industrialized country of former French West Africa. Before independence the factories of Dakar and Rufisque sent their goods to the other countries of the federation. Most manufacturing is centered on the processing of agricultural products. Phosphate, found in the vicinity of Thiès, is the only exploitable mineral.

Senegal's economic prospects, which seemed excellent at independence, became increasingly poor in the late 1960's. Annual peanut harvests declined sharply, largely because of drought conditions continuing into the 1970's. The removal of the French government subsidy for peanuts and the subsequent decline of approximately 20% in the payment per ton contributed to the peanut farmers' growing dissatisfaction. They responded by planting fewer acres in peanuts. Labor disturbances in the major cities and student rebellions after 1968 were symptoms of the country's economic problems.

When Senegal was the economic center of French West Africa it received the bulk of the exports of the western part of the federation,

MARC & EVELYNE BERNHEIM, FROM G. WOODFIN CAMP ASSOC.

Diembéring is a village in south Senegal's Casamance region, between Gambia and Portuguese Guinea.

A Senegalese musician on the island of Gorée. The decorated instrument he is holding is called a *kora*.

LOUISE E. JEFFERSON, FROM MONKMEYER

St.-Louis, near the mouth of the Senegal River, was formerly the capital of both Senegal and Mauritania.

either by road or via the Bamako-Dakar railroad. Senegal processed these exports and shipped them overseas. In addition, the federation's major administrative offices were located in Dakar, so that the Senegalese grew accustomed to the employment opportunities of a large government establishment. After the breakup of the federation, the other former French areas became much less dependent upon Senegalese ports, and they organized their own government establishments. Nevertheless, the Senegalese middle classes have continued to demand employment in government, and Senegal devotes a larger percentage of its annual budget to administration than does any other West African state.

Senegal has a relatively well-developed transportation network. There are about 2,400 miles (3,900 km) of surfaced roads, over half of which are paved. Railroads link the principal cities north of the Gambia River. Dakar, connected by rail with Bamako, the capital of Mali, is one of the major ports of Africa. Besides the international airport at Dakar, there are airports in several other cities and towns handling domestic flights.

History and Government. Little is known of the movements of African peoples into Senegal before 1000 A. D. Early agriculturists were present in relatively large numbers by the time of the rise of the kingdom of Ghana in the 8th century.

Early History. The Fulani-dominated kingdom of Tekrur on the middle Senegal River was converted to Islam in the 11th century. In the 13th century it challenged the Mali Empire for supremacy in the Western Sudan. By the 18th century the Fulani and Tukulor peoples had created the Islamic imamate of Futa Toro. Their theocratic practices influenced Muslim reformers throughout the Western Sudan.

The complex Wolof and Serer kingdoms were fully functioning throughout most of western and central Senegal by the 15th century. The Wolof kingdom of Jolof maintained a tenuous ascendancy over other Wolof states, including Walo, Bayol, and Cayor, until the 18th century. With the collapse of Jolof's control there were as many as 10 separate states in the area north of the Gambia River. These societies were relatively untouched by Islam until the religious wars of the 19th century, when the bulk of the Wolof population was converted.

European Penetration. Europeans first arrived off Cape Verde in the mid-15th century, and soon the Portuguese established a post at Arguin Island, near the coast of Mauritania. But the Senegambia region was not considered very profitable, and the Portuguese concentrated their efforts elsewhere. In the early 17th century the Dutch established a fortified trading station on the island of Gorée, near Dakar, but it was captured by the French in 1677. Gorée and a settlement at St.-Louis became the two main French outposts in the area.

The mercantilist warfare between Britain and France from the late 17th to late 18th century was carried on in Senegambia as in other parts of the world. Each succeeding war further impoverished the mercantile companies of both powers. But Senegambia was never an area that prompted expectations of great fortunes. Although the local kingdoms cooperated with European slave traders, relatively few slaves were shipped from the region even during the height of the slave trade in the 18th century.

French Control. The abolition of the slave trade by Britain in 1807, and afterward by other powers, began a period of reduced European involvement in the affairs of African kingdoms. For Senegal, this nonintervention ended in 1854 with the arrival of French Capt. (later Gen.) Louis Faidherbe, who built the foundations of the region's French colonial administration. He checked the westward advance of the Tukulor forces headed by al-Hajj Umar and intervened in favor of French traders in the affairs of the Wolof and Serer states.

By the end of the 1880's most of western Senegal had become a French protectorate. Senegal was made a colony with its present boundaries in 1895. From their bases in Senegal, the French destroyed the empires in the interior, thus gaining the bulk of their West African empire by 1900. One French failure was the loss of the vital communication link of the Gambia River, which was secured for Britain by a treaty in 1889. The boundaries drawn by that agreement remain those of independent Gambia.

French administration in Senegal differed from that of France's other African possessions. In the second half of the 19th century the inhabitants born in the four communes—Dakar, Rufisque, Gorée, and St.-Louis—were granted French citizenship. The communes elected their own municipal governments and together sent a deputy to the French Parliament. A policy of assimilation was followed more consistently in Senegal than elsewhere, which resulted in a proportionately greater number of educated Senegalese. The capital of French West Africa was at St.-Louis until it was transferred to Dakar in 1902. The Senegalese therefore had more political opportunities than their counterparts in other areas.

French citizenship was extended to all inhabitants of French West Africa in 1946, and Senegal, like the other colonies, became an overseas territory. It was represented in the French Parliament and had a territorial assembly. The two Senegalese deputies elected to the French Parliament—Léopold Senghor and Lamine Guèye—played a major role in Senegal's political development. The *loi-cadre* reforms of 1956 led to the establishment of universal suffrage in Senegal and greater powers for the territorial assembly.

Senegal approved the constitutional referendum of Sept. 28, 1958, creating the French Community and voted to join the community. In 1959 Senegal and the neighboring former French Soudan formed the Mali Federation, which became independent within the French Community on June 20, 1960. On August 20, Senegal, under the leadership of Senghor, seceded and declared itself a separate republic. In the following month Soudan became the Republic of Mali.

Independent Senegal. Léopold Senghor, heading the Union Progressiste Sénégalaise, was elected the first president of independent Senegal. One of the most articulate spokesmen for inter-African cooperation and the maintenance of economic and political ties with Europe, he shaped a strongly pro-French policy for Senegal. Gradually one-man, one-party rule gave way to a more democratic multiparty government backed by constitutional reforms in 1976 and 1978. Senghor survived an attempted coup in 1963 and student and labor strife in 1968. He remained the strong man of Senegal until he resigned in 1981, succeeded by Prime Minister Abdou Diouf.

In 1981, Senegalese troops helped thwart a coup attempt in Gambia, and in February 1982 the two countries officially merged as the Confederation of Senegambia.

HARRY A. GAILEY, *San Jose State College*

Bibliography

Behrman, Lucy, *Muslim Brotherhoods and Politics in Senegal* (Harvard Univ. Press 1970).
Cowan, Laing Gray, *Local Government in West Africa* (Columbia Univ. Press 1958).
Gellar, Sheldon, *Senegal* (Westview 1981).
Klein, Martin A., *Islam and Imperialism in Senegal: Sine-Saloum, 1847–1914* (Stanford Univ. Press 1968).
Schumacher, Edward J., *Politics, Bureaucracy, and Rural Development in Senegal* (Univ. of Calif. Press 1975).
Skurnik, W. A., *The Foreign Policy of Senegal* (Northwestern Univ. Press 1972).

SENEGAL RIVER, sen-ə-gôl′, in West Africa. The Senegal River, which forms the boundary between Senegal and Mauritania, flows into the Atlantic Ocean. Its headstreams, the Bafing and Bakoy rivers, rise on the northern slopes of the Fouta Djallon mountains in Guinea and unite at Bafoulabé in Mali to form the master stream. The 1,000-mile (1,600-km) course of the Senegal system forms a great curve embracing the dry plains of Fouta and Ferlo in Senegal.

Downstream from Bakel, below the influx of the tributary Falémé River, the Senegal divides into separate channels enclosing narrow islands, including the Île à Morfil, which is 300 miles (500 km) in length. The lower course has a very low gradient, and the tide runs upstream nearly 300 miles from the sea. This reach in particular is subject to widespread annual flooding and is a complex of lakes, marshes, and distributary channels. The mouth of the Senegal is a narrow estuary opening to the sea behind a great sandspit, the Langue de Barbarie, which is growing southward under the influence of the Canary Current. The city of St.-Louis, founded by the French in 1659 as a base for the penetration of West Africa along the Senegal River, is located on an island about 15 miles (25 km) up the estuary. It is increasingly difficult to reach from the sea because of obstructing sand bars.

In the high-water periods from August to mid-October, the Senegal River is navigable by small vessels above St.-Louis as far as Kayes in Mali, a distance of about 600 miles (1,000 km). From July to January small craft can always reach Matam in Senegal, about 400 miles (600 km) from the ocean. Podor in Senegal, 175 miles (280 km) from the sea, can be reached all year.

Difficulties of navigation have reduced the significance of the Senegal for modern transportation, but the river is increasingly important as a source of irrigation water. Rice is grown on its floodplain, and important water-control works have been installed in the Delta Irrigation Scheme downstream from Richard Toll, which is approximately 70 road miles (110 km) from St.-Louis.

HIBBERD V. B. KLINE, JR.
University of Pittsburgh

SENESCHAL, sen′ə-shəl, an official in medieval France. The term derives from the Old Teutonic words "seni" (old) and "skalke" (servant). The title was given to the senior servant in the royal household. A subordinate of the mayor of the palace during the Merovingian era, the seneschal increased in importance under the Carolingians. Under the Capetians he became the most powerful palace official. After 1127 the seneschal was chosen from among the barons of the royal family. The last was Thibaut V, Count of Blois, who died in 1191. Several of the great feudal lords, such as the dukes of Normandy, also had seneschals.

A. F. P., FROM PICTORIAL

Léopold Senghor, president of Senegal (1960–1980).

SENGHOR, saN-gôr', **Léopold Sédar** (1906–   ),
Senegalese poet and political leader, who became the first president of Senegal in 1960. He
was born in Joal, Senegal, on Oct. 9, 1906. He
was educated at mission schools and then at the
Dakar Lycée and in Paris on a scholarship. Senghor was the first African to pass the *agrégation,*
qualifying him to teach in a lycée. He taught in
lycées in France and joined the French Army at
the outbreak of World War II.

Senghor was elected to represent Senegal in
the French Constituent Assemblies in 1945 and
1946. From 1946 to 1958, he was continuously
reelected to the French National Assembly,
where he led a group of African deputies. In
1948, Senghor formed the Senegalese Democratic Bloc, which pressed for reforms that would
make the French Union a true federation of
equals. He was elected to the Senegalese Assembly in 1959, and when Senegal joined with
the Sudanese Republic to form the Federation of
Mali, Senghor became president of the federal
assembly. In August 1960, he took Senegal out
of the federation and in September was elected
president of the Republic of Senegal. He was
reelected in 1963 and every five years thereafter
until his resignation on Jan. 1, 1981.

Senghor is the philosopher of négritude, an
assertion of Negro-African values. His works of
poetry include *Chants d'ombre* (1945), *Hosties
noires* (1948), *Éthiopiques* (1956), *Nocturnes*
(1971), and *Collected Poems* (1977). *African Socialism* (1959) expressed his political views.

L. Gray Cowan
State University of New York at Albany

SENILITY is a term applied to the infirmities and
decrements in physical and psychological functioning regularly associated with advanced age.
Physically, the senile are characterized by
stooped posture, dry wrinkled skin, sparse hair,
and stiff joints. Muscle strength is diminished,

and a fine tremor of the hands is frequently
noticeable. Mentally, there is gradual impair-
ment of memory, shortened attention span, and
emotional instability. Physiological measurements of all the vital organs show decreased
functional capacity with increasing age. These
decrements are gradual, and concordant results
from many laboratories leave little doubt that
such changes usually begin in the third decade
of life, shortly after physical maturity has been
achieved. Thus senescence begins in the third
decade, but determination of the status of senility is arbitrary, made even more difficult by the
fact that different individuals age at different
rates.

The branch of science concerned with aging,
its causes and effects, is called gerontology. Senescence, the process of aging, as opposed to the
state of senility, can be viewed as the total of
those progressive, irreversible changes that occur with age in an organism, decreasing its powers of survival and adaptability. The cause or
causes of such changes remain unsolved, although many theories have been proposed. One
simple mechanical theory sees the mechanism of
senescence as the result of accumulated injury,
or wear and tear. Heredity has been thought by
many investigators to play a part, but direct evidence of aging processes as an inherent property
of living matter is lacking. Ionizing radiation,
because of its known destructive effects on living
tissues, has been implicated as a causal factor in
the mechanism of aging.

Many investigators have turned their attention to the cardiovascular system because of the
obviously critical part this system plays in supplying nutrients and oxygen to all the organs of
the body. It is true that alterations in cardiovascular function are the commonest physiological
changes in old age. It may be, however, that this
system simply "ages earlier"—that is, is more
vulnerable to those effects, whatever they are,
that produce irreversible changes.

Finally, the effect of psychosocial factors on
aging cannot be neglected. The elderly individual is aware of the opinions of his peers and
reacts to them. Where evaluation of the aged is
uniformly disparaging, to grow old is to be put in
an unenviable position. Those youth-centered
cultures that apply the stereotype of usefulness
to aged people are the very ones that have the
greatest "problem" with aging. While exhaus-
tive psychological examinations leave little
doubt that there is decreased ability of older persons to learn and to adapt, the equation "old person equals useless person" is manifestly untrue,
as it overlooks the vast experience that one accumulates during a lifetime.

Gustave Newman, M. D.
Center for the Study of Aging, Duke University

Further Reading: Freese, Arthur S., *The End of Senility*
(Arbor House 1978); Galton, Lawrence, *The Truth About
Senility: How to Avoid It* (T. Y. Crowell 1979); Miller,
Edgar, *Abnormal Ageing: The Psychology of Senile and
Presenile Dementia* (Wiley 1977); Nandy, Kalidas, and Sher-
win, Ira, eds., *The Aging Brain and Senile Dementia* (Ple-
num 1977); Pumer, Morton, *Vital Maturity: Living Longer
and Better* (Universe Bks. 1979).

SENIOR, sēn'yər, **Nassau William** (1790–1864),
English economist, best known for his introduction of the concept of "abstinence," or postponement of consumption, as a key element in the formation of capital. The son of a clergyman,
Senior was born in Berkshire on Sept. 26, 1790.
He was educated at Oxford and admitted to the

bar in 1819, but he was soon publishing articles on economic problems and became a professor of political economy at Oxford in 1825.

Following in the tradition of Adam Smith and the classical school, Senior sought to define economics in terms of a few basic, irrefutable laws. He insisted that economic theory be divorced from value judgments, considerations of human welfare, and other extraneous elements. His exclusive concern with economic dynamics led him to write a report that resulted in repressive amendments to Britain's poor law in 1834. He also opposed the factory acts of 1837, which limited to 12 hours the length of the working day in any factory whose labor force included children.

Recognizing that demand and supply determined the value of goods, Senior argued that supply was dependent on the costs of production and that these costs could be regarded in terms of the sacrifices necessary to make production possible—the labor of workers and the abstinence of capitalists. Abstinence, in this sense, referred to the willingness of the entrepreneur to forego, either temporarily or permanently, the unproductive use of his profits in order to accumulate capital for further production.

Senior's theories were summarized in his book *An Outline of the Science of Political Economy* (1836). He died in London on June 4, 1864.

SENLIS

SENLIS, sän-lēs′, is a town in France in Oise department. It is on the Nonette River, north of Chantilly Forest and 27 miles (43 km) northeast of Paris. Senlis is a popular resort for Parisians, and tourists are attracted by its numerous architectural treasures. The town was a royal residence from the time of Clovis I in the late 5th century until the late 16th century. Hugh Capet was chosen king by an assembly that met at Senlis in 987.

The center of the old town is surrounded by thick walls built during the Gallo-Roman era. In the old town is the cathedral of Notre Dame, one of the most beautiful Gothic structures in France. Begun in 1153, it was not completed until the 16th century. Near the cathedral are the remains of the royal château. There are many old churches, Renaissance houses, and Gallo-Roman ruins, including a 3d century arena. Population: (1968) 10,111.

SENNACHERIB

SENNACHERIB, sə-nak′ər-ib, was king of Assyria from 704 B. C. until his death in 681. His name in Assyrian was Sin-aḫḫē-erība, meaning "[The moon god] Sin has replaced [his dead] brothers." The English form of the name goes back to the Septuagint.

Military Campaigns. Sennacherib was the son and successor of Sargon II. Almost from the very beginning of his reign, the new King was occupied with quelling rebellions all over his wide realm. His main military campaigns were in Babylonia and Palestine.

The first four years of his reign were taken up with fighting in the south. In Babylonia, Marduk-apal-iddina (the Biblical Merodach-baladan) regained the throne from which he had been ousted by Sargon in 709, and with his allies, the Elamites, he mustered a large army to fight the Assyrians. However, he was defeated by Sennacherib, who triumphantly entered Babylon and established Bel-ibni on the Babylonian throne.

In 701, Sennacherib turned his attention to the west, especially to Palestine and Phoenicia, which upon the death of Sargon had succeeded partially in throwing off the yoke of Assyria. He first defeated the coastal cities of Phoenicia, including Sidon and Arwad (Aradus), and then proceeded south against the cities of Ashkelon (Ascalon), Joppa (Jaffa), and Ekron (Akir) and against Hezekiah, the king of Judah. According to Sennacherib's account, he laid siege to Jerusalem, shutting up Hezekiah in the city "like a bird in a cage." But he did not succeed in capturing Jerusalem, and he returned to Assyria after imposing heavy tribute on Hezekiah.

Accounts in the Old Testament and in the history of Herodotus (5th century B. C.), probably referring to the Palestinian campaign, say that Sennacherib was forced to retreat to Nineveh because of a plague that devastated his army. In II Kings 19:35 one reads: "It came to pass that night, that the angel of the Lord went out, and smote in the camp of the Assyrians an hundred fourscore and five thousand; and when they arose early in the morning, behold, they were all dead corpses." Similarly, Herodotus says (Book 2, sect. 141), that "there came in the night a multitude of field-mice, which devoured all the quivers and bowstrings of the enemy, and ate the thongs by which they managed their shields," as a consequence of which the Assyrians lost the use of their weapons and were defeated.

Sennacherib again marched on Babylon in 700 B. C., and in several successive years he fought the Babylonians and Elamites. His forces met the enemy in the Battle of Khalule in 691 B. C. and razed Babylon in 689, thus restoring peace to Assyria's southern possessions. The destruction of Babylon was thorough: the walls, temples, and houses were burned; the city was flooded with water from the canals; the images of the gods were smashed; and the people were struck down with the sword.

Rebuilding of Nineveh. Sennacherib's remaining eight years were apparently years of peace, if one discounts an occasional punitive expedition. During this period he devoted himself fully to making Nineveh a capital worthy of the great Assyrian empire. The old palace was torn down and replaced by a larger and more magnificent one. The streets of the capital were widened and straightened. The greatly enlarged city was surrounded by huge walls, an inner and an outer one, pierced by 15 gates. Parks were laid out in the city and planted with all kinds of trees. Large aqueducts were built to bring water from the mountains.

Sennacherib seems to differ from other Assyrian kings in his lack of interest in temple construction. This apparent lack of respect for the divine is well matched by his almost sacrilegious deeds in destroying and smashing the temples and images of Babylon.

Sennacherib's Death. Sennacherib was murdered in 681 B. C. by one or two of his sons as he was worshiping in the temple of Nineveh. Assyrian sources are not in accord on the number of his assassins; the Old Testament (II Kings 19:37) names two, Adrammelech and Sharezer. Esarhaddon, Sennacherib's faithful son, quickly overcame the rebels and ascended the throne.

I. J. GELB
*The Oriental Institute
University of Chicago*

Further Reading: Honor, Leo L., *Sennacherib's Invasion of Palestine* (AMS Press 1926); Olmstead, Albert *History of Assyria*, reprint (Univ. of Chicago Press 1960).

SENNAR, sen-när′, is a town in east-central Sudan. Situated on the Blue Nile River, it is 160 miles (260 km) southeast of Khartoum. The town is a rail center in a rich farming area.

The Sennar Dam, on the Blue Nile at the nearby village of Makwar, was completed in 1925. About 9,900 feet (3,000 meters) long and 119 feet (36 meters) high, it provides irrigation water for nearly one million acres (400,000 hectares) in the fertile Gezira region. The cotton grown there produces over one third of Sudan's revenue.

The old town of Sennar, now uninhabited, was the capital of the Funj sultanate, which ruled the area from the 16th to the 19th century. Population: (1965) 17,600.

SENNETT, sen′et, **Mack** (1884–1960), American motion picture producer-director of the silent era, whose name was synonymous with slapstick routines, notably custard pie fights and fantastic chases. He was born Michael Sinnott in Danville, Quebec, Canada, on Jan. 17, 1884. He began his motion picture career in New York City in 1909 as an actor with D. W. Griffith's Biograph Company but soon formed his own organization, the Keystone Company, and moved it to Hollywood. There he made about 1,000 films, with such stars as Charlie Chaplin, Mabel Normand, Marie Dressler, Buster Keaton, W. C. Fields, Harold Lloyd, Ben Turpin, and Wallace Beery. His best-known creations featured the Keystone Kops and the Mack Sennett Bathing Beauties.

Sennett's films followed much the same comedy pattern, but they had a quality of freshness and spontaneity that made them immensely popular. With the advent of talking pictures, the appeal of largely visual comedy waned, and Sennett's studio was closed in 1928. His biography *King of Comedy* appeared in 1954. He died in Woodland Hills, Calif., on Nov. 5, 1960.

Further Reading: Fowler, Gene, *Father Goose: The Story of Mack Sennett* (Covici 1934).

SENS, säNs, is a town in France, in Yonne department in Burgundy. It is on the Yonne River, 70 miles (113 km) southeast of Paris. There are fine examples of early Gothic and Renaissance architecture, including the Cathedral of St. Étienne, which dates mostly from the 12th century, and museums rich in medieval and classical remains. The cathedral's stained glass windows, dating from the 12th century to the 17th, are particularly striking. Manufactures include machinery, food products, and chemicals.

In ancient times the town was the capital of the Senones, a powerful Celtic tribe. After it was taken by the Romans, who called it Agendicum, it became one of the most important cities of Gaul. In later times it was the seat of several ecclesiastical councils. Population: (1968) 22,-658.

SENSE AND SENSIBILITY is a novel by Jane Austen, published in 1811. It relates the vicissitudes in love of two sisters, Elinor and Marianne Dashwood. Elinor loves and is loved by Edward Ferrars, but he feels himself honor bound by his earlier and now regretted engagement to Lucy Steele. Marianne is loved by the admirable Colonel Brandon, considerably her senior, but she prefers the charming and selfish John Willoughby, who jilts her to marry an heiress. Edward's arrogant mother, on learning of his engagement to Lucy, disinherits him in favor of his foppish younger brother Robert. The mercenary Lucy then elopes with Robert, leaving Edward free to marry Elinor. Marianne at last recognizes the folly of her romanticism and accepts Brandon as her husband.

In contrasting the difference between Elinor's sound "sense" and Marianne's romantic "sensibility," Jane Austen occasionally verges on didacticism. However, the book contains some of her neatest characterization and satiric comment.

DeLancey Ferguson
Formerly, Brooklyn College

Mack Sennett comedies featured the Keystone Kops, inept policemen who engaged in frantic chases.

CULVER PICTURES

POLICE PATR

POLICE DEPT.

SENSES AND SENSATION. Men have been concerned with the senses as long as they have asked questions about the nature of the world and been self-conscious about the limitations of their knowledge. If we admit that most, if not all, of our knowledge of the world comes from sensation, it is natural for us to ask what kind of filter our senses are. The legitimacy of the evidence that our senses provide remains a subject of lively controversy and will probably continue so as long as there are philosophers. But what concerns us here is the nature of the senses from the point of view of the physiologist or the psychologist.

A sensory system consists of a set of receptor cells, accessory structures that transform the energy of the physical stimulus before that energy impinges on the receptor cells, neural pathways leading from the receptor cells, and, finally, the areas in the central nervous system to which the neural pathways lead.

There is a great disparity in the amount known about the different sense modalities. Much research has been done in vision and hearing but relatively little in smell and taste. So incomplete is our understanding of the latter two senses that there is no general agreement about what their stimuli are. It was suggested by Lloyd H. Beck in 1950 that the stimulus for smell is the selective cooling of olfactory cells by molecules of odorous substances and that olfactory cells therefore are detectors of radiant energy. The stimuli for some taste sensations are better known than others. The hydrogen ion is probably the stimulus for sour, but common properties of sweet or of bitter stimuli have not been established.

Classification of the Senses. The senses can be classified in many ways. They may, for example, be classified by the kind of physical energy to which the end organs are sensitive, or by anatomical characteristics of the receptors themselves, or by the type of nerve that carries the impulses from the receptor. Thus, the question "How many senses are there?" has no single answer. The number depends on how one wishes to classify them.

Aristotle distinguished five senses: vision, hearing, touch, taste, and smell. Lucretius in *De rerum natura* discussed the senses in four categories: hearing, taste, smell, and vision as a form of touch. Sir Charles Scott Sherrington, in his classic *The Integrative Action of the Nervous System* (1906), used a functional classification. According to this scheme, there are four classes of senses: the proprioceptors, which give information about deep tissues within the body; the interoceptors, which, like taste, give information about the internal surface of the body; the exteroceptors, the skin senses, which give information about the external surface of the body; and the distance receptors, which, like vision and hearing, respond to objects at a distance.

A modern classification based more on anatomical differences considers four groups of senses. The *special senses* are those with specialized organs found in the head end of an organism. These include vision, hearing, smell, taste, and the vestibular sense, which is the sense of balance or equilibrium and whose organ is the nonauditory labyrinth in the inner ear. The *skin senses* include touch, skin pain, and the temperature senses. The *deep senses* include the muscle, tendon, and joint sensations together with deep pain and pressure. The *visceral senses* convey information about organic and visceral events.

Sensory Nerves. Since the sense organs differ so widely, responding as they do to different kinds of physical energy, the best place to find phenomena common to all the senses is in the sensory nerves—the neural pathways that lead from the sensory cells. The threshold of any sensory system is the least energy to which the system responds. When physical energy above the system's threshold impinges on a sense organ, the sense cells transform this energy into electrical impulses, action potentials, in the sensory nerves.

It has been demonstrated experimentally that the magnitude of impulses in a sensory nerve and the speed of conduction of these impulses along the nerve depend on the particular fiber and on its condition and not on the magnitude of the stimulus—provided that the nerve responds at all. This principle—the all-or-none law—puts a severe limitation on the means that sensory nerves can use to transmit information from sense organs. It means that a nerve fiber cannot show the strength of a stimulus by the strength of its response.

The accompanying diagrams illustrate the electrical activity caused by strong, moderate, and weak stimuli in single sensory nerves. Time is represented on the horizontal axis, and the voltage of the neural activity is represented by the height of the vertical spikes. The time between the onset of the stimulus and the first spike is called the latency of the nerve. In each case the stimulus begins at the time indicated by the arrow. Notice that the amplitude of the responses remains constant, but the frequency diminishes as the stimulus intensity decreases. This illustrates the all-or-none law.

Adaptation, another general sensory principle, is shown in long-continued stimuli. The fre-

ALL-OR-NONE LAW

Strong stimulus

Moderate stimulus

Weak stimulus

quency of responding decreases with the duration of the stimulus. This is adaptation, the system becoming less sensitive with continued stimulation. A common example of sense-organ adaptation is the apparent decrease in brightness shortly after a light is first turned on in a dark room.

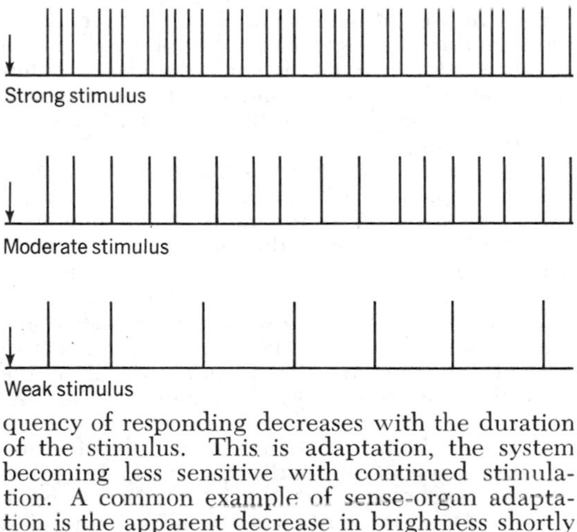

A single nerve fiber can transmit information about time (the onset of cessation of a stimulus) or about the amount of stimulation (encoded in the frequency of impulses in the fiber). The particular fiber or the number of fibers stimulated provides another kind of information. Finally, information may be conveyed in the temporal arrangement of the arrival of impulses in a cortical area from various fibers; that is, fibers firing asynchronously may convey information by

ADAPTATION

the degree of asynchrony. Thus, conceivably, the pattern of arrival of impulses at some point in the nervous system contains a fourth kind of information. Modulator and volley theories utilize this principle.

The German physiologist Johannes Müller in 1840 formulated a doctrine that has assumed prime importance in the physiology of the senses. Müller asserted that sensations are produced not directly by conditions of the outside world but by states of the nerves, that the specific sensation produced is determined by the nature of the sensory systems excited, and that each nerve is capable of being excited only by a particular class of stimuli. The function of a receptor system was defined by Sherrington as the lowering of the threshold for one kind of stimulus—the adequate stimulus—and raising of the threshold for others. Application of Müller's principles—the specific energy of nerves doctrine—gives us what is called the place theory of the senses. For example, in a sense organ, some cells may be sensitive to the low end of the stimulus continuum, some to the middle range, and others to the high end. Since each of these groups makes synaptic connections with different sensory nerves, information about the stimulus quality is conveyed by the particular fibers that are stimulated. These theories explain sensitivity to a range of the adequate stimulus in terms of the selective sensitivity of groups of receptors.

Weber's and Fechner's "Laws". On the basis of experiments on the minimum detectable differences of weights in the hand, the physiologist Ernst Heinrich Weber, in 1834, concluded that the just-noticeable difference in weight felt is proportional to the weight in the hand before the extra weight is added. For example, if an individual cannot detect an addition smaller than k grams added weight when he holds 10 grams in his hand, then he would be unable to detect an addition smaller than $10\ k$ grams when holding 100 grams.

In 1860, Gustav Fechner asserted as a general principle for the senses what is now known as Weber's law—that the ratio of the minimum detectable difference in the magnitude of a stimulus divided by the reference magnitude is constant. On the basis of further assumptions, Fechner derived a relation now called Fechner's law, which holds that the perceived or subjective magnitude of a stimulus is proportional to the logarithm of the physical magnitude of the stimulus.

These relations, although responsible for motivating much of the early experimental work in sensory psychology and physiology, later became subject to severe criticism. It was found that these "laws" break down—more seriously for some senses, less seriously for others. Moreover, it was recognized that the validity of the law depends on the scale in which the stimulus is measured. For example, if we study Weber's law in the temperature senses, and if the law holds in the centigrade scale, then it cannot be correct for the Fahrenheit scale, and vice versa. Nevertheless, the relations hold more than historical interest, because for many applied situations they provide convenient engineering rules of thumb for scales of stimuli often employed, in ranges of stimuli often encountered.

Sensitivity and its Significance. It seems to be rather generally true that for the range of stimuli to which they are maximally sensitive, the human special senses are as sensitive as they can be, and that under the conditions that provide maximal sensitivity for the human senses, no other animal's senses can surpass them. The threshold for the human eye, when it is most sensitive (after dark adaptation), is about four ten-billionths (4×10^{-10}) of an erg measured at the surface of the cornea, if the light stimulus is monochromatic with wavelength 510 millimicrons. These measurements were made by Selig Hecht, Simon Shlaer, and Maurice Henri Leonard Pirenne in 1942. Calculations based on absorption in various parts of the eye lead to the conclusion that only about 10 quanta of light need to be absorbed by the rods in the retina for threshold to be reached. A receptor could not be much more sensitive than this, and in an organism whose nervous system exhibits the slightest bit of "noise"—discharging without stimulation—increased sensitivity would be worse than useless. Moreover, it is probable that each of the 10 rods needs to absorb only a single quantum to become activated. No system can be more sensitive than this, and the limitation is not biological but physical.

The situation is similar for the human ear. Although the human ear hears vibrations of from about 16 to 20,000 cycles per second, its greatest sensitivity is reached at about 3,000 cycles per second. At this frequency it was found in 1935 that the extent of movement of the ear drum in response to a threshold tone is less than one billionth of a centimeter. The movement of the basilar membrane must be less than one one-hundred-billionth (10^{-11}) of a centimeter—a distance smaller than one one-thousandth of the diameter of a hydrogen atom.

From another point of view this sensitivity is equally amazing. Thermal noise is produced by the agitation of molecules in air at ordinary temperatures. The intensity of this noise between 1,000 and 6,000 cycles per second is not much below auditory threshold for an individual with good hearing. Here too an increased sensitivity would be of little use.

Since man reaches the useful limit of hearing in the neighborhood of 3,000 cycles per second, we should not expect other animals to hear better at this frequency. But at higher frequencies human hearing is relatively poor. Dogs, cats, and bats have auditory sensitivity far greater than man's—above 20,000 cycles per second.

From an evolutionary point of view the facts about maximal sensitivity seem eminently sensible. The region of greatest sensitivity for human daylight vision is in the neighborhood of 550 millimicrons wavelength—the yellow-green portion of the spectrum—and this is the region of maximum energy reaching the surface of the earth from the sun.

Man is the only animal to whom speech is important. His peak of maximum auditory sensitivity is lower in frequency than the peak for most other animals, but it lies in the region most important for the perception of speech, which is certainly one of the pinnacles of evolution's achievement.

PHILBURN RATOOSH
University of California, Berkeley
(Bibliography on next page)

Bibliography

Adrian, Edgar D., *The Basis of Sensation* (1928; reprint Hafner 1964).
Adrian, Edgar D., *The Physical Background of Perception* (Oxford 1967).
Boring, Edwin G., *Sensation and Perception in the History of Experimental Psychology* (Appleton 1942).
Case, James, *Sensory Mechanisms* (Macmillan 1966).
Geldard, Frank A., *The Human Senses* (Wiley 1953).
Granit, Ragnar, *Receptors and Sensory Perception* (Yale Univ. Press 1955).
Tamar, Henry, *Principles of Sensory Physiology* (Thomas C. C. 1971).

SENSITIVE PLANT, the common name of some species of *Mimosa* in the pea family, especially *M. sensitiva* and *M. pudica* of tropical America. These plants respond to the touch by rapidly folding their twice-pinnate leaves—a few leaflets if lightly touched, the whole leaf if strongly shocked. The leaves also "go to sleep" in the dark. The stimulus is apparently transferred by some chemical means, causing water to be lost from large cells in the swollen bases of leaflets and petioles, with release of the pressures that kept the leaf spread. Gradual recovery accompanies reentry of the water into the cells. *M. pudica*, the more common species in cultivation, is a short-lived prickly perennial usually grown as an annual.

SENSITIVITY TRAINING is the generic name for a wide variety of group interaction experiences offered to the public at large and to particular occupational groups. The term is synonymous with "T-groups," T standing for training. Encounter groups are derived from T-groups, but the former tend to emphasize more physical interaction. Most often under the aegis of organizations, T-groups are usually geared to common occupational or industrial problems, with the intent of having participants function more effectively in their jobs or roles.

Basic groups, usually 8 to 15 participants and one leader, may assemble regularly for periods ranging from a few hours a week to a weekend (marathon) of full-time interaction, to several weeks of daily group interaction. Groups generally aim to develop understanding of group dynamics, plus individual learning such as increased sensitivity to and recognition of other people's feelings; greater readiness to be direct and open about one's own feelings and perceptions of others ("owning one's own emotions"); and the capacity to give and receive perceptions of one's personal style of talking and interacting with others ("feedback").

History. The sensitivity training movement evolved from the work of social psychologists Kurt Lewin and Ronald Lippitt in 1946. To determine how applications of group dynamics could help workers implement the Connecticut fair employment practices act, observers studied the interactions of members of small groups, later pooling their observations. Excited by hearing their behavior described by the scientists, the persons observed began to participate in sharing their observations. Thus the process of interpersonal feedback began.

The emotional impact promised such great possibilities for individual growth and enhanced capacity to cope with human interaction that the staff founded the National Training Laboratories (NTL). The predominant organization in sensitivity training, NTL largely focused on T-groups in business, education, and social agencies.

While by no means uniform, NTL leaders, mostly educators and academic psychologists, generally refuse to give direction to group members, forcing participants to develop their own agenda. The way participants interact with one another becomes the subject of study, and discussion is mainly about the way people talk and the emotional factors that emerge when they do.

Criticism. While the groups regularly evoke strong emotional reactions, these outpourings are not synonymous with emotional growth or change. For the most part, participants are positive, even laudatory, about their experiences immediately after the group terminates. Their estimation of the value derived drops off markedly with time, and while they may have experienced subjective change, others around them usually fail to see it. Such changes that have been scientifically demonstrated seem to be in the learning of a new vocabulary to describe human interaction, a vocabulary characteristic of the movement. Much professional criticism has been voiced over the significant number of "emotional casualties" that can result from the process. See also ENCOUNTER GROUP.

BRUCE L. MALIVER
Postgraduate Center for Mental Health

Further Reading: Bradford, Leland P., et al., eds, *T-Group Theory and Laboratory Method* (Wiley 1964).

SENTA, sen'tä, is a city in Yugoslavia, in the autonomous province of Vojvodina, northern Serbia, about 80 miles (130 km) northwest of Belgrade. The Hungarian form of the name is Zenta. It is a trading center for an agricultural area, has natural gas wells nearby, and is a railroad center at the head of navigation on the Tisa River. Eugene of Savoy's victory at Senta over the Turks in 1697 led to the cession of the greater part of Hungary, Transylvania, and Croatia to Austria by the Peace of Karlowitz (1699). Population: (1963 est.) 22,000.

SENTENCE, in traditional grammar, a set of words so related as to express a complete thought. A sentence may contain one or more clauses. A *simple* sentence consists of one independent (main) clause; a *compound* sentence of two or more independent clauses; a *complex* sentence of one independent clause and one or more dependent clauses; and a *compound-complex* sentence of two or more independent clauses and one or more dependent clauses. See CLAUSE.

According to their use, sentences are classed as *declarative* (stating a fact), *interrogative* (asking a question), *exclamatory* (making a statement under the influence of strong feeling, or expressing a wish), and *imperative* (giving a command). A sentence usually has an expressed *subject* (a word or group of words referring to the person or thing that is talked about) and a *predicate* (a verb that, with its modifiers, asserts or predicates something about the subject). In an *elliptical* sentence, however, usually either the subject or the predicate is not expressed. This is especially common in an imperative or an exclamatory sentence (*Do it!* with *you* considered as understood; *What a fine day!* with *it is* understood), but there may also be ellipses in declarative and interrogative sentences (*John*, as an answer to the question *Who is there?* with *is there* understood; or *What?* with *did you say* or *happened* understood). Conventionalized exclamations or cries can also be considered as sentences (*Oh, no!* or *Ouch!*). See also GRAMMAR.

SENTENCE, the penalty or punishment imposed by a criminal court after a determination of a defendant's guilt. It is equivalent to a judgment in a civil case and may consist of an order prescribing a fine, a period of imprisonment for a specified number of days, months, or years; or the death penalty, in those countries that still retain it.

In the United States, the limits of punishment are prescribed by congress or by the state legislatures. They generally grant some flexibility to the judge or jury in deciding the exact sentence in each case. It is within the constitutional power of a legislative body, however, to make a specified penalty mandatory on conviction of a particular crime, without permitting the exercise of any discretion by the sentencing judge or jury.

The essence of a sentence is the kind and amount of punishment; that is, as a general rule, the time of commencement and termination of imprisonment are not regarded as a part of the sentence proper. Sentences for several offenses or for several counts of the same indictment may be *successive* (one starting after another ends) or *concurrent* (the convicted person having the privilege of serving on each day a portion of each sentence).

RICHARD L. HIRSHBERG
Attorney at Law

SENTIMENTAL JOURNEY, the last literary work by the English author Laurence Sterne, published in two volumes in 1768. It was the first half of a projected four-volume work that Sterne did not live to complete. The full title, *A Sentimental Journey Through France and Italy,* is therefore misleading. At the end of volume two, the author has only reached Lyon.

A Sentimental Journey, like *Tristram Shandy,* is an outcome of Sterne's tours of the Continent. He narrates his experiences in the person of Parson Yorick of *Tristram,* and he frequently alludes to other characters in the novel. Indeed, the itinerary of the *Journey* is outlined in volume seven of *Tristram.* The narrative method, too, with all its digressions, is the same, as is the humor, including sly bawdry. However, the great character creations of *Tristram* are lacking.

Sterne himself described *A Sentimental Journey* as "a quiet journey of the heart in pursuit of *Nature,* and those affections which arise out of her." He aimed "to teach us to love the world and our fellow creatures better than we do."

DELANCEY FERGUSON
Formerly, Brooklyn College

SENUSI. See SANUSI.

SEOUL, sōl, the capital and largest city of the Republic of Korea, is situated in the central-western part of the Korean peninsula, on the Han River about 20 miles (32 km) east of Inchon, its seaport. In 1948 the capital was separated from Kyonggi province and made the Special City of Seoul, which has provincial status.

Description. With lofty peaks to the north and green hills to the south, Seoul has a setting of great natural beauty. From the air the city presents a panorama combining the new and the old. A modern metropolis with skyscrapers, expressways, and Western-style hotels, it has retained its historic palaces, gates, and other treasures of Korea's past.

The city's main entrance is the South Gate. Leading from it to the Capitol is Taepyong Street, lined with modern government buildings, foreign legations, and newspaper offices. The commercial center of the city is Chongno Street, with many stores. Near the East Gate extends a large colorful market.

The buildings of the Toksu (Duksu) Palace are situated in the city's center. The grounds are now a public park. Two of the buildings, of Western design, house the National Museum, which contains masterpieces of Korean art. Other palaces are the Kyongbok, near the Capitol, and

Seoul, capital of the Republic of Korea. Building at lower right houses part of National Museum collection.

PAOLO KOCH, RAPHO GUILLUMETTE

the Changdok, behind which stretches the Secret Garden, with wooded slopes, ponds, and pavilions. Near the Changdok Palace are the municipal zoo and an amusement park.

Seoul has more than a dozen universities. Among them are Seoul National University and the country's leading private institutions of higher learning.

Economy. Linked by rail, highway, and air service with all parts of the Republic of Korea, Seoul is the economic heart of the nation. It has many food processing industries and produces a large percentage of the republic's farm implements and consumer goods, such as clothing and electrical appliances. Much of the manufacturing is concentrated in the Yongdungpo section, south of the Han River.

History. Developed early as a trading center, Seoul was made the capital of Korea in 1394 by King Taejo, the founder of the Yi dynasty. At that time the city was named Hansung. It remained the capital of the kingdom for five centuries. The South Gate and principal palace buildings were built during the first 200 years of the Yi dynasty.

The city underwent many changes after the opening of Korea to the West in the 1870's and during the period of Japanese occupation from 1910 to 1945. Under the occupation it was named Kyongsong (Keijo in Japanese).

When U. S. forces landed in Korea following the surrender of Japan in World War II, the city was the natural site for their headquarters. Renamed Seoul ("the capital"), it became the seat of the U. S. military government and subsequently the capital of the Republic of Korea, proclaimed in 1948.

Seoul was severely damaged during the Korean War (1950–1953), changing hands four times. But it regained its position as the political, economic, and cultural center of Korea and developed as one of the world's fastest-growing cities. Between 1949 and 1970 the population increased from 1,446,019 to 5,509,993.

KYUNG CHO CHUNG
Author of "New Korea" and "Korea Tomorrow"

SEPARATION OF POWERS, a founding principle of the U. S. government requiring separation of the executive, legislative, and judicial branches of government, which theoretically will check and balance one another. See CHECKS AND BALANCES; CONSTITUTION OF THE UNITED STATES; FEDERALISM; UNITED STATES: *Form and Constitution of the Federal Government.*

SEPARATISTS, in religion, those wishing to separate from an established church order. The term is more specifically applied to the Brownists, a group formed in 1580 in Norwich, England, by Robert Browne. Browne strove to organize his followers into churches modeled on New Testament examples, under congregational government, and free from civil regulation. He was soon joined by Robert Harrison and Henry Barrow (Barrowe).

Persecuted by civil and religious authorities, Browne and Harrison went into exile in the Netherlands in 1581. There, in 1582, Browne published his *Treatise of Reformation Without Tarrying for Any,* which expounds the congregational concept of church organization. Barrow and John Greenwood became leaders of a London congregation in 1586, but they and many of their followers were imprisoned. Restrictive measures instituted by John Whitgift, archbishop of Canterbury, culminated in the execution of Barrow and Greenwood in 1593. Sir Walter Raleigh estimated at that time that there were about 20,000 English Brownists. Public opinion forbade further separatist executions, but arrests continued, and many fled to the Netherlands. Of these, John Robinson's congregation in Leiden was outstanding. Several of its members were among those who sailed on the *Mayflower* in 1620 to establish a settlement in America.

By 1631 there were 11 separatist congregations in London. In 1640 the terms "Independent" and "Congregational" were applied to the movement. Under the Commonwealth its growth was unhindered. The Stuart Restoration brought renewed persecution, but the Toleration Act (1689) removed the worst repressions. By 1730 there were 380 congregations in England, and by 1811 there were 800. The Evangelical Revival moderated the more rigid Calvinism of the movement and established the separatists as Congregationalists.

The term "separatists" is also applied to those in Germany who refused to join the Evangelical Union, the forced uniting of the Lutheran and Reformed churches, effected by Frederick William III of Prussia in 1817. It is applied as well to those who before the union had refused to conform to the strict tenets of Lutheranism, particularly the Pietists. Often incorrectly identified as separatists are some of the groups in England led by Thomas Rose and John Rough who refused to revert to Roman Catholicism during the reign of Queen Mary I.

See also CONGREGATIONALISTS; MASSACHUSETTS–*History*; PURITANISM.

RICHARD E. WEBB
Formerly, British Information Services

SEPHARDIM, sə-fär′dim, Jews who were forced out of Spain after the inauguration of the Inquisition there in 1480. The name is also applied to their descendants, as distinguished from the Ashkenazim, or Jews who had settled in northern Europe. The name "Sephardim" derives from Sepharad, a city in Asia Minor where exiles from Jerusalem settled after the first destruction of the temple in 586 B. C. (Obadiah, verse 20). Later, the name was applied to Spain.

The Sephardim had a high degree of culture, and when they settled in other countries, they preserved their own language, Ladino, which is a mixture of Spanish and Hebrew, as well as their own ritual, customs, and literature. They took refuge first in Portugal, then in Morocco and the eastern Mediterranean region, Italy, and the Balkins. One of their outstanding centers was at Salonika in Macedonia, which retained its importance for them until it was destroyed by the Germans during World War II. Amsterdam, the Netherlands, was another of their cultural centers. They also spread throughout western Europe. The early Jewish emigrants to the American colonies were predominantly Sephardic.

The Sephardic ritual was derived from that of Babylonia, the Ashkenazic from that of Palestine. Some confusion exists in the use of the term, as it is sometimes applied to all non-Ashkenazic elements, which comprise some 15% of the world's total Jewish population. Many leaders in philosophy, science, literature, and the arts have been numbered among the Sephardim.

SEPIOLITE, sē'pē-ə-līt, is a hydrous magnesium silicate best known for its use in making pipes. The mineral has a smooth feel, and it is light and sufficiently porous to float on water when dry—hence its German name *meerschaum*, or "sea foam." It is easily carved and takes a good polish. The material is translucent and has an earthy luster, and it ranges from white to grayish, yellowish, or reddish white.

Sepiolite occurs as a compact mineral with a mixed fibrous and amorphous structure. It is found in nodular masses in association with other magnesium minerals such as magnesite or serpentine. The most notable sites are in Turkey, but it also occurs in Czechoslovakia, Greece, Morocco, Spain, the United States, and elsewhere.

Composition, $Mg_4(Si_6O_{15})(OH)_2 \cdot 6H_2O$; hardness, 2–2.5; specific gravity, 2; crystal system, probably monoclinic.

SEPOY MUTINY, sē'poi, a revolt (1857–1858) in the Indian Army that threatened British rule in India. It is also known as the Indian Mutiny.

Sepoy is an Anglo-Indian term for an Indian soldier who served in the Indian Army under British officers when India was under British rule. The East India Company employed Indian soldiers to fight under British leaders because of the difficulty of transporting troops from Europe and the high mortality among them due to the Indian climate.

Causes of the Mutiny. The Sepoy Mutiny is generally regarded as an expression of resentment against some aspects of British rule rather than as an organized attempt to gain independence. It was confined mainly to the "Bengal Army," which was actually recruited from Oudh and the North West Frontier. The soldiers from Madras, Bombay, the Punjab, and most of the large princely states, as well as the Sikhs and Gurkhas, remained loyal to Britain.

The British annexation of Oudh and other independent territories had alarmed both Muslim and Hindu leaders. The spread of Western ideas and Western education, British legislation aimed at social reform and the abolition of various Hindu practices, and the introduction of the railroad and the telegraph were threatening the traditional way of life. Attempts at Christianization by zealous missionaries had aroused bitter resentment. Military discipline had suffered because many of the best officers had been transferred to political positions, and British prestige had waned as a result of the defeat inflicted on British arms in the First Afghan War (1838–1842).

The event that actually sparked the revolt was the Army's adoption of the Enfield rifle and the rumor that the new cartridges were greased with animal fat. This was offensive to Hindus, for whom the cow was sacred, and to Muslims, who believed the pig was unclean. The British authorities hastened to issue an assurance that the cartridges were greased with vegetable fat, but the rumor had spread too far and the situation was out of hand.

The Mutiny. On May 9, 1857, 85 sepoys were imprisoned at Meerut for refusing to use the supposedly polluted cartridges. The next day they were set free by rebelling troops, who killed some of their officers and other Europeans. They then proceeded some 40 miles (60 km) to Delhi, which was inadequately protected by British troops. The sepoy garrison joined the mutineers, but the British blew up the arsenal to prevent its falling into rebel hands. Delhi fell with considerable bloodshed, and Bahadur Shah II, titular Mughul (Mogul) ruler, was proclaimed emperor of India by the victorious forces.

In order to restore their prestige, as well as for strategic reasons, it was essential for the British to regain control of Delhi. Forces from Ambala and Meerut took up a position on the ridge overlooking the city. Reinforcements from the Punjab joined them, and in September the city was retaken after a three-month siege. Bahadur Shah was deported and his sons were killed, ending the Mughul dynasty.

Another major disaster to the British in June and July was the fall of Kanpur (Cawnpore) to mutineers under Nana Sahib (Dandhu Panth) of Bithur, whose claims as adopted son of the peshwa of the Marathas had not been recognized by the British. The British forces had to surrender after holding out for three weeks, and, although promised safe conduct to Allahabad, they were slain. Their wives and children were also killed just before Sir Henry Havelock retook the city in July. This massacre greatly inflamed British resentment and led to extremely harsh reprisals.

Another important event of the revolt was the rebel siege of Lucknow. It was besieged in June, and at the beginning of July, Sir Henry Lawrence, the chief commissioner, was forced to take refuge in the residency, where he was killed. Sir John Eardley Wilmot Inglis took command of the garrison, which continued to resist attack with reinforcements under Sir Henry Havelock arriving in September and further reinforcements under Sir Colin Campbell in November. The city finally came completely under British control again in March 1858.

British control of these important centers made the outcome of the struggle fairly certain, but the revolt had spread through the Bengal Army in central India from Delhi to Calcutta, where the garrisons were thinly protected by British troops. Although the officers in some of the stations were able to preserve order, in others the troops rose and killed their officers and other Europeans. By June 1858, as a result of the campaign waged by Sir Hugh Rose against the rebelling forces under Tantia Topi (a Maratha Brahman) and Nana Sahib, no important city or fortress remained in the hands of the mutineers. Tantia Topi was captured and executed in April, and Nana Sahib was driven into the jungle, where he is believed to have perished.

The Results. Lord Canning, the governor general of India, was able to undo some of the harmful effects of the revolt by pursuing a policy of moderation after peace was restored. An important result of the mutiny was the transfer of the government of India from the East India Company to the British crown under the Government of India Act of 1858. See also INDIA—*Modern History.*

Bibliography
Chattopadhyaya, Haraprasad, *The Sepoy Mutiny, 1857: A Social Study and Analysis* (Bookland 1957).
Embree, Ainslee T., ed., *1857 in India: Mutiny or War of Independence?* (Heath 1963).
Metcalf, Thomas R., *The Aftermath of Revolt: India, 1857–1870* (Princeton Univ. Press 1964).
Sen, Surendra Nath, *Eighteen Fifty-Seven* (Luzac 1957).
Thompson, Edward J., *The Other Side of the Medal* Harcourt, Brace 1926).

SEPPUKU, Japanese ceremonial suicide. See HARA-KIRI.

SEPT-ÎLES, se-tēl', a town in eastern Quebec, Canada, is on a bay at the northwestern end of the Gulf of St. Lawrence, about 350 miles (563 km) northeast of Quebec. Sept-Îles is also known by the English translation of its name, Seven Islands.

The town consists of six islands and a part of the mainland. It is an important shipping center for the iron ore mined to the northwest. Sept-Îles was discovered by Jacques Cartier in 1535, settled in 1650, and incorporated in 1951. Population: 29,262.

SEPTEMBER is the ninth month of the Gregorian calendar. It derives its name in part from the Latin word *septem,* meaning "seven," since it was the seventh month of the Roman year, which began in March.

September has 30 days, and the autumnal equinox, marking the beginning of the fall season, occurs on September 22d. In the United States, Labor Day, which is celebrated on the first Monday of September, is traditionally regarded as the end of the summer season. The Jewish New Year, Rosh Hashanah, usually occurs in September. Michaelmas, the feast of the archangel Michael, is observed on September 29th.

The astrological signs for September are Virgo (August 23 to September 22) and Libra (September 23 to October 22). The birthstone for the month is the sapphire or the star sapphire.

In military history, September was an important month. World War II began and ended during September. Germany invaded Poland on Sept. 1, 1939, opening hostilities, and Britain and France declared war on Germany on September 3. Representatives of Japan signed surrender documents on board the USS *Missouri* on Sept. 2, 1945. During the American Revolution the Battle of Yorktown, which led to the surrender of the British forces under General Cornwallis, was fought during September 1781.

William Howard Taft, the 27th president of the United States and the only man to hold both the office of president and chief justice of the U. S. Supreme Court, was born on Sept. 15, 1855. Two presidents died in office as the result of assassin's bullets during September, James A. Garfield (Sept. 19, 1881) and William McKinley (Sept. 14, 1901).

SEPTIC TANK, an underground steel, concrete, or brick container for separating solids from a flow of sewage and decomposing them by the action of bacteria in the sewage. The liquid portion of the sewage usually is discharged from the tank to an underground disposal facility such as a tile field or cesspool. Septic tanks are considered acceptable for small buildings and single-family residences on large lots where the soil is suitable and public sewerage facilities are not available.

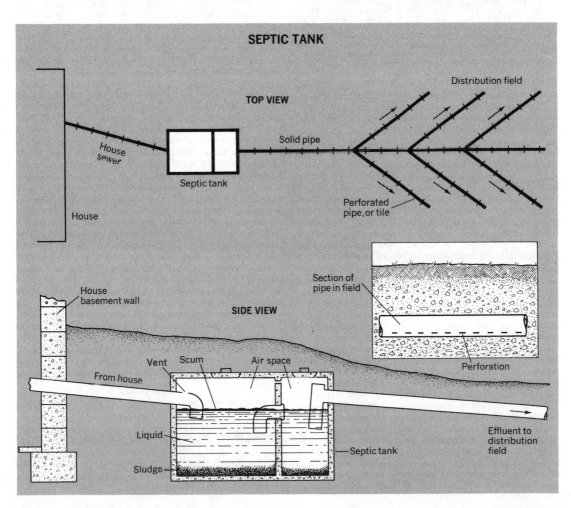

SEPTIC TANK

A septic tank should be capable of holding sewage from a building for at least 24 hours. Allowing for garbage grinders in kitchens, the U. S. Public Health Service recommends a minimum capacity of 750 gallons (2,840 liters) for single-family residences. Large-capacity tanks are economical because the interval between cleanings of accumulated sludge may be five or more years. Two-compartment tanks are preferred, and the second compartment should be about one third the capacity of the first.

The tile field or cesspool receiving the discharge from a septic tank should be located in sandy soil. Its bottom should be at least two feet (60 cm) above the highest ground water table or impervious soil. The disposal area should be far away and downhill from water wells because the outflow of a septic tank contains harmful bacteria. State and local regulations should be followed in selecting the location. Percolation tests should be made to determine the infiltrative capacity of the soil. Many local health departments can assist in this work.

The operation of a septic tank usually is not improved by the addition of chemicals. Vents for tank gases are not desirable except through the building plumbing. Water-repellent tissues or paper towels should not be flushed into the tank.

JOHN E. KIKER, JR.
Coauthor of "Sewerage Planning"

Further Reading: Imhoff, Karl, and others, *Disposal of Sewage and other Waterborne Wastes* (Ann Arbor Science 1971); Kiker, John E., Jr., *Subsurface Sewage Disposal*, Bulletin No. 23, Florida Engineering and Industrial Experiment Station (Univ. of Florida 1962); Salvato, Joseph A., Jr., *Environmental Sanitation* (Wiley 1958); U. S. Public Health Service, *Manual of Septic Tank Practice*, Publication No. 526 (USGPO 1967).

SEPTICEMIA, sep-tə-sē'mē-ə, or blood poisoning, is a condition in which disease-producing microorganisms invade the bloodstream and may produce symptoms such as high fever, chills, and weakness. See BLOOD POISONING.

SEPTIMIUS SEVERUS, Lucius. See SEVERUS, LUCIUS SEPTIMIUS.

SEPTUAGINT, sep'tū-ə-jənt, the oldest Greek version of the Old Testament. It is also called the Alexandrine version, or the Version of the Seventy, or simply indicated by the Roman numerals for 70–LXX. The legend of its origin, as given in the Epistle of Aristeas (100 B. C.) is that Ptolemy II Philadelphus, king of Egypt in the 3d century B. C., requested the Jewish high priest in Jerusalem to send 72 scholars, 6 from each of the 12 tribes, to Alexandria to translate the sacred Hebrew law into Greek. Their task was accomplished with miraculous speed and accuracy. In popular tradition the number became 70.

The historical facts underlying the legend are probably as follows: the version was made in Alexandria, beginning in the reign of Ptolemy II, for the use of the large numbers of Alexandrian Jews who were no longer familiar with Hebrew. The first portion to be translated was the Pentateuch; the Prophets followed, and eventually the Writings, that is, the Wisdom literature and the other books of the Old Testament. The latest parts were probably translated in the 1st century B. C. Certain books not found in the Palestinian or Hebrew canon and that now form part of the Aprocrypha, such as the Wisdom of Solomon, were added, perhaps as late as the beginning of the Christian era.

The varieties of style show that there must have been several translators. The language of the LXX is the Hellenistic Greek of Alexandria, based upon the Attic dialect. The most accurate work of translation is found in the Pentateuch, and next to it the Proverbs. The translation of the Psalms and the Prophets is paraphrastic. Jeremiah is well done, but Daniel is so bad that editors usually give in its place the text of Theodotion, who lived in the late 2d century A. D. It is thought that the Hebrew upon which the LXX was based was written in square characters, unpointed, that is, without vowels, without separation of words, and with many abbreviations. It once was supposed that the disagreements between the Greek and Hebrew texts could be explained by assuming that the LXX translated the Samaritan Pentateuch, but this is most unlikely. A more probable theory is that the ancient Hebrew text differed somewhat from the later Masoretic text and that the Greek text itself was changed slightly by copyists during the period prior to our oldest manuscripts.

The LXX is the original of most of the ancient versions of the Old Testament. Even where, as in the case of the Syriac, the translation was made directly from the Hebrew, the LXX has influenced the later form of the text, sometimes producing later revisions or recensions of it. It was the Bible of the earliest Greek-speaking church, to which the Greek New Testament was added. Thus it has remained the standard text of the Greek Orthodox Church ever since. Of 350 direct Old Testament quotations in the New Testament scarcely 50 disagree materially with the LXX. It was used by Philo Judaeus and Josephus in the 1st century A. D. and probably by Greek-speaking Jews in general for two centuries or more. However, it was abandoned by the Jews after it had been adopted by the Christians and had received a Christian interpretation. In its place far more literal translations were provided, but even these were soon abandoned. The synagogue services now use the Hebrew Old Testament almost exclusively.

As Origen, whose *Hexapla* in the 3d century A. D. is the first critical edition of the Alexandrian Greek Bible, was the first to see, the Septuagint is of very great value to the textual critic, as it testifies to the state of the text many centuries prior to the standard Hebrew of the medieval manuscripts. The Hebrew text has not altered very greatly, as the Dead Sea Scrolls of Isaiah found in 1947 seem to show. Even the mistakes of the LXX are useful, as showing which Hebrew words were misunderstood.

The leading manuscripts are the *Codex Vaticanus* in Rome, *Codex Alexandrinus* and *Codex Sinaiticus* in the British Museum, and the Washington and Chester Beatty fragments.

FREDERICK C. GRANT
Formerly, Union Theological Seminary

Bibliography
Hadas, Moses, ed., *Aristeas to Philocrates* (Harper 1951).
Hatch, E., and Redpath, H. A., *Concordance to the Septuagint* (Oxford 1897).
Swete, Henry B., *An Introduction to the Old Testament in Greek*, 1902 ed., rev. by H. St. J. Thackeray (KTAV 1971).
Swete, Henry B., *The Old Testament in Greek*, 3 vols (Cambridge 1907, 1909, 1912).
Thackeray, H. St. J., *The Septuagint and Jewish Worship* (Oxford 1921).

SEQUENCE, a succession of numbers arranged in a definite order. The individual numbers are called the *terms* of the sequence. The general notation for a sequence is $a_1, a_2, \ldots, a_n, \ldots$, where a_1 is the first term, a_2 is the second term, and so on. If the sequence terminates it is said to be a *finite* sequence. For example, $10,9,8,7,6,5,4,3,2,1$ is a finite sequence of ten terms. Here, $a_1 = 10$, $a_2 = 9$, and, in general, $a_n = 11 - n$, where $n = 1, \ldots, 10$. If the sequence does not terminate it is called an *infinite* sequence. For example, $1,4,9,\ldots,n^2,\ldots$ is an infinite sequence since n^2 is defined for all positive integers n. Henceforth in this article, the word "sequence" refers only to an infinite sequence.

Sequences are used in all branches of mathematics involving limits and approximation. (See also CALCULUS—*The Limit Concept.*) The concept of a sequence is also used in a basic way in many other diverse fields, as for example, in number theory, combinatorics, and logic.

Some Examples of Sequences. The simplest examples of sequences are those for which the nth term, a_n, is determined by a specific formula. For instance, if $a_n = n^2$ and $n = 1,2,3, \ldots$, we obtain $a_1 = 1$, $a_2 = 4$, $a_3 = 9$, and so on by substitution, giving the sequence of squares

$$1,4,9,16,\ldots a_n \ldots, \text{ where } a_n = n^2.$$

Similarly, if $b_n = 2^{n-1}$, we obtain the sequence

$$1,2,4,8,16,\ldots b_n \ldots, \text{ where } b_n = 2^{n-1}.$$

Some other examples are:

$$1,1/2,1/3,1/4,\ldots c_n \ldots, \text{ where } c_n = 1/n;$$
$$\frac{1}{2},\frac{1}{5},\frac{1}{10},\frac{1}{17},\ldots d_n \ldots, \text{ where } d_n = \frac{1}{n^2 + 1}.$$

Another useful way of generating a sequence is to give a rule that explains how to obtain any term from the value of the previous term. Then, once the first term is given, it is possible to generate all the terms of the sequence. For example, suppose that

$$a_{n+1} = a^2_n - 1, \text{ and } a_1 = 2.$$

For $n = 1$, we obtain $a_2 = a^2_1 - 1 = 2^2 - 1 = 3$. Similarly, $a_3 = a^2_2 - 1 = 3^2 - 1 = 8$, $a_4 = 64 - 1 = 63$, and so on. Thus we generate the sequence $2,3,8,63,3968,\ldots$, using the relation $a_{n+1} = a^2_n - 1$ and $a_1 = 2$. This method of defining a sequence is called the *recursive* method. It permits the calculation of any term because we have a starting point (here, $a_1 = 2$) and a general method of preceding to the next term (here, $a_{n+1} = a^2_n - 1$). We can similarly define a sequence recursively by defining any term in terms of the previous two terms, once the first two terms are given. The *Fibonacci* sequence, named after Leonardo Fibonacci, is the sequence

$$1,1,2,3,5,8,13,21,34,55,\ldots$$

In this case, each term after the second term is the sum of the previous two, and the sequence starts with the terms $1,1$. Thus, $a_1 = 1$, $a_2 = 1$, and $a_{n+2} = a_{n+1} + a_n$, where $n = 1,2,\ldots$.

An *arithmetic sequence* is one in which the difference of two consecutive terms is a constant d, called the *difference*. In symbols, $a_{n+1} - a_n = d$. If the first term is $a_1 = a$, then the successive terms are $a_2 = a + d$, $a_3 = (a + d) + d = a + 2d$, $a_4 = (a + 2d) + d = a + 3d$, and so on. Thus the nth term of an arithmetic sequence is $a_n = a + (n - 1)d$, where a is the first term, and d is the common difference. Note that in this case the recursion $a_{n+1} = a_n + d$ immediately leads to an explicit formula $a_n = a + (n - 1)d$.

Similarly, a *geometric sequence* is one in which the quotient of successive terms is a constant r, called the *ratio*. In symbols, $a_{n+1}/a_n = r$, or $a_{n+1} = a_n r$. If $a_1 = a$, then we obtain successively $a_2 = ar$, $a_3(ar)r = ar^2$, $a_4 = ar^3$, and so on. Thus the nth term of a geometric sequence is $a_n = ar^{n-1}$.

There is an easy method for computing the sum of the first n terms of an arithmetic series. Let the first term be a_1 equal to a, let the common difference be d, and let $L = a_n = a + (n - 1)d$ be the nth term. Then the sum S of the series is

$$S = a + (a + d) + \ldots + (L - d) + L.$$

Rewriting,

$$S = L + (L - d) + \ldots + (a + d) + a.$$

Adding these last two equations,

$$2S = (a + L) + (a + L) + \ldots + (a + L)$$
$$= n(a + L).$$

Thus, for an arithmetic series,

$$S = \frac{n}{2}(a + L),$$

where n = number of terms, a = first term, and L = last term. For example,

$$1 + 2 + 3 + \ldots + 100 = \frac{100}{2}(1 + 100) =$$
$$50 \times 101 = 5,050.$$

We can also find a simple expression for the sum of a geometric series. Let $a_1 = a$, and let r = ratio. Then

$$S = a + ar + ar^2 + \ldots + ar^{n-1}.$$

Multiplying by r,

$$rS = ar + ar^2 + \ldots + ar^{n-1} + ar^n.$$

Subtracting the last two equations,

$$(r - 1)S = ar^n - a = a(r^n - 1).$$

Hence, for a geometric series,

$$S = \frac{a(r^n - 1)}{r - 1},$$

where n = number of terms, a = first term, and r = ratio. Here, it is assumed that $r \neq 1$. See also SERIES.

A *harmonic sequence* is a sequence whose reciprocals form an arithmetic sequence. For instance, $2/3, 2/8, 2/13, 2/18, \ldots$, where $a_n = 2/(5n - 2)$, is a harmonic sequence because the reciprocals $1/a_n = (5n - 2)/2$ form an arithmetic sequence with $a = 3/2$ and $d = 5/2$. There is no simple formula for the sum of the first n terms of a harmonic sequence.

A sequence need not be defined by a simple formula. For example, the sequence of prime numbers $2,3,5,7,11,13,17,\ldots$ is an extremely important sequence. Here, $p_n = n$th prime. No simple formula exists for p_n, yet the computation of p_n for any given n is routine, though perhaps tedious. See also PRIME NUMBER.

Decimal Expansions. The infinite decimal expansion of any real number may be regarded as a sequence. For example, consider $\pi = 3.14159 \ldots$. If we take π to more and more decimal places we obtain the sequence 3, 3.1, 3.14, 3.141, $\ldots$. Each term of the sequence is an approximation to π, with the nth term, b_n, being within $1/10^{n-1}$ of π. Thus, b_n is very near π when n is large. Similarly, the decimal expansion of any real number b gives rise to a sequence b_n of finite decimal approximations to that real number b. A formula for b_n is $b_n = [10^{n-1}b]/10^{n-1}$, where $[x]$ is x rounded down to the nearest integer. For example, when $b = \pi$, we have $b_2 = [10\pi]/10 = [31.4..]/10 = 31/10 = 3.1$, as indicated previously.

Limit of a Sequence. Sometimes the term a_n will approach a fixed number a as n gets larger and larger. By using the notion of a limit, it is possible to clarify this idea and to make it precise. For example, if we take $a_n = (n - 1)/n$, we obtain the sequence $0, 1/2, 2/3, 3/4, \ldots$. If n is large, a_n is almost equal to 1 because $(n - 1)/n = 1 - (1/n)$, and $1/n$ is small. Suppose we wish to ensure that a_n is within 0.01 of 1. Then we need only choose n large enough to do this; in this case, it is required that n be larger than 100. Similarly, a_n is within 0.001 of 1 if n is larger than 1,000, and so on. In general, regardless of how small a positive number ε is, it is possible to find some number N (here $N = \dfrac{1}{\varepsilon}$) so that a_n is within ε of 1 when n is larger than N. This leads to the general definition of a limit of a sequence.

Definition. Let a_n be a sequence of numbers, and let a be a fixed number. We say that $a = \lim\limits_{n \to \infty} a_n$, or $a_n \to a$ as $n \to \infty$, provided the following condition holds: for any $\varepsilon > 0$, there is an integer N so that if $n > N$, we have $a - \varepsilon < a_n < a + \varepsilon$.

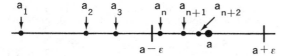

In the diagram, all the terms a_n, a_{n+1}, and so on of the sequence from some number $n > N$ onward are within the interval from $a - \varepsilon$ to $a + \varepsilon$. This result holds for any particular $\varepsilon > 0$, although as ε is made smaller, it may be necessary to take N larger. Thus, the statement $\lim\limits_{n \to \infty} a_n = a$ is the precise way of stating that a_n is as good an approximation of a as one wants, provided n is large enough. Less precisely, it states that a_n is close to a if n is large.

We can see how this concept is used in the following example, where it is desired to compute $\sqrt{3}$. It is known that if x is near $\sqrt{3}$, then $\dfrac{1}{2}\left(x + \dfrac{3}{x}\right)$ is a much better approximation. Thus, if we define

$$a_{n+1} = \frac{1}{2}\left(a_n + \frac{3}{a_n}\right), \text{ and } a_1 = 1,$$

we obtain better approximations to $\sqrt{3}$ as n increases. The following table gives a_n accurate to four decimal places.

n	1	2	3	4 and above
a_n	1	2	1.7500	1.7321

In fact, $\lim\limits_{n \to \infty} a_n = \sqrt{3}$. The table shows that a_n rapidly approaches its limit $\sqrt{3}$, and we can quickly find $\sqrt{3} = 1.7321$. This same method, where the successive terms a_n are the approximate solutions and the limit is the actual solution, can be used to find solutions of many equations. See also EQUATION.

It is not necessary for a sequence to have a limit. This is shown by the following examples:
(1) The sequence $1, -1, 1, -1, \ldots$, given by $a_n = (-1)^{n+1}$.

Here, the sequence oscillates between 1 and -1, but neither is a limit because the successive terms do not stay near either of them.
(2) The sequence $1, 4, 9, 16, \ldots$, given by $b_n = n^2$.
Here, the terms do not approach any value, but become and stay arbitrarily large. We write $b_n \to \infty$ as $n \to \infty$ in such a case.
(3) The sequence $1, -2, 3, -4, 5, -6, \ldots$, given by $c_n = (-1)^{n+1} n$.
The terms become arbitrarily large in size but fluctuate in sign. Here the absolute value $|c_n| \to \infty$. Some authors also write $c_n \to \pm \infty$ or even $c_n \to \infty$ in this case.
(4) The sequence $0, 1, 0, 2, 0, 3, \ldots$
The even terms go to infinity and the odd terms are 0. Here, there is no limit.

In general, if a_n is a sequence that has a limit a, it is said to *converge*. If the sequence does not have a limit, it is said to *diverge*.

Some Specific Sequences and Their Limits. Some examples of sequences and their limits are given in the following examples:

(1) $\lim\limits_{n \to \infty} \dfrac{1}{n} = 0$.

(2) $\lim\limits_{n \to \infty} 2^{1/n} = 1$.

This result is not immediately clear. However, a computation makes the result plausible: $2^1 = 2$, $2^{1/2} = 1.41, \ldots$, $2^{1/10} = 1.072, \ldots$, and $2^{1/100} = 1.007$.

(3) $\lim\limits_{n \to \infty} n^{1/n} = 1$.

This result is also not immediately clear. However, a computation makes the result plausible. For $n = 1,000$, $1,000^{1/1,000} = 1.0069$.

(4) $\lim\limits_{n \to \infty} \left(1 + \dfrac{1}{n}\right)^n = e = 2.71828\ldots$

This sequence is convergent but not very rapidly. For $n = 2$, we have $\left(1 + \dfrac{1}{2}\right)^2 = 2.25$. For $n = 10$, $(1.1)^{10} = 2.59$, while for $n = 100$, $(1.01)^{100} = 2.705$. The number e is one of the most important numerical constants in mathematics, occurring in many contexts. See also e.

There is an interesting interpretation of the sequence $\left(1 + \dfrac{1}{n}\right)^n$ and its limit e. If \$1 is invested at 100% interest, then \$2 will accumulate at the end of the year. But if the interest is compounded n times a year, the amount accumulated will be $\left(1 + \dfrac{1}{n}\right)^n$. Thus, e may be regarded as the amount accumulated in one year from \$1 at 100% interest, compounded continuously.

(5) $\lim\limits_{n \to \infty} a^n = 0$,

provided $-1 < a < 1$.
This result is useful in summing an *infinite* geometric series $a + ar + ar^2 + \ldots$. In fact, the sum to n terms is $\dfrac{a - ar^n}{1 - r}$. If $-1 < r < 1$, then this sum approaches the limit $\dfrac{a}{1 - r}$ as $n \to \infty$, since $r^n \to 0$ as $n \to \infty$. Thus, we write $a + ar + ar^2 + \ldots = \dfrac{a}{1 - r}$ $(-1 < r < 1)$.

MELVIN HAUSNER, *New York University*

Further Reading: Gelfand, S. I., *Sequences and Combinatorial Problems* (Gordon and Breach Science Publishers 1969).

SEQUOIA, si-kwoi'ə, the name commonly given to two genera of giant conifers—the true *Sequoia* and the closely related *Sequoiadendron*. Both are classified in the redwood family Taxodiceae. Although many species of both genera existed during the Miocene Epoch in many parts of the world, only one species of each genus survives. Those are the redwood (*Sequoia sempervirons*), found in western California and southwestern Oregon, and the big tree (*Sequoiadendron giganteum*), found only in central California. The major groves of these species are in Redwoods, Yosemite, Kings Canyon, and Sequoia national parks; in Muir Woods National Monument; and in various national and state forests. The trees, which include some of the largest and oldest in the world, were named for Sequoya, an Indian chief who devised a method of writing Cherokee.

The big tree was formerly classified as *Sequoia gigantea,* but the discovery in 1941 of fossils and in 1943 of living specimens of a formerly unknown species, the dawn redwood (*Metasequoia glyptostroboides*), necessitated a reclassification of the big tree, of various fossil trees formerly called *Sequoia,* and of fossils of the related swamp cypresses (*Taxodium*).

The Redwood. Distribution of the redwood is now limited to a fog belt about 30 miles (48 km) wide and 450 miles (725 km) long, following the Pacific coast from Curry county in southwestern Oregon to Salmon Creek Canyon in Monterey county, California. It is found at elevations ranging from sea level to 2,500 feet (762 meters), but the best stands, or groves, are on protected flats in sheltered, moist coastal plains. It is also grown as an ornamental in other parts of North America and in Europe.

The redwood is the tallest tree in the United States, often reaching a height of over 300 feet (90 meters). Its diameter may exceed 20 feet (6 meters). The younger trees have a pyramidal shape, but the older specimens have a narrow head and an irregularly buttressed base. The reddish brown, fibrous bark becomes deeply furrowed as the tree gets older and may attain a thickness of 1 foot (30 cm).

The leaves are linear, flat, and stiff and are twisted at the base to form a two-ranked flat spray. They are generally ¼ to 1¼ inches (6–32 mm) long and about ¹⁄₁₂ inch (2 mm) wide. Their color is deep yellowish green above and whitish underneath. The leaves live for three or four years and remain on the tree for an additional year or two after they have died. The relatively short branches are drooping, and the lateral branchlets are deciduous. The leaves at the tops of adult trees are short (ranging from ¼ to ½ inch, or 6 to 12 mm) and tapered.

The trees bear cones of both sexes but on different branches. The small staminate cones (catkins) are terminal on branchlets and consist of many spirally disposed stamens, each with two to five pollen sacs. Each terminal ovulate cone, with 14 to 24 scales, bears five to seven ovules and develops a woody apex. They are about 1 inch (25 mm) long, oval, pendulous, and reddish brown in color, and they mature in a single season. The russet brown seeds are about ⅙ inch (4 mm) long, elliptic, flattened, and narrowly margined. The embryo has two cotyledons. After shedding their seeds, cones may remain on the trees for several months. Reproduction of the trees by seeds is quite limited, but sprouts from stumps are common.

Giant sequoia (*Sequoiadendron giganteum*)

The redwood is the only known natural polyploid (hexaploid) in the Taxodiaceae family and one of the few recorded in conifers. The species probably resulted from hybridization of two, or possibly three, distinct ancestral species with an accompanying trebling of chromosomes.

The ages of various redwood trees have been greatly overestimated at 2,500 to 3,000 years. Their true ages are probably considerably less. Trees 300 feet (90 meters) high and 20 feet (6 meters) or more in diameter are most likely about 2,000 years old. Trees cut for commercial purposes are usually 400 to 800 years old.

The redwood is usually free of fungus diseases and highly resistant to attacks by termites and other insects. Fire does not damage old trees with a heavy bark but can kill or injure young trees. The exceedingly durable wood is soft, light, nonresinous, straight-grained, and easily worked. It varies in color from light cherry to dark mahogany. Butt logs contain the hardest and heaviest timber. The redwood has been the most important tree in the development of the lumber industry in California. It is used for building, industrial, and other purposes.

The Big Tree. Big trees occur in a discontinuous belt on the western slope of the Sierra Madre in central California. The belt stretches for 250 miles (400 km) from Placer county to Tulare county. The trees are grouped in some 70 groves that range from a few specimens to 1,000. The altitude of the groves ranges from 4,000 to

8,500 feet (1,200–2,600 meters). The area occupied by the big tree is marked by a climate with an annual rainfall of 45 to 60 inches (1,143–1,524 mm) and a snow cover of 2 to 10 feet (60–305 cm) for three to six months of the year.

The big tree is not as tall as the redwood but is certainly the most massive tree known, attaining a height of 100 to 325 feet (30–100 meters), a diameter of 5 to 30 feet (1.5–9 meters) 6 feet (1.8 meters) above ground level, and an estimated weight of more than 1,000 tons. The bottom limbs may branch off anywhere between 80 and 225 feet (24–69 meters). The crown of the big tree is usually round at the top but may appear broken with age. The bark, darker and browner than the redwood's, is deeply furrowed and from ½ to 2 feet (15–61 cm) thick.

The leaves are awl-like, ⅛ to ½ inch (3–13 mm) long, and densely grouped, exposing the tips only. On larger twigs, the leaves tend to be longer and are longest in seedlings. The male cones are terminal on branchlets, about ¼ inch (6 mm) long, scaly, and distributed all over the tree. The small, pale green female cones mature into woody, yellow-brown cones about 2 to 3 inches (50–76 mm) long. They are made up of 35 to 40 scales, each bearing four to six flat, thin, narrowly winged seeds that are shed in the second summer. The big tree reproduces solely from seed germinating on bare, exposed soil. The seed remains fertile for 20 years.

The age of the oldest big trees is estimated at about 3,500 years, although most are younger than 1,500 years. Big trees are second in age only to bristlecone pines, whose ages as established by ring counts range up to 4,600 years.

The wood of the big tree is weak, coarse-grained, and more brittle than that of the redwood. It was at one time sold as redwood for use in such things as fences and shingles, but it is no longer of any commercial importance.

THEODOR JUST
Formerly, Field Museum of Natural History

SEQUOIA NATIONAL PARK, si-kwoi'ə, is a preserved natural wild area on the western slopes of the Sierra Nevada in central California, about 55 miles (89 km) east of Fresno. The area was declared a national park in 1890 to protect the big trees (*Sequoiadendron giganteum*) of which there are hundreds with diameters of more than 10 feet (3 meters). The park stretches southward from the border of Kings Canyon National Park to the headwaters of the Tule River. Its eastern boundary is made up of the tallest peaks of the Sierra Nevada, including Mt. Whitney (14,494 feet, or 4,418 meters), the highest mountain in the 48 contiguous states.

Sequoia National Park is bisected by the Great Western Divide, a jagged granite ridge that runs through the park from north to south. On the east of the ridge are high mountain lakes of glacial origin and the Kern River Canyon, which runs parallel to the ridge for about 25 miles (40 km), attaining a depth of about 3,000 feet (915 meters). West of the ridge, at an altitude of from 4,000 to 8,000 feet (1,220–2,440 meters) are the Giant Forest and other groves of giant sequoia. See also SEQUOIA.

SEQUOYA, si-kwoi'ə (1770?–1843) was a Cherokee Indian scholar. His name is also spelled Sequoyah. He was born in Taskigi, Tenn. At maturity he assumed the name of George Guess after an American trader whom he believed to be his father. He was a silversmith among the Cherokees in Georgia, where he invented a system by which, employing 85 characters, every sound in the Cherokee language could be reduced to writing. This syllabary, approved by the Cherokee general council in 1821, enabled thousands of tribesmen to read and write. It was adopted by the missionaries, and was used in printing the *Cherokee Phoenix and Indian Advocate,* a weekly newspaper first published in 1828. In 1823 he carried the new learning to the western tribes in Arkansas and five years later he moved with them to Oklahoma. Sequoya died, possibly in Tamaulipas State, Mexico, in August 1843. His name is perpetuated in the sequoia tree.

SERAGLIO, sə-ral'yō, a palace of the Ottoman sultans. The term is derived from the Italian *serraglio,* meaning enclosure or palace, and refers generally to any sultan's palace, more especially to the harem, or women's quarters. The Seraglio was a term given by Westerners to Topkapı Sarayı, a former palace of the sultans in Istanbul. See also TOPKAPI SARAYI.

SERAO, sä-rä'ō, **Matilde** (1856–1927), Italian novelist and journalist. She was born in Patras, Greece, on March 7, 1856, the daughter of an Italian political exile and a Greek mother. She first attracted attention by a short story, *Novelle,* which she followed with a popular novel, *Fantasia* (1883). Her writing is characterized by vigor and realism, and in her later work a certain psychological insight is also apparent. Her most famous novels are *La virtú di Checchina* (1885), *Il paese di cuccagna* (1891; *The Land of the Cockayne*), *La conquista di Roma* (1885), and *La ballerina* (1899).

Matilde Serao married Eduardo Scarfoglio in 1885, and together they founded the newspaper *Il Corriere di Roma,* which was short-lived. Then, in Naples, they edited *Il Corriere di Napoli.* She separated from her husband in 1904 and subsequently founded *Il Mattino* and *Il Giorno.* She died in Naples on July 25, 1927.

SERAPE, sə-räp'ē, a kind of shawl traditionally worn by Mexican men, who fold it over the left shoulder. The serape, or sarape, made of a wool blanket, usually striped, derives from the pre-Columbian *poncho,* a rectangle with a slit for the head. Indian serapes may also be worn as ponchos for warmth. Those of Spanish Mexicans, without a slit, are purely decorative.

SERAPHIM, ser'ə-fim, are winged celestial creatures mentioned in the book of Isaiah (6:2). They are described as having six wings. In the vision of Isaiah, one of the Seraphim brought a burning coal and touched it to the prophet's lips to purify them, symbolically readying him for his prophetic role (Isaiah 6:6–7). They are also mentioned in a singular form (seraph) in other places in the Old Testament, such as Isaiah 30:6, Numbers 21: 6–8, and Deuteronomy 8:15. Similar descriptions are found in the literature and art of other ancient Middle Eastern religions. For example, in Mesopotamia, drawings of six-winged creatures holding a serpent in each hand have been discovered at Tell Halaf. In later Christian literature the seraphim had the highest rank among the angels, followed by the cherubim and thrones. See also ANGEL.

J. ALLAN CASH, FROM RAPHO GUILLUMETTE

The roofs of the Peć Monastery are outlined against the mountains of the Metohija region in southwestern Serbia.

SERBIA, sûr'bē-ɔ, is one of the six socialist republics that make up Yugoslavia. The Serbo-Croatian form of the name is Srbija or Srbiya. The republic constitutes the east central part of Yugoslavia. On the north it is bounded by Hungary and on the east by Rumania and Bulgaria. On the south its border meets that of Yugoslav Macedonia and then takes a northerly course along Albania until it meets the eastern edge of Montenegro. Also to the west are the republics of Bosnia and Hercegovina and of Croatia.

Serbia has an area of about 34,000 square miles (88,000 sq km). It consists of Serbia proper (the former kingdom of Serbia), with about 21,500 square miles (55,500 sq km); the autonomous province of Vojvodina, with about 8,300 square miles (21,500 sq km); and the autonomous region of Kosovo, with about 4,200 square miles (11,000 sq km).

Serbia has a total population (1971) of 8,436,547. The chief city is Belgrade, which is the capital and largest city of Serbia and of Yugoslavia and had a population of 1,204,271 in 1971. Other large cities, with their 1971 populations, include Novi Sad (214,048), Niš (193,320), and Subotica (146,755).

For the geography, topography, and economic development of Serbia, see YUGOSLAVIA.

HISTORY

There are several hypotheses about the origin of the word "Serb," and its exact etymology is obscure. One theory is that it comes from the Caucasian *ser*, meaning "man," with the plural suffix of *bi* of that language added. The name Serb was mentioned for the first time in the 6th century A. D. by the geographer Vibius Sequestrus. The first Serbs appeared at the beginning of the 6th century in Germany, in the Magde-burg and Anhalt regions. The German city of Zerbst (Serbište in Slavic) is a reminder of the early invasion. Serbs in the Balkan Peninsula are mentioned for the first time in 822 by Einhard, of Charlemagne's court, but the Byzantine Emperor Constantine VII Porphyrogenitus, writing in the 10th century, refers to Serbs as already being in the Illyric province by the middle of the 7th century.

The Serbs were one of the peoples of the Caucasus and lived on the eastern shores of the

SERBIA

0   100 Mi.

0   100 Km.

571

Sea of Azov. At the time of the barbarian invasions, they began to move with other Slavs toward the west, a progress that began as early as the 4th century. When the Huns invaded Europe in the 5th century, they were accompanied by Slavs. A century later the Slavs settled in Rumania and during the 7th century colonized the Balkan Peninsula by conquest.

They proceeded ruthlessly with their colonization, destroying several important cities that had been founded by the Romans—among them Singidunum (Belgrade), Viminacium (Kostolac on the Danube), Dioclea (Titograd in Montenegro), and Salona (Split in Dalmatia). Their democratic, clannish organization was concerned only with the direct interests of their particular tribe or clan. The tribes themselves had no deep sense of unity or consciousness of common interests. This seems to have been the main reason for their anarchic life and their resultant weakness in spite of numerical strength. It is also the reason the Slavs were slow in organizing their own states and the evident explanation of the fact that the first Slav states were organized by foreigners.

The Nemanya Dynasty. Rascia, the first Serb state, was founded in the mountains of southeastern Bosnia and northeastern Hercegovina and tended, from the 10th century, to expand eastward and southeastward toward the plains of Kosovo and the valleys of the Vardar and Morava rivers. At that time it centered principally on the Raska River, from which it originally took its name. The definite organization of the state was accomplished by Stephen Nemanya (Nemanja), who ruled from 1168 to 1196. He was one of the ablest and most outstanding rulers of Serbia and extended the nucleus of the state into the Morava and Vardar valleys. Nemanya was succeeded by his son Stephen, who received important support from another son, Rastko, later known as Saint Sava. Sava was an intelligent and energetic statesman and continued the work begun by his father. He founded the independent Serbian Orthodox Church that still bears his name, and his memory is revered by all Serbs.

The Nemanya dynasty ruled for two centuries, producing many powerful kings, who from the 14th century on made Serbia the strongest state in the Balkan Peninsula, prepared to take the place of the decadent Byzantine Empire. In 1330, Stephen Uroš III, one of the most famous of the Serbian kings, defeated the Bulgars in the Battle of Velbuzhd, driving them out of the Vardar Valley. In 1346, Stephen Dushan (Stephen Uroš IV), unlike his predecessors who were crowned kings of Serbia, assumed the title of emperor of the Serbs and Greeks. His campaigns against the Bulgars and Albanians were successful, and by the time he died in 1355 the Serbian empire stretched from the Danube to the Gulf of Corinth and from the Aegean to the Adriatic.

The economic and cultural progress of Serbia at this period was above the average European level. Many monasteries of Serbian-Byzantine architectural style—including Studenitca, Decani, and Gračanica—founded by several kings, bear witness to this highly developed Serbian culture. Dushan's code of laws (*Zakonik*), formulated in 1349–1354, shows the advanced social structure of the Serbian state.

Turkish Rule. Dushan's successor, Stephen Uroš V, lacked the energy and strength of his father, and the latter's conquests ended by becoming a source of weakness for the state. The Turkish drive toward Europe turned its might toward the Serbs, first defeating them at the Maritsa River in 1371 and then on the Plain of Kosovo in 1389, where the Serbian defenders fought courageously against far superior Turkish forces. In that battle the Serbian prince, Lazar, was killed, as was the Turkish sultan, Murad I. Kosovo was not only a battle where crowned heads fell. It marked as well the fall of the independent Serbian state. Serbia, as an Ottoman vassal, continued its precarious independence until 1459, its rulers retreating to the north on the Danube, seeking the protection of the Hungarian kings.

With the downfall of the Serbian state, the nation came under the Turkish yoke, where it remained for more than four centuries. It was not until 1804 that the Serbs began their struggle for liberation. During this long Turkish occupation, the Serbian Orthodox Church remained the only national institution not destroyed by the conquerors. It was active in keeping alive the traditions of the old state of the Nemanya and the glorious empire of Dushan, as well as faith in a better future. In the southeastern part of Serbia—Montenegro—the freedom-loving mountaineers retreated to their inaccessible mountains and successfully resisted all Turkish attempts at conquest.

After the Ottoman advance into Europe was stopped at Vienna in 1683, the Turks gradually retreated southward toward the Danube and Sava rivers. The Porte (Turkish government), however, was slowly losing control not only of its army but also of its governors in the distant provinces. More and more these officials resorted to terroristic methods to preserve their conquests. Under these conditions the Serbian people grew desperate, and finally, after several unsuccessful attempts, they started in 1804 the great national revolution against the Turks.

The Fight for Independence. The Serbs were led in this revolt by George Petrović, called Karageorge (Karadjordje, or "Black George"), whose family had emigrated to Serbia from Montenegro in the first part of the 18th century. Karageorge, a man of great courage and ability, had fought the Turks from his earliest youth. He was elected by the people as their leader at the outbreak of the revolt, and after a series of victories at Ivankovac (1805), Mišar (1806), and Belgrade (1806), he succeeded in freeing all the pashalik (province) of Belgrade from the Turks. In that same year Russia, which was also involved in a war with Turkey, concluded an alliance with Serbia that drew the attention of Europe to this former Ottoman province. Serbia enjoyed some autonomy and was self-governing. In the Treaty of Bucharest with Russia in 1812, there was a clause calling for the autonomy of Serbia and for moderate treatment of the population.

Turkey, however, taking advantage of the difficult situation of Russia, which was then at war with Napoleon, refused to honor these conditions and moved in force against the Serbs. Karageorge was forced to retreat to Austria in 1813, and the Turks regained control. The Serbs, however, started a second revolt in 1815, led this time by Miloš Obrenovich (Obrenović). Both revolts had originated in Shumadiya, the heart of Serbia. Karageorge returned to Serbia but was assassinated, with the approval of Miloš, in 1817. His death touched off a dynastic feud that continued into the 20th century.

If Karageorge is remembered as the greatest Serbian hero, Miloš is considered the most astute of Serbian diplomats. He succeeded in obtaining the autonomy of the country when in March 1826 the Porte signed a convention with Russia at Akkarman, by which Turkey bound itself to carry out within 18 months the provisions of the Treaty of Bucharest of 1812. Later, in the Treaty of Adrianople of 1829 with Russia, Turkey solemnly engaged itself to honor without delay its obligations toward Serbia, and also to evacuate its army from six counties belonging to the pashalik of Belgrade.

Autonomy. In 1830 the sultan issued a solemn personal letter guaranteeing Serbia's autonomy, under Russian protection, and recognizing Miloš Obrenovich as hereditary prince of Serbia. In 1833, Turkey finally ceded to Serbia the six counties of the pashalik of Belgrade that the Ottomans still occupied, and Miloš made a state visit to the sultan in 1835 to pay his respects and to thank him for fulfilling his promises.

Although Miloš was known as an able diplomat, in governing his country he used absolutist methods that earned him the hatred of his people. He was finally forced to abdicate in 1839. This popular disfavor extended also to his son Michael, who, after a short reign, abdicated in 1842. The People's Assembly (Skulpština) then called Karageorge's son Alexander Karageorgevich back to the throne. Alexander ruled from 1842 to 1858, a reign marked by considerable improvement in cultural life and the development of a state organization. During his reign Serbia moved a step forward toward full independence, when the Congress of Paris in 1856 confirmed the autonomy of Serbia as being guaranteed by all the great powers and not by Russia alone.

In 1858, Prince Alexander, who was engaged in a conflict with the party of "defenders of the constitution" (Ustavobranitelji), also had to abdicate and leave the country. The old autocrat Miloš Obrenovich, then living in exile in Rumania, was recalled to the throne of Serbia. His reign was short, however, as he died less than two years afterward.

Michael Obrenovich then reascended the throne (1860). He was a well-educated and liberal-minded prince. At this time Europe was dominated by the policy of nationalities encouraged by Napoleon III. National unification was in progress in Germany as well as in Italy. Fired by these examples, Michael formed ambitious plans for liberating the different nationalities still within the Turkish Empire. He entered into negotiations with the rulers of Greece, Rumania, and the neighboring principality of Montenegro, as well as with Serbian national leaders in Bosnia and Bulgaria, with the view to creating a vast alliance against the Ottoman Empire. He also established friendly relations with the Croat leaders, hoping to promote closer relations between Serbs and Croats. But his plans did not materialize before he was assassinated on June 10, 1868.

The reign of Michael, marked as it was by many diplomatic successes, proved another step toward the complete liberation of Serbia. The Turks had reserved the right to keep garrisons in Belgrade and several other cities, but by patient diplomatic action, supported by France, Britain, and Russia, Michael obtained from the Porte in 1867 the withdrawal of the garrisons from Serbia. The only evidence that Serbia was not as yet a fully independent state was the Turkish flag, which continued to fly beside the Serbian flag over the evacuated fortresses.

Independence. Michael was succeeded by his nephew Milan, during whose reign Serbia engaged in two wars with Turkey (1876 and 1877–1878) for the liberation of the Serbs from the Ottoman Empire. The first of these wars against the Turks was waged unsuccessfully by the Serbians and Montenegrins alone. In the second war the Serbians joined forces with the Russians and succeeded in liberating Niš and substantial territories in the south and southeast of Serbia. But the policy of Russia was to favor Bulgaria at the expense of Serbia in order to pave the way for Russian access to the Aegean Sea and the Mediterranean.

The Treaty of San Stefano (March 3, 1878) created a Great Bulgaria and deprived Serbia of almost all its military conquests. The Berlin Congress in 1878 nullified the Treaty of San Stefano and established a new status in the Balkans. Serbia was substantially enlarged in the south and southeast, but above all it was now recognized as a fully independent state. On the other hand, the Congress of Berlin decreed that Austria-Hungary should occupy the predominantly Serbian provinces of Bosnia and Hercegovina. This occupation led to new troubles in the Balkans and finally became one of the indirect causes of World War I. See also BERLIN CONGRESS; EASTERN QUESTION.

Establishment of the Kingdom. On March 6, 1882, Milan became monarch of the newly acclaimed kingdom of Serbia. In 1885, after the unification of Bulgaria with Eastern Rumelia, Milan attacked the Bulgars, fearing they would become the strongest state in the Balkans. In this war he was unsuccessful, and later he had to face difficulties at home. Finally, he was forced to abdicate in 1889 in favor of his son Alexander.

Alexander I Obrenovich was the most unpopular king in the history of Serbia, and his marriage to Draga Mashin, a commoner widow 10 years his senior, greatly increased his unpopularity. On June 10, 1903, Alexander and Queen Draga were assassinated. With this event the Obrenovich dynasty came to an end.

At Alexander's death, the Skulpština called Peter I Karageorgevich to the throne. He was the son of Alexander Karageorgevich and the grandson of Karageorge himself. Peter had spent most of his life in exile, where he had been imbued with liberal and democratic ideals. His reign marked the beginning of a new era for Serbia during which it made considerable progress. It developed a parliamentary system and democratic institutions and achieved significant economic and social progress. The new Serbia attracted not only its brothers under Turkish rule, but also the Serbs and Croats in Austria-Hungary. Austria-Hungary was afraid of Serbia's progressiveness, which it tried to arrest by annexing Bosnia and Hercegovina in 1908, while engaging in an economic war with the Serbs. Two years later it refused to renew the trade agreement with Serbia, forcing the Serbs to seek new markets for their exports. The Serbian government passed through this economic crisis successfully and directed its efforts toward the creation of a Balkan League for the liberation of the Balkans from the Turks.

The Balkan Wars (1912–1913). In October 1912, the Balkan League (Serbia, Montenegro, Bulgaria, and Greece) engaged in war against Turkey. The Turkish Army was defeated, and those parts of the Balkans still under Turkish rule were liberated after 500 years. The Serbian Army particularly distinguished itself in a series of victorious battles, including Kumanovo, Novi Pazar, Monastir (Bitolj), and also took a prominent part in the siege and capture of the great Turkish fortress of Adrianople (Edirne).

The Balkan allies, however, failed to agree on the division of the territory thus liberated from the Turks, and Bulgaria refused to submit the issue to arbitration by the czar of Russia according to the provisions of the treaty of alliance between Serbia and Bulgaria. Encouraged by Austria-Hungary, Bulgaria attacked Serbia on June 29, 1913, carrying hostilities against the Greeks also. Bulgaria, however, was defeated, first at Bregalnica, then in a number of other battles. With the entrance of Rumania into the war on the side of Serbia, Montenegro, and Greece, the Bulgarians sued for peace, which was concluded in Bucharest on Aug. 10, 1913. By the terms of the Treaty of Bucharest, Serbia was awarded extensive territories in the region of the Vardar Valley and in the southwest toward Albania. See also BALKANS—*History.*

World War I to the Present. This successful conclusion of the Balkan Wars increased Serbia's prestige with the South Slavs (Serbs, Croats, and Slovenes) in Austria-Hungary, but caused the Austrian Empire to look upon Serbia as a new menace to its own existence. On June 28, 1914, Austrian Archduke Francis Ferdinand was assassinated in the Bosnian city of Sarajevo by a Serbian revolutionary. Austria-Hungary used this as a pretext to declare war on Serbia on July 28, precipitating World War I.

During the war, the Serbian Army was brilliantly led by Prince Alexander, who, in 1914, had been appointed regent by his aged and ailing father, Peter I. Though vastly outnumbered by the enemy, the Serbians achieved remarkable successes, twice defeating the army of Austria-Hungary. For more than a year Serbia successfully resisted the invaders, and it was not until both the German and Bulgarian armies threw their might on the side of Austria-Hungary that the Serbs had to give ground. In the memorable and bloody retreat through the Albanian mountains, Alexander succeeded in bringing out of Serbia 200,000 of his soldiers. Aided and equipped by the Allies, this reorganized Serbian Army played an important part on the Salonika front and succeeded in breaking through the enemy lines at Dobropolje and Kajmakchalan (Kaimakĉalan) in September 1918.

In 1918, Serbia became part of the new Kingdom of Serbs, Croats, and Slovenes, which changed its name to the Kingdom of Yugoslavia in 1929. In 1941–1944, Serbia was ruled by a German occupation government. In 1945 it became part of the Communist-ruled People's Republic of Yugoslavia.

CONSTANTIN FOTITCH
Author of "The War We Lost"

Further Reading: Kerner, Robert Joseph, ed., *Yugoslavia* (Univ. of Calif. Press 1949); Stavrianos, Leften S., *The Balkans Since 1453* (Rinehart 1958).

SERBO-CROATIAN LANGUAGE. See SLAVIC LANGUAGES; YUGOSLAVIA—*Languages and Literature.*

SERENADE, originally a musical composition meant to be played or sung in the evening in the open air. The word is derived from the Italian *serenata,* meaning "evening song." Traditionally, a serenade was sung by a young swain under the window of his beloved, or, if he had no voice for singing, he hired an ensemble of musicians to play instrumental serenades. Because of the romantic nature of the serenade, the music was simple and melodic. Perhaps the most perfect example of the vocal serenade is *Deh, vieni alla finestra* from Mozart's *Don Giovanni.*

Instrumental composers adapted the serenade to their purposes. Important examples are two serenade trios by Beethoven, both in D major, and Brahms' serenades in D major, for full orchestra, and A major, for orchestra without violins. Particularly popular and melodious instrumental serenades are Tchaikovsky's Serenade for small orchestra and Serenade for string orchestra.

SERFS were members of the class of peasants who were bound to the land of their lord, which they cultivated. Serfs and villeins occupied a position between slaves and independent freemen. The villeins were free in Continental realms and had less onerous obligations than the serfs. In England the distinction between serf and villein was less clear, and the obligations were about the same. Above this mass of agricultural laborers were the lords, free craftsmen, and merchants. Serfdom is generally associated with western Europe during the Middle Ages, but it also appeared in other areas at other times.

Under the seignorial system of land tenure, called the manorial system in the British Isles, tenants held land in accordance with certain conditions. These conditions amounted to an almost complete surrender of personal liberties. A serf could not be sold, but he could be transferred along with the property to which he was attached. Serfs could not marry, change their occupation, or move without their lord's permission. To pay for working a lord's land, the serf was required to deliver a portion of his produce to the lord and had to use the lord's grain mills and other facilities. He also spent part of his time working on the lord's acreage and on such projects as roads and bridges.

Serfdom became less common as the medieval economy developed and as new lands were opened. Lords in new regions offered relatively easy obligations in order to attract colonists, while lords in established areas lightened the burdens so their serfs would not run away. The growth of a money economy also hastened the end of serfdom, in which payments were made in kind. During the 12th, 13th, and 14th centuries, serfdom declined in western Europe, although laws concerning serfdom often remained in legal codes.

Much of eastern Europe had been developed by colonists, and there was a tradition of a free peasantry. The nobility had more power than the monarchs, however, which allowed the nobility free rein over the peasants. By the 16th century the peasantry had been enserfed, and it did not regain its freedom until the late 18th century. In Russia, where types of bondage had existed since the 12th century, serfdom increased as the Muscovite state expanded in the 15th and 16th centuries. The Russian serfs were not formally freed until the Edict of Emancipation of 1861. See also SEIGNORIALISM.

SERGE, sûrj, is a durable twilled fabric with a smooth clear face and a diagonal rib on the front and back. It is made from worsted, wool, cotton, silk, or rayon. Worsted serge is used to make dresses, suits, coats, and caps. Rayon or silk serge is used to make coats, children's wear, dresses, men's suits, and sportswear. Serge holds a crease very well, and it drapes and clings well. However, it may develop a shine at points of wear.

SERGEANT, sär'jənt, in military land and air forces, a noncommissioned officer in one of the top grades of enlisted service. The grades of sergeant in the U. S. Army are—in ascending order—sergeant, staff sergeant, sergeant first class, master sergeant or first sergeant, and sergeant major. In the U. S. Air Force the rank equivalent to sergeant first class is technical sergeant, and in the U. S. Marine Corps it is gunnery sergeant.

In the British armed forces a sergeant, or serjeant, is the senior ranking noncommissioned officer, ranking above corporal. In the Royal Air Force a flight sergeant ranks above an army sergeant. The rank of sergeant is also used in police forces. In the United States a sergeant is below a captain, or in some cases a lieutenant, and in Britain he is below an inspector.

SERGEANT AT ARMS, sär'jənt, an executive and disciplinary officer of legislative bodies. In both houses of the Congress of the United States, his authority may not be ignored with impunity. In cases of disorder he carries the mace down the aisle of the House. If any member continues the disorder after this demonstration, he is guilty of contempt. The sergeant at arms also serves processes and, if necessary, summons absent members during sessions when their presence is necessary to constitute a quorum. In the House of Representatives he has charge of the members' payroll. The sergeants at arms are elected by the Congress.

SERGIPE, sər-zhē'pə, in eastern Brazil, is the smallest state of the republic, covering an area of 8,492 square miles (21,994 sq km). It is bordered on the north by the state of Alagoas across the São Francisco River, on the west and south by the state of Bahia, and on the east by the Atlantic Ocean. The coast is flat and sandy, but the interior consists of wooded hills, where iron ore and crystal quartz are found. Sergipe is drained by the São Francisco, and by the intermittently flowing Vasa Barris, Sergipe, and Cotinguiba rivers.

The chief crops cultivated in the state of Sergipe include cotton, sugarcane, cacao, rice, coffee, and corn. Stock raising and lumber are also important.

The capital and chief port of Sergipe is Aracaju, which is on the Sergipe River near its mouth on the Atlantic Ocean. The city's industries include tanneries, cotton mills, and sugar refineries. Other cities in the state include Estância, Propriá, and Itabiana.

The area was settled in the 16th century by planters from Bahia. It was held by the Dutch in 1624–1654, but otherwise remained a dependency of Bahia until 1821, and then became an independent captaincy. Sergipe became a province of the empire in 1824 and a state of the republic in 1889. Population: (1970) 900,119.

SERGIUS, sûr'jē-əs, **Saint** (c. 1315/1319–1392), Russian spiritual leader, who made the monastery of Trinity-Sergius (now Zagorsk) a center of Russian religious life. Varfolome (Bartholomew) Kirillovich was born of noble parentage in Rostov, Russia. His family moved to the village of Radonezh, whence he is often called Sergius of Radonezh. After his parents died he retired to a forest and led the life of hermit. In 1337 he took the vows of a monk, taking the name Sergius, and became abbot of Trinity monastery. His reputation for sanctity became widespread, and his monastery became a place of pilgrimage. Sergius died at his monastery in 1392. His feast is September 25.

SERGIUS I, sûr'jē-əs, **Saint** (died 701), pope from 687 to 701. Sergius was the scion of a Syrian family that had settled in Palermo, Sicily. He went to Rome during the reign (672–676) of Pope Adeodatus II and was ordained a priest. He succeeded Pope Conon on Dec. 15, 687, after a disputed election in which there were three claimants to the papacy.

Sergius refused to approve those decrees of the Council of Trullo (691) that he felt were contrary to the customs of Rome and denigrated its position in the church. Angered by the action, Emperor Justinian II arrested two papal advisers and ordered the arrest of Sergius, but the militia of Ravenna and Rome refused to carry out the order. Sergius died in Rome on Sept. 9, 701. His feast is September 9.

SERGIUS II, sûr'jē-əs (died 847), pope from 844 to 847. A Roman noble, Sergius was elected pope in January 844 and was consecrated without the approval of Emperor Lothair I, contrary to the provisions of the Constitutio Romana of Eugene II.

Lothair sent his son Louis to punish those responsible for the breach, but Sergius managed to mollify Louis and crowned him king of the Lombards. Sergius refused the demand of Louis' adviser, Drogo, bishop of Metz, that the Romans swear an oath of loyalty to Louis, but he insisted that they swear the oath to Lothair. Sergius is criticized for not sufficiently fortifying Rome before the Saracen attack of Aug. 23, 846, of which he had ample warning. He died in Rome on Jan. 27, 847.

SERGIUS III, sûr'jē-əs (died 911), pope from 904 to 911. He was born in Rome and became bishop of Cere. In 897 he failed in an attempt to seize the papacy. He succeeded in 904, becoming pope on January 29 by arranging the assassination of his predecessor, Leo V, and that of a rival claimant, Christopher. Sergius is reputed to have been the father of a son who later became Pope John XI, by Marozia, daughter of the powerful Theophylactus family. Sergius rebuilt the basilica of St. John Lateran, which had been destroyed by an earthquake. He died in Rome on April 14, 911.

SERGIUS IV, sûr'jē-əs (died 1012), pope from 1009 to 1012. He was born in Luna, Italy. He was bishop of Albano when elected pope on July 31, 1009. His reign was dominated by the Roman nobility, particularly John Crescentius II. Sergius died in Rome on May 12, 1012.

SERICULTURE. See SILK.

SERIES, in geology, is the collective term for rock strata deposited during a given geological epoch. A series may contain several rock *stages* and is in turn a subdivision of a *system.* The term is applied informally to a succession of rock formations having some common feature.

SERIES, in mathematics, a succession of terms considered to be known when the successive terms (first, second, third, and so on) are known. A sequence is also a succession of terms; the word *series* is used when the sums of the terms (rather than the individual terms) are under consideration. See also SEQUENCE.

A series is usually written with + or − signs separating successive terms. Typical series are

(i) $1 + 2 + 3 + 4 + \ldots$

and

(ii) $1 + \frac{1}{2} + \frac{1}{4} + \frac{1}{8} + \frac{1}{16} + \ldots$

Series that continue forever with no last term are known as infinite series and were formerly much used for calculation. The value of π, for example, can be found to as many decimal places as desired by means of series. However, they have been largely superseded in this role by iterative approximation programs carried out by calculating machines. Two types of infinite series, Fourier series and power series, are used for investigating the properties of certain functions: the function is expressed as the sum of a series whose individual terms are fairly simple. The most important use under this heading is for solving differential equations.

The study of infinite series has also a considerable didactic value. The concept of sum of an infinite number of terms is by no means the same as the concept of sum in elementary mathematics, and the investigation of its properties gives effective and interesting training in abstract reasoning.

How Series Are Specified. A series may be specified by specifying each term directly, or by showing how each term can be formed from previous terms. For example, series (ii) above can be specified by saying that the nth term is $(\frac{1}{2})^{n-1}$ or it may be specified *recursively* by saying that the first term is 1 and that from then on each term is half of the preceding term. The general problem of finding a formula for the nth term when the series is given in the second way is part of the calculus of finite differences.

For two elementary series (arithmetic and geometric) the results are well known and are given in the following section.

A well-known series that is always defined in the second way is the *Fibonacci series.* In one form of the series, the first term is zero, the second is 1, and from then on each term is the sum of the two preceding terms. In formulas,

$$u_1 = 0, \ u_2 = 1, \text{ and } u_r = u_{r-1} + u_{r-2} \text{ if } r > 2$$

where u_r denotes the rth term, and > means "greater than." Thus the series starts

$$0 + 1 + 1 + 2 + 3 + 5 + 8 + 13 + 21 + \ldots$$

It is of interest in geometry and biology. See also FIBONACCI SERIES.

The relation between successive terms ($u_r = u_{r-1} + u_{r-2}$ in this case) is called the *scale of relation* of the series. More generally, the scale of relation might be

$$u_r = a u_{r-1} + b u_{r-2} + \ldots + k u_{r-m}.$$

In this case, the series is a *recursive series of order m.*

Two Elementary Types of Series. If each term is greater than the one before it by a fixed amount d, then the series is an *arithmetic series,* and d is the *common difference.* If the first term is a then the nth term is $a + (n − 1)d$. Series (i) above is an arithmetic series whose common difference is 1.

If each term can be obtained by multiplying the one before it by a fixed number r, then the series is a *geometric series,* and r is the *common ratio.* If the first term is a, then the nth term is ar^{n-1}. Series (ii) above is a geometric series whose common ratio is $\frac{1}{2}$. Archimedes used a geometric series in finding the area of a segment of a parabola, as described subsequently.

FINITE SERIES

The sum of the first n terms of a series is called the nth *partial sum.* For each of the following series a formula for the partial sums is known.

The general arithmetic series:

$$a + (a + d) + (a + 2d) + \ldots + [a + (n − 1)d] = n[a + \tfrac{1}{2}(n − 1)d]$$

The general geometric series:

$$a + ar + ar^2 + \ldots + ar^{n-1} = a(1 − r^n)/(1 − r)$$

if $r \neq 1$. The sum is an if $r = 1$.

The series of integers:

$$1 + 2 + 3 + \ldots + n = \tfrac{1}{2}n(n + 1).$$

The series of squares:

$$1^2 + 2^2 + 3^2 + \ldots + n^2 = \tfrac{1}{6}n(n + 1)(2n + 1).$$

The series of cubes:

$$1^3 + 2^3 + \ldots + n^3 = \tfrac{1}{4}n^2(n + 1)^2.$$

Similar formulas are known for higher powers.

The first n terms of an infinite series form, of course, a finite series. There are also a few series that contain essentially only a finite number of terms, such as the following binomial-coefficient series of order n,

$$C(n,0) + C(n,1) + C(n,2) + \ldots + C(n,n)$$

whose sum is 2^n. See also COMBINATIONS AND PERMUTATIONS—*Relation to Binomial Theorem.*

The best-known technique for finding the sum of a finite series is the method of differences, which is described in several of the texts cited in the bibliography.

INFINITE SERIES

For a series with an infinite number of terms the fundamental question is: what is the sum of *all* the terms. But in elementary mathematics, the sum of an infinite number of terms is not even defined. Therefore we must first ask: how should the sum of an infinite number of terms be defined?

The clue to one possible answer (which is in fact the standard definition of the sum) lies in considering the successive partial sums. For example, the partial sums of

$$1 + \frac{1}{2} + \frac{1}{4} + \frac{1}{8} + \frac{1}{16} + \ldots$$

are

$$1, \ 1\tfrac{1}{2}, \ 1\tfrac{3}{4}, \ 1\tfrac{7}{8}, \ 1\tfrac{15}{16} \ldots$$

It is clear that these sums are getting closer and closer to 2. This fact is expressed more precisely in the following way: given any positive number ε (no matter how small) there is a number n such that the nth partial sum and all subsequent ones are within ε of 2. Thus the obvious number to take for the sum of the series is 2.

For any infinite series there may or may not be a number s with the above property: namely that, given any positive ε, there is a partial sum such that it and all subsequent ones are within ε of s. If there is such a number s, then the sum of the series is defined to be s. It is clear that for any series there cannot be more than one such number s. The proof of this fact is the first and simplest theorem of infinite series.

The analogy with the mathematical concept of limit is obvious to any student of the calculus. In fact, the sum of an infinite series can be defined by means of the concept of the limit of a sequence, as follows. The infinite sequence for the partial sums of the general form of an infinite series is:
$S_1 = a_1$, $S_2 = a_1 + a_2$, $S_3 = a_1 + a_2 + a_3$, $S_n = a_1 + a_2 + a_3 + \ldots + a_n, \ldots$. If the infinite sequence of partial sums $S_1, S_2, S_3, \ldots S_n, \ldots$ has a limit S, then S is the sum of the infinite series. That is, the sum S of an infinite series is defined to be
$$S = \lim_{n \to \infty} S_n$$
if this limit exists.

Another possible kind of behavior is exemplified by the series $1 + 1 + 1 + 1 + 1 + \ldots$. Here, the partial sums grow larger and larger. To be precise, given any number N (no matter how large) there is a partial sum such that it and all subsequent ones are greater than N. Under these circumstances, the sum of the series is defined to be $+\infty$. (If the sums grow similarly large and negative, the sum is defined to be $-\infty$.) Even if the terms of a series diminish, their sum may still be $+\infty$. For instance, the sum of $1 + \frac{1}{2} + \frac{1}{3} + \frac{1}{4} + \frac{1}{5} + \ldots$ is $+\infty$.

Other Methods of Summation. The definition of the sum of a series given earlier is reasonably obvious but is by no means the only possible one. The conditions a definition of sum must satisfy can be expressed informally as follows: when, in the calculations in which series usually occur, a series is replaced by its sum, correct results must nearly always be obtained. The theory will make the "nearly always" precise by specifying the calculations for which the series cannot be "replaced" by its sum. If the "usual calculations" include only addition, multiplication, and so on, the standard definition does well enough. If they are to include integration and differentiation, the standard definition is not strict enough, and "convergence" should be replaced by what is usually called "uniform convergence." For other purposes, it may be convenient to replace the definition by a less strict one, the most important of which is due to the Italian mathematician Ernesto Cesaro.

Terminology and Notation. The infinite series whose rth term is a_r is often written in the form
$$\sum_r a_r \text{ or (where there is no risk of ambiguity)}$$
as $\sum a_r$. Thus series (ii) could be written as $\sum (\frac{1}{2})^{r-1}$.

A series whose sum is a finite number is *convergent*, one whose sum is $+\infty$ is *positively divergent*, and one whose sum is $-\infty$ is *negatively divergent*. If there is a number M such that *every* partial sum is between $-M$ and M, the series is *bounded*. The word *divergent* is used differently by different writers. Sometimes it means "not convergent," and sometimes it means "either positively or negatively divergent." A bounded nonconvergent series is said to *oscillate finitely*. An unbounded series that is neither positively divergent nor negatively divergent is said to *oscillate infinitely*.

The sum of the series $\sum a_r$ is denoted by $\sum_{r=1}^{\infty} a_r$, though some writers use this symbol (improperly) to denote the series itself.

The series $\sum a_r$ is said to be *absolutely convergent* if $\sum |a_r|$ is convergent. ($|a|$ denotes either a or $-a$, whichever is positive. If $a = 0$, then $|a|$ is 0.) A series that is convergent but not absolutely convergent is *conditionally convergent*, and it can be proved that every absolutely convergent series must be convergent.

Examples of Infinite Series. (i) $1 + \frac{1}{2}^k + \frac{1}{3}^k + \frac{1}{4}^k + \ldots$ is absolutely convergent if $k > 1$, positively divergent if $k \leqslant 1$. (The symbol $>$ means "greater than," and the symbol $\leqslant$ means "less than or equal to.") If $k = 1$, this series is a harmonic series.

(ii) $1 + x + x^2 + x^3 + \ldots$ is a geometric series. It is absolutely convergent if $-1 < x < 1$ and its sum is $1/(1-x)$; it is positively divergent if $x \geqslant 1$. (The symbol $<$ means "less than," and the symbol $\geqslant$ means "greater than or equal to.")

(iii) $1 + x + x^2/2! + x^3/3! + \ldots$ (where $n!$ denotes the product of all the integers from 1 to n inclusive) is absolutely convergent and its sum is e^x where e is the base of natural logarithms. This series is called the *exponential series*.

(iv) $x - x^2/2 + x^3/3 - x^4/4 + \ldots$ is absolutely convergent if $-1 < x < 1$ and conditionally convergent if $x = 1$. Its sum is $\log_e(1 + x)$. The series is negatively divergent if $x \leqslant -1$.

Other sums of series are as follows:

(v) $\sum_{r=0}^{\infty} (-1)^r x^{2r+1}/(2r + 1)! = \sin x$

(vi) $\sum_{r=0}^{\infty} (-1)^r x^{2r}/(2r)! = \cos x$

(vii) $\sum_{r=0}^{\infty} (-1)^r x^{2r+1}/(2r + 1) = \arctan x$ if $-1 < x < 1$.

Convergence. It might be expected that the theory of infinite series would be mainly concerned with finding convenient formulas for the sums of various series, but only rarely can such a formula actually be found. In many investigations, however, it is enough to know whether or not a series has a finite sum, and the actual value of the sum is not of vital importance. Moreover, it is often possible to show that a given series has a sum, even though it is not possible to find a formula for it.

For instance, it is possible to show that every partial sum of the series

(i) $1 + 1/(1 \times 2) + 1/(2 \times 4) +$
$1/(3 \times 8) + 1/(4 \times 16) + \ldots +$
$1/(n \times 2^n) + \ldots$

is less than 2, because the partial sums of this series are less than those of $1 + \frac{1}{2} + \frac{1}{4} + \frac{1}{8} + \ldots$, which are obviously less than 2. With a little more work it can be shown that the partial sums of series (i) are all less than 1.8, or even that they are less than 1.695, and so on. In fact, there must be a *least* number with the property that the partial sums are all less than it. It is not hard to see that this number will be the sum of the series, although these considerations do not yield any way of finding a formula for this number. Thus a large part of the elementary theory of series is concerned with tests for convergence. Some of the best-known tests follow. In each case, the series $a_1 + a_2 + a_3 + \dots$ is being tested.

The nth Term Test. If a_n does not tend to zero as n tends to infinity, then the series is not convergent.

The Alternating Series Test. If the terms are alternately positive and negative, if each term is numerically smaller than the preceding term, and if a_n tends to zero as n tends to infinity, then the series is convergent.

The following tests apply only to series with no negative terms. They can be applied indirectly to more general series, by applying them to $|a_1| + |a_2| + |a_3| + \dots$. If this series is convergent, then the given series $a_1 + a_2 + a_3 + \dots$ is absolutely convergent.

The Boundedness Test. If there is a number k such that every partial sum is less than k, then the series is convergent.

Comparison Tests. If $0 \leqslant a_n \leqslant c_n$ for every n, and if $c_1 + c_2 + \dots$ is convergent, then $a_1 + a_2 + \dots$ is convergent. If $d_n \leqslant a_n$ for every n, and if $d_1 + d_2 + \dots$ is positively divergent, then $a_1 + a_2 + \dots$ is positively divergent. The discussion of the series $1 = 1/(1 \times 2) + \dots + 1/(n \times 2^n)$ earlier in the section is an example of comparison testing.

If the a_n and the c_n are all positive, and if $a_{n+1}/a_n \leqslant c_{n+1}/c_n$ for every n, and if $c_1 + c_2 + \dots$ is convergent, then so is $a_1 + a_2 + \dots$.

If the a_n and the d_n are all positive, and if $a_{n+1}/a_n \geqslant d_{n+1}/d_n$ for every n, and if $d_1 + d_2 + \dots$ is positively divergent, then so is $a_1 + a_2 + \dots$.

Cauchy's Root Test. If there is a number k, less than 1, such that $\sqrt[n]{a_n} \leqslant k$ for every n, then $a_1 + a_2 + \dots$ is convergent.

The Ratio Test. If every a_n is positive and if there is a number a, less than 1, such that $a_{n+1}/a_n < a$ for every n, then $a_1 + a_2 + \dots$ is convergent.

The Integral Test. If $a_n = \phi(n)$ for every positive integer n, where ϕ is a positive-valued, integrable, decreasing function, then $a_1 + a_2 + \dots$ is convergent if and only if the limit $\int_1^\infty \phi(x)\,dx$ exists.

Expansion in Series. As already pointed out, the first and most obvious problem in the theory of series is that of finding whether a given series has a sum. The converse problem is also of interest: given a function, to find a series of a convenient form that has the function as its sum. There are two particularly convenient forms of series for this purpose, the power series and the Fourier series.

Power Series. A series of the form

$$a_0 + a_1 x + a_2 x^2 + a_3 x^3 + \dots$$

is called a *power series in x*. Examples of power series whose sums are e^x, $\log_e(1 + x)$, $\sin x$, $\cos x$, and $\arctan x$ are given above under Examples of Infinite Series. Power series are particularly easy to handle. In the first place, their convergence behavior is simple. Except for a few that (like the exponential series) converge for every x, each power series in x has a *radius of convergence*, that is, a number r such that the series is absolutely convergent when $-r < x < r$, but fails to converge if $x > r$ or $x < -r$. In the second place, the elementary rules of algebra and of calculus apply to them as though they were polynomials. In particular, power series can be added, multiplied, differentiated, and integrated term by term.

It can be proved that the expansion of a given function in a power series is unique, that is to say, that if $\sum_{r=0}^\infty a_r x^r$ and $\sum_{r=0}^\infty b_r x^r$ both equal $f(x)$ for every x in some interval, then $a_r = b_r$ for every r.

If $\sum_{r=0}^\infty a_r x^r = f(x)$ in some interval containing zero, then $a_0 = f(0)$, $a_1 = f'(0)/1!$, $a_2 = f''(0)/2!$, and so on, where $f'(0)$ is the value of the first derivative of $f(x)$ at $x = 0$, $f''(0)$ is the value of the second derivative of $f(x)$ at $x = 0$, and so on.

This gives a method for finding the coefficients in the expansion in series of any function that has such an expansion. This method was used by Brook Taylor and Colin Maclaurin, and consequently power series are often referred to as *Taylor's series* or *Maclaurin's series*, especially when written in the form $\sum f^{(r)}(0)x^r/r!$. A Taylor series is a power series in $(x - a)$, and a Maclaurin series is a power series in x.

One important use of power series is in solving differential equations. Certain equations do not have solutions that can be expressed in terms of polynomials, or trigonometrical or exponential functions, but do have solutions expressible as the sum of a power series.

Fourier Series. A series that is expressed as $\sum_r [a_r \cos(rx) + b_r \sin(rx)]$ is called a *Fourier series*. Because the graphs of $y = a \cos(kx)$ and of $y = b \sin(kx)$ are each in the shape of a sine curve, the sum of the series, if it exists, can be regarded, informally, as the result of superposing an infinite number of sinusoidal vibrations. When a function f does have a Fourier expansion, that is to say, when

$$f(x) = \sum_{r=0}^\infty [a_r \cos(rx) + b_r \sin(rx)]$$

the coefficients a_r and b_r are given by the formulas

$$a_0 = \frac{1}{2\pi} \int_{-\pi}^{\pi} f(x)\,dx,$$

$$a_r = \frac{1}{\pi} \int_{-\pi}^{\pi} f(x)\cos(rx)\,dx,$$

$$b_r = \frac{1}{\pi} \int_{-\pi}^{\pi} f(x)\sin(rx)\,dx.$$

In fact, if f is any function for which these integrals exist, the a_r and b_r above are called the *Fourier coefficients* for f, and the Fourier series with these coefficients is called the *Fourier series for f*. The theory of Fourier series is concerned with distinguishing conditions under which a function is the sum of its Fourier series. Because sine and cosine are periodic with period 2π, it follows that such a function must have period 2π. The other conditions are concerned with the continuity of f and of its derivatives. Two examples of Fourier series are $\sin x - \frac{1}{2} \sin 2x + \frac{1}{3} \sin 3x - \ldots$, which has the sum $\frac{1}{2}x$ if $-\pi < x < \pi$; and

$$\frac{\pi}{2} - \frac{4}{\pi} \left(\frac{\cos x}{1^2} + \frac{\cos 3x}{3^2} + \frac{\cos 5x}{5^2} + \ldots \right),$$

which has the sum $|x|$ if $-\pi < x < \pi$. Fourier series are of much use in the study of wave motions. The analysis of a given wave motion (that is, of a given periodic function) into its constituent sinusoidal components (that is, into the individual terms of the Fourier series) is known as *Fourier analysis*.

Uniform Convergence. Each term of a power series in x is a function of x; therefore, in general, so is the sum. The same applies to Fourier series. Moreover, the power series is of interest for all values of x from $-r$ to r, where r is the radius of convergence. The Fourier series is of interest for values of x ranging from $-\pi$ to π.

In general, a series may be given in which each term is a function of x:

$$f_0(x) + f_1(x) + f_2(x) + \ldots$$

the series being convergent for every value of x between a given pair of numbers.

There is a stronger kind of convergence in such situations that some series have and some do not. It is known as *uniform convergence*, and its formal definition is as follows. A series whose terms are functions of x is *uniformly convergent* to $s(x)$ for $a < x < b$ if, given any positive number ε, there is a partial sum such that both it and all later partial sums $s_n(x)$ have the following property: the difference between $s_n(x)$ and $s(x)$ is less than ε for every x between a and b.

It is the phrase "for every x between a and b" that is important here and serves to distinguish uniform convergence from mere convergence. Diagrammatically, $s(x) - s_n(x)$ is the vertical distance between the graphs of $y = s(x)$ and $y = s_n(x)$, and so uniformity of convergence implies that this distance is less than ε not merely for one particular value of x but everywhere in the range of values considered. This clearly ensures that the graph of $y = s_n(x)$ as a whole should converge to the graph of $y = s(x)$.

Uniformly convergent series have the following important properties. The sum of a uniformly convergent series of continuous functions is itself continuous, and uniformly convergent series may be integrated and differentiated term by term.

A power series is uniformly convergent in any range between $-r$ and r, where r is its radius of convergence. Fourier series are uniformly convergent under certain not-too-restrictive conditions that are fulfilled in most practical cases.

Series With Complex Terms. If $c_1, c_2, c_3 \ldots$ are complex numbers, the series $c_1 + c_2 + c_3 + \ldots$ can be treated in the same way as a series of real numbers. The definition of sum is word-for-word the same, and it can be shown that the series has a sum if (and *only* if) the series of real parts considered separately and the series of imaginary parts considered separately each has a sum. Indeed, $(a_1 + ib_1) + (a_2 + ib_2) + \ldots$ has the sum $s + it$ if, and only if, $a_1 + a_2 + \ldots$ has the sum s and $b_1 + b_2 + \ldots$ has the sum t. This fact reduces the elementary theory of series of complex numbers to the elementary theory of series of real numbers.

Particularly important are power series. If z denotes a complex variable, a function f that has the property that $f(z)$ is the sum of a power series in $z - c$ is an *analytic function*, and such functions play a fundamental role in the theory of functions of a complex variable.

Asymptotic Series. Functions ϕ and ψ are *asymptotic* if $\phi(n)/\psi(n)$ tends to 1 as n tends to infinity. If $\psi(n)$ is the sum of the first n terms of a series, then the series is an *asymptotic expansion* of ϕ. Such expansions may be useful even if the series is not convergent. As an example, the harmonic series $1 + \frac{1}{2} + \frac{1}{3} + \ldots$, is an asymptotic expansion of the logarithm, because $\left(\sum_{r=1}^{n} 1/r \right) / \log_e n \to 1$.

HISTORICAL BACKGROUND

Zeno's Paradox. Perhaps the earliest problem involving an infinite series is the famous paradox about Achilles and the tortoise. It was posed by the Greek philosopher Zeno of Elea in the 5th century B. C. His argument may be put as follows.

Achilles can run 10 times as fast as a tortoise. In a race he gives the tortoise a start of, say, 100 feet. When he reaches the point at which the tortoise started, the tortoise will be 10 feet ahead of him. When he has run those 10 feet, the tortoise will be one foot ahead, and so on. From this argument, Zeno concluded that Achilles would always be behind the tortoise. Common sense, however, insists that if he runs 10 times as fast as the tortoise, he must eventually overtake it.

The usual modern explanation of the paradox is that the number of feet covered by Achilles in overtaking the tortoise is the sum of the infinite series $100 + 10 + 1 + \frac{1}{10} + \frac{1}{100} + \ldots$, which equals $111.11 \ldots$. Here, the infinite series arises in the explanation of the paradox rather than in Zeno's argument itself.

Archimedes' Method of Exhaustion. Much closer to the idea of infinite series is a procedure used by Archimedes to find the area of a segment of a parabola (see accompanying diagram). This procedure consisted of the following steps: (1) remove from the segment a triangle whose area is A units; (2) remove from what remains two triangles whose areas together amount to $(\frac{1}{4})A$ units; (3) remove from what now remains four triangles whose total area is one quarter of $(\frac{1}{4})A$ units; and (4) continue the procedure in this way so that the segment is gradually "exhausted." A modern mathematician would finish the calculation by saying that the area of the segment is the sum of the infinite series $A + (\frac{1}{4})A + (\frac{1}{4})^2A + \ldots$, which is $(\frac{4}{3})A$. This is, indeed, Archimedes' final result. However, he did not find the sum of the infinite series but instead proceeded indirectly.

Archimedes first proved that if each of the numbers $A, B, C, \ldots Z$ is one quarter of the preceding number, then $A + B + C + \ldots + Z = (\frac{4}{3})A - (\frac{1}{3})Z$. This is equivalent to the formula for summing a finite geometrical progression in which each term is one quarter of the preceding one. He then proved that the area of the segment could not be greater than $(\frac{4}{3})A$, nor less than $(\frac{4}{3})A$. His proof was as follows. If the area were greater than $(\frac{4}{3})A$, then, by removing enough triangles from the segment, he could ensure that the remaining area would be less than the amount by which the area of the segment exceeded $(\frac{4}{3})A$. Then the sum of the areas of the triangles, say $A + B + C + \ldots + Z$

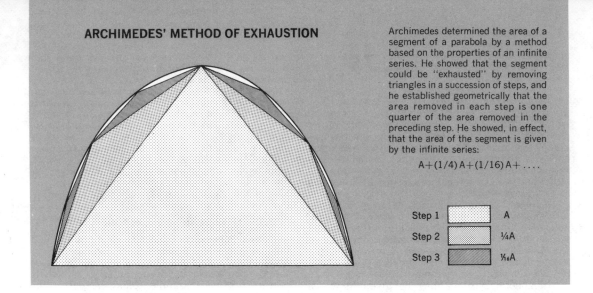

ARCHIMEDES' METHOD OF EXHAUSTION

Archimedes determined the area of a segment of a parabola by a method based on the properties of an infinite series. He showed that the segment could be "exhausted" by removing triangles in a succession of steps, and he established geometrically that the area removed in each step is one quarter of the area removed in the preceding step. He showed, in effect, that the area of the segment is given by the infinite series:

$$A + (1/4)A + (1/16)A + \ldots .$$

Step 1		A
Step 2		¼A
Step 3		⅟₁₆A

would have to be greater than $(\frac{4}{3})A$, which is impossible because this sum is $(\frac{4}{3})A - (\frac{4}{3})Z$. On the other hand, if the area of the segment were less than $(\frac{4}{3})A$, he could, by taking the procedure far enough, ensure that the area $(\frac{4}{3})Z$ would be less than the amount by which $(\frac{4}{3})A$ exceeded the area of the segment. Then the sum of the areas of triangles $A + B + C + \ldots + Z$ would be greater than the area of the segment, which is impossible.

The main difference between Archimedes' method and modern ones is that Archimedes assumes that the area that he is calculating exists. He therefore does not concern himself with the problem of whether an infinite series has a sum.

Developments to the End of the 19th Century. After Archimedes, little work was done on series until Johannes Kepler investigated areas and perimeters of elliptical segments. In *Nova stereometria doliorum vinariorum* (1615), he used the same mathematical techniques to find the volumes of wine casks. However, Kepler replaced Archimedes' method of exhaustion by the logically vaguer but intellectually more stimulating concept of "infinitely small."

Kepler's technique was carried further by Francesco Bonaventura Cavalieri in *Geometria indivisibilibus continuorum nova quadam promota* (1635), by John Wallis in *Arithmetica infinitorum* (1655), and by Isaac Newton. Newton found series that represented the areas of segments of circles and hyperbolas, as given in his *De analysi per aequationes numero terminorum infinitas* (1711). The formula for the terms of Taylor's series was discovered in 1712 by Brook Taylor and published in 1715 in *Methodus incrementorum directa et inversa*. This chapter of the history of mathematics, in which many elegant and useful results were obtained by logically untrustworthy methods, culminated in the works of Leonhard Euler, notably in his *Introductio in analysin infinitorum* (1748). However, Euler completely neglected the question of whether or not the series under investigation was convergent, despite the fact that Gottfried Wilhelm von Leibniz had recognized the essential distinction between series that converge and those that do not. Indeed, Leibniz had given a criterion for the convergence of a series of alternately positive and negative terms in 1705.

Equally important, and on equally shaky logical foundations, were the investigations of Jean Baptiste Joseph Fourier. He invented the Fourier series as a tool for the investigation of the flow of heat, as described in his *La Théorie analytique de la chaleur* (1822). However, physical intuition, instead of logical deduction, kept him clear of invalid results.

Meanwhile, pure mathematicians had been working toward a more logical theory. The modern definition of a limit and the definition of the sum of an infinite series in terms of a limit were introduced by Augustin Louis Cauchy in his *Cours d'analyse* (1821). However, only later did he recognize uniform convergence, which was discovered in 1847 by Sir George Gabriel Stokes. Not until then could the question of term-by-term integration and similar problems be properly treated. Even Karl Friedrich Gauss, who had given a careful treatment of a hypergeometric series in 1812, failed to appreciate this point.

In 1829, Peter Gustav Lejeune Dirichlet validated the use of Fourier series under certain conditions, and in 1837 he proved that rearranging an absolutely convergent series does not affect its sum. In 1886, Henri Poincaré introduced asymptotic expansion using divergent series. In 1882 and 1890, Otto Hölder and Ernesto Cesàro introduced more general types of limits.

See also FOURIER SERIES; TAYLOR'S THEOREM.

HUGH A. THURSTON
The University of British Columbia

Bibliography

Davis, Harold T., *Summation of Series* (Trinity Univ. Press 1962).
Dienes, Paul, *Taylor Series: An Introduction to the Theory of a Complex Variable* (Dover 1931).
Fichtenholz, G. M., *Infinite Series: Rudiments* (Gordon 1970).
Hardy, Godfrey H., *Course of Pure Mathematics*, 10th ed. (Cambridge 1952).
Hyslop, James M., *Infinite Series*, 4th ed. (Wiley 1954).
Knopp, Konrad, *Infinite Sequences and Series* (Dover 1956).
Markushevich, Alekser I., *Infinite Series* (Heath 1967).
Rainville, Earl D., *Infinite Series* (Macmillan 1967).
Stanaitis, O. E., *Introduction to Sequences, Series, and Improper Integrals* (Holden Day 1967).
Thomas, George D., *Infinite Series and Elementary Differential Equations* (Addison-Wesley 1969).

SERIGRAPHY. See SILK SCREEN PRINT.

SERINGAPATAM, sə-ring-gə-pə-tam', is a town in southeastern India, formerly the capital of the kingdom of Mysore. It is situated on an island in the Kaveri (Cauvery) River.

Seringapatam's massive fort, built in the 15th century, stands on the western end of the island. Within its walls are the ruins of a palace and mosque built by Tipu Sultan, Muslim ruler of Mysore. There is also an old Hindu temple. Just outside the fort is Tipu's graceful summer palace, now in ruins. At the eastern end of the island, the suburb of Ganjam contains the mausoleum of Tipu and his father, Hyder Ali.

Seringapatam was beseiged by the British in 1792 and again in 1799. During the second siege Tipu was killed when British troops stormed the fort, and Mysore was completely conquered. The town declined in importance after its capture by the British. Population: (1961) 11,423.

SERKIN, ser'kin, **Rudolf** (1903–   ), American pianist. He was born in Eger, Bohemia (now Cheb, Czechoslovakia), on March 28, 1903, the son of Russian parents. He ended a career as a child prodigy in 1915, when he went to Vienna to study—piano with Richard Robert and composition with Joseph Marx and Arnold Schoenberg. He resumed his concert career in 1920, including appearances with Adolph Busch's chamber music ensemble. From then on Serkin and Busch were closely linked professionally, and Serkin married Busch's daughter Irene. One of their sons, Peter, became an outstanding pianist.

Serkin emigrated to the United States in 1933, making his American debut that year in Washington, D. C. In 1934 he performed with the New York Philharmonic and toured the United States regularly thereafter. Serkin taught at the Curtis Institute of Music, Philadelphia, beginning in 1939, and became its director in 1968.

SERMON, a religious address delivered to the congregation at a service of worship. Examples are found in several religions, but chiefly in Judaism and Christianity. Many of the recorded addresses of the Old Testament prophets were sermons. In the New Testament, Jesus' teaching was frequently addressed to congregations in the synagogue, for example, Luke 4:16–30. Several sermons of Peter and Paul are also reported in the Acts of the Apostles, for example, chapters 2:14–36, 13:16–43.

Although philosophers lectured in their schools and the Stoic-Cynic street preachers delivered diatribes (exhortations to moral living), their influence on the early church did not compare with the example of the Jewish synagogue. In both church and synagogue the method was usually the same, involving an exposition of Holy Scripture ending with an exhortation and a prayer. The Jewish prayer was a *kaddish,* one of the oldest elements in the synagogue liturgy.

Many of the Christian Church Fathers have left collections of sermons, notably St. John Chrysostom in the East and St. Augustine in the West. Their sermons were read and copied for hundreds of years. In the West Augustine's sermons were frequently adapted to meet the needs of less well-educated congregations. In the Middle Ages there were "preaching friars" who often spoke out-of-doors, as at the preaching crosses in markets and villages. With the Reformation in the 16th century, even more stress was laid upon preaching, and the typical Protestant service was and still is chiefly centered in the sermon. In the Roman Catholic Church an increased emphasis has been placed on the sermon since the Second Vatican Council.

Although more emphasis is now being laid upon liturgical rites in all churches, the place of the sermon is still recognized, and will probably continue to be. Christianity, like Judaism and even Islam, is a religion of a book that needs to be explained, interpreted, and applied.

FREDERICK C. GRANT
Formerly, Union Theological Seminary

SERMON ON THE MOUNT, Jesus' discourse to the disciples and the multitude in the Gospel of Matthew 5–7. It is also found in briefer form in Luke 6:20–49, where it is virtually "the ordination sermon of the Twelve" (Luke 6:12–16). There are parallels to these teachings elsewhere in the Gospels, and many scholars hold that the nucleus of the sermon was preserved in the "Sayings Source" (called "Q" for *Quelle,* "source"), and that the evangelists, chiefly Matthew, elaborated it by adding relevant material from other sources. As a typical "sermon" of Jesus, it is unsurpassed in interest and importance.

The chief subjects are: (1) the Beatitudes (Matthew 5:3–10) followed by a special application to the disciples; (2) Jesus' purpose, to "fulfill" the Law, to widen or deepen its scope, rather than to annul or "destroy" it (Matthew 5:17–48); this is illustrated by several examples of the "fulfillment" of the ancient legislation; (3) Jesus' reinterpretation of the customary acts of piety prescribed by the scribes and their Pharisaic followers—almsgiving, prayer, and fasting (Matthew 6:1–18); this section includes the Lord's Prayer; (4) the importance of absolute sincerity and trust in God (Matthew 6:19–34); (5) various admonitions, as against censoriousness, imprudence in preaching, hesitation or reluctance in prayer, hypocrisy, merely verbal profession of faith, and concluding with the great parable of the two house builders (Matthew 7:1–27).

Many scholars have described this sermon as "the Charter of Christianity." However, it is best understood as a sermon, presupposing the current Jewish faith and practice but insisting upon a new approach, a new devotion, of the kind all Jesus' teachings expressed.

FREDERICK C. GRANT
Formerly, Union Theological Seminary

SEROV, sye'rəf, is a city in the USSR, in the central Ural Mountains, 190 miles (305 km) north of Sverdlovsk. It was known as Nadezhdinsk until 1939, when it was renamed in honor of a Soviet aviator. The city developed in the 1890's when ironworks were built to serve the area's mines. Industrialization intensified in the 1930's, and it became a center of metallurgical industries. Population: (1970) 100,000.

SEROW, sə-rō', any of a genus of goat antelopes found in eastern Asia from Japan and Taiwan to China and Tibet and south to Sumatra. Also known as *serau* and *sarau,* the serow is closely related to several other species, including the goral of Tibet, the mountain goat of North America, and the chamois of Europe.

Serows are rather goatlike in general appearance, with stout bodies and relatively short legs. They have long, coarse hair and a short mane but lack a beard. They also have short, sharply pointed, slightly curved horns and short, deerlike tails. Traveling singly or in small groups, serows frequent steep, rough, scrub- or tree-covered mountain slopes, usually at lower elevations. They are not very fast-moving but are sure-footed. They eat grass and leaves, often in protected thickets.

Serows make up the genus *Capricornis* of the family Bovidae. The best-known species is the Himalayan serow, *C. tahr,* a grizzled, reddish brown animal with a black head and neck, standing about 3 feet (90 cm) at the shoulders. It has been raised in captivity in the United States, where the female normally produces two kids in late spring. The Sumatran species, *C. sumatrensis,* is about the same size but grizzled black to grayish brown with brown legs. The Japanese species, *C. crispus,* is much smaller and grayer.

JOHN D. BLACK
Northeast Missouri State University

SERPENS, sûr′pənz, is a summer constellation of the Northern Hemisphere. In Greek mythology it represented a serpent held in the hands of the giant Ophiuchus, another constellation figure, usually identified with the god of medicine Asklepios (Roman Aesculapius). In modern sky charts Serpens consists of two disconnected sections, Serpens Caput (the head) and Serpens Cauda (the tail), separated by Ophiuchus.

The constellation is made up of rather faint stars, the brightest of which, Cor Serpentis, has a magnitude of 2.7. However, Serpens lies in a region that contains many star clusters, of which M5 is the brightest in northern skies. Three novae occurred in the boundaries of Serpens in the 20th century. Lying in Ophiuchus between the two parts of Serpens is Barnard's Star, a nearby 10th-magnitude star that has the largest proper motion of any star known. See also CONSTELLATION.

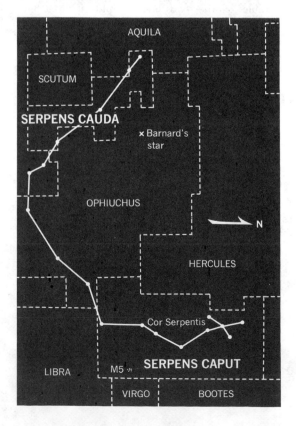

SERPENTINE, sûr′pən-tēn, is a hydrous magnesium silicate mineral. It exists in two major forms: a massive, platy variety called antigorite, and a fibrous, silky variety called chrysotile. The latter material is quarried from rocks and prepared commercially as asbestos. (See ASBESTOS.) The massive variety, which is translucent and has a somewhat waxy luster, is often used as an ornamental stone. The name serpentine derives from the "serpentlike" coloration of this variety, a mottled darker and lighter green. A naturally occurring mixture of the stone with marble is known as *verd antique* marble. Williamsite is an apple green, impure variety that is sometimes mistaken for jade. Other color variations such as yellow or brown are produced by veins of talc, magnesite, iron oxide, or other minerals present in the stone.

Serpentine is a common mineral that is found in both igneous and metamorphic rocks, often in association with chromite, garnierite, and magnetite. The mineral is formed by the hydration of olivine, enstatite, or other primary magnesium silicate minerals, or by the combined action of water and carbon dioxide on olivine alone. The fibrous variety is usually found as veins running through the massive form of the mineral. Large deposits are found in many European countries and in South Africa, while in the United States the mineral occurs in the northeastern states, Arizona, and California.

Composition, $Mg_6(Si_4O_{10})(OH)_8$; hardness, 2–5, but usually about 4; specific gravity, 2.65 in massive varieties, 2.2 in fibrous varieties; crystal system, monoclinic.

SERPUKHOV, syer-pōō′кнəf, is a city in the USSR, at the confluence of the Nara and Oka rivers, 60 miles (97 km) southwest of Moscow. Founded in the 14th century, it became one of the fortress towns protecting Moscow from southern attacks. There are remains of the old fortress. The city has been a textile center since the 19th century. Population: (1970) 124,000.

SERRA, ser′rä, **Junípero** (1713–1784), Spanish missionary in America. He was born on the island of Mallorca on Nov. 24, 1713. He entered the Franciscan order, became a priest, and won recognition as a professor of philosophy and as a pulpit orator. Serra obtained permission to become a missionary, and he arrived in Mexico City in 1750. He first served for nine years among the Pamé Indians of the Sierra Gorda in eastern Mexico.

In 1769, though in frail health, Serra traveled with a Spanish military party to the present site of San Diego, Calif., where he founded a mission. Under his leadership during the next 15 years, members of the Franciscan order established 9 (of an eventual total of 21) missions in California. Other mission sites, which constituted the first settlements in California, included San Luís Obispo and San Juan Capistrano. The first buildings were crude, and the more familiar adobe-brick or cut-stone buildings were erected later.

Serra died at Mission San Carlos Borromeo, near Monterey, which he had made his headquarters, on Aug. 28, 1784. At the time of his death his 9 missions claimed some 6,000 converts, the mission flocks and herds grazed thousands of acres, and the Indians were engaged in many crafts taught them by the Franciscans.

SERRAI, sá'râ, is a city in Greece, about 40 miles (65 km) northeast of Salonika. It is the capital of Serrai district (nomos). The city, which is on the approach to the strategic Rupel Pass leading to Bulgaria, was fortified by the Byzantines to protect the Salonika-Constantinople (Istanbul) route. From the 10th century to World War II it was attacked, at various times, by Bulgarians, Greeks, Serbs, and Turks. Population: (1971) 39,863.

SERRANO Y DOMINGUEZ, ser-rä'nō ē thō-mēng'gäth, **Francisco** (1810–1885), Spanish general and government leader. He was born in Anjonilla on Sept. 17, 1810, and entered the army as a boy of 12. He advanced rapidly and also became involved in politics. After the death of Ferdinand VII in 1833, Serrano supported the infant Isabella II, whose accession led to the First Carlist War (1833–1839). Serrano fought against the Carlists, who championed the claims of Don Carlos, Isabella's uncle. See also CARLISM.

Serrano participated actively in the tumultuous politics of Isabella's reign, at times holding high offices and at other times opposing the administration. In 1854 he took part in the successful uprising of Baldomero Espartero and Leopoldo O'Donnell. Serrano was appointed captain general of Cuba in 1859 and served until 1863, when he was made duke de la Torre. He returned to Spain and served in O'Donnell's government.

Isabella's opposition to progressive reforms caused her deposition in 1868. Serrano was a leader of the revolution against her and was appointed regent by the Cortes in 1869. When Amadeus took the throne in 1870, Serrano continued to be influential. The selection of Alfonso XII, Isabella's son, as the monarch in 1874 was followed by Serrano's fall from national prominence. He died in Madrid on Nov. 26, 1885.

SERTORIUS, sûr-tō'rē-əs, **Quintus** (c. 123–72 B. C.), Roman general. He distinguished himself as a soldier under Gaius Marius and was quaestor in Cisalpine Gaul in 90. During the Social War (90–88) between Marius and Lucius Cornelius Sulla, Sertorius aided Marius in seizing Rome. As Marius' representative he went to Spain in 83 or 82 and drove out Sulla's governor but was himself driven out of Spain into Mauretania, in Africa, in 81.

He successfully resisted efforts to dislodge him and in 80 returned to Spain, where his bravery, rude eloquence, and generous treatment of the native people won him a large following among both the native people and Romans. Marcus Perperna brought him reinforcements in 77, and Sertorius gained control of most of Spain.

Sertorius organized an independent government on the Roman model, headed by a senate of 300 members, and founded a school to educate the sons of local chiefs. To counteract the greater forces at the disposal of the Roman Senate he formed an alliance with the Mediterranean pirates and negotiated with Mithridates VI, King of Pontus. Despite the arrival of a formidable expedition led by Pompey the Great in 77, Sertorius maintained his position until 74. Thereafter, his support deteriorated, and jealousy among his subordinates led to his murder in 72.

SERUM HEPATITIS, hep-ə-tīt'əs, a type of viral hepatitis. See HEPATITIS.

SERUM SICKNESS is an illness that results from the injection of a drug or an animal serum into man. It usually begins six to 14 days following the injection but may appear within a few hours or be delayed four or five weeks.

Serum sickness is basically an allergic reaction. Since the late 19th century, serum from immunized animals has been used to protect people against certain bacterial diseases. The human tissues that receive such animal serum recognize it as foreign and produce antibodies to it. When a certain ratio of injected serum and circulating antibodies develops, serum sickness results. Fortunately serum sickness is infrequent today, since antimicrobial drugs have displaced animal serum in the treatment of the infectious diseases for which the serum was once used. Drugs, however, can produce the same reaction, and currently penicillin and its derivatives are the most common cause of serum sickness.

Serum sickness usually begins with an itchy red rash that appears initially at the site of the injection and then spreads over the entire body surface. Most patients develop a fever of 101° to 102° F (38°–39° C) and may experience headache, nausea, vomiting, tender swelling of lymph glands, a feeling of generalized lassitude, or pain and inflammation in the joints. The typical case is benign and self-limiting, disappearing spontaneously in three to seven days. Generally, bed rest, fluids, and aspirin for fever and pain are adequate treatment.

Infrequently serum sickness may involve the central nervous system and produce convulsions, confusion, or neuritis. Occasionally it produces kidney dysfunction, and in some persons it can cause shortness of breath, wheezing, cough, and perhaps shock. Any of these symptoms demands the immediate attention of a physician, but a fatal outcome to serum sickness is rare.

J. R. CALDWELL, M. D.
University of Florida College of Medicine

SERVAL, sûr'vəl, a large, wild cat, one of the commonest cats found in the brush and grasslands of Africa south of the Sahara. The serval stands about 20 inches (50 cm) tall at the shoulders and is about 3 feet (90 cm) long, not including its long tail. It has a fawn or tawny coat marked with rows of black spots and frequently blends in well with its surroundings. Servals are active

Serval (*Felis serval*)

both during the day and at night. They are among the fastest cats and actively hunt and run down guinea fowl and other birds as well as rodents, hares, young antelopes, and other small mammals. The serval, *Felis serval, or Leptailurus,* is a member of the cat family Felidae.

SERVAN-SCHREIBER, ser-vaᴎ′ shrī-bâr′, **Jean Jacques** (1924–   ), French journalist, author, and politician. He was born in Paris on Feb. 13, 1924. He studied at the École Polytechnique and joined General de Gaulle's Free French army as a pilot in 1943.

In 1953 he founded *L'Express,* a weekly newsmagazine that he edited until 1969. In 1970 he became president of Groupe-Express, publisher of a number of French magazines. The president of the Radical Socialist party, he was elected to the Chamber of Deputies in 1970.

Servan-Schreiber's best-known work is *Le Défi Américain* (1967; Eng. tr., *The American Challenge,* 1968), in which he attributes American economic leadership to its technological ability and managerial flexibility and Europe's secondary position to its artificial divisions into independent states. His other works include *Le Reveil de la France* (1969; Eng. tr., *The Spirit of May,* 1970) and *Ciel et terre* (1970; Eng. tr., *The Radical Alternative,* 1971).

SERVETUS, sûr-vē′təs, **Michael** (1511–1553), Spanish theologian and physician, who was executed as a heretic for his anti-Trinitarian views. He is also renowned as the discoverer of the pulmonary circulation sustem. Servetus was born in Tudela, Navarre. He was the son of a notary, who sent him to Toulouse to study civil law. Here Servetus became interested in the discussions of the Reformers and began to devote his attention to theology. Subsequently he found his way to Germany and there printed a strongly anti-Trinitarian tract, *De trinitatis erroribus* (1531), which was followed the next year by *Dialogorum de trinitate libri II.* But he found that the expression of his opinions, which finally came to include a denial of infant Baptism and of original sin, was as obnoxious to the Protestants as to Catholics, and he made his escape to France under the name of Michel de Villeneuve. He went to Paris in 1536, where he studied medicine and graduated as doctor. In Paris he seems to have encountered John Calvin for the first time. Having quarreled with the medical faculty at Paris, he left that city (1538), studied theology and Hebrew at Louvain, and practiced medicine in Avignon and Charlieu. He continued his medical studies at Montpellier and in 1541 settled in Vienne, becoming physician to the archbishop.

In 1553, Servetus published his matured theological system anonymously under the title of *Christianismi restitutio.* The magistrates of Vienne, however, discovered the identity of the author, and Servetus was tried and convicted of heresy but managed to escape from prison. Later readers discovered that in dealing with the problem of the relation of the Holy Spirit to regeneration, Servetus had incidentally described the course of the blood from the right ventricle of the heart through the lungs and back to the left ventricle.

He set out for Italy, but some fatal fascination made him go by way of Geneva, where he arrived on Aug. 13, 1553. On the following day he was arrested by the magistrates on a charge of blasphemy and heresy. His writings were checked for heresies, but the magistrates of Geneva were aware that this was extraordinary treatment of a person who was neither a subject nor a resident. They therefore consulted the magistrates of all the Protestant Swiss cantons, who referred the matter to their divines. The latter unanimously declared for punishment, Calvin being especially urgent and emphatic on the necessity for putting Servetus to death. Indeed Calvin had indicated earlier that if Servetus came to Geneva, he would do his best to prevent him from leaving alive. As Servetus refused to retract his opinions, he was condemned to death for heresy. He was burned at the stake on Oct. 27, 1553.

SERVICE, Robert W. (1874–1958), Canadian author, whose narrative verses about the Klondike gold rush gained him immense popularity.

Life. Robert William Service was born in Preston, England, on Jan. 16, 1874, and grew up in Glasgow, Scotland. After finishing high school he was apprenticed as a bank clerk but quickly grew bored. He emigrated to Canada, and for ten years he traveled up and down the Pacific Coast of Canada and the United States, working at various jobs and writing poetry. In 1905 he took a job as teller with a Canadian bank and was soon transferred to a branch bank in Whitehorse and, later, Dawson, in the Yukon.

Once in the North, Service began to turn out light narrative poems depicting life in that area, where gold prospectors, trappers, and frontier taverns still flourished. His first book of verses, *Songs of a Sourdough* (1907; later reprinted as *The Spell of the Yukon*), made him wealthy, and he resigned from his bank job in 1909. After three more years in the North, during which time he published *Ballads of a Cheechako* (1909) and *Rhymes of a Rolling Stone* (1912), he left Canada to work in the Balkans in World War I as a correspondent for the Toronto *Star.* During the war, he served as an ambulance driver—which gave him material for his *Ballads of a Red Cross Man* (1917)—and as a Canadian Army officer.

After the war, Service settled down to a life of leisure in France, broken only by a period of refuge in Canada during World War II. His later books include several novels, notably *The Roughneck* (1923) and *The House of Fear* (1927); two volumes of autobiography, *Ploughman of the Moon* (1945) and *Harper of Heaven* (1948); and some verse. But none of these later works approached the success or vigor of his early poems. He died in Lancieux, France, on Sept. 11, 1958.

Verse. Service's best verses are those describing the rugged life of the Yukon at the end of the gold rush. It has been suggested that he painted the characters in his works as much seedier than the people really were, but that does not affect the attractiveness of the colorful poems, which tell vivid stories in strong rhythms and contain a certain joyful zest. Service's most popular poem is probably *The Shooting of Dan McGrew,* which tells how "a bunch of the boys were whooping it up in the Malemute Saloon"· with the hero and the "lady that's known as Lou." Another immensely popular piece is the winsome *Cremation of Sam McGee.* Though Service may have lacked sophistication, he was the poet of a time and place for which his narrative rhythm and his romantic-heroic attitude were uniquely expressive.

SERVICE INDUSTRY, an industry whose utility consists of providing to consumers the services required in daily living. It does not produce physical goods. Hotels, repair shops, and professional consultants are examples. See INDUSTRY—*Services*.

SERVICEBERRY, a shadbush, or the berrylike fruit of the shadbush. See also SHADBUSH.

SERVIUS TULLIUS, sûr′vē-əs tul′ē-əs, was the 6th king of Rome (reigned 579–534 B. C.). Servius apparently was a Roman or Latin who married the daughter of the fifth king, Lucius Tarquinius Priscus, whom he succeeded in 579.

Servius' reign is said to have been marked by constitutional reforms and material progress, but the so-called Servian Reform probably did not develop until the 5th or 4th century, and the Servian Wall was not built until 378. Nevertheless, he concluded a treaty with the Latin League and probably erected public buildings in Rome. Tradition says that his murder was arranged by his daughter and Tarquinius Superbus, his son-in-law and successor.

SERVOMECHANISM, an electrochemical feedback control system. More specifically, a servomechanism is an automatic control system in which the operation of a high-power device is caused to follow closely the command of a low-power device. The high-power and low-power devices usually are located some distance apart. The ratio of the power controlled to the power in the control signal may often be a million million to one.

The high-power device is called the *controlled member.* The quantity being controlled usually is the position or the speed of this member. The low-power device is called the *command* or *reference device.* Its output is the command signal, which usually is a signal representing a position or a speed. Often, the command signal is an electrical signal (voltage) obtained from a radar echo, a pressure-sensing device, or even a light-sensitive device.

Servomechanisms have an important property that distinguishes them from other automatic control systems. In a servomechanism the operation of the high-power device is made a function of the *difference,* or error, between its desired state, or commanded state, and its existing state. In all servomechanisms the commanded state is con-

stantly or intermittently compared with the existing state of the controlled member. If there is an error, an adjustment is made. This error-sensing property of servomechanisms makes possible their remarkably high operating accuracy under widely diverse conditions.

Uses. Servomechanisms are important in manufacturing steel, machine tools, and chemicals; in steering ships, aircraft, or guided missiles; in printing color magazines; in scientific research; and in numerous other applications. They are applied daily to operations that man finds difficult or unpleasant. In response to a signal no greater than the twitch of a muscle, they control great masses. For instance, in many of the world's great observatories the light from a star is made to control the motion of a massive telescope to an accuracy of a few millionths of an inch.

Basic Principles. The use of feedback—the means by which the error-sensing property of a servomechanism is achieved—has given rise to the term *feedback control system.* In all servomechanisms a signal representing the existing state of the controlled member is fed back for comparison with the command signal to provide information about the difference or error. The error information is used as a signal to actuate the power-amplifying part of the system and to bring about the desired amount of control. All servomechanisms therefore comprise: (1) a means of measuring what is desired (desired state) and what is being accomplished (actual state); (2) a means of transmitting the desired measurement to the low-power command device, and a means of transmitting the actual measurement from the high-power controlled member; (3) a means for establishing the difference between the desired state and the actual state; and (4) a means of amplifying the difference signals and using them to control large amounts of power. The error-sensing and amplifying part of the system is often referred to as the brain, or nerve center.

Feedback. The principle of feedback is readily understood by an example from everyday life. Consider the situation in a schoolroom. Here, the textbook may be thought of as the command, the teacher may be thought of as the nerve center, and the student may be thought of as the controlled member.

The quantity being controlled is the student's depth of understanding of the textbook. If the educational process were limited to having the

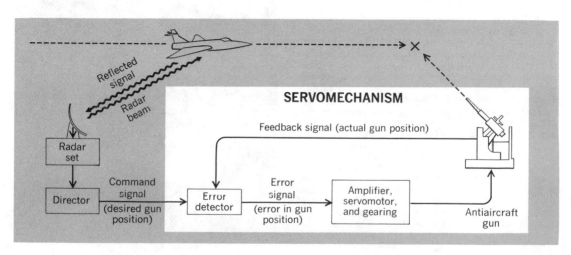

SERVOMECHANISM

Feedback signal (actual gun position)

Radar set

Reflected signal

Radar beam

Director

Command signal

(desired gun position)

Error detector

Error signal

(error in gun position)

Amplifier, servomotor, and gearing

Antiaircraft gun

teacher expound on the text while the student merely listened, we would not expect much learning because the teacher would have no means of knowing whether the student really understood or whether what was said was relevant to the learning process. It is for this reason that education makes use of the test or quiz. The teacher receives "feedback" by means of the quiz, which measures how well the student understands. If there is an error in understanding, the teacher can make an adjustment.

As a matter of fact, in our daily actions, we frequently operate in exactly the same manner as do servomechanisms—as systems in which the control action is a function of the difference between the desired state and the existing state, this difference being established by feedback from the controlled element to the nerve center of the system.

Typical Servo System. An antiaircraft gunfire control system is a typical servo system. In such a system, a servomechanism points the gun at a target aircraft. As shown in the accompanying simplified diagram, a radar set automatically tracks a target airplane and furnishes information about the target position to a director. The director computes where the gun should point so that the projectile and the target will collide after the projectile has traveled the necessary distance. The servomechanism compares the actual gun position with the gun position computed by the director. Any detected difference between the two positions results in a difference, or error, signal. This signal is amplified and used to actuate a servomotor, which drives the gun. The gun is driven until its pointing error is negligible.

Design and Performance. The designers of servomechanisms face many problems in putting together the elements that are to go into the system. For instance, when servomechanisms are used in an airplane, their scope is severely restricted by the necessity of combining reliability of operation with compactness in design. The equipment must operate reliably both on the ground at temperatures ranging from −40° F to 120° F (−40° C–50° C) and at altitudes ranging up to 60,000 feet. In industrial applications, a servomechanism can be bulkier and heavier equipment, but it must be no less reliable and must often cope with the hazards of contaminated or explosive atmospheres and stand a lot of abuse. Advances in engineering have been rapid since the end of World War II, and many truly remarkable systems have been designed.

The performance demanded of servomechanisms also taxes the ingenuity and creative resources of designers. The task is invariably one of designing equipment that will hold a close correspondence between control and command in the presence of widely varying loads and rapidly changing commands. Unless careful attention is paid to the mathematical theory of feedback systems, the performance will tend to become oscillatory—that is, the system will "hunt." Furthermore, the theory of servomechanisms stipulates this essential law of control for any servomechanism: in the presence of any steady error, the controlled quantity must be the time derivative of the error—that is, in a position control system a steady position error must establish a rate of change of position (velocity) at the output. Systems in which a steady position error establishes only position at the output are elementary gov-

ernors or regulators, not servomechanisms. See also AUTOMATIC CONTROL SYSTEM; FEEDBACK CONTROL SYSTEM.

GORDON S. BROWN[*]
Coauthor of "Principles of Servomechanisms"

Bibliography

Ahrendt, William R., and Savant, C. J., Jr., *Servomechanism Practice*, 2d ed. (McGraw 1960).
Bukstein, Edward J., *Basic Servomechanisms* (Holt 1963).
James, Hubert M., and others, *Theory of Servomechanisms* (Dover 1964).
Savant, C. J., Jr., *Control System Design*, 2d ed. (McGraw 1964).
Truxal, John G., *Automatic Feedback Control System Synthesis* (McGraw 1955).
Weiner, Norbert, *Cybernetics: Or Control and Communication in the Animal and the Machine* (MIT Press 1961).
Wilson, D. R., ed., *Modern Practice in Servo Design* (Pergamon 1971).

SESAME, ses'ə-mē, a rough, hairy, gummy annual plant, *Sesamum indicum,* about 2 feet (61 cm) high, with egg-shaped leaves tapering to a point, opposite below and alternate above, slightly toothed, and mucilaginous. The flowers are solitary in the axils, pale or rose-colored, five-parted, with irregular-lipped corolla, having the tube curved downward and dilated above the oblique base. Sesame, which has been known from ancient times, originated in the East, where it is cultivated for the pleasant, spicy taste of its black or white seeds. It is easily grown, can thrive in poor soil, and has become a popular crop for gardeners in the United States. The plant has been naturalized in the Southern states.

The very tiny, sweet, and oily seeds are used for food in the Orient and imported into Europe for crushing to extract the oil. The seeds yield half of their weight in the oil, which is yellow, limpid, inodorous, and keeps for years without becoming rancid. It is of great economic value. It can be employed instead of olive oil in many ways, as for culinary purposes (where it is often preferred as a polyunsaturated substitute for oil from animal fats), medicine (having a laxative effect), cosmetics, and soaps. It is also employed as an adulterant in olive oil and may itself be adulterated with peanut oil. The cake left after removal of the oil makes a good feed for cattle.

Flowers and leaves of sesame (*Sesame indicum*)

T. H. EVERETT

SESQUICENTENNIAL EXPOSITION, an exposition held at Philadelphia, Pa., from June 1 to Nov. 30, 1926, to commemorate the 150th anniversary of the signing of the Declaration of Independence. Among the outstanding buildings were the Palace of Liberal Arts and Manufactures and the Palace of Agriculture and Food Products. Guests included President and Mrs. Calvin Coolidge, Queen Marie of Rumania, and Prince Gustav Adolf of Sweden.

From the patriotic standpoint, the exposition achieved its purpose, but financially it was not a success, and the city of Philadelphia had to issue bonds to cover bills aggregating $5 million. The total cost was estimated at $18 million. The attendance was about 6 million.

SESSHU, ses-shōō (1420–1506), was the greatest Japanese master of ink painting. He studied under the landscape painter Shubun and was deeply influenced by Zen Buddhism. Like his colleagues he painted mainly Chinese landscapes in the Chinese manner, but during a stay in China he evolved an individual mode of expression based on direct observation of the scenery.

Sesshu's work is characterized by a love of nature that seems to be conveyed with a directness guided by intuitive understanding. This quality of capturing the inner essence of a subject is apparent in his paintings in two styles. The *shin* style is dominated by a vigorous, angular, and rather complex line and has strong contrasts of light and dark. Examples are the *Longer Landscape Scroll* (Mori Collection, Yamaguchi prefecture), which depicts the changing seasons, and the *Winter Landscape* (Tokyo National Museum). Exemplifying the explosive, very simplified *haboku* style is the much different landscape that Sesshu painted for his pupil Soen (Tokyo National Museum), in which dark ink is splashed over lighter ink that is still wet.

SESSIONS, sesh'ənz, **Roger Huntington** (1896–   ), American composer and teacher, who, according to Milton Babbitt, his student and a composer of electronic music, exerted a major influence on modern American music as a result of his "complete craftsmanship, artistic responsibility to the past and present, and . . . concern with compositional dynamics rather than with idiomatic superficialities."

Sessions was born in Brooklyn, N. Y., on Dec. 28, 1896. After graduating from Harvard in 1915, he attended Yale, where he studied composition under Horatio Parker. He later studied under Ernest Bloch and was his assistant in music theory at the Cleveland Institute of Music (1921–1925). Sessions subsequently became one of the leading American teachers of composition. His posts included those at Boston University (1933–1935); Princeton University (1935–1945; 1953–1965); the University of California, Berkeley (1945–1953); and Juilliard School of Music, New York (from 1965).

Sessions' compositions are in a variety of musical idioms. His music, although somewhat lyrical, is essentially intellectual and has not achieved widespread popularity. He wrote stage works, notably *The Black Maskers* (1923); symphonies; concertos; chamber music; and choral music. Among his books are *The Musical Experience of Composer, Performer and Listener* (1950), *Harmonic Practice* (1951), and *Reflections on the Music Life in the United States* (1956).

SESTINA, ses-tē'nə, an extremely intricate form of verse invented by Arnaut Daniel, a Provençal troubadour, toward the end of the 12th century, and adopted by Spanish, Portuguese, and Italian poets, notably Dante Alighieri and Petrarch. It consists of six six-line stanzas; the last word of each line of the first stanza is repeated as the last word of a line in each succeeding stanza, but in different order. Provençal poets set the rhyme scheme as follows: first stanza, 1,2,3,4,5,6; second, 6,1,5,2,4,3; third, 3,6,4,1,2,5; fourth, 5,3,2,6,1,4; fifth, 4,5,1,3,6,2; sixth, 2,4,6,5,3,1. After the sixth stanza there is a three-line envoy in which the six rhyme words are repeated, three at the end of the lines and three in the middle. It will be noted that in each stanza after the first, the first line ends with the same word as the last line of the preceding stanza, and the second line ends with the same word as the first line of the preceding stanza.

In France, the form was revived by the *Pléiade* poets, notably by Pontus de Thiard in the 16th century, and it was used extensively by Count Ferdinand de Gramont in the 19th century. In Germany, the sestina was adopted by various 17th and 19th century poets. Sir Edmund William Gosse awakened interest in the sestina among modern English poets in 1877, and Algernon Charles Swinburne employed it with remarkable success in later decades. Ezra Pound and W. H. Auden are among 20th century poets who have utilized this intricate verse form.

SESTOS, ses'təs, is a ruined town in Turkey, on the European shore of the Dardanelles (Hellespont). It is at the strait's narrowest point, opposite the ancient town of Abydos in Asia Minor. The site is just northeast of the modern Turkish town of Ecceabat.

It was the invasion point for Xerxes I in 480 B. C., when he and his army crossed the Hellespont over a bridge of boats and marched through Thrace, Macedonia, and Thessaly. Sestos also is the scene of the legendary romance of Hero and her lover Leander. Leander supposedly swam across the Hellespont from Abydos each night to meet her.

SESTRIERE, ses-trē-ā're, is an Alpine resort in northwestern Italy, close to the French border and 40 miles (65 km) west of Turin. It is situated at an altitude of 6,668 feet (2,032 meters), between the Chisone and Dora Riparia valleys. Sestriere is one of the leading winter sports centers in Europe and has a famous skiing school. It also attracts summer visitors. Cable cars ascend three nearby mountains to heights of more than 8,000 feet (2,440 meters). Population: (1967) 551.

SET, in the religion of ancient Egypt, was the god of evil. Originally worshiped as a deity of Upper Egypt, he was later assimilated into the Osiris myth as the murderer of his brother Osiris. According to the myth Set (Seth) was later killed in revenge by Osiris' son Horus.

The Hyksos rulers of Egypt identified Set with their warrior god Sutekh and built a temple to him at Avaris. Later dynasties believed him to be the enemy of all gods and destroyed all monuments to him. He was called Typhon by the Greeks.

SET DESIGN. See THEATER—*Theatrical Elements.*

SET THEORY. A set is a collection of things of any kind; they may be real or imagined, physical objects or abstract concepts. For example, we may speak of the set of all leaves on a particular tree or of the set of all good ideas the president of the United States has on a certain day.

History and Axiomatic Foundations. One of the earliest uses of sets probably was in connection with counting or tallying. The pebbles in a pile could be transferred one at a time to keep track of the number of repetitions of a certain event just as a shipwrecked sailor may carve notches in a stick to count the days that have passed. This is essentially a process of pairing off, in which we say that the number of objects in one set (the notches on the stick) equals the number of objects in the other set (the days) if for each object in one set there is a corresponding object in the other, and vice versa.

Surprisingly, the first logical difficulties in dealing with sets arose from this process of counting or tallying. In the last quarter of the 19th century, the German mathematician Georg Cantor applied this counting process to infinite sets (such as the set of all positive whole numbers 1, 2, 3, ...) and obtained some seemingly paradoxical results.

For example, the set of all natural numbers (the positive numbers 1, 2, 3, ...) can be paired off with the set of all even natural numbers or with the set of all rational numbers. (A rational number is one that can be expressed as an integer or as a quotient of integers; for instance, 1/2, and 3/2.) In this sense, the set of even natural numbers is "as numerous" as the seemingly larger set of all natural numbers and "as numerous" as the set of all rational numbers.

However, Cantor showed that the natural numbers could not be paired off with all the real numbers. (A real number is any rational or irrational number. See also IRRATIONAL NUMBER.) Thus there are at least two different sizes of infinite sets—that is, at least two different "numbers" (called transfinite numbers) must be used to denote the sizes of infinite sets. This was perhaps the first great discovery in the theory of infinite sets. Cantor used the first letter of the Hebrew alphabet—aleph—with a subscript zero ($\aleph_0$) to denote the size of the set of all natural numbers, and he used the letter c, for *continuum*, to denote the size of the set of all real numbers. Since the set of natural numbers can be paired with a set of some of the real numbers, the transfinite number c is definitely larger than $\aleph_0$. Cantor then wondered whether there were any transfinite numbers between $\aleph_0$ and c. He conjectured that there were none. This conjecture

became known as the *continuum hypothesis*. For 40 years neither he nor other workers were able to prove or disprove his conjecture. In a celebrated list of 50 mathematical problems drawn up by the German mathematician David Hilbert in 1900, the continuum hypothesis was first on the list.

The work mathematicians have done on the continuum hypothesis in about the last 75 years is reminiscent of that done on Euclid's parallel postulate over a period of about 2,000 years. The final results in the two cases are quite analogous.

In 1938, Kurt Gödel showed that it was not possible to use the concepts of set theory to disprove the continuum hypothesis. That is, he showed that if set theory including the continuum hypothesis is inconsistent, then there must be an inconsistency in set theory itself. Then in 1963, Paul Cohen of Stanford settled the other half of the question. He showed that the concepts of set theory could not be used to prove the continuum hypothesis. That is, he showed that if set theory including a denial of the continuum hypothesis is inconsistent, then there must be an inconsistency in set theory itself.

The two results of Gödel and Cohen show that the continuum hypothesis is independent of the other axioms of set theory; that is, it may be either affirmed or denied. They also proved this same independence for another one of the axioms, called the *axiom of choice*, which deals with the possibility of selecting a particular representative from each set of any family of nonempty sets. The independence of these results from the other axioms of set theory opens up the possibility of constructing several types of set theory—now called nonstandard set theory—in which one or the other of these results is denied, just as several types of non-Euclidean geometry arose from the denial of Euclid's parallel postulate. Thus Gödel's and Cohen's work plays a role in the development of set theory that is analogous to that played by the discovery of non-Euclidean geometries in the development of geometry. It is still too early to predict what applications may be found for nonstandard set theory.

Terminology. The basic concept in connection with sets is membership: s is an element, or member, of the set S; in symbols, $s \in S$. If s is not an element of S, one writes $s \notin S$. For example, 3 is an element of the set of positive whole numbers, but π is not an element of this set. A set S is defined if and only if for any object s it can be definitely determined either that s is an element of S or that s is not an element of S (and not both). Note that small letters are used to denote elements of sets, and capital letters to denote the sets themselves.

Two notations are in common use to describe a set. The set whose elements are the three numbers 3, 9, and 13 may be denoted by (3, 9, 13); the set of all even whole numbers may be denoted by {x | x is an even whole number}. The vertical bar in this notation may be read as "such that" so that the whole statement would read: all x such that x is an even whole number. This second type of notation is sometimes called *set-builder notation* because it provides the rule by which the set can be constructed.

In the axiomatic development of set theory it has been found that certain paradoxes can arise unless suitable restrictions on the size of a set are stipulated. This may be done in the discussion of a particular problem by finding, or being

The set of all even numbers can be paired off in a one-to-one correspondence with the set of all natural numbers and the set of all rational numbers.

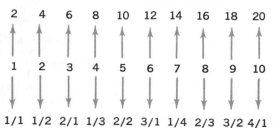

| 2 | 4 | 6 | 8 | 10 | 12 | 14 | 16 | 18 | 20 |

| 1 | 2 | 3 | 4 | 5 | 6 | 7 | 8 | 9 | 10 |

| 1/1 | 1/2 | 2/1 | 1/3 | 2/2 | 3/1 | 1/4 | 2/3 | 3/2 | 4/1 |

given, a set containing all the objects that are of interest in connection with that problem and then confining attention to elements of that set. Such a set is called a *universal set*, or *universe*, and all the sets arising in that discussion will be made up of (some of) the elements of that universal set. A set that has no elements is called an *empty set*, or *null set*, and is usually denoted by the symbol ϕ. The set of all Russian cosmonauts who went to the moon before 1950 is empty. An illustration of these concepts is provided by the following example: If the universal set is $\{x \mid x$ is a positive whole number$\}$, then the set $\{x \mid 5x < 12\}$ is $\{1, 2\}$; if the universal set is $\{3, 9, 13\}$, then the set $\{x \mid 5x < 12\}$ is empty.

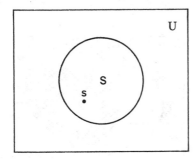

Venn diagram showing that s is a member of set S (s ε S), and S is a subset of U (S ⊂ U).

A Venn diagram provides a convenient schematic representation of a set that enables geometric intuition to suggest ideas that frequently prove to be useful. The universal set may be represented by all the points in an arbitrary geometrical figure—for example, a rectangle. Other sets of interest in the discussion would be represented by geometrical figures inside this rectangle. However, proofs of theorems must rest on the axioms of set theory and not merely on the picture provided by a Venn diagram.

Relations Between Sets. As stated above, membership is the basic concept in connection with sets. Two sets S and T are defined to be equal, written $S = T$, if and only if they have the same elements. For example, $\{1, 2, 3\} = \{x \mid x$ is a positive whole number less than 4$\}$. Since all empty sets are equal (they all have no elements), it is customary to speak of *the* empty set. The set S is a *subset* of T, written $S \subset T$, if and only if every element of S is an element of T. This includes the possibility that $S = T$. In fact, $S = T$ if and only if $S \subset T$ and $T \subset S$. If $S \subset T$ but $S \neq T$, then S is called a *proper subset* of T. The empty set is a subset of every set S since, if $\phi \subset S$ were false, there would have to be an object b such that $b \, \varepsilon \, \phi$ and $b \nmid S$. But there is no such object since the empty set has no elements.

Two sets S and T are called *equivalent* if and only if there is a correspondence between the sets such that each element of S corresponds to a unique element of T and each element of T corresponds to a unique element of S. Two finite sets are equivalent if and only if they have the same number of elements. As indicated above, surprising results occur with infinite sets. For example, the set $N = \{x \mid x$ is a positive whole number$\}$ is equivalent to its proper subset $E = \{x \mid x$ is a positive, even whole number$\}$. This

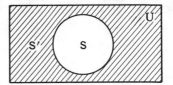

The complement of set S is S'.

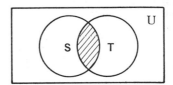

The union of set S and set T is S ∪ T.

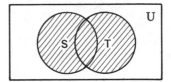

The complement of the union of set S and set T is (S ∪ T)'.

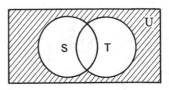

The intersection of set S and set T is S ∩ T.

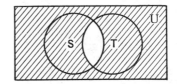

The complement of the intersection of set S and set T is (S ∩ T)'.

may be seen by letting the element n of N correspond to the element $2n$ of E. Any infinite set has a subset equivalent to the set N of positive whole numbers. A set is infinite if and only if it is equivalent to one of its proper subsets.

An important theorem is that the set $\mathscr{S}$ consisting of all the subsets of S has a higher cardinal number than does S, even if S is infinite. This theorem allows the construction of ever-higher orders of infinite sets, each consisting of the set of all subsets of the preceding set. The proof depends upon the fact that it is possible to define a subset A of S such that when the elements of S are paired off with the elements of $\mathscr{S}$, none can be paired off with A. Thus, $\mathscr{S}$ has at least one more element than S.

Operations with Sets. The *union* of two sets S and T, written $S \cup T$, is the set of all objects that are elements of at least one of the two sets. In

BASIC LAWS OF OPERATIONS WITH SETS

Commutative:	$S \cup T = T \cup S,$ $S \cap T = T \cap S$
Associative:	$S \cup (T \cup R) = (S \cup T) \cup R$ $S \cap (T \cap R) = (S \cap T) \cap R$
Idempotent:	$S \cup S = S, \ S \cap S = S$
Distributive:	$S \cap (T \cup R) = (S \cap T) \cup$ $(S \cap R)$ $S \cup (T \cap R) = (S \cup T) \cap$ $(S \cup R)$
Absorptive:	$S \cup (S \cap T) = S,$ $S \cap (S \cup T) = S.$

symbols, $S \cup T = \{x \mid x \ \varepsilon \ S \text{ or } x \ \varepsilon \ T \text{ or both}\}$. The *intersection* of two sets S and T, written $S \cap T$, is the set of all objects that are elements of both of the sets S and T. The two operations, union and intersection, have many properties in common with addition and multiplication of numbers, but there are also several important differences. The basic laws governing these operations are given in the box above.

The *complement* of a set S, written S', is the set of all objects that are not elements of S. In symbols, $S' = \{x \mid x \ \varepsilon \ S\}$. Of course, only elements of the universal set are considered. The complement of the complement of a set is the original set: $(S')' = S$.

Augustus De Morgan's laws give expressions for the complement of the union of two sets and the complement of the intersection of two sets: $(S \cup T)' = S' \cap T'$; $(S \cap T)' = S' \cup T'$.

DE MORGAN'S LAWS

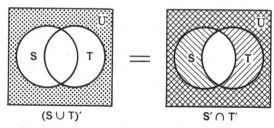

(S ∪ T)'   S' ∩ T'

First law: The complement of the union of two sets (shaded area in left diagram) equals the intersection of the complements of the sets (crosshatched area in right diagram).

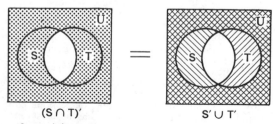

(S ∩ T)'   S' ∪ T'

Second law: The complement of the intersection of two sets (shaded area in left diagram) equals the union of the complements of the sets (entire shaded area in right diagram).

The empty set, ϕ, and the universal set, U, also have special properties with respect to these operations:

  (1) $S \cup \phi = S$, and $S \cap \phi = \phi$,
  (2) $S \cup U = U$, and $S \cap U = S$,
  (3) $\phi' = U$, and $U' = \phi$,
  (4) $S \cup S' = U$, and $S \cap S' = \phi$.

The operations of union and intersection may be extended to apply to any family of sets instead of to just two sets, and these extended operations have properties similar to those described above. The subset relation between two sets can be characterized in terms of union or in terms of intersection. In fact, $S \subset T$ if and only if $S \cup T = T$ or, equivalently, if and only if $S \cap T = S$. Using these rules, $\{[(S \cup T)' \cap S]' \cup T\}'$ can be simplified to just ϕ, for example.

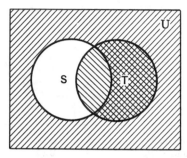

Crosshatched area is S' ∩ T. Entire shaded area, including crosshatches, is S' ∪ T. Unshaded area is (S' ∪ T)' = S ∩ T'.

Russell's Paradox. Among the paradoxes in set theory discovered about 1900, Bertrand Russell's is the simplest to describe. In fact, several questions of the parlor-game type are based on it. In an axiomatic development of set theory, such paradoxes are avoided by somehow restricting the size that a set can attain.

Since the elements of a set can be objects of any kind whatever, these elements may themselves be sets. For example, the elements of the set $\mathcal{S} = \{X \mid X \subset S\}$ are sets. Thus the possibility arises that a set A might be an element of itself, that is, $A \ \varepsilon \ A$. As an example, the set consisting of all those objects describable in exactly 12 words would be a member of itself. Sets coming readily to mind do not have this property. For example, the set N of all positive whole numbers is not, itself, a whole number, so $N \ \varepsilon \ N$. A set S might be called an *ordinary* set if $S \ \varepsilon \ S$, and an *extraordinary* set if $S \ \varepsilon \ S$.

Russell's paradox is concerned with the set R of all ordinary sets; that is, $R = \{S \mid S \ \varepsilon \ S\}$. The question arises: Is R ordinary or extraordinary? These two possibilities may be considered in turn. First, suppose R is an ordinary set, that is, $R \ \varepsilon \ R$. But this is exactly the condition required for membership in the set $R = \{S \mid S \ \varepsilon \ S\}$; that is $R \ \varepsilon \ R$. Thus, this possibility has led to a contradiction, and it must be rejected. Second, suppose R is an extraordinary set; that is, $R \ \varepsilon \ R$. But then R must satisfy the condition required of all objects that are elements of R; that is, $R \ \varepsilon \ R$. This possibility has also led to a contradiction. But there are no other possibilities, so either the first or second possibility (and not both) must describe the actual situation. The resolution of this difficulty lies in asking: Is R a set? In an axiomatic development, a set is required to satisfy certain conditions, or to be the result of applying certain prescribed processes. The object R considered above would fail to satisfy these requirements. It is not a set, so there is no reason to expect it to behave like a set. In particular, the relation ε of set membership has no meaning in connection with R.

Functions. A function may be defined in terms of ordered pairs. Intuitively, the ordered pair of the objects x and y, written (x,y), is just an arrangement of the objects x and y in which x is the first element and y is the second. It is not required that x and y be different. Equality between ordered pairs is defined by setting $(x,y) = (u,v)$ if and only if $x = u$ and $y = v$. In an axiomatic development, an ordered pair could be defined in any way consistent with this notion of equality. One such definition, in terms of set theory, is $(x,y) = \{ \{x\}, \{x,y\} \}$. That is, (x,y) is the set whose elements are the sets $\{x\}$ and $\{x,y\}$.

A function is a set f of ordered pairs such that no two different ordered pairs in the set have the same first element. In symbols, if $(x,y_1)\ \varepsilon\ f$ and $(x,y_2)\ \varepsilon\ f$, then $y_1 = y_2$. It is important to notice that this condition is not symmetric in x and y. The set X of all objects x that occur as a first element in some ordered pair in the function f is the *domain* of f, and the set Y of all second elements is the *range* of f. A set Y_1 that has Y as a subset is frequently convenient in describing the function. If $(x,y)\ \varepsilon\ f$, then y is the value of the function at x, written $y = f(x)$.

The function concept is used in all branches of pure and applied mathematics. Examples of functions abound, both in mathematics and in everyday life. For example, if the sets X and Y_1 are each taken to be the real numbers, then $f = \{(x,y) \mid y = x^2\}$ is a function. The domain of this function is X, the set of all real numbers; however, the range Y is the set of all nonnegative real numbers. For any positive number x, the value $f(x)$ of this function is the area of a square with side x units in length. The set $g = \{ (x,y \mid y = 0$ if x is rational, and $y = 1$ if x is irrational$\}$ is a function with domain X and range $\{0,1\}$. This function is a frequently used example in several branches of mathematics. The set $p = \{ (x,y) \mid y$ is the product of 6 times the smallest integer bigger than $x\}$ is a function. For reasonably small positive values of x, $p(x)$ is the postage required on a first-class letter weighing x ounces. If C is the set of chairs in a certain classroom, the set $\{ (c,s) \mid c\ \varepsilon\ C$ and s is the student sitting in $c\}$ would be of interest to the teacher. If two students are perched on the same chair, it is not a function.

The inverse of a function f, in symbols f^{-1}, is the set of ordered pairs obtained by interchanging the first and second elements in each ordered pair in f. In symbols, $f^{-1} = \{(x,y) \mid (y,x)\ \varepsilon\ f\}$. Of course, f^{-1} may fail to be a function. For example, $f = \{ (1,2), (3,2) \}$ is a function with domain $\{1,3\}$ and range $\{2\}$, but $f^{-1} = \{ (2,1), (2,3) \}$ is not a function since it contains two different ordered pairs with the same first element. A function whose inverse is also a function is said to be one-to-one. A one-to-one function may be used in tallying or as the correspondence between two sets S and T to prove that these sets are equivalent.

Applications. Some applications of set theory have already been mentioned. Most of modern mathematics can be developed from set theory. The function concept pervades all of mathematics. The family of all subsets of a given universal set U, together with the set operations of union, intersection, and complement, is a typical example of an algebraic structure called a Boolean algebra. This algebraic structure was first studied by George Boole around 1850 in connection with his work on logic. Since 1945, it has been used in the design of electronic computers. In probability theory, if the universal set U is finite, the probability that an element of U has a particular property p may be defined as the quotient of the number of elements in the set $P = \{x \mid x$ has the property $p\}$ divided by the number of elements in U. A generalization of this definition applies if U is infinite.

In logic, statements such as "x is round" or "$2x + 1 > 3$" are considered. If $p(x)$ is such a statement, the *truth set* P of $p(x)$ is the set of all objects which make the statement true. In symbols, $P = \{x \mid p(x)\}$. If, further, Q is the truth set of the statement $q(x)$, then the truth set for $p(x)$ and $q(x)$ is $P \cap Q$; the truth set for $p(x)$ or $q(x)$ is $P \cup Q$; the truth set for the contradiction of $p(x)$ is P'. This interplay allows logical questions about statements to be rephrased in terms of sets. The statement $p(x)$ implies the statement $q(x)$ if and only if $P \subset Q$; the statements $p(x)$ and $q(x)$ are equivalent if and only if $P = Q$.

A simple example will illustrate the use of truth sets. In a small village, there are 52 people, 25 males, 18 adults (that are 9 married couples), and 3 visitors (a father, a mother, and a boy). How many girls (female, not adult) are there in the village? Since there are no girls among the visitors, they may be removed from consideration leaving 49 people, 23 male, 16 adult (8 couples). If M and A are the sets of males and adults, respectively, the set of girls is $M' \cap A'$. Now $M' = (M' \cap A)\ \cup\ (M' \cap A')$. Also, M' has $49 - 23 = 26$ elements and $M' \cap A$ has 8 elements. Since $M' \cap A$ and $M' \cap A'$ have no elements in common, $M' \cap A'$ must have $26 - 8 = 18$ elements. Thus there are 18 girls in the village.

B. H. Arnold, *Oregon State University*

Bibliography

Fehr, Howard F., and others, *Introduction to Sets, Probability and Hypothesis Testing* (Heath 1964).
Kamke, E., *Theory of Sets* (Dover 1950).
National Council of Teachers of Mathematics, *Sets* (1964).
Pinter, Charles C., *Set Theory* (Addison-Wesley 1971).
Reigh, Mildred, *Introduction to Sets* (McGraw 1966).
Selby, Samuel, and Sweet, Leonard, *Sets, Relations, Functions*, 2d ed. (McGraw 1969).

SÈTE, set, is a Mediterranean seaport in France, in Hérault department, about 17 miles (27 km) southwest of Montpellier. Formerly called Cette, it is on a sandy strip of land between the Étang de Thau lagoon and the Gulf of Lions. It lies at the base of 591-foot (180-meter) Mont St.-Clair and is intersected by a network of canals.

After Marseille it is France's second Mediterranean port. Noted as a wine export center, Sète also manufactures chemicals, electrical equipment, and wine casks; produces vermouth; and refines petroleum. The port was built during the 17th century by Jean Baptiste Colbert, chief minister of finance under Louis XIV, and was fortified in the 18th century. It suffered heavy damage during World War II. Population: (1968) 40,220.

SETH, in the Old Testament, was the third son of Adam, born after Abel's death, according to Genesis 4:25. Another tradition, based on Genesis 5:3, does not mention Cain and Abel, thus making Seth the first-born son of Adam and Eve. He was the father of Enosh, and the genealogical table in I Chronicles 1:1 mentions him as an ancestor of Noah. Luke included him in the geneology of Christ (Luke 3:38). He was made the object of special reverence by a heretical Jewish sect called the Sethites.

SETI I, se'tē (reigned c.1303–1290 B. C.), was the second king of the 19th dynasty of Egypt. The son of Ramses I and father of Ramses II, Seti restored much of the territory and prestige that Egypt had lost during the end of the 18th dynasty. He fought successfully in Palestine and against the Libyans and made peace with the Hittites. He built much of the Hypostyle Hall at Karnak and his tomb at Thebes.

SÉTIF, sä-tēf', is a city in northeastern Algeria, in the department of the same name. It is situated at an altitude of about 3,600 feet (1,100 meters), in a cereal-growing region. Connected by rail with Algiers and Constantine, the city is a local trade and communications center. Its industries include carpet manufacturing and flour milling.

Known in ancient times as Sitifis, the city dates back to the 1st century A. D., when the Romans founded it as a veterans' colony. The modern city was built by the French on the ruins of the ancient town. Population: (1966) 98,337.

SETON, sē'tən, **Saint Elizabeth Ann** (1774–1821), American Roman Catholic religious leader, who was the first native-born North American to be canonized. She founded the first American community of the Daughters (or Sisters) of Charity of St. Vincent de Paul.

Elizabeth Ann Bayley was born in New York, N. Y., on Aug. 28, 1774. The well-educated, devoutly Episcopalian daughter of a noted physician, she married the merchant William Seton in 1794, had five children, and also found time to help the poor. When Seton lost his fortune and his health, she accompanied him on a therapeutic voyage to Italy in 1803 to visit friends, the Filicchi family, in Livorno. They consoled her at Seton's death six weeks later and introduced her to Catholicism. She returned to New York and joined the Roman Catholic Church in 1805.

Elizabeth's family and friends, who shared the strong anti-Catholic prejudice of that era, opposed her conversion and abandoned the practically destitute widow. In 1808 she accepted the invitation of Father L. W. V. Dubourg, superior of the Sulpicians, to found a girls' school in Baltimore. Several women offered their aid, and Dubourg and Bishop Carroll of Baltimore gave her a rule for a religious community. Mother Seton moved to Emmitsburg, Md., in 1809 and in 1812 adopted a modified rule of the Daughters of Charity. She and her congregation devoted themselves to care of the sick and the poor and especially to teaching, largely shaping the American parochial school system. Several other independent congregations are derived from that of Mother Seton. She died in Emmitsburg on Jan. 4, 1821, and was canonized in 1975. Her feast day is January 4.

Further Reading: Melville, Annabell, *Elizabeth Bayley Seton, 1774–1821* (Scribner 1960).

SETON, sē'tən, **Ernest Thompson** (1860–1946), American naturalist, illustrator, and writer. He was born Ernest Seton Thompson in South Shields, England, on Aug. 14, 1860, and was taken to Canada as a child. He studied art at the Royal Academy in London and gained his knowledge of animals and woodcraft in the wilds of Canada and the western United States.

The success of Seton's story collection *Wild Animals I Have Known* (1898; new ed., 1942) led him to write and illustrate some 40 other books. He also lectured widely and led scouting and woodcraft activities for young people. Among his works are the stories *The Trail of the Sandhill Stag* (1899), *The Biography of a Grizzly* (1900), and *The Lives of the Hunted* (1901) and his autobiography *The Trail of an Artist-Naturalist* (1940). He died in Santa Fe, N. Mex., on Oct. 23, 1946.

Anya Seton (1916–   ), his daughter, was a successful novelist, whose works include *My Theodosia* (1941), the story of Aaron Burr's daughter; and *Dragonwyck* (1944), a Gothic novel with a Hudson River setting.

Further Reading: Wiley, Farida A., ed., *Ernest Thompson Seton's America* (Devin-Adair 1954).

SETON HALL UNIVERSITY, sē'tən, is a private, Roman Catholic, coeducational institution of higher learning, with its main campus in South Orange, N. J. It was founded as Seton Hall College in Madison, N. J., in 1856, and the campus was moved to South Orange in 1860. It was renamed Seton Hall University in 1950.

Seton Hall grants bachelor's degrees in the schools of arts and sciences, education, nursing, and business administration. A college of the university in Paterson, N. J., offers a similar undergraduate program. A school of law is located in Newark. Graduate programs leading to master's degrees are available, and a doctoral program in chemistry is also provided. In the early 1970's, enrollment exceeded 9,000.

SETON-WATSON, se'tən-wot'sən, **Robert William** (1879–1951), British historian. He was born in Ayton, Perthshire, Scotland, on Aug. 20, 1879. He was educated at New College, Oxford (B. A., 1902; D. Litt., 1910), and he studied at the universities of Berlin, Paris, and Vienna. An expert on central Europe and the Balkans, he was professor of central European history at the University of London (1922–1945) and professor of Czechoslovak studies at Oxford (1945–1949). He founded the magazine *New Europe* (1916), and was joint editor, with Sir Bernard Pares, of the *Slavonic Review* (1922–1949). He died in Skye, Scotland, on July 25, 1951.

Seton-Watson's works include *The Southern Slav Question* (1911), *The Rise of Nationality in the Balkans* (1917), *Europe in the Melting Pot* (1919), *Slovakia Then and Now* (1931), *Britain in Europe, 1789–1914* (1937), *Britain and the Dictators* (1938), *From Munich to Danzig* (1939), and *History of the Czechs and Slovaks* (1943).

SETTER. Any of several breeds of dogs originally trained to crouch in a set position on finding game. See ENGLISH SETTER; GORDON SETTER; IRISH SETTER.

SETTIGNANO, Desiderio da. See DESIDERIO DA SETTIGNANO.

SETTLE, set'əl, **Elkanah** (1648–1724), English dramatist, chiefly remembered for his controversies with John Dryden. He was born in Dunstable, on Feb. 1, 1648, and studied for a time at Oxford. The first of his rather bombastic plays was *Cambyses, King of Persia* (1666), followed by *The Empress of Morocco,* which was performed twice at Whitehall Palace before being presented on the public stage in 1670. Dryden, who saw Settle as a threat to his position as the major court dramatist, criticized *The Empress* in a pamphlet composed with John Crowne and Thomas Shadwell. Settle replied with a pamphlet criticizing Dryden's play *Conquest of Granada,* and Dryden in turn satirized him in his poem *Absalom and Achitophel* (1681), referring to him as "Doeg." This evoked two more pamphlets from Settle.

In 1691, Settle was made poet laureate of London. He died in London on Feb. 12, 1724.

SETTLEMENT HOUSE, a social welfare agency or neighborhood center, staffed by trained and sympathetic workers who study the needs of a particular local community by participating in its life and by enlisting the assistance of local people. They devise and carry out a program of services to individuals, families, groups, and organizations that supplements and reinforces those of existing institutions.

History. The first university settlement, Toynbee Hall, was founded in east London in 1884 by Samuel Augustus Barnett, vicar of St. Jude's Parish and later canon of Westminster. His colleagues were men from Oxford and Cambridge universities. Barnett used the term "settlement" to describe a group of professional persons who live in a working-class neighborhood and identify themselves with its life as a means of understanding and improving conditions. He sought a way to bring people together across economic and social barriers, so that they might learn from each other and thereby build a richer life both for themselves and for the nation as a whole. The motivation of the early residents of Toynbee Hall was religious, but they conceived of the settlement as a nonsectarian agency. They became identified with the local community—its school, politics, and everyday life.

The settlement movement in the United States began with the establishment of Neighborhood Guild, now University Settlement, on the lower East Side of New York by Stanton Coit in 1886. Among noted pioneers in the movement were Jane Addams, cofounder in 1889 of Hull House in the slums of Chicago, and Lillian D. Wald, who with a colleague founded in 1893 a visiting nurse service that formed the nucleus of the Henry Street Settlement in New York City.

The National Federation of Settlements and Neighborhood Centers was founded in 1911 by settlements in the United States. Similar federations also exist in Austria, Canada, Denmark, Finland, France, Germany, Britain, the Netherlands, Norway, and Sweden. In 1926 the various national federations formally established the International Federation of Settlements, which would later be represented by observers at the United Nations.

Organization. Insofar as major objectives and policies are concerned, settlements are governed by boards of directors or trustees, representing the contributing public and sponsoring organizations and, in many cases, including members

NANCY HAYS, FROM MONKMEYER

The settlement house serves as a center of athletic and creative activities for neighborhood children.

from the neighborhoods served. The board is the legal entity that secures funds, acquires, holds, and disposes of real property, employs personnel, and exercises other powers in the name of the settlement.

The services of the settlement to the community are administered and performed by an employed staff under the direction of a head worker, as in the United States, or a warden in Britain chosen by the board. Some services are performed by volunteers under staff supervision.

The board may secure the necessary funds from a community chest, as is done in most U. S. cities, from individual contributors, from foundations and trust funds, from municipal or state governments, or in the form of fees, from the users of settlement services.

Services and Programs. Settlement houses, in their aims and operations, are based on the conviction that neighborhood environment affects the development of individual and family life, and that citizens working together can effect changes in their environment. Settlements attempt to influence this interaction through the introduction of skilled professional workers. The settlement workers view all individuals and families living in the neighborhood as the settlement's constituency, rather than merely those who participate in group activities under settlement auspices. The board and staff conceive their responsibility to be to a whole neighborhood, or district, which may include two or more neighborhoods, rather than to any single age, cultural, racial, or religious group within the community.

The "neighborhood," as the term is used by settlement workers, is the geographical area in which most of the functional needs of preadolescent children are met. Here are the family dwelling and usually the elementary school, the church, the grocery, pharmacy, and candy store. Here also is a play space for small children. The nature of neighborhood life is a major concern of settlements, because neighborhood environment affects greatly the character of family life and the development of children. The neighborhood is used as a laboratory, in which social needs are studied. Meeting these needs may involve the provision of specific services by the settlement or the assistance of other agencies.

The service programs of settlements vary with the culture, economic condition, educational experience, and social problems of the people in the respective neighborhoods. In general, the settlement's services consist of appraisal of needs, location of institutions and services available to meet these needs, assistance to persons in making use of services, and establishment of new services when necessary in order to demonstrate the need and ways of meeting it to the general community.

Specific services to individuals usually include counseling on personal problems, providing an opportunity for self-expression through one or more of the arts, and assistance in making use of community services. In addition, settlements are family agencies, extending recreational and informational services to all members of the family.

A continuing service of most settlements is the provision of opportunities for participation in group activities. The various groups meet during leisure hours. Some of them are designed to meet the members' needs for sociability and neighborliness. Others comprise persons who share an interest in art, music, handicrafts, cooking, or dramatics. Still others bring together persons who want to effect some change in the neighborhood, such as the establishment of a playground, the erection of a new school, the removal of health hazards, or public service improvements. These groups, especially in the United States, depend heavily on social workers.

The Individual Worker. The settlement worker identifies himself personally and professionally with the problems of the neighborhood in which he works. Many early settlements were established on the assumption that residence in the settlement's building, or at least in the immediate vicinity, was indispensable for the achievement of this identification. Later, a number of settlement workers questioned the necessity of residence in the settlement building. In Britain differences of opinion on this question resulted in the formation of two associations, the British Association of Residential Settlements, which insisted on residence, and the Educational Settlements Association, which did not require it. In both the United States and France, residential and nonresidential settlements have combined in single national federations. Differing views on the question of residence do not, however, indicate any substantial difference of opinion about the real identification of the staff with the social problems of the neighborhood.

From the beginning, settlement houses have sought to reform the social order in those respects in which it worked injustice or uncalled-for hardships on disadvantaged members of society. They are usually not content to perform palliative services. Rather, their emphasis is on the removal of conditions that cause hardships, though it is often necessary to give immediate help in emergencies. Settlements are firmly committed to democratic methods in bringing about social change: methods that include education, discussion, and citizens' activity through legitimate groups of their own choosing and creation.

JOHN McDOWELL, *Former Executive Director*
National Federation of Settlements
and Neighborhood Centers

SETÚBAL, sə-tōō'väl, is a seaport in south central Portugal and the capital of Setúbal district. It is on the Sado River estuary, 20 miles (32 km) southeast of Lisbon, and has a fine harbor. Muscatel wines, oranges, and salt are among its exports, and it has a major sardine canning industry. The town was a favorite royal residence in 1481–1495, under John II. Most of its historic buildings were destroyed in 1755 in an earthquake. Population: (1960) 44,435.

SEURAT, sû-rä', **Georges Pierre** (1859–1891), French painter, who was the originator of the neoimpressionist style, also called pointillism, or divisionism. Seurat replaced the irregular, spontaneous brushstrokes of the impressionists with carefully placed small dots of pure color, planned to fuse in the eye of the beholder and to create, at some distance, the effect of mixed colors with subtle gradations of hue and tone. The style was based on scientific theories of color and optics of the time, but Seurat added to these formulas a talent for stylization, an eye for the humorous and the bizarre, and a highly decorative sense of composition that made his personal vision the focus of a highly influential movement in modern art.

Life. Seurat was born on Dec. 2, 1859, in Paris, where he lived for most of his life. He studied at the École des Beaux-Arts in 1878–1879 and served a year of military duty before devoting himself to mastering drawing. His dark, rich drawing style, using a type of hard crayon on rough paper, emphasizes form rather than line. The rough paper caused a stippled effect suggestive of the pointillist technique that he was beginning to formulate in his paintings.

By the early 1880's, Seurat's research into the color theories of Michel Eugène Chevreul, Édouard Rood, and other scientists had led him to pointillism, apparent in its early stage in *The Bathers* (1884; National Gallery, London). This painting, exhibited at the Groupe des Artistes Indépendants in 1884, drew the admiration of Paul Signac, who became Seurat's close friend and follower. Camille Pissarro, another convert to neoimpressionism, brought Seurat into the last impressionist exhibit (1886), at which he showed *Sunday Afternoon on the Island of La Grande Jatte* (1885; Art Institute of Chicago). The movement grew, dominating the exhibits of the Société des Artistes Indépendants from 1884 through 1891. The critic Félix Fénélon became the spokesman for the movement, and Signac formulated its theories in his book *From Delacroix to Neo-Impressionism* (1899). After 1887, when Signac, Seurat, and Pissarro exhibited in Brussels, that city became a second center of neoimpressionism, attracting the allegiance of Henry van de Velde, Theo van Rysselberghe, and other painters. Seurat died in Paris on March 29, 1891, at the height of his career.

Work. Seurat's output was not large, since he worked slowly and methodically, often on very large canvases. His major paintings, besides

SEURAT'S *Sunday Afternoon on the Island of La Grande Jatte* (1888) silhouettes figures and uses the pointillist technique of applying color in dots.

The *Bathers* and the *Grand Jatte*, are *The Models* (1886; Barnes Foundation, Merion, Pa.); *The Chahut* (1889–1891; Kröller-Müller Museum, Otterloo); *The Parade* (1889; Metropolitan Museum, New York); and *The Circus* (1890–1891; Louvre, Paris). He also painted a number of landscapes from sketches made during summers spent at seaside resorts and about 160 small wood panels, mostly studies for his larger works.

ALFRED NEUMEYER, *Author of "The Search for Meaning in Modern Art"*

Further Reading: Dorra, Henri, and Rewald, John, *Seurat: Catalogue Raisonné* (1959); Herbert, Robert L., ed., *Seurat's Drawings* (Burns & MacEachern 1963); Homer, William, *Seurat and the Science of Painting* (Harvard Univ. Press 1964); Russell, John, *Seurat* (Burns & MacEachern 1965).

SEUSS, Dr. See GEISEL, THEODOR SEUSS.

SEVAN, Lake, se-vän', a lake in the Armenian republic of the USSR. It is the largest lake in the Caucasus and lies at an altitude of 6,285 feet (1,916 meters). The lake is noted for its fish, particularly Sevan trout, and has been developed as a recreation area. Hydroelectric projects initially reduced its area and lowered the water level, but Soviet engineers diverted river waters to halt the shrinkage.

SEVAREID, sev'ər-īd, **Eric** (1912–   ), American broadcaster and author. Arnold Eric Sevareid was born in Velva, N. Dak., on Nov. 26, 1912. He began his newspaper career as a copyboy on the Minneapolis *Journal* in 1931. After graduation from the University of Minnesota in 1935, he became a reporter on the Minneapolis *Star* (1936–1937) and later a reporter and city editor on the Paris edition of the New York *Herald-Tribune* (1938–1939). After joining the staff of the Columbia Broadcasting System as a European correspondent in 1939, he gained distinction for his coverage of World War II. After the war he continued as a CBS correspondent and news analyst in Washington, D. C., and elsewhere.

His book *Not So Wild a Dream* (1946) was praised as a fine piece of reporting, both of his own life and thought and of his war experiences. His other writings include *Canoeing with the Cree* (1935), an account of a canoeing adventure (for young readers), and *This Is Eric Sevareid* (1964), a collection of his newspaper columns and radio and television scripts dealing with conservation, politics, civil rights, and other subjects.

SEVASTOPOL, sev-əstō'pəl, is a city on the Black Sea in the USSR. It is in the southwest Crimea, in the Ukrainian republic. Another form of its name is Sebastopol. The city is on Sevastopol Bay, the Black Sea's best natural harbor, which is large and deep. The main section of the city is on a slope between the bay and its southern arm. The city is an important naval base and shipbuilding center, and there are some light manufacturing industries.

Southeast of the center of the city is the Malakhov fortress, which guarded approaches to the harbor and was a focal point during the Crimean War siege. The city has a museum devoted to the history of the city during the Crimean War (1854–1856). On a promontory west of the city is the site of the ancient Greek colony of Chersonesus. Founded in the 6th century B. C., the colony continued as a trading center under the Roman and Byzantine empires.

Sevastopol itself was originally the Tatar village of Akhtiar, founded in the 13th century, and was annexed under Catherine II the Great in 1783. Thereafter it was the principal Russian naval base on the Black Sea. It was besieged by Allied forces for 11 months during the Crimean War, the Russians retiring in September 1855, after the city had been destroyed. French and British engineers then blew up the docks and forts, which, by the Treaty of Paris (1856), were not to be rebuilt. These restrictions were annulled in 1871, and the docks and forts were restored. See also CRIMEAN WAR.

Since 1890, the port has been primarily a military base, guarding the Black Sea entrance to the Ukraine and to the Caucasus, and commercial trade has been limited. During World War II, Sevastopol underwent a siege, comparable to the one it experienced during the Crimean War, before falling to the Germans in July 1942. The city received a tremendous amount of damage when Soviet forces stormed it in 1944. Population: (1970) 229,000.

SEVEN CITIES OF CÍBOLA. See Cíbola, Seven Cities of.

SEVEN DEADLY SINS, seven vices that commonly give rise to numerous other sins. According to Saint Thomas Aquinas and other theologians, they are pride, covetousness, lust, envy, gluttony, anger, and sloth. The vices in themselves may not be particularly serious, but they frequently are the root cause of actions or omissions that are regarded as grave sins. They are considered "deadly" because they are directly opposed to the development of virtue.

SEVEN HILLS, a city in northern Ohio, in Cuyahoga county is about 10 miles (16 km) south of Cleveland, which it serves as a suburb. It is principally a residential community. Seven Hills was incorporated as a township in 1923. It became a village in 1927, and achieved the status of a city in 1961. During the 1960's the city grew rapidly, more than doubling its population in 10 years. It has a mayor-council form of government. Population: 13,650.

SEVEN PINES, Battle of, in the American Civil War, fought on May 31–June 1, 1862, about 9 miles (14 km) east of Richmond, Va. See Civil War–*The Military Campaigns.*

SEVEN SEAS is a phrase used to connote all of the seas and oceans of the world. The origin of the phrase is uncertain, but the number seven has had mystical significance to sea travelers since ancient times. As presently used, the phrase is usually taken to include the major divisions of the world ocean: the Antarctic, Arctic, North and South Atlantic, Indian, and North and South Pacific Oceans.

SEVEN SLEEPERS OF EPHESUS, ef'ə-səs, a legend widely disseminated in manuscripts of both Western and Eastern Christians, and even found in Mohammedan sources. The earliest preserved record of it is a Syriac text from the beginning of the 6th century. The story relates that during the persecution of the Christians under Emperor Decius (reigned 249–251), seven noble youths of Ephesus, having refused to worship pagan idols, concealed themselves in a nearby cavern, the entrance of which was closed by order of the Emperor. The persecuted youths immediately fell into a deep slumber, from which they were accidentally awakened in the reign of Theodosius II (reigned 408–450), after the lapse of two centuries. The stone blocking the entrance to their retreat having been removed by a shepherd, one of their number went to the city to purchase bread. He was astonished to see the Christian cross erected in the city, and the citizens were confounded by his antiquated dress and the obsolete money he offered in payment for bread. Suspected of having found a secret treasure, he was carried before a judge, to whom he related his miraculous story. The bishop of Ephesus, the magistrates, and even the Emperor himself hastened to the cave and found the sleepers still bearing the bloom of youth. Before they expired, one of them explained to the Emperor that God had caused them to fall asleep to demonstrate the proof of the resurrection.

SEVEN WEEKS' WAR. See Austro-Prussian War.

SEVEN WONDERS OF THE WORLD, a selection of seven ancient works of art and architecture, regarded by the Greek and Roman world of the Alexandrian epoch and later as awe-inspiring and preeminent in size or splendor. According to the most popular tradition they are: (1) the pyramids of Egypt; (2) the hanging gardens of Semiramis and the walls of Babylon; (3) the statue of the Olympian Zeus by Phidias, at Olympia; (4) the Colossus of Rhodes; (5) the temple of Artemis at Ephesus; (6) the Mausoleum at Halicarnassus; and (7) the Lighthouse at Alexandria. Only the pyramids have survived.

Egyptian Pyramids. About 80 pyramids built in ancient Egypt survive. Most are situated on the Nile's west bank near Cairo, and were erected in the period 2650–1800 B.C. by Egyptian monarchs to serve as their tombs. The earliest example, a step pyramid with six tiers, is that of King Djoser at Saqqara.

The largest pyramids are those at Giza, built for pharaohs of the Old Kingdom: Khufu (Cheops), Khafre (Chephren), and Menkaure (Mycerinus). The first of these, called the Great Pyramid because it is the largest, measures about 755 feet (230 meters) at the base on each of its four sides and covers nearly 13 acres (5.2 hectares). It originally reached a height of 481 feet (147 meters). It is now believed that 100,000 workers, employed only during the Nile flood season, could have built the Great Pyramid in 20 years.

Hanging Gardens of Babylon. Both the city walls and the hanging gardens that Greek travelers found so impressive were of the "new" city erected subsequent to Sennacherib's destruction of Babylon in 689 B.C. The Chaldean kings, Nabopolassar (reigned 626–605) and his son Nebuchadnezzar II (reigned 605–562) were builders of the mighty walls described by Herodotus and Ctesias in the 5th century B.C.

Herodotus ignores the hanging gardens, but other writers describe them as a series of terraces rising along the Euphrates bank and connected by marble stairways. Planted with a profusion of trees, shrubs, and flowers, the gardens were watered by fountains fed through pipes from cisterns in the topmost terrace. Nebuchadnezzar had the world's most celebrated gardens developed as an adjunct of his palace, but the Greeks ascribed them to Semiramis, a legendary queen of Babylon, daughter of the goddess Derceto.

Statue of Zeus by Phidias. Like the Athena statue for the Parthenon, Phidias' colossal statue of Zeus was a chryselephantine work, the flesh parts of ivory on a wood or stone core, the drapery and other ornaments of gold. The sculptor represented the god crowned with an olive wreath and seated on a cedarwood throne that was adorned with gold, ivory, ebony, and precious stones. In his right hand Zeus held an ivory and gold statue of Victory, in his left a scepter surmounted by an eagle. The statue was placed in the great temple of Zeus in the sacred grove at Olympia (completed in 457 B.C.) and nearly reached the room's 60-foot (18-meter) roof. Emperor Theodorus I removed it to Constantinople, where it was destroyed in a fire in 475 A.D.

Colossus of Rhodes. The statue of the sun, popularly called the Colossus of Rhodes, was designed by Chares of Lindus and erected overlooking the harbor of Rhodes. It required 12 years to build (292–280 B.C.) but survived only 56

**SEVEN WONDERS
OF THE
ANCIENT WORLD**

1. Egyptian Pyramids at Giza

2. Hanging Gardens of Babylon

3. Statue of Zeus at Olympia

4. Colossus of Rhodes

5. Temple of Artemis at Ephesus

6. Mausoleum at Halicarnassus

7. Lighthouse at Alexandria

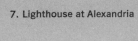

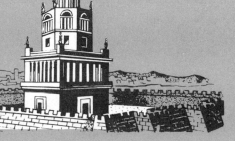

years before it fell during an earthquake in 224
B. C. The statue was upward of 105 feet (32
meters) tall. It is said that the fragments remained *in situ* for 896 years until a Muslim general, in 672 A. D., sold them to a Jew of Emesa.

Temple of Artemis. The famous temple dedicated to Artemis at Ephesus, chief of the 12
Ionian cities in Asia Minor, was designed and
built by the architect Chersiphron in the 6th century B. C. Croesus contributed to the building
fund. The temple was burned by Herostratus in
356 B. C., but it was rebuilt by the joint efforts
of all the Ionian states. It was again destroyed
when the Goths sacked the city in 262 A. D.
Fragments of the columns of the original temple
are in the British Museum.

Mausoleum at Halicarnassus. After the death in
353 B. C. of Mausolus, king of Caria in Asia
Minor, his widow, Queen Artemisia, determined
to commemorate him with the most costly memorial. The structure, designed by Pythius and
adorned by sculptures of Scopas and Praxiteles,
was destroyed by an earthquake before 1400 A. D.

Lighthouse at Alexandria. Erected about 270
B. C., in the reign of Ptolemy II Philadelphus, on
an islet off the harbor of Alexandria, this lighthouse (pharos) was the prototype of all the
similar structures built on the coasts of the Roman Empire.

SEVEN YEARS' WAR, a general European conflict from 1756 to 1763. A primary theme was
the struggle for supremacy in Germany between
Prussia under the ambitious Frederick II the
Great and Austria under Maria Theresa, but there
were also colonial wars between France and Britain for control of North America and India.
Britain, anxious to reduce France's power and to
protect Hannover, the crown's Continental possession, was Prussia's main ally. Austria was
aided by France, Russia, Sweden, most of the
German states of the Holy Roman Empire and
Spain. The basis of Austrian discontent during
this era was the settlement of the War of the
Austrian Succession in 1748, which had confirmed Frederick's possession of Silesia, formerly
an Austrian territory.

Open hostilities were preceded by a European
diplomatic revolution. Austria had long been
friendly with Britain and hostile toward French
ambitions. However, Count von Kaunitz, the
Austrian chancellor, believed that Austria first
had to defeat Prussia. Kaunitz therefore suggested an Austro-French alliance. Meanwhile,
Britain approached Frederick II and proposed an
alliance that would protect Hannover from France.
By the Convention of Westminster (1755), Frederick guaranteed Hannover's neutrality. France
then concluded the Treaty of Versailles, a defensive alliance, with Austria in 1756. Russia
offered to support Austria with troops, and Sweden and other states indicated that they opposed
Prussia.

Early Stages of the War. Anticipating attack,
Frederick seized the initiative in August 1756 by
invading neighboring Saxony, a rich area that he
used for financing future operations. Austria
tried to join forces with the Saxons, but Frederick
prevented this maneuver, and the isolated Saxons
capitulated in October.

Prussia's opponents gradually organized, and
in January 1757, Austria and Russia signed an
offensive alliance. This was followed in May by
a Franco-Austrian offensive alliance. Frederick,
facing superior forces, took the offensive again,
invading Bohemia in April and advancing to
Prague, where he routed a large Austrian army
in May. By June the Austrians had regrouped,
and under Field Marshal von Daun they advanced on Frederick. The Prussians turned from
Prague and met the Austrians at Kolin on June
18, 1757. Frederick suffered a sharp defeat and
retreated from Bohemia.

In the west the French pushed back an army
commanded by Britain's Duke of Cumberland,
defeating it at Hastenbeck in July and forcing it
to agree to disband. Frederick's difficulties were
compounded by Sweden's invasion of Pomerania
in September and by the arrival in East Prussia
of a huge Russian army, which inflicted a crushing defeat on the Prussians.

Surrounded and threatened, Frederick scored
notable victories at Rossbach and Leuthen in
late 1757 and at Zorndorf in August 1758. The
British and Hannoverians, previously ineffective,
improved after William Pitt came to power in
Britain and defeated the French at Krefeld in
June 1758. Frederick also suffered setbacks, and
these soon left him vulnerable. Daun defeated
the Prussians at Hochkirch in October 1758, and
the Austrian and Russian armies linked up in
1759. In August, Frederick attacked them at
Kunersdorf, receiving a sharp defeat that permitted Daun to take Dresden.

End of the War. During the last years of the
war, the Prussians were on the defensive, and
victories like Liegnitz and Torgau in 1760
were more than offset by coalition successes, like
the Russian burning of Berlin in 1760 and their
devastating incursions into Prussian territory. By
the end of 1761 it appeared that Prussia would
be defeated and dismembered. Fortunately for
Prussia, Empress Elizabeth of Russia died in January 1762, and her successor, Peter III, was a
devoted admirer of Frederick. Peter withdrew
the Russian troops, and, although he was soon
overthrown, his wife, Catherine II, kept the
Russians out of the conflict.

Inconclusive fighting preceded the armistice
agreements of late 1762, which were followed by
peace treaties in 1763. The Franco-British treaty
was signed in Paris on Feb. 10, 1763. It dealt
primarily with colonial affairs and made Britain
the preeminent colonial power. The Treaty of
Hubertusburg, signed by Prussia, Austria, and
Saxony on Feb. 15, 1763, confirmed Prussia as a
major European force. Although Prussia had
been on the verge of defeat, Frederick lost no
territory, as the treaty restored the prewar status
quo.

Colonial Wars. The struggle for supremacy in
North America pitted Britain against France.
War broke out in 1754 and continued intermit-
tently until settled by the Treaty of Paris. The
second major area of conflict was in India, where
Robert Clive decisively outmaneuvered his French
adversaries. See also FRENCH AND INDIAN WAR;
INDIA—*History*.

Further Reading: Dorn, Walter L., *Competition for
Empire, 1740–1763* (Harper 1940); Kennett, Lee, *French
Armies in the Seven Years' War* (Duke Univ. Press
1967); Savory, Reginald, *His Britannic Majesty's Army
in Germany During the Seven Years' War* (Oxford 1966).

SEVENTEEN-YEAR LOCUST, a type of cicada insect abundant in the northeastern part of the
United States. It has a 17-year life cycle, the
longest developmental cycle of any insect known.
See also CICADA.

SEVENTEENTH CENTURY. Most of the developments of the 17th century that were crucial in the molding of the modern world were neither begun nor completed between 1601 and 1700. Although many of these developments were European in origin or direction, each major sphere of the globe had an important and lasting impact on other spheres.

The Scientific Revolution, colonial expansion, and the growth of the slave trade are outstanding examples of how 17th century Europe shaped the world of subsequent times. But the revolution in science that overthrew the older conception of the universe depended on the work of thinkers and experimenters of the 16th century, and the principles formulated by Newton have been modified since his death in 1727. European direction of the African slave trade began in the 16th century, and the trade itself reached its height about 1800. Europe's colonial expansion, which started in the late 15th century, was accelerated in the 17th century, and during that period it was led by different peoples and assumed new forms. In both its positive and negative aspects it continued into the 20th century.

In the 17th century, Asian states from Ottoman Turkey to Japan had to make many adjustments because of the European presence on their land or maritime frontiers. But Asian influences on Europe were considerable. The role of Asia in the making of Europe before, during, and after the 17th century has been investigated extensively by the American scholar Donald F. Lach.

The fundamental part that Africa has played in the shaping of American societies, though more important in Brazil than in the future United States during the 17th century, is now receiving its due attention. The Brazilian scholar Gilberto Freyre pioneered in research on the African contribution to Brazil.

The great influence the Americas have had on the rest of the world was felt in the 17th century, although the North American continent was just being settled. American food plants and minerals were making their impact on Europe, Asia, and Africa. Of all these products, peanuts, potatoes, maize, tobacco, and chocolate were destined to affect the modern world far more than American gold and silver.

1. Europe

In the first half of the 16th century, Lutheranism had firmly entrenched itself in northern Germany and had spread to the Scandinavian countries so that the Baltic had become almost a Lutheran lake. In the second half of the same century, a group of interconnected conflicts in the neighborhood of the English Channel had failed to bring about the suppression of Calvinism in Britain, Holland, and France. From 1576, and more particularly from 1594, Catholicism in Germany had passed to the counteroffensive, and there its conflict was against aggressive Calvinism, while the Lutherans were becoming a conservative interest, anxious for peace.

WARFARE

When the 17th century opened, the forces of the Reformation and the Counter-Reformation seemed to be gathering themselves for a final struggle in Germany, where imperial authority was in eclipse and imperial institutions were now failing to function. The whole balance of the

Cathedra Petri (Chair of Peter), by the 17th century genius Bernini, is in the apse of St. Peter's, Rome.

Continent was in question, for a small margin seemed likely to decide whether the Austrian Habsburgs should lose their imperial position or should reassert their authority and combine with the Spanish Habsburgs to dominate Christendom. From the beginning of the 17th century, therefore, western Europe lay under the shadow of a great war. Plans for the establishment of perpetual peace symptomized the growing nervousness and combined with the "appeasement" policy of the Lutherans and of James I of England to give evidence of the horror that war inspired. Proposals for the reunion of Protestants and Catholics were brought out under the shadow of war by Hugo Grotius in Holland, for example, and later by John Durie in England.

Thirty Years' War. The Austrian Habsburgs were in decline at the opening of the century, but during the first decade they were planning to rescue their dynasty, and during the second decade the plans were being put into effect. In 1597 the Counter-Reformation had opened a remarkable new attack in Styria, and the Protestants, who had seemed to be consolidating their victories in the neighboring Habsburg territories, soon saw that they must be prepared to face actual warfare unless they were content to be put into definite retreat.

Beginning in Bohemia, extending to Germany, and moving from there into the region of the Baltic from 1624, the Thirty Years' War (1618–1648) brought the religious conflict in Europe to a climax and raised issues that were bound to affect the fate of the entire West. It gathered into itself all the regional controversies, local disputes, and international rivalries of Christendom and became a more general war than any that had

599

Louis XIV, the "Sun King," ruled France during much of the 17th century. Here, he receives the Great Condé.

preceded it. As long as the Habsburgs went on winning successes in the course of the struggle, their victory at each successive stage only had the effect of bringing into the conflict a new enemy, whose security seemed threatened by their latest advance. Fortunately for Europe, the Ottoman Turks were unable to take advantage of the distracted condition of the Christian countries in this period. The West made such marked improvements in military science during the course of the war that it proved decidedly superior to the East when the Turkish attacks were renewed in the latter half of the century.

The results of the war were: first, the rise of a vast Swedish empire, which went on expanding during most of the century until it comprised almost all the coast of the Baltic; second, the effective origin of the problem of Alsace-Lorraine and the passage of France from a defensive policy to that career of aggression which is associated with the reign of Louis XIV; and, third, the eclipse of the Spanish Habsburgs (who had come near to the domination of Europe in the 1580's) and the further reduction of Habsburg imperial power in Germany, with the result that the Austrian branch of the dynasty concentrated its attention in the future on the consolidation of its group of Danubian territories. The Peace of Westphalia, which concluded the war in 1648, was the first of the series of great international treaties which from that time onward periodically established an order and a territorial arrangement in Europe after a war involving the entire Continent.

Role of Louis XIV. Partly because the Spanish Habsburgs were in decline and Spain itself was economically undermined, partly also because the Austrian Habsburgs were distracted by the renewed attacks of the Turks, the French monarchy under Louis XIV (reigned 1643–1715) embarked on an aggressive course after 1661. Fear of its Continental ascendancy united many nations against it in the League of Augsburg (1686) and the Grand Alliance (1689). As he developed his career of conquest, Louis would cleverly isolate his enemy, reducing to a minimum the need for direct military action. The great development that he gave to the French diplomatic system and the practice of diplomacy had a marked effect on other countries, so that this branch of governmental activity advanced to a new stage. Furthermore, in the conflict against the France of Louis XIV, European statesmen became more conscious than ever before of the principle of the balance of power, and more scientific in their application of it.

MONARCHY

The 17th century marks a critical period in the history of European monarchy, for that institution had to meet a serious challenge in most of the countries of the Continent, as well as in England. This is the period when, in many monarchies and principalities, the conflict between the ruler and the parliamentary systems—the diets or estates—came to a point of critical decision. As in England, the conflict often involved the question of the king's right to keep a standing army and the right of the parliamentary estates to give or withhold their assent to taxation. Now, as at other periods, the needs of the government in time of war, and the growing burden of expense as the methods of warfare developed, had much to do with the development that was given to the structure of the modern state.

Position of the Assemblies. In the various countries of Europe and in many of the principalities of Germany the diets or estates had long held the princely ruler more tightly imprisoned than the English Parliament had done. The extremes to which this had been taken in Bohemia, Hungary, and other Habsburg territories had been from the start one of the main issues involved in the Thirty Years' War.

On the European continent, however, the assertion of "historic rights" against the ruler represented the obstructiveness of a selfish and reactionary nobility that controlled the proceedings in the "parliamentary" assemblies. It was the prince who sought to save the peasantry from the tyranny of its local lords and who represented the general welfare of society against the selfish private privileges of the nobility. It was the prince who more truly represented the community at large and tended to gain the support of the nonnoble classes. The whole general conflict has sometimes been described, therefore, as the struggle of "the State versus the Estates."

Even in the United Provinces of the Netherlands the provincial estates, as they opposed the monarchical and centralizing tendencies of the House of Orange, were reactionary, defending a system of local autonomy and resisting the attempt to weld the provinces into a state. Even in France, where the States General ceased to function after 1614, the Parlement of Paris, consciously attempting to imitate the procedures of the contemporary English Parliament, was in reality supporting ancient privilege and private rights that obstructed the work of government. The vicissitudes of the institution of monarchy, particularly toward the middle of the century, are illustrated by the conflict of the Habsburgs with the Bohemian nobility until 1620 and with the Hungarian nobility throughout the century, the bitter struggle of many German princes (including the Hohenzollern ruler of Brandenburg-Prussia) against their respective systems of estates, the English Civil War and Commonwealth (1642–1660), the French *Fronde* in the period 1648–1653, the "republican" regime of Johan De Witt in Holland (1653–1672), and the ascendancy of the nobles in Denmark and Sweden. The rebellion of Portugal against Spain in 1640 and the great rising of Catalonia in the same year raised similar questions of principle. And the sufferings caused by the Thirty Years' War produced repeated further insurrections on the part of a hungry peasantry, as, for example, the rebellions that took place in Sicily and Naples in 1647–1648.

The Forms of Monarchy. The necessities of war and the requirements of internal order, however, showed that monarchical authority was still indispensable. Most of all there was need for an authority to support the general welfare of society against nobles who refused to regard themselves as subjects, and against sectional groups that refused to bow to the authority of government. In France, where the king had sometimes acted as though he were merely the most privileged of the vested interests of the country, using his power to support one faction against another and sharing out the spoils amongst his favorites, Cardinal Richelieu (chief minister 1624–1642) taught the monarch a higher, superintending role, separating the king's conduct in his private life from his function as the personification of the idea of the state. From 1661, Louis XIV brought this conception of monarchy to its climax and turned it into a work of art, making himself at any rate the greatest "actor of majesty" that Europe had ever seen. Neither Louis nor the monarchs of the next generation succeeded, however, in making the further distinction between the dynastic interests of the royal family and the interests of the body politic as such. The Restoration of 1660 in England, the establishment in 1660–1665 of the most extreme royal absolutism in Denmark, the revival of the authority of the House of Orange in Holland (especially from 1672), the victory of

the Hohenzollern dynasty over the estates in Brandenburg-Prussia (as in 1663 and 1667), and the triumph of the royal power in Sweden in 1680–1682 all signalize the recovery of the principle of monarchy and the restoration of internal stability in the countries of western Europe.

In certain regions—for example, in Mecklenburg, in Poland, and to a considerable degree in Hungary—the monarch failed in the attempt to discipline the nobles into the modern idea of the state. In other regions—particularly in Brandenburg-Prussia and in the Russia of Peter the Great (sole ruler 1689–1725)—the ruler succeeded in turning the nobles into "servants of the state," but only by conniving with them in their oppression of the other classes of society and by giving them governmental authority on their own estates. In these countries there developed on the basis of military needs a secular, utilitarian type of monarchy, more ruthless in its methods than the religious monarchy of Louis XIV. In general the peasantry and the townsmen to the east of the Elbe River suffered in the 17th century a continuation of that decline which had been taking place in the 16th century, so that their position and prospects were worse than they had been in medieval times.

ARTISTIC, INTELLECTUAL, AND RELIGIOUS LIFE

The development of a "Catholic Renaissance" in France, the achievements of Catholic missionaries in all parts of the world, the wide establishment of the Jesuit order, and the victories of Count Tilly and Albrecht von Wallenstein in the early stages of the Thirty Years' War all contributed to a feeling of exultation in Rome at the time when the new Basilica of St. Peter's, the "greatest architectural wonder of the world," had at last been completed. St. Peter's was consecrated in 1626 and remained the real center of artistic activity in Rome throughout the century.

The life of the prosperous Dutch middle class was depicted by Jan Steen in *The Baptismal Party.*

During the pontificate (1623–1644) of Urban VIII, as well as during the reigns of his two successors, Rome was turned into a baroque city, chiefly under the inspiration of the sculptor and architect Lorenzo Bernini and the painter Pietro da Cortona.

The baroque style, greatly patronized by the Jesuits, seemed to express the exuberance of the Counter-Reformation, and it dominated European art for at least a century, spreading from Rome to Spain, Portugal, Austria, Catholic Germany, and Poland, although it had less influence in France and England. It was a dynamic style, seeking dramatic effects and loading churches with ornament and gilding, colored sculptures, and sensuous curves. Behind it was a spirit that seems to have affected painting and poetry, giving therefore a certain unified character to the culture of the time.

Northern Cultural Leadership. Culturally, the 17th century saw the end of the long period of Mediterranean leadership. In the closing decades of the century the remarkable advances that changed the character of Western civilization were centered around the English Channel.

At the beginning of the century Spain was still enjoying its "Golden Age" in literature, the arts, and even science—an age of great originality and of riotous individualism. The influence of Spain was quickly transmitted to the other countries of western Europe and had its part in the development of the culture of Versailles, the flowering of the arts in the reign of Louis XIV of France. At the beginning of the 17th century the genius of Galileo illustrated the important part still played by Italy in the world of science. In the second quarter of the century the Dutch came into their "Golden Age" with a burgher culture that blossomed in literature and art, as well as in technology. Holland acquired an ascendancy, particularly in the Protestant world, and greatly influenced England, for example, and governments such as that of the Great Elector in Brandenburg-Prussia.

The most remarkable transition in the history of Western civilization for over a thousand years, however, took place in the last quarter of the 17th century, at a time when the English, the Dutch, and the French—especially the French Huguenots—were bound together by a close system of intercommunications. They were building up a culture vastly different from that of the Renaissance or of 17th century Spain or of Louis XIV's court of Versailles. At this point in the story the success of the Scientific Revolution coincides with the palpable appearance of what we today would call the modern world.

The Scientific Revolution. It would be proper to regard most of the 17th century as still medieval, for it represented a world and an outlook packed with what we would call archaisms. At its opening men still pictured the physical universe in general in the way they had been doing for centuries. The Renaissance itself had had the effect of making all branches of thought more subservient to ancient Greece than had previously been the case. During most of the century, scholasticism still prevailed in the universities, even in the Protestant world. During most of the century, Aristotle was still the master in natural science, where the ancient syntheses and the ancient modes of explanation remained current.

The Newtonian Synthesis. A new star and a new comet in the later decades of the 16th century had shaken the bases of the ancient astronomy and made it difficult to believe that the planets were attached to crystalline spheres. The consideration of the problem of projectiles had created a similar disturbance in the ancient science of mechanics; for it was difficult to reconcile the behavior of cannon balls with the basic assumption of that science, the assumption that a body could not keep in motion unless its original mover kept on pushing it. These two fundamental problems in astronomy and mechanics became like levers that dislodged an ancient universe and installed a new one, transforming the methods of science and revolutionizing human society. But first there was a period in which the bases of science itself had to be completely reexamined, and the whole question of scientific method was overhauled by 1650 in the work of Galileo, in the writings of Sir Francis Bacon, and in the *Discourse on Method* by René Descartes.

A chain of inquirers from the time of Galileo and Johannes Kepler pursued the crucial problems in astronomy and mechanics and gradually disengaged the problem of gravitation, until in the 1670's a host of scientists in both England and France were touching the fringes of the final synthesis and bringing the scientific movement to its most exhilarating period. Galileo's way of mathematizing a problem and producing a formula had been geared to a more economical and strategic use of the experimental method. The effects of gravity, the path of falling bodies, the orbits of the planets, the pull of the stone on the sling that swirls it around, the irregularities in the movements of the planets as they came into proximity with one another, the more accurate measurement of celestial distances—these were the homely elemental problems that were being studied, and the results of earlier work on them were being refined and correlated.

The century had seen various attempts to create vast mythical "systems of the universe," which were born out of high flights of philosophical speculation. But a humbler approach to the problem of nature now produced such results in its treatment of a few pivotal points as to revolutionize man's picture of the universe and change forever his views about the way in which the problems of the physical world should be tackled. One imagined the moon being attracted to the earth like a falling apple; yet, if that were the case, why did it not drop completely into the earth? If, however, one imagined the moon as a stone swirling around the earth in an invisible sling, one could then ask whether the tendency of the moon to fall into the earth might not exactly counteract the tendency of the moon to press out of the sling, making a beeline into empty space.

It was Sir Isaac Newton—born in 1642, the year of Galileo's death—who worked out the correspondences. He showed with what nicety the heavenly bodies were mathematically balanced and developed on these lines a vast synthesis that presented a new system of the skies. Mechanics and astronomy were fused into a comprehensive whole; things terrestrial and things celestial were now comprised in a single fabric of explanation. One system of laws prevailed over the entire universe. For the first time science achieved a plausible and satisfactory explanation of a moving earth. For the first time the ideal to which so many of the 17th century scientists had been pressing—the ideal of a universe reduced to a

The Thirty Years' War ravaged central Europe from 1618 to 1648, killing a large part of Germany's population.

species of clockwork—seemed within reach. The new developments in scientific method were vindicated. And in a single stroke Newton completed the overthrow of the authority of both the ancient world and the medieval.

Other Developments in Science. It was the concentration on two pivotal problems that set human thought on a new path, and it was the developments in mechanics and astronomy that changed the very character of natural science. But other movements throughout the 17th century also helped to usher in a new scientific era. By 1600, Europe had at last appropriated and assimilated all that it had to learn from the scientific teaching of the ancient world. The 17th century saw the final example of the influence of ancient Greece: the old atomic theory was not only revived but was given a form that made it tenable for Christians. And, as Bacon had predicted, it led to a more subtle feeling for the complexity of the internal structure of matter, it generated new types of hypotheses, and it facilitated the quest for a mechanistic explanation of natural phenomena.

The 17th century saw the development of the important elementary scientific instruments—the telescope, the microscope, the thermometer, the pendulum clock, the barometer, the air pump, and the blowpipe. Certain anatomical discoveries at different dates in Padua enable one to see how slow had been the transmission, establishment, and recognition of scientific discoveries in the 16th century. The development of the periodical press in the 17th century, the increased facilities for scientific correspondence, the foundation of scientific societies (which helped to finance experiments and to publish results), and the rise of public interest in the work of scientists all transformed the system of scientific communication and greatly speeded up the European repercussions of work achieved in any locality. Technological needs, in such fields as shipbuilding, navigation, and hydraulics, gave a stimulus to many branches of inquiry.

If the universities resisted the new science a campaign was conducted against their ancient curriculum; other institutions provided centers for scientific research; and royalty patronized this work. Treatises were written in the vernaculars, and the appeal was made from the learned world to that new arbiter in the world of thought, the general reading public. Science was being popularized; for example, in 1686, the year before Newton's *Principia* transformed the system of the universe, Bernard Le Bovier de Fontenelle in France produced *The Plurality of Worlds, a* work that summed up the pre-Newtonian astronomy in a dialogue intended to be as diverting for fashionable ladies as the latest novel. The 17th century thus exhibited a great tidal rise of science, the effects of which were widely felt in the world at large.

Religion. The medieval character of much of the 17th century is illustrated by the leading part that religion played in the culture and the politics of the age. This feature is apparent equally in the England of Archbishop William Laud and the England of Oliver Cromwell. Sometimes it appears more clearly after 1600 than in the previous 50 years, as in the case of the remarkable "Catholic Renaissance" in 17th century France. Under these conditions, political theory itself was generally conducted within the framework of ecclesiastical thought, and it is within such a framework that one must consider Richelieu's doctrines of government as well as the conception of monarchy that was current in the France of Louis XIV. Also, it was within such a framework that there emerged a conception of *raison d'état* ("interest of state") that became significant in the 17th century.

Toleration, which in the 16th century had been not an ideal but a compromise—a recognized departure from the ideal, even sometimes a mere measure of *Realpolitik*—established itself more genuinely as a religious principle among some of the sects of the 17th century. It was only gradually, however, that even the various branches of

Protestantism learned to tolerate one another. And if freedom came to be enlarged during the course of the 17th century this was partly due to war-weariness and the rise of religious indifference, and partly to the desire of rulers to retain or recruit populations for purposes of economic recovery.

Because the state kept watch over the general mundane interests of society instead of merely behaving as the servant of one church against another, it tended to emerge above the rival faiths, and these tended to be viewed rather as mere parties within the state. The secular government increased its authority, emerging as the effective umpire or arbiter. The older idea of the nation as a religious society gave way, as the century proceeded, to the modern conception of the secular state.

Christianity itself grew unusually weak in the closing decades of the 17th century, perhaps because the religious conflicts had been too bitter and the fanaticism had been too intense. The scientific movement had come to its climax in Sir Isaac Newton without making any essential breach with religion. But the traditional religious outlook, like the traditional university teaching, had tended to lose credit in the accompanying controversies. Christianity also lost one of its great incidental supports in the general overthrow of authority that occurred—the discrediting of the customary appeal to the teaching that had been handed down from the past. Newton's achievement was to become—against the wish of Newton himself—the basis for a completely mechanistic view of the universe, and the churches at the end of the 17th century were not in the best condition for meeting the challenge presented by the new science.

Isaac Newton, a leader of the 17th century Scientific Revolution, investigating the principles of light.

SOCIAL AND ECONOMIC LIFE

The transition to the modern world was marked by a widespread process of secularization in society, in politics, and in all the realms of thought. The Scientific Revolution assisted this process, for its apostles had long been claiming that the methods of the new science could be transferred not merely from physics to chemistry and biology, but from the natural to the human sciences—to history, anthropology, politics, economics, and comparative religion. Here, too, the teaching of the past now lost its authority among a wide reading public. In France and England more scientific forms of inquiry, more methodical reference to statistics, and a more systematic collection of information affected the conduct and even the machinery of government.

A New World View. Before the end of the 17th century "the age of reason" had opened, the age of the French *philosophes* had begun. The results of the Scientific Revolution were being turned by literary minds into a new world view, a new attitude to life. Men were becoming aware that they now possessed a power of changing their environment, even those aspects of it that they had been disposed to regard as providentially ordained. And a world which had long believed that the Golden Age lay in the distant past and that human societies and civilizations suffered from a natural process of decline began to see a future that opened out to wider horizons and indefinite improvement. The transition to the idea of progress had begun.

The Bourgeoisie. The process of secularization covered a wider area than can be accounted for by the Scientific Revolution alone. It would seem to have been the natural accompaniment of the development of a more urbanized society in the countries around the English Channel. Not only in the United Provinces, but also in England and in the France of Louis XIV, one sees the bourgeoisie coming into the ascendancy in this period. This class produced the general reading public, to which the leaders of the scientific movement directed their appeal. The bourgeoisie was the section of society least submissive to tradition, least ready to accept mystery or mystification, and most apt to follow a worldly minded common sense. To meet its needs, literary style, which had been so ornamental, was pruned into simplicity and directness, as the scientists wished.

Trade and Competition. As in the time of the Renaissance, the region that held the cultural leadership and decided the character of the succeeding age was the region that was the most economically advanced. Expanding markets, provided partly by the New World and partly by the large-scale needs of greatly enlarged armies, had given great stimulus to economic advance, and in the United Provinces, England, and France overseas trade now came to assume great proportions. Holland had taken the lead in the movement and for a time was the shipping, trading, manufacturing, and financial center of Europe. Amsterdam was the commercial and financial capital of the Continent: the Dutch East India Company had been founded in 1602 and the Bank of Amsterdam in 1609. In the mid-1630's the tulip mania brought out in Holland a crisis of frenzied speculation, and by the end of the century England and France were moving toward similar crises. The closing decades of the 17th century saw bitter economic conflict between

The King's Mosque, in Isfahan, Iran, was built in 1611 for Shah Abbas the Great. He made Isfahan his capital and one of Persia's most beautiful cities.

the English, Dutch, and French, and it seemed that the wars of religion, which had ended in 1648 with the Peace of Westphalia, were to be followed by wars of trade.

In the United Provinces, England, and France, the developments in finance and speculation were altering the structure of the state itself. One can see this particularly in the great war of 1689–1697 between William III and Louis XIV, in part a conflict between financial systems.

The Changing World. The promoters of natural science throughout the century insisted on the utilitarian importance of science and on the possibilities of its practical application. Both in agriculture and in industry this led to a more methodical study of processes and materials, a closer concentration on the means by which technological progress could be achieved. The Scientific Revolution of the 17th century and the Agrarian and Industrial revolutions often regarded as products of the 18th century were actually proceeding together in the period 1601–1700. It is impossible to disentangle these strands of intellectual and social change or to say that any one of them would have reached the importance it achieved if the others had not been developing at the same time.

In reality, though, it was not merely science and man's attitude to the world that were changing. The world itself was being transformed before man's eyes. An environment that had looked much the same for thousands of years was now developing so quickly that people in western Europe began to realize they were living in a dynamic society.

SIR HERBERT BUTTERFIELD
Cambridge University

2. Asia, North Africa, and the Pacific

Scarcely a region of Asia was not rocked by deep change in the 17th century. Regimes, including imperial systems that had been founded in earlier centuries, either declined sharply or were swept away. The upheavals and unrest of the era were caused mainly by internal problems of the various states. But during this century European influences began to take on greater significance than ever before in many parts of Asia.

Ottoman Empire. As the 17th century opened, even the most casual observer could not fail to note that the once mighty Ottoman Turkish Empire was succumbing to political arteriosclerosis. Except for Murad IV (reigned 1623–1640), the sultans in Constantinople were little more than pompous figureheads. At the court, grasping viziers competed with venal eunuchs and harem favorites for power and privileges, while in the background hovered the Janissaries, reluctant to perform their traditional military functions.

Under such conditions state policies tended to become increasingly static and ultraconservative. More and more, imperial gratification was sought in glorification of the past. The decline of the authority of the Sublime Porte in the outlying sectors of the empire was underscored especially by the rise of virtually independent regimes in Tunisia and Algeria, whose pirate fleets menaced the shipping of the entire Mediterranean. And were it not for the absence of sufficiently strong and aggressive neighbors along the empire's eastern and northern frontiers, the imperial realm might have been despoiled of much more territory than actually was lost.

After 1639 Turkey's frontiers in the east remained stable, but from midcentury Ottoman arms suffered fateful setbacks in Europe. There Austria came to grips with the Ottoman giant. Successfully withstanding the second Turkish siege of Vienna in 1683, Austria took the offensive, and, by the Treaty of Karlowitz in 1699, the Ottoman Empire was compelled to relinquish most of Hungary to the Habsburgs. Further Ottoman retreats were still to come.

Iran (Persia). In the reign (1587–1629) of Abbas I of the Safavid dynasty, Iran recovered much of its former political and military might and cultural splendor. During these years Isfahan, the Safavid capital, was hailed as one of the most beautiful cities in the world by visitors from all over Europe and Asia.

After the death of Abbas, the dynasty entered into a generally unbroken decline that continued until its downfall about 100 years later. The lack of firm leadership invited aggression by Iran's neighbors. The Ottoman Turks seized large tracts of territory in the northwest and regained control of Baghdad, which had been captured by Abbas.

More fateful were the stirrings of the Afghans in the east. In the early 18th century they established their independence, and in 1722 they captured Isfahan.

India. At the opening of the 17th century the Mughul (Mogul) dynasty under Emperor Akbar commanded one of the mightiest empires the Indian subcontinent had ever known. But before the century came to a close serious cracks appeared in the Mughul regime and domain.

Akbar's two immediate successors, Jahangir (reigned 1605–1627) and Shah Jahan (reigned 1628–1658), were able monarchs. Upholding his sound and tactful administrative policies, they devoted themselves to the promotion of the economic well-being and cultural advancement of the imperial realm. The splendor of Mughul artistic expression is well exemplified in the painting and architecture of Shah Jahan's reign. Such magnificent edifices as the mausoleum at Agra, known as the Taj Mahal, and the overpowering Red Fort at Delhi date from his time.

Aurangzeb (reigned 1658–1707) was the last of the great Mughul emperors. He spent most of his reign in a vain attempt to reduce the entire subcontinent to his rule. Despite seemingly endless wars and campaigns, the west-central part of India and the far south were able to elude conquest. It was particularly unfortunate for Mughul interests that Aurangzeb clashed with such proud peoples as the Marathas, the Rajputs, and the Sikhs. They nurtured enmities that were to cost the Mughuls dearly in the 18th century. The

Khandita Nayaka, one of eight types of women in love, is the subject of a Rajput painting from Mewar, India.

bigoted Emperor also committed the blunder of upsetting the delicate religious understandings that the Mughuls, who were Muslims, had fashioned with the numerically superior Hindus. Without at least a semblance of Hindu-Muslim unity the Mughuls could not prevail for long.

In the 17th century the Portuguese, who had dominated the European trade with India, were reduced to a secondary role by the advent of traders from other Western nations. In the early years of the century the Dutch and English appeared on the scene. They were later followed by the French. These Europeans conducted their activities through East India companies, organizations that were progressively better directed and financed. For a long while they were primarily interested in trade and strove to avoid becoming entangled in local politics and wars. They scrambled to secure trading privileges and the right to establish "factories," or trading posts, from local princes in ports along the eastern and western Indian coasts. By the close of the century the English and French had outdistanced the Dutch in India and were serious rivals, disputing between themselves and vying for the favor and support of local Indian rulers. The struggle for greater stakes had begun.

China. By the early years of the 17th century most of the traditional symptoms of dynastic decline had become apparent in the Chinese Empire. Increasingly the regime of the Ming dynasty (1368–1644), pervaded by corruption and inefficiency, found itself incapable of meeting the challenges that had periodically heralded the downfall of a ruling house. Armies of peasant rebels roamed about the countryside. The most formidable, led by Li Tzu-ch'eng, actually captured the imperial capital, Peking, in 1644. While these internal upheavals were occurring, Manchu peoples to the northeast were on the march. Advancing south of the Great Wall, they ousted Li from Peking and went on to conquer all of China. Their new dynasty was designated the Ch'ing (1644–1912).

The Manchus devoted the first half century of their rule to consolidating their grip on the Chinese Empire. The essence of their policy was to uphold traditional Chinese institutions and customs while taking precautions to preserve as much as possible of their own way of life. By this approach the "barbarian" Manchus hoped to prevent their cultural absorption by their Chinese subjects. Fortunately for the Manchus, they received the strong cooperation of the Chinese scholar-bureaucratic class. As a result of Manchu policies, peace and prosperity were restored to much of China. In the late 17th century the population began to rise sharply, partly because of the introduction of new food plants—such as potatoes, peanuts, and maize—from the New World.

From the early years of their rule the Manchus set about to reconstruct the tributary system. This entailed inducing or compelling foreign rulers to acknowledge the overlordship of the Son of Heaven. First in status among the tributary states was Korea, which had actually been overrun by the Manchus shortly before their invasion of China. Even as a tributary state Korea continued to pursue its new policy of national isolation, which as late as the second half of the 19th century justified the country's designation as the Hermit Kingdom. Most other states bordering the Chinese Empire were drawn into the tributary system. On the maritime frontier, Japan refused to join, but not so the kingdom of Okinawa. In 1683 the large offshore island of Taiwan (Formosa) was forcibly annexed.

In the far northeast the Russians, having penetrated into the Amur Valley, were compelled to withdraw. The frontier of the Chinese and czarist empires was fixed by the Treaty of Nerchinsk (Nipchu) in 1689. The Manchus, like the Ming, found it increasingly necessary to deal with a new type of "barbarian." To the list of Europeans seeking trade with China, the Ch'ing dynasty now had to include the English, Dutch, and French, who sought, above all, the famed silks and porcelains of the Middle Kingdom.

Japan. In 1600, Tokugawa Ieyasu, vying for supreme political and military power in Japan, won an epochal victory over a coalition of feudal lords in the Battle of Sekigahara. Three years later he formally assumed the title of shogun, which was retained by his descendants for the next 265 years.

During the era of the Tokugawa shogunate the evolution of feudalism in Japan reached its peak and then entered its decline and ultimate demise. Ieyasu and his immediate successors spent many years in fashioning a sociopolitical system that has been called "centralized feudalism." It was designed to ensure the perpetuation of power in the hands of the Tokugawa family. Edo (now Tokyo) was made the headquarters of the Tokugawa Bakufu (military government), the fief system was reshuffled to facilitate shogunal control of the various daimyo, and these feudal lords were required to reside as semihostages in the shogun's capital for many months of each year. A new sociolegal system was developed, confirming many privileges of the samurai (warriors), notably their right to bear weapons.

The increasingly worrisome problem of the presence of European traders and missionaries in Japan was brought to a head at the approach of midcentury. In particular, the shogunate was uneasy about the activities of missionaries, especially of the Jesuits, who were patronized by the Portuguese. By 1639, after a series of repressive laws, a policy of national seclusion had been instituted. All foreigners, except the Dutch and Chinese, were ordered to leave the country forever, and Japanese themselves were forbidden to leave the country or to return from abroad without the permission of the shogunate. This policy was generally enforced for over 200 years.

The Tokugawa shogunate succeeded in establishing widespread peace and stability. Warfare practically disappeared from Japan for almost 250 years. An initial result was the general improvement of the economy and the steady rise in the size of the population. In the latter half of the century a trend toward urbanization and the growth of domestic trade set in. In the expanding cities, notably Edo and Osaka, great mercantile centers emerged, and the well-to-do merchants became patrons of a new style of living and culture. During these years the geisha house, wood-block printing, sumo wrestling, and the kabuki theater began to come into popular vogue. A high point of this bright and lively culture was reached in the Genroku era (1688–1703).

Southeast Asia. The 17th century was a stormy and turbulent era in mainland Southeast Asia. The Toungoo dynasty of Burma, established in 1486 and briefly displaced in 1599, was restored

METROPOLITAN MUSEUM OF ART, BEQUEST OF MRS. H. O. HAVEMEYER

Japanese painting of a woman is attributed to Moronobu, who also designed wood-block prints.

under the dynamic King Anaukpetlun in 1605. But after his death in 1628 the kingdom was ripped continuously by internal strife and foreign intrusions. Siam (now Thailand) was buffeted during this era by the rivalries of the Dutch, English, and French. In 1688 a palace revolt resulted in the smashing of the overweening French influence in Siam and the death of Constantine Phaulkon, a Greek adventurer who had acquired inordinate favor at the court. In Vietnam the internal struggles that had torn the kingdom apart in the 16th century were revived. Both the Trinh family dominating the north and the Nguyen family holding sway in the south professed loyalty to the Le dynasty.

Seventeenth century Dutch successes in Asia not only upset the directions and nature of East Indian (Indonesian) history and life but also vaulted the Netherlands to a place among the foremost European powers of the time. After initial probes into the Eastern trade during the preceding century, the Dutch responded decisively to the lure of the wealth of the East by chartering the Dutch East India Company in 1602. A private, monopolistic trading company enjoying broad political and military powers, it remained responsible for Dutch affairs in Asia, notably the East Indies, until its dissolution in 1795.

From an early time the company focused on the winning of a monopoly in the spice trade of the Indonesian archipelago. To this end it sought with much success to drive out its Portuguese and English rivals. From its headquarters at Batavia (now Djakarta) in Java, founded in 1619, it relentlessly extended its power and influence through the islands. Its successes in interfering in local political affairs and acquiring control over territories were facilitated by the absence of strong Indonesian regimes, except such states as Mataram and Bantam in Java, Atjeh in Sumatra, and Makassar in Sulawesi (Celebes). From its East Indian bases, the company forged a vast commercial empire reaching from the Persian Gulf to China and Japan.

In the 17th century the Spaniards were faced with the challenge of extending and maintaining their control of the Philippine archipelago. Encountering resistance from many local peoples, especially from the Moros in the south, they also had to contend with the attacks of the Dutch from East Indian bases. The Spaniards were ably assisted by missionary friars in their efforts to consolidate their power and cultural influence in the Philippines.

The Pacific. Credit for the European discovery of Australia is given to the Dutch navigator Willem Jansz, whose expedition sighted the Cape York Peninsula in 1606 and later made at least one landing on the continent. Australia was gradually shown to be an island. In 1606 the Spanish navigator Luis Vaez de Torres passed through the Torres Strait, which separates Australia from New Guinea, and in 1642–1643 the Dutch explorer Abel Tasman sailed from the Indian Ocean into the Pacific south of Australia, discovering Tasmania and New Zealand. The first British navigator to touch Australia was William Dampier in 1688.

HYMAN KUBLIN, *Brooklyn College*

3. Subsaharan Africa

In the 17th century a series of events in Subsaharan Africa set in motion forces destined to play increasingly influential roles in the future of Africa's peoples.

Rise of New States. A number of new states came into prominence, and in notable cases their nationals were able to maintain a powerful influence over the years, even into the postcolonial era of independent African nations. In West Africa, ancient Kanem-Bornu remained dominant in the savanna; but in the forest, Benin was joined by the expanding Yoruba empire of Oyo and the newly formed Ashanti Union, centered at Kumasi. Below the Zambezi River the kingdom of Mwene Mutapa (Monomotapa) lingered, although its former southern territories, around the site of Zimbabwe, had split off as the independent principality of Changamire late in the 15th century.

South of Lake Nyasa (Lake Malawi), the Malawi kingdom dominated the trade routes to the east coast, while on the Zambezi floodplain the Lozi state probably emerged during the early part of the 17th century. Farther north, between the Kasai and Lualaba tributaries of the Congo River, the Luba empire had taken shape late in the 16th century. About 1600 a member of its royal family, Cibinda Ilunga, founded the Lunda kingdom, which dominated the upper Kasai re-

gion for well over 250 years. Finally, it was in the 17th century that Buganda, on Lake Victoria, rose to prominence. Its expansion then and later came largely at the expense of its neighbor and former overlord, the kingdom of Bunyoro.

Both Ashanti and Buganda continued to grow in strength well into the 19th century. Their success was characterized by a powerful sense of national solidarity that enabled their people to maintain an uncommon influence on regional affairs into the colonial period and beyond. Similarly, the Lozi, the Yoruba, and the Shona of Mutapa have continued to command an important voice within their own regions of Africa.

Foreign Penetration. Other remarkable developments of the 17th century were external in origin. These included a contest between Portugal and the Omani Arabs for control of the East African coast; the rise of the Atlantic slave trade; the mission of Portuguese Jesuits at the court of Ethiopia; and the arrival of the Dutch at the site of Cape Town in 1652.

The struggle between Oman and Portugal in East Africa eventually restricted Portuguese authority to the Mozambique coast south of Cape Delgado, but otherwise merely substituted one foreign overlord for another. In Christian Ethiopia, the Portuguese succeeded for a time in winning the allegiance of the emperors to the pope, a move that precipitated bloody civil war and helped encourage a xenophobia that dominated Ethiopian affairs into the 19th century.

More portentous for the continent as a whole was the advent of large-scale slaving to provide labor for the emerging plantation colonies of the New World. After the Portuguese, the Dutch, then the French, British, and others began visiting West African waters in search of slaves. The French established themselves in Senegal, while the British and Dutch concentrated their posts on the Gold Coast. Over the years merchants of many nations participated in a commerce that brought an estimated 1.3 million slaves to the Americas during the 17th century. Many more perished in passage or resisting capture, but whatever the total loss, it fell far short of the massive transport of slaves across the Atlantic that was to occur in the 18th and early 19th centuries.

The arrival of the Dutch in South Africa was an event destined eventually to touch the lives of all who dwelt below the Limpopo River. Established initially as a provisioning station for ships passing to the East Indies, the Cape colony soon became the permanent residence of European settlers, who slowly spread outward during the second half of the 17th century. These *trekboer* frontiersmen developed a stubborn adherence to the land and a sense of racial and religious destiny—factors that formed the basis of the Boer character and helped create the Boers' national spirit. It was this spirit that finally gave birth to the apartheid society of South Africa.

ROBERT W. JULY, *Author of "A History of the African People"*

4. North America

At the beginning of the 17th century Europe stood on the threshold of the conquest and settlement of North America. The continent was to become a frequent battleground in the endless wars for national supremacy among England, France, Spain, and the Netherlands. As prizes were rich natural resources—hopefully gold and silver, certainly timber, fish, and furs.

Colonists arrive in Jamestown, Va., established in 1607 as the first permanent English settlement in America.

Spain had already established a foothold at St. Augustine, Fla., in 1565, but not until 1607 did the English found their first colony, at Jamestown, Va., near Chesapeake Bay. France followed the next year with an outpost on the St. Lawrence River at Quebec. The Dutch established New Amsterdam at the mouth of the Hudson River in 1624, just four years after the second English settlement, at Plymouth, Mass.

Struggle for Supremacy. In the early years of the century the various colonies struggled more often against the wilderness and Indians for survival than against each other. As a matter of policy the Spaniards, French, and Dutch preferred to establish military and trading posts, which attracted only a few settlers. The English, on the other hand, encouraged large-scale migration to their American colonies, and by 1660 the population of Anglo-America totaled over 75,000 on the mainland. But the Dutch settlements in the Hudson Valley divided the major English colonies on the Chesapeake from those in New England. Moreover, in Europe the merchants of Amsterdam threatened England's mercantile ambitions. In one of the subsequent naval wars between the two commercial powers, an English expedition captured New Amsterdam in 1664, and the colony was soon renamed New York.

Equally important to the growing strength of English America was the large tract of land between New York and Maryland that King Charles II granted to the young Quaker William Penn in 1681. Under Penn's dynamic leadership, Pennsylvania attracted thousands of Europeans seeking a fresh start in the New World. Meanwhile Charles had secured his southern boundary by granting the Carolinas to a group of court favorites. A prosperous settlement soon sprang up around Charles Town (now Charleston, S. C.), and Spain ultimately abandoned its northward expansion.

By the late 17th century only France remained to challenge English dreams of dominating the North American continent. While England gained a foothold on the shores of Hudson Bay, the French explorers Jacques Marquette, Louis Jolliet, and Sieur de La Salle carried the Bourbon flag far into the interior and down the Mississippi River. At stake was control of the continent's fur trade. Minor skirmishes between opposing forces finally broke out into full-scale conflict in 1689, when the parent nations in Europe clashed in the War of the League of Augsburg. Its American phase is named King William's War, for William III of England. This was the first of a series of wars that continued until 1763, with England finally victorious.

Economic Development. Competition for empire was not confined to military actions. The predominant economic theory of the 17th century—mercantilism—had as its goal the establishment of the self-sufficient empire, in which the mother country and its colonies would achieve national prosperity together, hopefully at the expense of their major rivals. Incorporating the principles of mercantilism, the English Navigation Acts of the 1660's excluded foreign vessels from trading within the empire, required the colonies to export certain commodities to the mother country only, and prohibited them from importing most manufactured articles from other countries.

Although seemingly restrictive, the Navigation Acts in fact stimulated the economic development of the American colonies. New England's merchants carried fish and timber to the West Indies, and Yankee shipbuilders sold many of their vessels to England. Tobacco growers in the Chesapeake region found a protected market for their crop in England, as did Carolina rice and indigo planters. The middle colonies prospered as suppliers of wheat and flour to their neighbors. By the end of the 17th century, England's North American colonies annually imported goods worth more than £300,000 from the mother country.

One measure of colonial prosperity was the fact that the population trebled in the last four decades of the century to more than 250,000. A major reason for this increase was the availability of land and jobs. The chronic shortage of labor attracted indentured servants—men and women who served as contract workers, mostly on farms and plantations, for a period of years in order to pay for their transatlantic passage. Many of them subsequently became landowners themselves. At the same time, however, the enslavement of Africans began to spread through the English colonies, although slavery in North America was still in its infancy in 1700.

——EVENTS OF THE SEVENTEENTH CENTURY——

1602—Dutch East India Company founded.
1603—Elizabeth I of England died; James I (James VI of Scotland) king of England (to 1625).
1603—Tokugawa shogunate established in Japan (to 1868).
1605—Death of Akbar, Mughul emperor from 1556.
1606—Dutch navigator Willem Jansz discovered Australia.
1607—Jamestown founded: first English settlement in Virginia.
1608—Champlain founded Quebec.
1610—Henry IV of France assassinated; Louis XIII king (to 1643).
1611—King James Bible (*Authorized Version*) Issued.
1611—English established their first trading station in India, at Masulipatam.
1613—Romanov dynasty founded in Russia.
1616—Deah of Shakespeare and Cervantes.
1618—Outbreak of Thirty Years' War.
1619—Founding of Batavia (Djakarta) by Dutch in Java.
1620—Pilgrims founded colony at Plymouth (Mass.).
1623—Murad IV Ottoman sultan (to 1640).
1624—Richelieu chief minister of France (to 1642).
1624—Dutch founded New Amsterdam (New York City).
1625—Charles I king of England (to 1649).
1625—Grotius published *De jure belli ac pacis*, pioneer work of international law.
1628—Harvey published his discovery of the circulation of the blood.
1628—Shah Jahan, Mughul emperor (to 1658).
1629—Bernini appointed chief architect of St. Peter's, Rome.
1629—Death of Abbas I of Iran (shah from 1587).
1630—Puritans founded Boston.
1632—Gustavus Adolphus of Sweden (king from 1611) killed at Battle of Lützen.
1634—Lord Baltimore founded colony In Maryland for Roman Catholic settlers.
1637—Descartes published *Discours de la méthode*.
1640—Frederick William elector of Brandenburg (to 1688); called the "Great Elector."
1640—Portugal independent after 60 years of Spanish rule.
1641—Dutch took Malacca from Portuguese.
1642—First Civil War in England (to 1646; Second Civil War, 1648).
1642—Mazarin chief minister of France (to 1661).
1642—Death of Galileo; birth of Newton.
1642—Tasman discovered Tasmania and New Zealand.
1643—Louis XIV king of France (to 1715).
1644—End of Ming dynasty in China; beginning of Ch'ing (Manchu) dynasty (to 1912).
1647—Religious experience of George Fox, founder of Society of Friends, or Quakers (c. 1652).
1648—Peace of Westphalia; end of Thirty Years' War.
1649—Charles I of England beheaded; England a republic (to 1660).
1652—Cape Town founded by the Dutch.
1654—Brazilians expelled the Dutch without help from Portugal.
1658—Aurangzeb, Mughul emperor (to 1707).
1660—Charles II king of England (to 1685); monarchy restored.
1661—Louis XIV of France assumed personal rule.
1664—English took Dutch colony of New Netherland (renamed New York in 1667).
1664—French East India Company founded.
1666—Great Fire of London.
1670—Charleston (S. C.) founded.
1681—William Penn received land grant comprising most of present Pennsylvania.
1683—Turkish siege of Vienna lifted.
1683—Taiwan became part of China.
1685—Revocation of Edict of Nantes (1598), protecting liberties of French Huguenots.
1687—Newton's *Principia mathematica* published.
1687—Parthenon badly damaged during Venetian bombardment of Turks in Athens.
1688—Glorious Revolution in England overthrew James II (king from 1685).
1688—Beginning of Genroku era (to 1703) In Japan: flowering of urban culture.
1689—William III and Mary II joint sovereigns of England. Bill of Rights enacted.
1689—William III, king of England and stadholder of the Netherlands, organized Grand Alliance against Louis XIV of France.
1689—Peter the Great sole czar of Russia (to 1725).
1689—Treaty of Nerchinsk fixed Russian-Chinese border west of the Amur River valley.
1690—Locke published *Essay Concerning Human Understanding*.
1694—Bank of England created.
1697—Charles XII king of Sweden (to 1718).
1699—Treaty of Karlowitz: Austria acquired Hungary from the Turks.

Social and Political Development. Free social and political institutions were equally important factors in attracting more Europeans to the English colonies in the latter half of the century. In the absence of a landed aristocracy, ordinary men had greater opportunity to advance according to their abilities. In the absence of an established church, children and adults alike were free to grow intellectually. And, most important, the absence of English interference in internal political affairs permitted the colonists to develop their own local and provincial governments. Property holders were fully represented in public affairs, and the basic rights of citizenship they had come to expect as Englishmen were guaranteed.

This progress was severely threatened by King James II in 1685, but the Glorious Revolution, which overthrew him in England in 1688, also had its counterpart in several of the American colonies. The net result was a gain for self-government, particularly in New York and Maryland, which had previously been dominated by their proprietors.

As English settlements continued to grow at the turn of the century, warfare against the French and the Indians once again erupted, but the weight of numbers inexorably favored the English. The southern plantations that raised the important cash crops demanded larger numbers of African slaves for labor, while the middle settlements attracted increasing numbers of Scotch-Irish and German immigrants. In New England, where the small family farm predominated, men were turning more often to the sea for their livelihood. The patterns of life for Americans in the years to follow had thus firmly established their roots in the 17th century.

BENJAMIN W. LABAREE, *Williams College*

5. Middle and South America

Exclusive exploitation of the Americas by Spain and Portugal, which those two powers regarded as their right, ended abruptly in the 17th century as the English, French, and Dutch began serious colony planting in North America and the Caribbean. Spain protested but was unable to frighten the newcomers. Portugal suffered Dutch occupation of its sugar-rich bulge of Brazil for 30 years, until Brazilians themselves rallied to drive out the intruders in the 1650's. Although the claims of the Iberian powers were flouted, with only two exceptions (Spain's loss of Jamaica to England and of Haiti to France) other European states had to content themselves with lands that Spain had not troubled, or lacked the manpower, to occupy.

Advancement of the Frontiers of Settlement. In the 17th century Spain posted a less spectacular but more enduring record than in the preceding century. It was written largely by missionaries. They prepared new frontiers for settlers, who planted Spain in large previously uncolonized areas of North and South America.

As the old century closed, New Spain jumped its frontier from north-central Mexico to the Pueblo Indian lands, which had been explored by Francisco Vásquez de Coronado. New Mexico was lost for a dozen years after 1680 because of the Pueblo Revolt, but Spain established a way-station in the great gap between Santa Fe and Chihuahua when refugees gathered at El Paso to await the reconquest of the upper Rio Grande country. Across the Sierra Madre the Jesuits pushed their mission frontier through Sinaloa and into Sonora along the west coast, and the Franciscans put another frontier along the lower Rio Grande, in Coahuila and Nuevo León.

In South America, Spaniards moved from Venezuela and Nueva Granada (Colombia) into the lands drained by Orinoco River system. Others climbed the higher Andes and prepared to descend into the Oriente, or eastern lowlands drained by the upper Amazon River system. In Chile they moved cautiously southward against the fierce Araucanians. Jesuits went up the rivers of the Plata system and founded their Reductions (mission villages) of Paraguay. Cattlemen took possession of the *pampa*. The older provinces supported this expansion.

The Portuguese operated their great *fazendas* (plantations) in the coastal areas of Brazil. But some few began a ranching industry in the northeast behind Bahia (now Salvador), which was then the capital. Missionaries edged up the Amazon. In the south the Paulistas, still seeking a sound base for the economy of their São Paulo, ranged inland in search of riches and raided the Paraguay Reductions for slaves.

Cultural and Economic Life. Institutionally the 17th century was a period of consolidation. Cities grew, reflecting the American prosperity in their often ornate churches, *conventos*, houses, and royal buildings. Universities, a dozen or more in Spanish America, passed on medieval patterns of learning; Jesuit *colegios*, as in Europe, introduced Renaissance interest in the ancient classics; lower schools drilled young Spaniards in the three R's; and mission schools brought to the Indians European crafts and skills, along with Christianity. Spanish and Portuguese America developed literary figures, no longer simply chroniclers. Mexico trained the dramatist Juan Ruiz de Alarcón and sent him on to greatness in Spain, but it kept Sor Juana Inés de la Cruz, "The Tenth Muse," and scholarly Carlos Sigüenza y Góngora; Lima boasted of the poet Pedro de Peralta and the satirist Juan del Valle y Caviedes. The century was also a time of cultural self-expression in Brazil, despite the lack of a university.

The American mines continued to yield treasure of gold, silver, and mercury, although output did not equal earlier figures. Stockraising was important in many areas, and cultivation, too, of European and American crops. Into plantation economies much African slave labor was introduced to replace or supplement the declining Indian labor force. Small-scale domestic industries came in from Europe, and Indian crafts, weaving, tile production, and pottery-making were fostered. Overseas trade was limited to designated Iberian and American ports, and intercolonial exchange was closely regulated. Within colonies, long distances and poor roads hampered large-scale commercial enterprise. The Manila galleons kept New Spain in contact with the Orient. Despite heavy royal taxation, American economic life was reasonably healthy.

Both Spain and Portugal closed the century with American empires that were strong enough to weather the serious international challenges of the age ahead and that were ready for the fertilization from the new ideas to come. They had passed on an enduring legacy of their institutions, cultures, languages, and religion to a sizable portion of two American continents.

JOHN FRANCIS BANNON
Saint Louis University

Bibliography

Argan, Giulio C., *The Europe of the Capitals: 1600–1700* (Skira 1965).

Aston, Trevor H., ed., *Crisis in Europe, 1560–1660* (Basic Bks. 1965).

Balandier, Georges, *Daily Life in the Kingdom of the Kongo* (Pantheon Bks. 1968).

Bannon, John F., *History of the Americas*, 2d ed. (McGraw 1963).

Bazin, Germain, *The Baroque* (N. Y. Graphic 1968).

Boxer, Charles R., *The Dutch Seaborne Empire, 1600–1800* (Knopf 1965).

Boxer, Charles R., *The Portuguese Seaborne Empire, 1415–1825* (Knopf 1970).

Brebner, John B., *Canada: A Modern History*, 2d ed. rev. by Donald C. Masters (Univ. of Mich. Press 1969).

Butterfield, Herbert, *The Origins of Modern Science, 1300–1800*, rev. ed. (Collier Bks. 196?).

Clark, George N., *Science and Social Welfare in the Age of Newton* (Oxford 1937).

Clark, George N., *The Seventeenth Century*, 2d ed. (Oxford 1947).

Cowie, Leonard W., *Seventeenth-Century Europe* (Bell, G. 1960).

Craven, Wesley F., *The Colonies in Transition, 1660–1713* (Harper 1968).

Davidson, Basil, *Black Mother: The Years of the African Slave Trade* (Little 1961).

Defourneaux, Mercelin, *Daily Life in Spain in the Golden Age* (Praeger 1971).

Dunn, Richard S., *The Age of Religious Wars, 1559–1689* (Norton 1970).

Erlanger, Philippe, *Louis XIV* (Praeger 1970).

Freyre, Gilberto, *The Masters and the Slaves*, 2d Eng. lang. ed., rev. (Knopf 1956).

Friedrich, Carl J., *The Age of the Baroque, 1610–1660* (Harper 1952).

Gibson, Charles, *Spain in America* (Harper 1966).

Goodrich, Luther C., *A Short History of the Chinese People*, 3d ed. (Harper 1953).

Grimmelshausen, Johann, *Simplicissimus* (Bobbs 1964). (A novel set in the Thirty Years' War, first published in 1669.)

Hall, Daniel G. E., *A History of South-East Asia*, 3d ed. (St. Martins 1968).

Haring, Clarence H., *The Spanish Empire in America* (Oxford 1947).

Hazard, Paul, *The European Mind: The Critical Years (1680–1715)* (Yale Univ. Press 1953).

James, W. J., *Habsburg and Bourbon, 1494–1789* (Harrap 1955).

July, Robert W., *A History of the African People* (Scribner 1970).

Lach, Donald F., *Asia in the Making of Europe*, 6 vols. (Univ. of Chicago Press 1965–   ).

Leonard, Irving A., *Baroque Times in Old Mexico* (Univ. of Mich. Press 1959).

Levron, Jacques, *Daily Life at the Court of Versailles* (Macmillan 1968).

McNeill, William H., *A World History*, 2d ed. (Oxford 1971).

Maland, David, *Culture and Society in Seventeenth-Century France* (Scribner 1970).

Maland, David, *Europe in the Seventeenth Century* (St. Martins 1966).

Nussbaum, Frederick L., *The Triumph of Science and Reason, 1660–1685* (Harper 1953).

Ogg, David, *Europe in the Seventeenth Century*, 8th ed., rev. (Macmillan 1962).

Packard, Laurence B., *The Commercial Revolution, 1400–1776: Mercantilism–Colbert–Adam Smith* (Holt 1927).

Pepys, Samuel, *Diary* (many editions).

Pomfret, John E., and Shumway, F. M., *Founding the American Colonies, 1583–1660* (Harper 1970).

Robertson, Alec, and Stevens, D. W., *The Pelican History of Music*, vol. 2: *Renaissance and Baroque* (Penguin 1964).

Sansom, George, *A History of Japan, 1615–1867* (Stanford Univ. Press 1963).

Spear, Percival, *India: A Modern History* (Univ. of Mich. Press 1961).

Steinberg, Sigfrid H., *The Thirty Years' War and the Conflict for European Hegemony* (Norton 1967).

Sykes, Percy M., *History of Persia*, 3d ed., vol. 2 (1930; reprint, Barnes & Noble 1969).

Tapié, Victor L., *The Age of Grandeur: Baroque Art and Architecture* (Grove 1960).

Vucinich, Wayne S., *The Ottoman Empire: Its Record and Legacy* (Van Nostrand 1965).

Whitehead, Alfred N., *Science and the Modern World* (Macmillan 1926).

Willey, Basil, *The Seventeenth Century Background* (Chatto 1934).

Wolf, John B., *Louis XIV* (Norton 1968).

Wright, Louis B., *The Atlantic Frontier: Colonial American Civilization* (Knopf 1947).

Zumthor, Paul, *Daily Life in Rembrandt's Holland* (Macmillan 1959).

LOUIS GOLDMAN FROM RAPHO GUILLUMETTE

The Dome of the Rock in Jerusalem, built in the 7th century, was the first domed mosque of Islamic architecture.

SEVENTH CENTURY. Of all periods in the history of the Western world, the 7th century A. D. seems at first glance most to deserve being called the dark age. In western Europe the cultural achievements of the great transmitters of ancient learning in the 6th century were fading into intellectual sterility. Pope Gregory I the Great (reigned 590–604) marked the transition by his apparent condemnation of the study of classical letters and his abject surrender to the miraculous. Although he revived the papal authority, the unity of Latin Christendom could still succumb, as the old Roman political unity had done, to the particularism of the barbarian kingdoms. These Germanic kingdoms showed little promise of rebuilding a universal law and order. The Lombards, having divided Italy, were unable to make it whole again. In Gaul and southern Germany the Merovingian rulers of the Franks became "do-nothing kings" (*rois fainéants*), their realm almost in dissolution. Anglo-Saxon England was a congeries of kingdoms frequently at war with one another. Spain, united under the Visigoths, nonetheless suffered from internal weaknesses that were soon to bring the kingdom's destruction. In these circumstances the change, long since evident, to an agrarian economy, society, and culture, was proceeding toward completion, bringing to an end the urban civilization of antiquity.

If in the eastern Mediterranean world the Roman Empire had survived the first onslaughts of German and Asian invaders, and under Justinian had enjoyed in the previous century a revival of power and cultural brilliance, it was now in the 7th century meeting with disaster. Under repeated attack from barbarian tribes of Slavs and Avars in the Balkans and from the more civilized peoples of western Asia, the empire—now Greek (Byzantine), as well as Roman—was almost continuously fighting for its life. The end of the Roman Empire and of the ancient Mediterranean civilization seemed to be at hand.

Such a picture of gloom, however, is not a just representation of Europe and the Mediterranean world in the century. Although a period of decline, the 7th century was also one of transition, of further change from the old to the new in the great and continuous process of history. It was, in fact, a time of political, religious, economic, and cultural movements of vital importance to the development of the ancient Mediterranean into the European civilization of the Middle Ages and the modern world. The Byzantine Empire, fighting valiantly, not only survived —a notable success in such an age—but became the center from which Greco-Roman culture and Greek Christianity spread later among the Slavic and Asian peoples of the Balkan Peninsula and of Russia. Its active economic life was to aid in the revival of trade and industry in the West.

Meanwhile, a vast movement developed in the southwestern quarter of Asia and across northern Africa. A great new religion arose— Islam—and it inspired the leadership of the Arabs in that amazing religious-political-economic expansion that produced a new world power. Successor to much of the Greco-Roman heritage as well as to the Asian, Islam was instrumental in restoring the unity of the Mediterranean world. And by taking Greek and Arabic learning into Spain and Sicily, the Muslims were soon to be a significant civilizing force in western Europe.

In East Asia, Buddhism was in an important phase of development in China. Under the T'ang dynasty the Chinese Empire and Chinese culture enjoyed a golden age of high achievement. During the 6th century, Buddhism had spread to Japan. In the 7th century a centralized Japanese state was coming into being on the model of T'ang China. In India and Southeast Asia, both Buddhism and Brahmanism showed creative strength.

Even in western Europe some creative activity was taking place. From Ireland and then from Rome, Latin Christian missionary work resulted in the conversion of the Germanic invaders of Britain, the organization of the English church, the foundation of new centers of learning, and the beginnings of Latin, Roman Christianity and culture in the Netherlands and Germany.

In the Western Hemisphere, centers of civilization flourished in Central America, Mexico, and Peru. The scarcity of chronological evidence precludes an account of these areas in the 7th century. For a summary of developments in the Americas before the 8th century, see INDIANS, AMERICAN.

GAINES POST
Princeton University

1. Europe and the Rise of Islam

For the future of European civilization the most important developments of the 7th century were undoubtedly the defense of the Byzantine Empire and the expansion of western Asia under the banner of Islam.

DEFENSE OF THE BYZANTINE EMPIRE

The ancient Roman Empire had been shattered in the west by the Germanic invasions and weakened in the east by the revived power of Iran (Persia) under the Sassanian dynasty. The efforts of Emperor Justinian (reigned 527–565) to regain what had been lost were rewarded with success in Italy, North Africa, and southern Spain. But the reconquest so devastated Italy that the Lombards were able to occupy the valley of the Po (Lombardy) and the Apennines, leaving the empire isolated territories: Venice, Ravenna, Rome, Naples, the southern tip of the peninsula, and Sicily. More unfortunate still was the consequence for the empire in the east, for the military effort in Italy had entailed the weakening of the eastern frontiers. The Slavs were pushing into the Balkans and Greece, while an Asian horde, the Avars, who had settled in the plain of Hungary, repeatedly threatened Constantinople. Meanwhile, Iran was generally on the offensive. The able Emperor Mauricius (reigned 582–602) checked the Persians and defeated the Avars and Slavs. But a mutiny of his army on the Danube and an uprising in Constantinople ended his life and resulted in new disasters in the reign of his successor, the brutal Phocas (reigned 602–610). Factional strife rent the great cities of the empire, and Khosrau (Chosroes) II Parvez of Iran occupied Roman Armenia, Mesopotamia, and Syria.

Victories of Emperor Heraclius. Salvation came from Emperor Heraclius (reigned 610–641), who obtained the throne when a rebellion started by his father against Phocas ended in success. But for several years longer the empire had to endure continued misfortune: renewed raids by Slavs and Avars, the capture by Khosrau of Jerusalem and the Holy Cross (reputedly the original cross on which Christ had suffered), and the Persian conquest of Egypt.

Then, aided by a great emotional response and crusading spirit in the name of the Mother of God, and by the loans (with interest) of the church and the leadership of Patriarch Sergius, Heraclius waged continuous war against the Persians, while Sergius and the magister Bonus brilliantly and finally defeated the Avars in their attempt to capture Constantinople (626). Heraclius in 628 reached the heart of Khosrau's realm, and recovered the Holy Cross, which was piously returned to Jerusalem except for fragments given to the Armenians or taken back to Constantinople.

Once more the Byzantine Empire had survived, largely because of the genius of Heraclius. But the effort against Iran and the Avars had been exhausting, and Iran itself was disastrously weakened. The high taxes for the costs of war and loans to the church aroused dissatisfaction.

Religious Controversy and Reaffirmation. More serious, perhaps, was the strong opposition to the orthodox empire and official church by the Monophysites, who dominated Egypt and Syria. Since the 5th century the Monophysites, believing in the one divine nature of Christ, had refused to accept the doctrine of the divine and human natures as defined by the Council of Chalcedon (451), for their monotheism was suspicious of anything that seemed to weaken the divine unity of the person of Christ. Patriarch Sergius and Heraclius in the edict *Ekthesis* (638) proposed as a compromise the doctrine of one divine will (monothelitism) in the two natures. Rejected by both sides, the doctrine of the Monothelites in any case came too late to serve the purpose of regaining the loyalty of Egypt and Syria. Finally, in 680–681, when these provinces had been irretrievably lost, the Council of Constantinople reaffirmed as orthodox the old doctrine of the two natures of Christ.

Religious dissension had split and helped destroy the power of the empire in the Middle East. These troubles explain why not even the ability of Heraclius, had his health remained, could have succeeded in the defense of the empire against a new enemy, the Arabs.

RISE OF ISLAMIC CIVILIZATION

In the epic ebb and flow of the history of the relations between Europe and Asia, the Persians had failed to end the long Greco-Roman-Byzantine hegemony over Anatolia, Syria, and Egypt that had begun with the conquests of Alexander the Great. Now, however, the internal weaknesses of the empire and the crippling of Iran opened the Fertile Crescent to a people who were ready to seize their opportunity. Inspired by a great religious leader, Mohammed, and by the desire for rich conquests, the Arabs became a great militant force and in the declining years of Heraclius embarked on their phenomenal expansion.

Nature of Islam. Mohammed, claiming divine inspiration, preached a religion founded on the belief in one God (Allah) and in Mohammed as his Prophet. His teachings included an improved moral and social code for the Arabs (for example, forgiveness of enemies, sobriety, and a moderation of polygamy), as it included the reward of paradise for all Muslims (the faithful, or "self-surrenderers") who practiced the virtues commanded, offered prayers daily in the direction of Mecca, observed the annual fast of Ramadan, made the pilgrimage to Mecca, and fought for the faith. The new religion was called Islam ("surrender"), and Islam came to mean the ensemble of Muslims and their civilization. Mohammed's sayings were soon embodied in the suras (chapters) of the Koran, the sacred book of Islam.

The Sutton Hoo Ship Burial in Suffolk, England—
the grave of a 7th century Saxon king—was laden
with treasures, including (*left*) an iron helmet with
a face mask and (*above*) a gold clasp.

Expansion of Islam. The success of the new religion was not immediate. But after the flight (hegira) in 622 from Mecca to Yathrib (Medina), Mohammed and his followers rapidly won numerous converts by defeating and plundering Meccan caravans and armies. They gained control of Mecca in 630 and were unifying Arabia by the time of the Prophet's death in 632.

Thereafter, within ten years, under able generals like Khalid and Amr Ibn al-As, the Arabs destroyed the army of Heraclius and occupied Syria, Palestine, and Egypt. They captured Ctesiphon, the Sassanian capital, and began the conquest of Asia eastward to the Oxus (Amu Darya) and Indus rivers. By the end of the 7th century, under the Umayyad caliphs of Damascus, the Arabs had completed the conquest of North Africa from Libya to the Strait of Gibraltar. A few years afterward the converted Moors of North Africa overthrew the Visigothic kingdom and occupied most of Spain.

Civilization of Islam. From central Asia westward to the Atlantic, under the authority of the caliphs, the civilization of Islam came into being. If Arabic was the universal official and literary language, the learning of Islam came from the conquered peoples, and thus the new civilization incorporated the ancient Mediterranean learning (the Greek above all, with borrowings from India and China) and transmitted it to the West. Although it began as a reaction against Europe and although Muslim and Christian hostility often recurred, Islam carried on to new heights the unity of the old Mediterranean civilization. Islam itself was a part of the Semitic religious movements that had brought forth Judaism and Christianity, and in turn it too was influenced by Greek philosophy. There was no deep conflict between East and West, between Asia and Europe.

CULTURAL AND ECONOMIC LIFE IN THE EAST

In the first overwhelming sweep of the Arabs, the Byzantine Empire lost all its non-European territories except Anatolia. Constans II (reigned 641–668), defeated by the Arabs in the East,

spent most of his time in Italy and Sicily. The opportune invention of "Greek fire"—probably a mixture of quicklime, naphtha, and pitch, with perhaps saltpeter—gave the Byzantines control of the seas in time to beat off the Muslim fleet and save Constantinople. But with the Arabs remaining a threat to Anatolia and the capital, a new danger appeared in the settlement of the Hunnic Bulgars across the lower Danube.

The military strength of the empire, based on reforms undertaken by Heraclius, enabled Constantinople to survive as the mighty fortress defending Europe on the east and as the center of Greek civilization. From that center, Greek letters and Greek Christianity were to help in civilizing Russia, and an active economic life was to help in the later revival of western Europe.

Preservation of Ancient Learning. In their different ways, therefore, Byzantines and Arabs during the 7th century preserved the ancient Mediterranean civilization and prepared the way for its development, when it entered the West, into medieval European civilization. Most of the creative work in this process would be done from the 9th to the 13th centuries. But in the 7th century Greek classical literature and learning, at least, were studied in the Byzantine Empire. Maximus the Confessor, by popularizing the Pseudo-Dionysius' Neoplatonic works on angelology, helped increase the mystical element of Greek Christianity and, indirectly, of Jewish and Muslim thought. The invention of "Greek fire" was a sign of continuing Greek technological genius. Already Greek philosophy, mathematics, and science had penetrated western Asia, and many of the works in these subjects were being translated into Syriac by Nestorian Christians in Syria, Mesopotamia, and Iran. The Syriac versions were later to be translated into Arabic.

Meanwhile, Indian mathematics reached a high level in the 7th century with the work of Brahmagupta. The so-called Hindu numerals were appearing in Mesopotamia, where Severus Sebokht was acquainted with them. This scholar was also a student of Aristotelian philosophy.

Thanks in part to him, Islam was destined to absorb, build on, and transmit Greek and Indian knowledge.

Economic Life. Like the cultural life of the century in the Middle East, the ancient economic life continued to exist, if it did not always flourish because of war and raids. But the Arabs and their subjects in Syria and Egypt and North Africa soon expanded trade between Asia and the Byzantine Empire and Spain. At times there was some interruption of the old commerce between the eastern Mediterranean and western Christendom, but internal troubles were a more important factor in the continuing economic decline in Italy and in Gaul. In fact, along with the Byzantines, the Arabs renewed the economic unity and prosperity of the Mediterranean world and in a few centuries stimulated the revival of trade and industry in the Latin West.

WESTERN EUROPE

No continuity of the ancient world was apparent in western Europe during the 7th century.

Localism. Italy was divided between the loosely knit Lombard kingdom and the scattered territories of the Byzantine Empire. A renewal of Greek culture in Sicily and the extreme south came with the settlement of many refugees from Greece and the East. The Lombard kings were not strong enough to conquer the whole peninsula, papal Rome in particular being a serious obstacle. The hardening of this localism in the 7th century explains why no power could make Italy more than a geographical expression until the 19th century.

As for the Roman Church, the achievements of Pope Gregory I the Great in the preceding period resulted in the survival of the papal control of the territory that was the nucleus of the later Patrimony of Peter, or Papal States. The popes held firm in doctrinal disputes with the patriarchs of Constantinople and the emperors, and their staunch adherence to the doctrine of the two natures of Christ won a definitive victory at the Council of Constantinople in 680–681. They did not, however, secure recognition as superiors of the patriarchs of Constantinople, and ultimately the great schism of the Eastern and Western churches resulted.

The kingdom of the Franks in Gaul and the valley of the Rhine was in danger of falling to pieces as the Merovingian dynasty was weakened by the power of the nobles and the loss of crown lands and revenues. Dagobert I (reigned 629–639) enjoyed great prestige but was the last of the line to rule more than nominally over the realm as a whole. The chief administrative officer of each division of the kingdom, the mayor of the palace, was becoming the actual ruler. One of these mayors, the Austrasian Pepin of Heristal, in his victory over Neustria at Tertry (687), won virtual control of the whole kingdom. His son, Charles Martel, in 732 repelled the Moors of Spain and was the founder of the great Carolingian dynasty.

In Spain the Visigothic kings were trying to establish a real public authority and a strong state. Indeed, the memory of the unity of Spain under these kings contributed to the rise of the tradition of an independent Spanish empire and to a feeling of nationalism during the reconquest of Spain from the Moors. Yet the monarchy was dominated by the clergy; and the dissatisfaction of great nobles and the unhappiness of the persecuted Jews soon made Visigothic Spain an easy prey for an invading Muslim force (711).

Roman Britain had disappeared. The native British were pushed into the extreme west or across the channel into Armorica (Brittany), and the several kingdoms of the Germanic Angles, Saxons, and Jutes showed as yet no promise of the unity that later became England.

The beautifully illuminated Lindisfarne Gospels, dating from the 7th century, are now in the British Museum.

The 7th century basilica of San Juan de Baños in Spain is the finest surviving example of Visigothic architecture.

Forces of Unity. Altogether, then, in western Europe the localism introduced by the Germanic invaders became permanent and defeated medieval efforts to revive the Roman ideal of political unity. The final outcome was nationalism. Yet some of the common Roman heritage in institutions and law was vaguely reappearing in these barbarian kingdoms. Frankish, Lombard, and Visigothic kings tried to rule with the old authority that Roman emperors had enjoyed, and to revive the idea of a public law and state superior to tribal distinctions and private rights. The *Edictus* (643) of the Lombard King Rothari asserted the royal power and codified the law. King Recceswinth in Spain issued a codification of the Roman and Visigothic laws—the *Liber Iudiciorum* (654)—thus replacing the Germanic personality of the law with the Roman ideal of a body of law common to all within the state.

But the Roman heritage survived and spread above all through the missionary strength of Latin Christianity. Latin, and even Greek, learning and literature had been flourishing in Irish monasteries, and by 615, Irish monks had carried their Christianity and Latin letters into Scotland, Northumbria, Bavaria, Gaul, and northern Italy. Saint Columbanus, about 612, founded the monastery of Bobbio, where the monks began the study of books that came from the old library of Cassiodorus. The bishops of Rome, however, now became the chief leaders of the movement. In 597, Gregory the Great began the papal policy of sending Benedictine monks from Rome to convert the Angles and Saxons to Roman Christianity. Gradually Benedictine monasticism superseded the Irish, and at the Synod of Whitby (664) the Irish accepted Roman practices (the dating of Easter and the tonsure of priests) and the authority of the popes. The unity of the Roman Church was firmly established.

In 668, Pope Vitalian (reigned 657–672) appointed the Greek scholar Theodore of Tarsus archbishop of Canterbury. Theodore began the organization of the English church. At the same time the African abbot Hadrian made Canterbury an important center of Latin learning, and Benedict Biscop founded the famous schools of Jarrow and Wearmouth. By the end of the 7th century,

finally, Anglo-Saxon monks were the successors of the Irish in missionary work on the Continent. Aided by Pepin of Heristal and Charles Martel, who wished to extend the power of the Franks, Willibrord and Winfrid (Saint Boniface) began the conversion of Frisia (the Netherlands) and Germany. The monasteries and churches founded by them and their disciples hastened the rise of an active agricultural life as well as learning, and the entrance of Germany into the world of Roman civilization.

Western Intellectual and Artistic Life. The religious and cultural unity of western Europe was now at hand, but as yet creative efforts in literature, learning, and the arts were poor and unoriginal. Archbishop Isidore of Seville, however, compiled an encyclopedia (the *Etymologies*). It reveals an extensive knowledge, still possible in Spain, of all fields of the learning that had survived about the world and man, about Christian doctrine, the Latin language and grammar, medicine, law, the natural sciences, and technology. The encyclopedia is elementary, but it became the standard work of reference in medieval education. In Ireland and Anglo-Saxon England the Latin poetry of monks like Aldhelm, though not great literature, reflected a competent knowledge of the classics. An anonymous treatise, *On the Twelve Abuses of the Age*, offers an intelligent discussion of the duty of the king to protect the weak, rule according to law and justice, and maintain the common welfare. Anglo-Saxon literature began with Caedmon's *Hymn of Creation*, based on the biblical story, and, possibly, with the first Germanic epic, *Beowulf*, although some scholars place the latter as late as the 10th century. Meanwhile, the schools of Wearmouth and Jarrow were educating Bede, whose mature Latin scholarship leads into the 8th century and the Carolingian renaissance.

CONCLUSION

Rome had stopped at the Rhine and the Danube. Barbarian kingdoms, even trade and piracy, and above all Irish, Roman, and Anglo-Saxon missionaries extended the universalism of Rome to northern Europe and thus limited the extreme particularism of politics, languages, and customs.

Indeed, by the end of the 7th century, Latin Christianity and civilization were the one unifying force in all western Europe. Under the leadership of Rome, Constantinople, and Islam, the ancient Mediterranean civilization was about to become European.

GAINES POST
Princeton University

2. India and Southeast Asia

The Indian subcontinent remained politically divided in the 7th century, with focal points of power at Kanauj in the north and at Badami and Kanchi in the south. Southeast Asia, a region in which Indian cultural influences were strong, saw the steady expansion of Kambuja on the mainland and of Śrivijaya in the islands to the south.

Political Developments in India. The Pushyabhuti family of Thanesar reached the height of its power under Harsha (reigned 606–647), the subject of the Sanskrit biography *Harshacharita*, by the court poet Bana. Early in his reign Harsha united Thanesar with the Maukhari kingdom of Kanauj and thus wielded absolute power in the Doab, or territory between the Ganges and Yamuna rivers. However, despite the extensive range of his political involvements, he failed in his self-imposed military mission. His southward expansion was checked by Pulakeshin II of Badami. In the east, Assam was friendly to Harsha, but in Bengal his enemy Shashanka remained unsubdued. The kingdoms of Lata, Malwa, and Rajasthan in the west were never really brought under Harsha's effective control. However, he laid a solid foundation for the future greatness of Kanauj. Harsha also established diplomatic links with China and sponsored Chinese Buddhist pilgrims. The travel record of the pilgrim Hsüantsang is basic source material on 7th century India.

In peninsular India, the Chalukyas of Karnataka, with their capital at Badami, and the Pallavas of Tamil Nadu, with their capital at Kanchi, grew in strength. A contemporary Sanskrit eulogy describes the Chalukya Pulakeshin II (reigned 610–642) as the "lord of eastern and western waters." Besides unifying hitherto fragmented Karnataka, he established pockets of Chalukya power in Gujarat and in Andhra, to the north and east. The crowning achievement of his career was, however, his victory over Harsha.

The strength of the Chalukyas was considerably sapped by a bitter struggle with the Pallavas. Pulakeshin was probably killed by the Pallava Narasimhavarman I (reigned about 630–668), who claimed to have destroyed Badami. Kanchi was captured in retaliation by the Chalukya Vikramaditya I (reigned 655–681). But neither power could win a decisive victory, and their hostility continued into the next century.

Political Developments in Southeast Asia. At the beginning of the 7th century the once powerful state of Funan, in what are now Cambodia and southern Vietnam, was on the wane. About 630 it was finally annexed by Iśanavarman, the ruler of Kambuja, in present southern Laos. Iśanavarman's active interest in the politics of the neighboring state of Champa, in central Vietnam, led to a matrimonial alliance between the two royal houses. The fall of Funan also served as an impetus to the Mons of present Thailand, who consolidated the principality of Dvaravati in the lower Chao Phraya Valley and sent embassies to China in 638 and 649. In the west, new states emerged in southern Burma. The 7th century traveler Hsüan-tsang mentions two of them, the Mon country of Ka-no-lang-ka and the Pyu principality of Shih-li-cha-ta-lo (Śrikshetra, near Prome).

Śrivijaya, on Sumatra, became the most powerful of the island kingdoms. By the close of the 7th century it had conquered Malayu (modern Djambi), extended its supremacy over Bangka Island, and sent an expedition against Java. From the second half of the century it sent regular embassies to China.

Cultural Developments. The crystallization of Indian regional kingdoms and their patronage of religious and cultural movements fostered the emergence of famed centers of art and learning. Buddhism had Harsha as its patron, and the growing Buddhist center of Nalanda (in present Bihar state) attracted pilgrims from Central Asia, Southeast Asia, and China. The rock-cut temples at Mahabalipuram (near Madras) were a product of Pallava royal inspiration. The Brahman and Jain centers of Badami and Aihole (both in northern Mysore state) sprang into prominence under the Chalukyas.

Indian culture continued to be the elitist ideal in Southeast Asia. Brahmanism was gaining ground, particularly in Kambuja. But Buddhism was perhaps more widespread. Chinese records show that in 605, during the Chinese sack of Champa, 1,350 Buddhist works were carried off to China. The 7th century Chinese traveler I-ching described Śrivijaya not only as a focal point of trade with China but also as the "center of Buddhist learning in the islands of southern seas."

BRAJADULAL CHATTOPADHYAYA
Jawaharlal Nehru University

3. China and Korea

The 7th century saw the reconstruction of the Chinese Empire as the major power of East Asia. This was the culmination of the work begun by Sui Wen Ti, who had reunited China in 589 after centuries of political division. Wen Ti also brought about the reconquest of Tonkin in 603, but the next year he was murdered and succeeded by his son Yang Kuang (Sui Yang Ti).

Political Developments. During his reign, Yang Ti carried out massive construction activities. The Great Wall was rebuilt, and the Grand Canal, a major transportation route, was opened. However, his reign ended in disaster as a result of overexpenditure on construction and a series of costly attempts to reconquer the Korean state of Koguryo. Rebellions destroyed him and the Sui dynasty in 618.

After a short civil war, Li Yüan (T'ang Kao Tsu) established the T'ang dynasty, which lasted from 618 to 907. His reign was brief, ending in a coup by his son Li Shih-min (T'ang T'ai Tsung), who forced his father to abdicate in 626. T'ai Tsung's reign was to set the T'ang dynasty on a firm foundation and to expand Chinese power as far west as Samarkand and Bukhara.

The power and prosperity of China during the 7th century resulted in part from the reestablishment of the "equal-field system" of land distribution under T'ai Tsung. Maximum limits on land ownership were established by law, and state-owned lands were to be distributed for life to small farmers. The system, which had been attempted before, was designed to break the

Pallava relief from a cave temple at Mahabalipuram, in Tamil Nadu state, India, depicts the goddess Durga destroying the buffalo-demon Mahisa. Durga, wife of Shiva, is often shown as a beautiful woman with many arms. Her mount is a lion.

power of great landlords and to solve the problem of poverty. It had some effect, although it could not have been enforced throughout the country.

T'ai Tsung was succeeded in 649 by Kao Tsung, who soon fell under the influence of a remarkable woman, the concubine Wu Chao. She became empress and gained control of the government in 664. Seven years after Kao Tsung's death in 683, she declared herself emperor of the Chou dynasty, which is not regarded as legitimate. Empress Wu became the only woman ever to rule China in her own right. During her reign (690–704), the civil service examination system took shape as the major route to government service.

The Empress continued T'ang expansionist policies. After the first unification of Tibet in 607, Chinese control of Central Asia had been challenged by the Tibetans. After 30 years of struggle, Tibetan power was broken in 699. Dur-

Relief from the tomb of Chinese Emperor T'ang T'ai Tsung shows one of his favorite battle chargers.

ing the 7th century, Chinese forces were also involved in Korean wars. Chinese troops assisted the state of Silla in bringing about the first unification of Korea in 668, after which the Koreans drove them out of the peninsula.

Cultural Developments. The 7th century was an important period of Buddhist development in China. The writings of Hui-neng are a major source for the study of early Ch'an (in Japanese, Zen) thought. Dozens of Chinese monks made pilgrimages to India, notably Hsüan-tsang, whose *Record of the Western Regions* is an important source for Indian history. He also made major contributions to Chinese Buddhism through his translations of Indian scriptures.

Other schools of thought flourished in China during the 7th century. Nestorian Christian priests and churches appeared in Ch'ang-an, the T'ang capital, and Iranian Mazdaist temples were also built there. The Manichaean scripture appeared in China by the end of the century. Taoism remained important, expressed by the anti-Buddhist Fu I.

T'ai Tsung was a poet and a writer on government, and he encouraged the development of scholarly work. Among the important scholars of the period was Liu Shih-chi, whose *Shih-t'ung (On History)* long influenced Chinese historiography.

Major developments occurred in sculpture. Paralleling the growth of Chinese influences on Buddhism was a kind of Sinicization of the Gandharan Buddhist sculpture that had become current in China after its spread from northwestern India. While Buddhist sculpture continued to flourish, secular work also became important. Fine bas-reliefs from the 7th century include those of T'ai Tsung's favorite horses, carved for his tomb. Beautifully glazed ceramic figurines of animals and people, now treasured by collectors, were made in vast quantities for burial purposes.

JAMES R. SHIRLEY
Northern Illinois University

4. Japan

In the 7th century, Japan underwent a series of reforms that changed it from a country loosely ruled by a group of territorially based tribes, or clans, to a centralized state modeled on China of the great T'ang dynasty (618–907).

The most important figure in the early stage of reform was Prince Shotoku, who served as regent for Empress Suiko (reigned 593–628) and was related by blood to the Soga, the most powerful ministerial family at court. In the early years of the 7th century, Shotoku dispatched the first official missions to China that were to play a major role in the process of Japanese cultural borrowing from the continent during the next few centuries. He instituted a system of "cap ranks" at court to encourage advancement on the basis of merit, not simply birth. And he reputedly compiled a 17-article "constitution" that enunciated, chiefly in the language of Chinese Confucianism, the need for ethical government in Japan.

The records tell little about the precise division of authority between Prince Shotoku and the Soga. But after the Prince's death in 622, the Soga appear to have become increasingly autocratic in their ways. Sovereigns, with whom they were tied to by marriage, were mere pawns in their hands, and the Soga may even have aspired to supplant the imperial dynasty.

In 645 the Soga were overthrown in a palace coup led by Prince Naka and Nakatomi Kamatari, who sponsored the epochal Taika ("Great Change") Reform. Inspired by the land system of T'ang China, the Taika reform was aimed primarily at nationalizing the agricultural land of Japan for the purpose of redistributing it in equal

FUJIHARA, FROM MONKMEYER

The 7th century pagoda of the Horyu-ji Temple in Nara, Japan, is one of the world's oldest wooden buildings.

Korean scroll painting of a 7th century court noble is now in the National Museum in Seoul.

PAOLO KOCH, FROM RAPHO GUILLUMETTE

EVENTS OF THE SEVENTH CENTURY

604—Death of Pope Gregory I the Great.
604—Traditional date of Shotoku Taishi's "constitution" in Japan.
606—Beginning of Harsha's reign in northern India (to 647).
607—First mission to China by envoys representing all of Japan.
607—Unification of Tibet.
618—Beginning of T'ang dynasty in China (to 907).
622—Flight (hegira) of Mohammed from Mecca to Yathrip (Medina).
626—T'ang T'ai Tsung emperor of China (to 649).
628—Byzantine Emperor Heraclius victorious over Khusrau (Chosroes) II of Iran.
629—Dagobert, last effective Merovingian king of the Franks (to 639).
632—Death of Mohammed.
636—Defeat of Byzantine Army by the Arabs in Battle of the Yarmuk ensured Arab conquest of Syria.
636—Death of Archbishop Isidore of Seville.
638—Fall of Jerusalem to the Arabs.
641—Decisive defeat of the Persians by the Arabs at Nihavand.
642—Fall of Alexandria to the Arabs.
643—*Edictus* of Rothari, Lombard law code, approved by assembly of warriors.
645—Return of Buddhist pilgrim Hsüan-tsang to China after ten years in India.
646—Taika Reform Edict issued in Japan.
654—*Liber Iudiciorum*, Roman-Visigothic law for Spain, promulgated.
661—Muawiya first caliph of Umayyad dynasty, with capital at Damascus.
664—Synod of Whitby ensured unity of Celtic and Roman Christianity under the papacy.
668—Unification of Korea.
669—Theodore of Tarsus, archbishop of Canterbury, arrived in Britain and began to organize English church under authority of Rome.
681—Sixth ecumenical council (Constantinople III) ensured final triumph of doctrine of the two natures of Christ.
687—Battle of Tertry gave Pepin of Heristal virtual control over the Franks.
690—Empress Wu usurped throne of China (reigned to 704).
698—Arabs captured and destroyed Carthage.

plots to members of the numerically preponderant peasantry. But the reform was extended during the ensuing decades of the 7th century to embrace as well a variety of institutional and social changes that were designed to remake Japan into a Chinese-style bureaucratic state. This state was ultimately defined and provided with a detailed set of administrative and penal laws in the Taiho ("Great Treasure") Code of 702. In 710 the seat of imperial authority, which had frequently been shifted about, was settled in the newly constructed and, for the age, opulent city of Nara.

Culturally, the 7th century was a time when the Japanese came to be exposed to the full glory and brilliance of Chinese civilization, especially as it was colored during this period by the religious doctrines and artistic styles of Buddhism. Surviving temple structures, statues, and paintings attest to the particularly profound impact of Buddhist art on the Japanese as they undertook the sweeping reforms that brought into being their first truly centralized state.

H. Paul Varley, *Columbia University*

Bibliography

Arberry, Arthur J., tr. and ed., *The Koran Interpreted*, 2 vols. (Macmillan 1955).

Bede, Saint, *Ecclesiastical History of the English People* (several editions).

Bieler, Ludwig, *Ireland: Harbinger of the Middle Ages* (Oxford 1963).

Blair, Peter, *An Introduction to Anglo-Saxon England* (Cambridge 1954).

Cantor, Norman, *Medieval History*, 2d ed. (Macmillan 1969).

Coedès, George, *The Indianized States of Southeast Asia* (East West Center Press 1968).

Duckett, Eleanor, *The Gateway to the Middle Ages* (Macmillan 1938).

Gibb, Hamilton A. R., *Mohammedanism*, 2d ed. (Oxford 1962).

Goodrich, Luther C., *A Short History of the Chinese People*, 3d ed. (Harper 1953).

Grousset, René, *The Empire of the Steppes: A History of Central Asia* (Rutgers Univ. Press 1970).

Hall, John W., *Japan from Prehistory to Modern Times* (Delacorte 1970).

Havighurst, Alfred F., ed., *The Pirenne Thesis: Analysis, Criticism, and Revision*, rev. ed. (Heath 1969).

Hitti, Philip K., *History of the Arabs*, 10th ed. (St. Martins 1970).

Laistner, Max L. W., *Thought and Letters in Western Europe, A. D. 500 to 900*, 2d ed. (Cornell Univ. Press 1957).

Latouche, Robert, *The Birth of Western Economy*, 2d ed. (Barnes & Noble 1967).

Latouche, Robert, *Caesar to Charlemagne: The Beginnings of France* (Barnes & Noble 1968).

Lewis, Bernard, *The Arabs in History*, 4th ed. (Hutchinson 1966).

Lopez, Robert S., *The Birth of Europe* (Evans, M. & Co. 1967).

Lot, Ferdinand, *The End of the Ancient World* (Knopf 1931).

Majumdar, Ramesh Chandra, *Hindu Colonies in the Far East*, 2d ed. (Mukhopadhyay 1963).

Majumdar, Ramesh Chandra, ed., *The History and Culture of the Indian People*: vol. 3, *The Classical Age*, 3d ed. (Bharatiya Vidya Bhavan 1970).

Moss, Henry St. L. B., *The Birth of the Middle Ages, 395–814* (Oxford 1935).

Ostrogorsky, George, *History of the Byzantine State*, rev. ed. (Rutgers Univ. Press 1969).

Pirenne, Henri, *Mohammed and Charlemagne*, new ed. (Barnes & Noble 1955).

Reischauer, Edwin O., and Fairbank, John K., *East Asia: The Great Tradition* (Houghton 1960).

Schnürer, Gustav, *The Church and Culture in the Middle Ages*, vol. 1 (St. Anthony Guild 1956).

Stenton, Frank, *Anglo-Saxon England*, 3d ed. (Oxford 1971).

Strayer, Joseph, and Munro, Dana, *The Middle Ages* (Appleton 1970).

Varley, Herbert Paul, *Japanese Culture: A Short History* (Praeger 1972).

Vasiliev, Alexander, *History of the Byzantine Empire*, 2d ed. (Univ. of Wis. Press 1952).

Wallace-Hadrill, John, *The Barbarian West, 400–1000* (Longmans 1952).

SEVENTH-DAY ADVENTISTS, a Christian evangelical movement that developed in the 19th century as an outgrowth of the general advent awakening. It is rooted in the Millerite movement of the 1840's and is in part distinguished by the observance of the seventh day (Saturday) sabbath as a memorial of God's creation and by faith in the imminent, personal return of Jesus.

The essence of Seventh-day Adventism is salvation by faith in God the Son, Jesus Christ, whose life and death provide for the restoration of man to his original relationship with God. For Adventists the Bible authentically records God's self-revelation in his saving acts by Jesus Christ, whose life demonstrated God's perfect will for man as enunciated in the moral law. Adventists expect the culmination of man's redemption in the return of Jesus Christ to begin his kingdom of glory. Events at the end of the present age will see the bestowal of immortality upon the redeemed, both living and resurrected, whose destiny has been determined by one phase of God's judgment. The destruction of sin and sinners follows the final phase of judgment and prepares for the creation of new heavens and a new earth, which completes the work of restoring man to God.

An authoritative voice in the Seventh-day Adventist movement from its beginning has been that of Ellen G. White, who claimed special revelations from God. She pioneered with such leaders as Hiram Edson, Joseph Bates, and her husband James White. Her counsels led to the formal organization of the Seventh-day Adventist Church in Battle Creek, Mich., in 1863, and continue to give direction in the development of the church. She wrote some 45 books and thousands of articles in such fields as education, health, and Christ-directed living.

Teaching redemption of the whole man, Adventists proscribe the use of "unclean" foods, alcoholic beverages, and tobacco, and the nonmedical use of drugs. They advocate a vegetarian diet and a balanced program of exercise and hygienic living. They carry on work in 185 countries and territories, operating over 325 medical units and supporting 450 colleges and secondary schools and nearly 4,000 elementary schools.

Adventist churches are organized along congregational lines within state conferences, union conferences, and world divisions of a general conference, with headquarters in Washington, D. C. Adventist membership exceeds 2 million.

Robert H. Pierson, *President General Conference of Seventh-day Adventists*

SEVERINI, sā-vā-rē̃'nē̃, **Gino** (1883–1966), Italian painter, a founder of the futurism movement. He was born in Cortona on April 7, 1883, but lived chiefly in Paris after 1906. He studied with the painter Giacomo Balla in Rome in 1900–1901 and there met Umberto Boccioni, who became the theoretician of futurism.

In 1910, Severini was a signer of the futurist manifesto, calling on artists to incorporate into their work the speed and dynamism inherent in modern life, and he took part in the first futurist exhibition in Paris in 1912. During the years 1915–1921 the cubist influence was evident in his works, and thereafter he sought an individual neoclassical idiom. One of his best-known works is *Dynamic Hieroglyphic of the Bal Tabarin* (1912; Museum of Modern Art, New York). He died in Paris on Feb. 26, 1966.

SEVERINUS, sev-ər-ī′nəs, **Saint** (died 482), monk who preached Christianity in Noricum (modern Austria). Severinus was probably of Roman origin, but he spent his early years as a monk in the East. He first preached in what is now Vienna and then turned his attention to the region of Comanges and Astura (modern Stockerau and Hainburg, Austria). He founded several monasteries, including one at Boiotro near Passau and another at Favina, where he died on Jan. 8, 482. His feast is January 8.

SEVERINUS, sev-ər-ī′nəs (died 640), reigned as pope from 638 to 640. Severinus, a native of Rome, was an elderly man at the time of his election as pope in the fall of 638. Emperor Heraclitus delayed his consecration until May 28, 640, when he gave up trying to win Severinus' acceptance of the *Ecthesis,* a work that supported the Monothelite heresy. Severinus died in Rome on Aug. 2, 640.

SEVERN RIVER, sev′ərn, one of the principal rivers of Great Britain. It rises in Montgomeryshire, Wales, flows east into England and then in a roughly semicircular course through Shropshire, Worcestershire, and Gloucestershire to empty into the Bristol Channel. The total length of the river is about 200 miles (320 km). Its major tributaries are the Vyrny, the Wye, and the Avon.

SEVERNA PARK, sə-vûr′nə, is an unincorporated area in central Maryland, in Anne Arundel county, on a peninsula jutting into Chesapeake Bay, 17 miles (27 km) south of Baltimore. It is a residential community, from which many persons commute to work in Baltimore, Annapolis, or Washington, D. C. It is governed by the county council. Population: 16,358.

SEVERNAYA ZEMLYA, syā′vyir-nə-yə zyim-lyà′, is an archipelago of the USSR in the Arctic Ocean. Its name means "northern land." Separating the Kara and Laptev seas, it lies north of the Taimyr Peninsula and is part of the Russian republic. Slightly less than half of its area of 14,300 square miles (37,000 sq km) is ice-covered. The four main islands are Komsomolets, Pioner, Oktyabrskaya Revolyutsiya, and Bolshevik.

SEVERSKY, Alexander P. De. See DE SEVERSKY, ALEXANDER PROCOFIEFF.

SEVERUS, Alexander. See ALEXANDER SEVERUS, MARCUS AURELIUS.

SEVERUS, sə-vēr′əs, **Lucius Septimius** (146–211), Roman emperor. He was born in Leptis Magna, North Africa, in 146. A member of a distinguished North African family that included senators, Severus entered the Senate about 173 and held a number of progressively more responsible offices and military commands before becoming consul in 190. During the tumultuous last years of the reign of Commodus, Severus and his brother Geta were allied with Pertinax, whose main rivals were Clodius Albinus and Pescennius Niger. Pertinax succeeded Commodus on Jan. 1, 193, but was assassinated in March. After the murder of Pertinax, Severus, who commanded a large army in Upper Pannonia, was proclaimed emperor by his troops. He immedi-

ALINARI, ART REFERENCE BUREAU

Lucius Septimius Severus, Roman emperor (146–211 A. D.)

ately marched to Rome to crush the partisans of Didius Julianus, who had meanwhile purchased the imperial purple from the Praetorian Guard. On his approach Julianus was deserted and murdered by his own soldiers. In professing that he had assumed the purple only to revenge the death of the virtuous Pertinax, Severus gained many adherents and was able to disband the Praetorians and replace them with loyal guards.

While Severus was victorious at Rome, Niger was in the east at the head of a powerful army, by which he also had been called to the purple. In an attempt to blunt the ambitions of one rival, Albinus, governor of Britain, Severus granted him the title of caesar before launching his campaign against Niger. Severus followed up a series of early victories with the decisive engagement in 194 on the plains of Issus, in which Niger was totally ruined by the loss of 20,000 men. After devastating some territory beyond the Euphrates River, Severus in 196 took Byzantium, which had shut its gates against him, after a protracted siege.

He then returned to Rome, resolved to destroy Albinus. Severus first attempted to have Albinus assassinated, but when this failed he marched against Albinus and defeated him in Gaul near Lugdunum (Lyon) in 197. After returning to Rome, Severus turned his attention to the east to repel an invasion of the Parthians. From Parthia he marched toward the more southern provinces and entered Egypt. Back in Rome he had the Arch of Septimius Severus built in 203 to commemorate the first ten years of his reign.

A rebellion in northern Britain called him away again in 208. After penetrating to the far north of Caledonia and losing a vast number of men, he returned southward and rebuilt or repaired the wall of Hadrian across the island from the Tyne River to the Solway Firth. He died in York in 211 and was succeeded by his sons Geta and Caracalla.

Further Reading: Birley, Anthony, *Septimius Severus: The African Emperor* (Doubleday 1972).

SEVIER, sə-vēr', **John** (1745–1815), American pioneer and first governor of the state of Tennessee. He was born in Rockingham county, Va., on Sept. 23, 1745. He founded the town of Newmarket, Shenandoah county, Va., became a celebrated Indian fighter, and in 1774 served as captain in the Virginia line during Lord Dunmore's War.

He had moved in 1772 with his wife and children, to the Watauga colony on the western slope of the Allegheny Mountains. At the beginning of the Revolution, he drafted a memorial to the legislature of North Carolina, requesting annexation to that colony; as a result, all of the present Tennessee was made a county of North Carolina and known as Washington district.

Sevier served in the North Carolina legislature and was appointed district judge at Watauga. Elected colonel of the trans-Allegheny forces, he commanded in many Indian fights, including those at Boyd's Creek (1779) and King's Mountain (1780). After the war, North Carolina found that the retention of the large section later known as Tennessee would involve obligations for a corresponding portion of the federal debt, and, therefore, the tract was made over to the central government.

The settlers then determined to organize an independent state and apply for admission to the Union. At a convention held on Aug. 23, 1784, Sevier was elected governor of the new State of Franklin, as it was called. North Carolina now recognized its mistake and granted Watauga a superior court, besides organizing the militia troops into a brigade with Sevier as brigadier. But Sevier entered office as governor on March 1, 1785, reorganized the military, established a superior court and concluded treaties with the Cherokees.

In 1787, North Carolina declared that the Franklin government was unlawful, subdued it, and briefly imprisoned Sevier. In 1796, however, Sevier was elected first governor of the new state of Tennessee. He served three terms (1796–1801), and another three (1803–1809). In 1811 he was elected a U. S. Representative. He died in office, while on an Indian territory survey in Alabama, on Sept. 24, 1815.

Further Reading: Driver, Carl, *John Sevier* (Univ. of N. C. Press 1932).

SEVIER LAKE, sə-vēr', in west central Utah, in Millard county is a salt water lake that is steadily shrinking. Lake Sevier is one of the residual salt lakes left by the Pleistocene Lake Bonneville. Once it was second in size only to the Great Salt Lake among this group, but it has gradually been reduced in size by evaporation and large-scale diversion for irrigation of the Sevier River, which flows into the lake from the north and would normally help counteract the evaporation losses. At its highest modern stage (1872–1873), Lake Sevier was 28 miles (45 km) long and 10 miles (16 km) wide. Now it has more the character of an enormous salt marsh. In dry years much of the bed is encrusted with salt deposits. The lake has no present outlet, but at an earlier stage in the recession of Lake Bonneville it drained into the Great Salt Lake through a river, the bed of which is still discernible.

The Franciscan missionaries Silvestre Vélez de Escalante and Francisco Atanasio Domínguez, Utah's first explorers, were told of the lake by Indians in 1776. It was early known as Lake Niera or Lake Buenaventura. Under the latter name it became confused in cartography and legend with the Great Salt Lake. Its present name derives from the Spanish *Severo,* corrupted by American traders to Sevier. The first recorded visit to Lake Sevier was made by a party of fur hunters in 1827.

SÉVIGNÉ, sā-vē-nyā', **Marquise de** (1626–1696), French literary figure, whose witty, eloquent letters to her daughter, Mme. de Grignan, earned her a prominent place in French literature. Marie de Rabutin-Chantal was born in Paris on Feb. 5, 1626. She was the daughter of the Baron de Chantal, was left an orphan at the age of six, and was reared chiefly under the guidance of her uncle, Philippe II de Coulanges. She was married in 1644 to the Marquis Henri de Sévigné, who was killed in a duel in 1651, leaving her with a son and a daughter. Her wealth, beauty, talent, and social position brought her offers of marriage. However, she chose to devote herself to her children, to reading, and to the brilliant social and literary circle of the Hôtel Rambouillet in Paris. Some innocent business letters from her, discovered among the papers of the superintendent of finance, Nicolas Fouquet, after his arrest for embezzlement in 1661, led to a minor scandal when it was rumored that the correspondence was love letters.

Mme. Sévigné was deeply attached to her daughter, who in 1669 married Count François de Grignan and shortly afterward accompanied him to Provence, where he had been appointed lieutenant governor. This separation resulted in the voluminous correspondence that, while not intended for publication, has been given to the world and has made Mme. de Sévigné famous as a personality, as a literary stylist, and as a recorder of the social life of the resplendent court of Louis XIV.

The bulk of Mme. de Sévigné's 1,700 letters cover the seven-year period following her separation from her daughter in 1671. In later life they were rarely apart. The correspondence abounds in delightful gossip, witty anecdote, clever remarks on men and topics of the day, and graceful delineations of the pleasures and the gaieties of Parisian society. They mirror the life of a person who in turn a noted court beauty, the brilliant wit of the Hôtel Rambouillet, a religious devotee, a woman of business endeavoring to meet the demands placed on her income by her extravagant son, an appreciative student of the Latin and French classics, and always a devoted mother, deploring the separation from her daughter. Mme. de Sévigné died at Grignan on April 17, 1696.

The letters were published first in 1726. Definitive is Louis J. N. Monmerqué's revised edition (14 vols., 1862–1868), supplemented by the *Lettres inédites,* prepared by Charles Capmas (2 vols., 1876). The first volume of a later French edition, edited by Émile Gerard-Gailly, appeared in Paris in 1953. Standard French biographies are by Paul Mesnard (in the Monmerqué edition of the letters) and Charles A. Walckenaer (5 vols., 1842–1852). An English edition of the letters is by Alfred E. Newton (7 vols., 1927). Selections in English, with biographical commentary, have been prepared by Richard Aldington (2 vols., 1937), Arthur S. Megaw (1946), and Violet Hammersley (1956), which has a preface by W. Somerset Maugham.

SEVILLE, sə-vil', is a city and province in southwestern Spain. The Spanish form of the name is *Sevilla.* It is situated on the Guadalquivir River, 337 miles (542 km) southwest of Madrid. It is the largest city in southern Spain and owes its size to its position at the head of navigation on the Guadalquivir, to the agriculture of the surrounding plain, and to the minerals of the Sierra Morena, to the north. The city contains some of the world's finest examples of medieval Islamic architecture and is an important focus of tourism.

Economy. Until the Spanish Civil War of 1936–1939, Seville's industries were mainly concerned with foodstuffs. More modern industries expanded rapidly after a plant was set up to build fighter planes during the Civil War. These include other aircraft industries, agricultural machinery, shipbuilding, and chemicals. The textile industry has grown in company with the extension of cotton growing in the Guadalquivir valley. Industry has been spurred by the designation of Seville as a growth center in Spain's national development plans. Seville is Spain's only inland port, handling some 2,000 vessels per year.

Plan of the City. The oldest part of Seville lies on the east bank of the Guadalquivir. It is characterized by narrow streets, archways, and whitewashed balconied houses, whose patios are the most sumptuous in Spain. The old city is at its most typical in the Santa Cruz district, the medieval Jewish quarter. The city's shops are mainly around the Town Hall and along the busy Sierpes and Campana streets. The modern residential and industrial districts lie to the north and east, beyond the arc of the former city walls, which were demolished in the 19th century. On the west side of the river are the districts of Remedios and Triana, the latter famous for its gypsies and flamenco art.

Important Buildings. Few cities in Spain offer so much variety of Moorish and Christian architecture as Seville. The greatest religious monument is the cathedral, which is a complex of buildings in various styles ranging from Mudéjar through Gothic to baroque. It stands on the site of the principal Moorish mosque, which in turn occupied the place of a Visigothic church. The main body of the cathedral was built in the French Gothic style in the 15th century and contains the tomb and library of Christopher Columbus. The side chapels and sacristies contain paintings by Zurbarán, Murillo, Valdés Leal, El Greco, and Goya.

Parts of the cathedral date from the Moorish period, including the courtyard called the Patio de los Naranjos. The most famous relic of the mosque is the Giralda tower, the former minaret that has become the symbol of Seville. The decorated brick minaret, which is 207 feet (63 meters) high, was built in 1184. It is crowned by a Renaissance bell tower added in the 16th century. The tower takes its name from the weather vane, a statue of Faith, which is known as the Giraldilla. The tower is ascended by a series of ramps up which a horse may be ridden.

Seville is rich in ornate Gothic and baroque churches. Several were built on the sites of mosques and preserve elements of Mudéjar architecture, especially in their minaretlike towers.

The most important civil building is the Alcázar Palace, a mixture of Morisco and Gothic styles. It is near the cathedral. Built by Peter I of Castile in the 14th century on the site of the

YAN, FROM RAPHO-GUILLUMETTE

The Moorish and Christian heritage of Seville blend in this doorway to the Casa de Pilatos, a 16th century residence modeled on Pilate's house in Jerusalem.

residence of the sultans, the work was directed by Moorish architects. The Torre del Oro ("Tower of Gold"), built in 1220 as part of the city ramparts, overlooks the port and at one time was used to store treasure from the Americas. The Casa de la Lonja, next to the cathedral, houses the Archives of the Indies, documents relating to Spanish America and the Philippines.

The Town Hall, dating from the first half of the 16th century, is an elaborate plateresque building. The neoclassical and baroque Tobacco Factory, now used by the University of Seville, was the setting for part of Bizet's *Carmen.* Among the outstanding private residences are the Palacio de las Dueñas of the dukes of Alba, and the Casa de Pilatos of the dukes of Medinaceli. Both palaces exemplify the Sevillan mixture of Mudéjar, Gothic, and Renaissance styles.

Of Seville's many parks, plazas, and gardens, the most noteworthy are the María Luisa Park, in the southern part of the city, and the Murillo, Las Delicias, and Alcázar gardens. The latter, although remodeled in the 14th century, retain a Moorish atmosphere, with their orange, lemon, palm and box trees; myrtles and jasmine; and artistic fountains and pools.

Some of the most noted painters of Spain's Golden Century—the 17th—are associated with Seville, including Zurbarán, Murillo, Velázquez, and Valdés Leal. Many of their famous works can be seen in the Provincial Fine Arts Museum and in the Caridad Hospital.

Cathedral exhibits Mudéjar, Gothic, and Baroque architectural styles. The Giralda tower (*upper right*) is a former minaret incorporated into the Christian structure and topped by a 16th century Renaissance bell tower.

Pimiento is characteristic of the narrow streets in the Santa Cruz district, once the heart of the Moorish city and subsequently the medieval Jewish quarter.

Five miles (8 km) from Seville, near Santiponce, are the ruins of the Roman city of Itálica, the birthplace of the emperors Trajan, Hadrian, and Theodosius. They include the largest amphitheater in Spain, with a capacity of 25,000 spectators.

History. Seville began as an Iberian settlement of marsh dwellings. It was later occupied by the Phoenicians and Carthaginians. From the 2d century B. C. to the 5th century A. D., first under the name of Hispalis and then of Julia Romula, it was a Roman commercial and administrative city, the capital of Baetica province. Julius Caesar resided in the city several times.

Seville was overrun by the Visigoths in 461 and by the Moors under Musa Ibn Nusayr in 712. The Moors gave the city the name Ixvillia, and it became the most important commercial center in the Iberian Peninsula.

Seville was reconquered by Christian forces under Ferdinand III, king of Castile and León, on Nov. 2, 1248. Its most prosperous period was the 16th and 17th centuries, when it enjoyed the monopoly of trade with the Spanish Empire in the New World. The population rose from 45,000 in 1520 to 121,900 in 1588, due to the growth of colonial trade. Three important organizations were established in the city: the Castilian Admiralty; the Universidad de Mercantes de Nuestra Señora del Buen Aire, a powerful mercantile association; and the Casa de Contratación de Indias, set up in the Alcázar by the Catholic monarchs Isabella and Ferdinand in 1503 to regulate colonial commerce. Most of the gold from the Americas was minted in Seville.

The city experienced a decline in the 18th and 19th centuries. The Casa de Contratación was transferred to Cádiz in 1720, and freedom to trade with the Americas was granted to other Spanish ports. In 1751 the city was damaged by an earthquake. Although attempts were made from 1794 on to revive Seville's commerce by improving navigation on the Guadalquivir, the Peninsular War and successive civil wars prevented the city's recuperation until the end of the 19th century. Testimony to Seville's recovery was the Ibero-American Exhibition of 1929, held in the María Luisa Park. The numerous pavilions of the exhibition, dedicated to the Spanish-American nations, are a permanent reminder of Seville's links with the New World, as are the annual Ibero-American trade fairs that were inaugurated in 1961.

The Province. Seville province has an area of 5,402 square miles (14,001 sq km). It is divided by the Guadalquivir River, which reaches the Atlantic in extensive marshes (the *Marismas*), which have been partially reclaimed for rice cultivation but are traditionally the home of fighting bulls and such wildlife as flamingos. To the north is the Sierra Morena, a mining area with pastures and chestnut woods, which separates the Guadalquivir valley from the Meseta of Castile. The Aljarafe plain, surrounding Seville, is covered with vineyards and olive groves. South of the Guadalquivir extend the rich soils of the Campiña, where the large farms grow cotton, grain, sugar beets, and sunflowers. Irrigation is of great importance along the river. Outside the capital there are few industries. Population: (1971) of the province, 1,434,900; (1967) of the city, 610,400.

JOHN NAYLON
Keele University

Sèvres porcelain: breakfast set (1758), decorated in blue; and vase (about 1758) with *rose Pompadour* ground.

SÈVRES, Treaty of, sâ'vrə, the peace agreement between Turkey and its World War I opponents, excluding the United States and the USSR, which followed a conference at San Remo, Italy. (See SAN REMO, CONFERENCE OF.) The treaty was signed in Sèvres, France, on Aug. 10, 1920.

From the Turkish viewpoint the treaty, which denied Turkey real sovereignty, was disastrous. Turkey lost its Middle Eastern provinces, which became mandates of France (Syria, including Lebanon) and of Britain (Iraq, Trans-Jordan). Some of European Turkey was ceded to Greece, and Italy received the Dodecanese Islands and Rhodes. Armenia's independence was guaranteed, and parts of Anatolia were removed from Turkish control. An international commission was to administer the demilitarized Bosporus and Dardanelles. Turkey never ratified the treaty, which was superseded by the Lausanne pacts. See LAUSANNE CONFERENCE OF 1922–1923.

SÈVRES PORCELAIN, sâ'vrə, is French porcelain made at Vincennes and, later, at Sèvres. Under the patronage of Louis XV, a porcelain factory was founded by private citizens at Vincennes in 1738. After much royal funding, the king in 1753 authorized the title "Manufacture Royale de Porcelaine de France" and the mark of crossed L's. The factory was transferred to Sèvres in 1756, and taken over by the King in 1759. He and Mme. de Pompadour amassed large collections of its table services, vases, clocks, figurines, and flowers on wire stems.

These articles were of soft-paste porcelain (*pâte tendre*) a mixture of clay and glassy materials in imitation of the hard-paste porcelain (*pâte dur*) made at Meissen. Soft paste was warmer and softer in looks but often wilted in firing and was easily scratched or broken.

Sèvres was characteristically decorated with white panels, painted with delicate flowers, birds, figures or scenes, surrounded by raised gilded frames, set off by brilliantly colored grounds, sometimes patterned in gold. These colors included dark blue, *bleu de roi* (bright blue), turquoise, yellow, and *rose Pompadour*. Figurines after Boucher designs or models by Falconet and other sculptors were at first glazed, then were in biscuit (unglazed). Wares of the 1750's and

1760's, in the rococo style, are generally considered aesthetically the best.

In 1772, soon after kaolin was discovered in France, Sèvres began to make hard-paste porcelain figurines and then services in the neoclassical style. The factory became state property in 1793. Production of soft-paste porcelain ended in 1804, and the factory made chiefly services in the gaudy Empire style with historical scenes. In the 1850's, soft paste was reintroduced, and new techniques were invented. In 1876 the factory was moved to Saint-Cloud.

SEWAGE, liquid or solid wastes carried off by sewers. See also WASTEWATER.

SEWALL, sōō'əl, **Samuel** (1652–1730), American judge and diarist. He was born in Bishopstoke, England, on March 28, 1652, of New England parents. He graduated from Harvard in 1671, and was ordained a minister. However, he turned to a secular career, started a printing press at Boston, studied law, and entered politics. In 1692 he was made a special commissioner to try the cases of alleged witchcraft in Salem, and joined in the sentence of condemnation against witches. When he realized his error, he made in 1697 a public confession in church, and afterward spent one day annually in fasting and prayer. He was appointed judge of the supreme court of Massachusetts, and from 1718 until 1728 was its chief justice.

Sewall was possibly the first person in America to attack Negro slavery, publishing *The Selling of Joseph* (1700), a three-page tract of much eloquence. But he is best known for his diary, a garrulous detail of every sort of minutiae, extending from 1674 to 1729. The diary naturally affords a most valuable source for the political and social history of the colony. It was first published in *Massachusetts Historical Collections* (1878–1882). An abridged edition, *Samuel Sewall's Diary*, edited by Mark Van Doren, first published in 1927, was reprinted by Russell and Russell in 1963. Among Sewell's other works were *A Memorial to the Kennebeck Indians* (1721) and *The Revolution in New England Justified* (1691), of which he was coauthor. He died in Boston on Jan. 1, 1730.

William H. Seward, Lincoln's secretary of state

SEWARD, sōō′ərd, **William Henry** (1801–1872), American political leader, who was secretary of state under Presidents Abraham Lincoln and Andrew Johnson. An able and innovative administrator, he retained the confidence of Europe during the Civil War. His determined pursuit of the purchase of Alaska, then regarded as "Seward's Folly," ultimately enriched the United States with its largest state.

Born in Florida, Orange county, N. Y., on May 16, 1801, Seward graduated from Union College in 1820, studied law, and began practicing in Auburn, N. Y., in 1823. Politics gradually lured him away from the legal profession, and in 1830 he was elected as an anti-Masonic candidate to the New York Senate.

Governor and Senator. Four years later, Seward failed in a gubernatorial bid, but in 1838 he was elected the first Whig governor of New York. Though his administration was made difficult by the internal dissensions of his party, it was also marked by important reforms, which increased Whig strength in the state. During his term many of the restrictions imposed on foreigners were removed, and the antirent troubles, arising from violent tenant protests against the semimanorial leasehold system prevailing in the Hudson Valley, were adjusted. A bill was passed securing for fugitive slaves a trial by jury with counsel furnished by the state. Also, the natural history and geological survey of the state was begun, and the state museum of natural history was established. Reelected in 1840, Governor Seward declined renomination in 1842. From 1843 to 1849 he handled his law practice, although he also lectured on political topics.

Elected to the U. S. Senate in 1849, Seward attained great influence as both a party leader and an adviser to President Zachary Taylor. In a speech of March 11, 1850, promoting the admission of California into the Union, he spoke of the exclusion of slavery from all new states as being demanded by "a higher law." This phrase, which greatly offended the Southern Democrats, became a battle cry of the abolitionist movement. Seward strongly opposed President Millard Fillmore's proslavery attitude, though many Whigs in Congress accepted it. Having been reelected senator in 1855, Seward took a leading part in the debate preceding the Civil War. In an address in Rochester, N. Y., in October 1858, he referred to the "irrepressible conflict," whose outcome would make the United States a nation either of all free labor or all slave.

Secretary of State. In 1860, Seward was the most prominent Republican candidate for the presidential nomination, receiving more votes than Lincoln on the first ballot at the Chicago convention. After Lincoln's nomination, however, Seward campaigned for him all over the North. Appointed secretary of state by Lincoln in 1861, he continued in this post through Johnson's administration. At first inclined to be bellicose and authoritarian, he steered the State Department admirably during the war years. He reorganized the diplomatic service, and by his dispatches and instructions to representatives abroad, he prevented Europe from yielding to pressures to support the Confederacy.

An important incident of his secretaryship was the conflict with Britain known as the "Trent Affair." A U. S. warship intercepted the British ship *Trent*, and two Confederate agents were seized. Britain demanded their restoration, which public opinion opposed. War was averted by Seward and Lincoln's skillful diplomacy. The United States released the prisoners while affirming Britain's recognition of the principle of exemption from search, a principle that the United States had contended for during the War of 1812. Seward also insisted on redress for U. S. citizens for depredations by the *Alabama* and other British ships used by the Confederacy.

Secretary Seward firmly asserted the Monroe Doctrine in relation to the French invasion of Mexico, but, by avoiding a provocative attitude that might have involved the United States in a foreign war, he was able to defer the decision to a more favorable time. Before the close of the Civil War he intimated to the French government the irritation felt in the United States in regard to the armed intervention in Mexico. Many dispatches on this subject were sent during 1865 and 1866, increasing in urgency, until the French forces were withdrawn.

Seward supported Lincoln's proclamation liberating the slaves in all localities in rebellion, and three years later he announced the abolition of slavery throughout the Union by constitutional amendment.

In the spring of 1865, Seward was thrown from his carriage, and his arm and jaw were fractured. While he was confined to his couch with these injuries, President Lincoln was assassinated, and on the same evening, April 14, one of the conspirators entered the chamber of the secretary and inflicted several knife wounds in his face and neck.

Seward recovered and resumed his duties in the Johnson administration. He sustained the President's reconstruction policy, thereby alienating the more powerful section of the Republican party and subjecting himself to bitter censure. He opposed the impeachment of the President in 1868. Meanwhile, in 1867, he had successfully negotiated the purchase of Alaska from

Russia. A treaty for the purchase of the Danish West Indies and an arrangement with Colombia to secure U. S. control of the Isthmus of Panama failed to win Senate approval.

After his retirement in March 1869, Seward visited Alaska, and in 1870 he went on a world tour. He returned to his home in Auburn, N. Y., where he died on Oct. 10, 1872.

Further Reading: Van Deusen, Glyndon G., *William Henry Seward* (Oxford 1967).

SEWARD, sōō′ərd, a city in southern Alaska, is situated on the Kenai Peninsula, at the head of Resurrection Bay on the Pacific Ocean, about 75 miles (120 km) south of Anchorage. Seward is an important transportation and supply center for the interior of Alaska. It is the southern terminus of the Alaska Railroad and of a major highway system. Its harbor is ice-free all year. Lumbering and fishing are carried on in the region, and oil strikes have been made nearby. The community was founded in 1902. Government is by council and manager. Population: 1,843.

SEWELL, sū′əl, **Anna** (1820–1878), English author, whose fame rests on her juvenile novel *Black Beauty.* She was born in Great Yarmouth, Norfolk, on March 30, 1820, the daughter of Mary Wright Sewell, a writer of didactic ballads and verses. An injury to an ankle in childhood made her virtually an invalid for life. She had always loved horses, and after reading an essay pleading for better treatment of horses, she decided to write a story incorporating the same plea indirectly. The work, her only book, was published in 1877 under the title *Black Beauty: The Autobiography of a Horse.*

Black Beauty became popular immediately, was widely translated, and eventually won acclaim as one of the most successful animal stories ever written. Anna Sewell died at Old Catton, near Norwich, on April 25, 1878.

SEWELL, sū′əl, **Jonathan** (1766–1839), Canadian judge. Born in Cambridge, Mass., in June 1766, he was educated at Bristol, England, and in 1785 settled in Canada. Sewell studied law, was called to the bar, and practiced in Quebec.

In 1795, Sewell was appointed attorney general and judge of the court of Vice-Admiralty. From 1808 to 1838 he was chief justice of Lower Canada (Quebec). He was president of the executive council in 1808–1829, and from 1809 he was speaker of the legislative council. As chief judge, he promulgated procedural rules in questions raised by law suits between British and French Canadians. Also he supported the repressive governor, Sir James Craig. Sewell was impeached by the assembly, but the British government dismissed both charges. He was author of *A Plan for the Federal Union of the British Provinces in North America* (1824). He died in Quebec on Nov. 12, 1839.

SEWELLEL, sə-wel′əl, a small, bulky, harsh-furred animal with tiny eyes and ears and a rudimentary tail. It superficially resembles a ground squirrel. Probably the most primitive of the living rodents, the sewellel, *Aplodontia rufa,* is the only species of the family Aplodontidae. It is found only in certain mountainous areas along the Pacific coast of North America, often living in communal burrows. It lives near water, is a strong swimmer, and feeds on succulent herbs.

SEWING is the joining together of two or more pieces of fabric or other material with needle and thread. Thousands of years ago, early man used a bone needle and animal sinew to sew skins together for clothing, tents, or other equipment. From that time all sewing was done by hand, at home or in professional workshops, until the invention of the sewing machine in the 19th century. In industrialized societies, most sewing, at home or in factories, is by machine, but fine hand sewing is needed for certain purposes.

Nonprofessional people of all ages sew for economy, individuality of style and fabric, or precision of fit or as a hobby. Their work ranges from a simple dress or cushion cover to an elaborate couturier-designed garment or furnishings with a custom-made look.

EQUIPMENT, MATERIALS, AND TECHNIQUES

The basic equipment, materials, and techniques for sewing, whether by hand or machine, for clothing or furnishings, are the same.

Equipment. Sewing, like any art or profession, requires proper equipment. Learn to use it skillfully, and thereby make sewing a pleasure.

Sewing Equipment. The *sewing machine,* which does the greater part of sewing on most articles, is undisputedly the most important piece of equipment. There are two types—the straight-stitch machine for straight stitching, and the zigzag machine, which will do both straight stitching and zigzag stitching for such tasks as finishing seams or making buttonholes. For either type, attachments are available—a zipper foot to permit stitching close to the zipper chain, a seam guide to help keep the stitching an even distance from the edge, a hemmer to turn and stitch narrow hems in one operation, a ruffler to make gathers, a buttonholer, a binder, and others. See also SEWING MACHINE.

There are many small pieces of sewing equipment. Scissors include *bent-handle shears* for cutting fabric, *trimming scissors* for trimming seams and for other small jobs, and *pinking shears* for finishing edges. Measuring tools consist of a plastic-coated, nonstretchable, 60-inch (150-cm) *tape measure;* a 6-inch (15-cm) *metal gauge* with slide indicator for a *yardstick* (meter stick) for fabric and straight surfaces; and an 18-inch (45-cm) plastic ruler for pattern adjustments.

Needles come in assorted sizes to suit different weights of fabric. For hand-sewing needles, the higher the number the finer the needle. For machine needles, the lower the number, the finer the needle. In hand sewing, needles of medium length are for general purposes, and short needles are for finishing details. A snugly fitting *thimble* protects the second finger, which guides the needle in hand sewing. *Pins* should be fine, sharp, and rustproof in order not to mark delicate fabrics. Among other useful tools are a *pincushion,* a *chalk pencil* or *tailor's chalk* to mark adjustments and hem widths, a *skirtmarker* to mark hemlines, and *dressmaker's tracing paper* and *tracing wheel* to transfer pattern markings to the wrong side of some fabrics.

Pressing Equipment. Pressing is an important part of sewing and likewise requires proper equipment and knowledge of its use. The basic equipment is a *steam iron,* with temperature control according to fabric, and an adjustable, padded *ironing board.* Other, optional equipment includes a *sleeveboard* for pressing sleeves and seams; a *press mitt* for darts and curved

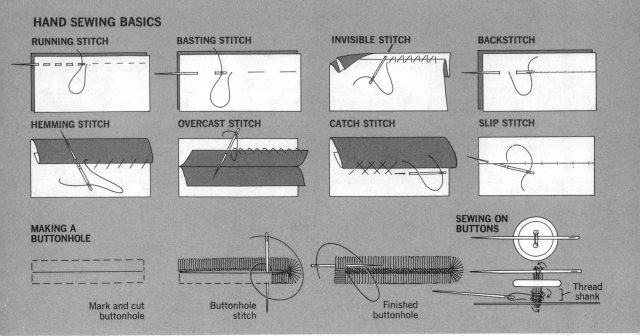

HAND SEWING BASICS

RUNNING STITCH **BASTING STITCH** **INVISIBLE STITCH** **BACKSTITCH**

HEMMING STITCH **OVERCAST STITCH** **CATCH STITCH** **SLIP STITCH**

MAKING A BUTTONHOLE

SEWING ON BUTTONS

Mark and cut buttonhole

Buttonhole stitch

Finished buttonhole

Thread shank

---

seams; a *tailor's ham* (firm cushion) for curved seams, darts, collars, and lapels; and an unpadded *seamboard,* or *point presser,* for seams in heavy fabrics, collar points, and other small, hard-to-reach areas. A *needleboard* is used for pressing pile fabrics. *Press cloths* of drill cloth for heavy fabric or of cheesecloth for light ones, often dampened, are placed over fabric to prevent shine. A *seam roll* for pressing seams open prevents seam edges from appearing on the right side of heavy fabrics. A wooden *pounding block* flattens steamed edges of tailored garments.

Thread and Notions—*Thread*. Thread should be two shades darker than the fabric because thread on the spool appears darker than a single strand. Mercerized cotton thread is suitable for stitching cotton, linen, wool, dull rayon, and cotton and synthetic blends. Silk thread is appropriate for stitching silk, wool, shiny rayon, and fine linen and for basting expensive fabrics, because it will not mar the fabric when pressed.

Synthetic thread, finer than most other kinds, is suitable for synthetic and knit fabrics. Cotton thread, in black or white and in many sizes, is for various weights of cotton. Buttonhole twist is a strong silk thread for handmade buttonholes, for attaching buttons, and for decorative top stitching.

***Notions*.** Notions, for constructing and finishing articles, are generally purchased to match the fabric and meet the construction requirements of a particular article. Some, however, such as snaps and hooks, may be kept on hand. *Bias seam binding* is to finish edges that fray, and *straight seam binding* is to finish straight edges and to stay (reinforce) waistlines. Closing devices include *zippers,* in a wide selection of lengths and colors; *snaps,* where closings are subject to little strain; *hooks and eyes,* where there is strain; and a variety of *buttons.* For stiffening, there are *grosgrain ribbon* to stay waistlines and interface waistbands, *cable cord* for filling corded seams and making frogs and button loops, and *belting* for backing fabric belts.

***Work Area*.** The work area should be large enough to arrange both sewing and pressing equipment conveniently and near each other. For laying out patterns and cutting fabric, a large smooth surface is essential. A folding cutting board or a bedboard can be used on a large table. The work area should be a place where, if you are interrupted, you can leave your work undisturbed.

***Fabric*.** Fabrics are available in many different weaves, textures, and finishes. They may be woven, knit, or pressed. Natural fibers are cotton, wool, linen, and silk. Among the many synthetic fibers are nylon, polyester, and acrylic. Frequently fabrics are a combination of natural and synthetic fibers. See TEXTILE—*Glossary.*

Fabric is chosen according to its use. For example, durable fabrics, such as double knit and bonded fabrics, are suitable for sportswear, day dresses, and suits. Stretch fabrics are primarily for sportswear. Medium and heavy-weight fabrics are appropriate for suits. Light and medium-weight fabrics are suitable for dresses. Fabrics that can be washed and worn with little or no

GRAIN LINES AND BIAS

Straighten grain by pulling fabric at opposite corners and cutting on crosswise grain line

True bias

Selvage

Lengthwise grain

Selvage

Crosswise grain

ironing are preferred for children's clothes. Fabrics for furnishings may be sturdy or delicate, depending on the style of the room and the use of the furnishings. They should, however, be closely woven so that they will keep their shape. Many fabrics are made expressly for certain purposes, such as giving body and shape through underlining, lining, and interfacing. Some fabrics, such as silk, which may slip off grain during cutting, and velvet, which has pile, need special handling.

Stitching—Hand Sewing. Hand sewing is a part of every well-made machine-sewn garment and of curtains and draperies with a custom-made look. Occasionally, an entire garment of delicate fabric may be hand sewn. The thread should be about 24 inches (60 cm) long and is usually single. Secure the thread at the beginning of the work by knotting it, and at the end by backstitching. The illustrations show the correct position of the needle and thread for various stitches and the direction in which to work.

Running stitches are for seams and tucks in delicate fabrics and for gathering. *Basting stitches* are used to hold two or more pieces of fabric together for final stitching. Basting is removed when it has served its purpose. For basting, use thread in a contrasting color to the fabric so that it can be seen easily. Use even basting for seams and areas where close control is needed, such as set-in sleeves and joining gathers. Use uneven basting for seams, center-line markings, and as a guide for top stitching. *Backstitches* are ideal for inserting zippers by hand and for joining lapped seams on the underside.

Hemming, or *whipping, stitches* are for hems where hem edges are finished by seam binding or edge stitching. *Invisible stitches* also are excellent for finished hems. They are below the hem edge and between the hem and skirt. The *slip stitch* is used when one edge is turned under, as in hems and suit linings. *Overcast stitches* are for finishing seam and hem edges that fray. *Catch stitches* can be made over cut edges that do not fray, such as hems and lapped seams in interfacing. *Buttonhole stitches* are to edge buttonholes in garments of delicate fabrics and in tailored suits and coats. *Padding stitches* are used in tailoring to hold two layers of fabric together to prevent slipping.

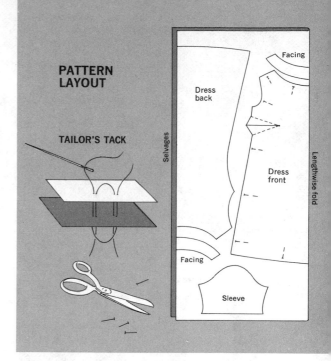

PATTERN LAYOUT

TAILOR'S TACK

Dress back

Facing

Dress front

Salvages

Lengthwise fold

Facing

Sleeve

To sew on buttons, use either a single or double thread. There should be space between the button and the fabric so that the fabric with the buttonhole in it will fit smoothly. For buttons with no metal shank, make one of thread.

Machine Sewing. Machine sewing is fast and durable and is used in practically all permanent stitching, except for finishing details. Machine stitching is ended by backstitching, that is, by sewing in the reverse direction about ½ inch (12 mm) to tie the threads.

MAKING GARMENTS

The general procedure is the same for making all garments, but in less complicated ones, some steps may be simplified or omitted.

Measurements and Patterns. Commercial patterns are made to fit standard body measurements. Several body measurements are required to determine correct pattern size. The pattern is larger than body measurements because it in-

SEAMS

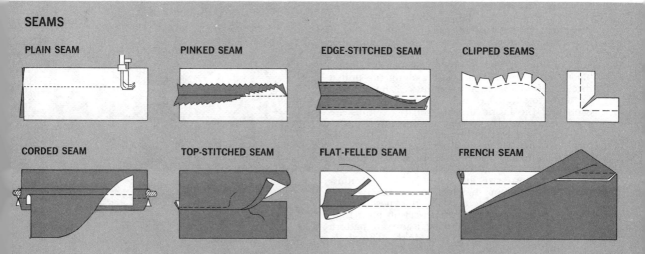

PLAIN SEAM

PINKED SEAM

EDGE-STITCHED SEAM

CLIPPED SEAMS

CORDED SEAM

TOP-STITCHED SEAM

FLAT-FELLED SEAM

FRENCH SEAM

PLEATS, GATHERS, AND DARTS

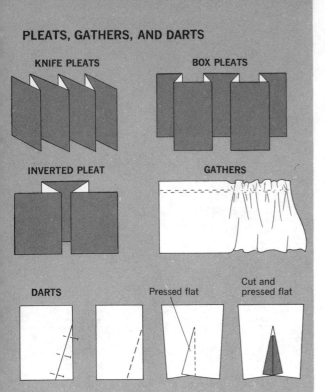

KNIFE PLEATS

BOX PLEATS

INVERTED PLEAT

GATHERS

DARTS   Pressed flat   Cut and pressed flat

seams and without diagonal darts. Plaids should be matched at the seam lines. The center of the plaid or a prominent lengthwise stripe should be in the center of the garment. If the plaid is even, that is, formed of evenly spaced identical stripes both lengthwise and crosswise, follow the pattern layout and cutting guide. If the plaid is uneven crosswise, that is, the crosswise stripes are dissimilar in color and in size, lay all pattern pieces in the same direction. If the plaid is uneven lengthwise or crosswise and lengthwise, the pattern must have center seams. For those uneven lengthwise, fold the fabric crosswise and lay all pattern pieces in the same direction. For those uneven crosswise and lengthwise, lay all pattern pieces in the same direction on a single thickness of fabric. Turn the pattern over to cut the second half.

Napped fabrics, such as suede cloth and cashmere, should be cut with the nap running down, that is, so that the fabric feels smooth when the fingers are brushed lightly over it. Pile fabrics, such as velvet and velveteen, should be cut with the pile running down for a smooth surface with a soft sheen or running up for a rough surface of richer color.

Pinning and Cutting. Generally, fabric is folded right sides together, except for pile and napped

cludes allowance for seams and darts and for ease (a few inches to permit freedom of movement) in such areas as bust, waist, hips, and length from shoulder to waist. When variations beyond those for allowances occur between the body measurements and the pattern, adjust the pattern.

Preparation of Fabric. The fabric must be prepared for pattern layout and cutting according to the grain. Lengthwise (warp) threads that run parallel to the selvages (the two woven sides of a piece of fabric) form the *lengthwise grain.* Crosswise (woof) threads that run from selvage to selvage form the *crosswise grain.* Garments cut on the *true grain* (that is, with the length parallel to the lengthwise grain) hold their shape. The diagonal formed by folding the crosswise grain parallel to the lengthwise grain is the *true bias.* Fabric cut on the true bias tends to stretch.

In order to cut fabric on the true grain, straighten the ends, then straighten the grain, if necessary. Straighten the ends by snipping through the selvage, grasping a crosswise thread and pulling it gently as you ease the fabric back on the thread, and cutting along the pulled thread. Fold the fabric lengthwise and pin the selvages together. If the straightened ends are even and the fabric lies flat, the two grains are at right angles. If the ends are uneven, straighten the fabric by gently pulling it on the true bias, working along the length of fabric.

Pattern Layout and Cutting—Layout. A pattern guide, with each pattern, shows the correct layout for pattern size and fabric width. It illustrates the direction in which to lay the pattern, when to use a double or single thickness of fabric, and when to lay a pattern section on a fold. The lengthwise grain marking is on all pattern pieces except those placed on fold. The grain line must be parallel to the selvage.

For plaid fabrics, choose a pattern with few

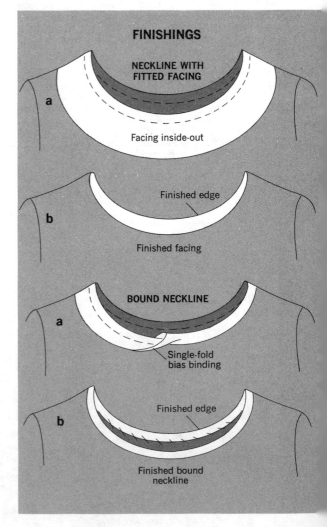

FINISHINGS

NECKLINE WITH FITTED FACING

a   Facing inside-out

b   Finished edge   Finished facing

BOUND NECKLINE

a   Single-fold bias binding

b   Finished edge   Finished bound neckline

SLEEVES

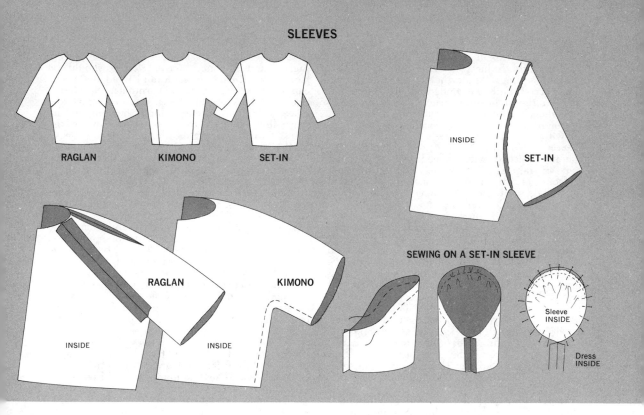

RAGLAN   **KIMONO**   **SET-IN**

INSIDE   **SET-IN**

RAGLAN   **KIMONO**

INSIDE   INSIDE

SEWING ON A SET-IN SLEEVE

Sleeve INSIDE

Dress INSIDE

---

fabrics and those, such as bonded fabrics, with the design only on the right side. Fold the fabric and pin the edges together along the selvages, the ends, and the fold. As each pattern piece is laid correctly on the fabric, pin it in place with sharp pins within the seam allowance. Pin with the fabric grain. Hold the fabric flat and cut with bent-handle shears. Cut notches marked on the pattern outward as you cut the fabric, and after the fabric is cut, cut them inward.

Markings. Pattern markings for darts and other details are the guide for joining the garment sections. Transfer all markings from the pattern to the fabric with tailor's tacks or tracing paper and wheel. When making tailor's tacks, use a different color thread for each symbol. Then match colors when joining sections.

Pressing. Press each detail after you stitch it in order to obtain a professional look. Pressing techniques vary with the fabric and construction detail. Regulate the heat control on the iron according to the fiber content of the fabric. On a scrap of the fabric, test the heat and amount of steam or moisture needed. Place garment sections smoothly, wrong side up, on the correct piece of equipment and cover with a press cloth. Place the iron lightly over the area to be pressed, allow steam to penetrate the fabric, and then lift the iron and move it to another area, following the lengthwise grain of the fabric. Do not overpress. Pile fabrics are placed over a needleboard and steamed rather than pressed.

Construction—Seams. The type of seam varies depending on the type of fabric and the style of the garment. The *plain seam* is appropriate for almost any type of fabric and is used more than any other. On most fabrics the seam edges must be finished by pinking the edges if possible, by edgestitching soft fabrics, or, for loosely woven fabrics that fray, by blind-stitch zigzag, binding, or overcasting.

Corded seams are decorative. Cut true-bias strips of matching or contrasting fabric. Cover the cord with the bias strip, using the zipper foot. Then stitch the covered cord into the seam. *Top-stitched seams* are decorative as well as functional. Baste the line for the top stitching to keep it an even distance from the edge. *Flat-felled seams*, suitable for shirts, slacks, and shorts, are durable because the edges are enclosed. Two lines of stitching are visible on the top side. *French seams*, used for sheer fabrics and lingerie, are narrow, with one seam enclosed within another.

Grading may be required for enclosed seams. Trim the seam allowances to different widths to reduce bulk, as, for example, in seams enclosed between the garment and the facing.

Curved seams, such as those enclosed in necklines and collars, are clipped so the edges will lie flat when the facing is turned to the underside. Grade the seam allowances. Then, on inward curves, clip into the seam allowance almost to the stitching. On outward curves, cut small notches in the seam allowances.

Darts, Gathers, and Pleats. Darts, gathers, and pleats are means to control fullness and give contour to a garment. *Darts* are suitable for almost any except sheer fabrics. Pin and baste darts before stitching. For a well-made dart, begin the stitching at the wide end and taper to the point with the last few stitches barely on the fold. Press darts flat, then press them to one side. In heavy fabric, slash darts through the center, and press them open. Overcast the edges if the fabric will fray.

Gathers are preferred for soft and sheer fabrics. Place the first line of stitching barely outside the seam line and the second line in the seam allowance ½ inch (12 mm) from the edge. At each end, and on the top side, anchor the threads by winding them around a pin. Pull the threads on the underside and ease the fabric back on the thread for the fullness required.

Pleats add fullness to skirts and are also a detail of styling. Mark the top fold with one color thread and the underfold with another. Then on the right side, match thread colors.

Finishing the Edges. The finish on the edge of a garment varies with the location of the edge and with the type of fabric.

Facing. Necklines and lapped openings are generally finished with shaped facings (second layers of fabric). Interfacing (fabric between the facing and the garment) should be included for added body and to prevent seams from stretching. Grade and clip these seams so they will lie flat. Then press.

Binding. A double-fold bias binding is excellent for finishing the edges of soft and sheer fabrics, because the edges are enclosed and do not show through. Trim off the seam allowance if binding is not suggested on the pattern. Stitch about ¼ inch (6 mm) from the edge to prevent the edge from stretching. Cut a strip of fabric on the true bias six times the finished width, and fold it lengthwise, wrong sides together. Stretch the folded bias slightly as you pin the edges to the right side of the neckline curve. Stitch barely below the first stitching. Press stitching only. Fold the binding over the seam edge to the stitching on the underside, and pin. Finish by hand.

Hems. Hems are the last step in finishing a garment. They vary in width according to the shape of the skirt at the hemline. A 3-inch (76-mm) hem is appropriate for a straight skirt; a circular hem is about 1 inch (25 mm) wide; and a 6- or 8-inch (152 or 203 mm) double-fold hem is frequently used in a sheer gathered skirt.

Mark the hemline an even distance from the floor with a skirtmarker or yardstick. Fold, pin, and baste on the marked line. Mark the hem an even width, then cut away the excess width. Hem edges should be finished on most fabrics. They may be pinked, bound, or overcast by machine, depending on the fabric. Hems should be invisible, and hand sewing is therefore preferred for the final stitching. However, the blind-stitch zigzag is frequently used for children's clothes and sportswear because of its durability.

Closings. Closings should be strong because they are subjected to strain. *Zippers,* preferred for dresses, skirts, shorts, and slacks, are generally concealed in a seam. The lapped application, with one line of stitching visible, is preferred for side and center closings. The slot seam, with the zipper centered under the seam, has two lines of stitching visible and is for center seam and sleeve closings. Instructions for inserting the zipper are given on the zipper package. The zipper may be sewn by machine or hand.

Snaps at the neckline and waistline hold the edges in place when closings have buttons. *Hooks and eyes* hold waistbands and necklines securely when these closings have zippers. *Snap-on-tape* is excellent for crotch closings in infants' clothing. A *continuous bound placket,* an opening from a cuff or waistband, is used for sleeves and gathered skirts.

Details—Collars. Interface collars for added body. The top collar should be slightly larger than the undercollar so that the finished collar can be shaped to lie smoothly. All seams in stitching and joining a collar to the neckline are enclosed. Therefore, for a smooth-fitting collar, the seams must be graded and clipped.

Sleeves. Three basic sleeve styles are set-in, raglan, and kimono. *Set-in sleeves* should be handled with care to shape and mold the sleeve cap as it is fitted into the armhole. Stitch the sleeve, right sides together. On the right side, place a line of stitches along the cap on the seam line between the notches to control the ease. Turn to the right side, and pin the sleeve in the armhole, right sides together, matching underarm seams, notches, and the center of the sleeve with the shoulder seam of the bodice. Draw the thread to ease the fullness to fit the armhole, distributing the ease evenly. Secure the thread ends, and then remove the sleeve from the armhole. Press the sleeve cap over a press mitt to shrink out the fullness and shape the cap. Pin the sleeve in the armhole, matching markings as before. Hand-baste, then stitch. Press only the seam allowance, and then turn it toward the sleeve.

Raglan sleeves, which fit smoothly along shoulder and arm unbroken by a seam, are easy to construct. They are often selected for coats because they fit nicely over other garments but are also used for dresses and blouses.

Kimono sleeves, cut in one piece with the bodice, fit better if they have *gussets* (shaped pieces of fabric inserted under the arm).

Waistlines. Waistline joinings should be stayed (reinforced) with straight seam binding or grosgrain ribbon to prevent stretching. Seam allowances are pressed downward on most skirts, upward if the skirt is pleated or gathered.

Lining, Underlining, Interlining, and Interfacing. A garment may have a *lining* or *underlining* of a special fabric to give it body, help hold its shape, and provide a custom-made look. Both are

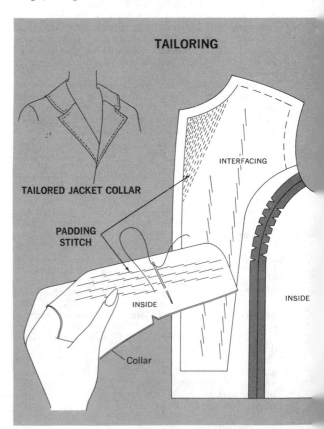

TAILORING

TAILORED JACKET COLLAR

PADDING STITCH

INTERFACING

INSIDE

INSIDE

Collar

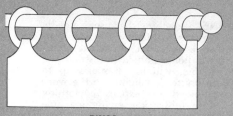

RINGS

PINCH PLEATS

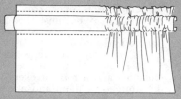

CASING

second thicknesses of fabric cut exactly the same as the garment. A *lining* is constructed separately from the garment and is then attached to it, at neck and waist, wrong side to wrong side. An *underlining* is basted to the wrong side of the garment section, and the two layers are handled as one in construction. *Interlining* is a third thickness of fabric placed between the lining and the outer fabric for warmth or added body. *Interfacing* is a third thickness of fabric placed between the garment section and the facing or hem for body. It should be chosen according to the fabric of the garment and for the effect desired.

Tailoring. In tailoring the garment is molded and shaped as it is being constructed. Tailoring requires greater knowledge of fabric and sewing techniques than does plain sewing. Tailored garments, such as suits and coats, are made of medium- or heavy-weight fabrics with complex inner construction, which involves hand sewing.

Many experts construct suit jackets of muslin to be sure of a perfect fit before cutting into expensive fabrics. Any adjustments made in the muslin shell are transferred to the pattern before cutting.

Mark the fabric with tailor's tacks. Underline each section to preserve the shape and add body. For best results, interface with hair canvas in such areas as front openings, extending across the chest and around armholes; across the shoulders and from neck to 3 inches (76 mm) below the armholes; collar; and hems. Seams and darts are handled as in any good sewing.

Try on the jacket, over the skirt and blouse, at frequent intervals to be sure it fits correctly before stitching. During each try-on, roll the lapels and collar as they will be worn, and lap and pin the front opening, matching center lines. Allow for the lining when fitting.

Lapels. Roll lapels with the interfacing on top and tack the interfacing to the roll line, which is from neck to top buttonhole, using the padding stitch. Roll lapels over the fingers as you work several rows of stitches in the lapels. Press over a tailor's ham. The interfacing along fronts and lapels should be ⅝ inch (15 mm) from the fabric edge. Pin previously shrunken ¼ inch (6 mm) tape over interfacing edge, and miter the corners. Hand-sew each edge in place. Baste both the front and back interfacing around neck and armholes. Lap seams at the shoulder and underarm, and catch-stitch together.

Undercollar. Tack interfacing to the undercollar as for lapels. Roll the collar as you work from roll line to neckline and then from roll line to seam line. Press over a tailor's ham. Sew the undercollar to the neckline. Trim seam allowances and press the seam open.

Front Facing and Top Collar. After joining the front facings and top collar to the jacket, press the seams, and then press them open over a seamboard and point presser. Trim seam allowance on jacket and undercollar to ¼ inch (6 mm) and on facing and top collar to ⅛ inch (3 mm). Cut diagonally across points, close to the stitching, and notch outward curves and clip into inward curves. Turn facing to the underside. Baste along the edges with silk thread, easing the facing under slightly below the lapels, and the garment under slightly along the lapels and collar. Press lapels and collar over the tailor's ham, and quickly use the pounding block to flatten the edges. Roll lapels and collar, and baste the facing in place on the underside.

Sleeves. Baste, stitch, and press the sleeves, either set-in or raglan, as described above.

Hems. Cut interfacing on the true bias 1 inch (25 mm) wider than the hems. Align one edge with the hemline, and catch-stitch each edge in place. Turn the hem over the interfacing, and baste and press. Catch-stitch hem to the interfacing.

Lining. Machine-stitch seams, leaving the shoulder open. Press basted darts and pleats, and then hand-sew a few inches along the pleats and center of darts with a fine catch stitch.

Turn jacket to the wrong side (except sleeves), and hand-sew lining to the jacket, making all stitches through seam allowance, facing, and interfacing of the jacket, never through the top fabric. Pin lining around the armholes. At the underarm, sew lining and jacket seam allowances together with a long basting stitch. Pin and baste the front shoulder in place, turn under the back shoulder seam allowance, lap and pin it over the front lining. Turn under seam allowances around the neck and along the front edges, and lap and pin them over the facing. Slip-stitch. Baste lining around armholes.

Turn under the lining hem, and pin it over the jacket hem. Baste ½ inch (12 mm) from lining fold. (This allows for ease in the lining.) Fold on the basting and hand-sew the under layer of the hem to the jacket hem and interfacing.

Slip the lining over the sleeve. Turn under the seam allowance, and lap and pin it over the armhole seam allowance; slip-stitch. Finish the sleeve hem the same as the jacket hem.

Add the couturier touch. Hand-sew the zipper in the skirt. Sew a chain weight where lining and hem join to preserve the lines of the jacket.

MAKING FABRIC FURNISHINGS

Curtains, slipcovers, bedspreads, and decorative pillows are not difficult to make. Style and fabric should be chosen with an eye to the shape, size, exposure, and purpose of the room and to the furniture in it. If furnishings are well constructed, they will have a custom-made look at considerable savings.

Seldom, if ever, can you find patterns for furnishings. You must therefore work with measurements. Accuracy is essential. Straightening fabric and making seams and darts are basically the same for furnishings as for clothing.

Curtains. There are many different styles of curtains and a rod for every style. Curtains may be unlined or lined and may vary from less than window length, as in café curtains, to floor length. They may be gathered or pleated and may be attached to the curtain rod by a casing (an opening through which the rod slips), rings, or hooks. Most have a heading at the top. Sheer curtains and heavier ones (also called draperies) may be hung on separate rods at the same window. See DRAPERY AND CURTAINS.

When measuring for length, allow enough fabric for the heading and hem. When estimating width, allow two and a half to three times the width of the window for sufficient fullness. Curtains should be cut on the lengthwise grain. You can piece the width if necessary but not the length. Stitch sheer and other unlined curtains with a French seam. For lined curtains, use a plain seam and hand-sew the lining in place. Use a strip of 3- to 6-inch (76–152 mm) crinoline to hold pleated headings erect.

Most curtains, except sheer tie-backs, should have a weighted tape sewn in the bottom hem so that they will hang evenly. More formal curtains may be finished at the top with a valence of fabric pleated or gathered and supported by a rod or shelf, or with a painted or fabric-covered cornice board.

Slipcovers. You must measure carefully the length and width of each section of a chair or other piece of furniture, allowing enough material for seams and hems. You will probably want to block out pieces of muslin according to your measurements and pin-fit them to the chair to get the exact shape for a pattern. Experts work directly with the slipcover fabric.

The pattern should be laid out so that lengthwise measurements follow the lengthwise grain of the fabric. Care must be taken to match plaids and stripes at the seam line or to center a floral panel on each section of pattern. Pin-fit the fabric pieces to the chair, right side out, to see that the design matches and that the cover fits. Remove the cover, and pin identifying pieces of paper to each section. Stitch the sections together. Corded seams are most popular.

The cover may be finished off with a straight, pleated, or gathered flounce. It is closed on a back corner or the center back with a zipper. If there is a cushion, it should be reversible. On both sides of the cushion, floral designs should be centered, and stripes should match the inside back and front of the chair.

GLADYS CUNNINGHAM
Author of "Singer Sewing Book"

Bibliography

Better Homes & Gardens, *Sewing Book* (Meredith 1961).
Bishop, Edna B., and Arch, Marjorie S., *Bishop Method of Clothing Construction* (Lippincott 1966).
Coats & Clark's Educational Bureau, *Coats & Clark's Sewing Book* (Western 1968).
Cunningham, Gladys, *Singer Sewing Book* (Western 1969).
McCall's Editors, *McCall's Sewing Book* (Random House 1968).
Margolis, A. P. *Dressmaking Book* (Doubleday 1967).
Perry, Patricia, ed., *Everything About Sewing* series (Butterick 1971–1972).
Perry, Patricia, ed., *Ready Set Sew* (Butterick 1971).
Perry, Patricia, ed., *Vogue Sewing Book* (Butterick 1970).

SEWING MACHINE, a machine that uses a needle and one or two threads to bind or decorate fabric or other material. It is an important labor-saving device in the home and in industry. The home sewing machine, which can make up to 1,500 stitches per minute, has lightened the work of women and provided less expensive clothing for the family. The industrial sewing machine is used in mass-producing clothing, shoes, luggage, pocketbooks, baseball gloves, awnings, tents, books, and other items. It makes the same basic stitches as a home machine but operates faster, making up to 5,000 stitches per minute. Both single-needle and multineedle machines are used, and they can meet almost any sewing requirement.

Sewing machines can be classified as chain-stitch or lockstitch machines. A chain-stitch machine works with only one thread that goes through the needle and the fabric. A "looper," or hook, pulls one looped stitch into the next, forming the chain stitch. Chain-stitch machines are used chiefly in sewing sacks, bags, or other items where an easily ripped stitch is desirable.

A lockstitch machine uses an eyepointed needle with a thread supply, and a shuttle-and-bobbin assembly with another thread supply. The machine sews two or more pieces together with a lockstitch, which consists of two threads that interlock in the material. Lockstitch machines are used mostly to sew clothing, leather goods such as luggage and shoes, upholstery, and books.

Most home sewing machines are either straight lockstitch machines or zigzag lockstitch machines. In the former, the needle moves up and down and sews straight stitches. In the latter, the needle not only moves up and down but also swings from side to side. As a result, it can sew in straight lines, zigzag patterns, or smooth curves.

Almost all home machines are powered by small electric motors with either foot- or knee-operated motor-speed controls. Some treadle-powered machines are still in use, mostly in rural areas or undeveloped countries.

STRAIGHT-STITCH MACHINES

The first popular straight-stitch machines had a long shuttle enclosing a long bobbin. The shuttle traveled forward along a curved raceway, carrying the bobbin thread through a loop of needle thread on the underside of the fabric. Then the fabric was advanced, which tightened the loop and interlocked the two threads in the middle of the fabric. This kind of machine, which is still manufactured, is simple, trouble free, and inexpensive. It has some limitations because it only sews straight and uses simple attachments such as a hemmer, binder, zipper foot, and, in some cases, a buttonholer.

Most straight-stitch machines are now made in Japan and feature an oscillating shuttle and round bobbin assembly based on a Singer model patented before 1900. This kind of straight-stitch machine differs from the long-shuttle machine in that the shuttle movement is forward and backward along a semicircular path, the bobbin is round, and the lockstitch is formed in a different way.

The modern machine sews forward and in reverse, darns, and uses attachments such as the hemmer, binder, ruffler, zipper and cording foot, quilting foot, and buttonholer. The template buttonholer is a precision attachment with nine different size templates that can be inserted in it, en-

SEWING MACHINE

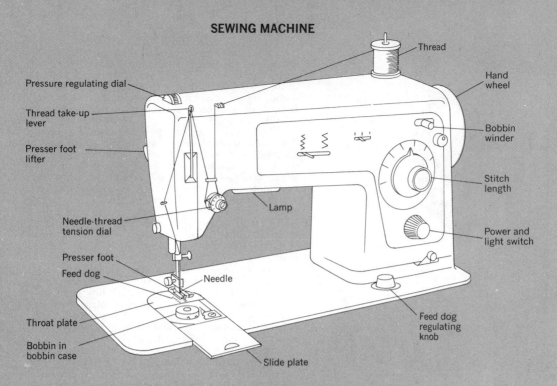

Thread

Hand wheel

Pressure regulating dial

Thread take-up lever

Presser foot lifter

Bobbin winder

Stitch length

Needle-thread tension dial

Lamp

Power and light switch

Presser foot

Feed dog

Needle

Throat plate

Feed dog regulating knob

Bobbin in bobbin case

Slide plate

HOW A STITCH IS MADE

A loop in the needle thread begins to form as the needle starts to rise. When the loop is large enough, the shuttle hook slips into the loop.

As the take-up lever slackens the needle thread to permit enlargement of the loop, the hook carries the enlarging loop around and under the bobbin case.

After the hook releases the enlarged loop, the take-up lever gradually tightens the needle-thread loop, which has completely encircled the bobbin thread.

The take-up lever keeps tightening the needle-thread loop until both the needle thread and the bobbin thread are joined in the material, forming the lockstitch.

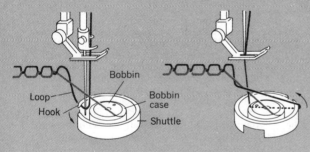

Loop

Bobbin

Bobbin case

Hook

Shuttle

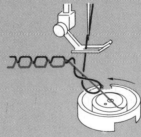

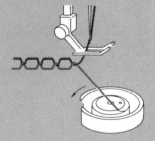

abling the sewer to make a wide variety of buttonhole sizes for every type of garment. Although semiautomatic and automatic zigzag machines have been gaining in popularity, many oscillating-shuttle, straight-stitch machines are still used by housewives who just darn, mend, and sew a few seams.

How a Straight-Stitch Machine Works. The basic operation of the straight-stitch sewing machine has changed little since its invention in the mid-19th century. There have been some variations, particularly in the design and movement of the shuttle. Most straight-stitch machines now have an oscillating shuttle, as described previously. However, some have a rotary hook shuttle, whose movement is circular, continuous, and smooth. The operations of oscillating-shuttle and rotary-shuttle machines are similar.

When a sewing cycle starts, the needle descends and carries thread down through the material, and the shuttle hook advances to meet the needle. Then the take-up lever slackens the tension of the thread, forming a loop in the needle thread. The shuttle hook enters the loop and enlarges it, while carrying the loop around the bobbin case. As a result of this motion, the upper (needle) thread encircles the lower (bobbin) thread. As the needle starts upward, the take-up lever tightens the upper thread around the lower thread. When the needle reaches its highest point of travel, both threads are joined together in the material, forming the lockstitch. Then the sewing cycle begins again.

Various thread-control devices guide the upper and lower threads during the sewing cycle. As the upper thread is unwound from a spool on the arm, it passes through a series of guides and then into disks that control the thread tension. The thread then passes through a check spring, which holds the upper thread until the

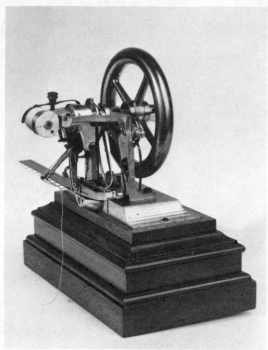

HOWE'S sewing machine had an eyepointed needle carrying one thread and a long shuttle carrying a second thread. It was the first patented lockstitch machine (1846).

needle enters the material, and then through the take-up lever, which allows the loop of upper thread to be formed so that the shuttle hook can pick it up. The contour of the shuttle keeps the upper thread in a loop until it encircles the lower thread, which is kept under tension.

The feed system moves in time with the sewing cycle. When the needle is descending, a toothed feed dog moves the material away from the operator, carrying the material into position for forming the stitch. As the needle enters the material, the feed dog drops below the needle plate surface, and the material is motionless while the stitch is formed. When the needle starts upward, the feed dog moves toward the operator, returning to its position for rising. As the needle rises, the feed dog rises and grips the material, and the sewing cycle begins again.

Every component of the sewing mechanism is activated by a main shaft that runs through the upper machine arm. A series of eccentric cams control the needle bar movement in the upper part of the machine as well as the shuttle-and-bobbin assembly and the feed system in the lower part of the machine. The feed reverse is simply an offset cam attached to the feed linking bar. When the reverse is activated, the cam moves the feed bar in the direction opposite to that of the forward direction.

ZIGZAG MACHINES

With a semiautomatic zigzag machine the operator can sew on buttons, make buttonholes, overcast seams, and blindstitch by pushing a button or moving a lever rhythmically with the right hand while sewing. An automatic machine controls the zigzag operation automatically by means of a set of built-in or inserted cams in the zigzag section. Special fingers ride the cams and move the needle bar along the contour of an individual cam. In this way, the machine can form a variety of stitch patterns. Some automatic zigzag machines also contain cams for control of the feed system and this increases sewing versatility.

Zigzag machines can perform more functions than straight-stitch machines but are more complicated and more expensive. Nevertheless, if the home seamstress is going to sew on knit material, double-knit material, stretch material, or any material requiring a stitch with elasticity, a zigzag machine is almost essential. Also, some zigzag machines have an open arm that is especially useful when sewing in sleeves, pant legs, socks, or other tubular clothing that has places that are hard to reach without ripping out a seam.

How a Zigzag Machine Works. In a zigzag machine, a hinged bracket holds the needle bar, which is activated by a connecting link from the zigzag control panel. When the control lever or button is moved, the needle bar responds not only by moving up and down but also by swinging from side to side.

Zigzag machines basically use the same kinds of shuttle-and-bobbin assemblies as those used on straight-stitch machines. There is at least one long-shuttle zigzag machine, and there are several oscillating-shuttle zigzag machines. However, most zigzag machines have a rotary shuttle. In some of these machines, such as the Bernina, the shuttle and bobbin are seated perpendicular to the sewing surface. In others, such as Singer Touch & Sew machines, the shuttle and bobbin are seated parallel to the sewing surface.

HISTORY

In 1790, Thomas Saint, an English cabinet-maker, obtained the first known patent on a sewing machine. His crude machine used a crochet-type hooked needle that carried the thread through a hole prepunched by an awl. Barthélemy Thimmonier made one of the first workable machines, which was patented in France in 1830. Several of his chain-stitch machines were used to sew French Army uniforms, but Thimmonier had fierce opposition from tailors, who burned his factory twice because they were afraid the machine would take their jobs. Thimmonier eventually went to America, where he received a patent in 1850. By that time, at least one lockstitch machine far superior to his chain-stitch machine had been invented.

In the United States, Walter Hunt devised a sewing machine about 1833. It had an eye-pointed needle attached to the end of an arm. Although Hunt never applied for a patent, his use of the eyepointed needle made possible the invention of a practical sewing machine.

Elias Howe was granted U. S. patent 4750 for his sewing machine on Sept. 10, 1846, after many years of development. Howe's machine had a curved eyepointed needle and a long shuttle that moved back and forth horizontally underneath the cloth. Howe had little success selling his machines in the United States, so he went to England. There he sold the English patent rights to William Thomas, a corset maker, who became a millionaire as a result.

Isaac M. Singer, another American, had become interested in the sewing machine after watching a friend try to repair several machines.

In 1851 he perfected a machine that had a long shuttle like Howe's. His machine also had a heart-shaped cam on the main shaft so that the needle bar could move straight up and down and carry a straight needle instead of a curved one like Howe's.

An American cabinetmaker, Allen B. Wilson, invented a rotary hook shuttle in 1851 and a four-motion feed in 1854. Wilson's shuttle had a continuous rotary motion, which provided a great increase in sewing speed. His four-motion feed had a plate with teeth that advanced the fabric in time with the needle movement. Both of his devices are still used on modern machines.

When Howe returned to the United States in 1849, he sued the Singer Company and others for patent infringements, and finally won at least one suit against Singer in 1854. In 1856, four manufacturers, including Singer, Howe, and Wilson, joined in an agreement to pool their patent rights. This so-called "Sewing Machine Combination" held most of the sewing machine patents until they expired in the 1870's.

Other American inventors who contributed to the success of the sewing machine include James E. Gibbs, who developed the single-thread chain stitch in 1856; Thomas White, founder of White Sewing Machine; and Will Free, founder of the Free Company.

In Europe, Pfaff started making sewing machines in 1862. A gun factory in Husqvarna, Sweden, built a machine in the late 1880's, and many other European manufacturers were making machines before 1900. The Japanese began to make sewing machines after 1900; their industry became a major one after World War II.

Early sewing machines were designed primarily for use in industry. For instance, garment factories used sewing machines on production lines in the early 1850's. Electric sewing machines had become important to the manufacturing trades by 1905. The first zigzag machine was built for industrial use before 1900. It was used mainly for sewing window blinds.

The first electric sewing machine for home use was marketed by the Singer Company in 1889, but home electric machines did not become popular until the 1920's. Since then, they have almost completely superseded hand- or foot-powered types.

Home zigzag machines were first introduced in the United States after World War II, mostly as a result of a lowered import tariff in accordance with the Marshall Plan for rebuilding Europe. Necchi machines from Italy came first in 1947; then came the Elna and Bernina from Switzerland; Pfaff, Adler, and Anker from Germany; and Husqvarna (Viking) from Sweden.

Zigzag machines changed the sewing practices of the home seamstress and brought a rebirth of home sewing unprecedented in history. Hand-finished sewing was all but eliminated because the machine could sew on buttons, make buttonholes, overcast seams, and blindstitch by pushing a button or moving a lever. Sewing creativity was further enhanced when zigzag machines were improved to sew designs and make buttonholes automatically.

WILLIAM EWERS
Author, "Sincere's Sewing Machine Service Book"

Further Reading: Ewers, William, *Sincere's Sewing Machine Service Book* (Sincere 1971); Ewers, William, *Sincere's Zig Zag Sewing Machine Service Book* (Sincere 1970); Ewers, William, and Baylor, H. W., *Sincere's History of the Sewing Machine* (Sincere 1970).

SEX is the sum of those differences among individuals by which distinction is made between partners engaged in sexual reproduction. Sex is known at all levels of biological organization, except among the viruses. Most commonly, individuals are one sex or the other, but there are some individuals, called hermaphrodites, in which male and female organs and functions coexist. Such hermaphroditism occurs in most plants, in many protozoans, in many invertebrates, and in certain fishes. Birds and mammals are sometimes born showing degrees of intersexuality, but not functional hermaphroditism.

By *sexual reproduction* is implied the transfer of genetic information as a preliminary to multiplication. In bacteria, pairs fuse, or conjugate, and a variable length of the single chromosome is passed from the "male," or donor, cell to the "female," or recipient, cell. In hermaphrodite protozoa, such as *Paramecium*, individuals conjugate, and each transfers a small "migratory" nucleus that unites with the partner's stationary nucleus. The conjugants, each now containing some genetic information from the other, then separate, and each divides to form several new individuals. In the higher plants and animals, genetic information is recombined through the mediation of specialized sex cells, called *gametes*. The *spermatozoon*, the male gamete, is commonly small and motile, while the *egg*, or *ovum*, the female gamete, is large and nonmotile. The gametes unite at *fertilization*.

Bacteria and protozoa can multiply without prior union, thus exhibiting *asexual reproduction*. Higher organisms can also increase by asexual reproduction and in several ways: by *subdivision*, as when a sea anemone "pulls itself in two"; by *budding*, as in plants and in animals like *Hydra*; and by *parthenogenesis*, the development of an unfertilized egg, a phenomenon known in numerous plants and animals.

The transfer of genetic material in sexual reproduction is only secondarily associated with multiplication. Primarily, it is part of a system of "genetic recombination" that makes possible biparental inheritance, natural selection, and the adaptive evolution of the race. The other essential part of this system is *meiosis*, which involves the reassortment, or shuffling, of maternal and paternal genes. Meiosis also entails reduction of the genes (and chromosomes) to half their number. It commonly takes place during *gametogenesis*, the formation of the germ cells, so that each gamete carries a half (*haploid*) complement of chromosomes. The union of gametes in fertilization reestablishes the full (*diploid*) complement characteristic of the species.

SEXUAL CHARACTERISTICS

The essential sexual difference between males and females lies in the kind of gamete they produce. In many lower invertebrates, the gonad is simply an aggregation of germ cells, which differentiate into gametes so that gonads and gametes are equally *primary sexual characteristics*. In higher organisms, cells of a different kind make up the bulk of the gonad. The gonad is, however, still distinctive—testis in the male, ovary in the female. Through developmental error or experimental intervention, germ cells of the opposite sex may enter the early gonad. In mammals, misplaced germ cells do not long survive, but in amphibians they can take part in gametogenesis.

Secondary sexual characteristics include all other distinguishing features of the genital tract in males and females, as well as differences in body form and size, pelage and plumage, and behavior. Structural differences constitute what is known as *sexual dimorphism.* The range of these differences is wide. In some species the sexes look identical, while in others there are wide differences. In the marine worm *Bonellia,* the reduced male lives within the female.

GENETIC BASIS OF SEX

In mammals, sex is determined by the sex chromosomes, labeled X and Y. The X chromosome is usually much larger than the Y and carries 60 or more genes, while the Y chromosome has very few genes. The female is the homogametic sex, having an XX sex chromosome make-up, and all eggs carry an X sex chromosome. The heterogametic male, having an XY sex-chromosome makeup, produces two kinds of spermatozoa: X-bearing spermatozoa and Y-bearing spermatozoa. More complex arrangements are seen in some bats, shrews, marsupials, and a gerbil in which the female's are XX and males are XYY, and in mongooses where females are XXXX and males are XXY.

The genes present on the sex chromosomes find expression in *sex-linked* characters, such as the quality of color vision and the rate of blood clotting. So-called *sex limited* characters, however, are due to genes found on the nonsex chromosomes (autosomes) that can be expressed in only one sex. For example, a common form of baldness results from an autosome that finds expression only in a male hormonal environment.

The sex-chromosome constitution determines whether the embryonic gonad develops into an ovary or a testis. This direct influence of the sex chromosomes appears to be exerted only on this tissue, with other organs and tissues coming under the action of the sex hormones produced by the gonads. Germ cells are not essential for testis differentiation and hormone production but do play an important role in differentiation and hormone production in the ovary. How sex chromosomes exert their effect is not clear, but there is no doubt that the Y chromosome is strongly male-determining. When the Y chromosome is lost during spermatogenesis or early in development, and an O-carrying spermatozoon (a spermatozoon with no sex chromosome) is produced and fertilizes the egg, the resulting XO individual is born female. Although the Y chromosome is strongly male-determining, it may not, however, be directly responsible for maleness: it may instead "switch on" a male-determining gene located on the X chromosome. This theory has been put forward to account for the male organs in "intersexual" female (XX) mice, goats, and pigs, in which the switching-on might be attributable to an autosomal gene.

Since numerous genes are on the X chromosome and human females are XX, a compensatory mechanism operates to avoid a double-dosage effect in females in contrast to males: one X chromosome is inactivated early in embryonic development. The inactive X forms a small dense body, "sex-chromatin," that identifies the nuclei of females as "sex-chromatin" positive. Males are "sex-chromatin negative." With cells obtained from the amniotic fluid surrounding a developing embryo through simple surgery (amniocentesis), it is possible to determine the sex of an unborn child by determining whether the cells are sex-chromatin negative or positive.

X and Y chromosomes were first noted in insects and are found in many other nonmammals. In birds, reptiles, and in some amphibians and fishes, the male is the homogametic sex and the female the heterogametic. Thus there are genes for maleness on X chromosomes and for femaleness on the Y chromosomes. Sometimes the altered relationship is stressed by giving the chromosomes different letters—for example, ZZ for a male and WZ for a female. In most insects, the males are the heterogametic sex. In the fruit fly *Drosophila,* sex is determined by the balance between the feminizing influence of the X chromosome and the masculinizing influence of autosomal genes, since in this particular case the Y chromosome is inert. In butterflies and moths, however, the male is homogametic. Other insects, such as the honeybee, depend on quite different means of sex determination. Diploid queens and workers come from fertilized eggs, while the haploid drones (males) derive from parthenogenetic development of unfertilized eggs.

The potency of the gene influence in sex determination differs. In mammals it seems to be absolute. Not only is the sex of the gonad permanent once it is established, but the germ cells in the gonads can develop only into gametes corresponding to their sex-chromosome constitution, and only if they are in the appropriate gonad. In birds, however, sex reversal is possible. In the domestic hen, for example, the left gonad normally develops into an ovary, while the right remains undetermined. If subsequently the ovary is destroyed by disease or removed, the remaining gonad develops into a testis, and the bird changes into a fully functional rooster. In amphibians, female germ cells placed in testes will form spermatozoa, and male germ cells placed in ovaries will form eggs. In some species, the development of the gonad can be reversed by hormone treatment. In hermaphroditic fish both types of sex organs and gametes may function simultaneously or sequentially, testifying to great complexity in the genic control. If the male function precedes, the hermaphroditism is said to be *protandrous,* while if the female function occurs first, the hermaphroditism is said to be *protogynous.* Among the numerous hermaphroditic invertebrates, a bisexual state may persist, as in pulmonate snails, or a complete reversal of sex may occur, influenced by age or changes in food availability or in water temperature, as in the slipper limpet (*Crepidula*). Oysters are prone to change their sex with the seasons. Other invertebrates may be sexually neutral at first and then be determined in one direction or the other by specific stimuli. In *Bonellia,* contact with the female's proboscis causes the larvae to develop as males, while without this contact they become females.

HORMONAL CONTROL OF SEX DIFFERENTIATION

The principal hormones controlling sex differentiation in mammals are those of the testis, which produces *androgens* (mainly testosterone), and the ovary, which secretes *estrogens* (mainly estradiol). In the embryo, testosterone directly stimulates the development of the Wolffian duct system, the forerunner of the male genital tract, but has no effect on the Mullerian duct system, the forerunner of the female genital tract. Yet experimental evidence clearly shows that the Mullerian system is inhibited in males—presumably by some as yet unidentified substances emanating from the testis. Spermatogenesis is promoted partly by testosterone but chiefly by gonadotrophins released by the pituitary gland. In females the ovary plays little or no role: the Mullerian duct system appears to differentiate spontaneously and the Wolffian duct system to regress. There is an innate tendency to femaleness in mammals, but the masculinizing effect of testosterone in males is exerted well before differentiation begins in females. Later, estradiol plays an essential role in the physiological activity of the female tract. Like spermatogenesis, oogenesis, the development of the ovum, is mainly under the control of pituitary gonadotrophins.

Although a similar general pattern of hormonal control exists in birds, the underlying (nonhormonal) tendency is toward maleness. This fact partly explains the sex reversal that can occur in hens and other female birds. On the other hand, while sex reversal can be induced in the male embryo with estrogens, the female is resistant to androgens. The typical male plumage of many birds is not a result of androgens since here again the innate tendency, apparently operating through pituitary hormones, is towards the male feather color and pattern, with the female arising from inhibition by estrogen. In a few amphibians sex can be completely and permanently reversed by administration of androgen or estrogen, provided treatment is started early enough.

COURSE OF SEXUAL DEVELOPMENT

In vertebrates the gonad primordium begins as a band of cells on either side of the body cavity of the late embryo. These cells develop to form a "genital ridge"; in humans this occurs in about the third week of pregnancy. At first the primordium contains no germ cells. These migrate into the tissue from a source external to the embryo proper. In mammals the source appears to be the basal part of the yolk sac. The germ cells multiply rapidly in the genital ridge, both in the surface layer, or epithelium, and in strands of tissue, the primitive sex cords, just beneath. The epithelium will later form the *cortex*, or outer part, of the gonad, and the primitive sex cords, the *medulla*, or inner part. The genital ridge becomes more protuberant, shorter, and rounder in cross section and is now termed the "indifferent gonad." The first signs of sex differences then become evident. In the male embryo the germ cells all move into the primitive sex cords, which enlarge, become hollow, and form the spermatogenic tubules of the testis. In the female the medulla disappears. The germ cells gather in the cortex, which increases greatly in thickness. There, they become oocytes and induce the formation of the follicles that characterize the ovary.

While the gonads are differentiating, two pairs of simple tubes, the Wolffian and Mullerian duct systems, develop initially side by side. The Wolffian duct system differentiates into the *epididymis, vas deferens,* and *seminal vesicle,* while the Mullerian system becomes the *oviduct, uterus,* and part of the *vagina.* At the end of the second month of development, the Wolffian system begins to degenerate in the female embryo, the Mullerian ducts in the male.

The human testis at birth is almost complete, but has not yet descended into the scrotum nor produced spermatozoa. Spermatogenesis begins in late childhood and reaches full activity during puberty. The human ovary at birth carries its complete stock of oocytes—between 500,000 and 1 million—and no more are formed in postnatal life. Each oocyte is surrounded by a single layer of flattened cells, constituting the primordial follicle. At puberty, oocytes start to grow in size, and the follicles enlarge greatly through multiplication of their cells. When the appropriate stage is reached, follicles open in the process known as *ovulation,* discharging their oocytes into the oviduct, where fertilization can occur.

Puberty is associated with the acquisition of full functional capacity in the genital systems of both sexes, and the development of other secondary sex characteristics such as typical changes in body form and behavior, together with the growth of beard in males, of breasts in females, and of pubic hair in a distinctive pattern in both sexes. See also EMBRYOLOGY.

ABERRANT SEXUAL TYPES

Various mishaps can intervene in gametogenesis or embryonic development and give rise to sexual anomalies. In man, eggs ready for fertilization may exhibit several abnormalities—they may, for example have no sex chromosome (O) or have two X chromosomes (XX). Fertilization with normal spermatozoa, carrying either an X chromosome or a Y chromosome, then yields embryos with XO, YO, XXX, or XXY constitutions. If spermatozoa showing corresponding abnormalities—that is, spermatozoa having no sex chromosome (O), having two X chromosomes, having an X and a Y chromosome (XY), or having two Y chromosomes—fertilize normal eggs (X), the resulting embryos are XO, XXX, XXY, or XYY. YO embryos are apparently inviable, but the other embryos do survive to birth and maturity, giving rise to recognized clinical conditions.

Patients with an XO sex chromosome makeup exhibit Turner's syndrome. They are short stocky women with physical defects, sometimes mental retardation, and are sex-chromatin negative. They lack secondary sexual development, and are sterile because they have little or no ovarian tissue. Triple-X women, formerly known as superfemales, have two sex-chromatin bodies in each nucleus. (Two of the X chromosomes are necessarily inactivated.) They are fertile but often mentally retarded. An XXY sex-chromosome makeup is known as Klinefelter's syndrome. Such patients are men though they are sex-chromatin positive. They have small testes, are infertile, and are often intellectually handicapped. Patients with the XYY makeup, often called supermales, were once thought to have criminal tendencies, but this theory is no longer accepted.

Aberrant sexual states in man that are not linked with sex chromosomal anomalies include conditions in which the patient has a testis on one side and an ovary or ovotestis on the other side. Such patients are called *gynandromorphs,* and they are usually sterile. How their asymmetric genital tract originates is not known. In a syndrome known as *testicular feminization,* the patients have the appearance of women, often most attractive women, and commonly seek medical advice because they do not menstruate or cannot conceive. In these cases, clinical examination reveals a lack of sex chromatin, usually a pair of poorly developed testes in the inguinal canal, and a short blind vagina. These cases are, in fact, men whose tissues cannot respond to testosterone and who have followed the innate mammalian tendency to femaleness. The fault seems to lie in the mutation of an autosomal gene.

In twin pregnancy in cattle, sheep, goats, and pigs the two placentas often fuse, uniting the blood circulations of the two fetuses. If the twins are sexually unlike, the female, known as a *free-martin*, becomes partly sex-reversed, and will generally be sterile. This most likely happens because an "inducer" substance in the testis of the male twin is carried over to the female twin and produces anomalous effects.

SEX RATIO

The sex ratio expresses the proportion of males to females and is usually stated as the number of males per 100 females. The sex ratio is commonly qualified according to time. The *primary sex ratio* is the ratio of fertilization, the *secondary sex ratio* is the ratio at birth, and the *tertiary ratio* is the ratio at adulthood.

The primary sex ratio has just been determined for the first time in a mammal—a mouse. It is 100, or an equal number of males and females at fertilization. Determination of the sex ratio at the blastocyst stage of embryonic development when the sex chromatin first becomes visible shows a ratio of about 100 for several laboratory animals. For many years it was thought that the primary sex ratio for man was probably well above this level, perhaps as high as 130. However, recent investigations on human embryos recovered surgically or through abortion consistently support the idea that in man the true primary sexual ratio is also about 100. There are, in fact, good reasons for believing that a significant divergence of the primary ratio from parity would be biologically hazardous to the species.

The secondary sex ratio in man is well documented. It varies a little among races, but the overall average is about 106, suggesting a small selective loss of females during gestation, or pregnancy. Various environmental agents may influence the secondary sex ratio through the rate of prenatal mortality. Postnatally, the loss is about equal for a number of years, so that the tertiary sex ratio for man is also about 106. After age 40, however, male loss is increasingly greater, and the ratio falls steadily so that at age 80 the ratio is less than 50—that is, there are fewer than 50 males per 100 females.

Many attempts have been made in man and other animals to find a means of altering the primary sex ratio at will. These attempts have included various treatments to the female and the treatment of semen used for artificial insemination. In general, the intention has been to alter the proportions of spermatozoa bearing the X or the Y sex chromosomes or to favor the passage of one or other kind of spermatozoon into the egg. However, no method has yet been shown to be effective and repeatable.

C. R. AUSTIN, *Cambridge University*

Bibliography

Allison, Anthony, ed., *The Biology of Sex* (1961; reprint, Penguin 1967).
Austin, Colin R., ed., *Sex Differentiation and Development* (Cambridge 1960).
Austin, Colin R., and Short, Roger V., eds., *Reproduction in Mammals*, vol. 1–6 (Cambridge 1972–1975).
Perry, John S., ed., "Intersexuality," *Journal of Reproduction and Fertility*, supplement no. 7 (1969).
Silver, Rae, Introduction by, *Hormones and Reproductive Behavior: Readings from Scientific American* (Freeman 1979).

SEX EDUCATION, instruction in the various physiological, psychological, and sociological aspects of sexual response and reproduction. Although most Americans favor some sort of sex instruction in public schools, this has become an intensely controversial issue because, unlike most subjects, sex education is concerned with an especially sensitive and highly personal part of human life.

Sex Education Programs and Their Goals. Sex-education courses vary widely in American public schools, but most involve two basic types of instruction: the teaching of human biology (the "facts of life") and discussions of such controversial sexual topics as contraception, promiscuity, masturbation, prostitution, abortion, homosexuality, rape, and responsible decision making about sex. Other topics in sex-education classes—often called "life sciences" or "family life" classes—include dating, sexual adjustment in marriage, child rearing, the integrity of the family, and divorce.

In some schools the entire program of sex education may consist of films that have biological or moralistic themes, followed by discussion sessions conducted by local physicians or public-health nurses. In others, professional people of the community may present lectures on sex-related themes, followed by question-and-answer periods during assembly programs or in after-school sessions. In some programs, family life and sex education form a course at a specific grade level, usually in connection with home-making classes. In still other programs, various aspects of human sexuality are considered in several courses, with the physiological aspects covered in science classes and the behavioral aspects falling under social studies or literature.

Some sex-education programs begin in the public elementary schools. A family-education program in Flint, Mich., for example, began in grade four, when pupils were taught the biological facts of reproduction. "Psychosocial and psychosexual concepts" were the themes in grades 10 to 12. Parents were encouraged to participate and were instructed in how to communicate with their children on sexual subjects.

An optional program conducted by the Falls Church, Va., public schools consisted of a sixth-grade life sciences course, a ninth-grade class, and a seminar for high-school juniors and seniors on human sexuality. Human anatomy and the human life cycle were taught, and there were unrestricted discussions about sexual matters.

Most sex education programs have as their principal goal helping teenagers make responsible decisions about their sex life. Those who favor such programs say that students are provided with knowledge that can help reduce the high rates of teenage pregnancy and venereal disease.

The Guttmacher Institute, a research organization in New York City, has estimated that over 1 million teenage girls become pregnant each year in the United States. At the same time, the institute estimated that four in ten girls who reached age 14 in 1981 would have at least one pregnancy while in their teens and that two in ten would give birth at least once. According to the federal Center for Disease Control, the incidence of gonorrhea among teenagers is nearly three times that of the general population.

State Policies. Only Maryland, New Jersey, and the District of Columbia require that sex education instruction be provided by local school boards. Kentucky requires that sex education be offered in health classes but does not specify how the program should be implemented. Local school districts are encouraged but not required to offer sex education courses in Delaware, Iowa, Kansas, Minnesota, Montana, Pennsylvania, and Utah. Twenty-two other states permit local school boards to make their own decisions, and the remaining states have no official policy concerning sex-education courses in public schools. Statutes banning public-school sex-education classes were repealed in Michigan in 1977 and in Louisiana in 1979.

Approximately one third of the high schools of the United States offer some sort of sex education course, but many teach little more than basic human anatomy. Dr. Melvin Zelnik of Johns Hopkins University reported in *Family Planning Perspectives* (vol. 12, 1980) that about two thirds of students aged 15 to 19 receive some type of sex education in school. Fewer than half have been instructed in methods of birth control, but the great majority have been informed about venereal disease and the menstrual cycle.

Opponents and Proponents. Many parents believe that sex education should not be taught in the classroom, but that responsibility for such instruction should remain with the parents or their priest, minister, or rabbi. Other opponents of sex education in the schools include the Pro-Family Forum, the Eagle Forum, and the Moral Majority.

Many opponents do not object to classroom instruction in human biology. They do object, however, to what they see as an unintended result of sex-education courses: potential encouragement of children to experiment with sexual activity while disregarding parental and religious moral teachings. Religious fundamentalists are not the only persons opposed to sex education in the schools. Others in the fields of medicine and education, particularly, feel that it is impossible to provide proper sex education in the atmosphere of the classroom.

On the other hand, those who favor sex education in the public schools consider such instruction as the only meaningful way of reducing the high rate of teenage pregnancy. Their argument is that there is value in giving teenage students a better knowledge of the risk of pregnancy, along with referral to services where contraception and other aid may be obtained. They claim that religious training and parental guidance in sexual matters have proved to be inadequate and that classroom instruction can provide teenagers with the skills they need to make sexual choices in today's complex world. Knowledge of sexual matters, they contend, is better obtained in the public-school classroom than from the teenagers' peers or the mass media.

An example of the controversial nature of introducing sex education in the public schools occurred in New Jersey. In 1980 the state board of education ordered local school districts to establish courses in sex education within the next three years. Instruction was to follow the board's guidelines and was to begin not later than the sixth grade and to extend through high school. In the ensuing debate in the New Jersey legislature, the state teachers and school boards associations and the New Jersey Right to Life Committee lobbied against the order, while the Junior League, Planned Parenthood, and the Ro-

man Catholic Church favored the measure. Opposition on the part of the teachers and school board associations was based primarily on the premise that the whole matter of sex education should be solely the responsibility of local school boards. The New Jersey Right to Life Committee opposed the measure because the guidelines proposed by the board of education would permit instruction in abortion as an alternative to childbirth. Eventually the state board of education revised its policy, dropping its list of required subjects and leaving the choice of subject matter to the local boards.

MARC LEEPSON
Staff Writer, Editorial Research Reports

Bibliography

Brown, Lorna, ed., *Sex Education in the Eighties* (Plenum Publications 1981).
Calderone, Mary S., and Johnson, Eric W., *The Family Book of Sexuality* (Harper 1981).
Call, Alice L., *Toward Adulthood: Sex Education* (Harper 1969).
Dallas, Dorothy M., *Sex Education in School and Society* (Humanities Press 1972).
Haims, Lawrence J., *Sex Education and the Public Schools* (Lexington Books 1973).
Johnson, Warren R., *Sex Education and Counseling of Special Groups* (Thomas, C. C. 1975).
Leepson, Marc, "Sex Education," *Editorial Research Reports*, vol. 2, no. 8, Aug. 28, 1981.
Lewis, Howard R. and Martha E., *The Parent's Guide to Teenage Sex and Pregnancy* (St. Martin's Press 1980).
McCary, James L., *A Complete Sex Education for Parents, Teenagers, and Young Adults* (Reinhold 1973).
Rogers, Rex, ed., *Sex Education: Rationale and Reaction* (Cambridge 1974).
Ross, Sidney S., *What Sex Education Is All About: A Guide for Parents* (Sidney Scott Ross 1979).
Sobran, Joseph, "Sex Education," *The Human Life Review*, winter 1981.
Stronck, David, ed., *Sex Education in the Science Classroom* (National Science Teachers 1981).

SEX HORMONE, hôr′mōn, any of several hormones that affect the growth or function of the reproductive organs or the development of secondary sexual characteristics. See ESTROGEN; HUMAN REPRODUCTION; TESTOSTERONE.

SEX THERAPY, a form of treatment, education, or counseling that deals with the sexual problems of individuals or couples. The demand for sexual counseling and the interest in human sexuality have been stimulated by a number of sources, particularly by the work of Alfred C. Kinsey and that of William Masters and Virginia Johnson. Open discussion of sexual functioning is now generally permissible; effective birth-control methods are widely available; abortion has been legalized in many places; and, at least in the Western world, sex-role behavior is becoming less stereotyped than in the past. Our civilization has known both sexual repression and sexual freedom. Even in the present relatively liberal period, many people are troubled by a variety of sexual problems, and they require both care and information.

Sexual problems can be symptomatic of physical problems, psychological conflicts, or interpersonal difficulties; they can be a side effect of the use of certain drugs; or they can be caused by a combination of these factors. Sexual function can be adversely affected by stress, by emotional disorders, or by a lack of sexual knowledge.

Beginning in the 1960's, a number of centers were established to treat the complaints of people having difficulty with their sexual functioning. Those complaints most frequently presented include impotence, premature or retarded ejaculation in men; lack of orgasmic response, vaginismus (vaginal spasms), and dyspareunia (painful coitus) in women; and general sexual incompatibility resulting from lack of desire in either a man or a woman.

Impotence is the condition in which a man cannot obtain or maintain an erection satisfactory for the purposes of coitus. In premature ejaculation the man becomes orgasmic and ejaculates before he wishes to. There is no specific time frame within which to define the dysfunction, but the diagnosis usually is made when the man regularly ejaculates before or immediately after entering the woman's vagina. In retarded ejaculation the man reaches climax during coitus only with great difficulty, if at all.

Lack of orgasmic response, also known as anorgasmia, is the inability of a woman to achieve orgasm by masturbation or coitus. Women who can achieve orgasm by either of those methods are not categorized as anorgasmic. A related complaint is inhibited sexual excitement; some women do not respond to sexual stimulation with vaginal lubrication or a sense of excitement. In vaginismus an involuntary muscle spasm constricts the vagina, preventing penetration by the penis. Dyspareunia is recurrent and persistent pain during intercourse. It is related to and may coincide with vaginismus.

Lack of sexual desire is experienced by both men and women who may not be hampered by any specific sexual problem once they are involved in the sex act. Lack of interest may be expressed by decreased frequency of coitus, perception of the partner as unattractive, or overt complaints of lack of desire.

A variety of approaches are used to treat sexual dysfunctions. Before entering sex therapy, however, a patient should have a thorough medical evaluation to determine whether a physical condition is causing or contributing to the problem.

Most sexual-counseling programs are modifications of the therapy originally developed by William Masters and Virginia Johnson. Masters and Johnson did pioneer research on physiological responses to sexual stimulation and designed a treatment method to deal with specific sexual complaints.

Many sex-therapy programs specialize in treating couples. Basic to this type of therapy is the premise that the most common sexual problems facing couples require the treatment of both partners. Both people are involved in the relationship in which there is sexual distress, and both, therefore, should participate in the therapy program. This type of therapy, sometimes called dual-sex therapy, is a behavioral, short-term approach that usually involves 20 to 30 sessions.

In a typical dual sex-therapy program, the relationship as a whole is treated, with emphasis on sexual functioning as part of that relationship. Treatment is directed at improving communication between the partners, and the psychological and physiological aspects of sexual functioning are discussed and explained. To help the couple with their particular problem, the therapist prescribes exercises for them to practice in the privacy of their own home. Beginning exercises focus on heightening sensory awareness to touch, sight, sound, and smell. Intercourse is forbidden in the early part of therapy to relieve the couple of the pressure of performance and to allow them to benefit fully from the initial exercises. The couple are instructed to use a variety of stimulating techniques before proceeding to intercourse. The exercises vary according to the couple's complaint, and special techniques are used to treat each of the different sexual dysfunctions. Following each home exercise period are therapy sessions in which problems and satisfactions, both sexual and related to other areas of the couple's lives, are discussed. Gradually, the couple gain confidence and learn or relearn to communicate, verbally and sexually.

Masters and Johnson report a high overall success rate with the varieties of sexual disorders they have treated, with the greatest success achieved in treating the problem of premature ejaculation.

Another effective treatment method is analytically oriented sex therapy, which integrates the techniques of sex therapy with the techniques of traditional psychotherapy. The combined approach is used by many psychiatrists in treating individual patients and people with problems that extend beyond the sexual area. Relaxation techniques, behavioral desensitization (unlearning old behavior patterns), hypnosis, group psychotherapy, and psychoanalytically oriented psychotherapy are also used in the treatment of sexual disorders. The reported success rate varies from approximately 60% to about 80% with all treatment methods.

One of the problems arising from the rapid growth of sex-therapy centers is the presence of charlatans in the field. Most competent and ethical sex therapists are licensed physicians or psychologists who have had additional training in sex therapy. Referrals for treatment usually are made through medical schools, psychiatric societies, hospitals, and mental-health centers.

VIRGINIA A. SADOCK, M. D.
New York University School of Medicine

Further Reading: Hogan, Douglas R., "The Effectiveness of Sex Therapy: A Review of the Literature," in *Handbook of Sex Therapy*, ed. by Joseph LoPiccolo and Leslie LoPiccolo (Plenum 1978); Sadock, V. A., "Treatment of Psychosexual Dysfunction," in *Comprehensive Textbook of Psychiatry*, ed. by H. I. Kaplan, A. M. Freedman, and B. J. Sadock, pp. 1799–1803 (Williams & Wilkins 1980).

SEXAGESIMAL SYSTEM, sek-sə-jes'ə-məl, a number system using 60 for a base instead of ten. It was introduced about 2000 B. C. by the Babylonians. They used a positional notation in writing numbers greater than 60, which apparently was chosen as a base because it has a wealth of factors (2, 3, 4, 5, 6, 10, 12, 15, 20, 30) and thereby is convenient in metrology. Thus the positional principle—a key advance in numeration—was first associated with the sexagesimal rather than the decimal system. As an example, the number 7,322 to the base 60 in modern notation would be written as $7,322 = 222_{60} = 2 \times (60)^2 + 2 \times (60)^1 + 2 \times (60)^0$, where the three 2's are read from left to right and $(60)^0 = 1$.

Sexagesimal fractions were used by Alexandrian astronomers, including Ptolemy, and this probably was one path that led to the present use of the base 60 for measures of time and angles. For instance, 60 seconds equals one minute and 60 minutes of arc equals one degree. See also NUMBER SYSTEMS AND NOTATIONS; NUMERALS.

SEXISM. See PREJUDICE AND DISCRIMINATION.

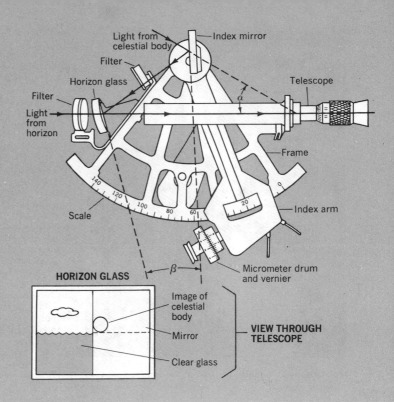

SEXTANT

A sextant (*right*) measures the angle α between the horizon and an observed celestial body. Angle α is twice angle β, which is the angle between the horizon glass and the index mirror mounted on the movable index arm. The size of angle β is measured by means of a scale on the sextant arc. Since a reading of angle α is desired, each degree number on the scale is made twice as great as the actual number of degrees along the arc. To use the sextant, the observer holds the instrument vertical and aligns the telescope by viewing the horizon through the clear glass (*left*). He moves the index arm to bring the image of a celestial body into view in the telescope and then rotates the micrometer drum to bring the bottom of the image to the horizon. The scale gives the angular elevation of the body.

SEXTANT, seks′tənt, an optical instrument for measuring the altitude, or angle of elevation, of a celestial body. It was invented independently by Thomas Godfrey, an American, and John Hadley, an Englishman, in 1730. The sextant derives its name from the fact that some instruments had a metal-frame arc of one sixth of a circle, or 60°. The instruments now are built with arcs of different degrees, but all of them commonly are called "sextants." Occasionally, the terms "octant," "quintant," or "quadrant" now are used for instruments having arcs of 45°, 72°, and 90°, respectively.

The sextant originally was used in marine navigation to help determine the position of a ship at sea. It still is used for this purpose, and in addition, it now is used in helping to determine the position of an airplane. Sextants used in air navigation differ significantly from those used in marine navigation. Consequently, modern instruments are grouped in two classes: marine sextants and air sextants.

Marine Sextants. As shown in the accompanying diagram, a marine sextant has a frame on which the other parts of the hand-held instrument are mounted. The arc portion of the frame has graduations marked in degrees. The index arm, moved by hand, is pivoted about the center of curvature of the graduated arc. The index mirror, mounted at the upper end of the index arm, rotates clockwise when the index arm is moved clockwise. The horizon glass is mounted in a fixed position on the frame, and at zero reading on the graduated arc the horizon glass and the index mirror are parallel. The horizon glass, which is viewed through the telescope, has a left half that is clear glass and a right half that is a mirror.

The light from a celestial body is reflected from the index mirror to the horizon-glass mirror, which in turn reflects this light into the telescope. The light from the horizon travels on a straight path through the clear glass part of the horizon glass and into the telescope. Filters in both light paths reduce light levels that would cause discomfort to the person looking through the telescope.

An observer determines the altitude of a celestial body by first holding the sextant frame in a position as nearly vertical as possible. He then uses the telescope to view the sea horizon through the clear glass part of the horizon glass, thereby establishing that the telescope is horizontal. The observer then moves the index arm along the graduated arc until the image of the celestial body is seen in the mirror portion of the horizon glass. Next, the observer rotates the micrometer drum until the bottom of this image is in line with the sea horizon. At that moment, the sextant scale reading and the precise time are recorded by the observer. By making two or more similar observations of a celestial body and by using data in navigation almanacs, the observer can determine the latitude and longitude of the ship's position.

Air Sextants. An air sextant performs the same function as a marine sextant but differs from the latter in significant ways. On an airplane, the natural horizon is very seldom visible for use as a reference line in celestial navigation. Therefore, a bubble level or some other gravity-responsive device is built into the optical system of the sextant to serve as an artificial horizon. However, a gravity-responsive device also responds to accelerations of the airplane, even in straight and level flight. These accelerations result in momentary deviations of the bubble reference from the true vertical. Consequently, a single observation could be in error by as much as 150 miles (240 km). Therefore, several observations are averaged by mechanical means over a period of one or two minutes. Under normal flying conditions, this procedure gives a position that is accurate to within about 5 miles (8 km).

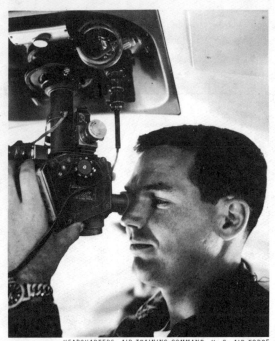

HEADQUARTERS, AIR TRAINING COMMAND, U. S. AIR FORCE

The periscopic bubble sextant is used in aircraft to establish position from sightings taken of the stars.

Most modern air sextants are periscopic. This form is demanded because the speed and altitude of modern aircraft deprive the crew of observation domes. The periscopic sextant can provide observations from about −10° to +92° of altitude of a celestial body through 360° in azimuth. These observations are made through a 1.375-inch (35-mm) diameter tube that extends 1.5 inches (38 mm) above the skin of the airplane.

The sextant is kept in a gimballed mount attached to the airplane. This mount gives the periscopic sextant a unique advantage over any hand-held sextant in that the former is capable of positive azimuthal positioning. With a rotatable compass rose in the mount, the periscopic sextant can be used to measure relative bearings and thus can check the aircraft magnetic compass by obtaining the true heading.

In an air sextant, an index prism performs the same function as the index mirror of the marine sextant. The index prism is rotatable, and its angle indirectly indicates the altitude of a celestial body. A knob controls the prism rotation and is coupled to a counter, which gives the altitude of the celestial body directly in degrees and minutes.

The light from the celestial body travels through objective and erecting lens systems and then through a fixed prism, which directs the light to the horizontal and focusable eyepiece. The bubble, which is in a transparent chamber mounted adjacent to the objective lens tube, is illuminated by daylight or by a lamp. The bubble image is passed through a lens to a corner reflector prism and back to a beam splitter, which reflects a portion of the light into the eyepiece. A measurement of the altitude of the celestial body is obtained by rotating the prism until the image of the celestial body lies in the center of the bubble image. See also NAVIGATION.

SEXUAL REPRODUCTION, Human. See HUMAN REPRODUCTION.

SEXUALLY TRANSMITTED DISEASE. See VENEREAL DISEASE.

SEYCHELLES, sā-shel′, an independent island republic in the Indian Ocean about 1,000 miles (1,600 km) east of Zanzibar. The archipelago consists of 92 islands and islets extending over some 600 miles (960 km) of ocean. Formerly a British crown colony, Seychelles became the independent Republic of Seychelles at midnight, June 28, 1976. Its capital, chief port, and largest city is Victoria, on Mahé.

The Land. Seychelles has an area of 107 square miles (278 sq km), comprising both granitic and coraline islands. Mahé, the largest and most important island, is 55 square miles (142 sq km) in area. Other principal islands are Praslin, La Digue, and Silhouette. The outlying Farquhar, Desroches, and Aldabra Islands, in the British Indian Ocean Territory since 1965, were returned to Seychelles when it became independent.

The archipelago lies near the equator, but its climate is tempered by the southeast trade winds from June to November. Temperatures on Mahé vary between 75° F and 85° F (24° C–29° C). Rainfall ranges from about 90 inches (2,300 mm) annually in Victoria to 140 inches (3,550 mm) a year on the slopes. The highest elevation is Morne Seychellois on Mahé, rising to almost 3,000 feet (900 meters).

The People. The population of the Seychelles was estimated to be 63,000 in 1979. Most of the Seychellois are descended from early French settlers and African slaves. Their principal language is Creole, but English is the official language. Over 90% of the people are Catholic.

Economy. The Seychelles' economy is heavily dependent on tourism and agriculture, primarily on export commodities. The major exports are copra, cinnamon, vanilla, patchouli (an oil used in manufacturing soap and perfume), and dried fish. Subsistence crops include bananas, sweet potatoes, and cassava.

History. The islands were discovered by Portuguese mariners in 1505, but remained unoccupied except by pirates until they were settled by the French in the mid-18th century. They were taken by Britain in 1794, became a dependency of the British colony of Mauritius in 1810, were formally ceded to Britain by the Treaty of Paris in 1814, and became a crown colony in 1903.

In 1977, a year after independence, the government was overthrown. The new constitution of 1979 set up a one-party socialist state.

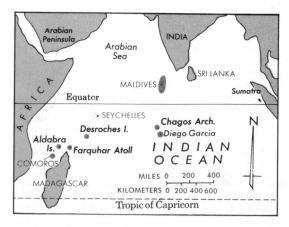

SEYMOUR, se'môr, Charles (1885–1963), American educator and historian. He was born in New Haven, Conn., on Jan. 1, 1885. He received B. A. degrees from Cambridge University and from Yale University, where he also obtained a Ph. D. At Yale from 1911, he taught history and served as provost and as president (1937–1950) of the university. He was chief of the Austro-Hungarian division of the American Commission at the Paris Peace Conference in 1919. He died in Chatham, Mass., on Aug. 11, 1963. An authority on World War I diplomacy, Seymour was curator of the World War documents collection at Yale. He edited *The Intimate Papers of Colonel House* (1926–1928), and wrote *American Diplomacy During the World War* (1934) and *American Neutrality, 1914–1917* (1935).

SEYMOUR, Edward. See SOMERSET, 1ST DUKE OF.

SEYMOUR, se'môr, Horatio (1810–1886), American political leader, who was the Democratic nominee for president of the United States in 1868. He was born in Pompey Hill, N. Y., on May 31, 1810, and was educated at Geneva Academy (now Hobart College) and at a military school in Middletown, Conn. He also studied law in Utica, N. Y., and was admitted to the bar. He was elected to the New York Assembly in 1841, served as mayor of Utica in 1842, and reentered the Assembly in 1843. Seymour served as governor of New York in 1853–1854 and again in 1863–1864. In his second term he upheld the supremacy of the Constitution and supported the restoration of the Union, but denied that the Civil War was the result of slavery or that slavery should be abolished to restore the Union. Nominated for president by the Democrats in 1868, he lost to Ulysses S. Grant. He died in Utica, N. Y., on Feb. 12, 1886.

SEYMOUR, se'môr, Jane (1509?–1537), third wife of Henry VIII of England. She was born probably in 1509 at Wolf Hall in Savernake, Wiltshire, the house of her father, Sir John Seymour. A former lady-in-waiting to Catherine of Aragon, she likewise served Anne Boleyn, Henry's second wife. From the date of Henry's first meeting with Jane Seymour on Sept. 10, 1535, he pursued her with gifts, but Jane discreetly rejected his proposals. Determined to marry Jane, Henry initiated the legal proceedings against Anne, for adultery, that led to her execution. Henry married Jane on May 30, 1536. She died giving birth to a son, the future Edward VI, at Hampton Court in October 1537. For a portrait of Jane Seymour, see HOLBEIN, HANS, THE YOUNGER.

SEYMOUR, se'môr, a town in southwestern Connecticut, in New Haven county, is on the Naugatuck River, about 10 miles (16 km) northwest of New Haven and 12 miles (19 km) south of Waterbury. Brass, copper, sheets, and wire cables are manufactured here.

The area was settled about 1680. In 1802, David Humphreys of Derby, Conn., brought back from Spain, where he had been serving as American minister, the first merino sheep in the United States, and opened a woolen mill here. The area became known as Humphreyville. In 1850 the settlement was incorporated as a town and renamed Seymour, in honor of Thomas H. Seymour, then governor of Connecticut. Seymour is governed by a board of selectmen. Population: 13,434.

SEYMOUR, se'môr, a city in southern Indiana, in Jackson county, is about 60 miles (96 km) southeast of Indianapolis. It is the trade center of an agricultural and stock-raising region. The city's industries include the making of heavy machinery, wood products, shoes, textiles, and paper and packaging materials, and also light manufacturing.

Seymour was founded in 1852 and was incorporated as a city in 1867. It has the mayor-council form of government. Population: 15,050.

SFAX, sfåks, is a seaport and the second-largest city of Tunisia. Located on the northern shore of the Gulf of Gabès, the city is opposite the Kerkenna Islands.

Sfax is connected by road and by rail with the other principal cities of Tunisia. Phosphates, which are mined at Gafsa to the southwest, are the chief export. Other exports include olive oil, sponges, and dates. The major industries are the processing of olive oil and fishing.

Little remains of the ancient, pre-Muslim city, which was called Taparura. Among the Islamic monuments of Sfax is the Great Mosque, built from the 9th to the 11th century. Population: (1966) 70,472.

SFORZA, sfôr'tsä, a celebrated Italian house that played an important part in the 15th and 16th centuries, gave six rulers to Milan, and formed alliances with most of the princely houses of Europe.

GIACOMUZZO (MUZIO) ATTENDOLO (1369–1424), the founder of the house, was from Cotignola in Romagna. His skill and courage made him one of the most powerful condottieri (mercenary captains) of Italy. His added name of Sforza ("the forcer") vouches for his great strength. Muzio served in the wars in the Papal States, Tuscany, and Naples and died as grand constable of Naples.

FRANCESCO I (1401–1466) and ALESSANDRO (1409–1473), two of his sons, were also condottieri and were even more successful. Alessandro gained control of Pesaro in 1445, and his descendants held the city until 1512. Francesco entered the service of the Visconti Duke of Milan and received the command of the Milanese forces in the war against Venice. In 1447 he laid claim to the states of Milan through his wife, Bianca Maria, although she was only the natural daughter of the last duke. To enforce his claim he concluded a treaty with Venice and advanced against the newly formed republic of Milan. In 1449 he laid siege to the city, which on March 3, 1450, was forced by famine to surrender. An able and autocratic ruler, Francesco consolidated the power of Milan, took Genoa, and lavishly patronized the arts.

ASCANIO (1455–1505), his son, was a patron of the arts who rose to become a cardinal.

GALEAZZO MARIA (1444–1476), also Francesco's son, succeeded his father. Although competent in some respects, he was a voluptuary and was known for his cruelty. He was murdered by republican conspirators.

GIAN GALEAZZO (1469–1494) was Galeazzo Maria's son and successor. Gian's mother, Bona of Savoy, served as regent until 1480. Bianca Maria, Galeazzo Maria's daughter, later married Emperor Maximilian I.

LUDOVICO (1451–1508), another son of Francesco, took over the Milanese government in 1480 and kept his nephew a virtual prisoner. Known as il Moro (the Moor), he was determined to retain the duchy. After Gian died in 1494, leaving a daughter, Bona, who married Sigismund I of Poland, Ludovico was formally chosen as duke. He and his wife, Beatrice Este, were both noted for their patronage of the arts, including their support of Leonardo da Vinci.

To buttress Milan against the Kingdom of Naples, Ludovico concluded an alliance with Charles VIII of France in 1494, which led to the French invasion of Italy. Although Ludovico subsequently turned against Charles, who had tenuous claims to Naples, he was confronted by another French invasion in 1499, led by Louis XII, who had succeeded Charles VIII on the throne of France. Despite Swiss aid, Ludovico in 1500 lost the duchy to Louis, who kept him prisoner in France.

MASSIMILIANO (1491–1530), his son, once more drove the French from his territories with the help of the Swiss. After his defeat in the Battle of Marignano in 1515, Massimiliano was obliged to cede his dominions to Francis I of France, in return for a pension. He spent the remainder of his life in France. Francis was afterward driven from Italy by Emperor Charles V.

FRANCESCO II (1492–1535), brother of Massimiliano, was invested with the duchy of Milan by Emperor Charles V in 1522. After Francesco's death, which marked the end of the male ducal line, France and Spain struggled for control of the duchy until 1559, when, by the Treaty of Cateau-Cambrésis, it passed to Spain. Several other branches of the family survived.

SFORZA, sfôr'tsä, **Carlo** (1872–1952), Italian foreign minister and a leading opponent of fascism. He was born in Montignoso di Lunigiana on Sept. 25, 1872, and was a descendant of the Renaissance Sforza family. A diplomat, Count Sforza was active in Balkan affairs during and after World War I. In 1919 he became a member of the Senate and in 1920 was made foreign minister. As foreign minister he negotiated a treaty with Yugoslavia and reached agreements with Czechoslovakia and Rumania.

In 1922 he resigned as ambassador to France in protest against Mussolini's assumption of power. Thereafter he was one of Mussolini's bitterest critics, refusing many overtures to join the Fascists. The suppression of all opposition parties in 1926 forced Sforza into exile, where he continued to work for a democratic Italy. After Italy's surrender in World War II, he returned to Rome in late 1943 and helped to establish the new government. He was foreign minister from 1947 to 1951, retiring because of ill health. He died in Rome on Sept. 4, 1952.

SHACKAMAXON, shak-ə-mak'sən, **Treaty of,** the compact, traditionally called the "Great Treaty," made by William Penn with the Delaware Indians at their village of Shackamaxon—now Kensington, a part of Philadelphia. Soon after his arrival in the province of Pennsylvania in the fall of 1682, Penn entered into negotiations with the Indians, seeking to establish friendly relations with them. At their meetings, the whites bore no arms, respecting the Indians' disapproval of hostile weapons. On June 23, 1683, under a great elm tree at Shackmaxon several engagements were signed by the chiefs and duly witnessed by whites and Indians. They granted to Penn and his heirs large areas of southeastern Pennsylvania.

The chief Indian representative was the sachem Tammanen, or Tammany. A century later Benjamin West commemorated the treaty in a painting, while Voltaire alluded to it as "the only treaty never sworn to and never broken."

SHACKLETON, Sir Ernest (1874–1922), British Antarctic explorer. He was born in Kilkee, Ireland, on Feb. 15, 1874. He was educated at Dulwich College, served in the merchant marine, and was a lieutenant in the Royal Navy Reserve. He was third lieutenant under Capt. Robert F. Scott in the National Antarctic Expedition in 1901–1904, and with Scott reached latitude 82°23'S on Jan. 9, 1909, a record farthest south at the time. He also ascended Mt. Erebus, 13,120 feet (4,000 meters) high, and on Jan. 16, 1909, he reached the South Magnetic Pole, determining its position as latitude 72°25'S, longitude 154°E.

Shackleton headed a third expedition in 1914, and contemplated a dog-team journey from the Weddell Sea to McMurdo Sound by way of the South Pole. Short of the wintering base, his ship, the *Endurance,* was caught in the Weddell Sea pack ice. Carried toward the north, it sank on Oct. 25, 1915.

The men drifted precariously northward on ice floes for months until they reached Elephant Island. While 22 men remained on the island, Shackleton and 5 companions traveled 1,200 miles (1,920 km) in a 22-foot (6-meter) whaleboat through the stormiest ocean in the world to South Georgia for help. After four attempts, the stranded men on Elephant Island were rescued by a Chilean warship on Aug. 25, 1916.

On his return to the Antarctic in the 1921–1922 season, Shackleton was stricken with a sudden heart attack and died at sea off South Georgia on Jan. 5, 1922. He was buried on a rugged mountaintop in South Georgia.

Shackleton was knighted in 1909. He was the author of *Heart of the Antarctic* (1919) and *Diary of a Troopship, South* (1919).

FINN RONNE
Captain, U. S. Naval Reserve (Retired)

SHAD, any of several herringlike fishes that are extremely important food fishes. In particular, the name is applied to *Alosa sapidissima.* This fish is found from Labrador to Florida and has been transplanted successfully to the Pacific coast, where it is now found from Alaska to southern California. It is also present, though rare, in the Lake Ontario basin. River names are often attached to the common name, and the species is sometimes called Delaware River shad or Hudson River shad.

Shads reach a maximum weight of 14 pounds (6.3 kg) and a length of 30 inches (75 cm). Generally, females are larger than males, the females averaging 4 to 5.5 pounds (1.8–2.5 kg), the male 2.5 to 4 pounds (1.1–1.8 kg). The shad is blue or blue-green on its back and upper sides, silvery below. Above the gill cover there is a dark spot, and frequently there are other spots along the base line of the blue color. The shad has a single, short, spineless dorsal fin consisting of about 15 rays and a deeply forked tail. The ventral edge of the body is sharply compressed. The toothless jaws fit into each other, a peak in the center of the lower jaw fitting into a notch on the upper. Shads feed on insects and insect larvae, very small fishes, and crustaceans. They are also known to eat minute plant forms.

NEW YORK STATE DEPARTMENT OF ENVIRONMENTAL CONSERVATION
Adult male shad (Alosa sapidissima)

The shad is primarily a marine fish, but goes into fresh water to spawn. The spawning migration starts when the water temperature reaches between 50° and 60° F (10°–16° C), the necessary temperature for their spawning. The males reach the spawning grounds first. During spawning the fish pair, swimming together. The eggs are deposited in the shallow water and sink to the bottom. The adults, having spawned, return to the sea. Spawning migration in the north begins toward the end of May, while in the south its peak is in February. A female averages about 28,000 eggs but has been known to produce as many as 156,000. The eggs hatch in about six days. The fry stay in fresh water until colder weather starts them toward the sea, by which time they are between 4 and 5 inches (10–12.5 cm) long. They become mature in their third or fourth year.

Because the shad is such a profitable fish commercially, millions of young are hatched artificially and released. There has been considerable depletion of the supply, however, by overfishing, as it is easy to net them when they are in great schools in the lower reaches of the rivers. Pollution has also depleted this population. They are taken in gill or trammel nets. The fish is eaten fresh and despite its innumerable small bones, is a delicious food fish. Shad roe, so popular in the East, is not so in the West, and most of the large catch taken in the Sacramento-San Joaquin region is shipped to eastern markets.

Two shads are found in Europe. The allis shad, *Clupea aloas,* is found in several of the larger rivers of Europe, but it is not numerous. The twaite shad, *Clupea finte,* occurs in the rivers of the British Isles and in the Mediterranean and Baltic seas and is known to be landlocked in lakes in Switzerland and northern Italy. In Germany the twaite shad is often called the *maifish* because it spawns in May.

CHRISTOPHER W. COATES*
The New York Aquarium

SHADBUSH, also called juneberry or serviceberry, any of a group of shrubs or small trees that are grown for their profuse white flowers or their bluish, berrylike fruit. Shadbushes are classified in the genus *Amelanchier,* which consists of about 25 members. Most are native to North America.

Shadbushes range in height from bushes 1 foot (0.3 meter) tall to trees 40 feet (12 meters) tall. They have oblong or oval leaves with slight serrations along the edges. Their attractive small white flowers appear in early spring, followed by the fruits, which are sweet and juicy. *A. laevis,* which grows to a height of 40 feet, is perhaps the most beautiful shadbush, but *A. humilis, A. stolonifera,* and *A. sanguinea* are superior for their fruits.

SHADDOCK, shad'ək, also called pomelo or pompelmous, a citrus fruit closely related to the grapefruit. Shaddocks grow in clusters on trees, also called shaddocks, that are native to Malaya and Polynesia. The shaddock typically is pear-shaped and much larger than a grapefruit, growing to the size of a watermelon and weighing 10 to 20 pounds (4.9–9 kg). Its yellow or pink rind is coarse and thick. The fruit has sections like those of the orange, and the pulp is pale yellow or reddish. The shaddock, *Citrus grandis,* is named after a Captain Shaddock, whose English ship took the seed from the East Indies to Barbados in 1696. See also GRAPEFRUIT.

SHADWELL, Thomas (c. 1641–1692), English dramatist and poet. He was born in Norfolk and educated at Cambridge and the Middle Temple. He married an actress, Anne Gibbs, for whom, in 1668, he wrote his first play, *The Sullen Lovers*— an adaptation of Moliére's *Les Fâcheux.* Some comments in the preface to the play opposing John Dryden's view on comedy began a long, bitter quarrel between the two that reached a climax when Dryden cruelly satirized Shadwell as a great dullard in *Mac Flecknoe* (1682). After the Revolution of 1688, Dryden lost his title of Poet Laureate to Shadwell, who also became royal historiographer. Shadwell died in London, probably as a result of an overdose of opium, on Nov. 16, 1692.

Shadwell's verse is of little merit, but his plays show a marvelous comic talent. He claimed to write in the style of Ben Jonson, caricaturing with biting humor the foibles of the Londoners of his day. Shadwell's best plays include *Epsom Wells* (1672); *The Libertine* (1676), with Don Juan as the hero; and *The History of Timon of Athens, the Man-Hater* (1678), a romanticized version of Shakespeare's tragedy.

SHAFFER, shaf'ər, **Peter** (1926–), English playwright, noted for the wide range of his talents. He was born in Liverpool on May 15, 1926. From 1944 to 1947, he and his twin brother, Anthony (also a dramatist), did their national service in the coal mines. Peter then entered Cambridge on a scholarship. After graduating in 1950 he went to New York City, where he worked for two years in the public library. He returned to London in 1954, worked for a music publisher, and wrote television and radio plays.

His first stage play, *Five Finger Exercise* (1958), was a popular and critical success in London and New York. *The Private Ear* and *The Public Eye* (1962), a pair of one-act plays, had modest runs in London and on Broadway. *The Royal Hunt of the Sun,* an epic drama about Pizarro's conquest of Peru, opened the 1964 Chichester Festival and had a brief New York run in 1965. The one-act plays *Black Comedy* and *White Lies* (1966) reveal Shaffer's mastery of farce.

Equus (1973), perhaps his most important and serious play, deals with a mentally disturbed stableboy obsessed with horses. *Amadeus* (1979), a tragicomic tour de force, imagines the Austrian composer Salieri's rivalry with Mozart.

SHAFTESBURY, shafts'bə-rē, **1st Earl of** (1621–1683), English political leader. Anthony Ashley Cooper was born in Wimborne St. Giles, Dorset, on July 22, 1621. He entered Exeter College, Oxford, in 1637, and went to study law at Lincoln's Inn in 1638. At the beginning of the Civil War he sided with the king's party, but finding himself distrusted by the court he went over to the Parliament, from which he received the command of the parliamentary forces in Dorsetshire. He was, nevertheless, a subscriber to the protestation that charged Cromwell, the Protector, with arbitrary government, though this fact did not prevent him from becoming one of his privy council. After the deposition of Richard Cromwell, Cooper planned privately to restore Charles II. He was one of the members of the convention who carried the invitation to the King and was soon after made a privy councillor and a commissioner for the trial of the regicides. In 1661 he was raised to the peerage, with the title Baron Ashley, and appointed chancellor of the exchequer and a lord of the treasury. But he opposed two of the leading measures favored by the crown, the corporation act in 1661 and the act of uniformity in 1662. He supported the Dutch war and issued illegal writs for the election of members of Parliament during a recess. In 1673 he supported the Test Act.

In 1672 he was created earl of Shaftesbury and lord high chancellor. His conduct on the bench was able and impartial. He had been in office less than a year when the seals were taken from him, probably through the influence of the duke of York, and from that moment he became one of the most powerful leaders of the opposition. He made use of the popish plot to force out of the earl of Danby's administration (1678) and produce the formation of a new one, in which he was himself briefly president of the council. In his hostility to the duke of York, Shaftesbury is thought to have entered an association with the duke of Monmouth for the purpose of supporting Monmouth's claims to the crown. Shaftesbury was committed to the Tower of London and tried for high treason, but the grand jury before whom the bill of indictment was laid ignored it. Fearing further prosecution, however, he fled to Amsterdam, Holland, where he died on Jan. 21, 1683.

SHAFTESBURY, shafts'bə-rē, **3d Earl of** (1671–1713), English moral philosopher. He did not create a complete philosophical system but concentrated on ethics and aesthetics.

Anthony Ashley Cooper, who became earl of Shaftesbury, was born at Exeter House, London, on Feb. 26, 1671. He was educated under the supervision of the philosopher John Locke. He attended Winchester College from 1683 to 1686, and then toured the Continent for two years. Cooper was elected a member of Parliament from the borough of Poole in Dorset in 1695. He served in The House of Commons until 1698, when he decided that he would not seek reelection because of ill health.

Cooper succeeded to his father's title in 1699. An independent-minded Whig, he played an active role in the House of Lords. He was made vice admiral of Dorset in 1701 but was deprived of his office in July 1702 when the Tories came to power. Shaftesbury then retired from public life. He left England in July 1711 because of ill health and died in Naples on Feb. 15, 1713.

Philosophy. Freedom of thought and inquiry were central to Shaftesbury's approach, and for him even atheism was an acceptable position. He was the first to use the term "moral sense" by which he meant an inclination toward or an affection for virtue. This "moral sense" he believed was natural to man. Virtue did not need either the fear of hell or the promise of heaven to exist, but rather was literally its own reward.

Although Shaftesbury was a regular attendant of the Church of England, his writings reveal him to have been a Deist. He objected to revealed religion on the grounds that by resorting to the miraculous it subverted the natural order and impugned the handiwork of a good and benevolent Creator.

Shaftesbury held that man is naturally a social being and that his natural virtue overrides his selfish inclinations. His thought owes much to the influence of the Cambridge Platonists, particularly in its stress on innate ideas. Thus Shaftesbury held that man has an innate aesthetic sense that depends on universal Platonic ideas of truth and beauty.

Writings. In his literary style Shaftesbury strove for elegance above all else. His writings consist of a series of essays and pamphlets that were collected and published in three volumes in 1711 under the title of *Characteristicks of Men, Manners, Opinions, Times.*

Further Reading: Green, Stanley, *Shaftesbury's Philosophy of Religion and Ethics: A Study of Enthusiasm* (Ohio Univ. Press 1967).

SHAFTESBURY, shafts'bə-rē, **7th Earl of** (1801–1885), English philanthropist and factory and mining reformer. Anthony Ashley Cooper was born on April 28, 1801, in London. He was educated at Harrow and Oxford, and was a member of the House of Commons for Woodstock, Dorchester, Dorsetshire, and Bath from 1826 to 1851, when he succeeded to the peerage. He supported the administrations of Liverpool and Canning. In 1828 he was appointed a commissioner of the board of control, and six years later he became a lord of the admiralty under Sir Robert Peel. From 1828, serving on an investigative lunacy committee, he constantly strove to improve the lunacy laws and administration, and it is largely due to his efforts that most of the worst abuses were removed. But his name is chiefly associated with his tireless and successful efforts to improve the condition of factory workers. About 1833 he first proposed a 10-hour limitation of their working-day, and in spite of opposition his proposal became law in 1847. In 1842 he promoted improvement of the condition of coal miners.

Though a Conservative, he supported the repeal of the corn laws. For 39 years, he acted as chairman of the Ragged School Union, and he was also identified with various movements for securing better housing accommodations for the working classes. He died in Folkestone, Kent, on Oct. 1, 1885.

SHAH, shä, is a Persian word meaning "king." When compounded as "shahanshah," it means "king of kings," or emperor. The shahs customarily wielded despotic power. At times the title was used by lesser princes or as a personal name or title. The title "shah" is borne by the sovereign of Iran and is also used in other countries of central and southern Asia.

SHAH JAHAN, shä jə-hän′ (1592–1666), was a Mughul (Mogul) emperor in India. He was born in Lahore on Jan. 5, 1592, and in his youth was known as Prince Khurram. The Prince was the favorite son of Emperor Jahangir, but the Empress used her influence to promote Khurram's youngest brother as the next ruler. Khurram then led a rebellion against Jahangir until the two were reconciled shortly before the Emperor's death in 1627. With the aid of his father-in-law, Asaf Khan, Khurram ascended the throne in 1628 with the title Shah Jahan. He was deposed by his son Aurangzeb in 1658 and died a prisoner in Agra on Jan. 22, 1666.

During the reign of Shah Jahan the Mughul Empire reached the height of its wealth and glory. He extended the Mughul dominions southward into the Deccan, annexing Ahmadnagar and reducing Bijapur and Golconda to tributaries. He was less successful in the west against the Persians. Shah Jahan is noted for the splendid monuments he had built at Agra and Delhi. Chief among them is the Taj Mahal at Agra—a mausoleum for his favorite wife, Arjumand Banu. The Emperor is also buried there.

SHAH NAMEH, shä nä-me′, is the Persian national epic. Its name means "Book of the Kings." It was written in the late 10th and early 11th centuries by the great poet Firdausi and consists of 60,000 rhymed couplets.

The epic sings the story of the Persians from their beginning under Gayūmarth, through the golden age of the reign of Jamshīd, and down to the conquest of the Sassanids by the Arabs and Islam in the 7th century. Written in almost pure Persian, studiously avoiding Arabic, it articulates the long-developing renaissance of the Persian spirit in its reaction to the Arab conquest and lays the foundation of the golden age of Persian culture that followed Firdausi.

SHAHN, shän, **Ben** (1898–1969), American painter and graphic artist, known for a highly individualized style, combining realism with abstraction, and for themes of social concern or protest. He was born in Kaunas, Lithuania, on Sept. 12, 1898, the son of a wood-carver. In 1906 he emigrated with his family to the United States, where he became a citizen in 1918. After serving as a lithographer's apprentice, he studied at New York University and the National Academy of Design and in 1925 went to Europe to study. He returned to the United States in 1929 and began the work that made him a major figure in contemporary art. He died in New York City on March 14, 1969.

Among Shahn's best-known works is the series of paintings *The Passion of Sacco and Vanzetti* (1931–1932; Whitney Museum of American Art, New York), a searing pictorial commentary on the trial and execution of the two Italian-born radicals. In 1933, Shahn assisted Diego Rivera with a mural project (never completed) in Rockefeller Center, New York City, and during the next decade he painted murals for a number of public buildings. His composition *Handball* (1939; Museum of Modern Art, New York) relates to the mural that he painted in the early 1940's for the Social Security (now Federal Security) Building, Washington, D. C. Other notable examples of his work are the paintings *Willis Avenue Bridge* (1940; Museum of Modern Art) and *Epoch* (1950; Philadelphia Museum of Art). In his

PHILADELPHIA MUSEUM OF ART

Epoch (1950) by the American artist Ben Shahn

later years Shahn devoted himself largely to book illustration and commercial art. His writings include *The Shape of Content* (1957).

Further Reading: Bush, Martin H., *Ben Shahn: The Passion of Sacco and Vanzetti* (Syracuse Univ. Press 1969); Morse, John D., ed., *Ben Shahn* (Praeger 1972); Soby, James T., ed., *Ben Shahn: His Graphic Art* (Braziller 1957); id., *The Paintings of Ben Shahn* (Braziller 1963).

SHAILENDRA, a pre-Muslim dynasty in Indonesia. See SAILENDRA.

SHAIVISM is a Hindu sect that recognizes Shiva (Śiva) as the supreme god. See SHIVA.

SHAKA, a Zulu warrior. See CHAKA.

SHAKER HEIGHTS, a city in northeastern Ohio, in Cuyahoga county, is situated east of Cleveland, of which it is a residential suburb.

About 1820, a society of Shakers established a colony within the limits of the present Shaker Heights. Property was owned in common. The Shaker Historical Society maintains a museum of Shaker furniture, tools, and household implements, and a library. See SHAKERS.

The society's membership eventually declined, and the colony was disbanded in 1889. The property was sold and the new owners developed it as a residential community. Shaker Heights was incorporated as a village in 1912 and became a city in 1931. It is governed by a mayor and council. Population: 32,487.

BROWN BROTHERS

SHAKER religious experiences were expressed through ring dancing (above), speaking in tongues, and trances.

SHAKERS

SHAKERS, a Christian sect that conducted one of the most successful experiments in religious communal living in 19th century America. The sect is known officially by several names: United Society of Believers in Christ's Second Appearing; the Millennial Church; and the Children of Truth, or Alethians, the latter derived from the Greek word for truth. The Shakers acquired their nickname from their practice of whirling, trembling, or shaking during religious services. They believed that a person could rid himself of sin or wicked habits by engaging in such ecstatic religious exercises.

Origins. The roots of American Shakerism can be traced to a group of English Quakers from Manchester, but particularly to the efforts of Ann Lee. Although she was baptized and married in the Church of England, Ann was attracted in 1758 to a religious sect of Shaking Quakers led by James and Jane Wardley. This group claimed to possess the Holy Spirit by whose presence and power they were able to speak in tongues (glossolalia), predict forthcoming events, and heal the sick. They also believed that the Second Coming of Christ would be in the form of a woman and that open and minutely detailed confession of one's innermost sins was a prerequisite both for salvation and membership.

Finding these views compatible with her own, Ann Lee spent the next 15 years with the Wardleys, zealously denouncing all conventional religious groups. Often she would disrupt a sedate Anglican worship service with her dancing, speaking in tongues, or irreverent accusations. After one such outburst in 1770, she was imprisoned. While in jail, she had a series of visions. In one she dreamed that the union of Adam and Eve was not for the divinely ordained purposes of procreation but, rather, for lustful self-indulgence. Therefore, she concluded, since sex was the principal cause of man's sin, sexual activity must be avoided at all costs. In still another revelation, Ann claimed to receive a command to go to America, which she obeyed in 1774.

Because of her enthusiasm, outspokenness, charismatic personality, and visionary experiences,

Ann Lee had emerged in England as a leader of the Shaking Quakers and was accorded the respectful title "Mother." However, it was in America that she really exhibited her leadership abilities. Almost singlehandedly she inspired the small band of believers that accompanied her to a wilderness settlement at Watervliet, N. Y., near Albany, to clear the wooded land for planting. Tirelessly she led a two-year evangelical mission throughout New England, teaching, praying, healing, and never once doubting that her religious message would catch on. Eventually it did, but only after her death in 1784.

High Point. Shakerism reached the peak of its development between 1830 and 1850 under the effective leadership of Elders James Whittaker and Joseph Meacham and Eldress Lucy Wright. During this period its membership grew to 6,000. Approximately 20 prominent Shaker societies were established, notably in Mt. Lebanon, N. Y., in Harvard and Hancock, Mass., in East Canterbury, N. H., in Enfield, Conn., and in Sabbathday Lake, Me. Still others were created in Ohio, Kentucky, Indiana, and Florida.

Among the reasons most frequently given to account for the expansion of Shakerism are these: (1) The missionary ardor of its adherence. Between 1801 and 1811, for example, Issachar Bates traveled thousands of miles on foot throughout the Ohio Valley, converting at least 1,000 settlers to Shakerism. (2) The simplicity of its creed. Converts were obliged to respond affirmatively to Jesus' admonition "If any man would come after me, let him deny himself, and take up his cross, and follow me (Matthew 16:24), with the understanding that such denial involved subjecting one's will to those in authority, living a disciplined life, and engaging in strenuous manual labor. (3) The fascination of its unorthodox modes of worship. Doubtless many people were attracted to Shakerism because of its variety of unconventional, yet deeply moving practices or experiences during religious services—for example, ring dances, trances, spiritual visitations, prophetic revelations, healings, and speaking in tongues. (4) The universality of its appeal. In a period when economic, racial, and class distinctions were rather pronounced in the United States, Shaker communism, which stressed that property and profit were to be held in common for the good of all, had a widespread appeal. So too did the Shakers' view that all men—adults or children, men or women, Indians or white men, pioneers or planters, "ignorant negro or learned Presbyterian divine"—deserved to be treated equally. Accordingly, in every Shaker society, women took their places as equals with men both in the spiritual and the temporal administration of the community.

Decline. After the Civil War, Shakerism began to decline. In 1874, Shaker membership had dwindled to 2,415, and 20 years later to 1,000. By the 1970's, the sect was virtually extinct. Some Shaker communities, as in Mt. Lebanon, N. Y., and Hancock, Mass., have been preserved for their historical interest. Unquestionably the gradual decline was caused by the Shaker practice of celibacy. Without marriages and thus without children, though some were adopted, the sect could grow only by a constant influx of converts, and that never happened. Its unrestrained mysterious rites of worship, its economy principally dependent upon agriculture and handicrafts, its almost total repudiation of a world out-

SHAKERS relied upon their own ingenuity and skill to provide for their needs. Their austerity of life and the simplicity of their designs can be seen in the furnishings of the elder's bedroom (*above*) and the kitchen (*top right*) at the Shaker Museum, Old Chatham, N. Y. The layout of the round stone Shaker barn (*right*) at Hancock, Mass., was designed for efficiency.

side the society, and its penchant for stifling the individuality of its members had little appeal to those living in and enjoying the benefits of a fast-changing industrial-capitalistic society.

Organization, Beliefs, and Practices. Shaker villages or communities usually consisted of at least two "families" of 30 persons, each of whom lived in a large house with separate entrances, stairways, and sleeping quarters in order to keep the sexes apart. The spiritual administration of each "family" or community was entrusted to four elders, two men and two women, who received their instructions from the ministry. The business affairs were the responsibility of the deacons or trustees, also generally two men and two women. While the deacons were accountable to the elders, the latter were answerable only to the ministry, which had ultimate supervision over the entire community. The ministry consisted of two elders and eldresses chosen from among the various "family" elders. As one Shaker writer put it, the ministry consisted of "the elders of the elders."

In addition to equality of the sexes, the other cardinal principles of Shakerism included celibacy, confession, and communal ownership of property. The Shakers never really forbade marriage, but they considered it less desirable than celibacy. They held the view that since Christ was not "an exponent of physical reproduction," his true followers must likewise live a sexually pure "virgin life."

Oral confession of sin before two witnesses was a prerequisite to salvation, and it was also required for admission in a Shaker society. Moreover, it was to be repeated as often as a member felt that he had sinned. Finally, since Shakers considered themselves to be a rebirth of the orig-

inal primitive pentecostal church of the Apostles (Acts 2:44–46), they believed that their worldly possessions were not really their own but God's and, therefore, ought to be "laid at the apostles' feet" as an irrevocable gift to the community to be equally distributed.

Doubtless the practices that were most characteristic of this sect were religious. Notable among these was the habit of sitting in silent meditation until overcome by a spiritual power that caused them to tremble or shake violently, and their spiritually symbolic marches and dances. However, they were equally well known for their industriousness and hospitality, their avoidance of extremes in dress and decoration, their pacifism, and their creative practicality. The beautiful simplicity of their furniture has made it highly prized. (See FURNITURE—*Shaker Furniture*.) The creative ability of the Shakers also was expressed through some of their ingenious inventions, including the circular (buzz) saw, washing machine, metal pen point, clothespin, and flat broom.

JOHN THOMAS NICHOL
Bentley College

Bibliography

Andrews, Edward D., *The People Called Shakers* (Dover 1963).
Andrews, Faith, *Shaker Furniture* (Peter Smith 1963).
Evans, F. W., *Shakers* (Appleton 1859).
Green, Calvin, and Wells, Seth, *A Summary View of the Millennial Church* (1848).
Johnson, Theodore E., *Hands to Work and Hearts to God* (Bowdoin Museum of Art 1969).
Mace, Aurelia G., *The Aletheia* (Knowlton and McLeary 1907).
Piercy, Caroline B., *The Valley of God's Pleasure* (Stratford House 1951).
Sears, Clara E., *Gleanings from Old Shaker Journals* (Houghton Mifflin 1916).
White, Anna, and Taylor, Leila, *Shakerism* (1904).

Mr. WILLIAM
SHAKESPEARES
COMEDIES,
HISTORIES, &
TRAGEDIES.

Published according to the True Originall Copies.

LONDON
Printed by Isaac Iaggard, and Ed. Blount. 1623.

Frontispiece of the First Folio (1623). The Droeshout engraving of Shakespeare is said to be a good likeness.

SHAKESPEARE, William (1564–1616), English dramatist and poet, who is generally considered to be the greatest of authors in any language, ancient or modern. Throughout the world, Shakespeare's plays are performed more frequently than those of any other playwright. Editions and translations of them continue to flow from the press 350 years after the publication of the first collected edition, and articles and books about Shakespeare appear in such numbers that no bibliography can pretend to give a complete list.

Some great authors, although classics in their own countries, are not readily exportable to other nations and cultures. Racine is nowhere so great as in France, or Cervantes in Spain, or Pushkin in Russia. But Shakespeare makes an essential appeal to all cultures. His *Macbeth*, for example, is a success in Bantu languages.

Shakespeare's language, like that of the King James Version of the Bible, has had a profound influence on everyday English speech, and speakers of English use expressions like "that's the rub" or "in one fell swoop" without being conscious that they are quoting Shakespeare. But more important, it is Shakespeare's language that conditions their idea of what poetry is. To fail to appreciate his finest passages—and there are hundreds that can be so classified—is to be virtually tone-deaf and imaginatively blind. For a while, in the 18th century, English poets seemed to feel that it was not Shakespeare's language, but Milton's, that was the language of poetry, and they wrote in the language of Milton as much as they could. But the fashion passed. One of the greatest English poets of the 19th century, John Keats, was also one of the most sensitive appreciators of Shakespeare.

Shakespeare seems not to depend on fashion. He survives all the changes because it is not only his language but also his insight into human character that capture attention. His Hamlet, his Lear, his Othello, his Brutus—all are tragic heroes of magnificent stature and nobility. His clowns and humorists—Falstaff and Touchstone, Bottom the Weaver and Launce with his dog—are irresistible. And his women—Juliet, Cleopatra, Lady Macbeth, Miranda—overwhelm us with admiration and wonder. It is, as Dryden said, that Shakespeare, "of all modern, and perhaps ancient poets, had the largest and most comprehensive soul."

LIFE AND CAREER

The date of Shakespeare's birth is not known. The earliest biographical record is an entry of his baptism in Holy Trinity Church, Stratford-upon-Avon, Warwickshire, on April 26, 1564. His father, John Shakespeare, first appears in the town records in 1552, when he was fined for not removing a dunghill from before his door in Henley Street. He became prominent in town affairs. He was elected a chamberlain of the Stratford corporation in 1561, alderman in 1565, and high bailiff (mayor) in 1568. He signed documents with a mark, but this is no longer supposed to prove that he was illiterate. From 1577 to his death in 1601, there are many signs in the records of financial troubles. He is excused from a levy for the poor, he sells his wife's inheritance, and he does not attend meetings of the corporation, so that another is appointed alderman in his place. Finally, in 1592 he is included in a list of nine who do not obey the law by going to church once a month, a note in the record signifying that this is for fear of process for debt. In 1596, however, he is described by the herald who made a rough draft of a coat of arms for him as a man who "hath lands and tenements of good wealth and substance."

The poet's mother was Mary, daughter of Robert Arden of Wilmcote, a wealthy landowner and relative of the aristocratic Ardens of Park Hall. Eight children were born to her, of whom William was the third child and oldest son. She died in Stratford in 1608.

Early Years. No records exist of Shakespeare in his early years, but something is known about the Stratford Grammar School, which he presumably attended. The curriculum of such a school would have been adequate to provide the poet with the basis for such classical learning as he had—perhaps more than Ben Jonson's "small Latin and less Greek" would suggest but rather less than some modern commentators suppose.

The two principal legends about his life in the country are that he was apprenticed to a butcher, for whom "when he killed a calf, he would do it in high style, and make a speech," and that he fled Stratford because he was caught deer poaching in the park of Sir Thomas Lucy of Charlecote. These stories cannot now be traced back farther than the late 17th century, about 100 years after the events are supposed to have happened.

Marriage. The first record of William Shakespeare after his christening is a license for marriage, Nov. 27, 1582, in the episcopal register of the diocese of Worcester. The bride's name is given as Anne Whateley of Temple Grafton. The next day a bond of £40 was entered to secure the marriage, without trouble, of Shakespeare and

Anne Hathway or Hathaway, of Stratford. The sum was posted by two yeoman friends of the bride's father, Richard Hathway of Shottery, parish of Old Stratford, whose will had been proved in the preceding July. Anne Whateley and Anne Hathway are probably the same person, and since the latter is traceable, the Whateley entry is probably a clerk's mistake. The special license to which these records refer provided for a marriage after only one asking of the banns. The usual three banns would have carried the wedding into a prohibited period on the church calendar and delayed it for about two months. This delay would have been undesirable because Anne was already pregnant. The baptismal register at Stratford records the christening on May 26, 1583, of Susanna, daughter of William Shakespeare. On Feb. 2, 1585, the same register records the christening of twins, Hamnet (a variant of Hamlet) and Judith, apparently named for a Stratford baker, Hamnet Sadler, a beneficiary and witness of the poet's will, and his wife Judith. Shakespeare's wife bore him no other children. She lived until 1623, and the inscription on her grave records the fact that she was then 67 years old, which would make her about eight years older than her husband.

"Missing" Years. Nothing is known of Shakespeare's life between the christening of the twins and the first record of his appearance in the theater in London as actor and playwright. Seven or eight years, from about 1584 to 1592, are blank so far as the records go. The actor William Beeston, whose father was a member of Shakespeare's company, many years later told John Aubrey, the antiquarian, that Shakespeare had been a schoolmaster in the country. Because of the academic flavor of such early plays as *The Comedy of Errors* and *Love's Labour's Lost*, this tradition has found favor with modern biographers. There is no record of Anne Shakespeare in London during her husband's stay there, nor is there anything in Stratford until 1597, when Shakespeare, an established man of the theater, bought New Place.

Career in London. In September 1592, Robert Greene, the dissipated university wit, died in poverty and misery in London, leaving a pamphlet called *A Groatsworth of Wit Bought with a Million of Repentance*. In an epilogue he warned three of his friends who wrote plays (probably Christopher Marlowe, George Peele, and Thomas Nash) against the players, who live on the efforts of writers and then neglect them in their hour of need. "Trust them not," he says, "for there is an upstart crow, beautified with our feathers, that with his *Tiger's heart wrapped in a player's hide*, supposes he is as well able to bombast out a blank verse as the best of you; and being an absolute *Johannes fac totum* is in his own conceit the only Shake-scene in a country." This evidently refers to a presumptuous actor, not a university man like Greene and his friends, who has dared to write blank-verse plays and is versatile enough to be a threat to them.

That the jack-of-all-trades is Shakespeare seems clear from the fact that the "Tiger's heart wrapped in a player's hide" is a parody of a line in *King Henry the Sixth*, Part 3, and from the pun on Shakespeare's name. Later in the year, Henry Chettle, who had seen Greene's pamphlet through the press, apologized in the preface to his own *Kind-Hart's Dreame*. Marlowe and

Memorial bust of Shakespeare in Holy Trinity Church, Stratford, where the poet was christened and buried.

Shakespeare had apparently resented the attacks in Greene's book. Marlowe, though warned against the players and Shakespeare, had been called an atheist and Machiavellian, and Chettle expressed the wish that he had moderated more of Greene's bitterness than he did. "With neither of them that take offense was I acquainted, and with one of them I care not if I never be. The other, whom at that time I did not so much spare, as since I wish I had. . . . I am as sorry as if the original fault had been my fault, because myself have seen his demeanour no less civil than he excellent in the quality he professes [profession he follows, that is, acting]. Besides, divers of worship have reported his uprightness of dealing, which argues his honesty, and his facetious grace in writing, that approves his art."

Player and Writer, 1592–1594. By the end of 1592, then, Shakespeare had become an actor, written plays, attracted the jealousy of a university-trained poet, and won the respect of Chettle and "divers of worship" for his civility, his honesty, and his excellence as player and writer. Why he left Stratford, and his wife and children, for London and how he got a start in the theater are unknown. The well-known legend that he began by holding gentlemen's horses at the playhouse door comes down from Sir William Davenant, the eccentric 17th century poet, playwright, and theater manager who sometimes claimed to be Shakespeare's bastard son. There are other legends that Shakespeare was first a "servant" in the theater or first a prompter's assistant, or call boy.

From 1592 to 1594 the theatrical companies were somewhat disorganized because of the plague, and it is during these years that Shake-

In the 1943 Broadway production of *Othello*, Paul Robeson (*right*), as the tragic Moor, confronts the wicked Iago, portrayed by José Ferrer.

speare presented himself as a poet. His two narrative poems *Venus and Adonis* and *The Rape of Lucrece* were published in 1593 and 1594.

Actor and Playwright. Sometime in 1594 the two principal acting companies of the later Elizabethan era were formed: the Lord Chamberlain's Men and the Lord Admiral's Men. Technically personal servants of these officials, the actors could wear livery, thereby securing protection against prosecution under the old statutes that classified players with rogues and vagabonds. They received also some prestige as retainers of the court, since the puritanical authorities of the City of London looked on players and theaters with disfavor. Furthermore, the patron's license was a useful introduction to the local authorities when the companies toured in the provinces. When they were at home, the players earned their living by producing plays in a public playhouse. Occasional performances at court, usually on holidays, carried prestige but did not provide a major share of their income. In March 1595, the Treasurer of the Royal Chamber notes payment of £20 to William Kemp (or Kempe), William Shakespeare, and Richard Burbage, servants to the Lord Chamberlain, for the presentation at court in Greenwich of two "comedies or interludes" during the previous Christmas holidays. Shakespeare was then a leading member of the company and a "sharer," or stockholder, who participated in the profits. It was a position of some dignity and of considerable promise financially. The Chamberlain's Men were to be the favorite court entertainers, giving 32 performances at court during Elizabeth's reign and becoming the King's Men on the accession of James I.

Shakespeare's position in the company and his financial obligations and returns may be inferred from various legal documents relating to suits against members of the company in 1610, 1615, and 1619. The company consisted of actor-sharers (of which Shakespeare must have been one in 1594–1595), hired men, and boys who played female parts and were assigned to the sharers on something like an apprenticeship basis. With the

acquisition of theater property, the Globe in 1599 and the Blackfriars in 1608, some members of the company became investors in real estate—landlords, or "housekeepers." As originally leased, the Globe Theatre was held in two moieties, or halves, one by Richard and Cuthbert Burbage and the other by Shakespeare, Augustine Phillips, Thomas Pope, John Heminge, and William Kemp. Shakespeare's interest was therefore a tenth, but it varied as members dropped out or new ones were added. He held one-seventh interest in the Blackfriars after it was acquired by the company. He was still holding his share of the Globe when the theater burned in 1613, but whether he retained his interests to the end of his life is uncertain. The most careful estimates of Shakespeare's income from theatrical sources give him about £50 annually to 1599, about £110 to 1608, and after retirement, about £60 to £70 from his interest as "housekeeper." His income from the theater almost certainly never went over £175 or £200 at the most. But in relation to the cost of living at that time, Shakespeare's income was quite comfortable.

Shakespeare's first obligation to the company was as an actor. He is listed among the principal actors of Jonson's *Every Man in his Humour* in 1598 and *Sejanus* in 1603, but he does not appear in the lists after that date. The First Folio edition of his own plays, 1623, lists him among the actors but does not specify the plays in which he took part. Legend has assigned to him the minor roles of Adam in *As You Like It* and the ghost in *Hamlet*. But his chief contribution to the company was the plays. He provided, alone or in collaboration, 38 plays between 1590–1591 and 1612–1613, and his work constitutes the most substantial part of the company's repertory for the period. His relations with his associates seem to have been very cordial. He received a small bequest in the will of Augustine Phillips, and he left money in his own will for memorial rings to Richard Burbage, Heminge, and Condell. The devotion of the two latter actors to his memory is obvious from the prefatory matter to the First Folio, which they edited.

Biographical Records, 1596–1613. Some details of Shakespeare's personal life during his first decade in London have come down to us. His son Hamnet was buried on Aug. 11, 1596, in Stratford. About the same time, John Shakespeare, the poet's father, applied to the College of Arms for a grant of arms, and a rough draft, drawn up by a herald, is dated Oct. 20, 1596. A note to a revised draft says that John Shakespeare possessed a pattern of the arms drawn up 20 years earlier, so this was apparently not the first time the poet's father had sought the insignia of a gentleman. It has been suggested that William must have prompted the revival of interest in arms, since his father was not at this time in prosperous circumstances, as he had been 20 years before, whereas the son was now increasing in wealth and status. The Shakespeare request was apparently granted, and the now familiar coat with the falcon and spear appears on the poet's monument in Stratford church. Three years later, leave to impale the arms of Arden was asked, but if this was granted, Shakespeare seems not to have made use of it.

In 1597 the records of the tax collectors give us some information about Shakespeare's London address. He is listed as one of the inhabitants of St. Helen's parish, Bishopsgate (a district not far from the Shoreditch theaters, The Theatre and The Curtain), who cannot be found to pay the tax, which for Shakespeare was 5s. The next year he is listed as owing 13s. 4d., and the collectors have traced him to the Bankside in Southwark, close to the site where the Globe Theatre was to be built. There, presumably, he paid his taxes, for his name does not appear as a delinquent in later rolls.

In 1597 he purchased New Place in Stratford, the house he was to repair, retire to when he left London, and hand on in his family as far as his granddaughter, his last lineal descendant. The prosperity that this transaction suggests is also indicated by a letter from Abraham Sturley of Stratford to Richard Quiney in which Shakespeare is said to be willing to purchase some land in Shottery and by a letter from Quiney to Shakespeare asking the loan of £30. This is the only letter to or from Shakespeare in existence. Quiney's other correspondence suggests that the loan was promptly made. Also in 1598 when an accounting was made of corn and malt in Stratford, in an attempt to check hoarding during a shortage of grain, Shakespeare was credited with 10 quarters, or 80 bushels. Only a dozen residents of Stratford had more. In the next year he invested in his share of the Globe Theatre. In 1602 he purchased 107 acres of arable land in Old Stratford for the sum of £320. His largest investment, however, was made in 1605. It was the purchase, for £440, of a moiety of certain tithes of three hamlets in Stratford. This produced, in 1611, an income of £60. In 1613, Shakespeare bought a gatehouse in Blackfriars, London, for £140.

Not much is known of Shakespeare's life in London aside from his work, and the few records we do have seem to raise as many questions as they answer. He was involved in two quarrels that got into the courts, but in neither case was he a principal. In 1596 he figured in a writ served by the sheriff against William Shakespeare, Francis Langley, Dorothy Soer, and Anne Lee, on the part of one William Wayte. Langley, who had built the Swan theater, had earlier been responsible for writs served on Wayte and his stepfather, William Gardiner, compelling them to keep the peace. Shakespeare's part in the quarrel does not seem clear, but somewhat fantastic applications of it to characters in his plays have been offered. In 1612 he was a witness in a suit brought by Stephen Belott, a wigmaker, against his father-in-law, Christopher Mountjoy, over a marriage portion. Shakespeare is shown to have known the French Huguenot Mountjoy family since about 1602, to have lived in their house in Cripplegate for a time in 1604, and to have served, at Mrs. Mountjoy's request, as an intermediary to persuade the apprentice Belott to marry his master's daughter. But his testimony was useless, since he could not remember what marriage portion had been agreed upon eight years earlier.

The little evidence we have concerning the habits and behavior of Shakespeare is somewhat contradictory. The Bankside was not a "respectable" district. The brothels and bear-baiting pits were there, and it was frequented by the sporting element rather than by sober citizens. John Manningham, a law student, entered in his diary on March 13, 1602, a story that Shakespeare overheard Richard Burbage making an assignation with a "citizen" at a performance of *King Richard the Third*. The actor was to announce himself as Richard the Third. Shakespeare got there first and was entertained, and when Burbage arrived and announced himself, the author sent down word that William the Conqueror was before Richard the Third. Against this gossip is the general statement of John Aubrey, who had it from Beeston, that Shakespeare "was not a company keeper" and "wouldn't be debauched." From the little we know, it must be concluded that he led a much more dignified and quiet life than did Marlowe, Greene, Peele, or Ben Jonson.

Last Years, 1613–1616. Shakespeare retired from active service as the leading playwright of the King's Men sometime in 1612 or 1613, leaving his position to the younger John Fletcher, with whom he collaborated on *King Henry the Eighth* and *The Two Noble Kinsmen*. The last years of his life have interested his imaginative biographers almost as much as the lost years of his youth, and the picture given usually tells more about the biographer than about the subject. The first biographer, Nicholas Rowe, said: "The latter part of his life was spent, as all men of good sense will wish theirs may be, in ease, retirement and the conversation of friends." Sir Sidney Lee and Lytton Strachey fill in other details from fancy. But if we turn to the Stratford records again, we find only that his brother Richard was buried in Feb. 4, 1613; he was given £5 in the will of John Combe, a wealthy Stratford moneylender, in 1614; his daughter Judith married the son of his old friend Richard Quiney in February 1616; and he drew up his own will in March 1616 and died on April 23 of that year.

The Will. The will is extant, and each of its three pages bears Shakespeare's signature. He left £300 to his daughter Judith, part of it as a marriage portion; £20 to his sister Joan and £5 to each of her three sons; £10 to the poor of Stratford; small remembrances to a few friends; his second-best bed to his wife; and the residuary estate to his daughter Susanna, who lived with the Shakespeares at New Place. Presumably, Susanna was to see that her mother was taken care of. It is apparent that Shakespeare wished to found a family of landed gentry, for he provides that the estate shall go to the male issue of his daughter Judith if Susanna and her daughter Elizabeth both fail to have a son. Susanna was the wife of Dr. John Hall, a prominent physician who left some manuscript casebooks in Latin, later translated and published, which mention illnesses of his wife, his daughter, and himself but none of his father-in-law. The Halls had no son, and their daughter Elizabeth married first Thomas Nash and later Sir John Bernard, but she died childless in 1670, the last direct descendant of the poet.

Shakespeare was buried on April 25, 1616. On his gravestone are four lines of doggerel verse:

Good friend, for Jesus' sake forbear
To dig the dust enclosed here!
Blest be the man that spares these stones
And curst be he that moves my bones.

Seventeenth century legend holds that Shakespeare wrote these lines himself and that the curse effectively prevented opening of the grave, "though his wife and daughter did earnestly desire to be laid in the same grave with him."

Portraits. The only two portraits of Shakespeare that have any authority are the bust on

In Franco Zeffirelli's film of *Romeo and Juliet* (1968), mourners bear the bodies of the tragic lovers.

his monument in the Stratford church, done by Gheerart Janssen sometime before 1623, and the engraving by Martin Droeshout, which serves as a frontispiece to the First Folio. It is not known whether either Janssen or Droeshout had ever seen their subject. Droeshout was only 15 when Shakespeare died. Neither portrait can be called a work of art, but presumably the bust was enough of a likeness to satisfy the family. The various paintings, some contemporary with him, that are claimed to be of Shakespeare serve the purpose of pacifying those who are revolted by the stolid expression of the bust and the engraving. But the safest thing to do is to follow the advice of Ben Jonson and "look not on his picture, but his book."

THE PLAYS

Shakespeare's first editors, his colleagues Heminge and Condell, divided his plays into comedies, histories, and tragedies, but they did not arrange them in order of composition. The first play in their Folio is *The Tempest,* a late play, and the last is *Cymbeline,* also a late play.

Chronology and Periods. The first serious attempt to ascertain the order in which the plays were written was made by Edmond (or Edmund) Malone in 1778. The effort was carried on in the 19th century by Frederick J. Furnivall, Frederick G. Fleay, and other members of the New Shakspere Society (1873–1894), which Furnivall founded. A generally accepted chronology of the 20th century is that of Edmund K. Chambers, shown in the accompanying table.

It is now conventional, though artificial, to divide Shakespeare's career into three periods—the Early Period, up until his company acquired the Globe Theatre in 1599; the Middle Period, from that time until they acquired the Blackfriars in 1608; and the Final Period.

656

Early Period. When he began, Shakespeare was an experimenter. He was entering a field in which John Lyly had created witty, sophisticated court comedies; Christopher Marlowe had charged his heroic melodramas with the mighty line of poetry that made forever obsolete the "Jigging veins of rhyming mother wits" (Marlowe's *Tamburlaine*); and Thomas Kyd had stunned the stage with his revenge play *The Spanish Tragedy.* George Peele and Robert Greene had written romantic plays of a mixed genre.

Shakespeare wrote four plays about the Wars of the Roses, making a kind of epic series out of *King Henry the Sixth,* Parts 1, 2, and 3, and *King Richard the Third.* The characterization is not profound, and the verse is often stiff and rhetorical, but these plays were to lead to the great accomplishments of *King Richard the Second, King Henry the Fourth,* and *King Henry the Fifth.* In these mature history plays Shakespeare blends history, patriotic feeling, great character portrayal, and even comedy in the most masterly way.

In tragedy, Shakespeare began with a Senecan horror thriller, *Titus Andronicus,* and wisely turned away from that to the romantic tragedy of *Romeo and Juliet,* a play of timeless beauty but a tragedy of fate rather than of character. In comedy, he began with a close imitation of Latin comedy, but he gradually introduced more and more of the romantic love element, which makes his great comedies at the end of this period— *Much Ado About Nothing, As You Like It,* and *Twelfth Night*—supreme of their kind.

Middle Period. An experiment with Roman material in *Julius Caesar* led to the great tragedies *Hamlet, Othello, King Lear,* and *Macbeth.* In these plays both character and fate have an influence on the outcome. Shakespeare's finest characterizations and his most profound vision of the nature of evil and the struggles of the human soul are to be seen here. Concurrently he wrote a group of "problem comedies," which are not so sunny as the great ones but search for meaning in troublesome moral dilemmas. Toward the end of this period he returned to classical subjects in *Antony and Cleopatra, Coriolanus,* and *Timon of Athens.*

Final Period. What was left for Shakespeare to exploit was the area of romance, very popular in his time both in fiction and in drama. He had used romantic elements in such earlier plays as *Two Gentlemen of Verona, As You Like It,* and *The Merchant of Venice* but had subordinated them to the requirements of comedy. Now—in *Pericles, Prince of Tyre; Cymbeline; The Winter's Tale;* and *The Tempest*—he chose plots with more wonder than probability in them and emphasized spectacle, song, and sensational effects. At the same time he created a marvelous series of innocent and persecuted heroines. Finally, perhaps after his retirement to Stratford about 1612, Shakespeare collaborated with his younger colleague John Fletcher on the history play *King Henry the Eighth* and on *The Two Noble Kinsmen,* based on the *Knight's Tale* in Chaucer's *Canterbury Tales.*

Quartos and Folios. That Shakespeare was an artist is obvious. The quality of the plays cannot be the result of accident. But this does not mean that he was writing for readers. He was writing for the stage. He and his company profited mainly from the production, not the publication, of his plays, and there is no evidence that he prepared any of them for the press. The question, then, of how his plays got from his own manuscript to our modern texts is of importance and interest.

Eighteen of Shakespeare's plays were published separately as quarto pamphlets. These were reprinted in the folio collection of 1623, and 18 unpublished plays were added. The editors of the folio, Shakespeare's associates Heminge and Condell, condemned the earlier quartos as "divers stolen and surreptitious copies, maimed and deformed by the frauds and stealths of injurious imposters." In the folio, it was claimed, these plays were given "cured and perfect of their limbs" and the unpublished plays "absolute in their numbers as he conceived them." For over two centuries these words were taken literally, but modern research has shown that usually the folio editors reprinted an earlier quarto when there was one. Often they used a recent quarto, with its accumulated misprints, rather than the earliest one. But they did often introduce changes, apparently from a playhouse manuscript. Furthermore, some of the quartos show signs of having been set up from Shakespeare's own manuscript or a faithful copy of it. Prejudice against the quartos is well justified, however, in the case of six, now always called the "bad quartos." They are the *Romeo and Juliet* of 1597, the *King Henry the Fifth* of 1600, the *Merry Wives* of 1602, the *Hamlet* of 1603, and the 1594–1595 editions of Parts 1 and 2 of *King Henry the Sixth.* These badly garbled texts certainly never came from the prompt copy or the author's manuscript. They were either taken down in faulty shorthand by an agent in the audience or, more probably, reconstructed from memory by an actor or other employee of the company. Sometimes the version on which the reconstruction was based may have been a shortened form used on tour in the provinces. And there is always the possibility that different texts of a play originated before and after revision by the author or someone else.

Manuscripts. No author's manuscript of a play in the folio has survived, but a strong case has been made for Shakespeare's hand as one of those in a play of composite authorship called *Sir Thomas More.* Most scholars believe that 147 lines on three pages of manuscript in the British Museum are in Shakespeare's own handwriting. If so, some confirmation has been found for the statement of the folio editors concerning their author's facility: "His mind and hand went together, and what he thought he uttered with that easiness that we have scarce received from him a blot in his papers." Ben Jonson's retort to this remark is characteristic and famous: "I *remember,* the Players have often mentioned it as an honour to *Shakespeare,* that in his writing, (whatsoever he penn'd) hee never blotted out line. My answer hath beene, would he had blotted a thousand. Which they thought a malevolent speech. I had not told posterity this, but for their ignorance, who choose that circumstance to commend their friend by, wherein he most faulted. And to justifie mine owne candor, (for I lov'd the man, and doe honour his memory (on this side Idolatry) as much as any.) Hee was (indeed) honest, and of an open, and free nature: had an excellent *Phantsie;* brave notions, and gentle expressions: wherein hee flow'd with that facility, that sometime it was necessary he should be stop'd: *Sufflaminandus erat;* as *Augustus* said of *Haterius.* His wit was in his owne power; would the rule of it had beene so too. . . ."

It is not surprising that no manuscripts of Shakespeare plays in the folio have survived. Twentieth century interest in original manuscripts should not be assumed to have existed in the 16th century. The author's manuscript, moreover, was of practical value as a working text of the play, and it would have been used rather than preserved. Upon completion of a play, the company had first to send it to the official

CHRONOLOGY OF THE PLAYS

The date of composition of Shakespeare's plays often cannot be fixed very precisely, but in some instances we have a definite date for a performance. The following chronology, from Edmund K. Chambers' *William Shakespeare* (1930), is generally accepted.

1590–1591	*Henry VI,* Parts 2 and 3
1591–1592	*Henry VI,* Part 1
1592–1593	*Richard III; Comedy of Errors*
1593–1594	*Titus Andronicus; Taming of the Shrew*
1594–1595	*Two Gentlemen of Verona; Love's Labour's Lost; Romeo and Juliet*
1595–1596	*Richard II; Midsummer Night's Dream*
1596–1597	*King John; Merchant of Venice*
1597–1598	*Henry IV,* Parts 1 and 2
1598–1599	*Much Ado About Nothing; Henry V*
1599–1600	*Julius Caesar; As You Like It; Twelfth Night*
1600–1601	*Hamlet; Merry Wives of Windsor*
1601–1602	*Troilus and Cressida*
1602–1603	*All's Well That Ends Well*
1604–1605	*Measure for Measure; Othello*
1605–1606	*King Lear; Macbeth*
1606–1607	*Antony and Cleopatra*
1607–1608	*Coriolanus; Timon of Athens*
1608–1609	*Pericles*
1609–1610	*Cymbeline*
1610–1611	*Winter's Tale*
1611–1612	*Tempest*
1612–1613	*Henry VIII; Two Noble Kinsmen*

Classic Shakespearean actors of the past include Sarah Siddons (*left*), in her great interpretation of Lady Macbeth; Edmund Kean (*above*), as Shylock in *The Merchant of Venice;* and John Barrymore (*right*), in his memorable portrayal of the villainous King Richard III.

licenser, who was the Master of the Revels. He read it and affixed his signature to the manuscript (for which he got a fee) if the play seemed to him to be free from offense. The main interest of this censorship was political. *Sir Thomas More* was not produced, for example, because the master found some of its speeches dangerous and would allow the play to appear only if considerable changes were made. Later, in King James' reign, there was a law against oaths, and the licenser was supposed to see that no profane matter crept in.

If the play met with his approval, the licenser signed a warrant on the last page, pocketed his fee, and returned the manuscript to the players. They then either had a transcript made or used the original for a director's copy. Notes of stage directions were made, sometimes with the names of the actors concerned. It is from such a note, carried over into print, that we know Will Kemp played Dogberry in *Much Ado About Nothing.* A "plot" or synopsis of scenes, with entrances noted, was drawn up to hang in the tiring-room, and the parts for the individual actors to memorize were copied out from the manuscript of the play.

Problems of direction in Elizabethan times— the difficulties an author had to overcome before his play was produced as he wished—can best be inferred from Hamlet's advice to the players. There Shakespeare shows a sensitiveness to diction ("Speak the speech, I pray you, as I pronounced it to you, trippingly on the tongue"), a dislike of extravagant overacting ("O, it offends me to the soul to hear a robustious, periwig-pated fellow tear a passion to tatters"), a love of "the modesty of nature," and an annoyance at interpolated gags by a comedian ("That's villainous, and shows a most pitiful ambition in the fool that uses it").

The Elizabethan theater did not have the system of long runs of plays familiar to us. The company kept several plays in repertory during a season, and when the manuscript was no longer needed as a prompt copy, it would be put away until some occasion for revival—a tour in the provinces or an opportunity to play at court— came about. If for any reason the players decided to publish a play, the published version might incorporate changes and notes previously made by players, as well as the printer's errors or emendations.

Sources. Shakespeare, like all other dramatists, drew not only upon life but upon books for his material. In several instances—notably *King John, The Taming of the Shrew, King Henry the Fourth, King Lear,* and *Hamlet*—he rewrote old plays. For his English historical plays he turned for material to Raphael Holinshed's *Chronicles of England, Scotland, and Ireland.* He found there plenty of historical detail, brief and formal characterization, and the prejudices about English history of the 15th century that favored the Tudor interest. He used his material with freedom, taking motives out of their context, altering the ages of characters—doing anything, in fact, that would increase the dramatic effectiveness of his play if it did not too seriously contradict general knowledge. History plays were popular in the decade following 1588 because of the renaissance of English patriotism after the Armada, and there are many indications that the Elizabethans considered the plays "true history," as educational as the chronicles and much more entertaining. In the history play, Shakespeare found opportunities for the study of character that served as preliminary exercises for his greatest achievements. Richard II, for instance, is a character who foreshadows Hamlet in part, and Richard III prefigures Iago.

Among great modern interpreters of Shakespeare are John Gielgud (*left*), in the title role of *Hamlet*; Katharine Hepburn (*above*), as the romantic Rosalind in the comedy *As You Like It*; and Laurence Olivier (*right*), in the motion picture *Henry V*, generally regarded as one of the finest screen adaptations of Shakespeare's plays.

A much richer book from the point of view of character portrayal provided him with the material for his Roman tragedies. This is Sir Thomas North's translation (1579) of Plutarch's *Lives*. Here Shakespeare got not only complex biographical analyses of the heroes of antiquity but also much that was useful for style. He versifies whole pages of North's prose, the most remarkable example of which is Enobarbus' description of Cleopatra's barge (*Antony and Cleopatra*, Act II, Scene 2). But there is still very great freedom in selection and utilization of material, and much that he uses is transformed by passing through the romantic imagination of the Englishman. Enobarbus is almost entirely Shakespeare's invention, and the citizens in *Julius Caesar* he saw not in a book but on the streets of London.

Twice Shakespeare dramatized English novels: *As You Like It* from Thomas Lodge's *Rosalynde* and *The Winter's Tale* from the *Pandosto* of Robert Greene, who years before had called Shakespeare an "upstart crow." Many of his plays depend, directly or indirectly, on Italian tales of love, adventure, and violence. Modern criticism has questioned whether there is always a unity between these adopted plots and the characters who enact them. If a disunity is found, it is only another evidence of the profound way in which character absorbed the playwright's mind, sometimes to the neglect of other matters.

Other great books, such as the English Bible and the *Essays* of Montaigne, have been shown to have strongly affected Shakespeare's thought and style. However "unlearned" he was supposed to have been, books played a large part in his education.

Question of Authorship. The question of the authorship of the plays now or formerly published under Shakespeare's name has turned in several directions and has had many ramifications. The first of these is the apocrypha—plays ascribed to Shakespeare in his lifetime or later but not now included in the canon (the authentic works). The second is the question of whether William Shakespeare of Stratford was actually the author of the plays of the canon or whether his name was merely put to plays that are the work of another man. The third is the question of whether the plays in the canon are collaborations, plays by other men slightly revised by Shakespeare, or plays drafted by Shakespeare and finished by other writers.

The canon of Shakespeare's dramatic works consists of the 36 plays published in the First Folio of 1623 plus two others, *Pericles* and *The Two Noble Kinsmen*, and part of a third, *Sir Thomas More*. Four plays that were fraudulently attributed to him in his lifetime—*Sir John Oldcastle, The London Prodigal, A Yorkshire Tragedy,* and *The Troublesome Reign of King John*—form part of the apocrypha. The rest of it consists of plays included in the second issue of the Third Folio in 1664, which had already been printed in quarto with the initials W. S. or other hint of Shakespearean authorship.

Many attempts—unconvincing to the great majority of Shakespearean scholars—have been made to show that William Shakespeare is a pseudonym for the real author of the plays in the canon, who was not the actor from Stratford. About 60 names have been proposed. The four favorites are Francis Bacon; Edward de Vere, 17th Earl of Oxford; William Stanley, 6th Earl of Derby; and Christopher Marlowe. Whether Shakespeare collaborated with others is a more respectable scholarly question. He is now thought to have done so in *King Henry the Eighth, The Two Noble Kinsmen,* and *Pericles,* as well as in part of *Sir Thomas More*.

THE POEMS

Shakespeare was as much a poet as a playwright. Fortunately, the existence of a poetic drama that, after Marlowe, was capable of the greatest expression poetically and dramatically made it unnecessary for Shakespeare to continue the career as a nondramatic poet that he had begun with *Venus and Adonis* and *The Rape of Lucrece*. The exception to this is his series of sonnets published in 1609. See SONNETS OF SHAKESPEARE.

Narrative Poems. Shakespeare's *Venus and Adonis* was entered for publication on April 18, 1593, by the printer Richard Field, a fellow townsman three years his senior, who had come up to London in 1579. The poem was dedicated to the young Earl of Southampton, a favorite patron of writers of amatory verse, and some sort of monetary acknowledgment was probably given by the nobleman, although the old legend that once he gave the poet £1,000 is incredible. The dedication refers to *Venus and Adonis* as "the first heir of my invention" (that is, his first published work), and Shakespeare promises "some graver labor" if this one is found acceptable. The promise was kept a year later by the dedication of *The Rape of Lucrece*, in which the poet says he has warrant of the Earl's disposition that makes this second offering assured of acceptance. "What I have done is yours," he says, "what I have to do is yours, being part in all I have, devoted yours"—lines that seem to suggest an intimacy greater than that reflected in the first dedication.

Sonnets and Lyrics. In 1599 a small anthology called *The Passionate Pilgrim* was issued by the publisher William Jaggard with the name of Shakespeare on the title page. Among the 20 poems are two sonnets by him and three excerpts from *Love's Labour's Lost*, but some of the other poems are known to be by other men and possibly all of them are. When the book reached a third edition in 1612, several selections from Thomas Heywood's *Troia Britanica* were added, and Heywood protested at the piracy, with the remark that Shakespeare was also vexed. This led to the issuance of a new title page without an author's name. In 1601 a genuine poem by Shakespeare, now called *The Phoenix and the Turtle*, appeared in Robert Chester's *Love's Martyr*, a collection of poems celebrating the love of Sir John Salusbury and his wife. Shakespeare's poem is a "metaphysical" one, in quatrains, and it has met with both strong condemnation and strong praise. Appended to the edition of the sonnets in 1609 was a poem called *The Lover's Complaint*. Modern critics doubt, on internal evidence, that it is by Shakespeare.

Not these miscellanea but the songs and other lyrical passages in the plays and the sonnets give Shakespeare the very highest rank as a lyric poet. When he wrote lyrics for music, his style became clear and limpid, however tortured and complex the play might be. The songs are commonly filled with pleasant details of nature, very English, but they never become prosy or pedestrian. They show the gaiety of the contemporary ballet or dancing song, the gravity of the motet, and the occasional epigrammatic quality of the madrigal. All of these part-songs had reached the height of their development in the poet's lifetime, and the modern song with accompaniment, the "air," was just coming in. Two of Shakespeare's songs can still be sung to contemporary musical settings. They are "It was a lover and his lass" (from *As You Like It*, Act 5, Scene 3), set by Thomas Morley in his *First Book of Airs* (1600), and "O mistress mine" (from *Twelfth Night*, Act II, Scene 3), set by Morley in his *Consort Lessons* (1599) and by William Byrd with elaborate variations for the virginals. The songs at the end of *Love's Labour's Lost*, beginning "When daisies pied and violets blue" and "When icicles hang by the wall," have been called by John Masefield the loveliest thing ever said about England. But most important of all, the songs always have a dramatic purpose and a dramatic effectiveness. The poet never releases his lyricism wantonly or idly.

SHAKESPEARE AS DRAMATIST

It is fortunate that the greatest of English poets flourished at a time when it was possible to write poetic drama for the popular theater. And Shakespeare above all was a man of the theater. He solved the problems confronting him as a playwright as brilliantly as he wrote poetry.

The Elizabethan Stage. The stage of Shakespeare's time was more plastic than ours. Spectators surrounded it on three sides, and there was no scenery in the modern sense. At the Globe, an outdoor theater, the stage was quite simple. It was a platform in front of a wall, with a door on either side leading to the tiring-room. Curtains were used to cover the doors or to enclose a space on the stage. A balcony above provided another level for acting. Posts held up a roof that partly covered the stage, and these could represent trees. There was a trapdoor for acting below the level of the stage, as in the graveyard scene in *Hamlet*. Properties were carried on and off stage in full view of the audience (bodies had to be carried off also).

Shakespeare's audiences were not given printed programs listing the time and place of each scene. The notation of time and place in modern editions is the anachronistic contribution of modern editors. If the location is important, it is mentioned in the lines, as in the first forest scene in *As You Like It*. But many scenes are unlocalized and may be imagined as taking place anywhere. Because of this and because there was no scene shifting, the pace of the play could be very rapid. This generalization of location created difficulty for the dramatist in the indication of dramatic time. But Shakespeare made of difficulty an opportunity, so that in *Othello*, for example, he is able to have two time schemes, contradictory but not noticeably so to the spectator, each of which has its subtle effect on the feeling and tension of the drama.

The closeness of the audience to the actors made the soliloquy and the aside much less artificial than they seem on the less intimate modern stage. These conventional devices were also means of achieving swiftness and directness, since conveying the same information by dialogue, however "natural" it might seem, would take much longer. But Shakespeare was not content with the soliloquy merely as an economical device: witness *Hamlet*.

The makeup of an Elizabethan repertory company was another source of limitations and opportunities for the playwright. Actors naturally specialized somewhat in such a company, and their individual peculiarities had to be allowed for. Happily, in Richard Burbage, the Chamberlain-King's Men had an actor of great versatility and talent for the leading roles, and in Will Kemp and Robert Armin, Shakespeare seems to have had two extraordinarily good clowns. The most peculiar aspect of the company to modern eyes was the necessity of using boys to play female parts. How could a heroine of any greatness be portrayed adequately by a boy? Shakespeare seized enthusiastically upon the romance device of a girl disguising herself as a boy, and in the comedies where the heroine is most important, Rosalind and Viola project their charm in disguise. Furthermore, his heroines derive their attractiveness not from physical charm but from wit and modesty, gaiety and purity. Even Cleopatra, the "serpent of old Nile," conquers Antony by keen insight and sensitive and brilliant dexterity of mind and temper rather than by elementary physical appeal.

There is little protest in Shakespeare at the limitations of his medium. In the Prologue to Act I of *King Henry the Fifth*, he refers to the theater as "this unworthy scaffold . . . this wooden O" and asks how it can represent the vast fields of France where Harfleur and Agincourt were won. And in Caesar's triumph (*Antony and Cleopatra*, Act V, Scene 2), Cleopatra imagines seeing some boy player with a squeaking voice acting the part of Cleopatra, but this is rather a fear of parody than of representation. In *As You Like It, Macbeth*, and *The Tempest,* Shakespeare uses the old idea of the world itself as a bare stage, with the actions of men and women merely the plot of a play, and he apparently felt that it was as futile to complain of the limitations of the theater as it would be to complain of the limitations of life itself. See also THEATER; THEATER ARCHITECTURE.

Mind and Opinions. Shakespeare's mind and opinions are not so inscrutable as some 19th century critics supposed them to be. Matthew Arnold was summing up a romantic point of view when he wrote of Shakespeare:

Others abide our question. Thou art free.
We ask and ask: Thou smilest and art still,
Out-topping knowledge.

Modern investigation and a somewhat more skeptical approach have yielded a credible picture of the man Shakespeare, however elusive the explanation of his genius remains. "He was not of an age, but for all time" wrote Jonson of him, and the statement is true in more than one sense. Shakespeare shows remarkably little interest in purely contemporary aspects of his age. It is surprising to find in all his works no reference to the watermen who plied their boats for hire across the Thames and were a common and colorful feature of London life, especially to one whose place of business was on the Surrey side. And it is even more curious that he never mentions tobacco.

The plays have been combed for references to contemporary events and persons, with meager results. There is a reference to Queen Elizabeth in *A Midsummer Night's Dream*, but Shakespeare does not comment on her death in 1603. There is a reference to Essex in one of the choruses of *King Henry the Fifth*, but it expresses a hope that was sadly disappointed. A passage in *The Merry Wives* glances at some farcical difficulties of a German traveler, Count Mömpelgart, in securing horses when he was on a visit to England. Macbeth includes a prophesy intended to flatter

CULVER PICTURES

In 1952 film of *Julius Caesar*, Brutus (James Mason) delivers his funeral oration, as Marc Antony (Marlon Brando) mourns the corpse of the slain Caesar.

King James. There may be other topical references not now recognizable, but even so, Shakespeare, in comparison with his fellows, is remarkably indifferent to the news of the day. Perhaps he shared the disdain of Rosencrantz, in *Hamlet*, who told how the boys' companies acted topical plays to score a cheap success: ". . . there is, sir, an eyrie of children, little eyases, that cry out on the top of question and are most tyrannically [outrageously] clapp'd for 't."

The poet's sensitiveness was touched, rather, by the Warwickshire countryside, the environment of his youth. Its native flowers and trees, the field sports, country people, and animals are always vividly evoked. His fairy lore is that of his native county, and he carries with him—to Belmont in Italy where Lorenzo and Jessica are wooing, to the woods near Athens where Theseus is celebrating his wedding, to the glassy stream in Denmark where Ophelia drowned—the five senses of an English country boy. Milton described him as "Fancy's child," warbling "his native wood-notes wild."

Even Shakespeare's political sympathies are conservative. He is most eloquent in praise of degree and rank (*Troilus and Cressida*, Act I, Scene 3); of the divinity of kingship (*King Richard the Second*); of feudal loyalty and devotion (*King Henry the Fifth*); and of "little England," not the great empire envisioned by a Raleigh or a Drake (*King Richard the Second*, Act II, Scene 1). He shows constant fondness for the tillers of the soil and distaste for the workmen of the city, glorified by Thomas Dekker and Thomas Heywood.

Imagery and Rhetoric. Investigation of Shakespeare's imagery has shown some interesting associations in that part of his mind below the level of consciousness. A beginning of this study was made by Walter Whiter in the 18th century, but his work was forgotten. Whiter pointed out that Shakespeare associated with the idea of flattery such miscellaneous items as dogs, candy, melting, stones, poison, and ice. When one item of this cluster sprang to mind, others were likely to accompany it. Moreover, this cluster persisted in his memory over a number of years. Its presence can be traced in *King Richard the Second, As You Like It, Timon of Athens,* and *Antony and Cleopatra.*

Modern researchers have uncovered many more image clusters, some of which seem peculiar to Shakespeare. In many instances a play has its own dominant imagery, such as light and darkness in *Romeo and Juliet,* animals in *Othello,* disease in *Hamlet,* cooking and food in *Troilus and Cressida,* and commercial transactions in *Cymbeline.* Certain images that pervade many plays are sometimes thought to have symbolic significance—for example, music and tempest. An ornithologist, Edward A. Armstrong, has found elaborate bird images and unexpected linkings of images. Caroline Spurgeon tried to classify the images to form a picture of Shakespeare's personality, and Wolfgang Clemen traced the development of imagery in the plays of different periods.

Shakespeare was trained in the discipline of rhetoric, and the verse of his early plays is especially rhetorical. The opening soliloquy of *King Richard the Third* and the laments of the nurse and the Capulets in *Romeo and Juliet* (Act IV, Scene 5) are examples. Shakespeare not only used elaborate, structured language but also made fun of it in *Love's Labour's Lost.* In his middle and later periods he abandoned the stiff rhetorical manner for more natural speech.

Like all Elizabethans, Shakespeare was fond of conceits, tricks with words and ideas, and puns. Samuel Johnson's remark in this connection is famous: "A quibble was to him the fatal Cleopatra for which he lost the world and was content to lose it." But Keats saw that the working out of conceits produced in the poet a kind of intensity that cast up many fine things, as if said unintentionally. In Shakespeare's mature style, what was once extraneous decoration—suited to the taste of the readers of Lyly—became metaphor of the richest sort. And metaphor is the essence of poetry. No description of Shakespeare's achievement as a poet could better his own, when he added to his passage on the lover and the madman as imaginers (*A Midsummer Night's Dream,* Act V, Scene 1) a portrait of the poet:

> The poet's eye, in a fine frenzy rolling,
> Doth glance from heaven to earth, from earth
>   to heaven;
> And as imagination bodies forth
> The forms of things unknown, the poet's pen
> Turns them to shapes, and gives to airy
>   nothing
> A local habitation and a name.

CRITICISM AND THEATRICAL HISTORY

Shakespeare did not succeed in founding a family. Neither was he the founder of a literary school of followers, as Spenser and Jonson were. There is ample evidence from the allusions to him even before 1600 that he was a popular writer, both as poet and as playwright. Jonson, the greatest critic of the age and a man opposed on principle to much in Shakespeare's kind of art, did him full justice. The references to him between 1590 and 1700, collected in *The Shakspere Allusion-Book* (rev. ed., 1932), fill two large volumes, and others have been found since.

Criticism. In general, Shakespeare's reputation has remained high. The Restoration period sometimes preferred Jonson for correctness and Beaumont and Fletcher for "the language of gentlemen." But Shakespeare was popular on the stage, and Dryden praised him highly and discriminatingly. In the 18th century a kind of Shakespeare idolatry set in, which lasted well into the 19th. This served in part as an attack on the rigid canons of neoclassic taste and an aid to the growing Romantic movement, but it should be remembered that Samuel Johnson, certainly no romantic, defended Shakespeare for violating the unities, even if he did regret that poetic justice was not always employed in the conclusions of the plays. The reaction against the idolatry has not lessened his fame or station among the world's great, and it has carried with it a tremendous amount of scholarly study, to which Americans and Germans have contributed as much as Englishmen—study that has thrown revealing light on the theater, the companies, the texts, and the man himself.

In the 19th century the most important critical evaluation of Shakespeare's work was done by the great romantics. Coleridge delivered 12 lectures on the plays in 1811–1812, and in *Biographia Literaria* (1817) he discussed the specific manifestations of poetic power in a critical analysis of *Venus and Adonis* and *The Rape of Lucrece.* Hazlitt's *Characters of Shakespeare's Plays* appeared in 1817. Charles Lamb, the best-read in Elizabethan literature of all the romantics, published in 1807 the first edition of *Tales from Shakespear, Designed for the Use of Young Persons.* Carlyle declared in his *On Heroes, Hero-Worship, and the Heroic in History* (1841) that Shakespeare was all art and no artifice, a claim that modern critics have refuted.

Andrew C. Bradley's *Shakespearean Tragedy* (1904) remains a classic, although Bradley's tendency to treat the characters as if they were real people has been resisted by many critics, notably Elmer E. Stoll. Harley Granville-Barker brought to Shakespeare criticism the knowledge and skill of a playwright, actor, and director. The scholarly studies of Sir Walter Greg, Sir Edmund K. Chambers, J. Dover Wilson, Frank P. Wilson, and Gerald E. Bentley, among others, have provided a sounder basis for critical appreciation. Since the mid-1900's the finding of mythical and symbolic meanings in Shakespeare has become fashionable. Among the notable proponents of this kind of criticism are G. Wilson Knight and Northrop Frye.

Theatrical History. The greatest actors of the English-speaking stage have uniformly attempted the major Shakespearean roles, and the plays have served for 300 years as the greatest test and greatest opportunity for actor, producer, and designer. After Burbage the next actor of first rank was Thomas Betterton. His devotion to Shakespeare led him to make a pilgrimage to Stratford and collect data, which he gave to Nicholas Rowe, the first biographer. He was famous as Hotspur, Brutus, Othello, Macbeth, and Lear, and he played Hamlet with great success until he was over 70. Many of the versions he used were "improved" for Restoration taste, but in his own acting versions he refused to paraphrase.

A *Comedy of Errors* in the 1963 production at Stratford, Ontario, was presented in a *commedia dell'arte* style. The stage of the Stratford Festival theater was designed to resemble the stages that were used during Shakespeare's lifetime.

In the mid-18th century, David Garrick dominated the stage, and he served as actor, producer, and adapter of Shakespeare. He failed in the parts of Othello and Iago, but his Lear and Hamlet were famous, and his comic talent was shown in his Benedick (in *Much Ado*).

Garrick's successor in the great tradition was John Philip Kemble, who was active from 1783 to 1817. He played most of the tragic heroes with success, but other members of his brilliant family equaled him. His sister Sarah, Mrs. Siddons, was the greatest of Lady Macbeths, and his niece Fanny Kemble won great fame for her Juliet. As a manager, Kemble revived some minor Shakespearean plays that had been long off the stage.

Edmund Kean exemplified romantic interpretation at its height. He appeared first at Drury Lane in January 1814, and for the younger generation he immediately supplanted Kemble. Praise of him by Leigh Hunt, Hazlitt, and Lamb has become literature. He was especially famous for his Shylock, Othello, and Richard III.

W. Charles Macready in the 1830's tried to keep alive the old system of large patent theaters but failed. Two of his actors were great: Helen Faucit, the finest actress of the romantic heroines, and Samuel Phelps, who, after being held back by Macready, came into his own with the failure of the big theaters and the repeal of the Licensing Act in 1843. At Sadler's Wells Theatre, Phelps presented Shakespeare for 20 years. He revived most of the plays, and he scorned "improved" texts.

As manager of the Princess' Theatre from 1850 to 1859, Charles Kean, the son of Edmund Kean, started the elaborate, scholarly, and heavy productions that continued through the age of Henry Irving and Beerbohm Tree. This smothering of the play by the production was stopped in the 20th century by the influence of Gordon Craig and Harley Granville-Barker.

Shakespearean roles have attracted all of the principal actors on the 20th century stage. Among the most eminent are Sir John Gielgud and Sir Lawrence Olivier, both of whom were stars at the famous Old Vic Theatre in London. Two major English companies have continued the great tradition of the Old Vic in presenting Shakespeare's plays—the Royal Shakespeare Company, with its main theater at Stratford-upon-Avon, and the National Theatre Company, which took over the Old Vic in 1963.

Summer festivals in which a number of Shakespearean plays are produced have sprung up since the 1950's. The Stratford Shakespearean Festival at Stratford, Ontario, Canada, established in 1953, was followed by the American Shakespeare Festival at Stratford, Conn. Others that continue to flourish annually are the Oregon Shakespearean Festival at Ashland, the San Diego (Calif.) National Shakespeare Festival; the Colorado University Shakespeare Festival at Boulder; the Great Lakes Shakespeare Festival at Lakewood, Ohio; the New York Shakespeare Festival in the outdoor Delacorte Theatre in Central Park, New York City; and the Champlain Shakespeare Festival in Burlington, Vt. See also the Index entry *Shakespeare, William,* and the articles on each of the plays and the poetical works.

HALLETT SMITH
Author of "Shakespeare's Romances"

Bibliography

Shakespeare's works are available in *Shakespeare: The Complete Works,* ed. by G. B. Harrison (Harcourt 1960); *The Complete Works of Shakespeare,* ed. by George Lyman Kittredge (Ginn 1936); and *William Shakespeare: The Complete Works,* ed. by Charles Jasper Sisson (Harper 1952). The individual plays are available in such series as The New Arden Shakespeare, ed. by Una Ellis-Fermor and others (Methuen and Harvard Univ. Press); The New Cambridge Shakespeare, ed. by Arthur Quiller-Couch and John Dover Wilson (Cambridge); The Pelican Shakespeare, general ed., Alfred Harbage (Penguin); and The Signet Classic Shakespeare, general ed., Sylvan Barnet (New Am. Lib.).

Life and Times

Bentley, Gerald E., *Shakespeare: A Biographical Handbook* (Yale Univ. Press 1961).
Chambers, Edmund K., *William Shakespeare: A Study of Facts and Problems,* 2 vols. (Oxford 1930).
Chute, Marchette, *Shakespeare of London* (Dutton 1949).

(*Bibliography continued on next page*)

Fripp, Edgar I., *Shakespeare, Man and Artist*, 2 vols. (Oxford 1938).

Frye, Roland M., *Shakespeare's Life and Times: A Pictorial Record* (Princeton Univ. Press 1967).

Raleigh, Walter, and others, eds., *Shakespeare's England: An Account of the Life and Manners of His Age*, 2 vols. (Oxford 1916).

Reese, Max M., *Shakespeare: His World and His Work* (St. Martins 1953).

Criticism

Armstrong, Edward A., *Shakespeare's Imagination: A Study of the Psychology of Association and Inspiration* (Drummond 1946).

Bradby, Anne, ed., *Shakespeare Criticism, 1919–1935* (Oxford 1936).

Bradley, Andrew C., *Shakespearean Tragedy* (Macmillan 1904).

Bullough, Geoffrey, ed., *Narrative and Dramatic Sources of Shakespeare*, 6 vols. (Columbia Univ. Press 1957–1966).

Charlton, H. B. *Shakespearean Comedy* (Cambridge 1938).

Charlton, H. B. *Shakespearean Tragedy* (Cambridge 1949).

Clemen, Wolfgang H., *The Development of Shakespeare's Imagery* (Methuen 1951).

Frye, Northrop, *Fools of Time: Studies in Shakespearean Tragedy* (Univ. of Toronto Press 1967).

Frye, Northrop, *A Natural Perspective: The Development of Shakespearean Comedy and Romance* (Columbia Univ. Press 1965).

Granville-Barker, Harley, *Prefaces to Shakespeare*, 4 vols. (Princeton Univ. Press 1946–1947).

Knight, G. Wilson, *The Crown of Life* (Oxford 1947).

Knight, G. Wilson, *The Imperial Theme* (Oxford 1931).

Knight, G. Wilson, *The Wheel of Fire* (Oxford 1930).

Muir, Kenneth, and Schoenbaum, Samuel, *A New Companion to Shakespearean Studies* (Cambridge 1971).

Ridler, Anne (Bradby), ed., *Shakespeare Criticism, 1935–1960* (Oxford 1963).

Smith, Hallett, *Shakespeare's Romances: A Study of Some Ways of Imagination* (Huntington Lib. 1972).

Spurgeon, Caroline F. E., *Shakespeare's Imagery and What It Tells Us* (Cambridge 1935).

Stoll, Elmer E., *Art and Artifice in Shakespeare* (Cambridge 1933).

Stoll, Elmer E., *Shakespeare and Other Masters* (Harvard Univ. Press 1940).

Stoll, Elmer E., *Shakespeare Studies* (Macmillan 1927).

Wilson, Frank P., *Marlowe and the Early Shakespeare* (Oxford 1949).

Wilson, Frank P., *Shakespeare and the New Bibliography*, new ed., rev. and ed. by Helen Gardner (Oxford 1970).

Wilson, Frank P., *Shakespearian and Other Studies*, ed. by Helen Gardner (Oxford 1969).

SHAKESPEARE'S SONNETS. See SONNETS OF SHAKESPEARE.

SHAKHTY, shäkн'tē, is a city in the USSR, in the Russian republic, 40 miles (64 km) northeast of Rostov. It was formerly known as Aleksandrovsk-Grushevski. It is a major coal-mining center for the eastern Donets Basin and produces high quality anthracite coal. Shakhty manufactures machinery, clothing, furniture, and food products. Population: (1970) 205,000.

SHAKTI, shäk'tē, in Hinduism, is the female generative principle, personified as the mother goddess Shakti, or Devi. *Shakti* (*śakti*) means "power"; *devī* means "goddess." The worship of the mother goddess as the paramount divinity is termed "Shaktism." It is one of the three main popular forms of Hinduism, the others being Shivaism and Vishnuism. Shaktism is particularly prevalent in Bengal and Assam.

Because the male principle is regarded as inactive and the female principle is considered active, Shakti is often regarded as the strength or potency of a male deity of whom she is the consort. Thus she has as many names as aspects. As the consort of Shiva, she is worshiped as the benevolent Parvati, as the destroyer Kali, and as the inaccessible Durga, with both benevolent and terrifying aspects. As the wife of Vishnu, she receives devotion as the gracious Lakshmi.

SHALE, any fine-grained sedimentary rock that is formed by the consolidation of beds of mud, clay, or silt. Such beds were deposited slowly over geological time. Shales consist primarily of clay minerals such as illite and montmorillonite that are mixed with fine particles of quartz and mica. As the quartz content increases, the shales grade into sandstones, while with increasing amounts of calcite they grade into marls or limestones. Because of the compression of the plate-like clay particles as the rocks were formed, shales usually have a thinly laminar structure, and they are dense and nearly impervious to water. If the beds are subjected to further pressure and are consequently forced to flow, the shales metamorphose into slates.

Shales are usually grayish, but if various pigmenting materials are present they may also be white, yellow, brown, red, green, or black. Iron-rich shales contain pyrite, siderite, or iron silicates, and shales rich in calcium are used in the manufacture of cement. Carbonate-rich shales may contain fossils, and rocks with a particularly high content of complex organic matter are known as *oil shales*. Such shales decompose when they are heated and yield oils that are a source of fuel, wax, and tar acids and bases.

The extensive deposits of oil shales around the world are considered important fuel reserves for the future. See OIL SHALE.

SHALLOT, shə-lot′, a perennial bulbous herb (*Allium ascalonicum*) of the lily family, closely related to onions and garlic. The bulbs are usually less than 2 inches (5 cm) long and 1 inch (2.5 cm) in diameter. They send up hollow small leaves that are often used for mixing with salads and dressings or are eaten alone. The bulbs are also similarly used.

Shallots are planted in early spring in rich soil about 4 inches (10 cm) apart, in rows 15 to 18 inches (38–46 cm) apart, and kept cleanly cultivated throughout the season. The leaves may be cut at any time and the bulbs taken up in autumn. They are dried like onions or garlic, and should be kept in a dry, cool place. From two to six bulbs are usually produced by each bulb planted.

In southern states of the United States, shallots are generally planted in the autumn, but in northern states they are planted in the spring. Shallots are less popular in the United States than in Europe.

SHALMANESER III, shal-mə-nē′zər, was an Assyrian king who reigned from 858 to 824 B.C. His name in Assyrian is Shulmanu-asharidu, "the god Shulman is chief." See also ASSYRIA—*Late Assyrian Empire.*

SHALYAPIN, Fyodor. See CHALIAPIN, FEODOR IVANOVICH.

SHAMANISM, shä′mən-izm, is a religion or cult in which the officiant goes into a trance state and is believed possessed by a spirit control that speaks and acts through him. Among the Tungus of Siberia, from whose language the word "shaman" comes, a shaman was responsible for the well-being of his territorial kin group. Though the position was often inherited, the final choice was made by spirits who informed a candidate of their interest during his first trance experience. Thereafter long training was required, often under the guidance of an established shaman, to develop effective control. Siberian shamans, like those of neighboring Central Asia, were called in to diagnose and cure illness, find lost property, and foretell the future. In both areas trance was induced by accelerating rhythms of a tambourine and of dancing.

In Africa, it is believed that a shaman often works while possessed by ancestor spirits. Among the Dayak of Borneo, hereditary shamanesses officiate at the re-interment ceremonies for the dead held every few years. In such religious contexts, the shaman is a respected priest and moral arbiter through whom the people can communicate with the spirits and gods of their pantheon.

Other types of shamanistic cults are found in different places in the world. The *zar* cult in North Africa and a similar cult in Turkestan flourish among upper-class Muslim women. In these cults a woman unhappy with her lot is believed possessed by an irresponsible, alien spirit, and the shamaness consulted prescribes a very expensive treatment, to be paid for by the patient's husband.

Shamanism has very ancient roots in China. In the early 20th century, shamans believed to be possessed by minor deities of the town participated in community ceremonies. There were also shamanesses with a clientele of unhappy girls and subordinate wives who had become possessed. In Japan, the priests of some Shinto and Buddhist sects were shamans or shamanesses licensed by the government after undergoing rigorous purificatory rites.

ELIZABETH E. BACON
Professor of Anthropology (Retired)
Michigan State University

Further Reading: Lewis, Ian M., *Ecstatic Religion* (Penguin 1971).

SHAMASH, shä′mäsh, was the sun god of Babylonia and Assyria. Inscriptions designate him as the offspring of Sin, the moon god, who in earlier, nomadic times was the dominant deity. With the development of agriculture the importance of the sun god grew, and he became one of a triad with Sin and Ishtar, the earth goddess.

To Shamash were attributed powers of justice and right. Evil was supposed to flee before the power of light. He was also the god of healing. His wife was Aya, who in inscriptions was called the "lady of mankind" and the "lady of the countries."

Shamash's children were Kettu (justice) and Mesharu (right), although they are also referred to with other minor sun gods, such as Bunene, as servitors of Shamash. But Ninib, the sun god of the morning and of spring, and Nergal, god of moon and summer, retained their powers under the headship of Shamash.

Shamash was worshipped principally at Sippar and Larsa. His sanctuary in both cities was called E-barra or E-babbara, "the shining house." Other temples of his worship were built in Babylon, Ur, Nippur, and Nineveh.

SHAMOKIN, shə-mō′kin, is a city in east-central Pennsylvania, in Northumberland county, about 45 miles (72 km) northeast of Harrisburg, the state capital. It is the industrial and commercial center of a region rich in anthracite coal deposits. Coal mining and the manufacture of textiles and clothing are the principal economic activities.

Coal was discovered in the area as early as 1770. Shamokin was settled by miners in 1835, and mining on a large scale began in 1840. The city is governed by a mayor and council. Population: 10,357.

SHAMROCK is a name derived from the Irish *seamrog*, meaning "trefoil," and it is applied to various trifoliate plants native to Ireland. Each is identified with the plant said to have been picked by Saint Patrick as a symbol to illustrate the doctrine of the Trinity. The shamrock is worn on Saint Patrick's Day, March 17, and has come to be regarded as the national plant of Ireland.

Among the plants known as shamrocks are black medic (*Medicago lupulina*); *Oxalis acetosella;* various clovers, such as the common red clover (*Trifolium pratense*); a trailing hop clover, with small leaves and yellow heads (*Timinus*); and the common low, white clover (*T. repens*).

SHAMYL, shä′mil (1797–1871), Muslim leader who opposed Russian rule in Dagestan, in the eastern Caucasus, which had passed to Russia in 1813. Shamyl, who was a well-educated man, was elected *imam* (political-religious leader) of Dagestan in 1834, and for the next 25 years he conducted a skillful guerrilla campaign against the Russians, while unifying the diverse peoples of the Caucasus.

In 1859 the Russians sent a large army against Shamyl, who was captured. He was allowed to make a pilgrimage to Mecca in 1870 and died, probably in Medina, Arabia, in March 1871.

SHAN, shän, an Asian people who live primarily in eastern Burma. The Shan are the third-largest ethnic group in Burma, and they constitute about 8% of the total population. Approximately two thirds of the Burmese Shan live in the semiautonomous Shan State, which occupies the east-central part of the country. The capital of the state is Taunggyi.

The Shan are related to the Siamese of Thailand and the Lao of Laos. The Shan language belongs to the Thai (Tai) family. The people are adherents of Theravada Buddhism. Their economy is based almost entirely on the cultivation of rice on irrigated land.

The Shan hold the cultivable land in the valleys of the Shan Plateau in eastern Burma, where they form the traditional ruling elite. As a result of poor communications across the Salween River, the western Shan generally established links with the Burmans, while the eastern Shan have maintained ties with their kinsmen in Thailand and Laos.

For centuries the Shan were ruled by a hereditary nobility, and the ancient families have retained much of their authority.

SHANG, shäng, an early Chinese dynasty that according to one tradition ruled from 1523 to 1028 B. C. The dynasty's rule marks the beginning of the Bronze Age in China and is known from written sources as well as archaeological remains. The Shang kings, who dominated a loose confederation of chiefdoms, may have controlled much of northern China. They were succeeded by their former vassals, the Chou. See also CHINA—*History.*

The northern district of Shanghai, with the Woosung (formerly Soochow) River in the foreground.

SHANGHAI, shang'hī', is China's largest city and greatest port. Dominating the estuary where the Yangtze River empties into the East China Sea, it serves as the gateway for the entire Yangtze Valley. The city is situated on the west bank of the Whangpoo (Huangpu, or Whampoa) River, 14 miles (23 km) south of its junction with the mouth of the Yangtze. The Woosung River (Soochow Creek) flows eastward through the city into the Whangpoo.

The City. Shanghai formerly was divided into two main areas: Old Shanghai and the "foreign settlements." In the 1930's construction of a third major section was begun north of the Woosung River.

The center of Old Shanghai was once surrounded by a wall 24 feet (7 meters) high, pierced by six gates. The section grew without planning, and the streets are narrow and the buildings crowded.

The section of the former foreign settlements lies a short distance north of Old Shanghai. It consists of the former French Concession and International Settlement. Within the section are many of Shanghai's best known localities: Nanking Road, with department stores, restaurants, and movie theaters; Huai Hai Lu, the Avenue Joffre of the former French Concession; Chung Shan Lu, once the Bund, a broad avenue along the Whangpoo River, lined with impressive buildings; and the People's Park and People's Square,

which occupy the site of the former racecourse.

The newest section of Shanghai is the City Center in the northern district. It was first developed in the 1930's before the war with Japan and was reconstructed after World War II.

Among the city's notable landmarks is the Lunghwa Temple in the southwest—a fine example of Chinese architecture. Also in the southwest is the Zikawei Observatory, established by French Jesuits. Old Shanghai contains the Wu Sing Ting, a famous zigzag bridge over an artificial lake. In the Western district is another landmark, the Ching An Temple.

Economy. Shanghai is one of China's most important industrial bases. The principal manufactures are textiles, iron and steel, ships, and tires. Other major products are pharmaceuticals, electrical equipment, bearings, fertilizer, chemicals, machine tools, heavy machinery, cement, and foodstuffs. The refining of petroleum and nonferrous metals and the production of thermal electric power are significant aspects of the city's industrial economy.

Shanghai is China's leading port for transpacific shipping. It also handles much of the coastal shipping from ports in Chekiang and Fukien provinces. The harbor is about 9 miles (14 km) long and has an average width of 1,500 feet (460 meters). Its major problem has been the silting of the Whangpoo River. The channel of the river at one point is only 750 feet (230 meters) wide with an average depth of 24 feet (7 meters). Oceangoing ships must wait for high tide before proceeding through the channel.

The Yangtze River provides the city's most important transportation link with central China. Railroads connect Shanghai with cities in the north and south. Hungchiao Airport, southwest of Shanghai, is served by international flights. Lunghwa Airport, south of the city, is used for domestic flights.

History. Although settled during the Sung dynasty (960–1279), Shanghai remained a fishing town of little importance until it was opened to foreign trade in the mid-19th century. Chinese capitalism, industry, and trade unionism were born in Shanghai, as was the Chinese Communist party (1921). The city also became a meeting ground for cultural interchange between East and West. A number of important political movements developed from labor and student organizations. By the start of the Sino-Japanese War (1937–1945), Shanghai had more than 30 institutions of higher education.

Because of Shanghai's stability relative to the troubled interior, the city had attracted capital, skills, and a large population. In 1936 it was China's principal center of trade, finance, and manufacturing, with 80% of the country's light industry and 25% of the heavy industry. One of the world's largest cities, it had a population of 4 million.

Political History. Shanghai began its development as a modern metropolis when it became one of the five "treaty ports" opened to foreign trade by the Treaty of Nanking (1842) following the Opium War with Britain. The British Settlement was established in 1843 north of the old Chinese city. In 1849, under the Whampoa (Whangpoo) Treaty, the French Concession was established west of the British Settlement. Around 1852 the United States leased land north of the Woosung River. This was merged with the British Settlement in 1863 to form the International Settlement.

Thirteen nations were eventually represented in the International Settlement, exercising government control through the Shanghai Municipal Council. In 1896, Japan secured a concession across the Woosung. In 1928 the Chinese government joined four Chinese districts together to form the Greater Shanghai Municipality.

Deteriorating relations between Japan and China resulted in a Chinese boycott of Japanese goods early in 1932. Japan took armed action in Shanghai to break the boycott but met with stubborn resistance from the 19th Route Army under Gen. Tsai Ting-kai. As a result an armistice was signed on May 5, 1932.

After the outbreak of the Sino-Japanese War in 1937, the Greater Shanghai Municipality was occupied by Japanese troops. Following the attack on Pearl Harbor in December 1941, Japan occupied the International Settlement as well. In 1943, during World War II, Britain and the United States agreed to return the International Settlement to China. Immediately after the war France signed a similar treaty.

Following World War II, the former foreign settlements and the Chinese city were unified under Chinese administration as the Greater Metropolitan Area of Shanghai, covering 345 square miles (894 sq km). The population, estimated at 4 million in 1945, grew to an estimated 6 million in 1949.

The Chinese Civil War reached Shanghai in 1949, and the city was occupied by Communist forces on May 26. Coming for the most part from rural bases in the interior, the Communists had a deep distrust of Shanghai. Their policy therefore was to diminish its importance and size and to liquidate its industrial base. During the early 1950's factories were dismantled and moved to interior cities. A drive was undertaken to move and disperse Shanghai's labor and excess population. However, in the mid-1950's this policy was reversed, and efforts to increase Shanghai's industrial base were initiated.

Under the Communist regime the area of Shanghai Municipality was increased to 2,200 square miles (5,700 sq km) and thus includes extensive rural districts. The municipality is under the direct control of the central government. Population: (1974 est.) 10,820,000.

LORENZO LO
Former Director, Board of Directors
St. John's University, Shanghai

SHANGRI-LA, shang-gri-lä′, is the imaginary land of eternal youth and peace described in James Hilton's novel *Lost Horizon* (1933). It is supposedly located in Tibet. The success of the novel and of the motion picture based on it made Shangri-La a popular term for any remote paradise or place whose location is unknown or kept secret. During World War II, when U. S. planes from the aircraft carrier *Hornet* made the first air attack on Japan (1942), President Roosevelt said they had taken off from Shangri-La.

SHANHAIKWAN, shän′hī′gwän′, is a town in northeastern China, at the eastern end of the Great Wall. It is situated in Hopei province, on the Gulf of Liaotung.

Shanhaikwan (Shanhaiguan) was important for centuries as a key defense point on the Manchurian border. Its name means "gate between the mountains and the sea." Population: (1953) 35,000.

SHANKAR, shän′kär, **Ravi** (1920–   ), Indian sitar player, who had a glowing and spectacular success in conveying his country's rather difficult musical heritage to the West. He was born in Varanasi (Benares) on April 7, 1920, of a talented Bengali family. When he was ten, Ravi, his mother, and brothers joined his older brother, the dancer Uday Shankar, in Paris. In 1935 he met the sarod player Ustad Allauddin Khan, considered India's finest musician. Three years later, 18-year-old Ravi gave up a successful dancing career to study rigorously with the guru in his small, primitive village in Maihar State. Though he was imbued with a consuming zeal to introduce the music of India to Western audiences, Ravi's start in 1956 was small. But by the 1960's, owing to consummate skill with the sitar and personal charm, his concerts, recordings, and films were attracting wide audiences in Europe and the United States.

SHANKAR, shän′kär, **Uday** (c. 1902–1977), Indian dancer, who was a foremost figure in arousing Western interest in Indian classical dance. Shankar studied Indian dance in India and ballet in London, where he graduated from the Royal College of Art (1923) and produced Indian plays and dances with his father. Anna Pavlova, who saw these works, asked him to stage and dance her ballet *Radha-Krishna* and persuaded him to give up painting for dance.

After successfully touring with Pavlova (1924–1928), Shankar returned to India to study further and to form his own troupe, which toured Europe and the United States. As a dancer he had great presence and brilliance, and as a choreographer, although he modified classical dance for theater, he brought it for the first time to Western attention. In 1938, with British and American support, he founded the Uday Shankar Indian Culture Center in Almora, India, to discover, film, and teach classical dance and music. It was closed during World War II but reopened in Calcutta in 1965. Shankar's wife Amala and his musician brother Ravi were part of his company. He died in Calcutta on Sept. 26, 1977.

SHANKARA, shung′kə-rä (c. 800 A. D.) was an Indian philosopher and saint, who was a leading representative of the Vedānta system of Hindu thought. He was born in the Malabar region of southern India to a Brahman family. The monasteries that he established in the four corners of India—at Sringeri, Dwarka, Puri, and Badrinath—continue to propagate his teachings.

Shankara—or Shankaracharya, "the Master Shankara"—regarded the revealed truth of the Upanishads as the highest message of the sacred literature of India. His rational interpretation of this revealed truth is presented in his commentaries on the Upanishads, the *Bhagavad Gītā*, and the *Brahmasūtra*, or *Vedāntasūtra*—Badarayana's codification of the thought of the Upanishads. Shankara set out to show that the Upanishads express a pure monism, or nonduality (*advaita*)—an identity between the individual soul and the supreme reality (Brahman). The inward perception of this identity is gained through knowledge and provides release from the less real world of phenomena and feeling. Religious actions and devotion have a subordinate role in this process. In general, they are the path to be taken by lesser aspirants. See also HINDUISM—*Uttara Mimamsa or Vedanta*; VEDANTA.

SHANNON, Claude E. (1916–   ), American applied mathematician, who in 1948 while working at Bell Telephone Laboratories developed a mathematical theory of communication later known as "information theory." It has fundamental importance in problems of communication, and it opened new paths of research in pure mathematics. Shannon analyzed a communication system in terms of an information source, a transmitter, a communication channel, a receiver, and a destination. He defined "information" as the degree of freedom the information source has in choosing among elements of a language to compose a given message.

Shannon was born in Gaylord, Mich., on April 30, 1916. He graduated from the University of Michigan in 1936 and from the Massachusetts Institute of Technology (Ph. D., 1940). After working for Bell Laboratories from 1941 to 1957, he became a professor of science at MIT in 1958. See also INFORMATION THEORY.

SHANNON RIVER, the longest river in the Republic of Ireland, with a total length of 254 miles (409 km). It rises at the foot of the Cuilcagh Mountains in County Cavan and flows southwest through Lough Allen, then takes an irregular course, generally south, to Lough Rea. From there it goes southwest to Lough Derg, then south to Limerick, where it becomes a tidal stream. Between here and its mouth, it expands and enters the Atlantic Ocean in a broad estuary.

The Shannon is the main river draining the Irish central lowland and is surrounded by bogs and marshes for much of its course. The lakes through which it passes are in part real lake basins and in part merely expansions of the river. The Shannon's chief tributary is the Suck, which meets it a little south of Athlone. Below Killaloe, falls that drop a total of 109 feet (33 meters) are utilized by a hydroelectric plant.

SHANSI, shän'shē', is a province in northern China, in the loess highlands between the Mongolian steppe to the north, the Hwang Ho (Yellow River) to the west and south, and the North China Plain to the east. The name Shansi, also spelled Shanxi, means "west of the mountains"— the Taihang range on the eastern border. The Great Wall forms the northern boundary.

Shansi has cold winters and hot summers. Level land constitutes only about 10% of the provincial area of about 60,700 square miles (157,100 sq km). Agriculture is concentrated in the valley of the Fen Ho, which flows southward into the Hwang Ho. The chief crops are millet, wheat, corn, kaoliang, and fruit, especially grapes. Cotton is grown in the south. The land is subject to soil erosion because of extensive deforestation, but progress in overcoming this problem has been made by planting trees, terracing, and digging canals.

The province is one of China's chief sources of coal, especially the area around Tatung in the north. Iron is also mined. The capital, Taiyüan, is one of the country's main iron and steel centers and a major producer of fertilizer, chemicals, and heavy machinery. Tatung manufactures cement, locomotives, and mining machinery.

Of particular religious and artistic interest are the Buddhist cave temples at Yünkang, near Tatung. The temples date from the Northern Wei dynasty (386–535 A. D.). Population: (1970) 18,000,000.

SHANTUNG, shän'dŏong', is a northern maritime province of China. The name, which is also spelled Shandong, means "mountainous east." Shantung has an area of about 59,200 square miles (153,300 sq km).

Geography. The flat northern and western parts of the province belong to the North China Plain. The western section is traversed by the Grand Canal. In the center and southeast are mountains reaching elevations of more than 5,000 feet (1,500 meters). This area is separated from the hilly Shantung Peninsula to the east by the valley of the Kiao (Chiao) River.

The peninsula, extending between the Po Hai gulf to its north and the Yellow Sea to its south, was once an island. It was joined to the mainland through a long process of alluvial deposition by the Hwang Ho (Yellow River), which has changed course on several occasions. The river now flows northeast through Shantung into the Po Hai but at times has reached the sea south of the peninsula. The Shantung Peninsula has several good harbors, and before World War II these played an important role in China's relations with foreign powers.

Economy. The economy of the flat northern and western areas is mainly agricultural, while that of the rest of the province is based on mining and fishing. About half of Shantung is farmland. The chief crops are wheat, sweet potatoes, corn, cotton, tobacco, peanuts, and a variety of fruits. The province is the main peanut-producing area of China. It is also famous for its wild silk (*tu-ssu,* or tussah), from which shantung fabric is made. Shantung's mineral wealth includes coal, iron, bauxite, and petroleum.

Tsingtao, the principal port and industrial center, produces textiles, locomotives, tires, and fertilizer. Tsinan, the capital, situated near the Hwang Ho, manufactures machine tools and fertilizer. Poshan and Tzupo are major mining centers. Agricultural industries form an important part of the provincial economy.

History. Tai Shan, near the city of Taian, has long been revered by Buddhists and Taoists as China's most sacred mountain. The town of Küfow (Chüfou) is the birthplace of Confucius and contains a large temple dedicated to him. The philosopher Mencius was also born in what is now Shantung.

Foreign penetration of Shantung began in 1858 when the port of Tengchow (now Penglai) was opened to Western trade. It was replaced by Chefoo (now Yentai) in 1863. In 1898, Germany obtained a lease on the territory around Kiaochow Bay, including Tsingtao, together with railroad and mining concessions. In the same year Great Britain leased the port of Weihaiwei (now Weihai). During World War I the Japanese seized the German interests, and when Japan's claims were recognized at the 1919 peace conference China refused to sign the Treaty of Versailles. As a result of the Washington Conference of 1922, Japan withdrew from Shantung and Britain later did also.

The entire province was occupied by Japanese troops in the Chinese-Japanese War of 1937–1945 despite a notable Chinese victory at Taierhchwang in 1938. During the war the Chinese broke the dikes of the Hwang Ho to stop the Japanese advance, and from 1938 to 1947, when the dikes were repaired, the river flowed south of Shantung into the East China Sea. Population: (1970 est.) 57,000,000.

SHANTUNG, shan-tung', is a plain-woven, ribbed-surface fabric used for lightweight to medium-weight dresses, blouses, and men's summer suits. The term "shantung" originally designated an all-silk fabric woven by hand in the Shantung province of China, but it now refers to any similar fabric made from silk, cotton, or rayon or other synthetic fibers. Italy and Belgium produce silk shantung, while England, France, India, and the United States produce cotton and synthetic-fiber shantung.

Shantung is characterized by a relatively large number of threads per inch in the lengthwise (warp) direction and a relatively small number of threads per inch in the crosswide (filling) direction. Also, the warp threads are fine, and the filling threads are coarse. With a plain weave, such a combination produces ribs running from edge to edge of the fabric. See also PONGEE.

ERNEST B. BERRY*
North Carolina State College

SHANTY. See CHANTEY.

SHAPIRO, shə-pēr'ō, **Karl Jay** (1913–   ), American poet, one of the leading voices of 20th century lyrical expression. His work has been praised for its great stylistic variety and powerful imagery. He was born in Baltimore, Md., on Nov. 10, 1913. He studied at Johns Hopkins University (1937–1939) and served in the U. S. Army throughout World War II. From 1950 to 1956 he edited *Poetry: A Magazine of Verse.* He also taught English at the universities of Nebraska, Illinois, and California (Davis) and was consultant in poetry to the Library of Congress in 1947–1948.

Shapiro's volumes of poetry include *Person, Place and Thing* (1942), *The Place of Love* (1943), *V-Letter* (1944), *Trial of a Poet* (1947), *Poems of a Jew* (1958), *The Bourgeois Poet* (1964), and *White-Haired Lover* (1968). He won the Pulitzer Prize for poetry (1945), as well as the Shelley Memorial Prize (1946) and two Guggenheim fellowships.

SHAPLEY, shap'lē, **Harlow** (1885–1972), American astronomer who helped to lay the foundation of the distance scale for the universe of galaxies. Shapley was born in Nashville, Mo., on Nov. 2, 1885. He obtained his doctorate from Princeton University in 1913, and through his researches as a graduate student he contributed to knowledge of stellar masses. In 1914 he went to Mt. Wilson Observatory. There he used the period-luminosity relation discovered by Henrietta Leavitt for cepheid variable stars and determined the distance to numerous globular clusters. Through this work he located the center of our galaxy (the Milky Way System) in the direction of the constellation Sagittarius, finding that the center lies at a distance of 30,000 to 40,000 light-years from our sun. Thus he did for the sun what Copernicus had done centuries earlier for the earth, removing it from its assumed location at the center of the known universe.

From 1921 to 1952, Shapley served as director of Harvard College Observatory. During those years he published (with Adelaide Ames) a catalog of bright galaxies, did extensive research on galaxy clusters, and discovered a new kind of dwarf galaxy. He was also very much a man of the world. He was instrumental in bringing hundreds of refugees to the United States from Nazi Germany, and he was one of the architects of the United Nations Educational, Scientific and Cultural Organization (UNESCO). His independent views on human freedom and international relations made him a target for Sen. Joseph McCarthy in the early 1950's, but he was completely exonerated of McCarthy's charges.

Shapley wrote many technical books and several works for a more general audience, including *Flights from Chaos* (1930), *Of Stars and Men* (1958), and *Beyond the Observatory* (1967). He died in Boulder, Colo., on Oct. 20, 1972.

BART J. BOK, *University of Arizona*

SHARECROPPING is a form of land tenure in which the tenant farms land for a share of the crop. The farmer provides the labor for his share of the income, usually about one half. The landlord supplies the land, living accommodations, and expenses for food, tools, seed, fertilizer, and other needs of the tenant.

The system flourished in the Southern United States after the Civil War, the tenants being both whites and Negroes. Sharecropping is also found in Latin America and elsewhere where it is considered an improvement over peasant status. *Metayage* is the term used to describe the sharecropping system that was dominant in France in the 18th century.

SHARETT, shä-ret', **Moshe** (1894–1965), Israeli prime minister. He was born in Kherson, Russia, on Oct. 15, 1894, and migrated to Palestine with his family in 1906. He studied in Constantinople (Istanbul) and London and returned to Palestine in 1925.

From 1931 until 1948, Sharett played an increasingly important role in the Zionist movement. He served as foreign minister from the formation of Israel in 1948, and he was instrumental in gaining Israel's admittance to the United Nations in 1949. In 1953, when David Ben-Gurion stepped down, Sharett became prime minister, holding the post until 1955, when Ben-Gurion returned. In 1956, disagreements with Ben-Gurion led to Sharett's resignation as foreign minister, but he retained his seat in the Knesset. From 1960 until his death he served as chairman of the World Zionist Executive. He died in Tel Aviv on July 7, 1965.

SHARI RIVER, shä'rē, in central Africa, is the principal river feeding Lake Chad. It is formed near the border between Chad and the Central African Republic border by the confluence of the Bamingui and Gribingui rivers.

The Shari (Chari) River flows northwest for about 700 miles (1,100 km) before entering the southern portion of Lake Chad in a wide delta. Its largest tributary is the Logone, which joins it near Fort-Lamy.

SHARIA, shə-rē'ə, in Islam, is the common word for the law. It means roughly "the path in which God wishes men to walk." See also ISLAM—*Law.*

SHARIF, shə-rēf', is an Arabic title derived from the Arabic word meaning "noble." The title, also written *sherif,* is applied to the descendants of Mohammed through Hasan, the son of Mohammed's daughter Fatima and of Ali. Sharifs are distinguished by green turbans. For centuries parts of the Middle East, including the holy city of Mecca, and North Africa were ruled by sharifs.

The tiger shark (*above*) is a man-eating member of the requiem shark family. One of the most dangerous man-eaters is the great white shark (*left*). The Atlantic nurse shark (*below*) somewhat resembles a catfish.

SHARK, a predatory fish that is represented by at least one species in each of the oceans and ocean-connected seas except the most northern polar seas and the waters immediately adjacent to Antarctica. The shark has always generated fear. Although the hazard to man from sharks is far less than that from most other kinds of marine accidents, large sharks of some species may maim or kill swimmers, and the psychological effects of such occurrences often curtail man's recreational use of the sea.

Classification and Evolution. Sharks are classified in the order Selachii, which together with the skates and rays of the order Batoidei makes up the class Elasmobranchi.

The earliest sharklike vertebrate fossils are from the Devonian Period of the Paleozoic Era. From its earliest appearance the shark line of evolution is distinct from the lines giving rise to the bony fishes and to the chimaeras. The teeth and spines of sharks are common fossils, but nearly complete skeletons are extremely rare, probably because of their cartilaginous nature. The evolutionary history of sharks, therefore, is understood only in its broadest outlines, and the relationship of modern sharks to the more primitive ones is somewhat speculative.

Kinds of Sharks. Scientists recognize about 275 species of sharks now living. The smallest is a streamlined, black and white shark of the genus Squaliolus. The adult male is about 6 inches (15 cm) long and the female about 8 inches (20 cm). The largest species is the whale shark (*Rhincodon typus*), which attains a length of 40 feet (12 meters) or more and a weight of some 26,000 pounds (11,800 kg). The most commonly known sharks include the spiny dogfish (*Squalus acanthias*), blue shark (*Prionace glauca*), nurse shark (*Ginglymastoma cirratum*), great hammerhead (*Sphyrna mokarran*), leopard shark (*Triakis semifasciata*), and thresher shark (*Alopius vulpinus*). For a listing of separate articles on the individual species of sharks, see the Index entry *Shark*.

If one kind of shark may be considered typical in the minds of most people, it is any one of the 25 or more species of requiem sharks of the genus *Carcharhinus*. The requiem sharks, which as adults range in length from 3 to 12 feet (1–3.7 meters), are so similar in general form that species can be recognized only by scrutiny of minor characteristics or by color or size differences. On the other hand, many species differ greatly from the requiem sharks. For example, the frilled shark (*Chlamydoselachus anguineum*) is eel-like; the angel sharks (*Squatina*) are flat and have winglike pectoral fins; and the sawsharks (*Pristiophoridae*) have long snouts armed with spines and superficially resemble the saw fishes (*Pristis*), which are rays, not sharks.

Physical Characteristics. Sharks, like skates and rays, have cartilaginous rather than bony skeletons. The skeletal cartilage is usually hardened by mineral deposits, but it lacks the architecture of true bone. Sharks have two pairs of fins, each pair supported by a girdle, and a segmentally constricted notochord. There are five to seven pairs of gill slits above or in front of the pectoral fins but never entirely below the plane of the pectorals. The skin is covered with scales of dermal origin, and the eyeballs are free from the upper edges of their orbits. For further information on the differences between sharks and other cartilaginous fishes, on the one hand, and bony fishes, on the other hand, see FISH—*Types of Fishes.*

Teeth. In proportion to their size, sharks have either large or powerful jaws variously armed with teeth suited to the feeding habits of their particular species. The teeth are not set in sockets but are attached in five or more transverse bands to tough ligaments on the surface of the jaw. One, two, or more of these bands of teeth are functional. Behind the functional teeth, several series of developing teeth are held in reserve, hidden beneath the skin on the inside of the mouth. New teeth originate in a germinal area behind the jaws and move gradually outward as they form and harden. The outer teeth drop off either singly or in bands to be replaced by teeth of the reserve series, thus providing the jaws with new teeth proportional in size to the growing shark as well as replacing worn or broken teeth. In some young, rapidly growing sharks new teeth may come into use every six weeks.

Adaptive Features. In order to reduce the pull of gravity, most sharks have large livers, containing high percentages of low specific gravity oils, that act as primary hydrostatic organs. Those sharks not restricted to a bottom habitat have large and stiff pectoral fins, which serve as hydrofoils to provide lift forward of the center of gravity. The downward directed sweep of the asymmetrical caudal fin gives them a balancing lift posteriorly. To avoid hydrodynamic instability with great loss in ability to swim efficiently underwater, the various lifting forces operating for the shark must be in balance and not so strong as to make the shark float.

The sharks—together with the skates, saltwater rays, and chimaeroids—are remarkable among vertebrates in retaining a relatively high level of urea as a normal constituent of the blood and body fluids. The high concentration of urea raises the osmotic pressure of the body fluids to a level comparable to that of seawater and thus greatly reduces the loss of fluids by osmosis.

Habitat. All sharks are marine dwelling, and although some may enter fresh water at the mouths of rivers or even travel upstream for great distances, none are known to complete their life cycles without returning to the sea. One large species, the bull shark (*Carcharhinus leucas*), is found in Lake Nicaragua, which it reaches by way of the San Juan River, but has not become adapted to permanent residence in fresh water and returns to the Caribbean Sea to breed.

Where seasonal changes in water temperatures are great, as in the near-surface waters of some temperate regions, sharks may be migratory. To reach water of suitable temperature they may merely move to a different depth, but some of the larger species make regular seasonal migrations of 100 to 1,000 miles (160–1,600 km). The extent and patterns of migrations are influenced variously in different regions by water temperature, food availability, and the species' habits in reproduction.

As a general rule, sharks tolerate a wide range of water pressures due to depth, and some are known to move freely between surface waters and depths of 1,200 feet (366 meters). About half the species are either restricted to depths of more than 600 feet (183 meters) or enter lesser depths rarely. The deepest ranges are unknown, but the species *Centroscymnus coelolepis* has been taken from about 8,000 feet (2,438 meters).

Feeding Habits. Most sharks are carnivorous, and feed on comparatively large prey. Depending

The common hammerhead, a dangerous and aggressive shark, is readily identified by its unusual head.

The strangely shaped monkfish, or anglefish, is a small shark that resembles a ray. It is not regarded as dangerous to swimmers.

COURTESY OF THE MUSEUM OF NATURAL HISTORY

COURTESY OF THE MUSEUM OF NATURAL HISTORY

upon their particular species, they may eat fish, squid, octopus, shellfish, turtles, seals, whales, or other sharks. But the adults of the two largest species—the whale shark and the basking shark (*Cetorhinus maximus*)—are exceptions. They feed principally on small microscopic organisms that they strain from seawater. By swimming slowly with their mouths open, they allow great volumes of water to enter their branchial chambers, where specialized gill rakers act as sieves to retain food as the water passes out through their gill slits.

Olfactory, auditory, and visual senses possibly together with other little-understood sensory structures, all play a part in the location and identification of the typical shark's food. Observations suggest that some of the larger voracious species, when present in groups near attractive prey and when stimulated through several senses, may respond by a frenzied and indiscriminate attack on the prey and even on each other. Such action is probably rare, however, and feeding sharks are usually cautious, and when alone, usually deliberate.

Reproduction. Fertilization is internal in all sharks, and the males have modifications of the pelvic fins known as *claspers* that function as intromittent organs. Many of the smaller sharks and also the huge whale sharks lay eggs. Each egg is enclosed in a leathery capsule, which at first is fully closed but later opens slightly to allow circulation of seawater. The circulation is produced by swimming movements of the developing embryo. In other species the egg capsules are retained within the mother's oviducts until they hatch, at which time both the young and the empty capsules are expelled.

In still other species the egg capsules are represented only by thin membranes that may either be absorbed or serve as temporary compartment walls within the oviducts. In requiem sharks, hammerheads, and related species, the yolk sac is modified after the nutrient yolk material is exhausted. The sac then forms a pseudoplacenta that adheres closely to the oviduct walls and allows transfer of nutrients through adjacent membranes from blood vessels of the mother to blood vessels of the embryo.

Embryonic development takes from six months to two years in species with known life histories. The number of young produced in one reproductive cycle varies from one to more than 100.

Fisheries. Sharks make up only about 0.5% of the world fishery production. Shark meat is little used in the United States or Canada, but in many other localities it is in strong demand either fresh, smoked, or dry-salted. The dried fins of certain large sharks are persistently in demand for use in shark-fin soup. Shark hides make very durable leather, but the low productivity of the fishery and high costs of processing prevent its extensive use.

STEWART SPRINGER
Mote Marine Laboratory
Sarasota, Florida

Bibliography

Bigelow, H. B., and Schroeder, W. C., *Fishes of the Western North Atlantic: Part 1, Lancelets, Cyclostomes, and Sharks* (Yale Univ. Press 1948).
Gilbert, Perry W., and others, eds., *Sharks, Skates, and Rays* (Johns Hopkins Press 1967).
Lineaweaver, Thomas H., III, and Backus, R. H., *The Natural History of Sharks* (Lippincott 1970).
Moy-Thomas, J. A., and Miles, R. S., *Paleozoic Fishes* (Saunders 1970).
Peyer, Bernhard, *Comparative Odontology*, tr. and ed. by Rainer Zangeri (Univ. of Chicago Press 1968).

SHARKSKIN is a smooth worsted fabric made in a twill or plain weave, with small designs produced by warp and filling yarns of different colors. It has a substantial feel, wears well, and sheds dirt readily. It is made in light to medium weights for suits. A plain-weave sharkskin made of rayon is a smooth crisp fabric with a dull finish. It is used for dresses and sportswear.

SHARON, shâr′ən, a town in eastern Massachusetts, in Norfolk county, is about 20 miles (32 km) south-southwest of Boston. Pacemakers used in heart surgery are manufactured here. Points of interest include the childhood home of Deborah Sampson, who enlisted in the Continental army during the American Revolution under the name of Robert Shurtleff, and Cobbs Tavern, a stopping place on the old Bay Road.

Sharon was settled in 1637. For many years it was part of Stoughton. It was incorporated as Sharon in 1765. Government is by town meeting. Population: 13,601.

SHARON, shar′ən, a city in western Pennsylvania, in Mercer county, is on the Shenango River, 70 miles (113 km) north of Pittsburgh. It is a business, industrial, and wholesale food center. The making and fabricating of steel and the manufacture of electrical equipment are the city's chief industries.

The area was first settled around 1800. A mill was built on the Shenango River in 1802. Sharon was laid out in 1815 and named for the plain in Biblical Palestine. It was incorporated as a city in 1918. Government is by a mayor and council. Population: 19,057.

SHARON, shâr′ən, **Plain of,** the coastal region of Israel along the Mediterranean Sea, extending from Mt. Carmel in the north to Jaffa in the south. It is about 50 miles (80 km) long and 8 to 10 miles (12–16 km) wide. In Old Testament times its largely marshy and sandy character made the land difficult to utilize. The rose of Sharon alluded to in the Song of Solomon (2:1) is a type of crocus that grows in the area.

SHARONVILLE, shâr′ən-vil, is a city in southwestern Ohio, in Hamilton county, about 20 miles (32 km) northeast of the center of Cincinnati. It is the site of a large automobile transmission plant. The community was founded in 1788 and was incorporated in 1911. Government is by mayor and council. Population: 10,108.

SHARP, Becky, the central character in the novel *Vanity Fair* by William Makepeace Thackeray. Becky is drawn as an unscrupulous and clever woman, who will abide no hindrance in her attempt to rise above her humble origin. One of the memorable heroines in English fiction, she is contrasted with the gentle, pretty, and somewhat witless Amelia Sedley.

SHARP, Cecil James (1859–1924), English musicologist and folk-music anthologist. He was born in London on Nov. 22, 1859. After graduating from Clare College, Cambridge, he went to Australia, where he was associate to the chief justice of South Australia (1883–1889). However, music was his first interest, and from 1889 to 1892 he was the organist of the Anglican cathedral at Adelaide. On his return to England, Sharp served as music master of the Ludgrove

MOUNT SHASTA, a dead volcano in northern California, offers a striking view of its twin peaks from the south.

Preparatory School (1893–1910) and principal of the Hampstead Conservatory (1896–1905). In 1911 he founded the English Folk Dance Society. He died in London on June 23, 1924.

English folk music was Sharp's particular field of study. Either in collaboration or alone he compiled more than a dozen books of songs and dance tunes. In pursuit of English folk music, he even visited the Appalachian Mountains of the United States, collecting songs imported by early immigrants from England. From this trip evolved his two-volume *English Folk Songs from the Southern Appalachian Mountains* (published posthumously, 1932), edited with Maud Karpeles.

SHARP, Granville (1735–1813), English abolitionist. He was born in Durham on Nov. 10, 1735. He studied law, but abandoned it to accept a place in the ordnance office in London. He befriended the Negro slave Jonathan Strong, who was ill and had therefore been turned away by his master. Sharp placed Strong in a hospital and, on his recovery, got work for him. Two years later Strong was claimed by his master, arrested, and imprisoned. Sharp then summoned master and slave before the lord mayor, who discharged the slave. The master still refused to release Strong, and Sharp's lawyers advised him to drop the fight after he was threatened with a countercharge for interfering with personal property. Sharp studied the law of personal liberty and interested himself in the cases of other slaves. The struggle was finally won before the King's Bench in 1772, when the ruling in the case of James Sommersett declared slavery illegal.

In 1777, Sharp resigned from the ordnance office because of his disapproval of the American war. Devoting himself to philanthropy, he was a founder of the Association for the Abolition of Slavery and of the Negro colony in Sierra Leone. An advocate of parliamentary reform, he opposed dueling and favored the extension of privileges to Ireland. He was a prolific pamphleteer on reform subjects. He died in London on July 6, 1813.

SHARP, James (1613–1679), Scottish ecclesiastic and archbishop of St. Andrews. Sharp was born in the Castle of Banff on May 4, 1613. He was educated at the University of Aberdeen and was appointed regent there. He held a professorship in St. Leonard's College, St. Andrews, and was then appointed minister at Crail, Fifeshire,

in 1648. In 1656 he was a representative from the Presbytery to Cromwell and he managed this mission so well that he was sent in 1660 to General Monk who was attempting to restore Charles II to the throne.

When Parliament established Episcopacy in 1661, Sharp was appointed professor of theology in St. Mary's College, St. Andrews and king's chaplain for Scotland. He now went over to the king's party, was consecrated archbishop of St. Andrews and primate of Scotland. In 1663 he secured the establishment of a high court commission. The harsh treatment by the court of those who favored Presbyterianism made Sharp an object of intense hatred throughout the country. On May 3, 1679, at Magus Muir, St. Andrews, he was dragged from his coach and beaten to death by a party of his enemies.

SHARPSBURG, Battle of, in the American Civil War. See ANTIETAM, BATTLE OF.

SHASTA, shas'tə, **Mount,** in northern California, in Siskiyou county, about 40 miles (64 km) south of the Oregon boundary. It is a spectacular peak, symmetrical in shape, rising to a height of 14,162 feet (4,280 meters). Because no mountain of comparable height is near, its appearance is especially impressive.

Mount Shasta is of volcanic origin, but is believed to be extinct, although vents of steam are observed on its sides. Five glaciers drop from the summit. One of these, the Whitney, is about 3 miles (5 km) long. The mountain was discovered in 1827 by Peter Skene Ogden and was first ascended in 1854 by E. D. Pearce. The city of Mount Shasta (population: 2,163) is a few miles southwest of the mountain.

SHASTA DAISY, shas'tə, any of several horticultural varieties of a plant, *Chrysanthemum maximus,* having large daisylike flowers. The Shasta daisy is named after Mt. Shasta. See also DAISY.

SHASTRI, shäs'trē, **Lal Bahadur** (1904–1966), Indian political leader, who succeeded Nehru as prime minister. He was born in Varanasi on Oct. 2, 1904. He received the title Shastri ("scholar") for excellence in religious studies.

Shastri joined Gandhi's movement of noncooperation with the British and was imprisoned several times. He became influential in local politics before India gained independence. After entering Parliament in 1952, he held cabinet posts under Nehru. When Nehru died in 1964, Shastri was chosen his successor.

Prime Minister Shastri continued India's policies of nonalignment in foreign affairs and moderate socialism at home. His handling of the war with Pakistan over Kashmir in 1965 won approval. He died in Tashkent, USSR, on Jan. 11, 1966, the day after signing an agreement to seek a peaceful solution to the Kashmir dispute.

SHATT AL-ARAB, shat'al-är'äb, is a river formed at Al Qurna in southeastern Iraq by the confluence of the Tigris and Euphrates rivers. An alternate spelling is Shat al-Arab. It flows southeasterly through a marshy region past Basra. From below Basra until it reaches the Persian Gulf, it forms the Iran-Iraq border. Its total length is about 120 miles (193 km).

SHAVUOT, shə-voo'ōt, is a Jewish feast that celebrates the giving of the law on Mt. Sinai. Originally, it was a harvest feast. See PENTECOST.

SHAW, Anna Howard (1847–1919), American minister and physician, who was a leader in the women's suffrage and temperance movements. Born in Newcastle-upon-Tyne, England, on Feb. 14, 1847, she went to the United States with her family at the age of four. The Shaws lived first in Lawrence, Mass., then in the Michigan wilderness. Anna managed to get an education at Albion College, Michigan, then took degrees in theology (1878) and medicine (1886) from Boston University. She was granted a local preacher's license by the Methodist Episcopal Church and was pastor of congregations at Hingham, Mass. (1878), and East Dennis, Mass. (1878–1885). Denied ordination by the New England Methodist Conference because of her sex, she was ordained in the Protestant Methodist Church on Oct. 12, 1880, the first woman ordained by that denomination.

In 1885, she resigned her pulpit to lecture for the Massachusetts Woman Suffrage Association. She was national superintendent of franchise for the Women's Christian Temperance Union in 1886–1892. Active in the National American Woman Suffrage Association, she was its president from 1904 to 1915. Her reputation as a lecturer and preacher was worldwide, and she was much honored. For her services to the Council of National Defense during World War I, she received the distinguished service cross. She died in Moylan, Pa., on July 2, 1919.

SHAW, Artie (1910–   ), American clarinetist and swing band-leader. He was born Arthur Arshawsky in New York City on May 23, 1910. As a boy he played clarinet in bands. Beginning as an orchestra leader in 1936, he became a leading exponent of swing and attained wide popularity as a clarinetist, ranking among such leading jazz figures as Louis Armstrong, Bix Beiderbecke, and Benny Goodman.

Shaw later became interested in writing and published a quasiautobiographical novel, *The Trouble with Cinderella* (1952), and various magazine articles. He lived in Spain for a time, as, according to some critics, a gesture of abdication from success. His instrumental works include *Concerto for Clarinet* and *Clarinet Method.* Three of his many marriages were to Lana Turner, Ava Gardner, and novelist Kathleen Winsor.

PICTORIAL PARADE
George Bernard Shaw, British playwright

SHAW, George Bernard (1856–1950), British playwright, critic, man of letters, socialist pamphleteer, and lecturer, who was one of the most influential figures in modern literature. He was almost 40 before he began to taste success. His career began with painful and fumbling slowness but culminated with his being named the 1925 Nobel laureate in literature, though he refused the prize. He continued to write almost until his death at 94, producing about 50 plays, many of them among the classics of Western theater.

Shaw's attitude to the drama and the stage was sharply unconventional. He believed in the theater as a place not for mere entertainment but for serious thought about man and society— "a temple of the ascent of man," he called it. The fact that his greatest successes were comedies in no way lessens the seriousness. For him, laughter was a means to clarity of thought, strength of purpose, and healthier feeling.

Shaw's medium was prose—pungently athletic, musical, resilient, witty. In analytical and argumentative force, it is unexcelled. His work is sometimes poetic, but his occasional attempts at verse make it clear that his decision to hold with prose was a wise one.

Early Life. Shaw was born in Dublin, Ireland, on July 26, 1856, of Anglo-Irish stock. His parents were unhappily married, and his mother left his father during Shaw's adolescence. Shaw later claimed that he had learned nothing creditable in the various schools he attended, but a great deal from visits to the National Gallery of Ireland and the theater, from the reading that he was allowed to pursue at will, and from the music in which the household was continuously involved. The two individuals who most influenced him as a boy were his mother, who was a singer and pianist, and George Vandeleur Lee, a conductor and music teacher, who was part of the Shaw ménage for many years. In 1876, after working for five years as a clerk in a real estate office, Shaw resigned and went to London, where his mother, sisters, and Lee had already gone.

For the next decade, Shaw's life was irregular, restless, and obscure as the family circumstances steadily declined. He read omnivorously at the British Museum, attended countless meetings of literary and debating societies, and assisted in the musical activities of Lee. He also adopted his lifelong habits of vegetarianism and teetotalism. In 1879 he wrote *Immaturity*, a long and clumsy novel, which nevertheless has flashes of self-portraiture and glimpses of the future master of prose debate. Four more novels followed: *The Irrational Knot, Love Among the Artists, Cashel Byron's Profession,* and *An Unsocial Socialist.* These were published in serial form in socialist magazines. The novels expressed their author's unconventional and mainly rationalistic views on religion, marriage, the arts, and society.

In 1882, Shaw's as yet unformed attitudes and ideas on socialism were suddenly given focus when he attended a lecture by the American economist Henry George, which led him to recognize that economics must be at the center of socialist thought. He set himself to master David Ricardo, Stanley Jevons, John Stuart Mill, and Karl Marx. In 1884 he joined the recently founded Fabian Society, of which he and Sidney and Beatrice Webb constituted the dynamic intellectual center for many years. He wrote tracts for the society, edited a volume of essays, and lectured and debated interminably. Although by the late 1890's his energies were increasingly directed to the theater, he never lost his belief in socialism as the only way to fundamental social betterment.

Shaw's religious thought developed in the same period. He had abandoned Christianity in his teens and become a rationalist and agnostic. In the 1880's he mingled in circles where evolutionary theory was much discussed, and in 1887 he read Samuel Butler's *Luck or Cunning?*, in which the mechanistic implications of Darwinism were attacked. Butler argued that evolution was the expression of a purposeful force of will in the universe, not the effect of mere mechanical causation and chance. Shaw's reading of Butler led to the formulation of his theory of a "Life Force" that, through biological change, continually seeks higher living forms through which to achieve its goal of perfect contemplation. This "religion," which owed much to William Blake, as well as to Butler, provided the philosophical basis of virtually all Shaw's writings after the mid-1890's, especially his plays.

Musical and Dramatic Criticism. In the mid-1880's, thanks to the efforts of the drama critic William Archer, Shaw began to earn a living through journalism—writing book reviews and accounts of concerts, art exhibitions, and plays. From 1888 to 1894 he reviewed the musical life of London, first under the pseudonym "Corno di Bassetto" and then under the initials G. B. S. Shaw's knowledge of music was vast. More than 30 years after his criticisms appeared, Ernest Newman called them "the most brilliant things that musical journalism . . . is ever likely to produce." Shaw felt that music, especially opera, was the noblest of the arts. His tastes were catholic, but his highest preference was for Mozart. He was an early Wagner enthusiast and wrote a long critical essay, *The Perfect Wagnerite* (1898). Shaw was also an early admirer of Sir Edward Elgar, and they shared a long friendship.

In 1895, Shaw became a dramatic critic for the *Saturday Review*, and for three and a half years he discussed the London theatrical scene. He mercilessly attacked the conventional plays of the period and challenged writers and producers to transform the theater into what he believed it ought to be: a place for the dramatic presentation and discussion of human problems. He scoffed at the universal unquestioning reverence for Shakespeare, which he called "Bardolatry," and he attacked Henry Irving, the actor who especially embodied it. In Shaw's view, drama had to find new and worthier courses, such as those that Ibsen was exploring. Ibsen had become a hero for Shaw, who wrote one of his major essays, *The Quintessence of Ibsenism* (1891) about him.

Early Plays and Marriage. Shaw's first three plays, *Widowers' Houses* (1892; dates of completion throughout), *The Philanderer* (1893), and *Mrs. Warren's Profession* (1893), deal with social questions such as slum landlordism and prostitution. His gift for satirical comedy appears fully in *Arms and the Man* (1894), a spoof on the romanticized view of war, and his first successful play. Its comic stripping away of illusions and pretensions pointed in the direction that his

PICTORIAL PARADE

George Bernard Shaw's *Pygmalion* was transformed into *My Fair Lady,* one of the most popular musicals of all time. This scene from the film version (1964) shows Eliza Doolittle (Audrey Hepburn, in hat) receiving instructions on how to be a lady from a short-tempered Professor Higgins (Rex Harrison).

plays of the next 20 years would take. Its initial success was limited, however, as was that of *Candida* (1894), though this later became one of his most popular comedies.

In 1898, Shaw married Charlotte Payne-Townshend, an Irish heiress and fellow Fabian. They lived in London for a time and then moved to Ayot St. Lawrence, Hertfordshire, their home for the rest of their lives. Their marriage, which was childless, lasted 45 years. Shaw was by now a public figure, but the quiet of Hertfordshire enabled him to write with prodigious industry.

Plays, 1895 to World War I. After *Candida*, virtually all of Shaw's plays dealt with social problems and problems of individual growth, seen in the light of his belief in the Life Force. *Candida* itself, with its mockery of conventional Victorian domesticity and its ending in which the young poet Marchbanks is liberated from illusion to carry out life's nobler purposes, set a pattern for several plays of "conversion." These plays, in which one or more of the protagonists is led to self-discovery and the possibility of self-fulfillment, include *The Devil's Disciple* (1897), *Captain Brassbound's Conversion* (1899), *The Shewing-Up of Blanco Posnet* (1909), and *Androcles and The Lion* (1912). In other plays, he explored the nature of the "great man" through whom the Life Force reaches forward in evolution: Napoleon, in *The Man of Destiny* (1895); Julius Caesar, in *Caesar and Cleopatra* (1898); and the rich munitions-maker Sir Andrew Undershaft, in *Major Barbara* (1905). In *Man and Superman* (1903), subtitled *A Comedy and a Philosophy*, Shaw affirmed his belief in the Life Force more fully and overtly than in any other play of this period. In all his plays, however, the theme of the Life Force provides only one of the major threads. His attacks on social ills were unceasing—on poverty, in *Major Barbara*; on questionable medical practices, in *The Doctor's Dilemma* (1906); on England's treatment of Ireland, in *John Bull's Other Island* (1904); and on the British class structure, in *Pygmalion* (1912). He also exposed some of the shams inherent in many social conventions and institutions, such as marriage, in *Getting Married* (1908) and in *Misalliance* (1910), and dealt with family relationships, the status of women, and other subjects in other plays.

The mood and action of these plays are those of high comedy, breaking occasionally into farce. The method is rather of discussion than of action, since Shaw's interest was much more in the high-spirited clash of ideas than in the depiction of events or the conflicts of passion. In their published form, many of the plays are accompanied by "prefaces," in which Shaw discussed the theater, himself, and a wide range of social and philosophical questions.

World War I and After. In the early weeks of World War I, Shaw published a pamphlet, *Common Sense about the War*, in which he castigated the diplomacy and militarism of all those who had made the war possible. Because he condemned the British and French as well as the Germans, he experienced a period of intense unpopularity, which waned only as he turned to pamphleteering for the cause of the Allies. The sense of near despair that he experienced in this period found expression in *Heartbreak House* (1916), which was much influenced by Chekhov. The play, with its country house setting that resembles a ship, its eccentric characters, and its brooding atmosphere of aimlessness and futility broken by episodes of farce, is unlike any other by Shaw.

In the later years of the war, Shaw wrote several short pieces in his former vein of burlesque comedy. Then came *Back to Methuselah* (1920), actually five plays in one, in which he propounds fully and imaginatively the theory of the Life Force, beginning back with the Garden of Eden and ending with a time ahead "as far as thought can reach," when the span of life has been extended to centuries and life itself has virtually become thought. It was followed by *Saint Joan* (1923), probably his most popular play. It is a study based on the life of Joan of Arc, exploring the forces in conflict around her by the Shavian devices of dramatic debate.

Shaw's continuing concern with economics and socialism was reflected in *The Intelligent Woman's Guide to Socialism and Capitalism* (1928) and in the later *Everybody's Political What's What?* (1944). It was also reflected in a lecture that he gave at the Metropolitan Opera House in New York in 1933, published later that year as *The Political Madhouse in America and Nearer Home*. In despair over the ineptitudes of parliamentary democracy, he praised communist Russia. For a time he became an admirer of such figures as Lenin, Stalin, and Mussolini. Some of the plays of his later years express these feelings, though the mood of high comedy continues to enliven them. They include *The Apple Cart* (1929), *The Millionairess* (1936), and *Buoyant Billions* (1947).

In his 95th year, Shaw fractured his thigh after falling from a tree that he was pruning in his garden. He died in Ayot St. Lawrence on Nov. 2, 1950. It is reported that on that night, theaters around the world were darkened in his honor.

J. PERCY SMITH
Author of "The Unrepentant Pilgrim"

Bibliography
Bentley, Eric, *Bernard Shaw* (New Directions 1947).
Chesterton, G. K., *George Bernard Shaw* (1909; reprint, Hill & Wang 1956).
Ervine, St. John Greer, *Bernard Shaw: His Life, Work and Friends* (Morrow 1956).
Meisel, Martin, *Shaw and the Nineteenth Century Theater* (Princeton Univ. Press 1963).
Purdom, C. B., *A Guide to the Plays of Bernard Shaw* (Methuen 1963).
Smith, J. Percy, *The Unrepentant Pilgrim* (Houghton 1965).

SHAW, Henry Wheeler. See BILLINGS, JOSH.

SHAW, Irwin (1913–   ), American novelist and playwright, whose works are characterized by dramatic intensity and sensitivity to the social milieu. Shaw was born in New York City on Feb. 27, 1913, and graduated from Brooklyn College in 1934. His earliest major works were plays, including *Bury the Dead* (1936), a strong plea for pacifism; *The Gentle People* (1939), a comedy about two Brooklynites who realize their dream of owning a boat in Florida by robbing and murdering without detection a gangster who was trying to extort "protection" money from them; *The Assassin* (1944), with a World War II setting; and *Children From Their Games* (1963), a comedy.

Shaw's most successful novel is *The Young Lions* (1948), the story about three soldiers; two Americans, one Jewish, the other Gentile, and a Nazi. Among his other novels are *Lucy Crown* (1956) and *Voices of a Summer Day* (1965).

SHAW, Lemuel (1781–1861), American judge. He was born in Barnstable, Mass., on Jan. 9, 1781. He graduated from Harvard University in 1800, and studied law in Boston, beginning his practice about 1804. Between 1811 and 1829, Shaw served in both houses of the state legislature. In 1822 he drew up the first charter, retained until 1913, for the city of Boston.

As chief justice of the Massachusetts supreme court, 1830–1860, Shaw won a high reputation by his thoughtful and scholarly decisions. He dealt with commercial and constitutional questions in such a way as to influence greatly the succeeding law on these subjects throughout the United States. His opinions on railroads, water power, and other public utilities were noted for the strength and solidity of their reasoning. Likewise, his charge to a jury was so thorough and specific as to be a model of clarity. He died in Boston on March 30, 1861.

SHAW, Robert (1916–   ), American conductor. He was born in Red Bluff, Calif., on April 30, 1916. After graduating from Pomona College in 1938, he founded the Collegiate Chorale, New York (1941–1954). He held a Guggenheim fellowship (1944), conducted the summer concerts of the San Diego Symphony (1953–1958), and was associate conductor of the Cleveland Orchestra (1956–1967). In 1966 he became conductor of the Atlanta Symphony Orchestra.

Shaw is best known as the founder (1948) and conductor of the Robert Shaw Chorale. This group, highly regarded for its precision and tone, performed with major symphony orchestras and made many popular recordings.

HERBERT WEINSTOCK
Coauthor of "Men of Music"

SHAWINIGAN, shə-win′i-gən, a city in southeastern Quebec, Canada, in St. Maurice county, in the foothills of the Laurentians, is on the St. Maurice River, 21 miles (34 km) northwest of Trois Rivières. The most powerful falls on the river are here, dropping 150 feet (45 meters) from a crest of rocks that gives the city its name, which is derived from an Algonkian word for "crest." The power from the falls has made Shawinigan an important industrial center. Its chief products are pulp and paper, chemicals, aluminum, cellophane, plastics, and textiles.

The earliest recorded mention of Shawinigan Falls was in 1651. In 1663 the area was hit by a severe earthquake. A slide was built at the falls to permit logs to pass down the river in 1852, and the first water and power mill here was founded in 1898. The community was incorporated as the village of Shawinigan Falls in 1901. It became a town in 1920 and a city in 1921. In 1958 the word "Falls" was dropped from its name. Population: 23,011.

SHAWINIGAN SUD, shə-win′i-gən sood, a village in southeastern Quebec, Canada, in Champlain county, is on the St. Maurice River, directly opposite Shawinigan. Although it is technically on the east bank of the river, a bend in the stream places it south of the city of Shawinigan. Shawinigan Sud is connected to Shawinigan by bridge and is part of its metropolitan area. It is chiefly a residential suburb. It was incorporated in 1912 and was known as Almaville until 1950. Population: 11,325.

SHAWL, a piece of fabric, usually rectangular, wrapped or draped about the body. Most shawls are worn over the upper torso, but some may also serve as a skirt or head covering.

Shawls, and closely related mantles and scarves, have been worn by many peoples throughout the world. Both men and women in ancient Mesopotamia, Persia, and Egypt wore shawls over their skirts, tunics, or coats. Greek shawls included the short chlamys for men and the long himation for men and women. From the himation developed various Roman shawls, including the man's toga and pallium and the woman's palla, worn over tunics. Similar garments were worn in Europe before and during the Middle Ages. A version of the Celtic shawl was the plaid worn by the peoples of northern Britain as a skirt and shawl in one, which developed into the Scottish Highland man's kilt and shoulder plaid.

Shawls were an indispensable item of Western women's dress in the 19th century and were especially graceful over long, full skirts. Woven or embroidered cashmere shawls, made of fine wool in Kashmir, were imported into Europe. They were copied in Paisley, Scotland. Wool, silk, and lace shawls, rectangular or triangular, were made in many cities for all classes. Silk shawls, gaily embroidered in China and fringed in Spain, became a distinctive element of Spanish dress. Fur and feather boas, scarves, and stoles are later variants of the shawl, which has generally been replaced by the coat.

Narrow, floating shawls were part of women's costumes in Han China. In the Islamic world, women have traditionally worn an outer shawl, mantle, or loose robe. In India, men wear shawls around the waist or over the shoulder. Hindu women wear the sari, a shawl and skirt in one. In pre-Columbian America, men and women wore shawls or mantles, tied on or in the form of a poncho. These garments evolved into the Mexican serape.

SHAWN, shôn, **Ted** (1891–1972), American dancer, choreographer, and teacher, who was a pioneer of modern dance. Edwin Myers Shawn was born in Kansas City, Mo., on Oct. 21, 1891. While a divinity student at the University of Denver, he learned to dance as therapy for paralysis caused by an overdose of diphtheria antitoxin. Making dance his career, he ran a studio in Los Angeles and toured the United States. Shawn became the partner of the dancer Ruth St. Denis in April 1914 and married her in August. In 1915 they founded the Denishawn company and school, through which American audiences and such modern dancers as Martha Graham were introduced to primitive and ethnic dance as a religious expression and as serious theater. Works such as *Xochitl, Invocation to the Thunderbird, Cosmic Dances of Shiva,* and *Four American Folk Dances* reflect Shawn's interest in both exotic and American themes. Instead of light melodies, he used the music of major composers, classical and modern, and commissioned special works.

After Shawn and St. Denis separated in 1932, Shawn formed a troupe of male dancers (1933–1940) to help overcome American prejudice against them. At Jacob's Pillow, a farm near Lenox, Mass., that he bought in 1930, he created an influential summer center for dance. Shawn died in Orlando, Fla., on Jan. 9, 1972.

SHAWNEE, shô-nē′, a city in northeastern Kansas, in Johnson county, is about 7 miles (11 km) southwest of the center of Kansas City, of which it is a residential suburb. Since 1950, when it was a tiny market town for a dairy and farming region, its population has increased about 2000%.

Shawnee was once known as Gum Springs and was the largest settlement in Kansas Territory for a time. Near the city a Shawnee Methodist mission was established in 1830. The community was founded in 1857 and was incorporated as a city in 1922. Government is by mayor and council. Population: 29,653.

SHAWNEE, shô-nē′, a city in central Oklahoma, the seat of Pottawatomie county, is on the North Canadian River, about 40 miles (64 km) east of Oklahoma City. It is largely residential, but there is some light industry, notably food processing and the making of electronic parts. Oklahoma Baptist University and St. Gregory's College (Roman Catholic) are in the city. The log building (1882) of the Shawnee Indian Mission is of historic note.

The Shawnee Indian Mission was established here in 1872. The town was laid out in 1892 and incorporated two years later. In the 1920's, despite tornado and flood disasters, the town grew rapidly after oil was discovered in the area, and reached a population of 35,000. During the Great Depression of the 1930's, however, the population declined and remained small until after World War II, when agricultural processing industries were established as mainstays of the city's economy. Shawnee has a council-manager form of government. Population: 26,506.

SHAWNEE INDIANS, shô-nē′, a North American tribe of Algonkian stock, originally situated in South Carolina, Tennessee, Pennsylvania, and Ohio. According to the tradition of the Delaware Indians, the Shawnees lived in the Ohio River valley before being driven south by the Iroquois; hence the name Shawnee ("Southerners"), from the Algonkian *shawun*, "south." By about 1669 the Shawnees were to be found as far south as the Gulf Coast and in Georgia, close to the region of the Spanish colonies in Florida. They were soon living in two bands, one on the Savannah River in South Carolina and another on the Cumberland River in Tennessee. These early migrations formed the pattern of tribal life for the next 200 years, during which the Shawnees became known as a roving people, though they were agriculturists living in villages and sometimes remaining in one location for several years to grow corn and other crops.

Colonial Period. During the years of colonial and Indian wars and of rivalries among the Spanish, English, and French traders along the Atlantic and the Gulf coasts (1674–1763), the Shawnees moved away from the Savannah, most of them going north to the Susquehanna River to be near their kinsmen, the Delaware, in Pennsylvania. Some Shawnee went south among the Creek Indians in Georgia and Alabama, where they were known as Sawanogi.

The Shawnees on the Cumberland began moving north about 1714, because of a war with the Chickasaw, who claimed northern Tennessee. The Cumberland Shawnees were located about 15 years later north of the Ohio River, where they were joined in 1754–1760 by their tribesmen from the Susquehanna River in the exodus of the Delaware tribe from Pennsylvania.

Migration and Removal. The Shawnees were allies of the French in the French and Indian War and sided with the British in the American Revolution. After the massacre of the Christian Delaware Indians at Gnadenhutten, Ohio, by whites on the frontier in 1782, a large part of the Shawnees left Ohio for the west. They were granted land in 1793 at Cape Girardeau, Mo., which at that time belonged to Spain. When this region passed to the United States as part of the Louisiana Purchase (1803), some bands moved southwest toward Spanish territory, settling in Oklahoma and Texas. These people were the nucleus of the tribal division known later as the Absentee Shawnees.

Those of the tribe who had remained at Cape Girardeau (Black Bob band) ceded their tract to the United States in 1825 and were assigned a reservation in Kansas, where they were joined by other Shawnee bands from different parts of the country after Congress passed the Indian Removal Act in 1830. They generally prospered but were compelled to sign a treaty in 1854, ceding their Kansas tract. They kept a small reserve, which they sold after the Civil War for white settlement. In 1869, most of the Shawnees (about 700) remaining in Kansas purchased the right of citizenship in the Cherokee Nation, now northeastern Oklahoma.

Absentee Shawnees had settled in the region of the mouth of the Little River, on both sides of the Canadian River in Oklahoma, when they were joined in 1854 by some Kansas Shawnees who were Southern sympathizers in the Methodist Church, South. During the Civil War, some tribal members served in the Confederate Army, others in the Union Army. The "Omnibus Treaty" with the United States in 1867 provided that the Absentee Shawnees might settle north of the Canadian River near their former locations, where they afterward shared a reservation with their kinsmen, the Potawatomi, in what is now mostly Pottawatomie county, Okla.

The Shawnees who remained in Ohio after 1793 were defeated by U. S. forces under Gen. Anthony Wayne at the Battle of Fallen Timbers in 1794 and surrendered most of their land by the Treaty of Greenville (1795). The Shawnee prophet Tenskwatawa, who advocated that the tribes unite in discarding the white man's civilization, was crushed by Gen. William Henry Harrison at the Battle of Tippecanoe in 1811. The celebrated war chief Tecumseh, commanding the Indian forces allied with the British in the War of 1812, was killed in battle with U. S. troops on the Thames River, in Ontario, Canada, in 1813. (See GREENVILLE, TREATY OF; TECUMSEH.)

After these reverses, the Ohio bands were reduced to three comparatively small reserves: Wapakoneta, Hog Creek, and Lewistown. These too were ceded to the United States, in 1831. The bands at Wapakoneta and Hog Creek left Ohio for the Shawnee reservation in Kansas. The Lewistown band, known as the Mixed Band of Seneca and Shawnee Indians, were assigned a tract of land in present Ottawa county, Okla., where they arrived late in 1832 after a long journey beset with difficulties. The Shawnees in Ottawa county have been called Eastern Shawnees since the "Omnibus Treaty" of 1867.

Citizens of Oklahoma since statehood was attained in 1907, most Shawnees have remained in that state, though some live among the Teton

Sioux in South Dakota. Some Indians of Shawnee descent have been noted among the Tuscarora in New York, descendants of an earlier migration.

Social Life. Shawnee villages on the western frontier were neat in appearance, with good log houses, fenced fields and orchards, and, in some cases, well-kept roads through the community. The tribal clan system was important in the different bands, and the tribal ceremonials, with their legends and lore, were observed. The people were known for their good sense, cheerful disposition, courage, and fine physique.

MURIEL H. WRIGHT, *Author of*
"A Guide to the Indian Tribes of Oklahoma"

Further Reading: Eggleston, Edward, and Seelye, Lillie Eggleston, *Tecumseh and the Shawnee Prophet* (1878); Foreman, Grant, *The Last Trek of the Indians* (Univ. of Chicago Press 1946); Josephy, Alvin M., *The Patriot Chiefs* (Viking 1961); Tucker, Glenn, *Tecumseh, Vision of Glory* (Bobbs 1956).

SHAYS, Daniel. See SHAYS' REBELLION.

SHAYS' REBELLION was an uprising, chiefly of farmers, in Massachusetts in 1786–1787. The revolt was the culmination of five years of restless dissatisfaction growing out of high taxes, heavy indebtedness, and declining farm prices. The legislature's repeal of the legal-tender status of paper money and its refusal to permit the offering of goods to satisfy debts meant that obligations had to be met with hard-to-obtain specie. Moreover, from excises the state paid 6% interest in specie on securities and promised redemption in full, although speculators had bought them at a fraction of their face value. Those who could not pay their debts faced trial by an inefficient and expensive court system. They saw their possessions auctioned to satisfy their creditors or were jailed for failure to pay even small sums.

Insurrection. Disaffection was widespread. Assembling in conventions in five counties in the summer of 1786, the people listed their demands for relief, also calling for amendment of the state constitution to reduce the costs of government. Mobs prevented the county courts and the Springfield session of the Massachusetts supreme court from conducting business. A hastily summoned legislature passed a tender-law, but did little else to adjust grievances.

Unappeased, insurgents, comprising perhaps one fifth of the people of several counties, took up arms and organized regiments, one of them captained by Daniel Shays, a former Revolutionary War officer who was blamed by some for the entire insurrection. Shays failed in an attempt to seize the federal arsenal at Springfield when his men quailed before a round or two of artillery fire on Jan. 25, 1787. Several other skirmishes took place in Hampshire county and in neighboring Berkshire county. Except for sporadic raids made over the state borders by dispersed insurgents, the fighting ended when the militia under Maj. Gen. Benjamin Lincoln routed Shays' forces at Petersham on Feb. 4, 1787.

Aftermath. When the legislature met again, it took repressive measures and assumed all the costs of the army raised by Gov. James Bowdoin and financed by private contributions. While significantly reducing court fees, it continued to pay interest on securities from excises and refused to issue paper money. In the spring election, the voters elected John Hancock governor. The new legislature, sympathetic to the rebels, reduced the poll and estate taxes and ended the indefinite jailing of debtors, but could accomplish little else that the Shaysites wanted.

Shays and 13 other leaders were condemned to death, but all were ultimately pardoned—Shays on June 13, 1788.

Shays' Rebellion increased class consciousness in Massachusetts and stirred up unrest in neighboring states. The demand for a stronger national government was sharpened as Congress, under the Articles of Confederation, had been unable to aid the state in suppressing the insurgents.

ROBERT J. TAYLOR, *Tufts University*

Further Reading: Taylor, Robert J., *Western Massachusetts in the Revolution* (Brown Univ. Press 1954).

SHCHEDRIN, Nikolai Evgrafovich. See SALTYKOV, MIKHAIL EVGRAFOVICH.

SHCHERBAKOV. See RYBINSK.

SHE STOOPS TO CONQUER is a comedy by Oliver Goldsmith, first presented at Covent Garden Theatre, London, in 1773. Its central feature, the mistaking of a gentleman's house for an inn, was undoubtedly an episode in Goldsmith's youthful career.

Goldsmith brilliantly evokes the atmosphere of a country house and rural life. At the same time he provides convincing portraits of the London characters. Their city manners are crossed with the forthrightness of nature. Raillery and repartee dwindle in importance before character and atmosphere. Squire Hardcastle is drawn without a stroke of overelaboration. Less sportive than his stepson, Tony Lumpkin, he digs as deeply into the memory. Tony and Mrs. Hardcastle are both unforgettable comic figures. The Hardcastles' delightful daughter, Kate, is as much a product of observation as Mrs. Millamant of Congreve's *The Way of the World* is a product of thought, and Maria of Sheridan's *The School for Scandal* is a product of the stage.

The refinements of sentimental comedy, which ruled the stage in Goldsmith's time, were repugnant to him as an instinctive artist. Before his playwrighting days, he had ridiculed "genteel comedy," and in the "low" passages of his first play, *The Good Natur'd Man* (1768), he had resolutely entered the lists against it. *She Stoops to Conquer* was his second and more successful play. Less artificial than the comedy of manners, the general class to which it belongs, it has in it more of Fielding's concern for fidelity to human nature than of Congreve's preoccupation with brilliance of wit and style.

SHEAR is the distortion of a solid resulting from applied forces that cause planes of the solid to slide relative to each other like cards in a pack. The applied forces, or shearing forces, act parallel to a plane, whereas tensile forces and compressive forces act perpendicular to a plane. As an example, shearing forces along two metal plates joined by a rivet tend to separate the rivet into two parts, with the planes of separation parallel to the direction of the applied forces. The shearing stress set up in a solid is the applied force divided by the area of the surface over which it acts. The shearing strain, which accompanies shearing stress, is the displacement of one plane of the solid relative to a parallel plane divided by the distance between the two planes. See also STRENGTH OF MATERIALS.

CULVER PICTURES

NORMA SHEARER, American film beauty, as she appeared in the title role of *Marie Antoinette* (1938)

SHEARER, Norma (1900–   ), American motion picture actress, known especially for her roles in films of the 1930's adapted from successful stage plays. She was born in Montreal, Canada, on Aug. 4, 1900, and was educated in the public schools of that city. She went to the United States in 1919 and became a naturalized citizen in 1931. In 1928 she was married to the Metro-Goldwyn-Mayer executive Irving Thalberg, who died in 1936. She began her film career in small parts in 1920 and first gained recognition for her role in the silent-film version of *He Who Gets Slapped* (1924), in which she appeared with Lon Chaney and John Gilbert. Among her first talking pictures was *The Last of Mrs. Cheney* (1929). In 1930 she won the Academy Award for her role in *The Divorcée*. Her best-known films after that date include *Strangers May Kiss* and *Private Lives* (both 1931); *Smilin' Through* and *Strange Interlude* (both 1932); *The Barretts of Wimpole Street* (1934); *Romeo and Juliet* (1936), an elaborate production planned for her by Thalberg; *Marie Antoinette* (1938); *The Women* (1939); *Idiot's Delight* (1939); and *We Were Dancing* (1942).

SHEARING, George Albert (1920–   ), Anglo-American jazz pianist and composer. He was born in London on Aug. 13, 1920. Blind from birth, he attended schools for the blind. He began his career as a pianist playing in various nightclubs, and he made his first recording in 1937. He then played with several British bands as soloist, and seven times, from 1941 to 1947, he won the Melody Maker award as top British pianist. In 1947, Shearing moved to the United States, becoming a citizen in 1956. There he played in clubs and with several groups, notably a five-man combo that included Margie Hyams (vibes), Chuck Wayne (guitar), Denzil Best (drums), and John Levy (bass).

Shearing, who has a so-called locked-hands piano style combined with vibes and guitar, wrote a number of successful songs. The best known is *Lullaby of Birdland* (1952).

SHEARS. See SCISSORS AND SHEARS.

SHEARWATER, any of several web-footed oceanic birds closely related to fulmars and petrels. Shearwaters are found over all the oceans, often coming to land only to nest. They are 12 to 25 inches (30–63 cm) long and have a wide wingspan. Their upper bills are sharply hooked and the lower bills have sharp downward hooks. Paired tubes run along the ridge of the upper bill carrying oxygen to the lungs. Rather somber in color, shearwaters are generally gray, black, or brown above and whitish below. They are highly migratory and are excellent fliers. In flight they flap and glide over the water, just skimming the surface and feeding on small aquatic animals they find close to the surface. The migratory abilities of the Manx shearwater (*Puffinus puffinus*) have been studied extensively and it is thought that the bird is able to use celestial bodies to navigate and find its home, even when thousands of miles away.

At breeding time, shearwaters often gather in large colonies. A typical nest is a cavity drilled in turf. Both parents incubate the single white egg for about seven weeks and care for the downy young, who remains in the nest for ten to 12 weeks and then plunges into the sea.

Shearwaters are classified in the family Procellaridae of the order Procellariiformes.

ERIC HOSKING, FROM NATIONAL AUDUBON SOCIETY

Manx shearwater (*Procellaria puffinus*)

SHEATHBILL, a pigeon-sized white bird found in the colder parts of the Southern Hemisphere, inhabiting remote snow- and ice-covered islands and shoreline of Antarctica. The two species— the white sheathbill (*Chionia alba*) and the lesser sheathbill (*C. minor*)—make up the family Chionididae of the order Charadriiformes. The sheathbill has a saddle-shaped horny sheath over the base of its short, stout bill, thornlike spurs on the bend of each rather long wing, a short tail, and short legs with slightly webbed feet. Sheathbills are strong fliers but spend most of their time on shore, eating seaweed and small crustaceans. They lay two or three white eggs blotched with brown or black in a nest hidden in a rock crevice or natural burrow. Both parents incubate the eggs and care for the young.

SHEBA, shē'bə, was a region in southern Arabia, the exact location of which is uncertain. Its people are known to have carried on extensive trade in biblical times. The Queen of Sheba is mentioned in the Old Testament as visiting King Solomon (reigned 962–922 B.C.) at Jerusalem "to test him with hard questions" (I Kings 10:2). The questions probably were riddles commonly used in Arab polite conversation. Most likely, her mission was for the purposes of trade, and the gifts exchanged were intended as a means of opening up trade relations.

Later Arab tradition contains many tales of the fabulous queen who married Solomon. The biblical account mentions nothing about a marriage, but states simply that she returned to her own land. Sabaeans apparently also dwelt in northwestern Arabia. They are mentioned in the records of the Assyrian king Tiglath-pileser IV in the 8th century B.C. The Abyssinians adopted some of the Arab tales and trace the lineage of their royal house to the Queen of Sheba.

SHEBOYGAN, she-boi'gən, a city in eastern Wisconsin, the seat of Sheboygan county, is situated on the western shore of Lake Michigan at the mouth of the Sheboygan River, 57 miles (91 km) north of Milwaukee. It is an industrial and port city on the edge of a rich dairy region. Sheboygan is noted for its sausages and cheeses, and is one of the largest exporters of cheese in the nation. Manufactured products include plastics, clothing, mirror plate, stainless steel, and leather goods.

The city's museums include the Sheboygan County Historical Society and the John Michael Kohler Arts Center. Sheboygan Indian Mound Park contains a group of Indian effigy burial mounds in the shapes of panthers and deer. The mound group, which date from between 500 and 750 A.D., is one of the few still intact.

The Sheboygan area was the site of a trading post in 1820 and of a sawmill in 1835. In 1836 prospectors built 20 frame buildings on the site, but these were torn down the following year. In 1838 traders began to come into the area and some farmers settled here. A town grew up, which became a convenient place for settlers to disembark and a winter home for lake sailors. The settlement was incorporated as a village in 1846. In the next few years immigrants flocked into Sheboygan, greatly increasing its population, and it was chartered as a city in 1853. Sheboygan is governed by a mayor and council. Population: 48,085.

SHECHEM, shē'kəm, was an ancient Canaanite city important in the patriarchal period and in later Jewish history. Modern archaeological investigations have identified Tell Balatah, 1.5 miles (2.4 km) east of Nablus and 40 miles (64 km) north of Jerusalem. The evidence indicates that it was inhabited as early as 4000 B.C. According to Genesis 12:6 and 33:18, both Abraham and Jacob visited it. After the conquest of Canaan, Joshua held a meeting of the Israelite tribes there (Joshua 24:1).

SHEEAN, shē'ən, **Vincent** (1899–1975), American writer. James Vincent Sheean was born in Pana, Ill., on Dec. 5, 1899, and studied at the University of Chicago. After working as a reporter for the New York *Daily News* and the Paris edition of the Chicago *Tribune*, he left regular employment as a journalist in 1925 but later accepted periodic assignments as a foreign correspondent. In World War II he served as an intelligence officer in the U.S. Army Air Force.

Although Sheean wrote fiction, he was more successful in his autobiographical, reportorial, and biographical works. *Personal History* (1935), relating his experiences in the 1920's, is a classic of first-person journalism and stimulated a host of imitators. *Not Peace But a Sword* (1939) concerns the Spanish Civil War and the origins of World War II. His biographies include *Lead, Kindly Light* (1949), about Gandhi; *Orpheus at Eighty* (1958), about Verdi; and *Dorothy and Red* (1963), about Dorothy Thompson and Sinclair Lewis. He died in Arcolo, Italy, on March 15, 1975.

SHEELER, Charles (1883–1965), American painter and photographer. He was born in Philadelphia, Pa., on July 16, 1883. He studied in Philadelphia at the School of Industrial Art from 1900 to 1903 and at the Pennsylvania Academy of Fine Arts from 1903 to 1906.

Sheeler visited Europe in 1904, 1905, and 1909, where he was influenced by modern art trends, particularly cubism, and he exhibited six paintings at the controversial Armory Show in New York in 1913. From 1912 on, he also worked in photography, ranging from fashion studies for *Vogue* magazine to an extensive survey of the Ford River Rouge plant in 1927. In 1920 he made an art film, *Mannahatta.*

One of the first American painters to exploit industrial forms, as in *American Landscape, 1930,* Sheeler has been grouped with a movement variously called the precisionists, the cubist-realists, and the immaculates. Sheeler's paintings resemble both photographs in realistic detail and abstract art in emphasis on geometric forms. He died in Dobbs Ferry, N.Y., on May 7, 1965.

Further Reading: Rourke, Constance, *Charles Sheeler, Artist in the American Tradition* (1938; reprint, Da Capo Press, Inc. 1969).

SHEEN, Fulton John (1895–1979), American Roman Catholic archbishop known for his radio and television sermons. Sheen was born in El Paso, Ill., on May 8, 1895. After graduation from St. Victor College in Bourbonnais, Ill., in 1917, he studied at St. Paul's Seminary, St. Paul, Minn., and was ordained a priest on Sept. 20, 1919. He acquired graduate degrees in philosophy from the Catholic University of America (1920) and the University of Louvain, Belgium (1923), and in theology from the Collegio Angelico in Rome (1924). He served as curate at St. Patrick's Church in Peoria, Ill., before beginning more than a quarter century of teaching the philosophy of religion at the Catholic University in 1926. On Nov. 1, 1950, he became national director of the Society for the Propagation of the Faith. On June 11, 1951, he was consecrated titular bishop of Caesariana and auxiliary bishop of New York. He was named bishop of Rochester, N.Y., in 1966, and titular archbishop of Newport, Wales, in 1969. He died in New York City, Dec. 9, 1979.

Bishop Sheen became a well-known television personality in the early 1950's through his program *Life Is Worth Living.* He had previously regularly been heard on *The Catholic Hour* on radio. He is the author of some 50 books, including *Life Is Worth Living* (1953) and *That Tremendous Lover* (1967).

The grasslands of eastern Colorado provide excellent conditions for the raising of sheep.

SHEEP, a group of cud-chewing, ruminant animals, closely related to goats, making up the genus *Ovis* of the cattle family, Bovidae. The term is applied most commonly to the demesticated varieties of sheep, *Ovis aries,* with which this article is concerned. There are also four main species of wild sheep found in mountainous regions of the Northern Hemisphere. For information on wild sheep, see separate articles on ARGALI; BIGHORN; MOUFLON; MOUNTAIN SHEEP; URIAL.

Sheep are distinguished from goats by several characteristics, including a generally stockier body, the presence of scent glands in the face and hind feet, and the absence of beards in males. See also GOAT.

With their small size, ease of handling, and ability to produce a wide variety of useful products such as fiber, hides, milk, and meat, as well as to serve as work animals, sheep were natural subjects for domestication by man. A large number of different types and breeds were developed over the centuries, in part as a result of isolation and in part as a result of adaptation to different kinds of climates and geographical conditions. Practically all breeds of sheep have been used for meat, while particular breeds are specialized producers of milk, wool, or fur. The use of sheep for meat, in particular, is becoming an increasingly important aspect of sheep breeding.

Domestication of Sheep. Sheep were among the very first animals to be domesticated, perhaps more than 8,000 years ago. The wild forms from which the domesticated varieties came were distributed at that time over a great arc of both mountainous and plains country in the Northern Hemisphere, and the present restriction of wild sheep to mountainous areas may represent a retreat before the advance of civilization. Although the earliest domestication most likely occurred in western Asia, present types of sheep appear to have traces of the Mediterranean mouflon as well as the Asian urial and argali.

By historical times, fleece sheep and fat-tailed sheep began to appear, as well as the more primitive wool varieties that resembled wild forms. The domestication of these animals permitted man to maintain a supply of high-quality protein food, and perhaps for the first time in his existence he obtained an adequate supply of fat in his diet. Since this new food supply was easily herded and moved, primitive societies were able to migrate more easily. Extensive pastoral nomadism in turn permitted the settlement of marginal grasslands, and the migration of the animals could be made to coincide with seasonal supplies of forage. In addition, wool processing was one of the first arts to be developed by man, and there is evidence of the use of wool in fabrics as early as 4000 B. C. Thus the domestication of sheep contributed in many ways to the development of civilization.

CHARACTERISTICS

The male sheep is called a *ram,* or *buck;* the female, a *ewe;* and the castrated male, a *wether.* Young sheep from birth to the age of 12 months are known as *lambs,* and from 12 to 24 months as *yearlings.* Sheep meat is called lamb or mutton according to the age of the animal at time of slaughter. This is usually determined by the break joint, a temporary cartilage just above the ankle. Carcasses and meat from lambs and some yearlings in which the forefeet are removed at this break joint are called lamb, and those from sheep in which the feet must be taken off at the ankle are called mutton.

General Description. Sheep are so variable in many characteristics that exact definition is difficult. There are tremendous differences in horns, face, ears, head, body, tail, color, and covering of hair and wool. The horns, if present, tend to grow backward and downward and then to curve forward in a spiral. They are covered by slight transverse elevations. Depending on the breed, horns may be present in rams only or in both sexes, or absent in both sexes. The muzzle is generally narrow and thin and is divided by a central cleft. The lips have great flexibility, enabling the sheep to graze selectively and close to the ground. In a majority of breeds suborbital glands open in the skin below the eyes, and a glandular pouch is found between the toes. Wattles may be present on the neck. Many domestic breeds have long tails, while wild types have short · tails, and some breeds have large, broad tails composed largely of fat.

The size and form of the sheep's body are determined by the skeleton and by the extent of muscling and fat deposition. The backbone normally consists of 7 cervical, 13 thoracic, 6 or 7 lumbar, 4 sacral (fused), and from 4 or 5 to more than 20 coccygeal vertebrae. There are usually 13 pairs of ribs, including 8 pairs attached directly to the breastbone, 4 pairs with cartilaginous extensions that join to attach to the breastbone, and 1 pair of floating ribs. The thoracic and lumbar vertebrae have vertical and transverse extensions which influence the shape and width of the back. There is great variability in the size and length of the leg bones. The front legs have no bony connection with the body, the shoulder blades being attached by muscles. The weight of a mature sheep may vary from about 80 to 400 pounds (36–180 kg), although weights in the lower parts of this range are commonest. Typical dimensions for ewes include a length of 44 inches (110 cm) from head to tail, a width of 12 inches (30 cm) in the middle, and a height of 26 inches (66 cm) at the shoulder. Again, however, breeds vary greatly in size.

The sheep has 20 temporary or lamb teeth and 32 permanent teeth, with 8 incisors in each case. Instead of teeth in the front of the upper jaw, there is a cartilaginous pad. Herbage is pressed between the incisors and the pad is torn loose by jerking the head. Age is indicated by the replacement of the lamb incisor teeth with larger permanent teeth. The central pair of incisors is generally replaced after one year, and successive pairs annually thereafter. After a sheep is four years old, the spread, wear, and loss of incisor teeth may be used to estimate age.

Like other ruminants, the sheep has a stomach with four compartments, adapted to regurgitation and cud chewing. The esophagus leads to the rumen or largest compartment, where food is stored prior to regurgitation for further chewing. The reticulum, with its honeycomb appearance, is a continuation of the rumen, and food also enters this portion prior to regurgitation. When the food is swallowed for the second time, it passes into the third stomach, the omasum, which has lengthwise leaves and connects directly with the abomasum, or true stomach.

Wool fiber is characteristically produced by most sheep, but some breeds have only short hair, and others, particularly primitive types, have a mixture of a hairy outer coat with wool. The color is normally white, although black and various shadings or spottings of black, brown, or red may occur. The sheep's skin, which is only about 0.08 inch (0.2 cm) thick, may also be pigmented. The skin contains sweat glands, sebaceous or oily glands, and the follicles from which hair and wool fibers grow, often arranged in a typical pattern. Primary follicles develop early in prenatal life, and each is associated with a sweat gland, an oily gland, and a smooth muscle. They usually occur in groups of three along with a variable number of secondary follicles. The latter develop late in fetal life and have only an oily gland. In different breeds the number of fibers may vary from less than 5,000 to over 60,000 per square inch (800–9,000 per sq cm), and variations within breeds and individuals also are large.

Life Cycle. Sheep mature at one to two years of age, but may not reach maximum productivity until they are three to five years old. Generally they do not live beyond the seventh to tenth year, but survival to 20 years has been reported.

A high proportion of sheep will breed at about 19 months of age. Rams often mature earlier than ewes. Up to four or five years, reproductive functions may improve with age. In temperate climates ewes normally breed only in the fall and early winter months, but the breeding season may extend over the entire year. Estrual, or heat, periods average 30 hours, but they may last up to several days. They generally recur at 17-day intervals. Ovulation normally takes place late in the heat period. The duration of pregnancy is almost five months, varying from 141 to 159 days.

Birth weights may vary from 4 to 18 pounds (1.8–8 kg), but average weights normally range from 8 to 10 pounds (3.6–4.5 kg). Ram lambs average heavier than ewe lambs, and singles heavier than twins. Generally the majority of lambs are born as singles, but twins are frequent, triplets are common, and multiple births of five or more have been reported. Since most ewes have only two functional teats, usually not more than two lambs are raised by the mother. Milk production may vary from less than one to more than four quarts, or liters, per day, gradually declining after the first few weeks. Lambs generally suckle for three to five months, but they begin to eat other food within a few weeks.

Habits. Sheep are typically timid and defenseless, tending to follow the leader and to flock together. They are sometimes thought to be stupid, but some mental abilities, such as their weather sense, are well developed. Some breeds are less gregarious than others and graze in small groups or even individually. Although sheep will graze on low ground, they like to graze uphill. Grazing occupies about half their time and commences in the early morning. They may lie down through the middle of the day and then resume grazing in the afternoon. At night they usually bed down or sleep on high ground. In bad weather they seek shelter, and in hot weather readily hunt shade. They prefer dry conditions and are vulnerable to cold or rain after shearing.

Sheep cannot protect themselves from predatory animals such as coyotes and dogs. Although

Australian Merino ram

Suffolk ram

Corriedale ewe and lambs

SHEEP BREEDS

Most sheep breeds are developed as wool or meat producers, although some have been selected for milk production, and a few are raised for their pelts. The Australian merino is one of the best fine-wool breeds, and the Romney marsh is a fine long-wool breed. The Hampshire and Suffolk are important meat breeds, and the Corriedale yields both meat and wool. The Karakul yields fur pelts.

they are wary and run when frightened, under domestication they are easy prey. Moreover, frightened sheep may pile up against obstructions and smother.

BREEDS OF SHEEP

There are more breeds, types, and varieties of sheep than of any other species of livestock. Many of the 952 breeds listed by some authorities are actually subbreeds or closely related breeds and types, but about a third of them are true, well-recognized breeds. Over 400 breeds have sufficient information available to permit their classification according to distinctive productive traits.

Wool is the most obvious characteristic on which to classify breeds of sheep. Fine-wool breeds generally are specialized for wool production and not well developed for meat. Highly specialized meat breeds tend to have medium or long wool, but some crossbreeds developed to produce dual-purpose sheep excel over other breeds in both wool and meat production. More specialized breeds are used for milk or fur. "Hair" breeds of sheep, which produce little or no wool or frequently shed their wool, are kept for meat alone. The somewhat primitive breeds have a coarse, mixed type of wool that is used for carpets.

Fine-Wool Breeds. About 10% of the classified breeds produce fine wool. These fine-wool breeds

in almost all cases are varieties of the Merino breed, of Spanish origin. Fineness varies from the superfine-wool Tasmanian Merino to the South Australian strong-wool Merino. The Rambouillet of the United States is well developed for meat production, as is the Mutton Merino of Germany. Types descended from or similar to the Australian Merino are found all over the world and generally produce the most valued white wool.

Fine-wool breeds tend to be relatively small in size in relation to fleece weight. They are angular in form and have a somewhat less developed meat conformation than other types of sheep, and the skin has a tendency to fold. The legs and sometimes the faces are covered with wool. Polled, or hornless, varieties occur, but horns in the male and horn knobs in the female are common. The fine-wool breeds also generally have long, thin tails. Reproductive rates tend to be low, but the breeding season is long, and some will breed at any time of the year. Gestation periods are quite long, averaging about 150 to 152 days. The sheep generally are slow in maturing but live long and are quite hardy. The fine-wool breeds thrive in a dry, warm climate.

Medium-Wool Breeds. Medium-wool breeds are noted for meat production, whereas their wool production is often minor and the fleece weight low. About 20% of all the breeds are in this group. The most common mutton-ram breeds in

Karakul ram

Romney marsh ram

Hampshire yearling ewe

Lincoln long-wool

the United States, the Hampshire and Suffolk, are typical of medium-wool types. Other medium-wool, meat-type breeds of British origin include the Cheviot, Clun Forest, Dorset Down, Dorset Horn, North Country Cheviot, Oxford, Ryeland, Shropshire, and Southdown. Medium-wool breeds in France include the Alpine, Cher Barrichon, Bluefaced Maine, Lot Causses, Central Pyrenean, Charmoise, French Alpine, Île-de-France, Limousin, Lourdes, Prealpes du Sud, Roussillon Red, Sologne, and Tarascon. Some other medium-wool breeds include the German Whiteheaded Mutton, German Blackheaded Mutton, Latvian and Lithuanian Blackheaded Mutton, Rygja of Norway, Serrai of Greece, and Tsigai of the Soviet Union and some border countries.

Medium-wool breeds vary tremendously in size: from the Southdown, with mature ewe weights of 90 to 180 pounds (40–80 kg), to the Suffolk, with corresponding weights of 150 to 260 pounds (68–118 kg). All are white, but some breeds have black or brownish faces and legs and possibly some black wool fibers. They mature early, and ewes can often be bred as lambs but are somewhat short-lived. Reproductive rates are medium to high, and the breeding season is medium to short in length. An exception is the Dorset Horn, which breeds in the spring as well as in the fall. Gestation periods are quite short, ranging from 142 to 146 days. Meat conformation is

generally excellent in this group, being thick and blocky, and an even covering of fat is likely.

Long-Wool Breeds. Long-wool breeds are noted for heavy fleeces. They are also noted for meat production and tend to be quite large in size. Only 16 breeds are classified as long-wool, and many of them originated in Britain. Best known from Britain are the Border Leicester, English Leicester, Lincoln, and Romney Marsh. Others include the Avranchin and Cotentin of France, Galway and Roscommon of Ireland, and Texel of the Netherlands.

The breeds vary in size of mature ewes from 118 to 200 pounds (54–91 kg) for Romney Marsh to 174 to 279 pounds (79–127 kg) for Border Leicester. Almost all are polled in both sexes, with the exception of horned males in the Whitefaced Dartmoor. All are white. As the group name indicates, the coarse wool fibers are long, varying from 5 to 16 inches (13–40 cm). Fleece weights range from about 6.6 to 20 pounds (3–9 kg). The sheep require ample feed conditions and thrive in medium to cool, humid climates. Lambing rates are generally high, but range from 105% to 145% for the Romney Marsh to 180% to 210% for the Avranchin.

Crossbreeds. Crossbred, dual-purpose types of sheep generally originated in the 20th century. Most are crosses of long-wool with fine-wool or medium-wool breeds. The 16 breeds classified in this group are medium to large in size. Their excellent white fleeces and good meat conformation lead to their superiority as ewe breeds to cross with mutton rams for market lambs. Best known are the Columbia, Montadale and Targhee of the United States, Corriedale and Perendale of New Zealand, and Polwarth of Australia. In western range areas of the United States, wool-type ewes are crossed with mutton rams such as the Suffolk or Hampshire Down. The blackface cross lambs may all be sold for slaughter, or ewe lambs may be shipped to farm areas to be crossed with other mutton breeds. Crosses among wool breeds are sometimes used to produce replacement range ewes.

Crossbreeds vary in size of mature ewes from 100 to 120 pounds (45–55 kg) for the Georgian and Polwarth to 130 to 224 pounds (59–102 kg) for the Columbia. Almost all are polled, except for some males in the Polwarth and Precoce breeds that are horned. The fiber lengths are medium, varying from 2.3 to 6 inches (6–15 cm). Fiber diameters are also medium but quite variable, while fleece weights are relatively heavy, ranging from 5.9 to 18 pounds (2.7–8.2 kg). Lambing rates are quite favorable, ranging up to 175%, and gestation lengths are somewhat intermediate, averaging about 147 to 149 days. The breeds do well over a wide range of feed and climatic conditions but are probably best suited to temperate climates.

Coarse-Wool Breeds. Carpet-wool, or coarse-wool, breeds of sheep are characterized not only by their wool but also by their great variability. They are frequent in the desert areas of Africa and the Middle and Far East, but they are also found in the cold humid regions of Iceland, Scotland, and northern Europe. All colors are represented. The sheep often have fat tails and fat rumps, but some breeds have short tails, and others have long, thin tails. They are generally small to medium in size. Lambing rates are fairly low.

Over 160 breeds have been classified in the coarse-wool group, although many of them are also used for milk or pelts, and all are used for meat. Only a few representative breeds can be listed here. These include the Navajo of the United States; Scottish Blackface types of Britain; Bordaleiro of Portugal; Churro and Segura of Spain; Thônes-Marthod of France; Valais Blacknose of Switzerland; Bergamo, Campanian Barbary, Sicilian Barbary, Lamon, and Varese of Italy; Dalmatian-Karst, Ovče Polje, Pirot, Piva, Sjenica, Solčava, and Zeta Yellow of Yugoslavia; Chios of Greece; Karayaka, Kivircik, and Daglic of Turkey; Arabi and Awassi of the Middle East; Doukkala, Tadla, and Zemmour of Morocco; Beni Guil, Berber, and Tunisian Barbary of North Africa; Macina of West Africa; and Ausimi and Barki of Egypt. Soviet coarse-wool breeds include the Balbas, Hissar, Kazakh Fat-rumped, Dagestan Mountain, Romanov, Saraja, and Voloshian. Indian coarse-wool breeds include the Bellary, Bhakarwal, Bikaneri, Hassan, Jalauni, Deccani, and Gurez. Those from Pakistan are the Bibrik, Kaghani, Kuka, Lohi, Rakhshani, and Thal, while such breeds from China include the Han-yang, Hu-yang, Kuche, Mongolian, Tan-Yang, Tibetan, and Tung-yang. Some breeds can be located by their names, such as the Algerian Arab, Cyprus Fat-tailed, Common Albanian, German Heath, Icelandic, Old Norwegian, Polish Heath, and Swedish Landrace.

Dairy Breeds. Fifty breeds of sheep have been classified as milk or dairy breeds. They tend to be medium in size, with angular bodies, and they are sometimes quite prolific. Some have lop ears. They are common in Mediterranean countries. Italy in particular has the greatest number of milk breeds, including the Altamura, Calabrian, Langhe, Lecce, Sardinian, and Sicilian. Other breeds include the Basque-Béarn and Lacaune of France, East Friesian of Germany, Lacho and Mancha of Spain, Racka of Hungary, Karnobat and Svishtov of Bulgaria, Istrian Milk and Valachian of Yugoslavia, Greek Zackel and Mytilene of Greece, and Damani of Pakistan.

Fur and Hair Breeds. Only a few breeds are kept for fur pelts, which are sometimes known as persian lamb since the pelts are taken from new-born lambs. All of these are found in the Soviet Union as well as in some other countries. Included are the Karakul and Malich, which have fat tails, and the Chushka, Reshetilovka, and Sokolka.

About 20 breeds are classified as hair breeds, although some short wool fibers may also be present. Their colors are quite variable. The breeds are kept primarily for meat and are adapted to the warm, humid tropics and subtropics. The Barbados is kept for hunting in Texas. Many are found in Africa, but some are present in the West Indies, South America, and the Middle and Far East. All are quite small, ranging from 50 to 155 pounds (20–70 kg) for mature ewe weights. Some of them breed the year round, but lambing rates are generally low.

Representative hair breeds include the Abyssinian of Ethiopia; Congo Long-legged; Madagascar, Masai, Somali, Sudanese, and Tanganyika Long-tailed of East Africa; Fulani, Tuareg, and West African Dwarf of West Africa; Blackheaded Persian, Dorper, Namaqua, and Ronderib Africander of South Africa; Mandya and Nellore of India; Jaffna of Ceylon; and Hejazi of the Middle East.

SHEEP RAISING

Sheep are widely distributed over the world, although they are kept mainly in temperate climates, most being found between the latitudes of 20° and 60° in both the Northern and Southern hemispheres. They are particularly adapted to desert and semiarid areas and to mountainous regions. The world's sheep population is roughly about a billion head. The principal sheep-raising nations, in order of importance are: Australia, the Soviet Union, New Zealand, Argentina, India, Republic of South Africa, Turkey, United States, Uruguay, United Kingdom, Brazil, Iran, and Spain. In the United States the vast majority of the sheep herds are located in the central and western parts of the country, almost equally divided between both areas. The leading states are Texas, Wyoming, California, Montana, South Dakota, Utah, Colorado, New Mexico, Idaho, Iowa, Ohio, Oregon, Minnesota, and Arizona.

Products. When sheep are kept mainly for the production of lamb meat, lambs are slaughtered at the age of 4 to over 12 months. Live weights run from 65 to over 100 pounds (30–45 kg) and carcass weights from 25 to 50 pounds (11–22 kg). Some lambs are slaughtered directly after weaning, while others are fed one to three months longer, usually on good pasture or on a ration high in concentrates. High-quality carcasses are plump and blocky, with the fat evenly distributed over most of the surface and liberally intermixed with the lean. Valuable cuts include loin and rib chops and leg of lamb.

Wool is an important source of income in many sheep-raising countries. Fleece weights range from 4 to 15 pounds (2–7 kg), or more, averaging slightly over 8 pounds (3.6 kg). Under exceptional feed conditions, rams may shear up to 35 pounds (16 kg). Wool is valued and graded according to fineness, length, and variability of clean wool, and freedom from foreign matter. Fine and medium wools are used largely for apparel fabrics and blankets, while longer, coarser wools are used mainly for rugs and carpets. See also WOOL.

In some European and Middle Eastern countries sheep are used for milk production as well as for meat and wool. Ewe milk has a higher fat content than cow's milk, averaging about 6%. Such milking breeds as the East Friesian may yield up to 130 gallons (490 liters) annually. Sheep are also valued in some areas for their manure. Sheepskins are used for a variety of lightweight leathers, and pelts may be tanned with the wool on for coats, robes, rugs, and slippers. Fur pelts are obtained from young Karakul lambs. See also LEATHER.

Methods of Production. In the western range areas of the United States, as a representative sheep-raising nation, an economic sheep-production unit usually includes several thousand head. In the warmer sections the sheep are kept in fenced pastures, but in the colder and more mountainous areas they are generally herded in bands of 1,000 to 2,500. Under the herding system sheep migrate considerable distances each year, being herded on ranges of intermediate elevation in the spring and fall, on the high mountain ranges in the summer, and on lower areas in winter. Supplemental feed is generally supplied on winter ranges, and in some areas sheep are fed hay for 100 days or more during the winter. Breeding usually occurs on the fall or winter ranges, and lambing on the winter feedlots or on the spring range. Shearing takes place in the spring either before or after lambing. Lambs are usually weaned and marketed for slaughter on leaving the summer ranges.

Farm sheep raising is carried on with diversified operations. Farm flocks are usually small, numbering 25 to 100 and rarely more than 500. Production methods vary considerably. The flocks may be kept on permanent or temporary pastures, but often they are used to keep down weeds and to consume waste roughages. Silage is frequently fed along with hay in the winter months.

Nutritive Requirements. Roughages make up about 95% of the feed requirements of sheep, and they supply most of the energy needs. The ration should contain 10% to 15% protein, the best source being leguminous plants. In some areas minerals such as calcium, phosphorus, iodine, copper, and cobalt must be supplied. Although sheep may do well without salt, they normally consume about 1 pound (0.45 kg) per month. It is not certain whether all vitamins are required by sheep. Vitamins D and E are generally available from natural sources, and vitamin C and the B complex are synthesized. Vitamin A is the most likely to be deficient, but ample amounts of the vitamin are usually supplied by green pasture, hay, or silage.

Sheep prefer short, fine forages, but they will consume a wide variety of grasses, legumes, weeds, herbs, and shrubs. Although legume hays are preferable, grass hays, corn or sorghum fodder, cereal hays, and straws are often fed. Nonleguminous hays may require protein and mineral supplements. Silages made from corn, sorghum, cereals, grasses, and other plants are satisfactory to replace part of the hay ration. Concentrates are fed sparingly to sheep. Common farm grains fed to sheep include oats, corn, barley, wheat, rye, and sorghum. Common protein supplements include the cake or oil meal made from soybeans, flaxseed, or cottonseed.

Sheep can exist for long periods with little or no water, but they do better if it is available. Depending on the weather and feed, from 1 to 8 quarts, or liters, may be consumed daily.

CLAIR E. TERRILL
United States Department of Agriculture

Bibliography

Briggs, Hilton M., *Modern Breeds of Livestock*, 3d ed. (Macmillan 1969).

Ensminger, M. Eugene, *Sheep and Wool Science*, 3d ed. (Interstate 1964).

Hafez, E. Saad Elsayed, ed., *Reproduction in Farm Animals*, 2d ed. (Lea & Febiger 1969).

Hafez, E. Saad Elsayed, ed., *Adaptation of Domestic Animals* (Lea & Febiger 1968).

Isaac, Erich, *Geography of Domestication* (Prentice-Hall 1970).

Mason, Ian L., *A Dictionary of Livestock Breeds*, rev. (Commonwealth Bureau of Animal Breeding and Genetics, Edinburgh 1969).

Von Bergen, Werner, ed., *Wool Handbook*, vol. 1 (Interscience 1963).

Zeuner, Frederick E., *A History of Domesticated Animals* (Harper 1963).

Wool fleeces are sheared with electrically powered clippers. An expert can shear about 100 sheep per day.

GRANT HEILMAN

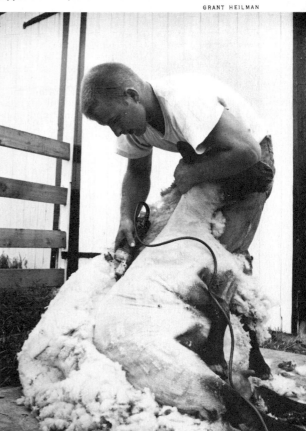

Sheepdogs such as the border collie shown here have been used for centuries by herders and drovers. A properly trained dog can take the place of several men.

WALTER CHANDOHA

SHEEP DOG, a working dog that is primarily bred to guard flocks of sheep. It is most often thought of as being chiefly bred from the Scotch border collie and used to shepherd flocks of sheep in Britain. But it is found in one guise or another in almost every country in the world. On Italy's Maremma plain, herding breeds of dog are produced primarily to guard sheep. In Germany the Alsatian or German shepherd dog has been bred to herd flocks of sheep, but elsewhere this breed of dog is more often used as a police dog, or as a "seeing-eye" dog for the blind.

The Scotch border collie is one of the most popular sheep dogs and has been outstanding in sheepherding trials since 1873. It is black, gray, or blue merle, with white spots, or black, white, and tan. Male dogs weigh up to 45 pounds (20 kg) and stand 18 inches (46 cm) at the shoulder. The skull is fairly broad, with a blunt muzzle; the coat is thick and rather long. The border collie has been exported all over the world, particularly to New Zealand and Australia, where two breeds have evolved: the kelpie, to herd sheep, and the Australian cattle dog, or heeler.

SHEEPSHEAD, a popular game and food fish (*Archosargus probatocephalus*) of the family Sparidae. Greenish in color with a laterally compressed body marked by seven vertical dark bands, it sometimes attains a length of 30 inches (76 cm) and a weight of 15 to 20 pounds (7–9 kg). It received its name from the resemblance of its teeth to those of a sheep. Sheepsheads are found along the Atlantic and Gulf coasts of North America from Cape Cod to Texas. They were once common in the region of New York but are no longer caught there. The sheepshead is most common in the vicinity of inlets. It is a bottom-dwelling species that feeds on crustaceans, mollusks, and plants. When numerous, sheepsheads sometimes prove destructive to oyster beds.

The sheepshead is a widely sought game fish, particularly in southern waters. It is fished for with strong lines and hooks baited with clam or soft-shelled crab, and it usually puts up a good fight before being landed.

The freshwater drumfish is also sometimes called sheepshead.

SHEFFIELD, shef'ēld, a city in northwestern Alabama, in Colbert county, is on the south bank of the Tennessee River, about 110 miles (176 km) northwest of Birmingham. Sheffield and the neighboring cities of Florence and Tuscambia form the center of the Muscle Shoals region of the Tennessee Valley Authority hydroelectric power development. Near Sheffield are several of the TVA dams, and the city's economic activities are largely associated with the TVA. The region has deposits of iron ore, limestone, phosphate, bauxite, rock asphalt, and clays.

Sheffield was founded in 1883 and was incorporated in 1885. It is governed by a commission. Population: 11,903.

SHEFFIELD, shef'ēld, a large industrial city in central England, is in the West Riding of Yorkshire, at the foot of the Pennines. It is on the Don River at its junction with four of its tributaries—the Sheaf, the Porter, the Rivelin, and the Loxley. It is about 160 miles (257 km) northwest of London, 40 miles (64 km) east of Manchester, and 50 miles (80 km) southwest of York. Sheffield is widely known for its plate and its cutlery.

Sheffield is one of the most important steel producing centers in Britain. The city's mills turn out every type of steel from armor plate and rails to rifle barrels and type. The cutlery and plating industries are also large. Smaller, but also important are snuff factories, confectionery works, food processing plants, iron and brass foundries, paper mills, and bookbinderies. Optical instruments, bicycles, chemicals and paints are also manufactured here.

Despite the heavy industry in Sheffield, there are many beautiful sections. The city lies in the rolling Pennine moors and is surrounded by heavily wooded dales. The suburbs are attractively built with many terraces and fine residences. Of particular interest in the city are the 12th century parish church and the Town Hall (built in 1897). The city museum has an extensive collection of cutlery and plate. Graves Art Gallery is also noteworthy. The University of Sheffield was founded in 1905.

Sheffield was a Roman station and was incorporated as a town in Anglo-Saxon times. In the first part of the 12th century, William de Lovetot, a Norman lord, built a castle and a parish church at the confluence of the Sheaf and the Don. Mary Stuart, Queen of Scots, was imprisoned at Sheffield Castle for 14 years.

The cutlery made at Sheffield was already well known in the 14th century. The local rivers were lined with water mills that gave the smiths power for grinding and forging. By 1700 the city had a monopoly on the English cutlery trade.

In 1740 a new type of hard steel was developed at Sheffield, and the city grew into the center of England's steel industry. In 1742, Thomas Boulsover, a local cutler, accidentally discovered how to plate copper with silver, and worked his discovery into a new industry, the Sheffield plate. (See SHEFFIELD PLATE.) Up until that time the town was small and insignificant. During the 19th century it grew rapidly, and by 1911 it was the largest city in Yorkshire. Population: (1971) of the city, 519,-703; of the metropolitan area, 730,000.

SHEFFIELD PLATE, shef'ēld, is metalware formed from a copper sheet to which a silver sheet has been soldered. In 1742 the cutler Thomas Boulsover in Sheffield, England, discovered that a thin sheet of silver could be soldered to a thicker sheet of copper and the two rolled out into a single sheet. He used his discovery to make buttons. About 1750 his apprentice, Joseph Hancock, applied the process to candlesticks, coffee pots, and other domestic wares. These Sheffield plate articles met the demands of the middle class, who were glad to replace their pewter with ware that looked like silver but was much less costly. Sheffield became the chief center of production, but Sheffield plate was also made in Birmingham by Matthew Bolton and others and in Scotland, Ireland, the Netherlands, Russia, and America. Parliament established hallmarks to distinguish it from sterling silver.

Although early Sheffield pieces were silvered on one side only, after 1765 both sides were silvered. To prevent the copper showing, the edges were at first soldered. Later, plated wire or sterling silver ornamentation in bands or gadroon or floral patterns was applied. Sterling silver inserts were made to permit engraving. The development of water- or steam-driven machinery for stamping, embossing, piercing, and other techniques made production cheaper than the hand process. Designs were generally copied from those of sterling silver, following the sequence of rococo-influenced Queen Anne and early Georgian, neoclassical late Georgian and Empire, and the ornate, florid Late style. Workmanship was of good quality. After about 1840, Sheffield plate was replaced by commercial electroplating. In the 20th century old Sheffield plate became a collector's item.

SHEIKH, shēk, is an Arabic word meaning "old man" and is used generally as a title of reverence. The word, also transliterated as *shaikh* and *shaykh*, has acquired a great variety of significations. Among the bedouins and other migratory tribes where patriarchal government prevails, the head of the tribe is called a sheikh. The superiors of Muslim religious and monastic orders are also called sheikhs. By extension, the term is applied to learned men and is used as a common title of courtesy.

SHEKEL, shek'əl, the ancient Hebrew measure of weight and, in later times, the unit of Israelite coins, usually of silver. The weight varied. In the postexilic period, the shekel weighed about 11.42 grams (0.403 ounce), and in 70 A.D. it weighed about 14.27 grams (0.5 ounce). The Israelites did not coin their own money until 110 B.C., when the shekel was made the unit of coinage. There were also half, quarter, and one-twentieth shekels.

SHELBURNE, shel'bərn, **Lord** (1737–1805), English prime minister. He inherited the earldom of Shelburne from his father. William Petty was born in Dublin, Ireland, on May 20, 1737. He entered Oxford University but two years later left and entered the army. While engaged in the campaign in Germany he was returned to the House of Commons for High Wycombe in 1760 and was reelected in 1761. However, the death of his father in 1761 elevated him to the House of Lords.

In 1764 he took his seat in the Irish House of Lords as Earl of Shelburne, and in 1766 took a leading part in the English Parliament in the repeal of the Stamp Act. Under William Pitt, Earl of Chatham, Shelburne became secretary of state for the Southern Department on July 23, 1766. In August the entire control of the administration of the colonies was placed in his hands. He endeavored to pursue a conciliatory policy toward the American colonies, but in this he was thwarted by his colleagues, and in January 1768 he was replaced by Lord Hillsborough.

When Lord North resigned in March 1782, Shelburne declined George III's invitation to form a new ministry, but acted as intermediary in pressing the post upon Rockingham. In Rockingham's cabinet he became secretary of state for home affairs and tried to introduce several economic reforms. Rockingham died in July of that year, and Shelburne accepted the duty of forming a government. In this ministry William Pitt the Younger, then only 23, became chancellor of the exchequer. In the debate on the change of ministry Shelburne declared that he still adhered to all the constitutional ideas that he had absorbed from his master in politics, Lord Chatham, and that he had not altered his opinion concerning American independence. But during the negotiations of the Peace of Paris he was reluctantly led to agree to the concession. The coalition of the prime minister, Lord North, and Charles James Fox against his government led to his resignation in 1783.

In 1784, Shelburne was created Marquis of Lansdowne in the English peerage. Disraeli said he was "the first great minister who comprehended the rising importance of the middle class." Shelburne died in London on May 7, 1805.

SHELBY, shel'bē, **Isaac** (1750–1826), American frontier soldier, who was the first governor of Kentucky. He was born at North Mountain, Md., on Dec. 11, 1750. In 1773, the family moved to what is now eastern Tennessee. Shelby was an officer in frontier fighting against the Indians, and in the early years of the Revolution he collected supplies for the Continental army.

As a colonel of militia, he was active against the British in the Carolinas. He was a leader in the victory at King's Mountain (Oct. 7, 1780) and planned the attack that defeated the British in the Battle of Cowpens (Jan. 17, 1781).

After the war, he moved to Kentucky, where he was a member of the conventions that prepared the way for Kentucky's admission to the Union as a state and that framed the state constitution. He was elected the state's first governor in 1792 and served four years.

In the War of 1812, he gathered 4,000 Kentucky volunteers as part of the American invasion of Canada. They won the Battle of the Thames over the British (Oct. 5, 1813). He received a gold medal from Congress for his services. In March 1817, President James Monroe offered Shelby the cabinet post of secretary of war, but he declined because of his age.

Shelby died on July 18, 1826, at his home, 'Traveler's Rest," at Danville, Ky. Counties in nine Southern and Midwestern states, and a number of towns have been named in his honor.

SHELBY, shel'bē, a city in southwestern North Carolina, the seat of Cleveland county, is situated near the foothills of the Blue Ridge Mountains, about 43 miles (68 km) west of Charlotte. It is the center of an agricultural region that produces cotton, fruit, dairy products, and beef cattle. The city's industries include the manufacture of textiles, hosiery, flour and baked goods, and lumber.

Shelby was chartered in 1843 and incorporated as a city in 1929. Government is by council and manager. Population: 15,310.

SHELBYVILLE, shel'bē-vil, a city in eastern Indiana, the seat of Shelby county, is on the Big Blue River, about 27 miles (43 km) southeast of Indianapolis. It makes electrical equipment, fiber glass, paper plastics, furniture, industrial heating equipment and parts for radio and television and for airplanes and rockets. Shelbyville was laid out in 1822. It was incorporated as a town in 1850 and chartered as a city in 1860. Government is by mayor and council. Population: 14,989.

SHELBYVILLE, shel'bē-vil, a city in northern Kentucky, the seat of Shelby county, is situated in an agricultural and stock-raising Bluegrass region, about 30 miles (48 km) east of Louisville. It has a large tobacco market and flour and feed mills, and is an important dairy center. The city's industry includes printing, metal processing, and the manufacture of fertilizers, utensils, and metal products.

Richard Boone, brother of Daniel Boone, the frontiersman, built a fort about 2 miles (3 km) from the present-day Shelbyville, but it was abandoned in 1781 after an Indian attack. Shelbyville itself was founded in 1792. It was named, as was the county, in honor of the first governor of Kentucky, Isaac Shelby. The city is governed by a mayor and council. Population: 5,308.

SHELBYVILLE, shel'bē-vil, a town in south central Tennessee, the seat of Bedford county, is on the Duck River, about 60 miles (96 km) south of Nashville. It is a dairy and poultry processing center with light industry. Textiles, pencils, metal goods, plastics, and leather are manufactured here. Printing is also important.

Shelbyville was platted in 1810 and incorporated in 1819. It was named for Col. Isaac Shelby, who in 1780 fought in the Revolutionary War Battle of King's Mountain and later became the first governor of Kentucky. Shelbyville was the scene of a number of skirmishes during the Civil War. The town is governed by a mayor and council. Population: 13,530.

SHELDON, Charles Monroe (1857–1946), American Congregationalist minister, whose religious novel *In His Steps* was an all-time best seller. Sheldon was born in Wellsville, N. Y., on Feb. 26, 1857. He studied at Brown University and graduated from Andover Theological Seminary in 1886. He was ordained a Congregationalist minister, and became a pastor in Waterbury, Conn. In 1889 he became pastor of the Central Congregational Church in Topeka, Kans.

As a means of attracting a congregation to his evening services he read a chapter a week from stories he wrote. *In His Steps,* the story of a congregation that consistently followed the teachings of Jesus, was first written for this purpose. It was published in serial form in *The Advance,* a Chicago religious journal, and then in book form in 1896. It sold more than 23 million copies and was translated into 23 languages. Sheldon resigned from his pastorate in 1919 and became editor in chief of the *Christian Herald,* a position he held until 1925. He remained a contributing editor while writing numerous other religious books. Sheldon died in Topeka, Kans., on Feb. 24, 1946.

SHELDRAKE, male duck of the genus *Tadorna.* In particular the name is applied to the common shelduck (*T. tadorna*) found along coastal regions of Europe. The name is also sometimes given to the merganser. See DUCK—*Kinds of Ducks.*

SHELDUCK, any of seven species of relatively large colorful ducks classified in the tribe Tadornini. See DUCK—*Kinds of Ducks.*

SHELEPIN, she-lye'pyēn, **Aleksandr Nikolayevich** (1918–   ), Soviet Communist leader. He was born in Voronezh. Shelepin, the son of an office worker, belongs to the first group of top Soviet officials born after the Russian Revolution.

Shelepin took graduate work in Moscow in the late 1930's, fought in the Red Army in Finland in 1939, and joined the Communist party in 1940. He rose rapidly in Komsomol, the party's youth organization, which he joined in 1941.

As head of Komsomol between 1952 and 1958, he mastered brilliantly the complex political and ideological shifts of the time. Despite his youth, he won Nikita Khrushchev's confidence, and his rise was spectacular. In December 1958 he became head of state security (the KGB) and, in November 1962, of the newly created party-state control commission. He began to build his own political machine by placing former subordinates from Komsomol in high positions.

Shelepin provided the organization required for the ousting of Khrushchev in October 1964 and was made a full member of the party's Presidium a month later. After 1964, however, Shelepin and his followers began to be gradually removed from key posts. In April 1975, Shelepin was removed from the Politburo.

GEORGE W. SIMMONDS
University of Detroit

SHELIFF RIVER. See CHÉLIFF RIVER.

SHELL, the hard, protective covering of various forms of plants, especially nuts and seeds; and of animals, such as turtles; the eggs of birds and reptiles; or the rigid "external skeleton" of some invertebrates, such as foraminifers, echinoderms, crustaceans, brachiopods, but especially of mollusks, which include clams, snails, and other sea shells. This article is restricted to the shells of the Mollusca, while the characteristic structures of other shells, tests, and exoskeletons are described under separate headings. See CRUSTACEA; ECHINODERM; EGG; MOLLUSCA.

Shells are produced as hard, limy exoskeletons by the vast majority of the mollusks, although some shells may be internal as in the cuttlefish, squids, a few clams, and many opisthobranch sea slugs, or are entirely absent as in most land slugs and all nudibranch sea slugs. Seashells are produced by five marine classes of mollusks: the gastropods (snails or univalves); the pelecypods (clams, mussels, oysters, or bivalves); and three minor groups—the scaphopods (tusk and tooth shells), the cephalopods (chambered nautilus), and amphineurans (chitons or coat-of-mail shells). It is estimated that about half the 100,000 living species of mollusks are from the seas, while the others are from freshwater (such as river mussels and pond and aquarium snails) or from terrestrial habitats (garden snails and tree snails).

Structure and Growth of Shells. The shell material is produced in the form of a liquid secretion mainly from glands located along the edge of the fleshy, capelike mantle, an organ found in all mollusks. The liquid calcium carbonate becomes crystallized to form additions to the hard shell when mixed with a colloidal albumen that is also produced by the mantle. Shell deposition is not continuous but occurs periodically during the life of the animal, sometimes every few days, weeks, or even seasonally. Growth is generally inhibited during unfavorable environmental conditions, such as abnormally cold or dry weather, paucity of food, or during and just after breeding periods. A minor amount of shell material is produced by other regions of the mantle for the purpose of repairing cracks and holes or encasing foreign particles. (See PEARL.) The foot in gastropods secretes a hard, operculum or trapdoor.

Shell growth begins early in the development of the larval form of the mollusk. In most snails the young already have two or three spiral shell whorls, known as nepionic or nuclear whorls, before they hatch from the egg capsule. In the young stages of many bivalves, the early free-swimming form, such as the spat, or young, of oysters, has two shelly valves that in a few days grow too large and heavy to permit further swimming. Additional growth occurs in clam shells along the free edge of the valve, and, in the case of snail shells, along the rim of the outer lip of the aperture. In the spiral forms of univalves, the shell may be thought of as a regularly increasing or expanding cone that is wound around an axis or the columella of the shell. The many different shapes of univalve shells are determined by genetic factors that, in turn, control the rate of expansion of the aperture and the degree and regularity of the plane in which the new whorls are added, and, to a lesser degree, by the major modifications in sculpturing. Water currents, waves, food, temperature, and other conditions may influence growth during the lifetime of an individual.

The span of life and maximum age of marine species are very imperfectly known. Undoubtedly many species live for only two, three, or four years. The common European periwinkle (*Littorina littorea*) found in New England has been kept alive in captivity for 20 years. Large specimens of the horse conch (*Fasciolaria gigantea*), the queen conch (*Strombus gigas*), and the cameo king conch (*Cassis*) probably represent ten to 25 years of growth. The nudibranch sea slugs are believed to be short-lived, and *Aeolis* and *Gonidoris* have been shown to survive only into the second year. It is believed that the giant clam (*Tridacna*) of the Indo-Pacific region lives for perhaps 100 years, but this has not been confirmed by experiments or accurate calculations. The average age of the Atlantic bay scallop (*Aequipecten irradians*) is about 16 months, while its maximum age only two or three years. The average age of a 5-inch (13.7 cm) pismo clam (*Tivela stultorum*) on the Pacific coast is about eight years; its maximum age is 25 years.

There are two fundamental types of sculpturing in spirally coiled gastropods: *spiral* and *axial*. The former is expressed as ridges, cords, threads, channels, and cut lines, which all follow the direction of growth of the shell, while in axial sculpturing the formation of ribs, ridges, and varices is parallel to the edge of the growing lip. In the bivalves, sculptural features that parallel the growing edge of the valve are spoken of as *concentric*. Some mollusks may produce remarkably smooth shells that resemble highly glossed porcelain, while others make ornately sculptured or grossly spined shells.

Marine Shells. The marine bivalves show remarkable diversity in shape and mode of life. Most, however, are sand dwellers and live just below the surface of the muddy sand, where they keep in contact with food-laden ocean water by means of two fleshy, tubular siphons. In the venus (*Venus*), surf (*Mactridae*), and lucine (*Lucina*) clams, the siphons are very short, while in others, such as the common soft-shelled clam (*Mya*) and the angel wing of Florida (*Barnea costata*), which live far below the surface, the siphons are encased in a very long muscular tube.

The oysters are without siphons or functional foot and remain attached to the hard substrate during adult life. The coon oyster lives among the branches of the mangrove trees of the tropics and is able to feed and breathe only during high tide. The distantly related thorny oysters (*Spondylus*) that live in fairly deep tropical waters are renowned for their vivid colors and long, delicate spines. Those from the Gulf of Mexico command high prices among shell collectors.

A number of bivalves have become specialized to the extent of making burrows in wood, compact clay, and soft stone. The elongate, brown date mussels (*Lithophaga*) secrete acid with which they etch out their homes in coral blocks. Their own shells are protected from the acid by a tightly fitting jacket of horny periostracum. The shipworms (*Teredo* and *Bankia*) destroy the wooden plankings of ships, wharf pilings, and manila hemp lines. The body of this clam resembles a long, white worm with the two cutting shells at one end and the siphons at the other. Strangest of the bivalves is the wateringpot shell (*Aspergillum*) of the East Indies and Indian Ocean, about 6 inches (15 cm) in length, which resembles the spout of a garden watering pot. The circular, swollen end of the calcareous tube is perforated with numerous small holes, and the only clamlike feature to the shell is two tiny valves on one side of the tube.

The ability to swim is rare among adult bivalves. Scallops (*Pecten*) include many species that can swim for several dozen feet at a time. The movement is accomplished by the rapid snapping of the two shelly valves. While the scallops always swim with their valves in a horizontal plane, the *Lima* file clams most frequently progress edgewise, that is, with the breadth of the valves vertical or slightly oblique. The long, colorful tentacles of the *Lima* keep the animal momentarily suspended in water while the valves are being opened in preparation for another "bite" forward.

Seashells vary greatly in size. The adults of some tiny *Rissoa* snails never exceed ⅓₂ of an inch (0.79 mm), while the horse conch (*Pleuroploca gigantea*) of the lower Florida Keys may reach a length of 2 feet (60 cm). Of equal size is the great spindle shell (*Megalotractus*) from the Great Barrier Reef off Australia. Among the marine clams, the amethyst gem clam (*Gemma gemma*) found in shallow, sand-bottomed bays of the eastern United States, is one of the smallest bivalves, barely exceeding ⅟₁₆ of an inch (1.5 mm). The largest known living shelled mollusk is the giant clam (*Tridacna gigas*) of the tropical Indo-Pacific region. It may reach a length of 4 feet (1.2 meters) and a total weight of 500 pounds (225 kg). Contrary to popular belief, it is not a man-eating clam but lives on single-celled seaweeds or algae that grow symbiotically within the tissues of its mantle. Apparently there has been no authenticated record of its having trapped and drowned a human.

Perhaps the oddest of the marine snails are the carrier shells (*Xenophora*) that gather and attach to themselves other dead shells, bits of coral, and stones. Viewed from above, the carrier shell resembles a pile of marine debris, and this peculiar habit is believed to be of camouflage or protective value to the animal. The animal holds the edge of its shell to the foreign object and secretes from the fleshy mantle liquid calcium carbonate that soon hardens to form the permanent attachment.

The four families of marine snails most sought after by collectors of sea shells are the cones (Conidae), cowries (Cypraeidae), volutes (Volutidae), and the olive shells (Olividae). The several hundred species of living cones are warm-water inhabitants, all of a standard inverted conic shape with little major variation in sculpture, but quite variable in their attractive color designs. Rarest of them is the famous glory-of-the-seas cone from the East Indies and the Philippines. There are only two dozen known specimens, all exhibiting a graceful, smooth spire and intricate yellow and red color markings. Specimens of this cone have been sold for up to $1,000. Several species of cones from the Indo-Pacific region are known to inflict a sting that is fatal to man.

The shell of the cowrie, of which there are about 160 living species, is well known for its highly glossed finish, smooth and rounded contours, and brightly hued color patterns. The small yellow money cowrie (*Cypraea moneta*) was for many centuries used as a form of money in Africa and southern Asia. It also played an important part in religious rites and was used as a symbol of fertility and life. The 4-inch (10-cm) long golden cowrie is a particularly choice collector's item because of its comparative rarity and unusual orange-cream color. It lives in the reefs of the Central Pacific from the Philippines to the Fiji Islands, but only in the latter area is it worn around the necks of native chiefs as a sign of high rank or royalty.

Collectors of fancy seashells are constantly in search of specimens of outstanding qualities, and although a number of species are well known for their high value or unusual beauty, the standards by which their rarity and attractiveness are judged are quite varied. For many conchologists rarity is gauged by the top price that a specimen may bring. For others the important judging point is the scarcity of the species in nature or perhaps the rarity of specimens in collections. Left-handed, double-mouthed, or distorted specimens, like misprints in stamps, are highly valued by many veteran collectors. There are literally hundreds of truly rare species, but most of these are deep-sea shells, some of which are known only from a single specimen. Most of these are small and not particularly attractive. The high-priced shells are found among the showy genera, like the cones, volutes, murex shells, scallops, and cowries. Some species may be considered rarities for years and command very high prices before they are collected in large quantities. The precious wentletrap (*Epitonium scalare*) of the West Pacific once was in such demand that Chinese traders found it profitable to make counterfeits out of rice paste. The species is now considered reasonably common and is low-priced, but genuine rice counterfeits are now rare and equal in value to the price of the first-known shell specimens.

Distribution. Seashells are found in every ocean, from the shoreline to the very deepest parts of the seas and from the polar regions to the tropics. Each major area in the world has sea shells unique to its waters, although a few species, particularly those that live at the surface of the ocean, are worldwide in distribution. The geographic boundaries of past geologic oceans and environmental conditions, especially water temperature and salinity, have been responsible for the formation of these faunal regions.

Largest and richest of these regions is the Indo-Pacific, a vast, tropical marine area extending from the western shores of Africa, through the Indian Ocean to Japan, Australia, and the Polynesian Islands. The area is known for its richness in number of species, particularly among such groups as the cowries, cones, terebras, turbans, and venus clams. Some showy genera are unique to the Indo-Pacific, such as the spider conchs (*Lambis*), the chambered nautilus, and the giant clams (*Tridacna*). Not all sections of the Indo-Pacific are excellent collecting grounds, either because of excessive fresh water, muddy conditions, or lack of sufficient nitrogenous foods. The richest areas are along the east coast of Africa from Kenya to Mozambique, the section off the coast of Queensland, Australia, several small areas throughout the East Indies, the Philippines, and the Ryukyu Islands.

Second to the Indo-Pacific in attractive seashells is the West Indian region that includes the Caribbean and the Antilles, from Bermuda to Florida and south to Brazil. Although not particularly rich in species, some genera possess large and attractive species, such as the triton trumpet (*Charonia*), the true conchs (*Strombus*), the helmet shells (*Cassis*), and the tulip shells (*Fasci-*

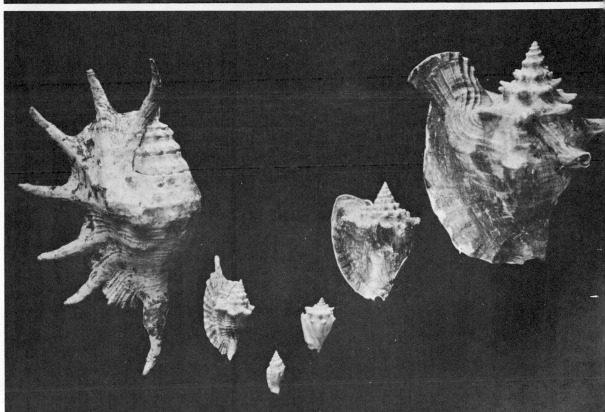

The widening of the lower whorl is demonstrated in these arrangements of spindles (*top*) and conchs (*bottom*).

SHELLS

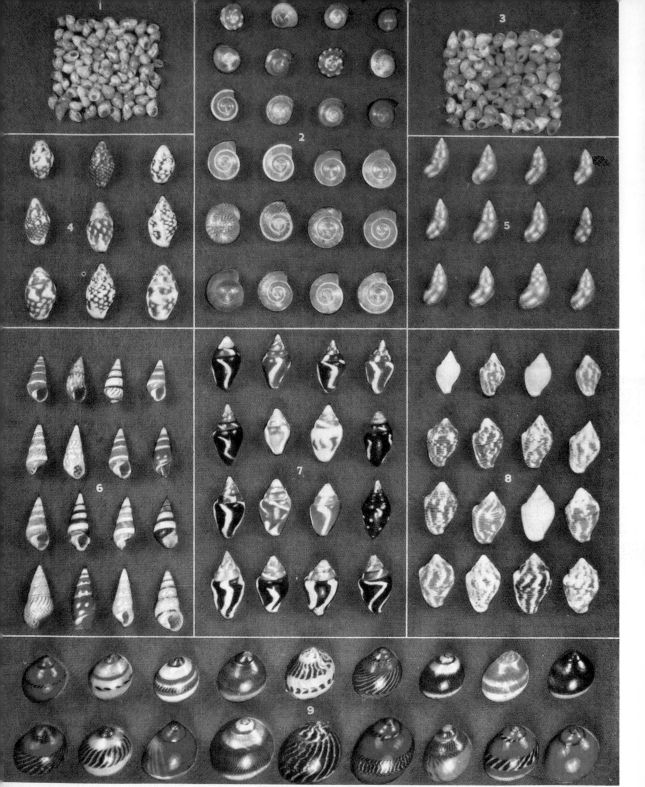

Tiny shells range in size from a half inch to a barely visible speck. Of all kinds known, about 90 percent are little, although the larger species usually make up the bulk of collections. The ones on this page (there are thousands much smaller) are: (1) *Tricolia tessellata* (Curacao); (2) *Umbonium vestiarium* (Indian Ocean); (3) *Tricolia affinis* (Martinique); (4) *Columbella pardalina* (Philippines); (5) *Cantharidus irisodontes* (Australia); (6) *Bankivia fasciata* (Australia); (7) *Columbella fulgurans* (Philippines); (8) *Columbella mercatoria* (Bermuda); (9) *Neritina communis* (Philippines). The two rows at the bottom, handsomest of sea snails, are marked like tooled leather.

SHELLS

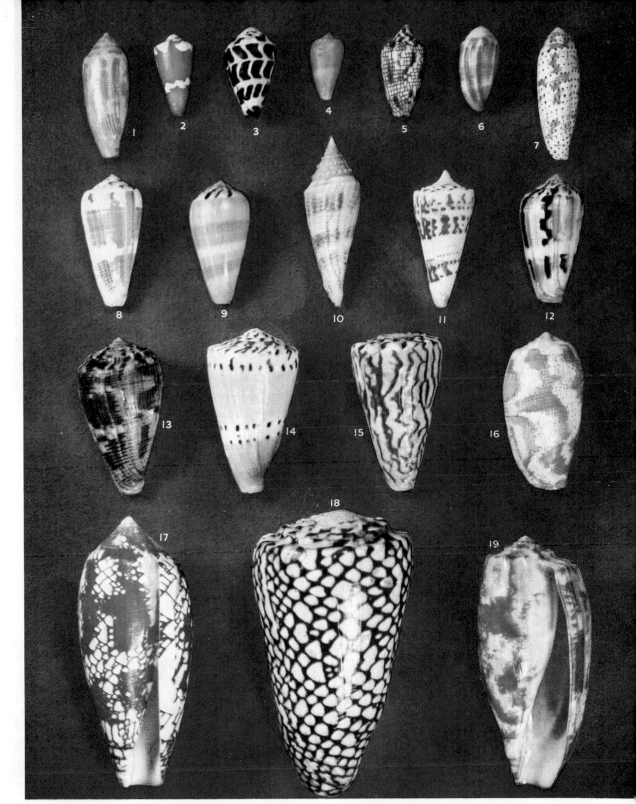

Collecting cones is dangerous, for some give poisonous stings when alive. For tracing the habitats of these, a world atlas is needed. All should be handled with care. While living (17) *Conus aulicus* (Philippines) and (19) *Conus geographus* (Moluccas) can inject a poison that causes great pain or even death. Others of the Conus group are: (1) *aureus* (Philippines); (2) *lithographus* (Ceylon); (3) *hebraeus* (Hawaii); (4) *rosaceus* (South Africa); (5) *lucidus* (Manta, Ecuador); (6) *glans* (Philippines); (7) *nussatella* (Red Sea); (8) *consol* (Singapore); (9) *fulmen* (Japan); (10) *d'Orbignyi* (Japan); (11) *monilis* (Indo-Pacific); (12) *achatinus* (Japan); (13) *purpurascens* (Acapulco, Mexico); (14) *mustelinus* (East Indies); (15) *princeps* (Acapulco, Mexico); (16) *tulipus* (Moluccas); (18) *marmoratus* (Philippines).

SHELLS

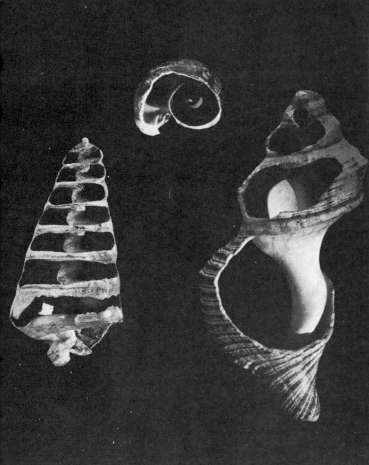

Above: An arrangement showing the divergent development of the outer lips of the conch and spider shells.

SHELLS

Left: Three shells broken to show the winding of the coil around the axis.

Below: Three types of screw shells.

Photographs from The American Museum of Natural History, New York *olaria*). The wentletraps (*Epitoniidae*), lucine clams, and marginellas are represented by numerous species.

The Mediterranean region is semitropical in nature and comparatively rich in species, about 2,000 in all being known. Generically it resembles the West Indian region. Other distinctive molluscan faunas are found in South Africa, the Patagonian region of South America, the tropical Pacific-Panamic area, the west coast of North America, and the New Zealand-Tasmanian region.

Freshwater Varieties. Freshwater shells are represented by only two of the classes of mollusks, the snails and the clams. The estimated 10,000 species exhibit remarkable variation in shape and sculpture, ranging from the 14-inch (35.5-cm) long river mussels of eastern China to the pinhead-sized amnicolid snails of American lakes and ponds. They live in a variety of habitats, some occurring in hot springs, the bottom of very deep lakes, within caves, or at the foot of waterfalls, while others can survive in hot, temporary ponds and drainage ditches of the tropics or in the frozen ponds of the polar regions.

The principal families of freshwater snails are the Viviparidae, the large, operculated apple snails that are sometimes used in aquaria; the Thiaridae, worldwide and abundant, turret-shaped, operculated snails; the Hydrobiidae, small, coiled shells usually less than a half inch (12.7 mm) in size, some of which carry serious parasitic diseases in the Orient; the Planorbidae, a worldwide group of pulmonate pond snails to which belongs the familiar red ramshorn of home aquaria; the Lymnaeidae pond and lake snails, some of which in the northern United States carry a parasitic disease known as swimmer's itch. The most conspicuous freshwater bivalves are the river mussels or unios, of which there are several dozen genera found in the major watersheds of the world. Many of them are large and have an attractive, lustrous interior. In the Mississippi drainage, there are many large species that, before the advent of plastics, were the major source of pearl buttons.

Land Varieties. Most of the land shells are pulmonate gastropods, that is, snails that have a modified lung, and they include the garden and woodland snails and the shell-less slugs. A few small species are gill-bearing, operculated prosobranch snails. Many of the land shells are as highly colored and as attractively designed as the most popular of the seashells. Numerous species, reaching 2 or 3 inches (51–76 mm) in size, dwell among the branches of high trees, such as the Philippine *Obba, Helicostyla,* and *Amphidromus* snails and the brightly colored *Liguus* tree snails of southern Florida and Cuba. The *Polymita* bush snails of Oriente province, Cuba, have the artificial appearance of having been painted in bright shades of red, orange, yellow, and black.

Largest of the land shells are the giant African snails of the genus *Achatina.* The largest species lives in the rain forests of Gabon and the Republic of the Congo, and its shell reaches a length of 8 inches (20 cm), while the extended foot upon which the snail crawls may stretch to over 12 inches (30 cm) in length. This snail is roasted and eaten by the natives. About half as large is the giant east African snail (*Achatina fulica*) that after World War II caused considerable alarm among agriculturalists in many of the western Pacific islands because of the damage it caused to garden plants. This prolific snail was carried by man first to the island of Mauritius sometime before 1800, to India in 1857, to the East Indies prior to 1927, and was finally spread, mainly by the Japanese, to Taiwan (Formosa), the Ryukyu Islands, and Micronesia during the 1930's and 1940's. It is now established in Hawaii.

The woodlands of North America contain many hundreds of interesting land shells. Most of them, however, are rather small and drab in color. The species inhabiting the mountainous areas are generally quite different from those living in the coastal regions, and a further faunal difference is evident between those of the western and eastern parts of the United States. Most of these snails prefer damp, shady areas where there is a certain degree of calcium carbonate in the soil and rocks. About 40 kinds of European snails and land slugs have been accidentally introduced into America, and of special note is one of the French edible snails (*Helix aspersa*), which is a considerable nuisance in California gardens.

R. Tucker Abbott
Academy of Natural Sciences, Philadelphia.

Bibliography

Abbot, R. Tucker, *Seashells of North America* (Western 1969).
Dance, S. Peter, *Rare Shells* (Univ. of Calif. Press 1969).
Johnstone, Kathleen Y., *Collecting Seashells* (Grosset 1970).
Hoyt, Murray, *Jewels from the Ocean Deep* (Putnam 1967).
Morris, Percy A., *Field Guide to the Shells of Our Atlantic and Gulf Coasts,* rev. ed., (Houghton 1951).
Morris, Percy A., *Field Guide to the Shells of the Pacific Coast and Hawaii* (Houghton 1966).

SHELLAC, shə-lak', is a resinous material commonly used in varnishes, polishing waxes, sealing waxes, binding agents, and stiffening agents. It is produced from lac, a resinous matter secreted by small insects that inhabit India and nearby South Asian regions. The insects feed on tree sap, transforming it into a resinous material that they deposit on twigs. These deposits are scraped off the twigs and dried to produce stick lac, which is ground and washed to obtain seed lac. The seed lac is melted, filtered, dried, and drawn into thin sheets; this product is called shellac. Shellac varnish is prepared by dissolving shellac in denatured alcohol. Shellac varnishes, which are quick drying and form a hard finish, are used chiefly on floors and furniture. Because they are not water-resistant, they should not be used to finish outdoor objects.

SHELLEY, Mary Wollstonecraft Godwin (1797–1851), English author of the famous horror novel *Frankenstein* (1818). She was born in London on Aug. 30, 1797, the daughter of William Godwin and Mary Wollstonecraft. In 1814 she eloped to Switzerland with Percy Bysshe Shelley and, after the death of his wife Harriet in 1816, was married to him. During their travels she wrote *Frankenstein,* which created a sensation.

After Shelley's death in 1822, she devoted herself to literary work, producing such novels as *Valperga* (1823), *The Last Man* (1826), and *Lodore* (1835). Her other works include *Journal of a Six Weeks' Tour* (1817), written with Shelley, and *Rambles in Germany and Italy* (1844). She also published some of Shelley's poetry and miscellaneous writings (1839, 1840, 1847). She died in London on Feb. 1, 1851. See also Frankenstein.

Percy Bysshe Shelley, a leading English Romantic poet

THE BETTMANN ARCHIVE

SHELLEY, Percy Bysshe (1792–1822), English poet, who was one of the greatest of the English Romantic poets. Among his most famous works are the verse drama *Prometheus Unbound;* the elegy on the death of John Keats, *Adonais;* and the lyrical poems *Ode to the West Wind* and *To a Skylark.*

Childhood and Youth. Shelley was born at Field Place, Warnham, Sussex, on Aug. 4, 1792. His father, Timothy Shelley, was a skillful agriculturalist and a Whig member of Parliament. His mother, Elizabeth Pilfold Shelley, was of a poetic and artistic inclination. As the eldest son and heir to his family's main estates, Percy Bysshe was regarded with great interest from birth. With him in mind, his grandfather, Sir Bysshe Shelley, built the mansion called Castle Goring, near Vorthing, on the southern coast. At the age of six the child began his classical education, and soon afterward he was taken on long rides round the farms to learn something of his future duties. On the millpond at Warnham he first showed the love of boats that was to last him for life. Indoors, he invented strange tales to entertain his sisters and composed his earliest verses. In 1802, Shelley was sent to a preparatory school, Sion House Academy, at Brentford, where he was tormented by the older boys. There also, perhaps because he felt persecuted, he was first filled with a sense of mission in the cause of liberty.

Shelley entered Eton in 1804. There harsh experiences continued, for his original ideas and eccentricities provoked some of his schoolfellows and he was nicknamed "Mad Shelley." However, in the end he had friends enough at Eton, where, in July 1810, he pronounced his Latin oration like other noteworthy classical scholars. His tales of terror and wonder, *Zastrozzi* and *St. Irvyne,* written while he was at school, were not specially uncommon at a time when such absurdities were vendible and several Etonians concocted them. *Zastrozzi,* published in 1810, brought £40—and vanished. An undertaking of deeper intention was a poem on human society called *Queen Mab,*

already in progress when Shelley went on to University College, Oxford, in 1810. He took with him also memories of scientific lectures and the conversation and benevolence of Dr. James Lind of Windsor, a heroic old voyager with many accomplishments. At this period Shelley was attached to his cousin Harriet Grove, and the only discord between them and their families was caused by "his letters on speculative subjects"— echoes of *Queen Mab.*

On April 10, 1810, Shelley was at Oxford for matriculation at his father's college, University College, and duly signed the form of words declaring that he accepted the Statutes and the Thirty-Nine Articles of the Church of England. In October he went into residence. His father accompanied him and recommended him as "already an author" to his old acquaintance Henry Slatter, a bookseller near University College. Shelley at once made friends with another freshman named Thomas Jefferson Hogg, who also had upset his family by his free thinking. The two made themselves conspicuous in University College by their aloofness and busied themselves with literary collaborations of small merit. Shelley produced *A Poetical Essay on the Existing State of Things* (1811), one of sundry youthful pamphlets of which there are no known copies.

However, both Shelley and Hogg were responsible for an anonymous tract that followed immediately after, *The Necessity of Atheism.* The point of this pamphlet was to demand from orthodoxy at Oxford or anywhere—for Shelley scattered it widely—logical proof of the accepted notion of the Deity. The logicians of Oxford replied by ordering the copies found in Slatter's shop (spread out there early one morning by Shelley) to be burned. They also traced the authorship and presently brought Shelley and Hogg to trial in their college. The two chose to refuse the possible leniency of the master and fellows and were expelled on March 25, 1811. Shelley sped round among his friends to say good-bye and to borrow money, and next morning, his ideas of four beautiful years at Oxford still hovering round him, he and Hogg were on the London coach.

First Marriage. The disaster caused consternation at Field Place. In the spring of 1811, Timothy Shelley consented to allow his son £200 a year. He could not prevent a new complication. The 19-year-old Shelley, visiting his sisters at school in Clapham, had met a girl named Harriet Westbrook, three years his junior. She was the daughter of John Westbrook, a vintner, who was apparently the proprietor of a club called the Cocoa Tree. When Shelley's daring talk had given Harriet a certain reputation among her schoolmates, and she wrote to him in distress, he decided to take her from school and marry her in Scotland. They were married on Aug. 28, 1811. Harriet was of exquisite appearance and in Shelley's view lacked only some of his opinions in order to be the perfect wife. Before long the happiness they had despite the deepening anger of Shelley's father was assailed by an attempt on Hogg's part to seduce Harriet. Eliza, Harriet's older sister by 12 years, who had once meant more to Shelley than Harriet, now became part of the household, which was often moved from place to place. In November 1811 they arrived in the Lake District, where Shelley met one of his idols, the poet Robert Southey. However, Southey was no longer against the established order of things: so fallen, so lost, he advised Shelley not to go to Ireland to help Catholic emancipation. But, of course, Shelley and his womenfolk went over to Dublin in February 1812. Instantly he scattered a broadside, *Address to the Irish People,* and at length angered a public meeting by his counsels of tolerance. This episode ended, after more printing, including a *Declaration of Rights,* in April, when he took the boat for Wales.

By this time Shelley and Harriet were receiving £400 a year from their families but could not readily find a home. A rose-clad cottage at Lynmouth, England, suited them. However, Shelley had printed an angry *Letter to Lord Ellenborough* about the recent prosecution of Daniel Eaton for publishing the third part of Thomas Paine's *Age of Reason.* He sent it out in bottles by sea and balloons by air and was kept under observation by the government. Shelley thereupon joined a philanthropist, William Madocks, M.P., in a project of land reclamation at Tremadoc on Cardigan Bay in Wales. Office work did not bother him, and in February 1813 he wrote, "When I come home to Harriet I am the happiest of the happy."

On the night of February 26 an attempt to shoot Shelley was made in his lonely villa, Tan yr Allt. Envy of a "stranger" may have been the motive. The Shelleys sought relief in a holiday in Ireland, but even there Shelley was planning the issue of his "progressive" poem *Queen Mab,* which tilted against official religion and marriage. He printed it privately and distributed it from John Westbrook's house on the north side of Hyde Park in 1813. It is a poem of impassioned vision, a mixture of wonder book and treatise, influenced by William Godwin's *Political Justice* and a mass of miscellaneous literature.

Shelley and Mary Wollstonecraft Godwin. In 1813, the Shelleys, with their first child, took a house at Bracknell, near Windsor. The novelist Thomas Love Peacock now became their friend. He accompanied them on an autumn tour to Scotland, after which they returned to Windsor. To Peacock's bewilderment, this proved to be the last period of Shelley's living with Harriet. Shelley had become one of William Godwin's supporters and obtained large sums of money for him. During his calls on Godwin, Shelley had met the philosopher's daughter Mary, whose mother, Mary Wollstonecraft, had been long dead. The result was that on July 28, 1814, Shelley and Mary, accompanied by Claire Clairmont, the daughter from a previous marriage of the second Mrs. Godwin, ran off to Switzerland. Shelley invited Harriet to join them, but by this time she had sickened of Godwin and his philosophy and refused.

Shelley was considerably relieved from the burden of his increasing financial difficulties by the death of Sir Bysshe in January 1815. Godwin, however, with his incessant need for money, had him at his mercy. After many wanderings, Shelley and Mary found a home at Bishopgate, again in the Windsor region. A Thames tour contributed to the picturesque beauty in Shelley's poem *Alastor, or the Spirit of Solitude,* published in 1816. Reading Wordsworth had also influenced him in the writing of this fine reverie.

On Jan. 24, 1816, a son, William, was born to Shelley and Mary. In May, Shelley took Mary, William, and Claire to Geneva. There he met Lord Byron, who found Shelley remarkably companionable. He even submitted to Shelley's tuition on the message of Wordsworth's poetry, which added subtlety to Canto III of Byron's *Childe Harold.* Byron also entered into an unhappy liaison with Claire. In England again, later in the year, Shelley sent his *Hymn to Intellectual Beauty* to Leigh Hunt, the editor of *The Examiner,* and was promptly acclaimed. He also became a guest at Hunt's Hampstead cottage at the same time that John Keats was similarly welcomed. However, this sunshine was abruptly darkened. In December 1816 the news reached Shelley that Harriet had been found drowned, and in March 1817 the custody of his two children by Harriet was awarded to Harriet's father.

Shelley married Mary Godwin on Dec. 30, 1816. Some consolation for Harriet's death was given by literary and musical evenings at Leigh Hunt's, where he met one of his most understanding friends, Horace Smith, stockbroker and man of letters. As for Keats, Shelley was as ever intensely willing to be of service to genius, but his advice irritated the younger poet. Keats declined Shelley's invitation to his Arcadian cottage, Albion House, at Great Marlow, in the beloved Thames Valley. However, the many others who did come were regaled with hospitality. Shelley was also an active friend of the poor in the district. His poetic and political energies did not diminish. An important prose work of the period was *A Proposal for Putting Reform to the Vote* (1817). His poem *Laon and Cyntha* (1817), in 12 cantos, is a visionary story, with tyranny as its terror and two idealists as its glory. The poem, renamed *The Revolt of Islam* (1818), was reviewed in the *Quarterly Review* in such a way as to expose Shelley's personal life to contempt.

Shelley in Italy. Poisonous tongues and illness urged the Shelleys out of England. With them, on March 12, 1818, went Claire and Allegra, Claire's illegitimate daughter by Byron. Again they went from one lodging to another. One of their stops was at Este, at a house lent by Lord Byron. Little Clara Shelley, their second child, died in consequence of the journey, and within a year William also died. Shelley's youngest son, Percy Florence, born in Florence in November 1819, was the only one of his children by Mary to survive. The magic of Italy had thus its sinister and tragic side for Shelley. However, Shelley made great artistic advances from his first sight of Lake Como and Milan. A new radiance was upon him. At Este he began to foresee his verse drama *Prometheus Unbound,* which can be considered as a revision of *Queen Mab* in its general creed. It is a transformation of commonplaces into enchantments. His scientific thought played its part in this "lyrical drama," with its prophecies of the intellectual and technical world to come. At Este, also, he composed one of his finest "hilltop poems," *Lines Written Among the Euganean Hills,* which includes a tribute to Byron, or rather the Byron of his imagination. In Naples and in Rome, Shelley brought *Prometheus Unbound* to three acts, and after some months happily added a fourth (1819) that is mainly a high carnival in honor of Greece's golden age, realized in modern forms.

Prometheus Unbound was written partly in the open air among the scented flowers then coloring the ruins of the Baths of Caracalla. Had Shelley written nothing more than his prose letters and notes concerning the natural and artistic delights of Italy, he still would be read.

Moving from Rome to Leghorn after his son's death, he exerted his poetic powers, particularly in the five-act tragedy *The Cenci* (1819). Its subjects of incest and murder horrified theater managers in London. Shelley's long *Masque of Anarchy,* a poem meant both to inspire and to moderate the leaders of socialism, was withheld by Leigh Hunt from publication until 1832, on grounds of its liability to law. In Florence, in October 1819, Shelley answered the wild unrest of the season with his autobiographical and self-less *Ode to the West Wind.* The year 1819 was, in fact, a particularly productive one for him in every form of composition that he knew—even in burlesque. His *Peter Bell the Third,* in part a hilarious parody of Wordsworth's poem *Peter Bell,* was thrown off nonchalantly. At this time also, Shelley wrote his incomparable ode *To a Skylark.* In 1820, Shelley again set forth as a comic writer in *Oedipus Tyrannus, or Swellfoot the Tyrant, a Tragedy in Two Acts,* ridiculing the unsuccessful married life of George IV.

Early in 1820 the Shelleys moved to Pisa, chiefly to be near the celebrated physician Vacca. In July, Shelley amusingly described a practical concern of his in the famous metrical *Letter to Maria Gisborne.* The concern, however, was not a joke. He had set his mind on establishing a steamboat service between Leghorn and Marseille and was employing Mrs. Gisborne's son Henry Reveley, an engineer, to build the first boat. The attempt, however, failed. His poem *The Witch of Atlas,* written in August 1820, is evidently here and there a fantasia on the inventions that steam, or electricity, can animate.

On August 16, Keats replied to Shelley's invitation that he be Shelley's guest when he came to Italy seeking a cure for consumption. The invitation was renewed when Keats landed at Naples in November. Circumstances prevented the acceptance, but Shelley's zeal for his friend, whose latest volume confirmed him in his opinion of Keats' imaginative power, did not stop at that. When he heard early in 1821 that Keats had died in Rome, he felt that the malice of anonymous reviewers had hastened his untimely end. Shelley wrote the long poem *Adonais,* a triumphal elegy for Keats, one of the finest in English literature. Other writings of 1820 and 1821 include *Defence of Poetry,* in prose, somewhat on the lines of the essay by Shelley's forerunner and kinsman Sir Philip Sidney; *Epipsychidion,* a Platonic exposition of love addressed to Emilia Viviani, an aristocratic Italian girl, then immured in a convent in Pisa; and *Hellas,* a lyrical drama inspired by the beginning of the Greek rebellion against the Turkish yoke in 1821. An unauthorized edition of *Queen Mab* drew from Shelley a public announcement that for him the poem was obsolete.

Last Year and Death. At Pisa in 1821, Shelley was joined by his cousin (and subsequent biographer) Tom Medwin, his schoolfellow Edward Williams, and, in autumn, by Lord Byron. Byron had proposed to found a new magazine, owned by himself and Shelley, with Leigh Hunt as an experienced editor. Shelley had persuaded Hunt to sail to Italy, hoping that he would join the company before 1821 ended. Hunt's ship was delayed. Edward Trelawny, an adventurer with a touch of genius, arrived first, and the Pisa circle flourished. But for the summer of 1822 the Shelleys and Williams removed to Lerici, where the two old Etonians lived largely on the sea, in their sailing boat the *Don Juan.* Shelley never-

theless was much engaged in hours of solitude on his new poem, a vision once again, *The Triumph of Life.* At the end of June, Hunt and his large family reached Leghorn. Shelley and Williams sped there in their boat to greet them. There, Shelley also confronted Byron, who appeared to be abandoning the proposed magazine. After some days, however, it seemed that this menace was past. On the homeward voyage from Leghorn to Lerici, Shelley's boat went down in a storm on July 8, 1822, and the poet and his friend Williams perished. Their bodies were found after some time and were cremated on the sands near Viareggio under the surveillance of Trelawny, Hunt, and Byron. Ultimately Shelley's ashes were buried in the *Adonais* cemetery, the Protestant Cemetery in Rome, near his child William.

Critique. Shelley's portrait painted by Amelia Curran in Rome, now at the National Portrait Gallery in London, remains fascinating, revealing one aspect of his nature, the angelic. His friends remarked on his coming and going like a spirit. But he was not only angelic. Wherever he went, except at Lord Byron's, he instantly took command of each and all. Byron perhaps even privately admitted (he has almost said as much) that Shelley was his master.

The dilemma of Shelley, the Sussex aristocrat who inherited liberalism, was to choose between action and poetry. Perhaps he might combine both, in order to do the world some service. Shelley's attitude toward his privileges as an inheritor was almost penitential—the master must be the servant. His funds were for others. He gave Leigh Hunt £1,400 in one stroke, pensioned Peacock, continually rescued Godwin, but somehow like an old-fashioned patron.

In England at that time, probably only Samuel Taylor Coleridge was Shelley's superior in learning and reading and his equal in comprehending and simplifying great subjects. The success of both as translators, Coleridge from Schiller, Shelley from Goethe, is still valid. Coleridge, the friend of Sir Humphry Davy, also knew what the sciences of his age were achieving, and Shelley was not far behind. With respect to literary ability, it appears that both Shelley and Coleridge were greatest when they were speaking to those of similar intellect. Horace Smith and Trelawny are among those who give some impression of Shelley in discourse. However, the amount of Shelley's recorded "table talk" is not so extensive as that of Coleridge because Shelley died so young.

Possibly the chief poetic gospel of Shelley was preached in three long poems. The first and one of the most remarkable was the undergraduate poem, *Queen Mab.* Yet, as he soon realized, it was crude in matter and manner. The theme was taken up again five or six years later in *Prometheus Unbound,* which is not likely to be mistaken for a college exercise. It is a tremendous work—a bioscope illusion, a ballet—yet it is still on the old theme of the coming race, perfectibility, science, and beauty for every man. *The Triumph of Life,* a pathetic sea-stained fragment, looks different. What remains of Shelley's last grand spectacle is the utter contrast to triumph, although that word may mean just "procession." Life, seen in this painting, is death-dealing. But the second vision and completion would surely have represented the glory and the joy of a re-organized world. In this bold unfinished poem

Shelley employs the realism that he has been said by some critics not to have. Toward his last days he was becoming more willing to disprove the "angelic" attack on him, as when in his *Peter Bell* he flayed the fashionable London of his early Grosvenor Square period. With all this, many will return to his simple and conceivably sentimental lyrics, which echo his friend Hunt's observation, "Music affected him deeply." These lovely lyrics are often of no importance in the history of literature except that they go on forever. "I arise from dreams of thee" is just one of dozens in which anthologists have delighted since 1822.

EDMUND BLUNDEN
Author of "Shelley: A Life Story"

Bibliography

Shelley's writings were collected and annotated by Mary Shelley in 1839 and 1840. A 10-volume edition by Roger Ingpen and Walter E. Peck, *The Complete Works of Percy Bysshe Shelley*, was published in 1926–1930 and revised in 1965. His *Complete Poetical Works* was edited by Thomas Hutchinson in 1904, with later editions in 1905, 1933, 1934, and 1961.

Baker, Carlos H., *Shelley's Major Poetry: The Fabric of a Vision* (Princeton Univ. Press 1948).

Blunden, Edmund, *Shelley: A Life Story* (Collins 1946).

Buxton, John, *Byron and Shelley: The History of a Friendship* (Macmillan, London, 1968).

Cameron, Kenneth N., ed., *Shelley and His Circle, 1773–1822*, 8 vols. (Oxford 1961–   ).

Dowden, Edward, *Life of Percy Bysshe Shelley* (Routledge 1951).

Gisborne, Mrs. Maria, *Maria Gisborne and Edward E. Williams, Shelley's Friends: Their Journals and Letters*, ed. by Frederick Jones (Univ. of Okla. Press 1951).

Hunt, Leigh, *Autobiography*, ed. by J. E. Morpurgo (Chanticleer 1949).

Lea, Frank A., *Shelley and the Romantic Revolution* (Routledge 1945).

Norman, Sylva, *Flight of the Skylark: The Development of Shelley's Reputation* (Univ. of Okla. Press 1954).

Reiter, Seymour, *Study of Shelley's Poetry* (Univ. of N. Mex. Press 1967).

Rogers, Neville, *Shelley at Work: A Critical Inquiry*, 2d ed. (Oxford 1967).

Schulze, Earl J., *Shelley's Theory of Poetry: A Reappraisal* (Mouton 1966).

Shawcross, John, *Shelley's Literary and Philosophical Criticism* (Folcroft 1909).

White, Newman, *The Unextinguished Hearth: Shelley and His Contemporary Critics* (1938; reprint, Octagon 1966).

Wolfe, Humbert, ed., *Life of Percy Bysshe Shelley*, 2 vols. (Dutton 1933).

SHELLFISH, broadly, are aquatic shelled invertebrates, many of which are popular foods. See CLAM; CRAB; CRUSTACEA; FISH AND SHELLFISH CULTURE; LOBSTER; MOLLUSCA; OYSTER; SHRIMP; SNAIL AND SLUG.

SHELTER. For primary articles on this basic human need, see BUILDING; HOUSE; HOUSING; URBAN PLANNING; and URBAN RENEWAL. For information on various types of structures, see articles such as CASTLES AND CHÂTEAUX; HOTEL; LAKE DWELLINGS; LOG CABIN; TENT; TEPEE; and TRAILER.

Additional information on types of shelters is provided in articles on various countries, peoples, and life styles, such as CAMPING; CAVE DWELLERS; ESKIMO; FRONTIER LIFE; GREECE—*Classical Art and Architecture;* and INDIANS, AMERICAN. For air raid and fallout shelters, see BOMB SHELTER and CIVIL DEFENSE.

SHELTER ISLAND is an island and township in southeastern New York, in Suffolk county. It is situated between the two prongs of the eastern end of Long Island, with Little Peconic Bay to the west and Gardiners Bay to the east. The irregularly-shaped island is roughly 7 miles (11 km) long and 6 miles (10 km) wide. There are three villages—Shelter Island in the center, Shelter Island Heights on the south shore, and Dering Harbor on the north. There are good harbors for yachts and small craft, and the island is a popular summer resort.

In 1637, Shelter Island, which was occupied by Manhanset Indians, became part of a grant made to William Alexander, Earl of Stirling. The following year, Lord Stirling's agent, James Farett, received Shelter Island as payment for his services. In 1641, Farett sold the island to four Royalists seeking asylum from Oliver Cromwell. One of them, Nathaniel Sylvester, built a manor house here, and his descendants were still living in it in the 20th century. During the New England persecution of Quakers, which began in 1656, the Sylvesters cared for those who sought refuge here. William Islip bought tracts from the Sylvesters in 1695 and 1706, and 1,000 acres (405 hectares) were purchased in 1700 by George Havens, whose descendants still live here. During the whaling period (1785–1850), many men from Shelter Island joined whaling ships sailing out of Sag Harbor, and when whaling declined they turned to menhaden fishing. The island became a fashionable resort for New Yorkers in 1871. Population: 2,071.

SHELTERBELT, a barrier of trees or shrubs, either natural or planted by man, that serves to protect soils or crops from damage by wind and rain. See WINDBREAK.

SHELTON, a city in southwestern Connecticut, in Fairfield county, is on the Housatonic River, 10 miles (16 km) west of New Haven and 10 miles northeast of Bridgeport. Shelton's industries manufacture textiles, apparel, sponge rubber, drawn wire, tacks, screw machine products, refractories, pins, and metal specialties.

Shelton was settled about 1697 as part of Stratford. A parish called Ripton was organized in 1724. The town of Huntington was incorporated in 1789. Its name was changed in 1919 to coincide with the city of Shelton. The city is governed by a mayor and board of aldermen. Population: 31,314.

SHEM, shem, was the eldest son of Noah, and brother of Ham and Japheth. According to the account in the book of Genesis, Shem was the ancestor of all the nations inhabiting southwest Asia (10:21–31), including the people of Elam (Persia).

SHEMA, shə-mä', is the most important prayer in Judaism. The recitation of its full text, consisting of the biblical passages Deuteronomy 6:4–9; 11:13–21 and Numbers 15: 37–41, is a religious duty that has to be performed as the central part of the daily morning and evening prayers. Almost always recited in Hebrew, the prayer is repeated again upon going to bed as the "Bedtime Shema." Its first sentence, "Hear (*Shema*), O Israel: the Lord our God, the Lord is one," is the Jewish confession of faith, said also on other ritual occasions, and is the last confession to be made prior to death. The exclamation "*Shema Yisrael!*" is the Jewish equivalent of "My God!"

RAPHAEL PATAI
Fairleigh Dickinson University

SHEN YEN-PING, shun'yen'bing' (1896–   ), Chinese novelist, short story writer, and critic, who is also known by his pseudonym Mao Tun. He first became involved in revolutionary politics in the 1920's, and after the establishment of the People's Republic in 1949 he served for a time as minister of culture.

Shen's sharply realistic fiction deals with themes of social criticism and revolution. His novels include the trilogy *Eclipse* (1928) and *Midnight* (1933).

SHENANDOAH, shen-ən-dō′ə, a borough in east central Pennsylvania, in Schuylkill county, is 37 miles (60 km) northwest of Allentown. Anthracite mining was long its chief industry, but a general decline in coal mining has made the town more dependent upon its other industries, notably the manufacture of wearing apparel, auto oil filters, cigars, mirrors, and plastics.

Shenandoah was settled in 1835. The town was platted in 1862, when large-scale coal mining began, and incorporated in 1866. The first Greek Catholic parish in the United States was organized here in 1884. Shenandoah has a mayor-council form of government. Population: 7,589.

SHENANDOAH, The, shen-ən-dō′ə, one of the vessels operated by the Confederates in the American Civil War to raid Union shipping. She was built in Glasgow, Scotland, in 1863 as the *Sea King,* for the route to India. Purchased by the Confederacy in 1864, she was taken over in October at Funchal, Madeira, by Capt. James I. Waddell and a Confederate crew. Fitted with six guns, she set out as a raider named *Shenandoah.*

She rounded the Cape of Good Hope and captured nine Union ships. After replenishing supplies at Melbourne, Australia, she headed north through the Pacific Ocean and crowned her career with a raid on the whaling fleet from New Bedford, Mass., in the Bering Sea, in June 1865, where she took or destroyed about 25 ships.

The Civil War had then been over for two months, but Waddell did not know until August, when he was in contact with a British ship. He sailed to Liverpool, England, and surrendered his ship to the British government. She was transferred to the United States and sold to the Sultan of Zanzibar. The United States received indemnity for some of the damage done by the *Shenandoah.* See ALABAMA CLAIMS.

SHENANDOAH NATIONAL PARK, shen-ən-dō′ə, in northern Virginia, about 75 miles (120 km) west of Washington, D. C., covers a striking section of the Blue Ridge Mountains. The Skyline Drive follows the crest of the ridge through the park with views of the Shenandoah Valley and the Piedmont country.

The park is about 75 miles long and from 2 to 13 miles (3 to 20 km) wide. Its area is more than 300 square miles (775 sq km). Sixty peaks in the park are over 3,000 feet (912 meters) high. Hawksbill Mountain (4,049 feet or 1,215 meters) is the highest.

Forest covers 95% of the park. Oaks predominate, with scattered hemlocks, pine, fir, spruce, maple, birch, sycamore, and elm. More than 900 species of wildflowers have been recorded. About 200 species of birds and more than 50 species of mammals are found. The most commonly seen are the turkey buzzard, the raven, the white-tailed deer, and the bobcat.

SHENANDOAH VALLEY, shen-ən-dō′ə, in northwestern Virginia, between the Allegheny Mountains to the west and the Blue Ridge to the east. It is famous for its beauty and fertility. Fruit orchards and rich pastures stretch for miles. The display of fruit blossoms in the spring draws thousands of visitors.

The valley is also notable for its historical associations. During the Civil War it was a major battleground.

Description. The valley runs northeastward from near Lexington, Va., to the Potomac River. It is about 150 miles (240 km) long and from 10 to 20 miles (16–32 km) wide. Its southern portion is divided down the middle by the ridge of Massanutten Mountain, which is about 45 miles (72 km) long and reaches a height of about 3,000 feet (912 meters).

The North Fork of the Shenandoah River flows in a northeasterly direction north of Massanutten Mountain, and the South Fork is south of the mountain. The forks join near Front Royal to form the Shenandoah River, which runs northeastward to empty into the Potomac at Harpers Ferry, W. Va. Geologically the valley is part of the Great Appalachian Valley, which continues northward as the Hagerstown Valley in Maryland and the Cumberland Valley in Pennsylvania.

The principal towns in the valley are Lexington, Waynesboro, Staunton, Harrisonburg, Luray, Front Royal, and Winchester. All are distribution centers for the produce of the region and for tourists.

History. Explorers from the colony of Virginia visited the Shenandoah Valley in the middle of the 17th century, but the venture that gave impetus to the valley's settlement was an expedition in 1716 conducted by Gov. Alexander Spotswood. He led a small party westward from Williamsburg, Va., into the wilderness and reached the crest of the Blue Ridge. From there they saw the vast, virgin expanse of the valley, laced with the two forks of the river. On a river bank they buried a bottle containing a document stating that the region had been annexed in the name of King George I of England. On his return to Williamsburg, Spotswood presented to each of his companions a miniature gold horseshoe. The company became known as the "Knights of the Golden Horseshoe."

Their accounts of the rich Shenandoah country spurred the movement of settlers. Three general areas of the valley were settled by different nationalities. The lower valley, from the Potomac for about 40 miles (64 km) southward, was occupied largely by English immigrants from tidewater Virginia. The central valley, from near Strasburg to Harrisonburg, was settled almost wholly by Germans. The upper valley, south of Harrisonburg, received mostly Scotch-Irish settlers from Pennsylvania.

Each part of the valley developed its own character. The people of the lower valley remained associated socially with the tidewater country and had slaves to work their plantations, on which tobacco was a major crop. They worshiped in the Church of England. Residents of the central valley, who cultivated diversified crops, lived quiet, self-contained lives. Their religion was Lutheran. The upper valley people, Presbyterian in their creed, were known for their independence, their staunch democracy, and their constant quest for new lands. They engaged in many battles with the Indians.

The Shenandoah Valley, looking toward Elkton, Va., from the Skyline Drive.

The Civil War. During the American Civil War (1861–1865), because the Shenandoah Valley was an important source of food for the Confederate armies and civilian population, it was known as "the granary of the Confederacy." But it was also a vital strategic area, providing a corridor for an army to invade the North or the South. This was more of an advantage for the Confederacy than for the Union, because the trend of the valley led toward Washington, D. C., and the populous centers of the North, but away from Richmond, Va., the Confederate capital, and other Southern centers. The valley was fought over for four years. Many of its towns were taken and retaken by both sides several times. This warfare culminated in the autumn of 1864, when Union armies systematically laid waste to the region.

The first major operation in the valley, the campaign of Confederate Gen. Thomas J. (Stonewall) Jackson in the spring of 1862, became a military classic. Driving his infantry up and down the valley with a speed that bewildered the Union forces, Jackson fought the battles of Kernstown (March 23), McDowell (May 8), Front Royal (May 23), Winchester (May 25), Cross Keys (June 8), and Port Republic (June 9). All but Kernstown were Confederate victories. The campaign engaged Union armies that might have aided the forces then besieging Richmond. Jackson himself, having accomplished this, took his own troops to help defend the capital.

In 1863, after the Confederate victory at the Battle of Chancellorsville (May 1–4), Gen. Robert E. Lee chose the valley as the route of his invasion of Pennsylvania. Gen Richard S. Ewell won the Second Battle of Winchester in mid-June. Lee's invasion ended in his defeat at Gettysburg (July 1–3), and Union troops that followed his retreat occupied the lower valley.

In the general movement planned by Union Gen. Ulysses S. Grant for the spring of 1864, Gen. Franz Sigel advanced up the valley as far as Staunton but was defeated at New Market (May 15) and had to withdraw. This battle is famous because the cadet corps of the Virginia Military Institute at Lexington was engaged. Gen. David Hunter led another Union force south up the valley in June until he was repulsed by Confederate Gen. Jubal A. Early.

With no opposition before him, Early led his small army down the valley, crossed the Po-tomac, and turned toward Washington. On July 11, he reached Fort Stevens, only 5 miles (8 km) from the White House. Grant's army was investing Richmond, and Washington was nearly defenseless. But Grant detached a corps, which reached Washington in time to repel Early, who retreated to the Shenandoah.

In the fall of 1864, Grant determined to eliminate the valley as a concentration area for Confederate troops and as a source of supply. Gen. Philip H. Sheridan routed the Confederates at Winchester (September 19) and drove them up the valley. As he pursued them, his troops sacked farms, burned barns, and destroyed crops. When he was finished, the valley was a wreck. Early surprised the Union army at Cedar Creek (October 19), in Sheridan's absence, but Sheridan reached the field to turn the tide and disperse the Confederates. This was the last major action in the valley.

SHENSI, shun'sē', is a province in north-central China. The name, also written Shan-hsi and Shǎnxi, means "west of the pass"—the Tungkwan (T'ung-kuan) Pass, which is the eastern entrance of the Wei Ho valley. The province has an area of about 75,600 square miles (195,-800 sq km). Its capital is Sian (Hsi-an) in the Wei Ho valley.

Geography. Shensi has four natural regions. (1) The north Shensi loess plateau has a strongly continental climate, subject to the dry winter monsoon but little influenced by the rain-bearing southeast summer monsoon. Cattle grazing is important in a 15-mile-wide belt along the Great Wall; in the rest of the area this is combined with the cultivation of drought- and frost-resistant crops. (2) The Wei Ho valley extends from Paoki (Pao-chi) in the west to the great eastward bend of the Hwang Ho (Yellow River). About 60% of Shensi's crops are harvested in this fertile heartland of the province, where the population density is very great. (3) The Tsinling (Ch'in-ling) Mountains, a forested area with an average elevation of 8,200 to 9,800 feet (2,500–3,000 meters) above sea level, extend over 930 miles (1,500 km) in an east-west direction south of the Wei Ho valley. They serve as a climatic demarcator, protect areas to the south from the cold dry northwest winter monsoons, and considerably weaken the effects of the southeast summer monsoon on areas to the north.

(4) The upper Han River valley south of the Tsinling Mountains is characterized by natural conditions similar to those in the Szechwan Basin. Unlike Shensi areas to the north, the valley produces sugar, tung oil, lacquer, and oranges. The region has a growing season of over 200 days and two harvests a year in a climate favorable to agriculture.

Economy. In agriculture, first place is taken by wheat (mostly in the Wei Ho valley), followed by millet (mainly in the north) and rice (mainly in the upper Han Valley). Cotton is the main industrial crop.

The rich coalfields in the vicinity of Tungchwan (T'ung-ch'uan) and Paishui north of the Wei Valley are the most important in China after those of Shansi. However, Shensi lacks iron ore. Yenchang (Yen-ch'ang) in northern Shensi is the center of its important petroleum-extraction industry and was China's first operating oilfield (1910).

Sian is an important industrial center, with large cotton-textile mills, and agricultural- and mining-machinery plants, chemical works for production of sulfates, nitrates, and hydrochloric acid, and the biggest thermoelectric station in northwest China. Paoki, at the head of the Wei Ho valley, is a city created by its position as a rail and highway hub. It has cotton-textile, flour, and paper mills, a match factory, and a machine-building plant. Sienyang (Hsien-yang), an important cotton-textile center, is the southern terminus of the rail spur to Tungch-wan, used to move coal to the Lunghai Railroad. Yaosien (Yao-hsien) is a major cement producer.

Shensi is a key area in the attempt to control the silting up of the Yellow River. The National People's Congress in 1955 approved a plan to control the river by constructing 46 dams on it, 17 of them in Shensi. Another important conservation measure was the creation of a 50,000-acre forest belt along the Great Wall, preventing wind-borne desert sands from penetrating the loess plateau and destroying farmlands.

Shensi occupies a pivotal position in interregional communications in China. The east-west Lunghai Railroad links up with the Lanchow-Sinkiang line; and the Paoki-Chengtu line, connecting Shensi and Szechwan, gives Shensi an important role in the development of southwest China.

Centers of Historical Interest. The valleys of the Wei Ho in Shensi and the middle Hwang Ho in Honan were the first centers of Chinese civilization. Sian is of great historic interest. The capital of the Chinese Empire was located at or near Sian during the Western Chou (about 1027–770 B.C.), Ch'in (221–206 B.C.), and Western Han (202 B.C.–9 A.D.) dynasties, as was the western capital for the Sui (581–618 A.D.) and T'ang (618–906 A.D.). Yenan in north Shensi is often called the "cradle of the Chinese Revolution," because from 1937 it served as capital of the Communist-held Shensi-Kansu-Ningsia Border Area. Population: (1970 est.) 21,000,000.

RICHARD SORICH, *Columbia University*

SHENSTONE, shen'stən, **William** (1714–1763), English poet, who also holds an important place in English landscape gardening. He was born at Halesowen, Worcestershire, on Nov. 13, 1714. After attending Oxford, where he began to write verse, he took over Leasowes, a family estate near Halesowen, and in 1745 began what was to be virtually his lifework—the beautifying of the grounds. He died there on Feb. 11, 1763.

Shenstone's best-known poems are *The School-Mistress,* one of the earliest 18th century imitations of Spenser, and *Pastoral Ballad,* which helped to revive interest in the ballad. His complete works appeared in *The Works in Verse and Prose of William Shenstone,* edited by Robert Dodsley (1764–1769).

Further Reading: Humphreys, Arthur R., *William Shenstone* (Macmillan 1937); Williams, Marjorie, *William Shenstone and His Friends* (Oxford 1933).

SHENYANG. See MUKDEN.

SHEOL, shē'ōl, is the abode of the dead in the Old Testament. All the dead went to sheol, which was conceived of as located variously under the earth, at the roots of the mountains, and the like. The dead led a shadowy, listless existence, but there is no notion in the Old Testament that sheol was a place of punishment. It was only in extrabiblical literature of the intertestamentary period that sheol came to be considered a place of punishment. Many scholars believe that the word *sheol* is derived from the Hebrew word meaning "ask," since the dead could be consulted as oracles.

SHEPARD, Alan B., Jr. See ASTRONAUTS.

SHEPHEARDES CALENDER, shep'ərdz, a series of 12 eclogues (pastoral poems) by the English poet Edmund Spenser. *The Shepheardes Calender* was published anonymously in 1579, with a dedication "To the noble and vertuous gentleman most worthy of all titles of learning and chevalrie, M. Philip Sidney." Each of the eclogues is accompanied by a commentary or glossary that gives the argument and the meaning of unusual words. The work purports to be written by E. K., a friend of the poet identified by some scholars as Edward Kirke, a college mate of Spenser, and by others as Spenser himself. The whole is introduced by a "General Argument" and an epistle to Master Gabriel Harvey of Cambridge. The *Calender* was an immediate success. It went through five editions during Spenser's lifetime, the first in 1579, and then in 1581, 1586, 1591, and 1597, and is regarded as one of the high-water marks of English poetry.

The Shepheardes Calender is descended from many sources. For its use of the eclogue form, its origins may be traced to Theocritus most of all, and in varying degrees to Bion, Vergil, Petrarch, Boccaccio, Giovan Battista Spagnoli, Jacopo Sannazzaro, and Clement Marot. For meters and rhythms, of which Spenser attempts a wide variety, his main sources are Chaucer in particular, Henry Howard, Earl of Surrey, Marot, and the old ballads. The language of the book marks Spenser as a daring innovator in poetic diction. It consists of words and forms from Lancashire and other dialects; of colloquialisms, old literary words, obsolete expressions, and the best of contemporary poetic diction; and of coinages in words and in forms, often happy, sometimes farfetched, of Spenser's own.

The single eclogues employ the traditional devices: the monologues, the two- and three-part dialogues, the singing contests, and the stories. The scheme of an eclogue for each month, following the general plan of country almanacs, was original. But this motif is followed only indifferently—in October not at all, quite fully in the January, February, November, and December divisions. In like manner the romance of Colin's love for Rosalynd also runs through some of the eclogues and is absent from the others. The two motifs combine to make the framework of the poem.

There is probably no single book in English that looks in so many poetic directions as *The Shepheardes Calender*. It is the work of a young writer possessed of enthusiasm, the splendor and excitement of the Renaissance, wide taste and reading, and one of the supreme lyrical gifts in all poetry for tone, rhythm, ornament, and the enveloping glamor of a beautiful and rare spirit and mentality. Most of Spenser's later work finds its beginnings in the *Calender*. Though he progressed far beyond it in every way, in profundity of content, in rhythm and imagery, the progression was in almost every case directly from the qualities of his first work. As the poet's poet, which he undoubtedly is, Spenser stands from the first revealed. In *The Shepheardes Calender* lovers of John Milton will find many of his qualities predicted, and to a varying extent the same is true of Shakespeare, Keats, Thomas Chatterton, Blake, Coleridge, Wordsworth, and Tennyson, to mention only a few of Spenser's debtors.

STARK YOUNG
Formerly, "The New Republic"

SHEPHERD'S PURSE is a common weed, *Capsella bursa-pastoris,* of the mustard family. Indigenous to Eurasia, it is now found the world over. It is an annual or winter annual, with a rosette of toothed or lobed basal leaves. The few stem leaves are arrowhead shaped, stalkless, and smooth edged or toothed. The usually branched stem may grow two feet (61 cm) tall. The slender-stalked flowers have four small white petals and six stamens and are borne in clusters that elongate as the seeds mature. The flattened pods are typically triangular, with a prominent vein on each face, and contain many orange-brown seeds. Young leaves of shepherd's purse may be used as a potherb or in salads.

JOHN W. THIERET
Southwestern Louisiana University

SHEPILOV, she-pē'lôf, **Dmitri Trofimovich** (1905–), Soviet Communist official. Little is known of him until World War II, when he was a political instructor in the Ukraine, where he became an associate of Nikita Khrushchev. From 1947 Shepilov worked in the propaganda section of the Communist party's Central Committee, and in 1952 he was made a full member of the committee. Later in the year he became editor of the influential newspaper *Pravda*. Shepilov accompanied Khrushchev on important diplomatic missions, including a trip to Peking in 1954, while editor. In 1956 he was made foreign minister. In 1957 he was accused of antiparty activities and stripped of his posts.

SHEPSTONE, shep'stən, **Sir Theophilus** (1817–1893), British South African official and diplomat. He was born near Bristol, England, on Jan. 8, 1817. At the age of three he was taken by his father, a missionary, to Cape Colony, where he was educated in mission schools.

Shepstone became headquarters interpreter of Bantu languages in Cape Town in 1835 and in the ensuing years held a number of positions dealing with the tribal groups in Natal. He was named secretary for native affairs in Natal in 1856. He had the respect of the Africans and opposed changes that, in the name of "civilization," would disrupt their tribal system. In 1873 he crowned Cetshwayo king of the Zulu and obtained assurances of his loyalty to Britain.

Shepstone was recalled to London for consultation in 1874 and again in 1876, when he was knighted. On his return he found the tribes in turmoil and the Boers in Transvaal embroiled in disputes with them. Early in 1877 he rode into Transvaal with a small staff and, by proclamation in April, brought it under British sovereignty. This act provoked considerable criticism, as did his opposition to the establishment of responsible government in Natal.

Shepstone retired from public life in 1880 but four years later took the place of Cetshwayo as Zulu ruler. He died in Pietermaritzburg, Natal, on June 23, 1893.

SHERATON, sher'ə-tən, **Thomas** (1751–1806), English furniture designer, who created a delicate, rectilinear, neoclassical style that inspired some of the best 18th century furniture. Sheraton was born in Stockton-on-Tees, county Durham. The son of a cabinetmaker, he seems to have learned his father's trade. He was a devout Baptist who, without a formal education, wrote religious works and preached in Baptist chapels all his life. Probably from about 1790, he lived in London, making a scanty living by teaching drawing and publishing books on religion and furniture design. He does not seem to have made much furniture. Only one signed piece, a bookcase, is known to be by Sheraton.

Sheraton's most important work is *The Cabinet-Maker and Upholsterer's Drawing Book,* published in four parts (1791–1794). A manual for cabinetmakers, it is filled with plates and full explanatory notes. The designs, some of them borrowed but most of them original, give an overall effect of simple grace, emphasizing rectilinear

Shepherd's purse (*Capsella bursa-pastoris*)

GRANT HEILMAN

Sheraton-style furniture is graceful and well proportioned. Characteristics include inlay (table, *left*) and carving (chairs, *above*).

lines and good proportion, in a refined and delicate neoclassical manner reminiscent of the Louis XVI and Adam styles. Mahogany and satinwood were the preferred woods. The chairs generally had square, cut-out backs, and the furniture legs, square or cylindrical in cross-section, were slender, tapering, and often reeded. Some pieces of furniture showed Sheraton's inventive turn. There was much fine carving, inlay, lacquering, and painting in such neoclassical motifs as lyres, urns, festoons, foliage scrolls, and circles and ovals set with shells, rosettes, or fans. *The Drawing Book*, widely copied in England and America, is the basis for Sheraton's great reputation and is what is referred to by the term "Sheraton style." The term "Sheraton" applied to furniture should be interpreted as Sheraton style.

Sheraton's later works consist of *The Cabinet Dictionary* (1803), which was arbitrary in its choice of terms, and *The Cabinet-Maker, Upholsterer, and General Artist's Encyclopedia,* of which one volume, A–C, appeared in 1805. Its plates were influenced by French Empire and English Regency styles. A marked departure from Sheraton's early work, they show heavy forms, eccentric ornament, and wild color. Sheraton died in poverty in London on Oct. 22, 1806.

Further Reading: Fastnedge, Ralph, *Sheraton Furniture* (Faber 1962).

SHERBROOKE, shûr′brŏŏk, a city in southern Quebec, Canada, the seat of Sherbrooke county, is situated at the confluence of the Magog and St. Francis rivers, 93 miles (150 km) east of Montreal and about 30 miles (48 km) north of the U. S. border at Norton, Vt. It is the commercial metropolis of the part of Quebec known as the Eastern Townships. Manufacturers produce a large variety of goods, including textiles, machinery, wearing apparel, rubber, soft drinks and processed foods, chocolate, superheaters, and hockey sticks.

The Université de Sherbrooke, a government-sponsored Roman Catholic institution, is here. The city also has a Roman Catholic cathedral, and St. Peter's, built in 1844, is one of the oldest Anglican churches in the Eastern Townships.

Sherbrooke was incorporated as a town in 1852 and as a city in 1875. Population: 74,075.

SHERIDAN, Philip Henry (1831–1888), Union general in the American Civil War. He was born in Albany, N. Y., on March 6, 1831, but when he was a boy his family moved to Somerset in Perry county, Ohio. He was appointed to the U. S. Military Academy at West Point in 1848 but did not graduate until 1853 because he was suspended in 1852 for an assault upon a cadet sergeant. Sheridan's early service was in Oregon, Washington Territory, and California.

Early in 1861, Sheridan was promoted to lieutenant and then to captain. His industry won him the regard of Gen. Henry W. Halleck, who assigned him to various administrative posts. When the Civil War began, he was chief quartermaster and commissary of the Union army of southwest Missouri.

He remained a captain and practically a noncombatant until May 25, 1862, when friends secured him command of the 2d Regiment of Michigan Volunteer Cavalry. As a cavalry commander, Sheridan quickly distinguished himself. On July 1, 1862, he defeated a greatly superior Confederate force at Booneville, Miss. This brought him promotion to brigadier general, U. S. Volunteers. Transferred in September to Gen. Don Carlos Buell's command, he showed himself an outstanding infantry division commander at the battles of Perryville and Stone's River, and was promoted major general of Volunteers on December 31. His conduct at the Battle of Chickamauga (Sept. 19–20, 1863) was criticized by some as more prudent than heroic, but he at least kept his division intact. He won great distinction in the assault on Missionary Ridge at Chattanooga (Nov. 25, 1863). In April 1864, Gen. Ulysses S. Grant (on Halleck's recommendation) selected Sheridan to command the cavalry corps of the Army of the Potomac.

Cavalry Command. In this new and demanding assignment, Sheridan had much to learn. During the Battle of the Wilderness, he failed to guard the flanks of the Union army, insisting that his mission was to seek out and destroy the Confederate cavalry. After some wrangling, Sheridan secured Grant's permission to "cut loose" on May 8, and launched a raid on Richmond, Va., which drew the Confederate cavalry under Gen. J. E. B. Stuart after him. He rejoined the Army of the Potomac on May 24 after riding completely around Gen. Robert E. Lee's army and winning four engagements, in one of which Stuart was killed. In the meantime, however, without cavalry, Grant had been forced to operate blindly in hostile countryside. Furthermore, the Confederate cavalry had not been seriously hurt. Led by Gen. Wade Hampton, it defeated Sheridan at Trevilian Station, Va., in June.

In August 1864, Grant entrusted Sheridan with the Federal command of the Shenandoah Valley. After careful preparations, he defeated Confederate forces under Gen. Jubal A. Early at Winchester and Fisher's Hill, then began to withdraw from the valley, systematically destroying or carrying off all supplies that could be useful to the Confederate armies.

Undaunted, Early surprised Sheridan's army at Cedar Creek on October 19, during Sheridan's absence. After initial success, the Confederate attack stalled, and Sheridan—riding furiously to rejoin his troops—led them forward in an overwhelming counterattack. Early in 1865, he again raided up the Shenandoah Valley to Charlottesville, destroying Early's tiny remaining force at Waynesboro en route.

Thereafter, he rejoined the Army of the Potomac before Richmond and became the cutting edge of Grant's final offensive, defeating Gen. George E. Pickett at Five Forks on April 1, and thereafter harrying and blocking Lee's retreating forces until their surrender at Appomattox Station on April 9.

Postwar Career. Sheridan emerged from the Civil War a major general of the regular Army. When hostilities ended, he was sent to Texas with a veteran army to restore order and bring pressure on the empire of Mexico, which Napoleon III had established with Austrian Archduke Maximilian as emperor. As military governor in Texas and Louisiana, his rule was so harsh that President Andrew Johnson relieved him in 1867, transferring him to the West, where he became responsible for Indian campaigns that took up most of his remaining active service. He became

Gen. Philip H. Sheridan during the Civil War

THE BETTMANN ARCHIVE

a lieutenant general in 1869; accompanied the Prussian Army as observer during the Franco-Prussian War of 1870; and in 1883 succeeded Gen. William T. Sherman as Army commander in chief. In 1888, shortly before his death, he was promoted general, U. S. Army.

Character. Sheridan was a professional soldier, never interested, like many of his fellow officers, in politics or business. His military virtues were energy, pugnacity, common sense, and a mastery of the administrative skills necessary for taking the best possible care of his command. He was always careful to secure accurate information concerning the enemy and the terrain, maintaining picked detachments of expert guides, scouts, and spies. Finally, he possessed a definite, natural, personal magnetism that bound his men to him, even though he enforced strict discipline. Of limited education himself, he improved the Army's sketchy military school at Fort Leavenworth. Some of his contemporaries found him uncooperative. Naturally, his positive nature made him enemies. His relief of Gen. Gouverneur K. Warren after Five Forks caused considerable ill feeling. As a subordinate, he was often set on having his own way and occasionally showed considerable skill in evading the spirit of his orders without openly disobeying them. But, above all, he was a fighter. Sheridan died at Nonquitt, Mass., on Aug. 5, 1888.

JOHN R. ELTING
Colonel, U. S. Army (Retired)

Further Reading: Hergesheimer, Joseph, *Sheridan* (Houghton 1931); O'Connor, Richard, *Sheridan the Inevitable* (Bobbs 1953); Sheridan, Philip Henry, *Personal Memoirs*, 2 vols. (1888); Stackpole, Edward J., *Sheridan in the Shenandoah* (Stackpole 1961).

SHERIDAN, Richard Brinsley (1751–1816), British playwright, politician, and orator. His plays moved away from the then popular sentimental comedies but remained rooted in the more stable traditions of English comedy. They show a thorough knowledge of the stage and provoke laughter with their intricately maneuvered action and disclosures of human foibles. *The Rivals* and *The School for Scandal* were among the funniest and most human plays of the 18th century, and they remain popular today.

Early Life. Sheridan was born in Dublin, Ireland, and baptized on Nov. 4, 1751. He was the third son of Thomas Sheridan, an actor and teacher of elocution, and his wife Frances Chamberlaine, author of a novel and two published plays. He was educated at Harrow school, where he was an indifferent and negligent student but popular with his classmates. In 1770 his father moved to Bath, where young Sheridan was introduced into the society that he was later to portray so delightfully in his comedies.

While in Bath, Sheridan also met the family of the well-known musician and composer Thomas Linley, whose daughter Elizabeth Ann was an accomplished and popular singer. These family contacts led to Sheridan's romantic courtship of Elizabeth, which resulted in their eloping to France to escape the unwelcome attentions to Elizabeth of one Thomas Matthews. They were secretly married in France, but their families had them brought home and separated. Sheridan fought two duels with Matthews. Finally, on April 13, 1773, Elizabeth and Sheridan were officially married with their parents' consent.

Author and Theater Manager. Soon after his marriage, Sheridan began his theater career.

THE BETTMANN ARCHIVE
Richard Brinsley Sheridan, British playwright

His first comedy, *The Rivals,* was produced in London at Covent Garden on Jan. 17, 1775. A failure the first night, it was withdrawn and subjected to "some severe prunings, trimmings and patchings," with the result that it was a great success on its second performance, on January 28. His next play was the two-act farce, *St. Patrick's Day,* first performed on May 2 at the same theater. *The Duenna,* a comic opera, with music by Thomas Linley and some songs probably arranged by Mrs. Sheridan, was well received at Covent Garden on Nov. 21, 1775, and became the favorite musical comedy of its day.

In June 1776 the great actor and theater manager David Garrick retired from the stage and sold his share of the Drury Lane Theatre to Sheridan, Linley, and James Ford, the fashionable "man midwife" (obstetrician). Already established as a playwright, Sheridan now embarked upon a career as a theater manager. In 1777 he and his associates secured the remaining half of the Drury Lane patent. Sheridan managed the theater, except for a brief period, until 1782. But he constantly neglected the business of running the theater and finally gave up the management to others, although he continued to hold his shares of the patent and to rely upon the theater for his living.

For his first contribution to the Drury Lane repertory, Sheridan adapted Sir John Vanbrugh's 1696 play *The Relapse,* which he presented under the title *A Trip to Scarborough* on Feb. 24, 1777. *The School for Scandal* followed on May 8, 1777. Immediately successful, it has ever since been regarded as the best comedy written in the 18th century. Sheridan's last original play, *The Critic,* a burlesque of bombastic tragedy and sentimental comedy, was performed at Drury Lane on Oct. 30, 1779.

Sheridan's career as an active playwright, then, lasted only five years. After a long period devoted to politics, however, he wrote an adaptation of an English translation of von Kotzebue's *Die Spanier in Peru* (*The Spanish in Peru*),

produced May 24, 1799, as *Pizarro.* He also contributed to several occasional entertainments performed at Drury Lane and wrote the *Verses to the Memory of Garrick,* spoken at the theater on March 11, 1779. See also RIVALS, THE; SCHOOL FOR SCANDAL.

Political and Social Life. Over 30 years of Sheridan's life were devoted to politics. He was a member of Parliament for Stafford (1780–1806), for Westminster (1806), and for Ilchester (1807–1812). Associated with Edmund Burke and Charles James Fox, who sought reform, he was generally in opposition, but he held office briefly as undersecretary for the northern department (of foreign affairs) in 1782, as secretary of the treasury in 1783, and as treasurer of the navy in 1806. A friend and supporter of the Prince of Wales (later George IV), he was appointed receiver general of the Duchy of Cornwall in 1804. One of the most eloquent orators in the Commons, he attracted large audiences, especially to his somewhat theatrical denunciations of Warren Hastings during the impeachment and trial of that colonial administrator in 1787–1788.

Sheridan's social career was equally spectacular. He was a member of the Literary Club, proposed by Samuel Johnson on March 14, 1777; he and his wife frequented the highest social circles; and he was intimate with the Prince of Wales, indulging in the extravagances and dissipations of the Carlton House set.

Last Years. Sheridan's wife died in 1792, leaving a son, Thomas. In 1795, Sheridan married Esther Jane Ogle, by whom he had another son, Charles Brinsley.

Always improvident, Sheridan accumulated enormous debts, and the destruction by fire of the Drury Lane playhouse on Feb. 24, 1809, precipitated his financial ruin. After the loss of his seat in Parliament, he was beset by his creditors, and bailiffs occupied his house, where he lay in his last illness. He refused to take advantage of opportunities to enrich himself by political patronage, and he died in relative poverty, in London, on July 7, 1816.

DOUGALD MACMILLAN
The University of North Carolina

Bibliography

Editions of Sheridan's Works include *The Plays & Poems of Richard Brinsley Sheridan,* ed. by Raymond Crompton Rhodes, 3 vols. (1928; reprint, 1962).
Gibbs, Lewis, *Sheridan, His Life and His Theatre* (1948; reprint, Kennikat 1970).
Moore, Thomas, *Memoirs of the Life of the Right Honourable Richard Brinsley Sheridan,* 2 vols. (Scholarly Press 1826).
Rhodes, Raymond Crompton, *Harlequin Sheridan: The Man and the Legends* (Oxford 1933).
Sadleir, Michael T., *The Political Career of Richard Brinsley Sheridan* (Folcroft Press 1912).
Sherwin, Oscar, *Uncorking Old Sherry: The Life and Times of Richard Brinsley Sheridan* (Burns & MacEachan 1960).

SHERIDAN, the largest city in northern Wyoming, the seat of Sheridan county, is situated about 150 miles (240 km) north of Casper and about 18 miles (28 km) south of the Montana boundary. Sheridan is the trading and supply center of a large farming and coal-mining area.

The community was named for Gen. Philip H. Sheridan, Union cavalry leader in the Civil War. It was incorporated as a town in 1884 and as a city in 1907. Government is by city manager. Population: 15,146.

SHERIF. See SHARIF.

SHERIFF, a senior executive officer of a county in jurisdictions that adhere to the British form of county administration. In the British commonwealth he is appointed; in the United States, he is generally elected, with a term usually from two to four years. In England the office antedates the Norman Conquest. As the king's chief man in the county, or shire, the Saxons called him *scyrereve,* that is, *shire keeper,* hence sheriff.

In addition to his judicial authority and his responsibility for executing royal writs, the sheriff was originally responsible for revenues, police, and jails. Magna Carta stripped him of his most important judicial power, and in the 16th century he was also stripped of his important military authority. The duties of the modern English office of sheriff include the regulating of parliamentary elections, executing of process issuing from the High Court and the criminal courts, the calling of jurors, and levying in cases of forfeitures of recognizances, or bonds.

In the United States, the duties of sheriffs, though far from uniform, have generally followed a traditional pattern. The sheriff has the duty of maintaining the peace in areas of a county that are not within the jurisdiction of a specified city police force. He makes arrests and takes bail. He also generally has the power to appoint deputies, but he cannot delegate this power of appointment. He serves summonses to initiate litigation and executes a variety of court orders, particularly for the summoning of juries and the execution of money or property judgments. In some places he also supervises elections and collects taxes.

The sheriff is usually bonded and is liable for erroneous or unauthorized seizures of property. He may be criminally liable for a willful and corrupt breach of duty, and is also usually liable for the wrongful acts of his appointed deputies. In making an execution sale, the sheriff in no way guarantees the validity of the title of the property sold unless he specifically purports to do so. The buyer takes no better title than the person against whom the execution is issued.

SHERLOCK HOLMES is the major character in a series of novels and short stories by Sir Arthur Conan Doyle. Holmes, probably the most famous detective in fiction, is able to solve the most baffling crimes through the process of deductive reasoning. He is assisted by his friend Dr. Watson, a bumbling physician with a good-natured and pompous personality, who serves as an excellent foil to the brilliant, somewhat brusque detective.

Holmes, who was originally named Sherringford Holmes and who lived in fictional quarters at 221b Baker Street, London, first appeared in the novel *A Study in Scarlet* (1887). His adventures were continued in other novels—*The Sign of the Four* (1890), *The Hound of the Baskervilles* (1902), and *The Valley of Fear* (1915)—and in a series of stories published in the *Strand Magazine.* He became a favorite motion picture hero, especially as portrayed by Basil Rathbone. See also DOYLE, SIR ARTHUR CONAN.

SHERMAN, James Schoolcraft (1855–1912), American political leader, who served as vice president of the United States. He was born in Utica, N. Y., on Oct. 24, 1855. He graduated from Hamilton College, was admitted to the bar, and began practice in Utica.

Entering politics as a Republican, Sherman served as mayor of Utica (1884) and in the U. S. House of Representatives (1887–1891, 1893–1909). A skillful politician, he allied himself with the conservative Republican leadership in the House. Interested primarily in parliamentary maneuver, Sherman is identified with little important legislation. He was elected vice president on the ticket with William Howard Taft in 1908. Renominated in 1912, Sherman died in Utica on Oct. 30, 1912, three days before the election, in which Taft was defeated.

SHERMAN, John (1823–1900), American political leader, who in a long public career won almost every honor except the presidency. He was born in Lancaster, Ohio, on May 10, 1823. His father, a member of the state supreme court, died in 1829, leaving his widow with 11 children to support. John, the eighth child, was three years younger than his favorite brother, William Tecumseh Sherman, the future general.

John left school at the age of 14 to go to work but then turned to the study of law under an uncle and his oldest brother, Charles. Admitted to the bar in 1844, he also entered business in lumbering and real estate. His marriage in 1848 to the daughter of a prominent Mansfield, Ohio, lawyer strengthened the social and professional foundations for his political career.

At first a Whig, Sherman joined the new Republican party and was elected to the U. S. House of Representatives in 1854. After 6 years in the House, Sherman was elected to the U. S. Senate, where he was to serve 32 years (1861–1877, 1881–1897), his membership there interrupted only by 4 years as secretary of the treasury under President Rutherford B. Hayes. As chairman of the Senate finance committee and later in the cabinet, Sherman emerged as the ablest financial expert in public life. In expenditures, he favored a "pay as you go" philosophy. Though he had supported legal tender status for greenbacks during the Civil War, Sherman later convinced bankers that the government should redeem its obligations in gold. He supported passage of the Specie Resumption Act in 1875, and while at the Treasury oversaw its successful implementation in 1879.

Back in the Senate, Sherman's skill at compromise resulted in 1890 in the adoption of two laws bearing his name: the antitrust act aimed at "conspiracy, in the restraint of trade" and the silver purchase act. Three times an aspirant for the presidential nomination (1880, 1884, 1888), Sherman failed to overcome his colorless personality and the opposition of inflationists.

President William McKinley, to make room in the Senate for his leading political adviser, Mark Hanna, named Sherman secretary of state in 1897. The aged Sherman, his memory failing, could not discharge his duties satisfactorily. Furthermore, he opposed the prevailing expansionist sentiment. After the United States declared war against Spain in 1898, McKinley obtained his resignation. Sherman died in Washington, D. C., on Oct. 22, 1900.

SHERMAN, Roger (1721–1793), American political leader and signer of the Declaration of Independence. He was born in Newton, Mass., on April 19, 1721. As a boy in Stoughton, Mass., he learned farming and shoemaking from his father. He supplemented brief elementary schooling by extensive self-education. Moving to New Milford, Conn., in 1743, he practiced farming, shoemaking, and surveying, and he and his brother William kept a general store.

In 1745, Roger became county surveyor, a lucrative position, and from 1750 to 1761 he prepared a series of annual almanacs. After studying law briefly he was admitted to the bar in 1754, and soon was elected justice of the peace, member of the county court, and representative in the legislature. In 1761, Sherman moved to New Haven, where until 1772 he kept a store. He represented New Haven in the legislature (1764–1766); was a member of the council (1766–1785); and served as an elected judge in the Superior Court (1766–1788).

Sherman disliked violent radical action, and in the mid-1760's he joined the moderate opposition to British regulation and in principle denied Parliament's right to make laws for America. During the Revolution he was a vigorous leader in Congress and in Connecticut's legislature, fighting persistently for sound money and adequate taxation. He served on the committee that drafted the Declaration of Independence, and was the only American to sign four historic documents: the Continental Association of 1774, the Declaration of Independence, the Articles of Confederation, and the Federal Constitution. In 1783 he and Richard Law prepared a revision of Connecticut's laws, published in 1784, and he was elected New Haven's first mayor in 1784. At the Philadelphia Convention of 1787 he decided that a stronger central government was required, and presented the famous "Connecticut Compromise" setting up two houses of Congress, one with representation equal for each state and the other proportional to population. Back home, he fought hard for ratification. He closed his distinguished career with two years in Congress as representative and two years as senator.

Sherman was conservative in religion and politics and very dubious of the masses' ability to govern themselves. His contemporaries noted his high intelligence, unswerving honesty, stern devotion to duty, and unusual awkwardness in manner. Thomas Jefferson described him as "a man who never said a foolish thing in his life," and John Adams called him "as honest as an angel and as firm in the cause of American independence as Mount Atlas." Sherman died in New Haven, Conn., on July 23, 1793.

ALBERT VAN DUSEN
University of Connecticut

SHERMAN, Stuart Pratt (1881–1926), American educator and literary critic. He was born in Anita, Iowa, on Oct. 1, 1881, and graduated from Williams College in 1903 and received a Ph.D. from Harvard in 1906. He taught, first at Northwestern University (1906–1907) and then at the University of Illinois (1907–1924). His *Matthew Arnold* and *On Contemporary Literature* (both 1917) were drawn from his university lectures.

In 1917, Sherman began a long, spirited, and witty literary quarrel with H. L. Mencken over the latter's pro-Nietschean views. He also at first opposed the aesthetic theories of Benedetto Croce but then adopted them in his own critical works *Americans* (1922), *The Genius of America* (1923), and *Points of View* (1924). In 1924 he became editor of *Books*, the literary supplement of the New York *Herald Tribune*. Sherman died near Manistee, Mich., on Aug. 21, 1926.

SHERMAN, William Tecumseh (1820–1891), American general, who was one of the greatest Union commanders in the Civil War. Possessing a quick and incisive mind and a strong personality, Sherman saw the war in broad strategic terms, and he comprehended its social, political, and economic aspects more clearly than did most military men.

Sherman was born on Feb. 8, 1820, at Lancaster, Ohio. He was named Tecumseh because his father admired the Shawnee Indian chief of that name. At the age of nine, he was adopted after his father's death by Thomas Ewing, who had been active in national politics. His foster mother insisted that "William" be prefaced to his name. Through his foster father's influence, Sherman was appointed to the U. S. Military Academy. He graduated in 1840, sixth in a class of 42, ranking highest in engineering, rhetoric, mental philosophy—and demerits.

Early Career. Commissioned July 1, 1840 as a 2d lieutenant in the 3d Artillery, Sherman was stationed in Florida and as a 1st lieutenant commanded a small detachment at Picolata. Transferred in 1842 to Fort Moultrie, S. C., Sherman spent four happy years in Charleston, captivated by the social life. In the Mexican War he was stationed in California and saw no fighting. In 1850 he returned to Washington, D. C., where his foster father was serving as secretary of the interior, and married his foster sister, Ellen Boyle Ewing.

As a captain in the commissary department, Sherman served in St. Louis, Mo., and New Orleans, La., but discouraged by his prospects and the "dull, tame life" of the Army, resigned from the service on Sept. 6, 1853. Next he represented the St. Louis banking firm of Lucas, Turner & Co., in San Francisco, but the panic in the goldfields during 1854–1855 doomed the San Francisco branch bank. He sought unsuccessfully to get back into the Army, and went to Kansas to manage real estate owned by his family. At Leavenworth during 1858–1859 he tried a brief fling as a lawyer, but was quickly betrayed by the temper that went with his red hair and beard. With the help of two army friends, Pierre G. P. Beauregard and Braxton Bragg, he secured appointment as superintendent of the state military academy at Alexandria, La.

An indulgent teacher devoted to his students, Sherman began to reveal that paternalistic streak that during the Civil War made him the idol of the Western armies. In dismay he watched secession sweep through the South, and when Louisiana left the Union in January 1861, Sherman resigned from the only job he ever really had liked, predicting that the South was rushing into disaster and writing his daughter that "men are blind and crazy." Irritated when President Abraham Lincoln shrugged off his advice about the situation in Louisiana, Sherman went to St. Louis resolved to sit out the war as president of the Fifth Street Railroad.

Civil War Service. Sherman was vigorously roused by the Confederate firing on Fort Sumter in April 1861. He regarded President Lincoln's call for 75,000 volunteers for three months' service as trifling with a desperate emergency. The Army was reaching for trained officers, and Sherman accepted a commission as a colonel.

He commanded a brigade at the First Battle of Bull Run (Manassas). That confused action, which ended in a panic of the Union troops, was

Sherman's first battle experience, and it convinced him that he was unfit for the responsibility of an independent command.

But Lincoln ignored Sherman's plea that he be spared such responsibility. He promoted Sherman to brigadier general and sent him to Kentucky to share a command with Gen. Robert Anderson, who had defended Fort Sumter in the war's first engagement.

Here Sherman was nervous and confused. He suffered under the delusion that his forces were about to be overwhelmed by superior Confederate power. He so unnerved those around him that the Cincinnati *Commercial* published a report that he was insane. He was called "Crazy" Sherman, and his army career seemed at an end. But Gen. Henry W. Halleck, in command at St.

THE BETTMANN ARCHIVE

GEN. WILLIAM TECUMSEH SHERMAN was one of the foremost soldiers in the American Civil War.

Louis, recognized Sherman's special talent in military planning and gave him another chance. Sherman worked on the plans for Gen. Ulysses S. Grant's campaign against Forts Henry and Donelson in early 1862. His admiration for Grant grew into a devoted friendship.

Under Grant, Sherman commanded brilliantly at the Battle of Shiloh (April 6–7, 1862). When Grant, in despair over criticism of his conduct of the battle, talked of leaving the Army, Sherman was able to persuade his friend to await a turn in fortune.

Promoted to major general, dating from May 1, 1862, Sherman played a principal role in the campaign under Grant that led to the siege and capture of Vicksburg. Sherman began with a failure in that campaign, when with an expedition of 32,000 men he floundered at Chickasaw Bluffs (Dec. 27–29, 1862). He cooperated with Gen. John A. McClernand in the capture of Fort Hindman, Ark. (Jan. 4–12, 1863), and thereafter commanded the 15th Corps for Grant (Jan. 4–Oct. 29, 1863) in the series of engagements that brought about the fall of Vicksburg on July 4, 1863. He opposed Grant's plan to cut loose from his base of supplies and live off the land as he swept around Vicksburg, coming at the city from the rear. Later in the war, Sherman taught his own armies to live off the country.

Sherman succeeded Grant as commanding general of the Department of Tennessee. Later, joining Grant in the Chattanooga campaign, Sherman held the flank against fierce assaults while Gen. George H. Thomas swept to victory on Missionary Ridge (Nov. 24–25, 1863). By forced marches Sherman pushed his troops to Knoxville just in time to save Gen. Ambrose E. Burnside, who was besieged there, from possible disaster (Dec. 3–4, 1863).

In Georgia and the Carolinas. When in March 1864, Grant became commander of all the Union armies, Sherman was assigned to command in the South, mounting a campaign to parallel Grant's drive in Virginia. With about 99,000 men, Sherman started from Chattanooga on May 7, and on Sept. 2 his men occupied Atlanta, the key city of the Deep South, after a siege. In this campaign Sherman's strategic skill was well displayed. He fought few major battles, but maneuvered to outflank his foe time after time.

From Atlanta, Sherman conducted his famous March to the Sea (Nov. 16–Dec. 22), leading 62,000 men in a broad swath through the heart of Georgia, ravaging the countryside. "I can make Georgia howl," he said, and the psychological impact of this march was devastating to the South.

When Sherman's army entered Savannah, he wired Lincoln: "I beg to present you, as a Christmas gift, the city of Savannah, with 150 heavy guns, plenty of ammunition, and 25,000 bales of cotton." On Jan. 15, 1865, Congress voted its thanks to Sherman for his "triumphal march."

In February 1865, Sherman headed north through the Carolinas, aiming at a junction with Grant's forces in Virginia, which would end the war. Confederates led by Gen. Joseph E. Johnston could offer only token resistance. The last battle was fought at Bentonville, N. C., on March 19–21. When Gen. Robert E. Lee surrendered to Grant in Virginia on April 9, Johnston's position was hopeless. Sherman accepted his surrender near Durham, N. C., on April 26. Sherman was sharply criticized for the generosity of the terms he offered.

Postwar Years. Commanding the military division of the Mississippi from 1865 to 1869, Sherman was promoted to lieutenant general (1866) and to full general (1869). When Grant was inaugurated president in 1869, Sherman became general in chief of the army, a post he held for 14 years.

Sherman remained a popular figure, known for his broad and positive views on public affairs. He was much in demand as a speaker, especially at veterans' meetings.

Periodically, a boom was begun to draft Sherman as a presidential candidate. His telegram in response to such an appeal from the Republican national convention in 1884 was a classic example of brief, forthright statement: "I will not accept if nominated, and will not serve if elected."

Sherman published his *Memoirs* in 1875. He died in New York City on Feb. 14, 1891.

Further Reading: Lewis, Lloyd, *Sherman, Fighting Prophet* (Harcourt 1958); Liddell Hart, Basil H., *Sherman* (Dodd 1929); Merrill, James M., *William Tecumseh Sherman* (Rand 1971); Williams, T. Harry, *McClellan, Sherman, and Grant* (Rutgers Univ. Press 1962).

SHERMAN, a city in northeastern Texas, the seat of Grayson county, is about 60 miles (96 km) north of Dallas and about 15 miles (24 km) south of the Oklahoma boundary. Sherman is a distributing point for farm crops, livestock, and oil, which are produced in the area. The city's industries manufacture electronic components, machinery, truck bodies, textiles, first aid supplies, and business forms. Food processing is important.

Austin College, a coeducational Presbyterian institution, is in Sherman. At Denison, 8 miles (12 km) to the northeast, is Dwight D. Eisenhower state park, which contains the birthplace of the former president. Lake Texoma, on the Red River at the Oklahoma border, provides a huge recreation area.

Sherman was settled in 1849 and incorporated as a town in 1854. Sherman became a city in 1895 and is governed by a city manager.

Sherman and Denison form a metropolitan area that covers the county. Population: (metropolitan area) 89,796; (city) 30,413.

SHERMAN ANTITRUST ACT, an act passed by the U. S. Congress in 1890 to combat monopoly and improper restraints on competition. Because of the increase in industrialization following the Civil War, and the inability of the common law and state legislation to curb concentrations of economic power and abuses of such power, Congress enacted on July 2, 1890, a statute that has come to be regarded as the country's economic constitution, an expression of national faith in free competitive enterprise. The act was named for U. S. Senator John Sherman (1823–1900), a former secretary of the treasury. With respect to activities affecting interstate and foreign commerce, the Sherman Act prohibits two broadly phrased practices: (1) contracts, combinations, and conspiracies in restraint of trade, and (2) monopolization and attempts and conspiracies to monopolize.

The proscription of various agreements in restraint of trade was judicially restricted in 1911 to unreasonable restraints of trade. Under this "rule of reason," the burden was placed on the party attacking a restrictive practice to prove that its detrimental effects on competition outweighed the business justifications supporting the practice. This dilution of the first of the Sherman Act's prohibitions was countered by two developments. First, Congress responded in 1914 with the Clayton Act, which applied more stringent standards to certain practices, such as exclusive dealing arrangements, contracts tying the sale of one product to another, and discriminatory pricing. In the same year, Congress created the Federal Trade Commission and authorized it to forbid "unfair" competitive practices. Second, the courts, operating within the "rule of reason," defined several categories of particularly obnoxious restraints as unreasonable per se, that is, unlawful without regard to their merits or demerits in the particular case. Practices thus condemned include agreements among different firms to fix prices or divide markets, group boycotts, and certain uses of patent rights to gain advantages with respect to unpatented articles. The trend is toward expansion of the classes of per se illegality and contraction of areas in which practices must be shown to be unreasonable in their particular economic setting. Certain kinds of resale price maintenance con-

tracts have been exempted by legislation from the ban of the Sherman Act.

The second of the Sherman Act's prohibitions, directed at monopolization, was used principally to challenge concentrations of economic power in a single business organization. Where a single firm achieved such dominance that it had control of more than 65% of a recognized industry or market, a charge of monopolization might be prosecuted, although not always successfully. But where dominance rested in several firms, a situation described as oligopoly, the charge of monopolization could not be sustained. And under the "rule of reason" the courts generally refused to find that merger agreements and other transactions leading to oligopolistic concentration constituted unreasonable restraints of trade. Again Congress responded, forbidding certain kinds of stock acquisitions in the Clayton Act of 1914 and, when this proved ineffective, enacting a still broader ban on mergers and related transactions in the Celler-Kefauver Amendment of 1950. Following this third attempt by Congress to limit undue concentration in industry, both the courts and the Federal Trade Commission have tended to outlaw all mergers showing even the slightest tendency toward oligopoly.

The Sherman Act, as supplemented by the Clayton and Federal Trade Commission acts, is enforced by criminal prosecutions carrying penalties of fine and imprisonment, government injunction suits, actions by injured private parties for injunctions and treble damages, and administrative proceedings by the Federal Trade Commission. See also ANTITRUST LAWS.

WILLIAM K. JONES
Law School, Columbia University

SHERPA, sher'pə, a people of Mongoloid racial stock inhabiting the high valleys of Solo and Khumbu in northern Nepal. They cultivate wheat, barley, and potatoes and herd sheep, goats, and yaks. Excellent mountain climbers and accustomed to high altitudes, the Sherpa are much sought after as guides and porters for Himalayan expeditions. The first climbers to reach the summit of Mt. Everest were the Sherpa Tenzing Norkay and the New Zealander Sir Edmund Hillary in 1953.

SHERRELWOOD, an unincorporated area of Adams county in north central Colorado, is about 10 miles (16 km) east of the foothills of the Rocky Mountains, and about 5 miles (8 km) north of the city of Denver. Sherrelwood was built up in the late 1960's as a residential suburb of Denver, with zoning laws aimed at keeping out industry. Population: 18,868.

SHERRINGTON, Sir Charles Scott (1857–1952), English neurophysiologist who shared the 1932 Nobel Prize in physiology or medicine with Edward Douglas Adrian for investigations of the nervous system. Sherrington was born in London on Nov. 27, 1857, and qualified in medicine at St. Thomas' Hospital in 1885. He worked in Europe with notable scientists such as Robert Koch and Rudolf Virchow before returning to a lectureship at St. Thomas'. In 1891 he was appointed superintendent of the Brown Institution in London, and thereafter he taught and did research at Liverpool and Oxford. He was knighted in 1922 and died in Eastbourne on March 4, 1952.

Sherrington's publications deal primarily with studies of the nervous system. He mapped out the motor nerve supply of muscles and showed that one third of these nerve fibers carry impulses back to the central nervous system. In 1897 he established the concept that when one set of muscles is stimulated, the opposing set is inhibited in reflex. He later investigated reflex processes in nerve cells of the spinal cord. Sherrington was also interested in pathology and was the first to use diphtheria antitoxin successfully in Britain. He was active in public health and scientific organization activities, and he served as president of the Royal Society from 1920 to 1925.

SHERRY is a fortified white wine, usually marketed in delicate blends. It is named for the city of Jerez, Spain, which dominates the original Sherry district in the southern province of Cádiz. The wines in the blend are made from the Palomino grape. During aging the sherries are blended by using the *solera* system, wherein a bottom tier of casks is replenished from a higher tier of casks containing younger wines and so on up in a series of 5 to 11 stages of blending. The blend is fortified · with brandy and sometimes sweetened or colored, guaranteeing a consistency in any given category of sherry.

The different categories of sherry have a wide range of taste and color. *Fino, Vino de Pasto,* and *Amontillado* are dry, nutty, and light; *Oloroso, Amoroso,* and *Golden* are medium dry; and *Cream* and *Brown* sherries are sweet and dark. Although sherry may be drunk as a dinner wine, the drier ones are usually served as before-dinner cocktails and the sweeter ones reserved for dessert or after dinner.

Sherry has been made in Spain since the Middle Ages. In the 16th century it became very popular in England under the name *sack* (Shakespeare's fat knight, Sir John Falstaff, drank quantities of sack), and today many of the largest distributors of sherry are English. Sherry is also made in the United States, South Africa, and Australia, where technological controls are used to develop the flavor.

'S HERTOGENBOSCH, ser'tō-кнən-bôs, is a city in the south central Netherlands and the capital of North Brabant province. The city, popularly known as Den Bosch, is at the confluence of the Dommel and Aa rivers and is linked by canal with the Maas (Meuse) River, slightly to the north. There is a magnificent 15th–16th century flamboyant Gothic cathedral with a 13th century tower and a 16th century city hall.

Its charter was granted in 1184 by Henry I, Duke of Brabant, after whom it was named. The French form of its name is Bois-le-Duc, and both the Dutch and French forms mean "the duke's woods." During the Eighty Years' War (1568–1648), when the Protestant Dutch revolted against Spanish rule, 's Hertogenbosch remained Catholic and loyal to Spain. It was besieged several times before it was captured in 1629. The Dutch painter Hieronymus Bosch was born in the city. Population: (1971) 81,401.

SHERWOOD, Robert E. (1896–1955), American playwright and journalist, the winner of four Pulitzer prizes, whose plays ranged from light comedy to heavy melodrama. Many of them were political, often supporting pacifism.

Life. Robert Emmet Sherwood was born in New Rochelle, N. Y., on April 4, 1896. His college studies were interrupted in 1917, when he enlisted in the 42d Battalion of the Canadian Black Watch to fight in World War I. He returned, embittered by the war, and went back to school, graduating from Harvard in 1918.

Sherwood was drama critic for *Vanity Fair* magazine in 1919–1920. He was associate editor (1920–1924) and editor (1924–1928) of *Life* magazine and at the same time was motion-picture editor of both *Life* and the New York *Herald* and literary editor of *Scribner's Magazine.*

During World War II, Sherwood served President Franklin D. Roosevelt as speech writer and literary adviser and also directed the overseas branch of the Office of War Information. Out of his White House experience came the book *Roosevelt and Hopkins* (1948), which ranks among the most important primary sources for the history of the Roosevelt era. In 1949 it was awarded both the Pulitzer and the Bancroft prizes for historical writing. Sherwood died in New York City on Nov. 14, 1955.

Plays. Sherwood's first play, *The Road to Rome* (1927), was an immediate success. Obviously indebted to George Bernard Shaw's *Caesar and Cleopatra,* it dealt imaginatively with Hannibal's halt before Rome in the Second Punic War. A dozen years later Sherwood remarked wryly that he had "tried in it every style of dramaturgy—high comedy, low comedy, melodrama, romance (both sacred and profane), hard-boiled realism, beautiful writing—and, of course, . . . a 'message.' That message was that I was opposed to war."

Some of these ingredients were used separately in succeeding plays: farcical comedy in *The Queen's Husband* (1928), romantic comedy in *Reunion in Vienna* (1931), and melodrama in *The Petrified Forest* (1934). *Waterloo Bridge* (1929) was his first serious effort to dramatize the plight of the idealist and man of good will in the years between the two world wars.

Robert E. Sherwood, American playwright

BROWN BROTHERS

Idiot's Delight (1936) pictured a polyglot group, mostly well meaning, trapped by the outbreak of war and drawn into its vortex. This play, which won a Pulitzer Prize, was prompted by the brutal swaggering of Mussolini's Fascists and Hitler's Nazis. The tragic dilemma of a man of peace who has to make war is further developed in Sherwood's second Pulitzer Prize play, *Abe Lincoln in Illinois* (1938).

Like many idealists of the 1930's, Sherwood had hoped that the Soviets might someday show the way to a better world order. The Stalin-Hitler alliance, followed by Russia's aggression against Finland, completed his disillusionment with the world. *There Shall Be No Night,* perhaps his strongest play, dramatized the problem of whether an intelligent man should remain intellectually detached or heroically risk his life to help others. This play was written in white heat in 1940, and brought him his third Pulitzer Prize. Sherwood's screenplay for *The Best Years of Our Lives* (1946), depicting disabled veterans adapting themselves to their estranged families after World War II, won an Academy Award.

DELANCEY FERGUSON
Formerly, Brooklyn College

SHERWOOD FOREST is an ancient forest in central England, known for its associations with the legends of Robin Hood. It is in the west of Nottinghamshire in a low, sandy district between Nottingham and Worksop, extending 25 miles (40 km) from north to south and 5 to 10 miles (8–16 km) from east to west. The town of Mansfield and several villages are within the ancient bounds, and coal is mined in the region.

In the 17th and 18th centuries, most of the trees were cut down for use in building. Only the northern section called the "Dukeries" was spared. Here, on ducal estates, vast gardens were cultivated around ancient oak and birch. In the 20th century the national government acquired about 12,500 acres (5,059 hectares) of the region for reforestation and planted many trees, mostly pines. Some oak, birch, beech, and bracken are still found in Sherwood Forest.

SHETLAND ISLANDS, a group of more than 100 islands, about 130 miles (209 km) northeast of the mainland of Scotland and some 50 miles (80 km) northeast of the Orkney Islands, at the same latitude as southern Greenland. The Shetland Islands constitute the Scottish county of Zetland and the northernmost part of the British Isles. The name Shetland, or Zetland, is believed to be derived from the Old Norse name for the islands, *Hjaltland.*

Many of the islands are very small, and even the larger ones are so shaped that no part of them is more than 3 miles (5 km) from the sea. The terrain is rugged and nearly treeless. There are spectacular seaside cliffs and irregular coastlines with long sea lochs, or voes. The climate is damp, and there is usually a strong wind, but the long winters are not extremely cold. Only about 20 of the islands are inhabited. Mainland, the largest island, has the only burghs—Lerwick, the county town, and Scalloway, a fishing center that was the ancient capital of the islands. Other major islands are Yell, Unst, Fetlar, Bressay, Whalsay, Muckle Roe, Papa Stour, Foula, West Burra, East Burra, Tondra, Fair Isle, and Noss (now a nature preserve).

In the 1970's, exploration for and exploitation of the rich oil deposits in the North Sea off the Shetlands spurred—and greatly altered—the economy of the islands. Traditionally, the breeding of the Shetland pony has been the chief economic activity. The Shetland sheepdog is also bred here. Sheep are raised, and their fine, light wool is knitted into beautiful patterns and exported. Fishing is also important to the traditional economy of the islands.

The Shetland Islands have been inhabited at least since the Bronze Age. At Jarlshof, a 17th century mansion on the southern tip of Mainland, excavations in the 1930's uncovered dwellings and artifacts from the Bronze and Iron Ages and extensive remains of a Viking settlement of the 10th–13th centuries. Sir Walter Scott named the site Jarlshof when he used it as the setting for his novel *The Pirate* (1822). Other places of interest on Mainland are the ruined castle in Scalloway and the Grind of the Navir, a gateway and staircase created by wave action. The caves on Papa Stour are also noteworthy.

In the 7th or 8th century Christian missionaries came to the Shetland Islands and began converting the inhabitants. In the 8th and 9th centuries, the islands were invaded by Norsemen, who ruled here until the 15th century. In 1469, Shetland was pledged to Scotland by Christian I of Denmark as a surety for a part of his daughter's dowry on her marriage to James III. The dowry was never paid, so Scotland annexed the islands in 1472. Population: (1972) of Zetland county, 17,731; of Lerwick, 6,282.

SHETLAND PONY, the smallest of all breeds of ponies. It is a native of the Shetland and Orkney islands lying to the north of Scotland. Of ancient origin, the Shetland has been used for a variety of pack and saddle purposes. Although small, it is strong for its size. The breed is now found in many European countries and the United States, where it has long been popular as a safe and gentle riding pony for children.

The Shetland pony, best known as a saddle horse and harness horse for children, is also trained for show.

The Shetland pony is generally about 9.3 hands (37 inches, or 91 cm) high, and may be any color, including dun, blue dun, piebald, and skewbald. It has a small head and ears, a small muzzle with open nostrils, and a thick mane and tail. Its coat in winter is thick, in summer fine and slick. It has a short, strong back, a deep girth, good withers, and shoulders that slope comfortably for the rider. Its compact little body has very hard, strong legs and small, open feet. See also HORSE—*Horse Breeds of the World*.

SHETLAND SHEEPDOG, a herding dog from the Shetland Islands that looks like a miniature Scotch or Rough collie. Its color is black, golden, or mahogany, with varying amounts of white or tan. The desirable height for "shelties" is 14 inches (35.5 cm), the weight 48 pounds (22 kg). Probably not many modern Shetland sheep-dogs are actively working flocks of sheep, as for many years they did, but from their heritage and background has evolved a remarkably trainable and obedient dog. There seems to be little doubt that the small working collie, from which was produced the larger modern show collie, was also the forebear of the Shetland sheepdog.

SHEVAT, shə-vät′, is the 5th month of the Jewish civil year and the 11th of the religious year. It has 30 days and falls in January-February of Gregorian calendar year. See JEWISH CALENDAR.

SHEWBREAD, shō′bred, was the 12 loaves of consecrated unleavened bread placed upon a table just before the Holy of Holies in the Jewish sanctuary as prescribed in Leviticus 20:5–9. Fresh loaves were set out in two piles on the table every Sabbath, and those removed were eaten by the priests. In an emergency, however, they incurred no blame in giving it to persons who were in a state of ceremonial purity, as in the instance of David and his men (I Samuel 21:4–6).

SHIA, an Islamic group that developed after Mohammed's death. See ISLAM—*The Shia*.

EVELYN M. SHAFER

The Shetland sheepdog, a miniature collie

SHIELD, one of the continental blocks of the earth's crust that have been relatively stable since the rocks solidified in Precambrian times. See GEOLOGY—*The Earth's History*.

SHIELD, a defensive device held by the hand or attached to the arm to ward off blows or projectiles. Throughout the world shields were used wherever people fought in open combat. They have been made of many kinds of materials—wood, leather, wickerwork, metals, cloth, and even turtle shells. The Chinese, for example, made remarkably effective shields of woven cane covered with cloth. In Europe, primitive shields usually were made of wood covered with animal hides, or of hides alone. Later, shields were reinforced with metal rings, covered with iron or bronze plates, or studded with metal nails. Shields were decorated with tribal or personal emblems, and from this developed the art of heraldry and blazonry. In ancient Greece, foot soldiers carried the *aspis*, a round shield of bull's hide overlaid with metal plates and with a boss

THE METROPOLITAN MUSEUM OF ART

St. George in armor on a 15th century shield from Saxony (*left*). Italian shield (*above*) dates from 16th century.

or metal projection in the center, or they bore the oval *sakos* made of wood or wickerwork covered with oxhides, or the heavy, rectangular *hoplon* which gave its name to their shock troops, or hoplites. The circular Roman shield of iron or brass was the *clypeus*, and the rectangular *scutum* was the defense of the legions. The oblong *pavoises* of the Gauls were so large they could be used as boats.

Early Saxon shields were made of light linden wood and leather with an iron reinforcing band, or *umbo*. Shields were hung from the neck by a strap called the *guige* or attached to the arm by two armlets. The big Norman shields were a modified ovate, narrowing to a point at the base. They were used in the conquest of England, as depicted in the Bayeux Tapestry, and also in the Crusades.

Shields were decorated, sometimes with gold and silver. They were hung on the sides of ships for defense and on the walls of banquet halls for ornament, and used as biers when they failed their bearers.

The *buckler, target,* and *targe* were small shields used to ward off blows. The *pavis* was a large convex shield used as a defense against archery at sieges. With the development of plate armor in the 13th century to replace chain mail, the shield may be said to have enveloped the warrior.

At the end of the 15th century with increasing use of firearms, armor became largely ceremonial, and shields developed into surprising gadgets: targes coalesced with gauntlets and sported built-in lanterns for night fighting. They sprouted hand cannons or blades from their bosses and had hooks with which to break the enemies' swords.

Heraldry reached its heyday with scalloped shields bent and curved into fanciful shapes obscuring their blazonry. The heraldic shield is called a *scutcheon*. It takes the form of a lozenge to display the arms of a widow or spinster. See also HERALDRY.

SHIGA, shē-gä, is a prefecture in Japan, situated in the southern part of Honshu island. It covers an area of 1,550 square miles (4,016 sq km), of which about 25% is occupied by Lake Biwa and the surrounding national park.

Shiga is an important agricultural and textile manufacturing region. Its capital is Otsu, which is also a major tourist center. Population: (1970) 889,768.

SHIGA NAOYA, shē-gä nä-ō-yä (1883–1971), Japanese novelist and short story writer. His works, often on the theme of family conflict, are marked by keen psychological insights and great subtlety of style. Among his major novels are *Han no hanzai* (1913; Han's Crime), which is about a disastrous marital relationship; *Wakai* (1917; Reconciliation), an autobiographical work about a conflict between a father and son; and *An'ya koro* (completed 1937; Journey into the Dark), a complex study of incestuous interrelationships.

Shiga was born in Miyagi, Japan, on Feb. 20, 1883. He was brought to Tokyo in 1885 and was educated there, attending Tokyo University for two years. His first story, *Aru asa* (One Morning) was published in 1908. Collections of his works appeared in 1931, 1937, and 1955. Shiga died in Tokyo on Oct. 21, 1971.

SHIGATSE, shē-gä'tse, is a town in southern Tibet, 135 miles (215 km) southwest of Lhasa. It is situated on the Nyang Chu near that river's confluence with the Tsangpo (upper Brahmaputra). Shigatse stands at the crossing of the two main trading routes of Tibet: one leading from China and Lhasa west to Leh in the Ladakh district of Kashmir; the other running south to Gangtok in Sikkim and then to Kalimpong, India.

An important trading center, Shigatse is the largest population center in Tibet after Lhasa. It has a fort dating from the 17th century. About a mile (1.5 km) south is the great Buddhist monastery of Tashi Lhunpo, which before the Chinese occupied Tibet in 1950 had more than 3,000 monks and was headed by the Panchen Lama, whose spiritual authority rivaled that of the Dalai Lama. Population: (1953) 26,000.

SHIGELLA, shi-gel'ə, a genus of nonmotile, gram-negative, rod-shaped bacteria that can cause intestinal disturbances in man and other animals. Infection with a strain of *Shigella* produces an acute infection known as bacillary dysentery or shigellosis. Some infections may be asymptomatic but most produce various intestinal symptoms ranging from mild diarrhea to severe and sometimes fatal dysentery. Infection with *C. dysenteriae* is particularly severe. It can be treated with a variety of antibiotics, though shigellae often become resistant to these drugs. If dysentery is severe, replacement of lost fluid and electrolytes may be necessary.

SHIH CHING. See FIVE CLASSICS.

SHIH HUANG-TI, shir' hwäng' dē (259–210 B.C.), was the first emperor of China. In 246, as King Cheng, he ascended the throne of Ch'in, one of seven states into which China was then divided. After uniting China by conquering the other states, he assumed the title Shih Huang-ti ("First August Sovereign") in 221.

The emperor established a centralized system of government, and organized China into provinces and prefectures. The Ch'in legal system and Ch'in weights and measures were extended throughout the empire, and the Chinese script was standardized. The Emperor erected a barrier against nomads from the north by linking up the walls built by the former states and thereby creating the Great Wall.

At the instigation of his adviser Li Ssu, Shih Huang-ti sought in 213 to suppress Confucianism and ensure Legalist orthodoxy by burning all books except those on medicine, agriculture, and divination. The Emperor died in 210, and the Ch'in dynasty fell four years later.

SHIH TZU, shē' tsōō', a toy dog similar to the Pekingese. The shih tzu was introduced from Tibet into China in the 16th century, when it was customary to present visiting Chinese officials with a pair of the little dogs. Thus the breed was established in China, where it presumably was occasionally crossed with Pekingese.

The dog's standard weight ranges to 18 pounds (8 kg). The head has long hair falling over the eyes, the coat is dense, the legs are short and sturdy, and the tail is heavily plumed and curled backward. The breed was virtually unknown in the West until a few dogs were imported to Britain in the 1930's. The breed was recognized by the American Kennel Club in 1969.

SHIHKIACHWANG, shir'jē-ä'jwäng', a city in China, is a major industrial center and the capital of Hopei province. Situated in the southwestern part of the province near the Shansi border, it is 160 miles (260 km) southwest of Peking.

Shihkiachwang (Shijiazhuang) is an important railroad hub, located at the junction of the Peking-Wuhan railroad with the lateral Taiyüan-Tehchow line. It was only a small settlement in the early 1900's and owes its development to the construction of the rail lines.

Located near a thickly populated cotton-producing region to the southeast, Shihkiachwang has become an important center of the cotton textile industry. Other industries include the manufacturing of machinery, iron and steel, cement, glass, and chemicals, and the processing of foodstuffs. Population: (1958) 623,000.

RICHARD SORICH, *Columbia University*

SHIITES, shē'īts, a group of Islamic sects that maintain, contrary to Sunnite belief, that Ali, Mohammed's son-in-law, and his descendants were the rightful successors of Mohammed. They are also called Shia. See ISLAM—*The Shia.*

SHIKOKU, shē-kō-kōō, is the smallest of the four main islands of Japan. Located in the southeastern part of the country, it is separated from Honshu by the Inland Sea on the north and the Kii Channel on the east and from Kyushu by the Bungo Channel on the west.

Shikoku has an area of 6,857 square miles (17,760 sq km). Its interior is mountainous, reaching a height of 6,499 feet (1,981 meters) at the summit of Mt. Ishizuchi, and is heavily forested with pine, Japan cedar, cypress, and bamboo. The island is drained by many rivers. Plums, pears, and oranges are cultivated in the uplands. Along the coasts and in the river valleys are fertile lowlands where rice, wheat, tobacco, and soybeans are grown.

About half of Shikoku's population is clustered in urban areas on or near the coasts. The chief cities are Matsuyama in the northwest, the capital of Ehime prefecture; Takamatsu and Tokushima in the northeast, respective capitals of Kagawa and Tokushima prefectures; and Kochi in the south, the capital of Kochi prefecture. The four prefectures, which comprise all of Shikoku and a few small offshore islands, have a population (1970) of 3,904,014.

SHILLONG, shi-lông', a city in northeastern India, is the capital of the states of Meghalaya and Assam. It is situated in Meghalaya, on the Shillong Plateau at an altitude of about 4,900 feet (1,500 meters). The city is a trading center, summer resort, and military base. It is connected by road with Gauhati, about 60 miles (100 km) to the north on the Brahmaputra River in Assam, and with Sylhet to the south in Bangladesh.

Shillong became the capital of Assam in 1874. When the substate of Meghalaya was created from Assam state in 1970, Shillong became the capital of Meghalaya as well, though it continued to be administered by Assam. In 1972, Meghalaya attained full statehood. Shillong was transferred to it but remained the capital of Assam pending the construction of a new administrative center for that state. Population: (1967) 84,000.

BURT GLINN, FROM MAGNUM

HILLSIDE TERRACES OF SHIKOKU were created by generations of Japanese farmers seeking to exact a full measure of productivity from the land.

SHILOH, shī′lō, was an important Israelite sanctuary in central Palestine in the mountains west of the Jordan River. Archaeological excavations confirm the biblical description of its location "on the north side of Bethel, on the east side of the highway that goeth up from Bethel to Shechem, and on the south side of Lebonah" (Judges 21:19). The site is 9 miles (14 km) north of Bethel and about 21 miles (34 km) north of Jerusalem. When the Israelites had conquered the land of Canaan about 1200 B. C., Joshua led the tribes to Shiloh, where the tabernacle was set up and lots were cast for the apportionment of the land (Joshua 18:1, 10). The area around Shiloh fell to Ephraim's lot (Joshua 16:5–8).

Shiloh became the headquarters of the Israelite tribes (Joshua 21:2; 22:9, 12), and the Ark was kept in the tabernacle there, where the Lord appeared to Samuel (I Samuel 3–4). During the war with the Philistines about 1050 B. C., the Ark was removed from Shiloh. The Philistines destroyed the town (Jeremiah 7:12–15) and established a garrison there (I Samuel 10:5). Judging from I Kings 14:2–4, the town was apparently rebuilt, for the prophet Ahijah dwelt there in the time of Jeroboam (about 922–901 B. C.).

SHILOH, Battle of, shī′lō, one of the most bitterly contested battles of the American Civil War, fought on April 6 and 7, 1862, in southern Tennessee, about 100 miles (160 km) southwest of Nashville. The first great battle of the war had been fought at Bull Run (Manassas) in Virginia in July 1861, nearly a year before. It had ended in a temporary stalemate in the eastern theater. In the West, Kentucky tried to remain neutral, but by the end of 1861 both sides had sent troops into the state.

In February 1862, Union Gen. Ulysses S. Grant captured forts Henry and Donelson on the Tennessee and Cumberland rivers in northern Tennessee near the Kentucky boundary, taking about 11,500 men and 40 guns. The whole Confederate line of defense across Kentucky gave way. The Confederates were forced to retreat to Murfreesboro, Tenn., southeast of Nashville, as other Union forces moved toward Nashville.

With the Southern press clamoring for his removal, Gen. Albert Sidney Johnston, commanding the Confederate forces in the region, began to assemble the scattered troops. He decided to designate Corinth, in the northeast corner of Mississippi, as the concentration point for the army.

Assembling of the Armies. By the end of March, Johnston and his second-in-command, Gen. Pierre G. T. Beauregard, managed to gather in Corinth more than 40,000 men, including a few units from as far away as the Gulf of Mexico. These were organized into three corps, commanded by Gens. Leonidas Polk, Braxton Bragg, and William J. Hardee. There was also a small reserve corps under Gen. John C. Breckinridge.

Meanwhile, Gen. Henry W. Halleck, who was Grant's department commander, had ordered Grant's troops to make a reconnaissance southward along the Tennessee River. They encamped near Pittsburg Landing, on the west side of the river, about 5 miles (8 km) north of the Mississippi boundary. There they awaited the arrival of another large Union force under Gen. Don Carlos Buell, which had been ordered southward from Nashville to join them.

Grant's army of 42,000 men was divided into six divisions. Five of these, a total of 37,000, were near Pittsburg Landing. One division, under Gen. Lew Wallace's command, was stationed 6 miles (9 km) to the north. Buell's army marching from Nashville was almost as large as Grant's; together they would far outnumber any concentration of forces that the Confederates could put in the field.

General Johnston saw that he must strike Grant's army before Buell arrived. The Confederates started northward from Corinth on the afternoon of April 3, intending to attack at dawn on the 5th, but a violent rainstorm turned the dirt roads into a sea of mud. The attack was postponed from the 5th to Sunday, April 6, but

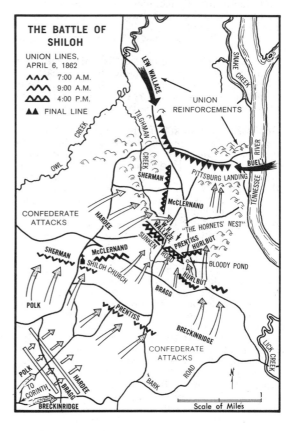

THE BATTLE OF SHILOH

UNION LINES, APRIL 6, 1862

∧∧∧ 7:00 A.M.
∧∧∧ 9:00 A.M.
∧∧∧ 4:00 P.M.
▲▲ FINAL LINE

on the 5th the leading division of Buell's army arrived on the other side of the Tennessee River, only 7 miles (11 km) away.

That night the armies encamped only 2 miles (3 km) apart, with the Union forces, whose advanced units were about 4 miles (6 km) west of the river, wholly unaware of their danger. Neither they nor their leaders expected an attack. They were not disposed for defense, nor had any trenches been dug for their protection. Early in the morning of April 6, a suspicious brigade commander in Gen. Benjamin M. Prentiss' Union division sent a small force forward to investigate the nearby woods. At dawn they exchanged shots with the Confederate outposts, but it was too late to give warning of the attack, which burst on the Union camps.

Confederate Attack. For the assault, General Johnston had chosen an unusual formation. He formed his troops in three lines, with Hardee's corps in front, Bragg's corps in a second parallel line, and then Polk's and Breckenridge's reserve corps.

The Confederates charged straight to their front into the divisions of Prentiss and Gen. William Tecumseh Sherman, who held the right flank near the Old Shiloh Church. They and Gen. John A. McClernand's division made a brief stand. Many men fought valiantly, but others broke and fled. When Grant, who had been absent from the field, arrived he found all five of his divisions fighting desperately in what seemed like a hopeless struggle. He had already sent for Buell's troops, and now he sent for Lew Wallace to join him.

The Union forces had retreated about halfway to the river to a new position, naturally strong, with open fields on each side and a sunken road in front. Here, in the center, in a position known to history as "The Hornets' Nest," the Confederates were halted for hours. They could not take it by assault, but gradually the Union troops on each flank were forced back. Johnston fell mortally wounded. Beauregard took command, and the attack continued.

Finally "The Hornets' Nest" was surrounded. Gen. William H. L. Wallace was killed trying to lead his division out. Prentiss was forced to surrender, but time was running out for the Confederates. They made a last attack on the Union left toward Pittsburg Landing to cut off the escape of the Union forces, but Buell's troops were now arriving.

Union Counterstroke. On the next day, Grant attacked. Of the soldiers who had fought on the first day, he had only about 7,000 effectives, but Lew Wallace had arrived with his 5,000, and Buell had supplied 20,000 more. To oppose these, the Confederates could muster only about 20,000 men. For hours they held the line in front of Shiloh Church, but at last they withdrew in good order from the field.

The Battle of Shiloh, the second great battle of the war, was a tremendous shock to the people of the North and the South. When the reports were published, they found that each side had lost about 25% of the troops engaged—the Confederates about 10,700, the Union more than 13,000. The people suddenly realized that this was to be a long and bloody war.

JOSEPH B. MITCHELL
Author of "Decisive Battles of the Civil War"

Further Reading: Catton, Bruce, *Terrible Swift Sword* (Doubleday 1963); Grant, Ulysses S., *Personal Memoirs,* 2 vols. in 1 (1894); Henry, Robert S., *The Story of the Confederacy* (Bobbs 1931); Horn, Stanley F., *The Army of Tennessee* (Bobbs 1941).

SHIMANE, shē-mä-nē, is a prefecture in Japan, situated in the southwestern part of Honshu island on the Sea of Japan. Its capital is Matsue. Shimane is a heavily forested region. Farming, stock raising, lumbering, and fishing are the principal economic activities. The prefecture has an area of 2,558 square miles (6,626 sq km). Population: (1970) 773,575.

SHIMAZAKI TOSON, shē-mä-zä-kē tō-sôn (1872–1943), Japanese author, who is best remembered for his novels, which depict the conflicts between the values of the past and of the Japan of his time. One of his most important works is the naturalistic novel *Hakai* (1906; *The Broken Promise*), about the problems of a schoolmaster belonging to the *Eta,* or outcast group, in Japan.

Other novels include *Ie* (1910; *The Family*) and *Shinsei* (1918; *The New Life*). His masterpiece is *Yoake Mae* (1935; *Before the Dawn*), a historical novel set in the enlightened Meiji period of the second half of the 19th century.

Shimazaki was born in Nagano, Japan, on March 25, 1872. He was educated in Tokyo and was a schoolmaster from 1896 to 1906. Thereafter he devoted himself to literature. His earliest works, lyrical, romantic poems on love and nature were published in 1907 as *Wakanashu* (*Collection of Young Leaves*). He died on Aug. 22, 1943.

SHIMIZU, shē-mē-zōō, is a port city in Japan, on Suruga Bay in central Honshu between Shizuoka and Mt. Fuji. The modern city was formed in 1924 by the amalgamation of three towns, but the port has been active since the 14th century as the chief outlet for the rich agricultural region around Shizuoka. Shimizu handles most of Japan's green tea exports. Other major exports are canned and frozen fish, mandarin oranges, and plywood. The city is also an industrial center, with a shipyard, an oil refinery, and factories producing aluminum and machinery.

The harbor is protected by a natural breakwater called Miho-no-Matsubara. This 3-mile (5-km) bar of white sand lined with ancient pines is celebrated in art and literature as the setting of the famous legend of the Feather Robe (*Hagoromo*). Population: (1970) 234,966.

ROBERT M. SPAULDING, JR.
University of Michigan

SHIMODA, shē-mō-dä, is a seaport in Japan, on the Izu Peninsula of Shizuoka prefecture, 85 miles (135 km) southwest of Tokyo. It is known chiefly for its connection with the opening of Japan to foreign intercourse in the 19th century.

Shimoda and Hakodate (on Hokkaido) were the ports opened to American ships by Commodore Matthew Perry's Treaty of Kanagawa signed on March 31, 1854. Later in 1854, Perry stopped at Shimoda and concluded a supplementary treaty. This visit is commemorated annually by a "Black Ship Festival." Russian Admiral Putyatin arrived at Shimoda at the end of 1854 to negotiate the first Russo-Japanese treaty.

American Consul General Townsend Harris lived in Shimoda in 1856–1857, opening the first foreign diplomatic establishment in Japan and obtaining a new treaty, which introduced the principle of extraterritoriality. The name "Treaty of Shimoda" is applied variously to Perry's supplementary treaty of June 17, 1854, the Putyatin treaty of Feb. 7, 1855, and the Harris treaty of June 17, 1857. The latter should not be confused with Harris' more important commercial treaty of July 29, 1858, which substituted Kanagawa (Yokohama) for Shimoda on the list of Japanese ports open to foreigners. Population: (1965) 28,645.

Further Reading: Statler, Oliver, *The Shimoda Story* (Random House 1969).

SHIMONOSEKI, shē-mō-nō-se-kē, a city in Japan, is a port on the southwestern tip of Honshu, commanding the Shimonoseki Strait between the Sea of Japan and the Inland Sea. It has long been a major fishing port and is famous for its globefish, which are highly poisonous unless cooked by experts. Shimonoseki's seafood processing, metalworking, chemical, and shipbuilding industries are well developed. The city is linked with Kitakyushu by a railroad tunnel and a two-level pedestrian-vehicular tunnel.

Known until 1902 as Akamagaseki (or popularly as Bakan), the city has figured prominently in Japanese history. There in 1185 the Taira clan was defeated in a naval battle by the Minamoto, who became dominant in Japan until 1333.

In 1863 the daimyo of Choshu ordered the Shimonoseki batteries to fire on all foreign ships. The following year, after a punitive attack by British, U. S., French, and Dutch warships, Japan paid an indemnity and opened the Shimonoseki strait to foreign ships. This episode had major repercussions in the domestic power struggle that ended in the Meiji Restoration of 1868. The treaty ending the first Chinese-Japanese War was signed in the city on Aug. 17, 1895. Population: (1970) 258,425.

ROBERT M. SPAULDING, JR.
University of Michigan

SHIN BUDDHISM, or *Jodo Shinshu*—the "True Pure Land" sect of Japanese Buddhism. See SHINRAN.

SHINER, shīn'ər, a common name for a number of small freshwater fishes of the family Cyprinidae, or carps, probably based on their silvery color. The family is an enormous one, widely distributed in the north temperate zones of Europe, Asia, Africa, and North America. As with the other Cyprinidae, the shiners are recognizable by having no jaw teeth, although they have a small number of throat teeth, and by their single dorsal fin in the middle of the back.

Some shiners live in ponds or lakes, often in or near weed beds. Others live in cool streams. Most of them eat small insects, small crustaceans, and vegetation.

SHINGLE, a thin piece of wood, slate, metal, or composite material laid in overlapping rows to cover the roof or walls of a building. Wood shingles are tapered, whereas other shingle materials generally are flat. In the United States, many houses are roofed with shingles, most of which are made of an asphalt composition, but some are made of wood, asbestos, aluminum, copper, ceramic tile, or slate.

Wood shingles were in use in the earliest American colonies. At that time, they were made of white pine, cedar, cypress, or the best available straight-grained wood. Wood shingles now are chiefly made of red cedar from the Pacific Northwest. They are about ⅜ inch (1 cm) thick at the butt end, 16, 18, and 24 inches (40, 46, and 61 cm) long, and of various widths as cut by power saws. Another type of shingle, called a shake, is split by hand. Shakes are ⅜ to 1¼ inches (1–3 cm) thick at the butt, 18 to 32 inches (46–81 cm) long, and up to 14 inches (36 cm) wide. Wood shingles are measured by the number covering a 100-square-foot (0.9-sq-meter) area with standard overlap of the shingles. Wood shingles were in almost universal use until about 1916 when more fire-resistant materials were developed.

Asphalt shingles are cut in single- to three-shingle widths from asphalt-saturated felt surfaced with mineral granules. Self-sealing and interlocking asphalt shingles are manufactured, the former having a factory-applied adhesive undercoating that softens in the sun and bonds to the shingle below. Asbestos shingles are a compound of asbestos, portland cement, and other minerals. Shingles containing asbestos and fiberglass generally provide extra durability and resistance to fire.

FRANK DORR*
Former Associate Editor of "Popular Science"

Red cedar shingles split by hand (*right*) give a rustic appearance to the roof of a home. Asphalt shingles (*below*), usually made with a crushed mineral surface, are popular, inexpensive, and easily installed.

JOHNS-MANVILLE

RED CEDAR SHINGLE BUREAU

SHINGLES. See HERPES ZOSTER.

SHINGON, shin-gôn, a Japanese Buddhist sect. See under BUDDHA AND BUDDHISM; JAPAN—*Religion and Philosophy.*

SHINN, Everett (1876–1953), American artist, a member of the "ashcan" school of painting. He was born in Woodstown, N.J., on Nov. 7, 1876, and studied at the Pennsylvania Academy of Fine Arts. Like other "ashcan" artists, he started his career as an illustrator for newspapers and magazines and for a time was art editor of *Ainslee's Magazine* and art director of *Cosmopolitan.* Beginning in 1902, he exhibited realistic oils and pastels of city waterfronts and street scenes. In 1908 he participated in the first exhibition of the "ashcan" school, also known as "The Eight."

Shinn's particular interest was the theater, and his paintings of vaudeville, ballet, and the circus are amusing and pleasant restatements of the art of Degas. He was a close friend of David Belasco, the theatrical producer, for whom he decorated the Belasco Theatre in New York City. He also worked for other stage personalities, including Henry Irving and Ethel Barrymore. In addition, Shinn opened his own theater in Greenwich Village, New York City, where he wrote, produced, and acted in amusing melodramas with such titles as *Lucy Moore, or the Prune Hater's Daughter, Wronged from the Start.* Shinn died in New York City on May 1, 1953.

Further Reading: DeShazo, Edith, with Richard Shaw, *Everett Shinn, 1876–1953: A Figure in His Time* (Potter, C. N., 1964).

SHINRAN, shin-rän (1173–1262), a Japanese priest who founded Shin Buddhism, or Jodo Shinshu—the "True Pure Land" sect. The Shin has the largest following of all the Japanese Buddhist sects.

Shinran was a disciple of Honen, the founder of the Jodo ("Pure Land") sect. Honen taught that rebirth in the Pure Land paradise could be attained through piety and the repetition of a simple prayer signifying absolute faith in the redeeming power of the Amida Buddha. Shinran carried this doctrine further by teaching that individual conduct or station has no bearing on salvation through pure faith. He discarded many religious taboos, including priestly celibacy, and was exiled to a remote province for having married. There he continued to preach.

The simplicity of Shinran's teaching has had a wide popular appeal on all levels of Japanese society. His faith now has adherents in many countries, including the United States.

SHINTO, shin'tō, a complex of ancient Japanese folk beliefs and rituals that developed into a national patriotic cult. In early Japan the diverse local practices did not constitute a religious system. There were groups of ritualists, abstainers and taboo experts, diviners, and reciters of tradition. Religion and magic centered in fertility rites and purifications. There were local and seasonal festivals, and shrines in honor of innumerable deities and supernatural forces, with legends of creation and descent of the gods to populate Japan.

History. In the 6th century A. D. Buddhism was imported from Korea, and by the 8th century Japan was eagerly adopting Chinese culture. As the vehicle of Chinese arts and learning, with its imposing architecture and sophisticated priesthood. Buddhism won enormous prestige. The indigenous beliefs, however, were too deeply rooted to yield easily. With the adoption of Chinese writing, the myths and lore—previously transmitted orally—were recorded in two books: *Kojiki* (712 A.D.) and *Nihongi* (720 A. D.). As the oldest surviving histories these became the chief documents of Shinto. The word Shinto was coined to distinguish the traditional religion from Buddhism. The colloquial term, *kami-no-michi,* means "divine-power-way." A political attempt was made to settle the conflict between Buddhism and Shinto by combining the two under the name Ryōbu Shintō (Two-aspect Shinto). Shinto deities were declared to be avatars of various Buddhas and Bodhisattvas, Shinto shrines were then merged with Buddhist temples, and priests performed rites of both religious. With the passage of time this political expedient

The 20th century American painter Everett Shinn, a member of the "ashcan" school, was particularly interested in the theater. *London Music Hall* (1918) is one of his many humorous portrayals of stage entertainment.

collapsed. In the 17th century scholars rediscovered the *Kojiki, Nihongi,* and other early documents, revived Shinto, and exalted the emperor as the descendant of the sun goddess
Amaterasu. Kamo Mabuchi, Motoori Norinaga,
and Hirata Atsutane laid the foundations of
modern Shinto. Their Shinto Revival provided
morale to carry Japan through the abolition of
feudalism, the disestablishment of Buddhism,
and the Meiji Restoration (1868). Shinto, together with a code of feudal morality later
named *Bushido,* was consciously remodeled into
the cult of fanatical loyalty and patriotism that
was inculcated in schools and in the army until
1945.

In the Meiji era (1868–1912), Shinto was
divided into State Shinto—defined as patriotic
ritual incumbent on all Japanese—and Sect or
Religious Shinto. Any government employee
might be called on to officiate at some ritual of
State Shinto, and all schoolchildren were compelled to participate regularly, regardless of their
religious affiliation. At the end of World War II,
State Shinto was abolished. Sect Shinto has expanded enormously. Popular cults include Ten-
rikyo, a faith-healing sect, Konkokyo, Kurozumi-
kyo, Odoru Shukyo, Mioshie, and Seicho-no-ie.
The former national shrines are now maintained
as historical monuments.

The Great Torii, a sacred wooden gateway, rises from
the Inland Sea at Itsukushima Shrine near Hiroshima.

CONSULATE GENERAL OF JAPAN

Beliefs and Practices. Shinto has little theology
and no congregational worship. Its unifying
concept is *kami,* inadequately translated as
"god." Kami comes close to the anthropological
concept of *mana,* that is, nonmoral supernatural
power, generally impersonal. Motoori's explanation of *kami* included the myriad deities of
heaven and earth, spirits of shrines, birds, beasts,
trees, seas, mountains, "anything whatsoever
which was outside the ordinary, which possessed
superior power or which was awe-inspiring . . .
evil and mysterious things if they are extraordinary and dreadful" as well as the sacred emperors, persons in authority, thunder, foxes,
wolves, and peaches (sex symbols). Ancient
local chieftains and the nobles of subsequent
times were *kami.* The emperor was "manifest-
kami." Ancestral spirits, brave warriors, sex,
beautiful scenery, magical objects such as mirrors, paper, and hair—all are *kami.* The Chinese
ancestor cult was so congenial to Shinto that it
was assimilated promptly and never regarded as
foreign.

Major Shinto shrines are dedicated to outstanding deities of heaven and earth, imperial
ancestors, and national heroes. Local shrines are
dedicated to various heavenly and earthly *kami,*
to clan ancestors, trees of unusual shape, symbols
of fertility, or to propitiation of dreaded evil
spirits. Individuals worship whenever they wish.
Local shrine festivals afford community holidays.
Shouting youths carry a portable shrine around
the district with stops for offerings and reading
of *norito* (ritual formulas) by priests. *Kagura*
(*kami*-dances), farces, and masked performers
entertain the crowd. The priesthood is hereditary. Priests of major shrines may be from noble
families. At local shrines priests serve only on
special occasions. Shinto priests are neither ascetics nor theologians. They perform rites of purification and of fertility, and formally present
newly married couples and infants to the *kami.*
Since death is polluting, funeral rites are left to
the Buddhists. Shinto ritualists used to intone
mystic formulas that guided craftsmen, especially
swordmakers, in their work.

Much of the art of early Japan depended on
Shinto ritual. Shrine architecture, simple and
dignified, derives from Indonesian sources.
Shrines contain no images or decorations other
than a mirror, symbol of the sun goddess, and
dishes for offerings to the *kami,* with straw ropes
and paper hangings to avert pollution. They
usually have a traditional entrance gate called
the *torii.* It was customary for every Japanese
home to contain a tiny Shinto shrine or god-
shelf, called the *kami-dana.* The family head
presented offerings to his ancestors and other
kami, and reported family events to the ancestors,
just as the emperor reported national events to
the sun goddess and imperial ancestors · at the
grand shrine of Ise. The ceremonial accession of
a new emperor is a major Shinto ritual.

DOUGLAS G. HARING
Syracuse University

Bibliography

Aston, W. G., tr., *Nihongi,* 2 vols. (1896).
Bunce, William K., *Religions in Japan* (Tuttle 1955).
Chamberlain, Basil H., tr., *The Kojiki,* 2d ed. (Thomp-
son, J. L. 1932).
Holtom, Daniel C., *Modern Japan and Shinto National-
ism,* rev. ed. (Univ. of Chicago Press 1947).
Sansom, George B., *Japan: A Short Cultural History*
(Century 1931).
Warren, Langdon, *The Enduring Art of Japan,* chapter 2
(Harvard Univ. Press 1952).

THE BETTMANN ARCHIVE

The American clipper *Dreadnought* was one of the many fast sleek cargo ships of the Age of Sail.

SHIP, a vessel powered by sail or fuel, designed for navigation on the sea or large bodies of water. A ship is distinguished from a boat by its size. By a common definition, a boat is small enough to be carried on a ship. A vessel that sails the ocean is called a ship. One that sails on rivers or on most lakes is called a boat.

A vessel's size is measured by its tonnage. Originally the term was a measure of its capacity, with one ton being roughly equal to one large wine barrel. Later, tonnage was refined into several categories. *Deadweight* tonnage is a ship's carrying capacity. *Displacement,* expressed in tons, is the weight of a vessel as it floats or the weight of the water it displaces. *Gross* tonnage is the total enclosed space in a ship, divided by

100 cubic feet (2.8 cu meters). *Net* tonnage is the gross tonnage of a ship, minus those areas required for propulsion machinery, fuel, and certain living quarters. In giving the tonnage of a vessel, the category is not always specified, but the figure indicates the vessel's size in relation to other vessels. These standards are applied to all ships.

For centuries, vessels sailed by using the wind, caught in some kind of sail. The history of the ship must begin with the era of sail.

Early in the 19th century, steam was applied successfully to navigation. The use of this power, employing various fuels, was refined over the years well into the 20th century. By the 1970's, experiments had been made with nuclear power for ships and with hybrid vessels that had some of the properties of an airplane. The search for faster and more efficient ways of using the world's oceans for communications was continuing.

1. Sailing Vessels

From the dawn of history, men have sailed ships in some fashion. Even in the mid-20th century, with sail practically obsolete except for sport, sailboats are numbered by the thousands. Pleasure craft are found, in season, along the coasts and on the lakes of much of the world, while in Asian and African waters Chinese junks or Arab dhows may be seen carrying on their ancient business. Sailing vessels dominated maritime activity, however, for only four centuries— from about 1460 to 1860.

The principal advantage of sail was that its motive power cost nothing. Mariners were spared backbreaking work at the oars. In later years, when steam had begun to compete with sail, operators saved fuel costs. On the other

Early sailing ships. At top left, the Oseberg ship from early Viking times; above, model of an ancient Egyptian ship found in a royal tomb; left, Phoenician merchant ship of 7th century.

hand, sailing vessels were uncertain instruments in battle and in commerce because they depended on the strength and direction of the wind. One was never sure how well, if at all, a vessel might be maneuvered nor when she might reach her destination. These disadvantages caused warships, in earlier times, to use slave labor at the oars. In the 19th century, navies and merchant fleets came to prefer to pay for coal rather than to gamble on the winds.

EARLY DEVELOPMENT

Man discovered early that it was a very simple matter to move a primitive boat along in the same direction as the wind. All that was needed was to hoist a section of skins, cloth, or the like on a stick, and with such a rude sail the boat would move along easily without having to be rowed. The sailing vessel proper, however, which could sail against the wind as well, took many centuries to develop. In order to progress along the water, into the direction from which the wind was blowing, it was necessary to discover how to tack, or approach by zigzags. It was a long time before the hulls, the masts and sails, and the "know-how" of the mariners were equal to that technique. No matter how skillful the sailors became, however, even the best-designed vessels could never be sailed directly into the wind within the final tenth of the 360° circle.

The exact steps in the early development of sailing vessels are still a matter of conjecture. Among the signposts along the way are the ancient Egyptian vessels pictured in carvings or drawings. These usually show both oars and a huge sail. At first, the Egyptians' navigation was principally on the Nile River. Gradually they

took to the adjacent seas. It seems certain that the sail was used only with a following wind and that otherwise the boatmen waited for a favorable breeze or rowed. It is known that the Cretans and Phoenicians carried on widespread maritime activity, but the technical aspects of their vessels still remain pretty much a mystery.

Greeks and Romans. By the time of the Greeks and Romans, vessels had fallen into two distinct types—the galley or warship, and the round ship or merchantman—which lasted for centuries on Mediterranean waters. The slender streamlined galley was not properly a sailing vessel. Its regular method of propulsion was by slave oarsmen, and its sail was used only to take advantage of a following wind. Particularly for fighting, the oars played an important role because the galley could be maneuvered in a definite direction at good speed, regardless of the direction of the wind. Often its beaklike ram was used to crush in the side of an enemy ship. On the other hand, the galley was of little use for protracted cruising or blockade duty because of the scant room for food, water, or other stores. Besides, human endurance could stand only so much labor at the oars. It was, therefore, customary to put into shore frequently. For naval purposes, the galley remained the dominant form of vessel in the Mediterranean all the way from the Greek victory over the Persians at Salamis in 480 B. C. down to the Battle of Lepanto, in which the Spaniards and Italians defeated the Turks in 1571 A. D., more than 2,000 years later.

Useful as those slender galleys were for warfare, they were no good for carrying cargoes in ordinary commerce. The cost of scores of slaves to man the oars would have been prohibitive and, more important, there would have been no room to stow the goods. Consequently, cargoes were transported in real sailing vessels. These round ships, as the name implies, were tubby affairs—the ratio of length to beam (breadth) was perhaps around five to two. They lay deeper in the water than the shallow galleys. They usually rose fairly high in the stern, but not in the bow. At first, they had only one mast, with one great sail. Later, around the time of Christ, they tended to have an additional small mast and sail in the bow, and sometimes also a small topsail. These rather clumsy vessels were steered with great oars like paddles, one on either side of the stern. They still could not head into the wind, but it seems that some of them could operate with the wind abeam (coming in on the side) without drifting too much to leeward away from the wind. In the early Middle Ages, many of the Mediterranean cargo ships seem to have adopted the triangular lateen sail instead of the clumsy old square sail. Sometimes they had two masts, with smaller sails, instead of one large one. The lateen rig, still used in Arab waters, became popular after the Muslim conquests in the 7th century.

Early Northern Ships. In the meantime, a distinct and separate development was going on in northern European waters. Because of the custom of sometimes burying important persons in their vessels, a few well-preserved northern hulls have been discovered, so that the exact features of their ships are better known than those of the Mediterranean merchantmen. The earliest find, dating from around 250 A. D., was at Nydam in Denmark. It showed three features that distinguished the northern from the southern vessels of that day, and for another thousand years to come. It was "clinker-built"—that is, its planks overlapped like clapboards—whereas the Mediterranean hulls were "carvel-built," with the edges of the planks fitted so that the surface was smooth. This Nydam boat was double-ended, with little difference between bow and stern, whereas the two ends in southern vessels were quite distinct. Finally, it had no deck. Presumably it was propelled by oars, as there is no indication of mast or sail. By 800 A. D., however, the northern vessels had definitely become sailing craft.

By this time, the Vikings or Northmen were pushing out onto the seas in many directions. As they raided and settled far and wide, they became known as Danes in England and Ireland, as Normans in France and Italy, and as Varangians in Russia. Theirs were among the very few ships of that day to venture out onto the high seas, westward to Iceland and Greenland, and by the year 1000 to North America.

Two of their vessels, dating from around 800 and 900 respectively, have been found at Oseberg and Gokstad near Oslo in Norway. Each had a large square sail, though oars were used on occasion. Each also had a real keel and a big steering oar operated with a tiller at the right-hand side of the stern. This arrangement led to the use of the term "steer-board" and then "starboard" to designate that side of a ship. The older Oseberg boat was 70 feet, 6 inches (21 meters) long and 16 feet, 9 inches (4 meters) wide, but only 5 feet, 3 inches (1.5 meters) deep, so that her "freeboard" above the waterline was uncomfortably low. The Gokstad boat of 900 A. D. was somewhat larger—the same beam but about 8 feet (2.4 meters) longer and, to make her more seaworthy, 18 inches (46 cm) deeper. There were still no decks on these boats, so the hardy Northmen had to travel in the open without shelter. The vessels with which William the Conqueror invaded England in 1066 were probably of this same general type.

Late Medieval Ships. Between about 1100 and 1460, several important changes occurred. Most significant of all, some unknown northern shipwright, possibly in the region of the Netherlands, developed the stern rudder around 1200. This was firmly attached to the stern post, in place of the old steering oar. It would help much in enabling vessels to sail to windward, a process that would be further aided by building deeper hulls. The low topsides of the Viking ships began to undergo a change also, around 1100, with the erection of superstructures called castles at the bow and stern. They were primarily military in purpose, though the structural influence spread to merchant vessels. Sea fighting in that day was at close range—"infantry combat on floating platforms," as it has been called. The castles could

William the Conqueror's fleet of warships under sail in a following wind during the 11th century.

CULVER PICTURES

Two English warships of the 16th century were the *Henry Grâce à Dieu (left)* and the *Great Harry*.

be defended even if the enemy boarded into the low waist. The superstructures of the tall ships were to give a topheavy look to most seagoing craft for centuries. The term "forecastle," often abbreviated to "fo'c'sle," lasted in maritime parlance to denote the forward part of the vessel where the crew were quartered. The topsides of ships did not return to a simple sheer line until the mid-19th century.

The eventual ship of the great "age of sail" resulted in no small part from the blending of northern and southern features during the later years of the Middle Ages. Probably the chief influence in this came from the Crusades. In those expeditions to the Holy Land between 1096 and 1291, the northerners usually found it most convenient to cross the Mediterranean in Italian vessels, but on some occasions they came down in their own vessels. Each region, therefore, had a chance to see what the other had produced in the way of ships. In the joint development, the north contributed the fixed rudder and the single great sail, whereas the south, with its decked, carvel-built ships, offered advances in hull building.

By 1400, the changes began to occur with rapidity. Until then, most ships still had one mast and one sail. A half century later, some had three masts—which would become the fore, main, and mizzen—and three sails. After that, sails became further subdivided—it was much easier to handle several small ones than a single great one.

By 1500, the new types of vessels were sufficiently seaworthy to be able to go anywhere. Some of these, prowling along distant sea lanes, were small caravels, such as the *Niña* and *Pinta* of Christopher Columbus' squadron. Others were full-rigged ships such as his *Santa María*. Those vessels, in which he ventured to America in 1492, were about the same in size and type as those with which Vasco da Gama opened up the sea route to India in 1497–1499. In each case, the flagships measured scarcely 150 tons.

While these vessels could tack against the wind, it was desirable to do as little tacking as possible because progress was slow and tedious. Later, in the days of steamships, mariners could plot their desired course on a chart by the shortest "great circle" route, and follow it regardless of the winds. In the days of sail, however, they preferred to follow the route that would give them favorable following winds, even though the mileage might be longer on the map. They knew that on a more direct run, with continual head winds, tacking would run up its own added mileage. Thus, on what became the most heavily traveled of all sea lanes—the 3,000-odd miles (4,800 km) of stormy North Atlantic between America and England—the prevailing westerly winds forced a sailing vessel to travel some 400 miles farther in going from Liverpool to New York than in going from New York to Liverpool.

The early mariners somehow discovered some of the major patterns of winds and currents. Columbus, dropping way down to the Canary Islands after leaving Spain, was borne across the Atlantic by the southeast trade winds to the West Indies. Then he followed what would later be identified as the Gulf Stream up the North American coast before heading back across the Atlantic. About the same time, Vasco da Gama stood out boldly into the Atlantic where the southeast trade winds bore him almost to the Brazilian bulge of South America, and then turned back across the South Atlantic to the Cape of Good Hope.

THE GREAT AGE OF SAIL

Heavy traffic quickly appeared on the routes discovered by Columbus and da Gama, for the voyages of exploration brought the establishment of colonies overseas. Spain and Portugal, pioneers in this, developed a pattern of annual sailings. The Spanish "plate fleets" included both merchantmen and warships to carry and to guard the precious homeward cargoes of silver from the mines of Mexico and Peru. Such convoys were among the most striking aspects of the great age of sail that lasted from about 1460 to 1860. Portugal, too, brought its cargoes of precious spices home from the East under heavy guard.

Naval Vessels. During the first half of the age of sail, the borderline between the cargo carriers and the fighting ships was in many cases not distinct, either in their structure or their behavior. At the same time, a few large warships were especially constructed for the sole business of fighting. The English had already launched a big warship in 1418 at Southampton. A century later, the Scots, Swedes, French, Spaniards, and Portuguese, as well as the English, were building war vessels that were huge for that day. Among these was Scotland's *Great Michael* and, soon afterward, England's *Henry Grâce à Dieu* of 1514, named for Henry VIII. Some of these became known as galleons and had beaks for ramming the enemy. Most of them were armed with several hundred light handguns or "murthering pieces," as they were sometimes called. These were all built with the idea that naval actions would continue to be fought at close range, with the vessels lying alongside each other.

The year 1588, however, signalized an important revolution in naval tactics, when close-range fighting gave way to the use of heavy guns at a distance. There had been some useful experimenting along that line by a group of English mariners, known as the "sea dogs," who had been harrying the Spanish shipping and colonies. Instead of the huge Spanish galleons, which were veritable "floating barracks" loaded with infantry, they had developed a lighter and more weatherly type of ship that could stand off and pound the enemy at a distance. That is what happened when Philip II of Spain sent his Invincible Armada against England in 1588. The English ships got to windward and poured shot into the Spaniards, who were unable to close with them.

From that time until the end of the age of sail, naval warfare was influenced by that experience. Sometimes in fleets of big capital ships, sometimes in individual frigates or lesser cruisers, warships normally fired at each other with smoothbore guns at ranges up to a quarter mile (400 meters) or so. Part of the success came from the ability to gain the weather gauge, to windward of the enemy. Obviously a vessel with the wind behind her had the chance to move in a wide arc in almost any direction. Her opponent was at a serious tactical disadvantage, since she could not move against the wind without tacking. In the earlier days, it had not mattered if the commander of a warship was a soldier with no experience in shiphandling, for he counted on a sailing master to lay the ship alongside the enemy for close-order action. Now, since it was necessary to move the ship in order to aim the guns, the naval commander had to be a shiphandler as well as a fighting man.

By the 18th century, naval warfare had become fairly standardized and static, not only in the types of ships but also in their fighting methods. The 17th century had seen a steady trend toward that situation: One important step was the construction of England's *Sovereign of the Seas* in 1637, almost exactly a half century after the Armada fight. One of the biggest ships yet built, she carried 100 guns on her two fighting decks. Except for her long, projecting beak, she had many of the features that would characterize capital ships for years to come. She was designed by Phineas Pett, first of a remarkable family of shipwrights. Other navies soon followed suit in their construction programs.

By 1689, when Britain and France started upon their "Second Hundred Years' War," a series of contests that lasted until 1815, naval ships and methods had reached a point beyond which there was little room for change. A veteran 80-year-old warship that fought in one action of the American Revolution was only slightly different from the latest products. Nelson's celebrated flagship *Victory* was 40 years old at the Battle of Trafalgar (1805) against the French and Spaniards.

The *Mayflower II* is a replica of the ship on which the Pilgrims sailed from England to America in 1620.

The *Victory*, Nelson's flagship, has been restored to look as she did at the Battle of Trafalgar in 1805.

The *Constitution*, a frigate that carried 44 guns, was one of the first six warships of the U. S. Navy and was authorized by an Act of Congress in 1794.

The experience of the Dutch wars between 1652 and 1672 had shown that little warships did not belong in big fights. A full-dress battle was a matter for the big capital ships that could absorb the sort of punishment that their guns could deal out. Some of those 17th century battles had been indiscriminate melees in which both fleets became all mixed up. To correct that, the fleets thereafter went into action with the ships following one another in a "line ahead" formation. Consequently, the major vessels big and strong enough to take part in such engagements became known as ships of the line or line-of-battle ships. They were gradually divided into several "rates," according to the number of guns they mounted. Biggest of all were the lofty first rates, with 100 guns or more, arranged on three fighting decks. Each navy had a few of these to serve as flagships, but they were too cumbersome for general duty. The same was true of the three-decked second rates, with 84 to 90 guns or so. The most useful, and consequently the most numerous, of the ships of the line were the two-decked third rates, often known as "74's" because of the usual number of their guns. They could sail well and fight well under most conditions. Below them came smaller two-decked fourth rates of 64 guns or so.

The Shift to Steam. In the world's navies, the coming of steam in the mid-19th century meant the speedy decline of sail. The exposed paddle-wheels of the early steamers were too vulnerable to enemy fire, but once the screw propeller demonstrated its effectiveness in the mid-1840's, the superior advantages of steam were obvious. Its particular value lay in the tactical maneuverability it gave in battle. It was now once more possible, as in ancient navies, to become free of winds and currents. The Crimean War (1854–1856) and the American Civil War (1861–1865) showed how useless sailing warships had become. Early steam machinery consumed so much coal, however, that vessels for some time continued to cruise under canvas. Many of the naval officers, moreover, resented both engines and engineers. Formerly they had had to match their wits against the wind to get where they wanted to go, but now they simply jangled a bell, and the engineer below did the rest. That spirit was so strong in the U. S. Navy in 1869, when European warships were fast abandoning sail, that propellers were cut down so that they would not interfere with the ships' sailing qualities, and orders were given that steam was to be used only in emergencies. By the end of the 19th century, however, all vestiges of sail had disappeared.

Early Merchantmen. In the meantime, the merchantmen were undergoing their own significant evolution. Though individually not so conspicuous as the great warships, they were far more numerous than men-of-war and more varied in type. Their carrying of cargoes, moreover, was quite as vital to the prosperity and well-being of the maritime nations as was the protection given by the navies.

By 1600, Holland was on the eve of its great years of achievement at sea, with a large, efficient, and widely diversified merchant marine. Sir Walter Raleigh tried to arouse the English to follow the example of the Dutch, who were able to provide ships specially fitted for the particular trade at hand. If special circumstances called for speed, fast vessels were available. But speed was expensive, and the Dutch did not waste fast ships where slow ones would do, or big ships where smaller ones would suffice. They even had vessels with flat enough bottoms so that, in ports where the tide ran far out, they could lie without damage on the sand or mud.

The English at that time had no such wide diversification among their merchantmen. The *Mayflower*, for instance, was a sort of tramp-of-all-work, a 180-ton ship with a high poop, when she was chartered to carry the Pilgrims to America. So, too, were the similar ships that brought pioneer settlers to Virginia, to Massachusetts Bay, and to Maryland. Their next lading might be wine from Bordeaux, hemp from Russia, or iron from Spain. Gradually, special types developed in addition to those general freighters. These ranged all the way from North Sea herring smacks, Thames lighters, and Newcastle colliers up to the pompously majestic East Indiamen, almost equal to warships in size and appearance.

Packets. One particular group of sailing vessels performed a very important new function in the 19th century, marking the beginning of the "line" principle in shipping—vessels sailing on regular schedules on particular runs. Before this, most vessels had been transients or tramps, picking up cargo wherever it could be found. Others, called "regular traders," followed a particular route between ports, but they did not have fixed sailing dates. The New York sailing packets to

The *Philadelphia,* a U. S. ship of the line in 1848. She was 247 feet from figurehead to stern gallery, 85 feet in extreme breadth, and carried 140 guns.

England and France, with their regular route and regular schedule, were thus the first real liners. Announcing that they would sail on time, "full or not full," they provided what came to be known as "berth service." This meant that shippers could send their exports to a packet pier, knowing that they would go with the next sailing. This became an essential feature of later steamship service.

Starting with the Black Ball Line in 1818, these tough ships served as the principal link between the New World and the Old, as they carried their passengers, mails, and fine freight across 3,000 miles (4,830 km) of the roughest seas in the world. Their Yankee captains kept driving them as fast as they could go, even through winter gales when most shipping stayed in port. Their object was not so much spectacular bursts of speed as steady, consistent performance. Because of the prevailing westerly winds, their average time from New York to Liverpool was around three weeks, but the return passage against the westerlies varied widely, averaging between five and six weeks. The packets gradually lost their unique importance after regular transatlantic steam navigation between England and America began in 1838.

Clippers. In the merchant marines of the world, the great age of sail did not suddenly end with the coming of steam. In contrast with naval vessels, sailing vessels reached their spectacular climax in the course of the 30 years after steam spanned the Atlantic in 1838. The clipper ships, first the American and then the British, set up speed records that far surpassed any earlier achievement. The *Flying Cloud,* the *Cutty Sark,* and the other "greyhounds of the sea" that made those records are still more widely remembered than any other merchantmen, although the packets rendered more useful and long-lasting service. The term "clipper," unlike "packet," did not denote a vessel with a special function, but simply one that was fast and, to use the modern word, streamlined. All the so-called clippers had speed and fine lines in common, but little else.

For several decades, the Americans had been interested in fast vessels. They had had real need for speed during the troubled years between 1775 and 1815, to dodge British cruisers that blockaded the coast or patrolled the seas during the American Revolution, the War of 1812, and the hectic intervening years of neutral trading.

Out of such circumstances grew the sharp, fast, slender "Baltimore clippers." These were generally little schooners with raking masts, useful in running the Royal Navy's blockade or preying upon British merchantmen as privateers.

The British, on their part, knowing that speed could be very expensive, seldom sought it in privately owned vessels. The government might build fast frigates and mail brigs, but the average shipowner was apt to be more interested in bluff-bowed, "burthensome" vessels that could carry plenty of cargo, even though they were slow.

After the beginning at Baltimore, American yards continued to build fast little schooners. Some were designed for honest purposes as pilot boats. Some of them became slavers, although by that time the slave trade was highly illegal, while others smuggled opium on the China coast.

The initial impulse for larger streamlined clippers grew out of the China tea trade, where there was a premium on speedy arrival. Some credit the 494-ton *Ann McKim,* built at Baltimore in 1839, with being the first large clipper. The centers of the new activity, however, were New York and Boston. By the mid-1840's, New York merchants were ordering the *Houqua, Rainbow,* and *Sea Witch,* which cut down the running time between Canton and New York. *Sea Witch* set an all-time record of 74 days in 1848–1849.

This new clipper type had its "bows turned inside out," to cut through the waves instead of butting through them as the older bluff-bowed, apple-cheeked ships had done. The clipper also had slendered lines aft, and its point of maximum beam was farther from the bow than previously. The clippers, moreover, were on the whole more heavily sparred than ordinary ships and carried much more canvas. This streamlining was achieved at the expense of carrying capacity. The extreme clippers could load much less cargo than a conventional ship of the same registered tonnage. They would pay only in situations that put a premium on speed.

Such a situation seemed to arise in 1849 with the news of the discovery of gold in California the year before. The "forty-niners" rushed out to San Francisco on any old craft that would float. In ordinary vessels, the 16,000-mile (25,000-km) trip around stormy Cape Horn took from 150 to 200 days. Food and supplies were almost nonexistent in the gold fields, and commanded high prices. Flour worth $5 or $6

The *Flying Cloud,* the most famous of American clippers, was designed by Donald McKay and launched in 1851. She set a record of 89 days from New York to San Francisco on her maiden voyage.

a barrel in New York fetched 10 times as much, with other items in the same generous proportion.

These conditions touched off a feverish epidemic of clipper construction that lasted four years, long after the initial profits had been skimmed. Altogether, some 350 clippers were built, of which 82 made the San Francisco run in 110 days or less, the criterion of a first-rate clipper. Many of the best ships were produced in New York's crack East River shipyards, but those turned out by Donald McKay, a gifted Nova Scotian trained in New York, at his East Boston yard have generally rated the superlatives. The three fastest Cape Horn runs to San Francisco were made in 89 days, and two of those were made by McKay's *Flying Cloud* in 1851 and 1854. Of the six vessels credited with making more than 400 miles a day, nearly all were McKay products.

Some records were made under the British flag, for when the California run became overstocked with new clippers, new opportunities arose under the Red Ensign of England. In 1849, Parliament repealed the old navigation laws. Not only could American ships now bring tea from China to London, but American ships could be purchased for British registry. The discovery of gold in Australia in 1851 provided a new, and more lasting, demand for fast ships. Two of McKay's finest clippers established records on that lengthy run. His *Lightning's* 63 days from Melbourne to Liverpool in 1853 was never equaled, while his *James Baines,* named for her owner, in 1854 set up two records—12 days from New York to Liverpool and then 63 days from Liverpool to Melbourne, a record that stood for 15 years.

The British began to build clippers of their own, for the China trade at first, with a later shift to the Australian run. Whereas the American vessels had wooden hulls, the British were composite, with iron frames and wooden planking. Four of these became celebrated for their swift runs—the *Ariel, Taeping, Thermopylae,* and *Cutty Sark.* They averaged around 900 tons, only about half the *Flying Cloud's* 1,782 tons.

From Sail to Steam. The completion of the *Cutty Sark* at Dumbarton, Scotland, in 1869 may be said to mark the end of an era. She made remarkable trips to and from China, and then Australia, for years to come, but by that time sail had started upon its long, losing fight against the rapid encroachments of steam. The opening of the Suez Canal in 1869 was a severe blow to the square-riggers, for even if they were towed through that 100-mile (160-km) ditch, they could scarcely make progress through the baffling winds of the Red Sea. With the distance from London to Bombay cut in half, and from London to the Far East reduced by one third as compared with the old voyage around the Cape of Good Hope, the steamers had a tremendous advantage. They could make two or three voyages a year while a clipper was making one. Even more serious than the Suez opening was the development, in the late 1860's, of the compound engine that radically cut down a steamer's consumption of coal, making the steamer economical for carrying bulk cargo. Steamers with this engine took over most of the busiest hauls, from Britain to the ports of Europe, the east coasts of the Americas, and Africa, in addition to the Suez route to India and the Far East.

That left for the square-riggers only a very few long runs where coal would be expensive and sometimes difficult to obtain. For a time, the choicest available service for sail was that to Australia and New Zealand, with general cargo outward and wool or grain in return. This run gave business to crack clippers like the *Cutty Sark* and *Thermopylae.* Before long, however, there ceased to be the urgency for speed on that run or any of the others open to the square-riggers. Many were kept busy, at low freight rates, hauling jute from Calcutta to Dundee, where it was made into burlap. There was also considerable business around Cape Horn to the west coasts of North and South America, especially for grain from California, lumber from Puget Sound, and nitrates from Chile. A number of secondhand square-riggers carried fish from Alaska down to Seattle. Since carrying capacity had become more important than speed, the extremely sharp clippers that had set up the records in midcentury gave way to more capacious vessels that might sometimes rate as medium clippers, carrying less lofty spars and not so much sail area.

The fisheries were a field where sail held its own until well into the 20th century. The very nature of the task meant that sail was well adapted to it. Much of the fishing was car-

The *John R. Bergen* is typical of the American schooners that sailed the coastal waters in the late 1800's.

ried on in local waters, but some hardy souls from Europe would sail all the way to the Grand Banks below Newfoundland, rich in codfish. Gradually motor vessels took over most of the shipping, but the Portuguese continued, even to mid-20th century, crossing to the Banks in their big schooners.

Some nations shifted from sail to steam more quickly and thoroughly than others. Just before the outbreak of World War I in 1914, one fifth of the world's tonnage was still under sail, but the proportion varied widely among the nations. Although the British had the second-largest sailing fleet, it was barely one twelfth of the total British tonnage, for steam had overtaken sail around 1883. At the other extreme was Finland, where sail composed 82% of the fleet. Ever since Britain had repealed its navigation laws in 1849, the Norwegians in particular had developed a flourishing tramp trade. Germany, like Britain, was shifting strongly to steam, but it had one of the most remarkable fleets of square-riggers —the Laeisz line of four- or five-masted steel barks, operating from Hamburg to the west coast of South America. The abnormally large proportion of sail in the French merchant marine was the result of a subsidy policy so liberal that it was said that a French square-rigger could sail around the world without a ton of cargo and still make money.

The United States was one of the last strongholds of sail. Its tonnage under sail held its own against steam until 1898, about 15 years after the change had come in Britain.

Lacking the industrial facilities of Britain at the time of the steam boom around 1870, the Americans allowed much of their overseas commerce to be taken over by foreign steamers. The chief employment on the high seas for their big "Down Easters," square-riggers mostly built in Maine and commanded by Maine men, was in the grain trade from California around Cape Horn to Europe. In the protected coastal trade, schooners found employment for years in hauling lumber, stone, lime, and above all, coal. There was still business for the original two-masted rig, while three-masters were coming in gradually. The pioneer four-master, the *William L. White*, was built in 1880, followed by the first five-master, the *Governor Ames* in 1888, and the six-master *George W. Wells* in 1900. One seven-master, the *Thomas W. Lawson*, was built in 1902 and wrecked five years later.

The five- and six-masters, built in Maine and operated from there, had a decade or two of lively business carrying coal from Hampton Roads, Va., to New England, but gradually steam took over that business. Also important in the American picture from about 1890 to 1910 were the graceful two-masted fishing schooners operating out of Gloucester, Mass. The Maritime Provinces of Canada also participated vigorously in the later days of sail, not only with similar fishing schooners but also with many freighters.

THE 20TH CENTURY

The last large-scale service of sail came during World War I. The United States for half a century had been depending upon British, German, and other foreign steamships to carry most of its exports and imports. The coming of the war swept the German ships off the seas and left the British too busy to make up for that lack. The Americans, suddenly realizing the need for ships of their own, found that they had few adequate seagoing steamships. Old sailing ships, barks, and schooners commanded high prices as they were swept into service on the distant runs to South America, Africa, and Australia. Even some new large schooners were built and reaped high profits. A few sailing vessels were sunk when caught by German raiders. One of the raiders was itself a big square-rigger, the *Seeadler* under the command of Count Felix von Luckner. This was the last important naval vessel to see action under sail.

By the middle of the 20th century, virtually the only big sailing vessels in active service were training ships for naval, coast guard, or merchant marine officers of various nations. The value of such training under canvas for future service in steam or diesel vessels was vigorously debated. The U. S. Naval Academy and the American merchant marine schools abandoned their square-rigged training ships, but the Coast Guard Academy at New London, Conn., still used its *Eagle*, while square-rigged training ships from other nations frequently visited American ports.

The most active sailing vessels actually paying their way by carrying cargo in the mid-20th century were the Chinese junks and the Arab dhows. The three-masted junks, with high free-

LATEEN

SCHOONER

SLOOP

BRIGANTINE

BRIG

The earliest sailing vessels had only a single mast with a single sail such as the lateen rig. As ships increased in size so did the number of masts, the amount of sail carried, and the complexity of the rig. The major types of rig in use during the great age of sail are shown above in simplified form.

The three basic European types were the full-rigged ship, the brig, and the sloop, with three, two, or one mast respectively. The full-rigged ship was square-rigged on all three of its masts, the fore, main, and mizzen. The brig's two masts, fore and main, were both square-rigged. The sloop's single mast was usually fore-and-aft rigged. In addition to adopting those three types, the American colonists early in the 18th century developed a fourth, the schooner, which was fore-and-aft rigged on all its masts—two at the outset and more later. Those four basic types were only a beginning, for modifications were numerous and sometimes bewildering. A bark was like a full-rigged ship except that her mizzenmast had the fore-and-aft instead of square rig. In a barkentine, only the foremast was square-rigged. In the same way, a brigantine was square-rigged on the foremast and fore-and-aft on the mainmast, but there were sometimes protracted disputes as to whether a particular vessel was a brigantine or a topsail schooner.

The square rig, in which the sails hung at right angles to the length of the ship, was probably the most beautiful feature ever developed in ships. In the square-riggers, each of the masts had its several separate sails, each suspended from a yard. In the medieval vessels, there had usually been simply one big square sail, but now there were at least three—the course, the topsail, and the topgallant sail, counting upwards from the deck. Some of the more elaborate rigs had royals still farther up on the masts,

Ships of The Age of Sail

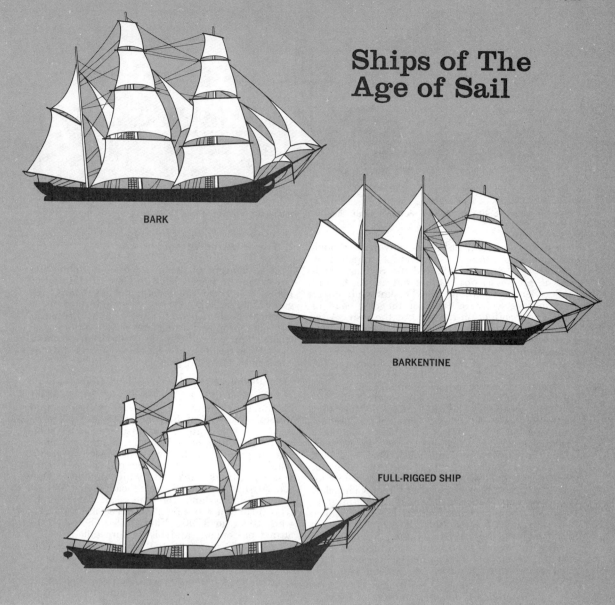

BARK

BARKENTINE

FULL-RIGGED SHIP

while skysails and moonsails were found in a few of the clippers at the end of the sailing-ship era. The only exception to that arrangement was that on the rear mast of a ship or brig, the bottom sail would be a fore-and-aft ''spanker'' instead of a square course. In the fore-and-aft rig, there would normally be one big sail, with sometimes a small topsail above it.

The square rig and the fore-and-aft each had its particular advantages, which is why each remained in vogue for so long. The square rig, caught more wind and gave better propulsion out on the high seas where there was plenty of wind. At the same time, it called for large crews, for men had to go aloft and climb out on each yard to let out or shorten sail. The fore-and-aft rig might not provide quite as much speed out at sea, but along the coast it gave a vessel a better chance of fighting clear when winds threatened to drive her onto a lee shore. In addition, the big fore-and-aft sails could be hoisted or lowered from the deck without anyone's having to go aloft, so they did not require as large a crew as a square-rigged vessel of the same size.

These considerations were kept in mind in picking the proper type of vessel for a particular service. On runs where frequent medium-sized cargoes were more desirable than a few big ones, brigs would be used instead of ships. Where speed was not essential, a ship operator could save on crew's wages by rerigging the mizzenmast to convert a ship into a bark. Many vessels that started as full-rigged ships on the strenuous packet runs, with their emphasis on speed, became barks when they shifted to whaling. The schooner was very useful along the coast where there was constant danger of being driven onto a lee shore.

BROWN BROTHERS

The *Clermont*, built by Robert Fulton, made her first commercial voyage from New York to Albany in 1807.

board and battened sails, are seaworthy, though clumsy in appearance. The dhows, propelled by one great lateen sail, followed the regular schedule of the monsoons, sailing out of Al Kuwait and other ports around the Persian Gulf either for the west coast of India or the east coast of Africa, depending on the time of the year. After swapping their dates and rugs for whatever they could get, they returned home with the semiannual shift in the direction of the winds. In rig and methods of navigation, the junks and the dhows differed little from their predecessors.

The widespread romantic appeal of sail has helped to preserve some old vessels—some because of what they did, and others because they represent once-important types. The Oseberg and Gokstad Viking boats have been mentioned. Among others are Britain's most famous warship, the *Victory*, at Portsmouth Dockyard, and the favorite American man-of-war, the *Constitution*, afloat at Boston Naval Shipyard. The clipper *Cutty Sark* is established at Greenwich below London. San Francisco has made a floating museum of a square-rigger built in 1887 and known successively as the *Balclutha, Star of Alaska,* and *Pacific Queen.* At Mystic, Conn., a number of such early vessels have been assembled—an 1841 whaler, a very old two-masted schooner, a later iron square-rigger, and several smaller vessels.

ROBERT G. ALBION
*Gardiner Professor Emeritus of Oceanic
History and Affairs, Harvard University*

Bibliography

General Histories

Anderson, Romola and R. C., *The Sailing Ship: 6000 Years of History,* rev. ed. (Norton 1963).
Chappelle, Howard I., *The Search for Speed Under Sail, 1700–1855* (Norton 1967).
Greenhill, Basil, and Giffard, Ann, eds., *The Merchant Sailing Ship: A Photographic History* (Praeger 1970).
Landstrom, Bjorn, *Sailing Ships* (Doubleday 1969).
Schauffelen, Otmar, *Great Sailing Ships Since 1628* (Praeger 1969).
Villiers, Alan, *Way of a Ship,* rev. ed. (Scribner 1970).

Special Studies

Albion, Robert G., *Square-Riggers on Schedule* (Princeton Univ. Press 1938).
Braynard, Frank O., *Famous American Ships* (Hastings House 1956).
Cutler, Carl, *Greyhounds of the Sea: The Story of the American Clipper Ship,* (U. S. Naval Inst. 1961).
Le Scal, Yves, *The Great Days of the Cape Horners* (New Am. Lib. 1967).
Longridge, Charles N., *The Anatomy of Nelson's Ships* (Marshall, Percival 1955).
McKay, Richard C., *Some Famous Sailing Ships and Their Builder, Donald McKay* (1928; reprint, 7 C's 1970).

2. Fuel-Powered Vessels

The concept of steam as a source of motive power can be traced back to Hero of Alexandria (50 A. D.). Learned men in medieval times regarded its adaptation to water transport as a practical goal. Theoreticians such as Leonardo da Vinci proposed using steam for various mechanical purposes. But the translation of these theoretical designs into the steam vessel did not come until the 19th century.

DEVELOPMENT OF POWER-DRIVEN SHIPS

As early as 1618, David Ramsey in England obtained a patent "to use divers newe apte formes or kindes of invencons, without horse or oxen, to rayse waters, and to make boates runn upon the water as swifte in calmes, and more safe in stormes, than boates full sayled in greate windes." But he never produced a real steam vessel. Others tinkered with designs. One scholar has listed 18 steamboat inventors between Ramsey and the American John Fitch, who floated a working steamboat on the Delaware River in 1790. Fitch failed, however, to attract passengers, and his venture failed.

By 1807 many of the mechanical problems that had plagued the early inventors had been solved, and Robert Fulton of New York launched his famous *Clermont,* more properly known as the *North River Steamboat,* on the Hudson River. She was the first wholly successful steamboat. Her first voyage from New York to Albany took only 32 hours, compared with the four days required by the average sloop.

The *Clermont* was 133 feet (41 meters) long and 13 feet (4 meters) wide. Fulton's engine was simple. It had a boiler about 20 feet (6 meters) long, made of copper. The steam that it generated went into a single cylinder. A piston transmitted the push from the cylinder to two paddle wheels on the boat's side. Each wheel was 15 feet (4.6 meters) in diameter, and each was fitted with eight paddles, each 4 feet (1.2 meters) long. The 20-horsepower engine drove the boat at 5 miles (8 km) an hour.

The *Clermont* burned both wood and coal. Most of the early U. S. steamboats used both these fuels. Much coal was imported and was expensive to use. Wood was plentiful and cheap.

The steamboat was here to stay. The early inventors almost always called the craft a "boat" or a "vessel," and rarely if ever used the term "ship." They did not envision applying steam power to oceangoing vessels.

The steamboats were designed to operate only on rivers and lakes and in harbors and channels, and to assist ships. Steamboats were more effective than sailing ships in overcoming the adverse tides in a harbor or a swift river current. They could tow wind-driven ships to a pier.

Nevertheless, one of the first steamboats went to sea successfully, under the pressure of economic necessity. Col. John Stevens built the *Phoenix* in Hoboken, N. J., in 1809, but the craft was compelled by Fulton's monopoly on the Hudson to go elsewhere. In June 1809 she sailed down the New Jersey coast to Philadelphia, taking 12 days for the trip. This was the first deep-sea passage by a steam-propelled craft. But the *Phoenix* was still a boat, because she was built for river service and could not have survived a storm at sea. She carried passengers on the Delaware River for many years.

Following these pioneers, an array of steam craft began to ply the inland and sheltered coastal waters of the United States. On the Hudson and Delaware rivers, along Long Island Sound and Chesapeake Bay, on the Great Lakes, and down the Ohio and Mississippi rivers the dreams of Fitch and Fulton came true.

In 1811 the steam-powered *New Orleans* sailed from Pittsburgh to New Orleans. In 1818 the paddler *Walk-in-the-Water* brought steam travel to the Great Lakes. Ferryboats and tugs began to dot the ports of Boston, New York, Philadelphia, Baltimore, Charleston, and Savannah. Special types of steamboats began to evolve for special purposes, notably the flat-bottomed three-decker *Washington*, the first true Mississippi River boat, which made her 25-day maiden voyage from New Orleans to Louisville, Ky., in 1817. The industrial growth and westward expansion of the United States found a vigorous ally in the steamboat.

Elsewhere, the use of the steamboat developed rapidly, especially in England, where it was part of the Industrial Revolution. This economic revolution had brought steam power to run railroads and machinery, pump water, and drive sawmills. Shipbuilders constructed huge steam tugs that looked like sailing passenger packets except for their tall stacks and protruding side paddles.

Steam at Sea. With the success of the steamboat on sheltered waters, imaginative engineers began to plan vessels that could sail the oceans. They faced many obstacles. Perhaps the principal one was the idea of a ship with a fire in its hull embarking on a long voyage out of sight of land. Fire was the great dread of mariners. Another problem was the cost of steam compared to that of sails. The wind in the sails cost nothing. But the venture to open sea was bound to come.

The first steam vessel to cross any ocean was the *Savannah*, which in May 1819 went from Savannah, Ga., to Liverpool, England, in 29 days. It was built by an American, Moses Rogers, specifically to discover if a steam vessel could make an ocean voyage. The vessel was 98 feet (30 meters) long, much shorter than Fulton's *Clermont*, but she was twice as broad across the beam. Her engine generated 90 horsepower and burned wood and coal.

The *Savannah* was equipped with sails as well, and actually used them on most of her ocean passage. In this combination of old and new motive powers, she was setting a pattern for oceangoing steam vessels for decades. Sails on steamships were not abandoned as auxiliary equipment until the end of the 19th century for several reasons.

All early steamships had to use salt water in their boilers. They had to stop often to clean the salt from the boilers, and at such times they resorted to sail. Condensers that could be counted on to distill enough fresh water to end the dependence on salt water were not developed until late in the 19th century.

Sails also were the salvation of many steamships that suffered broken propeller shafts or other mechanical accidents. A number of passenger liners reached port only because they had masts rigged for sail ready for an emergency.

The *Savannah* was a striking engineering success, with principles and features that were far ahead of her time, but she was an economic failure as a steamship. Shippers refused to send cargo in a vessel that had a fire in her hull. Passengers, too, were fearful of the fire and would not sail in her, in spite of the luxurious accommodations, with rosewood paneling and full-length mirrors. After one round trip to Europe, the *Savannah* was rebuilt as a sailing ship and was lost off Fire Island, N. Y., in 1821.

But the *Savannah* had proved that steamships were practical for ocean navigation. Ironically, her success brought reactions in Britain and Europe that were opposite from those in the United States. Abroad, the result was a boom in building steamships and establishing transoceanic ship service. In the United States, the *Savannah's* financial failure stimulated development of the sailing ship. The success of the passenger packets under sail and of the famous clipper ships that carried the American flag to every quarter of the globe in the mid-19th century delayed U. S. steamship development.

After the *Savannah's* voyage, construction of steamboats and steamships progressed rapidly in Britain and on the continent of Europe, in spite of the die-hards, especially in the navies, who resisted every advance. Steam packets built in Britain, France, and the Netherlands grew larger and larger. These and later steamships used coal as a fuel until the introduction of oil late in the 19th century.

Atlantic Crossings. A series of pioneers chugged across the Atlantic Ocean. The British *Rising Star*, under steam part of the way, made the first westward passage in 1822. The French *Caroline Brest* crossed in 1823 and the British-built *Curacao* in 1827. The Canadian *Royal William* sailed from Pictou, Nova Scotia, to Cowes, England, in 1833.

Britain began regular transatlantic steamship service in 1838, more than ten years before the American clipper ships astonished the world with their speed under sail. The first two scheduled vessels raced across the Atlantic. The *Sirius*, a converted packet with 360-horsepower engines—four times the power of the *Savannah*—sailed from Cork, Ireland. The new *Great Western*, built especially for the Atlantic run, sailed from Bristol, England. The *Sirius* took 18 days to cross; the *Great Western*, larger and faster, took 15 days. The two arrived in New York harbor only hours apart. Both vessels carried sails at sea and used them.

In 1840 the Cunard Line, which was to become famous, sent its first steamship, the *Britannia*, across the Atlantic. She was 207 feet (63 meters) long and 34 feet (10.4 meters) wide and

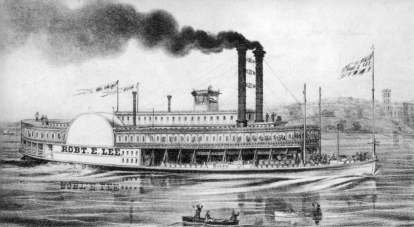

The *Robert E. Lee,* most famous of the Mississippi steamboats. She beat the *Natchez* in a 1,200-mile race from New Orleans to St. Louis in the record time of 3 days, 18 hours, and 14 minutes.

weighed 1,156 tons. She was nearly ten times as powerful as the *Savannah* and could steam 8½ knots, with its paddle wheels making 16 revolutions a minute.

Steamships on Other Oceans. Flags of many nations flew on oceans other than the Atlantic. Steamship lines that were to operate for more than a century were organized to link Britain, France, and the Netherlands with their overseas colonies. The steamship as a freight carrier came just at the right time. One steamship had four times the capacity of the largest sailing craft. As the empire nations exploited their new colonies ever more intensely and drew on their raw materials, the steamship was the indispensable line of communication.

The great Peninsular and Oriental Line from Britain to India began as a small company operating steam packets to the Spanish peninsula. The British India Company carried the men of empire to Africa, the Middle East, and the Orient. The rival Union and Castle lines were the principal links between Britain and Africa. The Royal Mail Line and the Pacific Line shared the business to South America and the West Indies. The French Cie. Des Messageries Maritimes plied between France and Indochina. The Rotterdamsche Lloyd sent its Dutch-built vessels throughout the world.

Iron Hull and Screw Propellers. The expanding world sea traffic impelled advances in ship design. The wooden hulls and paddle wheels of the early steamships were inadequate. In 1843 the *Great Britain* was launched. Designed by Isambard K. Brunel, she was the first vessel with an iron hull and watertight bulkheads and the first large vessel with a screw propeller.

Screw propulsion was not a new idea. John Stevens, builder of the *Phoenix,* had built a twin-screw vessel in the United States in 1804, but the principle was neglected. Designers had believed that a ship's engine should be amidships for the sake of stability and that a long propeller shaft dissipated engine power. Paddle wheels, it was thought, gave a ship more maneuverability.

U. S. Coastal Steamboats. While other nations were adapting the use of steam to global enterprises, the United States was advancing with equal vigor to develop steam transportation along its coasts, on the Great Lakes, and on inland rivers. The steamship played a vital role in the nation's rapid expansion, bearing passengers and freight between busy cities and into remote regions.

One of the most famous and successful U. S. coastal services was the Fall River Line, which operated an overnight run between New York and Fall River, Mass., where passengers took the train to Boston. Beginning in 1847 the line's ships ran for 90 years. As a comfortable, convenient link between two of the East Coast's great cities, it was a commercial triumph.

The Fall River steamers were among the largest steam-propelled craft in the world in their early years. They were from 300 to 500 feet (92–122 meters) long and 40 to 60 feet (12–18 meters) wide.

The *Savannah,* first steam vessel to cross the Atlantic. She was a full-rigged ship with steam as auxiliary power. Using her sails on most of the voyage, she made the crossing in 29 days.

The *Avalon,* a sternwheel steamboat that ran on the Mississippi River system well into the 20th century. Flat-bottomed sternwheelers are still used throughout the world on shallow inland waters.

In spite of their size, the Fall River craft were fast. In 1855 the *Metropolis* made the 180-mile (290-km) run from New York to Fall River in 8 hours, 51 minutes, with one long stretch at an average speed of 19 knots. The transatlantic speed record at this time was 13 knots.

During its long career, the Fall River Line pioneered in many aspects of convenience and safety afloat. Its vessels were the first to have electric lights on shipboard and to install a sprinkler system to prevent fires. The line never suffered a passenger fatality, although its ships steamed at full speed through fog and bad weather, in the crowded shipping lanes of Long Island Sound, without the benefit of any of today's navigational devices.

American coastal steamships achieved many advances in design and engineering. One of the most original and daring departures from convention was made by the Swedish-born American naval architect John Ericsson—later famous as the builder of the ironclad warship *Monitor*—who built the *John S. McKim* in 1844 for the Clyde Line, which ran between New York and Florida ports. Ericsson put the engine aft and was able to use a propeller to greater advantage.

The Clyde Line did not continue to build ships with engines aft, but its vessels led the way in other engineering aspects. They were among the first American ships to be built of iron, and later the company was the leader in switching to steel construction. A Clyde ship was the first in the United States to have a compound engine (two cylinders), and another was the first with a triple expansion engine. The Clyde Line flourished until after World War II.

Other notable companies in the long history of U. S. coastwise service were the Morgan and Mallory lines, which linked the East Coast with ports on the Gulf of Mexico; the Merchants & Miners Line, which lasted more than a century; and its rival, the Savannah Line. All of these were liquidated just before or after World War II because they could not compete with overland truck traffic.

Great Lakes Steamboats. The Great Lakes offered a convenient route for the traffic of American westward expansion, and passenger and freight ships traversed their waters before the mid-19th century. Their design advances kept pace with those of vessels elsewhere, from paddle wheel to propeller, from wood to iron, and finally to steel.

All the Great Lakes freight ships and most of the passenger ships had their engines aft. The dry cargo carriers had an unusual pilot house structure far forward that gave them a unique silhouette. A revolutionary hull design called the "whaleback" also appeared on the Great Lakes. Whalebacks looked like long, half-submerged cigars with small superstructures at each end. They were also known as pig boats. This type reached its climax in the big passenger ship *Christopher Columbus* (1892), which could carry 5,600 persons.

The early Great Lakes steamships, like those along the coasts and on the rivers, used the "walking beam" type of engine, which operated the paddle wheels. The engine's cylinders were vertical, and from them the pistons were linked fore and aft with a heavy iron beam structure topside that looked like two **A**'s connected bottom to bottom. Each pointed end was linked to an upright extension of the piston. First one end, then the other, would rise, giving the walking beam a continuous up-and-down motion. The center of the walking beam was fastened to the round shaft at whose two lower ends the paddle wheels were built, imparting to the paddles the steady turning power that moved the ship.

For many years, the motion of the walking beam amidships of a steamboat cutting the water was a visible sign of the wonders of steam propulsion. Later designs enclosed the walking beam in a high wooden deckhouse to make the ship look modern, and many admirers of the craft felt that some of the ship's beauty was gone. On many American river and lake boats, the engines were visible to passengers through large glass panels.

River Steamboats. Highly specialized types of steamboats evolved on the Ohio and Mississippi rivers, where sandbars were a peril. The boats had to be able to sag fore and aft and athwartships if they ran aground on a bar. The engine was on the lowest deck, which was built to accommodate the long horizontal piston that turned the paddle wheels. Many of these riverboats had one paddle wheel at the stern or mounted twin paddles far aft to provide more power.

These boats have been celebrated in song, story, and legend. Their appearance was spectacular. Twin smokestacks, sometimes 70 feet (21 meters) high, their tops decorated in fantastic fashion, belched smoke and sparks above the towering wooden superstructure, which bore gaily colored frills. The high stacks helped keep sparks from falling on the wooden decks. Their huge paddle wheels churned the water into foam.

The riverboats were a vital lifeline of U. S. travel and commerce. In the boom years before the Civil War, the total tonnage of steamboats on American rivers nearly surpassed the tonnage of the entire steam merchant fleet of Britain. The decks of the American boats were piled high

The *Puritan*, an iron-hulled steamer, ran the coastal waters from New York to Fall River.

with cotton bales and other merchandise. Their passenger spaces were richly furnished with handsome rugs, gold-framed paintings, tufted couches, and opulent drapes. Most cabins, however, were small and narrow.

Steamboats operated not only on the major rivers of the United States but on smaller ones as well. Small steam craft pushed westward up the Missouri and some of its tributaries. Many of the pioneers who opened the Far West traveled part way by steamboat. In a more modest fashion, river steamboats developed in other countries along the lines of the American vessels. Fleets of steamboats plied the Rhine, the Volga, the Nile, and the Amazon rivers.

U. S. Intercoastal Steamships. When California was occupied by U. S. forces in 1847, during the Mexican War, steamship designers recognized the need for big, ocean-type vessels to provide water transportation to the Pacific Coast. These ships had to make the long, rough passage around Cape Horn or take passengers to either end of the Isthmus of Panama, where they might cross overland to the other coast. The vessels built for these runs began the intercoastal route, which for more than a century was a major American steamer service. This development came just as American sailing ships were entering their golden age, the era of the clipper ships. Although iron-hulled ships were sailing the oceans, the early intercoastal craft were of wood. The vast forests of the United States encouraged the use of wood for a longer time than in the shipyards of the Old World.

The paddle-wheeler *California* was the first ship on the intercoastal run. She sailed from New York late in 1847. When she reached the western end of the Isthmus of Panama early in 1848, gold had been discovered in California, and hundreds of travelers clamored for passage to San Francisco. The gold rush and the ceding of California to the United States in 1848 by the treaty that ended the Mexican War brought a boom in shipbuilding for the Pacific Coast route. Steamships began to venture into the Pacific. The American paddle-wheeler *Monumental City* was the first to cross this ocean, sailing from San Francisco to Sydney, Australia, in 1853.

U. S. Ocean Steamships. Coincident with the intercoastal route, U. S. maritime interests experimented with service across the Atlantic,

which had become the province of foreign lines. These first American Atlantic passenger steamships were a failure. They used the basic steam plant, the paddle wheels, and the general outline of the earliest ocean steamships. American capital and American energy were directed to opening the Far West, and this "frontier" psychology raised the price of labor. American seamen demanded and received higher wages than the seamen of other nations. A program of federal subsidies could not keep the ships sailing, and finally the service collapsed. The success of the American clippers weakened the incentive to use steam on the seas, and the overlong reliance on sail hurt the American competitive position. Inland and coastal steam routes flourished, but U. S. ocean traffic languished.

The first American steamship on a regular transatlantic route was the *Washington*, of 1,700 tons. On her maiden voyage in 1847, she proved far inferior to the older *Britannia*, the Cunard Line's first steamship. Operated by the Bremen Line, her European terminus was at Bremerhaven, Germany. This line and a similar service to Le Havre, France, were federally subsidized.

The famous Collins Line, started in 1850, was the climax of the subsidy program. Its superb quartet of fast liners were outstanding ships. They introduced the straight stem in contrast to the clipper's gracefully curved bow with its bowsprit. With their speed and their luxurious passenger quarters, they attracted the best of the Atlantic passenger trade. They captured the Blue Ribbon, the mythical symbol of Atlantic speed supremacy. Four boilers burned 83 tons of coal a day on the *Baltic*, the fastest Collins ship, whose best crossing was made at an average speed of 13.3 knots. It would be 100 years before another U. S.-built steamship would win the Atlantic speed crown.

But the subsidy program ran into difficulties. It had been passed with the aid of many Southern congressmen, who began to wonder why they were supporting Northern capitalists. Why should their cotton be shipped to New York to go abroad? They wondered, too, if some of these fast ships might not be used as blockading auxiliaries in a war between the states, which had begun to loom as a possibility. The political problem was intensified by the fact that the Collins Line lost two of its first four ships in tragic accidents.

In 1858, the subsidy was withdrawn, and all major U. S. transatlantic passenger lines collapsed. The only regular freight lines carrying the American flag were sailing packet companies. The only American steamship line that survived at sea was the Pacific Mail Line, which had no competition and had established itself without a subsidy in the Pacific.

American ocean shipping suffered a grievous blow from the Civil War. The most prosperous unit of the merchant fleet, the whalers, was struck down by Confederate raiders. The clipper ships were halted. Many American ships sought refuge under other flags from the depredations of the raiders, and a law was passed by a vindictive Congress to prevent them from returning to American registry. While inland river, Great Lakes, and coastal shipping under the American flag flourished, ocean shipping was largely left to development by other nations.

European Ocean Steamships. During the mid-19th century, ship operators and designers of European countries expanded their services and made great advances in engineering. Fleets of cargo or passenger steamers flying the flags of Britain, the Netherlands, France, Germany, and Italy were busy in every ocean. Some steamship lines that were famous until well into the 20th century were organized at this time. The two German rivals, the Hamburg-American Line and the North German Lloyd, became by 1900 the two largest passenger lines in the Atlantic trade.

The Great Eastern. The most significant forward steps in design and engineering were embodied in the *Great Eastern,* built in Britain between 1854 and 1857. Designed by I. K. Brunel, builder of the *Great Western* and the *Great Britain,* she was the most extraordinary steamship ever built.

The *Great Eastern* was the largest ship built in the world for almost 50 years, and was ahead of her time in concept, construction, and facilities. She was 693 feet (210 meters) long and had a beam of 82 feet (25 meters). Her passenger capacity was 4,000.

The *Great Eastern* was built of iron. She had both paddle wheels and a screw propeller, five smokestacks, and also six masts rigged for both square and fore-and-aft sails. Her propeller was driven by a four-cylinder horizontal jet condensing type engine that could develop 6,500 horsepower at 55 revolutions per minute. But the steam pressure was only 25 pounds (11 kg) per square inch, which demonstrated one of the chief problems of that time in steam-engine construction. Engine joints and construction integrity at stress points were still so inadequate as to produce a minimum of power efficiency. The *Great Eastern's* paddle wheels were turned by another four-cylinder engine that could produce 3,000 horsepower with a steam pressure of only 15 pounds (7 kg). Neither power unit was strong enough to drive the ship at her anticipated speed.

Economically, the ship was a disaster. After running up a deficit of more than $5 million as a liner and troop carrier, the *Great Eastern* was assigned to one useful job. From her decks the first Atlantic cable was laid in 1865–1866. She was the only ship large enough to accommodate the entire length of the cable.

Advances in Ship Design. While Brunel was trying his great leap forward in design with the *Great Eastern* and subsequent ships, other designers were content to move more slowly, making minor improvements in their power units and evolving better hulls through trial and error. World trade was increasing rapidly. The opening of the Suez Canal in 1869 cut many days from the passage time from Europe to India and the Far East. The incentive to build larger and faster steamships was enormous.

In 1889 the building of the first major twin-screw liners, the *City of Paris* and the *City of New York,* for Britain's Inman Line foreshadowed the end of sail as auxiliary power to bring a steamship home after the single propeller was crippled. Two propellers seemed to be insurance against this emergency. The engines of the *City of Paris* developed 14,350 horsepower, compared to 90 for the little pioneer *Savannah,* and their steam pressure was 150 pounds (68 kg) per square inch, against 10 pounds (4.5 kg) for the *Savannah.* The Inman ships could make more than 20 knots. These most beautiful of all Atlantic liners had three stacks but retained the old-style clipper ship stems.

The *Great Eastern* was the largest ship in the world for almost 50 years. She was 693 feet long and accommodated 4,000 passengers. She was propelled both by paddle wheels and a screw propeller.

OCEAN LINERS

Aquitania (1912)

CUNARD STEAM-SHIP COMPANY LTD.

Queen Mary (1934)

CUNARD STEAM-SHIP COMPANY LTD.

Queen Elizabeth (1938)

CUNARD STEAM-SHIP COMPANY LTD.

Steam Turbines. The basic reciprocating engine style for steamships, which had been standard since the *Savannah*'s time, had been enlarged and made more efficient, but its principle had not been changed. Finally, there came a change in concept—the steam turbine, devised in 1884 by a British inventor, Charles A. Parsons.

The idea of the turbine is that steam turns a bladed shaft as air drives a windmill. The old direct action of cylinder, piston, and shaft is discarded. Steam in a turbine drives forward and astern shafts at speeds as high as 2,000 revolutions a minute. Parsons' turbine increased engine efficiency, reduced fuel consumption, and provided more space for cargo and passengers. Around 1900, steam propulsion at sea was being directed along new lines.

The Diesel Engine. Just as the great ship lines were changing from reciprocating engines to turbines, another major advance in power design was beginning. The diesel engine was being tested on the *Wandal*, a small cargo ship on the Caspian Sea. This was an internal-combustion engine that was economical to operate because it burned low-grade fuel. After using coal dust for a short time, the engineers adopted oil as the basic fuel.

The first seagoing diesel-powered ship was the Danish *Selandia*, launched in 1912. She was a 4,950-gross-ton vessel driven by a vertical, single-acting, four-cycle Burmeister and Wain diesel. The engine's value was proved by the *Selandia*'s 26,000-mile (41,600-km) run to Bangkok, Siam (now Thailand), via London and Antwerp without refueling. She required an engine-room crew of only eight men instead of the 25 needed on a coal burner of similar size.

The diesel engine is used in many types of vessels. Many of the world's largest tankers are diesel-driven, and about as many modern cargo ships have diesels as turbines. The diesel has not been adopted for ships of high speed, and relatively few large passenger ships have been built with diesel propulsion. The diesel has almost completely replaced old-style steam on tugs and other harbor-service vessels. Diesel-powered craft are known as "motor ships."

After the success of oil-powered diesel engines, the value of oil as a fuel for ships was appreciated. While lower grades of oil were used in diesels, higher grades were refined for use in turbines. By 1920, a great proportion of the world's shipping was powered by oil.

Size of Ships. In the late 18th century, the average ship's tonnage was less than 300 tons. During the 19th century, the figures rose rapidly. Sailing ships never exceeded 5,000 tons, but for steamers this was only the beginning.

The average cargo ship of the 19th century never exceeded 6,000 tons, but passenger ships increased dramatically in size. The 18,000 tons of the *Great Eastern* made her the largest ship in the world for almost 50 years, but by 1900, passenger ships measured over 20,000 tons.

In the first decade of the 20th century, passenger ships grew to nearly three times this size. Their expansion reached a peak in the 1930's, with the only three liners ever to exceed 80,000 tons: the British *Queen Mary* (81,000), the British *Queen Elizabeth* (83,000), and the French *Normandie* (83,000). After World War II, economy and efficiency of operation impelled the building of smaller liners. By the 1970's, the average liner or cruise ship measured 20,000 tons.

United States (1952)

France (1961)

The *Queen Elizabeth II*, last of the great ocean liners, was built in 1968.

The largest ships afloat today are the enormous oil tankers. Hundreds are over 200,000 tons, and many are over 300,000. Designers have projected tankers that might reach one million tons. Cargo ships have remained small. In the 1970's their average tonnage was a bit over 20,000 deadweight.

Appearance of Ships. The appearance of steamships has changed over the years with the larger size of the ships and changes in engine and hull design. The early ocean steamships looked like ordinary three-masted sailing ships, except for the paddle wheels and single smokestacks. Then two-stacked paddle steamers were built. On some the middle or main mast was eliminated.

In 1870 the White Star Line began placing the finest passenger cabins in a superstructure halfway between the ship's bow and stern. This was a radical innovation, for ever since Cleopatra's barge on the Nile, the choicest accommodations had been at the stern.

With the shift from paddle wheel to propeller power, the long sleek hull came into favor with steamship designers. Freighters rarely had more than one smokestack, but liners were built with two or three stacks. For a while, the four-stack liner caught the builders' imagination, as in the famous Cunarders *Mauretania* and *Lusitania* early in the 20th century, but only 14 of this type were built. The only five-stacker ever built was the *Great Eastern.*

When sails were eliminated by the introduction of twin-screws, a major structural evolution occurred. Without sails and their heavy yards, a ship's superstructure could be higher. Ever since the *Savannah*, the superstructure had been only one level of deckhouses, but now there was room for more levels. Ship superstructures mounted higher until 1914, when the 54,000-ton German *Vaterland* showed seven decks towering 80 feet (24 meters) above the hull proper.

Masts came to be vestigial remnants. They carried signal flags, and when wireless was invented they were used to string the antennae. After two generations of serving chiefly as decorations, they have been largely eliminated. The streamlined foremast, the only one that remains today on most vessels, has been moved from the bow deck to atop the pilot house and carries radar, wireless, and a searchlight.

The smokestack, one of the conspicuous features of any ship's silhouette, has often been a decorative structure. Around 1900 it was a proud symbol of the ownership of the line and carried various color designs and combinations. In the 1920's stacks became more commonplace. The squat stack of the diesel-powered vessel was a novelty. By the 1970's, the designers had turned back to colorful and unusual stacks, even in oil tankers and freighters.

LATE 20TH CENTURY SHIPS

In the 1970's cargo and passenger vessels were undergoing radical changes in design and operation to meet the demands of commerce and travel. The design of cargo ships and the methods of loading and stowing cargo were helping to meet the enormous volume of freight on the oceans. Passenger traffic, faced with airline competition, was turning to smaller, more luxurious cruise ships. Among the emerging new designs were craft that resembled a combination of surface ship and airplane and promised startling developments in the future, especially in speed.

Cargo Ships. Cargo ships may be broadly classified by the type of cargo they are designed to carry. *General cargo ships* may take any goods that are not handled by specialized ships. *Tankers* hold oil or other fluids. *Dry bulk carriers* convey coal, iron ore, or other materials that do not require containers. Refinements of these types, such as *multipurpose ships,* which can carry fluid and general cargoes on the same run, are in service for special purposes.

The concepts, construction, and use of general cargo ships have undergone drastic changes since the mid-20th century. From 1850 to 1960, the ordinary cargo ship remained relatively unchanged. A ship had two or three cargo holds forward of the engine and two aft. An array of masts, booms, and king posts, aided by great nets, lifted the cargo into and out of these holds. The cargo, in large shipments and small, of various sizes and shapes, was stowed as neatly as possible. Some mechanical unloading devices were evolved for bulk carriers such as ore ships on the Great Lakes, coal ships, and chemical carriers, but the loading and unloading techniques were not greatly changed since the days of ancient Rome. The freighter was larger and her engine more efficient, but her basic cargo deck plan might have been followed without difficulty by a shipowner before the Civil War.

An era of revolutionary change in cargo ships began in the 1960's. The three principal types that it produced are the container ship, the roll-on, roll-off ship, and the LASH ship.

Container Ships. A container ship has her engines, her superstructure, and her stack aft. Forward of the superstructure, the long hull is an empty space. This space is divided into compartments by vertical steel bulkheads. These compartments hold the cargo containers.

The containers are aluminum and steel boxes, usually 8 feet (2.4 meters) square and either 20 or 40 feet (6 or 12 meters) long. The larger container can carry as large a load as a railroad freight car. They are packed by the shipper at his plant and transported to a port by trucks.

At the pier, computer controls determine the loading order of the containers and their place in the ship, which depends on where they are to be unloaded. Four-story-high A-frame lifts pick up the containers and deftly deposit them in their designated hold in the ship. At their destination, the containers are unloaded by similar methods.

The size of the average container ship is about 25,000 tons—two or three times that of the freighter of the World War II period—and she is 600 to 700 feet (180–210 meters) long. Her average speed is 27 or 28 knots, twice as fast as the freighters of the late 1940's. Some container ships have achieved 33 knots. A container ship can carry up to four times as much cargo as a freighter built in 1960.

The increased cargo capacity, faster speed, and especially the efficient handling of cargo in the port created a revolution in shipping. A container ship can unload and load again in 24 hours, compared to up to four days for a conventional freighter. A container ship can be handled at one berth in port, instead of being shifted between piers to deal with different cargoes. One container ship, it has been estimated, can do the work of six ordinary freighters.

Building container ships is expensive, and old shipping lines with many freighters, confronted with a revolution, banded together. Rivals like the Cunard, Holland-America, and French lines joined to form the Atlantic Container Line. They sold dozens of old freighters and continued business with one fourth the number of new container ships.

Roll-on, Roll-off Ships. The roll-on, roll-off ship is a refinement of the container ship. Cargo containers are placed on wheeled conveyors like a flat-bed truck trailer. These conveyors are driven aboard ship through openings in her sides and stern and by ramps or elevators are stowed in their assigned places in the cargo holds. The driver's cab is detached from the conveyor and taken ashore, while the cargo and its wheeled conveyor remain to be driven off at the unloading port. This type of ship, usually about 700 feet (210 meters) long, is used also to carry vehicles and any cargo that can be rolled aboard.

LASH Ships. In the LASH vessels, which are about 800 feet (240 meters) long, the packaging principle is developed still further. LASH is the acronym of *Lighter Aboard SHip.* A number of lighters, or barges, each loaded with up to 300 tons of cargo, are hoisted aboard by a crane on wheels that is part of the ship. The crane moves the lighter forward into the shell of the ship. Since each lighter carries so much cargo and is put aboard in a matter of seconds, this procedure is remarkably efficient.

Tankers. The vessels that carry petroleum and other liquid products form the largest ship classification in the world today, and individual ships are the largest afloat. In general, they may be described as enormous floating tanks.

As an important commodity, oil has been carried in barrels on sluggish wind-driven craft across the Caspian Sea centuries ago. The idea of bulk oil transportation with the shell of the vessel forming the walls of a tank was untried until the little *Glückauf,* the prototype of the modern tanker, was built in Britain in 1886. Her engines were aft, so that three fourths of her length could be divided into an uninterrupted series of oil tanks. Her success as an oil carrier proved vital to the world's economy.

The *Glückauf* also set a pattern of ownership and registry that persists to modern times. She was owned by the Standard Oil Company, an American corporation, but was built in Britain and flew the German flag. Today, many of the world's large tanker fleets are American-controlled but fly the flags of Panama or Liberia. These flags, known as flags of convenience, denote the ship's registry and enable the owners to avoid various forms of regulation, taxes, and high labor costs. See FLAG OF CONVENIENCE.

The largest tankers of the early 1970's, measuring at least 1,100 feet (335 meters) long and 175 feet (53 meters) wide, can carry 300,000 tons of oil at a 20-knot speed on a trip of thousands of miles. Small tankers are used for short hauls along the coasts, and tank barges on rivers and lakes.

The U. S. tanker *Manhattan,* which was more than 1,000 feet (305 meters) long with a capacity of about 115,000 tons, made history in 1969. She conquered the ice of the Northwest Passage around the Arctic coasts of Canada and Alaska in a run from Chester, Pa., to Point Barrow, Alaska, to test the feasibility of bringing oil from the rich fields of northern Alaska to the ports of the eastern United States.

Dry Bulk Carriers. Dry bulk carriers were developed in the 19th century to carry iron ore

Container ship *Hawaiian Enterprise*

MODERN CARGO SHIPS

LASH ship *Doctor Lykes*

Tanker ship *Idemitsu Maru*

General cargo ship *Prudential Seajet*

through the Great Lakes to the steel mills in the eastern United States. These ships had the superstructure and bridge far aft. Forward of the superstructure, the vessel's hull was a huge hold to carry the ore. The ships averaged around 600 feet (180 meters) in length and took about 15,000 tons of cargo. Later models, up to 700 feet (210 meters), carried 25,000 tons.

Oceangoing bulk carriers are larger. Built on a design like those of the lake boats, they can take about 100,000 tons of cargo.

A new ship type called an O/O carrier, which can carry either ore or oil, appeared in the 1950's. Its capacity was about 250,000 tons. A decade later, an O/B/O ship was put into service to carry up to 150,000 tons of ore, non-liquid bulk cargo, or oil.

Tugs. One of the most familiar types of vessels, especially in harbors and on rivers and lakes, is the tugboat. Small tugs aid in docking large ships and propel strings of cargo-laden barges. Huge oceangoing tugs may tow some kinds of cargo barges on long voyages. Others assist in deep-sea salvage work. The steam tug has been largely replaced by diesel-powered craft with pilot-house control of the engines.

An innovation in the tug category has been the tug-barge. A barge of up to 20,000 tons is pushed by a large tug or "towboat," whose bow fits into a notch cut in the stern of the barge. This scheme has been considered as a way to cut costs on the oil tanker routes from the Gulf of Mexico north along the eastern coast of the United States. A large tug needs only a fifth of the crew required for a modern tanker.

Advanced Ship Types. Among the types of vessels that are still largely in an experimental stage are the air cushion vehicle, or hovercraft, and the hydrofoil. The hovercraft moves over water or any dense surface on a cushion of air. A typical craft can carry 15 passengers or 3½ tons of cargo at about 60 miles (100 km) an hour. A possible development in this field is a *surface effect ship* of up to 30,000 tons that could cross an ocean at speeds up to 115 miles (180 km) an hour. (See AIR CUSHION VEHICLE.) A hydrofoil is a small vessel with a curved or cambered surface on her bottom that creates a lift as it moves through the water. See HYDROFOIL.

Nuclear-Powered Ships. The first nuclear-powered cargo ship was launched at Camden, N. J., in 1958. She was christened the *Savannah*, after

739

The nuclear ship *Savannah* was the first ship to use nuclear energy to generate steam for her turbines. Launched in 1958, she cruised around the world carrying passengers and cargo, but she proved too expensive to operate as a regular commercial vessel.

MARITIME ADMINISTRATION

the first steamship to cross the Atlantic, in the hope that she would mark an advance over conventional oil-powered craft as her namesake had achieved over sail power.

But she proved too expensive to operate as a cargo ship. Her power plant ran the ship efficiently, but she required double the crew of an ordinary freighter, and her cargo space was limited, principally by the shielding 16 feet (5 meters) thick around her nuclear core. West Germany and Japan also built experimental nuclear vessels but met similar problems. Adapting nuclear power to ships that must pay their way may depend on solving problems of cost.

Passenger Ships. The 20th century has seen great changes in design and in use of passenger vessels. From late in the 19th century, ocean travel between Europe and the United States was heavy. American tourists flocked to Europe and the westward flow of immigrants to the United States amounted at times before World War I to one million a year. Many of these immigrants were crowded into cramped quarters on small ships, and others were accommodated in inexpensive quarters on large ships. The German *Vaterland* carried 2,700 third- and fourth-class passengers, who were jammed into one fifth of the ship's space. When the United States imposed restrictions on immigration in 1921, this inflow was reduced to a trickle. To fill their passenger spaces, the large liners had to popularize "cabin class" and "tourist class" accommodations.

The golden age of the transatlantic liner was from the 1920's until World War II. Scores of small passenger ships flying the flags of many nations made their scheduled runs, but the pride of the sea was the bevy of huge liners, most of them under the British, French, or German flags.

Among the most famous during these years were the British *Aquitania, Mauretania, Queen Mary,* and *Queen Elizabeth;* the French *Île de France* and *Normandie;* and the German *Bremen* and *Europa.* These ships were huge, all of them measuring over 40,000 tons, and they emphasized luxury and service for passengers. The two *Queens* and the *Normandie* were all more than 1,000 feet (304 meters) long. They could cross the Atlantic in five days. The original *Queen Elizabeth* was succeeded by the *Queen Elizabeth II,* a 963-foot (294-meter) vessel of 65,983 tons. Primarily intended for cruises, it made its maiden voyage in 1969.

The United States had never invested largely in the ocean passenger trade and did not share in the rich business of this period. In 1952, American shipbuilders introduced the *United States,* whose 35-knot speed made her the fastest liner afloat. But the best days of the ocean liner were over, and the *United States* was laid up in the late 1960's for lack of passengers. A subsidy program kept a few American passenger vessels at sea.

Immediately after World War II, the airplane took over the bulk of world travel across the oceans. By the 1970's, few ships carried passengers. Crowds of Muslim pilgrims went by sea on their way to Mecca, often as deck passengers, and there were many overnight passenger ferries on short hauls. But for longer trips, the big passenger ship appeared to be finished.

On coastal and inland waters, too, in the United States and other countries, the passenger steamboat was vanishing before the competition of the automobile. U. S. coastal passenger shipping ended with World War II, and the Great Lakes and river service halted not long afterward. In some countries, a few steamboats continued to carry passengers on excursions.

Yet the future of the passenger ship appeared secure. The cruise ship had captured the imagination and the patronage of the traveler for pleasure. Seldom exceeding 20,000 tons, these vessels operate on short vacation cruises and on long voyages around the world, touching at out-of-the-way ports. Their features include air-conditioned cabins, swimming pools, and sun decks covered by glass in inclement weather. All modern passenger ships have their engines aft.

Ships of the Future. The greatest potentials in the future of transoceanic shipping may lie in the development of new radical types of vessels. With 71% of the globe covered by oceans or seas, the effort will undoubtedly be made to fill the need for transportation over its waters. See also BOATS AND BOATING; WARSHIPS; and the Index entry *Ship.*

FRANK O. BRAYNARD
South Street Seaport Museum, New York City

Bibliography

Braynard, Frank O., *S. S. Savannah, The Elegant Steam Ship* (Univ. of Ga. Press 1963).
Brinnin, John Malcolm, *The Sway of the Grand Saloon* (Delacorte Press 1971).
Dunn, Laurence, *Passenger Liners*, rev. ed. (Coles 1965).
Kuechle, David, *The Story of the Savannah* (Harvard Univ. Press 1971).
LaDage, John H., *Merchant Ships: A Pictorial Study*, 2d ed. (Cornell Maritime 1968).
Nelson, Stewart B., *Oceanographic Ships Fore and Aft* (USGPO 1971).
Sawyer, Leonard Arthur, and Mitchell, E. H., *The Liberty Ships* (Cornell Maritime 1970).

SHIP REGISTRY ACT, an enactment of Aug. 18, 1914, that provided for the admission of foreign-built ships to American registry for foreign trade. Congress finally acknowledged, with the outbreak of World War I, that ever since the first Registry Act of September 1789, which confined American registry to ships built in the United States, there had been serious embarrassment to U. S. citizens who owned property at sea. They had been barred from trading with the United States under the American flag though they could do so with all other countries. Because of this policy, which carried prohibitory penalties, many American commercial firms operated foreign-built ships, which often could be built more cheaply abroad, under other flags. At the time of the Panama Canal Act of 1912, efforts were made to get rid of some technicalities, but it took the outbreak of war in Europe to get Congress to pass the Ship Registry Act of 1914. It granted the President discretionary powers, also, to suspend such provisions as that calling for all watch officers of vessels of the United States registered for foreign trade to be U. S. citizens.

SHIPIBO, shə-pē′bō, a South American Indian tribe of Panoan stock, living in the forested regions of the upper Ucayali River, Peru. Their existence was reported by Franciscan missionaries who visited them in 1651, but a mission established for them in 1764 was, after a brief period of success, massacred in 1767, and the Shipibos have since rarely come in contact with the whites. They are great wanderers and have no fixed places of migration. They are skilled boatmen and fishermen.

SHIPKA PASS, ship′kä, is a strategic pass through the Shipka range of the Balkan Mountains in Bulgaria. During the Russo-Turkish War (1877–1878), there was heavy fighting in the pass after the Russians took it from the Turks in July 1877. The Turks counterattacked in August, and fighting continued into September, with severe losses on each side. Both the Turks and the Russians then dug in, but the Turks surrendered in January 1878.

SHIPPING. See TRADE.

SHIP'S BELLS, a method of dividing time that is used aboard most oceangoing vessels to govern the activities of the crew. The 24-hour day is divided into 5 full watches and 2 dog watches: first watch (8 P.M. to midnight), midwatch (midnight to 4 A.M.), morning watch (4 to 8 A.M.), forenoon watch (8 A.M. to noon), afternoon watch (noon to 4 P.M.), first dog watch (4 to 6 P.M.) and second dog watch (6 to 8 P.M.). Bells are rung to indicate the passage of time within a watch or dog watch. A pair of rings marks the passage of an hour. Two pairs of bells and a single bell during the first watch would mean 2½ hours into the first watch, or 10:30 P.M. Eight bells mean the end of a full watch. Ship's bells were first used in the 15th century.

SHIP'S LOG. See LOG.

SHIPWORM, any of a genus of wormlike clams that burrow into wood. See TEREDO.

SHIPWRECKS. See DISASTERS—*Marine Disasters.*

SHIRAZ, shē-räz′, is a city in southwestern Iran and the capital of Fars province. It is in a high valley (5,200 feet or 1,585 meters), about 35 miles (56 km) southwest of the ancient ruins of Persepolis. Shiraz is a commercial and manufacturing center and is famous for its wines, carpets, and inlaid wood and metal products. The city is much praised in Persian poetry for its climate, wine, and rose gardens. In the northern part of the city are the tombs of the celebrated poets Hafiz and Saadi, both natives of Shiraz. Among the other points of interest are the Shah Cheragh mausoleum; the New Mosque, built in 1218; the Vakil Mosque; and the 17th century madrasa, or theological school.

A settlement existed at Shiraz in the 5th century B. C., but it did not become important until after the Arab invasions of the 7th century A. D. Timur (Tamerlane) sacked the city in 1393, but it recovered its prosperity under the Safavids. The Afghans sacked it in the early 18th century. In the late 18th century the Zand dynasty made Shiraz its capital, and many buildings date from the reign (1750–1779) of Karim Khan. Population: (1966) 269,865.

SHIRE, shīr, is an English term denoting an administrative district. It is still in general use in England and Wales, although it has been superseded in many areas by the modern term *county.* Thus Derbyshire, Glamorganshire, and Renfrewshire are counties. In the United States, counties are the first division of the state, but the use of the word shire has no significance as to division; it is merely a portion of a name. An example is Berkshire county, Mass. However, in England the suffix "shire" is in itself an indication that the division is a county.

It has been said that King Alfred (reigned 871–899) divided England into shires. However, although there exists in England a system of subdivisions known as shires, that theory seems at least doubtful. For the Saxon people were a collection of clans, and these clans were divided into families, two or three large families to a clan. The head of the family was the supreme lawgiver in the family, and he himself was under the leadership of the head of the clan, or tribal community. These tribal communities united to form what is known as *hundreds*, and the hundreds united to form *shires*. Thus the country, instead of being divided deliberately into shires, was formed by the union of many separate shires, each of which was, for practical purposes, an independent kingdom. Some of these small districts still exist: Norhamshire in Northumberland and Richmondshire in Yorkshire, for example. Apparently it was after this union of shires under one national head, not a spontaneous process but one of slow and at times retrogradal growth, that the shire took its position as a subordinate part of the kingdom. As such it had as its head the *shire-reeves*, whence is derived the modern term sheriff.

The shire-reeve, before the Norman Conquest, was one of the two heads of the shire organizations, the other being the *ealdorman* (or earl), whence comes the modern term, alderman. The ealdorman seems to have represented the old organization and dignity of the shire when it was an independent kingdom; he shared certain offices with the bishop. But the shire-reeve was more particularly the representative of the king, and after the Norman Conquest he became purely a royal officer, with his importance considerably curtailed. He held the sheriff's *tourn,* an annual court to which came the vassals of the king. The appeal from this court was to the king himself, and from this appeal came the growth of the *curia reqis,* or King's court, in its three branches: common pleas, King's bench, and exchequer. This court assessed taxes, also, and thus the sheriff became the financial head of the shire. From the time of the Plantagenet accession to the throne, the importance of the shire organization decreased. The modern sheriff is largely an aid to the county court. The duties of sheriff include taking charge of parliamentary elections, executing process emanating from the High Court and the criminal courts, the calling of jurors, and the collection of forfeited recognizances, or bonds. See also COUNTY.

Further Reading: Jolliffe, John E., *The Constitutional History of Medieval England: From the English Settlement to 1485,* 4th ed., repr. (Van Nostrand-Reinhold 1961); Sayles, George O., *The Medieval Foundations of England,* 2d rev. ed., repr. (A. S. Barnes 1961); Stenton, F. M., *Anglo-Saxon England,* 3d ed. (Oxford 1971).

SHIRE RIVER, shē'rā, in southeastern Africa, flowing about 250 miles (400 km) from Lake Malawi (Nyasa) to the Zambezi River. It issues from the southern end of the lake in Malawi and flows south into Mozambique, where it joins the Zambezi about 100 miles (160 km) from the Zambezi's mouth. The Shire flows through rich farmland. It is navigable below a 50-mile (80-km) stretch in Malawi known as the Murchison Rapids.

SHIRER, shīr'ər, **William Lawrence** (1904–), American newspaper correspondent, radio commentator, and author. He was born in Chicago, Ill., on Feb. 23, 1904, and graduated in 1925 from Coe College. After serving as a reporter for the Paris edition of the Chicago *Tribune* (1925–1926), he was European correspondent for the *Tribune* (1926–1933) and for the Universal News Service (1935–1937). From 1937 to 1941, Shirer was European representative for the Columbia Broadcasting System and from 1939 he also served as war correspondent and commentator for CBS. Later, he joined the Mutual Broadcasting System as a commentator (1947–1949).

Shirer's first book, *Berlin Diary: The Journal of a Foreign Correspondent, 1934–1941* (1941), became a best seller. In 1960 he published *The Rise and Fall of the Third Reich: A History of Nazi Germany,* which traces the history of Nazi Germany from its beginnings after World War I to its destruction in World War II. The book, also a best seller, won the National Book Award in 1961. In addition, Shirer wrote a number of novels and *The Sinking of the Bismarck* (1962), about the World War II German warship.

SHIRLEY, shûr'lē, **James** (1596–1666), English poet and playwright, who was one of the most significant dramatists to emerge after the accession of Charles I. Shirley was born in London on Sept. 18, 1596, and educated at Oxford and Cambridge. He took Anglican orders and became a schoolmaster at St. Albans. But he was soon converted to Roman Catholicism and in 1625 went to London, where he became a prolific writer for the stage and a favorite at the royal court. He spent the years 1636–1640 in Dublin, where some of his plays were produced. An act of Parliament suppressing the theaters in 1642 probably hindered his productivity after that time. He died on Oct. 29, 1666, of exposure during the great fire in London.

In addition to poetry, some of which was collected in *Poems* (1646), Shirley wrote more than 40 dramatic works, including comedies, tragedies, tragicomedies, and masques—all marked by sobriety, rectitude, and poetic grace. His best tragedies are *The Traitor* (1631) and *The Cardinal* (1641), the latter a play of love, politics, and revenge suggested by the contemporary career of Richelieu in France. Except for a measure of social restraint, Shirley's comedies, such as *The Witty Fair One* (1628) and *The Lady of Pleasure* (1635), have much in common with the best of Restoration comedy. *The Triumph of Peace,* an ingenious and elaborate masque written by Shirley and produced by Inigo Jones in 1634, is notable for its songs. But a later masque, *The Contention of Ajax and Ulysses* (first printed in 1659), contains the poem beginning "The glories of our blood and state/ Are shadows, not substantial things," for which Shirley is best known.

Further Reading: Armstrong, Ray L., *The Poems of James Shirley* (1941; reprint, Lansdowne Press 1971); Forsythe, Robert S., *The Relations of Shirley's Plays to the Elizabethan Drama* (Blom, B. 1914); Nason, Arthur H., *James Shirley, Dramatist* (Blom, B. 1967).

SHIRLEY, shûr'lē, **William** (1693–1771), American colonial governor. He was born in Preston, Sussex, England, and he studied law at Cambridge and practiced in London before emigrating to America in 1731. A lawyer and judge in Boston, he became a rival to Gov. Jonathan Belcher, whose commercial policies he opposed. Appointed royal governor of Massachusetts in 1741, Shirley set to work to strengthen the defenses of the colony in preparation for war with France. He planned the victorious expedition against Cape Breton Island in 1745. In 1749, he was appointed to a commission to settle the boundary between French North America and New England.

Resuming his gubernatorial duties in 1753, he negotiated an Indian treaty and erected several forts on the Kennebec River in anticipation of renewed war. In 1755, during the French and Indian War, Shirley was named commander in chief of the British forces in North America. He planned the expedition against Niagara but was unsuccessful largely because of dissension among the colonies. Accused of mismanagement and possible treason, he was superseded in his command and his governorship in 1756 and was summoned to England, where, however, charges were dismissed. Shirley was appointed governor of the Bahamas in 1761 but resigned in 1767 and retired to Roxbury, Mass., where he died on March 24, 1771.

SHIVA, shē'və, is the third deity in the great triad of Hindu gods, the other two being Brahma and Vishnu. The cult of Shiva is one of the most popular in modern Hinduism. His name, which is also rendered as Siva, signifies in Sanskrit "auspicious" or "of good omen." He typifies both destruction and reproduction, but is generally regarded as the deity in the character of destroyer. He is a later form of the Vedic god, Rudra. His worshipers assign to him the first place in the Trimurti, or triad. To them Shiva is Time, Justice, Water, the Sun, the Destroyer, and the Creator. He is represented in his characters of the god of regeneration and of justice as riding on a white bull, called Nandi.

In some representations, Shiva has five heads; three eyes, one on his forehead, indicative of his power of contemplation; two, four, eight, or ten hands; and, in the middle of his forehead, a crescent. His throat is dark blue; his hair of a light reddish color, thickly matted together and brought over his head so as to project like a horn from his forehead. He wears a garland of human skulls around his neck and, as a second necklace, a serpent; and holds a trident surmounted by a skull and one or two human heads.

Shiva is often represented as entirely covered with serpents, emblems of immortality. Among his weapons are a bow called *Ajakava*, a thunderbolt, and an ax. He resides on Mt. Kailas, a northern peak of the Himalayas. One of his principal attendants is Tandu, a teacher of dancing and mimicry, whence Shiva is the patron of dancers. He has more than 1,000 names, which are detailed· in the 69th chapter of the Siva Purana, one of the Sanskrit epics.

Shiva's spouse is called by many names in various parts of India. The most common of these include Kali, Durga, Pārvatī, and Chandi. Ganesha, the elephant-headed god, is also associated with him.

SHIVAJI, shē′vä-jē (1627–1680) was an Indian ruler who laid the foundations of Maratha power in western India. He was born near Poona in what is now Maharashtra state, the son of a tax official of the Muslim kingdom of Bijapur. Resolving to free his Hindu coreligionists from Muslim domination, Shivaji (Śivaji) raised an army that defeated the forces of Bijapur and defied the Mughul (Mogul) Emperor Aurangzeb. Although captured by the Mughuls, he escaped, resumed the war against them, and in 1674 was crowned an independent sovereign at Raigarh.

By the time of his death, Shivaji controlled a considerable territory on the western side of the Indian peninsula, as well as other parts of the south. He had developed an efficient administration and a powerful army, but he also encouraged a spirit of independence among the Marathas that was strong enough to enable them to withstand for 150 years all attempts to conquer them.

SHIVELY, shĭv′lē, is a city in northern Kentucky, in Jefferson county, about 5 miles (8 km) southwest of the center of Louisville. It has whiskey distilleries and tobacco storage warehouses. Shively was incorporated in 1939 and is governed by a mayor and council. Population: 19,223.

SHIVERING. See TEMPERATURE, BODY.

SHIZUOKA, shē-zoo̅-ō-kä, a city in Japan and the capital of Shizuoka prefecture, is situated on Suruga Bay midway between Tokyo and Nagoya. It grew rapidly in the 20th century chiefly because of its location in the center of an area producing 70% of Japan's tea. Ieyasu, the founder of the Tokugawa Shogunate, spent a third of his life in Shizuoka, and the ruins of his castle can still be seen.

Shizuoka prefecture is a major producer of oranges as well as tea. Its fishing and food processing industries are also important. The prefecture has an area of 3,000 square miles (7,769 sq km). Population: (1970) of the prefecture, 3,089,895; of the city, 416,378.

SHKLOVSKY, shklôf′skē, **Victor Borisovich** (1893–   ), Russian writer and critic, who was one of the chief advocates of the formalist theory of literature. The formalism movement stressed aesthetic rather than social or political values and encouraged the use of new words and literary devices to stimulate a fresh approach to Russian literature. Shklovsky's most important critical works include *About the Theory of Prose* (1925), *The Technique of the Writer's Craft* (1928), and studies of Leo Tolstoy (1928) and Fyodor Dostoyevsky (1957).

As a young man, Shklovsky opposed the Bolshevik government for a time and lived mostly in Germany for a few years. There he wrote an autobiographical work, *A Sentimental Journey* (1923), covering the years between 1917 and 1922. He returned to Russia shortly thereafter and became a strong supporter of the regime. In the 1920's he joined the Serapion Brothers, an organization of young Russian writers dedicated to freedom of literary expression. In his later years, Shklovsky modified his opinions to be more in accord with official dogma.

SHKODËR, shkō′dər, is a city in northern Albania, at the southern end of Lake Shkodër. The Italian form of the name is Scutari. Served by Shëngjin, an Adriatic port to the southeast, Shkodër is a regional trade center for wool, cotton, hides, tobacco, and dried fish. Its products include textiles, metal goods, and glass. There are picturesque mosques, a Venetian citadel, and a Roman Catholic cathedral.

In the 1st millenium B. C. it was an Illyrian capital. It was captured by the Romans in 168 B. C. During the Middle Ages it was held successively by the Serbs and Venetians. In the 15th century it was a stronghold of Skanderbeg, an Albanian national hero. It was taken by the Turks in 1479, but from the mid-1700's local rulers maintained virtual independence. After the Balkan Wars (1912–1913), it became part of Albania. Population: (1967 est.) 49,800.

The lake is the largest in the Balkans, with an area of about 146 square miles (376 sq km), and lies partly in Yugoslavia. Fed partly by the Morača River and drained by the Buenë (Bojana), it was once an inlet of the Adriatic Sea.

SHOCK, a state of circulatory collapse caused by acute loss of blood or fluids from the body; by expansion of blood vessels, causing blood to pool in parts of the body; or by damage to the heart, affecting the heart's ability to pump blood through the body, or by a decrease in function of all the cellular elements making up the circulatory system. In all cases the circulatory system is not functioning normally, and blood is not being pumped at the usual pressure and in the usual amount, resulting in a deficiency of blood flow to peripheral tissues. The initial symptoms of shock include weakness, weak thready pulse, low arterial pressure, pallor, sweating, rapid heart rate, nausea, restlessness, confusion, and apathy. Loss of consciousness may also occur.

The clinical picture of shock is produced in a variety of ways. (1) The heart cannot pump the needed blood because of the death of heart muscle from occlusion or blockage of the artery supplying the heart with blood. (2) The chambers of the heart cannot accept blood because they are compressed by an accumulation of fluid under pressure in the pericardium, the sac surrounding the heart. Since the heart cannot fill adequately, it cannot deliver blood normally. (3) An obstruction in the main artery connecting the heart and lungs can cause circulation to fail. (4) There is not enough blood to fill the circulatory system. This condition can result from hemorrhage; a loss of plasma and its associated protein, electrolytes, and water from capillaries injured by burns, infection, or chemical injury; or a loss of water and electrolytes from vomiting and diarrhea. (5) If the process of dying is slow, cell metabolism in the circulatory system fails and signs of circulatory insufficiency producing the picture of shock are present before breathing ceases. (6) An acute dilation of the small blood vessels, particularly those supplying the muscles, also causes a marked fall in arterial blood pressure, and if the patient is standing, a loss of consciousness.

In practice several of the above-mentioned mechanisms are usually simultaneously responsible for shock. For example, reflex arteriolar dilation from pain occurs in patients with diminished cardiac output resulting from a massive myocardial infarct, known popularly as a heart attack. Both the loss of blood and reflex arteriolar dilation are important in circulatory failure caused by penetrating wounds of the chest. Infection, with its adverse effect on cell metabolism, is a frequent complication in patients who have lost blood from trauma or are dehydrated.

The treatment of shock depends on the factors underlying the circulatory collapse. For example, if shock is due to loss of fluid, the fluid must be replaced; if it is due to heart malfunction, the cardiac problem must be treated. Because shock can be fatal, emergency treatment should be given until medical attention can be obtained. See ELECTRIC SHOCK; FIRST AID.

E. A. STEAD, JR., M. D.
Duke University

SHOCK, ELECTRIC. See ELECTRIC SHOCK.

SHOCK ABSORBER, any of several mechanical devices for absorbing the energy of sudden impacts. Spring-type shock absorbers, which are often made of rubber, generally are used to protect delicate instruments from direct impacts. Hydraulic shock absorbers, which basically consist of a piston and cylinder and a fluid such as oil, are used in airplane landing-gear systems and in automobiles.

An automobile has two front and two rear shock absorbers. The two front ones are mounted between the vehicle frame and the lower control arm, and the two rear ones are mounted between the vehicle frame and the axle housing. A typical hydraulic shock absorber used in an automobile is shown in the accompanying diagram. The shock absorber opposes the compression of a spring in the suspension system when the automobile hits a bump, and it opposes the rebound of the spring after the automobile has passed over the bump. This damping action on the oscillation of the suspension-system spring provides a smooth ride and helps keep the wheel firmly on the road at all speeds.

On a bump stroke, the piston rod and piston travel downward in the cylinder, forcing oil through the foot-valve assembly and into the oil reservoir. The controlled resistance that the oil encounters in passing through the foot-valve assembly produces the bump-damping force of the

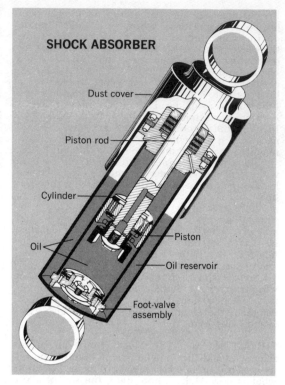

SHOCK ABSORBER

Dust cover
Piston rod
Cylinder
Oil
Piston
Oil reservoir
Foot-valve assembly

shock absorber. On a rebound stroke, the piston rod and piston travel upward in the cylinder, forcing the oil to escape downward through small passageways in the piston assembly. The controlled resistance that the oil encounters in flowing through these passageways produces the rebounding damping force of the shock absorber.

SHOCK THERAPY is a form of treatment for certain mental illnesses. It is most often used for treating severe depression, but it is also occasionally employed in dealing with certain types of schizophrenia. Since the development of the tranquilizers and antidepressant drugs, the use of shock therapy has declined somewhat, but some psychiatrists still favor it. One of its advantages is the speed with which it can produce results.

All types of shock therapy produce convulsions. These convulsions are effective in treating some mentally ill patients, but how the convulsions produce beneficial results is not understood. It had long been observed that patients in mental hospitals often lost all their symptoms if they experienced spontaneous convulsions. As a result, in the 1920's and 1930's physicians began to attempt to induce convulsions deliberately. Several chemicals were used to induce the convulsions, the most effective and safest of which is a synthetic camphor preparation, pentylenetetrazol, known as Metrazol, and which is still occasionally used. Insulin, in doses that lower the blood sugar enough to produce convulsions, has also been used.

The most common form of shock therapy, however, involves the passage of an electric current through the brain to produce convulsions. Known as electroshock therapy, or electroconvulsive therapy, this form of treatment is sometimes used together with antidepressant drugs. See also ELECTROSHOCK THERAPY.

SHOCK WAVE, a large-amplitude compressional wave that arises from a lightning stroke, a bomb blast or other intense explosion, or a supersonic flow over an airplane or other object in a fluid medium. A shock wave characteristically is a small disturbed region or wave front within which abrupt changes occur in the pressure, density, and velocity of the air or other fluid medium.

Because shock waves generally are not visible, special techniques must be used to display their presence. These techniques include schlieren photographs and shadowgraphs of supersonic flow over objects. Both of these techniques are commonly used in wind-tunnel tests in which supersonic flows are passed over stationary objects of various shapes. Such tests have shown that when the object has a blunt nose approximately like that of an airplane, the shock wave is approximately parabolic in shape.

See also HYDROGEN BOMB; SONIC BOOM.

Further Reading: Kirkwood, John G., *Shock and Detonation Waves* (Gordon 1968).

SHOCKLEY, William Bradford (1910–   ), American physicist who shared the 1965 Nobel Prize in physics with Walter Brattain and John Bardeen for their research on semiconductors and discovery of the transistor effect. Shockley was born in London, England, on Feb. 13, 1910, and his family moved to California in 1913. Attending the California and Massachusetts institutes of technology, he obtained his doctorate in 1936 and joined the Bell Telephone Laboratories in Murray Hill, N. J. During World War II he headed a research group studying antisubmarine operations and served as a consultant to the secretary of war. Shockley then returned to the Bell laboratories, where with Brattain and Bardeen he did his research on semiconductors.

Semiconductors, such as germanium, transmit electricity in one direction only and can function as rectifiers in transforming alternating to direct current. Shockley's team found that certain impurities improved the performance of such crystals, and in the late 1940's they developed a semiconductor system that amplified current as well. The compact solid-state device, called a transistor, quickly became of great importance in electronics. See TRANSISTOR.

Shockley later served the Defense Department in evaluating weapons systems. In 1958 he became director of the Shockley Semiconductor Laboratory and president of the Shockley Transistor Corporation. In 1963, Shockley was made a professor of engineering science at Stanford University.

Shockley became interested in controversial theories about the inheritance of intelligence in different racial groups, and in the 1960's he sought to have the National Academy of Sciences support research on this subject. The request was turned down, and Stanford later rejected his proposal to teach a course on the subject.

SHODDY is a low-quality fabric manufactured wholly or in part from reclaimed wool. Shoddy usually is made by tearing up reclaimed cloth, mixing the torn material with fleece wool or other fibers, and then respinning the resultant yarn. In the United States shoddy goods must have "reused" or "reprocessed" labels to guide the consumer in price versus quality decisions.

SHOE, a form of footgear that covers the foot up to the ankle and that is intended as a protection from cold, dampness, or rough terrain. In addition to shoes, other basic types of footgear are sandals, moccasins, boots, slippers, and mules.

The *sandal* has a flat sole of leather or wood fastened to the foot by straps, thongs, or a knob between the toes. The *moccasin* is distinguished by a sole that extends up around the foot to form some part or all of the upper section of the shoe. This is a primitive form of footgear that is still worn by hunters because of its flexibility and because it gives greater protection against dampness than shoes with a seam between the sole and the uppers. The *boot* consists of a sole and an upper part that extends above the ankle to protect the leg from cold, wetness, or dangerous conditions, such as snakebite or thorny plants. The *slipper* is a soft shoe, often intended for indoor wear, with uppers generally made of fabric and sometimes lined for winter wear with wool or fur. *Mules* are slippers that consist of a sole and an upper that covers only the toes.

Materials. Shoes have been made of various substances, depending on the raw material available and the varying climatic conditions in different parts of the world. Thus wooden shoes were worn in forested Europe; clogs (wooden soles with straps for support) in the warm Middle East, India, and Japan; tree bark moccasins in Scandinavia; and straw sandals and fabric shoes in Korea and China. The people of predominantly cold countries have always worn high boots, of which Russian boots in black or red leather are typical. The Laplanders' boots have moccasin feet with turned-up toes, and the people of Tibet, Bhutan, and Nepal in the Himalaya wear high boots made from the skin of the hairy yak.

Leather has been the principal material for making shoes. Undoubtedly the first material used for shoes and the most widely available, leather has also proved to have the most suitable qualities. Stone Age man was unable to cover himself with any other material as large as the skin of the animal he had killed for food, and it is probable that he also wrapped pieces of hide around his feet to protect them against the cold, the rough ground, or the sharp shards of flint from which he made his tools. When the hide dried and cracked, primitive man softened it with animal oils and fats—the first effort at leather dressing.

With the dawning of personal vanity, man began to experiment with vegetable dyes to alter the color of his skin clothes. In so doing, he chanced upon a method of preserving the hide from putrefying and by accident turned it into leather. Dressing and curing hides by natural oils and vegetable dyes were practiced until the 20th century, when tanning came to be done chemically with chromium salts. Vulcanized rubber has been increasingly used for footwear in the 20th century. Synthetic rubber, discovered during World War II by Waldo Semon, is now the most important shoemaking material, providing hardwearing, waterproof soles. Also, plastics are used, especially for uppers.

Shoes have always been made on a molded shape called a *last*, traditionally of maple wood, but now often made of plastic or aluminum. A wooden last of the Neolithic Period was found in Switzerland, and many iron lasts made by the Romans have been dug up in England. Compli-

SHOES AND OTHER FOOTGEAR

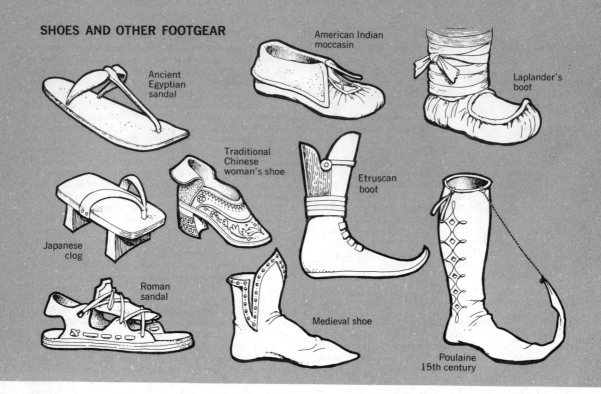

Ancient Egyptian sandal

American Indian moccasin

Laplander's boot

Traditional Chinese woman's shoe

Etruscan boot

Japanese clog

Roman sandal

Medieval shoe

Poulaine 15th century

cated machinery has been made to perform every process that was formerly done by hand in the making of a shoe, but great skill is still needed on the part of the operator to turn out a satisfactory machine-made article.

History. Until the age of cheap mass production, shoes were generally considered a mark of rank or prestige. Common men walked barefoot, and their feet became calloused, helping them to escape much of the discomfort that would result from not wearing shoes. The nobility, on the other hand, felt obliged to wear shoes as a proof of gentility, that they could not bear roughness or dirt. In China, in order to indicate their incapacity for physical work, upper-class parents bound their daughters' feet to prevent normal growth and to produce a small, twisted "lily foot." As a result, wealthy Chinese women could scarcely walk in their tiny shoes.

Early Shoes. Shoes were unnecesary in warm climates. In ancient Egyptian wall paintings only kings and priests are shown wearing sandals, made of plaited reeds or, as in the case of Tutankhamen, of finely tooled leather. People in cooler climates wore shoes much earlier. Egyptian wall paintings at Beni Hassan (2000 B.C.) and at Thebes (1450 B.C.) depict Syrians, and Minoans from Crete, wearing an assortment of elaborate sandals and boots. The meticulous art of the Assyrians has left us detailed designs of their elaborate and sophisticated sandals on the reliefs from Calah (modern Nimrud) and Nineveh (about 800 B.C.).

Ankle-high boots with turned-up toes were characteristic of the Hittite culture, and it has been suggested that the Etruscans may have come from the same stock because figures in Etruscan tomb paintings of a much later date wear identical boots. This curious design of turned-up, pointed toes, perhaps originally a symbol of the horn of the moon, has persisted in all the Muslim countries of the Middle East.

Classical Shoes. Greek sandals were developed from those of earlier Middle Eastern peoples, with many individual designs of straps over the instep and intricate lacing up the leg. To prevent the laces from slipping down, the heel piece was often extended for several inches up the back of the leg and was provided with eyelets through which the laces were passed after being twisted around the leg. Robert Graves writes in *The Greek Myths* that Greek warriors wore only one sandal—on the left foot, their shield side—because that foot was advanced during a hand-to-hand struggle and could be used for kicking an enemy in the groin. Thus the left was the hostile foot and was never set first on the threshold of a friend's house. The custom survives among modern soldiers, who begin marching with the left foot foremost.

Greek women appear to have worn *buskins,* soft boots that came up above the ankle. Greek vase paintings show women at their toilet holding such footgear. Further evidence that buskins were worn especially by women is provided by an Attic vase on which male actors, impersonating women, are shown putting on these soft boots.

The Romans wore more ornate sandals than the Greeks, with the uppers covering a great deal of the foot but still leaving the toes bare. They also wore the *calceus,* a shoe that covered the foot to the ankle like a modern shoe, and buskins that reached halfway up the calf. Roman senators wore black buskins with a crescent-shaped clasp of ivory or silver on the instep. Buskins were often open up the front, laced across, and lined with the skins of small animals, the heads and claws of which were allowed to hang down over the tops as ornament. Roman soldiers derived their title *caligati* from their strong sandals, or boots, called *caliga,* which were often studded with nails.

Early Medieval Shoes. In the less advanced cultures of northern Europe, people wore hose fitted

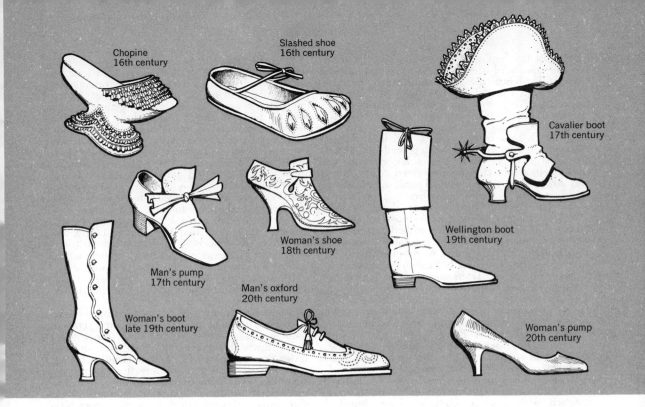

Chopine
16th century

Slashed shoe
16th century

Cavalier boot
17th century

Man's pump
17th century

Woman's shoe
18th century

Wellington boot
19th century

Woman's boot
late 19th century

Man's oxford
20th century

Woman's pump
20th century

with feet, like babies' leggings, as protection from cold and moisture. Over these they wore oblong pieces of leather bound to the feet by leather thongs. The thongs, laced through punched holes, two in the front and one at the back, drew up the corners of the leather sole over the toes and behind the heel. The thongs were then crisscrossed up the leg, over the baggy hose, in the fashion typical of the Anglo-Saxons, Gauls, Goths, or Franks.

In the cultural centers of the early Christian world, the craft of shoemaking became highly developed and important in the 4th century. Beautifully decorated shoes and boots can be seen in Byzantine and other early manuscripts and in contemporary statues, where the details of soles, uppers, and fastenings of shoes are clearly indicated. These early shoes generally covered the foot and were laced over a slit at the ankle that provided room for the foot to enter easily.

The Normans introduced into England neat ankle boots with contrasting bands around the tops. Robert, the eldest son of William the Conqueror, was nicknamed *Curta Ocrea*, meaning "short boot," but it is not known if this was because he originated the style or because he continued to wear such boots long after they had gone out of fashion. The most usual footwear in the 11th and 12th centuries was the closed shoe of soft leather or cloth, with a pointed toe that gradually lengthened as the elongated Gothic style became predominant in northern Europe.

14th and 15th Century Shoes. Boots, sometimes pulled over the knees, were first worn in the 14th century as a protection for the legs when riding horseback and continued in fashion through several centuries. The boots had no fastenings, and their loose tops were either turned over into cuffs or allowed to fall in creases, according to the stiffness of the material used.

From the end of the 14th century and all through the 15th, as headdresses and hats rose into points on the head, the toes of shoes also became more and more elongated to balance the design. The shoes of princes had toes that extended 24 inches (60 cm) beyond the foot, stuffed with fiber or straw to keep them in shape. These shoes were called *poulaines* or *crakows*, suggesting that the fashion may have originated in Poland. As these long points became inconvenient, they were sometimes tied up to the knees with chains. But the frequency of accidents caused by this exaggerated fashion and the mincing walk assumed by his nobles caused Edward IV, a man not given to fripperies, to enforce a sumptuary law restricting the length of the toe to 2 inches (5 cm).

During the 14th and the 15th centuries shoes were often made of such delicate materials that cloglike overshoes, called *pattens*, were introduced for outdoor wear. They were made of iron, wood, or even cork (for kings), and their toes and heels were thickened or fitted with pegs to lift the sole above wetness and dirt. The pattens, held on the foot by straps over the instep, could be easily slipped off by the wearer before he entered the house. Similar to pattens were *chopines*, high platforms, to which shoes or mules were permanently attached. In the 16th century, chopines became very high, like stilts. Hamlet, addressing one of the Players, says: "Your ladyship is nearer to heaven than when I saw you last, by the altitude of a chopine."

16th Century Shoes. A complete reversal of styles, from the pointed Gothic to the blunted German fashion, took place in the early 16th century. The toes of shoes were squared to match the wide costumes familiar to us from portraits by Holbein. Made of soft, embossed Italian leather, velvet, or cloth, the square toes were rolled over and back and often slashed to allow contrasting material to puff through the slits. In contrast to previous fashions, the uppers were very low cut and barely covered the toes and the backs of the heels, leaving the instep bare and giving the impression of a people stricken with the painful complaint of hammertoe. Again the law stepped in, this time restricting the width of shoes instead of their length.

By 1550 shoes had acquired a more natural shape, with toes more pointed, and had uppers that were higher over the instep, with the front often rising to a point. The sides, cut low to ease the foot into the shoes, evolved a little later into straps that were fastened with a buckle or a ribbon bow over the high front.

Heels had first been put on shoes by the 1590's. Perhaps they were introduced by Queen Elizabeth I of England, who wished to increase her small stature. Heels immediately became high fashion, and the bows or rosettes that decorated the straps or toes became more and more pronounced. It has been said that the people of medieval and Elizabethan England were better shod than those of other nations because the enormous amount of meat they consumed made leather more readily available and cheaper than in other countries of Europe.

17th Century Shoes. The mid-17th century saw the gradual squaring of the toe again, this time without a puff. Shoes had firm leather soles and heels, and the uppers extended over the instep, with a tongue or flap over which the side pieces fastened with a square buckle. These buckles grew larger, the tongues longer, and the heels higher as the century advanced. Enormous bows gradually replaced the buckles. In 1660, Louis XIV of France was presented with a pair of shoes with bows 16 inches (40 cm) across and with high red heels. Such shoes delighted the King and his court so much that the fashionable male world continued to totter on high heels and trip over wide bows for another 10 years. The high heels worn by Louis to enhance his rather meager height were curved, making them less clumsy looking than a straight heel. (A high curved heel is still called a Louis heel.)

The 17th century was also the era of the boot. Continental wars in the early part of the century made the boot the most practical footwear for men. In the swashbuckling period of *The Three Musketeers,* boot tops were widened, and loose stockings were festooned above them —a detail eventually so exaggerated that it produced the astonishing effect of manly figures in petticoat breeches with lace frills around their knees falling into wide boot tops.

18th Century Shoes. The end of the 17th century and the early 18th century (another period of war) saw the rise to popularity of the heaviest boot yet made. The *jackboot* (so called because a metal frame, or jack, held the leather tops from slipping down or creasing) had bucket tops and spurs carried on wide flaps over the instep. These boots were sometimes called *Ramillies* boots, after the Battle of Ramillies in the War of the Spanish Succession. Wide flaps covered the knees in some styles, but the leather behind the knee was cut away so that the knee could bend. Because long boots were expensive, the common soldier was given a cheaper imitation in the form of long gaiters, made of canvas coated with pipe clay, which covered the tops of his ankle boots and buttoned up the sides to well above the knees.

Shoemaking in the 18th century reached a peak of daintiness for formal wear with the use of brocades or soft kid, either embroidered or sewn with spangles. Shoes had pointed toes and high curved heels and were often ornamented with a diamond buckle over the tongue. Matching pattens were usually made with a thicker sole to prevent the delicate shoe fabric from becoming soiled. Women's shoes became more important as skirts were shortened in the 1780's. However, some Englishmen, countrymen at heart, would wear their riding boots on every occasion unless forcibly refused admittance.

19th and 20th Century Shoes. The Napoleonic Wars again made boots essential for men. On the British side, the famous *Wellington boot,* named after the general, was merely a long-fronted riding boot that became the fashionable wear for all officers. The French, Austrians, Poles, and Germans wore a shorter boot, with a scalloped front from which hung a tassel; it was worn with tight, braid-decorated breeches patterned after the romantic uniform of the Hessian hussars.

As breeches lengthened into trousers during the early 19th century, flat *pumps* often replaced boots for men, although sometimes the trousers were drawn down over the boot and strapped under the foot in a fashion that lasted for many years. In the epoch of prudery that occurred in the 19th century, women's feet suffered an eclipse under long skirts. Their shoes during this period remained unchanged in shape, resembling blunt-toed dancing shoes, until the 1860's when, for a short period of emancipation, little ankle boots were allowed to show under shortened crinolines.

It is usually assumed that the practice of making right and left feet in footwear began in the 19th century. However, this comfortable fashion was not unknown in classical and medieval times, but it is curious that it did not become a general practice sooner.

Mass production of shoes began in the mid-19th century and, with the clothing industry in general, was responsible for one of the worst forms of sweatshop labor. But mass production also enabled the poor to be better shod—many having been shoeless previously.

Ankle boots, laced up the front or with elastic gussets in the sides, continued to be worn by men through the late 19th century and until World War I. Men's clothes then became more youthful in appearance, partly as a result of the smart uniforms worn during the war. From that time on, *oxfords,* laced up the instep over a tongue and with or without toe caps, have been a universal fashion, in calf for day wear and in patent leather for the evening.

Women's shoes in the late 19th and early 20th centuries continued to have heels, usually of the low, curved Louis shape. They became more fancy as skirts were slightly shortened or held up to show the feet. High laced or buttoned boots were worn in winter and outdoors. Such boots with light kid uppers and patent leather vamps were fashionable with the slit hobble skirt about 1912. The much shorter skirts of the 1930's emphasized stockings and shoes, which became higher-heeled and single-strapped. Finally they developed into the court shoe, or opera pump, which has become a classic. Wedge soles—copied from the Chinese shoe in which the sole and heel are all one piece enabling the heel to be high but more stable—were introduced during World War II. The *platform shoe,* with a very thick sole and high, thick heel, was introduced in 1947.

The most disastrous fashion for both sexes was the narrow, pointed shoe that became the rage in the 1950's. When allied, in women's shoes, to the high "pin," or "spike" heel of wood around a metal rod, they spelled ruin for ankles, toes, and floors. But, with the usual persistence of a fashion that is much criticized on rational grounds, the style lasted several years before being replaced by its opposite—square toes and thick, medium-high heels. In men's shoes, casual attitudes toward grooming made suede shoes with crepe-rubber soles popular, in the mistaken theory that suede needs less care than shiny leather. Slip-on shoes began to replace the classic oxford. Both men and women wore sandals and Swedish clogs with contour-fitted soles.

During the 20th century different kinds of shoes have been carefully designed to serve specific needs. There were special shoes for sports —track, golf, cricket, football, tennis, rock-climbing, mountaineering—and for occupations—mining, diving, and firefighting. Many shoes, fashionable or utilitarian, were made of synthetic materials.

Customs and Folklore. Shoes have figured prominently in Eastern religious observances. Orthodox Jews, Muslims, and Hindus all remove their shoes before entering the holy places of their faith. The custom probably originated as a gesture of humility when shoes were so rare as to be considered a mark of dignity and the shoeless foot a sign of servitude.

Throwing a shoe at the bridal pair and tying shoes to the bridal car at weddings are relics of an ancient custom. The bride's parents once gave her shoes to the bridegroom as a sign that she had left their home forever and that he assumed dominion over her after the wedding.

Shoemakers have their own tutelary saint in Saint Crispin (martyred in 287), and through him their trade is called the "Gentle Craft." Crispin was a Christian missionary who practiced the trade of shoemaking by night and preached the Gospel by day. An angel, it is said, miraculously provided leather so that his shoes could be bought cheaply by the poor.

The psychological importance of shoes is apparent from their central place in many fairy tales and in folklore. Cinderella, the downtrodden, is singled out for fame and fortune through a tiny glass slipper into which only her foot would fit. In the 17th century, when the fashion for boots was at its peak, magic boots figure prominently in such tales as *Puss in Boots* and *Jack the Giant-Killer*. In *The Twelve Dancing Princesses*, the princesses' shoes are mysteriously worn out every morning—a symbol of rebellion against a tyrannical father. An old tale retold by the brothers Grimm, the story expresses the girls' wish to transfer their duty to the 12 handsome suitors who danced with them secretly through the night. Shoes are a good-luck symbol in the rather pious *History of Little Goody Two-Shoes*, possibly by Oliver Goldsmith. And *The Red Shoes* by Hans Christian Anderson, is a cautionary tale of shoes imbued with personality that finally dance out of control, carrying the wearer to her death.

MARGARET STAVRIDI
Author of "The History of Costume"

Further Reading: Boucher, François, *20,000 Years of Fashion* (Abrams 1966); Stavridi, Margaret, *The History of Costume,* 4 vols. (Plays 1970); Wilson, Eunice, *History of Shoe Fashions* (Pitman 1969).

ARTHUR W. AMBLER, FROM NATIONAL AUDUBON SOCIETY

The shoebill, a relative of the storks and herons.

SHOEBILL, a large grotesque storklike bird, whose very large swollen bill is shaped like an inverted wooden shoe and is equipped with a ridge that ends in a nail-like hook. The shoebill, *Balaeniceps rex,* also known as the whale-headed stork and as the bogbird, is the only member of the family Balaenicipitidae. Comparatively rare now, it is found along marshes of the White Nile south of the Sudan region. It stands about 40 inches (1 meter) tall on crane-like legs and is dull gray with a greenish sheen to its powdery feathers. Generally found in pairs or small groups, shoebills stand in shallow water and feed on fishes, frogs, and small crocodiles and turtles, sometimes using their unusual bills to dig food material from bottom mud.

SHOEMAKER, Willie (1931–   ), American jockey, who won more Thoroughbred races than any other rider. In 1970 he set a career record of 6,033 wins, breaking Johnny Longden's mark, and in 1981 he rode to his 8,000th victory. In five separate seasons he led all jockeys in wins, and his 485 firsts in 1953 set a season record. In reaching the 8,000 mark, he earned nearly $82 million for the owners of his mounts.

Shoemaker won the Kentucky Derby three times—on Swaps (1955), Tomy Lee (1959), and Lucky Debonair (1965)—missing another in 1957, when, riding Gallant Man, he misjudged the finish line and stood up too soon.

William Lee Shoemaker, nicknamed "the Shoe," was born in Fabens, Texas, on Aug. 19, 1931. He began to ride at the age of seven and was working with race horses at 14. He won his first race in 1949. Small even for a jockey, he seldom weighed more than 100 pounds (45 kg). Falls in 1968 and 1969 put him out of action, but he recovered to break Longden's record.

Shoemaker was elected to the National Museum of Racing Hall of Fame in 1958 and the Jockeys' Hall of Fame in 1959.

SHOGUN, shō'gən, is a Japanese title meaning "generalissimo." The shogun was originally a purely military official, who was commander in chief of the Army. The office became hereditary, and the shogun acquired nearly all the real powers of government. His military administration, or shogunate, was known as the *bakufu,* or "tent government," in contrast to the civil government at the imperial capital.

The shoguns were military dictators of Japan for most of the period from about 1192, the year that Minamoto Yoritomo received the title, until 1868, when Tokugawa Yoshinobu (Keiki), surrendered his governing power to the forces of the Emperor. See also JAPAN—*History.*

SHOLAPUR, shō'lä-pōōr, is a city in western India, in Maharashtra state about 220 miles (350 km) southeast of Bombay. The city is an industrial center, with cotton cloth as its chief manufacture. It is also the main marketing and distributing point for the agricultural products of Sholapur district, which grows jowar and rice as its chief food crops and cotton and peanuts as its principal industrial crops. Population: (1971) 398,122.

SHOLES, shōlz, **Christopher Latham** (1819–1890), American inventor, who was coinventor of a typewriter patented in 1868, an improved version of which became the first typewriter used by the public and by business. See also TYPEWRITER.

SHOLOKHOV, shō'lə-кнôf, **Mikhail Aleksandrovich** (1905–   ), Soviet author, who was awarded the Nobel Prize in 1965. He was the first Russian writer to receive the Nobel accolade in literature with Kremlin approval.

Sholokhov is best remembered for his monumental novel of Cossack life, *The Quiet Don,* written between 1926 and 1940. The background of this four-volume novel is the Russian Revolution, and its subject is the wavering loyalty of its lonely Cossack hero. The characters are vividly realized, and the violent historical panorama is excitingly portrayed. The book was widely popular in the West as well as in the Soviet Union. An English translation of the novel was published in two volumes: *And Quiet Flows the Don* (1934) and *The Don Flows Home to the Sea* (1940).

Sholokhov was born in Veshenskaya, Rostov oblast, on May 24 (May 11, Old Style), 1905, into a family of illiterate Cossack peasants. After working as a mason, handyman, soldier, and journalist, he turned to literature, confining his writing almost completely to descriptions of Cossacks and Cossack life. His first books were two volumes of stark and tragic short stories—*Tales of the Don* (1925) and *The Azure Steppe* (1926). While working on the *Don* tetralogy, Sholokhov also published *Virgin Soil Upturned* (1932), a propagandistic novel about farm collectivization that gained popularity in the Soviet Union. It appeared in English translation in 1935. A second part was published and translated in 1960.

Regarded in the Soviet Union as one of his country's greatest writers, Sholokhov was given many honors by his government. Chief among these were the Stalin Prize, the Order of the Fatherland, and the Lenin Prize.

Further Reading: Stewart, David Hugh, *Mikhail Sholokhov: A Critical Introduction* (Univ. of Mich. Press 1967).

SHOLOM ALEICHEM. See ALEICHEM, SHOLOM.

SHOOTING STAR. See METEOR.

SHORE, Jane (1445?–1527), mistress of Edward IV. She was born in London. She had remarkable beauty and charm, and it was said by Sir Thomas More that her influence with Edward was never exercised but for the benefit of others. Richard III, partly to revive among the citizens the memory of the licentiousness of his brother, whom he accused of being "the chief abettor of that witch Shore," determined to expose her to public ignominy by accusing her of witchcraft. He was unable to effect his purpose but directed her to be tried for adultery by the bishop of London's court, which condemned her to do public penance in a white shift at Saint Paul's. At length she was reduced to poverty, and she appears to have died in 1526 or 1527.

Her story appears in literature in Shakespeare's *Richard III*; in a tragedy, *Jane Shore* (1713), by Nicholas Rowe; and in many old English ballads.

SHORELINE, the dividing line between land and the water in rivers, lakes, or oceans. Shorelines are continually being modified by wave work, especially along the large bodies of water. Waves strike blows averaging several hundred pounds per square foot and, armed with sand and gravel, are powerful agents of erosion. They undermine cliffs and carve out sea caves. In many places, especially along the chalk cliffs of England and France where the rocks are soft, coasts are worn back at an average rate of several feet a year. For example, the island of Helgoland in the North Sea had a circumference of 120 miles (190 km) in 800 A. D., but today has a circumference of only 3 miles (5 km). It would probably be worn completely away were it not for artificial protection.

Beach Formations. The material thus worn away builds beaches. Where the debris is coarse, boulder or shingle beaches result. Where the debris is finer, sand beaches are formed. Much sand is drifted parallel to the coastline by shore, or littoral, currents, and where it drifts past some bend in the coast, the beach is prolonged into a spit extending past the bend out into deep waters. Because of the constant action of waves and tides the ends of spits are often curved into hooks, as at Sandy Hook on the New Jersey coast of the United States. If a spit or hook grows out so that it connects an island to the mainland, a tied island results. The sand link between the coast and the island is known as a tombolo.

On low, flat, gently sloping coasts, the waves break some distance from shore. Sand is heaped up at this point by the action of waves and undertow, and an offshore, or barrier, beach is formed. Between the beach and the mainland a lagoon or a tidal marsh is formed. This water tends to fill slowly with decaying vegetation and wash from the land, so that peat beds are often formed. Off the mouths of large rivers, deltas are built, and extensive mud flats, or tidal flats, occur. See also TIDAL MARSH.

Emergent and Drowned Coasts. Shorelines are profoundly modified by changes of water level, known as eustatic changes if they are worldwide changes in ocean level. In the latter case, because the ocean bottoms along continental

EVOLUTION OF AN EMBAYED SHORELINE

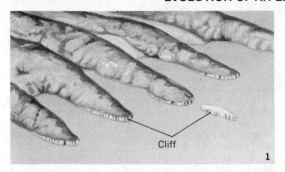

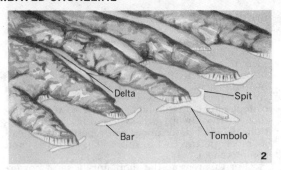

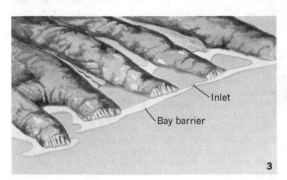

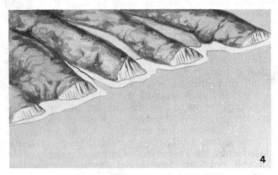

The embayed shoreline was originally produced either by subsidence of the coast or by the raising of sea level. Thereafter the surf began to cut away the headlands and islands, forming cliffs (1). Rivers in the bays formed deltas, while continuing sea erosion produced beaches, bars, spits, and tombolos in a variety of shapes (2).

As erosion progressed, the shoreline became much simpler through the cutting back of the headlands, while rivers continued to fill in bays with deposits of sediment (3). Eventually the headlands and bays were altogether eliminated (4). Any irregular shoreline tends to be reduced to a simple, regular form by the energy of wave action.

margins are often smooth, the uplift forms long straight coasts known as coasts of emergence. Along such coasts, abandoned beaches and wave-cut cliffs may be seen well above water level, testifying to the recent uplift. Such beaches are numerous on the coast of California. On a smaller scale, when lakes are drained or dry up, such abandoned beaches are also common. Such beach lines are seen clearly around the old shoreline of Great Salt Lake in the United States.

On the other hand, when a coast sinks, or is drowned or submerged, as it is usually called, the sea enters the river valleys, forming long, narrow and often branching bays, like Chesapeake Bay. The tops of former hills may become off-shore islands, as has happened at many points along the coast of Maine. In the diagram, various stages are shown of the evolution of a typical drowned coast. As the diagram suggests, in their earlier stages such drowned shores afford the best harbors. The famous Inside Passage to Alaska is the result of deep drowning of a very mountainous coast.

See also BEACH; DELTA; EROSION; GEOLOGY— *Geological Processes.*

Further Reading: Bascom, Willard, *Waves and Beaches* (Anchor Bks. 1964); King, Cuchlaine A. M., *Beaches and Coasts* (St. Martins 1960).

SHOREVIEW, a village in eastern Minnesota, in Ramsey county, is a northern suburb of St. Paul. It is built along the shores of a number of lakes, whose beaches attract many visitors. The village has some light industry, notably electronics and printing. Shoreview was incorporated in 1957. It is governed by a mayor and council. Population: 17,300.

SHOREWOOD, a village in southeastern Wisconsin, in Milwaukee county, is on the western shore of Lake Michigan, immediately north of the city of Milwaukee, of which it is a residential suburb. There is no industry.

The community, which is situated in the eastern part of the county, was incorporated in 1900 as East Milwaukee. In 1917, it was reincorporated as the village of Shorewood. It is governed by a village manager and a village board. Population: 14,327.

SHORT BALLOT. See BALLOT—*Short Ballot.*

SHORT CIRCUIT, an electrical path of very low impedance, usually provided by a fault that forms a circuit with less length and impedance than that of the normal circuit. The fault may arise from an electrical insulation failure, from mechanical damage, or from damage caused by rain or lightning. It usually results in a flow of excess current, which can damage wiring, appliances, or other electrical equipment. Protection against damage from short circuits commonly is provided by circuit breakers or fuses.

See also CIRCUIT BREAKERS; ELECTRIC WIRING —*Fuses* and *Circuit Breakers;* FUSE.

SHORT-EARED OWL. See OWLS.

SHORT-HORNED GRASSHOPPER, any of a large family, Acrididae, of long slender insects with powerful hind legs that are used for jumping. Members of the family are commonly known as grasshoppers, and those species that have a distinct migratory phase, as locusts. See GRASSHOPPER.

SHORT STORY, a literary form, the nature of which is implicit in the words comprising its name. As a story, it narrates a series of events or a single incident involving individuals in mental or physical activity. Thus, like all fiction, it portrays, and its success depends on the immediacy achieved between the reader and the subject portrayed. As a short story, however, it cannot effect this immediacy by the means common to the novel, such as leisurely characterization, detailed description, and repetition. Instead it must portray with mirrorlike swiftness and completeness.

For this reason, the short story is most powerful through graphic narration. This is not to say that its subject matter can be only simple and realistic. Of all literary forms, the short story is the least restricted in subject matter, for its length permits treatment of subjects that could not alone sustain interest in a longer form.

BEGINNINGS AND FIRST MASTERS

From earliest times the short story has served as allegory, fable, and moral example. It has drawn themes from matter supernatural and natural, romantic and realistic, grotesque and mundane. It has portrayed the abnormal as well as the representative personality, mental processes as well as physical action, and casual happening as well as arresting incident. All these have a place in the short story, provided they are translated into the concrete. Growing consciousness of this necessity has forged the techniques that have made possible significant short-story writing.

Evolution of Techniques. Something of these techniques was known to the earliest storytellers. Traces of their application can be seen, for example, in the ballad, which is a short story told in song. In its objectivity, impressionistic description, directness of portrayal, and totality of effect, the ballad anticipates the principles expounded and applied by the greatest modern short-story writers.

Significant, too, is the ballad's origin in verse form, which dictated its storytelling technique. Many tediously long stories have been told in verse. Nevertheless, verse is essentially disciplinary and is more conducive to artful brevity and compression than prose. It is more than coincidence that Edgar Allan Poe formulated his philosophy of the short story after he had studied balladry and his own method of poetic composition. It is also significant that Geoffrey Chaucer chose to cast his stories almost exclusively in poetic form and that Edmund Spenser, in an age that smothered the short story by its heavy prose rhetoric, found in verse the best medium for his allegorical stories. Similarly, such poets as Robert Burns, Samuel Taylor Coleridge, and John Keats produced stories in verse that might have been dictated by Poe's principles. And Robert Browning, in his dramatic monologues, achieved the character story ahead of the prose writers.

It has been essential to the development of the short story that, periodically, there should occur a turning back to folk literature and the rediscovery of effective techniques once applied instinctively, for writers often forget that a single clear picture is worth a multitude of words. The short story especially, because of its spatial limitation, must be a picture. Since it is a picture composed not of lines and color but of words, it can appeal only indirectly to the senses.

But what at first seems to be a deficiency is actually a source of strength, for the short story can appeal equally, if indirectly, to all the senses. Hence, in the short story, words achieve their maximum power when they create the illusion of sense impression. It is therefore not surprising that the short story is extinguished in an age that develops a rhetorical style impeding the direct presentation of scene. Nor is it surprising that the short story most naturally flourishes and develops in an age that expresses itself with simplicity and directness.

For this reason, the history of the short story reveals not so much a steadily ascending line of continuity as a series of peaks, which, until the 19th century, were widely separated in time. Each in a different way, Giovanni Boccaccio and Chaucer realized the rich possibilities of the form, but it was destined shortly to drop into obscurity. Over four centuries later, Poe brought it into a state of self-consciousness by propounding a technique that was applicable far beyond his own stories.

Next to further the development of the short story was the advent of modern realism. As in all stages of the history of the short story, the importance of realism lies not in subject matter, but in the writer's attitude toward his material. The realist desires to portray what he sees exactly as he sees it. Consequently, he will seek all means of graphic and direct portrayal. He will also keep himself out of his picture, and, as a result of this objectivity, his story will contain its own verisimilitude, which is more pertinent to its success than the realism of the subject matter. Combining realism of attitude with deliberate technique, Guy de Maupassant wrote stories that endure as perfect models of their type.

The short story advanced in proportion to the writer's endeavor to transcend the limitations of his form. Even after the accomplishments of Poe and Maupassant, spatial limitation remained provocative. Thus, the short-story writer next sought means to *suggest* more than his space allowed him actually to say. This stage is best represented by Anton Chekhov, whose potent influence still motivates experimentation.

The First Masters. The *Decameron* of Boccaccio and the *Canterbury Tales* of Chaucer, both written in the 14th century, show how individual creativeness could breathe life into the conventionalized forms that were already the heritage of the short story. These writers drew freely from the great spontaneous stream of storytelling that started with human history and flowed from the Orient through the Continent and on into England.

The frameworks of these two collections are in themselves evidence of the universal popularity of the short story as a prime and respected means of entertainment. The *Decameron* stories are told by a group of young ladies and young men to while away the time in the idyllic retreat that shelters them from the grim plague raging in Florence in 1348. Chaucer's pilgrims tell their stories to shorten their journey from London to Canterbury, where they will pay homage at the shrine of Saint Thomas à Becket. In all the stories thus told there is a spirit suggesting an effortless love of storytelling—a spirit soon to be lost as the story grew more literary and widened the gap between teller and listener.

Boccaccio drew chiefly upon the Milesian tale of the type loosely strung together in the *Golden*

Ass, the 2d century A. D. novel of Lucius Apuleius. But source, or even form, is of minor importance when set next to the vitality that Boccaccio brought to the short story. It was his zest for life, rather than an intellectual regard for technique, that forged his stories. The whole of the *Decameron* pulsates with emotion. Sometimes the motivating force is intense love or hate, but more often it is quite simply man's will to pleasure—the desire to attain satiation and then move on to new objects. His plots show clearly how satisfaction is achieved or denied, and Boccaccio had little need to probe beneath the surface picture or to individualize characters, for the basic drives of man are common to all. This first great human comedy suggests how the short story can survive, in spite of awkwardness of form, by virtue of the consistency and ardor of its creator's approach to life and his ability to portray this ardor directly.

Unlike Boccaccio, Chaucer was a virtuoso of short-story form. The variety of form in the *Canterbury Tales* makes it a great roundup of the medieval short story. For example, a chivalric romance is told by the Knight, a lai (tale of Celtic origin) is the Wife of Bath's contribution, and a saint's legend is piously related by the Prioress. Fabliaux (realistic satires, especially pointed at the clergy and women) are told by the Miller, the Reeve, the Shipman, the Friar, and the Merchant. The Nun's Priest's Tale is a fable. The exempla (short stories illustrating a general statement, usually of a didactic nature) told by the Monk and the Pardoner indicate variety within the same form, for the Monk relates a mere list of tragedies, whereas the Pardoner's tale of greed is at once so concrete and suggestive that its existence alone would prove Chaucer a master of the short-story form.

Boccaccio's essential realism made him objective, but Chaucer's objectivity is a conscious story technique. In the General Prologue, Chaucer makes a significant plea for realism, saying that the reader must allow him to tell the stories in the exact words of the pilgrims. The effect of this is the achievement of the necessary tone of each type—the ribaldry of the fabliau, the simple piety of the saint's legend, the delicacy of the lai—and, consequently, the removal of all traces of Chaucer the creator.

Hiatus, 15th–18th Centuries. The subsequent history of the short story comprises the efforts of writers to recover the height reached by Boccaccio and Chaucer. The short story lost favor in the full bloom of the Renaissance. It could neither compete with the long prose romances and the drama nor survive under the stylistic devices that puff up such writing as John Lyly's *Euphues* (1578). The writer's attention became fixed upon the techniques of expression, not those of portrayal, so that neither Chaucer's graphic clarity nor Boccaccio's direct realism was possible.

The advancement of science stimulated man's quest for certainty in communication, which was accompanied by a deliberate change to a simpler prose style. New directness and simplicity are seen first in such nonfiction writings as René Descartes' *Discourse on Method* (1637) and John Locke's *Essay Concerning Human Understanding* (1690). These tendencies regenerated the novel, but the short-story form had been buried too long to be quickly resurrected.

True, there were glimmerings of the short story in the periodicals, and these essay-stories were to help lead American writers to an awareness of short-story form. The English journalist-novelist Daniel Defoe also struck off at least one piece—*A True Relation of the Apparition of one Mrs. Veal . . .* (1705)—which, with its combination of realistic technique and ghostly theme, retains the power to interest. Chiefly, however, writers had forgotten what to do with the short story. Novelists, aware of short-story material, frequently incorporated it into their novels. A notable example is the extraneous Man of the Hill story in Henry Fielding's *Tom Jones* (1749).

EMERGENCE AS AN INDEPENDENT FORM

What was needed was the directive force of writers and critics willing to declare the short story an independent literary form. In this, America was to speak first.

Craftsmanship in America. Edgar Allan Poe remarked in 1842 that the only noteworthy short-story writers produced by America were Washington Irving and Nathaniel Hawthorne. Of course, Poe should have included his own name. Interestingly, this triumvirate was significantly influenced by German and English romanticism.

Irving and Hawthorne. It was the peculiar ability of Irving to borrow German legend and manipulate it so that it seemed indigenous to America. Except to the scholar, Rip Van Winkle does not betray his German origin. In fact, *Rip Van Winkle* and other tales with an American setting in *The Sketch Book* (1819–1820) and *Tales of a Traveller* (1824) created a body of American legend acceptable to even the most fastidious, for Irving wrote in the style of the 18th century English essayists.

Not unnaturally, then, his pieces sometimes contain more of the essay than of the story, and the somewhat apologetic title, *The Sketch Book,* suggests that Irving was not quite certain that the short story could stand on its own strength as a finished literary product. Even so, his humorous objectivity and occasional directness of portrayal made his tales something more than apologues. This new something was recognized by his first readers, and the great vogue of *The Sketch Book* led indirectly to the establishment of the many annuals, lady's books, and gift books that were soon to provide the first respectable home for the single short story.

With Hawthorne the short story gained in conciseness, chiefly because he saw it as a means to question and probe as well as to portray aimless scene and character. Hence his plots tightened into allegory, by which he could represent ideas in terms of concrete symbols. He was quite frank about his didactic concern, often indicating it in titles such as *The May-pole of Merry Mount, A Parable* and *Egotism, or the Bosom Serpent.* Too often the abstract idea is apparent in the concrete symbol, so that the stories seem remote.

One of Hawthorne's favorite themes concerns the man who experiments with life rather than participates in it, as in his stories *Wakefield* and *Dr. Heidegger's Experiment.* Hawthorne himself seems to be the scientist at work in the laboratory, preoccupied less with life than with the ideas abstracted from life. Though he achieves objectivity, it is the objectivity of the lecturer who shows slides to illustrate what he has to say. Only rarely can his presence be forgotten, for there is the sound of his voice or the shadow of his pointer. If illusion has been achieved, it is quickly shattered when the lights come up and he concludes without benefit of slides.

Poe as Theorist. Hawthorne's collection of stories *Twice-Told Tales* (1837; enl. ed., 1842) called forth the definitive review—in *Graham's Magazine* in 1842—in which Poe at last established the short story as an independent form. Because of its brevity and consequent emotional intensity and unity, Poe had already assigned the short lyric first place in poetry, and in his own stories he had evolved a distinctive technique aiming at the same qualities. Thus by 1842 he was ready to expound certain fundamental principles of short-story technique.

According to Poe, the short story (1) must be of such length as to be read in one sitting, (2) must create a single effect, (3) must not contain one word that in meaning or tone fails to point to that preconceived effect, and (4) must convey the impression of finality, so that the reader desires neither an opening other than that provided nor a continuation beyond the final sentence. These principles subordinate plot or theme to effect, thus setting up for the first time a criterion other than pure narration. Words are to be used for their emotive rather than intellectual power. Brevity is to be artful compression by the elimination of what detracts from the desired effect and the abstraction of what enhances it. Significantly, these principles are applicable to any subject matter. It is presentation alone that defines the form.

Poe as Writer. Poe's influence was not only that of theory, for he applied as well as formulated his principles. He served a very deliberate apprenticeship in short-story writing by producing parodies of the terror tale that flourished in England and the Continent. Parody writing taught him much, for the exaggerated stylistic devices he thus developed—in *Shadow: A Parable,* for example—became instrumental in creating the single effects of such characteristic tales as *The Fall of the House of Usher* (1839) and *The Masque of the Red Death, A Fantasy* (1842).

Poe's technique in theory and practice makes it clear that over and above his attraction for things of mystery and imagination was his rationalism. The fact that many of his tales were written to induce mood should not obscure the equally important fact that they were produced by the most objective approach to style and theme that had yet appeared in fiction writing. Starting with the single impression to be achieved, Poe isolated from the possible means of expression only those elements most productive of the desired effect. In a purely atmosphere sketch such as *Shadow,* he secured the effect wholly by stylistic devices, but in a plot story such as *Ligeia,* he extended the same isolating process to create incidents that would most effectively point the theme (power of the human will). In fact, Poe wrote his stories in the spirit of the detective who has solved the mystery but must carefully retrace his steps and reexamine the clues to construct a logical case. It is not surprising, then, that he should have put his technique to thematic use and thus created the detective story.

When Poe eliminated the supernatural from his stories, he originated a type of story distinct from the terror tale. In such stories, the reasoning process leading up to the solution of the mystery takes precedence over the mystery itself. Sometimes the ratiocination is almost mathematical, as in *The Gold Bug* (1843). Sometimes it deduces the nature of the mystery from knowledge of the character of the culprit, as in *The Purloined Letter* (1845). At other times it deduces the identity of the criminal from the nature of the crime, as in *The Murders in the Rue Morgue* (1841). The true hero is Reason, which Poe personified in his detective Dupin.

The modern detective story descended directly from Poe. But probably its lasting vogue is due to Dupin's first successor, Sherlock Holmes, created in the late 19th century by Sir Arthur Conan Doyle. Doyle mixed Poe's method with the personality of an Edinburgh professor and created a character who has become legend to all classes of readers. As Sherlock Holmes is a fuller-bodied character than Dupin, so is his foil, Dr. Watson, who succeeded Poe's vehicular first person (the narrator).

In his stories both of reason and of imagination, Poe sacrificed many time-honored elements of fiction for the sake of his single effect. It is perhaps because of this sacrifice that Poe's stories were influential in his own country only after a long delay and then in an indirect way. If, by concentrating on the single impression, he avoided the loose construction of Irving's stories and the didactic allegory of Hawthorne's tales, he also lost concreteness of character and places. He created memorable plots but not memorable people. His stories have the coloring of moods, not of localities. There is in his writing no intrinsic element to tie it to America. In contrast, it is instructive to note that Nikolai Gogol (born the same year as Poe, in 1809) exerted inestimable influence over Russian writers because of his portrayal of Russian people in Russian scenes. No American writer can say of any of Poe's tales what Maksim Gorky said of one of Gogol's: "We all spring from Gogol's *The Overcoat.*"

Realism. Paradoxically, though, Poe exerted great influence on the short story in general. The power of that influence came from the specific nature of his technique as applied in his own stories, as well as the concise formulation of his theory of technique. Familiarity with his work arose especially in France, first through the plagiarism of hack writers (possible because of the lack of international copyright laws) and then more legitimately through the excellent translation of his tales by Charles Baudelaire. Interestingly, the next major achievement in short-story writing came from France.

Maupassant. Although Guy de Maupassant (born in 1850, the year after Poe's death) knew and was impressed by Poe in translation, he was by temperament and association more sensitive to the realism that was already giving new form to the fiction of both Russia and France. Under the exacting tutelage of Gustave Flaubert, Maupassant served a seven-year literary apprenticeship. Flaubert was a realist, but over and above his conviction that the writer should draw his material from life was his belief that the true value of art lay in form and expression. Maupassant did not ape his master's fastidious craftsmanship, but from him he gained a sense of form that outlines his stories with the same definiteness as Poe's.

Thus Maupassant's realism is neither the spontaneous overflow of sensual delight that animates Boccaccio's tales nor the experimental and formless naturalism of Émile Zola and his disciples. Rather, it is the reshaping of the materials of life to illuminate the effect desired and to subordinate whatever is irrelevant to the effect. As he wrote in the preface to his novel *Pierre and Jean* (1888), "the realists of art ought rather to call themselves the illusionists." Striving for the effect of realism, Maupassant drew upon people and incidents, whereas Poe sought to achieve emotional effects by creating moods and atmospheres. Yet the techniques are essentially similar. For example, in the title story of his collection *Mademoiselle Fifi* (1882), Maupassant isolates the sadism of Baron van Eyrick in a series of illustrative incidents, just as Poe isolates human will power by portraying its triumph over death in *Ligeia*.

Maupassant was an ironist, but his expression of attitude is so embedded in plot and symbols that it seldom appears distinct from the actual narration. Both *A Piece of String* and *The Diamond Necklace* are constructed out of a juxtaposition of events and circumstances that not only constitute plot but suggest the irony of fate. Still another kind of irony is expressed by the juxtaposition of types of people, showing especially the shallowness of the falsely self-righteous individual in contrast to the moral strength and sincerity of the conventionally shunned one. *Boule-de-suif*, about a well-known prostitute, is an acknowledged masterpiece founded on such a contrast, and *The House of Tellier* is also created out of the meeting of the conventional and the unconventional.

Essential to Maupassant's form is his objectivity. His characters are known through their appearance and action. Their motives are not analyzed, and the inner recesses of their minds are not probed. Maupassant had contempt for analytical fiction, which he declared in his preface to *Pierre and Jean* to be "composed after the manner of the philosopher writing a book on psychology." The objective writer is the true realist, for he knows that "psychology ought to be concealed in a book, as it is concealed in reality, beneath the facts of existence." Thus in his stories he naturally achieved the brevity and concrete portrayal essential to the form, while the Victorian English writers fumbled in handling the short story because they could neither reduce the luxuriant verbiage nor sharpen the leisurely style fostered by their huge novels.

American Realists. Also because of Maupassant's objectivity, plot appears to dominate his stories. The true nature of his illusory realism was soon ignored, largely because it was too personal to be imitated. However, the sheer plot technique proved easily applicable. In America, this technique was studied by Henry Cuyler Bunner, whose *Made in France* (1893) is a collection of deliberate paraphrases of Maupassant's stories given a Yankee twist, further complications of plot, and the intensified surprise ending. In this way, certain elements of Poe's technique returned to exert force upon the American short story, finally producing a writer who attained a national popularity beyond that of any other short-story writer—O. Henry (William Sydney Porter).

The American short story also had received a strong impetus from Bret Harte, who had combined certain elements of the Poe-Maupassant technique with a theme from Dickens: beneath that rough exterior there beats a heart of gold. After the notoriety gained by *The Luck of the Roaring Camp* (1868), Harte exploited both the formula and the latent sentimentalism of this theme. His superficial realism, sentimentalism, and arresting plots were a winning combination, and it is little wonder that his influence was great.

Realism came falteringly to American fiction in devious ways. First it appeared in the form of the kind of indigenous humor immortalized by Mark Twain (Samuel Langhorne Clemens), who in at least one story, *The Man That Corrupted Hadleyburg* (1900), achieved a perfect blending of tragedy and comedy without either the sentimentalism of Harte or the sensationalism of Maupassant. Also, imported realism had an iconoclastic vogue in the 1870's, when translations of Ivan Turgenev began to appear in American magazines.

Essentially, however, a serious realism came to the American short story, not as a literary creed but as the writer's conviction that he had a moral obligation to tell the truth about the particular section of the country with which he was intimately associated. Local color had been used quite naturally by such late 19th and early 20th century writers as Harriet Beecher Stowe, Sarah Orne Jewett, and George Washington Cable. It was employed with technical deliberateness by Bret Harte. It served Mary E. Wilkins Freeman in her depiction of the less romantic aspects of New England life, and in Hamlin Garland it became a means of calling attention to the farmer's harsh and bitter struggle for existence in the Middle West. Although a new kind of social didacticism thus entered the short story, concreteness of portrayal was further developed.

Early Impressionism. An inevitable product of realism in the short story was impressionism, the rendering of immediate sense impression. With his insistence upon compression and effect, Poe had provided the foundation for impressionism. But in his own stories he was intent upon evoking an emotional response and had little interest in providing the graphic detail necessary to sense impression. Under the influence of realism, however, writers turned to the problem of achieving immediacy of sense objects. Instead of presenting an object as a whole, the impressionist depicts only its most suggestive physical details. His chief device is compressed imagery that evokes in the reader a reaction to the physical properties even before it results in a complete picture of the object. Because of its swiftness of description and the immediacy of object in which it results, impressionism is admirably suited to the short-story form.

The stories of both Ambrose Bierce and Stephen Crane contain well-developed impressionism, but the bitter irony of these writers prevented them from becoming forces of influence. Chiefly they point to the future, with Bierce anticipating William Faulkner and with Crane, especially in style, foreshadowing Ernest Hemingway. Significantly, these early impressionists were newspaper men. Journalism, with its emphasis on concrete, brief, and arresting reporting, influenced the short story near the end of the 19th century, as the perfection of motion pictures was to suggest new devices for swiftness of portrayal to 20th century writers.

Merging of Diverse Tendencies. In the end it was not undiluted realism that triumphed but realism mixed with romanticism and sentimentalism. Robert Louis Stevenson had continued the romantic tradition, and even such self-styled realists as Frank Norris and Jack London are revealed as romanticists when set against their contemporary Stephen Crane. The great summation of these diverse tendencies is the stories of Rudyard Kipling, the first influential British short-story writer of the modern period. Kipling borrowed promiscuously, but the resulting blend was so perfectly proportioned that it carried the mark of powerful originality. His stories in *Plain Tales from the Hills* (1888) reveal the technical devices of Poe, the sentimentalism of Harte, the realism of Maupassant, an impressionistic method of description developed by his own experience in journalism, and, finally, the romanticized setting, in India. So potent was this combination that practically all writers were attempting stories in the manner of Kipling before the turn of the century.

Genuine realism was thus retarded, but its technical lessons were retained. The means to achieve immediacy of object were known at last to all writers and applied to all types of subject matter. Technically, the short story had advanced as far as it could go in one direction. Boundless imitation of the old would have been inevitable if writers had not become aware that a new form of storytelling had arisen in Russia.

DEVELOPMENT UNDER NEW TECHNICIANS

From the time of Gogol, Russian realism never portrayed merely the external world but included the psychological moment as a natural datum of existence. This is apparent in Ivan Turgenev's *A Sportsman's Sketches* (1847–1852) and is a distinguishing mark of the great novels of his contemporaries Leo Tolstoy and Fyodor Dostoyevsky. When in fiction a thought is allowed a significance equal to that of a physical action, there is necessarily a lessening of formal plot. Both of these novelists wrote a few stories exhibiting this kind of realism, but it was left to Anton Chekhov to perfect from it a short-story form.

Chekhov as Master. Chekhov (born in 1860, eight years after Gogol's death) was by temperament an objective yet compassionate artist. As a result of this, as well as of the tradition of realism to which he fell heir, he wrote stories that at first seemed revolutionary in their lack of technique. But, on being translated, the same stories incited so many attempts in the Chekhov manner among English and American writers that the presence of applicable technique was clearly demonstrated.

Chekhov was a versatile writer, but his unique contribution is the story in which, according to the popular description, "nothing ever happens." For an understanding of his technique, it is instructive to compare his story *The Schoolmistress* with Maupassant's *Miss Harriet*. Both stories portray the lives of frustrated and futile spinsters. Through brief description of Miss Harriet's appearance and references to her past, Maupassant makes explicit the restricted nature of her life, as well as the fact that her present religious fanaticism is merely a perversion of repressed normal tendencies. She falls in love with the young painter who has been friendly to her out of curiosity, and she commits suicide in recognition of the futility of her passion. In tribute to her wasted life, the painter kisses the lips of the corpse.

Except for a few impressionistic details, Chekhov does not describe his schoolmistress. The latter thinks briefly about her past but not about momentous forces or events. She is no fanatic, and she holds a casual conversation with the wealthy, attractive gentleman she meets when riding along a road. A chain of thought causes her to think fleetingly of her life had she been his wife, but she is not in love with him. She rides on, arguing with some peasants, and again sees the man as she draws up to a railroad crossing. That is all. Instead of plot, this is a candid-camera shot of a representative moment. By seeing it, the reader becomes aware of the essence of this particular life and, through that, of the typical nature of that life.

Chekhov's technique is thus one of abstraction and implication. He abstracts from the individual what is most representative, and by this he implies the universal. The process of abstraction guides his choice of scene and dialogue, both of which are likely to appear aimless and casual because it is seldom the significant incident or the directed conversation that is representative. By this means, Chekhov (with the help of the reader) overcomes spatial limitations while yet retaining immediacy of object through graphic portrayal of the individual. To call Chekhov a less skillful craftsman than Maupassant is simply to state preference for a certain kind of story.

Other New Technicians. The British writer Katherine Mansfield was the first short-story writer to make direct application of Chekhov's technique. She was even more precise in the process of abstraction, and her impressionism gives greater concreteness to the depiction of the chosen moment. Also, her implications are often helped by concrete symbolism, such as the pear tree in *Bliss* (1920). At their best, her stories are as intense in their connotations as their surface pictures, and they convey a sense of the inevitable. But because she believed that every moment was equally representative, some of her stories naturally lack this intensity. In all instances, she wrote with precision, strictly adhering to her abstract form. "I feel as fastidious as though I wrote with acid," she once explained in refusing to cut a single line from a story.

Although the stories of Joseph Conrad, John Galsworthy, Arnold Bennett, Somerset Maugham, and Stephen Vincent Benét continued to exhibit the fine craftsmanship of the older traditions, more experimental writers were attracted to the new technique. James Joyce's only volume of short stories, *Dubliners*, fell in 1914 upon an unheeding world, but it represents a stage in the evolving concept of what makes a story. Scenes connected only by the slender unity indicated by the title of the collection are substituted for formal plot.

Five years after *Dubliners*, Sherwood Anderson's story collection *Winesburg, Ohio* appeared, revealing the same lack of formal plot. With Anderson the new technique entered the American story almost in disguise. In such a story as *I'm a Fool*, there is the sound of the storyteller's voice spinning a rambling yarn. Yet there is no more yarn than in Chekhov, and the rambling is artful. The process was completed by Ernest Hemingway, who told stories in the Chekhov manner with such simplicity of style that even greater concreteness was achieved. To ensure the reader's reaction to the object presented rather than to the writer's emotion, he pared off as much as possible the intellectual nature of words.

When writers were relieved of the spatial restrictions of formal plot, they were free to give to the short story a more significant content than it had ever before received. Also, writers as varied in attitude and style as Thomas Wolfe, Erskine Caldwell, James T. Farrell, John O'Hara, William Saroyan, Katherine Anne Porter, J. D. Salinger, and John Updike could apply the technique of abstraction and implication and yet retain high degrees of individuality.

Throughout the rapid development of the short story since the time of Poe, the broad premise of Poe's technique has been retained, for the short story must always aim at singleness and totality of effect. It is not strange that the course of this development, through realism, impressionism, and abstractionism, should parallel that of painting, for the two forms exist within similar spatial boundaries. As painting had to evolve ways to escape being merely photographic reproduction, the short story confronted the necessity of preserving concreteness of portrayal while suggesting more than is portrayed. It is this conscious search for technique that makes the short story something more than mere anecdote or skeletal novel.

RUBY V. REDINGER
Baldwin-Wallace College

Bibliography

Bates, Herbert E., *The Modern Short Story: A Critical Survey* (Nelson 1941).

Beachcroft, Thomas O., *The Modest Art. A Survey of the Short Story in English* (Oxford 1968).

Burnett, Whit and Hallie S., eds., *The Modern Short Story in the Making* (Hawthorn Bks. 1964).

Chekhov, Anton, *Letters on the Short Story, the Drama, and Other Literary Topics*, ed. by Louis S. Friedland (Blom, B., 1964).

Graves, Wallace, and Leary, William G., *From Word to Story* (Harcourt 1971).

Nagel, James, comp., *Vision and Value: A Thematic Introduction to the Short Story* (Dickenson Pub. 1970).

O'Faoláin, Seán, *The Short Story* (Collins 1948).

Peden, William H., *The American Short Story* (Houghton 1964).

Vaid, Krishna B., *Technique in the Tales of Henry James* (Harvard Univ. Press 1964).

Walker, Warren S., comp., *Twentieth-Century Short Story Explication: Interpretations, 1900–1966, of Short Fiction Since 1800*, 2d ed. (Shoe String 1968).

Wright, Austin M., *The American Short Story in the Twenties* (Univ. of Chicago Press 1961).

Selected Collections of Individual Authors

Aleichem, Sholom, *Collected Stories of Sholom Aleichem*, 2 vols. (Crown 1965).

Bierce, Ambrose, *The Collected Writings of Ambrose Bierce*, ed. by Clifton Fadiman (Citadel 1946).

Chekhov, Anton, *Selected Short Stories*, ed. by G. A. Birkett and Gleb Struve (Oxford 1951).

Doyle, Sir Arthur Conan, *The Annotated Sherlock Holmes*, 2 vols., ed. by William S. Baring-Gould (Potter, C. N., 1967).

Dreiser, Theodore, *Best Short Stories of Theodore Dreiser* (World Pub. 1956).

Gogol, Nikolai, *Taras Bulba and Other Tales*, intro. by Nikolay Andreyev (Dutton 1962).

Hemingway, Ernest, *Hemingway Reader*, ed. by Charles Poore (Scribner 1953).

James, Henry, *Stories of the Supernatural*, ed. by Leon Edel, rev. ed. (Taplinger 1970).

Kafka, Franz, *Selected Short Stories* (Modern Lib.)

Kipling, Rudyard, *Best Short Stories of Rudyard Kipling*, ed. by Randall Jarrell (Doubleday 1961).

Lardner, Ring, *Best Short Stories of Ring Lardner*, ed. by S. J. R. Sanders, rev. ed. (Scribner 1958).

London, Jack, *Best Short Stories of Jack London* (Doubleday 1953).

Mann, Thomas, *Stories of Three Decades*, tr. by H. T. Lowe-Porter (Knopf 1936).

Mansfield, Katherine, *Short Stories* (Knopf 1937).

Maugham, W. Somerset, *Complete Short Stories*, 2 vols. (Doubleday 1952).

Maupassant, Guy de, *Best Short Stories* (Garden City Pub. Co. 1945).

Maurois, André, *The Collected Stories of André Maurois*, tr. by Adrienne Foulke (Simon & Schuster 1967).

O'Connor, Flannery, *The Complete Stories of Flannery O'Connor* (Farrar, Straus 1971).

O'Connor, Frank, *Stories of Frank O'Connor* (Knopf 1952).

O'Hara, John, *Selected Short Stories* (Modern Lib.).

Parker, Dorothy, *The Collected Stories of Dorothy Parker* (Modern Lib.).

Poe, Edgar Allan, *The Complete Tales and Poems of Edgar Allan Poe* (Modern Lib.).

Porter, Katherine Anne, *The Collected Stories of Katherine Anne Porter* (Harcourt 1965).

Runyon, Damon, *Famous Stories* (Modern Lib.).

Salinger, J. D., *Nine Stories* (Little 1953).

Sillitoe, Alan, *The Loneliness of the Long-Distance Runner* (Knopf 1960).

Turgenev, Ivan, *Sportsman's Notebook*, tr. by Charles and Natasha Hepburn (Viking 1957).

Updike, John, *Pigeon Feathers and Other Stories* (Knopf 1962).

Welty, Eudora, *Selected Stories* (Modern Lib.).

Wharton, Edith, *Collected Short Stories*, 2 vols., ed. by R. W. B. Lewis (Scribner 1968).

Woolf, Virginia, *The Haunted House and Other Short Stories* (Harcourt 1944).

Miscellaneous Collections

Abrahams, William M., ed., *Fifty Years of the American Short Story: From the O. Henry Awards, 1919–1970*, 2 vols. (Doubleday 1970).

Abrahams, William M., ed., *Prize Stories: The O. Henry Awards* (Doubleday, annually).

Aldrich, Earl M., Jr., ed., *The Modern Short Story in Peru* (Univ. of Wis. Press 1966).

Allen, Dick, *Science Fiction: The Future* (Harcourt 1971).

Bergin, Thomas G., *Modern Italian Short Stories*, rev. ed. (Heath 1959).

Blacker, Irwin R., ed., *The Old West in Fiction* (Obolensky 1962).

Charles, Gerda, ed., *Modern Jewish Stories* (Prentice-Hall 1965).

Clarke, John H., ed., *American Negro Short Stories* (Hill & Wang 1967).

Colford, William E., ed. and tr., *Classic Tales from Modern Spain* (Barrons Educ. Ser. 1964).

Colquhoun, Archibald, and Rogers, Neville, eds., *Italian Regional Tales of the Nineteenth Century* (Oxford 1961).

Davis, Robert G., ed., *Ten Modern Masters: An Anthology of the Short Story*, 2d ed. (Harcourt 1959).

Decker, Clarence R., and Angoff, Charles, eds., *Modern Short Stories from Many Lands* (Manyland Bks. 1963).

Eggeling, Hans F., ed., *Modern German Short Stories* (Oxford 1929; 2d series 1933; 3d series 1954).

Ewers, John K., ed., *Modern Australian Short Stories* (Ginn 1966).

Flores, Angel, ed., *Nineteenth Century French Tales* (Doubleday 1960).

Foley, Martha, ed., *The Best American Short Stories* (Houghton; annually, 1942–1957).

Foley, Martha, and Burnett, David, eds., *The Best American Short Stories* (Houghton; annually, from 1958).

Green, Frederick C., ed., *French Short Stories of the 19th and 20th Centuries*, rev. ed. (Dutton 1961).

Grossman, William, ed. and tr., *Modern Brazilian Short Stories* (Univ. of Calif. Press 1967).

Guerney, Bernard G., comp. and tr., *New Russian Stories* (New Directions 1953).

Hughes, Langston, ed., *Best Short Stories of Negro Writers: An Anthology from 1899 to the Present* (Little 1967).

Isherwood, Christopher, ed., *Great English Short Stories* (Dell 1957).

Jenner, William J. F., ed., *Modern Chinese Stories*, tr. by the editor and Gladys Yang (Oxford 1970).

Jones, Gwyn, ed., *Welsh Short Stories* (Oxford 1956).

Knight, Damon, ed., *One Hundred Years of Science Fiction* (Simon & Schuster 1968).

Larson, Charles R., ed., *African Short Stories: A Collection of Contemporary African Writings* (Collier Bks. 1970).

McEvoy, Bernard L., ed., *Stories from Across Canada* (Lippincott 1967).

Modern Library, various collections, including *An Anthology of Famous American Stories; An Anthology of Famous British Stories; Best Russian Short Stories; Best Spanish Short Stories; Famous Science Fiction Stories; Great German Short Novels and Stories; Great Modern Short Stories; Great Tales of the American West; Stories of Modern Italy*.

Morris, Ivan I., ed., *Modern Japanese Stories: An Anthology* (Tuttle 1961).

Bibliography continued on following page

The New Yorker, three collections (Simon & Schuster 1940, 1952, 1962).

O'Brien, Edward J. H., ed., *The Best American Short Stories* (Houghton; annually, 1915–1941).

O'Brien, Edward J. H., ed., *Fifty Best American Short Stories, 1915–1939* (Houghton 1939).

Reid, James M., ed., *Scottish Short Stories* (Oxford 1963).

Rimanelli, Glose, and Ruberto, Roberto, eds., *Modern Canadian Stories* (Ryerson 1966).

Rowse, Alfred A., *Cornish Stories* (Macmillan 1967).

Saturday Evening Post editors, *Best Modern Short Stories from the Saturday Evening Post* (Curtis Bks. 1965).

Snow, Sir Charles Percy, and Johnson, Pamela H., *Winter's Tales: Stories from Modern Russia* (St. Martins 1962).

Stead, Christian K., ed., *New Zealand Short Stories*, 2d series (Oxford 1966).

West, Ray B., ed., *The Short Story in America, 1900–1950* (Regnery 1952).

Whitney, Thomas P., ed. and tr., *The New Writing in Russia* (Univ. of Mich. Press 1964).

Yarmolinsky, Avrahm, ed., *A Treasury of Great Russian Short Stories* (Macmillan 1944).

SHORTHAND is any brief, rapid method of writing that is used principally in recording the spoken word, ordinarily by substituting characters or abbreviations for the conventional letters and words. Many such methods of writing have been invented and used during ancient and modern times. Shorthand has had a long history, its development and use closely paralleling development and use of longhand. In fact, longhand as we know it is itself a kind of shorthand because it is a shorter and more dependable method of recording and communicating ideas than were the picture writing and ideographs that preceded it.

Ancient Use of Shorthand. There is considerable evidence that shorthand was in use before the beginning of the Christian era, abbreviated writing having been employed by the early Greeks to take down lectures and to record poems recited at such national meetings as the Olympic Games. Probably most people are now aware that Marcus Tullius Tiro, Cicero's freedman, reported the orations of Cicero and Cato the Younger as early as 63 B.C. What they may not know is that the Tironian notes seem to have contributed to the development of later shorthand systems.

Roman reporters known as *notarii* also became skilled in the use of the Tironian notes. One of their practices was to use the initial letters to express names and words in the proceedings they were reporting, and in order to save time the same practice was carried over into the transcripts. This practice of using longhand abbreviations is recognized today in such shortened forms as A. D. (anno Domini), N. B. (nota bene), and P. S. (postscriptum).

The early Christians seem to have made use of shorthand. It is thought that Saint Paul dictated many of his epistles to amanuenses—especially the Epistle to the Colossians. In this instance, Paul's friend Tychichus may have acted as the writer of shorthand, while Onesimus, the runaway slave, served as the transcriber.

Records show that a contract was made in Egypt, in 155 A. D., to teach a boy shorthand. In the 4th century the Roman scholar Decimus Magnus Ausonius wrote a poem to a young reporter, calling him a youth "skilled in swift shorthand." Also in the 4th century, Saint Augustine referred to an episcopal assemblage in Carthage at which eight stenographers were employed, apparently in relays of two each.

Thus shorthand in ancient times was used to record and preserve poems recited, orations delivered, meetings held—all of which might otherwise have been lost as soon as uttered. However, with the beginning of the Dark Ages, the art became practically nonexistent. For one thing, the Latin language, for which the Tironian notes had been invented, was becoming the lingua Romana, the foundation of the Romance languages of modern times. The Tironian notes in their original form were not well adapted to this language use. In addition, the superstition of the period regarded shorthand as a black art. And finally, reading and writing all but disappeared during this period—shorthand along with them.

Early Modern Use of Shorthand. While there are various evidences of interest in shorthand during the 15th and 16th centuries, probably the first important step toward its revival was taken by the Englishman Timothy Bright in 1588. Bright, sometimes called the father of modern shorthand, dedicated his book to Queen Elizabeth, who granted to her "well-beloved subject, Tymothe Brighte, Doctor of Physike," a patent for a "shorte and new kynde of writing by character to the furtherance of good learning." The patent restricted the publication and teaching rights of Bright's shorthand to him and his assigns for a period of 15 years. This matter of the "patent" is mentioned because it was used by later inventors as a means of retaining exclusive rights to the publication of their systems.

Other shorthand systems followed. Thomas Shelton's *Tachygraphical Alphabet and Directions,* published in 1626, was the system used by Samuel Pepys in his diary. In the 17th century, just as in the ancient period, shorthand was extensively used for the purpose of recording speeches, which might not have been preserved otherwise. At this time, the principal matter recorded consisted of sermons, so important as a part of the intellectual and religious awakening. Indeed, when during the reign of Charles II it was feared that printed Bibles would be suppressed, many people were engaged in copying the Bible in shorthand. Shorthand was also used extensively as "secret writing." It has been said that Pepys would never have revealed himself in his diary so completely if he had not believed that his "secret" writing protected him from the general public. In 1649, shorthand was used in reporting the court trial of John Lilburne. It has been indicated that the record was as nearly verbatim as can be determined after the passage of more than three centuries.

William Mason first published his system in 1672, printing later editions in 1682 and 1707. Mason's system of shorthand formed the basis of the famous Gurney system, the backbone of British shorthand for at least 200 years. In 1738, Thomas Gurney was appointed official reporter to the criminal court of Old Bailey, and the Gurney family firm became official reporters in the House of Lords and the House of Commons early in the 19th century. The Gurneys, who evidently felt that to teach their system widely would result in the setting up of undesirable competition to their highly lucrative monopoly of reporting, trained their own personnel and charged such high prices to others for their books that competition was discouraged. Another system was that of John Byrom, published in *The Universal English Short-Hand; or, the Way of Writing English in the Most Easy and Concise . . . Manner* (1767). The Byrom system was used by John and Charles Wesley.

Early Use in American Colonies. Shorthand was taken to the United States by the English settlers. Among the earliest of these was Roger Williams, founder of Rhode Island, while another instance was that of John Winthrop, son of the first Massachusetts governor and himself governor of Connecticut. Winthrop and his wife corresponded with each other in a combination of shorthand and longhand. Many of the early presidents of Harvard were writers of shorthand, and Thomas Jefferson recommended its use as a means of ready communication with those who knew the system, which at the same time would prevent other people from reading and understanding what had been written.

European Systems. From the 17th to the 19th century, shorthand was being developed in France, Germany, and elsewhere on the Continent. Of significance in this European development was the invention in 1834 of the first cursive system by Franz Xaver Gabelsberger. It appears that the Gabelsberger method influenced most Germanic and Scandinavian shorthand systems.

Uses and Requirements of Modern Shorthand. With the invention and practical use of the typewriter, shorthand became an important tool in business communication as well as in the long-established uses of reporting and personal writing. But stenographers, shorthand reporters, and those who use shorthand for personal writing and note taking do not require the same degree of speed and precision.

For present-day use, shorthand should meet these simple criteria: (1) It must be legible. (2) It must have possibilities of speed (more rapid than longhand) suitable to the purpose for which it is used. (3) The time required to master the system must be appropriate to the use for which it is intended. (4) It must be developed on principles that enable the user to write accurately enough to recognize and transcribe words he has not memorized.

Each use of shorthand has a different requirement for speed, but all require legibility. Shorthand for personal use needs only to be faster than longhand, and the writer sets his own speed. For business dictation purposes, shorthand must meet the speed requirements of the person dictating. Such requirements range from literally no words a minute, while the person dictating is thinking, to over 120 words a minute in spurts. The verbatim reporter must be able to record at speeds of over 200 words a minute for sustained periods, and in the case of court reporting, he must do this when the matter recorded comes from a variety of speakers with differing speech patterns. It is obvious that adaptations of the shorthand system used are necessary to meet these differing demands.

Modern Requirements. Longhand in any language meets all of the above criteria except that of speed. As for ancient and early methods of shorthand, they were valuable for the preservation of important material and the development of modern shorthand, but they were all characterized by a large proportion of arbitrary signs. The use of such signs means that the words they represent must be memorized by rote. The heavier such a memory load is, the less reliable is the system in the hands of the user and the less likely it is to meet the test of legibility.

The Gurney system, which has so remarkably stood the test of time, depended apparently upon the completeness of the outline (the shorthand representation of the word) for legibility, and upon extended experience with the system for proficiency in writing it. In order to become an expert writer of Gurney, the learner first became acquainted with the system, then spent a protracted period reading the notes of others—that is, he transcribed the notes taken by others of discourse he himself had not heard. He practiced assiduously to increase his own proficiency, and eventually became a reporter himself. That the Gurney system met the test of legibility is attested by the fact that, due to loss of an original transcript of a trial, Gurney notes were transcribed again by others 70 years later. That it had speed is evidenced by the fact that it met the gruelling demands of reporting for the House of Commons and the House of Lords. However, it is apparent that it did not meet the criterion of ease and speed in learning.

The basic method of representation in the early systems seems to have been relatively arbitrary. Representation of a given character or family of characters by a given sign seems to have been the most usual principle of construction. Little analysis was made of sounds and their consistent representation, of the relative frequency of sounds, or of their sequence in the language for which the shorthand system was designed.

Isaac Pitman Shorthand. The first commercially used phonetic system of shorthand was invented by Sir Isaac Pitman, whose shorthand manual was first published in 1837. To date it is the most prevalent system in the English-speaking world outside the United States. Pitman himself, somewhat overmodestly, said he did not invent anything or discover anything. Although he used some signs that had been employed by others, what he did that was original and important was to organize the principles for using the signs into a dependable system by which all words heard could be written.

In Isaac Pitman shorthand, the symbols used represent sounds. Light (unvoiced) sounds are represented by light strokes; heavy (voiced) sounds are represented by heavy strokes, thus:

p\   b\   f\   v\

These light and heavy strokes, straight and curved, represent the consonantal framework of the system. Hooks, circles, hoops, and shortening and lengthening of consonant strokes are used to increase the legibility of the system. Pitman uses a 12-vowel scale of light and heavy dots and dashes to represent as nearly as is practically possible the vowel sounds of English. This vowel scale is as follows (showing position in relation to consonant stroke):

ă   ah   ŏ   aw   ĕ   ā   ŭ   ō   ĭ   ē   ŏŏ   ōō

Vowels written at the beginning of a consonant stroke are first-place vowels, those written in the middle are second-place, and those written at the end are third-place. Thus the first vowel in the word determines the position in which the outline is written, whether above, on, or through the base line.

THE LORD'S PRAYER IN SHORTHAND
Matthew 6: 9-13, King James Version

Our Father which art in heaven,

Hallowed be thy name.

Thy kingdom come.

Thy will be done in earth, as it is in heaven.

Give us this day our daily bread.

And forgive us our debts, as we forgive our debtors.

And lead us not into temptation,

    but deliver us from evil:

For thine is the kingdom, and the power,

    and the glory, forever. Amen.

Isaac Pitman shorthand

Gregg shorthand

Speedwriting

---

are designed to correct earlier inconsistencies, some to improve speed or legibility. In other words, shortcuts developed by users are introduced into the system to improve speed. Such shortcuts are a delight to the experienced user of the system, but they tend to make it more elaborate and hence more difficult for the beginner to learn and less well adapted to personal use. In most cases, a separate reporting shorthand is developed, many of the shortcuts of which become incorporated into the basic system. By the 1880's, Isaac Pitman shorthand in England had gone through many editions and had undergone many elaborations. It had now become difficult to learn in the opinion of many persons.

Gregg Shorthand. In 1888, Irish-born John Robert Gregg produced his *Light-Line Phonography,* later known as Gregg shorthand. Early in life Gregg had been a shorthand student and enthusiast. He knew many systems, but his closest association was with Thomas Stratford Malone, whose method he taught. His own system was designed to be easier to learn and to write than the systems that had preceded it.

The characters of the Gregg system represent voiced and unvoiced sounds by differences in the length of strokes, thus:

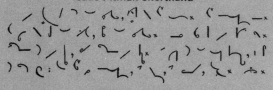

Vowels are represented by large and small circles and by hooks:

$\bigcirc$ = ā ă ah	o = ē ĕ ĭ
$\cap$ = ū o͝o o͞o	v = ō ŏ aw

All vowels are joined in the shorthand outline, as they are joined in the longhand word. Note the illustration at the end of this article.

At the time of its first publication in England, Gregg shorthand was not successful. Gregg went to the United States, and in 1893 the first American edition of his system was printed in Boston. Pitmanic systems were strongly entrenched in the East and in the vicinity of Ohio, where the headquarters of Benn Pitman had been set up. Gregg went to Chicago. From that time on the venture of Gregg shorthand was eminently successful. The system was simple. It was approximately phonetic—sufficiently so that words could be represented by signs that stood for sounds, but without being so finely discriminatory in sounds as to confuse the learner. It had the advantage of being written in one position on a ruled line, just as longhand is written. It was continuously spelled—that is, vowels were incorporated into the outline with the consonants, instead of being indicated by position or by the way of writing the consonant that preceded or followed the vowel. It was developed on a basis of principles that could be mastered. It could be written rapidly, was legible, and did not require an unreasonably long period to master.

Gregg believed in his system, and from his Chicago office he went out through the West, the Middle West, and the South, selling the system to the business schools and high schools. This was in the early 20th century, when such schools were introducing business courses. Because Gregg had to teach his system immediately to those who were to be teachers, the methodology

Benn Pitman Shorthand. Benjamin (Benn) Pitman, brother of Isaac, took Pitman shorthand to the United States and set up his publishing company in Cincinnati. The first edition in the United States, published in 1855, was the 9th edition of Isaac Pitman shorthand. After Jerome Howard joined the staff and made changes in the system, it became known as Pitman-Howard shorthand. Pitman-Howard retained the original vowel scale representation but modified the representation of certain consonants. This system was extensively used in the United States both for business and for reporting through the first quarter of the 20th century.

Evolution Pattern of Shorthand Systems. Shorthand systems seem to have a kind of common life history. The first stage of the system is simple—easy to learn, easy to use, but with relatively limited speed possibilities. A successful system goes through many editions, each designed to improve its utility. Some of the improvements of Gregg shorthand became a part of the system so far as teachers were concerned. Thus, because no shorthand of any kind was being taught in most of the schools of the Middle West, West, and South, and because Gregg was a good system with a good service, it soon became predominant in those areas. It is now the system most used in the United States.

In the early days of Gregg shorthand, it was thought by many that because of the length of the outlines, the system could not be used for verbatim reporting at high speeds. Charles Lee Swem destroyed this misconception when he became a championship shorthand reporter at the speed of 280.4 words per minute on court testimony. That this was not an instance of a particularly able person is evidenced by the continuing numbers of Gregg shorthand reporters.

From the early simple shorthand system published in the United States in 1893, Gregg evolved through various editions into an elaborate system subject to many of the criticisms that Gregg had originally intended to avoid.

During the periods when Pitman shorthand was being developed and used and when Gregg was developing his system, the people who were studying and practicing shorthand were interested in the art per se, and they were interested in comparing systems to find more rapid and more accurate methods of writing. They understood the language they were trying to represent in shorthand. The art was closely associated with good writing and speaking, a tool for scholarly pursuits. Thus the time required for mastery of the system was of less importance than its sensitivity in recording. Later both Pitman and Gregg had evolved to the place where they had higher speed potentials than were required for business office use, and the editors of both systems brought out new editions designed to simplify the learning. The Pitman Publishing Corporation in the United States published its *Basic Course in Pitman Shorthand* (1946), a book that presents the basic shorthand system unchanged in 50 simple lessons, which do not include many special phrase adaptations. The Gregg Publishing Company published an edition called *Gregg Shorthand Manual Simplified* (1949), the basic principle of which was to reduce the number of brief forms and abbreviating principles and return to the earlier method of writing outlines more completely. This assured legibility and, within limits, did not reduce the speed potential of the system.

Both Gregg and Pitman, because of their basic phonetic structure, have been adapted successfully to many foreign languages.

Machine Shorthand. In addition to the symbol systems of shorthand, other methods of short writing have been developed. Machine shorthand, after a relatively long period of non-acceptance, demonstrated itself to be a reporting system with a very high speed potential, with dependable legibility, and with relatively less time required for developing reporting skill. In machine shorthand, a keyboard of longhand type is used according to certain principles to represent words. The keys for a given word may be struck simultaneously, the impression being recorded on paper tape like adding machine tape, one word to a line. This one-stroke recording obviously makes for speed. Proceedings recorded by one reporter may easily be read by another who knows the system. The machine (Stenograph or Stenotype) is light, compact, easily portable,

and silent. The operator writes by touch. This enables him to watch the speaker, a very great advantage in reporting. Machine shorthand reporters now do most of the convention reporting and a large part of the court, legislative, and hearing reporting in the United States.

Abbreviated Longhand Systems. Longhand abbreviation systems have been developed increasingly in the United States. These are designed to provide legible methods of writing at relatively low speeds, sufficient for business and personal use. Speeds up to 120 words a minute for short periods are assured competent writers. Some systems—such as Speedwriting—use a combination of longhand letters and symbols, while others use only the longhand letters. Consonants are depended upon to provide the framework of the word. Important vowels are written, while obscure vowels are omitted. Short forms are used for words of high frequency. All in all, principles to be mastered are reduced to a minimum. It is believed by the inventors of abbreviated longhand systems that, since the learner needs only to adapt the longhand he already knows to the shorthand system, learning time may be reduced and legibility assured.

HELEN REYNOLDS
Formerly, New York University

Further Reading: Butler, Edward Henry, *The Story of British Shorthand* (Pitman 1951); Gregg, John Robert, *Selections from the Story of Shorthand* (Gregg 1941); Leslie, Louis A., *Methods for Teaching Gregg Shorthand* (Gregg 1953).

SHORTHORN, a breed of cattle. The heaviest of the beef breeds, it is widely distributed in the central and western United States. See CATTLE—*Breeds of Temperate Climates.*

SHORTWAVE RADIO, communication by radio using any wavelength in the range from about 100 meters to 10 meters (the frequency range from 3,000 kHz to 30,000 kHz). Shortwaves are commonly used for amateur radio communications, long-distance international broadcasting, and aeronautical radio. See also RADIO.

SHOSHONEAN INDIANS, shō-shō′nē-ən, are those who speak languages belonging to the Shoshonean stock of the Uto-Aztecan linguistic family. Many separate sociopolitical groups have been combined into four branches—the Plateau, Kern River, Southern California, and Pueblo—and eight divisions of the linguistic stock. Except for the Pima and Papago tribes of Southern Arizona, all speakers of the Uto-Aztecan languages in the United States belong to the Shoshonean stock. Aside from a few tribes, including the Hopi and Comanche, the Shoshoneans belong geographically to the semidesert, range, and sagebrush region of the Great Basin, or more exactly, the area between the Rocky Mountains and the Sierra Nevada.

SHOSHONI INDIANS, shō-shō′nē, the most northerly of the Shoshonean tribes, which are within the Uto-Aztecan linguistic stock. They occupied portions of Wyoming, Utah, Nevada, and Idaho, and their stronghold was the Snake River area in Idaho. The name means "in the valley," or "valley dwellers," and although the Shoshoni once ranged the plains, hostile tribes later pushed them into the mountains. Never great in numbers, the Shoshoni total fewer than 10,000 and reside mostly on reservations.

SOVFOTO

Dmitri Shostakovich, leading Soviet composer

SHOSTAKOVICH, shos-tə-kō'vich, **Dmitri** (1906–1975), Soviet composer, whose music—much of it inspired by Soviet history—gained recognition throughout the world and placed him high among the foremost creators of Western music in the 20th century.

Life. Dmitri Dmitriyevich Shostakovich was born in St. Petersburg (now Leningrad) on Sept. 25, 1906, the son of an engineer. From 1919 to 1925 he attended the Leningrad Conservatory, where he studied harmony and counterpoint with Maximillian Steinberg and composition with Aleksandr Glazunov, some of whose technical finesse was communicated to the young student.

Before he was 20 years old, Shostakovich had composed his first symphony, which was enormously successful. Other compositions followed, and in 1928 his opera *The Nose,* based on the classic story by Nikolai Gogol, was produced. His ballet *The Age of Gold* (1930) did not remain long in the dance repertoire, but a suite taken from it became a popular concert piece.

Shostakovich's second opera, *Lady Macbeth of the Mtsensk District* (1934), was applauded by its Muscovite audiences and widely performed in the United States and Europe, but two years later, in January 1936, the official Soviet newspaper, *Pravda,* condemned the opera and its composer for catering to decadent bourgeois tastes.

Accepting the criticism, Shostakovich remedied the situation by composing a number of works that could conceivably be played to the current watchwords. The Fourth Symphony he himself withdrew in 1936, after rehearsals, but with the Fifth Symphony (1937) he added another work to the permanent concert repertoire. Commemorating the 20th anniversary of the October Revolution, it carried the wry subtitle *A Soviet Artist's Reply to Just Criticism.* However, there is nothing diffident about the symphony itself, which, though uneven, rises to a noble largeness rarely heard in modern music. In 1937, evidently in favor with the government, Shostakovich was appointed a professor at the Leningrad Conservatory. At first he taught instrumentation, later composition.

Shostakovich fell afoul of the regime again, and in 1948 the Communist party central committee accused him, along with others, of "formalism," that is, art for art's sake. In 1949, however, Shostakovich was a Soviet delegate to the Cultural and Scientific Conference for World Peace, held in New York City. In 1956 he revised his disfavored opera *Lady Macbeth of the Mtsensk District.* It gained popularity under its new title, *Katerina Ismailova,* and in 1968 was made into a motion picture that was shown around the world. In 1958 the Khrushchev government, blaming Stalin's "subjective approach" to the arts, exonerated Shostakovich and his confreres.

In all, Shostakovich won three Stalin Prizes and a number of Lenin Prizes for his works. He also received many international awards, and in 1966 he was named a Hero of Socialist Labor, the highest honor bestowed on a Soviet composer, and was awarded the Order of Lenin. A member of the Communist party from 1960, he accepted the party's criticisms of his music and was generally considered the greatest Soviet composer of his time. He died in Kuntsevo, outside Moscow, on Aug. 9, 1975.

Works. Shostakovich composed more than a dozen symphonies. His youthful First Symphony is the tasteful, thoughtful work of one musically well read and already in command of distinctive rhythmic and melodic gifts. Less effective are his Second (*October Symphony,* 1927) and Third (*May First Symphony,* 1931), in which he attempted to put social meaning into his music. The Fifth Symphony is his finest, and with the First it is unmatched by any of the composer's later symphonies—not even by the highly publicized Seventh (*Leningrad Symphony*), written in 1941 during the siege of his beloved city.

As a chamber-music composer, Shostakovich most truly lived up to his undoubted genius, possibly because as such he could compose without bothering about the implications of what the notes say. The Piano Quintet (1940) is his masterpiece in this category. It is well shaped, has an impressive range of technical resource, and clings steadily to sincerity without neglecting variety of mood. He also wrote a Concerto for Piano, Trumpet, and Strings (1933), a Violin Concerto (1956), a Concerto for Piano and Orchestra (1957), a Cello Concerto (1959), a Sonata for Violin and Piano (1969), and numerous other instrumental pieces.

Shostakovich also composed a number of scores for motion pictures. These, although not artistically memorable, are effective because of their studied crudity and flair for the workaday. They often contain singable tunes. Other works include oratorios, tone poems, and songs.

WALLACE BROCKWAY
Coauthor of "Men of Music"

Further Reading: Martynov, Ivan I., *Dmitri Shostakovich: The Man and His Work,* tr. by T. Guralski (Greenwood 1947); Seroff, Victor Ilyich, and Galli-Shohat, Nadejda, *Dmitri Shostakovich: The Life and Background of a Soviet Composer* (Knopf 1943).

SHOT PUT. See TRACK AND FIELD.

SHOTGUN. See SMALL ARMS.

SHOTOKU TAISHI, shō-tō-kū tī-shē (574–622), was a Japanese prince who initiated reforms that by the 8th century gave Japan a centralized government on the model of China. In 592, Shotoku became regent for Empress Suiko, his aunt. With the aim of building a stronger central government he gradually increased the powers of the imperial family at the expense of the nobles. In 602 he introduced a system of court ranks that encouraged official advancement on the basis of merit rather than birth only. Two years later he issued a 17-article "constitution"—actually a code of injunctions setting forth principles of good government in Confucian terms. In 607 he sent the first of a series of Japanese missions to China that furthered the process of cultural borrowing over several centuries. Shotoku was a Buddhist, and in order to propagate that faith he sponsored the construction of temples, notably the Horyu-ji at Nara.

SHOTWELL, James Thomson (1874–1965), American historian, who played an important part in the movement to rethink traditional views of the past in the light of original source materials, and to rewrite history accordingly. He was a tireless worker for international peace.

Shotwell was born in Strathroy, Ontario, Canada, on Aug. 6, 1874. A graduate of the University of Toronto, he began teaching history at Columbia University in 1900, and received his Ph. D. there three years later. He was professor of history at the university from 1908 to 1942. He headed the division of history in the U. S. delegation at the Paris Peace Conference in 1919 and was instrumental in establishing the International Labor Organization at that time. From 1924 to 1948 he directed the division of economics and history of the Carnegie Endowment for International Peace, and in 1949–1950 he was president of the organization. The 150-volume *Economic and Social History of the World War,* published from 1921 to 1940 under the sponsorship of this organization, was carried to completion by Shotwell as general editor. He was president of the League of Nations Association of the United States from 1935 to 1939 and in the latter year organized the Commission to Study the Organization of Peace, serving as chairman until 1950. At the United Nations Charter Conference of 1945 he was chairman of the consultant experts in various fields. Shotwell died in New York City on July 15, 1965.

Among Shotwell's publications in the field of history and international affairs are: *The Religious Revolution of Today* (1913); *An Introduction to the History of History* (1922), revised as *The History of History* (vol. 1, 1939); *War as an Instrument of National Policy and Its Renunciation in the Pact of Paris* (1929); *Heritage of Freedom; the United States and Canada in the Community of Nations* (1934); *On the Rim of the Abyss* (1936); *The Great Decision* (1944); *The United States in History* (1956).

SHOULDER, in human anatomy, the highly mobile structure that joins the upper arm to the chest wall. Three bones compose the shoulder girdle: (1) the scapula, or shoulder blade, a large flat triangular-shaped bone lying posteriorly on the chest wall; (2) the clavicle, or collarbone, a long bone, located anteriorly nearly horizontal above the first rib; and (3) the humerus, the large long bone of the upper arm.

The shoulder is a ball-and-socket type of joint. The head of the humerus is a smooth hemisphere that rests in the cup of the glenoid cavity of the scapula. The entire joint is protected by heavy musculature, tendons and ligaments that are attached to the head of the humerus, enabling the upper arm to move rapidly up and down on the trunk or simultaneously to rotate internally and externally.

Because of its extreme mobility, the shoulder joint is subject to a variety of injuries, including dislocation and fracture. In a dislocation the head of the humerus is displaced either anteriorly or posteriorly in the socket of the joint. This painful injury weakens the capsule of the shoulder joint and is apt to recur unless open corrective surgery is done. Fractures also usually involve the head of the humerus. The fracture may be a split through the surgical neck of the bone or impacted against the glenoid fossa, or cavity.

There are two main bursae, fluid-filled sacs, in the region of the shoulder. The subdeltoid bursa is located under the deltoid muscle (the major muscle for lifting the arm), and the subacromial bursa is located under the long tendon of the biceps muscle. Bursitis, an inflammation of the bursa, can cause severe pain. Methods used to relieve the pain include aspiration, or removal of the fluid in the bursa, local cortisone injections to reduce inflammation, and local X-ray therapy.

REAUMUR S. DONALLY M. D.
Washington Hospital Center
Washington, D. C.

SHOWBOAT, a type of floating theater that plied United States inland waters during the 19th and early 20th centuries, stopping to give performances at various settlements along the way. These river theaters came into being to meet the need of early pioneers in the Midwest for theatrical and other entertainment. Settlement of the vast Mississippi basin, begun in the 18th century and greatly accelerated after the Louisiana Purchase of 1803, was almost entirely river borne. The migrants started hundreds of communities, many of them tiny, along and near the riverbanks. The only way organized entertainment could be brought to these scattered communities was with mobile playhouses—the showboats.

Beginning with small craft that merely drifted downstream, and progressing to palatial floating theaters that were pushed, rather than pulled, by steam "towboats," the showboats flourished until an encroaching civilization, particularly the movies, the automobile, and the radio, forced them out of business.

The showboat and its way of life were immortalized for Americans in Edna Ferber's novel *Showboat* (1926), which was made into a popular Broadway musical of the same name in 1927, with music by Jerome Kern and lyrics by Oscar Hammerstein 2d.

The Pre-Civil War Period. The first showboat—albeit an improvised one—was probably the *Noah's Ark,* an ordinary keelboat with a rude superstructure, on which a group of itinerant players under Noah Miller Ludlow drifted from Nashville, Tenn., down the Cumberland, Ohio, and Mississippi rivers, to Natchez, Miss., in the early winter of 1817. It is presumed that the actors presented plays at the river landings en route.

The first deliberately planned showboat was the *Floating Theatre,* built at Pittsburgh in 1831 by William Chapman, Sr., a British actor who had

SHOWBOATS, such as the *Goldenrod* (above), moored at St. Louis, are a fast-disappearing aspect of Americana. Melodrama (right) was an entertainment staple.

emigrated to the United States with his family four years before. It consisted of a 100-foot-long (30-meter) barge with a garagelike superstructure containing a tiny stage equipped with tallow candle footlights, and a pit and gallery with wooden benches seating 200. Presenting straight drama, with his family playing most of the roles, Chapman at first followed the practice of floating his drama boat down the Ohio and Mississippi each year during summer and early winter, selling it at New Orleans, and returning to Pittsburgh by steamer to build a new boat. Later he bought and put his show aboard a small steamboat (the *Steamboat Theatre*), which enabled him to return upriver under his own power and to enter tributaries. The Chapman troupe was active on the rivers until 1847.

Spurred by the Chapmans' success, dozens of small showboats swarmed over the Middle Western rivers in the 1840's and 1850's, offering entertainment ranging all the way from drama and vaudeville to minstrel shows, museums, and lectures. Unfortunately, some presented questionable shows, and these craft, along with gambling, whiskey, and medicine boats, brought disrepute to the showboating business before the Civil War put an end to all shows from the rivers.

An exception to this trend was provided by several well-run circus boats. The most spectacular of these was Gilbert R. Spaulding and Charles J. Rogers' *Floating Circus Palace*, built at Cincinnati. Nearly 200 feet long by 35 feet wide (30 by 10 meters), this huge one-ring circus amphitheater seated 3,400 in its dress circle and two galleries. The craft and its steam towboat housed nearly 100 performers, trainers, staff, and crew, plus 40 trained horses and other animals. It played the river cities in the period between 1851 and 1862.

The Post-Civil War Period. Showboating attained full maturity in the half century following the Civil War. The lead was set by Augustus Byron French of Palmyra, Mo., a pre-Civil War showboat entertainer, who in 1878, at the age of 45, married Callie Leach, 16, and built his first showboat, *The New Sensation*. In the years between 1878 and 1907, four more French-owned showboats rode the rivers, the last—following Captain

French's death in 1902—being captained by his widow, who had already, in 1888, become the first licensed woman pilot on the Mississippi.

Concentrating on wholesome vaudeville, the Frenches did much to rehabilitate the showboat business. They also established a showboat circuit of major rivers and their tributaries, setting a pattern for showboats generally—the upper Ohio in spring, the lower Ohio and upper Mississippi in summer, and the lower Mississippi in fall and early winter.

Many of the operating methods they followed also became standard, such as the advance-advertising by means of a speed launch preceding the showboat; the calliope that heralded the boat's approach for miles around; and the brightly uniformed band that paraded village streets on the morning of its arrival.

Among other notable showboaters were: Edwin A. Price, who owned eight showboats between 1887 and 1928, was noted for his eccentricities, and is reputed to have been the prototype for Capt. Andy Hawks in Edna Ferber's novel, *Showboat*; Ralph Emerson, the "Showboat King," who operated nine of them after the turn of the century; W. R. Markle, builder of the palatial showboats *New Grand Floating Palace*, *Sunny South*, and *Goldenrod* between 1901 and 1909; the Bryant family, particularly Sam Bryant and his son Billy, operators of *Princess* and *Bryant's New Showboat* between 1907 and 1942; and the Menke brothers—John William (Bill), H. J. (Harry),

B. F. (Ben), and C. J. (Charley)—who purchased and operated several famous showboats during the first half of the 20th century. A showboater with an off-beat circuit was James Adams, owner of the *S. S. Playhouse*, also known as the *James Adams Floating Theatre*, an oceangoing showboat that plied the Albemarle and Chesapeake regions of the Atlantic coast between the years 1906 and 1937.

During their heyday, showboats were popular and generally prosperous. So eager were the river folk for entertainment that a small landing would often produce an audience, including people from the hinterland, as big as the town itself. As time went on, the boats became bigger and more sumptuous, until a craft like the *Goldenrod*, the biggest ever built (200 feet long by 45 feet wide—61 by 14 meters—and seating 1,400), could boast central heating and luxury appointments rivaling those of land theaters.

From time to time, showboats offered almost every kind of theatrical entertainment—from drama, minstrelsy, and vaudeville to melodrama, musical comedy, and sophisticated plays of the 20th century. But beginning with the 1890's, melodrama became the chief ingredient. Among the favorites were such plays as Mrs. Henry Wood's *East Lynne* and Timothy Shay Arthur's *Ten Nights in a Barroom*.

Showboating reached its zenith in 1910, when 26 showboats were operating on Middle Western rivers. By 1928 the number had dwindled to 14, by 1938 to five. Ironically, in order to win attention from audiences made sophisticated by the movies, showboats in the end were often forced to burlesque the melodrama that had once been their mainstay played straight. A few showboats still ply the waterways, offering the traditional entertainment for which they were famous. These, however, are more historical curiosities than a viable system of entertainment, and they are fast disappearing.

Further Reading: Donovan, Frank R., *Riverboats of America* (Crowell 1966); Graham, Philip, *Showboats: The History of an American Institution* (Univ. of Texas Press 1951).

SHOWBREAD. See SHEWBREAD.

SHRAPNEL, shrap'nəl, **Henry** (1761–1842), British general, who invented the shrapnel shell. He was born on June 3, 1761, probably at Bradford-on-Avon, Wiltshire, England. He received a commission in the Royal Artillery in 1779 and served in Newfoundland, Gibraltar, the West Indies, and Flanders.

He devoted his talent for invention to improvements in ordnance. His greatest success was a spherical projectile filled with musket balls and black powder, which was exploded by a time fuse in midair, scattering the fragments over a wide area. Each could kill or wound a man, and the shrapnel was devastating against close-packed bodies of soldiers. It was widely used in the trench fighting of World War I. In modern armies it has been largely replaced by high-bursting-charge projectiles, in which the projectile fragments substitute for the steel balls.

Shrapnel was made a lieutenant general in 1837, but never won any special recognition for his invention. He died at Southampton, England, on March 13, 1842.

SHRAPNEL. See PROJECTILES.

SHREVEPORT, shrēv'pôrt, a city in northwestern Louisiana, the seat of Caddo parish (county), is on the Red River, 18 miles (29 km) east of the Texas border. Part of the city extends into Bossier parish. The area is one of the state's leading cotton regions, and is rich in oil and natural gas. Shreveport is an important manufacturing, distributing, and trading center. The principal industries include metal products, machinery, lumber, chemicals, petroleum, printing, stone, clay, glass, apparel, and food products. Several of the nation's largest natural gas companies have their headquarters here, and Barksdale Air Force Base is nearby.

Centenary College, a Methodist institution, offers a four-year degree program. Among the city's cultural groups are the Little Theatre, the Civic Opera, and the Shreveport Symphony. Museums include the Louisiana State Exhibit Museum—which contains work of local artists, amphibians and reptiles, and industrial and geological exhibits—and the R. W. Norton Art Gallery. The Louisiana State Fair is held in Shreveport each autumn. A spring festival, Holiday in Dixie, features dances, parades, and pageants.

The Shreveport area was settled about 1834, soon after Henry Miller Shreve cleared the Red River of a large driftwood jam that had been blocking navigation. The small settlement became a flourishing port, and was incorporated as a town in 1839. Cotton-growing thrived in the region. In 1863 the town became the Confederate capital of Louisiana. It was the last stronghold of the Confederacy during the Civil War. It was chartered as a city in 1871. In 1906, the discovery of oil at Caddo Lake on the Texas border stimulated the city's growth. Shreveport has a commission form of government. Population: of the metropolitan area, 376,710; of the city, 205,820.

SHREW, a small mouselike mammal of a group that includes the smallest living mammals. Shrews make up the family Soricidae of the order Insectivora. Although generally resembling small mice or moles, they have minute eyes and sharp-pointed snouts. Over 20 species are known from the United States, with related forms on every major continent except Australia. The great abundance of these small, burrow-inhabiting animals is not generally recognized, but they are the most plentiful mammals in the eastern United States.

The animal's reputation for bad temper is

Common shrew (*Sorex araneus castaneus*)

A pigmy shrew, *Sorex minutus* (top), attacks an earthworm. A shorttail shrew, *Blarina*, is below.

STEPHEN DALTON, FROM NATIONAL AUDUBON SOCIETY

KARL H. MASLOWSKI, FROM NATIONAL AUDUBON SOCIETY

based upon its restless activity and voracious appetite. Both these facts are explained by the exceedingly high rate of metabolism of the animal's tissues. In the tiny masked shrew (*Sorex cinereus*) the rate is four times as fast as in comparable amounts of mouse tissue. Shrews eat approximately 3.3 times their own weight every day. The food consists of insects and other invertebrate animals and occasionally small mammals. The water shrew (*S. palustris*) catches fish and insect larvae while swimming under water. Short-tailed shrews of the genus *Blarina* produce a poisonous venom in their submaxillary glands, apparently used for killing mice. Laboratory tests show that the poison will quickly kill mice or rabbits when injected into their blood streams, and a few cases of severe toxic symptoms in man following bites by *Blarina* shrews are authentically reported.

EDWARD S. HODGSON, *Tufts University*

SHREW MOLE, any of several species of primitive shrewlike moles of the family Talpidae, order Insectivora. The Asiatic shrew mole (*Uropsilus soricipes*) of western China and eastern Tibet is the most primitive of living moles. Its body form is essentially shrewlike with none of the charac-

teristic adaptations of fossorial (digging) types. The tail is about one half or slightly less than half the total length of 5 to 6 inches (12.7–15 cm). The eyes are small but normal in structure and function, and the external ears are better developed than in any other member of the family, reaching the height of the surrounding fur. Little is known of the habits of shrew moles.

There are several related species (*U. andersoni, Nasillus gracilis, N. investigator*) which differ from each other in minor details. All occur in the same region of China and Tibet and have been found at high altitudes ranging to 12,000 feet (3,650 meters) above sea level. The so-called shrew mole (*Neurotrichus gibbsii*) of the humid northwest coast of the United States is quite different. It is the smallest of true fossorial moles with forefeet specialized for digging. See INSECTIVORA; MOLE.

PHILIP HERSHKOVITZ
Field Museum of Natural History

SHREWSBURY, a municipal borough in central west England, the county town of Shropshire, is situated at a loop in the Severn River, about 140 miles (225 km) northwest of London. It is a communications center and has a large cattle market. Industry includes agricultural and industrial engineering, locomotive repairing, and brewing. Shrewsbury is one of England's finest medieval towns and is famous for its half-timbered houses and ancient bridges. Holy Cross and St. Mary's churches incorporate much Norman work. Existing portions of Shrewsbury Castle date from the time of Edward I. The county museum houses Roman remains from nearby Wroxeter (formerly the Roman settlement of Viroconium).

Because its location made it a gateway between England and Wales, Shrewsbury was always a military prize. After the Romans withdrew, it was known in Cymric (Welsh) as Pengwern until 778, when King Offa of Mercia seized it and renamed it Scrobbesbyrig. It was fortified by the Normans and was the site of numerous battles. Henry IV defeated Hotspur (Henry Percy) here in 1403, and Oliver Cromwell besieged it in 1644.

RICHARD E. WEBB
Formerly, British Information Services

SHREWSBURY, a town in central Massachusetts, in Worcester county, is immediately east of Worcester, of which it is a residential suburb. There is a little light industry. Lake Quinsigamond, on the town's western border, is a popular recreational area.

Shrewsbury was settled in 1722 and incorporated in 1727. The Revolutionary War leader Artemas Ward was born here in 1727, and his home is one of the town's points of interest. Shrewsbury is governed by a town manager and selectmen. Population: 22,674.

SHREWSBURY SCHOOL is an English public (private) secondary school in Shrewsbury, Shropshire. Ranking with Eton and Harrow among English public schools, it was founded in 1552 by Edward VI. Under Samuel Butler, headmaster from 1798 to 1836, it attained a reputation for classical scholarship. In 1882, Shewsbury was moved from its quarters opposite Shrewsbury castle to its present site south of the Severn River. Among its graduates are the novelist Charles Dickens and the poet Sir Philip Sidney.

ROBERT H. WRIGHT, FROM NATIONAL AUDUBON SOCIETY

Loggerhead shrike with grasshopper it has impaled

SHRIKE, shrīk, a predatory songbird of the family Laniidae, which is so named because of its shrieklike calls. The family numbers 67 species, which are restricted chiefly to the Old World. Only two breed in the New World: the great gray shrike (*Lanius excubitor*), called the northern shrike in North America, and the loggerhead shrike (*L. ludovicianus*). The latter is found only in North America, but the range of the great gray shrike encompasses also the greater part of Eurasia and North Africa. The family is divided into two subfamilies: the typical shrikes (Laniinae) with 25 species, and the bush shrikes (Malaconotinae) with 42. The latter is restricted to Africa with the exception of one species, the range of which extends also to southern Arabia.

All shrikes are predatory, feeding on small birds, small mammals (such as mice), lizards, or the larger insects, which they kill with their strongly hooked bills. Their feeding habits are not unlike those of the smaller birds of prey, although the shrikes are true songbirds. The typical shrikes differ from the bush shrikes by having, as a rule, a larger head and a stronger bill. They tend also to be more compactly built and to have a plainer plumage. In the bush shrikes the plumage is softer and often highly colored with bright red, orange, yellow, and green, with velvety black patches in some species. The two differ also in their hunting habits. The typical shrikes hunt in the open from an exposed perch, while the bush shrikes keep more to cover and secure a large part of their food by foraging through the trees and bushes.

Some authorities consider that the two groups are not closely related, and the true affinities of the bush shrikes remain uncertain. Some species of the typical shrikes have the curious habit of impaling unwanted or excess prey on a thorn or other sharp projection such as barbed wire, a habit that has earned them the odd name of "butcherbird."

CHARLES VAURIE
Curator, Department of Ornithology,
American Museum of Natural History

SHRIMP, any of several types of small aquatic animals that resemble crayfish but are of more slender build, with slender legs lacking large nippers. In tropical waters shrimps may reach the size of a small lobster. Their colors are mostly pale, subject to alteration with environmental conditions. The pink color of cooked shrimp is due to chemical change. The head bears stalked eyes and long feelers, and behind it the forward or thoracic part of the body is enclosed along the sides in a delicate shell (*carapace*). The thorax bears five pairs of slim walking legs. The rear part of the body forms the jointed abdomen, terminating in a tail fan employed to give a powerful backward stroke in swimming. On its under side the abdomen bears well-developed swimming paddles (*pleopods*) to which, in females, the eggs are glued during breeding. Shrimp eggs hatch into minute larvae that bear no resemblance to the adult, and a series of larval stages with intervening molts occurs before the typical shape appears.

Shrimps are common in shallow waters along seashores, and they also extend sparsely into fresh water. They feed on animal and vegetable matter and are in turn devoured as food by fish and other larger animals.

Shrimps make up the suborder Natantia of the crustacean order Decapoda ("ten-legged"). There are three types of shrimps. Commercial shrimps of the Atlantic coast, ranging from Virginia to Texas and Brazil, are of a type termed *penaeid*, having miniature nippers on the first three pairs of legs. Another type of edible shrimp, termed *caridean*, has nippers on the first two pairs of legs only. The third type of shrimp is the *stenopidean*, in which the first three pairs of legs bear pincers and at least one leg of the third pair is much larger than the other legs. Most commercially caught shrimp in North Amer-

Red-backed cleaning shrimp (*Hippolysmata grabhami*)

A. W. AMBLER, FROM NATIONAL AUDUBON SOCIETY

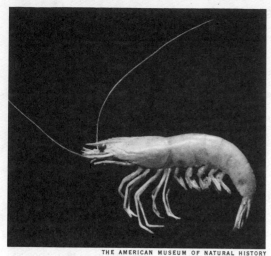

THE AMERICAN MUSEUM OF NATURAL HISTORY
Brown shrimp (*Penaeus aztecus*)

ica are in the penaeid group. They include *Peneus setiferus*, the major commercial shrimp of the Gulf Coast. *Crago septemspinosus*, the common shrimp of the North Atlantic region; *Crago franciscorum* of the west coast of North America; and *Palaemonetes vulgaris*, also known as the "prawn," are in the caridean group. In *Peneus* the largest pincers are on the third pair of legs, in *Crago* they are on the first pair of legs, and in *Palaemonetes* they are on the second pair. See also CRUSTACEA.

SHRIMP PLANT, a shrubby plant, *Beloperone guttata*, of the acanthus family, native to Mexico. It is cultivated outdoors in the southern United States and is grown as a houseplant farther north. About 2 to 3 feet (60–90 cm) tall, the plant is many branched from the base and has ovate, hairy leaves borne on weak stems. Its white and purple flowers are borne in spikes that are almost hidden beneath showy brick-red, heart-shaped bracts, which bear some resemblance to the shrimp. The plant requires a warm climate with direct sun and a rich, well-drained soil.

SHRIMPFISH, any of a family, Centriscidae, of fishes with compressed knifelike bodies covered by plates of transparent tortoiseshell armor. They are found in shallow waters from East Africa to Hawaii. The undersurface of the shrimpfish's body is very sharp—so sharp that the fish is often called a razorfish in Australia. The shrimpfish generally swims head down, but when disturbed, it turns the sharp edge of its body toward an intruder and swims in the more common horizontal position.

SHRINE, a place of worship and religious pilgrimage that is associated with a miracle or that houses the remains of a holy person or a sacred relic. The catacombs of Rome, in which Christian martyrs were buried, were early shrines. Places in Jerusalem associated with events in the life of Jesus and his death have been regarded as shrines. Appearances of the Virgin Mary have caused the erection of shrines, such as those at Lourdes, France, and Fátima, Portugal. The city of Mecca, in Saudi Arabia, is the great Islamic shrine.

SHRINERS, officially the Ancient Arabic Order of the Nobles of the Mystic Shrine for North America. The shriners are a service organization of North American Masons—a prerequisite to membership—but an order outside of Masonry itself. Though founded in 1872 as a fraternal order, the Shriners turned to philanthropy. They established 17 hospitals for crippled children and sponsored many activities raising money for charities. See also MASONS.

SHRIVER, Sargent (1915–   ), American public official. Robert Sargent Shriver, Jr., was born in Westminster, Md., on Nov. 9, 1915. He received a law degree from Yale University in 1941. After serving in the Navy during World War II, he became an assistant editor of *Newsweek* magazine. Engaged in 1946 by Joseph P. Kennedy to edit the letters of a son, Joseph, Jr., who had been killed during the war, Shriver was later named assistant general manager of the Kennedy-owned Merchandise Mart in Chicago. He married Kennedy's daughter Eunice in 1953 and served as presidential campaign adviser to her brother John F. Kennedy in 1960.

Invited by President Kennedy in 1961 to plan the organization of the Peace Corps, Shriver became its first director. A unique foreign assistance program, the Peace Corps was launched with a small group of trained volunteers who were sent to developing nations to teach and to aid in community development and agricultural projects. Under Shriver's capable leadership from 1961 to 1966, the Peace Corps expanded its program to 46 countries and its membership to 12,000. In 1964 President Lyndon B. Johnson also named Shriver director of the Office of Economic Opportunity, a new agency dedicated to eliminating poverty in the United States. As U. S. ambassador to France (1968–1970), he won friends with a "people-to-people" approach.

In 1972 the Democratic national committee named Shriver to run for vice president with Sen. George McGovern. The convention's choice, Sen. Thomas Eagleton, withdrew from the race after it was revealed that he had received electric shock treatments for depression. McGovern and Shriver lost in a landslide to President Nixon in November. Shriver failed in a bid for the Democratic presidential nomination in 1976.

SHROPSHIRE, shrop'shər, sometimes called *Salop*, is a county in central England, bordering Wales on the west, Cheshire on the north, Staffordshire on the east, Worcestershire on the southeast, and Herefordshire on the south. It is 1,347 square miles (3,489 sq km) in area and is bisected by the Severn River from northwest to southeast. North of the river lies a plain broken by occasional hills, chief of which is Wrekin, an extinct volcano. Ellesmere is the largest lake in this area. South of the Severn the terrain is mountainous. The highest peak is Stiperstones (1,731 feet). Shrewsbury is the county town.

Shropshire is chiefly agricultural, with dairying in the north and stock breeding in the south, home of the famous Shropshire sheep. Industry includes the manufacture of china, bricks, tile, aluminum products, toys, radios, wearing apparel, and carpeting.

The history of Shropshire has been turbulent because of its position next to the mountains of Wales. Stone Age, British, and Roman forts were located here. Shropshire was a part of the kingdom of Mercia. Offa's Dyke, built in the 8th century, as a defense against the Welsh by the Mercians, crosses the county. After the Norman Conquest, Shropshire's 30 or more castles were strongholds against Welsh raids until the passage of the Act of Union of England and Wales in 1536. Population: (1971) 336,934.

RICHARD E. WEBB
Formerly, British Information Services

SHROPSHIRE LAD, shrop'shər, a collection of 63 lyrics by A. E. Housman, first published in 1896. *A Shropshire Lad* is perhaps the most widely circulated volume of English verse since Edward FitzGerald's translation of the *Rubáiyát of Omar Khayyám* in 1859. Housman's themes are traditional: life is brief; nature is beautiful but indifferent; love is fickle.

Tersely stated, in subtle modulations of standard meters and stanza forms, these themes are summed up in a single declaration from the poem numbered 62:

> Therefore, since the world has still
> Much good, but much less good than ill,
> And while the sun and moon endure
> Luck's a chance, but trouble's sure,
> I'd face it as a wise man would,
> And train for ill and not for good.

Death is certain. Our only choice is between dying bravely and dying like a coward. The man who faces the worst possibilities of life may find that he has, like the Mithridates of the poem (probably Mithridates VI of Pontus), inoculated himself against poison. He is prepared to meet trouble when it comes. The wry humor, the preoccupation with disaster and death, the urge to act while there is still time, all build up to the statement of an austere stoicism.

DeLANCEY FERGUSON
Formerly, Brooklyn College

SHROVE TUESDAY, shrōv, is the day before Ash Wednesday, the first day of Lent. Originally, it had a strictly religious meaning as the day on which Christians confessed their sins and were absolved by a priest or in the Old English term, were "shriven." It later took on the character of a festival or carnival before the 40-day period of prayer and fasting known as Lent. Shrovetide, a longer observance, extends from the Sunday through the Tuesday before Ash Wednesday.

SHRUB is a general term applied to small woody plants that are branched from the base. This growth pattern is in contrast on one hand to herbs, which are characteristically softer and die back (that is, die in part, from the top of the plant toward its base) to the ground; and on the other hand to trees, in which there is one main woody stem. However, here as elsewhere, plants do not necessarily fit rigidly into these man-made categories. Some herbs, like certain of the chickweeds, do not die back completely, and others may have varying amounts of woody tissue, as in the cultivated geranium and the castor bean. Trees, such as the Japanese maple, may be branched practically from the base, and the gray birch often sends up numerous stems from old stumps.

Blueberries, huckleberries, blackberries, raspberries, and currants are shrubs of marked economic importance, while mountain laurel, firethorn, Japanese barberry, lilac, hydrangea, and the roses are among the most colorful and attractive ornamental plants. Most shrubs drop their leaves in autumn, but mountain laurel and great laurel (*Rhododendron maximum*) are evergreen. All the plants mentioned above are flowering plants. However, some conifers, like the American yew and certain varieties of the Oriental arborvitae and of the juniper, are also shrubby. Poison sumac, a shrub of moist habitats that has pinnate leaves with entire leaflets and white fruits, causes intense dermatitis. In common parlance, a shrub is a bush, and neither term is very specific.

EDWIN B. MATZKE
Columbia University

SHU CHING, or *Book of History,* one of the Five Classics of China. See also FIVE CLASSICS.

SHUBERT, shōō'bərt, **Lee** (1875–1953), American theatrical producer. He was born in Syracuse, N. Y., on March 15, 1875. As a young man he joined his brothers Sam and Jacob in the management of small theatrical companies, and by 1900 they held the lease of theaters in Syracuse and nearby towns. In the same year they took over the management of the Herald Square Theatre in New York City, where they formed the Shubert Theatrical Company. Before long they took control of the Hippodrome, the Lyric, and many other Broadway theaters.

After Sam died in 1906, Lee became president of the firm, which in the next half century produced over 500 plays and musicals and controlled or owned as many as 61 theaters outside New York. In 1907 the Shuberts joined their foremost rivals, Marc Klaw and Abe Erlanger, to form the United States Amusement Company, but the group was later dissolved. In 1908, Lee became business manager of New Theatre, an abortive attempt to establish a national theater.

Lee resigned the presidency of the Shubert company in 1931, although he retained control. In 1950 the U. S. government instituted proceedings against the company as having a monopoly over the American stage. Lee died in New York City on Dec. 25, 1953, and in 1956 the Shubert organization divested itself of a number of its playhouses.

SHUDRA, shōō'drə, the lowest of the four traditional Hindu social classes, or varnas. The Shudra (Śūdra) varna originally consisted of servants and slaves and apparently included the peoples of the ancient Indus Valley, or Harappan, civilization conquered by the Aryans. The Shudras came to be divided into "clean" and "unclean" occupational groups. Food touched by an "unclean" Shudra could not be used by a "clean" Shudra or a person whose caste had higher than Shudra status.

SHUFFLEBOARD is a game in which flat wooden or composition disks are pushed along a rectangular court by cues whose heads are curved to fit the disks. The objective is to land the disks in numbered areas on the court—preferably in the highest-numbered ones.

Early forms of the game—given such names as slidegroat, shovepenny, shovegroat—date back to 15th century England, and other variations were found in the early American colonies. Around the dawn of the 20th century shuffleboard became a popular shipboard pastime, and still remains so. Shipboard courts are not stan-

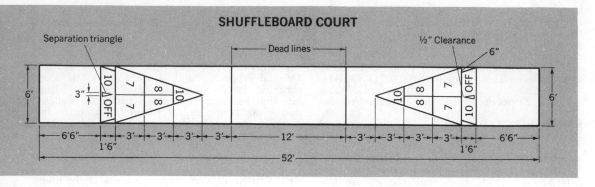

SHUFFLEBOARD COURT

dardized, varying in size with available accommodations, and the roll of a liner prevents the ocean-going variety of the sport from being as precise a one as that played on land.

By the mid-1920's the game as played on land had become, when played seriously, a standardized one with official rules and official competition. The disks, colored red or black, are between ¾ inch and an inch in thickness and 6 inches in diameter; the cues may be no longer than 6 feet 3 inches.

The court, made of concrete or terrazzo, is 52 feet long and 6 feet wide. In this court two large triangles point toward each other, their points being 18 feet apart. Each triangle is 9 feet in altitude, and its base extends across the entire 6-foot width of the court. In the apex of each triangle is a single area marked "10"; in the midsection are two areas marked "8", and in the base two areas marked "7", all areas being 3 feet in altitude. Behind the base of each triangle is another area, 1½ feet in altitude, marked "10 off."

Players must stand behind the baseline at the "10 off" area behind one triangle and aim for the areas in the other one, receiving points for landing their disks in the "10", "8", or "7" areas, and have 10 points deducted for landing in the "10 off" area. Their opponents are permitted to dislodge their disks from scoring areas and—a prime objective—to carom them into the "10 off" area. A game may be for 50, 75, or 100 points. Each player, or team of two players, has four disks of the same color. Opponents slide the disks alternately. Penalties are meted out for landing on certain lines, stepping over the baseline, for interference, and other violations.

Shuffleboard is basically a game of skill and is played by persons of all ages. In the United States two national tournaments are held annually, a summer one in Traverse City, Mich., and a winter one in various Florida cities. Florida may be considered the game's greatest stronghold, and St. Petersburg—favored resort city for those of advancing years—the shuffleboard capital. Its largest club, the Mirror Lake Club, has more than 100 courts, and there are thousands of active players in this city alone. In a nation with an increasing number of older persons, shuffleboard's popularity is on the increase too.

PARKE CUMMINGS
Author of "The Dictionary of Sports"

SHULTZ, George Pratt (1920–   ), American economist and public official. He was born in New York City on Dec. 13, 1920. After graduating in 1942 from Princeton University, where he majored in economics, he saw service in the Pacific area during World War II as an officer in the Marine Corps. Continuing his education after the war, he received a Ph.D. in industrial economics in 1949 from the Massachusetts Institute of Technology and then joined the MIT faculty. In 1955–1956 he took a leave of absence to serve as senior staff economist with President Eisenhower's Council of Economic Advisers. In 1957 he was appointed professor of industrial relations at the University of Chicago Graduate School of Business, and from 1962 to 1968 he served as dean of the school.

Concurrently with his academic duties, Shultz was called upon frequently as a consultant to government agencies and an arbitrator of industrial disputes. He became known as a moderate advocate of a free-market economy, an impartial and pragmatic industrial economist, and an expert labor mediator.

In December 1968, President-elect Nixon chose Shultz to be his secretary of labor, and he served in that post in 1969–1970. In June 1970 the president named him chairman of the new Office of Management and Budget, and on June 12, 1972, he succeeded John B. Connally as secretary of the treasury. A few months later, on Dec. 1, 1972, he was appointed by President Nixon to the additional post of presidential assistant in charge of a new cabinet-level Council on Economic Policy. He thus gained wide experience in handling international economic problems.

In 1974, Shultz left Washington to join the Bechtel Corporation, a large, international engineering and construction company in San Francisco. He became president of the firm in 1975 and was serving in that capacity in February 1981 when President Reagan called upon him to head a new 12-member Economic Policy Advisory Board. On June 25, 1982, President Reagan named him secretary of state to succeed Alexander M. Haig, Jr. He was confirmed by the Senate on July 15, 1982.

SHUSHAN. See SUSA.

SHUTE, shoot, Nevil, pen name of Nevil Shute Norway (1899–1960), English author and aeronautical engineer. He was born in Ealing on Jan. 17, 1899. After military service in France during World War I, he was graduated from Balliol College, Oxford, in 1922 and then became an aeronautical engineer. He assisted in the building of the rigid aircraft R100, on which he flew as chief engineer in a round trip between England and Canada in 1930. Shortly thereafter he founded an aircraft construction company and was its managing director until he resigned in 1938 to devote his entire time to writing. During World War II, Shute was a lieutenant commander and contributed to the development of a number of important weapons. After 1950 he lived in Australia, where he died, in Melbourne, on Jan. 12, 1960.

Beginning with *Marazan* (1926), Shute wrote more than 20 novels. *What Happened to the Corbetts?* (U. S. title *Ordeal,* 1939) foretold what an average British family was soon to suffer from air raids. *Pied Piper* (1942), which had a more favorable critical response than Shute's earlier works, was made into a popular motion picture, as was *On the Beach* (1957). In 1954 his autobiography *Slide Rule* was published. *Trustee from the Toolroom,* his last novel, was published posthumously in 1960.

SHUTTLE, Space. See SPACE SHUTTLE.

SHYLOCK, shī'lok, is a character in Shakespeare's *The Merchant of Venice.* A Jewish usurer, he lends Antonio, a merchant, 3,000 ducats on condition that if he is not repaid in three months, Antonio must surrender a pound of his own flesh. Shylock's purpose is defeated by Portia, Antonio's representative in court, who points out that if Shylock, as a Jew, sheds a drop of Christian blood, his life is forfeit.

Shylock is one of Shakespeare's most complex and perplexing characters. Early stage interpretations presented him as a buffoon; later, he was treated as a vicious and bloodthirsty villain; still later, as a tragic martyr. Perhaps, in a sense, he is a combination of all of these—intensely human, bearing the centuries-long burden of his people—a man who can say in one speech, "I will feed fat the ancient grudge I bear him," and in another, "Hath not a Jew hands, organs, dimensions, senses, affections, passions?" See also MERCHANT OF VENICE.

SI KIANG, she' jē-äng', the longest river in southern China. Si Kiang, or Hsi Chiang, means "West River." The main stream begins at the confluence of the Hungshui and Yü rivers, which rise in Yünnan province and meet at Kweiping in Kwangsi. It flows generally eastward through Kwangsi and empties into the South China Sea in Kwangtung, forming a large delta on the eastern side of which are Canton and Hong Kong.

The Si Kiang has a length of 1,250 miles (2,000 km), including the Hungshui. It is navigable from the sea to Wuchow in low water and to Kweiping in high water.

SI UNITS. See MEASURES AND MEASURING SYSTEMS.

SIAL, sī'al, is one of two major groups of rocks in the earth's crust. The term derives from *si*lica (silicon oxide) and *alu*mina (aluminum oxide), the dominant constituents of sial. The other major group of rocks is called sima, from its dominant minerals *si*lica, *i*ron oxides, and *mag*nesia (magnesium oxide).

Sial includes light rocks such as granites and sediments and has an average specific gravity of 2.7. Such rocks are primary constituents of the continental crust to depths of several miles. Sima includes basalts and still heavier dark rocks with specific gravities of up to 4. Such rocks underlie the ocean floor and are increasingly abundant in the lower portions of the continental crust. Basaltic lavas and volcanoes also occur on the earth's surface.

SIALKOT, si-äl'kōt, is a city in Pakistan, 65 miles (105 km) north of Lahore. It is a rail junction and a trade and manufacturing center. Its chief products are sporting goods, surgical equipment, and military supplies.

Sialkot has been identified with ancient Shakala (Śakala), capital of the Indo-Greek ruler Menander (Milinda) in the 2d century B. C. and of the Ephthalite, or Hun, leader Mihiragula in the 6th century A. D. Population: (1972) 185,000.

SIAM. See THAILAND.

SIAMANG, sē'ə-mang, a gibbon, *Hylobates syndactalus,* or *Symphalangus syndactylus,* found in Sumatra. The largest of the gibbons, it stands about 3 feet (90 cm) tall and has two or three toes partially united by a web. See GIBBON.

SIAMESE CAT, one of the most popular breeds of cat. See CAT–*Breeds.*

SIAMESE FIGHTING FISH, sī-ə-mēz', a small tropical freshwater fish of southeastern Asia. Like its relatives, the climbing perch and gourami of the family Anabantidae, the Siamese fighting fish, *Betta splendens,* has a special accessory breathing apparatus that enables it to live in oxygen-deficient waters that otherwise would be lethal.

In its native habitat, the Siamese fighting fish is a drab, small-finned fish. Years of selective breeding and cultivation have, however, yielded many brightly colored, graceful forms with very long veil-like dorsal, anal, and caudal fins, which have become popular in tropical fish aquaria. Males are also known for their fighting behavior, sometimes displayed in contests in Thailand.

Siamese fighting fish construct bubble nests. The male takes bubbles of air into his mouth, coats them with a sticky secretion, and blows them to the surface of the water to form a nest. After fertilizing the eggs as they are extruded from the female's body, the male blows them to the surface nest, where they hatch in a short time. The male also cares for the young during the brief period they remain in the nest.

Siamese fighting fish (*Betta splendens*)
SHAW, FROM ANNAN PHOTOS

SIAN, shē'än', a city in northern China, is the capital of Shensi province and for many centuries was the capital of all of China. It is situated near the Wei River and is on China's main east-west railroad.

Sian (Xian) has been a major trading and administrative center since ancient times. A modern industrial city, it has cotton mills, a large thermal power plant, and chemical works. Walls dating from the Ming dynasty (1368–1644) enclose a rectangle 2.5 miles (4 km) long by 1.5 miles (2.4 km) wide. There are walled suburbs at each of the four principal city gates.

Sian is the seat of Northwestern University and the Northwestern Institute of Technology. South of the city is the Shensi Provincial Museum, whose large collection of stone tablets includes the celebrated Nestorian monument, which dates from 781.

History. The city, then known as Changan (Ch'ang-an), became the imperial capital under the Western (Earlier) Han dynasty (202 B. C.–9 A. D.). It suffered varying fortunes in succeeding dynasties, but enjoyed prosperity under the T'ang (618–906), when as Siking—the western capital—it was one of two centers of the empire.

The name "Sian," adopted under the Ming dynasty, was replaced by Changan in 1913 and by Siking in 1932, but was restored in 1943. In 1900–1902 the city served as a refuge for the emperor and dowager empress following the Boxer Rebellion. It was here that Chiang Kai-shek was kidnapped in 1936 by the Manchurian military leader Chang Hsueh-liang, leading to Chiang's agreement for a united front with the Communists. Population: (1970 est.) 1,900,000.

SIANGTAN, shē-äng'tän', is a city in China, in Hunan province, on the Siang River, 20 miles (30 km) southwest of Changsha. Its name is also written *Xiangtan.* The city has engineering, textile, and food processing industries. About 30 miles (45 km) to the west is the village of Shaoshan, where Mao Tse-tung was born. Population: (1958 est.) 247,000.

SIBELIUS, si-bā'lē-əs, **Jean** (1865–1957), Finnish composer, who drew on the legacy of German romantic music to create his own individual style, which, untouched by 20th century innovations, became the spiritual voice of Finland's struggle for independence.

Life. Johan Julius Christian Sibelius was born in Hämeenlinna on Dec. 8, 1865. (He later adopted the name "Jean" when he acquired an uncle's calling cards.) His musical education began with piano lessons at the age of nine. By the next year he had written his first composition, and at 15 he began the study of the violin.

In 1886, after a year's study of law at the University of Helsingfors (now Helsinki), he devoted himself to music at the Helsingfors Conservatory (since 1939 the Sibelius Academy). There he studied under Martin Wegelius, who guided the young composer's talent with care, despite the fact that Sibelius was unsympathetic with his teacher's discipleship of Wagner. Following the completion of his work at the conservatory, he studied abroad, first in Berlin (1889) with Albert Becker and then in Vienna (1890) with Robert Fuchs and Karl Goldmark.

On his return to Finland in 1891, Sibelius found his Russian-dominated homeland undergoing a patriotic revival, as the Russian Pan-Slavic movement gained new momentum in Finland. His own patriotic sentiments were said to have infused two major works of 1892: the cantata, *Kullervo* (based on the Finnish epic *Kalevala*), which he never released for publication, and *A Saga,* a tone poem for orchestra, which he revised in 1901. In 1899 he composed the most openly patriotic of his works, the *Song of the Athenians* (for male voices, horn septet, and percussion), and the famous *Finlandia,* which became a symbol of Finnish nationalism.

Soon acclaimed as his country's leading composer, Sibelius was granted in 1897 a yearly pension from the government and in 1904 moved to a country home in Järvenpää, near Helsinki. Except for occasional visits to Europe, to England, and to the United States, where he taught briefly at the New England Conservatory, he remained in his homeland, continuing his creative work throughout the troubled years of World War I. By the end of the 1920's, however, his compositional activity had ebbed: his Seventh Symphony was completed in 1924, and his last published works date from 1929 and 1930. He died in Järvenpää on Sept. 20, 1957.

Music. Sibelius is universally known for his symphonic music, although he also composed many songs, choral works, piano pieces, and incidental works (including the well-known *Valse Triste*), one opera (unpublished), and much chamber music, of which only the string quartet *Voces Intimae* (1909) is widely known. Orchestral compositions include the *Four Legends* (1895; rev. later) made up of *Lemminkäinen and the Maidens, Lemminkäinen in Tuonela, The Swan of Tuonela* (originally composed in 1893), and *Lemminkäinen's Homecoming,* all based on runes of the *Kalevala;* the Violin Concerto (1903; rev. 1905); the symphonic fantasia, *Pohjola's Daughter* (1906); and the seven symphonies. The symphonies' majestic themes, somber orchestral colors, and romantic but conservative harmonies have evoked for generations of listeners the wild, natural scenery of the composer's native land.

Jean Sibelius, Finland's great national composer

CULVER PICTURES

The Yenisei River, in Eastern Siberia, is one of the great waterways flowing northward into the Arctic Ocean.

SIBERIA, sī-bir′ē-ə, in the Russian republic, is the vast Asian part of the Soviet Union, extending from the Ural Mountains to the Pacific Ocean, excluding the Kazakhstan republic and the republics that form Central Asia. Spanning 130 degrees of longitude between the Urals and the Bering Strait, Siberia covers an area of about 5 million square miles (13 million sq km) and had a population of 25.5 million in 1971. It is bounded on the north by the Arctic Ocean, on the west by the Urals, on the south by Kazakhstan, Outer Mongolia, and Manchuria, and on the east by the Pacific Ocean.

The entire Siberian region is best described in terms of its three major parts: Western Siberia, between the Urals and the Yenisei River; Eastern Siberia, between the Yenisei and the Pacific coastal ranges; and the Soviet Far East, along the Pacific coast.

WESTERN SIBERIA

Western Siberia, because it was the first area to be colonized and has the least rigorous climate, is the most populous and most developed section of Siberia.

Physical Features. Western Siberia comprises a great lowland plain extending from the semiarid steppe of Kazakhstan to the icy shores of the Arctic Ocean. It corresponds to the drainage basin of the Ob River, one of the great Siberian streams, rising in the Altai Mountains and flowing through the West Siberian Lowland to the Arctic Ocean. This lowland is one of the largest in the world, occupying an area of about 1 million square miles (2.5 million sq km).

Unlike the rolling Russian plain rising to 1,000 feet (300 meters) on the other side of the Ural Mountains, the West Siberian Lowland is level, without any perceptible elevations. The city of Omsk, 1,000 miles (1,610 km) from the sea, lies at a height of only 270 feet (82 meters) above sea level. The Trans-Siberian Railway traverses the southern part of the lowland.

Situated far from the moderating influence of the Atlantic Ocean, the West Siberian Lowland has a climate of greater continentality than the European USSR, with much colder winters

and a wide temperature range between winter and summer. For example, Tomsk, situated at the same latitude as Moscow, has the same average July temperature as the Soviet capital, but the average January temperature of Tomsk is −4° F (−20° C) compared with 13° F (−10° C) in Moscow. Snow remains on the ground in Tomsk for six months, from October through March, without a thaw.

The topographic uniformity of the West Siberian Lowland is broken only by a sequence of soil and vegetation zones. In the far north, along the shores of the Arctic Ocean, is a narrow tundra zone, with moss and lichen vegetation and waterlogged soils underlain by permanently frozen ground. South of a wooded tundra transition zone is the forest zone of coniferous trees. This zone, known as the taiga, covers about two thirds of the West Siberian Lowland. Vegetation consists chiefly of spruce, larch, fir, and Siberian stone pine, with birch and aspen along the southern margins. In spite of moderate rainfall, poor drainage and low evaporation produce bog conditions over most of the taiga.

The wooded steppe, which adjoins the birch-aspen zone of trees, occupies the southernmost part of Western Siberia. It is the most populous and economically most developed part of Siberia. Fertile black-earth soils favor agriculture, and in spite of the danger of recurrent drought the Soviet regime sponsored a major grain expansion program there in the mid-1950's. The wooded Ishim steppe, the wooded Baraba steppe, the Kulunda steppe, and the Altai foreland steppe are the leading agricultural areas of Western Siberia.

The predominantly low relief of the West Siberian plain is broken only in the southeast, where the Altai Mountains rise on the Soviet-Mongolian border. The Belukha peak, at 15,157 feet (4,620 meters), is the highest point of the Altai. The northern and western slopes of the mountains are covered with dense tree growth, followed by mountain meadows at higher elevations. The southeastern part of the Altai, situated in the rain shadow, is arid. The Altai Mountains give rise to the Ob River and its chief tributary, the Irtysh. Two northern outliers of the Altai enclose the Kuznetsk Basin, one of the leading coal-producing areas of the Soviet Union and the industrial heart of Siberia.

Population and Political Divisions. About 90% of Western Siberia's total population of 12,100,-000 lives in the wooded steppe section. The agricultural segment of the population is made up of Russians and Ukrainians who migrated from European Russia after the 1890's. The native population includes Finnic tribes in the forest and tundra zones and Turkic tribes in the Altai Mountains. The Finnic tribes are the Ostyaks (Khanty), Voguls (Mansi), and Samoyeds (Nentsy). Their principal occupations are hunting, fishing, and the raising of reindeer. The Altaic tribes are hunters and herdsmen.

Politically, Western Siberia is divided into five oblasts and one krai, some of which include autonomous areas based on the indigenous population. The six administrative units are Tyumen, Omsk, Novosibirsk, Tomsk, and Kemerovo oblasts and Altai krai. Tyumen oblast includes the autonomous areas known as the Khanty-Mansi and Yamel-Nenets national okrugs, while Altai krai includes the Gorno-Altai autonomous oblast.

Western Siberia's leading cities, with their 1970 populations, are Novosibirsk (1,161,000), Omsk (821,000), Novokuznetsk (499,000), Barnaul (439,000), Kemerovo (385,000), Tomsk (339,000), and Prokopyevsk (275,000).

Economy. The economy of Western Siberia combines major industrial operations based on local resources (Kuznetsk coal, ores, petroleum, natural gas, and timber) with extensive agriculture in the wooded steppe. The coal and iron ore of the Kuznetsk Basin have given rise to the iron and steel industry of Novokuznetsk, whose

Siberia, long primarily a supplier of raw materials, now has substantial metals industries. Bratsk aluminum plant uses power from huge hydroelectric works nearby.

SOVFOTO

steel output was doubled by construction of the West Siberian Steel Plant in the 1960's. Steel, in turn, supplies the raw material for the machinery centers that have developed in Western Siberia. They are Novosibirsk, Omsk, Tomsk, and Barnaul. Agricultural machinery and mining equipment form a large part of their output. As the Soviet Union's second-largest coal producer, the Kuznetsk Basin mined more than 100 million tons of coal annually in the early 1970's.

Oil and natural gas resources in the Ob River region are in the process of development, and the newly discovered Tyumen fields are the largest in the USSR. A pipeline from the oil field at Surgut to a major oil refinery at Omsk, which previously received crude oil by pipeline from the Volga-Urals fields in Europe, was completed in the 1960's. There are plans for the transmission of natural gas from the sub-Arctic part of Western Siberia to European Russia.

Western Siberia's agriculture specializes in the production of wheat and in dairying. Spring wheat takes up half of the total sown acreage and other grains, including rye and oats, an additional third. The sown share of industrial crops and fodder crops is 10% to 15%. The most important industrial crop, sunflowers, is associated with wheat in the steppe zone. Other crops are fiber flax, potatoes, and sugar beets.

Dairying is the most important branch of animal husbandry. Most of the milk is processed into butter. The greater stress on butter making is due in part to the lack of market for fresh milk and in part to the nature of the local fodder grasses, which tend to raise the butterfat content in the milk. Beef cattle and sheep are raised in more arid steppe sections, as well as in the Altai Mountains. Reindeer herding, hunting, and fishing are the modes of livelihood of the indigenous peoples of the sub-Arctic North.

Transportation. Railroads are found only in the southern part of Western Siberia. In addition to the main line of the Trans-Siberian Railway, there are a number of branch lines connecting Omsk and Tyumen, Tatarsk and Kulunda, and Novosibirsk and Barnaul. The South Siberian Railway, running parallel to and south of the Trans-Siberian, was completed in the early 1950's. The Middle Siberian, between the Trans-Siberian and the South Siberian, was built as a narrow-gauge railroad in the mid-1950's and was converted to broad gauge in the early 1970's. The Ob and Irtysh rivers play a major role as waterways during the ice-free navigation season, lasting about six months.

EASTERN SIBERIA

Eastern Siberia, lying between Western Siberia and the Soviet Far East, is the least populous and most inhospitable section of Siberia.

Physical Features. Eastern Siberia extends about 1,800 miles (2,900 km) from west to east and 1,500 miles (2,400 km) from south to north. In contrast to Western Siberia, Eastern Siberia has a general upland relief in which plateaus and mountains take up more than 75% of the total area. Lowlands are found only along the west bank of the Yenisei River, actually a continuation of the West Siberia Lowland, in the Vilyui River basin, and along the Arctic coast.

Eastern Siberia's climate is far more continental than Western Siberia's, with lower temperatures and precipitation. Frosts of −40° F (−40° C) are common throughout the region.

The Yakutsk region, a forbidding land with rich mineral deposits, is one of the coldest areas in Siberia. Many native Yakuts herd reindeer and hunt furbearing animals.

Over 180 days a year have subfreezing average temperatures.

The southern limit of permafrost, which in Western Siberia lies along the Arctic coast, bends sharply southward on crossing the Yenisei, enclosing virtually all of Eastern Siberia in the zone of permanently frozen subsoil. Both tundra and taiga occupy a far greater share of Eastern Siberia than of Western Siberia. Eastern Siberia has no continuous steppe belt but only isolated patches of wooded or treeless steppe in a few low-lying areas in the south. Eastern Siberia is, therefore, far less important as an agricultural area. On the other hand, the high-quality stands, chiefly larch, play a major role in timber supply.

Eastern Siberia corresponds to the drainage basin of the Yenisei River, one of the great Siberian waterways. It is navigable during the ice-free season of less than six months. All are being increasingly developed for summer navigation in connection with the Arctic sea route. In addition, these rivers offer a massive hydroelectric power potential estimated at 40% of the total Soviet waterpower supply. Development of these rivers began only in the mid-1950's with the construction of two giant hydroelectric stations along the Angara River, a tributary of the Yenisei, at Irkutsk and Bratsk. Construction of a third station on the Angara, at Ust-Ilimsk, was begun in the early 1970's. The first station on the Yenisei, at Krasnoyarsk, went into operation in 1967.

The mineral resources of Eastern Siberia are large and varied. Coal reserves (bituminous and lignitic) are almost twice as large as those of the Kuznetsk Basin. The most important coal reserves, in the far north of the Tunguska and Lena basins, are still inaccessible, but important coalfields are also found along the Trans-Siberian Railway in the south, notably in the Irkutsk-Cheremkhovo area. Ferrous metals include iron and manganese. The iron ore reserves found in Eastern Siberia are the largest between the Urals and the Pacific coast. Large salt deposits occur near Irkutsk and Yakutsk. Eastern Siberia is the leading Soviet region for production of gold and mica. There are also reserves of the base metals

(lead, zinc, and copper), graphite, diamonds, aluminum ore, and other minerals.

Population and Political Divisions. With a total area of 1.6 million square miles (4,125,000 sq km) and a population of 7,500,000 people, Eastern Siberia is the most sparsely settled part of the Soviet Union. Its average population density is five times less than even that of Western Siberia. The farm population is concentrated in the few steppe areas suitable for agriculture. Because of limited agricultural opportunities and the rapid industrialization, urban population greatly exceeds rural.

Russian settlers along the Trans-Siberian Railway have driven a wedge between the indigenous peoples. Unlike Western Siberia, the region has few Ukrainians. The indigenous peoples are found in greater numbers than in Western Siberia. Most numerous are the Buryats, a Mongol people, numbering about 250,000 and constituting an autonomous republic. South of the railroad are the Khakass and Tuvinians, both Turkic groups. In the northern forest zone are the Finnic Samoyeds and the Tungus.

Politically, Eastern Siberia falls into six major divisions. These are Krasnoyarsk krai, with the Khakass autonomous oblast and the Taimyr and Evenki national okrugs; the Tuva autonomous republic; Irkutsk oblast, with a Buryat national okrug; the Buryat autonomous republic; and Chita oblast, with another Buryat national okrug. The major cities, with their 1970 populations, are Krasnoyarsk (648,000), Irkutsk (451,000), Chita (242,000), Ulan-Ude (254,000), Angarsk (204,000), Bratsk (155,000), Norilsk (136,000), and Cheremkhovo (109,000).

Economy. The industrial development of Eastern Siberia, planned by the Soviet authorities in the 1930's, started to materialize only 20 years later. Industrialization of the region was contingent on the construction of major hydroelectric stations, whose power output was to be used for the exploitation of local resources. Construction of major stations at Irkutsk, Bratsk, and Krasnoyarsk provided the large amounts of low-cost electricity needed for the reduction of aluminum metal, and Eastern Siberia thus became the Soviet Union's leading aluminum producer. The region also supplies gold, nickel, tin, tungsten, lithium, beryllium, and other metals.

In agriculture, the sown area has been expanded to some extent, but far from the scale achieved in Western Siberia. Crops are restricted to the southern steppes in Krasnoyarsk krai and Irkutsk oblast. Grain (wheat and oats) is the leading crop. Animal husbandry increases in importance toward the east, particularly among the indigenous herding peoples (Khakass, Tuvinians, and Buryats). Reindeer raising, hunting, fishing, and sealing are major occupations in the forest zone and along the Arctic coast.

Transportation. The Trans-Siberian Railway is the backbone of the transportation system of the south, where population and economic activity are concentrated. Branches join Achinsk and Abakan, Krasnoyarsk and Yeniseisk. A major development in connection with the proposed industrial construction was the building of the Taishet-Ust-Kut railroad, completed in 1954. This line joins the Trans-Siberian at Taishet with the head of Lena River navigation at Ust-Kut, serving the hydroelectric city of Bratsk on its way. Another major branch leaves the Trans-Siberian at Ulan-Ude and (since 1955) leads through Outer Mongolia to China. This Soviet-Chinese railroad link is about 720 miles (1,160 km) shorter than the former route through Manchuria. Truck highways lead north into the forest zone from the Trans-Siberian line.

SOVIET FAR EAST

The Soviet Far East is characterized by the juxtaposition of mountains and sea, an abundance of natural resources, as yet largely undeveloped, and great remoteness from the economic and population centers of the rest of the USSR.

Physical Features. The Soviet Far East extends along the coast of the Pacific Ocean between Korea and the Bering Strait for a straight-line distance of 2,500 miles (4,000 km). This vast territory, covering an area of 2.4 million square miles (6.2 million sq km), is deeply indented by a number of arms of the Pacific Ocean, including the Bering Sea, the Sea of Okhotsk, and the Sea of Japan. The relief is mountainous, with ranges extending parallel to the coast.

Because of the great latitudinal extent of the region and the deep penetration of arms of the sea, it comprises a number of subregions of varying geographic characteristics. These subregions are the Maritime area, the Amur area, the Okhotsk littoral, the Kamchatka Peninsula, the Chukchi Peninsula, Sakhalin island, and the Lena River basin, corresponding to the Yakut autonomous republic. The Maritime and Amur areas, in the south, are the most populous and economically most developed subregions, connected with the rest of the Soviet Union by the Amur River and the Trans-Siberian Railway. The other areas are largely undeveloped, depending on sea routes for their links with the "mainland."

Most of the Soviet Far East lies in the monsoon climate zone. The winter monsoon, originating in Eastern Siberia, brings cold dry air. The summer monsoon, coming from the sea, brings moist air. Only the Chukchi Peninsula, in the far north, has a typical Arctic climate, influenced by the nearness of the Arctic Ocean and the cold Kamchatka ocean current. The tundra zone there occupies a wider belt than anywhere else in the USSR. North of the mouth of the Amur River, the growing season is less than three months. Because of the raw climate and the mountainous relief, normal agriculture is possible only in a few lowlands in the south, including the Zeya-Bureya plain along tributaries of the Amur and the Khanka Lake plain.

Except for the northern tundra, almost the entire Soviet Far East is forested. Eastern Siberian conifers (Daurian larch, Yeddo spruce, and Japanese stone pine) dominate in the north. In the south are broadleaf forests, the so-called Ussuri taiga, with the Amur linden, elm, ash, Manchurian walnut, and Korean pine. These forests harbor a multitude of fur-bearing animals, such as squirrels, sables, and foxes, which supply one of the major export products of the region. Fisheries, chiefly salmon, and the hunting of whales and seals are also important industries. Among mineral resources are coal, developed mainly in the Bureya Basin and near Vladivostok, oil (Sakhalin), tin and other rare metals (near Tetyukhe), and gold (Kolyma).

Population and Political Divisions. Native peoples, mainly small Siberian tribes, make up only 3% of the total population. Settlement of the region by Russians and Ukrainians is continuing, with more than 90% of the population concentrated in the south along the railroad and the Amur and Ussuri rivers. The region had 5,900,000 inhabitants in 1971. The urban population exceeds the rural, since a large share of the migrants go to the cities as industrial workers.

Politically, the Soviet Far East falls into the following divisions: Khabarovsk krai, which includes the so-called Jewish autonomous oblast (Birobidzhan); Maritime krai; Amur oblast; Sakhalin oblast; Kamchatka oblast; Magadan oblast; and the Yakut autonomous republic, which is based on the Yakuts, a Turkic people numbering about 250,000. The Chukchi and Koryak tribes are the only Siberian ethnic groups constituted in national okrugs. The Chukchi national okrug is part of Magadan oblast, and the Koryak national okrug part of Kamchatka oblast.

The chief cities are situated along the Trans-Siberian Railway and the main rivers, the Amur and the Ussuri. The major cities, with their 1970 populations, are Vladivostok (442,000), Khabarovsk (437,000), Komsomolsk (218,000), Petropavlovsk (173,000), Ussuriisk (formerly Voroshilov, 128,000), Blagoveshchensk (128,000), Yakutsk (108,000), Yuzhno-Sakhalinsk (106,000), and Nakhodka (105,000).

Economy. Because of its great distance from the heart of the Soviet Union, the Far East is more self-contained than other parts of the country. Much of the output of mining and manufacturing industries goes for local needs. Furs, gold, fish, and nonferrous metals are the key export items. The Mirny district of Yakutia is the Soviet Union's principal diamond producer. Agriculture, which is intended to meet local consumption, combines such typical Russian crops as wheat, oats, and rye with such Far Eastern crops as rice, soybeans, and kaoliang.

HISTORY

Siberia's earliest settlement and history were largely influenced by the region's natural vegetation zones. Indigenous Siberian tribes occupied the forest zone, while warlike Central Asian horsemen roamed the steppes. Southern Siberia came under the sway of Genghis Khan and his successors in the 13th century. The Golden

The streets of Norilsk are covered with ice and snow during May. Fur hats and coats are needed until June in this city north of the Arctic Circle.

Horde, one of the successors of the Mongol empire, controlled Western Siberia, while the Yuan dynasty of China under Kublai Khan laid a loose claim to Eastern Siberia and the Far East.

Russian Conquest and Settlement. The first Russian penetration of Siberia occurred in the 12th century, when Novgorod merchants crossed the northern Urals and traded with the Finnic tribes of the Ob River country. But it was not until the 16th century that the Russians began to move into Siberia in force. A small Cossack band under Yermak (or Ermak) Timofeyev crossed the middle Urals in 1581–1582 and conquered the Tatar khanate of Sibir, one of the remnants of the Golden Horde. Sibir (or Isker), near the site of modern Tobolsk, gave its name to the entire region.

Yermak's conquests were rapidly extended by private adventurers. Taking advantage of a net work of east-west tributary rivers and short portages, they advanced with surprising speed through the forest zone, establishing contacts and trading furs with the indigenous tribes. These enterprising Russian bands built wooden forts that have since become cities. They reached Tomsk in 1604, Krasnoyarsk in 1628, and Irkursk in 1652. The advance in the north began later, but, once started, progress there was even more rapid than in the south. Yakutsk was founded in 1632, and the shore of the Pacific was reached in 1640 on the Sea of Okhotsk. In half a century the entire Siberian forest domain of fur-trading tribes had been opened up by the Russians. Only in the south was the Russian advance slowed by the Mongol and Turkic nomad herders of the steppe and by China's outposts on the Amur River. After continued Cossack inroads along the Amur had been increasingly opposed by the Chinese, the Treaty of Nerchinsk (1689) fixed the border between the two empires, leaving the Amur lands to China.

During the 18th century, the Russians extended their Siberian holdings into the steppe, notably in the upper reaches of the Ob and Irtysh rivers. At the same time, they began the practice of exiling convicts to the newly acquired inhospitable land. However, it was only after the Decembrist Revolution of 1825 that the exile practice gained momentum. Major places of exile were Nerchinsk and Sretensk in the Chita area, Yakutsk and Vilyuisk, Krasnoyarsk, and Turukhansk. In 1858–1860 the Russians acquired the Amur lands from China.

The modern development and settlement of Siberia began only with the construction of the Trans-Siberian Railway. Work on that great enterprise started in 1891 and was completed through Manchuria in 1903. An all-Russian route was finished only in 1917. The construction of the railroad in Western Siberia spurred the migration of settlers from European Russia. Between 1890 and 1910 hundreds of thousands of peasants established themselves each year in the newly opened lands.

Since the Revolution. The Bolshevik Revolution in 1917 brought an era of confusion to Siberia. In 1918 the Trans-Siberian Railway was captured by Czechoslovak prisoners of war who sought to leave Russia via the Pacific. The Czechoslovaks suppressed early Bolshevik revolutionary centers along the railroad. At the same time a counterrevolutionary government at Omsk came under the control of Adm. Aleksandr V. Kolchak. Interventionist forces of Japan, Britain, France, and the United States landed at Vladivostok. In October 1919 the Red Army began an offensive against Kolchak's forces east of the Urals and in the course of 1920 gained control of Siberia east of Lake Baikal. By 1922 virtually the entire Siberian mainland was under Soviet control. Kamchatka followed in 1923 and northern Sakhalin in 1925. A pro-Bolshevik Far Eastern Republic, set up in 1920, joined the Russian republic in 1922.

When the Soviet regime launched its first five-year plan in 1928, Siberia, like the rest of the country, became the scene of intensive industrial construction. Development was centered in particular in the Kuznetsk Basin. Economic growth was spurred during World War II when many industrial enterprises were evacuated to Siberia from war-threatened areas and helped support the Soviet war effort. Siberia's territory was expanded in 1944 with the annexation of Tuva, which had had independent status since 1921. In 1945, southern Sakhalin and the Kuril Islands were acquired from Japan.

After the war, industrialization proceeded apace, with special attention to the development of the region around Lake Baikal. There the construction of giant hydroelectric stations in the 1950's and 1960's resulted in the growth of industries (for example, aluminum) requiring large amounts of electric power. In the vast West Siberian plain, the discovery of rich oil and natural gas deposits gave rise in the 1970's to a network of pipelines serving the industrial districts of southern Siberia and European Russia.

THEODORE SHABAD
Editor of "Soviet Geography"

Bibliography

Conolly, Violet, *Beyond the Urals: Economic Developments in Soviet Asia* (Oxford 1967).
Davies, Raymond A., and Steiger, A. J., *Soviet Asia* (Dial 1942).
Hooson, David J. M., *New Soviet Heartland* (Van Nostrand-Reinhold 1964).
Lessner, Erwin, *Cradle of Conquerors* (Doubleday 1955).
Mowat, Farley, *Siberians* (Little 1971).
Shabad, Theodore, *Basic Industrial Resources of the USSR* (Columbia Univ. Press 1969).
Shabad, Theodore, *Geography of the USSR* (Columbia Univ. Press 1951).
Thiel, Eich, *The Soviet Far East* (Praeger 1957).
Treadgold, Donald W., *The Great Siberian Migration* (Princeton Univ. Press 1957).

SIBERIAN HUSKY, a spitz-type sled dog. See HUSKY.

SIBYL, sib'əl, was the name given by the Greeks and Romans to a prophetess inspired by a god, usually Apollo. She was often associated with some shrine or temple, as at Delphi, where the sibyl, while in a trance, uttered prophetic sayings in unintelligible riddles. These utterances were translated by attendant priests, who might also write out the prophecies in Greek hexameter verse.

By the 4th century B. C., several such sibyls lived in various parts of the ancient world, and included the Cimmerian, Cumaean, Delphian, Erythraean, Libyan, Persian, Phrygian, Samian, Tiburtine, and Trojan (or Hellespontine) sibyls. Of these, the most famous was the Cumaean sibyl, who, according to legend, conducted Aeneas on his visit to the lower world and sold the Sibylline Books to Tarquinius Superbus, King of Rome. She lived in a cave in Mount Cuma near Cumae, a Greek colony in southern Italy. The sibyl's caves and the underground cavern still exist. Speaking tubes cut through the rock and skillfully arranged sounding boards made it seem that the prophetic voice came from the center of the earth and spoke from every side, just as Vergil describes it in the *Aeneid*. See also SIBYLLINE BOOKS.

SIBYLLINE BOOKS, sib'ə-lin, the three books of prophecies concerning Rome that the sibyl of Cumae sold to Lucius Tarquinius Superbus, the last king of Rome, in the late 6th century B. C. The legend is that the sibyl first offered nine books to Tarquin at a price so high that he refused to buy them. She then burned three of the books and offered the remaining six at the same price. Again Tarquin refused, whereupon the sibyl burned three more. Tarquin bought the last three books at the original price for the nine.

The books were placed in the care of a commission that consulted them in times of public danger. The books were kept in the temple of Jupiter on the Capitoline Hill, but were lost in the fire that destroyed the temple in 83 B. C. A new collection of sibylline verses was made and was apparently in existence until about 400 A. D.

SIBYLLINE ORACLES, sib'ə-lin, a collection of spurious prophecies attributed to the sibyl. They were composed in Greek hexameter verse between the 1st century B. C. and the 2d century A. D. Some portions were actually fragments of ancient oracles, but for the most part they were the work of learned Jews of Alexandria. Later Christian interpolations included prophecies concerning the Messiah and elements of Christian doctrine.

Many of the events prophesied had already taken place and thus lent credibility to prophecies about the future. The Jewish historian Josephus alludes to them favorably as do some early Christian writers such as Clement of Alexandria. The 13th century hymn *Dies Irae*, which was formerly used as the sequence in the Roman Catholic Mass for the dead, mentions the prophecies of the sibyl about the destruction of the earth by fire. The oracles were collected in some 14 books, 12 of which are extant.

SICILIAN VESPERS, si-sil'yən ves'pərz, a revolt of the Sicilians that began on March 30, 1282, and led to the expulsion of the Angevin ruler of Sicily, Charles I, and his replacement by Peter III of Aragón.

Restive under Angevin rule, the Sicilians were ripe for rebellion when a French soldier insulted a Sicilian woman in front of a church in Palermo at the hour of vespers. Riot led to revolution, and Peter, who laid claim to Charles' throne through his wife, invaded the island and accepted the crown. Though Sicilian grievances against the Angevin French were genuine, the rapidity with which the revolts spread was partially due to the careful planning of the Byzantine emperor Michael VIII Palaeologus, whose control of his eastern empire was threatened by Charles. The revolts forced Charles to abandon plans for conquering Constantinople and ultimately led to Aragonese control of Sicily, with the Angevins confined to southern Italy.

SICILIES, Kingdom of the Two, sis'ə-lēz, a former political and sovereign state of Italy consisting of the southern part of the Italian peninsula and the island of Sicily. After the fall of the Roman Empire, the area was occupied in whole or in part by the Ostrogoths, then the Byzantines, and then the Arabs. With the Norman conquest of the area, the pope in 1130 conferred on the Norman Roger II the title of King of Apulia, Calabria, and Sicily. This united kingdom lasted until 1282. In 1302 the Angevin heirs to the crown were confined to southern Italy, and the Aragonese occupied Sicily.

In 1442, Alfonso V of Aragón captured Naples from the Angevins and reunited the two kingdoms under his rule as Alfonso I of the Two Sicilies. The united kingdom was split again on his death. In 1504, Sicily was united with Naples under the Spanish crown and governed by viceroys.

The Peace of Utrecht (1713) gave Naples to Austria, and Sicily to Savoy. Spain recaptured Sicily in 1718, ceded it to Austria in 1720, then recaptured both Naples and Sicily in 1734. In 1759 the Spanish Bourbons established their rule there as a power independent of the Spanish crown. They retained control, except for a brief period during the Napoleonic era, until they were driven out of Sicily in 1860 and out of Naples in 1861. By popular vote the former kingdom became an integral part of Italy.

SICILY, sis′ə-lē, one of the 20 regions of Italy, is the largest and most populous island in the Mediterranean Sea. The Italian form of the name is *Sicilia.* The island has an area of 9,831 square miles (25,462 sq km) and a population of almost 5 million. At the Strait of Messina, Sicily is only about 2 miles (3 km) from the "toe" of the Italian mainland, and on the southwest it is about 90 miles (145 km) from Cape Bon in Tunisia.

In an effort to undercut separatist agitation, the Italian government granted regional autonomy to Sicily in May 1946. Palermo, the island's largest city, is the capital. Under the jurisdiction of Sicily are several adjacent isles and archipelagos: the Egadi Islands to the west, Ustica and the Lipari Islands to the north, the Pelagie Islands to the south, and Pantelleria to the southwest.

Sicily is made up of nine provinces: Agrigento, Caltanissetta, Catania, Enna, Messina, Palermo, Ragusa, Siracusa (Syracuse), and Trapani. The capitals of these provinces carry similar names and are among the island's principal population centers. Other cities of note include Augusta in the east, fast becoming one of Italy's busiest seaports, and Marsala in the west, a center of wine production.

Sicily's strategic location astride the sea-lanes of the Mediterranean, midway between Africa and Italy, has caused the island to be invaded time after time. Its cultural heritage is consequently one of the most complex in Europe. Written in stone in temples, theaters, cathedrals, and mosaics, this record is a source of continuing amazement and delight to visitors and residents alike.

Long the poor man of Italy, Sicily conjures up in the foreign mind an island of long hot summers that raise tempers to the breaking point; the home of the Mafia; a stronghold of male chauvinism and religious ceremonialism; a culture alien even to other Italians with its strains of Norman, Arabic, Greek, African, and other peoples; and a region almost as barren as a desert. Though this picture may be essentially true, these qualities are not so negative as they might seem. They must be construed in terms of the area's past, present, and even the future.

As a result of the discovery of oil and gas in the 1950's and the efforts of imaginative entrepreneurs, many of the island's traditional handicaps have been overcome. More economic progress has taken place since the 1950's than in all the previous centuries.

The People. Ethnically the island's people are a mixture of many elements—native Sicilians, Greeks, Carthaginians, Romans, Vandals, Ostrogoths, Arabs, Berbers, Normans, Spaniards, northern Italians, and others. Predominantly of the Mediterranean physical type, Sicilians are usually shorter than the people of northern Europe. Most have broad heads, olive complexion, dark hair and eyes, and in middle age they tend toward corpulence.

Sicilians share many of the traits common to Italians in general: a strong feeling of family loyalty; a tendency toward gregariousness; a sense of warm practical humanitarianism and a dislike for militarism; a love of music; a penchant for emotional display and "cutting a fine figure"; an inclination toward apathetic resignation rather than philosophical speculation about ultimate values; an attitude of skepticism; frequent selfishness and arrogance on the part of those in authority; and a vocal contempt for authority on the part of some others, though this often changes to deference and even servility in the presence of the authorities themselves. Long ruled by foreigners, Sicilians are more suspicious of outsiders than are northerners, and they have an inadequately developed sense of obligation to the state. This trait helps to explain their frequent "conspiracy of silence" (*omertà*) that is so vexing to officials investigating crime. Tax evasion is twice as bad in Sicily as in Piedmont in northwestern Italy. Quick-tempered and passionate, Sicilians insist on confining young, unmarried girls to very restricted lives.

The vast majority are Roman Catholics, but in Palermo and nearby Piano degli Albanesi there are a few thousand Uniates of the Byzantine rite, a breakaway sect from the Greek Orthodox Church and in communion with Rome. Religious traditions play a vital part in peasant life especially, though it is hard to distinguish between the influence of Christian beliefs and even older religious and social pressures. Many superstitions persist, including that of the "evil eye." All these patterns of behavior, however, are undergoing change in the face of increased education, industrialization, and social mobility.

The standard Italian language is understood by everyone, though regional dialects are often preferred for intimate conversation. In a few scattered pockets Albanian and Greek dialects are spoken.

In large cities most Sicilians live in apartments, and only the very rich can afford villas. Despite much construction since World War II,

SEM PRESSER, FROM BLACK STAR

Characteristic of the mountain villages of Sicily is this town of Montelepre, just outside Palermo.

serious housing shortages persist. Buildings are made almost entirely of masonry or cement. Many villages are built on hilltops, partly to escape the malaria that used to be prevalent in the lowlands. Living standards in inland towns often remain primitive. In rural areas it is not unusual for an entire family to live in a one- or two-room house, with occasionally a precious donkey sharing part of the abode. The colorfully painted carts drawn by feather-tufted horses of past centuries are fast disappearing.

The Sicilian diet tends to be starchier than that of northern Italy. The main meal, eaten after 1 P. M., usually begins with pasta, though poor people often must content themselves with thick soup. Pizza is popular, and bread is a staple. Olive oil is used for cooking and salads. Vegetables and fresh fruit form an important part of the diet. Relatively small amounts of meat and dairy products are consumed. In summer, frozen desserts are delicacies. Wine usually accompanies the meal. There is almost no drunkenness.

Stores and offices are generally open between 9 A. M. and 1 P. M., reopening late in the afternoon and closing by 8 P. M. The evening stroll (*passeggiata*) before supper is an enduring ritual. Vast crowds watch the professional football (soccer) games. Motion pictures and television are other popular forms of mass entertainment. Puppet shows still take place at festivals.

Education follows the lines of national practice, but the regional government has complete control over primary education. There is a shortage of schools, and the rate of illiteracy is double that of Italy as a whole. Universities are located in Palermo, Messina, and Catania, but more are needed. Provision is slowly being made for technical education.

Social services are organized like those on the mainland, but the standard of services is poor. A shortage of medical services persists.

Population. The 1969 estimate showed a population of 4,876,600, making Sicily the third most populous region of Italy and one of the most densely inhabited. Compared to northern Italy, Sicily has high birth and infant mortality rates, and these are especially high in the mining province of Caltanissetta. The chief characteristic of the distribution of population is the universal tendency to live in close-packed towns, often little better than rural slums, making it necessary for residents to travel many miles to work in the fields. There are three cities with populations in excess of 250,000: Palermo, Catania, and Messina.

In 1871, soon after the unification of Italy, Sicily's population was 2,584,000. It increased to 3,529,799 by 1901. In the next 20 years the population was relatively stationary because of heavy emigration overseas. The United States, Brazil, and Argentina were the major destinations, and Tunisia also received considerable numbers. After World War I, emigration was confined mostly to other European countries.

The economic resurgence of Europe that began in the 1950's caused a new wave of Sicilian emigrants—particularly unmarried men from the small towns—to seek jobs in industrial cities of the Po Valley, Germany, Switzerland, and elsewhere. Half a million have departed in this manner.

Many of Sicily's best scholars, artists, and administrators have also preferred to move north.

Such writers as Giuseppe Tomasi di Lampedusa, author of *The Leopard*, who remained in Sicily seemed eccentric in their unconcern for worldly success. Nor was there any compensating movement in reverse. University teachers from the mainland who received appointments in Sicily often commuted to work by air.

Mafia. Partially suppressed during the Fascist period, the Mafia enjoyed a restoration of power during the Anglo-American invasion of Sicily in 1943. When Allied military government officials were filling thousands of jobs vacated by Fascists, they often relied on local men who were part of the kinship networks. There had, of course, long been close ties between gangsters in America and in Sicily. Don Calogero Vizzini of Villalba, the best-known of the surviving Mafia leaders, who had been jailed by Mussolini, was immediately appointed to a position of trust. Until his death in 1954 he and his associates invoked all the old practices of clientage, banditry, terrorism, and *omertà* to build up enormous power.

As before, the center of the *mafiosi* was western Sicily, Trapani being considered the "capital." Soon the network spread into Palermo and the east. *Latifondisti* ("large estate owners") in the interior instinctively fell back on Mafia protection when peasants sought to seize parts of their estates in the postwar era. The Sicilian separatist movement of 1943–1945 and the subsequent establishment of regional autonomy opened up other possibilities for the *mafiosi*. In and around Palermo the Mafia fought all attempts to bring about industrialization, fearing that factory workers would be too concentrated, educated, and self-confident to be tractable. The result was that industrialists avoided Palermo. The worst phase of trouble in that city began in 1956, when open warfare broke out between a number of gangs for control of the food markets. Land speculation in the suburbs was another area of combat. Still later the drug traffic became important.

In 1962 the central and regional governments launched parliamentary investigations of the Mafia. Individuals like Danilo Dolci showed by practical example that the Mafia could be successfully resisted if ordinary men would cooperate against it.

The Land. Sicily's triangular shape gave it in ancient times the name Trinacria or Triquetra. Forming the three corners are Cape Faro (Peloro) in the northeast, Cape Passero in the southeast, and Cape Boeo (Lilibeo) in the west. The island is a detached part of the Italian Apennine and North African Atlas mountain ranges. The main chain runs from Cape Faro westward across two thirds of the island parallel with the north coast. Though seldom exceeding 5,000 feet (1,525 meters), the range sharply separates the interior from the northern shore. Mount Etna, the island's highest peak (about 10,700 feet, or 3,260 meters), and Stromboli and Vulcano offshore to the northeast are active volcanoes.

Except for the fertile plain along the eastern coast to the south of Catania and the beautiful Conca d'Oro near Palermo, most of Sicily's coastline consists of steep cliffs. Two thirds of the island is over 1,000 feet (300 meters) above sea level.

A depression from Termini Imerese on the Tyrrhenian Sea to Agrigento in the south sepa-

With only an autumn and winter rainy season, Sicily has depended on irrigation since the period of Arab rule.

rates western Sicily from the east. Much of the former zone is a high limestone plateau sown in wheat and other cereals. East of the depression stands the sulfur plateau. To the southeast are the low Iblei Mountains.

Sicily has several rivers but, except for the autumn and winter rainy season, most of them are dry. The situation caused by Sicily's severe lack of water is aggravated by deforestation and failure to systematize mountain torrents.

The climate is mild, even in winter. At the eastern coast resort of Taormina the average winter temperature is 55° F (13°C). Frost and snow are rare at low elevations, but the top of Etna remains blanketed in snow through June. Though summers are really not much hotter than in southern Italy or the Po Valley, a peculiarity of the Sicilian climate is the enervating sirocco, a hot, dry, often dust-laden wind that occasionally blows from Africa.

Man's influence has greatly changed the island's vegetation. Natural woodlands survive chiefly on the northern slopes and on Etna. Oaks, chestnuts, olive trees, and dwarf scrub (*macchia*) are typical. Animal life is not plentiful and resembles that of southern Italy and Sardinia.

The mountainous character of Sicily made railway construction very costly, but this challenge was successfully met after Italy's annexation of the island in 1860. During the Fascist era a network of highways was built, but many interior villages continued to be almost inaccessible. After World War II the road system was improved by the construction of a number of superhighways (*autostrade*).

Communications by water have always been important. Steamers ply daily between Naples and Palermo, and there is good service to Messina and Catania. Train and auto ferries link Messina to the mainland. In the early 1970's plans were being made for construction of a giant suspension bridge, capable of accommodating both trains and motor vehicles, across the Strait of Messina.

Places of Interest. For variety of architectural styles Palermo is probably the most exciting city, with palaces and churches belonging to the Arab-Norman, Renaissance, and baroque eras. Agrigento, in the south, is justly famed for its Doric monuments strung along the Valley of the Temples, a sight equaled only in Greece. Syracuse, on the east coast, has fine Greek theaters, temples, and statues. Segesta, in western Sicily, is the site of a superb unfinished Greek temple. Near the inland town of Piazza Armerina is the remarkable Villa Imperiale, dating from Diocletian's reign. And for natural beauty the resort of Taormina, with its Mt. Etna, is a favorite.

Agriculture. Despite the urban character of Sicily's population and impressive expansion of industry in postwar years, agriculture continued to be the foundation of the island's economy. About half of the working force is engaged in agriculture, but many of them are underemployed.

Production of wheat and grapes in Sicily dates from antiquity. Under Arab rule, irrigation was begun, and rice, cotton, sugarcane, citrus fruits, and saffron were introduced. But water shortages continue to bedevil Sicilian farmers despite efforts to build flood-control projects.

Producer of 10% of Italy's wheat and a third of the rye, Sicily has a higher proportion of arable land sown in these grains than any other region in the nation. Yet it ranks next to the lowest in productivity per acre because of climatic conditions and backward farming methods. Grain traditionally has been grown on the *latifondi*—large, extensively cultivated estates. These are often owned by absentee landlords and run on capitalistic lines by middlemen employing a few workers by the year (*salariati*) and large numbers of badly paid day-laborers (*braccianti*). Since World War II some of these lands, usually the poorest, have been expropriated by the government and redistributed to the peasants, but the task has proved difficult. To replace the *latifondi*, cooperatives are needed. These are hard to organize, especially in the west where the Mafia virtually has a veto.

The Temple of Concord, Agrigento, Sicily. Sicily has some of the most impressive Greek remains in existence, and this is one of the best preserved.

Nevertheless, some agricultural improvements have occurred. Although the area sown to wheat has declined, cereals continue to take up over half the arable land. Agricultural experts are encouraging farmers to shift to crops like grapes and tomatoes that require more intensive cultivation. As a result, the value of wine production had caught up with that of cereals by the early 1960's, while the amount of tomatoes grown more than tripled prewar figures. There was a twofold increase in the potato crop and a fivefold increase in artichokes. Sicily's lemon and orange harvest exceeds that of any other region in Italy but lags behind both Spain and Israel. One eighth of Italy's olive oil comes from Sicily. Flax is widely cultivated, and cotton has become increasingly important.

The island's coastal waters teem with fish, especially tuna. About one fourth of Italy's fishing boats sail from Sicilian ports.

Though the number of livestock has more than doubled since 1930, the figure (about 300,-000) remains low. The supply of fodder is poor, permanent meadows are scarce, and much of the pasture is suitable only for sheep or goats.

Industry. Prior to World War II, Sicily's industries were limited chiefly to sulfur mining and fruit processing. The Fascist regime tended to ignore the problem of industrial development. In any case, without coal or cheap electricity not much could be done. Thus at war's end Sicily had only 1.3% of Italy's industry, though it had 10% of the population.

The economic situation changed dramatically after World War II and especially after 1957, though northern Italy expanded at an even faster rate. The national government sponsored imaginative economic investment programs through such agencies as the *Cassa per il Mezzogiorno* (Fund for the South), subsidized the electric-power industry, and encouraged the hanging of high-voltage cables across the Strait of Messina.

The establishment of a regional parliament for Sicily in 1946 was also helpful in that legislation was enacted giving tax advantages to outside capital. Within 15 years the number of corporations on the island had risen from 218 to 1,576.

In the 19th century Sicily produced 90% of the world supply of sulfur. In the immediate postwar era it was hoped that the sulfur industry would again play an important part in the development of Sicily's economy. But in the decades that followed, it became apparent that this ailing industry with its deep mines and archaic methods could not compete with Canada and the United States.

The discovery of oil was the most startling event in postwar Sicily. Rejecting the antiforeign policies of the Fascist era, the regional government sensibly encouraged foreign companies to drill. In 1953 oil was struck near Ragusa. Soon after, another field was discovered in the sea off Gela. The first refinery was built at Augusta, later to be linked by pipeline to Ragusa. Alongside were built a thermoelectric plant, cement works, and factories for producing fertilizers, plastics, and other petrochemicals. In the decade after the discovery of oil, the tonnage handled in Sicilian ports increased sixfold. The port of Augusta had pushed ahead of Venice and Naples by 1964.

The discovery of methane gas made possible the development of Enna, one of the poorest of the provinces. By 1963 this was in quantity production, and pipelines were laid to the coast. Bronte was the site of a second find.

Thus Sicily came to possess the cheap energy that could facilitate greater industrialization. The new Sicily of industry was a phenomenon primarily of the eastern coast. The lack of industrialization in Palermo and the west, where the *mafiosi* remained troublesome, was one major qualification to Sicily's postwar success story. A second qualification was that the number of jobs lost in the decline of traditional industries was not fully offset by the new plants. Unemployment actually increased and would have been greater except for the migration of young men to the labor markets of the Po Valley and Europe. Despite Sicily's economic progress, the gap between it and the booming north grew greater.

CHARLES F. DELZELL
Vanderbilt University

History. The first people of historical record in Sicily were the Sicans (Sicani), who inhabited the island 11 centuries before Christ. The Sicans were driven out by the Sicels (Siculi), who gave the island its name.

Phoenician, Greek, Carthaginian, and Roman Occupation. Sicily was already a part of the Mycenean civilization of Crete before the arrival of the Phoenicians. Because of its geographical position and the fertility of its soil, the island attracted many navigators, including the Phoenicians. The Greeks founded Messina about 724 B.C. Some Corinthian Greeks had earlier built Syracuse farther south on the eastern coast. Moving westward, in 691 B.C., they also settled Gela on the southwestern coast of the island. By

635 B. C. the Greeks had driven the Phoenicians back to the western part of the island.

Under the Greeks, Sicily became highly civilized and prosperous. By the 5th century B. C., Syracuse was the most important and the strongest of all Greek cities, but its wealth and resources could not fail to invite conquest, and for years it fought off raids. Moving westward on the island, the Greeks tried to found other colonies, but they were unsuccessful because the Carthaginians had already established themselves there. With the political decline of Athens, Greek domination of Sicily came to an end.

The Carthaginians reduced Palermo to a pile of debris and occupied a large part of the island. Encouraged by the strife in Sicily, the Romans moved southward to the Strait of Messina, clashing with the might of Carthage. By the middle of the 2d century B. C., the Romans had gained complete mastery of the island.

From Ostrogothic to Hohenstaufen Rule. After the fall of the Roman Empire in 476 A. D., Sicily was occupied by the Ostrogoths. By the middle of the 6th century, however, Sicily came under the rule of the Byzantine emperors. In 827 the Saracens captured the island, and in time Palermo became a cultural center of the Arab Empire. In 1072 the Norman Robert Guiscard, Duke of Apulia and Calabria, and his brother Roger conquered Palermo. Roger completed the conquest of Sicily by 1091. In 1130, the antipope, Anacletus II, bestowed upon Roger's son, Roger II, the title of king of Apulia, Calabria, and Sicily.

In 1198 the Hohenstaufen Frederick, son of the Holy Roman Emperor Henry VI, became king of Sicily, inheriting the crown through his mother, Constance. He established his capital in Palermo, centralized Sicily's administration, and encouraged a 'great cultural outpouring. In 1220 the pope crowned him Holy Roman Emperor.

Angevin and Aragonese Rule. The death of Frederick II in 1250 struck a serious blow to the cultural development of Sicily. The pope conferred the crown on Charles I of Anjou, the brother of Louis IX, king of France. In the war that ensued, Manfred, son of Frederick II, was killed in battle in 1266. Thereupon Charles took possession of the kingdom. The Sicilians were not satisfied with the French feudal lords, especially after they transferred their capital from Palermo to Naples. The revolution of the Sicilian Vespers in 1282 ended the Angevin rule of Sicily.

In the struggle, the Sicilians were aided by Peter III, king of Aragón, who had married a daughter of Manfred. By the Peace of Caltabellotta in 1302, the unity of southern Italy was broken, for the Angevins retained possession of southern Italy, while the Aragonese occupied Sicily. With the exception of a brief period in the 15th century, Sicily and Naples were ruled separately until 1504. In that year the Spanish, in league with other powers, repulsed a French invasion of Italy, and Sicily was united with Naples under the Spanish crown.

Bourbon Sicily. During the early 18th century Sicily was handed from one power to another, as one of the rewards for victory or as a consolation prize in the great powers' struggle for supremacy in Europe. In 1713 it was awarded to Savoy. Spain conquered it in 1718 but was forced to cede it to Austria in 1720. The Spanish conquered it again in 1734. In 1759 the Bourbon king of Spain, Charles III, conferred the kingdoms of Naples and Sicily on his son Ferdinand

IV and decreed they should never again be united to the Spanish monarchy. The Bourbon kings of Naples and Sicily ruled thereafter, with the exception of a brief interval in the Napoleonic period, until the final battle for the unification of Italy began in 1860. In May of that year an insurrection broke out in Sicily against Bourbon rule. Giuseppe Garibaldi sailed from Genoa to assist the insurgents. The victory of his troops and the Sicilians was complete, and in 1861 the united kingdom of Italy was proclaimed, to be ruled by the House of Savoy.

In World War II, after the Allies had defeated Axis troops in North Africa, Sicily was invaded and conquered by the Allies in July–August 1943 and thereafter was used as a stepping-stone for the invasion of peninsular Italy.

HOWARD R. MARRARO
Formerly, Columbia University

Bibliography

Finley, Moses I., *History of Sicily: Ancient Sicily to the Arab Conquest* (Viking 1968).
Guido, Margaret, *Sicily: An Archaeological Guide* (Praeger 1967).
Lowe, Alfonso, *Barrier and the Bridge: Historic Sicily* (Norton 1971).
Mack Smith, Denis, *History of Sicily: Medieval Sicily* (Viking 1968).
Mack Smith, Denis, *History of Sicily: Modern Sicily after 1713* (Viking 1968).
Norwich, John J., *Kingdom in the Sun: 1130–1194* (Harper 1970).
Pantaleone, Michele, *Mafia and Politics* (Coward-McCann 1966).

MONREALE CATHEDRAL, near Palermo, was built in the latter part of the 12th century. It presents a harmonious combination of Byzantine and Western styles.

IAN GRAHAM, FROM PHOTO RESEARCHERS

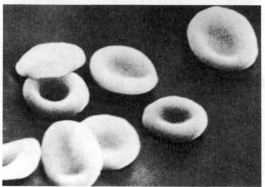

SICKLE-CELL ANEMIA, a common genetic disorder among peoples native to malarial regions, causes deoxygenated red blood cells (*top*) to take on a sickle shape. (*Bottom*) Normally shaped red blood cells.

SICKLE-CELL DISEASE, a group of hereditary disorders occurring in the black population of the United States and in parts of southern Europe, Africa, Asia, and Central and South America. The hallmark of the disorder is the presence of sickle-shaped red cells in the blood instead of normal disk-shaped cells.

Sickling disorders are caused by the presence of an abnormal hemoglobin in the red blood cell. Hemoglobin is a complex protein pigment containing iron found in the red blood cells and functioning primarily in the transport of oxygen to the tissues of the body. In sickle-cell disease, there is a minor chemical alteration in the makeup of the hemoglobin molecule. The small alteration is sufficient to make the hemoglobin crystallize into a rodlike shape when the blood loses oxygen, and these hemoglobin crystals distort the red cell, causing the sickle shape. The genes controlling hemoglobin formation are inherited from both parents. A person inheriting one sickle cell hemoglobin (HbS) gene and one normal adult hemoglobin gene (HbA) is a heterozygous carrier of the sickle-cell trait (SCT). A person inheriting a sickle-cell hemoglobin gene from each parent is homozygous for the condition and has the disease known as sickle-cell anemia (SCA). In the United States approximately one in ten black persons has the sickle-cell trait, while one in 400 has sickle-cell anemia.

Persons with the sickle-cell trait are usually without symptoms, although in certain situations that lead to inadequate oxygen levels they may experience abdominal pain and bleeding. These symptoms occur because the sickle cells block blood flow in small vessels, leading to tissue damage and destruction. Persons with sickle-cell anemia generally have marked anemia with jaundice, shortness of breath, and periodic episodes, called crises, marked by severe pains in the abdomen, bones, and muscles and often accompanied by fever and signs of infection.

Persons with the sickle-cell trait generally require no treatment, but a knowledge of the presence of the trait is an important aspect of family planning. Those with anemia may require special care during crises, which are treated by bed rest, antibiotics, drugs for pain, and at times, blood transfusions.

AMOZ CHERNOFF, M. D.
University of Tennessee Memorial Research Center

SICKLES, Daniel Edgar (1825–1914), American public figure. He was born at New York City on Oct. 20, 1825. He was admitted to the bar in 1846, served as a Democrat in the state legislature, and became city corporation counsel in 1853. He succeeded in obtaining the purchase of the land for Central Park in New York City.

He served in the state senate, and then in the U. S. House of Representatives (1857–1861). On Feb. 27, 1859, in Washington, D. C., he shot and killed Philip Barton Key, son of Francis Scott Key, author of *The Star-Spangled Banner,* whom he had accused of a liaison with his wife. Sickles was acquitted of murder on a plea of temporary aberration of mind—the first time this defense had been adopted in a court.

At the start of the Civil War, Sickles, although a Democrat, was authorized by President Lincoln to organize the Excelsior Brigade in New York for the Union army. As a brigadier general, he led it in the Peninsular campaign in 1862. Early in 1863, he was appointed major general to command the III corps, which fought at Chancellorsville (May 1–4, 1863).

Sickles was bold and impetuous. At the Battle of Gettysburg (July 1–3, 1863), Sickles led his corps forward from the Union defense line without orders to occupy a peach orchard which, he believed, was a better position. His move created a salient in the Union line, and his corps was scattered by a Confederate attack. Sickles lost his right leg in the fight.

After the war, Sickles was military governor of the Carolinas in 1867, but was relieved by President Andrew Johnson because of his harsh measures. He was U. S. minister to Spain (1869–1873) and served again in Congress (1893–1895). Sickles died in New York on May 3, 1914.

SICYON, sish′ē-ən, was a city in ancient Greece, about 10 miles (16 km) west of Corinth. Founded from Argos and under its rule for several centuries, Sicyon gained its independence about 660 B. C., and for more than a century was ruled by tyrants, reaching its greatest power under Cleisthenes. It was an ally to Sparta in the Peloponnesian War (431–404). In 251 it became a democracy under the leadership of its chief citizen, Aratus, and joined the Achaean League.

From the 6th to the 3d century B. C., the city was a center of art and philosophy and was famous for the beauty of its bronzes. The painters Apelles and Pamphilus and the sculptors Canachus and Lysippus flourished there. Several of the ancient structures, including the theater, agora, and stadium, have been excavated.

SIDDHARTHA, the given personal name of the historical Buddha. See BUDDHA AND BUDDHISM.

SIDDONS, sid'enz, **Sarah Kemble** (1755–1831), one of the greatest tragic actresses of the English stage. She was born in Brecon, Wales, on July 5, 1755, the eldest of the 12 children of Roger Kemble, actor-manager of a traveling theatrical company. She spent her childhood in his company and at the age of 18 married William Siddons, also a member of the troupe. In 1775, David Garrick engaged her for his company at the Drury Lane in London. After appearing there briefly without success, she returned to the provincial theaters and in Shakespearean and other roles soon began to display the dramatic power for which she became famous. On her return to the Drury Lane in 1782, she won acclaim as Isabella in Garrick's adaptation of Thomas Southerne's tragedy *The Fatal Marriage.* During the next 30 years she appeared in most of the great tragic roles, to the continued delight of audiences and critics. She made her formal farewell in the role in which she was said to be perfect—that of Lady Macbeth—at Covent Garden in 1812 but continued thereafter to make private or incidental appearances on the stage. She died in London on June 8, 1831.

Critics such as William Hazlitt and Leigh Hunt, along with other prominent persons of her day, praised Mrs. Siddons as a tragic actress without equal. She was a beautiful and extremely dignified woman, with a rich, resonant voice and a declamatory style that combined pathos, majesty, and minute refinement. Among portraits of her by famous painters, one of the best known is Sir Joshua Reynold's *Tragic Muse.*

Further Reading: Campbell, Thomas, *Life of Mrs. Siddons,* 2 vols. (1834; reprint, Blom, B.); Ffrench, Yvonne, *Mrs. Siddons: Tragic Actress* (rev. ed., Ryerson Press 1954); Manvell, Roger, *Sarah Siddons: Portrait of an Actress* (Putnam 1971); Parsons, Florence M., *Incomparable Siddons* (1909; reprint, Blom, B. 1969).

SIDEREAL TIME, sī-dēr'ē-əl, or "stellar time," is the system of time reckoning based on the earth's rotation with respect to the celestial sphere. See CALENDAR; DAY; TIME—*Measurement and Determination of Time.*

SIDERITE, sid'ər-īt, a carbonate of ferrous iron, is also known as chalybite or spathic iron. The name siderite derives from the Greek *sideros* ("iron"), while chalybite refers to an ancient people of Asia Minor who supposedly discovered ironworking. The mineral has been a significant ore of the metal in Austria, Britain, Germany, and Scotland.

Siderite crystals are transparent to translucent and have a glassy luster. Unlike other carbonates they are usually light to dark brown. The mineral is commonly found mixed with clays in concretions having concentric layers, a form known as clay ironstone. (See also CLAY IRONSTONE.) It also occurs in large, stratified formations in shales. Such formations often contain carbonaceous materials and are known as black-band ores. The mineral is also found in limestones, and crystalline siderite occurs in veins in association with ores of other metals such as pyrite and galena. When it is the predominant mineral in such veins, it may be mined.

Composition, $FeCO_3$; hardness, 3.5–4; specific gravity, 3.96 (pure siderite); crystal system, hexagonal.

SIDEWINDER, a small, pale-colored desert rattlesnake, *Crotalus cerastes,* of the southwestern United States that moves by throwing its body forward in a series of loops. See RATTLESNAKE; SNAKE.

SIDI-BEL-ABBES, sē-dē-bel-ə-bes' is a city in northwestern Algeria. It is situated on the Mekerra River, about 40 miles (65 km) south of Oran. Located in an important agricultural region, it is a leading commercial center and also has some light manufacturing. The city is linked by rail and highway with Oran and with Morocco to the southwest.

The French established a military post at Sidi-Bel-Abbes after their occupation of Algeria in the 19th century. The town later served as the headquarters of France's Foreign Legion. The legion was withdrawn when Algeria became independent in 1962. Once a walled town, the city now has a very modern appearance. Population: (1966) 91,527.

SIDMOUTH, Henry Addington, 1st Viscount. See ADDINGTON, HENRY.

SIDNEY, Algernon (1622–1683), English political leader and advocate of constitutional liberties. He was born at Penshurst Place, Kent, in 1622. Sidney served in 1642 as captain of a troop of horse in Ireland, and in the civil war espoused the cause of Parliament. He was returned to the Long Parliament in 1646 as member for Cardiff. In 1647 he was briefly appointed governor of Dublin, and in 1648–1650 was made governor of Dover.

In 1649, Sidney was appointed one of the commissioners for the trial of Charles I, but was not present at the trial and did not sign the warrant. His plan seems to have been the deposition of the king by an agreement of both houses. He protested against the Protectorate of Cromwell and held aloof from public affairs until the restoration of the Long Parliament by the army in 1659. In that year he was sent as a commissioner to negotiate a peace between Sweden and Denmark, and during his absence the Restoration took place. He remained in exile until 1677, when he was given leave to return to settle his private affairs.

Sidney was again drawn into politics, and made several unsuccessful attempts to enter Parliament. Following an accusation that he was the head of a great nonconformist plot, he vindicated himself, but his private letters show a deep sympathy for nonconformists and Scots as well as hatred for bishops and Roman Catholics. Sidney engaged in an intrigue with the French ambassador, through whom he endeavored to persuade Louis XIV to aid the establishment of a republic in England.

In 1683, Sidney formed one of the "council of six" in the "Ryehouse Plot" to organize a Scottish insurrection. He was arrested and sent to the Tower, charged with three overt acts of treason: consultations amounting to a conspiracy to levy war against the king; invitation to certain Scots to cooperate; and of having written a treasonable libel concerning the lawfulness of deposing kings. The law demanded two witnesses for high treason. The notorious Judge Jeffreys accepted the paper as the second witness, and on this faulty evidence Sidney was sentenced to death. He was executed on Tower Hill, London, on Dec. 7, 1683.

SIDNEY, Sir Philip (1554–1586), English poet, statesman, and soldier. Widely accomplished and highly polished, performing the most difficult task with seeming ease, he was a model of the perfect Renaissance gentleman. He was also one of the finest poets of the Golden Age of English literature.

Life. Sidney was born in Penshurst, Kent, on Nov. 30. 1554. After studying at Oxford and Cambridge, he made a tour of the Continent, as did most young gentlemen of his day. He returned to England in 1575 and soon became a favorite of Queen Elizabeth I, who in 1576 sent him on an embassy to Germany. In 1581, Sidney had a quarrel with the Earl of Oxford, and the Queen interposed to prevent a duel. Sidney then retired to Wilton, in Wiltshire, where he devoted himself to writing. He was knighted in 1583.

Sidney planned to sail with Sir Francis Drake in an expedition against the Spanish in America but was stopped by Elizabeth. She then named him governor of Flushing (Vlissingen, the Netherlands), where English troops were helping the Dutch to overthrow their Spanish rulers. In a battle at Zutphen, on Sept. 22, 1586, Sidney was badly wounded. After weeks of silent suffering, he died at Arnhem on Oct. 17, 1586. A month-long period of mourning was observed in England.

Writings. As was customary among gentlemen of the time, Sidney wrote only for the amusement of the court, passing around his manuscripts. His writings were published only after his death. He wrote verse, political tracts, masques, and translations of the Psalms and other works, but his masterpieces are the *Arcadia, The Defence of Poesie,* and *Astrophel and Stella.*

The *Arcadia* is a lengthy pastoral romance in prose with some songs and verses interpolated. It was written about 1581, but Sidney later began to revise and expand it, shaping it more like an epic. Unfortunately he died before completing the revision. The story of the romance is highly complex, and its prose style is studied and artificial. These characteristics made the work popular in its day, when such things were admired, but today it is read chiefly by scholars. Shakespeare used one of the subplots of the *Arcadia* as the Gloucester subplot of *King Lear.*

The *Defence of Poesie,* an essay, describes poetry as a partaking of the creative process. Sidney holds that by presenting ideals, poetry is a better teacher than history, which shows evil and error, and philosophy, which is dull. He also defends the classical idea of tragedy and criticizes his contemporaries for mixing comedy and tragedy. Shakespeare had not yet written by that time.

Astrophel and Stella is a series of 108 sonnets, with 11 songs interpolated. In it, Sidney disclaims all poetic devices, pretending to speak straight from the heart. In fact, though, he uses all of the devices and themes common to the sonnet. The poems tell something of a story as they progress—of Astrophel's love for Stella, who finally repulses him. *Astrophel and Stella* was the first such series in English, and the skill, vitality, and beauty of its poems were to be excelled only by Shakespeare in some of his sonnets. See also ARCADIA; DEFENCE OF POESIE.

Further Reading: Boas, Frederick S., *Sir Philip Sidney, Representative Elizabethan: His Life and Writings* (De Graff 1956); Greville, Fulke, *The Life of the Renowned Sir Philip Sidney,* ed. by Nowell Smith (Folcroft 1907); Wallace, Malcolm W., *The Life of Sir Philip Sidney* (1915; reprint, Octagon 1967).

SIDNEY, a city in western Ohio, the seat of Shelby county, is on the Miami River, 40 miles (66 km) north of Dayton. It is situated in a rich agricultural area. The city's industries include metal finishing and fabrication, refrigeration, and the manufacture of lathes, compressors, and road machinery.

In 1739 a trading post was set up in the area, but the first permanent settlement was not established until 1820, when Sidney was incorporated. The city was named after the Elizabethan English poet, statesman, and soldier Sir Philip Sidney. It has a council-manager form of government. Population: 17,657.

SIDON, sī′dən, was an ancient powerful city-state of Phoenicia, on the Lebanese coast of the Mediterranean Sea. The modern town is called Saida. Sidon reached its zenith of wealth and influence in the 2d millennium B. C., but from about 1000 its role was secondary to that of Tyre, 21 miles (34 km) to the south. Historians now generally agree that Sidon is the older of the two and that Tyre was colonized by Sidon. Both Tyre and Sidon were centers of commerce from which Phoenician seamen embarked on their voyages of trade and colonization throughout the Mediterranean Sea.

Sidonian artisans became widely renowned for their handiwork in precious metals and purple textiles, which were in great demand wherever Phoenician ships sailed. The city's glassware, linens, and perfumes were also famous. Sidonian trade has been traced as far back as the Egyptian Old Kingdom (3d millennium B. C.), and the city was mentioned in the Tell el-Amarna tablets of 14th century B. C. Egypt. Its merchants and skilled craftsmen were cited by Homer, Isaiah, and Ezekiel. Biblical references to Sidon, sometimes called Zidon, are numerous. Solomon used timber from Sidon in building his temple, and Jezebel, daughter of a king of Tyre, was of Sidonian origin. Saint Mark relates that Christ visited "the borders of Tyre and Sidon," and Saint Paul stopped to see friends here on his journey to Rome as a prisoner.

The successive empires that held sway in the Middle East are reflected in the town's history. Its wealth was a natural attraction for conquerors from Assyria, Babylonia, and Persia. Persian domination was ended in 333 B. C. with the arrival of Alexander, who took the city without a fight. Among the many sarcophagi unearthed at Sidon is one that depicts Alexander in battle and hunting scenes. In succeeding centuries Sidon was dominated by the Seleucids, Romans, and Byzantines. It was controlled periodically by the Crusaders from 1110, when it fell to Baldwin I, until 1291, when the Arabs regained it, but by that time the city had been so decimated by siege and warfare that it was no longer important, and it did not enjoy a commercial revival until the 17th century. In 1837 the city was decimated by an earthquake.

The modern Saida, 25 miles (40 km) south of Beirut and Lebanon's fourth largest city, is a fishing port and trade center for the nearby farm region, where fruits and nuts, cereals, cotton, and sugarcane are raised. Silt has rendered its once fine harbor unnavigable except for small coastal ships. It is the Mediterranean terminus for an oil pipeline from Saudi Arabia, and there are refineries and large storage tanks. Population: (1964 est.) 35,600.

SIDS. See SUDDEN INFANT DEATH SYNDROME.

SIEGBAHN, sēg'bän, **Karl Manne Georg** (1886–), Swedish physicist who won the 1924 Nobel Prize in physics "for his discoveries and research in the field of X-ray spectroscopy." His main work was the development of new methods and equipment to investigate the X-ray spectra of most of the elements from sodium to uranium and to obtain more precise measurements of the wavelengths of X rays.

Siegbahn was born in Örebro, Sweden, on Dec. 3, 1886. He received his doctorate from the University of Lund in 1911 and was director of the Nobel Institute of Physics from 1937 to 1964. The siegbahn unit is a standard length (10^{-11} cm) used to describe wavelengths of X rays.

SIEGE, sēj, a military operation conducted against a fortification or fortified area with the intention of capturing it. To be successful a siege must destroy or weaken the defending force and its protective works to an extent permitting successful assault, or it must compel surrender by destroying the will to resist of the besieged. In a successful siege the following elements are usually present: (1) adequate combat superiority on the part of the besieger to repel sorties and to ensure success in the final assault; (2) sufficient bombardment power to destroy or breach fortifications; (3) complete investment to prevent reinforcement and resupply; and (4) time to achieve capture before superior relieving forces can be employed by the defender.

Successful and unsuccessful sieges have played important parts in most of the wars of history, and in some they have been decisive. Throughout the ages siegecraft has progressed in cause and effect relationship with the art and science of fortifications. From early times men and nations have used fortifications to protect themselves. The history of siegecraft encompasses the development of means to overcome these defenses —from the earliest fence or palisade, the stone wall and feudal castle, the earth trench and masonry fort, to the modern steel and concrete fortress.

Siege Warfare to the 19th Century. Before the introduction of modern long-range artillery, sieges followed a fairly definite pattern. The besieging force would first completely encircle the fortified place—an act known as investment. A deliberate, systematic advance was made to the protective works. The protective works were breached by bombardment, ramming, and mining. Finally, the assault was made through the breach.

The ancients completed the investment by building a strong wall (circumvallation) to protect themselves from attacks from without. In this manner Julius Caesar besieged the Gauls at Alesia in 52 B.C. and, after defeating numerous attempts of relief by other Gallic tribes, captured the city. This decisive siege led to the incorporation of Gaul into the Roman Empire. Later investments were accomplished by building a series of strong points around the invested place with the intervals protected by terrain, field works, sentries, and patrols.

When investment in itself did not force capitulation, an advance to the walls, breaching operations, and a strong assault became necessary. Ingenious and elaborate devices were used to shield the attacking troops as they advanced their battering rams, pointed bores, and ballistas

close enough to breach the walls. In other instances strongly built towers as high as 150 feet (45 meters) were moved to where they could overlook the walls and fire down on the defenders, while others under protection from those in the towers scaled the walls or otherwise forced an entry.

The gradual emergence of gunpowder as an effective propellant for artillery enabled the besieger to breach and destroy the high walls of the medieval and feudal castle from a distance of several hundred yards, thereby minimizing the costly approach to assaulting distance. The decisive siege of Constantinople in 1453 by Mohammed II sounded the death knell of existing fortifications and ended the Byzantine Empire. Mohammed employed dozens of huge cannon, up to 30 inches (750 mm) in bore, which hurled stone balls of 200 to 600 pounds (90–270 kg). Unable to prevent or to repair the breaches made by these bombards, the valiant defenders finally succumbed to the overwhelming assaults of the Turks.

The Marquis de Vauban, the great 17th century French engineer, was largely responsible for the development and construction of the new low-walled, bastioned fortress designed to minimize the effects of artillery. (See *Fortifications*.) The besiegers' problem now was to get beyond the sloping glacis, through or over the counterscarp, across the deep protective ditch, and to breach the ground-level wall or scarp. Siege artillery had to neutralize the defenders' guns, then be advanced beyond or through the counterscarp where it could be employed against the scarp or wall, and all the while be reasonably protected against the defenders' fire and sorties. The solution, oddly enough, was largely due to the ideas of Vauban himself, and consisted of digging one's way forward by using the earth itself for protection.

Although used at an early date in the East, extensive trenching and mining operations did not begin in the West until the late 17th and early 18th centuries, when mercenary and conscript-type armies began to appear. The systematic approach to the fortifications then took on the form of digging a trench parallel to the line of investment, called the first parallel, then advancing toward the fortress by multiple zigzag trenches (saps). The forward edge of the saps were then connected, forming a second parallel. This process was repeated as often as necessary— usually at least three parallels were constructed— until the besiegers were close enough to commence breaching and to make the assault. The trenches and saps were usually 3 feet (1 meter) deep and 12 to 15 feet (4–5 meters) wide, the excavated earth being used to build up a protective parapet. The extremely dangerous sapping was the limiting factor. Highly skilled and well-paid sappers could progress only about 50 yards (45 meters) in 24 hours.

Vauban in his writings indicates that the first successful siege using these methods was the one he himself commanded against Maastricht in 1673. The War of the Spanish Succession (1701– 1714) saw the British, under the 1st Duke of Marlborough, successfully capture dozens of French forts by these methods, even though at heavy cost of life. From that time until the 19th century the belief prevailed that a besieger equipped with an adequate siege train, sufficient numbers of skilled sappers and miners, and strong assault forces could, at the price of severe casualties, take any fortress.

Siege Warfare to World War II. The development of long-range, high trajectory rifled artillery that fired a high explosive shell changed greatly the capabilities and limitations of both the besieged and the besieger. Only steel and concrete structures could withstand bombardment and then only if their strength kept pace with the ever-increasing explosive and penetrating power of projectiles. At the same time, defensive artillery and automatic weapons made the systematic approach to a fortress impossible. Increased ranges of howitzers and the expansion of urban areas coincident with the Industrial Revolution made it unfeasible and uneconomical to protect cities and towns by continuous fortifications.

In the years between the Franco-German War of 1870 and World War II, rings of relatively small, strong forts were built around key cities such as Verdun, Toul, Épinal, Liège, Namur, Antwerp, and Maubeuge, and others at key points between these city fortresses and in border areas to form a barrier. These forts were of steel and concrete, largely underground, with armor-protected guns, and placed so as to prevent artillery fire on the place to be defended, to delay the attacker's advance, and to channel him into unfavorable terrain.

Most of these forts were built to withstand bombardment by 9-inch (220 mm) howitzers, the largest known mobile siege piece of the time. Germany, however, during the opening phases of World War I employed artillery pieces up to 17-inch (420-mm) caliber against these forts and readily captured Liège, Namur, Maubeuge, and Antwerp, although not without delays that seriously affected their strategic plans. The lesson had been learned that any isolated fortress could be successfully taken in time by forces employing very heavy artillery. The resultant concept of defense utilizing huge field armies, artillery in depth, automatic weapons, and networks of trenches and other field fortifications led to the years of stalemated trench warfare on the Western Front. This trench warfare was itself a form of siege warfare characterized by tremendous artillery bombardments and extensive sapping and mining operations used to gain ground. The British used 3,500,000 artillery rounds over a 10-day period in June 1917 to bombard the German positions on Messines Ridge, and dug 20 mines and used a million pounds of explosive prior to their final assault.

World War II. Based on the lessons of World War I, fortifications built in the era between world wars were extended in depth, made physically stronger, built almost completely underground, and were interconnected or at least mutually supporting. The culmination was the French Maginot Line and its opposing German Westwall (also known as the Siegfried Line). Neither of these fortifications, nor other similar types, were besieged in the classic sense during World War II. The Allied operations against the Westwall in 1944 can be likened to siege warfare, however, in that intense air and artillery bombardment was used to soften resistance of each strong point to enable successful assault by tanks and infantry.

The war in Russia produced several important sieges, both successful and unsuccessful. From September 1941 until January 1944 the German and Finnish armies besieged the city of Lenin-

grad with its population of about 3,000,000. Although there is some doubt whether the Germans ever planned a final assault on the city, maximum efforts were expended to defeat the defending army and to force capitulation by large-scale aerial bombings and artillery bombardment with guns of up to 17-inch caliber. Contributing to the German failure was the fact that the city was never completely invested. Although a hazardous and difficult operation, supplies were continually brought to the city by boat across Lake Ladoga in the summer and over the ice in the winter. By January 1944 the Russians had marshaled a relief army to break the siege. It is estimated that Leningrad suffered over a million casualties in the 29 months of siege, but it never fell.

In July 1942, for the second time within a century (the first being during the Crimean War), the city and port of Sevastopol fell to a determined and violent siege. Shielded on almost two sides by the Black Sea, the land approaches were protected by a system of permanent and field fortifications modernized by Russia in 1939 to include 19 forts, 3,600 pillboxes, and extensive antitank traps and minefields. On June 2, 1942, the German and Rumanian forces began their bombardment by naval units, aircraft, and thousands of artillery pieces, one of which was the fantastic 35.4-inch (900-mm) "Big Dora," designed and built for use against the Maginot Line. By June 18 one of the principal forts had been taken by assault, and on July 1 the key fort, Fort Malakhov, fell. The city surrendered the next day.

Later Siege Techniques. Siege warfare in the era of Vauban was formalized and mathematical, but it is difficult to stereotype modern siege warfare. The elements of investment and assault are still present, but the deliberate methodical advance to assault position has been largely eliminated. Investment can often be accomplished by isolating the besieged area through ground and air firepower alone rather than by physical encirclement. The assault can be made from relatively great distances by armored and infantry forces aided by airpower, mobile artillery, and other supporting arms.

The development of modern tanks, trucks, aircraft, rockets, and missiles has given to opposing forces a degree of mobility and firepower hitherto unknown. These enable the besieger to invest rapidly and, by varying means, to bombard accurately from great distances and to assault speedily and in great strength. The besieged, however, can utilize the same developments for defense in greater depth, for rapid and powerful sorties, and to resupply over great distances even when encircled.

The influence of nuclear and thermonuclear weapons on siege warfare is difficult to predict. Foreseeably, a nuclear-armed attacker could, by making maximum use of the destructive power of such weapons, literally destroy any given fortification or fortified area. However, if complete destruction and contamination are unacceptable to the besieger for moral or political reasons, or because of contemplated future use, the employment of nuclear weapons in a siege may necessarily be limited and relegated to the role of powerful conventional artillery.

WILLIAM D. FALCK
Colonel, U. S. Army
Formerly, United States Military Academy

SIEGFRIED, sēg'frēd, in mythology, is a hero whose legend is a central theme in medieval folk tales. In Icelandic literature, where he is known as Sigurd, he is a main character in the *Poetic Edda* and in the 13th century *Volsunga Saga.* He frees the Valkyrie Brynhild (Brunhild) and is betrothed to her, but then, under the influence of a magic potion, marries Gudrun and helps Gudrun's brother Gunnar win Brynhild by means of a trick. When Brynhild discovers her betrayal, she instigates the murder of Sigurd by Gunnar's brother and then dies broken-hearted at his side.

The *Nibelungenlied,* a German epic written about 1200, was influenced by Icelandic sources but changes the story slightly. Siegfried, who is not engaged to Brunhild, wins her for Gunther (Gunnar) by performing prodigious feats while disguised as Gunther, and his death results from Brunhild's rage at the deception. The story of Siegfried was the inspiration of Wagner's *Der Ring des Nibelungen,* in which he is the main character in *Die Götterdämmerung* and *Siegfried.* See also BRUNHILD; GÖTTERDÄMMERUNG; NIBELUNGEN; NIBELUNGENLIED; SIEGFRIED (opera).

SIEGFRIED, zēKH'frēt, is the third of the four music dramas making up Richard Wagner's *Ring des Nibelungen.* It was first performed as a part of the first complete *Ring* cycle at Bayreuth, Germany, on Aug. 16, 1876.

The story is a continuation of the events in *Das Rheingold* and *Die Walküre.* Before *Siegfried* opens, Sieglinde has given birth to the hero Siegfried, and died. The child is raised by the dwarf Mime, who plans to trick the hero into getting for him the gold and magic ring now held by the giant Fafner, who has turned himself into a dragon the better to guard his treasure. The god Wotan, disguised as a Wanderer, tells Mime that only a hero who has not learned fear can win the gold. When Siegfried questions Mime he discovers that the dwarf has his father's shattered sword, Nothung. Singing a rousing song at the forge, Siegfried mends the magic sword.

In Act Two, after a beautiful pastoral known as *Forest Murmurs,* Siegfried kills Fafner and also Mime, whose treachery he discovers. A forest bird tells him of a sleeping maiden surrounded by fire. Siegfried takes the ring and follows the bird. In Act Three he meets Wotan and brutishly shatters the god's staff, a symbol of his divine power. The hero then crosses through the flames that surround the sleeping Brünhilde and wakes her with a kiss. The music drama ends with one of the most exciting duets in opera, and Siegfried places the ring on Brünhilde's finger.

SIEGFRIED LINE. See FORTIFICATIONS—*World War II;* SIEGE—*World War II.*

SIEMENS, zē'mɔns, a family of German inventors, electrical engineers, and industrialists.

ERNST WERNER VON SIEMENS (1816–1892) was born in Lenthe, near Hannover, on Dec. 13, 1816. After studying in Lübeck, he volunteered for the Prussian Army in 1838, attended the military academy in Berlin, and served as an artillery officer until 1848. While stationed in Berlin in 1847, he and a fellow engineer, Johann G. Halske, opened a small telegraphic repair shop. From this modest beginning came the great industrial firm of Siemens & Halske.

In its first year of operation, the company received a government order to construct the first telegraph cable system in Germany, extending from Berlin to Frankfurt am Main. In the years that followed, Siemens devoted his extraordinary inventiveness and energies to expanding the firm, at the same time working on a long list of inventions or new applications of scientific discoveries. As the company flourished it undertook vast electrical engineering projects, also producing new and improved telegraphic equipment. Branches were established in other German cities, and in 1858 Siemens and his brother William founded a subsidiary in England. This later evolved into the huge Siemens Brothers works established in Charlton, Kent.

It was the invention of the regenerative furnace that ensured the fortunes of the Siemens brothers. The furnace began with their efforts to apply the principle of Werner's regenerative steam engine and condenser to other basic manufacturing processes that required high temperatures. In 1856 another brother, Friedrich, built a furnace that embodied this principle, and William made further improvements. The next year the furnace was used for the melting and reheating of steel, and the idea was subsequently used in blast furnaces, glassmaking, and other industrial operations. Its foremost contribution to industrial science came in 1865 or 1866, when it was first employed to convert iron ore directly into steel. This process, which became known as the open-hearth process, revolutionized steelmaking and eventually spread throughout the world. A similar method of steel production, in which cast iron and wrought iron were combined and melted on an open hearth, was called the Siemens-Martin process. See STEEL—*Open-Hearth Process.*

Because of the close association of Werner and William, it is often difficult to attribute to any one of them a particular invention. However, among the major innovations with which Werner's name is associated in particular is an electroplating process, patented in 1842; a differential governor for steam engines and an anastatic process for reproducing printed matter, about 1844; a regenerative steam engine and condenser, already mentioned; a selenium photometer; and the electric dynamo. His epochal suggestion in 1847 that gutta-percha be used to insulate conductors overcame the difficulty of preserving electrical wire from moisture and made possible the first underground and submarine telegraph cables. The firm of Siemens & Halske laid the first major underwater cable from Dover to Calais in 1850 and several others in the years that followed, and in 1874 the London branch of the firm laid a transatlantic cable. In 1881, Werner built the world's first public-service electric street railway at Lichterfelde, a suburb of Berlin.

Werner and William both were involved in the development of the modern electrical dynamo, which transformed mechanical energy into electricity without the use of permanent magnets, and which marked the commercial birth of the electrical industry. The self-excitation principle seems to have been first discovered by Werner, who also contributed an important element in 1857 when he designed the shuttle winding for the armature, but it was William who published the results of their research in 1867. In the same year, similar announcements of the dynamo came in England from two other inventors, Sir Charles Wheatstone and Cromwell F. Varley, each of them working independently. The Siemens firm played a leading role in subsequent improvements of the machine. Werner died in Berlin on Dec. 6, 1892. His *Personal Recollections* were translated into English in 1893, and his *Scientific and Technical Papers* were published in English in 1892–1895.

SIR WILLIAM SIEMENS (1823–1883), brother of Werner, was born in Lenthe on April 4, 1823, and christened Karl Wilhelm Siemens. He left the commercial school at Lübeck in 1843 to continue his studies at Magdeburg, where his brother was stationed. At the Stolberg works there the two of them began their lifelong collaboration in technological study and experimentation that eventually created the great Siemens industrial empire. Later in 1843, Wilhelm was dispatched to England and succeeded in selling manufacturers there a new electroplating technique that Werner had devised. In 1844 he returned to England and took up permanent residence there, adopting the English form of his name and becoming a British subject in 1859. Although his first years there were unsuccessful, he did make progress in improving the regenerative steam engine and condenser that Werner had originally conceived. William's first commercial success followed his invention in 1851 of a water meter, whose wide acceptance proved highly profitable to him.

By 1858 the growing German firm of Siemens & Halske opened its branch in England, with William at the head. Concurrent with his interest in metallurgy, William also contributed to Werner's numerous accomplishments in electrical engineering, especially telegraphy. William's firm assisted with many of the important underground cable installations on the Continent and by itself undertook the laying of the Atlantic cable in 1874. For this and future projects, William ingeniously designed the cable ship *Faraday*.

Like his brother, William was one of the pioneers in the transmission of electrical power, and in 1883 he opened an electric railway in the north of Ireland. To him also must be given a share of credit in the development of the dynamo and of electric illumination. Thus in 1879 he invented an electric furnace of the arc type that, although neglected at first, proved to be a prototype of the arc furnace in standard use today in the iron and steel industries, in smelting, and in the production of the important nonferrous alloys. The 113 English patents taken out in his name include a pyrometer and the bathometer, used for measuring depths in water. William was elected a fellow of the Royal Society in 1862 and was knighted in 1883, a few months before his death in London on November 18 of that year. His *Collected Works*, edited by E. F. Bamber, were published in 3 volumes in 1889.

FRIEDRICH SIEMENS (1826–1904), another brother of Werner, was born in Menzendorf on Dec. 8, 1826. Working at William's firm in England, he was the first to conceive (1856) the idea of the regenerative furnace, which won wide application in the glassmaking industry and which his brothers developed into their famed steelmaking process. He died in Dresden on April 24, 1904.

CARL FRIEDRICH VON SIEMENS (1872–1941), one of Werner's sons, was born in Charlottenburg on Sept. 5, 1872. He served in a number of executive positions in the Siemens firm, heading the London division from 1902 to 1908 and becoming director in 1912 of the Siemens Schuckertwerke in Germany. Under his leadership the firm expanded and the branches of telephony and electrochemistry were separated. The Siemens Bauunion was created to handle the civil engineering branch of the works: subways, power plants, and hydroelectric installations. Siemensstadt, the concern's headquarters near Berlin, became a veritable city, employing some 100,000 workers at the start of World War II. Siemens died in Heindendorf on July 9, 1941. In the postwar era the firm played a role in West Germany's industrial resurgence, becoming a leading supplier of electronics equipment in addition to its other wide-ranging interests.

Further Reading: Kirby, Richard S., and others, *Engineering in History* (McGraw 1956); Siemens, Georg, *Geschichte des Hauses Siemens*, 3 vols. (1946–1952).

SIENA, syâ'nä, is a city in Italy in the region of Tuscany and is the capital of Siena province. The city is 30 miles (48 km) south of Florence on a plateau in the midst of hills covered with vineyards and olive groves. The atmosphere has changed little since the Middle Ages, and it has no important industries. In its landmarks and plan Siena is still a 14th century city, with narrow, irregular streets and small, picturesque squares lined with old palaces and medieval houses.

In the center of the city is a wide, shell-shaped square, Il Campo, dominated by the imposing Palazzo Pubblico with the tall and slender Torre del Mangia. This is the finest Gothic town hall in Tuscany. Among its works of art are Simone Martini's *Maestà* and frescoes by Ambrogio Lorenzetti. Also in the square are the Loggia della Mercanzia and the Fonte Gaia, a fountain by Jacopo della Quercia. His original fountain sculptures, now in the municipal museum, have been replaced by copies. The famous Corsa del Palio, a festival of medieval origin that consists of a parade and a horse race, is still held twice every summer in Il Campo. The paraders, in colorful medieval costumes, represent each of the city's 17 quarters (*contrade*), and in the horse race, each horse runs under the colors of one of the ten *contrade* chosen to take part in the race.

Siena's beautiful cathedral (12th–14th centuries) has a polychrome marble facade. The lower part, by Giovanni Pisano, is Romanesque. The upper part is a striking example of Italian Gothic. The walls and columns of the interior are covered with stripes of black and white marble, and the marble floor is beautifully inlaid. The sculptured pulpit is by Nicola Pisano, aided by his son Giovanni and others. The high altar is by Baldassare Peruzzi. The adjacent Piccolomini Library, founded about 1495 by Francesco Piccolomini (later Pope Pius III), has frescoes by Pinturicchio. Near the cathedral are the baptistery, with a beautiful baptismal font by Jacopo della Quercia and works by Donatello and Lorenzo Ghiberti, and the Museo dell'Opera del Duomo.

In the 14th century Bonsignori Palace is the art gallery, a collection of paintings of the Sienese School, which produced its greatest masters in the 13th and 14th centuries with Duccio di Buoninsegna, Simone Martini, Lippo Memmi, and Pietro and Ambrogio Lorenzetti. Other palaces of that period are the Piccolomini, Tolomei, Sansedoni, and Saracini. Scenes of the life of Saint Catherine of Siena are in the Church of San Domenico. Siena has fine cultural traditions dating back to the 13th century, when its university was founded.

Throngs gather in Piazza del Campo, Siena, to watch the Corsa del Palio, a re-creation of a medieval festival.

History. Siena was an Etruscan settlement long before Roman times, but its Etruscan name is unknown. It first appears in history under a Latin name as a Roman colony in the time of the Emperor Augustus. It was later held by Goths, Lombards, Franks, and local feudal lords, over whom the bishops of Siena finally gained ascendancy.

In the 12th century a free commune was formed, which gradually extended its power over the countryside and soon became the champion of the Ghibelline cause in Tuscany. Meanwhile the Guelph city of Florence also tried to enlarge its possessions. The ensuing political and economic rivalry soon led to a series of wars, fought with varying fortunes.

After its victory over Florence at Montaperti in 1260, Siena reached its highest intellectual, artistic, and economic development. In the 14th and 15th centuries, however, external wars and internal strife between Guelphs and Ghibellines and between the aristocratic and popular factions gradually weakened the republic. From 1497 to 1512, Pandolfo Petrucci held sole power and tried to restore order, but his son was forced into exile in 1516. French and Spaniards fought over Siena, and in 1554 troops of Emperor Charles V put the city under siege. After a long and gallant struggle to save their republican liberties the defenders were forced to capitulate in April 1555. Charles V invested his son Philip with Siena, but in 1559 the city passed to the Medici. It remained a part of the grand duchy of Tuscany until 1860, when it joined Piedmont, which later became part of a united Italy. Siena suffered very little during World War II.

The Province. The province is made up of the hills and mountains of the Tuscan Apennines between the Chianti Mountains in the northeast and the Monte Amiata group in the southwest. The valley farms yield olives, cereals, grapes, and other fruits. Much of the famous Chianti wine comes from the province. There are also quarries that yield travertine and a fine orange-colored marble. The principal cities, besides Siena, are San Gimignano, Montepulciano, and Poggibonsi. The area is 1,475 square miles (3,820 sq km). Population: (1969 est.) of the city, 54,200; of the province, 260,700.

SIENKIEWICZ, shen-kye'vich, **Henryk** (1846–1916), Polish novelist, who is best known for *Quo Vadis?* Sienkiewicz was born in Wola Odrzejska, near Lukow, Poland on May 4, 1846, and educated at the University of Warsaw. He published various critical articles while still a student, was for a time editor of *Słowo*, a journal published in Warsaw, and in 1872 published his first work of fiction, *Na Marne*, translated into English as *In Vain*. In 1876, Sienkiewicz went to the United States, where for a time he lived in California in a Polish colony founded by the famous Polish-American actress Helena Modjeska and her husband. His travels took him to most of the countries of Europe and even into central Africa.

Among Sienkiewicz' chief works are *With Fire and Sword* (1883), *The Deluge* (1886), and *Pan Michael* (1888)–the three forming a great patriotic trilogy dealing with Poland's struggle for freedom in the 17th century and regarded as Sienkiewicz' finest work, and the two distinguished psychological novels *Without Dogma* (1891) and *Children of the Soil* (1895). *Quo Vadis?* (1895; Eng. tr., 1896), a tale of Roman life under Nero, is by far his most popular work. It has been translated into nearly every language and was dramatized and filmed with great success.

In 1905, Sienkiewicz received the Nobel Prize for literature. During the early years of World War I he worked untiringly for the cause of Polish independence and for the International Red Cross. He died in Vevay, Switzerland, on Nov. 14, 1916.

791

The commercial center of Freetown, capital of Sierra Leone

SIERRA LEONE, sē-er'ə lē-ōn', is a republic in West Africa. Before it became independent in 1961, it consisted of a British colony and protectorate. The colony incorporated the rugged Sierra Leone ("Lion Mountain") Peninsula and other regions on the Atlantic Ocean, and the protectorate covered the remainder of the country. The name Sierra Leone was applied first to the peninsula, by the Portuguese explorer Pedro da Cintra in 1460.

Sierra Leone is inhabited by 18 distinct ethnic groups, which were divided among several dozen independent political units until 1896. In that year a protectorate was proclaimed by the British colonial government at Freetown, originally established to control settlements of Africans liberated from captivity. Freetown's Creole community, which had evolved a distinctive Afro-European culture, had also promoted the extension of British influence inland. The Creoles have continued to play leading roles in many spheres of Sierra Leonean life.

Beginning in the 1950's, a spectacular rise in the licit and illicit export of diamonds has provided Sierra Leone substantial earnings, but the long-term effect may have been to inhibit rather than to stimulate other productive developments. Since the nation became independent, both civilian and military governments have faced serious difficulties in their attempts to promote a more broadly based economic development and to unite the country's many ethnic groups in a stronger national consciousness.

The Land. Sierra Leone is a small country with a coastline of 210 miles (340 km) on the Atlantic. Its territory includes several offshore islands, such as Sherbro and the Banana and Turtle islands.

The coastal region consists mostly of mangrove swamps and a plain extending about 60 miles (100 km) inland. The flat coastline is broken south of the Rokel estuary by a range of hills almost 3,000 feet (900 meters) high, forming the Sierra Leone Peninsula. In the north and east the upland plateau regions average 1,000 to 2,000 feet (300–600 meters) in elevation, with several peaks exceeding 6,000 feet (1,800 meters). The highest point in Sierra Leone is Bintimani Peak, rising to 6,390 feet (1,948 meters) in the Loma Mountains.

The greater part of Sierra Leone lies within the West African rain forest, but most of the primary forest has long been cleared. The characteristic landscape in the south consists of cultivated farms interspersed with large areas of bush fallow and oil palms. In the higher and drier lands of the north and east there are large areas of savanna woodland where cattle raising is possible. But soil erosion, accelerated by the torrential rainfalls, is particularly serious in upland areas. Much of the land, it has been said, has the color and fertility of a brick.

INFORMATION HIGHLIGHTS

Official Name: Republic of Sierra Leone.

Head of State: President.

Head of Government: President.

Area: 27,700 square miles (71,740 sq km).

Boundaries: *North* and *east,* Guinea; *south,* Liberia; *west,* Atlantic Ocean.

Population: (1971 off. est.) 2,600,000; (1963 census) 2,180,355.

Capital: Freetown (1963 census) 127,917.

Major Languages: English (official), Mende, Temne, Krio (Creole).

Major Religions: Primal religions, Islam, Christianity.

Monetary Unit: Leone.

Weights and Measures: British system.

Flag: Tricolor of green, white, and blue horizontal stripes. See also FLAG.

National Anthem: "High we exalt thee, realm of the free."

Sierra Leone is traversed by more than a dozen substantial rivers, whose estuaries mostly terminate in mangrove swamps. These waterways, rarely navigable for distances sufficient to make them a commercial asset, have long impeded lateral communications. Although many bridges have been built since the 1950's some rivers can still be crossed only by ferry.

The climate is tropical, with average annual temperatures around 80° F (26° C). Humidity is generally high. Rainfall is heaviest on the coast, especially in the highlands of the Sierra Leone Peninsula, where it averages 200 inches (5,000 mm) annually. It amounts to about 120 inches (3,000 mm) at Freetown and less in the northeast. More than two thirds of the annual rainfall occurs between June and September.

The People. Most of Sierra Leone's people live in rural areas. Freetown is the capital and largest city. Other important towns include Bo, formerly the capital of the British protectorate, Kenema, and Makeni.

The largest ethnic groups are the Mende, who live mainly in the south, and the Temne, who inhabit the north. Together they comprise about 60% of Sierra Leone's population. Smaller groups include the Limba, Kono, Koranko, Sherbro, Susu, Loko, Mandingo, and Fulani. Most of the Creoles, descendants of the liberated Africans who settled in Freetown, continue to live in and around the city.

Way of Life. The traditional life of the indigenous farmers is being changed in varying degrees by the impact of commerce, mining, and Western ideas and technology. But many communities continue to practice the simple technique commonly termed "shifting cultivation," on land that is usually held in some form of collective tenure.

The power of the chiefs over their people, normally limited under customary law, was in many respects enlarged under colonial rule. Although subjected to administrative and legal supervision, the chiefs gained control of new revenues and powers of patronage. Since the advent of electoral politics, some chiefs have been able to use their office for further personal and political advantage, thus provoking the resentment of many farmers.

Secret societies, like the Poro, have long exercised important functions, settling disputes within and between chiefdoms, regulating traditional education, and exerting various forms of social control.

Ethnic loyalties remain strong among those people who have migrated to urban centers and to the diamond fields. Western education and participation in the modern economy have not eradicated older patterns of behavior. Even Creole culture, which is superficially British and Christian, incorporates many elements of diverse African origin and embraces an important Muslim community.

The majority of Sierra Leoneans practice primal religions, but those are frequently affected by Islamic or Christian influences. Islam and Christianity are expanding in many parts of the country. Perhaps 25% of the population is Muslim and 5% is Christian.

Language and Education. English is the official language of Sierra Leone. The Mende language is widely spoken by people in the south, and Temne is used in the north. The lingua franca is Creole, or *Krio*.

EPOQUE LTD., FROM BLACK STAR

Busy open market in Freetown offers morning shoppers a wide variety of fruits and vegetables.

Western education, pioneered by Christian missions and long concentrated in the colony area, has been extended since independence. By 1969 there were nearly 140,000 pupils in over 900 primary schools and about 17,000 in secondary, technical, and teacher-training institutions. Fourah Bay College, established as an Anglican seminary in the early 19th century, and Njala University College, founded in 1963, constitute the University of Sierra Leone.

SIERRA LEONE

0 _____ 100 Mi.

0 _____ 100 Km.

The Economy. Most Sierra Leoneans are engaged in agriculture, which is officially estimated to account for one third of the gross domestic product. The principal food crop is rice. But since labor was diverted from agriculture to diamond digging in the 1950's, Sierra Leone has had to import rice, which it formerly exported. The chief agricultural exports are palm kernels, coffee, cacao, piassava, and ginger.

The commercial economy depends heavily on the extraction of mineral resources. Nearly 60% of Sierra Leone's exports consist of diamonds, which have been mined in Kono district in the east since 1933 by the Sierra Leone Selection Trust. In the early 1950's illicit diggers began to take diamonds from alluvial deposits over wide eastern areas. Since their operations proved impossible to control, they were legalized and licensed after 1955, and the Government Diamond Office was established to buy the diamonds. It is not clear how long this diminishing resource will last.

Iron ore, mined at Marampa by the Development Company of Sierra Leone (DELCO), is the second most valuable export. Other iron ore deposits in Tonkolili district of central Sierra Leone have not yet been developed. There is also some mining of bauxite and rutile (titanium dioxide).

Sierra Leone is expanding and improving its road system to replace the inadequate narrow-gauge railroad connecting Freetown with Makeni and with Pendembu. Iron ore is shipped by a private railroad to the port of Pepel. The country's international airport is at Lungi, linked to Freetown by ferry across the broad Rokel estuary.

Freetown has one of the best natural harbors along the West African coast. Regular shipping services connect the city with British, European, Japanese, and American ports. Most of Sierra Leone's exports go to Britain, which supplies usually about 30% of Sierra Leone's imports. Japan, the United States, and several European countries are also important trading partners. There is little trade with other African states.

History and Government. During the mid-16th century, European writers described the invasion of the Sherbro River hinterland from the southeast by people called the Manes. They were probably ancestors of the modern Mende and Loko peoples, and with their arrival the ethnic pattern of settlement reached approximately its present form. There was a diversity of languages and cultures, and political authority was diffused. Most states were small, some having no centralized political institutions.

Fragmentation did not mean disorder. Relationships within and between states were regulated by mechanisms of some complexity and sophistication, like the Poro secret society. The needs of subsistence were adequately met by agriculture and by exploiting the resources of forests and rivers. Smiths worked in iron; carvers of wood and ivory won Portuguese patronage. However, the region remained somewhat sheltered from the main forces for change in precolonial Africa—long-range commerce and Islam.

Europeans began to buy slaves in Sierra Leone in the 16th century. Although the slave trade grew as American demand expanded, the average number of slaves exported from the Sierra Leone region never exceeded 2,000 annually. Europeans bought slaves from African or mulatto brokers in small consignments and were also interested in African produce, such as ivory, pepper, and subsequently hardwoods and dyewoods. The theocratic Muslim state established in Fouta Djallon (Futa Jalon) by 1775 began to channel slaves, gold, and hides to the coast in return for imported goods and kola nuts. The region therefore became more closely linked with long-distance overland trade routes, and Muslim influence spread more rapidly.

British Colony and Protectorate. After 1787, British abolitionists, under the leadership of Granville Sharp, settled over 2,000 freed Africans from Britain and the Americas at Freetown, hoping to promote the wide diffusion of Christianity, Western civilization, and commerce. The

A Sierra Leonean woman carries her baby in a sling while balancing a load of wood on her head.

settlement became a British crown colony in 1808, and the population was progressively swelled by the emancipation of Africans recaptured from slave ships.

Many of the immigrants, and their Creole descendants, achieved distinction in commerce, the churches, and the professions. Among the best known were Bishop Samuel Ajayi Crowther and the barrister Sir Samuel Lewis. This new community, whose distinctive culture synthesized diverse African and European elements, began to influence the whole West African coast as well as the immediate interior. Sierra Leoneans helped to diffuse Christianity, exchanged European manufactured goods for African produce, and spread knowledge of the English language and the power of the British Empire. Many Creole leaders hoped to build a new West African nation, some hoping for an alliance with Islam as represented by Samori Touré's inland Mandingo empire.

Partly stimulated by the activities of the Creoles, the colonial government hesitantly extended its authority inland and in 1896 proclaimed its protectorate over the interior of Sierra Leone. The introduction of a house tax, together with other new burdens, led to a rebellion in the protectorate in 1898. Many Creoles were killed during the uprising, and the British thereafter tended to restrict Creole activities in their new territories. Africans were more rarely appointed to responsible positions in the expanded government administration. Simultaneously, Creole businessmen suffered heavily from the competition of Lebanese immigrants and well-financed European merchants.

In 1924, colony residents were allowed for the first time to elect three members of the Legislative Council. After World War II, while many Creoles continued to treasure their status as British subjects, others began to cooperate with political leaders in the protectorate. In 1951 the British introduced a new constitution for the colony and protectorate, giving political power to the majority party. Elections held that year brought to power the protectorate-based Sierra Leone People's party (SLPP), led by Milton Margai, a Mende physician.

During the following decade of constitutional progress, old conflicts between the colony and protectorate became less important. Graver and more ominous problems were signaled by strikes and riots in Freetown, by widespread rebellions against the exactions of certain chiefs, and by the tendency of the diamond boom to jeopardize economic balance, social stability, and public order. The social problems underlying these difficulties remained unsolved when Sierra Leone became independent on April 27, 1961, with Sir Milton Margai as prime minister.

Independence. The unevenness of economic and social development partly neutralized the well-rooted liberal and constitutional principles with which Sierra Leonean leaders had approached national independence. The SLPP, drawing its principal strength from the chiefs, found it difficult to establish grass roots support. Successive opposition parties found it easier to win support by ethnic appeals to peoples dissatisfied with their share of government patronage than by formulating clear alternative policies. When Prime Minister Margai died in 1964, he was succeeded by his brother, Albert (later Sir Albert) Margai. The latter tried unsuccessfully to create a one-party state.

EPOQUE LTD., FROM BLACK STAR

Diamond-bearing gravel in Sierra Leone is sifted and washed to recover the precious stones.

In March 1967, a closely fought election appeared to give a majority to the All Peoples' Congress (APC) led by Siaka Stevens, a Limba trade unionist and former SLPP minister. The APC victory triggered successive military coups—first by Brig. David Lansana in the interest of Albert Margai, then by middle-ranking officers who formed the National Reformation Council (NRC). In April 1968 the NRC was overthrown by army privates and noncommissioned officers, who restored parliamentary government with Siaka Stevens as prime minister.

Stevens' administration did much to restore economic and social priorities ignored by the SLPP. But Sierra Leone's relative weakness in the international economy restricted growth, produced inflation, and bred new sources of discontent, which were reinforced by allegations of ethnic discrimination. In April 1971, after an attempted military coup, Sierra Leone became a republic, with Stevens as president.

Sierra Leone remained a member of the Commonwealth of Nations. It continued to practice a foreign policy of nonalignment within the Organization of African Unity.

JOHN D. HARGREAVES, *Author of*
"Prelude to the Partition of West Africa"

Bibliography

Cartwright, John, *Politics in Sierra Leone, 1947–1967* (Univ of Toronto Press 1970).
Fyfe, Christopher, *A Short History of Sierra Leone* (Longmans Ltd. 1962).
Fyfe, Christopher, ed., *Sierra Leone Inheritance* (Oxford 1964), an excellent documentary anthology.
Fyfe, Christopher, and Jones, Eldred, eds., *Freetown: A Symposium* (Oxford 1968).
Laan, H. L. van der, *The Sierra Leone Diamonds* (Oxford 1965).
McCulloch, Merran, *Peoples of the Sierra Leone Protectorate* (Int. African Inst. 1950).

JOSEF MUENCH

Peaks of the Sierra Nevada range rise above Bullfrog Lake in Kings Canyon National Park, California.

SIERRA MADRE, sē-er′ə mad′rē, is a city in south-western California, in Los Angeles county. It lies in the foothills of the San Gabriel Mountains, 17 miles (27 km) northeast of the center of Los Angeles. It makes emergency oxygen equipment and automobile crash test dummies.

Founded in 1881, it was incorporated in 1907. Government is by mayor and council. Population: 10,837.

SIERRA MADRE, syer′rä mä′thrä, the principal mountain range of Mexico. The Sierra Madre, which covers about 75% of the face of Mexico, is divided into three parts. The Sierra Madre Oriental and the Sierra Madre Occidental begin below the U. S. border and extend southward along Mexico's east and west coasts, clustering around the great central plateau. In the south they are met by the lower Sierra Madre del Sur. See also MEXICO—*The Land.*

SIERRA NEVADA, sē-erə nə-vad′ə, a mountain range in eastern California. It is the site of three national parks—Yosemite, Sequoia, and Kings Canyon—and of beautiful Lake Tahoe, whose clear, blue waters reach depths of more than 1,600 feet (490 meters). The name *Sierra Nevada* is Spanish for "snowy saw-toothed range."

The Sierra Nevada is a great granite block extending 430 miles (692 km) south from the Feather River to Tehachapi Pass. The uplift and tilting to the west of a huge segment of the earth's crust produced a long, gradual slope on the west and a near-vertical escarpment on the east. The peaks increase in altitude from Lake Tahoe (6,225 feet, or 1,898 meters) southward to Mt. Whitney (14,496 feet, or 4,418 meters), the highest peak in the United States outside Alaska. From Mt. Whitney, the altitude of the peaks gradually decreases to the south end of the range.

Awe-inspiring canyons have been deeply incised into the long western slope by a number of rivers, including the Feather, American, Tuolumne, Merced, San Joaquin, Kings, and Kern. On the shorter, steeper eastern slope many creeks descend to join the Owens, Walker, Carson, and Truckee rivers. Mountain glaciation played a part in shaping bold, impressive landscapes in the Sierra Nevada. Sheer cliffs, meadows, lakes,

and high leaping waterfalls, such as one sees in Yosemite Valley, add beauty to the range.

Rainfall increases with the elevation up to 4,500 feet (1,350 meters), then decreases to the crest of the range. Beyond the summit on the eastern slope, the rainfall is less. Winter snowfall is heavy. Annual amounts of 30 to 40 feet (9–12 meters) are normal near Lake Tahoe and Donner Pass, and seasonal snowfalls of up to 60 feet (18 meters) have been recorded.

Life zones occur in a belted arrangement. At the west base of the range, adjacent to the Sacramento and San Joaquin valleys, grasses and shrubs are dominant. At elevations of 3,000 to 4,000 feet (900–1,200 meters) grow great forests of commercially valuable timber, composed of yellow pine, sugar pine, incense cedar, and fir. In scattered groves within the forest is found the *Sequoia gigantea,* or "big tree," considered the largest member of the earth's flora. At 6,000 to 7,000 feet (1,800–2,150 meters) occur lodgepole pine, Jeffrey pine, and red fir. Near the 9,000-foot (2,750-meter) level, only the hardier specimens are found. Above the timber line the rocky terrain is essentially bare of vegetation. The dry east slopes support scattered trees in intermediate elevations, and at the foot of the range sagebrush and other shrubs merge with desert types of vegetation.

West slope rivers supply irrigation water to farmlands in the Sacramento and San Joaquin valleys and the Tulare Basin. California's largest cities secure municipal water from these rivers, and hydroelectric plants on the rivers and on the aqueducts that lead from them generate power for the state's farms and metropolitan areas.

The Sierra Nevada interposes a barrier 40 to 80 miles (65–130 km) wide to east-west travel. Vehicles can cross the range only over certain passes. Major highways use the following passes: Beckwourth (5,250 feet, or 1,600 meters), Donner (7,135 feet, or 2,175 meters), Carson (8,600 feet, or 2,620 meters), Ebbetts (8,800 feet, or 2,680 meters), Sonora (9,625 feet, or 2,935 meters), and Walker (5,248 feet, or 1,600 meters). A road over Tioga Pass (9,625 feet, or 3,030 meters) connects Yosemite Valley and Mono Lake, but it is usually closed by snow for 9 months of the year. The Western Pacific Railway crosses Beckwourth Pass, and the Southern Pacific goes over Donner Pass. Mountain trails used by hikers and pack trains cross the range. John Muir Trail along the mountain crest opens up the wilderness of the High Sierras.

The discovery of gold in the Sierra Nevada started the 1849 gold rush and attracted a large population to the foothill zone. But mining of gold and other metals is no longer important. Tourism is the largest industry of the region, and there are camping and recreation facilities of all sorts throughout the mountains. Both summer resorts and winter sports centers abound. Other economic activities include fruit growing, in the western foothills, and lumbering and grazing, on the intermediate slopes.

See also KINGS CANYON NATIONAL PARK; SEQUOIA NATIONAL PARK; TAHOE, LAKE; YOSEMITE NATIONAL PARK.

RUTH E. BAUGH
University of California, Los Angeles

Further Reading: Farquhar, Francis, *History of the Sierra Nevada* (Univ. of Calif. Press 1965); Matthes, François E., *The Incomparable Valley: A Geologic Interpretation of Yosemite*, ed. by Fritiof Fryxell (Univ. of Calif. Press 1950); Muir, John, *My First Summer in the Sierra* (1911; reprint, Berg 1972).

SIERRA NEVADA, syer'rä nä-vä'thä, the highest mountain range in Spain. It is in the south, in the provinces of Granada and Almería. It extends for about 60 miles (97 km) east and west, roughly parallel to and some 20 miles (32 km) north of the Mediterranean Sea. There are several glaciers, those on Veleta peak being the southernmost in Europe. Its highest peak, Mulhacén (11,411 feet or 3,478 meters), is perpetually covered with snow. Mica slate is its chief constituent, and vegetation is scanty except in the lower valleys.

SIEYÈS, syä-yâs', **Emmanuel Joseph** (1748–1836), French revolutionary leader. Sieyès typified one aspect of the many-faceted French Revolution—the confrontation of a man of thought with the complex and difficult requirements of practical politics. His skill as a propagandist helped to drive on the first revolutionary events of 1789 but his attempt a decade later to end the incessant turmoil of French political life with the aid of the sword served instead to inaugurate a long episode of military despotism under Napoleon.

He was born in Fréjus, in Provence, on May 3, 1748, the son of a minor official without independent wealth. Sieyès was sent into the church to make his career, although his personal preference ran to the life of a soldier. His intelligence made him a quick learner at the seminary of St.-Sulpice in Paris, but he gave his true interest not to theology but to the new ideas of the Enlightenment.

Skepticism toward religion did not keep him from taking holy orders (hence his courtesy title of *abbé*). He became a priest in 1773 and rose gradually through a series of church offices until in 1787 he became councilor for the estate of the clergy. Under the conditions of the time, when all higher ecclesiastical appointments had become the preserve of the nobility, he could not aspire to any position in the church beyond that of a skilled subordinate, whatever his ability and his energy.

French Revolutionary Years. The antipathy he had gradually acquired for the nobility found vent in 1788 during the political crisis that set the crown and the privileged orders against each other, with the commoners for the most part hostile to King Louis XVI. Sieyès contributed to the shift of the commoners' feeling against the aristocracy by two pamphlets published that year. But it was the stark argument and the hot hatred of his *Qu'est-ce que le tiers état?* (*What is the Third Estate?*), published early in 1789, that brought him fame and helped to strengthen anti-aristocratic feeling during the elections to the Estates-General. He was himself elected as a deputy for the third estate from Paris and played a significant part in the transformation of the Estates-General into the National Assembly. Indeed, though he did not originate the term "National Assembly," it was he who gave it currency.

Sieyès' qualities as a political theorist fertile in devising new constitutional arrangements did not compensate for his lack of oratorical skill and his stiffness in personal relations, and he began to lose his immense popularity. During the Reign of Terror, he was unmistakably hostile to the Jacobins, but his quiescence and his vote for the death of Louis XVI kept him safely from attention. Later, when asked what he had done during this period, he replied, *"J'ai vécu"* ("I stayed alive").

The fall of Maximilien Robespierre, the architect of the Reign of Terror, brought Sieyès back into public life in 1795. He became a member of the Committee of Public Safety, where he emphasized the need to consolidate and conclude the Revolution and to achieve peace. Elected to the Council of Five Hundred, he was one of the negotiators of peace with the Dutch at The Hague in 1795 and went as minister plenipotentiary to Berlin 1798, where he obtained the neutrality of Prussia.

The next year he became a member of the Directory, the executive authority in France, and as its leading figure took the initiative in a coup d'etat designed to consolidate its authority at the expense of the electorate and the representative assemblies. His military collaborator in this enterprise was Gen. Napoléon Bonaparte, recently returned from Egypt. To Sieyès' surprise, Bonaparte seized control of the government after the coup of 18–19 Brumaire (Nov. 9–10, 1799). Though Bonaparte rejected Sieyès' complex draft constitution and established his own system of personal rule, he accepted Sieyès' principle of putting the authority of the state beyond popular control.

Later Life. Sieyès acknowledged Bonaparte's mastery and was rewarded with a series of honors. He became president of the Senate and then a count of the empire (1808), receiving a farm at Versailles and two houses in Paris. Though Sieyès' active political career was concluded, his past came back to haunt him when Napoleon fell. He was proscribed in 1815 as a regicide and fled early the next year to Brussels, where he lived until the July Revolution of 1830 again toppled the Bourbons. He then returned to Paris, where he lived until his death on June 20, 1836. See also FRANCE—*History;* FRENCH REVOLUTION; NAPOLEON I.

HERBERT H. ROWEN, *Rutgers University*

Further Reading: Clapham, John H., *The Abbé Sieyès: An Essay in the Politics of the French Revolution* (1912); Neton, Albéric, *Sieyès (1748–1836), d'après des documents inédits*, 2d ed. (1901); Van Deusen, Glyndon G., *Sieyès: His Life and His Nationalism* (Columbia Univ. Press 1932).

SIGEBERT I, sēzh-bâr′ (535–575), Merovingian king of Austrasia, the northeastern part of the Frankish realm. He was the son of Clotaire I, who had divided the Frankish kingdom among his four sons at his death in 561. Sigebert repelled an invasion by the Avars in 562, and in 567 he inherited the lands of his brother Charibert.

His later years were occupied by wars with his half-brother Chilperic. Sigebert had married a Visigothic princess, Brunhilde, whose sister Galswintha married Chilperic, king of Neustria, which formed the western part of the Merovingian lands. Chilperic had Galswintha murdered so he could marry his mistress Fredegund, and Sigebert, supported by his brother Gontran, claimed Galswintha's lands in the name of Brunhilde. War ensued, and Sigebert forced Chilperic to retreat. He was about to be acclaimed king by Chilperic's subjects when he was assassinated in Vitry by emissaries of Fredegund.

SIGEBERT II, sēzh-bâr′ (601–613), Merovingian king of Austrasia, a kingdom in the northeastern part of the Frankish realm. He was the son of Theodoric (Thierry) II. When his father died in 613, Brunhilde, Sigebert's great-grandmother, proclaimed him king and herself regent. The Austrasian aristocracy rebelled and sought help from Clotaire II of Neustria. Clotaire captured Sigebert and Brunhilde and had them executed.

SIGEBERT III, sēzh-bâr′ (631–656), Merovingian king of Austrasia, the northeastern part of the Frankish realm. He was the son of Dagobert I, King of the Franks, who made Sigebert the king of Austrasia in 634. After his father's death in 639, Sigebert was guided by the Carolingian mayors of the palace, who were the effective rulers. Deeply pious, Sigebert actively promoted Christianity and founded several monasteries. His religious fervor was later rewarded with sainthood.

SIGEL, sē′gəl, **Franz** (1824–1902), German-born American general in the Civil War. He was born in Sinsheim, Baden, Germany, on Nov. 18, 1824. He graduated from the Karlsruhe military academy in 1843 and took part in local rebellions in 1848 and 1849 before emigrating to England (1851–1852) and to the United States. He taught school in New York City and became director of city schools in St. Louis, Mo.

At the beginning of the Civil War, Sigel worked successfully to rally the large German population in the North behind the Union cause. He organized an infantry regiment in Missouri and, as a brigadier general of volunteers, he fought in the Missouri campaigns of 1861 and at the Battle of Pea Ridge (March 7–8, 1862).

Two weeks later he was made a major general and in June received command of an army corps in Virginia. He fought at the Second Battle of Bull Run (Manassas), but his troops lost an important engagement at New Market, Va., in the Shenandoah Valley, on May 15, 1864.

After the war, Sigel was in turn pension agent, collector of internal revenue, and register in New York City. He was also publisher and editor of the *New Yorker Deutsches Volksblatt* and editor (1897–1900) of the *New York Monthly*. His influence was strong among German-descended citizens. Sigel died in New York on Aug. 21, 1902.

SIGHT. See Eye.

SIGISMUND, zē′gis-mō̄nt (1368–1437), Holy Roman emperor. He was born in Nuremberg on Feb. 15, 1368, the son of Emperor Charles IV. Sigismund received an unusually fine education at the court of Prague and his mastery of seven languages impressed his contemporaries. Sigismund succeeded to the margravate of Brandenburg on the death of Charles IV in 1378, while his elder brother Wenceslaus became king of Bohemia and was elected German emperor. In 1380, Sigismund was betrothed to Maria, the daughter and supposed heiress of Louis I the Great, king of Poland and Hungary. But on the death of King Louis in 1382 the Poles chose as their queen Jadwiga, Louis' younger daughter, who in 1386 became the wife of Jagiello, Grand Duke of Lithuania, thereby founding Poland's Jagiellonian dynasty. In Hungary, Sigismund found himself confronted by the opposition of Louis' widow and factions supported by foreign powers. In 1385 he married Maria and was crowned king of Hungary two years later.

The overthrow of the great Serbian kingdom by the Turks in 1389 made Hungary a frontier land and guardian of the west. Sigismund led an army against the Turks in 1396 but suffered a disastrous defeat at Nicopolis (Nikopol). He avoided capture by an adventurous flight into Greece, returning to Hungary to find himself faced with new civil war. At least the Turks failed to direct their chief attack against Hungary. They first turned against the Byzantine Empire and were soon occupied in defending themselves against the invasions of Timur (Tamerlane).

The shortcomings of his brother Wenceslaus, particularly his inactivity and failure to suppress the internal wars raging in Germany and to overcome the Great Western Schism of the church, induced the German princes to depose Wenceslaus as emperor in 1400, but his successor, Rupert of the Palatinate, also proved powerless to solve these grave problems.

Holy Roman Emperor. Rupert's death in 1410 brought Sigismund to the imperial throne the following year, and he gained general recognition by his coronation in Aachen (Aix-la-Chapelle) in 1414. His simultaneous success in convening a general Christian council at Constance for the reform of the church and the restoration of its unity led Sigismund to the height of his political power.

As the protector of the Council of Constance of 1414–1418, he was chiefly responsible for the deposition of the "popes" John XXIII, Benedict XIII, and Gregory XII and the elevation of Martin V to the papal throne in Rome. While the external unity of the church was thus restored, the council failed, in spite of the Emperor's efforts, to achieve a reform of the internal conditions of the church. The council attempted to end the movement that Jan Hus had begun among the Czech people. Sigismund, who had invited Hus to Constance and offered him a safe conduct, felt in accordance with ecclesiastical teaching that he was not bound by his word once Hus had been officially found to be a heretic. Hus died at the stake in Constance on July 6, 1415.

When, in 1419, Wenceslaus died and Bohemia fell to Sigismund, the Czechs rose against Sigismund, and 17 years of wars with the Hussites followed. Sigismund was unable to subdue the Hussite movement by force. He achieved the pacification of Bohemia only by making the Compact of Prague with the moderate Hussite groups, which were granted communion in both forms.

This concession Sigismund received from the Council of Basel in 1433. See also HUSSITES.

Although the Council of Basel (1431–1449) took place in the empire, Sigismund's influence on its deliberations was not significant. Since he spent most of his time and effort after 1418 in the defense of Hungary and the conquest of Bohemia, he could give only limited attention to the empire. In 1433 he was crowned again by Pope Eugene IV, without, however, becoming thereby the arbiter of the internal struggles within the church and the empire. In 1415 he had given the margravate of Brandenburg, together with the electoral dignity, to his chief paladin, Frederick of Hohenzollern. With Sigismund's death in Znaim (now Znojmo, Czechoslovakia) on Dec. 9, 1437, the Luxembourg dynasty became extinct. Hungary and Bohemia were inherited by his son-in-law, Albert V, Duke of Austria, who as Emperor Albert II opened the long succession of Habsburg rulers on the imperial throne.

HAJO HOLBORN
Author of "A History of Modern Germany"

SIGISMUND I, zē'gis-mŏont (1467–1548), king of Poland. He was born on Jan. 1, 1467, the son of Casimir IV. He succeeded his brother Alexander as grand duke of Lithuania and was elected king of Poland in 1506, thereby continuing the personal union between the two realms.

In contrast to his father and to his two brothers, the kings John Albert and Alexander, who reigned before him, Sigismund did not seek the support of the numerous and dynamic gentry (*szlachta*) and became dependent on the great nobles (magnates). During his reign the peasants lost most of their rights and came under the rule of the nobility. Sigismund conducted three inconclusive wars against Muscovy and lost in the dynastic rivalry with the Habsburgs over Bohemia and Hungary, ruled at the time by his brother Vladislav (Ulászló). East Prussia, where the Teutonic Knights were disintegrating, he failed to incorporate into Poland. Despite the wishes of the population, the King allowed the Knights to transform their territory into a secular principality under his Hohenzollern nephew, Albert, 1st Duke of Prussia, who became a vassal of Poland in 1525. However, the duchy of Masovia (Mazowsze), in central Poland, was incorporated into the kingdom in 1529.

Despite some setbacks, the Poland of Sigismund was the most powerful country in eastern Europe, rapidly expanding economically and culturally under the influence of the Italian Renaissance and the first impact of the Reformation. Long-standing ties with Italy were strengthened by Sigismund's second marriage, to Bona Sforza, daughter of the Duke of Milan. Sigismund died in Cracow on April 1, 1548.

SIGISMUND II, zē'gis-mŏont (1520–1572), king of Poland. The son of Sigismund I and Bona Sforza, he was born in Cracow on Aug. 1, 1520. He was recognized as future grand duke of Lithuania at his mother's insistence at the age of two and in 1530 was elected "king apparent" of Poland, while his father was still reigning. He acceded without difficulty to both thrones at his father's death in 1548.

The gentry (*szlachta*) expected him to take the lead in much-needed reforms—to curtail the prerogatives of the aristocracy and to create a firm administration with a treasury capable of financing the country's defense. These expectations did not materialize until later in his reign. At first, the King associated himself with the great nobles (magnates) by marrying Barbara Radziwill, a member of a powerful Lithuanian family, but she died in 1551.

The great achievement of Sigismund, known as Augustus, was the transformation in 1569 of the personal union of Poland and Lithuania into a formal union by the Union of Lublin. Simultaneously, western, or royal, Prussia, hitherto a fief of the kings, was incorporated into the kingdom. Earlier, in a war with Russia, he had gained control of Livonia, an area north of Lithuania. During the reign of Sigismund Augustus the Reformation made considerable progress in the towns, as well as among the landed gentry and a number of aristocratic families. After the Council of Trent and the reforms in the Roman Catholic Church, the Protestant denominations began losing ground. The King was pressed from both sides but decided in favor of religious freedom by leaving the matter to the personal choice of the people. Sigismund died childless in Knyszyn on July 6, 1572, and with him the male line of the Jagiellonian dynasty ended.

SIGISMUND III, zē'gis-mŏont (1566–1632), king of Poland and of Sweden. He was born in Gripsholm Castle, Sweden, on June 20, 1566, the son of King John III of Sweden and Catherine, sister of King Sigismund II of Poland. He was therefore tied to the Vasa dynasty of Sweden and the Jagiellonian dynasty of Poland. Sigismund's election to the Polish throne in 1587 was backed by the influential chancellor, Jan Zamojski, who hoped that a union with Sweden would enable Poland to dominate the Baltic Sea.

Sigismund became king of Sweden at the death of his father in 1592. His ardent Roman Catholicism estranged his Swedish subjects. Duke Karl, his uncle and the future King Charles IX, led the opposition to Sigismund, had himself proclaimed regent, and defeated Sigismund when the King landed in Sweden in 1598. Sigismund was deposed in 1599, but he refused to renounce his claims and plunged Poland into prolonged wars with Sweden.

Religious considerations also stood in the way of a personal or dynastic union between Poland and Russia. After the extinction of the Rurik dynasty in Russia and the resulting confusion and wars, Polish troops occupied Moscow. The Russian boyars offered the crown to Sigismund's son Vladislav (Władysław) in 1610, but the King refused his permission. He apparently wanted the crown for himself, yet made it impossible by rejecting the religious conditions of the Greek Orthodox boyars.

Sigismund, who transferred the Polish capital from Cracow to Warsaw in 1596, was not successful in his relations with the Polish gentry (*szlachta*). Their leader, Chancellor Zamojski, turned against the King, and after Zamojski's death in 1605, Sigismund was confronted by an aristocratic rebellion. Although victorious, Sigismund did not have enough influence to counteract the growing political anarchy mistakenly identified by the *szlachta* as its "golden freedom." Despite the King's strong pro-Catholic feelings, Poland remained neutral during the Thirty Years' War. He died in Warsaw on April 30, 1632.

SIGN LANGUAGE

SIGN LANGUAGE is a system of communication based on a code of hand and arm gestures, or signals. Other parts of the body may also be used. The gestures may be descriptive and intelligible or symbolic and esoteric. Sign languages may be utilitarian or theatrical for communication with people, or they may be ritualistic for communication with deities. They can convey information, issue commands, or tell stories. Fragmentary codes are common. Complete sign languages are still in use in parts of Asia and the Americas. Scholars believe that such systems may formerly have been widespread.

Utilitarian Sign Languages. Many useful signs supplement or replace speech and are, accordingly, arhythmic. Modern fragments include gestures of greeting, signals for traffic control, and hand signals for airplane pilots. A complete system is the deaf-and-dumb alphabet, which spells out words. See also DEAFNESS—*Education and Training of the Deaf.*

A most comprehensive system flourished among the American Indians of the Great Plains. It facilitated communication in trade or war between tribes of different languages. According to early explorers, tribes throughout North America employed a gesture code. During the Great Plains cultural florescence in the 18th and 19th centuries, the nomadic tribes refined the code. Since their dispersal and because of the prevalence of English speech, their sign language has been shrinking to showpieces and to Boy Scout projects.

Plains sign language expresses such concepts as prayer, rain, clouds, and lightning; objects like arrows, animals, and plants; human actions and emotions; and quantity, size, and speed. Details could vary with a speaker's personality, and they could incorporate new cultural objects such as horse or gun. The usefulness of the sign language extended to a related pictographic writing.

Ritual Codes. Gestures that convey requests to deities are ritualistic. American Indian rituals invoked supernaturals to effect cures, produce rain, or fulfill other desires. The codes of their sacred societies have remained secret. Today fragments remain in most tribes, as in the Iroquois and Chippewa. But in semipublic ceremonies of the New Mexico Pueblo Indians, two dance groups maintain ritual sign languages. Sacred clowns and singers in the corn or *tablita* dance gesticulate for rain. Their gestures illustrate song texts, which lure rain gods from the four sky directions to bring moisture down to the earth.

The Indians of the Pacific Northwest impersonate supernaturals, alternating fundamental, fixed gestures with rhythmic mime. To the south, the Indians of Central America do not gesticulate in their dances, but their ancestors apparently did. Ancient Maya and Aztec codices show gods and priests in ritual poses.

In Oceania the traditional Hawaiian hula dances were dedicated to the gods. They told legends or they brought tribute to eminent rulers. Modern hulas are secular. In Bali, Buddhist priests use a gesture code for incantations. Indonesia received from India a code for the enactment of sacred epics, the *Rāmāyaṇa* and *Mahābhārata.* The Hindu mudras or gestures came from the gods Brahma, Vishnu, and Siva. In Manipur the agrarian Laɪ Hairoba dance combines realistic mime with ritual gestures, such as rain-compelling motions.

Theatrical Codes. Gestures that are theatrical address spectators or even deities. The symbols of India and Hawaii combine theater with ritual. The Hindu mudras constitute an elaborate dance art, with body coordination. They were already codified when a sage, Bharata, recorded them two millennia ago. They include signs for gods; emotions, activities, and objects of daily life; and living creatures. The natya dance has sets of mudras for each hand and for both hands, with many variants of orientation. The kathakali school enacts long dramas with a vocabulary of 500 signs, expressing chanted words.

Many Indonesian dances, such as the Burmese pwe provide entertainment. They employ ornamental finger and hand poses. Japanese theater has achieved a peak of precision. The solemn No drama and popular Kabuki theater rely on symbolic poses, as in the monogatari (narration) and in the dammari (dumb show). Fan manipulation can depict violent sword play or fluttering, falling leaves.

In Asian theater, as in ritual languages, the gestures express metaphoric, poetic texts. They form a rhythmic counterpoint with footwork and music.

Comparisons. Many signs recur within the Plains-Pueblo and the Asia-Oceania areas. Some recur in all these areas with similar meanings. They may recur in modern culture, but often with other meanings. For example, the Amerindians describe lightning by a descending zigzag. The Plains sign for rain resembles the Pueblo hand motion, but the latter descends with a more sweeping arm gesture. The Hindu padma hand for lotus reappears in Hawaii. The Hindu pataka hand and the similar ardhachandra pose are widely diffused for consecration, palm focused on people or forces of sky or earth. In the Toxuit dance, Kwakiutl Indian women use this gesture with palms forward or up, to call up earth powers. Aztec priests hold the palm sideward. In the Orient-derived Catholic mass, priests bless with this pose. But a traffic policeman extends his palm to say "Stop." The chandrakala hand signifies the crescent moon in natya, hula, and Plains sign code. But an airplane pilot would read, "Alter heading as indicated."

Some gestures have a universal connotation, but the majority seem to reflect specific cultural concepts. Identical recurrence with the same meaning is significant, for it may support current theories of two-way Asia-America relationships. Archaeologists find evidence for interchange between Oceania and the American northwest coast, and between India and Central America after 100 A. D. The Plains and Pueblo codes developed locally to supply specific needs. But they may well owe impetus to Mexican influence and ultimately to India.

GERTRUDE PROKOSCH KURATH
*Dance Research Center
Ann Arbor, Mich.*

Bibliography

Bowers, Faubion, *The Dance in India* (Columbia Univ. Press 1953).

Brun, Theodore, *The International Dictionary of Sign Language* (Wolfe Pub. 1969).

Hunt, Jack, and Fahringer, Ray, *Student Pilot Handbook* (Books 1943).

Hutchinson, Ann, *Labanotation: A System for Recording Movement* (Phoenix House 1955).

Jensen, Hans, *Sign, Symbol, and Script,* 3d ed., tr. by George Unwin (Allen, G. 1970).

Jones, Harry, *Sign Language* (English Univs. 1968).

(*Bibliography continued on next page*)

Mallery, D. G., and others, *Sign Language Among North American Indians Compared with That Among Peoples of Deaf-Mutes* (1881; reprint, Humanities Press 1971).

Miyake, Syutaro, *Kabuki Drama* (Luzac 1938).

Shawn, Ted, *Gods Who Dance* (Dutton 1929).

Stokoe, William C., Jr., *Sign Language Structure* (Univ. of Buffalo, Dept. of Anthropology & Linguistics 1960).

Tomkins, William, *Universal Indian Sign Language of the Plains Indians of North America* (published by the author 1926).

Watson, David O., *Talk With Your Hands* (published by the author 1964).

SIGNAC, sē-nyȧk', **Paul** (1863–1935), French artist, who was a leading member of the neoimpressionist school, notable for a painting technique called "pointillism." In pointillism, minute juxtaposed dots (stipples or points) of pure pigment, applied to the canvas, fuse into solid colors to create a continuous image through an optical-illusion effect.

Life. Signac was born in Paris on Nov. 11, 1863. He was the son of wealthy parents, and his financial independence permitted him to follow his artistic interests. He was also a clever and astute conversationalist, and he was quickly accepted into the leading contemporary Parisian art circles.

Except for drawing classes, Signac had little formal training. His early works were in the impressionist style, influenced especially by Claude Monet. In 1884 he helped to organize the first Salon des Indépendants, where he met Georges Seurat.

Seurat had been making experiments in a number of painting styles, but, encouraged by Signac, he turned away from the brushstrokes of the impressionists to scientifically placed dots of high-intensity color, to become the leader of the pointillist movement. Seurat, in turn, influenced Signac, who also abandoned impressionism for the new technique. After Seurat's death in 1891, Signac became the acknowledged leader of the neoimpressionists, a group that at various times included Camille Pissarro, Henri Cross, and Maurice Denis among its members.

In 1899, Signac published *D'Eugène Delacroix au néo impressionisme*. This volume, which served as the neoimpressionists' manifesto, defined Signac's theories regarding the scientific division of light into its color components, tracing the historical origins of the pointillist technique and its practical uses. Signac's art was represented in all the exhibitions of the Société des Artistes Indépendants (until 1893), and from 1908 until his death, in Paris, on Aug. 15, 1935, he served as its president.

Work. Signac painted in both oil and watercolor. His oils, while technically precise in regard to color, lack warmth and spontaneity. This quality was particularly evident after 1900, when he abandoned the pointillist dots for small squares of color that give a mechanical mosaic effect. His watercolors, on the other hand, have freedom and life, with a rhythmic line and a vibrant tone that are missing in his oils.

Signac was an avid yachtsman, and his best efforts reflect this interest, with water playing a dominant part in most of his paintings. Significant works include *The Harbor of Saint Cast* (1890; private collection), *Sea Breeze* (1891; private collection), and *Port of St.-Tropez* (1894; Musée de l'Annonciade, St.-Tropez).

Further Reading: Herbert, Robert L., *Neo-Impressionism* (Solomon R. Guggenheim Foundation 1968); Rewald, John, *Post-Impressionism from Van Gogh to Gauguin* (Mus. of Modern Art 1956).

SIGNALING is the means and practice of communication in various commercial fields and in military operations by methods usually other than the direct human voice. Signals are most commonly expressed by visual, audible, or electrical means, utilizing such devices as lights, flags, smoke, sounds, telegraph, telephone, and radio. Among the chief uses of signals are railroad traffic control, road traffic control, and communications by and to ships, airplanes, and other vehicles. In military operations the entire system of transmitting information among the land, naval, and air forces employed, including the use of messengers, falls within the purview of signals and signaling.

MILITARY SIGNALING

The term *military signaling* is applied to all means used to transmit information within the military forces to direct or facilitate the activities of the many components of those forces. These means include visual and audible signals, electrical communications transmitted by both wire and radio waves, as well as messengers and trained animals. *Signal communication* is another term commonly used interchangeably with military signaling.

Signal communication is often described as the voice of command. The commander's voice must indeed have been used to control his troops in wars fought before the dawn of recorded history, just as the same means are used by squad leaders in modern wars. However, the commander's "voice" has taken many forms as the history of warfare has run its course. The voice of command has been a silent puff of smoke over the Italian hills during the time of Hannibal and the piercing note of a bugle in the American Civil War. Genghis Khan extended his voice on the wings of pigeons, and World War II commanders used radio communications.

Messengers. Probably the oldest means of transmitting orders, except the commander's voice, is the messenger. In the 4th century B. C., Persia's King Darius III established a system of couriers spanning his entire empire and used these to send orders to his armies. Riders and fresh mounts were stationed one day's ride apart to carry mes-

Alphabetical smoke signals are believed to have been used in the 2d century B. C. by the historian Polybius.

THE BETTMANN ARCHIVE

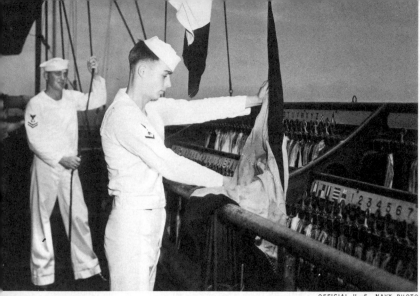

Navy signalmen prepare to hoist a signal using internationally recognized flags. The signal is based on the International Code of Signals by which only a few flags are used to convey a complete message.

sages in relays. In the 19th century, Napoleon kept at his headquarters "staff" officers who were in reality couriers used to transmit orders.

The messenger remains, as always, an important part of military signaling. He may walk or gallop as he did through countless early wars, ride on a bicycle or motorcycle as in World War I, in a jeep or light airplane as in and after World War II, or in a helicopter as in later wars. He is still important in modern armies.

Audible and Visual Signaling. In the fine army that Alexander the Great inherited from his father, Philip II of Macedon (reigned 359–336 B. C.), the commander's voice was supplemented by the trumpet. Standards, swords, and spears were all used to give visual signals to the troops. Alexander changed the custom of breaking camp at the sound of the trumpet to one of using visual signals from a mast near his headquarters when he found that the trumpets alerted the enemy.

Smoke signals were used by Alexander the Great in the 4th century B. C., and by Hannibal in the 3d. Torches were used for signaling at night. Smoke signals were also used by the primitive Indians of North America. In modern armies smoke signals, as well as bright-colored panels, are of definite value in marking the front lines for friendly airplanes flying overhead.

The musicians in the army of Julius Caesar in the 1st century B. C. were not taken along to improve morale but rather to assist the commander in controlling his troops. The cornu (horn) and the tuba were used to direct the infantry in battle movements, while the shrill notes of the lituus (trumpet) directed the cavalry. Caesar also used standards to signal his troops. The Gauls of Caesar's time communicated very rapidly with each other over long distances by means of a system of towers placed on hills, relaying shouts of "sonorous monosyllables" to convey intelligence.

In the Middle Ages, the horn of Roland, hero of the *Song of Roland*, signaled the ambush. Trumpeters were used in later armies, and by the mid-19th century the bugler was the commander's constant shadow. Napoleon supplemented his system of rapid coaches and mounted messengers with a system of semaphores mounted on towers to transmit urgent information between Paris and his armies in the field. The semaphores consisted of mechanical arms that could be raised

and lowered in the proper combinations to indicate specific letters of the alphabet.

Flag telegraphy, or wigwag, a system of signaling with flags, was developed in the mid-19th century by an American Army surgeon, Albert J. Myer, who drafted a memorandum on visual signal devices in 1856, and by two British officers, Capt. (later Sir) Francis Bolton of the army and Capt. (later Vice Admiral) Philip H. Colomb of the navy. This system was first used in combat in the American Civil War. Ironically, it was put to good use by the Confederates in the First Battle of Bull Run, when Gen. Pierre Gustave Toutant Beauregard's signal officer turned out to be a man who had helped Myer test his invention in 1859.

A forerunner of the modern tracer bullets may be found in the whistling arrows used in the 13th century by Genghis Khan to direct the fire of his archers against the enemy. An extremely noisy wooden rattle was used to warn of gas attack during World War I.

One final type of audible signaling deserves mention. At the Battle of Marengo on June 14, 1800, the detached corps of Gen. Louis Charles Antoine Desaix de Veygoux marched to the sound of the guns and arrived in time to save Napoleon's army from defeat. On the second day of the Battle of Gettysburg, July 2, 1863, Confederate Gen. Richard S. Ewell's attack was too late when he could not hear the sound of Gen. James Longstreet's guns, which was the agreed signal for his attack.

Electrical Communications. The practical demonstration of the electric telegraph by Samuel F. B. Morse in 1844 gave the military commander the capability of controlling huge forces over vast distances. The ability to send messages to any point on the earth's surface with virtually the speed of light was one of the truly revolutionary technological advances in warfare.

Wire Communications. Telegraphy was first used in the Crimean War (1853–1856), but its potential was first explored in depth during the American Civil War. President Abraham Lincoln in Washington was able to keep in close touch with military forces in several areas of operations. When a unified command was established by the North, Gen. Ulysses S. Grant could accompany one of his armies in the field and still supply strategic direction to armies operating in other the-

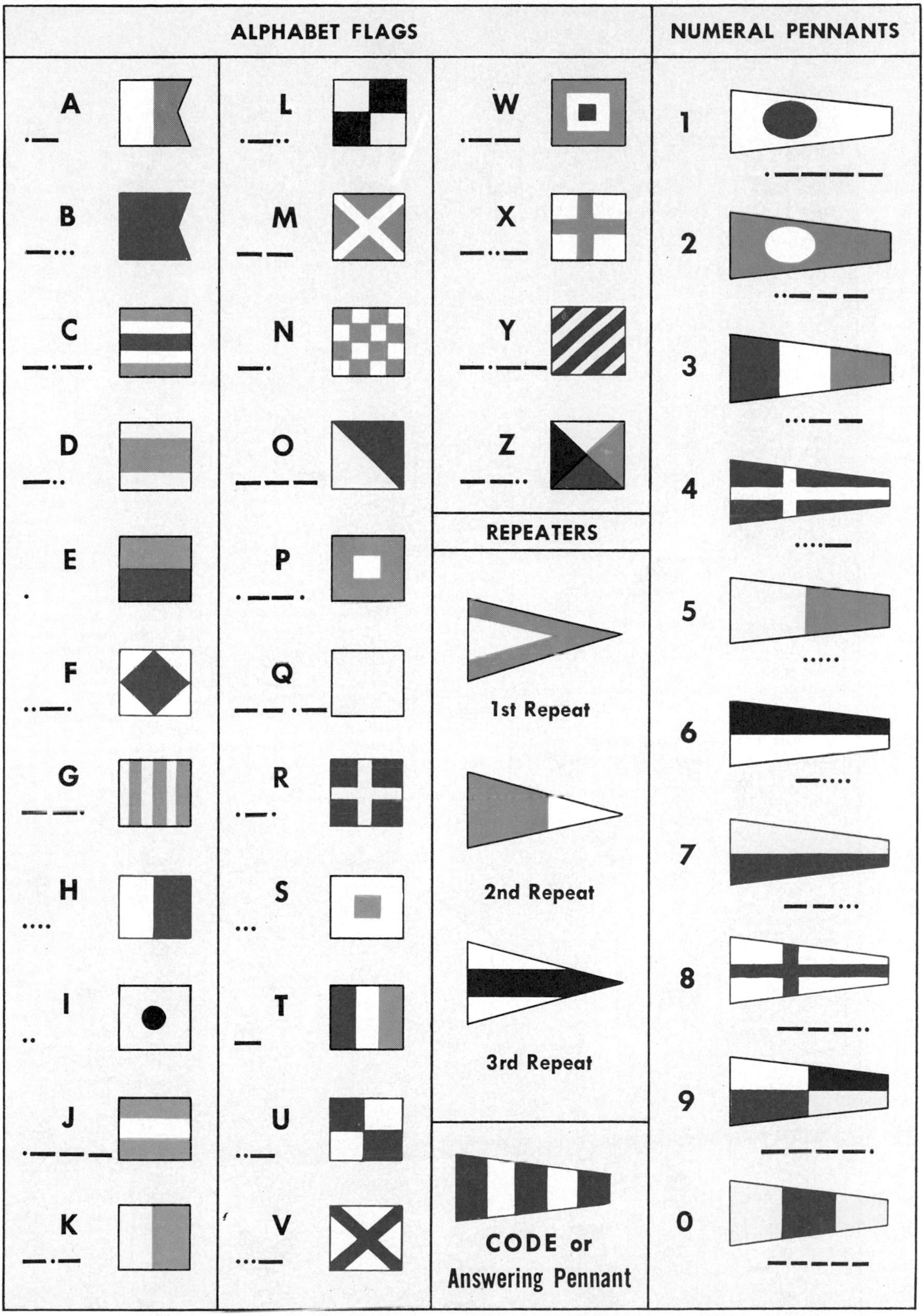

ALPHABET FLAGS

A	· —	L	· — · ·	W	· — —
B	— · · ·	M	— —	X	— · · —
C	— · — ·	N	— ·	Y	— · — —
D	— · ·	O	— — —	Z	— — · ·
E	·	P	· — — ·		
F	· · — ·	Q	— — · —		
G	— — ·	R	· — ·		
H	· · · ·	S	· · ·		
I	· ·	T	—		
J	· — — —	U	· · —		
K	— · —	V	· · · —		

REPEATERS

1st Repeat

2nd Repeat

3rd Repeat

CODE or
Answering Pennant

NUMERAL PENNANTS

1	· — — — —
2	· · — — —
3	· · · — —
4	· · · · —
5	· · · · ·
6	— · · · ·
7	— — · · ·
8	— — — · ·
9	— — — — ·
0	— — — — —

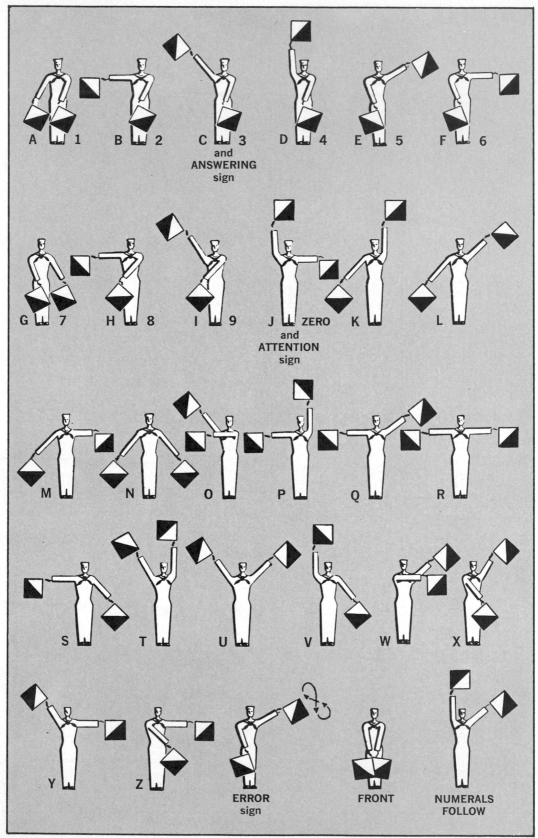

Adapted from "The Bluejacket's Manual," U.S. Naval Institute

Semaphore alphabet, numbers, and special signals.

aters by means of the telegraph. The telegraph also made it possible to control the railroads, which played such an important part in that war.

The field telephone was first used on a large scale in World War I. Telephones connected the higher headquarters, and telephone lines were laid all the way down to the front-line trenches. One of the major problems during the great battles was the maintenance of tactical control while telephones lines were continually being destroyed by massive artillery barrages. One of the valuable uses of field telephones during World War I was to effect liaison between infantry and artillery.

The telephone was the primary means of military signaling in World War II. Tremendous telephone wire and cable systems were constructed in all theaters of war to connect not only the operating forces but also the rear echelon installations of service and supply as well. Again, as in World War I, telephone lines went right down to the front lines, and in this war the signalmen were able to advance those lines as the armies moved forward.

Radio Communications. The most valuable supplement to wire communications in military operations was the radio. Radios had been used in World War I, but only at the higher levels of command, and they were not always reliable. But radio came into its own in World War II. Radios were used to direct bombers to their targets, to direct ground artillery fire from airplanes, and to coordinate tanks and infantry tactical elements in the attack. Radio networks were set up to support the telephone systems within the divisions, corps, and armies. Radios were also used to provide long-distance communications across all the world's oceans. The Allies, using radio, were able to coordinate the complex operations of the land, sea, and air forces in the amphibious assaults of the war—Normandy, Okinawa, and all the rest.

The radios used in World War II and in later wars ranged from the "walkie-talkie," weighing only a few pounds and effective for only a short distance near the foxholes, to large transmitters that beamed messages for hundreds and thousands of miles. It is the military radio in modern times that makes it possible for the commander to control all the elements of his command, no matter how scattered they are or how rapidly they may be moving.

PHILIP L. LANSING
United States Military Academy

MARINE SIGNALING

The term *marine signaling* applies to the methods of communicating between ships at sea and at anchor as well as between ships and shore stations. It includes visual media, radio, and sound-making devices.

History. Communication between ships at sea, especially between naval craft, always has been of critical importance. The origins of systematic marine signaling, however, can be traced back only to 1530, when a Spanish writer, Alonso de Chaves, mentions a formal procedure of signaling as in use in the Spanish Navy. At that time, no signal book had been developed. The fleet commander issued his own plan of signals in his combat or sailing orders. Also dating from 1530 is a British naval order directing the admiral's ship to fly a distinguishing flag, from which, perhaps,

comes the designation of flagship for such a vessel. Sir Walter Raleigh is credited with having promulgated the first detailed signal instructions for a naval force.

In 1715, Jonathan Greenwood made an unofficial attempt to compile a regulation signal book for the British Navy, but the book was not adopted generally. The first official signal book was published by Julian Corbett between 1782 and 1790.

A substantial step forward was taken in 1799 when the British Board of the Admiralty issued the first printed signal book. This book was especially important because all Royal Navy vessels possessed and used it. The alphabetical code developed by Rear Adm. Sir Home Riggs Popham was adopted by the Royal Navy in 1803.

In 1812, Popham improved this code by using alphabetical and numerical flags and increased the permutations of 3- and 4-flag hoists to a vocabulary of about 30,000 words, including geographical, technical, and logistical tables.

Special codes of signals for merchant ships were published in various countries early in the 19th century. Captain Frederick Marryat of the Royal Navy adapted Popham's system of signaling for use in the merchant service in 1817. The one most used by American vessels in the clippership era was revised in 1854 by Henry J. Rogers of Baltimore. In 1844, he patented a marine signaling system that was adopted by the U. S. Navy but by no foreign powers.

During a United States Navy fleet exercise, primary flight control personnel direct air operations from a post aboard the aircraft carrier U. S. S. *Franklin D. Roosevelt.*

OFFICIAL U. S. NAVY PHOTOGRAPH

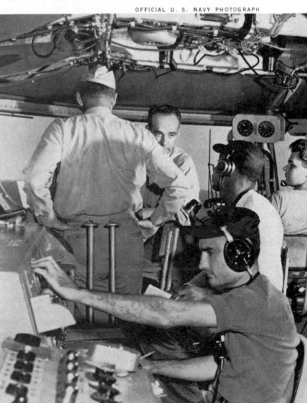

The first code book was produced in 1857 by a committee of the British Board of Trade. The code was intended only for the flag system of signaling and used 18 flags. In its first version the book was entitled *The Commercial Code of Signals*. A French version was published in 1858 under the name *Code commercial des signaux*. It was not until 1870 that the permanent name of *International Code of Signals* was adopted.

The first compilation was simple. Signals were made with up to four alphabetical flags at a hoist. Three-letter groups had meanings for such vital data as latitude, time, date, and weather and even had sets of letters to indicate numerals. After using this code for 30 years, the Board of Trade set up a committee in December 1887 to revise and bring the book up to date and to attempt to formulate a method of using the signals at night. The committee worked until 1897, but the new International Code of Signals was not put into general use until Jan. 1, 1902. The number of flags was increased from 18 to 26, one for each letter, and flag hoists were somewhat more complicated than under the 1857 code. The new code was not truly international and therefore did not prove entirely satisfactory during World War I.

The problem was subsequently referred by the British to the International Radio-telegraph Conference in 1927, and this body assumed responsibility for codes and signals. In 1931 the new *International Code of Signals*, in two volumes, one for visual signals and one for radio, was published. It was adopted on Jan. 1, 1934. Editions were published in English, French, German, Italian, Japanese, Norwegian, and Spanish.

Naval codes and signals are different from the International Code. Each nation has its own naval code book, but since the formation of the North Atlantic Treaty Organization, a NATO code also has been adopted. This code is common to all ships of the NATO nations. By hoisting the International Code pennant, however, a naval vessel notifies a merchant ship that her own language is being used and at the same time indicates to accompanying naval craft that the message is not to be in naval code.

Signaling With Flags. Visual signaling is accomplished by means of flags, flashing lights using Morse code, and by semaphore. Signals must be visible to the ship for which they are intended and therefore are displayed quite high on a ship. Flag hoists always are read from the top down. As a general rule in the merchant serice, only one hoist is shown at a time. When more than one hoist is displayed by a ship, the proper order is to read the flags on the masthead, then the fore triatic stay, the after triatic stay, the outer starboard yardarm, the inner starboard yardarm, the outer port yardarm, and the inner port yardarm, in that sequence.

Each alphabetical flag, when flown by itself ("singly"), is known as a single-letter signal and has a meaning. Single-letter signals are either very urgent or commonly used signals and are to be read by all ships that can observe them. The following are the single-letter signals of the International Code:

A	I am undergoing a speed trial.
B	I am taking in or discharging explosives.
C	Yes (affirmative).
D	Keep clear of me. I am maneuvering with difficulty.
E	I am directing my course to starboard.
F	I am disabled. Communicate with me.
G	I require a pilot.

H	I have a pilot on board.
I	I am directing my course to port.
J	I am going to send a message by semaphore.
K	You should stop your vessel instantly.
L	You should stop. I have something important to communicate.
M	I have a doctor on board.
N	No (negative).
O	Man overboard.
P	(Displayed at the foremast-head in harbor): All persons are to repair on board as the vessel is about to proceed to sea. (Displayed at sea): Your lights are out or burning badly.
Q	My vessel is healthy and I request free pratique.
R	The way is off my ship; you may feel your way past me.
S	My engines are going full speed astern.
T	Do not pass ahead of me.
U	You are standing into danger.
V	I require assistance.
W	I require medical assistance.
X	Stop carrying out your intentions and watch my signals.
Y	I am carrying mails.
Z	Calling a shore station.

Two-letter signals are used principally for distress warnings, navigation, and the maneuvering of ships.

Three-letter signal hoists are divided into six categories: points of the compass, to signal the direction of wind, tide, and current and never to signal a vessel's course; relative bearings representing points on the bow, beam, and quarter, and units of 10° to port and starboard; standard times (the time zones); model verb, to signal the affirmative, negative, and interrogative for any verb for which a code group is provided in the general code; punctuation and simplifying phrases, which always precede the signals to which they refer and consist of question mark and period; general code, which is the combination of letters to convey a word or phrase.

Four-letter signals beginning with the letter A are geographical signals. The names of 11,600 places are given in such signals. Four-letter words not beginning with A are signals for ships and their radio call signs. They are published in a book known as the "Beme List." The first letter—occasionally first two letters—of the group indicates the nationality of the ship. British ships use either G or M as the initial letter, American ships use K or W; ZK means the vessel is under New Zealand registry. In general, four-letter calls are assigned to vessels equipped with radio-transmitting apparatus; two-letter, four-digit calls are allocated to craft equipped with radio-telephone. American naval vessels use the letter N as the first letter of their calls, which are composed of four-letters.

The International Code consists of 26 mostly square alphabet flags, 1 answering pennant, 3 repeaters or substitute pennants, and 10 numeral pennants, 0 through 9. The purpose of the substitute pennants is to permit the use of a letter more than once in a group without having to keep additional sets of signal flags on board. For example, if the group consists of the letters KIKA, the hoist would consist of K, I, first substitute, and A. Should the group be KBBR, the hoist would be K, B, second substitute, and R.

Numeral pennants are used for four distinct types of signals: position signals, always prefixed by the letter P, to transmit latitude and longitude; time signals, always prefixed by the letter T, to convey the time in the 24-hour readings; bearing and bearing position signals, always prefixed by the letter X, to show bearing in degrees from true north, unless otherwise signaled; and course signals, which have no letter prefix.

Signal Lamps and Semaphore.

Signal Lamps and Semaphore. Supplementing these flag signals, which to a considerable extent depend upon prearranged codes, are the flexible devices of signal lamps and semaphore flags. Using the international Morse code, it is possible to transmit messages by light from ship to ship. A blinker tube over a flashlight gives short-range communication with maximum security at night. More powerful battery-operated signaling lights have been developed with ranges up to 2 miles (3 km) in broad daylight and perhaps 4 to 5 miles (6–8 km) at night. Naval craft are equipped with electric-arc searchlights that have shutters in front of the arc. The shutter can be opened and closed to signal the dot and dash of the Morse code over many miles in bright sunlight as well as at night. Usually the limit of range is the horizon, but at night the beam often can be seen well beyond the horizon. Where security of position is not important, the searchlight is an excellent means of sending messages. Signal lights on yardarms are used in the same manner, but the range is much less than with searchlights. Messages transmitted by Morse code can be entirely the sender's composition.

Semaphore flags are as flexible in use as the signal lights, but their range is limited. They can be used only under conditions of good visibility. For naval vessels steaming in column or lying at anchor, or from a shore signaling station to vessels not far away, the semaphore is quite useful. Since a signalman requires only a pair of flags that can be carried in one hand, this method is the most convenient devised for emergency communication.

Radio. For long-range communication, as well as transmission beyond the line of sight, radio is the preeminent medium. The first over-water radio signal was dispatched on May 7, 1898 from Bournemouth, Dorsetshire, England, to the Isle of Wight, 14 miles (22.5 km) away. Development was rapid and constant. Messages may be sent in Morse code, the most dependable and longest-range method, or by radiotelephone. Many rules have been formulated for the use of radio in preserving life at sea. Vessels manned with only one radio operator are required to have an automatic alarm (receiver) that will ring a bell when any emergency call is picked up. Lifeboats of many ships are equipped with emergency transmitting equipment. Using a frequency of 500 kilocycles, the hand-cranked transmitter sends an emergency signal of 12 4-second dashes each minute. An interval of a second occurs between each long dash. Shipboard receiving sets sound the automatic alarm when any 4 of the 12 dashes are picked up.

Radio lacks privacy. A number of devices have been developed to give a measure of security to messages. These include ultrafast automatic transmission from a prepunched tape, speech scramblers for the radiotelephone, and the use of complicated codes and ciphers.

Radiotelephone. The use of radiotelephone is becoming more common, and technical improvements have increased its range and strengthened its dependability. Particularly where language offers no barrier, the radiotelephone has become the preferred method of communication between ships.

Along the Atlantic Coast and on the Great Lakes and inland waterways of the United States, there is constant radiotelephone communication between ships and shore establishments. Towboats on the inland waterways have receiver-transmitters that are constantly tuned to a common wavelength, and the ships' pilots talk directly to each other. No radio operators are carried on these craft.

The versatility of the telephone cannot be matched. For emergencies, the code word is "Mayday," and it is used only in situations justifying broadcast of the SOS in code. Many proposals have been advanced to have all vessels at sea equipped with telephones in the same manner as the inland waterways' towboats, but the problem of overcoming language difficulties has not been solved.

Fog Signals. When visibility is reduced fog signals are used by ships, and visual warnings become ineffective. Ships are required by international rules of the road to have "an efficient whistle," "an efficient foghorn to be sounded by mechanical means," and an efficient bell. Power-driven ships under way are to sound a "prolonged blast" (four to six seconds in duration) at least once each two minutes. Power-driven vessels stopped and making no headway are required every two minutes to sound two prolonged blasts separated by an interval of one second. Vessels at anchor are to ring the bell rapidly for about five seconds at intervals of not more than one minute. In addition, anchored vessels must sound in succession one short blast, one prolonged blast, and one short blast. Similar, but not identical, rules apply to sailing vessels. There also is a complete body of rules governing craft using the inland waters of the United States, in which directives for procedure in making fog signals are set forth.

See also BUOY; LIGHTHOUSE; SEARCHLIGHT; SEMAPHORE.

LANE C. KENDALL
United States Maritime Service

Bibliography

Military Signaling

Colby, Carroll B., *The Signal Corps Today: Its History and Role in Modern Warfare* (Coward 1971).
Ropp, Theodore, *War in the Modern World* (Duke Univ. Press 1959). A short history of warfare in the last 500 years, including references to the influence of military signaling.
Terrett, Dulany, *The Signal Corps: The Emergency* (USGPO 1956). Part of the official history of the U. S. Army in World War II, which gives a brief history of the U. S. Army Signal Corps.
Thompson, George R., and others, *The Signal Corps: The Test* (USGPO 1957). A detailed history of Signal Corps operations from December 1941 to July 1943.

Marine Signaling

Broome, John E., *Make a Signal!* (De Graff 1956). A comprehensive survey of the art of signaling at sea, with special references to naval activity, written for the general reader.
Russell, P. J., *Sea Signalling Simplified for the Merchant Navy, Fishermen, Yachtsmen, Sea Cadets, etc.* (De Graff 1954). A guide to procedures in marine signaling, with a compact list of more or less common signals.

Official Publications

France, Service Hydrographique de la Marine, *Liste des signaux distinctifs et indicatifs internationaux des stations françaises* (Annually).
Great Britain, Board of Trade, *The International Code of Signals for the Use of All Nations*, 2 vols., 20th ed. (1936; vol. 1 reprinted 1951; vol. 2 reprinted 1954).
Great Britain, Hydrographic Office, *The Admiralty List of Radio Signals*, 5 vols. (Usually annually).
United States Hydrographic Office, *The 1931 International Code of Signals*, American ed., 2 vols. (USGPO 1933; reprinted, 1937). This publication contains, besides the complete list of official signals of the time, a brief history of marine signaling.

Luca Signorelli's *Conversion of Saint Paul,* a fresco in the Basilica della Santa Casa in Loreto, Italy.

SIGNORELLI, sē-nyō-rel'lē, **Luca** (c. 1441–1523), Italian painter, who was one of the great masters of the early Renaissance in Italy. As a predecessor of Michelangelo, he is significant particularly for his interest in the anatomy and action of the human figure and for pioneering its use as the dominant feature of monumental mural decoration.

Life. Luca d'Egido di Ventura de' Signorelli was born in Cortona. He was probably trained at Arezzo by Piero della Francesca. His early works are listed by Giorgio Vasari as having been painted in Arezzo churches, but they are lost. In 1475, Signorelli was working in Florence, probably under the influence of Andrea del Verrocchio and the brothers Antonio and Piero Pollaiuolo. By 1479 he was back in Cortona and held a number of political offices there. Outside commissions took him to Loreto (frescoes in the Sagrestia della Cura, about 1480); Rome (frescoes in the Sistine Chapel, 1482–1483); Florence (1491), as counsel for the projected façade of the cathedral and to paint several panels for Lorenzo the Magnificent; and Orvieto (1499–1506), to work on the frescoes of the Chapel of San Brizio in the cathedral.

In 1506, Signorelli went to Siena, where he made cartoons (never carried out) for floor mosaics in the cathedral and where he participated in fresco decorations of the Pandolfo Petrucci Palace, which were executed largely by Girolamo Genga. In 1508–1509 and in 1513, Pope Julius II called him to Rome, where he failed to receive a commission but had some contact with Michelangelo. In 1512 he was sent to Florence as ambassador of Cortona to celebrate the Medicis' return. From 1513 he lived mostly in Cortona, where he died on Oct. 16, 1523.

Works. Signorelli's work shows a consistent respect for the monumental tradition begun with Masaccio's revolutionary *Payment of the Tribute Money* (Brancacci Chapel, Florence)—a tradition developed through the future compositions of Paolo Uccello, Piero della Francesca, Antonio Pollaiuolo, and Melozzo da Forlì. His early frescoes in Loreto, compared to the relatively crude yet forceful figures of his predecessors, show a tendency to subordinate the figure composition to the architectural framework. The same feature appears in the frescoes of the Sistine Chapel, which may have been due in part to his close collaboration with the more restrained Il Perugino and the Florentines, Ghirlandaio and Sandro Botticelli, and in part to the panel-like character of this wall series.

Signorelli's most important works are the frescoes of the Brizio Chapel in the cathedral of Orvieto. Begun by Fra Angelico in 1447 and continued by Benozzo Gozzoli on the vaults of the chapel, the scheme involves a Christ Enthroned, surrounded by the celestial hosts of a Last Judgment. The frescoes extend to the walls of the two bays in free interpretations of such themes as the Fall of the Damned and Crowning of the Elect, and the Fall of the Antichrist and Resurrection. There are also decorative portraits of famous men of antiquity and scenes from Dante, Vergil, and Ovid. The striking combination of powerful, anatomically constructed figures, dynamically composed into an extended space and its architectural framework, is matched by an equally striking originality of content. Signorelli brilliantly combined the traditional Last Judgment theme with motives from Dante's *Divine Comedy* and from such didactic works as Girolamo Savonarola's sermons.

Signorelli's altar and easel paintings offer a more intimate and direct understanding of his development as a painter. The early *Flagellation* panel (Brera Museum, Milan) reveals an interest in light as a means of modeling forms, in luminosity of color, and in strong figures, as well as a tendency toward exaggerated movement. His development can be followed in the *Virgin Enthroned* altar (1484), painted for the Chapel of St. Onofrio in the cathedral of Perugia; the *Circumcision* altar (1492; National Gallery, London); and the famous *tondo* (Uffizi Gallery, Florence), with its scene of Madonna and Child enlivened by classical nude figures in the background. This latter panel, together with *Pan as God of Natural Life and Music* (destroyed in the Berlin Museum during World War II), done for Lorenzo the Magnificent just before his death in 1492, reflects Lorenzo's classical interests and those of his period.

LAURENCE SCHMECKEBIER, *Author of "Handbook of Italian Renaissance Painting"*

SIGNORET, sē-nyô-rā', **Simone** (1921–   ), French actress, sometimes described as having the "saddest face in French cinema" and known for her world-weary roles. Simone Henriette Charlotte Kaminker was born in Wiesbaden, Germany, on March 25, 1921, the daughter of a French Army officer. She attended schools in Paris and in the early 1940's worked there as a typist and a tutor in English and Latin while playing bit parts on the French stage and screen.

One of her first important motion picture roles was in *Macadam* (1946), for which she won the Prix Suzanne Bianchetti in 1947. She then appeared in such notable films as *La Ronde* (1954), *Diabolique* (1955), and *Witches of Salem* (1958). For her performance in *Room at the Top* (1959), she won the American Academy Award. Her later films include *The Day and the Hour* (1964); *Ship of Fools* (1965); *The Sleeping Car Murders* (1966), also starring her husband, Yves Montand; *The Sea Gull* (1968); *Le Chat* (1971); and *Madame Rosa* (1977). She has made numerous stage and television appearances and published an autobiography, *Nostalgia Isn't What It Used to Be* (1978).

SIGURD, zē'gŏort, is the name given in Icelandic sources to a mythological hero called Siegfried in German literature. See SIEGFRIED.

SIGURÐSSON, si'gûrths-son, **Jón** (1811–1879), Icelandic scholar and patriot. He was born in Rafnseyri on June 17, 1811. After graduating from secondary school, he served as a secretary to Bishop Steingrímur Jónsson. In 1833 he went to Copenhagen to study classical philology and history at the university, but he became ill and never finished his studies. In 1835 he turned instead to the study of his native language and literature. He was made a scholar of the foundation honoring Arne Magnússon, an Icelandic historian and archaeologist. Sigurðsson soon became the foremost scholar in his field.

When he went to Copenhagen, the Icelandic romantic poets and idealists had taken the lead in demanding political autonomy for Iceland and a reborn Althing (parliament) at Thingvellir, Iceland's historic capital. Sigurðsson took over this leadership but as a hardheaded realist who wanted the modern Althing as a representative body in Reykjavik rather than at Thingvellir. His plans were successful to a point: the Althing was reestablished in Reykjavik in 1845, and in 1874, Denmark's Christian IX conceded a partly autonomous constitution on the anniversary marking the millennium of the island's settlement.

Better than anyone else, Sigurðsson knew how to deal with his political adversaries, the Danes, by historical argumentation and to rally the Icelanders, both poets and practical men. His liberal periodical, *Ný Félagsrit* (1841–1873), served as a forum for Icelandic political thought. As president of the Icelandic Literary Society and an active member of the Arnamagnaean Foundation of the Society for Northern Antiquaries, he was also by far the most influential leader of Icelandic (Old Norse) studies during his lifetime. He himself edited many of the Icelandic sagas, a new *Diplomatarium Islandicum* (1857–1876), and a periodical devoted to Icelandic history and literature. He died in Copenhagen on Dec. 7, 1879.

STEFÁN EINARSSON, *Author of "History of Icelandic Prose Writers"*

SIHANOUK, sē'hȧ-nōŏk, **Prince Norodom** (1922–   ), Cambodian political leader, who obtained his country's independence from France in 1953 and subsequently headed the government until his overthrow in 1970. He was born in Phnom Penh on Oct. 31, 1922. At the age of 18 he was named king by the French governor general of Indochina following the death of King Sisowath Monivong, his grandfather, on April 23, 1941.

Sihanouk's reign was marked by the effects of the Japanese military occupation during World War II, by prolonged political instability resulting from the transformation of an absolute into a constitutional monarchy in 1947, and by his country's struggle for independence from France in 1945–1953. Sihanouk voluntarily abdicated on March 3, 1955, to free himself for a direct political role aimed at democratizing and stabilizing his country's government. He was succeeded as king by his father, Norodom Suramarit. On the latter's death in 1960, the National Assembly elected Prince Sihanouk to the newly created office of chief of state.

After 1955, as founder and leader of the Popular Socialist Community, a broad-front political movement, Sihanouk became Cambodia's dominant political figure. His domestic program emphasized rapid economic development within a socialistic framework, and internationally he followed a policy of neutralism. During the 1960's this policy resulted in increasing moral and diplomatic support for Communist China and North Vietnam.

The activities of the Vietnamese Communists in Cambodia and the economic stagnation caused by Sihanouk's nationalization policies led to his overthrow in 1970. While Sihanouk was in Moscow, Cambodian Premier Lon Nol and Prince Sisowath Sirik Matak ousted him from power on March 18. Sihanouk then proceeded to Peking and set up a government in exile. On July 5 a Cambodian military tribunal condemned him to death in absentia. In April 1975, after the fall of Cambodia to Khmer Rouge forces, he was named chief of state for life. However, he resigned on April 5, 1976, and retired from public life.

SIKESTON, sīks'tən, a city in southeastern Missouri, in New Madrid and Scott counties, is in the Mississippi River flood plain, about 150 miles (241 km) south of St. Louis and 25 miles (40 km) west of Cairo, Ill., where the Ohio River empties into the Mississippi. It is the grain and cotton market for the surrounding agricultural area. Sikeston's industry includes the manufacture of shoes, canvas products, toys, locks, and milk cartons.

The city was platted in 1860 by John Sikes, and incorporated in 1874. It has a mayor-council form of government. Population: 17,431.

SIKHOTE-ALIN RANGE, sē'кнô-tye ä-lēn', mountain system on the Pacific coast of the USSR, between the Ussuri and lower Amur rivers on the west and the Sea of Japan and the Tatar Strait on the east. About 700 miles (1,125 km) long, it consists of a series of parallel ranges extending in a southwest direction to the area of Vladivostok. Most of the peaks reach elevations of 2,500 to 3,500 feet (760 to 1,065 meters). The highest is Tardoki-Yani, 6,815 feet (2,077 meters). According to the character of the coast, the eastern slope of the system may be divided into two sections. The southern, from Peter the

Great Bay to Olga Gulf, is strongly dissected and has many indentations. The northern, from Olga Gulf to De-Kastri Bay, has undissected shores. The mountain system is covered with coniferous forest in the north and with Manchurian-type broadleaf forest in the south.

The range is very sparsely populated, and the only economic activities are fisheries along the coast and lumbering and mining inland.

THEODORE SHABAD
Editor of "Soviet Geography"

SIKHS, sēks, are followers of the Sikh religion, particularly of Guru Govind Singh, and, by extension, a communal group of East Punjab, India. The word *sikh* is derived from the Hindi meaning "disciples." The religion combines elements of Islam and Hinduism. The Sikhs have supplied some of the world's best soldiers. Jat Sikhs are efficient grain farmers, and after the partition of India in 1947 the number of Sikh moneylenders and businessmen increased.

Growth of Sikhism. Guru Nānak, founder of the Sikh religion and its first guru (teacher), was a 16th century Hindu mystic who had studied both Hinduism and Islam. The Punjab had been annexed by Sultan Mahmud of Ghazni, king of Afghanistan, early in the 11th century, but Muslim rule had alternated with periods of anarchy. When Nānak began teaching in 1499 there was almost complete lawlessness under the weak Lodi dynasty and the government was taking active measures to repress Hinduism. Nānak's doctrines in large part were a response to these chaotic conditions. The core of his beliefs was Hindu but he was undoubtedly greatly influenced by Islam. This mixture of faiths is evident throughout Sikhism, although the religion also contains strikingly original elements. Nānak believed in a monotheistic deity whom he designated Sat Nām ("true name") and who had created all men equal. This emphasis on equality contradicted Hindu caste practices and led him to denounce caste differences and to insist upon the dignity of labor. He reacted against ritual as practiced by both Hindus and Muslims, placing individual conduct before ritual.

Religious leadership was handed down from Nānak through a succession of gurus, listed here with their terms of guruship: Angad (1538–1552), Amardās (1552–1574), Rāmdās (1574–1581), Arjan Mal (Arjun, 1581–1606), Har Govind (Har Gobind, 1606–1645), Har Rāi (1645–1661), Har Kishan (1661–1664), Teg Bahādur (1664–1675), and Govind Singh (1675–1708). The most important of the early gurus was Arjan Mal, who completed the *Ādi Granth,* or first book of the holy scripture of the Sikhs, which contains sayings of Nānak; Kabīr, a predecessor of Sikhism; and other saints. Arjan Mal's Sikh organization finally became so strong that the Muslim ruler had him tortured and executed. The ninth guru, Teg Bahādur, was executed by the Mogul emperor Aurangzeb for refusing to renounce his faith, and Govind Singh, his son, became the tenth and last guru. He divided the concept of guruship into three parts: personal, which would end with him; religious, which would live forever in the *Granth;* and temporal, which he vested in the community, or Khālsā.

Guru Govind Singh set out to make the Sikhs into a fighting force and to strengthen the military and political aspects of the religion. He reaffirmed Nānak's doctrines of the equality of man and the dignity of labor so that women were allowed to participate in Sikh affairs, and in 1699 he instituted the ceremony of baptism. The first five persons baptized came from the five castes, thus symbolizing the unity of all castes. They took the name Singh (lion) and swore to observe the "five k's": not to cut hair or beard (*keś*); to wear a comb (*kanga*), shorts (*kach*), and iron bracelet (*kartha*); and to carry a sword (*kirpan*). Certain other rules of personal conduct, such as refraining from smoking, were also enjoined. Baptism was voluntary and could be repeated as an act of renewed dedication to Sikh ideals. The Khālsā (community of the pure) was said to exist wherever there were five baptized Sikhs, and priests (*granthis*) were merely professional readers of the scriptures. The foundations of a lay organization were thus established. Temples were important to the orthodox only because they were organized around the necessary nucleus of baptized Sikhs and housed the *Granth Sāhib*, an expanded version of the *Ādi Granth.*

Sikhism accepted the Hindu doctrine of reincarnation, but decried contemplation as a vehicle of grace. The main Sikh devotion was service: service to one's family, to Sikhism, to mankind, and finally, the greatest service of all, to God through martyrdom. God was worshiped as the cause of causes, and the relation to him was mystical and highly personal. Daily prayers were generally said in private, and service took the place of both ritual sacrifice and ritual purity. Mysticism was thus wedded to a worldly ethic. The Akāli, or Sikh holy man, was an itinerant fighter, and the ideal man was the saint-warrior.

The Sikh Empire. Guru Govind Singh was assassinated in 1708 by one of his Muslim retainers, and his two young sons were captured and cruelly executed at Sirhind. Bāndā led a rebellion to avenge these deaths, Sirhind was razed in 1710, and the following years saw constant struggle between the Sikhs and the weakening Mogul rulers. By 1802 a new military leader, Ranjit Singh, had united the Sikh *misls* or chieftainships and established his capital at Lahore. By this time the British had entered the Punjab, and in 1809 an agreement was signed recognizing the Sutlej River as the boundary between British India and the Sikh Empire. Ranjit Singh annexed Kashmir in 1819 and by 1834 had brought Peshawar within the empire. Despite the dissolute life led by Ranjit Singh in his last years, there is no doubt of his military genius, and he was highly respected by the British. Factional disputes weakened Sikh unity, and the Sikhs were defeated by the British in the two Sikh Wars of 1845–1846 and 1848–1849.

British Rule. The Sikhs cooperated with the British in reconstructing the central authority that had lapsed after Ranjit Singh's death. In the Indian Mutiny (1857–1858) they were loyal to Britain, and the British later recruited large numbers of Sikhs for the Indian Army and the police. The Singh Sabhā movement for furthering Sikh education received government approval and in 1902 culminated in an association called the Chief Khālsā Diwān, which took the lead in Sikh affairs. Discontent was brewing, however, and the revolutionary activities of the Ghadr party, which was formally organized in 1913 by Indians in the United States, were largely Sikh in inception, although they were repudiated by the Chief Khālsā Diwān. In World War I, Indian sentiment was strongly in support of Britain. On

April 13, 1919, the "Amritsar Massacre" occurred when Gen. Reginald Dyer ordered his troops to fire into a crowd composed largely of Sikhs, at Jāllianwālā Bagh, a square in the city, to make them disperse. According to the government estimate, some 1,500 people, including women and children, were left dead or dying. During the dispute over the management of Sikh shrines (1920–1925), the Sikhs followed the passive resistance being promulgated at the time by Mahatma Gandhi. Passive resistance was felt to be an additional test of Sikh personal hardihood, and it accorded with Sikh emphasis on martyrdom. During this dispute the Chief Khālsā Diwān lost prestige, and leadership passed to the Akāli party, which gained further support after the government conceded Sikh rights and established the Shiromani Gurdwara Prabandhak Committee (SGPC) to control Sikh shrines. After 1919, Sikh energies were turned more and more toward demands for Indian independence, although Sikhs were again loyal to Britain during World War II.

Sikh Partition. Viscount (later 1st Earl) Mountbatten of Burma, as the last viceroy of India, consulted Sikh leaders before declaring the government plans for the partition of India, and the Sikhs accepted the decision of the Boundary Commission made on Aug. 18, 1947. Hindu-Muslim riots had begun in Calcutta a year earlier, and from there they spread to Bihar. The first Sikhs were involved in the winter of 1946–1947 when rioting broke out in the North-West Frontier Province and the Punjab. It is estimated that there were between 200,000 and 500,000 casualties during the transfer of populations between West Pakistan and India, and Sikhs were actively engaged in the riots. By the spring of 1948 the Sikhs west of the boundary had joined their co-religionists in India.

The SGPC remained in control of Sikh shrines. The Communist party of the Punjab, founded by a branch of the old Chadrites, was composed largely of Sikhs, but the party weakened after both the Akāli Party and the Congress condemned their war policy as treason, and not until 1952 did it reemerge as a political force. The Patiala and East Punjab States Union of 1948–1956 was largely Sikh in population and played an increasingly prominent role in Sikh leadership. Although many Sikhs belonged to the Congress party, the Akāli party remained the all-Sikh political group. One of its leaders, Master Tara Singh, former president of the SGPC, several times expressed a demand for a separate Sikh state. The point at issue between leaders was the degree to which the Sikhs should participate in Hindu policy. Baptism became less frequent in the decade following partition, there was an increase in the number of *sahajdhari* or clean-shaven Sikhs, and Hindu influence became greater. There was also some growth in subsects that accepted the religious teaching of other gurus. Approximately 6 million Sikhs, however, whether baptized or not, still followed the teaching of Guru Govind Singh.

MARIAN W. SMITH
Formerly, University of London

Further Reading: Archer, John C., *The Sikhs in Relation to Hindus, Moslems, Christians, and Ahmadiyyas: A Study in Comparative Religion* (Princeton Univ. Press 1946); MacAuliffe, Max A., *The Sikh Religion: Its Gurus, Sacred Writings and Anthems*, 6 vols. (Clarendon 1909); Singh, Khushwant, *A History of the Sikhs*, 2 vols. (Princeton Univ. Press 1963–1966).

ALICE S. KANDELL, FROM RAPHO-GUILLUMETTE
A family in Sikkim. Most of the people of this small state of India are of Mongoloid stock.

SIKKIM, sik'im, formerly a protectorate of India in the eastern Himalaya, became a state of the Indian Union in 1975. It is bounded on the east by Bhutan, on the west by Nepal, and on the north by China. Sikkim's capital city is Gangtok.

The Land. Sikkim extends about 70 miles (110 km) from north to south and is 50 miles (80 km) wide. It has an area of 2,744 square miles (7,107 sq km). The terrain, almost entirely mountainous, ranges in altitude from about 750 feet (230 meters) in the south to 28,146 feet (8,579 meters) at the summit of Kanchenjunga. The climate varies from tropical to alpine, and rainfall generally exceeds 100 inches (2,500 mm) annually, falling mostly in the period from April to September.

The People. Sikkim's population of 204,760 (1971) is overwhelmingly of Mongoloid stock. About 70% of the people are Hindu (mainly Nepalese) and 30% Buddhist (mainly Lepcha, the principal indigenous group, and Bhotia). Though Lamaistic Buddhism is the state religion, its relative strength has steadily waned. Polyandry, once common, has also declined.

Economy. Agriculture, primarily of a subsistence nature, supports the bulk of the people. Maize is by far the most important crop. Rice, planted on hillside terraces with vertical extensions up to 3,000 feet (900 meters), is also important. Other crops are millet, buckwheat, wheat, barley, and potatoes. Orchards of bananas, oranges, apples, and cardamons provide some cash income.

Fairly rich superficial copper deposits in the south are worked by Nepalese using primitive hand methods. Magnetitic iron ores also occur but have not been exploited.

ALICE S. KANDELL, FROM RAPHO-GUILLUMETTE

Hillside terraces in mountainous Sikkim are planted with rice, one of the country's major food crops.

History and Government. The Lepchas of Sikkim are said to have been converted to Buddhism by lamas from Tibet in the 16th century, and the Sikkimese ruling family is believed to have originated in Tibet. British influence dates from 1816, when Britain forced the Gurkhas of Nepal to withdraw from Sikkim. In 1890, after a British military victory over Tibet, a convention was signed under which China recognized a British protectorate over Sikkim. British protection ended when India became independent in 1947. Under a treaty signed in 1950, Sikkim formally became a protectorate of India. Trade was primarily with India, and India maintained strategic roads to Tibet across the high passes of Jelep La and Natu La. Although internal affairs were administered by the chogyal (maharaja), assisted by executive and legislative councils, India was responsible for defense and foreign affairs.

In 1974 a civil revolt, with demands for more democratic government, resulted in India's sending in troops. In May it was agreed that a new National Assembly would be elected. With India's support, the assembly voted in April 1975 to abolish the monarchy and to make Sikkim a state of India. These moves were approved in a referendum in mid-April, and Sikkim was formally made the 22d state of India on May 16, 1975.

JOSEPH E. SCHWARTZBERG*
University of Minnesota

SIKORSKI, sē-kôr'skē, **Władysław** (1881–1943), Polish prime minister and general. He was born in Tuszów, near Sandomierz, Russian Poland, on May 20, 1881, and was educated at the Polytechnic Institute in Lwów (Lvov). He became a leader of Jozef Pilsudski's Polish legions in World War I and then commanded an army in the Polish campaign against the Bolsheviks in 1920, distinguishing himself in the defense of Warsaw. After World War I he was Poland's prime minister (1922–1923) and minister of war (1924–1925). Sikorski opposed Pilsudski's seizure of power in 1926 and subsequently declined in influence, retiring in 1928. He spent the next several years writing on military affairs.

In 1939, Sikorski became prime minister and war minister in the Polish government in exile, which he established in France. As Polish commander in chief, he raised an army, which was evacuated to Britain in 1940. He then organized Polish forces in various parts of the world and reorganized Polish air units in Britain, enabling them to participate effectively in the Battle of Britain. An agreement with the Soviet Union in 1941 for restoration of diplomatic relations and release of Polish prisoners for combat service against the Axis foundered in 1943, and Russo-Polish relations were severed.

Sikorski died in an airplane crash near Gibraltar on July 5, 1943, after inspecting Polish forces in the Middle East.

SIKORSKY, si-kôr'skē, **Igor I.** (1885–1972), Russian-American aeronautical engineer who pioneered in the design of helicopters and multiengine airplanes. Sikorsky was born in Kiev on May 25, 1885. After graduating from the Naval College at St. Petersburg (now Leningrad) in 1906 and the Institute of Technology at Kiev in 1908, he became chief engineer at a Russian aviation factory in 1912. In 1913, he built and flew the first multiengine airplane. During World War I, he made a fortune building four-engine bombers for the Russian Army but lost it when he fled Russia during the Revolution.

Sikorsky arrived in the United States in 1919 and in 1923 formed the Sikorsky Aero Engineering Corporation, which produced the 14-passenger S-29, one of the first twin-engine planes made in the United States. In 1928 his company became a division of United Aircraft Corporation, with Sikorsky as its engineering manager. In that post he developed several airplanes, including the S-40 (1931), the first large American four-engine flying clipper, and the S-42 (1935), which was used in pioneering commercial transpacific and transatlantic flights. In 1939 he developed the first American helicopter capable of sustained flight and satisfactory control. This helicopter, the VS-300, was the forerunner of a long line of helicopters bearing his name. Sikorsky retired, except as a consultant, in 1957. He died in Easton, Conn., on Oct. 26, 1972.

SILAGE, sī'lij, also called *ensilage,* is a moist livestock feed that is produced by the storage of moist forage, grain, or grain by-products in the presence of acids and an atmosphere with no oxygen. The crop is cut at a certain stage in its growth, as explained below. It is then placed in a silo, an airtight container that may take the form of a tall cylinder, a bunker, or a trench. There the plant cells and certain adhering microorganisms live only a few hours until they have exhausted the entrapped oxygen. However, other microorganisms are also present—anaerobic bacteria, which can live without oxygen. These bacteria multiply, living on the sugars and other carbohydrates in the stored product and converting them to organic acids. After one to three weeks of storage, a sufficient concentration of acids is generated to prevent any further growth of the bacteria. The result is silage, which will remain preserved almost indefinitely so long as oxygen is excluded.

Kinds and Uses. Indian corn and sorghums are the crops best suited for silage making, because they contain sufficient carbohydrates of the kinds that are readily converted to lactic and acetic acids. However, most forage crops can be successfully made into silage if their moisture content is lowered to about 70% before storing. Alfalfa, red clover, timothy, Napier grass, oats, bromegrass, sugarcane, beet tops, and sweet-corn stover are some of the important crops used. Moist grain, ears, and seed heads from corn, sorghum, oats, and other crops can be made into silage that has a much higher feed value than when the whole plant is used. Silage made from forage crops or mixtures of forage crops is commonly referred to as grass silage and offers a higher protein content than corn does.

Silages made from corn, sorghums, and forage crops are used as succulent roughages to replace or supplement hay and pasture in the rations of cattle and sheep. Average silage and hay have approximately the same feeding value, when determined on the basis of the dry matter they contain. Good silage is palatable, and when fed in combination with hay or poor pasture, it increases the roughage intake by cattle. It is much higher than hay in carotene—a source of vitamin A to livestock. In the spring and early summer, pastures usually grow faster than animals can graze them off, so the surplus growth is frequently made into silage. This in turn may be used to supplement pastures in the dry part of the summer when growth is retarded. However, silage is primarily used for winter feeding. Grain-type silages are more prevalent because they are adapted to large-scale, intensive feeding programs. Such programs are necessary in areas where labor and overhead costs are high and where relatively low prices of farm products permit only a small margin of profit.

Preparation. When silage is being made, corn, sorghums, and other grain crops are usually allowed to mature to the stage at which the crop contains 65% to 75% moisture. These crops are cut and chopped with a silage harvester, which performs both operations simultaneously. A trailing wagon or truck is used to collect the chopped material and haul it to the silo. The material is unloaded into the silo with a blower or other machinery, depending on the kind of silo. The filling is done either at the rate of 50 or more tons per day or by careful spreading and packing of the chopped material at slower rates. In both cases the aim is to keep the amount of entrapped air to a minimum.

High-quality leafy and succulent forage crops are cut and allowed to dry in the field to about 70% moisture before being chopped and placed in the silo. If this processing is not done first, the silage develops an objectionable odor, and portions at the bottom of the silo may become water-soaked and too acid to make palatable feed. Furthermore, silage made from crops with more than 75% moisture may lose 10% to 20% of its feeding value through seepage, because the plant juices are pressed out of the heavy forage by its own weight.

Losses of dry matter invariably occur in the making of silage, even though the seepage loss can be avoided. That is, carbohydrates are oxidized during the period when plant cells and microorganisms are exhausting the entrapped air of oxygen, and the anaerobic organisms are developing enough acidity to preserve the crop. This oxidation results in a 10% to 20% loss of dry matter from forages and a 3% to 5% loss from grains converted into silage. These are known as fermentation losses. In addition, a top loss of about 5% dry matter usually results from the development of molds on the exposed surfaces of the silage mass, unless it is sealed with an airtight cover of plastic film or other suitable material.

Lethal concentrations of carbon dioxide or nitrous oxide or both sometimes accumulate in tower- and pit-type silos when the silos are partially filled. These gases are given off as by-products during the depletion of oxygen and the development of acidity. Cautious workmen aerate a silo with the blower of the elevator before entering it after interruptions in the course of the filling operation. See also SILO.

ROBERT B. MUSGRAVE
Cornell University

Further Reading: Murdoch, John, *Making and Feeding Silage* (Farming Press 1961); U. S. Department of Agriculture, *Food and Life* (USGPO 1939); Wilson, Harold K., *Grain Crops*, 2d ed. (McGraw 1955).

SILAS, sī′ləs, was the companion of St. Paul on some of his missionary journeys and acted as a secretary to St. Peter. Silas was a Roman citizen and prominent in the affairs of the Jerusalem church. The Silas mentioned in Acts and the Silvanus named in the various epistles of Paul and I Peter are undoubtedly the same person. He was chosen by Paul to accompany him on his second missionary journey. He was beaten and imprisoned with Paul at Philippi (Acts 16: 12–40). When Paul went on to Athens from Borea, Silas remained there for a time and then rejoined him at Corinth, where I Thessalonians was composed. It opens with a greeting from "Paul, Silvanus, and Timothy." Some time later, Silas joined St. Peter and may have had a hand in the composition of I Peter in which he is mentioned (5:12). According to legend, Silas was the first bishop of Corinth.

SILAS MARNER, sī′ləs mär′nər, is a short novel by the English writer George Eliot, published in 1861. It is one of the most popular of her works. Its story has beauty and significance, and the skillful characterizations and narrative technique, as well as the author's moral insight, make this novel an unquestioned masterpiece of 19th century English fiction.

The story is laid in the typical English village of Ravelow, at a time "when the spinning wheels hummed busily in the farmhouses." Against a picturesque and realistic background of rural life and custom, George Eliot set the strange and alien figure of the weaver, Silas Marner, who went there as an outcast from a narrow religious community in the city, where he had been unjustly convicted of robbery. Utterly broken in spirit, bankrupt of his simple faith, and cut off from all kindly human interests, he became a miser, cherishing the ever-growing heap of his earnings at the loom as the sole object of his starved affections. When his gold was stolen by the vicious Dunstan Cass, younger son of the village squire, his life was left utterly barren and he became practically insane.

At this crisis the abandoned wife of Godfrey Cass, Dunstan's elder brother, perished in the snow before Marner's hut, and her child, Eppie, was found by Marner and welcomed as a providential gift sent to replace his stolen gold. The theme of the novel is the transformation in Marner's life, the restoration that comes to his simple and affectionate soul with this substitution of a human love, demanding care and sacrifice, in place of the miser's love of gold.

Interwoven with the story of Silas is that of Godfrey Cass, the good-hearted but weak and badly brought up father of Eppie. He paid for his unwillingness to accept the consequences of his unworthy marriage by seeing Eppie, when grown to womanhood, adhere to her foster father even after Godfrey and his second wife, Nancy, had told her the truth about her parentage and welcomed her to their childless home.

JAMES H. HANFORD
Author of "John Milton, Englishman"

SILENUS, sī-lē′nəs, in classical mythology, was the chief deity of certain woodland spirits, called sileni. The sileni are sometimes confused with Greek satyrs and Roman fauns. In literature and art Silenus appears as old and obese, bald but bearded, pug-nosed, with equine ears, legs, and tail, and carrying a wineskin. He is generally intoxicated and therefore, since he cannot trust his feet, usually riding or supported by other sileni. Silenus was a companion of Dionysus, the wine god, whom he reared and initiated in the joys of revelry. Since he knew important secrets and had prophetic gifts, he was often captured and held by inquirers until he answered their questions.

SILESIA, sī-lē′zhə, is an area in central Europe of economic and historical significance, over which European powers fought for centuries. The German form of the name is Schlesien, the Polish is Śląsk, and the Czech is Slezsko. Since World War II it has been almost entirely in the Katowice, Opole, Wrocław, and Zielona Góra administrative districts of south and southwestern Poland, but with smaller areas also in Czechoslovakia and East Germany.

In early 1938, when the great bulk of Silesia was part of Germany, German Silesia had a population of 4,800,000. Following annexations from Czechoslovakia and Poland, the area increased by more than 4,000 square miles (10,400 sq km) and the population to over 7,600,000 in 1941. As redistributed following World War II, Polish Silesia has an area of approximately 17,500 square miles (45,325 sq km) and Czech Silesia, which was restored after the war to its pre-1938 status, an area of 2,132 square miles (5,422 sq km).

The area known as Silesia extends, southeastward approximately 220 miles (355 km) along the Oder River Valley, with an approximate width of over 70 miles (115 km). The largest city is Wrocław (Breslau), lying roughly in the center and containing a university and an archbishopric. The population of Wrocław rose greatly when the Germans concentrated industry there

during World War II, but it declined drastically after its accession to Poland in the postwar redistribution. Besides the centrally flowing Oder River, the other great land feature is the Sudety range that extends along the southwest border of Silesia, which rises to 5,259 feet (1,603 meters).

Historically the area is divided into Upper and Lower Silesia. Upper Silesia is in the southeast, with Opole (Oppeln) as its chief city. This region is particularly important for heavy industry, including ironworks and steelworks, and for lead, zinc, and nickel mines. Lump and brown coal are mined, the former particularly in the Gliwice-Tarnowskie Góry Mysłowice (Gleiwitz-Tarnowitz-Myslowitz) triangle, which was second only to the Ruhr in German coal production. Lower Silesia is in the northwest, and its most important cities are Wrocław and Legnica (Liegnitz) in Polish Silesia, and Görlitz, across the Neisse River in East German Silesia. Lower Silesia has been notable for manufacturing and agriculture. In Wrocław, Legnica, and Görlitz, the textile industry has been important since the 18th century. Wrocław also produces cars, tools, power machines, and electrical equipment. There are well-developed road, rail, and canal systems.

Until World War II, Silesia as a whole had been able to produce enough meat, potatoes, bread, sugar, and dairy products to feed a population several times its size. This is a notable output for the amount of mining and industry and the generally heavy population density in the area. Rye, oats, wheat, and barley are the principal grains, while vegetables, fruits, and tobacco are also grown. Over one quarter of the land is forest.

Early History. The name Silesia is Germanic in origin, derived from the Silingae, a Vandal tribe that lived in the area in the approximate period 300 B.C.–350 A.D., when they migrated westward. They were replaced by a Slavic people, and by the year 1000 the Polish bishopric of Wrocław had been established. Although, there had been earlier Bohemian claims, Emperor Henry III in the 11th century awarded Silesia to a Polish duke, who paid tribute to Bohemia. The rightful inheritor, Vladislav (Władysław) was expelled by his brothers in 1146. In 1163, Emperor Frederick I Barbarossa invaded the territory and divided Vladislav's lands between his two surviving sons. This settlement marked the beginning of Upper and Lower Silesia.

In the 13th century the land took on a Germanic character with the coming of large

SILESIA

- Prussian Silesia before 1919
- Austrian Silesia before 1919
- Portion of Upper Silesia ceded to Poland in 1921
- Area now in East Germany

Silesia has many tiny villages sheltering in the valleys between its mineral-rich hills and mountains.

numbers of German colonists, who developed commerce and agriculture. Wrocław became important on the east-west trade route to Kiev. In the same century, however, the Tatars invaded Silesia, causing vast destruction. During the 14th century the Polish kings, under whom the land had been parceled into a number of principalities, renounced their claims in treaties of 1335, 1356, and 1372 and were replaced by Bohemian kings. However, this action amounted to little more than a change in overlordship, since the princes of Silesia remained of the same Polish family, the Piasts. Nevertheless, the political and religious connection with Bohemia was close, and the Hussite Wars of the early 15th century ravaged Silesia.

Between 1469 and 1490, Matthias Corvinus, King of Hungary, extended his rule over many of the towns of Silesia, though the countryside remained largely under Bohemia. Following the death of Louis II, king of Hungary and Bohemia, in the Battle of Mohács in 1526, Silesia came under the control of the Habsburgs, as Ferdinand, the brother-in-law of Louis II, inherited the crowns of Hungary and Bohemia. By this time the Lutheran movement was spreading, and Silesia, along with Bohemia, became Protestant. The work of the Counter Reformation, however, was successful, and it was not until 1648, after the ravages of the Thirty Years' War (1618–1648), that Calvinism and Lutheranism were both recognized as legal religions. The success of Charles XII of Sweden undid Catholic domination, and Emperor Joseph I was forced at Altranstädt (1707) to restore many churches to the Protestants.

The development of mining and textiles in the 17th and 18th centuries made Silesia one of the most valuable parts of the Habsburg realm. In 1740, in defiance of the Pragmatic Sanction of 1713, which legalized Habsburg succession through the female line, Frederick II of Prussia seized ·Silesia from Maria Theresa of Austria. Frederick's flimsy claim was based on a treaty of 1537 by one of the many Polish princes of Silesia with the state of Brandenburg. By 1742, Maria Theresa had been forced to cede all of Silesia, except Cieszyn (German, Teschen; Czech, Těšín), Opava (Troppau), and Krnov (Jägerndorf) to Prussia. This settlement was further stipulated by the Treaty of Dresden (1745) and in the Peace of Aix-la-Chapelle (1748) and was the principal result of the War of Austrian Succession. Prussian possession of Silesia was again reaffirmed after the Seven Years' War (1756–1763), and thereafter most of it remained under Prussia until after World War I.

Modern History. During the 19th century and the early 20th, Silesia played an important role in Germany's economic development, but, following Germany's defeat in World War I, Poland made claims to all of Silesia. In 1919 the newly constituted Czechoslovakia took over the Austrian parts of Silesia west of Cieszyn, this city being divided between Czechoslovakia and Poland by the settlement. Attention was now focused on Upper Silesia, and in 1920 an allied commission came to Opole, which became the scene of disorders. The French occupation forces, meanwhile, were both inadequate and pro Polish. On March 20, 1921, a plebiscite was held, with 707,-605 votes being cast for union with Germany and 479,359 for inclusion in Poland. Following more disorders the Council of the League of Nations took charge and divided Upper Silesia. While a considerable portion remained with Germany, the partition seriously affected the economic unity of the area. The cession of Katowice (Kattowitz), Chorzow (Königshütte), Lubliniec (Lublinitz), Pszczyna (Pless), Rybnik, and Tarnowskie Góry (Tarnowitz) to Poland brought with it at least two thirds of Silesia's steelworks, three quarters of the coal, and four fifths of German zinc, which was then one sixth of world production. The fact that many people in Upper Silesia spoke neither German nor Polish but a dialect called Wasserpolnisch further clouded the issue. A convention reached in Geneva in 1922, providing for minority rights for 15 years, could hardly be regarded as successful. After the Munich agreement of September 1938, Hitler took most of Czechoslovakian Silesia, and with Poland's collapse in 1939 the rest of Upper Silesia was reclaimed by Germany.

In early 1945 the Russians drove the Germans out of Silesia with accompanying atrocities equaling those of the Nazis. By summer the USSR, having taken eastern Poland, assigned much eastern German territory to Poland, including practically all of Silesia. The Poles now outdid the Russians in retribution against the Germans. In the last months of the war about two thirds of the German population moved westward, but many had returned when the Poles closed their new borders, including the Oder-Neisse line, which left the northwest corner of Silesia, including Görlitz, in East Germany. Meanwhile, Czechoslovakia recovered its areas that had been seized by Nazi Germany. As a result of great pressure, 3,150,000 Germans left Silesia after the war, mostly for West Germany, and only 700,000 remained. Many Poles moved to Silesia.

MARVIN L. BROWN, JR.
North Carolina State University

Further Reading: Kaeckenbeeck, Georges, *The International Experiment of Upper Silesia* (Oxford 1943); Kaps, Johannes, *The Tragedy of Silesia, 1945–1946*, tr. by Gladys H. Hartinger (Verlag Christ Unterwegs 1952–1953); Rose, William J., *The Drama of Upper Silesia* (Daye 1935).

SILHOUETTE, sil-ə-wet′, a flat monochrome image sharply outlined against a contrasting ground, especially a profile portrait cut out of black paper. Silhouetting as a painting technique was used in Stone Age cave art, Egyptian low reliefs, and black-figured Greek pottery. In 17th century Europe some painters did shadow portraits from the shadows cast by a head placed between a light and a wall.

In 18th century France, such portraits were cut out of paper, notably by the French finance minister Étienne de Silhouette, who made them as a hobby. As a result of his advocacy of economies to fill the depleted treasury, people wore coats without folds, used wooden instead of porcelain snuff boxes, and bought cut-paper portraits instead of painted miniatures. The term *à la Silhouette* meant "on the cheap," and the name was retained for the portraits.

Silhouettes were popular in the late 18th and the early 19th century, partly because, in a period of neoclassicism, they were believed to be in the Greek style. Most were portraits, but some were whole scenes. The usual method was freehand cutting of paper by such artists as Francis Torond and Auguste Edouart. Early English silhouettes were painted black on white, as, for example, those by John Miers. The silhouette style was later diluted by the use of color and painted details. Silhouettes were replaced by photography about 1850, but the style was used for early 20th century cartoon films. Silhouette-making is a part of some school art programs.

Further Reading: Lister, Raymond, *Silhouettes* (Pitman 1953); Mégroz, R. Louis, *Profile Art Through the Ages* (Philosophical Lib. 1949).

SILICA, sil′ə-kə, or silicon dioxide (SiO_2), is a very common compound in nature, both in free form as in quartz and in combined form as in the silicates. It is used in the manufacture of glass, water glass, ceramics, enamels, refractories, foundry molds, abrasives, concrete, mortar, and silicon carbide and other silicon compounds. In powdered form it is a filler in pharmaceuticals, cosmetics, and paper, and it also serves as a plasticizer in resins, an anticaking agent in foods, a thermal insulator, and a decolorizing and purifying agent.

Silica is colorless and tasteless and physiologically inert, although prolonged breathing of silica dust leads to silicosis. The compound is insoluble in water and most acids and alkalis, but it reacts with hydrogen fluoride and more slowly with heated phosphoric acid, and in amorphous and finely divided form it dissolves in alkalis. Silica crystals are hard and transparent and have a specific gravity of about 2.6, and they melt at about 1600°C (2900°F)—depending on the crystal system—to form a glass. In nature the different crystal systems of silica are represented by quartz (hexagonal), cristobalite (tetragonal), and tridymite (triclinic). Amorphous silica is represented by opal, chalcedony, flint, jasper, and diatomaceous earth. See separate entries on these subjects.

SILICA GEL, sil′ə-kə jel, is an amorphous and very adsorbent form of silica. It is used in chemical industries as an extracting agent, in chromatography, and as a dehumidifying and dehydrating material. See SILICA.

SILICATE, sil′ə-kāt, a chemical compound of silicon, oxygen, and metallic elements. Orthosilicates contain the SiO_4^{-4} group and metasilicates the SiO_3^{-2} group.

SILICATE MINERALS, sil′ə-kāt, the most important class of minerals, form over 90% of the earth's crust. Almost all igneous rock-forming minerals are silicates, and the approximately 800 members of the class represent about 40% of all the kinds of minerals known. The basic structural unit of silicates is a tetrahedron surrounding a silicon ion, with one oxygen ion at each of the tetrahedron's four corners. The units may be single, paired, or linked in rings or networks of rings. See ROCKS.

SILICON, sil′ə-kən, symbol Si, is a nonmetallic element of great importance to man. Present in stars and meteorites, it constitutes about 27.6% of the earth's crust by weight and is the second most abundant element on earth, after oxygen. It is found in animal skeletons and plant tissues and forms the cell walls of diatoms. The element does not occur naturally on earth in the free state. It was first isolated by the English chemist Sir Humphry Davy in 1800 and the French chemists Louis Thénard and Joseph Gay-Lussac in 1811, but was not identified as an element until 1826 by the Swedish chemist Jakob Berzelius. Crystalline silicon was first prepared by the French chemist Henri Sainte-Claire Deville in 1854.

Properties. Located in Group IVA of the periodic table, silicon is one of the carbon family of elements. Its atomic number is 14 and its atomic weight 28.086. In its crystalline form it is a black to dark gray, brittle solid with a high metallic luster. In its amorphous form it is dark brown. The element has a specific gravity of 2.33 and it is one of the harder solids, with a hardness of 7 on the Mohs scale. Silicon melts at 1410° C (2570° F) and boils at 2355° C (4271° F). Silicon is a poor conductor of electricity and it expands very little when it is heated. There are three stable isotopes in nature.

Silicon has a valence of +4. It is not a reactive element. Practically insoluble in water, it is unaffected by most acids except hydrofluoric acid. However, it combines with the halogens and reacts with alkalis, even in dilute solutions, to form silicates and hydrogen. Its affinity for hydrogen is weak, compared to that of carbon, and in nature the element is found mainly in combination with oxygen.

Preparation and Uses. Although silicon can be prepared in several ways, it is generally made commercially by heating the dioxide, silica (SiO_2), with coke in an electric furnace. Zone refining of the element yields very high-purity silicon, as does decomposition of silicon tetraiodide (SiI_4) and trichlorosilane ($SiHCl_3$). High-purity silicon is of great importance in the electronics industries. Doped with elements such as boron, gallium, phosphorus, and arsenic, it is used in making transistors, silicon diodes, and other semiconductors.

Silicon of ordinary purity is used in alloys, which the element forms with most metals. Such alloys include ferrosilicon, used in making very resistant silicon steels and metallic magnesium, and silicon copper, combined with tin to make the silicon bronze used in telephone and telegraph wires. The element is also combined with certain ceramic materials to make cermets and other special refractories, and it serves as a reducing agent of metallic oxides in some high-temperature reactions.

Compounds. Silicon occurs in the form of silica and silicates in rocks and in minerals such as sands, clays, and feldspars, to name a very few of these important natural compounds. In fact, the earth's crust may be thought of as essentially a network of silicon and oxygen atoms. Of the many silicon compounds in commercial use, only a few can be mentioned here. Among them are the silanes and their derivatives, such as monosilane (SiH_4) and disilane (Si_2H_6), and the organic polymers called silicones. Sodium silicate is better known as water glass, and silicon carbide is valued for its hardness. See CARBIDE; ROCKS; SILICA; SILICONE; WATER GLASS.

Further Reading: Hauser, Ernst A., *Silicic Science* (Van Nostrand 1955).

SILICON CARBIDE, sil′ə-kən kär′bīd, is a carbon-silicon compound with a hardness of 9. It is used as an abrasive, as a refractory material, and as a semiconductor. See CARBIDE; CARBORUNDUM.

SILICONE, sil′ə-kōn, any of a number of synthetic polymers composed of silicon, oxygen, and various hydrocarbon groups. The silicon and oxygen atoms in a silicone are arranged alternately in simple or branched chains or rings, with the hydrocarbon groups attached to the silicon atoms. Comparatively simple silicones are thin, clear liquids, but as the molecular chain becomes longer or branches, the polymers become more viscous. Silicone rubbers consist of long molecular chains with some cross linking, while silicone resins have a high degree of molecular complexity.

Silicones in general have a strong resistance to heat, moisture, and the action of many other chemicals, and they are excellent electrical insulators. They retain these properties over wide temperature ranges, their stability being comparable to that of silicate minerals. Depending on the hydrocarbon groups in the molecule, silicones serve as oils, greases, coolants, defoamers, adhesives, rubbers, resins, enamels, paints, or waterproofing materials, among other uses. Because they are physiologically inert, they are also of great importance as prosthetic materials in medicine. Silicone rubber is valued for its ability to remain flexible at low temperatures, but because it has a low tensile strength it is reinforced with powdered silica.

Silicones first became commercially important in World War II, although they were known of for several decades previously. The most common commercial processes used in making the polymers involve the direct reaction of silicon with an alkyl halide in the presence of a catalyst, with subsequent polymerization of the resulting compound. Another method is to react silicon tetrachloride ($SiCl_4$) with an appropriate Grignard reagent, an organometallic compound containing an alkyl radical, magnesium, and a halide. The product of the reaction is hydrolyzed and then polymerized.

Further Reading: Meals, Robert N., and Lewis, F. M., *Silicones* (Reinhold 1959); Noll, Walter, *Chemistry and Technology of Silicones* (Academic Press 1968).

SILICOSIS, sil-ə-kō′səs, a chronic disease of the lungs caused by the long-term ingestion of excessive amounts of silica (SiO_2). The disease is most commonly noted in coal, copper, and gold miners, stonecutters, tunnelers, granite workers, and those having to do with sandblasting, stone chipping and buffing, and certain glass, ceramic, and metallurgic processes. Pure silica, or sand, chokes the lymph nodes of the lungs, the normal body mechanism for removing such waste particles. Workers in the tuberculosis laboratory at Saranac Lake, N. Y., and others have demonstrated that silica particles less than 10 microns

$$(1 \text{ micron} = \text{approximately } \frac{1}{25,000} \text{ inch}) \text{ in size}$$

produce the greatest damage and usually occur in concentrations of greater than 15 million particles per cubic foot before significant penetration to the finer air passages occurs.

The disease is insidious and usually develops over a period of 15 or 20 years of mining activity. It produces a generalized nodular fibrosis of the lungs and predisposes to tuberculosis, pneumonia, emphysema, and bronchiectasis. The highest mortality results primarily from tuberculosis, which runs as high as 60 percent in advanced cases, but also from fibrosis and from emphysema, which strains the right side of the heart, causing pulmonary heart disease (*cor pulmonale*). The characteristic X-ray picture of diffuse nodularity, plus the industrial history, are essential in the diagnosis.

There is no specific treatment for silicosis. The efforts of industrial medicine are directed to early diagnosis and prevention. Protective masks, studies of silica concentration in confined spaces, and follow-up chest X-rays are most important.

REAUMUR S. DONALLY, M. D.
Washington Center Hospital

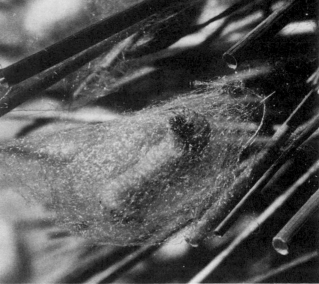

Silkworms are cultivated by feeding them on mulberry leaves (*top left*) until they are ready to spin their cocoons. In the unfinished cocoon (*top right*) the silkworm is clearly visible. The egg-shaped finished cocoons (*bottom*) are collected for processing in a silk factory.

SILK is a fine, lustrous fiber produced by silkworms and other insect larvae, generally to form their cocoons. The breeding of silkworms and the making of silk began in prehistoric times. China is generally credited with the first silk culture, although some claims have been made that it originated in India.

Development of the Silk Industry. Traditional Chinese accounts ascribe the cultivation of silkworms and the weaving of silk to the wife of the legendary emperor Huang-ti, who is supposed to have lived in the 3d millennium B.C. In any event, silk culture flourished by the time of the Shang dynasty (c.1523–1027 B.C.).

Aristotle and Pliny described the silkworm, but for centuries after silk fabrics were known in the West, the prevalent opinion was that silk was either a fleece that grew on a tree or the fiber from the inner bark of some tree or shrub. Some persons, deceived by the glossy, silky fibers of the seed vessels of *Asclepias* and the silk-cotton tree, believed that it was the product of one of these. A few came near the truth with the conjecture that silk was spun by a spider or beetle. So carefully did the Orient keep its secret that it was not exposed until 552 A.D., when two Nestorian monks, who had lived in China, concealed a small quantity of silkworm eggs and brought them to Constantinople.

From Constantinople, sericulture spread through the Balkan Peninsula, and Byzantine silks soon became prized in Europe for ecclesiastical vestments. Although the looms of Constantinople declined in the 8th and 9th centuries, those of Thebes and other Greek and Syrian cities increased their production and improved their methods of manufacture. The Greeks maintained their supremacy until 1204, when the Latin Empire of Constantinople was established. Meanwhile, the Arabs had introduced the industry into northern Africa, Spain, Portugal, and Sicily. Spanish and Sicilian production was substantial by the 11th century. When the Normans conquered Sicily, beginning about 1060, they encouraged the local silk industry. The second Norman ruler of Sicily, Roger II (reigned 1105–1154), invaded Greece in 1147 and took captive a number of silk weavers. He established them in Palermo and Calabria, where they were induced to teach the Greek methods of silk culture.

In the reign of Louis XI (1461–1483) silk was manufactured in Tours and later in Lyon, Montpellier, and Paris. Cocoons were first raised successfully in France in the reign of Francis I (1515–1547). The French silk industry, encouraged by successive rulers, expanded until 1685, when the revocation of the Edict of Nantes drove

In a Chinese silk factory workers sort cocoons (*top left*) before soaking them in hot water to soften the gum that coats the fiber. The cocoons are then unravelled and the fibers wound onto reels (*top right*). Skeins of silk are weighed and labeled before shipment (*bottom*).

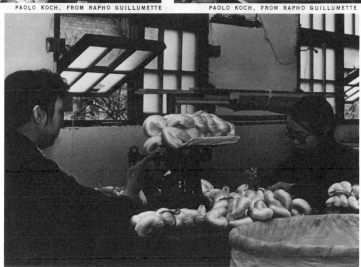

into exile about 400,000 Huguenots, many of whom were silk workers. Not for many years did the industry regain the ground it had lost, and then it was almost destroyed again during the French Revolution. Those Huguenots who settled in England tried to manufacture silk there, but without much success until 1718, when a new method of throwing was introduced. Thereafter, the English industry expanded rapidly, and English silks replaced French in the European market. The French industry revived with the aid of protective tariffs in the Napoleonic and Restoration periods. Conversely, the industry in England was almost ruined after 1860, when that country negotiated a commercial treaty that admitted French silks duty free. Silk manufacture also flourished in Switzerland and Germany in the 19th century. The Belgian and Dutch industries, dating from the late Middle Ages, remained productive during the 19th century. The Russian industry received a great impetus in the 1890's with the enactment of a protective tariff.

With the opening of the treaty ports in China in the mid-19th century, large quantities of raw silk began to reach world markets from Shanghai and Canton. China exported only its surplus, the great bulk of its raw silk being woven and sold in the home market. The same has been true of the minor producing areas in Asia. There has

been some export of Asian manufactured silks, particularly those of China, India, and Japan. In 1857, Japan entered the raw silk export field and rapidly assumed leadership.

The first silk mill in the United States was established in 1810 at Mansfield, Conn. However, the American industry did not prosper until protective tariffs on manufactured silk were introduced in the latter half of the 19th century.

The development of man-made fibers in the 20th century greatly reduced the demand for silk fabrics and hosiery. Japan is by far the principal consumer of raw silk, with the United States, Italy, India, France, South Korea, Switzerland, Germany, and Britain consuming relatively small amounts. The leading silk producers are Japan, China, the USSR, India, and South Korea.

Types of Silkworms. Any caterpillar that spins a fibrous cocoon that can be used to make cloth is known as a silkworm. By far the most important and most widely disseminated species of silkworm is *Bombyx mori*, which belongs to the family Bombycidae, a native of northern China or Bengal.

Among the less important species of silkworms, the following are probably best known. The Japanese oak silk moth (*Antheraea yamamai*) produces green-tinted silk, which is used in

Silk, which is a versatile fabric with many uses, is displayed for a customer in the showroom of a silk factory in Japan.

Japan and China for embroidery. A close relative, *Antheraea peryni*, is a native of northern China, where its large grayish brown cocoons are used for threads and various fabrics. Both wild and cultivated cocoons of *Antheraea assamensis* and *Antheraea paphia* are also used extensively in Asia, as is the silk of the ailanthus silkworm (*Philosamia cynthia*). Since the thread of the ailanthus silkworm cannot be reeled, the silk is obtained by carding. The moth has been introduced into Europe, Africa, and the eastern United States. The Syrian silkworm (*Pachypasa otus*) was the silkworm of Europe until long after the introduction of the Chinese silkworm and was cultivated extensively until 1875. The amount of silk produced by each cocoon is relatively small. Silk has been made from several common American silkworms, but quality and cost compare unfavorably with silk from the Chinese species. The cecropia moth (*Samia cecropia*), the largest North American moth, occurs over the whole of the United States and southern Canada. It produces a large cocoon of very strong silk. Glover's silkworm (*Samia gloveri*) is similar but does not occur in the East. The promethea moth (*Callosamia promethea*), common in the eastern half of the United States, has a cocoon much like that of *Philosamia cynthia*, and the quality of the silk is similar. The cocoons of the polyphemus moth (*Telea polyphemus*) and the io moth (*Automeris io*) are somewhat like those of the Chinese silkworm, but the silken strands are copiously glued together.

Silkworm Cultivation. In the cultivation of the silkworm the first requisite is an ample supply of foliage. This is usually obtained by growing mulberry trees far enough apart to give each tree ample space to develop its branches in all directions. The distance between trees varies from 15 to 40 feet (4.6–12 meters), depending on the variety and method of training.

During the winter, the silkworm eggs are kept at a temperature of less than 50° F (10° C) in a dry, circulating atmosphere. In the spring, they are placed in a room or incubator in which the temperature is raised gradually to about 73° F (23° C). In about 10 days the larvae emerge. They are then covered with sheets of perforated paper sprinkled with chopped mulberry leaves, which should be renewed about 9 times during the first 24 hours. Paper with larger perforation is necessary as the worms grow. When ready to spin, the worms should be supplied with brush, straw, or other material on which they can form their cocoons. At this time the temperature should be maintained at about 75° F (24° C) and the humidity close to 65%. Scrupulous cleanliness and abundant fresh air are essential at all times. The cocoons are sorted according to quality, size, and color. After grading they are heated to kill the pupas, which, if left alive, would break the thread many times as they emerged as adult silkworm moths.

Manufacture of Silk. The filament that the silkworm spins into a cocoon is so fine that several filaments must be reeled together to produce a thread thick enough to handle. This process is undertaken in large factories called *filatures*. There the cocoons are placed in basins of water near the boiling temperature. Filaments from as many cocoons as are needed to make the desired size of raw silk thread are then combined, twisted, and reeled into skeins. When the filament from one cocoon has become exhausted, it is replaced by another cocoon. The reeler adjusts the size of the thread by controlling the number of fresh and partially exhausted cocoons that are forming the thread. A single cocoon of good quality may furnish from 400 to 800 yards (365–730 meters) of reelable filament. Asian silks reeled by different filatures and the different qualities of silk from the same filature are designated by colorful labels called *chops*.

Silk that has been reeled is called *raw silk*. The damaged cocoons and the parts of each cocoon that cannot be reeled are called *waste silk*. Waste silk is combed and spun into spun silk or schappe yarns. Japanese raw silk is prepared for shipment in books containing from 25 to 30 tightly rolled skeins, which are then packed in bales weighing from 125 to 140 pounds (55–65 kg). Chinese silks are packed and shipped in a similar manner. Italian silks are packed in bales weighing 200 pounds (90 kg) or more.

The silk used in the manufacture of fabrics may be divided into three general classifications: (1) silk threads as they come from the filature, where several cocoon threads have been combined; (2) silk known as *organzine*, in which the original threads have been twisted and several of these twisted threads have been combined; and (3) silk known as *tram*, in which threads coming from the reeling machine have been very lightly twisted together.

When silk threads are woven as they come from the filature, without having been dyed, their natural gum gives them enough body to make them suitable for weaving. When they are dyed before weaving, the gum is removed in the dyeing process. To give these threads strength and cohesion, they must be twisted before dyeing. This process is called *throwing*. See also SILK-WORM; TEXTILES.

Bibliography

Carboni, Paolo, *Silk: Biology, Chemistry, Technology* (Chapman 1952).

Hollen, Norma, and Saddler, Jane, *Textiles*, 3d ed. (Macmillan, N.Y. 1968).

Leggett, William F., *The Story of Silk* (Little and Ives 1949).

Linton, George E., *Modern Textile Dictionary*, rev. ed. (Duell 1963).

Matsui, Shichiro, *The History of the Silk Industry in the United States* (Howes 1930).

Silk and Rayon Users Association, *The Silk Book* (1951).

Singer, Charles, and others, *A History of Technology*, vol. 4 (Oxford 1958).

SILK-COTTON TREE, a giant tropical tree, *Ceiba pentandra*, of the family Bombaceae. It occurs mostly in tropical America but grows also in Asia and Africa. The tree is cultivated in plantations, especially on the Indonesian island of Java, for its yield of the commercial fiber kapok.

The silk-cotton tree has a massive trunk with enormous twisting nearly horizontal branches. It may grow 100 to 150 feet (30–45 cm) tall and has planklike buttress roots that may extend 30 feet (9 meters) radially from the trunk. The tree's palmately compound leaves have seven 4- to 6-inch (10–15-cm) long leaflets. It bears striking white or pink, bell-shaped flowers in 6- to 8-inch (15–20-cm) long clusters.

The fruit of the silk-cotton tree is a large leathery capsule, about 3 to 6 inches (7.5–15 cm) long. The capsule is filled with seeds embedded in a mass of silky ivory-white fibers rising from the inner wall of the capsule. The fibers, usually known as kapok, are also called ceiba, silk cotton, or Java cotton. When dried, the short hollow kapok fibers are light and resilient. Although they are too brittle to be spun into yarn, they make an excellent filling for cushions, mattresses, and sleeping bags. Because of its buoyancy and impermeability to water, kapok was formerly used as a filling for life preservers. Oil from kapok seeds is used to make soap.

SILK SCREEN PRINT, an image made by rubbing paint on a surface through openings in a stencil or stencil-like film applied to a mesh screen. The silk-screen process, like stenciling, is a kind of surface printing as distinct from relief or intaglio methods. It deposits mat layers of paint on a surface rather than staining it, as in printing. The process as used by artists, generally requiring a silk screen and hand techniques, is called serigraphy. As used commercially, with different kinds of screen and often photography, it is called screen printing.

In silk screen printing, a screen of fine silk, nylon, cotton, or steel wire is stretched tightly over a rectangular wood or metal frame hinged to a board. The original drawing is placed under

Silk screen print in the modern abstract style, done by Sister Mary Corita (Corita Kent).

CORITA KENT

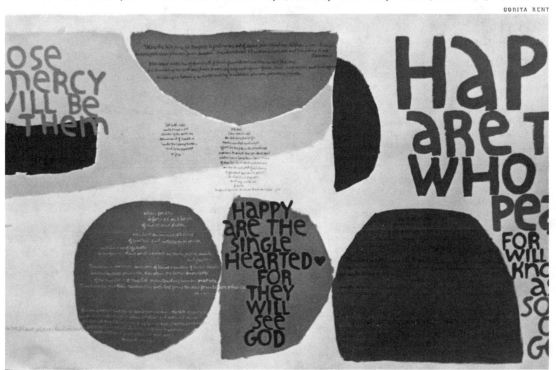

it. In the simplest processes the resist (not to be printed) areas of the design are painted on the screen with shellac, lacquer, or glue; or a stencil cut in thin vinyl or other film is applied to the screen. In a more sophisticated procedure, the areas to be printed are painted with tusche (lithographer's ink), the screen is entirely covered with a glue solution and dried, and the tusche is washed off the reverse side with kerosine, carrying along the glue over it. Alternatively, the screen may be covered with glue, the resist areas painted with black lacquer or shellac, and the glue washed off the printing areas. Similar effects can be achieved with photographic methods, and various techniques can be combined.

The surface to be printed is then placed under the frame, which, with the screen on the bottom, forms a shallow box into which a water or, usually, oil paint is poured. It is rubbed over the screen with a squeegee, remaining on top of the resist areas but penetrating the areas of uncovered mesh. Innumerable layers of color, opaque or transparent, may be built up, using a new stencil for each color. The screen can be cleaned and reused many times.

Silk-screen printing is a relatively modern development, and today the process is important industrially to print textiles, posters, signs, labels, bottles and other curved objects, and half-tone illustrations. In the late 1930's and the 1940's, American artists such as Harry Sternberg and Anthony Velonis made silk screen prints of the American scene. In the 1950's artists such as Glen Alps and Sister Mary Corita turned to more abstract, personal subjects. Multinational artists of the 1960's—Robert Rauschenberg, Bridget Riley, Victor Vasarely, Andy Warhol, and others—have taken a Pop art and minimal art approach to silk screen and have combined artists' and industrial techniques.

Further Reading: Shokler, Harry, *Artists Manual for Silk Screen Print Making* (Tudor 1961); Sternberg, Harry, *Silk Screen Color Printing* (McGraw 1942).

SILKWEED,
a type of weed found in North and South America and in Africa. See ASCLEPIAS.

SILKWORM,
any caterpillar that spins a cocoon of silky fiber that may be used for making cloth, especially *Bombyx mori*. There are several different strains of *Bombyx mori*, each with its own characteristics.

The silkworm moth has a short thick body, stout legs, and broad white wings crossed by several faint lines or by a pale bar on the front pair of wings. The female lays from 200 to 500 eggs, each about as large as a pinhead, singly on any convenient surface, gluing them there by a mucilaginous secretion. The eggs do not hatch until the following spring.

The young silkworm larva, about 0.25 inch (6.4 mm) long, soon consumes approximately its own weight of foliage daily and increases rapidly in size. It casts its skin four times, growing most rapidly after each month. It is fully grown in approximately six weeks, when it is about 3 inches (76 mm) long. It now ceases to feed, empties its alimentary tract, and seems to shrink in size.

The larva then begins spinning, first making an outer network known as the *floss,* and then winding the silk in a continuous thread around its body, which continues to decrease in size. The completed cocoon is considerably shorter than the caterpillar itself. The spinning operation lasts

about five days, during which time the insect usually produces from 2,000 to 3,000 feet (610–915 meters) of silk, which consists of two blended strands. These are produced by special glands, called *sericteries,* which extend nearly the whole length of the body and terminate in spinnerets situated in the mouth.

Within 15 to 20 days after the chrysalis has formed, the adult insect emerges, lays its eggs, and dies. It has been estimated that there are 20,000 to 40,000 eggs to an ounce. About 1 ounce of eggs will yield 100 pounds of cocoons or 9 pounds of raw silk. From 15 to 20 pounds of good mulberry leaves should yield 1 pound of cocoons. The food of the caterpillar is preferably the foliage of the white mulberry tree (*Morus alba*), but several other species are used. The Osage orange is occasionally used as a substitute but is said to produce an inferior grade of silk. Caterpillars also thrive on the leaves of lettuce and some other plants.

CHARLES HOWARD CURRAN, *Former Curator Department of Insects and Spiders American Museum of Natural History*

Further Reading: Cooper, Elizabeth K., *Silkworms and Science: The Story of Silk* (Harcourt 1961); Tazima, Yataro, *Genetics of the Silkworm* (Prentice-Hall 1964).

SILKY TERRIER,
a pet dog of British origin that was developed to its present standards in Australia. Australia had already developed the Australian terrier in the early 1900's (from the earlier Skye terriers) and had also brought in Yorkshire terriers from England. The silky terrier is principally a cross between the Australian and the Yorkshire terriers, with its silken coat owing probably to the Skye terriers in the Australian terriers' ancestry. The dog's head is wedge-shaped, and the ears are erect and set high on the head. The coat, which is flat, is a fine, glossy silk. The tail is set high and is devoid of plume. Adult dogs have a coat of 5 to 6 inches (about 12 to 15 cm) long. They weigh from 8 to 10 pounds (4–5 kg).

Many silkies began to appear in the United States and Canada in the early 1950's. In 1959 came American Kennel Club recognition, and by the 1970's the silky had become one of the 45 most popular breeds.

Silky terrier, a long-haired terrier from Australia.

EVELYN M. SHAFER

SILL, in geology, an igneous rock intrusion that lies between other rock strata rather than cutting across the strata, as in a dike. However, a sill may in fact cut across one or more layers of rock in the course of its extent. A sill is formed when a magma flow enters a channel of least resistance along a bedding plane, or lifts lighter sedimentary rocks and consolidates beneath them. Such features are usually of approximately uniform thickness.

SILLA, sil'ə, was an ancient Korean kingdom under which the Korean peninsula was united in the late 7th century. See also KOREA—*History*.

SILLANPÄÄ, sil'län-pa, **Frans Eemil** (1888–1964), Finnish novelist. He was awarded the Nobel Prize in literature in 1939 "for his exquisite art in painting the peasant life and nature of his country."

The only son of landless peasants, Sillanpää was born in Hämeenkyrö on Sept. 16, 1888. He borrowed money to study biology at the University of Helsinki, but left without taking his degree. His first novel, *Elämä ja aurinko* (1916; *Life and Sun*), which describes a summer love affair of two young people, was well received.

Sillanpää, however, did not achieve his mature style until his second novel, *Hurskas kurjuus* (1919; Eng. tr., *Meek Heritage*, 1938), which depicts the bleak life of a peasant and his pointless death in the Finnish civil war of 1918. The civil war provided the background for *Nuorena nukkunut* (1931; Eng. tr., *The Maid Silja*, 1933), the story of a farm servant girl. This is generally considered Sillanpää's best work. He also wrote many short stories, most of which have not been translated into English. One of his novels, *Miehen tie* (1932; *One Man's Way*), which deals with the relationship between two peasants, was made into a motion picture in Helsinki in 1940. His last novel was *Ihmiselon ihanuus ja kurjuus* (1945; *The Beauty and Misery of Human Life*). Sillanpää died in Helsinki on June 3, 1964.

Frans Sillanpää, Nobel Prize-winning Finnish novelist

CONSULATE GENERAL OF FINLAND

SILLIMAN, sil'ə-mən, **Benjamin** (1779–1864), American scientist and pioneer in science education who founded the *American Journal of Science [and] Arts* in 1819. Silliman was born in North Stratford (now Trumbull), Conn., on Aug. 8, 1779. He graduated from Yale in 1796, studied law, and was admitted to the bar. He was the first professor of chemistry and natural history at Yale, serving there from 1802 to 1853 and as professor emeritus until his death. After his appointment he continued his studies abroad, especially in geology. He became famous as a teacher, but it was even more through his public lectures that he helped popularize science study in the United States. He also exerted great influence as editor of his journal, which became one of the country's leading scientific periodicals and is still published under the title of the *American Journal of Science*. Silliman died in New Haven, Conn., on Nov. 24, 1864.

BENJAMIN SILLIMAN (1816–1885), his son, was born in New Haven on Dec. 4, 1816. He began teaching at Yale as an assistant to his father, succeeding to his post as professor in 1853. He also served first as assistant editor, then as editor, of his father's journal. With his father, he played an important part in establishing the Department of Philosophy and the Arts at Yale, and both father and son were original members of the National Academy of Sciences. He died in New Haven on Jan. 14, 1885.

Further Reading: Fulton, John F., and Thomson, Elizabeth H., *Benjamin Silliman, 1779–1864, Pathfinder in American Science* (reprint, Greenwood Press 1968).

SILLIMANITE, sil'ə-mə-nīt, is a comparatively rare aluminum silicate named in honor of Benjamin Silliman. Its transparent to translucent crystals are brown, pale green, or white and have a glassy luster. The mineral resembles andalusite and is found as a constituent of gneiss and schist, often together with corundum. There are notable localities in Brazil, central Europe, and the northeastern United States.

Composition, $AlAlO(SiO_4)$; hardness, 6–7; specific gravity, 3.23; orthorhombic.

SILLITOE, sil'ə-tō, **Alan** (1928–   ), English novelist and poet, one of the so-called "angry young men" of contemporary British fiction. He was born in Nottingham on March 4, 1928. After attending school there, he worked in local factories and served two years as a radio operator in the Royal Air Force. The years 1952–1956 he spent traveling and writing in France, Italy, and Spain.

Sillitoe's first novel, *Saturday Night and Sunday Morning* (1958), is a story of working-class life in present-day Nottingham. It is pervaded by a bitter awareness of social injustice. It was followed by *The Loneliness of the Long-Distance Runner* (1959), a collection of stories set in contemporary England. The title story was acclaimed as a major study of youthful rebellion against society. Among his other novels are *The General* (1960), an allegorical story about war; *Key to the Door* (1962), a sequel to his first novel; and *A Start in Life* (1970), a picaresque adventure set in Nottingham and London. His other works include the story collections *The Ragman's Daughter* (1963) and *Guzman, Go Home* (1969) and the verse collections *The Rats and Other Poems* (1960) and *Love in the Environs of Voronezh* (1968).

BETH BERGMAN

Beverly Sills as Cleopatra in Handel's *Giulio Cesare*

SILLS, Beverly, stage name of Belle Silverman (1929–   ), coloratura soprano and opera company director, who was regarded by many critics as the greatest singing actress of her day. She was born in Brooklyn, N. Y., on May 25, 1929. She made her opera debut at 17 with the Philadelphia Civic Opera. She then toured with the Charles Wagner Opera Company, and in 1953 made her debut with the San Francisco Opera.

Miss Sills joined the New York City Opera in 1955, but it was not until 1966, when she sang the role of Cleopatra in Handel's *Giulio Cesare,* that she became a star. Thereafter she sang such roles as Manon, Lucia di Lammermoor, Norma, Queen Elizabeth in Donizetti's *Roberto Devereux,* and the four women in *The Tales of Hoffman.* She made her debut at La Scala, Milan, in 1969 and at the Metropolitan in New York in 1975, meanwhile remaining a member of the company of the New York City Opera. On July 1, 1979, she became general director of the New York City Opera, although she continued to sing in opera in New York City and elsewhere.

SILO, a container for making and storing a livestock feed called silage. It may be a simple pit or trench called a tower. All types have walls to prevent air and moisture from passing into or out of the silage. Roofed silos exclude rain and snow.

The silo originated centuries ago as a shallow pit on a knoll or other well-drained site. In time the side walls of pits in porous soil were lined with stone, brick, concrete, or wood to prevent their caving in and to help exclude air. In regions where silage became mechanized on a large scale, trenches came to be preferred to pits because they could be more conveniently loaded with dump-type vehicles, and the silage could be packed by tractors. Removing the silage from one end can be mechanized with tractor loaders, or cattle can self-feed on silage by means of a rack on skids.

Trench Silos. Trench silos may be constructed partly or entirely above ground, with temporary or permanent walls to hold the silage while it is being packed. After final packing, temporary walls can be removed and used to construct another above-ground trench silo. When the temporary walls are removed, the crop is stored as cut or coarsely chopped so that the silage will bind and the mass will retain its oblong shape. Air is excluded by tight packing and by a covering of plastic or other airtight film.

Tower Silos. Tower silos are made of wood, tile, concrete, or steel. They are usually cylindrical structures. In the United States, the land of tower silos, most are about 15 feet (4.6 meters) in diameter and about 40 feet (12 meters) high. The diameter of a tower that is unloaded from the top must be small enough to remove at least three inches (7.6 cm) of silage every day to avoid spoilage from molding.

Cylindrical tower silos can be equipped with a mechanical unloading device that removes silage from the top and drops it down a large external chute, which keeps the silage from being scattered by the wind. Mechanical unloaders remove the silage uniformly, leaving the surface firm, smooth, and level; these conditions retard the development of molds. Gastight silos made of glass-coated steel are equipped with bottom unloaders. Such silos permit feeding and filling on a continuous or interrupted basis.

See also SILAGE.

ROBERT B. MUSGRAVE*
Cornell University

SILOAM, sī-lō′əm, a pool in Jerusalem mentioned in John 9:7 as the place where Jesus sent the man born blind to wash in order to receive his sight. The pool is the result of water carried from the spring of Gihon by means of a tunnel constructed during the reign of King Hezekiah (reigned about 715 to 687 B. C.) to protect the water supply of Jerusalem from the threatening armies of the Assyrian King Sennacherib. A reservoir existed at the spring from at least the time of King Ahaz (reigned about 734 to 715 B. C.) and is probably the "upper pool" mentioned in II Kings 18:17 and Isaiah 7:3. Hezekiah's 1,749-foot (533-meter) tunnel was restored in 1910. In the 5th century a Christian church was built on the site of the pool of Siloam, and later a mosque occupied the site. Consequently, only a small portion of the pool remains.

SILONE, sē-lō′nä, **Ignazio,** the pen name of Secondo Tranquilli (1900–1978), Italian author and political figure. He was born in Pescina on May 1, 1900. He became a Communist in 1917 and helped to found the Italian Communist party. He left the party in 1930, but because of his opposition to fascism in the 1920's he had to leave Italy in 1931. He resided in Switzerland until 1944, when he returned to Rome. He later served as a member of the executive committee of the Italian Socialist party (from 1941) and in 1945 became editor of its newspaper, *Avanti.*

Silone's novel *Fontamara,* published in an English translation in 1930 and not in Italy until 1947 because of its political viewpoint, is the story of peasant life under fascism. Silone revised the work in 1958, as he has done with other of his writings, refining its characters. His other books include *Pane e Vino* (1937; Eng. tr., *Bread and Wine,* 1937), which was revised as *Vino e Pane* (1955), and its sequel *Il seme sotto la neve* (1952; *The Seed Beneath the Snow*). He died in Geneva, Switzerland, on Aug. 22, 1978.

SILT is any loose sedimentary material consisting of rock particles finer than sand and grading into clay. One commonly accepted system gives the size range of coarse to fine silt particles as 0.06 mm (0.0024 inch) to 0.002 mm (0.00008 inch). The term silt is also applied to a soil in which 80% or more of the individual soil grains are silt-sized. Deposits of silts may consolidate over geological time to form siltstones.

SILURIAN PERIOD, si-lōŏr'ē-ən, in geology, the third period of the Paleozoic Era and the system of rocks formed in its time span of some 20 million years, beginning approximately 430 million years ago.

Determination of the Period. The name is derived from that of the Silures, an ancient tribe of south Wales. It was given to the formation in 1835 by the Scottish geologist Sir Roderick I. Murchison. (The sequence first so named, along the River Wye progressing downward from the base of the Old Red Sandstone, was later determined as of Devonian age.) At the same time the English geologist Adam Sedgwick, working in north Wales, was investigating rocks that he designated the Cambrian system. When it became apparent that the upper part of the rocks Sedgwick called Cambrian was composed of those that Murchison had included as the lowest part of his Silurian system, the rocks in question became the Lower Silurian of the survey that Murchison directed.

Subsequently the name Ordovician was applied to the controversial beds by an English geologist, Charles Lapworth, in 1879. The term included rocks now classed as in the Arenigian, Llanvirnian, Llandellian, Caradocian, and Ashgillian Series. The Tremadocian series was placed in the basal Ordovician in North America and Scandinavia, and the term Silurian was retained for the smaller Upper Silurian, which now includes Llandoverian, Wenlockian, Ludlovian, and Downtonian Series. Graptolites—floating colonial animals having minute individuals arranged along fine, ribbonlike, suspended structures—abound in some shales and were the diagnostic fossils in Lapworth's studies. In North America, the Silurian system is commonly divided into three series, the Albionian, Niagaran, and Cayugan. Certain scientists regard the first series as merely a stage of the second, to be followed by the Clintonian and Lockportian Stages.

Silurian Rocks in Europe. The Silurian in northwestern England and Wales consists of more than 2 miles (3 km) of graywackes and graptolite-bearing dark shales. Limestones are rich in corals, brachiopods, and bryozoans in the Wenlockian of western England. The island of Gotland off Sweden is so famous for its coralline limestones that the Silurian is called the Gotlandian system in several countries. The Caledonian orogeny, or period of mountain building, affected a belt extending through western Scandinavia into Scotland and Ireland at the period's close.

The Silurian was predominantly an age of aquatic life, although by the end of that time, plants and scorpions had established themselves on land. The coral reef community of the Middle Silurian depicted here shows: (1) stalked echinoderms, related to modern sea lilies; (2) a cephalopod mollusk, *Phragmoceras*; (3) honeycomb corals of the family Favositidae; (4) and (5) related tube and chain corals of the families Syringoporidae and Halysitidae; (6) a solitary coral; (7) a nautiloid mollusk with a shell like that of its surviving relative, the chambered nautilus; (8) and (9) two of the ubiquitous trilobites; (10) and (11) two brachiopods, *Pentameras* and *Leptaena*; and (12) a mollusk, *Cyrtorizoceras*.

The ancient arthropods known as eurypterids were common in seas of the Silurian Period. The one in the reconstruction at left is of the genus *Pterygotus*, which attained lengths of up to 9 feet (3 meters). The closest living relative is the horseshoe crab. Also seen are snail and brachiopod shells and segmented worms.

Silurian Rocks in North America. In the eastern United States, erosion progressively reduced lands formed in western New England by the Taconian orogeny at the beginning of the Silurian. Silurian rocks about 1 mile (1.5 km) thick were laid down in Pennsylvania and thereabout in a basin that subsided as it filled. The earliest Silurian rocks that are found there are conglomerates and sandstones, passing westward into shales. By the end of the period, however, limestones were widespread. Some of the principal mountains in the state consist of quartzite that is solidified early Silurian sandstone. The Atlantic coast has thick sequences accumulated in a region from Maine northwestward that was characterized by sediment-producing islands and volcanoes in the Silurian.

The Clintonian Stage is the source of iron ore in New York and the Appalachian Mountains south to the Alabama. Lockportian limestone representing Silurian coral reefs is found in a broad belt from Illinois to Ontario and New York and is quarried in Chicago and extensively in western Ohio. The reefs had separated deeper water receiving muds from eastern lands from clear water of poor circulation to the northwest. The same coralline limestone forms the falls at Niagara, the high escarpment of central Ontario, the peninsula between Lake Huron and Georgian Bay and the islands north of the lake, and the points separating Green Bay from Lake Michigan. The Mississippi River passes below Silurian bluffs in northwestern Illinois. Similar rocks are found south of Hudson Bay, in Manitoba, and in areas in arctic Canada, since in the Silurian Period world climates were not so rigorous as at the present time.

In the Late Silurian, or Cayugan, in northwestern New York, salts evaporated in lagoons having restricted access to open seas. The resulting salt and gypsum is the source for chemical industries about Syracuse. At the same time, southern Michigan sank nearly 1 mile (1.6 km) as limestone and salts accumulated in a basinlike depression there. Brine pumped from these beds in Michigan and Ontario is used in making ordinary table salt.

In western North America, Silurian rocks were never deposited in a large area centered in Colorado, Wyoming, and Montana. However, rocks of this period appear and thicken rapidly to a mile or so in the cordilleran geosyncline in western Utah and Nevada, in the same belt that subsided deeply in the preceding periods. The Silurian is the oldest system from which fossils have been identified in the Sierra Nevada of California. In southeastern Alaska, 2 miles (3 km) or more of graptolite-bearing shales and lavas succeeded by limestones indicate the continuing presence of volcanism in a geosynclinal belt along the Pacific coast. See also PALEOZOIC ERA.

MARSHALL KAY
Columbia University

Further Reading: Kummel, Bernhard, *History of the Earth*, 2d ed. (Freeman 1970).

SILVA, sil′və, **António José da** (1705–1739), Portuguese playwright. He was born in Rio de Janeiro, Brazil, on May 8, 1705. In 1712 he moved with his family to Lisbon, where he later studied law at the University of Coimbra. A Jew, Silva was imprisoned with other members of his family by the Inquisition in 1726, but after being tortured he renounced Judaism, was released, and became a successful lawyer. In 1739, Silva and his wife were arrested for secretly practicing Judaism. He was condemned to death and was strangled, in Lisbon, on Oct. 18, 1739, and his body was burned.

Silva, who is sometimes referred to in Portuguese literature as *O Judeu* ("the Jew"), wrote eight plays. *Guerras do Alecrim da Mangerona* (1737; *Wars Between the Rosemary and the Marjoram*) is regarded his best work. His plays, which mix dialogue with popular songs, are witty, satirical commentaries on the pretensions of contemporary society. They include *A Vida do grande D. Quixote de la Mancha* (1733; *The Life of Don Quixote*) and *Encantos de Medeia* (1735; *The Spells of Medea*).

Further Reading: Silva, António José da, *Obras Completas*, 4 vols., ed. by José P. Taveras (1957–1958).

ERA	PERIOD	
CENOZOIC	QUATERNARY	
	TERTIARY	
MESOZOIC	CRETACEOUS	
	JURASSIC	
	TRIASSIC	
PALEOZOIC	PERMIAN	
	CARBON-IFEROUS	PENNSYLVANIAN
		MISSISSIPPIAN
	DEVONIAN	
	SILURIAN	
	ORDOVICIAN	
	CAMBRIAN	
PRE-CAMBRIAN TIME		

SILVA, sēl'va, **José Asunción** (1865–1896), Colombian poet. He was born in Bogotá on Nov. 27, 1865. He spent the year 1886 in Europe, where he met many of the leading writers. Inspired by their work, for ten years after his return to Bogotá he wrote some of the finest modernist poetry in Spanish. But he could not find a publisher, and when, upon his father's death, he assumed support of the family, he struggled unsuccessfully to pay off the debts of the estate. Finally he found a publisher in France, but the ship carrying his manuscript was lost at sea. Then his dearly loved sister died. Plunged into melancholy by these successive misfortunes, he committed suicide, in Bogotá, on May 24, 1896.

Silva's most famous poem, *Nocturno III,* was an elegy for his sister. Other widely known poems are *Crepusculo (Twilight), Ante la estatua (Before the Statue),* and *El Dia de difuntos (The Day of the Dead).* His poetry, though marked by pessimism and tinged with irony, has a haunting sense of melody, and his freedom and flexibility in the use of verse forms did much to liberate the style of Spanish-American poetry.

SILVA XAVIER, Joaquim José da. See TIRADENTES.

SILVANUS, sil-vā'nəs, in Roman mythology, was a god of uncultivated land and, therefore, was associated with the unknown. Peasants made small sacrifices to him when entering his territory. As a woodland spirit, he was often identified with Pan, Silenus, the satyrs, and barbarian gods of untilled land. Silvanus also occurs as a title of Mars, the god of war.

SILVAS AMERICANAS, sēl'väs ä-mer-ē-kän'as, is the general title of a series of poems by the Venezuelan classical scholar Andrés Bello. The first part, *Alocución a la poesía—fragmentos de un poema inédito titulado América,* was published in the *Biblioteca Americana* (1823). The second part, *La agricultura de la zona tórrida,* appeared in the *Repertorio Americano* (1826). The *Alocución* is fragmentary in nature. The first section is directed to poetry, and the second deals with the contributions of Colombia to Spanish American independence. The *Agricultura,* a masterpiece of Spanish American poetry, describes the products and geography of Spanish America and exalts the joy of country living.

SILVER, Abba Hillel (1893–1963), American Zionist leader and Reform rabbi. Silver was born in Neinstadt, Lithuania, on Jan. 28, 1893, and in 1901 was taken to the United States, where his family settled in New York. In 1915 he was ordained a rabbi by Hebrew Union College and also graduated from the University of Cincinnati. He received his doctorate in divinity from Hebrew Union in 1925. He served as rabbi in Wheeling, W. Va., before becoming rabbi of the Temple in Cleveland, Ohio, in 1917, a position he held until his death, on Nov. 28, 1963, in Cleveland.

Rabbi Silver led the Zionist movement to a more politically active role in securing the establishment of a Jewish state in Palestine. As chairman (1946–1948) of the American Section of the Jewish Agency he planned the strategy of Zionism in its relations with both the United States and the United Nations, where he was chief spokesman for the Jewish Agency in the debate over the founding of Israel.

CANADIAN METAL MINING ASSOCIATION

Miners inspect a silver-bearing calcite vein in a silver mine in Ontario, Canada.

SILVER is a lustrous, white, corrosion-resistant metallic element. Outstanding properties of silver include its great electrical and thermal conductivity. Its symbol, Ag, is an abbreviation of the Latin name for the element, *argentum,* while the common name is derived from the Anglo-Saxon *seolfor.*

Silver was one of the metals known to ancient civilizations, along with gold, copper, iron, tin, lead, and mercury. Because pure silver is sometimes found in large masses, the metal could be used without complex separation and refinement processes, and it was in use in Egypt before 3500 B.C.

The leading silver-producing countries are the United States, Mexico, Canada, Peru, the USSR, and Australia. The combined output of North and South America accounts for about half the world's silver production.

Uses. The most important use of silver is as a monetary metal, both in the form of bullion and in coins. Sterling and plated silver are widely used in tableware and in jewelry. About one third of the silver consumed is in the form of photosensitive silver halides, which are used in photography. There are also many industrial applications of silver alloys. Corrosion-resistant alloys are used as lining materials in vessels and pipes. Other alloys are used in brazing because of their low melting points and good workability. Alloys with high electrical conductivity are used in electrical contacts. Silver alloys are important in dentistry for bridgework, pins, and fillings. The bactericidal properties of colloidal silver make it useful in medicine, and silver preparations are used as caustics, astringents, and antiseptics. Silver is also used as a catalyst in chemical reactions to promote the oxidation of organic compounds in the vapor state, such as the oxidation of ethyl alcohol to acetaldehyde.

Properties. Silver is a metal located in Group IB of the periodic table, along with copper

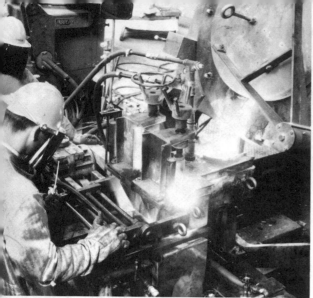

Silver-alloy melt is poured into equipment that casts two 1,000-pound bars simultaneously.

and gold. Its atomic number is 47, and its atomic weight is 107.87. The isotopes of silver, including artificially produced radioactive isotopes, range in weight from ^{102}Ag to ^{117}Ag. The only naturally occurring isotopes are ^{107}Ag, which makes up 52% of the silver found in nature, and ^{109}Ag, which accounts for 48%. Crystals of silver have a face-centered cubic lattice structure. The element melts at 960.8° C (1774.4° F) and boils at about 1950° C (4010° F). Its specific gravity is 10.50 at 20° C (68° F). The most common valence of silver is + 1, but the + 2 state is also found.

The electrical and thermal conductivities of silver are the highest of any element. It also has the highest optical reflectivity. When polished, silver will reflect about 95% of the light in the visible range of the spectrum. Silver is more malleable and ductile than any other element except gold. It is a relatively soft metal, and it scratches easily. Silver, which is intermediate in chemical reactivity between copper and gold, is a relatively inert metal that is resistant to common corrosive agents, such as oxygen, water, and dilute acids. However, it does combine readily with sulfur in the air or with hydrogen sulfide to form silver sulfide, Ag_2S, which is the black tarnish commonly seen on silverware. Silver is soluble in nitric acid, hot concentrated sulfuric acid, mercury, and fused alkali peroxides.

An unusual property of silver is its ability when molten to absorb large quantities of oxygen, even up to 20 times its own volume. However, as the liquid silver cools, most of the oxygen is released.

Occurrence. Silver is a rare metal, making up less than a hundred-millionth of the earth's crust. Although some silver is found as a native element, most occurs in compounds, such as sulfides, arsenides, antimonides, tellurides, bismuthides, and halides. The most common of the silver minerals is argentite, Ag_2S, which when pure contains 87% silver. Argentite occurs alone or dissolved in galena, PbS. Copper ores containing silver are chalcopyrite, $CuFeS_2$; chalcocite, Cu_2S; and bornite, Cu_5FeS_4.

More than two thirds of the silver produced is obtained as a by-product from ores of other metals, primarily lead and copper ores, with small amounts from zinc and gold ores. Although only a few ounces of silver may be recovered per ton of ore, the great value of the metal makes working of low-grade mines profitable. The remainder of the silver produced comes from high-grade ores, such as argentite and cerargyrite, AgCl, which is commonly known as horn silver.

Extraction. Silver is extracted from its ores by direct smelting, amalgamation, leaching, or cyanidation. The most common method of obtaining silver directly from its ores is the high-recovery *cyanidation process*. In this process, silver is dissolved from the ore by treatment with sodium cyanide solution. The dissolved silver is then precipitated by the addition of zinc or aluminum and an alkali to the solution.

In the *leaching method*, horn silver is dissolved in concentrated brine, and the silver is then precipitated out by the addition of copper. In the *amalgamation process*, horn silver is treated with mercury at room temperature. The ore is reduced to silver, which then dissolves in the mercury to form an amalgam. The mercury can be distilled off from the amalgam by heating.

Silver-bearing lead and copper ores are treated by *direct smelting*. When the ore is fused, the silver is absorbed by either the lead or the copper. Silver is extracted from lead by the *Parkes process*, in which 1% zinc is added to the molten crude lead. The zinc reacts with silver to form alloys with higher melting points and lower densities than the lead bath. Thus, these alloys float to the surface and are skimmed off. Zinc is removed from the alloys by distillation. Any lead remaining with the silver is removed by *cupellation*, a process in which the molten metal is heated in a blast of air on a cupel, or hearth, made of bone ash. The lead is converted to litharge, PbO, which flows over the edge of the cupel, leaving pure silver.

Silver is extracted from copper by the *Betts process*, in which copper is electrolytically refined. In this process silver is obtained from the sludge, or anode slime, deposited in the baths. Silver is dissolved out of the sludge with nitric acid and is then obtained in pure form by cathodic reduction.

Silver Alloys. Other metals are alloyed with silver to improve its mechanical strength and its resistance to wear and tarnish. The silver content of metals is expressed in terms of "fineness," or parts of silver per 1,000 parts of total metal. For example, sterling silver, which is the most familiar of the silver alloys, is 925 fine—that is, it contains 92.5% silver; the other 7.5% is copper. The addition of the copper to the silver increases the mechanical strength of the metal and lowers its melting point. Sterling silver is widely used for tableware, jewelry, and decorative articles.

Antimony and arsenic are alloyed with silver to improve its tarnish resistance. Cadmium is alloyed with silver to lower its melting point. These low-melting substances are used as brazing alloys and as jewelry solders. They are also used in electrical contacts. Copper-silver alloys can be worked and are used in the brazing of metals.

Iron-silver alloys are important because silver has a grain-refining and deoxidizing action on stainless steel, and consequently the stainless steel suffers less pit corrosion. Silver is alloyed with lead because it improves the resistance of lead to deformation. These alloys are used in soft solders and as anodes in the electrolytic refining of zinc. Silver-lead alloys containing 3% to 5% lead have excellent antifriction properties.

An alloy of tin and silver is used to form a dental amalgam, which is plastic for a short time before setting into a hard mass that is resistant to corrosion. Palladium and platinum increase the tarnish resistance of silver, and these alloys are also used in dental work because of their corrosion resistance.

Tin-silver alloys are used in valves in refrigeration equipment. Zinc-silver alloys are used for electrical contacts and in brazing. Alloys of silver and copper and zinc have low melting points, good flow characteristics, high strength, and good malleability, ductility, and corrosion resistance. These alloys are used in brazing.

Compounds. The most important compound of silver is silver nitrate, $AgNO_3$, which is used as the starting compound in the preparation of other silver compounds and in the manufacture of mirrors. The major use of silver nitrate is in the production of silver halides for photosensitive emulsions for films and papers in the photographic industry. Silver nitrate is a colorless salt that is very soluble in water. It is prepared by dissolving silver in nitric acid and then evaporating the solution. Traces of silver nitrate will blacken the skin as a result of the reduction of silver ions to metallic silver by proteins.

Silver carbonate, AG_2CO_3, is a light yellow salt produced by the addition of carbonic acid to silver oxide. It is useful in the synthesis of organic compounds. Silver chromate, Ag_2CrO_4, is a dark red powder that is also used in organic synthesis.

Silver bromide, $AgBr$, and silver chloride, $AgCl$, are the silver halides used in photosensitive emulsions. Silver bromide is a yellowish white solid, and silver chloride is white. Both are insoluble in water and soluble in sodium thiosulfate, which is commonly known as photographers' "hypo." Silver iodide, AgI, has a crystalline structure that very closely resembles that of ice, and it has been used in seeding clouds to furnish nuclei for ice formation in attempts at rainmaking.

In the compounds discussed previously the valence of silver is $+1$. Silver compounds in which the valence of the element is $+2$ are not stable in solution except in the form of complex ions. However, there are stable solid compounds, such as AgF_2 and AgO, in which the valence of silver is $+2$.

Silver Plating. Silver is one of the most commonly used metals for electroplating either metallic or nonmetallic materials. Plating is done to increase the reflectivity of the material or for decorative purposes. Silver is plated on metals from a sodium cyanide bath containing silver nitrate. Plastics can be silvered by the chemical reduction of a complex silver ion to metallic silver or by the deposition of silver by vacuum evaporation.

In the production of mirrors, silver is chemically deposited on one surface of the glass to increase its reflectivity. The silvering preparations consist of two solutions. One is an ammoniacal solution of silver nitrate, $Ag(NH_3)_2NO_3$, which also contains some potassium hydroxide. The other solution is a reducing agent, such as sugar, Rochelle salt, or formaldehyde. The reducing agent, when mixed with the silver solution, converts the silver-ammonia complex ion to metallic silver. The glass to be silvered is first thoroughly cleaned, and then the solutions are poured on it. If the ammoniacal silver solution is allowed to evaporate on standing, it can deposit a silver azide that is sensitive and explosive.

HERBERT LIEBESKIND, *The Cooper Union*

A mill rolls silver strip in various thicknesses and widths. Strip is used in making dishes, platters, trays, electrical contacts, and sea-water batteries.

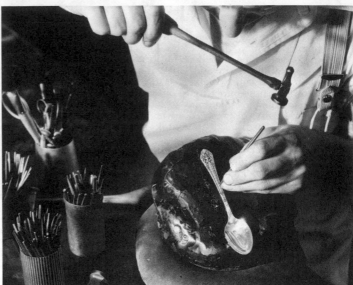

A metalworker forms a silver bowl by using a hand tool to press silver sheet against a revolving wooden form on the lathe spindle (*left*). Decorative patterns on a silver spoon are formed by indentations made with a hammer and chasing tools (*above*).

SILVER AS A MONETARY METAL

Silver has been used as money since the time of ancient Babylonia. For centuries it was the primary form of money. In the United States, bimetallism was officially adopted in 1792, when the mint was authorized to coin as much gold and silver as were offered. The silver dollar contained 371.25 grains and the gold dollar 24.75 grains, a ratio of 15 to 1.

The 19th Century. The bimetallic standard depended on a ratio of market prices of the two metals equal to their official mint ratio. In fact, however, the market price ratio was near 15.5:1 by 1803, when France adopted a 15.5:1 dual metal standard. The market ratio continued to creep up toward 16:1 by 1816, when England adopted this ratio for coinage. In 1834, after an extensive flow of gold to England, the U. S. Congress lowered the gold content of the dollar to 23.2 grains. Thus the mint ratio was increased to 16:1.

Rich gold discoveries in the mid-1800's led, however, to lowered gold prices and higher silver prices. As the discrepancy widened between official mint prices and market prices, bimetallism ceased to work. Silver was sold in the market for a higher price than it commanded at the mint. Silver coin was driven from circulation during the Civil War, and further coinage of silver dollars was prohibited by the Coinage Act of 1873. Europe and Latin America also abandoned the free coinage of silver in the 1870's. Silver circulated as money only in the form of subsidiary coinage. This was possible only because silver's value in subsidiary coins was considerably debased. The American half dollar, for example, contained 172.8 grains of silver instead of 185.625.

In the United States, silver shortly became involved in a contest between easy-money and tight-money adherents. In 1873 the relative prices of silver and gold shifted again. Discoveries of silver in Nevada lowered its price to below the old mint price of $1.293 an ounce. Silver-mine owners, farmers, and debtors, who wanted to increase the supply of money in circulation and thus bring about higher prices, began a campaign to restore bimetallism.

In 1878 and again in 1890, Congress voted to require substantial open-market silver purchases and to authorize treasury notes backed by silver. In 1896, however, sound-money forces won a decisive political victory over the advocates of "free silver." In 1900, Congress officially adopted a gold-coin monetary standard, eliminating silver from the definition.

The 20th Century. The silver-mine owners and their representatives continued to carry on the fight for silver early in the 20th century, and in World War I, when the price of silver again began to soar, they brought back silver dollars.

The Great Depression of the 1930's reawakened interest in silver. As a result of the London Monetary Conference of 1933, the United States agreed to buy 24 million ounces at 64.64 cents an ounce—half the traditional price but 50% more than the prevailing market price. Throughout the 1930's, senators favoring silver and congressional proponents of cheap money succeeded in having the government artificially maintain the price of silver by buying quantities of it, ostensibly for coinage but mostly for burial in the vaults of West Point.

During World War II the rationale for silver as a monetary metal again disappeared. As silver-using industries operated at full capacity, the price of silver rose rapidly. The public began to hoard silver coins in anticipation of the day when the market price of the silver content would exceed their face value. When this finally occurred in the early 1960's, the U. S. government took steps to eliminate silver from the money system.

The Treasury ceased to issue silver certificates—the paper money secured by silver. However, the reduced supply of $1 and $2 bills was filled by Federal Reserve notes. In 1965 the silver content of newly minted quarters and dimes was eliminated, and quarters and dimes thereafter consisted of a layer of copper between two layers of cupronickel. The silver content of the half dollar was reduced to 40%, and by 1970 it was eliminated entirely.

Silver became simply a precious metal, traded by industrial and commercial users and speculators. The market price soared to unprecedented heights in late 1979, reaching $50.35 per ounce in January 1980. Two months later the price had dropped to $10.80 per ounce.

E. BRUCE FREDRIKSON
Syracuse University

Bibliography

Butts, Allison, and Coxe, C., eds., *Silver: Economics, Metallurgy, and Use* (1967; reprint, Krieger 1975).

Polk, Judd, and Wilkins, M., eds., *Sterling: Its Meaning in World Finance* (1956; reprint, Arno 1978).

Rickenbacker, William, *Wooden Nickels: Or, the Decline and Fall of Silver Coins* (Arlington House 1966).

Turner, Dennis, and Blinn, Stephen H., *Trading Silver—Profitably* (Arlington House 1975).

Weinstein, Allen, *Prelude to Populism: Origins of the Silver Issue, 1867–1878* (Yale Univ. Press 1970).

Wills, Geoffrey, *Silver for Pleasure and Investment* (Arco 1970).

SILVER AGE, in Greek and Roman literature, one of the mythological ages of man. Following the Golden Age, it lay under the care of the god Jupiter. The phrase "silver age" is also applied to a period of Latin literature that extended from about 15 A.D. to 180 A.D. and included such notable writers as Martial, Tacitus, and Juvenal. See also AGES OF MAN.

SILVER BROMIDE. See SILVER—*Compounds.*

SILVER CHLORIDE. See SILVER—*Compounds.*

SILVER CHROMATE. See SILVER—*Compounds.*

SILVER FOX. See FOX.

SILVER IODIDE. See SILVER—*Compounds.*

SILVER NITRATE. See SILVER—*Compounds.*

SILVER SPRING, an unincorporated community in central Maryland, is about 7 miles (11 km) north of the capitol in Washington, D. C. Developed in the years immediately after World War II, it is primarily a residential suburb of Washington, but it has several scientific research laboratories.

The neighborhood of Silver Spring was the closest point to the center of Washington that was reached by Confederate Gen. Jubal Early's raiders in July 1864, and represented the most dangerous threat to the safety of the Union government. Population: 72,893.

SILVER SPRINGS, a group of springs in central Florida, in Marion county, about 5 miles (8 km) northeast of Ocala. The springs emerge from a subterranean stream in a vast cavern and flow together to form the Silver River, which empties into the Oklawaha River, a part of the state's inland waterway system. The clear waters keep a uniform temperature of 72° F (22° C).

Glass-bottomed boats allow tourists to see the plants and fish to the maximum depth of 81 feet (25 meters). The springs are surrounded by a large landscaped park.

SILVER TREE, an evergreen tree, *Leucadendron argentum,* named for its silvery white, silky leaves. Native to the Cape region of South Africa, the tree is cultivated as an ornamental plant in warm climates and in greenhouses.

The silver tree attains 40 feet (12 meters) in height. The leaves, which are crowded on the branches, have hardened tips and are stalkless. They measure 3 to 6 inches (7.5–15 cm) in length and ½ to 1¼ inches (12–30 mm) in width. The globular silver and yellow flowers are borne at the tips of the branches. Male and female flowers are on separate trees.

JOHN W. THIERET
University of Southwestern Louisiana

SILVER WEDDING. See WEDDING ANNIVERSARY.

SILVERBERRY, North American shrub or small tree, *Elaeagnus commutata.* See OLEASTER.

SILVERFISH, a soft-bodied, wingless insect that is a common household pest. Related to bristletails and firebrats, the silverfish (*Lepisma saccharina*) is within the family Lepismatidae, order Thysanura. It is about 0.5 inch (1.7 cm)

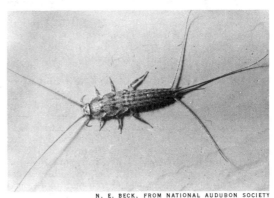

N. E. BECK, FROM NATIONAL AUDUBON SOCIETY
Silverfish, a common household insect pest

long and has long antennae and three tail-like appendages at the end of the abdomen. Its body is covered with gray or silvery scales.

Secretive, the silverfish lives and feeds on wallpaper, book bindings, paper, and fabrics, often causing considerable damage. It lays its comparatively few eggs in cracks, crevices, or folds of food material. Egg to adult development takes seven to nine months in the tropics but about two years in temperate regions. Silverfish are quick moving and not easily captured and thus have a long life-span.

SILVERIUS, sil-vēr'ē-əs, **Saint** (died about 537), pope from 536 to 537. Silverius became pope through the efforts of the Ostrogothic King Theodatus in early July of 536. His predecessor, Pope Agapetus I, had deposed Anthimus, patriarch of Constantinople, a favorite of the Byzantine Empress Theodora, for being a monophysite heretic. After failing to persuade Silverius to restore Anthimus, Theodora sent the deacon Vigilius to Rome with orders to the Byzantine commander, Belisarius, to condemn Silverius and install Vigilius as pope.

Charges of treason were brought against Silverius, and he was exiled to Patara in Lycia in

March of 537. Emperor Justinian ordered him returned to Rome for trial, but instead he was exiled on the island of Ponza, where he was forced to resign on Nov. 11, 537. He reportedly died of starvation there a short time later. His feast day is observed on June 20.

SILVERS, Phil (1912–   ), American comedy star of stage, screen, and television. He was born Philip Silversmith in Brooklyn, N. Y., on May 11, 1912, to Russian immigrant parents. He began his career as a boy tenor in vaudeville, then toured for several years with the Minsky burlesque troupe, and made his state debut in the musical *Yokel Boy* (1939). The next year he made his first motion picture, *The Hit Parade*, and in the period 1942–1945 appeared in some 20 films, always in subordinate roles.

After serving as an entertainer in the Mediterranean area during World War II, Silvers played the leading roles in the Broadway productions *High Button Shoes* (1947–1950) and *Top Banana* (1951–1952). The latter and its film version (1954), brought him wide acclaim. He was an even greater success as Sergeant Bilko in the television series of the 1950's *The Phil Silvers Show* (originally named *You'll Never Get Rich*). Later, he appeared in the Broadway production *Do-Re-Mi* (1960) and in such films as *A Funny Thing Happened on the Way to the Forum* (1966). In 1972 he starred in a Broadway revival of *A Funny Thing*.

SILVERSIDE, any of a family, Atherinidae, of slender fishes with a broad silvery band on each side. About 150 species occur in tropical and temperate waters throughout the world. Most are marine fishes, but some species live in brackish water and some in fresh water. Silversides range from 3 to more than 20 inches (7.5–50 cm) in length. They are generally greenish on the upper side and whitish below. They have small mouths with poorly developed teeth and feed on aquatic plants and small animals.

Some common U. S. species include the brook silverside (*Labidesthes sicculus*), the tidewater silverside (*Menidia beryllina*), the Mississippi silverside (*M. audens*), the jacksmelt (*Atherinopsis californiensis*), and the grunion (*Leuresthes tenuis*). See also GRUNION.

SILVERWARE. See FLATWARE; GOLDWORK AND SILVERWORK.

SILVESTER. See SYLVESTER.

SILVICULTURE, the improvement and ecological management of timber forests. See FORESTRY.

SIMA. See SIAL.

SIMBIRSK, syim-byĕrsk′, former name of the Russian city of Ulyanovsk. See ULYANOVSK.

SIMCOE, sim′kō, **John Graves** (1752–1806), British army officer, who was the first lieutenant governor of Upper Canada (Ontario). He was born in Cotterstock, Northumberland, on Feb. 25, 1752. Entering the army as an ensign in 1771, he served throughout the American Revolution, surrendering at Yorktown with Cornwallis. His *Journal of the Operations of the Queens Rangers* (1787) is an account of the force that he led. He became a member of the

House of Commons in 1790, and two years later returned to North America as lieutenant governor of Upper Canada.

On July 8, 1792, Simcoe established his capital at Newark (later Niagara), but moved it in 1793 to Toronto. He encouraged settlement by American Loyalists and assisted agricultural development of the country. During 1796–1797 he commanded the British forces fighting in Santo Domingo against both the French and Toussaint L'Ouverture. After returning to Britain he was appointed commander in chief in India. Simcoe died in Torbay, Devonshire, on Oct. 26, 1806, before assuming office.

SIMCOE, sim′kō, a town in southern Ontario, Canada, the seat of Norfolk county, is on the Lynn River, 6 miles (10 km) north of Lake Erie. The city's industries include canning, tobacco curing, and the manufacture of machinery, metal products, and textiles.

Simcoe was settled in the late 1700's and was named for John Simcoe, the first lieutenant governor of Upper Canada. The town was incorporated in 1875. Population: 14,326.

SIMENON, sĕm-nôn′, **Georges Joseph Christian** (1903–   ), Belgian-born novelist, who is most famous for his detective stories featuring Inspector Maigret. He was born in Liège on Feb. 13, 1903, and attended the Collège St.-Servais until the death of his father forced him to leave. He eventually took a job as a reporter on *La Gazette de Liège* and was assigned to cover the police court. He soon had his own column, which he wrote from 1919 to 1922.

Simenon then went to Paris, where he turned out hundreds of pulp novels and stories, writing under 17 different pseudonyms. In 1930 he created Inspector Maigret, who has been featured in more than 75 stories. Early Maigret works include *Le Crime du Inspecteur Maigret* (1932) and *Les Fiançialles de M. Hire* (1933).

Simenon's detective stories give an insight into day-to-day police work and are noted for their psychological awareness. They have been widely translated and have been adapted for films and broadcasting. Simenon has also written over 150 other novels dealing with various psychological and social themes, including *Lettre à mon juge* (1947; Eng. tr., *Act of Passion*, 1952) and *L'Ours en peluche* (1960). He moved to the United States in 1945, where he resided for over 10 years before returning to Europe, where he lived in France and Switzerland.

SIMEON, sim′ē-ən, was the second son of Jacob and Leah (Genesis 29:33), from whom the tribe of Simeon took its name. Simeon was held hostage in Egypt by his brother Joseph while his other brothers were sent back to Jacob with orders to return with their youngest brother Benjamin (Genesis 42:24, 36; 43:23). Joseph freed him when they brought him Benjamin.

According to Genesis 34, Simeon and his brother Levi avenged the violation of their sister Dinah by Shechem, the Hivite, son of the local ruler. They agreed to intermarry with the Hivites if they would be circumcised and then attacked their city while the males were still weak from the procedure. The tribes of Simeon and Levi settled in central Palestine but were forced to move south because of the opposition of superior Canaanite forces.

SIMEON I, sim'ē-ən (died 927), emperor of Bulgaria, brought the medieval Bulgarian empire to its height. He was the son of King Boris I, who retired in 889 in favor of his son Vladimir. Boris returned in 893, deposed the cruel Vladimir, and installed Simeon as king. Simeon extended his domain westward, gaining access to the Adriatic Sea and absorbing Serbian territory. His consuming ambition, however, was to crush the Byzantine Empire, and most of his campaigns, until he made peace in 924, were directed against it. In 925 he proclaimed himself emperor of the Bulgars and Greeks.

Educated in Constantinople, Simeon was an enthusiastic supporter of Greek culture. He encouraged the translation of Greek works into Slavonic and the development of an independent Bulgarian literature and culture.

SIMEON STYLITES, sim'ē-ən stī-lī'tēz, **Saint** (c. 390–459), Syrian ascetic, who was the first "Pillar Saint." Simeon was born in Cilicia and while still a young man moved to Antioch in Syria. He attracted a number of followers by his austere way of life. After about 10 years of leading the life of an anchorite, he built a pillar with a platform on top in 433, on which he remained for the rest of his life. He eventually raised it to a height of about 60 feet (18 meters). He carried on his ascetical practices and praying, and preached to the crowds of pilgrims who came to see him. His disciples provided for his simple needs. His feast is kept by Eastern Christians on September 1 and in the West on January 5.

SIMFEROPOL, syim-fər-ô'pəl-yə, a city in the USSR, is the capital of the Crimean oblast of the Ukrainian SSR. It is on the Salgir River, 40 miles (65 km) northeast of Sevastopol. There are machinery and food processing industries. The site of a settlement since ancient times, the city was called Ak-Mechet while under Tatar rule in the 15th-18th centuries. The Russians renamed it Simferopol when they annexed the Crimea in 1783. The city was the capital of the Crimean Tatar government in 1918 and of the White Russians under General Wrangel in 1920. From 1921 to 1946 it was the capital of the Crimean Autonomous SSR. Population: (1970) 250,000.

SIMHAT TORAH, sim-ĸнät' tō-rä', the Jewish festival that marks the end of the reading of the Torah or Pentateuch in each synagogue. It literally means "Rejoicing of the Law" and occurs on the last day of the Feast of Tabernacles (Sukkot). The usual observance includes the removal of the scrolls of the Torah from the ark and carrying them around the synagogue seven times to the accompaniment of singing and, particularly among Hasidic sects, with dancing. Congregation members read the last section of Deuteronomy and the first verses of Genesis.

SIMI VALLEY, si-mē', a city in southwestern California, in Ventura county, about 35 miles (56 km) northwest of the center of Los Angeles. It makes camper trailers, marine sanitary sewage units, liquid oxygen, toothpaste tubes, picture frames, and ladies' sportswear. Strathearn historical park and the Chumash Indians caves are nearby. Simi Valley was founded in 1850 and was incorporated in 1969. Government is by council and manager. Population: 77,500.

SIMILAR FIGURES. In plane geometry, two polygons are similar if the angles of one are equal to the corresponding angles of the other, and the corresponding sides are proportional. For example, in the accompanying diagram the figures ABCD and EFGH are similar because angle A equals angle E, angle B equals angle F, angle C equals angle G, angle H equals angle D, and

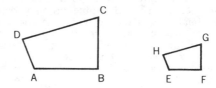

AB/EF = BC/FG = CD/GH = DA/HE. The constant ratio of any two corresponding sides of similar figures is called the ratio of similitude of the figures.

Two triangles are similar when two angles of one of them are equal respectively to two angles of the other. Therefore, a triangle is similar to any triangle cut off by a line parallel to one of its sides. Also, triangles whose corresponding sides are proportional are similar.

SIMILE. See FIGURES OF SPEECH.

SIMKHOVITCH, sim-kō'vich, **Mary Melinda Kingsbury** (1867–1951), American social worker. She was born at Chestnut Hill, Mass., on Sept. 8, 1867. Several years after graduating from Boston University in 1890, she became head worker at the College Settlement in New York City. In 1899 she married Vladimir Simkhovitch, a Columbia history professor.

In 1902, Mrs. Simkhovitch helped organize Greenwich House in Manhattan and, as its director for over 40 years, she developed it into an outstanding social and cultural center. She died in New York, N. Y. on Nov. 15, 1951.

SIMLA, sim'lə, is a town in India, in the state of Himachal Pradesh, 170 miles (270 km) north of Delhi. It is the capital of the state and the former summer capital of the British Indian government. Simla has an attractive location on a wooded ridge of the Himalaya at an altitude of about 7,150 feet (2,180 meters) above sea level. It is a popular resort, the largest in the area. Population: (1961) 42,947.

SIMMONS, Furnifold McLendel (1854–1940), American political leader. He was born near Pollocksville, N. C., on Jan. 20, 1854. He graduated from Trinity College (now Duke University) in 1873, and began to practice law. A Democrat, he served in the U. S. House of Representatives from 1887 to 1889. Later, as Democratic state chairman, Simmons dominated his party. He wrested control from a faction that included Negroes and won passage of a state constitutional amendment that effectively disfranchised Negroes.

In the U. S. Senate from 1901 to 1931, Simmons cosponsored the Underwood-Simmons tariff (1913), which lowered duties. He sought a compromise on the Treaty of Versailles. He opposed the election of Alfred E. Smith, a Democrat, for president in 1928, and two years later Simmons was defeated for renomination. He died in New Bern, N. C., on April 30, 1940.

SIMMONS COLLEGE is a liberal arts college, primarily for women, in Boston, Mass. It was founded in 1899 as Simmons Female College by a bequest of John Simmons. The present name was adopted in 1915.

Simmons was one of the first women's colleges in the United States to recognize the value of combining technical instruction, which would enable graduates to earn a living, with a liberal arts education. Toward this end, a basic liberal arts course is combined with a program of specialized professional study leading to a B. A. or a B. S. degree. Areas of professional study include publishing, library science, social science, education, social work, business, home economics, nursing and health services, and various interdisciplinary programs. Men are admitted to graduate study, leading to master's degrees. Enrollment in the early 1970's was over 2,200.

SIMMS, William Gilmore (1806–1870), American writer, who is remembered chiefly for novels based on Southern Indians and on border warfare between colonials and the British during the American Revolution. He was born in Charleston, S. C., on April 17, 1806, the son of an unsuccessful merchant. He served for a time as a pharmacist's apprentice and then studied law, which he later practiced until he established himself as a writer and man of letters. He died in Charleston on June 11, 1870.

Simms began his literary career as a poet and during his lifetime produced some 15 volumes of skillful but undistinguished verse. His fiction includes crime stories, such as *Martin Faber* (1833), and novels set in strange lands, such as *The Damsel of Darien* (1839) But he was at his best when writing historical romances set in the South. *The Yemassee* (1835), a tale of an Indian war, is considered his masterpiece. The many others are usually identified as members of series. *Guy Rivers* (1834) and *Beauchampe* (1842) are among those known as border romances. *The Partisan* (1835), *Mellichampe* (1836), and others belong to the group celebrating the American Revolution in South Carolina. In these works Simms is seen as the successor if not always the equal of Sir Walter Scott and James Fenimore Cooper. Simms also wrote short stories, plays, critical essays, histories of South Carolina, and biographies. See also YEMASSEE, THE.

Further Reading: Parks, Edd W., *William Gilmore Simms as Literary Critic* (Univ. of Ga. Press 1960); Ridgely, Joseph, *William Gilmore Simms* (Twayne 1963).

SIMON, sī-mən, **Saint,** one of the twelve Apostles of Jesus. His name appears in the list of Apostles in the gospels of Matthew (10:4), Mark (3:18), and Luke (6:15), but he is not mentioned elsewhere in the New Testament. According to the gospel of Luke, Simon was a member of the Zealots, a Jewish group that fanatically opposed the Romans. Later tradition made him the successor of James as bishop of Jerusalem. His feast is kept with that of St. Jude Thaddeus on October 28 in the West, but he is venerated alone in the East on May 10.

SIMON, sī'mən, **Neil** (1927–   ), American playwright and television writer, whose highly successful comedies often reflect his ability to see the comic incongruities of everyday life. Marvin Neil Simon was born in the Bronx, New York City, on July 4, 1927. He studied at New York University and began his career writing comedy for television. At first, he teamed with his brother Danny to produce materials for the Phil Silvers and Tallulah Bankhead shows, among others. He then wrote alone for television specials, notably those of Sid Caesar and Phil Silvers.

Simon's first play, *Come Blow Your Horn,* based on his and his brother's experiences in moving from their parents' home into a Manhattan bachelor apartment, opened on Broadway in 1961 and became a hit of two seasons' duration. It was followed by others equally successful—*Barefoot in the Park* (1963), *The Odd Couple* (1965), *Star Spangled Girl* (1966), *Plaza Suite* (1968), and *The Prisoner of Second Avenue* (1971). Simon also wrote the books for a number of popular musicals, including *Sweet Charity* (1966) and *Promises, Promises* (1968), and the film adaptation (1967) of his *Barefoot in the Park.*

SIMON FRASER UNIVERSITY, sī'mən frā'zər, is a nondenominational, publicly funded, coeducational institution of higher learning in Burnaby, British Columbia, Canada. It was founded by an act of the legislative assembly of British Columbia in 1963. Its campus is at the summit of Burnaby Mountain, seven miles (11 km) east of Vancouver.

Simon Fraser operates throughout the year on a trimester system. It has faculties of arts, education, and science and offers programs of study leading to bachelor's degrees in anthropology, biochemistry, biological sciences, physics, chemistry, commerce, economics, education, English, French, geography, German, history, kinesiology, mathematics, philosophy, physics, political science, psychology, Russian, sociology, and Spanish. Master's and doctoral degrees are also granted. In the early 1970's, enrollment was about 5,300.

SIMON LEGREE. See LEGREE, SIMON.

SIMON MACCABAEUS, sī'mən mak-ə-bē'əs (died 135 B. C.), Hasmonean ruler of Judea, who reigned from 141 to 135 B. C. He succeeded his brother Jonathan as high priest and was given the hereditary title of exilarch by the people. See also MACCABEES.

SIMON MAGUS, sī'mən mā'gəs, was a convert to Christianity who attempted to buy the power to work miracles from Peter and John (Acts 8:9–24). The sin of simony is named after him. See also SIMONY.

SIMON PETER. See PETER, SAINT.

SIMONE MARTINI. See MARTINI, SIMONE.

SIMONIDES OF CEOS, sī-mon'ə-dēz, sē'os (c. 556–c. 468 B. C.), Greek lyric poet. He was born in Iulis on the island of Ceos (modern Kea) in the Aegean Sea. Invited by Hipparchus (reigned 527 to 514 B. C.), tyrant of Athens, to visit that city, he there met the poets Anacreon and Lasus, Pindar's master. After the death of Hipparchus he went to Thessaly, where he won the favor of the Aleuads and Scopads, leading families of the region, whose victories in the games he afterward celebrated in poetry. Returning to Athens, Simonides won the prize in competition with Aeschylus for the best elegy honoring those who fell on the field of Marathon. About 476 B.C. he was invited to the court of Hiero at Syracuse, where he remained until his death.

Simonides, noted for his sweetness of disposition, appears to have been the chief favorite of Hiero in a court adorned by Pindar, Bacchylides, and Aeschylus. Poetic conception, pathos, and perfect power of expression are among the chief characteristics of his poetry. Pindar surpasses him, however, in vigor and originality. Simonides brought the elegy and epigram to a high degree of perfection, and in the dithyramb and triumphal ode he particularly distinguished himself. It is said that he was the first to sell his poems.

Further Reading: Bowra, Cecil M., *Greek Lyric Poetry*, 2d rev. ed. (Oxford 1961).

SIMONOV, sē'mə-nôf, **Konstantin Kirill Mikhailovich** (1915–1979), Russian novelist, dramatist, and poet. He was born in Petrograd (now Leningrad), Russia, on Nov. 28, 1915, and graduated from the Gorky Literary Institute in 1938. His experiences as a war correspondent during World War II provided much of his material. From 1950 to 1953 he edited *Literaturanaya Gazeta*, and in 1954 he became editor of the magazine *Novyi Mir*. Although he assumed an ambivalent position with regard to official criticism of other Russian writers, he was removed from his editorial post in 1957. He died on Aug. 28, 1979.

Simonov's first notable work was the poem *Ty pomnish, Aloisha, dorogi Smolenschchiny* (1941; Eng. tr., *You Remember, Aloisha*, 1956), in which the sufferings of wartime Russia are depicted. His best selling novel *Dni i nochi* (1944; Eng. tr., *Days and Nights*, 1945), set during the siege of Stalingrad, is an account of an ordinary man's defense of his homeland. Simonov's other works include *Russkiye lyudi* (1942; Eng. tr., *Russian People*, 1944) and *Zhivvye i miortvyye* (1959; Eng. tr., *The Living and the Dead*, 1962).

SIMONY, sī'mə-nē, is a transaction by which something sacred or spiritual is given or received for a pecuniary compensation, or a temporal benefit. The nature of simony is clearly illustrated in the story of Simon Magus in Acts 8:9–24, when it was committed for the first time.

Simon, a native of Samaria, was noted for his skill in magic. Attracted by the miracles wrought by the preachers of Christianity, he adopted the new faith and was baptized by Philip. Later, Peter and John came to the East to minister to the new converts. "Then laid they their hands on them and they received the Holy Spirit." When Simon saw this, he offered them money, saying "Give me also this power." Peter replied, "Your silver perish with you, because you thought you could obtain the gift of God with money."

Simony later assumed many forms, but it always implies an exchange of some material thing or temporal benefit for something spiritual that concerns God, principally, such as a purchased office or preferment in the church. During the Middle Ages the problem of simony was severe for the Church as it struggled to establish its rights and the extent of its authority as against those of civil powers.

In England, simony has been the subject of secular as well as ecclesiastical legislation, and in the Roman Catholic, Eastern Orthodox, and Protestant Episcopal Churches it is an ecclesiastical offense.

SIMPLE MACHINE, any one of several elementary devices, one or more of which is used in virtually all machinery. Traditionally, the group of simple machines includes the lever, the wheel and axle, the pulley, the inclined plane, the wedge, and the screw.

Generally, the purpose of a machine is to convert energy to work. In translational machines, including the lever, the pulley, the inclined plane, and the wedge, work is the product of force and distance. In rotational machines, including the wheel and axle and the screw, work is the product of the torque and the angle through which the object rotates while acted on by the torque. The torque is the product of the force producing rotation and the distance from the axis of rotation to the line of action of the force. See also BLOCK AND TACKLE; INCLINED PLANE; LEVER; PULLEY; SCREW; WEDGE; WHEEL AND AXLE.

SIMPLICIUS, sim-plish'ē-əs, **Saint** (died 483), pope from 468 to 483. Simplicius was born in Tivoli and became pope on March 3, 468. The problem of the Monophysite heresy dominated most of Simplicius' reign. When the imperial throne was usurped by Basiliscus in 475, the heresy was openly supported. Emperor Zeno returned to power in 477, and attempted a compromise by issuing the Henoticon (482), a letter that was orthodox on the surface but failed to mention the condemnation of the heresy by the Council of Chalcedon (451) or the Tome of Pope Leo, which stated the orthodox doctrine on the two natures in Christ. Simplicius died on March 10, 483 without taking any action on the Henoticon. His feast is March 10.

SIMPLON PASS, saN-plôN', an Alpine pass in Switzerland, at a height of 6,578 feet (2,005 meters). The pass, usually blocked by snow from December to May, is crossed by the Simplon road, which leads from Brig on the Rhône in Switzerland to Italy. Napoleon's engineers widened the Simplon road between 1800 and 1805 so that artillery could be taken over the Alps into Italy. The Simplon railroad tunnel, opened in 1906, is to the east of the pass.

SIMPSON, Sir George (1787?–1860), Canadian administrator. He was born in Loch Broom, Ross-shire, Scotland. In 1809 he went to work for a London firm engaged in the West Indian trade. Joining the Hudson's Bay Company in 1820, he was sent to Canada, where he helped achieve the merger of the Hudson's Bay and North West companies in 1821. He was soon made governor of the northern department of Rupert's Land.

From 1826 until he died, Simpson was governor in chief of all Hudson's Bay Company territories. He built a fur monopoly nearly spanning the continent, one that carried the company into a period of peace and unprecedented prosperity. Simpson, who was called "the little emperor," was an able administrator who traveled extensively throughout company territory, worked effectively with the personnel under his authority, and gave attention even to the tactical details of daily operations. He encouraged exploration.

Several editions of Simpson's journals and narratives have been published. He was made Knight Bachelor in 1841. His headquarters after 1833 were at Lachine, Lower Canada, near Montreal. He died there on Sept. 7, 1860.

SIMPSON, O. J. (1947–), American football player, who was rated one of the greatest running backs in collegiate and professional annals. Orenthal James Simpson, nicknamed "Juice," was born in San Francisco on July 9, 1947. A football and track star in high school and at the City College of San Francisco, he transferred to the University of Southern California. In 1967 he led USC to the Rose Bowl title and the national championship and in 1968 was awarded the Heisman Trophy as the best college player.

Drafted by the Buffalo Bills in 1969, he led the National Football League in rushing in 1972, 1973, 1975, and 1976, setting single-season records for rushing (2,003 yards) in 1973 and for touchdowns (23) in 1975. After knee surgery in 1977, his effectiveness waned. Traded to the San Francisco 49ers in 1978, he retired in 1979 and devoted himself to television commercials and acting in motion pictures.

SIMS, Thomas M., American fugitive slave, who was the subject of a celebrated case under the Fugitive Slave Act. He was born a slave, escaped from his master in Savannah, Ga., in 1851 and succeeded in reaching Boston, Mass. He was arrested there on April 3, 1851, and was held under the Fugitive Slave Act. The case aroused the abolitionists of Boston. Wendell Phillips, Theodore Parker, William Lloyd Garrison, and Thomas W. Higginson were prominent in the effort made to prevent his return to his master. A writ of habeas corpus was obtained after some difficulty, but was set aside, and Sims was eventually returned to his master in Savannah. He was afterward taken to Vicksburg, and in 1863 he escaped to Grant's army at Vicksburg. He became a messenger in the U. S. Department of Justice in 1877.

SIMS, William Sowden (1858–1936), American admiral, who instituted many naval reforms and commanded the U. S. fleet in European waters during World War I. He was born on Oct. 15, 1858, in Port Hope, Ontario, Canada. The family went to the United States in 1868, and Sims graduated from the U. S. Naval Academy in 1880.

As commander of the U. S. Asiatic fleet (1901–1902), he learned from Sir Percy Scott of the British Navy certain techniques of gunnery and ship design and became convinced that the U. S. Navy was deficient in these fields. Finding that his brother officers agreed with him and believing that any suggestions through Navy channels would be useless, he wrote his views directly to President Theodore Roosevelt, a strong Navy advocate. In 1902, Sims was named inspector of Navy target practice.

In this post, which gave him broad powers, and later as naval aide to Roosevelt, he promoted many reforms in gunnery, ship design, and Navy training. After a tour of sea duty, he was named in 1916 as head of the Naval War College, with the rank of rear admiral.

In April 1917, when the United States entered World War I, Sims was made a vice admiral and appointed to command the U. S. fleet that operated with the British Navy in European waters. Sims was largely influential in securing the adoption of the convoy system to protect vessels against German submarines.

Sims was promoted to admiral on Dec. 4, 1918, and again headed the Naval War College until he retired in 1922. He died in Boston, Mass., on Sept. 28, 1936.

SIMSBURY, a town in northern Connecticut, is on the Farmington River, 10 miles (16 km) northwest of Hartford. Tobacco is a major crop in the area. Many of Simsbury's residents are employed in Hartford. A factory here makes safety fuses. The Westminster School for boys and the Ethel Walker School for girls are in Simsbury. Stratton Brook state park is in the western part of the town.

Simsbury was settled in 1660 and was incorporated in 1670. The first copper coins in the American colonies were minted here in 1737. Simsbury is governed by a board of selectmen. Population: 21,161.

SIMULTANEOUS EQUATIONS. See EQUATION– *Equations in More Than One Variable.*

SIN, sēn, was the moon-god of Babylonia and Assyria, called Nanna by the Sumerians. His chief centers of worship were Ur and Harran. Sin was the "lamp of heaven and earth" and "lord of the months" and "lord of decisions." His symbol was the crescent. He was the father of the sun-god Shamash and of the goddess Ishtar.

SIN is the violation of what is believed to be prohibited by the command of God. It is a violation of conscience or the deliberate doing of what an individual believes to be evil. The concept of sin is to be found in primitive as well as advanced societies. Myths of the fall of man are common to many ancient societies and are similar to the one related in the Book of Genesis. Besides the corporate concept of sin inherent in myths of the fall of man, an individual concept of sin can also be found. It can be seen most clearly in the violation of taboos and of ritual rules. It was considered to be a violation of the numinous or the sacred.

Biblical Concepts. The ancient Israelites at first shared the notions of sin common to their neighbors. As the consciousness of their special relationship with God as expressed through the covenant made on Mt. Sinai developed, the concept of sin became considerably more personal. It came to be regarded as a direct offense against God. David, when finally convinced of his sin, says, "I have sinned against the Lord" (II Samuel 12:13). Sin was a revolt against God, who had a special relationship with the people of Israel and with each individual member. The prophets in particular helped to inculcate the idea, although the older notion of sin continued to exist.

The revolt against God, which sin was considered to be, resulted in a sense of guilt. But while there is a concept of guilt there is no psychological analysis or awareness of it in the Old Testament. Sin had a definite effect on the surrounding world. Evils in the world were conceived as the result of sin. In the Book of Genesis, the result of Adam's sin was that the earth was cursed.

The New Testament writers regarded sin as a state of man that Christ had come to heal. The state of sin was incompatible with the new relationship with God established by Christ (I John 3:9). Christ conquered sin, and through his grace the Christian can also conquer sin.

Theological Concepts. Theologians formalized and developed notions of sin found in the Old and New Testaments. The fall of Adam was believed to have been communicated to all men. Original sin was the result of Adam's sin and was an inclination toward sin and the common lot of all men. The redemption wrought by Christ made man whole and gave him the ability to overcome sin.

Various distinctions among the types of sin are made by theologians. Actual sins are real sins of thought, word, or deed. Sins are also divided according to their gravity. *Mortal* sins are sins that cut off the sinner completely from God because of the seriousness of the sin and the deliberateness and consciousness of the act. Lesser sins committed with less awareness are called *venial*. Venial sin does not cut the sinner off from God but lessens his receptivity to God's grace. Another distinction is that between *formal* and *material* sin. Formal sin is the conscious and deliberate doing of something known to be evil. Material sin is an act that is evil in itself but is not known to be so, and hence the individual is not culpable.

The traditional Roman Catholic notion of sin is based on a belief in the freedom of man and an understanding of sin as the conscious and deliberate violation of God's will. The traditional Protestant notion is based on a belief in the basic corruption of man by original sin. Unless man receives the Holy Spirit and has faith, which is a gift of God, the individual cannot even love God. Even when justified by God, sinfulness remains. Only in the next life will sin finally be taken away.

See also EVIL; ORIGINAL SIN.

SINAI, sī'nī, is a region forming the easternmost part of Egypt. A land bridge between Asia and Africa, it is bounded on the north by the Mediterranean Sea, on the east by the Gaza Strip, Israel, and the Gulf of Aqaba, and on the west by the Gulf of Suez and the Suez Canal. The southern portion is a triangular peninsula with its apex in the Red Sea.

The northern coast of Sinai is characterized by high sand dunes. A barren central plateau extends southward to a mountainous area culminating in Jebel Katherina, which reaches an altitude of 8,651 feet (2,637 meters). Nearby is Jebel Musa (7,497 feet, or 2,285 meters), which is traditionally identified with the Mt. Sinai mentioned in the Bible.

Sinai has a population of about 50,000. The modern importance of Sinai is due to its strategic location and to its deposits of manganese and petroleum. It was occupied by Israeli forces in 1956 and again in 1967. See also SINAI, MOUNT.

SINAI, Mount, sī'nī, the mountain where Moses received the Law and the Israelites entered into a covenant with God (Exodus 19:1 and following). Variant traditions refer to it as Horeb (Exodus 3:1, I Kings 19:8). Since early times, Christians have sought it in the southern part of the Sinai peninsula. Jebel Serbal (6,791 feet, or 2,070 meters) seems to have enjoyed favor first, but Jebel Musa, Arabic for the "Mount of Moses" (7,497 feet, or 2,285 meters), traditionally has been regarded as the mountain of the lawgiving. In the time of Byzantine Emperor Justinian I (reigned 527–565), the Monastery of St. Catherine was built at the foot of the mountain. The *Codex Sinaiticus,* a 4th century Greek text of the Old Testament and all of the New Testament, was discovered in the library of the monastery in 1844. In the 19th century, attention was shifted to Ras Safesh (6,300 feet, or 1,920 meters), which is situated at the northern end of the range, because there was room at its foot for a large encampment, such as is described in Exodus.

The location of the actual biblical mountain is unknown. A location anywhere in the Sinai peninsula rests on the assumption that the migrating Hebrews crossed the isthmus somewhere near Suez and then turned southward. This theory has been upset by strong evidence that the Ramses of Exodus 1:11 is a later pharaoh, Tanis, and that Migdol and Baal-zephon of Exodus 14:1 lay on or near the Mediterranean, the latter probably at Mons Casius. Lake Serbonis (modern Bardawil) then would be the sea that was crossed. Such a northern route suggests, as in Judges 11:16, that the Hebrews made Kadesh (Kadesh-barnea) their objective. Mountains easily reached from that place have been proposed—for example Jebel Helal or Jebel Araif. However, in I Kings 19:18, Mt. Horeb is conceived of as remote from the Beersheba area, and in Deuteronomy 1:2 it is an 11-day journey from Horeb to Kadesh-barnea. This would fit the distance to Jebel Musa and warrants a theory that a delegation went there from Kadesh-barnea. Arabia is also a strong contender for the laurels, because the Midian mentioned in Exodus 3:1 is the region east of the Gulf of Aqaba.

EMIL G. KRAELING
Author of "The Rand McNally Bible Atlas"

SINAI CAMPAIGN OF 1956. See ISRAELI-ARAB WARS.

SINALOA, sē-nä-lō'ä, is a state in northwest Mexico. Long and narrow in shape, Sinaloa extends some 350 miles (560 km) along the Gulf of California between the states of Sonora, to the northwest, and Nayarit, to the southeast. The eastern boundary that separates Sinaloa from Chihuahua and Durango lies in the outer ranges of the Sierra Madre Occidental.

The area of the state of Sinaloa comprises about 22,580 square miles (58,480 sq km). The chief cities are Culiacán, the capital, and Mazatlán, which is a fishing center, winter resort, and one of Mexico's busiest Pacific ports.

There are two fairly distinct climatic zones. The first is a humid, subtropical coastal strip that produces sugar cane, tobacco, coffee, cotton, rice, and tropical fruits, as well as winter vegetables that are canned and exported to the United States. The second and larger zone is that of the eastern uplands, a region of broad, wooded valleys, moderate rainfall, and temperate climate. Cereals and livestock are raised in this area, but its economic importance is due chiefly to its rich gold, silver, copper, lead, and iron mines. The forests yield both rubber and hardwoods for export. The principal streams are the Río del Fuerte and the Sinaloa, Culiacán, and Piaxtla rivers.

Industries, including leather works, sugar refineries, food canneries, textile plants, and foundries, are concentrated largely in Culiacán, in the central part of the state, and Mazatlán, in the south. Rail lines and highways run the length of the state, through Culiacán and Mazatlán, southeast to Guadalajara in Jalisco State, and north through Sonora to Nogales at the Arizona border. Sinaloa became a state in 1830. Population: (1970) 1,266,528.

The Mosque of Suleiman in Constantinople was designed by the Turkish architect Sinan and built in 1549–1557.

SINAN, si-nän', **Ibn Abd al-Mannan** (1489–1578 or 1588), Ottoman architect, who developed the centrally domed Ottoman Turkish mosque style. Muslim biographers credited him with about 360 mosques, palaces, public baths, hospitals, madrassas (schools), tombs, aqueducts, and fountains. He is called Koca Mimar ("the great architect") Sinan to distinguish him from two other architects of the same name.

Life. Sinan was born of Greek Christian parents in an Anatolian village near Kayseri on April 15, 1489. After travels with his grandfather, a builder, he trained as a Janissary in Constantinople (now Istanbul). During military campaigns Sinan became chief of artillery and built fortifications, a bridge of boats across Lake Van, and a bridge across the Danube. Later, as royal architect to Suleiman (Süleyman) the Magnificent and Selim II, he devoted himself to nonmilitary building. He died in Constantinople on July 17, 1578 or 1588.

Work. After the Ottoman conquest of Constantinople, Sinan and other Ottoman architects sought to adapt the style of the domed Byzantine masterpiece Hagia Sophia to the requirements of a mosque. Retaining the traditional colonnaded mosque court, he transformed the hitherto flat-roofed hypostyle prayer hall into a unified, light-filled open space under a huge central dome on piers. He achieved the transition from rectangle to circle with combinations of small domes and half domes and with pendentives (triangular sections of vaulting) often masked with stalactite ornament (rows of scallops). He balanced the dome with slender minarets at the corners of the building. The best examples of his work are the Şehzade (finished 1548), the Süleymaniye (1549–1557), both in Constantinople, and the Selimiye (1568–1574) in Edirne.

SINANTHROPUS, sə-nan'thrə-pəs, an extinct type of man, remains of which were first found in China in 1927. See also MAN, PREHISTORIC.

SINARQUISMO, si-när-kiz'mō, a Mexican fascistic movement. The word means "with order." Sympathetic to the Franco regime in Spain, the movement emerged in the late 1930's. It was supported financially by large landholders and wealthy businessmen. The *sinarquistas* deplored the excesses of the Mexican revolution, advocated an authoritarian government guided by Catholic principles, urged closer ties with Spain, and opposed communism and the United States. Axis agents exploited the movement during World War II. Supporters included Mexicans in small towns who were irritated by administrative misrule by government bureaucrats, and peasants, whose lot had not improved after the revolution.

The Sinarquismo movement claimed one million members in the early 1940's, but its ranks declined thereafter.

SINATRA, si-nä'trə, **Frank** (1917?–), American popular singer and actor. Francis Albert Sinatra was born in Hoboken, N. J., on Dec. 12, 1917 (1915, according to some sources), the only child of Italian-born parents. He attended local schools and worked for a time as copyboy on a newspaper. After winning a singing contest in 1937, he began his career as a singer in a Hoboken roadhouse and from 1939 to 1942 sang with Harry James' and Tommy Dorsey's bands. While with the latter, he developed the style of crooning that made him the bobby-soxers' idol and earned for him the sobriquet "the Voice." The success of his recordings and his popularity as a soloist (1943–1945) on the radio program *Your Hit Parade* brought him to the attention of Hollywood producers, and he made many musical films, such as *Anchors Aweigh* (1945), *Till the Clouds Roll By* (1947), and *On the Town* (1949).

When his popularity declined in the early 1950's, Sinatra turned to serious acting and won an Academy Award as the best supporting actor

Frank Sinatra, in *From Here to Eternity* (1953)

in the film *From Here to Eternity* (1953). He then starred in a long succession of films—including *The Man with the Golden Arm* (1956), *Some Came Running* (1959), and *Von Ryan's Express* (1965)—and became a leading television performer. These activities, together with investments in various business enterprises, made him one of the most successful figures in show business.

SINBAD was a legendary citizen of Baghdad, under the caliphs, who undertook seven wonderful voyages through the Indian Ocean and the Eastern seas. The adventures of Sinbad (or Sindbad) are reported in the story *Sindbad the Sailor* in *The Arabian Nights*. In the course of these voyages he discovered a roc's egg, a valley full of diamonds, and another full of dead elephants (from which he obtained a rich cargo of ivory), and he killed a monster (the Old Man of the Sea), who mounted his back and clung there. The stories probably embody the exaggerated experiences of Muslim navigators from Baghdad, Basra, and Siraf in the 8th to 10th centuries, when trade with India, China, and the islands of the Far East was at its height. In Arabic literature the story of Sinbad's adventures is not incorporated in *The Arabian Nights*.

PHILIP K. HITTI
Author of "History of the Arabs"

SINCLAIR, sin-klâr', **Upton** (1878–1968), American political figure and author, best known for his novels advocating social reform. Upton Beall Sinclair was born in Baltimore, Md., on Sept. 20, 1878. He was educated at the College of the City of New York and Columbia University. In 1902 he joined the Socialist party.

Sinclair's first novels were in traditional forms, but in 1904, with Socialist backing, he surveyed labor conditions in the Chicago meat-packing industry and wrote a dramatic exposition of them in *The Jungle* (1906), which created a sensation that led to the adoption of federal pure food laws. This novel, with its pairing of bitter attacks on existing industrial evils with demands for humanitarian and often Socialist reforms, provided a pattern for later novels, including *The Metropolis* (1908), *King Coal* (1917), and *Oil!* (1927). Similar in purpose were his studies of religion, journalism, education, and the arts, respectively, in *The Profits of Religion* (1918), *The Brass Check* (1919), *The Goslings* (1924), and *Mammonart* (1925).

Fitting actions to the ideals he expressed in his books, Sinclair was active in politics. In 1905 he founded the forerunner of the League for Industrial Democracy. His fight for free speech led to the founding in 1923 of the southern California branch of the American Civil Liberties Union. In 1934 he ran for governor of California as a Democrat, with the slogan EPIC—End Poverty in California. He lost the election after a savage campaign, but many of his ideas were adopted by professional politicians.

In 1940, Sinclair published *World's End*, the first of 11 novels centering on Lanny Budd, who always managed to be on hand when the great world decisions were being made. The series, which includes the Pulitzer-Prize-winning *Dragon's Teeth* (1942), provides a coherent history of Europe and America in the period of the world wars. *The Autobiography of Upton Sinclair* appeared in 1962. Sinclair died in Bound Brook, N. J., on Nov. 25, 1968.

Upton Sinclair, American novelist of social issues

The characters in Sinclair's novels were often stereotypes, and the works contained other artistic limitations, but they also contained many memorable scenes taken from life. His nonfiction, although slanted, displays a notable skill in collecting and organizing masses of data. Sinclair was a superb journalist, and his works constitute a significant record of 20th century American civilization.

DeLANCEY FERGUSON
Formerly, Brooklyn College

Further Reading: Dell, Floyd, *Upton Sinclair* (1927; reprint, AMS Press 1970); Warfel, Harry Redclay, *American Novelists of Today* (Am. Bk. 1951).

SIND, sind, is a province of Pakistan and a historic region of the Indian subcontinent. It became a province of Pakistan when that country was formed in 1947 but disappeared as an administrative unit in 1955 when the various provinces and regions of western Pakistan were amalgamated into one unit called West Pakistan. Its provincial status was revived by the Legal Framework Order of 1970, which set forth the basic principles of a projected new constitution for Pakistan.

Sind is bounded on the west by the province of Baluchistan, on the north by the province of Punjab, on the east and southeast by India, and on the southwest by the Arabian Sea. Its chief cities are Karachi, the capital, and Hyderabad. Karachi, the largest city in Pakistan and the national capital until 1960, was not included in Pakistan's earlier province of Sind. The present province has an area of 58,471 square miles (151,440 sq km) and a population (1961) of 8,468,712, over 90% Muslim.

The Land and Economy. In general, Sind corresponds to the lower Indus River valley, stretching from north to south in the form of the letter S. Physiographically, Sind can be divided into the western highlands of the Kirthar Range and the Kohistan area, rising to more than 6,000 feet (1,830 meters); the central valley, with the eastern and western valley regions and the delta regions; and the Thar Desert in the east. The climate is of the subtropical desert type, with scanty rainfall averaging 5 inches (125 mm) yearly.

As in the rest of Pakistan, the economy is predominantly agricultural and depends almost entirely on irrigation. The principal source of water is the Indus River, on which there are three irrigation dams ("barrages") in Sind: the Guddu, on the Punjab border; the Lloyd (Sukkur); and the Ghulam Muhammad, farthest south. The Lloyd Barrage controls a canal system whose total length, including subsidiary watercourses, extends 50,000 miles (80,000 km), or twice the length of the earth's circumference. Sind's principal crops are wheat, rice, cotton, oilseeds, sugarcane, and fruits. Sheep, cattle, camels, and poultry are raised, and there is a fishing industry. Manufacturing industries, concentrated in Karachi, produce textiles, cement, cardboard, chemicals, electric power and supplies, railroad equipment, and machinery and other metal products. Karachi, Pakistan's chief port, has an oil refinery and also is the center of printing and publishing. The artistic and cultural heritage of Sind is reflected in its superb examples of lacquerware, mirror embroidery, and exquisitely painted tilework.

History. Sind has a history of town life going back some 5,000 years, as attested by the numerous archaeological finds of modern times. The most important archaeological site is Mohenjo-daro, 180 miles (290 km) northeast of Karachi. The ruins of Mohenjo-daro, which was a flourishing city by about 2500 B.C., reveal a remarkably developed stage of civilization. The city had parallel streets, a planned drainage system, and grain storage facilities.

Sind's later history begins toward the end of the 6th century B.C., when the Persian king Darius I (the Great) sent the Greek explorer Scylax to survey the Indus Valley. In 325 B.C., Alexander the Great of Macedon conquered Sind from the north, but after his death in 323, Greek influence began to wane. The region flourished once again in the days of the Buddhist emperor Aśoka (Ashoka), who reigned about 274–237 B.C. In the 2d century B.C., following the disintegration of Asoka's empire, Sind was under the influence of Indo-Greek and Indo-Parthian dynasties. Later it was absorbed into the Kusham empire, which reached its height in the 1st or 2d century A.D. during the reign of Kanishka I, a great patron of Buddhism. At the close of the 4th century Sind was part of the empire of the Guptas, who effected a revival of Brahmanism in India.

Muslim rule in Sind began with the Arab conquest of the region in 711–712 by Muhammad Ibn Kasim. He had been sent by al-Hajjaj, governor of Iraq for the Umayyad caliph, to punish the Hindu ruler of Debal for interfering with shipping in the Arabian Sea. Sind remained under Arab rule for nearly 300 years. The next wave of Muslim conquest came in 1025–1026, when Mahmud of Ghazni marched through Sind to Somnath, in what is now the Indian state of Gujarat. Sind was annexed to the Delhi Sultanate in 1228, but after revolting 100 years later it maintained virtual independence under local Muslim rulers. The Mughul (Mogul) emperor Akbar, who was born in Sind, annexed it in 1591.

From 1783, after the breakup of the Mughul Empire, Sind was governed by amirs of the Tal-pura tribe, originally from Baluchistan. Sir Charles Napier conquered them for Britain in 1843, transmitting the news in a message reading *"Peccavi,"* Latin for "I have sinned." The conquest was later much criticized. However, Sind became united culturally and linguistically, as well as politically, under the British. It was administered as part of Bombay presidency until 1937, when it was made a separate province.

Regional Culture. Often referred to as a "cauldron of cultures," Sind has experienced an extraordinary mingling of populations since the days of Mohenjo-daro. At least 16 distinct types of peoples have left their mark on the region, producing a fusion of cultures, languages, arts, crafts, and life styles. Perhaps the greatest impact was that of the Arabs. Their influence—religious, social, and cultural—can be seen in modern times in the Sindhi language and customs, the Arab calendar, Arabic script, camel rearing, the wearing of long hair, and the cultivation of date palms.

Hyderabad, which was the provincial capital from 1947 to 1955, is the seat of the University of Sind. Tatta, 60 miles (100 km) east of Karachi, is noted for its great mosque, built by the Mughuls in the 17th century. It is considered to be the most complete surviving example of Iranian tilework in the Indian subcontinent.

SINDHIA, sin'dē-ə, a family of Maratha rulers in India. Their domain was Gwalior. See also GWALIOR.

SINDING, sin'ding, **Christian** (1856–1941), Norwegian composer and pianist. He was born in Kongsberg on Jan. 11, 1856, and studied in Christiania (now Oslo), at the Leipzig Conservatory, and in Berlin, Dresden, and Munich. He then began a distinguished career in Christiania, aided in later life by an annual grant from the Norwegian government.

Sinding first won recognition with his Piano Quintet in E Minor but subsequently composed in a wide variety of forms, especially for the piano and violin. His works include two violin concertos, a piano concerto, three symphonies, chamber music, an opera, choral music, and over 200 songs. However, it is as a piano composer that he is chiefly known, largely through his impressionistic piece *Frühlingsrauschen* (*Rustle of Spring*). His opera, *The Holy Mountain*, with a German libretto (*Der heilige Berg*) by Dora Duncker, was produced in 1914. In 1920–1921 he taught at the Eastman School of Music, Rochester, N.Y. Sinding died in Oslo on Dec. 3, 1941.

Sinding's two brothers, Otto Ludwig (1842–1909) and Stephen Abel (1846–1922), were well-known artists.

SINE. See TRIGONOMETRY.

SINE WAVE, a fundamental wave form. A sine wave is an undulating line, such as one representing a sine-wave voltage or current, in the shape of the sine curve $y = a \sin b x$. Sine waves are basic to harmonic analysis, since the graph of a body moving in simple harmonic motion takes the form of a sine wave. See also ELECTRICITY—*Alternating-Current Circuits;* FOURIER SERIES; GENERATOR, ELECTRIC—*Alternating-Current Generators;* HARMONIC ANALYSIS; TRIGONOMETRY—*Graphs of the Circular Functions.*

Government buildings in the City of Singapore were built by the British, who acquired the island in the early 19th century.

ANNAN PHOTO

SINGAPORE, sing'ə-pôr, is the smallest and most prosperous nation in Southeast Asia. Located off the southern tip of the Malay Peninsula, it stands athwart the northern passageway between the Indian and Pacific oceans. Thus it commands a strategic threshold that has been coveted for centuries as a world meeting ground and crossroads. Once a British colony, Singapore today is ruled by a disciplined socialist party. But its thriving port—one of the world's half-dozen largest in cargo tonnage handled—is operated on capitalist principles.

Singapore is one of history's rare examples of involuntary nationhood. On Aug. 9, 1965, Prime Minister Lee Kuan Yew wept as he reluctantly proclaimed independence in the wake of Singapore's unexpected eviction from the federation of Malaysia. The memory of an unwanted National Day is now partially eclipsed on August 9 by the simultaneous celebration of the anniversary of the founding of the city by Thomas Stamford Raffles in 1819.

The state's economy and politics received a severe jolt when Britain's Labour government decided to withdraw the British military presence in Singapore by the end of 1971. Diplomatic ef-

forts by Lee Kuan Yew to deflect the United Kingdom from this course succeeded only in creating the odd tableau of a leader of a new nation earnestly imploring a former colonizer to maintain a huge military base on its soil. The air and naval facility located on the island's north shore reverted to Singapore's control in 1971. But in the same year Britain's Conservative government, successor to the Labour government, agreed with Australia and New Zealand to cooperate in the defense of Singapore and Malaysia.

Rejected by Malaysia and partially abandoned by Britain, the reluctant Republic of Singapore faced the hazards of the 1970's while beginning a new era of lonely self-reliance.

The Land. Singapore is an oblong island connected to the southern point of the Malay Peninsula by a rail and road causeway 0.75 mile (1.2 km) long. Together with its 40 tiny adjacent islets, the republic occupies 226 square miles (585 sq km) of territory. At its greatest extent Singapore Island measures 27 miles (43 km) from east to west and 14 miles (22.5 km) from north to south. About 80 miles (130 km) north of the equator, it lies at the mouth of the funnel-shaped Strait of Malacca, the waterway between the

---

INFORMATION HIGHLIGHTS

Official Name: Republic of Singapore.
Head of State: President.
Head of Government: Prime Minister.
Legislature: Parliament.
Area: 226 square miles (585 sq km).
Boundaries: West and north, Johore Strait; east and south, Singapore Strait.
Highest Point: Bukit Timah—581 feet (177 meters).
Population: 2,122,456 (1970 census).
Capital: City of Singapore.
Major Languages: Malay, Chinese, Tamil, English.
Major Religions: Islam, Confucianism, Buddhism, Hinduism, Taoism, Christianity.
Monetary Unit: Singapore dollar.
Weights and Measures: British, Chinese, and local systems.
Flag: Red stripe on top, white stripe on bottom; crescent and five stars in white in the upper left corner. See also FLAG.
National Anthem: *Forward Singapore.*

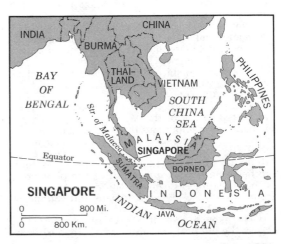

SINGAPORE

0 ——— 800 Mi.
0 ——— 800 Km.

BERNARD PIERRE WOLFF, FROM PHOTO RESEARCHERS

Fish market in the Chinese section of Singapore City. Singapore's population is predominantly Chinese.

island of Sumatra and Malaysia's west coast.

Singapore's topography is marked by low coastal indentations and gentle central hills. The climate is tropical. Temperature, relative humidity, and rainfall are high, and seasonal variation is slight. The jungle that once covered Singapore is now 85% cleared, so that little wildlife remains. The soil is generally low in fertility, and there are virtually no natural resources on the island.

The People. Singapore's population soared from 200 in 1819 to over 2 million by 1970. It is expected to pass 4 million before the end of the century. The government's vigorous family planning program lowered the birthrate by the early 1970's to 1.7% per year. Singapore's people are young and urban: almost half are under age 15, and 75% live in the city of Singapore on the island's southern shore.

Chinese make up 76% of the population, but this communal category is far from homogeneous. Five major Chinese dialects are spoken: Hokkien, Cantonese, Teochew, Hainanese, and Hakka. The Chinese also worship in many ways. Confucianism, Buddhism, Taoism, and Christianity all have Chinese adherents.

Malays compose 15% of the population. They are united in use of the Malay language and are virtually unanimous in their allegiance to the Muslim faith. Indians and Pakistanis account for 7% of the population. Most of them practice the Hindu or Muslim faith and use Tamil as their mother tongue. The remainder of the population is bewilderingly diverse, comprised of peoples from all over the globe. Eurasians and Europeans are the most numerous among them.

The government of Singapore is determined to use the cultural, linguistic, and religious diversity of its people to the advantage of all, fostering mutual respect and toleration for others as the cornerstone of a new Singaporean identity. Language policy designates Malay as the national language but accords equal and official status to Mandarin, Tamil, and English.

Singapore is proud of its high literacy rate and devotes more than one fourth of its budget to education. At the University of Singapore and Nanyang University, scholars sometimes grumble about the government's emphasis on vocational and technical training at the expense of theoretical studies, but government spokesmen insist that knowledge must have practical applications to problems of the nation's survival.

Health facilities and services are superb by any standard. There was a surplus of doctors in the early 1970's, and the island had 17 modern hospitals. Life expectancy was 70 years of age, which is high for the region. Physical fitness is encouraged in the schools and in competitive sports programs. Public sanitation is efficient and thorough. Stringent enforcement of antilitter laws keeps the streets remarkably clean.

Singapore's Housing and Development Board manages one of the world's most comprehensive experiments in public housing. By the 1970's, 30% of the population lived in public high-rise apartment complexes. Whole new satellite towns, such as Queenstown and Toa Payoh New Town, have been erected as self-sufficient communities. All races are encouraged to mingle in the new housing settlements. The island itself is being enlarged at a rate of 120 feet (36 meters) a week by landfill operations.

The Economy. Singapore has a superb natural harbor, and commerce is the traditional bulwark of the economy. Trade and services such as transport, banking, storage, repair, insurance, and communications have given Singaporeans the reputation of being the most highly skilled middlemen of Asia. Entrepôt activity has also brought prosperity unmatched by any nation in Asia except Japan.

Singapore's leaders recognize that the commercial sector alone cannot sustain the island's economic growth in the face of local population increases and accelerated competition from neighboring countries. Following recommendations made in 1961 by a UN industrial survey team, a crash industrialization program was augmented, and dramatic progress resulted. Several model industrial estates were established, with more envisaged for the future. The largest, at Jurong, is a thriving national showcase. Singapore's success in shifting to industry and attracting foreign investment can be attributed to aggressive planning, central location, political stability, and the availability of skilled manpower.

Vast oil deposits discovered during the late 1960's off the shores of Indonesia and Malaysia have given Singapore the windfall opportunity to serve as industry headquarters for Southeast Asia. Earnings from petroleum average $200 million a year.

Tourism and fishing are also of importance to the economy.

History and Government. Although Chinese chronicles and Malay legends recall a city named Temasek ("sea town") on the island during the 13th and 14th centuries, Singapore's modern history begins with an Englishman, Thomas Stamford Raffles. In 1819, Raffles acquired the island from the Malay Sultan of Johore on behalf of the

Large blocks of apartments have been built outside of Singapore City to house the expanding population.

British East India Company. With extraordinary foresight he laid the foundations for a great modern city, envisaging the transformation of a tiny fishing village into a free-trade emporium of global importance.

British Rule. After settling the Netherlands' conflicting claim to the island by the Anglo-Dutch Treaty of 1824, Britain allowed the administration of Singapore to pass from the East India Company to the British India office in 1858. The British colonial office began in 1867 to administer the island directly (along with Penang and Malacca) as the Crown Colony of the Straits Settlements. Even before 1869, when the opening of the Suez Canal markedly increased East-West commerce, Singapore was thriving as a major port. The island had already become an important link in Britain's eastern empire, supporting a population of approximately 100,000, mainly Chinese.

Britain developed a military and naval station at Singapore during the early decades of the 20th century and relied upon it as "the bastion of the Empire," the "Gibraltar of the East." During World War II the Japanese proved that Singapore was only a base and not a bastion. After racing down the Malay Peninsula in a brilliant campaign, Gen. Yamashita Tomoyuki took the "impregnable" island on Feb. 15, 1942, after a six-day siege. Conquest and occupation by the Japanese fundamentally disrupted the prewar society and marked the beginning of the end of British colonial rule.

When the British returned at the war's end, Singapore was made a separate crown colony. Penang and Malacca were joined to the federation of Malaya. The colony was granted internal self-government in 1959. The socialist People's Action party won 43 of the 51 legislative seats in the first general elections in 1959, thereby capturing decisive control of the government.

Independence and Federation. In September 1963, after a local referendum approving merger, Singapore achieved independence by becoming one of the 14 states in the new federation of Malaysia. Just 23 months later, on Aug. 9, 1965, severe internal conflict resulted in Singapore's separation from the federation. The island became an independent republic within the Commonwealth of Nations.

The Republic of Singapore. The republic's political system is based on the British model of parliamentary democracy. A 58-seat elected parliament is headed by the majority party leader, who, as prime minister, forms a cabinet that is responsible to Parliament. Lee Kuan Yew became Singapore's first prime minister in 1959. Parliament also elects a president for a four-year term to perform ceremonial duties.

Government by the People's Action party (PAP) has been characterized by an air of intense urgency. The action-oriented PAP has been driven by ideological socialism toward high goals and tight timetables. With British withdrawal of all but a token force from the area, with the U. S. disengagement from Vietnam, and with the increased acceptance among the world powers of the People's Republic of China, non-Communist Singapore feels it must race the clock to build enough autonomous vitality to withstand regional absorption or big-power hegemony. Britain's once total defense commitment to Singapore was replaced in 1971 with a token five-power arrangement involving Singapore, Malaysia, Britain, New Zealand, and Australia.

Singapore is deeply interdependent with Indonesia and the Malaysian federation in a Malay, Muslim archipelago that has a marked anti-Chinese atmosphere. PAP leaders are aware that some Malays view the success of Singapore as the partial fulfillment of the ancient Malay nightmare of Chinese domination. Such Malay fears contributed to Singapore's eviction from Malaysia and helped start and sustain racial rioting in Malaysia in 1969. Some of the sparks of the 1969 communal violence spilled over the causeway into Singapore before they were snuffed out with mass arrests.

SINGAPORE HARBOR, dotted with freighters and small craft, is one of Asia's busiest shipping centers.

Amid these threatening undercurrents, the leaders of Singapore are aware of future dangers and plan on the basis that the worst will happen. With the help of Israeli military advisers, the government has created an efficient self-defense system for the island. Compulsory national service is in force for all men and women between the ages of 18 and 45.

Modern Singapore has a cluster of impressive achievements. The island is prosperous, and the government is stable, efficient, and virtually free of corruption. Major credit must go to the hard-driving PAP, especially to the party's ambitious founder, the brilliant lawyer Lee Kuan Yew. Lee captains one of the world's most able cabinets and places heavy emphasis on intellectuals and university faculty. Despite the forms of British parliamentary democracy, he holds tight reign over a one-party state, practicing a highly disciplined form of "democracy." The PAP's only significant opposition—the Communist Barisan Socialist party—has been driven underground, to defection, or to political imprisonment. The PAP holds all 58 seats in Parliament.

The press is kept in line by government licensing, the labor unions are kept politically docile, and the intellectuals are harnessed into "practical" work in the interest of the state. But the PAP tempers its self-described "rugged society" or "competitive meritocracy" with enlightened impartiality and flexibility. Above all it legitimizes its rule with dramatically successful developmental results.

FELIX V. GAGLIANO
Ohio University

Further Reading: Josey, Alex, *Lee Kuan Yew* (Moore, D. 1968); Kahin, George McT., ed., *Governments and Politics of Southeast Asia*, rev. ed.: Part 4, "Malaya and Singapore," by J. Norman Parmer (Cornell Univ. Press 1964); Leasor, James, *Singapore: The Battle That Changed the World* (Doubleday 1968).

SINGER, Isaac Bashevis (1904–   ), American author, one of the greatest contemporary writers in Yiddish. He was born in Radzymin, Poland, on July 14, 1904, and grew up from 1908 in Warsaw. After receiving a traditional Jewish education, he turned to secular writing and in 1932 became coeditor of the Yiddish literary magazine *Globus,* which serialized his first novel, *Satan in Goray* (1935; Eng. tr., 1955). He immigrated to New York City in 1935 and became a U. S. citizen in 1943. In New York he wrote for the newspaper the *Jewish Daily Forward,* in which many of his subsequent works originally appeared in Yiddish. These, with dates of publication in English, include the novels *The Family Moskat* (1950), *The Magician of Lublin* (1960), *The Manor* (1967), and *The Estate* (1969) and the collections *Gimpel the Fool and Other Stories* (1957) and *The Seance and Other Stories* (1968). Among his other works is the autobiographical *In My Father's Court* (1966). He won the 1978 Nobel Prize in literature.

ISRAEL JOSHUA SINGER (1893–1944), the brother of Isaac Singer, was also a Yiddish writer. His best-known work is the novel *The Brothers Ashkenazi* (1936).

Further Reading: Allentuck, Marcia, ed., *Achievements of Isaac Bashevis Singer* (Southern Ill. Univ. Press 1969); Buchen, Irving, *Isaac Bashevis Singer and the Eternal Past* (N. Y. Univ. Press 1968); Siegel, Ben, *Isaac Bashevis Singer* (Univ. of Minn. Press 1969).

SINGER, Isaac Merrit (1811–1875), American inventor who developed the first practical home sewing machine. Singer was born in Pittstown, N. Y., on Oct. 27, 1811. He left home at the age of 12 and for many years was an itinerant mechanic. In 1851, Singer patented a sewing machine, organized I. M. Singer & Company, and began production of his machine.

Between 1851 and 1863, Singer received 20 patents for improvements on his machine, and by the 1860's his company was the world's leading manufacturer of sewing machines. Singer retired from active direction of the business in 1863 and spent his remaining years in Europe. He died in Torquay, England, on July 23, 1875. See also SEWING MACHINE—*History.*

SINGH, Govind. See GOVIND SINGH.

SINGING. See VOICE.

SINGING TOWER. See BOK SINGING TOWER.

SINGLE STANDARD, also known as *monometallism.* See BIMETALLISM.

SINGLE TAX, a reform proposed by the U. S. economist Henry George in his book *Progress and Poverty* (1879). George's proposal was "to abolish all taxation save that upon land values." This was developed not merely as a fiscal reform but as a method for achieving a more ambitious social goal, that of raising wages and establishing equal rights in land.

The term "single tax" was not used in *Progress and Poverty* but came into use some 10 years later. Actually, the name harks back to the *impôt unique* of the French physiocrats of the 18th century. They, too, visualized one tax upon land only, but George knew little of their work when he wrote *Progress and Poverty.*

Theory. The purpose of George's book was to explain the paradox of poverty accompanying progress, and to solve the riddle of why industrial depressions alternate with boom periods. George saw the answer to both problems in the monopolization of land—in its widest sense, including natural resources—by a few.

The rent of land increases with material progress, said George, and landowners reap the benefit while the wages of the landless are depressed. Rising rent encourages land speculation, which accelerates the process and leads to speculative rents that are so high that some in the ranks of labor and capital are unable to pay them and still employ themselves at a profit. These victims then stop producing, and a depression occurs. Though George recognized other causes of depression, such as monetary and credit situations, he maintained that land speculation was the basic and ever-present factor.

As his remedy for poverty and depressions, George said, "We must make land common property." He proposed to leave land titles undisturbed, but to take, through taxation, up to 100% of the economic rent of land, or the income exceeding that from the least productive land in use.

Criticisms and Applications. Early critics of George's single-tax proposal argued that it was unfair in placing the total burden of taxation on landowners, and particularly on rural landowners, many of whom were poor farmers. They also pointed out that since the tax applies to economic but not to business rents—rents due to improvements made on the land—the plan might founder over the difficulty of making distinctions between land and capital values.

Later opponents of the proposal tended to point to changed conditions. The single tax was conceived in a period when great fortunes were being made from land values in the United States. Subsequently, the income tax and other U.S. measures acted as levelers of these fortunes, and the rent of land became a smaller component of the national income, less able to bear the burden of increasingly heavy national budgets.

The single-tax idea made some progress in various parts of the world but usually only in partial applications. In the early 20th century some cities in western Canada began to tax land values more heavily than improvements. Provincial Alberta's generous income from oil-field royalties by the 1970's was largely the fruit of Georgist-inspired legislation early in the 20th century.

Some single-tax colonies arose in the United States, as in Fairhope, Ala., and Arden, Del. The single-tax idea was actually written into the Russian constitution during the short-lived regime of Alexander Kerensky (1917) before being swept away by revolution. And a national land-tax measure was enacted by Parliament in Britain in 1931, though it was never put into effect. See also GEORGE, HENRY.

SINGSPIEL, zing'shpēl, a type of opera, usually comic, loosely defined as a musical play consisting of spoken dialogue interspersed with songs. The term is German, meaning, literally, "sing-play." Popular in Germany in the second half of the 18th century, the *Singspiel* had much in common with English ballad opera and French *opéra comique.* Imitations of English ballad operas were, in fact, the beginnings of the German *Singspiel.* In the 1750's, J. C. Standfuss wrote music to German translations of Charles Coffey's librettos for *The Devil to Pay* and *The Merry Cobbler.* Johann Hiller's later version of *The Devil to Pay* was highly successful. Hiller then wrote several original *Singspiele* and became known as the father of the genre. Other composers, particularly Mozart, used the *Singspiel* format for works of great emotional intensity and complexity of style, and the genre as a relatively simple musical idiom declined.

SINHALESE, sin-hə-lēz', the majority people of Sri Lanka and their language. See also SRI LANKA—*The People.*

SINING, shē'ning', a city in northwestern China, is the capital of Chinghai province. It is situated at an altitude of 7,500 feet (2,300 meters) on the Sining River east of Koko Nor, a large lake. Sining (Xi-ning) is the focal point of Chinghai's transportation routes and lies within its best agricultural area. It serves as the marketing and shipment center for the products of the province, which include wool, hides, grains, and dairy products. Population: (1970 est.) 250,000.

SINKHOLE, a depression with the shape of a funnel or well that occurs in a land surface, most commonly in limestone regions. Sinkholes are also known as sinks, swallow holes, or dolines. They are formed by the enlargement of cracks or fractures in subterranean limestone by the dissolving action of groundwater or of streams trickling down from above, with a consequent slump of overlying soil to form a depression in the ground. Such depressions may communicate with underground limestone chambers hundreds of feet below. If such passages become blocked, the water draining into the sinkholes collects to form lakes. Some large sinkholes, also known as poljes, are produced by the collapse of cave roofs. The resulting depression may be several miles in diameter.

Sinkholes are not to be confused with the potholes produced by erosion of stream beds or the kettles formed by the melting of glacial ice.

SINKHOLES that have filled with accumulated water are prominent features of this Manitoba landscape.

ANNAN PHOTOS

SINKIANG, shin'jē-äng', is the largest administrative division of China. Formerly known as Chinese Turkestan and now styled the Sinkiang Uigur Autonomous Region, it is situated in the northwestern part of the country bordering Mongolia to the north, Soviet Central Asia to the west, Afghanistan and Kashmir to the southwest, and Tibet to the south. Its area is 635,800 square miles (1,646,700 sq km).

Geography and Economy. Sinkiang is a land of rainless deserts, fertile oases, and wide variations in altitude. It has mountain peaks rising more than 20,000 feet (6,000 meters) above sea level, and it contains the lowest point in China —the Turfan Depression, 505 feet (168 meters) below sea level. Flanked by mountain systems— the Altai on the north, the Tien Shan and Pamir on the west, and the Kunlun on the south— Sinkiang is cut off from moist winds blowing from the distant oceans. The average annual precipitation in most places is less than 15 inches (320 mm). The limited water supply largely determines the character and amount of vegetation and human activity.

A great portion of Sinkiang is occupied by the Tarim Basin, the interior of which is a sandy desert called the Takla Makan. Strung around the rim of the basin are oases containing ancient trading cities such as Kucha, Aqsu, Kashgar, Yarkand, and Khotan (Hotien). North of the Tarim Basin and separated from it by the eastern part of the Tien Shan is the Dzungarian Basin, which is ringed by a belt of grasslands and oases. One of its oasis cities is Urumchi (Tihwa), the capital of Sinkiang.

Agriculture flourishes where there is sufficient summer rainfall or water furnished by artesian wells or mountain snows. The important crops are grains, cotton, and fruit. The region has large herds of livestock and is China's principal source of wool. ,Petroleum, coal, and iron are extracted in the Dzungarian Basin. Industrial development is on a small scale, however, and is limited by insufficient transportation. The only railroad links Dzungaria with eastern China.

People and History. The Uigurs (Uighurs), a settled Muslim Turkic people, constitute a majority of Sinkiang's population. The nomadic Kazakhs, also Muslim and Turkic, are the next largest group. Other minorities include the Chinese, Hui (Muslim Chinese), Mongols, Kirghiz (a Turkic people), Tajiks (Iranian), and Sibo (Tungusic).

The ancient Silk Route from China to the west passed through the Tarim Basin in two branches. During the 1st millennium A. D., Indo-European languages were predominant in the basin, and the region had a highly developed Buddhist culture synthesizing Iranian, Indian, Greek, Chinese, and local elements. The Uigurs, arriving in the northern Tarim oases in the 9th century, produced a civilization that blended with the old culture.

The name Sinkiang—also written Xinjiang and Hsin-chiang—means "new borderland" in Chinese. The area came under permanent Chinese control in the 17th century, but close relations with the central government were not established until the 1930's. After 1949 new lands were brought under cultivation by irrigation projects, as in the Manas River valley, and industry was expanded. The government of the People's Republic began conducting nuclear tests in Sinkiang in the 1960's. Population: (1970 est.) 8,000,000.

SINKING FUND, an asset specifically earmarked for a known purpose. In corporate finance, its purpose is usually the "sinking" (payment) of an outstanding debt, although sinking funds may be set up for other reasons, such as the replacement of worn machinery.

Debt sinking funds are usually applied to bond issues and are generally mandatory—that is, they are created by contract when the bonds are issued. The corporation commits itself to make certain payments into the fund at stated intervals, guaranteeing that assets will be available to retire all or part of the debt. The contract may or may not stipulate that payments be in cash. In some cases, the payment amounts are not fixed but are based on a percentage of the company's gross income or net earnings.

A mandatory sinking fund increases the value of the bonds to which it applies. It usually cuts the issuing company's underwriting costs and may improve its credit status.

SINN FEIN, shin fān, an Irish nationalistic movement, the name of which may be translated as "Ourselves Alone." The movement had its roots in the 19th century revival of national consciousness reflected in the Gaelic League and in the Irish literary renaissance. It represented a conviction that the policy of Home Rule, pursued by the constitutional nationalists, was sterile. Sinn Fein was organized as a political party by Arthur Griffith in 1905. It grew rapidly among the people in Ireland after suppression of the Easter rising in Dublin in 1916.

In April 1919 a Sinn Fein Convention elected Eamon de Valera president of the organization. It set up a Dáil, or Assembly, declared an Irish republic and carried on government services while waging the Anglo-Irish civil war of 1920– 1921. The situation was confusing, with two Irish governments, and with many people preferring the Sinn Fein courts to the regular courts. The war ended with a treaty between the British government and Dáil Eireann, the Irish Assembly, whereby the Irish Free State was established in 1922. The Sinn Fein's power as a political party was shattered by a disagreement over the partition of Ireland, and de Valera founded a new party, Fianna Fail, in 1927. Sinn Fein lost its last four seats in the Dáil in the general election of 1961.

SINO-JAPANESE WARS. See CHINESE-JAPANESE WARS.

SINO-TIBETAN LANGUAGES, spoken in eastern Asia, are classified in three main families: the Chinese, including Mandarin and the Chinese "dialects"—actually affiliated languages; the Tibeto-Burman family, including Tibetan, Burmese, and Kachin; and the Thai (Tai) family, comprising Siamese, Laotian, Shan, and other languages. The relation of the Thai family to the other languages is probable but not certain.

The languages have several features in common. Roots words, as opposed to syntactical units, are monosyllabic. There is little or no inflection—compare English *love, love-d*—and affixes are not used, as in English *harm, harm-ful*. Syntax is highly dependent on word order, which in Latin, for example, it is not. Tone, the height and movement of the fundamental pitch of the voice, can differentiate words; thus Chinese *fei* (first tone), "fly"; *fei* (second tone), "fat."

SINOPE, si-nō'pē, a city in northern Turkey, was once the greatest city on the Black Sea. Its Turkish name is Sinop, and it is the capital of Sinop province. Although the city has a fine harbor, its topographic isolation has prevented it from developing commercially.

The city was founded in the 8th century B. C. by Milesians, and it became a flourishing port at the end of the caravan route from central Asia. From the 2d century it was the capital of the kings of Pontus. It was captured by the Romans in 70 B. C. and came under the Byzantines, the Greek empire of Trabzond, and the Seljuks before passing to the Ottomans in 1461. Diogenes was born in the city. Population: (1970) 15,100.

SINTER is a material deposited by mineral springs. The material sometimes consists of siliceous (silica-rich) sinter, a white to grayish form of opal that is also called geyserite or fiorite. Besides being laid down by the process of evaporation, siliceous sinter is also secreted by algae in springs. In limestone regions, the deposited material may instead consist of calcareous (calcite-rich) sinter. Such deposits are known as travertine, while a more porous variety is called tufa. Onyx marble, or Mexican onyx, is a banded form of spring-deposited calcite—and sometimes aragonite—that is used as an ornamental building material.

SINTERING is the joining of particles of a material, generally by applying heat at a temperature below the melting point of the material. Sintering is used to agglomerate metal particles in an ore, to join particles of metal powders, and to join particles of ceramic oxides. Sintering also is used in making cement and some kinds of glass. In general, the process of sintering has these characteristics: (1) The total surface area of the initial material decreases as the sintering proceeds. (2) The rate of sintering is greater with smaller particles than with larger ones. (3) The sintered product has greater strength and density than the initial material.

See also IRON—*Mining and Processing of Ore* (Sintering).

SINTRA, sēnn'trə, a town in Portugal, is on the slope of the Serra de Sintra, 12 miles (19 km) west northwest of Lisbon. It was formerly spelled Cintra. The town's mild climate and beautiful scenery and vegetation made it a favorite residence of Portuguese rulers. In the center of the town is the royal palace, built over several centuries. On a mountain above the town is the 19th century Palácio da Pena and, lower down, the ruins of a Moorish castle.

Two conventions were signed at Sintra, the first in 1509 when Portugal and Castile settled maritime differences. The second, signed by Portugal, Britain, and France in 1808, permitted a defeated French army to return home during the Peninsular Wars. Population: (1960) 19,930.

SINUIJU, sē-nōō-ē-jōō, is a city in North Korea, on the Yalu River opposite Antung, China. It is one of the main rail lines connecting the two countries. The city is a commercial and industrial center with forest product industries providing its chief manufacturing activity. Sinuiju was developed by the Japanese during their occupation of Korea (1910–1945). Population: (1967) 165,000.

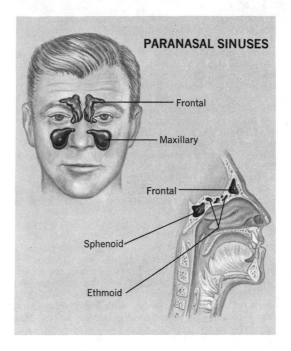

PARANASAL SINUSES
Frontal
Maxillary
Frontal
Sphenoid
Ethmoid

SINUS, sī'nəs, a cavity or hollow space that is usually filled with air or blood. There are many sinuses in bones and in various other organs and tissues of the body. In man, the most familiar sinuses are the paranasal sinuses, four pairs of air-filled cavities in the bones of the face. (See illustration.)

Several disorders may afflict the paranasal sinuses, the most important being sinusitis, an inflammation of the tissues lining the sinuses. The inflammation may be caused by allergy, by the inhalation of irritating substances such as fumes, gases, or other pollutants, or by infection, which may be viral or bacterial.

Since the cells lining the sinuses tend to secrete mucus that exits into the nose through openings connecting the sinus to the nasal passages, people who have small openings are prone to sinus problems caused by poor drainage. Poor drainage can also be caused by inflammation of the mucous membranes lining the sinuses, causing swelling that blocks the openings. Poor drainage increases the chance of infection and makes infection more difficult to cure.

Most people with mild irritation of the mucous membranes lining the sinuses have a postnasal drip, nasal discharge, or both, sometimes accompanied by sinus congestion and headache. These symptoms usually can be relieved with aspirin or other mild analgesics, antihistamines when allergy is involved, or nasal decongestants to shrink the swollen passages and promote better drainage. More serious problems occur when the sinuses become infected. When the infection is due to a virus as part of an upper respiratory infection the symptoms are usually mild and disappear within a few days. However, bacterial infection may complicate a cold or upper respiratory infection or may arise—particularly in the antra, or maxillary sinuses—from infection in the teeth or as a result of fracture of the bony floor of the antrum during dental extraction.

An acute infection usually causes local pain, tenderness, often swelling, and fever. X rays reveal that the air in the sinus is replaced by fluid or show thickening of the mucous membranes. Antibiotic treatment is usually given, but the sinuses may also have to be irrigated or even surgically drained. Untreated acute sinusitis may occasionally cause such serious complications as infection of the bone (osteomyelitis), infection of the tissues around the eye, meningitis, or brain abscess. Repeated infections or continual inflammations and irritations may cause a chronic postnasal drip and chronically congested or obstructed sinuses. In these cases minor irritants such as smoking or an increase in air pollution can trigger acute and painful headaches or congestion.

LOUIS J. VORHAUS, M. D.
Cornell University Medical College

SION, syôN, is the capital of Valais canton in Switzerland. Sion (German, *Sitten*) is located in the valley of the Rhône, on the north side of the river. It was known as Sedunum to the Romans. Two hills overlook this ancient town: the Tourbillon, on which there are the remains of a 13th century castle, and the Valère, which is crowned by the fortress-church of Notre Dame de Valère. The church was begun in the 11th century.

The town of Sion, which is a horticultural marketing center, contains the cathedral of Notre Dame du Glarier, with its Romanesque belfry, a 17th century town hall, and a luxurious 16th century private residence, the Maison Supersaxo. Population: (1970) 21,925.

SIOUX CITY, sōō, in northwestern Iowa, the seat of Woodbury county, is on the Missouri River, between the mouths of the Big Sioux and Floyd rivers. The boundary between Nebraska and South Dakota is directly across the Missouri.

Sioux City is the focal point of many major highways and railways, and is at the head of navigation on the Missouri. It is the distributing and industrial center of an area that extends into Nebraska, South Dakota, and southwestern Missouri. Meat packing and food processing are its chief industries. Fabricated metals and machinery are among its manufactures.

Morningside College, a coeducational institution associated with the Methodist Church, and Briar Cliff, also coeducational, a Roman Catholic college, are in Sioux City. The Sioux City Art Center has displays of contemporary American Midwestern paintings, and the Sioux City Public Museum exhibits Indian artifacts and historical collections.

Sioux City was laid out in 1854 and was incorporated in 1857. In the mid-19th century it was a supply center and a departure point for miners in the Black Hills of South Dakota and settlers bound for the Northwest. Sioux City is governed by a council and a city manager. Population: of city, 85,925; of metropolitan area, which extends into Nebraska, 82,003.

SIOUX FALLS, sōō, a city in southeastern South Dakota, in Minnehaha and Lincoln counties, is on the Big Sioux River, about 180 miles (288 km) southeast of Pierre. It is the seat of Minnehaha county and the state's largest city.

Situated only 14 miles (22 km) from the corner of three states—South Dakota, Minnesota, and Iowa—Sioux Falls is the trading center of a large agricultural and stock-raising area and an important distributing point, especially for farm machinery, automobiles, and trucks. Meat packing and the processing of food, chiefly dairy products, are leading economic activities.

Sioux Falls is the home of Augustana College, a coeducational Lutheran institution, and of Sioux Falls College, a coeducational Baptist school. Points of interest in the city include the Civic Fine Arts Association, which has a collection of paintings, the Pettigrew Museum of Natural Arts and History, and the Great Plains Zoo.

The first settlement on the city's site, begun in 1856, was abandoned after a series of Indian raids. In 1865 the deserted site was made a military post, and resettlement began. The community was incorporated as a village in 1877 and as a city in 1883. Government is by a city commission. Population: 81,343.

SIOUX INDIANS, a name given to the Dakota Indians of North America, a group embracing a number of tribes. See also DAKOTA INDIANS.

SIPHNOS, sif'nəs, is a Greek island in the Cyclades group in the Aegean Sea. Gold was mined on Siphnos (Sifnos) in ancient times. The island's mild climate and remains from the past attract tourists. There are towers dating from the classical period, and monasteries are scattered over the island. Mount Profitis Ilias rises to 2,936 feet (895 meters) in the mountainous interior, where the island's capital, Apollonia, is located. Population: (1961) 2,258.

SIPHON, sī'fən, a bent tube for transferring a liquid from one container to another one at a lower level. The tube is shaped like an inverted U, except that one arm is shorter than the other. The short-arm end is placed in the liquid to be transferred, and the long-arm end is placed in the lower container. When the siphon is operating, the liquid travels up through the short arm, through the bend, and down through the long arm.

The liquid flow can be started in several ways, as, for instance, by sucking air from the long arm until the flow of liquid starts. Liquid flows through the siphon because the net pressure at the short-arm end of the siphon (equal to atmospheric pressure less the pressure due to the column of liquid in the short arm) is greater than the net pressure at the long-arm end (equal to atmospheric pressure less the pressure due to the column of liquid in the long arm). For a siphon to operate, the vertical distance from the liquid level in the higher container to the top of the bend must be less than the distance to which the atmospheric pressure can raise a column of the liquid.

SIPPAR, si-pär', was an ancient Mesopotamian city on the east bank of the Euphrates River, situated about 20 miles (30 km) southwest of Baghdad, in present-day Iraq. The site is now named Abu Habba.

Sippar was a center for worship of the sun god Shamash. Its chief building was a temple dedicated to the deity. Extensive excavations, begun in 1881 by Hormuzd Rassam, have uncovered the temple and over 60,000 inscribed tablets. The famous victory stele of Naramsin was originally erected at Sippar. Removed by the Persians, it was rediscovered in modern times at Susa. See also SUMER.

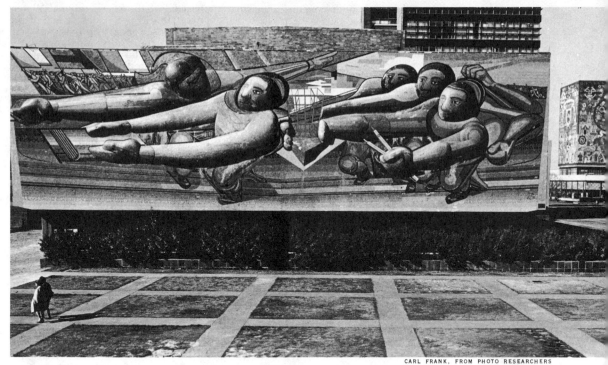

Siqueiros' mural for University City depicts students returning the fruits of knowledge to the motherland.

SIQUEIROS, sē-ke′ē-rōs, **David Alfaro** (1898–1974), Mexican muralist and easel painter, who conceived of art as a logical extension of his leftist political ideas. He was born in Chihuahua and began his studies at the San Carlos Academy of Fine Arts. In 1913 he joined Venustiano Carranza's revolutionary forces, rising to the rank of staff officer. From 1919 he traveled and studied in Europe, returning to Mexico in 1922, where he became a leader in the government-sponsored Syndicate of Technical Workers, Artists, and Sculptors, which emphasized the idea of a national people's art. After 1924, Siqueiros traveled in South America, Mexico, the USSR, and the United States, presenting his theories of art, but always more concerned with trade union work than with painting. During the Spanish Civil War he was an officer in the Republican army. He died in Cuernavaca on Jan. 6, 1974.

As a result of his political activity, Siqueiros' creative work was somewhat sporadic. He was, however, one of the most important personalities in the launching of the new movement in Mexican art, both as a technical innovator and as a theorist. His art, which is one of genuine social protest, expresses itself in strongly movemented forms, marked by a "dynamic realism" representative of the dynamic quality of contemporary life. He developed a bold, vigorous style that is sculptural in its modeling of form and uses a limited color range that depends on strong, vibrant contrasts of light and dark for effect.

Siqueiros was instrumental in reviving fresco painting in Mexican art, returning to native themes for his subject matter. Developing new techniques with the use of spray gun and Duco paint, he greatly speeded up the decoration of public buildings on a large scale, fulfilling one of his theories that his work (and thus his political ideas) should be seen by the greatest pos-

sible number of people. His notable murals include those for the Electrical Workers Union building, Mexico City (1939); the Escuela México, Chillán, Chile (1942); and the new University City buildings, near Mexico City (1952–1955).

Further Reading: De Micheli, Mario, *David Alfaro Siqueiros* (Abrams 1971).

SIR GEORGE WILLIAMS UNIVERSITY is a private, nondenominational, coeducational institution of higher learning in Montreal, Canada. It was founded as Sir George Williams College, as a result of educational efforts by the Young Men's Christian Association, and held its first classes in 1929. It was specifically chartered in 1948 and became a university in 1959.

Sir George Williams has faculties of arts, commerce, engineering, and pure science that offer courses leading to bachelor's and graduate degrees. Enrollment exceeds 5,500.

SIREN, sī′rən, a sound-producing device invented by the French physicist Charles Cagniard de la Tour in 1819. He devised the siren to determine the frequency, or number of vibrations per second, corresponding to a sound of any pitch.

Sirens are now used only as signals. The basic form is a circular disk rotated about a central axis by a motor, the disk being pierced with equally spaced holes in a concentric circle. A jet of air impinging on this circle is alternately cut off and then free to blow through a hole, thus sending a succession of compression pulses per revolution into the atmosphere. If there are ten holes and one jet of air, and the motor runs at 1,200 revolutions a minute, the pitch or frequency

of the tone will be $\dfrac{10 \times 1200}{60} = 200$ cycles per second. Also, a siren will sound under water when actuated by a jet of water.

The siren used by police and fire departments has a motor-driven centrifugal blower. Air issues radially from a number of slots around the rotor; they are all open or all closed as they pass across corresponding slots in a housing around them. As each slot has an area of a square inch or more, and as all open and close simultaneously, the intensity of the sound can become terrific. The motor is controlled by the drive of the car, and when the rotor speed rises and falls, the siren emits its familiar wailing tone.

RICHARD F. DEIMEL°
Author of "Mechanics of the Gyroscope"

SIREN, sī′rən, any of a small family, Sirenidae, of salamanders of the eastern United States. They are often found in streams, ditches, and other bodies of water, hiding among bottom rocks or in dense weeds. Sirens have elongated bodies— sometimes 3 feet (90 cm) long—and are generally eel-like in appearance, without hind limbs and having small forelimbs. They swim, breathing through permanent gills, searching for worms and other small aquatic invertebrates.

SIRENIAN, sī-rē′nē-ən, any of an order of large aquatic herbivorous mammals, including the manatee, dugong, sea cow, and several forms now extinct. See DUGONG; MANATEE; SEA COW.

SIRENS, sī′rənz, in Greek mythology, were sea nymphs living on an island, often located off southern Italy, who lured sailors to destruction by the charm of their singing. According to Homer, Odysseus escaped them by stopping his shipmates' ears with wax and having himself bound to the mast, so he could hear the song but not be drawn to shore. In another tale, the Argonauts passed safely because Orpheus' singing was more entrancing than the Sirens'. Defeated, the nymphs threw themselves into the sea and became rocks. Homer mentions two Sirens, later writers three or more. They are often depicted as part woman, part bird. In the Middle Ages they were thought to be the unhappy souls of the dead.

SIRHAN, sir-hän′, **Sirhan Bishara** (1944–   ), the assassin of Sen. Robert Kennedy in Los Angeles on June 5, 1968. An Arab born in Jerusalem on March 19, 1944, and reared as a Christian, he entered the United States as a permanent resident in 1957. Sirhan disliked Kennedy's support of Israel. Convicted in 1969 of murder and five counts of assault in the wounding of five other persons, he was sentenced to death, a punishment reduced in 1972 to life in prison.

SIRICA, si-rik′ə, **John Joseph** (1904–   ), American judge, who presided over the Watergate case. He was born in Waterbury, Conn., on March 19, 1904, the son of an Italian immigrant. He grew up in poverty, but was determined to be a lawyer, and in 1926 obtained an LL. B. from Georgetown University. He practiced law and was assistant U. S. attorney for the District of Columbia from 1930 to 1934.

In 1957, President Eisenhower named Sirica, a Republican, to the U. S. district court for the District of Columbia. Sirica was chief judge of the court from 1971 until 1974. In 1973 he presided at the trial of the seven original Watergate defendants. He did not believe some of the testimony, and imposed heavy provisional sentences to encourage the guilty men to aid the ongoing investigation. James McCord, a convicted burglar, implicated officials in President Nixon's administration. The truth gradually came out. Sirica also presided over related developments, including the dispute concerning Nixon's reluctance to give evidence to the prosecutor and Congress.

SIRICIUS, si-rish′ē-əs, **Saint** (died 399), pope from 384 to 399. Siricius was a native of Rome and a deacon. He became pope in 384, despite the rival candidacy of the antipope Damasus. In 390 he consecrated the Basilica of St. Paul on the Ostian Way, which had been rebuilt by Maximus, Emperor of the West. Little else is known of his reign except for his letters, which offer the first extant examples of papal decrees. Writing to Hemerius of Tarragona in 385, for example, he settled several disciplinary questions that had been referred to him, and in 390 he sent a letter, apparently directed to the Italian bishops, in which he points out abuses that had developed in the rite of ordination. These and his other letters emphasize the growing authority of Rome. The letters also reveal his awareness of his own authority. Siricius died in Rome on Nov. 26, 399. His feast is kept on November 26.

SIRIUS, sir′ē-əs, is the brightest star. Its magnitude of −1.42 is exceeded only by Mercury, Venus, Mars, and Jupiter at their brightest. Sirius is called the Dog Star because it lies in the constellation Canis Major, which in Greek mythology was the larger of the two dogs of Orion. The star was widely venerated by ancient civilizations. In Egypt it first appeared at dawn during the hottest time of year, and through the Romans this association led to the phrase "dog days." The bluish white star is 8.7 light-years away. It has a faint companion, a white dwarf. The two stars complete one revolution of each other in 50 years.

SIROCCO, sə-rok′ō, a hot, dusty wind that blows in from the Sahara Desert across northern Africa. The wind sometimes reaches the European shores of the Mediterranean Sea, by which time it has become humid. The sirocco is typical of warm cyclonic winds that have been heated by blowing across hot, dry surfaces. Similar winds occur in the summertime over the Great Plains of the United States. See also WINDS.

SISAL, sī′zəl, or sisal hemp (*Agave sisalina*), is a plant of the family Amaryllidaceae. The plant has erect stems up to 3 feet (0.9 meter) tall and 15 inches (38 cm) thick, bearing spirals of dark grayish green, waxy-surfaced, smooth-edged leaves that are 4 to 6 feet (1.2–1.8 meters) long. The stiff, parallel fibers of these leaves are important for making ropes, sacking, twine, sailcloth, and cable insulation because of their cohesion, elasticity, high tensile strength, and resistance to salt water.

Sisal is native to Mexico, although its exact origin is in dispute. Some authorities believe it to have occurred wild in Yucatán, where it is known as *yaxci*, while others consider it derived by mutation from plants of Mexican sisal, or henequen (*A. fourcroydes*), that were introduced into Florida in 1833. An inferior fiber is made from henequen. Sisal is now cultivated throughout the tropics, especially in Kenya and Tanzania, which together produce over half the world's supply, as well as in Angola, Brazil, Indonesia, Mexico, Mozambique, and Venezuela. Indonesian and Haitian sisal are considered the best because of the care taken in cultivation.

Cultivation. Sisal grows best in warm, moist climates on well-drained, loamy soil, but because of its great drought resistance it is often cultivated on dry, rocky soil, despite lower yields. Nursery plants 12 to 18 months old are planted out, usually at the beginning of the rainy season, at 4- to 8-foot (1.2–2.4 meter) intervals in rows 8 to 12 feet (2.4–3.6 meters) apart. They are set closer together in less favorable areas where the plants do not grow so large. Sisal is comparatively free from disease or insect attack and needs little or no care. Weeding should be done every three to four months in the first two years and less often thereafter. Suckers should also be removed occasionally.

Harvesting begins when the plant is three to five years old. The outer, older leaves are removed by a machine or with a knife. During its bearing life of five to eight years a plant produces about 275 leaves, the annual fiber yield per acre being 700 to 1,200 pounds (315–540 kg). When the plant is seven or eight year old, and occasionally as young as four, it produces a central spike 15 to 25 feet (4.6–7.6 meters) high. The spike bears a huge inflorescence of unpleasantly scented, greenish white, tubular flowers about 2.5 inches (6.3 cm) long. They seldom seed but give rise instead to bulbils, or small, bulblike, reproductive bodies, that number 1,500 to 4,000 per inflorescence. Growth diminishes after flowering, and the plant dies. However, if the unopened spike is cut off 4 feet (1.2 meters) above ground, the yield can be continued for several years.

Processing and Marketing. The harvested leaves are taken to a processing plant, where the fibers

Leaves of the sisal plant contain stiff, strong fibers that are extracted for use in making sacking and twine.

JANE LATTA

are extracted before they dry. This process is done by hand or by a machine that crushes the leaves and scrapes off the outer tissue. The pale yellow or white fibers, which are 40 to 50 inches (100–125 cm) long, are then washed, sometimes brushed to increase softness and luster, hung in the sun to dry, and graded. Finally they are put into bales of 230 to 600 pounds (100–270 kg) for shipment. See also AGAVE; FIBER.

Further Reading: Kirby, Richard H., *Vegetable Fibers: Botany, Cultivation, and Utilization* (Wiley 1963).

SISERA, sis'ər-ə, was the leader of a confederation of Canaanite kings defeated in a battle near Megiddo by Israelites under Deborah and Barak. The story of the battle is given in poetical form in the Song of Deborah in Judges 5 and later in prose in Judges 4. Sisera was slain after the battle while hiding in a tent. His city, Harosheth, was probably situated in the northwestern part of the plain of Esdraelon, near Megiddo. He is believed to have been the leader of an Illyrian people who migrated to Palestine.

SISINNIUS, si-sin'ē-əs (died 708), was pope in 708. Sisinnius, a Syrian by birth, was elected pope on Jan. 15, 708. Because of the threat of the Lombards and Muslims he ordered Rome's walls refortified. He died on Feb. 4, 708.

SISLER, sis'lər, **George Harold** (1893–1973), American baseball player. He was born in Manchester, Ohio, on March 24, 1893. Beginning his major league career as a first baseman for the St. Louis Browns in 1915, Sisler excelled both at bat and in the field, where he played with exceptional grace. In 1920 he won the batting title with an average of .407. He again led the league in 1922 with a .420, the third-highest season average in the 20th century. Finishing second that year, the Browns had their strongest team ever. But in 1923, a serious eye ailment that threatened blindness forced Sisler to retire. Returning to action in 1924, he did not match his earlier marks but still finished with a lifetime batting average of .340. He also led the league four times in stolen bases. Sisler ended his career in 1930 and was elected to the Baseball Hall of Fame in 1939. He died on March 26, 1973, in St. Louis, Mo.

SISLEY, sēs-lā', **Alfred** (1839–1899), French landscape painter, who was one of the foremost members of the impressionist school. He was born in Paris, the son of English parents, on Oct. 30, 1839. While a business apprentice in London, he studied the romantic landscapes of Turner and Constable. Returning to Paris in 1862, he entered, as an amateur, the studio of M. C. G. Gleyer, where he became a friend of the impressionist painters Renoir, Monet, and J. F. Bazille. In common with them and other impressionists, he rejected the academic studio approach in order to paint landscapes outdoors in Fontainebleau and other areas around Paris where the Barbizon painters had worked.

Supported by his merchant father, Sisley helped his impecunious friends, but after the failure of his father's business in 1871, he became a poverty-stricken professional painter. Although he contributed to four of the eight impressionist exhibitions, he received little recognition. From 1879 he lived in isolation in Moretsur-Loing, where he died on Jan. 29, 1899. A few years later his work was in demand.

Work. As an impressionist, influenced by the delicate, misty landscapes of Corot, Sisley sought to capture the mood of a particular place at a particular time of day and season of the year. He was concerned with the subtle effects of transparent atmosphere and of light reflected on water and leaves. Unlike Monet, however, he never dissolved the solidity of his objects in light. Examples of his work are *Boat During the Flood* (Louvre, Paris) and *Snow at Louveciennes* (Phillips Collection, Washington, D. C.).

SISMONDI, sēs-môN-dē′, **Simonde de** (1773–1842), Swiss economist and historian, one of the first economic theorists to attack the system of classical economics based on Adam Smith's ideas. Jean Charles Leonard Simonde de Sismondi was born in Geneva on May 9, 1773. He was educated for a banking career but fled with his parents to England when French revolutionary turmoil spread to Geneva in 1793. In 1794 the family moved to a small farm in Italy.

In his late 20's, Sismondi returned to Geneva, where he published *Treatise on Commercial Wealth* (1803) and other economic studies steeped in the Adam Smith tradition. He also produced a highly regarded 16-volume *History of the Italian Republics of the Middle Ages* (1807–1818).

A radical change in Sismondi's outlook became evident in his *New Principles of Political Economy* in 1819. The author, returning to England, had observed atrocious social conditions developing under unrestricted capitalism. Though he never questioned the sanctity of private property, Sismondi anticipated socialist thought by advocating government intervention to control the distribution of goods to guard against ruinous business cycles and the systematic exploitation of the poor. He also wrote a *History of the French* (29 vols., 1821–1844). He died in Geneva on June 25, 1842.

SISTERHOODS. See Religious Orders and Communities; Sisters of Charity; Sisters of Mercy.

SISTERS OF CHARITY, a number of congregations of religious women in the Roman Catholic Church. The majority follow adaptations of the rule that Saint Vincent de Paul prepared for the Sisters of Charity in France in 1633. The sisters were introduced into the United States in 1809 by Mother Elizabeth Bayley Seton, who adapted the rule of St. Vincent de Paul to suit the American scene. Several orders in the United States trace their origins to her work in Emmitsburg, Md. Their primary employment in the United States is as teachers in parochial schools, but they are also known for their charitable care of the poor, the sick, and the aged.

SISTERS OF MERCY, a congregation of religious women in the Roman Catholic Church, with pontifical approval, founded in Dublin, Ireland, in 1831 by Mother Mary Catherine McAuley. The works of the sisters are education on the primary, secondary, and collegiate levels; the administration of hospitals, orphanages, and homes for working girls; and other spiritual and corporeal works of mercy. The congregation has become one of the largest institutes of religious women in the world, numbering thousands of sisters, mostly in Ireland and the United States.

The first foundation of Sisters of Mercy in the United States was made in Pittsburgh, Pa., in 1843 by seven sisters from Carlow, Ireland. By the early 1970's there were more than 12,000 sisters in numerous mother houses scattered throughout the United States. Originally, the status of each mother house was that of an independent unit. In 1929, approximately half the membership in the United States amalgamated to form a single religious institute called the Sisters of Mercy of the Union. The remainder of the communities retained their autonomous organization. See also McAuley, Catherine.

Alfred Sisley's *Boat During the Flood* is an example of his impressionistic treatment of outdoor scenes in which the play of light is reflected in water.

SISTINE CHAPEL, sis'tēn, a 15th century papal chapel in the Vatican, with glorious frescoes by Michelangelo and other masters. It is used for papal ceremonies and elections.

The chapel was built by Giovannino de'Dolci between 1471 and 1484 for Sixtus IV, for whom it was named. It is a rectangular brick structure with six round-arched windows on each of the long walls and a low, barrel-vaulted ceiling. By 1483 it had been richly frescoed by Ghirlandaio, Botticelli, Perugino, Pinturicchio, and others. As one faces the altar, there are scenes from the life of Moses on the left wall, symbolizing man under the law; on the right, scenes from the life of Christ, symbolizing man under grace. Above, between the windows, are painted shell niches with figures of the popes. The original Assumption over the altar and the starry blue ceiling were later replaced by the work of Michelangelo.

Commissioned by Julius II, Michelangelo frescoed the ceiling in 1508–1512. The nine panels down the center, framed by huge nudes, carry the worshiper through pre-Mosaic history from the drunkenness of Noah back in time to the cosmic God separating light from darkness, a progression that suggests the neoplatonic doctrine of the return of the soul to God. In the curved area above the walls, pendentives, showing prophets and sibyls, alternate with lunettes showing the ancestors of Christ. These Christian themes are conveyed by massive figures derived from classical sculpture. In the magnificent *Last Judgment* painted over the altar for Paul III (1535–1541), Michelangelo reflected the Catholic Reformation and his own deepened piety.

SISYPHUS, sis'ə-fəs, in Greek mythology, was a man condemned to the unending punishment of rolling a heavy stone up a hill. Each time he got the stone to the top, it plunged down, and he had to begin again. Sisyphus, a king of Corinth and the founder of the Isthmian Games, angered Zeus, for reasons that vary in different tales, and the god sent death after Sisyphus. A clever trickster, Sisyphus bound death, and no one died until Ares released him. When Sisyphus died, after a long life, Hades kept the trickster eternally busy rolling his stone.

SITĀR, si-tär', a musical instrument of India. It is a member of the lute family, with a large body, long neck, and a varying number of strings. Sitar music has become popular in the West through the playing of Ravi Shankar and other sitārists. See INDIA—*Music.*

SITKA, sit'kə, is a city in southeastern Alaska, on Baranof Island, about 60 miles (96 km) south of Juneau. Sheltered by mountains from the north winds and benefited by the warm North Pacific Current, the city enjoys a milder climate than most of Alaska. Precipitation is high, but snowfall is not excessive. The seasonal fishing industry is the main economic activity.

A community college, affiliated with the University of Alaska and Sheldon Jackson Junior College, a Presbyterian institution, are in Sitka. The Sheldon Jackson Museum has anthropological exhibits. The Sitka National Monument, the site of the last stand of the Tlingit Indians against the Russian colonizers, is nearby.

Aleksandr Baranov, manager of the Russian-American Fur Company, established a trading post, Fort St. Michael, a few miles north of the

LEONARD VON MATT, FROM RAPHO GUILLUMETTE

The Sistine Chapel, with Michelangelo's *Last Judgment* over the altar and biblical scenes on the ceiling

present Sitka in 1799. It was destroyed by Indians in 1802. Two years later, Baranov drove the Indians from the site of Fort St. Michael and established a post, which he named New Archangel, on the site of Sitka. This became the principal northern Pacific port in North America. Iron and brass foundries cast cannon and bells. Some of the bells were sent to missions in California.

Sitka was the capital of Russian America until 1867, when Alaska was sold to the United States, and the capital of Alaska Territory until 1906, when the government was moved to Juneau. Population: 7,803.

SITTER, sit'ər, **Willem de** (1872–1934), Dutch astronomer and cosmologist who first applied Einstein's theory of relativity to the origin and expansion of the universe. De Sitter was born in Sneek, the Netherlands, on May 6, 1872. He studied mathematics at the University of Groningen, became a professor of theoretical astronomy at the University of Leiden in 1908, and was named director of the Leiden observatory in 1919.

From about 1897 to 1925, de Sitter studied the motion and orbits of four of Jupiter's satellites. During World War I, he published papers on Einstein's general theory of relativity, and this led to more widespread notice of the theory by British scientists. About 1930, he computed that the universe had a radius of 200 million light years and contained 80,000 million galaxies.

Dame Edith Sitwell, English poet

De Sitter also proposed that the universe is an expanding space-time continuum with motion and no matter. His works include *The Expanding Universe* (1930), *Kosmos* (1932), *On the Motion and Mutual Perturbation of the Material Particles in an Expanding Universe* (1933), and *The Astronomical Aspect of the Theory of Relativity* (1933). He died in Leiden on Nov. 20, 1934.

SITTING BULL (1834?–1890), was a chief of the Hunkpapa Sioux, whose success as a medicine man and as a fighter against the white men made him a great leader of his people. Sitting Bull (in Indian *Tatanka Yotanka*), bore the same name as his father, a subchief. The son was born on the Grand River in South Dakota. Accompanying his father, he fought against the Crow Indians when he was 14. During the 1860's and early 1870's he was active in the Plains Wars against the U. S. government.

Sitting Bull's refusal to go to a reservation in 1876 resulted in the sending of a military force against his camp on the Little Bighorn River in Montana. Thousands of warriors in the Sioux confederacy joined in the defense against the white troops. Before the battle, Sitting Bull reported a vision of soldiers falling into the Indian camp. It was interpreted as a portent of victory over the Army and was an inspiration to the Indians. On June 25, 1876, while other chiefs led the fighting against Gen. George Custer, Sitting Bull "made medicine"; that is, he invoked spiritual assistance. Despite the annihilation of Custer's command, Sitting Bull had to flee. He went to Canada with a band of followers but returned to the United States in 1881 when offered amnesty.

Confined to the Standing Rock reservation in North Dakota, Sitting Bull remained a symbol of opposition to the whites. When the Ghost Dance frenzy stirred Indian unrest in 1890, U. S. officials feared Sitting Bull would become a rallying point for the Indians. On December 15 he was arrested by Indian police, but during a scuffle

that immediately followed he and his son, Crow Foot, were shot to death. Sitting Bull was buried at Ft. Yates, N. Dak., but was reinterred near Mobridge, S. Dak., in 1953.

SITWELL, Dame Edith (1887–1964), English author, considered by some to be one of the finest English poets of the 20th century. Although a striking woman, she remained unmarried and reveled in being eccentric. She justified her eccentricity by describing it as "the ordinary carried to a high degree of pictorial perfection."

Edith Sitwell was born in Scarborough on Sept. 7, 1887. She was educated privately and became interested in poetry at an early age. In 1916 she helped found *Wheels*, a yearly anthology of modern verse, and for the next five years she and her brothers Osbert and Sacheverell were its chief contributors. In 1923, Miss Sitwell publicly recited her poetry sequence *Facade*, which had a musical accompaniment by William Walton. *Facade* was made into a ballet in 1931. In 1954, Queen Elizabeth II named Miss Sitwell a Dame of the Grand Cross of the British Empire. In 1955, Dame Edith became a Roman Catholic. She completed her autobiography, *Taken Care Of*, in April 1964, and she died, in London, on Dec. 9, 1964.

Although she was six feet tall, Edith Sitwell accentuated her height by wearing long, flowing, brightly colored gowns and capes. Her long, thin face was dominated by large, heavy-lidded eyes. She usually wore either elaborate, wide-brimmed hats or exotic turbans and adorned herself with an abundance of massive jewelry.

As a poet she was one of the master technicians of her time. She continually experimented

Sitting Bull, Indian leader of the Sioux

with poetic rhythms and sounds, producing poetry that was sometimes harshly dissonant and sometimes almost conventionally beautiful. She sought to communicate sensations rather than to describe them, and she avoided traditional imagery, considering it worn out and useless. Miss Sitwell's style progressed from fanciful, brilliant, and somewhat grotesque to serene and deeply religious. Her volumes of poetry include *Rustic Elegies* (1927), *Five Variations on a Theme* (1933), *Poems Old and New* (1940), *The Canticle of the Rose* (1949), *Gardeners and Astronomers* (1953), and *The Outcast* (1962). Miss Sitwell's critical works include *Alexander Pope* (1930), *Aspects of Modern Poetry* (1934), and *A Poet's Notebook* (1943). She also wrote two books on Queen Elizabeth I—*Fanfare for Elizabeth* (1946) and *The Queens and the Hive* (1962). *The English Eccentrics* (1933) is a collection of her essays.

Further Reading: Fifoot, Richard, *Bibliography of Edith, Osbert, and Sacheverell Sitwell* (Oxford 1963); Megroz, R. L., *Three Sitwells: A Biographical and Critical Study* (1927; reprint, Kennikat 1969); Lehrmann, John, *A Nest of Tigers: The Sitwells in Their Times* (Little 1969).

SITWELL, Sir Osbert (1892–1969), English poet and satirist, and brother of Edith and Sacheverell Sitwell. He was born in London on Dec. 6, 1892, and was educated at Eton. In 1912 he was commissioned in the Grenadier Guards and served in France during World War I. He left the army in 1919 for literary pursuits, and from then on his life was devoted to the conduct of (in his own words) "a series of skirmishes and hand-to-hand battles against the Philistine . . . though not without damage to himself." Upon the death of his father, Sir George, in 1943, Osbert Sitwell succeeded to the baronetcy. He died in Montagnana, Italy, on May 2, 1969.

Sir Osbert's literary style is elegant but involved, and his language is ostentatiously rich. His writing is full of humor, which in the early part of his career was often mistaken for a lack of seriousness. His early works include a book of satires, *The Winstonburg Line* (1920), and two volumes of poems, *Argonaut and Juggernaut* (1919) and *Out of the Flame* (1923). Sitwell became firmly established as a luminary of modern English letters with the publication of *Before the Bombardment* (1926), a novel portraying the declining and falsely confident society of the English upper and prosperous middle classes. His next work, *The Man Who Lost Himself* (1929), is one of the great fantastic novels of modern letters. It breaks all the classic rules and introduces an abundance of digressions, yet never loses shape. *Dumb Animals* (1930) is collection of brilliant short stories. In *Miracle on Sinai* (1933), the complexity of form of *The Man Who Lost Himself* is carried even farther.

Sir Osbert's best-known work is probably his autobiography. It appeared in five volumes: *Left Hand! Right Hand!* (1945), *The Scarlet Tree* (1946), *Great Morning* (1948), *Laughter in the Next Room* (1949), and *Noble Essences* (1950). The central character is Sir George, father of the eccentric Sitwell family, who was described by one critic as "on the verge of the incredible." He is portrayed with such loving care and humor that the work is likely to become one of the main literary memorials of its times.

Further Reading: See the *Further Reading* section of SITWELL, EDITH.

SITWELL, Sir Sacheverell (1897–   ), English writer and younger brother of Edith and Osbert Sitwell. He was born in Scarborough on Nov. 15, 1897, and brought up at the ancestral home in a Gothic atmosphere. He was educated at Eton and Oxford, and he devoted his life to travel and literature. He succeeded to the baronetcy upon the death of his brother in 1969.

Sir Sacheverell's books include many on art, notably *Southern Baroque Art* (1928), *The Gothick North* (1929), and *Southern Baroque Revisited* (1968). *All in a Summer Day* (1926) is an autobiographical fantasia, *Doctor Donne and Gargantua* (1930) is a notable narrative poem, and *Mauretania* (1930) is an account of travels in Morocco. His other works include *Primitive Scenes and Festivals* (1942), *British Architects and Craftsmen* (1945), and *Monks, Nuns, and Monasteries* (1965).

Further Reading: See the *Further Reading* section of SITWELL, EDITH.

SIVA. See SHIVA.

SIVAJI. See SHIVAJI.

SIVAN, sē-vän′, is the ninth month of the Jewish civil year and the third month of the religious year. The Feast of Weeks (Shavuot), which commemorates the giving of the Law, occurs on the 6th of Sivan. See JEWISH CALENDAR.

SIVAS, si-väs′, is a city in central Turkey, about 220 miles (354 km) east of Ankara on the banks of the Kızılırmak. It is the capital of Sıvas province, important for cereal growing and mineral deposits. The city is a trade center for the region. It was known in Roman times as Sebastia. Impressive mosques, caravansaries, and *madrasas* (religious schools) built by the Seljuk Turks in the 13th century can still be seen.

In September 1919, Mustafa Kemal (later Atatürk) held a conference at Sıvas, calling on the Turks to resist the Allies' attempt to dismember Turkey after World War I. Population: (1970) of the city, 132,500; (1965) of the province, 705,077.

SIVASH, syi-vȧsh′, a salt lagoon off the northeast coast of the Crimea in the Ukrainian SSR. It is also known as the Putrid Sea, the Gniloye More in Russian. Its area is about 1,000 square miles (2,590 sq km). Its western section lies between the Crimea and the Ukrainian mainland and its eastern section between the Crimea and the Arabat Spit, which separates the Sivash from the Sea of Azov. In the north the Sivash joins the Sea of Azov through the Genichesk Strait. Highly saline, stagnant, and shallow, the Sivash contains mineral salts that are a source of iodine, bromine, sodium, and magnesium.

SIWA, sē′wə, is an oasis in northwestern Egypt in the Western Desert near the Libyan border. It has an area of about 35 square miles (90 sq km) and the inhabitants are principally Berbers. Olives and dates are grown around the chief village, also called Siwa.

Siwa (Siwah) was the site of the oracle of Amon, which was consulted by Alexander the Great. Population: (1960) 3,839.

SIX NATIONS, a confederacy of Eastern North American Indian tribes. See IROQUOIS INDIANS.

KUNSTHISTORISCHES MUSEUM, VIENNA

Pieter Bruegel the Elder's *Peasant Dance* shows one aspect of the life led by most Europeans in the 16th century.

SIXTEENTH CENTURY. Between 1450 and 1650, Europe and the entire world lived through a single vast adventure whose great actions were often interlinked. A position at the very center of this adventure is what gives the 16th century its undeniable importance but also makes its true features hard to isolate. The century was neither a beginning nor an end of the experiences that mark it. It inherited these experiences and then passed them along to the century that followed. They outspanned the 16th century and controlled its course.

1. Europe

It is often said that the political history of the West was dominated from 1501 through 1600 by relentless conflicts among the modern states of England, France, and Spain. That is certainly true, but those states were forged by 15th century craftsmen—Henry VII of England (reigned 1485–1509), Louis XI of France (reigned 1461–1483), and, in Spain, Ferdinand and Isabella (Ferdinand II of Aragón: reigned 1479–1516; Isabella I of Castile: reigned 1474–1504). Even the house of Habsburg, so soon to play a leading role in European affairs, was already well settled in its fortunes, thanks to the wise and patient Emperor Frederick III (reigned 1440–1493). The power of the Ottoman Empire and the terror it so often induced in 16th century Europe were also legacies. The Ottoman Turks had taken Constantinople from the Christians in 1453.

During the half-century before 1500, Italy experienced, in Florence and then in Rome, the supreme blossomings of urban civilization that collectively are called the Renaissance. Humanism, too, flowered in the 15th century. But the years between 1450 and 1500 were also marked by religious disturbances, which were soon to cul-

minate in the Reformation, led by Martin Luther (1483–1546), John Calvin (1509–1564), and others.

Most of the techniques employed by 16th century craftsmen were also inherited, although the age brought them to a higher stage of perfection. The printer's art and decisive improvements in mining and metallurgy date from the second half of the 15th century. Artillery was a legacy of a still earlier age. But field artillery on movable carriages seems to have been first employed on a large scale in 1494, when Charles VIII of France descended on Italy.

Historians have recounted the pathetic plight of the Jews, who wandered despairingly from country to country in the 16th century as they were expelled from one state after another. But this new Exodus was also linked to the 15th century, notably to that day in 1492 when Ferdinand and Isabella stood under the walls of Granada and resolved to drive the Jews from Spain.

As the 16th century began in 1501, nine years had gone by since Columbus set sail on his first voyage of discovery; over three years since Vasco da Gama rounded the southern end of Africa; and nearly three years since da Gama's tiny fleet dropped anchor at Calicut, India. Thus two of the most important oceanic routes had already been discovered.

The 16th Century Achievement. One role of the 16th century was, therefore, that of an heir—careful to lose nothing of his patrimony, diligently adding to his wealth, and prudently solidifying his position. In the printing art the age was to produce the marvels of Johann Froben in Basel, Aldus Manutius in Venice, and the Estienne family and their many peers in Paris. The development of printing was an important factor in the spread of religious restiveness.

In Italy the 16th century was to foster and prolong the glow of the Renaissance. Leonardo da Vinci lived until 1519 and Raphael until 1520. The brilliance of Rome was not dimmed until 1527, when the city suffered frightful pillage at the hands of the Spanish and German troops of Charles, Duke of Bourbon. Florence was still at the height of its flowering and continued so until the pitiful siege by Emperor Charles V's forces in 1530. But Michelangelo, who worked in both cities, prolonged his career to 1564. As the century closed, a Renaissance of a kind was still shining brightly in Italy, this time in Venice and Bologna.

To its legacy the 16th century added much of its own creating, even if one considers only that great flowering of art called the baroque—cosmopolitan, imperial, even romantic, and destined largely to outlive the century. In seafaring, the age that was dowered in its cradle with a royal gift, the twin routes of the Atlantic and Indian oceans, added to these conquests the great highways of the Pacific. Vasco Núñez de Balboa reached the Pacific in 1513 after crossing the Isthmus of Panama, and Ferdinand Magellan crossed the ocean itself in 1520–1521. From the 1570's the Spaniards maintained a great sea track between Acapulco in New Spain (now Mexico) and Manila in the Philippines. The 16th century also filled in the charts of the Atlantic. Soon, to the profit of Europe, it covered the seas with a vast network of trade routes and added an impressive number of settlements and conquests on land—in sum, hardly more or less than all the peopled or accessible parts of the American continents. In technology, in building ports, in finding routes, in constructing ships, and in developing the science of war, the century had much to add. The wheel-lock mechanism for hand firearms was invented about 1520, and during the second half of the century the character of cavalry attack was transformed by the pistol.

The 17th Century Development. The 16th century left a vast wealth to the 17th century, which resumed and carried forward nearly all its enterprises. Thus, absolute monarchy was to attain its prime embodiment in Louis XIV of France, the Sun King (reigned 1643–1715). Yet the 16th century supplied the prototypes, notably in Emperor Charles V (reigned 1519–1556; as Charles I of Spain, 1516–1556) and, even more, in Philip II of Spain (reigned 1556–1598). The wars of religion that stained the 16th century with blood did not come to an end until 1648 with the Peace of Westphalia, after the unspeakable horrors of the Thirty Years' War. Likewise the baroque—that intricate, lavish art that has been called the style of the Catholic Counter-Reformation—although rooted in the second half of the 16th century, had its richest blossoming in the 17th.

Another of the glories of the 17th century, the Scientific Revolution, sprang from a soil well tilled by the 16th century. It arrived late, lagging behind the Renaissance in letters and the arts. The work of Galileo Galilei, Johannes Kepler, William Harvey, René Descartes, and Sir Isaac Newton after 1600 followed from the labors of 16th century astronomers, anatomists, and mathematicians.

The mathematical achievements of the 17th century would not have come so readily if certain typical equations of the third degree had not been solved by Scipione del Ferro, Niccolò Tartaglia, and Girolamo Cardano, or if Cardano's pupil Lodovico Ferrari had not gone on to solve for the first time an equation of the fourth degree. Or, to give a later example, from France, if François Viète had not ensured the victory of symbolic algebra—"specious algebra," as he called it—by attacking the problem of general solutions of equations and throwing a bridge from algebra across to geometry. The 17th century achievement is inconceivable without the many 16th century editions of the ancient Greek geometricians—in Latin, in the vernaculars, and in Greek itself. To cite only one example, Archimedes, the great geometrician of the ancient world, was not "reborn" until the 16th century.

In the sciences between 1501 and 1600, one could point to the tremendous labors of the anatomist Andreas Vesalius before Harvey; to the surgical innovations of Ambroise Paré; or to the triumphs of Nicolaus Copernicus and Tycho Brahe anticipating Kepler and the telescope. Experience, experiment, research, and theory accumulated in the 16th and 17th centuries to bring down the old cosmos—the world-scheme of Aristotle—and to usher in the age of modern science.

Woodcut by Albrecht Dürer illustrates a device used to give instruction in handling the problems of proportion and perspective. The woodcut is from one of the artist's theoretical treatises, *Underweysung der Messung.*

THE BETTMANN ARCHIVE   THE BETTMANN ARCHIVE   CULVER PICTURES

The three great monarchs of the first half of the 16th century were (*from left*): Henry VIII (painting by Hans Holbein the Younger); Francis I (painting by Jean Clouet); and Charles V (engraving after a painting by Titian).

SOCIAL AND ECONOMIC CONDITIONS

The 16th century in Europe was a time of economic expansion. Roughly from 1450 to 1650 there seems to have been a considerable increase in the population, as there was in China. Not until about the middle of the 16th century did Europe's population growth begin to entail severe economic hardships.

In the first half of the century, European intellectuals and humanists dreamed of an age of peace and prosperity. In a letter to a friend toward the beginning of 1517, the Dutch humanist Desiderius Erasmus, then in his late 40's, expressed a wish to be young again. "I anticipate the approach of a golden age," he wrote. In 1521, Martin Luther, on the eve of his struggles and triumphs, was equally optimistic.

Poverty and Social Unrest. This happy period—happy for the privileged classes—was not to last. After the middle of the 16th century the growth of population made its weight felt in a surplus of mouths to feed. Even before 1550 widespread revolts occurred among the peasants, who constituted nearly the whole of the population. The dramatic and epidemic uprising in the Peasants' War of 1524–1526 in Germany and Austria was put down in blood. On a much smaller scale France experienced an uprising in 1548–1549 over the *gabelle* (tax on salt) in Guienne and neighboring regions.

During the second half of the century the poor suffered even more, although they did not raise their voices so high in protest. Their rebellions were simple, isolated actions on the margins of history. But these instances of violence—such as the riots in the summer of 1594 by the Croquants, peasants of southwestern France, and the countless acts of brigandage in the Turkish Balkans, in Italy, and in Spain—all bespoke the growing wretchedness of the poor. Between 1550 and 1600 their misery was paraded through Venice, Florence, and Naples, through Valencia in Spain, and through many French cities—a spectacle the more terribly moving because of its monotony.

In Paris poverty was an incurable sore. There, massed together in the Hôtel-Dieu—the hospital accommodating all the sick, regardless of origin or ailment—beggars tended by barber-surgeons ended their wretched lives. Healthy beggars were chained by one foot to their neighbors and worn out working for a pittance on the town drains, which were choked with garbage, trash, and filth. A bad harvest or high prices, as in the summer of 1587, produced within a few days in Paris as many as 15,000 to 20,000 beggars demanding the king's bounty or the charity of city officials and the well-to-do.

Rise in Population. One acquires the strong impression that the growth of misery in Europe followed close on the rise in population. The price of wheat soared, and land sold at 10 to 20 times its former value. Too many hands offered their labor, and wages did not always keep pace with rising prices. The basic worth of a man was everywhere at a discount.

In Spain the population seems to have been dropping at the close of the 16th century, but in other countries it did not cease to grow or begin to recede until much later. In Germany population recession did not come until the beginning of the Thirty Years' War in 1618; in France, not until 1650. The surplus of human beings in relation to Europe's economic development goes far in accounting for a number of wars and much other violence during the 16th century. Underlying the wars of religion in Germany from 1546, in France from 1562, and in the Low Countries from 1566, were for grave political and social problems.

Growth of Cities. Europe's overseas expansion, material progress, and population rise in the 16th century account for the growth of cities, which became bigger, richer, and more wretched than ever. The age is crowded with urban outgrowths and changes. At Florence, a second town grew up, with new palaces away from the heart of the old city. The Florentine countryside was soon dotted with splendid villas. Venice and its environs took on the same complexion. On the Venetian mainland the villas of the rich rose along the quiet waters of the Brenta River, while in Venice itself business houses, markets, and public buildings multiplied. The same could be said of nearly every town in every region of

Europe, and one might even speak of a precocious urban luxury in the New World—in Mexico City and Lima, the Spanish viceregal capitals of New Spain and Peru. One could point to London being rebuilt in brick; or to Paris being rebuilt in stone, brick, and tile, overleaping the walls of Charles V and Philip Augustus and reaching out on both sides of the Seine.

Yet in the midst of these cities, who can fail to see the destitution of the poor, the fear at the heart of the owner, the deeds of theft and violence? And everywhere rose the gallows: in Paris at the Place Maubert and many other squares; near Paris, at Montfaucon. Among so many hanged, how many were poor? How many innocent?

Prosperity in 16th century Europe was the monopoly of a few privileged persons—heads of state, great landowners, princes of the church, and international businessmen. This last group was the life and soul of the commercial centers, such as Venice, Augsburg, Genoa, Lyon, Medina del Campo, Lisbon, Seville, and Antwerp. At its head stood the great banking and trading families of Genoa, Florence, and southern Germany, including the Fuggers and Welsers; and, after the first half of the century, a number of Spaniards and Portuguese, many of them Marranos, or converted Jews.

The dominance of the businessman in this age of commercial capitalism was not without its vicissitudes and catastrophes. The long sea voyages, however romantic, were business gambles. There were also sharp, passing crises of quite frequent occurrence, during which the banks were in desperate condition, as in 1580 and succeeding years. At such times, assets could not be readily mobilized and financial liquidity restored. Finally, businessmen had to fight the rise of prices, which gained momentum beyond any control in the last two decades of the century.

Rise in Prices. To be sure, the price rise was as nothing compared with those of later times, but it was the first of the great universal inflations, and the sharp upset of the market took the men of Europe by surprise. As in any inflation, the balance of personal luck frequently shifted. The flare-up of prices did not, of course, always indicate a real prosperity or any economically healthy rise. Yet, even aside from prices, all available statistics—for example, records of the amounts of goods shipped in trade—confirm that there was a general expansion of economic activity.

Was the source of these changes the arrival of precious metals from America, in amounts that glutted the market? According to the official figures of the customs at Seville, the port through which trade between Europe and Spanish America was funneled, between 1500 and 1650 some 180 tons of gold and 16,000 tons of silver arrived in Spain. During the first half of the 16th century, America supplied chiefly gold, but in the second half chiefly silver. It is easy to show that the inflation caused by gold, which affected only the highest levels of exchange, was slower and less extreme than the silver inflation, which struck the European economy at middle levels. The midcentury shift from gold "structures" to silver "structures" must have brought on a severe crisis for economic enterprises and, beyond them, for all states and societies in Europe.

The influx of precious metals was only one cause of the European price rise and the changes that came with it. Besides the gold and silver coins in circulation, there were fiduciary moneys—units such as the *livre tournois* in France—that were used in keeping accounts. These moneys of account were convertible into actual coins but were subject to risky manipulation and frequent devaluation. The rise in the standard of living must also be considered. More of the precious metals were required as the demand for goods increased and the level of economic life grew higher.

Trade and Commerce. Safe above the storm of prices, which so overwhelmed men of the 16th century, commerce went ahead by land and sea. In 1600 the fleets plying between Seville and America carried, at the highest estimate, a total of 50,000 tons of goods going and coming. There were also advances in agricultural production and industrial output. A huge international economy spread its network over the globe. Money from the New World found its way by stages to the Far East, producer of pepper, spices, silk, pearls, and chinaware. Baltic wheat by the boatload reached Portugal, Spain, and after 1590 the Mediterranean. Sugar came from Brazil and codfish from the Newfoundland banks. Europe brought home the products of the Levant and the Far East and, with them, luxury and extravagance for their own sakes.

Power shifted to the shores of the Atlantic, its towns, peoples, and states, to the detriment of the Mediterranean. In 1500, Venice had been dominant in trade. By 1550 the commercial and financial capital of Europe was Antwerp, with Lisbon, Seville, and Lyon as partners. In 1600, Amsterdam was on the threshold of its greatness.

Financial Practices. The new wealth in the world could hardly leave the princes of Europe indifferent. They fought for it, and it controlled their fates. Credit was misused on a huge scale. The kings of France borrowed recklessly in Paris and Lyon, and their creditors often advanced sums blindly. Almost everywhere the story was the same. In Italy, the governments of Genoa, Florence, and Venice exercised the prudence befitting investors and businessmen. But their restraint stood in contrast to the speculative madness that overtook the *asentistas* (contractors) to whom Emperor Charles V and King Philip II of Spain farmed out lucrative monopolies. German and Genoese moneylenders jostled one another offering their services, abandoned themselves to grandiose speculations, and transferred great sums of money, especially after 1566 to the Netherlands, where Spain was engaged in a struggle to retain control of one of its richest possessions.

These financial operations were marked by many sensational and bitter surprises, such as the near bankruptcy of the Spanish state in 1557, 1575, and 1596. Little by little the princes parceled out substantial resources in return for credit, pledging their revenues for years to come and disposing of their monopolies of trade and taxation. The king of Portugal sold off the pepper from the East Indies. Even the privilege of buying pepper in the Indies and selling it in Europe was farmed out by contracts, the possession of which was eagerly coveted.

Through the Casa de Contratación (House of Trade) in Seville, revenues from America were transmitted to the Spanish crown. Thus the king of Spain received, and later spent, much of the wealth produced by the West Indies and the silver mines of Mexico and Peru. In the end the

Martin Luther launched the Protestant Reformation in 1517 when he posted his 95 theses on indulgences.

prosperity of a whole century ebbed away between spendthrift princes, who ruined one another in wars of prestige and ambition, and traders, who were by no means always prudent. The only businessmen to survive were generally those who had had the foresight to buy land at the right moment. Certainly it was land that rescued the Fugger dynasty as well as many businessmen in Florence and elsewhere. Caught between the forced defaulting of governments and the continual strains of economic life, most businessmen who lacked this foresight eventually had to abandon their lives of luxury.

POWER POLITICS AND EMPIRE-BUILDING

Not all governments profited by the economic upsurge of the 16th century. The age brought a terrible test of strength of political structures. In this game the weakest organisms, such as the free towns that were so numerous in the 15th century, went to the wall. The only towns able to beat the game were those that had managed to take over their weaker neighbors at the start of the 15th century and feed on them. Venice had subjugated Bergamo, Verona, Brescia, and Padua. Genoa had subdued the towns along its Riviera, including its enemy Savona. Florence had set itself over the rest of Tuscany, notably over Pisa. Rome, under the rule of authoritarian popes, asserted strict control in the lands comprising the Patrimony of Saint Peter.

The Renaissance. If the Renaissance was brightest in Florence and later in Rome, that was largely because they had emerged as victors from such fratricidal struggles in the 15th century and at the start of the 16th. Venice, the solidest but perhaps the most materialistically minded of the victors, was not to experience the Renaissance until the very close of the 16th century. Its emblems were its bewitching courtesans and its

costly tables loaded with choice foods. The sumptuous gala dress of the Venetians is seen in the paintings of Titian, Paolo Veronese, and Tintoretto. In south Germany, Nuremberg was lighted by the artistic genius of Albrecht Dürer. And Augsburg, a town of financiers and silver mine owners, produced two famous portraitists, Hans Holbein the Elder and Hans Holbein the Younger.

The city and city-state were thus the frame for the Renaissance, as in ancient times the *polis* had been for the glory that was Greece. Wherever such cities were lacking, the movement wanted spontaneity. Those aspects of the Renaissance that were fostered by princes—as in France, Spain, and Poland—were like so many transplanted flowers. In 16th century Paris, the busy workshops were those connected with the completion or reconstruction of Gothic churches. The Renaissance made itself felt only in slight touches —in the making over of the Louvre, in the Fountain of the Innocents by Pierre Lescot and Jean Goujon, in certain tombs of St.-Denis, in the Château of Fontainebleau, and in other châteaus of the Paris region and the Loire Valley.

Conflict of States. Cities and city-states were not the only victims of the crisis of greed in the 16th century. States with insufficient means could not hold out against armies of mercenaries and the cannon of their enemies. Ever costlier wars flung onto the battlefields the poorest men in Europe: the Albanian cavalrymen of the Italian wars, Swiss mountaineers, German lansquenets from the Württemberg mountains, Frenchmen from the Pyrenees and the mountains of Dauphiné, lively mountain folk and peasants from Spain—all tirelessly rallying to the sound of the recruiter's drum. War underwent not only technical advances, in weaponry and tactics, but also an increase in manpower and matériel.

The kingdom of Naples had been simply obeying the laws of political physics when it succumbed to Charles VIII of France in 1495. The only element of doubt had been whether it would be devoured by the Turks, by the king of Aragón, who also ruled Sicily, or by the king of France, claimant of the rights of the 13th century Angevins. In the upshot it passed to Ferdinand II of Aragón in 1504. The same logic had demanded the fall of Milan. There, in 1495–1497, Leonardo da Vinci had painted *The Last Supper* in the convent adjoining the Church of Santa Maria delle Grazie. But cultural achievement availed Milan no more against French kings and Swiss looters than later against Spanish regiments. In the end, the city became a Habsburg dominion (1535). Logic further demanded the dismemberment of the small kingdom of Navarre, which straddled the Pyrenees. In 1512, Ferdinand II of Aragón annexed all but the minor portion lying north of the mountains. The same threat loomed over Ireland, Scotland, and all the politically weak. The threat became a reality even for glory-laden Portugal, which was forced to accept Philip II of Spain as its king in 1580.

What course did it seem a statesman should take in years of such insecurity and violent change? In *The Prince*, Niccolò Machiavelli set forth directions in precise terms, bearing on day-to-day, short-term tactics: calculate, recalculate, hold your breath, and you may gain the respite of a few days or a few hours, like Cesare Borgia, whose political career the author idealized. The long-term view, covering years and centuries, the careers of states and empires, was presented in *The Discourses*, Machiavelli's commentaries on the first 10 books of Livy's *History of Rome*. Although *The Prince* and much of *The Discourses* were written in 1513, *The Prince* was not published in Italian until 1532. It became the more famous of the two because, after the middle of the century, politicians read it closely. But they were not searching for the secret of the years that had unfolded since the century began; they were looking for lessons in treachery, hypocrisy, political opportunism, and cynicism. These were not the lessons set by the onetime secretary to the Council of Ten at Florence at the real heart of his book.

The political drama in which Machiavelli played out his part was a mere curtain raiser for the flaming Italy of the latter half of the century. Italy's internal wars hardly outlasted 1515, the year of the Battle of Marignano, a brilliant victory for the young French king, Francis I; or 1519, the date when Charles of Habsburg—already master of the Low Countries, the Austrian states, Spain, and Spanish America—was elected Holy Roman emperor.

Charles V. Charles was the contemporary of Francis I, Henry VIII of England, the Ottoman ruler Suleiman the Magnificent, Martin Luther, and Michelangelo. But it was in the new Emperor, born in 1500, that the century found its true man of destiny: one who was thoughtful yet visionary, shrewd but gallant, intelligent and calculating yet haunted by the extravagant and the romantic; a man devoured by the passion for glory; a man of action who was nonetheless a dreamer; the most powerful prince of his day but one who, face-to-face with his God and his conscience, was the most troubled, abject, and tormented Christian that ever lived. With him, there burst upon the stage of Europe and the world the modern empire, a coalition of diverse lands, seas, peoples, civilizations, and economies. Not even the empire of Suleiman the Magnificent bears comparison, though it stretched from the Persian Gulf to Algiers and beyond the Balkans to the gates of Vienna.

Charles V made his entry before history with fixed and startling ideas. His triumphs were peerless—Pavia (1525); Tunis (1535), Mühlberg (1547). His failures were still more stirring—Algiers, saved by a storm in 1541; the siege of Metz in 1552, abandoned in snows and sorrows. To restore a unified and close-knit Christendom, Charles hurled himself against indomitable opponents: the Valois kings of France; the Turks, allies of Francis I; the leaders of the Reformation. Luther's rebellion was unleashed in 1517. And Luther, whom the Emperor faced for only a brief moment at the Diet of Worms in 1521, was to thwart Charles' ambitions.

Exhausted and discouraged by his struggles, Charles abdicated in 1555–1556. He withdrew to a monastery in Spain, where he died in 1558. His son Philip received Spain, the Low Countries, and the Habsburg possessions in Italy, though not the crown of the Holy Roman emperors. Philip took up Charles' battle. But in his conflict with the Protestant English and Dutch he was defeated by default of Catholic France, which was torn by religious strife until 1598 and was, in any case, the traditional enemy of the Habsburgs.

The Maritime Struggle. On the Atlantic, Philip's game may not have been hopelessly lost by the defeat of the Spanish Armada, but it was hope-

BROWN BROTHERS

Saint Ignatius of Loyola founded the Society of Jesus in the 1530's and guided early Jesuit missionary work.

lessly compromised. In August 1588, the great fleet launched against England by the Spanish king was bested by the currents and storms of the North Sea and the ships of Queen Elizabeth I. This event brought to a head the vast religious war for world empire, although it did not end it.

Which were to win? Would it be the light, speedy, trim-rigged craft of the north, armed with effective artillery and exulting in profane names like *Eagle, Leopard, Raven,* and even *Crescent* and *Diana?* Or would it be the huge but slower vessels of the south, invoking the Virgin, Star of the Sea? The outcome was not settled by the end of 1600. The Invincible Armada was followed by other Spanish naval expeditions —in 1596, 1597, and 1601—though these, too, failed. The Spaniards controlled the Strait of Gibraltar; the English held the Channel. The Spaniards dominated the Atlantic when autumn storms began to threaten; the English commanded it as soon as the spring brought quiet seas. But a fleet must return to port, and the Spaniards held the most important island bases in the Atlantic: besides their own Canary Islands, they possessed between 1580 and 1640 the Portuguese Azores, Madeira, and the Cape Verde Islands. In America, they had lands and men. All this seemed to promise well for a long future.

EUROPE'S OVERSEAS EXPANSION

One must look to a farther horizon than the Atlantic and explore again the general question of the upsurge of Europe. Once before, from the 11th century to the middle of the 14th, Europe had felt an urgent flood of life. The disasters that came with the Black Death thwarted this advance. After a century of relapse, roughly 1350–1450, Europe resumed its forward march and this time subjected or tried to subject most of the world to European laws. From 1450 to 1650

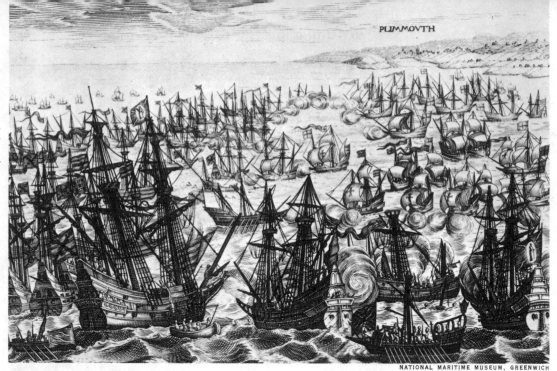

NATIONAL MARITIME MUSEUM, GREENWICH

The defeat of Spain's "Invincible Armada" by the English in 1588 opened the way for Britain's colonial expansion.

there is more to report than trial runs and first steps. Real successes, major triumphs, emerged.

The Oceans. The first real victory of Europe was over the vast salt wastes of water covering the globe. The triumphs were seafaring ventures: ships wafted to unknown shores, fleets homing from faraway lands. It is worthwhile to revive the picture in its setting of the world's ocean deserts and to watch in one's imagination as a fortune in wood, rigging, and cargoes moves past. A ship or a fleet sails on, its wake disappears, and loneliness resumes its reign over the sea. Let a vessel swerve from the appointed course and it is menaced by a thousand dangers, of which hunger and thirst loom largest. In 1558, Jean de Léry, a French Protestant, came home from the bay of Rio de Janeiro on a little Norman craft, a true floating coffin. The boat sailed slowly, aimlessly, after losing its way. First came the famine. "After we had eaten all the leather on board," he wrote, "even to the chest lids, we thought we were done for. A rat was worth more than an ox on land. The price went up to four crowns." But the story can be read a hundred and a thousand times over in the thrilling sea tales of the 16th century. Such words tell more than the important documents can of the fearful emptiness of the sea.

Hence arose the temptation—and the ease—of surprise attacks. By the end of the century the Portuguese had wrested from Asian rivals domination of the main shipping routes in the Indian Ocean. They maintained their control through their occupation of key ports: Goa, in India; Malacca, in Malaya; Hormuz, in the Persian Gulf. On the Atlantic, the only enemy a European faced was another European. After 1519 the sea highways between Europe and Spanish America took the form they maintained almost to the end of the era of sailing ships. Westward bound, vessels on the main route touched the Canaries and then, with the help of trade winds, crossed the ocean to the West Indies. On the return trip they followed the Gulf Stream from the tip of Florida to Newfoundland and then dropped through smooth seas to the Azores. On the Pacific, the Manila galleons plied due west from Acapulco to the Philippines, touching at Guam. They returned by way of the California coast.

Africa. The conquest of the seaways was only a start and a means. The victory had to be renewed and maintained: all that it meant was derived from other victories that it made possible, and these others plainly could not be won except on land. There were many ups and downs in this story. Africa was all but barred to Europeans: some regions, by dangerous endemic diseases; others, by deserts and unpeopled jungles; still others, by warlike peoples. The Europeans were satisfied to occupy a few points on the edge of the continent and to make more or less permanent settlements there.

During the 16th century, Europe's only profitable venture in Africa, apart from the buying of gold dust, was the trade in black slaves brought to the coast by warrior tribes. Of this business, the Portuguese trader was in command until the next century.

Asia. In Asia, once the first surprise attacks and successes were over, neither India, the East Indies, distant China, nor still more distant Japan was conquered in any literal sense. They were entered, exploited, and made a part of Europe's life, for Europe was always tempted by trade and trade operations. But the temptation never offered anything free. At Goa and Malacca, as in the Moluccas, the land of the clove—and in China, where one could buy as much of anything as one pleased, according to the Italian traveler Filippo Sassetti—the European economy and the traders and captains who represented it were made to pay hard cash for the luxury products of the East.

The East grew rich in this trade. A large part of the wealth of America—especially the silver from American mines, often in the form of Spanish silver pieces of eight reals—must have ended up in the towns of India and China. There is something awe-inspiring about this line of dependence stretching across the world from monsoon Asia to the mines of America. Upon the prosperity of those mines depended the firmness of Europe's grip on the foreign trade of Asia. Around 1630–1640 mineral production in the New World did in fact fall off. As a result, the trade lines between Europe and the Far East slackened.

America. Not until the middle of the 17th century was it possible to judge the 16th century European adventure in America. A few Spanish soldiers easily overthrew the Aztecs of Mexico and the Incas of Peru, the peoples that had dominated the most culturally advanced areas of the New World. Thanks to Indian labor the European conquerors could live on the land while laying the groundwork for a strong, mine-rich Spanish America and organizing a series of regular and powerful convoys between America and Seville.

Elsewhere the conquerors had to rest content with less distinguished lands and civilizations. Such was Portuguese Brazil in the 16th century. Yet, sugar plantations, worked by African slaves, soon brought prosperity, especially in the region of Recife and Bahia. In North America, the outlines of French and British colonization did not become clear until the 17th century.

CONCLUSION

The years from 1540 to 1560 produced remarkable changes in Europe. One may speak of a century serené and happy in its opening years, passing over to sadness, trouble, and despair toward its end. The change in the spirit of the times took France from the exuberance of François Rabelais and from Pierre de Ronsard and his fellow poets of the Pléiade to the solitary meditations of the essayist Michel de Montaigne; from the civil peace of the kingdom of Louis XII (reigned 1498–1515) and even of Francis I (reigned 1515–1547) to all the horrors of civil and religious war, of which the massacre of French Protestants on St. Bartholomew's Day (Aug. 24, 1572) is the gloomy symbol. But does this picture hold good for all of Europe? Can one draw such a contrast between the England of Sir Thomas More and the England of William Shakespeare? It would be wrong to force a generalization. On the whole, though, the first half of the 16th century was more peaceful but poorer in worldly goods than the second; the second half was marked by drama, extravagance, and a flood of money.

A more detailed account of the 16th century would be filled with the names of more great battles, princes, writers, artists, and religious leaders. But the story defies abridgment.

For example, the whole of the 16th century and the first half of the 17th were the golden age of Spanish literature. By 1600, Cervantes was at work on *Don Quixote,* and by 1603, Lope de Vega had written more than 200 plays, a small fraction of his total output. Portugal in the 16th century produced its great epic poet, Camões. He was one of many poets of various nationalities who were influenced by Ariosto, the foremost Italian narrative poet of the century. England, during Elizabeth's reign (1558–1603), attained distinction of the first rank in literature. The century spanned the careers of Spenser and Marlowe and launched those of Shakespeare and Ben Jonson.

Western Europe had great composers of polyphonic music, especially for voice, in men such as Josquin Després, Giovanni Gabrieli, Giovanni Palestrina, Roland de Lassus (Orlando di Lasso), and William Byrd. The panoramic landscapes of Pieter Bruegel the Elder were among the supreme achievements of Northern Renaissance painting in the Low Countries during the 16th century. In Spain, El Greco was working at Toledo. Of the Italian Renaissance painters, Correggio anticipated the baroque style, which was created toward the end of the century by Caravaggio and the Carracci family. In architecture, Andrea Palladio and Giacomo da Vignola were particularly influential.

The Renaissance spread eastward to Poland, which in the 16th century enjoyed an efflorescence of architecture, arts, and letters. In Russia, where a strong centralized state emerged under the leadership of Moscow, much building activity took place during the reign (1533–1584) of Ivan the Terrible. Expression was given to a national type of architecture that embraced both Byzantine and Italian influences.

Among the great religious figures of 16th century Europe were those of the Catholic reform movement known as the Counter-Reformation. Under this sadly ambiguous title one might sum up the mighty attack of the Jesuit troops under St. Ignatius of Loyola and their many missionary ventures in America. One might turn aside for a glance at the glories of mystic Spain: St. Teresa of Ávila and St. John of the Cross.

Too often, however, only the dramas of spirit and feeling in the 16th century are emphasized— its thought, its art, its religious life—and far less attention is paid to political developments and the realities of material life. This survey of the century in Europe has tried to show that there was a whole complex life that transcends the time limits of 1501 to 1600. There are really two different but continuous ages involved, dovetailing in the period 1540–1560. Although the Reformation has not been given a central place here, that is not because its influence is to be minimized. The whole century as it was really lived in Europe did experience a rising tide of religious life, both on the side of the old church and on that of the new churches. Reformation and Counter-Reformation did not form a time sequence but proceeded together step by step in their growth. The historical factors that led to Luther on one hand led to St. Ignatius on the other.

FERNAND BRAUDEL[*]
Collège de France

2. Asia, North Africa, and the Pacific

In the 16th century major upheavals and transformations occurred in various regions of Asia. Not only did some of the most powerful regimes in the long history of the East emerge, but their foremost rulers often sought, with much success, to extend their control over neighboring states and peoples. During this period Europeans began to penetrate the East. The Portuguese established firm bases in the Persian Gulf area, India, Malaya, Indonesia, and China; the Spaniards, in the Philippines. Attracted especially by the prospects of tapping new sources of wealth, the Europeans also sought to win converts to the Christian faith. Meanwhile, Islam, already dominant in the Middle East and strong in India, made headway in Southeast Asia.

Ottoman Empire. The empire of the Ottoman Turks, which had been growing for two centuries,

Japan's greatest surviving feudal castle, in Himeji, was begun by the warrior Toyotomi Hideyashi in 1581.

reached its zenith in the middle of the 16th century and then started a slow decline. Many of the political and military successes of the great sultans of the age actually rested upon the careful groundwork prepared by the somewhat colorless Bayezid II (reigned 1481–1512). Overhauling the political structure of the Ottoman regime, he also greatly strengthened the military and naval establishments. His fearsome son and successor, Selim I, managed in his brief reign (1512–1520) to expand the Ottoman domains considerably. By checking the Persians in the east, he consolidated the grip of the Ottoman Empire upon eastern Anatolia. But his greatest military triumph was the overwhelming of Egypt's Mamluk (Mameluke) rulers. Not only Egypt itself but also Syria and much of the Arabian peninsula were incorporated into the Ottoman Empire.

Suleiman I the Magnificent (reigned 1520–1566) then came to the helm of the empire. He was doubtless one of the mightiest monarchs of his time. His armies drove deep into and beyond the Balkan region in southeast Europe, captured Belgrade and Budapest, and laid siege to Vienna. Far to the east his armies conquered Iraq and its famed capital, Baghdad. With the aid of his fleets Suleiman was able to bring the islands of the eastern Mediterranean and lands in North Africa under his rule. After his death the vigor of the Ottoman Empire slowly waned.

The forward surge of the Ottomans in the 16th century won them a prestigious title in the world of Islam. When Selim I conquered the Mamluks in 1517, he became "Protector of the Holy Cities of Arabia"—Mecca and Medina. The Ottoman sultans also claimed to hold the office of caliph, by which they hoped to gain leadership of the entire community of Muslims.

During the 16th century the eastern Mediter-ranean, dominated by the Ottoman Empire, became relatively less important in world economic life. In large measure, this was due to the shift of centers of trade to the Atlantic seaboard and to the expansion of western European countries to Africa, the Americas, and Asia.

Iran (Persia). Several centuries of foreign domination of Iran were brought to a close with the founding of the Safavid dynasty in 1501. The first ruler, Shah Ismail I, labored until his death in 1524 to forge a new state system and to encourage unity among the diverse people of his domain. A key feature of his policies was the establishment of the Shiite sect of Islam as the state religion. In this unmistakable way the Iranian state was differentiated from Muslim regimes to the east and west.

Shah Abbas I (reigned 1587–1629) brought Iran to almost forgotten heights of power and splendor. His armies crushed the troublesome Uzbeks in the northeast and defeated the advancing forces of the Ottoman Turks in the west. In 1598, Abbas moved the imperial capital to Isfahan, which was soon transformed into one of the most magnificent cities of Asia.

India. The history of life of the Indian subcontinent were transformed by the rise of the Muslim Mughul Empire in the 16th century. Its creator was a Turko-Mongol prince, Babur, who invaded northwestern India from his base in Afghanistan. With his capture of Delhi in 1526, the Mughul Empire, comprising much of the Indian north and northwest, came into being. His son and successor, Humayun, was unable to maintain control of the domain and spent most of his reign (1530–1556) in exile.

The third Mughul ruler, Akbar (reigned 1556–1605), ranks among the greatest emperors India has known. A superb military leader, he devoted his life to the expansion of his realm, which by the time of his death embraced almost all of northern India. He is also known for his sound administrative policies and his efforts to eliminate religious divisiveness among his Muslim and Hindu subjects. To this end he vainly attempted to found a syncretic religion, which he designated *Din-i-Ilahi* (Divine Faith). The teachings of the main religions of the world—including those of Roman Catholicism, which had been made known to Akbar by pioneering Jesuits in India—were incorporated into this faith.

Mughul power was not extended significantly into peninsular India during the 16th century. There, a small number of constantly warring states managed to preserve their independence. The greatest of these states was the impressive Hindu kingdom of Vijayanagar, which had emerged in the middle of the 14th century. In 1565, Vijayanagar was overwhelmed by a coalition of the Deccan sultanates and entered on a precipitous decline.

Shortly after the arrival of the Portuguese mariner Vasco da Gama at Calicut in 1498, Portuguese traders began to visit India in growing numbers. In 1510, Viceroy Afonso de Albuquerque secured control over the tiny island of Goa on the west coast of the subcontinent. It soon blossomed into the headquarters of Portugal's mercantile enterprises in India and growing commercial empire in Asia. For the rest of the century the highly coveted goods of India were carried to Europe in the holds of Portuguese ships.

China. By the opening of the 16th century the Ming dynasty (1368–1644) had passed its prime. Already evident were those symptoms of political and social tension that had foreshadowed the decline and ultimate fall of preceding ruling houses. Especially noteworthy was the simmering dissatisfaction of the scholar-bureaucrat class, many of whose members still refused to reconcile themselves to the centralizing and at times despotic bent of the Ming. Equally galling to the bureaucratic elite was the rise to power and influence of overbearing eunuchs in the imperial government and court.

In the realm of foreign affairs, Ming China witnessed the appearance of many new problems during the 16th century. While the borders of the Chinese Empire had shrunk considerably during the earlier years of the dynasty, further advances by non-Chinese frontier peoples were generally arrested. More fateful were the activities of other "barbarians" in the long maritime border areas. Japanese pirates roamed Chinese waters and from time to time sacked coastal cities. Around 1513, Portuguese merchants started to arrive in Chinese ports from bases in India. They were the first in a continuous flow of Portuguese traders and missionaries who journeyed to the Middle Kingdom. The Spaniards, having hacked out bases in the not too distant Philippines, also undertook to establish trading relations with China. Both Portuguese and Spaniards strove to conduct missionary projects in China. A breakthrough was finally achieved by the Jesuit Matteo Ricci, who was permitted to enter mainland China in 1582.

In the 16th century, China experienced remarkable philosophical growth. The reinterpretation and reconceptualization of Confucianism, which had been given such impetus by Chu Hsi in the 12th century, found a peerless exponent in Wang Yang-ming (Wang Shou-jen). Inveighing against the rigidities of Confucian orthodoxy and exalting the individual and the dignity of man, he and his followers breathed new life into Chinese philosophical thought. The ideas of Wang Yang-ming and his disciples were also to exert a powerful influence upon Japanese thinkers of the 17th and 18th centuries.

Japan. The history of Japan during the 16th century comes within the Age of the Country at War (*Sengoku Jidai*). Following the Onin War (1467–1477), which attested to the passing of the manor system and the emergence of a new phase in the evolution of Japanese feudalism, strife wracked the entire archipelago for seemingly endless years. The consequence was the abject decline of the Ashikaga shogunate, the rise of a new type of territorial magnate—the daimyo—and, during the later years of *Sengoku Jidai*, the appearance of unprecedentedly powerful military barons—daimyo who successively contended for dominance of the Japanese islands. The turbulence of the era crested during the careers of three mighty warriors: Oda Nobunaga, Toyotomi Hideyoshi, and Tokugawa Ieyasu.

During his brief, violent life, Nobunaga established his supremacy in the area around the imperial capital, Kyoto, and in 1573 stripped the last Ashikaga shogun of his remaining powers, though not his title. Moreover, he smashed the military power of the Buddhist monasteries. After

Painting from *Khamsa*, a book by the Persian poet Nizami, written about 1525. The scene is a schoolroom.

Mosque of Suleiman the Magnificent, designed by the Ottoman architect Sinan, is still Istanbul's chief mosque.

Nobunga's death in 1582, Hideyoshi, the "Napoleon of Japan," reduced the entire archipelago to his control. Hoping to create an overseas empire, he sought to invade the Chinese Empire, but his armies were halted in adjoining Korea in two bloody campaigns (1592–1593 and 1597–1598). Following Hideyoshi's death in 1598, Ieyasu made a successful bid for mastery of Japan. The Battle of Sekigahara (1600) established his political and military hegemony.

The horizons of the Japanese people expanded tremendously during the 16th century. Their seamen plied the waters of East Asia in search of trade and ventured as far as Southeast Asia. Prominent among these seafarers were the Wako, samurai pirates who preyed on shipping and coastal cities west and south of Japan. During these years Europeans, notably the Portuguese, began to arrive in Japan to carry on trade and missionary activity.

Enlarged sources of wealth, derived from war, trade, and taxes, enabled daimyo and city merchants to live in great luxury and to patronize the arts. The new opulence characterized the Azuchi-Momoyama period, which is named after the magnificent but no longer existing castles built by Nobunaga and Hideyoshi. Among the artistic splendors of the age, the wall paintings and screens of the Kano school are outstanding.

Korea. The Yi dynasty, founded in 1392, had exhausted much of its innovative energies by the early years of the 16th century. During the reign (1506–1544) of Chungjong, concerted efforts were made to reestablish stability and promote reform, but with little lasting success. Before long, Korea was once again wracked by factional strife and disorder.

During the closing years of the century the country was devastated by the invasions of the Japanese warrior Toyotomi Hideyoshi. But Korea escaped foreign conquest, thanks to the intervention of Ming China and the opposition raised by the Korean Admiral Yi Sun-sin.

Siberia. A new era in the history of northern Asia opened in 1581 when the Cossack Yermak Timofeyev and a small band of his followers moved eastward across the Ural Mountains. Overwhelming the Tatar khanate of Sibir, they paved the way for an influx of trappers, merchants, and adventurers attracted by the riches of the fur trade. In the next 60 years the Russians raced across Siberia to the Pacific in search of new sources of pelts.

Southeast Asia. The 16th century was an age of widespread instability and strife in Southeast Asia. Burma, disunited for several centuries, was briefly welded together by the able Bayinnaung (reigned 1551–1581) of the Toungoo dynasty. The impact of Burmese military power was felt in neighboring Siam, then under the domination of the Thai state of Ayuthia (Ayutthaya). On at least two occasions Ayuthia was overwhelmed by Burmese invaders and reduced to vassalage. But in 1587 it recovered its independence under the leadership of Naresuen, who ascended the throne three years later. Vietnam was torn by a bloody struggle for power during most of the 16th century. The contenders were the Mac and Trinh families, the latter acting in behalf of weak kings of the Later Le dynasty. The Trinh triumphed in 1592 but were soon to be challenged by new rivals, the Nguyen.

In the island world of Southeast Asia momentous political and cultural shifts occurred. The Indonesian empire of Majapahit, with its center of power in eastern Java, continued to decline and soon disappeared. At the same time Islam, which had already penetrated Sumatra and the Malacca region of Malaya, began to inch steadily eastward into the Indonesian archipelago. Its spread was encouraged by local princes as an expression of protest and opposition to the domination of the rulers of older Hindu-Buddhist kingdoms. Internecine wars continued throughout the remainder of the century.

This internal upheaval was compounded by the arrival of a new power, the Portuguese, in the opening years of the century. In search of the source of the fabled spices of the East, they quickly established trading bases, reinforced by naval power, in Java and the Moluccas. The riches of the Indies transformed tiny Portugal into a major European state.

The successes of the Portuguese in Indonesia were rivaled by those of the Spaniards in the Philippines. Though Magellan had reached the islands in the early 16th century, it was not until 1565 that the Spaniards, sailing from the New World, were able to secure a permanent foothold in the archipelago. Slowly extending their power, they secured control of the strategic port of Manila in 1571. Not many years later, their galleons opened a new trade route to the West, in which the bullion of the Americas was exchanged for the wealth of the East. Soon after they were established in the Philippines, the Spaniards began to proselytize Christianity. As a result, the majority of Filipinos ultimately were converted to that faith.

The Pacific. Western exploration of the Pacific Ocean was initiated by the Spaniards in the early 16th century. After Magellan's westward crossing to the Philippines in 1520–1521, Spanish navigators such as López de Villalobos, López de Legazpi, Urdaneta, and Mendaña de Neyra conducted epochal voyages that demonstrated the immensity of the Pacific world. Portuguese navigators also participated in the exploration of the Pacific. Approaching from the Indian Ocean, they ventured into the waters to the southeast of Indonesia.

In 1578–1580, Francis Drake made the first British entry into the Pacific. Like the Spaniards and Portuguese, he was on the lookout for the rumored Terra Australis Incognita—the "unknown southern land," which was supposed to stretch to the South Pole, balancing Europe and Asia.

HYMAN KUBLIN, *Brooklyn College*

3. Subsaharan Africa

For most people of Subsaharan Africa the 16th century was the uneventful continuation of the bucolic life that African communities had followed for thousands of years. But the century also ended an era for some and began one for others.

The essential Africa lay in the countryside, with the farmer, cattleman, nomad, and hunter. Everywhere the African lived simply in small groups, his loyalties bound up in family ties, his government largely limited to village matters, and his routine shaped by the seasons of seedtime, growth, and harvest. Superimposed on this simple world were several events that at times gathered the common man into their vortex, yet only infrequently brought lasting changes to his life.

The Sudan. In the Western Sudan a column of Moroccan soldiers that had crossed the Sahara routed the forces of the Songhai empire in 1591, thereby shattering that powerful state, which had stood astride the Niger River for 150 years. This event seriously reduced both the influence of Islam in the region and the volume of trans-Saharan trade for two centuries. But to the east, near Lake Chad, Islam and trade continued to prosper. Ancient Kanem-Bornu reached the height of its authority under its brilliant *mai*, or ruler, Idris Alooma (reigned 1571–1603), while the neighboring states of Hausaland produced energetic rulers sympathetic to Islam.

Portuguese Penetration. Elsewhere in Africa a number of changes resulted from Portuguese imperialism. Having sailed around the continent in the 15th century, Portugal's mariners now proceeded to occupy and control African territory. Although held at bay on the Gold Coast and rebuffed by Benin, they nonetheless gained an influential position in the kingdom of Kongo, laid the groundwork for an ill-fated relationship with Ethiopia, and forcibly occupied the coastal emporia of East Africa.

By 1550 a half century of Portuguese slave trading and political interference in Kongo had reduced that powerful state to a wasted collection of warring factions. In East Africa, Portuguese conquest of the trading states from Sofala and Kilwa northward to Mombasa starved what had been a prosperous commercial network. Paradoxically, it also stifled what the Portuguese had sought to capture—the trade in gold with the interior kingdom of Mwene Mutapa (Monomotapa). Farther north, in 1541, Portuguese musketeers helped defend Christian Ethiopia against a Muslim invasion, setting the stage for Ethiopia's temporary conversion to Roman orthodoxy. A century later, the excessive zeal of Jesuit missionaries was to result in a revolt against them and the Ethiopian king who supported them.

South and East Africa. Deep in the interior beyond the influence of outsiders, two great popula-

J. ALLAN CASH, FROM RAPHO GUILLUMETTE

Fatehpur Sikri, near Agra, India, was Emperor Akbar's capital for 15 years. Mosque is entered from courtyard.

tion movements continued to unfold. One involved Bantu peoples; the other, Nilotic peoples.

The vast Bantu dispersion spilled southward, its vanguard probably reaching the Transkei in South Africa during the 16th century or earlier, having already crossed the Limpopo River to occupy the northern Transvaal. In the 16th century two crosscurrents emerged within the Bantu migration, both including cannibalism as well as conquest. In the west, the Jaga people suddenly erupted in mid-century in a military movement that swept up the Kongo state and lesser principalities. In East Africa, a similar migration by the Zimba ravaged the coast, virtually wiping out Kilwa and devastating Mombasa. What transformed the Jaga and Zimba into cannibalistic marauders remains a mystery, although population pressures may have been the catalyst.

The Nilotes, originating along the upper Nile, migrated southward over hundreds of years to interpenetrate with the Bantu in territories east and west of Lake Victoria. To the east, in the Great Rift Valley, the Nilotes were exemplified by proud pastoralists, such as the Nandi and Masai. West of Lake Victoria, Nilotes succeeded in founding a number of kingdoms, most notably Bunyoro, which dominated the area northwest of Lake Victoria during the 16th century.

ROBERT W. JULY, *Author of "A History of the African People"*

4. The Americas

The landfall of Columbus in 1492 added a new dimension to European development. This was expanded when Portugal's Vasco da Gama returned in 1499 from a successful voyage by sea to India. There was a flurry of interest in the discoveries on the part of powers other than Spain and Portugal—the Cabot voyages for England, the later one of Verrazzano for France. But during most of the 16th century the British and French were too much engrossed in domestic problems to do more than envy the good fortune

865

—— EVENTS OF THE SIXTEENTH CENTURY ——

1501—Safavid dynasty established in Iran (Persia).
1504—First dated edition of Amerigo Vespucci's printed letter *Mundus novus*, which established "New World" concept.
1507—First use of the name "America," on map drawn by Martin Waldseemüller.
1509—Henry VIII king of England (to 1547).
1509—Sebastian Cabot discovered Hudson Bay.
1511—Portuguese took Malayan port of Malacca, center of East Indian spice trade.
1513—Balboa crossed Panama, reached Pacific Ocean.
1513—Machiavelli wrote *The Prince.*
1515—Francis I king of France (to 1547).
1516—Accession of Habsburg to Spanish throne as Charles I (to 1556).
1517—Luther launched Protestant Reformation with 95 theses on indulgences.
1517—Turks conquered Egypt.
1519—Charles I of Spain elected Holy Roman Emperor as Charles V (to 1556).
1519—Cortés began Spanish conquest of Mexico.
1519—Death of Leonardo da Vinci.
1520—Suleiman I the Magnificent, Ottoman sultan (to 1566).
1520—Henry VIII and Francis I met on Field of Cloth of Gold to end Anglo-French hostility.
1522—First circumnavigation of the globe, begun by Magellan in 1519, completed by del Cano.
1524—Verrazzano explored Atlantic coast of North America for France.
1526—Babur defeated Delhi sultan at Panipat and established Mughul dynasty at Delhi.
1527—Rome sacked by Charles V's forces.
1529—Turks unsuccessfully besieged Vienna.
1532—Portuguese established permanent European settlement in Brazil, at São Vicente.
1533—Ivan IV the Terrible, began reign in Russia (to 1584).
1534—Act of Supremacy styled Henry VIII "Supreme Head in earth of the Church of England."
1535—Pizarro captured Inca capital, Cuzco, and founded Lima as Spanish capital of Peru.
1535—Cartier discovered St. Lawrence River.
1539—De Soto began exploration of southeastern United States for Spain (to 1542).
1540—Jesuit Order approved by Pope Paul III.
1540—Coronado began exploration of northern Mexico and U. S. Southwest for Spain (to 1542).
1541—Calvin established theocratic government in Geneva.
1542—St. Francis Xavier began mission to the East.
1543—Publication of Copernicus' *Revolutions of the Heavenly Orbs* and Vesalius' *Structure of the Human Body*: cornerstones of modern astronomy and anatomy.
1545—Council of Trent (to 1563) instituted reforms in Roman Catholic Church.
1555—Peace of Augsburg temporarily settled Catholic-Protestant conflict in Germany.
1556—Akbar, Mughul emperor in India (to 1605).
1556—Charles V resigned the imperial and Spanish crowns. Philip II king of Spain (to 1598).
1564—Death of Michelangelo: birth of Shakespeare.
1565—St. Augustine, Fla., oldest U. S. city, founded by Spaniards.
1568—Oda Nobunaga began process of unification of the feudatories of Japan.
1571—Turkish fleet defeated at Battle of Lepanto.
1571—Spaniards gained control of Manila.
1571—Idris Alooma, *mai* (ruler) of Kanem-Bornu in West Africa (to 1603).
1572—Massacre of French Protestants on St. Bartholomew's Day (August 24).
1580—Portugal came under Spanish rule (to 1640).
1580—Drake completed first British circumnavigation of the globe.
1580—Permanent foundation of Buenos Aires.
1581—United Provinces of the Netherlands declared independence from Spain.
1581—Russians began conquest of Siberia.
1582—Pope Gregory XIII established Gregorian Calendar (October 5/15).
1582—Oda Nobunaga assassinated; succeeded by Toyotomi Hideyoshi.
1582—Matteo Ricci began Jesuit mission in China.
1587—Kilwa, great trading center on East African coast, destroyed by the Zimba.
1588—Defeat of Spanish Armada by British.
1589—Henry IV king of France (to 1610); establishment of Bourbon dynasty.
1591—Moroccan force shattered power of the Songhai Empire of the Western Sudan.
1598—Edict of Nantes granted rights to Huguenots, ending Wars of Religion in France (from 1562).
1600—Battle of Sekigahara gave Tokugawa Ieyasu political and military hegemony in Japan.
1600—East India Company founded in London.

of the Spaniards and Portuguese. Except on the oceans, the Iberian powers were left largely undisturbed to conquer, explore, and exploit their lands overseas as defined by the Treaty of Tordesillas (1494). The treaty, which was based on prior discoveries, gave Spain most of the Americas and Portugal most of the East, all of Africa, and the eastern bulge of Brazil.

Spanish and Portuguese America. Spain, with priority of American opportunity, had lands bountifully endowed with precious-metal wealth—Mexico, Peru, and Colombia. Spain's lands proved capable of producing such widely marketable exotic commodities as tobacco and sugar and were ideal as well for transplanted Old World grains, fruits, and livestock. The numerous Indians provided a ready labor force, and because so many of them were farmers, they made it unnecessary for Spaniards overseas to depend on the homeland for basic sustenance. When the Indian populations declined, Spain was able to supplement the overseas labor force with hands from Africa. In addition, the home population was still fired by recent triumphs over the Moors and was eager for further expansion. Spain quickly put all these elements of good fortune to work and built an American empire.

Portugal's men and interests went primarily to the East. As a result, the potential of Brazil was not really discovered until the next century.

Long before the end of the 16th century most Spaniards who had gone to the Americas with a get-rich-quick-and-return idea had elected to stay, and others had come to participate in opportunities that the mother country would never be able to offer. The white men, everywhere in the minority, were aggressive and demanding. Little Spains dotted the New World. Capitals, viceregal and provincial, boomed, some achieving a magnificence that Spain's own cities could only envy. Mexico City and Lima even had their universities. Lesser cities included Guadalajara (in Mexico), Bogotá, Potosí (in Bolivia, then called Upper Peru), Santiago de Chile, and in the West Indies, Havana, Santo Domingo, and San Juan.

Almost from the beginning the long shadow of Spanish absolutism stretched across the Atlantic and had its viceroys in New Spain (Mexico) and Peru, captains-general and governors in the provinces, alcaldes and corregidores in the towns. Vestiges of self-government, inherited from medieval Spain, were snuffed out. The far-off yet fearsome crown regulated American affairs, political, social, economic, and even religious. It formulated all rules of governance and policy, imposed taxes and imposts, granted lands and the Indians upon them, screened Spaniards who thought to migrate, and contrived to exclude all foreigners, whatever their intent. Absolutism, paternalism, monopoly, and exclusivism were the guiding principles of the home authority, while the "three G's" (gold, glory, Gospel) impelled the colonials.

Church and state, long partners at home, worked in even closer union in America. The crown was dependent on the churchmen to help it fulfill its promises to the popes to effect the conversion of new subjects. Franciscans, Dominicans, Jesuits, and others served the Spaniards and the Indians on Spanish lands. Gradually the parish clergy grew numerous enough so that friars and padres could be released to carry the Christian message to the Indians on the ever-expanding frontiers.

Balboa stands above the waters of the Pacific Ocean, which he discovered on Sept. 25, 1513, later taking possession of it for Spain.

Challenges to Iberian Ascendancy. In the 16th century no rivals of the Iberian powers succeeded in planting colonies in the New World. The French tried three times—in the far north, in Florida, and in Brazil. The British were unsuccessful in Newfoundland and on the Carolina coast. The best that rivals could do was to harass the sealanes and raid the Caribbean and occasionally the Pacific coasts. Until Spain became disastrously overextended in Europe, as Philip II strove to keep all Europe Catholic, and until the English turned back Philip's "Invincible Armada," Spain's predominance, supported largely by American treasure, remained formidable on both sides of the Atlantic.

As the century closed, times were changing. Spain had created determined enemies. The English and Dutch were seasoning nationalist ambitions with a large dash of religious hatred, and Bourbon France was determined to redress the reverses of the Valois decades. Spain had posted an impressive record of achievement. The entire New World, however, was more than her too few millions could master.

JOHN FRANCIS BANNON
Saint Louis University

Bibliography

Allen, John W., *History of Political Thought in the Sixteenth Century,* 3d ed. (Barnes & Noble 1958).

Aston, Trevor H., ed., *Crisis in Europe, 1560–1660* (Basic Bks. 1965).

Balandier, Georges, *Daily Life in the Kingdom of the Kongo* (Pantheon Bks. 1968).

Bannon, John F., *History of the Americas,* 2d ed., vol. 1: *The Colonial Americas* (McGraw 1963).

Boas, Marie, *The Scientific Renaissance, 1450–1630* (Harper 1962).

Boxer, Charles R., *The Portuguese Seaborne Empire, 1415–1825* (Knopf 1970).

Braudel, Fernand, *Civilisation matérielle et capitalisme, XVᵉ–XVIIIᵉ siècles* (1967).

Bronowski, Jacob, *The Western Intellectual Tradition: From Leonardo to Hegel* (Harper 1960).

Butterfield, Herbert, *The Origins of Modern Science, 1300–1800,* rev. ed. (Collier Bks. 1962).

Cambridge University Press Syndics, *The New Cambridge Modern History:* vol. 1, *The Renaissance, 1493–1520,* ed. by G. R. Potter (1957); vol. 2, *The Reformation, 1520–1559,* ed. by G. R. Elton (1958); vol. 3, *The Counter-Reformation and Price Revolution, 1559–1610,* ed. by R. B. Wernham (1968).

Castiglione, Baldassare, *The Book of the Courtier* (many editions), first published in 1528.

Chabod, Federico, *Machiavelli and the Renaissance* (Harvard Univ. Press 1958).

Chastel, André, *The Age of Humanism: Europe, 1480–1530* (McGraw 1963).

Chastel, André, *The Crisis of the Renaissance: 1520–1600* (Skira 1968).

Daniel-Rops, Henri, *The Catholic Reformation* (Dutton 1962).

Davidson, Basil, *Black Mother: The Years of the African Slave Trade* (Little 1961).

Defourneaux, Mercelin, *Daily Life in Spain in the Golden Age* (Praeger 1971).

Dickens, Arthur G., *The Counter Reformation* (Harper 1969).

Dickens, Arthur G., *Reformation and Society in Sixteenth-Century Europe* (Harper 1966).

Dunn, Richard S., *The Age of Religious Wars, 1559–1689* (Norton 1970).

Durant, Will, *The Reformation* (Simon & Schuster 1957).

Durant, Will, *The Renaissance: A History of Civilization in Italy from 1304 to 1576* (Simon & Schuster 1953).

Elton, Geoffrey P., *Reformation Europe, 1517–1559* (Meridian Bks. 1964).

Gibson, Charles, *Spain in America* (Harper 1966).

Goodrich, Luther C., *A Short History of the Chinese People,* 3d ed. (Harper 1953).

Hall, Daniel, *A History of South-East Asia,* 3d ed. (St. Martins 1968).

Haring, Clarence H., *The Spanish Empire in America* (Oxford 1947).

Huizinga, Johan, *Erasmus* (Scribner 1924).

Jeannin, Pierre, *Merchants of the Sixteenth Century* (Harper 1971).

July, Robert W., *A History of the African People* (Scribner 1970).

Kirkpatrick, Frederick A., *The Spanish Conquistadores,* 2d ed. (Barnes & Noble 1967).

Koenigsberger, Helmut G., and Mosse, G. L., *Europe in the Sixteenth Century* (Longmans, Ltd. 1968).

Lach, Donald F., *Asia in the Making of Europe,* vol. 1 (Univ. of Chicago Press 1965).

Machiavelli, Niccolò, *The Prince* (many editions).

McNeill, William H., *A World History,* 2d ed. (Oxford 1971).

Mattingly, Garrett, *Armada* (Houghton 1959).

Mattingly, Garrett, *Renaissance Diplomacy* (Houghton 1955).

Merriman, Roger B., *Suleiman the Magnificent* (Cooper Square 1966).

More, Thomas, *Utopia* (many editions).

Morison, Samuel E., *The European Discovery of America* (Oxford 1971).

Nowell, Charles E., *The Great Discoveries and the First Colonial Empires* (Cornell Univ. Press 1954).

Penrose, Boies, *Travel and Discovery in the Renaissance* (Harvard Univ. Press 1952).

Rice, Eugene F., Jr., *The Foundation of Early Modern Europe, 1460–1559* (Norton 1970).

Robertson, Alec, and Stevens, D. W., *The Pelican History of Music,* vol. 2: *Renaissance and Baroque* (Penguin 1964).

Sansom, George, *A History of Japan, 1334–1615* (Stanford Univ. Press 1961).

Smith, Lacey B., *The Horizon Book of the Elizabethan World* (Am. Heritage 1967).

Spear, Percival, *India: A Modern History* (Univ. of Mich. Press 1961).

Sykes, Percy M., *History of Persia,* 3d ed., vol. 2 (1930; reprint, Barnes & Noble 1969).

Emperor Justinian led the Eastern Roman Empire to a glorious height in the 6th century. He is shown here in a mosaic in the choir of the Basilica of San Vitale, in Ravenna, Italy.

SIXTH CENTURY. The 6th century European-Mediterranean world was divided into three parts: the Eastern Roman, or Byzantine, Empire; the fragments of the Western Roman Empire, under Germanic rule; and the barbarian regions beyond the Rhine-Danube frontier of Roman civilization. The barbarian regions, inhabited mainly by nomadic peoples, extended all the way across Asia to the Great Wall of China.

East of the Byzantine Empire lay the civilizations of the ancient East: Iran, united under the Sassanian dynasty; India, completely disunited after the final disintegration of the Gupta empire; and China, united at the end of the century after 350 years of political fragmentation. An outer belt of civilized societies extended from northeastern Africa and Arabia to Southeast Asia and Japan.

In the then unknown Americas there were centers of civilization in Mexico, Central America, and the Andes of South America. Chronological evidence for a century-by-century discussion of the Mayan and other pre-Columbian societies is lacking. For a summary of early developments in the Western Hemisphere, see INDIANS, AMERICAN.

1. The European-Mediterranean World

The continuing existence and unusual vigor of the Eastern Roman Empire indicate the inaccuracy of the traditional concept that in 476 the Roman Empire fell. Edward Gibbon was accurate in placing the final fall of the Roman Empire in 1453, with the Turkish conquest of Constantinople.

THE BYZANTINE EAST

Reign of Justinian. The 6th century was a glorious period for the Eastern Empire. The central figure in this renaissance was Emperor Justinian I. From his accession in 527 until his death in 565 he labored successfully to maintain internal unity and to expand imperial frontiers. Effectively assisted by the general Belisarius, the jurist Tribonian, the financial expert John of Cappodocia, and his beloved Empress Theodora (died 548), the Emperor brought the Eastern Empire to a new magnificence.

Great buildings were erected, the most famous being the church of Hagia Sophia (Holy Wisdom). Designed by Anthemius of Tralles and Isidorus of Miletus, this building was a miracle of architectural genius and decorative splendor. Less spectacular was Justinian's legislative work—the *Corpus Juris Civilis*, or "Body of Law," also known as the Code of Justinian. It consisted of the *Codex* proper, a condensation of previous laws; the *Novellae*, or new laws; the *Digest*, or *Pandects*, judicial opinions; and the *Institutes*, a textbook of law. So effective was this all-embracing work that it became the authoritative handbook of civil law in both East and West.

Life in the Eastern Empire. Justinian's economic policies were vigorous but not very successful. Persian competition in Far Eastern trade was met by developing routes via the Black and Red seas. To bolster the silk industry, silkworms were imported. Business generally prospered, especially in luxury goods. On the other hand, imperial monopolies and controls hampered expansion. The chief beneficiaries of the apparent wealth of the empire seem to have been the court, the aristocrats, and the bureaucrats. Probably Justinian's greatest financial mistake was over-spending. On the lower levels, the lot of the populace was hard. There was grinding serfdom on the rural villas, poverty and disease in the cities.

At Constantinople, however, the populace shared the imperial luxury in two places: Hagia Sophia and the Hippodrome. Theirs, as well as Justinian's, was the spiritual exaltation of the airy dome of Hagia Sophia, "suspended by golden chains from Heaven," with "angels descending from on high to assist in the service." The Hippodrome saw all sorts of secular entertainment, especially chariot races. Organized groups, such as the "Greens" and the "Blues," followed with emotional frenzy the colors of their favorite charioteers. They even maintained permanent organizations, which took on a political aspect.

The most critical point in Justinian's career came in 532 when the Hippodrome groups burst into furious revolt, even setting up a rival emperor. Justinian would have abdicated had not Theodora shamed him and his officials into one last effort. Imperial prestige was restored, and when Theodora died her appreciative husband paid her memory the lasting tribute of never remarrying. This aspect of Theodora's character balances the scandalous tales concerning her cruelty, vanity, immoralities, and unbridled autocracy, as recounted by the court historian, Procopius. She was a determined woman who followed her convictions or prejudices. For ex-

Empress Theodora, Justinian's beloved wife, and her retinue. She was one of her husband's most trusted advisers. This mosaic, too, is in the Basilica of San Vitale in Ravenna, Italy.

ample, she sponsored the Monophysite sect, thus contributing to religious disunity. On the other hand, she aided unfortunate prostitutes.

More objective was Procopius' account of Justinian's wars and of the emperor's decision to appease the Persians along the Euphrates in order to reconquer Vandal Africa, Visigothic Spain, and Ostrogothic Italy. The problem of Persia was left to trouble his successors, along with the later menace of Arab expansion. By the end of the century the empire had powerful rivals on all frontiers, even in Italy, where Belisarius' conquests had fallen before the invading Lombards.

THE FRAGMENTED WEST

The British scholar Helen Waddell once wrote that 10th century Western civilization had "a bad name." So also had the 6th. But viewing the 6th century objectively, one finds good with bad. It was, for example, an age of reconstruction following a century of imperial disintegration and barbarian migrations. The Roman Empire of the West was no more, but its crumbling structure had been taken over by sturdy Germanic rulers. The result was a rough type of government characterized more by personal forcefulness than legality. Ruggedness had replaced bureaucracy. Outbursts of brutality on the part of rulers such as Clovis the Frank and Theodoric the Ostrogoth exemplify the worst in the new type of government. On the other hand, Theodoric's historic title "the Civilizer" and his restoration of order and prosperity to troubled Italy illustrate the possible blessings of vigorous Germanic rule.

Since the West comprised a number of independent kingdoms it may best be described by regions, specifically those loosely unified lands now known as Italy, Tunisia and Algeria, Spain, France, England, and Germany.

Italy. Italy was the last portion of the Western Empire to fall from the ineffective control of puppet emperors into the hands of Germanic invaders. Here was exemplified about the worst of disorder and retrogression in the 6th century West. For a time, however, after the 5th century ordeal of imperial anarchy, Italy enjoyed a restoration of peaceful civilized life under Theodoric the Great.

The Ostrogothic Kingdom. Theodoric established the Ostrogothic kingdom of Italy in 493, and ruled it much like a late Roman emperor of the more enlightened sort. To be sure, his Germanic warriors were an army of occupation that maintained order authoritatively, but in the civil service he employed experienced Romans such as Boethius, Symmachus, and Cassiodorus. Theodoric built a Roman-styled palace and mausoleum. He appreciated and encouraged Greco-Roman culture, having spent his earlier years in Constantinople as a guest-hostage of the emperor. He encouraged agriculture and industry, and the orderly peacefulness of his regime enabled Italy to recover much of the prosperity that had waned under the last emperors. It is said that for the first time in centuries Italy produced sufficient grain to export. Apparently, Theodoric's Italy experienced a revival of many aspects of earlier Roman civilization. There was, however, bitter religious strife, chiefly between the Arian Ostrogoths and the native Roman Athanasians, or orthodox Catholics. This discord between Christians constituted the weakest factor in his regime.

Eventually, Christian clerics and aristocratic Romans, longing for an orthodox, non-Germanic regime, plotted with Constantinople for reunion with the empire. Among those charged with treason were two of Theodoric's hitherto trusted ministers, Boethius and Symmachus. Theodoric struck hard. Both were cruelly executed—Boethius after a long imprisonment, during which he consoled himself by writing a noble work, *The Consolation of Philosophy.* Boethius also wrote theological treatises, and he is enrolled among the saints of the Roman Catholic Church.

Cassiodorus, who had not been involved, continued as the chief minister of state, even after Theodoric's death. Eventually he retired to his estates in the south to apply his ideals of education. There he established the Vivarium, a center where monks copied and studied not only religious works, but also the Greco-Roman classics. For example, in the realm of medicine, he advised those who could not read Greek to use the Latin translations of such writers as Dioscorides Pedanius, Galen, and Hippocrates. He warned against relying solely on human treatment: "Since medicine was created by God, . . . turn to Him." Such were the ideals of this new-style, 6th century university: the integration of Christian and pagan, of spiritual and rational. Unfortunately Cassiodorus' Italy was incapable of adopting such a reasonable compromise.

At Monte Cassino, Benedict of Nursia had wider success as the founder of a strictly religious institution for training Christians to serve the church singleheartedly. Their activities were confined to religious worship, religious reading, and labor in the Lord's field or vineyard. In desolate, ravaged Italy this simple program was destined to win the allegiance of religious men. Later, Benedictine monasticism captured the imagination of the entire West, its monasteries serving as centers of dynamic Christianity, religiously controlled education, charity, progressive agriculture, and peaceful community life.

Theodoric died in 526 leaving his daughter as regent of a small Germanic-Roman empire comprising Italy and the adjoining regions of the Adriatic and of southeastern France. Soon strife developed between the queen regent and the Gothic leaders, and between Gothic Italy and Constantinople. In 535, Emperor Justinian, having conquered Vandal North Africa, attacked Italy. The Ostrogoths fought stubbornly but vainly for 20 years against the Eastern armies. By mid-century the victors were in possession of a war-ravaged Italy that soon fell into the hands of a new band of migrant Germans, the barbaric Lombards. This new conquest of the Po Valley and the peninsula prostrated Italy.

Gregory the Great.

The future Pope Gregory I the Great (reigned 590–604) was gaining recognition as an able clerical administrator during this truly dark age of Italian history. It is against this somber background that Gregory emerges as a heroic figure. Born into a wealthy Roman family, well educated in both religious and secular learning, he escaped for a time from a hopeless world through monasticism. Turning the family estates into monasteries, he devoted himself so earnestly to ascetic practices that his health was impaired. Once, so the story goes, on seeing some English captives in the slave market he insisted that they were "angels, not Angles" and that he must go as a missionary to convert their fellow countrymen. The church had other plans for intelligent administrators, and he performed notable services for the pope, serving for years as envoy at Constantinople.

In 590, when Gregory became pope, a plague was raging in Rome. It is recorded that, as a result of expiatory processions ordered by Gregory, the plague ceased. Because the archangel Michael was seen above the tomb of Hadrian sheathing his sword of punishment, the name Castel Sant'-Angelo was given to the structure. Gregory's spiritual leadership was based on just such principles of implicit faith. He preached and wrote about miracles. His writings—such as the *Dialogues, Moralia,* and *Pastoral Care*—contain much that evokes charges of barbaric ignorance and medieval superstition from rational-minded moderns. Be that as it may, Gregory was neither a barbarian nor an ignoramus. He used most effectively the religious beliefs of his day for the strengthening of the church in its struggle for Christian unity, in Italy and elsewhere.

As head of the papal organization he showed a diplomatic finesse, a practical mindedness, and an invincible courage that justify his title "the Great." Asserting, as "Servant of the Servants of God," the supreme ecclesiastical authority of the successors of St. Peter, he extended the influence of the papacy through Italy and adjoining regions. He negotiated with Byzantine emperors, with Frankish kings, and with lesser rulers. With more or less success, he claimed authority over all Christian clergymen. Thus he laid the foundations for Roman Catholic unity. He sent Augustine to Kent on the mission that eventually made all England Roman Catholic. He vigorously supported Benedictine monasticism and Trinitarian Christianity in all parts of the West.

Practical mindedness of a different order characterized his letters concerning the administration of the papal estates in Italy and adjacent lands. Managers of estates were given detailed instructions on the most profitable handling of crops and livestock. Corrupt officials were threatened with severe punishment for mistreating the poor, widows, orphans, and serfs. Thus efficient agriculture and social justice were combined under the aegis of the papacy.

All in all, this one hardworking man seems to have done more than any other leader of the century to hold back the forces of anarchy that threatened to engulf Italy. Like his great 5th century predecessor Pope Leo I the Great, he stepped into the breach from which most men had fled. If there had been more Theodorics and Gregories, Italy might have reforged Roman, Germanic, and Christian forces into a more constructive civilization than that of the early Middle Ages.

North Africa.

What are now Tunisia and Algeria had been occupied by the Germanic Vandals under Gaiseric (Genseric) early in the 5th century. In the 6th century, enervated by Roman civilization, they were easily conquered by Emperor Justinian's "armada" (533–534). Their territory, along with Sicily, became part of the revived Roman Empire of the East, only to fall into the hands of the Arabs in subsequent centuries.

Spain.

Spain was ruled by Visigoths for about three centuries from the early 5th to early 8th century. The most orderly and unified part of this era was the 6th century. Gothic conquerors and Roman subjects had become unified in language, law, and customs. Common laws, eventually codified in the *Liber Iudiciorum* or *Fuero Juzgo* (654), were gradually replacing the separate Gothic and Roman codes. Intermarriage had accustomed the Goths to the native people's habits and language—a modified Latin, later to become Spanish.

As in Ostrogothic Italy, the Arian faith of the conquerors was a disturbing factor. But in 589 King Reccared formally adopted Trinitarian Catholicism. This act eliminated a pretext for rebellion on the part of malcontents and their Frankish partners in intrigue against the Visigothic regime.

France.

The Franks, like the Lombards, gave their name to the Roman regions that they occupied. From the lower Rhine Valley, late in the 5th century, two Frankish tribal federations, the Salians and the Ripuarians, had moved into the undefended Roman provinces of northern Gaul. In 486, Clovis I, chief of the Salians, defeated the last of the imperial generals at Soissons and gained control of the Seine Valley. Soon the Ripuarians and Alamanni of the middle Rhine were annexed to his expanding kingdom. Before Clovis' death he was master of most of France and was ruling autocratically, with an occasional touch of Roman formalism. Like his fellow Franks who maintained close contacts with their northern homeland, Clovis was more barbaric than his contemporary Theodoric "the Civilizer" in Italy.

Hagia Sophia, which still dominates the city of Istanbul, Turkey, is considered the finest achievement of 6th century Byzantine architecture. It was built as a church, later converted to a mosque, and is now a museum.

However, Clovis was an astute diplomat who read the signs of the times so accurately that he adopted, at the outset, the Roman Catholic faith of his subject peoples. This factor contributed much to the success of his arms and the permanence of his rule, for he and his successors enjoyed the support of the Christian clergy. Bishop Gregory of Tours, in his *History of the Franks,* explained Clovis' political successes as follows: "God brought low his enemies ... because he walked before Him with an upright heart."

Aside from such obvious prejudices, Gregory's history is a valuable detailed record of Frankish civilization. It was a rugged pioneer life, with much brutal conquest and exploitation. The Frankish court was a melee of intrigue and violence. It was, nevertheless, a world of political and economic opportunity, in which an attractive serving maid could become queen and a serf's son could rise to the position of royal physician.

From the pen of another writer comes a contrasting picture of quiet Christian community life in the south. Venantius Fortunatus was an Italian law student who migrated to Frankland from Lombard Italy. At Poitiers he found life so idyllic that he settled there, to write poetry and eventually to become bishop. He became acquainted with a former Frankish queen, Radegunda, who with her daughter had deserted rough court life for the peace and contentment (both spiritual and physical) of a Poitevin convent. In classical metric verse, Fortunatus described his visits with Radegunda, expressing his appreciation of a delicious dinner or praising her deeds of charity. He also composed inspiring hymns, notably the *Vexilla regis prodeunt* and *Pange lingua,* for occasions such as the installation of a newly acquired relic. Comparing the works of Fortunatus with those of Gregory of Tours, it is obvious that the more orderly and civilized aspects of imperial civilization flourished longer in the south than in the more completely Germanized regions of north Frankland. Already two distinct "Frances" are discernible.

Political life by the end of the century was in a turmoil. Although Clovis' kingdom after his death had continued to expand to the Atlantic,

the Pyrenees, the Mediterranean, the Alps, and the Rhine, there was constant internal conflict. Whenever a king died leaving several heirs, the kingdom was divided among them. Successive reunions and redivisions continued through the century. By 600 two distinct kingdoms were emerging in the north: Neustria, or West Frankland, in the northwest (the Seine Valley); and Austrasia, or East Frankland, in the northeast (the Rhine-Moselle Valley). In the south, Burgundy and Aquitaine continued as semidependent satellites, with a more highly Roman type of civilization. The century ended in a welter of strife between the two northern kingdoms, with the ferocious Queen Brunhilde of Austrasia playing a prominent role in these struggles after the assassination of her husband, King Sigebert, in 575.

Thus Frankish life in the late 6th century presents a paradox: civil war and brutal murder in Brunhilde's Frankland, peace and Christian gentility in Radegunda's Frankland. Everywhere, it might be noted, women among the upper classes played a prominent role. Among the middle and lower classes there seems to have been little variation from a common level of economic struggle and social degradation. In monastic and urban centers some local industry flourished, and there was considerable small-scale foreign trade, chiefly in luxury goods and largely carried on by Syrians, Jews, and Italians. Agricultural life was hard. Serfdom gave a certain security to tenure but little incentive. Church services and festivals brought occasional social diversion to the rank and file of the populace.

Britain. Roman Britain had been conquered by tribes of Angles, Saxons, and Jutes from the Continent in the mid-5th century. From footholds along the eastern coast of the island they slowly expanded inland, and by the end of the 6th century they were in possession of southeast Scotland and most of the east and central parts of England. Their tribal kingdoms (named from north to south) were Bernicia and Deira (later Northumbria), Mercia, East Anglia, and Middle Anglia (including the Northfolk and Southfolk), Essex (East Saxons), Kent (Jutes), Sussex, and Wessex. Occasionally these kingdoms were partially united, as under Æthelbert (Ethelbert) I of Kent (reigned 560–616). Wales, Scotland, and Ireland likewise comprised numerous loosely united, and usually warring, tribal kingdoms. Their peoples were Celtic. Most prominent were the Scoti, who made up a majority of the inhabitants of Ireland and Scotland.

For these two regions a partially unifying force was Christianity, introduced into Ireland in the 5th century by missionaries from Gaul, of whom St. Patrick was the most famous. During the second half of the 6th century, monastic missionaries such as St. Columba extended their influence to Scotland, where the island of Iona on the west coast became famous for its rugged piety and scholarship, including some knowledge of Greek. Scotch-Irish monastic culture was more advanced than that of England, thanks to the absence of devastating invasions.

This monastic culture produced the greatest religious leader of the British Isles in the 6th century, St. Columbanus. In 591, with 12 disciples, he set forth to bring the light of true Christian civilization to Gaul. He established strict monastic discipline and learning at Luxeuil in Burgundy, but having incurred the hostility of the Frankish rulers and clergy, he was exiled. His career indicates, once more, the constructive vigor of medieval monasticism—its mobility, freedom of expression, and international pioneering spirit. Like the leaders already described, Columbanus exemplifies an age that was far from stagnant.

Five years after Columbanus left Ireland to reconvert France, Pope Gregory's monastic mission, under Augustine, left Italy to reconvert England. Landing in Kent, the 40 missionaries were welcomed by the Christian queen, a Frankish princess. The pagan king of Kent, Æthelbert, permitted them to occupy the old Christian Church of St. Martin at Canterbury, where they courageously commenced their task. Soon Augustine's Roman-Benedictine Christianity was accepted by the king and his people. Eventually this Christian community became the archbishopric of Canterbury. By the end of the 7th century the new Christian organization had won the rest of England from its adherence to British and Scotch-Irish Christianity.

THE BARBARIAN NORTH

The vast regions beyond the Rhine-Danube frontier were inhabited by savage or semisavage tribes, usually nomadic. Those in Scandinavia were hardy Germanic peasants and seafaring men, whose Norse descendants in later centuries were destined to conquer far and wide. The Germanic tribes east of the Rhine and north of the upper and middle Danube—Saxons, Thuringians, Bavarians, Lombards, and Gepids—threatened the security of the Franks in Gaul and the Ostrogoths in Italy. The Franks conquered the Thuringians and brought the Bavarians under their suzerainty, but the Lombards established their power in Italy after the defeat of the Ostrogoths by the Byzantines.

East of the Elbe and north of the lower Danube were innumerable Slavic peoples, who tended to migrate into the settled regions of the old Roman Empire in southeastern Europe. Farther east, in the steppelands of southern Russia from the lower Dnieper River to the Caspian Sea, were groups of Huns—remnants of the Asian nomads who had ravaged Europe under Attila in the 5th century and subsequently retreated eastward. The Huns continued to raid the European provinces of the Eastern Roman Empire, although they were no longer a formidable threat.

In the second half of the 6th century new Asian nomads appeared in Europe. These were the Avars, who subjugated the Huns, Slavs, and Gepids, established an empire reaching from the Elbe and Danube to the Volga, and came into conflict with the Franks and Byzantines.

SOCIETY AND CULTURE

In summary, the 6th century Byzantine Empire carried on the Roman imperial tradition of centralized bureaucracy and militarism. In the West the Germanic successors of the emperors ruled despotically over smaller states but with less bureaucratic machinery. Their despotism was checked somewhat by the independent-spirited nobility. In economics, likewise, the Byzantine East carried on the imperial tradition of urban industry and commerce. In the West ruralism was dominant. There the villa (later the manor) provided a self-sufficient way of life for both aristocratic owners and peasant serfs. The standard of living was lower than in the East. However, peasants of all regions were ground down to bare existence, and in the East the proletarian masses lived in abject poverty except for governmental doles.

Socially, all regions were caste ridden, with imperial aristocrats dominant in the East and Germanic chieftains in the West. The cosmopolitan East had a flourishing middle class of merchants and lesser bureaucrats. The West had no proletariat which was comparable to that of the East.

Christianity gave the masses their chief gleam of hope. It provided release, inspiration, and social enjoyment. Church services were dramatic. Religious festivals were an occasion for both spiritual and social pleasure. The church also provided the chief impulses for literature and art. Immense structures such as Hagia Sophia in Constantinople, and small substantial chapels throughout the West, reflect the power of religion in human life as well as the regional variations in ecclesiastical architecture. Sculpture, mosaic, painting and the minor arts were similarly inspired and dominated by the church. There were splendid mosaics at Constantinople and Ravenna. Reliquaries and crucifixes were produced everywhere. The few extant manuscripts exemplify not only the primitive efforts of Westerners as compared with the finer work of Easterners, but also the devotion of dedicated scribes and illuminators. The mere mention of writers already described serves to indicate the clerical domination of learning and literature—religious treatises by Pope Gregory; the secular interests of Cassiodorus and Boethius; Gregory of Tours' history; and Fortunatus' poetry. For better or worse, cathedral and monastery were dynamic centers of a primitive but vigorous Western culture, which stands in rugged contrast to the splendid sophistication of Byzantine culture during the 6th century.

LOREN C. MACKINNEY
Author of "The Medieval World"

2. Inner Asia

For long periods before and after the 6th century nomadic Turco-Mongol peoples from the steppes of Inner Asia terrorized the settled lands and civilizations of Asia and Europe. In the mid-6th century a new Inner Asian power threatened the Chinese, Persian, and Eastern Roman empires. Called by the Chinese T'u-chüeh, from the Mongolian word *Türküt,* this people gave its name to the whole group of Turkic-speaking nations.

In 552 the T'u-chüeh defeated their Mongol overlords, the Juan-juan, who abandoned Mongolia to them. In alliance with the Persians, they defeated the Ephthalites (Hephthalites, or White Huns), who during the previous century had occupied what is now Soviet Central Asia and had invaded Iran and India. The T'u-chüeh menaced the northern frontiers of China and Iran and sent expeditions against the Byzantine outposts in the Crimea. In 582, however, they split into western and eastern kingdoms. The rivalry of the two groups enabled the Chinese to break their power in the 7th century.

The events in the Asian interior during the 6th century had important repercussions in Europe. Remnants of the Juan-juan, of the Ephthalites, or of both, were driven westward into Europe by the T'u-chüeh and became known as the Avars. The Byzantines induced the Avars to subjugate the Huns in south European Russia. Moving westward, the Avars overwhelmed the Slavs and came into conflict with the Franks. But they turned back from western Europe and allied with the Lombards to defeat the Gepids in Hungary. They then dispossessed the Lombards from the territory between the Danube and Sava rivers, impelling the Lombards to invade Italy. The Avars continued to trouble Europe until they were crushed by Charlemagne at the end of the 8th century.

3. Iran (Persia)

In the 6th century the Sassanian empire of Iran reached a new pinnacle of strength under Khosrau (Chosroes) I, whom Iranians today regard as the greatest of their pre-Islamic rulers. Yet within a century after his reign (531–579) the empire collapsed before the conquering Arabs under the banner of Islam.

Under Khosrau's weak predecessors since the late 4th century, the great noble families had grown in power and influence at the expense of imperial authority. The state religion, Zoroastrianism, had been undermined by the rise of a heretical movement known as Mazdakism, which had gained much popular support because it advocated the equal distribution of all wealth. Externally, the Byzantines to the west were always a threat, although in the 6th century Justinian adopted a defensive policy toward the Persians in order to reconquer the western Mediterranean. On Iran's northeastern frontier the nomadic Ephthalites had invaded Sassanian territories in the 5th century and still constantly interfered in Iranian internal affairs.

Khosrau's internal reforms were more important than his conquests. His policies were designed to restore the stability of the empire by strengthening its central authority. Khosrau ruthlessly suppressed the Mazdakites. To provide his government with an assured income, he reassessed the land and imposed taxes on land units rather than production. He sponsored a social revolution that had the effect of reducing the power of the great nobles and increasing that of the lesser nobles, whose service to the court determined their position. The Turks were largely responsible for removing the Ephthalites from

the northeast, and though the Turks presented a new threat from that direction, the Sassanians were able to bring some of the former Ephthalite territories under their control as a cushion against possible new invasion.

In Khosrau's time there was a revival of ancient Iranian customs and tradition. The legends forming the national epic—the *Shah Nameh,* known in the version completed by the poet Firdausi in the 11th century—were probably gathered during the Emperor's reign. There was also a revival of learning. Greek philosophers were welcomed to Khosrau's court after Justinian closed their academy in Athens in 529. Sanskrit books and the game of chess were brought to Iran from India at the Emperor's behest.

The great achievement of Khosrau I was to make the Sassanian empire a tightly organized structure with the king supreme. Khosrau II (reigned 591–628) enlarged the empire to its greatest extent. Taking advantage of Byzantine weakness, he conquered Syria, Egypt, and Anatolia, but by a dramatic reversal of fortune he was deposed and murdered after Emperor Heraclius suddenly took the offensive and struck at the heart of the Persian realm. Exhausted by this war, and with a population disaffected by the crushing taxes raised to finance it, the Sassanian empire was no match for the Arabs when they attacked in the 630's. After the defeat of the Sassanian Army, imperial authority and the religious hierarchy associated with it were discredited. Futile resistance continued locally for a time, led by the nobility. The great families had once commanded large military forces that might have prolonged the struggle, but since the reign of Khosrau I they had been replaced by less powerful nobles as the backbone of provincial and local authority.

4. Arabia and Ethiopia

In the century before the rise of Islam, Arab states flourished to the north of the Arabian Peninsula on the confines of the Eastern Roman and Sassanian empires, and in the southern part of the peninsula in what are now the two Yemens (Yemen Arab Republic and People's Democratic Republic of Yemen). During this period the history of South Arabia was closely linked with that of Ethiopia, on the other side of the Red Sea in Africa.

Arabia. The Ghassanid kingdom in southeastern Syria and the Lakhmid kingdom in Iraq were founded in the 3d century and reached their height in the 6th century. The Ghassanids, who developed the higher culture of the two, were under Byzantine influence; their enemies, the Lakhmids, were under the influence of Sassanian Iran. Both states had Christian populations. The kingdoms served as buffers between the bedouin Arabs to the south and the great empires to the north. The elimination of these buffers by the Byzantines and Persians at the beginning of the 7th century made it easier for Muslim armies to conquer the Middle East within a generation after Mohammed's death in 632.

South Arabia. From at least 1000 B.C. until about the end of the 2d century A.D. the pre-Muslim peoples of South Arabia controlled the international trade of the Red Sea and Indian Ocean, by which luxury products from India and East Africa reached the lands of the Mediterranean. Even afterward, they monopolized the shipment of goods northward by caravan. The

South Arabians developed a prosperous and sophisticated civilization based on trade and agriculture.

After the end of the 2d century B. C. the Himyar people dominated the region. By the 6th century A. D., Christianity and Judaism had won many converts in South Arabia. The East Roman and Persian empires sought to extend their influence to this area. In general the Christians favored the former, the Jews and pagans the latter.

A massacre of Christians at Najran in 523 precipitated a crisis. At the urging of the East Roman emperor, the Christian king of Aksum in Ethiopia invaded South Arabia and in 525 overthrew the Himyarite kingdom. The Ethiopian occupation lasted 50 years. During this time occurred a disaster called by later Arab historians "the bursting of the great dam," which was located at Marib. In 575 the Ethiopians were driven out by the Persians, who controlled Yemen until the rise of Islam in the 7th century.

By the 6th century the civilization of South Arabia had long been in decline. Arab historians attributed its decay to the destruction of the Marib Dam, but two other factors were more important: competition by the Romans in the Red Sea trade after their take-over of Egypt, and the divisive influence of Christianity and Judaism.

Ethiopia. The kingdom of Aksum (Axum) in northern Ethiopia represented a civilization that had arisen during the 1st millennium B. C., influenced by the culture of colonists from Arabia. Aksum had friendly relations with the East Roman Empire. It maintained contact with the Mediterranean world through its port of Adulis on the Red Sea. Although Christianity had been the official religion since the 4th century, it was not fully rooted among the people before the 6th century.

Until its defeat by the Persians in South Arabia in 575, Aksum had been expanding generally northward. In the 4th century it conquered both the Beja people of the deserts north of Ethiopia and the declining kingdom of Cush (Kush) in Sudan. Aksum's invasion of South Arabia in the 6th century was only one of several such expeditions across the Red Sea.

In the 7th century the Muslim Arab conquest of Arabia and Egypt cut Ethiopia's links with the Mediterranean world. Afterward the gravity center of Ethiopian civilization shifted southward, farther into the highlands, and Ethiopia remained isolated for the most part until the 19th century.

5. India and Southeast Asia

From the beginning of the 6th century the failing Gupta Empire of north India began to disintegrate more rapidly, and by the last quarter of the century its downfall was complete. The rest of India remained divided among small powers. In Southeast Asia, India exerted a strong cultural influence.

India. The internal dissensions that afflicted the Gupta Empire were reflected in its probable partition, but two other factors contributed to its collapse. One was a new and successful assault by the Ephthalites (White Huns, or Huna) from the northwest. The other was the rise of numerous local kingdoms in former Gupta territories.

The fresh Ephthalite thrust under Toramana, toward the close of the 5th century or the beginning of the 6th, gave the invaders a secure foothold in Kashmir, Punjab, Rajasthan, and Uttar Pradesh. At Eran in Madhya Pradesh, the ruling family transferred its allegiance from the Guptas to Toramana. Mihirakula, Toramana's successor, held extensive areas in north India and had his capital at Sialkot in Punjab. But indigenous resistance, first under the Malwa ruler Yashodharman and then under the Gupta king Narasimhagupta forced him to withdraw to the west of the Indus and into Kashmir.

Despite this success, the shattered Gupta Empire was not restored. Around 556, Valabhi in Gujarat became independent. The Gurjara-Pratihara kingdom, which sprang into prominence in a later period, emerged around Jodhpur in Rajasthan in the middle of the century. The Maukhari clan became powerful in southern Bihar and Uttar Pradesh, and the later Guptas contended for supremacy in roughly the same area. Toward the close of the century Prabhakaravardhana of Thanesar in Haryana laid the foundation of the future but brief prosperity of the Pushpabhuti line.

In peninsular India, Andhra, between the Krishna (Kistna) and Godavari rivers, was held throughout the century by the local Vishnukundin family. Farther south, between the Penner and Vellar rivers, were the early Pallavas, with their center at Kanchi in Tamil Nadu. In the Karnataka region and other parts of the western Deccan, the tiny kingdoms of the Kadambas, Gangas, Bhojas, Kalachuris, and early Rashtrakutas represented that area's decentralized polity in the early 6th century. The middle of the century, however, saw the rise of the Chalukyas of Badami in Karnataka. Their steady growth under such early rulers as Pulakeshin I (reigned about 535–566) and Kirtivarman I (reigned about 566–598) led to a bitter conflict with the Pallavas in the 7th century.

Southeast Asia. Although documentation is insufficient, a number of Indianized states are known to have existed in Southeast Asia during

Cave relief at Ellora, India, portrays Shiva and Parvati seated on Mt. Kailasa above the demon Ravana.

the 6th century. In the lower Irrawaddy Valley of Burma, the city of Pegu (Hamsavati) rose to prominence. Farther east, in the Malay Peninsula, was the kingdom the Chinese called Lang-ya-hsü, founded in the 2d century. Lang-ya-hsü sent embassies to China in 515, 523, 531, and 568. In Cambodia and southern Vietnam the kingdom of Funan prospered in the early 6th century under Jayavarman and Rudravarman. However, the Khmer state of Kambuja (Chenla) to the north was steadily growing in strength and was soon to effect the collapse of Funan. The kingdom of Champa in Vietnam had a fluctuating relationship with the Chinese court. In the second half of the 6th century relations with China deteriorated, and in 605 a Chinese general sacked the Cham capital.

Among the island kingdoms, Śrivijaya, centered at Palembang in southern Sumatra, had not yet attained greatness. The state that the Chinese called Kan-t'o-li was probably another kingdom in Sumatra. Its ruler Vijayavarman sent an embassy to China in 519. A kingdom in Bali also probably existed in the 6th century.

Apart from local traditions alluding to the Indian origin of the Southeast Asian kingdoms of the 6th century, there is more positive evidence of Indian influence. Sanskrit was the language used at court and in inscriptions. The religious media of Indian influence were Brahmanism and Mahāyāna Buddhism, the latter being perhaps the more dominant in this period.

BRAJADULAL CHATTOPADHYAYA
Jawaharlal Nehru University

6. China

At the beginning of the 6th century, China was still politically divided as it usually had been through the Six Dynasties period of the preceding three centuries. Until 589, when the Sui dynasty reunited China, a series of Chinese states ruled the Yangtze Valley, while the north was under the control of nomadic peoples. The strongest of these competing states in the 6th century was the Northern (Later) Wei dynasty (386–535) of the T'o-pa (Toba) Turks. Like other nomadic conquerors who in preceding centuries had enriched northern Chinese culture, they themselves were gradually assimilated. By the 6th century, Chinese control was being reasserted in northern China.

For nearly half a century, the Yangtze Valley was under the rule of a single emperor, the devout Buddhist Wu-ti (reigned 502–549) of the Liang dynasty. His court at Nanking was a flourishing center of Chinese literature and art. The Yangtze society was now growing out of its previous colonial social order, which had been established by Chinese refugees from the north. After the death of Liang Wu-ti, the south was divided into competing states.

In 581, Yang Chien (Sui Wen-ti, reigned 581–604), scion of an important family at the Northern Chou court, usurped the throne and created the Sui dynasty (581–618). He conquered the rest of China by 589, bringing to an end the long period of division. While maintaining the basic elements of the traditional imperial order, he reorganized the political system. Careful and frugal, he was faced not only by Chinese states in the south, but also by the T'u-chüeh empire to the north. Sui diplomacy was a factor in dividing the Tu-chüeh into eastern and western states in 582.

MUSEUM OF FINE ARTS, BOSTON, FRANCIS BARTLETT DONATION

The merciful Kuan-yin, depicted in a Chinese Buddhist sculpture, was in India the male savior Avalokiteshvara.

By the beginning of the century, Buddhism was thoroughly established as the dominant religion in China, but Chinese attitudes were beginning to reshape Indian Buddhism into Chinese forms. Ch'an (in Japanese, Zen) Buddhism, which is strongly Taoist in character, emerged in this century. Its origins are traditionally associated with the foreign monk Bodhidharma, said to have lived in China from 516 to 534. The T'ien-t'ai (in Japanese, Tendai) sect, which shows some Confucian influences, was founded in the 6th century by Hui Ssu and Chih I.

Chinese art and literature of the period both show evidence of the Buddhist impact. Magnificent rock carvings, as at the Lungmen caves, were done in the Gandharan style of northwestern India, introduced with Buddhism. Under Liang Wu-ti, the first collected translation of the Buddhist scriptures, the Tripitaka, was published. The most famous early anthology of Chinese literature, *Wen-hsüan*, was compiled about 530 by the Liang prince Hsiao T'ung.

JAMES R. SHIRLEY
Northern Illinois University

7. Korea and Japan

The 6th century was an age of great vitality throughout East Asia. The energy generated by the great process of reunification in China contributed also to important centralizing and reformist movements in Korea and Japan.

Korea. In the mid-6th century Korea was divided into three warring kingdoms—Koguryo in the north, Paekche in the southwest, and Silla in the southeast—as well as an enclave known as Kaya, at the southern end of the peninsula. Kaya was controlled until 562 by the Japanese, who called it Mimana.

Both Koguryo and Paekche were governed by aristocracies that had originated among the Tungusic peoples of Manchuria, and both had had long contact and familiarity with Chinese civilization. Silla, on the other hand, was a more remote and backward kingdom, ruled by native tribes and only indirectly exposed to the civilizing influences of China. Yet it was Silla that in the late 6th century and the 7th century emerged supreme militarily and came to unify all of Korea.

Japan. Tradition has it that Buddhism was formally introduced to Japan from Paekche in 552. The Japanese state consisted at the time of a group of territorially based and loosely organized clans headed by what was to become the imperial clan, or family, of later centuries. The introduction of Buddhism sparked a dispute at court over the larger issue of whether to undertake centralizing reforms along Chinese lines. Chief among the proponents of both Buddhism and reform was the ministerial family of Soga. In 587 the Soga defeated their more conservative opponents in battle and launched Japan upon a course that was to lead during the next century to the ostensible remodeling of the country as a "China in miniature."

Ironically, the Soga themselves eventually became an obstacle to the process of reform and were overthrown in a palace coup in 645. Although they had led the way in the acceptance of Buddhism, as both a religious and cultural force in Japanese life, and in the adoption of policies that allowed for a greater concentration of authority at court, the Soga continued to represent the vested interests of the old system of government by aristocratic clans. Intermarrying with the imperial family, they sought to dominate central affairs and may even have schemed to seize the throne for themselves.

Without the removal of the Soga from their commanding position in government, it would have been impossible for the progressives at court to implement the major land and administrative reforms of the late 7th and early 8th centuries. These reforms produced Japan's first great age of cultural flourishing in the period 710–784, when Nara was the imperial capital.

H. PAUL VARLEY
Columbia University

Bibliography

Barker, John W., *Justinian and the Later Roman Empire* (Univ. of Wis. Press 1966).
Bieler, Ludwig, *Ireland: Harbinger of the Middle Ages* (Oxford 1963).
Blair, Peter, *An Introduction to Anglo-Saxon England* (Cambridge 1954).
Cambridge University Press, *The Cambridge Medieval History:* vol. 2, *The Rise of the Saracens and the Foundation of the Western Empire* (1964).
Cantor, Norman, *Medieval History*, 2d ed. (Macmillan 1969).
Chapman, John, *Saint Benedict and the Sixth Century* (Sheed 1929).
Christensen, Arthur, *L'Iran sous les Sassanides* (Ejnar Munksgaard 1944).
Coedès, George, *The Indianized States of Southeast Asia*, ed. by Walter Vella (East West Center Press 1968).
Dill, Samuel, *Roman Society in Gaul in the Merovingian Age* (1926; reprint, Barnes & Noble 1966).
Doresse, Jean, *Ethiopia* (Putnam 1960).
Downey, Glanville, *Constantinople in the Age of Justinian* (Univ. of Okla. Press 1960).
Duckett, Eleanor, *The Gateway to the Middle Ages*, 3 vols. (Univ. of Mich. Press 1961).
Dudden, Frederick, *Gregory the Great*, 2 vols. (1905; reprint, Russell & Russell 1967).
Ghirshman, Roman, *Iran: From the Earliest Times to the Islamic Conquest* (Penguin 1954).
Gregory of Tours, *The History of the Franks*, 2 vols., tr. and intro. by O. M. Dalton (Oxford 1927).
Grousset, René, *The Empire of the Steppes: A History of Central Asia* (Rutgers Univ. Press 1970).
Hall, John W., *Japan from Prehistory to Modern Times* (Delacorte 1970).
Hitti, Philip K., *History of the Arabs*, chap. 5, 10th ed. (St. Martins 1970).
Hodgkin, Thomas, *Italy and Her Invaders, 376–814 A. D.* (1880–1889; reprint, Russell & Russell 1967).
Laistner, Max L. W., *Thought and Letters in Western Europe, A. D. 500 to 900*, 2d ed. (Cornell Univ. Press 1957).
Latouche, Robert, *Caesar to Charlemagne: The Beginnings of France* (Barnes & Noble 1968).
Lot, Ferdinand, *The End of the Ancient World* (Knopf 1931).
Majumdar, Ramesh, *Hindu Colonies in the Far East*, 2d ed. (Mukhopadhyay 1963).
Majumdar, Ramesh, ed., *The History and Culture of the Indian People:* vol. 3, *The Classical Age*, 3d ed. (Bharatiya Vidya Bhavan 1970).
Menéndez Pidal, Ramón, ed., *Historia de España:* vol. 3, *España visigoda*, 2d ed. (Espasa-Calpe).
Moss, Henry St. L. B., *The Birth of the Middle Ages, 395–814* (Oxford 1935).
Previté-Orton, Charles W., *The Shorter Cambridge Medieval History*, vol. 1 (Cambridge 1952).
Reischauer, Edwin, and Fairbank, John, *East Asia: The Great Tradition* (Houghton 1960).
Schnürer, Gustav, *The Church and Culture in the Middle Ages*, vol. 1 (St. Anthony Guild 1956).
Stenton, Frank, *Anglo-Saxon England*, 3d ed. (Oxford 1971).
Strayer, Joseph, and Munro, Dana, *The Middle Ages* (Appleton 1970).
Ullendorf, Edward, *The Ethiopians*, 2d ed. (Oxford 1965).
Wallace-Hadrill, John, *The Long-Haired Kings and Other Studies in Frankish History* (Methuen 1962).

EVENTS OF THE SIXTH CENTURY

507—Franks defeated Visigoths at Vouillé.
511—Death of Clovis I; division of Frankish kingdom.
520—Benedict of Nursia established monastery at Monte Cassino, Italy: mother foundation of the Benedictine order.
524—Execution of Boethius by Theodoric the Great.
525—Ethiopians conquered South Arabia.
526—Death of Theodoric the Great, founder (493) of Ostrogothic kingdom of Italy.
527—Justinian I, Byzantine emperor (to 565).
529—Academy at Athens closed by Justinian.
531—Khosrau (Chosroes) I, king of Persia (to 579).
534—Belisarius completed conquest of Vandal kingdom of North Africa for Justinian I (begun in 533).
534—Main body of *Corpus Iuris Civilis* (Justinian's Code) completed; new laws added to 565.
537—Dedication of Hagia Sophia (Blessed Wisdom) in Constantinople: most important surviving church of antiquity.
552—Traditional date of introduction of Buddhism to Japan.
552—T'u-chüeh (Turks) defeated Juan-juan and founded empire in Asian interior.
555—Byzantines completed conquest of Ostrogoths, begun by Belisarius in 535.
560—Æthelbert (Ethelbert) king of Kent (to 616): first Christian king to rule in England (converted by Augustine in 597).
563—Irish missionary Columba founded influential monastery on island of Iona, off Scottish coast.
568—Lombards invaded Italy.
575—Persians expelled Ethiopians from South Arabia.
589—China reunited under Sui dynasty, ending "age of political disunity" (from 220).
590—Gregory I the Great became pope (reigned to 604).
597—Augustine, apostle of England, landed in Kent and began conversion of the Anglo-Saxons.

SIXTUS I, siks'təs, **Saint** (died c. 125), pope from about 116 to about 125. Sixtus, a Roman, was the sixth pope. Most sources indicate that he reigned for about 10 years. A decree attributed to him, but which is probably of a later date, forbids the laity to handle the sacred vessels and requires the people to chant the "Sanctus" along with the priest at Mass. His feast day is observed on April 6.

SIXTUS II, siks'təs, **Saint** (died 258), pope in 257–258. Sixtus became pope in August 257, at the beginning of Emperor Valerian's persecutions. He upheld the validity of Baptism by heretics, as had his predecessors, but adopted a more conciliatory approach to variant practices. To this end he sent emissaries to Cyprian of Carthage, the principal advocate of the rebaptism of those baptized by heretics.

On Aug. 6, 258, Sixtus was arrested and beheaded, along with four deacons, while celebrating services in the cemetery of Praetextatus. His feast is kept on August 6.

SIXTUS III, siks'təs, **Saint** (died 440), pope from 432 to 440. Sixtus was a native of Rome and a priest at the time of his election to the papacy on July 31, 432.

Prior to his election as pope, Sixtus was suspected of sympathizing with the Pelagian heretics, but during his reign he opposed their views. He fostered the reconciliation of Cyril of Alexandria and John of Antioch, who had continued to dispute the decisions of the Council of Ephesus (431) on the two natures of Christ and the deposition of Nestorius. Sixtus opposed the attempts of the patriarch of Constantinople to extend his authority in Asia Minor. He was also responsible for the reconstruction of the Liberian basilica and its renaming as St. Mary Major. Sixtus died in Rome on Aug. 18, 440. He is venerated on August 18.

SIXTUS IV, siks'təs (1414–1484), pope from 1471 to 1484. Francesco Della Rovere was born in Celle, Italy, on July 21, 1414. Educated by the Franciscans, he joined the Conventual Franciscans and taught theology and philosophy at Bologna and Padua. He was elected minister general of his order in 1464 and named a cardinal in 1467. He was elected pope on Aug. 9, 1471, taking the name of Sixtus.

Sixtus was an inveterate nepotist and political meddler. He appointed his relatives to various posts and made cardinals of two nephews, Guiliano Della Rovere (the future Pope Julius II) and Pietro Riario. Sixtus was involved in the Pazzi family's conspiracy against the Medici family in 1478 and carried on a war with Florence (1478–1480). He turned on the Venetians, who had helped resist an invasion by the Neopolitans, and placed them under an interdict in 1483 because they refused to cease hostilities. His attempts to regain territory controlled by the Turks were fruitless.

Sixtus extended the privileges granted to the Conventual Franciscans and fostered the doctrine of the Immaculate Conception. A noted patron of arts and letters, he engaged in an extensive building program in Rome. He built and decorated the Sistine Chapel, enlisting the aid of famous artists such as Botticelli. He also reorganized the Vatican Library and opened it to scholars. Sixtus died in Rome on Aug. 12, 1484.

SIXTUS V, siks'təs (1520–1590), pope from 1585 to 1590. Felice Peretti was born in Grottammare, near Montalto, Italy, on Dec. 13, 1520. He joined the Franciscans in 1533, was ordained in 1547, and received his doctorate in theology from the University of Fermo in 1548. His preaching brought him to the attention of Roman officials in 1552. In 1557, Pope Paul II made him inquisitor of Venice, but his severity led to his recall in 1560. Pius V made him vicar general of the Franciscans and then bishop of Sant'Agata dei Goti in 1568. From that date he began to use Montalto as a surname. He was named a cardinal in 1570 and was transferred to the diocese of Fermo in 1571. When Cardinal Boncompagni became Pope Gregory XIII, Montalto retired to his villa. He was elected pope on April 24, 1585, as a compromise candidate, and took the name of Sixtus.

Gregory XIII had left the Papal States in a state of virtual chaos and with a sorely depleted treasury. Sixtus restored order by arresting and executing numerous bandits and marauders. By the sale of offices and new taxes he managed to increase revenues greatly. He encouraged new industries, particularly the production of silk and wool. Sixtus also engaged in an extensive building program, including the Lateran Palace and the completion of the dome of St. Peter's.

Sixtus carried out an extensive reform of church administration. In the bull *Postquam verus* of Dec. 3, 1586, he set the number of cardinals at 70 and imposed new regulations on them. He created 15 congregations in 1588 to carry on the administration of the church and the Papal States. He effectively enforced the decree of the Council of Trent against simony and plurality of benefices. He also silenced both the Dominicans and the Jesuits in their drawn-out controversy over grace.

His diplomatic efforts were complicated and extensive. The vacillation and ultimate assassination of Henry III of France forced Sixtus to ally himself with Philip II of Spain against Henry of Navarre. After the execution of Mary, Queen of Scots, in 1587, Sixtus aided in the building of the Armada. He died in Rome on Aug. 27, 1590.

SIZE is a glutinous material applied to canvas, paper, wood, plaster, textile yarns, and other products to reduce absorbency, make them receptive to a coating, or increase their strength. Size, or sizing, fills in pores of material but is not a smooth coating or glaze. It may be made of glue, gelatine, starch, casein, resins, shellac, or other adhesives.

In oil painting, canvas is sized with glue to protect it from oil paint. Wood panels are given a ground of gesso, a mixture of chalk or whiting and size. Paper is sized with gelatine or starch to make it less absorbent to ink. In gilding, glue size is applied to a gesso ground to hold gold leaf. Yarns are sized with starch to prevent friction in weaving.

SJÆLLAND, shel'län, an island of Denmark, lies east of the peninsula of Jutland, between the Kattegat and the Baltic Sea. Sjælland (or Zealand) is separated on the east from Sweden by the Øresund, at a distance of only 2.5 miles (4 km) at one point, and on the west from the island of Fyn by the Great (Store) Belt. It is the most densely populated part of Denmark. Copenhagen, the national capital, and the historic cities of Helsingør (Elsinore) and Roskilde are on the island. Administratively, the island is divided into five counties.

Sjælland is over 80 miles (130 km) long and up to 72 miles (115 km) wide, with a very irregular coastline. It has no mountains, but the surface is varied, with fertile fields and small hills intersected by canals. Much grain is produced, and there is excellent pasturage. Population: (1960) 1,973,108.

SKAGERRAK, skag′ə-rak, an arm of the North Sea, is a broad channel between Norway and Denmark. On the southeast it is connected with the Kattegat. The Skagerrak is about 150 miles (240 km) long and 70 to 90 miles (110–145 km) wide. Along the Danish coast it is shallow and has numerous sandbars, but along the Norwegian coast it reaches a depth of over 2,000 feet (610 meters).

SKAGWAY is a city in southeastern Alaska, in the Panhandle, at the northern end of Lynn Canal, about 75 miles (120 km) north-northwest of Juneau. It serves as the southern terminus of the Whitehorse and Yukon Railroad, which runs 111 miles (175 km) north to Whitehorse, Yukon Territory, Canada. Skagway was settled in 1897, during the Klondike gold rush. Population: 768.

SKALD, skäld, in Norwegian and Icelandic literature, one of the Scandinavian poets of the Viking period who composed and chanted lengthy poems, usually in honor of kings and heroes, or related tales about the gods. The term is Old Norse, meaning "poet." The skalds, or scalds, were skilled minstrels, adept in versification, and their work was highly ornate and placed great emphasis on form. Appearing first about the beginning of the 9th century in Norway, they reached their greatest development in the 10th and 11th centuries in Iceland, where they were found as late as the 13th century. They were usually attached to the court.

SKANDERBEG, skan′dər-beg (1404?–1468), was an Albanian chief and national hero. He was the fourth son of John Kastrioti (Castriota), a high official of Serbian origin, and his given name was George. An uncle, having married into one of the leading Albanian families, commanded the Albanian fortress of Krujë. When George was a boy, the Turks began to occupy Albania, and he was sent to Constantinople as a hostage. He was educated as a Muslim and given the name of Iskender and the title of bey, which were corrupted by his compatriots to Skanderbeg or Scanderbeg.

Under the Turks he had a distinguished record as an administrator and soldier, governing a *sanjak* (administrative district) and fighting in wars with the Serbs and Venice. While campaigning against the Hungarian János Hunyadi in 1443, Skanderbeg learned that his native land had revolted. He returned to Albania and took possession of the fortress of Krujë.

He then declared himself a Christian, rallied the Albanian clans into an organized league, and married the daughter of a local patriot chieftain. Skanderbeg took advantage of the rugged Albanian terrain and used highly mobile guerrilla forces to defeat almost annual expeditions sent by Murad II and Mohammed II. Venice subsidized him as an ally against the traditional enemy, and he also received the support of the papacy and the Kingdom of Naples.

Sultan Mohammed II, after many Turkish frustrations, finally concluded a ten-year armistice with Skanderbeg in 1461, acknowledging the independence of Albania and Epirus. Skan-

COMMON SKATE (*Raja erinacea*), generally a mottled brown on top (*left*), has conspicuous eyes and adjacent spiracles, or breathing holes, on top of its head. On its underside (*right*), which is generally whitish, there is a mouth, adjacent nostrils, and, slightly below, usually five paired gill openings.

PETER A. THOMAS, FROM NATIONAL AUDUBON SOCIETY

PETER A. THOMAS, FROM NATIONAL AUDUBON SOCIETY

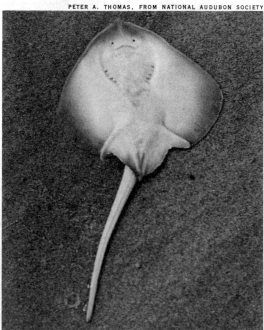

derbeg soon broke the truce, at the behest of Pope Pius II, who was organizing a crusade against the Turks. When the Pope died in 1464, and the crusade withered in the bud, Skanderbeg found himself abandoned by his Western allies. Mohammed himself unsuccessfully laid siege to Krujë in 1466, and Skanderbeg hurried to Rome to entreat the aid of Pope Paul II, but he was disappointed and received only a small subsidy. He returned to Albania and repulsed a second attempt by Mohammed to take Krujë in 1467. It was his last victory, and he died in the Venetian colony of Alessio (Lezhë) on Jan. 17, 1468. After his death Albanian resistance to the Turks fragmented, and the Ottomans were able to reconquer Albania by the end of the century.

SKÅNE, skō′nə, is the most southern region of Sweden. Also known as Scania, it borders on the Baltic Sea and the Øresund. It is Sweden's foremost agricultural region and comprises the counties of Kristianstad and Malmöhus. It has an area of 4,356 square miles (11,282 sq km). Skåne was long held by the Danes and was the scene of many Swedish-Danish conflicts before Denmark ceded it to Sweden in 1658. Population: (1968) 942,047. See also SWEDEN–*The Land.*

SKARN, in geology, a general term for silicate rocks formed by the replacement of limestones and marls with iron-rich garnets, pyroxenes, and amphiboles. Such rocks are considered waste in limestone quarries, and the term skarn was adopted from the Swedish word for rubbish.

SKATE, any of a family of flattened disk-shaped fish closely related to sharks and rays. Skates are found in temperate and tropical oceans and in some brackish water in most parts of the world. They generally live at depths of less than 600 feet (100 fathoms, or 185 meters) on sand, gravel, or mud bottoms, but a few species may occur at greater depths.

Skates range from about 20 inches to 8 feet (50 cm–2.5 meters) in length. Most are mottled brownish on top, whitish below. They have greatly expanded winglike pectoral fins that extend platelike around the head. Conspicuous eyes and spiracles, or breathing holes, are found on top of the head, and in some species there is an elongated nose. The mouth, on the underside of the head, is equipped with several rows of small teeth, which the skates use for feeding on bottom-dwelling invertebrates. Most species have a short tail that has two small dorsal fins. In some species electrogenic organs, which are capable of giving a low-voltage shock, are formed of modified muscle along the sides of the tail.

In male skates the pelvic fins are modified to form copulatory organs, called *claspers.* After copulation, the female lays rectangular eggs encased in a leatherlike keratin protective sheath. Each corner of this egg case, often known as a *mermaid's purse,* has a fingerlike extension or tendril by which it attaches itself to the bottom or some other object.

There are more than 100 species of skates. Most are classified in the genus *Raja* of the family Rajidae, order Rajiiformes. The most common species found along the American coast are the small hedgehog skate (*Raja erinacea*) of the Atlantic and the very large American Pacific skate (*R. binoculata*).

SKATING is gliding over a surface by means of skates. In ice skating the skates are short metal runners attached to boots or shoes. In roller skating, wheels replace the runners. This article deals with the sport of ice skating. See also HOCKEY.

The main divisions of the sport of ice skating include speed skating and figure skating. National and international competitions are held in both. According to the branch he chooses, a skater may exercise sheer physical prowess, creative ability, artistic sense, or a combination of all three. The opportunity for beauty of movement in modern figure skating is so great that this branch has been raised to an art form comparable to the dance.

Skating appeals to people of all ages, whether as a pleasant recreation, as a discipline with competition as its goal, or as a profession. Increasingly comprehensive coverage of national and international events by television and the accelerated building of artificial ice rinks are visible indications of the sport's growing worldwide popularity.

Equipment. Strictly speaking, the term "skate" should be confined to the metal runner, which consists of a blade attached to sole and heel plates by vertical stanchions. In the United States, however, the word "skate" is used loosely to mean the combination of boot and runner, the latter being referred to as the "blade."

The difference between speed, figure, and hockey skates lies in the structure of both the blade and the boot. The figure blade projects only slightly at the toe and heel, the bottom of the blade being ground to a complex curve from front to back, the major part of which corresponds to a circle having a radius of between 6 and 7 feet (1.8–2.1 meters). The rounded front section contains a series of sharp serrations known as "toe rakes" or "toe picks," which are used in certain types of spins and jumps. The beginner's tendency to catch these in the ice is due to the faulty return of the foot after the thrust. Running the length of the bottom of the blade is a groove known as the "hollow," which serves to divide the cutting section into two distinct edges. The figure boot is sturdy and relatively high both in the shaft and heel. A stiffened section known as the "counter" supports the arch of the foot.

For speed skating the blade is thin, has relatively little curvature from front to back, projects considerably in front of the toe of the boot, and is ground completely flat. The boot is low and quite flexible. The ice hockey boot is also somewhat low but is quite tough, having a reinforced toecap and a vertical leather section at the back to protect the Achilles tendon. The blade is thin, is sharply curved at the front and rear, and has a middle section varying in curvature according to the player's preference.

Women's figure skating attire normally consists of tan, semi-sheer nylon tights, a short skirt or dress, and matching pants. Skating costumes, usually in stretch materials, are also obtainable in the form of a leotard with a brief skirt attached. A sweater and gloves are advisable for cold rinks. Boots are usually white. Hair, if long, should be tied back, and scarves and hats are not recommended. Figure skating attire for men is informal except during tests and competitions, when one-piece suits made of a stretch material are usual. Boots are traditionally black.

Skaters in the Netherlands have used frozen waterways as winter roads for centuries.

For speed skating, black tights and black turtleneck sweaters are popular.

Skating for Recreation. A beginner's first object should be to learn to stroke correctly. A good stroke involves thrusting from the correct part of the blade, controlling knee action, and correctly transferring weight from one foot to the other, a subtle skill often taking several seasons to perfect. The following points should be observed in simple forward skating. The power thrust is made from the inside edge of the blade, never from the toe rake, and the direction of the thrust is sideways and slightly to the rear. A relatively upright posture is preserved throughout the thrust. When skating forward one should place his weight toward the rear of the blade. Backward skating should be learned as soon as possible. In the early stages the action consists of a two-footed movement.

Once a beginner decides what branch of skating most appeals to him—speed skating, figure skating, or hockey—practicing becomes more specialized. If figure skating is his goal, he should learn to make the curves, both forward and backward, on the inside and outside edges. He may also want to attempt the various jumps, spins, and general footwork, collectively known as "free style."

A skater may measure his progress in basic skating, figure skating, and free style by taking the official tests administered by the U. S. Figure Skating Association (USFSA). These consist of a series of 12 elementary tests available to the general public, plus a series of more advanced tests requiring membership in the USFSA, the eighth of which constitutes the gold medal and requires many years of hard training. It should be possible, however, for a reasonably athletic adult to master the 12 USFSA basic tests in one or two seasons if he is able to practice at least twice a week. The Ice Skating Institute of America (ISIA) is a professional organization consisting mainly of ice rink managements that aims at furthering recreational skating and technical knowledge of ice rink management. They administer a series of skating tests. The Professional Skaters Guild of America (PSGA) controls and classifies member professional figure skating instructors in the United States.

Amateur Competition. Amateur figure skating is regulated in the United States by the USFSA and speed skating by the American Skating Union (ASU). Both bodies are affiliated with the International Skating Union (ISU) and are members of the U. S. Olympic Committee. These regulating bodies organize championship competitions and trials, the results of which determine the composition of the teams representing the United States at the Olympic Winter Games and the world championship.

Figure skaters wishing to compete nationally must first qualify through regional and sectional competitions. It usually is necessary to join a local club affiliated with the USFSA in order to compete, but if no local club exists, it is possible to become a direct member of the USFSA. Selection of teams to compete internationally is based on the results of national competition. A speed skater may enter local competition by registering with his local association. International teams are selected at annual trials.

Speed Skating. Two forms of racing, known as Olympic style and American Pack or Mass Start style, exist in the United States. The basic difference is that in Olympic style racing the skater skates against the clock, while in the American Pack a number of skaters start together, competing against each other in a series of heats.

The Olympic Winter Games events and the world championship are held according to regulations laid down by the ISU. The distances are 500, 1,500, 5,000, and 10,000 meters for men, and 500, 1,000, 1,500, and 3,000 meters for women. Skaters reach speeds of over 28 miles (45 km) per hour in short races and maintain averages of over 25 miles (40 km) in longer events. The ISU also holds a competition known as the World Sprint Championship. A standard 400-meter track with two lanes is used, regulations permitting two skaters to skate simultaneously. At one point on the straightaway the tracks cross, thus enabling both skaters to take equal advantage of the inside track. Tracks used in American Pack style racing include the 6–lap (to the mile), the 8–lap, a 16–lap indoor track, and a 400–meter track adapted for this type of racing by the ASU. On occasions a 12–lap track is also used.

After a number of qualifying heats the winner of an American Pack style race is the skater who in the final round crosses the finishing line in the shortest time. The usual method of deciding the winner of the world championship is to take the total of each skater's times in seconds over all four distances, the longer distances having been proportionately reduced to reflect his time over 500 meters. The skater having the least number of seconds (points) against him is the winner. In the Olympic Winter Games each distance is treated as a separate event, and gold, silver, and bronze medals are awarded for each. The Olympic Games are not classified as championships.

Unlike the figure skater, the speed skater adopts a crouching posture, which reduces wind resistance and enables him to achieve a longer stroke. A strong rhythmic swing of the arms is used to increase momentum. As the tracks get smaller, increasing emphasis is laid on the ability to negotiate the curved ends of the track, such ability becoming of paramount importance on the 16–lap indoor track. The skater's lean to the inside of the circle may cause the edge of the boot to touch the ice. For this reason, and because all racing is in a counterclockwise direction, it is usual to set the blade well to the left edge of the boot.

The Olympic Winter Games held in Sapporo, Japan, in 1972 produced two outstanding American speed skaters. Anne Henning won the 500-

meter event in record time and earned a bronze medal in the 1,000 meters. Dianne Holum skated to the gold medal for the 1,500 meters, also establishing a new Olympic record, and won a silver medal in the 3,000-meter event.

Figure Skating. Figure skating is a wide and loosely used term embracing three branches: figures and free style, pair skating, and ice dancing. All branches had their origin in the curves and turns that can be made on correctly designed figure skates.

Fundamentals. A figure blade possesses two physical edges. The one farther from the center line of the body is called the outside edge, and the one nearer the center line is the inside edge. If a skater leans to one side so as to rock his blade over onto an edge he will make a curve in that direction. Four curves may be skated on each foot, each curve being known as an "edge." The names of the edges on the right foot are: the right forward outside (RFO), right forward inside (RFI), right back outside (RBO), and right back inside (RBI). The edges on the left foot are similarly designated. The foot on which the skater is at any moment skating is known as the skating foot, while the foot in the air is known as the free foot. Corresponding terms are used for other parts of the body, and thus reference is made to the free arm, skating shoulder, and so on. The size of a curve depends on the skater's height, speed, and degree of lean.

UPI

Grace of Champions: Dick Button (*above*) and Tenley Albright (*right*), both Olympic and world titleholders, seem suspended in air. Irina Rodnina and Aleksei Ulanov, a Russian couple, took 1972 Olympic gold medal in pairs.

TASS, FROM SOVFOTO

PICTORIAL PARADE

Peggy Fleming executes a rocker as judges watch critically during world figure skating championships.

Ard Schenk, record breaking Dutch skater, leans into a turn in 1972 world championships in Oslo.

Control of the edges is fundamental and vital to the proper performance of every movement contained in all branches of figure skating. The greatest difficulty confronting a beginner is the fact that his body tends to rotate in an uncontrolled manner in the direction of the edge being skated. When one skates a clockwise curve, for example, the body will rotate in a clockwise direction, soon producing an untenable position. To correct this the skater must learn to hold his body from the hips upward completely motionless both during and after the thrust, thereby preventing the slightest rotation of any part of his body in the direction of the curve, which is achieved solely by leaning. The hips are almost invariably the last part of the body to be brought under control, and the help of an expert instructor is usually necessary.

The body should be erect, with the hands and arms extended from the body at approximately hip level and the knees always preserving some degree of flexibility. The skating knee is very rarely completely straight. All balance should be controlled by the muscles of the skating leg and not by the upper part of the body. Having achieved initial control of the edges, the skater must then learn to rotate his body in a controlled fashion around its vertical axis. In this way the various turns may be made.

The simple movement of rocking from one edge to another without turning the body is known as a "serpentine" or "change of edge." For example, a skater might be on a clockwise curve and then rock his body over onto the opposite edge to take him in a counter-clockwise direction, thus producing a serpentine line. Turns may be made from forward skating to backward or from backward skating to forward. One-footed turns are known as "threes" and "brackets" when turned on the circumference of a circle and as "rockers" and "counters" when made at the rockover point—the point where a change of edge is made—of a serpentine line. Turns involving a change of foot are known as "mohawks" when made on the circumference of a circle and as "choctaws" when made on a serpentine line. When executing threes and rockers, the skater turns the skating foot in the natural direction of the initial curve, while brackets and counters require him to turn the foot in the opposite direction. The direction of rotation of mohawks and choctaws is governed by the character of the initial edge.

Competition. Since a blade leaves a white mark, or tracing, on clean ice, edges and turns are used to make various geometric drawings known as "figures," all of which are based on the two-circle figure eight form or the three-circle serpentine form. There are 69 such figures in the ISU schedule, but only a selection is used for any one competition. Judging, on a scale of one to six, is based on various considerations, including symmetry, cleanness of turns, correctness of form and—inasmuch as each figure must be skated three times without pause (triple repetition)—the ability to place one tracing on top of the preceding one.

In addition to their use in the actual figures, the turns and edges may, in conjunction with various spins and jumps from one edge to another, be used to produce over the whole ice surface a continuous and harmonious series of free style movements that, when performed to music for a specified length of time, are known as a "program." Two sets of marks are awarded, the first

Sunny winter weather attracts children and parents to a day of skating in Van Cortlandt Park, New York City.

for technical merit and the second for artistic impression. A short second free style program, containing compulsory free style moves, was introduced in 1973. Under the revised rules, free style skating counts for 40%, compulsory free style for 20%, and the figure section—also known as school figures—for 40% in competition.

One of the most attractive forms of skating to watch is pair skating, which consists of a free style program performed in unison by a mixed couple, with the addition of spectacular lifts by the man and various combined spins. There is a short second program containing compulsory moves. No figures are involved, and marking is on the same basis as for single skating.

The third branch, ice dancing, differs from pair skating in that a number of compulsory dances such as waltzes, foxtrots, and tangos must be performed, as well as an exhibition program known as "free dance," in which lifts, combined spins, and the separation of partners are severely restricted. Inventions for a compulsory type of dance may also be required. This branch of figure skating is not included in the Olympic Winter Games.

Famous names abound in figure skating, but undoubtedly those whose names are best known to the public are the former world champions Sonja Henie, Tenley Albright, Peggy Fleming, Dick Button, and Oleg and Ljudmila Protopopov, a great Russian pair.

Ice Shows. The origin of the ice show may be traced back to the formation in 1908 of a professional ice ballet company to perform at the Eispalast in Berlin. In 1915 this company, headed by Charlotte Oelschlagel, who later became famous simply as "Charlotte," was taken to the United States to appear at the New York City Hippodrome. The enormous success of this undertaking established the ice show as a popular form of entertainment.

Influenced by the success of Sonja Henie's movies and by the spectacular amateur charity carnivals staged in Canada and the United States, several enormous and elaborately costumed ice shows toured the major cities of North America in the late 1940's. Smaller shows, often performing on surfaces no larger than 20 by 20 feet (6 by 6 meters), were featured in hotels all over the continent. In Britain the emphasis was on large resident ice spectacles playing in the London arenas, concentrating for the most part on the presentation of the traditional English pantomimes —*Babes in the Wood, Robin Hood, Cinderella,* and others. In continental Europe smaller traveling shows played in theaters or under circus big tops.

The popularity of ice shows reached its peak in the early 1950's, during which the competition of television began to take serious toll, causing a severe retrenchment in the business, particularly among the smaller shows. In the United States this type of entertainment is almost entirely confined to the three large surviving companies: Ice Follies, Ice Capades, and Holiday on Ice.

History. Bone skates tied to the feet by thongs were known in prehistoric times and continued in use until at least the end of the 12th century. By the late 14th century, skates with iron blades set in wood were in general use in the Netherlands. Hollow grinding and curvature of the blade from front to back had been introduced by the end of the 18th century. During the early 19th century the blade was extended to the heel of the boot, thus facilitating backward skating. In 1848, E. W. Bushnell produced in Philadelphia the first all-metal skate, which was attached to the boot by clamps. The first skate to be screwed to the sole of the boot was invented by the American skater Jackson Haines. Subsequent important developments were the joining of the toe section of the blade to the sole plate and the introduction of toe rakes.

The early development of skating as a sport took place in the Netherlands, where skating was used for the practical purpose of getting from village to village along the frozen canals. A form of thrust from the outside edge, known as the "Dutch Roll," was used, and this skill plus the iron-bladed skate were taken back to London by King Charles II on his return from exile. Skating thus became a sport of the aristocracy, the aim being to skate with elegance and good manners. The first treatise on skating was written in 1772 by Robert Jones, an artillery lieutenant. The first half of the 19th century saw the rise of the stiff English school, which repudiated skating as an art, regarding it entirely as a science. During this period, however, many of the major turns were invented. This style was totally opposed to the flowing "continental" style introduced by Jackson Haines, which finally achieved official recognition with the founding in 1892 of the ISU, when it became officially known as the "international" style.

At some unestablished date between 1683 and 1742 the Edinburgh Skating Club, the first of its kind in the world, was founded. The first club organized in the United States was the Skating Club of the City and County of Philadelphia, which opened its doors in 1849. In 1861 it joined forces with the Humane Society and adopted its current name, Philadelphia Skating Club and Humane Society. The first artificial ice rink was opened in London in 1876 but closed down the same year owing to humidity problems. By the end of the 19th century, refrigeration problems had been solved and the number of artificial rinks was increasing rapidly.

ROBERT OGILVIE
Author of "Basic Ice Skating Skills"

Bibliography

Amateur Skating Union of the United States, *Official Handbook* (Amateur Skating Union).
Brown, Nigel, *Ice Skating, A History* (Barnes, A. S. 1959).
Lussi, Gustave, and Richards, Maurice, *Championship Figure Skating* (Barnes, A. S. 1951).
Ogilvie, Robert S., *Basic Ice Skating Skills* (Lippincott 1968).
Owen, Maribel Vinson, *The Fun of Figure Skating* (Harper 1960).
Richardson, T. D., *The Art of Figure Skating* (Barnes, A. S. 1962).
U. S. Figure Skating Association, *The Rulebook* (USFSA, biannually).
U. S. Figure Skating Association, *Evaluation of School Figure Errors,* 7th ed. (USFSA, 1970).

SKEAT, Walter William (1835–1912), English philologist, whose numerous works and able editing of early texts did much to create a general interest in philology. Skeat was born in London on Nov. 21, 1835. Educated at Christ's College, Cambridge (1858), he was lecturer in mathematics there (1864) and Erlington and Bosworth professor of Anglo-Saxon (1878–1912). He edited *Lancelot of the Laik* (1865) for the Early English Text Society, and in 1866 he began his great edition of *Piers Plowman* in three parallel texts, which he finished 20 years later. In 1872 his *Treatise on the Astrolabe* appeared, one of several studies preliminary to his seven-volume edition of Chaucer. The *Etymological Dictionary of the English Language* (1879–1884; rev. ed., 1910) was his most important work.

Skeat's other books include *Aelfric's Lives of Saints* (1881–1900), Chatterton's *Poems* (1871), *The Works of Chaucer* (1894–1895), and *The Student's Chaucer* (1895). He founded the English Dialect Society in 1873 and was its chief member during the 23 years of its existence. For it he prepared several provincial glossaries, and it was upon these and other publications of the society that Joseph Wright's *English Dialect Dictionary* (1896–1905) is based. A *Student's Pastime* (1896) consists of articles contributed to *Notes and Queries*. He also translated Johann Ludwig Uhland's *Songs and Ballads* (1864) and edited the *Anglo-Saxon Gospels* (1871–1887). Skeat died in Cambridge on Oct. 6, 1912.

SKEET SHOOTING. See TRAPSHOOTING.

SKELETON, the basic supporting framework of an animal. Although most animals have some kind of skeletal system, a skeleton is not essential to life, and many aquatic invertebrate animals do not have skeletons. A skeleton not only provides a supporting framework but also serves for the attachment of muscles and in many cases protects delicate internal organs.

Skeletons are composed of various substances, the most common being bone, cartilage, calcium deposits in the form of lime, and silica deposits. A skeleton may be rigid and immovable, as in a coral, or jointed, as in most higher animals.

There are two basic kinds of skeletons: an exoskeleton, or external skeleton, and an endoskeleton, or internal skeleton. An exoskeleton may be a shell or other covering enclosing all other body parts. It is typically associated with lower animals such as crustaceans and insects, but a type of exoskeleton is also found in a few higher animals, such as turtles and the armadillo. An endoskeleton is characteristic of vertebrates, but some invertebrates also have a loosely organized endoskeletal system.

INVERTEBRATES

Invertebrate skeletons vary greatly. Some simple animals, including protozoans, or one-celled animals, secrete calcium or silica that gives some form to their bodies. Most sponges have calcium or silica fibers or spicules (very small rods) that form a kind of internal mesh around which their various body cells cluster. In corals, brachiopods, mollusks, and echinoderms, the skeleton is usually composed of lime ($CaCO_3$) and grows at its margins, becoming thicker with age. The exoskeleton reaches its fullest development in the arthropods. All crustaceans, insects, and other arthropods are completely covered by a complex cuticle of several layers. An important constituent of the arthropod exoskeleton is chitin, a nitrogenous polysaccharide. The very hard arthropod exoskeleton has flexible joints that permit the animal to move. Once hardened, the exoskeleton cannot expand, which is a severe limitation to growth. To overcome this difficulty, arthropods undergo periodic molts of their entire skeleton, with their various body parts enlarging before a new exoskeleton hardens.

VERTEBRATES

The basic internal skeletal pattern is similar in all vertebrates. In some adult fishes the skeleton is composed of hyaline cartilage, but in all other adult vertebrates it is made largely of bone, supplemented by cartilage over joint surfaces and in some other places. The skeleton of all land vertebrates can be divided into a median animal skeleton, consisting of a skull, vertebral column, and thoracic basket, and a lateral, paired appendicular skeleton, consisting of a pectoral, or anterior, girdle supporting the upper, or fore, limbs and a pelvic, or posterior, girdle supporting the hind, or lower, limbs.

In all vertebrates the head skeleton consists of the cranium, or braincase, capsules for the sense organs of sight, smell, and hearing, and a visceral, or branchial arch, skeleton. In embryos this entire head skeleton is made of cartilage, but in all but sharks and rays, the cartilage is gradually replaced by bone. In aquatic animals, the branchial arch skeleton develops into parts of the gill system, while in land forms it contributes to the development of other organs,

VERTEBRATE SKELETONS

Vertebrate skeletons, unlike those of lower animals, are enclosed within soft tissues of the body and are therefore known as internal skeletons, or endoskeletons. Like external skeletons, the internal skeletons of vertebrates help provide support, protection, and greatly increased mobility. The backbone, skull, and some combination of ribs, pectoral girdle, and pelvic girdle provide a bony shield that supports and protects vital organs. The great mobility of the typical vertebrate results from the fact that the limb bones act as levers. As a result of leverage the muscles that connect the limb bones to each other and to the limb girdles have their speed of action greatly multiplied.

The basic skeletal plan of vertebrates—skull, backbone, ribs, limb girdles, and limbs—is subject to many modifications. In fish, for example, skeletal limb bones are absent and their functions are performed by fins. Most snakes lack both pectoral and pelvic girdles as well as limbs, although pythons have a vestigial pelvic girdle and hind limbs. Some modifications completely change the function of bones. For example, bones that supported the gills of ancient fish evolved into the bony ossicles found in man's middle ear.

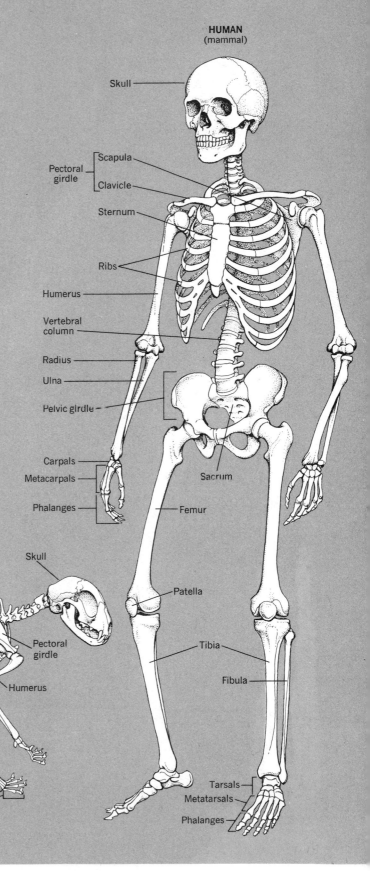

HUMAN
(mammal)

Skull

Pectoral girdle — Scapula, Clavicle

Sternum

Ribs

Humerus

Vertebral column

Radius

Ulna

Pelvic girdle

Carpals

Metacarpals

Phalanges

Sacrum

Femur

Patella

Tibia

Fibula

Tarsals

Metatarsals

Phalanges

CAT
(mammal)

Pelvic girdle

Vertebral column

Skull

Ribs

Pectoral girdle

Femur

Sternum

Humerus

Fibula

Ulna

Radius

Tibia

Carpals

Metacarpals

Tarsals

Metatarsals

Phalanges

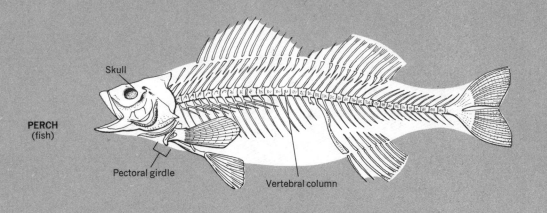

PERCH
(fish)

Skull

Pectoral girdle

Vertebral column

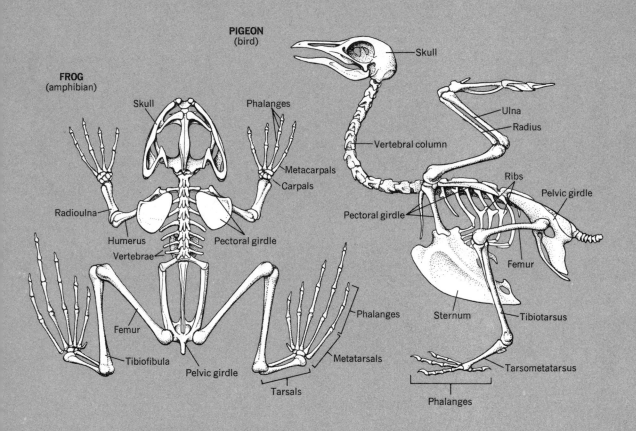

PIGEON
(bird)

Skull

Vertebral column

Ulna

Radius

Ribs

Pelvic girdle

Pectoral girdle

Femur

Sternum

Tibiotarsus

Tarsometatarsus

Phalanges

FROG
(amphibian)

Skull

Phalanges

Metacarpals

Carpals

Radioulna

Humerus

Pectoral girdle

Vertebrae

Femur

Phalanges

Tibiofibula

Metatarsals

Pelvic girdle

Tarsals

SNAKE
(reptile)

Vertebral column

Skull

Ribs

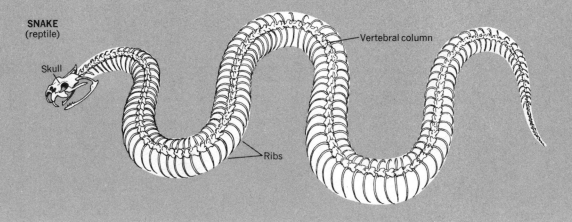

including parts of the jaw and some of the small bones of the ear. In mammals all three parts of the original head skeleton form a composite skull.

The vertebral column first appears as a slender gelatinous rod, the notochord, but in all vertebrates this original notochord is surrounded and supplanted by the spinal column. The spinal column, also termed spine or vertebral column, is composed of a series of bony segments, called vertebrae. The number and structure of the vertebrae differ greatly among the vertebrates. In fishes, the column has only two regions: trunk and tail. But in reptiles, amphibians, birds, and mammals, it is usually divided into five distinct regions: cervical, or neck; thoracic, or chest; lumbar, or lower back; sacral, or pelvic; and caudal, or tail.

The thoracic basket consists of the ribs and the sternum, or breastbone. The number of ribs and their exact structure and the size and structure of the sternum vary among the vertebrates. Birds, for example, have a sternum with a large median keel for the attachment of flight muscles.

The appendicular skeleton provides the framework and support for body appendages. In fishes these appendages are pectoral and pelvic fins, while in land vertebrates they are limbs. The parts of the pectoral, or shoulder, girdle and of the pelvic girdle, and the components of the limbs are homologous in amphibians, reptiles, birds, and mammals, though they are modified in various ways in adaptation to the animal's habitat and particular mode of life. In some cases there is a fusion of bones or a loss of limbs or digits, but in nearly all cases anatomical vestiges reveal the basic vertebrate skeletal plan.

HUMAN

The adult human skeleton is composed of 206 bones. These bones, which are joined by ligaments, provide basic structural support for the body, serve as a framework for the attachment of muscles, and protect many softer organs. As in other vertebrates, the human skeleton is divided into two parts: axial and appendicular.

Axial Skeleton. The human axial skeleton is composed of the skull, vertebral column, sternum, and ribs. The skull consists of 22 bones. Eight bones, including the frontal, two temporal, occipital, sphenoid, ethnoid, and two parietal, form the cranium that protects the brain. Fourteen facial bones provide structure and support for the mouth, nose, ears, and eyes.

The vertebral column is the main supporting structure in man and also functions to enclose and protect the spinal cord. It is composed of 33 segments, called vertebrae. Of these, the upper 24—7 cervical, 12 thoracic, and 5 lumbar —are movable, bony segments. The five sacral vertebrae are fused into a single large triangular bone, the sacrum, which is at the back of the pelvis. The last four (five) vertebrae are also fused into a single bone, the coccyx.

The breastbone, or sternum, is an elongated flattened bone that forms the middle portion of the front wall of the chest. The ribs are elastic arches of bone that make up a large part of the thoracic skeleton. In man there are 12 pairs of ribs. The first seven, sometimes called true ribs, are attached to the sternum in the front and to the vertebral column in the back, while the last five pairs are sometimes termed false ribs. The ribs protect the lungs. When muscles attached to the ribs contract, air is drawn into the lungs.

Appendicular Skeleton. The appendicular skeleton includes the shoulder girdle and the pelvic girdle. The shoulder girdle is made up of the scapula, or shoulder blade; the clavicle, or collarbone; and the upper limb. The scapula, a large flat triangular bone, forms the dorsal part of the shoulder girdle, while the clavicle, a long curved bone placed almost horizontally above the first rib, forms the ventral part.

The long upper arm bone is the humerus, which articulates with the scapula at the glenoid cavity. The forearm has two bones: the ulna and the radius. The ulna, or elbow bone, is found on the little-finger side of the arm. Its thicker proximal end forms a large part of the elbow joint. This bone decreases in size as it approaches the wrist, while the radius, found on the thumb side of the arm, becomes larger at the wrist end.

The skeleton of the hand comprises three parts: eight carpal, or wrist, bones; five slender metacarpal bones in the palm region; and 14 phalanges, or finger bones. There are two phalanges in the thumb and three in each other finger.

The pelvic girdle includes the bones of the pelvic and the lower limb. The pelvis is a bony, bowl-shaped cavity enclosing the lower internal abdominal organs and providing for the articulation of the bones of the upper leg. The pelvis is formed by the fusion of three bones: the ilium, the ischium, and the pubis.

The upper leg, or thigh, bone is the femur, the longest and strongest bone in the body. The head of the femur, called the acetabulum, forms a ball-and-socket joint, articulating with the ilium. The distal, or lower, end of the femur expands into a flattened region, the sides of which can be felt at the knee joint where the tibia, the larger of the two lower leg bones, articulates. In front of this joint, a flat, rounded, rather triangular bone, called the patella, forms the knee cap. The other lower leg bone is the fibula.

The structure of the foot is similar to that of the hand. There are seven tarsal, or ankle, bones; five metatarsal, or foot, bones; and 14 phalanges in the toes.

SKELTON, John (c. 1460–1529), English poet. He was born, probably in Norfolk, about 1460. Skelton studied at Oxford and at Cambridge and received the title of poet laureate from both institutions. He was a court poet at the court of Henry VII and served for a time as tutor to the future Henry VIII. In 1498, Skelton took holy orders and subsequently was appointed to the benefice of Diss in Norfolk. In the pulpit he was remarkable for his buffooneries and, according to the 17th century English antiquary and biographer Anthony Wood, was esteemed "fitter for the stage than for the pew or pulpit." However, his literary gifts were widely recognized, and Erasmus, one of the great figures of the age, declared him to be the *lumen et decus* ("light and ornament") of British letters.

The three most common subjects of Skelton's satire were the grammarian William Lily, the mendicant friars, and the powerful Cardinal Wolsey. His attacks on Wolsey at length aroused the resentment of that prelate. After an order for Skelton's apprehension was issued, he took refuge in Westminster Abbey, where he was protected until his death, not long before the fall of Wolsey. He died in London on June 21, 1529.

Among Skelton's most important works are the morality play *Magnyfycence;* three satires on Wolsey entitled *Why Come Ye Nat to Courte, Collyn Clout,* and *Speke, Parrot; The Tunnyng of Elynour Rummynge,* a burlesque about a group of drunken country sluts; and *Phyllyp Sparowe,* an elegy on the sparrow belonging to the "goodly maid" Jane Scroope that was killed by a cat. The last is one of the most poetic of his pieces. It is said that his own opinion of his works is reasonably just:

> Though my ryme be ragged,
> Tatter'd and jagged,
> It hath in it some pyth.

SKEPTICISM, in philosophy, is a critical attitude or methodology that questions the claims of knowledge made by philosophers and others. Skepticism has been known in various degrees, including the refusal to acknowledge that any knowledge is possible at all, the denial that any knowledge is valid if it is not derived from sense experience, and the denial of claims of knowledge in specific fields such as metaphysics, theology, or the sciences. Skepticism has contributed to the advancement of epistemology, or theories of knowledge, by forcing the critical analysis of all claims to knowledge and the rejection of unwarranted assumptions.

While skepticism is found in other early philosophers, the Roman Pyrrhonian school developed it to a high degree. The 3d century Greek philosopher Sextus Empiricus provided a famous series of rules for avoiding judgments in his *Adversus mathematicos* and the *Pyrrhoniarum hypotyposes.* In the 17th century René Descartes utilized a skeptical attitude in his search for a sound basis for all knowledge. In the 20th century skeptical attitudes are represented by the criticisms of metaphysics made by such philosophers as Rudolf Carnap and Bertrand Russell. See also EPISTEMOLOGY.

SKERRYVORE, sker′ē-vôr, a large rock in the Hebrides, off the west coast of Scotland, is about 11 miles (18 km) southwest of the island of Tiree. It is part of a dangerous reef in the fairway of vessels making for the Clyde and Mersey rivers. To reduce the increasing number of shipwrecks on the reef during the 19th century, a lighthouse was built on Skerryvore. It was designed and erected by Alan Stevenson, uncle of the author Robert Louis Stevenson. The tower is 138 feet (42 meters) high and contains 9 stories and a lightroom. When it was put into operation in 1844, the lighthouse had a range of 18 nautical miles, remarkable for its day.

SKETCH BOOK, a collection of miscellaneous writings by the American author Washington Irving. *The Sketch Book of Geoffrey Crayon, Gent.* was published in New York in seven numbers during 1819 and 1820. The collected edition brought out in 1820 in London contained two earlier essays—*Traits of Indian Character* and *Philip of Pokanoket*—which have been included in all subsequent editions. The entire collection was revised and given its final form in 1848. "I have preferred," Irving later explained, "adopting the mode of sketches and short tales rather than long works, because I choose to take a line of writing peculiar to myself." More explicitly, he wrote brief pieces to avoid the contagious and overwhelming influence of Sir Walter Scott.

Contents. In a miscellany like *The Sketch Book,* Irving was able to attempt several varieties of manner. *The Wife, The Broken Heart, The Widow and Her Son,* and *The Pride of the Village* fell in with a lachrymose tendency of the day and were long popular, but they have since lost most of their power to move. *Rural Life in England, The Country Church, Rural Funerals,* and *The Angler* are based upon actual observation; while not without sentimentalism, they have still a pleasant faded charm. The charm has not faded from such essays as *Westminster Abbey* and *Stratford-on-Avon,* clear, affectionate pictures of honorable places. But Irving is at his best as essayist when, his eye keenly on the object, he discards sentimentalism and speaks in his natural idiom—humor: this he does in *The Boar's Head Tavern, Eastcheap, Little Britain, John Bull,* and above all in the dainty series recounting the Christmas ceremonies at Bracebridge Hall.

Critique. About the whole book there is a delicate flavor of the past which has led some readers to think that past and present were confused in Irving's mind. The truth, however, is merely that his imagination was highly susceptible to history and tradition, and he was as naturally a maker of legends as a humorist. This is borne out by the tales in *The Sketch Book: The Spectre Bridegroom,* a merry parody, even to its bungling plot of the horrific narratives then lately brought from Germany; and the masterpieces of the volume, *Rip Van Winkle* and *The Legend of Sleepy Hollow.* Irving did not invent the central incidents of *Rip* and the *Legend;* one came from a German, one from an American source. Yet the two stories are as firmly localized in the Hudson Valley as if they had been founded on indigenous folk legends. Both are ascribed to Diedrich Knickerbocker. Both are mellow and rich in style, kindly and chuckling in humor, happy in characterization, and picturesque in description. The plots move with the accomplished ease of perfect leisure, and the landscapes have the golden look of perpetual autumn. Easily the two best short stories in English for the first three decades of the 19th century, they still unquestionably stand, after a 150 years busily given to the development of the short story type, among its undimned triumphs.

CARL VAN DOREN
Author of "The American Novel"

SKETCHING is making a rough, rapid drawing. A sketch may be a tentative, preparatory study for a finished work, or it may be a spontaneous expression of the artist valued for its own sake. See also DRAWING.

SKIDMORE COLLEGE is a private women's liberal arts college in Saratoga Springs, N. Y. It was founded as Skidmore School of Arts by Lucy Skidmore Scribner in 1911, and was reorganized in 1917 after receiving an absolute charter from the state. Its name was changed in 1925. In the early 1970's a new campus was being built near the original campus.

Skidmore offers programs leading to B. S. or B. A. degrees, in liberal arts, business, music, drama, physical education, psychology, and nursing. During their sophomore and junior years, students of nursing attend the Skidmore Department of Nursing in New York City. Interdisciplinary programs and a year of study abroad are also offered. Enrollment in the early 1970's was more than 1,800.

Cutting trails across a blanket of unmarked powder, downhill skiers in the Swiss Alps plummet down a slope.

SKIING. Skiing has been practiced for over 4,000 years, but it did not become a popular recreational sport until the 20th century. The two main types of competitive skiing are Alpine and Nordic. Alpine skiing consists of downhill and slalom racing, while Nordic embraces jumping and cross-country events.

Skis and Poles. A ski is a long, flat runner turned up at the front end. Skis are made of a variety of materials, including wood, plastic, metal, and combinations of the three. Styles range from long for downhill racing, to heavy for jumping, to light for cross country. Wood skis, for many years the only type, are usually available in the lower price ranges. Metal and plastic skis have increased greatly in popularity as improved production methods have brought price reductions.

All skis should be cambered, or arched slightly in the middle, so the skier's weight will be distributed evenly when he steps on the skis. Plastic running surfaces reduce friction and increase speed, while metal edges permit good control on turns. Skis must be strong but should also be flexible and resilient. Finally, they must be able to withstand great variations in climate.

For ordinary skiers, all-purpose skis are suitable for most types of slopes and snow conditions. A common rule for ski lengths has been the distance between the ground and the skier's hand raised above his head but many instructors recommend shorter skis for beginners. For experts and professionals, skis vary to meet the needs of a particular event. Downhill skis are longer and heavier than slalom skis, which are used for turning quickly. Cross-country skis, even lighter and narrower, are usually made of wood. Different waxes are used for different snow conditions. Jumping skis are long, wide, and heavy.

Two poles are used, with light metal, such as an aluminum alloy, the most popular construc-

tion, although steel and fiber glass poles are not uncommon. The tip of a pole is sharp, and about 5 inches (13 cm) above it is a circular ring, interlaced with webbing. The ring and webbing prevent the pole from sinking into deep snow. At the top of the pole is a thong that fits around the wrist, so that the pole will not be dropped. Poles are an aid in climbing and pushing off, and sometimes help maintain balance. Downhill poles are shorter than the cross-country variety. Those for the average skier reach midway between the waist and armpit.

Boots, Bindings, and Other Equipment. Advances in plastic techniques have revolutionized ski-boot construction since the late 1960's. Rigid, waterproof plastic boots, often with some leather parts, quickly surpassed all-leather boots in popularity. Double boots, consisting of a rigid outer boot and a more flexible inner one, are also available. Modern boots are fastened with buckles, which have almost completely replaced the traditional laced boots. Flexible, soft-leather boots are still preferred for cross-country skiing.

Until the 1950's, the only purpose of ski bindings was to hold the skier's feet firmly on the skis. However, injuries from falls were frequent, and designers developed several bindings that would release the feet in a fall and still provide good contact while skiing. Modern cross-country bindings hold the feet only at the toes. For Alpine skiing step-in bindings have practically replaced earlier release bindings that used cables. Safety straps, attached to the binding and the boot, are often used to prevent skis from "running away" when the boots are released from the bindings.

Ski clothing should be warm, lightweight, wind-resistant, and as moisture-proof as possible. Sunglasses and goggles help prevent eyestrain and protect the skier from ultraviolet rays. Various types of packs, in which to carry food, extra equipment, and clothing, are widely used.

Slalom, a move combining speed and agility, demands intense concentration as competitors slice through gates.

Alpine Skiing. The primary objective of the casual skier is to enjoy the downhill run and to reach the bottom of the slope safely. Control is of the utmost importance, and the skier should be able to stop or turn. Checks and turns of the snowplow and stem variety—the ski tips close together, the heels relatively far apart—are the most elementary. For more advanced skiers there are variations of the Christiania, or Christie, where skis are parallel, and weight shift and body rotation are used. Experts can accomplish jump turns and other acrobatic maneuvers in the air.

For downhill racing, speed is the most important requirement, although not at the sacrifice of control, as slopes are uneven. Skiers do not race en masse, but separately, and each contestant is timed. Record times are obviously no criterion, since snow conditions vary, as well as the slope and length of the descent. Racing speeds sometimes exceed 80 miles (128 km) per hour.

The slalom form of downhill racing calls for great turning ability. The skier races against time through a number of pairs of flagged poles, each pair known as a gate, placed on the course so the skier must take a serpentine zigzag path down the slope. The faster the skier can change course and check his speed, the better he will do, but if he takes too great risks, he may fall or miss going through a gate. Judgment and control, as well as speed, are therefore of the utmost importance. The giant slalom, combining characteristics of the downhill and the slalom, has a longer course than the regular slalom, with gates set further apart.

Nordic Skiing. Although the jumping part of Nordic skiing has always been popular, cross-country skiing was confined largely to Scandinavia until the late 1960's. For jumping, the ski is longer and heavier than other types and usually has three grooves in the bottom for better control. No poles are used. The skier glides down an elevated ramp, the in-run, and then takes off into the air, landing on the out-run, or sloping surface of the hill. He is marked for distance and for form, so the longest jump will not necessarily win first place. Jumps of over 540 feet (165 meters) have been made. Since the distance of the jump depends not only on the jumper's skill but also on the size of the slope and the snow conditions, records are not always meaningful. The most celebrated jumping meet is at Holmenkollen, Norway.

In cross-country racing the ski is somewhat narrower and lighter than the downhill ski. Bindings permit free up-and-down foot motion, and the boot soles are more flexible than downhill ones. Cross-country racing is over level terrain, climbs and descents, and the skier is often faced with obstacles like walls and wooded territory. When not skiing downhill, the competitor must depend on his stride and pole thrust to supply momentum, which makes cross country the most physically taxing type of skiing. In Sweden the long Dalarna cross-country race, which commemorates a historic journey of Gustav Vasa, attracts several thousand competitors.

Competition. Skiing is one of the most important sports in the Winter Olympic Games. For both men and women, the two basic divisions are Nordic and Alpine events. Women's Nordic events are limited to cross-country races, while the men's division includes a variety of cross-country and jumping events, plus the biathlon, a combination of skiing and shooting. A Nordic Combined title, recognizing jumping and skiing excellence, is awarded in the men's division. In the Alpine category, men and women each compete in downhill, slalom, and giant slalom race. An Alpine Combined title was part of the competition through the 1948 games and has been unofficially awarded since then.

World championships, originally held annually, have been staged every four years since 1950 and are under the auspices of the Federation Internationale de Ski (FIS). Topflight Alpine skiers compete for the World Cup, which is awarded annually to those who compile the most points in a series of international races. In addition, many countries stage national championships each year. Professional skiers hold a number of tournaments throughout the world.

History. Primitive skis over 4,000 years old have been found in Scandinavian bogs, and it is known that the Laplanders were early skiers. At the Battle of Oslo in 1200, Norwegian troops used skis, and military use of skis was made in other wars, including World Wars I and II. Ski lengths have varied greatly over the centuries, with skis as short as 3 feet (1 meter) being used in 16th century warfare.

In earlier times skiing was more often a military skill or a means of transportation than a sport. However, it assumed recreational status during the late 19th century, and in the 20th century it became a major winter sport wherever terrain and weather conditions permitted.

In 1862 the first officially recorded ski competition was held near Oslo, and in 1877 the Christiania Ski Club was organized in Norway. An indication of the country's importance in skiing progress is the large number of skiing terms that are in Norwegian. The Christiania—commonly shortened to Christie—designates a high-speed turn with parallel skis. Telemark, a turn in deep snow, and slalom are other skiing terms with Norwegian origins.

Scandinavians were instrumental in introducing the sport to the United States, with skis reported in the Middle West as early as 1840. The first ski club in the United States, eventually known as the Nansen Ski Club, was organized in 1882 in Berlin, N. H., for jumping and cross-country racing. In 1904 the National Ski Association was formed in Ishpeming, Mich. All the charter member clubs were from the Middle West.

Around 1880 skiing gained popularity in Austria and later in Switzerland, Germany, and France. In the late 19th century many Englishmen became ski enthusiasts during their travels on the Continent. The Ski Club of Great Britain, formed in 1903, became one of the world's largest. In general, West Europeans preferred downhill skiing to the jumping and cross-country racing favored by the Scandinavians.

Beginning in 1907, Hannes Schneider, an Austrian, began to teach skiing in the Arlberg section of the Alps. His Arlberg technique, which was an improvement of the methods of an instructor named Mathias Zdarsky, became extremely popular after World War I. Schneider taught a crouched style with forward lean that emphasized rotating the body into a turn. Schneider's techniques were relatively easy to learn and were instrumental in popularizing the sport. An additional spur was the development of rope tows, which eliminated the slow, arduous uphill climb and enabled skiers to make many more runs per day.

In North America, eastern Canadian colleges and the Dartmouth Outing Club in the United States made key contributions to early 20th century skiing. In 1931 the first snow train carried members of the Appalachian Mountain Club from Boston to the ski slopes of the White Mountains. This was followed by trains from New York, and many city dwellers were soon taking weekend or vacation excursions to ski resorts. In 1932 the Winter Olympics, held at Lake Placid, N. Y., did much to stimulate interest in the United States. Enthusiasts watched and read about jumping and cross country as well as downhill and slalom racing.

After World War II different types of techniques developed. The Austrians championed the wedeln, which emphasized short, connected parallel turns. Another school stressed counter-rotation of the body while turning. In an attempt to standardize instruction in the United States, the American Ski Technique was worked out and gained acceptance during the 1960's.

By the early 1970's there were approximately 4 million skiers, nearly half of them women, in the United States, compared with a total of 2 million about 20 years earlier. In addition to the traditional ski areas, some of them world famous, many new ski slopes open each year. Artificial snow-making machines supplement normal snow-

Cross country skiing, growing rapidly in popularity, permits skiers to wander from marked trails.

falls at many ski slopes and have allowed skiing to be introduced into some areas where natural conditions make the sport impossible. The Northeast and Far West, with the advantages of cold winters and mountainous terrain, continue to be the most popular ski areas, but the sport is also growing rapidly in the Midwest, and some trails have been carved out of the mountains in the Southeast. Cross-country skiing, which had been out of favor in the United States, surged in the early 1970's as skiers enjoyed lighter equipment and the freedom from lift lines and increasingly crowded downhill slopes.

Although the most dramatic growth has been in the United States, enthusiasm for the sport has increased in Europe, South America, Japan, and other areas that have suitable conditions. To serve the multitudes of new skiers, the manufacture of skis and other equipment has burgeoned, and resort complexes have multiplied.

PARKE CUMMINGS[*]
Author of "The Dictionary of Sports"

Bibliography

Bradley, David et al, *Expert Skiing* (Grosset 1963).

Caldwell, John, *New Cross-Country Ski Book* (Greene 1971).

Jerome, John, and others, *Sports Illustrated Book of Skiing*, rev. ed. (Lippincott 1971).

Lederer, William J., and Wilson, Joe P., *Complete Cross-Country Skiing and Touring* (Norton 1970).

Lund, Morten, *Ski, G. L. M.: The Fastest and Safest Way to Learn* (Dial 1970).

Scharff, Robert, and others, eds., *Ski Magazine's Encyclopedia of Skiing* (Harper 1970).

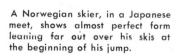

A Norwegian skier, in a Japanese meet, shows almost perfect form leaning far out over his skis at the beginning of his jump.

SKIKDA, skĕk-dä′, is a seaport city in northeastern Algeria, on the Mediterranean Sea at the mouth of the Safsaf River, about 40 miles (60 km) northeast of Constantine. It was formerly called Philippeville.

The city is an export center for the varied agricultural produce of the hinterland. Its industries include the processing of fish, grain, olive oil, and fruits and the manufacture of aluminum products. Its imports include construction materials and other manufactured products, which supply all of eastern Algeria.

Skikda occupies the site of ancient Phoenician and Roman settlements. It was known to the Romans as Rusicade. The remains of the Roman city include a theater and a cemetery. The modern city was founded by the French in 1838. Its name was changed from Philippeville to Skikda after the Algerian war of independence, which ended in 1962. Many of the city's numerous European inhabitants emigrated following the French withdrawal. Population: (1966) 72,742.

SKILTON, Charles Sandford (1868–1941), American composer. He was born in Northampton, Mass., on Aug. 16, 1868. After graduating from Yale in 1889, he studied music in Berlin and New York City. He taught music at Salem College in Salem, N. C., from 1893 to 1896 and at the State Normal School in Trenton, N. J., from 1897 to 1903. He then became a professor of music at the University of Kansas. He was also dean of the School of Fine Arts there until 1915.

In 1915, while teaching at the Haskell Institute, the government school for Indians near the university, Skilton became interested in Indian music, which influenced many of his own compositions. In 1915 he wrote *Two Indian Dances* for string quartet, expanded in 1920 into the *Suite Primeval* for orchestra. He also composed two operas using Indian tribal music: *Kalopin* (1927) and *The Sun Bride* (1930). Among his other works are incidental music for James M. Barrie's *Mary Rose* (1933), choral pieces, chamber music, and sketches for organ and piano. He died in Lawrence, Kans., on March 12, 1941.

SKIM MILK. See MILK.

Skimmer (*Rhyncops nigra*) and young.

SKIMMER, any of a family of birds related to gulls and terns and known for their habit of capturing small fishes and other aquatic animals by skimming the surface of water with the lower half of the bill immersed. Skimmers are from 15 to 20 inches (38–50 cm) long and have long knifelike bills, long pointed wings, short legs with small feet and slightly webbed toes, and short forked tails. They are generally black, brownish or grayish above, whitish below, and have brightly colored bills.

Skimmers breed in large colonies. They utter soft courtship cries, and the male often holds in his bill a stick that the female removes before mating. The nest is often a simple depression in the sand. The female alone usually incubates the two to five blotched, glossy eggs, but the male assists in feeding the young, which depend on their sand-coloring for protection.

Three species of skimmers—the American skimmer (*Rynchops nigra*), the African skimmer (*R. flavirostris*), and the Indian skimmer (*R. albicollis*)—make up the family Rynchopidae of the order Charadriiformes.